1997

42ND EDITION

INTERNATIONAL TELEVISION & VIDEO ALMANAC

Editor
JAMES D. MOSER

Managing Editor
TRACY STEVENS

British Editor
WILLIAM PAY

Canadian Editor
PATRICIA THOMPSON

QUIGLEY PUBLISHING COMPANY, INC.
159 WEST 53RD STREET • NEW YORK, NY 10019

(212) 247-3100

1997 42nd Edition
INTERNATIONAL TELEVISION & VIDEO ALMANAC

ISSN: 0539-0761
ISBN: 0-900610-58-1

PRINTED IN THE UNITED STATES OF AMERICA

TABLE OF CONTENTS

Index of Subjects 4A
Television Year in Review 13A
Statistics 17A
1996-97 Primetime Programs 22A
Syndicated Programs 26A
Who's Who 1
Obituaries (Oct. 1, 1995-Sept. 30, 1996) 411
Services 412
State and Local Film Commissions 441
Federal Government Film & Media Services 446
International Film & Television Festivals 449
The Trade Press 454
Organizations & Unions 459
Awards: Emmy, Golden Globe, Director & Writer's Guilds, BAFTA 467
Television Movies & Miniseries 1995-1996 472
Television Movies & Miniseries 1990-1995 481
Corporate Histories of the Networks 508
Companies & Personnel 512
Producers & Distributors 528
TV Stations 552
Network Affiliates 588
Station Representatives 595
State Broadcast Associations 298
Cable Networks 601
Cable System Operators 604
Direct Broadcast Satellite & Wireless Broadcasters 607
Home Video Companies 609
Consumer Electronics 613
Video Services 614
The Industry in Great Britain 622
The Industry in Select Foreign Countries 654

ALPHABETICAL
INDEX OF SUBJECTS

Company listings for the following sections are not included in this Index: The World Market, Video Services, The Industry in Great Britain. For these listings, please find the company in alphabetical order within the relevant section.

A

A.B. Enterprises/Beck International Corp....................... 528
ABC Inc. (American Broadcasting Company)
  Affiliate Listing 588
  Corporate History 508
  Corporate Listing & Personnel.......................... 512
  Disney/ABC Cable & International Television....... 513
  Distribution Co. 528
  Entertainment 512
  Primetime Programs 1996-97 .... 22A
  Television Center 435
  Television Network Group 512
  Video Publishing 514
A.C. Communications... 413
AC & R Advertising 413
A&E Home Video 609
A&E Television Network 601
A & M Video 609
AMC (American Movie Classics)........................... 601
A-Pix Entertainment 609
ASCAP... 460
ASI Market Research 427
AV Guide (publication) 454
Abrams, Bob, & Associates.................................. 413
Abrams/Gentile Entertainment 528
  Animation... 415
Absolute Post.. 422
Academy Players Directory................................... 454
Academy of Television Arts and Sciences............. 459
Academy of Television Arts and Sciences Awards.... 467
Access America 607
Acclaim 429
Action Jets F/X.. 429
Act III Television 528
Active Home Video.. 609
Action Jets F/X.. 429
Actor's Equity Association.................................... 459
Actors Group Agency 437
Adelphia Communications Corp............................. 604
Adler Media... 528
Admit One Video Presentations 609
Advanced Camera Systems................................... 429
Advanced Fire & Rescue Services 429
Advantage Audio.. 428
Adventure Film & Tape... 422
Advertising Age (publication) 454
Advertising & Publicity Services............................ 413
  Great Britain 645
Advertising Council 459
Advertising Research Foundation 459
Afghanistan 651
Albania 651
Algeria 651
Alias/Wavefront 429
Alice Entertainment.. 528
All American Television 528
All-Star Talent Agency.. 437
Alliance for Community Media 459
Alliance International 528
Alliance of Motion Picture and Television Producers.... 459
Allied Film & Video Services................................. 425
Alpha Cine Laboratory 425
AlphaStar Digital Television.................................. 607
Alter Image 422
Altered Anatomy Inc... 429
Alterian Studios... 429
Amblimation (see Dreamworks)
Amblin Entertainment.. 528
American Association of Advertising Agencies 459
American Cable Entertainment 604
American Cinema Editors 459
American Cinematographer (publication).................. 454
American Costume Corp.. 420
American Federation of Musicians.......................... 460
American Federation of Television and Radio Artists.... 460
American Guild of Musical Artists.......................... 460
American Guild of Variety Artists 460
American Humane Association 460
American Marketing Association 427

American Movie Classics....................................... 601
American Playhouse 529
American Premiere Magazine................................. 454
American Society of Cinematographers................... 460
American Society of Composers, Authors & Publishers.... 460
American Stock Photography................................. 433
American Telecasting, Inc..................................... 607
American Wireless Systems 607
Ammirati, Puris & Lintas 413
Anatomorphex.. 429
Angel Films 415
Angola... 651
Animal Makers 420
Animation.. 415
Animated Productions, Inc.................................... 529
Animotion.. 415
Antique & Classic Car Rentals.............................. 420
Archive Films, Inc.. 422
Archives for Advanced Media 425
Argentina 651
Armenia 653
Armstrong of Colorado.. 604
Art F/X 429
Arteffex 429
Artist Network 437
Arts & Entertainment Network 601
Asian Cinevision 460
Associated Actors and Artistes of America............. 460
Associated Media Images...................................... 433
Associated Press Broadcast Division..................... 529
Associated Production Music 428
Associated Television Int'l.................................... 529
Associations, U.S... 459
Association of America's Public Television Stations.... 461
Association of Independent Commercial Producers 461
Association of Independent Television Stations 461
Association of Independent Video & Filmmakers...... 461
Association of National Advertisers 461
Association of Talent Agents 461
Astral Home Entertainment................................... 609
Astro Color Lab... 425
Atlantis Films Ltd./Atlantis Releasing................... 529
Atomix.. 415
Audio Effects Company... 428
Austin/Simons & Associates 413
Australia 652
Austria.. 653
Authors' Guild.. 461
Authors League of America 461
Available Light, Inc.. 429
Avid Technology 422
Awards
  BAFTA (British Academy of Film & Television Arts)........ 470
  Directors Guild of America................................. 470
  Emmy (Daytime) 469
  Emmy (Primetime) 467
  Golden Globe 470
  Writers Guild of America................................... 470
Azerbaidzhan 654

B

BAFTA (British Academy of Film & Television Arts)
  Awards... 470
BBC Worldwide Americas 529
BBC Worldwide Television..................................... 529
BBDO Worldwide 413
BFS Limited 609
BMG Video... 609
BMI (Broadcast Music, Inc.)................................. 461
B.V.T.V. (Bob Vila Television)............................... 529
Backer, Spielvogel, Bates Worldwide Inc. 413
Baer Animations Company Inc............................... 415
Bagdasarian Prods. 415
Bahamas... 654
Bahrain 654
Baker & Taylor Video... 612
Baltimore Pictures.. 529

Bangladesh 654
Banner, Bob, Associates 529
Barbados 654
Barry, Ben, & Associates 529
Belarus 654
Belgium 654
Belisarius Prods. 529
Belize 655
Bell-Phillip TV Prods. 529
Benin 655
Benton Film Forwarding Company 425
Bermuda 655
Bickley/Warren Prods. 529
Bifrost LaserFX 429
Big Fights, Inc. 529
Big Sky Editorial 423
Big Time Picture Company, Inc. 423
Billboard 454
Biographies 1
Black Entertainment Television 601
Black/Marlens Company 529
Blade Communications 604
Blair, John, Communications, Inc. 595
Blockbuster Entertainment Corp. 611
Blue Sky Productions, Inc. 416
Blur Studio Inc. 416
Bobtown 416
Bochco, Steven, Prods. 529
Bodytech 429
Bohbot Entertainment 416
Bolivia 655
Bonded Film Storage 425
Book-of-the-Month Club, Inc. 612
Booth American Company 604
Booz, Allen & Hamilton 420
Bophuthatswana 655
Bosna-Herzegovinia 655
Boss Film Studios 429
Box, The 601
Boxoffice (publication) 454
Bozell, Inc. 413
Bramson & Assocs. 419
Bravo 601
Brazil 655
Bresnan Communications 604
Bright-Kauffman-Crane Prods. 530
Brillstein-Grey Entertainment 530
Broadcast (publication) 457
Broadcast Music, Inc. 461
Broadcast Pioneers Foundation 461
Broadcasters Associations 598
Broadcasting & Cable (publication) 454
Broadway Video Design 416
Broadway Video Entertainment 530
Brunei Darussalam 656
Budget Video, Inc. 612
Buena Vista Home Video 609
Buena Vista Imaging 429
Buena Vista International, Inc. 530
Buena Vista Television (see the Walt Disney Company)
Bulgaria 656
Burkina Faso 656
Burman Studios, Inc. 429
Burnett, Leo, & Company, Inc. 413
Burrud Productions, Inc. 530
Burson-Marsteller 413
Burundi 656
Buzzco Associates Inc. 416

C

CAI Wireless 607
CBS/Fox Video 609
CBC International 530
CBS, Inc (Columbia Broadcasting System)
    Affiliate Listing 589
    Corporate History 508
    Corporation & Personnel 514
    Enterprises 515
    Entertainment 514
    Entertainment Productions 531
    International 516
    Primetime Programs, 1996-97 .... 23A
    Studio Center 435
    Television Network 515
CBS/Group W Television Sales 595
CC/ABC National Television Sales 595
CC Studios 609
CEL Communications 531
CNBC 601
    Distribution 531
CNN (Cable News Network) 601
C-SPAN 601
C-TEC Cable Systems 604
Caballero Spanish Media 595
Cabin Fever Entertainment 609
Cable Films & Video 609

Cable Networks, Inc. 595
Cable News Network 601
Cable News Network/Headline News 601
Cable Networks 601
Cable Statistics 17A
Cable System Operators 604
Cable Television Advertising Bureau 462
Cable Television Information Center 462
Cable Video Store 601
Cablevision Industries, Inc. 604
Cablevision Systems Corp. 604
Cacioppo Production Design, Inc. 429
Calabash Productions 416
Calico Ltd. 416
California Communications, Inc. 423
Calvert Company, The 416
Cambodia 656
Camelot Entertainment Sales 531
Camera Equipment
    (Studio & Equipment Services) 435
Cameroon 656
Canada 656
Canadian Satellite Communications 607
Candid Camera, Inc. 531
Cannell, Stephen J., Prods. 531
Cannell Distribution Co. 531
Capitol Records Video 609
Caption Center 437
Captions, Inc. 437
Caroline Film Productions 531
Carsey-Werner Company, The 531
Carson Prods. 532
Cartoon Network, The 601
Casting Services 419
Casting Company, The 419
Casting Society of America 419
Castle Hill Television 532
Castle Rock Entertainment 532
Catholic Actors Guild 462
Celebrity Service International (publication) 455
Celluloid Studios 416
Central African Republic 658
Central Casting 419
Central Park Media 609
Century Communications Corp. 604
Certified Reports, Inc. 458
Certified Marketing Services, Inc. 427
Chad 658
Character Shop, The 429
Charter Communications 604
Chelsea Animation Company 416
Chicago Production Center 532
Children's Television Workshop 516
Chile 658
China 659
Chiodo Brothers Productions Inc. 416
Choice TV (see Fort Wayne Telsat, Inc.)
Christian Broadcasting Network 601
Chuck Jones Film Productions 416
Churchill Media 416
Cinar Films Inc. 531
Cine Tape, Inc. 423
Cinefex (publication) 455
Cinema Engineering Company 429
Cinema Guild 612
Cinema Network (CINENET) 429
Cinema Research Corp/Digital Resolution 429
Cinemax 601
Cinemorph Effects Group 429
Cinepix Animation 416
Cinesite Digital Film Center 430
Cinetel Productions 532
Cinevista 609
Cinnabar 430
Citadel Entertainment 532
Clark, Dick, Prods. 532
Classic Images 434
Clip Joint for Film 434
Coffey/Ballantine 416
Collins Entertainment Concepts Corp. 430
Colombia 659
Colossal Pictures 416
Columbia House Video 612
Columbia Pictures Television 532
Columbia TriStar Television 522
    Distribution 522
    International Television 523
    International Television Distribution 532
Columbia TriStar Home Video 609
Comcast Cable Communications 604
Comedy Central 601
Coming Attractions (publication) 455
Commercial Media Sales 596
Completion Guarantees/Bonding (Financial Services) 426
Composite Image Systems 430
Computer Film Company, The 430
Congo 659

Consolidated Film Industries, Inc. 423
Costa Rica 659
Costume Place, The 421
Consultants for Talent Payment, Inc. 420
Consumer News & Business Channel (CNBS) 601
Continental Cablevision 604
Continental Film Labs 425
Coproducers Corp 533
Cornell/Abood 416
Coronet Film & Video 609
Corporate Histories of the Networks 508
Corporation for Public Broadcasting 462
Cosgrove-Meurer Prods. 533
Costume Designers Guild Directory 455
Costumes and Uniforms 421
Country Music Television 601
Cox Cable Communications 604
Cramer Company, The 533
Creative Artists Agency 438
Creative Character Engineering 430
Creative Effects, Inc. 430
Creative Musical Services 428
Crest National Film & Videotape Labs 423
Criswell Productions 430
Croatia 659
Crosby, Bing, Prods. 533
Cruse & Company, Inc. 430
Crystal Pictures 533
Cuba 659
Culver Studios, The 423
Cutting Rooms (Editing Services) 422
Cyprus 660
Czech Republic 660

D

DDB Needham Worldwide, Inc. 413
DIC Enterprises, Inc. 533
DIC Entertainment 416
D.L.T. Entertainment 533
Daddy-O Productions 416
Daily Variety 455
Day Shades 430
De Filippo, Dom, Studio Inc. 430
De La Mare Engineering, Inc. 430
Della Femina, Travisano & Partners 413
Deluxe Laboratories, Inc. 425
Denmark 660
Dentsu, Inc. 413
dePasse Entertainment 533
Design F/X Co. 430
Di Bona, Vin, Prods. 533
Digiscope 430
Digital Domain 430
Digital Magic Company 430
Direct Effects 430
Directors Guild of America 462
  Awards 470
Directors Sound & Editorial Service 423
DirecTV 607
Discount Video Tapes, Inc. 612
Discovery Channel 601
Discovery Communications 533
Disney Channel 517
Disney Home Video (see Buena Vista Home Video)
Disney, Walt, Imagineering 430
Disney, Walt, Company 516
  Buena Vusta Pay Television 517
  Buena Vista Television 517
  Buena Vista Television Distribution 530
  Disney & Touchstone Television 516
  Disney Channel 517
  International Television 517
  Television Animation 516
  Television Animation Distribution 533
Djibouti 661
D'Ocon Films 416
Dolby Laboratories, Inc. 428
Dominican Republic 661
Dominion Video Satellite 607
Doremus & Company 413
Dramatists Guild 462
Dream Quest Images 430
Dream Theater 430
Dreamlight Images, Inc. 430
Dreamworks Feature Animations 416
Dreamworks TV Animations 416
Du Art Film Laboratories 425

E

E! Entertainment Television 601
  Distribution 534
E=MC2 Inc. 430
ESPN 602
ETD Entertainment Distribution 612
EUE/Screen Gem Prints 430
Eastman Kodak Company 517
Eastern Optical Effects 430
Easy Edit 423
Echo Film Services 423
Ecuador 661
Edelman Public Relations Worldwide 414
Edit Decisions, Inc. 423
Edit Point Post Production Systems 423
Editel 430
Editing Company, The 423
Editing Concepts 423
Editing Equipment 422
Editing Machine, The 423
Editing Services 422
Edwards, Ralph/Billett, Stu, Prods. 534
Efex Specialists 430
EFilm 430
Effective Engineering 430
Effects House, The 430
Effectsmith, The 430
Egypt 661
El Salvador 661
Electric Machine Entertainment 430
Electrofex 430
Electronic Industries Association 462
Electronic Media (publication) 455
Electronics (publication) 455
Electronics Now (publication) 455
Emmy Awards 467
Empire Burbank Studios 435
Encore 602
Encore Enterprises 416
Enoki Films U.S.A. Inc. 416
Entertainment Data, Inc. 427
Entertainment Partners 419
Entertainment Prods. 533
Epic Home Video 610
Episcopal Actors Guild 462
Estonia 661
Ethiopia 661
Exhibitor Relations Co. Inc. 427
ExpressVu, Inc. 607
Eyemark Entertainment 534
Eyepiece 457

F

FIM Technical Services/Special Effects 430
FX Networks, Inc. 602
Faith & Vision (F & V) 602
Falcon Cable TV 604
Family Channel 602
Fanch Communications, Inc. 604
Fantasy II Film Effects 430
Federal Communications Commission 447
Fiesta Sound 428
Film & Video Magazine 455
Film & Video Stock Shots 434
Film Commissions 441
Film Festivals 449
Film Journal, The 455
Film Preservation & Repair 425
Film Processing Labs 425
Film Quarterly (publication) 455
Film Roman, Inc. 534
Film Storage Vaults 425
Filmack Studios 425
Filmlife Inc., American Film Repair Institute 425
Filmroos, Inc. 534
Films, Made for TV 472
Filmservice Laboratories, Inc. 423
Filmtreat International Corp. 425
Filmtrix, Inc. 430
Financial Services 426
Fine Art Productions/Richie Suracci Pictures 430
Finland 661
Finnegan-Pinchuk Co. 534
Fioritto, Larry, Special Effects Services 430
First Run/Icarus Films 610
Fleischer Studios, Inc. 416
Flint Productions 416
Foote, Cone & Belding Communications 414
Fort Lee Film Storage & Service 425
Fort Wayne Telsat, Inc. 607
Foto-Kem, Foto-Tronics, Film-Video Lab 425
Four Point Entertainment 534
Four Star International 534
44 Blue Prods. 534
Fox, Inc.
  Affiliate Listing 590
  Animation Studios 416
  Broadcasting Co. 517
  Broadcasting Co. Distribution 534
  Corporate History 509
  Corporation & Personnel 517
  Primetime Programs, 1996-97 .... 23A
  Television Stations, Inc. 518
  Television Stations Prods. 534
  Twentieth Century Fox Television 518
  Video 610

Fox/Lorber Associates ... 535
Fox Lorber Home Video ... 610
Foxlab ... 535
Fox News Channel ... 602
France ... 662
Fred Wolf Films ... 416
Fremantle Corp., The ... 535
Fries, Chuck, Productions, Inc. ... 535
Fuji Photo Film U.S.A. ... 424
Full Moon Video ... 610

G

GB Entertainment Marketing Group ... 414
GGP/GGP Sports ... 535
GRB Entertainment ... 535
GTG Entertainment ... 535
Gabon ... 663
Gallup Organization, The ... 427
Gambia ... 663
Garden State Cable Television ... 604
Gateways to Space ... 416
Gear Wireless Cable ... 607
Genesis Entertainment ... 536
Georgia Cable TV ... 604
Germany ... 663
Ghana ... 665
Gilderfluke & Company ... 430
Glendale Studios ... 435
Globus Studios ... 430
Golden Book Video ... 610
Golden Globe Awards ... 470
Goldman, Danny, & Assoc. Casting ... 419
Goldwyn Entertainment Company ... 518
Goldwyn, Samuel, Television ... 536
Goodson, Mark, Productions ... 536
Goodtimes Home Video ... 610
Gothic Renaissance Prods. ... 536
Government Film Bureaus ... 446
Gracie Films ... 536
Grassroots Cable Systems ... 604
Gray-Schwartz Enterprises ... 536
Great Britain & Ireland ... 623
Advertising Agencies ... 645
Commercial Broadcasters & Government Units ... 626
Costume Suppliers ... 645
Equipment Companies ... 640
Financial Services ... 645
Home Video Distributors ... 649
Laboratories ... 642
Libraries, Film & Music ... 641
Multiple System Cable Operators ... 632
News Film Services ... 645
Producers, Distributors & Services ... 632
Production Services, Facilities ... 642
Recording Studios ... 642
Satellite-Cable Broadcasters ... 630
Services for Producers ... 640
Statistics ... 624
Studios ... 644
Titling-Special Effects ... 644
Trade/Government Units ... 646
Trade Publications ... 457
Year in Review ... 623
Greater Media, Inc. ... 604
Greatest Tales ... 417
Greece ... 665
Grey Advertising, Inc. ... 414
Greystone Communications ... 536
Griffin, Merv, Enterprises ... 536
Grinberg Film Libraries, Inc. ... 434
Group W Productions ... 417
Group W Television Sales ... 596
Grub Street Prods. ... 536
Grundy, Reg, Prods. ... 536
Guadaloupe ... 665
Gautemala ... 665
Guinea ... 665
Gunther-Wahl Productions ... 417
Guyana ... 665

H

HBO, Inc. ... 602
HBO Downtown Prods. ... 536
HBO Independent Prods. Inc. ... 536
HBO Studio Productions ... 431
HBO Video ... 610
HFWD Visual EFX ... 431
Haiti ... 665
Hallmark (Animation) ... 417
Hallmark Entertainment ... 536
Hamdon Entertainment ... 536
Hanna-Barbera Cartoons Inc. (Distribution) ... 536
Hanna Barbera Productions (Animation) ... 417
Hansard Enterprises ... 431
Hargrove, Dean, Prods. ... 537
Harmon Cable Communications ... 604
Harmony Gold, U.S.A. ... 537
Harpo Entertainment Group ... 537
Harpo Studios ... 436
Harrington, Righter & Parsons, Inc. ... 596
Harron Communications Corp. ... 604
Harvey Entertainment ... 417
Hearst Animation Productions ... 417
Hearst Entertainment ... 537
Heart of Texas Productions ... 417
Heartland Wireless Communications ... 607
Hemdale Home Video, Inc. ... 610
Henley, Arthur, Productions ... 537
Henson, Jim, Creature Shop ... 431
Henson, Jim, Productions (Animation) ... 417
Henson, Jim, Productions (Distribution) ... 537
Henson, Jim, Video ... 610
Hi-Tech Rentals ... 423
Hill, Walter, Productions ... 537
Hispanic Entertainment Specialist ... 427
History Channel, The ... 601
Hollywood Center Studios, Inc. ... 436
Hollywood Central Props ... 421
Hollywood Creative Directory, The ... 455
Hollywood Digital ... 431
Hollywood Film Co. ... 423
Hollywood Reporter, The ... 455
Hollywood Vaults, Inc. ... 425
Holographic Studios ... 431
Home Box Office, Inc. ... 602
Home Shopping Network, Inc. ... 602
Home Video Companies ... 609
Consumer and Trade Publications ... 454
Equipment Manufacturers ... 613
Direct Marketers ... 612
Major Video Retailers ... 611
Services ... 614
Wholesale Distributors ... 612
Home Vision ... 610
Honduras ... 665
Hong Kong ... 666
Hubley Studio ... 417
Hungary ... 666
Hunter Gratzner Industries, Inc. ... 431
Hutchins/Young & Rubicam ... 414
Hyperion Animation ... 417

I

IATSE ... 462
IATSE Official Bulletin (publication) ... 455
IFEX International ... 537
I.N.I. Entertainment Group, Inc. (Animation) ... 417
I.N.I. Entertainment Group, Inc. (Distribution) ... 537
IRS Video ... 610
ITC Entertainment Group ... 537
Iceland ... 666
Ilford Photo, Inc. ... 424
Image Bank Film & Photography Library ... 434
Image Creators, Inc. ... 431
Image Engineering, Inc. ... 431
Image Organization, Inc. ... 537
Image Technology (publication) ... 457
Imagination Studios ... 417
Imagine That ... 431
In Motion (publication) ... 455
Independent Film Channel ... 602
Independent-International Pictures ... 537
India ... 666
Indonesia ... 667
Industrial F/X Productions ... 431
Industrial Light & Magic (ILM) ... 431
Ingram Entertainment, Inc. ... 612
Ink Tank, The ... 417
Innovative Artists ... 438
Insight Communications, Co. ... 604
Institute of Electrical & Electronics Engineers ... 462
InterMedia Partners ... 604
International Alliance of Theatrical Stage Employees & Moving Picture Machine Operators of the U.S. & Canada (IATSE) ... 462
Production ... 463
International Council of the Academy of the National Academy of Television Arts and Sciences ... 464
International Creative Effects ... 431
International Creative Management ... 438
International Documentary (publication) ... 455
International Film Festivals & Markets ... 449
International Motion Picture Almanac ... 454
International Photographer (publication) ... 456
International Radio & Television Society ... 464
International Research & Evaluation ... 458
International Television & Video Almanac ... 454
Introvision International ... 431
Iran ... 667
Iraq ... 667
Israel ... 667
Italy ... 667
Ivory Coast ... 668

J

JEF Films 538
J.J. Sedelmaier Productions, Inc. 417
Jacobs, Michael, Productions 538
Jamaica 668
Japan 668
Jet FX 431
Jetlag Productions 417
Jones Effects Studio 431
Jones Intercable Inc. 605
Jones, Quincy/David Salzman Entertainment 538
Jordan 669
Journal of the Syd Cassyd Archives 456
Jumbo Pictures 417

K

KCET Studios 436
KTLA 602
Kagan, Paul, & Associates 458
Kaleidoscope Television 602
Katz American Television 596
Kaufman Astoria Studios 436
Kazhakhastan 669
Kelley, David E., Entertainment 538
Kennevik Media Properties, Inc. 538
Kenya 669
Kesser Post Production 423
King World Prods. 538
Kinderhook Research, Inc. 458
Kino International 610
Klasy-Csupo, Inc. 417
Konnigsberg Company, The 538
Kookanooka Toons 417
Korea, North 669
Korea, South 669
Krantz, Steve, Prods. 538
Krislin Company, The 417
Krofft, Sid & Marty, Picture Corp. 538
Kultur Intl. Films Ltd. 610
Kurtz & Friends 417
Kushner-Locke Co., The 538
Kuwait 669

L

L.A. Animation 417
LIVE Entertainment 610
Landsburg Co., Inc. 538
Langley Productions 538
Laos 669
Laser-Pacific Media Corporation 431
Latvia 669
Lazarus Lighting Design 431
Leach Entertainment Enterprises 538
Learning Channel, The 602
Lebanon 669
Lenfest Group 605
Leonard, Herbert B., Productions 539
Levine, Schneider Public Relations 414
Levinson Entertainment Ventures International 539
Lexington Scenery & Props. 431
Liberia 669
Liberty Studios Inc. 431
Liberty Cable Television 607
Libya 669
Lieberman, Jerry, Productions 417
Lifetime 602
Lighting Equipment (see Studio Equipment & Services)
Linker Systems 431
Linguatheque of L.A. 437
Lintas: Worldwide 414
Literary and Talent Agencies 437
Lithuania 670
Live Wire Productions 431
Longbow Prods. 539
LowTech, Inc. 431
Lucasfilm (see Industrial Light & Magic)
Luxembourg 670
Lyons Group 610

M

MCA Television 518
  Domestic Distribution/Sales 539
  International Television 519
  International Television Distribution/Sales 539
  MCA Television Entertainment 519
  Universal Television 519
MCA/Universal Home Entertainment 610
MG/Perin 540
MGM Animation 417
MGM Worldwide Television 519
MGM/UA Home Video, Inc. 610
MGM/UA Television Distribution 539
MMT Sales, Inc. 596
M.S. Distributing 612
MSNBC 602
MTM Entertainment, Inc. 519
  Distribution/Sales 540
MTM Enterprises 417
MTV Animation 418
MTV Productions 540
MTV Networks 602
M3D Productions 417
Macau 670
Macedonia 670
Madagascar 670
Made for TV Movies (Oct. 1, 1995-Sept. 30, 1996) 472
  1990-1996 481
Madison Square Garden Network 540
Magical Media Industries, Inc. 431
Magno Sound 423
Magno Visuals 426
Makeup & Effects Laboratories, Inc. 431
Malaysia 670
Mali 670
Malibu Distribution Worldwide 540
Marcus Cable Partners L.P. 605
Margolis, Jeff, Prods. 540
Market Research 427
Market Research Corp. of America 458
Marketing Group, The 414
Markets & Festivals 449
Marshall/Plumb Research Associates 420
Marvel Films 540
Marvel Films Animation 417
Matte World Digital 431
Matthews Productions 417
Matinee Entertainment 417
Mauritania 670
Mauritius 670
McCann Erickson Advertising 414
McCann Erickson Research 458
Medallion TV Enterprises, Inc. 540
Media Casting 419
Media General Company 605
MediaMax Productions 417
Melrose Titles & Optical Effects 431
Metro-Goldwyn-Mayer Inc. 519
  MGM Worldwide Television 519
Metrolight Studios 417
Mexico 670
Midcontinent Cable Co. 605
Miller/Boyett Prods. 540
Miller Imaging International, Inc. 431
Millimeter (publication) 456
Modern Props 421
Modern Talking Picture Service 540
Modus EFX Productions 431
Moffat Communications, Ltd. 605
Moffit-Lee Prods. 540
Mohave Weapns Systems 431
Moldova 671
Momentum International Marketing 414
Mongolia 671
Montage Group, Inc. 423
Moon Mesa Media 417
Monster Mecanix 431
Moore, Art, Inc. 596
Morgan Creek Productions 417
Morocco 671
Morris, William, Agency 439
Motion Artists, Inc. 431
Motion Picture Almanac (publication) 454
Motion Picture & Television Fund 464
Motion Picture Corporation of America 519
Movie Tech Inc. 423
Movies, Made for TV 472
Movies Unlimited 611
Moving Pictures (publication) 457
Mozambique 670
Muller Media 540
Multimedia Cablevision 605
Multimedia Entertainment 540
Museum of Television & Radio, The 464
Music, Music Libraries and Music Cutting
  (see Sound Services)
Musivision 418
Myanmar (Burma) 671
Myers, Julian & Associates 414

N

NATPE International 465
NBC, Inc. (National Broadcasting Company) 520
  Affiliate Listing 591
  Corporate History 509
  Corporation & Personnel 520
  International Distribution/Sales 540
  News Archives 434
  News Video Archives 541
  Primetime Programs, 1996-97 24A
  Productions 521

NBC Spot Television Sales 596
Namibia 671
National Academy of Television Arts and Sciences 464
National Association of Broadcasters 464
National Association of Television Program Executives 465
National Cable Television Association 465
National Captioning Institute 437
National Geographic Film Library 434
National Geographic Society Home Video 610
National Music Publishers' Association 465
National Photographic Laboratories 426
Nelvana Communications (Animation) 418
Nelvana Communications (Productions & Distribution) 541
Nepal 671
Nest Entertainment 418
Netherlands 671
Networks, Corporate Histories 508
New Age Casting 419
NewChannels Corp. 605
New Heritage Associates 605
New Line Home Video 611
New Line Television 521
New World Animation 418
New World Entertainment 521
International Distribution/Sales 541
Productions 541
New World Video 611
New York Choice Television 607
New York Women in Film & Television 465
New Yorker Video 611
New Zealand 672
Newsreel Access Systems, Inc. 434
Nickelodeon/Nick at Nite 541
Animation 418
Nielsen, A.C., Company 458
Nielsen Statistics, 1996 .... 20A
Northland Communications Corp. 605
Norway 672
Nostalgia Television 602
Nova Cable Management, Inc. 605
Noveck, Fima, Prods. 542
Novocom 431

O

OCS/Freeze Frame/Pixel Magic 432
Obituaries (Oct. 1, 1995—Sept. 30, 1996) 411
Ogilvy & Mather Inc. 414
O'Hara-Horowitz Productions 542
Oman 673
Omega Communications Inc. 605
Optic Nerve Studios 432
Optical House Inc. 432
Opticam, Inc. 418
Organizations-Great Britain 646
U.S. 459
Orion Home Video 611
Orion Pictures Corporation 521
Home Entertainment 521
Home Video 522
Television Entertainment 522
Television Entertainment Distribution/Sales 542
Ovation/Animation 418
Owen Magic Supreme 432

P

PBS, Inc. (Public Broadcasting Service) 522
Affiliate Listing 593
Corporate History 510
Corporation & Personnel 522
PBS Direct 612
PBS Home Video 611
P.F.M. Dubbing International 437
Pacific Coast Studio Directory 456
Pacific Data Images 418
Pacific International Enterprises, Inc. 542
Pacific Title & Art Studios 432
Pacific Title Archives 426
Pacific Title Digital 432
Pagano, Bialy, Manwiller 419
Pakistan 673
Palmer Video Corp. 612
Panama 673
Papazian-Hirsch Entertainment 542
Papau-New Guinea 673
Paragon Entertainment 542
Paraguay 673
Paramount Costume Company 422
Paramount Home Video 611
Paramount Pictures Stock Footage Library 434
Paramount Television Group 524
Distribution & Sales 542
International Television 525
Network Teleision Prods. 542
Paramount Recording Studios 428
Patchett-Kaufman Entertainment 542
Pathe Pictures 543
Performance Magazine 456
Performance World Special Effects 432
Period Props 422
Permanent Charities Committee
of the Entertainment Industries 465
Perennial Pictures Film Corp. 418
Perpetual Motion Pictures 432
Peru 673
Petry Television, Inc. 597
Philippines 673
Pinnacle EFX 432
Pixar Animation Studios 418
Playboy Entertainment Group 543
Playboy TV 602
Playhouse Pictures 432
Playlight Pictures 418
Poland 674
Polar Technologies USA 432
Polestar Films 418
Polygram Home Video 611
Polygram Television International 543
Popvision 607
Portugal 674
Post Group 424
Post Plus, Inc. 424
Post Time 424
Post-Newsweek Cable 605
Precision Post 424
Premiere Cable II Ltd. 605
Press, The 454
British Trade Publications 457
Canadian Trade Publications 457
Prevue Network 602
Prime Cable. 605
Prime Casting 419
Prime Time TV Shows 22A
PrimeStar Partners 607
Prism Entertainment Corp. 602
Prism Entertainment Home Video 611
Producer-Writers Guild of America Pension Plan 465
Producers & Distributors, TV 528
Producer's Masterguide (publication) 456
Programs
Films Made for TV 472
Network 22A
Syndication 26A
Program Syndication Services, Inc./Program Exchange 543
Prop Masters, Inc. 422
Prop Services West 422
Properties and Scenery (see Costume & Prop Rentals)
Publications Television & Home Video Trade 454
Publicity West 415
Pyramid Media 434

Q

QVC 602
Qatar 675
Quantel 432
Quarter Star Productions 418
Quigley Publishing Company 454
International Motion Picture Almanac 454
International Television & Video Almanac 454

R

R/C Models 432
R/Greenberg Assoc. Inc. 418
RGA/LA 432
Rainbow Casting 419
Rainbow Advertising Sales Corp. 597
Random House 611
Raleigh Studios 436
Raw Stock Manufacturers 424
Red Apple Films 418
Reel Directory, The 456
Reel EFX 432
Reel Thing, The 424
Reelistic FX 432
Regency Home Video 611
Rental Studios and Production Facilities
(see Studio Equipment & Services)
Rentrak Home Entertainment 612
Republic Pictures Corp. 543
Republic Pictures Home Video 611
Request Television 603
Retailers, Home Video 611
Rhino Home Video 611
Rhythm N'Hues 418
Rich Animation Studios 418
Rick Reinhart Pictures, Inc. 418
Rifkin & Associates 605
Riley Representatives 597
Roaring Mouse Entertainment 432
Rogers Cablesystems Ltd. 605
Romania 675

Ruby-Spears Productions (Animation) 418
Ruby-Spears Productions (Distribution & Sales) 543
Russian Federation 675
Rysher Entertainment 543

S

SESAC, Inc. 465
SFM Entertainment 543
SFX-Starlight Effects 432
SMPTE Journal 456
S.O.T.A. FX 432
SRW Inc. 605
ST Productions 418
Saatchi & Saatchi Advertising 415
Saban Entertainment (Animation) 418
Saban Entertainment (Distribution & Sales) 543
Safari Animation Effects 432
Sammons Communications 605
Saudi Arabia 676
Savalli Broadcast Sales 597
Scenery and Properties (see Costume & Prop Rentals)
Scenic Technologies 432
Schlatter, George, Productions 544
Sci-Fi Channel, The 603
Screen Actors Guild 465
Screen International Euroguide (publication) 457
Scripps Howard Cable 605
See 3 432
Seltel, Inc. 597
Senegal 676
Service Electric Cable Vision 605
Services
  Advertising & Publicity Representatives 413
  Animation 415
  Camera Equipment (Studio & Equipment Services 435
  Casting 419
  Completion Guarantees & Bonding (Financial Services) 426
  Consultants & Technical Services 420
  Costumes & Prop Rentals 420
  Cutting Rooms (Editing Services) 422
  Editing Equipment 422
  Editing Services 422
  Federal Government Film & Media Services 446
  Film & Video Stock 424
  Film Preservation & Repair 425
  Film Processing Labs 425
  Film Storage Vaults 425
  Financing Companies & Banking Services 426
  Lighting Equipment (Studio & Equipment Services 435
  Market Research 427
  Music, Music Libraries, Music Cutting
  (Sound Services) 425
  Properties & Scenery (Costume & Prop Rentals) 420
  Sound and Recording Services 425
  Special Effects 429
  Stock-Shot Film Libraries 433
  Studios & Equipment Services 435
  Subtitles & Captions 437
  Talent Agencies 437
  Theatrical Trailers 440
  Video 614
7th Level 418
Shapiro, Arnold, Prods. 544
Shaw Communications 605
Sherwood Animation 418
Shoot (publication) 456
Showtime Networks, Inc. 603
Shukovsky-English Prods. 544
Sideshow Productions 432
Sierra Leone 676
Sight & Sound Distributors 612
Silverbach-Lazarus Group 544
Silverman, Fred, Co. 544
Singapore 676
Single Frame Films 418
Skellington Productions 418
Slater, Mary Jo, Casting 419
Slovakia 676
Slovenia 676
Smith, Ron, Celebrity Look-Alikes 419
Society of Motion Picture & Television Engineers 466
Somalia 676
Songwriters Guild of America 466
Sony Television Entertainment 522
  Columbia TriStar Television 522
  Columbia TriStar Television Distribution 522
  Columbia TriStar International Television 523
Sony Pictures Imageworks (Animation) 418
Sony Pictures Imageworks (Special Effects) 432
Sound and Recording Services 425
Sound Thinking Music Research 428
Source, The, Stock Footage 434
South Africa 676
Southbay Makeup FX Studios 432
Spain 676
Spalla, Rick, Video Productions 544
Special Effects 429
Special Effects Systems 432
Special Effects Unlimited 432
Spectacor Films 544
Spectak Productions 432
Special Interest Video 612
Spelling Television 544
Spice 603
Splice is Nice 424
Spumco Inc. 418
Sri Lanka 678
Stalmaster, Lynn, & Assocs. 419
Startoons, Inc. 418
State Broadcast Associations 598
Station Representatives 595
Station Representatives Association 466
Stations-U.S. and Territories & Possessions 552
Statistics 17A
Stewart, Sande, Television, Inc. 544
Sticks & Stones 432
Stock-Shot-Film Libraries 433
Stokes/Kohne Associates 432
Streamline Pictures 418
Stock House, The 434
Stribling Productions 418
Studio Productions 432
Studio Wardrobe Department, The 422
Subtitles 437
Suburban Cable TV Co., Inc. 605
Sudan 678
Sullivan Company, The 544
Summit Communications Group Inc. 605
Sunbow Entertainment 544
Sunbow Productions 418
Suncoast Video 612
Suriname 678
Sweden 678
Switzerland 679
Synchronic Studios, Inc. 432
Syncrofim Services, Inc. 424
Syndicated TV Shows 26A
Syria 680

T

T&T Optical Effects 433
TBS 603
TCA Cable TV 605
TCI 605
TCI Cable Advertising 597
T.E.S.T. Kreashens 433
TKR Cable Co. 605
TMS/Yokuichi Corporation 418
TNN/The Nashville Network 603
TNT 603
TV Communications Network 607
TV Guide 456
TV-Rep, Inc. 597
Taffner Entertainment, Ltd. 544
Taiwan 680
Tajikistan 680
Talent and Literary Agencies 437
Talent Agency Inc., The 439
Talking Laser Company, The 433
Tanzania 680
Tape & Editorial Services, Inc. 424
Tape/Disc Business (publication) 456
Tape House, Inc. 424
Target & Response 415
Tatham Euro RSCG 415
Taweel-Loos & Co. Entertainment 418
Technicolor, Inc. 426
Technicreations 433
Tele-Communications, Inc. 605
Tele-Media 605
Telerep, Inc. 597
Telepictures Prods. 545
Television & Cable Factbook 456
Television & Video Almanac (publication) 454
Television Bureau of Advertising 466
Television Companies 508
Television Digest (publication) 456
Television Index (publication) 456
Television Producers & Distributors 528
Television Programs
  Movies & Miniseries, Oct. 1, 1995-Sept. 30, 1996 472
  Movies & Miniseries, 1990-1995 481
  Primetime, 1996-97 .... 22A
  Syndicated Shows 26A
Television Quarterly (publication) 456
Television Stations, US 552
Televisual (publication) 457
Teleworld, Inc. 545
Thailand 680
Theatre Authority, Inc. 466
Theatrical Trailers 440
3M Audio & Video Color Systems Division 424

3-D Video 433
Third Dimension Effects 433
Time Life Home Video 612
Time Warner Cable-Atlanta National Division 606
Time Warner Cable Group 606
Times Mirror Cable Television 606
Title House, Inc. 433
Todd-AO/Chace Preservation Services 426
Todd-AO Digital Images 433
Todd-AO/Editworks 428
Todd-AO Studios 424
Toei Animation Co. Ltd. 418
Togo 680
Toon Makers, Inc. 418
Tooniversal Co, The. 419
Touchstone Home Video (see Buena Vista Home Video)
Touchstone Television 545
Tower Video 612
Trade Publications 454
Trans World Intl. 545
Transvue TV Int'l. 545
Travel Channel, The 603
Triax Communications 606
Tribune Entertainment 545
Tri-Ess Sciences 433
Trinity Broadcasting Network 603
TriStar Television Production 545
Tunisia 680
Turkey 680
Turkmenistan 681
Turner Home Entertainment 611
Turner Intl 546
Turner Feature Animation 419
Turner Network Television (TNT) 603
Turner Program Services 523
Turner Television 523
  International 523
  Program Services 523
  Program Services Distribution & Sales 546
Twentieth Century Fox Television 518
21st Century Digital 433

U

UCLA Film & Television Archive 435
UPA Productions of America 546
UPN (see United Paramount Networks)
US Cable Corp. 606
U.S. Gov't. Film & Media Services 446
U.S. International Trade Commission 448
U.S. Satellite Broadcasting Co., Inc. 607
USA Network 603
UV/WGN 603
UV/WPIX 603
Uganda 681
Ukraine 681
United Arab Emirates 681
United Media 419
United Nations-Media Division 466
United Paramount Networks (UPN)
  Corporate History 511
  Primetime Programs, 1996-97 25A
United Video Cablevision 606
United Video Television 603
Universal Cartoon Studios 419
Universal Facilities Rental 422
Universal Studios Film Library 435
United Talent Agency 439
Universal Television 519
  Universal Television Productions 546
Univision Communications, Inc. 524
Univision Networks 603
Uruguay 681
Uzbekistan 681

V

VH-1 546
Variety (publication) 456
Variety's On Production (publication) 456
Varitel 433
Venezuela 681
Viacom Cable 606
Viacom, Inc. 524
  Cable 606
  International Distribution & Sales 546
  Productions 546
Vide-U Productions 419
Video Agency, The 433
Video Business (publication) 457
Video Dimensions, Inc. 433
Video Dimensions Home Video 612
Video Equipment Manufacturers (see Consumer Electronics)
Video Marketing & Distributing, Inc. 612
Video Monitoring Services of America 427
Video Store Magazine 457
Video Systems Magazine 457
Video Tape Library Ltd. 435
Video Tel 607
Video Week 457
Videocassette Recorders (see Consumer Electronics)
Videography Magazine 457
Videotape (see Film & Video Stock)
Vidmark 611
Vietnam 682
Viewer's Choice 603
Viewpoint Data Labs 433
Visionart 433
Visual Concept Engineering 433
Visual Impulse Productions 433
Voicecaster 419

W

WB Network 527
WEA, Corp. 611
WPIX 603
WSE Films, Inc. 419
WWOR-TV 603
Wald, Jeff, Entertainment 546
Warner Bros. Television 525
  Animation 546
  Corporation & Personnel 525
  Domestic Television 525
  Domestic Television Distribution & Sales 546
  International Television 526
  International Television Distribution & Sales 547
  Pay TV, Cable & Network 526
  Primetime Programs, 1996-97 25A
  Productions 548
  Telepictures Productions 526
  WB Television Network 527
Warner Home Video 611
Wax, Morton D., Public Relations 415
Wax Works/Video Works 612
Weapons Specialists 422
Weather Channel 603
Weiss Global Enterprises 548
West Coast Video Enterprises 612
West Glen Communications 611
Western Communications 606
Western Publishing Co., Inc. 611
Westlake Audio 428
Who's Who 1
Who's Who in Television (publication) 457
Wildfire Ultraviolet Visual Effects 433
Wilshire Court Prods. 548
Wind Dancer Prod. Group 548
Wireless Advantage 607
Wireless Cable International 607
Wireless Cable of Florida 607
Witt-Thomas Prods. 548
Wolf Films, Inc. 548
Wolf, Fred, Films Inc. 548
Wollin Production Services 424
Wolper Organization, The 548
Women in Communications 466
Women in Film 466
Wonderworks, Inc. 433
Worldvision Enterprises 548
Worldwide Intelligence 415
Worldwide Pants, Inc. 550
Worldwide Sports 419
Worldwide Television News 550
Writers & Artists Agency 439
Writers Guild of America 466
  Awards 470
Wunderfilm Design 433

X Y Z

Xaos 433
Y.L.S. Productions 433
Year in Review 13A
Yemen 682
Young, Adam, Inc. 597
Young & Rubicam 415
Yugoslavia 682
ZM Entertainment 550
Zaire 682
Zambia 682
Zen Entertainment 419
Zimbabwe 682

THE YEAR IN REVIEW
TELEVISION, CABLE, VIDEO AND NEW TECHNOLOGIES

1996 started off with the passage of the Telecommunications Act of 1996, a bill that will have wide ranging ramifications for the television, cable and telephone industries. Broadcasters will have access to a portion of the airways reserved for new digital services, but judgement has been reserved on the possible auction of those licenses. Makers of television sets will be required to include a "V-chip" in new televisions, allowing viewers the option of blocking access to material of violent or sexual nature. Companies may now own television stations covering 30 percent of the national population, as compared to the previous limit of 25 percent, and broadcasters are for the first time able to own cable companies. Most cable price regulations in smaller markets were ended, and cable companies and telephone companies will be allowed to merge. Full price deregulation is to be delayed for three years. Certain provisions of the bill regarding the electronic transmission of obscenity and abortion information were immediately challenged by civil libertarian groups and overturned by a federal judicial review panel.

BROADCAST

NBC won the ratings war for the 1995-96 season with a 11.7 overall rating and a 19% audience share. NBC's Thursday night programming block took the top Nielsens with "ER" rated the number one program, followed by the perennial hit "Seinfeld", "Friends" and newcomer "Caroline in the City". ABC came in second with an overall 10.6 rating and an 18% share, CBS third with a 9.6 rating and a 12% share, Fox fourth with a 7.3 rating and a 12% share, and new networks UPN and WB with 3.1/5 and 2.4/4 respectively. Overall, the major networks' ratings were down again, due most probably to cable services and the expanding roles of Fox, UPN and WB. The NBC coverage of the 1996 Summer Olympics, held in Atlanta, completely swamped all the other networks in the ratings.

The 1996 Emmy Awards for primetime again showed NBC's dominance as the top network winning 19 Emmys, cable programmer HBO 14, CBS 12, ABC 9 and FOX 5. Other winners were PBS with three Emmys, Showtime, TNT and TBS with 2 apiece, and WB, AMC, A&E and UPN with one apiece. For the complete Emmy Awards see the Awards section of this book.

Capital Cities/ABC, under the new Disney ownership, has become just plain old ABC again and named Jamie Tarses as president of ABC Entertainment, and Ted Harbert chairman of the network's entertainment division. Previously with NBC, Ms. Tarses was involved with the development of some of that network's top situation comedies.David Hill, formerly president of Fox Sports, was named president and CEO of Fox Television.

Digital television is on the way. Legislative bodies and industry groups spent much of 1996 attempting to hammer out compromises, concessions and concensuses regarding the high tech future of America's favorite medium. Although technologically feasible, digital television will require an enormous number of adjustments to take place, not the least of which will be to convince American consumers that their current television sets will soon be obsolete and need to be replaced with new digital receivers.

The spectrum of the airways that the FCC is proposing to reserve for digital television broadcasting is the frequencies between channels 7 through 51. The FCC proposes to auction off channels 60-69 to the wireless telecommunications industry. Broadcasters want all of the spectrum available for television broadcasting. Although single channel High Definition Television (HDTV) transmissions were the basis for the original plan, it has come to light that as many as four channels of standard-quality digital video broadcasts could be squeezed into these frequencies (multiplexing), with two additional non-video channels (text or other data) carried as well. The FCC has approved a digital standard which would allow broadcasters the choice of a single HDTV channel or a multiplexed signal. On a related note, Washington, D.C area NBC affiliate WRC-4 has been awarded the first HDTV test grant, for an experimental HDTV station to be operated by the Sarnoff Research Center.

Broadcasters have requested that each television station be allotted a second "transitional" channel to facilitate the switchover from the old broadcast standard, with no fees imposed and no time frame specified for the transition period. Some politicians and economists have pointed out that these frequencies are a potentially lucrative source of income and that the broadcasters should be willing to pay for the privilege of using these channels (with some estimating that the licenses could be auctioned off for as high as $70 billion). Broadcasters argue that such an auction could spell the end of free TV. The Clinton administration proposed a strict time frame of ten years for the transition between standard broadcast and any enhanced services, with the original broadcast frequencies to revert back to the government at the end of that period. A separate legislative draft proposes that broadcasters be required to pay refundable annual "transition" fees, based on the market value of the digital license, into a non-interest bearing escrow account to reserve their slots in the digital broadcast spectrum. If the transition to digital is accomplished within the allotted time frame, the transition fees will be refunded. In late June, the House and Senate majority leadership demanded that the FCC begin allotting the transitional licenses. The National Association of Broadcasters and proponents of the free allocation plan claim that it is absolutely necessary that broadcasters be given the green light so that consumer electronics manufacturers will feel confident enough to begin developing the new hardware that digital television will require.

In a late development, a group of software and computer companies including Microsoft, Apple and Dreamworks SKG challenged the technical standards for video developed for digital television, claiming that the proposed standards essentially froze out potential computer applications.

In order to head off a government-imposed rating system, the four major networks began developing a voluntary ratings system of their own. Executives from all major broadcasters, the National Association of

Broadcasters and the National Cable Television Association met with President Clinton to discuss the ratings plan, which will not take effect until January 1997. Jack Valenti of the MPAA, who has had experience with ratings systems with the CARA program, volunteered to help broadcasters come up with a plan. According to the early discussions, programs will be rated by the program distributors rather than a central ratings board and these ratings will trigger the V-chip by means not yet specified. Critics of the plan suggest that programs rated to show adult content, sex or violence will lose advertising dollars and that producers, leery of such financial risk, will be less likely to produce innovative programming. A Canadian experiment in the electronic blockage of rated programs blocks only those portions of the programs which are rated as objectionable, not the entire programs. Canadian broadcasters have also requested that any ratings be applicable to Canadian programming as well, so as not to develop conflicting standards.

The FCC has begun the process of mandating the broadcasting of educational children's programming. FCC Commissioner Reed Hundt has proposed a minimum of three hours per network per week. As usual, broadcasters balked, maintaining that the programs being aired at the current time are sufficiently educational and that government intrusion into programming decisions is unwarranted.

Television stations changed hands at an amazing rate in 1996, most probably as a direct result of the Telecommunications Act's ownership provisions. In late July, Rupert Murdoch's News Corporation, parent company of Fox Broadcasting, purchased station owner and syndicator New World Entertainment. The day the deal was announced, New World President Brandon Tartikoff tendered his resignation. This deal gives Fox, Inc. an additional 10 stations, bringing its total owned and operated station count to 22. The Tribune Company purchased 6 stations from Renaissance Communications in a deal estimated at $1.1 billion .Raycom Media purchased 7 stations owned by Aflac Inc. and agreed to acquire Ellis Communications, owner of 12 stations. In late September, the A. H. Belo Corporation arranged to purchase the Providence Journal, whose 9 stations combined with Belo's 6 TV stations make Belo the 10th largest station owner in the U.S.

In advertising, 1995 spot advertising was up 5% over 1994. Network advertising was up 2%, with syndication down 5%, and local advertising was up by 1%.

A study conducted by the Pew Research Center for the People and the Media found that 42% percent of Americans surveyed watch the networks' news broadcasts on a regular basis, down 5% from a year ago. The same study shows that among Americans under 30, only 22% watch the same network news. Some of the decline may be due to competition from cable news services such as CNN.

CABLE

NBC and Microsoft launched a 24-hour news cable channel, MSNBC on July 15, 1996, which was swapped in for the America's Talking channel (some cable carriers balked at the exchange until NBC threatened to pull all NBC programming from offending systems). MSNBC will reach at least 21 million households and is being carried over the Internet simultaneously. ABC, which had plans for a similar service, originally postponed any developments, then announced a late 1996 launch date. Fox, also planning a 24-hour news channel, reportedly offered to pay cable system operators $10 per subscriber to carry its news channel and entered into a stock-swap deal with TCI which would supply Fox's news channel to TCI's estimated 10 million subscribers in exchange for a 20% stake in the channel. In the same vein, Westinghouse Electric, the parent company of CBS, acquired the 24-hour Spanish-language news service Telenoticias in June. This is the network's first venture into the cable market. It will also position CBS strategically for a move into the potentially lucrative Latin American market. Other start-up cable channels, such as The Love Channel and The Animal Channel, are experiencing difficulties being allotted channels on cable systems. All of these problems are due to the lack of available channel slots on most cable systems, many of which have 70 or fewer channels available, most of which are filled by existing basic services, profitable premium and pay-per-view services, local broadcast channels and required programming. The advent of digital cable boxes, with channel capabilities in the multiple hundreds, in late 1996 may help alleviate this problem. TCI, Cox and Comcast will be the first national cable carriers to offer these converters in limited markets. In addition, third party vendors plan to offer digital converters with enhanced programming features. However, many in the industry believe that a large proportion of the newly available slots will be allotted to lucrative pay-per-view services. As if to illustrate this, Request Television, the nation's largest PPV supplier, will add 30 new PPV channels to its current 5.

In related cable news, Time Warner Cable in New York came under fire (and investigation) for its refusal to carry the new Fox News Channel. The mayor of New York, Rudolph Giuliani, offered to allow the cable system to replace one of the city's public access channels with the Fox channel, but the cable operator refused. The city then began retransmitting the new channel commercial free as an "educational" service on one of four municipal channels. Bloomberg News, another cable news channel not carried by Time Warner in New York, immediately requested (and got) similar retransmission. Critics of these actions included political opponents who claimed that the mayor's actions were intended only to curry favor with a major political supporter (Fox News is owned by Rupert Murdoch's News Corp., which also owns The New York Post, one of the major tabloids in New York and an editorial supporter of Giuliani, and local broadcaster WNYW) and members of the National Television Cable Association who criticized the deal as an attempt by a government agency to wield editorial influence over a cable franchises choice of programming. The bottom line is that such a dispute points up the lack of enough cable channels in some major markets to support all the new programming choices available.

In mid-July the FTC finally dropped any resistance to the proposed purchase of the Turner Broadcasting System by Time-Warner, after Time-Warner successfully blocked a lawsuit brought by investment partner U.S. West. The major sticking point for FTC approval was the minority share in Turner held by the largest company in the cable industry, Tele-Communications Inc. (TCI), which critics maintained would create a noncompetitive force in the cable industry. To head off any problems caused by this, TCI accepted a 10% nonvoting share in the stock of the combined company. In a related matter of concern for the FTC, the Time Warner cable companies agreed to carry CNN's competition, in the first instance the fledgling 24-hour news channel MSNBC, forestalling any claims of noncompetitive programming. Ted Turner, chairman of Turner was named to head HBO, CNN and other Time Warner/Turner cable networks. Shareholder approval of the merger came October 10, 1996. This merger has made Time-Warner the world's biggest entertainment company.

MCA disputed the launch of Viacom's new cable channel, TV Land, saying that the joint development deal regarding the USA Network between the two companies precluded the development of any new cable channels by either without the assent of the other. Viacom responded that the new service was merely a spin-off of Nickelodeon's Nick at Nite programming. In related news, Viacom's plans to spinoff its cable operations to TCI were approved by the IRS and the sale was finalized at an estimated price of $2.3 billion.

The WB Network, which is having a difficult time getting its programming into distribution around the country, has developed a system by which local cable operators can carry WB programming and insert their own ads. A hardware device allows stored digitized commercials to be synchronized with the transmission of WB signals. The FCC adopted new rules allowing telephone companies to begin offering television programming (Open Video Systems or OVS).

Cable customers were hit with large basic rate increases in the first quarter of 1996, averaging 9% among the top 5 cable corporations, with a 13% increase being imposed by TCI, the nation's largest cable provider.

In late February, the Supreme Court agreed to review the 1992 cable "must-carry" rule, a provision of the Cable Television Consumer Protection and Competition Act that requires cable television companies to carry local broadcast stations. In early October, a skeptical Court began hearing arguments. Several of the justices seemed to question broadcasters' assertion that cable systems function as a "gate-keeper" of the broadcast spectrum, and noted that since the inception of cable only 31 broadcasters out of 1600 had closed up shop. No final decision has been reached as of October 8th. Provisions of the new Telecommunications Act require that providers of adult programming completely scramble both video and audio signals so that they cannot be viewed or heard by minors. Playboy Enterprises has estimated that upgrading the scrambling technology to satisfy these requirements will cost nearly $5 million. In June, the Supreme Court ruled that cable operators could exercise "editorial" control over which programs could appear on the public access and leased-time access channels (both of which cable operators are required to carry), but disallowed the requirement for scrambling the signals of programming deemed "indecent".

SATELLITE BROADCASTING

Although direct satellite broadcasts are currently received by only a small percentage of television households satellite dishes are being touted by advertisers as an alternative to traditional cable services and consumer acceptance is growing. DirecTV is the nation's largest DBS provider, with 1.5 million subscribers, followed closely by Primestar and EchoStar. AT&T acquired a 2.5% share in DirecTV and began offering a 175-channel satellite service to its customers and satellite dishes through retail outlets such as The Sharper Image and Tower Records. MCI & Rupert Murdoch's News Corporation agreed to jointly develop a satellite broadcasting service, to be named American Sky Broadcasting (or ASkyB), and a telephone and data transmission service, to be named SkyMCI. Service should first be available in the Fall of 1997. The News Corporation also owns a 40 percent share in the

European satellite service British Sky Broadcasting (or BSkyB). Cable giant TCI created a separate corporation for its DBS company PrimeStar Partners., which will go public in the fourth quarter of 1996. Primestar boasts some 1.2 million subscribers and 100 channels. However, the FCC denied an application by TCI to use Canadian satellites to broadcast to American households, ostensibly for satellite licensing problems, but also citing the Canadian government's restrictive quotas on American programming.

If plans by the major media companies in Europe continue, the entire continental European Union will be served by digital satellite broadcasts in the next year, putting the E.U. ahead of of the U.S. in digital TV. (For more on the European plan, see the World Market section of this book.)

VIDEO

Bill Fields, former chief executive at Wal-Mart stores was hired as president of Blockbuster Video, a subsidiary of Viacom .It was estimated that a third of all of Viacom's income would come from Blockbuster. Golden Book Video purchased the family program library of Broadway Video Entertainment.

Looking forward to a digital future, Jack Valenti of the MPAA and Gary Shapiro of CEMA asked Congress to pass legislation that would preserve the rights of consumers to make recordings of broadcast, basic cable and certain pay-TV programs for their own use while protecting copyright holders by restricting home taping of pay-per-view programs and prerecorded media.

The roll-out of the new video platform, the DVD (Digital Video Disk) is scheduled for late 1996. Although the MPAA and CEMA have approved copyright protections and standards for this new medium, both the Recording Industry Association of America and the software industry's Information Technologies Industry Council have objected to certain of the provisions The current standard for the DVD calls for a single-sided disk that should be able to store nearly 4.7 gigabytes of information (the equivalent of one 133 minute movie) with two layers of information storage material and with a playback rate of an astounding 11 million bits of information per second that would partially replace the standard VHS videocassette and CD-ROM, and quite possibly the audio CD (priority has been given to the development of DVD playback machines which will allow the playback of current CDs). The two-layer (two-substrate) process will allow a much denser packing of data onto the disks, and improved lasers with smaller wavelengths will allow the encoding of data into smaller physical areas on the substrates. In order for movies to be stored on the DVD, all visual and audio data must be compressed. A variable-rate compression system called MPEG2 (the acronym stands for Motion Picture Engineering Group) will be utilized, allowing the playback of the film at different rates of data density according to the complexity of the scene without any degradation of the image and will allow the user to choose between a picture in the standard TV aspect ration of 4:3 or in the letterbox format of 16:9. Dolby AC-3 has been chosen as the sound standard for the DVD and will allow CD-quality audio playback. Initially, DVD players will retail in the high end of the consumer component price range (ranging between $700 to $1200), although prices are expected to drop within several years. DVD recorders and DVD-RAM (an erasable medium) are due by 1998. If the platform gains widespread acceptance, the implications for all of the facets of information technology are incredible. Future versions of the DVD could allow entire written libraries to be stored on one disk, and a DVD-RAM drive could be used across the entire spectrum of consumer electronic equipment, from TV, to audio, to game systems and to home computers. An important question remains whether consumers will embrace the new platform, and it may be useful to remember that the audio industry has attempted to introduce two new standard platforms in recent years, the MiniDisc and the DCC, neither of which has met with widespread consumer acceptance. Manufacturers planned to begin offering the DVD player for sale in the Fall of 1996, even though no movies were yet available.

NEW TECHNOLOGIES

The Telecommunications Bill of 1996 passed in February promised stiff regulations on material containing obscenity distributed on the Internet. A provision of the bill based on the 1873 Comstock Act would also prohibit the distribution of abortion information. These provisions were overturned by a Federal appellate court. The Encrypted Communications Privacy Act of 1996 outlines the standards by which electronic privacy and security can be assured. Without such encryption, financial services are unlikely to be appropriate for the Internet and the World Wide Web, and copyright protection cannot be applied. However, the Clinton administration insists that a "back door" escrow decryption key to such encryption technology be provided to law enforcement. Industry professionals claim that such technology will not be saleable overseas.

Germany restricted access to Internet sites featuring sexual material and Neo-Nazism, forcing American company Compuserve to block access to such areas for the entire German nation. In late February, H & R Block spun off its consumer on-line service, Compuserve. IBM and Sears, Roebuck & Company sold the on-line service Prodigy to a team of Prodigy managers and an investment company headed by former Viacom executive, Edward Bennett. In early March AT & T offered its customers low cost access to the Internet and World Wide Web, with MCI quickly following suit. However, with the proliferation of low-cost and/or flat rate Internet service providers (ISPs), commercial on-line services are finding it difficult to hold on to customers. America Online announced a discount for heavy users in late June to stem the erosion of its customer base. Some cable companies are entering the ISP business, albeit in a limited way. Both Time Warner and TCI cable companies have offered regional customers such service. PBS entered a joint venture with the Williams Companies to provide business education via the Internet. The planned venture will be called The Business Channel. In early August, a software failure closed down the online giant America On-Line for 19 hours.

Despite the commercial success of the Internet and the World Wide Web, even Bill Gates of Microsoft conceded that it was unlikely that full length films would be available via the Internet in the near future.

A Nielsen Media Research/ Commercenet report estimating Internet usage at 22 million Americans, 16 or older, was disputed by a number of academics, who suggested that Internet traffic was perhaps 20-25% lower than Nielsen had originally suggested. Nielsen's revised report shows that it is still apparent that nearly 20 million Americans utilize these new electronic means of communications regularly.

Sun Microsystems developed a prototype of a dedicated Internet access computer, planned to retail at less than $500. Oracle Systems also plans to market such a device. These stripped-down machines would have no internal hard drive, very little memory and restricted operating software, but would feature state-of-the-art networking capabilities. Software for these machines would be downloaded from the Internet or a local host computer. Microsoft introduced a new operating system, Windows CE, for communications, entertainment and portable computing devices.

Game industry giant Acclaim announced in April that they would no longer be developing cartridge-based games, citing the success of CD-based game titles. On the same front, Nintendo delayed the launch of its long-awaited 64- bit game player until September of 1996. The Sony PlayStation became the best-selling game system on the market, and a mid-year price reduction could assure the platform's dominance through the 1996 holiday season. Perhaps due to the growing predominance of the PlayStation, Sega's sales of its 32-bit game machine have been disappointing and Sega's chief executive Thomas J. Kalinske resigned. The 3DO game player neared the end of its life cycle and 3DO announced that they would focus on software production for other platforms.Increased competition for the big 3 video game manufacturers may come from multiple player games played on the Internet. Several game systems already feature modems.for this purpose and the Apple Pippin developed for the Japanese market can function both as a low-cost Internet access device and a game playing platform.

— JIM MOSER

STATISTICS

TELEVISION USAGE

	Total U.S. Households	TV Households	% with TV
1970	61,410,000	58,500,000	95.3
1980	77,900,000	76,300,000	97.9
1990	93,760,000	92,100,000	98.2
1991	94,800,000	93,100,000	98.2
1992	93,680,000	92,100,000	98.3
1993	94,710,000	93,100,000	98.3
1994	95,860,000	94,200,000	98.3
1995	97,060,000	95,400,000	98.3
1996	97,540,000	95,900,000	98.3

TELEVISION SETS

	In Home	Avg. # Sets Per Household	Avg. # Sets Per Multi-Set Household
1970	81,040,000	1.39	2.20
1980	128,190,000	1.68	2.36
1990	193,320,000	2.10	2.68
1991	193,200,000	2.08	2.67
1992	192,480,000	2.09	2.67
1993	200,565,000	2.15	2.72
1994	211,443,000	2.24	2.77
1995	217,067,000	2.28	2.80
1996	222,753,000	2.32	2.82

COLOR TV & MULTI-SET HOUSEHOLDS

	Color TV Households	%	Multi-Set Households	%
1970	20,910,000	35.7	18,840,000	32.2
1980	63,350,000	83.0	38,260,000	50.1
1985	77,660,000	93.2	48,220,000	56.8
1990	90,070,000	97.8	60,140,000	65.3
1991	91,300,000	98.3	60,040,000	64.5
1992	90,810,000	98.6	59,990,000	65.1
1993	91,520,000	98.3	62,560,000	67.2
1994	93,260,000	99.0	66,130,000	70.2
1995	94,446,000	99.0	67,639,000	70.9
1996	95,230,000	99.3	69,720,000	72.7

CABLE & VCR

	Cable Households	%	Pay Cable Households	%	VCR Households	%
1970	3,900,000	6.7	—	—	—	—
1980	15,200,000	19.9	5,200,000	6.8	840,000	1.1
1985	36,340,000	42.8	21,840,000	25.7	17,744,000	20.9
1990	51,900,000	56.4	27,120,000	29.4	63,181,000	68.6
1991	54,860,000	58.9	27,040,000	29.0	66,939,000	71.9
1992	55,490,000	60.2	25,990,000	28.2	69,075,000	75.0
1993	57,200,000	61.4	25,850,000	27.8	71,780,000	77.1
1994	58.750,000	62.4	26,070,000	27.7	74,420,000	79.0
1995	60,460,000	63.4	27,100,000	28.4	77,270,000	81.0
1996	62,580,000	65.3	30.360.000	31.7	78,830,000	82.2

TIME SPENT VIEWING

	1970	1980	1990	1993	1994	1995
Hours Viewing Television	5:56	6:36	6:53	7:13	7:16	7:17

PER-PERSON PER DAY ANNUAL AVERAGES

	1990	1991	1992	1993	1994	1995
Men	3:51	4:01	4:02	4:04	4:02	4:02
Women	4:28	4:36	4:40	4:41	4:39	4:38
Teens	3:15	3:16	3:10	3:07	3:05	3:02
Children	3:18	3:11	3:08	3:07	3:06	3:07

TV EXPENDITURES

TOTAL ADVERTISING VOLUME
(millions of dollars)

	1994	% of total	1995	% of total
TELEVISION	$34,167	22.8	$36,246	22.5
Newspapers	34,356	22.9	36,317	22.6
Magazines	7,916	5.3	8,580	5.3
Radio	10,529	7.0	11,338	7.0
Business Papers	3,358	2.2	3,559	2.2
All Others	54,820	39.8	59,689	40.4
Total Major Media	$150,030	100.0	160,920	100.0

TELEVISION ADVERTISING VOLUME
(millions of dollars)

	1993	% of total	1994	% of total	1995	% of total
Network TV	10,209	7.8	10.942	7.3	11,600	7.2
Spot TV	7,800	5.8	8,993	6.0	9,119	5.7
Nat. Synd*	1,576	1.0	1,734	1.2	2,016	1.2
Local TV	8,435	6.14	9,464	6.3	9,985	6.2
Cable Nets	1,970	1.3	2,321	1.5	2,670	1.7
Local Cable	594	.4	713	.5	856	.5
TELEVISION TOTAL	138,080	100.0	150,030	100.0	160,920	100.0

* includes WB & UPN for 1995

STATION TIME SALES
(millions of dollars)

	1992	1993	1994	1995
Network Compensation	375.0	370.0	396.0	632.0
Spot	6,750.0	6,973.0	8,040.0	8,152.0
Local	6,745.0	7,102.0	7,968.0	8,406.0
Total	13,870.0	14,445.0	16,008.0	17,190.0

LENGTH OF COMMERCIALS

Non-Network

Commercial Length	1991	1992	1993	1994
10 seconds	4.2%	4.2%	3.6%	3.4%
15 seconds	6.4	8.2	8.0	8.3
20 seconds	0.3	0.4	0.3	0.3
30 seconds	84.1	82.6	84.2	84.3
45 seconds	0.1	0.1	0.1	0.1
60 seconds	3.5	3.5	3.2	3.0
90 sec. or more	1.4	0.9	0.6	0.6

Network

Commercial Length	1991	1992	1993	1994
10 seconds	0.1%	0.1%	0.1%	0.1%
15 seconds	33.6	31.9	31.2	30.2
20 seconds	0.8	0.9	0.8	0.9
30 seconds	62.5	63.1	65.0	65.6
45 seconds	0.9	1.0	0.4	0.6
60 seconds	1.7	1.7	1.3	1.5
90 sec. or more	0.4	1.3	1.2	1.1

COMMERCIAL TELEVISION STATIONS

	VHF	UHF	TOTAL
1970	501	176	677
1980	516	218	734
1990	547	545	14,092
1991	547	551	1,098
1992	551	567	1,118
1993	552	585	1,137
1994	561	584	1,145
1995	562	599	1,163
1996	554	620	1,174

NETWORK TELEVISION COST TRENDS

Daytime (M-F)—Average Program

	# of Households Viewing Per Average Min.	Cost Per 30 Sec.	Cost Per 1000 Homes
1970	4,880,000	$4,000	$0.82
1975	5,550,000	5,200	0.94
1980	5,530,000	10,000	1.81
1985	5,460,000	14,700	2.69
1990	4,340,000	10,700	2.46
1991	4,350,000	10,400	2.39
1992	4,210,000	10,400	2.45
1993	4,420,000	11,100	2.50
1994	4,420,000	13,800	3.12

Nightime (M-S)—Average Program

	# of Households Viewing Per Average Min.	Cost Per 30 Sec.	Cost Per 1000 Homes
1970	11,430,000	$24,000	$2.10
1975	13,500,000	32,200	2.39
1980	15,240,000	57,900	3.79
1985	14,510,000	94,700	6.52
1990	12,540,000	122,200	9.74
1991	11,810,000	106,400	9.00
1992	12,020,000	93,700	7.79
1993	11,070,000	92,700	8.37
1994	12,710,000	97,200	7.64

Early Evening News (M-F)—Average Program

	# of Households Viewing Per Average Min.	Cost Per 30 Sec.	Cost Per 1000 Homes
1975	9,790,000	$12,400	$1.27
1980	11,490,000	25,700	2.23
1985	10,870,000	42,800	3.94
1990	9,570,000	51,800	5.41
1991	10,180,000	47,400	4.65
1992	9,420,000	43,400	4.61
1993	9,870,000	46,300	4.69
1994	10,600,000	47,200	4.45

Late Evening (M-F)—Average Program

	# of Households Viewing Per Average Min.	Cost Per 30 Sec.	Cost Per 1000 Homes
1975	5,170,000	$8,300	$1.61
1980	4,420,000	11,900	2.70
1985	4,260,000	14,700	3.45
1990	3,080,000	21,500	6.97
1991	2,970,000	16,500	5.57
1992	2,780,000	13,200	4.75
1993	2,970,000	15,800	5.31
1994	4,230,000	24,100	5.70

Source for all figures: TV Bureau of Advertising

NIELSEN RATINGS
TOP PRIMETIME PROGRAMS

The rating represents the percentage of 95.4 million tv households. The share is the percentage of tv sets in use turned to a show. Series which appear a second time on the list followed by the number 2 refer to shows which played more than once during the same weekly period. Ratings are for the 36 week season, 9/18/95 to 5/22/96.

		Network	Rating/Share			Network	Rating/Share
1	ER	NBC	22.0/36	50	The Pursuit of Happiness	NBC	10.0/15
2	Seinfeld	NBC	21.2/33	50	The X-Files	FOX	10.0/17
3	Friends	NBC	18.7/30	53	Beverly Hills, 90210	FOX	9.8/16
4	Caroline In the City	NBC	17.9/28	54	Step by Step	ABC	9.7/17
5	NFL Monday Night Football	ABC	17.1/29	55	CBS Tuesday Movie	CBS	9.6/15
6	Single Guy	NBC	16.7/26	55	Dr. Quinn, Medicine Woman	CBS	9.6/18
7	Home Improvement	ABC	16.2/25	55	The Fresh Prince of Bel Air	NBC	9.6/15
8	Boston Common	NBC	15.6/26	58	Murder, She Wrote	CBS	9.5/15
9	60 Minutes	CBS	14.2/24	59	In The House	NBC	9.4/17
10	NYPD Blue	ABC	14.1/24	59	Unsolved Mysteries	NBC	9.4/17
11	Frasier	NBC	13.6/21	61	Faculty	ABC	9.3/15
11	20/20	ABC	13.6/24	61	Hangin' With Mr. Cooper	ABC	9.3/16
13	Grace Under Fire	ABC	13.2/21	61	Melrose Place	FOX	9.3/14
14	Coach	ABC	12.9/20	64	Buddies	ABC	9.1/15
14	NBC Monday Night Movies	NBC	12.9/20	65	Almost Perfect	CBS	9.0/14
16	Roseanne	ABC	12.5/20	66	Good Company	CBS	8.9/14
17	The Nanny	CBS	12.4/20	66	Homicide: Life on the Street	NBC	8.9/16
18	Murphy Brown	CBS	12.3/18	66	Murder One	ABC	8.9/15
19	Primetime Live	ABC	12.3/21	69	Diagnosis Murder	CBS	8.8/15
20	Walker, Texas Ranger	CBS	12.3/22	70	Amer. Funniest Home Videos	ABC	8.7/15
21	Champs	ABC	12.2/18	70	CBS Wednesday Movie	CBS	8.7/15
21	NBC Sunday Night Movie	NBC	12.2/20	70	Dave's World	CBS	8.7/14
23	3rd Rock From the Sun	NBC	12.1/20	73	Nash Bridges	CBS	8.6/16
24	Chicago Hope	CBS	11.9/20	74	Bonnie	CBS	8.4/14
25	Can't Hurry Love	CBS	11.4/17	74	High Incident	ABC	8.4/13
25	CBS Sunday Movie	CBS	11.4/18	74	Muppets Tonight	ABC	8.4/15
25	Law and Order	NBC	11.4/20	77	Simpsons	FOX	8.3/13
25	Naked Truth	ABC	11.4/18	78	Married With Children	FOX	8.2/13
29	Amer. Funniest Home Videos 2	ABC	11.3/19	79	Jag	NBC	8.1/14
29	Dateline NBC/Tues.	NBC	11.3/19	79	Second Noah	ABC	8.1/13
29	Dateline NBC/Wed.	NBC	11.3/18	81	Aliens in the Family	ABC	8.0/14
32	The Dana Carvey Show	ABC	11.2/18	82	The Client	CBS	7.9/13
32	Fox NFL Sunday—Post Gun 2	FOX	11.2/20	83	48 Hours	CBS	7.8/13
34	Touched By An Angel	CBS	11.1/20	84	ABC Thursday Night Movie	ABC	7.7/12
35	Wings	NBC	11.0/18	84	Rescue: 911	CBS	7.7/12
36	If Not For You	CBS	10.9/16	86	The Louie Show	CBS	7.6/12
37	Mad About You	NBC	10.8/17	87	Bless This House	CBS	7.5/12
38	Hudson Street	ABC	10.7/17	87	Day One	ABC	7.5/12
39	ABC Sunday Night Movie	ABC	10.6/17	87	Matt Waters	CBS	7.5/11
39	Ellen	ABC	10.6/18	90	Before They Were Stars	ABC	7.4/12
39	News Radio	NBC	10.6/16	90	Dateline NBC/Sun.	NBC	7.4/14
42	Family Matters	ABC	10.5/19	90	World's Funniest Videos	ABC	7.4/12
42	The John Larroquette Show	NBC	10.5/17	93	Cops 2	FOX	7.3/13
44	Dateline NBC/Fri.	NBC	10.3/18	94	Due South	CBS	7.2/13
44	Lois & Clark	ABC	10.3/16	94	Marshal	ABC	7.2/12
46	ABC Monday Night Movie	ABC	10.2/16	96	The Jeff Foxworthy Show	ABC	7.1/13
46	High Society	CBS	10.2/15	96	Party of Five	FOX	7.1/11
48	Boy Meets World	ABC	10.1/18	98	Fox Tuesday Night Movie	FOX	7.0/11
48	The Drew Carey Show	ABC	10.1/16	98	Hope & Gloria	NBC	7.0/12
50	Cybill	CBS	10.0/16	98	Picket Fences	CBS	7.0/12

1996–1997
PRIMETIME PROGRAMS

ABC, CBS, FOX, NBC, UPN, WB

1996-97 PRIME TIME SHOWS

ABC-TV

Series Title	Day	Hr.	Mins.	Supplier	Production Principals	Cast Regulars & Semi-Regulars
America's Funniest Home Videos	Sun	7:00	60	Vin Di Bona Prods.	Vin Di Bona	Bob Saget
Boy Meets World	Fri	9:30	30	Touchstone TV/Michael Jacobs Prods.	Michael Jacobs, David Kendall	Ben Savage, Will Friedle, William Daniels, William Russ, Betsy Randle
The Drew Carey Show	Wed	9:30	30	Warner Bros. TV	Bruce Helford, Clay Graham	Drew Carey, Ryan Stiles, Christa Miller, Diedrich Bader.
Clueless	Fri	9:00	30	Paramount Network TV	Amy Heckerling, Pamela Pettler Twink Caplan	Stacey Dash, Rachel Blanchard, Elisa Donovan
Coach	Sat	9:00	30	Universal TV & Bungalow 78 Prods.	Barry Kemp, Craig T. Nelson Brad Johnson, Mark Ganzel	Craig T. Nelson, Jerry Van Dyke, Shelley Fabares, Clare Carey, Bill Fagerbakke, Ken Kimmins, Katherine Helmond
Common Law	Sat	9:30	30	Witt-Thomas Prods./ Warner Bros. TV	Paul Junger Witt, Tony Thomas Gary Levine, Rob LaZebnik	Greg Giraldo, Megyn Price, Gregory Sierra
Dangerous Minds	Mon	8:00	60	Touchstone TV	Jerry Bruckheimer, Ronald Bass Diane Frolov, Andrew Schneider	Annie Potts
Ellen	Wed	8:00	30	Touchstone TV/Black Marlens Co.	Dava Savel, Mark Driscoll, Vic Kaplan, Tracy Newman	Ellen DeGeneres, Joely Fisher, Arye Gross, Dave Higgins
Family Matters	Fri	8:00	30	Warner Bros. TV/Miller-Boyett Prods./Bickley-Warren Prods.	Thomas L. Miller, Robert L. Boyett, William Bickley, Michael Warren, David W. Duclon	Reginald VelJohnson, JoMarie Payton Noble, Rosetta LeNoire, Darius McCrary, Kellie Shanygne Williams
Grace Under Fire	Wed	9:00	30	Carsey-Werner Prods.	Chuck Lorre, Marcy Carsey, Tom Werner, Caryn Mandabach, Kevin Abbott, Brett Butler	Brett Butler, Casey Sander, Jon Paul Steuer, Kaitlin Cullum, Dylan Sprouse, Cole Sprouse, Tom Poston
High Incident	Tue	8:00	30	DreamWorks TV	Steven Spielberg, Charles Haid Ann Donahue, Art Monterastelli	David Keith, Blair Underwood
Home Improvement	Tue	9:00	30	Touchstone TV/Wind Dancer Prods.	Matt Williams, David McFadzean Charlie Hauck, Carmen Finestra, Elliot Shoenman, Bruce Ferber	Tim Allen, Patricia Richardson, Earl Hindman, Zachery Ty Bryan, Jonathan Taylor Thomas
Life's Work	Tue	8:30	30	Touchstone TV	Warren Bell	Lisa Ann Walter
Lois & Clark: The New Adventure of Superman	Sun	8:00	60	Warner Bros. TV & December 3rd. Prods.	Robert Singer, Brad Buckner Eugenie Ross-Leming	Teri Hatcher, Dean Cain, Lane Smith, Eddie Jones, K Callan, Justin Whalin
Murder One	Tue	9:00	60	Steven Bochco Prods.	Steve Bochco, Charles H. Eglee Michael Fresco, Joe Ann Fogle	Dylan Baker, Daniel Benzali, Barbara Bosson, Patricia Clarkson, John Fleck, Jason Gedrick, Michael Hayden, Stanley Tucci.
NYPD Blue	Tue	10:00	60	Steven Bochco Prods.	Steven Bochco, David Milch, Mark Tinker, Mike Robin	Dennis Franz, Jimmy Smits, James McDaniel, Gail O'Grady, Kim Delaney, Nicholas Turturro, Sharon Lawrence
Primetime Live	Wed	10:00	60	ABC News	Phyllis McGrady	Diane Sawyer, Sam Donaldson, Chris Wallace
Roseanne	Tue	8:00	30	Carsey-Werner Co./Full Moon-High Tide Prods.	Roseanne, Dan Palladino Stacie Lipp, Nancy Steen	Roseanne, John Goodman, Laurie Metcalf, Michael Fishman, Estelle Parsons, Martin Mull.
Relativity	Sat	10:00	60	Bedford Falls Co./ Twentieth Century TV	Marshal Herskovitz, Edward Zwick, Jason Katims	Kimberly Williams, David Conrad
Sabrina, The Teenage Witch	Fri	8:30	30	Viacom Prods.	Paula Hart, Nell Scovell	Melissa Joan Hart
Second Noah	Sat	8:00	60	MT2 Services, Inc./ Long Feather Ent./ New World Ent.	Pamela K. Long	Daniel Hugh Kelly, Betshy Brantley
Spin City	Tue	9:30	30	UBU Prods./ Lottery Hill Dreamworks	Gary David Goldberg	Michael J. Fox
Townies	Wed	8:30	30	Carsey-Werner Prods.	Matthew Carlson, Marcy Carsey, Tom Werner, Caryn Mandabach, Harvey Myman	Molly Ringwald, Jenna Elfman Lauren Graham
Turning Point	Wed	10:00	60	ABC News	Betsy West	Diane Sawyer, Forest Sawyer
20/20	Fri	10:00	60	ABC News	Victor Neufeld	Barbara Walters, Hugh Downs

CBS-TV

Series Title	Day	Hr.	Mins.	Supplier	Production Principals	Cast Regulars & Semi-Regulars
Almost Perfect	Wed	9:00	30	Paramount Network TV/ Levina & Isaacs Prods.	Ken Levine, David Isaacs, Robin Schiff	Nancy Travis, Kevin Kilner, David Clennon
Chicago Hope	Mon	10:00	60	Twentieth Television David E. Kelley Prods.	John Tinker, Bill D'Elia	Adam Arkin, Christine Lahti, Roxanne Hart, Mark Harmon, Hector Elizondo, Peter Berg.
Cosby	Mon	8:00	30	Carsey-Werner Prods./ LLC/Bill Cosby	Dr. Wiliam H. Cosby, Marcy Carsey, Tom Werner, Caryn Mandabach, Peter Tortorici	Bill Cosby, Phylicia Rashad, Doug E. Doug
Cybill	Mon	9:30	30	Carsey-Werner Prods.	Marcy Carsey, Tom Werner, Caryn Mandabach, Jay Daniel, Chuck Lorre, Cybill Shepherd	Cybill Shepherd, Christine Baranski, Tom Wopat, Alan Rosenberg, Alicia Witt, Deedee Pfeiffer
Dave's World	Fri	8:00	30	CBS Entertainment Prods.	Jonathon Axelrod, Harry Anderson James Widdoes, Tim O'Donnell	Harry Anderson, DeLane Matthews, Zane Carney, Andy Ducote, Shadoe Stevens, Meschach Taylor
Diagnosis Murder	Thu	8:00	60	Fred Silverman Co./Dean Hargrove Prods./Viacom	Fred Silverman, Dean Hargrove Dick van Dyke, Tom Chehak	Dick van Dyke
Dr. Quinn, Medicine Woman	Sat	8:00	60	CBS Ent./Sullivan Co.	Beth Sullivan, Carl Binder	Jane Seymour, Joe Lando, Chad Allen, Jessica Bowman, Shawn Toovey, Jonelle Allen
Early Edition	Sat	9:00	60	CBS Prods./Tristar TV	Bob Brush, Ian Abrams Lilah MMcCarthy	Kyle Chandler, Shanesia Davis, Fisher Stevens
Everybody Loves Raymond	Fri	8:30	30	Worldwide Pants/HBO Independent Prods.	Phil Rosenthal, Stu Smiley	Ray Romano, Patricia Heaton, Doris Roberts, Peter Boyle, Brad Garrett
EZ Streets	Wed	10:00	60	Universal TV	Paul Haggis, Mark Harris	Ken Olin, Daniel Rooney
48 Hours	Thu	10:00	60	CBS News	Susan Virinksy	Dan Rather, Harold Dow, Phil Jones, Erin Moriarty, Richard Schlesinger
Ink	Mon	8:00	30	Dreamworks SKG/ Shukovsky English Ent..	Diane English, Jeffrey Lane Ted Danson, Mary Steenburgen	Mary Steeburgen, Ted Danson
Moloney	Thu	9:00	60	Predawn Prods./Three Putt Prods./CBS/TriStar	Ronald Bass, Stephen Kronisch Clifton Campbell	Peter Srauss, Nestor Serrano, Wendell Pierce
Mr. & Mrs. Smith	Fri	9:00	60	Snackbar Ent./BPI & Warner Bros. TV	Kerry Lenhart, John J. Sakmar, Scott Bakula	Scott Bakula, Maria Bello
Murphy Brown	Mon	9:00	30	Warner Bros. TV/ Shukovsky- English Ent.	Bill Diamond, Candice Bergen Rob Bragin, Tom Seeley	Candice Bergen, Faith Ford, Charles Kimbrough, Joe Regalbuto, Grant Shaud, Lily Tomlin
The Nanny	Wed	8:00	30	TriStar TV/Sternin/ Fraser Ink	Robert Sternin, Prudence Fraser, Peter Marc Jacobsen	Fran Drescher, Charles Shaughnessy, Lauren Lane, Nicholle Tom, Madelin Zima
Nash Bridges	Fri	10:00	60	Off Duty Prods.	Carlton Cuse, Don Johnson	Don Johnson, Cheech Marin
Pearl	Wed	8:30	60	Witt-Thomas Prods.	Don Reo, Rhea Perlman, Paul Junger Witt, Tony Thomas	Rhea Perlman, Carol Kane, Malcolm McDowell
Promised Land	Tue	8:00	60	CBS & Moonwater Prods.	Martha Williamson	Gerald McRaney, Wendy Phillips Celeste Holm, Austin O'Brien Sarah Schuab, Eddie Karr
Public Morals	Wed	9:30	30	Steven Bochco Prods.	Jay Tarses	Donal Logue
60 Minutes	Sun	7:00	60	CBS News	Don Hewitt	Mike Wallace, Morley Safer, Ed Bradley, Steve Kroft, Lesley Stahl, Andy Rooney
Touched by an Angel	Sun	8:00	60	CBS & Moonwater Prods.	Martha Williamson	Della Reese, Roma Downey
Walker, Texas Ranger	Sat	10:00	60	Amadea Film Prods.	Chuck Norris, Aaron Norris	Chuck Norris, Clarence Gilyard

Fox

Series Title	Day	Hr.	Mins.	Supplier	Production Principals	Cast Regulars & Semi-Regulars
Beverly Hills 90210	Wed	8:00	60	Spelling TV	Aaron Spelling, E. Duke Vincent, Paul Waigner, Steve Wasserman, Jessica Kelin, Larry Molin	Jason Priestley, Jennie Garth, Ian Ziering, Brian Austin Green Tori Spelling, Tiffani-Amber
Cops	Sat Sat	8:00 8:30	30 30	Foxlab/Barbour/Langley	John Langley	
The Big Deal!	Sun	7:00	60	Stone Stanley Prods. & New World Ent.	David G. Stanley, Scott Stone	Mark DeCarlo
Living Single	Thu	8:30	30	SisterLee Prods./ Warner Bros. TV	Yvette Lee Bowser, Roger S.H. Schulman	Queen Latifah, Kim Fields Freeman, Erika Alexander, John Henton, T.C. Carson
Love and Marriage	Sat	9:30	30	Dorothy Parker Drank Here Prods./TriStar TV	Amy Sherman	Patricia Healy, Tony Denison, Adam Zolotin, Alicia Bergman, Adam Wylie

Series Title	Day	Hr.	Mins.	Supplier	Production Principals	Cast Regulars & Semi-Regulars
Lush Life	Mon	9:30	30	SisterLee Prods./ Warner Bros. TV	Yvette Lee Bowser	Lori Petty, Karyn Parsons
Married...With Children	Sat	9:00	30	Columbia Pictures TV	Pam Eells, Russel Marcus Vince Cheung, Ben Montanio	Ed O'Neill, Katey Sagal, Christina Applegate, David Faustino, Amanda Bearse, Ted McGinley
Martin	Thu	8:00	30	HBO Independent Prods.	Samm-Art Williams, Martin Lawrence, Bentley Kyle Williams	Martin Lawrence, Tisha Campbell, Tichina Arnold, Thomas Mikal Ford, Carl Payne
Melrose Place	Mon	8:00	60	Spelling TV	Aaron Spelling, Frank South E. Duke Vincent, Charles Pratt	Josie Bissett, Thomas Calabro, Heather Locklear, Marcia Cross, Grant Show, Andrew Shue
Millenium	Fri	9:00	60	20th Century Fox TV &	Chris Carter, Jorge Zamacona John P. Kousakis	Lance Henriksen, Megan Gallagher, Bill Smitrovich
Ned and Stacey	Sun	9:30	30	Hanley Prods./TriStar TV	Michael Weithorn	Thomas Haden Church, Debra Messing
New York Undercover	Thu	9:00	60	Wolf Films/Universal TV	Dick Wolf, Steve Smith	Malik Yoba, Patti D'Arbanville-Quinn, Michael DeLorenzo, Lauren Velez
Party Girl	Mon	9:00	30	Subway Prods. & Warner Bros. TV	Efrem Seeger	John Cameron, Christine Taylor Merrin Dungey
Party of Five	Wed	9:00	60	Columbia Pictures TV	Amy Lippman, Christopher Keyser, Ken Topolsky	Matthew Fox, Neve Campbell, Scott Wolf, Lacey Chabert, Taylor Porter, Paula Devicq
The Simpsons	Sun	8:00	30	Gracie Films/Twentieth TV	James L. Brooks, Matt Groening, Bill Oakley	Dan Castellaneta, Julie Kavner, Nancy Cartwright, Harry Shearer
Sliders	Fri	8:00	60	Universal TV		Jerry O'Connell, Sabrina Lloyd
The X-Files	Sun	9:00	60	FBC/ Twentieth TV	Chris Carter, R.W. Goodwin Howard Gordon	David Duchovny, Gillian Anderson

NBC-TV

Series Title	Day	Hr.	Mins.	Supplier	Production Principals	Cast Regulars & Semi-Regulars
Boston Common	Sun	8:30	30	Castle Rock TV & Komut Entertainment	David Kohan, Max Mutchnik	Anthony Clark, Hedy Burress Traylor Howard, Steve Paymer Tasha Smith, Vincent Ventresca
Caroline in the City	Tue	9:30	30	CBS Entertainment/ Barron/Pennette	Fred Barron, Marco Pennette,	Lea Thompson, Eric Lutes, Amy Pietz, Dotti Dartland, Malcomb Gets
Dark Skies	Sat	8:00	60	Bryce Zable Prods. & BetaFilm & Columbia	James D. Parriott, Bryce Zabel	Eric Close, Megan Ward, J.T. Walsh
Dateline NBC	Tue Fri Sun	10:00 9:00 7:00	60 60 60	NBC News	Neal Shapiro	Jane Pauley, Stone Phillips, Jon Scott, Deborah Roberts
ER	Thu	10:00	60	Constant c Prods./Amblin TV/Warner Bros. TV	Michael Crichton, John Wells Lydia Woodard, Carol Flint	Anthony Edwards, George Clooney, Sherry Stringfield, Noah Wyle, Eriq La Salle, Julianna Margulies
Frasier	Tue	9:00	30	Grub Street Prods./ Paramount TV	David Angell, Peter Casey, David Lee, Christopher Lloyd	Kelsey Grammer, John Mahoney, David Hyde Pierce, Peri Gilpin, Jane Leeves
Friends	Thu	8:00	30	Bright-Kauffman-Crane Prods./Warner Bros. TV	Kevin S. Bright, Marta Kauffman, David Crane Michael Borkow	Jennifer Aniston, Courteney Cox, Lisa Kudrow, Matt LeBlanc, Matthew Perry, David Schwimmer
The Jeff Foxworthy Show	Mon	8:00	30	Brillstein-Grey Comm.	Bernie Brillstein, Brad Grey Tom Anderson, Maxine Lapidus	Jeff Foxworthy
Homicide: Life on the Street	Fri	10:00	60	NBC Prods./Baltimore Pictures/FATIMA Prods./ MCEG Sterling Inc.	Barry Levinson, Tom Fontana	Richard Belzer, Andre Braugher, Clark Johnson, Yaphett Kotto, Kyle Secor, Melissa Leo, Reed Diamond
The John Larroquette Show	Tue	8:30	30	Witt-Thomas Prods.	Paul Junger Witt, Tony Thomas, Don Reo, John Larroquette	John Larroquette, Alison La Placa, Liz Torres, Gigi Rice, Chi McBride, Daryl "Chill" McDaniel, Lenny Clarke
Law & Order	Wed	10:00	60	Wolf Films/Universal TV	Dick Wolf, Rene Balcer Ed Sherin	Jerry Orbach, Sam Waterston, S. Epatha Merkerson, Jill Hennessy, Benjamin Bratt
Mad About You	Tue	8:00	30	Infront Prod./Nuance Prod./ TriStar TV	Danny Jacobson, Larry Charles Paul Reiser, Richard Day	Paul Reiser, Helen Hunt, Anne Elizabeth Ramsay, Leila Kenzle, John Pankow
Men Behaving Badly	Wed	9:30	30	Carsey-Werner Prods.	Matthew Carlson, Marcy Carsey Tom Werner, Caryn Mandabach	Ron Schneider, Ron Eldard, Justine Bateman
Mr. Rhodes	Mon	8:30	30	NBC Studios &	Mark Brazill, Jennifer Heath Peter Noah, Dave Becky	Tom Rhodes, Farrah Forke, Stephen Toblowsky, Ron Glass
NewsRadio	Wed	9:00	30	Brillstein-Grey Comm.	Paul Simms, Brad Grey, Bernie Brillstein	Dave Foley, Vicki Lewis, Phil Hartman, Stephen Root, Andy Dick, Maura Tierney, Khandi Alexander

Series Title	Day	Hr.	Mins.	Supplier	Production Principals	Cast Regulars & Semi-Regulars
The Pretender	Sat	9:00	60	MTM Entertainment & NBC Studios	Steven Long Mitchell, Tommy Thompson, Craig Van Sickle	Michael T. Weiss, Andrea Parker, Patrick Bauchau
Profiler	Sat	10:00	60	NBC Studios	Ian Sander, Kim Moses, Nancy Miller	Ally Walker, Robet Davi
Seinfeld	Thu	9:00	30	Castle Rock Entertainment	Larry David, George Shapiro, Howard West, Jerry Seinfeld	Jerry Seinfeld, Julia Louis-Dreyfus, Michael Richards, Jason Alexander
The Single Guy	Thu	8:30	30	Castle Rock/NBC Studios	Brad Hall, Sam Weisman Jay Kogen	Jonathan Silverman, Ernest Borgnine, Jessica Hecht, Ming-Na Wen, Joey Slotnick
Something So Right	Tue	8:30	30	Universal TV	Judd Pillot, John Peaslee Bob Tischler	Mel Harris, Jere Burns, Marne Patterson
Suddenly Susan	Thu	9:30	30	Warner Bros. TV	Gary Dontzig, Steven Peterman	Brooke Shields
3rd Rock From the Sun	Sun	8:00	30	Carsey-Werner Prods.	Marcy Carsey, Tom Werner, Caryn Mandabach, Bonnie Turner	John Lithgow, Jane Curtin
Unsolved Mysteries	Fri	8:00	60	Cosgrove/Muerer Prods.	John Cosgrove, Terry Dunn Meurer	Robert Stack
Wings	Wed	8:00	30	Grub Street Prods./ Paramount TV	David Angell, Peter Casey, David Lee, Howard Gewirtz, Mark Reisman, Ian Gurvitz	Tim Daly, Steven Weber, Crystal Bernard, Amy Yasbeck, David Schramm, Tony Shalhoub

UPN

Series Title	Day	Hr.	Mins.	Supplier	Production Principals	Cast Regulars & Semi-Regulars
The Burning Zone	Tue	9:00	60	Universal TV	James D, McAdams, Coleman Luck, Carleton Eastlake	Jefferey Dean Morgan, Tamlyn Tomita, James Black
Goode Behavior	Mon	9:00	30	Seven Mile Rd. Prods. & Paramount Network TV	Brian Pollack, Mert Rich, Bob Illes	Sherman Hemsley, Dorien Wilson
Homeboys in Outer Space	Tue	8:30	30	Sweet Lorraine Prods. & Touchstone TV	Ehrich Van Lowe	Flex, Darryl M. Bell
In The House	Mon	8:00	30	Quincy Jones/David Salzman Ent./NBC	Quincy Jones, David Salzman	LL Cool J, Alfonso Ribiero, Kim Wayans, Maia Campbell
Malcolm & Eddie	Mon	8:30	30	TriStar TV	Kim Weiskopf, Joel Madison	Malcolm-Jamal Warner, Eddie Griffin
Moesha	Tue	8:00	30	Big Ticket TV	Ralph Farquahr, Sara V. Finney Vida Spears	Brandy Norwood, William Allen Young, Marcus T. Paulk
The Sentinel	Wed	8:00	60	Pet Fly Prods. & Paramount Network TV	Danny Bilson, Paul DeMeo	Richard Burgi, Garrett Maggart
Sparks	Mon	9:30	30	MTM TV	Ed Weinberger, Bob Moloney	Robin Givens
Star Trek: Voyager	Wed	9:00	60	Paramount Network TV	Rick Berman, Jeri Taylor	Kate Mulgrew, Robert Beltran, Roxann Dawson, Jennifer Lien, Robert Duncan McNeill

WB

Series Title	Day	Hr.	Mins.	Supplier	Production Principals	Cast Regulars & Semi-Regulars
Brotherly Love	Sun	7:30	30	Witt-Thomas Prods. & Touchstone TV	Paul Junger Witt, Tony Thomas	Joey Lawrence, Andrew Lawrence, Matthew Lawrence
The Jamie Foxx Show	Wed	9:30	30	Warner Bros. TV	Bentley Evans, Marcus King	Jami Foxx, Garret Morris
The Steve Harvey Show	Mon	8:30	30	WB TV & Brillstein/ Grey Comm.	Bernie Brillstein, Brad Grey Winifred Harvey	Steve Harvey, Cedric the Entertainer
Kirk	Sun	7:00	30	Warner Bros. TV	Ross Brown, William Bickley, Susan Fales, Michael Warren	Kirk Cameron, Chelsea Noble, Louis Vanaria, Will Estes, Taylor Fry, Courtland Mead, Debra Mooney
Life With Roger	Sun	9:00	30	Warner Bros. TV	Howard Adler, Bob Griffard, Bob Keyes, Doug Keyes	Michael O'Malley, Maurice Godin
Nick Freno	Wed	8:30	30	Warner Bros. TV	Dennis Rinsler, Marc Warren	Mitch Mulaney
The Parent 'Hood	Mon	8:00	30	Warner Bros. TV	Marc Warren, Dennis Rinsler, Robert Townsend	Robert Townsend, Suzzanne Douglas, Kenny Blank
Savannah	Mon	9:00	60	Cherokee Rose Prods. & Spelling TV	Aaron Spelling, E. Duke Vincent, Jim Stanley, Connie Burge	Robyn Lively, Shannon Sturges, Jamie Luner
Seventh Heaven	Sun	8:00	60	North Shore Prods. &	Aaron Spelling, E. Duke Vincent Brenda Hampton	Stephen Collins, David Gallagher, Catherine Hicks, Barry Watson
Sister, Sister	Wed	8:00	30	Paramount Network TV & dePasse Entertainment	Suzanne de Passe, Brian Pollack Suzanne Coston, Mert Rich	Tim Reid, Jackee Harry, Tia Mowry, Tamera Mowry, Marques Houston
Unhappily Ever After	Sun	9:30	30	Walt Disney Studios	Ron Leavitt, Arthur Silver, Marcy Vosburgh, David Caplan	Geoff Pierson, Stephanie Hodge, Kevin Connolly, Nikki Cox
The Wayans Bros.	Wed	9:00	30	Warner Bros. TV	Phil Kelard, Tom Moore, Josh Goldstein, Eric Gould	Shawn Wayans, Marlon Wayans, John Witherspoon

SYNDICATED SHOWS, 1996

The following is a list of syndicated and off-network programming. An asterisk (*) indicates that the exact number of episodes is unavailable. Please contact the distributor for further information about availability and episodes. Additional programming, addresses and specific company information is listed in the Producers and Distributors section of this book.

NEW FIRSTRUN HALF HOUR STRIPS

Title	No. of Episodes	Distributor
Access Hollywood	195	New World/Genesis
Debt	*	Buena Vista
Decisions? Decisions	195	MG Perin
Deco Drive	195	Sunbeam
Hot Bench	195	Worldvision
Joe Perkins	*	Active Entertainment
Justice	195	MCA-TV
Lifeguard	195	Warner Bros.
Planet Hollywood Squares	*	King World
Real TV	195	Paramount
Strange Universe	195	Rysher
Swaps	195	Worldvision
The Beef	195	MTM

FIRSTRUN HALF HOUR STRIPS

Title	No. of Episodes	Distributor
American Journal	180	KingWorld
America's Most Wanted: Final Justice	195	Twentieth TV
CNN Headline News	260	Turner
Court TV: Inside America's Courts	260	New Line TV
A Current Affair	260	Twentieth TV
Day & Date	260	Group W
Entertainment Tonight	260	Paramount
Extra	260	Warner Bros.
First Business	*	Biznet
Hard Copy	195	Paramount
Inside Edition	260	KingWorld
Jeopardy	170	KingWorld
Juvenile Justice	210	Genesis
Lauren Hutton and..	195	TPS
L.A.P.D.	195	MGM
Real Stories - Highway Patrol	325	Genesis
Rescue 911	*	MTM
Shop Til You Drop	*	ACI
This Morning's Business	*	Paramount
Top Cops	*	Genesis
Wheel Of Fortune	195	KingWorld

NEW HOUR STRIPS

Title	No. of Episodes	Distributor
An Evening at the Improv	130	Western
Crook and Chase	195	Multimedia
Donna Willis, M.D.	195	20th Century Fox
He Says, She Says	195	MCA-TV
J & I	180	Maxan
Jim J & Tammy Faye	195	Worldvision
Later Today	260	Later Today TV Newsgroup
Loveline	175	New World/Genesis
Maureen O'Boyle	195	Warner Bros.
Off the Hook	195	KingWorld
Paget Brewster	195	Group W
Pat Bullard Show	195	Multimedia
Rosie O'Donnell	195	Warner Bros.
Scoop w/Sam & Dorothy	195	ACI
Teddy Carpenter	195	Tribune
The Bradshaw Difference	195	MGM

FIRSTRUN HOUR STRIPS

Title	No. of Episodes	Distributor
Donahue	210	Multimedia
George & Alana	195	Rysher
Geraldo	195	Tribune
Gordon Elliott	195	Twentieth TV
Jenny Jones	195	Warner Bros.
Mark Walberg Show	195	Genesis
Maury Povich	195	Paramount
Montel Williams	220	Paramount
Oprah Winfrey	240	KingWorld
Richard Bey	195	All American
Rolanda	195	KingWorld
Rush Limbaugh	200	Multimedia
Sally Jessy Raphael	225	Multimedia
Shirley	*	DLT
Stephanie Miller	*	Buena Vista
Tempestt Bledsoe	164	Columbia

NEW OFF-NETWORK HALF-HOURS

Title	No. of Episodes	Distributor
Boy Meets World	110	Buena Vista
Dave's World	*	CBS
Ellen	*	Buena Vista
Frasier	100	Paramount
Friends	100	Warner Bros.
Grace Under Fire	123	Carsey-Werner
Hangin' With Mr. Cooper	100	Warner Bros.
John Larroquette	*	Warner Bros.
Living Single	100	Warner Bros.
Mad About You	100	Columbia
Martin	100	Warner Bros.
The Nanny	*	Columbia

OFF-NETWORK HALF-HOURS

Title	No. of Episodes	Distributor
Alf	100	Warner Bros.
Amen	110	MCA-TV
America's Funniest Home Videos	115	MTM
Andy Griffith	249	Viacom
Benny Hill	*	DLT
Beverly Hillbillies	274	Viacom
Bewitched	117	Program Exchange
Blossom	110	Buena Vista
Brady Bunch	117	Program Exchange
California Dreams	65	Rysher
Charles In Charge	126	MCA-TV
Cheers	200	Paramount
Coach	120	MCA-TV
Cops	100	Twentieth TV
Cosby	140	Carsey-Werner
Dear John	90	Paramount
Designing Women	119	Columbia
Different Strokes	189	Columbia
Different World, A	100	Viacom
Dinosaurs	65	Buena Vista
Doogie Howser, M.D.	120	Twentieth TV
Empty Nest	166	Buena Vista
Family Matters	96	Warner Bros.
Family Ties	98	Paramount
Fresh Prince	96	Warner Bros.
Fury	*	Warner Bros.
Gilligan's Island	98	TPS
Gimme A Break	85	MCA-TV
Golden Girls	130	Buena Vista
Gomer Pyle	150	Viacom
Good Times	133	Columbia
Growing Pains	110	Warner Bros.
Happy Days Again	255	Paramount
Harry & The Hendersons	90	Warner Bros.
Head Of The Class	110	Warner Bros.
Hogan Family	97	Warner Bros.
Hogan's Heros	168	Viacom
Home Improvement	124	Buena Vista

Title	No. of Episodes	Distributor
Honeymooners	107	Viacom
I Dream Of Jeannie	109	Program Exchange
I Love Lucy	179	Viacom
The Jeffersons	253	Columbia
Laverne & Shirley	178	Program Exchange
Leave It To Beaver	234	MCA-TV
M*A*S*H	255	Twentieth TV
Mama's Family	95	Warner Bros.
Married w/Children	126	Columbia
Mr. Belvedere	110	Twentieth TV
Munsters	175	MCA-TV
Murphy Brown	*	Warner Bros.
New Adam-12	52	MCA-TV
New Dragnet	52	MCA-TV
Newhart	*	MTM
Night Court	*	Warner Bros.
Nine To Five	85	Twentieth TV
NYPD	49	Worldvision
Odd Couple	114	Program Exchange
Out Of This World	96	MCA-TV
Partridge Family	96	Program Exchange
Perfect Strangers	144	Warner Bros.
Rescue 911	*	MTM
Ropers	26	D.L.T.
Roseanne	147	Viacom
Russ Abbott Show	*	D.L.T.
Sanford & Son	136	Columbia
Saved By The Bell	100	Rysher
Seinfeld	108	Columbia
Small Wonder	96	Twentieth TV
Step By Step	96	Warner Bros.
The Simpsons	107	Twentieth TV
That Girl	136	Worldvision
Three Stooges	190	Columbia
Three's A Crowd	*	D.L.T.
Too Close For Comfort	122	D.L.T.
Top Cops	178	Genesis
227	116	Columbia
Victory At Sea	*	Republic
Webster	98	Paramount
What's Happening	131	Columbia
What's Happening Now	*	Columbia
Who's The Boss?	120	Columbia
WKRP In Cincinnati	90	MTM
Wonder Years, The	144	TPS

NEW OFF-NETWORK HOURS

Title	No. of Episodes	Distributor
Dr. Quinn, Medicine Woman	100	MTM
NYPD Bllue	100	20th Century Fox
The X-Files	97	20th Century Fox

OFF-NETWORK HOURS

Title	No. of Episodes	Distributor
A-Team	98	MCA-TV
Alias Smith & Jones	43	MCA-TV
Baretta	82	MCA-TV
Barnaby Jones	177	Worldvision
Baywatch (off-syndication)	107	All American
Ben Casey	153	Worldvision
Beverly Hills 90210	108	Worldvision
Big Valley	*	Genesis
Bonanza	260	Republic
Cannon	122	Viacom
Charlie's Angels	115	Columbia
CHIPs Patrol	138	TPS
Eight Is Enough	112	Warner Bros.
Fall Guy	*	Twentieth TV
Gunsmoke	402	Viacom
Hawaii 5-0	282	Viacom
Hill Street Blues	*	MTM
In The Heat Of The Night	137	MGM-TV
Knight Rider	90	MCA-TV
Matlock	177	Viacom
Mystery Movies	124	MCA-TV

Title	No. of Episodes	Distributor
Night Heat	96	Worldvision
Northern Exposure	85	MCA-TV
Perry Mason	271	Viacom
Remington Steele	*	MTM
Return Of The Saint	*	ITC
Saint, The	*	ITC
Simon & Simon	156	MCA-TV
Star Trek	127	Paramount
Star Trek: Next Generation	26	Paramount
St. Elsewhere	*	MTM
Streets Of San Franscisco	119	Worldvision
Super Dave	*	ACI
Tales From The Crypt (Off-cable/net)	80	Genesis
The Outer Limits (Off-cable)	49	MGM
T.J. Hooker	90	Columbia
21 Jump Street	107	Cannell Dist.
Vegas	68	Twentieth TV
Wild, Wild West	104	Viacom
Wiseguy	*	Cannell Dist.

NEW CHILDREN'S STRIPS

Title	No. of Episodes	Distributor
A.J.'s Time Travelers	40	Bohbot
All Dogs Go to Heaven	26	Claster
Apollo Kids	26	Western International
Flash Gordon	13	Hearst
Ghostwriter	26	Tradewinds
Mega Man	40	Summit Media
Name Your Adventure	40	Allan Entertainment
Pillow People	13	Summit Media
Richie Rich	13	Claster
Street Sharks	40	Bohbot
The Mask	40	Bohbot

CHILDREN'S STRIPS

Title	No. of Episodes	Distributor
Adventures Of Batman & Robin	*	FCN
Aladdin	*	Buena Vista
Animaniacs	*	FCN/Warner
Bananas In Pajamas	*	Sachs-Finley
Baywatch Bunch	*	All American
Bernstain Bears	26	Program Exchange
Blinky Bill	*	Sachs-Finley
Bobby's World	*	FCN
Bonkers	*	Buena Vista
Bozo's Bigtop	*	Larry Harmon
Bozo's Cartoons	*	Larry Harmon
Bullwinkle	98	Program Exchange
Darkwing Duck	65	Buena Vista
Dennis The Menace	78	Program Exchange
Dudley Do Right & Friends	38	Program Exchange
Exo Squad	*	MCA-TV
Flintstones	100	Turner
Flintstones	166	Program Exchange
Fox's Clubhouse	*	FCN
Garfield & Friends	73	Program Exchange
Gargoyles/Shnookums/Bonkers	*	Buena Vista
Goof Troop	65	Buena Vista
Highlander, Animated Series	*	Bohbot
Hulk Hogan's Rock N' Wrestling	*	Program Exchange
King Leonardo	38	Program Exchange
Laurel & Hardy Cartoons	*	Larry Harmon
Little Rascals	*	KingWorld
Mighty Max	*	Bohbot
Mighty Morphin Power Rangers	*	FCN
MGM Classics	*	Turner
Mutant League	*	Active Ent.
Popeye (New)	*	Hearst
Popeye (Original)	234	Turner
Rocky & His Friends	156	Program Exchange
Sailor Mood	*	Seagull
Scooby Doo Mysteries	110	Turner
Shnookums/Aladdin	*	Buena Vista
Space Kidettes	20	Program Exchange
The Littlest Pet Shop	*	Claster

Tale Spin	65	Buena Vista
Taz-Mania	*	FCN
Tennessee Tuxedo	140	Program Exchange
Three Stooges	156	Columbia
Timon & Pumba/Gargoyles	*	Buena Vista
Tom & Jerry	100	Turner
Topcat	*	Turner
Uncle Waldo's Cartoon Show	52	Program Exchange
Underdog	62	Program Exchange
V.R. Troopers	*	Saban
Warner Cartoons/Bugs	301	Turner
Woody Woodpecker	91	Program Exchange
World of Hanna Barbera	39	Turner
X-Men	*	FCN
Yogi & Friends	65	Program Exchange
Young Samson	20	Program Exchange

CHILDREN'S WEEKLY PROGRAMS

Title	No. of Episodes	Distributor
Adventures in Wonderland	*	Buena Vista
Amazin' Adventures	13	Bohbot
Amazin' Adventures 1	*	Bohbot
Amazin' Adventures 2	*	Bohbot
Baby Huey Show	*	Claster
Battletech	*	Saban
Bill Nye The Science Guy	*	Buena Vista
Biker Mice From Mars	65	Genesis
Blinky Bill	*	Sachs-Finley
Captain Planet	26	Turner
Children's Plus Network	67	Multimedia
Creatures of Delight	*	Active Ent.
Creepy Crawlers	*	Saban
Darkstalker	*	Summit Media
Disney Weekend	*	Buena Vista
Dragon Ball	*	Seagull
Family Theater Classics	*	New Line
Fantastic Four	26	Genesis
Feed Your Mind	*	Turner
Flintstones/Jetsons Hour	166	Turner
G.I. Joe	52	Claster
Gladiators 2000	*	Goldwyn
Happy Ness-Secret Of The Loch	*	Active Ent.
Ironman	26	Genesis
Jack Hanna's Animal Adventures	*	Litton
Jelly Bean Jungle	*	Active Ent.
Madison's Adventures	*	ITC
Magic Knight Rayearth	*	Summit Media
Marvel Action Universe	26	Genesis
Mega Man	*	Summit Media
Monster Force	*	MCA-TV
News For Kids	*	Mansfield
Nick News	*	Viacom
Not Just News	*	Twentieth TV
Phantom 2040	*	Hearst
Reality Check	*	Genesis
Shari Lewis Show	*	Peter Rodgers
Sing Me A Story At Belle's	*	Buena Vista
Stone Protectors	*	Sachs-Finley
Tenko & The Guardians Of The Magic	*	Saban
Warpspeed	*	Sunshine Kidvid Ent.
What's Up Network	*	MG/Perin, Inc.

NEW FIRSTRUN HALF-HOUR WEEKLIES

Title	No. of Episodes	Distributor
America's Dumbest Criminals	26	Active Entertainment
B. Smith Style	22	Telepictures
Backyard America	39	Kelly Entertainment
Better Than Ever	39	BKS/Bates
FDNY	26	Kelly Entertainment
Impact	26	Baruch/BET
Joan Embry	26	Western International
N Print	26	Taylor Foreman
PE-TV	26	Intersport
Power Animals	13	Summit Media

Ring Warriors	13	Summit Media
Secrets/Crypt Keeper's Haunted House	26	Samuel Goldwyn
WMAC	13	WMAC Masters

FIRSTRUN WEEKLY HALF HOURS

Title	No. of Episodes	Distributor
Action Man	*	Bohbot
Amazin Tails	26	Litton
American Adverturer	52	Associated TV
Babe Winkelman's Outdoor Secrets	*	Syndicom
Babe Winkelman's Good Fishing	*	Syndicom
Better Than Ever	*	BKS/Bates
Beverly Hills Beach Club	65	Seagull
Beyond Reality	*	ACI
Bob Vila's Home Again	*	Group W
Boogies Diner	*	MTM
Business Matters	*	Hearst
California Dreams	26	Rysher
Coast Guard	26	MG/Perin, Inc.
Computer Man, The	*	Pandora
Court TV: Inside America's Courts	*	New Line TV
Emergency Call	104	Genesis Ent.
Extremists, The	*	Litton
Feelin' Great	26	Telemarc
Fishing The West	*	Peregrine
George Michael's Sports Machine	*	ITC
Hard Copy/Weekend	*	Paramount
Hardy Boys Mysteries	13	New Line
Haven	52	Saban
Hitchhiker	85	Rysher
Hollywood People	*	DLT
Hot Hip & Country	*	Syndicom
Inside Edition/Weekend	52	KingWorld
Jack Hanna's Animal Adventures	*	Litton
Jeopardy/Weekend	52	KingWorld
Life Choices	*	U.S. Health Prod.
Main Floor	*	Litton
Martha Stewart Living	*	Group W
Motor Week	*	ITC
Nancy Drew Mysteries	13	New Line
Newsworthy	*	Newsworthy
Off The Record	*	Raycom
On Scene: Emergency Response	*	Group W
On The Road Again	*	Litton
Only In Hollywood	*	Peter Rodgers
Out Of The Blue	*	Tribune
Quest For The Dragon Star	*	Summit Media
Siskel & Ebert	46	Buena Vista
Super Dave	*	ACI
Sweet Valley High	52	Saban
Talk Music	*	Bohbot
This Is The NFL	26	Twentieth TV
This New House	*	Holigan Group
This Week In Motor Sports	*	Spectra
Tough Target	*	Grove
Trauma Center	26	Twentieth TV
Travel Center	*	Promark
24/Seven	*	BKS/Bates
U.S. Farm Report	*	Tribune
Wall Street Journal Update	*	Dow Jones
Weekend Travel Update	52	News Travel Net
Wheel Of Fortune/Weekend	52	KingWorld
Working Woman	*	Litton
Your Mind & Body	26	Warner Bros.

NEW FIRSTRUN WEEKLY HOURS

Title	No. of Episodes	Distributor
All You Need Is Love	22	All American
Beach Patrol	26	ITC
Bounty Hunters	24	Tradewinds
FX-The Series	22	Rysher
Lazarus Man	26	Turner
Mad Max/Road Warrior	22	Warner Bros.
Poltergeist	22	MGM
PSI Factor	22	Maxam

Robin Bubblehead's Pillow Talk	*	Active Entertainment
Sinbad	22	All American
Solutions/USA	52	Western International
Tarzan	22	Seagull
The Cape	22	MTM
The Ledge	*	Active Entertainment
The Wanderer	26	D.L. Taffner
Two	22	New World/Genesis
Viper	22	Paramount
Warriors of Wrestling	26	BKS Entertainment

FIRSTRUN WEEKLY HOURS

Title	No. of Episodes	Distributor
A Year To Remember American Gladiators	*	Samuel Goldwyn
American Gladiators	26	Samuel Goldwyn
American Wrestling Federation	*	Associated Television
Apollo Comedy Hour	26	Tribune
Babylon 5	22	Warner Bros.
Baywatch	107	All American
Baywatch Nights	22	All American
Beverly Hills 90210	108	Worldvision
Branson USA	*	Starcom
Current Affair Extra, A	52	Twentieth TV
Entertainers	*	CF Entertainment
Entertainment This Week	52	Paramount
Extra Weekend	*	Warner Bros.
Extraordinary, The	*	MG/Perin, Inc.
Flipper	22	Samuel Goldwyn
Forever Knight	26	Columbia
Gladys Knight Show	*	CF Entertainmenmt
HBO Comedy Showcase	*	Rysher
Hercules	26	MCA TV
High Tide	*	ACI
Highlander	22	Rysher
It's Showtime At The Apollo	*	Western Int'l.
Kung Fu: The Legend Continues	26	Warner Bros.
Land's End	22	Buena Vista
Lifestyles Of The Rich & Famous	22	Rysher
Lonesome Dove	26	Rysher
Music Scoupe	26	Select Media
Mystery Science Theater 3000	*	Tradewinds
Nancy Drew/Hardy Boys Mysteries	*	New Line
Night Stand	*	Worldvision
One West Waikiki	*	Rysher
The Outer Limits	*	MGM
Pointman	*	Warner Bros.
Real Stories of the Highway Patrol	325	Genesis
Renegade	*	Cannell
Save Our Streets	26	Kelly News & Ent.
Sightings	*	Paramount
Soul Train	26	Tribune
Star Trek: Deep Space 9	40	Paramount
Super Dave	20	ACI
Tales from the Crypt	80	Genesis
U.S. Customs: Classified	26	Cannell
The Wanderer	*	DLT Entertainmant
WCW Main Event	*	Turner Program Sales
WCW Pro Wrestling	*	Turner Program Sales
World of National Geographic	*	Turner Program Sales
Worldwide Wrestling	*	Turner Program Sales
WWF Superstars	52	World Wrestling Fed
WWF Wrestling Challenge	52	World Wrestling Fed
WWF Wrestling Spotlight	52	World Wrestling Fed

Source: Variety/Petrie Television

WHO'S WHO

IN THE ENTERTAINMENT WORLD

A

AARON, PAUL
Director, Producer, Writer. *B'way*: Salvation, Paris Is Out, '70 Girls '70, Love Me Love My Children.
PICTURES: A Different Story, A Force of One, Deadly Force, Maxie.
TELEVISION: *Movies*: The Miracle Worker, Thin Ice, Maid in America, When She Says No, Save the Dog!, In Love and War, Laurel Avenue (creator, writer, exec. prod.), Under One Roof (creator, writer), Grand Avenue (exec. prod.).

AARON, ROY H.
Arbitrator, Mediator, Entertainment Industry Consultant. b. Los Angeles, CA, April 8, 1929. e. UC Berkeley, BA; USC, LLB. Attorney in L.A. law firm of Pacht, Ross, Warne, Bernhard & Sears (1957-78). Joined Plitt Companies in 1978 as sr. v.p. & gen. counsel. In 1980 was named pres. & chief operating officer of Plitt Theatres, Inc. and related Plitt companies. 1985-93, pres. & CEO of Showscan Corp. 1993, business consultant, pres. of Plitt Entertainment Group Inc., chairman of Pacific Leisure Entertainment Group, L.L.C.

ABARBANEL, SAM X.
Producer, Writer, Publicist. b. Jersey City, NJ, March 27, 1914. e. Cornell U., U. of Illinois, B.S. 1935. Newspaperman in Chicago before joining NY exploitation dept. of Republic, then to studio as asst. publicity director. WWII in Europe with 103rd Div. After war became independent publicist and producer. Formed own co. in Spain, 1966. A founder of the Publicists Guild in Hollywood.
PICTURES: Argyle Secrets (co-prod.), Prehistoric Women (co-s.p., co-prod.), Golden Mistress (exec. prod.), Gunfighters of Casa Grande (assoc. prod.), Son of Gunfighter (assoc. prod.), Narco Men (prod.), Last Day of War (prod., co-s.p.), Summertime Killers (co-s.p).

ABEND, SHELDON
Executive. b. New York, NY, June 13, 1929. Maritime Labor-Rel. Negotiator, 1954-56; chmn., Maritime Union, 1954-56; head, exec. dir. Authors' Research Co. (est. 1957) representing estates of deceased authors. Independent literary negotiator, CC films, A.A.P., RKO General Inc., David O. Selznick, 7 Arts, Warner Bros., 1959-65; pres. American Play Co. Inc., Century Play Co. Inc., 1961-present. Est. Million Dollar Movie Play Library, 1962; pres. Amer. Literary Consultants est. 1965; exec. v.p. Chantec Enterprises Inc. 1969-72. Marketing literary consultant for Damon Runyon Estate. Copyright analyst and literary rights negotiator, United Artists Corp. Founder and chmn., Guild for Author's Heirs, 1970-72. Literary negotiator and prod. consultant for Robert Fryer, 1972. Founder, Copyright Royalty Co. for Authors' Heirs, 1974. Copyright consultant, Films, Inc. 1975; literary agent for Bway. play, Chicago, 1975. Owner of 53 classic RKO motion pictures for the non-theatrical markets, distributed by Films, Inc. Revived publishing of Damon Runyon stories in quality paperback. Published Cornell Woolrich mystery stories-all prod. by Alfred Hitchcock for TV & motion pictures, 1976. 1978, assoc. prod. of film, Why Would I Lie?; Originator of Million Dollar Movie Book Theatre and Million Dollar Movie Sound Track Co., 1980; assoc. prod. of B'way revival, Shanghai Gesture, 1981. Publ. 5 Cornell Woolrich books owned by S. Abend, 1982-83; Co-authored book, The Guardians; 1985, Romance of the Forties by Damon Runyon, 1986; 1985, founder and pres. American Concerts, Inc. and American Theatre Collections, Inc. Published Into the Night by Cornell Woolrich. Packaged m.p. Bloodhounds of Broadway 1988; co-author s.p. Ultimate Demand; 1990, stage adapt. of Bloodhounds of Broadway, Madam La Gimp. Exec. prod. adaptation of Cornell Woolrich stories for TV and movies. In 1990, won landmark copyright case before U.S. Supreme Court protecting Woolrich estate, also affecting other deceased authors, songwriters and their copywright renewals of their work. 1992, acquired Damon Runyon copyrights. 1993 Guys & Dolls handbook published by Viking.

ABRAHAM, F. MURRAY
Actor. b. Pittsburgh, PA, Oct. 24, 1939. r.n. Fahrid Murray Abraham. Attended U. of Texas, 1959-61; trained for stage at Herbert Berghof Studios with Uta Hagen. First NY acting job was as Macy's Santa Claus. Stage debut in Los Angeles in The Wonderful Ice Cream Suit, 1965. New York debut in The Fantasticks, 1966. Full professor of theatre at CUNY Brooklyn College. Honorary Doctorate, Ryder College.
THEATER: Antigone (NYSF, 1982), Uncle Vanya (Obie, LaMamma, etc.), The Golem (NYSF), Madwoman of Chaillot, Othello, Cyrano, A Life in the Theatre, Sexual Perversity in Chicago, Duck Variations, The David Show, Adaptation/Next, Don't Drink the Water, And Miss Reardon Drinks a Little, Where Has Tommy Flowers Gone?, A Christmas Carol, The Seagull, Landscape of the Body, 6 Rms Riv Vu, Survival of St. Joan, Scuba Duba, Teibele & Her Demon, The Ritz, Legend, Bad Habits, Frankie & Johnnie in the Claire De Lune, Twelfth Night, Macbeth, A Midsummer's Night Dream, Waiting for Godot, King Lear, Angels in America: Millenium Aproaches/Perestroika, Little Murders, A Month in the Country; also 5 Children's musicals, Theatreworks.
PICTURES: They Might Be Giants (debut, 1971), Serpico, The Prisoner of 2nd Avenue, The Sunshine Boys, All the President's Men, The Ritz, Madman, The Big Fix, Scarface, Amadeus (Academy Award, 1984), The Name of the Rose, Slipstream, The Favorite, Russicum (The Third Solution), The Betrothed, An Innocent Man, Beyond the Stars, Eye of the Widow, The Bonfire of the Vanities, Cadence, Mobsters, National Lampoon's Loaded Weapon 1, By the Sword, Last Action Hero, Sweet Killing, The Final Card, Surviving the Game, Nostradamus, Jamila, Quiet Flows the Dawn, Money, Dillinger and Capone, Mighty Aphrodite.
TELEVISION: *Series*: Love of Life, How to Survive a Marriage. *Movies*: Sex and the Married Woman, A Season of Giants, Journey to the Center of the Earth. *Guest*: Kojak, All in the Family. *Mini-Series*: Marco Polo, Dream West. *Special*: Largo Desolato.

ABRAHAMS, JIM
Producer, Writer, Director. b. Milwaukee, WI, May 10, 1944. e. U. of Wisconsin. Former private investigator. 1971, with friends David and Jerry Zucker, opened the Kentucky Fried Theatre in Madison, WI, a multimedia show specializing in live improvisational skits mixed with videotaped and film routines and sketches, with the threesome writing and appearing in most. Opened new theatre in Los Angeles in 1972 and developed large following. Co-wrote, co-dir., and co-exec. produced TV series Police Squad!
PICTURES: The Kentucky Fried Movie (co-s.p. with Zuckers), Airplane! (co-dir., co-exec. prod., co-s.p. with Zuckers), Top Secret! (co-dir., co-s.p., with Zuckers), Ruthless People (co-dir. with Zuckers), Big Business (dir.), The Naked Gun (exec. prod., co-s.p.), Cry-Baby (co-exec. prod.), Welcome Home Roxy Carmichael (dir.), The Naked Gun 2-1/2 (co-exec. prod.), Hot Shots! (dir., co-s.p.), Hot Shots Part Deux!. (dir., co-s.p.), Naked Gun 33 1/3: The Final Insult (co-exec. prod.).

ABRAHAMS, MORT
Producer. b. New York, NY. Dir. programming, prod., NTA, 1958-60; exec. prod. Cooga Mooga Prod. Inc., 1960-61. Producer: Target, The Corruptors 1961, Route 66, 1962-63; writer TV shows, 1963-64; prod., Kraft Suspense Theatre, 1965; prod., Man from U.N.C.L.E., 1965-66; exec. v.p., APJAC Prod. 1966. 1969, v.p. in chg. of prod., Rastar Prods.: 1971-74 exec. prod. American Film Theatre & v.p. Ely Landau Organization in charge of West Coast prod. Member of Faculty and producer-in-residence, Center for Advanced Film and TV Studies of A.F.I. Vice-pres. Alph Productions, 1993-present.
PICTURES: *Assoc. Prod.*: Doctor Doolittle, Planet of the Apes, Goodbye Mr. Chips. *Exec. Prod.*: Luther, Homecoming, The Man in the Glass Booth, The Greek Tycoon, Hopscotch, The Chosen

(exec. in chg. prod.), Beatlemania (exec. in chg. prod.), The Deadly Game, Arch of Triumph, The Holcroft Covenant, Seven Hours to Judgment (prod.).

ACKERMAN, BETTYE
Actress. b. Cottageville, SC, Feb. 28, 1928. e. Columbia U., 1948-52. Taught dancing 1950-54.
THEATER: No Count Boy, 1954; Tartuffe, Sophocles' Antigone and Oedipus at Colonus, The Merchant of Venice.
PICTURES: Face of Fire, Rascal, Ted & Venus.
TELEVISION: *Series*: Ben Casey. *Guest*: Alcoa Premiere, Alfred Hitchcock Presents, Perry Mason, Breaking Point, Hope-Chrysler Theatre, Bonanza, FBI Story, Mannix, Ironside, Medical Center, Columbo, Sixth Sense, Heat of Anger, Return to Peyton Place, The Rookies, Barnaby Jones, Police Story, Gunsmoke, Harry O, Streets of San Francisco, S.W.A.T., Petrocelli, Wonder Woman, Police Woman, Chips, 240-Robert, The Waltons, Dynasty, Falcon Crest, Me and Mom, Trapper John M.D. *Movies*: Companions in Nightmare, A Day for Thanks on Walton's Mountain, Confessions of a Married Man.

ACKLAND, JOSS
Actor. b. London, England, Feb. 29, 1928. e. Central Sch. of Speech Training & Dramatic Art. Spent time in Central Africa as a tea planter. Over 400 TV appearances. *Autobiography*: I Must Be in There Somewhere.
THEATER: The Old Vic (3 yrs.), Mermaid Theatre (artistic dir., 3 yrs.); Hotel in Amsterdam, Jorrocks Come as You Are, The Collaborators, A Streetcar Named Desire, The Madras House, Captain Brassbound's Conversion, Never the Sinner, Henry IV Parts I & II, Peter Pan (dramatic & musical versions), A Little Night Music, Evita, The Visit, etc.
PICTURES: Seven Days to Noon, Crescendo, Trecolonne in Cronaca, The House That Dripped Blood, The Happiness Cage, Villain, England Made Me, The Black Windmill, S.P.Y.S, The Little Prince, Royal Flash, Operation Daybreak, Who Is Killing the Great Chefs of Europe, Saint Jack, The Apple, Rough Cut, Lady Jane, A Zed and Two Noughts, The Sicilian, White Mischief, To Kill a Priest, It Couldn't Happen Here, Lethal Weapon 2, The Hunt for Red October, Object of Beauty, Bill and Ted's Bogus Journey, The Palermo Connection, The Mighty Ducks, Nowhere to Run, Mother's Boys, The Princess and the Goblin (voice), Miracle on 34th Street, Giorgino, Mad Dogs and Englishmen, A Kid in the Court of King Arthur, Occhio Pinocchio, Daisies in December, To the Ends of Time, Mighty Ducks 3, Surviving Picasso, Deadly Voyage, Firelight.
TELEVISION: *Movies/Specials*: Queenie, Shadowlands, The Man Who Lived at the Ritz, A Quiet Conspiracy, Jekyll and Hyde, First and Last, A Murder of Quality, A Woman Named Jackie, Ashenden, Voices in the Garden, Queenie, The Bible, Citizen X.

ADAM, KEN
Art Director, Prod. Designer. b. Berlin, Germany, Feb. 5, 1921. e. St. Pauls Sch., London; London U., student of architecture. 6 years war service as RAF pilot. Ent. m.p. ind. as draughtsman 1947 (This Was a Woman).
PICTURES: *Art Director*: The Devil's Pass, Soho Incident, Around the World in 80 Days. *Production Designer*: Spin a Dark Web, Night of the Demon, Gideon's Day, The Angry Hills, Beyond This Place, The Rough and the Smooth, In the Nick, Let's Get Married, Trials of Oscar Wilde, Dr. No, Sodom and Gomorrah, In the Cool of the Day, Dr. Strangelove, Goldfinger, Woman of Straw, Thunderball, The Ipcress File, Funeral in Berlin, You Only Live Twice, Chitty Chitty Bang Bang, Goodbye Mr. Chips, The Owl and the Pussycat, Diamonds Are Forever, Sleuth, The Last of Sheila, Barry Lyndon (Academy Award, 1975), Madam Kitty, The Seven Percent Solution, The Spy Who Loved Me, Moonraker, Pennies From Heaven (visual consult., assoc. prod.), King David, Agnes of God, Crimes of the Heart, The Deceivers, Dead-Bang, The Freshman, The Doctor, Company Business, Undercover Blues, Addams Family Values, The Madness of King George (Academy Award, 1994), Boys on the Side, Bogus.

ADAMS, BROOKE
Actress. b. New York, NY, Feb. 8, 1949. e. H.S. of Performing Arts; Inst. of American Ballet; Lee Strasberg. Made professional debut at age of six in Finian's Rainbow. Worked steadily in summer stock and TV until age 18. After hiatus resumed acting career.
THEATER: Split, Key Exchange, Linda Hur, The Heidi Chronicles, Lost in Yonkers. Helps run small summer theater upstate NY.
PICTURES: The Lords of Flatbush, Shock Waves (Death Corps), Days of Heaven, Invasion of the Body Snatchers, Cuba, A Man a Woman and a Bank, Tell Me a Riddle, Utilities, The Dead Zone, Almost You, Key Exchange, The Stuff, Man on Fire, The Unborn, Gas Food Lodging, The Baby Sitter's Club.
TELEVISION: *Movies*: F. Scott Fitzgerald and the Last of the Belles, The Daughters of Joshua Cabe Return, James Dean, Who is the Black Dahlia?, Murder on Flight 502, Nero Wolfe (pilot), Lace, Haunted, Special People, Lace II, The Lion of Africa, Bridesmaids, Sometimes They Come Back, The Last Hit.

Specials: Paul Reiser: Out on a Whim. *Series*: O.K. Crackerby. *Pilot*: A Girl's Life. *Guest*: Kojack, Family, Police Woman, Moonlighting.

ADAMS, CATLIN
Actress, Director. r.n. Barab. b. Los Angeles, CA, October 11, 1950. Began career as actress then studied directing at American Film Institute. Directorial debut: Wanted: The Perfect Guy. Also directed Little Shiny Shoes (short, written and prod. with Melanie Mayron), Stolen: One Husband (TV).
THEATER: Safe House, Scandalous Memories, Dream of a Blacklisted Actor, The Candy Store, Ruby Ruby Sam Sam, Bermuda Avenue Triangle (dir.).
PICTURES: *Actress*: The Jerk, The Jazz Singer. *Director*: Sticky Fingers (also co-s.p., co-prod.).
TELEVISION: *Specials*: How to Survive the 70's and Maybe Even Bump into a Little Happiness, She Loves Me She Loves Me Not. *Series*: Square Pegs. *Movies*: Panic in Echo Park, Freaky Friday. *Guest*: thirtysomething.

ADAMS, DON
Actor. b. New York, NY, April 13, 1926. Won Arthur Godfrey talent contest. Was nightclub impressionist before starting in TV.
PICTURES: The Nude Bomb, Jimmy the Kid, Back to the Beach.
TELEVISION: *Series*: Perry Como's Kraft Music Hall, The Bill Dana Show, Tennessee Tuxedo (voice), Get Smart (3 Emmy Awards, 2 Clio Awards), The Partners, Don Adams' Screen Test, Three Times Daley, Inspector Gadget (voice), Check It Out!, Get Smart (1995). *Movies*: The Love Boat, Get Smart Again!

ADAMS, EDIE
Actress, Singer. b. Kingston, PA, April 16, 1927. r.n. Edith Elizabeth Enke. e. Julliard Sch. of Music, Columbia Sch. of Drama.
THEATER: *NY*: Wonderful Town, Lil Abner (Tony Award), Mame.
PICTURES: The Apartment, Lover Come Back, Call Me Bwana, It's a Mad Mad Mad Mad World, Under the Yum Yum Tree, Love With the Proper Stranger, The Best Man, Made in Paris, The Oscar, The Honey Pot, Up in Smoke, The Happy Hooker Goes Hollywood, Boxoffice.
TELEVISION: *Series*: Ernie in Kovacsland, The Ernie Kovacs Show (1952-53), The Ernie Kovacs Show (1956), The Chevy Show, Take a Good Look (panelist), Here's Edie, The Edie Adams Show. *Movies*: Evil Roy Slade, Return of Joe Forrester, Superdome, Fast Friends, Make Me an Offer, A Cry for Love, Ernie Kovacs' Between the Laughter. *Guest*: Miss U.S. Television, Three to Get Ready, Kovacs on the Corner, Kovacs Unlimited, Jack Paar, Ed Sullivan Show, Perry Como Show, Pat Boone Show, G.E. Theatre, Colgate Comedy House, Dinah Shore Show, Palace, Bob Hope Show. *Specials*: Cinderella, Tales of the City.

ADAMS, GERALD DRAYSON
Writer. b. Winnipeg, Manitoba, 1904. e. Oxford U. Export exec. 1925-30; literary agt. 1931-45. Member: Screen Writers' Guild.
PICTURES: Magnificent Rogue, Plunderers, Gallant Legion, Big Steal, Dead Reckoning, Battle of Apache Pass, Son of Ali Baba, Flaming Feather, Flame of Araby, Lady from Texas, Steel Town, Untamed, Frontier, Duel at Silver Creek, Princess of the Nile, Three Young Texans, Gambler from Natchez, Wings of the Hawk, Between Midnight and Dawn, Taza Son of Cochise, Gambler from Natchez, Chief Crazy Horse, Golden Horde, Prince Who Was a Thief, Sea Hornet, Three Bad Sisters, Duel on the Mississippi, Black Sleep, War Drums, Gun Brothers, Affair in Reno, Frontier Rangers, Gold Glory & Custer, Kissin' Cousins, Harum Scarum.
TELEVISION: *Series*: Maverick, G.E. Theatre, Northwest Passage, Broken Arrow, Cheyenne, 77 Sunset Strip.

ADAMS, JULIE
Actress. r.n. Betty May Adams. b. Waterloo, IA, Oct. 17, 1926. e. jr. coll., Little Rock, AK. Coll. dramatics; m.p. debut in Red Hot and Blue (as Betty Adams); Star of Tomorrow, 1953.
PICTURES: Red Hot and Blue (debut, 1949), The Dalton Gang, Crooked River, Hostile Country, West of the Brazos, Colorado Ranger, Fast on the Draw, Marshal of Heldorado. As Julie Adams: Hollywood Story, Finders Keepers, Bend of the River, Bright Victory, Treasure of Lost Canyon, Horizons West, Lawless Breed, Mississippi Gambler, Man From the Alamo, The Stand of Apache River, Wings of the Hawk, The Creature From the Black Lagoon, Francis Joins the WACS, The Looters, One Desire, The Private War of Major Benson, Six Bridges to Cross, Away All Boats, Four Girls in Town, Slim Carter, Slaughter on 10th Avenue, Tarawa Beachhead, Gunfight at Dodge City, Raymie, Underwater City, Tickle Me, Valley of Mystery, The Last Movie, McQ, Psychic Killer, The Wild McCullochs, Killer Inside Me, Goodbye Franklin High, The Fifth Floor, Black Roses.
TELEVISION: *Series*: Yancy Derringer, General Hospital, The Jimmy Stewart Show, Code Red, Capitol. *Movies*: The Trackers, Go Ask Alice, Code Red, Backtrack, The Conviction of Kitty Dodds. *Guest*: Murder She Wrote.

ADAMS, MASON
Actor. b. NY, NY, Feb. 26, 1919. e. U. Wisconsin. B.A., 1940; M.A., 1941. Trained for stage at Neighborhood Playhouse.

Began on radio in 1946, spending nearly two decades in starring role of Pepper Young's Family. B'way debut: Get Away Old Man (1943).
THEATER: Career Angel, Public Relations, Violet, Shadow of My Enemy, Inquest, The Sign in Sidney Brustein's Window, Tall Story, The Trial of the Catonsville Nine, Foxfire, Checking Out, Danger Memory, The Day Room, The Rose Quartet.
PICTURES: God Told Me To, Raggedy Ann and Andy (voice), Northstar, The Final Conflict, F/X, Toy Soldiers, Son-in-Law, Houseguest.
TELEVISION: Series: Lou Grant, Morningstar/Eveningstar, Knight and Dave. Movies: The Deadliest Season, And Baby Makes Six, The Shining Season, Flamingo Road, The Revenge of the Stepford Wives, The Kid with the Broken Halo, Adam, Passions, Solomon Northrup's Odyssey, The Night They Saved Christmas, Who is Julia?, Under Siege, Rage of Angels: The Story Continues, Perry Mason, Jonathan: The Boy Nobody Wanted, Buying a Landslide, Assault at West Point, Not of This Earth.

ADAMS, MAUD
Actress. r.n. Maud Wikstrum. b. Lulea, Sweden, Feb. 12, 1945. Formerly a model. Film debut as model in The Boys in the Band.
PICTURES: The Boys in the Band, The Christian Licorice Store, U-Turn, Mahoney's Estate, The Man With the Golden Gun, Rollerball, Killer Force, The Merciless Man, Tattoo, Octopussy, Target Eagle, Jane and the Lost City, The Women's Club, A Man of Passion, The Favorite, Soda Cracker.
TELEVISION: Movies: Big Bob Johnson and His Fantastic Speed Circus, The Hostage Tower, Playing for Time, Nairobi Affair, The Case of the Wicked Wives. Series: Chicago Story, Emerald Point, N.A.S.

ADAMS, TONY
Producer. b. Dublin, Ireland, Feb. 15, 1953. Began career as asst. to dir. John Boorman and was associated with Burt Reynolds prior to joining Blake Edwards as a prod., 1971. Then president, Blake Edwards Entertainment; Pres. & CEO, The Blake Edwards Company, 1988.
PICTURES: Assoc. Prod.: Return of the Pink Panther, The Pink Panther Strikes Again. Exec. Prod.: Revenge of the Pink Panther. Prod.: ''10'', S.O.B., Victor/Victoria, Trail of the Pink Panther, Curse of the Pink Panther, The Man Who Loved Women, Micki & Maude, That's Life, A Fine Mess, Blind Date, Sunset, Skin Deep, Switch, Son of the Pink Panther.
TELEVISION: Julie Andrews (series and specials), Justin Case, Peter Gunn, Julie.

ADDISON, JOHN
Composer. b. West Chobham, Surrey, England, March 16, 1920. e. Wellington and Royal Coll. of Music. Entered m.p. ind. in 1948. Professor, Royal Coll. of Music, 1948-53. Member of bd. of governors of AMPAS 1980-89.
THEATER: The Amazons, Popkiss, The Entertainer, The Chairs, Luther, Midsummer Night's Dream, The Broken Heart, The Workhouse Donkey, Hamlet, Semi-Detached, The Seagull, Saint Joan of the Stockyards, Listen to the Mockingbird, Cranks (revue), Antony & Cleopatra, I Claudius, Twelfth Night, Bloomsbury, Antony and Cleopatra (LA Theatre Centre). Ballets: Carte Blanche (at Sadlers Wells and Edinburgh Fest.), Cat's Cradle (Marquis de Cuevas, Paris, Monte Carlo).
PICTURES: Seven Days to Noon, The Man Between, The Maggie, Make Me An Offer, Private's Progress, Reach for the Sky, Lucky Jim, I Was Monty's Double, Carlton Brown of the F. O., The Entertainer, School for Scoundrels, A Taste of Honey, The Loneliness of the Long Distance Runner, Tom Jones (Academy. Award, Grammy Award, 1963), Guns at Batasi, Girl With Green Eyes, The Loved One, Torn Curtain, A Fine Madness, I Was Happy Here, The Honey Pot, Smashing Time, The Charge of the Light Brigade, Start the Revolution Without Me, Country Dance (Brotherly Love), Mr. Forbush and the Penguins, Sleuth, Luther, Dead Cert, Ride a Wild Pony, Seven-Per-Cent Solution, Swashbuckler, Joseph Andrews, A Bridge Too Far (Brit. Acad. Anthony Asquith Award), The Pilot, High Point, Strange Invaders, Grace Quigley, Code Name: Emerald, To Die For.
TELEVISION: Sambo and the Snow Mountains, Detective, Hamlet, The Search for Ulysses, Way of the World, Back of Beyond, Black Beauty, The Bastard, Deadly Price of Paradise, Love's Savage Fury, Like Normal People, The French Atlantic Affair, Mistress of Paradise, Eleanor First Lady of The World, Charles and Diana: A Royal Love Story, Mail Order Bride, Thirteen at Dinner, Dead Man's Folly, Mr. Boogedy, Something in Common, Firefighter, Amazing Stories, Bride of Boogedy, Strange Voices. Mini-series: Centennial, Pearl, Ellis Island, Beryl Markham: A Shadow on the Sun, Phantom of the Opera. Series: Nero Wolfe, Murder She Wrote (Emmy Award).

ADELMAN, GARY
Executive. b. Los Angeles, CA, March 16, 1944. e. California State U., Long Beach State Coll. 1969, asst. on feature, The Masterpiece; assoc. prod. on The Candy Snatchers. Produced first feature film, The Severed Arm, 1974. Assisted Winston

Hock in development of 3-D process, 1975. 1976-93, pres. & COO of Monarch Prods. Post-prod. consultant for Jerry Gross Organization. 1983, founder and partial owner of New Image Releasing, Inc., new prod. & dist. co. Had post of secty./treas. 1987, named v.p., chg. prod., All-American Group. 1990, assoc. prod. on Nobody's Perfect.

ADELMAN, JOSEPH A.
Executive. b. Winnipeg, Manitoba, Can., Dec. 27, 1933. e. NYU, B.A., 1954; Harvard Law Sch., J.D., 1957, graduated cum laude. Attorney, United Artists Corp., New York, 1958; named west coast counsel, Hollywood, 1964; named exec. asst. to the v.p. in charge of prod. 1968; named v.p., west coast business and legal affairs, 1972; appointed executive v.p., Association of Motion Pictures and Television Producers, 1977; appointed v.p. in chg. of business affairs, Paramount Pictures Corp., 1979; co-founder and exec. v.p. Kidpix, Inc. since 1984; founder and CEO of Kidpix Theaters Corp. since 1985; appointed senior v.p. for business/legal affairs, Color Systems Technology, Inc. 1986; named pres. of CST Entertainment, 1987. Appointed managing dir., Broadway Video Entertainment, 1990. CEO, Intl. Entertainment Enterprises 1991. Admitted to NY, California and U.S. Supreme Court bars; member, Phi Beta Kappa; Alumni Achievement Award, NYU, 1982; American Bar Association; Los Angeles Copyright Society; Academy of Motion Picture Arts and Sciences; bd. of dirs., AMPTP, 1969-1979; National Assn. of Television Programming Executives.; bd. of trustees, Theatre Authority, 1970-79.

ADELSON, GARY
Producer. b. 1954. e. UCLA (B.A.). Son of Merv Adelson. Joined Lorimar Prods. 1970 as prod. asst. on TV movie Helter Skelter. In 1989, formed Adelson/Baumgarten Prods. with Craig Baumgarten.
PICTURES: The Last Starfighter, The Boy Who Could Fly, In The Mood, Tap, Hard to Kill, Hook, Universal Soldier, Nowhere to Run, Blank Check, It Could Happen to You, Jade.
TELEVISION: Helter Skelter (prod. asst.), Sybil (assoc. prod.), Eight Is Enough (prod.), The Blue Knight (prod.). Exec. prod.: Too Good To Be True, Our Family Business, Cass Malloy, John Steinbeck's The Winter of Our Discontent, Lace, Detective in the House, Lace II, Studio 5B (series), Glitz.

ADELSON, MERV
Producer. b. Los Angeles, CA, Oct. 23, 1929. e. UCLA. Pres., Markettown Builders Emporium, Las Vegas 1953-63; managing partner Paradise Dev. 1958-; pres. Realty Holdings 1962-; Bd. chmn., Lorimar Inc. 1969-86; chmn. bd. dirs. & CEO, Lorimar Telepictures 1986-.
PICTURES: Twilight's Last Gleaming, The Choirboys, Who Is Killing the Great Chefs of Europe?, Avalanche Express, The Big Red One.
TELEVISION: Series: The Waltons, Eight Is Enough, Dallas, Kaz, The Waverly Wonders, Knots Landing. Movies/Mini-Dir.: Sybil, A Man Called Intrepid, The Blue Knight, Helter-Skelter.

ADJANI, ISABELLE
Actress. b. Germany, June 27, 1955.
PICTURES: Faustine and the Beautiful Summer, The Slap, The Story of Adele H. (Acad. Award nom.), The Tenant, Barocco, Violette and Francois, The Driver, Nosferatu—The Vampire, The Bronte Sisters, Clara et les Chics Types, Possession, Quartet, Next Year If All Goes Well, One Deadly Summer, Antonieta, Deadly Circuit, Subway, Ishtar, Camille Claudel (also co-prod.; Acad. Award nom.), Toxic Affair, Queen Margot, Diabolique.

ADLER, ALLEN
Executive Producer. b. New York, NY, 1946. e. Princeton U., B.A.; Harvard Business Sch., M.B.A. Started with Standard & Poor's Inter-Capital; then joined Alan Hirschfield at American Diversified Enterprises; next to Columbia Pictures 1973 as corporate officer. 1979, named sr. v.p., Columbia. 1981, teamed with Daniel Melnick in IndieProd Co.
PICTURE: Making Love.

ADLON, PERCY
Director, Writer, Producer. b. Munich, Germany, June 1, 1935. e. Munich Univ. m. Eleonore Adlon, with whom he has worked on several film projects. Created more than forty tv documentaries.
PICTURES: Celeste, The Last Five Days (dir. only), The Swing, Sugarbaby, Bagdad Cafe, Rosalie Goes Shopping, Salmonberries, Younger and Younger.
TELEVISION: The Guardian and His Poet (Adolf Grimme Award).

AGAR, JOHN
Actor. b. Chicago, IL, Jan. 31, 1921. In service WWII.
PICTURES: Fort Apache (debut, 1948), Adventure in Baltimore, I Married a Communist, Sands of Iwo Jima, She Wore a Yellow Ribbon, Breakthrough, Woman on Pier 13, Magic Carpet, Along the Great Divide, Woman of the North Country, Man of Conflict, Bait, Rocket Man, Shield for Murder, Golden Mistress, Revenge of the Creature, Hold Back Tomorrow, Tarantula, Star in the

3

Dust, The Lonesome Trail, The Mole People, Flesh and the Spur, Daughter of Dr. Jekyll, Cavalry Command, The Brain from Planet Arous, Attack of the Puppet People, Ride a Violent Mile, Joe Butterfly, Jet Attack, Frontier Gun, Invisible Invaders, Raymie, Hand of Death, Lisette, Journey to the 7th Planet, Of Love and Desire, The Young and the Brave, Law of the Lawless, Stage to Thunder Rock, Young Fury, Waco, Johnny Reno, Curse of the Swamp Creature, Zontar: The Thing from Venus, Women of the Prehistoric Planet, St. Valentine's Day Massacre, Big Jake, Chisum, King Kong, Perfect Bride, Miracle Mile, Nightbreed, Fear, Invasion of Privacy, Body Bags, Pandora Directive (CD-ROM).

AGOGLIA, JOHN J.
Executive. Worked for 14 years for CBS Entertainment in New York, becoming v.p. business affairs. Joined NBC in 1979 as v.p., program and talent negotiations. 1980, named sr. v.p. business affairs; 1984, exec. v.p. NBC Prods.; 1986, exec. v.p., business affairs NBC-TV Network; 1987, in charge of foreign marketing relating to NBC Productions products. Appointed pres. of NBC Enterprises, 1990. Named pres. of NBC Prods., May 1993.

AGUTTER, JENNY
Actress. b. Taunton, Devonshire, England, Dec. 20, 1952. e. Elmhurst Ballet Sch. Received Variety Club of Great Britain Most Promising Artiste Award, 1971.
THEATER: School for Scandal, Rooted, Arms and the Man, The Ride Across Lake Constance, The Tempest, Spring Awakening, Hedda, Betrayal. Member, Royal Shakespeare Co.-King Lear, Arden of Taversham, The Body. Breaking the Silence, Shrew (Los Angeles), Love's Labour's Lost, Mothers and Daughters.
PICTURES: East of Sudan (debut, 1964), Ballerina (tv in U.S.), Gates of Paradise, Star!, I Start Counting, Walkabout, The Railway Children, Logan's Run, The Eagle Has Landed, Equus (BAFTA Award, 1977), Dominique, China 9 Liberty 37, The Riddle of the Sands, Sweet William, The Survivor, Amy, An American Werewolf in London, Secret Places, Dark Tower, King of the Wind, Dark Man, Child's Play 2, Freddie as F.R.O. 7 (voice), Blue Juice.
TELEVISION: The Great Mr. Dickens, The Wild Duck, The Cherry Orchard, The Snow Goose (Emmy Award, 1972), As Many as Are Here Present, A War of Children, The Man in the Iron Mask, A House in Regent Place, There's Love and Dove, Kiss Me and Die, A Legacy, The Waiting Room, Six Million Dollar Man, School Play, The Mayflower, Voyage of the Pilgrims, Beulah Land, Love's Labour's Lost, This Office Life, Magnum, The Two Ronnies, Silas Marner, The Twilight Zone, Murder She Wrote, No a Penny More Not a Penny Less, Dear John, The Equalizer, The Outsiders, Breaking the Code, Boon, Love Hurts, Heartbeat, The Buccaneers, September.

AIELLO, DANNY
Actor. b. New York, NY, June 20, 1936.
THEATER: Lampost Reunion (Theatre World Award), Wheelbarrow Closers, Gemini (Obie Award), Knockout, The Floating Light Bulb, Hurlyburly (LA Drama Critics Award), The House of Blue Leaves.
PICTURES: Bang the Drum Slowly (debut, 1973), The Godfather Part II, The Front, Fingers, Blood Brothers, Defiance, Hide in Plain Sight, Fort Apache the Bronx, Chu Chu and the Philly Flash, Deathmask, Once Upon a Time in America, Old Enough, The Purple Rose of Cairo, Key Exchange, The Protector, The Stuff, Radio Days, The Pick-Up Artist, Man on Fire, Moonstruck, The January Man, Crack in the Mirror, Do the Right Thing (LA, Chicago & Boston Film Critics Awards; Acad. Award nom.), Russicum (The Third Solution), Harlem Nights, Jacob's Ladder, Once Around, Hudson Hawk, The Closer, 29th Street, Ruby, Mistress, The Cemetery Club, The Pickle, Me and the Kid, The Professional, Ready to Wear (Pret-a-Porter), City Hall, Power of Attorney, He Ain't Heavy, Two Much, 2 Days in the Valley, Mojave Moon.
TELEVISION: Movies: The Last Tenant, Lovey: A Circle of Children Part 2, A Question of Honor, Blood Feud, Lady Blue, Daddy, Alone in the Neon Jungle, The Preppie Murder. Series: Lady Blue. Special: Family of Strangers (Emmy Award), Lieberman in Love.

AIMEE, ANOUK
Actress. r.n. Franccoise Soyra Dreyfus. b. Paris, France, April 27, 1932. Studied dancing at Marseilles Opera, acting at Bauer-Therond dramatic school, Paris. Started in films as teenager billed as Anouk.
PICTURES: La Maison Sous la Mer (debut, 1946), La Fleur de l'age, Les Amants De Verone, The Golden Salamander, Noche de Tormenta, Le Rideau Cramoisi, The Man Who Watched the Trains Go By (Paris Express), Contraband Spain, Forever My Heart, Les Mauvaises Rencontres, Ich Suche Dich, Nina, Stresemann, Pot Bouille, Montparnasse 19, Tous Peuvent Me Tuer, Le Tete Contre Les Murs, The Journey, Les Dragueurs, La Dolce Vita, Le Farceur, Lola, L'Imprevu, Quai Notre-Dame, Il Giudizio Universale, Sodom and Gomorrah, Les Grand Chemins, 8 1/2, Il Terrorista, Il Successo, Liola, Le Voci Bianche,

La Fuga, La Stagione del Nostro Amore, A Man and a Woman (Acad. Award nom.), Lo Sacandalo, Il Morbidonne, Un Soir Un Train, The Model Shop, Justine, The Appointment, Si C'Etait d Refaire, Mon Premier Amour, Salto nel Vuoto (Leap Into the Void), Tragedy of a Ridiculous Man, What Makes David Run?, Le General de l'Armee Morte, Success is the Best Revenge, Viva la Vie, A Man and A Woman: 20 Years Later, Arrivederci e Grazie, La Table Tournante, The House of the Lord, Dr. Bethune, Rabbit Face, Ready to Wear (Pret-a-Porter).

ALBECK, ANDY
Executive. b. U.S.S.R., Sept. 25, 1921. Industry career began in 1939 with Columbia Pictures Intl. Corp. 1947, Central Motion Picture Exchange. 1949, Eagle Lion Classics, Inc. Joined UA in 1951 in intl. dept., functioning in the area of operations. After filling a number of key posts, named asst. treas. in 1970. In 1972 became v.p. of UA and its subsidiary, UA Broadcasting, Inc. 1973, appt. pres. of UA Broadcasting and in 1976 named sr. v.p. operations. Named UA Corp. pres. & chief exec. officer in 1978. Retired, 1981.

ALBERGHETTI, ANNA MARIA
Singer, Actress. b. Pesaro, Italy, May 15, 1936. d. Daniele Alberghetti, cellist. Concert debut in 1948 in Pesaro, then toured Italy, Scandinavia, Spain; Am. debut Carnegie Hall, 1950, sang with NY Philharmonic Society, Phila. Symphony, on television. B'way stage debut: Carnival, 1962 (Tony Award).
PICTURES: The Medium (debut, 1951), Here Comes the Groom, The Stars Are Singing, The Last Command, Duel at Apache Wells, Ten Thousand Bedrooms, Cinderfella.
TELEVISION: Guest: Toast of the Town, Cavalcade of Stars, Arthur Murray Show, Bob Hope, Eddie Fisher, Red Skelton, Dinah Shore, Desilu Playhouse, G.E. Theatre, Chevy Show, Dupont Show, Voice of Firestone, Colgate Hour, Climax, Loretta Young, Ford Jubilee, Perry Como.

ALBERT, EDDIE
Actor. r.n. Eddie Albert Heimberger. b. Rock Island, IL, April 22, 1908. e. U. of Minnesota. Son is actor Edward Albert. Performer on Radio NBC.
THEATER: B'way: Brother Rat, Say Darling, The Music Man, Room Service, The Boys from Syracuse, Seven Year Itch, Our Town, No Hard Feelings, Reuben Reuben, Miss Liberty, You Can't Take It With You.
PICTURES: Brother Rat (debut, 1938), On Your Toes, Four Wives, Brother Rat and a Baby, Angel from Texas, My Love Came Back, Dispatch from Reuter's, Four Mothers, The Wagons Roll at Night, Out of the Fog, Thieves Fall Out, The Great Mr. Nobody, Treat 'em Rough, Eagle Squadron, Ladies' Day, Lady Bodyguard, Bombadier, Strange Voyage, Rendezvous With Annie, Perfect Marriage, Smash-Up, Time Out of Mind, Hit Parade of 1947, Dude Goes West, You Gotta Stay Happy, Fuller Brush Girl, You're in the Navy Now, Meet Me After the Show, Carrie, Actors and Sin, Roman Holiday (Acad. Award nom.), Girl Rush, I'll Cry Tomorrow, Oklahoma!, Attack, Teahouse of the August Moon, The Sun Also Rises, The Joker is Wild, Orders to Kill, Gun Runners, The Roots of Heaven, Beloved Infidel, The Young Doctors, Two Little Bears, Madison Avenue, Who's Got the Action?, The Longest Day, Captain Newman M.D., Miracle of the White Stallions, The Party's Over, Seven Women, The Heartbreak Kid (Acad. Award nom.), McQ, The Take, The Longest Yard, Escape to Witch Mountain, The Devil's Rain, Hustle, Whiffs, Birch Interval, Moving Violations, Yesterday, The Concorde -- Airport 79, Foolin' Around, How to Beat the High Cost of Living, Take This Job and Shove It, Yes Giorgio, Dreamscape, The Act, Stitches, Head Office, The Big Picture, Brenda Starr.
TELEVISION: Series: Leave It To Larry, Nothing But the Best, Saturday Night Revue, Green Acres, Switch!, Falcon Crest, General Hospital. Movies & Specials: The Yeagers, Benjamin Franklin, The Borrowers, Killer Bees, Nutcracker, Anything Goes, Crash, The Word, Evening in Byzantium, Pirates Key, Living in Paradise, Oklahoma Dolls, The Plan, Peter and Paul, Goliath Awaits, Concord, Beyond Witch Mountain, Rooster, Demon Murder Case, Coalfire, In Like Flynn, Dress Gray, Mercy or Murder?, War and Remembrance, Return to Green Acres, The Girl from Mars, The Barefoot Executive. Guest: The Fall Guy, Love Boat, Highway to Heaven, Falcon Crest, Murder She Wrote, thirtysomething, Ray Bradbury Theatre, Twilight Zone, Time Trax, Golden Palace, Dr. Quinn–Medicine Woman.

ALBERT, EDWARD
Actor. b. Los Angeles, CA, Feb. 20, 1951. e. UCLA. Son of actor Eddie Albert and late actress Margo. Was prod. asst. on Patton in Spain. Has appeared with father on radio and TV shows. Is photographer and has exhibited work in L.A.
THEATER: Room Service, Our Town, The Glass Menagerie, Hamlet.
PICTURES: The Fool Killer (debut, 1965), Wild Country, Butterflies Are Free, Forty Carats, Midway, The Domino Principle, Purple Taxi, The Greek Tycoon, When Time Ran Out, The Squeeze, Galaxy of Terror, Butterfly, The House Where Evil Dwells, A Time to Die, Ellie, Getting Even (Hostage: Dallas),

Distortions, Terminal Entry, The Rescue, Mind Games, Fist Fighter, Shoot Fighter, Fight to the Death, Broken Trust, The Ice Runner, Demon Keeper, Guarding Tess.
TELEVISION: *Series*: The Yellow Rose, Falcon Crest. Host: Viva, Different Point of View, On Call. *Guest*: Beauty and the Beast, Houston Knights, Murder She Wrote, Police Story, Hitchhiker, The Love Boat, The Rookies. *Movies*: Killer Bees, Death Cruise, The Millionaire, Silent Victory: The Kitty O'Neil Story, Black Beauty, Blood Feud, The Girl from Mars, Sight Unseen, Body Language. *Mini-Series*: The Last Convertible. *Specials*: Daddy Can't Read, Orson Welles' Great Mysteries (BBC).

ALBRIGHT, LOLA
Actress. b. Akron, OH, July 20, 1925. e. Studied piano 12 years. Switchboard operator and stenographer NBC; stenographer with WHAM and bit player; photographers' model. Screen debut in The Pirate, 1948.
PICTURES: The Pirate (debut, 1947), Easter Parade, Julia Misbehaves, The Girl From Jones Beach, Tulsa, Champion, Bodyhold, Beauty on Parade, The Good Humor Man, When You're Smiling, Sierra Passage, The Killer That Stalked New York, Arctic Flight, The Silver Whip, The Treasure of Ruby Hills, The Magnificent Matador, The Tender Trap, The Monolith Monsters, Pawnee, Oregon Passage, Seven Guns to Mesa, A Cold Wind in August, Kid Galahad, Joy House (The Love Cage), Lord Love a Duck, The Way West, Where Were You When the Lights Went Out?, The Impossible Years, The Money Jungle.
TELEVISION: *Series*: Peter Gunn, Peyton Place. *Guest*: Switch, The Eddie Capra Mysteries, Quincy, Airwolf. *Movies*: Helicopter Spies, How I Spent My Summer Vacation, Delta County USA, Terraces.

ALCAINE, JOSE LUIS
Cinematographer. b. Tangier, Algeria, Dec. 26, 1938. e. Spanish Cinema Sch., Madrid. After graduation joined Madrid's Studio Moros doing commercials.
PICTURES: El Puente, El Sur, Taseo, Rustlers' Rhapsody, Bluebeard Bluebeard, Women on the Verge of a Nervous Breakdown, The Mad Monkey, Tie Me Up Tie Me Down, Ay Carmela, Lovers.

ALDA, ALAN
Actor, Writer, Director r.n. Alphonso D'Abruzzo b. New York, NY, Jan. 28, 1936. e. Fordham U., 1956. Son of actor Robert Alda. Studied at Cleveland Playhouse on Ford Foundation Grant; performed with Second City, then on TV in That Was The Week That Was. For work as director, writer and actor on M*A*S*H won 5 Emmys, 2 Writers Guild Awards, 3 Directors Guild Awards, 6 Golden Globes, 7 People's Choice Awards, Humanitas Award (for Writing).
THEATER: *B'way*: Only in America, The Owl and The Pussycat, Purlie Victorious, Fair Game For Lovers (Theatre World Award), The Apple Tree (Tony nom.), Jake's Women (Tony Award nom.). *London*: Our Town.
PICTURES: Gone Are The Days (debut, 1963), Paper Lion, The Extraordinary Seaman, Jenny, The Moonshine War, The Mephisto Waltz, To Kill a Clown, Same Time Next Year, California Suite, The Seduction of Joe Tynan (also s.p.), The Four Seasons (also dir., s.p.), Sweet Liberty (also dir., s.p.), A New Life (also dir., s.p.), Crimes and Misdemeanors (D.W. Griffith Award, NY Film Critics Award), Betsy's Wedding (also dir., s.p.), Whispers in the Dark, Manhattan Murder Mystery, Canadian Bacon, Flirting With Disaster, Everyone Says I Love You.
TELEVISION: *Series*: That Was the Week That Was, M*A*S*H (11 years), Scientific American Frontiers (PBS, host). *Movies*: The Glass House, Playmates, Isn't It Shocking?, Kill Me If You Can (Emmy nom.), And the Band Played On, Jake's Women, White Mile. *Specials*: Free to Be You and Me, 6 Rms Riv Vu (also dir.), Life's Big Questions (host). *Series creator*: We'll Get By, The Four Seasons. *Guest*: Phil Silvers Show, The Nurses, Route 66, Trials of O'Brien, Coronet Blue, Carol Burnet Show. *Pilots*: Where's Everett, Higher and Higher.

ALDREDGE, THEONI V.
Costume Designer. b. Salonika, Greece, Aug. 22, 1932. m. actor Tom Aldredge. e. American School, Athens; Goodman Theatre School, Chicago, 1949-52.
THEATER: B'way: Sweet Bird of Youth, That Championship Season, Sticks and Bones, Two Gentlemen of Verona, A Chorus Line, Annie (Tony Award), Ballroom, Much Ado About Nothing, Barnum (Tony Award), Dream Girls, Woman of the Year, Onward Victoria, La Cage aux Folles (Tony Award), 42nd Street, Merlin, Private Lives, The Corn is Green, The Rink, Blithe Spirit, Chess, Gypsy, Oh Kay!, The Secret Garden, High Rollers.
PICTURES: You're A Big Boy Now, No Way to Treat a Lady, Uptight, Last Summer, I Never Sang for My Father, Promise at Dawn, The Great Gatsby (Acad. Award, 1974), Network, Semi-Tough, The Cheap Detective, The Fury, Eyes of Laura Mars (Sci Fi. Acad. Honor), The Champ, The Rose, Can't Stop the Music, Circle of Two, Loving Couples, A Change of Seasons, Middle Age Crazy, Rich and Famous, Annie, Monsignor, Ghostbusters, Moonstruck, We're No Angels, Stanley & Iris, Other People's Money, Addams Family Values.

ALEANDRO, NORMA
Actress. b. Buenos Aires, Argentina, Dec. 6, 1936. Sister is actress Maria Vaner. As child, performed in parents, in theater troupe. In Argentina performed in every theatrical genre and epoch. Was also director. Has written published short stories (1986) and poems and screenplay for Argentinian film, Los Herederos. Was in exile in Uruguay (18 months) and Spain 1976-82 because of the military junta in Argentina. Before exile had made 12 films; after return in 1982 starred in theatre and 7 films.
THEATER: U.S.: About Love and Other Stories (one-woman show, toured South America, then at La Mama and later off-B'way at Public Theater 1986); The Senorita de Tacna (written for her by Mario Vargas-Llosa, 1987).
PICTURES: The Official Story (Cannes Film Fest. Award, 1986), Gaby: A True Story (Acad. Award nom.), Cousins, Vital Signs, The Tombs.
TELEVISION: *Movies*: Dark Holiday, One Man's War.

ALEXANDER, JANE
Actress. b. Boston, MA, Oct. 28, 1939. r.n. Jane Quigley. m. director Edwin Sherin. Mother of actor Jace Alexander. e. Sarah Lawrence Coll., U. of Edinburgh. Stage career includes appearances on B'way; at Arena Stage, Washington D.C.; Kennedy Center, D.C.; Music Center, L.A.; and Shakespeare Festival at Stamford, Conn. Appointed chairwoman of the National Endowment for the Arts, 1993.
THEATER: *NY*: The Great White Hope (Tony & Theatre World Awards, 1969), 6 Rms Riv Vu, Find Your Way Home, Hamlet, The Heiress, First Monday in October, Goodbye Fidel, Losing Time, Monday After the Miracle, Old Times, Night of the Iguana, Approaching Zanzibar, Shadowlands, The Visit, The Sisters Rosensweig.
PICTURES: The Great White Hope (debut, 1970), A Gunfight, The New Centurions, All the President's Men, The Betsy, Kramer vs. Kramer, Brubaker, Night Crossing, Testament, City Heat, Square Dance, Sweet Country, Glory.
TELEVISION: *Movies*: Welcome Home Johnny Bristol, Miracle on 34th St., This is the West That Was, Death Be Not Proud, Eleanor and Franklin, Eleanor and Franklin: The White House Years, A Circle of Children, Lovey: A Circle of Children Part II, A Question of Love, Playing for Time (Emmy Award), In the Custody of Strangers, When She Says No, Calamity Jane, Malice in Wonderland, Blood & Orchids, In Love and War, Open Admissions, A Friendship in Vienna, Daughter of the Streets, Stay the Night. *Specials*: Mountain View, A Marriage: Georgia O'Keeffe and Alfred Stieglitz. *Pilot*: New Year.

ALEXANDER, JASON
Actor. r.n. Jay Scott Greenspan. b. Newark, NJ, Sept. 23, 1959. e. Boston Univ.
THEATER: *NY*: Merrily We Roll Along, Forbidden Broadway, The Rink, Personals, Stop the World, Light Up the Sky, Broadway Bound, Jerome Robbins' Broadway (Tony, Drama Desk & Outer Critics' Circle Awards, 1989), Accomplice. *Regional*: Give 'em Hell Harry.
PICTURES: The Burning (debut, 1981), Brighton Beach Memoirs, The Mosquito Coast, Pretty Woman, White Palace, Jacob's Ladder, I Don't Buy Kisses Anymore, Coneheads, The Paper, North, Blankman, For Better or Worse (also dir.), The Last Supper, Dunston Checks In, The Hunchback of Notre Dame (voice).
TELEVISION: *Series*: E/R, Everything's Relative, Seinfeld, Duckman (voice). *Movies*: Senior Trip, Rockabye, Favorite Son, Bye Bye Birdie. *Guest*: Newhart, Dream On. *Special*: Sexual Healing.

ALEXANDER, RALPH
Executive. Began career with Universal Pictures in sales, 1949; various sls. jobs with 20th Century Fox and Lorimar. 1981-82, v.p., theatrical foreign sls., Filmway Pictures; 1982-84, v.p., sls. for Latin America & Southeast Asia, Embassy Pictures Intl. 1984, exec. v.p., multi-media foreign sls. for Robert Meyers Intl. Nov., 1985, joined Dino De Laurentiis Corp. as intl. sls. dir. in chg. all foreign sls. theatrical and ancillary rights except tv. 1986, promoted to v.p., intl. sls., DEG; pres. marketing and sales, Kings Road Intl.; 1989; joined Scotti Bros. Pictures as pres. intl. sales and marketing, 1989.

ALGAR, JAMES
Producer, Writer, Director. b. Modesto, CA, June 11, 1912. e. Stanford U., B.A., M.A. journalism. Entire career since 1934 with Walt Disney Prods. Wrote and co-produced Great Moments with Mr. Lincoln; New York World's Fair; Circarama, America the Beautiful, Circle Vision 1958 Brussels World's Fair, Disneyland, Hall of Presidents, Disney World, Florida. Shares in nine Oscars.
PICTURES: *Animator*: Snow White. *Director*: Fantasia, Bambi, Adventures of Ichabod & Mr. Toad, White Wilderness, Jungle Cat, Ten Who Dared, The Legend of Lobo, The Incredible Journey, The Gnome-Mobile, Rascal. *Documentaries*: True-Life Adventures: Seal Island, The Living Desert, Vanishing Prairie, The African Lion, Secrets of Life.

TELEVISION: *Producer:* Run Light Buck Run, The Not So Lonely Lighthouse Keeper, One Day on Beetle Rock, Wild Heart, Along the Oregon Trail, The Best Doggoned Dog in the World, One Day at Teton Marsh, Solomon the Sea Turtle, Manado the Wolverine, Wild Geese Calling, Two Against the Arctic, Bayou Bay, Secrets of the Pond, Boy Who Talked to Badgers, Big Sky Man.

ALIN, MORRIS
Editor, Writer, Publicist, Lyricist. e. City Coll. of New York. Came into m.p. industry as auditor of Hunchback of Notre Dame roadshow oper., 1924; asst. sls. prom. mgr. Universal, 1926-27; slsmn., Universal, 1927; assoc. editor. The Distributor, MGM publication, 1927; editor, 1928-33; writer, publicist, MGM Studio, 1933-34; writer, publicist, Hollywood, New York, 1935-38; rejoined Universal. 1938, editor, Progress (Univ. publication); twice winner of International Competition on Industrial Journalism; senior publicist and Progress editor, Universal, 1961-67; editor Enterprise Press, 1968; member, executive Enterprise Press 1973; American Guild of Authors and Composers, American Society of Composers, Authors and Publishers, National Academy of Popular Music, and Motion Picture Pioneers.

ALLAND, WILLIAM
Producer. b. Delmar, DE, March 4, 1916. e. Baltimore. Acted in semi-professional groups; with Orson Welles' Mercury Theatre as actor, stage mgr.; asst. prod. Mercury Theatre radio series. Served in U.S. Air Force, WWII; then radio writer; prod., Universal, 1952; Paramount, 1960; Allied Artists, 1963.
PICTURES: *Actor:* Citizen Kane (also dialogue dir.), Macbeth. *Producer:* The Raiders, Flesh and Fury, Stand At Apache River, It Came From Outer Space, The Lawless Breed, Creature From The Black Lagoon, Johnny Dark, This Island Earth, Dawn At Socorro, Four Guns To The Border, Chief Crazy Horse, Revenge Of The Creature, Tarantula, The Creature Walks Among Us, The Mole People, Gun for a Coward, Land Unknown, Deadly Mantis, The Lady Takes a Flyer, As Young As We Are, The Party Crashers, Colossus of New York, Raw Wind in Eden, The Space Children, Look In Any Window (also dir.), The Lively Set, Treasure of the Lost Canyon, The Rare Breed, The Black Castle, Battle Over Citizen Kane.

ALLEN, COREY
Director, Actor. r.n. Alan Cohen. b. Cleveland, OH, June 29, 1934. e. UCLA, 1951-54; UCLA law sch. 1954-55. Actor turned dir. starred in Oscar-winning UCLA student film, appeared in 20 plays at Players Ring, Players Gallery and other L.A. theaters. TV: Perry Mason, Alfred Hitchcock Presents. With partner John Herman Shaner, prod. Freeway Circuit Theatre. Led Actors Workshop with actor Guy Stockwell for 10 years.
PICTURES: *Actor:* Rebel Without a Cause, Key Witness, Sweet Bird of Youth, Private Property, Party Girl, The Chapman Report. *Director:* The Erotic Adventures of Pinocchio, Thunder and Lightning, Avalanche.
TELEVISION: *Series Director:* This is the Life, Mannix, High Chaparral, Dr. Kildare, Streets of San Francisco (DGA nom.), Ironside, Barnaby Jones, Police Woman, Rockford Files, Quincy, Dallas, Lou Grant, McClain's Law, Family Novak, T.J. Hooker, Paper Chase: The Second Year, Hill Street Blues (Emmy), Road Home, Deep Space Nine. *Pilots:* Man Undercover, Capitol, Simon and Simon, Whiz Kids, Murder She Wrote, Code Name: Foxfire, Star Trek: The Next Generation. Unsub. *Movies:* See the Man Run, Cry Rape!, Yesterday's Child, Stone (pilot), Man in the Santa Claus Suit, The Return of Frank Cannon, Code Name: Foxfire (pilot), Brass, Destination America, Beverly Hills Cowgirl Blues, The Last Fling, Ann Jillian Story, Stalking Back.

ALLEN, DAYTON
Performer. b. New York, NY, Sept. 24, 1919. e. Mt. Vernon H.S. Motion picture road shows, 1936-40; disc jockey, WINS, N.Y., 1940-41; writer, vaudeville comedy bits, 1941-45; then radio comic, puppeteer and voices; TV since 1948; film commercials; shows include voices on Terrytoons, Deputy Dawg, Heckle & Jeckle, Lancelot Link: Secret Chimp, Lariat Sam, Oaky Doky, Bonny Maid Varieties, Howdy Doody (voices of Mr. Bluster, Flubadub, The Inspector & many others), Jack Barry's Winky Dink, The Steve Allen Show. 130 Dayton Allen 5 minute shows (synd.) Acted in film The Cotton Club.

ALLEN, DEBBIE
Actress, Choreographer. b. Houston, TX, Jan. 16, 1950. Sister is actress Phylicia Rashad. e. Howard U.
THEATER: Ti-Jean and His Brothers (debut, 1972), Purlie, Raisin, Ain't Misbehavin', West Side Story (revival), Sweet Charity (revival, Tony Award, 1986), Carrie (choreographer).
PICTURES: The Fish That Saved Pittsburgh (1979), Fame, Ragtime, Jo Jo Dancer Your Life is Calling, Blank Check.
TELEVISION: *Series:* The Jim Stafford Show, 3 Girls 3, Fame (series; 3 Emmys as choreographer, 1 nom. as actress), A Different World (prod., dir), In the House. *Mini-Series:* Roots-The Next Generation. *Movies:* The Greatest Thing That Almost Happened, Ebony, Ivory and Jade, Women of San Quentin,

Celebrity, Polly-Comin' Home (dir.), Stompin' at the Savoy (also dir.). *Specials:* Ben Vereen-His Roots, Loretta Lynn in Big Apple Country, Texaco Star Theater—Opening Night, The Kids from Fame, John Schneider's Christmas Holiday, A Tribute to Martin Luther King Jr.—A Celebration of Life, Motown Returns to the Apollo, The Debbie Allen Special (also dir., chor.), Sinbad Live (Afros and Bell Bottoms), Academy Awards (choreographer: 1991-96).

ALLEN, DEDE
Film Editor. r.n. Dorothea Carothers Allen b. Cleveland, OH, 1924. Once a messenger at Columbia Pictures, moved to editing dept., then to commercials and features.
PICTURES: Odds Against Tomorrow (1959), The Hustler, America America, Bonnie and Clyde, Rachel Rachel, Alice's Restaurant, Little Big Man, Slaughterhouse 5, Serpico, Night Moves, Dog Day Afternoon, The Missouri Breaks, Slap Shot, The Wiz, Reds (also exec. prod.), Harry and Son, Mike's Murder, The Breakfast Club, Off Beat, The Milagro Beanfield War (co-ed.), Let It Ride (co-ed.), Henry and June. The Addams Family.

ALLEN, JAY PRESSON
Writer, Producer. r.n. Jacqueline Presson. b. Fort Worth, TX, March 3, 1922. m. prod. Lewis M. Allen.
THEATER: *Writer:* The First Wife, The Prime of Miss Jean Brodie, Forty Carats, Tru (also dir.), The Big Love (also dir.).
PICTURES: *Writer:* Marnie, The Prime of Miss Jean Brodie, Cabaret, Travels with My Aunt, Funny Lady, Just Tell Me What You Want (also prod.), It's My Turn (exec. prod. only), Prince of the City (also exec. prod.), Deathtrap (also exec. prod.).
TELEVISION: *Series:* Family (creator), Hot House (also exec. prod.).

ALLEN, IOAN
Executive. b. Stafford, England, Oct. 25, 1938. e. Rossall School and Dartmouth Naval College, England. Artist management and record production, 1964-1969. Responsible for origination and development of the Dolby Stereo film program. Past Fellow of Society of Morion Picture & Television Engineers, Audio Engineering Society and the British Kinematographic Sound & Television Society. President, International Theatre Equipment Association. U.S. correspondent on the International Standards Organization cinematographic subcommittee. Adjunct professor at USC School of Cinema-Television. Vice president of Dolby Laboratories. Recipient of Scientific & Technical Awards–Academy of Motion Picture Arts & Sciences, 1979 and 1987. Received an Oscar in 1989 for work in Dolby Laboratories film program. 1985 recipient of Samuel L. Warner Award for contribution to motion picture sound.

ALLEN, JOAN
Actress. b. Rochelle, IL, Aug. 20, 1956. Founding member of Steppenwolf Theatre Co., in Chicago where she performed in over 20 shows.
THEATER: *Chicago includes:* A Lesson from Aloes, Three Sisters, The Miss Firecracker Contest, Cloud 9, Balm in Gilead, Fifth of July, Reckless, Earthly Possessions. *Off B'way:* The Marriage of Bette and Boo, And a Nightingale Sang (Clarence Derwent, Drama Desk, Outer Critics' Circle and Theatre World Awards). *B'way debut:* Burn This (1987, Tony Award), The Heidi Chronicles.
PICTURES: Compromising Positions (debut, 1985), Manhunter, Peggy Sue Got Married, Tucker: The Man and His Dream, In Country, Ethan Frome, Searching for Bobby Fischer, Josh and S.A.M., Mad Love, Nixon, The Crucible, The Ice Storm.
TELEVISION: *Special:* All My Sons. *Mini-Series:* Evergreen. Movie: Without Warning: The James Brady Story.

ALLEN, KAREN
Actress. b. Carrollton, IL, Oct. 5, 1951. e. George Washington U., U. of Maryland. Auditioned for theatrical company in Washington, DC and won a role in Saint, touring with it for 7 months. Spent several years with Washington Theatre Laboratory Co. Moved to NY, acting in student films at NYU and studying acting with Lee Strasberg at Theatre Institute.
THEATER: *NY:* Monday After the Miracle (B'way debut, 1982; Theatre World Award), Extremities, The Miracle Worker, The Country Girl. *Williamstown (MA) Theatre:* Tennessee Williams-- A Celebration, The Glass Menagerie.
PICTURES: National Lampoon's Animal House (debut, 1978), Manhattan, The Wanderers, Cruising, A Small Circle of Friends, Raiders of the Lost Ark, Shoot the Moon, Split Image, Until September, Starman, Terminus, The Glass Menagerie, Backfire, Scrooged, Animal Behavior, Secret Places of the Heart, Sweet Talker, Exile, Malcolm X, The Sandlot, Ghost in the Machine.
TELEVISION: *Movies:* Lovey: A Circle of Children Part II, Secret Weapon, Challenger, Voyage, Down Home. *Guest:* Alfred Hitcock Presents (1986). *Mini-Series:* East of Eden.

ALLEN, LEWIS M.
Producer. b. Berryville, VA, June 27, 1922. e. Univ. of VA. m. writer-producer Jay Presson Allen.

PICTURES: The Connection, The Balcony, Lord of the Flies, Fahrenheit 451, The Queen (exec. prod.), Fortune and Men's Eyes, Never Cry Wolf, 1918 (exec. prod.), Valentine's Day (exec. prod.), Swimming to Cambodia, O.C. & Stiggs (exec. prod.), End of the Line (co-prod.), Miss Firecracker (exec. prod.).

ALLEN, MEL
TV commentator b. Birmingham, AL, Feb. 14, 1913. e. U. of Alabama, A.B. 1932; U. Alabama Law Sch., LL.B. 1936. Started as sportscaster in Birmingham, while in law school; speech instructor in U. Ala. 1935-37; to N.Y. 1937, as staff announcer CBS to 1943; served in U.S. Army WWII in infantry until the war ended, then before discharge was transferred to work on NBC Army Hour; sportscasting throughout U.S., joined N.Y. Yankees, 1946, concurrently narrating many shorts incl. How to Make a Yankee, appearing on radio & video and in Babe Ruth Story; sports commentator Fox Movietonews; voted best sportscaster in Motion Picture Daily-Fame radio. TV polls; Monitor, NBC; NCAA TV College Football, NBC; World Series (1938-64), CBS-NBC; Rose Bowl (1951-62), NBC; Sports Broadcasters Hall Of Fame.

ALLEN, NANCY
Actress. b. New York, NY, June 24, 1950. e. H.S. Performing Arts, N.Y.
PICTURES: The Last Detail (debut, 1973), Carrie, I Wanna Hold Your Hand, 1941, Home Movies, Dressed to Kill, Blow Out, Strange Invaders, The Buddy System, The Philadelphia Experiment, The Last Victim (Forced Entry), Not for Publication, Terror in the Aisles, Sweet Revenge, Robocop, Poltergeist III, Limit Up, Robocop 2, Robocop 3.
TELEVISION: Movies: The Gladiator, Memories of Murder, Acting on Impulse, The Man Who Wouldn't Die.

ALLEN, REX
Actor. b. Wilcox, AZ, Dec. 31, 1922. e. Wilcox H.S., 1939. Vaudeville & radio actor; WLS, Chicago, 5 yrs.; was rodeo star appearing in shows through U.S.
PICTURES: Arizona Cowboy, Hills of Oklahoma, Under Mexicali Stars, Thunder in God's Country, Rodeo King & the Senorita, I Dream of Jeannie, Last Musketeer, South Pacific Trail, Old Overland Trail, Down Laredo Way, Phantom Stallion, For the Love of Mike, Tomboy and the Champ. Narrator: The Legend of Lobo, The Incredible Journey, Charlotte's Web.
TELEVISION: Guest: Perry Como Special. Voice only: commercials, Wonderful World of Color. Series: Frontier Doctor, Five Star Jubilee.

ALLEN, STEVE
Performer. b. New York, NY, Dec 26, 1921. m. actress Jayne Meadows. Attended Arizona St. Univ. U.S. Army 1942; radio shows, Los Angeles; TV, N.Y., 1950. On NY stage in The Mikado. Composer or lyricist of numerous songs including This Could Be the Start of Something Big, Pretend You Don't See Her, South Rampart St. Parade, Picnic, Houseboat, On the Beach, Sleeping Beauty, Bell Book and Candle, Gravy Waltz, Impossible; score for B'way musicals Sophie, and TV musicals: The Bachelor, and Alice in Wonderland.
AUTHOR: Fourteen For Tonight, Steve Allen's Bop Fables, The Funny Men, Wry On the Rocks, The Girls on the Tenth Floor, The Question Man, Mark It and Strike It, Not All of Your Laughter, Not All of Your Tears, Bigger Than a Breadbox, A Flash of Swallows, The Wake, Princess Snip-Snip and the Puppykittens, Curses, Schmock-Schmock!, Meeting of Minds, Ripoff, Meeting of Minds-Second Series, Rip-off, Explaining China, The Funny People, Talk Show Murders, Beloved Son: Story of the Jesus Cults, More Funny People, How To Make a Speech and How To Be Funny, Murder on the Glitter Box, The Passionate Non-smoker's Bill of Rights, Dumbth and 81 Ways to Make Americans Smarter, Murder in Manhattan, Steve Allen on the Bible, Religion and Morality, The Public Hating, Murder in Vegas, Hi-Ho Steverino!: My Adventures in the Wonderful Wacky World of TV, The Murder Game, More Steve Allen on the Bible, Religion & Morality Book II, Make 'em Laugh, Reflections, Murder on the Atlantic, The Man Who Turned Back the Clock and Other Short Stories.
PICTURES: Down Memory Lane (debut, 1949), I'll Get By, The Benny Goodman Story, The Big Circus, College Confidential, Don't Worry We'll Think of a Title, Warning Shot, Where Were You When the Lights Went Out?, The Comic, The Sunshine Boys, Heart Beat, Amazon Women on the Moon, Great Balls of Fire!, The Player, Casino.
TELEVISION: Series: The Steve Allen Show (1950-52), Songs for Sale, Talent Patrol, What's My Line, Steve Allen Show, Tonight, Steve Allen Show (1956-61), (1962-64), (1964-67), I've Got a Secret, Steve Allen Comedy Hour (1967), Steve Allen Show (1967-69), I've Got a Secret (1972-73) Steve Allen's Laugh Back, Meeting of Minds, Steve Allen Comedy Hour (1980-81), Life's Most Embarrassing Moments. Movies: Now You See It Now You Don't, Stone, The Gossip Columnist. Mini-Series: Rich Man Poor Man.

ALLEN, TIM
Actor. r.n. Timothy Allen Dick. b. Denver, CO, June 13, 1953. e. W. Michigan Univ., Univ. of Detroit (studied acting). Worked as

creative dir. for adv. agency before becoming stand up comedian. Made stand up tv debut on Showtime Comedy Club All-Stars, 1988. Author: Don't Stand Close to a Naked Man (1994).
PICTURES: Comedy's Dirtiest Dozen, The Santa Clause, Toy Story (voice), Jungle2Jungle.
TELEVISION: Series: Home Improvement. Specials: Tim Allen: Men Are Pigs (also writer), Tim Allen Rewrites America (also exec. prod., writer).

ALLEN, WILLIAM
Executive. e. USC Cinema/TV Sch., Pepperdine Univ. 1979, exec. trainee in CBS Entertainment division, eventually serving as assoc. program exec. in the Comedy Series Programming Dept., mngr./dir. of the CBS Comedy Program Developemnt Dept. 1986- 87, joined MTM as sr. v.p., Comedy Programming; 1987-88, sr. v.p. creative affairs; 1989-91, exec. v.p. MTM Television. 1992, named President of MTM Television.

ALLEN, WOODY
Actor, Director, Writer. r.n. Allan Stewart Konigsberg. b. New York, NY, Dec. 1, 1935. e. NYU, 1953; City Coll. NY, 1953. Began writing comedy at age 17, contributing to various magazines (Playboy, New Yorker) and top TV comedy shows incl. Sid Caesar (1957), Art Carney (1958-59), Herb Shriner (1953). Appeared in nightclubs starting in 1961 as stand-up comic; later performed as a jazz musician at Michael's Pub, NY. Special Award, Berlin Film Fest., 1975.
AUTHOR: Getting Even, Without Feathers, Side Effects.
THEATER: Author: Play It Again Sam (also actor), Don't Drink The Water, The Floating Lightbulb, Central Park West (from Death Defying Acts).
PICTURES: Actor-Screenplay: What's New Pussycat?, What's Up Tiger Lily? (also dubbed and compiled footage; assoc. prod.), Casino Royale (actor only). Director/Screenplay/Actor: Take the Money and Run, Bananas, Play It Again Sam (actor, s.p. only), Everything You Always Wanted to Know About Sex* But Were Afraid to Ask, Sleeper, Love and Death, The Front (actor only), Annie Hall (Academy Awards for Best Director and Original Screenplay, 1977), Interiors (dir., s.p. only), Manhattan, Stardust Memories, A Midsummer Night's Sex Comedy, Zelig, Broadway Danny Rose, The Purple Rose of Cairo (dir., s.p. only), Hannah and Her Sisters (Academy Award for Best Original Screenplay, 1986), Radio Days (dir., s.p., narrator only), September (dir., s.p. only), King Lear (actor only), Another Woman (dir., s.p. only), New York Stories (Oedipus Wrecks segment), Crimes and Misdemeanors, Alice (dir., s.p. only), Scenes From a Mall (actor only), Shadows and Fog, Husbands and Wives, Manhattan Murder Mystery, Bullets Over Broadway (dir., s.p. only), Mighty Aphrodite, Everyone Says I Love You (dir. & actor).
TELEVISION: Movies: Don't Drink the Water (also dir., writer), The Sunshine Boys. Specials: The Best on Record, Gene Kelly in New York New York, The Woody Allen Special (also writer, co-dir.), Woody Allen Looks at 1967 (Kraft Music Hall; also writer), Plimpton: Did You Hear the One About ...? Guest: Hullabaloo, Andy Williams, Hippodrome.

ALLEY, KIRSTIE
Actress. b. Wichita, KS, Jan. 12, 1955. m. actor Parker Stevenson. e. KS State U., U. of Kansas. On L.A. stage in Cat on a Hot Tin Roof.
PICTURES: Star Trek II: The Wrath of Khan (debut, 1982), Blind Date, Champions, Runaway, Summer School, Shoot to Kill, Loverboy, Look Who's Talking, Madhouse, Sibling Rivalry, Look Who's Talking Too, Look Who's Talking Now, Village of the Damned, It Takes Two.
TELEVISION: Series: Masquerade, Cheers (Emmy Award, 1991), Untitled. Movies: Sins of the Past, A Bunny's Tale, Stark: Mirror Image, Prince of Bel Air, Infidelity, David's Mother (Emmy Award, 1994). Mini-Series: North and South, North and South Book II. Guest: The Love Boat, The Hitchhiker.

ALLYSON, JUNE
Actress. r.n. Ella Geisman. b. Westchester, NY, Oct. 7, 1917. Started as chorus girl. Voted one of ten top money-making stars in Motion Picture Herald-Fame poll, 1955.
THEATER: B'way: Sing Out the News, Panama Hattie, Best Foot Forward, 40 Carats. Tour: No No Nanette.
PICTURES: Best Foot Foward (debut, 1943), Girl Crazy, Thousands Cheer, Meet the People, Two Girls and a Sailor, Music for Millions, Her Highness and the Bellboy, The Sailor Takes a Wife, Two Sisters From Boston, Till the Clouds Roll By, Secret Heart, High Barbaree, Good News, The Bride Goes Wild, The Three Musketeers, Words and Music, Little Women, The Stratton Story, Meet the People, Reformer and the Redhead, Right Cross, Too Young to Kiss, Girl in White, Battle Circus, Remains to be Seen, Executive Suite, Glenn Miller Story, Woman's World, Strategic Air Command, The Shrike, McConnell Story, Opposite Sex, You Can't Run Away From It, Interlude, My Man Godfrey, Stranger in My Arms, They Only Kill Their Masters, Blackout, That's Entertainment III.
TELEVISION: Series: DuPont Show With June Allyson. Guest: Murder She Wrote, Misfits of Science. Movies: See the Man Run, Letters from Three Lovers, Curse of the Black Widow, Vega$, Three on a Date, The Kid With the Broken Halo. Special: 20th Century Follies.

ALMODOVAR, PEDRO
Director, Writer. b. La Mancha, Spain, Sep. 25, 1951. Grew up in Calzada de Calatrava. At 17 moved to Madrid where worked 10 years for telephone co. while writing comic strips and articles for underground newspapers and working as actor with independent theater co., Los Goliardos. Upon the end of Francoist repression in 1975, made Super-8 experimental films starring friends. Wrote fiction, sang with rock band and created character of porn star, Patty Diphusa, whose fictionalized confessions he published in the magazine La Luna.
PICTURES: Pepi Lucy Bom and Other Girls on the Heap (debut, 1980), Labyrinth of Passion, Dark Habits, What Have I Done to Deserve This?, Matador, Law of Desire, Women on the Verge of a Nervous Breakdown, Tie Me Up! Tie Me Down!, High Heels, Kika.

ALMOND, PAUL
Producer, Director, Writer. b. Montreal, Canada, April 26, 1931. e. McGill U., Balliol Coll., Oxford U. 1954-66 produced and directed over a hundred television dramas in Toronto, London, N.Y., and Hollywood.
PICTURES: Backfire, Isabel, Act of the Heart, Journey, Final Assignment, Ups and Downs, Captive Hearts, The Dance Goes On.

ALONSO, MARIA CONCHITA
Actress, Singer. b. Cuba, 1957. Family moved to Venezuela when she was five. 1971, named Miss Teenager of the World. 1975, Miss Venezuela. 6th runner up, Miss World. Appeared in four feature films and 10 soap operas before coming to U.S. Recorded several albums as singer: 5 gold albums, 1 platinum, 3 Grammy noms.
THEATER: B'way: Kiss of the Spider Woman.
PICTURES: Fear City, Moscow on the Hudson, Touch and Go, A Fine Mess, Extreme Prejudice, The Running Man, Colors, Vampire's Kiss, Predator 2, McBain, The House of the Spirits, Roosters, Caught.
TELEVISION: An American Cousin (RAI mini-series). Specials: Viva Miami!, The Night of the Super Sounds (host). Guest: One of the Boys. Movies: Teamster Boss: The Jackie Presser Story, MacShayne: The Final Roll of the Dice, Texas.

ALONZO, JOHN A
Cinematographer, Director. b. Dallas, TX, 1934.
PICTURES: Bloody Mama, Vanishing Point, Harold and Maude, Get to Know Your Rabbit, Lady Sings the Blues, Sounder, Pete-n-Tillie, Hit, The Naked Ape, Conrack, Chinatown, Farewell My Lovely, The Fortune, I Will ... I Will ... For Now, Once Is Not Enough, The Bad News Bears, Black Sunday, Beyond Reason, Close Encounters of the Third Kind (addtl. photog.), Which Way Is Up?, Casey's Shadow, FM (dir. only), The Cheap Detective, Norma Rae, Tom Horn, Back Roads, Zorro the Gay Blade, Blue Thunder, Cross Creek, Scarface, Out of Control, Terror in the Aisles, Runaway, Jo Jo Dancer Your Life Is Calling, Nothing in Common, 50 Years of Action, Real Men, Overboard, Physical Evidence, Steel Magnolias, Internal Affairs, The Guardian, Navy Seals, Housesitter, Cool World, The Meteor Man, Clifford.
TELEVISION: Champions: A Love Story, Belle Star (also dir.), Blinded By the Light (also dir.), The Kid From Nowhere (also dir.), Roots: The Gift, Knights of the City.

ALTERMAN, JOSEPH GEORGE
Executive. b. New Haven, CT., Dec. 17, 1919. e. Wesleyan U., B.A., 1942; Inst. for Organization Management, Yale U. 1957-59. Exec. assist., SoundScriber Corp., 1945-48; district mgr., Industrial Luncheon Service, 1948-55; asst. secretary and admin. Secretary, Theatre Owners of America, 1955; Exec. dir. and vice pres., Natl. Assn. of Theatre Owners, 1966; Exec. v.p. COMPO., 1970. Retired 1988 from NATO. Consultant m.p. industry, conventions and meetings. Chmn. bd. governors, Institute for Learning in Retirement, Albertus Magnus College.

ALTMAN, ROBERT
Director, Writer, Producer. b. Kansas City, MO, Feb. 20, 1925. e. U. of Missouri. Early film writer credits: Bodyguard (co-story), Corn's-a-Poppin (co-s.p.). Made industrial films and documentaries for the Calvin Company in Kansas City, before dir. first indept. feature in 1957. Received D.W. Griffith Lifetime Achievement Award from Directors Guild of America, 1994.
THEATER: NY: Two By South, Come Back to the Five and Dime Jimmy Dean Jimmy Dean. Operas: The Rake's Progress, McTeague.
PICTURES: Director: The Delinquents (also s.p., prod.), The James Dean Story (also co-prod., edit.), Countdown, That Cold Day in the Park, M*A*S*H (Cannes Film Fest. Golden Palm Award, 1970; Acad. Award nom.), Brewster McCloud, McCabe & Mrs. Miller (also co-s.p.), Images (also s.p.), The Long Goodbye, Thieves Like Us (also co-s.p.), California Split (also co-prod.), Nashville (also prod.; NY Film Critics, Natl. Society of Film Critics & Natl. Board of Review Awards for Best Director & Picture, 1975; Acad. Award noms. for dir. & picture), Buffalo Bill and the Indians: Or Sitting Bull's History Lesson (also co-s.p., prod.), Three Women (also s.p., prod.), A Wedding (also co-s.p.,

prod., co-story), Quintet (also co-s.p., prod., co-story), A Perfect Couple (also co-s.p., prod.), Health (also co-s.p., prod.), Popeye, Come Back to the Five and Dime Jimmy Dean Jimmy Dean, Streamers (also co-prod.), Secret Honor (also prod.), Fool for Love, Beyond Therapy (also co-s.p.), O.C. and Stiggs (also co-prod.), Aria (dir. Les Boreades sequence; also s.p.), Vincent & Theo, The Player (BAFTA & Cannes Film Fest. Awards for Best Director, 1991; Acad. Award nom.), Short Cuts (also co-s.p.; Acad. Award nom. for dir.), Ready to Wear/Pret-a-Porter (also co-s.p.). Producer: The Late Show, Welcome to L.A., Remember My Name, Rich Kids, Mrs. Parker and the Vicious Circle, Kansas City.
TELEVISION: Series (dir., writer, &/or prod. episodes): The Roaring Twenties, The Millionaire, Bonanza, Bus Stop, Combat, Kraft Mystery Theatre (Nightmare in Chicago: Once Upon a Savage Night), The Gallant Men (pilot). Specials: Two by South (also prod.), The Laundromat, The Dumb Waiter (also prod.), Tanner '88 (also co-exec. prod.; Emmy Award for dir. episode The Boiler Room, 1989), The Room, The Real McTeague, Black and Blue. Movie: The Caine Mutiny Court-Martial (also co-prod.).

ALVARADO, TRINI
Actress. b. New York, NY, 1967. e. Fordham U. m. actor Robert McNeill. Began performing at age 7 as flamenco dancer with her parents' troupe. Prof. acting debut at 9 in stage musical Becca.
THEATER: Runaways, Yours Anne, Maggie Magalita, I Love You I Love You Not, Reds, The Magic Show, Godspell.
PICTURES: Rich Kids (debut, 1989), Times Square, Mrs. Soffel, Sweet Lorraine, Satisfaction, The Chair, Stella, American Blue Note, The Babe, American Friends, Little Women, Frighteners.
TELEVISION: Movies: Dreams Don't Die, Prisoner Without a Name, Nitti. Specials: Private Contentment, Unicorn Tales, A Movie Star's Daughter, Stagestruck, Sensibility and Sense. Guest: Kay O'Brien, Kate and Allie.

ALVIN, JOHN
Actor. r.n. John Alvin Hoffstadt; b. Chicago, IL, Oct. 24, 1917. e. Pasadena Playhouse, CA. Attended Morgan Park Military Acad. On radio Chicago & Detroit; on N.Y. stage Leaning on Letty, Life of the Party. Screen debut 1944 in Destination Tokyo. Under contract four years to Warner Bros., featured in 25 films.
PICTURES: Destination Tokyo, Objective Burma, San Antonio, The Beast With Five Fingers, Night and Day, Cheyenne, Missing Women, Two Guys from Texas, Bold Frontiersman, Train to Alcatraz, Shanghai Chest, Carrie, April In Paris, Roughly Speaking, The Very Thought of You, Shadow of a Woman, Three Strangers, Romance on the High Seas, Torpedo Alley, Irma La Douce, Marnie, Inside Daisy Clover, The Legend of Lylah Clare, They Shoot Horses Don't They?, They Call Me Mr. Tibbs, Somewhere in Time, Beethoven's 2nd, Milk Money.
TELEVISION: Meet Millie, Burns and Allen, Death Valley Days, Asphalt Jungle, Climax, Dragnet, Jack Benny Show, My Three Sons, The Texan, Adventures in Paradise, Rawhide, Rifleman, Omnibus, Wells Fargo, Alfred Hitchcock, Mannix, I Spy, Legend of Lizzie Borden, All in the Family, McDuff, Lineup, My Favorite Husband, Family Affair, Get Smart, The Incredible Hulk, The Lucy Show, Ironside, Nightstalker, MASH, Lou Grant Show, Hart to Hart, Yellow Rose, Dennis the Menace (2 Hour Pilot), Murder She Wrote, Monster Squad, House of Evil, Aftermath, General Hospital, Starsky & Hutch, Policewoman, Amazing Stories, Capitol, Passions, The Quest, Visions/KCET, Rachel Sweet Rachel, Swallows Came Back, Return to Green Acres, Moving Target, From Out of the Night, The Walkers, The Bold and the Beautiful.

AMATEAU, ROD
Director. b. New York, NY, Dec. 20, 1923. U.S. Army, 1941; 20th Century-Fox; 2nd unit dir.
PICTURES: The Statue, Where Does It Hurt?, The Wilby Conspiracy, Drive-In, Lovelines, Garbage Pail Kids (also s.p., prod.), Sunset (story only).
TELEVISION: Series: Schlitz Playhouse of Stars, Four Star Playhouse, General Electric Theatre, Private Secretary, Dennis Day Show, Lassie, Ray Milland Show, Bob Cummings Show, Burns & Allen Show (also prod.), Dobie Gillis. Movies: Uncommon Valor, High School U.S.A., Swimsuit (prod.).

AMES, LOUIS B.
Executive. b. St. Louis, MO, Aug. 9, 1918. e. Washington U., St. Louis. m. Jetti Ames. Began as music consultant and staff director of musical programs for NBC; music dir. 1948, WPIX; 1951 appt. program mgr., WPIX; assoc. prod., Today, NBC TV, 1954; feature editor Home, 1957; Adm.-prod. NBC Opera, 1958; dir. cultural prog. N.Y. World's Fair, 1960-63; dir. RCA Pavillion, N.Y. World's Fair, 1963-65; 1966 dir., Nighttime, TV; 1969, dir. of programming N.W. Ayer & Sons, Inc. 1973 Mgr. Station Services, Television Information Office. NYC.

AMIEL, JON
Director. b. London, Eng., 1948. e. Cambridge. Was in charge of the Oxford & Cambridge Shakespeare Co., then literary mngr. for Hampstead Theatre Club where he started directing. Became story edit. for BBC, then director.

PICTURES: Silent Twins, Queen of Hearts, Tune in Tomorrow, Sommersby, Copycat.
TELEVISION: A Sudden Wrench, Gates of Gold, Busted, Tandoori Nights (series), The Singing Detective (mini-series).

AMIN, MARK
Executive. Chairman & Acting CEO, TriMark Pictures.

AMIS, SUZY
Actress. b. Oklahoma City, OK, Jan. 5, 1962. e. Heritage Hall, Oklahoma City. At 16 was introduced on the Merv Griffin Show by Eileen Ford whose modeling agency she worked for, as "The Face of the Eighties." After modeling and living in Europe, made film debut in Fandango (1985). Off-B'way debut: Fresh Horses (Theatre World Award).
PICTURES: Fandango, The Big Town, Plain Clothes, Rocket Gibraltar, Twister, Where the Heart Is, Rich in Love, Watch It, The Ballad of Little Jo, Two Small Bodies, Blown Away, The Usual Suspects, Nadja.

AMOS, JOHN
Actor. b. Newark, NJ, Dec. 27, 1941. e. East Orange H.S., Colorado State U, Long Beach City Col. Inducted as honorary Master Chief Petty Officer in U.S. Navy 1993. Worked as professional football player, social worker (heading the Vera Institute of Justice in NY) and advertising copywriter before writing television comedy material (for the Leslie Uggams Show) and performing as stand-up comedian in Greenwich Village. Has also dir. theatre with Bahamian Rep. Co. Artistic dir.: John Harms Theatre, Englewood, NJ.
THEATER: L.A.: Norman Is That You? and Master Harold...And the Boys, Split Second, The Emperor Jones. B'way: Tough to Get Help. NYSF: Twelfth Night. Off-B'way: The Past is the Past. Regional: Fences, Halley's Comet (also writer).
PICTURES: Vanishing Point (debut, 1971), Sweet Sweetback's Baadasssss Song, The World's Greatest Athlete, Let's Do It Again, Touched By Love, The Beastmaster, Dance of the Dwarfs, American Flyers, Coming to America, Lock Up, Die Hard 2, Ricochet, Two Evil Eyes (The Black Cat), Mac, Night Trap (Mardi Gras for the Devil).
TELEVISION: Series: Mary Tyler Moore, The Funny Side, Maude, Good Times, Hunter, South by Southwest, 704 Hauser. Mini-Series: Roots. Movies: The President's Plane is Missing, Future Cop, Cops and Robin, Willa, Alcatraz-The Whole Shocking Story, Bonanza-the Next Generation. Pilots: Clippers, 704 Hauser Street; many guest appearances incl. Bill Cosby Show, Love American Style, Sanford and Son, The Love Boat, Cosby Show. Special: Without a Pass.

AMSTERDAM, MOREY
Actor, Producer, Writer, Composer, Musician. b. Chicago, IL, Dec. 14, 1914. e. U. of California, Berkeley. Boy soprano. Radio KPO. Night club performer, Chicago, 1929; comedian, singer, musician. Rube Wolf Orchestra; comedian, Optimistic Doughnuts Program, 1930; writer, performer with, Al Pearce Gang, 1932; writer, MGM, 1937; co-writer, m.p. Columbia, Universal; writer, performer, USO Shows, 1942-43; Owner, the Playgoers Club; v.p. International Pictures. Songs: Rum and Coca Cola, Why Oh Why Did I Ever Leave Wyoming, Yak A Puk, etc.
PICTURES: It Came From Outer Space, Machine Gun Kelly, Murder Inc., Gay Purr-ee (voice), Beach Party, Muscle Beach Party, Don't Worry ... We'll Think of a Title, The Horse in the Gray Flannel Suit, Won Ton Ton the Dog Who Saved Hollywood.
TELEVISION: Series: Stop Me If You've Heard This One, Morey Amsterdam Show, Broadway Open House, Battle of the Ages, Who Said That?, Keep Talking, Dick Van Dyke Show. Can You Top This? (also exec. prod.). Movies: Sooner or Later, Side By Side.

ANDERSON, GERRY
Hon. F.B.K.S., Producer, Director, Writer. b. London, England, 1929. Entered industry in 1946. Chmn./man. dir. Gerry Anderson Productions, Ltd. Over 320 pictures produced for TV worldwide. 1981 Co-founded Anderson Burr Pictures. 1982 prod. Terrahawks in association with London Weekend Television; second series, Terrahawks, 1984; Space Police pilot for series in assoc. with TVS, 1985-6; Dick Spanner stop motion series for Channel Four 1987. Entered commercials as a dir.: numerous commercials incl. Royal Bank of Scotland, Children's World, Domestos, Shout, Scotch Tape, etc. 1992 Anglo Russian Cartoon Series Astro Force and lecture tour An Evening with Garry Anderson.
PICTURES: Thunderbirds Are Go, Thunderbird 6, Journey to the Far Side of the Sun.
TELEVISION: Series: The Adventures of Twizzle, Torchy, The Battery Boy, Four Feather Falls, Supercar, Fireball XL5, Stingray, Thunderbirds, Captain Scarlet, Joe 90, The Secret Service, The Protectors, UFO, Space 1999, Terrahawks, Dick Spanner, Space Precinct.

ANDERSON, HARRY
Actor. b. Newport, RI, Oct. 14, 1952. m. actress-magician Leslie Pollack. Performed magic show prior to plays at Oregon

Shakespeare Festival. Also opening act for Kenny Rogers, Debbie Reynolds and Roger Miller in Las Vegas. Owner of magic shop in Ashland OR. Received Stage Magician of Year Award, National Acad. of Magician Arts and Sciences.
PICTURE: The Escape Artist.
TELEVISION: Series: Night Court (Emmy nom.), Our Time, Dave's World. Movies: Spies, Lies and Naked Thighs; The Absent-Minded Professor, Stephen King's It. Guest: Cheers, The Tonight Show, David Letterman, Saturday Night Live, Wil Shriner. Specials: Comic Relief, Harry Anderson's Sideshow (also exec. prod., writer), Comic Relief II, The Best of Gleason, Magic with the Stars, Nell Carter: Never Too Old to Dream, Hello Sucker.

ANDERSON, J. WAYNE
Executive. b. Clifton Forge, VA, Feb. 19, 1947. e. USA Signal School (1965-67); USN Service Schools (1967). USMC, 1965-69; opened and operated 1st military 35mm m.p. theatre, DaNang, Vietnam, 1967-69; R/C Theatres, dist. mgr., 1971-75; v.p., 1976-83; pres./COO, 1983-present; bd. of dirs., Maryland Permanent Bank & Trust co., 1988-present, chairman, 1992-present. Member of NATO, bd. of dirs., 1987-present, technical advancement committee, 1981-present; chmn., 1991-present; Inter-Society for the Enhancement of Theatrical Presenation, 1986-present; Huntsman Bd. of dirs., 1979-83; pres., 1982-83; NRA, 1970-life; Will Rogers Inst., 1988-present; Presidential Task Force, 1990-life.

ANDERSON, KEVIN
Actor. b. Illinois, Jan. 13, 1960. e. Goodman School. Member of Chicago's Steppenwolf Theatre where he starred in Orphans. Moved with the play when it transferred to New York (1985) and later starred in the London production, as well as the film version.
THEATER: NY: Orphans (Theatre World Award), Moonchildren, Brilliant Tracers, Orpheus Descending. London: Sunset Boulevard.
PICTURES: Risky Business (debut, 1983), Pink Nights, A Walk on the Moon, Orphans, Miles From Home, In Country, Sleeping With the Enemy, Liebestraum, Hoffa, The Night We Never Met, Rising Sun.
TELEVISION: Movies: Orpheus Descending, The Wrong Man. Special: Hale the Hero.

ANDERSON, LONI
Actress. b. St. Paul, MN, Aug. 5. 1946. e. U. of Minnesota. Taught school before acting.
PICTURES: Stroker Ace, The Lonely Guy (cameo), All Dogs Go to Heaven (voice), Munchie.
TELEVISION: Series: WKRP in Cincinnati, Partners in Crime, Easy Street, Nurses. Specials: Christmas in Opryland, Shaun Cassidy Special, Bob Hope specials, etc. Movies: The Magnificent Magnet of Mesa, Three on a Date, The Jayne Mansfield Story, Sizzle, Country Gold, My Mother's Secret Life, A Letter to Three Wives, Stranded, Necessity, A Whisper Kills, Too Good to Be True, Sorry Wrong Number, Coins in the Fountain, White Hot: The Mysterious Murder of Thelma Todd, The Price She Paid, Gambler V: Playing for Keeps.

ANDERSON, MELISSA SUE
Actress. b. Berkeley, CA, Sept. 26, 1962. Took up acting at suggestion of a dancing teacher. Did series of commercials; guest role in episode of Brady Bunch; episode of Shaft. Gained fame as Mary Ingalls on Little House on the Prairie series (Emmy nom.).
PICTURES: Happy Birthday to Me, Chattanooga Choo Choo, Dead Men Don't Die.
TELEVISION: Series: Little House on the Prairie. Movies: Little House on the Prairie (pilot), The Loneliest Runner, James at 15 (pilot), Survival of Dana, Midnight Offerings, Advice to the Lovelorn, An Innocent Love, First Affair, Dark Mansions. Special: Which Mother is Mine? (Emmy Award, 1980).

ANDERSON, MICHAEL
Director. b. London, England, Jan. 30, 1920. e. France, Germany. Ent. m.p. industry as actor, 1936. Son is actor Michael Anderson Jr.
PICTURES: Private Angelo (debut, 1949; co-dir. with Peter Ustinov), Waterfront, Hell Is Sold Out, Night Was Our Friend, Will Any Gentleman?, The Dam Busters, 1984, Around the World in 80 Days, Yangtse Incident (Battle Hell), Chase a Crooked Shadow, Shake Hands With the Devil (also prod.), The Wreck of the Mary Deare, All the Fine Young Cannibals, The Naked Edge, Flight From Ashiya, Wild and Wonderful, Operation Crossbow, The Quiller Memorandum, The Shoes of the Fisherman, Pope Joan, Doc Savage: The Man of Bronze, Conduct Unbecoming, Logan's Run, Orca, Dominique (Avenging Spirit), Murder By Phone, Second Time Lucky, Separate Vacations, Jeweller's Shop, Millenium.
TELEVISION: Mini-Series: The Martian Chronicles, Sword of Gideon, Young Catherine. Movies: Regina Vs. Nelles, The Sea Wolf, Harry Oakes, Rugged Gold, Captain's Courageous, 20,000 Leagues Under the Sea.

ANDERSON, MICHAEL, JR.
Actor. b. London, England, Aug. 6, 1943. Father is director Michael Anderson. Ent. films as child actor, 1954.
PICTURES: The Moonraker, Tiger Bay, The Sundowners, In Search of the Castaways, Play It Cool, Reach For Glory, Greatest Story Ever Told, Dear Heart, Major Dundee, The Glory Guys, The Sons of Katie Elder, The Last Movie, Logan's Run.
TELEVISION: Series: The Monroes. Mini-Series: Washington Behind Closed Doors, The Martian Chronicles. Movies: The House That Would Not Die, In Search of America, The Family Rico, The Daughters of Joshua Cabe, Coffee Tea or Me? Shootout in a One-Dog Town, Kiss Me Kill Me, The Million Dollar Face, Making of a Male Model, Love Leads the Way.

ANDERSON, RICHARD
Actor. b. Long Branch, NJ, Aug. 8, 1926. e. University H.S., W. Los Angeles. Served in U.S. Army, WWII. Began acting career in summer theatre in Santa Barbara and Laguna Playhouse where spotted by MGM executives who signed him to six yr. contract. Appeared in 26 films for MGM before leaving studio. Spokesperson for Kiplinger Washington Letter since 1985.
PICTURES: 12 O'Clock High, The People Against O'Hara, Scaramouche, The Story of Three Loves, Escape from Fort Bravo, Forbidden Planet, The Search for Bridey Murphy, Paths of Glory, The Long Hot Summer, Curse of the Faceless Man, Compulsion, A Gathering of Eagles, Johnny Cool, Seven Days in May, Seconds, The Ride to Hangman's Tree, Tora! Tora! Tora!, Macho Callahan, Doctors' Wives, Play It As It Lays, The Honkers, The Player, The Glass Shield, An American in Saigon.
TELEVISION: Series: Mama Rosa, Bus Stop, The Lieutenant, Perry Mason, Dan August, The Six Million Dollar Man, The Bionic Woman (Emmy nom.), Dynasty, Cover-Up. Guest: Ironside, The Big Valley, Mannix, My Friend Tony, The Mod Squad, Land of the Giants, The FBI, Gunsmoke. Movies: Along Came a Spider, Kane & Abel, The Return of the Six Million Dollar Man and the Bionic Woman, Pearl, Perry Mason Returns, Hoover vs. the Kennedys, Emminent Domain, Danger High, Stranger on My Land, The Bionic Showdown: The Six Million Dollar Man & The Bionic Woman (also co-prod.), Return of the Six Million Dollar Man and the Bionic Woman III, Kung Fu Revisted, Bionic Breakdown: The Six Million Dollar Man & The Bionic Woman (exec. prod.), Bionic Ever After? (also co-exec. prod.), In A Lake Of The Forest.

ANDERSON, RICHARD DEAN
Actor. b. Minneapolis, MN, Jan. 23, 1950. Planned to become professional hockey player. Became a street mime and jester. Performed with his own rock band, Ricky Dean and Dante.
PICTURES: Young Doctors in Love, Odd Jobs.
TELEVISION: Series: General Hospital (1976-81), Seven Brides for Seven Brothers, Emerald Point N.A.S., MacGyver, Legend. Movies: Ordinary Heroes, In the Eyes of a Stranger, Through the Eyes of a Killer, MacGyver: Lost Treasure of Atlantis (also co-exec. prod.), MacGyver: Trail to Doomsday, Beyond Betrayal, Past the Bleachers.

ANDERSON, SYLVIA
Producer, Writer (Pinewood Studios). b. London, England. e. London U. Entered m.p. ind. 1960. First pub. novel, Love and Hisses. UK rep for Home Box Office of America.
TELEVISION: series created include: Thunderbirds, U.F.O., Space 1999.

ANDERSON, WILLIAM H.
Producer. b. Utah, October 12, 1911. e. Compton Coll. Firestone Rubber Co.; Universal Credit Co. Producer & Member of Bd. of Dirs. at Walt Disney Prods.
PICTURES: Old Yeller, Swiss Family Robinson, The Happiest Millionaire, The Computer Wore Tennis Shoes, The Barefoot Executive, $1,000,000 Duck, Superdad, The Strongest Man in the World, The Apple Dumpling Gang, Treasure of Matecumbe, The Shaggy D.A.
TELEVISION: Series: Zorro, Pop Warner Football. Wonderful World of Disney Movies: Zorro, Texas John Slaughter, Daniel Boone, The Swamp Fox, Johnny Shiloh, Mooncussers, Bristle Face, The Scarecrow of Romney Marsh, The Legend of Young Dick Turpin, Willie and the Yank, A Boy Called Nuthin', The Young Loner, The Wacky Zoo of Morgan City, The Mystery of Dracula's Castle, The Bull from the Sky (co-prod.), Great Sleeping Bear Sled Dog Race (co-prod.).

ANDERSSON, BIBI
Actress. b. Stockholm, Sweden, Nov. 11, 1935. e. Royal Dramatic Theatre School (Kungliga Dramatiska Teatern).
PICTURES: Dum-Bom (debut, 1953), Sir Arne's Treasure, Smiles of a Summer Night, The Seventh Seal, Wild Strawberries, The Magician, Brink of Life, The Face, The Devil's Eye, Square of Violence, Pleasure Garden, The Swedish Mistress, Not to Mention These Women, My Sister My Love, Persona, Duel at Diablo, A Question of Rape, Black Palm Trees, The Girls, Story of a Woman, The Passion of Anna, The Kremlin Letter, The Touch, Scenes From a Marriage, It Is Raining on Santiago, Blondy (Vortex), The Hounds of Spring, I Never

Promised You a Rose Garden, An Enemy of the People, Quintet, The Concorde: Airport '79, Prosperous Times, The Marmalade Revolution, Black Crows, Exposed, The Hill on the Other Side of the Moon, Babette's Feast, Manika, Fordringsagare.
TELEVISION: Wallenberg—A Hero's Story.

ANDRESS, URSULA
Actress. b. Bern, Switzerland, Mar. 19, 1936. To Rome as teen where she landed roles in Italian films.
PICTURES: Sins of Casanova (debut, 1954), An American in Rome, The Tempest Has Gone, La Catena dell'Odio, Anyone Can Play, Dr. No, Four for Texas, Fun in Acapulco, Nightmare in the Sun, She, The Tenth Victim, What's New Pussycat?, Up to His Ears, Once Before ! Die, The Blue Max, Casino Royale, The Southern Star, Perfect Friday, Red Sun, Africa Express, Scaramouche, The Sensuous Nurse, Slave of the Cannibal God, Tigers in Lipstick, The Fifth Musketeer, Primitive Desires, Four Tigers in Lipstick, Clash of the Titans, Reporters, Mexico in Flames, Class Meeting.
TELEVISION: Mini-Series: Peter the Great. Series: Falcon Crest. Movies: Man Against the Mob.

ANDREWS, ANTHONY
Actor. b. London, England, Dec. 1, 1948. e. Royal Masonic Sch., Herts. Regional stage debut, 1967.
PICTURES: Take Me High/Hot Property (debut, 1973), Operation Daybreak, Under the Volcano, The Holcroft Covenant, The Second Victory, The Lighthorsemen, Hanna's War, Lost in Siberia, Haunted (also co-prod.).
TELEVISION: A Beast With Two Backs, Romeo and Juliet, A War of Children, QB VII, Upstairs Downstairs, Danger UXB, Brideshead Revisited, Ivanhoe, The Scarlet Pimpernel, Sparkling Cyanide, A.D., Bluegrass, Suspicion, The Woman He Loved, Columbo Goes to the Guillotine, Daniel Steel's Jewels.

ANDREWS, JULIE
Actress, Singer. r.n. Julia Wells. b. Walton-on-Thames, England. Oct 1, 1935. m. dir./writer Blake Edwards. debut, Eng. Starlight Roof Revue London Hippodrome, 1948.
AUTHOR: Mandy, Last of the Really Great Whangdoodles (1973).
THEATER: NY: The Boy Friend, My Fair Lady, Camelot, Putting It Together, Victor/Victoria.
PICTURES: Mary Poppins (debut, 1964; Academy Award), The Americanization of Emily, The Sound of Music (Acad. Award nom.), Hawaii, Torn Curtain, Thoroughly Modern Millie, Star!, Darling Lili, The Tamarind Seed, ``10,'' S.O.B, Victor/Victoria (Acad. Award nom.), The Man Who Loved Women, That's Life, Duet for One, A Fine Romance.
TELEVISION: Specials: High Tor, Julie and Carol at Carnegie Hall, The Julie Andrews Show, An Evening with Julie Andrews and Harry Belafonte, The World of Walt Disney, Julie and Carol at Lincoln Center, Julie on Sesame Street, Julie Andrews' Christmas Special, Julie and Dick in Covent Garden, Julie Andrews and Jackie Gleason Together, Julie Andrews: My Favorite Things, Julie Andrews:The Sound of Christmas, Julie and Carol: Together Again. Series: The Julie Andrews Hour (1972-73), Julie. Movie: Our Sons.

ANGERS, AVRIL
Actress, Comedienne, Singer. b. Liverpool, England, April 18. Stage debut at age of 14; screen debut in 1947 in Lucky Mascot (The Brass Monkey).
THEATER: The Mating Game, Cockie, Murder at the Vicarage, Little Me, Norman, Is That You?, Blithe Spirit, Oklahoma!, Gigi, The Killing of Sister George, Cards on the Table, When We Are Married, Cinderella, Easy Virtue, Post Mortem, Crazy for You.
PICTURES: Miss Pilgrim's Progress, Don't Blame the Stork, Women Without Men, Green Man, Devils of Darkness, Be My Guest, Three Bites of the Apple, The Family Way, Two a Penny, The Best House in London, Staircase, There's a Girl in My Soup, Forbush and the Penguins, Gollocks, Confessions of a Driving Instructor, Dangerous Davies.
TELEVISION: How Do You View, Friends and Neighbors, Dear Dotty, Holiday Town, Charlie Fainsbarn Show, Arthur Askey Show, All Aboard, The Gold Hunter, Bob Monkhouse Show, Before The Fringe, Hudd, Coronation Street, Dick Emery Show, Dad's Army, Bright Boffins, The More We Are Together, The Millionairess, Liver Birds, Looks Familiar, No Appointment Necessary, The Songwriters, All Creatures Great and Small, Coronation Concert, Minder, Smuggler, Just Liz, Give Us a Clue, Are You Being Served, Trelawney of the Wells, Cat's Eye, C.A.B., Rude Health, Victoria Wood Playhouse, Common As Muck.

ANHALT, EDWARD
Writer. b. New York, NY. Mar. 28, 1914. e. Columbia U.
PICTURES: Bulldog Drummond Strikes Back, Panic in the Streets (Academy Award for Best Original Story, 1950), Red Mountain, The Member of the Wedding (also prod.), The Sniper, My Six Convicts, Eight Iron Men, Not as a Stranger, The Pride and the Passion, The Young Lions, In Love and War, The Restless Years, The Sins of Rachel Cade, The Young Savages, Girls Girls Girls, A Girl Named Tamiko, Wives and Lovers,

Becket (Academy Award for Best Adapted Screenplay, 1964), The Satan Bug, Boeing-Boeing, Hour of the Gun, In Enemy Country, The Boston Strangler, The Madwoman of Chaillot, Jeremiah Johnson, The Man in the Glass Booth, Luther, Escape to Athena, Green Ice, The Holcroft Covenant.
TELEVISION: Peter the Great, QB VII, Contract on Cherry Street, Day That Christ Died, The Neon Empire, The Take, Alexander the Great, The Life and Times of Santa Claus, The Apostles.

ANNAUD, JEAN-JACQUES
Writer, Director. b. Draveil, France, Oct. 1, 1943. Began career as film director in French army, making educational pictures. Also directed 500 commercials. Received 1989 cinema prize from French Acad. for career's work. Directed IMAX film Wings of Courage.
PICTURES: *Director*: Black and White in Color (also s.p., winner of Best Foreign Language Film Oscar, 1978), Coup de Tete (Hothead), Quest for Fire (Cesar Award for best dir., 1982), The Name of the Rose, The Bear (also co-s.p.: Cesar Award for best dir., 1989), The Lover.

ANN-MARGRET
Actress, Singer, Dancer. r.n. Ann-Margret Olsson. b. Valsjobyn, Sweden, April 28, 1941. m. Roger Smith, actor, dir., prod. e. New Trier H.S., Winnetka, IL; Northwestern U. Radio shows, toured with band; worked with George Burns in Las Vegas. TV debut, Jack Benny Show, 1961.
PICTURES: Pocketful of Miracles (debut, 1961), State Fair, Bye Bye Birdie, Viva Las Vegas, Kitten With a Whip, The Pleasure Seekers, Bus Riley's Back in Town, Once A Thief, The Cincinnati Kid, Made in Paris, Stagecoach, The Swinger, Murderer's Row, The Prophet, The Tiger and the Pussycat, Rebus, Criminal Affair, RPM, C. C. & Company, Carnal Knowledge (Acad. Award nom.), The Outside Man, The Train Robbers, Tommy (Acad. Award nom.), The Last Remake of Beau Geste, The Twist, Joseph Andrews, The Cheap Detective, Magic, The Villain, Middle Age Crazy, I Ought To Be in Pictures, Lookin' to Get Out, The Return of the Soldier, Twice in a Lifetime, 52 Pick-up, A Tiger's Tail, A New Life, Newsies, Grumpy Old Men, Grumpier Old Men.
TELEVISION: *Specials*: The Ann-Margret Show, From Hollywood With Love, Dames at Sea, When You're Smiling, Ann-Margret Smith, Ann-Margret Olsson, Memories of Elvis, Rhinestone Cowgirl, Hollywood Movie Girls. *Movies*: Who Will Love My Children?, A Streetcar Named Desire, The Two Mrs. Grenvilles, Our Sons, Nobody's Children, Following Her Heart. *Mini-series*: Queen, Scarlett, Seduced By Madness: The Diane Borchardt Story.

ANSARA, MICHAEL
Actor. b. Lowell, MA, April 15, 1922. e. Pasadena Playhouse. Served in U.S. Army; then summer stock, little theatre, road shows.
PICTURES: Soldiers Three, Only the Valiant, The Robe, Julius Caesar, Sign of the Pagan, Bengal Brigade, New Orleans Uncensored, Diane, Lone Ranger, Sol Madrid, Daring Game, Dear Dead Delilah, The Bears and I, Mohammad Messenger of God, The Manitou, Gas, Access Code, Knights of the City. Lethal (KGB: The Secret War).
TELEVISION: *Series*: Broken Arrow, Law of the Plainsman, Buck Rogers in the 25th Century. *Mini-series*: Centennial. *Guest*: The Westerner, Lost in Space, Simon and Simon, Gavilan, George Burns Comedy Week, Hunter, Hardcastle and McCormick. *Movies*: How I Spent My Summer Vacation, Powderkeg, A Call to Danger, Ordeal, Shootout in a One-Dog Town, Barbary Coast, The Fantastic World of D.C. Collins.

ANSPACH, SUSAN
Actress. b. New York, NY, Nov. 23, 1945. e. Catholic U., Washington, DC. After school returned to N.Y. and in 3 years had performed in 11 B'way and off-B'way prods. Moved to Los Angeles and entered films.
PICTURES: The Landlord (debut, 1970), Five Easy Pieces, Play It Again Sam, Blume in Love, The Big Fix, Running, The Devil and Max Devlin, Gas, Montenegro, Misunderstood, Blue Monkey, Into the Fire, Blood Red, Back to Back.
TELEVISION: *Movies*: I Want to Keep My Baby, The Secret Life of John Chapman, Rosetti & Ryan, Mad Bull, The Last Giraffe, Portrait of an Escort, The First Time, Deadly Encounter, Cagney & Lacey: The Return. *Mini-series*: Space. *Series*: The Yellow Rose, The Slap Maxwell Story.

ANSPAUGH, DAVID
Director, Producer. b. Decatur, IN, Sept. 24, 1946. e. Indiana U., 1965-70; U. of Southern CA, 1974-76. School teacher, Aspen, CO 1970-74.
PICTURES: *Director*: Hoosiers (debut, 1986), Fresh Horses, Rudy, Moonlight and Valentino.
TELEVISION: *Series*: Hill St. Blues (assoc. prod. 1980-81; prod.-dir. 1981-82; prod.-dir. 1983-84, dir. 1985; DGA Award: 1983, 2 Emmy Awards for producing: 1982, 1983), St. Elsewhere (dir.), Miami Vice (dir.). *Movies*: Deadly Care, In the Company of Darkness.

ANTHONY, LYSETTE
Actress. b. London, England, 1963. Stage work incl. Bristol Old Vic, 1988-90.
PICTURES: Krull, The Emperor's New Clothes, Without a Clue, 29 Days in February, Switch, Husbands and Wives, The Pleasure Principle, Look Who's Talking Now, The Advocate, Dr. Jekyll and Ms. Hyde, Dead Cold, Dracula: Dead and Loving It.
TELEVISION: *Series*: Lovejoy (BBC), Three Up Two Down (BBC), Campion, Dark Shadows. *Movies/Specials*: Ivanhoe, Oliver Twist, Dombey and Son, Jemima Shore, Night Train to Murder, The Bretts, Princess Daisy, The Lady and the Highwayman (Dangerous Love), Jack the Ripper, A Ghost in Monte Carlo, Sweet Danger.

ANTHONY, MICHELE
Executive. e. George Washington U.; USC, J.D. Currently exec. v.p., Sony Music Entertainment. Bd. member of the Rock and Roll Halle of Fame, Tock the Vote, Sloan Kettering Cancer Center.

ANTHONY, TONY
Actor, Producer, Writer. b. Clarksburg, WV, Oct. 16, 1939. e. Carnegie Mellon.
PICTURES: Force of Impulse, Pity Me Not, The Wounds of Hunger, A Stranger in Town, The Stranger Returns, A Stranger in Japan, Come Together, Blindman, Pete Pearl and the Pole, Let's Talk About Men, Get Mean, Treasure of the Four Crowns, Comin' at Ya, For Better or For Worse.

ANTON, SUSAN
Actress. b. Oak Glen, CA, Oct. 12, 1950. Concert & night club singer. Country album & single Killin' Time went top 10 on Country charts, received Gold Record in Japan. On B'way in Hurlyburly (debut, 1985), The Will Rogers Follies. Off-B'way in X-mas a Go-Go. Vegas, hon. chmn. of Amer. Cancer Soc., Calif. Special Olympics, & hon. capt. U.S. Woman's Olympic Volleyball Team.
PICTURES: Goldengirl, Spring Fever, Cannonball Run II, Options (cameo), Making Mr. Right, Lena's Holiday.
TELEVISION: *Series*: Stop Susan Williams (Cliff Hangers); Presenting Susan Anton. *Movie*: The Great American Beauty Contest. *Guest*: Quantum Leap, Blossom, Murder She Wrote, Night Court, The Famous Teddy Z, Circus of the Stars.

ANTONIO, LOU
Actor, Writer, Producer, Director. b. Oklahoma City, OK, Jan. 23. e. U. of OK. Two Emmy Nominations for TV Movies.
THEATER: *Actor*: The Buffalo Skinner (Theatre World Award), The Girls of Summer, The Good Soup, The Garden of Sweets, Andorra, The Lady of the Camellias, The Ballad of the Sad Cafe, Ready When You Are, C.B. *Dir*.: Private Lives (w Taylor/Burton).
PICTURES: *Actor*: The Strange One, Splendor in the Grass, America America, Hawaii, Cool Hand Luke, The Phynx. *Also*: Mission Batangas (s.p.), Micki and Maude (exec. prod.).
TELEVISION: *Actor*: *Guest*: Picket Fences, Chicago Hope. *Series*: Snoop Sisters, Dog and Cat, Making It, Piece of Blue Sky, The Power and the Glory, Danny Thomas Hour, Partners in Crime, Sole Survivor, Where the Ladies Go, Star Trek. *Director*: *Mini-series*: Rich Man, Poor Man (co-dir.), Breaking Up Is Hard to Do, The Star Maker. *Movies*: Lanigan's Rabbi, Someone I Touched, Something for Joey, The Girl in the Empty Grave, The Critical List, Silent Victory-The Kitty O'Neil Story, A Real American Hero, The Contender, We're Fighting Back, Something So Right, A Good Sport, Threesome, Rearview Mirror, Face to Face, The Outside Woman (also prod.), Dark Holiday (also exec. prod.), Between Friends, Mayflower Madam, One Terrific Guy, Pals, 13 at Dinner, This Gun for Hire, Lies Before Kisses, The Last Prostitute, The Rape of Dr. Willis, A Taste for Killing, Nightmare in the Daylight.

ANTONIONI, MICHELANGELO
Director, Writer. b. Ferrara, Italy, Sept. 29, 1913. e. Bologna U. Film critic on local newspaper, then script writer and asst. director. First films as director were short documentaries including: Gente del Po (1943-47), N.U., L'Amorosa Menzogna, Superstizione, Sette canne un vestito, followed by later works La Villa dei Mostri, La Funivia del Faloria, Kumbha Mela, Roma, Noto, Mandorli, Vulcano, Stromboli, Carnevale. Received honorary Academy Award, 1995.
PICTURES: *Dir.-Writer*: Story of a Love Affair (feature debut as dir., 1950), The Vanquished, Lady Without Camelias (Camille Without Camelias), Love in the City (segment: When Love Fails), The Girl Friends, The Outcry, L'Avventura, The Night, Eclipse, The Red Desert, I tre Volti/Three Faces of a Woman (dir. only; segment: Prefazione), Blow-Up (Acad. Award nom. for dir.), Zabriskie Point, Chung Kuo (documentary), The Passenger, The Oberwald Mystery, Identification of a Woman, The Crew, Beyond the Clouds (co-dir., co-s.p., with Wim Wenders).

ANTONOWSKY, MARVIN
Executive. b. New York, NY, Jan. 31, 1929. e. City Coll. of New York, B.A., M.B.A. Joined Kenyon and Eckhart in 1957 for which was media research dir.; named marketing v.p. With Norman, Craig, & Kummel as v.p., mktg. services. 1965, became v.p. in

chg. of media research and spot buying at J. Walter Thompson. In 1969 joined ABC-TV as v.p. in chg. research. Left to become v.p. in chg. of programming at NBC-TV. 1976, sr. v.p., Universal-TV. 1979, joined Columbia Pictures as pres., mktg. & research. Rejoined MCA/Universal Pictures as pres, mktg., Nov. 1983. Formed Marvin Antonowsky & Assoc. marketing consultancy firm, 1989. Rejoined Columbia Pictures in 1990 as exec. v.p. and asst. to chmn. 1993, joined Price Entertainment as exec. v.p.

ANWAR, GABRIELLE
Actress. b. Laleham, England, 1970.
PICTURES: Manifesto (debut, 1989), If Looks Could Kill, Wild Hearts Can't Be Broken, Scent of a Woman, For Love or Money, The Three Musketeers, Body Snatchers, Things to Do in Denver When You're Dead, Innocent Lies, The Grave.
TELEVISION: Movies: First Born, In Pursuit of Honor. Specials: The Storyteller, Summer's Lease, Dead-End for Delia (Fallen Angels).

APFEL, EDWIN R.
Writer, Executive. b. New York, NY, Jan. 2, 1934. e. Franklin and Marshall Coll., B.A., 1955. Mktg. exec.: Metro-Goldwyn-Mayer, Verve Records, Embassy Pictures. Freelance copywriter. 1990, writer, Edward R. Murrow: This Reporter, Amer. Masters (PBS). 1992, council member, WGA East.

APPLEGATE, CHRISTINA
Actress. b. Hollywood, CA, Nov. 25, 1972.
PICTURES: Jaws of Satan (debut, 1980), Streets, Don't Tell Mom the Babysitter's Dead, Across the Moon, Wild Bill, Nowhere.
TELEVISION: Series: Washingtoon, Heart of the City, Married... With Children. Movies: Grace Kelly, Dance 'til Dawn. Guest: Quincy M.E., Charles in Charge, The New Leave It to Beaver, Amazing Stories, 21 Jump Street.

APTED, MICHAEL
Director, Producer. b. Aylesbury, Eng., Feb. 10, 1941. e. Cambridge. Broke into show business at Granada TV in England in early 1960's as trainee, researcher and finally director. In 1965 was producer-director for local programs and current affairs; then staff drama dir. for TV series, plays and serials. In late 1960's left Granada to freelance.
PICTURES: 14 Up, Triple Echo, Stardust, 21 Up, The Squeeze, Agatha, Coal Miner's Daughter, Continental Divide, Gorky Park, P'Tang Yang, Kipperbang, Firstborn, Bring on the Night, 28 Up, Critical Condition, Gorillas in the Mist, Class Action, 35 Up, Thunderheart, Incident at Oglala, Bram Stoker's Dracula (exec. prod. only), Blink, Nell, Moving the Mountain, Extreme Measures.
TELEVISION: Director: Another Sunday and Sweet F.A., Follyfoot, Joy The Style of the Countess, The Reporters, Buggins' Ermine, Jackpoint, Kisses at 50, High Kampf, Poor Girl, Wednesday Love, The Collection, The Long Way Home (doc.), Stronger Than the Sun, My Life and Times, Crossroads, New York News (pilot). Exec. Producer: Criminal Justice, Age 7 in America, Intruders, Strapped.

ARAU, ALFONSO
Director, Actor. b. Mexico. e. Univ. of Mexico. Studied drama there and with Saki Sano in Mexico; UCLA film school; studied pantomime in Paris.
PICTURES: Actor: The Wild Bunch, El Topo, Used Cars, Romancing the Stone, Three Amigos, Walker, Posse. Director: The Barefoot Eagle, Clazonian Inspector, Mojado Power (Wetback Power), Chido One, Like Water for Chocolate (Mexico's Ariel Award), A Walk in the Clouds.
TELEVISION: Series: El Show de Arau.

ARCAND, DENYS
Director. b. Deschambault, Quebec, Canada, June 25, 1941. e. U. of Montreal, 1963. While still history student, co-prod. Seul ou avec D'Autres (1962). Joined National Film Board of Canada, where began making documentary shorts (Champlain, Les Montrealistes and La Route de l'ouest) forming a trilogy dealing with colonial Quebec. In 1970 socio-political doc. about Quebec textile workers, On Est au Coton, generated controversy resulting in the NFB banning film until 1976.
PICTURES: On Est au Coton (doc.), Un Maudite Galette (1st fiction feature, 1971). Dir.-Writer: Quebec: Duplessis et Apres... (doc.), Rejeanne Padovani, Gina, Le Crime d'Ovide Plouffe, The Decline of the American Empire, Night Zoo (actor only), Jesus of Montreal (Cannes Film Fest. jury prize, 1989), Leolo (actor only), Love and Human Remains.
TELEVISION: Duplessis (s.p., 1977 series), Empire Inc. (series, dir.).

ARCHER, ANNE
Actress. b. Los Angeles, CA. Daughter of actress Marjorie Lord and actor John Archer. Married Terry Jastrow, TV network sports producer-director and pres. Jack Nicklaus Prods.
THEATER: A Coupla White Chicks Sitting Around Talking (off-B'way, 1981), Les Liaisons Dangereuses (Williamstown Fest., 1988).

PICTURES: The Honkers (debut, 1972), Cancel My Reservation, The All-American Boy, Trackdown, Lifeguard, Paradise Alley, Good Guys Wear Black, Hero at Large, Raise the Titanic, Green Ice, Waltz Across Texas (also co-story), The Naked Face, Too Scared to Scream, The Check Is in the Mail, Fatal Attraction (Acad. Award nom.), Love at Large, Narrow Margin, Eminent Domain, Patriot Games, Body of Evidence, Family Prayers, Short Cuts, Clear and Present Danger, There Goes My Baby (narrator), Mojave Moon.
TELEVISION: Series: Bob and Carol and Ted and Alice, The Family Tree, Falcon Crest. Movies: The Blue Knight, The Mark of Zorro, The Log of the Black Pearl, A Matter of Wife...and Death, The Dark Side of Innocence, Harold Robbins' The Pirate, The Sky's No Limit, A Different Affair, A Leap of Faith, The Last of His Tribe, Nails, Jane's House, Because Mommy Works (also co-prod.), The Man in the Attic. Mini-Series: Seventh Avenue. Special: Leslie's Folly.

ARCHERD, ARMY
Columnist, TV commentator. r.n. Armand Archerd. b. New York, NY, Jan. 13, 1922. m. actress Selma Archerd. e. UCLA, grad. '41, U.S. Naval Academy Post Graduate Sch., 1943. Started as usher at Criterion Theatre, N.Y., while in high school. After grad. UCLA, worked at Paramount studios before entering Navy. Joined AP Hollywood bureau 1945, Herald-Express, Daily Variety as columnist, 1953. M.C. Hollywood premieres, Emmys and Academy Awards. President, founder Hollywood Press Club. Awards from Masquers, L.A. Press Club, Hollywood Foreign Press Club, and Newsman of the Year award from Publicists Guild, 1970; Movie Game. TV series; People's Choice, co-host. 1987 received Hollywood Women's Press Club Man of the Year Award.

ARDANT, FANNY
Actress. b. Monte Carlo, 1949. Majored in political science in college. Served a 5-year apprenticeship in the French theater acting in Polyeucte, Esther, The Mayor of Santiago, Electra and Tete d'Or. TV debut in Les Dames de la Cote.
PICTURES: Les Chiens (debut, 1979), Les uns et les Autres, The Woman Next Door, The Ins and Outs, Life Is a Novel, Confidentially Yours, Benevenuta, Desire, Swann in Love, Love Unto Death, Les Enrages, L'Ete Prochain, Family Business, Affabulazione, Melo, The Family, La Paltoquet, Three Sisters, Australia, Pleure pas My Love, Adventure of Catherine C., Afraid of the Dark, Rien Que des Mensonges, La Femme du Deserteur, Amok, Colonel Chabert, Beyond the Clouds, Ridicule.

ARGENTO, DARIO
Director, Writer. b. Rome, Italy, 1940. Son of prod. Salvatore Argento.
PICTURES: Today It's Me...Tomorrow It's You (co-s.p.), Cemetery Without Crosses (co-s.p.), Once Upon a Time in the West (co-s.p.), Commandos (co-s.p.), Zero Probability (co-s.p.), The Five Man Army (co-s.p.), One Night at Dinner (co-s.p.), Sex Revolution (s.p.), Legion of the Damned (co-s.p.), Seasons of Love (co-s.p.), Bird With the Crystal Plumage (dir., s.p.), Cat O'Nine Tails (dir., s.p., story), Four Flies on Grey Velvet (dir., s.p.), Five Days in Milan (dir., co-s.p.), Deep Red (dir., s.p.), Suspiria (dir., co-s.p., music), Dawn of the Dead (co-prod., music), Inferno (dir., s.p., story), Tenebrae (Unsane; dir. s.p., story), Creepers (dir., prod., s.p.), Demons (prod., co-s.p.), Demons 2: The Nightmare is Back (s.p., prod.), Opera (Terror at the Opera; dir., s.p.), The Church (prod., s.p., story), Two Evil Eyes (episode: The Black Cat; dir., prod., s.p.), Devil's Daughter (prod., s.p.), Innocent Blood (actor), Trauma (dir., prod., co-s.p.).
TELEVISION: Series: Door Into Darkness (It.).

ARKIN, ADAM
Actor. b. Brooklyn, NY, Aug. 19, 1956. Father is actor Alan Arkin. Made acting debut in short film prod. by father, People Soup.
THEATER: I Hate Hamlet (Theatre World Award), Four Dogs and a Bone.
PICTURES: Made for Each Other, Baby Blue Marine, Improper Channels (s.p.), Under the Rainbow, Chu Chu and the Philly Flash, Full Moon High, The Doctor.
TELEVISION: Series: Busting Loose, Teachers Only, Tough Cookies, A Year in the Life, Northern Exposure, Chicago Hope. Mini-Series: Pearl. Specials: Mark Twain's America: Tom Edison, The Fourth Wise Man. Movies: It Couldn't Happen to a Nicer Guy, All Together Now, In the Line of Duty: Hunt for Justice.

ARKIN, ALAN
Actor, Director, b. New York, NY, March 26, 1934. e. Los Angeles City Col., Los Angeles State Col., Bennington (VT) Col. m. actress-author Barbara Dana. Father of actor Adam Arkin. Was member of folk singing group The Tarriers; then one of the original members of Chicago's Second City improvisational group. Directed short films T.G.I.F., People Soup (Acad. Award nom.). Author: Tony's Hard Work Day, The Lemming Condition, Halfway Through the Door, The Clearing, Some Fine Grandpa.

THEATER: *Off-B'way:* Second City, Man Out Loud, From the Second City. *B'way:* Enter Laughing (Tony & Theatre World Awards, 1963), Luv. *Director:* Eh?, Little Murders, White House Murder Case (Obie Award), Joan of Lorraine, Rubbers and Yanks Three, The Sunshine Boys, The Sorrows of Stephen, Room Service.
PICTURES: Calypso Heat Wave (debut, 1957), The Russians Are Coming The Russians Are Coming (Golden Globe Award, Acad. Award nom.), Woman Times Seven, Wait Until Dark, Inspector Clouseau, The Heart Is a Lonely Hunter (NY Film Critics Award, Acad. Award nom.), Popi, The Monitors, Catch-22, Little Murders (also dir.), Deadhead Miles, Last of the Red Hot Lovers, Freebie and the Bean, Rafferty and the Gold Dust Twins, Hearts of the West (NY Film Critics Award), The 7 Per Cent Solution, Fire Sale (also dir.), The In-Laws (also exec. prod.), The Magician of Lublin, Simon, Improper Channels, Chu Chu and the Philly Flash, Full Moon High, The Last Unicorn (voice), The Return of Captain Invincible, Joshua Then and Now, Bad Medicine, Big Trouble, Coupe de Ville, Edward Scissorhands, Havana, The Rocketeer, Glengarry Glen Ross, Indian Summer, So I Married an Axe Murderer, North, The Jerky Boys, Steal Big Steal Little, Mother Night.
TELEVISION: *Series:* Harry. *Movies:* The Defection of Simas Kurdirka, The Other Side of Hell, A Deadly Business, Escape from Sobibor, Cooperstown, Taking the Heat, Doomsday Gun. *Specials:* The Love Song of Barney Kempinski, The Fourth Wise Man, A Matter of Principle, Fay (pilot; dir.), Twigs (dir.), The Emperor's New Clothes (Faerie Tale Theatre), The Visit (Trying Times; dir.), The Boss (Trying Times; dir.), Necessary Parties (also co-writer, co-prod.). *Guest:* East Side/West Side, St. Elsewhere.

ARKOFF, SAMUEL Z.
Producer, Executive. b. Fort Dodge, IA, June 12, 1918. e. U. of Colorado, U. of Iowa, Loyola U. Law Sch. Chairman & president of the Samuel Z. Arkoff Company (formed 1980) and Arkoff Int'l Pictures (formed 1981). Served in USAF as cryptographer WWII. Co-founder American Releasing, 1954, and American International Pictures, 1955. Pres. and chmn. of bd. AIP until 1979. 1963, named with partner James H. Nicholson Producers of the Year by Allied States Assoc. of MP Theatre Owners; 1964, Master Showmen of the Decade by the Theatre Owners of America; 1971, he and Nicholson named Pioneers of the Year by the Foundation of the MP Pioneers, Inc. Since appointment in 1973, has served as intl. v.p. of Variety Clubs Intl. V.p., Permanent Charities Committee. Member of the bd. of Trustees of Loyola Marymount U., L.A., in 1979.
PICTURES: *Exec. Producer or Producer:* Reform School Girl, Motorcycle Gang, Machine Gun Kelly, The Bonnie Parker Story, The Fall of the House of Usher, The Pit and the Pendulum, Tales of Terror, Master of The World, Premature Burial, Panic in the Year Zero, The Raven, Beach Party, Haunted Palace, Comedy of Terrors, Bikini Beach, Masque of the Red Death, Muscle Beach Party, Pajama Party Tomb of Ligeia, Wild Angels, Devil's Angels, The Trip, Three in the Attic, Wild in the Streets, The Oblong Box, Scream and Scream Again, Murders in the Rue Morgue, Cry of the Banshee, Bloody Mama, Wuthering Heights, The Abominable Dr. Phibes, Frogs, Blacula, Dillinger, Heavy Traffic, Hennessy, Cooley High, Food of the Gods, Futureworld, The Great Scout and Cathouse Thursday, The Land That Time Forgot, The People That Time Forgot, At the Earth's Core, Island of Dr. Moreau, Our Winning Season, The Amityville Horror, C.H.O.M.P.S., Dressed to Kill, How to Beat the High Cost of Living, The Final Terror, Up the Creek.

ARKUSH, ALLAN
Director. b. Jersey City, NJ, Apr. 30, 1948. e. Franklin & Marshall, NYU. Film Sch. With New World Pictures as film, music and trailer editor 1974-9. Co-directed Hollywood Boulevard and Death Sport and was 2nd unit dir. of Grand Theft Auto before directing on own. Dir. rock videos with Bette Midler and Mick Jagger, Elvis Costello, Christine McVie.
PICTURES: Hollywood Boulevard (co-dir., co-edit.), Deathsport (co-dir.), Rock 'n' Roll High School (also story), Heartbeeps, Get Crazy, Caddyshack II, Shake Rattle and Rock.
TELEVISION: *Series:* Fame, St. Elsewhere, L.A. Law, Moonlighting (Emmy nom.), Shannon's Deal (spv. prod.), Tattinger's, Twilight Zone, Mann & Machine, I'll Fly Away, Middle Ages, Johnny Bago, Central Park West (co-exec. prod.). *Pilots:* The Bronx Zoo, Capital News (prod.), Parenthood (co-exec. prod.), Body of Evidence, Moon Over Miami (exec. prod.). *Movies:* XXX & OOOs (co-exec. prod.), Young at Heart, Desert Breeze (co-exec. prod.).

ARLEDGE, ROONE
Executive. b. Forest Hills, NY, July 8, 1931. e. Columbia U. Entered industry with Dumont Network in 1952; joined U.S. Army, 1953, serving at Aberdeen Proving Ground in Maryland, where produced and directed radio programs. Joined NBC in 1954 where held various production positions. In 1960 went to ABC where created ABC's Wide World of Sports in April, 1961. Named v.p. in chg. of ABC Sports. Created ABC's Wide World of Sports in April, 1961. Named pres. of ABC News in 1968; pres. of ABC News and Sports, 1977. Holds four George Foster Peabody Awards for sports reporting; 19 Emmy awards.

ARLING, ARTHUR E.
Cinematographer. b. Missouri, Sept. 2, 1906. e. N.Y. Inst. of Photography. Entered m.p. Fox studio 1927 as asst. cameraman, 2nd cameraman 1931; operative cameraman on Gone With the Wind which won the Academy Award for technicolor photography 1939. Lt. Comdr. U.S.N.R., WWII. Member: Amer. Soc. of Cinematographers.
PICTURES: The Yearling (Academy Award, 1946), Homestretch, Captain from Castile, Mother Was a Freshman, You're My Everything, Wabash Avenue, My Blue Heaven, Call Me Mister, Belles on Their Toes, The Glass Slipper, Three for the Show, Love Me or Leave Me, I'll Cry Tomorrow, Ransom, Great American Pastime, Tammy & the Bachelor, Pay the Devil, Story of Ruth, Pillow Talk, Lover Come Back, Notorious Landlady, Boys Night Out, My Six Loves, Ski Party, Once Before I Die.

ARMSTRONG, BESS
Actress. b. Baltimore, MD, Dec. 11, 1953. m. producer John Fiedler. e. Brown U.
PICTURES: The House of God (debut, 1979), The Four Seasons, Jekyll and Hyde—Together Again, High Road to China, Jaws 3-D, Nothing in Common, Second Sight, Mother Mother, The Skateboard Kid.
TELEVISION: *Series:* On Our Own, All is Forgiven, Married People, My So-Called Life. *Movies:* Getting Married, How to Pick Up Girls, Walking Through the Fire, 11th Victim, This Girl for Hire, Lace, Take Me Home Again, She Stood Alone: The Tailhook Scandal, Stolen Innocence. *Special:* Barefoot in the Park.

ARMSTRONG, GILLIAN
Director. b. Melbourne, Australia, Dec. 18, 1950. e. Swinburne Coll. Among 1st class in dirs. course at National Aust. Film & TV School, Sydney. Worked as art dir. on a number of films. Dir. numerous shorts (One Hundred a Day, The Singer and the Dancer) and documentaries (A Busy Kind of Bloke, Bingo Bridesmaids and Braces) before turning to features.
PICTURES: My Brilliant Career (Australian Film Inst. Award), Starstruck, Mrs. Soffel, Hard to Handle, High Tide, Fires Within, The Last Days of Chez Nous, Little Women.

ARMSTRONG, GORDON
Executive. b. East Orange, NJ, Nov. 26, 1937. e. Arizona State U., graduate studies at NYU. Joined 20th Century-Fox in 1970 as nat. pub. dir. In 1975 was appointed dir. of adv.-pub.-promo. for Dino De Laurentiis Corp. In 1978, became vice pres., world-wide marketing for the company; 1980, named v.p., adv.-pub.-prom., Universal Pictures; 1984, named exec. v.p., mktg. MCA Recreation. 1991, pres. mktg., Morgan Creek Prods. Pres., Entertainment Marketing Group, 1993. V.P., sales and mktg., ATTICA Cybernetics 1995. V.P., sales and mktg., Doubleclick Network 1996.

ARNALL, ELLIS GIBBS
Lawyer, executive. b. Newnan, GA, March 20, 1907. e. Mercer U., U. of the South. A.B. 1928, D.C.L. 1947; U. of Georgia LL.B. 1931; Atlanta Law Sch., LL.D. 1941; Piedmont Coll., LL.D 1943; Bryant Coll., LL.D. 1948. Georgia state rep. from Coweta County, 1936-38; asst. Attorney-General (GA) 1938-42; Attorney-General (GA) 1942-43; Governor of GA 1943-47; pres. Dixie Life Insurance Co.; pres., Columbus Natl Life Insurance Co.; sr. mem. law firm Arnall Golden & Gregory; pres. Georgia State Jr. Chamber of Commerce 1939. Author: The Shore Dimly Seen (1946), What The People Want (1948). Member U.S. Natl. Com. on UNESCO; member U.S. delegation to 4th annual conference UNESCO, Paris, 1949; SIMPP (pres. 1948, 1952); pres. Indept. Film Prod. Export Corp., 1953; bd. of dir., exec. com., U.S. Nat'l Comm. for UNESCO, 1964-65; AMPAS.

ARNAZ, JR., DESI
Actor, Singer. b. Los Angeles, CA, Jan. 19, 1953. e. Beverly Hills H.S. Son of Lucille Ball and Desi Arnaz. Sister is actress Lucie Arnaz. Gained fame as rock singer and musician with the Dino, Desi and Billy group. Video: A Day at the Zoo. Regional theatre includes Sunday in New York, Grease, Promises Promises, Alone Together, I Love My Wife, Is There Life After High School?, Love Letters, The Boys Next Door.
PICTURES: Red Sky at Morning (debut, 1971), Marco, Billy Two Hats, Joyride, A Wedding, House of the Long Shadows, The Mambo Kings.
TELEVISION: *Series:* Here's Lucy, Automan. *Movies:* Mr. & Mrs. Bo Jo Jones, Voyage of the Yes, She Lives, Having Babies, Flight to Holocaust, Black Market Baby, To Kill a Cop, The Courage and the Passion, How to Pick Up Girls, Crisis in Mid-Air, Gridlock, Advice to the Lovelorn, The Night the Bridge Fell Down. *Guest:* The Love Boat, Fantasy Island, Paul Reiser: Out on a Whim, Matlock.

ARNAZ, LUCIE
Actress. b. Los Angeles, CA, July 17, 1951. Daughter of Lucille Ball and Desi Arnaz. m. actor Laurence Luckinbill. Brother is actor Desi Arnaz Jr. B'way: They're Playing Our Song (Theatre World Award), Lost in Yonkers. National touring companies:

13

Whose Life is It Anyway?, Educating Rita, My One and Only, Social Security. Nightclubs: Lucie Arnaz-Latin Roots, Irving Berlin in Concert-In Sicily.
PICTURES: Billy Jack Goes to Washington, The Jazz Singer, Second Thoughts.
TELEVISION: Series: Here's Lucy, The Lucy Arnaz Show, Sons and Daughters. Pilot: One More Try. Movies: Who is the Black Dahlia, The Mating Season, The Washington Mistress, Who Gets the Friends? Special: Lucy & Desi: A Home Movie (host, co-exec. prod., co-dir.).

ARNESS, JAMES
Actor. r.n. James Aurness. b. Minneapolis, MN, May 26, 1923. e. Beloit Coll. Brother of actor Peter Graves. Served in U.S. Army; worked in advertising, real estate. Started in films in late 1940's appearing under his real name.
PICTURES: The Farmer's Daughter (debut 1947), Rose Are Red, The Man From Texas, Battleground, Sierra, Two Lost Worlds, Wyoming Mail, Wagon Master, Double Crossbones, Stars in My Crown (1st billing as James Arness), Cavalry Scout, Belle le Grand, Iron Man, The People Against O'Hara, The Girl in White, The Thing, Carbine Williams, Hellgate, Big Jim McLain, Horizons West, Lone Hand, Ride the Man Down, Island in the Sky, Veils of Bagdad, Hondo, Her Twelve Men, Them!, Many Rivers to Cross, Flame of the Islands, The Sea Chase, The First Travelling Saleslady, Gun the Man Down, Alias Jesse James (cameo).
TELEVISION: Series: Gunsmoke (20 years), How the West Was Won, McClain's Law. Movies: The Macahans, The Alamo: 13 Days to Glory, Gunsmoke: Return to Dodge, Red River, Gunsmoke: The Last Apache, Gunsmoke: To the Last Man, Gunsmoke: The Long Ride (also exec. prod.). Mini-Series: How the West Was Won.

ARNOLD, EDDY
Singer. b. Henderson, TN, May 15, 1918. Radio performer, Nashville, TN; recording star since 1946; records include That's How Much I Love You, Anytime, Bouquet of Roses (on the Country Music charts longer than any record in the history of country music), Make the World Go Away. Holds the record for most Country Records on the charts. Elected to Country Music Hall of Fame (1966); Entertainer of the Year (1967), Pioneer Award from Acad. of Country Music (1984), President's Award from Songwriter's Guild (1987).
TELEVISION: Series: Eddy Arnold Show (1952-3), Eddy Arnold Time, Eddy Arnold Show (1956), The Kraft Music Hall (1967-71). Hosted Music from the Land, Tonight Show, more than 20 specials.

ARNOW, TED J.
Executive. b. Brooklyn, NY. e. St. Johns U., Washington and Lee U. Served as dir. of recreation for 262nd General Hospital in Panama. Veteran of over 50 yrs. in amusement industry. Was v.p. for adv., pub., & promo. for Loew's Theatres. Member: Motion Picture Pioneers, Variety Clubs, Will Rogers Hospital; former pres. of AMPA (Assoc. M.P. Advertisers). Retired.

ARQUETTE, PATRICIA
Actress. b. Chicago, IL, Apr. 8, 1968. m. actor Nicolas Cage. Sister of actress Rosanna Arquette and actors Richmond, Alexis and David Arquette. Prof. debut in children's version of Story Theatre. Studied acting with Milton Katselis.
PICTURES: A Nightmare on Elm Street 3: Dream Warriors (debut, 1987), Pretty Smart, Time Out, Far North, Prayer of the Rollerboys, The Indian Runner, Ethan Frome, Trouble Bound, Inside Monkey Zetterland, True Romance, Holy Matrimony, Ed Wood, Beyond Rangoon, Infinity, Flirting With Disaster, The Secret Agent, Nightwatch.
TELEVISION: Movies: Daddy, Dillinger, Wildflower, Betrayed by Love. Special: The Girl With the Crazy Brother. Guest: The Edge (Indian Poker), thirtysomething, Tales From the Crypt.

ARQUETTE, ROSANNA
Actress. b. New York, NY, Aug. 10, 1959. Granddaughter of humorist Cliff Arquette (Charlie Weaver). Daughter of actor-producer Lewis Arquette. Sister of actress Patricia Arquette and actors Richmond, Alexis and David Arquette. Prof. debut in children's version of Story Theatre. Studied acting in San Francisco. Role in LA play led to bit parts on tv then regular role as Shirley Jones' teenage daughter on series Shirley (1979).
PICTURES: More American Graffiti (debut, 1979), Gorp, S.O.B., Baby It's You, Off the Wall, The Aviator, Desperately Seeking Susan, Silverado, After Hours, 8 Million Ways To Die, Nobody's Fool, Amazon Women on the Moon, The Big Blue, New York Stories (Life Lessons), Flight of the Intruder, Wendy Cracked a Walnut, The Linguini Incident, Fathers and Sons, Nowhere to Run, Pulp Fiction, Search and Destroy, Gone Fishin, Crash.
TELEVISION: Series: Shirley. Movies: Having Babies II, The Dark Secret of Harvest Home, Zuma Beach, The Ordeal of Patty Hearst, A Long Way Home, The Wall, The Executioner's Song, Johnny Belinda, One Cooks the Other Doesn't, The Parade, Survival Guide, Promised a Miracle, Sweet Revenge,

Separation, Son of the Morning Star, Black Rainbow, In the Deep Woods, The Wrong Man, Nowhere to Hide. Specials: Mom and Dad Can't Hear Me, A Family Tree (Trying Times).

ARTHUR, BEATRICE
Actress. r.n. Bernice Frankel. b. New York, NY, May 13, 1926. Franklin Inst. of Sciences & Art. Studied with Erwin Piscator at New School for Social Research; first stage role as Lysistrata; professional stage debut in Dog Beneath the Skin, 1947.
THEATER: Gas, Yerma, No Exit, Six Characters in Search of an Author, The Taming of the Shrew, (1948) The Owl and the Pussycat, The Threepenny Opera (1953 revival), The ShoeString Revue, What's the Rush?, Nature's Way, Ulysses in Nighttown, Gay Divorcee, Fiddler on the Roof, Mame (Tony Award, 1966), The Floating Light Bulb, Night of the 100 Stars.
PICTURES: That Kind of Woman, Lovers and Other Strangers, Mame, History of the World Part I.
TELEVISION: Debut: Once Upon a Time (1951), Numerous guest appearances. Series: Caesar's Hour, Maude (Emmy Award, 1977), Amanda's, Golden Girls (Emmy Award, 1988). Specials: All Star Gala at Ford's Theater (host), Jay Leno's Family Comedy Hour. Movie: My First Love.

ARTHUR, KAREN
Director. b. Omaha, NB, Aug. 24, 1941. 1950-68: ballet dancer, choreographer and musical comedy singer, dancer and actress. 1968-75: actress, film, TV and theatre. 1970-95, film, tv director.
PICTURES: Actress: A Guide for the Married Man, Winning. Director: Legacy (1975, Int'l Film Critics & Josef Von Sternberg Awards, 1975), The Mafu Cage, Lady Beware.
TELEVISION: Movies: Charleston, Victims for Victims: The Theresa Saldana Story (Christopher Award), A Bunny's Tale, The Rape of Richard Beck, Evil in Clear River (Christopher Award), Cracked Up, Bridge to Silence, Fall from Grace, Bump in the Night, Shadow of a Doubt, The Secret, The Disappearance of Christina, Against Their Will: Women in Prison. Mini-Series: Love and Betrayal: The Mia Farrow Story, Crossings, Return to Eden, The Jacksons: An American Dream, Dead by Sunset. Pilots: Tin Man, Blue Bayou. Episodes: Rich Man Poor Man Book II, Emerald Point, Boone, Two Marriages, Hart to Hart, Remington Steele, Cagney & Lacey (Emmy Award, 1985).

ARTZ, BOB
Theatre executive. b. Spokane, WA, Aug 21, 1946. e., B.T.A. Pasadena Playhouse College of Theatre Arts. Began in 1968 as doorman; then asst. mgr. to mgr. with National General Theatre Corporation. Joined Plitt Theatres in 1978 as dist. mgr. and ad/pub. director, West Coast. Joined General Cinema Theatres in 1986 as reg. marketing dir.; Western region. Became dir., film marketing in 1993. National dir., Entertainment Marketing & Operations in 1996. Member of Variety Club; Life Member: Pasadena Playhouse Alumni & Assoc.

ASH, RENE
Producer. b. Brussels, Belgium, March 14, 1939; e. U. of Omaha. Member of the Publicists Guild since 1968; Eastern v.p. of Pub Guild 1973-1981; Author of The Film Editor in Motion Pictures & Television. Employed with I.A.T.S.E. 1968-1979, prior to which was assoc. editor, Greater Amusements; various articles published in foreign film magazines; editor-in-chief, Backstage 1979-80; pres., Cinereal Pictures, 1984-85; co-pres., Eagle Films Corp., 1985-94; pres. Rea Film Prods.

ASHER, JANE
Actress. b. London, England, April 5, 1946.
PICTURES: Mandy (Crash of Silence; debut, 1952), Third Party Risk, Dance Little Lady, Adventure in the Hopfields, The Quatermass Experiment (The Creeping Unknown), Charley Moon, Greengage Summer (Loss of Innocence), The Girl in the Headlines, The Winter's Tale, Deep End, The Buttercup Chain, Henry VIII and His Six Wives (from the BBC series the Six Wives of Henry VIII), Runners, Success Is the Best Revenge, Dream Child, Paris By Night, Closing Numbers.
TELEVISION: Movies/Specials: Brideshead Revisited, Voyage 'Round My Father, East Lynne, The Mistress, Wish Me Luck, Tonight at 8:30, The Volunteer.

ASHLEY, ELIZABETH
Actress. b. Ocala, FL, Aug. 30, 1939. e. Studied ballet LA State U., 1957-58; grad. Neighborhood Playhouse, 1961. Author: Postcards From the Road.
THEATER: Take Her She's Mine (1962 Tony & Theatre World Awards), The Highest Tree, Barefoot in the Park, Ring 'Round the Bathtub, The Skin of Our Teeth, Legend, Cat on a Hot Tin Roof (B'way revival), Caesar and Cleopatra, Agnes of God, The Milk Train Doesn't Stop Here Anymore, When She Danced.
PICTURES: The Carpetbaggers (debut, 1964), Ship of Fools, The Third Day, The Marriage of a Young Stockbroker, Paperback Hero, Golden Needles, Rancho DeLuxe, 92 in the Shade, The Great Scout and Cathouse Thursday, Coma, Windows, Paternity, Split Image, Dragnet, Vampire's Kiss, Dangerous Curves, Lost Memories.

TELEVISION: *Series*: Evening Shade. *Movies*: Harpy, The Face of Fear, When Michael Calls, Second Chance, The Heist, Your Money or Your Wife, The Magician, One of My Wives is Missing, The War Between the Tates, A Fire in the Sky, Svengali, He's Fired She's Hired, Stagecoach, Warm Hearts Cold Feet, The Two Mrs. Grenvilles, Blue Bayou, Reason for Living: The Jill Ireland Story, Love and Curses... and All That Jazz, In the Best Interest of the Children. *Pilot*: Tom and Joann. *Guest*: Miami Vice, Hunter, Murder She Wrote, B.L. Stryker.

ASHLEY, JOHN
Actor, Producer. r.n. John Atchley. b. Kansas City, MO, Dec. 25, 1934. e. Oklahoma State U., B.A., 1956. Career started in Tulsa Little Theatre, 1956.
PICTURES: Dragstrip Girl (debut, 1957), Motorcycle Gang, Suicide Battalion, Beach Party, How to Stuff a Wild Bikini.
TELEVISION: *Series*: Straightaway. *Guest*: Men of Annapolis, Sheriff of Cochise, Frontier Doctor, Matinee Theatre, Jefferson Drum. *Movie*: Something is Out There (co-exec. prod.). *Series Prod*: The A-Team, Werewolf, Hardball, Raven, Walker: Texas Ranger.

ASHTON, JOHN
Actor. b. Springfield, MA, Feb. 22, 1948. e. USC (BA in theatre).
THEATER: The Last Meeting of the Knights of the White Magnolia (L.A. Drama Critics Circle Award), True West (Drama-Logue Award), A Flea in Her Ear (L.A. Drama Critics Circle Award).
PICTURES: Oh God!, Breaking Away, Borderline, Honky Tonk Freeway, Adventures of Buckaroo Banzai, Beverly Hills Cop, The Last Resort, King Kong Lives, Some Kind of Wonderful, Beverly Hills Cop II, She's Having a Baby, Midnight Run, I Want to Go Home, Curly Sue, Little Big League, Trapped in Paradise, The Shooter.
TELEVISION: *Series*: Dallas, Breaking Away, Hardball. *Guest*: M*A*S*H*, Police Squad!, The Twilight Zone. *Movies*: Elvis and the Beauty Queen, A Death in California, The Deliberate Stranger, I Know My First Name is Steven, Dirty Work, Stephen King's The Tommyknockers. *Mini-Series*: The Rhinemann Exchange. Love Lies and Murder.

ASNER, EDWARD
Actor. b. Kansas City, MO, Nov. 15, 1929. e. U. of Chicago, where affiliated with campus acting group. Served two years with U.S. Army in France. Returned to Chicago to join Playwright's Theatre Club. Moved to N.Y. NY Shakespeare Festival (1960) and American Shakespeare Festival (1961). In 1961 moved to Hollywood to become active in films and TV. National pres. Screen Actors Guild (1981-85), Prod. TV & feature projects through his company, Quince. Winner of numerous humanitarian awards.
THEATER: *B'way debut*: Face of a Hero, Born Yesterday (1989). *Off-B'way*: Ivanov, Threepenny Opera, Legend of Lovers, The Tempest, Venice Preserved.
PICTURES: Kid Gallahad (debut, 1962), The Slender Thread, The Satan Bug, The Venetian Affair, El Dorado, Gunn, Change of Habit, Halls of Anger, They Call Me Mister Tibbs, The Todd Killings, Skin Game, Gus, Fort Apache-The Bronx, O'Hara's Wife, Daniel, Pinocchio and the Emperor of the Night (voice), Moon Over Parador (cameo), JFK, Happily Ever After (voice), Cat's Don't Dance (voice).
TELEVISION: *Series*: Slattery's People, The Mary Tyler Moore Show (3 Emmy Awards: 1971, 1972, 1975), Lou Grant (3 Emmy Awards: 1978, 1980), Off the Rack, The Bronx Zoo, The Trials of Rosie O'Neill, Fish Police (voice), Hearts Afire, Thunder Alley. *Movies*: The Doomsday Flight, Daughter of the Mind, The House on Greenapple Road, The Old Man Who Cried Wolf, The Last Child, They Call It Murder, Haunts of the Very Rich, The Police Story, The Girl Most Likely To..., The Imposter, Death Scream, Hey I'm Alive, Life and Assassination of the Kingfish, The Gathering, The Family Man, A Small Killing, Anatomy of an Illness, Vital Signs, Kate's Secret, The Christmas Star, A Friendship in Vienna, Not a Penny More Not a Penny Less, Good Cops Bad Cops, Switched at Birth, Silent Motive, Yes Virginia There Is a Santa Claus, Cruel Doubt, Gypsy, Heads. *Mini-Series*: Rich Man Poor Man (Emmy Award, 1976), Roots (Emmy Award, 1977), Tender Is the Night.

ASPEL, MICHAEL
Radio/TV Presenter. b. London, England, Jan. 12, 1933. Entered industry 1954. Early career: BBC Radio as actor/presenter. BBC TV as announcer/newsreader. Presentations incl: Miss World, Crackerjack, Give Us A Clue, Ask Aspel, Family Favourites, Child's Play, ITV Telethon 1988, 1990 & 1992, Aspel and Company, This Is Your Life; BAFTA Awards, Strange ... But True? Awarded OBE in 1993.

ASSANTE, ARMAND
Actor. b. New York, NY, Oct. 4, 1949. e. American Acad. of Dramatic Arts. Appeared with regional theatre groups incl. Arena Stage (D.C.), Long Wharf (New Haven), and Actor's Theatre of Louisville.

THEATER: *B'way*: Boccaccio, Comedians, Romeo and Juliet, Kingdoms. *Off-B'way*: Why I Went Crazy, Rubbers, The Beauty Part, Lake of the Woods, Yankees 3 Detroit 0.
PICTURES: Paradise Alley, Prophecy, Little Darlings, Private Benjamin, Love and Money, I the Jury, Unfaithfully Yours, Belizaire the Cajun, The Penitent, Animal Behavior, Q & A, Eternity, The Marrying Man, The Mambo Kings, 1492: Conquest of Paradise, Hoffa, Fatal Instinct, Trial by Jury, Judge Dredd, Striptease.
TELEVISION: *Movies*: Human Feelings, Lady of the House, The Pirate, Sophia Loren-Her Own Story, Rage of Angels, Why Me?, A Deadly Business, Stranger in My Bed, Hands of a Stranger, Jack the Ripper, Passion and Paradise, Fever, Blind Justice, Kidnapped, Gotti. *Mini-Series*: Napoleon and Josephine: A Love Story, Evergreen. *Series*: The Doctors (1975).

ASSEYEV, TAMARA
Producer. e. Marymont College; UCLA (MA, theatre arts). Began career as asst. to Roger Corman, working on 8 films with him. In 1967 started to produce films independently. Then co-produced films with Alex Rose, starting with Drive-In. In 1966 at 24, became youngest member of Producers Guild of Amer. Member: Costume Council, LA City Museum; founding member LA Museum of Contemporary Art.
PICTURES: The Wild Racers, Paddy, The Arousers, TheHistory of Atlantic Records, Co-produced with Ms. Rose:Drive-In, I Wanna Hold Your Hand, Big Wednesday, Norma Rae.
TELEVISION: *Movies (exec. prod.)*: Penalty Phase, After the Promise, A Shadow on the Sun (also actress), The Secret Life of Kathy McCormick, The Hijacking of the Achille Lauro, Murder By Moonlight.

ASTIN, JOHN
Actor. b. Baltimore, MD, March 30, 1930. e. Washington and Jefferson Coll., Washington Drama Sch., Johns Hopkins U., grad. B.A., U. of Minnesota Graduate School. Father of actors Sean and Mackenzie Astin. First prof. job., Off-B'way, Threepenny Opera; B'way debut, Major Barbara; dir., co-prod., A Sleep of Prisoners, Phoenix Theatre; during 1955-59, did voices in cartoons, commercials. Prod. & dir. short subject Prelude.
THEATER: The Cave Dwellers, Ulysses in Nighttown, Tall Story, Lend Me a Tenor, H.M.S. Pinafore.
PICTURES: The Pusher (debut, 1958), West Side Story, That Touch of Mink, Move Over Darling, The Wheeler Dealers, The Spirit is Willing, Candy, Viva Max!, Bunny O'Hare, Get to Know Your Rabbit, Every Little Crook and Nanny, The Brothers O'Toole, Freaky Friday, National Lampoon's European Vacation, Body Slam, Teen Wolf Too, Return of the Killer Tomatoes, Night Life, Gremlins 2, Killer Tomatoes Eat France, Stepmonster, The Silence of the Hams, Frighteners, Harrison Bergeron.
TELEVISION: *Series*: I'm Dickens... He's Fenster, The Addams Family, The Pruitts of Southampton, Operation Petticoat, Mary, The Addams Family (voice for animated series), The Adventures of Brisco County Jr. *Guest*: Batman, The Flying Nun, Bonanza, Odd Couple, Night Gallery, Partridge Family, Police Woman, Love Boat, Night Court. Specials: Harry Anderson's Sideshow, Halloween With the Addams Family. *Movies*: Two on a Bench, Evil Roy Slade, Skyway to Death, Only with Married Men, The Dream Makers, Operation Petticoat (also dir.), Rossetti and Ryan: Men Who Love Women (dir. only), Huck and the King of Hearts. *Pilots*: Phillip and Barbara, Ethel Is an Elephant.

ASTIN, SEAN
Actor. b. Santa Monica, Feb. 25, 1971. parents are actors John Astin and Patty Duke. Brother is actor Mackenzie Astin. First acting job at 7 opposite mother in Afterschool Special Please Don't Hit Me Mom. Directed short films On My Honor, Kangaroo Court (Acad. Award nom.).
THEATER: Lone Star (L.A.).
PICTURES: The Goonies (debut, 1985), White Water Summer, Like Father Like Son, Staying Together, The War of the Roses, Memphis Belle, The Willies, Toy Soldiers, Encino Man, Where the Day Takes You, Rudy, Safe Passage, The Low Life.
TELEVISION: *Movies*: The Rules of Marriage, The Brat Patrol. *Pilot*: Just Our Luck.

ATHERTON, WILLIAM
Actor. b. New Haven, CT, June 30, 1947. While in high school became youngest member of Long Wharf Theatre Co. Given scholarship to Pasadena Playhouse; then switched to Carnegie Tech Sch. of Drama in 1965. In college years toured with USO prods in Europe and in stock and industrial shows. Came to NY where first prof. job was in nat'l co. of Little Murders.
THEATER: The House of Blue Leaves, The Basic Training of Pavlo Hummel, The Sign in Sidney Brustein's Window, Suggs (Theatre World Award, Outer Circle Critics Award, Drama Desk Award), Rich and Famous, Passing Game, Happy New Year, The American Clock, Three Acts of Recognition, The Caine Mutiny Court-Martial, Child's Play, Loco Motives.
PICTURES: The New Centurions (debut, 1972), Class of '44, The Sugarland Express, The Day of the Locust, The Hindenburg, Looking for Mr. Goodbar, Ghostbusters, Real Genius, No Mercy, Frank and Jesse, Die Hard, Die Hard 2, Grim Prairie Tales, Oscar, The Pelican Brief, Bio-Dome.

TELEVISION: *Mini-Series*: Centennial. *Movies*: Tomorrow's Child, Malibu, Intrigue, Buried Alive, Diagnosis of Murder, Chrome Soldiers, Robin Cook's Virus, Broken Trust. *Guest*: The Equalizer, Twilight Zone, Murder She Wrote, Tales From the Crypt, *Special*: The House of Mirth.

ATKINS, CHRISTOPHER
Actor. b. Rye, NY, Feb. 21, 1961. e. Dennison U., Ohio. Early modeling jobs before being hired for theatrical film debut in The Blue Lagoon (1980).
PICTURES: The Blue Lagoon, The Pirate Movie, A Night in Heaven, Beaks, Mortuary Academy, Listen to Me, Shakma, King's Ransom, Dracula Rising, Die Watching, Exchange Lifeguards, A Bullet Down Under, Trigger Fast, It's My Party.
TELEVISION: *Movies*: Child Bride of Short Creek, Secret Weapons, Fatal Charm. *Series*: Dallas. *Guest*: The Black Stallion. *Also*: The Black Rose, Miami Killer, The Floating Outfit, Deadman's Island, Angel Flight Down.

ATKINSON, ROWAN
Actor, Writer. b. England, Jan. 6, 1955. e. Newcastle U., Oxford.
THEATER: Rowan Atkinson in Revue (also writer), Not in Front of an Audience, The Nerd, Rowan Atkinson at the Atkinson (also writer; NY), Mime Gala, The Sneeze.
PICTURES: The Secret Policeman's Ball (also co-s.p.), The Secret Policeman's Other Ball, Never Say Never Again, The Tall Guy, The Witches, Hot Shots Part Deux, Four Weddings and a Funeral, The Lion King (voice).
TELEVISION: *Series*: Not the Nine O'Clock News (also writer; BAFTA Award for acting), Blackadder. *Specials*: Just for Laughs II, Live from London, Blackadder II, Blackadder the Third, Blackadder Goes Forth, Blackadder IV, Blackadder's Christmas Carol, The Appointments of Dennis Jennings, Mr. Bean (also writer), Mr. Bean Rides Again, The Thin Blue Line.

ATTENBOROUGH, DAVID
Broadcaster. b. London, England, May 8, 1926; e. Wyggeston Sch., Leicester; Clare Coll., Cambridge. Early career, editor in educational publishing house, ent. BBC-TC Sept. 1952. Prod. Zoo Quest series, Travellers Tales, Adventure and other prog., travel, Eastward with Attenborough, The Tribal Eye, Life on Earth, The Living Planet, The First Eden, The Trials of Life. Controller BBC-2, 1965-68; Dir. of Prog. BBC-TV, 1969-72.

ATTENBOROUGH, BARON RICHARD (SAMUEL)
1993, Life Peer of Richmond Upon Thames; Kt 1976; CBE 1967. Actor, Producer, Director. b. Cambridge, England, Aug. 29, 1923. m. 1945 Sheila Beryl Grant Sim. e. Wyggeston Grammar Sch., Leicester. Leverhulme Scholarship to Royal Acad. of Dramatic Art, 1941 (Bancroft Medal). First stage appearance in Ah Wilderness (Palmers Green, 1941). West End debut in Awake and Sing (1942), then The Little Foxes, Brighton Rock. Joined RAF, 1943; seconded to RAF Film Unit, and appeared in training film Journey Together, 1945; demobilized, 1946. Returned to stage, 1949, in The Way Back (Home of the Brave), To Dorothy a Son, Sweet Madness, The Mousetrap (original cast: 1952-54), Double Image, The Rape of the Belt. 1959 formed Beaver Films with Bryan Forbes; 1960 formed Allied Film Makers.
PICTURES: *Actor*: In Which We Serve (debut, 1942), Schweik's New Adventures, The Hundred Pound Window, Journey Together, A Matter of Life and Death (Stairway to Heaven), School for Secrets (Secret Flight), The Man Within (The Smugglers), Dancing With Crime, Brighton Rock (Young Scarface), London Belongs to Me (Dulcimer Street), The Guinea Pig, The Lost People, Boys in Brown, Morning Departure (Operation Disaster), Hell Is Sold Out, The Magic Box, Gift Horse (Glory at Sea), Father's Doing Fine, Eight O'Clock Walk, The Ship That Died of Shame, Private's Progress, The Baby and the Battleship, Brothers in Law, The Scamp, Dunkirk, The Man Upstairs, Sea of Sand (Desert Patrol), Danger Within (Breakout), I'm All Right Jack, Jet Storm, SOS Pacific, The Angry Silence (also co-prod.), The League of Gentlemen, Only Two Can Play, All Night Long, The Dock Brief (Trial & Error), The Great Escape, Seance on a Wet Afternoon (also prod.; San Sebastian Film Fest. & Brit. Acad. Awards for Best Actor), The Third Secret, Guns at Batasi (Brit. Acad. Award), The Flight of the Phoenix, The Sand Pebbles (Golden Globe Award), Dr. Dolittle (Golden Globe Award), The Bliss of Mrs Blossom, Only When I Larf, The Magic Christian, David Copperfield (TV in U.S.), The Last Grenade, A Severed Head, Loot, 10 Rillington Place, Ten Little Indians (And Then There Were None), Rosebud, Brannigan, Conduct Unbecoming, The Chess Players, The Human Factor, Jurassic Park, Miracle on 34th Street. *Producer*: Whistle Down the Wind, The L-Shaped Room. *Director*: Oh! What a Lovely War (also prod.; 16 Intl. Awards incl. Golden Globe and BAFTA UN Award), Young Winston (Golden Globe), A Bridge Too Far (Evening News Best Drama Award, 1977), Magic, Gandhi (also prod.; 8 Oscars, 5 BAFTA Awards, 5 Golden Globes, DGA Award, 1982), A Chorus Line, Cry Freedom (also prod.; Berlinale Kamera, 1987; BFI Award for Tech. Achievement), Chaplin (also prod.), Shadowlands (also prod.; BAFTA Award for Best British Film of 1993), In Love and War.

AUBERJONOIS, RENE
Actor. b. New York, NY, June 1, 1940. e. attended Carnegie Mellon U.
THEATER: *Includes*: Dark of the Moon, Beyond the Fringe, Tartuffe, King Lear, Fire, Julius Caesar, Charley's Aunt, Coco (Tony Award, 1970), Tricks, The Ruling Class, Twelfth Night, The Good Doctor (Tony nom.), Break a Leg, The New York Idea, Every Good Boy Deserves Favor; Richard III, The Misanthrope, Flea in Her Ear, Big River (Tony nom.), Metamorphosis, City of Angels (Tony nom.).
PICTURES: Lilith (debut, 1964), Petulia, M*A*S*H*, Brewster McCloud, McCabe and Mrs. Miller, Pete 'n Tillie, Images, Hindenberg, The Big Bus, King Kong, Eyes of Laura Mars, Where the Buffalo Roam, The Last Unicorn (voice), 3:15, Walker, Police Academy 5: Assignment Miami Beach, My Best Friend is a Vampire, The Little Mermaid (voice), The Feud, Star Trek VI: The Undiscovered Country (unbilled), The Player, Little Nemo (voice), The Ballad of Little Jo.
TELEVISION: *Series*: Benson (Emmy nom.), Star Trek: Deep Space Nine. *Movies*: The Birdmen, Shirts/Skins, Panache, Dark Secret of Harvest Home, Wild Wild West Revisited, More Wild Wild West, Smoky Mountain Christmas, The Christmas Star, Gore Vidal's Billy the Kid, Longarm, A Connecticut Yankee in King Arthur's Court, Absolute Strangers, Ned Blessing: The True Story of My Life, Wild Card. *Mini-Series*: The Rhineman Exchange. *Specials*: Faerie Tale Theatre (The Frog Prince, Sleeping Beauty), King Lear, Legend of Sleepy Hollow (Emmy nom.), Fort Necessity, Incident at Vichy, The Booth, The Cask of Amontillado, Ashenden (BBC), The Lost Language of Cranes (BBC). *Episode Director*: Marble Head Manor, Star Trek: Deep Space Nine.

AUDRAN, STEPHANE
Actress. b. Versailles, France, Nov. 8, 1938. Former wife of French star Jean-Louis Trintignant and director Claude Chabrol.
PICTURES: Les Cousins (debut under direction of Chabrol, 1959), Les Bonnes Femmes, Bluebeard, The Third Lover, Six in Paris, The Champagne Murders, Les Biches, La Femme Infidele, The Beast Must Die, The Lady in the Car, Le Boucher, Without Apparent Motive, Dead Pigeon on Beethoven Street, La Rupture, Just Before Nightfall, The Discreet Charm of the Bourgeoisie, Blood Wedding, The Devil's Advocate, Le Cri de Couer, Vincent Francois Paul and the Others, The Black Bird (U.S. film debut), Ten Little Indians, The Silver Bears, Eagle's Wing, The Big Red One, Coup de Torchon (Clean Slate), La Cage ux Folles III: The Wedding, Cop au Vin, Babette's Feast, Seasons of Pleasure, Faceless, Body-To-Body, Sons, Manika: The Girl Who Lived Twice, Quiet Days in Clichy, Mass in C Minor, Betty, Poulet au Vinaigre, Au Petit Marguery.
TELEVISION: Mistral's Daughter, The Blood of Others, The Sun Also Rises, Poor Little Rich Girl: The Barbara Hutton Story, Champagne Charlie.

AUERBACH, NORBERT T.
Executive. b. Vienna, 1923. Educated in U.S. and served with U.S. Army Intelligence in Europe during WWII. Joined m.p. business in 1946 after grad. UCLA. (business admin.). First asst. dir. at Service Studios in CA. Moved to N.Y. to join domestic sales dept. of Film Classics. Joined Columbia Pictures in foreign dept. In 1950 assigned to Paris office, where remained for over decade, except for 18 mos. in Portugal as mgr. Returned to Paris in 1953 and filled number of exec. sls. positions for Columbia, ultimately rising to continental mgr. 1961, left Columbia to produce films in France. Resumed career in dist. as continental mgr. at Paris office of United Artists. 1966 returned to prod. to make The Thief of Paris. 1967, joined Seven Arts Prods. heading theatrical and TV sls. operations in Paris. When Seven Arts acquired Warner Bros., he became continental sls. mgr. for Warners in Paris. 1968, set up European prod. and dist. org. for CBS Cinema Center Films, operating from London. 1972, moved to L.A. as v.p., foreign mgr. for CCF. Returned to London in 1973 to be consultant in prod. and dist. Rejoined UA in 1977 as sls. mgr. for Europe and the Middle East. Named sr. v.p. & foreign mgr. in 1978. Named pres. & COO, Jan. 1981; pres., CEO, Feb. 1981. Co-pres., United Int'l Pictures, London, until 1982. In 1983, formed packaging and financing Co., Eliktra, Inc. 1982, acting pres. and chief exec. officer of Almi Distribution Corp. Now Almi consultant, Exec. v.p. American Screen Co.

AUGUST, BILLE
Director. b. Denmark, 1948. e. trained in advertising photography, Danish Film School, grad. 1971, cinematography. As cinematographer shot: Miesta ei voi raiskata (Men Can't Be Raped), Karleken, The Grass is Singing. Became dir. 1978 with short Kim G. and dramas for Danish TV.
PICTURES: Honning Maane/In My Life (also sp.), Zappa (also s.p.), Twist and Shout (also s.p.), Pelle the Conquerer (also s.p.), The Best Intentions (Cannes Film Festival Palm d'Or Award, 1992), The House of the Spirits.

AUMONT, JEAN-PIERRE
Actor. b. Paris, France, Jan. 5, 1911. e. Conservatoire of Drama. Roles French stage and films. In 1943 enlisted in Free French Army. Film debut, Jean de la Lune, 1932.

THEATER: *U.S.*: Tovarich, Incident at Vichy, Hostile Witness, Carnival, Camino Real, Murderous Angels, Gigi, A Talent for Murder.
PICTURES: Hotel du Nord, Assignment in Brittany, The Cross of Lorraine, Heartbeat, Song of Scheherazade, Siren of Atlantis, Affairs of a Rogue, Wicked City, Lili, Life Begins Tomorrow, Gay Adventure, Charge of the Lancers, Hilda Crane, The Seventh Sin, John Paul Jones, The Enemy General, The Devil at 4 O'Clock, Carnival of Crime, Five Miles to Midnight, Cauldron of Blood, Castle Keep, Day for Night, Turn the Other Cheek, The Happy Hooker, Mahogany, Catherine & Co., Entire Days Among the Trees, Cat and Mouse, Blackout, Two Solitudes, Something Short of Paradise, Nana, Sweet Country, The Free Frenchman, Senso, A Star for Two, Becoming Colette, Giorgino, Jefferson in Paris.
TELEVISION: Sins, Windmills of the Gods, A Tale of Two Cities, Young Indiana Jones.

AURELIUS, GEORGE M.
Executive. b. Grasston, MN, Sept. 16, 1911. e. U. of Minnesota. Ent. m.p. ind. 1927 as usher Finkelstein & Ruben, St. Paul; asst. mgr. 1929-30; to Warner Theatres, New York 1931; mgr. Moss' B'way; Minnesota Amusement Co. 1932-41; city mgr. Publix-Rickards-Nace. Paramount-Nace Theatres, Tucson, Ariz. 1941-46; v.p. ABC Theatres of Arizona, Inc. 1949-67; pres. ABC North Central Theatres, Inc., 1967-72; v.p., ABC Intermountain Theatres, Inc., v.p. ABC Theatres of California, Inc. 1972-1974; Mgmt. Consulting and ShoWest Convention & Trade Show since 1975, named exec. dir., 1979. Retired 1985.

AUSTIN, RAY
Baron Devere-Austin of Delvin, Lord of Bradwell. Producer, Director, Writer. b. London, England, Dec. 5, 1932. Has written, produced and directed many TV series, specials and movies. Lecturer, film & tv techniques, etc., 1978-93. Lecturer U. of VA.
PICTURES: Virgin Witches, House of the Living Dead, Fun & Games (One Woman And A 1,000 Men).
TELEVISION: *Director of Series:* Avengers, The Champions, Department S, Randall & Hopkirk, Ugliest Girl in Town, Journey into the Unknown, Magnum P.I., Simon and Simon, House Calls, Kings Crossing, Fall Guy, Lime Street (pilot), Spencer for Hire, Haven Help Us, JAG. *Writer:* Department S (also prod.). *Producer/Director.* The Perfumed Garden. *Director:* It's the Only Way to Go, Fun and Games, Space 1999, New Avengers, Hawaii Five-O, Sword of Justice, Webb, Barnaby Jones, Hardy Boys, Wonder Woman, Salvage, B.J. and the Bear, Hart to Hart, The Yeagers, Man Called Sloane, From Here to Eternity, Bad Cats, Westworld, Tales of the Gold Monkey (2-hr. pilot), The Return of the Man from U.N.C.L.E. *Director/Writer:* Randall & Hopkirk, Black Beauty, Zany Adventures of Robin Hood, The Master, Hart to Hart (series), V, Air Wolf, Lime Street (pilot and episodes), Spenser for Hire (several episodes), Magnum P.I. (season premiere 2-hr. episode); Return of the Six Million Dollar Man (pilot); Our House (episodes), Dirty Dozen, Alfred Hitchcock Presents, A Fine Romance, Zorro, Boys of Twilight, Crossroads, Highlander, High Tide, Heaven Help Us.

AUTANT-LARA, CLAUDE
Director. Began career as scenic designer for French films in early 1920s; then asst. dir. to Rene Clair. First solo venture experimental film, 1923; in Hollywood, 1930-32. dir. Parlor, Bedroom and Bath, Incomplete Athlete.
PICTURES: Devil in the Flesh, Seven Deadly Sins (segment), Red Inn, Oh Amelia, Game of Love, Ciboulette, Red and the Black.

AUTEUIL, DANIEL
Actor. b. Algeria, Jan. 24, 1950. Parents were lyric opera singers in roving troupe. Lived in Avignon. Performed in Amer. prod. in Paris of Godspell. Then did musical comedy for 2 years. Provided voice of baby for French print of U.S. film Look Who's Talking.
PICTURES: L'Aggression/Sombres Vacanes, Attention Les Yeaux, La Nuit de Saint-Germain des Pres, Monsieuer Papa, L'Amour Viole (Rape of Love), Les Heroes n'ont pas Froid aux Oreilles, A Nous Deux, Bete Mais Discipline, Les Sous-Doues, La Banquiere, Clara et les Chic Types, Men Prefer Fat Girls, Pour 100 Briques t'as Plus Rien Maintentant, Que les Gros Salaires Levent le Doigt!!!, L'Indic, P'tit Con, The Beast, L'Arbalete, Palace, L'Amour en Douce, Jean de Florette, Manon of the Spring, Romuald and Juliette (Mama There's a Man in Your Bed), A Few Days With Me, My Life is Hell, L'Elegant Criminel, Un Coeur en Hiver (A Heart in Winter), Ma Saison Preferee (My Favorite Season), The Separation, According to Pereira, The Eighth Day (Best actor, Cannes 1996).

AUTRY, GENE
Actor. b. Tioga, TX, Sept. 29, 1907. Railroad telegrapher at Sapulpa, OK, 1925; became radio singer and recording artist (Columbia Records) 1928; screen debut 1934 at Mascot Pictures (later became Republic) as screen's first singing cowboy. Starred in 89 feature films and 91 half hour TV films. The Gene Autry Show, 1950-55. Formed Flying A Productions, pro-

duced Annie Oakley, The Range Rider, Buffalo Bill, Jr. and Adventures of Champion TV series. Wrote or co-wrote over two hundred songs, recorded 635 records, has 12 Gold Records, and 6 platinum records, including all-time best seller, Rudolph the Red-Nosed Reindeer. Voted top money making Western star 1937-42, and in top Western stars 1936, 1946-54; first Western star to be in top ten money makers from 1939-42. Served in U.S.A.A.F. as flight officer, 1942-45; on USO tour overseas 3 mos.; immediately thereafter resumed radio career with former sponsor, the Wm. Wrigley Co., formed Gene Autry Productions, Inc., star of Madison Square Garden Rodeo first in 1940; composed & recorded song Here Comes Santa Claus; Be Honest With Me (Acad. Award nom.); owner KSCA FM radio station, California Angels baseball team and chairman of the board of Gene Autry Western Heritage Museum. The only entertainer with five stars on the Hollywood Walk of Fame for radio, recordings, movies, tv and live performances, theatrical and rodeo. Hosted Melody Ranch Theatre on the Nashville Network, 1988-89. TV Specials incl. Biography, 1994; Gene Autry: Melody of the West, 1995.
PICTURES: In Old Santa Fe (debut, 1934), Tumbling Tumbleweeds, The Singing Vagabond, The Big Show, Oh Susannah, The Old Corral, Boots and Saddles, Manhattan Merry-Go-Round, Gold Mine in the Sky, Rhythm of the Saddle, Mexicali Rose, In Old Monterey, South of the Border, Rancho Grande, Melody Ranch, Back in the Saddle, Sierra Sue, Stardust on the Sage, Sioux City Sue, Saddle Pals, Robin Hood of Texas, The Last Round-Up, The Cowboy and the Indians, Cow Town, Mule Train, The Blazing Sun, Valley of Fire, Apache Country, Barbed Wire, Wagon Team, Saginaw Trail, Last of the Pony Riders, Alias Jesse James (cameo), many others.

AVALON, FRANKIE
Singer, Actor. r.n. Francis Thomas Avalone. b. Philadelphia, PA, Sept 18, 1940. e. South Philadelphia H.S. Trumpet prodigy age 9 yrs. Recording contract, Chancellor Records, Inc., 1957; Gold Record: Venus 1959; Gold Album: Swingin' on a Rainbow, 1959.
PICTURES: Jamboree (debut, 1957), Guns of the Timberland, The Alamo, Alakazam the Great (voice), Voyage to the Bottom of the Sea, Sail a Crooked Ship, Panic in the Year Zero, Beach Party, The Castilian, Drums of Africa, Operation Bikini, Bikini Beach, Pajama Party, Muscle Beach Party, How to Stuff a Wild Bikini, Beach Blanket Bingo, Ski Party, I'll Take Sweden, Sgt. Deadhead, Dr. Goldfoot and the Bikini Machine, Fireball 500, The Million Eyes of Su-Muru, Skidoo, Horror House, The Take, Grease, Back to the Beach, Troop Beverly Hills.
TELEVISION: *Series:* Easy Does It... Starring Frankie Avalon. *Guest:* Ed Sullivan, Perry Como, Pat Boone, Arthur Murray, Dick Clark Shows, Milton Berle, Golden Circle Spectacular, Dinah Shore Show, Steve Allen Show, The Patty Duke Show, Hullabaloo, Happy Days.

AVEDON, DOE
Actress, b. Old Westbury, NY, 1928. Bookkeeper, then actress.
THEATER: Young and the Fair, My Name Is Aquilon.
PICTURES: The High and the Mighty, Deep in My Heart, The Boss.
TELEVISION: *Series:* Big Town.

AVILDSEN, JOHN G.
Director, Cinematographer, Editor. b. Chicago, IL, Dec. 21, 1935. m. actress Tracy Brooks Swope. e. NYU. After service in Army made film with friend, Greenwich Village Story, then joined ad agency to write, direct, photograph & edit industrial films. Entered m.p. industry as ass't cameraman on Below the Hill, then first theatrical short, Smiles. Asst. dir: Black Like Me; prod. mgr.: Mickey One, Una Moglie Americana; 2nd unit dir.: Hurry Sundown. Produced, photographed & edited a short, Light, Sound, Diffuse. Returned to industry to make industrial films for ad agencies before resuming theatrical career.
PICTURES: Turn on to Love (debut feature, dir., photo.), Out of It (assoc. prod., dir. of photog.). *Director:* Sweet Dreams (aka Okay, Bill; also photo., edit.), Guess What We Learned in School Today? (also photo., edit.), Joe (also photo.), Cry Uncle (also photo., edit.), The Stoolie (also photo.), Save the Tiger, W. W. and the Dixie Dancekings, Foreplay (also edit., photo.), Rocky (Academy Award, 1976), Slow Dancing in the Big City (also prod., edit.), The Formula, Neighbors (also supv. edit.), Traveling Hopefully (documentary; Acad. Award nom.), A Night in Heaven (also edit., cinematographer), The Karate Kid (also edit.), The Karate Kid Part II (also edit.), Happy New Year, For Keeps, (also edit.), Lean On Me (also edit.), The Karate Kid Part III (also co-edit.), Rocky V (also co-edit.), The Power of One (also edit.), Steal This Video (documentary), 8 Seconds, Save The Everglades (documentary).
TELEVISION: From No House to Options House (2 On the Town, Emmy Award).

AVNET, JON
Producer, Director. b. Brooklyn, NY, Nov. 17, 1949. e. U. of PA, Sarah Lawrence Coll. Began career as director of off-B'way prods. Produced and directed low-budget film, Confusion's

Circle, which brought a directing fellowship at American Film Institute. Joined Weintraub/Heller Prods. as assoc. prod., where met Steve Tisch, with whom formed Tisch/Avnet Prods. Formed Avnet/Kerner Co., 1986.
PICTURES: Checkered Flag or Crash (assoc. prod.), Outlaw Blues (assoc. prod.), *Producer:* Coast to Coast, Risky Business, Deal of the Century (exec. prod.), Less Than Zero, Men Don't Leave, Funny About Love, Fried Green Tomatoes (also dir., co-s.p.), The Mighty Ducks, The Three Musketeers (co-exec. prod.), When a Man Loves a Woman, The War (also dir.), Miami Rhapsody (co-exec. prod.), Up Close and Personal (also dir.).
TELEVISION: *Producer:* No Other Love, Homeward Bound, Prime Suspect, Something So Right, Silence of the Heart, Calendar Girl Murders, Call to Glory (pilot and series), The Burning Bed, In Love and War (also exec. prod.), Between Two Women (also dir., co-s.p.). *Exec. Prod.:* Side By Side, My First Love, Breaking Point, O Do You Know the Muffin Man?, Heatwave, Backfield in Motion, The Nightman, The Switch, For Their Own Good.

AXEL, GABRIEL
Director. b. Denmark, 1918. e. France, then studied acting at Danish National Conservatory. Returned to France where joined the Paris theater co. of Louis Jouvet as stagehand. Worked as actor in Copenhagen boulevard theater where made directing debut. Went on to dir. Danish TV, mostly classic plays.
PICTURES: Golden Mountains (debut, 1957), Crazy Paradise, The Red Mantle, Danish Blue, Babette's Feast (also s.p.; Academy Award for Best Foreign-Language Feature, 1988), Christian (also s.p.).

AXELMAN, ARTHUR
Executive. b. Philadelphia, PA, Dec. 10, 1944. e. Florida Atlantic U., B.A., 1969. Entered NY offices of William Morris Agency, June 1972; transferred to Bev. Hills offices, 1976, as literary agent. Founded company's original TV Movie dept., 1977. Appointed v.p. in 1980, sr. v.p. in 1991. Among clients represented while overseeing network sales, negotiation, packaging, development, etc. of some 100 TV movies have been EMI TV, Bob Banner, Edward S. Feldman, Lee Grant, Thom Mount, Edward Anhalt, Zev Braun, Marvin Worth, Gilbert Cates, Jerry London, Jeremy Kagan, Dick Berg, Patty Duke, Finnegan-Pinchuk Prods.

AXELROD, GEORGE
Writer, Producer, Director. b. New York, NY, June 9, 1922. Stage mgr., actor, summer stock, 1940-41; radio writer, 1941-52.
Novels: Beggar's Choice, Blackmailer; co-writer, nightclub musical: All About Love, 1951. *Memoirs:* Where Am I Now When I Need Me?
THEATER: *B'way:* The Seven Year Itch, Will Success Spoil Rock Hunter?, Visit to a Small Planet, Once More with Feeling, Goodbye Charlie (also dir.).
PICTURES: *Writer:* Phffft, The Seven Year Itch, Bus Stop, Breakfast at Tiffany's, The Manchurian Candidate (also co-prod.), Paris When It Sizzles (also co-prod.), How to Murder Your Wife, Lord Love a Duck (also dir., prod.), The Secret Life of an American Wife (also dir., prod.), The Lady Vanishes, The Holcroft Covenant, The Fourth Protocol.

AXELROD, JONATHAN
Writer, Producer. b. New York, NY, July 9, 1950. Stepson of writer George Axelrod. Started as on-set "gofer" before writing screenplays. 1978-80, v.p. primetime drama dev.; ABC Entertainment; 1980-82, v.p. exec. dir. in chg. dev. ABC Ent.; 1983-85 exec. v.p., Columbia Pictures TV; 1985-87, pres. New World Pictures; 1987-, co-owner, Camden Artists; 1989, exec. v.p. Ventura Entertainment Group. 1990-93, pres. & CEO Producers Entertainment Group. Exec. Prod. of Hollywood Detective series. 1993-, exec. prod. of Dave's World.

AYKROYD, DAN
Actor, Writer. b. Ottawa, Canada, July 1, 1952. m. actress Donna Dixon. Member of Toronto Co. of Second City Theater. Worked as mgr. of Club 505, after-hours Toronto nightclub 1970-73. Performed and recorded (Briefcase Full of Blues, Made in America) with John Belushi as the Blues Brothers. Co-owner, Hard Rock Cafe.
PICTURES: Love at First Sight (debut, 1977; also co-s.p.), Mr. Mike's Mondo Video, 1941, The Blues Brothers (also co-s.p.), Neighbors, It Came From Hollywood, Doctor Detroit, Trading Places, Twilight Zone—The Movie, Indiana Jones and the Temple of Doom (cameo), Ghostbusters (also co-s.p.), Nothing Lasts Forever, Into the Night, Spies Like Us (also co-s.p.), One More Saturday Night (exec. prod. only), Dragnet (also co-s.p.), The Couch Trip, The Great Outdoors, Caddyshack II, My Stepmother Is an Alien, Ghostbusters II (also co-s.p.), Driving Miss Daisy (Acad. Award nom.), Loose Cannons, Nothing But Trouble (also dir., s.p.), Masters of Menace, My Girl, This Is My Life, Sneakers, Chaplin, Coneheads (also co-s.p.), My Girl 2, North, Exit to Eden, Tommy Boy, Casper (cameo), Canadian Bacon (cameo), Getting Away With Murder, Sgt. Bilko, Celtic Pride, My Fellow Americans.

TELEVISION: Coming Up Rosie (Canada), Saturday Night Live 1975-79 (writer and performer; Emmy Award for writing: 1977). Steve Martin's Best Show Ever (performer, writer). Guest: Tales from the Crypt (Yellow).

AYRES, GERALD
Producer, Writer. e. Yale U. where had four plays produced. Became B'way play doctor and then joined Columbia Pictures as freelance reader. Named story editor; exec. asst. to v.p. Mike Frankovich; then v.p. in chg. creative affairs in Hollywood. Left in 1970 to become independent. Formed Acrobat Films.
PICTURES: *Producer:* Cisco Pike, The Last Detail, Foxes (also s.p.), Rich and Famous (s.p. only; WGA Award, 1981).
TELEVISION: *Movies (writer):* Stormy Weathers (co-writer), Crazy in Love (ACE Award nom.), Liz: The Elizabeth Taylor Story.

AYRES, LEW
Actor. b. Minneapolis, MN, Dec. 28, 1908. Toured Mexico with own orchestra; then with Henry Halstead's Orchestra. Served as medical corpsman & asst. chaplain WWII.
PICTURES: The Sophmore (debut, 1929), The Kiss, All Quiet on the Western Front, Common Clay, East is West, Doorway to Hell, Up for Murder, Many a Slip, Spirit of Notre Dame, Heaven on Earth, Impatient Maiden, Night World, Okay America, State Fair, Don't Bet on Love, My Weakness, Cross Country Cruise, Let's Be Ritzy, She Learned About Sailors, Servants' Entrance, Lottery Lover, Silk Hat Kid, Leathernecks Have Landed, Panic on the Air, Shakedown, Lady Be Careful, Murder With Pictures, The Crime Nobody Saw, Last Train from Madrid, Hold 'Em Navy, King of the Newsboys, Scandal Street, Holiday, Rich Man Poor Girl, Young Dr. Kildare (and subsequent film series), Spring Madness, Ice Follies of 1939, Broadway Serenade, These Glamour Girls, The Golden Fleecing, Maisie Was a Lady, Fingers at the Window, Dark Mirror, Unfaithful, Johnny Belinda (Acad. Award nom.), The Capture, New Mexico, No Escape, Donovan's Brain, Altars to the East (also dir., prod., narrator), Advise and Consent, The Carpetbaggers, The Biscuit Eater, The Man, Battle for the Planet of the Apes, End of the World, Damien-Omen II, Battlestar Galactica.
TELEVISION: *Series:* Frontier Justice (host), Lime Street. *Movies:* Hawaii Five-O (pilot), Marcus Welby M.D. (pilot), Earth II, She Waits, The Stranger, The Questor Tapes, Heatwave, Francis Gary Powers, Suddenly Love, Salem's Lot, Letters from Frank, Reunion, Of Mice and Men, Under Siege, Hart to Hart: Crimes of the Hart.

AZARIA, HANK
Actor. b. Forest Hills, NY. e. Tufts Univ.
PICTURES: Pretty Woman, Cool Blue, Quiz Show, Birdcage.
TELEVISION: *Series:* The Simpsons (voice), Herman's Head, If Not for You. *Guest:* Fresh Prince of Bel-Air, Growing Pains, Mad About You.

AZNAVOUR, CHARLES
Singer, Songwriter, Actor. b. Paris, France, May 22, 1924. r.n. Shahnour Varenagh Aznavourian. Studied dance and drama as a child and was performing at the age of 10. Encouraged by Edith Piaf, became one of France's leading performers by the mid-1950s and an international concert star by the 1970s. Has also composed music for film.
PICTURES: Adieu Cherie (1947), C'est arrive a 36 Chandelles, Les Dragueurs, Shoot the Piano Player, Le testament d'Orphee, Le Passage du Rhin, Un taxi pour Tobrouk, Horace 62, Tempo di Roma, Les Quatres Verites, Le Rat'd Amerique, Pourquoi Paris?, Paris in August, Candy, The Games, The Adventurers, The Blockhouse, Ten Little Indians, The Twist, Sky Riders, Ciao Les Mecs, The Tin Drum, The Magic Mountain, Hatter's Ghosts, What Makes David Run?, Edith and Marcel, Long Live Life!, Mangeclous, Friend to Friend, Il Maestro, Double Game.

B

BABENCO, HECTOR
Director. b. Buenos Aires, Argentina, Feb. 7, 1946. Early years spent in Mar del Plata. Left home at 17 and traveled throughout European capitals for 8 years working as a writer, house-painter, salesman, and, in Rome, as an extra at Cinecitta. Moved to Sao Paulo, Brazil where he made several short documentaries, before turning to features in 1975.
PICTURES: Rei Da Noite (King of the Night; debut, 1975), Lucio Flavio—Passageiro da Agonia, Pixote (also co-s.p.), Kiss of the Spider Woman, Ironweed, Besame Mucho (prod. only), At Play in the Fields of the Lord (also co-s.p.).

BACALL, LAUREN
Actress. r.n. Betty Joan. b. New York, NY, Sept. 16, 1924. e. American Acad. Dram. Arts. Was m. Jason Robards, late Humphrey Bogart. *Autobiographies:* By Myself (1979), Now (1994).
THEATER: *B'way:* Cactus Flower, Goodbye Charlie, Applause (Tony Award), Woman of the Year. London/Australia: Sweet Bird of Youth.

PICTURES: To Have and Have Not (debut, 1944), Two Guys From Milwaukee (cameo), Confidential Agent, The Big Sleep, Dark Passage, Key Largo, Young Man With a Horn, Bright Leaf, How to Marry a Millionaire, Woman's World, Cobweb, Blood Alley, Written on the Wind, Designing Woman, Gift of Love, Flame Over India, Shock Treatment, Sex and the Single Girl, Harper, Murder on the Orient Express, The Shootist, Health, The Fan, Appointment With Death, Mr. North, Innocent Victim, Misery, A Star for Two, All I Want for Christmas, Ready to Wear (Pret-a-Porter), The Mirror Has Two Faces.
TELEVISION: Specials: The Girls in Their Dresses, Blithe Spirit, The Petrified Forest, Applause, Bacall on Bogart, A Foreign Field (BBC). Movies: Perfect Gentlemen, Dinner at Eight, A Little Piece of Sunshine (BBC), The Portrait, From the Mixed Up Files of Mrs. Basil E. Frankweiler.

BACH, CATHERINE
Actress. b. Warren, Ohio, March 1, 1954.
PICTURES: The Midnight Man, Thunderbolt and Lightfoot, Hustle, Cannonball Run II, Tunnels (Criminal Act), Music City Blues, Driving Force, Street Justice.
TELEVISION: Series: The Dukes of Hazzard (1979-85), The Dukes (cartoon, voice), African Skies. Guest on many specials. Movies: Matt Helm, Strange New World, Murder in Peyton Place, White Water Rebels.

BACHARACH, BURT
Composer, Conductor, Arranger. b. Kansas City, MO, May 12, 1928. e. McGraw U., Mannes Sch. of Music, Music Acad. of the West. Studied with composers Darius Milhaud, Henry Cowell, and Bohuslav Martinu. Has conducted for Marlene Dietrich, Vic Damone. As a performer albums include: Burt Bacharach; Futures, Man! His Songs. Book: The Bacharach-David Song Book (1978).
THEATER: Promises Promises (Tony Award, 1969).
PICTURES: Lizzie, The Sad Sack, The Blob, Country Music Holiday, Love in a Goldfish Bowl, Wives and Lovers, Who's Been Sleeping in My Bed?, Send Me No Flowers, A House Is Not a Home, What's New Pussycat?, Alfie, Made in Paris, After the Fox, Promise Her Anything, Casino Royale, The April Fools, Butch Cassidy and the Sundance Kid (2 Academy Awards: Best Original Score & Best Song: Raindrops Keep Fallin' on My Head; 1969), Something Big, Lost Horizon, Arthur (Academy Award for Best Song: Arthur's Theme; 1981), Night Shift, Best Defense, Tough Guys, Baby Boom, Arthur 2 on the Rocks.
TELEVISION: Special: Singer Presents Burt Bacharach (Emmy Award for Best Variety Special, 1971).

BACK, LEON B.
Exhibitor. b. Philadelphia, PA, Oct. 23, 1912. e. Johns Hopkins U., B.E., 1932; U. of Baltimore, LL.B., 1933. Entered m.p. ind. as mgr. for Rome Theatres, Inc., Baltimore, Md., 1934; booker, ass't buyer, 1936; ass't to gen. mgr. 1939; U.S. Navy 1944-46; v.p., gen. mgr., Rome Theatres, 1946; Allied MPTO of Md. 1952-55; nat'l dir. Allied States, 1952-55; nat'l secy. 1954; Pres. NATO of Maryland 1969-80; Pres. USO Council, Greater Baltimore 1969-75; Chairman, board of trustees, Employees Benefit Trust for Health & Welfare Council of Central Maryland, 1970-79.

BACON, KEVIN
Actor. b. Philadelphia, PA, July 8, 1958. m. actress Kyra Sedgwick. Studied at Manning St. Actor's Theatre. Apprentice at Circle-in-the-Square in N.Y. B'way debut in Slab Boys with Sean Penn. Narrated short film A Little Vicious.
THEATER: B'way: Slab Boys. Off-B'way: Getting Out (debut), Album, Forty Deuce (Obie Award), Poor Little Lambs, Flux, Men Without Dates, The Author's Voice, Loot, Road, Spike Heels.
PICTURES: National Lampoon's Animal House (debut, 1978), Starting Over, Hero at Large, Friday the 13th, Only When I Laugh, Forty Deuce, Diner, Footloose, Enormous Changes at the Last Minute, Quicksilver, White Water Summer (Rites of Summer), End of the Line, Planes Trains and Automobiles, She's Having a Baby, Criminal Law, The Big Picture, Tremors, Flatliners, Queens Logic, He Said/She Said, Pyrates, JFK, A Few Good Men, The Air Up There, The River Wild, Murder in the First, Apollo 13, Balto (voice), Sleepers.
TELEVISION: Movies: The Gift, The Demon Murder Case, The Tender Age (The Little Sister), Lemon Sky, Losing Chase (dir. only). Series: Search for Tomorrow, The Guiding Light. Special: Mr. Roberts.

BADHAM, JOHN
Director. b. Luton, Eng., Aug. 25, 1939. Raised in Alabama. e. Yale U., B.A.; Yale Drama School, M.F.A. Sister is actress Mary Badham. Landed first job at Universal Studio mailroom; later was Universal tour guide, a casting dir. and assoc. prod. to William Sackheim. Twice nominated for Emmy Awards for TV movies. Recipient of George Pal Award.
PICTURES: The Bingo Long Traveling All-Stars and Motor Kings (debut 1976), Saturday Night Fever, Dracula (Best Horror Film award, Science Fiction/Fantasy Academy), Whose Life Is It Anyway? (San Rafael Grand Prize), Blue Thunder, War Games (Best Directing award, Science Fiction/Fantasy Academy),

American Flyers, Short Circuit, Stakeout (also exec. prod.), Disorganized Crime (exec. prod. only), Bird on a Wire, The Hard Way, Point of No Return, Another Stakeout (also exec. prod.), Drop Zone (also exec. prod.), Nick of Time (also prod.).
TELEVISION: Movies: Night Gallery (assoc. prod. only), Neon Ceiling (assoc. prod. only), The Impatient Heart, Isn't It Shocking?, The Law, The Gun, Reflections of Murder, The Godchild, The Keegans, Relentless: Mind of a Killer (co-exec. prod. only). Series episodes: The Senator (also assoc. prod.), Kung Fu, Night Gallery, Streets of San Francisco, The Doctors, Owen Marshall - Counsellor at Law, Sunshine, Nichols, Sarge, The Sixth Sense, Cannon.

BAILEY, JOHN
Cinematographer. b. Moberly, MO, August 10, 1942. m. film editor Carol Littleton. e. U. of Santa Clara, Loyola U., U.S.C., U. of Vienna. Lecturer, American Film Institute, 1982, 1984, 1994.
PICTURES: Premonition, End of August, Legacy, The Mafu Cage (visual consult.), Boulevard Nights, Winter Kills (add. photog.), American Gigolo, Ordinary People, Honky Tonk Freeway, Continental Divide, Cat People, That Championship Season, Without a Trace, The Big Chill, Racing With the Moon, The Pope of Greenwich Village, Mishima, Silverado, Crossroads, Brighton Beach Memoirs, Light of Day, Swimming to Cambodia, Tough Guys Don't Dance (visual consult.), Vibes, The Accidental Tourist, My Blue Heaven, The Search for Signs of Intelligent Life in the Universe (also dir.), A Brief History of Time, Groundhog Day, In the Line of Fire, China Moon (dir. only), Nobody's Fool, Mariette in Ecstasy (dir. only).
TELEVISION: Battered City in Fear.

BAILEY, ROBIN
Actor. b. Hucknall (Nottingham), Eng., Oct. 5, 1919. e. Henry Mellish School, Nottingham.
THEATER: Barrets of Wimpole Street, Theatre Royal, Nottingham, 1938.
PICTURES: School for Secrets (1946), Private Angelo, Portrait of Clare, His Excellency, Gift Horse, Folly to Be Wise, Single Handed, Sailor of the King, The Young Lovers, For Better, For Worse, Catch Us If You Can, The Whisperers, Spy with a Cold Nose, You Only Live Twice, The Eliminator, Blind Terror, Down by the Riverside, Nightmare Rally, The Four Feathers, Jane and the Lost City.
TELEVISION: Olive Latimer's Husband, Seven Deadly Sins, The Power Game, Public Eye, Person to Person, Troubleshooters, Armchair Theatre, Split Level, The Newcomers, Discharge of Trooper Lusby, Brett, Owen M.D., Solidarity, General Hospital, Murder Must Advertise, Vienna 1900, Justice, The Pallisers, The Couch, Way of the World, Upstairs, Downstairs, Walk with Destiny, North and South, A Legacy, The Velvet Glove, Crown Court, Took and Co., The Good Companions, Cupid's Darts, Sorry, I'm a Stranger Here Myself, Call My Bluff, Jane, Potter, Tales from a Long Room, Sharing Time, Bleak House, Charters and Caldicott, Looks Familiar, On Stage, Rumpole of the Bailey, I Didn't Know You Cared, Number 27, Tinniswood's North Country, Tales From Hollywood, Bed, Dalziel and Pascoe.

BAIO, SCOTT
Actor. b. New York, NY, Sept. 22, 1961. Started career at 9 doing commercials and voice-overs.
PICTURES: Bugsy Malone, Skatetown USA, Foxes, Zapped!, I Love New York.
TELEVISION: Series: Blansky's Beauties, Happy Days, Who's Watching the Kids?, We're Movin' (host), Joanie Loves Chachi, Charles in Charge, Baby Talk, Diagnosis Murder. Specials: Luke Was There, Muggsy, Stoned, How to Be a Man, Gemini, The Truth About Alex. Guest: Hotel, The Fall Guy, Full House. Movies: The Boy Who Drank Too Much, Senior Trip, Alice in Wonderland.

BAKER, BLANCHE
Actress. r.n. Blanche Garfein. b. New York, NY, Dec. 20, 1956. Daughter of actress Carroll Baker and dir. Jack Garfein. e. Wellesley, Coll., studied acting with Uta Hagen. Acting debut, White Marriage, Yale Repertory Co. (1978), Regional Theater. B'way debut in Lolita (1981).
PICTURES: The Seduction of Joe Tynan (debut, 1979), French Postcards, Sixteen Candles, Raw Deal, Cold Feet, The Handmaid's Tale, Livin' Large, Bum Rap, Dead Funny.
TELEVISION: Mini-Series: Holocaust (Emmy Award, 1978). Movies: Mary and Joseph, The Day the Bubble Burst, The Awakening of Candra, Nobody's Child. Special: Romeo & Juliet.

BAKER, CARROLL
Actress. b. Johnstown, PA, May 28, 1931. e. schools there and St. Petersburg (FL) Junior Coll. Career started as dancer in nightclubs. Actors' Studio N.Y. Stage debut: Escapade. Then, All Summer Long. Autobiography: Baby Doll.
PICTURES: Easy to Love (debut, 1953), Giant, Baby Doll, The Big Country, But Not for Me, The Miracle, Bridge to the Sun, Something Wild, How the West Was Won, The Carpetbaggers, Station Six Sahara, Cheyenne Autumn, The Greatest Story Ever Told, Sylvia, Mister Moses, Harlow, Jack of Diamonds, The

Sweet Body of Deborah, Paranoia, A Quiet Place to Kill, Captain Apache, The Harem, Honeymoon, My Father's Wife, Bloodbath (The Sky Is Falling), Andy Warhol's Bad, The World is Full of Married Men, Watcher in the Woods, Star 80, The Secret Diary of Sigmund Freud, Native Son, Ironweed, Red Monarch, Kindergarten Cop, Blonde Fist, Cybereden.
TELEVISION: *Specials*: Rain, On Fire, Sharing Time, Coward's: What Mad Pursuit. *Guest*: Tales from the Crypt. *Movies*: Hitler's SS: Portrait in Evil, On Fire, Judgment Day: The John List Story, Men Don't Tell, A Kiss to Die For.

BAKER, DIANE
Actress. b. Hollywood, CA, Feb. 25, 1938. e. USC.
PICTURES: The Diary of Anne Frank (debut, 1959), The Best of Everything, Journey to the Center of the Earth, Tess of the Storm Country, The Wizard of Baghdad, Hemingway's Adventures of a Young Man, 300 Spartans, Nine Hours to Rama, Stolen Hours, The Prize, Straight Jacket, Marnie, Mirage, Sands of Beersheba, The Horse in the Grey Flannel Suit, Krakatoa — East of Java, Baker's Hawk, The Pilot, The Silence of the Lambs, The Closer, The Joy Luck Club, Twenty Bucks, Imaginary Crimes, The Net, The Cable Guy.
TELEVISION: *Series*: Here We Go Again. *Movies*: Dangerous Days of Kiowa Jones, Trial Run, The D.A.: Murder One, The Old Man Who Cried Wolf, Do You Take This Stranger?, Sarge: The Badge or the Cross, Congratulations It's a Boy!, A Little Game, Killer By Night, Police Story (pilot), A Tree Grows in Brooklyn, The Dream Makers, The Last Survivors, Fugitive Family, The Haunted, Perry Mason: The Case of the Heartbroken Bride. *Mini-Series*: The Blue and the Gray.

BAKER, DYLAN
Actor. b. Syracuse, NY. e. Southern Methodist Univ. (BFA), Yale Sch. of Drama (MFA).
PICTURES: Ishtar (debut, 1987), Planes Trains and Automobiles, The Wizard of Loneliness, The Long Walk Home, Delirious, Passed Away, Love Potion No. 9, Life With Mikey, Radioland Murders, Disclosure, The Stars Fell on Henrietta.
TELEVISION: *Series*: Murder One. *Movies*: The Murder of Mary Phagan, Love Honor and Obey: The Last Mafia Marriage. *Mini-Series*: Return to Lonesome Dove. *Guest*: Spenser: For Hire, Miami Vice, Law and Order.
THEATER: *B'way*: Eastern Standard (Theatre World Award), La Bete (Tony nom.). *Off-B'way*: Not About Heroes (Obie Award).

BAKER, GEORGE
Actor, Writer. b. Varna, Bulgaria, April 1, 1931. e. Lancing College, Sussex. Stage debut Deal Repertory Theatre, 1946.
AUTHOR: The Fatal Spring, Imaginary Friends, Going for Broke, The Marches of Wales, The Hopkins, Just a Hunch, Sister, Dear Sister, From Doom With Death, Mouse in the Corner, The Strawberry Tree, Talking About Mira Beau, Dead on Time, The Last Silence.
PICTURES: The Intruder (debut, 1953), The Dam Busters, The Ship That Died of Shame, Woman for Joe, The Feminine Touch, A Hill in Korea (Hell in Korea), No Time for Tears, These Dangerous Years (Dangerous Youth), The Moonraker, Tread Softly Stranger, Lancelot and Guinevere (Sword of Lancelot), Curse of the Fly, Mister Ten Per Cent, Goodbye Mr. Chips, Justine, The Executioners, On Her Majesty's Secret Service, A Warm December, The Fire Fighters, The Spy Who Loved Me, Thirty-Nine Steps, A Nightingale Sang in Berkeley Square, Hopscotch, North Sea Hijack (ffolkes), For Queen and Country.
TELEVISION: Fan Show, Ron Raudell's programme 1956, Guinea Pig, Death of a Salesman, The Last Troubadour, The Square Ring, Nick of the River, Mary Stuart, Probation Officers, Far Away Music, It Happened Like This, Boule de Suif, Maigret, Zero One, Rupert Henzau, Miss Memory, Any Other Business, The Navigators, Common Ground, Alice, The Queen and Jackson, The Big Man Coughed and Died, Up and Down, Call My Bluff, The Baron, St. Patrick, Love Life, Seven Deadly Virtues, The Prisoner, The Sex Games, Z Cars, Paul Temple, Candida, Fenn Street, Man Outside, The Persuaders, Main Chance, Ministry of Fear, Bowler, Voyage in the Dark, Dial M for Murder, Zodiac, The Survivors, I, Claudius, Print Out, Goodbye, Darling, Chinese Detective, Triangle, Minder, Hart to Hart, Goodbye Mr. Chips, Woman of Substance, The Bird Fancier, Robin of Sherwood, Time after Time, If Tomorrow Comes, Coast to Coast, Dead Head, The Canterville Ghost, Room at the Bottom, Ruth Rendell Mysteries (From Doon With Death; adap.), Journey's End, No Job for a Lady, Little Lord Fauntleroy.

BAKER, JOE DON
Actor. b. Groesbeck, TX, Feb. 12, 1936. e. North Texas State Coll., B.B.A., 1958. Began career on N.Y. stage, in Marathon 33 and Blues for Mr. Charlie. L.A. stage in The Caine Mutiny Court Martial.
PICTURES: Cool Hand Luke (debut, 1967), Guns of the Magnificent Seven, Adam at Six A.M., Wild Rovers, Welcome Home Soldier Boys, Junior Bonner, Walking Tall, Charley Varrick, The Outfit, Golden Needles, Mitchell, Framed, Checkered Flag or Crash, Speedtrap, The Pack, Wacko, Joysticks, The Natural,

Fletch, Getting Even (Hostage Dallas), The Living Daylights, The Killing Time, Leonard Part 6, Criminal Law, The Children, Cape Fear, The Distinguished Gentleman, Reality Bites, Panther, The Underneath, Congo, The Grass Harp, Goldeneye.
TELEVISION: *Movies*: Mongo's Back in Town, That Certain Summer, To Kill a Cop, Power, The Abduction of Kari Swenson, Edge of Darkness (BBC mini-series), Defrosting the Fridge (BBC), Citizen Cohn, Complex of Fear. *Series*: Eischeid. *Guest*: In the Heat of the Night.

BAKER, KATHY
Actress. B. Midland, TX, June 8, 1950. Raised in Albuquerque, NM. e. UC/Berkeley. Stage debut in San Francisco premiere of Fool for Love, won Obie and Theatre World Awards for New York debut in same. Also appeared in Desire Under the Elms, Aunt Dan and Lemon.
PICTURES: The Right Stuff (debut, 1983), Street Smart (Natl. Society of Film Critics Award), Permanent Record, A Killing Affair, Clean and Sober, Jacknife, Dad, Mr. Frost, Edward Scissorhands, Article 99, Jennifer Eight, Mad Dog and Glory, To Gillian on her 37th Birthday.
TELEVISION: *Series*: Picket Fences (2 Emmy Awards: 1993, 1995). Movies: Nobody's Child, The Image, One Special Victory, Lush Life. *Guest*: Amazing Stories.

BAKER, RICK
Makeup Artist, Performer. b. Binghamton, NY, Dec. 8, 1950. Started as assist. to makeup artist Dick Smith before creating his own designs in 1972. Frequent film appearances in makeup, usually as gorillas. Worked on Michael Jackson's video Thriller.
PICTURES: *Actor*: The Thing With Two Heads, King Kong, The Kentucky Fried Movie, The Incredible Shrinking Woman, Into the Night. *Makeup Design*: Schlock, Zebra Force, It's Alive, The Incredible Melting Man, Star Wars (2nd unit), It Lives Again, The Howling (consultant), Funhouse, An American Werewolf in London (Academy Award, 1981), Videodrome, Greystoke: The Legend of Tarzan Lord of the Apes (also costume design; Acad. Award nom.), Ratboy, Harry and the Hendersons (Academy Award, 1987), Coming to America (Acad. Award nom.), Gorillas in the Mist (also assoc. prod.), Missing Link, Wolf, Ed Wood (Academy Award, 1994), Batman Forever (also designed monster bat), The Nutty Professor. Other: Tanya's Island (beast design), Starman (transformation scenes), Cocoon (consultant), My Science Project (Tyrannosaurus Rex sequences consultant), Max My Love (chimpanzee consultant), Gremlins 2: The New Batch (co-prod., f/x supervisor), Baby's Day Out (baby f/x), Just Cause (special bodies), Little Panda (panda suits).
TELEVISION: *Makeup Design*: *Series*: Werewolf, Beauty and the Beast, Harry and the Hendersons. *Movies*: The Autobiography of Miss Jane Pittman (Emmy Award), An American Christmas Carol, Something Is Out There.

BAKER, ROY
Producer, Director. b. London. e. Lycaee Corneille, Rouen; City of London School. Ass't dir. with Gainsborough 1934-40; served in Army 1940-46.
PICTURES: Operation Disaster, Don't Bother to Knock, Inferno, One That Got Away, A Night to Remember, The Singer Not the Song, Flame in the Streets, Quartermass and the Pit, The Anniversary, Vampire Lovers, Dr. Jekyll and Mr. Hyde, Asylum (Paris Grand Prix), Seven Golden Vampires.
TELEVISION: The Human Jungle, The Saint, Gideon's Way, The Baron, The Avengers, The Champions, Department S., The Persuaders, Danger UXB, Minder.

BAKER, DR. WILLIAM F.
Executive. b. 1944. e. Case Western Reserve U., B.A., M.A., Ph.D. Began broadcasting career in Cleveland while still a student. Joined Scripps-Howard Broadcasting, 1971. Joined Group W as v.p. and general mgr., WJZ-TV, 1978; served as pres. and CEO, Group W Productions; pres. of Group W. Television, 1979; chmn., Group W Satellite Communications, 1981; 1983, carried Explorers Club flag to top of world, becoming one of few in history to visit both North and South Poles; April 1987, appointed pres. and CEO, WNET/Thirteen, N.Y. PBS station.

BAKER, WILLIAM M.
Executive. b. Newark, NJ, Dec. 26, 1939. e. University of Virginia 1961. Joined FBI in 1965. From 1987 to 1989, took a haitus from the FBI to serve as dir. of Public Affairs for the CIA. Retired from position as asst. dir., Criminal Investigative Division of FBI in 1991. Currently pres. and CEO Motion Picture Assoc. and exec. v.p., Motion Picture Assoc. of America.

BAKSHI, RALPH
Animator, Writer, Director. b. Haifa, Israel, Oct. 29, 1938. Began career at Terrytoons at age 18 as cell painter and animator, then creative dir. 1966, headed Paramount Cartoons. Pres., Bakshi Prods.
PICTURES: *Director*: Fritz the Cat (also s.p.), Heavy Traffic (also s.p.), Coonskin (also s.p.), Wizards (also s.p., prod.), The Lord of the Rings, American Pop (also co-prod.), Hey Good Lookin' (also s.p., prod.), Fire and Ice (also co-prod.), Cool World.

TELEVISION: Mighty Mouse: The New Adventures (creator), This Ain't Bebop (Amer. Playhouse, dir., s.p.), The Cool and the Crazy (dir., writer).

BAKULA, SCOTT
Actor. b. St. Louis, MO, Oct. 9, 1955. e. Kansas Univ.
THEATER: NY: Marilyn: An American Fable, Three Guys Naked from the Waist Down, Romance/Romance (Tony nom.). LA: Nite Club Confidential.
PICTURES: Sibling Rivalry, Necessary Roughness, Color of Night, A Passion to Kill, My Family/Mi Familia, Lord of Illusions.
TELEVISION: Series: Gung Ho, Eisenhower & Lutz, Quantum Leap (Emmy noms., Golden Globe Award), Murphy Brown, Mr. & Mrs. Smith. Movies: The Last Fling, An Eye for an Eye, In the Shadow of a Killer, Mercy Mission: The Rescue of Flight 771, Nowhere to Hide, The Invaders.

BALABAN, BOB
Actor, Director. b. Chicago, IL, Aug. 16, 1945. Began studying with Second City troupe while still in high school. Attended Colgate U. and NYU while appearing on Broadway in Plaza Suite.
THEATER: You're a Good Man Charlie Brown, The Inspector General, Who Wants to Be the Lone Ranger?, The Basic Training of Pavlo Hummel, The Children, The White House Murder Case, Some of My Best Friends, The Three Sisters, The Boys Next Door, Speed-the-Plow, Some Americans Abroad.
PICTURES: Actor: Midnight Cowboy (debut, 1969), Me Natalie, The Strawberry Statement, Catch-22, Making It, Bank Shot, Report to the Commissioner, Close Encounters of the Third Kind, Girlfriends, Altered States, Prince of the City, Absence of Malice, Whose Life Is It Anyway?, 2010, In Our Hands (doc.), End of the Line, Dead-Bang, Alice, Little Man Tate, Bob Roberts, For Love or Money, Greedy, Pie in the Sky. Director: Parents, My Boyfriend's Back, The Last Good Time (also co-s.p.).
TELEVISION: Movies: Marriage: Year One, The Face of Fear, Unnatural Pursuits, The Late Shift. Series: Miami Vice, Late Shift, Seinfeld. Director: Tales From the Darkside, Amazing Stories, Penn & Teller's Invisible Thread.

BALDWIN, ADAM
Actor. b. Chicago, IL, Feb. 27, 1962. While in high school in Winnetka, was chosen by director Tony Bill for role in My Bodyguard.
THEATER: Album (Chicago).
PICTURES: My Bodyguard (debut, 1980), Ordinary People, D.C. Cab, Reckless, Hadley's Rebellion, Bad Guys, 3:15, Full Metal Jacket, The Chocolate War, Cohen and Tate, Next of Kin, Predator 2, Guilty By Suspicion, Radio Flyer, Where the Day Takes You, Deadbolt, Bitter Harvest, Eight Hundred Leagues Down the Amazon, Wyatt Earp, Independence Day.
TELEVISION: Movies: Off Sides, Poison Ivy, Welcome Home Bobby, Murder in High Places, Cruel Doubt, Cold Sweat, Sawbones. Special: The Last Shot.

BALDWIN, ALEC
Actor. r.n. Alexander Rae Baldwin III. b. Massapequa, NY, April 3, 1958. m. actress Kim Basinger. e. George Washington U., NYU. Brother of actors Stephen, William and Daniel Baldwin. Trained at Lee Strasberg Theatre Inst. and with Mira Rostova, Elaine Aiken. Started career in daytime TV on serial The Doctors. Member, The Creative Coalition.
THEATER: A Midsummer Night's Dream, The Wager, Summertree, A Life in the Theatre (Hartman), Study in Scarlet (Williamstown). NY: Loot (B'way debut; Theatre World Award, 1986), Serious Money, Prelude to a Kiss, A Streetcar Named Desire.
PICTURES: Forever Lulu (debut, 1987), She's Having a Baby, Beetlejuice, Married to the Mob, Working Girl, Talk Radio, Great Balls of Fire!, The Hunt for Red October, Miami Blues, Alice, The Marrying Man, Prelude to a Kiss, Glengarry Glen Ross, Malice, The Getaway, The Shadow, Heaven's Prisoners (also exec. prod.), The Juror, Loosking For Richard, Ghost of Mississippi.
TELEVISION: Series: The Doctors (1980-2), Cutter to Houston, Knots Landing. Movies: Sweet Revenge, Love on the Run, Dress Gray, The Alamo: 13 Days to Glory. Guest: Hotel, Saturday Night Live.

BALDWIN, DANIEL
Actor. b. Long Island, NY, 1961. e. Nassau Comm. Col., Ball St. Univ. Brother of actors Alec, William and Stephen Baldwin.
PICTURES: Born on the Fourth of July, Harley Davidson and the Marlboro Man, Knight Moves, Car 54 Where Are You?, Lone Justice, Mullholland Drive.
TELEVISION: Series: Sydney, Homicide: Life on the Street. Movies: Too Good to Be True, L.A. Takedown, The Heroes of Desert Storm, Ned Blessing: The True Story of My Life, Attack of the 50 Foot Woman. Special: Curse of the Corn People. Guest: Family Ties, Charles in Charge, The Larry Sanders Show.

BALDWIN, STEPHEN
Actor. b. Long Island, NY, 1966. Brother of actors Alec, William and Daniel Baldwin. Stage debut in Off-B'way prod. Out of America.

PICTURES: The Beast, Born on the Fourth of July, Last Exit to Brooklyn, Crossing the Bridge, Bitter Harvest, Posse, New Eden, 8 Seconds, Threesome, A Simple Twist of Fate, Mrs. Parker and the Vicious Circle, Fall Time, The Usual Suspects, Under the Hula Moon, Bio-Dome, Fled.
TELEVISION: Series: The Young Riders. Movies: Jury Duty: The Comedy, Dead Weekend. Specials: The Lawrenceville Stories, In a New Light: Sex Unplugged (co-host). Guest: Family Ties, Kate and Allie, China Beach.

BALDWIN, WILLIAM
Actor. b. Massapequa, NY, Feb. 21, 1963. e. SUNY/Binghamton. Degree in political science; worked in Washington on staff of rep. Thomas J. Downey. Brother of actors Alec, Stephen and Daniel Baldwin. With Ford Model agency, appearing in tv ads while studying acting. Member, The Creative Coalition.
PICTURES: Born on the Fourth of July (debut, 1989), Internal Affairs, Flatliners, Backdraft, Three of Hearts, Sliver, A Pyromaniac's Love Story, Fair Game, Curdled.
TELEVISION: Movie: The Preppie Murder.

BALE, CHRISTIAN
Actor. b. Pembrokeshire, Wales, Jan. 30, 1974. Acting debut at age 9 in U.S. Pac-Man commercial. London stage debut following year in The Nerd.
PICTURES: Empire of the Sun, Land of Faraway, Henry V, Newsies, Swing Kids, Prince of Jutland, Little Women, Pocahontas (voice), The Secret Agent, Portrait of a Lady.
TELEVISION: Specials/Movies: Heart of the Country (BBC), Anastasia: The Mystery of Anna (U.S.), Treasure Island (released theatrically in U.K.), A Murder of Quality.

BALLARD, CARROLL
Director. b. Los Angeles, Oct. 14, 1937. e. UCLA. Prod. of 1967 film Harvest. Camera operator on Star Wars.
PICTURES: The Black Stallion (debut, 1979), Never Cry Wolf, Nutcracker: The Motion Picture, Wind.

BALLARD, KAYE
Actress. b. Cleveland, OH, Nov. 20, 1926. r.n. Catherine Gloria Balotta. Began career as impressionist-singer-actress, toured vaudeville. 17 recordings incl. The Fanny Brice Story, Peanuts, Oklahoma (w/ Nelson Eddy), Unsung Sondheim, Then & Again. Appeared in short film Walking to Waldheim.
THEATER: Three to Make Ready, Carnival, Molly, The Pirates of Penzance, Hey Ma It's Me, Working 42nd Street at Last, Chicago, Touch & Go (London), Nymph Errant (concert version), Hello Dolly, She Stoops to Conquer, Funny Girl, High Spirits, Crazy Words Crazy Times: The Cole Porter-Irving Berlin Revue, Beloved Enemies.
PICTURES: The Girl Most Likely, A House is Not a Home, Which Way to the Front?, The Ritz, Freaky Friday, Falling in Love Again, Pandemonium, Tiger Warsaw, Modern Love, Eternity, The Missing Elephant (Due South).
TELEVISION: Series: Henry Morgan's Great Talent Hunt, The Perry Como Show, The Mothers-in-Law, The Doris Day Show, The Steve Allen Comedy Hour, What a Dummy. Movies: The Dream Merchants, Alice in Wonderland. Guest appearances incl. over 100 spots on The Tonight Show. Pilot: Makin' Out.

BALLHAUS, MICHAEL
Cinematographer. b. Berlin, Germany, August 5, 1935.
PICTURES: Deine Zartlichkeiten, Two of Us, Whity, Beware of a Holy Whore, Tschetan, The Indian Boy, The Bitter Tears of Petra von Kant, Fox and his Friends, Mother Kusters Goes to Heaven, Summer Guests, Satan's Brew, I Only Want You To Love Me, Adolf and Marlene, Chinese Roulette, Bolweiser (The Stationmaster's Wife), Willie and the Chinese Cat, Women in New York, Despair, The Marriage of Maria Braun, Germany in Autumn, German Spring, The Uprising, Big and Little, Malou, Looping, Baby It's You, Friends and Husbands, Dear Mr. Wonderful, Magic Mountain, Edith's Diary, Aus der Familie der Panzereschen, The Autograph, Heartbreakers, Old Enough, Reckless, After Hours, Under the Cherry Moon, The Color of Money, The Glass Menagerie, Broadcast News, The House on Carroll Street,The Last Temptation of Christ, Working Girl, Dirty Rotten Scoundrels, The Fabulous Baker Boys, GoodFellas, Postcards from the Edge, Guilty by Suspicion, What About Bob?, The Mambo Kings, Bram Stoker's Dracula, The Age of Innocence, Quiz Show, Outbreak, Sleepers.

BALSAM, MARTIN
Actor. b. New York, NY, Nov. 4, 1919. e. New School for Social Research. Daughter is actress Talia Balsam. NY stage debut Ghost for Sale, 1941.
THEATER: Lamp at Midnight, The Wanhope Building, High Tor, A Sound of Hunting, Macbeth, Sundown Beach, The Closing Door, You Know I Can't Hear You When the Water's Running (Tony Award, 1968), Cold Storage (Obie Award).
PICTURES: On the Waterfront (debut, 1954), Twelve Angry Men, Time Limit, Marjorie Morningstar, Al Capone, Middle of the Night, Psycho, Ada, Breakfast at Tiffany's, Cape Fear,

Everybody Go Home!, The Conquered City, Who's Been Sleeping in My Bed?, The Carpetbaggers, Youngblood Hawke, Seven Days in May, Harlow, The Good Guys and the Bad Guys (Academy Award for Best Supporting Actor, 1965), After the Fox, Hombre, Me Natalie, The Good Guys and the Bad Guys, Trilogy, Catch-22, Tora! Tora! Tora!, Little Big Man, The Anderson Tapes, Confessions of a Police Captain, The Man, The Stone Killer, Summer Wishes Winter Dreams, The Taking of Pelham One Two Three, Murder on the Orient Express, Mitchell, Season for Assassins, All The President's Men, Two-Minute Warning, The Sentinel, Silver Bears, Cuba, There Goes the Bride, Cry Onion, The Salamander, The Goodbye People, Innocent Prey, St. Elmo's Fire, Death Wish III, The Delta Force, Whatever It Takes, Private Investigations, Two Evil Eyes (The Black Cat), Cape Fear (1991), The Silence of the Hams.
TELEVISION: *Series*: Archie Bunker's Place. *Guest*: Actors Studio Theatre, US Steel Hour, Mr. Peepers, Alfred Hitchcock Presents, Arrest and Trial. *Movies*: Hunters Are For Killing, The Old Man Who Cried Wolf, Night of Terror, A Brand New Life, Six Million Dollar Man, Trapped Beneath the Sea, Miles to Go Before I Sleep, Death Among Friends, The Lindbergh Kidnapping Case, Raid on Entebbe, Contract on Cherry Street, The Storyteller, Siege, Rainbow, The Millionaire, The Seeding of Sarah Burns, House on Garibaldi Street, Aunt Mary, Love Tapes, People vs. Jean Harris, Little Gloria, Happy at Last, I Want to Live, Murder in Space, Kids Like These. *Mini-Series*: Space, Queenie. *Specials*: Cold Storage, Grown Ups.
(d. February 13, 1996)

BANCROFT, ANNE
Actress. r.n. Anna Maria Italiano. b. New York, NY, Sept. 17, 1931. m. director-comedian Mel Brooks. e. American Acad. of Dramatic Arts. Acting debut on TV, Studio One as Anne Marno in Torrents of Spring.
THEATER: Two For the Seesaw (Tony Award, Theatre World Award: 1958), The Miracle Worker (Tony Award, 1960), Mother Courage, The Devils, A Cry of Players, Golda, Duet For One, Mystery of the Rose Bouquet, The Little Foxes.
PICTURES: Don't Bother to Knock (debut, 1952), Tonight We Sing, Treasure of the Golden Condor, The Kid from Left Field, Gorilla at Large, Demetrius and the Gladiators, The Raid, New York Confidential, Life in the Balance, The Naked Street, The Last Frontier, Walk the Proud Land, Nightfall, The Restless Breed, The Girl in Black Stockings, The Miracle Worker (Academy Award for Best Actress, 1962), The Pumpkin Eater, The Slender Thread, Seven Women, The Graduate, Young Winston, The Prisoner of Second Avenue, The Hindenburg, Lipstick, Silent Movie, The Turning Point, Fatso (also dir., s.p.), The Elephant Man, To Be or Not to Be, Garbo Talks, Agnes of God, 'night Mother, 84 Charing Cross Road, Torch Song Trilogy, Bert Rigby You're a Fool, Honeymoon in Vegas, Love Potion No. 9, Point of No Return, Malice, Mr. Jones, How to Make an American Quilt, Home for the Holidays, Dracula–Dead & Loving It, The Sunchaser.
TELEVISION: *Mini-Series*: Jesus of Nazareth, Marco Polo. *Specials*: I'm Getting Married, Annie and the Hoods, Annie: The Women in the Life of a Man (also dir.); Emmy Award for Best Variety Special, 1970), Mrs. Cage, The Mother. *Movies*: Broadway Bound, Oldest Living Confederate Widow Tells All, The Mother, Homecoming.

BAND, ALBERT
Producer, Director. b. Paris, France, May 7, 1924. e. Lyceum Louis le Grand, won French-English Literature Prize 1938; entered film industry as cutter Pathe Lab.; prod. ass't to John Huston at MGM; first screen credit adaptation Red Badge of Courage novel; first direction, The Young Guns; formed Maxim Productions, Inc., Sept. 1956; prod. Recently formed Albert Band Intl. Prods., Inc.
PICTURES: The Young Guns, I Bury the Living, Face of Fire, The Avenger, Grand Canyon Massacre, The Tramplers, The Hellbenders (prod. only), A Minute to Pray a Second to Die, Little Cigars, Dracula's Dog, She Came to the Valley, Metalstorm: The Destruction of Jared-Syn, Swordkill, Buy and Cell (exec. prod. only), Troll, Terrorvision, Ghoulies II, Robotjox.

BAND, CHARLES
Producer-Director. b. Los Angeles, CA, Dec. 27, 1951. e. Overseas Sch. of Rome. Son of Albert Band. Formed Media Home Ent., 1978; formed Empire Ent. 1983; formed Full Moon Ent., 1988; formed Moonbeam Productions, 1993.
PICTURES: *Prod.*: Mansion of the Doomed, Cinderella, End of the World, Laserblast, Fairytales, Swordkill, Dungeonmaster, Eliminators. *Dir.-Prod.*: Crash, Parasite, Metalstorm, Trancers, Pulsepounders, Meridian (Kiss of the Beast), Crash & Burn, Trancers II, Dr. Mordrid. *Exec. Prod.*: Tourist Trap, Day Time Ended, Ghoulies, Re-Animator, Zone Troopers, Troll, Terrorvision, Crawlspace, Dolls, From Beyond, The Caller, Spellcaster, Cellar Dweller, Ghoulies II, Enemy Territory, Deadly Weapon, Robot Jox, Prison, Buy & Cell, Ghost Town, Catacombs, Arena, Puppet Master, Shadowzone, Puppet Master II, The Pit and the Pendulum, Subpecies, Puppet Master III, Arcade, Dollman, Netherworld, Bad Channels, Trancers III,

Shrunken Heads, Oblivion, Dr. Mordrid, Robot Wards, Subspecies II, Mandroid, Invisible, Prehysteria, Remote, Dragonworld, Beanstalk, Pet Shop, Prehysteria II.

BANDERAS, ANTONIO
Actor. b. Malaga, Spain, Aug. 10, 1960. e. School of Dramatic Art, Malaga. Moved to Madrid in 1981 where he made his stage debut in Los Tarantos. Other theatre incl. The City and the Dogs, Daughter of the Air, The Tragedy of Edward II of England.
PICTURES: Labyrinth of Passion (debut, 1982), Pesantas Positzas, Y Del Seguro... Libranos Senor!, Pestanas Positzas, El Senor Galindez, El Caso Almeria, Los Zancos, Casa Cerrado, La Corte de Faraon, Requiem por un Campesino Espanol, 27 Horas, Puzzle, Matador, Asi Como Habian Sido, Law of Desire, The Pleasure of Killing, Baton Rouge, Bajarse Al Moro, Women on the Verge of a Nervous Breakdown, Si Te Dicen Que Cai, Tie Me Up! Tie Me Down!, Contra el Viento, La Blanca Paloma, Truth or Dare, The Mambo Kings, Philadelphia, Dispara, Of Love and Shadows, The House of the Spirits, Interview With the Vampire, Miami Rhapsody, Desperado, Four Rooms, Never Talk to Strangers, Two Much, Assassins, Evita.
TELEVISION: La llave de Hierro, Fragmentos de Interior, La Mujer de Tu Vida.

BANDY, MARY LEA
Director, Dept. of Film, Museum of Modern Art. b. Evanston, IL, June 16, 1943. e. Stanford U., B.A., 1965. Asst. editor, Harry Abrams and Museum of Modern Art. Director (1980-93), Chief Curator (1993-), Dept. of Film, Museum of Modern Art Editor of MOMA film publications incl.: Rediscovering French Film (1983). Member: Advisory Board, AFI's National Center for Preservation of Film and Video; Film Advisory Comm., American Federation of Arts; Advisory Comm. on Film, Japan Society; Advisory Comm. NY State Motion Picture and Television Advisory Board. Co-president, National Alliance of Media Arts Center, 1986-87, 1987-88. Bd. mem.: Intl. Film Seminars, MacDowell Colony, Natl. Film Preservation Board, Library of Congress, Advisory Board, Film Foundation, Board of Directors, Third World Newsreel.

BANJERJEE, VICTOR
Actor. b. Calcutta, India, Oct. 15, 1946. Was instrumental in forming the first Screen Extras Union in India, presently founding secretary. Won international recognition for A Passage to India. *Stage*: Pirates of Penzance, An August Requiem (director, 1981), Desert Song, Godspell.
PICTURES: The Chess Players (debut), Hullabaloo, Madhurban, Tanaya, Pratidan, Prarthana, Dui Prithri, Kalyug, Arohan, Jaipur Junction (German), A Passage to India, Foreign Body, The Home and the World, Hard to Be a God, Bitter Moon, World Within World Without.
TELEVISION: *Movie*: Dadah Is Death.

BANNEN, IAN
Actor. b. Airdrie, Scotland, June 29, 1928. Early career Shakespeare Memorial Theatre (now RSC), Stratford-on-Avon.
THEATER: A View From the Bridge, The Iceman Cometh, Long Days Journey Into Night, Sergeant Musgrave's Dance. Royal Shakespeare Thea. Co. 1961-62: Toys in the Attic, Hamlet, As You Like It (with Vanessa Redgrave), Romeo and Juliet, Othello, The Blood Knot, Devil's Disciple, The Iceman Cometh, Hedda Gabler, Translations (Drama Critics Award, 1981); Riverside Mermaid Theatres, 1983; Moon for the Misbegotten (London, Boston, Broadway), All My Sons.
PICTURES: Private's Progress (debut, 1956), The Third Key (The Long Arm), Battle Hell (Yangtse Incident), Miracle in Soho, The Birthday Present, Behind the Mask, A Tale of Two Cities, She Didn't Say No, The French Mistress, Carlton-Browne of the F.O. (Man in Cocked Hat), On Friday at 11, A French Mistress, The Risk (Suspect), Macbeth, Station Six Sahara, Psyche 59, Mister Moses, Rotten to the Core, The Hill, The Flight of the Phoenix (Acad. Award nom.), Penelope, Sailor From Gibraltar, Lock Up Your Daughters!, Too Late the Hero, The Deserter, Fright, Doomwatch, The Offence (BAFTA nom.), The Macintosh Man, The Driver's Seat, The Voyage, Bite the Bullet, From Beyond the Grave, Sweeney!, Inglorious Bastards, Ring of Darkness, The Watcher in the Woods, Eye of the Needle, Night Crossing, Gandhi, The Prodigal, Gorky Park, Defense of the Realm, Lamb, Hope and Glory (BAFTA nom.), The Courier, The Match, Ghost Dad, Crossing the Line (The Big Man), George's Island, The Gamble, Damage, A Pin for the Butterfly, Braveheart, Dead Sea Reels.
TELEVISION: Johnny Belinda, Jane Eyre, Jesus of Nazareth, Tinker Tailor Soldier Spy, Dr. Jekyll and Mr. Hyde, Fifteen Streets, Murder in Eden, Ashenden, Uncle Vanya, The Sound and the Silence, The Treaty, Doctor Finlay, The Politician's Wife, Original Sin.

BANNER, BOB
Producer, Director. b. Ennis, TX, Aug. 15, 1921. e. Southern Methodist U., B.A., 1939-43; Northwestern U., M.A., 1946-48. U.S. Naval Reserve 1943-46; faculty, Northwestern U., 1948-50; staff dir., NBC-TV in Chicago, 1949-50. Pres., Bob Banner Assocs. Visiting Prof.: Southern Methodist U.

TELEVISION: Garroway at Large (dir.), Fred Waring Show (prod., dir.), Omnibus (dir.), Nothing But the Best (prod. dir.), Dave Garroway Show (prod. dir), Dinah Shore Show, Garry Moore Show (exec. prod.), Candid Camera TV Show (exec. prod.), Carnegie Hall Salutes Jack Benny (exec. prod.), Julie & Carol at Carnegie Hall, Carol & Co., Jimmy Dean Show, Calamity Jane, Once Upon a Mattress, The Entertainers, Kraft Summer Music Hall, Carol & Co., Ice Follies, Carol Burnett Show, Peggy Fleming at Madison Square Garden, John Davidson at Notre Dame, Here's Peggy Fleming, Peggy Fleming at Sun Valley, The American West of John Ford, Love! Love! Love!—Hallmark Hall of Fame, To Europe with Love, Peggy Fleming Visits the Soviet Union, Perry Como's Lake Tahoe Holiday, Perry Como's Christmas In Mexico, Perry Como's Hawaiian Holiday, Perry Como's Spring In New Orleans, Don Ho Show, Perry Como Las Vegas Style, Perry Como's Christmas in Austria, All-Star Anything Goes, Peggy Fleming and Holiday on Ice at Madison Square Garden, Julie Andrews, One Step Into Spring, Leapin' Lizards, It's Liberace, Perry Como's Easter By The Sea, Ford Motor Company's 75th Anniversary; Gift of Music, specials starring Bob Hope, Julie Andrews, Andy Williams, Los Angeles Music Center 25th Anniversary. *Movies*: Mongo's Back in Town, The Last Survivors, Journey From Darkness, My Sweet Charlie, Bud and Lou, Yes Virginia There is a Santa Claus, Crash Landing, With Murder in Mind, The Sea Wolf, Angel Flight Down. *Series*: Almost Anything Goes, Solid Gold, Star Search, It's Showtime at the Apollo, Uptown Comedy Club.

BAR, JACQUES JEAN LOUIS
Executive, Producer, Exhibitor. b. Chateauroux, France, Sept. 12, 1921. e. Lycaees Lakanal and Saint Louis, France. Formed Citae-Films S.A., 1947; CIPRA in assoc. with MGM, 1961; S.C.B., Bourges, 8 cinemas; S.C.M., Le Mans, 9 cinemas. Hollywood films: Bridge to the Sun, Once A Thief, Guns for San Sebastian. Prod. 57 films in France, Spain, Italy, Switzerland, Japan and Brazil 1948-89.
PICTURES: Where the Hot Wind Blows, Bridge to the Sun, Rififi in Tokyo, A Very Private Affair, Swordsmen of Siena, Monkey in Winter, The Turfist, Any Number Can Win, The Day and the Hour, Joy House, Guns for San Sebastian, Last Known Address, The Homecoming, Dancing Machine, The Candidate, Once a Thief, My Father the Hero.

BARANSKI, CHRISTINE
Actress. b. Buffalo, NY, May 2, 1952. e. Juilliard Sch. of Music & Dramatic Arts.
THEATER: *NY*: Private Lives, One Crack Out, Says I Says He, Shadow of a Gunman, Hide and Seek (B'way debhut, 1980), Company, Coming Attractions, Operation Midnight Climax, A Midsummer Night's Dream (Obie Award, 1982), Sally and Marsha, The Real Thing (Tony Award, 1984), Hurlyburly, It's Only a Play, The House of Blue Leaves, Rumors (Tony Award, 1989), Elliot Loves, Nick and Nora, Lips Together Teeth Apart, The Loman Family Picnic.
PICTURES: Soup for One (debut, 1982), Lovesick, Crackers, Nine 1/2 Weeks, Legal Eagles, The Pick-Up Artist, Reversal of Fortune, The Night We Never Met, Life With Mikey, Addams Family Values, New Jersey Drive, Jeffrey, Birdcage.
TELEVISION: *Series*: Cybill (Emmy Award, 1995). *Movie*: Playing for Time. *Special*: The Addams Chronicles.

BARBEAU, ADRIENNE
Actress. b. Sacramento, CA, June 11, 1947. e. Foothill Col.
THEATER: *B'way*: Fiddler on the Roof, Grease (Tony nom., Theatre World Award). *L.A.*: Women Behind Bars, Strange Snow, Pump Boys & Dinettes, Drop Dead. Canadian Premiere: Lost in Yonkers. Regional: Love Letters, Best Little Whorehouse in Texas.
PICTURES: The Fog, Cannonball Run, Escape From New York, Swamp Thing, Creepshow, The Next One, Back to School, Open House, Two Evil Eyes, Cannibal Women & the Avocado Jungle of Death, Father Hood.
TELEVISION: *Series*: Maude, Batman (voice). *Movies*: The Great Houdinis, Having Babies, Red Alert, Return to Fantasy Island, Crash, Someone's Watching Me!, The Darker Side of Terror, The Top of the Hill, Valentine Magic on Love Island, Tourist, Charlie and the Great Balloon Chase, Seduced, Bridge Across Time, Blood River, Double Crossed, The Burden of Proof, The Parsley Garden, Jailbreakers, Bram Stoker's Burial of the Rats. *Guest*: Quincy, 8 Is Enough, Tony Orlando and Dawn, The David Frost Special, Bobby Vinton Show, FBI, Head of the Class, Love Boat, Hotel, Twilight Zone, Murder She Wrote, Dream On, Daddy Dearest, The Carlin Show, Babylon 5.

BARBER, FRANCES
Actress. b. Wolverhampton, Eng., May 13, 1957. e. Bangor U.; grad. studies in theatre, Cardiff U. Stage experience with fringe theaters including improvisational troupe Hull Truck Theatre Company, Glasgow Citizens and Tricycle Theatre (Killburn) before joining Royal Shakespeare Co. (Camille, Hamlet).
PICTURES: The Missionary (debut, 1982), A Zed and Two Noughts, White City, Castaway, Prick Up Your Ears, Sammy and Rosie Get Laid, We Think the World of You, The Grasscutter, Chamber ga part (Separate Bedrooms), Young Soul Rebels, Secret Friends.

TELEVISION: Clem, Jackie's Story, Home Sweet Home, Flame to the Phoenix, Reilly, Ace of Spies, Those Glory, Glory Days; Hard Feelings, Behaving Badly, The Nightmare Years.

BARBERA, JOSEPH R.
Executive. b. New York, NY, Mar. 24, 1911. e. NYU, American Institute of Banking. After schooling joined Irving Trust Co. in N.Y.; started submitting cartoon drawings to leading magazines selling one to Collier's. Joined Van Buren Assocs. as sketch artist, later going to work in animation dept. of MGM Studios. At MGM met William Hanna, who became his lifelong business associate. Made first animated short together in 1937, starting the famous Tom & Jerry series which they produced for 20 years. Left MGM in 1957 to form Hanna-Barbera Productions to make cartoons for TV. Hanna-Barbera became a subsidiary of Taft Ent. Co. in 1968 with both men operating the studio under long-term agreements with Taft. Taft and the studio were sold to Great American Broadcasting, 1988. Hanna-Barbera Prods. acquired by Turner Bdcstg. System, 1991. Barbera is co-founder, chmn. Team received Governor's Award from the Academy of Television Arts & Sciences, 1988.
PICTURES: Hey There It's Yogi Bear, A Man Called Flintstone, Charlotte's Web, C.H.O.M.P.S., Heidi's Song, Jetsons: The Movie, The Flintstones (exec. prod. of live action film; also cameo appearance).
TELEVISION: *Series*: The Huckleberry Hound Show (Emmy Award), Quick Draw McGraw, Yogi Bear, The Flintstones, The Jetsons, Top Cat, Jonny Quest, Scooby-Doo, Smurfs. *Specials/Movies*: The Gathering (Emmy Award), I Yabba Dabba Do!, Hollyrock-a-Bye Baby.

BARBOUR, ALAN G.
Writer, Editor, Publisher. b. Oakland, CA, July 25, 1933. e. Rutgers U. m. Catherine Jean Callovini, actress, Teacher, AADA, American Mime Theatre. U.S. Army, worked as computer programmer. Formed Screen Facts Press in 1963, Screen Facts Magazine. Compiled, edited: The Serials of Republic, The Serials of Columbia, Great Serial Ads, The B Western, Serial Showcase, Hit the Saddle, The Wonderful World of B-Films, Days of Thrills and Adventure, Serial Quarterly, Serial Pictorial, Karloff—A Pictorial History, Errol Flynn—A Pictorial Biography, A Pictorial History of the Serial, A Thousand and One Delights, Cliffhanger, The Old-Time Radio Quiz Book. Direct Mktg. Div., RCA Records. Mgr., A & R, RCA, BMGVideo Club.

BARBOUR, MALCOLM
Executive. b. London, England, May 3, 1934. e. Radley Coll., Oxford, England, A.B., Columbia Coll. At NBC was press info. asst., 1958-59; asst. magazine ed., 1959-62; assoc. mag. ed., 1962-64; sr. mag. ed., 1964-65; mgr. of magazine pub., National Broadcasting Co., 1965-67; pub. mgr., Buena Vista, 1967-68; Eastern story ed., Walt Disney Prod., 1968-69; dir. of adv. & pub. relations, Buena Vista, 1969. Partner, Producers Creative Services, 1976-79. President, The International Picture Show, 1980-81 (Tim Conway comedies The Billion Dollar Hobo and They Went That-A-Way & That-A-Way; Slayer. Distributor: Soldier of Orange, The Magic of Lassie, The Visitor, etc.). President, Barbour/Langley Productions, 1982-present. Producer, Geraldo Rivera specials: American Vice, Innocence Lost, Sons of Scarface, Murder: Live from Death Row, Satan Worship. Producer, Jack Anderson specials. Writer-Producer, Cocaine Blues. Co-screenplay, P.O.W. The Escape. *Exec. producer*: Cops, Code 3, Inside the KGB, Cop Files, Deadly Sins (also writer).

BARDOT, BRIGITTE
Actress. b. Paris, France, Sept. 28, 1934. e. Paris Conservatory. Studied ballet, before becoming model. Studied acting with Rene Simon. On stage in L'Invitation au Chateau. Awarded French Legion of Honor, 1985. Active in the movement to preserve endangered animals. Created the Brigitte Bardot Foundation for animal protection, April 1986.
PICTURES: Le Trou Normand (debut, 1952), Nanina la Fille san Voiles, Les Dents Longues, Act of Love, Le Portrait de Caroline Cherie, Helen of Troy, Futures Vedettes, Les Grandes Maneuvres, Doctor at Sea, La Lumiere d'En Face (The Light Across the Street), Cette Sacre Gamine (Mam'zelle Pigalle), Mi Figlio Nerone, En Effeuillant la Marguerite (Please Mr. Balzac), The Bride is Much Too Beautiful, And God Created Woman, Une Parisienne, The Night Heaven Fell, En Cas de Malheur, Le Femme et le Pantin, Babette Goes to War, Come Dance With Me, La Verite (The Truth), La Bride sur le Cou, Les Amours Celebres, A Very Private Affair, Love on a Pillow, Contempt, A Ravishing Idiot, Dear Brigitte, Viva Maria, Masculine-Feminine, Two Weeks in September, Spirits of the Dead (Histories Extraordinaires), Shalako, Les Femmes, L'Ours et la Poupee, Les Novices, Boulevard du Rhum (Rum Runner), Les Petroleuses (The Legend of Frenchie King), Ms. Don Juan, L'Historie Tres Bonne et Tres Joyeuse de Colinot Troussechemise.

BARE, RICHARD L.
Producer, Director. b. Turlock, CA, Aug. 12, 1925. Started as dir. for Warners. SDG Best Dir. TV award, 1959. *Author*: The Film Director (Macmillan, 1971). Pres., United National Film Corp.
PICTURES: *Dir.*: Smart Girls Don't Talk, Flaxy Martin, This Side of the Law, House Across The Street, This Rebel Breed, Girl on the Run, Return of Frontiersman. *Dir.-Prod.-Writer*: Wicked Wicked, Story of Chang & Eng, City of Shame, Sudden Target, Purple Moon.
TELEVISION: 77 Sunset Strip, Maverick, So This is Hollywood, The Islanders, Dangerous Robin, This Rebel Breed, Twilight Zone, Bus Stop, Adventures in Paradise, The Virginian, Kraft Theatre, Run For Your Life, Green Acres, Farraday and Son, Westwind.

BAREN, HARVEY M.
Executive. b. New York, NY, Nov. 25, 1931. e. State U. of New York. Served in U.S. Army, 1952-54; United Artists Corp., 1954-59 (contract dept., print dept., booker—NY branch); asst. to general sls. mgr., Magna Pictures Corp., 1959-61; road show mgr., national sales coordinator, 20th Century-Fox, 1961-71; asst. general sales manager, Allied Artists Pictures, 1971-79; v.p., gen. sls. mgr., Nat'l. Screen Service, 1978-79; v.p., gen. sls. mgr., Cannon Pictures, 1979-80. 1980, pres. of Summit Feature Distributors; 1983, exec. V.P., dir., MGM/UA Classics; 1986, joined New Century/Vista as v.p., sls. admin. 1991, pres. Sea Movies Inc.

BARENHOLTZ, BEN
Executive. b. Kovel, Poland, Oct. 5, 1935. *Asst. theatre manager*: RKO Bushwick, Brooklyn, 1959-60. Manager: Village Theatre (Fillmore East), N.Y., 1966-68. *Owner-operator*: Elgin Cinema, 1968-75, originated Midnight Movie concept with El Topo. *President-owner*: Libra Film Corp., 1972-84. 1984-1992, v.p. & partner: Circle Releasing (which launched and distributed The Family Game, Therese, Blood Simple and prod. Raising Arizona). Pres. Barenholtz Prods. Inc.
PICTURES: *Exec. Prod.*: Miller's Crossing, Barton Fink, Cheat, White Man's Burden (Bleeding Hearts), Georgia.

BARISH, KEITH
Producer. b. Los Angeles, CA. Background in finance. Founded Keith Barish Prods. in 1979. 1984-88 in partnership with Taft Broadcasting Co., Entertainment Div. Founder and chmn. of Planet Hollywood. Appeared in film Last Action Hero.
PICTURES: *Exec. prod.*: Endless Love, Sophie's Choice (prod.), Kiss Me Goodbye, Misunderstood, Nine 1/2 Weeks, Big Trouble in Little China, Light of Day (prod.), The Running Man, The Monster Squad, Ironweed (prod.), The Serpent and the Rainbow, Her Alibi, Firebirds, The Fugitive.
TELEVISION: *Movie*: A Streetcar Named Desire (exec. prod.).

BARKER, BOB
TV host. b. Darrington, WA, Dec. 12. e. Springfield Central H.S., Drury Coll. News writer, announcer, disc jockey KTTS until 1949. News editor, staff announcer, Station WWPG. Pres. Bob Barker Prod., Inc. 1966 started as M.C. for both Miss USA Pageant and Miss Universe Pageant. 1970, first time as M.C. of both Rose Bowl Parade and Pillsbury Bakeoff. Series (emcee or host): The End of the Rainbow, Truth or Consequences (daytime: 1956-65; nighttime synd: 1966-74), Lucky Pair (prod.), That's My Line (1980-1), The Price Is Right (exec. prod. & m.c.; 1972-; received several Emmy Awards as host). *Narrator*: 500 Festival Parade, Indianapolis 1969-81.

BARKER, CLIVE
Writer, Producer, Director. b. Liverpool, England, Oct. 5, 1952. e. Liverpool Univ. Moved to London at twenty-one, forming theatre company. Began writing short stories which were subsequently published as Books of Blood (Vols. 1-3 & Vols. 4-6). *Novels*: Damnation Game, Weaveworld, The Great and Secret Show, Imajica, The Thief of Always, Everville, Sacrament. Also painter with exhibitions in NY, California. *Books*: Clive Barker: Illustrator, The Art of Clive Barker, Incarnations. *Plays*: History of the Devil, Colossus, Frankenstein In Love
PICTURES: Rawhead Rex (from his story), Transmutations (from his story), Hellraiser (dir., s.p.; from his novella The Hellbound Heart), Hellbound: Hellraiser II (co-exec. prod.; from his story), Nightbreed (dir., s.p.; from his novel Cabal), Sleepwalkers (actor), Hellraiser III: Hell on Earth (exec. prod.; from his story), Candyman (exec. prod.; from his story The Forbidden), Candyman: Farewell to the Flesh (exec. prod.; from his story), Lord of Illusions (dir., s.p., co-prod.; from his story The Last Illusion).

BARKER, MICHAEL W.
Executive. b. Nuremberg, Germany, Jan. 9, 1954. e. U. of Texas at Austin, B.S. in International Communications, 1976. Joined Films Inc. 1979-80, then United Artists 1980-83, first as non-theatrical sales manager, then as national sales manager of UA Classics. Co-founder and v.p., Sales & Marketing for Orion Classics, a div. of Orion, 1983-1992. Co-founder and co-pres., Sony Pictures Classics, 1992-present. Member, board of directors of BAFTA New York and Independent Features Project.

BARKETT, STEVE
Actor, Director, Producer, Film Editor, Writer. b. Oklahoma City, OK, Jan. 1, 1950. Exhibited and scored over 52 feature length classic silent films 1966-1968 as dir. of two film series at the Okla. Art Ctr. and Science and Arts Fdn., prior to coming to LA in 1970. Toured in stage prod. 1971-72: Pajama Tops, Winnie the Pooh. Exec. in several non-theatrical releasing cos., incl. Independent Film Associates and Thunderbird Films. From 1968 to 1974 was active in film preservation and restoration work on early silent and sound films. 1978 founded The Hollywood Book and Poster Company. Est. The Nautilus Film Co., 1978. Founded and operated Capt. Nemo's Video (1985-87). Co-wrote and performed 42 episodes of Capt. Nemo's Video Review for radio (1987).
PICTURES: *Actor*: The Egyptians are Coming, Corpse Grinders, Dillinger, Night Caller, Cruise Missile, Beverly Hills Vampire, Wizard of the Demon Sword, Bikini Drive-In, Cyber Zone, Hard Bounty, Masseuse, Star Hunter. *Prod./Dir./S.P./Edit.*: Collecting, Empire of the Dark, Angels of Death. *Editor only*: Hurricane Express. *Spcl. Fx. only*: Warlords, Sorceress. *Actor/Dir./ S.P./Prod./Edit.*: The Movie People, Cassavetes, The Aftermath, Angels of Death, Empire of the Dark. *Actor/FX*: Dark Universe, Dinosaur Island, Attack of the 60's Centerfold, Invisible Mom.

BARKIN, ELLEN
Actress. b. Bronx, NY, Apr. 16, 1954. e. Hunter Coll.; Actors Studio.
THEATER: Irish Coffee (debut, Ensemble Studio Theatre), Shout Across the River, Killings Across the Last, Tobacco Road, Extremities, Eden Court.
PICTURES: Diner (debut, 1982), Tender Mercies, Daniel, Eddie and the Cruisers, Harry and Son, The Adventures of Buckaroo Banzai Across the Eighth Dimension, Enormous Changes at the Last Minute, Terminal Choice, Desert Bloom, Down by Law, The Big Easy, Siesta, Made in Heaven (unbilled), Sea of Love, Johnny Handsome, Switch, Man Trouble, Mac, This Boy's Life, Into the West, Bad Company, Wild Bill, Mad Dog time.
TELEVISION: *Series*: Search for Tomorrow. *Movies*: Kent State, We're Fighting Back, Parole, Terrible Joe Moran, Act of Vengeance, Clinton and Nadine. *Special*: Faerie Tale Theatre (The Princess Who Never Laughed).

BARLOW, PHIL
Executive. President, Buena Vista Pictures Distribution.

BARNHOLTZ, BARRY
Executive. b. St. Louis, MO, Oct. 12, 1945. e. California State U., Northridge; USC; UCLA; W.L.A.U. (studied law). Concert promotions in So. Calif. 1963-71; with Medallion TV as v.p. in chg. sls.; Barnholtz Organization, representing independent prod. cos. for feature films for cable. Founder, sr. v.p. of Vidmark Inc., and Trimark Films.

BARON, STANLEY N.
Executive. President, Society of Motion Picture and Television Engineers.

BARR, ANTHONY
Producer, Director, Actor. r.n. Morris Yaffe. b. St. Louis, MO, March 14, 1921. e. Washington U., B.S. 1942. Actor, asst. stage mgr., 1944-46; stage mgr., Katherine Dunham Dancers, 1946-47; teacher, actor, dir. in chg. Film Actors' Workshop, Professional Theatre Workshop, Hollywood; v.p. current prime time series, ABC-TV; v.p., current dramatic program production, CBS-TV; v.p., CBS Entertainment Prods.
THEATER: Jacobowsky and the Colonel, Winters' Tale, Embezzled Heaven.
PICTURES: *Actor*: People Against O'Hara, Border Incident, The Hollywood Story, The Mozart Story. *Co-prod.*: Dime with a Halo.
TELEVISION: *Director*: Art Linkletter's Houseparty, About Faces. *Assoc. dir.*: Climax, Shower of Stars. *Prod.*: Climax, Summer Studio One. *Assoc. prod.*: Climax, Playhouse 90, Pursuit, G.E. Theatre, The Law and Mr. Jones, Four-Star.
AUTHOR: Acting for the Camera, 1982.

BARRAULT, MARIE-CHRISTINE
Actress. b. Paris, France, March 21, 1944. m. director Roger Vadim.
PICTURES: My Night at Maud's, Le Distrait (The Daydreamer), Lancelot of the Lake, The Aspern Papers, Les Intrus, La Famille Grossfeld, Chloe in the Afternoon, John Glueckstadt, Cousin Cousine (Acad. Award nom.), By the Tennis Courts, Perceval, The Medusa Touch, Tout est a nous, Femme Entre Chien et Loup, Ma Cherie, Stardust Memories, Table for Five, Josephs Tochter, A Love in Germany, Les Mots Pour le Dire, Swann in Love, Grand Piano, Prisonnieres, Un Etae de orages, Savage State, Necessary Love.

BARRETT, RONA
News Correspondent b. New York, NY, Oct. 8, 1936. e. NYU (communications major). Created the column, Rona Barrett's Young Hollywood, which led to featured column in 1960 in Motion Picture Magazine and a nationally syndicated column

distributed to 125 newspapers by the North American Newspaper Alliance. Turned to TV; initial appearances on ABC Owned Stations in 5 cities, providing two-minute reports for local newscasts. Resulted in Dateline Hollywood a network morning prog., co-hosted by Joanna Barnes. In 1969 created first daily syndicated TV news segment for Metromedia. 1975, became arts and entertainment editor for ABC's Good Morning America. 1980, joined NBC News. Publ. and exec. editor, newsletter, The Rona Barrett Report. 1985, pres., Rona Barrett Enterprises, Inc., sr. corresp., Entertainment Tonight; Mutual Radio Network. 1988: creator of original novels for television, for NBC prods. Appeared in films Sextette, An Almost Perfect Affair.

BARRIE, BARBARA
Actress. b. Chicago, IL, May 23, 1931. e. U. of TX, B.F.A., 1953. Trained for stage at Herbert Berghof Studio. NY stage debut, The Wooden Dish (1955). *Author*: Lone Star (1990), Adam Zigzag (1994).
THEATER: The Crucible, The Beaux Stratagem, The Taming of the Shrew, Conversations in the Dark, All's Well That Ends Well, Happily Never After, Horseman Pass By, Company, The Selling of the President, The Prisoner of Second Avenue, The Killdeer, California Suite, Big and Little, Isn't It Romantic, Torch Song Trilogy, Fugue, After Play.
PICTURES: Giant (debut, 1956), The Caretakers, One Potato Two Potato (best actress, Cannes Film Fest, 1964), The Bell Jar, Breaking Away (Acad. Award nom.), Private Benjamin, Real Men, End of the Line, The Passage.
TELEVISION: *Series*: Love of Life, Diana, Barney Miller, Breaking Away, Tucker's Witch, Reggie, Double Trouble, Love of Life, Big City Story. *Guest appearances*: Ben Casey, The Fugitive, Dr. Kildare, Alfred Hitchcock Presents, The Defenders, Mary Tyler Moore Show, Lou Grant, Trapper John, M.D., Babes, Kojak, Island Son, thirtysomething. *Movies*: Tell Me My Name, Summer of My German Soldier, To Race the Wind, The Children Nobody Wanted, Not Just Another Affair, Two of a Kind, The Execution, Vital Signs, Winnie, My First Love, Guess Who's Coming for Christmas?, The Odd Couple: Together Again, My Breast. *Specials*: To Be Young Gifted and Black, Barefoot in the Park, What's Alan Watching?, Lovejoy: The Lost Colony, My Summer As a Girl. *Mini-Series*: 79 Park Avenue, Backstairs at the White House, Roots: The Next Generation, Scarlett.

BARRON, ARTHUR RAY
Executive. b. Mt. Lake, MN, July 12, 1934. e. San Diego State U. 1956-60, B.S. Accounting. Certified public acc't, Calif., 1960. Coopers & Lybrand, 1960-63; Desilu Productions, Inc., 1963-67; v.p. finance and admin., Paramount TV, 1967-70; v.p. finance, Paramount Pictures Corp., 1970; sr. v.p. finance and admin., 1971; exec. v.p., finance & admin., 1974; exec. v.p. 1980; exec. v.p., Gulf & Western Industries, entertainment & communications group, 1983; promoted to pres., 1984-88. Chmn, Time Warner Enterprises, 1990.

BARRY, GENE
Actor. r.n. Eugene Klass. b. New York, NY, June 14, 1919. e. New Utrecht H.S., Brooklyn.
BROADWAY: Rosalinda, Catherine Was Great, Happy Is Larry, Bless You All, The Would-Be Gentleman, La Cage aux Folles (Tony nom.).
PICTURES: Atomic City (debut, 1952), The Girls of Pleasure Island, The War of the Worlds, Those Redheads From Seattle, Alaska Seas, Red Garters, Naked Alibi, Soldier of Fortune, The Purple Mask, The Houston Story, Back From Eternity, China Gate, The 27th Day, Forty Guns, Thunder Road, Hong Kong Confidential, Maroc 7, Subterfuge, The Second Coming of Suzanne, Guyana: Cult of the Damned.
TELEVISION: *Series*: Our Miss Brooks, Bat Masterson, Burke's Law (1963-66), The Name of the Game, Burke's Law (1994-95). *Movies*: Prescription Murder, Istanbul Express, Do You Take This Stranger?, The Devil and Miss Sarah, Ransom for Alice!, A Cry for Love, The Girl the Gold Watch and Dynamite, Adventures of Nellie Bly, Turn Back the Clock. *Mini-Series*: Aspen.

BARRY, JOHN
Composer, Arranger, Conductor. r.n. John Barry Prendergast. b. York, England, 1933. Started as rock 'n' roll trumpeter. Artist and prod., CBS Records.
PICTURES: Beat Girl, Never Let Go, The L-Shaped Room, The Amorous Mr. Prawn, From Russia With Love, Seance on a Wet Afternoon, Zulu, Goldfinger, The Ipcress File, The Knack, King Rat, Mister Moses, Thunderball, The Chase, Born Free (2 *Academy Awards*: Best Music Scoring and Best Song: title song, 1966), The Wrong Box, The Quiller Memorandum, The Whisperers, Deadfall, You Only Live Twice, Petulia, The Lion in Winter (Academy Award, 1968), Midnight Cowboy, The Appointment, On Her Majesty's Secret Service, Monte Walsh, The Last Valley, They Might Be Giants, Murphy's War, Walkabout, Diamonds Are Forever, Mary Queen of Scots, Alice's Adventures in Wonderland, The Public Eye (Follow Me), A Doll's House, The Tamarind Seed, The Dove, The Man With the Golden Gun, The Day of the Locust, Robin and Marian, King Kong, The Deep, The Betsy, Hanover Street, Moonraker, The

Black Hole, Starcrash, Game of Death, Raise the Titanic, Somewhere in Time, Inside Moves, Touched By Love, Body Heat, The Legend of the Lone Ranger, Frances, Hammett, High Road to China, Octopussy, The Golden Seal, Mike's Murder, Until September, The Cotton Club, A View to a Kill, Jagged Edge, Out of Africa (Academy Award, 1985), Howard the Duck, Peggy Sue Got Married, The Living Daylights, Hearts of Fire, Masquerade, A Killing Affair, Dances With Wolves (Academy Award, 1990), Chaplin, Indecent Proposal, Deception, My Life, The Specialist.
TELEVISION: Elizabeth Taylor in London, Sophia Loren in Rome.

BARRYMORE, DREW
Actress. b. Los Angeles, CA, Feb. 22, 1975. Father is actor John Barrymore, Jr. (John Drew Barrymore). At 11 months appeared in first commercial. *Author*: Little Girl Lost (1990).
PICTURES: Altered States (debut, 1980), E.T.: The Extra Terrestrial, Firestarter, Irreconcilable Differences, Cat's Eye, See You in the Morning, Far From Home, No Place to Hide, Waxwork II, Poison Ivy, Motorama, Doppelganger, Wayne's World 2, Bad Girls, Inside the Goldmine, Boys on the Side, Mad Love, Batman Forever, Everyone Says I Love You, Scream.
TELEVISION: *Series*: 2000 Malibu Road. *Movies*: Bogie, Suddenly Love, Babes in Toyland, Conspiracy of Love, The Sketch Artist, Guncrazy (also released theatrically), The Amy Fisher Story. *Specials*: Disneyland's 30th Anniversary, Night of 100 Stars II, Con Sawyer and Hucklemary Finn, 15 & Getting Straight.

BARRYMORE, JOHN DREW
Actor. b. Beverly Hills, CA, June 4, 1932. r.n. John Blythe Barrymore Jr. e. St. John's Military Acad., various public and private schools. Son of actors John Barrymore and Delores Costello. Daughter is actress Drew Barrymore. Started acting at age 18 under the name John Barrymore Jr.
PICTURES: Sundowners (debut, 1950), High Lonesome, Quebec, The Big Night, Thunderbirds, While the City Sleeps, Shadow on the Window, Never Love a Stranger, High School Confidential, Night of the Quarter Moon, The Cossacks, The Night They Killed Rasputin, The Pharaoh's Woman, The Trojan Horse, The Centurion, Invasion 1700, War of the Zombies.

BART, PETER
Executive. b. Martha's Vineyard, MA, July 24, 1932. e. Swarthmore Coll. and The London School of Economics. Eight years as corrp. for New York Times and wrote for such magazines as Harper's, The Atlantic, Saturday Review, etc. Joined Paramount Pictures in 1965. Named exec. ass't to Robert Evans, exec. in charge of world-wide prod. Appointed v.p. prod. Resigned 1973 to develop and produce own films for Paramount. Appointed pres. Lorimar Films, 1978. Resigned, 1979, to be indept. prod. 1983, joined MGM as sr. v.p., prod., m.p. div. Resigned, 1985, to be indep. prod. Editor, Variety. *Novels*: Thy Kingdom Come (1983), Destinies (1979), Fade Out. PICTURES: *Producer*: Islands in the Stream, Fun with Dick and Jane, Revenge of the Nerds (exec. prod.), Youngblood, Revenge of the Nerds II.

BARTEL, PAUL
Director, Writer, Actor. b. New York, NY, Aug. 6, 1938. e. UCLA, B.A. At 13 spent summer working at UPA Cartoons. Later at UCLA won acting and playwriting awards and prod. animated and doc. films. Awarded Fulbright schl. to study film dir. at Centro Sperimentale di Cinematograpfia in Rome where dir. short Progetti (presented Venice Fest., 1962). Then at Army Pictorial Center, L.I. City. Asst. dir. military training films and writer-dir. monthly news dec. series, Horizontos for U.S. Information Agency. Directed short film The Naughty Nurse. Appeared in 1984 short film Frankenweenie.
PICTURES: *Actor*: Hi Mom!, Private Parts (also dir. debut), Big Bad Mama (2nd unit. dir. only), Death Race 2000 (dir. only), Cannonball (also dir., co-s.p.), Eat My Dust!, Hollywood Boulevard, Grand Theft Auto, Mr. Billion, Piranha, Rock 'n' Roll High School, Heart Like a Wheel, Eating Raoul (also dir., s.p.), Trick or Treats, White Dog, Get Crazy, Not for Publication (also dir., s.p.), Lust in the Dust (dir. only), Into the Night, Sesame Street Presents Follow That Bird, Chopping Mall, Killer Party, The Longshot (dir. only), Munchies, Amazon Women on the Moon, Mortuary Academy, Out of the Dark (also exec. prod.), Scenes From the Class Struggle in Beverly Hills (also dir., s.p.), Pucker Up and Bark Like a Dog, Far Out Man, Gremlins 2: The New Batch, The Pope Must Die, Liquid Dreams, Desire and Hell at Sunset Motel, Posse, Grief, The Jerky Boys, The Usual Suspects, Red Ribbon Blues.
TELEVISION: *Actor*: Alfred Hitchcock Presents, Fame, L.A. Law, Acting on Impulse (movie), A Bucket of Blood (movie). *Director*: Amazing Stories (The Secret Cinema, Gershwin's Truck; also writer, actor), The Hustler of Muscle Beach.

BARTKOWIAK, ANDRZEJ
Cinematographer. b. Lodz, Poland, 1950. Attended Polish Film School. Moved to US in 1972, gaining experience in TV commercials and low-budget features. Protege of Sidney Lumet, for whom did several Pictures.

PICTURES: Deadly Hero, Prince of the City, Deathtrap, The Verdict, Daniel, Terms of Endearment, Garbo Talks, Prizzi's Honor, The Morning After, Power, Nuts, Twins, Q&A, Hard Promises, A Stranger Among Us, Falling Down, Guilty As Sin, Speed, A Good Man in Africa, Losing Isaiah, Species, Jade.

BARTY, BILLY
Actor. b. Millsboro, PA, Oct. 25, 1924. e. LA City Col., LA State U. Began performing at age 3 appearing as Mickey Rooney's little brother in the Mickey McGuire shorts. Founded Little People of America, 1957; Billy Barty Foundation, 1975.
PICTURES: Golddigers of 1933, Footlight Parade, Roman Scandals, Gift of Gab, A Midsummer Night's Dream, Nothing Sacred, The Clown, The Undead, Billy Rose's Jumbo, Roustabout, Harum Scarum, Pufnstuf, The Day of the Locust, The Amazing Dobermans, W.C. Fields and Me, Foul Play, Firepower, Hardly Working, Under the Rainbow, Night Patrol, Legend, Tough Guys, Body Slam, Rumplestiltskin, Willow, Lobster Man From Mars, UHF, The Rescuers Down Under (voice), Life Stinks.
TELEVISION: Series: Ford Festival, The Spike Jones Show, Circus Boy, Club Oasis, Ace Crawford—Private Eye. Movies: Punch and Jody, Twin Detectives.

BARUCH, RALPH M.
Executive. b. Frankfurt, Germany, Aug. 5, 1923. e. The Sorbonne. m. Jean Ursell de Mountford. Administrative aide, SESAC, Inc. 1944-48; account exec., DuMont Television Network, 1950-54; account exec., CBS Films, 1954; account supervisor, 1957; dir. int'l sales, 1959; CBS Group President 1961-70; pres. and CEO Viacom International, 1971-1983, chairman from 1983-1987 and is currently a consultant to Viacom International. Trustee of Lenox Hill Hospital. Chairman Emeritus of the National Academy of Cable Programming and recipient of the Academy's first Governor's Award. Past-president of the International Radio & Television Society and was honored by an IRTS gold medal award. Founder and fellow of the International Council of the National Academy of Television Arts & Sciences. Recipient of an Emmy Award. Former dir., Executive Committee of the National Cable Television Assoc. Co-founder of C-Span. Recipient of the Vanguard Award, three NCTA President's Awards and NCTA Chairman of the Year Award. Chairman of the USIA's Television Communications Board of Advisors under Pres. Reagan. Elected to the Broadcasting/Cable Hall of Fame in 1992. Appointed to New York City Cultural Affairs Advisory Comm. Member of New York Yacht Club.

BARWOOD, HAL
Writer, Producer, Director. e. U. of Southern California Sch. of Cinema. Has written scripts in collaboration with Matthew Robbins, Barwood branching out into producing with Corvette Summer in 1978 and directing with Warning Sign in 1985.
PICTURES: Screenplays (all with Robbins): The Sugarland Express, The Bingo Long Traveling All-Stars and Motor Kings, MacArthur, Corvette Summer (also prod.), Dragonslayer (also prod.), Warning Sign (also dir.).

BARYSHNIKOV, MIKHAIL
Dancer, Actor. b. Riga, Latvia, Jan. 27, 1948. Joined Kirov Ballet, Leningrad, 1969-74; defected to U.S. With American Ballet Theatre 1974-78; New York City Ballet Company 1978-79; named director of the American Ballet Theatre. B'way stage debut, Metamorphosis (1989).
PICTURES: The Turning Point (debut, 1977; Acad. Award nom.), That's Dancing!, White Nights (also co-choreog.), Dancers (also choreog.), Company Business, The Cabinet of Dr. Ramirez.
TELEVISION: Baryshnikov at the White House (Emmy Award, 1979), Bob Hope on the Road to China, Baryshnikov on Broadway (Emmy Award, 1980), AFI Salute to Fred Astaire, Baryshnikov in Hollywood, AFI Salute to Gene Kelly, David Gordon's Made in USA, All Star Gala at Ford's Theater, Dance in America: Baryshnikov Dances Balanchine (Emmy Award, 1989).

BASCH, BUDDY
Print Media Syndicater, Publicist, Producer. b. South Orange, NJ, June 28, 1922. e. Columbia U. Began career as youngest radio editor in U.S. at 15; since written for national mags, syndicates, wire services, and newspapers. Edit. & pub. Top Hit Club News for 7 yrs. Joined Donahue and Coe 1940 on m.p. accounts, U.S. Army in Europe 1942-45. 1945-67: own publicity and promotion office, working on m.p. company accounts and stars such as Burl Ives, Dinah Shore, Tony Martin, Danny Kaye, Peter Lorre, Tony Bennett, Gloria De Haven, McGuire Sisters, Rhonda Fleming, Sammy Davis, Jr., Anna Maria Alberghetti, Polly Bergen, Meyer Davis, The Beatles, Glenn Miller and Tommy Dorsey Orchestras. Produced many shows for radio, TV and stage in New York, Newark, Chicago, Hartford. Asst. to publisher, The Brooklyn Eagle 1962. 1966 formed Buddy Basch Feature Syndicate, covering assignments on show business, travel, health, medicine, food, human interest and general subjects for N.Y. Daily News, A.P., Grit Magazine, Travel/Holiday,

Frontier Magazine, Kaleidoscope, True, United Features, Gannett Westchester-Rockland Newspapers, Bergen (NJ) Record, Argosy, N.A.N.A., Womens' News Service, Today Magazine, Christian Science Monitor, New York Post, Inflight Magazine, Deseret News, California Canadian, Diversion. Provided Associated Press with worldwide exclusives on a number of national and intl. events. Member: Friars Club since 1959. Organized & appointed permanent chairman, VIP Reception and Security for Friars luncheons and dinners since 1970. Served as Chairman of Elections (6 times). Member of Admission Comm. and House Committee. Contributing ed. Friars Epistle.

BASINGER, KIM
Actress. b. Athens, GA, Dec. 8, 1953. m. actor Alec Baldwin. e. Neighborhood Playhouse. Began career as Ford model in New York.
PICTURES: Hard Country (debut, 1981), Mother Lode, Never Say Never Again, The Man Who Loved Women, The Natural, Fool for Love, 9-1/2 Weeks, No Mercy, Blind Date, Nadine, My Stepmother is an Alien, Batman, The Marrying Man, Final Analysis, Cool World, The Real McCoy, Wayne's World 2, The Getaway.
TELEVISION: Series: Dog and Cat, From Here to Eternity. Mini-Series: From Here to Eternity. Movies: Dog and Cat (pilot), The Ghost of Flight 401, Katie: Portrait of a Centerfold, Killjoy. Guest: Charlie's Angels.

BASS, RONALD
Writer. b. Los Angeles, CA. e. Yale, Harvard Law School. Entered industry as entertainment lawyer, while writing novels: The Perfect Thief, Lime's Crisis, The Emerald Illusion.
PICTURES: Code Name: Emerald, Black Widow, Gardens of Stone, Rain Man (Academy Award, 1988), Sleeping With the Enemy, The Joy Luck Club, When a Man Loves a Woman, Dangerous Minds, Waiting to Exhale.
TELEVISION: Series: Dangerous Minds, Moloney.

BASS, SAUL
Director, Producer. b. New York, NY, May 8, 1920. e. Arts Students League. Pres., Saul Bass/Herb Yager & Assoc. Directed short films, m.p. titles/prologues/epilogues, TV commercials. Directorial feature debut in 1974 with Phase IV.
PICTURES: Shorts: The Searching Eye, From Here to There, Why Man Creates (Academy Award, 1968), Notes on the Popular Arts (Acad. Award nom.), The Solar Film (Acad. Award nom.), Bass on Titles, Quest. Feature sequences: Grand Prix, Psycho. Full Features: Carmen Jones, The Big Knife, The Seven Year Itch, The Man With The Golden Arm, Johnny Concho, Saint Joan, Around the World in 80 Days, The Pride and the Passion, Bonjour Tristesse, Cowboy, Vertigo, The Big Country, Anatomy of a Murder, Psycho, Ocean's Eleven, Spartacus, Exodus, West Side Story, Advise and Consent, Walk on the Wild Side, It's a Mad Mad Mad Mad World, Bunny Lake Is Missing, That's Entertainment Part 2, The Human Factor, Broadcast News, Big, The War of the Roses, Goodfellas, Cape Fear, Mr. Saturday Night, The Age of Innocence.
(d. April 25, 1996)

BASSETT, ANGELA
Actress. b. New York, NY, Aug. 16, 1958. Moved to St. Petersburg, FL, at 5 yrs. old. e. Yale.
THEATER: B'way: Ma Rainey's Black Bottom, Joe Turner's Come and Gone. Off-B'way: Colored People's Time, Antigone, Black Girl, Henry IV Part 1. Regional: Beef No Chicken.
PICTURES: F/X (debut, 1986), Kindergarten Cop, Boyz N the Hood, City of Hope, Critters 4, Innocent Blood, Malcolm X, Passion Fish, What's Love Got to Do With It (Acad. Award nom.; Golden Globe Award), Strange Days, Waiting to Exhale, Vampire in Brooklyn.
TELEVISION: Movies: Line of Fire: The Morris Dees Story, The Jacksons: An American Dream. Guest: Cosby Show, 227, thirtysomething, Tour of Duty, Equal Justice.

BATEMAN, JASON
Actor. b. Rye, NY, Jan. 14, 1969. Brother of actress Justine Bateman. Son of prod.-theatrical mgr. Kent Bateman. Started career in commercials until cast in Little House on the Prairie at 12 (1981).
PICTURES: Teen Wolf Too, Necessary Roughness, Breaking the Rules.
TELEVISION: Series: Little House on the Prairie, Silver Spoons, It's Your Move, Valerie (Valerie's Family, The Hogan Family), Simon, Chicago Sons. Movies: The Fantastic World of D.C. Collins, The Thanksgiving Promise, Can You Feel Me Dancing, The Bates Motel, Moving Target, A Taste for Killing, Confessions: Two Faces of Evil, This Can't Be Love, Hart to Hart: Secrets of the Hart. Mini-Series: Robert Kennedy and His Times. Specials: Just a Little More Love, Candid Camera: Eat! Eat! Eat!

BATEMAN, JUSTINE
Actress, b. Rye, NY, Feb. 19, 1966. Brother is actor Jason Bateman. Father, prod.-theatrical mgr. Kent Bateman.

THEATER: Lulu, Self-Storage, The Crucible, Love Letters, Carnal Knowledge, Speed-the-Plow.
PICTURES: Satisfaction, The Closer, Primary Motive, Deadbolt, The Night We Never Met, God's Lonely Man, Kiss & Tell.
TELEVISION: *Series*: Family Ties, Men Behaving Badly. *Guest*: Tales from the Dark Side, One to Grow On, It's Your Move, Glitter. *Movies*: Right to Kill?, Family Ties Vacation, Can You Feel Me Dancing?, The Fatal Image, In the Eyes of a Stranger, The Hunter, Terror in the Night, Another Woman, A Bucket of Blood. *Specials*: First the Egg, Whatta Year... 1986, Fame Fortune and Romance, Candid Camera: Eat! Eat! Eat!, Merry Christmas Baby, A Century of Women.

BATES, ALAN
Actor. b. Allestree, Derbyshire, England, Feb. 17, 1934. e. Herbert Strutt Grammar Sch.; after natl. service with the RAF studied at RADA with Albert Finney, Peter O'Toole and Tom Courtenay. Professional stage debut 1955 with the Midland Theatre Co. in You and Your Wife.
THEATER: *London stage*: The Mulberry Tree, Look Back in Anger (also NY, Moscow), Long Day's Journey Into Night, Poor Richard, Richard III, In Celebration, Hamlet, Butley (also NY; Tony Award, 1973), The Taming of the Shrew, Life Class, Otherwise Engaged, The Seagull, Stage Struck, A Patriot for Me, One for the Road, Victoria Station, Dance of Death, Yonadab, Melon, Much Ado About Nothing, Ivanov, Stages, The Showman, Simply Disconnected, Fortune's Fool.
PICTURES: The Entertainer (debut, 1960), Whistle Down the Wind, A Kind of Loving, The Caretaker (The Guest), The Running Man, Nothing But the Best, Zorba the Greek, Georgy Girl, King of Hearts, Far From the Madding Crowd, The Fixer (Acad. Award nom.), Women in Love, Three Sisters, The Go-Between, A Day in the Death of Joe Egg, Impossible Object (Story of a Love Story), Butley, In Celebration, Royal Flash, An Unmarried Woman, The Shout, The Rose, Nijinsky, Quartet, The Return of the Soldier, Britannia Hospital, The Wicked Lady, Duet for One, A Prayer for the Dying, We Think the World of You, Mr. Frost, Hamlet, Force Majeure, Dr. M (Club Extinction), Shuttlecock, Secret Friends, Silent Tongue, Losing Track, The Grotesque.
TELEVISION: The Thug, A Memory of Two Mondays, The Jukebox, The Square Ring, The Wind and the Rain, Look Back in Anger, Three on a Gasring, Duel for Love, A Hero for Our Time, Plaintiff & Defendant, Two Sundays, The Collection, The Mayor of Casterbridge, The Trespasser, Very Like a Whale, Voyage Round My Father, An Englishman Abroad, Separate Tables, Dr. Fischer of Geneva, One for the Road, Pack of Lies, Oliver's Travels, Hard Times.

BATES, KATHY
Actress. b. Memphis, TN, June 28, 1948. e. S. Methodist U. Regional theatre incl. D.C. and Actor's Theatre in Louisville.
THEATER: Vanities (Off-B'way debut, 1976), Semmelweiss, Crimes of the Heart, The Art of Dining, Goodbye Fidel (B'way debut, 1980), Chocolate Cake and Final Placement, Fifth of July, Come Back to the 5 & Dime Jimmy Dean Jimmy Dean, 'night Mother (Tony nom., Outer Critics Circle Award), Two Masters: The Rain of Terror, Curse of the Starving Class, Frankie and Johnny in the Clair de Lune (Obie, L.A. Drama Critics Award), The Road to Mecca.
PICTURES: Taking Off (debut, 1971), Straight Time, Come Back to the 5 & Dime Jimmy Dean Jimmy Dean, Two of a Kind, Summer Heat, My Best Friend is a Vampire, Arthur 2 on the Rocks, Signs of Life, High Stakes (Melanie Rose), Men Don't Leave, Dick Tracy, White Palace, Misery (Academy Award, Golden Globe & Chicago Film Critics Awards, 1990), At Play in the Fields of the Lord, Fried Green Tomatoes, Shadows and Fog, The Road to Mecca, Prelude to a Kiss, Used People, A Home of Our Own, North, Dolores Claiborne, Angus, Diabolique, The War at Home.
TELEVISION: *Movies*: Johnny Bull, No Place Like Home, Roe vs. Wade, Hostages, Curse of the Starving Class, The Late Shift. *Mini-Series*: Murder Ordained, The Stand. *Guest*: The Love Boat, St. Elsewhere, Cagney and Lacey, L.A. Law, China Beach. *Special*: Talking With (also dir.).

BATTY, PETER
Producer, Director, Writer. b. Sunderland, England, June 18, 1931. e. Bede Grammar Sch. and Queen's Coll., Oxford. Feature-writer both sides Atlantic 1954-58. Joined BBC TV 1958 dir. short films. Edited Tonight programme 1963-4. Exec. prod. ATV 1964-68. Awarded Grand Prix for doc. at 1965 Venice and Leipzig festivals. Official entries 1970 and 1971 San Francisco and Melbourne festivals. Nominated Intl. Emmy, 1986. Own company since 1968 prod. TV specials, series, commercials.
TELEVISION: The Quiet Revolution, The Big Freeze, The Katanga Affair, Sons of the Navvy Man, The Fall and Rise of the House of Krupp, The Road to Suez, The Suez Affair, Battle for the Desert, Vietnam Fly-In, The Plutocrats, The Aristocrats, Battle for Cassino, Battle for the Bulge, Birth of the Bomb, Search for the Super, Operation Barbarossa, Farouk: Last of the Pharaohs, Superspy, Spy Extraordinary, Sunderland's Pride and Passion, A Rothschild and His Red Gold, The World of Television, The Story of Wine, The Rise and Rise of Laura Ashley, The Gospel According to Saint Michael, Battle for Warsaw, Battle for Dien Bien Phu, Nuclear Nightmares. A Turn Up in A Million, Il Poverello, Swindle!, The Algerian War, Fonteyn and Nureyev: The Perfect Partnership, The Divided Union, A Time for Remembrance, Swastika Over British Soil. Contributed 6 episodes to Emmy-winning World at War series.

BAUER, STEVEN
Actor. b. Havana, Cuba, Dec. 2, 1956. r.n. Steve Echevarria. Moved with family to Miami at age 3. e. Miami Dade Jr. Coll. where studied acting. Breakthrough came with selection for role in Que Pasa U.S.A.? for Public TV. Signed by Columbia TV and moved to California.
PICTURES: Scarface, Thief of Hearts, Running Scared, The Beast, Wildfire, Gleaming the Cube, Bloody Murder!, Raising Cain, Woman of Desire, Improper Conduct, Stranger by Night, Wild Side.
TELEVISION: *Series*: Wiseguy. *Guest*: The Rockford Files, From Here to Eternity, One Day at a Time, Hill Street Blues. *Movies*: Doctors' Private Lives, She's in the Army Now, Nichols and Dymes, An Innocent Love, Sword of Gideon, Sweet Poison, False Arrest, Drive Like Lightning. *Mini-Series*: Drug Wars: The Camarena Story.

BAUM, MARTIN
Executive. b. New York, NY, March 2, 1924. Pres., ABC Pictures; previously partner Baum & Newborn Theatrical Agency; head of West Coast office General Artists Corp., head of m.p. dept., Ashley Famous Agency; pres., Martin Baum Agency; sr. exec. v.p. Creative Management Assoc.; pres., Optimus Productions, Inc., producing Bring Me the Head of Alfredo Garcia, The Wilby Conspiracy, The Killer Elite. Partner with Michael Ovitz, Ron Meyer, Rowland Perkins, Bill Haber in Creative Artists Agency, Inc.

BAUMGARTEN, CRAIG
Executive. b. Aug. 27, 1949. Partner in independent prod. co., New America Cinema. Joined Paramount. Pictures as prod. exec.; named v.p., prod. In 1980 went to Keith Barish Prods., of which was pres. three years. In 1983 appt. exec. v.p. & exec. asst. to the pres. & CEO, Columbia Pictures. Resigned 1985; joined Lorimar Motion Pictures as pres. Joined 20th Century Fox m.p. div. as exec. v.p. of production Oct. 1987. Resigned. 1989 formed Adelson/Baumgarten Prods. with Gary Adelson. Co-Producer: Hard to Kill, Hook, Universal Soldier, Nowhere to Run, Blank Check, It Could Happen to You, Jade, The Shooter, Esmeralda. 1994, formed Baumgarten/Prophet Entertainment Inc.

BAXTER, BILLY
Executive. b. New York, NY, Feb. 8, 1926. e. Holy Cross, 1948. Mgr., Ambassador Brokerage Group, Albany, 1957-58; Bill Doll & Co., 1959-63; organ., prod., radio show, Earl Wilson Celebrity Column, 1962; prod. Broadway show, Mandingo, with Franchot Tone, 1962; dir. of promotion, spec. events, Rumrill Ad Agency, 1963-64; dir. of promotion, exploitation, Landau Co., 1964-65; dir. of adv. and pub., Rizzoli Co., 1965-66. Consultant on special events to the Philip Morris Corp. and American Express.
PICTURES: *Coprod.*: Love and Anarchy, Daughters-Daughters, Outrageous, One Man, Dawn of the Dead. *Prod.*: Diary of the Cannes Film Festival with Rex Reed, 1980. *Prod.-dir.* documentaries: Artists of the Old West, Remington & Russell, Buffalo Bill Cody (1988).

BAXTER, KEITH
Actor. b. Monmouthshire, Wales, April 29, 1933. e. Wales, entered Royal Acad. of Dramatic Art in 1951. 1952-55 in national service; returned to RADA. Did years of repertory work in Dublin, Croydon, Chichester, London's West End, and New York. Biggest stage hit in Sleuth, both London and N.Y. Later in Corpse (London, NY).
PICTURES: The Barretts of Wimpole Street, Peeping Tom, Chimes at Midnight, With Love in Mind, Ash Wednesday, Berlin Blues.
TELEVISION: For Tea on Sunday, Hold My Hand Soldier, Saint Joan.

BAXTER, MEREDITH
Actress. b. Los Angeles, CA, June 21, 1947. e. Interlochen Arts Academy. On stage in Guys and Dolls, Butterflies Are Free, Vanities, Country Wife, Talley's Folly, Love Letters, Diaries of Adam & Eve.
PICTURES: Ben, Stand Up and Be Counted, Bittersweet Love, All the President's Men, Jezebel's Kiss.
TELEVISION: *Series*: The Interns, Bridget Loves Bernie, Family, Family Ties, The Faculty. Movies: Cat Creature, The Stranger Who Looks Like Me, Target Risk, The Imposter, The Night That Panicked America, Little Women, The Family Man, Beulah Land, Two Lives of Carol Letner, Take Your Best Shot, The Rape of Richard Beck, Kate's Secret, The Long Journey Home (also co-exec. prod.), Winnie: My Life in the Institution, She Knows Too

Much, The Kissing Place, Burning Bridges, Bump in the Night, A Mother's Justice, A Woman Scorned: The Betty Broderick Story, Her Final Fury: Betty Broderick—The Last Chapter, Darkness Before Dawn (also co-exec. prod.), For the Love of Aaron, One More Mountain, My Breast (also co-exec. prod.), Betrayed: A Story of Three Women (also co-exec. prod.). Specials: The Diaries of Adam and Eve, Vanities, Other Mothers (Afterschool Special).

BAXTER, STANLEY
Actor. b. Glasgow, Scotland, May, 1926. e. Hillhead H.S., Glasgow. Principal comedian in Howard & Wyndham pantomimes. Summer revues. Televised regularly on BBC-TV, and also frequent broadcaster. M.P. debut 1955 in Geordie.
THEATER: The Amorous Prawn, On the Brighter Side, Chase Me Comrade (Australia), Cinderella, What the Butler Saw, Phil The Fluter, Mother Goose Pantomime seasons 1970-74. Jack & The Beanstalk, Cinderella, Mother Goose, Aladdin, Cinderella.
PICTURES: Geordie (debut, 1955), Very Important Person, Crooks Anonymous, The Fast Lady, Father Came Too, Joey Boy.
TELEVISION: Baxter on (series) 1964; The Confidence Course, The World of Stanley Baxter, Stanley Baxter Show, Time for Baxter, The Stanley Baxter Big Picture Show, The Stanley Baxter Moving Picture Show, Part III, Stanley Baxter's Christmas Box, Bing Crosby's Merrie Olde Christmas, Stanley Baxter's Greatest Hits, Baxter on Television, Stanley Baxter Series, The Stanley Baxter Hour, Children's Royal, Stanley Baxter's Christmas Hamper, Stanley Baxter's Picture Annual, 1986; Mr. Majeika (series, 1988-89), Fitby, Stanley Baxter Is Back.

BEACHAM, STEPHANIE
Actress. b. Casablanca, Morocco, Feb. 28, 1947. e. RADA. On London stage in The Basement, On Approval, London Cuckolds, etc.
PICTURES: The Games, Tam Lin, The Nightcomers, Dracula A.D., And Now the Screaming Stars, House of Whipcord, Schizo, The Confessional, Horror Planet (Inseminoid), The Wolves of Willoughby Chase, Troop Beverly Hills.
TELEVISION: Series: Tenko (PBS), The Colbys, Dynasty, Sister Kate, seaQuest DSV. Movies/Specials: Napoleon & Josephine: A Love Story, Lucky/Chances, Secrets, To Be the Best, Foreign Affairs, Marked Personal, Jane Eyre, A Sentimental Education.

BEAL, JOHN
Actor, r.n. James Alexander Bliedung. b. Joplin, MO, Aug. 13, 1909. e. Wharton Sch., U. of PA. Author-Illustrator: Actor Drawing. Served in USAAF, WWII.
THEATER: B'way: Another Language, She Loves Me Not, Voice of the Turtle, Teahouse of the August Moon, The Crucible, A Little Hotel on the Side, The Master Builder, The Seagull, Three Men on a Horse. Off B'way: Long Day's Journey into Night, Our Town.
PICTURES: Another Language (debut, 1933), Hat Coat and Glove, The Little Minister, Les Miserables, Laddie, Break of Hearts, M'Liss, We Who Are About to Die, The Man Who Found Himself, Border Cafe, Danger Patrol, Double Wedding, Madame X, Beg Borrow or Steal, Port of Seven Seas, I Am the Law, The Arkansas Traveler, The Cat and the Canary, The Great Commandment, Ellery Queen and the Perfect Crime, Doctors Don't Tell, Atlantic Convoy, One Thrilling Night, Edge of Darkness, Let's Have Fun, Key Witness, So Dear to My Heart, Alimony, Song of Surrender, Chicago Deadline, Messenger of Peace, My Six Convicts, Remains to Be Seen, The Country Parson, The Vampire, That Night, The Sound and the Fury, Ten Who Dared, The House That Cried Murder, Amityville 3-D, The Firm.
TELEVISION: Movies: The Legend of Lizzie Borden, Eleanor and Franklin: The White House Years, Jennifer: A Woman's Story. Specials: The Necklace, Hit the Deck, The Easter Angel.

BEALS, JENNIFER
Actress. b. Chicago, IL, Dec. 19, 1963. Started as fashion model before making film debut in small role in My Bodyguard, 1980.
PICTURES: My Bodyguard, Flashdance, The Bride, Split Decisions, Vampire's Kiss, Layover, Rider in the Dark, The Lizard's Tale, Sons, Jackal's Run, A Reasonable Doubt, Dr. M, Blood and Concrete, In the Soup, Day of Atonement, Caro Diario, Mrs. Parker and the Vicious Circle, Arabian Knight (voice), Devil in a Blue Dress, Four Rooms.
TELEVISION: Series: 2000 Malibu Road. Specials: The Picture of Dorian Grey, Cinderella (Faerie Tale Theatre). Movies: Terror Strikes the Class Reunion, Indecency, Night Owl.

BEAN, ORSON
Actor. b. Burlington, VT, July 22, 1928. r.n. Dallas Burrows. Performed in nightclubs as comic and on Broadway (Never Too Late, Will Success Spoil Rock Hunter?, Subways Are for Sleeping, Roar of the Grease Paint, the Smell of the Crowd, Ilya Darling.) Author: Me and the Orgone. Founder, administrator, dir. 15th St. School, NY.
PICTURES: How to Be Very Very Popular (debut, 1955), Anatomy of a Murder, Lola, Forty Deuce, Innerspace, Instant Karma.

TELEVISION: Series: The Blue Angel (host), I've Got a Secret (panelist), Keep Talking, To Tell the Truth (panelist), Mary Hartman Mary Hartman, One Life to Live, Dr. Quinn: Medicine Woman. Special: Arsenic and Old Lace.

BEAN, SEAN
Actor. b. Sheffield, Yorkshire, England, Apr. 17, 1958.
THEATER: Romeo and Juliet, Fair Maid of the West, Midsummer Night's Dream, Who Knew Mackenzie and Gone, Deathwatch, Last Days of Mankind.
PICTURES: Winter Flight, Caravaggio, Stormy Monday, War Requiem, The Field, Patriot Games. Shopping, Black Beauty, Goldeneye, When Saturday Comes.
TELEVISION: Troubles, Small Zones, 15 Street, My Kingdom for a Horse, Winter Flight, Samson & Delilah, The True Bride, Prince, Tell Me That You Love Me, Clarissa, Scarlett, Jacob.

BEART, EMMANUELLE
Actress. b. Gassin, France, Aug. 14, 1965. Moved to Montreal at age 15. Returned to France and enrolled in drama school.
THEATER: La Repetition ou l'Amour Puni, La Double Inconstance.
PICTURES: Premiers Desirs, L'Enfant Trouve, L'Amour en Douce, Manon of the Spring, Date With an Angel, A Gauche en Sortant de L'Ascenseur, Les Enfants du Desordre, Capitaine Fracasse, La Belle Noiseuse, J'Embrasse Pas, Un Coeur en Hiver (A Heart in Winter), Ruptures, Divertimento, L'Enfer (Hell), Une Femme Francaise, Nelly & Mr. Arnaud, Mission Impossible.
TELEVISION: Zacharius, Raison Perdue.

BEATTY, NED
Actor. b. Lexington, KY, July 6, 1937. Worked at Barter Theatre in Virginia appearing in over 70 plays 1957-66 and with Arena Stage, Washington D.C. 1963-71. Broadway debut: The Great White Hope.
PICTURES: Deliverance (debut, 1972), The Life and Times of Judge Roy Bean, The Thief Who Came to Dinner, The Last American Hero, White Lightning, Nashville, W.W. and the Dixie Dance Kings, All the President's Men, The Big Bus, Network, Mikey and Nicky, Silver Streak, Exorcist II: The Heretic, Gray Lady Down, The Great Georgia Bank Hoax, Superman, Alambrista!, Promises in the Dark, 1941, Wise Blood, American Success Company, Hopscotch, The Incredible Shrinking Woman, Superman II, The Toy, Touched, Stroker Ace, Back to School, The Big Easy, The Fourth Protocol, The Trouble With Spies, Switching Channels, Rolling Vengeance, The Unholy, Midnight Crossing, After the Rain, Purple People Eater, Physical Evidence, Time Trackers, Big Bad John, Chattahoochee, A Cry in the Wild, Repossessed, Blind Vision, Going Under, Hear My Song, Prelude to a Kiss, Ed and His Dead Mother, Rudy, Black Water, Radioland Murders, Just Cause.
TELEVISION: Series: Szysznyk, The Boys, Homicide: Life on the Street. Special: Our Town (1977). Movies: Footsteps, Marcus-Nelson Murders, Dying Room Only, The Execution of Private Slovik, Attack on Terror: The FBI vs. the Ku Klux Klan, The Deadly Tower, Tail Gunner Joe, Lucan, A Question of Love, Friendly Fire, Guyana Tragedy: The Story of Jim Jones, All God's Children, The Violation of Sarah McDavid, Splendor in the Grass, Pray TV, A Woman Called Golda, Kentucky Woman, Hostage Flight, Go Toward the Light, Spy, Last Train Home, Back to Hannibal, The Tragedy of Flight 103: The Inside Story, Trial: The Price of Passion, T Bone N Weasel. Guest: Murder She Wrote, M*A*S*H, Rockford Files, Alfred Hitchcock, B.L. Stryker, Roseanne. Mini-Series: Celebrity, The Last Days of Pompeii, Robert Kennedy and His Times.

BEATTY, WARREN
Actor., Producer, Director, Writer. r.n. Henry Warren Beaty. b. Richmond, VA, March 30, 1937. Sister is actress Shirley MacLaine. m. actress Annette Bening. e. Northwestern U. Studied with Stella Adler. Small roles on television; on stage in Compulsion (winter stock, North Jersey Playhouse.) Broadway debut: A Loss of Roses (Theatre World Award).
PICTURES: Splendor in the Grass (debut, 1961), The Roman Spring of Mrs. Stone, All Fall Down, Lilith, Mickey One, Promise Her Anything, Kaleidoscope, Bonnie and Clyde (also prod.), The Only Game in Town, McCabe and Mrs. Miller, $ (Dollars), The Parallax View, Shampoo (also prod., co-s.p.), The Fortune, Heaven Can Wait (also prod., co-dir., co-s.p.), Reds (also prod., dir., co-s.p.; Academy Award for Best Director 1981), Ishtar (also prod.), Dick Tracy (also prod., dir.), Bugsy (also co-prod.), Love Affair (also prod, co-s.p.).
TELEVISION: Series: The Many Loves of Dobie Gillis (1959-60). Guest: Kraft Television Theatre, Studio One, Suspicion, Alcoa Presents, One Step Beyond, Wagon Train.

BECK, ALEXANDER J.
Executive. b. Ung. Brod, Czechoslovakia, Nov. 5, 1926. e. Charles U., Prague, NYU. Owns 500 features and westerns for foreign distribution and library of 1400 shorts. Importer and exporter; Pres., chairman of bd. Alexander Beck Films, 1955; formed Albex Films and A.B. Enterprises, 1959; formed & pres. Beckman Film Corp., 1960; formed Alexander Beck

Productions, 1964. In 1969 formed Screencom Int'l Corp., 1986, formed Beck Int'l Corp., 1987; formed Challenger Pictures Corp., 1988.

BECK, JACKSON
Actor-announcer-narrator. b. New York, NY. TV and radio commercials, children's records, comm. industrial films; Narrator.

BECK, MICHAEL
Actor. b. Memphis, TN, Feb. 4, 1949. e. Millsaps Coll. on football scholarship (quarterback). Became active in college theatre. In 1971 attended Central Sch. of Speech and Drama, London; studied 3 years, following which toured England with repertory companies for 2 years. Returned to U.S.; cast as lead in independent film, Madman (shot in Israel in 1977).
PICTURES: Madman, The Warriors, Xanadu, Megaforce, War Lords of the 21st Century, The Golden Seal, Triumphs of a Man Called Horse.
TELEVISION: Mini-Series: Holocaust, Celebrity. Movies: Mayflower: The Pilgrim's Adventure, Alcatraz: The Whole Shocking Story, Fly Away Home, The Last Ninja, Rearview Mirror, Chiller, Blackout, Only One Survived, The Reckoning, Houston: Legend of Texas, Deadly Game, Deadly Aim, Stranger at My Door, Fade to Black. Series: Houston Knights.

BECKER, HAROLD
Director. Dir. documentaries, Eugene Atget, Interview with Bruce Gordon, Blind Gary Davis, Signet, Ivanhoe Donaldson.
PICTURES: The Ragman's Daughter (debut, 1972), The Onion Field, The Black Marble, Taps, Vision Quest, The Boost, Sea of Love, Malice (also co-prod.), City Hall (also co-prod.).

BEDELIA, BONNIE
Actress. b. New York, NY, March 25, 1946. e. Hunter Coll.
THEATER: Enter Laughing, The Playroom, My Sweet Charlie (Theatre World Award).
PICTURES: The Gypsy Moths (debut, 1969), They Shoot Horses Don't They?, Lovers and Other Strangers, The Strange Vengeance of Rosalie, The Big Fix, Heart Like a Wheel, Death of an Angel, Violets Are Blue, The Boy Who Could Fly, The Stranger, Die Hard, The Prince of Pennsylvania, Fat Man and Little Boy, Die Hard 2, Presumed Innocent, Needful Things.
TELEVISION: Series: Love of Life (1961-7), The New Land. Movies: Then Came Bronson, Sandcastles, A Time for Love, Hawkins on Murder (Death and the Maiden), Message to My Daughter, Heatwave!, A Question of Love, Walking Through the Fire, Salem's Lot, Tourist, Fighting Back, Million Dollar Infield, Memorial Day, Alex: The Life of a Child, The Lady from Yesterday, Somebody Has to Shoot the Picture, Switched at Birth, A Mother's Right: The Elizabeth Morgan Story, The Fire Next Time, Judicial Consent, Legacy of Sin: The William Coit Story. Special: The Gift. Guest: Fallen Angels (The Quiet Room).

BEGLEY, ED, JR.
Actor. b. Los Angeles, CA, Sept. 16, 1949. Son of late actor Ed Begley. Debut in a guest appearance on My Three Sons at 17.
THEATER: NY: The Cryptogram.
PICTURES: The Computer Wore Tennis Shoes (debut, 1970), Now You See Him Now You Don't, Showdown, Superdad, Cockfighter, Stay Hungry, Citizens Band (Handle With Care), Blue Collar, The One and Only, Goin' South, Hardcore, Battlestar Gallactica, The In-Laws, The Concorde: Airport '79, Private Lessons, Cat People, Eating Raoul, Get Crazy, This Is Spinal Tap, Streets of Fire, Protocol, Transylvania 6-5000, Amazon Women on the Moon, The Accidental Tourist, Scenes From the Class Struggle in Beverly Hills, She-Devil, Meet the Applegates, Dark Horse, Greedy, Even Cowgirls Get the Blues, Renaissance Man, The Pagemaster, Batman Forever.
TELEVISION: Series: Roll Out, St. Elsewhere (1982-88), Parenthood, Winnetka Road. Guest: Room 222, Love American Style, Happy Days, Columbo, M*A*S*H, Barnaby Jones, Doris Day Show, Mary Hartman Mary Hartman, Faerie Tale Theatre. Movies: Family Flight, Amateur Night at the Dixie Bar and Grill, Elvis, Hot Rod, A Shining Season, Rascals and Robbers - The Secret Adventures of Tom Sawyer and Huck Finn, Tales of the Apple Dumpling Gang, Voyagers, Not Just Another Affair, Still the Beaver, An Uncommon Love, Insight/The Clearing House, Roman Holiday, Spies Lies & Naked Thighs, Not a Penny More Not a Penny Less, In the Best Inerest of the Child, The Big One: The Great Los Angeles Earthquake, Chance of a Lifetime, The Story Lady, In the Line of Duty: Siege at Marion, Exclusive, Running Mates. Cooperstown, World War II: When Lions Roared, Columbo: Undercover, Incident at Deception Ridge, The Shaggy Dog. Specials: Mastergate, Partners.

BELAFONTE, HARRY
Actor, Singer, Producer. b. New York, NY, March 1, 1927. Trained for stage at the Actors Studio, New Sch. for Social Research and American Negro Theatre. Professional debut, Royal Roost nightclub, N.Y., Village Vanguard, 1950. Broadway debut: John Murray Anderson's Almanac, 1953. Recording, concert artist. Emmy Award for Tonight With Harry Belafonte 1961.

THEATER: Juno and the Paycock, John Murray Anderson's Almanac. (Tony Award, 1953), Three for Tonight, A Night With Belafonte, To Be Young Gifted and Black (prod.), Asinamali (co-prod.).
PICTURES: Bright Road (debut, 1953), Carmen Jones, Island in the Sun, Odds Against Tomorrow, The World the Flesh and the Devil, The Angel Levine, Buck and the Preacher, Uptown Saturday Night (also prod.), Beat Street (prod. only), The Player, Ready to Wear (Pret-a-Porter), White Man's Burden, Kansas City.
TELEVISION: Series: Sugar Hill Times. Movie: Grambling's White Tiger. Many variety specials.

BELAFONTE, SHARI
Actress. b. New York, NY, Sept. 22, 1954. Daughter of actor-singer Harry Belafonte. e. Carnegie-Mellon U., BFA, 1976. Worked as publicist's asst. at Hanna Barbera Prods. before becoming successful model (appearing on more than 200 magazine covers and in numerous TV commercials).
PICTURES: If You Could See What I Hear, Time Walker, Murder One Murder Two, The Player.
TELEVISION: Series: Hotel. Pilot: Velvet. Guest: Hart to Hart, Code Red, Trapper John M.D., Different Strokes, The Love Boat, Matt Houston. Movies: The Night the City Screamed, The Midnight Hour, Kate's Secret, Perry Mason: The Case of the All-Star Assassin, French Silk. Host: Big Hex of Little Lulu, AM Los Angeles, Living the Dream: a Tribute to Dr. Martin Luther King, Jr.

BELFER, HAL B.
Executive Producer, Director, Choreographer. b. Los Angeles, CA, Feb. 16. e. USC; U. of CA (writing). Head of choreography depts. at both 20th Century-Fox and Universal Studios. Dir. of entertainment, in Las Vegas, Riviera and Flamingo Hotels. Prod., musical shows for Mexico City, Aruba, Puerto Rico, Montreal, Las Vegas. Dir., TV commercials and industrials. H.R. Pufnstuf TV series. Producer-director-choreographer: Premore, Inc. Develop TV specials and sitcom, tape and film. Exec. prod., Once Upon a Tour and Dora's World, Rose on Broadway, Secret Sleuth, Inn by the Side of the Road, Imagine That! Special staging Tony The Pony Series and prod., segment of What a Way to Run a Railroad; TV specials. Talent development programs, Universal Studios, 20th Century-Fox. Personal management and show packager; 1982, exec. prod., Enchanted Inn (TV Special), Cameo Music Hall I, Stage mgr.: Promises, Promises, A Chorus Line (Sahara Hotel, Las Vegas). Created Hal Belfer Associates Talent and Production Consultant.

BEL GEDDES, BARBARA
Actress. r.n. Barbara Geddes Lewis. b. New York, NY, Oct 31, 1922. Father was Norman Bel Geddes, scenic designer. B'way debut in Out of the Frying Pan; toured USO camps in Junior Miss, 1941; voted Star of Tomorrow, 1949. Author-illustrator children's books: I Like to Be Me (1963), So Do I (1972). Also designer of greeting cards for George Caspari Co.
THEATER: Out of the Frying Pan, Deep Are the Roots, Burning Bright, The Moon Is Blue, Living Room, Cat on a Hot Tin Roof, The Sleeping Prince, Silent Night Holy Night, Mary Mary, Everything in the Garden, Finishing Touches.
PICTURES: The Long Night (debut, 1947), I Remember Mama (Acad Award nom.), Blood on the Moon, Caught, Panic in the Streets, Fourteen Hours, Vertigo, The Five Pennies, Five Branded Women, By Love Possessed, Summertree, The Todd Killings.
TELEVISION: Live TV in 1950s: Robert Montgomery Presents (The Philadelphia Story), Schlitz Playhouse of the Stars; several Alfred Hitchcock Presents episodes (incl. Lamb to the Slaughter), Our Town. Series: Dallas (Emmy Award, 1980).

BELL, TOM
Actor. b. Liverpool, England, 1932. Early career in repertory and on West End stage. First TV appearance in Promenade.
PICTURES: The Concrete Jungle (The Criminal; debut, 1960), Echo of Barbara, Payroll, The Kitchen, H.M.S. Defiant (Damn the Defiant!), A Prize of Arms, The L-Shaped Room, Ballad in Blue (Blues for Lovers), He Who Rides a Tiger, Sands of Beersheba, In Enemy Country, The Long Day's Dying, Lock Up Your Daughters, All the Right Noises, The Violent Enemy, Quest for Love, Straight on Till Morning, Royal Flash, The Sailor's Return, Stronger Than the Sun, The Innocent, Wish You Were Here, Resurrected, The Magic Toy Shop, The Krays, Let Him Have It, Feast of July.
TELEVISION: No Trams to Lime Street, Love on the Dole, A Night Out, The Seekers, Long Distance Blue, Summer Lightning, Hard Travelling, White Knight, The Virginian, The Rainbow, Prime Suspect, The Cinder Path.

BELLAMY, EARL
Producer, Director. b. Minneapolis, MN, March 11, 1917. e. Los Angeles City Coll. President, The Bellamy Productions Co.
PICTURES: Seminole Uprising (debut, 1955), Blackjack Ketchum: Desperado, Toughest Gun in Tombstone, Stagecoach to Dancers' Rock (also prod.), Fluffy, Gunpoint, Munster Go Home!, Incident at Phantom Hill, Three Guns for Texas,

Backtack, Sidecar Racers, Seven Alone, Part 2: Walking Tall, Against a Crooked Sky, Sidewinder 1, Speedtrap, Magnum Thrust.
TELEVISION: Bachelor Father, Wells Fargo, Lone Ranger, Alcoa Premiere, Arrest and Trial, The Virginian, The Crusaders, Schlitz Playhouse, Rawhide, The Donna Reed Show, Andy Griffith Show, Wagon Train, Laramie, Laredo, I Spy, Mod Squad, Medical Center.

BELLFORT, JOSEPH
b. New York, NY, Sept. 20, 1912. e. NYU, Brooklyn Law Sch. Joined RKO Service Corp., Feb., 1930; trans. to RKO Radio Pictures, legal dept., 1942; joined RKO Fgn. dept., 1944; handled Far Eastern division, 1946; then asst. to European gen. mgr.; gen. European mgr., 1949-1958; gen. sales mgr. National Screen Service, 1959; home office supv., Europe & Near East, 20th Century-Fox, 1963; home office intl. mgr., 20th Century-Fox, 1966; asst. v.p. & foreign mgr. 20th Cent.-Fox, 1967; v.p. 20th Century-Fox, Intl. Corp. & Inter-America, Inc. 1968; named sr. v.p., 1975. Resigned from Fox, 1977 to become v.p., Motion Picture Export Assn. of America in New York. Retired 1983.

BELLOCCHIO, MARCO
Director, Writer. b. Piacenza, Italy, Nov. 9, 1939. e. Academy of Cinematografia, Rome (studying acting, then film directing); Slade School of Fine Arts, London 1959-63.
PICTURES: Fist in His Pocket (debut, 1965), China Is Near, Amore e Rabbia (segment: Discutiamo Discutiamo), Nel Nome del Padre (In the Name of the Father), Slap the Monster on the Front Page (also co-s.p.), Madmen to Be Released, Triumphal March, Il Gabbiano (The Seagull), The Film Machine, Leap Into the Void, The Eyes and the Mouth, Henry IV, Devil in the Flesh, The Sabba's Vision, The Conviction, The Butterfly's Dream.

BELMONDO, JEAN-PAUL
Actor. b. Neuilly-sur-Seine, France, April 9, 1933. e. private drama school of Raymond Girard, and the Conservatoire d'Art Dramatique. Formed a theater group with Annie Girardot and Guy Bedos.
THEATER: Jean Marais' production of Caesar and Cleopatra, Treasure Party, Oscar, Kean, Cyrano de Bergerac, Tailleur pour Dames.
PICTURES: A Pied a Cheval et En Voiture (By Foot Horse and Car), Look Pretty and Shut Up, Drole de Dimanche, Les Tricheurs, Les Copains du Dimanche, Charlotte et Son Jules, A Double Tour, Breathless, Classe Tous Risques, Moderato Cantabile, La Francaise et l'Amour, Les Distractions, Mademoiselle Ange, La Novice, Two Women, La Viaccia, Une Femme Est une Femme, Leon Morin, Pretre, Les Amours Celebres, Un Singe en Hiver, Le Doulos, L'Aine des Ferchaux, La Mer A Boire, Banana Peel, That Man From Rio, Cent Mille Dollars au Soleil, Echappement Libre, La Chasse a l'Homme, Dieu a Choisi Paris, Weekend a Zuydcocte, Par Un Beau Matin d'Ete, Up to His Ears, Is Paris Burning?, Casino Royale, The Thief of Paris, Pierrot le Fou, The Brain, Love Is a Funny Thing, Mississippi Mermaid, Borsalino, A Man I Like, The Burglars, Tender Scoundrel, Inheritor, Stavisky, Fear Over the City, L'Animal, The Professional, Ace of Aces, The Vultures, Happy Easter, Hold Up, Le Solitaire, Itinerary of a Spoiled Child (also prod.), L'Inconnu dans la Maison, Les Miserables, Desire.

BELSON, JERRY
Producer, Director, Writer. With Garry Marshall, writer of The Dick Van Dyke Show, prod. of The Odd Couple. Co-authoring the Broadway play The Roast (1980).
PICTURES: How Sweet It Is (prod., s.p.), The Grasshopper (s.p., prod.), Smile (s.p.), Fun With Dick and Jane (s.p.), Smokey and the Bandit II (s.p.), Student Bodies (exec. prod.), The End (s.p.), Jekyll and Hyde Together Again (dir.), Surrender (dir., s.p.), For Keeps (prod.), Always (co-s.p.).
TELEVISION: Series: The Dick Van Dyke Show, The Odd Couple, The Tracey Ullmann Show (co-creator, co-exec. prod.; Emmy Awards). Special: Billy Crystal: Midnight Train to Moscow (co-writer; Emmy Award).

BELUSHI, JAMES
Actor. b. Chicago, IL, June 15, 1954. e. DuPage Coll., Southern Illinois U. Brother was late actor John Belushi. Began at Chicago's Second City Theatre.
THEATER: Sexual Perversity in Chicago, The Pirates of Penzance, True West, Conversations With My Father, Baal.
PICTURES: Thief (debut, 1981), Trading Places, The Man with One Red Shoe, Salvador, About Last Night, Jumpin' Jack Flash, Little Shop of Horrors, Number One With a Bullet (co-s.p. only), The Principal, Real Men, Red Heat, Who's Harry Crumb? (cameo), K-9, Homer and Eddie, Wedding Band (cameo), Taking Care of Business, Mr. Destiny, The Palermo Connection, Only the Lonely, Masters of Menace (cameo), Curly Sue, Once Upon a Crime, Diary of a Hitman (cameo), Traces of Red, Last Action Hero (cameo), The Pebble and the Penguin (voice), Destiny Turns on the Radio, Separate Lives, Canadian Bacon (cameo), Race the Sun, Jingle All the Way.

TELEVISION: Series: Who's Watching the Kids?, Working Stiffs, Saturday Night Live. Specials: The Joseph Jefferson Awards, The Best Legs in the 8th Grade, Cinemax's Comedy Experiment's Birthday Boy (also prod., writer). Mini-Series: Wild Palms. Movies: Royce, Parallel Lives, Sahara.

BELZER, RICHARD
Actor, Comedian. b. Bridgeport, CT, Aug. 4, 1944.
PICTURES: The Groove Tube (debut, 1974), Fame, Author Author, Night Shift, Scarface, America, Flicks, The Wrong Guys, Freeway, Fletch Lives, The Big Picture, The Bonfire of the Vanities, Off and Running, Mad Dog and Glory, Girl 6, Get on the Bus.
TELEVISION: Series: The Late Show (host), Homicide: Life on the Street. Specials: On Location: Richard Belzer in Concert (also writer), Belzer on Broadway (also writer, exec. prod.). Movies: Not of This Earth, Prince for a Day.

BENBEN, BRIAN
Actor. b. Winchester, VA, June 18. Raised in Marlboro, NY. m. actress Madeleine Stowe. In regional and alternative theatre before making B'way debut in Slab Boys.
TELEVISION: Series: The Gangster Chronicles, Kay O'Brien, Dream On (Cable ACE Award, 1992). Special: Conspiracy: The Trial of the Chicago 8.
PICTURES: Clean and Sober (debut, 1988), Dangerous Obsession (Mortal Sins), I Come in Peace, Radioland Murders.

BENDICK, ROBERT
Indep. documentary prod., dir. b. New York, NY, Feb. 8, 1917. e. NYU, White School Photography. U.S. Air Force, W.W.II. Documentary and still cameraman before joining CBS Television as cameraman and dir., 1940; rejoined CBS Television as dir. special events, 1946; promoted dir. news & special events; acting program dir. 1947; res. out. '51. Collab with Jeanne Bendick on Making the Movies, Electronics for Young People, Television Works Like This, Filming Works Like This, 1971; Prod. Peabody Award-winning U.N. show The U.N. in Action; v.p., Cinerama Prod., co-prod. This Is Cinerama; co-dir., Cinerama Holiday; prod. Dave Garroway Show Today, prod., Wide Wide World 1955-56, NBC prod. dir. C.V. Whitney Pict., June, 1956; Merian C. Cooper Ent., 1957; prod. NBC, 1958. Prod.; Garroway Today Show, Bob Hope 25 Yrs. of Life Show, 1961; Bell Telephone Threshold Science Series, Groucho Marx, Merrily We Roll Along, US Steel Opening New York World's Fair, 1964. Prod. First Look Series 1965 (Ohio St. Award); prod. & dir. American Sportsman, ABC; prod., pilot, Great American Dream Machine (NET) (Emmy Award, 1971 and 1972); 1975, Co-exec. prod., Dick Cavett—Feeling Good. pres. Bendick Assoc. Inc.,; prod. of education audio-visual systems, Bd. of Governors, N.Y. Academy of TV Arts and Sciences. 1976, co-author with Jeanne Bendick, TV Reporting. Consultant, Warner Qube Cable Co.; 1978, produced/directed, Fight for Food (PBS). Program consultant to Times-Mirror Cable Co., L.A. Produced segment ABC 20/20. Member awards committee, National TV Acad. Arts & Science. Co-author with Jeanne Bendick of Eureka It's Television (1993). Inducted into Natl. TV Academy Arts & Science, NY chapter, Silver Circle, 1994.

BENEDICT, DIRK
Actor. r.n. Dirk Niewoehner. b. Helena, MT, March 1, 1945. e. Whitman Coll., Walla Walla, WA. Enrolled in John Fernald Academy of Dramatic Arts, Rochester, MI, after which had season with Seattle Repertory Theatre; also in summer stock at Ann Arbor, MI. Broadway debut, 1970, Abelard and Heloise. Author: Confessions of a Kamikaze Cowboy, And Then We Went Fishing. Film debut, Georgia, Georgia, 1972.
PICTURES: Ssssss, W, Battlestar Galactica, Scavenger Hunt, Ruckus, Underground Aces, Body Slam, Blue Tornado, Shadow Force, Cahoots, Tales From the Crypt Presents Demon Knight, Alaska, The Feminine Touch.
TELEVISION: Guest: Love Boat, Murder She Wrote, Hawaii Five-O. Series: Chopper One, Battlestar Galactica, The A Team, Movies: Journey from Darkness, The Georgia Peaches, Scruples, Trenchcoat in Paradise.

BENEDICT, PAUL
Actor, Director. b. Silver City, NM, Sept. 17, 1938. Acted with the Theatre Company of Boston, Arena Stage, D.C.; Trinity Rep., Providence; Playhouse in the Park, Cincinnati; Center Stage, Baltimore; A.R.T., Cambridge.
THEATER: NY: Little Murders, The White House Murder Case, Bad Habits, It's Only a Play, Richard III, The Play's the Thing. LA: The Unvarnished Truth, It's Only a Play. Director: Frankie & Johnnie in the Clair de Lune, Bad Habits, The Kathy and Mo Show, Beyond Therapy, Geniuses, Any Given Day.
PICTURES: They Might Be Giants (debut, 1971), Taking Off, Up the Sandbox, Jeremiah Johnson, The Front Page, The Goodbye Girl, This Is Spinal Tap, Arthur 2 on the Rocks, Cocktail, The Chair, The Freshman, Sibling Rivalry, The Addams Family.
TELEVISION: Series: Sesame Street (1969-74), The Jeffersons, Mama Malone. Movies: Hustling, Baby Cakes, Attack of the 50 Ft. Woman. Mini-Series: The Blue and the Gray. Guest: Kojak, Maude, All in the Family, Harry-O.

BENING, ANNETTE
Actress. b. Topeka, KS, May 29, 1958. Raised in San Diego. e. San Francisco St. Univ. Acted with San Francisco's American Conservatory Theatre. m. actor Warren Beatty.
THEATER: Coastal Disturbances (Tony Award nom., Theatre World & Clarence Derwent Awards), Spoils of War.
PICTURES: The Great Outdoors (debut, 1988), Valmont, Postcards from the Edge, The Grifters (Natl. Society of Film Critics Award, Acad. Award nom., 1990), Guilty by Suspicion, Regarding Henry, Bugsy, Love Affair, The American President, Richard III, Mars Attacks.
TELEVISION: Guest: Miami Vice, Wiseguy. Pilot: It Had to Be You. Movies: Manhunt for Claude Dallas, Hostage.

BENJAMIN, RICHARD
Actor, Director. b. New York, NY, May 22, 1939. m. actress Paula Prentiss. e. Northwestern U.
THEATER: Central Park productions of The Taming of the Shrew, As You Like It; toured in Tchin Tchin, A Thousand Clowns, Barefoot in the Park, The Odd Couple. Broadway debut in Star Spangled Girl (Theatre World Award, 1966), also in The Little Black Book, The Norman Conquests. Directed London productions of Barefoot in the Park.
PICTURES: Actor: Goodbye Columbus, Catch-22, Diary of a Mad Housewife, The Marriage of a Young Stockbroker, The Steagle, Portnoy's Complaint, The Last of Sheila, Westworld, The Sunshine Boys (Golden Globe Award), House Calls, Love at First Bite, Scavenger Hunt, The Last Married Couple in America, Witches' Brew, How to Beat the High Cost of Living, First Family, Saturday the 14th. Director: My Favorite Year, Racing with the Moon, City Heat, The Money Pit, Little Nikita, My Stepmother Is an Alien, Downtown, Mermaids, Made in America, Milk Money, Mrs. Winterbourne.
TELEVISION: Series: He and She (with Paula Prentiss, 1967), Quark. Special: Arthur Miller's Fame. Movies: No Room to Run (Australia), Packin' It In.

BENNETT, ALAN
Author, Actor. b. Leeds, England, May 9, 1934. e. Oxford U. With Jonathan Miller, Dudley Moore and Peter Cook co-authored and starred in satirical revue Beyond the Fringe in London (1961) and on B'way (special Tony Award, 1963).
THEATER: Forty Years On (actor, author), Getting On, Habeas Corpus (also actor), The Old Country, Enjoy, Kafka's Dick, Single Spies (also dir.), The Madness of George III.
PICTURES: Actor: Pleasure at Her Majesty's, The Secret Policeman's Other Ball, Long Shot, Dream Child (voice), Little Dorrit. Writer: A Private Function, Prick Up Your Ears, The Madness of King George, The Wind in the Willows (voice).
TELEVISION: Famous Gossips, On the Margin (also actor), An Evening With, A Day Out, Sunset Across the Bay, A Little Outing, A Visit from Miss Prothero, Me—I'm Afraid of Virginia Wood, Doris and Doreen, The Old Crowd, Afternoon Off, All Day on the Sands, The Insurance Man, Talking Heads (6 TV monologues), One Fine Day, Our Winnie, A Woman of No Importance, Rolling Home, Marks, An Englishman Abroad, Intensive Care (also actor), 102 Boulevard Haussmann, Poetry in Motion.

BENNETT, BRUCE
Actor. r.n. Herman Brix. b. Tacoma, WA, May 19, 1909. e. U. of Washington.
PICTURES: My Son Is Guilty, Lone Wolf Keeps a Date, Atlantic Convoy, Sabotage, Underground Agent, The More the Merrier, Sahara, Mildred Pierce, The Man I Love, A Stolen Life, Nora Prentiss, Cheyenne, Dark Passage, Treasure of the Sierra Madre, Smart Girls Don't Talk, Task Force, The Second Face, The Great Missouri Raid, Angels in the Outfield, Sudden Fear, Dream Wife, Dragonfly Squadron, Robber's Roost, Big Tipoff, Hidden Guns, Bottom of the Bottle, Strategic Air Command, Danger Signal, Silver River, Younger Brothers, Without Honor, Mystery Street, The Last Outpost, Three Violent People, The Outsider, Deadhead Miles, The Clones.

BENNETT, HARVE
Producer. r.n. Harve Fischman. b. Chicago, IL, Aug. 17, 1930. e. UCLA. Quiz Kids radio show, 5 yrs.; newspaper columnist, drama critic; freelance writer; Assoc. prod., CBS-TV; freelance TV writer; prod. of special events. CBS-TV; dir., Television film commercials; program exec., ABC, vice pres., programs west coast, ABC-TV.
PICTURES: Star Trek II: The Wrath of Khan (exec. prod., co-story), Star Trek IV: The Voyage Home (prod., co-s.p.), Star Trek V: The Final Frontier (prod., co-story).
TELEVISION: Pres., Bennett-Katleman. Productions at Columbia Studios. Series: Mod Squad (prod., writer), The Young Rebels (creator-writer), Six Million Dollar Man (exec. prod.), Bionic Woman (exec. prod.). American Girls (exec. prod.). From Here to Eternity, Salvage 1, Time Trax (exec. prod.). Mini-Series: Rich Man Poor Man. Movies: A Woman Named Golda (exec. prod.; Emmy Award), The Jesse Owens Story (exec. prod.), Crash Landing: The Rescue of Flight 232 (writer).

BENNETT, HYWEL
Actor, Director. b. Garnant, South Wales, Apr. 8, 1944. Early career National Youth Theatre where he played many leading Shakespearean roles followed by extensive work in British theatre. 1971-81: directed numerous stage productions.
PICTURES: The Family Way (debut, 1967), Drop Dead My Love, Twisted Nerve, The Virgin Soldiers, The Buttercup Chain, Loot, Percy, Endless Night, Alice in Wonderland, Murder Elite, War Zone.
TELEVISION: Where The Buffalo Roam, Malice Aforethought, Tinker Tailor Soldier Spy, series, Artemis 81, Myself A Mandarin, Frankie and Johnnie, Check Point Chiswick, Twilight Zone, The Idiot, The Traveller, Death of a Teddy Bear, Three's One, Pennies From Heaven, Shelley (series), The Critic, The Consultant, Absent Friends, The Secret Agent, A Mind to Kill, Virtual Murder, The Other Side of Paradise.

BENSON, HUGH
Producer. Exec. Prod., Screen Gems; exec. prod., MGM Television. On staff Col.-TV, pilots and long form.
PICTURES: Nightmare Honeymoon (prod.), Logan's Run (assoc. prod.), Billy Jack Goes to Washington (prod.).
TELEVISION: Producer: Contract On Cherry St., Child Stealers, Goldie and the Boxer, A Fire in the Sky, Shadow Riders, Confessions of a Lady Cop, The Dream Merchants, Goldie and the Boxer Go to Hollywood, Goliath Awaits, The Blue and the Gray, Hart to Hart, Master of Ballantrae, Anna Karenina, The Other Lover, I Dream of Jeannie 15 Yrs. Later, Miracle of the Heart: A Boy's Town Story, Crazy Like a Fox, In the Heat of the Night (pilot and series), Daughter of the Streets, Back to Hannibal: Tom and Huck Return, Danielle Steele's Fine Things, Danielle Steele's Changes, Shadow of a Stranger, Diana: Her True Story, Danielle Steele's Message From 'Nam, A Season of Hope, Liz: The Elizabeth Taylor Story.

BENSON, ROBBY
Actor, Writer, Director. r.n. Robert Segal. b. Dallas, TX, Jan. 21, 1956. m. actress Karla DeVito. Father is Jerry Segal, novelist and screenwriter, mother is Ann Benson, veteran of Dallas stage and nat'l summer stock and nat'l spokesperson for Merrill Lynch. Appeared in commercials and summer stock at age 5. B'way debut at age 12 in Zelda. Dir. debut 1989, White Hot (a.k.a. Crack in the Mirror). Composed music for Diana Ross, Karla DeVito and soundtrack of film The Breakfast Club.
THEATER: NY: Zelda, The Rothschilds, Dude, The Pirates of Penzance. Regional: Oliver!, Evita, The King and I, King of Hearts, Do Black Patent Leather Shoes Really Reflect Up?
PICTURES: Jory (debut, 1973), Jeremy, Lucky Lady, Ode to Billy Joe, One on One (also co-s.p. with father), The End, Ice Castles, Walk Proud (also co-s.p. & co-composer with father), Die Laughing (also prod., co-s.p., co-composer), Tribute, National Lampoon Goes to the Movies, The Chosen, Running Brave, Harry and Son, City Limits, Rent-a-Cop, White Hot (also dir.), Modern Love (also dir., s.p., composed songs), Beauty and the Beast (voice), Betrayal of the Dove (s.p. only), At Home with the Webbers, Deadly Exposure.
TELEVISION: Movies: Death Be Not Proud, The Death of Richie, Remember When, Virginia Hill Story, All the Kind Strangers, Two of a Kind, California Girls, Invasion of Privacy, Homewrecker, Precious Victims. Specials: Our Town, The Last of Mrs. Lincoln. Series: Search for Tomorrow, Tough Cookies. Guest: One Day at a Time, Alfred Hitchcock Presents (1985). Episode Director: True Confessions (3 episodes), Thunder Alley, Evening Shade, Good Advice, Muddling Through, Monty, Dream On, Friends, Family Album. Pilot Director: Bringing Up Jack, George Wendt Show, Game Night.

BENTON, ROBERT
Writer, Director. b. Waxahachie, TX, 1932. e. U. of Texas, B.A. Was art director and later consulting ed. at Esquire Magazine where he met David Newman, a writer-editor, and formed writing partnership. Together wrote a monthly column for Mademoiselle (10 years). Benton made directorial debut with Bad Company, 1972.
THEATER: It's a Bird... It's a Plane... It's Superman (libretto), Oh! Calcutta (one sketch).
PICTURES: Co-writer (with Newman): Bonnie and Clyde, There Was a Crooked Man, What's Up, Doc?. Co-writer: Superman (with Mario Puzo and Tom Mankiewicz). Director/Writer: Bad Company, The Late Show, Kramer vs. Kramer (Academy Awards for Best Director and Adapted Screenplay, 1979), Still of the Night, Places in the Heart (Academy Award for Best Original Screenplay, 1984), Nadine, The House on Carroll Street (co-exec. prod. only), Billy Bathgate (dir. only), Nobody's Fool.

BERENGER, TOM
Actor. b. Chicago, IL, May 31, 1950. e. U. of Missouri (drama). Studied acting at H.B. Studios. Acted in regional theatres and off-off-Broadway. Plays include Death Story, The Country Girl, National Anthems, The Rose Tattoo, Electra, Streetcar Named Desire, End as a Man (Circle Rep.).
PICTURES: The Sentinel (debut, 1977), Looking for Mr. Goodbar, In Praise of Older Women, Butch and Sundance: The

Early Days, The Dogs of War, Beyond the Door, The Big Chill, Eddie and the Cruisers, Fear City, Rustler's Rhapsody, Platoon (Acad. Award nom.), Someone to Watch Over Me, Shoot to Kill, Betrayed, Last Rites, Major League, Born on the Fourth of July, Love at Large, The Field, Shattered, At Play in the Fields of the Lord, Sniper, Sliver, Gettysburg, Major League 2, Chasers, Last of the Dogmen, The Substitute.
TELEVISION: *Series*: One Life to Live (1975-76). *Movies*: Johnny We Hardly Knew Ye, The Avenging Angel, Body Language. *Mini-Series:* Flesh and Blood, If Tomorrow Comes. *Special:* Dear America: Letters Home From Vietnam (reader).

BERENSON, MARISA
Actress. b. New York, NY, Feb. 15, 1947. Granddaughter of haute couture fashion designer Schiaparelli. Great niece of art critic and historian Bernard Berenson. Former model.
PICTURES: Death in Venice (debut, 1971), Cabaret, Barry Lyndon, Casanova & Co., Killer Fish, S.O.B., The Secret Diary of Sigmund Freud, La Tete Dans Le Sac, L'Arbalete, Desire, Quel Treno da Vienna, Il Giardino Dei Cigliegi, Winds of the South, White Hunter Black Heart, Night of the Cyclone, The Cherry Orchard, Flagrant Desire.
TELEVISION: *Movies*: Tourist, Playing for Time, Notorious. *Mini-Series*: Sins, Hemingway. Also: Lo Scialo, Blue Blood, Have a Nice Night, L'Enfant Des Loups, Oceano, Hollywood Detective, Bel Ami, Murder She Wrote (guest).

BERESFORD, BRUCE
Director, Writer. b. Sydney, Australia, Aug. 16, 1940. e. U. of Sydney, B.A. 1962. Worked as teacher in London, 1961. Film editor, East Nigerian Film Unit, 1966; sect. and head of prod., British Film Inst. Production Board, 1966-71.
PICTURES: *Director*: The Adventures of Barry McKenzie (also co-s.p.), Barry McKenzie Holds His Own (also prod., co-s.p.), Don's Party, The Getting of Wisdom, Money Movers, Breaker Morant (also s.p.), The Club, Puberty Blues, Tender Mercies, King David, The Fringe Dwellers (also s.p.), Crimes of the Heart, Aria (sequence), Her Alibi, Driving Miss Daisy, Mister Johnson (also co-s.p.), Black Robe, Rich in Love, A Good Man in Africa, Silent Fall, The Last Dance.
TELEVISION: *Movie*: Curse of the Starving Class (writer, exec. prod.)

BERG, DICK
Writer, Producer. b. New York, NY. e. Lehigh U. 1942; Harvard Business Sch. 1943. Prior to 1960 writer for TV shows Playhouse 90 Studio One, Robert Montgomery Presents, Kraft Television Playhouse. 1961-69 prod., writer for Universal Studios; exec. prod. The Chrysler Theatre, Alcoa Premiere, Checkmate. Created and wrote Staccato (series). 1971-85: prod., writer of over 50 TV movies via his Stonehenge Prods. TV films won 15 Emmies, 23 nominations. Twice elected pres. National Acad. of Television Arts and Sciences.
PICTURES: *Prod.*: Counterpoint, House of Cards, Banning Shoot (also s.p.), Fresh Horses.
TELEVISION: Prod. and/or writer: *Mini-Series*: A Rumor of War, The Martian Chronicles, The Word, Space, Wallenberg: A Hero's Story. Movies: Rape and Marriage: The Rideout Case, An Invasion of Privacy, Thief, Footsteps, Firehouse, American Geisha, Class of '63, Louis Armstrong, Chicago Style, Everybody's Baby: The Rescue of Jessica McClure (exec. prod.)

BERG, JEFF
Executive. b. Los Angeles, CA, May 26, 1947. e. U of California, Berkeley, B.A., 1969. V.P., head lit. div., Creative Mgt. Associates, Los Angeles, 1969-75; v.p., m.p. dept., International Creative Associates, 1975-80; pres., 1980-. Dir., Joseph Intl. Industries. Named chmn. ICM.

BERG, PETER
Actor. b. New York, NY, 1964. e. Malcalester Col., St. Paul, MN.
PICTURES: Miracle Mile, Heart of Dixie, Race for Glory, Shocker, Genuine Risk, Crooked Hearts, Late for Dinner, A Midnight Clear,Aspen Extreme, Fire in the Sky, Girl 6, The Great White Hype.
TELEVISION: *Series*: Chicago Hope. *Movies*: Rise and Walk: The Dennis Byrd Story, The Last Seduction (also released theatrically).

BERGEN, CANDICE
Actress. b. Beverly Hills, CA, May 9, 1946. m. late dir. Louis Malle. Father was late ventriloquist Edgar Bergen. e. U. of PA. Modeled during college; freelance photo-journalist. Autobiography: Knock Wood (1984). B'way debut in Hurlyburly.
PICTURES: The Group (debut, 1966), The Sand Pebbles, The Day the Fish Came Out, Live for Life, The Magus, The Adventurers, Getting Straight, Soldier Blue, Carnal Knowledge, The Hunting Party, T. R. Baskin, 11 Harrowhouse, The Wind and the Lion, Bite the Bullet, The Domino Principle, A Night Full of Rain, Oliver's Story, Starting Over (Acad. Award nom.), Rich and Famous, Gandhi, Stick.
TELEVISION: *Series*: Murphy Brown (5 Emmy Awards: 1989, 1990, 1992, 1994, 1995). *Mini-Series*: Hollywood Wives. *Movies*:

Arthur the King, Murder: By Reason of Insanity, Mayflower Madam. *Specials*: Woody Allen Special, Moving Day (Trying Times).

BERGEN, POLLY
Singer, Actress. r.n. Nellie Burgin b. Knoxville, TN, July 14, 1930. e. Compton Jr. Coll., CA. Prof. debut radio at 14; in light opera, summer stock; sang with orchestra and appeared in night clubs; Columbia recording star; on B'way stage, John Murray Anderson's Almanac, Champagne Complex, First Impressions. Bd. chmn. Polly Bergen Co.; chmn. Culinary Co., Inc.; co-chmn. Natl. Business Council for Equal Rights Amendment; Humanitarian Award: Asthmatic Research Inst. & Hosp., 1971; Outstanding Mother's Award, 1984.
PICTURES: At War With the Army (debut, 1950), That's My Boy, Warpath, The Stooge, Half a Hero, Cry of the Hunted, Arena, Fast Company, Escape from Fort Bravo, Belle Sommers, Cape Fear, The Caretakers, Move Over Darling, Kisses for My President, A Guide for the Married Man, Making Mr. Right, Mother Mother, Cry-Baby, Dr. Jekyll and Ms. Hyde.
TELEVISION: *Series*: Pepsi-Cola Playhouse (host 1954-55), To Tell the Truth (panelist), The Polly Bergen Show, Baby Talk.*Guest*: G.E. Theatre, Schlitz Playhouse, Playhouse 90, Studio One, Perry Como, Ed Sullivan Show, Bob Hope Show, Bell Telephone, Wonderful World of Entertainment, Dinah Shore Show, Dean Martin Show, Andy Williams Show, Red Skelton Show, Mike Douglas Show. *Special*: The Helen Morgan Story (Emmy Award, 1958). *Movies*: Death Cruise, Murder on Flight 502, Telethon, How to Pick Up Girls, The Million Dollar Face, Born Beautiful, Velvet, Addicted to His Love, She Was Marked For Murder, The Haunting of Sarah Hardy, My Brother's Wife, Lightning Field, Lady Against the Odds, Perry Mason: The Case of the Skin-Deep Scandal, Leave of Absence (also story, co-exec. prod.). *Mini-Series*: 79 Park Avenue, The Winds of War, War and Remembrance.

BERGER, HELMUT
Actor. r.n. Helmut Steinberger. b. Salzburg, Austria, May 29, 1943. e. Feldkirk College and U. of Perugia. First film, small role in Luchino Visconti's The Witches (Le Streghe) in 1966.
PICTURES: The Young Tigers, The Damned, Do You Know What Stalin Did To Women?, The Garden of the Finzi-Continis, Dorian Gray, A Butterfly with Bloody Wings, The Greedy Ones, The Strange Love Affair, Ludwig, Ash Wednesday, Conversation Piece, The Romantic Englishwoman, Orders to Kill, Madam Kitty, Merry-Go-Round, Code Name: Emerald, The Glass Heaven, Faceless, The Betrothed, The Godfather Part III.

BERGER, RICHARD L.
Executive. b. Tarrytown, NY, Oct. 25, 1939. e. Cornell U., UCLA 1963, B.S. In 1964 joined acct. dept., 20th Century-Fox; promoted to exec. position in Fox-TV. Was dir. of programming, then v.p. of programs. Appt. asst. v.p. prod. 20th-Fox. Left in 1975 to join CBS-TV as v.p. dramatic development. Returned to 20th-Fox in 1977 as v.p., domestic prod., 20th Century-Fox Pictures. Joined Disney as pres. Walt Disney Pictures; resigned 1984. Named sr. v.p., United Artists Corp., promoted to pres. MGM/UA Film Group, 1988.

BERGER, SENTA
Actress. b. Vienna, Austria, May 13, 1941. Studied ballet, then acting at VIenna's Reinhardt Seminar. Debuted in German films as teen.
PICTURES: Die Lindenwirtin vom Donanstrand (debut, 1957), The Journey, Katia, The Good Soldier Schweik, The Secret Ways, Sherlock Holmes and the Deadly Necklace, The Testament of Dr. Mabuse, The Victors, Major Dundee, The Glory Guys, Cast a Giant Shadow, Bang! Bang! You're Dead, The Poppy Is Also a Flower, The Quiller Memorandum, To Commit a Murder, The Treasure of San Gennaro, The Ambushers, Diabolically Yours, If It's Tuesday This Must Be Belgium, De Sade, When Women Had Tails, Percy, The Scarlet Letter, Merry-Go-Round, White Mafia, The Swiss Conspiracy, Cross of Iron, Nest of Nipers, The Two Lives of Mattia Pascal, The Flying Devils, Swiss Cheese.

BERGERAC, JACQUES
Actor. b. Biarritz, France, May 26, 1927. Career includes Five Minutes with Jacques Bergerac on radio; in the theatre, on tour in Once More with Feeling; on most major network TV shows.
PICTURES: Twist of Fate, The Time is Now, Strange Intruder, Come Away With Me, Les Girls, Gigi, Man and His Past, Thunder in the Sun, Hypnotic Eye, A Sunday in Summer, Fear No More, Achilles, A Global Affair, Taffy and the Jungle Hunter, The Emergency Operation, Lady Chaplin, The Last Party, One Plus One.

BERGIN, PATRICK
Actor. b. Ireland, 1954.
PICTURES: Those Glory Glory Days, Taffin, The Courier, Mountains of the Moon, Sleeping With the Enemy,.Love Crimes, Highway to Hell, Patriot Games, Map of the Human Heart, Double Cross.

TELEVISION: *Movies:* Act of Betrayal, Robin Hood, They, Frankenstein. *Specials:* Morphine and Dolly Mixtures (BBC), The Real Carlotte. *Guest:* Twilight Zone: Lost Classics.

BERGMAN, ALAN
Songwriter. b. Brooklyn, NY. e. U. of North Carolina, UCLA. m. Marilyn Bergman with whom he collaborates.
THEATER: Ballroom, Something More, The Lady and the Clarinet.
PICTURES: Lyrics for: Harlow, Harper, In the Heat of the Night, Fitzwilly, The Thomas Crown Affair (Academy Award for Best Song: The Windmills of Your Mind, 1968), John and Mary, The Happy Ending, Gaily Gaily, The Magic Garden of Stanley Sweetheart, Move, Pieces of Dreams, Wuthering Heights, Doctor's Wives, Sometimes a Great Notion, Pete 'n' Tillie, The Life and Times of Judge Roy Bean, Breezy, 40 Carats, The Way We Were (Academy Award for title song, 1973), Summer Wishes Winter Dreams, Harry and Walter Go to New York, Ode to Billy Joe, A Star Is Born, Same Time Next Year, The Promise, And Justice for All, A Change of Seasons, Back Roads, Author Author, Yes Giorgio, Best Friends, Tootsie, Never Say Never Again, Yentl (Academy Award for song score, 1983), The Man Who Loved Women, Micki and Maude, The January Man, Major League, Shirley Valentine, Welcome Home, Switch, For the Boys.
TELEVISION: Queen of the Stardust Ballroom (Emmy Award), Hollow Image, Sybil (Emmy Award); and themes for Bracken's World, Maude, The Sandy Duncan Show, Good Times, Alice, The Dumplings, Nancy Walker Show, The Powers That Be, Brooklyn Bridge, etc.

BERGMAN, ANDREW
Writer, Director, Producer. b. Queens, NY, 1945. e. Harpur Coll., magna cum laude; U. of Wisconsin, Ph.D, history, 1970. Worked as publicist at United Artists. Author: We're in the Money, a study of Depression-era films, and the mysteries: The Big Kiss-Off of 1944, Hollywood and Levine, Sleepless Nights. Also wrote Broadway comedy, Social Security.
PICTURES: *Writer:* Blazing Saddles, The In Laws, So Fine (also dir.) Oh God You Devil, Fletch, The Freshman (also dir.), Soapdish, Honeymoon in Vegas (also dir.), It Could Happen to You (dir. only), The Scout, Striptease (also dir.). *Exec. Prod.:* Chances Are, Undercover Blues, Little Big League.

BERGMAN, INGMAR
Writer, Director. b. Uppsala, Sweden, July 14, 1918. e. Stockholm U. Directed university play prods.; wrote & dir. Death of Punch, 1940; first theatrical success, dir., Macbeth, 1940; writer-director, Svensk Film-industri, 1942-present; first s.p, Frenzy, 1943; first directorial assignment, Crisis, 1945; chief prod., Civic Malmo, 1956-60. Directed Swedish prod. Hamlet for stage at Brooklyn Acad. of Music, 1988.
PICTURES: *Writer only:* Torment, Woman Without a Face, Eva, The Last Couple Out, Pleasure Garden, Best Intentions, Sunday's Children. *Dir.-Writer:* Crisis It Rains on Our Love, A Ship to India, Night is My Future (dir. only), Port of Call, The Devil's Wanton, Three Strange Loves, To Joy, This Can't Happen Here (dir. only), Summer Interlude (Illicit Interlude), Secrets of Women, Summer With Monika, The Naked Night (Sawdust and Tinsel), A Lesson in Love, Dreams (Journey Into Autumn), Smiles of a Summer Night, The Seventh Seal, Wild Strawberries, Brink of Life, The Magician, The Virgin Spring (dir. only), The Devil's Eye, Through a Glass Darkly, Winter Light, The Silence, All These Women, Persona, Stimulantia (episode), Hour of the Wolf, Shame, The Ritual, The Passion of Anna, The Touch, Cries and Whispers, Scenes from a Marriage, The Magic Flute, Face to Face, The Serpent's Egg, Autumn Sonata, From the Life of the Marionettes, Fanny and Alexander, After the Rehearsal.
U.S. TELEVISION: The Lie.

BERGMAN, MARILYN
Songwriter. b. Brooklyn, NY. e. NYU. m. Alan Bergman with whom she collaborates. Became pres. of ASCAP, 1994.
THEATER: Ballroom, Something More, The Lady and the Clarinet.
PICTURES: Lyrics for: Harlow, Harper, In the Heat of the Night, Fitzwilly, The Thomas Crown Affair (Academy Award for Best Song: The Windmills of Your Mind, 1968), John and Mary, The Happy Ending, Gaily Gaily, The Magic Garden of Stanley Sweetheart, Move, Pieces of Dreams, Wuthering Heights, Doctor's Wives, Sometimes a Great Notion, Pete 'n' Tillie, The Life and Times of Judge Roy Bean, Breezy, 40 Carats, The Way We Were (Academy Award for title song, 1973), Summer Wishes Winter Dreams, Harry and Walter Go to New York, Ode to Billy Joe, A Star Is Born, Same Time Next Year, The Promise, And Justice for All, A Change of Seasons, Back Roads, Author Author, Yes Giorgio, Best Friends, Tootsie, Never Say Never Again, Yentl (Academy Award for song score, 1983), The Man Who Loved Women, Micki and Maude, The January Man, Major League, Shirley Valentine, Welcome Home, Switch, For the Boys.
TELEVISION: Queen of the Stardust Ballroom (Emmy Award), Hollow Image, Sybil (Emmy Award); and themes for Bracken's World, Maude, The Sandy Duncan Show, Good Times, Alice, The Dumplings, Nancy Walker Show, The Powers That Be, Brooklyn Bridge, etc.

BERKOFF, STEVEN
Actor, Director, Writer. b. London, Eng., Aug. 3, 1937. e. studied drama in London and Paris. Founder of London Theatre Group. Author of plays, East, West, Greek Decadence, Sink the Belgrano, Kvetch (London, NY). Staged, adapted and toured with: Kafka's In the Penal Colony, The Trial and Metamorphosis; Agamemnon, The Fall of the House of Usher. Starred in Hamlet and Macbeth. NY theater: Director: Kvetch (also writer, actor), Coriolanus, Metamorphosis (starring Baryshnikov). Also dir. Roman Polanski in Metamorphosis in Paris.
PICTURES: *Actor:* Nicholas and Alexandra, A Clockwork Orange, Barry Lyndon, The Passenger, Outland, McVicar, Octopussy, Beverly Hills Cop, Rambo: First Blood II, Revolution, Underworld, Absolute Beginners, Under the Cherry Moon, The Krays, Decadence (also dir., s.p.), Fair Game.
TELEVISION: Beloved Family, Knife Edge, War and Remembrance, A Season of Giants, Intruders.

BERLE, MILTON
Actor. r.n. Milton Berlinger. b. New York, NY, July 12, 1908. e. Professional Children's Sch., N.Y. Early appearances as child actor incl. film Tillie's Punctured Romance. In vaudeville; on N.Y. stage (Ziegfeld Follies 1936, Life Begins at 8:40, etc.): nightclubs; concurrently on radio & screen. Author: Out of My Trunk (1945), Earthquake (1959), Milton Berle: An Autobiography (1974).
PICTURES: New Faces of 1937, Radio City Revels, Tall Dark and Handsome, Sun Valley Serenade, Rise and Shine, A Gentleman at Heart, Whispering Ghosts, Over My Dead Body, Margin for Error, Always Leave Them Laughing, Let's Make Love, The Bellboy (cameo), It's a Mad Mad Mad Mad World, The Loved One, The Oscar, Don't Worry We'll Think of a Title, The Happening, Who's Minding the Mint?, Where Angels Go... Trouble Follows, For Singles Only, Can Hieronymus Merkin Ever Forget Mercy Humppe and Find True Happiness?, Lepke, Won Ton Ton the Dog Who Saved Hollywood, The Muppet Movie, Cracking Up, Broadway Danny Rose, Driving Me Crazy, Storybook.
TELEVISION: *Series:* Texaco Star Theatre, Kraft Music Hall TV Show, Jackpot Bowling, Milton Berle Show. *Guest:* Doyle Against the House, Dick Powell Show, Chrysler TV special, Lucy Show, F Troop, Batman, Love Boat, many others. *Movies:* Seven in Darkness, Evil Roy Slade, Legend of Valentino, Side By Side.

BERLINGER, WARREN
Actor, b. Brooklyn, NY, Aug. 31, 1937. e. Columbia U.
THEATER: Annie Get Your Gun, The Happy Time, Bernardine, Take A Giant Step, Anniversary Waltz, Roomful of Roses, Blue Denim (Theatre World Award), Come Blow Your Horn, How To Succeed in Business Without Really Trying, (London) Who's Happy Now?, California Suite (1977-78 tour).
PICTURES: Teenage Rebel, Three Brave Men, Blue Denim, Because They're Young, Platinum High School, The Wackiest Ship in the Army, All Hands on Deck, Billie, Spinout, Thunder Alley, Lepke, The Four Deuces, I Will I Will... for Now, Harry and Walter Go to New York, The Shaggy D.A., The Magician of Lublin, The Cannonball Run, The World According to Garp, Going Bananas, Outlaw Force, Ten Little Indians, Hero, Crime and Punishment, Feminine Touch, That Thing You Do!.
TELEVISION: *Series:* Secret Storm (serial), The Joey Bishop Show, The Funny Side, A Touch of Grace, Operation Petticoat, Small & Frye, Shades of L.A. *Guest:* Alcoa, Goodyear, Armstrong, Matinee Theatre, The London Palladium, Kilroy, Bracken's World, Columbo, Friends. *Movies:* The Girl Most Likely To..., The Red Badge of Courage, Ellery Queen, Wanted: The Sundance Woman, Sex and the Single Parent, The Other Woman, Trial By Jury, Death Hits the Jackpot.

BERMAN, BRUCE
Executive. President of Worldwide Production, Warner Bros. Pictures.

BERMAN, PANDRO S.
Producer. b. Pittsburgh, PA, March 28, 1905. Son of late Harry M. Berman, gen. mgr. Universal, FBO. Asst. dir. film ed., FBO; film & title ed. Columbia Studios; chief film ed. RKO, later asst. to William Le Baron & David Selznick; became prod. 1931 (RKO). A Champion of Champions Producer in Fame ratings. Joined MGM 1940.
PICTURES: What Price Hollywood?, Symphony of Six Million, Morning Glory, The Gay Divorcee, Of Human Bondage, Roberta, Alice Adams, The Informer, Quality Street, Top Hat, Follow the Fleet, Winterset, Stage Door, Vivacious Lady, Carefree, Room Service, Gunga Din, Bachelor Mother, The Hunchback of Notre Dame, Ziegfeld Girl, Honky Tonk, Rio Rita, The Seventh Cross, National Velvet, Dragon Seed, The Picture of Dorian Grey, Marriage Is a Private Affair, Undercurrent, Sea of Grass, The Three Musketeers, Madame Bovary, Father of the Bride, Father's Little Dividend, The Prisoner of Zenda, Ivanhoe,

All the Brothers Were Valiant, Knights of the Round Table, The Long Long Trailer, Blackboard Jungle, Bhowani Junction, Tea and Sympathy, Something of Value, The Brothers Karamazov, The Reluctant Debutante, Butterfield 8, Sweet Bird of Youth, The Prize, A Patch of Blue, Justine, Move.

BERMAN, STEVEN H.
Executive. b. Middletown, OH, March 22, 1952. e. Ohio U., B.F.A. in playwriting, 1974; USC, Annenberg Sch. of Communication studied management, 1977. Special research projects Paramount and ABC TV, 1977. Account exec., Gardner Advertising, 1978. Development exec., CBS Television, 1979-82. Dir. of comedy dev., CBS Television, 1982-84. Five years at CBS in series development, comedy and drama. Vice pres., dramatic dev., Columbia Pictures TV, 1984-85. Sr. v.p., Creative Affairs, Columbia Pictures TV, 1985-87. Exec. v.p., Columbia TV, div. of Columbia Entertainment TV, 1987-90. Indept. prod., Columbia Pictures TV, 1990-present.

BERNARD, MARVIN A.
Executive. b. New York, NY, Oct. 1, 1934. e. NYU. Lab technician to v.p. in charge of sales, Rapid Film Technique, Inc., 1949-63; developed technological advances in film rejuvenation and preservation, responsible for public underwriting; 1964-69; real estate sales & investments in Bahamas, then with Tishman Realty (commercial leasing div.); est. B-I-G Capital Properties; v.p. and operating head of International Filmtreat 1970-1973; authored Film Damaged Control Chart, a critical analysis of film care and repair, 1971; founded Filmlife Inc. with latest chemical/mechanical and technical advancement in field of film rejuvenation and preservation. 1973-75 bd. chmn. and chief executive officer of Filmlife Inc., motion picture film rejuvenation, storage and distribution company. Feb. 1975 elected president in addition to remaining bd. chairman. 1979 consultant to National Archives of U.S. on m.p. preservation. 1981 dev. m.p. rejuvenation and preservation for 8mm and S8mm. 1986 introduced this technology to private home movie use before and after transfer to videotape. 1987, active mem. of awards comm. for tech. achievements, National Acad. TV Arts & Sciences. Recognition as leading authority and m.p. conservator from Intl. Communications Industries Assn. (ICIA), 1988. 1989, Filmlife became 1st national film to video transfer lab in U.S.; elected to Princeton Film Preservation Group. Established Film/Video Hospital, repairing broken tapes & videocassettes, Aug. 1990.

BERNARD, TOM
Executive. Co-President, Sony Pictures Classics.

BERNHARD, HARVEY
Producer. b. Seattle, WA, March 5, 1924. e. Stanford U. In real estate in Seattle, 1947-50; started live lounge entertainment at the Last Frontier Hotel, Las Vegas, 1950. Partner with Sandy Howard, 1958-60; v.p. in chg. prod., David L. Wolper Prods., dividing time between TV and feature films, 1961-68; with MPC, v.p., chg. prod., 1968-70. Now pres. of Harvey Bernhard Ent., Inc.
PICTURES: The Mack (1973), The Omen, Damien—Omen II, The Final Conflict, The Beast Within, Ladyhawke (exec. prod.), The Goonies (prod.), The Lost Boys.

BERNHARD, SANDRA
Actress, Comedian, Singer. b. Flint, MI, June 6, 1955. Moved to Scottsdale, AZ at 10. Began career in Los Angeles 1974 as stand-up comedian while supporting herself as manicurist in Beverly Hills. Has written articles for Vanity Fair, Interview, Spin, recorded and written lyrics for debut album I'm Your Woman (1985) and starred in one-woman off-B'way show Without You I'm Nothing (1988). Published collection of essays, short stories and memoirs, Confessions of a Pretty Lady (1988). Frequent guest on Late Night with David Letterman and Robin Byrd Show.
PICTURES: Cheech and Chong's Nice Dreams (debut, 1981), The King of Comedy, Sesame Street Presents: Follow That Bird, The Whoopee Boys, Track 29, Heavy Petting, Without You I'm Nothing, Hudson Hawk, Inside Monkey Zetterland, Dallas Doll.
TELEVISION: Series: The Richard Pryor Show, Roseanne. Movie: Freaky Friday.

BERNSEN, CORBIN
Actor. b. North Hollywood, CA, Sept. 7, 1954. m. actress Amanda Pays. Son of actress Jeanne Cooper. e. UCLA, B.A. theater arts; M.F.A playwriting. Teaching asst. at UCLA while working on playwriting degree. 1981 studied acting in NY while supporting self as carpenter and model (Winston cigarettes). Built own theater in loft. Formed theatre co. Theatre of the Night.
PICTURES: Three the Hard Way (debut, 1974), Eat My Dust!, King Kong, S.O.B., Hello Again, Bert Rigby You're a Fool, Major League, Disorganized Crime, Shattered, Frozen Assets, The Killing Box, Savage Land, Major League 2, Trigger Fast, A Brilliant Disguise, The New Age, Radioland Murders, Tales From the Hood, The Great White Hype, The Dentist, Menno's Mind, Circuit Breaker.

TELEVISION: Series: Ryan's Hope, L.A. Law, A Whole New Ballgame. Movies: Breaking Point, Line of Fire: The Morris Dees Story, Dead on the Money, Grass Roots, Love Can Be Murder, Beyond Suspicion, I Know My Son is Alive, Where Are My Children?, Voice From Within, Dangerous Intentions, In the Heat of the Night: By Duty Bound, Bloodhounds. Guest: Anything But Love, Roc, The Larry Sanders Show, Love and War, The Nanny, Night Watch, Seinfeld, Dear John.

BERNSEN, HARRY
Producer, Executive. b. Chicago, IL, June 14, 1935. Served in US Marine Corp., 1953-55. Had own agency, Continental Management, 1956-70. Became producer, 1970.
THEATER: Prod.: Beyond the Rainbow, The Boys in Autumn.
PICTURES: Fool's Parade (assoc. prod.), Something Big (assoc. prod.), Three the Hard Way (prod.), Take a Hard Ride (prod.), Fatal Inheritance (prod.).
TELEVISION: Movie: The Awakening Land (exec. prod.). ABC After School Specials, 1982-88 (exec. prod.).

BERNSTEIN, ARMYAN
Director, Writer, Producer.
PICTURES: Thank God It's Friday (s.p.), One From the Heart (co-s.p.), Windy City (dir. s.p.), Cross My Heart (dir., co-s.p.), Satisfaction (co-exec. prod.), The Commitments (co-exec. prod.), A Midnight Clear (co-exec. prod.), The Baby-sitters Club (co-exec. prod.).

BERNSTEIN, BOB
Executive. Began public relations career 1952 at DuMont TV Network, followed by 2 yrs. as press agent for Liberace. With Billboard Magazine as review editor 3 yrs. Joined Westinghouse Bdg. Co. as p.r. director 1959. In 1963 named p.r. director for Triangle Publications, serving in various capacities to 1971. Joined Viacom Intl. as director of information services. In 1975 formed own co., March Five Inc., p.r. and promotion firm.

BERNSTEIN, ELMER
Composer, Conductor. b. New York, NY, April 4, 1922. Scholarship, Juilliard. e. Walden Sch., NYU., U.S. Army Air Force radio unit. After war 3 yrs. recitals, musical shows, United Nations radio dept; pres., Young Musicians Found.; 1st v.p. Academy of Motion Picture Arts & Sciences; co-chmn. music branch. Music dir. Valley Symphony. Recording artist, United Artists. More than 90 major films. Pres. of Composers & Lyricists Guild of America.
THEATER: How Now Dow Jones?
PICTURES: Never Wave at a WAC, Sudden Fear, Robot Monster, Cat Women of the Moon, It's a Dog's Life, Man With the Golden Arm, Storm Fear, The View From Pompey's Head, The Ten Commandments, Fear Strikes Out, Desire Under the Elms, Drango, The Naked Eye, Sweet Smell of Success, The Tin Star, Anna Lucasta, The Buccaneer, God's Little Acre, Kings Go Forth, Some Came Running, The Miracle, The Story on Page One, From the Terrace, The Magnificent Seven, The Rat Race, By Love Possessed, The Commancheros, Summer and Smoke, The Young Doctors, Birdman of Alcatraz, Walk on the Wild Side, A Girl Named Tamiko, To Kill a Mockingbird, The Great Escape, The Caretakers, Hud, Kings of the Sun, Rampage, Love With the Proper Stranger, The Carpetbaggers, Four Days in November, The World of Henry Orient, The Hallelujah Trail, The Reward, Seven Women, Cast a Giant Shadow, Hawaii, Thoroughly Modern Millie (Academy Award, 1967), I Love You Alice B. Toklas, The Scalphunters, True Grit, The Gypsy Moths, Midas Run, Where's Jack?, Cannon for Cordoba, The Liberation of L.B. Jones, A Walk in the Spring Rain, Doctor's Wives, See No Evil, Big Jake, The Magnificent Seven Ride, Cahill U.S. Marshall, McQ., Gold, The Trial of Billy Jack, Report to the Commissioner, From Noon Till Three, The Incredible Sarah, The Shootist, Slap Shot, National Lampoon's Animal House, Bloodbrothers, Meatballs, The Great Santini, Saturn 3, The Blues Brothers, Airplane!, Zulu Dawn, Going Ape, Stripes, An American Werewolf in London, Honky Tonk Freeway, The Chosen, Five Days One Summer, Airplane II: The Sequel, Spacehunter, Trading Places, Class, Bolero, Ghostbusters, The Black Cauldron, Spies Like Us, Legal Eagles, Three Amigos, Amazing Grace and Chuck, Leonard Part 6, Da, Funny Farm, The Good Mother, Slipstream, My Left Foot, The Grifters, The Field, Oscar, A Rage in Harlem, Rambling Rose, Cape Fear (adapt.), The Babe, The Cemetery Club, Mad Dog and Glory, Lost in Yonkers, The Age of Innocence, The Good Son, I Love Trouble, Roommates, Canadian Bacon, Devil in a Blue Dress.
TELEVISION: Specials: Hollywood: The Golden Years, The Race for Space: Parts I & II, D-Day, The Making of the President—1960 (Emmy Award), Hollywood and the Stars, Voyage of the Brigantine Yankee, Crucifiction of Jesus, NBC Best Sellers Theme (1976). Series: Julia, Owen Marshall, Ellery Queen, Serpico, The Chisholms. Movies: Gulag, Guyana Tragedy.

BERNSTEIN, FRED
Executive. Was sr. v.p. of business affairs and prod. of worldwide prod. for Columbia Pictures in 1980's before serving as sr. v.p. of MCA Inc.'s Motion Picture Group, 1987-94. Named pres. of Coumbia TriStar Motion Pictures, 1994.

BERNSTEIN, JACK B.
Executive. b. New York, NY, May 6, 1937. e. City U. of New York, B.A., sociology. U.S. Army-Europe, 1956-58; research bacteriologist, 1959-61. Entered industry in 1962 with S.I.B. Prods., Paramount, as v.p. gen. mgr.; 1964-66, v.p. gen. mgr. C.P.I. Prods, 1966-73 prod. mgr. asst. dir., free lance. 1973-1982, assoc. prod. exec. prod. at several studios. 1983-86, v.p. worldwide prod., Walt Disney Pictures; 1987, sr. v.p., worldwide prod., United Artists Pictures; 1988-90, sr. v.p. worldwide prod., MGM Pictures. Member: DGA, Friars, Academy of MP Arts & Sciences; Academy of TV Arts & Sciences, AFI.
PICTURES: Asst. dir.: Hearts of the West. Prod. mngr.: Silver Streak. Assoc. Prod.: The Other Side of Midnight, The Fury, Butch and Sundance: The Early Days, Six Pack, Unfaithfully Yours. Exec. Prod.: North Dallas Forty, Monsignor, The Beast Within. Co-Prod.: The Mambo Kings, Under Siege.

BERNSTEIN, JAY
Producer, Personal manager. b. Oklahoma City, OK, June 7, 1937. e. Pomona Coll. 1963-76, pres. of Jay Bernstein Public Relations, representing over 600 clients. Formed Jay Bernstein Enterprises, acting as personal manager for Farrah Fawcett, Suzanne Somers, Kristy McNichol, Susan Hayward, Donald Sutherland, Bruce Boxleitner, Robert Conrad, Susan Saint James, Robert Blake, William Shatner, Linda Evans, Cicely Tyson, etc. Past pres., Bernstein Thompson Entertainment Complex, entertainment and personal mgt. firm.
PICTURES: Exec. prod.: Sunburn, Nothing Personal.
TELEVISION: Exec. prod. *Movies*: The Return of Mike Hammer, Mickey Spillane's Margin for Murder; Wild, Wild, West, Revisited; More Wild, Wild West. Murder Me Murder You, More Than Murder, The Return of Mike Hammer, Murder Takes All, The Diamond Trap, Final Notice, Double Jeopardy. *Series*: Bring 'Em Back Alive, Mike Hammer, Houston Knights.

BERNSTEIN, WALTER
Director, Writer. b. New York, NY. Aug. 20, 1919. e. Dartmouth. Wrote for New Yorker Magazine; in W.W.II was roving correspondent for Yank Magazine. Returned to New Yorker after war. Wrote TV scripts; published book Keep Your Head Down (collection of articles).
PICTURES: *Writer*: Kiss the Blood Off My Hands (co-s.p.), That Kind of Woman, Heller in Pink Tights, A Breath of Scandal (co-s.p.), Paris Blues, The Magnificent Seven (uncredited), Fail Safe, The Money Trap, The Train, The Molly Maguires, The Front, Semi-Tough, The Betsy (co-s.p.), An Almost Perfect Affair, Yanks, Little Miss Marker (dir. debut), The House on Carroll Street.

BERNSTEIN, WILLIAM
Executive. b. New York, NY, Aug. 30, 1933. e. New York U., B.A. 1954; Yale U., L.L.B. 1959. Joined United Artists as an attorney in 1959. 1967-72, v.p., business affairs. Promoted to senior v.p., 1972. Executive v.p., Orion Pictures, 1978-91. Pres. and CEO Orion Pictures, 1991-92. Exec. v.p., Paramount Pictures 1992-present. Member, A.B.A., A.M.P.A.S.

BERRI, CLAUDE
Director, Actor, Producer. b. Paris, July 1, 1934. r.n. Claude Langmann. Started as actor, playing roles in French films and on stage in the 1950s. Began dir. career with short film Jeanine, followed by Le Poulet (The Chicken; also prod.; Academy Award for best live action short subject, 1965). 1963, created Renn Productions. 1973, became partner in AMLF distribution co.
PICTURES: *Director*: The Two of Us (feature debut, 1967), Marry Me Marry Me (also s.p., actor), Le Pistonne (The Man with Connections), Le Cinema de Papa (Cinema of My Father; also prod.), Le Sex Shop (also s.p.), Male of the Century (also s.p., actor), The First Time (also s.p.), Tess (prod.), Inspecteur la Bavure (prod.), Je Vous Aime (prod., s.p.), In a Wild Moment, Je Vous Aime (I Love You), Le Maitre d' Ecole (The Schoolmaster; also prod., s.p.), A Quarter to Two Before Jesus Christ (prod.), L'Africain (prod.), Banzai (prod.), L'Homme Blesse (prod.), Tchao Pantin (also prod., s.p.), Jean la Florette, Manon of the Spring, The Bear (exec. prod.), Valmont (exec. prod.), Uranus (also s.p., prod.), Germinal (also prod., co-s.p.).

BERRIDGE, ELIZABETH
Actress. b. New Rochelle, NY, May 2, 1962. Studied acting at Lee Strasberg Inst., Warren Robertson Theatre Workshop.
THEATER: *NY*: The Vampires, The Incredibly Famous Willy Rivers, Outside Waco, Ground Zero Club, Cruise Control, Sorrows and Sons, Crackwalker, Coyote Ugly, Briar Patch. *Regional*: Tuesday's Child, Hedda Gabler, Lulu, Venus and Thumbtacks.
PICTURES: Natural Enemies, The Funhouse, Amadeus, Smooth Talk, Five Corners, When the Party's Over.
TELEVISION: *Series*: One of the Boys, The Powers That Be, The John Larroquette Show. *Movies*: Silence of the Heart, Home Fires Burning, Montana.

BERRY, HALLE
Actress. b. Cleveland, OH, 1968. Named Miss Teen Ohio, Miss Teen All-American, runner up to Miss U.S.A.

PICTURES: Jungle Fever, Strictly Business, The Last Boy Scout, Boomerang, Father Hood, The Program, The Flintstones, Losing Isaiah, Race the Sun, Girl 6, Executive Decision, Rich Man's Wife.
TELEVISION: *Movie*: Solomon and Sheba. *Mini-Series*: Queen.

BERRY, JOHN
Director. b. New York, NY, 1917. Directed films in Hollywood mid and late '40s; went abroad during McCarthy era in U.S. where worked in French film industry. Later went to London to do stage work, acting as well as directing. Returned to U.S. to do stage work; returned to Hollywood to do TV.
PICTURES: Cross My Heart, From This Day Forward, Miss Susie Slagle's, Casbah, Tension, He Ran All the Way, CCa Va Barder, The Great Lover, Je Suis un Sentimental, Tamango, On Que Mambo, Claudine, Maya, The Bad News Bears Go to Japan, Thieves, Il y a maldonne, 'Round Midnight (actor only), A Man in Love (actor only), La Voyage a Paimpol (also prod.), Captive in the Land (also prod.).
TELEVISION: One Drink at a Time, Farewell Party, Mr. Broadway, Sister Sister (also prod.), Angel on My Shoulder, Honeyboy, Legitimate Defense.

BERRY, KEN
Actor. b. Moline, IL, Nov. 3, 1933.
PICTURES: Two for the Seesaw, Hello Down There, Herbie Rides Again, The Cat from Outer Space.
TELEVISION: *Movies*: Wake Me When the War Is Over, The Reluctant Heroes, Every Man Needs One, Letters from Three Lovers, Love Boat II. *Series*: The Ann Sothern Show, Bob Newhart Show (1962), F Troop, Mayberry RFD, Ken Berry Wow Show, Mama's Family. *Guest*: Dick Van Dyke Show, Hazel, Lucy Show, Carol Burnett, Sonny & Cher, etc.

BERTINELLI, VALERIE
Actress. b. Wilmington, DE, April 23, 1960. m. musician Eddie Van Halen. Dramatic training at Tami Lynn Academy of Artists in California. Made early TV appearances in the series, Apple's Way, in commercials, and in public service announcements. Started own prod. company to acquire properties for self.
PICTURE: Number One with a Bullet.
TELEVISION: *Movies*: Young Love First Love, The Promise of Love, The Princess and the Cabbie, I Was a Mail Order Bride, The Seduction of Gina, Shattered Vows, Silent Witness, Rockabye, Pancho Barnes, In a Child's Name, What She Doesn't Know, Murder of Innocence. *Specials*: The Secret of Charles Dickens, The Magic of David Copperfield. *Series*: One Day at a Time, Sydney, Cafe Americain. *Mini-Series*: I'll Take Manhattan.

BERTOLUCCI, BERNARDO
Director, Writer. b. Parma, Italy, May 16, 1940. e. Rome U. Son of Attilio Bertolucci, poet and film critic. At age 20 worked as asst. dir. to Pier Paolo Pasolini on latter's first film, Accatone: in 1962 made debut film, The Grim Reaper, from script by Pasolini. 1962 published poetry book: In Cerca del Mistero. 1965-66: directed and wrote 3-part TV documentary: La vie del Petrolio for Ital. Oil co. in Iran. Collaborated on s.p. Ballata de un Milliardo, Sergio Leone's Once Upon a Time in the West, L'inchiesta. Produced films Sconcerto Rock, Io con te non ci sto piu, Lost and Found.
PICTURES: *Director-Writer*: The Grim Reaper, Before the Revolution, Love and Rage (episode: Agony), Partner, The Spider's Strategem, The Conformist, Last Tango in Paris, 1900, Luna, Tragedy of a Ridiculous Man, The Last Emperor (Academy Awards for Best Director & Screenplay, 1987), The Sheltering Sky, Little Buddha, Stealing Beauty.

BESCH, BIBI
Actress. b. Vienna, Austria, Feb. 1, 1942. Mother was actress Gusti Huber. Daughter is actress Samantha Mathis. Raised in Westchester County, NY. Appeared on soap daytime dramas as Secret Storm, Love is a Many-Splendored Thing, and Somerset.
THEATER: *NY Stage*: Fame, The Chinese Prime Minister, Here Lies Jeremy Troy, Once for the Asking.
PICTURES: The Pack, Hardcore, The Promise, Meteor, The Beast Within, Star Trek II: The Wrath of Khan, The Lonely Lady, Date With an Angel, Kill Me Again, Tremors, Steel Magnolias, Betsy's Wedding, My Family/Mi Familia, California Myth, Lonely Hearts, Distance, Black Harvest.
TELEVISION: *Series*: Secrets of Midland Heights, The Hamptons, The Jeff Foxworthy Show. *Movies*: Victory at Entebbe, Peter Lundy and the Medicine Hat Stallion, Betrayal, Transplant, The Plutonium Incident, The Sophisticated Gents, Death of a Centerfold: The Dorothy Stratten Story, Secrets of a Mother and Daughter, The Day After, Lady Blue, Crazy From the Heart, Doing Time on Maple Drive, Abandoned and Deceived, Wounded Heart, Rattled, White Dwarf, A.C.E.S., Orleans, Home Video. *Mini-Series*: Backstairs at the White House. *Special*: The Last Shot.
(d. September 7, 1996)

BESSON, LUC
Director, Writer, Producer. b. Paris, France, March 18, 1959.
PICTURES: Le Dernier Combat (dir., prod., s.p.), Le Grand
Carnaval (2nd unit dir.), Subway (dir., prod., s.p.), Kamikaze
(prod., s.p.), Taxi Boy (tech. advis.), The Big Blue (dir., s.p.,
lyrics, camera op.), La Femme Nikita (dir., s.p., song), The
Professional (dir., prod., s.p.).

BEST, BARBARA
Publicist. b. San Diego, CA, Dec. 2, 1921. e. U. of Southern
California, AB, 1943. Pub., 20th Century-Fox, 1943-49; reporter,
San Diego Journal, 1950 Stanley Kramer Co. 1950-53; own
agency, Barbara Best & Associates, 1953-66; 1966 exec. v.p.
Jay Bernstein Public rel.; Freeman and Best, 1967-74; Barbara
Best Inc. publ. rel. 1975-85; Barbara Best Personal
Management, current.

BEST, JAMES
Actor. b. Corydon, IN, July 26, 1926. Magazine model; on stage;
in European roadshow cast of My Sister Eileen; served as M.P.
with USAAF, WWII.
PICTURES: One Way Street (debut, 1950), Commanche
Territory, Winchester 73, Peggy, Kansas Raiders, Air Cadet,
Cimarron Kid, Target Unknown, Apache Drums, Ma & Pa Kettle
at the Fair, Steel Town, Francis Goes to West Point, Battle at
Apache Pass, Flat Top, About Face, The Beast from 20000
Fathoms, Seminole, The President's Lady, City of Bad Men,
Column South, Riders to the Stars, The Raid, The Caine Mutiny,
Return from the Sea, They Rode West, Seven Angry Men, The
Eternal Sea, A Man Called Peter, Forbidden Planet, Calling
Homicide, When Gangland Strikes, Come Next Spring, Gaby,
The Rack, Man on the Prowl, Hot Summer Night, Last of the
Badmen, Verboten!, The Naked and the Dead, The Left Handed
Gun, Cole Younger - Gunfighter, The Killer Shrews, Ride
Lonesome, Cast a Long Shadow, The Mountain Road, Shock
Corridor, Black Gold, The Quick Gun, Black Spurs,
Shenandoah, Three on a Couch, First to Fight, Firecreek, The
Brain Machine, Sounder, Ode to Billy Joe, Gator (also assoc.
prod.), Nickelodeon, Rolling Thunder, The End (also assoc.
prod.), Hooper.
TELEVISION: Series: Dukes of Hazzard. Movies: Run Simon
Run, Savages, The Runaway Barge, The Savage Bees. Guest:
Alfred Hitchcock Presents, Twilight Zone, The Andy Griffith
Show, Hawkins, Enos, In the Heat of the Night, etc. Mini-Series:
Centennial.

BETHUNE, ZINA
Actress, Dancer, Singer. b. New York, NY, Feb. 17, 1950. B'way:
Most Happy Fella, Grand Hotel. National tours: Sweet Charity,
Carnival, Oklahoma!, Damn Yankees, Member of the Wedding,
The Owl and The Pussycat, Nutcracker. New York City Ballet
(Balanchine), Zina Bethune & Company Dance Theatre,
Bethune Theatredanse. Special performance at the White
House and Kennedy Center.
PICTURES: Sunrise At Campobello, Who's That Knocking at My
Door, The Boost.
TELEVISION: Series: The Guiding Light, The Nurses, Love of
Life. Guest: Lancer, Cains Hundred, Naked City, Route 66, Little
Women, Santa Barbara, Judy Garland Show, Jackie Gleason
Show, Gunsmoke, Dr. Kildare, Emergency, Planet of The Apes,
Police Story, Chips, Hardy Boys, Dirty Dancing. Movies:
Nutcracker: Money Madness Murder (also choreographer),
Party of Five. Specials: The Gymnast (An ABC Afterschool
Special), Heart Dancing, From the Heart.

BETTGER, LYLE
Actor. b. Philadelphia, PA, Feb. 13, 1915. e. Haverford School,
Philadelphia, American Acad. of Dramatic Art, N.Y. m. Mary
Rolfe, actress. Started in summer stock; in road cos. of Brother
Rat, Man Who Came to Dinner.
THEATER: John Loves Mary, Love Life, Eve of St. Mark, The
Male Animal, Sailor Beware, The Moon is Down.
PICTURES: No Man of Her Own, Union Station, First Legion,
Greatest Show on Earth, The Denver & Rio Grande,
Vanquished, Forbidden, The Great Sioux Uprising, All I Desire,
Drums Across the River, Destry, Carnival Story, Sea Chase,
Showdown at Abilene, Gunfight at OK Corral, Town Tamer,
Johnny Reno, Nevada Smith, Return of The Gunfighter,
Impasse, The Hawaiians, The Seven Minutes.
TELEVISION: Court of Last Resort, Grand Jury, Hawaii 5-0,
Police Story, Bonanza, Combat, Gunsmoke, etc.

BEVILLE, HUGH M., JR.
Executive. b. April 18, 1908. e. Syracuse U., NYU (MBA). To
NBC 1930 statistician, chief statistician; Research mgr., dir.,
research; U.S. Army 1942-46; dir. of research and planning
for NBC, v.p., planning and research, 1956; v.p., planning,
1964; consultant, 1968; professor Business Admin.,
Southampton Coll., 1968. Exec. dir., Broadcast Rating
Council, 1971-82, author-consultant, contributing editor,
TV/Radio Age, 1982-85. Author, Audience Ratings; Radio,
Television, Cable, 1985, Elected member, Research Hall of
Fame, 1986.

BEY, TURHAN
Actor. b. Vienna, Austria, March 30, 1922. Came to U.S. in
1930's studying acting at Ben Bard's School of Dramatic Arts,
Pasadena Playhouse.
PICTURES: Footsteps in the Dark (debut, 1941), Burma
Convoy, Raiders of the Desert, Shadows on the Stairs, The Gay
Falcon, Junior G-Men of the Air (serial), The Falcon Takes Over,
A Yank on the Burma Road, Bombay Clipper, Drums of the
Congo, Destination Unknown, Arabian Nights, The Unseen
Enemy, The Mummy's Tomb, Danger in the Pacific, Adventures
of Smilin' Jack (serial), White Savage, The Mad Ghoul,
Background to Danger, Follow the Boys, The Climax, Dragon
Seed, Bowery to Broadway, Ali Baba and the 40 Thieves, Frisco
Sal, Sudan, Night in Paradise, Out of the Blue, The Amazing Mr.
X, Adventures of Casanova, Parole Inc., Song of India,
Prisoners of the Casbah, Stolen Identity (prod. only), Healer,
Possessed by the Night.
TELEVISION: Guest: Seaquest, Murder She Wrote, Babylon 5

BEYMER, RICHARD
Actor. r.n. George Richard Beymer, Jr., b. Avoca, IA, Feb. 21,
1939. e. N. Hollywood H.S., Actors Studio. Performer, KTLA,
Sandy Dreams, Fantastic Studios, Inc., 1949, Playhouse 90.
PICTURES: Indiscretion of an American Wife (debut, 1953), So
Big, Johnny Tremain, The Diary of Anne Frank, High Time, West
Side Story, Bachelor Flat, Five Finger Exercise, Hemingway's
Adventures of a Young Man, The Longest Day, The Stripper,
Grass (Scream Free!), Cross Country, Silent Night Deadly Night
3: Better Watch Out, My Girl 2.
TELEVISION: Series: Paper Dolls, Twin Peaks. Movies:
Generation, With a Vengeance. Guest: The Virginian, Walt
Disney (Boston Tea Party), Dr. Kildare, Man from U.N.C.L.E.,
Moonlighting, Murder She Wrote, The Bronx Zoo.

BIALIK, MAYIM
Actress. b. Dec. 12, 1976.
PICTURES: Pumpkinhead (debut, 1988), Beaches.
TELEVISION: Series: Blossom. Movies: Blossom in Paris, Don't
Drink the Water. Specials: Earth Day Special, Sea World Mother
Earth Celebration (host), Surviving a Break-Up, The Kingdom
Chums: Original Top Ten (voice), I Hate the Way I Look, For Our
Children: The Concert (host). Pilot: Molly. Guest: Webster, Facts
of Life, MacGyver, Empty Nest, The John Larroquette Show.

BICK, JERRY
Producer. b. New York, NY, April 26, 1923. e. Columbia U.,
Sorbonne. Taught English at U. of Georgia, before entering film
industry in pub. dept. of MGM, N.Y. Opened own literary agency
in Hollywood after stint with MCA. Began career as producer in
London; debut film, Michael Kohlhaas, 1969. 1986-89, exec. v.p.
worldwide prod., Heritage Entertainment.
PICTURES: The Long Goodbye, Thieves Like Us, Russian
Roulette, Farewell My Lovely (exec. prod.), The Big Sleep,
Against All Odds (exec. prod.), Swing Shift.

BIEHN, MICHAEL
Actor. b. Anniston, AL, July 31, 1956. Raised in Lincoln, NB, and
Lake Havisu, AZ. At 18 years moved to Los Angeles and stud-
ied acting with Vincent Chase. First professional job in 1977 in
TV pilot for Logan's Run.
PICTURES: Grease (debut, 1978), Coach, Hog Wild, The Fan,
The Lords of Discipline, The Terminator, Aliens, The Seventh
Sign, Rampage, In a Shallow Grave, The Abyss, Navy Seals,
Time Bomb, K2, DeadFall, Tombstone, Deep Red, Jade.
TELEVISION: Series: The Runaways. Guest: Logan's Run, Hill
Street Blues, Police Story, Family. Movies: Zuma Beach, A Fire
in the Sky, China Rose, Deadly Intentions, A Taste for Killing,
Strapped. Pilots: James at 15, The Paradise Connection.

BIGELOW, KATHRYN
Director, Writer. b. 1951. e. SF Art Inst., Columbia. Studied to
be painter before turning to film with short Set-Up, 1978. Was
script supervisor on Union City; appeared in film Born in Flames.
PICTURES: The Loveless (feature debut as co-dir. with Monty
Montgomery, 1981; also co-s.p.), Near Dark (also co-s.p.), Blue
Steel (also co-s.p.), Point Break, Strange Days.
TELEVISION: Mini-Series: Wild Palms (co-dir.).

BIKEL, THEODORE
Actor. b. Vienna, Austria, May 2, 1924. Moved to Palestine
(Israel) as teen where he made stage debut in The Russian
Milkman. Studied acting at Royal Academy of Dramatic Arts in
London. London stage debut in 1948. Autobiography: Theo
(1995).
THEATER: Tonight in Samarkland, The Lark, The Rope
Dancers, The Sound of Music, Cafe Crown, Fiddler on the
Roof.
PICTURES: The African Queen, Melba, Desperate Moment, The
Divided Heart, The Little Kidnappers, The Vintage, The Pride
and the Passion, The Enemy Below, Fraulein, The Defiant Ones
(Acad. Award nom.), I Want to Live, The Angry Hills, The Blue
Angel, A Dog of Flanders, My Fair Lady, Sands of the Kalahari,
The Russians Are Coming the Russians Are Coming, Sweet

November, My Side of the Mountain, Darker Than Amber, 200 Motels, The Little Ark, Prince Jack, Dark Tower, See You in the Morning.
TELEVISION: The Eternal Light, Look Up and Live, Who Has Seen the Wind?, The Diary of Anne Frank, Killer by Night, Murder on Flight 502, Victory at Entebbe, Testimony of Two Men, Loose Change.

BILBY, KENNETH W.
Executive. b. Salt Lake City, UT, Oct. 7, 1918. e. Columbia U., U. of Arizona, B.A. With N.Y. Herald-Tribune, 47-50; author, New Star in the Near East, 1950; pub. rel. rep. to RCA Victor, Camden, NJ, 1950-54; exec. v.p. National Broadcasting Co., N.Y., 1954-60; v.p. public affairs, RCA, 1960-62, exec. v.p., 1962-75; exec. v.p. corporate affairs, 1976-present.

BILL, TONY
Director, Producer, Actor. b. San Diego, CA, Aug. 23, 1940. e. Notre Dame U. Founded Bill/Phillips Prods. with Julia and Michael Phillips, 1971-73; Tony Bill Prods. 1973-92; Barnstorm Films, 1993-; Acad. of M.P. Arts & Sciences, bd. of govs., bd of trustees, chmn. prods. branch.
PICTURES: Director: My Bodyguard (debut, 1980), Six Weeks, Five Corners (also co-prod.), Crazy People, Untamed Heart (also co-prod.), A Home of Our Own. Prod.: Hearts of the West (exec. prod.), Harry and Walter Go to New York, Boulevard Nights (exec. prod.), Going in Style, Little Dragons (also actor). Co-producer: Deadhead Miles, Steelyard Blues, The Sting (Academy Award for Best Picture, 1973), Taxi Driver. Actor: Come Blow Your Horn (debut, 1963), Soldier in the Rain, Marriage on the Rocks, None But the Brave, You're a Big Boy Now, Ice Station Zebra, Never a Dull Moment, Castle Keep, Flap, Shampoo, Heartbeat, Pee-wee's Big Adventure, Less Than Zero.
TELEVISION: Director: Dirty Dancing (pilot), Love Thy Neighbor, Next Door (movie), One Christmas (movie). Actor: Special: Lee Oswald - Assassin (BBC). Series: What Really Happened to the Class of '65? Movies: Haunts of the Very Rich, Having Babies II, The Initiation of Sarah, With This Ring, Are You in the House Alone?, Portrait of an Escort, Freedom, Washington Mistress, Running Out, The Killing Mind. Guest: Alfred Hitchcock Presents (Night Caller, 1985). Mini-Series: Washington Behind Closed Doors.

BILLS, ELMER E.
Executive. b. Salisbury, MO, July 12, 1936. e. University of Missouri, B.S. Partner B & B Theatres, Inc.

BILSON, BRUCE
Director. b. Brooklyn, NY, May 19, 1928. e. UCLA, BA, Theater Arts, 1950. m. actress Renne Jarrett. Father was prod. George Bilson, son is prod.-dir. Danny Bilson, daughter is prod. Julie Ahlberg. Asst. film ed. 1951-55; USAF photo unit 1952-53; asst. dir. 1955-65 including Andy Griffith Show, Route 66. Assoc. prod. The Baileys of Balboa. Dir. since 1965 of more than 380 TV shows. Emmy Award, Get Smart, DGA nom. The Odd Couple.
PICTURES: The North Avenue Irregulars, Chattanooga Choo Choo.
TELEVISION: Series: The Sentinel, Touched by an Angel, Viper, The Flash, Dinosaurs, Barney Miller, Get Smart (Emmy Award, 1968), Hogan's Heroes, House Calls, Alice, Private Benjamin, Life With Lucy, Spenser: For Hire, Hotel, Dallas, Hawaii Five-O, Dynasty, The Fall Guy, Nightingales. Movies/pilots: The Odd Couple, The Dallas Cowboys Cheerleaders, BJ and the Bear, The Misadventures of Sheriff Lobo, Half Nelson, Finder of Lost Loves, The Girl Who Came Gift Wrapped, The Ghosts of Buxley Hall, The New Gidget, Barefoot in the Park, The Bad News Bears, Harper Valley PTA.

BINDER, STEVE
Producer, Director, Writer. b. Los Angeles, CA, Dec. 12. e. Univ. of Southern California. 1960-61 announcer in Austria and Germany with AFN, Europe. Prof. of Cinema, Univ. Southern CA. Mem.: DGA, Producers Guild of America, Writers Guild of America, NARAS, ATAS.
PICTURES: Director: The T.A.M.I. Show, Give 'Em Hell Harry!, Melissa.
TELEVISION: Prod./Dir.: Steve Allen Show (1963-65, 1973), Elvis Presley Comeback Special, Barry Manilow Special (also writer, Emmy Award, 1977), Diana Ross '81 (also writer), Ringling Bros & Barnum Bailey Circus (also writer), Pee-wee's Playhouse, Big Fun on Swing Street, Barry Manilow, Pee-wee's Playhouse Christmas Special (prod.), A Tribute to Sam Kinison. Dir.: Diana Ross Sings Jazzy Blues, Diana Ross—World Tour, Diana Ross in Central Park (Cable Ace Award), Diana, The International Special Olmpics, 6th Anniversary of the Grand Ole Opry, The First Annual ESPY Awards. Exec. Prod/Dir.: Disney's Greatest Hits on Ice, John Denver's Montana X-Mas Skies, One Night With You. Exec. Prod.: Pee-wee's Playhouse.

BIONDI, JR. FRANK J.
Executive. b. Jan. 9, 1945. e. Princeton U.; Harvard U., MBA (1968). Various investment banking positions 1968-74; asst.

treas. Children's TV Workshop 1974-78; v.p. programming HBO 1978-82; pres. HBO 1983, then chmn. & chief exec. off. 1984 joined Coca-Cola Co. as exec. v.p., entertainment business arm. Resigned 1987 to join Viacom International as pres. and CEO. Pres, MCA, 1996.

BIRCH, THORA
Actress. b. California. Began acting at age 4. First appeared in commericals.
PICTURES: Paradise, All I Want for Christmas, Patriot Games, Hocus Pocus, Monkey Trouble, Clear and Present Danger, Now and Then, Alaska.
TELEVISION: Series: Parenthood, Day by Day. Guest: Amen, Doogie Howser M.D.

BIRKIN, JANE
Actress. b. London, England, Dec. 14, 1946. Daughter is actress Charlotte Gainsbourg. Sister of director-writer Andrew Birkin. Was subject of Agnes Vardas` 1988 documentary Jane B. par Agnes V.
PICTURES: Blow-Up, Kaleidoscope, Wonderwall, Les Chemins de Katmandou, La Piscine, Cannabis, Romance of a Horse Thief, Trop jolies pour etre honnetes, Dark Places, Projection Privee, La Moutarde me monte au nex, Le Mouton Enrage, 7 Morts sur Ordonnance, Catherine et Cie, La Course a l'echalote, Je T'Aime Moi Non Plus, Seriex comme let plaisir, Le Diable au Coeur, L'Animal, Death on the Nile, Au bout du bout du banc, Melancolie Baby, La Miel, La Fille Prodigue, Evil Under the Sun, L'Ami de Vincent, Circulez u'a rien a voir, Love on the Ground, le Garde du Corps, The Pirate, Beethoven's Nephew, Dust, Leave All Fair, la Femme de ma vie, Comedie!, Kung Fu Master (also story), Soigne ta droite, Daddy Nostalgia, Between the Devil and the Deep Blue Sea.

BIRNBAUM, ROGER
Producer, Executive. b. Teaneck, NJ. e. Univ. of Denver. Was v.p. of both A&M Records and Arista records before becoming m.p. producer. Headed Guber/Peters Company, then named pres. of worldwide prod., United Artists; pres. of worldwide prod. and exec. v.p. of 20th Century Fox. Left Fox in 1993 to become co-founder of Caravan Pictures.
PICTURES: Producer/Exec. Producer: The Sure Thing, Young Sherlock Homes, Who's That Girl, The Three Musketeers, Angie, Angels in the Outfield, A Low Down Dirty Shame, Houseguest, Tall Tale, While You Were Sleeping, Dead Presidents, Powder, Celtic Pride.

BIRNEY, DAVID
Actor. b. Washington, DC, April 23, 1940. e. Dartmouth Coll., B.A., UCLA, M.A. Phd. Southern Utah St. (hon.). Following grad. sch. and the Army spent 2 yrs. in regional theatre, Amer. Shakespeare Festival, Hartford Stage Co., Barter Theatre, to N.Y. where appeared in Lincoln Center prod. of Summertree (Theatre World Award). Appeared for two yrs. on TV daytime series, Love Is a Many Splendored Thing, doing other stage roles in same period. Theatre panelist, Natl. Endowment for the Arts; Board Member, Hopkins Center, Dartmouth College; Board of Foundation for Biomedical Research.
THEATER: NY debut NY Shakespeare Fest (Comedy of Errors); 3 seasons Lincoln Center Rep. Many NY and regional credits incl: Amadeus, Benefactors, Man and Superman, Macbeth, Hamlet, Richard II, III, Romeo & Juliet, Much Ado About Nothing, King John, Titus Andronicus, Major Barbara, Biko Inquest, Playboy of the Western World, The Miser, Antigone, My Fair Lady, Camelot, Love Letters, Present Laughter.
PICTURES: Caravan to Vaccares, Trial by Combat, Oh God Book II, Prettykill, Nightfall.
TELEVISION: Series: Bridget Loves Bernie, Serpico, St. Elsewhere, Glitter, Live Shot, Beyond 2000 (host), Raising Kids (host), Great American TV Poll (host). Mini-Series: Night of the Fox, Seal Morning, Adam's Chronicles, Testimony of Two Men, Master of the Game, Valley of the Dolls, The Bible. Movies: Murder or Mercy, Bronk, Serpico: The Deadly Game, Someone's Watching Me!, High Midnight, Only With Married Men, OHMS, Mom The Wolfman & Me, The Five of Me, The Long Journey Home (also co-exec. prod.), Love and Betrayal, Always Remember I Love You, Touch and Die, Keeping Secrets. Specials: Missing: Have You Seen This Person? Drop Everything and Read, 15 and Getting Straight, Mark Twain's The Diaries of Adam and Eve (co-prod.). Guest appearances in series & anthology shows.

BISSET, JACQUELINE
Actress. b. Weybridge, England, September 13, 1944. e. French Lycaee, London. After photographic modeling made film debut in The Knack, 1965.
PICTURES: The Knack... and How to Get It (debut, 1965), Cul de Sac, Two For the Road, Casino Royale, The Cape Town Affair, The Sweet Ride, The Detective, Bullitt, The First Time, Secret World, Airport, The Grasshopper, The Mephisto Waltz, Believe in Me, Stand Up and Be Counted, The Life & Times of Judge Roy Bean, The Thief Who Came to Dinner, Day for Night, Le Manifique, Murder on the Orient Express, End of the Game,

The Spiral Staircase, St. Ives, Sunday Woman, The Deep, The Greek Tycoon, Secrets, Who Is Killing the Great Chefs of Europe?, Together? (I Love You I Love You Not), When Time Ran Out, Rich and Famous, Inchon, Class, Under the Volcano, High Season, Scenes From the Class Struggle in Beverly Hills, La Maison de Jade, Wild Orchid, The Maid, A Judgment in Stone.
TELEVISION: *Movies*: Forbidden, Anna Karenina, Choices, Leave of Absence. *Mini-Series*: Napoleon and Josephine: A Love Story.

BLACK, ALEXANDER F.
Publicist. b. New Rochelle, NY, Dec. 27, 1918. e. Brown U., BA, 1940. Joined Universal 1941. U.S. Navy 1942-45, Lt. Sr. Grade. Rejoined Universal 1946 serving in various capacities in Foreign Department, becoming director of foreign publicity for Universal International Films, Inc. in 1967; 1974, named exec. in chg. intl. promotion for MCA-TV.

BLACK, KAREN
Actress. b. Park Ridge, IL, July 1, 1942. r.n. Karen Ziegler. e. Northwestern U. Left school for NY to join the Hecscher House, appearing in several Shakespearean plays. In 1965 starred in Playroom, which ran only 1 month but won her NY Drama Critic nom. as best actress.
THEATER: Happily Never After, Keep It in the Family, Come Back to the Five and Dime Jimmy Dean Jimmy Dean.
PICTURES: You're a Big Boy Now (debut, 1966), Hard Contact, Easy Rider, Five Easy Pieces (Acad. Award nom.), Drive He Said, A Gunfight, Born To Win, Cisco Pike, Portnoy's Complaint, The Pyx, Little Laura and Big John, Rhinoceros, The Outfit, The Great Gatsby, Airport 1975, Law and Disorder, Day of the Locust, Nashville, Family Plot, Crime and Passion, Burnt Offerings, Capricorn One, Killer Fish, In Praise of Older Women, The Squeeze, The Last Word, Chanel Solitaire, Come Back to the Five and Dime Jimmy Dean Jimmy Dean, Killing Heat (The Grass is Singing), Can She Bake a Cherry Pie?, Martin's Day, Bad Manners (Growing Pains), Cut and Run (Amazon: Savage Adventure), Invaders from Mars, Flight of the Spruce Goose, It's Alive III, Hostage, Eternal Evil, The Invisible Kid, Out of the Dark, Homer and Eddie, Night Angel, Miss Right, Dixie Lanes, Sister City, Zapped Again, Twisted Justice, Over Exposure, The Children, Mirror Mirror, Haunting Fear, Quiet Fire, Children of the Night, Hotel Oklahoma, Killer's Edge, Club Fed, Evil Spirits, Moon Over Miami, The Legend of the Rollerblade 7, Hitz (Judgment), FInald Judgment (Mrs. Sorrel), Caged Fear, Bound & Gagged: A Love Story, The Player, Rubin & Ed, The Trust, The Double O Kid, Sister Island, Plan 10 From Outer Space, The Wacky Adventures of Dr. Boris & Mrs. Duluth, Odyssey, Every Minute Is Goodbye, A Thousand Stars, Children of the Corn III: The Fever, Crime Time.
TELEVISION: *Movies*: Trilogy of Terror, The Strange Possession of Mrs. Oliver, Mr. Horn, Power, Where the Ladies Go, Because He's My Friend, Full Circle Again (Canadian TV). *Guest*: In the Heat of the Night.

BLACK, NOEL
Director. b. Chicago, IL, June 30, 1937. e. UCLA, B.A., 1959; M.A. 1964. Made short film Skaterdater.
PICTURES: Pretty Poison (debut, 1968), Cover Me Babe, Jennifer on My Mind, Mirrors, A Man a Woman and a Bank, Private School, Mischief (s.p., exec. prod.).
TELEVISION: Trilogy, The American Boy, The World Beyond, I'm a Fool, The Golden Honeymoon, The Electric Grandmother, The Doctors Wilde, Meet the Munceys, Eyes of the Panther, The Hollow Boy. *Movies*: Mulligan's Stew, The Other Victim, Prime Suspect, Happy Endings, Quarterback Princess, Deadly Intentions, Promises to Keep, A Time to Triumph, My Two Loves, Conspiracy of Love, The Town Bully. *Mini-series*: Deadly Intentions.

BLACK, STANLEY
Composer, conductor, musical director. OBE. b. London, Eng. Resident conductor, BBC, 1944-52. Musical director 105 feature films and Pathe Newsreel music: Music dir. Associated British Film Studios 1958-64. Guest conductor, Royal Philharmonic Orchestra and London Symphony. Orchestra: many overseas conducting engagements including (1977) Boston Pops and Winnipeg Symphony. Associated conductor Osaka Philharmonic Orchestra. Exclusive recording contract with Decca Record Co. since 1944.
PICTURES: Crossplot, The Long the Short and The Tall, Rattle of a Simple Man, The Young Ones, Hell Is a City, Top Secret, Valentino.

BLACKMAN, HONOR
Actress. b. London, England, 1926. Stage debut. The Gleam 1946.
PICTURES: Fame Is the Spur (debut, 1947), Quartet, Daughter of Darkness, A Boy A Girl and a Bike, Diamond City, Conspirator, So Long at the Fair, Set a Murderer, Green Grow the Rushes, Come Die My Love, Rainbow Jacket, Outsiders, Delavine Affair, Three Musketeers, Breakaway, Homecoming, Suspended Alibi, Dangerous Drugs, A Night to Remember, The

Square Peg, A Matter of Who, Present Laughter, The Recount, Serena, Jason & the Golden Fleece, Goldfinger, The Secret of My Success, Moment to Moment, Life at the Top, A Twist of Sand, Shalako, Struggle for Rome, Twinky (Lola), The Last Grenade, The Virgin and the Gypsy, Fright, Something Big, Out Damned Spot, Summer, Cat and the Canary.
TELEVISION: African Patrol, The Witness, Four Just Men, Probation Officer series, Top Secret, Ghost Squad, Invisible Man, The Saint, The Avengers series, Voice of the Heart, The Upper Hand (series).

BLADES, RUBEN
Actor, Composer, Singer, Writer. b. Panama City, Panama, July 16, 1948. e. U. of Panama (law and political science, 1974), Harvard U., L.L.M., 1985. Has recorded more than 14 albums, winning 2 Grammy Awards (1986, 1988). With his band Seis del Solar has toured U.S., Central America and Europe. President of Panama's Papa Egoro political party.
PICTURES: *Actor*: The Last Fight (debut, 1982), Crossover Dreams (also co-s.p.), Critical Condition, The Milagro Beanfield War, Fatal Beauty, Homeboy, Disorganized Crime, The Lemon Sisters, Mo' Better Blues, The Two Jakes, Predator 2, Homeboy, The Super, Life With Mikey, A Million to Juan, Color of Night. Music: Beat Street, Oliver & Company, Caminos Verdes (Venezuela), Q&A, Scorpion Spring.
TELEVISION: *Guest*: Sesame Street. *Movies*: Dead Man Out (ACE Award), One Man's War, The Josephine Baker Story (Emmy nom.), Crazy from the Heart (Emmy nom.), The Heart of the Deal, Miracle on I-880.

BLAIN, GERARD
Actor, Director. b. Paris, Oct. 23, 1930. Began his professional career in 1943 as an extra in Marcel Carne's The Children of Paradise. Appeared on stage in Marcel Pagnol's Topaze (1944). Military service in a parachute regiment. In 1955 Julien Duvivier gave him his first major role in Voici le Temps des Assassins (Murder a la Carte). By 1969 had appeared in more than 30 stage and film roles before becoming a director and co-author.
PICTURES: Les Mistons (1957), Le Beau Serge, Les Cousins. In Italy: The Hunchback of Rome, L'Ora di Roma, I Defini, Run with the Devil, Young Husbands. In Germany: The American Friend, L'Enfant de l'Hiver. As director and author or co-author: Les Amis, Le Pelican (also actor), Un Enfant dans la Foule, Un Second Souffle, Le Rebelle, Portrait sur Michel Tournier, Pierre et Djemila.

BLAIR, JANET
Actress. b. Blair, PA, April 23, 1921. r.n. Martha Janet Lafferty. With Hal Kemp's Orchestra; toured in South Pacific, 1950-52.
PICTURES: Three Girls About Town (debut, 1941), Blondie Goes to College, Two Yanks in Trinidad, Broadway, My Sister Eileen, Something to Shout About, Once Upon a Time, Tonight and Every Night, Tars and Spars, Gdallant Journey, The Fabulous Dorseys, I Love Trouble, The Black Arrow, Fuller Brush Man, Public Pigeon No. 1, Boys Night Out, Burn Witch Burn, The One and Only Genuine Original Family Band, Won Ton Ton the Dog Who Saved Hollywood.
TELEVISION: *Series*: Leave it to the Girls (panelist), Caesar's Hour, The Chevy Show, The Smith Family. *Special*: Arabian Nights, Tom Sawyer. *Guest*: Bell Telephone Hour, Ed Sullivan, Murder She Wrote, etc.

BLAIR, LINDA
Actress. b. St. Louis, MO, Jan. 22, 1959. Model and actress on TV commercials before going into films.
PICTURES: The Sporting Club (debut, 1971), The Exorcist, Airport '75, Exorcist II: The Heretic, Roller Boogie, Wild Horse Hank, Hell Night, Ruckus, Chained Heat, Savage Streets, Savage Island, Red Heat, Night Patrol, Night Force, Silent Assassins, Grotesque, Witchery, The Chilling, Bad Blood, Moving Target, Up Your Alley, Repossessed, Aunt Millie's Will, Zapped Again, Dead Sleep, Double Blast, Temptress.
TELEVISION: *Movies*: Born Innocent, Sarah T._Portrait of a Teenage Alcoholic, Sweet Hostage, Victory at Entebbe, Stranger in Our House, Calendar Girl Cop Killer? The Bambi Bembenek Story, Perry Mason: The Case of the Heartbroken Bride. *Guest*: Fantasy Island, Murder She Wrote.

BLAIR, STEWART
Executive. b. Scotland. e. Univ. of Glasgow. Was v.p. of Chase Manhattan Bank N.A. in NY, before joining Tele-Communications Inc. in 1981. Served as vice-chmn. & CEO of United Artists Entertainment Company. 1992, appointed chmn. of CEO of United Artists Theatre Circuit Inc. Bd. member of Foundation of Motion Picture Pioneers, exec. v.p. of Will Rogers Memorial Fund.

BLAKE, JEFFREY
Executive. President, Sony Pictures Releasing.

BLAKE, ROBERT
Actor. b. Nutley, NJ, Sept. 18, 1933. r.n. Michael Gubitosi. Started as a child actor in Our Gang comedies as Mickey

Gubitosi, also appeared as Little Beaver in Red Ryder series. Later was Hollywood stunt man in Rumble on the Docks and The Tijuana Story. First adult acting job was at the Gallery Theater in Hatful of Rain.
PICTURES: I Love You Again (debut, 1940, as Bobby Blake), Andy Hardy's Double Life, China Girl, Mokey, Salute to the Marines, Slightly Dangerous, The Big Noise, Lost Angel, Red Ryder series (as Little Beaver), Meet the People, Dakota, The Horn Blows at Midnight, Pillow to Post, The Woman in the Window, A Guy Could Change, Home on the Range, Humoresque, In Old Sacramento, Out California Way, The Last Round-Up, Treasure of the Sierra Madre, The Black Rose, Blackout (also co-prod.), Apache War Smoke, Treasure of the Golden Condor, Veils of Bagdad, The Rack, Screaming Eagles, Three Violent People, Beast of Budapest, Revolt in the Big House, Pork Chop Hill, The Purple Gang, Town Without Pity, PT 109, The Greatest Story Ever Told, The Connection, This Property Is Condemned, In Cold Blood, Tell Them Willie Boy is Here, Ripped-Off, Corky, Electra Glide in Blue, Busting, Coast to Coast, Second-Hand Hearts, Money Train.
TELEVISION: Series: The Richard Boone Show, Barretta (Emmy Award, 1975), Hell Town (also exec. prod.). Movies: The Big Black Pill (also creator & exec. prod.), The Monkey Mission (also creator & exec. prod.), Of Mice and Men (also exec. prod.), Blood Feud, Murder 1--Dancer 3 (also exec. prod.), Heart of a Champion: The Ray Mancini Story, Judgment Day: The John List Story. Guest: One Step Beyond, Have Gun Will Travel, Bat Masterson.

BLAKELY, SUSAN
Actress. b. Frankfurt, Germany, Sept. 7, 1950, where father was stationed in Army. Studied at U. of Texas. m. prod., media consultant Steve Jaffe. Became top magazine and TV commercial model in N.Y.
PICTURES: Savages (debut, 1972), The Way We Were, The Lords of Flatbush, The Towering Inferno, Report to the Commissioner, Shampoo, Capone, Dreamer, The Concorde—Airport '79, Over the Top, Dream a Little Dream, My Mom's a Werewolf, Russian Holiday.
TELEVISION: Series: Falcon Crest, The George Carlin Show. Mini-Series: Rich Man Poor Man. Movies: Secrets, Make Me an Offer, A Cry For Love, The Bunker, The Oklahoma City Dolls, Will There Really Be A Morning?, The Ted Kennedy Jr. Story, Blood & Orchids, April Morning, Fatal Confession: A Father Dowling Mystery, Broken Angel, Hiroshima Maiden, Ladykillers, Sight Unseen, The Incident, End Run, Dead Reckoning, Murder Times Seven, And the Sea Will Tell, Sight Unseen, Blackmail, Wildflower, Against Her Will: An Incident in Baltimore, Intruders, No Child of Mine, Honor Thy Father and Mother: The True Story of the Menendez Murders. Special: Torn Between Two Fathers. Guest: Step by Step. Pilot: Dad's a Dog.

BLAKLEY, RONEE
Actress, Singer. b. Stanley, ID, 1946. Wrote and performed songs for 1972 film Welcome Home Soldier Boys.
PICTURES: Nashville (debut, 1975; Acad. Award nom.), The Private Files of J. Edgar Hoover, The Driver, Renaldo and Clara, Good Luck Miss Wyckoff (Secret Yearnings/The Sin), The Baltimore Bullet, A Nightmare on Elm Street, Return to Salem's Lot, Student Confidential, Someone to Love.

BLANC, MICHEL
Actor. b. France, 1952.
PICTURES: Que la Fete Commence, The Tenant, Les Bronzes, The Adolescent, Les Bronzes font du Ski, Le Cheval d'Orgueil, Walk in the Shadow, Les Fugitives, Evening Dress, Menage, I Hate Actors!, Story of Women, Monsieur Hire, Chambre a Part, Strike It Rich, Uranus, Merci la Vie, Prospero's Books, The Favor the Watch and the Very Big Fish, Ready to Wear (Pret-a-Porter), Grosse Fatigue (also dir., s.p.), The Grand Dukes, The Monster.

BLANCO, RICHARD M.
Executive. b. Brooklyn, NY. e. electrical engineering, Wentworth Institute. J.C., 1925-27; bus. admin., U. of CA, 1939-40; U.S. Govt. Coll., 1942. Superv. Technicolor Corp., 1931-56; organ. and operator Consumer Products, Kodachrome film process., Technicolor, 1956-62; dir. of MP Govt. and theatre sales, NY & DC, 1963-65; gen. mgr. of Technicolor Florida photo optns. at Kennedy Space Center.; prod. doc. & educ. films for NASA, 1965; v.p. of tv div., Technicolor Corp. of America; 1967 elected corporate v.p. Technicolor, Inc.; 1971 pres., Technicolor Graphic Services, Inc.; 1974, elected chmn. of bd. of Technicolor Graphic Services; 1977, elected to bd. of dirs. of Technicolor Inc.

BLANK, MYRON
Circuit executive. b. Des Moines, IA, Aug. 30, 1911. e. U. of Michigan. Son of A. H. Blank, circuit operator. On leaving coll. joined father in operating Tri-States and Central States circuits. On leave 1943-46 in U.S. Navy, officer in charge visual educ. Now pres. Central States Theatre Corp. pres. TOA, 1955; chmn. bd. TOA Inc. 1956-57; exec. chmn. of NATO. Pres. of Greater Des Moines Comm. Built Anne Blank Child Guidance Center-Raymond Blank Hospital for Children. Endowed chair for gifted

and talented children at Univ. of Iowa; permanent scholarship at Watzman Inst., Israel. Sturdevant Award from NATO, Humanitarian Award from Variety Club in 1980. Partial scholarship for 80 students annually for 3-week seminar at Univ. of Iowa.

BLATT, DANIEL
Producer. e. Philips Andover Acad., Duke U., Northwestern U Sch. of Law.Independent producer since 1976; prior posts: resident counsel, ABC Pictures; exec. v.p. Palomar Pictures.
PICTURES: I Never Promised You a Rose Garden, Winter Kills, The American Success Company, The Howling, Independence Day, Cujo, Restless, The Boost.
TELEVISION: Movies: Circle of Children, Zuma Beach, The Children Nobody Wanted, Sadat, V—The Final Battle, Badge of the Assassin, Raid on Entebbe, Sacred Vows, A Winner Never Quits, Sworn to Silence, Common Ground. Series: V, Against the Law.

BLATTY, WILLIAM PETER
Writer, Director, Producer. b. New York, NY, Jan. 7, 1928. e. George Washington U., Seattle U. Worked as editor for U.S. Information Bureau, publicity dir. for USC and Loyola U. before becoming novelist and screenwriter. Novels include John Goldfarb Please Come Home (filmed), Twinkle Twinkle Killer Kane, The Exorcist, Legion (filmed as Exorcist III).
PICTURES: The Man From the Diner's Club, A Shot in the Dark, Promise Her Anything, What Did You Do in the War Daddy?, Gunn, The Great Bank Robbery, Darling Lili, The Exorcist (also prod./Academy Award for Best Adapted Screenplay, 1973), The Ninth Configuration (a.k.a. Twinkle Twinkle Killer Kane; also dir., prod.), The Exorcist III (also dir.).

BLAU, MARTIN
Executive. b. New York, NY, June 6, 1924. e. Ohio U., 1948. Employed on newspapers in OH, TX, WV. Pub. dept., Columbia Pictures, 1951; asst. pub. mgr. 1959; pub. mgr., Columbia Int'l, 1961; admin. asst. to v.p. of adv. & pub. Columbia Pictures, 1966. Dir. adv. and publicity, Columbia Pictures Int'l, 1970; v.p., 1971; sr. v.p., 1985. Retired, 1988.

BLAY, ANDRE
Executive. In 1979, sold Magnetic Video to 20th Century Fox, named pres., CEO, 20th Century Fox Home Video; 1981, formed The Blay Corporation; 1982, joined with Norman Lear and Jerry Perenchio, founders of Embassy Communications, as chairman and CEO of Embassy Home Entertainment; 1986, when Embassy sold to Nelson Group, left to form Palisades Entertainment Group with Elliott Kastner.
PICTURES: Exec. Prod.: Prince of Darkness, They Live, Homeboy, The Blob, A Chorus of Disapproval.

BLECKNER, JEFF
Director, Producer. b. Brooklyn, NY, Aug. 12, 1943. e. Amherst College, BA., 1965; Yale Sch. of Drama, MFA 1968. Taught drama at Yale, also participated in the theater co. 1965-68. 1968-75 theater dir. NY Shakespeare Fest. Public Theatre (2 Drama Desk Awards, Tony nom. for Sticks and Bones); Basic Training of Pavlo Hummel (Obie Award, 1971), The Unseen Hand (Obie Award). Began TV career directing The Guiding Light, 1975.
TELEVISION: Hill Street Blues (Emmy Award, DGA Award, 1983), Concealed Enemies (Emmy Award, 1984), Daddy, I'm Their Momma Now (Emmy nom.), Do You Remember Love (Christopher, Humanitas, Peabody Awards, Emmy nom.), Fresno, Terrorist on Trial, Brotherly Love, My Father My Son, Favorite Son, Mancuso F.B.I. (exec. prod.), Lifestories (exec. prod.), Last Wish, In Sickness and In Health, The Round Table (pilot), 7th Avenue (pilot), Serving In Silence (Emmy nom.), A Father For Charlie. Mini-series: In The Best of Families, Beast.

BLEES, ROBERT
Writer, Producer. b. Lathrop, MO, June 9, 1925. e. Dartmouth, Phi Beta Kappa. Writer/photographer, Time and Life Magazines. Fiction: Cosmopolitan, etc. Exec. boards of Writers Guild, Producers Guild. Executive consultant, QM Prods.; BBC (England). Trustee, Motion Picture & TV Fund. Expert witness, copyright and literary litigation, U.S. Federal Court, California Superior Court.
PICTURES: Magnificent Obsession, Autumn Leaves, The Glass Web.
TELEVISION: Producer. Combat!, Bonanza, Bus Stop, Kraft Theater. Writer also: Alfred Hitchcock, Cannon, Barnaby Jones, Harry O, Columbo. Co-creator: The New Gidget.

BLEIER, EDWARD
Executive. b. New York, NY, October 16, 1929. e. Syracuse U., 1951, C.U.N.Y., grad. courses. Reporter/sportscaster: Syracuse and NY newspapers/stations: 1947-50. Prog. service mgr., DuMont Television Network, 1951; v.p., radio-television-film, Tex McCrary, Inc. 1958. American Broadcasting Company, 1952\-57; 1959-68 v.p. in chg. pub. relations (marketing, advertising, publicity), & planning, broadcast div.; v.p. in chg. of daytime sales & programming; v.p./gen. sales mgr., ABC-TV Network. U.S. Army

39

Psy. War School; Ex-chmn., TV Committee, NASL; Trustee, NATAS; founder-director & vice-chmn., International TV Council (NATAS); past-pres., IRTS; trustee, Keystone Center for Scientific & Environmental Policy, Council on Foreign Relations; ATAS; AMPAS; guest lecturer at universities. Chmn., Steering comm., Aspen B'dcaster's Conference. 1969-present: Warner Bros. Inc.: Pres, pay-TV, cable & network features.

BLIER, BERTRAND
Director. b. Paris, France, 1939. Son of late actor Bernard Blier. Served as asst. dir. to Georges Lautner, John Berry, Christian-Jaque, Denys de la Paatelliere and Jean Delannoy for two years before dir. debut.
PICTURES: Hitler Connais Pas (debut, 1963), Breakdown, C'Est une Valse (s.p. only), Going Places, Femme Fatales (Calmos), Get Out Your Handkerchiefs (Academy Award for Best Foreign-Language Film, 1978), Buffet Froid, Beau-pere, My Best Friend's Girl, Notre Historie, Menage, Too Beautiful for You.

BLOCK, WILLARD
Executive. b. New York, NY, March 18, 1930.; e. Columbia Coll., Columbia U. Law Sch., 1952. Counter-Intelligence Corps., U.S. Army, 1952-54, account exec., Plus Marketing, Inc. 1954-55; joined sales staff, NBC Television Network, 1955-57; sales staff, CBS Enterprises, Inc., 1957; intl. sales mgr, 1960; dir., intl. sales, 1965; v.p., 1967; v.p., Viacom Enterprises, 1971; pres., 1972; v.p. MCA-TV, 1973; v.p., gen. mgr., Taft, H-B International, Inc.; pres. Willard Block, Ltd.; 1979, named pres., Viacom Enterprises; 1982-89, pres. Viacom Worldwide Ltd. Currently consultant to Sumitomo Corp., TCI, Starsight Telecast; member bd. dirs. Starsight Telecast.

BLOODWORTH-THOMASON, LINDA
Producer, Writer. b. Poplar Bluff, MO, 1947. With husband Harry Thomason co-owner of Mozark Productions.
TELEVISION: *Series*; M*A*S*H (writer), Rhoda (writer), Flithy Rich (prod.), Lime Street (co-exec. prod., creator), Designing Women (co-exec. prod., creator, writer), Evening Shade (co-exec. prod., creator, writer), Women of the House. Pilots: Dribble (prod.), Over and Out (writer), London and Davis in New York (prod.)

BLOOM, CLAIRE
Actress. r.n. Claire Blume. b. London, England, Feb. 15, 1931. To U.S. in 1940 during London evacuation. Returned to England in 1943. e. Guildhall School of Music & Drama, Central Sch. Stage debut with Oxford Rep 1946 in It Depends What You Mean. Other Stage work: The White Devil (London debut), The Lady's Not for Burning, Ring Round the Moon, A Streetcar Named Desire; at Stratford-on-Avon, Old Vic seasons, etc. B'way: Rashomon, A Doll's House, Hedda Gabler, Vivat Vivat Regina. Author: Limelight and After: The Education of an Actress (1982).
PICTURES: The Blind Goddess (debut, 1948), Limelight, Innocents in Paris, The Man Between, Richard III, Alexander the Great, The Brothers Karamazov, The Buccaneer, Look Back in Anger, The Royal Game (Schachnovelle/ Brainwashed), The Wonderful World of the Brothers Grimm, The Chapman Report, The Haunting, 80000 Suspects, High Infidelity, Il Maestro di Vigevano, The Outrage, The Spy Who Came in From the Cold, Charly, The Illustrated Man, Three Into Two Won't Go, A Severed Head, Red Sky at Morning, A Doll's House, Islands in the Stream, Clash of the Titans, Deja Vu, Sammy and Rosie Get Laid, Crimes and Misdemeanors, The Princess and the Goblin (voice), Mighty Aphrodite, Daylight.
TELEVISION: *Specials/Movies (US/UK)*: Cyrano de Bergerac, Caesar and Cleopatra, Misalliance, Anna Karenina, Wuthering Heights, Ivanov, Wessex Tales, An Imaginative Woman, A Legacy, In Praise of Love, The Orestaia, Henry VIII, Backstairs at the White House, Brideshead Revisited, Hamlet, Cymbeline, King John, Ann and Debbie, The Going Up of David Lev, Ellis Island, Separate Tables, Florence Nightingale, The Ghost Writer, Time and the Conways, Shadowlands, Liberty, Promises to Keep, The Belle of Amherst, Hold the Dream, Anastasia, Queenie, Intimate Contact, Beryl Markham: A Shadow on the Sun, Oedipus the King, The Lady and the Highwayman, The Camomile Lawn, The Mirror Crack'd From Side to Side, It's Nothing Personal, Barbara Taylor Bradford's Remember.

BLOOM, MARCIE
Executive. Co-President, Sony Pictures Classics.

BLOOM, VERNA
Actress. b. Lynn, MA, Aug. 7, 1938. e. Boston U. Studied drama at Uta Hagen-Herbert Berghof School. Performed with small theatre groups all over country; then started repertory theatre in Denver. Appeared on Broadway in Marat/Sade (played Charlotte Corday), Brighton Beach Memoirs.
PICTURES: Medium Cool (debut, 1969), The Hired Hand, High Plains Drifter, Badge 373, National Lampoon's Animal House, Honkytonk Man, After Hours, The Journey of Natty Gann, The Last Temptation of Christ.

TELEVISION: *Movies*: Where Have All the People Gone?, Sarah T.: Portrait of a Teenage Alcoholic, The Blue Knight, Contract on Cherry Street, Playing for Time, Rivkin–Bounty Hunter, Gibbsville.

BLOUNT, LISA
Actress. b. Fayetteville, AK, July 1, 1957. e. Univ. of AK. Auditioned for role as extra in film September 30, 1955 and was chosen as the female lead.
PICTURES: September 30, 1955, Dead and Buried, An Officer and a Gentleman, Cease Fire, What Waits Below, Radioactive Dreams, Prince of Darkness, Nightflyers, South of Reno,Out Cold, Great Balls of Fire, Blind Fury, Femme Fatale, Cut and Run, Stalked.
TELEVISION: *Series*: Sons and Daughters. *Pilot*: Off Duty. *Movies*: Murder Me Murder You, Stormin' Home, The Annihilator, Unholy Matrimony, In Sickness and in Health, An American Story, Murder Between Friends, Judicial Consent. *Guest*: Moonlighting, Magnum P.I., Starman, Murder She Wrote, Hitchhiker, Picket Fences.

BLUM, HARRY N.
Executive. b. Cleveland, OH, Oct. 3, 1932. e. U. of Michigan, B.B.A., LL.B. Toy & hobby industry executive, gen. mngr. Lionel division of General Mills, management consultant, and venture capital and money manager before entering industry. Now heads The Blum Group, entertainment financing, packaging, production and worldwide distrib.
PICTURES: Executive Action (assoc. prod.), The Land That Time Forgot (assoc. prod.), At the Earth's Core (exec. prod.), Drive-In (assoc. prod.), Diamonds (exec. prod.), The Bluebird (assoc. prod.), Obsession (prod.), Skateboard (prod.), The Magician of Lublin (exec. prod.), Duran Duran—Arena (exec. prod.), Young Lady Chatterly II (exec. prod.), Eminent Domain (exec. prod.).

BLUM, MARK
Actor. b. Newark, NJ, May 14, 1950. Studied drama at U. of Minnesota and U. of Pennsylvania. Also studied acting with Andre Gregory, Aaron Frankel and Daniel Seltzer. Extensive Off-B'way work after debut in The Cherry Orchard (1976).
THEATER: *NY*: Green Julia, Say Goodnight Gracie, Table Settings, Key Exchange, Loving Reno, Messiah, It's Only a Play, Little Footsteps, Cave of Life, Gus & Al (Obie Award), Lost in Yonkers (Broadway). *Regional*: Brothers (New Brunswick, NJ), Close Ties (Long Wharf), The Cherry Orchard (Long Wharf), Iago in Othello (Dallas). *Mark Taper Forum*: American Clock, Wild Oats, Moby Dick Rehearsed and An American Comedy.
PICTURES: Desperately Seeking Susan, Just Between Friends, Crocodile Dundee, Blind Date, The Presidio, Worth Winning.
TELEVISION: *Series*: Sweet Surrender, Capitol News. *Pilot*: Critical Condition. *Guest*: Miami Vice, St. Elsewhere, Roseanne. *Movies*: Condition: Critical, Indictment: The McMartin Trial.

BLUMOFE, ROBERT F.
Producer. b. New York, NY, Sept. 23, 1909. e. Columbia Coll., AB, Columbia U. Sch. of Law, JD. v.p., West Coast oper., U.A., 1953-66; indept. prod.; pres. RFB Enterprises, Inc; American Film Institute, director, AFI—West, 1977-81. Now indep. prod.

BLUTH, DON
Animator, Director, Producer, Writer. b. El Paso, TX, Sept. 13, 1938.e. Brigham Young U. Animator with Walt Disney Studios 1956 and 1971-79; animator with Filmation 1967; Co-founder and director with Gary Goldman and John Pomery, Don Bluth Productions, 1979-85; animator, Sullivan Studios, 1986. Joined Fox Animation as dir./prod., 1995.
PICTURES: *Animation director*: Robin Hood, The Rescuers, Pete's Dragon, Xanadu. *Director/Co-Producer*: The Secret of NIMH (also co-s.p.), An American Tail, The Land Before Time, All Dogs Go to Heaven (also co-story), Rock-a-Doodle, Hans Christian Andersen's Thumbelina (also s.p.), A Troll in Central Park, The Pebble and the Penguin (presenter).
TELEVISION: Banjo the Woodpile Cat (prod., dir., story, music and lyrics).

BLYTH, ANN
Actress. b. Mt. Kisco, NY, Aug. 16, 1928. e. New Wayburn's Dramatic Sch. On radio in childhood; with San Carlos Opera Co. 3 years; Broadway debut in Watch on the Rhine.
PICTURES: Chip Off the Old Block (debut, 1944), The Merry Monahans, Babes on Swing Street, Bowery to Broadway, Mildred Pierce (Acad. Award nom.), Swell Guy, Brute Force, Killer McCoy, A Woman's Vengeance, Another Part of the Forest, Mr. Peabody and the Mermaid, Red Canyon, Once More My Darling, Free for All, Top o' the Morning, Our Very Own, The Great Caruso, Katie Did It, Thunder on the Hill, I'll Never Forget You, Golden Horde, One Minute to Zero, The World in His Arms, Sally and Saint Anne, All the Brothers Were Valiant, Rose Marie, The Student Prince, King's Thief, Kismet, Slander, The Buster Keaton Story, The Helen Morgan Story.
TELEVISION: *Guest*: Lux Video Theatre (A Place in the Sun).

BOCHCO, STEVEN
Producer, Writer. b. New York, NY, Dec. 16, 1943. m. actress Barbara Bosson. e. Carnegie Tech, MFA. Won MCA fellowship in college, joined U-TV as apprentice. His shows typically feature several interwoven plots and characters, deal with social issues, and shift from comedy to drama within an episode. Awards incl. Humanitas, NAACP Image, Writers Guild, George Foster Peabody, & Edgar Allen Poe Awards.
PICTURES: Co-Writer: The Counterfeit Killer, Silent Running.
TELEVISION: Writer and story ed.: Name of the Game, Columbo, McMillan and Wife; Delvecchio (writer-prod.), Paris (exec. prod.), Richie Brockelman (co-creator), Turnabout (writer), Invisible Man (writer), Vampire (writer), Hill St. Blues (creator, prod.), Emmys 1981, 1982, 1983, 1984), Every Stray Dog and Kid (exec. prod.), Bay City Blues (exec. prod., writer, creator), L.A. Law (Emmy Awards: 1987, 1989), Hooperman, Cop Rock, NYPD Blue (Emmy Award, 1995), Byrds of Paradise, Murder One, Public Morals.

BOCHNER, HART
Actor, Director. b. Toronto, Ontario, Oct. 3, 1956. Son of actor Lloyd Bochner. e. U. of San Diego. Wrote, prod., dir. short film The Buzz (1992) starring Jon Lovitz. Directed film PCU (1994).
PICTURES: Islands in the Stream (debut, 1977), Breaking Away, Terror Train, Rich and Famous, The Wild Life, Supergirl, Making Mr. Right, Die Hard, Apartment Zero, Mr. Destiny, Mad at the Moon, Batman: Mask of the Phantasm (voice), The Innocent, High School High (dir.).
TELEVISION: Movies: Haywire, Having It All, Fellow Traveller, Complex of Fear. Mini-Series: East of Eden, The Sun Also Rises, War and Remembrance, And the Sea Will Tell, Children of the Dust. Special: Teach 109.

BOCHNER, LLOYD
Actor. b. Toronto, Canada, July 29, 1924. Father of actor Hart Bochner.
PICTURES: Drums of Africa, The Night Walker, Sylvia, Tony Rome, Point Blank, The Detective, The Horse in the Gray Flannel Suit, Tiger by the Tail, Ulzana's Raid, The Man in the Glass Booth, The Lonely Lady, Millenium, The Naked Gun 2 1/2, Morning Glory, It Seemed Like A Good Idea At The Time, Hot Touch, The Crystal Cage, Berlin Lady, Landslide, Lolita's Affair, The Dozier Case, Fine Gold.
TELEVISION: Series: One Man's Family, Hong Kong, The Richard Boone Show, Dynasty. Movies: Scalplock, Stranger on the Run, Crowhaven Farm, They Call It Murder, Satan's School for Girls, Richie Brockelman: Missing 24 Hours, Terraces, Immigrants, A Fire in the Sky, The Best Place to Be, The Golden Gate Murders, Mary and Joseph: A Story of Faith, Mazes & Monsters, Blood Sport, Race For the Bomb, Double Agent, Eagle One, Our Man First. Guest: Fantasy Island, Masquerade, The A-Team, Hotel, Crazy Like a Fox, Greatest Heroes of the Bible, Murder She Wrote, Designing Women, Hart To Hart, Who's The Boss, Golden Girls, The Love Boat, etc..

BODE, RALF
Cinematographer. b. Berlin, Germany. Attended Yale where was actor with drama school and acquired degree in directing. Received on-job training teaching combat photography and making films for Army at Ft. Monmouth. First professional job in films was gaffer on Harry, followed by long association with director John G. Avildsen, for whom served as gaffer and lighting designer on Guess What We Learned in School Today, Joe, and Cry Uncle. Later dir. of photography for Avildsen on Inaugural Ball and as East Coast dir. photo. for Rocky.
PICTURES: Saturday Night Fever, Slow Dancing in the Big City, Rich Kids, Coal Miner's Daughter, Dressed to Kill, Raggedy Man, A Little Sex, Gorky Park, First Born, Bring on the Night, Violets Are Blue, Critical Condition, The Big Town, The Accused, Distant Thunder, Cousins, Uncle Buck, One Good Cop, Love Field, Made in America, George Balanchine's The Nutcracker, Bad Girls, Safe Passage, Don Juan DeMarco.
TELEVISION: PBS Theatre in America, working as lighting designer and dir. of photo. Also many TV commercials. Movie: Gypsy.

BOETTICHER, BUDD
Director, Writer. Producer. r.n. Oscar Boetticher, Jr. b. Chicago, IL, July 29, 1916. e. Culver Military Acad., Ohio State U. bullfighter Novillero; then technical dir., Blood and Sand, 1941; asst. dir., Hal Roach studios and Columbia 1941-44; became feature director at Columbia in 1944; dir. Eagle Lion, 1946; dir., Universal; independ. prods., 1954. Autobiography: When in Disgrace.
PICTURES: As Oscar Boetticher: Behind Locked Doors, Assigned to Danger, Black Midnight, Killer Shark, Wolf Hunters. As Budd Boetticher: The Bullfighter and the Lady (also co-story), The Sword of D'Artagnan, The Cimarron Kid, Bronco Busters, Red Ball Express, Horizons West, City Beneath the Sea, Seminole, The Man from the Alamo, Wings of the Hawk, East of Sumatra, The Magnificent Matador (also story), The Killer Is Loose, Seven Men From Now, Decision at Sundown, The Tall T, Buchanan Rides Alone, Ride Lonesome (also prod.),

Westbound, The Rise and Fall of Legs Diamond, Comanche Station (also prod.), Arruza (also prod., co-s.p.), A Time For Dying (also s.p.), My Kingdom For a... (also s.p.).

BOGARDE, SIR DIRK
Actor. b. Hampstead, London, March 28, 1921. r.n. Derek Van Den Bogaerde. e. Allen Glens Coll., Glasgow & University Coll., London. Knighted, Feb. 1992. Started theatrical career with Amersham Repertory Co., then London stage; in Army in WWII. Commander des arts et des Lettres, France, 1990. Hon. Doc. Lit.: St. Andrews Univ., Sussex Univ. Top ten British star: 1953-54, 1956-64; number one British money-making star 1955, 1957, 1958, 1959; Variety Club Award—Best Performance 1961-64.
THEATER: U.K.: Power With Glory (1947), Point of Departure, The Shaughraun, The Vortex, Summertime, Jezebel.
PICTURES: Come on George (debut as extra, 1939), Dancing With Crime, Esther Waters, Quartet, Once a Jolly Swagman, Dear Mr. Prohack, Boys in Brown, The Blue Lamp, So Long at the Fair, Blackmailed, Woman in Question, Hunted (Stranger in Between), Penny Princess, The Gentle Gunman, Appointment in London, Desperate Moment, They Who Dare, The Sleeping Tiger, Doctor in the House, For Better or Worse, The Sea Shall Not Have Them, Simba, Doctor at Sea, Cast a Dark Shadow, Spanish Gardener, III Met by Moonlight (Night Ambush), Doctor at Large, Campbell's Kingdom, A Tale of Two Cities, The Wind Cannot Read, The Doctor's Dilemma, Libel, The Angel Wore Red, Song Without End, The Singer Not the Song, Victim, H.M.S. Defiant (Damn the Defiant), We Joined the Navy (cameo), The Password Is Courage, I Could Go on Singing, The Mind Benders, The Servant (BFA Award, 1964), Hot Enough for June (Agent 8 3/4), Doctor in Distress, The High Bright Sun (McGuire Go Home), King and Country, Darling (BFA Award, 1965), Modesty Blaise, Accident, Our Mother's House, Sebastian, The Fixer, Justine, Oh! What a Lovely War, The Damned, Death in Venice, The Serpent (Night Flight From Moscow), The Night Porter, Permission to Kill, Providence, A Bridge Too Far, Despair, Daddy Nostalgia.
TELEVISION: The Little Moon of Alban, Blithe Spirit, Upon This Rock, The Patricia Neal Story, May We Borrow Your Husband?, The Vision.
AUTHOR: A Postillion Struck by Lightning (1977), Snakes and Ladders (1978), An Orderly Man (1983), Backcloth, A Particular Friendship, Great Meadow, A Short Walk From Harrods. Novels: A Gentle Occupation, Voices in the Garden, West of Sunset, Jericho, A Period of Adjustment, Cleared For Take Off (autobiography).

BOGART, PAUL
Director. b. New York, NY, Nov. 13, 1919. Puppeteer-actor with Berkeley Marionettes 1946-48; TV stage mgr., assoc. dir. NBC 1950-52; won numerous Christopher Awards; recipient homage from French Festival Internationale Programmes Audiovisuelle, Cannes '91.
PICTURES: Marlowe (debut, 1969), Halls of Anger, Skin Game, Cancel My Reservation, Class of '44 (also prod.), Mr. Ricco, Oh God! You Devil, Torch Song Trilogy.
TELEVISION: U.S. Steel Hour, Kraft Theatre, Armstrong Circle Theatre, Goodyear Playhouse, The Defenders (Emmy Award, 1965), All in the Family (Emmy Award, 1978), The Golden Girls (Emmy Award, 1986). Specials: Ages of Man, Mark Twain Tonight, The Final War of Ollie Winter, Dear Friends (Emmy Award, 1968). Secrets, Shadow Game (Emmy Award, 1970), The House Without a Christmas Tree, Look Homeward Angel, The Country Girl, Double Solitaire, The War Widow, The Thanksgiving Treasure; The Adams Chronicles, Natica Jackson. Movies: In Search of America, Tell Me Where It Hurts, Winner Take All, Nutcracker: Money, Madness and Murder, Broadway Bound, The Gift of Love, The Heidi Chronicles.

BOGDANOVICH, PETER
Director, Producer, Writer, Actor. b. Kingston, NY, July 30, 1939. e. Collegiate Sch., Stella Adler Theatre Sch., N.Y. 1954\-58. Stage debut, Amer. Shakespeare Festival, Stratford, CT, followed by N.Y. Shakespeare Festival, 1958. Off-Bway: dir./prod.: The Big Knife, Camino Real, Ten Little Indians, Rocket to the Moon, Once in a Lifetime. Film critic and feature writer, Esquire, New York Times, Village Voice, Cahiers du Cinema, Los Angeles Times,New York Magazine, Vogue, Variety, etc. 1961–. Owner: The Holly Moon Company Inc. (L.A.), 1992-present.
PICTURES: Voyage to the Planet of the Prehistoric Women (dir., s.p., narrator; billed as Derek Thomas), The Wild Angels (2nd unit dir., co-s.p., actor). Director: Targets (also prod., co-s.p., actor), The Last Picture Show (also co-s.p.; N.Y. Film Critics' Award, best s.p.; British Academy Award, best s.p. 1971), Directed by John Ford (also s.p., interviewer), What's Up Doc? (also prod., co-s.p.; Writer's Guild of America Award, best s.p., 1972), Paper Moon (also prod.; Silver Shell, Mar del Plata, Spain 1973), Daisy Miller (also prod.; Best Director, Brussels Festival, 1974), At Long Last Love (also prod., s.p.), Nickelodeon (also co-s.p.), Saint Jack (also co-s.p., actor; Pasinetti Award, Critics Prize, Venice Festival, 1979), Opening Night (actor only), They All Laughed (also co-s.p.), Mask,

Illegally Yours (also prod.), Texasville (also co-prod., s.p.), Noises Off (also co-exec. prod.), The Thing Called Love. TELEVISION: *Special*: The Great Professional: Howard Hawks (co-dir., writer, interviewer; BBC). *Series*: CBS This Morning (weekly commentary; 1987-89). *Guest*: Northern Exposure (actor). AUHTOR: The Cinema of Orson Welles (1961), The Cinema of Howard Hawks (1962), The Cinema of Alfred Hitchcock, (1963), John Ford (1968; enlarged 1978), Fritz Lang in America, (1969), Allan Dwan—The Last Pioneer (1971), Pieces of Time (1973, enlarged 1985), The Killing of the Unicorn: Dorothy Stratten: 1960-1980 (1984), This Is Orson Welles (1992). Also edit., intro. writer to annual Year and a Day Engagement Calendar (1991-).

BOGOSIAN, ERIC
Actor, Writer. b. Woburn, MA, Apr. 24, 1953. e. studied 2 years at U. of Chicago, then Oberlin, theater degree, 1976. In high school, acted in plays with Fred Zollo (now prod.) and Nick Paleologus (now MA congressman). Moved to NY and worked briefly as gofer at Chelsea Westside Theater. Then joined downtown performance space, the Kitchen, first acting in others pieces, then creating his own incl. character Ricky Paul, a stand-up comedian in punk clubs. Theater pieces include: The New World, Men Inside, Voices of America, FunHouse, Drinking in America (Drama Desk and Obie Awards), Talk Radio, Sex Drugs Rock & Roll, Pounding Nails in the Floor With My Forehead (Obie Award), SubUrbia (author only). Book: Notes From Underground.
PICTURES: Special Effects, Talk Radio (also s.p.; Silver Bear Award 1988 Berlin Film Fest.), Sex Drugs Rock & Roll (also s.p.), Naked in New York, Dolores Claiborne, Under Siege 2: Dark Territory, Arabian Knight (voice).
TELEVISION: *Guest*: Miami Vice, Twilight Zone, Law & Order, The Larry Sanders Show. *Movies*: The Caine Mutiny Court Martial, Last Flight Out, Witch Hunt. *Special*: Drinking in America.

BOLAM, JAMES
Actor. b. Sunderland, England. Ent. ind. 1960.
PICTURES: The Kitchen, A Kind of Loving, Loneliness of the Long Distance Runner, HMS Defiant, Murder Most Foul, In Celebration.
TELEVISION: Likely Lads, When The Boat Comes In, Only When I Laugh, The Beiderbecke Affair, Father Matthews Daughter, Room at the Bottom, Andy Capp, The Beiderbecke Tapes, The Beiderbecke Connection, Second Thoughts.

BOLOGNA, JOSEPH
Actor, Writer. b. Brooklyn, NY., Dec. 30, 1938. e. Brown U. m. actress-writer Renee Taylor. Service in Marine Corps and on discharge joined ad agency, becoming director-producer of TV commercials. Collaborated with wife on short film, 2, shown at 1966 N.Y. Film Festival. Together they wrote Lovers and Other Strangers, Broadway play, in which both also acted. Wrote s.p. for film version. Both wrote and starred in Made for Each Other, and created and wrote TV series, Calucci's Dept.
PICTURES: Lovers and Other Strangers (co.-s.p. only), Made for Each Other (also co.-s.p.), Cops and Robbers, Mixed Company, The Big Bus , Chapter Two, My Favorite Year, Blame It on Rio , The Woman in Red, Transylvania 6-5000, It Had to Be You (also co-dir., co-s.p.), Coupe de Ville, Jersey Girl, Alligator II: The Mutation, Love Is All There Is.
TELEVISION: *Series*: Calucci's Dept. (creator, co-writer only), Rags to Riches, Top of the Heap. *Movies*: Honor Thy Father, Woman of the Year (also co-writer), Torn Between Two Lovers, One Cooks The Other Doesn't, Copacabana, A Time To Triumph, Prime Target, Thanksgiving Day, Citizen Cohn, The Danger of Love: The Carolyn Warmus Story, Revenge of the Nerds IV: Nerds in Love. *Special*: Acts of Love and Other Comedies (Emmy Award, 1974). *Mini-Series*: Sins.

BONANNO, LOUIE
Actor. b. Somerville, MA, Dec. 17, 1961. e. Bentley Coll., Waltham, MA, BS-economics, finance; AS accountancy, 1983. Moved to NY, 1983 to study at Amer. Acad. of Dramatic Arts. Toured U.S. 1985-86 as Dangermouse for MTV/Nickelodeon. In L.A. appeared as stand-up comedian. Stage debut in The Head.
PICTURES: Sex Appeal (debut, 1986), Wimps, Student Affairs, Cool as Ice, Auntie Lee's Meat Pies.
TELEVISION: Eisenhower & Lutz (series), 227, Tour of Duty, TV 101, Santa Barbara, New York Story.

BOND, DEREK
Actor, Scriptwriter. b. Glasgow Scotland, Jan. 26, 1920. e. Haberdasher' Askes Sch., London. Stage debut in As Husbands Go, 1937; served in Grenadier Guards H.M. Forces 1939-46, awarded Military Cross; author of Unscheduled Stop, Two Young Samaritans, Ask Father Christmas, Packdrill, Double Strung, Order to Kill, The Riverdale Dam, Sentence Deferred, The Mavroletty Fund. Many TV appearances. Pres., British Actors Equity, 1984-86. Author: Steady Old Man.
PICTURES: The Captive Heart (debut, 1946), Nicholas Nickleby, Joanna Godden, Uncle Silas, Scott of the Antarctic, Marry Me,

Poets Pub, Weaker Sex, Broken Journey, Christopher Columbus, Tony Draws a Horse, Quiet Woman, Hour of Thirteen, Distant Trumpet, Love's a Luxury, Trouble in Store, Svengali, High Terrace, Stormy Crossing, Rogues Yarn, Gideon's Day, The Hand, Saturday Night Out, Wonderful Life, Press For Time, When Eight Bells Toll, Intimate Reflections, Vanishing Army.

BONET, LISA
Actress. b. Los Angeles, CA, Nov. 16, 1967. First gained recognition on The Cosby Show as Denise Huxtable at the age of 15.
PICTURES: Angel Heart, Dead Connection, Bank Robber, New Eden.
TELEVISION: *Series*: The Cosby Show, A Different World. *Guest*: Tales From the Dark Side. *Special*: Don't Touch.

BONET, NAI
Actress, Producer. Worked in entertainment field since age of 13, including opera, films, TV, stage, night clubs and records.
PICTURES: *Actress*: The Soul Hustlers, The Seventh Veil, Fairy Tales, The Soul of Nigger Charlie, The Spy with the Cold Nose, John Goldfarb Please Come Home, etc. Wrote and starred in Nocturna and Hoodlums.
TELEVISION: Johnny Carson Show, Merv Griffin Show, Joe Franklin Show, Beverly Hillbillies, Tom Snyder Show.

BONHAM-CARTER, HELENA
Actress. b. London, England, May 26, 1966. Great granddaughter of Liberal Prime Minister Lord Asquith. e. Westminster. Appeared on BBC in A Pattern of Roses; seen by director Trevor Nunn who cast her in Lady Jane, 1986, theatrical film debut. On London stage in Trelawny of the Wells.
PICTURES: Lady Jane, A Room with a View, Maurice (cameo), Francesco, La Mascheral (The Mask), Getting It Right, Hamlet, Where Angles Fear to Tread, Howards End, Mary Shelley's Frankenstein, Mighty Aphrodite.
TELEVISION: *Guest*: Miami Vice. *Movies*: A Hazard of Hearts (U.S.), The Vision, Beatrix Potter, Fatal Deception: Mrs. Lee Harvey Oswald, Dancing Queen.

BONO, SONNY
Singer, Actor, Director, Writer. b. Detroit, MI, Feb. 16, 1935. r.n. Salvatore Bono. Started writing songs at age 16; entered record business with Specialty Records as apprentice prod. Became ass't. to Phil Spector, rock music prod. and did background singing. Recorded albums with former wife Cher, made two feature films and formed nightclub act with her. CBS comedy-variety series began as summer show in 1971 and made regular later that year. Elected Mayor, Palm Springs, CA 1988. Published autobiography in 1991. Elected to Congress, 1995.
PICTURES: Wild on the Beach (debut, 1965), Good Times (also wrote songs), Chastity (prod., s.p. only), Escape to Athena, Airplane II: The Sequel, Troll, Hairspray, Under the Boardwalk.
TELEVISION: *Series*: The Sonny & Cher Comedy Hour, The Sonny Comedy Revue. *Movies*: Murder on Flight 502, Murder in Music City, Top of the Hill. *Guest*: Shindig, Hullabaloo, Man from U.N.C.L.E., Love American Style, Murder She Wrote, Parker Lewis Can't Lose.

BOOKMAN, ROBERT
Executive. b. Los Angeles, CA, Jan. 29, 1947. e. U. of California, Yale Law Sch. Motion picture literary agent, IFA 1972-74, ICM 1974-79. 1979-84, ABC Motion Pictures v.p., worldwide production; 1984-6, Columbia Pictures, exec. v.p., world-wide prod. 1986, Creative Artists Agency, Inc., as motion picture literary and directors' agent.

BOONE, PAT
Singer, Actor. b. Jacksonville, FL, June 1, 1934. e. David Lipscomb Coll., North Texas State Coll., grad. magna cum laude, Columbia U. Winner of Ted Mack's Amateur Hour TV show; joined Arthur Godfrey TV show, 1955. Most promising new male star, Motion Picture Daily-Fame Poll 1957. One of top ten moneymaking stars, M.P. Herald-Fame Poll, 1957. Daughter is singer Debbie Boone. Author: Twixt Twelve and Twenty, Between You & Me and the Gatepost, The Real Christmas, others.
RECORDINGS: Ain't That a Shame, I Almost Lost My Mind, Friendly Persuasion, Love Letters in the Sand, April Love, Tutti Frutti, many others.
PICTURES: Bernardine (debut, 1957), April Love, Mardi Gras, Journey to the Center of the Earth, All Hands on Deck, State Fair, The Main Attraction, The Yellow Canary, The Horror of It All, Never Put It in Writing, Goodbye Charlie, The Greatest Story Ever Told, The Perils of Pauline, The Cross and the Switchblade, Roger and Me.
TELEVISION: *Series*: Arthur Godfrey and His Friends, The Pat Boone-Chevy Showroom (1957-60), The Pat Boone Show (1966-8). *Movie*: The Pigeon.

BOORMAN, JOHN
Director, Producer, Writer. b. London, Eng., Jan. 18, 1933. Wrote film criticism at age of 17 for British publications incl. Manchester Guardian; founder TV Mag. Day By Day; served in National Service in Army; Broadcaster and BBC radio film critic

1950-54; film editor Independent Television News; prod. documentaries for Southern Television; joined BBC, headed BBC Documentary Film Unit 1960-64, indep. doc. about D.W. Griffith; chmn. Natl. Film Studios of Ireland 1975-85; governor Brit. Film Inst. 1985-.
PICTURES: *Director.* Catch Us If You Can (Having a Wild Weekend; debut, 1965), Point Blank, Hell in the Pacific, Leo the Last (also co-s.p.), Deliverance (also prod.; 2 Acad. Award noms.), Zardoz (also prod., s.p.), Exorcist II: The Heretic (also co-prod.), Excalibur (also exec. prod., co-s.p.), Danny Boy (exec. prod. only), The Emerald Forest (also prod.), Hope and Glory (also prod., s.p., actor; 3 Acad. Award noms., Nat'l Film Critics Awards for dir., s.p.; L.A. Film Critics Awards for picture, s.p., dir.; U.K. Critics Awards for picture), Where the Heart Is (also prod., co-s.p.), I Dreamt I Woke Up (also s.p., actor), Two Nudes Bathing (also s.p., prod.), Beyond Rangoon (also co-prod.).
TELEVISION: *Series:* Citizen '63 (dir.), The Newcomers (dir.).

BOOTH, MARGARET
Film editor. b. Los Angeles, CA, 1898. Awarded honorary Oscar, 1977.
PICTURES: Why Men Leave Home, Husbands and Lovers, Bridge of San Luis Rey, New Moon, Susan Lenox, Strange Interlude, Smilin' Through, Romeo and Juliet, Barretts of Wimpole Street, Mutiny on the Bounty, Camille, etc. Supervising editor on Owl and the Pussycat, The Way We Were, Funny Lady, Murder by Death, The Goodbye Girl, California Suite, The Cheap Detective (also assoc. prod.), Chapter Two (also assoc. prod.), The Toy (assoc. prod. only), Annie, The Slugger's Wife (exec. prod. only).

BOOTHE, POWERS
Actor. b. Snyder, TX, 1949. e. Southern Methodist U. On Broadway in Lone Star.
PICTURES: The Goodbye Girl, Cruising, Southern Comfort, A Breed Apart, Red Dawn, The Emerald Forest, Extreme Prejudice, Stalingrad, Rapid Fire, Tombstone, Blue Sky, Sudden Death, Nixon.
TELEVISION: *Series:* Skag, Philip Marlowe. *Movies:* Skag, Plutonium Incident, Guyana Tragedy--The Story of Jim Jones (Emmy Award, 1980), A Cry for Love, Into the Homeland, Family of Spies, By Dawn's Early Light, Wild Card, Marked for Murder, Web of Deception.

BORGE, VICTOR
Comedian, Pianist. b. Copenhagen, Denmark, Jan. 3, 1909. Child prodigy at age 8. Awarded scholarship to study in Berlin and Vienna. Later became humorous concert artist. Wrote and starred in musical plays and films in Denmark. Fled Nazis in 1940, came to America. Appeared on Bing Crosby radio show, concert and nightclub tours, tv variety shows. One-man Broadway shows: Comedy in Music, 1953, 1965, 1977, 1989. Guest conductor with major symphonies around the world. Recent recording, The Two Sides of Victor Borge. Author: My Favorite Intermissions and My Favorite Comedies in Music. Awarded Medal of Honor by Statue of Liberty Centennial Comm. Knighted by 5 Scandinavian countries, honored by U.S. Congress and U.N. Created Thanks to Scandinavia Scholarship Fund, Dana College, Univ. of Conn., SUNY—Purchase Scholarships. Recent video: Onstage with Victor Borge.

BORGNINE, ERNEST
Actor. b. Hamden, CT, Jan. 24, 1917. e. Randall Sch. of Dramatic Art, Hartford, CT. Joined Barter Theatre in Virginia. Served in U.S. Navy; then little theatre work, stock companies; on Broadway in Harvey, Mrs. McThing; many TV appearances. Honors: 33rd Degree of the Masonic Order, Order of the Grand Cross, from same. Named honorary Mayor of Universal City Studios.
PICTURES: China Corsair (debut, 1951), The Mob, Whistle at Eaton Falls, From Here to Eternity, The Stranger Wore a Gun, Demetrius & the Gladiators, Johnny Guitar, Bounty Hunter, Vera Cruz, Bad Day at Black Rock, Marty (Academy Award for Best Actor, 1955), Run for Cover, Violent Saturday, Last Command, Square Jungle, Catered Affair, Jubal, Best Things in Life are Free, Three Brave Men, The Vikings, Badlanders, Torpedo Run, Rabbit Trap, Season of Passion, Man on a String, Pay or Die, Go Naked in the World, Barabbas, McHales's Navy, Flight of the Phoenix, The Oscar, Chuka, The Dirty Dozen, Ice Station Zebra, Legend of Lylah Clare, The Split, The Wild Bunch, The Adventurers, Suppose They Gave a War and Nobody Came?, A Bullet for Sandoval, Bunny O'Hare, Willard, Rain for a Dusty Summer, Hannie Caulder, The Revengers, Ripped Off, The Poseidon Adventure, Emperor of the North Pole, The Neptune Factor, Manhunt, Law and Disorder, Sunday in the Country, The Devil's Rain, Hustle, Shoot, Love By Appointment, The Greatest, Crossed Swords, Convoy, Strike Force, Diary of Madam X, The Black Hole, The Double McGuffin, The Ravagers, When Time Ran Out, High Risk, Super Fuzz, Escape from New York, Deadly Blessing, Young Warriors, Codename: Wild Geese, Skeleton Coast, Spike of Bensonhurst, The Opponent, Any Man's Death, Laser Mission, Turnaround, Captain Henkel, Real Men Don't Eat Gummy Bears, Moving Target, The Last Match, Mistress, All Dogs Go to Heaven 2 (voice).

TELEVISION: *Series:* McHale's Navy, Air Wolf, The Single Guy. *Movies:* Sam Hill: Who Killed the Mysterious Mr. Foster?, The Trackers, Twice in a Lifetime, Future Cop, Jesus of Nazareth, Fire!, The Ghost of Flight 401, Cops and Robin, All Quiet on the Western Front, Blood Feud, Carpool, Love Leads the Way, Last Days of Pompeii, The Dirty Dozen: The Next Mission, Alice in Wonderland, The Dirty Dozen: The Deadly Mission, Treasure Island (Ital. TV), The Dirty Dozen: The Fatal Mission, Jake Spanner-Private Eye, Appearances, The Burning Shore, Mountain of Diamonds (Ital TV). *Guest:* Philco Playhouse, General Electric Theater, Wagon Train, Laramie, Zane Grey Theater, Alcoa Premiere, The Love Boat, Little House on the Prairie, Murder She Wrote, Home Improvement. *Specials:* Billy the Kid, Legend in Granite: The Vince Lombardi Story.

BORIS, ROBERT
Writer, Director. b. NY, NY, Oct. 12, 1945. Screenwriter before also turning to direction with Oxford Blues, 1984.
PICTURES: *Writer.* Electra Glide in Blue, Some Kind of Hero, Doctor Detroit, Oxford Blues (also dir.), Steele Justice (dir.), Buy and Cell (dir.).
TELEVISION: Birds of Prey, Blood Feud, Deadly Encounter, Izzy and Moe, Frank and Jesse (also dir.).

BORODINSKY, SAMUEL
Executive. b. Brooklyn, NY, Oct. 25, 1941. e. Industrial Sch. of Arts & Photography. Expert in film care and rejuvenation. Now exec. v.p., Filmtreat International Corp. Previously with Modern Film Corp. (technician) and Comprehensive Filmtreat, Inc. & International Filmtreat (service manager).

BOSCO, PHILIP
Actor. b. Jersey City, NJ, Sept. 26, 1930. e. Catholic U., Washington, DC, BA. drama, 1957. Studied for stage with James Marr, Josephine Callan and Leo Brady. Consummate stage actor (in over 100 plays, 61 in NY) whose career spans the classics (with NY Shakespeare Fest. and American Shakespeare Fest, CT.), 20 plays with Arena Stage 1957-60, to modern classics as a resident actor with Lincoln Center Rep. Co. in the 1960s, winning Tony and Drama Desk Awards for the farce Lend Me a Tenor, 1988. Recipient: Clarence Derwent Award for General Excellence, Outer Critics Circle Award & Obie for Lifetime Achievement.
THEATER: Auntie Mame (B'way debut, City Center revival, 1958), Measure for Measure, The Rape of the Belt (Tony nom.), Donnybrook, Richard III, The Alchemist, The East Wind, The Ticket of Leave Man, Galileo, Saint Joan, Tiger at the Gates, Cyrano de Bergerac, Be Happy for Me, King Lear, The Miser, The Time of Your Life, Camino Real, Operation Sidewinder, Amphitryon, In the Matter of J. Robert Oppenheimer, The Good Woman of Setzuan, The Playboy of the Western World, An Enemy of the People, Antigone, Mary Stuart, The Crucible, Enemies, Mrs. Warren's Profession, Henry V, The Threepenny Opera, Streamers, Stages, The Biko Inquest, Whose Life Is It Anyway? A Month in the Country, Don Juan in Hell, Inadmissible Evidence, Ah! Wilderness, Man and Superman, Major Barbara, The Caine Mutiny Court Martial, Heartbreak House (Tony nom.), Come Back Little Sheba, Loves of Anatol, Be Happy for Me, Master Class, You Never Can Tell, A Man for All Seasons, Devil's Disciple, Lend Me a Tenor (Tony Award, 1989), The Miser, Breaking Legs, An Inspector Calls, The Heiress, Moon Over Buffalo.
PICTURES: Requiem for a Heavyweight, A Lovely Way to Die, Trading Places, The Pope of Greenwich Village, Walls of Glass, Heaven Help Us, Flanagan, The Money Pit, Children of a Lesser God, Suspect, Three Men and a Baby, Another Woman, Working Girl, The Luckiest Man in the World, Dream Team, Blue Steel, Quick Change, True Colors, FX2, Shadows and Fog, Straight Talk, Angie, Milk Money, Nobody's Fool, Safe Passage, It Takes Two.
TELEVISION: *Series:* TriBeCa. *Specials:* Prisoner of Zenda, An Enemy of the People, A Nice Place to Visit, Read Between the Lines (Emmy Award). *Guest:* Nurses, Trials of O'Brien, Law and Order, Spenser: For Hire, The Equalizer, Against the Law, Janek. *Movies:* Echoes in the Darkness, Second Effort, Internal Affairs, Murder in Black and White, The Return of Eliot Ness, Against the Wall, The Forget-Me-Not Murders, Attica: Line of Fire, Janek: A Silent Betrayal, Young at Heart.

BOSLEY, TOM
Actor. b. Chicago, IL, Oct. 1, 1927. e. DePaul U. Had roles on radio in Chicago and in stock productions before moving to New York. Appeared off-Broadway and on road before signed to play lead in Fiorello! for George Abbott on Broadway. First actor to win Tony, Drama Critics, ANTA and Newspaper Guild awards in one season for that role.
PICTURES: Love with the Proper Stranger, The World of Henry Orient, Divorce American Style, Yours Mine and Ours, The Secret War of Harry Frigg, To Find a Man, Mixed Company, Gus, O'Hara's Wife, Million Dollar Mystery, Wicked Stepmother.
TELEVISION: *Specials:* Alice in Wonderland (1953), Arsenic and Old Lace, The Drunkard, Profiles in Courage. *Guest:* Focus, Naked City, The Right Man, The Nurses, Route 66, The Perry

Como Show. *Series*: That Was the Week That Was, The Debbie Reynolds Show, The Dean Martin Show, Sandy Duncan Show, Wait Til Your Father Gets Home (voice), Happy Days, That's Hollywood (narrator), Murder She Wrote, Father Dowling Mysteries. *Movies*: Marcus Welby M.D.: A Matter of Humanities (pilot), Night Gallery, A Step Out of Line, Vanished, Congratulations It's a Boy!, Mr. & Mrs. Bo Jo Jones, Streets of San Francisco (pilot), No Place to Run, Miracle on 34th Street, The Girl Who Came Gift Wrapped, Death Cruise, Who Is the Black Dahlia?, Last Survivors, The Night That Panicked America, Love Boat, Testimony of 2 Men, Black Market Baby, With This Ring, The Bastard, The Triangle Factory Fire Scandal, The Castaways on Gilligan's Island, The Rebels, Return of the Mod Squad, For the Love of It, Jesse Owens Story, Fatal Confession: A Father Dowling Mystery, The Love Boat: A Valentine Voyage.

BOSTWICK, BARRY
Actor. b. San Mateo, CA, Feb. 24, 1945. e. USIU Sch. of Performing Arts, San Diego, BFA in acting; NYU Grad. Sch. of the Arts. Made prof. stage debut while in coll. working with Walter Pidgeon in Take Her She's Mine. Joined APA Phoenix Rep. Co. making his B'way debut in Cock-A-Doodle Dandy.
THEATER: Salvation, House of Leather, Soon, The Screens, Colette, Grease (created role of Danny Zuko, 1972), They Knew What They Wanted, The Robber Bridegroom (Tony Award, 1977), She Loves Me, L'Historie du Soldat, Nick and Nora.
PICTURES: The Rocky Horror Picture Show, Movie Movie, Megaforce, Eight Hundred Leagues Down the Amazon, Weekend at Bernie's 2, Spy Hard.
TELEVISION: *Series*: Foul Play, Dads. *Movies*: The Chadwick Family, The Quinns, Murder By Natural Causes, Once Upon a Family, Moviola — The Silent Lovers, Red Flag: The Ultimate Game, Summer Girl, An Uncommon Love, Deceptions, Betrayed by Innocence, Body of Evidence, Addicted to His Love, Parent Trap III, Till We Meet Again, Challenger, Captive, Between Love and Hate, Praying Mantis, Danielle Steel's Once in a Lifetime, The Return of Hunter, The Secretary. *Mini-Series*: Scruples, George Washington, I'll Take Manhattan, War and Remembrance. *Specials*: A Woman of Substance, You Can't Take It With You, Working.

BOSUSTOW, NICK
Producer. b. Los Angeles, CA, March 28, 1940. e. Menlo Coll., CA, administration. MCA, intl. sales, 1963. Pres., Stephen Bosustow Productions, 1967; pres., ASIFA-West; Academy Award '70 best short, Is It Always Right to Be Right?; 1973 Acad. Award nom., The Legend of John Henry. TV specials: The Incredible Book Escape, Misunderstood Monsters, A Tale of Four Wishes, Wrong Way Kid (Emmy, 1984); The Hayley Mills Story Book (series). 1973, pres., Bosustow Entertainment, Inc.

BOSWALL, JEFFERY
Producer, Director, Writer. b. Brighton, Eng., 1931. e. Taunton House School, Montpelier Coll., Brighton. Started career as an ornithologist for the Royal Society for the Protection of Birds. Joined BBC in 1958 as radio producer, moving to TV 1964 making films in diverse locations (Ethiopia and Antarctica). Contributed to 50 films as wildlife cameraman. Co-founder of British Library of Wildlife Sounds. 1987: returned to RSPB. Head of Film and Video Unit, 1987. 1992, sr. lecturer in Biological Film & Video, Derby Univ. Chairmanship BKSTS Intl Wildlife Filmmakers' Symposium.
AUTHOR: Birds for All Seasons. Ed. Look and Private Lives. Contrib.: Times, Countryman, the Field, Wildlife and Countryside, BBC Wildlife, Scientific Film, Journal of the Society of Film and TV Arts, Image Technology. Has written for scientific journals and writes annual update for Encyclopedia Britannica on ornithology.
TELEVISION: 18 films in the Private Lives series of which 4 (about the Kingfisher, Cuckoo, Starling and Jackass Penguin) won intl awards. Animal Olympians, Birds For All Seasons, Where the Parrots Speak Mandarin, Wildlife Safari to Ethiopia.

BOTTOMS, JOSEPH
Actor. b. Santa Barbara, CA, April 22, 1954. Brother of Sam and Timothy Bottoms. Did plays in jr. high school in Santa Barbara and then with community theatre.
PICTURES: The Dove (debut, 1974), Crime and Passion, The Black Hole, Cloud Dancer, King of the Mountain, Blind Date, Open House, Born to Race, Inner Sanctum.
TELEVISION: *Movies*: Trouble Comes to Town, Unwed Father, Stalk the Wild Child, The Intruder Within, Side By Side: The True Story of the Osmond Family, I Married Wyatt Earp, The Sins of Dorian Gray, Time Bomb, Braker, Island Sons, Cop Killer, Gunsmoke: To the Last Man, Treacherous Crossing, Liar's Edge. *Mini-Series*: Holocaust, Celebrity. *Special*: Winesburg Ohio. *Guest*: Owen Marshall, Murder She Wrote.

BOTTOMS, SAM
Actor. b. Santa Barbara, CA, Oct. 17, 1955. Brother of Timothy, Joseph and Ben Bottoms. Co-prod. documentary Picture This. Appeared in documentary Hearts of Darkness.

PICTURES: The Last Picture Show (debut, 1971), Class of '44, Zandy's Bride, The Outlaw Josey Wales, Apocalypse Now, Bronco Billy, Hunter's Blood, Gardens of Stone, After School, Ragin' Cajun, Dolly Dearest, In 'n Out, North of Chiang Mai, Prime Risk, The Trust, Sugar Hill.
TELEVISION: *Series*: Santa Barbara. *Movies*: Savages, Cage Without a Key, Desperate Lives, Island Sons. *Mini-Series*: East of Eden. *Guest*: Greatest Heroes of the Bible, Murder She Wrote, Doc Elliot, Eddie Capra, Lucas Tanner.

BOTTOMS, TIMOTHY
Actor. b. Santa Barbara, CA, Aug. 30, 1951. Brother of actors Joseph and Sam Bottoms. Early interest in acting; was member of S.B. Madrigal Society, touring Europe in 1967. Sang and danced in West Side Story local prod. With brother Sam co-prod. documentary Picture This about making of the Last Picture Show and Texasville.
PICTURES: Johnny Got His Gun (debut, 1971), The Last Picture Show, Love and Pain and the Whole Damn Thing, The Paper Chase, The White Dawn, The Crazy World of Julius Vrooder, Operation Daybreak, A Small Town in Texas, Rollercoaster, The Other Side of the Mountain: Part 2, Hurricane, The High Country, Tin Man, The Census Taker, Hambone and Hillie, In the Shadow of Kilimanjaro, The Sea Serpent, The Fantasist, Invaders from Mars, The Drifter, Mio in the Land of Faraway, Return to the River Kwai, A Case of Law, Texasville, Istanbul, I'll Met By Moonlight, Top Dog.
TELEVISION: *Special*: Look Homeward Angel. *Mini-Series*: The Money Changers, East of Eden. Movies: The Story of David, The Gift of Love, A Shining Season, Escape, Perry Mason: The Case of the Notorious Nun. Island Sons. *Series*: Land of the Lost.

BOULTING, ROY
Producer, Director, Writer. b. Bray, Buckinghamshire, England, Nov. 21, 1913. Twin brother of collaborator, producer/director John Boulting (d: 1985). e. McGill U., Montreal. Capt., Brit. Army, WWII. Dir. Charter Film, Charter Film Prod. Ltd. London; dir. British Lion Films, Ltd., 1958. 1977, co-author with Leo Marks of play, Favourites, Danny Travis, 1978.
PICTURES: *Producer*: Trunk Crime (feature debut, 1939), Inquest, Pastor Hall, Thunder Rock, Fame Is the Spur, The Guinea Pig, Singlehanded (Sailor of the King), High Treason, Josephine and Men, Run for the Sun, Brothers in Law, Happy Is the Bride, Carlton-Browne of the F.O. (Man in a Cocked Hat), A French Mistress, The Family Way, Twisted Nerve, There's a Girl in My Soup, Soft Beds and Hard Battles (Undercovers Hero), The Number. *Director*: Journey Together, Brighton Rock (Young Scarface), Seven Days to Noon, The Magic Box, Crest of the Wave (Seagulls Over Sorrento; co-dir., co-prod.), Private's Progress (also co-s.p.), Lucky Jim, I'm All Right Jack (also co-s.p.), The Suspect (The Risk; co-dir., co-prod.), Heaven's Above (also co-.sp.), Rotten to the Core.
TELEVISION: Agatha Christie's The Moving Finger (BBC).

BOUQUET, CAROLE
Actress. b. Neuilly-sur-Seine, France, Aug. 18, 1957. e. Sorbonne, Paris, Paris Conservatoire. Also model for Chanel No. 5 perfume.
PICTURES: That Obscure Object of Desire (debut, 1977), Buffet Froid, Il Cappotto di Astrakan, For Your Eyes Only, Bingo Bongo, Mystere, Nemo, Le Bon Roi Dagobert, Rive Droite Rive Gauche, Special Police, Double Messieurs, Le Mal d'aimer, Jenatsch, Bunker Palace Hotel, New York Stories, Too Beautiful for You, Grosse Fatigue, A Business Affair.

BOUTSIKARIS, DENNIS
Actor. b. Newark, NJ, Dec. 21, 1952. e. Hampshire Col.
THEATER: *Off-B'way*: Another Language (debut, 1975), Funeral March for a One Man Band, All's Well That Ends Well, Nest of the Wood Grouse, Cheapside, Rum and Coke, The Boys Next Door, Sight Unseen. *B'way*: Filomena, Bent, Amadeus.
PICTURES: The Exterminator, Batteries Not Included, Crocodile Dundee II, The Dream Team, Talent for the Game, The Boy Who Cried Bitch, Boys on the Side.
TELEVISION: *Series*: Nurse, Stat, The Jackie Thomas Show, Misery Loves Company. *Movies*: Victim of Love: The Shannon Mohr Story, Love and Betrayal: The Mia Farrow Story.

BOWIE, DAVID
Singer, Actor. b. Brixton, South London, England, Jan. 8, 1947. r.n. David Robert Jones. m. model-actress Iman. Broadway debut: The Elephant Man (1980).
PICTURES: The Virgin Soldiers (debut, 1969), Ziggy Stardust and the Spiders from Mars (1973; U.S. release 1983), The Man Who Fell to Earth, Just a Gigolo, Radio On, Christiane F, Cat People (performed song), The Hunger, Yellowbeard (cameo), Merry Christmas Mr. Lawrence, Into the Night, Absolute Beginners (also songs), Labyrinth (also songs), When the Wind Blows (songs), The Last Temptation of Christ, Imagine—John Lennon, The Linguini Incident, Twin Peaks: Fire Walk With Me, Basquiat.
TELEVISION: *Specials*: Christmas With Bing Crosby, The Midnight Special, Glass Spider Tour.

BOWSER, EILEEN
Curator, Film Archivist, Historian. b. Ohio, Jan. 18, 1928. e. Marietta Coll., B.A., 1950; U. of North Carolina, M.A., history of art, 1953. Joined Dept. of Film, Museum of Modern Art, 1954. Curator, Dept. of Film (1976-1993). Organized major exhib. of the films of D.W. Griffith, Carl-Theodor Dreyer, Art of the Twenties, recent acquisitions and touring shows. On exec. comm. of Federation Internationale des Archives du Film 1969-91, v.p. FIAF 1977-85; pres. FIAF Documentation Commission 1972-81. Film Archives Advisory Comm. since 1971. Assoc. of Univ. Seminars on Cinema and Interdisciplinary Interpretation. Publications: The Transformation of Cinema: 1907-15, Vol II, History of the American Film Series, The Movies, David Wark Griffith, Biograph Bulletins 1908-1912. A Handbook for Film Archives. Has written numerous articles on film history.

BOX, BETTY, OBE
Producer. b. Beckenham, Kent, England, 1920. Assisted Sydney Box in prod. 200 propaganda films in W.W.II. Assoc. prod. Upturned Glass.
PICTURES: Dear Murderer, When the Bough Breaks, Miranda, Blind Goddess, Huggett Family series. It's Not Cricket, Marry Me, Don't Ever Leave Me, So Long At the Fair, The Clouded Yellow, Appointment With Venus (Island Rescue). Venetian Bird (The Assassin), A Day to Remember, Doctor in the House, Mad About Men, Doctor at Sea, The Iron Petticoat, Checkpoint, Doctor at Large, Campbell's Kingdom, A Tale of Two Cities, The Wind Cannot Read, The 39 Steps, Upstairs and Downstairs, Conspiracy of Hearts, Doctor in Love, No Love for Johnnie, No, My Darling Daughter, A Pair of Briefs, The Wild and the Willing, Doctor in Distress, Hot Enough for June (Agent 8 3/4), The High Bright Sun (McGuire Go Home), Doctor in Clover, Deadlier Than the Male, Nobody Runs Forever (The High Commissioner), Some Girls Do, Doctor in Trouble, Percy, The Love Ban, Percy's Progress (It's Not the Size That Counts).

BOXLEITNER, BRUCE
Actor. b. Elgin, IL, May 12, 1950. m. actress Melissa Gilbert. After high school enrolled in Chicago's Goodman Theatre, staging productions and working with lighting and set design in addition to acting.
PICTURES: Six-Pack Annie, The Baltimore Bullet, Tron, The Crystal Eye, Breakaway, Diplomatic Immunity, Kuffs, The Babe.
TELEVISION: Series: How the West Was Won, Bring 'Em Back Alive, Scarecrow and Mrs. King, Babylon 5. Movies: The Chadwick Family, A Cry for Help, The Macahans, Kiss Me—Kill Me, Murder at the World Series, Happily Ever After, Wild Times, Kenny Rogers as The Gambler, Fly Away Home, Bare Essence, I Married Wyatt Earp, Kenny Rogers as The Gambler: The Adventure Continues, Passion Flower, Angel in Green, Kenny Rogers as the Gambler: The Legend Continues, Red River, The Town Bully, From the Dead of Night, The Road Raiders, Till We Meet Again, Murderous Vision, The Secret, Perfect Family, Double Jeopardy (also co-exec. prod.), House of Secrets, Gambler V: Playing for Keeps, Danielle Steel's Zoya. Mini-Series: How the West Was Won, East of Eden, The Last Convertible. Special: Wyatt Earp: Return to Tombstone.

BOYER, PHIL
TV Executive. b. Portland, OR, Dec. 13, 1940. e. Sacramento State U. Began broadcasting career as 12-year-old in Portland, establishing nation's first youth radio facility—a 5-watt facility in the basement of his home. At 16 began working at KPDQ, Portland; two years later joined KPTV, Portland, as announcer. In 1960 joined KEZI-TV, Eugene, OR, heading prod. and prog. depts. In 1965 named staff prod.-dir. for KCRA, TV, Sacramento, CA, becoming prod. mgr. in 1967 and prog. mgr. in 1969. In 1972 joined KNBC-TV, Los Angeles, as prog. dir. In 1974 named v.p., programming, of ABC Owned TV Stations; 1977, v.p.-gen. mgr., WLS-TV, Chicago; 1979, v.p.-gen. mgr. of WABC-TV, NY, 1981; v.p., gen mgr., ABC-owned TV station div.; 1984, joined ABC Video Enterprises as v.p. intl. dev.; 1986 named sr. v.p., intl and prog. dev., CC/ABC Video Ent.

BOYETT, ROBERT LEE
Producer. e. Duke U., B.A.; Col. U., M.A., marketing. Began career in media and mkt. research at Grey Advertising, Inc. Was program development consultant for PBS. In 1973 joined ABC as dir. of prime time series TV, East Coast. In 1975 named ABC TV v.p. & asst. to v.p. programs for West Coast. In 1977 joined Paramount Pictures in newly created position of v.p., exec. asst. to pres. & chief operating officer. In 1979, joined Miller-Milkis-Boyett Productions to produce for Paramount Television.
TELEVISION: Exec. prod.: Laverne and Shirley, Happy Days, Bosom Buddies, Mork and Mindy, Valerie, Perfect Strangers.

BOYLE, BARBARA D.
Executive. b. New York, NY, Aug. 11, 1935. e. U. of California, Berkeley, B.A., 1957; UCLA, J.D., 1960. Named to bar: California, 1961; New York, 1964; Supreme Court, 1964. Atty. in busn. affairs dept. & corp. asst. secty., American Intl. Pictures, Los Angeles, 1965-67; partner in entertainment law firm, Cohen & Boyle, L.A., 1967-74; exec. v.p. & gen. counsel, COO, New

World Pictures, L.A., 1974-82. Sr. v.p. worldwide prod., Orion Pictures, L.A., 1982-86; exec. v.p., prod., RKO Pictures, L.A., 1986-87. President, Sovereign Pictures, L.A., 1988-92; Boyle-Taylor Prods., 1993 to present. Co-chmn. 1979-80, Entertainment Law Symposium Advisory Committee, UCLA Law Sch. Member, AMPAS, Women in Film (pres., 1977-78, mem. of bd., chairperson 1981-84), Women Entertainment Lawyers Assn., California Bar Assn., N.Y. State Bar Assn., Beverly Hills Bar Assn., Hollywood Women's Political Committee, American Film Institute. Bd. mem.: Women Director's Workshop, Independent Feature Project/West, Los Angeles Women's Campaign Fund. Founding mem. UCLA Sch. of Law's Entertainment Advisory Council (& co-chairperson 1979 & 80).

BOYLE, LARA FLYNN
Actress. b. Davenport, IA, Mar. 24, 1970. e. Chicago Academy for the Visual and Performing Arts. First studied acting at the Piven Theatre. Professional debut at age 15 in tv mini-series Amerika.
PICTURES: Poltergeist III (debut, 1988), How I Got Into College, Dead Poets Society, May Wine, The Rookie, The Dark Backward, Mobsters, Wayne's World, Where the Day Takes You, The Temp, Eye of the Storm, Equinox, Red Rock West, Threesome, Baby's Day Out, The Road to Wellville, Farmer & Chase, Cafe Society, The Big Squeeze.
TELEVISION: Series: Twin Peaks. Mini-Series: Amerika. Movies: Terror on Highway 91, Gang of Four, The Preppie Murder, The Hidden Room, Past Tense, Jacob.

BOYLE, PETER
Actor. b. Philadelphia, PA, Oct. 18, 1933. e. LaSalle Coll. Was monk in Christian Bros. order before leaving in early 60s to come to N.Y. Acted in off-Broadway shows and joined The Second City in Chicago. Also did TV commercials.
THEATER: NY: Shadow of Heroes, Paul Sills' Story Theatre, The Roast, True West, Snow Orchid.
PICTURES: The Virgin President (debut, 1968), The Monitors, Medium Cool, Joe, Diary of a Mad Housewife, T.R. Baskin, The Candidate, Steelyard Blues, Slither, The Friends of Eddie Coyle, Kid Blue, Ghost in the Noonday Sun, Crazy Joe, Young Frankenstein, Taxi Driver, Swashbuckler, F.I.S.T., The Brink's Job, Hardcore, Beyond the Poseidon Adventure, Where the Buffalo Roam, In God We Trust, Outland, Hammett, Yellowbeard, Johnny Dangerously, Turk 182, Surrender, Walker, The In Crowd, Red Heat, The Dream Team, Speed Zone, Funny, Men of Respect, Solar Crisis, Kickboxer 2, Honeymoon in Vegas, Nervous Ticks, Malcolm X, The Shadow, The Santa Clause, Bulletproof Heart, Born to Be Wild, While You Were Sleeping.
TELEVISION: Series: Comedy Tonight, Joe Bash. Mini-Series: From Here to Eternity. Movies: The Man Who Could Talk to Kids, Tail Gunner Joe, Echoes in the Darkness, Disaster at Silo 7, Guts and Glory: The Rise and Fall of Oliver North, Challenger, In the Line of Duty: Street War, Taking the Heat, Royce. Specials: 27 Wagons Full of Cotton, Conspiracy: The Trial of the Chicago Eight. Guest: Cagney & Lacey, Midnight Caller, X-Files (Emmy Award, 1996). Pilot: Philly Heat.

BRABOURNE, LORD JOHN
Producer. b. London, England, Nov. 9, 1924.
PICTURES: Harry Black and the Tiger, Sink the Bismarck, H.M.S. Defiant (Damn the Defiant!), Othello, The Mikado, Up the Junction, Romeo and Juliet, Dance of Death, Peter Rabbit and Tales of Beatrix Potter, Murder on the Orient Express, Death on the Nile, Stories from a Flying Trunk, The Mirror Crack'd, Evil Under the Sun, A Passage to India, Little Dorrit.

BRACCO, LORRAINE
Actress. b. Brooklyn, NY, 1955. m. actor Edward James Olmos. At 16 began modelling for Wilhelmina Agency appearing in Mademoiselle, Seventeen, Teen magazine. Moved to Paris where modelling career continued and led to TV commercials. After making her film debut in Duo sur Canape became a disc jockey on Radio Luxembourg, Paris. 1983 produced a TV special on fashion and music. In Lincoln Center workshop performance of David Rabe's Goose and Tom Tom, 1986.
PICTURES: Cormorra, The Pick-up Artist, Someone to Watch Over Me, Sing, The Dream Team, On a Moonlit Night, Good Fellas (Acad. Award nom.), Talent for the Game, Switch, Medicine Man, Radio Flyer, Traces of Red, Being Human, The Basketball Diaries, Hackers.
TELEVISION: Movies: Scam, Getting Gotti.

BRACKEN, EDDIE
Actor. b. New York, NY, Feb. 7, 1920. e. Prof. Children's Sch. for Actors, N.Y. m. Connie Nickerson, actress. Vaudeville & night club singer: stage debut in Lottery, 1930.
THEATER: Lady Refuses, Iron Men, So Proudly We Hail, Brother Rat, What A Life, Too Many Girls, Seven Year Itch, Shinbone Alley, Teahouse of the August Moon, You Know I Can't Hear You When The Water's Running, The Odd Couple, Never Too Late, Sunshine Boys, Hotline to Heaven, Hello Dolly, Damn Yankees, Sugar Babies, Show Boat, The Wizard of Oz.

PICTURES: Too Many Girls (debut, 1940), Life With Henry, Reaching for the Sun, Caught in the Draft, The Fleet's In, Sweater Girl, Star Spangled Rhythm, Happy Go Lucky, Young and Willing, The Miracle of Morgan's Creek, Hail the Conquering Hero, Rainbow Island, Bring on the Girls, Duffy's Tavern, Hold That Blonde, Out of This World, Ladies' Man, Fun on a Weekend, The Girl From Jones Beach, Summer Stock, Two Tickets to Broadway, About Face, We're Not Married, Slight Case of Larceny, Wild Wild World (narrator), Shinbone Alley (voice), National Lampoon's Vacation, Preston Sturges: The Rise and Fall of an American Dreamer, Oscar, Home Alone 2: Lost in New York, Rookie of the Year, Baby's Day Out.
TELEVISION: Series: I've Got a Secret (panelist), Make the Connection (panelist), Masquerade Party (host, 1957).Guest: Goodyear Playhouse, Studio One, Climax, Murder She Wrote, Blacke's Magic, Amazing Stories, Tales of the Dark Side, Golden Girls, Wise Guy, Empty Nest, Monsters. Movies: The American Clock, Assault at West Point.

BRADEN, WILLIAM
Executive, Producer. b. Alberta, Canada, June 2, 1939. e. U.S., Vancouver, B.C. and abroad. Began career as stuntman in Hollywood, and has worked in all aspects of industry Worked for Elliott Kastner as prod. exec. and with Jeffrey Bloom, of Feature Films, Inc., as prod. exec. and v.p. in chg. of prod. Also with Dunatai Corp., as head of film and TV prod. With Completion Bond Co. one yr. as prod. exec., Australia then with Filmaker Completion as pres. 4 years. Now indep. prod.
PICTURES: Pyramid (assoc. prod., prod. supv.), Russian Roulette (prod. exec.), 92 in the Shade (prod. exec.), Breakheart Pass (prod. exec.), Dogpound Shuffle (asst. dir.), Dublin Murders (supvr. re-edit), He Wants Her Back (prod.), Goldengirl (prod. exec.), Running Scared (prod.), Death Valley (asst. dir.), The Seduction (prod. exec.), Slapstick of Another Kind (prod. exec.).
TELEVISION: Requiem for a Planet (series, prod./creator). Specials: Nothing Great is Easy (exec. prod.), King of the Channel (exec. prod.), I Believe (prod.), If My People... (prod.), America: Life in the Family (dir./prod.). Also various Movies of the Week for networks and many industrial and doc. films.

BRADFORD, JESSE
Actor. b. 1980. Made first appearance as infant in Q-tip commercial.
PICTURES: Falling in Love (debut, 1984), Prancer, Presmued Innocent, My Blue Heaven, The Boy Who Cried Bitch, King of the Hill, Far From Home: The Adventures of Yello Dog, Hackers.
TELEVISION: Movie: The Boys. Special: Classified Love. Guest: Tribeca.

BRADLEY, ED
Newscaster. b. Philadelphia, Pa., June 22, 1941. e. Cheyney State Coll, B.S. Worked way up through the ranks as local radio reporter in Philadelphia 1963-67 and NY 1967-71. Joined CBS News as stringer in Paris bureau, 1971; then Saigon bureau. Named CBS news correspondent, 1973. Became CBS News White House corr. and anchor of CBS Sunday Night News, 1976-81; principal corr. and anchor, CBS Reports, 1978-81; co-editor and reporter 60 Minutes since 1980. Recipient: Alfred I. duPont-Columbia University and Overseas Press Club Awards, George Foster Peabody and Ohio State Awards, George Polk Award.
TELEVISION: Special reports: What's Happened to Cambodia, The Boat People, The Boston Goes to China, Blacks in America—With All Deliberate Speed, Return of the CIA, Miami... The Trial that Sparked the Riot (Emmy Award), The Saudis, Too Little Too Late (Emmy Award), Murder—Teenage Style (Emmy Award, 1981), In the Belly of the Beast (Emmy Award, 1982), Lena (Emmy Award, 1982).

BRAEDEN, ERIC
Actor. b. Kiel, Germany, Apr. 3, r.n. Hans Gudegast. Awarded Federal Medal of Honor by pres. of Germany for promoting positive, realistic image of Germans in America.
PICTURES: Morituri, Dayton's Devils, 100 Rifles, Colossus: The Forbin Project, Escape from the Planet of the Apes, Lady Ice, The Adulteress, The Ultimate Thrill, Herbie Goes to Monte Carlo, The Ambulance.
TELEVISION: Series: The Rat Patrol, The Young and the Restless (People's Choice Award, Soap Opera Award, 2 Emmy noms.). Movies: Honeymoon With a Stranger, The Mask of Sheba, The Judge and Jake Wyler, Death Race, Death Scream, The New Original Wonder Woman (pilot), Code Name: Diamond Head, Happily Ever After, The Power Within, The Aliens Are Coming, Lucky, The Case of the Wicked Wives.

BRAGA, SONIA
Actress. b. Maringa, Parana, Brazil, 1950. Began acting at 14 on live children's program on Brazilian TV, Gardin Encantado. Stage debut at 17 in Moliere's Jorge Dandin, then in Hair! Starred in many Brazilian soap operas including Gabriella, as well as a prod. of Sesame Street in Sao Paulo.
PICTURES: The Main Road, A Moreninha, Captain Bandeira Vs. Dr. Moura Brasil, Mestica, The Indomitable Slave, The Couple,

Dona Flor and Her Two Husbands, Gabriella, I Love You, A Lady in the Bus, Kiss of the Spider Woman, The Milagro Beanfield War, Moon Over Parador, The Rookie, Roosters.
TELEVISION: Movies: The Man Who Broke 1000 Chains, The Last Prostitute, The Burning Season. Guest: The Cosby Show, Tales From the Crypt.

BRANAGH, KENNETH
Actor, Director, Producer, Author. b. Belfast, Northern Ireland, Dec. 10, 1960. m. actress Emma Thompson. Moved to Reading, England at 9. e. RADA. Went from drama school into West End hit Another Country, followed by Gamblers, The Madness, Francis. Royal Shakespeare Co.: Love Labors Lost, Hamlet, Henry V. Left Royal Shakespeare Company to form his own Renaissance Theater Co. with actor David Parfitt for which he wrote a play Public Enemy (also produced Off-B'way), wrote-directed Tell Me Honestly, directed Twelfth Night, produced-directed-starred in Romeo & Juliet, and played Hamlet, Benedick and Touchstone in a sold-out nationwide tour and London season. L.A.: King Lear, A Midsummer Night's Dream. Author: Beginning (1990). Received BAFTA's Michael Balcon Award for Outstanding Contribution to Cinema (1993). Made Oscar nominated short film Swan Song.
PICTURES: High Season (debut, 1987), A Month in the Country, Henry V (also dir., adapt.; BAFTA & Natl. Board of Review Awards for Best Director, 1989), Dead Again (also dir.), Peter's Friends (also dir., prod.), Swing Kids, Much Ado About Nothing (also dir., adapt.), Mary Shelley's Frankenstein (also dir., co-prod.), In the Bleak Mid-Winter (dir., s.p. only), Anne Frank Remembered (narrator), Othello, Hamlet (also dir, prod..).
TELEVISION: The Boy in the Bush (series), The Billy Plays, Maybury, To the Lighthouse, Coming Through, Ghosts, The Lady's Not For Burning, Fortunes of War (mini-series) Thompson (series), Strange Interlude, Look Back in Anger.

BRANDAUER, KLAUS MARIA
Actor. b., Altaussee, Austria, June 22, 1944. m. film and TV dir.-screenwriter Karin Mueller. e. Acad. of Music and Dramatic Arts, Stuttgart, W. Germany. Was established in the German and Austrian theater before film debut.
PICTURES: The Salzburg Connection (debut, 1972), Mephisto (Cannes Film Fest. Award, 1981). Never Say Never Again, Colonel Redl, Out of Africa, The Lightship, Streets of Gold, Burning Secret, Hanussen, Hitlerjunge Salomon, Das Spinnennetz (The Spider's Web) The French Revolution, The Russia House, White Fang, The Resurrected, Seven Minutes (also dir.), Becoming Colette, Felidae (voice).
TELEVISION: Quo Vadis?

BRANDIS, JONATHAN
Actor. b. Danbury, CT, April 13, 1976. Started as print model at age 4; followed by several tv commercials.
PICTURES: Fatal Attraction, Stepfather 2, Never Ending Story II: The Next Chapter, Ladybugs, Sidekicks.
TELEVISION: Series: seaQuest DSV. Movies: Poor Little Rich Girl, Stephen King's IT, Good King Wenceslas.

BRANDO, MARLON
Actor. b. Omaha, NB, April 3, 1924. Sister is actress Jocelyn Brando. e. Shattuck Military Acad., Faribault, MN. Studied acting at New School's Dramatic Workshop, NY, with Stella Adler; played stock in Sayville, Long Island. Broadway debut: I Remember Mama, followed by Truckline Cafe, Candida, A Flag Is Born, A Streetcar Named Desire. Voted one of top ten Money-Making Stars, M.P. Herald-Fame poll, 1954-55. Autobiography: Brando: Songs My Mother Taught Me (1994).
PICTURES: The Men (debut, 1950), A Streetcar Named Desire, Viva Zapata!, Julius Caesar, The Wild One, On the Waterfront (Academy Award, 1954), Desiree, Guys and Dolls, The Teahouse of the August Moon, Sayonara, The Young Lions, The Fugitive Kind, One-Eyed Jacks (also dir.), Mutiny on the Bounty, The Ugly American, Bedtime Story, The Saboteur—Code Name: Morituri, The Chase, The Appaloosa, A Countess From Hong Kong, Reflections in a Golden Eye, Candy, The Night of the Following Day, Burn!, The Nightcomers, The Godfather (Academy Award, 1972), Last Tango in Paris, The Missouri Breaks, Superman, Apocalypse Now, The Formula, A Dry White Season, The Freshman, Christopher Columbus: The Discovery, Don Juan DeMarco, Divine Rapture, The Island of Dr. Moreau.
TELEVISION: Mini-Series: Roots: The Next Generations (Emmy Award, 1979).

BRANDON, MICHAEL
Actor. b. Brooklyn, NY. e. AADA. Appeared on B'way in Does Tiger Wear a Necktie?
PICTURES: Lovers and Other Strangers, Jennifer on My Mind, Four Flies on Grey Velvet, Heavy Traffic (voice), FM, Promises in the Dark, A Change of Seasons, Rich and Famous.
TELEVISION: Series: Emerald Point, Dempsey & Makepeace, Home Fires. Movies: The Impatient Heart, The Strangers in 7A, The Third Girl From the Left, Hitchhike!, The Red Badge of Courage, Queen of the Stardust Ballroom, Cage Without a Key, James Dean, Scott Free, Red Alert, The Comedy Company, A

Vacation in Hell, A Perfect Match, Between Two Brothers, The Seduction of Gina, Deadly Messages, Rock 'n' Roll Mom, Dynasty: The Reunion, Not in My Family, Moment of Truth: Murder or Memory?

BRANDT, RICHARD PAUL
Executive. b. New York, NY, Dec. 6, 1927. e. Yale U., BS, Phi Beta Kappa. Chmn. Trans Lux Corp.; chmn., Brandt Theatres; dir., Presidential Realty Corp.; chmn. emeritus & trustee, American Film Institute; trustee, American Theatre Wing; member, Tony Awards Management Comm.; vice-chmn. & trustee, College of Santa Fe.

BRAUNSTEIN, GEORGE GREGORY
Producer. b. New York, NY, May 23, 1947. e. Culver Military Acad., U. of California, B.A., biology, chemistry, 1970. U. W.L.A. Law School, J.D. 1987. Father is Jacques Braunstein (Screen Televideo Prods. At War with the Army, Young Lions, etc.).
PICTURES: Train Ride to Hollywood, Fade to Black, Surf II, And God Created Woman, Out Cold, Don't Tell Her It's Me.

BRAVERMAN, CHARLES
Producer, Director. b. Los Angeles, CA, March 3, 1944. e. Los Angeles City Coll., U. of Southern California, B.A. m. Kendall Carly Browne, actress. Child actor, 1950-57. Two time Emmy winner.
PICTURES: Dillinger, Soylent Green, Same Time Next Year (all montages, titles), Can't Stop the Music (titles), Hit and Run (prod./dir.).
TELEVISION: An American Time Capsule, The Smothers Brothers Racing Team Special, How to Stay Alive, David Hartman... Birth and Babies, Breathe a Sigh of Relief, The Television Newsman, Getting Married, The Making of a Live TV Show, Televisionland, Nixon: Checkers to Watergate, Braverman's Condensed Cream of Beatles, Two Cops, Peanuts to the Presidency: The Jimmy Carter Campaign, The Making of Beatlemania, Willie Nelson Plays Lake Tahoe, Tony Bennett Sings, What's Up, America?, The Big Laff Off, Engelbert at the MGM Grand, Oscar's First 50 Years, Frankie Valli Show, The Sixties, Showtime Looks at 1981, Roadshow, Kenny Rodger's America, St. Elsewhere, DTV (Disney Channel), Crazy Like a Fox, Dreams, The Richard Lewis Special, Prince of Bel Air, Brotherhood of Justice, The Wizard; Heart of the City, Rags to Riches, The New Mike Hammer, Sledge Hammer!, Gabriel's Fire, Life Goes On, Beverly Hills 90210, FBI: Untold Stories, Final Shot: The Hank Gathers Story, Melrose Place, Northern Exposure (DGA nom.), Haunted Lives II.

BRECHER, IRVING
Writer, Director. b. New York, NY, Jan. 17, 1914. e. Roosevelt H.S. in Yonkers. Yonkers Herald reporter; network programs writer for Milton Berle, Willie Howard, Al Jolson, etc., m.p. writer since 1937.
PICTURES: At the Circus, Go West, Du Barry Was a Lady, Shadow of the Thin Man, Best Foot Forward, Meet Me in St. Louis, Summer Holiday, Yolanda and the Thief, Life of Riley (also dir.), Somebody Loves Me (also dir.), Cry for Happy, Sail a Crooked Ship (also dir.), Bye Bye Birdie.
TELEVISION: The People's Choice, The Life of Riley.

BREGMAN, MARTIN
Producer, Writer. b. New York, NY, May 18, 1931. m. actress Cornelia Sharpe. e. Indiana U., NYU. Began career as business and personal mgr. to Barbra Streisand, Faye Dunaway, Candice Bergen, Al Pacino, etc. Chairman NY Advisory Council for Motion Pictures, Radio and TV (co-founder, 1974).
PICTURES: Producer: Serpico, Dog Day Afternoon, The Next Man, The Seduction of Joe Tynan, Simon, The Four Seasons, Eddie Macon's Run, Venom, Scarface, Sweet Liberty, Real Men, A New Life, Sea of Love, Nesting, Betsy's Wedding, Whispers in the Dark, The Real McCoy, Carlito's Way, The Shadow, Gold Diggers: The Secret of Bear Mountain, Matilda.
TELEVISION: Prod.: S*H*E (movie), The Four Seasons (series).

BRENNAN, EILEEN
Actress. b. Los Angeles, CA, Sept. 3, 1935. e. Georgetown U., American Acad. of Dramatic Arts, N.Y. Daughter of silent film actress Jean Manahan. Big break came with lead in off-Broadway musical, Little Mary Sunshine (Obie & Theatre World Awards, 1960).
THEATER: The Miracle Worker (tour), Hello Dolly! (Broadway), and revivals of The King and I, Guys and Dolls, Camelot, Bells Are Ringing; also An Evening with Eileen Brennan, A Couple of White Chicks Sitting Around Talking.
PICTURES: Divorce American Style (debut, 1967), The Last Picture Show (BAFTA nom.), Scarecrow, The Sting, Daisy Miller, At Long Last Love, Hustle, Murder by Death, FM, The Cheap Detective, The Last of the Cowboys (The Great Smokey Roadblock), Private Benjamin (Acad. Award nom.), Pandemonium, The Funny Farm, Clue, Sticky Fingers, Rented Lips, The New Adventures of Pippi Longstocking, It Had to Be You, Stella, Texasville, White Palace, Joey Takes a Cab, I Don't Buy Kisses Anymore, Reckless.

TELEVISION: Series: Rowan & Martin's Laugh-In, All My Children, 13 Queens Boulevard, A New Kind of Family, Private Benjamin (Emmy Award, 1981), Off the Rack. Specials: Working, In Search of Dr. Seuss. Movies: Playmates, My Father's House, The Night That Panicked America, The Death of Richie, When She Was Bad..., My Old Man, When the Circus Came to Town, Incident at Crestridge, Going to the Chapel, Deadly Intentions... Again?, Taking Back My Life: The Nancy Ziegenmeyer Story, Poisoned by Love: The Kern County Murders, Precious Victims, My Name Is Kate, Take Me Home Again, Freaky Friday, Trail of Tears. Mini-Series: The Blue Knight, Black Beauty. Guest: Taxi, Magnum P.I., Newhart, All in the Family, Murder She Wrote.

BREST, MARTIN
Director. b. Bronx, NY, Aug. 8, 1951. e. NYU Sch. of Film. m. producer Lisa Weinstein. Made award-winning short subject, Hot Dogs for Gauguin (featuring Danny DeVito). Accepted into fellowship program at American Film Institute, making first feature, Hot Tomorrows (dir., prod., s.p.), as AFI project. Appeared in Fast Times at Ridgemont High, Spies Like Us. Produced film Josh and S.A.M.
PICTURES: Going in Style (also s.p.), Beverly Hills Cop, Midnight Run (also prod.), Scent of a Woman (also prod.).

BRIALY, JEAN-CLAUDE
Actor. b. Aumale, Algeria, March 30, 1933. e. Strasbourg U. (philosophy) also attended drama classes at Strasbourg Conservatoire. Made several short films with Jacques Rivette and Jean-Luc Godard.
PICTURES: Paris Does Strange Things, Elevator to the Gallows, Les Cousins, Three Faces of Sin, A Woman Is a Woman, Seven Capitol Sins, The Devil and Ten Commandments, Two Are Guilty, Nutty Naughty Chateau, Carless Love, Male Hunt, Circle of Love, King of Hearts, The Oldest Profession, Shock Troops, The Bride Wore Black, Claire's Knee, A Murder is a Murder, The Phantom of Liberty, Catherine et Cie, The Accuser, L'Annee Sainte, Robert and Robert, Eglantine, Les Violets Clos, L'oiseau Rare, Un Amour De Pluie, Bobo Jacco, L'oeil Du Maitre, La Banquiere, La Nuit de Varennes, Cap Canaille, Le Demon Dan L'Isle, Edith and Marcel, Sarah, Stella, The Crime, Papy Fait de la Resistance, Pinot, Simple Flic, Comedie été.

BRICKMAN, MARSHALL
Writer, Director. b. Rio de Janeiro, Brazil, Aug. 25, 1941. e. U. of Wisconsin. Banjoist, singer, writer with folk groups The Tarriers and The Journeymen before starting to write for TV. Appeared in films Funny and That's Adequate.
PICTURES: Co-writer (with Woody Allen): Sleeper, Annie Hall (Academy Award, 1977), Manhattan, Manhattan Murder Mystery. Director-Writer: Simon (dir. debut, 1980), Lovesick, The Manhattan Project (also prod.). Co-Writer: For the Boys, Intersection.
TELEVISION: Writer: Candid Camera 1966, The Tonight Show 1966-70. Specials: Johnny Carson's Repertory Co. in an Evening of Comedy (1969), Woody Allen Special, Woody Allen Looks at 1967. Prod.: Dick Cavett Show (1970-72, Emmy Award).

BRICKMAN, PAUL
Writer, Director. b. Chicago, IL. e. Claremont Men's Coll. Worked as camera asst., then story analyst at Paramount, Columbia, and Universal.
PICTURES: Handle With Care (Citizen's Band; assoc. prod., s.p.), The Bad News Bears in Breaking Training (s.p.), Risky Business, (dir., s.p.), Deal of the Century (s.p., co-exec. prod.), That's Adequate (interviewee), Men Don't Leave (dir., co-s.p.).

BRICUSSE, LESLIE
Composer, Writer. b. London, England, Jan. 29, 1931. e. Cambridge Univ.
THEATER: Book, music and lyrics (with Anthony Newley): Stop the World—I Want to Get Off, The Roar of the Greasepaint--The Smell of the Crowd, The Good Old Bad Old Days, The Travelling Music Show. Also: Pickwick (lyrics), Over the Rainbow (lyrics), Sherlock Holmes (book, songs), Jekyll and Hyde (book, lyrics).
PICTURES: Wrote songs for: Goldfinger, Penelope, In Like Flint, Gunn, A Guide for the Married Man, Doctor Dolittle (also s.p.; Academy Award for best song: Talk to the Animals, 1967), Sweet November, Goodbye Mr. Chips, Scrooge (also s.p., exec. prod.), Willy Wonka and the Chocolate Factory, Revenge of the Pink Panther, Superman, The Sea Wolves, Sunday Lovers (s.p. only for An Englishman's Home segment), Victor/Victoria (Academy Award, 1982), Santa Claus, That's Life, Home Alone, Hook, Tom & Jerry: The Movie.
TELEVISION: Series Theme Songs: Hart to Hart, I'm a Big Girl Now. Specials: Peter Pan, Babes in Toyland.

BRIDGES, ALAN
Director. b. England, Sept. 28, 1927. Started dir. for the BBC before moving into feature films.

PICTURES: An Act of Murder (debut, 1965), Invasion, Shelley, The Hireling, Out of Season, Summer Rain, The Return of the Soldier, The Shooting Party, Displaced Persons, Apt Pupil, Secret Places of the Heart, Fire Princess.
TELEVISION: The Father, Dial M For Murder, The Intrigue, The Ballade of Peckham Rye, The Initiation, Alarm Call: Z Cars, The Fontenay Murders, The Brothers Karamazov, The Idiot, Days to Come, Les Miserables, Born Victim, The Wild Duck, The Lie, Brief Encounter, Forget Me Not Lane, Double Echo, Saturday, Sunday Monday, Crown Matrimonial.

BRIDGES, BEAU
Actor. r.n. Lloyd Vernet Bridges III. b. Hollywood, CA, Dec. 9, 1941. e. UCLA, U. of Hawaii. Father is actor Lloyd Bridges, brother is actor Jeff Bridges.
PICTURES: Force of Evil (debut, 1948), No Minor Vices, The Red Pony, Zamba, The Explosive Generation, Village of the Giants, The Incident, For Love of Ivy, Gaily Gaily, The Landlord, Adam's Woman, The Christian Licorice Store, Hammersmith Is Out, Child's Play, Your Three Minutes Are Up, Lovin' Molly, The Other Side of the Mountain, Dragonfly (One Summer Love), Swashbuckler, Two-Minute Warning, Greased Lightning, Norma Rae, The Fifth Musketeer, The Runner Stumbles, Silver Dream Racer, Honky Tonk Freeway, Night Crossing, Love Child, Heart Like a Wheel, The Hotel New Hampshire, The Killing Time, The Wild Pair (also dir.), Seven Hours to Judgement (also dir.), The Iron Triangle, Signs of Life, The Fabulous Baker Boys, The Wizard, Daddy's Dyin'...Who's Got the Will?, Married to It, Sidekicks.
TELEVISION: Series: Ensign O'Toole, United States, Harts of the West. Guest: Sea Hunt, Ben Casey, Dr. Kildare, Mr. Novak, Combat, Eleventh Hour, Cimarron Strip, Amazing Stories, The Outer Limits. Movies: The Man Without a Country, The Stranger Who Looks Like Me, Medical Story, The Four Feathers, Shimmering Light, The President's Mistress, The Child Stealer, The Kid from Nowhere (also dir.), Dangerous Company, Witness for the Prosecution, The Red-Light Sting, Alice in Wonderland, Outrage!, Fighting Choice, The Thanksgiving Promise (also dir., co-prod.), Everybody's Baby: The Rescue of Jessica McClure, Just Another Secret, Women & Men: Stories of Seduction (The Man in the Brooks Brothers Shirt), Guess Who's Coming for Christmas?, Without Warning: The James Brady Story (Emmy Award, 1992), Wildflower, Elvis and the Colonel, The Man With 3 Wives, The Positively True Adventures of the Alleged Texas Cheerleader-Murdering Mom (Emmy Award, 1993), Secret Sins of the Fathers (also dir.), Kissinger and Nixon, Losing Chase.

BRIDGES, JEFF
Actor. b. Los Angeles, CA, Dec. 4, 1949. Appeared as infant in 1950 film The Company She Keeps. Made acting debut at age 14 in the TV series Sea Hunt starring his father, Lloyd Bridges. Studied acting at Herbert Berghof Studio, NY. Mil. service in Coast Guard reserves. Brother is actor-director Beau Bridges. Composed and performed song for film John and Mary. Named Male Star of the Year (1990) by NATO.
PICTURES: Halls of Anger (debut, 1970), The Yin and Yang of Mr. Go, The Last Picture Show (Acad. Award nom.), Fat City, Bad Company, The Iceman Cometh, The Last American Hero, Lolly-Madonna XXX, Thunderbolt and Lightfoot (Acad. Award nom.), Hearts of the West, Rancho Deluxe, Stay Hungry, King Kong, Somebody Killed Her Husband, The American Success Company, Winter Kills, Heaven's Gate, Cutter's Way (Cutter and Bone), Tron, The Last Unicorn (voice only), Kiss Me Goodbye, Against All Odds, Starman (Acad. Award nom.), Jagged Edge, 8 Million Ways to Die, The Morning After, Nadine, Tucker: The Man and His Dream, See You in the Morning, Cold Feet, The Fabulous Baker Boys, Texasville, The Fisher King, The Vanishing, American Heart (also co-prod.), Fearless, Blown Away, Wild Bill, White Squall, The Mirror Has Two Faces.
TELEVISION: Movies: Silent Night, Lonely Night; In Search of America, The Thanksgiving Promise (cameo). Special: Faerie Tale Theatre (Rapunzel). Guest: Lloyd Bridges Show, The FBI, Most Deadly Game.

BRIDGES, LLOYD
Actor. b. San Leandro, CA, January 15, 1913. e. UCLA. Went into stock from college dramatics. Formed off-B'way theater, the Playroom Club. With wife taught drama at private sch. in Darien, CT when signed stock contract with Columbia. B'way stage: Dead Pigeon, Oh Men! Oh Women!, Heart Song, Cactus Flower, Man of La Mancha.
PICTURES: They Dare Not Love, Honolulu Lu, The Lone Wolf Takes a Chance, Cadets on Parade, Son of Davy Crockett, I Was a Prisoner of Devil's Island, Here Comes Mr. Jordan, The Medico of Painted Sprgins, Our Wife, Two Latins From Manhattan, Harmon of Michigan, Three Girls About Town, The Royal Mounted Patrol, Harvard Here I Come, You Belong to Me, The Wife Takes a Flyer, Underground Agent, North of the Rockies, West of Tombstone, Blondie Goes to College, Sing for Your Supper, Shut My Big Mouht, Canal Zone, Stand By All Networks, Tramp Tramp Tramp, Alias Boston Blackie, Hello Annapolis, Sweetheart of the Fleet, Meet the Stewarts, Flight

Lieutenant, Riders of the Northland, Atlantic Convoy, The Talk of the Town, Spirit of Stanford, A Man's World, Pardon My Gun, Commandos Strike at Dawn, Sahara, The Heat's On, Hail to the Rangers, The Crime Doctor's Strangest Case, Destroyer, Two-Man Submarine, Louisiana Hayride, Once Upon a Time, She's a Soldier Too, The Master Race, Saddle Leather Law, A Walk in the Sun, Strange Confession, Secret Agent X-9 (serial), Miss Susie Slage's, Abilene Town, Canyon Passage, Ramrod, The Trouble With Women, Unconquered, Secret Service Investigator, Sixteen Fathoms Deep, Moonrise, Red Canyon, Hideout, Home of the Brave, Calamity Jane and Sam Bass, Trapped, Rocketship XM, Try and Get Me (The Sound of Fury), The White Tower, Colt .45, Little Big Horn, Three Steps North, The Whistle at Eaton Falls, Last of the Comanches, High Noon, Plymouth Adventure, The Tall Texan, The Kid From Left Field, City of Bad Men, The Limping Man, Pride of the Blue Grass, Apache Woman, Wichita, The Deadly Game (Third Party Risk), Wetbacks, The Rainmaker, Ride Out for Revenge, The Goddess, Around the World Under the Sea, Attack on the Iron Coast, The Daring Game, The Happy Ending, To Find a Man, Running Wild, Deliver Us From Evil, The Fifth Musketeer, Bear Island, Airplane!, Airplane II: The Sequel, Weekend Warriors, The Wild Pair, Tucker: The Man and His Dream, Cousins, Winter People, Joe Versus the Volcano, Hot Shots!, Honey I Blew Up the Kid, Hot Shots Part Deux!, Blown Away.
TELEVISION: Series: Police Story, Sea Hunt, The Lloyd Bridges Show, The Loner, San Francisco International Airport, Joe Forrester, Paper Dolls, Capitol News, Harts of the West. Movies: Tragedy in a Temporary Town, The Fortress, The People Next Door, Paper Dolls, Silent Night, Lonley Night, The Thanksgiving Promise, She Was Marked For Murder, Cross of Fire, Leona Helmsley: The Queen of Mean, In the Nick of Time, Devlin, Secret Sins of the Father, The Other Woman. Mini-series: Roots, Disaster on the Coastliner, East of Eden, Movieola, The Blue and the Gray, George Washington, Dress Gray, North & South Book II. Special: Cinderella... Frozen in Time, Nothing Lasts Forever. Guest: Bigelow Theatre, Kraft Suspense Theatre, Robt. Montgomery Present, CBS Playhouse, Alcoa Hour, Philco Playhouse, U.S. Steel Hour, Climax Playhouse 90

BRIGHT, RICHARD
Actor. b. Brooklyn, NY, June 11. e. trained for stage with Frank Corsaro, John Lehne and Paul Mann.
THEATER: The Balcony (1959), The Beard, The Salvation of St. Joan, Gogol, The Basic Training of Pavlo Hummel, Richard III, Kid Twist, Short Eyes as well as regional theater.
PICTURES: Odds Against Tomorrow, Lion's Love, Panic in Needle Park, The Getaway, Pat Garrett and Billy the Kid, The Godfather, The Godfather II, Rancho Deluxe, Marathon Man, Citizens Band, Looking For Mr. Goodbar, On the Yard, Hair, The Idolmaker, Vigilante, Two of a Kind, Once Upon a Time in America, Crackers, Crimewave, Cut and Run, Brighton Beach Memoirs, 52-Pick-up, Time Out, Red Head, The Godfather III.
TELEVISION: Series: Lamp Unto My Feet, Armstrong Circle Theater, The Verdict Is Yours, Kraft Television Theatre, Studio One, Cagney and Lacey, Beacon Hill, Hill Street Blues, From These Roots. Movies: A Death of Innocence, The Connection, The Gun, Cops and Robin, Sizzle, There Must Be A Pony, Penalty Phase. Mini-series: From Here to Eternity, Skag.

BRIGHT, RICHARD S.
Executive. b. New Rochelle, NY, Feb. 28, 1936. e. Hotchkiss Sch., 1953-54; Wharton Sch. of Finance, U. of Pennsylvania, 1954-58. With U.S. Army Finance Corp., 1959-60. Was corporate exec. prior to founding Persky-Bright Organization in 1973, private investment group to finance films. Now bd. chmn, Persky-Bright Productions, Inc.
THEATER: A History of the American Film, Album (Off-B'way, co-prod.).
PICTURES: Last Detail, Golden Voyage of Sinbad, For Pete's Sake, California Split, The Man Who Would Be King, Funny Lady, The Front, and Equus. Financing/production services for: Hard Times, Taxi Driver, Missouri Breaks, Bound for Glory, Sinbad and the Eye of the Tiger, Hair, Body Heat, Still of the Night. Executive Producer: Tribute.
TELEVISION: The President's Mistress (co-producer).

BRILLSTEIN, BERNIE
Producer, Talent Manager. b. New York, NY. 1931. e. NYU, B.S. advertising. Manager whose clients have incl. Lorne Michaels, John Belushi, Jim Henson and the Muppets. Chairman and chief exec. officer, Lorimar Film Entertainment. Founder, chmn., pres., The Brillstein Company. Co-partner of Brillstein-Grey Entertainment and Brillstein-Grey Communications.
PICTURES: Exec. Prod.: The Blues Brothers, Up the Academy, Continental Divide, Neighbors, Doctor Detroit, Ghostbusters, Spies Like Us, Summer Rental, Armed and Dangerous, Dragnet, Ghostbusters II.
TELEVISION: Exec. prod.: Burns and Schreiber Comedy Hour, Buckshot, Open All Night, Show Business, Sitcom, Buffalo Bill, Jump, The Faculty, The Real Ghostbusters (exec. consultant), It's Garry Shandling's Show, The Days and Nights of Molly Dodd, The "Slap" Maxwell Show, The Boys (pilot), The

Wickedest Witch, Normal Life, The Larry Sanders Show, Newsradio, Def Comedy Jam—Prime Time, Hightower 411, Just Shoot Me.

BRIMLEY, WILFORD
Actor. b. Salt Lake City, UT, Sept. 27, 1934. Formerly a blacksmith, ranch hand and racehorse trainer; began in films as an extra and stuntman. Also acted as A. Wilford Brimley. Original member of L.A. Actors Theatre.
PICTURES: True Grit, Lawman, The China Syndrome, The Electric Horseman, Brubaker, Borderline, Absence of Malice, Death Valley, The Thing, Tender Mercies, Tough Enough, High Road to China, 10 to Midnight, Hotel New Hampshire, Harry and Son, The Stone Boy, The Natural, Country, Cocoon, Remo Williams: The Adventure Begins, American Justice, End of the Line, Cocoon: The Return, Eternity, The Firm, Hard Target, Last of the Dogmen.
TELEVISION: Movies: The Oregon Trail, The Wild Wild West Revisited, Amber Waves, Roughnecks, Rodeo Girl, The Big Black Pill, Ewoks: The Battle for Endor, Murder in Space, Thompson's Last Run, Act of Vengeance, Gore Vidal's Billy the Kid, Blood River, Tom Clancy's Op Center. Series: Our House, Boys of Twilight. Guest: The Waltons.

BRINKLEY, DAVID
TV news correspondent. b. Wilmington, NC, July 10, 1920. e. U. of North Carolina, Vanderbilt U. Started writing for hometown newspaper. Joined United Press before entering Army, WWII. After discharge in 1943, joined NBC News in Washington as White House corr. Co-chmn. for many years with late Chet Huntley on NBC Nightly News. Then began David Brinkley's Journal. Moved to ABC to host This Week with David Brinkley.

BRISKIN, MORT
Producer, Writer. b. Oak Park, IL, 1919. e. U. of Southern California; attended Harvard and Northwestern law schools, being admitted to the bar at 20. Practiced law before entering m.p. industry in management with such stars as Mickey Rooney. Turned to production and also wrote screenplays for 16 of his 29 films. Created nine TV series as prod. or exec. prod. of some 1,350 TV segments of which he wrote more than 300.
PICTURES: The River, The Magic Face, No Time for Flowers, The Second Woman, Quicksand, The Big Wheel, The Jackie Robinson Story, Ben, Willard, Walking Tall, Framed.
TELEVISION: Sheriff of Cochise, U.S. Marshal, The Texan, Grand Jury, The Walter Winchell File, Official Detective, Whirlybirds.

BRITTANY, MORGAN
Actress. r.n. Suzanne Cupito. b. Hollywood, CA, Dec. 5, 1951.
PICTURES: Gypsy, The Birds, Marnie, Yours Mine and Ours, Gable and Lombard, Sundown: The Vampire in Retreat, The Prodigal, Last Action Hero, The Saint.
TELEVISION: Series: Dallas, Glitter, Melrose Place. Guest: B. L. Stryker. Movies: Amazing Howard Hughes, Delta County U.S.A., The Initiation of Sarah, Samurai, Stunt Seven, Death on the Freeway, The Dream Merchants, Moviola: The Scarlett O'Hara War, The Wild Women of Chastity Gulch, LBJ: The Early Years, Perry Mason: The Case of the Scandalous Scoundrel, National Lampoon's Favorite Deadly Sins.

BRITTON, TONY
Actor, b. Birmingham, England, 1924. e. Thornbury Grammar Sch., Glos. Early career as clerk and in repertory; TV debut, 1952, The Six Proud Walkers (serial); m.p. debut, 1955, Loser Takes All.
THEATER: The Guv'nor, Romeo and Juliet, The Scarlet Pimpernel, The Other Man, The Dashing White Sergeant, Importance of Being Earnest, An Ideal Husband, School for Scandal, A Dream of Treason, That Lady, The Private Lives of Edward Whiteley, Affairs of State, The Night of The Ball, Gigi, The Seagull, Henry IV Part 1, Kill Two Birds, Cactus Flower, A Woman of No Importance, The Boston Story, Lady Frederick, My Fair Lady, Move Over Mrs. Markham, No No Nanette, Dame of Sark, The Chairman, Murder Among Friends, The Seven Year Itch, St. Joan, The Tempest, King Lear, A Man for All Seasons.
PICTURES: Birthday Present, Behind the Mask, Operation Amsterdam, The Heart of a Man, The Rough and the Smooth, The Risk, The Horsemasters, Stork Talk, The Break, There's a Girl in My Soup, Forbush and The Penguins, Sunday Bloody Sunday, Night Watch, The Day of the Jackal.
TELEVISION: The Man Who Understood Women, Ooh La La, Call My Bluff, The Nearly Man, Friends and Brothers. Series: Melissa, Father Dear Father, Robins Nest, Don't Wait Up.

BROADBENT, JIM
Actor. b. England. Member of the National Theatre and the Royal Shakespeare Company. Wrote and starred in short film A Sense of History (Clermont-Ferrand Intl. Film Fest. Award).
THEATER: The Recruiting Officer, A Winter's Tale, The Government Inspector, A Flea in Her Ear, Goose Pimples.
PICTURES: The Shout (debut, 1978), The Passage, Breaking Glass, The Dogs of War, Time Bandits, Brazil, The Good Father,

Superman IV: The Quest for Peace, Life Is Sweet, Enchanted April, The Crying Game, Widow's Peak, The Wedding Gift, Princess Caraboo, Bullets Over Broadway, Rough Magic, The Secret Agent, Richard III.
TELEVISION: Not the Nine O'Clock News, Gone to Seed, Sense of History (also writer), Murder Most Horrid, Gone to the Dogs, Only Fools and Horses, The Victoria Wood Show, Silas Marner, Blackladder, Birth of a Nation.

BROADHEAD, PAUL E.
Executive. e. Univ. of MS. Founder of Paul Broadhead & Assocs. real estate development. 1984, sold his interests in that company. Became chmn. of bd. of Theatre Properties, Cinemark USA.

BROADNAX, DAVID
Actor, Producer, Writer. b. Columbus, GA, Dec. 16.
PICTURES: Actor: The Landlord, Come Back Charleston Blue, Sharpies (also prod., co-s.p.), Zombie Island Massacre (also prod., story).
TELEVISION: As the World Turns, Another World, Edge of Night, Love Is a Many Splendored Thing, Search for Tomorrow, Saturday Night Live.

BROCCOLI, ALBERT "CUBBY"
Producer. b. New York, NY, April 5, 1909. e. City Coll. of New York. Agriculturist in early years; entered m.p. ind. as asst. director, 20th Century-Fox, 1938. Worked with theatrical agent Charles Feldman 1948-51; prod., Warwick Films 1951-60; prod, Eon Prods., Ltd. since 1961. Thalberg Award, 1982.
PICTURES: Red Beret (Paratrooper), Hell Below Zero, Black Knight, Prize of Gold, Cockleshell Heroes, Safari, Zarak, April in Portugal, Pickup Alley, Fire Down Below, Arrivederci Roma, Interpol, How to Murder a Rich Uncle, Odongo, High Flight, No Time to Die, The Man Inside, Idle on Parade, Abandon of Africa, Bandit of Zhobe, Jazz Boat, Killers of Killimanjaro, In the Nick, Let's Get Married, The Trials of Oscar Wilde, Johnny Nobody, Carolina, Dr. No, Call Me Bwana, From Russia with Love, Goldfinger, Thunderball, You Only Live Twice, Chitty Chitty Bang Bang, On Her Majesty's Secret Service, Diamonds Are Forever, Live and Let Die, The Man with the Golden Gun, The Spy Who Loved Me, Moonraker, For Your Eyes Only, Octopussy, A View to a Kill, The Living Daylights, Licence to Kill, Goldeneye.
(d. June 27, 1996)

BROCKMAN, MICHAEL
Executive. b. Brooklyn, NY, Nov. 19, 1938. e. Ithaca Coll. Became v.p., daytime programming, ABC Entertainment, 1974; later v.p., tape prod. operations and admin. Left to become v.p., daytime programs, NBC Entertainment, 1977-1980. Became v.p. programs, Lorimar Prods. 1980-82; v.p. daytime and children's prog. CBS Entertainment, 1982-89. 1986, title changed to v.p. daytime, children's and late night. Became pres. ABC daytime, children's & late night entertainment 1989-90. Joined Mark Goodson Prods. as v.p. 1991. Became sr. v.p. in 1993. Pres., M. Brockman Broadcast, 1995.

BRODERICK, MATTHEW
Actor. b. New York, NY, Mar. 21, 1962. Son of late actor James Broderick and writer-dir./artist Patricia Broderick. Acted in a workshop prod. of Horton Foote's Valentine's Day with his father (1979).
THEATER: NY: Torch Song Trilogy, Brighton Beach Memoirs (Tony & Theatre World Awards, 1983), Biloxi Blues, The Widow Claire, How to Succeed in Business Without Really Trying (Tony Award, 1995).
PICTURES: Max Dugan Returns (debut, 1983), WarGames, Ladyhawke, 1918, On Valentine's Day, Ferris Bueller's Day Off, Project X, Biloxi Blues, Torch Song Trilogy, Glory, Family Business, The Freshman, Out on a Limb, The Night We Never Met, The Lion King (voice), The Road to Wellville, Mrs. Parker and the Vicious Circle, Arabian Knight (voice), Infinity (also dir., co-prod.), The Cable Guy, Infinity (also dir.).
TELEVISION: Specials: Master Harold... and the Boys, Cinderella (Faerie Tale Theatre), The Year of the Generals (voice), A Simple Melody. Movie: A Life in the Theatre. Guest: Lou Grant.

BRODNEY, OSCAR
Writer. b. Boston, MA, 1906. e. Boston U., LL.B., 1927; Harvard, LL.M., 1928. Atty., MA Bar, 1928-35.
PICTURES: She Wrote the Book, If You Knew Susie, Are You With It?, For the Love of Mary, Mexican Hayride, Arctic Manhunt, Yes Sir, That's My Baby, Double Crossbones, Gal Who Took the West, South Sea Sinner, Comanche Territory, Harvey, Frenchie, Francis Goes to the Races, Little Egypt, Francis Covers the Big Town, Willie and Joe Back at the Front, Scarlet Angel, Francis Goes to West Point, Walking My Baby Back Home, Sign of the Pagan, Black Shield of Falworth, Captain Lightfoot, The Spoilers, Purple Mask, Lady Godiva, Day of Fury, Star in the Dust, Tammy and the Bachelor, When Hell Broke Loose, Bobbikins (also prod.), Tammy Tell Me True, The Right Approach, All Hands on Deck, Tammy and the Doctor, The Brass Bottle, I'd Rather Be Rich.

49

BRODSKY, JACK
Producer. b. Brooklyn, NY, July 3, 1932. e. George Washington H.S. Writer for N.Y. Times. Joined 20th-Fox publicity in N.Y. in 1956. Left in 1961 to head national ad-pub for Filmways. Joined Rastar Productions to work on Funny Girl; later named v.p. in charge of prod. In 1976 named v.p. in chg. film prod. prom., Rogers & Cowan; 1978, Columbia Pictures v.p. of adv., pub., promo.; 1979, named exec. v.p. of Michael Douglas' Big Stick Productions; 1983; joined 20th-Fox as exec. v.p., worldwide adv., pub., exploit. Resigned 1985 to resume career as producer.
PICTURES: Little Murders, Everything You Always Wanted To Know About Sex But Were Afraid to Ask (exec. prod.), Summer Wishes Winter Dreams, The Jewel of the Nile, Dancers (co-exec. prod., actor), King Ralph, Scenes From a Mall (actor), Rookie of the Year (co-exec. prod.).
AUTHOR: The Cleopatra Papers, with Nat Weiss.

BROKAW, CARY
Executive, Producer. b. Los Angeles, CA, June 21, 1951. e. Univ. of CA/Berkeley, UCLA Grad. Sch. Worked at several positions at 20th Century Fox before serving as exec. v.p. for Cineplex Odeon Corp. 1983 became co-chmn., pres. of Island Alive; 1985, became co-chmn., pres. & CEO of Island Pictures. Formed Avenue Entertainment Pictures in 1987, becoming chmn. & CEO.
PICTURES: Executive Producer. Trouble in Mind, Down by Law, Nobody's Fool, Slamdance, Pascali's Island, Signs of Life, Cold Feet, Drugstore Cowboy, After Dark My Sweet, The Object of Beauty, Sex Drugs Rock & Roll, The Player, American Heart. Producer: Short Cuts, Restoration, Voices From a Locked Room.
TELEVISION: Movies: In the Eyes of a Stranger, Amelia Earhart: The Final Flight, See Jane Run, Stranger in Town.

BROKAW, NORMAN R.
Executive. b. New York, NY, April 21, 1927. Joined William Morris Agency as trainee in 1943; junior agent, 1948; sr. agent, company exec. in m.p. and TV, 1951; 1974, v.p., William Morris Agency, World Wide all areas. 1981, named exec. v.p. & mem. of bd., William Morris Agency, worldwide; 1986, named co-chmn. of bd., WMA, worldwide. 1989, named pres. & CEO, William Morris Inc. worldwide. 1991, named Chmn. of Board of CEO. Member Acad. of TV Arts & Sciences, AMPAS. Member bd. of dir. of Cedars-Sinai Medical Center, Los Angeles; pres., The Betty Ford Cancer Center. Clients include former President and Mrs. Gerald R. Ford, Bill Cosby, Gen. Alexander Haig, Priscilla Presley, Andy Griffith, Dr. C. Everett Koop, Marcia Clark, Christopher Darden.

BROKAW, TOM
TV Host, Anchorman. b. Yankton, S.D., Feb. 6, 1940. e. U. of South Dakota. Newscaster, weatherman, staff announcer KTIV, Sioux City, IA, 1960-62. Joined KMTV, NBC affiliate in Omaha, in 1962; 1965, joined WSB-TV, Atlanta. Worked in L.A. bureau of NBC News, anchored local news shows for KNBC, NBC station (1966-73). In 1973 named NBC News' White House correspondent; was anchor of NBC Saturday Night News. Named host of Today show in August, 1976. In 1982 co-anchor, NBC Nightly News. Co-anchor 1993 series NBC newsmagazine, Now With Tom Brokaw & Katie Couric. Special: Conversation with Mikhail S. Gorbachev.

BROLIN, JAMES
Actor, Director. b. Los Angeles, CA, July 18, 1940. r.n. James Bruderlin. e. UCLA. Son is actor Josh Brolin. Debut in Bus Stop (TV series); named most promising actor of 1970 by Fame and Photoplay magazines. Winner, Emmy and Golden Globe Awards. Also nominated for 3 additional Emmys and 2 Golden Globes.
PICTURES: Take Her She's Mine (debut, 1963), John Goldfarb Please Come Home, Goodbye Charlie, Dear Brigitte, Von Ryan's Express, Morituri, Fantastic Voyage, Way ... Way Out, The Cape Town Affair, Our Man Flint, The Boston Strangler, Skyjacked, Westworld, Gable and Lombard, The Car, Capricorn One, The Amityville Horror, Night of the Juggler, High Risk, Pee-wee's Big Adventure, Bad Jim, Super High Score, Ted & Venus, Gas Food Lodging, Cheatin' Hearts (also exec. prod.), Back Stab.
TELEVISION: Series: Marcus Welby M.D. (Emmy Award, 1970), Hotel, Angel Falls, Extreme. Movies: Marcus Welby M.D. (A Matter of Humanities), Short Walk to Daylight, Class of '63, Trapped, Steel Cowboys, The Ambush Murders, Mae West, White Water Rebels, Cowboy, Beverly Hills Cowgirl Blues, Hold the Dream, Intimate Encounters, Voice of the Heart, Finish Line, Nightmare on the 13th Floor, And the Sea Will Tell, Deep Dark Secrets, The Sands of Time, Visions of Murder, Gunsmoke: The Long Ride, The Calling, Parallel Lives, A Perry Mason Mystery: The Case of the Grimacing Governor, Terminal Virus. Special: City Boy (PBS). Director: Hotel (12 episodes), The Young Riders.

BROMHEAD, DAVID M.
Executive. b. Teaneck, NJ, Jan. 7, 1960. e. Leighton Park Sch., Reading, England, 1973-78. Overseas sls. exec., Rank Film Dist., 1980; joined New World Pictures, 1984, dir. intl. dist.; named dir., TV dist., 1986.

BRON, ELEANOR
Actress, Writer. b. Stanmore, Middlesex, Eng., 1938. Started career in Establishment Club, London, and on American tour. Leading lady on British TV show Not So Much a Programme—More a Way of Life. Author of Double Take, The Pillowbook of Eleanor Bron, Life and Other Punchers.
THEATER: The Doctor's Dilemma, Howards End, The Prime of Miss Jean Brodie, Hedda Gabler, The Duchess of Malfi, The Madwoman of Chaillot.
PICTURES: Help!, Alfie, Two for the Road, Bedazzled, The Turtle Diary, Thank You All Very Much, Women in Love, The Millstone, Little Dorrit, Black Beauty, A Little Princess.
TELEVISION: Movies: The Day Christ Died, The Attic: The Hiding of Anne Frank, Intrigue, Changing Step, The Blue Boy. Series: Where Was Spring? (also co-wrote), After That This. Guest: Rumpole of the Bailey, Yes Minister, Absolutely Fabulous.

BRONDFIELD, JEROME
Writer. b. Cleveland, OH, Dec. 9, 1913. e. Ohio State U., 1936. Reporter, ed. on Columbus Dispatch, Associated Press, story ed., script head, RKO Pathe, Oct., 1944; writer, dir. & supvr. of many doc. shorts incl. This Is America series; TV writer; short story writer; collab. s.p., Below the Sahara; s.p. Louisiana Territory; doc. film writer; Author, Woody Hayes, The 100-Yard War, Knute Rockne, The Man and the Legend. Sr. editor, Scholastic, Inc.

BRONFMAN, EDGAR, JR.
Executive. Joined Seagram 1982 as asst. to officeof the pres.; served as mng. dir. of Seagram Europe until he was appointed pres. of The House of Seagram, 1984-88; became pres. & COO in 1989. June 1994 named pres. & CEO of The Seagram Company Ltd. Upon acquisition of MCA Inc. was named acting chairman, 1995.

BRONSON, CHARLES
Actor. b. Ehrenfeld, PA, Nov. 3, 1921. r.n. Charles Buchinsky. Worked as a coal miner. Served in Air Force (1943-46) as tail gunner on B29s in Pacific. Studied acting at Pasadena Playhouse. Started in films billed under real name. Guest in numerous TV shows in addition to those below.
PICTURES: You're in the Navy Now (debut, 1951), The People Against O'Hara, The Mob, Red Skies of Montana, My Six Convicts, The Marrying Kind, Pat and Mike, Diplomatic Courier, Bloodhounds of Broadway, House of Wax, The Clown, Miss Sadie Thompson, Crime Wave, Tennessee Champ, Riding Shotgun, Apache, Drum Beat (lst billing as Charles Bronson), Vera Cruz, Big House U.S.A., Target Zero, Jubal, Run of the Arrow, Machine Gun Kelly, Gang War, Showdown at Boot Hill, When Hell Broke Loose, Ten North Frederick, Never So Few, The Magnificent Seven, Master of the World, A Thunder of Drums, X-15, Kid Galahad, The Great Escape, Four for Texas, The Sandpiper, The Battle of the Bulge, This Property Is Condemned, The Dirty Dozen, Villa Rides, Guns for San Sebastian, Farewell Friend, Once Upon a Time in the West, Rider on the Rain, You Can't Win Em All, The Family, Cold Sweat, Twinky (Lola), Someone Behind the Door, Red Sun, Chato's Land, The Mechanic, The Valachi Papers, The Stone Killer, Chino, Mr. Majestyk, Death Wish, Breakout, Hard Times, Breakheart Pass, From Noon Till Three, St. Ives, The White Buffalo, Telefon, Love and Bullets, Caboblanco, Borderline, Death Hunt, Death Wish II, Ten to Midnight, The Evil That Men Do, Death Wish 3, Murphy's Law, Assassination, Death Wish 4: The Crackdown, Messenger of Death, Kinjite: Forbidden Subjects, The Indian Runner, Death Wish V: The Face of Death.
TELEVISION: Series: Man With a Camera, Empire, Travels of Jamie McPheeters. Guest: Philco Playhouse (adventure in Java), Medic, A Bell for Adano, Gunsmoke, Have Gun Will Travel, Meet McGraw, The FBI, The Fugitive, The Virginian. Movies: Raid on Entebbe, Act of Vengeance, Yes Virginia There Is a Santa Claus, The Sea Wolf, Donato and Daughter, A Family of Cops.

BROOK, PETER
Director. b. London, England, March 21, 1925. e. Magdalen Coll., Oxford. To London 1943 to dir. his first play, Doctor Faustus; other stage incl. Man and Superman, Marat/Sade, A Midsummer Night's Dream, etc.
PICTURES: The Beggar's Opera (debut, 1953), Moderato Cantabile (also co-s.p.), Lord of the Flies (also s.p., edit), The Persecution and Assassination of Jean-Paul Marat as Performed by the Inmates of the Asylum of Charenton Under the Direction of the Marquis de Sade, Tell Me Lies (also prod.), King Lear (also s.p.), Meetings With Remarkable Men (also s.p.), The Tragedy of Carmen, Swann in Love (s.p. only), The Mahabharata.

BROOKS, ALBERT
Director, Writer, Actor. r.n. Albert Einstein. b. Los Angeles, CA, July 22, 1947. e. Carnegie Tech. Son of late comedian Harry Einstein (Parkyakarkus). Brother is performer Bob Einstein. Sports writer KMPC, L.A. 1962-63. Recordings: Comedy Minus One, A Star is Bought (Grammy nom.).

PICTURES: *Actor*: Taxi Driver, Real Life (also dir., co-s.p.), Private Benjamin, Modern Romance (also dir., co-s.p.), Twilight Zone—The Movie, Terms of Endearment (voice), Unfaithfully Yours, Lost in America (also dir., co-s.p.), Broadcast News (Acad. Award nom.), Defending Your Life (also dir., s.p.), I'll Do Anything, The Scout (also co-s.p.), Mother (also dir.).
TELEVISION: *Series*: Dean Martin Presents the Golddiggers, Saturday Night Live (prod., dir. short films 1975-76), Hot Wheels (voices), The Associates (wrote theme song). *Specials*: Milton Berle's Mad Mad Mad World of Comedy, General Electric's All-Star Anniversary. *Guest*: Love American Style, The Odd Couple, Ed Sullivan Show, Tonight Show, others.

BROOKS, JAMES L.
Director, Producer, Writer. b. North Bergen, NJ, May 9, 1940. e. NYU. Copyboy for CBS News, N.Y.; promoted to newswriter. 1965 moved to L.A. to work for David Wolper's documentary prod. co. In 1969 conceived idea for series, Room 222; formed partnership with fellow writer Allan Burns. Together they created Mary Tyler Moore Show in 1970. 1977, established prod. co. on Paramount lot with other writers, producing and creating the series, The Associates and Taxi. Formed Gracie Films. Directed play Brooklyn Laundry, in L.A.
PICTURES: Real Life (actor), Starting Over (s.p., co-prod.), Modern Romance (actor), Terms of Endearment (dir., prod., s.p.; Academy Awards for Best Picture, Director and Screenplay, 1983), Broadcast News (dir., prod., s.p.), Big (co-prod.), Say Anything (exec. prod.), The War of the Roses (co-prod.), I'll Do Anything (dir., prod., s.p.).
TELEVISION: *Movie*: Thursday's Game (writer, prod., 1971). Series: The Mary Tyler Moore Show (co-creator, writer, exec. prod.; 2 Emmy Awards for writing: 1971, 1977; 3 Emmy Awards as exec. prod.: 1975, 1976, 1977), Rhoda (writer, prod.), The New Lorenzo Music Show (writer), Lou Grant (co-exec. prod.). Series (co-creator, and/or exec. prod.): Taxi (3 Emmy Awards as exec. prod.: 1979, 1980, 1981), Cindy, The Associates, Cheers, Tracey Ullman Show (Emmy Award as exec. prod., 1989), The Simpsons (2 Emmy Awards as exec. prod.: 1990, 1991), Sibs, Phenom, The Critics.

BROOKS, JOSEPH
Producer, Director, Writer, Composer, Conductor. Well-known for composing music for TV commercials before turning to producing, directing, writing and scoring theatrical feature, You Light Up My Life, in 1977. Winner of 21 Clio Awards (advertising industry), Grammy, Golden Globe, People's Choice, Amer. Music Awards; created music for 100 commercials. Has also composed for theatrical films. Winner of Cannes Film Festival Advertising Award.
PICTURES: *Scores*: The Garden of the Finzi-Continis, Marjoe, Jeremy, The Lords of Flatbush. *Prod.-Dir.-Writer-Composer*: You Light Up My Life (Academy Award for Best Song: title song, 1977), If Ever I See You Again (also actor).

BROOKS, MEL
Writer, Director, Actor. b. Brooklyn, NY, June 28, 1926. r.n. Melvin Kaminsky. m. actress Anne Bancroft. e. VA Military Inst. 1944. U.S. Army combat engineer 1944-46. As child, did impressions and was amateur drummer and pianist. First appearance as actor in play Separate Rooms in Red Bank, NJ. Was also social dir. of Grossinger's Resort in the Catskills. Became writer for Sid Caesar on TV's Broadway Review and Your Show of Shows. Teamed with Carl Reiner on comedy record albums: The 2000 Year Old Man, The 2000 and 13 Year Old Man. Founded Brooksfilms Ltd., 1981. Won Academy Award for Best Short Subject (animated): The Critic (also, s.p., narrator). Co-writer of Shinbone Alley.
THEATER: *Writer*: New Faces of 1952 (sketches), Shinbone Alley (book), All-American (book).
PICTURES: New Faces (co-s.p.), The Producers (dir., s.p.; Academy Award for Best Original Screenplay, 1968), The Twelve Chairs (dir., s.p., actor), Blazing Saddles (dir., co-s.p., actor), Young Frankenstein (dir., co-s.p.; Acad. Award nom. for s.p.), Silent Movie (dir., co-s.p., actor), Frances (exec.-prod), High Anxiety (dir., prod., co-s.p., actor), The Muppet Movie (actor), History of the World Part 1 (dir., prod., s.p., actor, lyrics), To Be or Not To Be (exec-prod., actor), Spaceballs (dir., prod., co-s.p., actor), My Favorite YEar (exec.-prod.), Look Who's Talking Too (voice), Life Stinks (dir., prod., co-s.p., actor), Robin Hood: Men in Tights (dir., prod., co-s.p., actor), The Silence of the Hams (actor), The Little Rascals (actor), They Fly II (exec.-prod.), Dracula: Dead and Loving It (dir., prod., co-s.p., actor). *Prod.*: The Elephant Man, The Doctor and the Devils, The Fly, 84 Charing Cross Road, Solarbabies, The Vagrant.
TELEVISION: *Special*: The Sid Caesar-Imogene Coca-Carl Reiner-Howard Morris Special (co-writer; Emmy Award, 1967). *Series*: Get Smart (co-creator, co-writer), When Things Were Rotten (co-creator, co- writer, prod.), The Nutt House (prod., co-writer).

BROSNAN, PIERCE
Actor. b. Navan, County Meath, Ireland, May 16, 1953. Left County Meath, Ireland for London at 11. Worked as commercial

illustrator, then joined experimental theater workshop and studied at the Drama Center. On London stage (Wait Until Dark, The Red Devil Battery Sign, Filumenia, etc.)
PICTURES: The Mirror Crack'd (debut, 1980), The Long Good Friday, Nomads, The Fourth Protocol, Taffin, The Deceivers, Mister Johnson, The Lawnmower Man, Entangled, Mrs. Doubtfire, Love Affair, Goldeneye, Mars Attacks, The Mirror Has Two Faces.
TELEVISION: *Series*: Remington Steele, Frame-Up (NBC Friday Night Mystery). *Movies/Specials*: Murphy's Stroke, The Manions of America, Nancy Astor, Noble House, Around the World in 80 Days, The Heist, Murder 101, Victim of Love, Live Wire, Death Train (Detonator), The Broken Chain, Don't Talk to Strangers, Alistair MacLean's Night Watch.

BROUGH, WALTER
Producer, Writer. b. Phila. PA, Dec. 19, 1935. e. La Salle U. (B.A.), USC (M.A.). Began career with Stage Society Theatre, LA. Currently CEO, Orb Enterprises, Inc.
PICTURES: Gabriella, A New Life, No Place to Hide, Run Wild Run Free, The Desperadoes, Funeral for an Assassin (also prod.), On a Dead Man's Chest (also prod.), Jed and Sonny (also prod.).
TELEVISION: Doctor Kildare, The Fugitive, Branded, Name of the Game, Mannix, Mission Impossible, The Magician, Man From Atlantis, Police Story, Wildside, Heart of the City (also prod.), Thunder Guys (pilot), Spencer for Hire (also co-prod.), Law & Harry McGraw, New Mission Impossible (also co-prod.), Over My Dead Body, Hunter, Tequila & Bonetti, Sirens.

BROUGHTON, BRUCE
Composer. b. Los Angeles, CA , March 8, 1945. e. U. of Southern California, B.M., 1967. Music supvr., CBS-TV, 1967-77. Since then has been freelance composer for TV and films. Member of Academy of TV Arts & Sciences Society of Composers & Lyricists (past pres.), AMPAS (governor). Nominated 15 times for Emmy. Nominated for Grammy for Young Sherlock Holmes.
PICTURES: The Prodigal, The Ice Pirates, Silverado (Acad. Award nom.), Young Sherlock Holmes, Sweet Liberty, The Boy Who Could Fly, Square Dance, Harry and the Hendersons, Monster Squad, Big Shots, Cross My Heart, The Rescue, The Presidio, Last Rites, Moonwalker, Jacknife, Betsy's Wedding, Narrow Margin, The Rescuers Down Under, All I Want for Christmas, Honey I Blew Up the Kid, Stay Tuned, Homeward Bound: The Incredible Journey, So I Married an Axe Murderer, For Love or Money, Tombstone, Holy Matrimony, Baby's Day Out, Miracle on 34th Street.
TELEVISION: *Series*: Hawaii Five-0, Gunsmoke, Quincy, How the West Was Won, Logan's Run, The Oregon Trail, Buck Rogers (Emmy Award), Dallas (Emmy Award), Dinosaurs (theme), Capitol Critters (theme), Tiny Ton Adventures (Emmy Award). *Movies*: The Paradise Connection, Desperate Voyage, The Return of Frank Cannon, Desperate Lives, Killjoy, One Shoe Makes It Murder, The Master of Ballantrae, MADD, The Candy Lightner Story, Cowboy, A Thanksgiving Promise, The Old Man and the Sea, O Pioneers! (Emmy Award). Mini-*Series*: The Blue and the Gray, The First Olympics—Athens: 1896 (Emmy Award), George Washington II, Tiny Toon Adventures.

BROUMAS, JOHN G.
Executive. b. Youngstown, OH, Oct. 12, 1917. e. Youngstown. Usher, Altoona Publix Theatres, 1933, usher to asst. mgr., Warner Thea. 1934-39; mgr. Grand 1939-40; mgr. Orpheum 1940-41. WWII active, Officer Chemical Corps, commanding officer 453rd Chem. Battalion (Reserve); Life member Reserve Officers Assoc.; Gen. mgr. Pitts & Roth Theatres 1946-54; pres., Broumas Theatres; v.p. NATO, 1969; bd. of dir. of NATO of VA, MD, D.C.; pres., Broumas Theatre Service 1954-82; bd. chmn., Showcase Theatres 1965-82; past pres. & bd. chmn. Maryland Theatre Owners; v.p. & bd. of dir., Virginia Theatre Owners; bd. of dir. NATO of D.C.; pres. B.C. Theatres; Past dir. and mem. Motion Picture Pioneers; Advisory Council; Will Rogers Memorial Hospital; Washington, D.C. Variety Club, Tent No. 11, bd. of gov. 1959, 1st asst. chief. barker, 1964 & 71, chief barker 1965-66, 1972, and 1978-79, and bd. chmn., 1980; lecturer, Georgetown Univ., 1972-; Life Patron, Variety Clubs Int'l, 1978 Life Liner, Variety Clubs Intl.; member: Screen Actors Guild. 1994.

BROWN, BLAIR
Actress. b. Washington, DC, 1948. e. National Theatre Sch. of Canada.
THEATER: *NY*: The Threepenny Opera (NY Shakespeare Fest), Comedy of Errors, The Secret Rapture, Arcadia. Acted with Old Globe, San Diego; Stratford, Ont. Shakespeare Fest.; Guthrie Theatre MN; Arena Stage, Wash.; Long Wharf, New Haven; Shaw Festival.
PICTURES: The Paper Chase, The Choirboys, One-Trick Pony, Altered States, Continental Divide, A Flash of Green, Stealing Home, Strapless, Passed Away.
TELEVISION: *Series*: The Days and Nights of Molly Dodd, Talk It Over (discussion). *Mini-series*: Captains and the Kings, James Michener's Space, Arthur Hailey's Wheels, Kennedy. *Movies*:

The 3,000 Mile Chase, The Quinns, And I Alone Survived, The Child Stealer, The Bad Seed, Hands of a Stranger, Eleanor and Franklin: The White House Years, Extreme Close-Up, Those Secrets, Majority Rule, Rio Shannon (pilot), The Day My Parents Ran Away, Moment of Truth: To Walk Again, The Gift of Love. *Specials*: School for Scandal, The Skin of Your Teeth, Lethal Innocence.

BROWN, BRYAN
Actor. b. Sydney, Australia, June 23, 1947. m. actress Rachel Ward. Began acting professionally in Sydney. Worked in repertory theatres in England with the National Theatre of Great Britain. Returned to Australia to work in films while continuing stage work with Theatre Australia.
PICTURES: Love Letters From Teralba Road (debut, 1977), The Irishman, Weekend of Shadows, Newsfront, Third Person Plural, Money Movers, Palm Beach, Cathy's Child, The Odd Angry Shot, Breaker Morant, Blood Money, Stir, Winter of Our Dreams, Far East, Give My Regards to Broad Street, Parker (Bones), The Empty Beach, F/X, Tai-Pan, Rebel, The Good Wife, Cocktail, Gorillas in the Mist, Shall We Dance, FX2 (also co-exec. prod.), Sweet Talker (also co-wrote story), Prisoners of the Sun, Blame It on the Bellboy.
TELEVISION: *Mini-Series*: Against the Wind, A Town Like Alice, The Thorn Birds. *Movies*: The Shiralee (Aust.), Dead in the Water, Devlin, The Last Hit.

BROWN, CLANCY
Actor. b. Ohio. e. Northwestern Univ.
PICTURES: Bad Boys (debut, 1983), The Adventures of Buckaroo Banzai, The Bride, Highlander, Extreme Prejudice, Shoot to Kill, Season of Fear, Blue Steel, Waiting for the Light, Ambition, Past Midnight, Pet Sematary II, Thunder Alley, The Shawshank Redemption, Dead Man Walking, Donor Unknown, Female Perversions.
TELEVISION: *Series*: Earth 2. *Movies*: Johnny Ryan, Love Lies & Murder, Cast a Deadly Spell, Desperate Rescue: The Cathy Mahone Story, Bloodlines, Last Light.

BROWN, DAVID
Executive, Producer. b. New York, NY, July 28, 1916. m. writer-editor Helen Gurley Brown. e. Stanford U., A.B., 1936; Columbia U. Sch. of Journalism, M.S., 1937. Apprentice reporter, copy-editing, San Francisco News & Wall Street Journal, 1936; night ed. asst. drama critic, Fairchild Publications, N.Y., 1937-39; edit. dir. Milk Research Council, N.Y., 1939-40; assoc. ed., Street & Smith Publ., N.Y., 1940-43; assoc. ed., exec. ed., then ed.-in-chief, Liberty Mag., N.Y., 1943-49; edit. dir., nat'l education campaign, Amer. Medical Assn., 1949; assoc. ed., mng. ed., Cosmopolitan Mag., N.Y., 1949-52; contrib. stories & articles to many nat'l mags.; man. ed., story dept., 20th-Fox, L.A., Jan., 1952; story ed. & head of scenario dept., 1953-56; appt'd. member of exec. staff of Darryl F. Zanuck, 1956; mem. of exec. staff, 20th-Fox studios, and exec. studio story editor, 1956-60; Prod. 20th-Fox Studios, Sept. 1960-62; Editorial v.p. New American Library of World Literature, Inc., 1963-64; exec. story opers., 20th Century-Fox, 1964-67; vp. dir. of story operations, 1967; exec. v.p., creative optns. and mem. bd. of dir., 1969-71. Exec. v.p., mem. bd. of directors Warner Bros., 1971-72; partner and director, The Zanuck/Brown Co., 1972-88. Pres., Manhattan Project Ltd., 1988-; mem., bd. of trustees, American Film Institute, 1972-80. Recipient with Richard D. Zanuck of the Mo. Pic. Acad. of Arts & Sciences' Irving G. Thalberg Memorial Award. Books: Brown's Guide to Growing Gray, Delacorte, Let Me Entertain You, Morrow, The Rest of Your Life is the Best of Your Life, Barricade.
PICTURES: Ssssssss, The Sting (Academy Award for Best Picture, 1973), The Sugarland Express, The Black Windmill, Willie Dynamite, The Girl from Petrovka, The Eiger Sanction, Jaws, MacArthur, Jaws 2, The Island, Neighbors, The Verdict, Cocoon, Target, Cocoon: The Return, Driving Miss Daisy (exec. prod.), The Player, A Few Good Men, The Cemetery Club, Watch It, Canadian Bacon.

BROWN, GEORG STANFORD
Actor, Director. b. Havana, Cuba, June 24, 1943. Acted on stage with the New York Shakespeare Fest. in the 1960s. Gained fame as one of the rookie cops in the 1970s TV series, The Rookies, before turning to TV directing.
THEATER: All's Well That Ends Well, Measure for Measure, Macbeth, Murderous Angels, Hamlet, Detective Story.
PICTURES: The Comedians, Dayton's Devils, Bullitt, Colossus: The Forbin Project, The Man, Black Jack (Wild in the Sky), Stir Crazy, House Party 2.
TELEVISION: *Series*: The Rookies. *Movies*: The Young Lawyers, Ritual of Evil, The Rookies (pilot), Dawn: Portrait of a Teenage Runaway, The Night the City Screamed, The Kid With the Broken Halo, In Defense of Kids, The Jesse Owens Story, Murder Without Motive. *Dir. of movies*: Grambling's White Tiger, Kids Like These, Alone in the Neon Jungle, Stuck With Each Other, Father & Son: Dangerous Relations. *Dir. of episodes*: Charlie's Angels, Starsky and Hutch, Dynasty, Hill Street Blues, Great American Hero, Cagney & Lacey (Emmy Award, 1986).

BROWN, HIMAN
M.P. Producer, Director, b. New York, NY, July 21, 1910. e. City Coll. of New York, St. Lawrence U. Radio & TV package prod. since 1927 include: Inner Sanctum, Thin Man, Bulldog Drummond, Dick Tracy, Terry and the Pirates, Joyce Jordan MD, Grand Central Station, CBS Radio Mystery Theatre, pres. Production Center, Inc.
PICTURES: That Night, Violators, The Stars Salute, The Price of Silence, The Road Ahead.

BROWN, JIM
Actor. b. St. Simons Island, GA, Feb. 17, 1936. e. Manhasset H.S., Syracuse U. For nine years played football with Cleveland Browns; in 1964 won Hickock Belt as Professional Athlete of the year. Founder, Black Economic Union.
PICTURES: Rio Conchos (debut, 1964), The Dirty Dozen, Ice Station Zebra, The Split, Riot, Dark Of The Sun, 100 Rifles, Kenner, El Condor, The Phynx, ... tick ... tick ... tick ..., The Grasshopper, Slaughter, Black Gunn, I Escaped from Devil's Island, The Slams, Slaughter's Big Rip-Off, Three the Hard Way, Take a Hard Ride, Adios Amigo, Mean Johnny Barrows, Kid Vengeance, Fingers, One Down Two to Go (also exec. prod.), Richard Pryor: Here and Now (exec. prod. only), Pacific Inferno (also exec. prod.), Abducted, The Running Man, I'm Gonna Git You Sucka, L.A. Heat, Crack House, Twisted Justice, The Divine Enforcer, Original Gangstas, Mars Attacks.
TELEVISION: *Movie*: Lady Blue.

BROWN, WILLIAM
Executive. b. Ayr, Scotland, June 24, 1929. e. Ayr Acad., U. of Edinburgh, where graduated Bachelor of Commerce, 1950. Served to Lt., Royal Artillery, 1950-52. Sales mgr. for Scotland Television Ltd. in London, 1958-61, sales dir. 1961-63. Deputy mng. dir. of Scottish Television Ltd. at Glasgow 1963-66, mng. dir. 1966-90. Deputy chmn. 1974-91. Chmn. from 1991. Chmn. Scottish Amicable Life Assurance Society Ltd., 1989-94. Dir., Radio Clyde (now Scottish Radio Holdings) 1973-. Chmn., Scottish Arts Council, 1992-. Dir.: ITN, 1972-77, 1987-90; Channel 4 Co Ltd. 1980-84; Scottish Opera Theatre Royal Ltd. 1974-90. Chmn.: Council, Indept. TV Cos. Assn. 1978-80. C.B.E., 1971. Ted Willis Award 1982. Gold Medal, Royal TV Society 1984. Hon. Doctorates: Edinburgh U. (1990), Strathclyde U. (1992).

BROWNE, ROSCOE LEE
Actor, Director, Writer. b. Woodbury, NJ, May 2, 1925. e. Lincoln U., PA; postgraduate studies in comparative literature and French at Middlebury Coll., VT, Columbia U., N.Y. Taught French and lit. at Lincoln U. until 1952. National sales rep. for Schenley Import Corp. 1946-56; United States' intl. track star and a member of ten A.A.U. teams. Twice American champion in the 1000-yard indoor competition, twice all-American and, in 1951 in Paris, ran the fastest 800 meters in the world for that year. Professional acting debut, 1956, in Julius Caesar at the NY Shakespeare Fest.; published poet and short story writer. Trustee: Millay Colony Arts, NY; Los Angeles Free Public Theatre.
THEATER: *NY*: The Ballad of the Sad Cafe, The Cool World, General Seeger, Tiger Tiger Burning Bright!, The Old Glory, A Hand Is on the Gate (dir., actor), My One and Only. *Off-Broadway*: The Connection, The Blacks, Aria da Capo, Benito Cereno (Obie Award), Joe Turner's Come and Gone (L.A., S.F., Pittsburgh), Two Trains Running.
PICTURES: The Connection (debut, 1961), Black Like Me, The Comedians, Uptight, Topaz, The Liberation of L. B. Jones, Cisco Pike, The Cowboys, The World's Greatest Athlete, Superfly T.N.T., The Ra Expeditions (narrator), Uptown Saturday Night, Logan's Run, Twilight's Last Gleaming, Nothing Personal, Legal Eagles, Jumpin' Jack Flash, Oliver & Company (voice), Moon 44, The Mambo Kings, Naked in New York, Brother Minister: The Assassination of Malcolm X (narrator), Babe (voice), The Pompatus of Love, Last Summer in the Hamptons.
TELEVISION: *Series*: McCoy, Miss Winslow and Son, Soap, Falcon Crest. *Movies*: The Big Ripoff, Dr. Scorpion, Lady in a Corner, Columbo: Rest in Peace Mrs. Columbo, Meeting of Minds (Peabody Award), A Connecticut Yankee in King Arthur's Court (Peabody Award). *Guest*: All in the Family, Maude, Barney Miller, Soap, Head of the Class, The Cosby Show (Emmy Award, 1986), Falcon Crest. *Mini-Series*: King, Space.

BROWNING, KIRK
TV Director. b. New York, NY, March 28, 1921. e. Brooks School, Andover, MA, Avon Old Farms, Avon, CT., and Cornell U. 1940. Reporter for News-Tribune in Waco, TX; with American Field Service, 1942-45; adv. copywriter for Franklin Spier, 1945-48; became floor mgr. NBC-TV 1949; app't asst. dir. NBC-TV Opera Theatre in 1951 directing NBC Opera Theatre, TV Recital Hall, and Toscanini Simulcasts.
TELEVISION: Trial of Mary Lincoln, Jascha Heifetz Special, Harry and Lena, NBC Opera Theatre, Producers Showcase, Evening with Toscanini, Bell Telephone, The Flood, Beauty and the Beast, Lizzie Borden, World of Carl Sandburg, La Gioconda (Emmy Award, 1980), Big Blonde, Working, Ian McKellan Acting Shakespeare, Fifth of July, Alice in Wonderland, Live From the Met—Centennial.

BROWNLOW, KEVIN
Film Historian, Writer, Director, Film Editor. b. Crowborough, Eng., June 2, 1938. e. University College Sch. Asst. ed./editor, World Wide Pictures, London, 1955-61; film editor, Samaritan Films, 1961-65; film editor, Woodfall Films, 1965-68. Director, Thames Television 1975-90. Dir., Photoplay Productions 1990-present.
PICTURES: It Happened Here (dir. with Andrew Mollo) 1964, Charge of the Light Brigade (editor), Winstanley (with Andrew Mollo), Napoleon (restoration of 1927 film, re-released 1980).
TELEVISION: Charm of Dynamite (dir., ed.), All with David Gill: Hollywood (dir., writer), Unknown Chaplin (dir., prod.; Emmy Award), Buster Keaton: A Hard Act to Follow (prod.; 2 Emmy Awards), Harold Lloyd—The Third Genius, D.W. Griffith: Father of Film, Cinema Europe—The Other Hollywood.
AUTHOR: How It Happened Here (1968), The Parade's Gone By... (1968), Adventures with D.W. Griffith (editor, 1973), The War the West and the Wilderness (1979), Hollywood: The Pioneers (1980), Napoleon: Abel Gance's Classic Film (1983), Behind the Mask of Innocence (1990), David Lean–A Biography (1996).

BRUBAKER, JAMES D.
Producer. b. Hollywood, CA, March 30, 1937. e. Eagle Rock H.S. Transportation coordinator for 15 years before becoming unit prod. mgr., 1978-84. Then assoc. prod., exec. prod. & prod.
PICTURES: Assoc. Prod.: True Confessions, Rocky III, Rhinestone. Unit Prod. Mgr.: New York New York, Comes a Horseman, Uncle Joe Shannon, Rocky II, Raging Bull, True Confessions (also assoc. prod.), Rocky III (also assoc. prod.), Staying Alive, Rhinestone (also assoc. prod.), K-9, Problem Child, Mr. Baseball. Exec. Prod.: The Right Stuff, Beer, Rocky IV, Cobra, Over the Top, Problem Child (also prod. mgr.), Brain Donors (also prod. mgr.), A Walk in the Clouds.
TELEVISION: Movie: Running Mates (prod.)

BRUCE, BRENDA
Actress. b. Manchester, England, 1922. e. privately. London stage debut: 1066 and All That.
THEATER: Gently Does It (1953), This Year Next Year, Happy Days, Woman in a Dressing Gown, Victor Eh!, Merry Wives of Windsor, The Revenger's Tragedy, Little Murders, Winter's Tale, Pericles, Twelfth Night, Hamlet.
PICTURES: Millions Like Us (debut, 1944), Night Boat to Dublin, I See a Dark Stranger (The Adventuress), They Came to a City, Carnival, Piccadilly Incident, While the Sun Shines, When the Bough Breaks, My Brother's Keeper, Don't Ever Leave Me, The Final Test, Law and Disorder, Behind the Mask, Peeping Tom, Nightmare, The Uncle, That'll Be the Day.
TELEVISION: Mary Britton series, Return to Heaven, Wrong Side of the Park, The Lodger, The Monkey and the Mohawk, Love Story, A Piece of Resistance, Give the Clown His Supper, Knock on Any Door, The Browning Version, Death of a Teddy Bear, Softly, Softly, The Girl, Happy, Family at War, Budgie.

BRUCKHEIMER, BONNIE
Producer. b. Brooklyn, NY. Started in advertising and public relations eventually working for treasurer of Columbia Pictures. Later worked as asst. to Arthur Penn and Ross Hunter. Became partner with Bette Midler in All Girl Productions, 1985.
PICTURES: Big Business (assoc. prod.), Beaches, Stella, For the Boys, Hocus Pocus, Man of the House.
TELEVISION: Movie: Gypsy (exec. prod.).

BRUCKHEIMER, JERRY
Producer. b. Detroit, MI. e. U. of Arizona. Was art dir./prod. of TV commercials before becoming producer of films. 1983, formed Don Simpson/Jerry Bruckheimer Prods. with the late Don Simpson and entered into deal with Paramount Pictures to produce; company moved over to Walt Disney in early 1990's.
PICTURES: Assoc. Prod.: The Culpepper Cattle Company, Rafferty and the Gold Dust Twins. Producer: Farewell My Lovely, March or Die, Defiance, American Gigolo, Thief, Cat People (exec. prod.), Young Doctors in Love, Flashdance, Thief of Hearts, Beverly Hills Cop, Top Gun, Beverly Hills Cop II, Days of Thunder, The Ref, Bad Boys, Crimson Tide, Dangerous Minds, The Rock.
TELEVISION: Exec Prod: Dangerous Minds (series).

BRYAN, DORA
Actress. b. Southport, Lancashire, Eng., Feb. 7, 1924. e. Council Sch. Stage debut 1935.
PICTURES: The Fallen Idol (debut, 1949), No Room at the Inn, Once Upon a Dream, Blue Lamp, Cure for Love, Now Barabas, The Ringer, Women of Twilight, The Quiet Woman, The Intruder, You Know What Sailors Are, Mad About Men, See How They Run, Cockleshell Heroes, Child in the House, Green Man, Carry on Sergeant, Operation Bullshine, Desert Mice, The Night We Got the Bird, A Taste of Honey, Two a Penny, Apartment Zero.
TELEVISION: Virtual Murder, Casualty, Presenting Frank Subbs, Heartbeat.

BUCHHOLZ, HORST
Actor. b. Berlin, Germany, Dec. 4, 1933. e. high school. In radio and stage plays. Started in films dubbing foreign movies. Work with Berlin's Schiller Theatre result in film debut in French film.
PICTURES: Marianne (debut, 1955), Emil and the Detectives, Himmel Ohne Sterne (Sky Without Stars), Regine, Teenage Wolfpack, The King in Shadow, The Confessions of Felix Krull, The Legend of Robinson Crusoe, Mompti, Endstation Liebe, Nasser Asphalt, Resurrection, Das Totenschiff, Tiger Bay (English-language debut, 1959), The Magnificent Seven, Fanny, One Two Three, Nine Hours to Rama, The Empty Canvas, Andorra, Marco the Magnificent, That Man in Istanbul, Johnny Banco, Cervantes (The Young Rebel), L'Astragale, How When and With Whom, La Sauveur, La Columba non deve Volare, The Great Waltz, The Catamount Killing, Women in Hospital, The Amazing Captain Nemo, From Hell to Victory, Avalanche Express, Aphrodite, Sahara, Fear of Falling, Code Name: Emerald, And the Violins Stopped Playing, Escape From Paradise, Aces: Iron Eagle III, Far Away So Close.
TELEVISION: Movies: The Savage Bees, Raid on Entebbe, Return to Fantasy Island, Berlin Tunnel 21, Family Affairs, The Lion of Granada, Come Back to Kampen. Mini-Series: The French Atlantic Affair.

BUCKLEY, BETTY
Actress. b. Fort Worth, TX, July 3, 1947. e. Texas Christian U., BA. Studied acting with Stella Adler. NY Stage debut: 1776 (1969); London debut: Promises Promises. Appeared in interactive short film Race for Your Life.
THEATER: Johnny Pott, What's a Nice Country Like You Doing in a State Like This?, Pippin, I'm Getting My Act Together and Taking It on the Road, Cats (Tony Award, 1983), Juno's Swans, The Mystery of Edwin Drood, Song and Dance, Carrie, The Fourth Wall, The Perfectionist, Sunset Boulevard (London/B'way; Olivier Award nom.).
PICTURES: Carrie (debut, 1976), Tender Mercies, Wild Thing, Frantic, Another Woman, Rain Without Thunder, Wyatt Earp.
TELEVISION: Series: Eight is Enough. Movies: The Ordeal of Bill Carney, Roses Are for the Rich, The Three Wishes of Billy Grier, Babycakes, Bonnie & Clyde: The True Story (Emmy nom.), Betrayal of Trust. Specials: Bobby and Sarah, Salute to Lady Liberty, Taking a Stand (Afterschool Special; Emmy nom.), Stephen Sondheim Carnegie Hall Gala. Mini-Series: Evergreen. Guest: L.A. Law, Tribeca.

BUCKLEY, DONALD
Executive. b. New York, NY, June 28, 1955. e. C.W. Post Coll, NY, Sch. of Visual Arts. Ad. mgr., United Artists Theatres, 1975-78; acct. exec., Grey Advertising, 1978-80. Joined Warner Bros. in 1980 as NY adv. mgr.; 1986, promoted to east. dir. of adv./promo. for WB; 1988, named eastern dir. of adv. and publicity. 1991, promoted to v.p., East Coast Adv. & Publicity. 1996, promoted to v.p., Advertising & Publicity/v.p. Warner Bros. On-Line.

BUJOLD, GENEVIEVE
Actress. b. Montreal, Canada, July 1, 1942. e. Montreal Conservatory of Drama. Worked in a Montreal cinema as an usher; American TV debut: St. Joan.
THEATER: The Barber of Seville, A Midsummer Night's Dream, A House...A Day.
PICTURES: La Guerre est Finie, La Fleur de L'Age, Entre La Mer et L'eau Douce, King of Hearts, The Thief of Paris, Isabel, Anne of the Thousand Days, Act of the Heart, The Trojan Women, The Journey, Kamouraska, Earthquake, Swashbuckler, Obsession, Alex and the Gypsy, Another Man Another Chance, Coma, Murder by Decree, Final Assignment, The Last Flight of Noah's Ark, Monsignor, Tightrope, Choose Me, Trouble in Mind, The Moderns, Dead Ringers, False Identity, Secret Places of the Heart, A Paper Wedding, An Ambush of Ghosts, Mon Amie Max.
TELEVISION: Specials: Saint Joan, Antony and Cleopatra. Movies: Mistress of Paradise, Red Earth White Earth.

BULLOCK, SANDRA
Actress. b. Arlington, VA, 1964. Raised in Germany; studied piano in Europe. e. East Carolina Univ., drama major. First prof. acting job in NY in Off-B'way prod. No Time Flat.
PICTURES: Who Shot Patakango?, Love Potion No. 9, When the Party's Over, The Vanishing, The Thing Called Love, Demolition Man, Speed, Me and the Mob, While You Were Sleeping, The Net, Two If by Sea, A Time to Kill, In Love and War.
TELEVISION: Series: Working Girl. Movies: The Preppie Murder, Bionic Showdown: The Six Million Dollar Man and the Bionic Woman, Jackie Collins' Lucky/Chances.

BURGHOFF, GARY
Actor. b. Bristol, CT, May 24, 1943. Winner of Student Hallmark Award while in high school, 1961. Also wildlife artist, with work exhibited in many U.S. galleries.
THEATER: NY: You're a Good Man Charlie Brown, The Nerd. Other: Finian's Rainbow, Bells Are Ringing, Sound of Music, The Boy Friend, Romanoff and Juliet, Whose Life Is It Anyway?

PICTURES: M*A*S*H*, B.S. I Love You, Small Kill (also co-dir.).
TELEVISION: *Series*: The Don Knotts Show, M*A*S*H (Emmy Award, 1977). *Guest*: Good Guys, Name of the Game, Love American Style, Fernwood 2-Night, Sweepstakes, Love Boat, Fantasy Island. *Movies*: The Man in the Santa Claus Suit, Casino. *Special*: Twigs.

BURKE, ALFRED
Actor. b. London, England, 1918.
PICTURES: Touch and Go, The Man Upstairs, The Angry Silence, Moment of Danger, The Man Inside, No Time To Die, Children of the Damned, The Nanny, One Day in the Life of Ivan Denisovitch, Law and Disorder, Yangtse Incident, Interpol, Bitter Victory.
TELEVISION: The Crucible, Mock Auction, Parole, No Gun, No Guilt, The Big Knife, Parnell, The Strong Are Lonely, Home of the Brave, The Birthday Party, The Watching Eye, Public Eye (series).

BURKE, DELTA
Actress. b. Orlando, FL, July 30, 1956. e. LAMDA. m. actor Gerald McRaney. Competed in Miss America contest as Miss Florida, prior to studying acting in England.
TELEVISION: *Series*: The Chisholms, Filthy Rich, 1st & Ten, Designing Women, Delta (also co-exec. prod.), Women of the House (also exec. prod.). *Movies*: Charleston, A Last Cry for Help, Mickey Spillane's Mike Hammer: Murder Me Murder You, A Bunny's Tale, Where the Hell's That Gold?!!? Love and Curses... And All That Jazz (also co-exec. prod.), Day-o.

BURNETT, CAROL
Actress, Singer. b. San Antonio, TX, April 26, 1933. Daughter is actress Carrie Hamilton. e. Hollywood H.S., UCLA. Introduced comedy song, I Made a Fool of Myself Over John Foster Dulles, 1957; regular performer Garry Moore TV show, 1959-62. Recipient outstanding commedienne award Am. Guild Variety Artists, 5 times; TV Guide award for outstanding female performer 1961, 62, 63; Peabody Award, 1963; 5 Golden Globe awards for outstanding comedienne of year; Woman of Year award Acad. TV Arts and Scis. Voted one of the world's 20 most admired women in 1977 Gallup Poll. First Annual National Television Critics Award for Outstanding Performance, 1977. Best Actress Award at San Sebastian Film Fest. for film A Wedding, 1978. Inducted Acad. of Television Arts and Sciences Hall of Fame, 1985. *Author*: Once Upon a Time (1986).
THEATER: *NY*: Once Upon a Mattress (debut, 1959; Theatre World Award), Fade Out-Fade In, Moon Over Buffalo. *Regional*: Calamity Jane, Plaza Suite, I Do I Do, Same Time Next Year.
PICTURES: Who's Been Sleeping in My Bed? (debut, 1963), Pete 'n' Tillie, The Front Page, A Wedding, H.E.A.L.T.H., The Four Seasons, Chu Chu and the Philly Flash, Annie, Noises Off.
TELEVISION: *Series*: Stanley, Pantomime Quiz, The Garry Moore Show (Emmy Award, 1962), The Entertainers, The Carol Burnett Show (1967-78; in syndication as Carol Burnett & Friends), Carol Burnett & Company, Carol & Company, The Carol Burnett Show (1991). *Specials*: Julie & Carol at Carnegie Hall, Carol and Company (Emmy Award for previous 2 specials, 1963), An Evening with Carol Burnett, Calamity Jane, Once Upon a Mattress, Carol + 2, Julie & Carol at Lincoln Center, 6 Rms Riv Vu, Twigs, Sills & Burnett at the Met, Dolly & Carol in Nashville, All-Star Party for Carol Burnett, Burnett Discovers Domingo, The Laundromat, Carol Carl Whoopi & Robin, Julie & Carol—Together Again, The Carol Burnett Show: A Reunion (also co-exec. prod.), Men Movies & Carol. *Movies*: The Grass Is Always Greener Over the Septic Tank, Friendly Fire, The Tenth Month, Life of the Party: The Story of Beatrice, Between Friends, Hostage, Seasons of the Heart. *Mini-Series*: Fresno. *Guest*: Twilight Zone, The Jack Benny Program, Get Smart, The Lucy Show, Fame, Magnum P.I.

BURNETT, CHARLES
Director, Writer, Cinematographer. b. Vicksburg, MI, 1944. e. LA Community Col., UCLA.
PICTURES: *Director*: Killer of Sheep (also prod., s.p., photog., edit.), My Brother's Wedding (also prod., s.p., photog.), To Sleep With Anger (also s.p.), The Glass Shield (also s.p.). Cinematographer: Bless Their Little Hearts (also s.p.), Guest of Hotel Astoria.

BURNS, GEORGE
Actor. r.n. Nathan Birnbaum. b. New York, NY, Jan. 20, 1896. In vaudeville as singer in children's quartet, later as roller skater, then comedian; formed team Burns & (Gracie) Allen, 1925, marrying Gracie in 1926. Team performed many years on Keith and Orpheum vaudeville circuits, then on screen in Paramount short subjects, on radio in England; in 1930 began long career on American radio. Feature picture debut 1932 in The Big Broadcast. Books: I Love Her—That's Why, Living It Up: Or They Still Love Me in Altoona!, How to Live to Be 100—or More! The Ultimate Diet, Sex and Exercise Book, Dr. Burns' Prescription for Happiness, Dear George: Advice and Answers from America's Leading Expert on Everything from A to Z, Gracie, Wisdom of the 90s.

PICTURES: The Big Broadcast (debut, 1932), International House, College Humor, Six of a Kind, We're Not Dressing, Many Happy Returns, Love in Bloom, Here Comes Cookie, Big Broadcast of 1936, Big Broadcast of 1937, College Swing, College Holiday, A Damsel in Distress, College Swing, Honolulu, The Solid Gold Cadillac (narrator), The Sunshine Boys (Academy Award for Best Supporting Actor, 1975), Oh God!, Sgt. Pepper's Lonely Hearts Club Band, Movie Movie, Just You and Me Kid, Oh God! Book II, Oh God! You Devil, 18 Again, Radioland Murders.
TELEVISION: *Series*: The George Burns & Gracie Allen Show (1950-58), The George Burns Show, Wendy and Me, George Burns Comedy Week. *Movie*: Two of a Kind. *Specials*: Grandpa Will You Run With Me?, Disney's Magic in the Magic Kingdom (host), A Conversation With... George Burns (Emmy Award, 1990); and numerous others.
(d. March 1, 1996)

BURNS, KEN
Producer, Director, Cinematographer, Writer. b. July 29, 1953. e. Hampshire Col. Producer and director of the following documentaries: Brooklyn Bridge (also photog., edit.; Acad. Award nom.), The Shakers: Hands to Work Hearts to God (also co-writer), The Statue of Liberty (also photog.; Acad. Award nom.), Huey Long (also co-writer), Thomas Hart Benton (also photog.), The Congress, The Civil War (also photog., co-writer; numerous awards incl. Peabody and Emmy), Lindbergh (co-prod. only), Empire of the Air: The Men Who Made Radio (also photog., music dir.), Baseball (co- writer, prod., dir.). Co-author: Shakers: Hands to Work Hearts to God: The History and Visions of the United Society of Believers in Christ's Second Appearance from 1774 to Present, The Civil War: An Illustrated History, Baseball: An Illustrated History. Appeared in film Gettysburg.

BURNS, RALPH
Musical Conductor, Composer. b. Newton, MA, June 29, 1922.
PICTURES: Lenny, Cabaret (Academy Award, 1972), Lucky Lady, New York New York, Movie Movie, All That Jazz (Academy Award, 1979), Urban Cowboy, Annie, My Favorite Year, Jinxed, Kiss Me Goodbye, Star 80, National Lampoon's Vacation, Perfect, Bert Rigby You're a Fool.
TELEVISION: *Specials*: Baryshnikov on Broadway, Liza and Goldie Special. *Movies*: Ernie Kovacs—Between the Laughter, After the Promise, Sweet Bird of Youth.

BURRILL, TIMOTHY
Producer, Executive. b. North Wales, June 8, 1931. e. Eton Coll., Sorbonne U., Paris. Grenadier Guards 2 yrs, then London Shipping Co. Ent. m.p. ind. as resident prod. mgr. Samaritan Films working on shorts, commercials, documentaries, 1954. Ass't. dir.: The Criminal, The Valiant Years (TV series), On The Fiddle, Reach for Glory, War Lover, Prod. mgr: The Cracksman, Night Must Fall, Lord Jim, Yellow Rolls Royce, The Heroes of Telemark, Resident prod. with World Film Services. 1970 prod. two films on pop music for Anglo-EMI. 1972 first prod. administrator National Film School in U.K. 1974 Post prod. administrator The Three Musketeers. Prod. TV Special The Canterville Ghost; assoc. prod, That Lucky Touch; UK Administrator, The Prince and the Pauper; North American Prod. controller, Superman; 1974-1983 council member of BAFTA; mng. dir., Allied Stars (Breaking Glass, Chariots of Fire); 1979-80 V. chmn. Film BAFTA; 1980-83 chmn. BAFTA; 1981-92, Gov. National Film School, executive BFTPA mem. Cinematograph Films Council. 1982-88 Gov Royal National Theatre; 1987-93, chmn., Film Asset Developments, Formed Burrill Prods, 1979-; chmn. First Film Foundation. Exec. member PACT, 1991. Vice-chmn. (film) PACT, 1993.
PICTURES: *Prod.*: Privilege, Oedipus the King, A Severed Head, Three Sisters, Macbeth (assoc. prod.), Alpha Beta, Tess (co-prod.), Pirates of Penzance (co-prod.), Supergirl, The Fourth Protocol, To Kill a Priest (co-prod.), Return of the Musketeers (tv in U.S.), Valmont, The Rainbow Thief, The Lover, Bitter Moon, Sweet Killing.

BURROWS, JAMES
Director, Producer. b. Los Angeles, CA, Dec. 30, 1940. e. Oberlin, B.A.; Yale, M.F.A. Son of late Abe Burrows, composer, writer, director. Directed off-B'way.
PICTURE: Partners.
TELEVISION: *Series* (director): Mary Tyler Moore, Bob Newhart, Laverne and Shirley, Rhoda, Phyllis, Tony Randall Show, Betty White Show, Fay, Taxi (2 Emmy Awards: 1980, 1981), Lou Grant, Cheers (also prod.; 4 Emmy Awards as producer: 1983, 1984, 1989, 1991; 2 Emmy Awards as director: 1983, 1991), Dear John, Night Court, All is Forgiven (also exec. prod.), The Fanelli Boys, Frasier (Emmy Award, 1994), Friends, NewsRadio, Men Behaving Badly, Chicago Sons. *Movie*: More Than Friends.

BURROWS, ROBERTA
Executive. e. Brandeis U; Academia, Florence, Italy. Career includes freelance writing for natl. magazines: GQ, Italian Bazaar, US, Family Circle, and post as dir. of pub. for Howard Stein Enterprises and with Rogers & Cowan and Billings

Associates. Joined Warner Bros. as sr. publicist 1979; named dir. east coast publicity, 1986. Resigned 1989 to dev. novelty products. Proj. co-ordinator at Orion Pictures in NY for The Silence of the Lambs, Little Man Tate, Married to It, Bill & Ted's Bogus Journey. Columnist, Max publication.

BURSTYN, ELLEN
Actress. b. Detroit, MI, Dec. 7, 1932. r.n. Edna Rae Gilhooley. Majored in art; was fashion model in Texas at 18. Moved to Montreal as dancer; then N.Y. to do TV commercials (under the name of Ellen McRae), appearing for a year on the Jackie Gleason show (1956-57). In 1957 turned to dramatics and won lead in B'way show, Fair Game. Then went to Hollywood to do TV and films. Returned to N.Y. to study acting with Lee Strasberg; worked in TV serial, The Doctors. Co-artistic dir. of Actor's Studio. 1982-85. Pres. Actors Equity Assn. 1982-85. On 2 panels of Natl. Endowment of the Arts and Theatre Advisory Council (NY).
THEATER: *NY*: Same Time Next Year (Tony Award, 1975), 84 Charing Cross Road, Shirley Valentine, Shimada. L.A.: Love Letters. Regional: The Trip to Bountiful.
PICTURES: *As Ellen McRae*: For Those Who Think Young (debut, 1964), Goodbye Charlie, Pit Stop. *As Ellen Burstyn*: Tropic of Cancer, Alex in Wonderland, The Last Picture Show, The King of Marvin Gardens, The Exorcist, Harry and Tonto, Alice Doesn't Live Here Anymore (Academy Award, 1974), Providence, A Dream of Passion, Same Time Next Year, Resurrection, Silence of the North, The Ambassador, In Our Hands (doc.), Twice in a Lifetime, Hanna's War, Dying Young, The Color of Evening, The Cemetery Club, When a Man Loves a Woman, Roommates, The Baby-sitters Club, How to Make an American Quilt, The Spitfire Grill.
TELEVISION: *Movies*: Thursday's Game, The People Vs. Jean Harris, Surviving, Act of Vengeance, Into Thin Air, Something in Common, Pack of Lies, When You Remember Me, Mrs. Lambert Remembers Love, Taking Back My Life: The Nancy Ziegenmeyer Story, Grand Isle, Shattered Trust: The Shari Karney Story, Getting Out, Getting Gotti, Trick of the Eye, My Brother's Keeper, Follow the River. *Special*: Dear America: Letters Home From Vietnam (reader). *Series*: The Doctors, The Ellen Burstyn Show. *Guest*: Cheyenne, Dr. Kildare, 77 Sunset Strip, Perry Mason, The Iron Horse.

BURTON, KATE
Actress. b. Geneva, Switzerland, Sept. 10, 1957. e. Brown Univ. (B.A.), Yale Drama Sch. Daughter of late Richard Burton. m. stage manager Michael Ritchie. Worked at Yale Repertory Theatre, Hartford, Stage Co., the Hartman, Huntington Theatre, Williamstown, Berkshire Theatre festivals, The O'Neil Playwright's Conference, Pray Street Theatre.
THEATER: Present Laughter (debut, 1982; Theatre World Award), Alice in Wonderland, Winners, The Accrington Pals, Doonesbury, The Playboy of the Western World, Wild Honey, Measure For Measure, Some Americans Abroad (Drama Desk nom.), Jake's Women, London Suite, Company.
PICTURES: Big Trouble in Little China (debut, 1986), Life With Mikey, August, First Wives Club.
TELEVISION: *Mini-Series*: Ellis Island, Evergreen. *Movies*: Alice in Wonderland, Uncle Tom's Cabin, Love Matters, Mistrial, Notes For My Daughter. *Series*: Home Fires, Monty.

BURTON, LEVAR
Actor. b. Landstuhl, W. Germany, Feb. 16, 1957. e. U. of Southern California. Signed to play role of Kunta Kinte in TV mini-series, Roots, while still in school. Has hosted Public TV children's shows, Rebop, and Reading Rainbow.
PICTURES: Looking for Mr. Goodbar, The Hunter, The Supernaturals, Star Trek: Generations, Star Trek: First Contact.
TELEVISION: *Mini-Series*: Roots. *Special*: Almos' a Man. *Movies*: Billy: Portrait of a Street Kid, Battered, One in a Million: The Ron Leflore Story, Dummy, Guyana Tragedy: The Story of Jim Jones, The Acorn People, Grambling's White Tiger, The Jesse Owens Story, A Special Friendship, Roots: The Gift, Firestorm: 72 Hours in Oakland, Parallel Lives. *Series*: Star Trek: The Next Generation, Reading Rainbow (PBS; host, co-exec. prod.).

BURTON, TIM
Director, Producer. b. Burbank, CA, Aug. 25, 1958. Cartoonist since grade school in suburban Burbank. Won Disney fellowship to study animation at California Institute of the Arts. At 20 went to Burbank to work as apprentice animator on Disney lot, working on such features as The Fox and the Hound, The Black Cauldron. Made Vincent, 6-minute stop-motion animation short on his own which was released commercially in 1982 and won several film fest. awards. Also made Frankenweenie, 29 minute live-action film. Appeared in film Singles. Wrote and illustrated children's book based on The Nightmare Before Christmas.
PICTURES: *Director*: Pee-wee's Big Adventure, Beetlejuice, Batman, Edward Scissorhands (also co-story), Batman Returns (also co-prod.), Ed Wood (also co-prod.), Mars Attacks (also prod.). Co-Prod.: The Nightmare Before Christmas (also story), Cabin Boy, James and the Giant Peach, Mars Attacks.

TELEVISION: *Episode Director*: Aladdin (Faerie Tale Theatre), Alfred Hitchcock Presents, Amazing Stories (Family Dog). *Exec. Prod. for animated series*: Beetlejuice, Family Dog.

BUSBY, Ann
Executive. Senior v.p., MCA Motion Picture Group.

BUSCEMI, STEVE
Actor. b. Brooklyn, NY, 1957. Started as standup comedian in New York City, also wrote and acted in numerous one-act plays in collaboration with Mark Boone Jr. Acted in many plays by John Jesurun and worked briefly with the Wooster Group; worked as fireman. Studied acting at Lee Strasberg Inst. in NY.
PICTURES: The Way It Is/Eurydice in the Avenue, No Picnic, Parting Glances, Sleepwalk, Heart, Kiss Daddy Good Night, Call Me, Force of Circumstance, Vibes, Heart of Midnight, Bloodhounds of Broadway, Borders, New York Stories (Life Lessons), Slaves of New York, Mystery Train, Tales from the Dark Side, Miller's Crossing, Barton Fink, Billy Bathgate, Crisscross, In the Soup, Reservoir Dogs, Trusting Beatrice, Rising Sun, Twenty Bucks, Ed and His Dead Mother, The Hudsucker Proxy, Floundering, Airheads, Me and the Mob, Pulp Fiction, Billy Madison, Desperado, Somebody to Love, The Search for One-Eye Jimmy, Living in Oblivion, Things to Do in Denver When You're Dead, Pistolero, Fargo, Kansas City, Trees Lounge.
TELEVISION: *Mini-Series*: Lonesome Dove. *Movie*: The Last Outlaw. *Guest*: Miami Vice, The Equalizer, L.A. Law, Mad About You, Homicide: Life on the Streets.

BUSCH, H. DONALD
Exhibitor. b. Philadelphia, PA, Sept. 21, 1935. e. U. of Pennsylvania, physics, math, 1956; law school, 1959. 1960 to 1987 practiced law, anti-trust & entertainment. 1984, pres., Budco Theatres, Inc. 1975-87, pres., Busch, Grafman & Von Dreusche, P.C. 1987, pres. & CEO, AMC Philadelphia, Inc. Member: NATO chmn. (1990-91), chmn. emeritus, 1992; Showeast, gen. chmn., 1990-1. Will Rogers Memorial Fund (dir.) 1988, pres. of NATO, Pennsylvania. 1995, dir. Motion Picture Pioneers, Inc.

BUSEY, GARY
Actor, Musician. b. Goose Creek, TX, June 29, 1944. e. Coffeyville Jr. Coll. A.B., 1963; attended Kansas State Coll, OK State U. Played drums with the Rubber Band 1963-70. Also drummer with Leon Russell, Willie Nelson (as Teddy Jack Eddy).
PICTURES: Angels Hard as They Come (debut, 1971), Didn't You Hear?, Dirty Little Billy, The Magnificent Seven Ride, The Last American Hero, Lolly Madonna XXX, Hex, Thunderbolt and Lightfoot, The Gumball Rally, A Star Is Born, Straight Time, Big Wednesday, The Buddy Holly Story (Natl. Society of Film Critics Award; Acad. Award nom., 1978), Foolin' Around, Carny, Barbarosa, D.C. Cab, The Bear, Insignificance, Stephen King's Silver Bullet, Let's Get Harry, Eye of the Tiger, Lethal Weapon, Bulletproof, Act of Piracy, Predator 2, My Heroes Have Always Been Cowboys, Hider in the House, Point Break, The Player, Under Siege, South Beach, The Firm, Rookie of the Year. Surviving the Game, Chasers, Breaking Point, Drop Zone, Man With a Gun, Black Sheep, Carried Away.
TELEVISION: *Series*: The Texas Wheelers. *Guest*: High Chaparral (debut, 1970), Gunsmoke, Saturday Night Live, The Hitchhiker (ACE Award). *Movies*: Bloodsport, The Execution of Private Slovik, The Law, Wild Texas Wind, Chrome Soldiers. *Mini-Series*: A Dangerous Life, The Neon Empire.

BUSFIELD, TIMOTHY
Actor. b. Lansing, MI, June 12, 1957. e. East Tennessee State U; Actor's Theatre of Louisville (as apprentice and resident). Founded Fantasy Theatre in Sacramento, 1986, a professional acting co., which performs in Northern CA schools, providing workshops on playwriting for children and sponsors annual Young Playwrights contest.
THEATER: Richard II, Young Playwrights Festival (Circle Rep.), A Tale Told, Getting Out (European tour), Green Mountain Guilds Children Theatre, Mass Appeal, The Tempest, A Few Good Men (B'way). Founded & co-prod. The "B" Theatre, 1992, prods. Mass Appeal, Hidden in This Picture.
PICTURES: Stripes, Revenge of the Nerds, Revenge of the Nerds II, Field of Dreams, Sneakers, The Skateboard Kid, Striking Distance, Little Big League, Quiz Show.
TELEVISION: *Series*: Reggie, Trapper John M.D., thirtysomething (Emmy Award, 1991; also dir. 3 episodes), Byrds of Paradise, Champs. *Guest*: Family Ties, Matlock, Paper Chase, Love American Style, After M.A.S.H, Hotel. *Movies*: Strays, Calendar Girl-Cop-Killer?: The Bambi Bembenek Story, Murder Between Friends, In the Shadow of Evil, In the Line of Duty: Kidnapped.

BUTTONS, RED
Actor. r.n. Aaron Chwatt. b. New York, NY, Feb. 5, 1919. Attended Evander Child H.S. in the Bronx. Singer at the age of 13; comic, Minsky's. Served in U.S. Army, during WWII; in Army stage prod. and film version of Winged Victory. Received Golden

Globe Award noms. for Harlow and They Shoot Horses Don't They?; Best Comedian Award for The Red Buttons Show. Performed in most major Variety nightclubs shows.
PICTURES: Winged Victory (1944, debut), 13 Rue Madeleine, Footlight Varieties of 1951, Sayonara (Academy Award fo Best Supporting Actor, 1957; also Golden Globe Award), Imitation General, The Big Circus, One Two Three, The Longest Day, Gay Purr-ee (voice), Five Weeks in a Balloon, Hatari!, A Ticklish Affair, Your Cheatin' Heart, Harlow, Up From the Beach, Stagecoach, They Shoot Horses Don't They?, Who Killed Mary What's 'er Name?, The Poseidon Adventure, Gable and Lombard, Viva Knievel!, Pete's Dragon, Movie Movie, C.H.O.M.P.S., When Time Ran Out..., 18 Again!, The Ambulance, It Could Happen to You.
TELEVISION: Series: The Red Buttons Show (1952-55), The Double Life of Henry Phyfe, Knots Landing. Movies: Breakout, The New Original Wonder Woman, Louis Armstrong: Chicago Style, Telethon, Vega$, The Users, Power, The Dream Merchants, Leave 'Em Laughing, Reunion at Fairborough, Alice in Wonderland, Hansel & Gretel.
oot Boy With Cheek, Hold It, The Admiral Had a Wife, Winged Victory, Tender Trap, Play It Again Sam, The Teahouse of the August Moon, Red Buttons on Broadway, Finian's Rainbow.

BUZZI, RUTH
Actress. b. Westerly, RI, July 24, 1939. e. Pasadena Playhouse Col. of Theatre Arts. On Country Music charts with You Oughta Hear the Song. Has received 5 Emmy nominations; Golden Globe winner, AGVA Variety Artist of the Year, 1977, Rhode Island Hall of Fame, Presidential commendation for outstanding artist in the field of entertainment, 1980, NAACP Image Award.
THEATER: Sweet Charity (Broadway), 4 off-Broadway shows incl. A Man's A Man, Little Mary Sunshine, Cinderella, Wally's Cafe, 18 musical revues and Las Vegas club act.
PICTURES: Record City, Freaky Friday, The Apple Dumpling Gang Rides Again, The North Avenue Irregulars, The Villian, Surf Two, Skatetown USA, Chu Chu and the Philly Flash, The Being, The Bad Guys, Dixie Lanes, Up Your Alley, Diggin' Up Business, My Mom's a Werewolf, It's Your Life Michael Angelo, The Trouble Makers (orig. title: The Fight Before Christmas).
TELEVISION: Series: Rowan & Martin's Laugh-In, The Steve Allen Comedy Hour, Donny & Marie, The Lost Saucer, Betsy Lee's Ghost Town Jamboree, Carol Burnett's The Entertainers, Days of Our Lives, Sesame Street; semi-regular on 12 other series including Flip, Tony Orlando & Dawn, That Girl, Glen Campbell's Goodtime Hour, Leslie Uggums Show, The Dean Martin Variety Hour; guest on many TV series and specials including Medical Center, Adam 12, Trapper John M.D., Love Boat, They Came from Outer Space, Major Dad, Alice, Here's Lucy, Saved by the Bell, etc. Movie: In Name Only. Many cartoon voice-over series and over 150 on-camera commercials.

BYGRAVES, MAX
Comedian, Actor. b. London, England, October 16, 1922. e. St. Joseph's R.C. School, Rotherhithe. After RAF service, touring revues and London stage. TV debut in 1953, with own show. Autobiography: I Wanna Tell You A Story, 1976. Novel: The Milkman's on His Way, 1977. Received O.B.E., New Year's Honours 1983.
PICTURES: Skimpy in the Navy (debut, 1949), Bless 'em All, Nitwits on Parade, Tom Brown's Schooldays, Charley Moon, A Cry from the Streets, Bobbikins, Spare the Rod, The Alf Garnett Saga.
TELEVISION: Roamin' Holiday (series).

BYRD, CARUTH C.
Production Executive. b. Dallas, TX, March 25, 1941. e. Trinity U, San Antonio. Multi-millionaire businessman, chmn. of Caruth C. Byrd Enterprises, Inc., who entered entertainment industry forming Communications Network Inc. in 1972. Was principal investor in film Santee (1972) and in 1973 formed Caruth C. Byrd Prods. to make theatrical features. 1983, chmn., Lone Star Pictures. 1987, formed Caruth C. Byrd Television. Formed Caruth C. Byrd Entertainment Inc. May, 1989. Concerts incl. Tom Jones, Natalie Cole, B.J. Thomas, Tammy Wynette, Seals & Croft, Eddie Rabbit, Helen Reddy, Jim Stafford, Tanya Tucker and many more.
PICTURES: Murph the Surf, The Monkeys of Bandapur (both exec. prod.), Santee, Sudden Death, Hollywood High II, Lone Star Country, Trick or Treats.
TELEVISION: Fishing Fever, Kids Are People Too, Tribute to Mom and Dad, Back to School, Texas 150: A Celebration Special.

BYRNE, DAVID
Actor, Singer, Director. b. Dumbarton, Scotland, May 14, 1952. Moved to Baltimore at 7. e. Rhode Island Sch. of Design studying photography, performance and video, and Maryland Inst. Coll. of Art 1971-72. Prod. and dir. music videos. Awarded MTV's Video Vanguard Award, 1985. Best known as the lead singer and chief songwriter of Talking Heads. Composed and performed original score for choreographer Twyla Tharp's The Catherine Wheel (B'way). Wrote music for Robert Wilson's The Knee Plays.

PICTURES: Stop Making Sense (conceived and stars in concert film), True Stories (director, s.p., narrator), The Last Emperor (music, Academy Award, 1987), Married to the Mob (music), Heavy Petting, Between the Teeth (also co-dir.). Also contributed music to such films as Times Square, The Animals' Film, King of Comedy, America is Waiting, Revenge of the Nerds, Down and Out in Beverly Hills, Dead End Kids, Cross My Heart.
TELEVISION: A Family Tree (Trying Times), Alive From Off-Center (also composed theme), Survival Guides; Rolling Stone Magazine's 20 Years of Rock and Roll.

BYRNE, GABRIEL
Actor. b. Dublin, Ireland, 1950. e. University Coll., Ireland. Worked as archaeologist, then taught Spanish at girls' school. Participated in amateur theater before acting with Ireland's Focus Theatre, an experimental rep. co. and joining Dublin's Abbey Theatre Co. Cast in long-running TV series the Riordans. Also worked with National Theater in London. Author: Pictures in My Head (1994).
PICTURES: On a Paving Stone Mounted, The Outsider, Excalibur, Hanna K, The Keep, Defence of the Realm, Gothic, Lionheart, Siesta, Hello Again, Julia and Julia, A Soldier's Tale, The Courier, Miller's Crossing, Shipwrecked, Dark Obsession (Diamond Skulls), Cool World, Point of No Return, Into the West (also assoc. prod.), A Dangerous Woman, In the Name of the Father (co-prod. only), Prince of Jutland, A Simple Twist of Fate, Trial by Jury, Little Women, The Usual Suspects, Frankie Starlight, Dead Man, Last of the High Kings (also co-s.p.)Mad Dog Time.
TELEVISION: Series: The Riordans, Branken. Movies/ Specials: Wagner, The Search for Alexander the Great, Treatment, Joyce, Mussolini, Christopher Columbus, Lark in the Clear Air (also dir., writer), Buffalo Girls.

BYRNES, EDD
Actor. b. New York, NY, July 30, 1933. e. Harren H.S. Prof. debut, Joe E. Brown's Circus Show; appeared on stage in Tea and Sympathy, Picnic, Golden Boy, Bus Stop, Ready When You Are C.B., Storm in Summer.
PICTURES: Reform School Girl, Darby's Rangers, Up Periscope, Marjorie Morningstar, Yellowstone Kelly, Girl on the Run, The Secret Invasion, Wicked Wicked, Grease, Stardust, Go Kill and Come Back, Payment in Blood, Troop Beverly Hills.
TELEVISION: Series: 77 Sunset Strip, Sweepstake$. Has appeared in over 300 TV shows incl.: Matinee Theatre, Crossroads, Jim Bowie, Wire Service, Navy Log, Oh Susanna!, Throb, Rags to Riches, Murder She Wrote. Movies: The Silent Gun, Mobile Two, Telethon, Vega$, Twirl.

BYRON, KATHLEEN
Actress. b. London, England, Jan. 11, 1922. e. London U., Old Vic. co. student, 1942. Screen debut in Young Mr. Pitt, 1943.
PICTURES: Silver Fleet, Black Narcissus, Matter of Life and Death, Small Back Room, Madness of the Heart, Reluctant Widow, Prelude to Fame, Scarlet Thread, Tom Brown's Schooldays, Four Days, Hell Is Sold Out, I'll Never Forget You, Gambler and the Lady, Young Bess, Night of the Silvery Moon, Profile, Secret Venture, Hand in Hand, Night of the Eagle, Hammerhead, Wolfshead, Private Road, Twins of Evil, Craze, Abdication, One of Our Dinosaurs Is Missing, The Elephant Man, From a Far Country, Emma.
TELEVISION: The Lonely World of Harry Braintree, All My Own Work, Emergency Ward 10, Probation Officer, Design for Murder, Sergeant Cork, Oxbridge 2000, The Navigators, The Worker, Hereward the Wake, Breaking Point, Vendetta, Play To Win, Who Is Sylvia, Portrait of a Lady, Callan, You're Wrecking My Marriage, Take Three Girls, The Confession of Mariona Evans, Paul Temple, The Worker, The Moonstone, The Challengers, The Golden Bowl, The Edwardians, The New Life, Menace, The Rivals of Sherlock Holmes, The Brontes, On Call, Edward VII, Sutherland's Law, Crown Court, Anne of Avonlea, Heidi, Notorious Woman, General Hospital, North & South, Angelo, Within these Walls, Jubilee, Z Cars, Tales from the Supernatural, Secret Army, An Englishman's Castle, The Professionals, Forty Weeks, Emmerdale Farm, Blake Seven, The Minders, Together, Hedda Gabler, Nancy Astor, God Speed Co-operation, Take Three Women, Reilly, Memoirs of Sherlock Holmes, Moon And Son, The Bill, Casualty, Portrait of a Marriage, Gentlemen & Players.

BYRUM, JOHN
Writer, Director. b. Winnetka, IL, March 14, 1947. e. New York U. Film School. First job as gofer on industrial films and cutting dailies for underground filmmakers. Went to England where wrote 1st s.p., Comeback. From 1970-73, was in NY writing and re-writing scripts for low-budget films.
PICTURES: Writer: Mahogany, Inserts (also dir.) Harry and Walter Go to New York, Heart Beat (also dir), Sphinx, Scandalous, The Razor's Edge (also dir.), The Whoopee Boys (also dir.), The War at Home (also dir.).
TELEVISION: Movie: Murder in High Places (dir., writer). Series: Alfred Hitchcock Presents (1985), Middle Ages (creator, writer, exec. prod.), South of Sunset (creator, writer, exec. prod.), Winnetka Road (creator, writer, exec. prod.).

C

CAAN, JAMES
Actor. b. Bronx, NY, March 26, 1940. e. Hofstra U. Studied with Sanford Meisner at the Neighborhood Playhouse. Appeared off-B'way in La Ronde, 1961. Also on B'way in Mandingo, Blood Sweat and Stanley Poole.
PICTURES: Irma La Douce (debut, 1963), Lady in a Cage, The Glory Guys, Red Line 7000, El Dorado, Games, Countdown, Journey to Shiloh, Submarine X-1, The Rain People, Rabbit Run, T.R. Baskin, The Godfather (Acad. Award nom.), Slither, Cinderella Liberty, The Gambler, Freebie and the Bean, The Godfather Part II, Funny Lady, Rollerball, The Killer Elite, Harry and Walter Go To New York, Silent Movie, A Bridge Too Far, Another Man Another Chance, Comes a Horseman, Chapter Two, Hide in Plain Sight (also dir.), Thief, Bolero, Kiss Me Goodbye, Gardens of Stone, Alien Nation, Dick Tracy, Misery, The Dark Backward, For the Boys, Honeymoon in Vegas, The Program, Flesh & Bone, A Boy Called Hate, Things to Do in Denver When You're Dead, Bottle Rocket, Eraser, Bulletproof.
TELEVISION: Much series guest work (Naked City, Route 66, Wagon Train, Ben Casey, Alfred Hitchcock Presents, etc.) 1962-69. Movie: Brian's Song (Emmy nom.).

CACOYANNIS, MICHAEL
Producer, Director, Writer. b. Cyprus, June 11, 1922. Studied law in London, admitted to bar at age 21. Became a producer of BBC's wartime Greek programs while attending dramatic school. After acting on the stage in England, left in 1952 for Greece, where he made his first film, Windfall in Athens, with his own script. While directing Greek classical plays, he continued making films.
PICTURES: Director/Writer: Windfall in Athens (Sunday Awakening; debut, 1954), Stella, Girl in Black, A Matter of Dignity (The Final Lie), Our Last Spring (Eroica), The Wastrel, Electra, Zorba the Greek, The Day the Fish Came Out, The Trojan Women, Attila '74, Iphigenia, Sweet Country, Up Down and Sideways.

CAESAR, IRVING
Author, Composer, Publisher. b. New York, NY, July 4, 1895. e. City Coll. of New York. Abroad with Henry Ford on Peace Ship, WWI; songwriter since then, songs with George Gershwin, Sigmund Romberg, Vincent Youmans, Rudolph Friml and others; songwriter for stage, screen and radio, including Swanee, Tea for Two, Sometimes I'm Happy, I Want to Be Happy, Lady Play Your Mandolin, Songs of Safety, Songs of Friendship, Songs of Health and Pledge of Allegiance to the Flag.

CAESAR, SID
Actor. b. Yonkers, NY, Sept. 8, 1922. Studied saxophone at Juilliard School; then appeared in service revue Tars and Spars. Cast by prod. Max Liebman in B'way revue Make Mine Manhattan in 1948. Voted best comedian in M.P. Daily's TV poll, 1951, 1952. Best Comedy Team (with Imogene Coca) in 1953. Received Sylvania Award, 1958. Formed Shelbrick Corp. TV, 1959. Appeared in B'way musical Little Me (1962), Off-B'way & B'way revue Sid Caesar & Company (1989). Author: Where Have I Been? (autobiography, 1982).
PICTURES: Tars and Spars (debut, 1945), The Guilt of Janet Ames, It's a Mad Mad Mad Mad World, The Spirit Is Willing, The Busy Body, A Guide for the Married Man, Airport 1975, Silent Movie, Fire Sale, Grease, The Cheap Detective, The Fiendish Plot of Dr. Fu Manchu, History of the World Part 1, Grease 2, Over the Brooklyn Bridge, Cannonball Run II, Stoogemania, The Emperor's New Clothes.
TELEVISION: Series: Admiral Broadway Revue, Your Show of Shows (Emmy Award for Best Actor, 1952), Caesar's Hour (Emmy Award for Best Comedian, 1956), Sid Caesar Invites You (1958), As Caesar Sees It, The Sid Caesar Show. Movies: Flight to Holocaust, Curse of the Black Widow, The Munsters' Revenge, Found Money, Love Is Never Silent, Alice in Wonderland, Freedom Fighter, Side By Side, The Great Mom Swap. Guest: U.S. Steel Hour, G.E. Theatre, The Ed Sullivan Show, Carol Burnett Show, Lucy Show, That's Life, Love American Style, When Things Were Rotten, The Love Boat, Amazing Stories, others. Specials: Tiptoe Through TV, Variety—World of Show Biz, Sid Caesar and Edie Adams Together, The Sid Caesar Imogene Coca Carl Reiner Howard Morris Special, Christmas Snow.

CAGE, NICOLAS
Actor. b. Long Beach, CA, Jan. 7, 1964. r.n. Nicholas Coppola. Nephew of dir. Francis Ford Coppola. Joined San Francisco's American Conservatory Theatre at age 15. While attending Beverly Hills High School won role on tv pilot Best of Times.
PICTURES: Fast Times at Ridgemont High (debut, 1982; billed as Nicholas Coppola), Valley Girl, Rumble Fish, Racing with the Moon, The Cotton Club, Birdy, The Boy in Blue, Peggy Sue Got Married, Raising Arizona, Moonstruck, Vampire's Kiss, Fire Birds, Wild at Heart, Tempo di Mecidere (Time to Kill), Zandalee, Honeymoon in Vegas, Amos & Andrew, DeadFall, Red Rock

West, Guarding Tess, It Could Happen to You, Trapped in Paradise, Kiss of Death, Leaving Las Vegas (Academy Award, Chicago Film Critics Award, Nat'l Society of Film Critics Award; Golden Globe Award), The Rock.

CAINE, MICHAEL
Actor. r.n. Maurice Micklewhite. b. London, England, March 14, 1933. Asst. stage mgr. Westminster Rep. (Sussex, UK 1953); Lowestoft Rep. 1953-55. London stage: The Room, The Dumbwaiter, Next Time I'll Sing For You (1963). Author: Michael Caine's Moving Picture Show or: Not Many People Know This Is the Movies, Acting on Film, What's It All About? (autobiography, 1993). Awarded C.B.E., 1992. Video: Michael Caine—Acting on Film.
PICTURES: A Hill in Korea (debut, 1956; aka Hell in Korea), How to Murder A Rich Uncle, The Key, Two-Headed Spy, Blind Spot, Breakout (Danger Within), Foxhole in Cairo, Bulldog Breed, The Day the Earth Caught Fire, Solo for Sparrow, Zulu, The Ipcress File, Alfie (Acad. Award nom.), The Wrong Box, Gambit, Funeral in Berlin, Hurry Sundown, Woman Times Seven, Billion Dollar Brain, Deadfall, The Magus, Play Dirty, The Italian Job, The Battle of Britain, Too Late the Hero, The Last Valley, Get Carter, Kidnapped, Zee and Company (X,Y & Zee), Pulp, Sleuth (Acad. Award nom.), The Black Windmill, The Destructors (The Marseille Contract), The Wilby Conspiracy, Peeper, The Romantic Englishwoman, The Man Who Would Be King, Harry and Walter Go to New York, The Eagle Has Landed, A Bridge Too Far, The Silver Bears, The Swarm, California Suite, Ashanti, Beyond the Poseidon Adventure, The Island, Dressed to Kill, The Hand, Victory, Deathtrap, Educating Rita (Acad. Award nom.), Beyond the Limit, Blame It on Rio, The Jigsaw Man, The Holcroft Covenant, Hannah and Her Sisters (Academy Award for Best Supporting Actor, 1986), Water, Sweet Liberty, Mona Lisa, Half Moon Street, Jaws—The Revenge, The Whistle Blower, The Fourth Protocol (also exec. prod.), Surrender, Without a Clue, Dirty Rotten Scoundrels, A Shock to the System, Mr. Destiny, Bullseye!, Noises Off, The Muppet Christmas Carol, On Deadly Ground.
TELEVISION: Series: Rickles (1975). In more than 100 British teleplays 1957-63 incl. The Compartment, The Playmates, Hobson's Choice, Funny Noises with Their Mouths, The Way with Reggie, Luck of the Draw, Hamlet, The Other Man. Movies: Jack the Ripper, Jekyll and Hyde, Blue Ice, World War II: When Lions Roared.

CALHOUN, RORY
Actor. r.n. Francis Timothy McCown. b. Los Angeles, CA, Aug. 8, 1922. e. Santa Cruz H.S. Worked as logger, miner, cowpuncher, firefighter before becoming actor.
PICTURES: (as Frank McCown): Something for the Boys (debut, 1944), The Bullfighters, Sunday Dinner for a Soldier, Nob Hill, The Great John L, Where Do We Go From Here?; (as Rory Calhoun): The Red House, Adventure Island, That Hagen Girl, Miraculous Journey, Massacre River, Sand, Return of the Frontiersman, A Ticket to Tomahawk, County Fair, Rogue River, I'd Climb the Highest Mountain, Meet Me After the Show, With a Song in My Heart, Way of a Gaucho, The Silver Whip, Powder River, How to Marry a Millionaire, Yellow Tomahawk, River of No Return, A Bullet Is Waiting, Dawn at Socorro, Four Guns to the Border, The Looters, Ain't Misbehavin', Treasure of Pancho Villa, The Spoilers, Red Sundown, Raw Edge, Flight to Hong Kong, Utah Blaine, Hired Gun, The Domino Kid, The Big Caper, Ride Out for Revenge, Apache Territory, The Saga of Hemp Brown, Thunder in Carolina (Hard Drivin'), The Colossus of Rhodes, Marco Polo, Treasure of Monte Cristo (The Secret of Monte Cristo), Gun Hawk, The Young and the Brave, A Face in the Rain (also co-exec. prod.), Black Spurs, Young Fury, Operation Delilah, Finger on the Trigger, Our Man in Baghdad, The Emerald of Artatama, Apache Uprising, Dayton's Devils, Operation Cross Eagles, Night of the Lepus, Blood Black and White, Won Ton Ton the Dog Who Saved Hollywood, Mule Feathers, Kino the Padre on Horseback, Love and the Midnight Auto Supply, Just Not the Same Without You, Bitter Heritage, The Main Event, Motel Hell, Angel, Rollerblade Warriors, Avenging Angel, Hell Comes to Frogtown, Bad Jim, Fists of Steel, Pure Country.
TELEVISION: Series: U.S. Camera, The Texan, Capitol. Mini-Series: The Blue and the Gray, The Rebels. Movies: Flight to Holocaust, Flatbed Annie and Sweetie Pie: Lady Truckers. Guest: The Road Ahead, Day Is Done, Bet the Wild Queen, Zane Grey Theater, Killer Instinct, Land's End (pilot), Champion, Hart to Hart, Police Woman, Movin' On, Alias Smith & Jones.

CALLAN, MICHAEL
Actor, Singer, Dancer. b. Philadelphia, PA, Nov. 22, 1935. Singer, dancer, Philadelphia nightclubs; to New York in musicals including The Boy Friend and West Side Story; dancer at Copacabana nightclub; in short-run plays, Las Vegas: That Certain Girl, Love Letters.
PICTURES: They Came to Cordura (debut, 1958) The Flying Fontaines, Because They're Young, Pepe, Mysterious Island, Gidget Goes Hawaiian, 13 West Street, Bon Voyage, The Interns, The Victors, The New Interns, Cat Ballou, You Must Be Joking!, The Magnificent Seven Ride!, Frasier the Sensuous

Lion, Lepke, The Photographer, The Cat and The Canary, Record City, Double Exposure (also prod.), Chained Heat, Freeway, Leprechaun III.
TELEVISION: Series: Occasional Wife, Superboy. Guest: Murder She Wrote, Superboy, etc. Movies: In Name Only, Donner Pass: The Road to Survival, Last of the Great Survivors. Mini-Series: Blind Ambition, Scruples.

CALLEY, JOHN
Executive. b. New Jersey, 1930. Was dir. of nighttime programming and dir. of programming sales at NBC, 1951-57; prod. exec. & TV prod., Henry Jaffe Enterprises, 1957; in charge of radio & tv for Ted Bates Adv. Agency, 1958; 1960-69, Filmways Inc., exec. v.p. & prod.; 1970, exec. v.p. in chg. of worldwide prod., Warner Bros.; pres. of Warner Bros. 1975-80. Retired from industry for 13 yrs. 1993 appointed pres. of United Artists.

CALLOW, SIMON
Actor, Writer, Director. b. London, June 15, 1949. e. Queens, U. of Belfast, The Drama Centre. Originated role of Mozart in London premiere of Amadeus and Burgess/Chubb in Single Spies. Author: Being an Actor, Acting in Restoration Comedy, Charles Laughton: A Difficult Actor, Shooting the Actor, Orson Welles: The Road to Zanadu.
THEATER: London: Plumber's Progress, The Doctor's Dilemma, Soul of the White Ant, Blood Sports, The Resistible Rise of Arturo Ui, Amadeus, Restoration, The Beastly Beatitudes of Balthazar B, Titus Andronicus (Bristol Old Vic), Faust. Shakespeare's Sonnets. Director: Loving Reno, The Infernal Machine (also translator), Jacques and His Master (also trans.; L.A.), Single Spies, Shades, My Fair Lady (Natl. tour), Shirley Valentine (London, NY), Carmen Jones.
PICTURES: Amadeus, A Room With a View, The Good Father, Maurice, Manifesto, Postcards From the Edge, Mr. and Mrs. Bridge, The Ballad of the Sad Cafe (dir. only), Howards End (unbilled), Four Weddings and a Funeral, Street Fighter, Jefferson in Paris, Ace Ventura: When Nature Calls, James and the Giant Peach.
TELEVISION: Man of Destiny, La Ronde, All the World's a Stage, Wings of Song, The Dybbuk, Instant Enlightenment, Chance of a Lifetime (series), David Copperfield, Honour, Profit and Pleasure, Old Flames, Revolutionary Witness: Palloy.

CALVET, CORINNE
Actress. r.n. Corinne Dibos. b. Paris, France, April 30, 1925. e. U. of Paris School of Fine Arts, Comedie Francaise. On French stage and radio; screen debut in French films, then to U.S. in 1949. Author: Has Corinne Been a Good Little Girl?, The Kirlian Aura.
PICTURES: La Part de L'Ombre (debut, 1946), Nous ne Sommes pas Maries, Petrus, La Chateau de la Derniere Chance, Rope of Sand (U.S. debut), When Willie Comes Marching Home, My Friend Irma Goes West, Quebec, On the Riviera, Peking Express, Sailor Beware, Thunder in the East, What Price Glory?, Powder River, Flight to Tangier, The Far Country, So This Is Paris, The Adventures of Casanova (Sins of Casanova), The Girls of San Frediano, Four Women in the Nihgt, Bonnes a Tuer (One Step to Eternity), Napoleon, Plunderers of Painted Flats, Bluebeard's Ten Honeymoons, Hemingway's Adventures of a Young Man, Apache Uprising, Pound, Too Hot to Handle, Dr. Heckle and Mr. Hype, The Sword and the Sorcerer, Side Roads.
TELEVISION: Movies: The Phantom of Hollywood, She's Dressed to Kill, The French Atlantic Affair.

CAMERON, JAMES
Director, Writer. b. Kapuskasing, Ontario, Canada, Aug. 16, 1954. e. Fullerton Junior Col. (physics). 1990, formed Lightstorm Entertainment.
PICTURES: Piranha II—The Spawning (dir.), The Terminator (dir., s.p.), Rambo: First Blood Part II (co-s.p.), Aliens (dir., s.p.), The Abyss (dir., s.p.), Terminator 2: Judgment Day (dir., co-s.p., prod.), Point Break (exec. prod.), True Lies (dir., co-s.p., prod.), Strange Days (co-prod., co-s.p., story).

CAMERON, JOANNA
Actress, Director. r.n. Patricia Cameron. b. Aspen, CO, Sept. 20, 1951. e. U. of California, Sorbonne, Pasadena Playhouse, 1968. Guinness Record: Most network programmed TV commercials. TV Director: Various commercials, CBS Preview Special, closed circuit program host U.S.N., all TV equipped ships—actress and dir. Documentaries: Razor Sharp (prod., dir.), El Camino Real (dir., prod.).
PICTURES: How To Commit Marriage (debut), B.S. I Love You, Pretty Maids All in a Row.
TELEVISION: Movies: The Great American Beauty Contest, Night Games, It Couldn't Happen to a Nicer Guy, High Risk, Swan Song. Series: Isis. Guest: The Survivors, Love American Style, Daniel Boone, Mission Impossible, The Partners, Search, Medical Center, Name of the Game, The Bold Ones, Marcus Welby, Petrocelli, Columbo, Switch, MacMillan, Spiderman. Specials: Bob Hope Special, Bob Hope 25th NBC Anniversary Special; numerous commercials.

CAMERON, KIRK
Actor. b. Canoga Park, CA, Oct. 12, 1970. m. actress Chelsea Noble. Sister is actress Candace Cameron. Started doing TV commercials at age 9.
PICTURES: The Best of Times, Like Father, Like Son, Listen to Me.
TELEVISION: Series: Two Marriages, Growning Pains, Kirk. Movies: Goliath Awaits, Starflight: The Plane That Couldn't Land, A Little Piece of Heaven, Star Struck, The Computer Wore Tennis Shoes. Specials: The Woman Who Willed a Miracle, Andrea's Story. Ice Capades with Kirk Cameron.

CAMP, COLLEEN
Actress. b. San Francisco, CA, 1953. Spent 2 years as a bird trainer at Busch Gardens before being noticed by an agent and cast on TV. TV debut on the Dean Martin Show. Assoc. prod. on Martha Coolidge's film The City Girl. Sang several songs in They All Laughed and made Billboard charts with song One Day Since Yesterday.
PICTURES: Battle for the Planet of the Apes (debut, 1973), Swinging Cheerleaders, Death Game (The Seducers), Funny Lady, Smile, The Gumball Rally, Cats in a Cage, Game of Death, Apocalypse Now, Cloud Dancer, They All Laughed, The Seduction, Valley Girl, Smokey and the Bandit III, Rosebud Beach Hotel, The Joy of Sex, Police Academy II, Doin' Time, D.A.R.Y.L., Clue, Walk Like a Man, Illegally Yours, Track 29, Wicked Stepmother, My Blue Heaven, Wayne's World, The Vagrant, Un-Becoming Age, Sliver, Last Action Hero, Greedy, Naked in New York, Die Hard With a Vengeance, The Baby-sitter's Club.
TELEVISION: Movies: Amelia Earhart, Lady of the House, Sisterhood, Addicted to His Love, Backfield in Motion, For Their Own Good. Mini-Series: Rich Man Poor Man Book II. Series: Dallas. Guest: Happy Days, Dukes of Hazzard, WKRP in Cincinnati, Magnum PI, Murder She Wrote, Tales from the Crypt. Guest: George Burns Comedy Week. Special: Going Home Again.

CAMP, JOE
Producer, Director, Writer. b. St. Louis, MO, Apr. 20, 1939. e. U. of Mississippi, B.B.A. Acct. exec. McCann-Erickson Advt., Houston 1961-62; owner Joe Camp Real Estate 1962-64; acct. exec. Norsworthy-Mercer, Dallas 1964-69; dir. TV commercials; founder and pres. Mulberry Square Prods, 1971-present. Author: Underdog.
PICTURES: Dir./Prod./Writer: Benji, Hawmps, For the Love of Benji, The Double McGuffin, Oh Heavenly Dog, Benji the Hunted.
TELEVISION: Specials: The Phenomenon of Benji (dir., writer, prod.), Benji's Very Own Christmas Story (dir., prod., writer), Benji at Work (prod., writer), Benji at Marineland (dir., writer), Benji Zax and the Alien Prince (dir.).

CAMPANELLA, TOM
Executive. b. Houston, TX, 1944. e. City U. of NY. Joined Paramount Pictures 1968 as asst. business mgr.; later worked for corporate div. and Motion Picture Group. Named exec. dir., nat'l adv. 1979, made v.p., nat'l adv. 1982, appt. sr. v.p., adv., for M.P. Group of Paramount, 1984. Appointed exec. v.p., adv. & promo., 1990.

CAMPBELL, BRUCE
Actor, Producer. b. Birmingham, MI, 1958.
PICTURES: The Evil Dead (debut, 1983; also exec. prod.), Crimewave (also co-prod.), Evil Dead 2 (also co-prod.), Maniac Cop, Moontrap, Darkman, Maniac Cop 2, Sundown: The Vampire in Retreat, Mindwarp, Lunatics: A Love Story (also prod.), Waxwork II: Lost in Time, Army of Darkness (also co-prod.), The Hudsucker Proxy, Congo.
TELEVISION: Series: The Adventures of Brisco County Jr.

CAMPBELL, GLEN
Actor, Singer. b. Delight, AK, April 22, 1936. After forming local band became studio guitarist in Hollywood on records for such performers as Frank Sinatra and Elvis Presley. Won two Grammy awards for record By the Time I Get to Phoenix, 1967. Appeared frequently on Shindig on TV.
PICTURES: The Cool Ones, True Grit, Norwood, Any Which Way You Can, Rock a Doodle (voice).
TELEVISION: Series: The Smothers Brothers Comedy Hour, The Glen Campbell Goodtime Hour, The Glen Campbell Music Show; many specials. Movie: Strange Homecoming.

CAMPBELL, MICHAEL L.
Executive. b. Knoxville, TN, Jan. 22, 1954. Worked for White Stores, Inc. in a management position until 1982. Founded first theatre venture, Premiere Cinemas in 1982. Premiere grew to 150 screens and was sold to Cinemark in 1989. Founded Regal Cinemas in 1989. President and CEO Regal Cinmeas, Inc which has more than 1200 screens. Named Coopers & Lybrand regional entreprenuer of the year, 1993. Dir. NATO and serves on NATO executive committee.

CAMPBELL, WILLIAM
Actor. b. Newark, NJ, Oct. 30, 1926. e. Feagin Sch. of Drama. Appeared in summer stock; B'way before film debut.
PICTURES: The Breaking Point (debut, 1950), Breakthrough, Inside the Walls of Folsom Prison, Operation Pacific, The People Against O'Hara, Holiday for Sinners, Battle Circus, Small Town Girl, Code Two, The Big Leaguer, Escape from Fort Bravo, The High and the Mighty, The Fast and the Furious, Man Without a Star, Cell 2455— Death Row, Battle Cry, Running Wild, Man in the Vault, Backlash, Love Me Tender, Walk the Proud Land, Eighteen and Anxious, The Naked and the Dead, Money Women and Guns, The Sheriff of Fractured Jaw, Natchez Train, Night of Evil, The Young Racers, The Secret Invasion, Dementia 13, Hush Hush Sweet Charlotte, Blood Bath, Track of the Vampire, Pretty Maids All in a Row, Black Gunn, Dirty Mary Crazy Larry.
TELEVISION: Series: Cannonball, Dynasty, Crime Story. Pilot: The Heat: When You Lie Down With Dogs. Movie: Return of the Six Million Dollar Man and the Bionic Woman.

CAMPION, JANE
Director, Writer. b. Wellington, New Zealand, 1955. e. Victoria Univ. of Wellington (BA, anthropology, 1975), Sydney Coll. of Arts (BA, painting, 1979). Attendend Australian Sch. of Film & TV in early 1980's, where she debuted as dir. & writer with short film Peel (1982; Palme d'Or at Cannes Film Fest., 1986). Other short films: A Girl's Own Story, Passionless Moments, After Hours, Two Friends.
PICTURES: Director-Writer: Sweetie (feature debut, 1989; Australian Film Awards for Best Director & Film; LA Film Critics New Generation Award, American Indept. Spirit Award), An Angel at My Table (Venice Film Fest. Silver Lion Award, Indept. Spirit Award), The Piano (Academy Award, WGA, LA Film Critics, NY Film Critics, & Natl. Society of Film Critics Awards for best screenplay; LA Film Critics & NY Film Critics Awards for best director; Cannes Film Fest. Award for best film), The Portrait of a Lady.

CANBY, VINCENT
Journalist, Critic. b. Chicago, IL, July 27, 1924. e. Dartmouth Coll. Navy officer during WWII. Worked on newspapers in Paris and Chicago. Joined Quigley Publications in 1951 in editorial posts on Motion Picture Herald. Reporter for Weekly Variety 1959-1965. Joined New York Times film news staff, 1965; named film critic, 1969. Author: Living Quarters (1975); End of the War (play, 1978); Unnatural Scenery (1979); After All (play, 1981); The Old Flag (1984).

CANNELL, STEPHEN J.
Writer, Producer. b. Los Angeles, CA, Feb. 5, 1942. e. U. of Oregon, B.A., 1964. After coll. worked at father's decorating firm for 4 years while writing scripts in evening. Sold 1st script for Adam 12, 1966. Asked to serve as head writer at Universal Studios. Chief exec. officer, Stephen J. Cannell Prods. TV prod. co. he formed 1979. Also formed The Cannell Studios, parent co. 1986. Natl. chmn., Orton Dyslexia Society. Received Mystery Writers award 1975; 4 Writers Guild Awards. Acted in films: Identity Crisis, Posse.
TELEVISION: The Rockford Files (creator, writer, prod.; Emmy Award), The Jordan Chance, The Duke, Stone, 10 Speed and Brownshoe, Nightside, Midnight Offerings, The Greatest American Hero, The Quest, Them. Prod.: The A-Team, Hardcastle and McCormick, The Rousters, Riptide, Brothers-in-Law, Creator/Prod.: Baa Baa Black Sheep, Richie Brockelman, Hunter, Wise Guy, 21 Jump Street, J.J. Starbuck, Sonny Spoon, Sirens (co-exec. prod.), Unsub (exec. prod., writer, pilot), Booker (exec. prod.), Top of the Hill (exec. prod.), Scene of the Crime (exec.-prod., creator), The Commish (exec. prod.), Traps, Greyhounds (exec. prod., writer), Hawkeye, Marker (exec. prod., creator), Renegade (exec. prod., creator), U.S. Customs Classified (exec. prod., host).

CANNON, DYAN
Actress. r.n. Samille Diane Friesen. b. Tacoma, WA, Jan. 4, 1937. e. U. of Washington. Studied with Sanford Meisner. Modelled before becoming actress. Directed, produced and wrote short film Number One (Acad. Award nom.).
THEATER: B'way: The Fun Couple, Ninety-Day Mistress. Tour: How to Succeed in Business Without Really Trying.
PICTURES: The Rise and Fall of Legs Diamond (debut, 1960), This Rebel Breed, Bob & Carol & Ted & Alice (Acad. Award nom.), Doctors' Wives, The Anderson Tapes, The Love Machine, The Burglars, Such Good Friends, Shamus, The Last of Sheila, Child Under a Leaf, Heaven Can Wait (Acad. Award nom.), Revenge of the Pink Panther, Honeysuckle Rose, Coast To Coast, Deathtrap, Author Author, Caddyshack II, The End of Innocence (also dir., prod., s.p.), The Pickle.
TELEVISION: Mini-Series: Master of the Game. Movies: The Virginia Hill Story, Lady of the House, Having It All, Arthur the King, Jenny's War, Rock 'n' Roll Mom, Jailbirds, Christmas in Connecticut, Based on an Untrue Story, A Perry Mason Mystery: The Case of the Jealous Jokester. Guest: Playhouse 90.

CANNON, WILLIAM
Writer, Producer, Director. b. Toledo, OH, Feb. 11, 1937. e. Columbia Coll., B.A., 1959; M.B.A., 1962. Dir. Off-B'way, Death of a Salesman, Pirates of Penzance, 1960. Wrote, prod., dir., Square Root of Zero, Locarno and San Francisco Film Festivals, 1963-65; Distrib., Doran Enterprises, Ltd.; writer Knots Landing, Heaven on Earth, Author, Novel, The Veteran, 1974; Publisher, Highlife and Movie Digest, 1978; The Good Guys, 1987. Co-inventor: Cardz (TM), 1988.
PICTURES: Writer: Skidoo, Brewster McCloud, Hex.

CANOVA, DIANA
Actress. b. West Palm Beach, FL, June 1, 1952. Daughter of actress Judy Canova and musician Filberto Rivero. NY theater: They're Playing Our Song (1981). People's Choice award, favorite female performer, 1981.
THEATER: B'way revival of Company.
PICTURE: The First Nudie Musical.
TELEVISION: Series: Dinah and Her New Best Friends, Soap, I'm a Big Girl Now, Foot in the Door, Throb, Home Free. Guest: Ozzie's Girls (debut), Happy Days, Love Boat, Fantasy Island, Hotel, Chico and the Man, Barney Miller, Murder She Wrote. Movies: The Love Boat II, With This Ring, Death of Ocean View Park, Night Partners.

CANTON, ARTHUR H.
Motion Picture Producer. b. New York, NY. e. NYU, Columbia U. Capt. USAF. Pres., Canton-Weiner Films, indep. films importers, 1947; Van Gogh (Academy Award for best 2-reel short subject, 1949); MGM Pictures, eastern div. publicity mgr., executive liaison, advertising-publicity, Independent Productions; public relations executive, v.p.; pres., Blowitz, Thomas & Canton Inc., 1964; pres., Arthur H. Canton Co. Inc.; prod. exec., Warner Bros., 1968-70; advertising-publicity v.p., Columbia Pictures, 1971; exec. v.p. of advertising and publicity, Billy Jack Productions, 1974-76. Co-founder of Blowitz & Canton Co. Inc., 1976, chmn of bd. Now pres. of Arthur H. Canton Co. Member Academy of Motion Picture Arts and Sciences.

CANTON, MARK
Executive. b. New York, NY, June 19, 1949. e. UCLA, 1978. v.p., m.p. dev., MGM; 1979, exec. v.p., JP Organization; 1980, v.p. prod., Warner Bros.; named sr. v.p., 1983 and pres. worldwide theatrical prod. div., 1985; v.p. worldwide m.p. production, 1989; appointed chmn. of Columbia Pictures, 1991. Promoted to chmn. of Columbia TriStar Motion Pictures, 1994. Resigned, 1996.

CAPRA, FRANK, JR.
Executive. Son of famed director Frank Capra. Served in various creative capacities on TV series (Zane Grey Theatre, Gunsmoke, The Rifleman, etc.). Associate producer on theatrical films (Planet of the Apes, Play It Again Sam, Marooned, etc.). Joined Avco Embassy Pictures, 1981, as v.p., worldwide production. In July, 1981, became pres. of A-E. Resigned May, 1982 to become indep. producer. Now with Pinehurst Industry Studios, NC.
PICTURES: Producer: Born Again, The Black Marble, An Eye for an Eye, Vice Squad, Firestarter, Marie. Exec. prod.: Death Before Dishonor.

CAPSHAW, KATE
Actress. b. Ft. Worth, TX, 1953. r.n. Kathleen Sue Nail. e. U. of Missouri. m. director Steven Spielberg. Taught school before moving to New York to try acting.
PICTURES: A Little Sex (debut, 1982), Indiana Jones and the Temple of Doom, Best Defense, Dreamscape, Windy City, Power, SpaceCamp, Black Rain, Love at Large, My Heroes Have Always Been Cowboys, Love Affair, Just Cause, Duke of Groove (short), How to Make an American Quilt.
TELEVISION: Series: The Edge of Night, Black Tie Affair. Movies: Missing Children: A Mother's Story, The Quick and the Dead, Her Secret Life, Internal Affairs, Next Door.

CARA, IRENE
Singer, Actress. b. New York, NY, March 18, 1959. Off-B'way shows include The Me Nobody Knows, Lotta. On B'way in Maggie Flynn, Ain't Misbehavin', Via Galactica. Received Academy Award for co-writing theme song from Flashdance, 1983.
PICTURES: Aaron Loves Angela, Sparkle, Fame, D.C. Cab, City Heat, Certain Fury, Killing 'em Softly, Paradiso, Busted Up, Maximum Security, Happily Ever After (voice).
TELEVISION: Series: Love of Life, The Electric Company. Mini-Series: Roots—The Next Generation. Movies: Guyana Tragedy, Sister Sister, For Us the Living. Special: Tribute to Martin Luther King, Jr.

CARDIFF, JACK
Cinematographer, Director. b. Yarmouth, Eng., Sept. 18, 1914. Early career as child actor, before becoming cinematographer, then dir. in 1958.

PICTURES: *Cinematographer:* A Matter of Life and Death (Stairway to Heaven), Black Narcissus (Academy Award, 1947), The Red Shoes, Scott of the Antarctic, Black Rose, Under Capricorn, Pandora and the Flying Dutchman, The African Queen, The Magic Box, The Master of Ballantrae, The Barefoot Contessa, The Brave One, War and Peace, Legend of the Lost, The Prince and the Showgirl, The Vikings, The Journey, Fanny, Scalawag, Crossed Swords (The Prince and the Pauper), Death on the Nile, Avalanche Express, The Fifth Musketeer, A Man a Woman and a Bank, The Awakening, The Dogs of War, Ghost Story, The Wicked Lady, Scandalous, Conan the Destroyer, Cat's Eye, Rambo: First Blood II, Blue Velvet, Tai-Pan, Million Dollar Mystery. Director: Intent to Kill (debut, 1958), Beyond This Place, Scent of Mystery, Sons and Lovers, My Geisha, The Lion, The Long Ships, Young Cassidy (co-dir.), The Liquidator, Dark of the Sun, Girl on a Motorcycle, Penny Gold, The Mutations, Ride a Wild Pony.
TELEVISION: *As cinematographer:* The Far Pavillions, The Last Days of Pompeii.

CARDINALE, CLAUDIA
Actress. b. Tunis, No. Africa, April 15, 1939. Raised in Italy. Studied acting at Centro Sperimentale film school in Rome. Debuted 1956 in short French film Anneaux d'Or.
PICTURES: Goha (feature debut, 1957), Big Deal on Madonna Street, The Facts of Murder, Upstairs and Downstairs, The Battle of Austerlitz, Il Bell' Antonio, Rocco and His Brothers, Senilita, Girl With a Suitcase, The Love Makers, Cartouche, The Leopard, 8 1/2, Bebo's Girl, The Pink Panther, Circus World, Time of Indifference, The Magnificent Cuckold, Sandra, Blindfold, Lost Command, The Professionals, Don't Make Waves, Mafia, The Queens, Day of the Owl, The Hell With Heroes, Once Upon a Time in the West, A Fine Pair, The Butterfly Affair, The Red Tent, The Legend of Frenchy King, Conversation Piece, Escape to Athena, The Salamander, Careless, Immortal Bachelor, History, The French Revolution, Hiver '54, L'abbe Pierre, Mother, 588 Rue Paradis, Women Only Have One Thing on Their Minds...
TELEVISION: Princess Daisy, Jesus of Nazareth.

CAREY, HARRY JR.
Actor. b. Saugus, CA, May 16, 1921. e. Newhall, CA, public school, Black Fox Military Acad., Hollywood. m. Marilyn Fix. Appeared in Railroads on Parade at 1939-40 NY World's Fair. Summer stock, Skowhegan, ME., with father; page boy, NBC, New York; U.S. Navy 1941-46.
PICTURES: Rolling Home (debut, 1946), Pursued, Red River, Three Godfathers, She Wore a Yellow Ribbon, Wagonmaster, Rio Grande, Copper Canyon, Warpath, Wild Blue Yonder, Monkey Business, San Antone, Island in the Sky, Gentlemen Prefer Blondes, Beneath the 12-Mile Reef, Silver Lode, The Outcast, Long Gray Line, Mister Roberts, House of Bamboo, The Great Locomotive Chase, The Searchers, The River's Edge, Rio Bravo, The Great Imposter, Two Rode Together, Alvarez Kelly, Bandolero, The Undefeated, Dirty Dingus Magee, Big Jake, Something Big, One More Train To Rob, Cahill: U.S. Marshal, Take a Hard Ride, Nickelodeon, The Long Riders, Endangered Species, Mask, Crossroads, The Whales of August, Cherry 2000, Illegally Yours, Breaking In, Bad Jim, Back to the Future Part III, The Exorcist III, Tombstone.
TELEVISION: Movies: Black Beauty, The Shadow Riders, Wild Times, Once Upon a Texas Train. Guest: Gunsmoke, Rifleman, Laramie, Wagon Train, Have Gun Will Travel, John Ford's America, Legends of the American West. Disney Series: Spin & Marty. Special: Wyatt Earp: Return to Tombstone.

CARIOU, LEN
Actor. b. St. Boniface, Manitoba, Canada, Sept. 30, 1939. e. St. Paul's Col.
THEATER: NY stage: House of Atreus, Henry V, Applause (Theatre World Award), Night Watch, A Sorrow Beyond Dreams, Up from Paradise, A Little Night Music, Cold Storage, Sweeney Todd—The Demon Barber of Fleet Street (Tony Award), Master Class, Dance a Little Closer, Teddy & Alice, Measure for Measure, Mountain, The Speed of Darkness, Papa.
PICTURES: A Little Night Music, One Man, The Four Seasons, There Were Times Dear, Lady in White, Never Talk to Strangers.
TELEVISION: Movies: Who'll Save Our Children?, Madame X, Surviving, Miracle on Interstate 880, Class of '61, The Sea Wolf, Witness to the Execution, Love on the Run, The Man in the Attic. Specials: The Master Builder, Juno and the Paycock, Kurt Vonnegut's Monkey House (All the King's Men).

CARLIN, GEORGE
Actor, Comedian. b. New York, NY, May 12, 1937. Stand-up comedian and recording artist; received 1972 Grammy Award for Best Comedy Album: FM & AM. Has released 15 comedy albums between 1960-90. Has guested on many TV shows including Talent Scouts, On B'way Tonight, Merv Griffin Show, Saturday Night Live. Author: Sometimes a Little Brain Damage Can Help (1984).
PICTURES: With Six You Get Eggroll, Car Wash, Americathon (narrator), Outrageous Fortune, Bill & Ted's Excellent Adventure, Bill and Ted's Bogus Journey, The Prince of Tides.

TELEVISION: Series: Kraft Summer Music Hall, That Girl, Away We Go, Tony Orlando and Dawn, Shining Time Station, The George Carlin Show. Movies: Justin Case, Working Trash. Appeared in 8 HBO comedy specials.

CARLINO, LEWIS JOHN
Writer, Director. b. New York, NY, Jan. 1, 1932. e. U. of Southern California. Early interest in theatre, specializing in writing 1-act plays. Winner of Obie award (off-B'way play). Won Rockefeller Grant for Theatre, the Int'l. Playwriting Competition from British Drama League, Huntington Hartford Fellowship.
THEATER: Cages, Telemachus Clay, The Exercise, Double Talk, Objective Case, Used Car for Sale, Junk Yard.
PICTURES: Writer: Seconds, The Brotherhood, The Fox (co-s.p.), A Reflection of Fear, The Mechanic (also prod.), Crazy Joe, The Sailor Who Fell From Grace With the Sea (also dir.), I Never Promised You a Rose Garden (co-s.p.), The Great Santini (also dir.), Resurrection, Class (dir. only), Haunted Summer.
TELEVISION: Honor Thy Father, In Search of America, Where Have All the People Gone?

CARLTON, RICHARD
Executive. b. New York, NY, Feb. 9, 1919. e. Columbia U., Pace Inst. Columbia Pictures 1935-41; U.S. Army 1941-45; National Screen Serv. 1945-51; Sterling Television 1951-54; U.M. & M. TV Corp. 1955; v.p. in charge of sales, Trans-Lux Television Corp. 1956; exec. v.p., Television Affiliates Corp., 1961; exec. v.p. Trans-Lux Television Corp.; v.p. Entertainment Div. Trans-Lux Corp., 1966. Pres., Schnur Appel, TV, Inc. 1970; Deputy Director, American Film Institute, 1973. Pres., Carlton Communications Corporation, 1982; exec. dir., International Council, National Academy of Television Arts and Sciences, 1983-93. Became writer/consultant, 1994.

CARMEN, JULIE
Actress. b. New York, NY, Apr. 4, 1954. Studied acting at Neighborhood Playhouse. On NY stage in The Creation of the Universe, Cold Storage, Zoot Suit. Also acted with INTAR and the New Conservatory Theater. Recipient of 1992 National Council of La Raza Pioneer Award.
PICTURES: Night of the Juggler, Gloria, Man on the Wall, Comeback, Blue City, The Penitent, The Milagro Beanfield War, Fright Night 2, Kiss Me a Killer, Paint It Black, Cold Heaven, In the Mouth of Madness.
TELEVISION: Series: Condo, Falcon Crest. Movies: Can You Hear the Laughter?: The Story of Freddie Prinze, Three Hundred Miles for Stephanie, She's in the Army Now, Fire on the Mountain, Neon Empire, Manhunt: Search for the Night Stalker, Billy the Kid, Drug Wars: The Cocaine Cartel, Finding the Way Home, Curacao.

CARMICHAEL, IAN
Actor. b. Hull, England, June 18, 1920. e. Scarborough Coll., Bromsgrove Sch. Stage debut: R.U.R. 1939. B'way debut: Boeing-Boeing (1965). One of the top ten British money making stars Motion Picture Herald Fame Poll 1957, 1958.
PICTURES: Bond Street (debut, 1948), Trottie True (Gay Lady), Mr. Prohack, Time Gentlemen Please, Ghost Ship!, Miss Robin Hood, Meet Mr. Lucifer, Betrayed, The Colditz Story, Storm Over the Nile, Simon and Laura, Private's Progress, The Big Money, Brothers in Law, Lucky Jim, Happy Is the Bride, Left Right and Center, I'm All Right Jack, School for Scoundrels, Light Up the Sky, Double Bunk, The Amorous Prawn, Hide and Seek, Heavens Above, The Case of the 44's, Smashing Time, The Magnificent Seven Deadly Sins, From Beyond the Grave, The Lady Vanishes, Dark Obsession (Diamond Skulls).
TELEVISION: New Faces, Twice Upon a Time, Passing Show, Tell Her The Truth, Lady Luck, Give My Regards to Leicester Square, Jill Darling, Don't Look Now, Regency Room, Globe Revue, Off the Record, Here and Now, The Girl at the Next Table, Gilt and Gingerbread, The Importance of Being Earnest, Simon and Laura, 90 Years On, The World of Wooster (series), The Last of the Big Spenders, The Coward Revue, Odd Man In, Bachelor Father (series), Lord Peter Wimsey (series), Alma Mater, Comedy Tonight, Song by Song, Country Calendar, Down at the Hydro, Obituaries, Strathblair, The Great Kandinsky. Guest: Under The Hammer, Bramwell.

CARNEY, ART
Actor. b. Mt. Vernon, NY, Nov. 4, 1918. Started as band singer with the Horace Heidt Orchestra. On many radio shows before and after war. Served in U.S. Army, 1944-45. Regular on Morey Amsterdam's radio show which eventually moved to television.
THEATER: The Rope Dancers. B'way: Take Her She's Mine, The Odd Couple, Lovers, The Prisoner of Second Avenue.
PICTURES: Pot o' Gold (debut, 1941), The Yellow Rolls Royce, A Guide for the Married Man, Harry and Tonto (Academy Award for Best Actor, 1974), W. W. and the Dixie Dancekings, Won Ton Ton the Dog Who Saved Hollywood, The Late Show, Scott Joplin, House Calls, Movie Movie, Ravagers, Sunburn, Going in Style, Defiance, Roadie, Steel, St. Helens, Take This Job and Shove It, Better Late Than Never, Firestarter, The Naked Face, The Muppets Take Manhattan, Night Friend, Last Action Hero.

TELEVISION: *Series*: The Morey Amsterdam Show, Cavalcade of Stars, Henry Morgan's Great Talent Hunt, The Jackie Gleason Show (1951-55; 2 Emmy Awards: 1953, 1954), The Honeymooners (Emmy Award, 1955), The Jackie Gleason Show (1956-57), The Jackie Gleason Show (1966-70; 2 Emmy Awards: 1967, 1968), Lanigan's Rabbi. *Guest*: Studio One, Kraft Theatre, Playhouse 90, Alfred Hitchcock Presents (Safety for the Witness), Sid Caesar Show, Twilight Zone (Night of the Meek), Bob Hope Chrysler Theater (Timothy Heist), Danny Kaye Show, Men From Shiloh, Batman, Carol Burnett Show, Jonathan, Winters Show, Faerie Tale Theatre (The Emperor's New Clothes). *Specials*: Peter and the Wolf, Harvey, Our Town, Charley's Aunt, Art Carney Meets the Sorcerer's Apprentice, Very Important People, Jane Powell Special: Young at Heart, Man in the Dog Suit, The Great Santa Claus Switch. Movies: The Snoop Sisters, Death Scream, Katherine, Letters From Frank, Terrible Joe Moran (Emmy Award, 1984), The Night They Saved Christmas, A Doctor's Story, Izzy and Moe, Blue Yonder, Where Pigeons Go to Die.

CARNEY, FRED
Producer, Director. b. Brooklyn, NY, June 10, 1914. e. Mt. Vernon H.S., 1932. Actor on B'way & summer stock; prod. mgr. for radio show, Truth or Consequences; asst. to prod.-dir of Kraft TV Theatre, 3 yrs.; dir., Kraft, Pond's Show; creator-prod., Medical Horizons; dir., Lux Video Theatre; prod. commercials at Cunningham & Walsh. Assoc. Prod. Everybody's Talking for ABC-TV. Ass't. exec. dir., Hollywood Chpt., Nat'l Acad. TV; Assoc. prod. 40th Acad. Award show, ABC-TV Arts & Sciences.

CARON, GLENN GORDON
Writer, Director, Producer. Started as tv writer for James L. Brooks, Steve Gordon. Prod. of tv series Breaking Away. Formed prod. co., Picturemaker Productions, 1985.
PICTURES: *Director*: Clean and Sober (debut, 1988), Wilder Napalm, Love Affair.
TELEVISION: *Series*: Moonlighting (creator, prod., writer).

CARON, LESLIE
Actress, Dancer. b. Paris, France, July 1, 1931. e. Convent of Assumption, Paris; Nat'l Conservatory of Dance, Paris 1947-50; joined Roland Petit's Ballet des Champs Elysees where she was spotted by Gene Kelly who chose her as his co-star in An American in Paris. Also with Ballet de Paris.
THEATER: Orvet, Ondine, Gigi (London), 13 Rue de l'Amour, The Rehearsal, Women's Games, On Your Toes, One For the Tango.
PICTURES: An American in Paris (debut, 1951), The Man With a Cloak, Glory Alley, The Story of Three Loves, Lili (Acad. Award nom.; BFA Award), The Glass Slipper, Daddy Long Legs, Gaby, Gigi, The Doctor's Dilemma, The Man Who Understood Women, The Subterraneans, Austerlitz, Fanny, Guns of Darkness, Three Fables of Love, The L-Shaped Room (Acad. Award nom.; BFA Award), Father Goose, A Very Special Favor, Promise Her Anything, Is Paris Burning?, Head of the Family, The Beginners, Madron, Chandler, Purple Night, Valentino, The Man Who Loved Women, Golden Girl, Contract, Imperative, The Unapproachable, Dangerous Moves, Warriors and Prisoners, Courage Mountain, Damage, Funny Bones, Let It Be Me.
TELEVISION: *Mini-Series*: QB VIII, Master of the Game. *Guest*: Love Boat, Tales of the Unexpected, Carola, Falcon Crest. *Movie*: The Man Who Lived at the Ritz. *Special*: The Sealed Train.

CARPENTER, CARLETON
Actor. b. Bennington, VT, July 10, 1926 e. Bennington H.S., Northwestern U. (summer scholarship). Began career with magic act, clubs, camps, hospitals in New Eng.; then toured with carnival; first N.Y. stage appearance in Bright Boy. Appeared in nightclubs, nightclubs; as magazine model. TV debut, Campus Hoopla show. Screen debut Lost Boundaries (also wrote song for film, I Wouldn't Mind). Member: SAG, AFTRA, AEA, ASCAP, Dramatists Guild, Mystery Writers of Amer. (ex.-treas., bd. mem.).
THEATER: *NY*: Career Angel, Three To Make Ready, The Magic Touch, The Big People, Out of Dust, John Murray Anderson's Almanac, Hotel Paradiso, Box of Watercolors, A Stage Affair, Greatest Fairy Story Ever Told, Something for the Boys, Boys in the Band, Dylan, Hello Dolly!, Light Up the Sky, Murder at Rutherford House, Rocky Road, Apollo of Bellac, Sweet Adaline, Geo. White's Scandals, Life on the L.I.E. Miss Stanwyck is Still in Hiding, Good Ole Fashioned Revue, What is Turning Gilda So Grey?, Crazy for You, Many Thousands Gone.
PICTURES: Lost Boundaries (debut, 1949), Summer Stock, Father of the Bride, Three Little Words, Two Weeks With Love, The Whistle at Eaton Falls, Fearless Fagan, Sky Full of Moon, Vengeance Valley, Up Periscope, Take the High Ground, Some of My Best Friends Are..., The Prowler, Simon, Byline, Cauliflower Cupids, The Bar, Carnegie Hall.
TELEVISION: Over 6,000 shows (live & filmed) since 1945.

CARPENTER, JOHN
Director, Writer, Composer. b. Carthage, NY, Jan. 16, 1948. e. U. of Southern California. At U.S.C. became involved in film

short, Resurrection of Bronco Billy, which won Oscar as best live-action short of 1970. Also at U.S.C. began directing what ultimately became Dark Star, science fiction film that launched his career.
PICTURES: *Director*: Dark Star (also co-s.p., music), Assault on Precinct 13 (also s.p., music), Halloween (also s.p., music), The Fog (also co-s.p., music), Escape from New York (also co-s.p., music), The Thing, Christine (also music), Starman, Big Trouble in Little China (also music), Prince of Darkness (also music, and s.p. as Martin Quatermass), They Live (also music, and s.p. as Frank Armitage), Memoirs of an Invisible Man, In the Mouth of Madness (also co-music), Village of the Damned (also s.p., co-music). Other: Eyes of Laura Mars (co-sp., co-story), Halloween II (co- s.p., co-prod., co-music), Halloween III: Season of the Witch (co-prod., co-music), The Philadelphia Experiment (co-exec. prod.), Black Moon Rising (co-s.p., story), The Silence of the Hams (actor).
TELEVISION: *Movies* (director): Elvis, Someone Is Watching Me (also writer), John Carpenter Presents Body Bags (also co-exec. prod., actor). Movies (writer): Zuma Beach, El Diablo, Blood River.

CARPENTER, ROBERT L.
Executive. b. Memphis, TN, March 20, 1927. Joined Universal Pictures in 1949 as booker in Memphis exchange; promoted to salesman, 1952, then branch mgr., 1958; 1963 named Los Angeles branch mgr. 1971, moved to New York to become asst. to gen. sales mgr. Named gen. sls. mgr. 1972, replacing Henry H. Martin when latter became pres. of Universal. Left in 1982 to become consultant and producer's rep. 1984, joined Cannon Releasing Corp. as east. div. mgr. Left in 1989 to become consultant and producers rep.

CARR, MARTIN
Producer, Director, Writer. b. New York, NY, Jan. 20, 1932. e. Williams Coll.
AWARDS: Winner of 5 Emmys; 3 Peabody awards; 2 Du-Pont Col. Journalism awards; Robert F. Kennedy award; Sidney Hillman award; Writers Guild Award.
TELEVISION: PBS Smithsonian World (exec. prod.). For CBS prod., wrote and dir. CBS Reports: Hunger in America, The Search for Ulysses, Gauguin in Tahiti, Five Faces of Tokyo, Dublin Through Different Eyes. For NBC prod., wrote and dir. NBC White Paper: Migrant, NBC White Paper: This Child Is Rated X. Also directed drama, dance, music, opera specials and daytime serial for CBS-TV. ABC Close-Up. The Culture Thieves. PRS Global Paper: Waging Peace, ABC News 20/20; NBC, The Human Animal.

CARRADINE, DAVID
Actor. b. Hollywood, CA, Dec. 8, 1936. e. San Francisco State U. Son of late actor John Carradine. Brother of actors Keith and Robert Carradine. Began career in local repertory; first TV on Armstrong Circle Theatre and East Side, West Side; later TV includes Shane series and Kung Fu; N.Y. stage in The Deputy, Royal Hunt of the Sun (Theatre World Award).
PICTURES: Taggart, Bus Riley's Back in Town, Too Many Thieves, The Violent Ones, Heaven With a Gun, Young Billy Young, The Good Guys and the Bad Guys, The McMasters, Macho Callahan, Boxcar Bertha, Two Gypsies, You and Me (also dir.), A Country Mile (also prod.), Mean Streets, The Long Goodbye, Death Race 2000, Cannonball, Bound for Glory, Thunder and Lightning, The Serpent's Egg, Gray Lady Down, Deathsport, Circle of Iron, Fast Charlie: The Moonbeam Rider, The Long Riders, Cloud Dancer, Americana (also dir., prod.), Q, Trick or Treats, Safari 3000, Lone Wolf McQuade, Warrior and the Sorceress, On the Line, P.O.W. The Escape, Armed Response, The Misfit Brigade, Open Fire, Animal Protector, Warlords, Crime Zone, Night Children, Wizards of the Lost Kingdom 2, Sundown: The Vampire in Retreat, Crime of Crimes, Nowhere to Run, Tropical Snow, Future Force, Think Big, Bird on a Wire, Sonny Boy, Project Eliminator, Evil Toons, Dune Warriors, Kill Zone, Try This One on For Size, Animal Instincts, Capital Punishment, First Force, Roadside Prophets, Double Trouble, Distant Justice, Waxworks II, Midnight Fear, Night Rhythms, Southern Frontier, Crazy Joe, Hollywood Dream.
TELEVISION: *Movies*: Maybe I'll Come Home in the Spring, Kung Fu (1972 pilot), Mr. Horn, Johnny Belinda, Gaugin the Savage, High Noon Part II, Jealousy, The Bad Seed, Kung Fu: The Movie, Oceans of Fire, Six Against the Rock, The Cover Girl & the Cop, I Saw What You Did, Brotherhood of the Gun, The Gambler Returns: Luck of the Draw, The Eagel and the Horse. *Mini-series*: North & South Books I & II. Series: Shane, Kung Fu, Kung Fu: The Legend Continues. *Guest*: Darkroom, Amazing Stories.

CARRADINE, KEITH
Actor. b. San Mateo, CA, Aug. 8, 1949. e. Colorado State U. Daughter is actress Martha Plimpton. Son of late actor John Carradine, brother of David and Robert Carradine. First break in rock opera Hair. Theater: Wake Up It's Time to Go to Bed, Foxfire, The Will Rogers Follies.

PICTURES: A Gunfight (debut, 1971), McCabe and Mrs. Miller, Hex, Emperor of the North Pole, Thieves Like Us, Antoine et Sebastien, Run Joe Run, Idaho Transfer, Nashville (also composed songs; Academy Award for best song: I'm Easy, 1975), You and Me, Lumiere, Welcome to L.A. (also composed songs), The Duellists, Pretty Baby, Sgt. Pepper's Lonely Heart Club Band (cameo), Old Boyfriends, An Almost Perfect Affair, The Long Riders, Southern Comfort, Choose Me, Maria's Lovers (also composed song), Trouble in Mind, The Inquiry (The Investigation), Backfire, The Moderns, Street of No Return, Cold Feet, Daddy's Dyin'...Who's Got the Will?, The Ballad of the Sad Cafe, Crisscross, The Bachelor, Andre, Mrs. Parker and the Vicious Circle, The Tie That Binds, Wild Bill.
TELEVISION: Movies: Man on a String, Kung Fu, The Godchild, A Rumor of War, Scorned and Swindled, A Winner Never Quits, Murder Ordained, Eye on the Sparrow, Blackout, Stones for Ibarra, My Father My Son, The Revenge of Al Capone, Judgment, Payoff, In the Best of Families: Marriage Pride & Madness, Is There Life Out There?, Trial by Fire Mini-Series: Chiefs. Guest: Bonanza, Love American Style.

CARRADINE, ROBERT
Actor. b. Hollywood, CA, March 24, 1954. Son of late actor John Carradine; brother of Keith and David Carradine.
PICTURES: The Cowboys (debut, 1972), Mean Streets, Aloha Bobby and Rose, Jackson County Jail, The Pom Pom Girls, Cannonball, Massacre at Central High, Joyride, Orca, Blackout, Coming Home, The Long Riders, The Big Red One, Heartaches, Tag: The Assassination Game, Wavelength, Revenge of the Nerds, Just the Way You Are, Number One With a Bullet, Revenge of the Nerds II: Nerds in Paradise, Buy and Cell, All's Fair, Rude Awakening, The Player, Bird of Prey, Escape From L.A.
TELEVISION: Series: The Cowboys. Movies: Footsteps, Rolling Man, Go Ask Alice, The Hatfields and the McCoys, The Survival of Dana, The Sun Also Rises, Monte Carlo, The Liberators, I Saw What You Did, The Incident, Clarence, Doublecrossed, Revenge of the Nerds III: The Next Generation, Body Bags, The Disappearance of Christina, Revenge of the Nerds IV: Nerds in Love (also co-prod.), A Part of the Family. Guest: Alfred Hitchcock Presents (1985), The Hitchhiker, Twilight Zone (1986). Specials: Disney's Totally Minnie, As Is.

CARRERA, BARBARA
Actress. b. Nicaragua, Dec. 31, 1951. Fashion model before film career; had bit in film Puzzle of a Downfall Child.
PICTURES: The Master Gunfighter, Embryo, The Island of Dr. Moreau, When Time Ran Out, Condorman, I the Jury, Lone Wolf McQuade, Never Say Never Again, Wild Geese II, The Underachievers, Love at Stake, Wicked Stepmother, Loverboy, Spanish Rose, Night of the Archer, Tryst, Oh No Not Her (Love Is All There Is), Moscow Connection, Ghost Ships of the Kalahari, Love Is All There Is.
TELEVISION: Mini-Series: Centennial, Masada, Emma: Queen of the South Seas. Series: Dallas. Movies: Sins of the Past, Murder in Paradise, Lakota Moon, The Rockford Files.

CARRERE, TIA
Actress. r.n. Althea Janairo. b. Honolulu, HI, 1967. Was prof. model before turning to acting. Received NATO/ShoWest award for Female Star of 1994.
PICTURES: Zombie Nightmare (debut, 1987), Aloha Summer, Fatal Mission, Instant Karma, Showdown in Little Tokyo, Harley Davidson and the Marlboro Man, Wayne's World, Rising Sun, Wayne's World 2, True Lies, Jury Duty, My Generation, The Immortals.
TELEVISION: Series: General Hospital. Mini-Series: James Clavell's Noble House. Movies: The Road Raiders, Fine Gold. Guest: The A-Team, MacGyver, Tales From the Crypt.

CARREY, JIM
Actor. b. Newmarket, Ontario, Canada, Jan. 17, 1962. Began performing act at Toronto comedy clubs while teenager. Moved to LA at 19, performing at the Comedy Store.
PICTURES: Finders Keepers (debut, 1984), Once Bitten, Peggy Sue Got Married, The Dead Pool, Earth Girls Are Easy, Pink Cadillac, High Strung, Ace Ventura: Pet Detective (also co-s.p.), The Mask, Dumb and Dumber, Batman Forever, Ace Ventura: When Nature Calls, The Cable Guy.
TELEVISION: Series: The Duck Factory, In Living Color. Movies: Mickey Spillane's Mike Hammer—Murder Takes All, Doin' Time on Maple Drive. Special: Jim Carrey's Unnatural Act. Canadian TV: Introducing Janet, Copper Mountain: A Club Med Experience.

CARROLL, DIAHANN
Actress, Singer. b. New York, NY, July 17, 1935. r.n. Carol Diahann Johnson. m. singer Vic Damone. Started singing as teen, winning 1st place on tv's Chance of a Lifetime talent show resulting in engagement at Latin Quarter nightclub in New York. Autobiography: Diahann! (1986).
THEATER: B'way: House of Flowers, No Strings (Tony Award, 1962), Agnes of God.

PICTURES: Carmen Jones (debut, 1954), Porgy and Bess, Goodbye Again, Paris Blues, Hurry Sundown, The Split, Claudine (Acad. Award nom.), The Five Heartbeats.
TELEVISION: Series: Julia, The Diahann Carroll Show, Dynasty. Movies: Death Scream, I Know Why the Caged Bird Sings, Sister Sister, From the Dead of Night, Murder in Black and White, A Perry Mason Mystery: The Case of the Lethal Lifestyle. Mini-Series: Roots: The Next Generations; many specials; guest appearances incl. The Naked City, Andy Williams, Judy Garland, Dean Martin Shows.

CARROLL, GORDON
Producer. b. Baltimore, MD, Feb. 2, 1928. e. Princeton U. Advtg. exec., Foote, Cone & Belding, 1954-58; Ent. industry, Seven Arts Prods., 1958-61; v.p., prod., Jalem Prods., 1966-1969; independent producer to present.
PICTURES: How to Murder Your Wife, Luv, Cool Hand Luke, The April Fools, Pat Garrett and Billy the Kid, Alien, Blue Thunder, The Best of Times, Aliens, Red Heat, Alien 3.

CARROLL, PAT
Actress. b. Shreveport, LA, May 5, 1927. e. Immaculate Heart Coll., L.A, Catholic U., Washington, DC. Joined U.S. Army in capacity of Civilian Actress Technician. Night club entertainer in N.Y., 1950.
THEATER: Catch a Star (debut, 1955), Gertrude Stein Gertrude Stein (Drama Desk, Outer Critics Circle, Grammy Awards), Dancing in the End Zone, The Show Off. Shakespeare Theatre at the Folger: Romeo and Juliet (Helen Hayes Award), The Merry Wives of Windsors (as Falstaff; Helen Hayes Award), Mother Courage (Helen Hayes Award), H.M.S. Pinafore, Volpone.
PICTURES: With Six You Get Eggroll, The Brothers O'Toole, The Last Resort, The Little Mermaid (voice).
TELEVISION: Series: Red Buttons Show, Saturday Night Revue, Caesar's Hour (Emmy Award, 1957), Masquerade Party (panelist), Keep Talking, You're in the Picture (panelist), Danny Thomas Show, Getting Together, Busting Loose, The Ted Knight Show, She's the Sheriff. Specials: Cinderella, Gertrude Stein. Guest: Carol Burnett, Danny Kaye, Red Skelton, many others. Movie: Second Chance.

CARSEY, MARCY
Producer. b. Weymouth, MA, Nov. 21, 1944. e. Univ. NH. Was actress in tv commercials, tour guide at Rockefeller Center. Served as exec. story editor, Tomorrow Ent., 1971-74; sr. v.p. for prime time series, ABC-TV, 1978-71; founded Carsey Prods., 1981; owner, Carsey-Werner Co., 1982-.
TELEVISION: Series (exec. prod.): Oh Madeline, The Cosby Show, A Different World, Roseanne, Chicken Soup, Grand, Davis Rules, Frannie's Turn, You Bet Your Life (synd.), Grace Under Fire, Cybill, Cosby (1996-), Men Behaving Badly, Townies. Pilots: Callahan, I Do I Don't. Special: Carol Carl Whoopi and Robin. Movie: Single Bars Single Women.

CARSON, JEANNIE
Actress. b. Yorkshire, England, 1928. Became Amer. Citizen, 1966. Founded Hyde Park Festival Theatre with husband William "Biff" McGuire, 1979. Has taught a musical drama class at U. of WA. Awards: TV Radio Mirror, 1st Recipient of the Variety Club Theatre Award in England.
THEATER: U.K.: Ace of Clubs, Love From Judy, Starlight Roof, Casino Reviews, Aladdin. U.S.: The Sound of Music, Blood Red Roses, Finian's Rainbow (revival). Tours: Camelot, 110 in the Shade, Cactus Flower. Also extensive work with the Seattle Repertory Theatre as actress, and dir. with Seattle Bathhouse Theatre.
PICTURES: A Date with a Dream (debut, 1948), Love in Pawn, As Long as They're Happy, An Alligator Named Daisy, Mad Little Island (Rockets Galore), Seven Keys.
TELEVISION: Best Foot Forward, Little Women, Berkeley Square, The Rivals, Frank Sinatra Show, Heidi, What Every Woman Knows, Jimmy Durante Show, Pat Boone Show, A Kiss for Cinderella. Series: Hey Jeannie, Jeannie Carson Show.

CARSON, JOHNNY
Host, Comedian. b. Corning, IA, Oct. 23, 1925. e. U. of Nebraska, B.A. 1949. U.S. Navy service during WWII; announcer with station KFAB, Lincoln, Neb.; WOW radio-TV, Omaha, 1948; announcer, KNXT-TV, Los Angeles, 1950; then hosted own program, Carson's Cellar (1951-53); latter resulted in job as writer for Red Skelton Show. 1958 guest hosting for Jack Paar on The Tonight Show led to his becoming regular host 4 years later. President, Carson Productions. Recipient: ATAS Governor's Award, 1980. Author: Happiness Is a Dry Martini (1965).
PICTURES: Movies: Looking for Love, Cancel My Reservation.
TELEVISION: Series: Earn Your Vacation (emcee; 1954), The Johnny Carson Show (daytime, 1955; later moved to nighttime, 1955-56), Who Do You Trust? (1957-62), The Tonight Show Starring Johnny Carson (1962-92). Guest: Playhouse 90, U.S. Steel Hour, Get Smart, Here's Lucy, etc. Pilot: Johnny Come Lately.

CARTER, DIXIE
Actress. b. McLemoresville, TN, May 25, 1939. m. actor Hal Holbrook. e. U. of Tennessee, Knoxville, Rhodes Coll.; Memphis, Memphis State U. Off-B'way debut, A Winter's Tale with NY Shakespeare Fest (1963). London debut, Buried Inside Extra (1983). Lincoln Center musicals: The King & I, Carousel, The Merry Widow. Video: Dixie Carter's Unworkout.
THEATER: Pal Joey (1976 revival), Jesse and the Bandit Queen (Theatre World Award), Fathers and Sons, Taken in Marriage, A Coupla White Chicks Sitting Around Talking, Buried Inside Extra, Sextet, Pal Joey.
PICTURE: Going Berserk.
TELEVISION: Series: The Edge of Night, On Our Own, Out of the Blue, Filthy Rich, Diff'rent Strokes, Designing Women. Movies: OHMS, The Killing of Randy Webster, Dazzle, Gambler V: Playing for Keeps, A Perry Mason Mystery: The Case of the Lethal Lifestyle.

CARTER, JACK
Actor, r.n. Jack Chakrin. b. New York, NY, June 24, 1923. e. New Utrecht H.S., Brooklyn Coll., Feagin Sch. of Dramatic Arts. Worked as comm. artist for adv. agencies. Debut B'way in Call Me Mister, 1947; starred in TV Jack Carter Show, NBC Sat. Nite Revue. Hosted first televised Tony Awards. Seen on most major variety, dram. programs, incl. Ed Sullivan Show. Emmy nom. 1962 for Dr. Kildare seg. Played most major nightclubs. On B'way in Top Banana, Mr. Wonderful, Dir. several Lucy Shows. TV incl. specials, HA Comedy Special, Top Banana, Girl Who Couldn't Lose.
PICTURES: The Horizontal Lieutenant, Viva Las Vegas, The Extraordinary Seaman, The Resurrection of Zachary Wheeler, Red Nights, Hustle, The Amazing Dobermans, Alligator, The Octagon, History of the World Part 1, Heartbeeps (voice), The Arena, Deadly Embrace, In the Heat of Passion, Social Suicide, The Opposite Sex, W.A.R., Natl. Lampoon's Last Resort.
TELEVISION: Series: American Minstrels of 1949, Cavalcade of Stars, The Jack Carter Show. Movies: The Lonely Profession, The Family Rico, The Sex Symbol, The Great Houdinis, The Last Hurrah, Human Feelings, Rainbow, The Gossip Columnist, The Hustler of Muscle Beach, For the Love of It. Guest: Blossom, Empty Nest, Nurses, Murder She Wrote, Time Trax, Burke's Law, New Adventures of Superman.

CARTER, LYNDA
Actress. b. Phoenix, AZ, July 24. r.n. Lynda Jean Cordoba. e. Arcadia H.S. Wrote songs and sang professionally in Ariz. from age of 15; later toured 4 yrs. with rock 'n roll band. Won beauty contests in Ariz. and became Miss World-USA 1973. Dramatic training with Milton Katselas, Greta Seacat, and Sandra Seacat.
PICTURE: Lightning in a Bottle.
TELEVISION: Series: Wonder Woman, Hawkeye. Specials: The New Original Wonder Woman Specials; 5 variety specials, Hawkeye. Movies: The New Original Wonder Woman, A Matter of Wife... and Death, Baby Brokers, Last Song, Hotline, Rita Hayworth: The Love Goddess, Stillwatch (also exec. prod.), Mickey Spillane's Mike Hammer, Murder Takes All, Danielle Steel's Daddy, Posing: Inspired By 3 Real Stories, She Woke Up Pregnant, A Secret Between Friends.

CARTER, NELL
Actress. b. Birmingham, AL. Sept. 13, 1948.
THEATER: Hair, Dude, Don't Bother Me I Can't Cope, Jesus Christ Superstar, Ain't Misbehavin' (Tony & Theatre World Awards, 1978), Ain't Misbehaving (1988 revival), Hello Dolly! (L.A.).
PICTURES: Hair, Quartet, Back Roads, Modern Problems, Bebe's Kids (voice), The Grass Harp.
TELEVISION: Series: Lobo, Gimme a Break, You Take the Kids, Hangin' With Mr. Cooper. Specials: Baryshnikov on Broadway, The Big Show, An NBC Family Christmas, Ain't Misbehavin' (Emmy Award), Christmas in Washington, Nell Carter, Never Too Old To Dream, Morton's By the Bay (pilot). Movies: Cindy, Maid for Each Other, Final Shot: The Hank Gathers Story.

CARTLIDGE, WILLIAM
Director, Producer. b. England, June 16, 1942. e. Highgate Sch. Ent. m.p. ind. 1959. Early career in stills dept., Elstree Studio. Later worked as an asst. dir. on The Young Ones, Summer Holiday, The Punch & Judy Man, The Naked Edge. As 1st asst. dir. on such pictures as Born Free, Alfie, You Only Live Twice, The Adventurers, Young Winston, Friends. As assoc. prod., Paul and Michelle, Seven Nights in Japan, The Spy Who Loved Me, Moonraker. Prod.: Educating Rita, Not Quite Paradise, Consuming Passions, Dealers, The Playboys. Producer of Haunted, Incognito.

CARTWRIGHT, VERONICA
Actress. b. Bristol, Eng., 1949. m. writer-dir. Richard Compton. Sister is actress Angela Cartwright. Began career as child actress. Stage: The Hands of Its Enemies (Mark Taper Forum, LA 1984), The Triplet Connection (off-B'way).
PICTURES: In Love and War (debut, 1958), The Children's Hour, The Birds, Spencer's Mountain, One Man's Way, Inserts,

Goin' South, Invasion of the Body Snatchers, Alien, Nightmares, The Right Stuff, My Man Adam, Flight of the Navigator, Wisdom, The Witches of Eastwick, Valentino Returns, False Identity, Man Trouble, Candyman: Farewell to the Flesh.
TELEVISION: Series: Daniel Boone. Guest: Leave It to Beaver, Twilight Zone. Mini-series: Robert Kennedy and His Times. Movies: Guyana Tragedy—The Story of Jim Jones, The Big Black Pill, Prime Suspect, Intimate Encounters, Desperate for Love, A Son's Promise, Hitler's Daughter, Dead in the Water, It's Nothing Personal, My Brother's Keeper. Specials: Who Has Seen the Wind?, Bernice Bobs Her Hair, Tell Me Not the Mournful Numbers (Emmy Award), Joe Dancer, Abby My Love, On Hope.

CARUSO, DAVID
Actor. b. Queens, NY, Jan. 7, 1956.
PICTURES: Without Warning (debut, 1980), An Officer and a Gentleman, First Blood, Thief of Hearts, Blue City, China Girl, Twins, King of New York, Hudson Hawk, Mad Dog and Glory, Kiss of Death, Jade.
TELEVISION: Series: N.Y.P.D. Blue. Movies: Crazy Times, The First Olmypics—Athens 1896, Into the Homeland, Rainbow Drive, Mission of the Shark, Judgment Day: The John List Story. Guest: Crime Story, Hill Street Blues.

CARVER, STEVE
Director. b. Brooklyn, NY, April 5, 1945. e. U. of Buffalo; Washington U., MFA. Directing, writing fellow, Film Inst. Center for Advanced Studies, 1970. (Writer, dir. films Patent and the Tell-Tale Heart). Teacher of filmmaking art and photo. Florissant Valley Col., MO 1966-68. News photographer, UPI. Instructor, film and photography, Metropolitan Ed. Council in the Arts; St. Louis Mayor's Council on the Arts, Give a Damn (dir., prod.); asst. dir. Johnny Got His Gun; writer, editor with New World Pictures. Member: Sierra Club, Natl. Rifle Assn.
PICTURES: Arena, Big Bad Mama, Capone, Drum, Fast Charlie, The Moonbeam Rider, Steel, An Eye for an Eye, Lone Wolf McQuade (also prod.), Oceans of Fire, Jocks (also co-s.p.), Bulletproof (also co-s.p.), River of Death, Crazy Joe, The Wolves.

CARVEY, DANA
Actor. b. Missoula, MT, Apr. 2, 1955. e. San Francisco State Coll. Won San Francisco Stand-Up Comedy Competition which led to work as stand-up comedian in local S.F., then L.A. comedy clubs. TV debut as Mickey Rooney's grandson on series, One of the Boys, 1982. Received American Comedy Award (1990, 1991) as TV's Funniest Supporting Male Performer.
PICTURES: Halloween II, Racing With the Moon, This is Spinal Tap, Tough Guys, Moving, Opportunity Knocks, Wayne's World, Wayne's World 2, Clean Slate, The Road to Wellville, Trapped in Paradise.
TELEVISION: Series: One of the Boys, Blue Thunder, Saturday Night Live (Emmy Award, 1993). Specials: Superman's 50th Anniversary (host), Salute to Improvisation, Wayne & Garth's Saturday Night Live Music a Go-Go. Guest: The Larry Sanders Show. Pilots: Alone at Last, Whacked Out.

CASEY, BERNIE
Actor. b. Wyco, WV, June 8, 1939. e. Bowling Green U. Played pro-football with San Francisco 49ers and L.A. Rams.
PICTURES: Guns of the Magnificent Seven (debut, 1969), Tick...Tick...Tick, Boxcar Bertha, Black Gunn, Hit Man, Cleopatra Jones, Maurie, Cornbread Earl and Me, The Man Who Fell to Earth, Dr. Black/Mr. Hyde, Brothers, Sharky's Machine, Never Say Never Again, Revenge of the Nerds, Spies Like Us, Steele Justice, Rent-a-Cop, I'm Gonna Git You Sucka, Backfire, Bill and Ted's Excellent Adventure, Another 48 HRS, Under Siege, The Cemetery Club, Street Knight, The Glass Shield.
TELEVISION: Series: Harris and Company, Bay City Blues. Movies: Brian's Song, Gargoyles, Panic on the 5:22, Mary Jane Harper Cried Last Night, It Happened at Lake Wood Manor, Ring of Passion, Love is Not Enough, Sophisticated Gents, Hear No Evil, The Fantastic World of D.C. Collins. Mini-Series: Roots— The Next Generations, The Martian Chronicles.

CASS, PEGGY
Actress. b. Boston, MA, May 21, 1924. On B'way in Burlesque, Bernardine, Auntie Mame (Tony & Theatre World Awards, 1957), A Thurber Carnival, Don't Drink the Water, Front Page, Plaza Suite, Last of the Red Hot Lovers, Once a Catholic, 42nd Street, The Octette Bridge Club.
PICTURES: The Marrying Kind (debut, 1952), Auntie Mame (Acad. Award nom.), Gidget Goes Hawaiian, The Age of Consent, If It's Tuesday This Must Be Belgium, Paddy.
TELEVISION: Series: The Jack Paar Show, Keep Talking, The Hathaways, To Tell the Truth, The Doctors (1978-79), Women in Prison. Movie: Danielle Steel's Zoya. Guest: Garry Moore Show, Barbara Stanwyck Show, Tales from the Darkside, Major Dad.

CASSEL, ALVIN I.
Executive. b. New York , NY, July 26. e. U. of Michigan, B.A., 1938. Capt. in U.S. Army European Theatre, 1941-45. Surveyed Central Africa for MGM, 1946-50, then assumed duties as asst.

mgr. for MGM South Africa. Continued with MGM in West Indies, 1950-51 and Philippines, 1951-57. In 1957 joined Universal as mgr./supvr. for Southeast Asia; back to MGM in 1963 as supvr. S.E. Asia; 1967, with CBS Films as Far East supvr. In 1972, established Cassel Films to secure theatrical films for foreign distributors, principally in Far East. 1979, consultant for Toho-Towa co. of Japan and other Far East distributors.

CASSEL, JEAN-PIERRE
Actor. b. Paris, France, Oct. 27, 1932. Began as dancer, attracting attention of Gene Kelly at Left Bank nightspot, resulting in film debut. Also appeared in plays before becoming established as leading French screen star.
PICTURES: The Happy Road (debut, 1956), A Pied a Cheval et en Voiture, Le Desorde et la Nuit, Love Is My Profession, The Love Game, The Joker, Candide, The Five-Day Lover, Seven Capital Sins, La Gamberge, The Elusive Corporal, Arsene Lupin contre Arsene Lupin, Cyrano and D'Artagnan, The Male Companion, High Infidelity, La Ronde, Those Magnificent Men in Their Flying Machines, Is Paris Burning?, The Killing Game, The Bear and the Doll, Oh! What a Lovely War, The Army of the Shadows, The Rupture, The Boat on the Grass, Baxter!, The Discreet Charm of the Bourgeoisie, The Three Musketeers, Le Mouton Enrage, Murder on the Orient Express, Who Is Killing the Great Chefs of Europe?, Chouans! Grandeson, From Hell to Victory, La Ville des Silence, The Green Jacket, Ehrengard, The Trout, Vive la Sociale! Tranches de Vie, Mangeclous, The Return of the Musketeers, Mr. Frost, Vincent & Theo, The Favor the Watch and the Very Big Fish, Between Heaven and Earth, Petain, Blue Helmet, L'Enfer, Ready to Wear (Pret-a-Porter), La Ceremonie (A Judgment in Stone).
TELEVISION: Casanova (U.S.), The Burning Shore, Notorious, Warburg, Young Indiana Jones Chronicles, From Earth and Blood, Elissa Rhais.

CASSEL, SEYMOUR
Actor. b. Detroit, MI, Jan. 22, 1937. As a boy travelled with a troupe of burlesque performers including his mother. After high school appeared in summer stock in Michigan. Studied acting at American Theatre Wing and Actor's Studio. After joining a workshop taught by John Cassavetes, began a long creative association with the director-actor. B'way: The World of Suzy Wong, The Disenchanted.
PICTURES: Murder Inc., Shadows, Too Late Blues, Juke Box Racket, The Killers, The Sweet Ride, Coogan's Bluff, Faces (Acad. Award nom.), The Revolutionary, Minnie and Moskowitz, Black Oak Conspiracy, Death Game (The Seducers), The Killing of a Chinese Bookie, The Last Tycoon, Scott Joplin, Opening Night, Valentino, Convoy, California Dreaming, Ravagers, Sunburn, The Mountain Men, King of the Mountain, I'm Almost Not Crazy...John Cassavetes-The Man and His Work (doc.), Love Streams, Eye of the Tiger, Survival Game, Tin Men, Johnny Be Good, Plain Clothes, Colors, Track 29, Wicked Stepmother, Dick Tracy, White Fang, Cold Dog Soup, Mobsters, Diary of a Hitman, Honeymoon in Vegas, In the Soup, Trouble Bound, Indecent Proposal, Boiling Point, Chain of Desire, Chasers, There Goes My Baby, When Pigs Fly, Hand Gun, It Could Happen to You, Tollbooth, Dark Side of Genius, Imaginary Crimes, Things I Never Told You, Dead Presidents, The Last Home Run, Dream for an Insomniac, Four Rooms, Cameleone.
TELEVISION: Movies: The Hanged Man, Angel on My Shoulder, Blood Feud, I Want to Live, Beverly Hills Madame, Sweet Bird of Youth, My Shadow, Dead in the Water, Face of a Stranger. Pilot: Rose City. Special: Partners. Series: Good Company.

CASSIDY, DAVID
Actor, Singer. b. New York, NY, April 12, 1950. Son of late actor Jack Cassidy; brother of Shaun and Patrick. Composed and performed theme song for The John Larroquette Show.
THEATER: B'way: The Fig Leaves Are Falling (debut, 1968), Joseph and the Amazing Technicolor Dreamcoat, Blood Brothers. Regional: Little Johnny Jones, Tribute. London: Time.
PICTURES: Instant Karma, The Spirit of '76.
TELEVISION: Series: The Partridge Family, David Cassidy-Man Undercover. Movie: The Night the City Screamed. Guest: The Mod Squad, Bonanza, Adam-12, Ironside, Marcus Welby M.D., Police Story (Emmy nom.), The Love Boat, Alfred Hitchcock Presents, The Flash.

CASSIDY, JOANNA
Actress. b. Camden, NJ, Aug. 2, 1944. e. Syracuse U.
PICTURES: Bullitt (debut, 1968), Fools, The Laughing Policeman, The Outfit, Bank Shot, The Stepford Wives, Stay Hungry, The Late Show, Stunts, The Glove, Our Winning Season, Night Games, Blade Runner, Under Fire, Club Paradise, The Fourth Protocol, Who Framed Roger Rabbit, 1969, The Package, Where the Heart Is, Don't Tell Mom the Babysitter's Dead, All-American Murder, May Wine, Vampire in Brooklyn, Chain Reaction.
TELEVISION: Series: Shields and Yarnell, The Roller Girls, 240-Robert, Family Tree, Buffalo Bill, Code Name: Foxfire, Hotel

Malibu. Movies: She's Dressed to Kill, Reunion, Invitation to Hell, The Children of Times Square, Pleasures, A Father's Revenge, Nightmare at Bitter Creek, Wheels of Terror, Grass Roots, Taking Back My Life, Live! From Death Row, Perfect Family, Barbarians at the Gate, Stephen King's The Tommyknockers, The Rockford Files: I Still Love L.A, Sleep Baby Sleep. Mini-Series: Hollywood Wives. Special: Roger Rabbit and the Secrets of Toontown (host), Other Mothers (Afterschool Special). Pilot: Second Stage. Guest: Taxi, Love Boat, Hart to Hart, Charlie's Angels, Lou Grant.

CASSIDY, PATRICK
Actor. b. Los Angeles, CA, Jan. 4, 1961. Son of late actor Jack Cassidy and actress-singer Shirley Jones.
THEATER: NY: The Pirates of Penzance, Leader of the Pack, Assassins. Regional: Conrack.
PICTURES: Off the Wall, Just the Way You Are, Fever Pitch, Nickel Mountain, Love at Stake, Longtime Companion, I'll Do Anything.
TELEVISION: Series: Bay City Blues, Dirty Dancing. Movies: Angel Dusted, Midnight Offerings, Choices of the Heart, Christmas Eve, Dress Gray, Something in Comon, Follow Your Heart, Three on a Match, How the West Was Fun. Mini-Series: Napoleon and Josephine: A Love Story. Pilot: The Six of Us.

CASTLE, NICK
Writer, Director. b. Los Angeles, CA, Sept. 21, 1947. e. Santa Monica Coll., U. of Southern California film sch. Son of late film and TV choreographer Nick Castle Sr. Appeared as child in films Anything Goes, Artists and Models. Worked with John Carpenter and other USC students on Acad. Award-winning short, The Resurrection of Bronco Billy.
PICTURES: Skatedown USA (s.p.), Tag: The Assassination Game (Kiss Me Kill Me; dir., s.p.), Escape from New York (co-s.p.), The Last Starfighter (dir.), The Boy Who Could Fly (dir.), Tap (dir., s.p.), Hook (co-story), Dennis the Menace (dir.), Major Payne (dir.), Mr. Wrong (dir.).

CATES, GILBERT
Director, Producer. r.n. Gilbert Katz. b. New York, NY, June 6, 1934. e. Syracuse U. Brother is dir.-prod. Joseph Cates. Began TV career as guide at NBC studios in N.Y., working way up to prod. and dir. of game shows (Camouflage, Haggis Baggis, Mother's Day, etc.). Created Hootenanny and packaged and directed many TV specials. Pres. Directors Guild of America 1983-87. Awarded DGA's Robert B. Aldrich award 1989. Dir. short film The Painting.
PICTURES: Rings Around the World (debut, 1966), I Never Sang for My Father (also prod.), Summer Wishes Winter Dreams, One Summer Love (Dragonfly; also prod.), The Promise, The Last Married Couple in America, Oh God!—Book II (also prod.), Backfire.
TELEVISION: Specials: International Showtime (1963-65 exec. prod.-dir.), Electric Showcase Specials (dir.-prod.) Academy Awards (prod.; Emmy Award, 1991), After the Fall (prod., dir.). Movies: To All My Friends on Shore (dir., prod.), The Affair (dir.), Johnny, We Hardly Knew Ye (prod., dir.), The Kid from Nowhere (prod.), Country Gold (dir.), Hobson's Choice (dir.), Burning Rage (dir., prod.), Consenting Adult (dir.), Fatal Judgement, My First Love (dir), Do You Know the Muffin Man (dir.), Call Me Anna (dir., prod.), Absolute Strangers (dir., exec. prod.), In My Daughter's Name (co-exec. prod.), Confessions: Two Faces of Evil.
THEATER: Director: Tricks of the Trade, Voices, The Price (Long Wharf Theatre). Producer: Solitaire/Double Solitaire, The Chinese and Mr. Fish, I Never Sang for My Father, You Know I Can't Hear You When the Water's Running.

CATES, JOSEPH
Producer, Director. r.n. Joseph Katz. b. 1924. e. NYU. Brother is dir. Gilbert Cates. Father of actress Phoebe Cates. One of first producers and dirs. of live TV with Look Upon a Star, 1947. Prod., Jackie Gleason Cavalcade of Stars, game shows, ($64,000 Question, $64,000 Challenge, Stop the Music, Haggis Baggis), NBC Spectaculars (1955-60), High Button Shoes, The Bachelor, Accent on Love, Gene Kelly, Ethel Merman, Victor Borge, Yves Montand shows.
THEATER: Prod. on B'way: What Makes Sammy Run?, Joe Egg, Spoon River Anthology, Gantry, Her First Roman.
PICTURES: Director: Who Killed Teddy Bear, The Fat Spy, Girl of the Night.
TELEVISION: Series: International Showtime (Don Ameche Circuses). Prod.-dir. of spectaculars and special programs, 1955-88: Johnny Cash, David Copperfield, Steve Martin; Anne Bancroft: The Woman in the Life of Man (Emmy Award as exec. prod., 1970), Jack Lemmon and Fred Astaire: S'Wonderful S'Marvelous S'Gershwin (Emmy Award as exec. prod., 1972), Annual Ford Theater Salutes to the President, Country Music Awards Show, Miss Teen Age America, Junior Miss pageants, Tony Awards 1992, International Emmies, The Ford Theatre Salute to the President, The 1993 Monte Carlo Circus Festival. Movies: Prod.: The Quick and the Dead, The Last Days of Frank and Jessie James, The Cradle Will Fall, Special People.

CATES, PHOEBE
Actress. b. New York, NY, July 16, 1962. e. Juilliard. Father is prod-dir. Joseph Cates. m. actor Kevin Kline. Dance prodigy and fashion model before launching acting career. NY stage debut The Nest of the Wood Grouse (1984).
PICTURES: Paradise (debut, 1982), Fast Times at Ridgemont High, Private School, Gremlins, Date With an Angel, Bright Lights Big City, Shag, Heart of Dixie, I Love You to Death (unbilled), Gremlins 2: The New Batch, Drop Dead Fred, Bodies Rest and Motion, My Life's in Turnaround, Princess Caraboo.
TELEVISION: Movies: Baby Sister, Lace, Lace II. Special: Largo Desolato.

CATON-JONES, MICHAEL
Director. b. Broxburn, Scotland, 1958.
PICTURES: Scandal (debut, 1989), Memphis Belle, Doc Hollywood (also cameo), This Boy's Life, Rob Roy (also exec. prod.).

CATTRALL, KIM
Actress. b. Liverpool, Eng., Aug. 21, 1956. e. American Acad. of Dramatic Arts, N.Y. Started stage career in Canada's Off-B'way in Vancouver and Toronto; later performed in L.A. in A View from the Bridge, Agnes of God, Three Sisters, etc. On B'way in Wild Honey. Chicago Goodman Theatre in the Misanthrope. Regional: Miss Julie (Princeton).
PICTURES: Rosebud (debut 1975), The Other Side of the Mountain Part II, Tribute, Ticket to Heaven, Porky's, Police Academy, Turk 182, City Limits, Hold-Up, Big Trouble in Little China, Mannequin, Masquerade, Midnight Crossing, Palais Royale, Honeymoon Academy, The Return of the Musketeers, Brown Bread Sandwiches, Bonfire of the Vanities, Star Trek VI: The Undiscovered Country, Split Second, Double Vision, Breaking Point, Unforgettable, Live Nude Girls, Where Truth Lies.
TELEVISION: Series: Angel Falls. Movies: Good Against Evil, The Bastard, The Night Rider, The Rebels, The Gossip Columnist, Sins of the Past, Miracle in the Wilderness, Running Delilah, Tom Clancy's Op Center, Above Suspicion, The Heidi Chronicles, Two Golden Balls. Mini-Series: Scruples, Wild Palms.

CAULFIELD, MAXWELL
Actor. b. Glasgow, Scotland, Nov. 23, 1959. m. actress Juliet Mills. First worked as a dancer at a London nightclub. After coming to NY in 1978, ran the concession stand at the Truck and Warehouse Theatre. Won a Theatre World Award for Class Enemy.
THEATER: Entertaining Mr. Sloane, Salonika, Journey's End, Sleuth, The Elephant Man, An Inspector Calls, Sweet Bird of Youth, The Woman In Black.
PICTURES: Grease 2, Electric Dreams, The Boys Next Door, The Supernaturals, Sundown: The Vampire in Retreat, Mind Games, Alien Intruder, Midnight Witness, Ipi/Tombi, In a Moment of Passion, Calendar Girl, Gettysburg, Inevitable Grace, Empire Records, Prey of the Jaguar.
TELEVISION: Series: The Colbys. Movies: The Parade, Till We Meet Again, Blue Bayou, The Rockford Files.

CAVANAUGH, ANDREW
Executive. Held positions with Norton Simon, Inc. and Equitable Life Insurance Co. before joining Paramount Pictures in 1984 as v.p., human resources. 1985, appt. sr. v.p., administration, mng. personnel depts. on both coasts. Also oversees corp. admin. function for Paramount.

CAVANI, LILIANA
Director. b. near Modena, in Emilia, Italy, Jan. 12, 1937. e. U. of Bologna, diploma in classic literature, 1960; Ph.D. in linguistics. In 1960 took courses at Centro Sperimentale di Cinematografia in Rome where made short films Incontro Notturno and L'Evento. 1961 winner of RAI sponsored contest and started working for the new second Italian TV channel, 1962-66 directing progs. of serious political and social nature incl. History of 3rd Reich, Women in the Resistance, Age of Stalin, Philippe Petain–Trial at Vichy (Golden Lion Venice Fest.), Jesus My Brother, Day of Peace, Francis of Assisi. Has also directed operas Wozzeck, Iphigenia in Tauris and Medea on stage; also dir. opera liriche: Cardillac, Jenufa, Traviata, Vestale, Cena Delle Beffe, Iphigenia in Tauride, Medea.
PICTURES: Galileo, I Cannibali, Francesco d'Assisi, L'Ospite, Milarepa, Night Porter, Beyond Good and Evil, The Skin, Oltre la Porta, The Berlin Affair, Francesco, Sans Pouvoir le Dire.

CAVETT, DICK
Actor, Writer. b. Kearny, NE, Nov. 19, 1936. e. Yale U. Acted in TV dramas and Army training films. Was writer for Jack Paar and his successors on the Tonight Show. Also wrote comedy for Merv Griffin, Jerry Lewis, Johnny Carson. In 1967 began performing own comedy material in night clubs. On TV starred in specials Where It's At (ABC Stage 67) and What's In.
THEATER: B'way: Otherwise Engaged, Into the Woods.

PICTURES: Annie Hall, Power Play, Health, Simon, A Nightmare on Elm Street 3, Beetlejuice, Moon Over Parador, After School, Funny, Year of the Gun, Forrest Gump.
TELEVISION: Series: This Morning (ABC daytime talk show, 1968), The Dick Cavett Show (ABC primetime talk show, summer 1969), The Dick Cavett Show (ABC late night talk show, 1969-72: Emmy Award, 1972), ABC Late Night (talk show, 1973-74; Emmy Award, 1974), The Dick Cavett Show (CBS primetime variety; 1975), Dick Cavett Show (talk show: PBS, 1977-82; USA, 1985-86; CBS, 1986), The Edge of Night (1983), The Dick Cavett Show (CNBC talk show: 1989). Author: Cavett (with Christopher Porter) 1974.

CAZENOVE, CHRISTOPHER
Actor. b. Winchester, Eng., Dec. 17, 1945. m. Angharad Rees. e. Eton, Oxford U., trained at Bristol Old Vic Theatre School. West End theater includes Hamlet (1969), The Lionel Touch, My Darling Daisy, The Winslow Boy, Joking Apart, In Praise of Rattigan, The Life and Poetry of T.S. Eliot, The Sound of Music. B'way debut: Goodbye Fidel (1980).
PICTURES: There's a Girl in My Soup, Royal Flash, East of Elephant Rock, The Girl in Blue Velvet, Zulu Dawn, Eye of the Needle, From a Far Country, Heat and Dust, Until September, Mata Hari, The Fantastist, Hold My Hand I'm Dying, Three Men and a Little Lady, Aces: Iron Eagle III, The Proprietor.
TELEVISION: Series: The Regiment, The Duchess of Duke Street, Dynasty, A Fine Romance, Tales From the Crypt. Specials/Movies: The Rivals of Sherlock Holmes (1971), Affairs of the Heart, Jennie: Lady Randolph Churchill, The Darkwater Hall Mystery, Ladykillers—A Smile Is Sometimes Worth a Million, The Red Signal, Lou Grant, The Letter, Jenny's War, Lace 2, Kane and Abel, Windmills of the Gods, Shades of Love, Souvenir, The Lady and the Highwayman, Tears in the Rain, Ticket to Ride (A Fine Romance), To Be the Best.

CELENTINO, LUCIANO
Producer, Director, Writer. b. Naples, Italy, 1940. e. Rome, Paris, London. Ent. ind. 1959. Wrote, prod., dir. many plays incl: Infamita di Questa Terra, Black Destiny, Honour, Stranger's Heart, Youth's Sin, Wanda Lontano Amore. Stage musicals such as Songs...Dots...And Fantasies, Night Club's Appointment, Filumena, Serenada, Mamma. Since 1964, film critic of Il Meridionale Italiano. From 1962, co-writer and first asst. director to Luigi Capuano and Vittorio De Sica. In 1972, formed own company, Anglo-Fortunato Films. Co-wrote, prod., dir. Blood Money. Dir. Bandito (in Italy). Wrote and dir. Toujours, Parole, Jackpot; 1988: Panache (dir.), 1989: Was There a Way Out? (prod., wrote, dir.), Hobo.

CELLAN-JONES, JAMES
Director. b. Swansea, Wales, July 13, 1931. e. St. John's Coll., Cambridge. Best known for his adaptations of classic novels for the BBC and PBS (shown on Masterpiece Theatre). Won Nymphe d'Or at Monaco Festival.
PICTURE: The Nelson Affair, Chou Chou, Une Vie de Debussy.
TELEVISION: The Scarlet and the Black, The Forsyte Saga, Portrait of a Lady, The Way We Live Now, Solo, The Roads to Freedom, Eyeless In Gaza, The Golden Bowl, Jennie (DGA series award), Caesar and Cleopatra, The Adams Chronicles, The Day Christ Died, The Ambassadors, Unity Mitford, Oxbridge Blues (also prod.), Sleeps Six (also prod.), The Comedy of Errors, Fortunes of War, You Never Can Tell, Arms and the Man, A Little Piece of Sunshine, A Perfect Hero (also prod.), The Gravy Train Goes East, Maigret, Harnessing Peacocks, Brighton Belles.

CHABROL, CLAUDE
Director. b. Paris, France, June 24, 1930. Worked as newsman for Fox, then writer for Cahiers du Cinema. A founding director of the French New Wave.
PICTURES: Le Beau Serge, The Cousins, A Double Tour, Les Bonnes Femmes, Les Godelureaux, The Third Lover, Seven Capital Sins, Ophelia, Landru, Le Tigre Aime la Chair Fraiche, Marie-Chantal Contre le Docteur Kah, Le Tigre Se Parfume a la Dunamite, Paris vu par... Chabrol, La Ligne de Demarcation, The Champagne Murders, The Route to Corinth, Les Biches, La Femme Infidele, This Man Must Die, Le Boucher, La Rapture, Ten Days' Wonder, Just Before Nightfall, Dr. Popaul, Les Noces Rouges, Nada, The Blood of Others, The Horse of Pride, Alouette je te plumera, Poulet au Vinaigre, Inspector Lavardin, Masques, Le Cri du Hibou, Story of Women, Clichy Days (Quiet Days in Clichy), The Lark (actor only), Doctor M (Club Extinction), Madame Bovary, Betty, L'Enfer (Hell; also s.p.), Through the Eyes of Vichy, A Judgment in Stone (also co-s.p.).

CHAKERES, MICHAEL H.
Executive b. Ohio. e. Wittenberg U, 1935. Pres. and chmn. of bd. of Chakeres Theatres of Ohio and Kentucky. U.S. Army AF 1942-45. Bd. of Dir.: National NATO, NATO of Ohio, Will Rogers Hospital, Motion Picture Pioneers, Society National Bank, Wittenberg U., Springfield Foundation, Variety Club of Palm Beach, Tent No. 65. Member: Masonic Temple, Scottish Rite, I.O.O.F., AHEPA, Leadership 100, ARCHON-Order of St. Andrew, Rotary Club, City of Hope, University Club.

CHAKIRIS, GEORGE
Actor. b. Norwood, OH, Sept. 16, 1933. Entered m.p. industry as chorus dancer.
PICTURES: Song of Love (debut, 1947), The Great Caruso, The 5000 Fingers of Dr. T, Give a Girl a Break, Gentlemen Prefer Blondes, There's No Business Like Show Business, White Christmas, Brigadoon, The Girl Rush, Meet Me in Las Vegas, Under Fire (1st acting role), West Side Story (Academy Award for Best Supporting Actor, 1961), Two and Two Make Six, Diamond Head, Bebo's Girl, Kings of the Sun, Flight From Ashiya, 633 Squadron, McGuire Go Home! (The High Bright Sun), Is Paris Burning?, The Young Girls of Rochefort, The Big Cube, The Day the Hot Line Got Hot, Why Not Stay for Breakfast?, Jekyll and Hyde... Together Again, Pale Blood.
TELEVISION: Series: Dallas (1985-86). Guest: Fantasy Island, CHiPs, Matt Houston, Scarecrow and Mrs. King, Hell Town, Murder She Wrote. Movie: Return to Fantasy Island. Specials: You're the Top, Highways of Melody, Kismet, Notorious Woman (PBS).

CHAMBERLAIN, RICHARD
Actor. r.n. George Richard Chamberlain. b. Los Angeles, CA, March 31, 1935. Studied voice, LA Conservatory of Music 1958; acting with Jeff Corey. Founding mem. City of Angels, LA Theater Company. Became TV star in Dr. Kildare series, 1961-66. Founded prod. co. Cham Enterprises. Had hit record Three Stars Will Shine Tonight (them from Dr. Kildare) in 1962.
THEATER: Breakfast at Tiffany's, Night of the Iguana, Fathers & Sons, Blithe Spirit.
PICTURES: The Secret of the Purple Reef (debut, 1960), A Thunder of Drums, Twilight of Honor, Joy in the Morning, Petulia, The Madwoman of Chaillot, Julius Caesar, The Music Lovers, Lady Caroline Lamb, The Three Musketeers, The Towering Inferno, The Four Musketeers, The Slipper and the Rose, The Swarm, The Last Wave, Murder by Phone (Bells), King Solomon's Mines, Alan Quartermain and the Lost City of Gold, The Return of the Musketeers (tv in U.S.), Bird of Prey.
TELEVISION: Specials: Hamlet, Portrait of a Lady, The Woman I Love, The Lady's Not for Burning. Movies: F. Scott Fitzgerald and the Last of the Belles, The Count of Monte Cristo, The Man in the Iron Mask, Cook and Perry: The Race to the Pole, Wallenberg: A Hero's Story, Casanova, Aftermath: A Test of Love, The Night of the Hunter, Ordeal in the Arctic. Mini-Series: Centennial, Shogun, The Thorn Birds, Dream West, The Bourne Identity. Series: Dr. Kildare, Island Son (also co-exec. prod.) Host: The Astronomers. Guest: Gunsmoke, Thriller, The Deputy, Alfred Hitchcock Presents.

CHAMBERS, EVERETT
Producer, Writer, Director. b. Montrose, CA; Aug. 19, 1926. e. New School For Social Research, Dramatic Workshop, N.Y. Entered industry as actor; worked with Fred Coe as casting dir. and dir., NBC, 1952-57; Author: Producing TV Movies.
PICTURES: Actor: Too Late Blues. Writer: Tess of the Storm Country, Run Across the River, The Kiss (short; dir.: Acad. Award nom.), The Lollipop Cover (also prod., dir.; Chicago Film Fest.), Private Duty Nurses, A Girl to Kill For.
TELEVISION: Producer: Series: Johnny Staccato (also writer), Target the Corrupters, The Dick Powell Theatre, The Lloyd Bridges Show (also writer), Peyton Place, Columbo, Future Cop, Timeslip (exec. prod., writer; 1985 Christopher & A.W.R.T. Awards), Lucan (also writer), Airwolf, Partners in Crime, Rin Tin Tin K-9 Cop (also creative consultant). Movies: Beverly Hills Madam, A Matter of Sex (exec. prod.), Will There Really Be a Morning?, Berlin Tunnel 21 (sprv. prod.), Night Slaves (also writer), Moon of the Wolf, Trouble Comes to Town, The Great American Beauty Contest, Can Ellen Be Saved? (also writer), Jigsaw John, Street Killing, Nero Wolfe, Twin Detectives (also writer), The Girl Most Likely to..., Sacrifice the Queen, Paris Conspiracy, Family Secret, Incident in a Small Town (spv. prod.). Co-writer: The Perfect Town for Murder, Last Chance (pilot).

CHAMPION, JOHN C.
Director, Producer, Writer. b. Denver, CO, Oct. 13, 1923. e. Stanford U., Wittenberg Coll. p. Lee R. Champion, Supreme Court judge. Entered m.p. in Fiesta; did some radio work; in stock at MGM briefly; co-pilot Western Air Lines, Inc., 1943; served in U.S. Army Air Force, air transport command pilot 1943-45; public relations officer AAF; writer & prod. for Allied Artists; v.p. prod. Commander Films Corp.; press. Champion Pictures, Inc.; prod., MGM, Warner, Paramount, Universal, Member: SAG, SWG, SIMPP, SPG; TV Academy, Prod. Writer, Mirisch-U.A.; prod. TV Laramie series; created McHales Navy; author, novel, The Hawks of Noon, 1965; National Cowboy, Hall of Fame Award, 1976.
PICTURES: Panhandle, Stampede, Hellgate, Dragonfly Squadron, Shotgun, Zero Hour, The Texican, Attack on the Iron Coast, Submarine X-1, The Last Escape, Brother of the Wind, Mustang Country (dir-prod-writer).

CHAMPION, MARGE
Dancer, Actress, Choreographer. b. Los Angeles, CA, Sept. 2, 1921. r.n. Marjorie Celeste Belcher. e. Los Angeles public

schools. Father was Ernest Belcher, ballet master. Was model for Snow White for Disney's animated feature. Debuted in films as Marjorie Bell. Made debut with former husband Gower Champion as dancing team; team was signed by MGM; voted Star of Tomorrow, 1952.
THEATER: Blossom Time, Student Prince (LA Civic Opera), Dark of the Moon. Beggar's Holiday (NY), 3 for Tonight (NY), nvitation to a March (tour). Director: Stepping Out, Lute Song (Berkshire Theatre Fest. 1989), She Loves Me, No No Nanette.
PICTURES: Honor of the West (debut, 1939), The Story of Vernon and Irene Castle, Sorority House, Mr. Music, Show Boat, Lovely to Look At, Everything I Have Is Yours, Give a Girl a Break, Three for the Show, Jupiter's Darling, The Swimmer, The Party, The Cockeyed Cowboys of Calico County. Choreographer only: The Day of the Locust, Whose Life Is It Anyway?.
TELEVISION: Series: Admiral Broadway Revue, Marge and Gower Champion Show. Guest: GE Theatre, Chevy Show, Bell Telephone Hour, Ed Sullivan, Shower of Stars, Fame. Movie: Queen of the Stardust Ballroom (choreographer; Emmy Award, 1975).

CHAN, JACKIE
Actor, Director, Writer. r.n. Chan Kwong-Sang. b. Hong Kong, Apr. 7, 1955. Trained in acrobatics, mime and martial arts at Peking Opera Sch. Was child actor in several films; later became stuntman before being launched as action star by prod.-dir. Lo Wei.
PICTURES: Little Tiger From Canton, New Fist of Fury, Shaolin Wooden Men, To Kill With Intrigue, Snake in the Eagle's Shadow, Snake & Crane Arts of Shaolin, Magnificent Bodyguards, Drunken Master (Drunk Monkey in the Tiger's Eyes), Spiritual Kung Fu, The Fearless Hyena, Dragon Fist, The Young Master (also dir., co-s.p.), Half a Loaf of Kung Fu, The Big Brawl, The Cannonball Run, Dragon Lord (also dir., co-s.p.), Winners and Sinners, The Fearless Hyena Part 2, Cannonball Run II, Project A (also co-dir., co-s.p.), Wheels on Meals, My Lucky Stars, The Protector, Twinkle Twinkle Lucky Stars, Heart of the Dragon (First Mission), Police Story (also dir., co-s.p.), Armour of God (also dir., co-s.p.), Project A Part 2 (also dir., co-s.p.), Dragons Forever, Police Story II (also dir., co-s.p.), Mr. Canton and Lady Rose (Miracle; also dir., co-s.p.), Armour of God II: Operation Condor (also dir., co-s.p.), Island of Fire, Twin Dragons, Police Story III: Super Cop (also dir., co-s.p.), City Hunter, Crime Story, Project S, Drunken Master II, Rumble in the Bronx.

CHANCELLOR, JOHN
TV Anchorman, News Reporter. b. Chicago, IL, 1927. e. U. of Illinois. After military service joined Chicago Sun-Times (1948) and after two years moved to NBC News as Midwest corr. In 1948, assigned to Vienna bureau. Subsequently reported from London; was chief of Moscow bureau before appt. as host of Today program for one year (1961). Left NBC 1965-67 to become dir. of Voice of America. In recent yrs. anchorman for special coverage of moon landings, political conventions, inaugurations etc. Anchorman, NBC Nightly News, 1970-82. Now sr. commentator, NBC News, delivering news commentaries on NBC Nightly News.

CHANNING, CAROL
Actress. b. Seattle, WA, Jan. 31, 1921. e. Bennington Coll.
THEATER: B'way: Gentlemen Prefer Blondes, Lend an Ear (Theatre World Award), Hello Dolly! (Tony Award, 1964), Show Girl, Lorelei. Tour: Legends.
PICTURES: Paid in Full (debut, 1950), The First Traveling Saleslady, Thoroughly Modern Millie (Acad. Award nom.), Skidoo, Shinbone Alley (voice), Sgt. Pepper's Lonely Hearts Club Band (cameo), Happily Ever After (voice), Hans Christian Andersen's Thumbelina (voice), Edie & Pen.
TELEVISION: Specials: Svengali and the Blonde, Three Men on a Horse, Crescendo, The Carol Channing Special; many guest appearances incl. Omnibus, George Burns Show, Lucy Show, Carol Burnett Show, The Love Boat.

CHANNING, STOCKARD
Actress. r.n. Susan Stockard. b. New York, NY, Feb. 13, 1944. e. Radcliffe Coll., B.A., 1965. With Theater Co. of Boston, experimental drama company, 1967.
THEATER: Two Gentlemen of Verona, No Hard Feelings, Vanities (Mark Taper Forum, LA), They're Playing Our Song, The Lady and the Clarinet, Golden Age, The Rink, Joe Egg (Tony Award, 1985), Love Letters, Woman in Mind, House of Blue Leaves, Six Degrees of Separation, Four Baboons Adoring the Sun.
PICTURES: The Hospital (debut, 1971), Up the Sandbox, The Fortune, The Big Bus, Sweet Revenge, Grease, The Cheap Detective, The Fish That Saved Pittsburgh, Safari 3000, Without a Trace, Heartburn, The Men's Club, A Time of Destiny, Staying Together, Meet the Applegates, Married to It, Six Degrees of Separation (Acad. Award nom.), Bitter Moon, Smoke, To Wong Foo—Thanks for Everything—Julie Newmar, Up Close and Personal, Moll Flanders, Edie and Pen.

TELEVISION: *Series*: Stockard Channing in Just Friends, The Stockard Channing Show. *Movies*: The Girl Most Likely To..., Lucan, Silent Victory: The Kitty O'Neil Story, Not My Kid, The Room Upstairs, Echoes in the Darkness, The Perfect Witness, David's Mother. *Guest*: Medical Center, Trying Times (The Sad Professor). *Special*: Tidy Endings.

CHAPIN, DOUG
Producer. Began career as actor; then switched to film production, making debut with When a Stranger Calls, 1979.
PICTURES: Pandemonium, American Dreamer, What's Love Got to Do With It,.
TELEVISION: *Movies*: Belle Starr, Missing Pieces, Second Sight.

CHAPLIN, CHARLES S.
Executive. b. Toronto, Ont., Canada, June 24, 1911. Studied law. Entered m.p. ind. in 1930 as office boy with United Artists; then office mgr. booker, St. John, N.B., 1933; br. mgr. 1935; to Montreal in same capacity, 1941; 1945-62, Canadian gen. mgr.; v.p. Canadian sls. mgr., 7 Arts Prod., 1962; CEO, v.p., dir. TV sls., Europe-Africa, Middle East-Socialist countries, 1968-70; v.p., WB-7 Arts, 1970-72; exec. v.p. intl. film dist., NTA (Canada) Ltd., Toronto Intl. Film Studios, 1972-80; pres., Charles Chaplin Enterprises, specializing in theatrical and TV sls. and prod. Pres.: B'nai Brith, Toronto Bd. of Trade, various charitable org., many trade assns., past pres. Canadian M.P. Dist. Assn., Chmn. m.p. section Com. Chest, chmn. publ. rel. comm. & past-chmn., M.P. Industry Council; Natl. Board Council Christians & Jews, etc. Representing many indept. producers in Europe, Canada, Far East, South America, etc.

CHAPLIN, GERALDINE
Actress. b. Santa Monica, CA, July 3, 1944. e. Royal Ballet School, London. Father was actor-director Charles Chaplin. Starred in over 20 European productions, including seven with Spanish filmmaker, Carlos Saura. On NY stage in The Little Foxes.
PICTURES: Limelight (debut, 1952), Par un Beau Matin d'Ete, Doctor Zhivago, Andremo in Citta, A Countess from Hong Kong, Stranger in the House (Cop-Out), I Killed Rasputin, Peppermint Frappe, Stres es Tres Tres, Honeycomb, Garden of Delights, The Hawaiians, Sur un Arbre Perche, Z.P.G. (Zero Population Growth), Innocent Bystanders, La Casa sin Fronteras, Ana and the Wolves, The Three Musketeers, Le Marriage a la Mode, The Four Musketeers, Summer of Silence, Nashville, Elisa My Love, Noroit, Buffalo Bill and the Indians or Sitting Bull's History Lesson, Welcome to L.A., Cria, In Memorium, Une Page d'Amour, Roseland, Remember My Name, Los Ojos Vendados, The Masked Bride, L'Adoption, A Wedding, The Mirror Crack'd, Le Voyage en Douce, Bolero, Life Is a Bed of Roses, Love on the Ground, The Moderns, White Mischief, Mama Turns 100, The Return of the Musketeers (tv in U.S.), I Want to Go Home, The Children, Buster's Bedroom, Chaplin, The Age of Innocence, Words Upon the Window Pane, Home for the Holidays, Jane Eyre.
TELEVISION: *Specials*: The Corsican Brothers, My Cousin Rachel, The House of Mirth, A Foreign Field. *Mini-Series*: The World. *Movie*: Duel of Hearts.

CHAPLIN, SAUL
Musical Director, Producer. b. Brooklyn, NY, Feb. 19, 1912. e. NYU, 1929-34. Wrote vaudeville material, 1933-36; songwriter Vitaphone Corp.; other, 1934-40; Columbia, 1940-48; MGM, from 1948; songs include: Bei Mir Bist Du Schoen, Shoe Shine Boy, Anniversary Song.
PICTURES: *Scoring/Musical Director/Arranger*: Argentine Nights, Crazy House, Countess of Monte Cristo, An American in Paris (Academy Award, 1951), Lovely to Look At, Give a Girl a Break, Kiss Me Kate, Seven Brides for Seven Brothers (Academy Award, 1954), Jupiter's Darling, Interrupted Melody, High Society, Les Girls (assoc. prod.), Merry Andrew (assoc. prod.), Can-Can (assoc. prod.), West Side Story (Academy Award, 1961), The Sound of Music (assoc. prod.), Star! (prod.), Man of La Mancha (assoc. prod.), That's Entertainment II (co-prod.).

CHAPMAN, MICHAEL
Cinematographer, Director. b. New York, NY, Nov. 21, 1935. m. writer-dir. Amy Jones. Early career in N.Y. area working on documentaries before becoming camera operator for cinematographer Gordon Willis on The Godfather, Klute, End of the Road, The Landlord. Also camera operator on Jaws.
PICTURES: *Cinematographer*: The Last Detail, White Dawn, Taxi Driver, The Front, The Next Man, Fingers, The Last Waltz, Invasion of the Body Snatchers, Hardcore, The Wanderers, Raging Bull, Dead Men Don't Wear Plaid, Personal Best, The Man With Two Brains, Shoot to Kill, Scrooged, Ghostbusters II, Quick Change, Kindergarten Cop, Whispers in the Dark, Rising Sun, The Fugitive. *Director*: All the Right Moves, The Clan of the Cave Bear.
TELEVISION: Death Be Not Proud, King, Gotham. *Dir.*: The Annihilator (pilot).

CHARBONNEAU, PATRICIA
Actress. Stage appearances with Actors Theatre of Louisville, KY. Also in NY in My Sister in This House.
PICTURES: Desert Hearts, Manhunter, Stalking Danger, Call Me, Shakedown, Brain Dead, Captive, The Owl, K2.
TELEVISION: *Series*: Crime Story. *Pilots*: C.A.T. Squad, Dakota's Way. *Guest*: Spenser: For Hire, The Equalizer, Wiseguy, UNSUB, Matlock. *Movies:* Disaster at Silo 7, Desperado: Badlands Justice.

CHARISSE, CYD
Dancer, Actress. r.n. Tula Ellice Finklea. b. Amarillo, TX, March 8, 1921. e. Hollywood Prof. Sch. m. Tony Martin, singer. Toured U.S. & Europe with Ballet Russe starting at age 13. Began in films as bit player using the name Lily Norwood. Signed contract with MGM in 1946. Named Star of Tomorrow 1948. B'way debut 1991 in Grand Hotel.
PICTURES: Something to Shout About (debut, 1943; billed as Lily Norwood), Mission to Moscow; Ziegfeld Follies (1st film billed as Cyd Charisse), The Harvey Girls, Three Wise Fools, Till the Clouds Roll By, Fiesta, Unfinished Dance, On an Island with You, Words and Music, Kissing Bandit, Tension, East Side West Side, Mark of the Renegade, Wild North, Singin' in the Rain, Sombrero, The Band Wagon, Brigadoon, Deep in My Heart, It's Always Fair Weather, Meet Me in Las Vegas, Silk Stockings, Twilight for the Gods, Party Girl, Five Golden Hours, Black Tights, Two Weeks in Another Town, The Silencers, Maroc 7, Won Ton Ton the Dog Who Saved Hollywood, Warlords of Atlantis, That's Entertainment III.
TELEVISION: *Movies*: Portrait of an Escort, Swimsuit, Cinderalla Summer; many specials.

CHARLES, MARIA
Actress. b. London, England, Sept. 22, 1929. Trained at RADA. London stage debut 1946 in Pick Up Girl.
THEATER: *London*: Women of Twilight, The Boy Friend, Divorce Me Darling!, Enter A Free Man, They Don't Grow on Trees, Winnie the Pooh, Jack the Ripper, The Matchmaker, Measure for Measure, Annie (1979-80), Fiddler on the Roof, Steaming, Peer Gynt, The Lower Depths, When We Are Married, Follies, Party Piece, School for Scandal, Driving Miss Daisy, Hay Fever, Blithe Spirit. *Dir.*: Owl and the Pussycat. *Dir./prod.*: The Boy Friend, 40, Starting Here Starting Now.
PICTURES: Folly To Be Wise, The Deadly Affair, Eye of the Devil, Great Expectations, The Return of the Pink Panther, Cuba, Victor/Victoria, Savage Hearts, The Fool.
TELEVISION: The Likes of 'Er, The Moon and the Yellow River, Down Our Street, Easter Passion, Nicholas Nickleby, The Voice of the Turtle, The Fourth Wall, The Good Old Days, Turn Out the Lights, Angel Pavement, The Ugliest Girl in Town, Other Peoples Houses, Rogues Gallery, The Prince and the Pauper, Crown Court, Bar Mitzvah Boy, Secret Army, Agony, Never the Twain, La Ronde, Shine of Harvey Moon, Sheppey, La Ronde, Brideshead Revisited, A Perfect Spy, Casualty, The Fallout Guy, Lovejoy, Anna, Agony Again.

CHARTOFF, ROBERT
Producer. b. New York, NY., Aug. 26, 1933. e. Union College, A.B.; Columbia U., LL.B. Met Irwin Winkler through mutual client at William Morris Agency (N.M.) and established Chartoff-Winkler Prods. Currently pres., Chartoff Prods., Inc.
PICTURES: Double Trouble, Point Blank, The Split, They Shoot Horses Don't They?, The Strawberry Statement, Leo the Last, Believe in Me, The Gang That Couldn't Shoot Straight, The New Centurions, Up the Sandbox, The Mechanic, Thumb Tripping, Busting, The Gambler, S*P*Y*S, Breakout, Nickelodeon, Rocky, New York New York, Valentino, Comes a Horseman, Uncle Joe Shannon, Rocky II, Raging Bull, True Confessions, Rocky III, The Right Stuff, Rocky IV, Beer, Rocky V, Straight Talk.

CHASE, BRANDON
Producer, Director. President MPA Feature Films, Inc.; newscaster-news director NBC-TV 1952-57. Executive director Mardi Gras Productions, Inc. and member of Board of Directors. Now pres., Group I Films, Ltd., and V.I. Prods., Ltd.
PICTURES: The Dead One, The Sinner and the Slave Girl, Bourbon Street Shadows, Verdict Homicide, Face of Fire, Four for the Morgue, Mission To Hell, The Wanton, Harlow, Girl In Trouble, Threesome, Wild Cargo, Alice in Wonderland, The Models, The Four of Us, Against All Odds, The Giant Spider Invasion, House of 1000 Pleasures, The Rogue, Eyes of Dr. Chaney, Alligator, Crash!, Take All of Me, The Psychic, UFOs Are Real, The Actresses, The Sword and the Sorcerer.
TELEVISION: Wild Cargo (series prod.-dir.); This Strange and Wondrous World (prod.-dir.), Linda Evans: Secrets to Stay Young Forever.

CHASE, CHEVY
Actor. r.n. Cornelius Crane Chase. b. New York, NY, Oct. 8, 1943. e. Bard Coll.; B.A. Studied audio research at CCS Institute. Worked as writer for Mad Magazine 1969. Teamed with Kenny Shapiro and Lane Sarasohn while still in school to collaborate on material for underground TV, which ultimately

became off-off-Broadway show and later movie called Groove Tube. Co-wrote and starred in Saturday Night Live on TV, winning 2 Emmys as continuing single performance by a supporting actor and as writer for show. Wrote Paul Simon Special (Emmy Award, 1977).
PICTURES: The Groove Tube (debut, 1974), Tunnelvision, Foul Play, Caddyshack, Oh Heavenly Dog, Seems Like Old Times, Under the Rainbow, Modern Problems, National Lampoon's Vacation, Deal of the Century, Fletch, National Lampoon's European Vacation, Sesame Street Presents Follow That Bird (cameo), Spies Like Us, Three Amigos!, The Couch Trip (cameo), Funny Farm, Caddyshack II, Fletch Lives, National Lampoon's Christmas Vacation, L.A. Story (cameo), Nothing But Trouble, Memoirs of an Invisible Man, Hero (unbilled), Last Action Hero (cameo), Cops and Robbersons, Man of the House.
TELEVISION: Series: Saturday Night Live, The Chevy Chase Show.

CHASE, STANLEY
Producer. b. Brooklyn, NY, May 3. e. NYU, B.A.; Columbia U, postgraduate. m. actress/artist Dorothy Rice. Began career as assoc. prod. of TV show Star Time; story dept., CBS-TV; then produced plays Off-B'way and on B'way, winner Tony and Obie awards for The Threepenny Opera. Joined ABC-TV as dir. in chg. programming; prod., Universal Pictures & TV; exec. consultant, Metromedia Producers Org.; prod. & exec. Alan Landsburg Productions. Formed Stanley Chase Productions, Inc. in 1975, which heads as pres.
THEATER: B'way Producer: The Potting Shed, The Cave Dwellers, A Moon for the Misbegotten, European Tour: Free and Easy. Off-B'way: The Threepenny Opera.
PICTURES: The Hell with Heroes, Colossus: The Forbin Project, Welcome to Blood City, High-Ballin', Fish Hawk, The Guardian, Mack the Knife.
TELEVISION: Inside Danny Baker (pilot), Al Capp special (prod., writer), Happily Ever After (pilot; prod., writer), Bob Hope Presents the Chrysler Theatre series, Jigsaw (pilot), Fear on Trial (Emmy nom.), Courage of Kavik: The Wolf Dog (exec. prod.), An American Christmas Carol, Grace Kelly.

CHASMAN, DAVID
Executive. b. New York, NY, Sept. 28, 1925. e. Sch. of Industrial Art, 1940-43; Academie De La Grande-Chaumiere, 1949-50. Monroe Greenthal Co., Inc. 1950-53; Grey Advertising Agency, Inc., 1953-60. Freelance consultant to industry 1950-60; worked on pictures for UA, 20th-Fox, Columbia, Samuel Goldwyn, City Film; Adv. mgr. United Artists, 1960; exec. dir. adv., United Artists, 1962; exec. production, United Artists, London, 1964; v.p. in prod. United Artists, 1969; v.p. of west coast operations, U.A. 1970; sr. v.p. in charge of prod., U.A. 1972; president, Convivium Productions Inc., 1974. Joined Columbia 1977, named exec. v.p. worldwide theatrical prod. 1979. Joined MGM 1980; named exec. v.p.-worldwide theatrical prod.
PICTURES: Exec. prod.: Brighton Beach Memoirs, The Secret of My Success.

CHAUDHRI, AMIN QAMAR
Director, Producer, Cinematographer, Editor. b. Punjab, India, April 18, 1942. e. Hampstead Polytechnic, London, City U. of New York. Pres., Filmart Enterprises Ltd. & Filmart Int'l Ltd., Pres./CEO, Continental Film Group Ltd. Pres./CEO, Continental Entertainment Group, Ltd., Heron Int'l Pictures, Ltd.
PICTURES: Director: Kashish, Khajuraho, Eternal, Urvasi, Konarak, The Land of Buddha. Producer: Night Visitors, Diary of a Hit Man. Producer/Director: Once Again, An Unremarkable Life, Tiger Warsaw, The Last Day of School, Gunga Din, Golden Chute, Wings of Grey, Call It Sleep. Cinematography: Right On, Sweet Vengeance, The Hopefuls, The Wicked Die Slow, Who Says I Can't Ride a Rainbow, Black Rodeo, Medium Is the Message, Death of a Dunbar Girl, Kashish, The Last Day of School.
TELEVISION: Reflections of India (prod.-dir.), Wild Wild East (camera), Nehru (edit.), Medium is the Message (photog.), America... Amerika (prod., dir.).

CHAYKIN, MAURY
Actor. b. Brooklyn, NY, July 27, 1949. e. Univ. of Buffalo. Formed theatre co. Swamp Fox; later acted with Buffalo rep. co., Public Theatre in NY. Moved to Toronto in 1980.
PICTURES: The Kidnapping of the President, Death Hunt, Soup for One, Of Unknown Origin, Harry and Son, Highpoint, Mrs. Soffel, Turk 182!, Meatballs III, The Bedroom Window, Wild Thing, Stars and Bars, Caribe, Iron Eagle II, Twins, Millennium, Breaking In, Where the Heart Is, Mr. Destiny, Dances With Wolves, George's Island, My Cousin Vinny, Leaving Normal, The Adjuster, Hero, Sommersby, Money for Nothing, Josh and S.A.M., Beethoven's 2nd, Camilla, Whale Music (Genie Award), Unstrung Heroes, Devil in a Blue Dress, Cutthroat Island.
TELEVISION: Special: Canada's Sweetheart: The Saga of Hal Banks (Nellie Award)

CHELSOM, PETER
Director, Writer. b. Blackpool, England. Studied acting at London's Central School of Drama. Acted with Royal

Shakespeare Co., Royal Natl. Theatre, Royal Court Theatre. Dir. at Central School of Drama, taught acting at Actors Ints. and at Cornell Univ. Wrote and directed short film Treacle for Channel 4/British Screen. Director of many commercials for television in London and U.S.
PICTURES: Hear My Song (dir., story, co-s.p.), Funny Bones (dir., co-prod., co-s.p.).

CHEN, JOAN
Actress. r.n. Chen Chong. b. Shanghai, China, 1961. Studied acting with actress Zhang Rei Fang at Shanghai Film Studio. Debuted as teenager in Chinese films. Moved to U.S. in 1981.
PICTURES: Little Flower, Awakening, Dim Sum: A Little Bit of Heart, Tai-Pain, The Last Emperor, The Blood of Heroes, Turtle Beach, When Sleeping Dogs Lie, Night Stalker, Heaven and Earth, Golden Gate, On Deadly Ground, Temptation of a Monk, The Hunted, Red Rose/White Rose, Judge Dredd, Wild Side, Precious Find.
TELEVISION: Series: Twin Peaks. Movie: Shadow of a Stranger. Guest: Miami Vice.

CHER
Singer, Actress. r.n. Cherilyn Sarkisian. b. El Centro, CA, May 20, 1946. Began singing as backup singer for Crystals and Ronettes then with former husband Sonny Bono in 1965; first hit record I Got You Babe, sold 3 million copies. Made two films and then debuted nightclub musical-comedy act in 1969. CBS comedy-variety series started as summer show in 1971; became regular series the following December. NY stage debut: Come Back to the Five and Dime Jimmy Dean Jimmy Dean (1982).
PICTURES: Wild on the Beach (debut, 1965), Good Times, Chastity, Come Back to the Five and Dime Jimmy Dean Jimmy Dean, Silkwood, Mask, The Witches of Eastwick, Suspect, Moonstruck (Academy Award for Best Actress, 1987), Mermaids, The Player, Ready to Wear (Pret- a-Porter), Faithful.
TELEVISION: Series: Sonny & Cher Comedy Hour (1971-74), Cher, The Sonny and Cher Show (1976-77). Specials: Cher, Cher... Special, Cher and Other Fantasies, Cher: A Celebration at Caesar's Palace, Cher at the Mirage. Movie: If These Walls Could Speak. Guest: Shindig, Hullabaloo, Hollywood Palace, The Man from U.N.C.L.E., Laugh-In, Glen Campbell, Love American Style.

CHERMAK, CY
Producer, Writer. b. Bayonne, NJ, Sept. 20, 1929. e. Brooklyn Coll., Ithaca Coll.
TELEVISION: Writer, prod., exec. prod.: Ironside, The Virginian, The New Doctors, Amy Prentiss, Kolchak: The Night Stalker, Barbary Coast, CHiPS. Movie: Murder at the World Series (prod., s.p.).

CHERNIN, PETER
Executive. Chairman, Fox, Inc. Formerly pres., Fox Broadcasting.

CHERTOK, JACK
Producer. b. Atlanta, GA, July 13, 1906. Began career as script clerk, MGM; later asst. cameraman, asst. dir., head of music dept., short subjects prod. (including Crime Does Not Pay, Robert Benchley, Pete Smith series). Feature prod. MGM 1939-42 (The Penalty, Joe Smith, American, Kid Glove Killer, The Omaha Trail, Eyes in the Night, etc.). In 1942, apptd. Hollywood prod. chief, Co-Ord. Inter-Amer. Affairs, serving concurrently with regular studio work. Left MGM in 1942 and prod. for Warner Bros. to late 1944; Produced The Corn is Green and Northern Pursuit for Warner Bros. Pres. Jack Chertok TV, Inc.
TELEVISION: Prod.: My Favorite Martian, Lone Ranger, Sky King, Cavalcade, Private Secretary, My Living Doll, Western Marshal, The Lawless Years.

CHETWYND, LIONEL
Executive, Writer, Director. b. London, England, 1940. m. actress Gloria Carlin. Emigrated to Canada, 1948. e. Sir George Williams U., Montreal, BA, economics; BCL-McGill U., Montreal. Graduate Work-Law, Trinity Coll. Oxford. Admitted to bar, Province of Quebec, 1968. C.B.C., TV-Public Affairs and Talks, 1961-1965. CTV network 1965-67. Controller commercial TV and film rights, Expo '67. Freelance writer and consultant 1961-68. Asst. mng. dir. Columbia Pictures (U.K.) Ltd. London 1968-72. Asst. mng. dir. Columbia-Warner UK, 1971. Story and book for musical Maybe That's Your Problem, 1971-1973. Then Bleeding Great Orchids (staged London, and Off-B'way). Also wrote The American 1776, official U.S. Bi-centennial film and We the People/200 Constitutional Foundation. Former mem. of NYU grad. film sch. faculty, lecturer on screenwriting at Frederick Douglass Ctr. Harlem. Mem of Canadian Bar Assc. Served on bd. of gov., Commission on Battered Children, and the Little League.
PICTURES: The Apprenticeship of Duddy Kravitz (s.p.; Acad. Award nom.), Morning Comes (dir., s.p.), Two Solitudes (prod., dir., s.p., Grand Award Salonika), Quintet (s.p.), The Hanoi Hilton (dir., s.p.), Redline, (dir., s.p.).

TELEVISION: Johnny We Hardly Knew Ye (prod., s.p.; George Washington Honor Medal, Freedom Fdn.), It Happened One Christmas (s.p.), Goldenrod (prod., s.p.), A Whale for the Killing (s.p.), Miracle on Ice (s.p.; Christopher Award), Escape From Iran: The Canadian Caper (s.p.), Sadat (s.p.); NAACP Image Award), Children in the Crossfire (s.p.), To Heal a Nation (writer, exec. prod.), Evil in Clear River (exec. prod.; Christopher Award), So Proudly We Hail (exec. prod., dir., s.p.), The Godfather Wars (s.p.), Heroes of Desert Storm, Reverse Angle (PBS; exec. prod., writer), Doom's Day Gun, The Bible... Jacob, The Bible... Joseph.

CHINICH, MICHAEL
Producer. b. New York, NY. e. Boston U. Began career as casting agent in N.Y.; moved to L.A. to join MCA-Universal Pictures as executive in casting. Named head of feature film casting; then prod. v.p.
PICTURES: *Casting dir.*: Dog Day Afternoon, Coal Miner's Daughter, Animal House, Melvin and Howard, The Blues Brothers, Mask, Midnight Run, Twins, Ghostbusters II, Kindergarten Cop, Dave, Junior. *Exec. Prod.*: Pretty in Pink, Ferris Bueller's Day Off, Some Kind of Wonderful, Planes Trains and Automobiles (co-exec. prod.), Commandments.

CHOMSKY, MARVIN J.
Director, Producer. b. Bronx, NY, May 23, 1929. e. Syracuse U., B.S.; Stanford U., M.A. Started in theatre business at early age as art dir. with such TV credits as U.S. Steel Hour, Playhouse 90, Studio One, etc. Later worked with Herbert Brodkin who advanced him to assoc. prod. with such TV shows as The Doctors and The Nurses. Brought to Hollywood in 1965 as assoc. prod. for Talent Associates, producing series of TV pilots. Art dir.: The Bubble.
PICTURES: Evel Knievel, Murph the Surf, Mackintosh and T.J., Good Luck Miss Wycoff, Tank.
TELEVISION: *Series*: The Wild Wild West, Gunsmoke, Star Trek, Then Came Bronson. *Movies*: Assault on the Wayne, Mongo's Back in Town, Family Flight, Fireball Forward, Female Artillery, The Magician, The F.B.I. Story: The F.B.I. Vs. Alvin Karpas, Mrs. Sundance, Attack on Terror: The F.B.I. Vs. the Ku Klux Klan, Kate McShane, Brink's: The Great Robbery, Law and Order, A Matter of Wife and Death, Victory at Entebbe, Little Ladies of the Night, Roots (co-dir.), Danger in Paradise, Holocaust (Emmy Award, 1978), Hollow Image, King Crab, Attica (Emmy Award, 1980), Inside the Third Reich (Emmy Award, 1982), My Body My Child, The Nairobi Affair, I Was a Mail Order Bride, Robert Kennedy and His Times, Evita Peron (also prod.), Peter the Great (also prod.; Emmy Award as prod., 1986), The Deliberate Stranger (also prod.), Anastasia: The Mystery of Anna (also prod.), Billionaire Boys Club (also spv. prod.), Angel in Green, I'll Be Home for Christmas (also prod.), Brotherhood of the Rose (also prod.), Telling Secrets, Strauss Dynasty (also prod.), Hurricane Andrew (also prod.), Catherine the Great (also prod.).

CHONG, RAE DAWN
Actress. b. Vancouver, Canada, 1962. Father is director-comedian Tommy Chong. Debut at 12 in The Whiz Kid of Riverton (TV). B'way debut 1991 in Oh Kay!
PICTURES: Stony Island (debut, 1978), Quest for Fire, Beat Street, The Corsican Brothers, Choose Me, Fear City, City Limits, American Flyers, Commando, The Color Purple, Soul Man, The Squeeze, The Principal, Walking After Midnight, Tales From the Darkside, Far Out Man, The Borrower, Amazon, Chaindance, Time Runner, When the Party's Over, In Exile, Boulevard, Boca, Hideaway, The Break.
TELEVISION: *Movies*: The Top of the Hill, Badge of the Assassin, Curiosity Kills, Prison Stories: Women on the Inside, Father & Son: Dangerous Relations.

CHONG, TOMMY
Actor, Writer, Director. b. Edmonton, Alta., Canada, May 24, 1938. Daughter is actress Rae Dawn Chong. Was guitar player with various Canadian rhythm and blues combinations, before teaming with Richard (Cheech) Marin in improvisational group. Has made comedy recordings.
PICTURES: Up in Smoke, Cheech and Chong's Next Movie (also dir., co-s.p.), Cheech and Chong's Nice Dreams (also dir., co-s.p.), Things Are Tough All Over, It Came from Hollywood, Still Smokin', Yellowbeard, The Corsican Brothers (also dir., s.p.), After Hours, Tripwire (cameo), Far Out Man (also dir., s.p.), The Spirit of 76, FernGully (voice), National Lampoon's Senior Trip.
TELEVISION: Trial and Error (co-exec. prod.).

CHOOLUCK, LEON
Producer, Director. b. New York, NY, March 19, 1920. e. City Coll. of New York, 1938. Production, distribution, editing Consolidated Film Industries Ft. Lee 1936-40; staff sgt., Army Pictorial Service as news photographer 1941-45; prod. for Regal Films (Fox) Clover Prods. (Col.), Hugo Haas Prods. and Orbit Pro. (Col), 1957-58; dir. Highway Patrol, 1958. Prod. mgr., Captain Sinbad, prod. sprv. Encyclopedia Britannica Films, in Spain, 1964; prod. supv., U.S. Pictures, Battle of the Bulge; v.p.

Fouad Said Cinemobile Systems, 1969-70; ABC Pictures 1970-71 (Grissom Gang, Kotch). 1983-present, consultant, intl. film services.
PICTURES: Hell on Devil's Island, Plunder Road, Murder by Contract, City of Fear (prod.), The Fearmakers, Day of the Outlaw, Bramble Bush, Rise and Fall of Legs Diamond (assoc. prod.), Studs Lonigan, Three Blondes in His Life (dir.), El Cid, Midas Run (assoc. prod.), Payday; Three the Hard Way, Take a Hard Ride, Apocalypse Now, Loving Couples, Square Dance. Wonders of China for Disney Circlevision Epcot (supv.).
TELEVISION: Prod. supv.: 1/4 hr. Fireside Theatre, Stoney Burke, The Outer Limits (assoc. prod.), I Spy (assoc. prod.), Lock Up (dir.). *Specials*: Strange Homecoming, James Mitchener's Dynasty, Judge Horton and the Scottsboro Boys, Pearl, A Rumor of War, Murder in Texas, Love Boat, Dynasty, Breakdown (Alfred Hitchcock), On Wings of Eagles.

CHOW, RAYMOND
O.B.E. Producer. b. Hong Kong, 1927. e. St. John's U., Shanghai. Worked for Hong Kong Standard; then joined the Hong Kong office of the U.S. Information Service. In 1959 joined Shaw Brothers as head of publicity, became head of production before leaving in 1970 to start Golden Harvest to produce Chinese-language films in Hong Kong. Kung-fu films featuring Bruce Lee put Harvest into int'l market. Started English-language films in 1977, beginning with The Amsterdam Kill and The Boys in Company C. Named Showman of the Year 1984 by NATO. Awarded O.B.E. in 1988.
PICTURES: Armour of God, The Big Boss (and subsequent Bruce Lee films), The Cannonball Run (and Part II), High Road to China, Lassiter, Miracles, Mr. Boo (a.k.a. The Private Eyes; and many subsequent Michael Hui films), Painted Faces, Police Story (and Part II), Project A (and Part II), Rouge, Teenage Mutant Ninja Turtles (and Part II), The Reincarnation of Golden Lotus.

CHRISTIANSEN, ROBERT W.
Producer. b. Porterville, CA. e. Bakersfield Coll. Spent 3 years in Marine Corps. Worked on Hollywood Reporter in circulation and advertising. Joined Cinema Center Films; prod. asst. on Monte Walsh and Hail Hero. Co-produced first feature in 1970, Adam at Six A.M., with Rick Rosenberg, with whom co-produced all credits listed.
PICTURES: Adam at Six A.M., Hide in Plain Sight.
TELEVISION: *Features*: Suddenly Single, The Glass House, Gargoyles, A Brand New Life, The Man Who Could Talk to Kids, The Autobiography of Miss Jane Pittman, I Love You...Goodbye, Queen of the Stardust Ballroom, Born Innocent, A Death in Canaan, Strangers, Robert Kennedy and His Times, Kids Don't Tell, As Summers Die, Gore Vidal's Lincoln, Red Earth, White Earth, The Heist, A House of Secrets and Lies, The Last Hit, Heart of Darkness, Tad, Kingfish: A Story of Huey P. Long, Redwood Curtain.

CHRISTIE, JULIE
Actress. b. Chukua, Assam, India, April 14, 1941. Father had tea plantation in India. e. in Britian, at 16 studied art in France, then attended Central Sch. of Music & Drama in London. 3 yrs. with Frinton-on-Sea Rep., before TV debut in A for Andromeda. Birmingham Rep.; Royal Shakespeare Co.; East European and American tour. NY stage: Uncle Vanya. London stage: Old Times.
PICTURES: Crooks Anonymous (debut, 1962), Fast Lady, Billy Liar, Young Cassidy, Darling (Academy Award & BFA Award, 1965), Dr. Zhivago, Farenheit 451, Far From the Madding Crowd, Petulia, In Search of Gregory, The Go-Between, McCabe and Mrs. Miller, Don't Look Now, Shampoo, Nashville (cameo), Demon Seed, Heaven Can Wait, Memoirs of a Survivor, The Return of the Soldier, Heat and Dust, Golddiggers, Power, Miss Mary, La Memoire tatourée (Secret Obsession), Fools of Fortune, Dragonheart, Hamlet.
TELEVISION: Debut: A is for Andromeda (UK series, 1962), Sins of the Fathers (Italian TV), Separate Tables, Dadah Is Death (Amer. TV debut, 1988), The Railway Station Man.

CHRISTOPHER, DENNIS
Actor. b. Philadelphia, PA, Dec. 2, 1955. e. Temple U. NY stage debut, Yentl the Yeshiva Boy (1974). Other NY theater: Dr. Needle and the Infectious Laughter Epidemic, The Little Foxes, Brothers, Exmass, A Pound on Demand, Advice from a Caterpillar. Regional theater incl. Balm in Gilead, American Buffalo. Appeared in 1991 short The Disco Years.
PICTURES: Blood and Lace, Didn't You Hear?, The Young Graduates, Fellini's Roma, Salome, 3 Women, September 30, 1955, A Wedding, California Dreaming, The Last Word, Breaking Away, Fade to Black, Chariots of Fire, Don't Cry It's Only Thunder, Alien Predator, Flight of the Spruce Goose, Jake Speed, Friends, A Sinful Life, Circuitry Man, Dead Women in Lingerie, Doppelganger, Circuitry Man II: Plughead Rewired.
TELEVISION: *Movies*: The Oregon Trail, Stephen King's IT, False Arrest, Willing to Kill: The Texas Cheerleader Story, Curacao, Deadly Invasion: The Killer Bee Nightmare. *Specials*: Bernice Bobs Her Hair, Jack and the Beanstalk (Faerie Tale

Theatre), Cristabel. *Guest*: Trapper John M.D., Tales of the Unexpected, Stingray, Cagney & Lacey, Moonlighting, Hooperman, The Equalizer, Matlock, Murder She Wrote, Monsters, Civil Wars, Dark Justice, The Watcher, The Cosby Mysteries.

CHRISTOPHER, JORDAN
Actor, Musician. b. Youngstown, OH. Oct. 23, 1941. e. Kent State U. Led rock 'n' roll group, The Wild Ones. B'way debut, Black Comedy, 1967.
PICTURES: Return of the Seven, The Fat Spy, The Tree, Angel Angel Down We Go, Pigeons, Brainstorm, Star 80, That's Life!
TELEVISION: *Series*: Secrets of Midland Heights.

CHUNG, CONNIE
TV News Anchor. r.n. Constance Yu-Hwa Chung. m. anchor Maury Povich. b. Washington, D.C., Aug. 20, 1946. e. U. of Maryland, B.S. Entered field 1969 as copy person, writer then on-camera reporter for WTTG-TV, Washington; 1971, named Washington corr.; CBS News; 1976, anchor KNXT, Los Angeles; 1983, anchor, NBC News at Sunrise; anchor, NBC Saturday Nightly News and news specials; 1989 moved to CBS as anchor, Sunday Night Evening News; anchor and reporter, Saturday Night with Connie Chung (later Face ot Face With Connie Chung). Received Emmy Award for Shot in Hollywood (1987), Interview With Marlon Brando (1989); 2 additional Emmy Awards: 1986, 1990. Became co-anchor with Dan Rather, of CBS Evening News, 1993-95. Prime time series: Eye to Eye With Connie Chung, 1993. Many other awards incl. Peabody, 2 LA Emmy Awards, Golden Mike, Women in Business Award, etc.

CILENTO, DIANE
Actress. b. Queensland, Australia, April 2, 1934. e. Toowoomba. Went to New York and finished schooling and then American Acad. of Dramatic Art. First theatre job at 16; toured U.S. with Barter Co.; returned to London and joined Royal Acad. of Dramatic Art; several small parts and later repertory at Manchester's Library Theatre.
THEATER: *London stage*: Tiger at the Gates (also NY: Theatre World Award), The Third Secret, The Four Seasons, The Bonne Soup, Heartbreak House. NY: The Big Knife, Orpheus, Altona, Castle in Sweden, Naked, Marys, I've Seen You Cut Lemons.
PICTURES: Wings of Danger (Dead on Course; debut, 1952), Moulin Rouge, Meet Mr. Lucifer, All Halloween, The Angel Who Pawned Her Harp, The Passing Stranger, Passage Home, The Woman for Joe, The Admirable Crichton (Paradise Lagoon), The Truth About Women, Jet Storm, Stop Me Before I Kill! (The Full Treatment), I Thank a Fool, The Naked Edge, Tom Jones (Acad. Award nom.), Rattle of a Simple Man, The Third Secret, The Agony and the Ecstacy, Hombre, Negatives, Z.P.G. (Zero Population Growth), Hitler: The Last Ten Days, The Wicker Man, The Tiger Lily, The Boy Who Had Everything, Duet for Four.
TELEVISION: La Belle France (series), Court Martial, Blackmail, Dial M for Murder, Rogues Gallery, Rain, Lysistrata, The Kiss of Blood, For the Term of His Natural Life.

CIMINO, MICHAEL
Writer, Director. b. New York, NY, 1943. e. Yale U. BFA, MFA. Was tv commecial director before becoming screen writer.
PICTURES: Silent Running (co-s.p.), Magnum Force (co-s.p.). Director: Thunderbolt and Lightfoot (also s.p.), The Deer Hunter (also co-wrote story, co-prod.; Academy Awards for Best Picture & Director, 1978.), Heaven's Gate (also s.p.), Year of the Dragon (also co-s.p.), The Sicilian (also co-prod.), Desperate Hours (also co-prod.), The Sunchasers (also co-s.p., co-prod.).

CIPES, ARIANNE ULMER
Executive. b. New York, NY, July 25, 1937. e. Royal Acad. of Dramatic Art, London, U. of London. Daughter of film director Edgar G. Ulmer. Actress, then production and dubbing, Paris; CDC, Rome; Titra, New York; 1975-77, v.p., Best International Films (international film distributor), Los Angeles; 1977 co-founder and sr. v.p./sales & services of Producers Sales Organization, 1981, named exec. v.p., American Film Marketing Assn. 1982, founded AUC Films, consulting and intl. and domestic sales-producers rep.

CIPES, JAY H.
Executive. b. Mt. Vernon, NY, Dec. 14, 1928. e. Cornell U. 1960-66, independent producer-packager-distributor European features for U.S. TV sales; 1967, producer, 20th Century-Fox TV; 1970, producer, Four Star TV; 1971, marketing exec. Technicolor, Inc.; 1973, v.p., marketing, Technicolor, Inc.; 1979 sr. v.p., director worldwide marketing, Technicolor, Inc. Professional Film Division. 1992, indept. consultant to prod. & post-prod. facilities.

CLARK, BOB
Director, Writer, Producer. b. New Orleans, LA, Aug. 5, 1939. e. Hillsdale Coll.
PICTURES: *Director*: The She Man, The Emperor's New Clothes, Children Shouldn't Play with Dead Things (credited as Benjamin Clark), Deathdream (Dead of Night), Deranged (prod.

only), Black Christmas (Silent Night Evil Night), Breaking Point, Murder by Decree, Tribute, Porky's (also s.p., prod.), Porky's II—The Next Day (also s.p., prod.), A Christmas Story (also s.p., prod.), Rhinestone, Turk 182, From the Hip (also co-s.p.), Loose Cannons (also co-s.p.), It Runs in the Family (also co-s.p.).
TELEVISION: *Movies*: The American Clock, Derby. *Series* episode: Amazing Stories (Remote Control Man).

CLARK, CANDY
Actress. b. Norman, OK, June 20. Was successful model in N.Y. before landing role in Fat City, 1972. Off-B'way debut 1981: A Couple of White Chicks Sitting Around Talking; followed by It's Raining on Hope Street. Appeared in short Blind Curve.
PICTURES: Fat City (debut, 1972), American Graffiti (Acad. Award nom.), I Will I Will... For Now, The Man Who Fell To Earth, Citizens Band (Handle With Care), The Big Sleep, When You Comin' Back Red Ryder, More American Graffiti, National Lampoon Goes to the Movies, Q, Blue Thunder, Amityville 3-D, Hambone and Hillie, Cat's Eye, At Close Range, The Blob, Original Intent, Deuce Coupe, Cool as Ice, Buffy the Vampire Slayer, Radioland Murders.
TELEVISION: *Movies*: James Dean, Amateur Night at the Dixie Bar and Grill, Where the Ladies Go, Rodeo Girl, Johnny Belinda, Cocaine and Blue Eyes, The Price She Paid.

CLARK, DANE
Actor. b. New York, NY, Feb. 18, 1915. e. Cornell U., St. John's. In radio series 2 yrs.; on N.Y. stage (Of Mice and Men, Dead End, The Country Girl, Brecht on Brecht, The Number, The Fragile Fox, A Thousand CLowns, Mike Downstairs, etc.). Natl. Co. of Two for the Seesaw.
PICTURES: The Glass Key (debut, 1942), Sunday Punch, Pride of the Yankees, Tennessee Johnson, Action in the North Atlantic, Destination Tokyo, The Very Thought of You, Hollywood Canteen, Pride of the Marines, God Is My Co-Pilot, Her Kind of Man, A Stolen Life, That Way With Women, Deep Valley, Embraceable You, Moonrise, Whiplash, Without Honor, Backfire, Barricade, Never Trust a Gambler, Fort Defiance, Highly Dangerous, Gambler and the Lady, Go Man Go, Blackout, Paid to Kill, Thunder Pass, Port of Hell, Toughest Man Alive, Massacre, The Man is Armed, Outlaw's Son, Blood Song, The Woman Inside, Last Rites.
TELEVISION: *Series*: Wire Service, Bold Venture, Perry Mason (1973-4). *Specials*: No Exit, The Closing Door, The French Atlantic Affair. *Guest*: Twilight Zone, I Spy, Mod Squad, Cannon, Hawaii 5-O, Murder She Wrote, Police Story, Highway to Heaven, The Rookies, many others. *Movies*: The Face of Fear, The Family Rico, Say Goodbye Maggie Cole, The Return of Joe Forrester, Murder on Flight 502, James Dean, Condominium. *Mini-Series*: Once an Eagle, The French Atlantic Affair.

CLARK, DICK
Performer; Chairman, CEO, dick Clark Prods., Inc. b. Mt. Vernon, NY, Nov. 30, 1929. e. Syracuse U. graduated 1951, summer announcer WRUN, Utica 1949, staff announcer WOLF, Syracuse 1950. After grad. 1951, took regular job with WOLF. Rejoined WRUN, Utica, then joined WKTV, Utica. Announcer WFIL Philadelphia 1952. *Author*: Your Happiest Years, 1959; Rock, Roll & Remember, 1976; To Goof or Not to Goof, 1963; Dick Clark's Easygoing Guide to Good Grooming, 1986; The History of American Bandstand, 1986. Formed dick clark productions, 1956, TV and motion picture production with in-person concert division, cable TV programing dept.Host of two weekly synd. radio programs: Countdown American and Rock Roll & Remember. Founder and principal owner of Unistar Communications Group. Took company public in January, 1987 (NASDAQ: DCPI), serves as chmn. & CEO.
PICTURES: *Actor*: Because They're Young (debut, 1960), The Young Doctors, Killers Three. *Producer*: Psychout, The Savage Seven, Remo Williams: The Adventure Begins.
TELEVISION: *Host*: American Bandstand (also exec. prod.; Emmy Award as exec. prod., 1983), The Dick Clark Beechnut Show, Dick Clark's World of Talent, Record Years, Years of Rock. $25,000 Pyramid (3 Emmy Awards as host: 1979, 1985, 1986), $100,000 Pyramid, The Challengers. *Producer*: Where The Action Is, Swinging Country, Happening, Get It Together, Shebang, Record Years, Years of Rock. *Executive Producer*: American Music Awards, Academy of Country Music Awards, Dick Clark's New Year's Rockin' Eve, ACE Awards, Daytime Emmy Awards, Golden Globe Awards, Soap Opera Awards, Superstars and Their Moms, Caught in the Act (pilot). *Series*: TV's Bloopers & Practical Jokes, Puttin' on the Hits, Puttin' on the Kids, Dick Clark's Nitetime, Inside America, In Person From the Palace, Getting in Touch, Live! Dick Clark Presents! *Movies*: Elvis, Man in the Santa Claus Suit, Murder in Texas, Reaching for the Stars, The Demon Murder Case, The Woman Who Willed a Miracle (Emmy Award, 1983), Birth of the Beatles, Copacabana, Promised a Miracle, The Town Bully, Liberace, Backtrack, Death Dreams, Elvis and the Colonel, Secret Sins of the Family. *Specials*: Live Aid—An All-Star Concert for African Relief, Farm Aid III, Super Bloopers & New Practical Jokes, American Bandstand's 33 1/3 Celebration,

America Picks the No. 1 Songs, You Are the Jury, Thanks for Caring, Supermodel of the World, Freedom Festival '89, What About Me I'm Only Three, 1992 USA Music Challenge.

CLARK, DUNCAN C.
Executive. b. July, 1952, Sutton, Surrey, England. Entered industry in 1972. Appointed dir. of publicity and adv., CIC, Jan. 1979, taking up similar post in 1981 for United Artists. On formation of U.I.P. in 1982, appt. dir., pub. and adv., & deputy mng. dir., 1983. 1987 appt. v.p. adv. & pub., Columbia Pictures Intl (NY). In 1987, sr. v.p. intl marketing for Columbia (Burbank); appt. sr. v.p., Columbia Tri-Star Film Distribs., Inc., (NY). Relocated to corp. headquarters in Culver City, 1991. Appointed exec. v.p. Worldwide Marketing, Aug. 1994.

CLARK, GREYDON
Producer, Director, Writer. b. Niles, MI, Feb. 7, 1943. e. Western Michigan U., B.A., theatre arts, 1963. Heads own company, World Amusement Corp., Sherman Oaks, CA.
PICTURES: Writer: Satan's Sadists, Psychic Killer. Dir.-writer: Mothers Fathers and Lovers, Bad Bunch. Prod.-writer-dir.: Satan's Cheerleaders, Hi-Riders, Angel's Brigade, Without Warning, Joysticks (prod., dir. only), Uninvited (dir. only), Skinheads.

CLARK, HILARY J.
Executive. e. U. of Southern California, B.A., 1976. Began industry career 1978 as ad-pub admin. in co-op adv. dept., Buena Vista Dist. Co. Promoted to mgr. of natl. field pub & promo., 1980. Acted as unit publicist on numerous films (Explorers, Sylvester, Swing Shift, Twilight Zone, Crossroads, etc.) before returning to BV 1986 as natl. pub. dir. for Walt Disney Pictures. Became exec. dir. of Natl. Publicity for Disney and Touchstone Pictures, 1988; v.p. Intl. Publicity for Buena Vista Intl., 1990.

CLARK, MATT
Actor, Director. b. Washington, DC, Nov. 25, 1936.
THEATER: NY: A Portrait of the Artist as a Young Man, The Subject Was Roses, The Trial of the Catonsville Nine; Regional: One Flew Over the Cuckoo's Nest, Tonight We Improvise.
PICTURES: Black Like Me (debut, 1964), In the Heat of the Night, Will Penny, The Bridge at Remagen, Macho Callahan, Homer (co-s.p. only), Monte Walsh, The Beguiled, The Grissom Gang, The Cowboys, The Culpepper Cattle Company, The Great Northfield Minnesota Raid, Jeremiah Johnson, The Life and Times of Judge Roy Bean, Emperor of the North Pole, The Laughing Policeman, Pat Garrett and Billy the Kid, White Lightning, The Terminal Man, Hearts of the West, Outlaw Blues, Kid Vengeance, The Driver, Dreamer, Brubaker, An Eye for an Eye, Legend of the Lone Ranger, Ruckus, Some Kind of Hero, Honkytonk Man, Love Letters, The Adventures of Buckaroo Banzai, Country, Tuff Turf, Return to Oz, Let's Get Harry, Da (dir. only), The Horror Show, Back to the Future Part III, Cadence, Class Action, Frozen Assets, Fortunes of War, The Harvest, Candyman: Farewell to the Flesh.
TELEVISION: Series: Dog and Cat, The Jeff Foxworthy Show. Mini-Series: The Winds of War, War and Remembrance. Movies: The Execution of Private Slovik, The Great Ice Rip-Off, Melvin Purvis: G-Man, This is the West That Was, The Kansas City Massacre, Dog and Cat (pilot), Lacy and the Mississippi Queen, The Last Ride of the Dalton Gang, The Children Nobody Wanted, In the Custody of Strangers, Love Mary, Out of the Darkness, The Quick and the Dead, The Gambler III: The Legend Continues, Terror on Highway 91, Blind Witness, Deceptions, Dead Before Dawn, Barbarians at the Gate. Specials: Shadow of Fear, Andrea's Story. Pilots: The Big Easy, Highway Honeys, Traveling Man. Guest: Hardcastle and McCormick, Midnight Caller, Bodies of Evidence. Director: Midnight Caller, My Dissident Mom (Schoolbreak Special).

CLARK, PETULA
Actress, Singer. b. Ewell, Surrey, England, Nov. 15, 1932. On British stage in The Sound of Music, Candida, Someone Like You (also composer, co-writer). B'way debut in Blood Brothers (1993). Starred in own BBC TV series 1967-8. Winner of two Grammy Awards, 1964 (Best Rock and Roll Recording: Downtown), 1965 (Best Contemporary R & R Vocal Performance Female: I Know a Place).
PICTURES: Medal for the General (debut, 1944), Strawberry Roan, Murder in Reverse, I Know Where I'm Going, London Town (My Heart Goes Crazy), Vice Versa, Easy Money, Here Come the Huggets, Vote for Hugget, Don't Ever Leave Me, The Huggets Abroad, The Romantic Age (Naughty Arlette), Dance Hall, White Corridors, Madame Louise, The Card (The Promoter), Made In Heaven, The Gay Dog, The Runaway Bus, The Happiness of Three Women, Track the Man Down, That Woman Opposite (City After Midnight), Six-Five Special, A Couteaux Tires (Daggers Drawn), Questi Pazzi Pazzi Italiani, The Big T.N.T. Show, Finian's Rainbow, Goodbye Mr. Chips, Never Never Land.

CLARK, SUSAN
Actress. r.n. Nora Golding. b. Sarnid, Ontario, Canada, March 8, 1943. Trained at Royal Acad. of Dramatic Art, London and Stella Adler Academy.
PICTURES: Banning (debut, 1967), Coogan's Bluff, Madigan, Tell Them Willie Boy Is Here, Colossus: The Forbin Project, Skullduggery, Skin Game, Valdez Is Coming, Showdown, The Midnight Man, Airport 1975, Night Moves, The Apple Dumpling Gang, The North Avenue Irregulars, Murder by Decree, City on Fire, Promises in the Dark, Double Negative, Nobody's Perfekt, Porky's.
TELEVISION: Series: Webster. Movies: Something for a Lonely Man, The Challengers, The Astronaut, Trapped, Babe (Emmy Award, 1976), McNaughton's Daughter, Amelia Earhart, Jimmy B. and Andre (also co-prod.), The Choice, Maid in America (also co-prod.), Snowbound: The Jim and Jennifer Stolpa Story, Tonya and Nancy: The Inside Story, Butterbox Babies. Specials: Hedda Gabler, Double Solitaire.

CLAYBURGH, JILL
Actress. b. New York, NY, April 30, 1944. m. playwright David Rabe. e. Sarah Lawrence Coll. 1966. Former member of Charles Playhouse, Boston.
THEATER: The Nest (off-B'way), The Rothschilds, Jumpers, Pippin, In the Boom Boom Room, Design For Living.
PICTURES: The Wedding Party (debut, 1969), The Telephone Book, Portnoy's Complaint, The Thief Who Came to Dinner, Terminal Man, Gable and Lombard, Silver Streak, Semi-Tough, An Unmarried Woman (Acad. Award nom.), Luna, Starting Over (Acad. Award nom.), It's My Turn, First Monday in October, I'm Dancing as Fast as I Can, Hannah K, Where Are The Children?, Shy People, Beyond the Ocean, Whispers in the Dark, Rich in Love, Day of Atonement, Naked in New York.
TELEVISION: Series: Search For Tomorrow. Movies: The Snoop Sisters (Female Instinct), Miles To Go, Hustling, The Art of Crime, Griffin and Phoenix, Who Gets the Friends?, Fear Stalk, Unspeakable Acts, Reason for Living: The Jill Ireland Story, Trial: The Price of Passion, Firestorm: 72 Hours in Oakland, Honor Thy Father and Mother: The True Story of the Menedez Murders, For the Love of Nancy, The Face on the Milk Carton. Guest: Medical Center, Rockford Files, Saturday Night Live.

CLEESE, JOHN
Actor, Writer. b. Weston-Super-Mare, England, Oct. 27, 1939. e. Clifton Coll., Cambridge U. Began acting with Cambridge University Footlights revue. With classmate Graham Chapman wrote for British TV. Co-creator of Monty Python's Flying Circus. Co-author (with psychiatrist Robin Skynner): Families and How to Survive Them (1983), Life and How to Survive It (1995).
PICTURES: Interlude (debut, 1968), The Bliss of Mrs. Blossom, The Best House in London, The Rise and Rise of Michael Rimmer (also co-s.p.), The Magic Christian (also co-s.p.), The Statue, And Now for Something Completely Different (also co-s.p.), Monty Python and the Holy Grail (also co-s.p.), The Life of Brian (also co-s.p.), The Great Muppet Caper, Time Bandits, The Secret Policeman's Other Ball, Monty Python Live at the Hollywood Bowl (also co-s.p.), Monty Python's The Meaning of Life (also co-s.p.), Yellowbeard, Privates on Parade, Silverado, Clockwise, A Fish Called Wanda (also co-s.p., exec. prod.), BAFTA Award, Writer's Guild of America nom., Oscar nom.), The Big Picture (cameo), Erik the Viking, An American Tail: Fievel Goes West (voice), Splitting Heirs, Mary Shelley's Frankenstein, The Swan Princess (voice), Rudyard Kipling's The Jungle Book.
TELEVISION: Special: Taming of the Shrew. Series: The Frost Report, At Last the 1948 Show, Monty Python's Flying Circus, Fawlty Towers. Guest: Cheers (Emmy Award, 1987).

CLEMENS, BRIAN
Writer, Producer, Director. b. Croydon, England. Early career in advertising then wrote BBC TV play. Later TV filmed series as writer, script editor and features. Script editor Danger Man; Won Edgar Allen Poe Award for Best TV Thriller of 1962 (Scene of the Crime for U.S. Steel Hour). Various plays for Armchair Theatre; ATV Drama 70; Love Story. Winner two Edgar Allan Poe Awards, Cinema Fantastique award for best s.p.
PICTURES: The Tell-Tale Heart, Station Six-Sahara, The Peking Medallion, And Soon The Darkness, The Major, When The Wind Blows, See No Evil, Dr. Jekyll and Sister Hyde, Golden Voyage of Sinbad, Watcher in the Woods, Stiff, Highlander 2, Justine (France), Bugs (UK).
TELEVISION: Wrote and prod.: The Avengers (2 Emmy noms.), The New Avengers, The Professionals, Escapade (U.S.), Perry Mason, Loose Cannon, Fther Dowling..

CLENNON, DAVID
Actor. b. Waukegan, IL. e. Univ. of Notre Dame, Yale Drama School.
THEATER: NY: Unseen Hand, Forensic and the Navigators, As You Like It, Little Eyolf, Medal of Honor Rag, The Cherry Orchard. Regional: Blood Knot, Loot, Marat/Sade, Beyond Therapy, others.
PICTURES: The Paper Chase, Bound for Glory, The Greatest, Coming Home, Gray Lady Down, Go Tell the Spartans, On the

Yard, Being There, Hide in Plain Sight, Missing, The Escape Artist, The Thing, Ladies and Gentlemen the Fabulous Stains, The Right Stuff, Hannah K., Star 80, Falling in Love, Sweet Dreams, Legal Eagles, He's My Girl, The Couch Trip, Betrayed, Downtown, Man Trouble, Light Sleeper, Matinee, Two Crimes.
TELEVISION: *Series:* Rafferty, Park Place, thirtysomething, Almost Perfect. *Movies:* The Migrants, Crime Club, Helter Skelter, Gideon's Trumpet, Marriage is Alive and Well, Reward, Special Bulletin, Best Kept Secrets, Blood and Orchids, Conspiracy: The Trial of the Chicago 8, Nurses on the Line: The Crash of Flight 7, Black Widow Murders, Original Sins, Tecumseh: The Last Warrior. *Guest:* Alfred Hitchcock Presents, Murder She Wrote, Barney Miller, Dream On (Emmy Award, 1993). *Special:* The Seagull.

CLIFFORD, GRAEME
Director. b. England. Worked as film editor on such films as Don't Look Now, The Rocky Horror Picture Show, The Man Who Fell to Earth, F.I.S.T., The Postman Always Rings Twice, before turning to directing.
PICTURES: Frances, Burke & Wills, Gleaming the Cube, Deception, Past Tense.
TELEVISION: The New Avengers, Barnaby Jones, Faerie Tale Theatre, The Turn of the Screw, Twin Peaks, Crossroads.

CLOONEY, GEORGE
Actor. b. Augusta, KY, 1962. Father is tv newscaster-host Nick Clooney. Aunt is singer Rosemary Clooney. e. Northern KY Univ.
PICTURES: Return of the Killer Tomatoes, Red Surf, Unbecoming Age, From Dusk Till Dawn, Batman and Robin.
TELEVISION: *Series:* E/R, The Facts of Life, Roseanne, Sunset Beat, Baby Talk, Sisters, ER.

CLOONEY, ROSEMARY
Singer, Actress. b. Maysville, KY, May 23, 1928. Was singer with sister Betty on radio and with Tony Pastor's band. Won first place on Arthur Godfrey's Talent Scouts in early 1950's. Had first million selling record in 1951 with Come on-a My House. Son is actor Miguel Ferrer. *Autobiography:* This for Remembrance (1977).
PICTURES: The Stars Are Singing (debut, 1953), Here Come the Girls, Red Garters, White Christmas, Deep in My Heart, Radioland Murders.
TELEVISION: *Series:* Songs for Sale, The Johnny Johnston Show, The Rosemary Clooney Show (1956-57), The Lux Show Starring Rosemary Clooney (1957-58). *Movie:* Sister Margaret and the Saturday Night Ladies. *Guest:* Ed Sullivan, Steve Allen, Perry Como's Kraft Music Hall, Red Skelton, Dick Powell Show, Bing Crosby, Hardcastle and McCormick, ER.

CLOSE, GLENN
Actress. b. Greenwich, CT, Mar. 19, 1947. e. Coll. of William and Mary. Began performing with a repertory group Fingernails, then toured country with folk-singing group Up With People. Professional debut at Phoenix Theatre, New York. Also accomplished musical performer (lyric soprano).
THEATER: *NY:* Love for Love, Rules of the Game, Member of the Wedding, Rex, Uncommon Women and Others, The Crucifer of Blood, Wine Untouched, The Winter Dancers, Barnum, Singular Life of Albert Nobbs (Obie Award), The Real Thing (Tony Award, 1984), Childhood, Joan of Arc at the Stake, Benefactors, Death and the Maiden (Tony Award, 1992), Sunset Boulevard (Tony Award, 1995). *Regional:* King Lear, Uncle Vanya, The Rose Tattoo, A Streetcar Named Desire, Brooklyn Laundry, Sunset Boulevard.
PICTURES: The World According to Garp (debut, 1982), The Big Chill, The Natural, The Stone Boy, Greystoke: The Legend of Tarzan Lord of the Apes (dubbed voice), Jagged Edge, Maxie, Fatal Attraction, Light Years (voice), Dangerous Liaisons, Immediate Family, Reversal of Fortune, Hamlet, Meeting Venus, Hook (cameo), The Paper, The House of the Spirits, Anne Frank Remembered (voice), Mary Reilly, Mars Attacks, 101 Dalmatians.
TELEVISION: *Movies:* Too Far To Go, The Orphan Train, Something About Amelia, Stones for Ibarra, Sarah: Plain and Tall, Skylark (also co-exec. prod.), Serving in Silence: The Margarethe Cammermeyer Story (Emmy Award, 1995; also co-exec. prod.). *Specials:* The Elephant Man, Broken Hearts Broken Homes (host, co-exec. prod.).

COATES, ANNE V.
Film editor, Producer. b. Reigate, Surrey, Eng. e. Bartrum Gables Coll. m. late dir. Douglas Hickox. Worked as nurse at East Grinstead Plastic Surgery Hospital. Recipient of 1995 A.C.E. Career Achievement award.
PICTURES: Pickwick Papers, Grand National Night, Forbidden Cargo, To Paris With Love, The Truth About Women, The Horse's Mouth, Tunes of Glory, Don't Bother to Knock, Lawrence of Arabia (Academy Award, 1962; also ACE nom.), Becket (Acad. Award & ACE noms.), Young Cassidy, Those Magnificent Men in Their Flying Machines (co-ed.), Hotel Paridiso, Great Catherine, The Bofors Guns, The Adventurers, Friends, The Public Eye, The Nelson Affair, 11 Harrowhouse, Murder on the Orient

Express (BAFTA nom.), Man Friday, Aces High, The Eagle Has Landed, The Medusa Touch (prod. & sprv. ed.), The Legacy, The Elephant Man (Acad. Award nom., BAFTA nom.), The Bushido Blade, Ragtime (co-ed.), The Pirates of Penzance, Greystoke: The Legend of Tarzan Lord of the Apes, Lady Jane, Raw Deal, Masters of the Universe, Farewell to the King (co-ed.), Listen to Me, I Love You to Death, What About Bob?, Chaplin, In the Line of Fire (Acad. Award nom., A.C.E. nom., BAFTA nom., G.B.F.E. award), Pontiac Moon, Congo, Striptease.

COBE, SANDY
Executive, Producer, Distributor. b. New York, NY, Nov. 30, 1928. e. Tulane U., B.A., fine arts. U.S. Army WWII & Korea, combat photographer; produced 11 features for Artmark Pictures, N.Y. General Studios, exec. v.p., distribution; First Cinema Releasing Corp., pres. Formed Sandy Cobe Productions, Inc., producer, packager, European features for U.S. theatrical & television. 1974 pres., Intercontinental Releasing Corporation, domestic and foreign distribution of theatrical features; 1989, named chmn. of bd. and CEO. Member, dir. of bd., American Film Marketing Assn., Dir. of bd., Scitech Corp. USA, 14 year mem., Academy of Television Arts and Sciences, 32nd degree Mason, Shriner, Variety Club Int'l. Special commendations from: Mayor of Los Angeles, California State Senate, City and County of L.A., California Assembly and Senate, and Governor of CA.
PICTURES: Terror on Tour (prod.), Access Code (exec. prod.), A.R.C.A.D.E. (prod.), Terminal Entry (exec. prod.), Open House (prod.).

COBE, SHARYON REIS
Executive, Producer. b. Honolulu, HI, e. U. of Hawaii, Loyola Marymount U. Dancer Fitzgerald, & Sample, N.Y. United Air Lines, N.Y.; v.p., story editor, Gotham Publishing N.Y.; v.p., distribution-foreign sales, World Wide Film Distributors, L.A.; pres. and chief operating officer, Intercontinental Releasing Corp., L.A. Member of Variety Clubs Intl., Industry Rltns. Com., Amer. Film Mktg. Assoc., Indpt. Feature Projects West. (tent 25), Women in Film.
PICTURES: Home Sweet Home (prod. mgr.), To All a Good Night (assoc. prod.), Access Code (co-prod.), Terminal Entry (prod.), Open House (exec. in chg. of prod.).

COBLENZ, WALTER
Producer.
PICTURES: The Candidate, All the President's Men, The Onion Field, The Legend of the Lone Ranger, Strange Invaders, Sister Sister, 18 Again!, For Keeps, The Babe.
TELEVISION: *Movie:* Jack Reed: Badge of Honor, House of Secrets, Not Our Son.

COBURN, JAMES
Actor. b. Laurel, NB, Aug. 31, 1928. e. Los Angeles City Coll., where he studied drama. Also studied with Stella Adler in NY for 5 years. Served in U.S. Army. First acting role in coast production of Billy Budd. Later to New York, where he worked on TV commercials, then in live teleplays on Studio One, GE Theatre, Robert Montgomery Presents. Summer stock in Detroit before returning to Hollywood. Commercial: Remington Rand.
PICTURES: Ride Lonesome (debut, 1959), Face of a Fugitive, The Magnificent Seven, Hell Is for Heroes, The Great Escape, Charade, The Americanization of Emily, The Loved One, Major Dundee, A High Wind in Jamaica, Our Man Flint, What Did You Do in the War Daddy?, Dead Heat on a Merry-Go-Round, In Like Flint, Waterhole No. 3, The President's Analyst, Duffy, Candy, Hard Contract, Last of the Mobile Hot-Shots, The Carey Treatment, The Honkers, Duck You Sucker, Pat Garrett and Billy the Kid, The Last of Sheila, Harry in Your Pocket, A Reason to Live—A Reason to Die, The Internecine Project, Bite the Bullet, Hard Times, Sky Riders, The Last Hard Men, Midway, Cross of Iron, California Suite (cameo), The Muppet Movie, Goldengirl, Firepower, The Baltimore Bullet, Loving Couples, Mr. Patman, High Risk, Looker, Martin's Day, Death of a Soldier, Phoenix Fire, Walking After Midnight, Train to Heaven, Young Guns II, Hudson Hawk, The Player, Hugh Hefner: Once Upon a Time (narrator), Deadfall, Sister Act 2: Back in the Habit, Maverick, The Nutty Professor, Eraser.
TELEVISION: *Series:* Klondike, Acapulco, Darkroom (host), Hollywood Stuntmakers (host), Fifth Corner. *Movies:* Draw!, Sins of the Fathers, Malibu, The Dain Curse, Valley of the Dolls, Crash Landing: The Rescue of Flight 232, The Hit List, Greyhounds, The Avenging Angel, Ray Alexander: A Menu for Murder, The Set Up. *Specials:* Pinocchio (Faerie Tale Theater), Mastergate. *Pilot:* Silver Fox.

COCA, IMOGENE
Actress. b. Philadelphia, PA, Nov. 18, 1908. p. the late Joe Coca, orchestra leader, and Sadie Brady, vaudevillian. At 11, debut tap dancer in New York vaudeville; solo dancer B'way musicals; as comedienne, in New Faces of 1934; with former husband, Bob Burton, in Straw Hat Revue in 1939, and others through 1942. New York night clubs, Cafe Society and Le Ruban

Bleu, Palmer House, Chicago; Park Plaza, St. Louis, and at Tamiment resort. Seen on early experimental TV telecasts in 1939.1949 to TV via B'way Revue, co-starring with Sid Caesar. Emmy Award, 1951. Returned to B'way in Musical On the Twentieth Century.
PICTURES: Under the Yum Yum Tree, Promises! Promises!, Rabbit Test, National Lampoon's Vacation, Nothing Lasts Forever, Buy and Cell, Papa Was a Preacher.
TELEVISION: Series: Buzzy Wuzzy (host, 1948), Admiral Broadway Revue (1949), Your Show of Shows (1950-54). Imogene Coca Show (1954-55), Sid Caesar Invites You (1958), Grindl (1963-64), It's About Time (1966-67). Special: Ruggles of Red Gap. Guest: Fireside Theatre, Hollywood Palace, Love American Style, Moonlighting. Movies: Alice in Wonderland, Return of the Beverly Hillbillies.

COCCHI, JOHN
Writer, Critic. b. Brooklyn, NY, June 19, 1939. e. Fort Hamilton H.S., 1957; Brooklyn College, A.A.S., 1961. U.S. Army, 1963-65. Puritan Film Labs, manager, 1967-69. Independent-International Pictures, biographer-researcher, 1969. Boxoffice Magazine, critic, reporter, columnist, 1970-79. Co-author: The American Movies Reference Book (Prentice-Hall). Contributor: Screen Facts, Film Fan Monthly, Films in Review. Actor in: The Diabolical Dr. Ongo, Thick as Thieves, Captain Celluloid vs. the Film Pirates. Worked on dubbing: Dirtymouth, 1970. Author of film books incl. The Westerns: a Movie Quiz Book, Second Feature, Best of the B Films. Now free lance writer, researcher, agent. Recent credits: contributor to books, 500 Best American Films, 500 Best British and Foreign-Language Films. Consultant to Killiam Shows, Prof. Richard Brown, Photofest, Star Magazine; research chief for American Movie Classics channel, 1984-present.

COEN, ETHAN
Producer, Writer. b. St. Louis Park, MN, Sep. 21, 1957. e. Princeton U. Co-wrote s.p. with brother, Joel, XYZ Murders (renamed Crimewave).
PICTURES: Producer/Co-Writer: Blood Simple (also co-edited under pseudonym Roderick James), Raising Arizona, Miller's Crossing, Barton Fink, The Hudsucker Proxy, Fargo (Best director, Cannes 1996).

COEN, GUIDO
Producer, Executive. In 1959 became production exec. Twickenham Studios, 1963 Appt. a dir. there, then producer and executive prod. series pictures for Fortress Films and Kenilworth Films.
PICTURES: One Jump Ahead, Golden Link, The Hornet's Nest, Behind the Headlines, Murder Reported, There's Always a Thursday, Date with Disaster, The End of the Line, The Man Without a Body, Woman Eater, Kill Her Gently, Naked Fury, Operation Cupid, Strictly Confidential, Dangerous Afternoon, Jungle Street, Strongroom, Penthouse, Baby Love, One Brief Summer, Burke and Hare, Au Pair Girls, Intimate Games.

COEN, JOEL
Director, Writer. b. St. Louis Park, MN, Nov. 29, 1954. e. Simon's Rock College, MA; studied film at NYU. m. actress Frances McDormand. Was asst. editor on Fear No Evil and Evil Dead. Co-wrote with brother, Ethan, s.p. for XYZ Murders (renamed Crime Wave.) Cameo role in film Spies Like Us, 1985.
PICTURES: Director/Co-Writer: Blood Simple (also co-editor, under pseudonym Roderick Jaynes), Raising Arizona, Miller's Crossing, Barton Fink (also co-editor, as Roderick Jaynes), The Hudsucker Proxy, Fargo (Best director, Cannes 1996).

COHEN, ELLIS A.
Producer, Writer. b. Baltimore, MD, Sept. 15, 1945. e. Baltimore Jr. Coll., A.A. 1967, Univ. of W. LA, mini-law sch., 1992. 1963, talent coord., Cerebral Palsy Telethon, WBAL-TV, Baltimore; 1964, p.r. asst. Campbell-Ewald Adv. Agency, L.A.; 1966, and retail mgr. 1968-69, talent booking; 1968, journalist & editor 1969-72, pr & adv. Camera Mart, NY; 1972-74 creator & editor-in-chief, TV/New York Magazine,; 1974-76 dir., world-wide pub./adv.; William Morris Agency, Prod., NY Emmy Awards Telecast (1973 & 1974). WOR-TV (prod.), chmn., exec. prod. of TV Academy Celebrity drop-in luncheon series; 1972, talent coordinator Bob Hope's Celebrity Flood Relief Telethon. Exec. prod., 1976 Democratic Nat'l Conv. Gala. 1978, Account Exec., Solters & Roskin P.R., L.A.; 1978 director of TV Network Boxing Events, Don King Prod., NY; 1979 ,Prod., Henry Jaffe Ent., Inc., 1980, prod.-writer, CBS Entertainment & pres. Ellis A. Cohen Prods. Since 1983, pres., Hennessey Ent., Ltd. Novel: Avenue of the Stars, (1990). Non-fiction: Dangerous Evidence (1995). Member, WGA, Producers Guild of America, World Affairs Council, Friars Club, Amer. Newspaper Guild, Intl. Press Corp., Israeli Press Corp., Academy of TV Arts & Sciences, SAG. Comm. Public Interest for NYC; Natl. Writers Union.
TELEVISION: Movies: Aunt Mary (prod., story); First Steps (prod.), Love Mary (prod.). Specials: NY Area Emmy Awards (prod. 1973 and 1974).

COHEN, IRWIN R.
Exhibition Executive. b. Baltimore, MD, Sept. 4, 1924. e. U. of Baltimore, (LLB) 1948, admitted to Maryland and U.S. Bar same year. Active limited practice. R/C Theatres outgrowth of family business started in 1932. One of founders of Key Federal Bank, chairman of board Loan Comm., director and member of exec. comm. Pres. NATO of Virginia 1976-78, chairman 1978-80. Director, member of exec. comm., treasurer, chairman of finance comm. National NATO. Member of Motion Picture Pioneers, Will Rogers Hospital, and various other orgs.

COHEN, LARRY
Director, Producer, Writer. b. New York, NY, July 15, 1946. e. CCNY. Started as writer for TV series incl. Kraft Mystery Theatre, The Defenders, Arrest and Trial. Creator of series Branded, The Invaders, Cool Million, Blue Light, Cop Talk.
PICTURES: Daddy's Gone A-Hunting (co-s.p.), El Condor (s.p.), Bone (Housewife; dir., prod., s.p.), Black Caesar (dir., prod., s.p.), It's Alive (dir., prod., s.p.), Demon (God Told Me To; dir., prod., s.p.), The Private Files of J. Edgar Hoover (dir., prod., s.p.), It Lives Again (dir., prod., s.p.), Success (American Success Company; story), Full Moon High (prod., dir., s.p.), Q (dir., prod., s.p.), I The Jury (s.p.), Perfect Strangers (Blind Alley; dir., prod., s.p.), The Man Who Wasn't There (story), Special Effects (dir., s.p.), Scandalous (story), The Stuff (exec. prod., dir., s.p.), Spies Like Us (actor), It's Alive III: Island of the Alive (exec. prod., dir., s.p.), Return to Salem's Lot (dir., exec. prod., s.p.), Best Seller (s.p.), Deadly Illusion (s.p.), Maniac Cop (prod., s.p.), Wicked Stepmother (dir., exec. prod., s.p.), Maniac Cop II (prod., s.p.), The Ambulance (dir., s.p.), The Apparatus (dir., s.p.), Guilty As Sin (s.p.), Original Gangstas (story), Invasion of Privacy (writer).
TELEVISION: Movies: Cool Million (Mask of Marcella; writer), Man on the Outside (writer), Shootout in a One Dog Town (co-writer, story) Desperado: Avalanche at Devil's Ridge (writer), As Good as Dead (dir., writer, prod.), 87th Precint–Ice (writer). Series: NYPD Blue (writer).

COHEN, PAUL
Executive. b. New York, NY, Apr. 16, 1948. e. Hofstra U.; New School for Social Research; Jungian Inst. NY. Started in industry as exec. prod., distributor, screenwriter, producer for Masada Prods. Served as v.p. of Grand Slam Prods., exec. prod. for Moonbeam Assocs. Head of Analysis Films, 1976-84. Founded Aries Film Releasing, 1989, becoming pres. & CEO.
PICTURES: Caligula, My Brilliant Career, Maniac, Basket Case, The Chosen, Butterfly, The Innocent, Mephisto, The Icicle Thief, My Twentieth Century, Superstar: The Life and Times of Andy Warhol, Overseas, The Story of Boys and Girls, Thank You and Goodnight, Lovers, Bad Lieutenant.

COHEN, ROB
Producer, Director. b. Cornwall-on-the-Hudson, NY, March 12, 1949. e. Harvard U. BA. Formerly exec. v.p. in chg of m.p. and TV for Motown. Started as dir. of m.p. for TV at 20th Century-Fox. Joined Motown at age of 24 to produce films. Headed own production co. 1985, appt. pres., Keith Barish Prods.
PICTURES: Mahogany (prod.), The Bingo Long Traveling All-Stars (prod.), Scott Joplin (prod.), Almost Summer (prod.), Thank God It's Friday (prod.), The Wiz (prod.), A Small Circle of Friends (dir.), Scandalous (dir., co-s.p.), The Razor's Edge (prod.), The Legend of Billie Jean (prod.), Light of Day (co-prod.), The Witches of Eastwick (co-exec. prod.), The Monster Squad (co-exec. prod.), Ironweed (co-exec. prod.), The Running Man (co-exec. prod.), The Serpent and the Rainbow (exec. prod.), Disorganized Crime (prod.), Bird on a Wire (prod.), The Hard Way (prod.), Dragon: The Bruce Lee Story (dir., co-s.p., actor), Dragonheart.
TELEVISION: Miami Vice (dir.), Cuba and Claude (exec. prod.), Vanishing Son (exec. prod.).

COHEN, ROBERT B.
Executive. e. George Washington U., B.A., Southern Texas Sch. of Law. 1980-84. Atty. for Pillsbury Madison's Sutro and for Greenberg, Glusker, Fields, Clamans and Machtinger (L.A.). Was asst. gen. counsel for Columbia Pictures. Joined Paramount 1985 as sr. atty. for M.P. Group. to oversee legal functions for assigned feature films; 1988 named v.p. in charge of legal affairs, Motion Picture Group of Paramount; 1990, named sr. v.p. legal affairs, motion picture group, Paramount.

COHEN, SID
Executive. e. Univ. of RI Col. of Business. Served as western div. mngr. for WB tv distrib. in 1970's. 1979-84, v.p. feature planning & sls. develop. for domestic tv distrib. div. of Paramount Pictures Corp. There he created the first satellite- delivered feature-film package for free over-the-air tv on a regularly scheduled natl. basis. 1985-91, pres. of domestic tv distrib. at King World Prods. Sept. 1991, became pres. of MGM Domestic TV Distrib.

COHN, ROBERT
Producer. b. Avon, NJ, Sept. 6, 1920. e. U. of Michigan, B.A., 1941. p. Jack Cohn. Joined Columbia as asst. dir. In WWII, as

Signal Corps film cutter. Air Corps Training Lab. unit mgr., combat aerial m.p. camera man with 13th A.A.F. Awarded: DFC, Air Medal & 3 clusters, Purple Heart. Assoc. prod. Lone Wolf In London, 1947; prod. Adventures in Silverado, 1948, all Col. Headed Robert Cohn prod. unit at Columbia, pres. International Cinema Guild. Columbia European prod.: exec. Columbia Studios. Hollywood: formed Robert Cohn Prod.
PICTURES: Black Eagle, Rusty Leads the Way, Palomino, Kazan, Killer That Stalked New York, The Barefoot Mailman, Mission Over Korea, The Interns, The New Interns, The Young Americans.

COLBERT, CLAUDETTE
Actress. r.n. Lily Chauchoin. b. Paris, Sept. 13, 1905. e. public schools, Paris, New York; Art Students League, N.Y. On N.Y. stage (debut, Wild Wescotts; followed by Marionette Man, We've Got to Have Money, Cat Came Back, Kiss in a Taxi, Ghost Train, The Barker, Dynamo, etc.). First screen role in For the Love of Mike (silent); voted one of ten top Money Making Stars in Fame Poll, 1935, '36, '47.
PICTURES: The Hole in the Wall (talkie debut, 1929), The Lady Lies, The Big Pond, Young Man of Manhattan, Manslaughter, Honor Among Lovers, The Smiling Lieutenant, Secrets of a Secretary, His Woman, The Wiser Sex, Misleading Lady, The Man From Yesterday, Make Me a Star (cameo), The Phantom President, The Sign of the Cross, Tonight is Ours, I Cover the Waterfront, Three Cornered Moon, The Torch Singer, Four Frightened People, It Happened One Night (Academy Award for Best Actress, 1934), Cleopatra, Imitation of Life, The Gilded Lily, Private Worlds, She Married Her Boss, The Bride Comes Home, Under Two Flags, Maid of Salem, I Met Him in Paris, Tovarich, Bluebeard's Eighth Wife, Zaza, Midnight, It's a Wonderful World, Drums Along the Mohawk, Boom Town, Arise My Love, Skylark, Remember the Day, The Palm Beach Story, No Time for Love, So Proudly We Hail, Practically Yours, Since You Went Away, Guest Wife, Tomorrow Is Forever, Without Reservations, The Secret Heart, The Egg and I, Sleep My Love, Family Honeymoon, Bride for Sale, Three Came Home, The Secret Fury, Thunder on the Hill, Let's Make It Legal, Outpost in Malaya (Planter's Wife), Daughters of Destiny, Si Versailles m'etait Conte, Texas Lady, Parrish.
THEATER: Marriage Go Round, Irregular Verb to Love, The Kingfisher, Aren't We All?
TELEVISION: Movie: The Two Mrs. Grenvilles.
(d. July 30, 1996)

COLBY, RONALD
Producer, Director, Writer. b. New York, NY. e. Hofstra U., NYU. Began career as playwright at Cafe La Mama and Caffe Cino; performed in off-B'way shows; spent year as actor-writer in residence at Pittsburgh Playhouse. Served as dialogue coach and asst. to Francis Coppola; was v.p. of Zoetrope Studios. Directed several documentaries and short films.
PICTURES: The Rain People (prod.), Hammett (prod.), Some Kind of Wonderful (exec. prod.), She's Having a Baby (exec. prod.).
TELEVISION: Margaret Bourke-White (co-prod.)

COLE, GARY
Actor. b. Park Ridge, IL, Sept. 20. e. Illinois State, theater major. Dropped out of coll. after 3 years and moved to Chicago where he tended bar, painted houses and worked with Steppenwolf Theatre group. In 1979 helped to form Remains Theatre, left in 1986 to become ensemble member of Steppenwolf.
PICTURES: Lucas, In the Line of Fire, The Brady Bunch Movie.
TELEVISION: Series: Midnight Caller, American Gothic. Movies: Heart of Steel, Fatal Vision, Vital Signs, Those She Left Behind, The Old Man and the Sea, Son of the Morning Star, The Switch, When Love Kills: The Seduction of John Hearn, A Time to Heal, Fall from Grace. Mini-Series: Echoes in the Darkness.

COLE, GEORGE
Actor. b. London, Eng., Apr. 22, 1925. e. secondary sch. Surrey. Stage debut in White Horse Inn, 1939; m.p. debut in Cottage to Let, 1941.
PICTURES: Henry V, Quartet, My Brother's Keeper, Laughter in Paradise, Scrooge, Lady Godiva Rides Again, Who Goes There (Passionate Sentry), Morning Departure (Operation Disaster), Top Secret (Mr. Potts Goes to Moscow), Happy Family, Will Any Gentleman, Apes of the Rock, The Intruder, Happy Ever After (Tonight's the Night), Our Girl Friday (Adventures of Sadie), Belles of St. Trinian's, Prize of Gold, Where There's a Will, Constant Husband, Quentin Durward, The Weapon, It's a Wonderful Life, Green Man, Bridal Path, Too Many Crooks, Blue Murder at St. Trinians, Don't Panic Chaps, Dr. Syn, One Way Pendulum, Legend of Young Dick Turpin, The Great St. Trinian's Train Robbery, Cleopatra, The Green Shoes, Vampire Lovers, Fright, The Bluebird, Mary Reilly.
TELEVISION: Life of Bliss, A Man of Our Times, Don't Forget To Write, The Good Life, Minder (series), Root Into Europe (series), My Good Friend (series), An Independent Man (series).

COLEMAN, DABNEY
Actor. b. Austin, TX, Jan. 3, 1932. e. VA Military Inst. 1949-51; U. Texas 1951-57; Neighborhood Playhouse School Theater 1958-60.
PICTURES: The Slender Thread (debut, 1965), This Property Is Condemned, The Scalphunters, The Trouble With Girls, Downhill Racer, I Love My Wife, Cinderella Liberty, The Dove, The Towering Inferno, The Other Side of the Mountain, Bite the Bullet, The Black Streetfighter, Midway, Rolling Thunder, Viva Knievel, North Dallas Forty, Nothing Personal, How to Beat the High Cost of Living, Melvin and Howard, Nine to Five, On Golden Pond, Modern Problems, Young Doctors in Love, Tootsie, WarGames, The Muppets Take Manhattan, Cloak and Dagger, The Man with One Red Shoe, Dragnet, Hot to Trot, Where the Heart Is, Short Time, Meet the Applegates, There Goes the Neighborhood, Amos & Andrew, The Beverly Hillbillies, Clifford.
TELEVISION: Movies: Brotherhood of the Bell, Savage, Dying Room Only, The President's Plane is Missing, Bad Ronald, Attack on Terror: The FBI Versus the Ku Klux Klan, Returning Home, Kiss Me Kill Me, Maneaters Are Loose!, More Than Friends, Apple Pie, When She Was Bad, Murrow, Guilty of Innocence, Sworn To Silence (Emmy Award, 1987), Baby M, Maybe Baby, Never Forget, Columbo and the Murder of a Rock Star, Judicial Consent, In the Line of Duty: Kidnapped, Devil's Food. Mini-Series: Fresno. Series: That Girl, Bright Promise, Mary Hartman Mary Hartman, Apple Pie, Forever Fernwood, Buffalo Bill, The Slap Maxwell Story, Drexell's Class, Madman of the People. Special: Plaza Suite, Texan.

COLEMAN, GARY
Actor. b. Zion, IL, Feb. 8, 1968. Gained fame as star of TV's Diff'rent Strokes.
PICTURES: On the Right Track, Jimmy the Kid.
TELEVISION: Series: Diff'rent Strokes. Guest: America 2-Night, Good Times, The Jeffersons, Lucy Moves to NBC, The Big Show, etc. Movies: The Kid from Left Field, Scout's Honor, The Kid With the Broken Halo; The Kid with the 200 I.Q., Fantastic World of D.C. Collins, Playing With Fire.

COLEMAN, NANCY
Actress. b. Everett, WA, Dec. 30, 1912. e. U. of Washington. In radio serials; on NY stage in Susan and God, Liberty Jones, Desperate Hours, 1955; American Theatre Guild Rep. Co. tour of Europe and So. America, 1961.
PICTURES: Dangerously They Live, Kings Row (debut, 1941), The Gay Sisters, Desperate Journey, Edge of Darkness, In Our Time, Devotion, Her Sister's Secret, Violence, Mourning Becomes Electra, That Man from Tangier, Slaves.
TELEVISION: Valiant Lady, Producers Showcase, Kraft Theatre, Philco Playhouse, Robert Montgomery Presents, Lux Theatre, Alcoa Hour, Theatre Guild Playhouse, Play of the Week, Silver Theatre, Adams Chronicles.

COLEMAN, THOMAS J.
Executive. b. Connecticut, Apr. 13, 1950. e. Boston U. Pres., Twalzo Music Corp., 1972-73; v.p., natl. sls. mgr., United Intl. Pictures, 1973-74; founded Atlantic Releasing Corp., 1974; Atlantic Television, Inc., 1981. All Atlantic corps. consolidated into Atlantic Entertainment Group, 1986. Co. has distributed over 100 films and produced 30 features and TV movies. Sold Atlantic, March, 1989. Formed Independent Entertainment Group, named chmn. Feb., 1992 formed Rocket Pictures.
PICTURES: Producer or Exec. Prod.: Valley Girl, Alphabet City, Roadhouse, Night of the Comet, Starchaser, Teen Wolf, Extremities, The Men's Club, Modern Girls, Nutcracker, Teen Wolf Too (exec. prod.), Cop (exec. prod.), Patty Hearst (exec. prod.), 1969 (exec. prod.), Bad Golf Made Easier (exec. prod.), Fluke (exec. prod.), A New York Minute (exec. prod.).

COLER, JOEL H.
Executive. b. Bronx, NY, July 27, 1931. e. Syracuse U., B.A., journalism. Worked as adv. asst. NBC; acct. exec. Grey advertising. Joined 20th Century-Fox 1964 as adv. coordinator Fox Intl.; 1967, named intl. adv./pub. mgr. 1974, named v.p. dir., intl. adv./pub. Nov. 1990, named v.p. publicity/promotions Fox Intl. 1991, v.p. Worldwide Distrib. Services. 1984, memb. L.A. Olympic Org. Com. Left Fox in 1992 to form Joel Coler & Friends intl. mktg. consultants.

COLIN, MARGARET
Actress. b. Brooklyn, NY, 1958. Raised on Long Island. Studied acting at Stella Adler Conservatory, Juilliard, Hofstra U. Left Hofstra to pursue acting career in Manhattan where she was cast in daytime TV series The Edge of Night. NY Theatre incl. work at Ensemble Studio, Geva Theatre and Manhattan Theatre Club (Aristocrats, Sight Unseen).
PICTURES: Pretty in Pink, Something Wild, Like Father Like Son, Three Men and a Baby, True Believer, Martians Go Home, The Butcher's Wife, Amos & Andrew, Terminal Velocity, Independence Day.
TELEVISION: Series: The Edge of Night, As the World Turns, Foley Square, Leg Work, Sibs. Movies: Warm Hearts Cold Feet,

The Return of Sherlock Holmes, The Traveling Man, Good Night Sweet Wife: A Murder in Boston, In the Shadow of Evil. *Guest*: Chicago Hope.

COLLERAN, BILL
Producer, Director. b. Edgerton, WI, Nov. 6, 1922. Story department 20th Century-Fox 1945-46; Director Louis de Rochemont 1946-50; stage mgr. NBC 1951; assoc. dir. The Hit Parade 1952-53; dir. The Hit Parade, various TV specs. 1954-56; dir. Cinerama Windjammer film 1956; tv specs. with Bing Crosby, Frank Sinatra, Debbie Reynolds 1957-60; exec. Prod. Judy Garland Show, Dean Martin Show, 1965-66; dir. Richard Burton's Hamlet film; prod. Popendipity ABC-TV spec. and various other TV specs. and series 1967-77. 1978-83, prod., dir., writer for Hill-Eubanks Group and Little Joey, Inc.; 1984-86, dir. music video for Simba; developing film and TV projects for own production co. 1988, semi-retired.

COLLET, CHRISTOPHER
Actor. b. New York, NY, March 13, 1968. Started acting in commercials as teenager.
THEATER: *NY*: Off-B'way: Coming of Age in SoHo, An Imaginary Life, Unfinished Stories. B'way: Torch Song Trilogy, Spoils of War. Regional: The Lion in Winter, The Old Boy, Pterodactyls.
PICTURES: Sleepaway Camp (debut, 1983), Firstborn, The Manhattan Project, Prayer of the Rollerboys.
TELEVISION: *Movies*: Right to Kill?, Stephen King's The Langoliers. *Specials*: Pigeon Feathers, First Love and Other Sorrows, Welcome Home Jelly Bean. *Guest*: The Equalizer, The Cosby Show.

COLLINS, GARY
Actor. b. Boston, MA, Apr. 30, 1938.
TELEVISION: *Series*: The Wackiest Ship in the Army, The Iron Horse, Sixth Sense, Born Free, Hour Magazine (host), Home. *Movies*: Quarantined, Getting Away from It All, Houston We've Got a Problem, The Night They Took Miss Beautiful, The Kid From Left Field, Jacqueline Susann's Valley of the Dolls, Danielle Steel's Secrets. *Mini-Series*: Roots.
PICTURES: The Pigeon That Took Rome, The Longest Day, Cleopatra, Stranded, Angel in My Pocket, Airport, Killer Fish, Hangar 18.

COLLINS, JOAN
Actress. b. London, Eng., May 23, 1933. e. Francis Holland Sch., London. Sister is writer Jackie Collins. Made stage debut in A Doll's House, Arts Theatre 1946. Author: Past Imperfect (autobiography, 1978), Katy, A Fight For Life, Joan Collins Beauty Book, Prime Time, Love & Desire & Hate, My Secrets, Too Damn Famous. On London, LA and NY stage in Private Lives. Video: Secrets of Fitness and Beauty (also exec. prod.)
PICTURES: I Believe in You (debut, 1951), Lady Godiva Rides Again, Judgment Deferred, Decameron Nights, Cosh Boy, The Square Ring, Turn the Key Softly, Our Girl Friday (Adventures of Sadie), The Good Die Young, Land of the Pharaohs, Virgin Queen, Girl in the Red Velvet Swing, Opposite Sex, Sea Wife, Island in the Sun, Wayward Bus, Stopover Tokyo, The Bravados, Rally Round the Flag Boys, Seven Thieves, Esther and the King, Road to Hong Kong, Warning Shot, Can Hieronymus Merkin Ever Forget Mercy Humppe and Find True Happiness?, If It's Tuesday This Must Be Belgium, Subterfuge, The Executioner, Up in the Cellar, Quest for Love, Inn of the Frightened People, Fear in the Night, Tales from the Crypt, Tales That Witness Madness, Dark Places, Alfie Darling, The Devil Within Her, The Bawdy Adventures of Tom Jones, Empire of the Ants, The Big Sleep, The Stud, Zero to Sixty, The Bitch, Game of Vultures, Sunburn, Homework, Nutcracker, Decadence, In the Bleak Mid-Winter, Decadence, In The Bleak Midwinter.
TELEVISION: *Series*: Dynasty. *Movies*: The Cartier Affair, The Making of a Male Model, Her Life as a Man, Paper Dolls, The Wild Women of Chastity Gulch, Drive Hard Drive Fast, Dynasty: The Reunion. *Specials*: Hansel and Gretel (Faerie Tale Theater), Mama's Back. *Mini-Series*: The Moneychangers, Sins, Monte Carlo (also exec. prod.), Annie.

COLLINS, PAULINE
Actress. b. Exmouth, Devon, Eng., Sept. 3, 1940. m. actor John Alderton (Thomas on Upstairs, Downstairs). e. Central School of Speech and Drama. Stage debut A Gazelle in Park Lane (Windsor, 1962). Best known to US audiences as Sarah in Upstairs, Downstairs.
THEATER: Passion Flower Hotel (London debut, 1965), The Erpingham Camp, The Happy Apple, The Importance of Being Earnest, The Night I Chased the Women with an Eel, Come as You Are, Judies, Engaged, Confusions, Romantic Comedy, Woman in Mind, Shirley Valentine (in London won Olivier Award as best actress, in NY won Tony, Drama Desk and Outer Critics Circle Awards.)
PICTURES: Secrets of a Windmill Girl, Shirley Valentine, City of Joy, My Mother's Courage.

TELEVISION: *Series*: Upstairs Downstairs, Thomas and Sarah, Forever Green, No—Honestly (all with husband), Tales of the Unexpected, Knockback, Tropical Moon Over Dorking.

COLLINS, STEPHEN
Actor. b. Des Moines, IA, Oct. 1, 1947. Appeared off-B'way in several Joseph Papp productions before B'way debut in Moonchildren, followed by No Sex We're British, The Ritz, Loves of Anatol, Censored Scenes from King Kong. Off-B'way: Twelfth Night, The Play's the Thing, Beyond Therapy, One of the Guys, The Old Boy, Putting It Together. Author of play Super Sunday (Williamstown Fest.), and novel Eye Contact (1994).
PICTURES: All the President's Men, Between the Lines, The Promise, Fedora, Star Trek: The Motion Picture, Loving Couples, Brewster's Millions, Jumpin' Jack Flash, Choke Canyon, The Big Picture, Stella, My New Gun.
TELEVISION: *Series*: Tales of the Gold Monkey, Tattinger's (revamped as Nick & Hillary), Working it Out. *Movies*: Brink's: The Great Robbery, The Henderson Monster, Dark Mirror, Threesome, Weekend War, A Woman Scorned: The Betty Broderick Story, The Disappearance of Nora, Barbara Taylor Bradford's Remember, A Family Divided. *Mini-Series*: The Rhinemann Exchange, Hold the Dream, Inside the Third Reich, Chiefs, The Two Mrs. Grenvilles, A Woman Named Jackie, Scarlett.

COLT, MARSHALL
Actor, Writer. b. New Orleans, LA, Oct. 26. e. Tulane U., B.S. Physics; Pepperdine U., M.A. Clinical Psychology; Fielding Inst., PhD. candidate student, Clinical Psychology. Combat tour in Southeast Asia during Vietnam War. Captain, U.S. Naval Reserve. Stage productions: (Hotel Universe, Who's Afraid of Virginia Woolf?, Zoo Story, Killer's Head, etc.).
PICTURES: Bimbo (short), North Dallas Forty, Those Lips, Those Eyes, Jagged Edge, Flowers in the Attic, Illegally Yours, Deceptions.
TELEVISION: *Guest*: Family, Paper Chase, Streets of San Francisco, Barnaby Jones, Murder She Wrote. *Series*: McClain's Law, Lottery! *Movies*: Colorado C-1, Sharon: Portrait of a Mistress, Once an Eagle, To Heal a Nation, Mercy or Murder, Guilty of Innocence.

COLTRANE, ROBBIE
Actor. b. Glasgow, Scotland, 1950. Ent. ind. 1977.
THEATER: San Quentin theatre workshop, Oxford Theatre Group, Citizens Theatre, Traverse Theatre, Borderline Theatre, Hampstead Theatre, Bush Theatre; one man shows: Your Obedient Servant,Mistero Buffo.
PICTURES: Bad Business (dir.); Flash Gordon, Death Watch, Subway Riders, Britannia Hospital, Scrubbers, Ghost Dance, Krull, National Lampoon's European Vacation, Caravaggio, Defence of the Realm, Chinese Boxes, The Supergrass, Mona Lisa, Eat the Rich, Bert Rigby You're a Fool, Wonderland (The Fruit Machine), Let It Ride, Henry V, Slipstream, Nuns on the Run, Perfectly Normal, The Pope Must Die, Triple Bogey on a Par 5 Hole, Oh What a Night, The Adventures of Huck Finn, Goldeneye.
TELEVISION: 1981 Take Two, Seven Deadly Sins, Keep It in the Family, Kick Up The Eighties, The Green Door, The Sheep Stealer, House With Green Shutters, The Lost Tribe, Alfresco, Laugh? I Nearly Paid My Licence Fee, Comic Strip Presents Five Go Mad in Dorset, Beat Generation, Susie, Gino, The Bullshitters, Miner's Strike, Tutti Frutti, Danny the Champion of the World (theatrical release in Europe), Jealousy (also dir., co-writer), Space Sluts From Planet Sex, French and Aunders, The Lenny Henry Show, Robbie Coltrane Special, Mistero Buffo (series), Alive & Kicking, The Secret Ingredients, The Bogie Man, Rednose of Courage, A Tour of the Western Isles, Coltrane in a Cadillac (also co-writer), Cracker (BAFTA & Cable ACE Awards).

COLUMBUS, CHRIS
Director, Writer: b. Spangler, PA, 1959. Grew up in Ohio. Started making short super 8 films in high school, studied screenwriting at New York U. Film Sch., graduated 1980. Sold first s.p., Jocks, while at college. Wrote for and developed TV cartoon series, Galaxy High School.
PICTURES: *Writer*: Reckless, Gremlins, The Goonies, Young Sherlock Holmes, Little Nemo: Adventures in Slumberland (co-s.p.). *Director*: Adventures in Babysitting (debut, 1987), Heartbreak Hotel (also s.p.), Home Alone, Only the Lonely (also s.p.), Home Alone 2: Lost in New York, Mrs. Doubtfire, Nine Months (also co-prod.).
TELEVISION: Amazing Stories, Twilight Zone, Alfred Hitchcock Presents.

COMDEN, BETTY
Writer. b. Brooklyn, NY, May 3, 1919. e. Erasmus Hall, NYU sch. of ed., B.S. Nightclub performer and writer with The Revuers, 1939-44. NY City Mayor's Award Art and Culture, 1978. Named to Songwriters Hall of Fame, 1980. NYU Alumnae Assn.'s Woman of Achievement award, 1987. Kennedy Center Honors for Life Achievement, 1991.

THEATER: With Adolph Green: writer book, sketches & lyrics for B'way shows: On the Town (book, lyrics, actress, 1944), Billion Dollar Baby (bk., Lyrics), Bonanza Bound! (bk., lyrics), Two on the Aisle (sketches and lyrics), Wonderful Town (lyrics; Tony Award, 1953), Peter Pan (lyrics), Bells Are Ringing (bk., lyrics), Say Darling (lyrics), A Party With Comden and Green (bk., lyrics, star; 1959 and 1977); Do Re Mi (lyrics), Subways Are For Sleeping (bk., lyrics), Fade Out-Fade In (bk., lyrics), Leonard Bernstein's Theatre Songs, Hallelujah, Baby (lyric; Tony Award, 1968), Applause (book; Tony Award, 1970), Lorelei (revision to book), By Bernstein (book and some lyrics), On the Twentieth Century (2 Tony Awards, book and lyrics, 1978); A Doll's Life (bk., lyrics), The Will Rogers Follies (Tony Award, 1991). Actress only: Isn't It Romantic.
PICTURES: *Writer with Adolph Green*: Good News, Take Me Out to the Ballgame (lyricst), On the Town, Barkleys of Broadway, Singin' in the Rain (also lyrics), The Band Wagon (also lyrics), It's Always Fair Weather (also lyrics), Auntie Mame, Bells Are Ringing (also lyrics), What a Way to Go, The Addams Family (lyrics). Actress only: Greenwich Village, Garbo Talks, Slaves of New York.

COMO, PERRY
Singer. r.n. Pierino Como. b. Canonsburg, PA, May 18, 1912. e. Canonsburg local schools; joined Carlone Band, then Ted Weems Orchestra, 1936-42; played many night clubs; records for RCA Victor. Voted Best Male vocalist M.P. Daily, TV poll, 1952-56; radio poll, 1954. Best TV performer M.P.D. Fame poll 1957. Recipient of Emmy Awards: Best Male Singer (1954, 1955), Best Emcee (1955), Best Male Personality (1956), Best Actor in a Musical or Variety Show (1956).
PICTURES: Something for the Boys (debut, 1944), Doll Face, If I'm Lucky, Words and Music.
TELEVISION: *Series*: The Chesterfield Supper Club, The Perry Como Show (1950-61), The Kraft Music Hall (1961-63); numerous annual holiday specials.

COMPTON, JOYCE
Actress. b. Lexington, KY, Jan. 27, 1907. e. Tulsa U. r.n. Olivia Joyce Compton. Screen debut in Ankles Preferred.
PICTURES: The Awful Truth, Spring Madness, Sky Murder, Turnabout, A Southern Yankee, If I Had a Million, Christmas in Connecticut, Artists and Models Abroad, Rustlers of Red Dog, The White Parade, Wild Party, Three Sisters, Sorry Wrong Number, Mighty Joe Young, Grand Canyon, Jet Pilot, The Persuader, Girl in the Woods, many others.

CONAWAY, JEFF
Actor. b. New York, NY, Oct. 5, 1950. Started in show business at the age of 10 when he appeared in M'way production, All the Way Home. Later toured in Critics Choice before turning to fashion modeling. Toured with musical group, 3 1/2, as lead singer and guitarist. Entered theatre arts program at NYU. Film debut at 19 in Jennifer on My Mind.
THEATER: Grease, The News.
PICTURES: Jennifer on My Mind (debut, 1971), The Eagle Has Landed, Pete's Dragon, I Never Promised You a Rose Garden, Grease, The Patriot, Elvira: Mistress of the Dark, Cover Girl, Tale of Two Sisters, The Sleeping Car, A Time to Die, Total Exposure, Almost Pregnant, In a Moment of Passion, Alien Intruder.
TELEVISION: *Series*: Taxi, Wizards and Warriors, Berrenger's, The Bold and the Beautiful. *Guest*: From Sea to Shining Sea (1974), Joe Forrester, The Mary Tyler Moore Show, Happy Days, Movin' On, Barnaby Jones, Kojak, Mickey Spillane's Mike Hammer. *Movies*: Having Babies, Delta County, U.S.A., Breaking Up Is Hard to Do, For the Love of It, Nashville Grab, The Making of a Male Model, Bay Coven, The Dirty Dozen: The Fatal Mission, Ghost Writer, Eye of the Storm.

CONDON, CHRIS J.
Producer, Director, Motion Equipment Designer. b. Chicago, IL, Dec. 7, 1922. e. Davidson Inst., U. of Southern California. U.S. Air Force 1943-46. Founded Century Precision Optics, 1948. Designed Athenar telephoto lenses, Century Super wide-angle lenses and Duplikins. Co-founded StereoVision International, Inc. 1969 specializing in films produced in new 3-D process. Member SMPTE. Lecturer and consultant on motion picture optics and 3-D motion picture technology.
PICTURES: The Wild Ride, The Surfer, Girls, Airline, The New Dimensions.

CONN, ROBERT A.
Executive. b. Philadelphia, PA, Jan. 16, 1926. e. Lehigh U. 1944; U. of Pennsylvania, 1948. 1st Lt. Days of Eden Army Security Agency, 1944-46, 1951-52; band & act. dept., MCA, 1952-53; dir. of adv. & prom. Official Films NY 1954; head of Official Films Philadelphia sales office serving PA, Baltimore, Washington, Cleveland and Detroit, 1956. Eastern Reg. Sls. Mgr. Flamingo Films, 1957; acct. exec. Dunnan and Jeffrey, Inc., 1961; v.p., Dunnan and Jeffrey, 1962; pres., adv. mgr., Suburban Knitwear Co., 1963; exec. v.p. Rogal Travel Service, 1964-68. 1968-78, pres. RAC Travel, Inc., Jenkintown, PA. and

pres. Royal Palm Travel, Inc. Palm Beach, Florida, 1978; Rosenbluth Travel Service, 1979; v.p., natl. retail mktg., E.F. Hutton & Co. (N.Y.), 1983.

CONNELLY, JENNIFER
Actress. b. New York, NY, Dec. 1970. e. Yale, Stamford U.
PICTURES: Once Upon a Time in America (debut, 1983), Creepers, Labyrinth, Seven Minutes in Heaven, Etoile, Some Girls, The Hot Spot, Career Opportunities, The Rocketeer, Of Love and Shadows (De Amor y de Sombra), Higher Education, Mulholland Drive.
TELEVISION: *Movie:* The Heart of Justice.

CONNERY, SEAN
Actor. b. Edinburgh, Scotland, Aug. 25, 1930. r.n. Thomas Connery. Worked as a lifeguard and a model before landing role in chorus of London prod. of South Pacific, 1953. Prod. dir., The Bowler and the Bonnet (film doc.), I've Seen You Cut Lemons (London stage). Director of Tantallon Films Ltd. (First production: Something Like the Truth). Recipient of Golden Globe Cecil B. Demille Award, 1996.
PICTURES: No Road Back (debut, 1957), Time Lock, Hell Drivers, Action of the Tiger, Another Time Another Place, Darby O'Gill and the Little People, Tarzan's Greatest Adventure, Frightened City, On the Fiddle (Operation Snafu), The Longest Day, Dr. No, From Russia With Love, Marnie, Woman of Straw, Goldfinger, The Hill, Thunderball, A Fine Madness, You Only Live Twice, Shalako, The Molly Maguires, The Red Tent, The Anderson Tapes, Diamonds Are Forever, The Offence, Zardoz, Murder on the Orient Express, The Terrorists, The Wind and the Lion, The Man Who Would Be King, Robin and Marian, The Next Man, A Bridge Too Far, The Great Train Robbery, Meteor, Cuba, Outland, Time Bandits, Wrong Is Right, Five Days One Summer, Sword of the Valiant, Never Say Never Again, Highlander, The Name of the Rose, The Untouchables (Academy Award, best supporting actor, 1987), The Presidio, Memories of Me (cameo), Indiana Jones and the Last Crusade, Family Business, The Hunt for Red October, The Russia House, Robin Hood: Prince of Thieves (cameo), Highlander 2: The Quickening, Medicine Man (also exec. prod.), Rising Sun (also exec. prod.), A Good Man in Africa, Just Cause (also exec. prod.), First Knight, Dragonheart (voice), The Rock.
TELEVISION: Requiem for a Heavyweight, Anna Christie, Boy with the Meataxe, Women in Love, The Crucible, Riders to the Sea, Colombe, Adventure Story, Anna Karenina, Macbeth (Canadian TV).

CONNICK, HARRY, JR.
Musician, Actor. b. New Orleans, LA, Sept. 11, 1967. Began performing with Bourbon Street jazz combos at age 6. Studied classical piano. Albums: Harry Connick, Twenty, When Harry Met Sally..., Lofty's Roach Souffle, We are in Love (Grammy Award, 1991), Blue Light Red Light, Twenty Five, Eleven, When My Heart Finds Christmas, She. Acting debut in Memphis Belle (1990). B'way debut 1990 in An Evening with Harry Connick Jr.
PICTURES: When Harry Met Sally... (special musical performances and arrangements), Memphis Belle (actor), The Godfather Part III (performed theme song), Little Man Tate (actor), Sleepless in Seattle (performed song), Copycat (actor), Independence Day (actor).
TELEVISION: *Specials*: Swinging Out With Harry, The Harry Connick Jr. Christmas Special, Swinging Out Live, The New York Big Band Concert. *Guest*: Cheers.

CONNORS, MIKE
Actor. r.n. Krekor Ohanian. b. Fresno, CA, Aug. 15, 1925. e. UCLA. Film debut in Sudden Fear (1952) as Touch Connors.
PICTURES: Sudden Fear (debut, 1952), Sky Commando, 49th Man, Island in the Sky, Day of Triumph, Five Guns West, The Twinkle in God's Eye, Oklahoma Woman, Swamp Woman, The Day the World Ended, The Ten Commandments, Flesh and Spur, Shake Rattle and Rock, Voodoo Woman, Live Fast Die Young, Suicide Battalion, Panic Button, Seed of Violence, Good Neighbor Sam, Where Love Has Gone, Harlow, Situation Hopeless–But Not Serious, Stagecoach, Kiss the Girls and Make Them Die, Avalanche Express, Nightkill, Too Scared to Scream, Fist Fighter, Friend to Friend.
TELEVISION: *Series*: Tightrope, Mannix (Golden Globe Award), Today's FBI, Crimes of the Century (host). *Movies*: High Midnight, Beg Borrow or Steal, The Killer Who Wouldn't Die, Revenge for a Rape, Long Journey Back, The Death of Ocean View Park, Casino, Hart to Hart Returns. *Mini-Series*: War and Remembrance.

CONRAD, ROBERT
Actor, Director. r.n. Conrad Robert Falk. b. Chicago, IL, March 1, 1935. e. public schools, Northwestern U. Prof. debut, nightclub singer. Formed Robert Conrad Productions, 1966 (later A Shane Productions, then Black Sheep Productions).
PICTURES: Thundering Jets (debut, 1958), Palm Springs Weekend, Young Dillinger, The Bandits (also dir.), Murph the Surf (Live a Little Steal a Lot), The Lady in Red, Wrong Is Right, Moving Violations, Uncommon Courage, Jingle All Way.

TELEVISION: *Series*: Hawaiian Eye, Wild Wild West, The D.A., Assignment Vienna, Baa Baa Black Sheep, The Duke, A Man Called Sloane, High Mountain Rangers, Jesse Hawkes, Search and Rescue. *Guest*: Lawman, Maverick, 77 Sunset Strip. *Mini-Series*: Centennial. *Movies*: Weekend of Terror, The D.A.: Conspiracy to Kill, Five Desperate Women, Adventures of Nick Carter, The Last Day, Smash-Up on Interstate 5, Wild Wild West Revisited, Breaking Up Is Hard To Do, More Wild Wild West, Coach of the Year, Will: G. Gordon Liddy, Confessions of a Married Man, Hard Knox, Two Fathers' Justice, Assassin, Charley Hannah, The Fifth Missile, One Police Plaza, High Mountain Rangers (also dir., co-story), Glory Days (also dir.), Anything to Survive, Mario and the Mob, Sworn to Vengeance, Two Fathers: Justice for the Innocent, Search and Rescue.

CONSTANTINE, MICHAEL
Actor. b. Reading, PA, May 22, 1927.
PICTURES: The Hustler, Hawaii, Skidoo, Justine, If It's Tuesday This Must Be Belgium, Peeper, Voyage of the Damned, The North Avenue Irregulars, Pray for Death, In the Mood, Prancer, My Life, The Juror, Thinner.
TELEVISION: *Series*: Hey Landlord, Room 222 (Emmy Award, 1970), Sirota's Court. *Mini-Series*: 79 Park Avenue, Roots: The Next Generations. *Movies*: Suddenly Single, Deadly Harvest, Say Goodbye Maggie Cole, The Bait, Death Cruise, The Night That Panicked America, Conspiracy of Terror, Wanted: The Sundance Woman, The Pirate, Crisis in Mid-Air, The Love Tapes.

CONTE, JOHN
Actor, Singer. b. Palmer, MA, Sept. 15, 1915. e. Lincoln H.S., Los Angeles. Actor, Pasadena Playhouse; radio anncr., m.c.; Armed Forces, WWII. Pres. KMIR-TV, Channel 36, Desert Empire Television Corp., Palm Springs, NBC Affiliate.
THEATER: On B'way in Windy City, Allegro, Carousel, Arms and the Girl.
PICTURES: Thousands Cheer, Lost in a Harem, Trauma, Man With the Golden Arm, The Carpetbaggers.
TELEVISION: *Series*: Van Camp's Little Show (1950-52), Mantovani. *Specials*: Max Liebman Spectaculars and dramatic shows, host and star of NBC Matinee Theatre, TV Hour of Stars.

CONTI, BILL
Composer. b. Providence, RI, April 13, 1942. Studied piano at age 7, forming first band at age 15. e. Louisiana State U., Juilliard School of Music. Moved to Italy with jazz trio where scored first film, Candidate for a Killing. Was: music supvr. on Blume in Love for Paul Mazursky.
PICTURES: Harry and Tonto, Next Stop Greenwich Village, Rocky, Handle With Care, Slow Dancing in the Big City, An Unmarried Woman, F.I.S.T., The Big Fix, Paradise Alley, Uncle Joe Shannon, Rocky II, A Man a Woman and A Bank, Goldengirl, The Seduction of Joe Tynan, The Formula, Gloria, Private Benjamin, Carbon Copy, Victory, For Your Eyes Only, I The Jury, Rocky III, Neighbors, Split Image, Bad Boys, That Championship Season, Unfaithfully Yours, The Right Stuff (Academy Award, 1983), Mass Appeal, The Karate Kid, The Bear, Big Trouble, Gotcha, Beer, Nomads, F/X, The Karate Kid II, A Prayer for the Dying, Masters of the Universe, Baby Boom, Broadcast News, For Keeps, A Night in the Life of Jimmy Reardon, Betrayed, Cohen and Tate, Big Blue, Lean On Me, The Karate Kid Part III, Lock Up, The Fourth War, Backstreet Dreams, Rocky V, Necessary Roughness, Year of the Gun, A Captive in the Land, The Adventures of Huck Finn, Bound By Honor, By the Sword, Rookie of the Year, 8 Seconds, Bushwhacked, Spy Hard.
TELEVISION: Kill Me If You Can, Stark, North and South, The Pirate, Smashup on Interstate 5, Papa & Me, Napoleon and Josephine, Murderers Among Us: The Simon Wiesenthal Story. *Series themes*: Cagney and Lacy, Dynasty, Falcon Crest, The Colbys, Kenya, Heartbeat, Lifestyles of the Rich and Famous, Emerald Point N.A.S., Dolphin Cove, The Elite, Instant Recall, Inside Edition.

CONTI, TOM
Actor. b. Paisley, Scotland, Nov. 22, 1941. Trained at Royal Scottish Academy of Music, Glasgow. Did repertory work in Scotland before London stage debut appearing with Paul Scofield in Savages, 1973.
THEATER: *London*: Devil's Disciple, Whose Life Is It Anyway?, They're Playing Our Song, Romantic Comedy, Two Into One, Italian Straw Hat, Jeffrey Bernard is Unwell. *Director*: Before the Party, The Housekeeper. NY: Whose Life Is It Anyway? (Tony Award, 1979), Last Licks (dir.), Present Laughter (dir.), Chapter Two.
PICTURES: Galileo (debut, 1975), Eclipse, The Duellists, The Haunting of Julia (Full Circle), Merry Christmas Mr. Lawrence, Reuben Reuben (Acad. Award nom.), American Dreamer, Miracles, Saving Grace, Beyond Therapy, The Gospel According to Vic, That Summer of White Roses, Shirley Valentine, Someone Else's America.
TELEVISION: Mother of Men (1959), The Glittering Prizes, Madame Bovery, Treats, The Norman Conquests, The Wall, Nazi

Hunter, The Quick and the Dead, Roman Holiday, The Dumb Waiter, Faerie Tale Theater (The Princess and the Pea), Fatal Judgement, Blade on the Feather, Voices Within: The Lives of Truddi Chase, The Wright Verdicts (series).

CONVERSE, FRANK
Actor. b. St. Louis, MO, May 22, 1938. e. Carnegie-Mellon. Early training on stage in New York. Active in repertory theatres. Two seasons with Amer. Shakespeare Fest.
THEATER: The Seagull, Death of a Salesman, Night of the Iguana, A Man for All Seasons, The House of Blue Leaves, First One Asleep Whistle, Arturo Ui, The Philadelphia Story (1980 revival), Brothers, A Streetcar Named Desire (1988 revival), Design for Living, The Crucible, Hobson's Choice, The Ride Down Mount Morgan, etc.
PICTURES: Hurry Sundown, Hour of the Gun, The Rowdyman, The Pilot, The Bushido Blade, Spring Fever, Everybody Wins, Primary Motive.
TELEVISION: *Movies*: Dr. Cook's Garden, A Tattered Web, In Tandem, Killer on Board, Cruise Into Terror, Sgt. Matlovich Vs. the U.S. Air Force, Marilyn: The Untold Story, The Miracle of Kathy Miller, Anne of Green Gables—The Sequel, Alone in the Neon Jungle. *Guest*: Mod Squad, Medical Center, Wonderworks, Guests of the Nation. *Series*: Coronet Blue, N.Y.P.D., Movin' On, The Family Tree, Dolphin Cove, One Life to Live.

CONWAY, GARY
Actor. r.n. Gareth Carmody. b. Boston, MA, Feb. 4, 1936. e. U. of California at L.A. As college senior was chosen for title role in Teen-Age Frankenstein. After graduating served in military at Ford Ord, CA. In 1960 began contract with Warner Bros., appearing in films and TV. Has also appeared on stage. Has given several one-man shows as painter and is represented in public and private collections.
PICTURES: I Was a Teenage Frankenstein, Young Guns of Texas, Once Is Not Enough, The Farmer (also prod.), American Ninja (also s.p.), Over The Top, American Ninja III: Blood Hunt (s.p.).
TELEVISION: *Series*: Burke's Law, Land of the Giants. *Movie*: The Judge and Jake Wyler. *Guest*: 77 Sunset Strip, Columbo, Police Story, Love Boat.

CONWAY, KEVIN
Actor. b. New York, NY, May 29, 1942.
THEATER: *Actor*: One Flew Over the Cuckoo's Nest, When You Comin' Back Red Ryder? (Obie & Drama Desk Awards), Of Mice and Men, Moonchildren, Life Class, Saved, The Elephant Man, Other Places, King John (NYSF), Other People's Money (Outer Critics Circle Award; also L.A. prod.), The Man Who Fell in Love with His Wife, Ten Below, On the Waterfront. *Director*: Mecca, Short Eyes (revival), One Act Play Fest (Lincoln Center), The Milk Train Doesn't Stop Here Anymore (revival), The Elephant Man (tour), Other People's Money (Chicago, L.A. & S.F.).
PICTURES: Believe in Me, Portnoy's Complaint, Slaughterhouse Five, Shamus, F.I.S.T., Paradise Alley, The Fun House, Flashpoint, Homeboy, The Sun and the Moon (dir., prod.), Funny Farm, One Good Cop, Rambling Rose, Jennifer Eight, Gettysburg, The Quick and the Dead, Lawnmower Man II.
TELEVISION: *Series*: All My Children. *Movies*: Johnny We Hardly Knew Ye, The Deadliest Season, Rage of Angels, The Lathe of Heaven, Attack on Fear, Something About Amelia, Jesse, When Will I Be Loved?, Breaking the Silence, The Whipping Boy. *Specials*: The Scarlet Letter, The Elephant Man. *Mini-Series*: Streets of Laredo.

CONWAY, TIM
Actor. b. Willoughby, OH, Dec. 15, 1933. e. Bowling Green State U. After 2 yrs. Army service joined KYW-TV in Cleveland as writer-director and occasional performer. Comedienne Rose Marie discovered him and arranged audition for the Steve Allen Show on which he became regular. In 1962 signed for McHale's Navy, series. Also has done night club appearances.
PICTURES: McHale's Navy (debut, 1964), McHale's Navy Joins the Air Force, The World's Greatest Athlete, The Apple Dumpling Gang, Gus, The Shaggy D.A., Billion Dollar Hobo, The Apple Dumpling Gang Rides Again, The Prize Fighter, The Private Eyes (also co-s.p.), Cannonball Run II, The Longshot, Dear God.
TELEVISION: *Series*: The Steve Allen Show, McHale's Navy, Rango, The Tim Conway Show (1970), The Tim Conway Comedy Hour, The Carol Burnett Show (3 Emmy Awards as actor: 1973, 1977, 1978; Emmy Award as writer: 1976), The Tim Conway Show (1980-81), Ace Crawford: Private Eye, Tim Conway's Funny America. *Guest*: Hollywood Palace, and shows starring Garry Moore, Carol Burnett, Red Skelton, Danny Kaye, Dean Martin, Cher, Doris Day, Coach (Emmy Award, 1996). *Movie*: Roll Freddy Roll.

COOGAN, KEITH
Actor. b. Palm Springs, CA, Jan. 13, 1970. e. Santa Monica City Col. Grandson of late actor Jackie Coogan. Formerly acted as Keith Mitchell. Appeared in shorts All Summer in a Day and The Great O'Grady.

PICTURES: The Fox and the Hound (voice), Adventures in Babysitting, Hiding Out, Under the Boardwalk, Cousins, Cheetah, Book of Love, Toy Soldiers, Don't Tell Mom the Babysitter's Dead, Forever, In the Army Now, A Reason to Believe.
TELEVISION: Series: The MacKenzies of Paradise Cove, The Waltons, Gun Shy. Movies: A Question of Love, Million Dollar Infield, Kid With the Broken Halo, Battered, Memorial Day, Spooner. Specials: Wrong Way Kid, The Treasure of Alpheus T. Winterborn, Rascal, Over the Limit, A Town's Revenge. Guest: Growing Pains, Silver Spoons, Fame, CHips, The Love Boat, Mork and Mindy, 21 Jump Street, 8 is Enough, Fantasy Island, Just the Ten of Us, Sibs, Tales From the Crypt, others. Pilots: Norma Rae, Apple Dumpling Gang, Wonderland Cove.

COOK, FIELDER
Director, Producer. b. Atlanta, GA, Mar. 9, 1923. e. Washington & Lee U., B.A.; U. of Birmingham, Eng., post grad. Served with 7th Amphibious Force, WWII.
PICTURES: Patterns (debut, 1956), Home Is the Hero, A Big Hand for the Little Lady (also prod.), How to Save a Marriage and Ruin Your Life, Prudence and the Pill (co-dir.), Eagle in a Cage, From the Mixed Up Files of Mrs. Basil E. Frankweiler.
TELEVISION: Movies: Sam Hill: Who Killed the Mysterious Mr. Foster?, Goodbye Raggedy Ann (also exec. prod.), Homecoming, Miracle on 34th Street, This is the West That Was, Miles to Go Before I Sleep, Judge Horton and the Scottsboro Boys, Beauty and the Beast, A Love Affair: The Eleanor and Lou Gehrig Story, Too Far to Go (also released theatrically), I Know Why the Caged Bird Sings, Gaugin the Savage, Family Reunion, Will There Really Be a Morning?, Why Me?, A Special Friendship. Mini-Series: Evergreen. Specials: The Hands of Carmac Joyce, Teacher Teacher, The Rivalry, Valley Forge, The Price (Emmy Award), Harvey, Brigadoon (also prod.; 2 Emmy Awards), Seize the Day, Third and Oak: The Pool Hall, A Member of the Wedding. Pilots: Ben Casey, The 11th Hour, The Waltons.

COOK, RICHARD
Executive. b. Bakersfield, CA, Aug. 20, 1950. e. USC. Began career 1971 as Disneyland sls. rep.; promoted 1974 to mgr. of sls. Moved to studio in 1977 as mgr.; pay TV and non-theatrical releases. 1980, named asst. domestic sls. mgr., for Buena Vista; 1981 promoted to v.p. & asst. gen. sls. mgr.; 1984, promoted to v.p. & gen. sls. mgr., B.V.; 1985, appt. sr. v.p., domestic distribution. 1988: appt. pres. Buena Vista Pictures Distribution. 1994, pres., Worldwide Marketing, Buena Vista Pictures Marketing. 1996 named chmn., Walt Disney Motion Picture Group.

COOKE, ALISTAIR
Journalist, Broadcaster. b. Manchester, Eng., Nov. 20, 1908. e. Jesus Coll., Cambridge U.; Yale U.; Harvard U. Film crit. of BBC 1934-37. London corr. NBC 1936-37. BBC commentator in U.S. since 1937. Commentator on radio show Letters From America, starting in 1945. Chief Amer. corr., Manchester Guardian, 1948-72; English narrator, The March of Time, 1938-39. Became U.S. citizen in 1941. Peabody award winner for International reporting, 1952, 1973-83. Hon. Knighthood, KBE, 1973.
AUTHOR: Douglas Fairbanks, Garbo & The Night Watchmen, A Generation on Trial, One Man's America, Christmas Eve, The Vintage Mencken, etc. America, 1973; Six Men, 1977; Talk About America, 1968; The Americans, 1979; Above London (with Robert Cameron), 1980; Masterpieces, 1981; The Patient Has the Floor, 1986, America Observed, 1988; Fun and Games with Alistair Cooke, 1995.
PICTURES: Narrator: Sorrowful Jones, The Three Faces of Eve, Hitler—The Last Ten Days
TELEVISION: Series: Omnibus (host; 1952-61), m.c. prod. U.N.'s International Zone (host, prod.; Emmy Award, 1958); Masterpiece Theatre (host, 1971-92). Special doc.: America: A Personal History of The United States (writer and narrator; 5 Emmy Awards, 1973; Franklin Medal, Royal Society of Arts, 1973).

COOLIDGE, MARTHA
Director, Writer, Producer. b. New Haven, CT, Aug. 17, 1946. e. Rhode Island Sch. of Design. NYU Inst. of Film and TV grad. sch. m. writer Michael Backes. Dir. short films while in school. Wrote and prod. daily children's tv show Magic Tom in Canada Worked on commercials and political doc. film crews. Prod., dir. and writer of docs. which have won festival awards, including Passing Quietly Through; David: Off and On (American Film Fest.), Old Fashioned Woman (CINE Golden Eagle Award, Blue Ribbon Award, American film festival), Bimbo (short), Magic Tom in Canada. First feature film Not a Pretty Picture (won Blue Ribbon Award, Amer. Film Fest.) Helped start assn. of Indep. Video and Filmmakers, Inc. As an AFI/Academy Intern worked with Robert Wise on his film Audrey Rose, 1976. Wrote orig. story that was filmed as the The Omega Connection. DGA, member of bd. of dirs.; WIF, member bd. of dirs. Acted in films Beverly Hills Cop III.
PICTURES: The City Girl, Valley Girl, Joy of Sex, Real Genius, Plain Clothes, That's Adequate (interviewee), Rambling Rose (IFP Spirit Award, 1991), Lost in Yonkers, Angie, Three Wishes.

TELEVISION: The Twilight Zone, Sledge Hammer (pilot), House and Home (pilot). Movies: Trenchcoat in Paradise, Bare Essentials, Crazy in Love.

COONEY, JOAN GANZ
Executive, Producer. b. Phoenix, AZ, Nov. 30, 1929. e. U. of Arizona. After working as a reporter in Phoenix, moved to NY in 1953 where she wrote soap-opera summaries at NBC. Then was publicist for U.S. Steel Hour. Became producer of live weekly political TV show Court of Reason (Emmy Award) and documentaries (Poverty, Anti-Poverty and the Poor) before founding Children's Television Workshop and Sesame Street in 1969. Currently chmn., exec. committe, CTW.

COOPER, BEN
Actor. b. Hartford, CT, Sept. 30, 1930. e. Columbia U. On stage in Life with Father (1942); numerous radio, TV appearances starting from 1945.
PICTURES: Side Street (debut, 1950), Thunderbirds, The Woman They Almost Lynched, A Perilous Journey, Sea of Lost Ships, Flight Nurse, The Outcast, Johnny Guitar, Jubilee Trail, Hell's Outpost, The Eternal Sea, The Last Command, Headline Hunters, The Rose Tattoo, Rebel in Town, A Strange Adventure, Duel at Apache Wells, Outlaw's Son, Chartroose Caboose, The Raiders, Gunfight at Comanche Creek, Arizona Raiders, Waco, The Fastest Gun Alive, Red Tomahawk, One More Train to Rob, Support Your Local Gunfighter.

COOPER, HAL
Director, Performer. b. New York, NY, Feb. 22, 1923. e. U. of Michigan. m. Marta Salcido; child actor in various radio prog. starting in 1932; featured Bob Emery's Rainbow House, Mutual, 1936-46; asst. dir. Dock St. Theatre, Charleston, SC, 1946-48.
TELEVISION: Your School Reporter, TV Baby Sitter, The Magic Cottage (writer, prod.). Director: Valiant Lady, Search for Tomorrow, Portia Faces Life, Kitty Foyle (also assoc. prod.), Indictment (also prod.), The Happy Time (also assoc. prod.), For Better or Worse (also prod.), The Clear Horizon, Surprise Package (also assoc. prod.), Dick Van Dyke Show, The Art Linkletter Show (also prod.), The Object Is, Death Valley Days, I Dream of Jeannie, That Girl, I Spy, Hazel, Gidget, Gilligan's Island, NYPD, Mayberry, Courtship of Eddie's Father, My World and Welcome to It, The Brady Bunch, The Odd Couple, Mary Tyler Moore, All in the Family. Exec. prod./Director: Maude, Phyl and Mikky, Love, Sidney, Gimme a Break, Empty Nest, Dear John, The Powers That Be.

COOPER, JACKIE
Actor, Director, Producer. b. Los Angeles, CA, Sept. 15, 1922. Began theatrical career at age of 3 as m.p. actor; was member of Our Gang comedies (first short was Boxing Gloves in 1929). First starring role in 1931 in Skippy. Worked at every major studio, always with star billing. At 20 enlisted in Navy. After three-yr. tour of duty went to N.Y. to work in live TV. Appeared in 3 plays on B'way stage and in Mr. Roberts on natl. tour and in London. Directed as well as acted in live and filmed TV. Served as v.p. in chg. of TV prod., for Screen Gems, 1964-69, when resigned to return to acting, directing, producing. 2 Emmy Awards for directing M*A*S*H and The White Shadow. Retired 1989.
PICTURES: Fox Movietone Follies (feature debut, 1929), Sunny Side Up, Skippy (Acad. Award nom.), Young Donovan's Kid, Sooky, The Champ, When a Feller Needs a Friend, Divorce in the Family, Broadway to Hollywood, The Bowery, Lone Cowboy, Treasure Island, Peck's Bad Boy, Dinky, O'Shaughnessy's Boy, Tough Guy, The Devil Is a Sissy, Boy of the Streets, White Banners, Gangster's Boy, That Certain Age, Newsboys' Home, Scouts to the Rescue (serial), Spirit of Culver, Streets of New York, What a Life, Two Bright Boys, The Big Guy, The Return of Frank James, Seventeen, Gallant Sons, Life With Henry, Ziegfeld Girl, Glamour Boy, Her First Beau, Syncopation, Men of Texas, The Navy Comes Through, Where Are Your Children?, Stork Bites Man, Kilroy Was Here, French Leave, Everything's Ducky, The Love Machine, Stand Up and Be Counted (dir. only), Chosen Survivors, Superman, Superman II, Superman III, Superman IV: The Quest for Peace, Surrender.
TELEVISION: Series: People's Choice (also directed 71 episodes), Hennesey (also dir. 91 epsiodes), Dean Martin Comedy World (host), Mobile One. Movies: Shadow on the Land, Maybe I'll Come Home in the Spring, The Astronaut, The Day the Earth Moved, The Invisible Man, Mobile Two, Operation Petticoat. Director: Having Babies III, Rainbow, White Mama, Rodeo Girl, Sex and the Single Parent, The Ladies, Deacon Street Deer, Perfect Gentlemen, Marathon, Leave 'Em Laughing, Rosie (also prod.), Glitter, The Night They Saved Christmas, Izzy and Moe.

COOPER, JEANNE
Actress. r.n. Wilma Jean Cooper. b. Taft, CA, Oct. 25. e. College of the Pacific, Pasadena Playhouse. Son is actor Corbin Bernsen. Recipient: 3 Soap Update MVP Awards, Soap Opera Digest, Pasadena Playhouse Woman of the Year and Hollywood Entertainment Museum Award.

THEATER: The Miracle Worker, Plain and Fancy, Picnic, On the Town, The Big Knife, Tonight at 8:30, Dark Side of the Moon, Plaza Suite.
PICTURES: Man From the Alamo, 13 West Street, The Redhead From Wyoming, Let No Man Write My Epitaph, The Glory Guys, Kansas City Bomber, All-American Boy, Frozen Assets.
TELEVISION: Series: Bracken's World, The Young and the Restless (1973-).

COOPER, SHELDON
Executive. e. Indiana U. Joined WGN Television, 1950 holding various positions in prod. including floor mgr., dir., prod.; 1961, named mgr. prod.; 1961 became exec. prod. for station; 1964, named asst. prog. mgr.; 1965, mgr. of dept.; 1966, v.p. prog. dev. with WGN Continental Productions Co.; elected to bd. of dir., Continental Broadcasting Co. and appointed station mgr., WGN TV, April 1974.; 1975, named v.p. and gen. mrg.; WGN Continental Broadcasting.; 1977, dir., broadcasting; 1979, pres. and gen. mgr., WGN Television; 1982, chief exec. of newly formed Tribune Broadcasting Co. and dir. of Tribune Co. Syndicate, Inc., 1982-present. One of founders of Operation Prime Time, consortium of independent stations. Awarded Emmys: 1960 as television's man of the year behind the cameras and 1964 for continuing excellence as writer, prod., executive, WGN TV. Chmn., Assoc. of Independent TV Stations, Inc. (INTV), 1980 and 1981; National v.p., Muscular Dystrophy Assoc.; 1980, on bd. National Assoc. of TV Prog. Executives (NATPE); first v.p., Chicago chap. Acad. of TV Arts and Sciences; v.p., trustee of national chap.

COOPERMAN, ALVIN
Producer. b. Brooklyn, NY. Prod., Untouchables, 1961-63; exec. dir., Shubert Theatre Ent. 1963; v.p., special programs, NBC, 1967-68; exec. v.p., Madison Square Garden Center, 1968-72; pres., Madison Square Garden Center, Inc.; founder , Madison Sq. Garden Prods. and Network; chmn. of the board, Athena Communications Corp.; pres., NY Television Academy, 1987-89.
TELEVISION: Producer. Romeo and Juliet (Emmy nom.), Pele's Last Game, The Fourth King, Amahl and the Night Visitors, Live from Studio 8H—A Tribute to Toscanini (Emmy Award), Live from Studio 8H—An Evening with Jerome Robbins and the New York City Ballet (Emmy Award), Live from Studio 8H—Caruso Remembered, Ain't Misbehavin' (Emmy nom.), NAACP Image Award), Pope John Paul II, My Two Loves, Safe Passage, Family Album, U.S.A. (26 half hrs.), Witness to Survival (26 half hrs.), Mobs and Mobsters, Follow The River, Susan B. Anthony Slept Here (docu.).

COPPOLA, FRANCIS FORD
Director, Writer, Producer. b. Detroit, MI, April 7, 1939. Raised in NYC. Son of late composer Carmine Coppola. Sister is actress Talia Shire. e. Hofstra U, B.A., 1958; UCLA, 1958-68, M.F.A., cinema. While at UCLA was hired as asst. to Roger Corman as dialogue dir., sound man and assoc. prod. 1969; est. American Zoetrope, (later Zoetrope Studios), a prod. center in San Francisco. Publisher, City (magazine, 1975-6). Appeared in documentary Hearts of Darkness: A Filmmaker's Apocalypse.
PICTURES: Tonight for Sure (dir., prod.), The Playgirls and the Bellboy (co-dir., co-s.p. of addtl. sequences for U.S. version), Premature Burial (asst. dir.), Tower of London (dialog. dir.), Battle Beyond the Sun (adapt.), The Young Races (sound, 2nd unit dir.), The Terror (assoc. prod., 2nd unit dir.), Dementia 13 (dir., s.p.), Is Paris Burning? (co-s.p.), This Property Is Condemned (co-s.p.), You're a Big Boy Now (dir., s.p.), The Wild Races (2nd unit dir.), Reflections in a Golden Eye (s.p.), Finian's Rainbow (dir.), The Rain People (dir., s.p.), Patton (co-s.p.; Academy Award, 1970), THX 1138 (exec. prod.), The Godfather (dir., co-s.p.; Academy Award for Best Screenplay, 1972), American Graffiti (exec. prod.), The Great Gatsby (s.p.), The Conversation (dir., co-prod., s.p.), The Godfather Part II (dir., co-s.p., prod.; Academy Awards for Best Picture, Director & Screenplay, 1974), Apocalypse Now (dir., prod., co-s.p., cameo), The Black Stallion (exec. prod.), Kagemusha (co-exec. prod.), One From the Heart (dir., co-s.p.), Hammett (exec. prod.), The Escape Artist (co-exec. prod.), The Black Stallion Returns (exec. prod.), The Outsiders (dir.), Rumble Fish (dir., exec. prod., co-s.p.), The Cotton Club (dir., co-s.p.), Mishima (co-exec. prod.), Peggy Sue Got Married (dir.), Gardens of Stone (dir., co-prod.), Tough Guys Don't Dance (co-exec. prod.), Lionheart (exec. prod.), Tucker: The Man and His Dream (dir.), New York Stories (Life Without Zoe; dir., co-s.p.), The Godfather Part III (dir., co-s.p., prod.), Wind (co-exec. prod.), Bram Stoker's Dracula (dir., co-prod.), The Secret Garden (exec. prod.), Mary Shelley's Frankenstein (prod.), Don Juan DeMarco (exec. prod.), My Family/Mi Familia (exec. prod.), Haunted (co-exec. prod.), Jack.
TELEVISION: Movies: The People (exec. prod.), White Dwarf (co- prod.), Tecumseh: The Last Warrior (co-exec. prod.). Special: Rip Van Winkle (Faerie Tale Theatre; dir.). Series: The Outsiders (exec. prod.).

CORBIN, BARRY
Actor. b. Dawson County, TX, Oct. 16, 1940. e. Texas Tech. Univ.
PICTURES: Urban Cowboy, Stir Crazy, Any Which Way You Can, Dead and Buried, The Night the Lights Went Out in Georgia, The Best Little Whorehouse in Texas, Six Pack, Honkytonk Man, The Ballad of Gregorio Cortez, WarGames, The Man Who Loved Women, Hard Traveling, What Comes Around, My Science Project, Nothing in Common, Under Cover, Off the Mark, Permanent Record, Critters 2: The Main Course, It Takes Two, Who is Harry Crumb?, Short Time, Ghost Dad, The Hot Spot, Career Opportunities.
TELEVISION: Series: Boone, Spies, Northern Exposure, The Big Easy. Mini-Series: The Thorn Birds, Lonesome Dove. Movies: Rage, This House Possessed, The Killing of Randy Webster, Murder in Texas, Bitter Harvest, A Few Days in Weasel Creek, Fantasies, Prime Suspect, Travis McGee, Flight #90: Disaster on the Potomac, The Jesse Owens Story, Fatal Vision, I Know My First Name is Steven, Last Flight Out, The Chase, Conagher, The Keys, Robin Cook's Virus. Guest: Call to Glory, Murder She Wrote, Hill Street Blues, Matlock.

CORD, ALEX
Actor. r.n. Alexander Viespi. b. Floral Park, NY, May 3, 1933. Early career in rodeo; left to become actor. Studied at Shakespeare Academy (Stratford, Conn.) and Actor's Studio (N.Y.). Spent two yrs. in summer stock; in 1961 went on tour with Stratford Shakespeare Co. Author of novel Sandsong. Co-founder of Chuckers for Charity polo team which has raised more than $2 million for various charities. Champion rodeo team roper and cutting horse rider.
PICTURES: Synanon (debut, 1965), Stagecoach, A Minute to Pray A Second to Die, The Brotherhood, Stiletto, The Last Grenade, The Dead Are Alive, Chosen Survivors, Inn of the Damned, Sidewinder One, Grayeagle, Jungle Warriors, Street Asylum.
TELEVISION: Series: W.E.B., Cassie & Company, Airwolf. Movies: The Scorpio Letters, Hunter's Man; Genesis II, Fire !, Beggerman Thief, Goliath Awaits, The Dirty Dozen: The Fatal Mission.

CORDAY, BARBARA
Executive. b. New York, NY, Oct. 15, 1944. Began career as publicist in N.Y. and L.A. Turned to writing for TV; named v.p., ABC-TV, in chg. of comedy series development. 1982-84, headed own production co. in association with Columbia Pictures TV; June, 1984-87 pres.; Columbia Pictures TV; 1988, appointed CBS Entertainment, exec. v.p. primetime programs. Member: Caucus of Writers, Producers & Directors; Hollywood Women's Coalition.
TELEVISION: Writer: American Dream (pilot), Cagney and Lacey (also co-creator).

COREY, JEFF
Actor. b. New York, NY, Aug. 10, 1914. e. Feagin Sch. of Dram. Art. On stage in Leslie Howard prod. of Hamlet, 1936; Life and Death of an American, In the Matter of J. Robert Oppenheimer, Hamlet-Mark Taper Forum, King Lear, Love Suicide at Schofield Barracks.
PICTURES: All That Money Can Buy, Syncopation, The Killers, Ramrod, Joan of Arc, Roughshod, Black Shadows, Bagdad, Outriders, The Devil and Daniel Webster, My Friend Flicka, Canyon City, Singing Guns, Seconds, In Cold Blood, Golden Bullet, Boston Strangler, True Grit, Butch Cassidy and The Sundance Kid, Beneath the Planet of the Apes, Getting Straight, Little Big Man, They Call Me Mister Tibbs, Clear and Present Danger, High Flying Lowe, Catlow, Something Evil, Premonition, Shine, Rooster, Oh God!, Butch and Sundance: The Early Days, Up River, Conan the Destroyer, Cognac, Messenger of Death, Bird on a Wire, The Judas Project, Deception, Beethoven's 2nd, Surviving the Game, Color of Night.
TELEVISION: Guest: The Untouchables, The Beachcomber, The Balcony, Yellow Canary, Lady in a Cage, Outer Limits, Channing, The Doctors and the Nurses, Perry Mason, Gomer Pyle, Wild Wild West, Run for Your Life, Bonanza, Iron Horse, Judd for Defense, Garrisons Gorillas, Gunsmoke, Hawaii Five O, Star Trek, The Psychiatrist, Night Gallery, Alias Smith and Jones, Sixth Sense, Hawkins, Owen Marshall, Police Story, Bob Newhart Show, Six Million Dollar Man, Doctors Hospital, Starsky and Hutch, Land of the Free, Kojak, McCloud, Captains Courageous, Bionic Woman, Barney Miller, One Day at a Time, The Pirate, Lou Grant, The Powers of Jonathan Starr, Cry for the Strangers, Today's FBI, Knots Landing, Archie Bunker's Place, Faerie Tale Theatre, Night Court, Helltown (series), Morning Star/Evening Star (series), New Love American Style, Starman, The A Team, A Deadly Silence (movie), Roseanne, Wolf, Jake and the Fatman, Rose and the Jackal, To My Daughter, Payoff, Sinatra, The Marshal, Home Court, Picket Fences.

CORMAN, GENE
Producer. r.n. Eugene H. Corman. b. Detroit, MI, Sept. 24, 1927. e. Stanford U. Went to work for MCA as agent 1950-57; left to produce his first feature film, Hot Car Girl. Partner with brother

Roger in Corman Company and New World Distributors. Vice pres. 20th Century Fox Television, 1983-87; exec. v.p. worldwide production, 21st Century Film Corp.
PICTURES: Attack of the Giant Leeches, Not of This Earth, Blood and Steel, Valley of the Redwoods, Secret of the Purple Reef, Beast from Haunted Cave, Cat Burglar, The Intruder, Tobruk, You Can't Win Em All, Cool Breeze, Hit Man, The Slams, Von Richthofen and Brown, I Escaped from Devil's Island, Secret Invasion, Vigilante Force, F.I.S.T. (exec. prod.), The Big Red One, If You Could See What I Hear, Paradise, A Man Called Sarge.
TELEVISION: What's In It For Harry, A Woman Called Golda (Emmy and Christopher Awards as prod.), Mary and Joseph, a Love Story, Blood Ties.

CORMAN, ROGER WILLIAM
Executive, Director, Producer, Writer, Distributor. b. Detroit, MI, April 5, 1921. e. Stanford U. 1947; Oxford U., England 1950. U.S. Navy 1944; 20th Century-Fox, production dept., 1948, story analyst 1948-49; Literary agent, 1951-52; story, s.p., assoc. prod., Highway Dragnet. Formed Roger Corman Prod. and Filmgroup. Prod. over 200 feature films and dir. over 60 of them. Formed production-releasing company, org., New World Pictures, Inc., 1970. Formed prod. co., Concorde, 1984; distribution co., New Horizons, 1985. On TV acted in film Body Bags. *Author:* How I Made a Hundred Movies in Hollywood and Never Lost a Dime.
PICTURES: *Director:* Five Guns West (dir. debut, 1955), Apache Woman, Swamp Women, The Day the World Ended, The Oklahoma Woman, The Gunslinger, It Conquered the World, Not of This Earth, Naked Paradise (Thunder Over Hawaii), Attack of the Crab Monsters, Rock All Night, Teenage Doll, Carnival Rock, Sorority Girl, Saga of the Viking Women and Their Voyage to the Waters of the Great Sea Serpent, The Undead, War of the Satellites, She Gods of Shark Reef, Machine Gun Kelly, Teenage Caveman, I Mobster, A Bucket of Blood, The Wasp Woman, Ski Troop Attack, House of Usher, The Little Shop of Horrors, The Last Woman on Earth, Creature From the Haunted Sea, Atlas, The Pit and the Pendulum, The Intruder, The Premature Burial, Tales of Terror, Tower of London, The Raven, The Terror, X—The Man With the X Ray Eyes, The Haunted Palace, The Young Racers, The Secret Invasion, The Masque of the Red Death, Tomb of Ligeia, The Wild Angels, The St. Valentine's Day Massacre, The Trip, Target: Harry (credited as Henry Neill), Bloody Mama, Gas-s-s-s, Von Richtofen and Brown, Frankenstein Unbound. Producer: Boxcar Bertha, Big Bad Mama, Death Race 2000, Eat My Dust, Capone, Jackson County Jail, Fighting Mad, Thunder & Lightning, Grand Theft Auto, I Never Promised You A Rose Garden, Deathsport, Avalanche, Battle Beyond the Stars, St. Jack, Love Letters, Smokey Bites the Dust, Galaxy of Terror, Slumber Party Massacre Part II, Death Stalker, Barbarian Queen, Munchies, Stripped To Kill, Big Bad Mama II, Sweet Revenge (co-exec. prod.), The Drifter (exec. prod.), Daddy's Boys, Singles (exec. prod.), Crime Zone (exec. prod.), Watcher (exec. prod.), The Lawless Land (exec. prod.), Stripped to Kill 2 (exec. prod.), The Terror Within, Lords of the Deep (also actor), Two to Tango, Time Trackers, Heroes Stand Alone, Bloodfist, Silk 2, Edgar Allan Poe's The Masque of Red Death, Hollywood Boulevard II (exec. prod.), Rock and Roll High School Forever (exec. prod.), Bloodfist II (prod.), Haunted Symphony, Midnight Tease, One Night Stand (exec. prod.). *Actor:* The Godfather Part II, Cannonball, The Howling, The State of Things, Swing Shift, The Silence of the Lambs, Philadelphia.
TELEVISION: *Movie Series:* Roger Corman Presents (exec. prod.)

CORNELL, JOHN
Producer, Director, Writer. b. Kalgoorlie, Western Australia, 1941. m. actress Delvene Delancy. Grew up Bunbury. e. studied pharmacy for two years in Perth. Won internship at Western Australian Newspapers at 19, becoming columnist then London editor at 26. As Melbourne prod. of TV show, A Current Affair, discovered bridge rigger Paul Hogan. Put him on show, became his manager and formed JP Productions with him in 1972. Prod. and appeared on The Paul Hogan Show. Formed movie co. with Hogan, Rimfire Films.
PICTURES: Crocodile Dundee (prod., co-s.p.), Crocodile Dundee II (prod., dir., editor), Almost an Angel (dir., prod.).

CORNFELD, STUART
Producer. b. Los Angeles, CA. e. U. of California, Berkeley. Entered America Film Institute's Center for Advanced Film Studies as producing fellow, 1975. Joined Brooksfilm as asst. to Mel Brooks on High Anxiety. Assoc. prod., History of the World Part I.
PICTURES: Fatso, The Elephant Man, (exec. prod.), National Lampoon's European Vacation (co-prod.), Girls Just Want to Have Fun (exec. prod.), The Fly, Moving, The Fly II (exec. prod.), Hider in the House (co-prod.), Kafka, Wilder Napalm.

CORRI, ADRIENNE
Actress. r.n. Adrienne Riccoboni. b. Glasgow, Scotland, Nov. 13, 1933. e. RADA at 13; parts in several stage plays including The Human Touch. Numerous TV appearances.

PICTURES: The Romantic Age (Naughty Arlette; debut, 1949), The River, Quo Vadis, The Little Kidnappers, The Sinners, Devil Girl From Mars, Meet Mr. Callaghan, Lease of Life, Make Me an Offer, Triple Blackmail, The Feminine Touch, Behind the Headlines, The Shield of Faith, Three Men in a Boat, Second Fiddle, The Surgeon's Knife, The Big Chance, Corridors of Blood, The Rough and the Smooth (Portrait of a Sinner), The Tell-Tale Heart, Sword of Freedom, The Hellfire, Dynamite Jack, Sword of Lancelot, A Study in Terror, Bunny Lake Is Missing, Doctor Zhivago, Woman Times Seven, The Viking Queen, Africa—Texas Style!, The File of the Golden Goose, Cry Wolf, Moon Zero Two, Vampire Circus, A Clockwork Orange, Madhouse, Rosebud, Revenge of the Pink Panther, The Human Factor.

CORT, BUD
Actor. r.n. Walter Edward Cox. b. New Rochelle, NY, March 29, 1950. e. NYU School of the Arts. Stage debut in Wise Child, B'way. L.A. theatre includes Forget-Me-Not Lane, August 11 1947, Endgame (Dramalogue Award), Demon Wine, The Seagull. Founding member of L.A. Classical Theatre. Theatrical film debut as extra in Up the Down Staircase 1967. Television debut in The Doctors.
PICTURES: Sweet Charity, M*A*S*H, Gas-s-s-s, The Traveling Executioner, Brewster McCloud, Harold and Maude, Die Laughing, Why Shoot the Teacher?, She Dances Alone, Hysterical, Electric Dreams (voice), Love Letters, The Secret Diary of Sigmund Freud, Maria's Lovers, Invaders from Mars, Love at Stake, The Chocolate War, Out of the Dark, Brain Dead, Going Under, Ted and Venus (also dir., co-s.p.), Girl in the Cadillac, Heat, Theodore Rex.
TELEVISION: *Special:* Bernice Bobs Her Hair. *Guest:* Faerie Tale Theatre (The Nightingale), The Hitchhiker (Made for Each Other), The New Twilight Zone, Midnight Caller. *Movies:* Brave New World, The Bates Motel, And the Band Played On.

CORT, ROBERT W.
Executive. e. U. of Pennsylvania (Phi Beta Kappa). Moved into feature prod. after having worked primarily in marketing/advertising. Joined Columbia Pictures as v.p., 1976; elevated to v.p., adv./pub./promo. Named exec. v.p. of mktg. for 20th-Fox, 1980. Moved into feature prod. as senior v.p., 1981. In 1983 named exec. v.p., prod., 20th-Fox Prods. 1985, joined Interscope Communications as pres.
PICTURES: *Prod.:* Critical Condition, Outrageous Fortune, Revenge of the Nerds II, Three Men and a Baby, The Seventh Sign, Cocktail, Bill & Ted's Excellent Adventure (exec. prod.), Renegades (exec. prod.), Blind Fury (exec. prod.), An Innocent Man, The First Power (exec. prod.), Bird on a Wire, Arachnophobia, Three Man and a Little Lady, Eve of Destruction, Class Action, Bill & Ted's Bogus Journey, Paradise, The Hand That Rocks the Cradle, The Cutting Edge, FernGully, The Gun in Betty Lou's Handbag, Out on a Limb, Jersey Girl, Holy Matrimony, Imaginary Crimes, Operation Dumbo Drop, The Tie That Binds, Mr. Holland's Opus.
TELEVISION: *Movies (co-exec. prod.):* A Mother's Courage (Emmy Award), A Part of the Family, Body Language.

CORTESE, VALENTINA
Actress. b. Milan, Italy, Jan. 1, 1924. Started career at 15 in Orizzonte Dipinto while studying at Rome Acad. of Dramatic Art. Following several appearances in European films brought to Hollywood by 20th Century-Fox, 1949; billed in U.S. films as Valentina Cortesa. Experience on dramatic stage in variety of roles inc. Shakespeare, O'Neill, Shaw.
PICTURES: Orrizonte Dipinto (debut, 1940), Primo Amore, A Yank in Rome, A Bullet for Strefano, Les Miserables, The Glass Mountain (English-language debut, 1950), Black Magic, Malaya, Thieves Highway, Shadow of the Eagle, The House on Telegraph Hill, Secret People, Lulu, Forbidden Women (Angels of Darkness), The Barefoot Contessa, Le Amiche, Magic Fire, Calabuch, Barabbas, The Evil Eye, The Visit, The Possessed, Juliet of the Spirits, Black Sun, The Legend of Lylah Clare, The Secret of Santa Vittoria, First Love, Give Her the Moon, The Assassination of Trotsky, Brother Sun Sister Moon, Day for Night (Acad. Award nom.), Tendre Dracula, Widow's Nest, When Time Ran Out, La Ferdinanda, Blue Tango, The Adventures of Baron Munchausen, The Betrothed, Young Toscanini, Buster's Bedroom.

CORTEZ, STANLEY
Director of Photography. r..n. Stanislaus Krantz. b. New York, NY, Nov. 4, 1908. e. NYU. Brother was late actor Ricardo Cortez. Began working with portrait photographers (Steichen, Pirie MacDonald, Bachrach, etc.), N.Y. Entered film indust. with Paramount; to Hollywood as camera asst. and later 2nd cameraman, various studios; pioneer in use of montage. Served Signal Corps WWII. Received Film Critics of Amer. award for work on Magnificent Ambersons. Under personal contract to David O. Selznick, Orson Welles, Walter Wanger, David Wolper. Contributor, Encyclopedia Britannica.
PICTURES: Four Days Wonder, The Forgotten Women, Alias the Deacon, Love Honor and Oh Baby!, Meet the Wildcat, The

Black Cat, Badlands of Dakota, Bombay Clipper, Eagle Squadron, The Magnificent Ambersons (Acad. Award nom.), Flesh and Fantasy, Since You Went Away (Acad. Award. nom.) Smash Up—The Story of a Woman, Secret Beyond the Door, Man on the Eiffel Tower, The Admiral Was a Lady, Fort Defiance, Abbott & Costello Meet Captain Kidd, Stronghold, Diamond Queen, Neanderthal Man, Shark River, Riders to the Stars, The Night of the Hunter, Man from Del Rio, Three Faces of Eve, Top Secret Affair, The Angry Red Planet, Thunder in the Sun, Dinosaurus, Back Street, Shock Corridor, Nightmare in the Sun, The Naked Kiss, Young Dillinger, Ghost in the Invisible Bikini, Blue, The Bridge at Remagen, Another Man Another Chance, Damien: Omen II (special photog.), When Time Ran Out (special photog.).

CORWIN, BRUCE CONRAD
Exhibitor. b. Los Angeles, CA, June 11, 1940. e. Wesleyan U. Pres., Metropolitan Theatres Corp.; Past pres., Variety Children's Charities Tent 25; Board of Trustees U.C.S.B. Foundation; pres. emeritus, L.A. Children's Museum; chmn., Coro Natl. Board of Governors; Past President of the Foundation of Motion Picture Pioneers.

CORWIN, NORMAN
Writer, Producer, Director. b. Boston, MA, May 3, 1910. Sports ed. Greenfield, Mass. Daily Recorder, 1926-29; radio ed., news commentator, Springfield Republican & Daily News, 1929-36; prog. dir., CBS, 1938. Author of Thirteen by Corwin, More by Corwin, Untitled & Other Plays, The Plot to Overthrow Christmas, Dog in the Sky, Overkill and Megalove, Prayer for the 70's, Holes in a Stained Glass Window, Trivializing America; taught courses at UCLA, USC, San Diego State U. Faculty, U.S.C. Sch. of Journalism, 1980-; sec., M.P. Academy Foundation, 1985. First v.p., Motion Picture Acad., 1989. Inducted into Radio Hall of Fame, Chicago Museum, 1993. Writer-host Academy Leaders (PBS). Chmn. Doc. Award Com., Motion Picture Acad. 1965-91; elected to bd. of gov., 1980; first v.p., 1988-89; chmn., writers' exec. comm., M.P. Academy; co-chmn. scholarship com., M.P. Academy; mem.: Film Advisory Bd.; bd. of trustees, Advisory Board, Filmex; bd. of dirs., WGA. Books incl. Directors Guild Oral History, Years of the Electric Ear, Norman Corwin's Letters.
THEATER: The Rivalry, The World of Carl Sandburg, The Hyphen, Overkill and Megalove, Cervantes. Together Tonight: Jefferson Hamilton and Burr.
PICTURES: Once Upon a Time, The Blue Veil, The Grand Design, Scandal in Scourie, Lust for Life (Acad. Award nom. best adapt. s.p.), The Story of Ruth.
TELEVISION: Inside the Movie Kingdom, The FDR series, The Plot to Overthrow Christmas, Norman Corwin Presents, The Court Martial of General Yamashita, Network at 50.

COSBY, BILL
Actor, Comedian. b. Philadelphia, PA, July 12, 1938. e. Temple U., U. of Mass., Ed.D. Served in United States Navy Medical Corps. Started as night club entertainer.
AUTHOR: The Wit and Wisdom of Fat Albert, Bill Cosby's Personal Guide to Power Tennis, Fatherhood, Time Flies.
COMEDY ALBUMS: Bill Cosby Is a Very Funny Fellow... Right! (Grammy Award, 1964), I Started Out As a Child (Grammy Award, 1965), Why Is There Air? (Grammy Award, 1966), Wonderfulness (Grammy Award, 1967), Revenge (Grammy Award, 1967), To Russell My Brother Whom I Slept With (Grammy Award, 1969), Bill Cosby Is Not Himself These Days, Rat Own Rat Own Rat Own, My Father Confused Me... What Must I Do? What Must I Do?, Disco Bill, Bill's Best Friend, Cosby and the Kids, It's True It's True, Bill Cosby - Himself, 200 MPH, Silverthroat, Hooray for the Salvation Army Band, 8:15 12:15, For Adults Only, Bill Cosby Talks to Kids About Drugs, Inside the Mind of Bill Cosby.
RADIO: The Bill Cosby Radio Program.
PICTURES: Hickey and Boggs (debut, 1972), Man and Boy, Uptown Saturday Night, Let's Do It Again, Mother Jugs and Speed, A Piece of the Action, California Suite, The Devil and Max Devlin, Bill Cosby Himself, Leonard Part VI (also co-prod., story), Ghost Dad, The Meteor Man, Jack.
TELEVISION: Series: I Spy (3 Emmy Awards for Best Actor: 1966, 1967, 1968), The Bill Cosby Show (1969-71), The New Bill Cosby Show (1972-73), Fat Albert and the Cosby Kids, Cos, The New Fat Albert Show (Emmy Award, 1981), The Cosby Show (1984-92), A Different World (exec. prod. only), You Bet Your Life, Here and Now (exec. prod. only), The Cosby Mysteries, Cosby (also prod., 1996-). Specials: The Bill Cosby Special, The Second Bill Cosby Special, Fat Albert Easter Special (voice), Cosby Salutes Alvin Ailey. Movies: To All My Friends on Shore (also exec. prod., story, music), Top Secret, The Cosby Mysteries (also co-exec. prod.), I Spy Returns (also co-exec. prod.).

COSMATOS, GEORGE PAN
Director, Producer, Writer. b. Tuscany, Italy, Jan. 4, 1947. e. London U., London Film School. Asst. on such films as Exodus, Zorba the Greek.

PICTURES: Director: Restless (also co-prod., s.p.), Massacre in Rome (also co-s.p.), The Cassandra Crossing (also co-s.p.), Escape to Athena (also co-s.p.), Of Unknown Origin, Rambo: First Blood Part II, Cobra, Leviathan, Tombstone, The Shadow Conspiracy.

COSTA-GAVRAS (CONSTANTIN)
Director, Writer. r.n. Konstaninos Gavras. b. Athens, Greece, Feb. 13, 1933. French citizen. e. Studied at the Sorbonne; Hautes Etudes Cinematographique, (IDHEC). Was leading ballet dancer in Greece before the age of 20. Worked as second, then first assistant to Marcel Ophuls, Rene Clair, Rene Clement and Jacques Demy. Pres. of the Cinematheque Francaise, 1982-87. Appeared as actor in film Madame Rosa.
PICTURES: Director: The Sleeping Car Murders (also s.p.; debut, 1965), Un Homme De Trop/Shock Troops (also s.p.), Z (also co-s.p.; 2 Acad. Award noms.), The Confession, State of Siege (also co- s.p.), Special Section (also co-s.p.), Clair de Femme (also s.p.), Missing (also co-s.p.; Academy Award for Best Adapted Screenplay, 1982; Palm d'Or at Cannes Film Fest.), Hannah K. (also prod.), Family Business (also s.p.), Betrayed, Music Box (Golden Bear, Berlin Festival, 1989), The Little Apocalypse.

COSTNER, KEVIN
Actor. b. Lynwood, CA, Jan. 18, 1955. e. CA. State U, Fullerton majored in marketing. Acted with South Coast Actors' Co-op, community theater gp. while at coll. After grad. took marketing job which lasted 30 days. Early film work in low budget exploitation film, Sizzle Beach, 1974. Then one line as Luther Adler in Frances. Role in The Big Chill was edited from final print. 1989, set up own prod. co. Tig Prods. at Raleigh Studios.
PICTURES: Sizzle Beach U.S.A., Shadows Run Black, Night Shift, Chasing Dreams, Table for Five, Testament, Stacy's Knights, The Gunrunner, Fandango, Silverado, American Flyers, The Untouchables, No Way Out, Bull Durham, Field of Dreams, Revenge (also exec. prod.), Dances With Wolves (also dir., co-prod.; Academy Awards for Best Picture & Director, 1990), Robin Hood: Prince of Thieves, JFK, The Bodyguard (also co-prod.), A Perfect World, Wyatt Earp (also co-prod.), Rapa Nui (co-prod. only), The War, Waterworld (also co-prod.), Tin Cup.
TELEVISION: Special: 500 Nations (co-exec. prod., host)

COUNTER, J. NICHOLAS III
Executive. Pres., Alliance of Motion Picture and Television Producers.

COURIC, KATIE
Newscaster. b. Arlington, VA, Jan. 7, 1957. e. Univ. of VA. Started as desk asst. at ABC News, then assignment editor for CNN, reporter for WTVJ, NBC affiliate in Miami. Moved to NBC's Washington D.C. station WRC. Became natl. correspondent for The Today Show, 1989, then co-host 1991-present. Served as co-host of Macy's Thanksgiving Day Parade, 1991-present. Co-host of nighttime series Now With Tom Brokaw & Katie Couric.

COURTENAY, TOM
Actor. b. Hull, England, Feb. 25, 1937 e. University Coll., London, Royal Acad. of Dramatic Art, 1960-61; Old Vic.
THEATER: Billy Liar, Andorra, Hamlet, She Stoops to Conquer, Otherwise Engaged (N.Y. debut), The Dresser, Poison Pen, Uncle Vanya, Moscow Stations, etc.
PICTURES: The Loneliness of the Long Distance Runner (debut, 1962), Private Potter, Billy Liar, King and Country, Operation Crossbow, King Rat, Doctor Zhivago (Acad. Award nom.), The Night of the Generals, The Day the Fish Came Out, A Dandy in Aspic, Otley, One Day in the Life of Ivan Denisovich, Catch Me a Spy, The Dresser (Acad. Award nom.), Happy New Year, Leonard Part VI, Let Him Have It, The Last Butterfly.
TELEVISION: Series: The Lads, Ghosts, Private Potter. Movies/Specials: I Heard the Owl Call My Name, Jesus of Nazareth, Absent Friends, Chekhov in Yalta, Redemption, The Old Curiosity Shop.

COURTLAND, JEROME
Actor, Producer, Director. b. Knoxville, TN, Dec. 27, 1926. Began career in 40s as actor, then turned to directing and producing.
PICTURES: Actor: Kiss and Tell, Man from Colorado, Battleground, The Barefoot Mailman, The Bamboo Prison, Tonka, Black Spurs. Director: Run, Cougar, Run, Diamond on Wheels. Producer: Escape to Witch Mountain, Ride a Wild Pony, Return from Witch Mountain, Pete's Dragon.
TELEVISION: Actor: The Saga of Andy Burnett, Tonka. Director: Hog Wild (also co-prod.), Harness Fever. Knots Landing, Dynasty, Hotel, Love Boat, Fantasy Island.

COUSTEAU, JACQUES-YVES, CAPTAIN
Producer. b. St. Andre de Cubzac, Gironde, June 11, 1910. e. French Naval Acad. Trained as Navy flier, switched to Gunnery office and started diving experiments. 1943 with Emile Gagnan conceived and released Aqua-Lung, first regulated compressed air breathing device for deep sea diving. After WWII org.

Experimental Diving Unit, performed oceanographic research. 1951 perfected first underwater camera equipment for TV. Founded environmental org. The Cousteau Society 1973. Awarded Chevalier de la Legion d Honneur for work in Resistance. Member National Acad. of Sciences. Elected to the Academie Francaise.
PICTURES: 20 short documentaries 1942-56; The Silent World (Academy Award, 1957; Grand Prize Cannes, 1956); The Golden Fish (Academy Award, short subject, 1959), World Without Sun (Academy Award, 1965), Voyage to the Edge of the World.
TELEVISION: Nearly 100 TV films on his series: The World of Jacques-Yves Cousteau, The Undersea World of Jacques Cousteau (2 Emmy Awards, 1972), Oasis in Space, The Cousteau Odyssey series, Cousteau/Amazon, Cousteau: Mississippi (Emmy Award, 1985), Rediscovery of the World series (exec. prod.).

COUTARD, RAOUL
Cinematographer. b. Paris, France, Sept. 16, 1924. Spent 4 years in Vietnam working for French Military Info. Service, later a civilian photographer for Time and Paris-Match. During WWII worked in photo labs. After war returned to France and formed prod. co. making documentaries. Joined Jean-Luc Godard as his cinematographer on Breathless (1960). His use of hand-held camera and natural light established him as a seminal camera-man of the French New Wave, working with Godard, Truffaut and later with Costa Gavras. Director: Hoa Binh (1971).
PICTURES: Breathless, Shoot the Piano Player, Lola, Jules and Jim, The Army Game, My Life to Live, Love at Twenty (segment), Les Carabiniers, Contempt, Alphaville, The Soft Skin, Male Companion, Pierrot le Fou, Made in USA, Weekend, Sailor From Gibraltar, The Bride Wore Black, Z, The Confession, Le Crabe Tambour, Passion, First Name: Carmen, Dangerous Moves, Salt on the Skin, La Garce, Max My Love, Burning Beds, Let Sleeping Cops Lie, Bethune: The Making of a Hero.

COWAN, WARREN J.
Publicist. b. New York, NY, Mar. 13. e. Townsend Harris H.S., UCLA, graduated 1941. Entered public relations, 1941, with Alan Gordon & Associates; three yrs. Air Force; joined Henry C. Rogers office in 1945; became partner, 1949, and changed name to Rogers & Cowan Public Relations; advisor, Rogers & Cowan, Inc., 1960; pres., Rogers & Cowan, Inc., 1964; named bd. chmn., 1983. Retired as Rogers & Cowan chmn. in 1992. 1994, started new P.R. company, Warren Cowan & Assocs. Served as natl. communications chmn. for United Way of America. On advisory bd. of the Natl. Assoc. of Film Commissioners; 2nd Decade Council of American Film Inst. On bd. L.A. County High School for the Arts, Scott Newman Center, Young Musicians Foundation.

COX, ALEX
Director, Writer. b. Liverpool, Eng., Dec. 15, 1954. Studied law at Oxford U. where he dir. and acted in plays for school drama society. Studied film prod. Bristol U. Received Fulbright Scholarship to study at UCLA film school, 1981.
PICTURES: Repo Man (also s.p.), Sid and Nancy (also co-s.p.), Straight to Hell (also co-s.p.), Walker (also co-editor), Highway Patrolman, The Glimmer Man.

COX, BRIAN
Actor. b. Dundee, Scotland, June 1, 1946. e. London Acad. of Music & Dramatic Art. Acted with Royal Lyceum Edinburgh and Birmingham Rep. Theatre; also season with Royal Shakespeare Company. Video: Acting and Tragedy. Author: The Lear Diaries, Salem in Moscow.
THEATER: The Master Builder, King Lear, Richard III, Fashion, Rat in the Skull (Olivier Award; also B'way), Titus Andronicus (Olivier Award), Penny for a Song, Misalliance.
PICTURES: Nicholas and Alexandra, In Celebration, Manhunter, Shoot for the Sun, Hidden Agenda, Prince of Jutland, Iron Will, Rob Roy, Braveheart, Chain Reaction.
TELEVISION: Inspector Morse, Therese Raquin, Pope John Paul II, Florence Nightingale, Beryl Markham: A Shadow on the Sun, Murder by Moonlight, Six Characters in Search of an Author, Picasso, The Negotiator, The Big Battalions, Bach, Bothwell, Churchill's People, Master of Ballantrae, Lost Language of Cranes, The Changeling, Secret Weapon.

COX, COURTENEY
Actress. b. Birmingham, AL, June 15, 1964. Left AL to pursue modelling career in NY. Dir. Brian DePalma selected her to be the young woman who jumps out of audience and dances with Bruce Springsteen in his music video Dancing in the Dark. This break led to featured role in short-lived TV series Misfits of Science (1985-86).
PICTURES: Masters of the Universe, Down Twisted, Cocoon: The Return, Mr. Destiny, Blue Desert, Shaking the Tree, The Opposite Sex, Ace Ventura—Pet Detective, Scream.
TELEVISION: Series: Misfits of Science, Family Ties, The Trouble With Larry, Friends. Movies: I'll Be Home for Christmas, Roxanne: The Prize Pulitzer, Till We Meet Again, Curiosity Kills, Battling for Baby, Topper, Sketch Artist II: Hands That See.

COX, RONNY
Actor. b. Cloudcroft, NM, July 23, 1938. e. Eastern New Mexico Univ.
PICTURES: The Happiness Cage (debut, 1972), Deliverance, Hugo the Hippo (voice), Bound for Glory, The Car, Gray Lady Down, Harper Valley P.T.A., The Onion Field, Taps, The Beast Within, Some Kind of Hero, Courage (Raw Courage), Beverly Hills Cop, Vision Quest, Hollywood Vice Squad, Steele Justice, Beverly Hills Cop II, Robocop, One Man Force, Loose Cannons, Martians Go Home!, Total Recall, Scissors, Captain America, Past Midnight.
TELEVISION: Series: Apple's Way, Spencer, St. Elsewhere, Cop Rock, Sweet Justice. Movies: The Connection, A Case of Rape, Who Is the Black Dahlia?, Having Babies, Corey: For the People, The Girl Called Hatter Fox, Lovey: A Circle of Children Part II, Transplant, When Hell Was in Session, Fugitive Family, Courage of Kavik: The Wolf Dog, The Last Song, Alcatraz—The Whole Shocking Story, Fallen Angel, Two of a Kind, The Jesse Owens Story, The Abduction of Kari Swenson, Baby Girl Scott, In the Line of Duty: The FBI Murders, The Comeback, When We Were Young, With Murder in Mind, Perry Mason: The Case of the Heartbroken Bride, A Part of the Family. Mini-Series: Favorite Son. Specials: Our Town, Chicago 7 Trial.

COYOTE, PETER
Actor. r.n. Peter Cohon. b. New York, NY, 1942. Studied with San Francisco Actors Workshop. Theatre includes The Minstrel Show (dir.), Olive Pits (also co-writer), The Red Snake, True West, The Abduction of Kari Swenson, Baby Girl Scott.
PICTURES: Die Laughing (debut, 1980), Tell Me a Riddle, Southern Comfort, The Pursuit of D.B. Cooper, E.T.: The Extra Terrestrial, Endangered Species, Timerider, Cross Creek, Slayground, Stranger's Kiss, Heartbreakers, The Legend of Billie Jean, Jagged Edge, Outrageous Fortune, A Man in Love, Stacking, Heart of Midnight, The Man Inside, Crooked Hearts, Exposure, Bitter Moon, Kika, That Eye The Sky, Moonlight and Valentino, Unforgettable.
TELEVISION: Movies: Alcatraz: The Whole Shocking Story, The People vs. Jean Harris, Isabel's Choice, Best Kept Secrets, Scorned and Swindled, Time Flyer, Child's Cry, Sworn to Silence, Echoes in the Darkness, Unconquered, A Seduction in Travis County, Living a Lie, Keeper of the City, Breach of Conduct. Buffalo Girls. Special: Abraham Lincoln: A New Birth of Freedom (voice).

CRAIG, MICHAEL
Actor. r.n. Michael Gregson. b. Poona, India, Jan. 27, 1929. At 16 joined Merchant Navy. 1949 returned to England and made stage debut in repertory. M.P. debut as extra, 1949.
PICTURES: Passport to Pimlico (debut, 1949), The Magic Box, The Cruel Sea, Malta Story, The Love Lottery, Passage Home, The Black Tent, Yield to the Night, Eye-Witness, House of Secrets, High Tide At Noon, Sea of Sand, Sapphire, Upstairs and Downstairs, The Angry Silence, Cone of Silence, Doctor In Love, Mysterious Island, Payroll, No My Darling Daughter, A Pair of Briefs, A Life for Ruth, The Iron Maiden, Captive City, Summer Flight, Stolen Flight, Of a Thousand Delights, Life at the Top, Modesty Blaise, Star!, Twinky, The Royal Hunt of the Sun, Brotherly Love (Country Dance), A Town Called Bastard, The Fourth Mrs. Anderson, Vault of Horror, Inn of the Damned, Ride a Wild Pony, The Irishman, Turkey Shoot, Stanley, Appointment With Death.

CRAIN, JEANNE
Actress. b. Barstow, CA, May 25, 1925. Model; crowned Miss Long Beach of 1941: Camera Girl of 1942.
PICTURES: The Gang's All Here (debut, 1943), Home in Indiana, In the Meantime Darling, Winged Victory, State Fair, Leave Her to Heaven, Margie, Centennial Summer, You Were Meant for Me, Apartment for Peggy, Letter to Three Wives, The Fan, Pinky, Cheaper by the Dozen, I'll Get By (cameo), Take Care of My Little Girl, People Will Talk, Model and the Marriage Broker, Belles on Their Toes, O. Henry's Full House, City of Bad Men, Dangerous Crossing, Vicki, Duel in the Jungle, Man Without a Star, The Second Greatest Sex, Gentlemen Marry Brunettes, Fastest Gun Alive, Tattered Dress, The Joker is Wild, Guns of the Timberland, Queen of the Nile, Twenty Plus Two, Madison Avenue, Pontius Pilate, Hot Rods to Hell, Skyjacked, The Night God Screamed.

CRAMER, DOUGLAS S.
Executive. e. Northwestern U., Sorbonne, U. of Cincinnati, B.A.; Columbia U.M.F.A. m. Joyce Haber, columnist. Taught at Carnegie Inst. of Tech., 1954-55; Production asst. Radio City Music Hall 1950-51; MGM Script Dept. 1952; Manag. Dir. Cincinnati Summer Playhouse 1953-54. TV supvr. Procter and Gamble 1956-59; Broadcast supvr. Ogilvy Benson and Mather adv. 1959-62; v.p. program dev. ABC-TV 1962-66; v.p. program dev. 20 Cent.-Fox TV 1966; exec. v.p. in chg. of prod., Paramount TV, 1968-71; exec. v.p. Aaron Spelling Prods. 1976-89; pres. Douglas S. Cramer Co, 1989-.
THEATER: Call of Duty, Love is a Smoke, Whose Baby Are You.
TELEVISION: Exec. prod.: Bridget Loves Bernie, QB VII, Dawn:

Portrait of a Runaway, Danielle Steel's Fine Things, Kaleidoscope, Changes, Message from Nam, Daddy, Palamino, Once in a Lifetime, Trade Winds, Lake Success. *Co-exec. prod.*: Love Boat (1977-86), Vegas (1978-81), Wonder Woman, Dynasty, Matt Houston, Hotel, Colbys.

CRAVEN, GEMMA
Actress. b. Dublin, Ireland, June 1, 1950. e. Loretto Coll. Studied acting at Bush Davies School. London stage debut, Fiddler on the Roof (1970).
THEATER: *London*: Audrey, Trelawny, Dandy Dick, They're Playing Our Song, Song and Dance, Loot, A Chorus of Disapproval, Three Men on a Horse, Jacobowsky and the Colonel, The Magistrate, South Pacific, The London Vertigo, Private Lives, Present Laughter.
PICTURES: Kingdom of Gifts, Why Not Stay for Breakfast, The Slipper and the Rose, Wagner, Double X: The Name of the Game, Words Upon the Windowpane, Still Life.
TELEVISION: Pennies From Heaven, Must Wear Tights, She Loves Me, Song by Song by Noel Coward, Song by Song by Alan Jay Lerner, East Lynne, Robin of Sherwood, Treasure Hunt, Gemma Girls and Gershwin, Boon, The Bill, The Marshal.

CRAVEN, WES
Director, Writer. b. Cleveland, OH, Aug. 2, 1939. e. Wheaton Coll., B.A.; Johns Hopkins, M.A. (philosophy). Worked as humanities prof. prior to film.
PICTURES: The Last House on the Left (also s.p., ed.), The Hills Have Eyes (also s.p., ed.), Deadly Blessing, Swamp Thing (also s.p.), A Nightmare on Elm Street (also s.p.), The Hills Have Eyes Part II (also s.p.), Deadly Friend, A Nightmare on Elm Street III: Dream Warriors (co-s.p., co-exec. prod. only), The Serpent and the Rainbow, Shocker (also exec. prod., s.p.), The People Under the Stairs (also s.p., co-exec. prod.), Wes Craven's New Nightmare (also actor, s.p.), Vampire in Brooklyn, The Fear (actor only), Scream.
TELEVISION: *Series*: Twilight Zone (1985, 7 episodes: Word Play, A Little Peace and Quiet, Shatterday, Chameleon, Dealer's Choice, The Road Less Traveled, Pilgrim Soul). The People Next Door (exec. prod.). *Movies*: A Stranger in Our House, Invitation to Hell, Chiller, Casebusters, Night Visions (also exec. prod., co-writer), Laurel Canyon (exec. prod. only), Body Bags (actor only).

CRAWFORD, MICHAEL
O.B.E. Actor. b. Salisbury, England, Jan.19, 1942. r.n. Michael Dumbell-Smith. Early career as boy actor in children's films, as a boy soprano in Benjamin Britten's Let's Make an Opera and on radio. Later star of TV's Not So Much a Programme, More a Way of Life. Solo albums: Songs from the Stage and Screen, With Love, Performs Andrew Lloyd Weber, A Touch of Music in the Night. Appeared for MGM Grand in production EFX.
THEATER: Come Blow Your Horn, Traveling Light, The Anniversary, White Lies and Black Comedy (N.Y.), No Sex Please We're British, Billy, Same Time Next Year, Flowers for Algernon, Barnum, The Phantom of the Opera (London: Laurence Olivier Award; New York: Tony, Drama Desk, Drama League & Outer Circle Critics Awards, 1988; also L.A.), The Music of Andrew Lloyd Weber (U.S., Canada, U.K. & Australia).
PICTURES: Soap Box Derby (debut, 1957), Blow Your Own Trumpet, A French Mistress, Two Living One Dead, Two Left Feet, The War Lover, The Knack... and How to Get It, A Funny Thing Happened on the Way to the Forum, The Jokers, How I Won the War, Hello Dolly!, The Games, Hello-Goodbye, Alice's Adventures in Wonderland, Condorman, Once Upon a Forest (voice).
TELEVISION: Still Life, Destiny, Byron, Move After Checkmate, Three Barrelled Shotgun, Home Sweet Honeycomb, Some Mothers Do 'ave 'em, Chalk and Cheese, BBC Play for Today, Private View, Barnum.

CRENNA, RICHARD
Actor. b. Los Angeles, CA, Nov. 30, 1927. e. Belmont H.S., USC.
RADIO: Boy Scout Jamboree, A Date With Judy, The Hardy Family, The Great Gildersleeve, Burns & Allen, Our Miss Brooks.
PICTURES: Red Skies of Montana (debut, 1951), Pride of St. Louis, It Grows on Trees, Our Miss Brooks, Over-Exposed, John Goldfarb Please Come Home, Made in Paris, The Sand Pebbles, Wait Until Dark, Star!, Midas Run, Marooned, The Deserter, Doctors' Wives, Red Sky at Morning, Catlow, A Man Called Noon, Dirty Money (Un Flic), Jonathan Livingston Seagull (voice), Breakheart Pass, The Evil, Wild Horse Hank, Death Ship, Stone Cold Dead, Body Heat, First Blood, Table for Five, The Flamingo Kid, Rambo: First Blood Part II, Summer Rental, Rambo III, Leviathan, Hot Shots! Part Deux, A Pyromaniac's Love Story (unbilled), Jade, Sabrina.
TELEVISION: *Series*: Our Miss Brooks, The Real McCoys, Slattery's People, All's Fair, It Takes Two, Pros & Cons. *Movies*: Footsteps, Thief, Passions, A Case of Deadly Force, The Day the Bubble Burst, Centennial, The Rape of Richard Beck (Emmy Award, 1985), Doubletake, The Price of Passion, Police Story: The Freeway Killings, Plaza Suite, Kids Like These, On Wings of

Eagles, Internal Affairs, Blood Brothers: The Case of the Hillside Stranglers, Murder in Black and White, Stuck with Each Other, Montana, Last Flight Out, Murder Times Seven, And the Sea Will Tell, Intruders, Terror on Track 9, A Place to Be Loved, The Forget-Me-Not Murders, Jonathan Stone: Threat of Innocence, Janek: A Silent Betrayal, In the Name of Love: A Texas Tragedy.

CRICHTON, CHARLES
Director. b. Wallasey, Eng., Aug. 6, 1910. e. Oundle & Oxford.
PICTURES: For Those in Peril (debut, 1944), Painted Boats (The Girl on the Canal), Dead of Night (Golfing segment), Hue and Cry, Against the Wind, Another Shore, Train of Events (Orchestra Conductor segment), Dance Hall, The Lavender Hill Mob, Hunted (The Stranger in Between), The Titfield Thunderbolt, The Love Lottery, The Divided Heart, Man in the Sky (Decision Against Time), Floods of Fear (also s.p.), The Battle of the Sexes, The Boy Who Stole a Million (also co-s.p.), The Third Secret, He Who Rides a Tiger, Tomorrow's Island (also s.p.), A Fish Called Wanda (also story; 2 Acad. Award noms.).
TELEVISION: The Wild Duck, Danger Man, The Avengers, Man in a Suitcase, The Strange Report, Shirley's World, Black Beauty, The Protectors, Space 1999, Return of the Saint, Dick Turpin 1 & 2 Series, Smuggler, Video Arts Shorts.

CRICHTON, MICHAEL
Writer, Director. r.n. John Michael Crichton. b. Chicago, IL, Oct. 23, 1942. e. Harvard U. Medical School (M.D.), 1969. Postdoctoral fellow, Salk Inst. for Biological Sciences, La Jolla, 1969-70. Visiting writer, MIT, 1988. Recipient Edgar Award, Mystery Writers Amer.: A Case of Need (1968), The Great Train Robbery (1980). Named medical writer of year, Assn. of Amer. Med. Writers: Five Patients (1970). Received Scientific and Technical Achievement Academy Award, 1995.
AUTHOR: *Novels*: (as John Lange): Odds On, Scratch One, Easy Go (The Last Tomb), The Venom Business, Zero Cool, Grave Descend, Drug of Choice, Binary. (as Jeffery Hudson): A Case of Need (filmed as The Carey Treatment). (as Michael Douglas, with brother Douglas Crichton): Dealing or the Berkeley-to-Boston Forty-Brick Lost-Bag Blues (filmed). (as Michael Crichton): The Andromeda Strain (filmed), The Terminal Man (filmed), The Great Train Robbery, Eaters of the Dead, Congo, Sphere, Jurassic Park, Rising Son, Disclosure, The Lost World. Non-Fiction (as Michael Crichton): Five Patients, Jasper Johns, Electronic Life, Travels.
PICTURES: Westworld (dir., s.p.), Coma (dir., s.p.), The Great Train Robbery (dir., s.p.), Looker (dir., s.p.), Runaway (dir., s.p.), Physical Evidence (dir.), Jurassic Park (co-s.p.), Rising Sun (co-s.p.), Disclosure (co-prod.), Congo (co-s.p.), Twister (co- s.p., co-prod.).
TELEVISION: *Movie*: Pursuit (dir.; based on Binary). *Series*: ER (creator, co-exec. prod.; Emmy Award, 1996). *Pilot*: ER (Writers Guild Award, 1996).

CRIST, JUDITH
Journalist, Critic. b. New York, NY, May 22, 1922. e. Hunter College, Columbia U. School of Journalism. Joined NY Herald Tribune, serving as reporter, arts editor, assoc. drama critic, film critic. Contributing editor COlumbia Magazine. Continued as film critic for NY World Journal Tribune, NBC-TV Today Show, New York Magazine, NY Post, Saturday Review, TV Guide, WWOR-TV. Teaches at Col. Grad. School of Journalism.
AUTHOR: The Private Eye the Cowboy and the Very Naked Girl, Judith Crist's TV Guide to the Movies, Take 22: Moviemakers on Moviemaking.

CRISTALDI, FRANCO
Producer. b. Turin, Italy, Oct. 3, 1924. Owner, prod. Vides Cinematografica; President of Italian Producer's Union.
PICTURES: White Nights, The Strawman, The Challenge, Big Deal On Madonna Street, Kapo, The Dauphins, Salvatore Giuliano, The Assassin, Divorce Italian Style, The Organizer, Bebo's Girl, Seduced and Abandoned, Time of Indifference, Sandra, A Rose for Every-One, China Is Near, A Quiet Couple, The Red Tent, New Paradise Cinema.
TELEVISION: Marco Polo.

CROMWELL, JAMES
Actor. b. Los Angeles, CA, Jan. 27. Father was director John Cromwell, mother was actress Kate Johnson. e. Carnegie Mellon Univ.
PICTURES: Murder by Death, The Cheap Detective, The Man With Two Brains, House of God, Tank, Revenge of the Nerds, Oh God You Devil, Explorers, A Fine Mess, Revenge of the Nerds II: Nerds in Paradise, The Rescue, Pink Cadillac, The Runnin' Kind, The Babe, Babe, Eraser, The People vs. Larry Flynt, Star Trek: First Contact.
TELEVISION: *Series*: All in the Family, Hot L Baltimore, The Nancy Walker Show, The Last Precinct, Easy Street, Mama's Boy. *Mini-Series*: Once an Eagle. *Movies*: The Girl in the Empty Grave, Deadly Game, A Christmas Without Snow, The Wall, Spraggue, The Shaggy Dog. *Guest*: M*A*S*H, Dallas, L.A. Law, Star Trek: The Next Generation, Hill Street Blues.

CRONENBERG, DAVID
Writer, Director. b. Toronto, Ont., May 15, 1943. e. U. of Toronto. In college produced two short movies on 16mm. 1971, to Europe on a Canadian Council grant where in 1975 he shot his first feature, They Came From Within (Shivers).
PICTURES: *Director*: They Came From Within (Shivers; also s.p.), Rabid (also s.p.), Fast Company, The Brood (also s.p.), Scanners (also s.p.), Videodrome, The Dead Zone, The Fly (also co-s.p., cameo), Dead Ringers (also co-prod., co-s.p.), Naked Lunch (also s.p.), M. Butterfly, Crash. *Actor*: Into the Night, Nightbreed, Trial by Jury, Henry & Verlin.

CRONKITE, WALTER
Correspondent. b. St. Joseph, MO, Nov. 4, 1916. e. U. of Texas. Reporter and editor Scripps-Howard News Service, TX; radio reporter; U.P. correspondent. WW II corres. British Isles, N. Africa. Foreign Correspondent, France, Belgium, Netherlands, Soviet Union. Joined CBS as Washington news correspondent, 1950; anchorman and mng. editor, CBS Evening News, 1962-81; special correspondent, CBS News, 1981-present. Many TV shows including You Are There, Twentieth Century, Eyewitness to History: CBS Reports: 21st Century, Walter Cronkite's Universe. Past nat'l pres. & mem. bd. Trustees, Acad. TV Arts & Sciences. Mng. editor of CBS Evening News 1963-81; Special corres., Children of Apartheid, Walter Cronkite at Large. 1993, formed prod. company with John Ward, Cronkite Ward & Company, which has produced more than 25 award winning documentary hours for the Discovery Channel, PBS and others. Host/commentator of The Cronkite Reports, on the Discovery Channel which investigates current, global news issues. Other Cronkite Ward & Co. productions: Great Books series for the Learning Channel and Understanding: Science programs for the Discovery Channel. Supplied voice for 1995 B'way revival of How to Succeed in Business Without Really Trying.

CRONYN, HUME
Actor, Writer, Director. b. London, Ont., Canada, July 18, 1911. Was married to late actress Jessica Tandy. e. Ridley Coll., McGill U., Amer. Acad. of Dramatic Art.
THEATER: *Actor N.Y. plays*: High Tor, Escape This Night, Three Men on a Horse, Boy Meets Girl, Three Sisters, Mr. Big, The Survivors, Now I Lay Me Down to Sleep (dir.), Hilda Crane (dir.), The Fourposter (dir.), Madam Will You Walk, The Honeys, A Day by the Sea, The Man in the Dog Suit, The Egghead (dir.), Triple Play (dir. and toured with wife), Big Fish Little Fish (also in London), The Miser, The Three Sisters, Hamlet, The Physicists, Slow Dance on The Killing Ground (prod.), appeared at the White House, Hear America Speaking, Richard III, The Miser, A Delicate Balance (1966 and tour, 1967), The Miser, Hadrian VII (tour), Caine Mutiny Court Martial, Promenade All, Krapp's Last Tape, Happy Days, Act Without Words, Coward In Two Keys, concert recital Many Faces Of Love, Noel Coward in Two Keys (National tour), Merchant of Venice and A Midsummer Night's Dream (Stratford Festival Theatre) Canada, The Gin Game (with Miss Tandy; Long Wharf Thea., New Haven, B'way, 1977, co-prod. with Mike Nichols; also toured U.S., Toronto, London, U.S.S.R., 1978-79). Foxfire (co-author, actor, at Stratford, Ont., 1980, Minneapolis, 1981 and N.Y., 1982-83); Traveler in the Dark (Amer. Repertory Theatre, Cambridge, MA), Foxfire (Ahmanson, LA 1985-86), The Petition (NY 1986).
PICTURES: Shadow of a Doubt (debut, 1943), Phantom of the Opera, The Cross of Lorraine, Lifeboat, The Seventh Cross (Acad. Award nom.), Main Street After Dark, The Sailor Takes a Wife, A Letter for Evie, The Green Years, The Postman Always Rings Twice, Ziegfeld Follies, The Secret Heart (narrator), The Beginning or the End, Brute Force, Rope (adapt. only), The Bride Goes Wild, Top o' the Morning, Under Capricorn (adapt. only), People Will Talk, Crowded Paradise, Sunrise at Campobello, Cleopatra, Hamlet, Gaily Gaily, The Arrangement, There Was a Crooked Man, Conrack, The Parallax View, Honky Tonk Freeway, Rollover, The World According to Garp, Impulse, Brewster's Millions, Cocoon, Batteries Not Included, Cocoon: The Return, The Pelican Brief, Camilla, Marvin's Room.
TELEVISION: *Series*: The Marriage. *Movies*: The Dollmaker (co-writer only), Foxfire (also co-writer), Day One, Age-old Friends, Christmas on Division Street, Broadway Bound (Emmy Award, 1992), To Dance With the White Dog (Emmy Award, 1994).

CROSBY, CATHY LEE
Actress. b. Los Angeles, CA, Dec. 2. e. Grad. of U. of Southern California. Studied with Lee Strasberg. Author of Let The Magic Begin.
THEATER: Downside Risk, Almost Perfect (Off-B'way debut), Jellyroll Shoes, They Shoot Horses, Don't They? (wrote, dir. starred in 1st theatrical adapt. Hollywood Amer. Legion), Zoot Suit—The Real Story (writer, dir., actress, adapter, Beverly Hills).
PICTURES: The Laughing Policeman (debut, 1973), Trackdown, The Dark, Coach, Training Camp (s.p.), San Sebastian (s.p.), Call Me By My Rightful Name, The Player.
TELEVISION: *Movies*: Wonder Woman, Keefer, Roughnecks, World War III, Intimate Strangers, One Child, North & South III: Heaven and Hell, Untamed Love (also co-exec. prod.). *Series*: That's Incredible. *Specials*: A Spectacular Evening in Egypt,

Battle of the Network Stars, Circus of the Stars, Bob Hope Specials, Get High on Yourself, Bob Hope: USO Tour of Lebanon & the Mediterranean.

CROSBY, KATHRYN
Actress. r.n. Olive Kathryn Grandstaff. b. Houston, TX, Nov. 25, 1933. e. U. of Texas, Queen of Angels Sch. of Nursing, Immaculate Heart Col. m. late actor-singer Bing Crosby. Author: Bing and Other Things, My Life With Bing.
THEATER: Mama's Baby Boy, The Enchanted, Sunday in New York, Sabrina Fair, The Guardsman, Guys and Dolls, Same Time Next Year, The Crucible, Cyrano de Bergerac, Tonight at 8:30, The Cocktail Hour, Oh Coward, I Do I Do, The Heiress, The Seagull, many others.
PICTURES: Forever Female, Rear Window, Living It Up, Sabrina, Arrowhead, Casanova's Big Night, Unchained, Cell 2455 Death Row, Tight Spot, Five Against the House, Reprisal, Guns of Fort Petticoat, The Phenix City Story, Wild Party, Mister Cory, Gunman's Walk, The Librarian, Anatomy of a Murder, The Brothers Rico, Operation Mad Ball, The Seventh Voyage of Sinbad, The Big Circus.
TELEVISION: *Guest*: Bob Hope Chrysler Theatre, Bing Crosby Christmas Specials, Suspense Theatre, Ben Casey, The Kathryn Crosby Show (KPIX-TV, San Francisco). Movie: The Initiation of Sarah.

CROSBY, MARY
Actress. b. Los Angeles, CA, Sept. 14, 1959. e. U Tx. Daughter of performers Kathryn Crosby and the late Bing Crosby. Formerly acted as Mary Frances Crosby. Appeared from an early age in several TV variety specials with her parents.
PICTURES: The Last Plane Out, The Ice Pirates, Tapeheads, Body Chemistry, Corporate Affairs, Eating, The Berlin Conspiracy, Desperate Motive (Distant Cousins).
TELEVISION: *Series*: Brothers and Sisters, Dallas. *Movies*: With This Ring, A Guide for the Married Woman, Midnight Lace, Golden Gate, Confessions of a Married Man, Final Jeopardy, Stagecoach. *Mini-Series*: Pearl, Hollywood Wives, North and South Book II.

CROSS, BEN
Actor. r.n. Bernard Cross. b. London, England, Dec. 16, 1947. e. Royal Acad. of Dramatic Art. Worked as stagehand, prop-master, and master carpenter with Welsh Natl. Opera and as set builder, Wimbledon Theatre.
THEATER: The Importance of Being Earnest (Lancaster, debut, 1972), I Love My Wife, Privates on Parade, Chicago, Lydie Breeze (NY debut, 1982), Caine Mutiny Court Martial.
PICTURES: A Bridge Too Far (debut, 1977), Chariots of Fire, The Unholy, The Goldsmith's Shop, Paperhouse, The House of the Lord, Eye of the Widow, Haunted Symphony, The Ascent, First Knight.
TELEVISION: *Movies/Specials*: Melancholy Hussar of the German Legion (1973, BBC), The Flame Trees of Thika, The Citadel, The Far Pavilions, Coming Out of the Ice, The Assisi Underground, Arthur Hailey's Strong Medicine, Steal the Sky, Pursuit, Twist of Fate, Nightlife, She Stood Alone, Diamond Fleece, Live Wire, Deep Trouble, Cold Sweat. *Series*: Dark Shadows (1991).

CROUSE, LINDSAY
Actress. b. New York, NY, May 12, 1948. Daughter of playwright Russel Crouse. e. Radcliffe.
THEATER: Was member of Circle Repertory Co. NY. Hamlet, Twelfth Night, Richard II, Childe Byron, Reunion (Obie Award). NY: Serenading Louie, The Shawl, The Stick Wife, The Homecoming (B'way debut; Theatre World Award). Member of L.A. Matrix Theatre Co.: The Tavern, Habeus Corpus.
PICTURES: All the President's Men (debut, 1976), Slap Shot, Between the Lines, Prince of the City, The Verdict, Daniel, Iceman, Places in the Heart, House of Games, Communion, Desperate Hours, Being Human, Bye Bye Love, The Indian in the Cupboard, The Arrival.
TELEVISION: *Movies*: Eleanor and Franklin, Chantilly Lace, Final Appeal, Out of Darkness, Parallel Lives. *Mini-Series*: The Kennedys of Massachusetts. *Specials*: Kennedy's Children, Lemon Sky, Between Mother and Daughter. *Pilot*: American Nuclear.

CROWE, CAMERON
Writer, Director. b. Palm Springs, CA, July 13, 1957. e. Calif. St. Univ., San Diego. Began career as journalist and editor for Rolling Stone. Adapted his book Fast Times at Ridgemont High into Writers Guild Award nominated screenplay for 1982 film.
PICTURES: American Hot Wax (actor). *Writer*: Fast Times at Ridgemont High, The Wild Life (also co-prod.), Say Anything (also dir.), Singles (also dir.), Singles (also dir.), Jerry Maguire (also dir.).
TELEVISION: *Series*: Fast Times (creative consultant).

CROWE, KEN
Executive. b. Sewickley, PA, Sep. 3, 1939. e. San Diego U. CPA, public accounting, Coopers & Lybrand, 1968-77; Mann

Theatres, treas./CFO, 1977-86; Paramount Mann Theatres, sr. v.p./CFO, 1986-88; Cinamerica Theatres, exec. v.p./CFO, 1988-present. Member of Motion Picture Pioneers, AICPA, FEI, Variety Club of So. Calif and Sertoma.

CROWE, RUSSELL
Actor. b. New Zealand, 1964. Raised in Australia. Worked as professional musician while appearing on Australian stage in Bad Boy Johnny and the Profits of Doom, Blood Brothers, Rocky Horror Show.
PICTURES: For the Moment, The Silver Brumby, Hammers Over the Anvil, Prisoners of the Sun, Love in Limbo, For the Moment, Proof (Australian Film Inst. Award), The Efficiency Expert, Romper Stomper (Australian Film Inst. Award), The Quick and the Dead, The Sum of Us, Virtuosity, Rough Magic, No Way Back.

CRUEA, EDMOND D.
Executive. b. Jersey City, NJ, June 3. Joined Grand Natl. Pictures, LA, 1935; Monogram Pictures, 1938-41, LA & Seattle; U.S. Army Signal Corps., 1942-46; Monogram Pictures, Seattle, 1946; branch mgr. & district mgr. Allied Artists, 1950-65 (Seattle, Portland, San Francisco, LA); v.p. & gen. sls. mgr., Allied Artists, 1965-71; dir. distribution, Abkco Films div. of Abkco Industries Inc., 1971-3; pres. Royal Dist. Corp, 1974; joined Film Ventures Intl. 1976 as exec. v.p. succeeding to pres. & COO in 1976. Co-founded New Image Releasing Inc., 1982, as pres. & CEO. 1985, v.p. theatrical, Cinetel Films; 1987 theatrical distrib. con-sultant, Sony Pictures (NY) and Shining Armour Commun (London). Acquisitions & distrib. consultant to Columbia TriStar Home Video, Triumph Pictures and Healing Arts Documentary Prods.; 1995, chmn. and CEO Global International Films Inc.

CRUISE, TOM
Actor. r.n. Thomas Cruise Mapother IV. b. Syracuse, NY, July 3, 1962. m. actress Nicole Kidman. Acted in high school plays; secured role in dinner theatre version of Godspell. Studied act-ing at Neighborhood Playhouse, before landing small part in Endless Love. Received American Cinema Award for Distinguished Achievement in Film, 1991.
PICTURES: Endless Love (debut, 1981), Taps, Losin' It, The Outsiders, Risky Business, All the Right Moves, Legend, Top Gun, The Color of Money, Cocktail, Rain Man, Born on the 4th of July (Golden Globe Award, Acad. Award nom., 1989), Days of Thunder (also co-wrote story), Far and Away, A Few Good Men, The Firm, Interview With the Vampire, Mission: Impossible.
TELEVISION: Director: The Frightening Framis (episode of series Fallen Angels).

CRYER, JON
Actor. b. New York, NY, Apr. 16, 1965. Son of actor David Cryer and songwriter-actress Gretchen Cryer. On B'way stage in Brighton Beach Memoirs.
PICTURES: No Small Affair (debut, 1984), Pretty in Pink, Morgan Stewart's Coming Home, O.C. and Stiggs, Superman IV: The Quest for Peace, Hiding Out, Dudes, Penn and Teller Get Killed, Hot Shots!, The Pompatus of Love.
TELEVISION: Series: The Famous Teddy Z, Partners. Special: Kurt Vonnegut's Monkey House. Movie: Heads.

CRYSTAL, BILLY
Actor, Writer, Producer, Director. b. Long Island, NY, Mar. 14, 1947. e. Marshall U., Nassau Commun. Col., NYU (BFA in tv & film direction). Father, Jack, produced jazz concerts; family owned Commodore jazz record label. Worked with Alumni Theatre Group at Nassau Commun. College. Later teamed with two friends (billed as We the People, Comedy Jam, 3's Company) and toured coffee houses and colleges. Became stand-up comedian on own, appearing at Catch a Rising Star, The Comedy Story and on TV. Album: Mahvelous!. Book: Absolutely Mahvelous!
PICTURES: Rabbit Test (debut, 1978), Animalympics (voice), This Is Spinal Tap, Running Scared, The Princess Bride, Throw Mama From the Train, Memories of Me (also co-prod., co-s.p.), When Harry Met Sally..., City Slickers (also exec. prod.), Mr. Saturday Night (also dir., prod., co-s.p.), City Slickers II: The Legend of Curly's Gold (also prod., co-s.p.), Forget Paris (also dir., prod., co-s.p.), Hamlet.
TELEVISION: Series: Soap, The Billy Crystal Comedy Hour (also writer), Saturday Night Live (also writer), Sessions (cre-ator, exec. prod. only). Guest: Saturday Night Live with Howard Cosell, Tonight Show, Dinah, Mike Douglas Show, That Was the Year That Was, All in the Family, Love Boat. Specials include: Battle of the Network Stars, Billy Crystal: A Comic's Line (also writer), A Comedy Salute to Baseball (also writer), On Location: Billy Crystal - Don't Get Me Started (also dir., writer), The Three Little Pigs (Faerie Tale Theatre), The Lost Minutes of Billy Crystal, Midnight Train to Moscow (also exec. prod., co-writer; Emmy Award 1990). Movies: SST—Death Flight, Human Feelings, Breaking Up Is Hard to Do, Enola Gay: The Men the Mission and the Atomic Bomb. Host: Grammy Awards (Emmy Awards for hosting, 1988, 1989), Academy Awards (Emmy Award for hosting, 1991; Emmy Award for co-writing, 1992).

CULBERG, PAUL S.
Executive. b. Chicago, IL, June 14, 1942. Began career in record industry, holding positions with Elektra Records & Wherehouse Record; 1977-80; v.p. sls. mktg., Cream Records.; 1980-82, dir. sls. Paramount Home Video; 1982, v.p. sls. mktg., Media Home Entertainment; 1984-89, pres., New World Video; 1989-present, COO, RCA Columbia/TriStar Home Video.

CULKIN, MACAULAY
Actor. b. New York, NY, Aug. 26, 1980. Acting debut at 4 yrs. old in Bach Babies at NY's Symphony Space. Appeared in several TV commercials. Studied ballet at George Ballanchine's School of American Ballet and danced in NY productions of H.M.S. Pinafore and The Nutcracker. Received Comedy Award and Youth in Film Award for role in Home Alone. Appeared in Michael Jackson video Black and White.
THEATER: NY: Afterschool Special, Mr. Softee, Buster B. and Olivia.
PICTURES: Rocket Gibraltar (debut, 1988), See You in the Morning, Uncle Buck, Jacob's Ladder, Home Alone, Only the Lonely, My Girl, Home Alone 2: Lost in New York, The Good Son, George Balanchine's The Nutcracker, Getting Even With Dad, The Pagemaster, Richie Rich.
TELEVISION: Guest: The Equalizer, Saturday Night Live, Bob Hope Christmas Special.

CULLUM, JOHN
Actor. b. Knoxville, TN, Mar. 2, 1930. e. Univ. of TN. Son is actor John David (J.D.) Cullum.
THEATER: NY: Camelot, On a Clear Day You Can See Forever (Theatre World Award, Tony nom.), Hamlet, Man of La Mancha, 1776, Shenandoah (Tony Award, Drama Desk & Outer Circle Critics Awards, 1975), The Trip Back Down, On the Twentieth Century (Tony Award, 1978), Deathtrap, Private Lives, Doubles, The Boys in Autumn, Aspects of Love, Showboat.
PICTURES: All the Way Home, 1776, The Prodigal, The Act, Marie, Sweet Country.
TELEVISION: Series: Buck James, Northern Exposure. Guest: Quantum Leap (also dir.). Movies: The Man Without a Country, The Day After, Shoot Down, With a Vengeance.

CULP, ROBERT
Actor, Writer, Director. b. Berkeley, CA, Aug. 16, 1930. e. Stockton, College of the Pacific, Washington U., San Francisco State; to N.Y. to study with Herbert Berghof (played Potzo in 1st U.S. prod. of Waiting for Godot. Starred in off-Bwdy prod. He Who Gets Slapped. Best Actor of the Year in an off-Bwdy Play; motion picture debut, 1962; P.T. 109; television guest appear-ances in Rawhide, Wagon Train, Bob Hope Presents the Chrysler Theatre; wrote and acted in Rifleman, Cain's Hundred, The Dick Powell Show.
THEATER: Bway: The Prescott Proposals, A Clearing in the Woods, Diary of a Scoundrel.
PICTURES: PT 109 (debut, 1963), Sunday in New York, Rhino!, Bob & Carol & Ted & Alice, The Grove, Hannie Caulder, Hickey & Boggs (also dir., uncredited co-s.p.), A Name for Evil, The Castaway Cowboy, Inside Out (Golden Heist), Sky Riders, Breaking Point, The Great Scout and Cathouse Thursday, Goldengirl, National Lampoon Goes to the Movies, Turk 182!, Big Bad Mama II, Silent Night Deadly Night 3: Better Watch Out, Pucker Up and Bark Like a Dog, Timebomb, The Pelican Brief, Panther.
TELEVISION: Series: Trackdown, I Spy (also wrote pilot and 6 shows; Emmy noms. as writer and actor), The Greatest American Hero (also wrote 2 shows). Guest: The Cosby Show. Movies: Sammy The Way Out Seal, The Raiders, The Hanged Man, See the Man Run, A Cold Night's Death, Outrage!, Houston We've Got a Problem, Strange Homecoming, A Cry for Help, Flood, Spectre, Last of the Good Guys, Women in White, Hot Rod, The Dream Merchants, The Night the City Screamed, Killjoy, Thou Shalt Not Kill, Her Life as a Man, The Calendar Girl Murders, Brothers-in-Law, The Blue Lightning, The Gladiator, The Key to Rebecca, Combat High, Voyage of Terror: The Achille Lauro Affair, Columbo Goes to College, I Spy Returns.

CUMMINGS, CONSTANCE
C.B.E. Actress. b. Seattle, WA, May 15, 1910. r.n. Constance Cummings Halverstadt. p. D.V. Halverstadt, attorney, and Kate Cummings, concert soprano; m. Benn Levy, English playwright. Was chorus girl in The Little Show and also appeared in June Moon. B'way debut: Treasure Girl, 1928; London debut: Sour Grapes, 1934. Joined National Theatre Co. 1971.
THEATER: Recent work: A Long Day's Journey into Night (with Laurence Olivier), The Cherry Orchard, Wings (Tony & Obie Awards 1979), The Chalk Garden, Tete a Tete.
PICTURES: The Criminal Code (debut, 1931), The Love Parade, Lover Come Back, Guilty Generation, Traveling Husbands, The Big Timer, Behind the Mask, Movie Crazy, Night After Night, American Madness, The Last Man, Washington Merry-Go-Round, Attorney for the Defense, Heads We Go (The Charming Deceiver), Channel Crossing, Billion Dollar Scandal, Broadway Through a Keyhole, The Mind Reader, Glamour, Looking for Trouble, This Man Is Mine, Remember Last Night?, Seven

Sinners (Doomed Cargo), Strangers on a Honeymoon, Busman's Honeymoon (Haunted Honeymoon), This England, The Foreman Went to France (Somewhere in France), Blithe Spirit, Into the Blue, Three's Company, The Scream, John and Julie, The Intimate Stranger (Finger of Guilt), The Battle of the Sexes, Sammy Going South (A Boy 10 Feet Tall), In the Cool of the Day.
TELEVISION: Touch of the Sun, Clutterbuck, The Last Tycoon, Ruth, Late Summer, Long Day's Journey Into Night, Jane Eyre, Wings, Agatha Christie's Dead Man's Folly.

CUMMINS, PEGGY
Actress. b. Prestatyn, North Wales, Dec. 18, 1925. e. Alexandra Sch., Dublin, Gate Theatre, Dublin. Starred in Let's Pretend on London Stage 1938, followed by Junior Miss, Alice in Wonderland, Peter Pan.
PICTURES: Dr. O'Dowd (debut, 1939), Salute John Citizen, Old Mother Riley—Detective, Welcome Mr. Washington, English Without Tears (Her Man Gilbey), The Late George Apley, Moss Rose, Green Grass of Wyoming, Escape, That Dangerous Age (If This Be Sin), Gun Crazy, My Daughter Joy (Operation X), Who Goes There (Passionate Sentry), Street Corner (Both Sides of the Law), Meet Mr. Lucifer, Always a Bride, The Love Lottery, To Dorothy a Son (Cash on Delivery), The March Hare, Carry on Admiral, Night of the Demon, Hell Drivers, The Captain's Table, Your Money or Your Wife, Dentist in the Chair, In the Doghouse.
TELEVISION: The Human Jungle, Looks Familiar.

CUNNINGHAM, SEAN S.
Producer, Director. b. New York, NY, Dec. 31 1941. e. Franklin & Marshall, B.A.; Stanford U., M.F.A. Worked briefly as actor, moving into stage-managing. Became producer of Mineola Theatre (Long Island, NY) and took several productions to B'way. Formed Sean S. Cunningham Films, Ltd., 1971. Produced commercials, industrial film, documentaries, features.
PICTURES: Together (prod., dir.), Last House on the Left (prod.), The Case of the Full Moon Murders (prod.), Here Come the Tigers (prod., dir.), Kick (prod., dir.), Friday the 13th (prod., dir.), A Stranger Is Watching (prod., dir.), Spring Break (prod., dir.), The New Kids (prod., dir.), House (prod.), House II: The Second Story (prod.), Deepstar Six (prod., dir.), The Horror Show (House III; prod.), House IV (prod.), My Boyfriend's Back (prod.), Jason Goes to Hell: The Final Friday (prod.).

CURRY, TIM
Actor. b. Cheshire, England, Apr. 19, 1946. e. Birmingham U. Albums: Read My Lips, Fearless, Simplicity.
THEATER: Hair, A Midsummer Night's Dream, The Rocky Horror Show, Travesties, Amadeus (Tony nom.), The Pirates of Penzance, Me and My Girl (U.S. tour), The Art of Success, My Favorite Year (Tony nom.).
PICTURES: The Rocky Horror Picture Show (debut, 1975), The Shout, Times Square, Annie, The Ploughman's Lunch, Blue Money, Clue, Legend, Pass the Ammo, The Hunt for Red October, Oscar, FernGully... The Last Rainforest (voice), Passed Away, Home Alone 2: Lost in New York, National Lampoon's Loaded Weapon 1, The Three Musketeers, The Shadow, Lovers' Knot, The Pebble and the Penguin (voice), Congo, The Muppet Treasure Island, Lover's Knot.
TELEVISION: Movies: Oliver Twist, Stephen King's IT. Voice work—series: Peter Pan and the Pirates (Emmy Award, 1991), Captain Planet and the Planeteers, Fish Police. Specials: The Life of Shakespeare, Three Men in a Boat, Rock Follies, City Sugar. Guest: Dinosaurs (voice), Earth 2.

CURTIN, JANE
Actress. b. Cambridge, MA, Sept. 6, 1947. e. Northeastern U. On stage in Proposition, Last of the Red Hot Lovers, Candida. Author, actress off-B'way musical revue Pretzel 1974-75.
PICTURES: Mr. Mike's Mondo Video, How to Beat the High Cost of Living, O.C. and Stiggs, Coneheads.
TELEVISION: Series: Saturday Night Live (1974-79), Kate & Allie (Emmy Awards: 1984, 1985), Working It Out. Movies: What Really Happened to the Class of '65, Divorce Wars—A Love Story, Suspicion, Maybe Baby, Common Ground. Special: Candida.

CURTIS, DAN
Producer, Director. b. Bridgeport, CT, Aug. 12, 1928. e. U. of Bridgeport, Syracuse U., B.A. Was sales exec. for NBC and MCA before forming own company, Dan Curtis Productions, which he now heads. Producer/owner of CBS Golf Classic (1963-73).
PICTURES: Dir.-Prod.: House of Dark Shadows, Night of Dark Shadows, Burnt Offerings (also co-s.p.), Me and the Kid.
TELEVISION: Producer: Series: Dark Shadows (ABC daytime serial, 1966-71), Dark Shadows (prime time series, 1991). Movies: Director: The Night Stalker, Frankenstein, The Picture of Dorian Gray. Producer-Director: The Night Strangler, The Norliss Tapes, Scream of the Wolf, Dracula, Melvin Purvis: G-Man, The Turn of the Screw, The Great Ice-Rip Off, Trilogy of Terror, Kansas City Massacre, Curse of the Black Widow, When Every

Day Was the Fourth of July (also co-story). Director: The Last Ride of the Dalton Gang, The Long Days of Summer, Mrs. R's Daughter, Intruders (also co-exec. prod.). Mini-Series (prod./dir.): The Winds of War, War and Remembrance (also co-writer).

CURTIS, JAMIE LEE
Actress. b. Los Angeles, CA, Nov. 22, 1958. m. actor-director Christopher Guest. Daughter of Janet Leigh and Tony Curtis. e. Choat Rosemary Hall, CT; Univ. of the Pacific. While in school won contract with Universal Studios appearing in small parts in several tv shows.
PICTURES: Halloween (debut, 1978), The Fog, Prom Night, Terror Train, Halloween II, Roadgames, Trading Places, Love Letters, Grandview USA, Perfect, Amazing Grace and Chuck, A Man in Love, Dominick and Eugene, A Fish Called Wanda, Blue Steel, Queens Logic, My Girl, Forever Young, My Girl 2, Mother's Boys, True Lies, House Arrest, Death Fish.
TELEVISION: Special: Tall Tales (Annie Oakley). Series: Operation Petticoat (1977-78), Anything But Love (Golden Globe Award). Movies: Operation Petticoat (pilot), She's in the Army Now, Death of a Centerfold: The Dorothy Stratten Story, Money on the Side, As Summers Die, The Heidi Chronicles. Pilot: Callahan. Guest: Quincy, Nancy Drew Mysteries.

CURTIS, TONY
Actor. r.n. Bernard Schwartz. b. New York, NY, June 3, 1925. Daughter is actress Jamie Lee Curtis. e. Seward Park H.S. In U.S. Navy, amateur dramatics, N.Y., started Empire Players Theatre, Newark, NJ; with Dramatic Workshop, Cherry Lane Theatre, Junior Drama workshop of Walt Whitman School; first prod. work with Stanley Woolf Players; m.p. debut unbilled in Criss-Cross; signed with U-I. Star of Tomorrow, 1953. Author: Tony Curtis: The Autobiography (1993).
PICTURES: Criss Cross (debut, 1948), City Across the River, The Lady Gambles, Johnny Stool Pigeon, Francis, Sierra, I Was a Shoplifter, Winchester 73, Sierra, Kansas Raiders, Prince Who Was a Thief, Flesh and Fury, Son of Ali Baba, No Room for the Groom, Houdini, All American, Forbidden, Beachhead, Johnny Dark, Black Shield of Falworth, 6 Bridges to Cross, So This Is Paris, Purple Mask, Square Jungle, Rawhide Years, Trapeze, Mister Cory, Midnight Story, Sweet Smell of Success, The Vikings, Kings Go Forth, The Defiant Ones (Acad. Award nom.), The Perfect Furlough, Some Like It Hot, Operation Petticoat, Who Was That Lady?, The Rat Race, Spartacus, Pepe (cameo), The Great Impostor, The Outsider, Taras Bulba, 40 Pounds of Trouble, The List of Adrian Messenger, Captain Newman, M.D., Paris When it Sizzles, Wild and Wonderful, Sex and the Single Girl, Goodbye Charlie, The Great Race, Boeing-Boeing, Chamber of Horrors (cameo), Not With My Wife You Don't!, Arrivederci Baby!, Don't Make Waves, On My Way to the Crusades I Met a Girl Who—(The Chastity Belt), The Boston Strangler, Rosemary's Baby (voice), Those Daring Young Men in Their Jaunty Jalopies (Monte Carlo or Bust), Suppose They Gave a War and Nobody Came, You Can't Win 'Em All, Lepke, The Last Tycoon, Casanova & Co., The Manitou, The Bad News Bears Go to Japan, Sextette, Little Miss Marker, The Mirror Crack'd, Brainwaves, King of the City, Insignificance, Club Life, The Last of Philip Banter, Balboa, Midnight, Lobster Man From Mars, The High-Flying Mermaid, Prime Target, Center of the Web, Naked in New York, The Reptile Man, The Immortals, The Celluloid Closet.
TELEVISION: Series: The Persuaders, McCoy, Vega$, Hollywood Babylon (host). Movies: The Third Girl from the Left, The Count of Monte Cristo, Vega$, The Users, Moviola: The Scarlett O'Hara War, Inmates: A Love Story, Harry's Back, The Million Dollar Face, Mafia Princess, Murder in Three Acts, Portrait of a Showgirl, Tarzan in Manhattan, Thanksgiving Day, Christmas in Connecticut, A Perry Mason Mystery: The Case of the Grimacing Governor.

CUSACK, JOAN
Actress. b. Evanston, IL, Oct. 11, 1962. Brother is actor John Cusack. e. U. of Wisconsin, Madison. Studied acting at Piven Theatre Workshop, Evanston, IL. While in coll. joined The Ark, local improvisational comedy group.
THEATER: Road, Brilliant Traces (Theatre World Award for both), Cymbeline, The Celestial Alphabet Event, 'Tis Pity She's a Whore, A Midsummer Night's Dream.
PICTURES: My Bodyguard (debut, 1980), Class, Sixteen Candles, Grandview U.S.A., The Allnighter, Broadcast News, Stars and Bars, Married to the Mob, Working Girl (Acad. Award nom.), Say Anything..., Men Don't Leave, My Blue Heaven, The Cabinet of Dr. Ramirez, Hero, Toys, Addams Family Values, Corrina Corrina, Nine Months, Mr. Wrong.
TELEVISION: Series: Saturday Night Live (1985-86). Special: The Mother.

CUSACK, JOHN
Actor. b. Evanston, IL, June 28, 1966. Sister is actress Joan Cusack. Member of Piven Theatre Workshop in Evanston for 10 years beginning when he was 9 years old. Appeared on several tv commercials as teen. Formed Chicago theatrical company, New Criminals.

PICTURES: Class (debut, 1983), Sixteen Candles, Grandview U.S.A., The Sure Thing, The Journey of Natty Gann, Better Off Dead, Stand By Me, One Crazy Summer, Hot Pursuit, Eight Men Out, Tapeheads, Say Anything..., Fat Man and Little Boy, The Grifters, True Colors, Shadows and Fog, Roadside Prophets, The Player, Bob Roberts, Map of the Human Heart, Money for Nothing, Bullets Over Broadway, The Road to Wellville, Floundering, City Hall.

D

D'ABO, OLIVIA
Actress. b. England. Parents, singer Michael d'Abo, actress Maggie London.
THEATER: LA: Scenes From an Execution, It's a Girl.
PICTURES: Conan the Destroyer, Bolero, Bullies, Into the Fire, Beyond the Stars, The Spirit of 76, Point of No Return, Wayne's World 2, Bank Robber, Greedy, Clean Slate, The Last Good Time, The Big Green, Kicking and Screaming.
TELEVISION: Series: The Wonder Years, The Single Guy.
Movies: Not My Kid, Crash Course, Midnight's Child.

DAFOE, WILLEM
Actor. r.n. William Dafoe. b. Appleton, WI, July 22, 1955. Worked with experimental group Theatre X on the road before coming to New York. Built sets and debuted with the Wooster Group at the Performing Garage playing (literally) a chicken heart in Elizabeth Le Compte's Nayatt School. Current member of the Wooster Group, performing with them frequently in U.S. and Europe. For them appeared in independent film The Communists Are Comfortable.
PICTURES: Heaven's Gate (debut, 1980), The Loveless, The Hunger, Streets of Fire, Roadhouse 66, To Live and Die in L.A., Platoon (Acad. Award nom.), Off Limits, The Last Temptation of Christ, Mississippi Burning, Triumph of the Spirit, Born on the Fourth of July, Cry-Baby, Wild at Heart, Flight of the Intruder, White Sands, Light Sleeper, Body of Evidence, Faraway So Close!, Clear and Present Danger, Tom and Viv, The Night and the Moment, The English Patient.

DAHL, ARLENE
Actress, Writer, Designer. b. Minneapolis, MN, Aug. 11, 1928. e. MN Business Coll.; U. of Minnesota, summers 1941-44; Minneapolis. Coll. of Music. m. Marc A. Rosen. Mother of actor Lorenzo Lamas. At age 11, played heroine of children's adventure serials on radio. Internationally syndicated beauty columnist, Chgo. Tribune-N.Y. News Syndicate, 1951-71; Pres. Arlene Dahl Enterprises, 1951-75; Sleepwear Designer, A.N. Saab & Co., 1952-57; Natl. Beauty Advisor, Sears Roebuck & Co., 1970-75; v.p. Kenyon & Eckhart Advg. Co., pres., Women's World Div., Kenyon-Eckhart, 1967-72; Fashion Consultant, O.M.A. 1975-78, Int'l. Director of S.M.E.I., 1973-76, Designer, Vogue Patterns 1978-85. Pres., Dahlia Parfums Inc., 1975-80, pres., Dahlia Prods., 1978-81; pres. Dahlmark Prods. 1981-. Publs: Always Ask a Man, 1965, Your Beautyscope, 1969, Secrets of Hair Care, 1971, Secrets of Skin Care, 1973, Your Beautyscope 1977-78, Beyond Beauty, 1980, Lovescopes, 1983. Honrs. include: 8 Motion Picture Laurel Awards, 1948-63; Hds. of Fame Award, 1971, Woman of the Year, N.Y. Adv. Council, 1969. Mother of the Year, 1979; Coup de Chapeau, Deauville Film Fest 1983. Received star on Hollywood Walk of Fame. Lifetime Achievement Award Filmfest 1994.
THEATER: B'way: Mr. Strauss Goes to Boston (debut, 1946), Cyrano de Bergerac, Applause. Major US tours include: Questionable Ladies, The King and I, One Touch of Venus, I Married an Angel, Mame, Pal Joey, Bell Book and Candle, The Camel Bell, Life With Father, A Little Night Music, Lilliom, Marriage Go Round, Blithe Spirit, Forty Carats, Dear Liar, Murder Among Friends.
PICTURES: My Wild Irish Rose (debut, 1947), The Bride Goes Wild, A Southern Yankee, Ambush, Reign of Terror (The Black Book), Scene of the Crime, The Outriders, Three Little Words, Watch the Birdie, Inside Straight, No Questions Asked, Caribbean, Jamaica Run, Desert Legion, Here Come the Girls, Sangaree, The Diamond Queen, Wicked as They Come, Fortune is a Woman, Bengal Brigade, Woman's World, Slightly Scarlet, She Played With Fire, Journey to the Center of the Earth, Kisses for My President, Les Ponyettes, DuBle en Liasse, Le Chemin du Katmandu. The Landraiders, A Place to Hide, Night of the Warrior.
TELEVISION: Max Factor Playhouse, Lux Television Theater, Pepsi Cola Playhouse, Opening Night, Arlene Dahl's Beauty Spot, Hostess, Model of the Year Show, Arlene Dahl's Starscope, Arlene Dahl's Lovescopes, One Life to Live (1981-84), Night of One Hundred Stars, Happy Birthday Hollywood, Who Killed Max Thorn?, Love Boat, Love American Style, Fantasy Island, Burke's Law, Renegade.

DAHL, JOHN
Director, Writer. b. Montana. e. Univ. of MT, Montana St. In collaboration with David Warfield made 30 minute rock musical, Here Come the Pugs and indept. feature, The Death Mutants.

PICTURES: Private Investigations (co-s.p.), Kill Me Again (dir., co-s.p.), Red Rock West (dir., co-s.p.), The Last Seduction (dir.), Unforgettable (dir., co-s.p.)

DALE, JIM
Actor. b. Rothwell, Northhamptonshire, England, Aug. 15, 1935. Debut as solo comedian at the Savoy, 1951. Joined National Theatre Co. in 1969 playing in Love's Labour's Lost, The Merchant of Venice, The National Health, The Card. U.S. theater: Mark Taper Forum: Comedians, Scapino. NY Theater: Taming of the Shrew, Scapino, Barnum (Tony and Drama Desk Awards, 1980), Joe Egg (Tony Award nom.), Me and My Girl, Privates on Parade, Travels With My Aunt. Has written songs and music for films: Twinky, Shalako, Joseph Andrews, Georgy Girl (Acad. Award nom.). Many tv appearances. Director: Asprin and Elephants.
PICTURES: Six-Five Special (debut, 1958), Raising the Wind, Nurse on Wheels, The Iron Maiden, Carry on Cabby, Carry on Jack, Carry on Spying, Carry on Cleo, The Big Job, Carry on Cowboy, Carry on Screaming, Don't Lose Your Head, The Winter's Tale, The Plank, Follow That Camel, Carry on Doctor, Lock Up Your Daughters, Carry on Again Doctor, The National Health, Digby—The Biggest Dog in the World, Joseph Andrews, Pete's Dragon, Hot Lead Cold Feet, Unidentified Flying Oddball, Scandalous, Carry on Columbus.
TELEVISION: Movie: The American Clock.

DALEY, ROBERT
Producer. e. UCLA. Began career in pictures at Universal International and TV at Desilu.
PICTURES: Play Misty For Me, Dirty Harry (exec. prod.), Joe Kidd, High Plains Drifter, Breezy, Magnum Force, Thunderbolt and Lightfoot, The Eiger Sanction, The Outlaw Josey Wales, The Enforcer, The Gauntlet, Every Which Way But Loose, Escape from Alcatraz (exec. prod.), Any Which Way You Can (exec. prod.), Bronco Billy (exec. prod.), Stick (exec. prod.), Real Genius (exec. prod.).
TELEVISION: The Untouchables, Ben Casey, The FBI, 12 O'Clock High, The Invaders, etc.

DALSIMER, SUSAN
Executive. Editor for E.P. Dutton before joining Lorimar Prods., as v.p. of east coast development. Left to become consultant for original programming at Home Box Office. 1987, named v.p., creative affairs, east coast, for Warner Bros. 1994, v.p., publishing for Miramax Films.

DALTON, TIMOTHY
Actor. b. Colwyn Bay, No. Wales, March 21, 1946. Started acting at Natl. Youth Theatre, then studied at RADA. Prof. stage debut in Richard III and As You Like It at Birmingham Rep.
THEATER: Coriolanus, The Merchant of Venice, Richard III, The Doctor's Dilemma, St. Joan, Macbeth, Henry IV, Henry V, The Samaritan, Black Comedy, White Liars, Lunatic Lover and Poet, Love Letters (1991).
PICTURES: The Lion in Winter (debut, 1968), Cromwell, The Voyeur, Wuthering Heights, Mary Queen of Scots, Permission to Kill, Sextette, Agatha, Flash Gordon, El Hombre Que Supo Amar, Anthony and Cleopatra, Chanel Solitaire, The Doctor and the Devils, The Living Daylights, Brenda Starr, Hawks, Licence to Kill, The King's Whore, The Rocketeer, Naked in New York, Saltwater Moose.
TELEVISION: Mini-Series: Centennial, Mistral's Daughter, Sins, Scarlett, Framed. Movies: The Master of Ballantrae, Lie Down With Lions, Field of Blood. Specials: The Three Princes, Five Finger Exercise, Candida, Daerie Tale Theater: The Emperor's New Clothes (narr.), Nature: In The Company of Wolves (docu.). Series: Sat'day While Sunday, Judge Dee, Hooked International, Charlie's Angels: Fallen Angel, Tales From the Crypt: Werewolf Concerto, Survival Factor Series (narr.).

DALTREY, ROGER
Singer, Actor. b. London, England, March 1, 1944. Lead vocalist in The Who.
PICTURES: Woodstock, Tommy, Lisztomania, The Legacy, The Kids Are Alright, McVicar (also prod.), Mack the Knife, The Teddy Bear Habit, Father Jim, If Looks Could Kill, Buddy's Song, Lightning Jack.
TELEVISION: Movie: Forgotten Prisoners: The Amnesty Files.

DALY, ANN
Executive. Pres., Domestic Home Video, Buena Vista Home Video.

DALY, JIM
Executive Director, Rank Organisation Plc. b. 1938. Managing director of Film and Television division which includes: Pinewood Studios, Rank Film Laboratories, Odeon Cinemas, Rank Film Distributors, Deluxe Hollywood, Deluxe Toronto, Rank Advertising Films, Rank Theatres, Rank Video Services, Rank Video Services America, Rank Video Services Europe, Film House Company, Rank Brimar, Rank Cintel, Strand Lighting, Rank Taylor Hobson. Appt. exec. dir., Rank Org. 1982.

DALY, JOHN
Executive. b. London, England, July 16, 1937. After working in journalism joined Royal Navy. On leaving Service after three years, trained as underwriter with an Assurance Company. In 1966 became David Hemmings manager and in 1967 formed the Hemdale Company with Hemmings (who later sold interest) Chmn. Hemdale Holdings Ltd.
PICTURES: Images, Sunburn (co-prod., co-s.p.), High Risk, Going Ape, Deadly Force, Carbon Copy, Yellowbeard, The Terminator, The Falcon and the Snowman, Salvador, River's Edge, At Close Range, Hoosiers, Platoon, Best Seller, Shag (exec. prod.), Vampire's Kiss (exec. prod.), Miracle Mile (prod.), Criminal Law (co-exec. prod.), War Party (prod.), The Boost, Out Cold (exec. prod.), Staying Together (exec. prod.).

DALY, ROBERT A.
Executive. b. New York, NY, Dec. 8, 1936. e. Brooklyn Coll., Hunter Coll. Joined CBS-TV in 1955; dir. of program acct.; dir. of research and cost planning; dir. of business affairs. Later named v.p., business affairs, NY; exec. v.p. of network on April, 1976. Named president, CBS Entertainment, Oct. 1977. In Oct. 1979 became responsible for CBS Theatrical Films as well as the TV operation. In 1980, appointed co-chmn. and co-chief exec. officer of Warner Bros. Sole title holder since Jan., 1982.

DALY, TIM
Actor. b. New York, NY, March 1, 1956. m. actress Amy Van Nostrand. Son of late actor James Daly, brother of actress Tyne Daly. e. Bennington Coll., B.A. Acted in summer stock while in college. Moved to NY where had own rock and roll band. Has performed in cabaret at Williamstown Theater Festival.
THEATER: Fables for Friends, Oliver Oliver, Mass Appeal, Bus Stop, Coastal Disturbances (Theatre World Award).
PICTURES: Diner, Just the Way You Are, Made in Heaven, Spellbinder, Love or Money, Year of the Comet, Caroline at Midnight, Dr. Jekyll and Ms. Hyde, Denise Calls Up, The Associate.
TELEVISION: Special: The Rise and Rise of Daniel Rocket. Mini-Series: I'll Take Manhattan, Queen. Series: Ryan's Four, Almost Grown, Wings. Movies: I Married a Centerfold, Mirrors, Red Earth White Earth, In the Line of Duty: Ambush in Waco, Dangerous Heart, Witness to the Execution. Guest: Midnight Caller, Hill Street Blues, Alfred Hitchcock Presents.

DALY, TYNE
Actress. r.n. Ellen Tyne Daly. b. Madison, WI, Feb. 21, 1946. Daughter of late actor James Daly and actress Hope Newell; brother is actor Timothy Daly.
THEATER: The Butter and Egg Man, That Summer That Fall, Skirmishes, The Black Angel, Rimers of Eldritch, Ashes, Three Sisters, Come Back Little Sheba (L.A., 1987), Gypsy (Tony Award, 1990), Queen of the Stardust Ballroom, The Seagull, On the Town, Call Me Madam (in concert).
PICTURES: John and Mary, Angel Unchained, Play It As It Lays, The Adulteress, The Enforcer, Telefon, Speedtrap, Zoot Suit, The Aviator, Movers & Shakers.
TELEVISION: Series: Cagney & Lacey (4 Emmy Awards), Christy (Emmy Award, 1996). Movies: In Search of America, A Howling in the Woods, Heat of Anger, The Man Who Could Talk to Kids, Larry, The Entertainer, Better Late Than Never, Intimate Strangers, The Women's Room, A Matter of Life or Death, Your Place or Mine, Kids Like These, Stuck With Each Other, The Last to Go, Face of a Stranger, Columbo: A Bird in the Hand, Scattered Dreams: The Kathryn Messenger Story, The Forget-Me-Not Murders, Columbo: Undercover, Cagney & Lacey: The Return, Cagney & Lacey: Together Again, Bye Bye Birdie. Guest: Medical Center, Columbo, Ray Bradbury Theatre, Wings.

DAMON, MARK
Executive. b. Chicago, IL, April 22, 1933. e. UCLA, B.A. literature, M.A. business administration. Actor: 1958 under contract to 20th Century Fox, 1960 winner Golden Globe Award-Newcomer of the Year; early career includes The Fall of The House of Usher, The Longest Day; 1961 moved to Italy, stayed 16 years appearing in leading roles in 50 films; 1974 head of foreign dept. for PAC, a leading film distributor in Italy; 1976 returned to the U.S. as exec. prod. of The Choirboys and in charge of its foreign distribution; 1979 founder and pres. of Producers Sales Organization, intl. distribution org. 1987 formed Vision Int'l.; 1993, formed MDP Worlwide, intl. prod. & distrib. co.
PICTURES: The Arena (prod.), Exec. prod. or co-exec. prod.: The Choirboys, The Neverending Story, Das Boot, Nine 1/2 Weeks (prod.), Short Circuit, Flight of the Navigator, Lost Boys, High Spirits, Bat 21 (co-prod.), Wild Orchid (prod.), Wild Orchid II: Two Shades of Blue, The Jungle Book.

DAMONE, VIC
Singer, Actor. r.n. Vito Farinola. b. Brooklyn, NY, June 12, 1928. m. actress-singer Diahann Carroll. e. Lafayette H.S., Brooklyn. Winner Arthur Godfrey talent show, 1947; then night clubs, radio, theatres. U.S. Army, 1951-53.
PICTURES: Rich Young and Pretty (debut, 1951), The Strip, Athena, Deep in My Heart, Hit the Deck, Kismet, Hell to Eternity.
TELEVISION: Series: The Vic Damone Show (1956-57), Lively Ones (1962-63), The Vic Damone Show (1967).

DAMSKI, MEL
Director. b. New York, NY, July 21, 1946. e. Colgate U., AFI. Worked as reporter, journalism professor. USC Cinema instructor.
PICTURES: Yellowbeard, Mischief, Happy Together.
TELEVISION: Series: M*A*S*H, Lou Grant, Dolphin Cove. Movies: Long Journey Back, The Child Stealer, Word of Honor, The Legend of Walks Far Woman, American Dream, For Ladies Only, Making the Grade, An Invasion of Privacy, Badge of the Assassin, A Winner Never Quits, Attack on Fear, Hero in the Family, Murder by the Book, Hope Division, The Three Kings, Everybody's Baby: The Rescue of Jessica McClure, Back to the Streets of San Francisco.

DANA, BILL
Actor, Writer. b. Quincy, MA, Oct. 5, 1924. In night clubs and on TV.
PICTURES: Actor: The Busy Body, The Barefoot Executive, The Nude Bomb (also s.p.).
TELEVISION: Series: The Steve Allen Show (performer, head writer, 1961), The Bill Dana Jose Jimenez Show (star, writer), Spike Jones Show (prod., writer, performer), Milton Berle Show (prod., writer, performer), No Soap Radio, Zorro and Son. Writer: All in the Family. Movies: The Snoop Sisters, Rosetti & Ryan: Men Who Love Women, A Guide for the Married Woman, Murder in Texas. Actor: Facts of Life, Too Close for Comfort, Golden Girls, Hollywood Palace, St. Elsewhere.

DANCE, CHARLES
Actor. b. Worcestershire, Eng., Oct. 10, 1946. e. Plymouth Coll. Art., Leicester Coll. of Art (graphic design degree). After first working as a West End theatre stagehand, made acting debut in 1970 in a touring company of It's a Two-Foot-Six-Inches-above-the-Ground World. Worked in provincial repertory theaters. Joined the Royal Shakespeare Company 1975-80: Hamlet, Richard III, As You Like It. Lead in Henry V (1975, N.Y.), Coriolanus (Paris, London, Stratford).
THEATER: revival of Irma La Douce (West End), Turning Over (London's Bush Theatre).
PICTURES: The Spy Who Loved Me (debut, 1977), For Your Eyes Only, Plenty, The Golden Child, Good Morning Babylon, White Mischief, The Hidden City, Pascali's Island, Alien 3, The Valley of Stone, Last Action Hero, China Moon, Century, Kabloonak, Exquisite Tenderness, Shortcut to Paradise, Undertow, Michael Collins, Space Truckers, In the Presence of Mine Enemies.
TELEVISION: Very Like a Whale, The McGuffin, The Jewel in the Crown, Edward VII, The Fatal Spring, Little Eiolf, Frost in May, Nancy Astor, Saigon—The Last Day, Out On a Limb, BBC's The Secret Servant, Rainy Day Woman, Out of the Shadows, First Born, Goldeneye, Phantom of the Opera (mini-series).

D'ANGELO, BEVERLY
Actress. b. Columbus, OH, Nov. 15, 1954. Studied visual arts and was exchange student in Italy before working as cartoonist for Hanna-Barbera Studios in Hollywood. Toured Canada's coffeehouse circuit as singer and appeared with rock band called Elephant. Joined Charlotte Town Festival Company. B'way debut in rock musical, Rockabye Hamlet. Off-B'way: Simpatico (Theatre World Award).
PICTURES: The Sentinel (debut 1977). Annie Hall, First Love, Every Which Way But Loose, Hair, Highpoint, Coal Miner's Daughter, Honky Tonk Freeway, Paternity, National Lampoon's Vacation, Finders Keepers, National Lampoon's European Vacation, Big Trouble, Maid to Order, In the Mood, Aria, Trading Hearts, High Spirits, National Lampoon's Christmas Vacation, Daddy's Dyin', Pacific Heights (unbilled), The Miracle, The Pope Must Die, Man Trouble, Lonely Hearts, Lightning Jack, Eye for an Eye, Edie and Pen, Pterodactyl Woman from Beverly Hills.
TELEVISION: Mini-Series: Captains and the Kings. Movies: A Streetcar Named Desire, Doubletake, Slow Burn, Hands of a Stranger, Trial: The Price of Passion, A Child Lost Forever, The Switch, Judgment Day: The John List Story, Jonathan Stone: Threat of Innocence, Menendez: A Killing in Beverly Hills. Special: Sleeping Beauty (Faerie Tale Theater).

DANES, CLAIRE
Actress. b. New York, NY, April 12, 1979. e. Professional Performing Arts School, NY; Lee Strasberg Studio. Acting career began with off-off-B'way appearances in Happiness, Punk Ballet and Kids on Stage.
PICTURES: Dreams of Love (debut), Thirty (short), The Pesky Suitor (short), Little Women, Romeo and Juliet, To Gillian on Her 37th Birthday, Polish Wedding.

TELEVISION: *Series*: My So Called Life. *Guest*: Law and Order. *Movies*: No Room for Opal, The Coming Out of Heidi Leiter.

DANGERFIELD, RODNEY
Actor, Comedian. r.n. Jacob Cohen. b. Babylon, NY, Nov. 22, 1921. Performer in nightclubs as Jack Roy 1941-51. Worked as businessman 1951-63, before becoming stand-up comedian. Founder Dangerfields' Nightclub, 1969. Regular appearances on Dean Martin Show, 1972-3. Appeared in TV movie Benny and Barney: Las Vegas Undercover.
PICTURES: The Projectionist, Caddyshack, Easy Money (also co-s.p.), Back to School, Moving, Rover Dangerfield (voice, exec. prod., s.p., co-story, co-wrote songs), Ladybugs, Natural Born Killers, Casper (cameo), Meet Wally Sparks (also co-s.p.).

DANIEL, SEAN
Executive. b. Aug. 15, 1951. e. California Inst. of Arts film school. BFA, 1973. Was journalist for Village Voice before starting m.p. career as documentary filmmaker and asst. dir. for New World Pictures. In 1976 joined Universal Pictures as prod. exec.; 1979, named v.p., then pres., production. Resigned March, 1989 to become pres., The Geffen Co., film div., resigned from Geffen, Nov. 1989. 1990, with Jim Jacks started own prod. co. Alphaville, in partnership with Universal Pictures.
PICTURES: Pure Luck, American Me, CB4, Hard Target, Heart and Souls, Tombstone.

DANIELS, JEFF
Actor. b. Athens, Georgia. Feb. 19, 1955. e. Central Michigan U. Apprentice with Circle Repertory Theatre, New York. Established Purple Rose Theatre Co. in Chelsea, Michigan. Playwright: The Kingdom's Coming, The Vast Difference.
THEATER: Brontosaurus, Short-Changed Review, The Farm, Fifth of July, Johnny Got His Gun (Obie Award), Lemon Sky, The Three Sisters, The Golden Age, Redwood Curtain.
PICTURES: Ragtime (debut, 1981), Terms of Endearment, The Purple Rose of Cairo, Marie, Heartburn, Something Wild, Radio Days, The House on Carroll Street, Sweet Hearts Dance, Checking Out, Arachnophobia, Welcome Home Roxy Carmichael, Love Hurts, The Butcher's Wife, There Goes the Neighborhood, Rain Without Thunder, Gettysburg, Speed, Terminal Velocity, Dumb & Dumber, 2 Days in the Valley, Fly Away Home, 101 Dalmations.
TELEVISION: *Movies*: A Rumor of War, Invasion of Privacy, The Caine Mutiny Court Martial, No Place Like Home, Disaster in Time, Teamster Boss: The Jackie Presser Story, Redwood Curtain. *Specials*: Fifth of July, The Visit (Trying Times). *Guest*: Breaking Away (pilot), Hawaii 5-0.

DANIELS, PAUL
TV performer, Magician. b. South Bank, England, Apr. 6, 1938. Early career starring in British and overseas theatres. 1983, Magician Of The Year Award by Hollywood's Academy of Magical Arts. 1985, his BBC TV special awarded Golden Rose of Montreux trophy. Presenter of Every Second Counts and Paul Daniels Magic Show. Devised children's TV series, Wizbit and radio series Dealing With Daniels, Secret Magic and Game Show Wipeout.

DANIELS, WILLIAM
Actor. b. Brooklyn, NY, Mar 31, 1927. m. actress Bonnie Bartlett. e. Northwestern U. Traveled around NY area as part of The Daniels Family song and dance troupe. Appeared with family on experimental TV in 1941. Stage debut in Life with Father. Brought to national attention in A Thousand Clowns in original B'way play and film version.
THEATER: The Zoo Story, On a Clear Day You Can See Forever, 1776, Dear Me, The Sky Is Falling, A Little Night Music.
PICTURES: Ladybug Ladybug, A Thousand Clowns, Two for the Road, The Graduate, The President's Analyst, Marlowe, 1776, The Parallax View, Black Sunday, Oh God!, The One and Only, Sunburn, The Blue Lagoon, All Night Long, Reds, Blind Date, Her Alibi.
TELEVISION: *Series*: Captain Nice, The Nancy Walker Show, Freebie and the Bean, Knight Rider (voice), St. Elsewhere (Emmy Awards, 1985, 1986), Boy Meets World. *Guest*: East Side/West Side, For the People, Toma, The Rockford Files. *Movies*: Rooster, Rehearsal for a Murder, Murdock's Gang, A Case of Rape, Sarah T.—Portrait of a Teenage Alcoholic, One of Our Own, Francis Gary Powers, Killer on Board, The Bastard, Big Bob Johnson and His Fantastic Speed Circus, Sgt. Matlovich Vs. the U.S. Air Force, The Rebels, City in Fear, Damien: The Leper Priest, Million Dollar Face, Drop Out Father, The Little Match Girl, Knight Rider 2000 (voice), Back to the Streets of San Francisco. Mini-series: Blind Ambition, The Adams Chronicles.

DANNER, BLYTHE
Actress. b. Philadelphia, PA, Feb. 3, 1943. e. Bard Coll. m. writer-producer Bruce Paltrow. Daughter is actress Gwyneth Paltrow. Appeared in repertory cos. in U.S. before Lincoln Center (N.Y.) productions of Cyrano de Bergerac, Summertree, and The Miser (Theatre World Award for last).
THEATER: *NY*: Butterflies Are Free (Tony Award, 1971), Major Barbara, Twelfth Night, The Seagull, Ring Around The Moon, Betrayal, Blithe Spirit, A Streetcar Named Desire, Much Ado About Nothing, Sylvia. Williamstown: Picnic.
PICTURES: To Kill a Clown (debut, 1972), 1776, Lovin' Molly, Hearts of the West, Futureworld, The Great Santini, Man Woman and Child, Brighton Beach Memoirs, Another Woman, Mr. and Mrs. Bridge, Alice, The Prince of Tides, Husbands and Wives, To Wong Foo—Thanks for Everything—Julie Newmar, Homage.
TELEVISION: *Movies*: Dr. Cook's Garden, F. Scott Fitzgerald and The Last of the Belles, Sidekicks, A Love Affair: The Eleanor and Lou Gehrig Story, Too Far to Go, Eccentricities of a Nightingale, Are You in the House Alone?, Inside the Third Reich, In Defense of Kids, Helen Keller: The Miracle Continues, Guilty Conscience, Money Power Murder, Judgment, Never Forget, Cruel Doubt, Getting Up and Going Home, Oldest Living Confederate Widow Tells All, Leave of Absence. Series: Adam's Rib, Tattingers (revamped as Nick & Hillary). *Specials*: To Confuse the Angel, George M, To Be Young Gifted and Black, The Scarecrow., Kiss Kiss Dahlings.

DANSON, TED
Actor. b. San Diego, CA, Dec. 29, 1947. e. Kent Sch., Stanford U., Carnegie-Mellon U, 1972. m. actress Mary Steenburgen. Studied at Actors Inst. New York stage debut, The Real Inspector Hound, 1972; 1978, mgr. and teacher, Actors Inst., L.A. Television debut, The Doctors. Founded Amer. Oceans Campaign; bd. mem. Futures for Children.
PICTURES: The Onion Field (debut, 1979), Body Heat, Creepshow, Little Treasure, Just Between Friends, A Fine Mess, Three Men and a Baby, Cousins, Dad, Three Men and a Little Lady, Made in America, Getting Even With Dad, Pontiac Moon (also co-exec. prod.), Loch Ness.
TELEVISION: An Affectionate Look at Fatherhood (special). *Series*: Somerset, Cheers (2 Emmy Awards: 1990, 1993), Ink (also co-exec. prod.). *Movies*: The Women's Room, Once Upon a Spy, Our Family Business, Cowboy, Something About Amelia, When the Bough Breaks (also prod.), We Are the Children, Mercy Mission: The Rescue of Flight 771, On Promised Land, Fight For Justice, The Canterville Ghost, Gulliver's Travels. *Guest*: Laverne & Shirley, Magnum P.I., Taxi, Saturday Night Live.

DANTE, JOE
Director. b. Morristown, NJ. Managing editor for Film Bulletin before going to Hollywood to work in advertising, creating campaigns for many films. Became protege of Roger Corman, co-directing Hollywood Boulevard. Edited film Grand Theft Auto; co-wrote story for Rock 'n' Roll High School.
PICTURES: *Director*: Piranha (also co-editor), The Howling (also co-editor), Twilight Zone-The Movie (dir. segment), Gremlins, Explorers, Innerspace, Amazon Women on the Moon (co-dir.), The 'Burbs, Gremlins II (also cameo), Matinee. Actor: Cannonball, Slumber Party Massacre, Eating Raoul, Sleepwalkers, Beverly Hills Cop III, The Silence of the Hams.
TELEVISION: Amazing Stories, Eerie Indiana. *Movie*: Runaway Daughters.

D'ANTONI, PHILIP
Producer. Director. b. New York, NY, Feb. 19, 1929. e. Fordham U., business administration. Joined CBS in mailroom, advanced into prod., sales development, prog. analysis, mkt. rsrch. Became indep. radio-TV repr. in 1954 for two years; then joined Mutual Broadcasting as sales manager; later, exec. v.p. Resigned in 1962 to form own prod. co. Made theatrical film debut with Bullitt as producer; directing debut with The Seven Ups. Heads D'Antoni Prods.
PICTURES: *Producer*: Bullitt, The French Connection (Academy Award for Best Picture, 1971). *Prod.-Dir.*: The Seven Ups.
TELEVISION: Movin' On (series) Elizabeth Taylor in London, Sophia Loren in Rome, Melina Mercouri in Greece, Jack Jones Special, This Proud Land. Movies: Mr. Inside/Mr. Outside, The Connection, Strike Force, In Tandem, Rubber Gun Squad, Cabo.

DANZ, FREDRIC A.
Executive. b. Seattle, WA, Feb. 28, 1918. Is chairman of Sterling Recreation Organization Co., Seattle; member, Foundation of M.P. Pioneers; v.p., Variety Club Intl.

DANZA, TONY
Actor. b. Brooklyn, NY, Apr. 21, 1951. e. U. of Dubuque, IA on a wrestling scholarship. After grad. professional boxer before tested for role in TV pilot (Fast Lane Blues) which he won. Back to New York and fighting until called to coast to appear as Tony Banta in Taxi series. On L.A. & NY Stage: Wrong Turn at Lungfish.
PICTURES: Hollywood Knights, Going Ape, Cannonball Run II, She's Out of Control, Mob Justice, Angels in the Outfield, The Jerky Boys (co-exec. prod. only).

TELEVISION: *Series*: Taxi, Who's the Boss, Baby Talk (voice), The Mighty Jungle (voice), George (co-exec. prod. only), Hudson Street (also co-exec. prod.). *Movies*: Murder Can Hurt You!, Doing Life (also exec. prod.), Single Bars Single Women, Freedom Fighter (also co-exec. prod.), The Whereabouts of Jenny (also co-exec. prod.), Dead and Alive (also co-exec. prod.), Deadly Whispers.

D'ARBANVILLE-QUINN, PATTI
Actress. b. New York, NY, 1951. Grew up in Greenwich Village. Landed first job as baby in Ivory Soap commercials. In early teens worked as disc jockey where discovered by Andy Warhol and cast in small role in film Flesh. Moved to Paris at 15 where she became successful model and was featured in book Scavullo on Beauty. Made film debut in Gerard Brach's 1969 film La Maison. Fluent in French, worked in French films until 1973 when moved to Los Angeles. Won Dramalogue Award for John Patrick Shanley's Italian-American Reconciliation (L.A., 1987).
PICTURES: La Maison, La Saigne, The Crazy American Girl, Rancho DeLuxe, Bilitis, Big Wednesday, The Main Event, Time After Time, The Fifth Floor, Hog Wild, Modern Problems, Contract: Kill, The Boys Next Door, Real Genius, Call Me, Fresh Horses, Wired.
TELEVISION: *Movies*: Crossing the Mob, Blind Spot. *Mini-Series*: Once an Eagle, New York Undercover. *Guest*: Crime Story, R.E.L.A.X., Tough Cookies, Charlie's Angels, Barnaby Jones, Miami Vice, Murder She Wrote.

DARBY, KIM
Actress. r.n. Deborah Zerby. b. Hollywood, CA, July 8, 1948. e. Swanson's Ranch Sch., Van Nuys H.S. Studied at the Desilu Workshop in Hollywood. Professional debut on the Mr. Novak TV series; screen debut as extra in Bye Bye Birdie.
PICTURES: Bus Riley's Back in Town, The Restless Ones, True Grit, Generation, Norwood, The Strawberry Statement, The Grissom Gang, The One and Only, Better Off Dead, Teen Wolf Too, Halloween: The Curse of Michael Myers.
TELEVISION: *Movies*: The Karate Killers, Ironside (pilot), The People, Streets of San Francisco (pilot), Don't Be Afraid of the Dark, Story of Pretty Boy Floyd, This Was the West That Was, Flatbed Annie & Sweetiepie: Lady Truckers, Enola Gay, Embassy. *Mini-Series*: Rich Man Poor Man, The Last Convertible. *Guest*: Eleventh Hour, Gunsmoke. *Special*: Flesh and Blood.

DARK, JOHN
Producer. Pres. of J.D.Y.T. Producciones S.L., Coin Film City.
PICTURES: Light Up the Sky, Wind of Change, Loss of Innocence (Greengage Summer), The 7th Dawn, Casino Royale, Half a Sixpence, Bachelor of Arts, There's a Girl in My Soup, From Beyond the Grave, Madhouse, Land That Time Forgot, At the Earth's Core, The People That Time Forgot, Warlords of Atlantis, Arabian Adventure, Slayground, Shirley Valentine, Stepping Out.

DARREN, JAMES
Actor. b. Philadelphia, PA, June 8, 1936. e. Thomas Jefferson h.s., South Philadelphia h.s. Studied acting with Stella Adler, NYC.
PICTURES: Rumble on the Docks (debut, 1956), The Brothers Rico, The Tijuana Story, Operation Mad Ball, Gunman's Walk, Gidget, The Gene Krupa Story, Because They're Young, All the Young Men, Let No Man Write My Epitaph, Guns of Navarone, Gidget Goes Hawaiian, Diamond Head, Gidget Goes to Rome, For Those Who Think Young, The Lively Set, Venus in Furs, The Boss' Son.
TELEVISION: *Series*: The Time Tunnel, T.J. Hooker. *Guest*: Police Story, Hawaii Five-0, Vega$, Baa Baa Blacksheep, One Day at a Time. *Movies*: City Beneath the Sea, Police Story, The Lives of Jenny Dolan, Turnover Smith, Scruples. *Director of episodes*: T.J. Hooker, The A Team, Stingray, Werewolf, Hardball, Hunter, Tequila and Bonetti, Raven, Silk Stalkings, Walker: Texas Ranger.

DARRIEUX, DANIELLE
Actress. b. Bordeaux, France, May 1, 1917. e. Lycee LaTour, Conservatoire de Musique.
THEATER: Coco, The Ambassador (B'way).
PICTURES: Le Bal (debut, 1932), La Crise Est Finis, Mayerling, Tarass Boulba, Port Arthur, Un Mauvais Garcon, Club de Femmes, Abus de Confiance, Mademoiselle ma Mere, The Rage of Paris, Katia, Retour a l'Aube, Battlement de Coeur, Premier Rendezvous, Caprices, Adieu Cherie, Au Petit Bonheur, Bethsabee, Ruy Blas, Jean de le Lune, Occupe-toi d'Amelie, La Ronde, Rich Young and Pretty, Five Fingers, Le Plaisir, La Verite sur Bebe Donge, Adorable Creatures, Le Bon Dieu sans Confession, The Earrings of Madame De, Le Rouge et le Noir, Bonnes a Tuer, Napoleon, Alexander the Great, A Friend of the Family, Loss of Innocence (Greengage Summer), Les Lions sont Laches, Les Bras de lat Nuit, Bluebeard (Landru), Patate, Le Coup de Grace, L'Or du Duc, Le Dimanche de la Vie, The Young Girls of Rochefort, La Maison de Campagne, Scene of the Crime, A Few Days With me.

DARTNALL, GARY
Executive. b. Whitchurch, England, May 9, 1937. e. Kings Col., Taunton. Overseas div., Associate British Pathe. European rep., 1958-60; Middle & Far East rep., Lion Intl. Films; U.S. rep., 1962; pres. Lion Intl. 1963; U.S. rep., Alliance Intl. Films Distributors Ltd., and London Indept. Prods. Ltd.; pres. Alliance Intl. Films Corp. and Dartnall Films Ltd., 1966; mng. dir., Overseas div. Walter Reade Org., 1969; pres. EMI Film Distribs., 1971; vice chmn. EMI TV Programs Inc., 1976; pres. EMI Videograms Inc., 1979; pres. VHO Programs Inc. & VHD Disc Mfg. Co, 1980; chmn. Thorn EMI Cinemas; CEO, Thorn EMI Screen Entertainment Ltd. 1987; acquired Southbrook Intl. TV and formed Palladium Inc., chmn. & CEO.

DASSIN, JULES
Director, Writer, Actor. b. Middletown, CT, Dec. 18, 1911. Was married to late actress Melina Mercouri. Actor on dramatic stage several years; radio writer. Joined MGM, 1940, as dir. short subjects; later dir. features.
PICTURES: *Director*: Nazi Agent, Affairs of Martha, Reunion in France, Young Ideas, The Canterville Ghost, A Letter for Evie, Two Smart People, Brute Force, The Naked City, Thieves' Highway, Night and the City, Rififi (also co-s.p., actor), He Who Must Die (also co-s.p.), Where the Hot Wind Blows (also co-s.p.), Never on Sunday (also actor, prod., s.p.), Phaedra (also prod., co-s.p., actor), Topkapi (also prod.), 10:30 p.m. Summer (also prod., co-s.p.), Survival (also co-prod.), Uptight (also prod., co-s.p.), Promise at Dawn (also actor, prod., s.p.), The Rehearsal, A Dream of Passion (also s.p., prod.), Circle of Two.
PLAYS: Ilya Darling, Medicine Show, Magdalena, Joy to the World, Isle of Children, Two's Company, Heartbreak House, Threepenny Opera, Sweet Bird of Youth, A Month in the Country, Who's Afraid of Virginia Woolf?, The Road to Mecca, Death of a Salesman.

DAVENPORT, NIGEL
Actor. b. Cambridge, England, May 23, 1928. e. Trinity Coll., Oxford. Began acting after stint in British military at 18 years. First 10 years of professional career in theatre. Majority of screen work in British films in 1960s and 70s.
PICTURES: Look Back in Anger (debut, 1959), Desert Mice, Peeping Tom, The Entertainer, Lunch Hour, In the Cool of the Day, Operation Snatch, Return to Sender, Ladies Who Do, The Third Secret, Sands of the Kalahari, A High Wind in Jamaica, Where the Spies Are, Life at the Top, A Man for All Seasons, Sebastian, The Strange Affair, Play Dirty, Sinful Davey, The Virgin Soldiers, The Royal Hunt of the Sun, The Mind of Mr. Soames, The Last Valley, No Blade of Grass, Villain, Mary Queen of Scots, L'Attentat, Living Free, Charley-One-Eye, Phase IV, La Regenta, Stand Up Virgin Soldiers, The Island of Dr. Moreau, Zulu Dawn, The Omega Connection, Nighthawks, Chariots of Fire, Greystoke: The Legend of Tarzan Lord of the Apes, Caravaggio, Without a Clue, The Circus Trap.
TELEVISION: A Christmas Carol, Dracula, The Picture of Dorian Gray, The Ordeal of Dr. Mudd, Masada, The Upper Crust.

DAVIAU, ALLEN
Cinematographer. b. New Orleans, LA, June 14, 1942. Started as still photographer and stage lighting designer. Received Gold Clio Award for Tackle (Levi's 501).
PICTURES: Harry Tracy, E.T.: The Extra-Terrestrial (Acad. Award nom.), Twilight Zone: The Movie (co-photog.), Indiana Jones and the Temple of Doom (Calif. unit), The Falcon and the Snowman, The Color Purple (Acad. Award nom.), Harry and the Hendersons, Empire of the Sun (Acad. Award nom.; BAFTA & ASC Awards), Avalon (Acad. Award nom.), Defending Your Life, Bugsy (Acad. Award nom.; ASC Award), Fearless, Congo.
TELEVISION: *Movies*: Rage, Legs. *Special*: The Boy Who Drank Too Much. *Series*: Amazing Stories (pilot).

DAVID, KEITH
Actor. b. New York, NY, June 4, 1954. e. Juilliard.
THEATER: *NY*: The Pirates of Penzance, A Midsummer Night's Dream, Waiting for Godot, Miss Waters to You, La Boheme, Coriolanus, Titus Andronicus, A Map of the World, The Haggadah, Alec Wilder: Clues to a Life, Boesman & Lena, Jelly's Last Jam, Hedda Gabler, Seven Guitars.
PICTURES: The Thing, Platoon, Hot Pursuit, Braddock: Missing in Action III, Off Limits, Stars and Bars, Bird, They Live, Road House, Always, Men at Work, Marked for Death, Final Analysis, Article 99, Reality Bites, The Puppet Masters, The Quick and the Dead, Clockers, Dead Presidents, Johns, Dead Cold (prod.), Marked Man (prod.), Daddy's Girl (prod.), The Dentist (prod.), The Nurse (prod.), The Stranger In The House (prod.), Voodoo (exec. prod.), Serial Killer (prod./dir.), Flipping.
TELEVISION: *Movies*: Ladykillers, Murder in Black and White, There Are No Children Here. *Mini-Series*: Roots: The Next Generations. *Special*: Hallelujah. *Guest*: The Equalizer, A Man Called Hawk, New York Undercover.

DAV-DAV

DAVID, PIERRE
Executive, Producer. b. Montreal, Canada, May 17, 1944. e. U. of Montreal. Joined radio sta. CJMS 1966 as pub. rel. & spec. events dir., 1969, while running Mutual Broadcasting Network of Canada's live entertainment div., created new film dist. co. Mutual Films. 1972 added prod. unit and as prod. or exec. prod., prod. and dist. 19 French-lang. Canadian films. With filmmaker Roger Corman est. Mutual Pictures of Canada, Ltd to dist. films in English Canada; 1978 teamed Mutual Films with Victor Solnicki and Claude Heroux to prod. Eng.-lang. m.p. Pioneered 3-picture concept for Canadian m.p. investors. Moved to L.A. 1983 where became pres., Film Packages Intl. where prod. exec. on Platoon. Then joined Larry Thompson Org. as partner involved in dev. and/or prod. of m.p., Jan., 1987, named chmn. of bd. and chief exec. officer, Image Org., Inc. intl. dist. co. formed by David and Rene Malo. Also pres. Lance Entertainment, prod. co.
PICTURES: *Prod.*: The Brood, Hog Wild, Scanners, Dirty Tricks, Gas, The Funny Farm, Visiting Hours, Videodrome, Going Berserk, Of Unknown Origin, Covergirl, Breaking All the Rules, For Those I Loved, Blind-Fear (co-prod.), The Perfect Bride, Hot Pursuit, The Perfect Weapon, Bounty Tracker, Distant Cousins, Deep Cover, Marital Outlaw, Stalked, Open Fire, The Force, The Secretary, Scanner Cop 2, The Wrong Woman. *Exec. Prod.*: Quiet Cool, Scanners II: The New Order, Desire and Hell at Sunset Motel, Martial Law, Scanners III, Dolly Dearest, Mission of Justice, Deadbolt, Internal Affairs, Twin Sisters, Pin, The Neighbor, The Paperboy. *Prod.-Dir.*: Scanner Cop.

DAVID, SAUL
Producer. b. Springfield, MA., June 27, 1921. e. Classical H.S., Springfield; Rhode Island Sch. of Design. Started in radio, newspaper work and as editorial director for Bantam Books. Worked for Columbia Pictures, 1960-62; Warner Bros., 1962-63; 20th Century-Fox, 1963-67, Universal, 1968-69; Executive story editor at MGM, 1972. Author: The Industry.
PICTURES: Von Ryan's Express, Our Man Flint, Fantastic Voyage, In Like Flint, Skullduggery, Logan's Run, Ravagers (exec. prod.).
(d. June 7, 1996)

DAVIDOVICH, LOLITA
Actress. b. Ontario, Canada, 1961. Also acted under the name Lolita David.
PICTURES: Class, Adventures in Babysitting, The Big Town, Blaze, The Object of Beauty, JFK, The Inner Circle, Raising Cain, Leap of Faith, Boiling Point, Younger and Younger, Cobb, For Better or Worse, Now and Then, Jungle2Jungle.
TELEVISION: *Movies*: Two Fathers' Justice, Prison Stories: Women on the Inside (Parole Board), Keep the Change, Indictment: The McMartin Trial.

DAVIDSON, JOHN
Actor, Singer. b. Pittsburgh, PA, Dec. 13, 1941. e. Denison U. In numerous school stage prods. before coming to N.Y. in 1964 to co-star with Bert Lahr in B'way show, Foxy. Signed as regular on The Entertainers with Carol Burnett.
PICTURES: The Happiest Millionaire, The One and Only Genuine Original Family Band, The Concorde—Airport '79, The Squeeze, Edward Scissorhands.
TELEVISION: *Special*: The Fantasticks. *Guest*: The FBI, The Interns, Owen Marshall, The Tonight Show, (also frequent guest host). *Series*: The Entertainers, Kraft Summer Music Hall, The John Davidson Show (1969), The Girl With Something Extra, The John Davidson Show (1976), The John Davidson Talk Show (1980), That's Incredible, New Hollywood Squares, Time Machine (game show), Incredible Sunday, The $100,000 Pyramid. *Movies*: Coffee Tea or Me?, Shell Game, Roger & Harry: The Mitera Target, Dallas Cowboys Cheerleaders II.

DAVIDSON, MARTIN
Director, Writer. b. New York, NY, Nov. 7, 1939.
PICTURES: The Lords of Flatbush, Almost Summer, Hero at Large, Eddie and the Cruisers, Heart of Dixie (also exec. prod.), Hard Promises.
TELEVISION: *Series*: Our Family Honor, Call to Glory, Law and Order, My Life and Times, Picket Fences, Chicago Hope. *Movies*: Long Gone, A Murderous Affair: The Carolyn Warmus Story, Follow the River.

DAVIES, JOHN HOWARD
Producer, Director. b. London, England, March 9, 1939. e. Haileybury, I.S.C. and Grenoble Univ. Former child actor played leading roles in Oliver Twist, The Rocking Horse Winner, Tom Brown's Schooldays.
TELEVISION: *Prod./Dir.*: Monty Python's Flying Circus, Steptoe and Son, Fawlty Towers, The Good Life, The Goodies, The Other One, No Job for a Lady, Mr. Bean.

DAVIS, ANDREW
Director. b. Chicago, IL. e. Univ. of IL. Former journalist and photographer before landing job as asst. cameraman on 1969 film Medium Cool. Was dir. of photog. on several tv commercials and documentaries.

DAVIS, CARL
Composer. b. New York, NY, Oct. 28, 1936. e. Queens Coll., Bard Coll. and New England Coll. of Music. Worked as pianist with Robert Shaw Chorale and wrote music for revue Diversions (1958) and Twists (London), Moved to England 1961 writing incidental music for Joan Littlewood's Theatre Workshop Co., Royal Shakespeare Co. and National Theatre. Other theater music includes Jonathan Miller's Tempest, Forty Years On, and the musical The Vackees. Best known for composing new scores for silent classics (Napoleon, The Crowd, Greed, Intolerance, etc.) for screenings at which he conducts and for Thames TV The Silents series. Concert work: Paul McCartney's Liverpool Oratorio.
PICTURES: The Bofors Gun, Up Pompeii, Rentadick, Man Friday, The Sailor's Return, Birth of the Beatles, The French Lieutenant's Woman, Praying Mantis, The Aerodrome, Champions, Weather in the Streets, George Stevens: A Filmmaker's Journey, King David, The Rainbow, Scandal, Girl in a Swing, Fragments of Isabella, Frankenstein Unbound, Diary of a Madman, Raft of the Medusa, The Voyage.
TELEVISION: That Was the Week That Was, Hollywood, the Pioneers, World at War, Mayor of Casterbridge, Lorna Doone, Unknown Chaplin, Buster Keaton—A Hard Act to Follow, Treasure Island, The Snow Goose, Our Mutual Friend, Naked Civil Servant, Silas Marner, The Accountant, Secret Life of Ian Fleming, Why Lockerbie?, Buried Mirro, A Christmas Carol, Royal Collection, Hotel du Lac, Black Velvet Gown.

DAVIS, COLIN
Executive. Held executive positions in Canada in adv., bdcst., & p.r. with several companies, including Procter & Gamble, Young & Rubicam. Joined MCA TV Canada as v.p. & gen. mgr., 1977. Named dir. intl. sls., 1978. In 1986 appt. pres., MCA TV Int'l.

DAVIS, FRANK I.
Executive. b. Poolesville, MD, Feb. 18, 1919. e. U. of Maryland, A.B., 1941; Harvard Law School, LL.B., 1948. Law firm, Donovan, Leisure, Newton, Lombard and Irvine, 1948-50; v.p., gen. counsel Vanguard Films, 1951; v.p., gen. counsel, Selznick Releasing Org., 1951-53; pres., The Selznick Company, 1953-55; v.p., Famous Artists Corp., 1956-62; v.p. George Stevens Productions Inc., 1962-65; exec. prod., The Greatest Story Ever Told; v.p. in charge of m.p. affairs, Seven Arts, 1966; exec. in chg. talent and exec. asst. to v.p. in chg. prod., MGM, 1967; dir. m.p. business affairs, MGM, 1970; v.p., business affairs, MGM, 1972; sr. v.p., motion picture business affairs, MGM/UA, 1983, exec. v.p., business affairs, MGM Pictures, 1986-88; sr. exec. v.p., business affairs, Pathe Entertainment Inc., 1989-90; sr. exec. v.p. of bus. affairs, MGM, 1990.

DAVIS, GEENA
Actress. r.n. Virginia Elizabeth Davis. b. Wareham, MA, Jan. 21, 1957. e. Boston U. Acted with Mount Washington Repertory Theatre Co., NH. Was NY model before winning role Tootsie, 1982.
PICTURES: Tootsie (debut, 1982), Fletch, Transylvania 6-5000, The Fly, Beetlejuice, The Accidental Tourist (Academy Award, supporting actress, 1988), Earth Girls Are Easy, Quick Change, Thelma & Louise, A League of Their Own, Hero, Angie, Speechless (also prod.), Cutthroat Island, The Long Kiss Goodnight.
TELEVISION: *Series*: Buffalo Bill (also wrote one episode), Sara. *Movie*: Secret Weapons. *Guest*: Family Ties, Riptide, Remington Steele, Saturday Night Live, Trying Times (The Hit List).

DAVIS, GEORGE W.
Art Director, b. Kokomo, IN, Apr. 17, 1914. e. U. of Southern California.
PICTURES: The Ghost and Mrs. Muir, House of Stranger, All About Eve, David and Bathsheba, The Robe (Academy Award, 1953), Love Is a Many-Splendored Thing, Funny Face, The Diary of Anne Frank (Academy Award, 1959), The Time Machine, Butterfield 8, Cimarron, Period of Adjustment, Mutiny on the Bounty, The Wonderful World of the Brothers Grimm, Twilight of Honor, How the West Was Won, The Americanization of Emily, The Unsinkable Molly Brown, A Patch of Blue, Mr. Buddwing, Point Blank, The Shoes of the Fisherman, The Gypsy Moths, Brewster McCloud, Wild Rovers, etc

DAVIS, JOHN
Executive, Producer. e. Bowdoin Col., Harvard Bus. Sch. Served as v.p. at 20th Century Fox before forming Davis Entertainment.

PICTURES: Predator, Three O'Clock High, License to Drive, Little Monsters, The Last of the Finest, Shattered, Storyville, The Firm, The Thing Called Love, Fortress, Gunmen, Grumpy Old Men, Richie Rich, The Hunted, Waterworld, The Grass Harp, Courage Under Fire.
TELEVISION: *Movies:* Tears and Laughter: The Joan and Melissa Rivers Story, The Last Outlaw, This Can't Be Love.

DAVIS, JUDY
Actress. b. Perth, Australia, 1955. m. actor Colin Friels. Left convent school as teenager to become a singer in a rock band. Studied at West Australia Inst. of Technology and National Inst. of Dramatic Art, Sydney. Worked with theatre companies in Adelaide and Sydney and at Royal Court Theatre, London. Los Angeles stage debut Hapgood.
PICTURES: High Rolling (debut, 1977), My Brilliant Career, Hoodwink, Heatwave, Winter of Our Dreams, The Final Option, A Passage to India (Acad. Award nom.), Kangaroo, High Tide, Georgia, Alice, Impromtu, Barton Fink, Naked Lunch, Where Angels Fear to Tread, Husbands and Wives (Acad. Award nom.), On My Own (Australian Film Inst. Award), The Ref, The New Age.
TELEVISION: Rocket to the Moon, A Woman Called Golda, One Against the Wind, Serving in Silence: The Margarethe Cammermeyer Story (Emmy Award, 1995).

DAVIS, LUTHER.
Writer, Producer. b. New York, NY, Aug. 29, 1921. e. Yale, B.A.
THEATER: *Writer.* Kiss Them for Me, Kismet (Tony Award), Timbuktu! (also prod.), Grand Hotel (Tony nom.). Co-Prod.: Eden Court, Not About Heroes.
PICTURES: *Writer.* The Hucksters, B.F.'s Daughter, Black Hand, A Lion Is in the Streets, The Gift of Love, Holiday for Lovers, The Wonders of Aladdin, Lady in a Cage (also prod.), Across 110th Street.
TELEVISION: *Writer/Prod.:* Kraft Suspense Theatre and many pilots for series (Run for Your Life, Combat, The Silent Force, Eastside, Westside, etc.). *Specials:* Arsenic and Old Lace (also prod.), The People Trap (prod.). *Movies:* Daughter of the Mind, The Old Man Who Cried Wolf.

DAVIS, MAC
Singer, Songwriter, Actor. b. Lubbock, TX, Jan 21, 1942. e. Emory U., Georgia State Coll. Employed as ditch digger, service station attendant, laborer, probation officer and record company salesman before gaining fame as entertainer-singer in 1969. Recording artist and composer of many popular songs. On B'way 1992 in The Will Rogers Follies.
PICTURES: North Dallas Forty, Cheaper to Keep Her, The Sting II.
TELEVISION: *Series:* The Mac Davis Show. *Movies:* Brothers-In-Law, What Price Victory?, Blackmail.

DAVIS, MARTIN S.
Executive. b. New York, NY, Feb. 5, 1927. U.S. Army, 1943-46; joined Samuel Goldwyn Prod., Inc., 1946; with pub. dept. Allied Artists, 1955; Paramount Pictures, 1958. as dir. sales and marketing then dir. adv., pub. expl. 1960; v.p. in chg. of home office and asst. to pres.; 1963; exec. v.p., 1966; exec. comm. & bd. of dir. Member of Bd., Gulf & Western, 1967, named sr. v.p. 1969; elected Exec. v.p. and mem. exec. comm. Gulf & Western, 1974; elected CEO and chmn. of bd. and chmn. exec. comm. 1983; CEO & managing partner Wellspring Associates, LLC, 1995. Member: bd. trustees, Montefiore Medical Center, Thomas Jefferson Memorial Foundation; Chmn,. NYC Chap, Natl. Multiple Sclerosis Society; bd. of trustees Carnegie Hall. Co-chmn. of Corp. Advisory Committee of the Barbara Bush Foundation for Family Literacy. Board of directors, National Amusements, Inc.

DAVIS, OSSIE
Actor, Writer, Director. b. Cogdell, GA, Dec. 18, 1917. e. Howard U., Washington, DC. m. actress Ruby Dee. Studied acting in N.Y. with Rose McLendon Players, leading to Broadway debut in 1946 in Jeb. For years thereafter was one of best-known black actors on Broadway stage (Anna Lucasta, Jamaica, The Green Pastures, Wisteria Tree, A Raisin in the Sun, I'm Not Rappaport.) Wrote and starred in Purlie Victorious, repeating role for film version. Directed and appeared with Ms. Dee in her musical Take It From the Top. Co-hosted Ossie Davis and Ruby Dee Story Hour on radio (3 years). Published plays: Purlie Victorious, Langston, Escape to Freedom, Curtain Call, Mr. Aldredge, Sir.
PICTURES: *Actor.* No Way Out, Fourteen Hours, The Joe Louis Story, Gone Are the Days, The Cardinal, Shock Treatment, The Hill, Man Called Adam, The Scalphunters, Sam Whiskey, Slaves, Let's Do It Again, Hot Stuff, House of God, Harry and Son, Avenging Angel, School Daze, Do the Right Thing, Joe Versus the Volcano, Jungle Fever, Gladiator, Malcolm X (voice), Grumpy Old Men, The Client, I'm Not Rappaport, Get on the Bus. *Director:* Cotton Comes to Harlem (also co-s.p.), Black Girl, Gordon's War, Countdown at Kusini (also actor, prod.).

TELEVISION: *Writer.* East Side/West Side, The Eleventh Hour. *Guest:* Name of the Game, Night Gallery, Bonanza, etc. *Specials:* Martin Luther King: The Dream and the Drum, With Ossie and Ruby (also co-prod.), Today is Ours (writer, dir.). *Movies:* All God's Children, Don't Look Back, Roots: The Next Generations, King, Teacher Teacher, The Ernest Green Story, Ray Alexander: A Taste for Justice, Ray Alexander: A Menu for Murder, The Android Affair. *Series:* B.L. Stryker, Evening Shade, John Grisham's The Client. *Mini-Series:* Queen, Stephen King's The Stand.

DAVIS, PETER
Author, Filmmaker. b. Santa Monica, CA, Jan. 2, 1937. e. Harvard Coll., 1955-57. Parents were screenwriter Frank Davis, and novelist-screenwriter Tess Slesinger. Writer-interviewer, Sextant Prods., FDR Series, 1964-65. Host: The Comers, PBS 1964-65. Author: Hometown (1982), Where Is Nicaragua? (1987), If You Came This Way (1995), articles for Esquire, NY Times Mag., The Nation, NY Woman, TV Guide.
PICTURES: Hearts and Minds (prod., dir.; Academy Award, best documentary, 1975; Prix Sadoul, 1974), Jack (writer/prod.).
TELEVISION: *Writer-prod.:* Hunger in America (assoc. prod., WGA Award, 1968), The Heritage of Slavery, The Battle of East St. Louis, (Saturday Review Award, 1970; 2 Emmy nom.), The Selling of the Pentagon (WGA, Emmy, Peabody, George Polk, Ohio State, Sat. Review Awards, 1971), 60 Minutes (segment prod.), Middletown (series, prod., Dupont Citation, Emmy noms. 1983), The Best Hotel on Skidrow (ACE Award noms., 1992).

DAVIS, PRESTON A.
Executive. b. Norfolk, VA. Served in US Army. 1976, joined ABC as engineer in Washington DC, later becoming sprv. of Electronic News Gathering; 1979, became tech. mngr. of ENG; 1983, named tech. mngr. then manager of ENG for southeast region, Atlanta; 1986, promoted to gen. mngr. ENG Operations, New York; 1988, named v.p. TV Operations, Broadcast Operations & Engineering, East Coast; 1993, named pres. of Broadcast Operations and Engineering for ABC Television Network Group.

DAVIS, ROGER H.
Executive. Chairman, Motion Picture and Television Fund.

DAVIS, SAMMI
Actress. b. Kidderminster, Worcestershire, Eng., June 21, 1964. Convent-educated before taking drama course. Performed in stage prods. with local drama society in Midlands, then Birmingham Rep. and Big Brum Theatre Co. Plays include The Home Front, The Apple Club, Nine Days, Databased, Choosey Susie. London stage debut: A Collier's Friday.
PICTURES: Mona Lisa, Lionheart, Hope and Glory, A Prayer for the Dying, Consuming Passions, The Lair of the White Worm, The Rainbow, The Horseplayer, Shadow of China, Four Rooms.
TELEVISION: Auf Wiedersehn Pet, The Day After the Fair, Pack of Lies, Chernobyl: The Final Warning, The Perfect Bride, Indecency, Spring Awakening. *Series:* Homefront.

DAVISON, BRUCE
Actor. b. Philadelphia, PA, June 28, 1946. e. Pennsylvania State U., NYU. debut, Lincoln Center Repertory prod. of Tiger at the Gates, 1967.
THEATER: NY: King Lear (Lincoln Center), The Elephant Man, Richard III (NY Shakespeare Fest.), The Glass Menagerie, The Cocktail Hour. *Regional:* Streamers (LA Critics Award), The Caine Mutiny Court-Martial, The Normal Heart, To Kill a Mockingbird, A Life in the Theatre, The Front Page, Downside, Breaking the Silence.
PICTURES: Last Summer (debut, 1969), The Strawberry Statement, Willard, Been Down So Long It Looks Like Up To Me, The Jerusalem File, Ulzana's Raid, Mame, Mother Jugs and Speed, Grand Jury, Short Eyes, Brass Target, French Quarter, High Risk, A Texas Legend, Lies, Crimes of Passion, Spies Like Us, The Ladies Club, The Misfit Brigade, Longtime Companion (NY Film Critics, Natl. Society of Film Critics, & Golden Globe Awards, 1990; Acad. Award nom.), Steel and Lace, Short Cuts, An Ambush of Ghosts, Six Degrees of Separation, Far From Home: The Adventures of Yellow Dog, The Cure, The Baby-sitters Club, Homage, Grace of My Heart, The Crucible.
TELEVISION: *Movies:* Owen Marshall: Counsellor at Law (A Pattern of Morality), The Affair, The Last Survivors, Deadman's Curve, Summer of My German Soldier, Mind Over Murder, The Gathering, Tomorrow's Child, Ghost Dancing, Poor Little Rich Girl: The Barbara Hutton Story, Lady in a Corner, Stolen: One Husband, Live! From Death Row, Desperate Choices: To Save My Child, A Mother's Revenge, Someone Else's Child, Down Out and Dangerous. *Specials:* Taming of the Shrew, The Lathe of Heaven, The Wave. *Guest:* Medical Center, Marcus Welby, Love American Style, Police

Story, Lou Grant, Murder She Wrote, Alfred Hitchcok Presents (1985), Amazing Stories. *Series*: Hunter, Harry and the Hendersons.

DAVISON, DALE
Executive. b. North Hollywood, CA, March 21, 1955. e. U.C.L.A., B.A., 1978. Entered the motion picture industry in 1973 working for Pacific Theatres. Employed with Great Western Theatres 1974-77 as manager, dir. of concessions, and asst. vice pres. Partner with Great Western Theatres, 1978-1984. Founder and CEO, CinemaCal Enterprises, Inc., 1985-present.

DAVISON, JON
Producer. b. Haddonfield, NJ, July 21, 1949. e. NYU Film School. 1972, joined New World Pictures as natl. dir. of publ./adv.; 1972, named in charge of prod.; 1980, became indep. prod.
PICTURES: Hollywood Boulevard, Grand Theft Auto, Piranha, Airplane!, White Dog, Twilight Zone—The Movie (episode), Top Secret! Robocop, Robocop 2, Trapped in Paradise.

DAWBER, PAM
Actress, Singer. b. Detroit, MI, Oct. 18, 1954. m. actor Mark Harmon. e. Farmington H.S., Oakland Community Coll. Worked as model and did commercials. First professional performance as singer in Sweet Adeleine at Goodspeed Opera House, East Haddam, CT.
THEATER: Regional: My Fair Lady, The Pirates of Penzance, The Music Man, She Loves Me, Love Letters.
PICTURES: A Wedding, Stay Tuned.
TELEVISION: *Series*: Mork and Mindy, My Sister Sam. *Movies*: The Girl the Gold Watch and Everything, Remembrance of Love, Through Naked Eyes, Last of the Great Survivors, This Wife For Hire, Wild Horses, Quiet Victory: The Charlie Wedemeyer Story, Do You Know the Muffin Man, The Face of Fear, The Man With 3 Wives, Web of Deception, Trail of Tears. *Specials*: Kennedy Center Honors, Salute to Andy Gibb, Night of the 100 Stars, 3rd Annual TV Guide Special.

DAY, DORIS
Singer, Actress. r.n. Doris Kappelhoff. b. Cincinnati,c OH, Apr. 3, 1924. e. dancing, singing. Toured as dancer; radio and band singer; screen debut in Romance on the High Seas, 1948. Voted one of Top Ten Money-Making Stars in Motion Picture Herald-Fame poll, 1951-52. Best female vocalist. M. P. Daily radio poll, 1952.
PICTURES: Romance on the High Seas (debut, 1948), My Dream is Yours, It's a Great Feeling, Young Man With a Horn, Tea for Two, Storm Warning, West Point Story, Lullaby of Broadway, On Moonlight Bay, I'll See You in My Dreams, Starlift, The Winning Team, April in Paris, By the Light of the Silvery Moon, Calamity Jane, Lucky Me, Young at Heart, Love Me or Leave Me, The Man Who Knew Too Much, Julie, The Pajama Game, Teacher's Pet, Tunnel of Love, It Happened to Jane, Pillow Talk (Acad. Award nom.), Please Don't Eat the Daisies, Midnight Lace, Lover Come Back, That Touch of Mink, Bill Rose's Jumbo, The Thrill of It All, Move Over Darling, Send Me No Flowers, Do Not Disturb, Glass Bottom Boat, Caprice, The Ballad of Josie, Where Were You When the Lights Went Out?, With Six You Get Eggroll.
TELEVISION: *Series*: The Doris Day Show (1968-73), Doris Day's Best Friends (educational cable show; 1985-86).

DAY, LARAINE
Actress. r.n. Laraine Johnson. b. Roosevelt, UT, Oct. 13, 1920. e. Long Beach Polytechic H.S., Paramount Studio School. In school dramatics; with Players Guild, Long Beach, Calif.; toured in church prod. Conflict; Professionally on stage in Lost Horizon, The Women, Time of the Cuckoo, Angel Street.
PICTURES: Stella Dallas (debut, 1937 as Laraine Johnson), Scandal Street, Border G-Men, Young Dr. Kildare (and subsequent series), And One Was Beautiful, My Son My Son, Foreign Correspondent, The Trial of Mary Dugan, The Bad Man, Unholy Partners, Fingers at the Window, Journey for Margaret, Mr. Lucky, The Story of Dr. Wassell, Bride by Mistake, Those Endearing Young Charms, Keep Your Powder Dry, The Locket, Tycoon, My Dear Secretary, I Married a Communist (Woman on Pier 13), Without Honor, The High and the Mighty, Toy Tiger, Three for Jamie Dawn, The Third Voice.
TELEVISION: Appearances include Climax, Playhouse 90, Alfred Hitchcock, Wagon Train, Let Freedom Ring, Name of the Game, FBI, Sixth Sense, Medical Center, Murder on Flight 504 (movie), Fantasy Island, Love Boat, Lou Grant, Airwolf, Hotel, Murder She Wrote.

DAY, ROBERT
Director. b. England, Sept. 11, 1922. Started as cinematographer before turning to direction.
PICTURES: *Director*: The Green Man (debut, 1956), Stranger's Meeting, Grip of the Strangler (The Haunted Strangler), First Man Into Space, Bobbikins, Two-Way Stretch, Tarzan the Magnificent (also co-s.p.), The Rebel (Call Me

Genius), Corridors of Blood, Operation Snatch, Tarzan's Three Challenges (also co-s.p.), She, Tarzan and the Valley of Gold, Tarzan and the Great River, Tarzan and the Jungle Boy (prod. only), The Man with Bogart's Face.
TELEVISION: *Pilots include:* Banion, Kodiak, Dan August, Sunshine, Switch, Logan's Run, Kingston, Dallas, Matlock. Movies include: Ritual of Evil, The House of Greenapple Road, In Broad Daylight, Having Babies, The Grass Is Always Greener Over the Septic Tank, Peter and Paul, Running Out, Scruples, Cook and Peary—The Race to the Pole, Hollywood Wives, The Lady from Yesterday, Diary of a Perfect Murder, Celebration, Higher Ground, Walking Through the Fire.

DAY-LEWIS, DANIEL
Actor. b. London, England, Apr. 29, 1957. Son of late C. Day-Lewis, poet laureate of Eng., and actress Jill Balcon. Grandson of late Sir Malcolm Balcon who prod. Hitchcock's Brit. films. e. Bristol Old Vic. Theatre School. First professional job at 12 as ruffian scratching cars with broken bottle in film, Sunday Bloody Sunday. Then acted with Bristol Old Vic and Royal Shakespeare Co. Appeared in West End in, among others, Dracula, Another Country, Romeo and Juliet, A Midsummer Night's Dream, Hamlet (Natl Theater, 1989).
PICTURES: Gandhi, The Bounty, A Room With a View, My Beautiful Laundrette, The Unbearable Lightness of Being, Stars and Bars, Nanou, Eversmile New Jersey, My Left Foot (Academy Award, 1989; also BAFTA, NY Film Critics, L.A. Film Critics, Natl. Society of Film Critics Awards), The Last of the Mohicans, The Age of Innocence, In the Name of the Father, The Crucible.
TELEVISION: *BBC Movies/Specials*: A Frost in May, How Many Miles to Babylon?, My Brother Jonathan, The Insurance Man, History of Hamlet (host).

DEAKINS, ROGER
Cinematographer. b. Devon, England, May 24, 1949. Accepted into National Film School in 1972. Working as professional filmmaker from 1975 directing and photographing documentary films including Around the World With Ridgeway, Zimbabwe, Eritrea—Behind the Lines, When the World Changed, Worlds Apart S.E. Nuba, Worlds Apart Rajgonds. Photographed first feature, Another Time Another Place in 1982.
PICTURES: 1984, The Innocent, Sid & Nancy, Shadey, Defense of the Realm, White Mischief, Personal Services, Stormy Monday, Pascali's Island, The Kitchen Toto, Mountains of the Moon, Air America, The Long Walk Home, Barton Fink, Homicide, Thunderheart, Passion Fish, The Secret Garden, The Hudsucker Proxy, The Shawshank Redemption (Acad. Award nom.; ASC Award), Fargo, Courage Under Fire.

DEAN, EDDIE
Actor. r.n. Edgar Dean Glosup. b. Posey, TX, July 9, 1907. 1930-33 in radio throughout middle west; 1934 National Barn Dance, Station WLS; 1935 on CBS & NBC with same program. Featured male singer on TV KTLA Western Varieties 1944-55. Came to Hollywood in 1936; since then has starred in many westerns. Featured performer in western series for PRC in 1945. Voted one of the ten best money making Western Stars in Motion Picture Herald-Fame Poll 1936-47; recording artists, personal appearances, rodeos, fairs, etc.; 1966 v.p. Academy of Country & Western Music; 1967-68 on Bd. of Dir. of Academy of Western Music, Calif. Winner, Pioneer Award of Academy of Country Music, 1978. In 1983 named ACM v.p.; also v.p. in 1985. Recorded video cassette 1986, A Tribute to Eddie Dean. Received two gold records in 1995 for co-writing of "Hillbilly Heaven."

DEAN, JIMMY
Performer. b. Plainview, TX, Aug. 10, 1928. Joined armed forces, 1946-49; first appeared in various clubs in Wash., 1949; then appeared on Town and Country Jamboree; toured Caribbean and Europe with his troupe; appeared in Las Vegas. TNN/Music City News Country Music Awards, Songwriter of the Year Awards.
SONGS: *Composer*: Big Bad John, Little Black Book, I.O.U., To a Sleeping Beauty, PT-109, Dear Ivan.
PICTURES: Diamonds Are Forever, Big Bad John.
TELEVISION: *Series*: The Jimmy Dean Show (1957; 1963-66), Daniel Boone, J.J. Starbuck. *Specials*: Sunday Night at the Palladium (London), Celebrities Offstage. *Movies*: The Ballad of Andy Crocker, Rolling Man, The City.

DEAN, MORTON
Television Newsman. b. Fall River, MA, Aug. 22, 1935. e. Emerson Coll. News dir., N.Y. Herald Tribune Net, 1957; corr. WBZ, 1960, corr. WCBS-TV, 1964; anchor, WCBW-TV News, 1967; corr., CBS News, 1967; anchor, CBS Sunday Night News, 1975; anchor, Sunday edition CBS Evening News, 1976; co-anchor, Independent Network News, 1985.

DEARDEN, JAMES
Writer, Director. b. London, Eng. Sept. 14, 1949. Son of late British director Basil Dearden. e. New Coll., Oxford U. Entered

film industry in 1967 as production runner. After editing commercials and documentaries, and working as asst. dir., wrote, prod. and dir. first short film, The Contraption (Silver Bear Award, 1978 Berlin Film Fest.). 1978, began dir. commercials and made short, Panic (Cert. of Merit, 1980 Chicago Film Fest.). 1979, made 45-min film Diversion, which became basis for Fatal Attraction (Gold Plaque, best short drama, 1980 Chicago Film Fest.).
PICTURES: Fatal Attraction (s.p.), Pascali's Island (dir., s.p.), A Kiss Before Dying (dir., s.p.).
TELEVISION: The Cold Room (dir., writer, Special Jury Prize, dir., 1985 Fest. Intl. d'Avoriaz du Film Fantastique).

De BONT, JAN
Cinematographer, Director. b. Holland, Oct. 22, 1943. Trained at Amsterdam Film Acad. Recipient of Kodak Camera Award and Rembrandt Award.
PICTURES: Cinematographer: Turkish Delight, Cathy Tippel, Max Havelaar, Soldier of Orange, Private Lessons (U.S. debut, 1981), Roar, I'm Dancing as Fast as I Can, Cujo, All the Right Moves, Bad Manners, The Fourth Man, Mischief, The Jewel of the Nile, Flesh + Blood, The Clan of the Cave Bear, Ruthless People, Who's That Girl, Leonard Part 6, Die Hard, Bert Rigby You're a Fool, Black Rain, The Hunt for Red October, Flatliners, Shining Through, Basic Instinct, Lethal Weapon 3. Director: Speed (debut, 1994), Twister.
TELEVISION (Photography): Movie: The Ray Mancini Story. Episode: Tales from the Crypt (Split Personality).

De BROCA, PHILIPPE
Director, Writer. b. Paris, France, Mar. 15, 1933. e. Paris Technical School of Photography and Cinematography.
PICTURES: Director/Writer: Les Jeux de l'Amour (The Love Game), The Joker, The Five Day Lovers, Seven Capitol Sins (dir. segment only), Cartouche (also actor), Les Veinards (segment), That Man From Rio, Male Companion (Un Monsieur de Compagnie), Les Tribulations d'un Chinois en Chine (Up to His Ears), King of Hearts (also prod.), Devil by the Tail, Give Her the Moon, Chere Louise, Le Magnifique, Dear Inspector (also s.p.), The Skirt Chaser, Someone's Stolen the Thigh of Jupiter, The African, Louisiana (TV in U.S.), The Gypsy, Chouans! (dir., co-s.p.), Scheherazade.

De CAMP, ROSEMARY
Actress. b. Prescott AZ, Nov. 14, 1913.
PICTURES: Cheers for Miss Bishop (debut, 1941), Hold Back the Dawn, Jungle Book, Yankee Doodle Dandy, Eyes in the Night, The Commandos Strike at Dawn, Smith of Minnesota, Without Men, This is the Army, The Merry Monahans, Bowery to Broadway, Blood on the Sun, Practically Yours, Rhapsody in Blue, Pride of the Marines, Danger Signal, Too Young to Know, From This Day Forward, Nora Prentiss, Night Unto Night, The Life of Riley, Look for the Silver Lining, Story of Seabiscuit, The Big Hangover, Night Into Morning, On Moonlight Bay, Scandal Sheet, Treasure of Lost Canyon, By the Light of the Silvery Moon, Main Street to Broadway, So This Is Love, Many Rivers to Cross, Strategic Air Command, 13 Ghosts, Saturday the 14th.
TELEVISION: Series: The Life of Reilly (with Jackie Gleason), The Bob Cummings Show, That Girl. Guest: Death Valley Days, Partridge Family, Love American Style, Police Story, Rockford Files, Days of Our Lives, Misadventures of Sheriff Lobo, Love Boat, B.J. & the Bear. Mini-Series: Blind Ambition. Movie: The Time Machine.

De CAPRIO, AL
Producer, Director. e. Brooklyn Tech., NYU. Started as radio engineer, cameraman, tech. dir., prod. & dir. CBS; dir. series episodes of Sgt. Bilko, Car 54 Where Are You?, Musical specials for ABC, CBS, NBC; v.p. exec. prod. dir., MPO Videotronics, Pres. World Wide Videotape; retired.

De CARLO, YVONNE
Actress. b. Vancouver, B.C., Sept. 1, 1922. e. June Roper School of Dance, British Columbia; Fanchon & Marco, Hollywood. Specialty dancing at Florentine Gardens, Earl Carroll's; m.p. debut in This Gun for Hire, 1942. One-woman club act and 7-person club act. Autobiography, Yvonne (1987).
THEATER: B'way: Follies.
PICTURES: This Gun for Hire (debut, 1942), Harvard Here I Come, Youth on Parade, Road to Morocco, Let's Face It, The Crystal Ball, Salute for Three, For Whom the Bell Tolls, True to Life, So Proudly We Hail, The Deerslayer, Practically Yours, Salome Where She Danced, Frontier Gal, Brute Force, Song of Scheherazade, Slave Girl, Black Bart, Casbah, River Lady, Criss Cross, Gal Who Took the West, Calamity Jane and Sam Bass, Buccaneer's Girl, The Desert Hawk, Tomahawk, Hotel Sahara, Silver City, Scarlet Angel, San Francisco Story, Hurricane Smith, Sombrero, Sea Devils, Fort Algiers, Captain's Paradise, Border River, Passion, Tonight's the Night, Shotgun, Magic Fire, Flame of the Islands, Ten Commandments, Raw Edge, Death of a Scoundrel, Band of Angels, Timbuktu, McLintock!, A Global Affair, Law of the Lawless, Munster Go Home, Hostile Guns, The Power, Arizona Bushwackers, The Seven Minutes, Play

Dead, It Seemed Like a Good Idea at the Time, Won Ton Ton the Dog Who Saved Hollywood, Blazing Stewardesses, Satan's Cheerleaders, Nocturna, Silent Scream, Guyana Cult of the Damned, The Man With Bogart's Face, Liar's Moon, American Gothic, Cellar Dweller, Mirror Mirror, Oscar, The Naked Truth.
TELEVISION: Series: The Munsters. Movies: The Girl on the Late Late Show, The Mark of Zorro, The Munsters' Revenge, A Masterpiece of Murder. Guest: Bonanza, Man From U.N.C.L.E., Murder She Wrote, Hollywood Sign (special), Johnny Carson, Merv Griffin, Steve Allen, David Frost, Perry Como, Tales from the Crypt, Dream On.

De CORDOVA, FREDERICK
Director. b. New York, NY, Oct. 27, 1910. e. Northwestern U., B.S. 1931. Gen. stage dir. Shubert enterprises, N.Y., 1938-41; same for Alfred Bloomingdale Prods., N.Y., and prod. Louisville (Ky.) Amphitheatre 1942-43. Dir., program planning, Screen Gems, 1964. Author: Johnny Came Lately, 1988.
PICTURES: Dialogue Director: San Antonio, Janie, Between Two Worlds. Director: Too Young to Know (debut, 1945), Her Kind of Man, That Way with Women, Love and Learn, Always Together, Wallflower, For the Love of Mary, The Countess of Monte Cristo, Illegal Entry, The Gal Who Took the West, Buccaneer's Girl, Peggy, The Desert Hawk, Bedtime for Bonzo, Katie Did It, Little Egypt, Finders Keepers, Here Come the Nelsons, Yankee Buccaneer, Bonzo Goes to College, Column South, I'll Take Sweden, Frankie and Johnny.
TELEVISION: Series (prod., dir.): The Burns and Allen Show, December Bride, Mr. Adams and Eve, George Gobel Show, The Jack Benny Program, The Smothers Bros. Show, My Three Sons (dir.), Tonight Show (prod.; 6 Emmy Awards).

DeCUIR, JR., JOHN F.
Art Director, Production Designer. b. Burbank, CA, Aug. 4, 1941. e. U. of Southern California, bachelor of architecture, 1965. Son of John F. De Cuir, Sr. 1966-68, U.S. Coast Guard (holds commission with rank of Lt. Commander, USCGR). 1968-72, project designer, Walt Disney World, Walt Disney Prods. 1972-74, dir. of design, Six Flags Corp. 1974-9, project designer, EPCOT, Walt Disney Prods. 1980-86, pres., John F. De Cuir, Jr. Design Consultants, Inc.; 1987-pres., Cinematix Inc.
PICTURES: Illustrator: Cleopatra, The Honey Pot. Design Concepts: The Agony and the Ecstasy. Art Director: Raise the Titanic, Ghostbusters. Special Effects Consultant: Dead Men Don't Wear Plaid, Monsignor. Producer: Jazz Club, The Baltimore Clipper, The Building Puzzle. Prod. Designer: Fright Night, Top Gun, Apt Pupil, Elvira Mistress of the Dark, Turner & Hooch, True Identity, Sleepwalkers, Sister Act 2: Back in the Habit.
TELEVISION: Art Director: Frank Sinatra Special—Old Blue Eyes Is Back, Annual Academy Awards Presentation 1971, Double Agent. Production Design: Double Switch, Earth * Star Voyager.

DEE, RUBY
Actress. b. Cleveland, OH, Oct. 27, 1924. r.n. Ruby Ann Wallace. e. Hunter Coll. m. actor-dir.-writer Ossie Davis. Worked as apprentice at Amer. Negro Theatre, 1941-44, studied at Actor's Workshop. Stage appearances include Jeb, Anna Lucasta, The World of Sholom Aleichem, A Raisin in the Sun, Purlie Victorious, Wedding Band, Boseman and Lena, Hamlet, Checkmates.
PICTURES: No Way Out, The Jackie Robinson Story, The Tall Target, Go Man Go!, Edge of the City, St. Louis Blues, Take a Giant Step, Virgin Island, A Raisin in the Sun, Gone Are the Days, The Balcony, The Incident, Up Tight, Buck and the Preacher, Black Girl, Countdown at Kusini, Cat People, Do the Right Thing, Love at Large, Jungle Fever, Cop and a Half, Just Cause.
TELEVISION: Movies: Deadlock, The Sheriff, It's Good to Be Alive, I Know Why the Caged Bird Sings, All God's Children, The Atlanta Child Murders, Go Tell it on the Mountain, Windmills of the Gods, The Court-Martial of Jackie Robinson, Decoration Day (Emmy Award, 1991), The Ernest Green Story. Specials: Actor's Choice, Seven Times Monday, Go Down Moses, Twin-Bit Gardens, Wedding Band, To Be Young Gifted and Black, Long Day's Journey into Night, Edgar Allan Poe: Terror of the Soul (narrator). Mini-Series: Roots: The Next Generation, Gore Vidal's Lincoln, The Stand. Series: Peyton Place, With Ossie and Ruby, Middle Ages.

DEE, SANDRA
Actress. r.n. Alexandra Zuck. b. Bayonne, NJ, April 23, 1942. Modeled, Harry Conover and Huntington Hartford Agencies, N.Y., 1954-56; signed long term exclusive contract, U-I, 1957.
PICTURES: Until They Sail (debut, 1957), The Reluctant Debutante, The Restless Years, Stranger in My Arms, Imitation of Life, Gidget, The Wild and the Innocent, A Summer Place, The Snow Queen (voice), Portrait in Black, Romanoff and Juliet, Come September, Tammy Tell Me True, If a Man Answers, Tammy and the Doctor, Take Her She's

Mine, I'd Rather Be Rich, That Funny Feeling, A Man Could Get Killed, Doctor You've Got to Be Kidding!, Rosie, The Dunwich Horror.
TELEVISION: *Movies:* The Daughters of Joshua Cabe, Houston We've Got a Problem, The Manhunter, Fantasy Island (pilot). *Guest:* Steve Allen Show, Night Gallery, Love American Style, Police Woman.

DEELEY, MICHAEL
Producer. b. London, Eng. August 6, 1932. Ent. m.p. ind. 1951 and TV, 1967, as alt. dir. Harlech Television Ltd. Film editor, 1951-58. MCA-TV 1958-61, later with Woodfall as prod. and assoc. prod. Assoc. prod. The Knack, The White Bus, Ride of the Valkyrie. Great Western Investments Ltd.; 1972; Great Western Festivals Ltd.; 1973, mng. dir. British Lion Films Ltd. 1975, purchased BLF, Ltd. Appt. Jnt. man. dir. EMI Films Ltd., 1977; pres., EMI Films, 1978, Member Film Industry Interim Action Committee, 1977-82; Deputy Chairman, British Screen Advisory Council, 1985. Appt. Chief Executive Officer, Consolidated Television Production & Distribution Inc., 1984.
PICTURES: *Prod.:* One Way Pendulum, Robbery, The Italian Job, Long Days Dying (exec. prod.), Where's Jack, Sleep Is Lovely, Murphy's War, The Great Western Express, Conduct Unbecoming, The Man Who Fell to Earth, Convoy, The Deer Hunter (Academy Award for Best Picture, 1978), Blade Runner.
TELEVISION: *Movie:* A Gathering of Old Men (exec. prod.).

DE FINA, BARBARA
Producer. Started as prod. asst. before working at various jobs for such filmmakers as Woody Allen and Sidney Lumet. Became assoc. prod. of development for King/Hitzig Prods., working on Happy Birthday Gemini, Cattle Annie and Little Britches. Was unit mgr./assoc. prod. on Prince of the City. First worked with Martin Scorsese on The King of Comedy as unit mgr. Produced music video Bad.
PICTURES: *Producer:* The Color of Money, The Last Temptation of Christ, New York Stories (segment: Life Lessons), GoodFellas (exec. prod.), The Grifters (exec. prod.), Cape Fear, Mad Dog and Glory, The Age of Innocence, Casino.

De HAVILLAND, OLIVIA
Actress b. Tokyo, Japan, July 1, 1916. e. California schools and Notre Dame Convent, Belmont. Acting debut, Max Reinhardt's stage prod., A Midsummer Night's Dream; going to Warner Bros. for film debut in m.p. version, 1935. Won Warner Bros. role in The Snake Pit (NY Film Critics & Look Awards), The Heiress (NY Film Critics, Women's Natl. Press Club & Look Awards). Autobiography: Every Frenchman Has One (1962).
THEATER: A Midsummer Night's Dream (Hollywood Bowl). B'way: Romeo and Juliet (1951), A Gift of Time. U.S. Tour: Candida (1951-52).
PICTURES: A Midsummer Night's Dream (debut, 1935), Alibi Ike, The Irish in Us, Captain Blood, Anthony Adverse, The Charge of the Light Brigade, Call It a Day, It's Love I'm After, The Great Garrick, Gold is Where You Find It, The Adventures of Robin Hood, Four's a Crowd, Hard to Get, Wings of the Navy, Dodge City, The Private Lives of Elizabeth and Essex, Gone With the Wind, Raffles, My Love Came Back, Santa Fe Trail, Strawberry Blonde, Hold Back the Dawn, They Died With Their Boots On, The Male Animal, In This Our Life, Princess O'Rourke, Thank Your Lucky Stars, Government Girl, The Well Groomed Bride, To Each His Own (Academy Award, 1946), Devotion, Dark Mirror, The Snake Pit, The Heiress (Academy Award, 1949), My Cousin Rachel, That Lady, Not as a Stranger, Ambassador's Daughter, Proud Rebel, Libel, Light in the Piazza, Lady in a Cage, Hush ... Hush Sweet Charlotte, The Adventurers, Pope Joan, Airport '77, The Swarm, The Fifth Musketeer.
TELEVISION: *Special:* Noon Wine (Stage 67). *Movies & Mini-series:* The Screaming Woman, Roots: The Next Generations, Murder is Easy, Charles & Diana: A Royal Romance, North & South Book II, Anastasia, The Woman He Loved.

DELANY, DANA
Actress. b. New York, NY, Mar. 13, 1956. e. Phillips Acad., Wesleyan U.
THEATER: B'way: Translations, A Life. *Off-B'way:* Blood Woman.
PICTURES: Almost You, Where the River Runs Black, Masquerade, Moon Over Parador, Patty Hearst, Housesitter, Light Sleeper, Batman: Mask of the Phantasm (voice), Tombstone, Exit to Eden, Live Nude Girls.
TELEVISION: *Series:* Love of Life, As the World Turns, Sweet Surrender, China Beach (2 Emmy Awards: 1989, 1992). *Guest:* Moonlighting, Magnum P.I. *Movies:* A Promise to Keep, Donato and Daughter, The Enemy Within, Choices of the Heart: The Margaret Sanger Story. *Mini-Series:* Wild Palms. *Specials:* Texan, Fallen Angels (Good Housekeeping).

De LAURENTIIS, DINO
Producer, Executive. b. Torre Annunziata, Italy, Aug. 8, 1919. Took part in Rome Experimental Film Center; dir., prod. chmn.

of the bd. and CEO, De Laurentiis Entertainment Group Inc.; founded in 1984 the DEG Film Studios in Wilmington, NC. Resigned 1988. Started Dino De Laurentiis Communications, 1990.
PICTURES: L'amore Canta, Il Bandito, La Figlia del Capitano, Riso Amaro, La Lupa, Anna, Ulysses, Mambo, La Strada, Gold of Naples, War and Peace, Nights of Cabiria, The Tempest, Great War, Five Branded Women, Everybody Go Home, Under Ten Flags, The Best of Enemies, The Unfaithfuls, Barabbas, The Bible, Operation Paradise, The Witches, The Stranger, Diabolik, Anzio, Barbarella, Waterloo, The Valachi Papers, The Stone Killer, Serpico, Death Wish, Mandingo, Three Days of the Condor, Drum, Face to Face, Buffalo Bill and the Indians, King Kong, The Shootist, Orca, White Buffalo, The Serpent's Egg, King of the Gypsies, The Brink's Job, Hurricane, Flash Gordon, Halloween II, Ragtime, Conan the Barbarian, Fighting Back, Amityville II: The Possession, Halloween III: Season of the Witch, The Dead Zone, Amityville 3-D, Firestarter, The Bounty, Conan the Destroyer, Stephen King's Cat's Eye, Red Sonja, Year of the Dragon, Marie, Stephen King's Silver Bullet, Raw Deal, Maximum Overdrive, Tai-Pan, Blue Velvet, The Bedroom Window, Crimes of the Heart, King Kong Lives, Million Dollar Mystery, Weeds, Desperate Hours, Kuffs, Once Upon a Crime, Body of Evidence, Army of Darkness, Unforgettable, Assassins, Dragonheart.
TELEVISION: *Movie:* Solomon and Sheba.

De LAURENTIIS, RAFFAELLA
Producer. Daughter of Dino De Laurentiis. Began career as prod. asst. on father's film Hurricane. Independent producer.
PICTURES: Beyond the Reef, Conan the Barbarian, Conan the Destroyer, Dune, Tai-Pan, Prancer, Dragon: The Bruce Lee Story, Trading Mom, Dragonheart, Backdraft (exec. prod.), Daylight (exec. prod.).
TELEVISION: *Series:* Vanishing Son.

De La VARRE, ANDRE, JR.
Producer, Director. b. Vienna, Austria, Oct. 26, 1934. Prod. Grand Tour travelogues; producer of promotion films for KLM, Swissair, tourist offices, recent productions: Bicentennial films for state of Virginia, city of Charleston, NY state; winner, Atlanta Film Festival, Sunset Travel Film Festival; Burton Holmes Travelogue subjects; Corporate Incentive Videos, V-P-R Educational Films; producer, director, lecturer, narrator.

DEL BELSO, RICHARD
Marketing Executive. b. Albany, NY, Aug. 9, 1939. e. Fordham U, 1961, NYU, 1965. Began career in adv./research dept. at Benton & Bowles Advertising, NY. Served as research dept. group head for Kenyon and Eckhart; group head for Grudin/Appell/Haley Research Co. (now known as A/H/F/ Marketing Research, Inc.). Two years as assoc. dir. of mktg., research for Grey Advertising (N.Y.). Joined MCA/Universal in 1976 as assoc. dir., mktg. research. In 1980 named v.p. & dir. of mktg. research for Warner Bros; became worldwide v.p. of mktg. research, 1984; named sr. v.p. worldwide theatrical film market research, 1990.

De LELLIS, BOB
Executive. President, Fox Video.

De LINE, DONALD
Executive. President, Touchstone Pictures.

DELON, ALAIN
Actor. b. Sceaux, France, Nov. 8, 1935. Discovered by Yves Allegret. Served in French Navy as a Marine. Worked as cafe waiter, heavy-load carrier.
PICTURES: When a Woman Gets Involved (debut, 1957), Be Beautiful and Keep Quiet, 3 Murderesses, Christine, Le Chemin Des Ecoliers, Plein Soleil (Purple Noon), Quelle Joie de Vivre!, Rocco and His Brothers, Famous Loves, Eclipse, The Leopard, The Devil and the 10 Commandments, Any Number Can Win, The Black Tulip, The Felines (Joy House), L'Insoumis (also prod., co-s.p.), The Yellow Rolls Royce, Once a Thief, Lost Command, Is Paris Burning?, Texas Across the River, The Adventurers, Spirits of the Dead, Samaurai, Diabolically Yours, Girl on a Motorcycle, Goodbye Friend, The Swimming Pool, Jeff (also prod.), The Sicilian Clan, Borsalino, The Red Circle, Madly (also prod.), Doucement Les Basses, Red Sun, The Widow Cuderc, Assassination of Trotsky, Dirty Money, The Teacher, Scorpio, Shock Treatment, The Burning Barn, Big Guns, Two Men in the City, La Race des Seigneurs, Les Seins de Glace, Borsalino & Company (also prod.), Zorro, Police Story, The Gypsy, Mr. Klein (also prod.), Like a Boomerang (also prod., s.p.), The Gang (also exec. prod.), Armaggedon, L'Homme Presse, Mort d'un Pourri (also s.p.), Attention Les Enfants Regardent, The Concorde - Airport 79, The Doctor, Teheran 43, Three Men to Destroy (also prod.), For a Cop's Honor (also dir, s.p., prod.), The Shock (also s.p.), The Cache (also prod., dir., s.p.), Swann in Love, Our Story, Military Police (also exec. prod., s.p.), The Passage (also

prod.), Let Sleeping Cops Lie (also prod., co-s.p.), New Wave, Dancing Machine, The Return of Casanova, Un Crime... L'Ours en Peluche.

DELPY, JULIE
Actress. b. Paris, France, 1970. Made acting debut as teenager for dir. Jean-Luc Godard.
PICTURES: Detective (debut, 1985) Bad Blood, King Lear, Beatrice, The Dark Night, Europa Europa, Voyager, The Three Musketeers, White, Killing Zoe, Younger and Younger, Before Sunrise.

DEL ROSSI, PAUL R.
Executive. b. Winchester, MA, Oct. 19, 1942. e. Harvard Coll, 1964; Harvard Business Sch., 1967. Sr. v.p., The Boston Co., 1977-1980; sr. consultant, Arthur D. Little, Inc.; presently pres. & CEO, General Cinema Theatres.

DeLUCA, MICHAEL
Executive, Writer. b. Brooklyn, Aug., 1965. Left NYU to take intern job at New Line Cinema; became story editor before becoming production exec. in 1989. 1993 named pres. of production of New Line.
PICTURES: Writer: Freddy's Dead: The Final Nightmare, In the Mouth of Madness, Judge Dredd (story).

De LUISE, DOM
Comedian, Actor. b. Brooklyn, NY, Aug. 1, 1933. e. Tufts Coll. m. actress Carol Arthur. Sons: Peter, Michael, David. Spent two seasons with Cleveland Playhouse. Launched TV career on The Garry Moore Show with character, Dominick the Great, a bumbling magician.
THEATER: Little Mary Sunshine, Another Evening With Harry Stoones, All in Love, Half-Past Wednesday, Too Much Johnson, The Student Gypsy, Last of the Red Hot Lovers, Here's Love, Little Shop of Horrors, Die Fledermus (NY Met. Opera: 2 seasons), Peter and the Wolf.
PICTURES: Fail Safe (debut, 1964), Diary of a Bachelor, The Glass Bottom Boat, The Busy Body, What's So Bad About Feeling Good?, Norwood, The Twelve Chairs, Who Is Harry Kellerman...?, Every Little Crook and Nanny, Blazing Saddles, The Adventure of Sherlock Holmes' Smarter Brother, Silent Movie, The World's Greatest Lover, The End, The Cheap Detective, Sextette, The Muppet Movie, Hot Stuff (also dir.), The Last Married Couple in America, Fatso, Wholly Moses, Smokey and the Bandit II, History of the World Part I, The Cannonball Run, The Best Little Whorehouse in Texas, The Secret of NIMH (voice), Cannonball Run II, Johnny Dangerously, Haunted Honeymoon, An American Tail (voice), Spaceballs (voice), A Taxi Driver in New York, Going Bananas, Oliver & Company (voice), All Dogs Go To Heaven (voice), Loose Cannons, Driving Me Crazy, Fievel Goes West (voice), Munchie (voice), The Skateboard Kid (voice), Happily Ever After (voice), Robin Hood: Men in Tights, The Silence of the Hams, A Troll in Central Park (voice), All Dogs Go to Heaven 2 (voice).
TELEVISION: Series: The Entertainers, The Dean Martin Summer Show, Dom DeLuise Show, The Barrum-Bump Show, The Glenn Campbell Goodtime Hour, The Dean Martin Show, Lotsa Luck, Dom DeLuise Show (synd.), The New Candid Camera, Fievel's American Tails (voice). Movies: Evil Roy Slade, Only With Married Men, Happy (also exec. prod.), Don't Drink the Water, The Tin Soldier. Guest: The Munsters, Please Don't Eat the Daises, Ghost and Mrs. Muir, Medical Center, Amazing Stories, Easy Street, B.L. Stryker.

del VALLE, JOHN
Publicist. b. San Francisco, CA, Mar. 23, 1904. e. U. of California. Adv., edit. staff various newspapers including asst. drama ed. S.F. Call-Bulletin, L.A. Mirror; adv.-publicity dir. San Francisco Fox Theatre 1933-36; publicist, Paramount Studio, 1936-42; dir. pub., adv. Arnold Prod. 1946; Chaplin Studios, 1947; Nat Holt Prod., 1948-52; Editor, TV Family mag., N.Y., 1952-53; adv. pub. dir. Century Films, 1954; pub. rel. Academy M.P. Arts & Sciences, 1965; publicist, various U.A. indep. film prod., 1955-56; unit publicist, Paramount, 1956; TC-F 1957-62, Para., 1962-63; Universal 1964-65; Mirisch Corp.-UA Filming, Hawaii, 1965; pub. rel. and editor, Atomics Int'l div. North American Rockwell, 1966-71; present, freelance writer. NY Times Op. Ed. (1985), Gourmet Mag. (1989), others.

DEMME, JONATHAN
Director, Writer, Producer. b. Rockville Centre, NY, Feb. 22, 1944. e. U. of Florida. First job in industry as usher; was film critic for college paper, The Florida Alligator and the Coral Gable Times. Did publicity work for United Artists, Avco Embassy; sold films for Pathe Contemporary Films; wrote for trade paper, Film Daily, 1966-68. Moved to England in 1969; musical co-ordinator on Irving Allen's EyeWitness in 1970. In 1972 co-prod and co-wrote first film, Angels Hard As They Come. Appeared in film Into the Night.
PICTURES: Hot Box (prod., co-s.p.), Black Mama White Mama (story). Director: Caged Heat (also s.p.), Crazy Mama (also s.p.), Fighting Mad (also s.p.), Citizen's Band (Handle

With Care), Last Embrace, Melvin and Howard, Swing Shift, Stop Making Sense, Something Wild (also co-prod.), Swimming to Cambodia, Married to the Mob, Miami Blues (prod. only), The Silence of the Lambs (Academy Award, 1991), Cousin Bobby, Philadelphia (also co-prod.), Devil in a Blue Dress (exec. prod. only).
TELEVISION: Specials: Who Am I This Time?, Accumation With Talking plus Water Motor, Survival Guides, A Family Tree (Trying Times series, PBS), Haiti: Dreams of Democracy. Movie: Women & Men 2 (A Domestic Dilemma; prod. only).
VIDEO: UB40, Chrissie Hynde, Sun City Video of Artists United Against Apartheid, Suzanne Vega's Solitude Standing.

DE MORNAY, REBECCA
Actress. b. Santa Rosa, CA, Aug. 29, 1962. Spent childhood in Europe, graduating from high school in Austria. Returned to America, enrolling at Lee Strasberg's Los Angeles Institute; apprenticed at Zoetrope Studios.
THEATER: Born Yesterday (Pasadena Playhouse), Marat/Sade (Williamstown Fest.).
PICTURES: Risky Business, Testament, The Slugger's Wife, Runaway Train, The Trip to Bountiful, Beauty and the Beast, And God Created Woman, Feds, Dealers, Backdraft, The Hand That Rocks the Cradle, Guilty as Sin, The Three Musketeers, Never Talk to Strangers.
TELEVISION: Movies: The Murders in the Rue Morgue, By Dawn's Early Light, An Inconvenient Woman, Blindside, Getting Out.

DEMPSEY, PATRICK
Actor. b. Lewiston, ME, Jan. 13, 1966. e. St. Dominic Regional h.s. in Lewiston where he became State downhill skiing champion. Juggling, magic and puppetry led to performances before Elks clubs and community orgs. Cast by Maine Acting Co. in On Golden Pond. In 1983 acted in Torch Song Trilogy in San Francisco and toured in Brighton Beach Memoirs. NY Theatre debut, 1991 in The Subject Was Roses.
PICTURES: Heaven Help Us (debut, 1985), Meatballs III, Can't Buy Me Love, In the Mood, In a Shallow Grave, Some Girls, Loverboy, Coupe de Ville, Happy Together, Run, Mobsters, For Better and For Worse (R.S.V.P.), Face the Music, Bank Robber, With Honors, Outbreak.
TELEVISION: Movies: A Fighting Choice, JFK: Reckless Youth, Bloodknot. Series: Fast Times at Ridgemont High. Special: Merry Christmas Baby.

De MUNN, JEFFREY
Actor. b. Buffalo, NY, Apr. 25, 1947. e. Union Col. Studied acting at Old Vic Theatre in Bristol, Eng.
THEATER: NY: Comedians, A Prayer for My Daughter, Modigliani, Augusta, Hands of Its Enemy, Chekhov Sketchbook, A Midsummer Night's Dream, Total Abandon, Country Girl, Bent, K-2, Sleight of Hand, Spoils of War, One Shoe Off, Hedda Gabler.
PICTURES: You Better Watch Out (Christmas Evil), The First Deadly Sin, Resurrection, Ragtime, I'm Dancing as Fast as I Can, Frances, Windy City, Enormous Changes at the Last Minute, Warning Sign, The Hitcher, The Blob, Betrayed, Blaze, Newsies, Eyes of an Angel, The Shawshank Redemption, Safe Passage, Killer, Phenomenon.
TELEVISION: Movies: The Last Tenant, Sanctuary of Fear, King Crab, Word of Honor, I Married Wyatt Earp, The Face of Rage, Sessions, When She Says No, Windmills of the Gods, Lincoln, Doubletake, A Time to Live, Who Is Julia?, Young Harry Houdini, Price of Justice, Switch, Elysian Fields, The Haunted, Treacherous Crossing, Jonathan: The Boy Nobody Wanted, Barbarians at the Gate, Crash: The Fate of Flight 1502, Settle the Score, Under the Influence, Betrayal of Trust, Citizen X, Down Came a Blackbird, Hiroshima, Almost Golden: The Jessica Savitch Story. Specials: Mourning Becomes Electra, Peacemaker (Triple Play II), Sensibility and Sense, The Joy That Kills, Teacher, Pigeon Feathers, Many Mansions, Wild Jackasses, Ebbie.

DENCH, DAME JUDI
Actress. b. York, England, Dec. 9, 1934. Studied for stage at Central Sch. of Speech and Drama. Theatre debut Old Vic, 1957. Created a Dame in 1988 Honours List. Recent Theatre: Cymbeline, Juno and the Paycock, A Kind of Alaska, The Cherry Orchard, The Plough and the Stars, Importance of Being Earnest, Pack of Lies, Mr. and Mrs. Nobody, Antony and Cleopatra, The Sea, Coriolanus, The Gift of the Gorgon, The Seagull. Director: Much Ado About Nothing, Look Back in Anger, Boys from Syracuse, Romeo and Juliet, Absolute Hell, A Little Night Music.
PICTURES: The Third Secret (debut, 1964), He Who Rides a Tiger, A Study in Terror, Four in the Morning, A Midsummer Night's Dream (RSC Prod.), Luther, Dead Cert, Wetherby, A Room With a View, 84 Charing Cross Road, A Handful of Dust, Henry V, Jack and Sarah, Goldeneye.
TELEVISION: Major Barbara, Pink String and Sealing Wax, Talking to a Stranger, The Funambulists, Age of Kings, Jackanory, Hilda Lessways, Luther, Neighbours, Parade's

End, Marching Song, On Approval, Days to Come, Emilie, The Comedy of Errors (RSC Prod.), Macbeth (RSC Prod.), Langrishe Go Down, On Giant's Shoulders, Love in a Cold Climate, Village Wooing, A Fine Romance (series), The Cherry Orchard, Going Gently, Saigon—Year of the Cat, Ghosts, Behaving Badly, Torch, Can You Hear Me Thinking?, Absolute Hell, As Time Goes By (series).

DENEAU, SIDNEY, G.
Sales executive. Head film buyer Fabian Theatres; U.S. Army 1942-46; gen. mgr. Schine Theatres 1947; v.p., gen. sales mgr., Selznick Releasing Orgn., 1949; 1956; v.p. asst. gen. sls. mgr., Para. Film Dist., 1958; exec. v.p., Rugoff Theatres, 1964. Resigned, September, 1969 to engage in own theatre consultant business.

DENEUVE, CATHERINE
Actress. r.n. Catherine Dorleac. b. Paris, France, Oct. 22, 1943. Sister was the late Francoise Dorleac. Made screen debut as teen using adopting mother's maiden name.
PICTURES: Les Collegiennes (debut, 1956), Wild Roots of Love, L'homme a Femmes, The Doors Slam, La Parisienne (segment: Sophie), Vice and Virtue, Satan Leads the Dance, Vacances Portugaises, Les Plus Belles Escroqueries du Monde, The Umbrellas of Cherbourg (Cannes Film Fest. Award, 1964), Male Hunt (La Chasse a l'Homme), Male Companion, La Costanza della Ragione, Repulsion, Le Chant du Monde, La Vie de Chateau (A Matter of Resistance), Who Wants to Sleep?, Les Creatures, The Young Girls of Rochefort, Belle de Jour (Venice Film Fest. Award, 1967), Benjamin, Manon 70, Mayerling, La Chamade (Heartbeat), The April Fools, Mississippi Mermaid, Don't Be Blue, Tristana, Donkey Skin, Henri Langolis, Liza, It Only Happens to Others, Dirty Money, Melampo, The Slightly Pregnant Man, Touche Pas a la Femme Blanche, La Grande Bourgeoise, Zig-Zag, La Femme aux Bottes Rouges, Hustle, Lovers Like Us, Act of Agression, The Beach Hut, Second Chance, March or Die, Ecoute voir, L'Argent des Autres, When I Was a Kid I Didn't Dare, Anima Persa, An Adventure for Two, Ils Sont Grandes ces Petits, Courage--Let's Run, The Last Metro, Je vous Aime, Choice of Arms, Hotel des Ameriques, Reporters, Daisy Chain, Le Choc, The African, The Hunger, Le Bon Plaisir, Fort Saganne, Love Songs, Let's Hope It's a Girl, Le Mauvaise Herbe, Scene of the Crime, Agent Trouble, A Strange Place to Meet (also prod.), Hotel Panique, The Man Who Loved Zoos, Frequency Murder, Helmut Newton: Frames From the Edge (doc.), The White Queen, Indochine (Acad. Award nom.), Ma Saison Preferee (My Favorite Season), The Chess Game, The Convent.

DENHAM, MAURICE
O.B.E., 1992: Actor. b. Beckenham, Kent, England, Dec. 23, 1909. e. Tonbridge Sch. Started theatrical career with repertory com. 1934. Served in W.W.II. Played in numerous plays, films & radio shows.
PICTURES: Blanche Fury, London Belongs To Me, It's Not Cricket, Traveller's Joy, Landfall, Spider and the Fly, No Highway in the Sky, The Net, Time Bomb, Street Corner (Both Sides of the Law), Million Pound Note (Man With a Million), Eight O'Clock Walk, Purple Plain, Simon and Laura, 23 Paces to Baker Street, Checkpoint, Carrington V.C. (Court Martial), Doctor at Sea, Night of the Demon, Man With a Dog, Barnacle Bill, The Captain's Table, Our Man in Havana, Sink the Bismark, Two-Way Stretch, Greengage Summer, Invasion, Quartette, The Mark, HMS Defiant, The Very Edge, Paranoiac, The Set Up, Penang, The King's Breakfast, Downfall, Hysteria, The Uncle, Operation Crossbow, Legend of Dick Turpin, The Alphabet Murders, The Night Callers, The Nanny, Those Magnificent Men in Their Flying Machines, Heroes of Telemark, After the Fox, The Torture Garden, The Long Duel, The Eliminator, Danger Route, Attack on the Iron Coast, The Best House in London, Negatives, The Midas Run, Some Girls Do, The Touch of Love, The Virgin and the Gypsy, Bloody Sunday, Countess Dracula, Nicholas and Alexandra, The Day of the Jackal, Luther, Shout at the Devil, Julia, The Recluse, From a Far Country, Mr. Love, The Chain, Monsignor Quixote, Murder on the Orient Express, 84 Charing Cross Road.
TELEVISION: Uncle Harry, Day of the Monkey, Miss Mabel, Angel Pavement, The Paraguayan Harp, The Wild Bird, Soldier Soldier, Changing Values, Maigret, The Assassins, Saturday Spectacular, Vanishing Act, A Chance in Life, Virtue, Somerset Maugham, Three of a Kind, Sapper, Pig in the Middle, Their Obedient Servants, Long Past Glory, Devil in The Wind, Any Other Business, The Retired Colourman, Sherlock Holmes (series), Blackmail, Knock on Any Door, Danger Man, Dr. Finley's Casebook, How to Get Rid of Your Husband, Talking to a Stranger, A Slight Ache, From Chekhov with Love, Home Sweet Honeycomb, St. Joan, Julius Caesar, Golden Days, Marshall Petain, The Lotus Eaters, Fall of Eagles, Carnforth Practice. The Unofficial Rose, Omnibus, Balzac, Loves Labour Lost, Angels, Huggy Bear, The Portrait, The Crumbles Murder, A Chink In The Wall, Porridge, For God's Sake, Bosch, Marie Curie, Upchat Line, Secret Army, My Son, My Son, Edward and Mrs. Simpson, Gate of Eden,

Potting Shed, Double Dealer, Minder, Agatha Christie Hour, Chinese Detective, The Old Men at the Zoo, The Hope and the Glory, Luther, Love Song, Mr. Palfrey, The Black Tower, Boon, Rumpole, All Passions Spent, Trial of Klaus Barbie, Miss Marple, Tears in the Rain, Behaving Badly, Seeing in the Dark, Inspector Morse: Fat Chance, La Nonna, Lovejoy, Memento Mori, Sherlock Holmes, The Last Vampire, Peak Pratice, Bed, The Bill, Prisoner In Time, Pie In The Sky.

De NIRO, ROBERT
Actor. b. New York, NY, Aug. 17, 1943. Studied acting with Stella Adler and Lee Strasberg; 1988, formed Tribeca Film Center in NY. Co-Prod. of film Thunderheart.
THEATER: One Night Stand of a Noisy Passenger (Off-B'way), Cuba and His Teddy Bear (Public Theater and B'way; Theatre World Award).
PICTURES: The Wedding Party (debut, 1969), Greetings, Sam's Song (The Swap), Bloody Mama, Hi Mom, Born to Win, Jennifer on My Mind, The Gang That Couldn't Shoot Straight, Bang the Drum Slowly, Mean Streets, The Godfather Part II (Academy Award, best supporting actor, 1974), Taxi Driver, The Last Tycoon, New York New York, 1900, The Deer Hunter, Raging Bull (Academy Award, 1980), True Confessions, The King of Comedy, Once Upon a Time in America, Falling in Love, Brazil, The Mission, Angel Heart, The Untouchables, Midnight Run, Jacknife, We're No Angels, Stanley and Iris, GoodFellas, Awakenings, Guilty by Suspicion, Backdraft, Cape Fear, Mistress (also co-prod.), Night and the City, Mad Dog and Glory, This Boy's Life, A Bronx Tale (also dir., co-prod.), Mary Shelley's Frankenstein, Casino, Heat, Marvin's Room (also exec. prod.), The Fan, Sleepers, Stolen Flower, Copland, Great Expectations.
TELEVISION: Specials: Night of 100 Stars, Dear America: Letters Home From Vietnam (reader).

DENISON, MICHAEL
C.B.E., Actor. b. Doncaster, York, Eng., Nov. 1, 1915. e. Harrow, Magdalen Coll., Oxford and Webber Douglas Sch. m. Dulcie Gray, actress, 1939. Served overseas, Capt. Intelligence Corps, 1940-46. Debuted on stage 1938 in Charlie's Aunt.
THEATER: Ever Since Paradise, Rain on the Just, Queen Elizabeth Slept Here, Fourposter, Dragon's Mouth, Bad Samaritan; Shakespeare Season Stratford-on-Avon; Edinburgh Festival; Meet Me By Moonlight, Let Them Eat Cake, Candida, Heartbreak House, My Fair Lady (Australia), Where Angels Fear to Tread, Hostile Witness, An Ideal Husband (1965, 1992, 1996), On Approval, Happy Family, No. 10, Out of the Question, Trio, The Wild Duck, The Clandestine Marriage, The Dragon Variation, At the End of the Day, The Sack Race, Peter Pan, The Black Mikado, The First Mrs. Fraser, The Earl and the Pussycat, Robert and Elizabeth, The Cabinet Minister, Old Vic Season: Twelfth Night, Lady's Not for Burning, Ivanov, Bedroom Farce, The Kingfisher, Relatively Speaking, Coat of Varnish, Capt. Brassbound's Conversion, School for Scandal, Song at Twilight, See How They Run, The Tempest, Ring Round the Moon, The Apple Cart, Court in the Act, You Never Can Tell, The Chalk Garden, Joy, Dear Charles, Best of Friends, The Importance of Being Earnest, Pygmalion, The Schoolmistress, Two of a Kind.
PICTURES: Tilly of Bloomsbury, (debut, 1939), Hungry Hill, My Brother Jonathan, The Blind Goddess, The Glass Mountain, Landfall, The Franchise Affair, The Magic Box, Angels One Five, The Importance of Being Earnest, Tall Headlines, There Was a Young Lady, Contraband Spain, The Truth About Women, Faces in the Dark, Shadowlands.
TELEVISION: Marco Millions, The Second Man, What's My Line, Milestones, Waiting for Gillian, Olympia, The Sun Divorce, Rain on the Just, East Lynne, Who Goes Home?, Festival Fever, Boyd QC (80 episodes: 1956-63), The Inside Chance, Frankie Howerd Sketch, The Importance of Being Earnest, Dear Octopus, Village Wooing, Compere for Joan Sutherland, Funeral Games, Unexpectedly Vacant, The Twelve Pound Look, The Provincial Lady, Subject: This Is Your Life (1977, and with Dulcie Gray, 1995), Crown Court, Private Schultz, Blood Money, Bedroom Farce, The Critic, Scorpion, Good Behavior, Rumpole, Cold Warrior, Howard's Way.

DENNEHY, BRIAN
Actor. b. Bridgeport, CT, July 9, 1939. e. Columbia U. In Marine Corps five years, including Vietnam. After discharge in 1965 studied with acting coaches in N.Y., while working at part time jobs as a salesman, bartender, truck driver.
THEATER: Streamers, Galileo (Goodman Th.), The Cherry Orchard, Translations.
PICTURES: Looking for Mr. Goodbar, Semi-Tough, F.I.S.T., Foul Play, 10, Butch and Sundance: The Early Days, Little Miss Marker, Split Image, First Blood, Never Cry Wolf, Gorky Park, Finders Keepers, River Rat, Cocoon, Silverado, Twice in a Lifetime, F/X, Legal Eagles, The Check Is in the Mail, Best Seller, The Belly of an Architect, Return to Snowy River Part II, Miles From Home, Cocoon: The Return, The Last of the Finest, Presumed Innocent, FX2, Gladiator, Seven Minutes, Tommy Boy, The Stars Fell on Henrietta, Midnight Movie.

TELEVISION: *Series:* Big Shamus Little Shamus, Star of the Family, Birdland. *Movies*: Johnny We Hardly Knew Ye, It Happened at Lake Wood Manor, Ruby and Oswald, A Death in Canaan, A Real American Hero, Silent Victory: The Kitty O'Neil Story, The Jericho Mile, Dummy, The Seduction of Miss Leona, A Rumor of War, Fly Away Home, Skokie, I Take These Men, Blood Feud, Off Sides, Acceptable Risks, Private Sessions, The Lion of Africa, A Father's Revenge, Day One, Perfect Witness, Pride and Extreme Prejudice, Rising Son, A Killing in a Small Town, In Broad Daylight, The Burden of Proof, To Catch a Killer, Diamond Fleece, Teamster: The Jackie Presser Story, Deadly Matrimony, Foreign Affairs, Murder in the Heartland, Prophet of Evil: The Ervil LeBaron Story, Final Appeal, Jack Reed: Badge of Honor (also co-exec. prod.), Leave of Absence, Jack Reed: Search for Justice (also dir., co-writer). *Mini-Series:* Evergreen. *Guest:* M*A*S*H, Lou Grant, Cagney and Lacey, Hunter, Tall Tales (Annie Oakley). *Special:* Dear America: Letter Home From Vietnam (reader).

DENVER, BOB
Actor. b. New Rochelle, NY, Jan. 9, 1935. e. Loyola U.
PICTURES: A Private's Affair, Take Her She's Mine, For Those Who Think Young, Who's Minding the Mint? The Sweet Ride, Did You Hear the One About the Travelling Saleslady?, Back to the Beach.
TELEVISION: *Series*: The Many Loves of Dobie Gillis, Gilligan's Island, The Good Guys, Dusty's Trail. *Movies*: Rescue from Gilligan's Island, The Castaways on Gilligan's Island, The Harlem Globetrotters on Gilligans Island, The Invisible Woman, High School USA, Bring Me the Head of Dobie Gillis. Also: Far Out Space Nuts, Scamps.

DENVER, JOHN
Singer, Actor. r.n. Henry John Deutschendorf. b. Roswell, NM, Dec. 31, 1943. Records, concerts, nightclubs.
PICTURES: Oh, God!, Fire and Ice (narrator).
TELEVISION: *Specials*: An Evening with John Denver (Emmy Award for Outstanding Special, 1975), Rocky Mountain Christmas, John Denver and the Muppets, Rocky Mountain Holiday, Salute to Lady Liberty, Jacques Costeau--The First 75 Years, Julie Andrews...The Sound of Christmas, John Denver's Christmas in Aspen. *Movies*: The Christmas Gift, Foxfire, Higher Ground (co-exec. prod., co-music, actor).

De PALMA, BRIAN
Director, Writer, Producer. b. Newark, NJ, Sept. 11, 1940. e. Columbia U.,B.A.; Sarah Lawrence, M.A. While in college made series of shorts, including Wotan's Wake, winner of Rosenthal Foundation Award for best film made by American under 25. Also judged most popular film of Midwest Film Festival (1963); later shown at San Francisco Film Festival. Dir.: The Responsive Eye (doc., 1966).
PICTURES: *Director:* Murder a La Mod (also s.p., edit.), Greetings (also co-s.p. ed.), The Wedding Party (also co-s.p., ed.), Hi Mom (also co-story, s.p.), Dionysus in '69 (also co-prod., co-photog., co-ed.), Get To Know Your Rabbit, Sisters (also co-s.p.), Phantom of the Paradise (also co-s.p.), Obsession (also co-story), Carrie, The Fury, Home Movies (also s.p., co-prod.), Dressed to Kill (also s.p.), Blow Out (also s.p.), Scarface, Body Double (also prod., s.p.), Wiseguys, The Untouchables, Casualties of War, The Bonfire of the Vanities (also prod.), Raising Cain (also s.p.), Carlito's Way, Mission: Impossible.

DEPARDIEU, GÉRARD
Actor. b. Chateauroux, France, Dec. 27, 1948. Studied acting at Theatre National Populaire in Paris. Made film debut at 16 in short by Roger Leenhardt (Le Beatnik et Le Minet). Acted in feature film by Agnes Varda (uncompleted).
PICTURES: Le Cri du Cormoran le Soir au-dessis des Jonques, Nathalie Granger, A Little Sun in Cold Water, Le Tueur, L'Affaire Dominici, Au Renedez-vous de la mort joyeuse, La Scoumone, Rude Journee our la Reine, Deux Hommes dans la Ville, The Holes, Going Places, Stavisky, Woman of the Granges, Vincent Francois Paul and the Others, The Wonderful Crook, 7 Morts sur ordonnance, Maitresse, Je t'Aime Moi Non Plus, The Last Woman, 1900, Barocco, Rene la Canne, Baxter Vera Baxter, The Truck, Tell Him I Love Him, At Night All Cats Are Gray, Get Out Your Handkerchiefs, The Left-Handed Woman, Bye Bye Monkey, Violanta, Le Sucre, Les Chiens, L'Ingorgo, Buffet Froid, Temporale Rosy, Mon Oncle d'Amerique, Loulou, The Last Metro, Inspector Blunder, I Love You, Choice of Arms, The Woman Next Door, Le Chevre. The Return of Martin Guerre, The Big Brother, Danton, The Moon in the Gutter, Les Comperes (also co-prod.), Fort Saganne, Le Tartuffe (also dir., co-s.p), Rive Droie Rive Gauche, Police, One Woman or Two, Menage, Ru du depart, Jean De Florette (also co-prod.), Under Satan's Sun (also co-prod.), A Strange Place for an Enounter (also co-prod.), Camille Claudel (also co-prod.), Dreux, Too Beautiful for You (also co-prod.), I Want to Go Home, Cyrano de Bergerac (also co-prod), Green Card, Uranus, Thanks for Life,

Mon Pere ce Heros (My Father the Hero), 1492: Conquest of Paradise, Tous les Matins du Monde (All the Mornings of the World), Helas Pour Moi (Oh Woe is Me), Une Pure Formalite (A Pure Formality), Germinal, My Father the Hero, Colonel Chabert, La Machine, Elisa, Les Anges Gardiens, The Horseman on the Roof, Bogus, Le Garcu, Hamlet.

DEPP, JOHNNY
Actor. b. Owensboro, KY, June 9, 1963. Raised in Miramar, FL. Played lead guitar with band The Kids, with whom he moved to L.A. in 1983. With no prior acting experience made film debut in A Nightmare on Elm Street.
PICTURES: A Nightmare on Elm Street (debut, 1984), Private Resort, Platoon, Cry-Baby, Edward Scissorhands, Freddy's Dead: The Final Nightmare (cameo), What's Eating Gilbert Grape, Arizona Dream, Ed Wood, Don Juan DeMarco, Dead Man, Nick of Time, Divine Rapture, Donnie Brasco.
TELEVISION: *Series*: 21 Jump Street. *Movie*: Slow Burn. *Guest*: Lady Blue.

DEREK, BO
Actress. r.n. Mary Cathleen Collins. b. Torrance, CA., Nov. 20, 1956. Discovered by actor-turned-filmmaker John Derek, whom she married.
PICTURES: Orca (debut, 1977), 10, A Change of Seasons, Fantasies (And Once Upon a Time), Tarzan The Ape Man (also prod.), Bolero (also prod.), Ghosts Can't Do It (also prod.), Hot Chocolate, Sognando la California (California Dreaming), Woman of Desire, Tommy Boy.
TELEVISION: *Movie*: Shattered Image.

DEREK, JOHN
Actor, Producer, Director, Cinematographer. b. Hollywood, CA, August 12, 1926. m. actress Bo Derek. Acting debut as bit player 1945 in I'll Be Seeing You, billed as Derek Harris. Made producer debut 1963 with Nightmare in the Sun, directorial debut 1966 with Once Before I Die.
PICTURES: *Actor:* I'll Be Seeing You (debut, 1945), A Double Life, Knock on Any Door, All the King's Men, Rogues of Sherwood Forest, Saturday's Hero, Mask of the Avenger, Scandal Sheet, The Family Secret, Thunderbirds, Mission Over Korea, The Last Posse, Prince of Pirates, Ambush at Tomahawk Gap, Sea of Lost Ships, The Outcast, The Adventures of Hajji Baba, Prince of Players, Run for Cover, An Annapolis Story, The Leather Saint, The Ten Commandments, Omar Khayyam, Fury at Showdown, High Hell, Prisoner of the Volga, Exodus, Nightmare in the Sun (also prod.), Once Before I Die (also dir., prod.), A Boy ... a Girl, Childish Things (also dir.). *Director-Cinematographer:* Fantasies (And Once Upon a Time), Tarzan The Ape Man, Bolero (also s.p.), Ghosts Can't Do It.
TELEVISION: *Series*: Frontier Circus.

DERN, BRUCE
Actor. b. Chicago, IL, June 4, 1936. e. U. of Pennsylvania. Daughter is actress Laura Dern. Studied acting with Gordon Phillips, member, Actor's Studio, 1959 after N.Y. debut in Shadow of a Gunman. Broadway: Sweet Bird of Youth, Orpheus Descending, Strangers. Film Award: Natl. Society of Film Critics (Drive He Said, 1971), People's Choice (Coming Home, 1978), Genie (Middle Age Crazy, 1980), Silver Bear (That Championship Season, 1982).
PICTURES: Wild River (debut, 1960), Marnie, Hush...Hush Sweet Charlotte, The Wild Angels, The St. Valentine's Day Massacre, Waterhole No. 3, The Trip, The War Wagon, Psych-Out, Rebel Rousers, Hang 'Em High, Will Penny, Number One, Castle Keep, Support Your Local Sheriff, They Shoot Horses Don't They?, Cycle Savages, Bloody Mama, The Incredible Two-Headed Transplant, Drive He Said, Silent Running, Thumb Tripping, The Cowboys, The King of Marvin Gardens, The Laughing Policeman, The Great Gatsby, Smile, Posse, Family Plot, Won Ton Ton the Dog Who Saved Hollywood, The Twist (Folies Bourgeoises), Black Sunday, Coming Home (Acad. Award nom.), The Driver, Middle Age Crazy, Tattoo, Harry Tracy: Desperado, That Championship Season, On the Edge, The Big Town, World Gone Wild, 1969, The 'Burbs, After Dark My Sweet, Diggstown, Wild Bill, Down Periscope, Mulholland Falls, Last Man Standing.
TELEVISION: *Series*: Stoney Burke. *Mini-Series*: Space. *Movies*: Sam Hill: Who Killed the Mysterious Mr. Foster?, Toughlove, Roses Are for the Rich, Uncle Tom's Cabin, Trenchcoat in Paradise, The Court-Martial of Jackie Robinson, Into the Badlands, Carolina Skeletons, It's Nothing Personal, Deadman's Revenge, Amelia Earhart: The Final Flight, A Mother's Prayer. *Guest*: Naked City, Ben Casey, The Virginian, Twelve O'Clock High, The Big Valley, Gunsmoke, The FBI, Land of the Giants, Saturday Night Live, Fallen Angels (Murder Obliquely).

DERN, LAURA
Actress. b. Los Angeles, CA, Feb. 10, 1967. Daughter of actors Diane Ladd and Bruce Dern. At age 5 appeared with

mother on daytime serial The Secret Storm. Was an extra in several of her father's films and her mother's Alice Doesn't Live Here Anymore. Studied acting at RADA appearing on stage in Hamlet, A Midsummer Night's Dream.
THEATER: NY: The Palace of Amateurs. LA: Brooklyn Laundry.
PICTURES: White Lightning (debut, 1973), Alice Doesn't Live Here Anymore, Foxes, Ladies and Gentlemen: The Fabulous Stains, Teachers, Mask, Smooth Talk, Blue Velvet, Haunted Summer, Fat Man and Little Boy, Wild at Heart, Rambling Rose (Acad. Award nom.), Jurassic Park, A Perfect World, Devil Inside, Citizen Ruth.
TELEVISION: Movies: Happy Endings, Three Wishes of Billy Greer, Afterburn (Golden Globe Award), Down Came a Blackbird. Special: The Gift (dir., co-story only). Guest: Fallen Angels (Murder Obliquely).

DE SANTIS, GREGORY JOSEPH
Producer, Writer, Director. b. Los Angeles, CA, July 12, 1955. e. Durham Univ., Canaan Coll. President, Millenium Mulitmedia.
PICTURES: Prod.: The Companion, Car Trouble, Pass the Buck, Die Sister Die!, Diary of a Surfing Film, Firepower, The Forest.
TELEVISION: Prod.: Volleyball: A Sport Come of Age, The Nature Series, Caribou Crossing, California Day, Midnight Son, Lightning, Mysterious River.

DESCHANEL, CALEB
Cinematographer, Director. b. Philadelphia, PA, Sept. 21, 1944. m. actress Mary Jo Deschanel. e. Johns Hopkins U., U. of Southern California Film Sch. Studied at Amer. Film Inst., interned under Gordon Willis then started making commercials, short subjects, docs.
PICTURES: Cinematographer: More American Graffiti, Being There, The Black Stallion, Apocalypse Now (2nd unit photog.), The Right Stuff, Let's Spend the Night Together (co-cinematographer), The Natural, The Slugger's Wife, It Could Happen to You, Flying Wild. Director: The Escape Artist, Crusoe.

De TOTH, ANDRE
Writer, Director, Producer. b. Hungary. Dir.-writer European films, 1931-39; U.S. assoc. Alexander Korda prod., 1940; dir. Columbia, 1943; assoc. David Selznick, 1943; assoc. Hunt Stromberg-UA, 1944-45; staff dir., Enterprise 1946-47; dir., 20th-Fox, 1948-49; collab. story, The Gunfighter; assoc., Sam Spiegel, Horizon Pictures, Columbia, 1962; Harry Saltzman, Lowndes Prod., U.A. 1966-68; National General, 1969-70.
PICTURES: Passport to Suez, None Shall Escape, Pitfall, Slattery's Hurricane, Springfield Rifle, Thunder Over the Plains, House of Wax, The Stranger Wore a Gun, Bounty Hunter, Tanganyika, The Indian Fighter, Monkey on My Back, Two Headed Spy, Day of the Outlaw, Man on a String, Morgan The Pirate, The Mongols, Gold for the Caesars, Billion Dollar Brain (exec. prod. only), Play Dirty (also exec. prod.), El Condor (prod. only), The Dangerous Game.

DEUTCH, HOWARD
Director. b. New York, NY. e. Ohio State U. m. actress Lea Thompson. Son of music publisher Murray Deutch. Spent almost 10 yrs. working in various film media, including music videos and film trailer advertising, before feature directorial debut with Pretty in Pink, 1986.
PICTURES: Pretty in Pink, Some Kind of Wonderful, The Great Outdoors, Article 99, Getting Even With Dad, Grumpier Old Men.
TELEVISION: Tales from the Crypt (2 episodes; ACE Award for Dead Right).

DEUTCHMAN, IRA J.
Executive. b. Cherry Point, NC, Mar. 24, 1953. e. Northwestern U., B.S., majoring in film. Began career with Cinema 5, Ltd. serving, 1975-79, as non-theatrical sls. mgr.; dir. theatrical adv./pub./dir. acquisitions. Joined United Artists Classics, 1981 as dir. of adv./pub. 1982, left to become one of the founding partners in Cinecom Intl. Films, where headed mktg./dist. div. from inception. Resigned, Jan. 1989 to form the Deutchman Company, Inc., a production company and marketing consultancy firm. Founded and served as pres. of Fine Line Features, a division of New Line Cinema, and sr. v.p. of parent corp, 1991-95. Currenly, pres. of Redeemable Features, a New York-based prod. company. Adjunct prof. Columbia U. film dept. On advisory bds. Sundance U.S. Film Festival and the Sundance Institute.
PICTURES: Exec. Prod.: Swimming to Cambodia, Matewan (assoc. prod.), Miles From Home (co-exec. prod.), Scenes from the Class Struggle in Beverly Hills, Straight Out of Brooklyn, Waterland, The Ballad of Little Jo, Mrs. Parker and the Vicious Circle.

DEUTCHMAN, LAWRENCE SCOT
Executive. b. Bronx, NY, Dec. 10, 1960. e. Rutgers U. Wrote, prod. & dir. Mythbusters campaign. 1986-92, various positions: Entertainment Industries Council, Inc.; wrote, prod., co-dir. That's a Wrap campaign. 1986-88, board member, Public

Interest Radio & Television Educational Society. 1987-88, wrote, exec. prod., post-prod. sprv., Buckle Up educational & music video (CINE Golden Eagle). 1989: EIC: An Industry in Action (writer, prod., dir.); Campaigns: Natl. Red Ribbon, Office for Substance Abuse Prevention (writer, dir., exec. prod.), Stop the Madness (co-writer, prod.). 1990, developed: Vince & Larry: The Amazing Crash Test Dummies (series, NBC), Drug Proofing Your Kids (tv special); Campaigns: Alcoholism Runs in Families, Texas Prevention Partnership (dir., exec. prod.), They Do as You Do (writer, exec. prod.). 1991: The Inhalant Problem in Texas docum. (co-exec. prod.), Inhalants: The Silent Epidemic award-winning drama (writer, co-exec. prod.), KBVO Fox Kids Club segments (writer, prod., set designer), The Incredible Crash Dummies toy property (co-creator), Ollie Odorfree property (creator). 1992-present: Pres., Dynamic Commun. Intl. Inc.; v.p. prod. & mktg., EIC. 1993: Hollywood Gets M.A.D.D. tv special (co-prod., TBS, TNT, synd.). 1994: Dinorock Time tv series (exec. prod., writer.); 1994-present, s.r., vp. prod. & mktg, EIC.

DEUTSCH, STEPHEN
Producer. b. Los Angeles, CA, June 30, 1946. e. UCLA, B.A.; Loyola Law Sch., 1974. Son of late S. Sylvan Simon. Stepson of Armand Deutsch. Private law practice before joining Rastar 1976 as asst. to Ray Stark; 1977, sr. v.p., Rastar; prod. head for SLM Inc. Film Co. entered independent prod. 1978.
PICTURES: Somewhere in Time, All the Right Moves, Russkies (co-exec. prod.), She's Out of Control, Bill & Ted's Excellent Adventure (exec. prod.), Lucky Stiff, Bill and Ted's Bogus Journey (co-exec. prod.), Body of Evidence (exec. prod.).

DEVANE, WILLIAM
Actor. b. Albany, NY, Sept. 5, 1939. Appeared in some 15 productions with N.Y. Shakespeare Festival, also B'way & off-B'way shows before heading to California for films and TV.
PICTURES: The Pursuit of Happiness (debut, 1970), The 300 Hundred Year Weekend, Lady Liberty, McCabe and Mrs. Miller, Glory Boy (My Old Man's Place), Irish Whiskey Rebellion, Report to the Commissioner, Family Plot, Marathon Man, Bad News Bears in Breaking Training, Rolling Thunder, The Dark, Yanks, Honky Tonk Freeway, Testament, Hadley's Rebellion, Vital Signs.
TELEVISION: Series: From Here to Eternity, Knots Landing, Phenom, The Monroes. Movies: Crime Club, The Bait, Fear on Trial, Red Alert, Black Beauty, Red Flag: The Ultimate Game, The Other Victim, Jane Doe, With Intent to Kill, Timestalker, Murder C.O.D., Nightmare in Columbia County, Obsessed, The President's Child. Prophet of Evil: The Ervil LeBaron Story, Rubdown, For the Love of Nancy, Falling From the Sky!: Flight 174, Robin Cook's Virus, Alistair MacLean's Night Watch. Special: The Missiles of October. Mini-Series: A Woman Named Jackie.

De VITO, DANNY
Actor, Director, Producer. b. Asbury Park, NJ, Nov. 17, 1944. m. actress Rhea Perlman. e. Oratory Prep Sch. Studied at American Acad. of Dramatic Arts. Wilfred Acad. of Hair and Beauty Culture. At 18 worked as hair dresser for 1 yr. at his sister's shop. NY stage in The Man With a Flower in His Mouth (debut, 1969), Down the Morning Line, The Line of Least Existence, The Shrinking Bride, Call Me Charlie, Comedy of Errors, Merry Wives of Windsor (NYSF). Three By Pirandello. Performance in One Flew Over the Cuckoo's Nest led to casting in the film version. Prod. short films: The Sound Sleeper (1973), Minestrone (1975).
PICTURES: Lady Liberty (debut, 1971), Hurry Up or I'll Be 30, Scalawag, One Flew Over the Cuckoo's Nest, Deadly Hero, The Van, The World's Greatest Lover, Goin' South, Going Ape, Terms of Endearment, Romancing the Stone, Johnny Dangerously, The Jewel of the Nile, Head Office, Wiseguys, Ruthless People, My Little Pony (voice), Tin Men, Throw Momma from the Train (also dir.), Twins, The War of the Roses (also dir.), Other People's Money, Batman Returns, Hoffa (also dir., co-prod.), Jack the Bear, Last Action Hero (voice), Look Who's Talking Now (voice), Reality Bites (co-prod. only), Renaissance Man, Pulp Fiction (co-exec. prod. only), Junior, Get Shorty (also co-prod.), Sunset Park (prod.), Matilda (also dir., co-prod.), Mars Attacks.
TELEVISION: Series: Taxi (Emmy & Golden Globe Awards, 1981; also dir. episodes), Mary (dir. only). Movies: Valentine, The Ratings Game (also dir.). Specials: All the Kids Do It (Afterschool Special), A Very Special Christmas Party, Two Daddies? (voice), What a Lovely Way to Spend an Evening (dir.), The Selling of Vince DeAngelo (dir.). Guest: Police Woman, Saturday Night Live, Amazing Stories (also dir.), The Simpsons (voice).

DEVLIN, DEAN
Actor, Writer, Producer. Began career azs an actor, appearing numerous film and television projects, as well as B'way production of There Must Be a Pony. Met Roland Emmerich while acting in Moon 44. Joined Emmerich as a partner at Centropolis Films.
PICTURES: Writer: Universal Soldier. Co-writer/prod.: Stargate, Independence Day.

De WITT, JOYCE
Actress. b. Wheeling, WV, April 23, 1949. e. Ball State U., B.A., theatre; UCLA, MFA in acting. Classically trained, worked in theater since 13 as actress and dir.
TELEVISION: *Series*: Three's Company. *Guest*: Baretta, The Tony Randall Show, Most Wanted, Risko, Finder of Lost Loves. *Movies*: With This Ring, Spring Fling.

DEY, SUSAN
Actress. b. Pekin, IL, Dec. 10, 1952. Signed as magazine teen model at age 15. Made professional TV debut at 17, appearing in The Partridge Family 1970.
PICTURES: Skyjacked (debut, 1972), First Love, Looker, Echo Park, That's Adequate.
TELEVISION: *Series*: The Partridge Family, Loves Me Loves Me Not, Emerald Point N.A.S., L.A. Law, Love and War. *Movies*: Terror on the Beach, Cage Without a Key, Mary Jane Harper Cried Last Night, Little Women, The Comeback Kid, The Gift of Life, Malibu, Sunset Limousine, I Love You Perfect, Bed of Lies, Lies and Lullabies (also co-prod.), Whose Child Is This? The War for Baby Jessica, Beyond Betrayal, Deadly Love.

DE YOUNG, CLIFF
Actor. b. Inglewood, CA, Feb. 12, 1947. e. California State Coll., Illinois State U. On stage in Hair, Sticks and Bones, Two By South, The Three Sisters, The Orphan.
PICTURES: Harry and Tonto, Blue Collar, Shock Treatment, Independence Day, The Hunger, Reckless, Protocol, Secret Admirer, F/X, Flight of the Navigator, Fear, Pulse, Rude Awakening, Glory, Flashback, Crackdown, Dr. Giggles, Carnosaur II, Final Frontier, The Craft, The Substitute.
TELEVISION: *Series*: Sunshine, Robocop. *Special*: Sticks and Bones. *Mini-Series*: Centennial, Master of the Game, Captains and the Kings, King, Robert Kennedy and His Times, Andersonville, Seduced By Madness. *Movies*: Sunshine, The 3000 Mile Chase, The Lindbergh Kidnapping Case, Scared Straight: Another Story, Invasion of Privacy, The Seeding of Sarah Burns, The Night That Panicked America, This Girl for Hire, The Awakening of Candra, Deadly Intentions, Sunshine Christmas, Fun and Games, Where Pigeons Go to Die, Fourth Story, Criminal Behavior, Love Can Be Murder, The Tommyknockers, Precious Victims, Heaven & Hell: North and South Book III, JAG, Element of Truth.

DIAMANT, LINCOLN
Executive, Biographer, Historian. b. New York, NY, Jan. 25, 1923. e. Columbia Coll., A.B. cum laude 1943. Cofounder, Columbia U. radio station. WKCR-FM; served in Wash. as prod., Blue Network (NBC), then in NY as CBS newswriter; 1949 joined World Pub. Co. as adv. and promo. dir.; 1952-69 worked in creative/TV dept. McCann-Erickson, Grey, then Ogilvy & Mather ad agencies (winning 6 Clio Awards). Prod. Lend Us Your Ears (Met. Museum Art broadcast series); founder, pres., Spots Alive, Inc., broadcast adv. consultants, 1969; Author, The Broadcast Communications Dictionary, Anatomy of a Television Commercial, Television's Classic Commercials, biography of Bernard Romans, Chaining the Hudson (Sons of Revolution Book Award), Stamping Our History, Yankee Doodle Days. Contrib., to Effective Advertising, to Messages and Meaning; New Routes to English; columnist Back Stage/Shoot. Member, Broadcast Pioneers, Acad. TV Arts & Sciences; v.p. Broadcast Advertising Producer's Society of America. Adjunct faculty member, Pace U.; Hofstra U. Fellow, Royal Society of Arts.

DIAMOND, BERNARD
Theatre Executive. b. Chicago, IL, Jan. 24, 1918. e. U. of Indiana, U. of Minnesota. Except for military service was with Schine Theatre chain from 1940 to 1963, working up from ass't. mng., booker, buyer, dir. of personnel to gen. mgr. Then joined Loews Theatres; last position, exec. v.p. Retired, 1985.

DIAMOND, NEIL
Singer, Songwriter. b. Brooklyn, NY, Jan. 24, 1941. Many concert tours.
PICTURES: Jonathan Livingston Seagull (music), Every Which Way But Loose (music), The Last Waltz (actor), The Jazz Singer (actor, music).
TELEVISION: *Specials*: Neil Diamond... Hello Again, I Never Cared for the Sound of Being Alone, I'm Glad You're Here With Me Tonight, Greatest Hits Live, Neil Diamond's Christmas Special.

DIAZ, CAMERON
Actress. Began career as model for Elite. Feature debut was in The Mask. Received ShoWest 1996 Female Star of Tomorrow Award.
PICTURES: The Mask, Feeling Minnesota, Head Above Water, The Last Supper, She's the One.

DI CAPRIO, LEONARDO
Actor. b. Hollywood, CA, Nov. 11, 1974. Started acting at age 14 in commercials and educational films. Appeared in short film The Foot Shooting Party.

PICTURES: Critters III (debut, 1991), Poison Ivy, This Boy's Life, What's Eating Gilbert Grape (Natl. Board of Review, Chicago Film Critics & LA Film Critics Awards, Acad. Award nom.), The Quick and the Dead, The Basketball Diaries, Total Eclipse, Marvin's Room, Romeo and Juliet.
TELEVISION: *Series*: Growing Pains, Parenthood.

DICKERSON, ERNEST
(A.S.C.): Cinematographer, Director. b. Newark, NJ, 1952. e. Howard U., architecture, NYU, grad. film school. First job, filming surgical procedures for Howard U. medical school. At NYU film school shot classmate Spike Lee's student films Sarah, and Joe's Bed Stuy Barbershop: We Cut Heads. Also shot Nike commercial and several music videos including Bruce Springsteen's Born in the U.S.A., Patti LaBelle's Stir It Up and Miles Davis' Tutu; and Branford Marsalis' Royal Garden Blues directed by Spike Lee. Admitted into Amer. Soc. of Cinematographers in 1989.
PICTURES: *Cinematographer:* The Brother From Another Planet, She's Gotta Have It (also cameo), Krush Groove, School Daze, Raw, Do the Right Thing, Def By Temptation, The Laser Man, Mo' Better Blues, Jungle Fever, Sex Drugs Rock & Roll, Cousin Bobby (co-photog.), Malcolm X. *Director:* Juice (also co-s.p., story), Surviving the Game, Tales Fromt he Crypt Presents Demon Knight.
TELEVISION: Do it Acapella (dir.; PBS).

DICKINSON, ANGIE
Actress. r.n. Angeline Brown. b. Kulm, ND, Sept. 30, 1931. e. Immaculate Heart Coll., Glendale Coll., secretarial course. Beauty contest winner.
PICTURES: Lucky Me (debut in bit part, 1954), Man With the Gun, The Return of Jack Slade, Tennessee's Partner, The Black Whip, Hidden Guns, Tension at Table Rock, Gun the Man Down, Calypso Joe, China Gate, Shoot Out at Medicine Bend, Cry Terror, I Married a Woman, Rio Bravo, The Bramble Bush, Ocean's 11, A Fever in the Blood, The Sins of Rachel Cade, Jessica, Rome Adventure, Captain Newman M.D., The Killers, The Art of Love, Cast a Giant Shadow, The Chase, The Poppy is Also a Flower, The Last Challenge, Point Blank, Sam Whiskey, Some Kind of a Nut, Young Billy Young, Pretty Maids All in a Row, The Resurrection of Zachary Wheeler, The Outside Man, Big Bad Mama, Klondike Fever, Dressed to Kill, Charlie Chan and the Curse of the Dragon Queen, Death Hunt, Big Bad Mama II, Even Cowgirls Get the Blues, The Maddening, Sabrina, The Sun, The Moon and The Stars.
TELEVISION: *Series*: Police Woman, Cassie & Co. *Movies*: The Love War, Thief, See the Man Run, The Norliss Tapes, Pray for the Wildcats, A Sensitive Passionate Man, Overboard, The Suicide's Wife, Dial M for Murder, One Shoe Makes It Murder, Jealousy, A Touch of Scandal, Stillwatch, Police Story: The Freeway Killings, Once Upon a Texas Train, Prime Target, Treacherous Crossing, Danielle Steel's Remembrance. *Mini-Series*: Pearl, Hollywood Wives, Wild Palms.

DICKINSON, WOOD
Executive, Exhibitor. r.n. Glen Wood Dickinson III. b. Fairway, KS, Sept. 14, 1952. e. Texas Christian U (BFA Communications, MA Film). CEO and pres. Dickinson, Inc. and Dickinson Operating Company, Inc., commonly known as Dickinson Theatres.

DILLER, BARRY
Executive. b. San Francisco, CA, Feb. 2, 1942. Joined ABC in April, 1966, as asst. to v.p. in chg. programming. In 1968, made exec. asst. to v.p. in chg. programming and dir. of feature films. In 1969, named v.p., feature films and program dev., east coast. In 1971, made v.p., Feature Films and Circle Entertainment, a unit of ABC Entertainment, responsible for selecting, producing and scheduling The Tuesday Movie of the Week, The Wednesday Movie of the Week, and Circle Film original features for airing on ABC-TV, as well as for acquisition and scheduling of theatrical features for telecasting on ABC Sunday Night Movie and ABC Monday Night Movie. In 1973, named v.p. in chg. of prime time TV for ABC Entertainment. In 1974 joined Paramount Pictures as bd. chmn. and chief exec. officer. 1983, named pres. of Gulf & Western Entertainment and Communications Group, while retaining Paramount titles. Resigned from Paramount in 1984 to join 20th Century-Fox as bd. chmn. and chief. exec. officer. Named chmn. & CEO of Fox, Inc. (comprising 20th Fox Film Corp., Fox TV Stations & Fox Bdcstg. Co.), Oct., 1985. Named to bd., News Corp. Ltd., June, 1987. Resigned from Fox in Feb., 1992. Named CEO of QVC Network Inc. TV shopping concern. Resigned QVC in 1995. CEO and bd. chair, Silver King Communications, Inc, Aug. 1995. Bd. chairman, Home Shopping Network, Nov. 1995.

DILLER, PHYLLIS
Comedienne, Actress. b. Lima, OH, July 17, 1917. r.n. Phyllis Ada Driver. e. Sherwood Music Sch., 1935-37; Bluffton Coll., OH, 1938-39. Started as publicist at San Francisco radio sta-

tion before becoming nightclub comic at the age of 37.
Recordings: Phyllis Diller Laughs, Are You Ready for Phyllis
Diller?, Great Moments of Comedy, Born to Sing. Performed
with many U.S. symphonies, 1971-90.
AUTHOR: Phyllis Diller's Housekeeping Hints, Phyllis Diller's
Marriage Manual, Phyllis Diller's The Complete Mother, The
Joys of Aging and How to Avoid Them.
THEATER: Hello Dolly! (B'way), Everybody Loves Opal,
Happy Birthday, The Dark at the Top of the Stairs, Subject to
Change, The Wizard of Oz, Nunsense, Cinderella.
PICTURES: Splendor in the Grass (debut, 1961), Boy Did I
Get a Wrong Number!, The Fat Spy, Mad Monster Party
(voice), Eight on the Lam, Did You Hear the One About the
Traveling Saleslady?, The Private Navy of Sgt. O'Farrell, The
Adding Machine, The Sunshine Boys (cameo), A Pleasure
Doing Business, Pink Motel, Pucker Up and Bark Like a Dog,
Dr. Hackenstein, Friend to Friend, The Nutcracker Prince
(voice), The Boneyard, Wisecracks, Happily Ever After (voice),
The Perfect Man, The Silence of the Hams.
TELEVISION: Series: Showstreet, The Pruitts of Southampton,
The Beautiful Phyllis Diller Show. Specials: The Phyllis Diller
Special, An Evening With Phyllis Diller, Phyllis Diller's 102nd
Birthday Party. Guest: Laugh In, Love American Style, The
Muppet Show, The Love Boat, CHiPs, etc.

DILLMAN, BRADFORD
Actor. b. San Francisco, CA, April 14, 1930. m. actress-model
Suzy Parker. e. Yale U., 1951. Studied at Actors Studio.
Author: Inside the New York Giants.
THEATER: The Scarecrow (1953), Third Person, Long Day's
Journey into Night (premiere; Theatre World Award), The Fun
Couple.
PICTURES: A Certain Smile (debut, 1958), In Love and War,
Compulsion, Crack in the Mirror, Circle of Deception,
Sanctuary, Francis of Assisi, A Rage to Live, The Plainsman,
Sergeant Ryker, Helicopter Spies, Jigsaw, The Bridge at
Remagen, Suppose They Gave a War and Nobody Came,
Brother John, The Mephisto Waltz, Escape from the Planet of
the Apes, The Resurrection of Zachary Wheeler, The Iceman
Cometh, The Way We Were, Chosen Survivors, 99 and
44/100% Dead, Gold, Bug, Mastermind, The Enforcer, The
Lincoln Conspiracy, Amsterdam Kill, The Swarm, Piranha,
Love and Bullets, Guyana: Cult of the Damned, Sudden
Impact, Treasure of the Amazon, Man Outside, Lords of the
Deep, Heroes Stand Alone.
TELEVISION: Series: Court-Martial, King's Crossing, Dynasty.
Movies: Fear No Evil, Black Water Gold, Longstreet, Five
Desperate Women, Revenge, Eyes of Charles Sand, The
Delphi Bureau, Moon of the Wolf, Deliver Us From Evil,
Murder or Mercy, Disappearance of Flight 412, Adventures of
the Queen, Force Five, Widow, Street Killing, Kingston: The
Power Play, The Hostage Heart, Jennifer: A Woman's Story,
Before and After, The Memory of Eva Ryker, Tourist, The
Legend of Walks Far Woman, Covenant, Heart of Justice.

DILLON, KEVIN
Actor. b. Mamaroneck, NY, Aug. 19, 1965. Younger brother of
actor Matt Dillon. Stage work includes Dark at the Top of the
Stairs, The Indian Wants the Bronx.
PICTURES: No Big Deal, Heaven Help Us, Platoon, Remote
Control, The Rescue, The Blob, War Party, Immediate Family,
The Doors, A Midnight Clear, No Escape.
TELEVISION: Movie: When He's Not a Stranger. Special: Dear
America: Letters Home from Vietnam (reader). Guest: Tales
From the Crypt.

DILLON, MATT
Actor. b. New Rochelle, NY, Feb. 18, 1964. Discovered at age
14 in junior high school by casting dir. who cast him in Over
the Edge. Brother is actor Kevin Dillon.
THEATER: NY: The Boys of Winter (B'way debut, 1985).
PICTURES: Over the Edge (debut, 1979), Little Darlings, My
Bodyguard, Liar's Moon, Tex, The Outsiders, Rumble Fish,
The Flamingo Kid, Target, Rebel, Native Son, The Big Town,
Kansas, Bloodhounds of Broadway, Drugstore Cowboy, A Kiss
Before Dying, Singles, Mr. Wonderful, The Saint of Fort
Washington, Golden Gate, To Die For, Frankie Starlight,
Beautiful Girls, Grace of My Heart, Albino Alligator.
TELEVISION: Movie: Women & Men 2: In Love There Are No
Rules (Return to Kansas City). Specials: The Great American
Fourth of July and Other Disasters, Dear America: Letters
Home From Vietnam (reader).

DILLON, MELINDA
Actress. b. Hope, AR, Oct. 13, 1939. e. Chicago Sch. of
Drama, Art Inst., Goodman Theatre. Launched career on
Broadway in original prod. of Who's Afraid of Virginia Woolf?
(Theatre World Award, Tony Award nom., Drama Critics
Award).
PICTURES: The April Fools (debut, 1969), Bound for Glory
(People's Choice Award), Slap Shot, Close Encounters of the
Third Kind (Acad. Award nom.), F.I.S.T., Absence of Malice
(Acad. Award nom.), A Christmas Story, Songwriter, Harry

and the Hendersons, Staying Together, Spontaneous
Combustion, Capt. America, The Prince of Tides, Sioux City,
To Fong Woo–Thanks for Everything Julie Newmar, How to
Make an American Quilt, Dorothy Day, The Effects of Magic.
TELEVISION: Series: Paul Sills Story Theatre. Guest: Twilight
Zone, The Defenders, Bonanza, East Side West Side, The
Paul Sand Show, The Jeffersons, Good Morning America, The
Today Show, Dick Cavett Show, Dinah Shore Show, Picket
Fences, The Client. Mini-Series: Space. Movies: Critical List,
Transplant, Marriage is Alive and Well, The Shadow Box,
Fallen Angel, Hellinger's Law, Right of Way, Shattered Spirits,
Shattered Innocence, Nightbreaker, Judgment Day: The John
List Story, Slow Bleed, State of Emergency, Confessions: Two
Faces of Evil, Naomi & Wynonna: Love Can Build a Bridge.

Di PIETRA, ROSEMARY
Executive. Joined Paramount Pictures in 1976, rising through
ranks to become director-corporate administration. 1985, promoted to exec. dir.-corporate administration.

DiNOVI, DENISE
Producer. b. Canada. Started as journalist, reporter, film crit-
ic in Toronto before entering film industry as unit publicist.
1980, joined Montreal's Film Plan production co. as co-prod.,
assoc. prod. and exec. in charge of prod. working on such
movies as Visiting Hours, Going Berserk, Videodrome.
Became exec. v.p. of prod. at New World, then head of Tim
Burton Prods., 1989-92.
PICTURES: Heathers, Edward Scissorhands, Meet the
Applegates, Batman Returns, The Nightmare Before
Christmas, Cabin Boy, Ed Wood, James and the Giant Peach.

DISHY, BOB
Actor. b. Brooklyn, NY. e. Syracuse U.
THEATER: Damn Yankees, From A to Z, Second City, Flora
the Red Menace, By Jupiter, Something Different, The
Goodbye People, The Good Doctor, The Unknown Soldier at
His Wife, The Creation of the World and Other Business, An
American Millionaire, Sly Fox, Murder at Howard Johnson's,
Grown Ups, Cafe Crown.
PICTURES: The Tiger Makes Out, Lovers and Other
Strangers, The Big Bus, I Wonder Who's Killing Her Now?,
The Last Married Couple in America, First Family, Author!
Author!, Brighton Beach Memoirs, Critical Condition, Stay
Tuned, Used People, My Boyfriend's Back, Don Juan
DeMarco.
TELEVISION: Series: That Was the Week That Was. Specials:
Story Theatre (dir.), The Cafeteria. Guest: The Comedy Zone.
Movies: It Couldn't Happen to a Nicer Guy, Thicker Than
Blood: The Larry McLinden Story.

DISNEY, ROY E.
Producer, Director. Writer, Cameraman, Film editor. b. Los
Angeles, CA, Jan. 10, 1930. e. Pomona Coll., CA. 1951 start-
ed as page, NBC-TV. Asst. film editor Dragnet TV series.
1952-78, Walt Disney Prods., Burbank, Calif., various capaci-
ties; vice chmn. of the board, The Walt Disney Co.; bd. chmn.,
Shamrock Holdings, Inc., bd. dir., Walt Disney Co.
PICTURES: Perri, Mysteries of the Deep, Pacific High.
TELEVISION: Walt Disney's Wonderful World of Color, The
Hound That Thought He Was A Raccoon, Sancho, The
Homing Steer, The Silver Fox and Sam Davenport, Wonders
of the Water World, Legend of Two Gypsy Dogs, Adventure in
Wildwood Heart, The Postponed Wedding, Zorro series, An
Otter in the Family, My Family is a Menagerie, Legend of El
Blanco, Pancho, The Fastest Paw in the West, The Owl That
Didn't Give A Hoot, Varda the Peregrine Falcon, Cristobalito,
The Calypso Colt, Three Without Fear, Hamade and the
Pirates, Chango, Guardian of the Mayan Treasure, Nosey the
Sweetest Skunk in the World, Mustang!, Call It Courage,
Ringo the Refugee Raccoon, Shokee the Everglades Panther,
Deacon the High-Noon Dog, Wise One, Whale's Tooth, Track
of African Bongo, Dorsey the Mail-Carrying Dog.

DIXON, BARBARA
Executive. b. Pasadena CA. e. USC, grad. degree from Johns
Hopkins U. Served as staff member of Senate Judiciary
Committee and was dir. of legislation for Sen. Birch Bayh,
1974-79. Left to become dir. of Office of Government & Public
Affairs of Natl. Transportation Safety Board. Named v.p.,
Fratelli Group, p.r. firm in Washington; took leave of absence
in 1984 to serve as deputy press secty. to Democratic V.P.
candidate, Geraldine Ferraro. In 1985 joined Motion Picture
Assn. of America as v.p. for public affairs.

DIXON, DONNA
Actress. b. Alexandria, VA, July 20, 1957. m. actor-writer Dan
Aykroyd. e. Studied anthropology and medicine, Mary
Washington U. Left to become a model, both on magazine
covers and in TV commercials (Vitalis, Max Factor, Gillette).
PICTURES: Dr. Detroit, Twilight Zone--The Movie, Spies Like
Us, The Couch Trip, It Had To Be You, Speed Zone, Lucky Stiff,
Wayne's World.

TELEVISION: *Series*: Bosom Buddies, Berrenger's. *Movies*: Mickey Spillane's Margin for Murder, No Man's Land, Beverly Hills Madam. *Specials*: Women Who Rate a "10," The Shape of Things, The Rodney Dangerfield Show: I Can't Take it No More.

DIXON, WHEELER WINSTON
Educator, Writer, Filmmaker. b. New Brunswick, NJ, March 12, 1950. e. Rutgers U. In 1960s asst. writer for Time/Life publications; also writer for Interview magazine. 1976, directed TV commercials in NY. One season with TVTV, Los Angeles, as post-prod. suprv. 1978, formed Deliniator Films, Inc., serving as exec. prod./dir. Since 1988 has directed film program at Univ. of Nebraska, where holds rank of tenured full prof. and chair, Film Studies Prog.; received Rockefeller Foundation grant. Author: The `B' Directors, 1985; The Cinematic Vision of F. Scott Fitzgerald, 1986; PRC: A History of Producer's Releasing Corp., 1986; books on Freddie Francis, Terence Fisher, Reginald Le Borg, 1992-93. Prod., dir. with Gwendolyn Audrey-Foster: Women Who Made the Movies (video). Books: The Early Film Criticism of Francois Truffaut, Re-Viewing British Cinema, 1900-92, It Looks at You, 1994. Prod/Dir: What Can I Do?, Squatters. 1992, guest programmer at the British Film Inst./Natl. Film Theatre. 1993, Distinguished Teaching Award. Invited lecturer at Yale, 1995.

DMYTRYK, EDWARD
Director. b. Grand Forks, B.C., Canada, Sept. 4, 1908. Entered employ Paramount 1923, working as messenger after school. Film editor 1930-39. One of the ``Hollywood Ten'' who was held in contempt by the House UnAmerican Activities Comm. 1947. The only one to recant. Autobiography: It's a Hell of a Life But Not a Bad Living (1979).
PICTURES: The Hawk (debut, 1935), Television Spy, Emergency Squad, Golden Gloves, Mystery Sea Raider, Her First Romance, The Devil Commands, Under Age, Sweetheart of the Campus, The Blonde From Singapore, Confessions of Boston Blackie, Secrets of the Lone Wolf, Counter-Espionage, Seven Miles From Alcatraz, Hilter's Children, The Falcon Strikes Back, Behind the Rising Sun, Captive Wild Woman Tender Comrade, Murder My Sweet, Back to Bataan, Cornered, Till the End of Time, Crossfire (Acad. Award nom.), So Well Remembered, Obsession (The Hidden Room), Give Us This Day, Mutiny, The Sniper, Eight Iron Men, The Juggler, The Caine Mutiny, Broken Lance, The End of the Affair, The Left Hand of God, Soldier of Fortune, The Mountain (also prod.), Raintree County, The Young Lions, Warlock (also prod.), The Blue Angel, The Reluctant Saint (It.), Walk on the Wild Side, The Carpetbaggers, Where Love Has Gone, Mirage, Alvarez Kelly, Shalako, Anzio, Bluebeard, The Human Factor, He Is My Brother.

DOBSON, KEVIN
Actor. b. New York, NY, Mar. 18, 1943.
PICTURES: Love Story, Bananas, Klute, The Anderson Tapes, The French Connection, Carnal Knowledge, Midway, All Night Long.
TELEVISION: *Series*: Kojak, Shannon, Knots Landing (also dir. 9 episodes). *Movies*: The Immigrants, Transplant, Orphan Train, Hardhat and Legs, Reunion, Mark I Love You, Mickey Splillane's Margin for Murder, Money Power Murder (also prod.), Casey's Gift: For Love of a Child, Sweet Revenge, Fatal Frienship, Dirty Work, House of Secrets and Lies, The Conviction of Kitty Dodds, If Someone Had Known. *Guest*: The Nurses, The Doctors, Greatest Heroes of the Bible.

DOCTOROW, ERIC
Executive. Pres., Home Video Division of Viacom, Inc. Worldwide Video.

DOERFLER, RONALD J.
Executive. e. Fairleigh Dickinson Univ. Became CPA in 1967. 1972, received M.B.A. from Fairleigh Dickinson. Joined Capital Cities 1969 as asst. controller. Became treas. in 1977; v.p. & CFO, 1980. 1983, named sr. v.p.,.then sr. v.p. & CFO.

DOHERTY, SHANNEN
Actress. b. Memphis, TN, April 12, 1971. On stage in The Mound Builders.
PICTURES: Night Shift, The Secret of NIMH (voice), Girls Just Want to Have Fun, Heathers, Freeze Frame, Blindfold, Mall Rats.
TELEVISION: *Series*: Little House on the Prairie, Our House, Beverly Hills 90210. *Movies*: The Other Lover, Obsessed, Jailbreakers, A Burning Passion: The Margaret Mitchell Story. *Mini-Series*: Robert Kennedy and His Times. *Pilot*: His and Hers. *Guest*: 21 Jump Street.

DOLGEN, JONATHAN L.
Executive. b. New York, NY, Apr. 27, 1945. e. Cornell U., NYU Sch. of Law. Began career with Wall Street law firm, Fried, Frank, Harris, Shriver & Jacobson. In 1976 joined Columbia Pictures Industries as asst. gen. counsel and deputy gen.

counsel. 1979, named sr. v.p. in chg. of worldwide business affairs; 1980, named exec. v.p. Joined Columbia m.p. div., 1981; named pres. of Columbia Pay-Cable & Home Entertainment Group. Also pres. Columbia Pictures domestic operations, overseeing Music Group. 1985, joined 20th-Fox in newly created position of sr. exec. v.p. for telecommunications. Became pres. of Sony Motion Picture Group, 1991. Appointed chmn. Viacom Entertainment Group, 1994.

DONAHUE, ELINOR
Actress. b. Tacoma, WA, Apr. 19, 1937.
PICTURES: Mr. Big, Tenth Avenue Angel, Unfinished Dance, Three Daring Daughters, Love is Better Than Ever, Girls Town, Pretty Woman, Freddy's Dead: The Final Nightmare.
TELEVISION: *Series*: Father Knows Best, The Andy Griffith Show, Many Happy Returns, The Odd Couple, Mulligan's Stew, Please Stand By, Days of Our Lives,The New Adventures of Beans Baxter, Get a Life. *Pilot*: The Grady Nutt Show. *Guest*: One Day at a Time, Sweepstakes$, The Golden Girls. *Movies*: In Name Only, Gidget Gets Married, Mulligan's Stew (pilot), Doctors' Private Lives, Condominium, High School U.S.A. *Special*: Father Knows Best Reunion.

DONAHUE, PHIL
Television Host. b. Cleveland, OH, Dec. 21, 1935. e. Notre Dame, BBA. m. actress Marlo Thomas. Worked as check sorter, Albuquerque Natl. Bank, 1957, then as announcer at KYW-TV & AM, Cleveland; then at. WABJ radio, Adrian, MI; morning newscaster WHIO-TV. Interviews with Jimmy Hoffa and Billy Sol Estes picked up nationally by CBS. Host of Conversation Piece, phone-in talk show. Debuted The Phil Donahue Show, daytime talk show in Dayton, Ohio, 1967. Syndicated 2 years later. Moved to Chicago, 1974. Host, Donahue, now in 165 outlets in U.S. In 1979 a mini-version of show became 3-times-a-week segment on NBC's Today Show. Winner of several Emmys. Books: Donahue: My Own Story (1980), The Human Animal (1985).

DONAHUE, TROY
Actor. r.n. Merle Johnson, Jr. b. New York, NY, Jan. 27, 1937. e. Bayport H.S., N.Y. Military Acad. Columbia U., Journalism. Directed, wrote, acted in school plays. Summer stock, Bucks County Playhouse, Sayville Playhouse; contract, Warner Brothers, 1959.
PICTURES: Man Afraid (debut, 1957), The Tarnished Angels, This Happy Feeling, The Voice in the Mirror, Live Fast Die Young, Monster on the Campus, Summer Love, Wild Heritage, The Perfect Furlough, Imitation of Life, A Summer Place, The Crowded Sky, Parrish, Susan Slade, Rome Adventure, Palm Springs Weekend, A Distant Trumpet, My Blood Runs Cold, Blast-Off! (Those Fantastic Flying Fools), Come Spy With Me, Sweet Savior, Cockfighter, Seizure, The Godfather Part II, Tin Man, Grandview U.S.A., Low Blow, Cyclone, Deadly Prey, American Revenge, Dr. Alien (I Was a Teenage Sex Mutant), Sexpot, Hard Rock Nightmare, Bad Blood, John Travis, Solar Survivor, The Chilling, The Housewarming, Deadly Spy Games, Assault of the Party Nerds, Deadly Diamonds, Deadly Embrace, Cry-Baby, Double Trouble.
TELEVISION: *Series*: Hawaiian Eye, Surfside 6. *Guest*: Matt Houston. *Movies*: Split Second to an Epitaph, The Loneliest Profession, Malibu.

DONALDSON, ROGER
Director. b. Ballarat, Australia, Nov. 15, 1945. Emigrated to New Zealand at 19. Established still photography business; then began making documentaries. Directed Winners and Losers, a series of short dramas for NZ-TV.
PICTURES: Sleeping Dogs (also prod.), Smash Palace (also s.p. prod.), The Bounty, Marie, No Way Out, Cocktail, Cadillac Man (also prod.), White Sands, The Getaway, Species.

DONEN, STANLEY
Director, Producer, Choreographer. b. Columbia, SC, April 13, 1924. e. USC. Former dancer, B'way debut 1940 in chorus of Pal Joey starring Gene Kelly. Assisted Kelly as choreog. on stage prod. of Best Foot Forward; hired by MGM to repeat duties in film version. Choreographer or co-choreographer on such films as Cover Girl, Holiday in Mexico, This Time for Keeps, A Date With Judy, Take Me Out to the Ballgame (also co-story credit).
PICTURES: *Director*: On the Town (debut, 1949; co-dir. with Gene Kelly), Royal Wedding, Singin' in the Rain, co-choreog. with Gene Kelly), Fearless Fagan, Love Is Better Than Ever, Give a Girl a Break (also co-choreog.), Seven Brides for Seven Brothers, Deep in My Heart (also co-choreog.), It's Always Fair Weather (co-dir., co-choreog. with Gene Kelly), Funny Face, The Pajama Game (co-dir., co-prod. with George Abbott), Kiss Them for Me. *Director-Producer*: Indiscreet, Damn Yankees (co-dir., co-prod. with George Abbott), Once More With Feeling, Surprise Package, The Grass Is Greener, Charade, Arabesque, Two for the Road, Bedazzled, Staircase, The Little Prince, Lucky Lady (dir. only), Movie Movie, Saturn 3, Blame It on Rio.

DONIGER, WALTER
Writer, Director, Producer. b. New York NY. e. Valley Forge Military Academy, Duke U., Harvard U. Graduate Business Sch. Entered m.p. business as writer later writer-prod-dir. Wrote documentaries in Army Air Forces M.P. Unit in W.W.II. WGA award nominee and other awards.
PICTURES: Rope of Sand, Desperate Search, Cease Fire, Safe At Home (dir.), House of Women (dir.), Duffy of San Quentin (dir.), Along the Great Divide, Tokyo Joe, Alaska Seas, Steel Cage (dir.), Steel Jungle (dir.), Hold Back the Night, Guns of Fort Petticoat, Unwed Mother (dir.), Stone Cold (exec. prod.).
TELEVISION: *Series*: Delvecchio, Mad Bull, Switch, Moving On, Baa Baa Blacksheep, McCloud, The Man and the City, Sarge, Owen Marshall, Peyton Place, Mr. Novak, The Greatest Show on Earth, Travels of Jaimie McPheeters, Outlaws, Hong Kong, Checkmate, Bat Masterson, The Web, Bold Venture, Tombstone Territory, Maverick, Rough Riders, Lockup, Dick Powell, The Survivors, Bracken's World, Bold Ones, Kung Fu, Barnaby Jones, Marcus Welby, Lucas Tanner, etc.

DONNELLY, DONAL
Actor. b. Bradford, Eng. July 6, 1931. Studied for theatre at the Dublin Gate Theatre.
THEATER: *NY Theatre*: Philadelphia Here I Come (B'way debut, 1966), Joe Egg, Sleuth (NY and U.S. tour), The Elephant Man, The Faith-Healer, The Chalk Garden, My Astonishing Self, Big Maggie, Execution of Justice, Sherlock's Last Case, Ghetto, Dancing at Lughnasa, Translations.
PICTURES: Rising of the Moon (1957), Gideon's Day, Shake Hands With the Devil, Young Cassidy, The Knack, Up Jumped a Swagman, The Mind of Mr. Soames, Waterloo, The Dead, The Godfather Part III, Squanto: A Warrior's Tale, Korea.
TELEVISION: Juno and the Paycock (BBC, 1958), Home Is the Hero, The Venetian Twins, The Plough and the Stars, Playboy of the Western World, Sergeant Musgrave's Dance, Yes-Honestly (series).

DONNELLY, RALPH E.
Executive. b. Lynbrook, NY, Jan. 20, 1932. e. Bellmore, NY public school; W. C. Mepham H.S., 1949. Worked for Variety (publication) as writer, 1950; Long Island Press as daily columnist, 1951; joined Associated Independent Theatres, 1953, as gen. mgr.; later film buyer; in 1973 left to become independent buyer and booker for Creative Films; film buyer and v.p., RKO/Stanley Warner Theatres, 1976-79; pres. & gen. mgr. for Cinema 5 Ltd. circuit, N.Y., 1980-87; 1987-93, exec. v.p. City Cinemas, N.Y. Now chmn. of Cinema Connection.

DONNER, CLIVE
Director. b. London, Eng., Jan 21, 1926. Ent. m.p. ind. 1942. Asst. film ed. Denham Studios, 1942. Dir. London stage: The Formation Dancers, The Front Room Boys, Kennedy's Children (also NY). *Film editor*: A Christmas Carol (Scrooge), The Card (The Promoter), Genevieve, Man With a Million (The Million Pound Note), The Purple Plain, I Am a Camera.
PICTURES: The Secret Place (debut, 1957), Heart of a Child, Marriage of Convenience, The Sinister Man, Some People, The Caretaker (The Guest), Nothing But the Best, What's New Pussycat?, Luv, Here We Go Round the Mulberry Bush (also prod.), Alfred the Great, Old Dracula (Vampira), The Nude Bomb, Charlie Chan and the Curse of the Dragon Queen, Stealing Heaven.
TELEVISION: Danger Man, Sir Francis Drake, Mighty and Mystical, British Institutions, Tempo, Spectre, The Thief of Baghdad, Oliver Twist, Rogue Male, The Scarlet Pimpernel, Arthur the King, To Catch a King, Three Hostages, She Fell Among Thieves, A Christmas Carol, Dead Man's Folly, Babes in Toyland, Not a Penny More Not a Penny Less, Coup de Foudre (Love at First Sight), Terror Strikes the Class Reunion (For Better or Worse), Charlemagne.

DONNER, RICHARD
Director. b. New York, NY, 1939. Began career as actor off-B'way. Worked with director Martin Ritt on TV production of Maugham's Of Human Bondage. Moved to California 1958, directing commercials, industrial films and documentaries. First TV drama: Wanted: Dead or Alive.
PICTURES: X-15 (debut, 1961), Salt and Pepper, Twinky (Lola), The Omen, Superman, Inside Moves, The Final Conflict (exec. prod. only), The Toy (also exec. prod.), Ladyhawke (also prod.), The Goonies (also prod.), Lethal Weapon (also prod.), The Lost Boys (exec. prod. only), Scrooged (also prod.), Lethal Weapon 2 (also prod.), Delirious (exec. prod. only), Radio Flyer, Lethal Weapon 3 (also prod.), Free Willy (co-exec. prod. only), Maverick (also prod.), Tales From the Crypt Presents Demon Knight (co-exec. prod. only), Assassins (also prod.).
TELEVISION: *Series episodes*: Have Gun Will Travel, Perry Mason, Cannon, Get Smart, The Fugitive, Kojak, Bronk, Gilligan's Island, Man From U.N.C.L.E., Wild Wild West, Tales From the Crypt, Two Fisted Tales, Twilight Zone, The Banana Splits, Combat. *Movies*: Lucas Tanner (pilot), Sarah T.: Portrait

of a Teen-Age Alcoholic, Senior Year, A Shadow in the Streets, Tales From the Crypt (exec. prod.; also dir. episode: Dig That Cat... He's Real Gone).

D'ONOFRIO, VINCENT PHILLIP
Actor. b. Brooklyn, NY, 1960. Studied acting with the American Stanislavsky Theatre in NY, appearing in Of Mice and Men, The Petrified Forest, Sexual Perversity in Chicago, and The Indian Wants the Bronx.
THEATER: *B'way*: Open Admissions.
PICTURES: The First Turn On! (debut, 1984), Full Metal Jacket, Adventures in Babysitting, Mystic Pizza, Signs of Life, The Blood of Heroes, Crooked Hearts, Dying Young, Fires Within, Naked Tango, JFK, The Player, Desire, Household Saints, Mr. Wonderful, Being Human, Ed Wood, Imaginary Crimes, Stuart Saves His Family, Strange Days, Feeling Minnesota.

DONOHOE, AMANDA
Actress. b. England, 1962. e. Francis Holland Sch. for Girls, Central Sch. of Speech & Drama. Member of Royal Exchange Theatre in Manchester. B'way dbut 1995 in Uncle Vanya.
PICTURES: Foreign Body (debut, 1986), Castaway, The Lair of the White Worm, The Rainbow, Tank Malling, Diamond Skulls (Dark Obsession), Paper Mask, The Madness of King George.
TELEVISION: *Series*: L.A. Law (Golden Globe Award). *Movies*: Married to Murder, Shame, It's Nothing Personal (also co-exec. prod.), The Substitute, Shame II: The Secret (also co-exec. prod.). *Special*: Game Set and Match (Mystery!).

DONOVAN, ARLENE
Producer. b. Kentucky. e. Stratford Coll., VA. Worked in publishing before entering industry as asst. to late dir. Robert Rosen on Cocoa Beach, uncompleted at his death. Worked as story editor, Columbia Pictures. 1969-82, literary head of m.p. dept. for ICM; involved in book publishing as well as stage and screen projects.
PICTURES: Still of the Night, Places in the Heart, Nadine, The House on Carroll Street (co-exec. prod.), Billy Bathgate.

DONOVAN, HENRY B.
Executive, Producer. b. Boston, MA. Entered m.p. ind. for RKO Pathe Studios, property master, special effects dir., unit mgr., asst. dir., prod. mgr.; worked on over 310 pictures; Harry Sherman, Hopalong Cassidy features (for Paramount). 10 yrs., U.S. Army Signal Corps, as head of dept. of California studios prod. training m.p.; pres.: Telemount Pictures, Inc. Prod., dir., writer Cowboy G Men (TV series). Wrote: Corkscrewed (novel), 7 Zane Grey westerns for Paramount.
PICTURES: Hopalong Cassidy Features, Gone with the Wind, Becky Sharp, Our Flag (dir.), Magic Lady (13 one-reel features), others. Cowboy G Men (prod., writer; 39 films).
TELEVISION: programming, financing, distribution. Global Scope; International TV; Dist., Financing, programming; sls. consultant, Intl. TV & motion pictures. Cable TV & distribution & program development, collector of movie memorabilia; DBS TV programming & financing: production software. Worldwide TV consultant. Created Silicon Valley for satellite B.D. Frontier Lawyer: Historical United States of America.

DONOVAN, TATE
Actor. b. New York, NY, 1964. Raised in New Jersey. Studied acting at USC. Worked as still photographer for two Mutual of Omaha documentaries.
THEATER: Ruffian on the Stair, The American Plan, The Rhythm of Torn Stars, Bent. B'way: Picnic.
PICTURES: SpaceCamp, Clean and Sober, Dead Bang, Memphis Belle, Love Potion No. 9, Ethan Frome, Equinox, Holy Matrimony.
TELEVISION: *Series*: Partners. *Movies*: Not My Kid, Into Thin Air, A Case of Deadly Force, Nutcracker: Money Madness Murder. *HBO Special*: Vietnam War Stories.

DOOHAN, JAMES
Actor. b. Vancouver, B.C., Canada, Mar. 3, 1920. WWII capt. in Royal Canadian Artillery. 1946 won scholarship to Neighborhood Playhouse in NY and later taught there. 1953, returned to Canada to live in Toronto, becoming engaged in acting career on radio, TV and in film. Then to Hollywood and chief fame as Chief Engineer Scott in TV series, Star Trek.
PICTURES: The Wheeler Dealers, The Satan Bug, Bus Riley's Back in Town, Pretty Maids All in a Row, Star Trek—The Motion Picture, Star Trek II: The Wrath of Khan, Star Trek III: The Search for Spock, Star Trek IV: The Voyage Home, Star Trek V: The Final Frontier, Star Trek VI: The Undiscovered Country, Double Trouble, National Lampoon's Loaded Weapon 1, Star Trek: Generations.
TELEVISION: *Series*: Star Trek. *Guest*: Hazel, Bonanza, The Virginia, Gunsmoke, Peyton Place, The Fugitive, Marcus Welby MD, Ben Casey, Bewitched, Fantasy Island, etc. Movie: Scalplock.

DOOLEY, PAUL
Actor. b. Parkersburg, WV, Feb. 22, 1928. Began career on
NY stage in Threepenny Opera. Later member of Second City.
B'way credits include The Odd Couple, Adaptation/Next, The
White House Murder Case, Hold Me, etc. Co-creator and
writer for The Electric Company on PBS. Owns co. called All
Over Creation.
PICTURES: What's So Bad About Feeling Good? (debut,
1968), The Out-of-Towners, Death Wish, The Gravy Train,
Slap Shot, A Wedding, A Perfect Couple, Breaking Away, Rich
Kids, Popeye, Health (also co-s.p.), Paternity, Endangered
Species, Kiss Me Goodbye, Strange Brew, Going Berserk,
Sixteen Candles, Big Trouble, O.C. and Stiggs, Monster in the
Closet, Last Rites, Flashback, Shakes the Clown, The Player,
My Boyfriend's Back, A Dangerous Woman, The Underneath,
God's Lonely Man.
TELEVISION: Specials: Faerie Tale Theater, The Firm,
Traveler's Rest, Tales of the City. Movies: The Murder of Mary
Phagan, Lip Service, Guts and Glory: The Rise and Fall of
Oliver North, When He's Not a Stranger, The Court Martial of
Jackie Robinson, Guess Who's Coming for Christmas?, White
Hot: The Mysterious Murder of Thelma Todd, Cooperstown,
Mother of the Bride, State of Emergency, The Computer Wore
Tennis Shoes. Series: The Dom DeLuise Show, Coming of
Age. Guest: Dream On, ALF, The Golden Girls, thirtysome-
thing, Mad About You, Evening Shade, Coach, Wonder Years,
The Boys, L.A. Law, The Mommies, Star Trek: Deep Space
Nine, many others.

DORAN, LINDSAY
Executive. b. Los Angeles, CA. e. U. of California at Santa
Cruz. Moved to London where was contributing author to The
Oxford Companion to Film and the World Encyclopedia of
Film. Returned to U.S. to write and produce documentaries
and children's programs for Pennsylvania public affairs station
WPSX-TV. Career in m.p. industry began in story dept. at
Embassy Pictures which she joined in 1979; 1982 promoted to
dir. of development; then v.p., creative affairs. 1985, joined
Paramount Pictures as v.p., production, for M.P. Group. 1987,
promoted to senior v.p., production. 1989, appointed pres.,
Mirage Productions.

DORFF, STEPHEN
Actor. b. July 29, 1973. Started acting at age 9.
PICTURES: The Gate (debut, 1987), The Power of One, An
Ambush of Ghosts, Judgment Night, Rescue Me, BackBeat,
S.F.W., Reckless, Innocent Lies, I Shot Andy Warhol.
TELEVISION: Series: What a Dummy. Movies: I Know My First
Name Is Steven, Always Remember I Love You, Do You Know
the Muffin Man?, A Son's Promise. Guest: Empty Nest,
Roseanne, The Outsiders, Married... With Children, Empty
Nest.

DORTORT, DAVID
Executive Producer. b. New York, NY, Oct. 23, 1916. e. City
Coll. of New York. Served U.S. Army, 1943-46. Novelist and
short story writer, 1943-49. Also TV writer. Now pres. of
Xanadu Prods., Aurora Enterprises, Inc., and Bonanza
Ventures, Inc. & Pres. TV branch, WGA, West, 1954-55; TV-
radio branch, 1955-57; v.p. PGA, 1967; pres. 1968. Chmn.,
Caucus for Producers, Writers and Directors, 1973-75. Pres.,
PGA, 1980-81; campaign dir., Permanent Charities Comm.,
1980-81; chmn., Interguild Council 1980-81. Received
WGA/West noms. for TV work on An Error in Chemistry
(Climax), and The Ox-Bow Incident (20th Century Fox Hour).
Author: novels include Burial of the Fruit, The Post of Honor.
PICTURES: The Lusty Men, Reprisal, The Big Land, Cry in
the Night, Clash by Night, Going Bananas (exec. prod.).
TELEVISION: Creator and exec. prod.: Bonanza, High
Chaparral, The Chisholms, Hunter's Moon, Bonanza: Legends
of the Ponderosa. Producer: The Restless Gun, The Cowboys.
Creator, story and exec. prod.: Bonanza: The Next Generation.

DOUGHERTY, MARION
Executive. e. Penn St. U. Gained fame as casting director.
Casting dir. on series Naked City, Route 66. Formed own co.
in 1965. Acted as co-executive producer on Smile, 1975. In
1977 named v.p. in chg. talent for Paramount Pictures. In 1979
joined Warner Bros. as sr. v.p. in chg. talent to work with production dept. and producers and directors.
CASTING: A Little Romance, Urban Cowboy, Honky Tonk
Freeway, Reds, Firefox, Honkytonk Man, The World According
to Garp, Sudden Impact, The Man With Two Brains, The Killing
Fields, Swing Shift, The Little Drummer Girl, Lethal Weapon
(also 2 & 3), Batman, Batman Returns, Forever Young, Falling
Down.

DOUGLAS, ILLEANA
Actress. Grandfather was actor Melvyn Douglas. Directed
short films The Perfect Woman (Aspen Film Fest. prize, 1994),
Boy Crazy—Girl Crazier.
THEATER: NY: Takes on Women, As Sure as You Live, Black
Eagles.

PICTURES: Hello Again, New York Stories (Life Lessons),
GoodFellas, Guilty By Suspicion, Cape Fear, Alive, Household
Saints, Grief, Quiz Show, Search and Destroy, To Die For,
Grace of My Heart.

DOUGLAS, KIRK
Actor, Producer, Director. r.n. Issur Danielovitch (changed to
Demsky). b. Amsterdam, NY, Dec. 9, 1916. m. Anne Buydens,
pres. of Bryna Prod. Co. Father of Michael, Joel, Peter, Eric. e.
St. Lawrence U, B.A, AADA. Stage debut in New York: Spring
Again. U.S. Navy during W.W.II; resumed stage work. Did
radio soap operas. Signed by Hal B. Wallis for film debut.
Autobiography: The Ragman's Son (1988). Novels: Dance
With the Devil, The Secret, Last Tango in Brooklyn. Recipient
of U.S. Presidential Medal of Freedom, 1981. Career achieve-
ment award, National Board of Review, 1989. Received AFI
Lifetime Achievement Award, 1991.
THEATER: Spring Again, Three Sisters, Kiss and Tell, Trio,
The Wind is Ninetry, Star in the Window, Man Bites Dog, One
Flew Over the Cuckoo's Nest, The Boys of Autumn.
PICTURES: The Strange Love of Martha Ivers (debut, 1946),
Out of the Past, I Walk Alone, Mourning Becomes Electra, The
Walls of Jericho, My Dear Secretary, Letter to Three Wives,
Champion, Young Man with a Horn, The Glass Menagerie,
Ace in the Hole (The Big Carnival), Along the Great Divide,
Detective Story, The Big Trees, The Big Sky, Bad and the
Beautiful, Story of Three Loves, The Juggler, Act of Love,
20,000 Leagues Under the Sea, Ulysses, Man Without a Star,
The Racers, The Indian Fighter (also prod.), Lust for Life, Top
Secret Affair, Gunfight at the OK Corral, Paths of Glory, The
Vikings (also prod.), Last Train from Gun Hill, The Devil's
Disciple, Strangers When We Meet, Spartacus (also prod.),
The Last Sunset, Town Without Pity, Lonely Are the Brave
(also prod.), Two Weeks in Another Town, The Hook, List of
Adrian Messenger (also prod.), For Love or Money, Seven
Days in May (also prod.), In Harm's Way, The Heroes of
Telemark, Cast a Giant Shadow, Is Paris Burning?, The Way
West, The War Wagon, A Lovely Way to Die, The Brotherhood
(also prod.), The Arrangement, There Was a Crooked Man, A
Gunfight, Summertree (prod. only), The Light at the Edge of
the World (also prod.), Catch Me a Spy, Scalawag (also dir.,
prod.), Master Touch, Once is Not Enough, Posse (also dir.,
prod.), The Chosen, The Fury, The Villain, Saturn III, Home
Movies, The Final Countdown, The Man from Snowy River,
Eddie Macon's Run, Tough Guys, Oscar, Welcome to Veraz,
Greedy.
TELEVISION: Movies: Mousey, The Money Changers, Draw!
(HBO), Victory at Entebbe, Remembrance of Love, Amos,
Queenie, Inherit the Wind, The Secret, Take Me Home Again.
Guest: The Lucy Show, Tales From the Crypt (Yellow).
Specials: Legend of Silent Night, Dr. Jekyll & Mr. Hyde.

DOUGLAS, MICHAEL
Actor, Producer. b. New Brunswick, NJ, Sept 25, 1944. p. Kirk
Douglas and Diana Dill. e. Black Fox Military Acad., Choate,
U. of California. Worked as asst. director on Lonely Are the
Brave, Heroes of Telemark, Cast a Giant Shadow; after TV
debut in The Experiment (CBS Playhouse), appeared off-
Broadway in City Scene, Pinkville (Theatre World Award).
Produced 1993 Off-B'way show The Best of Friends.
PICTURES: Hail Hero (debut, 1969), Adam at 6 A.M.,
Summertree, Napoleon and Samantha, One Flew Over the
Cuckoo's Nest (co-prod. only; Academy Award for Best
Picture, 1975), Coma, The China Syndrome (also prod.),
Running (also exec. prod.), It's My Turn, The Star Chamber,
Romancing the Stone (also prod.), Starman (exec. prod. only),
A Chorus Line, The Jewel of the Nile (also prod.), Fatal
Attraction, Wall Street (Academy Award; Natl. Board of Review
Award, 1987), Black Rain, The War of the Roses, Flatliners
(co-exec. prod. only), Shining Through, Radio Flyer (co-exec.
prod. only), Basic Instinct, Falling Down, Made in America (co-
exec. prod. only), Disclosure, The American President, The
Ghost and the Darkness.
TELEVISION: Series: Streets of San Francisco. Guest: The
FBI, Medical Center. Movies: Streets of San Francisco (pilot),
When Michael Calls.

DOUGLAS, MIKE
TV host. r.n. Michael Delaney Dowd, Jr. b. Chicago, IL, Aug.
11, 1925. Started career singing with bands in and around
Chicago. 1950-54 featured singer with Kay Kyser's band. In
1953 became host of WGN-TV's Hi Ladies in Chicago; also
featured on WMAQ-TV, NBC, Chicago, as singer and host.
Moved to Hollywood in late '50s, working as piano bar singer.
In 1961 hired as host for new show on station KYW-TV in
Cleveland, owned by Westinghouse Bdg. Co., featuring
celebrity guests. This became the Mike Douglas Show which
was later nationally syndicated and moved base of operations
to Philadelphia, then Los Angeles. Ran 21 years til Mid-1982.
Books: The Mike Douglas Cookbook (1969), Mike Douglas My
Story (1978), When the Going Gets Tough.
PICTURES: Gator, Nasty Habits, The Incredible Shrinking
Woman.

DOURIF, BRAD
Actor. b. Huntington, WV, Mar. 18, 1950. Studied with Stanford Meisner. Stage actor, three years with Circle Repertory Co., NY (When You Comin' Back Red Ryder?), before films and TV.
PICTURES: Split, One Flew Over the Cuckoo's Nest (Acad. Award nom., Golden Globe & BAFTA Awards, 1975), Group Portrait with Lady, Eyes of Laura Mars, Wise Blood, Heaven's Gate, Ragtime, Dune, Impure Thoughts, Istanbul, Blue Velvet, Fatal Beauty, Child's Play, Mississippi Burning, Medium Rare, The Exorcist: 1990, Spontaneous Combustion, Grim Prairie Tales, Sonny Boy, Graveyard Shift, Child's Play II, Hidden Agenda, Dead Certain, Jungle Fever, The Horseplayer, Body Parts, Child's Play 3, Common Bonds, Scream of Stone, Critters 4, London Kills Me, Diary of the Hurdy Gurdy Man, Murder Blues, Final Judgment, Amos & Andrew, Trauma, Color of Night, Murder in the First.
TELEVISION: *Movies*: Sgt. Matlovitch vs. the U.S. Air Force, Guyana Tragedy—The Story of Jim Jones, I Desire, Vengeance: The Story of Tony Cimo, Rage of Angels: The Story Continues, Desperado: The Outlaw Wars, Class of '61, Escape From Terror: The Teresa Stamper Story, Escape to Witch Mountain. *Mini-Series*: Studs Lonigan, Wild Palms. *Specials*: Mound Builders, The Gardener's Son. *Guest*: Miami Vice, The Hitchhiker, Spencer for Hire, Tales of the Unexpected, Moonlighting, The Equalizer, Murder She Wrote, Babylon 5, Voyager.

DOWN, LESLEY-ANNE
Actress. b. London, England, March 17, 1954. At age of 10 modeled for TV and film commercials, leading to roles in features. Film debut at 14 in The Smashing Bird I Used to Know (billed as Lesley Down).
THEATER: Great Expectations, Hamlet, etc.
PICTURES: The Smashing Bird I Used to Know (debut, 1969), All the Right Noises, Countess Dracula, Assault, Pope Joan, Scalawag, From Beyond the Grave, Brannigan, The Pink Panther Strikes Again, The Betsy, A Little Night Music, The Great Train Robbery, Hanover Street, Rough Cut, Sphinx, Nomads, Scenes from the Goldmine, Mardi Gras for the Devil, Death Wish V: The Face of Death, Munchie Stikes Back, The Unfaithful.
TELEVISION: *Series*: Upstairs, Downstairs, Dallas. *Movies*: Agatha Christie's Murder is Easy, Hunchback of Notre Dame, The One and Only Phyllis Dixey, Arch of Triumph, Indiscreet, Lady Killers, Night Walk. *Mini-Series*: North and South Books I & II & III, Last Days of Pompeii. *Specials*: Unity Mitford. Heartbreak House. Pilots: Shivers, 1775.

DOWNEY, ROBERT, JR.
Actor. b. New York, NY, April 4, 1965. Father is indep. filmmaker Robert Downey. Film debut at age 5 in his father's film Pound.
PICTURES: Pound (debut, 1970), Greaser's Palace, Jive, Up the Academy, Baby Its You, Firstborn, Tuff Turf, Weird Science, To Live and Die in L.A., Back to School, America, The Pick-Up Artist, Less Than Zero, Johnny B. Good, Rented Lips, 1969, True Believer, Chances Are, That's Adequate, Air America, Too Much Sun, Soapdish, Chaplin (Acad. Award nom., BAFTA Award), Hail Caesar, Heart and Souls, The Last Party, Short Cuts, Natural Born Killers, Only You, Restoration, Danger Zone, Home for the Holidays, Richard III.
TELEVISION: *Series*: Saturday Night Live. *Mini-Series*: Mussolini: The Untold Story. *Special*: Dear America (reader).

DOWNS, HUGH
Broadcaster. b. Akron, OH, Feb. 14, 1921. e. Bluffton Coll., 1938. Wayne U., 1941. Col. U., N.Y., 1955; Supervisor of Science Programming, NBC's Science Dept. one yr.; science consultant for Westinghouse Labs., Ford Foundation, etc.; chmn. of bd., Raylin Prods., Inc. Today, Chairman, U.S. Committee for UNICEF. Chm. of bd. of governors, National Space Society. Books: Thirty Dirty Lies About Old Age, Rings Around Tomorrow, School of Stars, Yours Truly Hugh Downs, On Camera: My Ten Thousand Hours on Television, Perspectives, Fifty to Forever.
TELEVISION: *Series*: Kukla Fran & Ollie (announcer), Home, Sid Caesar (announcer), The Jack Paar Show, Concentration, The Tonight Show (announcer, 1962), Today. *Host*: 20/20, Over-Easy (Emmy Award, 1981), Live From Lincoln Center.
RADIO: NBC's Monitor, ABC's Perspectives.

DOYLE, KEVIN
Executive. b. Sydney, Australia, June 21, 1933. e. N. Sydney Tech. HS., Aust. Jr. exec., asst. adv. & pub. div., 20th Century-Fox, Aust., 1947-59; adv. & pub. dir., Columbia Pictures Aust., 1960-66; international ad/pub. mgr.; Columbia Pictures Int'l, N.Y. 1966; intl. pub./promo. mgr.; 1980; 1987, Columbia Int'l. rep., Coca-Cola promotions/mktg. sub-committee; int'l pub./promo. mgr. Columbia Tri-Star Film Distributors Inc., 1988; int'l pub./promo. dir. Columbia/Tri-Star Film distrib. Inc. 1990. Retired 1992.

DOYLE-MURRAY, BRIAN
Actor, Writer. b. Chicago, IL., Oct. 31. Brother is comedian Bill Murray. Started as member of Chicago's Second City improv. troupe, before joining the Organic Theatre of Chicago and the Boston Shakespeare Co. Appeared Off-B'way in The National Lampoon Show and on radio on weekly National Lampoon Show.
PICTURES: Caddyshack (also co-s.p.), Modern Problems, National Lampoon's Vacation, Sixteen Candles, The Razor's Edge, Legal Eagles, Club Paradise (also co-s.p.), Scrooged, The Experts, How I Got Into College, Ghostbusters II, National Lampoon's Christmas Vacation, Nothing But Trouble, JFK, Wayne's World, Groundhog Day, Cabin Boy, Jury Duty, Multiplicity.
TELEVISION: *Series*: Saturday Night Live (also writer), Get a Life, Good Sports, Bakersfield P.D. *Movies*: Babe Ruth, My Brother's Keeper. *Special*: Texan.

DRAGOTI, STAN
Director. b. New York, NY, Oct. 4, 1932. e. Cooper Union and Sch. of Visual Arts. 1959 hired as sketch at ad agency, promoted to sr. art dir., later TV dept. and art dir. of Young & Rubicam. Studied acting HB Studios. Directed Clio Award-winning TV commercials (including I Love New York campaign).
PICTURES: Dirty Little Billy (debut, 1972; also co-prod., co-s.p.), Love at First Bite, Mr. Mom, The Man With One Red Shoe, She's Out of Control, Necessary Roughness.

DRAI, VICTOR
Producer. b. Casablanca, Morocco, July 25, 1947. e. Lycee de Port Lyautey, 1957-63. In real estate in Los Angeles 1976-82; clothing designer/mfg. in Paris, France, 1969-76. Began producing features in 1984, The Woman in Red.
PICTURES: The Man with One Red Shoe, The Bride, Weekend at Bernie's, Folks!, Weekend at Bernie's 2.

DRAZEN, LORI
Executive. Began career as asst. to dir. of adv. for Orion Pictures; creative dept. mgr., Kenyon & Eckhardt; gen. mgr., Seiniger Advertising; joined Warner Bros. 1985 as v.p., worldwide adv. & pub. services.

DREYFUSS, RICHARD
Actor. b. Brooklyn, NY, Oct. 29, 1947. e. Beverly Hills H.S.; San Fernando Valley State Coll. 1965-67. Prof. career began at Gallery Theatre (L.A.) in In Mama's House. Co-Exec. Prod. of film Quiz Show.
THEATER: Journey to the Day, Incident at Vichy, People Need People, Enemy Line, Whose Little Boy Are You, But Seriously, Major Barbara, The Time of Your Life, The Hands of Its Enemy (L.A.), The Normal Heart, Death and the Maiden, others.
PICTURES: The Graduate, Valley of the Dolls, The Young Runaways, Hello Down There, Dillinger, American Graffiti, The Second Coming of Suzanne, The Apprenticeship of Duddy Kravitz, Jaws, Inserts, Close Encounters of the Third Kind, The Goodbye Girl (Academy Award, 1977), The Big Fix (also co-prod.) The Competition, Whose Life Is It Anyway?, The Buddy System, Down and Out in Beverly Hills, Stand by Me, Tin Men, Stakeout, Nuts, Moon Over Parador, Let It Ride, Always, Postcards from the Edge, Once Around, Rosencrantz and Guildenstern Are Dead, What About Bob?, Lost in Yonkers, Another Stakeout, Silent Fall, The American President, Mr. Holland's Opus, James and the Giant Peach, Night Falls on Manhattan, Mad Dog Time.
TELEVISION: *Series*: Karen. *Host*: American Chronicles. *Guest*: Love on a Rooftop, Occasional Wife, The Big Valley, Room 222, Judd for the Defense, Mod Squad, The Bold Ones. *Special*: Funny You Don't Look 200 (host, co-prod., co-writer). *Movies*: Two for the Money, Victory at Entebbe, Prisoner of Honor (also prod.), The Last Word.

DROMGOOLE, PATRICK
Director, Producer, Executive. b. Iqueque, Chile, Aug. 30, 1930; e. Dulwich Coll., University Coll., Oxford. Joined BBC Radio as dir. 1954, later directing TV plays for BBC and ABC, incl. Armchair Theatre, Frontier, Dracula, Mystery Imagination. Joined HTV as West Country Programme Controller, 1968; dir. award-winning dramas; Thick as Thieves, Machinegunner. Developed Company's drama output and promoted policy of international pre-sales with such dramas as Jamaica Inn, Separate Tables, Catholics, Kidnapped, Robin of Sherwood, Arch of Triumph, Mr. Halpern and Mr. Johnson, Jenny's War, Codename Kyril, Wall of Tyranny, Strange Interlude, The Woman He Loved, Grand Larceny, Maigret. Made Fellow of RTS, 1978; chief exec. HTV Group since 1988. Fellow of RSA, 1989.
THEATER: *Director*: incl. first plays of Charles Wood, Joe Orton, David Halliwell, Colin Welland; Peter O'Toole in Man and Superman.
PICTURES: Two Weak South, Hidden Face, Dead Man's Chest, Anthony Purdy Esq., Point of Dissent, The Actors, King of the Wind (exec. prod.), Visage du Passe (dir.), Meutres en Douce.

DRU, JOANNE
Actress. r.n. Joanne La Cock. b. Logan, WV, Jan. 31, 1923. Sister of Peter Marshall. John Robert Powers model: on stage as showgirl in Hold on to Your Hats; a Samba Siren at Ritz Carlton & Paramount; with theatrical group under Batami Schneider.

PICTURES: Abie's Irish Rose (debut, 1946), Red River, She Wore a Yellow Ribbon, All the King's Men, Wagonmaster, 711 Ocean Drive, Vengeance Valley, Mr. Belvedere Rings the Bell, My Pal Gus, Return of the Texan, Pride of St. Louis, Thunder Bay, Outlaw Territory, Forbidden, Siege at Red River, Duffy of San Quentin, Southwest Passage, Three Ring Circus, Day of Triumph, Hell on Frisco Bay, The Warriors, Sincerely Yours, Drango, Light in the Forest, Wild and the Innocent, September Storm, Sylvia, Super Fuzz.
TELEVISION: Series: Guestward Ho. Guest: Ford Theatre, Schlitz Playhouse, Playhouse 90, Climax, Lux Video Theatre, David Niven Show, The Green Hornet, Marcus Welby M.D.
(d. September 10, 1996)

DRURY, JAMES
Actor. b. New York, NY, Apr. 18, 1934. e. New York U. Acting debut at age 8 in biblical play for children at Greenwich Settlement Playhouse. Performed on stage while youngster. Signed by MGM in 1955, working one day in each of seven movies that year, including Blackboard Jungle. Then got two-year contract at 20th-Fox. Gained fame as hero of TV series, The Virginian, which had nine-year run.
PICTURES: Forbidden Planet, Love Me Tender, Bernardine, Toby Tyler, Pollyana, Ten Who Dared, Ride the High Country, The Young Warriors.
TELEVISION: Series: The Virginian, Firehouse. Movies: Breakout, Alias Smith and Jones, The Devil and Miss Sarah, The Gambler Returns: Luck of the Draw.

DUBAND, WAYNE
Executive. b. Sydney, Australia, Feb. 13, 1947. Joined Warner Bros. 1969 as mgr. trainee in Australia. 1973, transferred to South Africa as mgr. dir.; 1977 gen. mgr. of CIC/Warner Bros. joint venture, also managing the CIC theatre operation there. 1980, named exec. asst. to Myron D. Karlin, pres. WB Intl., in Burbank. 1981, mgr. dir. of Warner/Columbia joint venture in France. 1985, appt. v.p. of sls. for WB Intl. division. 1987, appt. senior v.p. for Warner Bros. Intl. division. 1992, appt. pres. Intl. Theatrical div., WB Intl.

DUBE, JACKSON E.
Executive. b. New York, NY. e. U. of North Carolina. m. Pat Lavelle, actress. USAF 1942-45 Radar-Gunner, AAF, Italy. Writer: Television and Sponsor Magazine 1947-48; reviews of recorded music. 1947-51, Consol Film Inds. Penthouse Prods. Dist.: E. sales mgr. Atlas Tel. Corp. 1951-54; vp & gen. mgr., Craftsman Film Greatest Fights of the Century 1954; vp, Conquest Prods. CBS Net. Docus. 1954-57. TV and radio dir. Cote Fischer & Rogow Adv., 1957-59; exec. vp, Bon Ami Film; dist.: UA Feats. abroad 1959-63; prod's rep. Le Vien Prods.— Finest Hours King's Story; Eastern sales mgr. Desilu, 1964-67; exec. vp, UCC Films; dist. RKO feature Library abroad, 1969-70; pres. JED Rrns. Corp. Dist. London Films, Rank chi-dren's features, 1967-88. Consultant: New Century Ent., Windsor Pdns., Rurner Program Services, 1985-88. Agent for Weiss Global, Medallion TV Enterprises, Turner International, Morin International, 1988-92. Agent for Aries S.A. and Sidney Beckerman Prods. Agent for Otto Preminger Films Ltd. JED Productions Corp. owner or partner in remake rights to 125 US feature motion pictures 1992 to present.

DUBS, ARTHUR R.
Executive, Producer, Director, Writer, President and Owner of Pacific International Enterprises, b. Medford, OR, Feb. 26, 1930. e. Southern Oregon State Coll. Founded Pacific International Enterprises, 1969.
PICTURES: Producer-Director: American Wilderness, Vanishing Wilderness, Wonder of It All. Exec. Prod.: Challenge to Be Free. Prod.: Adventures of the Wilderness Family, Wilderness Family Part 2 (also s.p.), Mountain Family Robinson (also s.p.), Across the Great Divide, Sacred Ground, Mystery Mansion, Dream Chasers (also co-dir.). Co-Prod.: Windwalker.

DUCHOVNY, DAVID
Actor. b. New York, NY, Aug. 7, 1960. e. Yale. Was teaching asst. at Yale before landing first acting job in beer commercial.
PICTURES: Working Girl (debut, 1988), New Year's Day, Bad Influence, Julia Has Two Lovers, Don't Tell Mom the Babysitter's Dead, The Rapture, Ruby, Venice/Venice, Chaplin, Kalifornia.
TELEVISION: Series: Twin Peaks, The X Files.

DUDELHEIM, HANS RUDOLF
Communications Executive. b. Berlin, Germany, June 17, 1927. e. Sch. of Photography Berlin, School of Radio & TV NY. Film editor, ABC, 1951-66. Prod/Dir/Edit.: Cinema Arts Assn. 1966-90; served as pres. Founder, 1961, Cinema Arts Film Soc. Editor of documentaries: Saga of Western Man, Comrade Student, Sublimated Birth (also prod.), Kent State, Sigmund Freud, IBM Motivation Project, The Forgotten Pioneers of Hollywood, Painting With Love. Producer: Sesame Street, 60 Minutes: Ranaissance Community, American Dream Machine, Voyage of the Barba Negra. Presently film and video consul-tant.

DUDIKOFF, MICHAEL
Actor. b. Torrance, CA, Oct. 8, 1954.
PICTURES: Making Love, I Ought to Be in Pictures, Tron, Bachelor Party, Bloody Birthday, American Ninja, Radioactive Dreams, Avenging Force, American Ninja II: The Confrontation, Platoon Leader, River of Death, American Ninja 4: The Annihilation, Midnight Ride, Human Shield, Rescue Me, Virtual Assassin.
TELEVISION: Mini-Series: North and South Book II. Movie: The Woman Who Sinned. Series: Star of the Family, Cobra. Pilot: Sawyer and Finn. Guest: Happy Days, Dallas.

DUFFY, JAMES E.
Executive. b. Decatur, IL, April 2, 1926. e. Beloit Coll. Radio announcer, then reporter; joined publicity dept., ABC in 1949; named dir. of adv. & promo., then account exec. for Central division of ABC Radio Network; dir. of sales ABC Radio, 1957; central div. account exec., ABC TV Network, 1955; natl. dir. of Sales, ABC Radio central division, 1960; v.p., ABC Radio Network, 1961; exec. v.p. & natl. dir. of sales, 1962; v.p. in charge of sales, ABC TV Network, 1963; pres., ABC TV Network, 1970-85; pres., communications, 1985-86; v.p. Capital Cities/ABC, Inc.; pres., communications, ABC Network & Bdgst. Divisions.

DUFFY, PATRICK
Actor. b. Townsend, MT, March 17, 1949. e. U. of Washington. Became actor-in-residence in state of Washington, where per-formed with various statefunded groups. Acted off-B'way Taught mime and movement classes in summer camp in Seattle. Moved to L.A. and began TV acting career.
PICTURE: Vamping (also co-exec prod.).
TELEVISION: Specials: The Last of Mrs. Lincoln, Freedom Festival '89 (host). Movies: The Stranger Who Looks Like Me, Hurricane, Man From Atlantis, Enola Gay, Cry for the Strangers, Strong Medicine, Alice in Wonderland, Too Good to Be True, Unholy Matrimony, Murder C.O.D, Children of the Bride, Danielle Steel's Daddy, Texas. Series: Man from Atlantis, Dallas, Step By Step. Guest: Switch, George Burns' Comedy Week.

DUGAN, DENNIS
Actor, Director. b. Wheaton, IL, Sept. 5, 1946. m. actress Joyce Van Patten. Studied acting at Goodman Theatre School.
THEATER: NY: A Man's Man, The House of Blue Leaves. LA: Once in a Lifetime, Rainbows for Sales, Estonia, The Dining Room, The Kitchen.
PICTURES: Night Call Nurses, The Day of the Locust, Night Moves, Smile, Harry and Walter Go to New York, Norman ... Is That You?, Unidentified Flying Oddball, The Howling, Water, Can't Buy Me Love, She's Having a Baby, The New Adventures of Pippi Longstocking, Parenthood, Problem Child (also dir.), Brain Donors (dir. only), Happy Gilmore (dir. only).
TELEVISION: Series: Richie Brockelman: Private Eye, Empire, Shadow Chasers. Movies: Death Race, The Girl Most Likely To..., Last of the Good Guys, Country Gold, The Toughest Man in the World, Columbo: Butterfly in Shades of Grey. Mini-Series: Rich man Poor Man. Guest: Hooperman, Moonlighting, M*A*S*H, The Rockford Files, Scene of the Crime, Making a Living, Hill Street Blues. Pilots: Alice, Father O Father, Did You Hear About Josh and Kelly?, Full House, Channel 99. Director: Hunter, Sonny Spoon, Wiseguy, Moonlighting, The Shaggy Dog (movie).

DUGGAN, ERVIN S.
Executive. Started as reporter for the Washington Post in early 1960's. As member of President Lydon Johnson's staff helped define government's role in supporting public broad-casting with the Public Broadcasting Act of 1967. Served as special asst. to Senators Lloyd Bentsen and Adlai Stevenson III, Health Education and Welfare Secretary Joseph Califano; and as member of the State Dept. Policy Planning Staff. 1981-90, managed communications and consulting firm. Served 4 years as Commissioner of the Federal Communications Commission. Feb. 1994 joined PBS as pres. and CEO.

DUIGAN, JOHN
Director, Writer. Lived in England and Malaysia before mov-ing to Sydney, Australia. e. Univ. of Melbourne, philosophy, M.A. Taught for several years at Univ. of Melbourne and Latrobe U. before entering films. Directed and wrote experi-mental short, The Firm Man (1974). Novels: Badge, Players, Room to Move.
PICTURES: Dir.-Writer: Trespassers, Mouth to Mouth, Winter of Our Dreams (Australian Writers Guild Award), Far East, The Year My Voice Broke (Australian Acad. Award for best dir., s.p.) Romero (dir. only), Flirting, Wide Sargasso Sea, Sirens (also actor), The Journey of August King.
TELEVISION: Mini-Series: Vietnam (co-dir.). Movie: Fragments of War: The Story of Damien Parer.

DUKAKIS, OLYMPIA
Actress. b. Lowell, MA, June 20, 1931. m. actor Louis Zorich. e. Boston U., B.A., M.F.A. Founding mem. of The Charles

Playhouse, Boston, establishing summer theatre 1957-60. Taught acting at NYU: 1967-70 as instructor, 1974-83 as master teacher, and at Yale U. 1976. With husband conceived and guided artistic dev. of Whole Theatre of Monclair, NJ, 1977-90; producing artistic dir. Adapted plays for her co. and dir. theater there; also at Williamstown Theatre Fest. and Delaware Summer Fest. Appeared in more than 100 plays on B'way, Off-B'way and in regional and summer theater.
THEATER: Who's Who in Hell, The Aspern Papers, Night of the Iguana, The Breaking Wall, Curse of the Starving Class, Snow Orchid, The Marriage of Bette and Boo (Obie Award), Social Security.
PICTURES: Lilith, Twice a Man, John and Mary, Made for Each Other, Death Wish, Rich Kids, The Wanderers, The Idolmaker, National Lampoon Goes to the Movies, Flanagan, Moonstruck (Academy Award, best supporting actress, 1987), Working Girl, Look Who's Talking, Steel Magnolias, Dad, In the Spirit, Look Who's Talking Too, The Cemetery Club, Over the Hill, Look Who's Talking Now, Naked Gun 33 1/3: The Final Insult (cameo), I Love Trouble, Jeffrey, Mighty Aphrodite, Mr. Holland's Opus.
TELEVISION: Specials: The Rehearsal, Sisters, Last Act is a Solo, A Century of Women. Series: Search for Tomorrow, One of the Boys. Movies: Nicky's World, The Neighborhood, FDR-The Last Year, King of America, Lucky Day, Fire in the Dark, Sinatra, Young at Heart. Mini-Series: Tales of the City.

DUKE, BILL
Actor, Director. b. Poughkeepsie, NY, Feb. 26, 1943. e. Boston Univ., NY Univ. Sch. of the Arts. Recieved AFI Best Young Director Award for short The Hero (Gold Award, Houston Film Festival). Has written poetry, short stories for children. Member bd. of dirs. American Film Institute.
PICTURES: Actor: Car Wash, American Gigolo, Commando, Predator, No Man's Land, Action Jackson, Bird on a Wire, Street of No Return, Menace II Society. Director: A Rage in Harlem, Deep Cover, The Cemetery Club, Sister Act 2: Back in the Habit.
TELEVISION: Actor: Movies: Love is Not Enough, Sgt. Matlovich Vs. the U.S. Air Force. Series: Palmerstown U.S.A. Director: Series: A Man Called Hawk, Cagney & Lacey, Hill Street Blues, Miami Vice, Dallas. Specials: The Killing Floor, A Raisin in the Sun, The Meeting. Movie: Johnnie Mae Gibson.

DUKE, PATTY
Actress. r.n. Anna Marie Duke. b. New York, NY, Dec. 14, 1946. e. Quintano Sch. for Young Professionals. Mother of actors Sean and Mackenzie Astin. Pres., Screen Actors Guild, 1985-88. Author: Surviving Sexual Assault (1983), Call Me Anna (1987).
THEATER: The Miracle Worker (Theatre World Award), Isle of Children.
PICTURES: I'll Cry Tomorrow (debut as extra 1955), The Goddess, Happy Anniversary, The 4-D Man, The Miracle Worker (Academy Award, best supporting actress, 1962), Billie, Valley of the Dolls, Me Natalie, The Swarm, By Design, Something Special, Prelude to a Kiss.
TELEVISION: Series: The Brighter Day, The Patty Duke Show, It Takes Two, Hail to the Chief, Karen's Song, Amazing Grace. Guest: Armstrong Circle Theatre, The SS Andrea Doria, U.S. Steel Hour, All's Fair. Specials: The Prince and the Pauper, Wuthering Heights, Swiss Family Robinson, Meet Me in St. Louis, The Power and the Glory. Movies: My Sweet Charlie (Emmy Award, 1970), Two on a Bench, If Tomorrow Comes, She Waits, Deadly Harvest, Nightmare, Look What's Happened to Rosemary's Baby, Fire!, Rosetti & Ryan: Men Who Love Women, Curse of the Black Widow, Killer on Board, The Storyteller, Having Babies III, A Family Upside Down, Women in White, Hanging by a Thread, Before and After, The Miracle Worker (Emmy Award, 1980), The Women's Room, Mom The Wolfman and Me, The Babysitter, Violation of Sarah McDavid, Something So Right, September Gun, Best Kept Secrets, Fight for Life, Perry Mason: The Case of the Avenging Angel, A Time to Triumph, Fatal Judgment, Everybody's Baby: The Rescue of Jessica McClure, Amityville: The Evil Escapes, Call Me Anna, Always Remember I Love You, Absolute Strangers, Last Wish, Grave Secrets: The Legacy of Hilltop Drive, A Killer Among Friends, Family of Strangers, No Child of Mine, A Matter of Justice, One Woman's Courage, Cries From the Heart. Mini-Series: Captains and the Kings (Emmy Award, 1977), George Washington. Host: Fatal Passions, Angels: The Mysterious Messengers.

DUKES, DAVID
Actor. b. San Francisco, CA, June 6, 1945.
THEATER: B'way: Don Juan, The Great God Brown, Chemin de Fer, The Visit, Holiday, School for Wives, The Play's the Thing, Love for Love, Rules of the Game, Dracula, Travesties, Frankenstein, Bent, Amadeus, M. Butterfly, Love Letters, Someone Who'll Watch Over Me, Broken Glass.
PICTURES: The Strawberry Statement, The Wild Party, A Little Romance, The First Deadly Sin, Only When I Laugh,

Without a Trace, The Men's Club, Catch the Heat, Rawhead Rex, Date With an Angel, Deadly Intent, See You in the Morning, The Handmaid's Tale, Me and the Kid, Fled.
TELEVISION: Series: Beacon Hill, All That Glitters, Sisters, The Mommies. Mini-Series: 79 Park Avenue, Space, George Washington, The Winds of War, War and Remembrance, Kane & Abel. Specials: Strange Interlude, Cat on a Hot Tin Roof. Movies: Go West Young Girl, A Fire in the Sky, Some Kind of Miracle, The Triangle Factory Fire Scandal, Mayflower—The Pilgrim Adventure, Margaret Sanger— Portrait of a Rebel, Miss All-American Beauty, Sentimental Journey, Turn Back the Clock, Snowkill, Held Hostage: The Sis and Jerry Levin Story, The Josephine Baker Story, Wife Mother Murderer, She Woke Up, Look at It This Way (BBC), Spies. Guest: All in the Family, The Jeffersons, Once Day at a Time, Barney Miller, Hawaii 5-0, Police Story, Police Woman, Cannon, etc.

DULLEA, KEIR
Actor. b. Cleveland, OH, May 30, 1936. e. Rutgers Univ., San Francisco State Coll., Sanford Meisner's Neighborhood Playhouse. Acted as resident juvenile at the Totem Pole Playhouse in PA. NY theatre debut in the revue Sticks and Stones, 1956; appeared in stock co. prods. at the Berkshire Playhouse and Philadelphia's Hedgerow Theatre, 1959; off-Broadway debut in Season of Choice, 1969. Won San Francisco Film Festival Award for performance in film David and Lisa, 1963.
THEATER: Dr. Cook's Garden, Butterflies Are Free, Cat on a Hot Tin Roof, P.S. Your Cat is Dead, The Other Side of Paradise.
PICTURES: The Hoodlum Priest (debut, 1961), David and Lisa, The Thin Red Line, Mail Order Bride, The Naked Hours, Bunny Lake Is Missing, Madame X, The Fox, 2001: A Space Odyssey, De Sade, Pope Joan, Paperback Hero, Il Diavolo nel Cervello, Paul and Michelle, Black Christmas (Silent Night Evil Night), Leopard in the Snow, Welcome to Blood City, The Haunting of Julia (Full Circle), Because He's My Friend, The Next One, Brainwaves, Blind Date, 2010.
TELEVISION: Movies: Black Water Gold, Law and Order, Legend of the Golden Gun, Brave New World, The Hostage Tower, No Place to Hide. Special: Mrs. Miniver.

DUNAWAY, FAYE
Actress. b. Bascom, FL, Jan. 14, 1941. e. Texas, Arkansas, Utah, Germany, U. of Florida. Awarded a Fulbright scholarship in theatre. Boston U. of Fine Applied Arts. With Lincoln Center Rep. Co. for 3 years. NY Stage: A Man for All Seasons, After the Fall, Hogan's Goat (Theatre World Award), The Curse of an Aching Heart.
PICTURES: Hurry Sundown (debut, 1967), The Happening, Bonnie and Clyde, The Thomas Crown Affair, The Extraordinary Seaman, A Place for Lovers, The Arrangement, Puzzle of a Downfall Child, Little Big Man, The Deadly Trap, Doc, Oklahoma Crude, The Three Musketeers, Chinatown, The Towering Inferno, The Four Musketeers, Three Days of the Condor, Network (Academy Award, 1976), Voyage of the Damned, Eyes of Laura Mars, The Champ, The First Deadly Sin, Mommie Dearest, The Wicked Lady, Ordeal by Innocence, Supergirl, Barfly, Midnight Crossing, Burning Secret, The Handmaid's Tale, Wait Until Spring Bandini, The Gamble, On a Moonlit Night, Scorchers, Double Edge, The Temp, Arizona Dream, Don Juan DeMarco, Drunks, Dunston Checks In, Albino Alligator, The Chamber.
TELEVISION: Movies: The Woman I Love, The Disappearance of Aimee, Evita, Peron, 13 at Dinner, Beverly Hills Madam, The Country Girl, Casanova, The Raspberry Ripple, Cold Sassy Tree, Silhouette, Columbo: It's All in the Game (Emmy Award, 1994), A Family Divided. Mini-Series: Ellis Island, Christopher Columbus. Specials: Hogan's Goat, After the Fall, Supergirl: The Making of the Movie (host), Inside the Dream Factory (host). Series: It Had to Be You.

DUNCAN, LINDSAY
Actress. Stage actress with National Theatre, Royal Shakespeare Company.
THEATER: Plenty, The Provok'd Wife, The Prince of Homburg, Top Girls, Progress, The Merry Wives of Windsor, Les Liaisons Dangereuses (RSC, West End, Broadway; Theatre World Award), Cat On A Hot Tin Roof, Hedda Gabler, A Midsummer Night's Dream, Cryptogram.
PICTURES: Loose Connections, Samson & Delilah, Prick Up Your Ears, Manifesto, The Reflecting Skin, Body Parts, City Hall, A Midsummer Night's Dream.
TELEVISION: Reilly, Ace of Spies, Dead Head (serial), Traffik, A Year in Provence, The Rector's Wife, G.B.H., Jake's Progress.

DUNCAN, SANDY
Actress. b. Henderson, TX, Feb. 20, 1946. m. singer-dancer Don Correia. e. Len Morris Coll.
THEATER: The Music Man (NY debut, 1965); The Boyfriend, Ceremony of Innocence (Theatre World Award), Your Own Thing, Canterbury Tales, Peter Pan, Five Six Seven Eight Dance!, My One and Only.

PICTURES: $1,000,000 Duck, Star Spangled Girl, The Cat from Outer Space, Rock a Doodle (voice), The Swan Princess (voice).
TELEVISION: *Series*: Funny Face, The Sandy Duncan Show, Valerie's Family (later called The Hogan Family). *Movies*: My Boyfriend's Back, Miracle on Interstate 880. *Mini-Series*: Roots. *Specials*: Pinocchio, Sandy in Disneyland, The Sandy Duncan Special.

DUNING, GEORGE
Composer, Conductor, Arranger. b. Richmond, IN, Feb. 25, 1908. e. Cincinnati Conservatory of Music, U. of Cincinnati. Music dir. Aaron Spelling Prods., 1970-71, Bobby Sherman Show, Movies of the Week. Board of Directors, ASCAP, 1969-83. V.P. ASCAP, 1977-79. Society for Preservation of Film Music Career Achievement Award, 1987; Indiana Composer of the Year, 1993.
PICTURES: Down to Earth, The Guilt of Janet Ames, Johnny O'Clock, To the Ends of the Earth, Jolson Sings Again, The Eddy Duchin Story, From Here to Eternity, Picnic, Pal Joey, Cowboy, The Last Angry Man, The World of Susie Wong, Devil at 4 O'Clock, The Notorious Landlady, Toys in the Attic, Ensign Pulver, Dear Brigitte, Any Wednesday, Terror in the Wax Museum, The Man with Bogart's Face.
TELEVISION: No Time for Sergeants, Wendy and Me, The Farmer's Daughter, Big Valley, The Long Hot Summer, The Second Hundred Years, Star Trek, Mannix, Then Came Bronson.

DUNLAP, RICHARD D.
Producer, Director. b. Pomona, CA, Jan. 30, 1923. e. Yale U., B.A., 1944; M.F.A., 1948. U.S. Navy 1943-46; Instructor, English dept., Yale U., 1947-48; Prod.-dir., Kraft TV Theatre, 3 years; Dir, Assoc. Prod., Omnibus, 3 seasons; Dir., 25 half-hr. Dramatic Film Shows. Frank Sinatra Specials, Prod.-Dir., 11 Academy Award Shows, 4 Emmy Award Shows.

DUNNE, DOMINICK
Producer. Writer. b. Hartford, CT, Oct. 29, 1925. e. Canterbury Sch., 1944; Williams Col., 1949. Son is actor-prod. Griffin Dunne. Began career as stage manager at NBC-TV; then produced shows for CBS Studio One. Later exec. prod. at 20th-Fox TV, v.p. at Four Star. Novels: The Winners, The Two Mrs. Grenvilles, People Like Us, An Inconvenient Woman, A Season in Purgatory, Fatal Charms, The Mansions of Limbo.
PICTURES: The Boys in the Band (exec. prod.), The Panic in Needle Park, Play It as It Lays, Ash Wednesday.

DUNNE, GRIFFIN
Actor, Producer. b. New York, NY, June 8, 1955. Son of prod.-writer Dominick Dunne. foremerly m. actress Carey Lowell. Formed Double Play Prods. with Amy Robinson. Studied at Neighborhood Playhouse and with Uta Hagen. On Stage in Album, Marie and Bruce, Coming Attractions, Hotel Play, Search and Destroy (B'way debut; Theatre World Award).
PICTURES: *Actor*: The Other Side of the Mountain (debut, 1975), Chilly Scenes of Winter (also prod.), The Fan, American Werewolf in London, Cold Feet, Almost You, Johnny Dangerously, After Hours (also co-prod., Golden Globe nom.), Who's That Girl, Amazon Women on the Moon, Big Blue, Me and Him, Once Around (also co-prod.), My Girl, Straight Talk, Big Girls Don't Cry... They Get Even, The Pickle, Naked in New York, Quiz Show, I Like It Like That, Search and Destroy. *Producer only*: Baby It's You, Running on Empty, White Palace. *Director/Writer*: Duke of Groove (short, Oscar nom.).
TELEVISION: *Movies*: The Wall, Secret Weapon, Love Matters, The Android Affair, Love Matters (Ace nom.). *Specials*: Lip Service, Trying Times: Hunger Chic, Partners. *Pilot*: Graham.

DURNING, CHARLES
Actor. b. Highland Falls, NY, Feb. 28, 1923. e. NYU. Studied acting on the G.I. Bill. Prof. stage debut, 1960. Made several appearances with Joseph Papp's NY Shakespeare Festival.
THEATER: That Championship Season, Knock Knock, Au Pair Man, In the Boom Boom Room, The Happy Time, Indians, Cat on a Hot Tin Roof (Tony Award, 1990), Queen of the Stardust Ballroom, Inherit the Wind.
PICTURES: Harvey Middleman—Fireman (debut, 1965), I Walk the Line, Hi Mom!, The Pursuit of Happiness, Dealing: or the Berkeley-to- Boston Forty-Brick Lost-Bag Blues, Deadhead Miles, Sisters, The Sting, The Front Page, Dog Day Afternoon, The Hindenburg, Breakheart Pass, Harry and Walter Go to New York, Twilight's Last Gleaming, The Choirboys, An Enemy of the People, The Fury, The Greek Tycoon, Tilt, The Muppet Movie, North Dallas Forty, Starting Over, When a Stranger Calls, Die Laughing, The Final Countdown, True Confessions, Sharky's Machine, The Best Little Whorehouse in Texas (Acad. Award nom.), Tootsie, To Be or Not to Be (Acad. Award nom.), Two of a Kind, Hadley's Rebellion, Mass Appeal, Stick, The Man With One Red Shoe, Stand Alone, Big Trouble, Tough Guys, Where the River Runs Black, Solarbabies, Happy New Year, The Rosary Murders, A

Tiger's Tail, Cop, Far North, Cat Chaser, Dick Tracy, V. I. Warshawski, Brenda Starr, Etolie, Fatal Sky, The Music of Chance, The Hudsucker Proxy, I.Q., Home for the Holidays, The Last Supper, The Grass Harp, Spy Hard.
TELEVISION: *Series*: Another World (1972), The Cop and the Kid, Eye to Eye, Evening Shade. *Mini-Series*: Captains and the Kings, Studs Lonigan, The Kennedys of Massachusetts, A Woman of Independent Means. *Specials*: The Rivalry, The Dancing Bear, Working, Mr. Roberts, Side by Side (pilot), P.O.P. (pilot), Eye to Eye, Tales from Hollywood, Normandy (narrator), Texan, Leslie's Folly. *Movies*: The Connection, The Trial of Chaplain Jensen, Queen of the Stardust Ballroom, Switch, Special Olympics, Attica, Perfect Match, Crisis at Central High, The Best Little Girl in the World, Dark Night of the Scarecrow, Death of a Salesman, Kenny Rogers as The Gambler III—The Legend Continues, The Man Who Broke 1000 Chains, Case Closed, Unholy Matrimony, Prime Target, It Nearly Wasn't Christmas, Dinner at Eight, The Return of Eliot Ness, The Story Lady, The Water Engine, Roommates. *Guest*: Madigan, All in the Family, Barnaby Jones, Hawaii Five-O, Amazing Stories.

DURWOOD, EDWARD D.
Executive. e. Univ. of KS, B.S., 1975; M.B.A., 1985. Started with AMC Entertainment in 1976 as asst. film buyer, then head film buyer of Midwest Division. 1983, promoted to v.p. of AMC; 1985, with Real Estate Dept.; 1989, exec. v.p.; 1989 elected pres. & vice-chmn. of AMC.

DURWOOD, RICHARD M.
Executive. b. Kansas City, MO, Aug. 18, 1929. e. Brown U., A.B. Pres. Crown Cinema Corp.
MEMBER: Motion Picture Assn. of Kansas City (pres.), United Motion Pictures Assn. (pres. 1972-73), Young NATO (chmn., 1968-69), Past Chief Barker, Tent No. 8. Past mem., exec. comm., National NATO.

DURWOOD, STANLEY H.
Executive. b. 1920. e. Harvard Coll., B.S. Air Force navigator 3 years. Chmn. of bd. American Multi-Cinema Inc. Member: Harvard Club of Kansas City; Harvard Club of New York. On board of United Missouri Bankshares.

DUSSAULT, NANCY
Actress. b. Pensacola, FL, Jun. 30, 1936. e. Northwestern U.
THEATER: *B'way*: Street Scene, The Mikado, The Cradle Will Rock, Do Re Mi (Theatre World Award), Sound of Music, Carousel, Fiorello, The Gershwin Years, Into the Woods. *L.A. stage*: Next in Line.
PICTURE: The In-Laws.
TELEVISION: *Special*: The Beggars Opera. *Host*: Good Morning America. *Series*: The New Dick Van Dyke Show, Too Close for Comfort (The Ted Knight Show).

DUTTON, CHARLES S.
Actor. b. Baltimore, MD, Jan. 30, 1951. e. Towson St., Yale Sch. of Drama.
THEATER: *Yale Rep*: The Works, Beef No Chicken, Astopovo, Othello. *NY*: Ma Rainey's Black Bottom (Theatre World Award, 1983), Joe Turner's Come and Gone, The Piano Lesson.
PICTURES: No Mercy, Crocodile Dundee II, Jacknife, An Unremarkable Life, Q & A, Mississippi Masala, Alien3, The Distinguished Gentleman, Menace II Society, Rudy, Foreign Student, A Low Down Dirty Shame, Cry the Beloved Country, Nick of Time, The Last Dance, A Time to Kill, Get on the Bus.
TELEVISION: *Series*: Roc. *Guest*: Miami Vice, The Equalizer, Cagney and Lacey. *Movies*: Apology, The Murder of Mary Phagan, Jack Reed: Search for Justice, The Piano Lesson, Zooman. *Special*: Runaway.

DUVALL, ROBERT
Actor. b. San Diego, CA, Jan. 5, 1931. e. Principia College, IL. Studied at the Neighborhood Playhouse, NY.
THEATER: *Off-B'way*: The Days and Nights of Bee Bee Fenstermaker, Call Me By My Rightful Name, A View From the Bridge (Obie Award, 1965). *B'way*: Wait Until Dark, American Buffalo.
PICTURES: To Kill a Mockingbird (debut, 1962), Captain Newman M.D., Nightmare in the Sun, The Chase, Countdown, The Detective, Bullitt, True Grit, The Rain People, M*A*S*H, The Revolutionary, THX-1138, Lawman, The Godfather, Tomorrow, The Great Northfield Minnesota Raid, Joe Kidd, Lady Ice, Badge 373, The Outfit, The Conversation, The Godfather Part II, Breakout, The Killer Elite, The Seven Percent Solution, Network, We're Not the Jet Set (dir., co-prod. only), The Eagle Has Landed, The Greatest, The Betsy, Invasion of the Body Snatchers (cameo), Apocalypse Now, The Great Santini, True Confessions, The Pursuit of D.B. Cooper, Tender Mercies (Academy Award, 1983; also co-prod, songwriter), Angelo My Love (dir., prod., s.p. only), The Stone Boy, The Natural, Bellizaire the Cajun (cameo; also creative consultant), The Lightship, Let's Get Harry, Hotel Colonial, Colors, The Handmaid's Tale, A Show of Force, Days of

Thunder, Rambling Rose, Convicts, Newsies, Falling Down, The Plague, Geronimo: An American Legend, Wrestling Ernest Hemingway, The Paper, Something to Talk About, The Stars Fell on Henrietta, The Scarlet Letter, A Family Thing (also co-prod.), Phenomenon.
TELEVISION: *Movies*: Fame Is the Name of the Game, The Terry Fox Story, Stalin. *Mini-Series*: Ike, Lonesome Dove. *Guest*: Great Ghost Tales, The Outer Limits, Naked City, Route 66, The Defenders, Alfred Hitchcock Presents, Twilight Zone, Combat, Wild Wild West, The FBI, Mod Squad.

DUVALL, SHELLEY
Actress, Producer. b. Houston, TX, July 7, 1949. Founded Think Entertainment, TV prod. co. Appeared in 1984 short film Frankenweenie.
PICTURES: Brewster McCloud (debut, 1970), McCabe and Mrs. Miller, Thieves Like Us, Nashville, Buffalo Bill and the Indians, Three Women (Cannes Fest. Award, 1977), Annie Hall, The Shining, Popeye, Time Bandits, Roxanne, Suburban Commando, The Underneath, Portrait of a Lady.
TELEVISION: *Actress*: Bernice Bobs Her Hair, Lily, Twilight Zone, Mother Goose Rock 'n' Rhyme, Faerie Tale Theatre (Rumpelstiltskin, Rapunzel), Tall Tales and Legends (Darlin' Clementine). *Exec. Producer*: Faerie Tale Theatre, Tall Tales and Legends, Nightmare Classics, Dinner at Eight (movie), Mother Goose Rock 'n' Rhyme, Stories from Growing Up, Backfield in Motion (movie), Bedtime Stories, Mrs. Piggle-Wiggle.

DYSART, RICHARD A.
Actor. b. Brighton, MA, Mar. 30, 1929. e. Emerson Coll., B.S., M.S., L.L.D.(honorary). Univ. of Maine, PhD (honorary). Off-B'way in The Quare Fellow, Our Town, Epitaph for George Dillon, Six Characters in Search of an Author, on B'way in A Man for All Seasons, All in Good Time, The Little Foxes, A Place without Doors, That Championship Season, Another Part of the Forest.
PICTURES: Petulia, The Lost Man, The Sporting Club, The Hospital, The Terminal Man, The Crazy World of Julius Vrooder, The Day of the Locust, The Hindenberg, Prophecy, Meteor, Being There, An Enemy of the People, The Thing, The Falcon and the Snowman, Mask, Warning Signs, Pale Rider, Wall Street, Back to the Future Part III.
TELEVISION: *Movies*: The Autobiography of Miss Jane Pittman, Gemini Man, It Happened One Christmas, First You Cry, Bogie, The Ordeal of Dr. Mudd, Churchill and the Generals (BBC), People Vs. Jean Harris, Bitter Harvest, Missing, Last Days of Patton, Children--A Mother's Story, Malice in Wonderland, Day One, Bobby and Marilyn: Her Final Affair, Truman, A Child Is Missing. *Special*: Sandburg's Lincoln, Jay Leno's Family Comedy Hour, Concealed Enemies (PBS), Charlie Smith and the Fritter Tree (PBS), Moving Target. *Mini-Series*: War and Remembrance. *Series*: L.A. Law (Emmy Award, 1992).

DZUNDZA, GEORGE
Actor. b. Rosenheim, Germany, 1945. Spent part of childhood in displaced-persons camps before he was moved to Amsterdam in 1949. Came to NY in 1956 where he attended St. John's U. as speech and theater major.
THEATER: King Lear (NY Shakespeare Fest., debut, 1973), That Championship Season (tour, 1973), Mert and Phil, The Ritz, Legend, A Prayer for My Daughter.
PICTURES: The Happy Hooker, The Deer Hunter, Honky Tonk Freeway, Streamers, Best Defense, No Mercy, No Way Out, The Beast, Impulse, White Hunter Black Heart, The Butcher's Wife, Basic Instinct, Crimson Tide, Dangerous Minds.
TELEVISION: *Series*: Open All Night, Law and Order. *Movies*: The Defection of Simas Kudirka, Salem's Lot, Skokie, A Long Way Home, The Face of Rage, The Last Honor of Kathryn Beck, When She Says No, The Rape of Richard Beck, Brotherly Love, The Execution of Raymond Graham, Something is Out There, The Ryan White Story, Terror on Highway 91, What She Doesn't Know, The Enemy Within. Guest: Starsky and Hutch, The Waltons.

E

EASTWOOD, CLINT
Actor, Producer, Director. b. San Francisco, CA, May 31, 1930; e. Oakland Technical H.S., Los Angeles City Coll. Worked as a lumberjack in Oregon before being drafted into the Army, Special Services 1950-54. Then contract player at Universal Studios. Starred in TV series Rawhide, 1958-65. Formed Malpaso Productions, 1969. Made a Chevalier des Lettres by French gov., 1985. Mayor, Carmel, CA, 1986-88. Best Director for Bird: Hollywood Foreign Press Assoc., Orson Award. Made Commandeur de Ordre des Arts & Lettres by French Government, 1994. Received Irving G. Thalberg Award, 1995. Received American Film Institute Life Achievement Award, 1996.
PICTURES: Revenge of the Creature (debut, 1955), Francis in the Navy, Lady Godiva, Tarantula, Never Say Goodbye, Away

All Boats, The First Traveling Saleslady, Star in the Dust, Escapade in Japan, Ambush at Cimarron Pass, Lafayette Escadrille, A Fistful of Dollars, For a Few Dollars More, The Witches, The Good The Bad and The Ugly, Hang 'Em High, Coogan's Bluff, Where Eagles Dare, Paint Your Wagon, Kelly's Heroes, Two Mules For Sister Sara, Beguiled, Play Misty For Me (also dir.), Dirty Harry, Joe Kidd, Breezy (dir. only), High Plains Drifter (also dir.), Magnum Force, Thunderbolt & Lightfoot, The Eiger Sanction (also dir.), The Outlaw Josey Wales (also dir.), The Enforcer, The Gauntlet (also dir.), Every Which Way But Loose, Escape from Alcatraz, Bronco Billy (also dir.), Any Which Way You Can, Firefox (also dir., prod.), Honky Tonk Man (also dir., prod.), Sudden Impact (also dir., prod.), Tightrope (also prod.), City Heat, Pale Rider (also dir., prod.), Heartbreak Ridge (also dir., prod.), The Dead Pool (also prod.), Bird (dir. only), Thelonius Monk: Straight, No Chaser (exec. prod. only), Pink Cadillac, White Hunter Black Heart (also dir., prod.), The Rookie (also dir.), Unforgiven (also dir., prod.; Acad. Awards for Best Picture & Director; L.A. Film Critics Awards for Best Actor, Director & Picture; Natl. Society of Film Critics Awards for Best Director & Picture; Golden Globe Award for Best Director; DGA Award, 1992), In the Line of Fire, A Perfect World (also dir.), Casper (cameo), The Bridges of Madison County (also dir., prod.), The Stars Fell on Henrietta (co-prod. only), Absolute Power (also dir., prod.).
TELEVISION: *Series*: Rawhide. *Specials*: Fame Fortune and Romance, Happy Birthday Hollywood, Clint Eastwood: The Man From Malpaso, Don't Pave Main Street: Carmel's Heritage. *Dir.*: Amazing Stories (Vanessa in the Garden). *Guest*: Navy Log, Maverick, Mr. Ed, Danny Kaye Show.

EBERSOL, DICK
Executive. 1968, started at ABC as Olympic Television researcher; 1974, joined NBC as dir. of weekend late-night programming; named v.p. late night programming; 1977, became v.p. of Comedy Variety and Event Programming; 1981-85, served as exec. prod. of series Saturday Night Live; 1983, formed his own production company, No Sleep Productions, creating Friday Night Videos, Saturday Night's Main Event, Later With Bob Costas; 1989, named pres. of NBC Sports; served as exec. prod. of NBC's coverage of the 1992 Barcelona Summer Olympics.

EBERTS, JOHN DAVID (JAKE)
Producer, Financier. b. Montreal, Canada, July 10, 1941. e. McGill Univ., Harvard. President Goldcrest, founder & CEO 1976-83, 1985-6; 1984 joined Embassy Communications Intl. 1985 founded and chief exec. of Allied Filmmakers. Film Prods. Award of Merit 1986; Evening Standard Special Award 1987. Publication: My Indecision Is Final (1990).
PICTURES: Chariots of Fire, Gandhi, Another Country, Local Hero, The Dresser, Cal, The Emerald Forest, The Name of the Rose, Hope and Glory, Cry Freedom, The Adventures of Baron Munchausen, Driving Miss Daisy, Dances With Wolves, Black Robe, Get Back, City of Joy, A River Runs Through It, Super Mario Bros., No Escape, Arabian Knight.

EBSEN, BUDDY
Actor. r.n. Christian Ebsen, Jr. b. Belleville, IL, April 2, 1908. e. U. of Florida, Rollins Coll. Won first Broadway role as dancer in Ziegfeld's Whoopee in 1928. Sister, Vilma, became dancing partner and they played nightclubs and did road tours. Went to Hollywood and appeared in Broadway Melody of 1936 with Vilma then in many musicals as single. Later became dramatic actor and appeared on TV. Co-wrote title song for film Behave Yourself.
PICTURES: Broadway Melody of 1936 (debut, 1935), Born to Dance, Captain January, Banjo on My Knee, Yellow Jack, Girl of the Golden West, My Lucky Star, Broadway Melody of 1938, Four Girls in White, Parachute Battalion, They Met in Argentina, Sing Your Worries Away, Thunder in God's Country, Night People, Red Garters, Davy Crockett--King of the Wild Frontier, Davy Crockett and the River Pirates, Between Heaven and Hell, Attack!, Breakfast at Tiffany's, The Interns, Mail Order Bride, The One and Only Genuine Original Family Band, The Beverly Hillbillies.
TELEVISION: *Series*: Davy Crockett, Northwest Passage, The Beverly Hillbillies, Barnaby Jones, Matt Houston. *Guest*: Hawaii Five-O, Gunsmoke. *Movies*: Stone Fox, The Daughters of Joshua Cabe, Horror at 37000 Feet, Smash-Up on Interstate 5, The President's Plane is Missing, Leave Yesterday Behind, The Paradise Connection, Fire on the Mountain, The Return of the Beverly Hillbillies, The Bastard, Tom Sawyer, Stone Fox, Working Trash. *Special*: The Legend of the Beverly Hillbillies.
THEATER: Flying Colors, Yokel Boy, The Male Animal, Ziegfeld Follies, Take Her She's Mine, Our Town, The Best Man.

ECKERT, JOHN M.
Producer, Production Executive. b. Chatham, Ontario, Canada, e. Ryerson Polytechnical Inst., 1968-71 (film major). Member: DGA, DGC.

PICTURES: Power Play (assoc. prod.), Running (co-prod.), Middle Age Crazy (co-prod.), Dead Zone (unit prod. mgr.), Cats Eye (exec. in charge of prod.), Silver Bullet (assoc. prod.), Home Is Where the Heart Is (prod.), Millenium (suprv. prod.), Deep Sleep (prod.), Car 54 Where Are You? (s.p., prod.), Legends of the Fall (unit prod. mngr.), The Scarlet Letter (unit prod. mngr.), Flying Wild (assoc. prod.).
TELEVISION: Terry Fox Story (assoc. prod.), Special People (prod., Christopher Award), Danger Bay (series supv. prod., 1985-87), Family Pictures (unit prod. mngr.), Getting Gotti (prod.).

EDEN, BARBARA
Actress. b. Tucson, AZ, Aug. 23, 1934. r.n. Barbara Jean Huffman. e. San Francisco Conservatory of Music. Pres. Mi-Bar Productions. Dir. Security National Bank of Chicago.
PICTURES: Back From Eternity (debut, 1956), The Wayward Girl, A Private's Affair, From the Terrace, Twelve Hours to Kill, Flaming Star, All Hands on Deck, Voyage to the Bottom of the Sea, Five Weeks in a Balloon, Swingin' Along (Double Trouble), The Wonderful World of the Brothers Grimm, The Yellow Canary, The Brass Bottle, The New Interns, Ride the Wild Surf, 7 Faces of Dr. Lao, Quick Let's Get Married, The Amazing Dobermans, Harper Valley PTA, Chattanooga Choo Choo.
TELEVISION: Series: How to Marry a Millionaire, I Dream of Jeannie, Harper Valley P.T.A., A Brand New Life, Dallas. Movies: The Feminist and the Fuzz, A Howling in the Woods, The Woman Hunter, Guess Who's Sleeping in My Bed, The Stranger Within, Let's Switch, How to Break Up a Happy Divorce, Stonestreet: Who Killed the Centerfold Model?, The Girls in the Office, Condominium, Return of the Rebels, I Dream of Jeannie: 15 Years Later, The Stepford Children, The Secret Life of Kathy McCormick (also co-prod.), Your Mother Wears Combat Boots, Opposites Attract, Her Wicked Ways, Hell Hath No Fury, I Still Dream of Jeannie, Visions of Murder, Eyes of Terror, Dean Man's Island (also co-prod.).

EDWARDS, ANTHONY
Actor. b. Santa Barbara, CA, July 19, 1962. Grandfather designed Walt Disney Studios in the 1930s and worked for Cecil B. De Mille as conceptual artist. Joined Santa Barbara YHouth Theatre; acted in 30 plays from age 12 to 17. At 16 worked professionally in TV commercials. 1980 attended Royal Acad. of Dramatic Arts, London, and studied drama at USC. On NY stage 1993 in Ten Below.
PICTURES: Fast Times at Ridgemont High (debut, 1982), Heart Like a Wheel, Revenge of the Nerds, The Sure Thing, Gotcha!, Top Gun, Summer Heat, Revenge of the Nerds II (cameo), Mr. North, Miracle Mile, How I Got Into College, Hawks, Downtown, Delta Heat, Pet Sematary II, The Client.
TELEVISION: Series: It Takes Two, Northern Exposure, ER. Movies: The Killing of Randy Webster, High School U.S.A., Going for the Gold: The Bill Johnson Story, El Diablo, Hometown Boy Makes Good. Specials: Unpublished Letters, Sexual Healing.

EDWARDS, BLAKE
Director, Writer, Producer. r.n. William Blake McEdwards. b. Tulsa, OK, July 26, 1922. m. actress Julie Andrews. e. Beverly Hills H.S. Coast Guard during war. Film acting debut, Ten Gentlemen from West Point (1942).
RADIO: Johnny Dollar, Line-up; writer-creator: Richard Diamond.
PICTURES: Writer only: Panhandle, Stampede, Sound Off, All Ashore, Cruising Down the River, Rainbow Round My Shoulder, Drive a Crooked Road, The Atomic Kid (story), My Sister Eileen, Operation Mad Ball, Notorious Landlady, Soldier in the Rain. Producer only: Waterhole $NO3. Director: Bring Your Smile Along (also s.p.), He Laughed Last (also s.p.), Mister Cory (also s.p.), This Happy Feeling (also s.p.), The Perfect Furlough (also s.p.), Operation Petticoat, High Time, Breakfast at Tiffany's, Experiment in Terror, Days of Wine and Roses, The Pink Panther (also s.p.), A Shot in the Dark (also s.p., prod.), The Great Race (also s.p., prod.), What Did You Do in the War Daddy? (also s.p., prod.), Gunn (also prod.), The Party (also s.p., prod.), Darling Lili (also s.p., prod.), Wild Rovers (also s.p., prod.), The Carey Treatment (also s.p., prod.), The Tamarind Seed (also s.p.), The Return of the Pink Panther (also s.p., prod.), The Pink Panther Strikes Again (also s.p., prod.), Revenge of the Pink Panther (also s.p., prod.), "10" (also co-prod., s.p.), S.O.B. (also co-prod., s.p.), Victor/Victoria (also co-prod., s.p.), Trail of the Pink Panther (also co-prod., co-s.p.), The Curse of the Pink Panther (also co-prod., s.p.), The Man Who Loved Women (also prod., co-s.p.), Micki and Maude, A Fine Mess (also s.p.), That's Life (also co-prod.), Blind Date, Sunset (also s.p.), Skin Deep (also s.p.), Switch (also s.p.), Son of the Pink Panther (also s.p.).
TELEVISION: City Detective (prod., 1953), The Dick Powell Show (dir.), Creator: Dante's Inferno, Mr. Lucky, Justin Case (exec. prod., dir., writer), Peter Gunn (exec. prod., dir., writer), Julie (exec. prod., dir.). Specials: Julie! (prod., dir.), Julie on Sesame St. (exec. prod.), Julie and Dick in Covent Garden (dir.).

EDWARDS, JAMES H.
Executive. President & CEO, Storey Theatres, Inc. b. Cedartown, GA, Aug. 14, 1927. e. Georgia State. U.S. Navy, 1948-50. With Ga. Theatre Co., 1950-1952; Storey Theatres, 1952-present. Formerly pres. & chmn., NATO of GA; formerly pres., Variety Club of Atlanta. Former dir. at large, Nat'l. NATO. Director, numerous theatre cos.

EDWARDS, RALPH
Producer, Emcee. b. Merino, CO, June 13, 1913. e. U. of California, Berkeley. Began career in radio in 1929 as writer-actor-producer-announcer at station KROW, Oakland. Later joined CBS & NBC Radio in New York as announcer. Originated, produced and emceed Truth or Consequences, This Is Your Life and The Ralph Edwards Show for both radio & TV.
PICTURES: Seven Days Leave, Radio Stars on Parade, Bamboo Blonde, Beat the Band, I'll Cry Tomorrow, Manhattan Merry-go-round, Radio Stars of 1937.
TELEVISION: Producer/Creator: It Could Be You, Place the Face, About Faces, Funny Boners, End of the Rainbow, Who in the World, The Woody Woodbury Show. Producer/Host: This Is Your Life (specials for NBC). Producers: Wide Country, Name That Tune, Cross Wits, Knockout. Producer (with partner, Stu Billett): The People's Court, So You Think You Got Troubles?, Family Medical Center, Love Stories, Superior Court, Bzzz.

EGGAR, SAMANTHA
Actress. b. London, Eng., March 5, 1939. e. student Webber-Douglas Dramatic Sch., London; Slade Sch. of Art.
PICTURES: The Wild and the Willing, Dr. Crippen, Doctor in Distress, Psyche '59, The Collector (Acad. Award nom.), Return From the Ashes, Walk Don't Run, Doctor Dolittle, The Molly Maguires, The Lady in the Car With Glasses and a Gun, The Walking Stick, The Grove, The Light at the Edge of the World, The Dead Are Alive, The Seven Percent Solution, The Uncanny, Welcome to Blood City, The Brood, The Exterminator, Demonoid, Why Shoot the Teacher?, Curtains, Hot Touch, Loner, Ragin' Cajun, Dark Horse, Inevitable Grace, The Phantom.
TELEVISION: Series: Anna and the King. Movies: Double Indemnity, All The Kind Strangers, The Killer Who Wouldn't Die, Ziegfeld: the Man and His Women, The Hope Diamond, Love Among Thieves, A Ghost in Monte Carlo. A Case for Murder. Mini-Series: For the Term of His Natural Life, Davy Crockett, Great Escapes: Secrets of Lake Success. Guest: Columbo, Baretta, Love Story, Kojak, McMillan & Wife, Streets of San Francisco, Starsky and Hutch, Hart to Hart, Murder She Wrote, Finder of Lost Loves, George Burns Comedy Week, Lucas Tanner, Hotel, Fantasy Island, Magnum P.I., Stingray, Tales of the Unexpected, Heartbeat, Love Boat, 1st & Ten, Outlaws, Alfred Hitchcock Presents, Matlock, L.A. Law, Star Trek: The Next Generation. Specials: Man of Destiny, Hemingway Play.

EGOYAN, ATOM
Director. b. Cairo, Egypt, 1960. Raised in Victoria, British Columbia, Canada. e. Univ. of Toronto. Made short films, one of which, Open House appeared on tv series Canadian Reflections. Appeared in film Camilla.
PICTURES: Next of Kin (feature debut, 1984), Family Viewing, Speaking Parts, The Adjuster, Calendar, Exotica.
TELEVISION: In This Corner, Looking for Nothing, Gross Misconduct: The Life of Brian Spencer, Twilight Zone, Alfred Hitchock Presents (The Final Twist).

EICHHORN, LISA
Actress. b. Reading, PA, Feb. 4, 1952. e. Queen's U. Kingston, Canada and Eng. for literature studies at Oxford. Studied at Royal Acad. of Dramatic Art.
THEATER: The Hasty Heart (debut, LA). NY: The Common Pursuit, The Summer Winds, The Speed of Darkness, Down the Road, Any Given Day.
PICTURES: Yanks, The Europeans, Why Would I Lie?, Cutter and Bone, Weather in the Streets, Wild Rose; Opposing Force, Moon 44, Grim Prairie Tales, The Vanishing, King of the Hill, A Modern Affair.
TELEVISION: Series: All My Children (1987). Movies: The Wall, Blind Justice, Devlin. Mini-Series: A Woman Named Jackie.

EIKENBERRY, JILL
Actress. b. New Haven, CT, Jan. 21, 1947. e. Yale U. Drama Sch. m. actor Michael Tucker.
THEATER: B'way: All Over Town, Watch on the Rhine, Onward Victoria, Summer Brave, Moonchildren. Off-B'way: Lemon Sky, Life Under Water, Uncommon Women and Others, Porch, The Primary English Class.
PICTURES: Between the Lines, The End of the World in Our Usual Bed in a Night Full of Rain, An Unmarried Woman, Butch and Sundance: The Early Days, Rich Kids, Hide in Plain Sight, Arthur, The Manhattan Project.

TELEVISION: *Movies*: The Deadliest Season, Orphan Train, Swan Song, Sessions, Kane & Abel, Assault and Matrimony, Family Sins, A Stoning in Fulham Country, My Boyfriend's Back, The Diane Martin Story, The Secret Life of Archie's Wife, An Inconvenient Woman, Living a Lie, A Town Torn Apart, Chantilly Lace, Parallel Lives, Without Consent, Rugged Gold, The Other Woman. *Series*: L.A. Law, The Best of Families (PBS). *Specials*: Uncommon Women & Others, Destined to Live (prod., host), A Family Again, On Hope.

EILBACHER, LISA
Actress. b. Saudi Arabia, May 5. Moved to California at age 7; acted on TV as child.
PICTURES: The War Between Men and Women (debut, 1972), Run for the Roses (Thoroughbred), On the Right Track, An Officer and a Gentleman, Ten to Midnight, Beverly Hills Cop, Deadly Intent, Leviathan, Never Say Die, The Last Samurai.
TELEVISION: *Series*: The Texas Wheelers, The Hardy Boys Mysteries, Ryan's Four, Me and Mom. *Movies*: Bad Ronald, Panache, Spider Man, The Ordeal of Patty Hearst, Love for Rent, To Race the Wind, This House Possessed, Monte Carlo, Deadly Deception, Joshua's Heart, Blind Man's Bluff, Deadly Matrimony, The Return of Hunter. *Mini-Series*: Wheels, The Winds of War. *Guest*: Wagon Train, Laredo, My Three Sons, Gunsmoke, Combat.

EISNER, MICHAEL D.
Executive. b. Mt. Kisco, NY, March 7, 1942. e. Denison U., B.A. Started career with programming dept. of CBS TV network. Joined ABC in 1966 as mgr. talent and specials. Dec., 1968 became dir. of program dev., east coast. 1968, named v.p., daytime programming, ABC-TV. 1975 made v.p., prog. planning and dev. 1976 named sr. v.p., prime time production and dev., ABC Entertainment. 1976, left ABC to join Paramount Pictures as pres. & chief operating officer. 1984, joined The Walt Disney Company as chmn. & CEO.

EKBERG, ANITA
Actress. b. Malmo, Sweden, Sept. 29, 1931. Came to U.S. in 1951 as Miss Universe contestant. Worked as model before becoming actress appearing in small roles at Universal.
PICTURES: Mississippi Gambler, Abbott & Costello Go to Mars, Take Me to Town, The Golden Blade, Blood Alley, Artists and Models, Man in the Vault, War and Peace, Back from Eternity, Hollywood or Bust, Zarak, Pickup Alley, Valerie, Paris Holiday, The Man Inside, Screaming Mimi, Sign of the Gladiator, La Dolce Vita, The Dam on the Yellow River (Last Train to Shanghai), Little Girls and High Finance, Behind Locked Doors, The Last Judgment, The Mongols, Boccaccio '70, Call Me Bwana, 4 for Texas, L'Incastro, Who Wants to Sleep?, The Alphabet Murders, Way Way Out, How I Learned to Love Women, Woman Times Seven, The Glass Sphinx, The Cobra, Malenka the Vampire (Fangs of the Living Dead), If It's Tuesday This Must Be Belgium, The Clowns, Valley of the Widows, Killer Nun, Daisy Chain, Intervista.
TELEVISION: *Movies*: Gold of the Amazon Women, S*H*E.

EKLAND, BRITT
Actress. b. Stockholm, Sweden, Oct. 6, 1942. Was model before debuting in European films.
PICTURES: Short Is the Summer (debut, 1962), Il Commandante, After the Fox, The Double Man, The Bobo, The Night They Raided Minsky's, Stiletto, Cannibals, Machine Gun McCain, Tintomara, Percy, Get Carter, A Time for Loving, Endless Night, Baxter, Asylum, The Wicker Man, Ultimate Thrill, The Man With the Golden Gun, Royal Flash, Casanova & Co., High Velocity, Slavers, King Solomon's Treasure, The Monster Club, Satan's Mistress (Demon Rage), Hellhole, Fraternity Vacation, Marbella, Moon in Scorpio, Scandal, Beverly Hills Vamp, The Children.
TELEVISION: *England*: Carol for Another Christmas, Too Many Thieves, A Cold Peace. *USA: Guest*: Trials of O'Brien, McCloud, Six Million Dollar Man. *Movies*: Ring of Passion, The Great Wallendas, The Hostage Tower, Valley of the Dolls 1981, Dead Wrong.

ELAM, JACK
Actor. b. Miami, AZ, Nov. 13, 1916. e. Santa Monica Jr. Coll., Modesto Jr. Coll. Worked in Los Angeles as bookkeeper and theatre mgr.; civilian employee of Navy in W.W.II; Introduction to show business was as bookkeeper for Sam Goldwyn. Later worked as controller for other film producers. Given first acting job by producer George Templeton in 1948; has since appeared in over 100 films.
PICTURES: Wild Weed (debut, 1949), Rawhide, Kansas City Confidential, Rancho Notorious, Ride Vaquero, Appointment in Honduras, The Moonlighter, Vera Cruz, Cattle Queen of Montana, The Far Country, Moonfleet, Kiss Me Deadly, Artists and Models, Gunfight at the OK Corral, Baby Face Nelson, Edge of Eternity, Girl in Lovers Lane, The Last Sunset, The Comancheros, The Rare Breed, The Way West, Firecreek, Never a Dull Moment, Once Upon a Time in the West, Support

Your Local Sheriff, Rio Lobo, Dirty Dingus Magee, Support Your Local Gunfighter, The Wild Country, Hannie Caulder, Last Rebel, Pat Garrett and Billy the Kid, Hawmps, Grayeagle, Hot Lead Cold Feet, The Norsemen, The Villain, The Apple Dumpling Gang Rides Again, The Cannonball Run, Jinxed, Cannonball Run II, The Aurora Encounter, Big Bad John, Suburban Commando.
TELEVISION: *Series*: The Dakotas, Temple Houston, The Texas Wheelers, Struck by Lightning, Detective in the House, Easy Street. *Movies*: The Over-the-Hill Gang, The Daughters of Joshua Cabe, Black Beauty, Once Upon a Texas Train, Where the Hell's That Gold!!!?.

ELEFANTE, TOM
Executive. Began career as usher at Loews Riviera in Coral Gables, FL; progressed through ranks to asst. mgr., mgr. & Florida division mgr. 1972, joined Wometco Theatres as gen. mgr. 1975, returned to Loews Theatres as southeast div. mgr.; 1979, named natl. dir. of concessions, moving to h.o. in New York. 1987, appt. sr. v.p. & gen. mgr., Loews. Served as pres. and chmn. of NATO of Florida. 1990, then pres. of NATO of NY.

ELFAND, MARTIN
Executive. b. Los Angeles, CA, 1937. Was talent agent for ten years with top agencies; joined Artists Entertainment Complex in 1972. First film project as producer: Kansas City Bomber, first venture of AEC, of which he was sr. v.p. In 1977 joined Warner Bros. as production chief.T
PICTURES: *Prod.*: Dog Day Afternoon, It's My Turn, An Officer and a Gentleman, King David, Clara's Heart. *Exec. prod.*: Her Alibi.

ELFMAN, DANNY
Composer. b. Los Angeles, CA, May 29, 1953. Member of rock band Oingo Boingo, recorded songs for such films as The Tempest, Fast Times at Ridgemont High, 16 Candles, Beverly Hills Cop, Weird Science, Texas Chainsaw Massacre 2, Something Wild. Appeared in Hot Tomorrows, Back to School.
PICTURES: Forbidden Zone, Pee-wee's Big Adventure, Back to School, Wisdom, Summer School, Beetlejuice, Midnight Run, Big-Top Pee-wee, Hot to Trot, Scrooged, Batman, Nightbreed, Dick Tracy, Darkman, Edward Scissorhands, Pure Luck, Article 99, Batman Returns, Sommersby, The Nightmare Before Christmas (also vocalist), Black Beauty, Dolores Claiborne, To Die For, Dead Presidents, Mission: Impossible, The Frighteners.
TELEVISION: *Series*: Pee-wee's Playhouse, Sledgehammer, Fast Times, Tales from the Crypt, The Simpsons, The Flash, Beetlejuice, segments of Amazing Stories (Mummy Dearest, Family Dog), Alfred Hitchcock Presents (The Jar).

ELG, TAINA
Actress, Dancer. b. Helsinki, Finland, March 9, 1930. Trained and performed with Natl. Opera of Finland. Attended Sadler's Wells Ballet Sch. Toured with Swedish Dance Theatre, then Marquis de Cuevas Ballet.
THEATER: Look to the Lilies, Where's Charley?, The Utter Glory of Morrissey Hall, Strider, Nine.
PICTURES: The Prodigal (debut, 1955), Diane, Gaby, Les Girls, Watusi, Imitation General, The 39 Steps, The Bacchae, Liebestraum, The Mirror Has Two Faces.
TELEVISION: *Movie*: The Great Wallendas. *Mini-Series*: Blood and Honor: Youth Under Hitler (narrator). *Special*: O! Pioneers.

ELIAS, HAL
Executive. b. Brooklyn, NY, Dec. 23, 1899. Publicity dir., State Theatre, Denver; western exploitation mgr., MGM; adv. dept., pub. dept., MGM, Culver City studios; Head, MGM cartoon studio (Tom and Jerry); UPA Pictures, Inc., vice-pres. studio mgr.: Hollywood Museum; bd. dir., Academy of Motion Picture Arts & Sciences, 35 years; treasurer, AMPAS 1976-1979. Academy Oscar, 1979, for dedicated and distinguished service to AMPAS.

ELIZONDO, HECTOR
Actor. b. New York, NY, Dec. 22, 1936. m. actress Carolee Campbell. Studied with Ballet Arts Co. of Carnegie Hall and Actors Studio. Many stage credits in N.Y. and Boston.
THEATER: The Prisoner of Second Avenue, Dance of Death, Steambath (Obie Award), The Great White Hope, Sly Fox, The Price.
PICTURES: The Fat Black Pussycat, Valdez Is Coming, Born to Win, Pocket Money, Deadhead Miles, Stand Up and Be Counted, The Taking of Pelham One Two Three, Report to the Commissioner, Thieves, Cuba, American Gigolo, The Fan, Young Doctors in Love, The Flamingo Kid, Private Resort, Nothing in Common, Overboard, Beaches, Leviathan, Pretty Woman (Golden Globe nom.), Taking Care of Business, Necessary Roughness, Frankie and Johnny, Final Approach, Samantha, There Goes the Neighborhood, Being Human, Beverly Hills Cop III, Getting Even With Dad, Exit to Eden, Perfect Alibi, Dear God, Turbulence.
TELEVISION: *Series*: Popi (1976), Casablanca, Freebie and

the Bean; A.K.A. Pablo (also dir.), Foley Sq, Down and Out in Bevery Hills, Fish Police (voice), Chicago Hope. *Guest*: The Wendie Barrie Show (1947), The Impatient Heart, Kojack, the Jackie Gleason Show, All in the Family, The Pirates of Dark Water (voice), Tales of the Crypt. *Movies*: The Impatient Heart, Wanted: The Sundance Woman, Honeyboy, Women of San Quentin, Courage, Out of the Darkness, Addicted to His Love, Your Mother Wears Combat Boots, Forgotten Prisoners: The Amnesty Files, Finding the Way Home, Chains of Gold, The Burden of Proof. *Mini-Series*: The Dain Curse. *Specials*: Medal of Honor Rag, Mrs. Cage.

ELKINS, HILLARD
Producer. b. New York, NY, Oct. 18, 1929. e. NYU, B.A., 1951. Exec., William Morris Agy., 1949-51; exec. v.p., Gen. Artists Corp., 1952-53; pres., Hillard Elkins Mgmt., 1953-60; Elkins Prods. Intl. Corp., N.Y., 1960-71; Elkins Prods. Ltd., 1972-; Hillard Elkins Entertainment Corp., 1974; Media Mix Prods., Inc., 1979-82.
MEMBER: Academy of Motion Picture Arts & Sciences, Acad. of TV Arts & Sciences, Dramatists Guild, League of New York Theatres, American Fed. of TV & Radio Artists.
THEATER: Come On Strong, Golden Boy, Oh Calcutta!, The Rothschilds, A Doll's House, An Evening with Richard Nixon, Sizwe Banzi Is Dead, etc.
PICTURES: Alice's Restaurant, A New Leaf, Oh Calcutta!, A Doll's House, Richard Pryor Live in Concert, Sellers on Sellers.
TELEVISION: The Importance of Being Earnest, The Deadly Game, Princess Daisy, The Meeting (exec. prod.), Father & Son: Dangerous Relations.

ELKINS, SAUL
Producer. b. New York, NY, June 22, 1907. e. City Coll. of New York, B.S., 1927. Radio writer, dir., prod. 1930-2; dir., prod. stock co. touring Latin America 1932-34; writer Fox Films, 20th Century-Fox; writer RKO, Columbia 1937-42; writer, dial-dir., dir. Warner Bros. 1943-7; prod. Warner Bros. since 1947. Member: AMPAS, Screen Writer's Guild. Exec. prod., Comprenetics, Inc. Dir., Pioneer Prods., 1982.
PICTURES: Younger Brothers, One Last Fling, Homicide, House Across the Street, Flaxy Martin, Barricade, Return of the Frontiersmen, This Side of the Law, Colt .45, Sugarfoot, Raton Pass, The Big Punch, Smart Girls Don't Talk, Embraceable You.

ELLIOTT, CHRIS
Actor, Writer. b. New York, NY, May 31, 1960. Father is comedian Bob Elliott. Was performer in improv. theatres, summer stock; also tour guide at Rockefeller Center. Became writer/performer for David Letterman starting in 1982. *Author*: Daddy's Boy: A Son's Shocking Account of Life With a Famous Father (1989).
PICTURES: Manhunter (debut, 1986), The Abyss, Hyperspace, Groundhog Day, CB4, Cabin Boy (also co-story), Kingpin.
TELEVISION: *Series*: Late Night With David Letterman (also co- writer; 2 Emmy Awards for writing: 1984, 1985), Nick and Hillary, Get a Life (also creator, co-writer, prod.). *Specials*: Late Night With David Letterman Anniversary Specials (also co-writer; 2 Emmy Awards for writing: 1986, 1987), Chris Elliott's FDR: One-Man Show (also writer, prod.).

ELLIOTT, LANG
Producer, Director. b. Los Angeles, CA, Oct. 18, 1949. Began acting in films at an early age, influenced by his uncle, the late actor William Elliott (known as Wild Bill Elliott). Employed by, among others the McGowan Brothers. Turned to film production; co-founded distribution co., The International Picture Show Co., serving as exec. v.p. in chg. of financing, production & distribution. In 1976 formed TriStar Pictures, Inc. to finance and distribute product. In 1980 sold TriStar to Columbia, HBO and CBS. 1982, formed Lang Elliott Productions, Inc. Co-founded Longshot Enterprises with actor Tim Conway to prod. films and home videos, 1985. Videos include Dorf on Golf (the first made-for-home-video comedy), 'Scuse Me!, Dorf and the First Olympic Games. Formed Performance Pictures, Inc., in 1989, a prod. & distrib. company. Received Academy Award nom. for Soldier of Orange and The Magic of Lassie.
PICTURES: *Prod*: Ride the Hot Wind, Where Time Began, The Farmer, The Billion Dollar Hobo, They Went That-a-Way & That-a-Way, The Prize Fighter. *Prod.-dir.*: The Private Eyes, Cage, Cage II, and over 40 other pictures.
TELEVISION: Experiment in Love (prod.), Boys Will Be Boys (writer).

ELLIOTT, SAM
Actor. b. Sacramento, CA, Aug. 9, 1944. m. actress Katharine Ross. e. U. of Oregon.
PICTURES: Butch Cassidy and the Sundance Kid (debut in bit, 1969), The Games, Frogs, Molly and Lawless John, Lifeguard, The Legacy, Mask, Fatal Beauty, Shakedown, Road House, Prancer, Sibling Rivalry, Rush, Gettysburg, Tombstone.

TELEVISION: *Movies*: The Challenge, Assault on the Wayne, The Blue Knight, I Will Fight No More Forever, The Sacketts, Wild Times, Murder in Texas, Shadow Riders, Travis McGee, A Death in California. The Blue Lightning, Houston: The Legend of Texas, The Quick and the Dead, Conagher (also co-writer, exec. prod.), Fugitive Nights: Danger in the Desert, Buffalo Girls, The Ranger the Cook and a Hole in the Sky. *Series*: Mission: Impossible, The Yellow Rose. *Mini-Series*: Once and Eagle, Aspen (The Innocent and the Damned). *Guest*: Lancer, The FBI, Gunsmoke, Streets of San Francisco, Hawaii 5-0, Police Woman. *Pilot*: Evel Knievel.

ELWES, CARY
Actor. b. London, England, Oct. 26, 1962. e. Harrow. Studied for stage with Julie Bovasso at Sarah Lawrence, Bronxville, NY.
PICTURES: Another Country (debut 1984), Oxford Blues, The Bride, Lady Jane, The Princess Bride, Glory, Days of Thunder, Leather Jackets, Hot Shots!, Bram Stoker's Dracula, The Crush, Robin Hood: Men in Tights, Rudyard Kipling's The Jungle Book, Twister.

EMMERICH, ROLAND
Director, Writer, Exec. Producer. b. Germany. Studied production design in film school in Munich. First film was student production, The Noah's Ark Principle, which opened the 1984 Berlin Film Festival and was sold to more than 20 countries. Formed Centropolis Film Productions.
PICTURES: *Co-s.p./Dir.*:Making Contact (a.k.a. Joey; dir. only), Ghost Chase, Eye of the Storm (prod. only), Moon 44, Universal Soldier, Stargate, Independence Day.

ENGEL, CHARLES F.
Executive. b. Los Angeles, CA, Aug. 30. e. Michigan State U., UCLA. Son of writer-producer Samuel G. Engel. Pgm. devel., ABC-TV, 1964-68; v.p. Univ.-TV, 1972; sr. v.p., 1977; exec. v.p., 1980; pres., MCA Pay-TV Programming, 1981. ACE Award, 1988 for outstanding contribution to cable; v.p. Universal TV, exec. in chg. ABC Mystery Movie, 1989. Sr. v.p. 1992 in chg. Columbo, Murder She Wrote, SeaQuest, The Rockford Files. Founding member board of governors, the National Academy of Cable Programming. Member, Television Academy.
TELEVISION: The Aquarians (exec. prod.), Run a Crooked Mile (exec. prod.), Road Raiders (prod.), ABC Mystery Movie (exec. in chg. of prod.).

ENGELBERG, MORT
Producer. b. Memphis, TN. e. U. of Illinois, U. of Missouri. Taught journalism; worked as reporter for UPI, AP. Worked for US government, including USIA, Peace Corps., Office of Economic Opportunity; President's Task Force on War on Poverty. Left gov. service in 1967 to become film unit publicist, working on three films in Europe: Dirty Dozen, Far From the Madding Crowd, The Comedians. Returned to U.S.; appt. pub. mgr. for United Artists. Sent to Hollywood as asst. to Herb Jaffe, UA head of west coast prod., which post he assumed when Jaffe left. Left to join indep. prod., Ray Stark.
PICTURES: Smokey and the Bandit, Hot Stuff, The Villain, The Hunter, Smokey and the Bandit II, Smokey and the Bandit III, Nobody's Perfekt, The Heavenly Kid, The Big Easy, Maid to Order, Dudes, Three For the Road, Russkies, Pass the Ammo, Trading Hearts, Fright Night Part 2, Rented Lips, Remote Control.

ENGLANDER, MORRIS K.
Executive. b. New York, NY, July 5, 1934. e. Wharton Sch., U. of Pennsylvania. With General Cinema Corp. circuit before joining RKO Century Warner Theatres 1984 as exec. v.p., develp.; later co-vice chmn. of circuit. 1986, sr. real estate advisor, American Multi-Cinema. 1988: v.p. real estate Hoyts Cinemas Corp.; 1990 COO of Hoyts; pres. & COO of Hoyts. 1991.

ENGLUND, ROBERT
Actor. b. Glendale, CA, June 6, 1949. e. UCLA, RADA. First significant role was in the Cleveland stage production of Godspell, 1971.
PICTURES: Buster and Billie, Hustle, Stay Hungry, Death Trap (Eaten Alive), The Last of the Cowboys, St. Ives, A Star is Born, Big Wednesday, Bloodbrothers, The Fifth Floor, Dead and Buried, Galaxy of Terror, Don't Cry It's Only Thunder, A Nightmare on Elm Street, A Nightmare on Elm Street Part 2: Freddy's Revenge, Never Too Young to Die, A Nightmare on Elm Street 3: Dream Warriors, A Nightmare on Elm Street 4: The Dream Master, 976-EVIL (dir. only), A Nightmare on Elm Street: The Dream Child, Phantom of the Opera, The Adventures of Ford Fairlane, Danse Macabre, Freddy's Dead: The Final Nightmare, Eugenie, Wes Craven's New Nightmare, The Mangler, The Paper Route, Vampyre Wars, Killer Tongue, Regeneration.
TELEVISION: *Series*: Downtown, V, Freddy's Nightmares, Nightmare Cafe. *Specials and Movies*: Hobson's Choice, Young Joe: The Forgotten Kennedy, The Ordeal of Patty

Hearst, The Courage and the Passion, Mind Over Murder, Thou Shalt Not Kill, The Fighter, Journey's End, Starflight: The Plane That Couldn't Land, I Want to Live, Infidelity, A Perry Mason Mystery: The Case of the Lethal Lifestyle, Robin Cook's Mortal Fear, The Unspoken Truth. *Mini-Series*: V, North and South Book II. *Host*: Horror Hall of Fame.

EPHRON, NORA
Writer, Director. b. New York, NY, May 19, 1941. e. Wellesley Col. Daughter of writers Henry and Phoebe Ephron. m. writer Nicholas Pileggi. *Author*: Heartburn, Crazy Salad, Scribble Scribble. Appeared in films Crimes and Misdemeanors, Husbands and Wives.
PICTURES: *Writer*: Silkwood, Heartburn, When Harry Met Sally... (also assoc. prod.), Cookie (also exec. prod.), My Blue Heaven (also exec. prod.), This is My Life (also dir.), Sleepless in Seattle (also dir.), Mixed Nuts (also dir.), Michael (also dir.).
TELEVISION: *Movie (writer)*: Perfect Gentlemen.

EPSTEIN, JULIUS J
Screenwriter. b. New York, NY, Aug. 22, 1909. e. Pennsylvania State U. Worked as publicist before going to Hollywood where began writing. Had long collaboration with twin brother, Philip G. Epstein. Under contract with Warner Bros. over 17 years.
PICTURES: In Caliente, Broadway Gondolier, Four Daughters, Daughters Courageous, Four Wives, Saturday's Children, No Time for Comedy, The Strawberry Blonde, The Bride Came C.O.D., The Man Who Came to Dinner, The Male Animal, Casablanca (Academy Award, 1943), Arsenic and Old Lace, Mr. Skeffington (also co-prod.), Romanc on the High Seas, My Foolish Heart, Forever Female, The Last Time I Saw Paris, Young at Heart, The Tender Trap, Kiss Them for Me, Take a Giant Step (also prod.), Tall Story, Fanny, Light in the Piazza, Send Me No Flowers, Return From the Ashes, Any Wednesday (also prod.), Pete n' Tillie (also prod.), Jacqueline Susann's Once Is Not Enough, Cross of Iron, House Calls, Reuben Reuben (also co-prod.).

EPSTEIN, MEL
Producer. b. Dayton, OH, Mar. 25, 1910; e. Ohio State U. Adv. & edit. depts. on newspapers; entered m.p. ind. as player in 1931; then asst. dir., unit prod. mgr., second unit & shorts dir.; U.S. Army Signal Corps (1st Lt.); apptd. Paramount prod., 1946. Now retired.
PICTURES: Whispering Smith, Hazard, Copper Canyon, Dear Brat, Branded, The Savage, Alaska Seas, Secret of the Incas.
TELEVISION: Broken Arrow, Men into Space, The Islanders, Asphalt Jungle, Rawhide, Long Hot Summer, The Monroes, Custer, Lancer (pilot), Lancer (unit mngr., series), Medical Center (series).

ERDMAN, RICHARD
Actor, Director. b. Enid, OK, June 1, 1925. e. Hollywood H.S.
PICTURES: *Actor*: Janie, Objective Burma, Time of Your Life, Four Days Leave, The Men, Cry Danger, Jumping Jacks, Happy Time, The Stooge, Stalag 17, The Power and the Prize, Saddle the Wind, Namu The Killer Whale. *Director*: Bleep, The Brothers O'Toole. *Writer-Prod.*: The Hillerman Project.
TELEVISION: Ray Bolger Show, Perry Mason, Police Story, Tab Hunter Show, Alice, Bionic Woman, One Day at a Time, Playhouse of Stars, Twilight Zone, The Lucy Show, Lou Grant, Cheers, Wings. *Movie*: Jesse. *Director*: The Dick Van Dyke Show, Mooch (special). *Writer-Prod.*: More Than a Scarecrow.

ERICSON, JOHN
Actor. b. Detroit, MI, Sept. 25, 1926. e. American Acad. of Dramatic Arts. Appeared in summer stock; then Stalag 17 on Broadway.
PICTURES: Teresa (debut, 1951), Rhapsody, The Student Prince, Green Fire, Bad Day at Black Rock, The Return of Jack Slade, The Cruel Tower, Oregon Passage, Forty Guns, Day of the Bad Man, Pretty Boy Floyd, Under Ten Flags, Slave Queen of Babylon, 7 Faces of Dr. Lao, Operation Atlantis, The Money Jungle, The Destructors, Treasure of Pancho Villa, The Bamboo Saucer (Collision Course), Heads or Tails, Bedknobs and Broomsticks, Hustle Squad, Crash, Final Mission, Alien Zone, Project Saucer, Golden Triangle, Queens Are Wild, Hustler Squad, $10,000 Caper.
TELEVISION: *Series*: Honey West. *Movies*: The Bounty Man, Hog Wild, Hunter's Moon, House on the Rue Riviera, Tenafly. *Mini-Series*: Robert Kennedy and His Times, Space. *Specials*: Saturday's Children, Heritage of Anger, The Innocent Sleep. *Guest*: Marcus Welby, Mannix, Streets of San Francisco, Fantasy Island, Bonanza, Medical Center, Route 66, Murder She Wrote, Police Story, General Hospital, Air Wolf, Gunsmoke, Police Woman, The FBI, One Day at a Time, Magnum P.I.

ERMAN, JOHN
Director. b. Chicago, IL, Aug. 3, 1935. e. U. of California. Debut as TV director, Stoney Burke, 1962.
PICTURES: Making It, Ace Eli and Rodger of the Skies, Stella.

TELEVISION: *Movies*: Letters From Three Lovers, Green Eyes, Alexander the Other Side of Dawn, Just Me and You, My Old Man, Moviola (This Year's Blonde; Scarlett O'Hara War; The Silent Lovers), The Letter, Eleanor: First Lady of the World, Who Will Love My Children? (Emmy Award, 1983), Another Woman's Child, A Streetcar Named Desire, Right to Kill?, The Atlanta Child Murders, An Early Frost, The Two Mrs. Grenvilles (also sprv. prod.), When the Time Comes, The Attic: The Hiding of Anne Frank (also prod.), David (also sprv. prod.), The Last Best Year (also sprv. prod.), The Last to Go (also prod.), Our Sons, Carolina Skeletons, Breathing Lessons (also prod.), The Sunshine Boys (also prod.). *Mini-Series*: Roots: The Next Generations (co-dir.), Queen (also co-prod.), Scarlett (also prod.).

ESBIN, JERRY
Executive. b. Brooklyn, NY, 1931. Started in mailroom at Columbia at 17 and worked for nc. nearly 25 years. Then joined American Multi Cinema. Joined Paramount Pictures in 1975 as mgr. of branch operations; later named v.p., asst. sls. mgr. In 1980 named v.p., gen. sls. mgr. 1981, v.p., domestic sls. & mktg. 1981, joined United Artists as sr. v.p., mktg. & dist.; 1982, named pres., MGM/UA m.p. dist. & mktg. div; 1983, sr. v.p., domestic dist., Tri-Star Pictures; 1985, promoted to exec. v.p.; 1989, joined Loews Theaters as sr. exec. v.p. and chief oper. officer, also in 1989 named pres. as well as chief operating officer, Loews Theater Management Corp.

ESMOND, CARL
Actor. b. Vienna, Austria, June 14, 1906. e. U. of Vienna. On stage Vienna, Berlin, London (Shakespeare, Shaw, German modern classics). Acted in many European films under the name Willy Eichberger. Originated part of Prince Albert in Victoria Regina (London). On screen in Brit. prod. incl. Blossom Time, Even Song, Invitation to the Waltz. To U.S. in 1938. Guest star on many live and filmed TV shows. US stage incl. The Woman I Love, Four Winds. Appeared in Oscar nom. docum. Resisting Enemy Interrogation.
PICTURES: Dawn Patrol, First Comes Courage, Little Men, Sergeant York, Panama Hattie, Seven Sweethearts, Address Unknown, Margin for Error, Master Race, Ministry of Fear, Experiment Perilous, Story of Dr. Wassell. The Catman of Paris, Smash-up, Story of a Woman, Casablanca, Climax, Slave Girl, Walk a Crooked Mile, The Navy Comes Through, Sundown, Lover Come Back, This Love of Ours, Without Love, Mystery Submarine, The Desert Hawk, The World in His Arms, Thunder in the Sun, From the Earth to the Moon, Brushfire, Kiss of Evil, Agent for H.A.R.M., Morituri.
TELEVISION: My Wicked Wicked Ways. *Guest*: The Man From Uncle, Lassie, The Big Valley, Treasury Agent, etc.

ESPOSITO, GIANCARLO
Actor. b. Copenhagen, Denmark, April 26, 1958. Made B'way debut as child in 1968 musical Maggie Flynn.
THEATER: *B'way*: Maggie Flynn, The Me Nobody Knows, Lost in the Stars, Seesaw, Merrily We Roll Along, Don't Get God Started. *Off-B'way*: Zooman and the Sign (Theatre World Award, Obie Award), Keyboard, Who Loves the Dancer, House of Ramon Igleslas, Do Lord Remember Me, Balm in Gilead, Anchorman, Distant Fires, Trafficking in Broken Hearts.
PICTURES: Running, Taps, Trading Places, The Cotton Club, Desperately Seeking Susan, Maximum Overdrive, Sweet Lorraine, School Daze, Do the Right Thing, Mo'Better Blues, King of New York, Harley Davidson and the Marlboro Man, Night on Earth, Bob Roberts, Malcolm X, Amos & Andrew, Fresh, Smoke, The Usual Suspects, Kla$h, Blue in the Face, Reckless.
TELEVISION: *Series*: Bakersfield P.D. *Movies*: The Gentleman Bandit, Go Tell It on the Mountain, Relentless: Mind of a Killer. *Special*: Roanok. *Guest*: Miami Vice, Spencer: For Hire, Legwork.

ESSEX, DAVID
Actor, Singer, Composer. b. Plaistow, London, Eng. July 23, 1947. e. Shipman Sch., Custom House. Started as a singer-drummer in East London band. 1967: Joined touring Repertory Co. in The Fantasticks, Oh, Kay, etc. 1970: West End debut in Ten Years Hard, 1972: Jesus Christ in Godspell, Che in Evita; Lord Byron in Childe Byron, 1983-84: Fletcher Christian in own musical Mutiny! on album and stage. International recording artist. Variety Club of Great Britain show business personality of 1978. Many gold & silver disc intl. awards. 1989, Royal Variety performance. World concerts since 1974.
PICTURES: Assault, All Coppers Are..., That'll Be the Day, Stardust, Silver Dream Racer (also wrote score), Shogun Mayeda.
TELEVISION: Top of the Pops, Own Specials, The River (also composed music), BBC series. U.S.: Merv Griffin, Johnny Carson, Dinah Shore, American Bandstand, Midnight Special, Grammy Awards, Salute To The Beatles, Don Kirshner's Rock Concert, A.M. America, Phil Everly in Session, Paul Ryan Show.

113

ESSEX, HARRY J.
Writer. b. New York, NY, Nov. 29, 1915. e. St. John's U., Brooklyn, B.A. With Dept. Welfare. Wrote orig. story, Man Made Monster, for Universal. During W.W.II in U.S. Army Signal Corps; scenarist, training films on combat methods, censorship. Novels: I Put My Right Foot In, Man and Boy, Marina.
THEATER: Something for Nothing, Stronger Than Brass, Neighborhood Affair, One for the Dame, Fatty, Twilight, When the Bough Breaks, Dark Passion, Casa D'Amor, I Remember It Well, Maurice Chevalier.
PICTURES: Boston Blackie and the Law, Dangerous Business, Desperate, Bodyguard, He Walked by Night, Dragnet, Killer That Stalked New York, Wyoming Mail, The Fat Man, Undercover Girl, Las Vegas Story, Models Inc., Kansas City Confidential, The 49th Man, It Came From Outer Space, I the Jury (also dir.), Creature from the Black Lagoon, Southwest Passage, Devil's Canyon, Mad at the World (also dir.), Teen-age Crime Wave, Raw Edge, Lonely Man, The Sons of Katie Elder, Man and Boy, Octoman, The Cremators (also prod., dir.), The Amigos.
TELEVISION: Untouchables, The Racers, Alcoa Hour, Westinghouse, Desilu; story consultant and head writer: Target, The Corruptors, The Dick Powell Show, Bewitched, I Dream of Jeannie, Kraft Suspense Theatre, Hostage Flight.

ESTEVEZ, EMILIO
Actor, Director, Writer. b. New York, NY, May 12, 1962. Father is actor Martin Sheen; brother is actor Charlie Sheen. Made prof. debut at age 20 in tv movie starring his father, In the Custody of Strangers.
PICTURES: Tex (debut, 1982), The Outsiders, Nightmares, Repo Man, The Breakfast Club, St. Elmo's Fire, That Was Then This is Now (also s.p.), Maximum Overdrive, Wisdom (also dir., s.p.), Stakeout, Young Guns. Men at Work (also dir., s.p.), Young Guns II, Freejack, The Mighty Ducks, National Lampoon's Loaded Weapon 1, Another Stakeout, Judgment Night, D2: The Mighty Ducks, The Jerky Boys (co- exec. prod. only), The War at Home, Mighty Ducks 3.
TELEVISION: Movies: In the Custody of Strangers. Nightbreaker.

ESTRADA, ERIK
Actor. r.n. Enrique Estrada. m. actress Peggy Rowe. b. New York, NY, Mar. 16, 1949. Began professional career in Mayor John Lindsay's Cultural Program, performing in public parks. Joined American Musical Dramatic Acad. for training. Feature film debut in The Cross and the Switchblade (1970).
PICTURES: The New Centurions, Airport '75, Midway, Trackdown, Where Is Parsifal?, Lightblast, The Repentant, Hour of the Assassin, The Lost Idol, A Show of Force, Night of the Wilding, Twisted Justice, Caged Fury, Guns, Spirits, Do or Die, The Divine Enforcer, Alien Seed, Night of the Wilding, National Lampoon's Loaded Weapon 1, The Last Riders, Gang Justice.
TELEVISION: Series: CHiPS. Guest: Hawaii Five-0, Six Million Dollar Man, Police Woman, Kojak, Medical Center, Hunter, Alfred Hitchcock Presents (1988), Cybill. Movies: Fire!, Honeyboy, The Dirty Dozen: The Fatal Mission, She Knows Too Much, Earth Angel.

ESZTERHAS, JOE
Writer. Author of novel Charlie Simpson's Apocalypse (nom. National Book Award, 1974), Nark!, and novelization of F.I.S.T.
PICTURES: F.I.S.T., Flashdance, Jagged Edge, Big Shots, Betrayed, Checking Out, Music Box (also exec. prod.), Basic Instinct, Nowhere to Run (co-sp., co-exec. prod.), Sliver (also co-exec. prod.), Jade (exec. prod. only), Hearts of Fire.

ETTINGER, EDWIN D.
Publicist. b. New York, NY, 1921. Entered m.p. ind. as office boy, MGM; pub. rel. and publ. for industrial, comm. clients, 1946-52; joined Ettinger Co., pub. rel., 1952; pub. rel. dir., Disneyland Inc., 1955; marketing dir., Disneyland, 1955-65; v.p., M.C.A. Enterprises, Inc., 1965-66; Board chmn. & CEO Recreation Environments, Inc., 1967-70; Board chmn. & CEO Recreations Inc., 1967-70; Pres., Ettinger, Inc., 1975-85; semi-retired in 1985.

ETTLINGER, JOHN A.
Producer, Director, Distributor. b. Chicago, IL, Oct. 14, 1924. e. Peddie Inst., Cheshire Acad. Signal Corps Photog. Center, 1942-45; with Paramount Theatres Corp., 1945-47; dir., KTLA, Paramount TV Prod., Inc., Los Angeles, 1948-50; radio-TV dir., Nat. C. Goldstone Agency, 1950-53; pres. Medallion TV Enterprises, Inc.; TV prod., View the Clue, Greenwich Village, High Road to Danger, Sur Demande, Star Route, Las Vegas Fights, Celebrity Billiards; Pres., KUDO-FM, Las Vegas.

EVANS, BARRY
Actor, Director. b. Guildford, England, 1943. Trained Central School. Repertory: Barrow, Nottingham, Chester, Royal Court,

Nat. Theatre, Hampstead Th. Club, Chips with Everything, London and B'way Young Vic. Theatre Clwyd Mold.
PICTURES: The White Bus, Here We Go 'Round the Mulberry Bush, Alfred the Great, Die Screaming, Marriane, The Adventures of a Taxi-Driver, Under the Doctor.
TELEVISION: Redcap, Undermined, The Baron, The Class, Armchair Theatre, Love Story, Doctor in the House, Doctor at Large, Short Story, Crossroads, Mind Your Language, Dick Emery Show.

EVANS, GENE
Actor. b. Holbrook, AZ, July 11, 1924. e. Colton H.S. Started career in summer stock, Penthouse Theatre, Altadena, CA. Screen debut: Under Colorado Skies, 1947.
PICTURES: Crisscross, Larceny, Berlin Express, Assigned to Danger, Mother Was a Freshman, Sugarfoot, Armored Car Robbery, Steel Helmet, I Was an American Spy, Force of Arms, Jet Pilot, Fixed Bayonets, Mutiny, Park Row, Thunderbirds, Donovan's Brain, Golden Blade, Hell and High Water, Long Wait, Cattle Queen of Montana, Wyoming Renegades, Crashout, Helen Morgan Story, Bravados, Sad Sack, The Hangman, Operation Petticoat, Support Your Local Sheriff, War Wagon, Nevada Smith, Young and Wild, Ballad of Cable Hogue, There Was a Crooked Man, Support Your Local Gunfighter, Camper John, Walking Tall, People Toys, Pat Garrett and Billy the Kid, Magic of Lassie, Blame It on the Night.
TELEVISION: Series: My Friend Flicka, Matt Helm, Spencer's Pilots. Movies: Kate Bliss & Ticker Tape Kid, Fire, The Sacketts, Shadow Riders, Travis McGee, The Alamo: 13 Days to Glory, Once Upon a Texas Train, Casino, Concrete Cowboys, Shootout in a One-Dog Town.

EVANS, LINDA
Actress. b. Hartford, CT, Nov. 18, 1942. e. Hollywood H.S., L.A. TV commercials led to contract with MGM.
PICTURES: Twilight of Honor (debut, 1963), Those Calloways, Beach Blanket Bingo, The Klansman, Mitchell, Avalanche Express, Tom Horn.
TELEVISION: Series: The Big Valley, Hunter, Dynasty. Movies: Nakia, Nowhere to Run, Standing Tall, Gambler: The Adventure Continues, Bare Essence, The Last Frontier, I'll Take Romance, Dynasty: The Reunion, The Gambler Returns: Luck of the Draw. Mini-Series: North & South Book II, Dazzle.

EVANS, RAY
Songwriter. b. Salamanca, NY, Feb. 4, 1915. e. Wharton Sch. of U. of Pennsylvania. Musician on cruise ships, radio writer spec. material. Hellzapoppin', Sons o' Fun. Member: exec. bd. Songwriters Guild of America, Dramatists Guild, West Coast advisory bd. ASCAP., bd., Myasthenia Gravis Fdn. CA chap., Songwriters Hall of Fame, Motion Picture Acad. Received star on Hollywood Blvd. Walk of Fame.
SONGS: To Each His Own, Golden Earrings, Buttons and Bows (Academy Award, 1948), Mona Lisa (Academy Award, 1950), Whatever Will Be Will Be (Academy Award, 1956), A Thousand Violins, I'll Always Love You, Dreamsville, Love Song from Houseboat, Tammy, Silver Bells, Dear Heart, Angel, Never Let Me Go, Almost in Your Arms, As I Love You, In the Arms of Love, Wish Me a Rainbow.
PICTURES: The Paleface, Sorrowful Jones, Fancy Pants, My Friend Irma, Aaron Slick From Punkin Crick, Son of the Paleface, My Friend Irma Goes West, The Night of Grizzly, Saddle the Wind, Isn't It Romantic, Capt. Carey U.S.A., Off Limits, Here Come the Girls, Red Garters, Man Who Knew Too Much, Stars Are Singing, Tammy, Houseboat, Blue Angel, A Private's Affair, All Hands on Deck, Dear Heart, The Third Day, What Did You Do in the War Daddy?, This Property Is Condemned.
BROADWAY MUSICALS: Oh Captain! Let It Ride!, Sugar Babies.
TELEVISION THEMES: Bonanza, Mr. Ed, Mr. Lucky, To Rome With Love.

EVANS, ROBERT
Producer. b. New York, NY, June 29, 1930. Son is actor Josh Evans. Radio actor at age 11; went on to appear in more than 300 radio prog. (incl. Let's Pretend, Archie Andrews, The Aldrich Family, Gangbusters) on major networks. Also appeared on early TV. At 20 joined brother, Charles, and Joseph Picone, as partner in women's clothing firm of Evan-Picone, Inc., 1952-67. In 1957 signed by Universal to play Irving Thalberg in Man of a Thousand Faces after recommendation by Norma Shearer, Thalberg's widow. Guest columnist NY Journal American, 1958. Independent prod. at 20th Century-Fox. 1966-76, with Paramount Pictures as head of prod., then exec. v.p. worldwide prod. (supervising Barefoot in the Park, Rosemary's Baby, Barbarella, Goodbye Columbus, Love Story, The Godfather I & II, The Great Gatsby, etc.). Resigned to become indep. prod. again; with exclusive contract with Paramount. Autobiography: The Kid Stays in the Picture (1994).
PICTURES: Actor: Man of a Thousand Faces, The Sun Also Rises, The Fiend Who Walked the West, The Best of

Everything. *Producer*: Chinatown, Marathon Man, Black Sunday, Players, Urban Cowboy, Popeye, The Cotton Club, The Two Jakes, Sliver, Jade, The Phantom.
TELEVISION: *Actor*: Elizabeth and Essex (1947), Young Widow Brown, The Right to Happiness. *Prod.*: Get High on Yourself.

EVERETT, CHAD
Actor. r.n. Raymond Lee Cramton. b. South Bend, IN, June 11, 1937. e. Wayne State U., Detroit. Signed by William T. Orr, head of TV prod. for Warner Bros. to 7-year contract. Appeared in many TV series as well as films. Next became contract player at MGM (1963-67). Received star on Hollywood Walk of Fame.
PICTURES: Claudelle Inglish (debut, 1961), The Chapman Report, Rome Adventure, Get Yourself a College Girl, The Singing Nun, Made in Paris, Johnny Tiger, The Last Challenge, Return of the Gunfighter, First to Fight, The Impossible Years, Firechasers, Airplane II: The Sequel, Fever Pitch, Jigsaw, Heroes Stand Alone, Official Denial.
TELEVISION: *Series*: The Dakotas, Medical Center, Hagen, The Rousters, McKenna, Dark Skies (narr. of pilot). *Guest*: Hawaiian Eye, 77 Sunset Strip, Surfside Six, Lawman, Bronco, The Lieutenant, Redigo, Route 66, Ironside, Hotel, Murder She Wrote, Shades of L.A., Cybil. *Movies*: Intruder, The Love Boat, Police Story, Thunderboat Row, Malibu, The French Atlantic Affair, Mistress in Paradise, Journey to the Unknown, In the Glitter Palace. *Mini-Series*: Centennial.

EVERETT, RUPERT
Actor. b. Norfolk, England, 1959. e. Ampleforth Central School for Speech & Drama. Apprenticed with Glasgow's Citizen's Theatre. Originated role of Guy Bennett in Another Country on London stage in 1982 and made feature film debut in screen version in 1984. Author: Are You Working Darling?
PICTURES: Another Country, Real Life, Dance with a Stranger, Duet for One, Chronicle of a Death Foretold, The Right Hand Man, Hearts of Fire, The Gold-Rimmed Glasses, Jigsaw, The Comfort of Strangers, Inside Monkey Zetterland, Ready to Wear (Pret-a-Porter), The Madness of King George, Dunston Checks In, Cemetary Man.
TELEVISION: Arthur the King, The Far Pavilions, Princess Daisy.

EVERSON, WILLIAM K.
Writer. b. Yeovil, Eng., April 8, 1929. Pub. dir., Renown Pictures Corp., Ltd., London, 1944; film critic; m.p. journalist; in armed forces, 1947-49; thea. mgr.; pub. & booking consultant, Monseigneur News Theatres, London, 1949; pub. dir., Allied Artists Inc. Corp., 1951; prod.; writer Paul Killiam Dorg., 1956. Writer-editor-researcher on TV series Movie Museum and Silents Please, also on TV specials and theatrical features Hollywood the Golden Years, The Valentino Legend, The Love Goddesses and The Great Director. Lecturer, archival consultant, American Film Institute representative. Film History instructor at NYU, The New School and Sch. of Visual Arts, all in NY. Also, Harvard U.
AUTHOR: The Western, The Bad Guys, The American Movie, The Films of Laurel & Hardy, The Art of W. C. Fields, Hal Roach, The Detective in Film, Classics of the Horror Film, Claudette Colbert.
(d. April 14, 1996)

EVIGAN, GREG
Actor. b. South Amboy, NJ, Oct. 14, 1953. Appeared on NY stage in Jesus Christ Superstar and Grease.
PICTURES: Stripped to Kill, DeepStar Six.
TELEVISION: *Series*: A Year at the Top, B.J. and the Bear, Masquerade, My Two Dads, P.S. I Luv U, Tek War. *Movies*: B.J. and the Bear (pilot), Private Sessions, The Lady Forgets, Lies Before Kisses, Tek War, Tek Justice, One of Her Own, Tek Lab, Tek Lords. *Guest*: One Day at a Time, Barnaby Jones, Murder She Wrote, New Mike Hammer, Matlock.

F

FABARES, SHELLEY
Actress. b. Los Angeles, CA, Jan. 19, 1944. r.n. Michele Marie Fabares. m. actor Mike Farrell. Earned gold record for 1962 single Johnny Angel.
PICTURES: Never Say Goodbye, Rock Pretty Baby, Marjorie Morningstar, Summer Love, Ride the Wild Surf, Girl Happy, Hold On!, Spinout, Clambake, A Time to Sing, Hot Pursuit, Love or Money.
TELEVISION: *Series*: Annie Oakley, The Donna Reed Show, The Little People (The Brian Keith Show), The Practice, Mary Hartman Mary Hartman, Highcliffe Manor, One Day at a Time, Coach. *Guest*: Twilight Zone, Mr. Novak, Love American Style, The Rookies, Marcus Welby, Hello Larry. *Movies*: U.M.C., Brian's Song, Two for the Money, Sky Hei$t, Pleasure Cove, Friendships Secrets & Lies, The Great American Traffic Jam (Gridlock), Memorial Day, Class Cruise, Deadly Relations, The Great Mom Swap.

FAHEY, JEFF
Actor. b. Olean, NY, Nov. 29, 1956. Family moved to Buffalo when he was 10 years old. Was member of Joffrey Ballet for 3 years. Appeared on B'way in Brigadoon (1980), tour of Oklahoma!, Paris prod. of West Side Story, and London prod. of Orphans.
PICTURES: Silverado (debut, 1985), Psycho III, Split Decisions, Backfire, Outback, True Blood, Out of Time, Last of the Finest, Impulse, White Hunter Black Heart, Body Parts, Iron Maze, The Lawnmower Man, Wrangler, Woman of Desire, Freefall, Wyatt Earp, Temptation.
TELEVISION: *Series*: One Life to Live, The Marshal. *Movies*: Execution of Raymond Graham, Parker Kane, Curiosity Kills, Iran: Days of Crisis, Sketch Artist, In the Company of Darkness, The Hit List, Blindsided, Quick, Sketch Artist II: Hands That See, Virtual Seduction.

FAIMAN, PETER
Director. b. Australia. Entered entertainment business through TV, involved early in production-direction of major variety series in Australia. Assoc. prod.-dir. of over 20 programs for The Paul Hogan Show and two Hogan specials filmed in England (1983). Developed Australia's most popular and longest-running national variety program, The Don Lane Show. Responsible for creative development of the TV Week Logie Awards on the Nine Network. For 4 years headed Special Projects Division of the Nine Network Australia. Resigned to establish own prod. co., Peter Faiman Prods. Fty. 1984. Made m.p. theatrical film debut as director of Crocodile Dundee, followed by Dutch.

FAIRBANKS, DOUGLAS, JR.
K.B.E., (Hon.) D.S.C., M.A., (Oxon), (Hon.) D.F.I., Westminster (Fulton, MO), (Hon.) LL.D (Denver). **Actor, Producer, Executive**. b. New York, NY, Dec. 9, 1909. e. Pasadena (CA) Polytech. Sch.; Harvard Mil. Acad., Los Angeles; Bovee and Collegiate Sch., N.Y.; was also tutored in Paris, London. Son of late Douglas Fairbanks. Began as screen actor 1923 in Stephen Steps Out; thereafter in more than 80 pictures. On U.S. stage from 1926. Formed own film prod. co. 1935; commissioned Lieut. (j.g.) USNR, 1940; Appt. Presidential envoy to certain South Amer. nations by Pres. Roosevelt. Helped org. British War Relief and was natl. chmn., Committee for CARE. W.A. White Committee to Defend America 1939-41. Promoted through ranks to Capt., USNR, Now retired. Awarded U.S. Silver Star, Combat Legion of Merit with "V" Attachment; Knight Commander of Order of British Empire, 1949. Distinguished Service Cross, Knight of Justice of Order of St. John of Jerusalem; French Legion of Honor, Croix de Guerre with Palm, etc. Chairman, American Relief for Korea. Entered TV film prod., 1952. Autobiographies: The Fairbanks Album (1975; with Richard Schickel), The Salad Days (1988), A Hell of a War (1993). FYI: republished in England, 1995.
THEATER: U.S.: Young Woodley, Saturday's Children, Present Laughter, Out on a Limb, Sleuth, The Pleasure of His Company (also U.K., Ireland, Canada, Australia, Hong Kong), The Winding Journey, Moonlight in Silver, My Fair Lady, The Secretary Bird.
PICTURES: (since sound): The Forward Pass, The Careless Age, The Show of Shows, Party Girl, Loose Ankles, The Little Accident, The Dawn Patrol, Little Caesar, Outward Bound, One Night at Susie's, Chances, I Like Your Nerve, Union Depot, It's Tough to Be Famous, Love is a Racket, Parachute Jumper, Morning Glory, Life of Jimmy Dolan, The Narrow Corner, Captured, Catherine the Great, Success at Any Price, Mimi, The Amateur Gentleman (also prod.), Man of the Moment, Accused, When Thief Meets Thief, The Prisoner of Zenda, Joy of Living, Having Wonderful Time, The Rage of Paris, The Young in Heart, Gunga Din, The Sun Never Sets, Rulers of the Sea, Green Hell, Safari, Angels Over Broadway, The Corsican Brothers, Sinbad the Sailor, That Lady in Ermine, The Exile, The Fighting O'Flynn, State Secret, Mr. Drake's Duck, Another Man's Poison (prod. only), Chase a Crooked Shadow (prod. only), Ghost Story.
TELEVISION: *Series*: Douglas Fairbanks Presents (also prod.). *Guest*: The Rheingold Theatre (also prod.), The Chevy Show, Route 66, Dr. Kildare, The Love Boat, B.L. Stryker. *Special*: The Canterville Ghost (ABC Stage '67). *Movies*: The Crooked Hearts, The Hostage Tower.

FAIRBANKS, JERRY
Executive Producer. b. San Francisco, CA, Nov. 1, 1904. Cameraman, 1924-29; prod., shorts, Universal, 1929-34; prod., Popular Science, Unusual Occupations, Speaking of Animals Series, Para., 1935-49; Winner two Acad. Awards; set up film div., NBC, 1948; formed, NBC Newsreel, 1949; devel. Zoomar Lens and Multicam System; formed Jerry Fairbanks Prods., 1950.
PICTURES: The Last Wilderness, Down Liberty Road, With This Ring, Counterattack, Collision Course, Land of the Sea, Brink of Disaster, The Legend of Amaluk, North of the Yukon, Damage Report, The Boundless Seas.
TELEVISION: Public Prosecutor (first film series for TV); other series: Silver Theatre, Front Page Detective, Jackson and Jill, Hollywood Theatre, Crusader Rabbit.

FAIRCHILD, MORGAN
Actress. b. Dallas, TX, Feb. 3, 1950. e. Southern Methodist U.
PICTURES: Bullet for Pretty Boy, The Seduction, Pee-wee's Big Adventure, Red-Headed Stranger, Campus Man, Sleeping Beauty, Midnight Cop, Deadly Illusion, Phantom of the Mall, Body Chemistry 3: Point of Seduction, Freaked, Virgin Hunters, Naked Gun 33 1/3: The Final Insult.
TELEVISION: Series: Search for Tomorrow, Flamingo Road, Paper Dolls, Falcon Crest, Roseanne. Movies: The Initiation of Sarah, Murder in Music City, Concrete Cowboys, The Memory of Eva Ryker, Flamingo Road (pilot), The Dream Merchants, The Girl the Gold Watch and Dynamite, Honeyboy, The Zany Adventures of Robin Hood, Time Bomb, Street of Dreams, The Haunting of Sarah Harding, How to Murder a Millionaire, Menu for Murder, Writer's Block. Perry Mason: The Case of the Skin-Deep Scandal, Based on an Untrue Story. Mini-Series: 79 Park Avenue, North and South Book II.

FAIRCHILD, WILLIAM
Writer, Director. b. Cornwall, England, 1918. e. Royal Naval Coll., Dartmouth. Early career Royal Navy.
AUTHOR: A Matter of Duty, The Swiss Arrangement, Astrology for Dogs, Astrology for Cats, Catsigns (U.S.), The Poppy Factory, No Man's Land (U.S.), Tierra de Nadie (Spain).
THEATER: Sound of Murder, Breaking Point, Poor Horace, The Pay-Off, The Flight of the Bumble B.
PICTURES: Writer: Morning Departure, Outcast of the Islands, The Gift Horse, The Net, Newspaper Story, Malta Story (also dir.), Passage Home, Value For Money, John and Julie (also dir.), The Extra Day (also dir.), The Silent Enemy (also dir.), Star!, Embassy, The Darwin Adventure, Invitation to the Wedding, Bruno Rising, The Promise, Statues in a Garden. Director only: The Horsemasters (tv in U.S.).
TELEVISION: The Man with the Gun, No Man's Land, The Signal, Four Just Men, Some Other Love, Cunningham 5101, The Break, The Zoo Gang, Lady with a Past.

FALK, PETER
Actor. b. New York, NY, Sept. 16, 1927. e. New Sch. for Social Research, B.A., 1951; Syracuse U. M.F.A. Studied with Eva Le Galliene and Sanford Meisner. Worked as efficiency expert for Budget Bureau State of CT.
THEATER: Off-B'way: Don Juan (debut, 1956), The Iceman Cometh, Comic Strip, Purple Dust, Bonds of Interest, The Lady's Not for Burning, Diary of a Scoundrel. On Broadway: Saint Joan, The Passion of Josef D., The Prisoner of Second Avenue. Regional: Light Up the Sky (L.A.), Glengarry Glen Ross (tour).
PICTURES: Wind Across the Everglades (debut, 1958), The Bloody Brood, Pretty Boy Floyd, The Secret of the Purple Reef, Murder Inc. (Acad. Award nom.), Pocketful of Miracles (Acad. Award nom.), Pressure Point, The Balcony, It's a Mad Mad Mad World, Robin and the 7 Hoods, Italiano Brava Gente (Attack and Retreat), The Great Race, Penelope, Luv, Anzio, Castle Keep, Machine Gun McCann, Operation Snafu, Husbands, A Woman Under the Influence, Murder by Death, Mikey and Nicky, The Cheap Detective, The Brink's Job, Opening Night, The In-Laws, The Great Muppet Caper, All the Marbles, Big Trouble, Happy New Year, The Princess Bride, Wings of Desire, Vibes, Cookie, In the Spirit, Tune in Tomorrow, The Player, Faraway So Close!, Roommates.
TELEVISION: Series: The Trials of O'Brien, Columbo (1971-77; Emmy Awards: 1972, 1975, 1976), Columbo (1989, also co-exec. prod.; Emmy Award, 1990). Guest: Studio One, Kraft Theatre, Alcoa Theatre, N.T.A. Play of the Week, Armstrong Circle Theatre, Omnibus, Robert Montgomery Presents, Brenner, Deadline, Kraft Mystery Theatre, Rendezvous, Sunday Showcase, The Untouchables, Dick Powell Show (The Price of Tomatoes; Emmy Award, 1962), Danny Kaye Show, Edie Adams Show, Bob Hope Chrysler Theatre. Movies: Prescription: Murder, A Step Out of Line, Ransom for a Dead Man, Griffin and Phoenix: A Love Story, Columbo Goes to College, Caution: Murder Can Be Hazardous to Your Health, Columbo and the Murder of a Rock Star, Death Hits the Jackpot, Columbo: No Time to Die, Columbo: A Bird in the Hand (also exec. prod.), Columbo: It's All in the Game (also writer, exec. prod.), Columbo: Butterfly in Shades of Grey (also exec. prod.), Columbo: Undercover, Columbo: Strange Bedfellows (also exec. prod.). Specials: The Sacco-Vanzetti Story, The Million Dollar Incident, Brigadoon, A Hatful of Rain, Clue: Movies Murder and Mystery.

FARBER, BART
Executive. Joined United Artists Corp. in early 1960s when UA acquired ZIV TV Programs. Served as v.p. United Artists Television and United Artists Broadcasting. 1971 named v.p. in charge of legal affairs of the cos. 1978, named sr. v.p.—TV, video and special markets; indep. consultant, TV, Pay TV, home video. 1982, joined Cable Health Network as v.p., legal & business affairs; 1984, v.p., business & legal affairs, Lifetime Network; 1986, independent communications consultant.

FARENTINO, JAMES
b. Brooklyn, NY, Feb. 24, 1938. e. American Acad. of Dramatic Arts.

THEATER: B'way: Death of a Salesman, A Streetcar Named Desire (revival, 1973; Theatre World Award). Off-B'way: The Days and Nights of Bebe Fenstermaker, In the Summerhouse. Regional: One Flew Over the Cuckoo's Nest (Jos. Jefferson, Chas. MacArthur & Chicago Drama Critics League Awards), California Suite, The Best Man, Love Letters.
PICTURES: Psychomania (Violent Midnight), Ensign Pulver, The War Lord, The Pad ... And How to Use It (Golden Globe Award, 1966), The Ride to Hangman's Tree, Banning, Rosie!, Me Natalie, The Story of a Woman, The Final Countdown, Dead and Buried, Her Alibi, Bulletproof.
TELEVISION: Series: The Lawyers (The Bold Ones), Cool Million, Dynasty, Blue Thunder, Mary, Julie. Guest: Naked City, daytime soap operas, Laredo, Route 66, The Alfred Hitchcock Hour, Ben Casey, Twelve O'Clock High. Special: Death of a Salesman, DOS Pasos USA. Mini-Series: Sins, Jesus of Nazareth (Emmy nom.). Movies: Wings of Fire, Sound of Anger, The Whole World is Watching, Vanished, Longest Night, Family Rico, Cool Million, The Elevator, Crossfire, Possessed, Silent Victory: The Kitty O'Neil Story, Son Rise: A Miracle of Love, Evita Peron, That Secret Sunday, Something So Right (Emmy nom.), The Cradle Will Fall, License to Kill, A Summer to Remember, That Secret Sunday, Family Sins, The Red Spider, Who Gets the Friends?, Common Ground, In the Line of Duty: A Cop for the Killing, Miles From Nowhere, When No One Would Listen, Secrets of the Sahara (Italy), One Woman's Courage, Honor Thy Father and Mother: The True Story of the Menendez Murders, Dazzled. Pilot: American Nuclear.

FARGAS, ANTONIO
Actor. b. Bronx, NY, Aug. 14, 1946. Studied acting at Negro Ensemble Co. and Actor's Studio.
THEATER: The Great White Hope, The Glass Menagerie, Mod Hamlet, Romeo and Juliet, The Slave, Toilet, The Amen Corner.
PICTURES: The Cool World (debut, 1964), Putney Swope, Pound, Believe in Me, Shaft, Cisco Pike, Across 110th Street, Cleopatra Jones, Busting, Foxy Brown, Conrack, The Gambler, Cornbread Earl and Me, Next Stop Greenwich Village, Car Wash, Pretty Baby, Up the Academy, Firestarter, Streetwalkin', Night of the Sharks, Shakedown, I'm Gonna Git You Sucka, The Borrower, Howling VI: The Freaks, Whore.
TELEVISION: Series: Starsky and Hutch, All My Children. Movies: Starsky and Hutch (pilot), Huckleberry Finn, Escape, Nurse, The Ambush Murders, A Good Sport, Florida Straits, Maid for Each Other, Percy and Thunder. Guest: Ironside, The Bill Cosby Show, Sanford and Son, Police Story, Kolchak The Night Stalker, Miami Vice, Kojak.

FARGO, JAMES
Director. b. Republic, WA, Aug. 14, 1938. e. U. of Washington, B.A.
PICTURES: The Enforcer, Caravans, Every Which Way But Loose, Forced Vengeance, Born to Race, Voyage of the Rock Aliens, Riding the Edge (also actor).
TELEVISION: Tales of the Gold Monkey, Gus Brown and Midnight Brewster, The Last Electric Knight, Hunter, Snoops, Sky High.

FARINA, DENNIS
Actor. b. Chicago, IL, Feb. 29, 1944. Served 18 years with Chicago police before being introduced to producer-director Michael Mann who cast him in film Thief. Celebrity Chmn. of Natl. Law Enforcement Officers Memorial in Washington, D.C.
THEATER: A Prayer for My Daughter, Streamers, Tracers, Bleacher Bums, Some Men Need Help, The Time of Your Life.
PICTURES: Thief (debut, 1981), Jo Jo Dancer Your Life Is Calling, Manhunter, Midnight Run, Men of Respect, We're Talkin' Serious Money, Mac, Another Stakeout, Striking Distance, Romeo Is Bleeding, Little Big League, Get Shorty, Eddie.
TELEVISION: Series: Crime Story. Mini-Series: Drug Wars: Columbia. Movies: Six Against the Rock, Open Admissions, The Hillside Stranglers, People Like Us, Blind Faith, Cruel Doubt, The Disappearance of Nora, One Woman's Courage, The Corpse Had a Familiar Face, Bonanza: Under Attack, Out of Annie's Past. Guest: Miami Vice, Hunter, Tales from the Crypt. Special: The Killing Floor.

FARLEY, CHRIS
Actor. b. Madison, WI, 1960. e. Marquette Univ. Started with The Ark Improv. Theatre Group; performed comedy at Main Stage at Second City in Chicago where he met producer Lorne Michaels.
PICTURES: Coneheads (debut, 1993), Wayne's World 2, Airheads, Bill Madison (cameo), Tommy Boy, Black Sheep.
TELEVISION: Series: Saturday Night Live.

FARNSWORTH, RICHARD
Actor. b. Los Angeles, CA, Sept. 1, 1920. Active as stuntman for 40 years before turning to acting.
PICTURES: Comes a Horseman, Tom Horn, Resurrection, The Legend of the Lone Ranger, Ruckus, Waltz Across Texas, The Grey Fox, The Natural, Rhinestone, Into the Night, Sylvester, Space Rage, The Two Jakes, Misery, Highway to Hell, The Getaway, Lassie.

TELEVISION: *Series*: Boys of Twilight. *Movies*: Strange New World, A Few Days in Weasel Creek, Travis McGee, Ghost Dancing, Anne of Green Gables, Chase, Wild Horses, Red Earth White Earth, Good Old Boy, The Fire Next Time.

FARR, FELICIA
Actress. b. Westchester, NY, Oct. 4, 1932. e. Pennsylvania State Coll. m. Jack Lemmon. Stage debut: Picnic (Players Ring Theatre).
PICTURES: Timetable, Jubal, Reprisal, The First Texan, The Last Wagon, 3:10 to Yuma, Onionhead, Hell Bent for Leather, Kiss Me Stupid, The Venetian Affair, Kotch, Charley Varrick, That's Life!, The Player.

FARR, JAMIE
Actor. r.n. Jameel Joseph Farah. b. Toledo, OH, July 1, 1934. e. Columbia Coll. Trained for stage at Pasadena Playhouse. PICTURES: Blackboard Jungle (debut, 1955), The Greatest Story Ever Told, Ride Beyond Vengeance, Who's Minding the Mint?, With Six You Get Eggroll, The Gong Show Movie, Cannonball Run, Cannonball Run II, Happy Hour, Scrooged, Speed Zone, Curse II: The Bite.
TELEVISION: *Series*: The Chicago Teddy Bears, M*A*S*H (also dir. episodes), The Gong Show (panelist), The $1.98 Beauty Show (panelist), After M*A*S*H (also dir. episodes). *Guest*: Dear Phoebe, The Red Skelton Show, The Dick Van Dyke Show, The Danny Kaye Show, The Love Boat, The New Love American Style, Murder She Wrote. *Movies*: The Blue Knight, Amateur Night at the Dixie Bar and Grill, Murder Can Hurt You!, Return of the Rebels, For Love or Money, Run Till You Fall.

FARRELL, HENRY
Writer. Author of novels and screenplays
PICTURES: Whatever Happened to Baby Jane? Hush ... Hush Sweet Charlotte, What's the Matter with Helen?
TELEVISION: *Movies*: How Awful About Allan, The House That Would Not Die, The Eyes of Charles Sand.

FARRELL, MIKE
Actor, Producer. b. St. Paul, MN, Feb. 6, 1939. m. actress Shelley Fabares.
PICTURES: Captain Newman M.D., The Americanization of Emily, The Graduate, Targets. *Prod.*: Dominick and Eugene.
TELEVISION: *Series*: Days of Our Lives, The Interns, The Man and the City, M*A*S*H. *Specials*: JFK: One Man Show (PBS), The Best of Natl. Geographic Specials (host/narrator). *Movies*: The Longest Night, She Cried Murder!, The Questor Tapes, Live Again Die Again, McNaughton's Daughter, Battered, Sex and the Single Parent, Letters from Frank, Damien: The Leper Priest, Prime Suspect, Memorial Day, Choices of the Heart, Private Sessions, Vanishing Act, A Deadly Silence, Price of the Bride, The Whereabouts of Jenny, Memorial Day (also prod.), Incident at Dark River (also prod.), Silent Motive (also prod.), Hart to Hart: Old Friends Never Die. *Director*: Run Till You Fall.

FARROW, MIA
Actress. b. Los Angeles, CA, Feb. 9. 1945. r.n. Maria de Lourdes Villiers Farrow. d. of actress Maureen O'Sullivan and late dir. John Farrow. e. Marymount, Los Angeles, Cygnet House, London.
THEATER: The Importance of Being Earnest (debut, Madison Ave. Playhouse, NY, 1963); Royal Shakespeare Co. (Twelfth Night, A Midsummer Night's Dream, Ivanov, Three Sisters, The Seagull, A Doll's House), Mary Rose (London), Romantic Comedy (B'way debut, 1979).
PICTURES: Guns at Batasi (debut, 1964), A Dandy in Aspic, Rosemary's Baby, Secret Ceremony, John and Mary, See No Evil, The Public Eye, Dr. Popaul (High Heels), The Great Gatsby, Full Circle (The Haunting of Julia), Avalanche, A Wedding, Death on the Nile, Hurricane, A Midsummer Night's Sex Comedy, The Last Unicorn (voice), Zelig, Broadway Danny Rose, Supergirl, The Purple Rose of Cairo, Hannah and Her Sisters, Radio Days, September, Another Woman, New York Stories (Oedipus Wrecks), Crimes and Misde-meanors, Alice (Natl. Board of Review Award, 1990), Shadows and Fog, Husbands and Wives, Widow's Peak, Miami Rhapsody, Reckless.
TELEVISION: *Series*: Peyton Place. *Specials*: Johnny Belinda, Peter Pan. *Movie*: Goodbye Raggedy Ann.

FAWCETT, FARRAH
Actress. b. Corpus Christi, TX, Feb. 2, 1947. e. U. of Texas. Picked as one of the ten most beautiful girls while a freshman; went to Hollywood and signed by Screen Gems. Did films, TV shows, and made over 100 TV commercials. Off B'way debut: Extremities (1983).
PICTURES: Love Is a Funny Thing, Myra Breckinridge, Logan's Run, Somebody Killed Her Husband, Sunburn, Saturn 3, Cannonball Run, Extremities, See You in the Morning, Man of the House.
TELEVISION: *Series*: Charlie's Angels, Good Sports. *Guest*: Owen Marshall Counselor at Law, The Six Million Dollar Man, Rockford Files, Harry-O. *Movies*: Three's a Crowd, The Feminist

and the Fuzz, The Great American Beauty Contest, The Girl Who Came Gift-Wrapped, Murder on Flight 502, Murder in Texas, The Burning Bed, Red Light Sting, Between Two Women, Nazi Hunter: The Beate Klarsfeld Story, Poor Little Rich Girl: The Barbara Hutton Story, Margaret Bourke-White, Small Sacrifices, Criminal Behavior, The Substitute Wife, Children of the Dust.

FAY, PATRICK J.
Director, Producer. b. June 7, 1916. e. Carnegie Tech. Dumont TV Network, 10 years. Director of over 100 Army training films; also dir. IBM Industrials.
AUTHOR: Melba, The Toast of Pithole, The Last Family Portrait in Oil, Coal Oil Johnny, French Kate, No Pardon in Heaven, An Ill Wind, Tighten Your G-String, As It Was in the Beginning (Television 50 Yrs. Ago).
PICTURES: Director for RCA, General Electric H.G. Peters Company, Bransby Films. *Screenplays*: Sanctuary, The Burning of New York City, Johnson's Island.
TELEVISION: Bishop Sheen, Broadway to Hollywood, Cavalcade of Stars, Manhattan Spotlight, Life is Worth Living, Front Row Center, Ilona Massey Show, Alec Templeton Show, Maggi McNellis Show, Key to Missing Persons, Kids and Company, Confession (also prod.), The Big Picture.

FAYE, ALICE
Actress, Singer. r.n. Alice Jeanne Leppert. b. New York, NY, May 5, 1912. m. bandleader-actor-singer Phil Harris. Started dancin and singing in choruses as teen; hired by Rudy Vallee as singer for his band which resulted in movie debut at Fox, 1934.
PICTURES: George White's Scandals (debut, 1934), She Learned About Sailors, Now I'll Tell, 365 Nights in Hollywood, George White's 1935 Scandals, Every Night at Eight, Music Is Magic, Poor Little Rich Girl, Sing Baby Sing, King of Burlesque, Stowaway, On the Avenue, Wake Up and Live, You Can't Have Everything, You're a Sweetheart, In Old Chicago, Sally Irene and Mary, Alexander's Ragtime Band, Tail Spin, Hollywood Cavalcade, Barricade, Rose of Washington Square, Lillian Russell, Little Old New York, Tin Pan Alley, That Night in Rio, The Great American Broadcast, Weekend in Havana, Hello Frisco Hello, The Gang's All Here, Four Jills in a Jeep (cameo), Fallen Angel, State Fair, Won Ton Ton the Dog Who Saved Hollywood (cameo), The Magic of Lassie.

FEHR, RUDI
Editor, Executive. b. Berlin, Germany, July 6, 1911. m. Maris Wrixon, actress. Started career with Tobis-Klangfilm, Berlin. Joined Warner Bros. editorial department, 1936. Became producer, 1952; promoted to executive, 1956; Post Production Exec. Warner Bros.; WB title changed to dir. of editorial & postprod. operations. Now retired; is consultant to industry.
PICTURES: *Editor*: Invisible Enemies, Honeymoon for Three, Desperate Journey, Watch on the Rhine, The Conspirators, Humoresque, Possessed, Key Largo, The Inspector General, House of Wax, Dial M for Murder, One From the Heart, Prizzi's Honor.

FEINGOLD, BEN
Executive. President, Columbia TriStar Home Video.

FEINSTEIN, ALAN
Actor. b. New York, NY, Sept. 8, 1941.
THEATER: *NY*: Malcolm, Zelda, A View from the Bridge (NY Drama Desk Award), As Is, A Streetcar Named Desire.
PICTURE: Looking for Mr. Goodbar.
TELEVISION: *Series*: Edge of Night, Love Of Life, Search for Tomorrow, Jigsaw John, The Runaways, The Family Tree, Berrenger's. *Movies*: Alexander: The Other Side of Dawn, Visions, The Hunted Lady, The Users, The Two Worlds of Jenny Logan, On Fire. *Mini-Series*: Masada.

FEITSHANS, BUZZ
Executive. b. Los Angeles, CA. e. USC. Started in film business as editor. Worked for 10 years at American-International as supvr. of prod. In 1975 formed A-Team Productions with John Milius. With Carolco Pictures: producer, 1981-6; exec. v.p. for mo. pic. production, member bd. dir. 1986-90. 1990\-, v.p. for Cinergi Prods.; 1994, pres. of Cinergi.
PICTURES: *Producer*: Dillinger, Act of Vengeance, Foxy Brown, Big Wednesday, Hardcore, 1941, Extreme Prejudice (exec. prod.), Conan the Barbarian, First Blood, Uncommon Valor, Rambo II, Red Dawn, Rambo III, Total Recall, Tombstone (exec. prod.), Color of Night.

FELDMAN, COREY
Actor. b. Reseda, CA, July 16, 1971. Has been performing since the age of 3 in over 100 commercials, television (Love Boat, Father Murphy, Foul Play, Mork and Mindy, Eight Is Enough, Alice, Gloria) and films.
PICTURES: Time After Time, The Fox and the Hound (voice), Friday the 13th—The Final Chapter, Gremlins, Friday the 13th—A New Beginning, The Goonies, Stand by Me, Lost Boys, License to Drive, The 'Burbs, Dream a Little Dream, Teenage Mutant Ninja Turtles (voice only), Rock 'n' Roll High School

Forever, Edge of Honor, Meatballs 4, Round Trip to Heaven, Stepmonster, Blown Away, National Lampoon's Loaded Weapon 1, Lipstick Camera, National Lampoon's Last Resort, Maverick, Dream a Little Dream 2, A Dangerous Place, Evil Obsession, Tales From the Crypt: Bordello of Blood.
TELEVISION: *Series*: The Bad News Bears, Madame's Place.
Movies: Willa, Father Figure, Kid with a Broken Halo, Still the Beaver, Out of the Blue, When the Whistle Blows, I'm a Big Girl Now, Exile. *Specials*: 15 & Getting Straight, How to Eat Like a Child.

FELDMAN, EDWARD S.
Producer. b. New York, NY, Sept. 5, 1929. e. Michigan State U. Trade press contact, newspaper and mag. contact, 20th Century Fox, 1950; dir. info. services, Dover Air Force Base. 1954-56; publ. coordinator, The World of Suzie Wong, 1960; joined Embassy, dir. of publicity, 1969; v.p. in chg., adv. & pub, 7 Arts Prods., 1962; v.p. exec. asst. to head prod. Warner-7 Arts Studio 1967; pres., m.p. dept., Filmways, 1970; Formed Edward S. Feldman Co., 1978.
PICTURES: What's the Matter With Helen? (exec. prod.), Fuzz (exec. prod.), Save the Tiger (exec. prod.), The Other Side of the Mountain (prod.), Two-Minute Warning (prod.), The Other Side of the Mountain Part 2 (prod.), The Last Married Couple in America (co-prod.), Six Pack (co-exec. prod.), The Sender (prod.), Hot Dog ... The Movie! (co-prod.), Witness (prod.), Explorers (co-prod.), The Golden Child (co-prod.), The Hitcher (exec. prod.), Near Dark (exec. prod.), Wired (prod.), Green Card (exec. prod.), The Doctor (exec. prod.), Honey I Blew Up the Kid (prod.), Forever Young (exec. prod.), My Father the Hero (exec. prod.), The Jungle Book (prod.).
TELEVISION: *Exec. Prod.*: Moon of the Wolf, My Father's House, Valentine, 300 Miles for Stephanie, Charles and Diana: A Royal Love Story, 21 Hours at Munich, King, Not in Front of the Children, Obsessed with a Married Woman.

FELDON, BARBARA
Actress. b. Pittsburgh, PA, Mar. 12, 1941. e. Carnegie Tech. Former fashion model, also appeared in many commercials. On NY stage in Past Tense, Cut the Ribbons.
PICTURES: Fitzwilly, Smile, No Deposit No Return.
TELEVISION: *Series*: Get Smart, The Marty Feldman Comedy Machine, The Dean Martin Comedy Hour (host), Special Edition (host), The 80's Woman (synd.; host), Get Smart (1995). *Movies*: Getting Away From It All, Playmates, What Are Best Friends For?, Let's Switch, A Guide for the Married Woman, Sooner or Later, A Vacation in Hell, Before and After, Children of Divorce, Get Smart Again!

FELDSHUH, TOVAH
Actress. b. New York, NY, Dec. 27, 1953. e. Sarah Lawrence Col., Univ. of MN. For humanitarian work received the Israel Peace Medal and the Eleanor Roosevelt Humanitarian Award.
THEATER: *NY*: Cyrano, Straws in the Wind, Three Sisters, Rodgers and Hart, Yentl (Theatre World Award), Sarava, The Mistress of the Inn, Springtime for Henry, She Stoops to Conquer, Lend Me a Tenor, A Fierce Attachment, Sarah and Abraham, Six Wives, Hello Muddah! Hello Fadduh!
PICTURES: White Lies, Nunzio, The Idolmaker, Cheaper to Keep Her, Daniel, Brewster's Millions, The Blue Iguana, A Day in October, Comfortably Numb.
TELEVISION: *Series*: As the World Turns, Mariah. *Movies*: Scream Pretty Peggy, The Amazing Howard Hughes, Terror Out of the Sky, The Triangle Factory Fire Scandal, Beggarman Thief, The Women's Room, Citizen Cohn, Sexual Considerations. *Specials*: Dosvedanya Mean Goodbye, Saying Kaddish. *Mini-Series*: Holocaust. Guest: LA Law, Law and Order, etc.

FELL, NORMAN
Actor. b. Philadelphia, PA, March 24, 1924. e. Temple U. Studied acting with Stella Adler. Member, Actors Studio. Professional debut at Circle-in-the-Square Theatre in N.Y. in Bonds of Interest. Summer Stock; appearances on TV; moved to Hollywood in 1958 to begin theatrical film career.
PICTURES: Pork Chop Hill, Ocean's Eleven, The Rat Race, Inherit the Wind, It's a Mad Mad Mad World, The Graduate, Bullitt, If It's Tuesday This Must Be Belgium, Catch-22, The Stone Killer, Rabbit Test, The End, On the Right Track, Paternity, Stripped to Kill, C.H.U.D.II: Bud the Chud, The Boneyard, For the Boys, Hexed.
TELEVISION: Over 150 live plays from NY and some 200 shows filmed in Hollywood. *Series*: Joe and Mabel, 87th Precinct, Dan August, Needles and Pins, Three's Company, The Ropers, Teachers Only. *Guest*: Matt Houston, Crazy Like a Fox, Simon and Simon, It's Garry Shandling's Show, The Boys (pilot). *Mini-Series*: Rich Man Poor Man, Roots: The Next Generations. *Movies*: The Hanged Man, There's a Crowd, The Heist, Thursday's Game, Death Stalk, Richie Brockelman, Moviola: This Year's Blonde, For the Love of It, Uncommon Valor, The Jessie Owens Story.

FELLMAN, DANIEL R.
Executive. b. Cleveland, OH, March 14, 1943. e. Rider Coll., B.S., 1964. Paramount Pictures, 1964-69; Loews Theatres,

1969-71; Cinema National Theatres, 1971-76; 1976-78, pres., American Theatre Mgmt. Joined Warner Bros. in 1978, named exec. v.p. Warner Bros. domestic distribution, Jan. 1993. President Variety Club Tent 35, 1977-78. Bd. member, Will Rogers Foundation; Chairman, Foundation of Motion Picture Pioneers.

FELLMAN, NAT D.
Executive. b. New York, NY, Feb. 19, 1910. Started as office boy, Warner Bros. Pictures, 1928; transferred to Warner Bros. Theatres, asst. to chief booker; handled pool, partnership operations; head buyer, booker for Ohio zone, 1941; asst. to chief film buyer in New York, 1943; apptd. chief film buyer, 1952; exec. asst. to v.p. and gen. mgr., Stanley Warner Theatres, 1955; asst. gen. mgr., Stanley Warner Theatres, 1962; acting gen. mgr., Stanley Warner Theatres, July, 1964; Stanley Warner Theatres, v.p. and gen. mgr., 1965; v.p., NGC Theatre Corp. and division mgr. Fox Eastern Theatres, 1968; v.p. National General Corp., and pres., National General Theatres, 1969; 1974, formed Exhibitor Relations Co., operations consultant; sold it and retired in 1982. Served as vice pres., Variety Clubs International and NATO, Chmn., presidents' advisory comm.

FENADY, ANDREW J.
Producer, Writer. b. Toledo, OH, Oct. 4, 1928. e. U. of Toledo, 1946-50. Radio-prod.-actor-writer. *Novels*: The Man With Bogart's Face, The Secret of Sam Marlow, The Claws of the Eagle, The Summer of Jack London, Mulligan, Runaways.
PICTURES: Stakeout on Dope Street, The Young Captives, Ride Beyond Vengeance, Chisum, Terror in the Wax Museum, Arnold, The Man with Bogart's Face.
TELEVISION: *Series*: Confidential File, The Rebel, Branded, Hondo. *Movies*: The Woman Hunter, Voyage of the Yes, The Stranger, The Hanged Man, Black Noon, Sky Heist, Mayday 40,000 Ft., The Hostage Heart, Mask of Alexander, Masterpiece of Murder, Who Is Julia?, Jake Spanner—Private Eye, The Love She Sought, Yes Virginia There Is a Santa Claus, The Sea Wolf.

FENN, SHERILYN
Actress. b. Detroit, MI, Feb. 1, 1965.
PICTURES: The Wild Life (debut, 1984), Just One of the Guys, Out of Control, Thrashin', The Wraith, Zombie High, Two Moon Junction, Crime Zone, True Blood, Meridian: Kiss of the Beast, Wild at Heart, Backstreet Dreams, Ruby, Desire and Hell at Sunset Motel, Diary of a Hit Man, Of Mice and Men, Three of Hearts, Boxing Helena, Fatal Instinct.
TELEVISION: *Series*: Twin Peaks. *Movies*: Silence of the Heart, Dillinger, Spring Awakening, Liz: The Elizabeth Taylor Story. *Guest*: Cheers, 21 Jump Street, Heart of the City. *Specials*: Tales From the Hollywood Hills (A Table at Ciro's), Divided We Stand, A Family Again.

FENNEMAN, GEORGE
M.C., Announcer. b. Peking, China, Nov. 10, 1919. e. San Francisco State U.
PICTURES: The Thing, How to Succeed in Business Without Really Trying.
TELEVISION: *Series*: You Bet Your Life, Surprise Package, Anybody Can Play, Tell It to Groucho, Your Funny Funny Films, Talk About Pictures, On Campus, Donny & Marie (announcer). *Commercials*: Spokesman for Home Savings of America/ Savings of America.

FERRARA, ABEL
Director, Writer. b. Bronx, NY, 1951. Moved to Peekskill, NY, as teenager where he made short films with future writer Nicholas St. John. Traveled to England, worked for the BBC. Returned to U.S. to attended SUNY/Purchase, making short Could This Be Love, which received some theatrical distribution. Has used the pseudonymn Jimmy Laine.
PICTURES: Driller Killer (also actor, s.p. songs), Ms. 45 (also actor), Fear City, China Girl (also songs), Cat Chaser, King of New York, Bad Lieutenant (also co-s.p.), Dangerous Game, Body Snatchers, The Addiction, The Funeral.

FERRARO, JOHN E.
Executive. b. Greenwich, CT, July 20, 1958. e. Emerson College, B.S. in Mass Communications, 1980. Joined Paramount Pictures Corp. 1980. 1983-84, story analyst, Paramount TV. 1984-85 supervisor, Drama Development. 1985-87 manager, Current Programs & Special Projects. 1987-88, dir. Drama Development. 1988, exec. dir., Acquisitions, Paramount Pictures. 1990, v.p., acquisitions & co-productions.

FERRAZZA, CARL J.
Executive. b. Cleveland, OH, Aug. 29, 1920. e. Catholic U. of America, Washington, DC. Started career 1945: as asst. mgr. & mgr. for Loews Theatres. 1952, joined Cincinnati Theatre Co., first as mgr. for Keith's Theatre, Cincinnati, and after prom. dir. for circuit. 1963, field rep. for United Artists, covering midwest. 1968, UA prom. mgr., N.Y. 1975-83, dir. of field activities, MGM/UA; 1984, joined Orion Pictures Distributing Corp. as v.p. promotional and field activities.

FERRELL, CONCHATA
Actress. b. Charleston, WV, Mar. 28, 1943. e. Marshall Univ.
THEATER: NY: The Three Sisters, Hot L Baltimore, Battle of
Angels, The Sea Horse (Theatre World, Obie & Vernon Rice
Drama Desk Awards), Wine Untouched. LA: Getting Out, Picnic.
PICTURES: Deadly Hero, Network, Heartland, Where the River
Runs Black, For Keeps?, Mystic Pizza, Edward Scissorhands,
Family Prayers, True Romance, Samurai Cowboy, Heaven and
Earth.
TELEVISION: Series: Hot L Baltimore, B.J. and the Bear,
McClain's Law, E/R, Peaceable Kingdom, L. A. Law, Hearts
Afire. Movies: The Girl Called Hatter Fox, A Death in Canaan,
Who'll Save My Children?, Before and After, The Seduction of
Miss Leona, Reunion, Rape and Marriage: The Rideout Case,
Life of the Party: The Story of Beatrice, Emergency Room,
Nadia, The Three Wishes of Billy Grier, North Beach and
Rawhide, Samaritan: The Mitch Snyder Story, Eye on the
Sparrow, Your Mother Wears Combat Boots, Goodbye Miss 4th
of July, Opposites Attract, Deadly Intentions... Again?, Backfield
in Motion. Guest: Good Times, Love Boat, Lou Grant, St.
Elsewhere, Frank's Place, Murder She Wrote, Who's the Boss?,
Matlock. Specials: The Great Gilly Hopkins, Portrait of a White
Marriage, Runaway Ralph, Picnic.

FERRER, MEL
Actor, Producer, Director. r.n. Melchoir Ferrer. b. Elberon, NJ,
Aug. 25, 1917. e. Princeton U. During coll. and early career spent
summers at Cape Cod Playhouse, Dennis, MA; then writer in
Mexico, authored juvenile book, Tito's Hats; later ed. Stephen
Daye Press, VT. Left publishing upon reaching leading-man sta-
tus at Dennis; on B'way as dancer in You'll Never Know,
Everywhere I Roam, others; also in Kind Lady, Cue For Passion;
then to radio, serving apprenticeship in small towns; prod.-dir. for
NBC Land of the Free, The Hit Parade, and Hildegarde program.
Entered m.p. ind., 1945, when signed by Columbia as dial. dir.:
The Girl of the Limberlost; later, returned to Broadway, leading
role, Strange Fruit; signed by David Selznick as producer-actor,
on loan to John Ford as prod. asst. on The Fugitive; then to RKO
for Vendetta.
THEATER: Kind Lady, Cue for Passion, Strange Fruit, Ondine,
The Best Man (L.A., 1987).
PICTURES: Actor: Lost Boundaries (debut, 1949), Born to Be
Bad, The Brave Bulls, Rancho Notorious, Scaramouche, Lili,
Saadia, Knights of the Round Table, Oh Rosalinda!, Proibito
(Forbidden), War and Peace, Paris Does Strange Things, The
Sun Also Rises, The Vintage, Fraulein, The World the Flesh and
the Devil, L'Homme a Femmes, The Hands of Orlac, Blood and
Roses, Legge di Guerra, Devil and the 10 Commandments, The
Longest Day, The Fall of the Roman Empire, Paris When It
Sizzles (cameo), Sex and the Single Girl, El Greco (also prod.),
El Senor de la Salle, The Black Pirate, The Girl From the Red
Cabaret, Brannigan, The Tempter (The Antichrist), Death Trap
(Eaten Alive), Hi-Riders, Pyjama Girl, Island of the Fish Men,
The Norsemen, Yesterday's Tomorrow, The Visitor, The Fifth
Floor, Nightmare City, Lili Marleen, Deadly Game, Screamers,
Mad Dog Anderson. Director: The Girl of the Limberlost (debut,
1945), The Secret Fury, Vendetta (co-dir.), Green Mansions,
Cabriola (Every Day Is a Holiday; also exec. prod., co-s.p.).
Producer: Wait Until Dark, The Night Visitor, A Time for Loving,
Embassy, W.
TELEVISION: Series: Behind the Screen, Falcon Crest. Movies:
One Shoe Makes It Murder, Seduced, Outrages, Dream West,
Peter the Great, Christine Cromwell, A Thanksgiving Promise
(prod.). Special: Mayerling.

FERRER, MIGUEL
Actor. b. Santa Monica, CA, Feb. 7, 1954. m. actress Leilani
Sarelle. Son of actor Jose Ferrer and singer Rosemary Clooney.
Began performing as a drummer. With actor Bill Mumy created
comic book The Comet Man.
PICTURES: Heartbreaker (debut, 1983), Lovelines, Star Trek III:
The Search for Spock, Flashpoint, Robocop, Deepstar Six,
Valentino Returns, Revenge, The Guardian, Twin Peaks: Fire
Walk With Me, Point of No Return, Hot Shots! Part Deux,
Another Stakeout, It's All True (narrator), The Harvest, Blank
Check.
TELEVISION: Series: Twin Peaks, Broken Badges, On the Air.
Guest: Miami Vice, Hill Street Blues, Cagney & Lacey,
Shannon's Deal. Pilot: Badlands 2005. Mini-Series: Drug
Wars: The Camarena Story, The Stand. Movies: Downpayment
on Murder, C.A.T. Squad, Guts & Glory: The Rise and Fall of
Oliver North, Murder in High Places, In the Shadow of a Killer,
Cruel Doubt, Scam, Royce, Incident at Deception Ridge, Jack
Reed: Search for Justice, A Promise Kept: The Oksana Baiul
Story, The Return of Hunter, In the Line of Duty: Hunt for
Justice.

FIEDLER, JOHN
Executive. Launched m.p. career in 1975 working in commercials and industrial and ed. films. Joined Technicolor as sr. exec.
in prod. svcs. in mktg. Joined Rastar 1980 as v.p., prod. dev. and
asst. to Guy McElwaine, pres. & CEO. Joined Paramount as v.p.
in prod.; then to Tri-Star Pictures in same post. Resigned to join

Columbia Pictures as exec. v.p., worldwide prod., 1984, then
pres. of prod. 1986. 1987, left to become independent prod.
1989 named pres. of prod., Rastar IndieProd.
PICTURES: The Beast, Tune in Tomorrow (prod.).

FIELD, DAVID M.
Executive. b. Kansas City, MO, Apr. 22, 1944. e. Princeton U.
Worked as reporter on city desk at Hartford (CT) Courant. In
1968 with NBC News in N.Y. and Washington, DC. Entered film
school at U. of Southern California (L.A.) after which joined
Columbia Pictures as west coast story editor. In 1973 went to
ABC-TV Network as mgr., movies of the week. 1975, moved to
20th-Fox as v.p., creative affairs. Joined United Artists in 1978;
named sr. v.p.—west coast production. Left in 1980 to become
20th-Fox exec. v.p. in chg. of worldwide production 1983,
resigned to enter independent production deal with 20th-Fox,
Consultant, Tri-Star Pictures. Wrote and produced Amazing
Grace and Chuck, 1987.

FIELD, SALLY
Actress. b. Pasadena, CA, Nov. 6, 1946. m. prod. Alan
Greisman. Daughter of Paramount contract actress Maggie
Field Mahoney. Stepdaughter of actor Jock Mahoney. e. Actor's
Studio 1973-75. Acting classes at Columbia studios. Picked over
150 finalists to star as lead in TV series, Gidget, 1965.
PICTURES: The Way West (debut, 1967), Stay Hungry, Smokey
and the Bandit, Heroes, The End, Hooper, Norma Rae
(Academy Award, 1979), Beyond the Poseidon Adventure,
Smokey and the Bandit II, Back Roads, Absence of Malice, Kiss
Me Goodbye, Places in the Heart (Academy Award, 1984),
Murphy's Romance (also exec. prod.), Surrender, Punchline,
Steel Magnolias, Not Without My Daughter, Soapdish, Dying
Young (co-prod. only), Homeward Bound: The Incredible
Journey (voice), Mrs. Doubtfire, Forrest Gump, Eye for an Eye,
Homeward Bound II: Lost in San Francisco (voice).
TELEVISION: Series: Gidget, The Flying Nun, Alias Smith and
Jones, The Girl With Something Extra. Movies: Maybe I'll Come
Home in the Spring, Marriage Year One, Mongo's Back in Town,
Home for the Holidays, Hitched, Bridger, Sybil (Emmy Award,
1977). Mini-Series: A Woman of Independent Means (also co-
exec. prod.). Host: Barbara Stanwyck: Fire and Desire. Guest:
Hey Landlord, Marcus Welby M.D., Bracken's World. Special: All
the Way Home.

FIELD, SHIRLEY-ANNE
Actress. b. London, Eng., June 27. Ent. films after repertory
experience. Under contract to Ealing-M.G.M. 1958.
THEATER: The Lily White Boys, Kennedy's Children, Wait Until
Dark, The Life and Death of Marilyn Monroe, How the Other Half
Loves.
PICTURES: It's Never Too Late, The Silken Affair, The Good
Companions, Horrors of the Black Museum, Upstairs and
Downstairs, Beat Girl, The Entertainer, Man in the Moon, Once
More With Feeling, Peeping Tom, Saturday Night and Sunday
Morning, These Are the Damned, The War Lover, Kings of the
Sun, Alfie, Doctor in Clover, Hell Is Empty, With Love in Mind,
House of the Living Dead (Doctor Maniac), My Beautiful
Laundrette, Getting It Right, The Rachel Papers, Shag, Hear My
Song, At Risk, Carrington.
TELEVISION: U.S.: Bramwell, Santa Barbara, Anna Lees, Lady
Chatterly.

FIELD, TED
Producer. r.n. Frederick W. Field. e. U. of Chicago, Pomona Coll.
Started career as one of owners of Field Enterprises of Chicago;
transferred to west coast, concentrating on movies and records.
Founded Interscope Communications, diversified co., which
develops and produces theatrical films; Interscope Records,
1990.
PICTURES: Revenge of the Nerds, Turk 182, Critical Condition,
Outrageous Fortune, Three Men and a Baby, The Seventh Sign,
Cocktail, Bill & Ted's Excellent Adventure (exec. prod.),
Renegades (exec. prod.), Innocent Man, The First Power (exec.
prod.), Bird on a Wire, Three Men and a Little Lady, Paradise,
The Hand That Rocks the Cradle, The Cutting Edge, FernGully,
The Gun in Betty Lou's Handbag, Out on a Limb, Jersey Girl,
Holy Matrimony, Imaginary Crimes, Operation Dumbo Drop, The
Tie That Binds, Mr. Holland's Opus.
TELEVISION: The Father Clements Story (co-exec. prod.).
Everybody's Baby: The Rescue of Jessica McClure (co-exec.
prod.), My Boyfriend's Back, A Mother's Courage: The Mary
Thomas Story (co-exec. prod.), Crossing the Mob, Murder
Ordained, Foreign Affairs (co-exec. prod.), A Part of the Family
(co-exec. prod.), Body Language (co-exec. prod.).

FIELDS, ALAN
Executive. Spent five years with Madison Square Garden
before joining Paramount Pictures. Career there included various positions: v.p. for pay-TV and Home Video TV. Spent two
years at studio lot in L.A. as part of network TV organization.
1981, named bd. director for Paramount Pictures (U.K.) in
London, serving as liaison to United Intl. Pictures and Cinema
Intl. Corp., serving on operating committees of both. 1985, appt.

v.p., Entertainment & Communications Group of Gulf & Western Industries, Inc., parent co. of Paramount; C.O.O., exec. v.p. Madison Square Garden Corp.

FIELDS, FREDDIE
Executive. b. Ferndale, NY, July 12, 1923. Vice-pres., member of bd. of directors, MCA-TV, MCA Canada Ltd., MCA Corp.; mem., Pres. Club, Wash., D.C.; pres., Freddie Fields Associates Ltd., 1960; Founder pres., chief exec. officer Creative Management Assoc. Ltd. Agency, Chicago, Las Vegas, Miami, Paris, Los Angeles, N.Y., London, Rome, 1961. Was exclusive agent of Henry Fonda, Phil Silvers, Judy Garland, Paul Newman, Peter Sellers, Barbra Streisand, Steve McQueen, Woody Allen, Robert Redford, Ryan O'Neal, Liza Minnelli and others. In 1975 sold interest in CMA (now International Creative Mgt.) but continued as consultant. Produced for Paramount Pictures. 1977: Looking for Mr. Goodbar. American Gigolo, Citizen's Band; Victory. In 1983 named pres. and COO, MGM Film Co. Resigned 1985 to become independent producer for MGM/UA.
PICTURES: Fever Pitch. Poltergeist II, Crimes of the Heart, Millenium, Glory. Exec. Prod. of The Montel Williams Show.

FIENNES, RALPH
Actor. b. Suffolk, England, Dec. 22, 1962. e. Chelsea College of Art & Design, RADA. Stage work with the Royal Shakespeare Co. includes King Lear, Troilus and Cressida, Love's Labour's Lost. B'way debut in Hamlet (Tony & Theatre World Awards, 1995).
PICTURES: Wuthering Heights (tv in U.S.), The Baby of Macon, Schindler's List (Acad. Award nom.; Natl. Society of Film Critics, NY Film Critics & BAFTA Awards), Quiz Show, Strange Days, The English Patient.
TELEVISION: Prime Suspect, A Dangerous Man: Lawrence After Arabia, The Cormorant (theatrical release in U.S.).

FIERSTEIN, HARVEY
Actor, Writer. b. New York, NY, June 6, 1954. e. Pratt Inst.
THEATER: Actor: Andy Warhol's Pork, The Haunted Host, Pouf Positive. Actor-Writer: Torch Song Trilogy (NY & London; Tony Awards for best actor & play; Theatre World Award), Safe Sex. Writer: Spookhouse, La Cage Aux Folles (Tony Award), Legs Diamond.
PICTURES: Garbo Talks, The Times of Harvey Milk (narrator), Torch Song Trilogy (also s.p.), The Harvest, Mrs. Doubtfire, Bullets Over Broadway, Dr. Jekyll & Ms. Hyde, Independence Day.
TELEVISION: Movies: The Demon Murder Case (voice), Apology. Series: Daddy's Girls. Guest: Miami Vice, The Simpsons (voice), Cheers, Murder She Wrote. Specials: Tidy Endings, In the Shadow of Love.

FIGGIS, MIKE
Director, Writer, Musician. b. Kenya, 1949. At age 8 family moved to Newcastle, England. Studied music before performing with band Gas Boad; joined experimental theatre group The People Show in early 70's as musician. Began making indept. films including Redheugh, Slow Fade, Animals of the City. Made 1-hr. film The House for U.K.'s Channel 4.
PICTURES: Director: Stormy Monday (debut, 1988; also s.p., music), Internal Affairs (also music), Liebestraum (also s.p., music), Mr. Jones, Leaving Las Vegas (also s.p., music; IFP Independent Spirit Award, 1996; Nat'l Society of Film Critics Award).

FINCH, JON
Actor. b. London, England, Mar. 2, 1943. Came to acting via backstage activities, working for five years as company manager and director.
PICTURES: The Vampire Lovers (debut, 1970), The Horror of Frankenstein, Sunday Bloody Sunday, L'affaire Martine Desclos, Macbeth, Frenzy, Lady Caroline Lamb, The Final Programme (The Last Days of Man on Earth), Diagnosis: Murder, Une Femme Fidele, The Man With the Green Cross, El Segundo Poder, Battle Flag, El Mister, Death on the Nile, La Sabina, Gary Cooper Which Art in Heaven, Breaking Glass, The Threat, Giro City (And Nothing But the Truth), Plaza Real, Streets of Yesterday, Game of Seduction, The Voice, Beautiful in the Kingdom, Mirror Mirror, Darklands.
TELEVISION: The Martian Chronicles (U.S.), Peter and Paul, The Rainbow, Unexplained Laughter, Dangerous Curves, Maigret, Beautiful Lies, Make or Break, The Oddjob Man (series), Sherlock Homes, Counterstrike (series), Mary Queen of Scots, Riviera, White Men Are Cracking Up, A Love Renewed, Merlin of the Crystal Cave, Richard II, Henry IV, Much Ado About Nothing, South of the Border, Hammer House of Horrors, Ben Hall (series).

FINESHRIBER, WILLIAM H., JR.
Executive. b. Davenport, IA, Nov. 4, 1909. e. Princeton U., B.A., 1931. Pub., CBS, 1931-34; mgr. Carnegie Hall, N.Y., 1934-37; script writer, dir., music comm., dir. of music dept., CBS, 1937-40; dir. of short wave programs, CBS, 1940-43; gen. mgr. CBS program dept. 1943-49; v.p. in charge of programs MBS, 1949-51; exec. v.p. & dir., MBS, 1951-53; v.p. & gen. mgr. of networks, NBC, 1953-54; v.p. in charge of Radio Network, NBC, 1955; v.p. Television Programs of America, 1956; director International operations, Screen Gems, 1957; v.p., Motion Picture Assoc. of America and Motion Picture Export Assoc. of America, 1960; bd. of dir., NARTB: exec. comm., bd. of dir., R.A.B; v.p. Radio Pioneers. Author, Stendhal the Romantic Rationalist.

FINLAY, FRANK
Actor. C.B.E. b. Farnworth, Eng., Aug. 6, 1926. Rep. in Troon, 1951, Halifax and Sunderland, 1952-3, before winning Sir James Knott Scholarship to RADA. e. Studied acting at RADA. Appeared with Guildford Repertory Theatre Co. 1957. London stage debut: The Queen and the Welshman, 1957. Broadway debut, Epitaph for George Dillon, 1958.
THEATER: Work with Royal Court, Chichester Fest., National Theatre includes: Sergeant Musgrave's Dance, Chicken Soup with Barley, Roots, Platonov, Chips with Everything, Saint Joan, Hamlet, Othello, Saturday Sunday Monday, Plunder, Watch It Come Down, Weapons of Happiness, Tribute to a Lady, Filumena (and N.Y.), Amadeus, The Cherry Orchard, Mutiny, Beyond Reasonable Doubt, Black Angel, A Slight Hangover.
PICTURES: The Loneliness of the Long Distance Runner (debut, 1962), The Longest Day, Life for Ruth (Walk in the Shadow), Private Potter, Doctor in Distress, Underworld Informers, The Comedy Man, Agent 8 3/4 (Hot Enough for June), The Wild Affair, A Study in Terror, Othello (Acad. Award nom.), The Sandwich Man, The Jokers, The Deadly Bees, Robbery, I'll Never Forget What's 'is Name, The Shoes of the Fisherman, Inspector Clouseau, Twisted Nerve, The Molly Maguires, Cromwell, The Body (narrator), Assault (The Devil's Garden), Gumshoe, Danny Jones, Sitting Target, Neither the Sea Nor the Sand, Shaft in Africa, The Three Musketeers, The Four Musketeers, The Wild Geese, Murder by Decree, Enigma, The Ploughman's Lunch, The Return of the Soldier, The Key, 1919, Lifeforce, The Return of the Musketeers (tv in U.S.), King of the Wind, Cthulhu Mansion.
TELEVISION: The Adventures of Don Quixote, Casanova, Candide, Julius Caesar, Les Miserables, This Happy Breed, The Lie, The Death of Adolph Hitler, Voltaire, The Merchant of Venice, Bouquet of Barbed Wire, 84 Charing Cross Road, Saturday Sunday Monday, Count Dracula, The Last Campaign, Thief of Bagdad, Betzi, Sakharov, A Christmas Carol, Arch of Triumph, The Burning Shore, In the Secret State, Verdict of Erebus, Mountain of Diamonds, Encounter, Stalin.

FINNEY, ALBERT
Actor. b. Salford, England, May 9, 1936. Studied for stage at Royal Acad. Dramatic Art making his West End debut 1958 in The Party. Appeared at Stratford-Upon-Avon 1959, playing title role in Coriolanus, etc.
THEATER: The Lily White Boys, Billy Liar, Luther (also NY), Much Ado About Nothing, Armstrong's Last Goodnight, Love for Love, Miss Julie, Black Comedy, A Flea in Her Ear, Joe Egg (NY), Alpha Beta, Krapp's Last Tape, Cromwell, Chez Nous, Hamlet, Tamburlaine, Uncle Vanya, Present Laughter. National Theatre, The Country Wife, The Cherry Orchard, Macbeth, The Biko Inquest, Sergeant Musgrave's Dance (also dir.), Orphans, Another Time (also Chicago), Reflected Glory.
PICTURES: The Entertainer (debut, 1960), Saturday Night and Sunday Morning, Tom Jones, The Victors, Night Must Fall (also co-prod.), Two for the Road, Charlie Bubbles (also dir.), The Picasso Summer (tv in U.K.), Scrooge, Gumshoe, Alpha Beta (tv in U.K.), Murder on the Orient Express, The Adventure of Sherlock Holmes' Smarter Brother (cameo), The Duellists, Wolfen, Looker, Loophole, Shoot the Moon, Annie, The Dresser, Under the Volcano, Orphans, Miller's Crossing, The Playboys, Rich in Love, The Browning Version, A Man of No Importance, The Run of the Country.
TELEVISION: The Claverdon Road Job, The Miser, Pope John Paul II, Endless Game, The Image, The Green Man.

FIORENTINO, LINDA
Actress. b. Philadelphia, PA, 1960. e. Rosmont Col. To New York, 1980, studing acting at Circle in the Square Theatre School.
PICTURES: Vision Quest (debut, 1985), Gotcha!, After Hours, The Modrens, Queens Logic, Shout, Chain of Desire, The Last Seduction, Bodily Harm, Jade, Unforgettable, Men in Black.
TELEVISION: Movies: The Neon Empire, Acting on Impulse, The Desperate Trail.

FIRSTENBERG, JEAN
Director. The American Film Institute.

FIRTH, COLIN
Actor. b. Grayshott, Hampshire, Eng., Sept. 10, 1960. Studied acting at the Drama Centre at Chalk Farm. On stage in Doctor's Dilemma, Another Country, Desire Under the Elms.
PICTURES: Another Country, 1919, A Month in the Country, Apartment Zero, Valmont, Wings of Fame, The Pleasure Principle, Femme Fatale, Playmaker, The Advocate, Circle of Friends.

TELEVISION: *Series*: Lost Empires. *Movies*: Camille, Dutch Girls, Tumbledown, Hostages. *Special*: Tales from the Hollywood Hills (Pat Hobby Teamed With Genius).

FIRTH, PETER
Actor. b. Bradford, Yorkshire, Oct. 27, 1953. Appeared in local TV children's show where casting director spotted him and got him role in series, The Flaxton Boys. Moved to London and worked in TV, first in children's show, later on dramas for BBC. Breakthrough role in Equus at National Theatre, 1973 which he repeated in film.
THEATER: Equus (Theatre World Award), Romeo and Juliet, Spring Awakening, Amadeus.
PICTURES: Diamonds on Wheels (debut, 1972; tv in U.S.), Brother Sun Sister Moon, Daniel and Maria, Equus (Acad. Award nom.), Joseph Andrews, Aces High, When You Comin' Back Red Ryder, Tess, Lifeforce, Letter to Brezhnev, Trouble in Paradise, White Elephant, A State of Emergency, Born of Fire, The Tree of Hands, Prisoner of Rio, Burndown, The Hunt for Red October, The Rescuers Down Under (voice), The Perfect Husband, White Angel, Shadowlands, An Awfully Big Adventure.
TELEVISION: *Series*: The Flaxon Boys, Home and Away, Country Matters. *Movies and specials*: Here Comes the Doubledeckers, Castlehaven, The Sullen Sisters, The Simple Life, The Magistrate, The Protectors, Black Beauty, Arthur, Her Majesty's Pleasure, the Picture of Dorian Gray, Lady of the Camillias, The Flip Side of Domenic Hide, Blood Royal, Northanger Abbey, The Way, The Truth: the Video, The Incident, Children Crossing, Prisoner of Honor, Married to Murder, The Laughter of God, Murder in Eden, Brighton Boy.

FISCHER, JOSEPH A.
Executive. Executive v.p., MCA Motion Picture Group.

FISHBURNE, LAURENCE
Actor. b. Augusta, GA, July 30, 1961. Raised in Brooklyn. Landed role on daytime serial One Life to Live at age 11. On NY stage in Short Eyes, Two Trains Running (Tony and Theatre World Awards), Riff Raff (also wrote and directed).
PICTURES: Cornbread Earl and Me (debut, 1975), Fast Break, Apocalypse Now, Willie and Phil, Death Wish II, Rumble Fish, The Cotton Club, The Color Purple, Quicksilver, Band of the Hand, A Nightmare on Elm Street 3: Dream Warriors, Gardens of Stone, School Daze, Red Heat, King of New York, Cadence, Class Action, Boyz N the Hood, Deep Cover, What's Love Got to Do With It (Acad. Award nom.), Searching for Bobby Fischer, Higher Learning, Bad Company, Just Cause, Othello, Fled, Hoodlums.
TELEVISION: *Series*: One Life to Live, Pee-wee's Playhouse. *Guest*: M*A*S*H, Trapper John, M.D., Spenser: For Hire, Tribeca (Emmy Award, 1993). *Movies*: A Rumor of War, I Take These Men, Father Clements Story, Decoration Day, The Tuskegee Airmen.

FISHER, AL
Executive. b. Brooklyn, NY. Entered m.p. industry as office boy, Fox Metropolitan Theatres; U.S. Army Provost Marshal General's Office, 1942-46; Universal Pictures, mgr., Park Avenue Theatre, N.Y. & Copley Plaza Theatre, Boston, 1946; Eagle Lion Film Co., mgr., Red Shoe's Bijou Theatre, N.Y., 1947; Stanley Kramer Prods., exploitation, Cyrano de Bergerac, 1951; press agent, 1951; prod., Bway show, Daphine, 1952; joined United Artists Corporation, 1952, named dir. of exploitation; now freelancing as producer's repr.

FISHER, CARRIE
Actress, Writer. b. Beverly Hills, CA, Oct. 21, 1956. e. London Central Sch. of Speech & Drama. Daughter of actress Debbie Reynolds and singer Eddie Fisher. On Broadway in the chorus of revival of Irene (1972; with mother); later in Censored Scenes from King Kong. *Author*: Postcards From the Edge (1987), Surrender the Pink (1990), Delusions of Grandma (1994).
PICTURES: Shampoo (debut, 1975), Star Wars, Mr. Mike's Mondo Video, The Empire Strikes Back, The Blues Brothers, Under the Rainbow, Return of the Jedi, Garbo Talks, The Man with One Red Shoe, Hannah and Her Sisters, Hollywood Vice Squad, Amazon Women on the Moon, Appointment with Death, The 'Burbs, Loverboy, She's Back, When Harry Met Sally..., The Time Guardian, Postcards From the Edge (s.p. only), Sibling Rivalry, Drop Dead Fred, Soapdish, This Is My Life.
TELEVISION: *Movies*: Leave Yesterday Behind, Liberty, Sunday Drive, Sweet Revenge. *Specials*: Come Back Little Sheba, Classic Creatures: Return of the Jedi, Thumbelina (Faerie Tale Theatre), Paul Reiser: Out on a Whim, Two Daddies? (voice), Trying Times (Hunger Chic), Carrie Fisher: The Hollywood Family (also writer). *Guest*: Laverne and Shirley, George Burns' Comedy Week.

FISHER, EDDIE
Singer. b. Philadelphia, PA, Aug. 10, 1928. Daughter is actress Carrie Fisher. Band, nightclub, hotel singer; discovered by Eddie Cantor, 1949; U.S. Army, 1951-53; many hit records include Wish You Were Here, Lady of Spain; radio & TV shows, NBC.

PICTURES: Bundle of Joy, Butterfield 8, Nothing Lasts Forever.
TELEVISION: *Series*: Coke Time With Eddie Fisher (1953-57), The Eddie Fisher Show (1957-59).

FISHER, FRANCES
Actress. b. Milford-on-Sea, England, May 11. Father was intl. construction supervisor. Raised in Colombia, Canada, France, Brazil, Turkey. Made stage debut in Texas in Summer and Smoke.
THEATER: *NY*: Fool for Love, Desire Under the Elms, Cat on a Hot Tin Roof, The Hitch-Hikers, Orpheus Descending, A Midsummer Night's Dream.
PICTURES: Can She Bake a Cherry Pie? (debut, 1983), Tough Guys Don't Dance, The Principal, Patty Hearst, Bum Rap, Heavy Petting, Pink Cadillac, Lost Angels, Welcome Home Roxy Carmichael, L.A. Story, Unforgiven, Babyfever, The Stars Fell on Henrietta, Waiting for Guffman, Female Perversion.
TELEVISION: *Series*: The Edge of Night (1976-81), The Guiding Light (1985), Strange Luck. *Movies*: Broken Vows, Devlin, Lucy & Desi: Before the Laughter, The Other Mother. *Pilots*: Elysian Fields. *Guest*: The Equalizer, Matlock, Newhart.

FISHER, GEORGE M.C.
Executive. b. Anna, IL. e. Univ. of IL, Brown Univ. Worked in research and devlop. at Bell Labs before joining Motorola in 1976, eventually becoming pres. & CEO in 1988. 1990, elected chmn. & CEO. Named chmn., pres. & CEO of Eastman Kodak Company, Dec. 1993.

FISHER, LUCY
Executive. b. Oct. 2, 1949. e. Harvard U., B.A. Exec. chg. creative affairs, MGM; v.p., creative affairs, 20th Century Fox; v.p., prod., Fox. 1980, head of prod., Zoetrope Studios; 1980-82, v.p., sr. prod. exec., Warner Bros.; 1983, sr. v.p. prod., WB. Joined Columbia TriStar in March, 1996 as vice chmn.

FISK, JACK
Director. b. Ipava, IL, Dec. 19, 1934. e. Cooper Union-Pa. Acad. of the Fine Arts. m. actress Sissy Spacek. Began in films as designer; turning to direction with Raggedy Man (1981).
PICTURES: *Director*: Raggedy Man, Violets Are Blue, Daddy's Dyin', ... Who's Got the Will? *Art Director*: Badlands, Phantom of the Paradise, Carrie, Days of Heaven, Heart Beat.

FITZGERALD, GERALDINE
Actress. b. Dublin, Ireland, Nov. 24, 1914. e. Dublin Art Sch. Mother of director Michael Lindsay-Hogg. On stage Gate Theat., Dublin; then in number of Brit. screen prod. including Turn of the Tide, Mill on the Floss. On N.Y. stage in Heartbreak House. Founded Everyman Street Theatre with Brother Jonathan Ringkamp.
THEATER: Sons and Soldiers, Portrait in Black, The Doctor's Dilemma, King Lear, Hide and Seek, A Long Day's Journey Into Night, (1971), Ah, Wilderness, The Shadow Box, A Touch of the Poet, Songs of the Streets (one woman show), Mass Appeal (dir. only), The Lunch Girls (dir.).
PICTURES: Blind Justice (debut, 1934), Open All Night, The Lad, The Aces of Spades, Three Witnesses, Lieutenant Daring RN, Turn of the Tide, Radio Parade of 1935, Bargain Basement (Department Store), Debt of Honor, Cafe Mascot, The Mill on the Floss, Wuthering Heights (U.S. debut, 1939; Acad. Award nom.), Dark Victory, A Child Is Born, 'Til We Meet Again, Flight from Destiny, Shining Victory, The Gay Sisters, Watch on the Rhine, Ladies Courageous, Wilson, The Strange Affair of Uncle Harry, Three Strangers, O.S.S., Nobody Lives Forever, So Evil My Love, The Late Edwina Black (The Obsessed), 10 North Frederick, The Fiercest Heart, The Pawnbroker, Rachel Rachel, The Last American Hero, Harry and Tonto, Cold Sweat, Echoes of a Summer, The Mango Tree, Bye Bye Monkey, Lovespell (Tristan and Isolde), Arthur, Blood Link, Easy Money, Poltergeist II, Arthur 2: On the Rocks.
TELEVISION: *Series*: Our Private World, The Best of Everything. *Movies*: Yesterday's Child, The Quinns, Dixie: Changing Habits, Do You Remember Love?, Circle of Violence, Night of Courage, Bump in the Night. *Mini-Series*: Kennedy. *Specials*: The Moon and Sixpence, Street Songs.

FITZGERALD, TARA
Actress. b. England, 1968. e. London's Drama Centre, 1990. THEATER: *London*: Our Song. *NY*: Hamlet.
PICTURES: Hear My Song (debut, 1991), Sirens, A Man of No Importance, The Englishman Who Went Up a Hill But Came Down a Mountain.
TELEVISION: The Black Candle, The Camomile Lawn, Anglo-Saxon Attitudes, Six Characters in Search of an Author, Fall From Grace.

FLAGG, FANNIE
Actress, Writer. b. Birmingham, AL, Sept. 21, 1944. e. Univ. of AL. Studied acting at Pittsburgh Playhouse, Town & Gown Theatre. Had her own live 90 minute tv show in Birmingham. To NY where she wrote and appeared in revues for Upstairs at the Downstairs Club. *Comedy albums*: Rally 'Round the Flagg, My

Husband Doesn't Know I'm Making This Phone Call. *Author:* Coming Attractions: A Wonderful Novel (Daisy Fay and the Miracle Man), Fried Green Tomatoes at the Whistle Stop Cafe, Fannie Flagg's Original Whistle Stop Cafe Cookbook.
THEATER: *B'way:* Patio Porch, Come Back to the Five and Dime Jimmy Dean Jimmy Dean, The Best Little Whorehouse in Texas.
Regional: Private Lives, Gypsy, Mary Mary, Tobacco Road, Old Acquaintance, etc.
PICTURES: Five Easy Pieces (debut, 1970), Some of My Best Friends Are..., Stay Hungry, Grease, Rabbit Test, My Best Friend Is a Vampire, Fried Green Tomatoes (also co-s.p.; Acad. Award nom. for s.p.).
TELEVISION: *Series:* The New Dick Van Dyke Show, Match Game P.M., Liar's Club, Harper Valley P.T.A. *Movies:* The New Original Wonder Woman, Sex and the Married Woman. *Pilots:* Comedy News, Home Cookin'. *Producer:* Morning Show.

FLATTERY, THOMAS L.
Executive-Lawyer b. Detroit, MI, Nov. 14, 1922. e. U.S. Military Acad., West Point, B.S., 1944-47; UCLA, J.D., 1952-55; USC, LL.M. 1955-65. Radioplane Company, staff counsel and asst. contract admin. 1955-7. Gen'l counsel and asst. sec'y, McCulloch Corp., CA, 1957-64; sec. & corp. counsel, Technicolor, Inc., 1964-70; v.p., sec. & gen. counsel, Amcord, Inc. 1970-72; v.p., sec. & gen. counsel, Schick Inc., 1972-75; counsel asst. sec., C.F. Braun & Co., 1975-76; sr. v.p., sec. & gen. counsel PCC Technical Industries, Inc. 1976-86; v.p., gen. counsel & sec., G & H Technology, Inc. 1986.-93. Attorney at law, 1993.

FLAXMAN, JOHN P.
Producer. b. New York, NY, March 3, 1934. e. Dartmouth U., B.A. 1956. 1st Lt. U.S. Army, 1956-58. Ent. m.p. industry in executive training program, Columbia Pictures Corp., 1958-63; exec. story consultant, Profiles in Courage, 1964-65; head of Eastern Literary Dept., Universal Pictures, 1965; writer's agent, William Morris Agency, 1966; partner with Harold Prince in Media Productions, Inc. 1967; founded Flaxman Film Corp., 1975. President-Tricorn Productions 1977; pres. Filmworks Capital Corp., 1979-83; Becker/Flaxman & Associates, 1979-83; pres., Cine Communications, 1983-present. Producer Off-Broadway, Yours, Anne (1985). Co-prod. with NY Shakespeare Fest., The Petrified Prince.
PICTURES: Something for Everyone, Jacob Two-Two Meets the Hooded Fang.
TELEVISION: The Caine Mutiny Court-Martial (prod.).

FLEISCHER, RICHARD
Director. b. Brooklyn, NY, Dec. 8, 1916. e. Brown U., B.A.; Yale U., M.F.A. Son of animator Max Fleischer. Stage dir.; joined RKO Pathe 1942. Dir. and wrote This Is America shorts, prod./dir. Flicker Flashbacks. Author: Just Tell Me When to Cry.
PICTURES: Child of Divorce (debut, 1946), Banjo, Design for Death (also co-prod.); Academy Award for Best Feature-Length Documentary, 1948), So This Is New York, Bodyguard, Follow Me Quietly, Make Mine Laughs, The Clay Pigeon, Trapped, Armored Car Robbery, The Narrow Margin, The Happy Time, Arena, 20000 Leagues Under the Sea, Violent Saturday, Girl in the Red Velvet Swing, Bandido, Between Heaven and Hell, The Vikings, These Thousand Hills, Compulsion, Crack in the Mirror, The Big Gamble, Barabbas, Fantastic Voyage, Doctor Dolittle, The Boston Strangler, Che!, Tora! Tora! Tora!, 10 Rillington Place, The Last Run, See No Evil, The New Centurions, Soylent Green, The Don Is Dead, The Spikes Gang, Mr. Majestyk, Mandingo, The Incredible Sarah, Crossed Swords (The Prince and the Paupre), Ashanti, The Jazz Singer, Tough Enough, Amityville 3-D, Conan the Destroyer, Red Sonja, Million Dollar Mystery, Call From Space (Showcan).

FLEMING, JANET BLAIR
Executive. b. Ottawa, Canada, November 29, 1944. e. Carlton U., Ottawa, Canada, B.A. Secretary to Canada's Federal Minister of Transport 1967-72; 1973-77, asst. to Sandy Howard—business affairs; 1977, co-founder and v.p./sales & admin. of Producers Sales Organization; 1981, named sr. v.p., admin.; 1982, sr. v.p., acquisitions; 1983, exec. v.p., Skouras Pictures; 1985 promoted to pres., intl. div.; 1987-88 mgr. Lift Haven Inn, Sun Valley, ID; 1989-present, owner/partner Premiere Properties (prop. management, Sun Valley, ID).

FLEMING, RHONDA
Actress. r.n. Marilyn Louis. b. Los Angeles, CA, Aug. 10. m. Ted Mann (Mann Theatres). e. Beverly Hills H.S. Member, several charity orgs. Bd. of Dir. trustee of World Opportunities Intl. (Help the Children). Alzheimer Rsch., Childhelp USA, bd. of trustees of the UCLA Foundation, etc. Opened Rhonda Fleming Mann Resource Center for Women with Cancer at UCLA Medical Center, 1994. Many awards incl. Woman of the Year Award from City of Hope 1986 & 1991, and for Operaton Children, etc. Stage incl. The Women (B'way), Kismet (LA), The Boyfriend (tour), one woman concerts.
PICTURES: Spellbound, Abiline Town, Spiral Staircase, Adventure Island, Out of the Past, A Connecticut Yankee in King

Arthur's Court, The Great Lover, The Eagle and the Hawk, The Redhead and the Cowboy, The Last Outpost, Cry Danger, Crosswinds, Little Egypt, Hong Kong, Golden Hawk, Tropic Zone, Pony Express, Serpent of the Nile, Inferno, Those Redheads from Seattle, Jivaro, Yankee Pasha, Tennessee's Partner, While the City Sleeps, Killer Is Loose, Slightly Scarlet, Odongo, Queen of Babylon, Gunfight at the OK Corral, Buster Keaton Story, Gun Glory, Bullwhip, Home Before Dark, Alias Jesse James, The Big Circus, The Crowded Sky, The Patsy (cameo), Won Ton Ton The Dog Who Saved Hollywood, The Nude Bomb.
TELEVISION: *Guest:* Wagon Train, Police Woman, Love Boat, McMillian and Wife, Legends of the Screen, Road to Hollywood, Wildest West Show of Stars. *Movies:* The Last Hours Before Morning, Love for Rent, Waiting for the Wind.

FLEMYNG, ROBERT
Actor. b. Liverpool, England, Jan. 3, 1912. e. Halleybury Coll. Stage debut: Rope, 1931.
PICTURES: Head Over Heels (debut, 1937), Bond Street, The Guinea Pig, The Conspirators, The Blue Lamp, Blackmailed, The Magic Box, The Holly and the Ivy, Cast a Dark Shadow, Man Who Never Was, Funny Face, Let's Be Happy, Wisdom's Way, Blind Date, A Touch of Larceny, Radtus (Italian), The King's Breakfast, The Deadly Affair, The Spy with the Cold Nose, The Quiller Memorandum, Deathhead Avenger, Oh! What a Lovely War, Battle of Britain, Cause for Alarm, Young Winston, The Darwin Adventure, Travels with My Aunt, Golden Rendezvous, The Medusa Touch, The Four Feathers, The Thirty-Nine Steps, Paris By Night, Kafka.
TELEVISION: appearances in England, U.S. inc.: Rainy Day, Playhouse 90, Wuthering Heights, Browning Version, After the Party, Boyd Q.C., They Made History, Somerset Maugham Show, Woman in White, The Datchet Diamonds, Probation Officer, Family Solicitor (series), Man of the World, Zero One, Compact (serial), Day by the Sea, The Living Room, Hawks and Doves, Vanity Fair, The Inside Man, The Doctor's Dilemma, The Persuaders, Major Lavender, Public Eye, Florence Nightingale, Edward VIII, Spy Trap, The Venturers' Loyalties, The Avengers, Crown Court, Enemy at the Door, Rebecca, Edward and Mrs. Simpson, The Ladykiller, Professionals, Fame Is the Spur, Crown Court, Spider's Webb, Executive Suite, Small World, Perfect Scoundrels, Short Story.

FLETCHER, LOUISE
Actress. b. Birmingham, AL, July 22, 1934. e. U. of North Carolina, B.A. Came to Hollywood at age 21; studied with Jeff Corey. Worked on TV shows (including Playhouse 90, Maverick). Gave up career to be a mother for 10 yrs.; returned to acting in 1973. Board of Directors: Deafness Research Foundation, 1980- . Honorary Degrees: Doctor of Humane Letters from Gallaudet U. and West Maryland Col. Advisory board: The Caption Center, The Nat'l Institute on Deafness and Other Communication Disorders.
PICTURES: Thieves Like Us, Russian Roulette, One Flew Over the Cuckoo's Nest (Academy Award, 1975), Exorcist II: The Heretic, The Cheap Detective, Natural Enemies, The Magician of Lublin, The Lucky Star, The Lady in Red, Strange Behavior, Mamma Dracula, Brainstorm, Strange Invaders, Firestarter, Once Upon a Time in America, Overnight Sensation, Invaders from Mars, The Boy Who Could Fly, Nobody's Fool, Flowers in the Attic, Two Moon Junction, Best of the Best, Shadow Zone, Blue Steel, Blind Vision, The Player, Georgino, Tollbooth, Return to Two Moon Junction, Virtuosity.
TELEVISION: *Series:* Boys of Twilight. *Movies:* Can Ellen Be Saved?, Thou Shalt Not Commit Adultery, A Summer to Remember, Island, Second Serve, J. Edgar Hoover, The Karen Carpenter Story, Final Notice, Nightmare on the 13th Floor, In a Child's Name, The Fire Next Time, The Haunting of Seacliff Inn, Someone Else's Child. *Guest:* Twilight Zone, Tales from the Crypt, Civil Wars, Deep Space Nine, Dream On, VR5.

FLINN, JOHN C.
Publicist. b. Yonkers, NY, May 4, 1917. e. U. of California. p. late John C. Flinn, pioneer m.p. executive. In pub. dept. David O. Selznick, 1936-39; unit publicist, then head planter, Warner, 1936-46; joined Monogram as asst. to nat'l adv. & pub. head & pub. mgr. 1946; apptd. nat'l dir. of pub. & adv. of Allied Artists Pictures, 1951; apptd studio dir. adv. & pub., Columbia, 1959; v.p., Jim Mahoney & Assocs. (p.r. firm) 1971. Joined MGM West Coast publ. dept. as publ. coordinator, 1973; rejoined Columbia Pictures in 1974 as studio publ. dir.; 1979, promoted to dir. industry relations. Joined MGM/UA publ. staff, 1988 to work on m.p. academy campaign for Moonstruck. Engaged by Paramount 1988-89 to assist in Acad. Award campaigns. Retired.

FLOREA, JOHN
Producer, Director, Writer. b. Alliance, OH, May 28, 1916. Served as photo journalist with Life magazine, 1940-50; assoc. editor Colliers magazine, 1950-53. Prod.-dir. with David Gerber 1979-84.
PICTURES: A Time to Every Purpose, The Astral Factor, The Invisible Strangler, Hot Child in the City.

TELEVISION: *Dir. several episodes*: Sea Hunt series, 1957-60; Bonanza, Outlaws, Outpost (pilot), The Virginian, Honey West, Daktari, Gentle Ben, Cowboy in Africa, High Chapparal, Flipper, Destry Rides Again, Not For Hire, Ironside, Highway Patrol, V, Target, Everglades, (also prod.), CHiPS, MacGyver. Prod.-dir. of film Islands of the Lost. With Ivon Tors Films. Nominated as one of the Top 10 directors in America by DGA for 1968 Mission Impossible episode. Dir. several Ironside episodes. Doc: Kammikazi, Attack Hawaiian Hospitality, Million Dollar Question, Marineland, Brink of Disaster. (Valley Freedom Award), Dangerous Report, (for CIA), The Runaways (Emmy Award), Down the Long Hills, Dark Canyon.

FLYNN, JOHN
Director, Writer. b. Chicago IL. e. George Washington U, Stanford, UCLA, B.A. (Eng.). Worked in mailroom at MCA then with p.r. firm. Began career as trainee script supvr. for dir. Robert Wise on West Side Story. Soon working as ass't. dir. on MGM-TV shows. Made dir. debut with The Sergeant, 1969.
PICTURES: The Jerusalem File, The Outfit (also s.p.), Rolling Thunder, Defiance, Touched, Best Seller, Lock Up, Brainscan.
TELEVISION: Marilyn—The Untold Story (dir.).

FOCH, NINA
Actress. b. Leyden, Holland, April 20, 1924. Daughter of Consuelo Flowerton, actress, & Dirk Foch, symphony orch. conductor. Adjunct Prof., USC, 1966-67; 1978-80, Adjunct professor, USC Cinema-TV grad. sch. 1986-; sr. faculty, American Film Inst,, 1974-77; bd. of Governors, Hollywood Acad. of Television Arts & Sciences, 1976-77; exec. Comm. Foreign Language Film Award, Acad. of Motion Picture Arts & Sciences, 1970-. Cochmn., exec. comm. Foreign Language Film Award 1983-.
PICTURES: The Return of the Vampire (debut, 1943), Nine Girls, Cry of the Werewolf, She's a Soldier Too, She's a Sweetheart, Shadows in the Night, I Love a Mystery, Prison Ship, Song to Remember, My Name is Julia Ross, Boston Blackie's Rendezvous, Escape in the Fog, The Guilt of Jane Ames, Johnny O'Clock, The Dark Past, Johnny Allegro, Undercover Man, St. Benny the Dip, An American in Paris, Young Man With Ideas, Scaramouche, Sombrero, Fast Company, Executive Suite (Acad. Award nom.), Four Guns to the Border, The Ten Commandments, Illegal, You're Never Too Young, Three Brave Men, Cash McCall, Spartacus, Such Good Friends, Salty, Mahogany, Jennifer, Rich and Famous, Skin Deep, Sliver, Morning Glory.
TELEVISION: *Series*: Q.E.D. (panelist), It's News to Me (panelist), Shadow Chasers. *Movies*: Outback Bound, In the Arms of a Killer, The Sands of Time. *Mini-series*: War and Remembrance. *Special*: Tales of the City. Guest star, most major series incl. Studio One, Playhouse 90, US Steel Hour, L.A. Law, Dear John, Hunter; talk shows, specials.

FOGARTY, JACK V.
Executive, Producer, Writer. b. Los Angeles, CA. e. UCLA. Management, MGM, 1960-62; exec. prod. mgr., Cinerama, Inc., 1962-64; assoc. prod., The Best of Cinerama, 1963; est. own p.r. firm, 1965; pres., AstroScope, Inc., 1969-74.
TELEVISION: *Writer/prod.*: The Rookies, S.W.A.T., Charlie's Angels, Most Wanted, Barnaby Jones, A Man Called Sloane, Trapper John, T.J. Hooker, Crazy Like a Fox, The Equalizer, Jake and the Fatman, Murder She Wrote, Charlie's Angels (story edit.). *Exec. Story consultant*: Most Wanted, A Man Called Sloane, Sheriff Lobo, T.J. Hooker. *Producer*: T.J. Hooker, Jessie.

FOLEY, JAMES
Director. b. New York, NY. E. NYU, USC. While at USC directed two short films, Silent Night and November which brought him attention. Directed two Madonna videos: Live to Tell and Papa Don't Preach.
PICTURES: Reckless, At Close Range, Who's That Girl, After Dark My Sweet, Glengarry Glen Ross, A Day to Remember, Fear, Two Bits, The Chamber.

FOLSEY, GEORGE, JR
Producer, Editor. b. Los Angeles, CA, Jan. 17, 1939. Son of late cinematographer George Folsey Sr. e. Pomona Coll., B.A., 1961.
PICTURES: *Editor*: Glass Houses, Bone, Hammer, Black Caesar, Schlock, Trader Horn, Bucktown, J.D.'s Revenge, Norman... Is That You?, Tracks, The Chicken Chronicles, The Kentucky Fried Movie, National Lampoon's Animal House, Freedom Road, The Great Santini (addt'l editing), The Blues Brothers (also assoc. prod.). *Producer*: An American Werewolf in London, Twilight Zone—The Movie (assoc. prod.); Trading Places (exec. prod. & 2nd unit dir.), Into the Night (co-prod.), Spies Like Us (co-prod.), Clue (co-exec. prod.), Three Amigos, Coming to America (co-prod., co-editor), Greed (co-exec. prod.), Grumpier Old Men.
VIDEO: Michael Jackson's Thriller (co-prod., editor).

FONDA, BRIDGET
Actress. b. Los Angeles, CA, Jan. 27, 1964. Daughter of actor Peter Fonda. Grew up in Los Angeles and Montana. e. NYU the-

ater prog. Studied acting at Lee Strasberg Inst., and with Harold Guskin. Starred in grad. student film PPT. Workshop stage performances include Confession and Pastels.
PICTURES: Aria (Tristan and Isolde sequence; debut, 1987), You Can't Hurry Love, Light Years (voice), Scandal, Shag, Strapless, Frankenstein Unbound, The Godfather Part III, Drop Dead Fred (unbilled), Doc Hollywood, Leather Jackets, Out of the Rain, Iron Maze, Single White Female, Singles, Army of Darkness, Point of No Return, Bodies Rest and Motion, Little Buddha, It Could Happen to You, The Road to Wellville, Camilla, Rough Magic, Balto (voice), City Hall.
TELEVISION: *Specials*: Jacob Have I Loved (Wonderworks), The Edge (The Professional Man). *Guest*: 21 Jump Street.

FONDA, JANE
Actress. b. New York, NY, Dec. 21, 1937. e. Emma Willard Sch., Troy, NY. Active in dramatics, Vassar. Father was late actor Henry Fonda. Brother is actor Peter Fonda. m. executive Ted Turner. Appeared with father in summer stock production, The Country Girl, Omaha, NB. Studied painting, languages, Paris. Art Students League, N.Y. Appeared in The Male Animal, Dennis, MA. Modeled, appeared on covers, Esquire, Vogue, The Ladies Home Journal, Glamour, and McCall's, 1959. Appeared in documentaries: Introduction to the Enemy, No Nukes.
THEATER: There Was A Little Girl (Theatre World Award), Invitation to a March, The Fun Couple, Strange Interlude.
PICTURES: Tall Story (debut, 1960), Walk on the Wild Side, The Chapman Report, Period of Adjustment, In the Cool of The Day, Sunday in New York, The Love Cage (Joy House), La Ronde (Circle of Love), Cat Ballou, The Chase, La Curee (The Game is Over), Any Wednesday, Hurry Sundown, Barefoot in the Park, Barbarella, Spirits of the Dead, They Shoot Horses Don't They? (Acad. Award nom.), Klute (Academy Award, 1971), F.T.A. (also prod.), Tout va Bien, Steelyard Blues, A Doll's House, The Bluebird, Fun With Dick and Jane, Julia (Acad. Award nom.), Coming Home (Academy Award, 1978), Comes a Horseman, California Suite, The China Syndrome (Acad. Award nom.), The Electric Horseman, Nine To Five, On Golden Pond (Acad. Award nom.), Rollover, Agnes of God, The Morning After (Acad. Award nom.), Leonard Part 6 (cameo), Old Gringo, Stanley and Iris.
TELEVISION: *Specials*: A String of Beads, Lily--Sold Out, The Helen Reddy Special, I Love Liberty, Tell Them I'm a Mermaid, Fonda on Fonda (host), A Century of Women (narrator). *Movie*: The Dollmaker (Emmy Award, 1984). *Series*: 9 to 5 (exec. prod. only).

FONDA, PETER
Actor, Director. b. New York, NY, Feb. 23, 1939. e. studied at U. of Omaha. Son of late actor Henry Fonda. Sister is actress Jane Fonda; daughter is actress Bridget Fonda.
PICTURES: Tammy and the Doctor (debut, 1963), The Victors, Lilith, The Young Lovers, The Wild Angels, Trip, Spirits of the Dead, Easy Rider (also co-s.p., prod.), Idaho Transfer (dir.), The Last Movie, The Hired Hand (also dir.), Two People, Dirty Mary Crazy Larry, Open Season, Race With the Devil, 92 in the Shade, Killer Force, Fighting Mad, Futureworld, Outlaw Blues, High Ballin!, Wanda Nevada (also dir.), Cannonball Run (cameo), Split Image, Certain Fury, Dance of the Dwarfs, Mercenary Fighters, Jungle Heat, Diajobu My Friend, Peppermint Frieden, Spasm, The Rose Garden, Fatal Mission, Family Spirit, Reckless, South Beach, Bodies Rest & Motion, DeadFall, Molly & Gina, Love and a .45, Nadja.
TELEVISION: *Movies*: A Reason to Live, The Hostage Tower, A Time of Indifference, Sound, Certain Honorable Men, Montana.

FONER, NAOMI
Writer, Producer. b. New York, NY. e. Barnard Col., Columbia U. m. dir. Stephen Gyllenhaal. Was media dir. of Eugene McCarthy's 1968 political campaign, then prod. asst. & researcher at PBS. 1968 joined Children's Television Workshop on staff of Sesame Street. Later helped develop series The Electric Company, 3-2-1 Contact. Creator and co-prod. of series The Best of Families. Wrote teleplay Blackout for PBS series Visions.
PICTURES: *Writer:* Violets Are Blue, Running on Empty (Golden Globe Award, Acad. Award nom.; also exec. prod.), A Dangerous Woman (also prod.), Losing Isaiah (also prod.).

FONTAINE, JOAN
Actress. b. Tokyo, Oct. 22, 1917. r.n. Joan de Beauvior de Havilland. e. American School in Japan. Sister is actress Olivia de Havilland. Started on stage in L.A., Santa Barbara and San Francisco in Kind Lady; then as Joan Fontaine in Call it a Day (L.A.), where she was spotted and signed to contract by prod. Jesse Lasky. Gave screen contract to RKO. On B'way in Tea and Sympathy (1954). *Author:* No Bed of Roses (1978) Appeared in The Lion in Winter at Vienna's English Speaking Theatre 1979.
PICTURES: No More Ladies (debut, 1935), Quality Street, You Can't Beat Love, Music for Madame, Maid's Night Out, A Damsel in Distress, Blonde Cheat, The Man Who Found Himself, The Duke of West Point, Sky Giant, Gunga Din, Man of Conquest, The Women, Rebecca (Acad. Award nom.), Suspicion (Academy Award, 1941), This Above All, The Constant Nymph

(Acad. Award nom.), Jane Eyre, Frenchman's Creek, Affairs of Susan, From This Day Forward, Ivy, The Emperor Waltz, Letter From an Unknown Woman, Kiss the Blood Off My Hands, You Gotta Stay Happy, Born to Be Bad, September Affair, Darling How Could You?, Something to Live For, Othello (cameo), Ivanhoe, Decameron Nights, Flight to Tangier, The Bigamist, Casanova's Big Night, Serenade, Beyond a Reasonable Doubt, Island in the Sun, Until They Sail, A Certain Smile, Voyage to the Bottom of the Sea, Tender Is the Night, The Devil's Own.
TELEVISION: Crossings, Dark Mansions, Cannon, The Users, Bare Essence, Good King Wenceslas, etc.

FOOTE, HORTON
Writer. b. Wharton, TX, March 14, 1916. Actor before becoming playwright. Plays include Only the Heart, The Chase, Trip to Bountiful, Traveling Lady, Courtship, 1918, The Widow Claire, Habitation of Dragons, Lily Dale, Valentine's Day, Dividing the Estate, Talking Pictures, The Roads to Home, Night Seasons.
PICTURES: Storm Fear, To Kill a Mockingbird (Academy Award, 1962), Baby the Rain Must Fall, The Chase, Hurry Sundown, Tomorrow, Tender Mercies (Academy Award, 1983), 1918 (also co-prod.), The Trip to Bountiful (also co-prod.), On Valentine's Day, Convicts, Of Mice and Men.
TELEVISION: Only the Heart, Ludie Brooks, The Travelers, The Old Beginning, Trip to Bountiful, Young Lady of Property, Death of the Old Man, Flight, The Night of the Storm, The Roads to Home, Drugstore: Sunday Night, Member of the Family, Traveling Lady, Old Man, Tomorrow, The Shape of the River, The Displaced Person, Barn Burning, The Habitation of Dragons.

FORBES, BRYAN
Actor, Writer, Producer, Director. b. Stratford (London), July 22, 1926. m. actress Nanette Newman. Former head of prod., man. dir., Associated British Prods. (EMI). Stage debut, The Corn Is Green (London), 1942; screen debut, The Small Back Room, 1948. Pres.: National Youth Theatre of Great Britain, 1985-; Pres.: Writers Guild of Great Britain, 1988-91.
AUTHOR: Short stories: Truth Lies Sleeping. Novels: The Distant Laughter, Familiar Strangers (U.S.: Stranger), The Rewrite Man, The Endless Game, A Song at Twilight (U.S.: A Spy at Twlight), The Twisted Playground, Partly Cloudy, Quicksand. Novelizations: The Slipper and the Rose, International Velvet. Non-Fiction: Ned's Girl (bio. of Dame Edith Evans) That Despicable Race (history of the British acting tradition). Autobiographies: Notes for a Life, A Divided Life.
THEATER: Director. Macbeth, Star Quality, Killing Jessica, The Living Room.
PICTURES: Actor. Tired Men, The Small Back Room All Over the Town, Dear Mr. Prohack, Green Grow The Rushes, The Million Pound Note (Man With a Million), An Inspector Calls, The Colditz Story, Passage Home, Appointment in London, Sea Devils, The Extra Day, Quatermass II, It's Great To be Young, Satellite in the Sky, The Baby and The Battleship, Yesterday's Enemy, The Guns of Navarone, A Shot in The Dark, Of Human Bondage, Restless Natives. Writer: The Cockleshell Heroes, The Black Tent, Danger Within, I Was Monty's Double (also actor), The League of Gentlemen (also actor), The Angry Silence (also prod., actor), Man in the Moon, Only Two Can Play, Station Six Sahara, Of Human Bondage (also actor), Hopscotch, Chaplin. Director-Writer: Whistle Down the Wind (dir. only), The L-Shaped Room (also actor), Seance on a Wet Afternoon (also prod.), King Rat, The Wrong Box, The Whisperers, Deadfall, The Madwoman of Chaillot (dir. only), The Raging Moon (Long Ago Tomorrow; also actor), The Stepford Wives (dir., actor), The Slipper and the Rose (also actor), International Velvet (also actor), Sunday Lovers (co-dir. only), Better Late Than Never (Menage a Trois), The Naked Face. Exec. Prod.: Hoffman, Forbush and the Penguins, The Railway Children, Peter Rabbit and the Tales of Beatrix Potter, The Go-Between, And Soon The Darkness, On The Buses, Dulcima.
TELEVISION: Actor. Johnnie Was a Hero, The Breadwinner, French Without Tears, Journey's End, The Gift, The Road, The Heiress, December Flower, First Amongst Equals. Writer/Dir.: I Caught Acting Like The Measles (documentary on the life of Dame Edith Evans) Goodbye Norma Jean and Other Things (documentary on the life of Elton John) Jessie, The Endless Game.

FORD, GLENN
Actor. r.n. Gwylin Ford. b. Quebec, Canada, May 1, 1916. Moved to Southern California as child. On stage with various West Coast theatre cos.; featured in The Children's Hour 1935; Broadway in Broom for a Bride, Soliloquy. Signed contract for film career with Columbia Pictures, 1939. Served in U.S. Marine Corps 1942-45.
PICTURES: Heaven With a Barbed Wire Fence (debut, 1940), My Son Is Guilty, Convicted Women, Men Without Souls, Babies for Sale, Blondie Play Cupid, The Lady in Question, So Ends Our Night, Texas, Go West Young Lady, The Adventures of Martin Eden, Flight Lieutenant, Destroyer, The Desperadoes, A Stolen Life, Gilda, Gallant Journey, Framed, The Mating of Millie, The Return of October, The Loves of Carmen, The Man from Colorado, Mr. Soft Touch, The Undercover Man, Lust for Gold,

The Doctor and the Girl, The White Tower, Convicted, The Flying Missile, The Redhead and the Cowboy, Follow the Sun, The Secret of Convict Lake, Green Glove, Young Man with Ideas, Affair in Trinidad, Time Bomb (Terror on a Train), The Man from the Alamo, Plunder of the Sun, The Big Heat, Appointment in Honduras, Human Desire, The Americano, The Violent Men, Blackboard Jungle, Interrupted Melody, Trial, Ransom, The Fastest Gun Alive, Jubal, The Teahouse of the August Moon, 3:10 to Yuma, Don't Go Near the Water, Cowboy, The Sheepman, Imitation General, Torpedo Run, It Started With a Kiss, The Gazebo, Cimarron, Cry for Happy, Pocketful or Miracles, The Four Horsemen of The Apocalypse, Experiment in Terror, Love Is a Ball, The Courtship of Eddie's Father, Advance to the Rear, Fate Is the Hunter, Dear Heart, The Rounders, The Money Trap, Is Paris Burning?, Rage, A Time for Killing, The Last Challenge, Day of the Evil Gun, Heaven With a Gun, Smith!, Santee, Midway, Superman, The Visitor, Virus, Happy Birthday to Me, Border Shootout, Raw Nerve.
TELEVISION: Series: Cade's County, Friends of Man (narrator), The Family Holvak, When Havoc Struck (narrator). Movies: Brotherhood of the Bell, The Greatest Gift, Punch and Jody, The 3000 Mile Chase, Evening in Byzantium, The Sacketts, Beggarman Thief, The Gift, Final Verdict. Mini-Series: Once an Eagle.

FORD, HARRISON
Actor. b. Chicago, IL, July 13, 1942. e. Ripon Coll. Started acting in summer stock at Williams Bay, WI, in Damn Yankees, Little Mary Sunshine. Moved to L.A. where he acted in John Brown's Body. Signed by Columbia Studios under seven-year contract. Took break from acting to undertake carpentry work which included building Sergio Mendes' recording studio. Returned to acting in American Graffiti.
PICTURES: Dead Heat on a Merry-Go-Round (debut, 1966), Luv, A Time for Killing, Journey to Shiloh, Zabriskie Point, Getting Straight, American Graffiti, The Conversation, Star Wars, Heroes, Force 10 from Navarone, Hanover Street, The Frisco Kid, More American Graffiti (cameo), Apocalypse Now, The Empire Strikes Back, Raiders of the Lost Ark, Blade Runner, Return of the Jedi, Indiana Jones and the Temple of Doom, Witness (Acad. Award nom.), The Mosquito Coast, Frantic, Working Girl, Indiana Jones and the Last Crusade, Presumed Innocent, Regarding Henry, Patriot Games, The Fugitive, Jimmy Hollywood (cameo), Clear and Present Danger, Sabrina, Devil's Own.
TELEVISION: Movies: The Intruders, James A. Michener's Dynasty, The Possessed. Guest: The Virginian, Ironside, The FBI, Love American Style, Gunsmoke, The Young Indiana Jones Chronicles. Special: Trial of Lt. Calley.

FORMAN, SIR DENIS
O.B.E., M.A.: Executive. b. Moffat, Dumfriesshire, Scot., Oct. 13, 1917. e. Loretto Sch., Musselburgh, Pembroke Coll., Cambridge. Served in Argyll & Sutherland Highlanders, W.W.II. Entered film business 1946, production staff Central Office of Information, 1947; Chief Production Officer C.O.I. 1948; appointed dir. of the British Film Inst., 1949; joined Granada Television Ltd., 1955. Jnt. Mng. Dir., 1965 chmn., British Film Inst., bd. of Gov., 1971-73. Chmn. Granada T.V. 1975-87. Chmn. Novello & Co. 1972. Fellow, British Acad. Film & TV Arts, 1976. Dep. chmn. Granada Group, 1984-90, consultant, 1990-96. Deputy chmn. Royal Opera House, 1983-92.

FORMAN, JEROME A.
Executive. b. Hood River, Oregon, June 20, 1934. e. U Arizona. 1966, became gen. mgr. Forman and United Theatres of the Northwest. 1971, joined Pacific Theatres; 1972, appointed v.p. & gen. mgr.; 1978-87, exec. v.p.; 1987-present, pres. One of the original founders of the ShoWest Convention. Currently chmn. emeritus, NATO of Calif. Presently 1991 chmn. NATO. 1991 elected chmn. bd. of Will Rogers Memorial Fund. Board member of the Foundation of the Motion Picture Pioneers.

FORMAN, MILOS
Director. b. Caslav, Czechoslovakia, Feb. 18, 1932. Trained as writer at Czech Film Sch. and as director at Laterna Magika. Directed short films Audition (Competition), If There Were No Music. Won Int'l. attention with first feature length film Black Peter, 1963. Emigrated to U.S. after collapse of Dubcek govt. in Czechoslovakia, 1969. Appeared as actor in films Heartburn, New Year's Day.
PICTURES: Peter and Pavla/Black Peter (also co-s.p.); Czech Film Critics & Grand Prix Locarno Awards), Loves of a Blonde (also co- s.p.), The Firemen's Ball (also co-s.p.), Taking Off (U.S. debut, 1971), Visions of Eight (Decathalon segment), One Flew Over the Cuckoo's Nest (Academy Award, 1975), Hair, Ragtime, Amadeus (Academy Award, 1984), Valmont, The People vs. Larry Flynt.

FORREST, FREDERIC
Actor. b. Waxahachie, TX, Dec. 23, 1936. e. Texas Christian U., U. of Oklahoma, B.A. Studied with Sanford Meisner and Lee Strasberg. Began career off-off B'way at Caffe Cino in The

Madness of Lady Bright then off-B'way in Futz, Massachusetts Trust and Tom Paine, all with La Mama Troupe under direction of Tom O'Horgan. Moved to Hollywood in 1970.
PICTURES: Futz (debut, 1969), When the Legends Die, The Don Is Dead, The Conversation, The Gravy Train, Permission to Kill, The Missouri Breaks, It Lives Again!, Apocalypse Now, The Rose (Acad. Award nom.), One From the Heart, Hammett, Valley Girl, The Stone Boy, Return, Where Are the Children?, Stacking, Tucker: The Man and His Dream, Valentino Returns, Music Box, The Two Jakes, Cat Chaser, Rain Without Thunder, Falling Down, Trauma, Chasers, One Night Stand.
TELEVISION: Movies: Larry, Promise Him Anything, Ruby and Oswald, Calamity Jane, Right to Kill?, The Deliberate Stranger, Quo Vadis, Little Girl Lost, Saigon: Year of the Cat (U.K.), Best Kept Secrets, Who Will Love My Children? A Shadow on the Sun, Margaret Bourke-White, Citizen Cohn, The Habitation of Dragons, Against the Wall. Mini-Series: Die Kinder.

FORREST, STEVE
Actor. b. Huntsville, TX, Sept. 29, 1925. r.n. William Forrest Andrews. Brother of late actor Dana Andrews. e. UCLA, 1950. Acted at La Jolla Playhouse; appeared on radio, TV; m.p. debut in Crash Dive billed as William Andrews.
PICTURES: Crash Dive (debut, 1942), The Ghost Ship, Geisha Girl, Sealed Cargo, Last of the Comanches, The Bad and the Beautiful (1st billing as Steve Forrest), Dream Wife, Battle Circus, The Clown, The Band Wagon, So Big, Take the High Ground, Phantom of the Rue Morgue, Prisoner of War, Rogue Cop, Bedevilled, The Living Idol, It Happened to Jane, Heller in Pink Tights, Five Branded Women, Flaming Star, The Second Time Around, The Longest Day, The Yellow Canary, Rascal, The Wild Country, The Late Liz, North Dallas Forty, Mommie Dearest, Sahara, Spies Like Us, Amazon Women on the Moon.
TELEVISION: Movies: The Hatfields and the McCoys, Wanted: The Sundance Women, The Last of the Mohicans, Testimony of Two Men, Maneaters are Loose, Hollywood Wives, Gunsmoke: Return to Dodge, Columbo: A Bird in the Hand. Series: The Baron, S.W.A.T., Dallas.

FORSTATER, MARK
Producer. b. Philadelphia, PA, 1943. e. City Coll. of New York, Temple U. In 1967 moved to England; studied at U. of Manchester and London Intl. Film School. First job in industry with Anglia TV on program, Survival. Began producing in 1970 with British Film Institute. Set up Chippenham Films to make documentaries. Moved into features in 1974 with Monty Python and the Holy Grail.
PICTURES: The Odd Job, Marigolds in August, The Grass Is Singing, Xtro, Paint It Black, Wherever She Is, The Wolves of Willoughby Chase, Death of a Schoolboy, Streets of Yesterday, Wherever You Are (exec. prod.). Shorts: The Glitterball, Wish You Were Here, The Silent Touch, Between the Devil and the Deep Blue Sea, Provocateur.
TELEVISION: The Cold Room, Forbidden, Separation, Grushko, Doing Rude Things.

FORSTER, ROBERT
Actor. b. Rochester, NY, July 13, 1941. e. Heidelberg Coll., Alfred U., Rochester U., B.S.
THEATER: Mrs. Dally Has a Lover, A Streetcar Named Desire, The Glass Menagerie, 12 Angry Men, The Sea Horse, One Flew Over the Cuckoo's Nest, The Big Knife.
PICTURES: Reflections in a Golden Eye (debut, 1967), The Stalking Moon, Medium Cool, Justine, Cover Me Babe, Pieces of Dreams, Journey Through Rosebud, The Don is Dead, Stunts, Avalanche, The Black Hole, Lady in Red (unbilled), Crunch, Alligator, Vigilante, Walking the Edge, Hollywood Harry (also prod., dir.), The Delta Force, Committed, Esmeralda Bay, Heat from Another Sun, The Banker, Peacemaker, Diplomatic Immunity, 29th Street, In Between, Badge of Silence, Maniac Cop 3: Badge of Silence, South Beach, Cover Story, Body Chemistry 3: Point of Seduction.
TELEVISION: Series: Banyon, Nakia, Once a Hero. Movies: Banyon, The Death Squad, Nakia, The City, Standing Tall, The Darker Side of Terror, Goliath Awaits, In the Shadow of a Killer, Sex Love and Cold Hard Cash. Pilots: Checkered Flag, Mickie & Frankie.

FORSYTH, BILL
Director. Writer. b. Glasgow, Scotland, July 29, 1946. At 16 joined film co. For next 10 years made industrial films, then documentaries. Joined Glasgow Youth Theater.
PICTURES: Director-Writer: That Sinking Feeling (debut, 1979; also prod.), Gregory's Girl, Local Hero, Comfort and Joy, Housekeeping, Breaking In, Rebecca's Daughters, Being Human.
TELEVISION: Andrina.

FORSYTHE, JOHN
Actor. b. Penn's Grove, NJ, Jan. 29, 1918. r.n. John Freund. Former commentator for Brooklyn Dodgers, prior to becoming actor. Debuted on tv in 1947.
THEATER: Mr. Roberts, All My Sons, Yellow Jack, Teahouse of the August Moon, and others.

PICTURES: Destination Tokyo (debut, 1943), The Captive City, It Happens Every Thursday, The Glass Web, Escape From Fort Bravo, The Trouble With Harry, The Ambassador's Daughter, Everything But the Truth, Kitten With a Whip, Madame X, In Cold Blood, The Happy Ending, Topaze, Goodbye and Amen, And Justice for All, Scrooged.
TELEVISION: Series: Bachelor Father, The John Forsythe Show, To Rome With Love, Charlie's Angels (voice only), Dynasty, The Powers That Be. Movies: See How They Run, Shadow on the Land, Murder Once Removed, The Letters, Lisa—Bright and Dark, Cry Panic, Healers, Terror on the 40th Floor, The Deadly Tower, Amelia Earhart, Tail Gunner Joe, Never Con a Killer, Cruise Into Terror, With This Ring, The Users, A Time for Miracles, Sizzle, The Mysterious Two, On Fire, Opposites Attract, Dynasty: The Reunion. Guest: Studio One, Kraft Theatre, Robert Montgomery Presents.

FORSYTHE, WILLIAM
Actor. b. Brooklyn, NY.
THEATER: A Streetcar Named Desire, A Hatful of Rain, Othello, Julius Caesar, 1776, Hair, Godspell.
PICTURES: King of the Mountain, Smokey Bites the Dust, Once Upon a Time in America, Cloak and Dagger, Savage Dawn, The Lightship, Raising Arizona, Extreme Prejudice, Weeds, Patty Hearst, Dead Bang, Torrents of Spring, Dick Tracy, Career Opportunities, Out for Justice, Stone Cold, Sons, American Me, The Waterdance, The Gun in Betty Lou's Handbag, Relentless 3, Direct Hit, The Immortals, Virtuosity, Things to Do in Denver When You're Dead, The Substitute, Palookaville.
TELEVISION: Series: The Untouchables (1993). Movies: The Miracle of Kathy Miller, The Long Hot Summer, Cruel Doubt, Willing to Kill: The Texas Cheerleader Story, A Kiss to Die For, Gotti. Guest: CHiPs, Fame, Hill Street Blues. Mini-Series: Blind Faith.

FORTE, FABIAN
Singer, Actor. b. Philadelphia, PA, Feb. 6, 1943. e. South Philadelphia H.S. At 14, signed contract with Chancellor Records. Studied with Carlo Menotti. Formerly billed simply as Fabian.
RECORDS: Turn Me Loose, Tiger, I'm a Man, Hound Dog Man, The Fabulous Fabian (gold album).
PICTURES: Hound Dog Man (debut, 1959), High Time, North to Alaska, Love in a Goldfish Bowl, Five Weeks in a Balloon, Mr. Hobbs Takes a Vacation, The Longest Day, Ride the Wild Surf, Dear Brigitte, Ten Little Indians, Fireball 500, Dr. Goldfoot and the Girl Bombs, Thunder Alley, Maryjane, The Wild Racers, The Devil's Eight, A Bullet for Pretty Boy, Lovin' Man, Little Laura and Big John, Disco Fever, Kiss Daddy Goodbye, Get Crazy.
TELEVISION: Movies: Getting Married, Katie: Portrait of a Centerfold, Crisis in Mid-Air. Guest: Bus Stop, Love American Style, Laverne & Shirley, The Love Boat.

FOSSEY, BRIGITTE
Actress. b. Tourcoing, France, Mar. 11, 1947. After debut at the age of 5 in Rene Clement's Forbidden Games (1952) returned to school, studying philosophy and translating. Rediscovered by director Jean-Gabriel Albicocco and cast in Le Grand Meaulnes (1967).
PICTURES: Forbidden Games (debut, 1952), The Happy Road, Le Grand Meaulnes (The Wanderer), Adieu l'Ami, M Comme Mathieu, Raphael ou le DeBauche, Going Places, La Brigade, The Blue Country, Femme Fetales, The Good and the Bad, The Man Who Loved Women, The Swiss Affair, Quintet, Mais ou et donc Orincar, The Triple Death of the Third Character, A Bad Son, The Party, Chanel Solitaire, A Bite of Living, Imperativ, The Party-2, Enigma, Au nom de tous les Meins, Scarlet Fever, A Strange Passion, A Case of Irresponsibility, The Future of Emily, The False Confidences, Cinema Paradiso.

FOSTER, CHRISTINE
Executive. r.n. Mary Christine Foster. b. Los Angeles, CA, March 19, 1943. e. Immaculate Heart Coll, B.A. 1967. UCLA MJ, 1968. Teacher while member of Immaculate Heart Community, 1962-65. Teacher, Pacific U., Tokyo, 1968; dir., research and dev. Metromedia Producers Corp., 1968-71; dir., dev. & prod. services, Wolper Org. 1971-76; mgr.; film progs. NBC TV 1976-77; v.p. movies for TV & mini-series, Columbia Pictures TV, 1977-81; v.p. series programs, Columbia TV, 1981; v.p. prog. dev., Group W. Prods. 1981-87; v.p., The Agency, 1988-90; agent, Shapiro-Lichtman Talent Agency, 1990-. Member: exec. comm. Humanitas Awards, 1986-; exec. comm. Catholics in Media, 1993-; Activities Committee, Acad. of TV Arts & Sciences, 1989-91; L.A. Roman Catholic Archdiocesan Communications Comm., 1986-89; Women in Film, bd. of dirs., 1977-78; teacher UCLA Extension, 1987-. Foreign and domestic university and public group lecturer and speaker.

FOSTER, DAVID
Producer. b. New York, NY, Nov. 25, 1929. e. Dorsey H.S., U. of Southern California Sch. of Journalism. U.S. Army, 1952-54; entered public relations field in 1952 with Rogers, Cowan &

Brenner; Jim Mahoney, 1956; Allan, Foster, Ingersoll & Weber, 1958; left field in 1968 to enter independent m.p. production. Partner in Turman-Foster Co.
PICTURES: *Produced* (with Mitchell Brower): McCabe and Mrs. Miller, The Getaway. Produced (with Lawrence Turman): The Nickel Ride (exec. prod.), The Drowning Pool, The Legacy, Tribute (exec. prod.), Caveman, The Thing, Second Thoughts, Mass Appeal, The Mean Season, Short Circuit, Running Scared, Full Moon in Blue Water, Short Circuit II, Gleaming the Cube, The Getaway (1993), The River Wild.
TELEVISION: Jesse (co-exec. prod), Between Two Brothers, Surrogate Mother.

FOSTER, JODIE
Actress. r.n. Alicia Christian Foster. b. Los Angeles, CA, Nov. 19, 1962. e. Yale U. Started acting in commercials including famous Coppertone ad. Acting debut on Mayberry, R.F.D. TV series (1968). Followed with many TV appearances, from series to movies of the week.
PICTURES: Napoleon and Samantha (debut, 1972), Kansas City Bomber, Tom Sawyer, One Little Indian, Alice Doesn't Live Here Anymore, Taxi Driver (Acad. Award nom.), Echoes of a Summer, Bugsy Malone, Freaky Friday, The Little Girl Who Lives Down the Lane, Il Casotto (The Beach Hut), Moi fleur bleue (Stop Calling Me Baby!), Candleshoe, Foxes, Carny, O'Hara's Wife, The Hotel New Hampshire, Mesmerized (also co-prod.), Siesta, Five Corners, Stealing Home, The Accused (Academy Award, 1988), The Silence of the Lambs (Academy Award, 1991), Little Man Tate (also dir.), Shadows and Fog, Sommersby, Maverick, Nell (Acad. Award nom.; also co-prod.), Home for the Holidays (dir., co-prod. only), Hate, Contact.
TELEVISION: Series: Bob & Carol & Ted & Alice, Paper Moon. Guest: The Courtship of Eddie's Father, Gunsmoke, Julia, Mayberry R.F.D., Ironside, My Three Sons. Specials: Alexander, Rookie of the Year, Menace on the Mountain, The Secret Life of T.K. Dearing, The Fisherman's Wife. Movies: Smile Jenny--You're Dead, The Blood of Others, Svengali, Backtrack.

FOSTER, JULIA
Actress. b. Lewes, Sussex, England, 1941. First acted with the Brighton Repertory Company, then two years with the Worthing, Harrogate and Richmond companies. 1956, TV debut as Ann Carson in Emergency Ward 10.
THEATER: The Country Wife, What the Butler Saw.
PICTURES: Term of Trial (debut, 1962), The Loneliness of the Long Distance Runner, Two Left Feet, The Small World of Sammy Lee, The System (The Gir Getters), The Bargee, One Way Pendulum, Alfie, Half a Sixpence, All Coppers Are ..., The Great McGonagall.
TELEVISION: A Cosy Little Arrangement, The Planemakers, Love Story, Taxi, Consequences, They Throw It at You, Crime and Punishment, The Image.

FOSTER, MEG
Actress. b. Reading, PA, May 14, 1948. e. N.Y. Neighborhood Playhouse.
PICTURES: Adam at 6 A.M. (debut, 1970), Thumb Tripping, Welcome to Arrow Beach (Tender Flesh), A Different Story, Once in Paris, Carny, Ticket to Heaven, The Osterman Weekend, The Emerald Forest, Masters of the Universe, The Wind, They Live, Leviathan, Relentless, Stepfather 2, Blind Fury, Tripwire, Jezebel's Kiss, Diplomatic Immunity, Dead One: Relentless II, Project Shadowchaser, Immortal Combat.
TELEVISION: Movies: The Death of Me Yet, Sunshine, Things In This Season, Promise Him Anything, James Dean, Sunshine Christmas, Guyana Tragedy, Legend of Sleepy Hollow, Desperate Intruder, Best Kept Secrets, Desperate, Back Stab, To Catch a Killer. Series: Sunshine, Cagney & Lacey. Guest: Here Come the Brides, Mod Squad, Men at Law, Hawaii Five-O, Murder She Wrote, Miami Vice. Mini-Series: Washington: Behind Closed Doors. Special: The Scarlet Letter.

FOWKES, RICHARD O.
Executive. b. Yonkers, NY, April 15, 1946. e. NYU, Geo. Washington U. Staff attorney for The Dramatists Guild, 1973-77; joined Paramount as assoc. counsel, 1977-80; moved to UA (NYC) as prod. attorney from 1980-82; returned to Paramount as v.p., legal & bus. affairs., MoPic division (LA) 1983; promoted to sr. v.p., bus. affairs & acquisitions, 1989; promoted to sr. v.p. in charge of bus. affairs, 1994.

FOWLER, HARRY
Actor. b. London, England, Dec. 10, 1926. e. West Central Sch., London. Stage debut, Nothing Up My Sleeve (London) 1950; Screen debut, 1941.
PICTURES: Demi-Paradise, Don't Take It to Heart, Champaine Charlie, Painted Boats, Hue and Cry, Now Barabbas, The Dark Man, She Shall Have Murder, The Scarlet Thread, High Treason, The Last Page, I Believe in You, Pickwick Papers, Top of the Form, Angels One Five, Conflict of Wings (Fuss Over Feathers), A Day to Remember, Blue Peter, Home and Away, Booby Trap, Town on Trial, Lucky Jim, Birthday Present, Idle on Parade, Don't Panic Chaps, Heart of a Man, Crooks Anonymous, The

Longest Day, Lawrence of Arabia, Flight from Singapore, The Golliwog, Ladies Who Do, Clash By Night, The Nanny, Life at the Top, Start the Revolution Without Me, The Prince and The Pauper, Fanny Hill, Chicago Joe and the Showgirl.
TELEVISION: Stalingrad, I Remember the Battle, Gideon's Way, That's for Me, Our Man at St. Mark's, Dixon of Dock Green, Dr. Finlay's Case Book, I Was There, Cruffs Dog Show, The Londoners, Jackanory, Get This, Movie Quiz, Get This (series), Going a Bundle, Ask a Silly Answer, London Scene, Flockton Flyer, Sun Trap, The Little World of Don Camillo, World's End, Minder, Dead Ernest, Morecambe Wise Show, Gossip, Entertainment Express, Fresh Fields, Supergram, A Roller Next Year, Harry's Kingdom, Body Contact, Davro's Sketch Pad, The Bill, In Sickness and in Health, Casualty, Leaves on the Line, Young Indiana Jones Chronicles, Southside Party, London Tonight.

FOWLEY, DOUGLAS
Actor. b. New York, NY, May 30, 1911. e. St. Francis Xavier's Mil. Acad., N.Y. In stock; operated dramatic sch. N.Y.; on screen in bit parts. From 1934 in regular roles.
PICTURES: Battleground, Just This Once, This Woman Is Dangerous, Singin' in the Rain, Man Behind the Gun, Slight Case of Larceny, Naked Jungle, Casanova's Big Night, Lone Gun, The High and the Mighty, Three Ring Circus, Texas Lady, Broken Star, Girl Rush, Bandido, Nightmare in the Sun, The North Avenue Irregulars, From Noon Till Three, The White Buffalo.
TELEVISION: The Moneychangers, Starsky and Hutch, Sunshine Christmas, Oregon Trail. Series: The Life and Legend of Wyatt Earp, Pistols and Petticoats, Gunsmoke.

FOX, EDWARD
Actor. b. London, England, April 13, 1937. Comes from theatrical family; father was agent for leading London actors; brother is actor James Fox.
PICTURES: The Mind Benders (debut, 1962), Morgan!, The Frozen Dead, The Long Duel, The Naked Runner, The Jokers, I'll Never Forget What's 'is Name, The Battle of Britain, Oh! What a Lovely War, Skullduggery, The Go-Between, The Day of The Jackal, A Doll's House, Galileo, The Squeeze, A Bridge Too Far, The Duellists, The Big Sleep, Force 10 from Navarone, The Cat and the Canary, Soldier of Orange, The Mirror Crack'd, Gandhi, Never Say Never Again, The Dresser, The Bounty, Wild Geese II, The Shooting Party, Return From the River Kwai, A Feast at Midnight, A Month by the Lake, Prince Valiant.
TELEVISION: Edward and Mrs. Simpson, A Hazard of Hearts, Anastasia: The Mystery of Anna, Quartermaine's Terms, They Never Slept, Shaka Zulu, Robin Hood, The Crucifer of Blood.

FOX, JAMES
Actor. b. London, England, May 19, 1939. Brother is actor Edward Fox. Ent. films as child actor in 1950 as William Fox. Left acting in 1973 to follow spiritual vocation. Returned to mainsteam films in 1982. B'way debut 1995 in Uncle Vanya.
PICTURES: The Miniver Story (debut, 1950; as William Fox), The Magnet, One Wild Oat, The Lavender Hill Mob, Timbuktu, The Queen's Guards, The Secret Partner, She Always Gets Their Man, What Every Woman Wants, The Loneliness of the Long-Distance Runner; Tamahine (1st film billed as James Fox), The Servant, Those Magnificent Men in Their Flying Machines, King Rat, The Chase, Thoroughly Modern Millie, Arabella, Duffy, Isadora, Performance, No Longer Alone, Runners, Greystoke: The Legend of Tarzan, A Passage to India, Pavlova, Absolute Beginners, The Whistle Blower, Comrades, High Season, The Mighty Quinn, Farewell to the King, The Boys in the Island, The Russia House, Patriot Games, Afraid of the Dark, The Remains of the Day.
TELEVISION: The Door, Espionage, Love Is Old, Love Is New, Nancy Astor, Country, New World, Beryl Markham: A Shadow on the Sun, Sun Child, She's Been Away (BBC; shown theatrically in U.S.), Never Come Back, Slowly Slowly in the Wind, Patricia Highsmith Series, As You Like It, A Question of Attribution, Heart of Darkness, Fall from Grace, Hostage, Doomsday Gun, Headhunters, The Old Curiosity Shop.

FOX, MICHAEL J.
Actor. b. Edmonton, Alberta, Canada, June 9, 1961. r.n. Michael Andrew Fox. m. actress Tracy Pollan. Appeared in Vancouver TV series Leo and Me, and on stage there in The Shadow Box. Moved to Los Angeles at age 18.
PICTURES: Midnight Madness (debut, 1980), The Class of 1984, Back to the Future, Teen Wolf, Light of Day, The Secret of My Success, Bright Lights Big City, Casualties of War, Back to the Future Part II, Back to the Future Part III, The Hard Way, Doc Hollywood, Homeward Bound: The Incredible Journey (voice), Life With Mikey, For Love or Money, Where the Rivers Flow North, Greedy, Coldblooded (also co-prod.), Blue in the Face, The American President, Homeward Bound II: Lost in San Francisco (voice), The Frighteners, Mars Attacks.
TELEVISION: Series: Palmerstown U.S.A., Family Ties (3 Emmy Awards), Spin City. Guest: Lou Grant, The Love Boat, Night Court, Trapper John M.D., Tales from the Crypt (The Trap; also

dir.). *Specials*: Teachers Only, Time Travel: Fact Fiction and Fantasy, Dear America: Letters Home From Vietnam (reader), James Cagney: Top of the World (host). *Movies*: Letters From Frank, High School USA, Poison Ivy, Family Ties Vacation, Don't Drink the Water. *Director*: Brooklyn Bridge (episode).

FOX, RICHARD
Executive. b. New York, NY, Feb. 24, 1947. Joined Warner Bros. Intl. as mgt. trainee in October 1975, working in Australia and Japan. 1977, named gen. mgr. of Columbia-Warner Dist., New Zealand. Joined WB in Tokyo, 1978\-1981. Joined WB in L.A. as exec. asst. to Myron D. Karlin, pres. of WB Intl., 1981; appt. v.p., sls. 1982; 1983, promoted to exec. v.p. of intl. arm; 1985, named pres. of WB Intl., assuming post vacated by Karlin. 1992, promoted to exec. v.p., Intl. Theatrical Enterprises, WB.

FOX, RICHARD A.
Executive. b. Buffalo, NY, Jan 5, 1929. e. U. of Buffalo, 1950. Chmn., Fox Theatres Management Corp. Pres., Nat'l NATO 1984-86; chmn., Nat'l NATO 1986-1988.

FOXWELL, IVAN
Producer, Writer. b. London, Eng., Feb. 22, 1914. Entered m.p. ind. 1933 as technician with British & Dominions Film Corp., subsequently with Paramount British & London Films; Assoc. with Curtis Bernhardt in Paris 1937 becoming producer & collaborating on story, s.p. of Carefour, Le Train pour Venise, De Mayerling Sarajevo, others. WWII with BEF and AEF 1939-46. Returned to British films 1947. Director, Foxwell Film Prods. Ltd. PICTURES: *Producer*: No Room at the Inn (also co-s.p.), Guilt Is My Shadow (also co-s.p.), Twenty-Four Hours of a Woman's Life, The Intruder (also co-s.p.), Manuela, A Touch of Larceny, Tiara Tahiti, The Quiller Memorandum, Decline and Fall (also s.p.). TELEVISION: The Intruder (co-writer), The Colditz Story (prod.).

FOXWORTH, ROBERT
Actor. b. Houston, TX, Nov. 1, 1941. e. Carnegie-Mellon U. Began acting at age 10 at Houston Alley Theatre and stayed with stage part-time while completing formal education. Returned to theatre on full-time basis after graduation. Made TV debut in Sadbird, 1969.
THEATER: *NY*: Henry V, Terra Nova, The Crucible (Theatre World Award), Love Letters, Candida. *Regional*: Antony & Cleopatra, Uncle Vanya, Cyrano de Bergerac, Who's Afraid of Virginia Woolf?, Othello, Habeus Corpus, The Seagull, Macbeth. PICTURES: Treasure of Matecumbe (debut, 1976), The Astral Factor, Airport '77, Damien: Omen II, Prophecy, The Black Marble, Beyond the Stars.
TELEVISION: *Series*: The Storefront Lawyers, Falcon Crest. *Movies*: The Devil's Daughter, Frankenstein, Mrs. Sundance, The Questor Tapes (pilot), The FBI Story: The FBI Vs. Alvin Karpis, James Dean, It Happened at Lakewood Manor, Death Moon, The Memory of Eva Ryker, Act of Love, Peter and Paul, The Return of the Desperado, Double Standard, Face to Face, The Price of the Bride, With Murder in Mind, For Love and Glory. *Specials*: Hogan's Goat, Another Part of the Forest.

FRAKER, WILLIAM A.
Cinematographer, Director. b. Los Angeles, CA, 1923. e. U. of Southern California Film Sch. Worked as camera operator with Conrad Hall; moved to TV before feature films. Photographed and co-prod. doc. Forbid Them Not.
PICTURES: *Cinematographer:* Games, The Fox, The President's Analyst, Fade In, Rosemary's Baby, Bullitt, Paint Your Wagon, Dusty and Sweets McGee, The Day of the Dolphin, Rancho Deluxe, Aloha Bobby and Rose, Lipstick, The Killer Inside Me, Gator, Exorcist II--The Heretic, Looking for Mr. Goodbar, American Hot Wax, Heaven Can Wait, Old Boyfriends, 1941, The Hollywood Knights, Divine Madness, Sharky's Machine, The Best Little Whorehouse in Texas, WarGames, Irreconcilable Differences, Protocol, Fever Pitch, Murphy's Romance, SpaceCamp, Burglar, Baby Boom, Chances Are, An Innocent Man, The Freshman, Memoirs of an Invisible Man, Honeymoon in Vegas, Tombstone (also co-assoc. prod.), Street Fighter, Father of the Bride II. *Director:* Monte Walsh, Reflection of Fear, Legend of the Lone Ranger.
TELEVISION: Stony Burke, Outer Limits, Ozzie and Harriet, Daktari, B.L. Stryker: The Dancer's Touch (dir.).

FRANCIOSA, ANTHONY
Actor. b. New York, NY, Oct. 25, 1928. e. Ben Franklin h.s. in NY. Erwin Piscator's Dramatic Workshop (4-year scholarship). First stage part in YWCA play; joined Off-Broadway stage group; stock at Lake Tahoe, CA, Chicago and Boston.
THEATER: *B'way*: End as a Man, The Wedding Breakfast, A Hatful of Rain (Theatre World Award, Tony nom.), Rocket to the Moon, Grand Hotel. *Tour*: Love Letters.
PICTURES: A Face in the Crowd (debut, 1957), This Could Be The Night, A Hatful of Rain (Acad. Award nom.), Wild Is The Wind, The Long Hot Summer, The Naked Maja, Career, The Story on Page One, Go Naked in the World, Senilita (Carless), Period of Adjustment, Rio Conchos, The Pleasure Seekers, A

Man Could Get Killed, Assault on a Queen, The Swinger, Fathom, In Enemy Country, The Sweet Ride, A Man Called Gannon, Ghost in the Noonday Sun, Across 110th Street, The Drowning Pool, Firepower, The World is Full of Married Men, Death Wish II, Julie Darling, Ghost in the Noonday Sun, Death Is in Fashion, Tenebrae, Help Me Dream, The Cricket, A Texas Legend, Backstreet Dreams, Death House, Brothers in Arms, Double Threat, City Hall.
TELEVISION: *Series*: Valentine's Day, The Name of the Game, Search, Matt Helm, Finder of Lost Loves. *Movies*: Fame is the Name of the Game, Deadly Hunt, Earth II, The Catcher, This is the West That Was, Matt Helm, Curse of the Black Widow, Side Show, Till Death Do Us Part, Ghost Writer. *Mini-Series*: Aspen, Wheels. *Guest*: Kraft Theatre, Philco Playhouse, Danger, Naked City, Arrest & Trial, Playhouse 90, etc.

FRANCIS, ANNE
Actress b. Ossining, NY, Sept. 16, 1932. Child model; radio, TV shows as child & adult; on B'way in Lady in the Dark.
PICTURES: Summer Holiday (debut, 1948), So Young So Bad, Whistle at Eaton Falls, Elopement, Lydia Bailey, Dream Boat, A Lion Is in the Streets, Rocket Man, Susan Slept Here, Rogue Cop, Bad Day at Black Rock, Battle Cry, Blackboard Jungle, The Scarlet Coat, Forbidden Planet, The Rack, The Great American Pastime, The Hired Gun, Don't Go Near the Water, Crowded Sky, Girl of the Night, Satan Bug, Brainstorm, Funny Girl, Hook Line and Sinker, More Dead Than Alive, The Love God?, Impasse, Pancho Villa, Survival, Born Again, The High Fashion Murders, The Return, Little Vegas.
TELEVISION: *Series*: Honey West, My Three Sons, Dallas, Riptide. *Guest*: Partners in Crime, Crazy Like a Fox, Jake and the Fatman, Twilight Zone, Finder of Lost Loves, Golden Girls, Matlock, Murder She Wrote, Burke's Law. *Movies*: Wild Women, The Intruders, The Forgotten Man, Mongo's Back in Town, Fireball Forward, Haunts of the Very Rich, Cry Panic, FBI Vs. Alvin Karpis, The Last Survivors, A Girl Named Sooner, Banjo Hackett, Little Mo, The Rebels, Beggarman Thief, Detour to Terror, Rona Jaffe's Mazes and Monsters, Poor Little Rich Girl: The Barbara Hutton Story, Laguna Heat, My First Love, Love Can Be Murder, Fortune Hunter.

FRANCIS, ARLENE
Actress. r.n. Arlene Francis Kazanjian; b. Boston, MA, Oct. 20, 1908. e. Convent of Mount St. Vincent Acad., Riverdale, NY; Finch Finishing Sch.; Theatre Guild Sch., NY. m. Martin Gabel, late actor. *Author*: That Certain Something (1960); Arlene Francis--A Memoir (1978).
THEATER: The Women (1937), Horse Eats Hat (Mercury Theater), Danton's Death, All That Glitters, Doughgirls, The Overtons, Once More With Feeling, Tchin-Tchin, Beekman Place, Mrs. Dally, Dinner at Eight, Kind Sir, Lion in Winter, Pal Joey, Who Killed Santa Claus?, Gigi, Social Security.
PICTURES: Murders in the Rue Morgue, Stage Door Canteen, All My Sons, One Two Three, The Thrill of It All, Fedora.
TELEVISION: Soldier Parade 1949-55, Blind Date, What's My Line; Home, Arlene Francis Show, Talent Patrol, etc.
RADIO: Arlene Francis Show, Emphasis, Monitor, Luncheon at Sardis.

FRANCIS, CONNIE
Singer. r.n. Constance Franconero. b. Newark, NJ, Dec. 12, 1938. Appeared, Star Time when 12 years old; won Arthur Godfrey's Talent Scout Show, 12 years old. Autobiography: Who's Sorry Now (1984). Regular on series The Jimmie Rodgers Show, 1959. Gold Records: Who's Sorry Now, My Happiness. Numerous vocalist awards.
PICTURES: Where the Boys Are, Follow the Boys, Looking For Love.

FRANCIS, FREDDIE
Producer, Director, Cinematographer. b. London, 1917. Joined Gaumont British Studios as apprentice to stills photographer; then clapper boy at B.I.P. Studios, Elstree; camera asst. at British Dominion. After W.W.II returned to Shepperton Studios to work for Korda and with Powell and Pressburger as cameraman.
PICTURES: *Director*: Two and Two Make Six (A Change of Heart/The Girl Swappers; debut, 1962), Paranoiac, Vengeance, The Evil of Frankenstein, Nightmare, Traitor's Gate, Hysteria, Dr. Terror's House of Horrors, The Skull, The Psychopath, The Deadly Bees, They Came from Beyond Space, Torture Garden, Dracula Has Risen from the Grave, Mumsy Nanny Sonny and Girly, Trog, Tales from the Crypt, The Creeping Flesh, Tales That Witness Madness, Son of Dracula, Craze, The Ghoul, Legend of the Werewolf, The Doctor and the Devils, Dark Tower. *Cinematographer:* Moby Dick (second unit photo., special effects), A Hill in Korea (Hell in Korea), Time Without Pity, Room at the Top, The Battle of the Sexes, Saturday Night and Sunday Morning, Sons and Lovers (Academy Award, 1960), The Innocents, Night Must Fall, The Elephant Man, The French Lieutenant's Woman, Dune, Memed My Hawk, Clara's Heart, Her Alibi, Brenda Starr, Glory (Academy Award, 1989), Man in the Moon, Cape Fear, School Ties, Princess Caraboo.
TELEVISION: *Movie*: A Life in the Theatre.

FRANCIS, KEVIN
Producer, Executive. b. London, England, 1949. Produced It's Life, Passport, Troubl with Canada, Persecution, The Ghoul, Legend of the Werewolf, etc. Executive produ. The Masks of Death, Murder Elite, A One-Way Ticket to Hollywood, etc. 1976, prod. Film Technique Educational course for BFI. 1972-94, CEO Tyburn Prods. Ltd. 1994-present, Ar;ington Productions Ltd.

FRANKENHEIMER, JOHN
Director. b. Malba, NY, Feb. 19, 1930. e. Williams Coll. Actor, dir., summer stock; radio-TV actor, dir., Washington, DC; then joined CBS network in 1953. Theater: The Midnight Sun (1959). PICTURES: The Young Stranger (debut, 1957), The Young Savages, Birdman of Alcatraz, All Fall Down, The Manchurian Candidate (also co-prod.), Seven Days in May, The Train, Seconds, Grand Prix, The Fixer, The Extraordinary Seaman, The Gypsy Moths, I Walk the Line, The Horsemen, The Impossible Object (Story of a Love Story), The Iceman Cometh, 99 and 44/100% Dead, French Connection II, Black Sunday, Prophecy, The Challenge, The Holcroft Covenant, 52 Pick-Up, Dead-Bang, The Fourth War, Year of the Gun, The Island of Dr. Moreau.
TELEVISION: Series dir.: I Remember Mama, You Are There, Danger, Climax, Studio One, Playhouse 90, Du Pont Show of the Month, Ford Startime, Sunday Showcase. Specials: The Comedian, For Whom the Bell Tolls, The Days of Wine and Roses, Old Man, The Turn of the Screw, The Browning Version, The Rainmaker. Movies: Against the Wall (Emmy Award, 1994), The Burning Season (Emmy Award, 1995; also co-prod.). Mini-Series: Andersonville (Emmy Award, 1996).

FRANKLIN, BONNIE
Actress. b. Santa Monica, CA, Jan. 6, 1944. e. Smith College & UCLA. On B'way: Applause (Theatre World Award, Tony nom. Outer Critics Circle award), Dames At sea, Your Own Thing. Off-B'way in Frankie and Johnny in the Claire de Lune.
TELEVISION: Series: One Day at a Time. Movies: The Law, A Guide for the Married Woman, Breaking Up Is Hard to Do, Portrait of a Rebel: Margaret Sanger, Your Place or Mine, Sister Margaret and Saturday Night Ladies, Shalom Sesame.

FRANKLIN, MICHAEL HAROLD
Executive. b. Los Angeles, CA, Dec. 25, 1923. e. U. of California, A.B., USC, LL.B. Admitted to CA bar, 1951; pvt. practice in L.A. 1951-52; atty. CBS, 1952-54; atty. Paramount, 1954-58; exec. dir. Writers Guild Am. West, Inc. 1958-78; natl exec. dir., Directors Guild of America 1978-. Mem. Am. Civil Liberties Union, Los Angeles Copyright Soc.

FRANKLIN, PAMELA
Actress. b. Tokyo, Japan, Feb. 4, 1950. Attended Elmshurst Ballet Sch., Camberley, Surrey.
PICTURES: The Innocents (debut, 1961), The Lion, The Third Secret, Flipper's New Adventure, The Nanny, Our Mother's House, The Prime of Miss Jean Brodie, The Night of the Following Day, And Soon the Darkness, Necromancy, Ace Eli and Rodger of the Skies, The Legend of Hell House, The Food of the Gods.
TELEVISION: Movies: The Horse Without a Head (theatrical in U.K.), See How They Run, David Copperfield (theatrical in U.K.), The Letters, Satan's School for Girls, Crossfire, Eleanor and Franklin.

FRANKLIN, RICHARD
Director, Producer, Writer. b. Melbourne, Australia, July 15, 1948. e. USC (Cinema, 1967).
PICTURES: Director: The True Story of Eskimo Nell (also co-prod., co-s.p.), Patrick (also co-prod., co-s.p.), The Blue Lagoon (co-prod. only), Road Games (also prod., co-s.p.), Psycho II, Cloak and Dagger, Into the Night (actor only), Link (also prod.), FX2, Hotel Sorrento (also prod.).
TELEVISION: Pilots: Beauty and the Beast, A Fine Romance. Movie: Running Delilah.

FRANKLIN, ROBERT A.
Executive. b. New York, NY, April 15. e. U. of Miami, B.B.A., 1958; Columbia Pacific U., M.B.A., 1979; Ph.D., 1980 majoring in marketing. Before entering film industry worked with House of Seagram, Canada Dry Corp., J. M. Mathes Adv. 1967, joined 20th Century-Fox as dir. of mkt. planning. Formed RP Marketing Intl. (entertainment consulting firm) in 1976 and World Research Systems (computer software marketer). 1981 joined MPAA; 1983, named v.p., admin. & info. services. 1986, named v.p. worldwide market research. Chmn., MPAA research comm.; member, AMA and ESOMAR.

FRANZ, ARTHUR
Actor. b. Perth Amboy, NJ, Feb. 29, 1920. e. Blue Ridge Coll., MD. U.S. Air Force. Radio, TV shows.
THEATER: A Streetcar Named Desire, Second Threshold.
PICTURES: Jungle Patrol (debut, 1948), Roseanna McCoy, The Red Light, The Doctor and the Girl, Sands of Iwo Jima, Red Stallion in the Rockies, Three Secrets, Tarnished, Abbott and Costello Meet the Invisible Man, Flight to Mars, Submarine Command, Strictly Dishonorable, The Sniper, Rainbow 'Round My Shoulder, The Member of the Wedding, Eight Iron Men, Invaders From Mars, Bad for Each Other, The Eddie Cantor Story, Flight Nurse, The Caine Mutiny, Steel Cage, Battle Taxi, New Orleans Uncensored, Bobby Ware Is Missing, Beyond a Reasonable Doubt, The Wild Party, Running Target, The Devil's Hairpin, Back From the Dead, The Unholy Wife, Hellcats of the Navy, The Young Lions, The Flame Barrier, Monster on the Campus, Atomic Submarine, The Carpetbaggers, Alvarez Kelly, Anzio, The Sweet Ride, The Human Factor, Sister of Death, That Championship Season.
TELEVISION: Movies: Murder or Mercy, Jennifer: A Woman's Story, Bogie.

FRANZ, DENNIS
Actor. b. Chicago, IL, Oct. 28, 1944. Started in Chicago Theatre.
PICTURES: Stony Island, Dressed to Kill, Blow Out, Psycho II, Body Double, A Fine Mess, The Package, Die Hard 2, The Player, American Buffalo.
TELEVISION: Series: Chicago Story, Bay City Blues, Hill Street Blues, Beverly Hills Buntz, Nasty Boys, N.Y.P.D. Blue (Emmy Award, 1994, 1996). Movies: Chicago Story (pilot), Deadly Messages, Kiss Shot, Moment of Truth: Caught in the Crossfire (also co-prod.), Texas Justice.

FRASER, BRENDAN
Actor. b. Indianapolis, IN, 1968. Raised in Holland, Switzerland, Canada. e. Actors' Conservatory, Cornish College of the Arts, Seattle. Member of Laughing Horse Summer Theatre in Ellensburg, WA.
THEATER: Waiting for Godot, Arms and the Man, Romeo and Juliet, A Midsummer Night's Dream, Moonchildren, Four Dogs and a Bone.
PICTURES: Dogfight (debut, 1991), Encino Man, School Ties, Twenty Bucks, Younger and Younger, With Honors, Airheads, The Scout, Now and Then, The Passion of Darkly Noon, Mrs. Winterbourne.
TELEVISON: Movie: Guilty Until Proven Innocent. Pilot: My Old School.

FRAZIER, SHEILA E.
Actress, Producer. b. Bronx, NY, Nov. 13. e. Englewood, NJ. Was exec. sect'y. and high-fashion model. Steered to acting career by friend Richard Roundtree. Studied drama with N.Y. Negro Ensemble Co. and New Federal Theatre, N.Y., also with Bob Hickey at H.B. Studios, N.Y. Currently owrking as a TV producer.
PICTURES: Super Fly (debut), Superfly T.N.T., The Super Cops, California Suite, What Does It Take?, Three the Hard Way, The Hitter, I'm Gonna Git You Sucker.
TELEVISION: Movie: Firehouse. Mini-Series: King. Series: The Lazarus Syndrome.

FREARS, STEPHEN
Director. b. Leicester, Eng., June 20, 1941. e. Cambridge, B.A in law. Joined Royal Court Theatre, working with Lindsay Anderson on plays. Later assisted Karel Reisz on Morgan: A Suitable Case for Treatment, Albert Finney on Charlie Bubbles, and Lindsay Anderson on If ... Worked afterwards mostly in TV, directing and producing. First directorial credit was 30-minute film The Burning, 1967.
PICTURES: Gumshoe (dir. debut 1971), Bloody Kids, The Hit, My Beautiful Laundrette, Prick Up Your Ears, Sammy and Rosie Get Laid, Dangerous Liaisons, The Grifters, Hero (GB: Accidental Hero), The Snapper, Mary Reilly, The Van.
TELEVISION: A Day Out (1971), England Their England, Match of the Day, Sunset Across the Bay, Three Men in a Boat, Daft as a Brush, Playthings, Early Struggles, Last Summer, 18 Months to Balmoral Street, A Visit from Miss Protheroe, Abel's Will, Cold Harbour, Song of Experience; series of six Alan Bennett plays; Long Distance Information, Going Gently, Loving Walter, Saigon: Year of the Cat, December Flower.

FREDERICKSON, H. GRAY, JR.
Producer. b. Oklahoma City, OK, July 21, 1937. e. U. of Lausanne, Switzerland, 1958\-59; U. of Oklahoma. B.A., 1960. Worked one yr. with Panero, Weidlinger & Salvatori Engineering Co., Rome Italy. In 1979 named v.p. of feature films, Lorimar Films.
PICTURES: Candy, Inspector Sterling, Gospel 70, An Italian in America, The Man Who Wouldn't Die, The Good, the Bad and the Ugly, Intrigue in Suez, How to Learn to Love Women, God's Own Country, Wedding March, An American Wife, Natika, Echo in the Village, Little Fauss and Big Halsey, Making It, The Godfather (assoc. prod.), The Godfather Part II (co-prod; Academy Award for Best Picture, 1974), Hit (exec. prod.), Apocalypse Now (co.-prod.; Acad. Award nom.), One From the Heart, The Outsiders, UHF, The Godfather Part III (co-prod.), Ladybugs (exec. prod.), Bad Girls (story), Heaven's Prisoners.
TELEVISION: Producer: The Return of Mickey Spillane's Mike Hammer, Houston Nights, Staying Afloat.

FREEDMAN, JERROLD
Director, Writer. b. Philadelphia, PA, Oct.29, 1942. e. Univ. of PA. Novel: Against the Wind.
PICTURES: Kansas City Bomber, Borderline, Native Son.
TELEVISION: *Director-Writer*: Blood Sport, Betrayal, Some Kind of Miracle, Legs, This Man Stands Alone. *Director*: The Streets of L.A., The Boy Who Drank Too Much, Victims, The Seduction of Gina, Best Kept Secrets, Seduced, Family Sins, Unholy Matrimony, The Comeback, Night Walk, A Cold Night's Death, The Last Angry Man, Goodnight Sweet Wife: A Murder in Boston, Condition: Critical.

FREEMAN, AL, JR.
Actor. b. San Antonio, TX, March 21, 1934. e. LA City Coll.
THEATER: The Long Dream (1960), Kicks and Co., Tiger Tiger Burning Bright, Trumpets of the Lord, Blues for Mister Charlie, Conversation at Midnight, Look to the Lilies, Are You Now or Have You Ever Been?, The Poison Tree.
PICTURES: Torpedo Run, Black Like Me, Dutchman, Finian's Rainbow, The Detective, Castle Keep, The Lost Man, A Fable (also dir.), Seven Hours to Judgement, Malcolm X.
TELEVISION: *Movies*: My Sweet Charlie, Assault at West Point. *Mini-Series*: Roots: The Next Generations, King. *Series*: Hot L Baltimore, One Life to Live (Emmy Award, 1979).

FREEMAN, JOEL
Producer. b. Newark, NJ, June 12, 1922. e. Upsala Coll. Began career at MGM studios, 1941. Air Force Mot. Pic. Unit 1942-46. Became assist. dir. at RKO, 1946. 1948 returned to MGM as asst. dir.; later assoc. prod. 1956 entered indep. field as prod. Supv. on various features and TV series. 1960 to Warner Bros., assoc. producing Sunrise at Campobello, The Music Man and Act One. After such films as Camelot and Finian's Rainbow, became studio exec. at Warners. Presently senior v.p. prod., New Century Entertainment Corp.
PICTURES: *Producer*: The Heart Is a Lonely Hunter, Shaft, Trouble Man, Love at First Bite, Octagon, The Kindred.

FREEMAN, KATHLEEN
Actress. b. Chicago, IL, Feb. 17, 1919.
PICTURES: Casbah (debut, 1948), The Saxon Charm, The Naked City, Behind Locked Doors, Mr. Belvedere Goes to College, The Reformer and the Redhead, A Life of Her Own, The House by the River, Lonely Hearts Bandits, Appointment With Danger, A Place in the Sun, The Company She Keeps, O. Henry's Full House, Singin' in the Rain, Talk About a Stranger, Love Is Better Than Ever, She's Back on Broadway, The Affairs of Dobie Gillis, Half a Hero, Athena, Artists and Models, The Far Country, The Midnight Story, Kiss Them for Me, Houseboat, The Fly, The Missouri Traveler, The Buccaneer, North to Alaska, The Ladies Man, The Errand Boy, Madison Avenue, The Nutty Professor, The Disorderly Orderly, Mail Order Bride, Point Blank, Hook Line and Sinker, The Good Guys and the Bad Guys, Myra Breckinridge, The Ballad of Cable Hogue, Which Way to the Front?, Support Your Local Gunfighter, Stand Up and Be Counted, Where Does It Hurt?, Unholy Rollers, Your Three Minutes Are Up, The Strongest Man in the World, The Norsemen, The Blues Brothers, Heartbeeps, The Best of Times, Malibu Bikini Shop, Dragnet, Innerspace, In the Mood, The Willies, Gremlins 2: The New Batch, Joey Takes a Cab, Dutch, FernGully ... The Last Rainforest (voice), Little Nemo: Adventures in Slumberland (voice), Hocus Pocus, Naked Gun 33 1/3: The Final Insult, At First Sight.
TELEVISION: *Series*: Topper, Mayor of the Town, It's About Time, Funny Face, Lotsa Luck. *Movies*: But I Don't Want to Get Married!, Call Her Mom, Hitched, The Daughters of Joshua Cabe Return, The Last Ride of the Dalton Gang.

FREEMAN, MORGAN
Actor. b. Memphis, TN, June 1, 1937. e. LA City Coll. Served in Air Force 1955-59 before studying acting. Worked as dancer at NY's 1964 World's Fair. Broadway debut in Hello Dolly! with Pearl Bailey. Took over lead role in Purlie. Became known nationally when he played Easy Reader on TV's The Electric Company (1971-76).
THEATER: *NY*: Ostrich Feathers, The Nigger Lovers, Hello Dolly!, Scuba Duba, Purlie, Cockfight, The Last Street Play, The Mighty Gents (Drama Desk & Clarence Derwent Awards), Coriolanus (Obie Award), Julius Caesar, Mother Courage, Buck, Driving Miss Daisy (Obie Award), The Gospel at Colonus (Obie Award), The Taming of the Shrew.
PICTURES: Who Says I Can't Ride a Rainbow? (debut, 1972), Brubaker, Eyewitness, Death of a Prophet, Harry and Son, Teachers, Marie, That Was Then...This Is Now, Street Smart (NY & LA Film Critics & Natl. Board of Review Awards; Acad. Award nom., 1987), Clean and Sober, Lean on Me, Johnny Handsome, Glory, Driving Miss Daisy (Natl. Board of Review & Golden Globe Awards; Acad. Award nom., 1989), The Bonfire of the Vanities, Robin Hood: Prince of Thieves, The Power of One, Unforgiven, Bopha (dir. only), The Shawshank Redemption (Acad. Award nom.), Outbreak, Seven, Moll Flanders, Chain Reaction.

TELEVISION: *Movies*: Hollow Image, Attica, The Marva Collins Story, The Atlanta Child Murders, Resting Place, Flight For Life, Roll of Thunder Hear My Cry, Charlie Smith and the Fritter Tree, Clinton and Nadine. *Series*: The Electric Company, Another World (1982-4). *Specials* (narrator): The Civil War, Follow the Drinking Gourd, The Promised Land.

FREEZER, HARLENE
Executive. Pres., New York Women in Film & Television.

FRESCO, ROBERT M.
Writer. b. Burbank, CA, Oct. 18, 1928. e. Los Angeles City Coll. Newspaperman. Los Angeles, 1946-47; U.S. Army, 1948-49; staff writer, Hakim Prod., 1950-51; various screenplays, 1951-56.
PICTURES: Tarantula, They Came to Destroy the Earth, Monolith.
TELEVISION: Scripts for Science Fiction Theatre, Highway Patrol.

FREWER, MATT
Actor. b. Washington, D. C., Jan. 4, 1958. Raised in Victoria, British Columbia. Studied drama at the Bristol Old Vic Theatre, appearing in Romeo and Juliet, Macbeth, Waiting for Godot, Deathtrap.
PICTURES: The Lords of Discipline (debut, 1983), Supergirl, Spies Like Us, Ishtar, The Fourth Protocol, Far From Home, Speed Zone, Honey I Shrunk the Kids, Short Time, The Taking of Beverly Hills, Twenty Bucks, National Lampoon's Senior Trip, Lawnmower Man II.
TELEVISION: *BBC*: Tender is the Night, Robin of Sherwood; assoc. *U.S. Series*: Max Headroom, Doctor Doctor, Shaky Ground, The Pink Panther (voice), Outer Limits. *Movie*: The Positively True Adventures of the Alleged Texas Cheerleader-Murdering Mom, The Day My Parents Ran Away, Kissinger and Nixon. *Mini-Series*: The Stand. *Guest*: Miami Vice. Specials: Long Shadows, In Search of Dr. Seuss.

FRICKER, BRENDA
Actress. b. Dublin, Ireland, Feb. 17, 1945. Appeared in short film The Woman Who Married Clark Gable. Theatre work includes appearances with the RSC, Royal Court Theatre, and The National Theatre.
PICTURES: Quatermass Conclusion, Bloody Kids, Our Exploits at West Poley, My Left Foot (Academy Award, best supporting actress, 1989), The Field, Utz, Home Alone 2: Lost in New York, So I Married an Axe Murderer, Angels in the Outfield, A Man of No Importance, Moll Flanders, A Time to Kill.
TELEVISION: *Series*: Casualty. *Specials*: Licking Hitler, The House of Bernarda Alba, The Ballroom Romance. *Mini-Series*: Brides of Christ, The Sound and the Silence, A Woman of Independent Means.

FRIEDBERG, A. ALAN
Executive. b. New York, NY, Apr. 13, 1932. e. Columbia Coll., B.A. 1952, Junior Phi Beta Kappa, Summa Cum Laude; Harvard Law School 1955. Past pres. and chmn. of bd. NATO, currently memb. of exec. committee. V.P. Foundation of Motion Picture Pioneers. 1990, named chmn. Loews Theatre Mgmt. Co. Retired.

FRIEDKIN, JOHN
Executive. b. New York, NY, Dec. 9, 1926. e. Columbia Univ. Entered industry in New York as publicist for Columbia Pictures; spent eight years at Young & Rubicam adv. agency. Formed Sumner & Friedkin with Gabe Sumner as partner; left to join Rogers & Cowan, where named v.p. In 1967 resigned to join 20th-Fox, moving to California in 1972 when home offices were transferred. Appointed Fox v.p. worldwide publ. & promo. In 1979 joined Warner Bros. as v.p., adv. pub. for intl. div; 1988, joined Odyssey Distributors Ltd. as sr. v.p., intl. marketing. 1990, formed indept. marketing firm.

FRIEDKIN, WILLIAM
Director, Writer. b. Chicago, IL, Aug. 29, 1939. m. producer Sherry Lansing. Joined WGN-TV, 1957, worked for National Education TV, did TV documentaries before feature films. Dir. B'way play Duet for One.
PICTURES: *Director*: Good Times (debut, 1967), The Night They Raided Minsky's, The Birthday Party, The Boys in the Band, The French Connection (Academy Award, 1971), The Exorcist, Sorcerer (also prod.), The Brink's Job, Cruising (also s.p.), Deal of the Century, To Live and Die in L.A. (also co-s.p.), Rampage (also s.p.), The Guardian (also co-s.p.), Blue Chips, Jade.
TELEVISION: *Movies*: C.A.T. Squad (also exec. prod.), C.A.T. Squad: Python Wolf, Jailbreakers. *Special*: Barbra Streisand: Putting It Together. *Series*: Tales From the Crypt (On a Dead Man's Chest).

FRIEDMAN, JOSEPH
Executive. b. New York, NY. e. City Coll. of New York, 1940-42, NYU, 1946-47. U.S. Navy 3 yrs. Asst. to nat'l dir. field exploita-

tion, Warner Bros. Pictures, 1946-58; nat'l exploitation mgr., Paramount 1958-60; exec. asst. to dir. of adv., publicity & exploitation, Para., 1961; dir. adv. & pub., Paramount 1964; v.p., Para., 1966; v.p. in charge of mktg., 1968; v.p., adv., and p.r., Avco Embassy, 1969; v.p., p.r. American Film Theatre, 1973; v.p., adv. and p.r., ITC, motion picture div., 1976, pres., Joseph Friedman Mktg. & Adv., Inc., 1977. Exec. dir. New Jersey M.P. & T.V. Commission, 1978; v.p. worldwide adv./pub. /promo., Edie & Ely Landau, Inc., 1980; exec. dir., NJ Motion Picture & Television Commission, 1981.

FRIEDMAN, PAUL
Executive. e. Princeton U. Woodrow Wilson Sch. of Public & Intl. Affairs, Columbia Sch. of Journalism. 1967, joined NBC News as newswriter in NY; 1970-75, served as reporter for WRC-TV in D.C., field prod. for The Huntley-Brinkley Report, sr. prod. for NBC Weekend Nightly News, exec. prod. of News 4 New York, sr. prod. NBC Nightly News; 1976-79, was exec. prod. of Today; 1982, joined ABC News as sr, prod. in London; there became dir. of news coverage for Europe, Africa, Middle East, while as operating the ABC News Bureaus in those areas; 1988-92, exec. prod. of World News Tonight With Peter Jennings; Jan. 1993 named exec. v.p. of ABC News.

FRIEDMAN, ROBERT L.
Executive. b. Bronx, NY, March 1, 1930. e. DeWitt Clinton H.S, Bronx. Started as radio announcer and commentator with Armed Forces Radio Service in Europe and U.S. sr. v.p., distrib. & mktg., United Artists Corp.; pres. domestic distribution, Columbia Pictures. 1984, named pres., AMC Entertainment Int'l Inc. 1992, named pres. of AMC Entertainment - the Motion Picture Group. On Century City bd. of dirs.; chmn. of Entertainment Industry Council. Member: M.P. Associates Foundation, Phila., pres. 2 yrs.; Variety Club (on board) M.P. Pioneers; (on board) area chmn. Distrib., chmn., Will Rogers Hospital Foundation, American Film Inst., Academy of M.P. Arts & Sciences.

FRIEDMAN, SEYMOUR MARK
Director. b. Detroit, MI, Aug. 17, 1917. e. Magdalene Coll., Cambridge, B.S. 1936; St. Mary's Hospital Medical Sch., London. Entered m.p. ind. as asst. film ed. 1937; 2nd asst. dir. 1938; 1st asst. dir. 1939, on budget pictures; entered U.S. Army 1942; returned to ind. 1946; dir. Columbia Pictures 1947. Vice president & executive production for Columbia Pictures Television, division of Columbia Pictures Industries, 1955. Member: Screen Directors Guild.
PICTURES: To the Ends of the Earth, Rusty's Birthday, Prison Warden, Her First Romance, Rookie Fireman, Son of Dr. Jekyll, Loan Shark, Flame of Calcutta, I'll Get You, Saint's Girl Friday, Khyber Patrol, African Manhunt, Secret of Treasure Mountain.

FRIEDMAN, STEPHEN
Producer, Writer. b. March 15, 1937. e. U. of Pennsylvania, Harvard Law School. Worked as lawyer for Columbia Pictures (1960-63) and Ashley-Famous Agency. 1963-67: Paramount Pictures. Formed and heads Kings Road Productions.
PICTURES: Producer: The Last Picture Show, Lovin' Molly (also s.p.), Slap Shot, Bloodbrothers, Fast Break, Hero at Large, Little Darlings, Eye of the Needle, All of Me, Creator, Enemy Mine, Morgan Stewart's Coming Home, The Big Easy, There Goes the Neighborhood.

FRIELS, COLIN
Actor. b. Scotland, e. Australia Natl. Inst. of Dramatic Art. m. actress Judy Davis. First began acting with the State Theatre Co. of So. Australia and the Sydney Theatre Co. Theatre includes Sweet Bird of Youth and Hedda Gabler. TV includes special Stark.
PICTURES: Buddies, Monkey Grip, For the Term of His Natural Life, Kangaroo, Malcolm, High Tide, Ground Zero, Grievous Bodily Harm, Warm Nights on a Slow Moving Train, Darkman, Class Action, Dingo, A Good Man in Africa., Angel Baby, Back of Beyond.

FRIENDLY, FRED W.
Producer, Journalist, Writer, Educator. r.n. Fred Wachenheimer. b. New York, NY, October 30, 1915. e. Cheshire Acad., Nichols Junior Coll. U.S. Army, Information and Education Section 1941-45. Editor and correspondent for China, Burma and India for CBI Roundup 1941-45. President, CBS News 1964-66: Edward R. Murrow Professor of Broadcast Journalism, Columbia U., 1966-present; advisor on TV, Ford Foundation, 1966-; member: Mayor's Task Force on CATV and Telecommunications, NYC, 1968; teacher and director: Television Workshop, Columbia U. Sch. of Journalism. RADIO Producer-writer-narrator: Footprints in the Sand of Time, 1938; co-prod. Hear It Now, 1951. Ten George Foster Peabody Awards; DeWitt Carter Reddick Award, 1980; See It Now (35 major awards incl. Overseas Press Club, Page One Award, New York Newspaper Guild, National Headliners Club Award, 1954); CBS Reports (40 major awards). Honorary L.H.D. degrees: U. of Rhode Island, Grinnell U., Iowa U. Military: Legion of Merit

medal, Soldier's Medal for heroism, 4 Battle Stars.
AUTHOR: See It Now (1955); Due to Circumstances Beyond Our Control (1967); The Good Guys, the Bad Guys and the First Amendment: Free Speech vs. Fairness in Broadcasting (1976), Minnesota Rag: The Dramatic Story of the Landmark Supreme Court Case that Gave New Meaning to Freedom of the Press (1981); The Constitution: That Delicate Balance (1984); The Presidency and the Constitution (1987).

FRIES, CHARLES W.
Executive, Producer. b. Cincinnati, OH. e. Ohio State U., B.S. Exec.-prod., Ziv Television; v.p., prod., Screen Gems; v.p., prod., Columbia Pictures; exec. v.p., prod. and exec. prod., Metromedia Prod. Corp., 1970-74; pres., exec. prod., Alpine Prods. and Charles Fries Prods. 1974-83; chmn. & pres., Fries Entertainment, 1984. Nat'l. treas., TV Academy; pres., Alliance TV Film Producers; exec. comm., MPPA. Chmn., Caucus of Producers, Writers and Directors, board of governors and exec. comm. of Academy of TV Arts and Sciences. Bd. trustees, secretary, Exec. committee & vice-chmn., American Film Institute. V.P. & dir. of the Center Theatre Group.
PICTURES: Prod.: Cat People, Flowers in the Attic, Troop Beverly Hills, Screamers.
TELEVISION: Movies: Toughlove, The Right of the People, Intimate Strangers, Bitter Harvest, A Rumor of War, Blood Vows: The Story of a Mafia Wife, The Alamo: 13 Days to Glory, Intimate Betrayal, Drop Out Mother, Crash Course, Supercarrier, Bridge to Silence, The Case of the Hillside Strangler, Deadly Web. Small Sacrifices, The Martian Chronicles. Specials: It's Howdy Doody Time: A 40 Year Celebration.

FRONTIERE, DOMINIC
Executive, Composer. b. New Haven, CT, June 17, 1931. e. Yale School of Music. Studied composing, arranging and conducting; concert accordionist, World's Champion Accordionist, 1943; An Hour with Dominic Frontiere, WNHC-TV, New Haven, 3 years, 1947; exec. vice-pres., musical dir., Daystar Prods. Composer or arranger over 75 films.
PICTURES: Giant, Gentlemen Prefer Blondes, Let's Make Love, High Noon, Meet Me in Las Vegas, 10,000 Bedrooms, Hit the Deck, Marriage-Go-Round, The Right Approach, One Foot in Hell, Hero's Island, Hang 'Em High, Popi, Barquero, Chisum, A for Alpha, Cancel My Reservation, Hammersmith is Out, Freebie and the Bean, Brannigan, The Gumball Rally, Cleopatra Jones and the Casino of Gold, The Stunt Man, Modern Problems, The Aviator.
TELEVISION: Composer-conductor: The New Breed, Stoney Burke, Bankamericard commercials (Venice Film Fest. Award for best use of original classical music for filmed TV commercials), Outer Limits, Branded, Iron Horse, Rat Patrol, Flying Nun, The Invaders, Name of the Game, That Girl, Twelve O'Clock High, Zig Zag, The Young Rebel, The Immortal, Fugitive, The Love War. Movie: Washington Behind Closed Doors.

FUCHS, LEO L.
Independent producer. b. Vienna, June 14, 1929. Moved to U.S., 1939. e. Vienna and New York. U.S. Army cameraman 1951-53; int'l. mag. photographer until entered motion pictures as producer with Universal in Hollywood in 1961.
PICTURES: Gambit, A Fine Pair, Sunday Lovers, Just the Way You Are.

FUCHS, MICHAEL
Executive. b. New York, NY, March 9, 1946. e. Union Coll., NYU Law School (J.D. degree). Show business lawyer before joining Home Box Office in 1976, developing original and sports programming. Named chmn. and CEO of HBO in 1984. 1982-87, v.p. Time Inc. in NY; 1987-1995, exec. v.p. Time Inc.

FUEST, ROBERT
Director. b. London, 1927. Early career as painter, graphic designer. Ent. TV industry as designer with ABC-TV, 1958. 1962: directing doc., commercials. 1966: Wrote and dir. Just Like a Woman, 1967-68; dir. 7 episodes of The Avengers, 1969: wrote and directed 6 episodes of The Optimists.
PICTURES: And Soon the Darkness, Wuthering Heights, Doctor Phibes, Doctor Phibes Rides Again (also s.p.), The Final Programme (also s.p., design), The Devil's Rain, The Geller Effect (s.p. only), The New Avengers, The Gold Bug, Revenge of the Stepford Wives, The Big Stuffed Dog, Mystery on Fire Island, Aphrodite, Worlds Beyond, Cat's Eyes.

FULLER, SAMUEL
Director, Writer, Producer, Actor. b. Worcester, MA, Aug. 12, 1912. m. actress Christa Lang. Copy boy, N.Y. Journal; reporter, rewrite man, N.Y. Graphic, N.Y Journal, San Diego Sun; journeyman reporter many papers. Writer of many orig. s.p.; in U.S. Army, 16th Inf. 1st U.S. Inf. Div. 1942-45.
AUTHOR: Crown of India, 144 Piccadilly Street, Dead Pigeon on Beethoven Street, The Rifle, The Big Red One, The Dark Page, La Grande Melee (Battle Royal), Pecos Bill and the Soho Kid, Once Upon Samuel Fuller (Stories of America; interview book).
PICTURES: Director-Writer: I Shot Jesse James, Baron of

Arizona, The Steel Helmet (also prod.), Fixed Bayonets, Park Row (also prod.), Pickup On South Street, Hell and High Water, House of Bamboo, Run of the Arrow (also prod.), China Gate (also prod.), Forty Guns, Verboten!, The Crimson Kimono (also prod.), Underworld U.S.A. (also prod.), Merrill's Marauders, Shock Corridor (also prod.), The Naked Kiss (also prod.), Dead Pigeon on Beethoven Street, The Big Red One, White Dog (also actor), Thieves After Dark, Street of No Return (also actor, edit.), Tini Kling. Actor: The Last Movie, The American Friend, Scott Joplin, 1941, Hammett, State of Things, Slapstick of Another Kind, Return to Salem's Lot, Helsinki Napoli All Night Long, Sons, Somebody to Love, Tigrero: A Movie That Was Never Made.

FUNT, ALLEN
Producer, Performer. b. New York, NY, Sept. 16, 1914. e. Cornell U. Best known as producer and creator of Candid Camera series which originated on radio in 1947 as Candid Microphone which inspired theatrical film shorts. TV version began in 1948 as Candid Mike, changed in 1949 to Candid Camera which played off and on until 1960 when became regular series on CBS, lasting until 1967. Revived briefly in early '70s and again in mid '80s in new format; then syndicated as The New Candid Camera. Joined in 1988 by son Peter Funt as host and prod. Specials: Candid Camera Christmas Special, Candid Camera: Eat! Eat! Eat!, Candid Camera on Wheels, Candid Camera's Vacation, Candid Camera Getting Physical, Candid Camera Goes to the Doctor, Candid Camera's Sporting Life. Produced and starred in film, What Do You Say to a Naked Lady?, Candid Camera's 50th Anniversary.

FURIE, SIDNEY J.
Director, Writer, Producer. b. Toronto, Canada, Feb. 28, 1933. Ent. TV and films 1954. Canadian features include: Dangerous Age, A Cool Sound from Hell. Also dir. many Hudson Bay TV series. To England 1960. 1961 appt. exec. dir. Galaworldfilm Productions, Ltd.
PICTURES: The Snake Woman, Doctor Blood's Coffin, Wonderful to Be Young, Night of Passion (also prod., s.p.), The Young Ones, The Leather Boys, Wonderful Life, The Ipcress File, The Appaloosa, The Naked Runner, The Lawyer, Little Fauss and Big Halsy, Lady Sings the Blues, Hit!, Sheila Levine Is Dead and Living in New York, Gable and Lombard, The Boys in Company C, The Entity, Purple Hearts (also prod., s.p.), Iron Eagle, Superman IV: The Quest For Peace, Iron Eagle II (also co-s.p.), The Taking of Beverly Hills, Ladybugs, Hollow Point, Iron Eagle IV.

FURLONG, EDWARD
Actor. b. Glendale, CA, Aug. 2, 1977. Discovered by casting agent for Terminator 2, having no previous acting experience. Appeared in Aerosmith video Livin' on the Edge.
PICTURES: Terminator 2: Judgment Day (debut, 1991), Pet Sematary 2, American Heart, A Home of Our Own, Brainscan, Little Odessa, The Grass Harp, Before and After.

FURMAN, ROY L.
Attorney, Executive. b. New York, NY, April 19, 1939. e. Brooklyn Coll., A.B. 1960; Harvard U., L.L.B. 1963. Pres., Furman Selz. Chmn., Film Society of Lincoln Center.

FURST, AUSTIN O.
Executive. e. Lehigh U., B.S. in economics/marketing. Began career in mktg. dept., Proctor and Gamble; 1972, joined Time Inc. as dir., new subscription sales for Time magazine; later joined Time Inc.'s new magazine dev. staff for People magazine; named circulation mgr., People magazine, 1974; 1975 named pres., Time Inc.'s Computer Television Inc., a pay-per-view hotel operation and was responsible for successful turnaround and sale of co.; 1976, v.p., programming, Home Box Office; named exec. v.p. HBO, 1979; 1981 established Vestron after acquiring home video rights to Time/Life Video Library; chmn. and CEO, Vestron, Inc.

G

GABOR, ZSA ZSA
Actress. r.n. Sari Gabor. b. Hungary, Feb. 6, 1918. e. Lausanne, Switzerland. Stage debut in Europe. Author: Zsa Zsa's Complete Guide to Men (1969), How to Get a Man How to Keep a Man and How to Get Rid of a Man (1971), One Lifetime is Not Enough (1991). As accomplished horsewoman has won many prizes in various intl. horse shows. Stage work incl. 40 Carats, Blithe Spirit.
PICTURES: Lovely to Look At, We're Not Married, Moulin Rouge, The Story of Three Loves, Lili, Three Ring Circus, The Most Wanted Man in the World, Death of a Scoundrel, Girl in the Kremlin, The Man Who Wouldn't Talk, Touch of Evil, Queen of Outer Space, Country Music Holiday, For the First Time, Pepe, Boys' Night Out, Picture Mommy Dead, Arrivederci Baby, Jack of Diamonds, Won Ton Ton the Dog

Who Saved Hollywood, Frankenstein's Great Aunt Tillie, A Nightmare on Elm Street 3, The Naked Gun 2 1/2: The Smell of Fear, Happily Ever After (voice).

GAIL, MAX
Actor. b. Grosse Ile, MI, Apr. 5, 1943. e. William Coll. B.A. Economics, Univ. of Mich M.B.A.
THEATER: NY: The Babe, One Flew Over the Cuckoo's Nest (also S.F.). LA: Visions of Kerouac.
PICTURES: The Organization, Dirty Harry, D.C. Cab, Heartbreakers, Pontiac Moon, Mind Lies, Sodbusters, Ox and the Eye, Lords of Tanglewood.
TELEVISION: Series: Barney Miller, Whiz Kids, Normal Life. Mini-Series: Pearl. Movies: The Priest Killer, Like Mom Like Me, Desperate Women, The 11th Victim, The Aliens Are Coming, Fun and Games, Letting Go, The Other Lover, Killer in the Mirror, Intimate Strangers, Can You Feel Me Dancing?, Tonight's the Night, Man Against the Mob, The Outside Woman, Ride With the Wind, Robin Cook's Mortal Fear, Naomi & Winona: Love Can Build a Bridge, Secret Agent (prod.), Wrong Side of the Fence (prod.).

GALE, BOB
Writer, Producer. b. St. Louis, MO, May 25, 1951. e. USC Sch. of Cinema. Joined with friend Robert Zemeckis to write screenplays, starting with episode for TV series, McCloud. Also co-wrote story for The Nightstalker series. Turned to feature films, co-writing with Zemeckis script for I Wanna Hold Your Hand, on which Gale also acted as associate producer. Exec. prod. of CBS animated series Back to the Future. Wrote and directed interactive feature Mr. Payback.
PICTURES: I Wanna Hold Your Hand (co-s.p., co-assoc. prod.), 1941 (co-s.p.), Used Cars (prod., co-s.p.), Back to the Future (co-prod., s.p.), Back to the Future Part II (prod., co-s.p.), Back to the Future Part III (prod., s.p.), Trespass (co-exec. prod., co-s.p.), Tales From the Crypt: Bordello of Blood (co-s.p.).
TELEVISION: Series: Back to the Future (animated; exec. prod.), Tales From the Crypt (wrote, dir. House of Horror).

GALE, GEORGE
Executive. b. Budapest, Hungary, May 26, 1919. e. Sorbonne U., Paris, France. Feature editor, Budapest Ed., U.S. Army Pictorial Service. Feature and TV editor MGM, Hal Roach, Disney Studios; prod. and prod. exec. Ivan Tors; American National Enterprises, Inc. Producer and director. Supervised the production of over 30 features for tv syndication and numerous theatrical features. Member ACE and Academy of Motion Picture Arts and Sciences. Formed George Gale Productions, Inc. in 1976.

GALLAGHER, PETER
Actor. b. New York, NY, Aug. 19, 1955. e. Tufts Univ.
THEATER: NY: Hair (1977 revival), Grease, A Doll's Life (Theatre World Award), The Corn is Green, The Real Thing (Clarence Derwent Award), Long Day's Journey Into Night (Tony Award nom.; also London), Guys & Dolls. Also: Another Country, Pride & Prejudice (both Long Wharf).PICTURES: The Idolmaker (debut, 1980), Summer Lovers, Dream Child, My Little Girl, High Spirits, Sex Lies and Videotape, Tune in Tomorrow, Late for Dinner, The Cabinet of Dr. Ramirez, The Player, Bob Roberts, Watch It, Malice, Short Cuts, Mother's Boys, The Hudsucker Proxy, Mrs. Parker and the Vicious Circle, While You Were Sleeping, The Underneath, Cafe Society, The Last Dance, To Gillian on Her 37th Birthday.
TELEVISION: Series: Skag. Movies: Skag, Terrible Joe Moran, The Caine Mutiny Court-Martial, The Murder of Mary Phagan, I'll Be Home for Christmas, Love and Lies, An Inconvenient Woman, White Mile. Specials: The Big Knife, Long Day's Journey Into Night, Private Contentment, Guys & Dolls: Off the Record.

GALLIGAN, ZACH
Actor. b. New York, NY, Feb. 14, 1964. e. Columbia U.
PICTURES: Gremlins, Nothing Lasts Forever, Waxwork, Mortal Passions, Rising Storm, Gremlins II, Zandalee, Lost in Time, Round Trip to Heaven, All Tied Up, Waxwork II, Warlock: The Armageddon, Ice, Caroline at Midnight, The First to Go.
TELEVISION: Movies: Jacobo Timerman: Prisoner Without a Name Cell Without a Number, Surviving, Psychic, For Love and Glory. Specials: The Prodigious Hickey, The Return of Hickey, The Beginning of the Firm, A Very Delicate Matter, The Hitchhiker: Toxic Shock. Mini-Series: Crossings. Pilot: Interns in Heat. Guest: Tales From the Crypt (Strung Along), Melrose Place, Extreme.

GAMBON, MICHAEL
Actor. b. Dublin, Ireland, Oct. 19, 1940. Ent. Ind. 1966. Early experience in theatre. 1985-87 Acting at National Theatre and London's West End. 1988: in Harold Pinter's Mountain Language.
PICTURES: Othello, The Beast Must Die, Turtle Diary, Paris By Night, The Rachel Papers, A Dry White Season, The Cook

the Thief His Wife and Her Lover, Mobsters, Toys, Clean Slate, The Browning Version, Squanto: A Warrior's Tale, A Man of No Importance, Bullet to Beijing, The Innocent Sleep, Nothing Personal.
TELEVISION: Uncle Vanya, Ghosts, Oscar Wilde, The Holy Experiment, Absurd Person Singular, The Singing Detective (serial), The Heat of the Day, The Storyteller, Maigret Sets a Trap.

GAMMON, JAMES
Actor. b. Newman, IL, Apr. 20. e. Boone H.S., Orlando, FL. Former television cameraman. First acting role was small part on Gunsmoke. Head of Los Angeles' Met Theatre for 10 years.
THEATER: The Dark at the Top of the Stairs (L.A. Critics Circle Award, best actor), Bus Stop (L.A. Drama Critics award, best director), Curse of the Starving Class (NY, L.A.), A Lie of the Mind (NY, L.A.).
PICTURES: Cool Hand Luke (debut, 1967), Journey to Shiloh, Macho Callahan, A Man Called Horse, Macon County Line, Black Oak Conspiracy, Urban Cowboy, Any Which Way You Can, Smithereens, Vision Quest, Sylvester, Silverado, Silver Bullet, Made in Heaven, Ironweed, The Milagro Beanfield War, Major League, Revenge, Coupe de Ville, I Love You to Death, Leaving Normal, Crisscross, The Painted Desert, Running Cool, Cabin Boy, Vegas Vice, Natural Born Killers, Wild Bill.
TELEVISION: *Series*: Bagdad Cafe. *Guest*: Bonanza, The Wild Wild West, Cagney & Lacey, The Equalizer, Crime Story, Midnight Caller. *Movies*: Kansas City Massacre, Rage, Women of San Quentin, M.A.D.D.: Mothers Against Drunk Drivers, Hell Town, The Long Hot Summer, Roe vs. Wade, Dead Aim, Conagher, Stranger at My Door, Men Don't Tell, Truman. *Mini-Series*: Lincoln.

GANIS, SIDNEY M.
Executive. b. New York, NY, Jan. 8, 1940. e. Brooklyn Coll. Staff writer, newspaper and wire service contact, 20th Century-Fox 1961-62; radio, TV contact and special projects, Columbia Pictures 1963-64. Joined Seven Arts Prod. 1965 as publicity mgr.; 1967, appt. prod. publicity mgr. Warner-7 Arts, Ass't prod., There Was a Crooked Man, 1969. Studio publicity dir., Cinema Center Films, 1970. Director of Ad-Pub for Mame, Warner Bros., 1973; Director of Advertising, Warner Bros., 1974; named WB v.p., worldwide adv. & pub., 1977; 1979, sr. v.p., Lucasfilm, Ltd.; 1982 Emmy winner, exec. prod., best documentary, The Making of Raiders of the Lost Ark. 1986, joined Paramount Pictures as pres., worldwide mktg; 1986, named pres., Paramount Motion Picture Group. 1988, elected trustee University Art Museum, Berkeley, CA. 1991, appointed exec. v.p., Sony Pictures Ent. Exec. v.p., pres. mktg. & distrib., Columbia Pictures, 1992. Elected to bd. of govs. AMPAS, 1992. Vice chmn., Columbia Pictures, 1994. Pres., worldwide mktg., Columbia TriStar.

GANZ, BRUNO
Actor. b. Zurich, Switzerland, March 22, 1941.
THEATER: Member of the Berlin Theater troupe, Schaubuhne. Hamlet (1967), Dans La Jungle Des Villes, Torquato Tasso, La Chevauchee Sur Le Lac de Constance, Peer Gynt.
PICTURES: Der Sanfte Lauf (1967), Sommergaste, The Marquise of O, Lumiere, The Wild Duck, The American Friend, The Lefthanded Woman, The Boys from Brazil, Black and White Like Day and Night, Knife in the Head, Nosferatu the Vampyre, Return of a Good Friend, 5% Risk, An Italian Woman, Polenta, La Provinciale, La Dame Aux Camelias, Der Erfinder, Etwas Wird Sichtbar, Circle of Deceit, Hande Hoch, Logik Der Gerfuhls, War and Peace, In the White City, System Ohne Schatten, Der Pendler, Wings of Desire, Bankomatt, Strapless, The Last Days of Chez Nous, Especially on Sunday, Faraway So Close!
TELEVISION: Father and Son (German TV).

GANZ, LOWELL
Writer, Producer, Director. b. New York, NY, Aug. 31, 1948. e. Queens Col. Worked as staff writer on tv series The Odd Couple. Met writing partner Babaloo Mandel at The Comedy Store in the early 1970s. Was co-creator Laverne & Shirley. First teamed with Mandel on script for 1982 comedy Night Shift.
PICTURES: *Writer*: Night Shift, Splash (Acad. Award nom.; also actor), Spies Likes Us, Gung Ho, Vibes, Parenthood (also actor), City Slickers, A League of Their Own (also actor), Mr. Saturday Night (also actor), Greedy (also actor), City Slickers II: The Legend of Curly's Gold, Forget Paris, Multiplicity.
TELEVISION: *Writer-Exec. Prod* (series): The Odd Couple, Happy Days, Busting Loose, The Ted Knight Show, Makin' It, Joanie Loves Chachi, Gung Ho, Knight and Dave, Parenthood. *Producer*: Laverne & Shirley (also writer).

GANZ, TONY
Producer. b. New York, NY. e. studied film at Harvard U. Produced documentaries for PBS in N.Y. Moved to L.A. 1973

where in charge of dev., Charles Fries Productions. Then joined Ron Howard Productions 1980. Left to form own prod. co. with Deborah Blum.
PICTURES: Gung Ho, Clean and Sober, Vibes.
TELEVISION: *Series*: American Dream Machine, Maximum Security (exec. prod.). *Movies*: Bitter Harvest, Into Thin Air.

GARCIA, ANDY
Actor. b. Havana, Cuba, Apr. 12, 1956. r.n. Andres Arturo Garcia Menendez. Family moved to Miami Beach in 1961. e. Florida International U, Miami. Spent several years acting with regional theaters in Florida; also part of improv. group. Music producer of album: Cachao Master Sessions Vol. I (Grammy Award), Chachao Master Sessions Vol II (Grammy nom.).
PICTURES: The Mean Season, 8 Million Ways to Die, The Untouchables, Stand and Deliver, American Roulette, Black Rain, Internal Affairs, A Show of Force, The Godfather Part III (Acad. Award nom.), Dead Again, Hero, Jennifer Eight, Cachao... Como Su Ritmo No Hay Dos (Like His Rhythm There Is No Other; also dir., co-prod.), When a Man Loves a Woman, Steal Big Steal Little, Things to Do in Denver When You're Dead, Night Falls on Manhattan, Death in Granada.
TELEVISION: *Movie*: Clinton and Nadine.

GARDINER, PETER R.
Executive. b. Santa Monica, CA, Apr. 25, 1949. Independent still photographer and industrial filmmaker before joining Paramount, 1973, in feature post-prod. 1979, joined Warner Bros. as asst. dir., corporate services. 1987, promoted to v.p., opns., WB corporate film-video services. 1993, promoted to v.p. Warner Bros. corp. film & video services.

GARDNER, ARTHUR
Producer. b. Marinette, WI, June 7. e. Marinette h.s. Entered m.p. ind. as actor, in orig. cast All Quiet on the Western Front, 1929. Juvenile leads in: Waterfront, Heart of the North, Assassin of Youth, Religious Racketeer; production, asst. dir. King Bros. 1941, then asst. prod. U.S. Air Force 1st Motion Picture Unit, 1943-45. Formed Levy-Gardner-Laven Prods. with Jules Levy, Arnold Laven, 1951.
PICTURES: (Asst. dir.): Paper Bullets, I Killed That Man, Rubber Racketeers, Klondike Fury, I Escaped From the Gestapo, Suspense; *Asst. prod.*: Gangster, Dude Goes West, Badmen of Tombstone, Gun Crazy, Mutiny, Southside 1-1000. *Prod.*: Without Warning, Vice Squad, Down Three Dark Streets, Return of Dracula, The Flame Barrier, The Vampire, The Monster that Challenged the World. Geronimo, The Glory Guys, Clambake, Scalphunters, Sam Whiskey, Underground, McKenzie Break, The Honkers, Hunting Party, Kansas City Bomber, White Lightning, McQ, Brannigan, Gator, Safari 3000.
TELEVISION: The Rifleman, Robert Taylor's Detectives, Law of the Plainsman, The Big Valley.

GARFIELD, ALLEN
Actor. b. Newark, NJ, Nov. 22, 1939. r.n. Allen Goorwitz. e. Upsala Col, Actors Studio. Worked as journalist for Newark Star Ledger and Sydney Morning Herald (Australia) prior to becoming an actor. Has also acted as Allen Goorwitz. Life Member of the Actors Studio, NYC.
PICTURES: Greetings, Putney Swope, Hi Mom!, The Owl and the Pussycat, Bananas, Believe in Me, Roommates, The Organization, Taking Off, Cry Uncle!, You've Got to Walk it Like You Talk It or You'll Lose That Beat, Get to Know Your Rabbit, The Candidate, Top of the Heap, Deadhead Miles, Slither, Busting, The Conversation, The Front Page, Nashville, Gable and Lombard, Mother Jugs & Speed, The Brink's Job, Skateboard, Paco, One-Trick Pony, The Stunt Man, Continental Divide, One from the Heart, The State of Things, The Black Stallion Returns, Get Crazy, Irreconcilable Differences, Teachers, The Cotton Club, Desert Bloom, Beverly Hills Cop II, Rich Boys, Let it Ride, Night Visitor, Dick Tracy, Club Fed, Until the End of the World, Jack and His Friends, Family Prayers, The Patriots, The Glass Shadow, Miracle Beach, Sketches of a Strangler, Destiny Turns on the Radio, Diabolique.
TELEVISION: *Movies*: Footsteps, The Marcus-Nelson Murders, The Virginia Hill Story, Serpico: The Deadly Game, The Million Dollar Rip-Off, Nowhere to Run, Ring of Passion, Leave 'Em Laughing, Citizen Cohn, Killer in the Mirror, Incident at Vichy, Judgment: The Trial of Julius and Ethel Rosenberg. *Guest*: Law and Order, Equal Justice, Eddie Dodd, Jack's Place, Taxi, etc.

GARFINKLE, LOUIS
Writer, Director, Producer. b. Seattle, WA, February 11, 1928. e. U. of California, U. of Washington, U. of Southern California (B.A., 1948). Writer KOMO Seattle, 1945; Executive Research, Inc., 1948; writer, educ. doc. screenplays, Emerson Films, EBF. 1948-50; s.p. You Can Beat the A-Bomb (RKO), 1950; writer-dir. training films, info. films, Signal Photo, 1950-53; copy, Weinberg Adv., 1953; head of doc. research in TV, U. of California, Berkeley, 1954-55; staff, Sheilah Graham Show,

1955; formed Maxim Prod. Inc. with Albert Band, 1956. Co-creator Collaborator Interactive Computer Software to asst. in writing stories for screen & TV, 1990; formed Collaborator Systems Inc. with Cary Brown and Francis X. Feighan, 1991. Received Best Screenwriting Tool Award from Screen Writers Forum, 1991. Member: AMPAS, WGA West, ATAS, Dramatists Guild, Board of Advisers Filmic Writing Major, USC School of Cinema & TV.
PICTURES: *Screenplay*: The Young Guns (also story), I Bury the Living (also story, co-prod.), Face of Fire (also co-prod.), Hellbenders, A Minute to Pray A Second to Die, The Love Doctors (also story, prod.), Beautiful People, The Models (also story), The Doberman Gang (also story), Little Cigars (also story), The Deer Hunter (story collab.; Acad. Award nom.).
TELEVISION: *Writer*: 712 teleplays for Day in Court, Morning Court, Accused, 1959-66. *Co-writer-creator*: Direct Line (pilot), June Allyson Show, Threat of Evil, Death Valley Days, Crullers At Sundown, Captain Dick Mine, No. 3 Peanut Place (pilot).

GARFUNKEL, ART
Singer, Actor. b. New York, NY, Nov. 5, 1942. e. Columbia Coll. Began singing at age 4. Long partnership with Paul Simon began in grade school at 13 in Queens, NY; first big success in 1965 with hit single, Sound of Silence. Partnership dissolved in 1970. Winner of 4 Grammy Awards.
PICTURES: Catch-22 (debut, 1970), Carnal Knowledge, Bad Timing/A Sensual Obsession, Good to Go, Boxing Helena.

GARLAND, BEVERLY
Actress. b. Santa Cruz, CA, Oct. 17, 1930. r.n. Beverly Fessenden. e. Glendale Coll., 1945-47.
PICTURES: D.O.A., The Glass Web, Miami Story, Bittercreek, Two Guns and a Badge, Killer Leopard, The Rocket Man, Sudden Danger, Desperate Hours, Curucu: Beast of the Amazon, Gunslinger, Swamp Woman, The Steel Jungle, It Conquered the World, Not of This Earth, Naked Paradise, The Joker is Wild, Chicago Confidential, Badlands of Montana, The Saga of Hemp Brown, Alligator People, Stark Fever, Twice Told Tales, Pretty Poison, The Mad Room, Where the Red Fern Grows, Airport 1975, Roller Boogie, It's My Turn, Death Falls, Haunted Symphony.
TELEVISION: *Series*: Mama Rosa, Pantomime Quiz, The Bing Crosby Show, My Three Sons, Scarecrow & Mrs. King, Decoy. *Guest*: Twilight Zone, Dr. Kildare, Medic (Emmy nom.), Magnum P.I., Remington Steele, Lois and Clark. *Movies*: Cutter's Trail, Say Goodbye Maggie Cole, Weekend Nun, Voyage of the Yes, Unwed Father, Healers, Day the Earth Moved, This Girl for Hire, The World's Oldest Living Bridesmaid, Finding the Way Home.

GARNER, JAMES
Actor. r.n. James Baumgarner. b. Norman, OK, April 7, 1928. e. Norman H.S. Joined Merchant Marine, U.S. Army, served in Korean War. Prod. Paul Gregory suggested acting career. Studied drama at N.Y. Berghof School. Toured with road companies; Warner Bros. studio contract followed.
PICTURES: Toward the Unknown (debut, 1956), The Girl He Left Behind, Shoot Out at Medicine Bend, Sayonara, Darby's Rangers, Up Periscope, Alias Jesse James (cameo), Cash McCall, The Children's Hour, Boys' Night Out, The Great Escape, The Thrill of It All, The Wheeler Dealers, Move Over Darling, The Americanization of Emily, 36 Hours, The Art of Love, Mister Buddwing, A Man Could Get Killed, Duel at Diablo, Grand Prix, Hour of the Gun, The Pink Jungle, How Sweet It Is, Support Your Local Sheriff, Marlowe, A Man Called Sledge, Support Your Local Gunfighter, Skin Game, They Only Kill Their Masters, One Little Indian, The Castaway Cowboy, Health, The Fan, Victor/Victoria, Tank, Murphy's Romance (Acad. Award nom.), Sunset, The Distinguished Gentleman, Fire in the Sky, Maverick, My Fellow Americans.
TELEVISION: *Series*: Maverick, Nichols, The Rockford Files, Bret Maverick, Man of the People. *Movies*: The Rockford Files (pilot), The New Maverick (pilot), The Long Summer of George Adams, The Glitter Dome, Heartsounds, Promise (also exec. prod.), Obsessive Love, My Name Is Bill W. (also exec. prod.), Decoration Day, Barbarians at the Gate, The Rockford Files: I Still Love L.A. (also co-exec. prod.), The Rockford Files: A Blessing in Disguise (also co-exec. prod.). *Mini-Series*: Space. *Specials*: Sixty Years of Seduction, Lily for President.

GARR, TERI
Actress. b. Lakewood, OH, Dec. 11, 1949. Began career as dancer, performing S.F. Ballet at 13. Later appeared with L.S. Ballet and in original road show co. of West Side Story. Several film appearances as a dancer incl. Fun in Acapulco, Viva Las Vegas, What a Way to Go, Roustabout, etc. Did commercials; appeared in film Head written by a fellow acting student, Jack Nicholson. Career boosted by appearance on TV as semi-regular on The Sonny and Cher Show.
PICTURES: Maryjane, Head, The Moonshine War, The Conversation, Young Frankenstein, Won Ton Ton the Dog Who Saved Hollywood, Oh God!, Close Encounters of the Third

Kind, Mr. Mike's Mondo Video, The Black Stallion, Witches' Brew, Honky Tonk Freeway, One from the Heart, The Escape Artist, Tootsie (Acad. Award nom.), The Sting II, The Black Stallion Returns, Mr. Mom, Firstborn, Miracles, After Hours, Full Moon in Blue Water, Out Cold, Let It Ride, Short Time, Waiting for the Light, The Player, Mom and Dad Save the World, Dumb & Dumber, Ready to Wear (Pret-a-Porter), Michael.
TELEVISION: *Series regular*: Shindig, The Ken Berry "Wow" Show, (1972), Burns and Schreiber Comedy Hour, Girl With Something Extra, The Sonny and Cher Comedy Hour, The Sonny Comedy Revue, Good and Evil, Good Advice, Women of the House. *Movies*: Law and Order, Doctor Franken, Prime Suspect, Winter of Our Discontent, To Catch a King, Intimate Strangers, Pack of Lies, A Quiet Little Neighborhood A Perfect Little Murder, Stranger in the Family, Deliver Them From Evil: The Taking of Alta View, Fugitive Nights: Danger in the Desert. *Specials*: The Frog Prince (Faerie Tale Theatre), Drive She Said (Trying Times), Paul Reiser: Out on a Whim, Mother Goose Rock 'n' Rhyme, The Whole Shebang, Aliens for Breakfast. *Mini-Series*: Fresno. *Guest*: Tales from the Crypt (The Trap), The Larry Sanders Show.

GARRETT, BETTY
Singer, Actress. b. St. Joseph, MO, May 23, 1919. e. scholarships: Annie Wright Seminary, Tacoma, WA; Neighborhood Playhouse, N.Y. Sang in night clubs, hotels, Broadway shows: Call Me Mister (Donaldson Award, 1946), Spoon River Anthology, A Girl Could Get Lucky, Meet Me in St. Louis (1989). Motion Picture Herald, Star of Tomorrow, 1949. Starred in one woman show, Betty Garrett and Other Songs, beginning in 1974 and touring through 1993 (Bay Area Critics & LA Drama Critics Awards); also in autobiographical show, No Dogs or Actors Allowed (Pasadena Playhouse, 1989), So There! (with Dale Gonyear; Pasadena Playhouse, 1993). Given Life Achievement Award by Los Angeles Drama Critics Circle, 1995.
PICTURES: The Big City (debut, 1948), Words and Music, Take Me Out to the Ball Game, Neptune's Daughter, On the Town, My Sister Eileen, Shadow on the Window.
TELEVISION: *Series*: All in the Family, Laverne and Shirley. *Guest*: Love Boat, Black's Magic, Somerset Gardens, Murder She Wrote, Harts of the West, The Good Life. *Movies*: All the Way Home, Who's Happy Now.

GARSON, GREER
Actress. b. County Down, Northern Ireland, Sept. 29, 1908. e. London U., B.A. cum laude; post grad. studies, Grenoble U. France. After early career in art research and editing for Encyclopaedia Britannica and market research with Lever's Intl. Advertising Service became actress with Birmingham Rep. Co. starring in 13 West End prods. before lured to Hollywood by MGM, 1938. Screen debut 1939 in Goodbye, Mr. Chips. Academy Award best actress, 1942 Mrs. Miniver. Voted one of the ten best Money-Making Stars in Motion Picture Herald-Fame Poll 1942-46 inclusive. Photoplay Mag. Gold Medal 1944-45 and top British Award 1942, 1943, 1944. Numerous other awards incl. L.A. Times Woman of the Year, Woman of the World Award from Intl. Orphans, Inc. 1987 Gov. Award for contrib. to arts NM, 1988 USA Film Fest. Master Screen Artist. Active in civic and benevolent activities. With late husband Col. E.E. (Buddy) Fogelson, awarded Dept. of Interior's citation for environmental preservation efforts. Founded Fogelson Museum NM 1987. Established The Greer Garson Theatre and Fogelson Library Center at the College of Santa Fe; founding donor for Fogelson Forum at Dallas Presbyterian Hospital, Garson Communications Center at Col. of Santa Fe, Fogelson Pavillion in Dallas. Donor for The Greer Garson Theatre at Southern Methodist Univ., Dallas.
THEATER: Stage debut Birmingham (England) Rep. theat. 1932 in Street Scene; London debut 1935 in Golden Arrow (opposite Laurence Olivier); continued London stage to 1938 (Vintage Wine, Mademoiselle, Accent on Youth, Page from a Diary, Old Music, etc.).
PICTURES: Goodbye Mr. Chips (debut, 1939), Remember?, Pride and Prejudice, Blossoms in the Dust, When Ladies Meet, Mrs. Miniver (Academy Award, 1942), Random Harvest, Madame Curie, The Youngest Profession (cameo), Mrs. Parkington, Valley of Decision, Adventure, Desire Me, Julia Misbehaves, That Forsyte Woman, The Miniver Story, The Law and the Lady, Scandal at Scourie, Julius Caesar, Her Twelve Men, Strange Lady in Town, Sunrise at Campobello, Pepe, The Singing Nun, The Happiest Millionaire.
TELEVISION: *Specials*: The Little Foxes, Crown Matrimonial, My Father Gave Me America, The Little Drummer Boy, Holiday Tribute to Radio City, Perry Como's Christmas in New Mexico, A Gift of Music (host), Bicentennial Tribute to Los Angeles. *Movie*: Little Women.
(d. April 6, 1996)

GARY, LORRAINE
Actress. b. New York, NY, Aug. 16, 1937. r.n. Lorraine Gottfried. m. executive Sidney J. Scheinberg. e. Columbia Univ.

PICTURES: Jaws, Car Wash, I Never Promised You a Rose Garden, Jaws 2, Just You and Me Kid, 1941, Jaws-The Revenge.
TELEVSION: Movies: The City, The Marcus-Nelson Murders, Partners in Crime, Pray for the Wildcats, Man on the Outside, Lanigan's Rabbi, Crash.

GASSMAN, VITTORIO
Actor. b. Genoa, Italy, Sept. 1, 1922. e. Acad. of Dramatic Art, Rome. Stage actor, 1943; m.p. debut, 1946.
PICTURES: Daniele Cortis, Mysterious Rider, Bitter Rice, Lure of Sila, The Outlaws, Anna, Streets of Sorrow; to U.S., Cry of the Hunted, Sombrero, The Glass Wall, Rhapsody, Girls Marked Danger, Mambo, War and Peace, World's Most Beautiful Woman, Tempest, The Love Specialist, The Great War, Let's Talk About Women, Il Successo, The Tiger, Woman Times Seven, Ghosts-Italian Style, Scent of a Woman, Viva Italia!, A Wedding, Quintet, Immortal Bachelor, The Nude Bomb, Sharky's Machine, Tempest, I Picari, The Family, The Sleazy Uncle, The House of the Lord, The Hateful Dead, To Forget Palermo, Los Alegres Picaro, Scheherzade, The Long Winter, Sleepers.

GATES, WILLIAM H.
Executive. b. 1957. Started computer programming at age 13. 1974, developed BASIC for the first microcomputer, MITS Altair. 1975, with Paul Allen formed Microsoft to develop software for personal computers. Chmn. & CEO of Microsoft Corp. leading provider of worldwide software for personal computers.

GATWARD, JAMES
Executive. b. London, England. Ent. Ind. 1957. Early career as freelance drama prod. dir. in Canada, USA, UK (with ITV & BBC). Prod. dir. various intern. co-productions in UK, Ceylond, Australia, Germany. Currently chief executive and Dep. chmn. TVS Television Ltd., chmn. Telso Communications Ltd., dir. of ITN, Channel Four, Super Channel, Oracle Teletext.

GAVIN, JOHN
Executive, Diplomat, Former Actor. b. Los Angeles, CA, April 8, 1932. m. actress Constance Towers. e. St. John's Military Acad., Villanova Prep at Ojai, Stanford Univ., Naval service: air intelligence officer in Korean War. Broadway stage debut: Seesaw, 1973. 1961-73 public service experience as spec. advisor to Secretary Gen. of OAS, performed gp. task work for Dept. of State and Exec. Office of the President. Pres. Screen Actors Guild, 1971-73. Named U.S. Ambassador to Mexico, 1981-86. Partner in Gavin & Dailey, a venture capital firm; Pres., Gamma Services Corp. (Intl. Consultants); dir., Atlantic Richfield Co., Dresser Industries, Pinkerton, Inc., The Hotchkiss and Wiley Funds, International Wire Group Co. Consultant to Dept. of State and serves pro-bono on several boards.
PICTURES: Behind the High Wall (debut, 1956), Four Girls in Town, Quantez, A Time to Love and a Time to Die, Imitation of Life, Psycho, Midnight Lace, Spartacus, A Breath of Scandal, Romanoff and Juliet, Tammy Tell Me True, Back Street, Thoroughly Modern Millie, The Madwoman of Chaillot, Pussycat Pussycat I Love You.
TELEVISION: Movies: Cutler's Trail, The New Adventures of Heidi, Sophia Loren: Her Own Story. Series: Destry, Convoy. Mini-Series: Doctors' Private Lives.

GAY, JOHN
Writer. b. Whittier, CA, April 1, 1924. e. LA City Coll.
PICTURES: Run Silent, Run Deep, Separate Tables, The Happy Thieves, Four Horsemen, The Courtship of Eddie's Father, The Hallelujah Trail, The Last Safari, The Power, No Way to Treat a Lady, Soldier Blue, Sometimes a Great Notion, Hennessey, A Matter of Time.
TELEVISION: Amazing Howard Hughes, Kill Me If You Can, Captains Courageous, Red Badge of Courage, All My Darling Daughters, Les Miserables, Transplant, A Private Battle, A Tale of Two Cities, The Bunker, Berlin Tunnel 21, Stand By Your Man, Dial "M" For Murder, The Long Summer of George Adams, A Piano for Mrs. Cimino, The Hunchback of Notre Dame, Ivanhoe, Witness for the Prosecution, Samson and Delilah, Fatal Vision, Doubletake, Uncle Tom's Cabin, Outlaw Six Against the Rock, Around the World in 80 Days, Blind Faith, Cruel Doubt.

GAYNOR, MITZI
Actress. r.n. Francisca Mitzi Von Gerber. b. Chicago, IL, Sept. 4, 1931. e. Powers Professional H.S., Hollywood. Studied ballet since age four; was in L.A. Light Opera prod. Roberta. Stage: Anything Goes (natl. co., 1989).
OPERA: Fortune Teller, Song of Norway, Louisiana Purchase, Naughty Marietta, The Great Waltz.
PICTURES: My Blue Heaven (debut, 1950), Take Care of My Little Girl, Golden Girl, We're Not Married, Bloodhounds of Broadway, The I Don't Care Girl, Down Among the Sheltering Palms, There's No Business Like Show Business, Three

Young Texans, Anything Goes, The Birds and the Bees, The Joker Is Wild, Les Girls, South Pacific, Happy Anniversary, Surprise Package, For Love or Money.
TELEVISION: Specials: Mitzi, Mitzi's Second Special, The First Time, A Tribute to the American Housewife, Mitzi and a Hundred Guys, Roarin' in the 20s, Mitzi...Zings Into Spring, What's Hot What's Not.

GAZZARA, BEN
Actor. b. New York, NY, Aug. 28, 1930. e. Studied at CCNY 1947-49. Won scholarship to study with Erwin Piscator; joined Actor's Studio, where students improvised a play, End as a Man, which then was performed on Broadway with him in lead. Screen debut (1957) in film version of that play retitled The Strange One.
THEATER: Jezebel's Husband, End as a Man, Cat on a Hot Tin Roof, A Hatful of Rain, The Night Circus, Epitaph for George Dillon, Two for the Seesaw, Strange Interlude, Traveler Without Luggage, Hughie, Who's Afraid of Virginia Woolf, Dance of Death, Thornhill, Shimada.
PICTURES: The Strange One (debut, 1957), Anatomy of a Murder, The Passionate Thief, The Young Doctors, Convicts Four, Conquered City, A Rage to Live, The Bridge at Remagen, Husbands, The Neptune Factor, Capone, Killing of a Chinese Bookie, Voyage of the Damned, High Velocity, Opening Night, Saint Jack, Bloodline, They All Laughed, Inchon, Tales of Ordinary Madness, Road House, Quicker Than the Eye, Don Bosco, A Lovely Scandal, Girl from Trieste, Il Camorrista, Tattooed Memory, Beyond the Ocean (also dir., s.p.), Forever, Farmer & Chase, The Shadow Conspiracy.
TELEVISION: Series: Arrest and Trial, Run for Your Life. Movies: When Michael Calls, Maneater, QB VII, The Death of Ritchie, A Question of Honor, An Early Frost, A Letter to Three Wives, Police Story: The Freeway Killings, Downpayment on Murder, People Like Us, Lies Before Kisses, Blindsided, Love Honor & Obey: The Last Mafia Marriage, Parallel Lives, Fatal Vows: The Alexandria O'Hara Story.

GEARY, ANTHONY
Actor. b. Coalville, UT, May 29, 1947. e. U. of Utah.
PICTURES: Blood Sabbath (debut, 1969), Johnny Got His Gun, Private Investigations, Penitentiary III, You Can't Hurry Love, Pass the Ammo, Dangerous Love, It Takes Two, UHF, Night Life, Crack House, Night of the Warrior, Scorchers.
TELEVISION: Series: Bright Promise, General Hospital (1978-83; 1990-). Guest: The Young and the Restless, Osmond Family Holiday Special, Sunset Beat, Murder She Wrote, Hotel, All in the Family, Streets of San Francisco. Movies: Intimate Agony, Sins of the Past, The Imposter, Kicks, Perry Mason: The Case of the Murdered Madam, Do You Know the Muffin Man?

GEBHARDT, FRED
Producer, Writer, Exhibitor. b. Vienna, Austria, Mar. 16, 1925. e. Schotten Gymnasium, Vienna, UCLA, 1939. Usher Boyd Theatre, Bethlehem, PA; Mgr., Rivoli Thea. L.A.; 1944; 18 yrs. mgr. many theatres. Fox West Coast, then Fine Arts Theatre. Writer, prod.: 12 To the Moon, The Phantom Planet; prod., Assignment Outer Space, Operation M; s.p., All But Glory, The Starmaker, Shed No Blood, Fortress in Heaven, Eternal Woman. Pres., Four Crown Prods., Inc.; recipient of Medal of Americanism, D.A.R., 1963; Honorary Lifetime Member, P.T.A., Young Man of The Year Award, 1956, 24 Showmanship Awards; Mem. Acad. M.P. Arts and Sciences, Ind. M.P. Prod. Assoc.
AUTHOR: Mental Disarmament, All But Glory, Starmaker, Shed No Blood, The Last of the Templars.

GEDRICK, JASON
Actor. b. Chicago, IL, Feb. 7, 1965.
PICTURES: Massive Retaliation (debut, 1984), The Zoo Gang, The Heavenly Kid, Iron Eagle, Stacking, Promised Land, Rooftops, Born on the Fourth of July, Backdraft, Crossing the Bridge.
TELEVISION: Series: Class of 96, Murder One.

GEESON, JUDY
Actress. b. Arundel, Sussex, England, Sept. 10, 1948. e. Corona Stage Sch. Began professional career on British TV, 1960.
THEATER: Othello, Titus Andronicus, Two Gentlemen of Verona, Section Nine, An Ideal Husband.
PICTURES: To Sir with Love, Berserk, Here We Go Round the Mulberry Bush, Prudence and the Pill, Hammerhead, Three into Two Won't Go, The Oblong Box, Two Gentlemen Sharing, The Executioner, Nightmare Hotel, 10 Rillington Place, Doomwatch, Fear in the Night, It's Not the Size That Counts, Brannigan, Diagnosis Murder, The Eagle Has Landed, Carry On England, Dominique, Horror Planet, The Plague Dogs (voice).
TELEVISION: Dance of Death, Lady Windermere's Fan, Room with a View, The Skin Game, Star Maidens, Poldark, She, The Coronation, Murder She Wrote, Astronomy (Triple Play II). Movie: The Secret Life of Kathy McCormick.

GEFFEN, DAVID
Executive, Producer. b. Brooklyn, NY, Feb. 21, 1943. Began in mailroom of William Morris Agency before becoming agent there and later at Ashley Famous. With Elliott Roberts founded own talent management co. for musicians. Founded Asylum Records, 1970. Pres. then chmn. Elektra-Asylum Records 1973-76. Sold co. to Warner Communications for whom he headed film prod. unit. Vice-chmn. Warner Bros. Pictures, 1975; exec. asst. to chmn., Warner Communications, 1977; Member music faculty Yale U., 1978. Formed Geffen Records 1980 and Geffen Film Co. Producer of Broadway shows Master Harold... and the Boys, Cats, Good, Dreamgirls, Social Security, Chess. 1990, sold record co. to MCA, Inc. With Steven Spielberg and Jeffrey Katzenberg formed Dreamworks entertainment company, 1995.
PICTURES: Personal Best, Risky Business, Lost in America, After Hours, Little Shop of Horrors, Beetlejuice (exec. prod.), Men Don't Leave, Defending Your Life, M. Butterfly, Interview With the Vampire.

GELBART, LARRY
Writer. b. Chicago, IL, Feb. 25, 1928. Began at age 16 writing for Danny Thomas on Fanny Brice Show. Followed by Duffy's Tavern, Bob Hope and Jack Paar radio shows.
THEATER: The Conquering Hero, A Funny Thing Happened on the Way to the Forum (with Burt Shevlove; Tony Award, 1962), Sly Fox, Mastergate, City of Angels (Tony Award, 1990), Power Failure.
PICTURES: The Notorious Landlady, The Thrill of It All, The Wrong Box, Not With My Wife You Don't, The Chastity Belt, A Fine Pair, Oh God!, Movie Movie, Neighbors, Tootsie, Blame It on Rio.
TELEVISION: Series: Caesar's Hour, M*A*S*H (Emmy Award, 1974; also co-prod.), United States. Movie: Barbarians at the Gate (Cable Ace Award, 1993). Special: Mastergate.

GELFAN, GREGORY
Executive. b. Los Angeles, CA, Aug. 7, 1950. Was entertainment atty. with Kaplan, Livingston et. al., and Weissmann, Wolff et. al. before joining Paramount Pictures in 1983 as dir. of business affairs. 1985, named v.p., business affairs, for M.P. Group of Paramount; 1989 promoted to sr. v.p. in chg. of business affairs. 1994, named exec. v.p. in chg. of business & legal affairs, 20th Century Fox.

GELLER, BRIAN L.
Executive. b. New York, NY, Feb. 3, 1948. e. Queens Coll. Entered industry with Columbia Pictures as sls. trainee in 1966, leaving in 1968 to go with American Intl. Pictures as asst. branch mgr. In 1969 joined Cinemation Industries as eastern div. sls. mgr.; 1978, left to become gen. sls. mr. of NMD Film Distributing Co. 1982, named dir. of dist., Mature Pictures Corp. 1983, gen. sls. mgr., Export Pix.; with Cinema Group as east. sls. mgr.; joined Scotti Brothers Pictures as national sales, mgr. Member of Motion Picture Bookers Club of N.Y.; Variety Tent 35, Motion Picture Pioneers.

GENDECE, BRIAN
Producer, Executive. b. St. Louis, MO, Dec. 3, 1956. e. Drury Coll., Springfield, MO. 1981-85, Director of Business Affairs, Weinstein/Skyfield Productions and Skyfield Management. 1986-87, dir. of business affairs, Cannon Films; 1987-89, dir. creative affairs, Cannon Films; 1989 co-pres., Sheer Entertainment; indie first look Epic Prods.; 1991 owner The Gendece Film Co.; 1991-93, prod./dir., 21st Century Film; 1993-96, dir. of mktg., Raleigh Film and Television Studios.
THEATER: Jack Klugman as Lyndon.
PICTURES: Runaway Train, Salsa, Rope Dancin', The Hunters, The American Samurai, Ceremony.
VIDEO: Bad Habits, Shape Up with Arnold, Laura Branigan's Your Love, How to Become a Teenage Ninja, L.A. Raiders' Wild Wild West, The Making of Crime and Punishment.

GEORGE, GEORGE W.
Writer, Producer. b. New York, NY, Feb.8, 1920. e. Williams Coll. U.S. Navy, 1941-44; screen-writer since 1948. President, Jengo Enterprises, dev. theatrical and m.p. projects.
THEATER: Prod.: Dylan, Any Wednesday, Ben Franklin in Paris, The Great Indoors, Happily Never After, Night Watch, Via Galactica, Bedroom Farce, Program for Murder (also co-author).
PICTURES: Writer: The Nevadan, Woman on Pier 13, Peggy, Mystery Submarine, Red Mountain Experiment, Alcatraz, Fight Town, Smoke Signal, Desert Sands, Uranium Boom, Halliday Brand, Doc, The James Dean Story, The Two Little Bears. Prod.: The James Dean Story, A Matter of Innocence, Twisted Nerve, Hello-Goodbye, Night Watch, Rich Kids, My Dinner With Andre.
TELEVISION: Climax, Screen Gems, Loretta Young Show, The Rifleman, Peter Gunn, The Real McCoys, Adventures in Paradise, Hong Kong, Follow the Sun, Bonanza.

GEORGE, LOUIS
Executive. b. Karavas, Kyrenia, Cyprus, June 7, 1935. e. Kyrenia Business Acad., Cyprus (honored 1951). Emigrated to U.S. in 1952. After brief stint in Foreign Exchange Dept. of City National Bank, New York, served in U.S. Army, 1953-55. Entered industry in 1956 as theatre manager with Loew's Theatres in N.Y. metro area, managing Metropolitan, Triboro, New Rochelle, between 1958-66. 1966 joined MGM as dir. of intl. theatre dept. 1969 promoted to dir. of world-wide non-theatrical sales. 1972-74 served as regional dir. of MGM Far East operations. 1974 left MGM to establish Arista Films, Inc., an indep. prod./dist. co. Pres. & CEO, Arista Films, Inc. Also bd. member, American Film Marketing Assn., chmn. Copywright and Film Security Committee of the Assn.
PICTURES: Slaughterhouse Rock, Buying Time, Violent Zone (exec. prod.), Angels Brigade, Final Justice, Surf II, Crackdown.

GEORGE, SUSAN
Actress, Producer. b. Surrey, England, July 26, 1950. m. actor-prod. Simon MacCorkindale. e. Corona Acad.
PICTURES: Billion Dollar Brain, The Sorcerers, Up the Junction, The Strange Affair, The Looking Glass War, All Neat in Black Stockings, Twinky (Lola), Spring and Port Wine, Eye Witness (Sudden Terror), Die Screaming Marianne, Fright, Straw Dogs, Sonny and Jed, Dirty Mary Crazy Larry, Mandingo, Out of Season, A Small Town in Texas, Tintorera, Tomorrow Never Comes, Enter the Ninja, Venom, The House Where Evil Dwells, Jigsaw Man, Lightning: The White Stallion, Stealing Heaven (exec. prod. only), That Summer of White Roses (also exec. prod.), The House That Mary Bought (also exec. prod.).
TELEVISION: Swallows and Amazons, Adam's Apple, Weaver's Green, Compensation Alice, The Right Attitude, Dracula, Lamb to the Slaughter, Royal Jelly, Masquerade, Czechmate, Hotel, Blacke's Magic, Jack the Ripper, Castle of Adventure, Cluedo, Stay Lucky.

GERALD, HELEN
Actress. b. New York, NY, Aug. 13. e. U. of Southern California, 1948. Stage: Italian Teatro D'Arte, Les Miserables, The Civil Death, Feudalism.
PICTURES: The Gay Cavalier, The Trap, Tarzan and the Leopard Woman, Cigarette Girl, Meet Miss Bobby Socks, G.I. War Brides, Gentleman's Agreement, A Bell for Adano, Tomorrow Is Forever, Janie, Grand Prix, The Sandpiper, Make Mine Mink, Best of Everything.
TELEVISION: Robert Montgomery Presents, Frontiers of Faith, Valiant Lady, Kraft Theatre, Gangbusters, Adventures of The Falcon, Schlitz Playhouse of Stars, This Is the Answer, Man from U.N.C.L.E., Run for Your Life, Perry Mason.

GERARD, GIL
Actor. b. Little Rock, AK, Jan. 23, 1943. e. Arkansas State Teachers Coll. Appeared in over 400 TV commercials. On stage in I Do! I Do!, Music Man, Stalag 17, Applause, etc.
PICTURES: Some of My Best Friends Are (1971), Man on a Swing, Hooch (also co-prod.), Airport '77, Buck Rogers in the 25th Century, Soldier's Fortune.
TELEVISION: Series: The Doctors, Buck Rogers in the 25th Century, Nightingales, Sidekicks, E.A.R.T.H. Force, Code 3 (host). Movies: Ransom for Alice, Killing Stone, Help Wanted: Male, Not Just Another Affair, Hear No Evil, Johnny Blue (pilot), For Love or Money, Stormin' Home, International Airport, Final Notice, The Elite, Last Electric Knight.

GERARD, LILLIAN
Publicist, Writer. b. New York, NY, Nov. 25, 1914. e. Baruch, CCNY, Columbia U. Publicity, Rialto Theatre, 1936; publicity-adv. Filmarte Theatre, 1938, Gerard Associates, 1938-47; V.P. and managing dir. of Paris Theatre, 1948-62; publicity-adv. dir., Rugoff Theatres, 1962. Film consultant to Times Films, Lopert Films, Landau Co., 1962-65. Adjunct Professor, Film, 1968-70, Columbia U., Sch. of the Arts, Special Projects Co-Ordinator, Museum of Modern Art, 1968-80. Now associated with Philip Gerard in Gerard Associates.

GERARD, PHILIP R.
Executive. b. New York, NY, Aug. 23, 1913. e. City Coll. of New York, B.B.A. 1935; Columbia U. Publicity dir. Mayer-Burstyn 1936-39; Gerard Associates, 1939-41; in public relations U.S. War Dept. 1942-44; with MGM 1944-48; with Universal Pictures since 1948; Eastern pub. mgr., 1950-59; Eastern ad. and pub. dir., Dec. 1959-68; N.Y. Production Exec., 1968-76. As of Jan. 1, 1977 formed Gerard Associates, film consultants on marketing, production and acquisitions. N.Y.C. Board member of CSS/RSVP (Retired Seniors Volunteer Program); Community Service Society. Member: Visitor's Day Comm., New York Hospital; volunteer at the International Center.

GERBER, DAVID
Executive. b. Brooklyn, NY. e. U. of the Pacific. m. actress Laraine Stephens. Joined Batten, Barton, Durstine and Osborn ad agency in N.Y. as TV supvr. Left to become sr. v.p. of TV at General Artists Corp. 1956, named v.p. in chg. sales at 20th-Fox TV where sold and packaged over 50 prime-time

series and specials. Entered indep. prod. with The Ghost and Mrs. Muir, followed by Nanny and the Professor. 1970 was exec. prod. of The Double Deckers, children's series made in England. 1972 joined Columbia Pictures Television as indep. prod.; 1974 was named exec. v.p. worldwide prod. for CPT. 1976 returned to indep. prod. 1985, joined MGM/UA TV broadcasting group in chg. world-wide prod. 1986 named president, MGM/UA Television. 1988-92, chmn & CEO, MGM/UA Television Prods. group.
TELEVISION: *Exec. prod.*: Cade's County, Police Story (Emmy, best dramatic series), Police Woman, The Lindbergh Kidnapping Case, Joe Forrester, The Quest and Gibbsville, To Kill a Cop, Power, Medical Story, Born Free, Beulah Land, The Night the City Screamed, Follow the North Star, Nothing Lasts Forever.

GERBER, MICHAEL H.
Executive. b. New York, NY, Feb. 6, 1944. e. St. Johns U., B.A., 1969; St. Johns U. School of Law, J.D., 1969. Atty. for Screen Gems, 1969-71; asst. secy. & asst. to gen. counsel, Columbia Pictures Industries, 1971-74; corporate counsel and secretary, Allied Artists Pictures, 1974, v.p. corporate affairs, Allied Artists, 1978; v.p., business affairs, Viacom Intl. 1980-86; 1986-89, sr. v.p.; 1989-93, pres., first run, intl. distrib. & acquisitions, Viacom Enterprises.

GERE, RICHARD
Actor. b. Philadelphia, PA, Aug. 29, 1949. e. U. of Massachusetts. Started acting in college; later joined Provincetown Playhouse and Seattle Repertory Theatre. Composed music for productions of these groups.
THEATER: *B'way*: Grease, Soon, Habeas Corpus, Bent (Theatre World Award), A Midsummer Night's Dream (Lincoln Center). *Off-B'way* in Killer's Head. *London*: Taming of the Shrew (with Young Vic).
PICTURES: Report to the Commissioner (debut, 1975), Baby Blue Marine, Looking for Mr. Goodbar, Days of Heaven, Bloodbrothers, Yanks, American Gigolo, An Officer and a Gentleman, Breathless, Beyond the Limit, The Cotton Club, King David, Power, No Mercy, Miles From Home, Internal Affairs, Pretty Woman, Rhapsody in August, Final Analysis (also co-exec. prod.), Sommersby (also co-exec. prod.), Mr. Jones (also co-exec. prod.), Intersection, First Knight, Primal Fear.
TELEVISION: *Movies*: Strike Force, And the Band Played On. *Guest*: Kojak. *Pilot*: D.H.P.

GERTZ, IRVING
Composer, Musical director. b. Providence, RI, May 19, 1915. e. Providence Coll. of Music, 1934-37. Assoc. with Providence Symph. Orch., comp. choral works for Catholic Choral Soc.; music dept., Columbia, 1939-41; U.S. Army, 1941-46; then comp. arranger, mus. dir. for many cos. incl. Columbia, Universal International, NBC, 20th Century Fox. Compositions: Leaves of Grass, Serenata for String Quartet, Divertimento for String Orchestra, Tableau for Orchestra.
PICTURES: Bandits of Corsica, Gun Belt, Long Wait, The Fiercest Heart, First Travelling Saleslady, Fluffy, Nobody's Perfect, Marines Let's Go!, It Came from Outer Space, The Man from Bitter Ridge, Posse from Hell, The Creature Walks Among Us, The Incredible Shrinking Man, Hell Bent for Leather, Seven Ways from Sundown, Francis Joins the WACS, Raw Edge, East of Sumatra, A Day of Fury, To Hell and Back, Cult of the Cobra, Plunder Road, Top Gun, Tombstone Express, The Alligator People, Khyber Patrol, The Wizard of Baghdad. Fluffy, Marines, Let's Go!
TELEVISION: *Orig. theme & scores*: America, The Golden Voyage, Across the Seven Seas, The Legend of Jesse James, Daniel Boone, Voyage to the Bottom of the Sea, Peyton Place, Land of the Giants, Lancer, Medical Center, Boutade for Wood-Wind Quartet, Salute to All Nations, A Village Fair, Liberty! Liberte! (for symphony orchestra).

GERTZ, JAMI
Actress. b. Chicago, IL, Oct. 28, 1965. e. NYU. Won a nationwide talent search competition headed by Norman Lear to cast TV comedy series Square Pegs. Following series studied at NYU drama school. Los Angeles theater includes Out of Gas on Lovers' Leap and Come Back Little Sheba. On NY stage in Wrong Turn at Lungfish. Also appeared in the Julian Lennon music video Stick Around.
PICTURES: Endless Love (debut, 1981), On the Right Track, Alphabet City, Sixteen Candles, Mischief, Quicksilver, Crossroads, Solarbabies, The Lost Boys, Less Than Zero, Listen to Me, Renegades, Silence Like Glass, Don't Tell Her It's Me, Sibling Rivalry, Jersey Girls, Twister.
TELEVISION: *Series*: Square Pegs, Dreams, Sibs. *Guest*: Diff'rent Strokes, The Facts of Life. *Movie*: This Can't Be Love.

GETTY, BALTHAZAR
Actor. b. California, Jan. 22, 1975. Spotted by talent agent while at Bel Air Prep School, winning lead role in remake of Lord of the Flies.

PICTURES: Lord of the Flies (debut, 1990), Young Guns II, My Heroes Have Always Been Cowboys, The Pope Must Die, December, Where the Day Takes You, Red Hot, Natural Born Killers, White Squall.
TELEVISION: *Special*: The Turn of the Screw.

GETTY, ESTELLE
Actress. b. New York, NY, July 25, 1923. e. attended New School for Social Research. Trained for stage with Gerald Russak and at Herbert Berghof Studios. Worked as comedienne on Borscht Belt circuit and as actress with Yiddish theatre. Founder Fresh Meadows Community theater. Also worked as acting teacher and coach and secretary. Author, If I Knew What I Know Now... So What? (1988).
THEATER: The Divorce of Judy and Jane (off-B'way debut, 1971), Widows and Children First, Table Settings, Demolition of Hannah Fay, Never Too Old, A Box of Tears, Hidden Corners, I Don't Know Why I'm Screaming, Under the Bridge There's a Lonely Place, Light Up the Sky, Pocketful of Posies, Fits and Starts, Torch Song Trilogy (off-B'way, B'way and tour, Drama Desk nom., 1982, Helen Hayes Award, best supp. performer in a touring show).
PICTURES: The Chosen, Tootsie, Protocol, Mask, Mannequin, Stop Or My Mom Will Shoot.
TELEVISION: *Series*: The Golden Girls (Golden Globe Award, Emmy Award, 1988), The Golden Palace, Empty Nest. *Movies*: No Man's Land, Victims for Victims: The Teresa Saldana Story, Copacabana. *Guest*: Cagney and Lacey, Nurse, Baker's Dozen, One of the Boys, Fantasy Island.

GETZ, JOHN
Actor. e. Univ Iowa, Amer. Conservatory Theatre (SF). Appeared on B'way in They're Playing Our Song, M. Butterfly. LA stage: Money & Friends.
PICTURES: Tattoo, Thief of Hearts, Blood Simple, The Fly, The Fly II, Born on the Fourth of July, Men at Work, Don't Tell Mom the Babysitter's Dead, Curly Sue, A Passion to Kill.
TELEVISION: *Series*: Rafferty, Suzanne Pleshette is Maggie Briggs, MacGruder & Loud, Mariah. *Movies*: Killer Bees, A Woman Called Moses, Kent State, Rivkin: Bounty Hunter, Muggable Mary: Street Cop, Not in Front of the Children, Concrete Beat, The Execution, In My Daughter's Name, Betrayal of Trust, Untamed Love, Awake to Danger. *Mini-Series*: Loose Change.

GHOSTLEY, ALICE
Actress. b. Eve, MO, Aug. 14, 1926. e. Univ. of OK.
THEATER: New Faces of 1952, Sandhog, Trouble in Tahiti, Maybe Tuesday, A Thurber Carnival, The Sign in Sidney Brustein's Window (Tony Award, 1965), Stop Thief Stop, Annie, The Beauty Part, Livin' The Life, Nunsense, Come Blow Your Horn, Bye Bye Birdie, Arsenic and Old Lace, Shangri-La.
PICTURES: New Faces (debut, 1954), To Kill a Mockingbird, My Six Loves, Ace Eli and Rodger of the Skies, Gator, Rabbit Test, Grease, Not for Publication, Viva Ace, The Flim Flam Man, With Six You Get Egg Roll, The GRaduate, Blue Sunshine, Record City.
TELEVISION: *Series*: The Jackie Gleason Show (1962-64), Captain Nice, The Jonathan Winters Show, Bewitched, Mayberry R.F.D., Nichols, The Julie Andrews Hour, Temperatures Rising, Designing Women. *Movie*: Two on a Bench. *Specials*: Cinderella, Twelfth Night, Shangri-La, Everybody's Doin' It. *Guest*: Please Don't Eat the Daisies, Get Smart, Love American Style, Hogan's Heroes, The Odd Couple, What's Happening!, Good Times, Gimme a Break, The Golden Girls, The Client, Cybill, etc.

GIANNINI, GIANCARLO
Actor. b. Spezia, Italy, Aug. 1, 1942. Acquired degree in electronics but immediately after school enrolled at Acad. for Drama in Rome. Cast by Franco Zeffirelli as Romeo at age of 20. Subsequently appeared in a play also directed by Zeffirelli, Two Plus Two No Longer Make Four, written by Lina Wertmuller.
PICTURES: Rita la Zanzara, Arabella, Anzio, Fraulein Doktor, The Secret of Santa Vittoria, Love and Anarchy, The Seduction of Mimi, Swept Away by an Unusual Destiny in the Blue Sea of August, Seven Beauties, How Funny Can Sex Be?, A Night Full of Rain, The Innocent, Buone Notizie (also prod.), Revenge, Travels with Anita, Lili Marleen, Lovers and Liars, La Vita e Bella, Picone Sent Me, Immortal Bachelor, American Dreamer, Fever Pitch, Saving Grace, New York Stories (Life Without Zoe), I Picari, The Sleazy, Uncle, Snack Bar Budapest, Oh King, Blood Red, Brown Bread Sandwiches, Killing Time, Short Cut, Once Upon a Crime, A Walk in the Clouds.
TELEVISION: Sins, Jacob.

GIANOPULOUS, JIM
Executive. Pres., Fox International Theatrical Distribution, Twentieth Century Fox, Inc.

GIBBS, DAVID
Executive. b. 1944. Ent. motion picture industry 1961, Kodak research, worked as a photographer for Kodak 1963-66.

Lectured at Harrow College of Technology and Kodak Photographic School until 1972. Left Kodak, 1975, after three years as a market specialist to join Filmatic Laboratories. Appt. asst. man. director, 1977, becoming chmn. and man. director, 1988. Member of RTS, SMPTE and IVCA. Past Chmn. BISFA 1988-90. Past president of the British Kinematograph, Sound and Television Society.

GIBBS, MARLA
Actress. b. Chicago, IL, June 14, 1931. e. Cortez Peters Business School, Chicago. Worked as receptionist, switchboard operator, travel consultant (1963-74) before co-starring as Florence Johnston on the Jeffersons (1974-85). Formed Marla Gibbs Enterprises, Los Angeles, 1978. Member of CA State Assembly, 1980. Image Award NAACP, 1979-83.
PICTURES: Black Belt Jones, Sweet Jesus, Preacher Man.
TELEVISION: Series: The Jeffersons, Checking In, 227. Movies: The Missing Are Deadly, Tell Me Where It Hurts, Nobody's Child. Mini-Series: The Moneychangers. Special: You Can't Take It With You.

GIBSON, DEREK
Executive. b. Huyton, England, July 7, 1945. e. Wigan Col. Head of Prod. at Astral Bellevue Pathe, 1979-80; v.p. Sandy Howard Prods.; Pres. Hemdale Film Group., 1982-present.
PICTURES: Prod./Exec.: The Terminator, Hoosiers, Salvador, Platoon (Academy Award winner for Best Picture, 1986), River's Edge, Best Seller, Criminal Law.

GIBSON, HENRY
Actor. b. Germantown, PA, Sept. 21, 1935. e. Catholic U. of America. Appeared as child actor with stock companies, 1943-57; B'way debut in My Mother My Father and Me, 1962.
PICTURES: The Nutty Professor, Kiss Me Stupid, The Outlaws Is Coming, Charlotte's Web (voice), The Long Goodbye, Nashville (Nat'l Soc. Film Critics Award, 1975), The Last Remake of Beau Geste, Kentucky Fried Movie, A Perfect Couple, The Blues Brothers, Tulips, Health, The Incredible Shrinking Woman, Monster in the Closet, Brenda Starr, Inner Space, Switching Channels, The 'Burbs, Night Visitor, Gremlins II, Tune in Tomorrow, Tom and Jerry: The Movie (voice), A Sailor's Tattoo, Biodome.
TELEVISION: Series: Rowan and Martin's Laugh-In (1968-72). Movies: Evil Roy Slade, Every Man Needs One, The New Original Wonder Woman (pilot), Escape from Bogen County, The Night They Took Miss Beautiful, Amateur Night at the Dixie Bar & Grill, For the Love of It, Nashville Grab, Long Gone, Slow Burn, Return to Green Acres, Return to Witch Mountain. Mini-Series: Around the World in 80 Days.

GIBSON, MEL
Actor, Director. b. Peekskill, NY, Jan. 3, 1956. Emigrated in 1968 to Australia with family. Attended Nat'l Inst. of Dramatic Art in Sydney; in 2nd yr. was cast in his first film, Summer City. Graduated from NIDA, 1977. Joined South Australian Theatre Co. in 1978, appearing in Oedipus, Henry IV, Cedoona. Other plays include Romeo and Juliet, No Names No Pack Drill, On Our Selection, Waiting for Godot, Death of a Salesman.
PICTURES: Summer City (Coast of Terror; debut, 1977), Mad Max, Tim, Chain Reaction (unbilled), Attack Force Z, Gallipoli, The Road Warrior (Mad Max II), The Year of Living Dangerously, The Bounty, The River, Mrs. Soffel, Mad Max Beyond Thunderdome, Lethal Weapon, Tequila Sunrise, Lethal Weapon 2, Bird on a Wire, Air America, Hamlet, Lethal Weapon 3, Forever Young, The Man Without a Face (also dir.), Maverick, Braveheart (also dir., co-prod.; Academy Award, 1996; Golden Globe, 1996), Casper (cameo), Pocahontas (voice), Ransom.
TELEVISION: Series: The Sullivans, The Oracle. Specials: The Ultimate Stuntman: A Tribute to Dar Robinson, Australia's Outback: The Vanishing Frontier (host). Guest host: Saturday Night Live.

GIELGUD, SIR JOHN
Actor. b. London, England, Apr. 14, 1904. e. Westminster Sch., Lady Benson's Sch. (dram.), London; Royal Acad. of Dramatic Art. Knighted, 1953. Autobiography: Early Stages (1983). Honorary degrees: Oxford, London, St. Andrews, Brandeis (U.S), Assoc. Legion of Honor.
THEATER: Began stage career in Shakespearean roles; on London stage also in the Constant Nymph, The Good Companions, Dear Octopus, The Importance of Being Earnest, Dear Brutus, etc., various Shakespearean seasons, London & N.Y. 1988: The Best of Friends.
PICTURES: Who is the Man? (debut, 1924), The Clue of the New Pin; Insult (sound debut, 1932), The Good Companions, Secret Agent, The Prime Minister, Julius Caesar (1953), Romeo and Juliet, Richard III, Around the World in 80 Days, The Barretts of Wimpole Street, Saint Joan, Hamlet, Becket (Acad. Award nom.), To Die in Madrid (narrator), The Loved One, Chimes at Midnight (Falstaff), Sebastian, Assignment to Kill, The Charge of the Light Brigade, The Shoes of the Fisherman, Oh What a Lovely War, Julius Caesar (1971),

Eagle in a Cage, Lost Horizon, Galileo, 11 Harrowhouse, Gold, Murder on the Orient Express, Aces High, Providence, Portrait of the Artist as a Young Man, Joseph Andrews, Murder by Decree, Caligula, The Human Factor, The Elephant Man, The Formula, Sphinx, Lion of the Desert, Arthur (Academy Award , best supporting actor, 1981), Chariots of Fire, Priest of Love, Gandhi, The Wicked Lady, Invitation to the Wedding, Scandalous, The Shooting Party, Plenty, Time After Time, Whistle Blower, Appointment With Death, Bluebeard Bluebeard, Arthur 2 on the Rocks, Getting It Right, Strike It Rich, Prospero's Books, Shining Through, The Power of One, First Knight, Haunted, Shine, The Leopard Son (narrator), Hamlet.
TELEVISION: Specials/Movies/Mini-Series: A Day by the Sea, The Browning Version, The Rehearsal, Great Acting, Ages of Man, Mayfly and th Frog, Cherry Orchard, Ivanov, From Chekhov With Love, St. Joan, Good King Charles' Golden Days, Conversation at Night, Hassan, Deliver Us from Evil, Heartbreak House, Brideshead Revisited, The Canterville Ghost, The Hunchback of Notre Dame, Inside the Third Reich, Marco Polo, The Scarlet and the Black, The Master of Ballantrae, Wagner, The Far Pavillions, Camille, Romance on the Orient Express, Funny You Don't Look 200, Oedipus the King, A Man For All Seasons, War and Remembrance, Summer Lease (Emmy Award, 1991), The Best of Friends, Inspector Alleyn: Hand in Glove, Leave All Fair, Ages of Man, John Gielgud: An Actor's Life, Lovejoy: The Lost Colony, Scarlett.

GILBERT, ARTHUR N.
Producer. b. Detroit, MI, Oct. 17, 1920. Lt., U.S.M.C., 1941-45. e. U. of Chicago, 1946. Special Agent, FBI, 1946-53; world sales dir., Gen. Motors, Cadillac Div., 1953-59; investments in mot. pictures and hotel chains, 1959-64; exec. prod., Mondo Hollywood, 1965; exec. prod. Jeannie-Wife Child, 1966; assoc. prod., The Golden Breed, 1967; commissioned rank of Colonel U.S.M.C., 1968; 1970-80, exec. prod. Jaguar Pictures Corp; Columbia, 1981-86; Indi Pic. Corp. Also account exec. and v.p. Pacific Western Tours. v.p., Great Basion Corp. Bev. Hills 1987-9; v.p., Lawrence 3-D TV 1990-present; v.p. Cougar Prods. Co. 1990-91. Producer in development at Jonte Prods. of Paris/London, 1992-94.
PICTURES: The Glory Stompers, Fire Grass, Cycle Savages, Bigfoot, Incredible Transplant, Balance of Evil.

GILBERT, BRUCE
Producer. b. Los Angeles, CA, March 28, 1947. e. U. of California. Pursued film interests at Berkeley's Pacific Film Archive; in summer involved in production in film dept. of San Francisco State U. Founded progressive pre-school in Bay Area. Became story editor in feature film division of Cine-Artists; involved in several projects, including Aloha, Bobby and Rose. Formally partnered with Jane Fonda in IPC Films, Inc., then pres., American Filmworks.
PICTURES: Coming Home (assoc. prod.), The China Syndrome (exec. prod.). Producer: Nine to Five, On Golden Pond, Rollover, The Morning After, Man Trouble, Jack the Bear.
TELEVISION: Series: Nine to Five (exec. prod.). Movies: The Dollmaker (exec. prod.), By Dawn's Early Light (writer, exec. prod.).

GILBERT, LEWIS
Producer, Writer, Director, Former Actor. b. London, England, Mar. 6, 1920. In RAF, W.W.II. Screen debut; 1932; asst. dir. (1930-39) with London Films, Assoc. British, Mayflower, RKO-Radio; from 1939-44 attached U.S. Air Corps Film Unit (asst. dir., Target for Today). In 1944 joined G.B.I. as writer and dir. In 1948, Gainsborough Pictures as writer, dir.; 1949; Argyle Prod. 1950; under contract Nettlefold Films, Ltd. as dir.
PICTURES: Actor: Under One Roof, I Want to Get Married, Haunting Melody. Director: The Little Ballerina, Marry Me (s.p. only), Once a Sinner, Scarlet Thread, There Is Another Sun, Time Gentlemen Please, Emergency Call, Cosh Boy, Johnny on the Run, Albert R.N., The Good Die Young, The Sea Shall Not Have Them, Reach for the Sky, Cast a Dark Shadow, The Admirable Crichton, Carve Her Name with Pride, A Cry from the Street, Ferry to Hong Kong, Sink the Bismarck, Light Up the Sky, The Greengage Summer, H.M.S. Defiant, The Patriots, Spare the Rod, The Seventh Dawn, Alfie, You Only Live Twice, The Adventurers, Friends (also prod., story), Paul & Michelle (also prod., story), Operation Daybreak, Seven Nights in Japan, The Spy Who Loved Me, Moonraker, Educating Rita (also prod.), Not Quite Paradise, Shirley Valentine (also prod.), Stepping Out (also co-prod.), Haunted (also s.p.).

GILBERT, MELISSA
Actress. b. Los Angeles, CA, May 8, 1964. m. actor Bruce Boxleitner. Made debut at age of 3 in TV commercial. Comes from show business family: father, late comedian Paul Gilbert; mother, former dancer-actress Barbara Crane. Grandfather,

Harry Crane created The Honeymooners. NY Off-B'way debut A Shayna Madel (1987; Outer Critics Circle & Theatre World Awards).
PICTURES: Sylvester (debut, 1985), Ice House.
TELEVISION: Series: Little House on the Prairie, Stand By Your Man, Sweet Justice. Guest: Gunsmoke, Emergency, Tenafly, The Hanna-Barbera Happy Hour, Love Boat. Movies: Christmas Miracle in Caulfield U.S.A., The Miracle Worker, Splendor in the Grass, Choices of the Heart, Choices, Penalty Phase, Family Secrets, Killer Instincts, Without Her Consent, Forbidden Nights, Blood Vows: The Story of a Mafia Wife, Joshua's Heart, Donor, The Lookalike, With a Vengeance, Family of Strangers, With Hostile Intent, Shattered Trust: The Shari Karney Story, House of Secrets, Dying to Remember, Babymaker: The Dr. Cecil Jacobson Story, Against Her Will: The Carrie Buck Story, Cries From the Heart, A Touch of Truth, Danielle Steel's. Zoya.

GILER, DAVID
Producer, Writer, Director. b. New York, NY. Son of Bernie Giler, screen and TV writer. Began writing in teens; first work an episode for ABC series, The Gallant Men. Feature film career began as writer on Myra Breckenridge (1970).
PICTURES: Writer: The Parallax View, Fun with Dick and Jane, The Blackbird (also dir.), Southern Comfort (also prod.). Prod.: Alien, Rustlers' Rhapsody, Let It Ride, Alien³.
TELEVISION: Writer: The Kraft Theatre, Burke's Law, The Man from U.N.C.L.E., The Girl from U.N.C.L.E., Tales From the Crypt (exec. prod.).

GILLIAM, TERRY
Writer, Director, Actor, Animator. b. Minneapolis, MN, Nov. 22, 1940. e. Occidental Coll. Freelance writer and illustrator for various magazines and ad agencies before moving to London. Animator for BBC series Do Not Adjust Your Set, We Have Ways of Making You Laugh. Member, Monty Python's Flying Circus (1969-76). Books incl. numerous Monty Python publications. Honorary degrees: DFA Occidental Col. 1987, DFA Royal Col. of Art 1989.
PICTURES: And Now for Something Completely Different (animator, co-s.p., actor), Monty Python and the Holy Grail (co-dir., co-s.p., actor, animator), Jabberwocky (dir., co-s.p.), Life of Brian (actor, co-s.p., animator), The Do It Yourself Animation Film, Time Bandits (prod., dir., co-s.p.), Monty Python Live at the Hollywood Bowl (actor, co-s.p., animator, designer), The Miracle of Flight (animator, s.p.), Monty Python's The Meaning of Life (co-s.p., actor, animator), Spies Like Us (actor), Brazil (co-s.p., dir.), The Adventures of Baron Munchausen (dir., co-s.p.), The Fisher King (dir.), Twelve Monkeys (dir.).
TELEVISION: Series: Monty Python's Flying Circus (also animator, dir.), Do Not Adjust Your Set, We Have Ways of Making You Laugh, The Mart Feldman Comedy Machine, The Last Machine (1995).

GILMORE, WILLIAM S.
Producer. b. Los Angeles, CA, March 10, 1934. e. U. of California at Berkeley. Started career in film editing before becoming asst. dir. and prod. mgr. at Universal Studios, where worked on 20 feature films. Headed prod. for Mirisch Co. in Europe; then to Zanuck/Brown Co. as exec. in chg. prod. Sr. v.p./prod. of Filmways Pictures, supervising literary development, prod. and post-prod.
PICTURES: Jaws (prod. exec.), The Last Remake of Beau Geste, Defiance, Deadly Blessing, Tough Enough, Against All Odds, White Nights, Little Shop of Horrors, The Man in the Moon, The Player, A Few Good Men, Watch It, The Sandlot, Curse of the Starving Class.
TELEVISION: Just You and Me, One in a Million--The Ron Leflore Story, The Legend of Walks Far Woman, S.O.S. Titanic, Another Woman's Child, Women and Men, Women and Men 2.

GILROY, FRANK D.
Writer, Director. b. New York, NY, Oct. 13, 1925. e. Dartmouth; postgrad. Yale School of Drama. TV writer: Playhouse 90, US Steel Hour, Omnibus, Kraft Theatre, Lux Video Theater, Studio One. B'way playwright.
AUTHOR: Plays: Who'll Save the Plowboy?, The Subject Was Roses (Pulitzer Prize & Tony Award, 1965), The Only Game in Town, Present Tense, The Housekeeper, Last Licks, Any Given Day. Novels: Private, Little Ego (with Ruth Gilroy), From Noon to 3. Book: I Wake Up Screening!: Everything You Need to Know About Making Independent Films Including a Thousand Reasons Not To (1993).
PICTURES: Writer: The Fastest Gun Alive, The Gallant Hours, The Subject Was Roses, The Only Game in Town. Dir.-Writer: Desperate Characters (also prod.), From Noon Till Three, Once in Paris, The Gig, The Luckiest Man in the World.
TELEVISION: Writer-Dir.: Nero Wolfe, Turning Point of Jim Malloy.

GILULA, STEPHEN
Executive. b. Herrin, IL, Aug. 20, 1950. e. Stanford U. UA Theatre Circuit, film booker for San Francisco area, 1973; Century Cinema Circuit, film buyer, LA, 1974. Co-founder,

Landmark Theatre Corp., 1974; serving as pres., 1982-present. Landmark merged with Samuel Goldwyn Co. in 1991. Chmn. NATO of California/Nevada, 1991-present; also on bd. of dirs. of NATO, 1992-present.

GIMBEL, ROGER
Producer, Executive. b. March 11, 1925. e. Yale. Began tv prod. career as creative chief of RCA Victor TV, then became assoc. prod. of the Tonight Show for NBC; named head of prog. dev. of NBC daytime programming; then prod. of the 90-minute NBC Tonight Specials, including The Jack Paar Show and the Ernie Kovacs Show. Became prod. and co-packager of the Glen Campbell Goodtime Hour for CBS, 1969; v.p. in chg. of prod. for Tomorrow Entertainment, 1971. Formed his own prod. co., Roger Gimbel's Tomorrow Enterprises, Inc., 1975; prod. Minstrel Man. Became U.S. pres. of EMI-TV, 1976. Received special personal Emmy as exec. prod. of War of the Children, 1975. Produced 33 movies for TV under the EMI banner and won 18 Emmys. In 1984, EMI-TV became The Peregrine Producers Group, Inc., of which he was pres. & COO. 1987, spun off Roger Gimbel Prods. as an independent film co; 1988-89, pres./exec. prod., Carolco/Gimbel Productions, Inc. 1989-96, pres. & exec. prod. of Roger Gimbel Prods Inc. in association with Multimedia Motion Pictures Inc.
TELEVISION: Movies/Specials: The Autobiography of Miss Jane Pittman, Born Innocent, Birds of Prey, Brand New Life, Gargoyles, Glass House, In This House of Brede, I Heard the Owl Call My Name, I Love You Goodbye, Larry, Miles to Go Before I Sleep, Queen of the Stardust Ballroom, Tell Me Where It Hurts, The Man Who Could Talk to Kids, Things in Their Season, A War of Children (Emmy Award), The Amazing Howard Hughes, Deadman's Curve, Steel Cowboy, Betrayal, The Cracker Factory, Survival of Diana, Can You Hear the Laughter?, S.O.S. Titanic, Walks-Far Woman, Sophia Loren: Her Own Sotory, Manions of America, A Question of Honor, The Killing of Randy Webster, Broken Promise, A Piano for Mrs. Cimino, Deadly Encounter, Aurora, Rockabye, Blackout, Apology, Montana, Shattered Dreams, Chernobyl: The Final Warning, Desperate Rescue: The Cathy Mahone Story, Murder Between Friends, etc.

GINNA, ROBERT EMMETT, JR.
Producer, Writer. b. New York, NY, Dec. 3, 1925. e. U. of Rochester, Harvard U., M.A. In U.S. Navy, WWII. Journalist for Life, Scientific American, Horizon, 1950-55; 1958-61, contributor to many magazines. Staff writer, producer, director NBC-TV, 1955-58; v.p., Sextant, Inc.; dir., Sextant Films Ltd., 1961-64. Founded Windward Productions, Inc., Windward Film Productions, Ltd., 1965. Active in publishing 1974-82; sr. ed. People; ed. in chief, Little Brown; asst. mgr., Life. Resumed pres., Windward Prods, Inc., 1982; publishing consultant.
PICTURES: Young Cassidy (co-prod.), The Last Challenge (co-s.p.), Before Winter Comes (prod.), Brotherly Love (prod.).

GINNANE, ANTHONY I.
Executive, Producer. e. Melbourne U (law), 1976. 1977 formed joint venture with financier William Fayman for Australian film production and distribution. 1981 established company Film and General Holdings Inc. for locating film projects/financing.
PICTURES: Producer or Exec. Prod: Sympathy in Summer (debut, 1970; also dir.), Fantasm, Patrick, Snapshot, Thirst, Harlequin, Race for the Yankee Zephyr, Strange Behavior, Turkey Shoot, Prisoners, Second Tim Lucky, Mesmerized, Dark Age, Slate Wyn & Me, Initiation, High Tide, The Lighthorsemen, Time Guardian, Incident at Raven's Gate, The Everlasting Secret Family, The Dreaming, Grievous Bodily Harm, Boundaries of the Heart, Killer Instinct, Savage Justice, Outback, A Case of Honor, Siege of Firebase Gloria, Driving Force, Demonstone, Fatal Sky, No Contest, Screamers, Bonjour Timothy.

GINSBERG, SIDNEY
Executive. b. New York, NY, Oct. 26, 1920. e. City Coll. of New York, 1938. Entered m.p. ind., as asst. mgr., Loew's Theatres; joined Trans-Lux 1943, as theatre mgr.; film booker; helped form Trans-Lux Distributing Corp., 1956; asst. to pres., Trans-Lux Dist. Corp.; asst. vice-pres., Trans-Lux Picture, Distributing and TV Corp., 1961, V.P. Trans-Lux Dist. Corp., 1967, V.P. in charge of worldwide sales, 1969. Haven International Pictures, Inc., Haven Int'l 1970; IFIDA gov., 1970, v.p. sales, Scotia International Films, Inc., 1971; exec. v.p., Scotia American Prods; 1977, pres., Rob-Rich Films Inc.; 1979, exec. v.p., A Major Studio, Inc.; 1980, exec. v.p., The Health and Entertainment Corp. of America; 1982, sr. acct. rep., 3M-Photogard; 1984, pres., Rob-Rich Films.

GINSBURG, LEWIS S.
Distributor, Importer, Prod. b. New York, NY, May 16, 1914. e. City Coll. of New York, 1931-32. Columbia U., 1932-33. Ent. film industry, tabulating dept., United Artists, 1933; sls. contract dept. 1934; asst. to eastern district mgr., 1938; slsmn.,

New Haven exch., 1939. Army, 1943. Ret. to U.S., then formed first buying & booking service in Connecticut, 1945-55; in chg., New England Screen Guild Exchanges, 1955; TV film distr., 1955; Formed & org. International Film Assoc., Vid-EX Film Distr. Corp., 1961. Prod., TV half-hour series; vice-pres. in chg., dist., Desilu Film Dist. C., 1962; organized Carl Releasing Co., 1963; Walter Reade-Sterling Inc., 1964-65; formed L.G. Films Corp.; contract and playdate mgr., 20th Fox, 1965-68. Cinerama Releasing Corp. Adm. Ass't to sales mgr., 1968-69; 20th Cent.-Fox. Nat'l sales coordinator, 1969-present. 1970, 20th Century-Fox, Asst. to the Sales Mgr. 1971, Transnational Pictures Corp., v.p. in chg. of dist., pres., Stellar IV Film Corp., 1972.

GIRARDOT, ANNIE
Actress. b. Paris, France, Oct. 25, 1931. Studied nursing. Studied acting at the Paris Conservatory, made her acting debut with the Comedie Franccaise. Has acted on the French stage and in reviews in the Latin Quarter.
PICTURES: Trezie a Table (debut, 1955), Speaking of Murder, Inspector Maigret, Love and the Frenchwoman, Rocco and His Brothers, Le Rendezvous, Crime Does Not Pay, Vice and Virtue, The Organizer, La Bonne Soupe (Careless Love), Male Companion, The Dirty Game, The Witches, Live for Life, Les Galoises Bleues, Dillinger Is Dead, The Seed of Man, Trois Chambres a Manhattan (Venice Film Fest. Award), The Story of a Woman, Love Is a Funny Thing, Shock!, Where THere's Smoke, Juliette et Juliette, The Slap, It Is Raining in Santiago, No Time for Breakfast (Cesar Award), Dear Inspector, The Skirt Chaser, Traffic Jam, Jupiter's Thigh, Five Days in June, La Vie Continue, Prisonniers, Comedie D'Amour, Girls With Guns, Les Miserables.

GISH, ANNABETH
Actress. b. Albuquerque, NM, Mar. 13, 1971. e. Duke U ('93). Started acting at age 8; appeared in several TV commercials in Iowa.
PICTURES: Desert Bloom, Hiding Out, Mystic Pizza, Shag, Coupe de Ville, Wyatt Earp, The Red Coat, Nixon, The Last Supper, Beautiful Girls.
TELEVISION: Series: Courthouse. Movies: Hero in the Family, When He's Not a Stranger, The Last to Go, Lady Against the Odds, Silent Cries. Mini-Series: Scarlett.

GIVENS, ROBIN
Actress. b. New York, NY, Nov. 27, 1964. e. Sarah Lawrence Col., Harvard Univ. Graduate Sch. of Arts & Sciences. While at college became model, made appearances on daytime dramas The Guiding Light and Loving.
PICTURES: A Rage in Harlem (debut, 1991), Boomerang, Foreign Student, Blankman.
TELEVISION: Series: Head of the Class, Angel Street, Courthouse, Sparks, Sparls and Sparks. Movies: Beverly Hills Madam, The Women of Brewster Place, The Penthouse, Dangerous Intentions.

GLASER, PAUL MICHAEL
Actor, Director. b. Cambridge, MA, March 25, 1943. e. Tulane U., Boston U., M.A. Did five seasons in summer stock before starting career in New York, making stage debut in Rockabye Hamlet in 1968. Appeared in numerous off-B'way plays and got early TV training as regular in daytime series, Love of Life and Love Is a Many Splendored Thing.
PICTURES: Actor: Fiddler on the Roof, Butterflies Are Free, Phobia. Director: Band of the Hand, The Running Man, The Cutting Edge, The Air Up There, Kazaam (also prod., story).
TELEVISION: Series: Starsky and Hutch. Guest: Kojak, Toma, The Streets of San Francisco, The Rockford Files, The Sixth Sense, The Waltons. Movies: Trapped Beneath the Sea, The Great Houdinis, Wait Till You Mother Gets Home!, Princess Daisy, Jealousy, Attack on Fear, Single Bars Single Women, Amazons (dir. only).

GLAZER, WILLIAM
Executive b. Cambridge, MA. e. State U. of New York, Entered m.p. ind. with Ralph Snider Theatres 1967-69; General Cinema Corp. 1969-71; Loews Theatres 1971-73; Joined Sack Theatres 1973 as Dist. mgr.; 1974 Exec. Asst. to Pres.; 1976 Gen. Mgr.; 1980 V.P. Gen. Mgr.; 1982 Exec. V.P. Member of SMPTE; NATO (Bd of Dir); Theatre Owners of New England Bd of Dir, also pres.; 1982-1985.

GLEASON, LARRY
Executive. b. Boston, MA, Apr. 30, 1938. e. Boston Coll., M.A., 1960. Held various positions, western div., mgr., General Cinema Corp.; 1963-73; gen. mgr., Gulf States Theatres, New Orleans, 1973-74; pres., Mann Theatres, 1974-85; joined DeLaurentiis Entertainment Group as pres., mktg./dist., 1985. Named sr. v.p., Paramount Pictures Corp, theatrical exhibition group, 1989. Named pres. Paramount Pictures Corp. theatrical exhib. group, 1991. Joined MGM/UA as pres. of Worlwide Distrib., 1994. Foundation of Motion Picture Pioneers v.p. Member, Variety Club, Will Rogers Foundation.

GLEN, JOHN
Director. b. Sunbury on Thames, Eng., May 15, 1932. Entered industry in 1947. Second unit dir.: On Her Majesty's Secret Service, The Spy Who Loved Me, Wild Geese, Moonraker (also editor). Editor: The Sea Wolves.
PICTURES: For Your Eyes Only (dir. debut, 1981), Octopussy, A View to a Kill, The Living Daylights, Licence to Kill, Aces: Iron Eagle III, Christopher Columbus: The Discovery.
TELEVISION: Series: Space Precinct (7 episodes).

GLENN, CHARLES OWEN
Executive. b. Binghamton, NY, March 27, 1938. e. Syracuse U., B.A., U. of PA. Capt., U.S. Army, 1961-63. Asst. to dir. of adv., 20th Cent. Fox, 1966-67; asst. adv. mgr., Paramount, 1967-68; acct. spvsr. & exec., MGM record & m.p. div., 1968-69; nat'l adv. mgr., Paramount, 1969-70; nat'l. dir. of adv., Paramount, 1970-71; v.p. adv.-pub.-prom., 1971-73; v.p. marketing, 1974; v.p. prod. mktg., 1975; joined American Intl. Pictures as v.p. in chg. of adv./creative affairs, 1979. 1980, when Filmways took AIP over he was named their v.p. in chg. worldwide adv./pub./promo.; joined MCA/Universal in 1982 as exec. v.p., adv.-promo.; 1984, appt. Orion Pictures adv.-pub.-promo. exec. v.p.; 1987, appt. Orion mktg. exec. v.p. 1989 recipient Outstanding Performance Award Leukemia Society of Amer. for completing NYC Marathon. 1993, pres. mktg., Bregman/Baer Prods. Featured actor in 1993 film Philadelphia. Member: Exec. comm. public relations branch, Academy of M.P. Arts & Sciences. Holder of NATO mktg. exec. of year (1983) award, Clio Award for U.S. adv. of Platoon; Variety Club, Motion Picture Pioneers, Screen Actors Guild.

GLENN, SCOTT
Actor. b. Pittsburgh, PA, Jan. 26, 1942. e. William & Mary Coll. Worked as U.S. Marine, newspaper reporter before going to New York to study drama at Actors Studio in 1968.
THEATER: Off-B'way: Zoo Story, Fortune in Men's Eyes, Long Day's Jack Street, Journey into Night. B'way: The Impossible Years, Burn This, Dark Picture.
PICTURES: The Baby Maker (debut, 1970), Angels Hard as They Come, Hex, Nashville, Fighting Mad, More American Graffiti, Apocalypse Now, Urban Cowboy, Cattle Annie and Little Britches, Personal Best, The Challenge, The Right Stuff, The Keep, The River, Wild Geese II, Silverado, Verne Miller, Man on Fire, Off Limits, Miss Firecracker, The Hunt for Red October, The Silence of the Lambs, My Heroes Have Always Been Cowboys, Backdraft, The Player, Night of the Running Man, Tall Tale, Reckless, Edie and Pen, Courage Under Fire, Carla's Song, Courage Under Fire, Edue & Pen.
TELEVISION: Movies: Gargoyles, As Summers Die, Intrigue, The Outside Woman, Women & Men 2, Shadowhunter, Slaughter of the Innocents, Past Tense.

GLENNON, JAMES M.
Cinematographer. b. Burbank, CA, Aug. 29, 1942. e. UCLA. m. actress Charmaine Glennon. Focus Awards judge 1985-; bd. or dirs., UCLA Theatre Arts Alumni Assoc. 1985-. ASC - member of American Society of Cinematographers, AMPAS.
PICTURES: Return of the Jedi, El Norte, The Wild Life, Smooth Talk, Flight of the Navigator, Time of Destiny, A Show of Force, December, The Gift.
TELEVISION: Lemon Sky (American Playhouse), Laurel Ave, DEA (pilot), Bakersfield (pilot), Judicial Consent.

GLESS, SHARON
Actress. b. Los Angeles, CA, May 31, 1943. m. producer Barney Rosenzweig. London stage: Misery.
PICTURES: Airport 1975, The Star Chamber.
TELEVISION: Series: Marcus Welby M.D., Faraday and Co., Switch, Turnabout, House Calls, Cagney and Lacey (2 Emmy Awards, Golden Globe Award), The Trials of Rosie O'Neill (Golden Globe Award). Mini-Series: Centennial, The Immigrants, The Last Convertible. Movies: The Longest Night, All My Darling Daughters, My Darling Daughters' Anniversary, Richie Brockelman: Missing 24 Hours, The Flying Misfits, The Islander, Crash, Whisper in the Gloom (Disney), Hardhat and Legs, Moviola: The Scarlett O'Hara War, Revenge of the Stepford Wives, The Miracle of Kathy Miller, Hobson's Choice, The Sky's No Limit, Letting Go, The Outside Woman, Honor Thy Mother, Separated by Murder, Cagney & Lacey: The Return, Cagney & Lacey: Together Again.

GLICK, PHYLLIS
Executive. b. New York, NY. e. Queens Coll. of C.U.N.Y. Began career with Otto-Windsor Associates, as casting director; left to be independent. 1979, joined ABC-TV as mgr. of comedy series development; promoted 1980 to director, involved with all comedy series developed for network. 1985, joined Paramount Pictures as exec. dir., production, for M.P. Group; 1989, co-exec. prod., Living Dolls.

GLOBUS, YORAM
Producer. b. Israel, Came to U.S. 1979. Has co-produced many films with cousin and former partner Menahem Golan.

Sr. exec. v.p., Cannon Group; Pres. and CEO Cannon Entertainment and Cannon Films; 1989 named chmn. and C.E.O Cannon Entertainment and officer of Cannon Group Inc.; then co-pres. Pathe Communications Corp. and chmn. and C.E.O. Pathe Intl. Left MGM/Pathe in 1991.
PICTURES: All as producer or exec. prod. with Menahem Golan: Sallah; Trunk to Cairo; My Margo; What's Good for the Goose; Escape to the Sun; I Love You, Rosa; The House on Chelouch Street; The Four Deuces; Kazablan; Diamonds; God's Gun; Kid Vengeance, Operation Thunderbolt, The Uranium Conspiracy, Savage Weekend, The Magician of Lublin, The Apple, The Happy Hooker Goes to Hollywood, Dr. Heckyl and Mr. Hype, The Godsend, New Year's Evil, Schizoid, Seed of Innocence, Body and Soul, Death Wish II, Enter the Ninja, Hospital Massacre, The Last American Virgin, Championship Season, Treasure of Four Crowns, 10 to Midnight, Nana, I'm Almost Not Crazy..., John Cassavetes: The Man and His Work, The House of Long Shadows, Revenge of the Ninja, Hercules, The Wicked Lady, Sahara, The Ambassador, Bolero, Exterminator 2, The Naked Face, Missing in Action, Hot Resort, Love Streams, Breakin', Grace Quigley, Making the Grade, Ninja III-The Domination, Breakin' 2: Electric Boogaloo, Lifeforce, Over the Brooklyn Bridge, The Delta Force, The Assisi Underground, Hot Chili, The Berlin Affair, Missing in Action 2-The Beginning, Rappin', Thunder Alley, American Ninja, Mata Hari, Death Wish 3, King Solomon's Mines, Runaway Train, Fool for Love, Invasion U.S.A., Maria's Lovers, Murphy's Law, The Naked Cage, P.O.W.: The Escape, The Texas Chainsaw Massacre, Part 2, Invaders from Mars, 52 Pick-Up, Link, Firewalker, Dumb Dicks, The Nutcracker: The Motion Picture, Avenging Force, Hashigaon Hagadol, Journey to the Center of the Earth, Prom Queen, Salome, Otello, Cobra, America 3000, American Ninja 2: The Confrontation, Allan Quartermain and the Lost City of Gold, Assassination, Beauty and the Beast, Down Twisted, Duet for One, The Emperor's New Clothes, The Hanoi Hilton, The Barbarians, Dutch Treat, Masters of the Universe, Number One with a Bullet, Rumpelstiltskin, Street Smart, UnderCover, The Assault, Hansel and Gretel, Going Bananas, Snow White, Sleeping Beauty, Tough Guys Don't Dance, Shy People, Dancers, Red Riding Hood, King Lear, Braddock: Missing in Action III, Too Much, Die Papierene Brucke, Field of Honor, Barfly (exec. prod.), Surrender (exec. prod.), Death Wish 4: The Crackdown (exec. prod.), Gor (exec. prod.), Business as Usual (exec. prod.), Over the Top, Superman IV: The Quest for Peace. Prod.: Delta Force, Operation Crackdown, Manifesto, Stranglehold, Delta Force II, Cyborg, Step By Step. Exec. prod.: The Kitchen Toto, Doin' Time on Planet Earth, Kickboxer, Kinjite, A Man Called Sarge, The Rose Garden, The Secret of the Ice Cave.

GLOVER, CRISPIN
Actor. b. New York, NY, 1964. e. Mirman School. Trained for stage with Dan Mason and Peggy Feury. Stage debut, as Friedrich Von Trapp, The Sound of Music, Los Angeles, 1977. Wrote books, Rat Catching (1987), Oak Mot (1990), Concrete Inspection (1992), What It Is and How It Is Done (1995). Recorded album The Big Problem Does Not Equal the Solution- The Solution Equals Let it Be.
PICTURES: My Tutor, Racing with the Moon, Friday the 13th-The Final Chapter, Teachers, Back to the Future, At Close Range, River's Edge, Twister, Where the Heart Is, Wild at Heart, The Doors, Little Noises, Rubin and Ed, Thirty Door Key, What's Eating Gilbert Grape, Chasers, Even Cowgirls Get the Blues, Crime and Punishment, Dead Man, What Is It? (dir. and wrote), The People vs. Larry Flynt.
TELEVISION: Movie: High School U.S.A. Special: Hotel Room (Blackout).

GLOVER, DANNY
Actor. b. San Francisco, CA, July 22, 1947. e. San Francisco State U. Trained at Black Actors Workshop of American Conservatory Theatre. Appeared in many stage productions (Island, Macbeth, Sizwe Banzi Is Dead, etc.). On N.Y. stage in Suicide in B Flat, The Blood Knot, Master Harold... and the Boys (Theatre World Award).
PICTURES: Escape from Alcatraz (debut, 1979), Chu Chu and the Philly Flash, Out (Deadly Drifter), Iceman, Places in the Heart, Witness, Silverado, The Color Purple, Lethal Weapon, Bat-21, Lethal Weapon 2, To Sleep with Anger (also co-exec. prod.), Predator 2, Flight of the Intruder, A Rage in Harlem, Pure Luck, Grand Canyon, Lethal Weapon 3, Bopha!, The Saint of Fort Washington, Maverick (cameo), Angels in the Outfield, Operation Dumbo Drop.
TELEVISION: Mini-Series: Chiefs, Lonesome Dove, Queen. Movies: Face of Rage, Mandela, Dead Man Out. Series: Storybook Classics (host), Civil War Journal (host). Specials: And the Children Shall Lead, How the Leopard Got Its Spots (narrator), A Place at the Table, A Raisin in the Sun, Override (dir. only), Shelley Duvall's Tall Tales and Legends: John Henry. Guest: Lou Grant, Palmerstown U.S.A., Gimme a Break, Hill Street Blues, Many Mansions.

GLOVER, JOHN
Actor. b. Kingston, NY, Aug. 7, 1944. e. Towson State Coll., Baltimore.
THEATER: On regional theatre circuit; Off-B'way in A Scent of Flowers, Subject to Fits, The House of Blue Leaves, The Selling of the President, Love! Valour! Compassion! (also B'way; Tony Award, 1995). With APA Phoenix Co. in Great God Brown (Drama Desk Award), The Visit, Don Juan, Chermin de Fer, Holiday. Other NY stage: The Importance of Being Earnest, Hamlet, Frankenstein, Whodunnit, Digby. L.A.: The Traveler (L.A. Drama Critics Award), Lips Together Teeth Apart.
PICTURES: Shamus, Annie Hall, Julia, Somebody Killed Her Husband, Last Embrace, Success, Melvin and Howard, The Mountain Men, The Incredible Shrinking Woman, A Little Sex, The Evil That Men Do, A Flash of Green, 52 Pick-Up, White Nights, Something Special, Masquerade, A Killing Affair, Rocket Gibraltar, The Chocolate War, Scrooged, Meet the Hollowheads, Gremlins 2: The New Batch, Robocop 2, Ed and His Dead Mother, Night of the Running Man, In the Mouth of Madness, Schemes, Automatics, Batman and Robin.
TELEVISION: Movies: A Rage of Angels, The Face of Rage, Ernie Kovacs-Between the Laughter, An Early Frost (Emmy nom.), Apology, Moving Target, Hot Paint, Nutcracker: Money Madness and Murder (Emmy nom.), David, The Traveling Man (ACE nom.), Twist of Fate, Breaking Point, El Diablo, What Ever Happened to Baby Jane?, Dead on the Money, Drug Wars: The Cocaine Cartel, Grass Roots, Majority Rule, Assault at West Point. Specials: An Enemy of the People, Paul Reiser: Out on a Whim, Crime and Punishment (Emmy nom.). Mini-Series: Kennedy, George Washington. Series: South Beach. Guest: L.A. Law (Emmy nom.), Frasier (Emmy nom.)

GLYNN, CARLIN
Actress. b. Cleveland, OH, Feb. 19, 1940. m. actor-writer-dir. Peter Masterson. Daughter is actress Mary Stuart Masterson. e. Sophie Newcomb College, 1957-58. Studied acting with Stella Adler, Wynn Handman and Lee Strasberg in NY. Debut, Gigi, Alley Theatre, Houston, TX 1959. NY stage debut Waltz of The Toreadors, 1960. On stage in The Best Little Whorehouse in Texas (Tony, Eleanora Duse & Olivier Awards), Winterplay, Alterations, Pal Joey (Chicago; Jos. Jefferson Award), The Cover of Life, The Young Man From Atlanta (winner, Pulitzer Prize for Drama, 1995). Adjunct professor at Columbia U film sch. Resource advisor at the Sundance Inst.
PICTURES: Three Days of the Condor, Continental Divide, Sixteen Candles, The Trip to Bountiful, Gardens of Stone, Blood Red, Night Game, Convicts.
TELEVISION: Series: Mr. President. Mini-Series: A Woman Named Jackie.

GODARD, JEAN-LUC
Writer, Director. b. Paris, France, Dec. 3, 1930. e. Lycee Buffon, Paris. Journalist, film critic Cahiers du Cinema. Acted in and financed experimental film Quadrille by Jacques Rivette, 1951. 1954: dir. first short, Operation Beton, followed by Une Femme Coquette. 1956, was film editor. 1957: worked in publicity dept. 20th Century Fox.
PICTURES: Director/Writer: Breathless (A Bout de Souffle; feature debut, 1960), Le Petit Soldat, A Woman Is a Woman, My Life to Live, Les Carabiniers, Contempt, Band of Outsiders, The Married Woman, Alphaville, Pierrot le Fou, Masculine-Feminine, Made in USA, Two or Three Things I Know About Her, La Chinoise, Weekend, Sympathy for the Devil, Le Gai Savoir, Tout a Bien (co-dir.), Numero Deux, Every Man For Himself, First Name Carmen, Hail Mary, Aria (Armide segment), King Lear, Keep Up Your Right (also edit, actor), Nouvelle Vogue (New Wave), Helas Pour Moi (Oh Woe is Me), Germany Year, J.L.G. by J.L.G., The Kids Play Russian.

GOLAN, MENAHEM
Producer, Director, Writer. b. Tiberias, Israel, May 31, 1929. e. NYU. Studied theater dir. at Old Vic Theatre London, m.p. prod. at City Coll, NY. Co-founder and prod. with cousin Yoram Globus, Golan-Globus Prods., Israel, then L.A., 1962. Later Noah Films, Israel, 1963, Ameri-Euro Pictures Corp, before buying controlling share in Cannon Films, 1979. Sr. exec. v.p., Cannon Group; chmn. of bd., Cannon Entertainment and Cannon Films. 1988, dir. and sr. exec. v.p. Cannon Group, chmn. and head of creative affairs, Cannon Entertainment when it became div. of Giancarlo Parretti's Pathe Communications Corp. Resigned March, 1989 to form 21st Century Film Corp as chmn. and CEO.
PICTURES: Director/co-writer: Kasablan, Diamonds, Entebbe (Operation Thunderbolt), Teyve and His Seven Daughters, What's Good for the Goose? Lepke, The Magician of Lublin, The Goodsend, Happy Hooker Goes to Hollywood, Enter the Ninja. Producer-Writer-Director: Mack the Knife, Hanna's War. Producer-Director: The Uranium Conspiracy, Delta Force, Over the Brooklyn Bridge, Over the Top. Producer/Exec. prod.: Sallah, Runaway Train, Sallah, Fool For Love, Maria's Lovers, Cobra, Evil Angels, I Love You Rosa, Body and Soul, also:

Deathwish II, The Last American Virgin, That Championship Season, House of Long Shadows, Revenge of the Ninja, Hercules, The Movie Tales (12 children's fairy tales films), The Wicked Lady, Cobra, Barfly (exec. prod.), Breakin', Missing in Action, Dancers (prod.), Surrender (exec. prod.), Death Wish 4: The Crackdown (exec. prod.), King Lear (prod.), Too Much (prod.), Powaqquatsi (exec. prod.), Mercenary Fighters (prod.), Doin' Time on Planet Earth (prod.), Manifesto (prod.), Kinjite (exec. prod.), Messenger of Death (exec. prod.), Alien From L.A. (prod.), Hero and the Terror (exec. prod.), Haunted Summer (exec. prod.), A Cry in the Dark (exec. prod.), Delta Force-Operation Crackdown (prod.), A Man Called Sarge (exec. prod.), Stranglehold: Delta Force II (prod.), Cyborg (prod.), The Rose Garden (exec. prod.), Rope Dancing (exec. prod.), The Phantom of the Opera.

GOLCHAN, FREDERIC
Producer. b. Neuilly sur Seine, France, Nov. 20, 1955. e. UCLA Film School, HEC in Paris, NYU Bus.Sch. Journalist/photographer for various European magazines. Worked for American Express, 1979-80. Started indept. investment banking firm, 1980-84. Started own production co., 1985. Directed Victory of the Deaf.
PICTURES: Flagrant Desire, Quick Change, Intersection, The Associate.
TELEVISION: Freedom Fighter, Home by Midnight, In The Deep Woods.

GOLD, ERNEST
Composer, Conductor. b. Vienna, Austria, July 13, 1921. e. State Acad. for Music and Performing Arts, Austria 1937-38; private study, 1939-49 in U.S. Worked as song writer 1939-42 and taught in private schools, 1942. Composed first score for Columbia Pictures, 1945. Musical dir., Santa Barbara Symphony, 1958-59. Taught at UCLA, 1973 and 1983-90 (adult ed.). Gold record for soundtrack of Exodus, 1968. Received star on Walk of Fame on Hollywood Blvd., 1975. Elected to bd. of govs., AMPAS, 1984.
PICTURES: Smooth as Silk, Wyoming, Witness for the Prosecution, The Pride and the Passion, Too Much Too Soon, On the Beach (Acad. Award nom.), Exodus (Academy Award, 1960), Inherit the Wind, The Last Sunset, Judgment at Nuremberg, Pressure Point, A Child Is Waiting, It's a Mad Mad Mad Mad World (Acad. Award nom.), Ship of Fools, The Secret of Santa Vittoria (Acad. Award nom.), The Wild McCullochs, Cross of Iron, Fun With Dick and Jane, Good Luck Miss Wyckoff, The Runner Stumbles, Tom Horn.
TELEVISION: Small Miracle, Wallenberg: a Hero's Story.

GOLDBERG, FRED
Executive. b. New York, NY, Aug. 26, 1921. e. Pace Col., Sch. of Marketing & Advertising. Expl. Paramount, 1946; asst. expl. mgr. trade contact, syndicate contact, NY newspaper contact promotion mgr., 1946-52; asst. publ. mgr. RKO, 1952; natl. publ. mgr., IFE, 1953; v.p. Norton and Condon, pub., 1953; returned to IFE Sept. 1954 as natl. pub. mgr.; head of NY office, Arthur Jacobs, then Blowitz-Maskel, 1956; exec. asst. to dir. pub., adv. UA Corp., 1958; exec. dir., adv. pub. exploitation, UA Corp., 1961; named v.p., 1962; sr. v.p., 1972; sr. v.p., dir. of mrkt., 1977. Left in 1978 to be consultant with Diener, Hauser & Bates Agency. In 1979 joined Columbia Pics. as sr. v.p. in chg. of adv./pub. Left in 1981 to form new company. Became teacher of M.P. Marketing & Distrib. at Univ. of Miami's Sch. of Communications. Author: Motion Picture Marketing & Distribution.

GOLDBERG, LEONARD
Executive, Producer. b. Brooklyn, NY, Jan. 24, 1934. e. Wharton ch., U. of Pennsylvania. Began career in ABC-TV research dept.; moved to NBC-TV research div.; 1961 joined BBD&Q ad agency in charge of overall bdcst. coordinator. In 1963 rejoined ABC-TV as mgr. of program devel. 1964-66, v.p., Daytime programs. 1966 named VP in chg of network TV programming. Resigned in 1969 to join Screen Gems as VP in chg. of prod. Left for partnership with Aaron Spelling in Spelling/Goldberg Prods.; later produced TV and theatrical films under own banner, Mandy Prods. 1986, named pres., COO, 20th Century Fox. Resigned, 1989. Elected to the board of Spectradyne Inc.
PICTURES: Prod.: All Night Long, WarGames, Space Camp, Sleeping With the Enemy, The Distinguished Gentleman, Aspen Extreme.
TELEVISION: Series: The Rookies, SWAT, Starsky and Hutch, Charlie's Angels, Family, Hart to Hart, T.J. Hooker, Fantasy Island, Paper Dolls, The Cavanaughs, Class of '96. Movies: Brian's Song, Little Ladies of the Night, The Legend of Valentino, The Boy in the Plastic Bubble, Something About Amelia, Alex: The Life of a Child, She Woke Up.

GOLDBERG, WHOOPI
Actress. b. New York, NY, Nov. 13, 1949. r.n. Caryn Johnson. e. Sch. for the Performing Arts. Began performing at age 8 in N.Y. with children's program at Hudson Guild and Helena Rubenstein Children's Theatre. Moved to San Diego, CA, 1974, and helped found San Diego Rep. Theatre appearing in Mother Courage, Getting Out. Member: Spontaneous Combustion (improv. group). Joined Blake St. Hawkeyes Theatre in Berkeley, partnering with David Schein. Went solo to create The Spook Show, working in San Francisco and later touring U.S. & Europe. 1983 performance caught attention of Mike Nichols which led to B'way show (for which she received a Theatre World Award) based on it and directed by him. Founding member of Comic Relief benefits. Theatrical film debut in The Color Purple (1985; Image Award NAACP, Golden Globe).
THEATER: small roles in B'way prods. of Pippin, Hair, Jesus Christ Superstar. 1988: toured in Living on the Edge of Chaos.
PICTURES: The Color Purple (debut, 1985; Acad. Award nom.), Jumpin' Jack Flash, Burglar, Fatal Beauty, The Telephone, Clara's Heart, Beverly Hills Brats (cameo), Homer and Eddie, Ghost (Academy Award, best supporting actress, 1990), The Long Walk Home, Soapdish, House Party 2 (cameo), The Player, Sister Act, Wisecracks, Sarafina!, The Magic World of Chuck Jones, National Lampoon's Loaded Weapon 1 (cameo), Made in America, Sister Act 2: Back in the Habit, Naked in New York (cameo), The Lion King (voice), The Little Rascals, Corrina Corrina, Star Trek: Generations, Theodore Rex, The Pagemaster (voice), Liberation (narrator), Boys on the Side, Moonlight and Valentino, The Celluloid Closet, Bogus, Eddie, The Associate, Ghosts of Mississippi.
TELEVISION: Series: Star Trek: The Next Generation, Bagdad Cafe, The Whoopi Goldberg Show (synd. talk show). Specials: Whoopi Goldberg Direct From Broadway, Comic Relief, Carol Carl Whoopi and Robin, Scared Straight: 10 Years Later, Funny You Don't Look 200, Comedy Tonight (host), My Past is My Own (Schoolbreak Special), Free to Be... a Family, The Debbie Allen Special, Cool Like That Christmas (voice). Guest: Moonlighting (Emmy nom.), A Different World. Movie: Kiss Shot.

GOLDBLUM, JEFF
Actor. b. Pittsburgh, PA, Oct. 22, 1952. Studied at Sanford Meisner's Neighborhood Playhouse in New York. On B'way in Two Gentlemen of Verona, The Moony Shapiro Songbook. Off-B'way: El Grande de Coca Cola, City Sugar, Twelfth Night.
PICTURES: Death Wish (debut, 1974), California Split, Nashville, Next Stop Greenwich Village, St. Ives, Special Delivery, The Sentinel, Annie Hall, Between the Lines, Remember My Name, Thank God It's Friday, Invasion of the Body Snatchers, Threshold, The Big Chill, The Right Stuff, The Adventures of Buckaroo Banzai, Into the Night, Silverado, Transylvania 6-5000, The Fly, Beyond Therapy, Vibes, Earth Girls Are Easy, Twisted Obsession, The Tall Guy, Mr. Frost, The Player, Deep Cover, The Favor the Watch and the Very Big Fish, Fathers and Sons, Jurassic Park, Hideaway, Nine Months, Powder, The Great White Hype, Independence Day, Mad Dog Time.
TELEVISION: Movies: The Legend of Sleepy Hollow, Rehearsal for Murder, Ernie Kovacs: Between the Laughter, The Double Helix (BBC), Framed, Lush Life. Series: Tenspeed and Brownshoe, Future Quest (host). Guest: The Blue Knight, It's Garry Shandling's Show.

GOLDEN, HERBERT L.
b. Philadelphia, PA, Feb. 12, 1914. e. Temple U., 1936, B.S. Reporter, rewrite man. asst. city ed., Philadelphia Record, 1933-38; joined Variety, 1938; on leave of absence, 1942-43, when asst. to John Hay Whitney and Francis Alstock, directors, M.P. Division, Coordinator of Inter-American Affairs (U.S.); in U.S. Navy, 1943-46; then returned to Variety. m.p. ed. Consultant on motion pictures, Good Housekeeping magazine McGraw-Hill Publications, American Yearbook. Ent. Ind. Div. Bankers Trust Co., NY, 1952; named v.p. 1954-56; v.p. & mem. of bd. United Artists Corp., 1958; member of board, MPAA, 1959; pres., Lexington Int., Inc. investments, 1962; mem. bd., chmn. exec. com., Perfect Photo Inc., 1962; 1965 sect. & mem. bd. Century Broadcasting Corp; chmn. G & G Thea. Corp.; pres. Diversifax Corp., 1966; consult. Pathe Lab, 1967; Mem. bd. Childhood Prod. Inc., Music Makers Group, Inc., Cinecom Corp. pres., Vere/Swiss Corp., 1977; mem. bd., Coral Reef Publications, Inc., 1977. Returned to Bankers Trust, 1979, to head its Media Group (service to film and TV industries). Retired, 1992.

GOLDEN, JEROME B.
Executive, Attorney. b. New York, NY, Nov. 26, 1917. e. St. Lawrence U., LL.B., 1942. Member legal dept., Paramount Pictures, Inc., 1942-50; United Paramount Theatres, Inc., 1950-53; ABC, Inc., 1953; secy., ABC, 1958-86; v.p., ABC, 1959-86. Consultant.

GOLDEN, PAT
Casting Director, Director. b. Pittsburgh, PA, July 21, 1951. e. U Pittsburgh, Carnegie-Mellon U. Has directed plays for theatre incl. Homeboy at Perry St. Th. in NY. Was in casting dept. of NY Shakespeare Festival Public Th. Served as assoc.

prod. on PBS series The Negro Ensemble Company's 20th Anniversary. Assoc. prod.: Hallelujah (PBS); dir.: House Party 2 documentary, My Secret Place (tv pilot).
PICTURES: Ragtime, Beat Street, Krush Groove, The Killing Fields, Blue Velvet, Platoon (Awarded Casting Society of America Award), Dear America, The Handmaid's Tale, House Party 2 (assoc. prod.), Voyager, Posse.

GOLDENSON, LEONARD H.
Executive. b. Scottsdale, PA, December 7, 1905. e. Harvard Coll., B.A., Harvard Law School, LL.B. Practiced law, NY; counsel in reorg. Paramount theatres in New England, 1933-37; 1937 apptd. asst. to v.p. Paramount in charge theat. operations; became head of theat. operations, 1938; elected pres. Paramount Theat. Service Corp., v.p. Paramount Pictures, 1938; dir. Paramount Pictures, 1942 (also pres. various Paramount theat. subsids) Pres., CEO & dir. United Paramount Theatres, Inc., 1950, and of American Broadcasting-Paramount Theatres, Inc., 1953, result of merger of ABC and United Paramount Theatres, Inc.; chmn. of bd. & CEO of ABC to 1986. Then chmn. of exec. comm. & dir. Capital Cities/ABC, Inc. 1972; mem., International Radio and TV Society, Natl. Acad. of TV Arts & Sciences, Broadcast Pioneers, Motion Picture Pioneers; founder/member of Hollywood Museum; grad. dir. of Advertising Council, Inc.; Trustee Emeritus Museum of TV & Radio; Hon. Chmn. Acad. of TV Arts & Sciences.

GOLDMAN, BO
Writer. b. New York, NY, Sept. 10, 1932. e. Princeton U., B.A., 1953. Wrote lyrics for B'way musical version of Pride and Prejudice entitled First Impressions (1959). Assoc. prod. & script editor for Playhouse 90 1958-60; writer-prod., NET Playhouse 1970-71, Theater in America 1972-74.
PICTURES: One Flew Over the Cuckoo's Nest (co-s.p.; WGA & Academy Awards, 1975), The Rose (co-s.p.), Melvin and Howard (NY Film Critics, WGA & Academy Awards, 1980), Shoot the Moon, Swing Shift (uncredited), Little Nikita (co-s.p.), Dick Tracy (uncredited), Scent of a Woman (Golden Globe Award, Acad. Award nom.), First Knight (co-s.p.), City Hall (co-s.p.).

GOLDMAN, EDMUND
Executive, Producer. b. Shanghai, China, Nov. 12, 1906. e. Shanghai and San Francisco. Entered ind. as asst. mgr., for Universal in Shanghai, 1935-36; named mgr. Columbia Pictures' Philippine office, 1937. 1951 named Far East. supvr. for Columbia, headquartering in Tokyo. 1953-91 indep. m.p. dist., specializing in foreign marketing, representing indep. producers and distributors. Retired, 1991.
PICTURES: Surrender Hell (prod.), The Quick and the Dead (exec. prod.).

GOLDMAN, MICHAEL F.
Executive. b. Manila, Philippines, Sept. 28, 1939. e. UCLA, B.S. in acct., 1962 California C.P.A. certificate issued June, 1972. In 1962 incorporated Manson International, which was sold in 1986. Incorporated Quixote Prods., 1979. Also owner and sole proprietor Taurus Film co. of Hollywood, founded 1964. Co-founder and first chief financial officer of American Film Marketing Association, sponsor of First American Film Market in Los Angeles in 1981; v.p. of AFMA 1982 and 1983, President AFMA 1984 and 1985. Chmn. AFMA, 1992-3. AFMA bd. mbr., 1981-87, 1988-present; Co-founder, Cinema Consultants Group, 1988. Produced feature, Jessi's Girls in 1975. Founded Manson Interactive, 1995. Member A.M.P.A.S. since 1979. Director, Foundation of Motion Picture Pioneers.

GOLDMAN, MITCHELL
Executive. Pres., of Theatrical Distribution, New Line Distribution, Inc.

GOLDMAN, STEVE
Executive. e. Univ. of IL. 1980, joined Paramount as Midwest division mngr., Chicago. Then served in NY as v.p. Eastern regional mngr. 1983, to Hollywood office. 1985, exec. v.p., sls. & mktg. 1989, exec. v.p. 1992, pres. Paramount Domestic Television. 1995, named exec. v.p. of Paramount Television Group.

GOLDMAN, WILLIAM
Writer. b. Chicago, IL, Aug. 12, 1931. e. Oberlin College, B.A., Columbia U., M.A. Novels include The Temple of Gold, Your Turn to Curtsy, My Turn to Bow, Soldier in the Rain (filmed), Boys and Girls Together, The Thing of It Is, No Way to Treat a Lady (filmed), Father's Day, The Princess Bride (filmed), Marathon Man (filmed), Magic (filmed), Tinsel, Control, Heat (filmed), The Silent Gondoliers, The Color of Light, Brothers. Non-fiction: The Season, Adventures in the Screen Trade, Wait Until Next Year (w/Mike Lupica), Hype and Glory.
PICTURES: Harper, Butch Cassidy and the Sundance Kid (Academy Award, 1969), The Hot Rock, The Stepford Wives, The Great Waldo Pepper, All the President's Men (Academy Award, 1976), Marathon Man (based on his novel), A Bridge Too Far, Magic (based on his novel), Heat (based on his novel), The Princess Bride (based on his novel), Misery, Memoirs of an Invisible Man (co-s.p.), Year of the Comet, Chaplin (co-s.p.), Maverick, The Ghost and the Darkness.

GOLDSMITH, JERRY
Composer. b. Los Angeles, CA, Feb. 10, 1929. e. Los Angeles City Coll. Studied piano with Jacob Gimpel and music composition, harmony, theory with Mario Castelnuovo-Tedesco. With CBS radio first with own show (Romance) and then moved on to others (Suspense). Began scoring for TV, including Climax, Playhouse 90, Studio One, Gunsmoke, etc. Emmy Awards for QB VIII, Masada, Babe, The Red Pony, Star Trek Voyager Theme.
PICTURES: Black Patch (debut, 1957), Lonely Are the Brave, Freud (Acad. Award nom.), The Stripper, The Prize, Seven Days in May, Lilies of the Field, In Harm's Way, Von Ryan's Express, Our Man Flint, A Patch of Blue (Acad. Award nom.), The Blue Max, Seconds, Stagecoach, The Sand Pebbles (Acad. Award nom.), In Like Flint, Planet of the Apes (Acad. Award nom.), The Ballad of Cable Hogue, Tora! Tora! Tora!, Patton (Acad. Award nom.), The Wild Rovers, The Other, Papillon (Acad. Award nom.), The Reincarnation of Peter Proud, Chinatown (Acad. Award nom.), Logan's Run, The Wind and the Lion (Acad. Award nom.), The Omen (Academy Award, 1976), Islands in the Stream, MacArthur, Coma, Damien: Omen II, The Boys From Brazil (Acad. Award nom.), The Great Train Robbery, Alien, Star Trek-The Motion Picture (Acad. Award nom.), The Final Conflict, Outland, Raggedy Man, The Secret of NIMH, Poltergeist (Acad. Award nom.), First Blood, Twilight Zone—The Movie, Psycho II, Under Fire (Acad. Award nom.), Gremlins, Legend (European ver.), Explorers, Rambo: First Blood II, Poltergeist II: The Other Side, Hoosiers (Acad. Award nom.), Extreme Prejudice, Innerspace, Lionheart, Rent-a-Cop, Rambo III, Criminal Law, The 'Burbs, Leviathan, Star Trek V: The Final Frontier, Total Recall, Gremlins 2: The New Batch (also cameo), The Russia House, Not Without My Daughter, Sleeping With the Enemy, Medicine Man, Basic Instinct (Acad. Award nom.), Mom and Dad Save the World, Mr. Baseball, Love Field, Forever Young, Matinee, The Vanishing, Dennis the Menace, Malice, Rudy, Six Degrees of Separation, Angie, Bad Girls, The Shadow, The River Wild, I.Q., Congo, First Knight, Powder, City Hall, 2 Days in the Valley, Executive Decision, Powder, Chain Reaction.

GOLDSMITH, MARTIN M.
Writer. b. New York, NY, Nov. 6, 1913. Bush pilot, playwright, novelist, screenwriter.
AUTHOR: Novels: Double Jeopardy, Detour, Shadows at Noon, Miraculous Fish of Domingo Gonzales. Play: Night Shift.
PICTURES: Detour, Blind Spot, Narrow Margin, Mission Over Korea, Overland Pacific, Hell's Island, Fort Massacre, Bat Masterson, It Happens Every Thursday, Shakedown.
TELEVISION: Playhouse 90, Goodyear Playhouse, Twilight Zone.

GOLDSMITH, MARVIN F.
Executive. b. Brooklyn, NY. e. NY Inst. of Tech. Started as page at CBS, eventually becoming film editor. Was tv group supervisor with Batten Barton Durstine & Osborne. 1973, joined ABC as mgr. nighttime sales proposals; 1976-78, account exec. in sports sales, then v.p. prime time sales proposals, then v.p. Eastern Sales. 1986, promoted to sr. v.p., natl. sls. mngr.; 1989, became sr. v.p. gen. sls. mngr. 1992, promoted to pres., sls. & marketing, ABC Television Network.

GOLDSTEIN, MILTON
Executive. b. New York, NY, Aug. 1, 1926. e. NYU, 1949. In exec. capac., Paramount; foreign sales coord., The Ten Commandments, Psycho; v.p. foreign sales, Samuel Bronston org.; asst. to Pres., Paramount Int'l, special prods., 1964; Foreign sales mgr., 1966; v.p., world wide sales, 1967, Cinerama; Sr. v.p. Cinema Center Films, 1969; pres., Cinema Center Films, 1971; v.p. Theatrical Mktg. & Sales, Metromedia Producers Corp., 1973; in March, 1974, formed Boasberg-Goldstein, Inc., consultants in prod. and dist. of m.p.; 1975, named exec. vice pres., Avco Embassy Pictures; 1978, named exec. v.p. & chief operating officer, Melvin Simon Prods. 1980, named pres.; 1985, pres. Milt Goldstein Enterprises, Inc.; 1990, chairman and ceo, HKM Films. 1991, pres., Introvision movies.

GOLDSTONE, JAMES
Director. b. Los Angeles, CA. June 8, 1931. e. Dartmouth Coll., B.A., Bennington Coll., M.A. Film editor from 1950. Writer, story editor from 1957. Dir. starting from 1958.
PICTURES: Jigsaw (debut, 1968), A Man Called Gannon, Winning, Brother John, Red Sky at Morning, The Gang That Couldn't Shoot Straight, They Only Kill Their Masters, Swashbuckler, Rollercoaster, When Time Ran Out.

TELEVISION: Pilots: Star Trek, Ironside, Iron Horse, The Senator, etc. Specials-Movies: A Clear and Present Danger (Emmy nom.), Eric (Virgin Islands Int'l. Film Fest. Gold Medal). Journey from Darkness (Christopher Award). Studs Lonigan (miniseries 1978), Kent State, (Emmy, best dir., special), Things in Their Season, Calamity Jane, The Sun Also Rises, Dreams of Gold, Earthstar Voyager.

GOLDTHWAIT, BOBCAT (BOB)
Comedian, Actor. b. Syracuse, NY, May 1, 1962. Performed with comedy troupe The Generic Comics in early 1980's. Album: Meat Bob.
PICTURES: Police Academy 2: Their First Assignment (debut, 1985), One Crazy Summer, Police Academy 3: Back in Training, Burglar, Police Academy 4: Citizens on Patrol, Hot to Trot, Scrooged, Shakes the Clown (also dir., s.p.), Freaked, Radioland Murders, Destiny Turns on the Radio, Hercules.
TELEVISION: Series: Capitol Critters (voice), Unhappily Ever After (voice). Specials: Bob Goldthwait: Don't Watch This Show, Share the Warmth, Is He Like That All the Time? (also dir., writer), Bob Saget: In the Dream Suite, Comic Relief, Medusa: Dare to Be Truthful. Guest: Tales From the Crypt, Married... With Children, The Larry Sanders Show, E.R., Beavis and Butthead, Comic Relief, The John Laroquette Show.

GOLDWATER, CHARLES
Executive, Exhibitor. b. New Orleans, LA. e. Boston U., B.S. Broadcasting & Film. Began career with Walter Reade Organization as usher in 1971-74, promoted to manager. Sack Theatres/USA Cinemas 1974-88, began as manager, promoted to s.v.p. & general manager. National Amusements, exec. dir. Project Development, 1988-90. Loews/Sony Theatres, sr. v.p. & general manager, 1990-1995. Currently pres. & CEO, Cinamerica/Mann Theatres. NATO bd. of dir. 1987-present. Chmn. CARA/Product Committee, 1991-present. General chmn. Showeast 1992-1995; chmn of the bd. Showeast, 1995-present. Bd. of directors, Motion Picture Pioneers, Will Riogers Organization, Theatre Owners of New England. Past bd. of directors, Variety Clubs of New England & New York.

GOLDWYN, SAMUEL, JR.
Producer, Director. b. Los Angeles, CA, Sept. 7, 1926. e. U. of Virginia. Father of actor Tony Goldwyn. U.S. Army, 1944; following war writer, assoc. prod., J. Arthur Rank Org.; prod. Gathering Storm on London stage; returned to U.S., 1948; assoc. prod., Universal; recalled to Army service, 1951; prod., dir., Army documentary films including Alliance for Peace (Edinburgh Film Festival prize); prod. TV shows, Adventure series for CBS, 1952-53; prod. TV series, The Unexpected, 1954; pres., The Samuel Goldwyn Company, 1955-. Also established Samuel Goldwyn Home Entertainment, and Goldwyn Pavilion Cinemas.
PICTURES: Prod.: Man With the Gun, The Sharkfighters, The Proud Rebel, The Adventures of Huckleberry Finn, The Young Lovers (also dir.), Cotton Comes to Harlem, Come Back Charleston Blue, The Golden Seal, Mystic Pizza (exec. prod.), Stella.
TELEVISION: The Academy Awards, 1987, 1988; April Morning (co-exec. prod.).

GOLDWYN, TONY
Actor. b. Los Angeles, CA, May 20, 1960. e. Brandeis U., London Acad. of Music & Dramatic Art.
THEATER: Digby, The Foreigner, The Real Thing, Pride and Prejudice, The Sum of Us, Spike Heels, Inherit the Wind.
PICTURES: Friday the 13th Part VI: Jason Live (debut, 1986), Gaby-A True Story, Ghost, Kuffs, Traces of Red, The Pelican Brief, Reckless, The Substance of Fire, Nixon, The Substance of Fire.
TELEVISION: Movies: Favorite Son, Dark Holiday, Iran: Days of Crisis, Taking the Heat, Love Matters, Doomsday Gun, The Last Word, The Boys Next Door, Truman. Mini-Series: A Woman of Independent Means. Special: The Last Mile. Guest: L.A. Law, Tales from the Crypt.

GOLINO, VALERIA
Actress. b. Naples, Italy, Oct. 22, 1966. Raised in Athens, Greece. Was model at age 14 before being discovered by dir. Lina Wertmuller for film debut.
PICTURES: A Joke of Destiny (debut, 1983), Blind Date, My Son Infinitely Beloved, Little Fires, Dumb Dicks, Storia d'Amore (Love Story), Last Summer in Tangiers, The Gold-Rimmed Glasses, Three Sisters, Big Top Pee-wee, Rain Man, Torrents of Spring, The King's Whore, Traces of an Amorous Life, Hot Shots!, The Indian Runner, Hot Shots! Part Deux, Clean Slate, Immortal Beloved, Leaving Las Vegas, Four Rooms.

GONZALEZ-GONZALEZ, PEDRO
Actor. r.n. Ramiro Gonzalez-Gonzalez. b. Aguilares, TX, May 24, 1925. Comedian in San Antonio Mexican theatres.
PICTURES: Wings of the Hawk, Ring of Fear, Ricochet

Romance, The High and the Mighty, Strange Lady in Town, Bengazi, I Died a Thousand Times, Bottom of the Bottle, The Sheepman, Gun the Man Down, Rio Bravo, The Young Land, The Adventures of Bullwhip Griffin, The Love Bug, The Love God, Hellfighters, Hook Line and Sinker, Chisum, Support Your Local Gunfighter, Zachariah, Six-Pack Annie, Won Ton Ton the Dog Who Saved Hollywood, Dreamer, Lust in the Dust, Uphill All the Way, Deception.
TELEVISION: Guest: O'Henry Playhouse, Felix the Fourth, Ann Southern Show, No Time for Sergeants, Gunsmoke, Perry Mason, The Monkees, Love American Style, Adam 12, Farmer's Daughter, Danny Kaye Show, National Velvet, Bachelor Father, Bonanza, The Fall Guy, Moonlighting, many others. Movies: Donor, Ghost Writer, Bates Motel (pilot).

GOOD, CHARLES E.
Executive. b. 1922. Joined Buena Vista in 1957 in Chicago office; progressed from salesman to branch mgr. and then district mgr. Later moved to Burbank as domestic sales mgr. in 1975; 1978, named v.p. & general sales mgr.; 1980, appointed pres., BV Distribution Co. Resigned presidency 1984; became BV consultant until retirement, 1987.

GOODALL, CAROLINE
Actress. b. London, England, Nov. 13, 1959. e. Natl Youth Theatre of Great Britain; Bristol Univ. On stage with Royal Court Theatre, Royal Natl. Theatre, Royal Shakespeare Co. Toured Australia in Richard III for RSC, 1986.
PICTURES: Every Time We Say Goodbye (debut, 1986), Hook, The Silver Brumby, The Webbers' 15 Minutes, Cliffhanger, Schindler's List, Disclosure, Hotel Sorrento, White Squall.
TELEVISION: Movies (Australia): Cassidy, Ring of Scorpio, The Great Air Race, Diamond Swords (Fr.). Mini-Series: After the War. Guest: Remington Steele, Tales of the Unexpected, Quantum Leap, The Commish, Rumpole of the Bailey, Poirot: Curse of the Western Star.

GOODING, CUBA, JR.
Actor. b. Bronx, NY, Sept. 2, 1968. Son of rhythm and blues vocalist Cuba Gooding. Raised in California. Prof. debut as dancer backing up Lionel Richie at 1984 Olympic Games. Recipient of NAACP Image Awards for Boyz in the Hood and tv movie Murder Without Motive. Voted by NATO/Showest as Newcomer of the Year, 1992.
PICTURES: Coming to America (debut, 1988), Sing, Boyz in the Hood, Hitz, Gladiator, A Few Good Men, Judgment Night, Lightning Jack, Outbreak, Losing Isaiah, Jerry Maguire.
TELEVISION: Movies: Murder Without Motive: The Edmund Perry Story, Daybreak, The Tuskegee Airmen. Special: No Means No.

GOODMAN, DAVID Z.
Writer. e. Queens Coll., Yale School of Drama.
PICTURES: Lovers and Other Strangers, Straw Dogs, Farewell My Lovely, Logan's Run, Eyes of Laura Mars, Man Woman and Child (co.-s.p.).

GOODMAN, JOHN
Actor. b. Afton, MO, June 20, 1952. e. Southwest Missouri State U. Moved to NY in 1975 where he appeared on stage (incl. A Midsummer Night's Dream) and in commercials. On Broadway in Loose Ends, Big River. L.A. stage in Antony and Cleopatra.
PICTURES: Eddie Macon's Run (1983, debut), The Survivors, Revenge of the Nerds, C.H.U.D., Maria's Lovers, Sweet Dreams, True Stories, Raising Arizona, Burglar, The Big Easy, The Wrong Guys, Punchline, Everybody's All-American, Sea of Love, Always, Stella, Arachnophobia, King Ralph, Barton Fink, The Babe, Matinee, Born Yesterday, We're Back! A Dinosaur's Story (voice), The Flintstones, Pie in the Sky, Mother Night.
TELEVISION: Series: Roseanne. Movies: The Face of Rage, Heart of Steel, The Mystery of Moro Castle, Murder Ordained, Kingfish: A Story of Huey P. Long (also co-prod.), A Streetcar Named Desire. Mini-Series: Chiefs. Guest: The Equalizer, Moonlighting.

GOODRICH, ROBERT EMMETT
Executive. b. Grand Rapids, MI, June 27, 1940. e. U. of Michigan, B.A., 1962; J.D., 1964; NYU. LL.M, 1966. Pres. & Secty., Goodrich Quality Theaters, Inc. 1967-present, developed circuit from father's one theater to 154 screens at 19 locations in 9 Mich. cities, 4 Indiana cities, 2 Illinois cities. Owns and operates 6 FM/AM radio stations in Grand Rapids, MI, Muskegon, MI. Member: NATO; Will Rogers Inst. advisory comm; bd., Mich. Millers Mutual Insurance Co.; State of MI Bar Assn.

GOODWIN, RICHARD
Producer. b. Bombay, India, Sept. 13, 1934. e. Rugby. Entered film world by chance: while waiting to go to Cambridge U. took temporary job as tea boy at studio which led to 20-year-long association with producer Lord Brabourne.

PICTURES: *Prod. Mgr.*: The Sheriff of Fractured Jaw, Carve Her Name with Pride, The Grass Is Greener, Sink the Bismarck, HMS Defiant. *Prod.*: The Tales of Beatrix Potter. *Co-Prod.*: Murder on the Orient Express, Death on the Nile, The Mirror Crack'd, Evil Under the Sun, A Passage to India, Little Dorrit.

GOODWIN, RONALD
Composer, Arranger, Conductor. b. Plymouth, Eng., Feb. 17, 1925. e. Pinner County Grammar Sch. Early career: arranger for BBC dance orchestra; mus. dir., Parlophone Records; orchestra leader for radio, TV and records. Fut. m.p. ind., 1958. Many major film scores. Guest cond. R.P.O., B.S.O., Toronto Symph. Orch. New Zealand Symphony Orch., Sydney Symphony Orch. Royal Scottish Natl. Orch., BBC Scottish Symphony Orch., BBC Welsh Symphony Orch., BBC Radio Orch., BBC Concert Orch., London Philharmonic Orch., Gothenberg Symphony Orch., Norwegian Opera Orch. & Chorus, Halle Orchestra, Singapore Symphony Orch., Australian Pops Orch, Detroit Symphony Orchestra, Danish Radio Orchestra, Odense Symphony Orch., Norrkoping Symphony Orch.
PICTURES: Whirlpool, I'm All Right Jack, The Trials of Oscar Wilde, Johnny Nobody, Village of the Damned, Murder She Said, Follow the Boys, Murder at the Gallop, Children of the Damned, 633 Squadron, Murder Most Foul, Murder Ahoy, Operation Crossbow, The ABC Murders, Of Human Bondage, Those Magnificent Men in Their Flying Machines, The Trap, Mrs. Brown, You've Got a Lovely Daughter; Submarine X-1, Decline and Fall, Where Eagles Dare, Monte Carlo or Bust, Battle of Britain, The Executioner, The Selfish Giant, Frenzy, Diamonds on Wheels, The Little Mermaid, The Happy Prince, One of Our Dinosaurs Is Missing, Escape From the Dark, Born to Run, Beauty and the Beast, Candleshoe, Force Ten from Navarone, Spaceman and King Arthur, Clash of Loyalties, Valhalla.

GORDON, ALEX
Producer. b. London, Eng., Sept. 8, 1922. e. Canford Coll., Dorset, 1939. Writer, m.p. fan magazines, 1939-41; British Army, 1942-45; pub. dir. Renown Pictures Corp., 1946-47; P.R. and pub. rep. for Gene Autry, 1948-53; v.p. and prod. Golden State Productions, 1954-58; prod. Alex Gordon Prods., 1958-66; producer Twentieth Century-Fox Television, 1967-76; film archivist/preservationist, 1976-84; v.p., Gene Autry's Flying A Pictures, 1985.
PICTURES: Lawless Rider, Bride of the Monster, Apache Woman, Day the World Ended, Oklahoma Woman, Girls in Prison, The She-Creature, Runaway Daughters, Shake Rattle and Rock, Flesh and the Spur, Voodoo Woman, Dragstrip Girl, Motorcycle Gang, Jet Attack, Submarine Seahawk, Atomic Submarine, The Underwater City, The Bounty Killer, Requiem for a Gunfighter.
TELEVISION: Movie of the Year, Golden Century, Great Moments in Motion Pictures.

GORDON, BERT I.
Producer, Director, Writer. b. Kenosha, WI, Sept. 24, 1932. e. Univ. of WI. Started on tv as commercial prod.
PICTURES: *Dir./Prod.*: Serpent Island (debut, 1954), King Dinosaur, Beginning of the End, Cyclops (also s.p.), The Amazing Colossal Man (also co-s.p.), Attack of the Puppet People (also story), War of the Colossal Beast, The Spider, Tormented, The Boy and the Pirates, The Magic Sword (also story), Village of the Giants (also story), Picture Mommy Dead, How to Succeed With Sex (dir., s.p.), Necromancy (also s.p.), The Mad Bomber (also s.p.), The Police Connection (also s.p.), The Food of the Gods (also s.p.), Empire of the Ants (also s.p.), The Coming (also s.p.), Satan's Princess, Malediction.

GORDON, BRUCE
Executive. b. Sidney, Australia, Feb. 4, 1929. Began career in Australian entertainment industry 1952 with Tivoli Circuit, live theatre chain; acted as advance man, front-of-house mgr., adv. dir.; promoted to busn. mgr., 1958. Named Tivoli membr. bd. of management, 1960-62. Joined Desilu Studios in 1962, developing Far East territories; promoted 1968 when Paramount acquired Desilu to mng. dir. Para. Far East opns. Named to bd. of TV Corp., 1969, operator of Channel 9 TV stns. & co.'s theatres in Sydney, Melbourne. Dir. on bd. of Academy Investments, operator of Perth theatre chain; responsible for building Perth Entertainment Centre. Named pres., Paramount TV Intl. Services, Ltd., 1974, in New York office. 1981, pres. Intl. Television of Paramount Pictures.

GORDON, CHARLES
Executive, Producer. b. Belzoni, MS. Began career as a talent agent with William Morris Agency. Left to write and develop television programming creating and producing 5 pilots and 3 series. Left TV to enter motion picture production in partnership with brother Lawrence Gordon. President and chief operating officer, The Gordon Company.

PICTURES: *Exec. prod.*: Die Hard, Leviathan. *Co-prod.*: Night of the Creeps, The Wrong Guys, Field of Dreams, K-9, Lock Up, The Rocketeer, The Super, Unlawful Entry, Waterworld. TELEVISION: *Writer-creator.* When the Whistle Blows. *Exec. prod.*: The Renegades. *Exec. prod.-creator.* Just Our Luck, Our Family Honor.

GORDON, DON
Actor. b. Los Angeles, CA, Nov. 13, 1926. r.n. Donald Walter Guadagno. Served, U.S. Navy, 1941-45. Studied acting with Michael Chekhov. e. Columbia U. Theatre includes On an Open Roof, Stockade.
PICTURES: Bullitt, The Lollipop Cover (best actor, Chicago Film Fest.), W.U.S.A., The Last Movie, Papillon, The Gambler, Out of the Blue, The Final Conflict, The Beast Within, Lethal Weapon, Skin Deep, The Exorcist III, The Borrower.
TELEVISION: *Series*: The Blue Angels, Lucan, The Contender. *Guest*: The Defenders, Remington Steele, Charlie's Angels, Twilight Zone, Simon & Simon, Outer Limits, MacGyver, etc. *Movies*: Happiness is a Warm Clue, Street Killing, Confessions of a Married Man.

GORDON, KEITH
Actor, Director, Writer. b. Bronx, NY, Feb. 3, 1961.
THEATER: A Traveling Companion, Richard III, Album, Back to Back The Buddy System, Third Street.
PICTURES: *Actor*: Jaws 2 (debut, 1978), All That Jazz, Home Movies, Dressed to Kill, Christine, The Legend of Billie Jean, Static (also co-s.p., co-prod.), Back to School, I Love Trouble. *Director-Writer*: The Chocolate War, A Midnight Clear, Mother Night.
TELEVISION: *Mini-Series*: Studs Lonigan, Wild Palms (co-dir.). *Movies*: Kent State, Single Bars Single Women, Combat High. *Special*: My Palikari (Amer. Playhouse).

GORDON, JEROME
Executive, Exhibitor. b. Newport News, VA, Mar. 1, 1915. Began movie career at age 10 as usher in father's theatre. At age 18, owned and operated two theatres. Spent one year in theater decorating business in Philadelphia. Worked for Fox West Coast circuit in Los Angeles, 1937-40. Returned to VA and developed small theater circuit with brothers. Served as pres. of Virginia NATO for 4 yrs. 1975-; exec. dir., Virginia NATO; 1976-, exec. dir., Maryland & D.C. NATO. Coordinated Mid-Atlantic NATO convention from 1975 until it merged with ShowEast in 1989. Currently exec. dir., Mid-Atlantic NATO. 1978-86, spec. asst. to pres., NATO; coordinated campaigns to pass Anti-Blind Bidding Laws in individual states. Edited Regional Presidents' NATO Handbook. Member, bd. of dirs., NATO; chmn., NATO Membership Development Committee. Exec. Committee, ShowEast. Recipient of Distinguished Service Award, ShowEast, 1992; B.V. Sturdivant Award, NATO ShowEast, 1992.

GORDON, LAWRENCE
Producer, Executive. b. Belzoni, MS, March 25, 1936. e. Tulane U. (business admin.). Assist. to prod. Aaron Spelling at Four Star Television, 1964. Writer and assoc. prod. on several Spelling shows. 1965, joined ABC-TV as head of west coast talent dev; 1966, TV and motion pictures exec. with Bob Banner Associates; 1968 joined AIP as v.p. in charge of project dev.; 1971 named v.p., Screen Gems (TV div. of Columbia Pictures) where he helped dev. Brian's Song and QB VII. Returned to AIP as v.p. worldwide prod. Formed Lawrence Gordon Prods. at Columbia Pictures; 1984-86, pres. and COO 20th Century Fox. Currently indep. prod. with 20th Century Fox. Producer of B'way musical Smile.
PICTURES: Dillinger (1973), Hard Times, Rolling Thunder, The Driver, The End, Hooper, The Warriors, Xanadu, Paternity, Jekyll and Hyde, Together Again, 48 Hours, Streets of Fire, Brewster's Millions, Lucas, Jumpin' Jack Flash, Predator, The Couch Trip, The Wrong Guys, Die Hard, Leviathan (exec. prod.), K-9, Field of Dreams, Lock Up, Family Business, Another 48 HRS, Die Hard 2, Predator 2, The Rocketeer, Used People.
TELEVISION: (Co-creator and co-exec. prod.) Dog and Cat, Matt Houston, Renegades, Just Our Luck, Our Family Honor.

GORDON, RICHARD
Producer. b. London, Eng., Dec. 31, 1925. e. U. of London, 1943. Served in Brit. Royal Navy, 1944-46; ed. & writer on fan magazines & repr. independent American cos. 1946, with publicity dept. Assoc. Brit. Pathe 1947; org. export-import business for independent, British and American product; formed Gordon Films, Inc., 1949; formed Amalgamated prod., 1956; formed Grenadier Films, Ltd. 1971. 1992, prod. of A Tribute to Orson Welles.
PICTURES: The Counterfeit Plan, The Haunted Strangler, Fiend Without a Face, The Secret Man, First Man into Space, Corridors of Blood, Devil Doll, Curse of Simba, The Projected Man, Naked Evil, Island of Terror, Tales of the Bizarre, Tower of Evil, Horror Hospital, The Cat and the Canary, Inseminoid.

GORDON, STUART
Director, Writer. b. Chicago, IL, Aug. 11, 1947. e. Univ. of WI. Worked at commercial art studio prior to founding Broom Street Theater in Madison, WI. Later founder and prod. dir. of Organic Theater Co. in Madison, then Chicago, 1969-85. Was fight choreographer on 1976 film The Last Affair.
PICTURES: *Director.* Re-Animator (also co-s.p.), From Beyond (also co-s.p.), Dolls, Robot Jox (also wrote story), Honey I Shrunk the Kids (co-story only), The Pit and the Pendulum, Honey I Blew Up the Kid (exec. prod., co-story only), Fortress, Body Snatchers (co-s.p. only), Castle Freak (also co-story), Space Truckers (dir., prod., co-story).
TELEVISION: *Director.* Bleacher Bums (special), Daughter of Darkness (movie).

GORDY, BERRY
Executive. b. Detroit, MI, Nov. 28, 1929. Was working on auto assembly line in Detroit when decided to launch record co., Motown. In 1961 wrote song, Shop Around; recording by Smokey Robinson made it his first million dollar record. Expanded into music publishing, personal mgt., recording studios, film and TV, also backing stage shows. Former Bd. chmn., Motown Industries. Chmn. The Gordy Co. Received Business Achievement Award, Interracial Council for Business Opportunity, 1967; Whitney M. Young Jr. Award, L.A. Urban League, 1980; Inducted into Rock and Roll Hall of Fame, 1988. Recipient of NARAS Trustee Award, 1991. Author of To Be Loved (1994). Member BMI, NAACP, A.M.P.A.S., DGI, NARAS.
PICTURES: Lady Sings the Blues (prod.), Bingo Long Traveling All-Stars and Motor Kings (exec. prod.), Mahogany (dir.), Almost Summer, The Last Dragon (exec. prod.).

GORE, MICHAEL
Composer, Producer. b. New York City, New York, March 5, 1951. e. Yale University and studied in Paris with composer Max Deustch. Began writing pop songs for his sister singer Lesley Gore; as a staff songwriter for Screen Gems-Columbia; and as a producer of classical recordings for CBS Records. Prod. for Philips Classics recording of The King and I (with Julie Andrews, Ben Kingsley). Wrote Whitney Houston's hit single All the Man That I Need.
PICTURES: Fame (2 Academy Awards for Best Score and Title Song, 1980), Terms of Endearment, Footloose, Pretty in Pink, Broadcast News, Defending Your Life, The Butcher's Wife, Mr. Wonderful.
TELEVISION: Generations (theme); Fame (theme).

GORING, SIR MARIUS
Actor. b. Newport, Isle of Wight, May 23, 1912. e. Cambridge U., Universities of Frankfurt-on-Main, Munich, Vienna, Paris. Early career with Old Vic; stage debut 1927, Jean Sterling Rackinlay's Children's Matinees. 1940-46 served with H. M. Forces and Foreign Office.
PICTURES: Rembrandt, Dead Men Tell No Tales, Flying 55, Consider Your Verdict, Spy in Black, Pastor Hall, The Case of the Frightened Lady, The Big Blockade, The Night Raider, Lilli Marlene, Stairway to Heaven, Night Boat to Dublin, Take My Life, Red Shoes, Mr. Perrin and Mr. Traill, Odette, Pandora and the Flying Dutchman, Circle of Danger, Highly Dangerous, So Little Time, The Man Who Watched Trains Go By, Rough Shoot, The Barefoot Contessa, Break in the Circle, Quentin Durward, Ill Met by Moonlight, The Moonraker, Family Doctor, Angry Hills, Whirlpool, Treasure of St. Teresa, Monty's Double, Beyond the Curtain, Desert Mice, The Inspector, Girl on a Motorcycle, Subterfuge, Zeppelin.
TELEVISION: Numerous appearances, Sleeping Dog, Man in a Suitcase, Scarlet Pimpernel, The Expert.

GOROG, LASZLO
Writer. b. Hungary, Sept. 30, 1903. e. U. of Sciences, Budapest. Playwright, short story writer, asst. editor, Budapest, 1928-39.
PICTURES: Tales of Manhattan, The Affairs of Susan, She Wouldn't Say Yes, The Land Unknown, Mole People.
TELEVISION: 4 Star, Dupont, The Roaring Twenties, 77 Sunset Strip, Maverick, etc.

GORSHIN, FRANK
Actor. b. Pittsburgh, PA, Apr. 5, 1933. Also nightclub comic and impresionist. On B'way stage in Jimmy.
PICTURES: Hot Rod Girl, Dragstrip Girl, Invasion of the Saucer Men, Portland Exposse, Warlock, Bells Are Ringing, Studs Lonigan, Where the Boys Are, The Great Impostor, Ring of Fire, The George Raft Story, Sail a Crooked Ship, That Darn Cat, Ride Beyond Vengeance, Batman, Skidoo, Record City, Underground Aces, The Uppercrust, Hot Resort, Uphill All the Way, Hollywood Vice Squad, Midnight, Beverly Hills Bodysnatchers, Hail Caesar, The Meteor Man, Twelve Monkeys.
TELEVISION: *Series:* ABC Comedy Hour (The Kopycats), The Edge of Night. *Movies:* Sky Heist, Death on the Freeway, Goliath Awaits, A Masterpiece of Murder. *Guest:* Hennessey,

The Detectives, Have Gun Will Travel, The Defenders, Naked City, The Munsters, Batman, Police Woman, SWAT, The Fall Guy, Murder She Wrote, etc.

GORTNER, MARJOE
Actor, Producer. b. Long Beach, CA, Jan. 14, 1944. Was child evangelist, whose career as such was basis for Oscar-winning documentary film, Marjoe. Acted in films and TV; turned producer in 1978 for When You Comin' Back Red Ryder?
PICTURES: Earthquake, Bobbie Joe and the Outlaw, The Food of the Gods, Viva Knievel, Sidewinder One, Acapulco Gold, Starcrash, When You Comin' Back Red Ryder?, Mausoleum, Jungle Warriors, Hellhole, American Ninja III: Blood Hunt, Wild Bill.
TELEVISION: *Movies:* The Marcus-Nelson Murders, Pray for the Wildcats, The Gun and the Pulpit, Mayday at 40000 Feet. *Guest:* Police Story, Barnaby Jones, The A-Team. *Series:* Falcon Crest.

GOSSETT, LOUIS, JR.
Actor. b. Brooklyn, NY, May 27, 1936. e. NYU, B.S. Also nightclub singer during 1960s.
THEATER: Take a Giant Step (debut, 1953), The Desk Set, Lost in the Stars, A Raisin in the Sun, Golden Boy, The Blacks, Blood Knot, The Zulu and the Zayda, My Sweet Charlie, Carry Me Back to Morningside Heights, Murderous Angels (L.A. Drama Critics Award).
PICTURES: A Raisin in the Sun (debut, 1961), The Bushbaby, The Landlord, Skin Game, Travels With My Aunt, The Laughing Policeman, The White Dawn, The River Niger, J.D.'s Revenge, The Deep, The Choirboys, An Officer and a Gentleman (Academy Award, best supporting actor, 1982), Jaws 3-D, Finders Keepers, Enemy Mine, Iron Eagle, Firewalker, The Principal, Iron Eagle II, Toy Soldiers, The Punisher, Aces: Iron Eagle III, Diggstown, Monolith, Flashfire, Blue Chips (unbilled), A Good Man in Africa, Iron Eagle IV, Inside.
TELEVISION: *Series:* The Young Rebels, The Lazarus Syndrome, The Powers of Matthew Star, Gideon Oliver. *Movies:* Companions in Nightmare, It's Good to Be Alive, Sidekicks, Delancey Street, The Crisis Within, Don't Look Back, Little Ladies of the Night, To Kill a Cop, The Critical List, This Man Stands Alone, Sadat, The Guardian, A Gathering of Old Men, The Father Clements Story, Roots: The Gift, El Diablo, Sudie and Simpson, The Josephine Baker Story, Carolina Skeletons, Father & Son: Dangerous Relations (also co-exec. prod.), Ray Alexander: A Taste for Justice, A Father for Charlie (also co-exec. prod.), Curse of the Starving Class, Zooman, Ray Alexander: A Menu for Murder. *Mini-Series:* Roots (Emmy Award, 1977), Backstairs at the White House. Return to Lonesome Dove. *Specials:* Welcome Home, A Triple Play: Sam Found Out, Zora Is My Name, The Century Collection Presents Ben Vereen: His Roots. *Guest:* The Mod Squad, Bill Cosby Show, Partridge Family, The Rookies, Love American Style, Police Story, Rockford Files, many others.

GOTTESMAN, STUART
Executive. b. New York, NY, June 11, 1949. Started career in mailroom of Warner Bros., 1972; later named promo. asst. to southwestern regional fieldman; promoted to that post which held for 10 years. 1987, named WB dir. field activities; 1990, appointed to WB national field operations.

GOTTLIEB, CARL
Writer, Director, Actor. b. New York, NY, March 18. e. Syracuse U., B.S., 1960. Directed short film The Absent-Minded Waiter.
PICTURES: *Actor.* Maryjane, M*A*S*H, Up the Sandbox, Cannonball, The Sting II, Johnny Dangerously, The Committee, Into the Night, Clueless. *Director.* Caveman (also co-s.p.), Amazon Women on the Moon (co-dir.). *Co-Writer:* Jaws (also actor), Which Way Is Up?, Jaws II, The Jerk (also actor), Doctor Detroit, Jaws 3-D.
TELEVISION: *Writer:* Smothers Bros. Comedy Hour (Emmy Award, 1969), The Odd Couple, Flip Wilson, Bob Newhart Show, The Super, Crisis at Sun Valley, The Deadly Triangle. *Director:* Paul Reiser: Out on a Whim, Partners In Life, Campus Cops. *Director-Co-creator:* Leo & Liz in Beverly Hills. *Co-creator:* George Burns' Comedy Week.

GOTTLIEB, MEYER
Executive. Pres. & COO, The Samuel Goldwyn Company.

GOUGH, MICHAEL
Actor. b. Malaya, Nov. 23, 1917. e. Rose Hill Sch., in Kent, England, and at Durham School. Studied at Old Vic School in London; first stage appearance in 1936 at Old Vic Theatre. N.Y. stage debut 1937 in Love of Women. London debut in 1938 in The Zeal of Thy House. Won 1979 Tony Award for Bedroom Farce.
PICTURES: Blanche Fury (debut, 1947), Anna Karenina, Saraband for Dead Lovers, The Small Back Room, The Man in the White Suit, Rob Roy, The Sword and the Rose, Richard III,

Reach for the Sky, Horror of Dracula (Dracula), Horrors of the Black Museum, The Horse's Mouth, Konga, Candidate for Murder, I Like Money (Mr. Topaze), The Phantom of the Opera, Black Zoo, Dr. Terror's House of Horrors, The Skull, Berserk, They Came From Beyond Space, A Walk With Love and Death, Women in Love, Trog, Julius Caesar, The Go-Between, Savage Messiah, Legend of Hell House, Horror Hospital (Computer Killers), Galileo, The Boys from Brazil, Venom, The Dresser, Top Secret!, Oxford Blues, Out of Africa, Caravaggio, Memed My Hawk, The Fourth Protocol, The Serpent and the Rainbow, Batman, Strapless, Let Him Have It, Blackeyes, Batman Returns, Little Nemo (voice), The Age of Innocence, Wittgenstein, Uncovered, Batman Forever.
TELEVISION: The Search for the Nile, Six Wives of Henry VIII, QB VII, Shoulder to Shoulder, The Citadel, Smiley's People, Brideshead Revisited, Mistral's Daughter, Lace II, Inside the Third Reich, To the Lighthouse, Suez, Vincent the Dutchman, Heart Attack Hotel, After the War, The Shell Seekers, Children of the North, Dr. Who, Sleepers.

GOULD, ELLIOTT
Actor. r.n. Elliott Goldstein. b. Brooklyn, NY, August 29, 1938. e. Professional Children's Sch., NY 1955. Vaudeville: appeared at Palace Theater, 1950. Broadway debut in Rumple (1957). Son is actor Jason Gould.
THEATER: Say Darling, Irma La Douce, I Can Get It for You Wholesale, On the Town (London), Fantasticks (tour), Drat the Cat, Little Murders, Luv (tour), Hit the Deck (Jones Beach), Rumors, Breakfast With Les & Bess.
PICTURES: Quick Let's Get Married (debut, 1965), The Night They Raided Minsky's, Bob & Carol & Ted & Alice (Acad. Award nom.), M*A*S*H, Getting Straight, Move, I Love My Wife, Little Murders (also prod.), The Touch, The Long Goodbye, Busting, S*P*Y*S!, California Split, Who?, Nashville (cameo), Whiffs, I Will I Will... For Now, Harry and Walter Go to New York, Mean Johnny Barrows, A Bridge Too Far, Capricorn One, Matilda, The Silent Partner, Escape to Athena, The Muppet Movie, The Last Flight of Noah's Ark, The Lady Vanishes, Falling in Love Again, The Devil and Max Devlin, Dirty Tricks, The Naked Face, Over the Brooklyn Bridge, The Muppets Take Manhattan, Inside Out, My First 40 Years, Lethal Obsession (Der Joker), The Telephone, The Big Picture, Dangerous Love, Night Visitor, The Wounded King, The Lemon Sisters, Judgment, Dead Men Don't Die, Bugsy, Strawanser, The Player, Exchange Lifeguards, Wet and Wild Summer, Naked Gun 33 1/3: The Final Insult (cameo), White Man's Burden, The Glass Shield, Kicking and Screaming, A Boy Called Hate, Johns.
TELEVISION: Specials: Once Upon A Mattress, Come Blow Your Horn, Jack and the Beanstalk (Faerie Tale Theater), Paul Reiser: Out on a Whim, Prime Time, Out to Lunch, Casey at the Bat (Tall Tales & Legends), Guest: Twilight Zone, Electric Company, Saturday Night Live, George Burns Comedy Week, Ray Bradbury Theatre, The Hitchhiker, Friends. Movies: The Rules of Marriage, Vanishing Act, Conspiracy: The Trial of the Chicago 8, Stolen: One Husband, Somebody's Daughter, Bloodlines: Murder in the Family. Series: E/R, Together We Stand, Sessions (HBO).

GOULD, HAROLD
Actor. b. Schenectady, NY, Dec. 10, 1923. e. SUNY, Albany, B.A. Cornell U., MA., Ph.D. Instructor of theatre and speech, 1953-56, Randolph Macon's Woman's Col., Lynchburg, VA. Asst. prof. drama and speech, 1956-60, Univ. of Calif., Riverside. Acted with Ashland, OR Shakespeare Fest. in 1958 and Mark Taper Forum (The Miser, Once in a Lifetime). Won Obie Award for Off-B'way debut in The Increased Difficulty of Concentration, 1969. ACE Award for Ray Bradbury Theatre. L.A. Drama Critics Award, 1994.
THEATER: The House of Blue Leaves, Fools, Grown Ups, Artist Descending a Staircase, I Never Sang for My Father, Freud (one man show), Love Letters, Incommunicado, King Lear (Utah Shakespearean Fest.), Mixed Emotions, Old Business, The Tempest (Utah Shakespearean Fest.), Substance of Five (San Diego Olde Globe).
PICTURES: Two for the Seesaw, The Couch, Harper, Inside Daisy Clover, Marnie, An American Dream, The Arrangement, The Lawyer, Mrs. Pollifax: Spy, Where Does It Hurt?, The Sting, The Front Page, Love and Death, The Big Bus, Silent Movie, The One and Only, Seems Like Old Times, Playing for Keeps, Romero, Flesh Suitcase, Killer.
TELEVISION: Series: Rhoda (Emmy nom.), Park Place, Foot in the Door, Under One Roof, Singer and Sons, Golden Girls, Feather and Father Gang. Movies: To Catch a Star, Moviola (Emmy nom.), Washington Behind Closed Doors, Aunt Mary, Better Late Than Never, King Crab, Have I Got a Christmas for You, Man in the Santa Claus Suit, I Never Sang For My Father, Get Smart Again!, Mrs. Delafield Wants to Marry (Emmy nom.), Love Bug II, Fox Hope. Special: The Sunset Gang. Guest: Police Story (Emmy nom.), Tales from the Hollywood Hills: The Closed Set, Ray Bradbury Theater (Emmy nom.).

GOULET, ROBERT
Singer, Actor. b. Lawrence, MA., Nov. 26, 1933. e. Edmonton; scholarship, Royal Conservatory of Music. Sang in choirs, appeared with numerous orchestras; disk jockey, CKUA, Edmonton; pub. rel., Rogo & Rove,Inc.
THEATER: NY: Camelot (as Lancelot; Theatre World Award), The Happy Time (Tony Award, 1968), Camelot (as King Arthur; 1993 revival). Regional: numerous tours including I Do I Do, Carousel, On a Clear Day You Can See Forever, Kiss Me Kate, South Pacific, The Fantasticks, Camelot (as King Arthur).
PICTURES: Gay Purr-ee (voice), Honeymoon Hotel, I'd Rather Be Rich, I Deal in Danger, Atlantic City, Beetlejuice, Scrooged, The Naked Gun 2 1/2: The Smell of Fear, Mr. Wrong.
TELEVISION: Series: Robert Goulet Show, Blue Light. Guest: The Ed Sullivan Show, Garry Moore, The Enchanted Nutcracker, Omnibus, The Broadway of Lerner and Loewe, Rainbow of Stars, Judy Garland Show, Bob Hope Show, The Bell Telephone Hour, Granada-TV special (U.K.), Jack Benny, Dean Martin, Andy Williams, Jack Paar, Red Skelton, Hollywood Palace, Patty Duke Show, The Big Valley, Mission : Impossible, Police Woman, Cannon, Murder She Wrote, Mr. Belvedere, Fantasy Island, Matt Houston, Glitter, WKRP in Cincinnati. Pilot: Make My Day. Specials: Brigadoon, Carousel, Kiss Me Kate. Movie: Based on an Untrue Story.

GOWDY, CURT
Sportscaster. b. Green River, WY, July 31, 1919. Basketball star at U. of Wyoming. All-Conference member; graduated U. of Wyoming. 1942. Officer in U.S. Air Force WWII, then became sportscaster. Voted Sportscaster of the Year, 1967, Nat'l Assn. of Sportswriters Broadcasters. Best Sportscaster, Fame, 1967. Did play-by-play telecasts for 16 World Series, 7 Super Bowls, 12 Rose Bowls, 8 Orange Bowls, 18 NCAA Final 4 college basketball championships. In 1970 was the first individual from the field of sports to receive the George Foster Peabody Award. Hosted the American Sportsman outdoor TV show on ABC for 20 years. (Received 8 Emmy Awards). Inducted into the Sportscasters Hall of Fame in 1981, the Fishing Hall of Fame in 1982, and the Baseball Hall of Fame in 1984, Pro Football Hall of Fame in 1992.

GRADE, LORD LEW
Executive. r.n. Louis Winogradsky. b. Tokmak, Russia, Dec. 25, 1906. Brother of Lord Bernard Delfont. Came to Eng. 1912. Was first a music hall dancer until 1934 when he became an agent with Joe Collins, founding Collins and Grade Co. Joint managing dir. Lew & Leslie Grade Ltd. theatrical agency until 1955; Chmn. & mng. dir., ITC Entertainment Ltd. 1958-82; Chmn. & chief exec., Associated Communications Corp. Ltd., 1973-82; pres. ATV Network Ltd., 1977-82; chmn.; Stoll Moss Theatres Ltd., 1969-82; chmn. & chief exec., Embassy Communications International Ltd., 1982-85; chmn. & chief exec., The Grade Co. 1985-; Dir. Euro Disney S.C.A. Paris 1988, v.p. British Olympic Assn. Fellow BAFTA, 1979, KCSS 1979. Chairman for Life Active--I.T.C., 1995. Consultant to Polygram Entertainment Group. Autobiography: Still Dancing (1988).
NY THEATER: Prod.: Merrily We Roll Along, Starlight Express, Sly Fox.

GRADE, MICHAEL
Executive. b. London, England, March 8, 1943. e. Stowe. Entered industry 1966. Early career as newspaper columnist, became an executive at London Weekend Television then Embassy Television in Hollywood. Joined BBC Television, 1983 as controller of BBC 1 and director of Programmes (TV), 1986. Joined Channel 4 as chief executive, 1988.

GRAFF, RICHARD B.
Executive. b. Milwaukee, WI, Nov. 9, 1924. e. U. of Illinois. Served U.S. Air Force; Universal Pictures 1946 to 1964 in Chicago, Detroit, Chicago and NY home office as asst. to genl. sales mgr.; 1964 joined National General in Los Angeles. 1967 became v.p. and general sales mgr. of National General Pictures, formed and operated company. 1968, exec. v.p. in charge of world-wide sales and marketing. 1968 made v.p. of parent company; v.p. general sales mgr. AIP in 1971; 1975, pres. Cine Artists Pictures; 1977, pres. Richard Graff Company Inc; 1983, pres. of domestic distribution, MGM/UA. 1987, pres., worldwide distribution, Weintraub Entertainment Group. 1990, pres. The Richard Graff Company, Inc.

GRAFF, TODD
Actor, Writer. b. New York, NY, Oct. 22, 1959. e. SUNY/Purchase.
THEATER: NY: Baby (Tony nom., Theatre World Award), Birds of Paradise. Author: The Grandma Plays, Sheila Levine.
PICTURES: Actor: Sweet Lorraine (also composed songs), Five Corners, Dominick & Eugene, The Abyss, An Innocent Man, Opportunity Knocks, City of Hope. Writer: Used People, The Vanishing (also co-prod.), Fly by Night (also actor), Angie (also co-prod., cameo).
TELEVISION: Special: Vietnam War Story.

GRANET, BERT
Producer, Writer. b. New York, NY, July 10, 1910. e. Yale U. Sch. of Fine Arts (47 workshop). From 1936 author s.p. orig. & adapt. numerous pictures. Exec. prod.: Universal, 1967-69, CBS, Desilu Studios.
PICTURES: Quick Money, The Affairs of Annabel, Mr. Doodle Kicks Off, Laddie, A Girl a Guy and a Gob, My Favorite Wife, Bride by Mistake, Sing Your Way Home, Those Endearing Young Charms, The Locket, Do You Love Me?, The Marrying Kind, Berlin Express, The Torch, Scarface Mob.
TELEVISION: Desilu (1957-61), Twilight Zone (pilot), The Untouchables (pilot), Scarface Mob; Loretta Young Show (1955-56), Walter Winchell File 1956-57, Lucille Ball-Desi Arnaz Show 1957-60, Westinghouse Desilu Playhouse, The Great Adventure.

GRAMMER, KELSEY
Actor. b. St. Thomas, Virgin Islands, Feb. 20, 1955. e. Juilliard. Acting debut on tv in Another World. On B'way in Sunday in the Park With George. Supplied voice for Disney/Mickey Mouse short Runaway Brain.
PICTURE: Down Periscope.
TELEVISION: Series: Cheers, Frasier (2 Emmy Awards, 1994, 1995; Golden Globe, 1996), Fired Up (exec. prod.). Guest: Simpsons (voice). Movies: Dance 'Til Dawn, Beyond Suspicion, The Innocent.

GRANGER, FARLEY
Actor. b. San Jose, CA, July 1, 1925. e. Hollywood. U.S. Armed Forces 1944-46. Joined Eva Le Gallienne's National Rep. Co. in 1960s (The Sea Gull, The Crucible, Ring Round the Moon).
PICTURES: The North Star (debut, 1943), The Purple Heart, Rope, Enchantment, The Live By Night, Roseanna McCoy, Side Street, Our Very Own, Edge of Doom, Strangers on a Train, Behave Yourself, I Want You, O. Henry's Full House, Hans Christian Andersen, Story of Three Loves, Small Town Girl, Senso, Naked Street, Girl in the Red Velvet Swing, Rogue's Gallery, Something Creeping in the Dark, They Call Me Trinity, Replica of a Crime, Amuk, The Slasher, The Redhead with the Translucent Skin, Kill Me My Love, Planet Venus, Night Flight From Moscow, Man Called Neon, Arnold, Savage Lady, The Co-ed Murders, Deathmask, The Prowler, The Imagemaker.
TELEVISION: Series: One Life to Live (1976-7), As the World Turns (1986-8). Movies: The Challengers, The Lives of Jenny Dolan, Widow, Black Beauty. Guest: Playhouse of Stars, U.S. Steel Hour, Producer's Showcase, Climax, Ford Theatre, Playhouse 90, 20th Century Fox Hour, Robert Montgomery Presents, Arthur Murray Dance Party, Wagon Train, Masquerade Party, Kojak, 6 Million Dollar Man, Ellery Queen.

GRANATH, HERBERT A.
Executive. e. Fordham U. Started with ABC TV in sales, marketing and production. 1979, became v.p. of Capital Cities/ABC Video Enterprises Inc.; 1982-93, served as pres. of same; Oct. 1993, named pres. ABC Cable and International Broadcast Group, sr. v.p. Capital Cities/ABC Inc.

GRANT, DAVID MARSHALL
Actor. b. New Haven, CT, June 21, 1955. e. Yale School of Drama.
THEATER: NY: Sganarelle, Table Settings, The Tempest, Bent, The Survivor, Making Movies, Angels in America: Millenium Approaches/Perestroika. Regional: Bent (also dir.), Once in a Lifetime, Lake Boat, Free and Clear, True West, The Wager, Rat in the Skull, Snakebit (author).
PICTURES: French Postcards (debut, 1979), Happy Birthday Gemini, The End of August, American Flyers, The Big Town, Bat 21, Air America, Strictly Business, Forever Young.
TELEVISION: Series: thirtysomething. Movies: Kent State, Legs, Sessions, Dallas: The Early Years, What She Doesn't Know, Citizen Cohn, Through the Eyes of a Killer. Special: A Doonesbury Special (voice). Pilot: Graham. Host: The Legend of Billy the Kid.

GRANT, HUGH
Actor. b. London, Eng., Sept. 9, 1960. e. New Coll., Oxford U. Acted with OUDS before landing role in Oxford Film Foundation's Privileged. Acted at Nottingham Playhouse and formed revue group, The Jockeys of Norfolk.
PICTURES: Privileged (debut, 1982), Maurice, White Mischief, The Lair of the White Worm, The Dawning, Remando al Viento (Rowing With the Wind), Bengali Night, Impromptu, Crossing the Line, The Remains of the Day, Night Train to Venice, Sirens, Four Weddings and a Funeral (BAFTA & Golden Globe Awards), Bitter Moon, The Englishman Who Went Up a Hill But Came Down a Mountain, Nine Months, An Awfully Big Adventure, Restoration, Sense and Sensibility, Extreme Measures (also prod.).
TELEVISION: Mini-Series: The Last Place on Earth. Series: The Demon Lover, Ladies in Charge. Movies/Specials: The

Detective, Handel: Honour, Profit and Pleasure, Jenny's War, The Lady and the Highwayman, Champagne Charlie, 'Til We Meet Again, Our Sons (U.S.), The Changeling.

GRANT, LEE
Actress. r.n. Lyova Rosenthal. b. New York, NY, Oct. 31, 1931. m. producer Joseph Feury. Daughter is actress Dinah Manoff. At 4 was member of Metropolitan Opera Company; played princess in L'Orocolo. Member of the American Ballet at 11. e. Juilliard Sch. of Music, studied voice, violin and dance. At 18 with road co. Oklahoma as understudy. Acting debut: Joy to the World.
THEATER: acted in a series of one-acters at ANTA with Henry Fonda. Detective Story (Critics Circle Award, 1949), Lo and Behold, A Hole in the Head, Wedding Breakfast; road co. Two for the Seesaw, The Captains and the Kings; toured with Electra, Silk Stockings, St. Joan, Arms and the Man, The Maids (Obie Award), Prisoner of Second Avenue.
PICTURES: Detective Story (debut, 1951; Acad. Award nom.), Storm Fear, Middle of the Night, Affair of the Skin, The Balcony, Terror in the City, Divorce American Style, In the Heat of the Night, Valley of the Dolls, Buona Sera Mrs. Campbell, The Big Bounce, Marooned, The Landlord (Acad. Award nom.), There Was a Crooked Man, Plaza Suite, Portnoy's Complaint, The Internecine Project, Shampoo (Academy Award, best supporting actress, 1975), Voyage of the Damned (Acad. Award nom.), Airport '77, Damien: Omen II, The Swarm, The Mafu Cage, When You Comin' Back Red Ryder, Little Miss Marker, Charlie Chan and the Curse of the Dragon Queen, Visiting Hours, Teachers, The Big Town, Defending Your Life, Under Heat. Dir.: Tell Me a Riddle, Willmar Eight, Staying Together.
TELEVISION: Series: Search for Tomorrow (1953-4), Peyton Place (Emmy Award, 1966), Fay. Guest: Studio One, The Kraft Theatre, Slattery's People, The Fugitive, Ben Casey, The Nurses, The Defenders, East Side/West Side, One Day at a Time, Bob Hope Show (Emmy nom.). Movies: Night Slaves, The Love Song of Bernard Kempenski, BBC's The Respectful Prostitute, The Neon Ceiling (Emmy Award, 1971), Ransom for a Dead Man, Lt. Schuster's Wife, Partners in Crime, What Are Best Friends For?, Perilous Voyage, The Spell, Million Dollar Face, For Ladies Only, Thou Shalt Not Kill, Bare Essence, Will There Really Be A Morning?, The Hijacking of the Achille Lauro, She Said No, Something to Live For: The Alison Gertz Story, In My Daughter's Name, Citizen Cohn. Mini-Series: Backstairs at the White House, Mussolini--The Untold Story. Special: Plaza Suite. Director: Nobody's Child, Shape of Things, When Women Kill, A Matter of Sex, Down and Out in America, No Place Like Home, Following Her Heart.

GRANT, RICHARD E.
Actor. b. Mbabane, Swaziland, May 5, 1957. e. Cape Town U., South Africa (combined English and drama course). Co-founded multi-racial Troupe Theatre Company with fellow former students and members of Athol Fugard and Yvonne Bryceland's Space Theatre, acting in and directing contemporary and classic plays. Moved to London 1982 where performed in fringe and rep. theater. Nominated most promising newcomer in Plays and Players, 1985, for Tramway Road.
PICTURES: Withnail and I, Hidden City, How to Get Ahead in Advertising, Killing Dad, Mountains of the Moon, Henry and June, Warlock, L.A. Story, Hudson Hawk, The Player, Bram Stoker's Dracula, Franz Kafka's It's A Wonderful Life (short), The Age of Innocence, Ready to Wear (Pret-a-Porter), Jack and Sarah, Twelfth Night.
TELEVISION: Series: Sweet Sixteen. Movies/Specials: Honest Decent and True, Lizzie's Pictures, Codename Kyril, Thieves in the Night (also released theatrically), Here Is the News, Suddenly Last Summer, Hard Times, Bed.

GRASGREEN, MARTIN
Executive. b. New York, NY, July 1, 1925. Entered m.p. ind. 1944, Columbia Pictures in contract dept. Promoted to travelling auditor 1947. Appt. office mgr. Omaha branch 1948; salesman Omaha, 1950. To Indianapolis, 1952, as city salesman; transferred to Cleveland as sales mgr., 1953. Left Columbia in 1960 to become 20th-Fox branch mgr. in Cleveland. Transferred to Philadelphia in 1965 as branch mgr.; transferred to NY in 1967 as Eastern dist. mgr. Resigned in 1970 to form Paragon Pictures, prod.-dist. co. 1975, formed Lanira Corp., representing producers for U.S. sales and dist. of films in U.S. Retired 1980.

GRASSHOFF, ALEX
Director. b. Boston, MA, Dec. 10, 1930. e. USC. 3 Acad. Award nominations for feature documentaries; Really Big Family; Journey to the Outer Limits; Young Americans (Acad. Award, 1968).
PICTURES: A Billion For Boris, J.D. and the Salt Flat Kid, The Last Dinosaur, The Jailbreakers.
TELEVISION: Series: The Rockford Files, Toma, Chips, Night Stalker, Barbary Coast, Movin' On. Specials: The Wave (Emmy Award), Future Shock (1973 Cannes Film Fest. Awards), Frank Sinatra, Family and Friends.

147

GRASSO, MARY ANN
Executive. b. Rome, NY, Nov. 3, 1952. e. U. of Calif., Riverside, B.A. art history, 1973; U. of Oregon, Eugene, Master of Library Science, 1974. Dir., Warner Research Collection, 1975-85; mgr., CBS-TV, docu-drama, 1985-88; Instructor 1980-88 UCLA Extension, American Film Institute. exec. dir. National Association of Theater Owners, 1988-present. Member: Acad. Motion Picture Arts & Sciences, Friends of the Motion Picture Pioneers, American Society of Association Executives , Phi Beta Kappa. Woman of Achievement, BPOA Awarded 1984. TV credits: The Scarlet O'Hara Wars, This Year's Blonde, The Silent Lovers, A Bunnies Tale, Embassy.

GRAVES, PETER
Actor. r.n. Peter Aurness. b. Minneapolis, MN, March 18, 1926. e. U. of Minnesota. Brother of actor James Arness. Played with bands, radio announcer, while at school; U.S. Air Force 2 yrs.; summer stock appearances.
PICTURES: Rogue River (debut, 1950), Fort Defiance, Red Planet Mars, Stalag 17, East of Sumatra, Beneath the 12-Mile Reef, Killers From Space, The Raid, Black Tuesday, Wichita, Long Gray Line, Night of the Hunter, Naked Street, Fort Yuma, Court Martial of Billy Mitchell, It Conquered the World, The Beginning of the End, Death in Small Doses, Poor White Trash (Bayou), Wolf Larsen, A Rage to Live, Texas Across the River, Valley of Mystery, The Ballad of Josie, Sergeant Ryker, The Five Man Army, Sidecar Racers, Parts: The Clonus Horror, Survival Run, Airplane!, Savannah Smiles, Airplane II: The Sequel, Number One With a Bullet, Addams Family Values.
TELEVISION: Series: Fury, Whiplash, Court-Martial, Mission Impossible, New Mission: Impossible. Movies: A Call to Danger, The President's Plane is Missing, Scream of the Wolf, The Underground Man, Where Have All the People Gone?, Dead Man on the Run, SST-Death Flight, The Rebels, Death on the Freeway, The Memory of Eva Ryker, 300 Miles for Stephanie, If It's Tuesday It Still Must Be Belgium. Mini-Series: Winds of War, War and Remembrance. Host/narrator: Discover! The World of Science, Biography.

GRAVES, RUPERT
Actor. b. Weston-Super-Mare, England, June 30, 1963. Before film debut worked as a clown with the Delta travelling circus in England.
THEATER: The Killing of Mr. Toad, 'Tis Pity She's a Whore, St. Ursula's in Danger, Sufficient Carbohydrates, Amadeus, Torch Song Trilogy, Candida, Pitchfork Disney, History of Tom Jones, A Madhouse in Goa, A Midsummer Night's Dream, Design for Living.
PICTURES: A Room with a View, Maurice, A Handful of Dust, The Children, Where Angels Fear to Tread, Damage, The Madness of King George, The Innocent Sleep, Different for Girls.
TELEVISION: Vice Versa, All for Love, A Life of Puccini, Fortunes of War, The Plot to Kill Hitler, The Sheltering Desert, Union Matters, Starting Out, Royal Celebration, Good and Bad at Games, Inspector Morse, Doomsday Gun.

GRAY, COLEEN
Actress. r.n. Doris Jensen. b. Staplehurst, NB, Oct. 23, 1922. e. Hamline U., B.A. summa cum laude, 1943, Actor's Lab. m. Fritz Zeiser. Member: Nat'l Collegiate Players, Kappa Phi, a capella choir, little theatres, 1943-44.
PICTURES: State Fair (debut, 1945), Kiss of Death, Nightmare Alley, Fury at Furnace Creek, Red River, Sleeping City, Riding High, Father Is a Bachelor, Apache Drums, Lucky Nick Cain, Models Inc., Kansas City Confidential, Sabre Jet, Arrow in the Dust, The Fake, The Vanquished, Las Vegas Shakedown, Twinkle in God's Eye, Tennessee's Partner, The Killing, Wild Dakotas, Death of a Scoundrel, Frontier Gambler, Black Whip, Star in the Dust, The Vampire, Hell's Five Hours, Copper Sky, Johnny Rocco, The Leech Woman, The Phantom Planet, Town Tamer, P.J., The Late Liz, Cry from the Mountain.
TELEVISION: Series: Window on Main Street, Days of Our Lives, (1966-67), Bright Promise (1968-72). Guest: Family Affair, Ironside, Bonanza, Judd for the Defense, Name of the Game, The FBI, The Bold Ones, World Premiere, Mannix, Sixth Sense, McCloud, Tales from the Dark Side. Movies: Ellery Queen: Don't Look Behind You, The Best Place to Be.

GRAY, DULCIE
C.B.E., F.L.S., F.R.S.A. Actress b. Malaya, Nov. 20, 1919. e. Webber Douglas Sch. Stage debut 1939, Aberdeen, Hay Fever, Author: Love Affair (play), 18 detective novels, book of short stories. 8 radio plays; co-author with husband Michael Denison, An Actor and His World; Butterflies on My Mind, The Glanville Women, Anna Starr; Mirror Image, Looking Forward Looking Back.
THEATER: Over 50 West End plays including Little Foxes, Brighton Rock, Dear Ruth, Rain on the Just, Candida, An Ideal Husband (1965, 1962, 1996 London & NY), Where Angels Fear to Tread, Heartbreak House, On Approval, Happy Family, No. 10, Out of the Question, Village Wooing, Wild

Duck, At The End of the Day, The Pay Off, A Murder Has Been Announced, Bedroom Farce, A Coat of Varnish, School for Scandal, The Living Room, Tartuffe, Cavell, Pygmalion, The School Mistress (Chicester), Two of a Kind.
PICTURES: Two Thousand Women, A Man About the House, Mine Own Executioner, My Brother Jonathan, The Glass Mountain, They Were Sisters Wanted for Murder, The Franchise Affair, Angels One Five, There Was a Young Lady, A Man Could Get Killed, The Trail of the Pink Panther, The Curse of the Pink Panther, The Black Crow.
TELEVISION: Milestones, The Will, Crime Passionel, Art and Opportunity, Fish in the Family, The Governess, What the Public Wants, Lesson in Love, The Happy McBaines, Winter Cruise, The Letter, Tribute to Maugham, Virtue, Beautiful Forever, East Lynne, Unexpectedly Vacant, The Importance of Being Earnest, This Is Your Life (1977; and with Michael Denison, 1995), Crown Court, Making Faces, Read All About It, The Voysey Inheritance, Life After Death, The Pink Pearl, Britain in the Thirties, Rumpole (The Old Boy Net.), Cold Warrior, Hook, Line and Sinker, Howard's Way (series; 6 yrs.), Three Up, Two Down, The Time and the Place.

GRAY, LINDA
Actress. b. Santa Monica, CA, Sept. 12, 1940.
PICTURES: Under the Yum Yum Tree, Palm Springs Weekend, Dogs, Fun With Dick and Jane, Oscar.
TELEVISION: Series: Dallas, Model Inc. Guest: Touched By an Angel. Movies: The Big Ripoff, Murder in Peyton Place, The Grass is Always Greener Over the Septic Tank, Two Worlds of Jennie Logan, Haywire, The Wild and the Fire, Not in Front of the Children, The Entertainers, Highway Heartbreaker, Moment of Truth: Why My Daughter?, Bonanza: The Return, To My Daughter with Love, Accidental Meeting, Moment of Truth: Broken Pledges.

GRAY, SPALDING
Performance artist, Actor, Writer. b. Barrington, RI, June 5, 1941. Began career as actor in 1965 at Alley Theater, Housten, then off-B'way in Tom Paine at LaMama Co. In 1969 joined the Wooster Group, experimental performance group. Has written and performed autobiographical monologues (Three Places in Rhode Island, Sex and Death to the Age 14, Swimming to Cambodia, Monster in a Box, Gray's Anatomy) throughout U.S, Europe and Australia. Taught theater workshops for adults and children and is recipient of Guggenheim fellowship. Artist in resident Mark Taper Forum, 1986-87. B'way debut: Our Town (1988).
PICTURES: Actor: Almost You, The Killing Fields, Hard Choices, True Stories, Swimming to Cambodia (also s.p.), Stars and Bars, Clara's Heart, Beaches, Heavy Petting, Straight Talk, Monster in a Box (also s.p.), The Pickle, King of the Hill, Twenty Bucks, The Paper, Bad Company, Beyond Rangoon, Drunks, Diabolique.
TELEVISION: Special: Terrors of Pleasure (HBO). Movies: The Image, To Save a Child, Zelda.

GRAY, THOMAS K.
Executive, producer. b. New York City, N. Y., July 1, 1945. e. U. of Arizona, B.A., post grad work at American Graduate School of Int'l Management, Phoenix. Began career as management trainee with United Atists film exchange in Spain, 1970, and year later became managing director, UA, Chile. Also managing director for UA, New Zealand, 1972; Columbia, 1973; South and East Africa, 1974. Joined Cinema Int'l Corp., London, as exec. assist. to co-chairman, 1974, and moved up to managing director of CIC/Warner, South Africa, 1976. Returned to UA as vice pres. Far East, Latin America, Africa and Australia, 1977. Joined Golden Communications Overseas Ltd., London, as vice pres. foreign sales, 1980. With Golden Harvest Films, Inc. since 1984 as sr. vice. pres., production. Executive in charge of prod. for Golden Harvest features: Flying, The Protector, China O'Brien, China O'Brien II, A Show of Force, Teenage Mutant Ninja Turtles, Best of Martial Arts (prod.), Teenage Mutant Ninja Turtles II: Secret of the Ooze (prod.), Teenage Mutant Ninja Turtles III. 1992, pres. and CEO of Rim Film Distribution Inc.

GRAYSON, KATHRYN
Actress, Singer. r.n. Zelma Hedrick. b. Winston-Salem, NC, Feb. 9, 1923. e. St. Louis schools.
THEATER: Camelot, Rosalinda, Merry Widow, Kiss Me Kate, Showboat.
PICTURES: Andy Hardy's Private Secretary (debut, 1941), The Vanishing Virginian, Rio Rita, Seven Sweethearts, Thousands Cheer; Anchors Aweigh, Ziegfeld Follies, Two Sisters from Boston, Till the Clouds Roll By, It Happened in Brooklyn, The Kissing Bandit, That Midnight Kiss, The Toast of New Orleans, Grounds for Marriage, Show Boat, Lovely to Look At, The Desert Song, So This Is Love, Kiss Me Kate, The Vagabond King.
TELEVISION: Guest: GE Theatre (Emmy nom.), Playhouse 90, Lux Playhouse, Murder She Wrote. Special: Die Fliedermaus.

GRAZER, BRIAN
Producer. b. Los Angeles, CA, July 12, 1951. e. U. of Southern California. Started as legal intern at Warner Bros.; later script reader (for Brut/Faberge) & talent agent. Joined Edgar J. Scherick-Daniel Blatt Co.; then with Ron Howard as partner in Imagine Films Entertainment. Received NATO/ShoWest Producer of the Year Award, 1992.
PICTURES: Night Shift, Splash (also co-story), Real Genius, Spies Like Us, Armed and Dangerous (also co-story), Like Father Like Son, Vibes, The 'Burbs, Parenthood, Cry-Baby (co-exec. prod.), Kindergarten Cop, The Doors (co-exec. prod.), Closet Land (co-exec. prod.), Backdraft (exec. prod.), My Girl, Far and Away, Housesitter, Boomerang, CB4 (co-exec. prod.), Cop and a Half, For Love or Money, My Girl 2, Greedy, The Paper, The Cowboy Way, Apollo 13, Fear, Sgt. Bilko, The Nutty Professor.
TELEVISION: Movies: Zuma Beach, Thou Shalt Not Commit Adultery, Splash Too. Series (executive prod.): Shadow Chasers, Take Five, Ohara, Parenthood. Special: Poison (prod.)

GREEN, ADOLPH
Writer, Actor. b. New York, NY, Dec. 2, 1915. m. actress-singer Phyllis Newman. Began career in the cabaret act The Revuers with partner Betty Comden and Judy Holliday (1944).
THEATER: Wrote book, sketches and/or lyrics for many Broadway shows including: On the Town (also actor), Billion Dollar Baby, Bonanza Bound! (also actor), Two on the Aisle, Wonderful Town (Tony Award for lyrics, 1953), Peter Pan (Mary Martin), Say Darling, Bells Are Ringing, A Party with Comden and Green (1959 & 1977), Do Re Mi, Subways Are For Sleeping, Fade Out Fade In, Halleujah Baby (Tony Awards for lyrics & best musical, 1968), Applause (Tony Award for book, 1970), Lorelei: Or Gentlemen Still Prefer Blondes (new lyrics), By Bernstein (book), On the Twentieth Century (Tony Awards for book & lyrics, 1978), A Doll's Life, The Will Rogers Follies (Tony Award for lyrics, 1991).
PICTURES: Writer (with Betty Comden): Good News, On the Town, The Barkleys of Broadway, Take Me Out to the Ball Game (co-lyrics), Singin' in the Rain, The Band Wagon, It's Always Fair Weather, Auntie Mame, What a Way to Go. Actor: Greenwich Village, Simon, My Favorite Year, Lily in Love, Garbo Talks, I Want to Go Home.

GREEN, GUY
Director. b. Somerset, Eng. Nov. 5, 1913. Joined Film Advertising Co. as projectionist & camera asst. 1933; camera asst., Elstree Studios (BIP) 1935; started as camera operator on films including One of Our Aircraft Is Missing, In Which We Serve, This Happy Breed. 1944: Director of Photography; Dir of Allied Film Makers Ltd.
PICTURES: Dir. of Photography: The Way Ahead, Great Expectations (Academy Award, 1947), Oliver Twist, Captain Horatio Hornblower, I Am a Camera. Director: River Boat (debut, 1954), Portrait of Alison, Tears for Simon, House of Secrets, The Snorkel, Desert Patrol (Sea of Sand), The Angry Silence, The Mark, Light in the Piazza, Diamond Head, A Patch of Blue (also co-exec. prod., s.p.), Pretty Polly (A Matter of Innocence), The Magus, A Walk in the Spring Rain (also co-exec. prod.), Luther, Once Is Not Enough, The Devil's Advocate.
TELEVISION: (U.S.) Incredible Journey of Dr. Meg Laurel; Isabel's Choice; Jennifer: A Woman's Story; Arthur Hailey's Strong Medicine, Jimmy B. and Andre, Inmates.

GREEN, JACK N.
Cinematographer. b. San Francisco. Started as camera operator for Bruce Surtees.
PICTURES: Camera operator: Fighting Mad, Firefox, Honky Tonk Man, Risky Business, Sudden Impact, Tightrope, Beverly Hills Cop, City Heat, Pale Rider, Ratboy. Cinematographer: Heartbreak Ridge, Like Father Like Son, The Dead Pool, Bird, Pink Cadillac, Race for Glory, White Hunter Black Heart, The Rookie, Deceived, Unforgiven, Rookie of the Year, A Perfect World, Bad Company, The Bridges of Madison County, The Net, The Amazing Panda Adventure, Twister.

GREEN, JOSEPH
Executive, Producer, Director. b. Baltimore, MD, Jan. 28, 1938. e. U. of Maryland, B.A. Since 1970 has headed own distribution co. Joseph Green Pictures and released its library of 150 features to theatres, TV and cable.
PICTURES: The Brain that Wouldn't Die (dir., s.p.), The Perils of P.K. (assoc. prod., dir.), Psychedelic Generation (prod., dir., s.p.).

GREEN, MALCOLM C.
Theatre Executive. b. Boston, MA, Mar. 1, 1925. e. Harvard Coll. Began career as asst. mgr., Translux Theatre, Boston & Revere Theatre, Revere, MA. Treas., Interstate Theatres, 1959-64. Film Buyer, Interstate, 1959-72. Formed Theatre Management Services in 1972 with H. Rifkin and P. Lowe and Cinema Centers Corp. with Rifkin and Lowe families in 1973.

Treas., Cinema Center, & pres., Theatre Mgmt. Services. Cinema Center grew to 116 theatres in 6 Northeast states, sold to Hoyts Cinemas Corp., 1986. Sr. v.p., Hoyts Cinemas Corp. 1986-89. Pres., Theatre Owners of New England, 1964-65; chmn bd., 1965-69; treas., 1970-84. Pres., NATO, 1986-88, Chmn Bd, 1988-90. Dir., Natl. Assoc. Theatre Owners. Chmn., NATO of New York State. Director, Vision Foundation. Dir., The Lyric Stage, Boston 1990-94; dir. & v.p., New Hampshire Music Festival, 1988-1996.

GREENAWAY, PETER
Director, Writer. b. Newport, Wales, Apr. 5, 1942. Trained as a painter, first exhibition was at Lord's Gallery in 1964. Started making short films and documentaries in 1966, including: A Walk Through H, The Falls, Act of God, Vertical Features Remake. Directorial feature debut in 1982. Author of numerous books including, 100 Objects to Represent the World, The Physical Self, Les Bruits des Nuages.
PICTURES: The Draughtsman's Contract, A Zed and Two Noughts, The Belly of an Architect, Drowning By Numbers, The Cook The Thief His Wife and Her Lover, Prospero's Books, The Baby of Macon, The Pillow Book.
TELEVISION: Death in the Seine, series of 9 Cantos from Dante's Inferno in collaboration with painter Tom Phillips, MIs for Man Music Mozart, Darwin.

GREENE, CLARENCE
Producer, Writer. b. New York, NY, 1918. e. St. John's U., L.L.B. Author of play Need a Lawyer. Formed Greene-Rouse prods. with Russell Rouse; Acad. Oscar co-orig. story Pillow Talk. Acad. award nom. co-orig. s.p. The Well. Two Writers Guild nominations. Writers Guild award outstanding teleplay, One Day in the Life of Ivan Denisovitch. Co-prod., writer TV series Tightrope.
PICTURES: Prod., collab. s.p.: The Town Went Wild, D.O.A., The Well, The Thief, Wicked Woman, New York Confidential, A House Is Not a Home, The Oscar. Prod.: Unidentified Flying Objects, The Gun Runners, Fastest Gun Alive, Thunder in the Sun, The Caper of the Golden Bulls, D.O.A. (story, 1988).

GREENE, DAVID
Director, Writer. b. Manchester, Eng., Feb. 22, 1921. Early career as actor. To U.S. with Shakespeare company early 1950's; remained to direct TV in Canada, New York and Hollywood.
PICTURES: The Shuttered Room, Sebastian, The Strange Affair, I Start Counting, Godspell, Gray Lady Down, Hard Country (prod., dir.).
TELEVISION: The Defenders. Movies: The People Next Door, Mdame Sin, Count of Monte Cristo, Friendly Fire, The Trial of Lee Harvey Oswald, A Vacation in Hell, The Choice, World War III, Rehearsal For Murder, Take Your Best Shot, Ghost Dancing, Prototype, Sweet Revenge, The Guardian, Fatal Vision (Emmy nom.), Guilty Conscience, This Child Is Mine, Vanishing Act, Miles to Go, Circle of Violence, The Betty Ford Story, After the Promise; Inherit the Wind, Liberace: Behind the Music, Red Earth, White Earth; The Penthouse (dir., exec. prod.), Small Sacrifices (Peabody Award), Honor Thy Mother.

GREENE, ELLEN
Actress, Singer. b. Brooklyn, NY, Feb. 22. e. Ryder Coll. After coll. joined musical road show. Appeared in cabaret act at The Brothers & the Sisters Club and Reno Sweeney's, NY. Off-B'way debut, Rachel Lily Rosenbloom. B'way in the The Little Prince and The Aviator. With NY Shakespeare Fest. in the Boom Boom Room, The Sorrows of Steven, The Threepenny Opera (Tony nom.). Film debut Next Stop, Greenwich Village (1976). Off-B'way co-starred in musical Little Shop of Horrors 1982, repeated role in film. Also Off-B'way in Weird Romance. L.A. stage: David's Mother.
PICTURES: Next Stop Greenwich Village (debut, 1976), I'm Dancing as Fast as I Can, Little Shop of Horrors, Me and Him, Talk Radio, Pump Up the Volume, Stepping Out, Rock a Doodle (voice), Fathers and Sons, Naked Gun 33 1/3: The Final Insult, Wagons East!, The Professional.
TELEVISION: Special: Rock Follies. Movie: Glory Glory. Mini-Series: Seventh Avenue. Pilot: Road Show.

GREENE, GRAHAM
Actor. b. Six Nations Reserve, Ontario, Canada. Member of the Oneida tribe. First show business job as audio technician for several rock bands. Began acting in theater in England.
THEATER: Diary of a Crazy Boy, Coming Through Slaughter, Crackwalker, Jessica, Dry Lips Oughta Move to Kapuskasing.
PICTURES: Running Brave, Revolution, Powwow Highway, Dances With Wolves (Acad. Award nom.), Thunderheart, Clearcut, Savage Land, Rain Without Thunder, Benefit of the Doubt, Maverick, North, Camilla, Die Hard With a Vengeance.
TELEVISION: U.S.: Series: Northern Exposure. Movies: Unnatural Causes, The Last of His Tribe, Cooperstown, Huck and the King of Hearts, Rugged Gold. Guest: Adderly, L.A. Law. Canada: Series: 9B, Spirit Bay. Movies: Murder Sees the Light, The Great Detective, Street Legal.

GREENFIELD, LEO
Executive. b. New York, NY, April 26, 1916. e. St. John's U, Coll. of Arts & Sciences. v.p., gen. sales mgr. Buena Vista, 1962; Columbia road show sales mgr. 1966; v.p.-gen. sales mgr., Cinerama Rel. Corp. 1966; pres.-gen. sales mgr., Warners, 1969; sr. v.p. worldwide distribution, MGM 1975; v.p. distribution & marketing, Marble Arch Productions, 1978; exec. v.p. Associated Film Distribution, 1979; pres., distribution, F/M, 1986; pres., dist., Kings Road Entertainment, 1987; pres., Greenlee Assoc., 1988.

GREENHUT, ROBERT
Producer. b. New York, NY. e. Univ. of Miami. Began career as prod. asst. on Arthur Hiller's The Tiger Makes Out, 1967. Worked as prod. manager and asst. director on such films as Pretty Poison, The Night They Raided Minsky's, Where's Poppa?, The Owl and the Pussycat, Husbands, Born to Win, Panic in Needle Park, The Last of the Red Hot Lovers. Received Crystal Apple from city of NY and Eastman Kodak Award for lifetime achievement.
PICTURES: Huckleberry Finn (assoc. prod.), Lenny (assoc. prod.), Dog Day Afternoon (assoc. prod.), The Front (assoc. prod.), Annie Hall (exec. prod.), Interiors (exec. prod.), Hair (assoc. prod.), Manhattan (prod.), Stardust Memories (prod.), Arthur (prod.), A Midsummer Night's Sex Comedy (prod.), The King of Comedy (exec. prod.), Zelig (prod.), Broadway Danny Rose (prod.), The Purple Rose of Cairo (prod.), Hannah and Her Sisters (prod.), Heartburn (prod.), Radio Days (prod.), September (prod.), Big (exec. prod.), Another Woman (prod.), Working Girl (exec. prod.), New York Stories (prod.), Crimes and Misdemeanors (prod.), Quick Change (prod.), Postcards From the Edge (co-exec. prod.), Alice (prod.), Regarding Henry (exec. prod.), Shadows and Fog (prod.), A League of Their Own (prod.), Husbands and Wives (prod.), Manhattan Murder Mystery (prod.), Renaissance Man (prod.), Wolf (co-exec. prod.), Bullets Over Broadway (prod.), Mighty Aphrodite (prod.), Everyone Says I Love You (prod.), The Preacher's Wife (prod.).
TELEVISION: Movie: Don't Drink the Water.

GREENWALD, ROBERT
Director, Producer, Teacher. b. New York, NY, Aug. 28, 1948. e. Antioch Coll., New School for Social Research. Teaches film and theatre at NYU, New Lincoln, New School. Formed Robert Greenwald Prods.
THEATER: A Sense of Humor, I Have a Dream, Me and Bessie.
PICTURES: Director: Xanadu, Sweet Hearts Dance (also exec. prod.), Hear No Evil.
TELEVISION: Prod.: The Desperate Miles, 21 Hours at Munich, Delta Country USA, Escape From Bogen County, Getting Married, Portrait of a Stripper, Miracle on Ice, The Texas Rangers, The First Time. Exec. prod.: My Brother's Wife, Hiroshima, Zelda, The Portrait, Daddy, Scattered Dreams, Murder in New Hampshire, Death in Small Doses. Director: Sharon: Portrait of a Mistress, In the Custody of Strangers, The Burning Bed, Katie: Portrait of a Centerfold, Flatbed Annie and Sweetpie: Lady Truckers, Shattered Spirits (also exec. prod.), Forgotten Prisoners, A Woman of Independent Means (also co-exec. prod.).

GREENWOOD, BRUCE
Actor. b. Noranda, Quebec, Canada, Aug. 14, 1956. e. Univ. of British Columbia, London Sch. of Speech and Learning, AADA. Worked in Canadian theater and as lead singer/guitarist with blues/rock band in Vancouver before arriving in LA in 1983.
PICTURES: Bear Island (debut, 1980), First Blood, Malibu Bikini Shop, Another Chance, Wild Orchid, Passenger 57, Exotica, Paint Cans, Dream Man.
TELEVISION: Series: Legmen, St. Elsewhere, Knots Landing, Hardball, Nowhere Man. Movies: Peyton Place: The Next Generation, Destination: America, In the Line of Duty: The FBI Murders, Perry Mason: The Case of the All-Star Assassin, Spy, Summer Dreams: The Story of the Beach Boys, The Great Pretender, Rio Diablo, Adrift, The Heart of a Child, Bitter Vengeance, Treacherous Beauties, The Companion, Servants of Twilight, Little Kindappers, Twist of Fate, Woman on the Run: The Lawrencia Bembenek Story, Jazzle, The Judds: Love Can Build a Bridge. Guest: Hitchhiker, Jake and the Fatman, Road to Avonlea.

GREER, JANE
Actress. b. Washington, DC, Sept. 9, 1924. r.n. Bettyjane Greer. Orchestra singer; photograph as WAC on Life Magazine cover won screen debut in Pan-Americana (as Bettejane Greer).
PICTURES: Pan American (debut, 1945), Two O'Clock Courage, George White's Scandals; Dick Tracy (1st film as Jane Greer), Falcon's Alibi, Bamboo Blonde, Sunset Pass, Sinbad the Sailor, They Won't Believe Me, Out of the Past, Station West, Big Steal, You're in the Navy Now, The Company She Keeps, You For Me, The Prisoner of Zenda, Desperate

Search, The Clown, Down Among the Sheltering Palms, Run for the Sun, Man of a Thousand Faces, Where Love Has Gone, Billie, The Outfit, Against All Odds, Just Between Friends, Immediate Family.
TELEVISION: Movie: Louis L'Amour's The Shadow Riders. Guest: Murder She Wrote, Twin Peaks.

GREGORY, JOHN R.
Executive, Producer, Writer. b. Brooklyn, NY, Nov. 19, 1918. e. Grover Cleveland H.S., 1935, New Inst. of M.P. & Telev., 1952; Sls., adv. dept. Fotoshop, Inc., N.Y., 1938-42; Spec. Serv., Photo. instructor, chief projectionist, supv., war dept. theatres, U.S. Army, 1942-46; sls. mgr., J. L. Galef & Son, N.Y.; 1948-49, gen. mgr., Camera Corner Co.; 1949-58, pres.; City Film Center, Inc., 1957; exec. v.p., Talent Guild of New York, 1958; pres., Teleview Prods., Inc., 1961; executive producer, City Film Productions, 1970. Executive post-production supervisor, Jerry Liotta Films, 1977. Author of many articles in nat'l publications dealing with m.p. practices and techniques; tech. editor, Better Movie-Making magazine, 1962; editor, pub., National Directory of Movie-Making Information, 1963; assoc. ed., Photographic Product News, 1964; contrib. editor, U.S. Camera. M.P. columnist, contributing ed. Travel and Camera magazine, 1969; Advisory panelist, Photo-methods (N.Y.), 1975. Consultant, Photographic Guidance Council, 1957, assoc. Society of M.P. & Television-Engineers, 1952.

GREIST, KIM
Actress. b. Stamford, CT, May 12, 1958. e. New Sch. for Social Research.
THEATER: Second Prize: Two Months in Leningrad, Twelfth Night (NY Shakespeare Fest.).
PICTURES: C.H.U.D. (debut, 1984), Brazil, Manhunter, Throw Momma from the Train, Punchline, Why Me?, Homeward Bound: The Incredible Journey, Houseguest, Homeward Bound II: Lost in San Francisco.
TELEVISION: Guest: Miami Vice, Tales From the Darkside, Chicago Hope (recurring). Movies: Payoff, Duplicates, Roswell.

GREY, JENNIFER
Actress. b. New York, NY, Mar. 26, 1960. Father is actor Joel Grey. Appeared as dancer in Dr. Pepper commercial before making NY stage debut in Off-B'way play Album. B'way in The Twilight of the Golds.
PICTURES: Reckless (debut, 1984), Red Dawn, The Cotton Club, American Flyers, Ferris Bueller's Day Off, Dirty Dancing, Bloodhounds of Broadway, Stroke of Midnight (If the Shoe Fits), Wind.
TELEVISION: Movies: Murder in Mississippi, Criminal Justice, Eyes of a Witness, A Case for Murder.

GREY, JOEL
Actor, Singer, Dancer. b. Cleveland, OH, April 11, 1932. r.n. Joel Katz. Father was performer Mickey Katz; daughter is actress Jennifer Grey. e. Alexander Hamilton H.S., L.A. Acting debut at 9 years in On Borrowed Time at Cleveland Playhouse. Extensive nightclub appearances before returning to theatre and TV.
THEATER: NY: Come Blow Your Horn, Stop the World—I Want to Get Off, Half a Sixpence, Harry: Noon and Night, Littlest Revue, Cabaret (Tony Award, 1967), George M!, Goodtime Charley, The Grand Tour, Cabaret (1987, B'way revival). Regional: Herringbone.
PICTURES: About Face (debut, 1952), Calypso Heat Wave, Come September, Cabaret (Academy Award, best supporting actor, 1972), Man on a Swing, Buffalo Bill and the Indians or Sitting Bull's History Lesson, The Seven Percent Solution, Remo Williams: The Adventure Begins..., Kafka, The Player, The Music of Chance, The Fantasticks.
TELEVISION: Specials: Jack and the Beanstalk, George M! Guest: Maverick, December Bride, Ironside, Night Gallery, The Burt Bacharach Show, The Tom Jones Show, The Englebert Humperdinck Show, The Carol Burnett Show, The Julie Andrews Hour, Dallas, Brooklyn Bridge. Movies: Man on a String, Queenie.

GREY, VIRGINIA
Actress. b. Los Angeles, CA, March 22, 1917. Screen career started 1927 with Uncle Tom's Cabin.
PICTURES: Misbehaving Ladies, Secrets, Dames, The Firebird, The Great Ziegfeld, Rosalie, Test Pilot, The Hardys Ride High, Hullaballoo, Blonde Inspiration, The Big Store, Grand Central Murder, Idaho, Strangers in the Night, Blonde Ranson, Unconquered, Who Killed Doc Robbin, The Bullfighter and the Lady, Highway 301, Slaughter Trail, Desert Pursuit, Perilous Journey, Forty-Niners, Target Earth, Eternal Sea, Last Command, Rose Tattoo, All That Heaven Allows, Crime of Passion, Jeanne Eagles, The Restless Years, No Name on the Bullet, Portrait in Black, Tammy Tell Me True, Back Street, Bachelor In Paradise, Black Zoo, The Naked Kiss, Love Has Many Faces, Madame X, Rosie, Airport.

GRIECO, RICHARD
Actor. b. Watertown, NY, 1966. Started with Elite Modeling Agency. Studied acting at Warren Robertson Theatre Workshop appearing in prods. of Orphans, Golden Boy. As musician released album Waiting for the Sky to Fall.
PICTURES: Born to Ride, If Looks Could Kill, Mobsters, Tomcat: Dangerous Desires, Bolt.
TELEVISION: Series: One Life to Live, 21 Jump Street, Booker, Marker. Movies: Sin and Redemption, A Vow to Kill

GRIEM, HELMUT
Actor. b. Hamburg, Germany, 1940. e. Hamburg U.
PICTURES: The Girl From Hong Kong, The Damned, The Mackenzie Break, Cabaret, Ludwig, Children of Rage, Desert of the Tartars, Voyage of the Damned, Germany in Autumn, The Glass Cell, Sgt. Steiner (Breakthrough), Berlin Alexanderplatz, Malou, La Passante, The Second Victory.
TELEVISION: Mini-Series: Peter the Great.

GRIER, DAVID ALAN
Actor. b. Detroit, MI, June 30, 1955. e. Univ. of MI, Yale. Acted with Yale Rep.
THEATER: NY: A Soldier's Play, The First (Theatre World Award), Richard III, Dreamgirls, The Merry Wives of Windsor.
PICTURES: Streamers (debut, 1983), A Soldier's Story, Beer, From the Hip, Amazon Women on the Moon, Off Limits, I'm Gonna Git You Sucka, Me and Him, Loose Cannons, Almost an Angel, The Player, Boomerang, In the Army Now, Blankman, Tales From the Hood, Jumanji.
TELEVISION: Series: All Is Forgiven, In Living Color, The Preston Episodes (also co-exec. prod.).

GRIER, PAM
Actress. b. Winston-Salem, NC, 1949.
PICTURES: The Big Doll House, Big Bird Cage, Black Mama White Mama, Cool Breeze, Hit Man, Women in Cages, Coffy, Scream Blacula Scream, Twilight People, The Arena, Foxy Brown, Bucktown, Friday Foster, Sheba Baby, Drum, Greased Lightning, Fort Apache The Bronx, Tough Enough, Something Wicked This Way Comes, The Vindicator, On the Edge, Stand Alone, The Allnighter, Above the Law, The Package, Class of 1999, Bill & Ted's Bogus Journey, Posse, Original Gangstas, Mars Attacks.
TELEVISION: Mini-Series: Roots: The Next Generations. Movie: A Mother's Right: The Elizabeth Morgan Story. Guest: Miami Vice, Crime Story, Pacific Station, Frank's Place, The Cosby Show, Night Court, In Living Color, Sinbad Show, Fresh Prince of Bel Air.

GRIFFIN, MERV
Executive, Singer, Emcee. b. San Mateo, CA, July 6, 1925. e. U. of San Francisco, Stanford U. Host of The Merv Griffin Show, KFRC-Radio, 1945-48; vocalist, Freddy Martin's orch., 1948-52; recorded hit song I've Got a Lovely Bunch of Coconuts; contract Warner Bros., 1952-54; Prod. Finian's Rainbow, City Center, NY, 1955. Chairman, Merv Griffin Prods.
PICTURES: By the Light of the Silvery Moon, So This Is Love, Boy From Oklahoma, Phantom of the Rue Morgue, Hello Down There, Two Minute Warning, The Seduction of Joe Tynan, The Man With Two Brains, The Lonely Guy, Slapstick of Another Kind.
TELEVISION: Series: The Freddy Martin Show (vocalist), Summer Holiday, Morning Show, The Robert Q. Lewis Show, Keep Talking (emcee), Play Your Hunch (emcee), Saturday Prom, The Merv Griffin Show (1962-63), Talent Scouts, Word for Word, The Merv Griffin Show (1965-86; Emmy Award for writing, 2 Emmy Awards for hosting), Secrets Women Never Share (exec. prod., host, 1987). Creator: Jeopardy, Wheel of Fortune.

GRIFFITH, ANDY
Actor. b. Mount Airy, NC, June 1, 1926. e. U. of North Carolina. Began career as standup comedian, monologist, recording artist (What It Was Was Football, 1954). TV acting debut in U.S. Steel Hour production of No Time for Sergeants, which he later played on Broadway and film.
THEATER: B'way: No Time for Sergeants (Theatre World Award), Destry Rides Again.
PICTURES: A Face in the Crowd (debut, 1957), No Time for Sergeants, Onionhead, The Second Time Around, Angel in My Pocket, Hearts of the West, Rustler's Rhapsody, Spy Hard.
TELEVISION: Series: The Andy Griffith Show, The Headmaster, The New Andy Griffith Show, Salvage One, Matlock. Movies: Strangers in 7A, Go Ask Alice, Pray for the Wildcats, Winter Kill, Savages, Street Killing, Girl in the Empty Grave, Deadly Games, Salvage, Murder in Texas, For Lovers Only, Murder in Coweta County, The Demon Murder Case, Fatal Vision, Crime of Innocence, Diary of a Perfect Murder, Return to Mayberry, Under the Influence, Matlock: The Vacation (also co-exec. prod.), The Gift of Love, Gramps. Mini-Series: Washington Behind Closed Doors, Centennial, From Here to Eternity, Roots: The Next Generations.

GRIFFITH, MELANIE
Actress. b. New York, NY, Aug. 9, 1957. m. Anotnio Banderas. Mother is actress Tippi Hedren. Moved to Los Angeles at 4. e. Catholic academies until Hollywood Prof. Sch., 1974. Did some modeling before being cast in Night Moves at 16. Studied acting with Stella Adler, Harry Mastrogeorge and Sandra Seacat.
PICTURES: The Harrad Experiment (debut, 1973), Smile, Night Moves, The Drowning Pool, One on One, Joyride, Underground Aces, Roar, Fear City, Body Double, Something Wild, Cherry 2000, The Milagro Beanfield War, Stormy Monday, Working Girl (Acad. Award nom.), In the Spirit, Pacific Heights, The Bonfire of the Vanities, Paradise, Shining Through, A Stranger Among Us, Born Yesterday, Milk Money, Nobody's Fool, Now and Then, Two Much, Mulholland Falls, Lolita.
TELEVISION: Series: Carter Country. Mini-Series: Once an Eagle. Movies: Daddy I Don't Like It Like This, Steel Cowboy, The Star Maker, She's in the Army Now, Golden Gate, Women & Men: Stories of Seduction (Hills Like White Elephants), Buffalo Girls. Guest: Vega$, Miami Vice, Alfred Hitchcock Presents.

GRILLO, BASIL F.
Executive. b. Angel's Camp, CA, Oct. 8, 1910. e. U. of California, Berkeley, A.B. Certified public accountant, exec. v.p., dir., Bing Crosby Ent., Inc., 1948-57; bus. mgr., Bing Crosby, 1945; co-organizer, dir., 3rd pres., & treas., Alliance of T.V. Film Producers, 1950-54; exec. prod., BCE, Inc., shows incl. Fireside Thea., Rebound, Royal Playhouse, The Chimps; dir., KCOP, Inc., 1957-60; dir. KFOX, Inc., 1958-62; pres., dir., Bing Crosby Prods., 1955-72; dir., Seven Leagues Ent., Inc., 1958; dir. Electrovision Prods., 1970, CEO, Bing Crosby Enterprises.

GRIMALDI, ALBERTO
Producer. b. Naples, Italy, Mar. 28, 1925. Studied law, serving as counsel to Italian film companies, before turning to production with Italian westerns starring Clint Eastwood and Lee Van Cleef. Is owner of P.E.A. (Produzioni Europee Associate, s.r.l.).
PICTURES: For a Few Dollars More, The Good the Bad and the Ugly, The Big Gundown, Three Steps in Delirium, A Quiet Place in the Country, The Mercenary, Satyricon, Burn!, The Decameron, Man of the East, The Canterbury Tales, Last Tango in Paris, Bawdy Tales, Arabian Nights, Salo or the 100 Days of Sodom, Burnt Offerings, Fellini's Casanova, 1900, Illustrious Corpses, Lovers and Liars, Hurricane Rosy, Ginger and Fred.

GRIMES, GARY
Actor. b. San Francisco, CA, June 2, 1955. Family moved to L.A. when he was nine. Made film debut at 15 in Summer of '42, 1971. Voted Star of Tomorrow in QP poll, 1971.
PICTURES: Summer of '42, The Culpepper Cattle Company, Cahill: U.S. Marshal, Class of '44, The Spikes Gang, Gus.
TELEVISION: Mini-Series: Once an Eagle.

GRIMES, TAMMY
Actress. b. Boston, MA, Jan. 30, 1934. Daughter is actress Amanda Plummer. e. Stephens Coll, The Neighborhood Playhouse. Recipient: Woman of Achievment Award (ADL), Mother of the Year Award, Mayor's Outstanding Contribution to the Arts Award (NYC). Member: bd. dirs. & v.p. of the Upper East-Side Historic Preservation District (NYC).
THEATER: Look After Lulu (Theatre World Award, 1959), Clerambard, The Littlest Revue, Stratford (Ont.) Shakespeare Fest., Bus Stop, The Cradle Will Rock, The Unsinkable Molly Brown (Tony Award, 1961), Rattle of a Simple Man, High Spirits, Private Lives (Tony Award, 1970), Trick, California Suite, 42nd Street, Tartuffe, A Month in the Country, The Guardsman, The Millionairess, Imaginary Invalid, The Importance of Being Earnest, Mademoiselle Columbe, Blythe Spirit, Waltz of the Toreadors, Molly, Taming of the Shrew, Orpheus Descending, Tammy Grimes: A Concert in Words and Music, A Little Night Music, Pygmalion.
PICTURES: Three Bites of the Apple (debut, 1967), Play It as It Lays, Somebody Killed Her Husband, The Runner Stumbles, Can't Stop the Music, The Last Unicorn (voice), The Stuff, No Big Deal, America, Mr. North, Slaves of New York, A Modern Affair.
TELEVISION: Specials: Omnibus, Hollywood Sings, Hour of Great Mysteries, Four Poster. Guest: St. Elsewhere, The Young Riders. Series: The Tammy Grimes Show. Movies: The Other Man, The Horror at 37,000 Feet, The Borrowers, You Can't Go Home Again, An Invasion of Privacy.

GRISSMER, JOHN
Executive, Producer, Director. b. Houston, TX, Aug. 28, 1933. e. Xavier U., B.S., 1955; Catholic U., M.F.A., dramatic writing, 1959. Taught drama courses, directed student productions at U. of CT & American U., Washington, DC. Produced and co-wrote House That Cried Murder, 1973; co-produced,

wrote and directed Scalpel; directed Nightmare at Shadow Woods. Partner in P.J. Productions Co. & North Salem Prods., Inc. Guest Director, Xavier Univ. Theatre.

GRIZZARD, GEORGE
Actor. b. Roanoke Rapids, NC, April 1, 1928. e. U. of North Carolina, B.A., 1949. Has been member of Arena Stage, Washington, D.C., APA repertory company and Tyrone Guthrie resident company in Minneapolis.
THEATER: The Desperate Hours. (B'way debut, 1955), The Happiest Millionaire (Theatre World Award), The Disenchanted, Face of a Hero, Big Fish, Little Fish, Who's Afraid of Virginia Woolf?, The Glass Menagerie, You Know I Can't Hear You When the Water's Running, The Gingham Dog, Inquest, The Country Girl, The Creation of the World and Other Business, Crown Matrimonial, The Royal Family, California Suite, Man and Superman, Another Antiqone, Show Boat, A Delicate Balance (Tony Award, 1996).
PICTURES: From the Terrace, Advise and Consent, Warning Shot, Happy Birthday Wanda June, Comes a Horseman, Firepower, Seems Like Old Times, Wrong Is Right, Bachelor Party.
TELEVISION: Movies: Travis Logan D.A., Indict & Convict, The Stranger Within, Attack on Terror: The FBI vs. the Ku Klux Klan, The Lives of Jenny Dolan, The Night Rider, Attica, Not In Front of the Children, The Deliberate Stranger, Underseige, That Secret Sunday, International Airport, Embassy, The Shady Hill Kidnapping, Oldest Living Graduate (Emmy Award, 1980), Perry Mason: The Case of the Scandalous Scoundrel, David, Caroline?, Iran: Days of Crisis, Not in My Family, Triumph Over Disaster: The Hurricane Andrew Story. Special: Enemy of the People. Mini-Series: The Adams Chronicles, Robert Kennedy and His Times, Queen, Scarlett.

GRODIN, CHARLES
Actor, Director, Writer. b. Pittsburgh, PA, April 21, 1935. e. U. of Miami. After time with Pittsburgh Playhouse studied acting with Uta Hagen and Lee Strasberg; began directing career in New York 1965 as asst. to Gene Saks. Has appeared in some 75 plays all over the country. Has also written scripts, produced plays. Books: It Would Be So Nice If You Weren't Here, How I Get Through Life, We're Ready for You Mr. Grodin.
THEATER: Tchin-Tchin (B'way debut, 1962), Absence of a Cello, Same Time Next Year, It's a Glorious Day... All All That (dir., co-author), Lovers and Other Strangers (dir.), Thieves (prod., dir.), Unexpected Guests (prod., dir.), Price of Fame (also author), One of the All-Time Greats (author).
PICTURES: Sex and the College Girl (debut, 1964), Rosemary's Baby, Catch-22, The Heartbreak Kid, 11 Harrowhouse (also adapt.), King Kong, Thieves, Heaven Can Wait, Real Life, Sunburn, It's My Turn, Seems Like Old Times, The Incredible Shrinking Woman, The Great Muppet Caper, The Lonely Guy, The Woman in Red, Movers and Shakers (also s.p., co-prod.), Last Resort, Ishtar, The Couch Trip, You Can't Hurry Love, Midnight Run, Taking Care of Business, Beethoven, Dave, So I Married an Axe Murderer, Heart and Souls, Beethoven's 2nd, Clifford, It Runs in the Family (My Summer Story).
TELEVISION: Specials (writer): Candid Camera (also dir.), The Simon & Garfunkel Special, Paul Simon Special (also dir.; Emmy Award for writing, 1978). Specials (dir.): Acts of Love and Other Comedies, Paradise (also prod.). Actor: Guest: The Defenders, My Mother the Car, The FBI, Guns of Will Sonnett, The Big Valley. Specials: Grown Ups, Love Sex and Marriage (also writer), Charley's Aunt. Movies: Just Me and You, The Grass Is Always Greener Over the Septic Tank. Mini-Series: Fresno. Series: Charles Grodin (talk).

GROSBARD, ULU
Director. b. Antwerp, Belgium. Jan. 9, 1929. e. U. of Chicago, B.A. 1950, M.A. 1952. Trained at Yale Sch. of Drama 1952-53. Asst. dir. to Eliza Kazan on Splendor in the Grass, 1961; asst. dir.: West Side Story, The Hustler, The Miracle Worker. Unit mgr.: The Pawnbroker.
THEATER: The Days and Nights of Beebee Fenstermaker, The Subject Was Roses, A View From the Bridge, The Investigation, That Summer—That Fall, The Price, American Buffalo, The Woods, The Wake of Jamie Foster, The Tenth Man.
PICTURES: The Subject Was Roses (debut, 1968), Who Is Harry Kellerman and Why Is He Saying Those Terrible Things About Me? (also co-prod.), Straight Time, True Confessions, Falling in Love, Georgia (also co-prod.).

GROSS, KENNETH H.
Executive. b. Columbus, OH, Feb. 12, 1949. e. New School for Social Research, U. of London. Conducted film seminars at New School and active in several indep. film projects. Published film criticism in various journals and magazines. Joined ABC Ent. 1971. Named supvr. of feature films for ABC-TV. Appt. mgr. of feature films, 1974. Promoted 1975 to program exec., ABC Ent. Prime Time/West Coast. Promoted to

exec. prod., movies for TV, ABC Ent. 1976 in L.A.; 1978, with literary agency F.C.A. as partner in L.A.; 1979 prod. for Lorimar; then with Intl. Creative Mgt; 1982, formed own literary talent agency, The Literary Group; 1985, merged agency with Robinson-Weintraub & Assoc. to become Robinson-Weintraub-Gross & Assoc. 1993, founding partner of Paradigm, a talent and literary agency.

GROSS, MARY
Actress. b. Chicago, IL, March 25, 1953. Brother is actor Michael Gross. e. Loyola U. Is also student of the harp. In 1980 discovered by John Belushi who saw her perform as resident member of Chicago's Second City comedy troupe, where she won Chicago's Joseph Jefferson Award as best actress for the revue, Well, I'm Off to the Thirty Years War. First came to national attention as regular on Saturday Night Live, 1981-85.
PICTURES: Club Paradise, The Couch Trip, Casual Sex?, Big Business, Feds, Troop Beverly Hills, The Santa Clause.
TELEVISION: Series: Saturday Night Live, The People Next Door. Specials: Comic Relief I, The Second City 25th Anniversary Reunion.

GROSS, MICHAEL
Actor. b. Chicago, IL, June 21, 1947. m. casting dir. Elza Bergeron. Sister is actress Mary Gross. e. U. Illinois, B.A., Yale School of Drama, M.F.A.
THEATER: NY Shakespeare Fest. (Sganarelle, An Evening of Moliere Farces, Othello). Off-B'way: Endgame, No End of Blame (Obie Award), Put Them All Together, Geniuses, Territorial Rites. B'way: Bent, The Philadelphia Story. L.A. stage: Hedda Gabler, The Real Thing, Love Letters, Money & Friends.
PICTURES: Just Tell Me What You Want, Big Business, Tremors, Midnight Murders, Cool as Ice, Alan & Naomi, Tremors II: Aftershocks.
TELEVISION: Series: Family Ties. Movies: A Girl Named Sooner, FDR: The Last Year, Dream House, The Neighborhood, Little Gloria Happy at Last, Cook and Peary-The Race to the Pole, Summer Fantasy, Family Ties Vacation, A Letter to Three Wives, Right to Die, In the Line of Duty: The FBI Murders, A Connecticut Yankee in King Arthur's Court, Vestige of Honor, In the Line of Duty: Manhunt in the Dakotas, With a Vengeance, Snowbound: The Jim and Jennifer Stolpa Story, In the Line of Duty: The Price of Vengeance, Avalanche, Awake to Danger, Deceived by Trust.

GROSSBART, JACK
Producer. b. Newark, NJ, Apr. 18, 1948. e. Rutgers Univ. Was agent , 1975-80, then personal manager, Litke-Grossbart Mgmt., 1980-87. Became tv prod., Jack Grossbart Prods., 1987.
TELEVISION: Movies (exec. prod./prod.): Shattered Vows, The Seduction of Gina, Rockabye, Killer in the Mirror, Something in Common, Dangerous Affection, Echoes in the Darkness, She Was Marked for Murder, The Preppie Murder, Joshua's Heart, Lies Before Kisses, Honor Bright, Last Wish, Something to Live For: The Alison Gertz Story, A Jury of One, Comrades of Summer, The Woman Who Loved Elvis, One of Her Own, Leave of Absence. Series (exec. prod.): Sydney, Cafe Americain.

GROSSBERG, JACK
Producer, Executive. b. Brooklyn, NY, June 5, 1927. Member: AMPAS.
PICTURES: Requiem for a Heavyweight, Pretty Poison, The Producers, Don't Drink the Water, Take the Money and Run, Bananas, Everything You Always Wanted To Know About Sex, Sleeper, A Delicate Balance, Luther, Rhinoceros, Leadbelly, King Kong, The Betsy, Fast Break, A Stranger is Watching, Brainstorm, Strange Brew, Touch and Go, The Experts, Little Monsters.

GROSSMAN, ERNIE
Executive. b. New York, NY, Sept. 19, 1924. Still dept., press-book edit., asst. field mgr., Warner Bros., 1940-58; Studio publicist, 1958-60; exploitation, promo. mgr. field dept., 1960-64; nat'l mgr., pub., exploit., promo.; 1964-67 exec. co-ord. advt., pub. & promo., Warner-7 Arts, 1967; WB nat'l supv. ad.-pub., 1970. exec. assist. to Richard Lederer, 1971-72; 1973 nat'l dir. of Pub. & Promotion, Warner Bros. Inc.; 1977, natl. dir. of adv.-pub.; 1980-85, natl. dir. promo. 1987, named southwest special events dir. Retired, 1994.

GRUEN, ROBERT
Executive. b. New York, NY, Apr. 2, 1913, e. Carnegie Mellon U., B.A. Stage designer, 1934-35; designer, 20th-Fox, 1936; prod. exec., National Screen Service Corp., 1936; head, Robert Gruen Associates, ind. design org., 1940; nat. pres. Industrial Designers Inst., 1954-55; dir. and v.p., National Screen Service Corp. since 1951; senior v.p. 1975-78; dir., NSS Corp., Continental Lithograph and NSS, Ltd., 1978-85. Retired 1985.

GRUENBERG, ANDY
Executive. b. Minneapolis, MN, March 10, 1950. e. University of Wisconsin. Held various sales positions with 20th Century Fox and Warner Bros. from 1976 to 1984. Joined Columbia Pictures as general sales mgr. Lorimar Pictures s.v.p. and general sales mgr. 1985-89. Hemdale Prods. pres. of distribution, 1989-91. Joined MGM/UA in 1991, currently exec. v.p. of distribution.

GRUENBERG, LEONARD S.
Executive. b. Minneapolis, MN, Sept. 10, 1913, e. U. of Minnesota. Began as salesman Republic Pictures, Minneapolis, 1935; with RKO in same capacity, 1936; promoted to city sales mgr. St. Louis, 1937, then branch mgr., Salt Lake City, 1941; later that year apptd. Rocky Mt. Dist. Mgr. (hqts., Denver, CO); 1946 Metropolitan, div. mgr., v.p. NTA, v.p. Cinemiracle Prods.; Pres., Chmn. of bd., Sigma III Corp., 1962. Chmn. of bd., Filmways, 1967. Chmn. of bd. Gamma III Dist. Co. & Chmn of bd. and Pres. Great Owl Corp., 1976. Member Variety Club, Sigma Alpha Mu Fraternity; Lieut. Civil Air Patrol, Lieut. Comdr., U.S.N.R.

GRUSIN, DAVID
Composer, Conductor, Performer. b. Littleton, CO, June 26, 1934. Directed music for the Andy Williams Show on TV for 7 yrs in the 1960s, where met Norman Lear and Bud Yorkin, producers of the series, who signed him to score their first feature film, Divorce, American Style (1967).
PICTURES: Waterhole No. 3, The Graduate, Candy, The Heart Is a Lonely Hunter, Winning, Where Were You When the Lights Went Out?, Generation, A Man Called Gannon, Tell Them Willie Boy Is Here, Adam at 6 A.M., Halls of Anger, The Gang That Couldn't Shoot Straight, The Pursuit of Happiness, Shoot Out, Fuzz, The Great Northfield Minnesota Raid, The Friends of Eddie Coyle, The Midnight Ride, W.W. and the Dixie Dancekings, The Yakuza, Three Days of the Condor, Murder By Death, The Front, Fire Sale, Mr. Billion, Bobby Deerfield, The Goodbye Girl, Heaven Can Wait, And Justice for All, The Champ, The Electric Horseman, My Bodyguard, Absence of Malice, On Golden Pond, Reds, Author! Author!, Tootsie, Scandalous, Racing with the Moon, The Pope of Greenwich Village, The Little Drummer Girl, Falling in Love, Goonies, The Milagro Beanfield War (Acad. Award, 1988), Clara's Heart, Tequila Sunrise, A Dry White Season, Havana, The Bonfire of the Vanities, For the Boys, The Firm, Mulhalland Falls.
TELEVISION: *Movies*: Deadly Dream, Prescription: Murder, Scorpio Letters, Eric, The Family Rico, The Death Squad; themes to many series.

GUBER, PETER
Producer. b. 1942. e. Syracuse U., B.A.; U. at Florence (Italy), S.S.P.; Sch. of Law, J.D., L.L.M. Recruited by Columbia Pictures as exec. asst. in 1968 while at NYU. Graduate Sch. of Business Adm. With Col. seven yrs. in key prod. exec. capacities, serving last three as studio chief. Formed own company, Peter Guber's Filmworks, which in 1976 was merged with his Casablanca Records to become Casablanca Record and Filmworks where he was co-owner & chmn. bd. 1980 formed Polygram Pictures later bringing in Jon Peters as partner. 1983 sold Polygram and formed Guber-Peters. 1988 merged co. with Burt Sugarman's Barris Industries to form Guber-Peters-Barris Entertainment Co. Co-chmn. & man. dir. 1989 took full control of co. with Sugarman's exit and addition of Australia's Frank Lowy as new partner. 1989 became CEO of Columbia Pictures Ent.; 1992 became chairman and CEo of Sony Pictures Ent. Awards: Producer of Year, NATO, 1979; NYU Albert Gallatin Fellowship; Syracuse U Ardent Award. Visiting prof., & chmn. producer's dept., UCLA Sch. of Theater Arts. Member of NY, CA and Wash. DC Bars. *Books:* Inside the Deep, Above the Title.
PICTURES: The Deep (first under own banner), Midnight Express. Co-Prod. with Jon Peters: An American Werewolf in London, Missing, Flashdance (exec. prod.), D.C. Cab (exec. prod.), Endless Love, Vision Quest (exec. prod.), The Legend of Billie Jean, Head Office, Clan of the Cave Bear, Six Weeks (exec. prod.), The Pursuit of D.B. Cooper (exec. prod.), Clue (exec. prod.), The Color Purple (exec. prod.), The Witches of Eastwick (prod.), Innerspace (exec. prod.), Who's That Girl (exec. prod.), Gorillas in the Mist (exec. prod.), Caddyshack II, Rain Man (exec. prod), Batman (prod.), Johnny Handsome, Tango and Cash (prod.), Batman Returns, This Boy's Life (exec. prod.), With Honors (prod.).
TELEVISION: Mysteries of the Sea (doc. Emmy Award). *Exec. prod.:* Television and the Presidency, Double Platinum, Dreams (series). *Movies*: Stand By Your Man, The Toughest Man in the World (exec. prod.), Bay Coven, Oceanquest, Brotherhood of Justice, Nightmare at Bitter Creek, Finish Line.

GUEST, CHRISTOPHER
Actor, Writer, Composer. b. New York, NY, Feb. 5, 1948. m. actress Jamie Lee Curtis. Brother is actor Nicholas Guest. Wrote the musical score and acted in National Lampoon's Lemmings off-B'way. On B'way in Room Service, Moonchildren.

PICTURES: The Hospital (debut, 1971), The Hot Rock, Death Wish, The Fortune, Girlfriends, The Last Word, The Long Riders, Heartbeeps, This Is Spinal Tap (also co-s.p.), Little Shop of Horrors, Beyond Therapy, The Princess Bride, Sticky Fingers, The Big Picture (dir. co-s.p., story), A Few Good Men, Waiting for Guffman (also dir.).
TELEVISION: *Series*: Saturday Night Live (1984-5). *Movies*: It Happened One Christmas, Haywire, Million Dollar Infield, A Piano for Mrs. Cimino, Attack of the 50 Ft. Woman (dir.). *Specials*: The TV Show, The Chevy Chase Special (also writer), The Billion Dollar Bubble, Lily Tomlin (also writer, Emmy Award, 1976), A Nice Place to Visit (writer only), Spinal Tap Reunion (also co-writer). *Mini-Series*: Blind Ambition.

GUEST, LANCE
Actor. b. Saratoga, CA, July 21, 1960. e. UCLA.
PICTURES: Halloween II, I Ought To Be in Pictures, The Last Starfighter, Jaws-The Revenge, The Wizard of Loneliness.
TELEVISION: *Series*: Lou Grant, Knots Landing. *Guest*: St. Elsewhere. *Movies*: Confessions of a Married Man. *Specials*: One Too Many, My Father My Rival, The Roommate. *Mini-Series*: Favorite Son.

GUEST, VAL
Writer, Director, Producer. b. London, England, 1911. e. England and America. Journalist with Hollywood Reporter, Zit's Los Angeles Examiner and Walter Winchell. Debuted as dir. & writer of 1942 short film The Nose Has It.
PICTURES: *Director/Writer*: Miss London Ltd. (feature debut, 1943), Murder at the Windmill, Miss Pilgrim's Progress, The Body Said No, Mr. Drake's Duck, Happy Go Lovely, Another Man's Poison, Penny Princess, The Runaway Bus, Life With the Lyons, Dance Little Lady, Men of Sherwood Forest, Lyons in Paris, Break in the Circle, It's A Great Life, The Quatermass Experiment (The Creeping Unknown), They Can't Hang Me, The Weapon, It's a Wonderful World, Quatermass II (Enemy From Space), The Abominable Snowman, Carry on Admiral, The Camp on Blood Island, Up the Creek, Further Up the Creek, Yesterday's Enemy, Expresso Bongo (also prod.), Life Is a Circus, Hell Is a City, Full Treatment (Stop Me Before I Kill; also prod.), The Day the Earth Caught Fire (also prod.), Jigsaw (also prod.), 80,000 Suspects (also prod.), The Beauty Jungle (Contest Girl; also co-prod.), Where the Spies Are (also co-prod.), Casino Royale (co-dir.), Assignment K, When Dinosaurs Ruled the Earth, Tomorrow, The Persuaders, Au Pair Girls, Confessions of a Window Cleaner, Killer Force (Diamond Mercenaries; dir. only), The Boys in Blue.
TELEVISION: Space 1999, The Persuaders, The Adventurer, The Shillingbury Blowers, The Band Played On, Sherlock Holmes & Dr. Watson, Shillingbury Tales, Dangerous Davies, The Last Detective, In Possession, Mark of the Devil, Child's Play, Scent of Fear.

GUILLAUME, ROBERT
Actor. b. St. Louis, MO, Nov. 30, 1937. e. St. Louis U., Washington U. Scholarship for musical fest. in Aspen, CO. Then apprenticed with Karamu Theatre where performed in operas and musicals. B'way plays and musicals include Fly Blackbird, Kwamina, Guys and Dolls, Purlie, Jacques Brel is Alive and Well and Living in Paris, Cyrano. In L.A. in Phantom of the Opera.
PICTURES: Super Fly T.N.T. (debut, 1973), Seems Like Old Times, Prince Jack, They Still Call Me Bruce, Wanted Dead or Alive, Lean On Me, Death Warrant, The Meteor Man, The Lion King (voice), First Kid.
TELEVISION: *Series*: Soap (Emmy Award, 1979), Benson (Emmy Award, 1985), The Robert Guillaume Show, Saturdays, Pacific Station, Fish Police (voice), Happily Ever After... Fairytales for Every Child. *Guest*: Dinah, Mel and Susan Together, Rich Little's Washington Follies, Jim Nabors, All in the Family, Sanford and Son, The Jeffersons, Marcus Welby, M.D., Carol & Company, Sister Kate, A Different World. *Mini-Series*: North and South. *Movies*: The Kid From Left Field, The Kid with the Broken Halo, You Must Remember This, The Kid with the 100 I.Q. (also exec. prod.), Perry Mason: The Case of the Scandalous Scoundrel, The Penthouse, Fire and Rain, Greyhounds, Children of the Dust. *Specials*: Purlie, 'S Wonderful 'S Marvellous 'S Gershwin, John Grin's Christmas, Martin Luther King: A Look Back A Look Forward, Living the Dream: A Tribute to Dr. Martin Luther King Jr. (host), The Debbie Allen Special, Carol & Company, Sister Kate, Story of a People (host), Mastergate, Cosmic Slop. *Pilot*: Driving Miss Daisy.

GUILLERMIN, JOHN
Director, Producer, Writer. b. London, England, Nov. 11, 1925. e. City of London Sch., Cambridge U. RAF pilot prior to entering film industry.
PICTURES: *Director*: Torment (debut; 1949; also co-prod., s.p.), Smart Alec, Two on the Tiles, Four Days, Song of Paris, Miss Robin Hood, Operation Diplomat (also co-s.p.), Adventure in the Hopfields, The Crowded Day, Dust and Gold, Thunderstorm, Town on Trial, The Whole Truth, I Was Monty's

Double, Tarzan's Greatest Adventure (also co-s.p.), The Day They Robbed the Bank of England, Never Let Go (also co-story), Waltz of the Torreadors, Tarzan Goes to India (also co-s.p.), Guns at Batasi, Rapture, The Blue Max. P.J. (U.S. debut, 1968), House of Cards, The Bridge of Remagen, El Condor, Skyjacked, Shaft in Africa, The Towering Inferno, King Kong, Death on the Nile, Mr. Patman, Sheena, King Kong Lives, The Favorite.
TELEVISION: Movie: The Tracker.

GUINNESS, SIR ALEC
Actor. r.n. Alec Guinness. b. London, Eng., April 2, 1914. e. Pembroke Lodge, Southbourne & Roborough Sch., Eastbourne. Studied acting at Fay Compton Studio of Dramatic Art. Created C.B.E. 1955; Knighted 1959. C.H., 1994. Honorary degrees in literature: Oxford, 1977; Canterbury, 1991. Stage debut: London, 1934. First film appearance was extra in 1934 in Evensong. Special Academy Award, 1980, for services to film. Autobiography: Blessings in Disguise (1985). Also author of Blessings in Disguise, and My Name Escapes Me.
THEATER: Libel! (walk-on debut, 1934), Queer Cargo, Hamlet (1934), Noah, Romeo & Juliet (1935), The Seagull, Love's Labour's Lost, As You Like It, The Witch of Edmonton, Hamlet (1937), Twelfth Night (1937), Henry V, Richard III, School for Scandal, The Three Sisters, The Merchant of Venice (1937), The Doctor's Dilemma, Trelawny of the Wells, Hamlet (1938), Henry V, The Rivals, The Ascent of F.6, Romeo and Juliet (1939), Great Expectations (1939), Cousin Muriel, The Tempest, Thunder Rock, Flare Path (B'way), Heart of Oak, The Brothers Karamazov, Vicious Circle, King Lear, An Inspector Calls, Cyrano de Bergerac, The Alchemist, Richard II, Saint Joan, The Government Inspector, Coriolanus, Twelfth Night (1948; also dir.), The Human Touch, The Cocktail Party (Edinburgh; B'way), Hamlet (1951; also dir.), Under the Sycamore Tree, All's Well That Ends Well, Richard III, The Prisoner, Hotel Paradiso, Ross, Exit the King, Dylan (B'way; Tony Award, 1964), Time Out of Mind, Voyage Round My Father, Habeas Corpus, A Family and a Fortune, Yahoo (also author), The Old Country, The Merchant of Venice (1984), A Walk in the Woods.
PICTURES: Great Expectations (debut, 1946), Oliver Twist, Kind Hearts and Coronets, A Run for Your Money, Last Holiday, The Mudlark, The Lavender Hill Mob (Acad. Award nom.), The Man in the White Suit, The Card (The Promoter), Malta Story, The Captain's Paradise, Father Brown (The Detective), To Paris With Love, The Prisoner, The Ladykillers, The Swan, The Bridge on the River Kwai (Academy Award, 1957), Barnacle Bill (All at Sea), The Horse's Mouth (also s.p.; Acad. Award nom. for s.p.), The Scapegoat (also co-prod.), Our Man in Havana, Tunes of Glory, A Majority of One, H.M.S. Defiant (Damn the Defiant!), Lawrence of Arabia, The Fall of the Roman Empire, Situation Hopeless But Not Serious, Doctor Zhivago, Hotel Paradiso, The Quiller Memorandum, The Comedians, Cromwell, Scrooge, Brother Sun Sister Moon, Hitler: The Last Ten Days, Murder by Death, Star Wars (Acad. Award nom.), The Empire Strikes Back, Raise the Titanic!, Lovesick, Return of the Jedi, A Passage to India, A Handful of Dust, Little Dorrit (Acad. Award nom.), Kafka.
TELEVISION: Movies/Specials/Mini-Series: The Wicked Scheme of Jebel Deeks, Twelfth Night, Conversation at Night, Solo, Little Gidding, The Gift of Friendship, Caesar and Cleopatra, Little Lord Fauntleroy, Tinker Tailor Soldier Spy (mini-series; BAFTA Award), Smiley's People (mini-series; BAFTA Award), Edwin, Monsignor Quixote, Tales From Hollywood, A Foreign Field, Eskimo Day.

GULAGER, CLU
Actor. b. Holdenville, OK, Nov. 16, 1928. Father, John Gulager, cowboy entertainer. e. Baylor U. Starred at school in original play, A Different Drummer, where spotted by prod. of TV's Omnibus; invited to New York to recreate role on TV.
PICTURES: The Killers, Winning, The Last Picture Show, Company of Killers, McQ, The Other Side of Midnight, A Force of One, Touched by Love, The Initiation, Lies, Into the Night, Prime Risk, The Return of the Living Dead, Hunter's Blood, The Hidden, Tapeheads, Uninvited, I'm Gonna Git You Sucka, Teen Vamp, My Heroes Have Always Been Cowboys, The Killing Device.
TELEVISION: Series: The Tall Man, The Virginian, The Survivors, San Francisco International Airport, MacKenzies of Paradise Cove. Movies: San Francisco International, Glass House, Footsteps, Smile Jenny You're Dead, Houston We've Got a Problem, Hit Lady, Killer Who Wouldn't Die, Charlie Cobb: Nice Night for a Hanging, Ski Lift to Death, Sticking Together, A Question of Love, Willa, This Man Stands Alone, Kenny Rogers as The Gambler, Skyward, Living Proof: The Hank Williams Jr. Story, Bridge Across Time. Mini-Series: Once an Eagle, Black Beauty, King, North and South II, Space.

GUMBEL, BRYANT
Announcer, News Show Host. b. New Orleans, LA, Sept. 29, 1948. e. Bates Coll. Started as writer for Black Sports

Magazine, NY, 1971; sportscaster, then sports dir., KNBC, Los Angeles. Sports host NBC Sports NY 1975-82. Now host on Today Show, New York (Emmy Awards, 1976, 1977).
TELEVISION: Super Bowl games, '88 Olympics, Games People Play, The R.A.C.E.

GUMPERT, JON
Executive. e. Cornell U. Law Sch. Sr. v.p., business affairs, MGM/UA Entertainment; pres., World Film Services, Inc., indep. prod. co. in N.Y. 1985, named v.p., business affairs, Warner Bros; 1986 sr. v.p. Vista Films. Named sr. v.p. legal bus. affairs, Universal Pictures 1990. Named exec. v.p., legal business affairs, Universal Pictures, 1994.

GUNSBERG, SHELDON
Executive. b. Jersey City, NJ, Aug. 10, 1920. e. St. Peters Coll., New Jersey State Normal, NYU. With Night of Stars, Madison Sq. Garden, 1942; for. pub., 20th-Fox 1942; United Artists, 1945-47; Universal, roadshows. Rank product, asst. adv., pub. dir., 1947-54; v. pres., Walter Reade Theatres; exec. v.p. & dir., Walter Reade Org. 1962; Made chief operating officer, 1971; president, and Chief Executive Officer, 1973; chmn. & CEO, 1984. Member: Film Society of Lincoln Center: bd. of dirs. (1955-present), chmn., bldg. committee, Walter Reade Theatre (1986-92), exec. v.p. (1987-90).

GUNTON, BOB
Actor. b. Santa Monica, CA, Nov. 15, 1945. e. UCal. Served in army during Vietnam War. Prof. acting debut at Cumberland County Playhouse in Tennese U.S.A.
THEATER: Off-B'way: Who Am I? (debut, 1971), How I Got That Story (Obie Award), Tip Toes, The Death of Von Richtofen. B'way: Happy End (debut, 1977), Working, Evita (Drama Desk Award; Tony nom.), Passion, King of Hearts, Big River, Rozsa, Sweeney Todd (Drama Desk Award; Tony nom.).
PICTURES: Rollerover (debut, 1981), Static, Matewan, The Pick-Up Artist, Cookie, Born on the Fourth of July, Glory, JFK, Patriot Games, The Public Eye, Jennifer Eight, Demolition Man, The Shawshank Redemption, Dolores Claiborne, Ace Ventura: When Nature Calls, Broken Arrow.
TELEVISION: Series: Comedy Zone, Hot House, Courthouse. Movies: Lois Gibbs and the Love Canal, A Woman Named Jackie, Finnegan Begin Again, Ned Blessing, Dead Ahead: The Exxon Valdez Disaster, Murder in the Heartland, Sinatra. Mini-Series: Wild Palms.

GURIAN, PAUL R.
Executive, Producer. b. New Haven, CT, Oct.18, 1946. e. Lake Forest Coll., U. of Vienna, NYU. Started producing films in 1971 with Cats and Dogs, a dramatic short which won prizes at Chicago Int. Film Fest and Edinburgh Fest. In 1977 formed Gurian Entertainment Corp., to acquire film properties for production.
PICTURES: Cutter and Bone, Peggy Sue Got Married, The Seventh Sign (exec. prod.).
TELEVISION: The Garden Party (PBS program), Profile Ricardo Alegria (short), Bernice Bobs Her Hair (shown at 1977 N.Y. Film Festival)

GUTTENBERG, STEVE
Actor. b. Brooklyn, NY, Aug. 24, 1958. e. Sch. of Performing Arts, N.Y. Off-B'way in The Lion in Winter; studied under John Houseman at Juilliard; classes with Lee Strasberg and Uta Hagen. Moved to West Coast in 1976; landed first TV role in movie, Something for Joey. B'way debut 1991 in Prelude to a Kiss.
PICTURES: Rollercoaster, The Chicken Chronicles, The Boys from Brazil, Players, Can't Stop the Music, Diner, The Man Who Wasn't There, Police Academy, Police Academy 2: Their First Assignment, Cocoon, Bad Medicine, Police Academy 3: Back in Training, Short Circuit, The Bedroom Window, Police Academy 4: Citizens on Patrol (also prod. assoc.), Amazon Women on the Moon, Surrender, Three Men and a Baby, High Spirits, Cocoon: The Return, Don't Tell Her It's Me, Three Men and a Little Lady, The Big Green, Home for the Holidays, It Takes Two.
TELEVISION: Guest: Police Story, Doc. Series: Billy, No Soap Radio. Movies: Something for Joey, To Race the Wind, Miracle on Ice, The Day After. Specials: Gangs (co-prod.), Pecos Bill: King of the Cowboys.

GYLLENHAAL, STEPHEN
Director. b. Pennsylvania. e. Trinity Col, CT. Started career in NYC making industrial films. Directed short film Exit 10.m.. writer-producer Naomi Foner.
PICTURES: Waterland, A Dangerous Woman, Losing Isaiah.
TELEVISION: Movies: The Abduction of Kari Swenson, Promised a Miracle, Leap of Faith, Family of Spies, A Killing in a Small Town, Paris Trout.

H

HAAS, LUKAS
Actor. b. West Hollywood, CA, Apr. 16, 1976. Kindergarten school principal told casting dir. about him which resulted in film debut in Testament. NY theater debut in Mike Nichols' Lincoln Center production of Waiting for Godot (1988). Appeared in AFI film The Doctor.

PICTURES: Testament (debut, 1983), Witness, Solarbabies, Lady in White, The Wizard of Loneliness, See You in the Morning, Music Box, Rambling Rose, Convicts, Alan and Naomi, Leap of Faith, Warrior Spirit, Boys, Johns, Palookaville, Mars Attacks!, Everyone Says I Love You.
TELEVISION: *Movies*: Love Thy Neighbor, Shattered Spirits, The Ryan White Story, The Perfect Tribute. *Guest*: Amazing Stories (Ghost Train), Twilight Zone, The Young Indiana Jones Chronicles. *Pilot*: Brothers-in-Law. *Specials*: A Place at the Table, My Dissident Mom, Peacemaker (Triple Play II).

HACK, SHELLEY
Actress. b. Greenwich, CT, July 6, 1952. e. Smith Coll. and U. of Sydney, Australia. Made modeling debut at 14 on cover of Glamour Magazine. Gained fame as Revlon's Charlie Girl on TV commercials.
PICTURES: Annie Hall, If Ever I See You Again, Time After Time, The King of Comedy, Troll, The Stepfather, Blind Fear, Me Myself and I, The Finishing Touch.
TELEVISION: *Series*: Charlie's Angels, Cutter to Houston, Jack and Mike. *Movies*: Death on the Freeway, Trackdown: Finding the Goodbar Killer, Found Money, Single Bars Single Women, Bridesmaids, Casualty of War, Taking Back My Life: The Nancy Ziegenmeyer Story, Not in My Family, The Case of the Wicked Wives, Falling From the Sky: Flight 174, Freefall, Frequent Flyer.

HACKER, CHARLES R.
Executive. b. Milwaukee, WI, Oct. 8, 1920. e. U. of Wisconsin. Thea. mgr., Fox Wisc. Amuse. Corp., 1940; served in U.S.A.F., 1943-45; rejoined Fox Wisconsin Amusement Corp.; joined Standard Theatres Management Corp. 1947, on special assignments; apptd. district mgr. of Milwaukee & Waukesha theatres 1948; joined Radio City Music Hall Corp. as administrative asst. July, 1948; mgr. of oper., 1952; asst. to the pres., Feb. 1957; v.p., Radio City Music Hall Corp., 1964; appointed executive vice president and chief operating officer, February 1, 1973. Pres., Landmark Pictures, May, 1979. Treas. Will Rogers Memorial Fund, 1978-95. Award: Quigley Silver Grand Award for Showmanship, 1947. Member: U.S. Small Business Admin. Region 1, Hartford Advisory Council 1983-93.

HACKETT, BUDDY
Actor. r.n. Leonard Hacker. b. Brooklyn, NY, Aug. 31, 1924. Prof. debut, borscht circuit.
THEATER: *B'way*: Call Me Mister, Lunatics and Lovers, I Had a Ball.
PICTURES: Walking My Baby Back Home (debut, 1953), Fireman Save My Child, God's Little Acre, Everything's Ducky, All Hands on Deck, The Music Man, The Wonderful World of the Brothers Grimm, It's a Mad Mad Mad Mad World, Muscle Beach Party, The Golden Head, The Good Guys and the Bad Guys (cameo), The Love Bug, Loose Shoes, Hey Babe!, Scrooged, The Little Mermaid (voice).
TELEVISION: *Series*: School House, Stanley, Jackie Gleason Show, Jack Paar Show, You Bet Your Life (1980), Fish Police (voice). *Movie*: Bud and Lou.*Specials*: Entertainment 55, Variety, The Mama Cass TV Program, Plimpton: Did You Hear the One About...?, Jack Frost (voice), Circus of the Stars, Buddy Hackett—Live and Uncensored.

HACKFORD, TAYLOR
Director, Producer. b. Santa Barbara, CA, Dec. 31, 1944. e. USC, B.A. (international relations). Was Peace Corps volunteer in Bolivia 1968-69. Began career with KCET in Los Angeles 1970-77. As prod.-dir. won Oscar for short, Teenage Father, 1978. Theatrical film debut as director with The Idolmaker (1980).
PICTURES: *Director*: The Idolmaker, An Officer and a Gentleman. *Dir./Prod.*: Against All Odds, White Nights, Chuck Berry: Hail! Hail! Rock 'n' Roll (dir. only), Everyone's All-American, Bound By Honor/Blood In Blood Out, Dolores Claiborne. Prod.: La Bamba. *Exec. Prod.*: Rooftops, The Long Walk Home, Sweet Talker, Queens Logic, Defenseless, Mortal Thoughts.

HACKMAN, GENE
Actor. b. San Bernardino, CA, Jan. 30, 1930. First major broadway role in Any Wednesday. Other stage productions include: Poor Richard, Children from Their Games, A Rainy Day in Newark, The Natural Look, Death and the Maiden. Formed own production co., Chelly Ltd.
PICTURES: Mad Dog Coll (debut, 1961), Lilith, Hawaii, A Covenant With Death, Bonnie and Clyde (Acad. Award nom.), First to Fight, Banning, The Split, Riot, The Gypsy Moths, Downhill Racer, Marooned, I Never Sang for My Father (Acad. Award nom.), Doctors' Wives, The Hunting Party, The French Connection (Academy Award, 1971), Cisco Pike, Prime Cut, The Poseidon Adventure, Scarecrow, The Conversation, Zandy's Bride, Young Frankenstein, Night Moves, Bite the Bullet, French Connection II, Lucky Lady, The Domino Principle, A Bridge Too Far, March or Die, Superman, All Night Long, Superman II, Reds, Eureka, Under Fire, Uncommon Valor, Misunderstood, Target, Twice in a Lifetime, Power, Hoosiers, Superman IV, No Way Out, Another Woman, Bat-21, Split Decisions, Full Moon in

Blue Water, Mississippi Burning (Acad. Award nom.), The Package, Loose Cannons, Postcards From the Edge, Narrow Margin, Class Action, Company Business, Unforgiven (Academy Award, Natl. Soc. of Film Critics, NY Film Critics, BAFTA, LA Film Critics & Golden Globe Awards, best supporting actor, 1992), The Firm, Geronimo: An American Legend, The Quick and the Dead, Crimson Tide, Get Shorty, Birdcage, Extreme Measures, The Chamber.
TELEVISION: *Guest*: U.S. Steel Hour, The Defenders, Trials of O'Brien, Hawk, CBS Playhouse's My Father My Mother, The F.B.I., The Invaders, The Iron Horse. *Movie*: Shadow on the Land.

HADLOCK, CHANNING M.
Marketing. TV Executive. b. Mason City, IA. e. Duke U., U. of North Carolina. Newspaperman, Durham, NC Herald, war corr., Yank; NBC, Hollywood; television prod.-writer, Cunning-ham & Walsh Adv.; v.p. account supr. Chirug & Cairns Adv.; v.p. Marketing Innovations; dir. mktg. Paramount Pictures; mktg. svcs, Ogilvy & Mather; mktg, Time Life Books.

HAGERTY, JULIE
Actress. b. Cincinnati, OH, June 15, 1955. Studied drama for six years before leaving for NY where studied with William Hickey. Made acting debut in her brother Michael's theatre group in Greenwich Village called the Production Company.
THEATER: The Front Page (Lincoln Center), The House of Blue Leaves (Theatre World Award, 1986), Wild Life, Born Yesterday (Phil. Drama Guild), The Years, Three Men on a Horse, Wifey, A Cheever Evening.
PICTURES: Airplane! (debut, 1980), A Midsummer Night's Sex Comedy, Airplane II: The Sequel, Lost in America, Goodbye New York, Bad Medicine, Beyond Therapy, Aria, Bloodhounds of Broadway, Rude Awakening, Reversal of Fortune, What About Bob?, Noises Off, The Wife.
TELEVISION: *Series*: Princesses. Specials: The Visit (Trying Times). House of Blue Leaves, Necessary Parties. *Movie*: The Day the Women Got Even.

HAGGAR, PAUL JOHN
Executive. b. Brooklyn, NY, Aug. 5, 1928. e. LA h.s. Veteran of over 40 yrs. with Paramount Pictures, working way up from studio mail room to become apprentice editor in 1953; promoted to asst. editor 1955; music editor, 1957. 1968, named head of post-prod. for all films and TV made by Paramount. 1985, named sr. v.p., post-prod. for the Motion Picture Group.

HAGGARD, PIERS
Director. b. London, 1939. e. U. of Edinburgh. Son of actor Stephen Haggard; great grandnephew of author Rider Haggard. Began career in theatre in 1960 as asst. to artistic dir. at London's Royal Court. Named director of Glasgow Citizens' Theatre, 1962. 1963-65 worked with the National Theatre, where co-directed Hobson's Choice and The Dutch Courtesan. Has directed many prize winning TV commercials.
PICTURES: Wedding Night (debut, 1969; also co-s.p.), Blood on Satan's Claw (Satan's Skin), The Fiendish Plot of Dr. Fu Manchu, Venom, A Summer Story.
TELEVISION: *Series*: Pennies from Heaven, Quatermass, Return to Treasure Island, Centrepoint, Space Precinct. *Specials/Movies*: A Triple Play: Sam Found Out (Liza Minnelli special), The Fulfillment of Mary Gray, Back Home, Quatermass Conclusion, Chester Cycle of Mystery Plays, Mrs. Reinhardt, Knockback, Visitors, Heartstones, I'll Take Romance, Four Eyes and Six-Guns, Eskimo Day, Heartstones.

HAGMAN, LARRY
Actor. b. Fort Worth, TX, Sept. 21, 1931. e. Bard Coll. Son of late actress Mary Martin. First stage experience with Margo Jones Theatre in the Round in Dallas. Appeared in N.Y. in Taming of the Shrew; one year with London production of South Pacific. 1952-56 was in London with US Air Force where produced and directed show for servicemen. Returned to N.Y. for plays on and off B'way: God and Kate Murphy (Theatre World Award), The Nervous Set, The Warm Peninsula, The Beauty Part.
PICTURES: Ensign Pulver, Fail Safe, In Harm's Way, The Group, The Cavern, Up in the Cellar, Son of Blob (aka: Beware! The Blob; also dir.), Harry and Tonto, Stardust, Mother Jugs and Speed, The Big Bus, The Eagle Has Landed, Checkered Flag or Crash, Superman, S.O.B., Nixon.
TELEVISION: *Series*: The Edge of Night, I Dream of Jeannie, The Good Life, Here We Go Again, Dallas. *Movies*: Three's a Crowd, Vanished, A Howling in the Woods, Getting Away from It All, No Place to Run, The Alpha Caper, Blood Sport, What Are Best Friends For?, Sidekicks, Hurricane, Sarah T.-Portrait of a Teenage Alcoholic, The Big Rip-Off, Return of the World's Greatest Detective, Intimate Strangers, The President's Mistress, Last of the Good Guys, Deadly Encounter, Staying Afloat, In the Heat of the Night: Who Was Geli Bendl? (dir. only), Dallas: Who Killed Jr?. *Special*: Applause.

HAHN, HELENE
Executive. b. New York, NY. e. Loyola U. Sch. of Law. Instructor of entertainment law at Loyola. Attorney for ABC before joining

Paramount in 1977 in studio legal dept. 1979, moved to business affairs; promoted to dir. 1980, v.p., 1981; sr. v.p., 1983. Left in 1985 to join Walt Disney Pictures as sr. v.p., business & legal affairs for m.p. division. 1987, promoted to exec. v.p., Walt Disney Studios.

HAID, CHARLES
Actor, Director, Producer. b. San Francisco, CA, June 2, 1943. e. Carnegie Tech. Appeared on NY stage in Elizabeth the First. Co-produced Godspell. Prod. & dir. short film The Last Supper.
PICTURES: Actor: The Choirboys, Who'll Stop the Rain, Oliver's Story, House of God, Altered States, Square Dance (co-exec. prod. only), Cop, The Rescue, Nightbreed, Storyville. Director: Iron Will.
TELEVISION: Series: Kate McShane, Delvecchio, Hill Street Blues, Cop Rock (prod. only). Movies: The Execution of Private Slovik, Remember When, Things in Their Season, Kate McShane (pilot), Foster and Laurie, A Death in Canaan, The Bastard, Death Moon, Twirl, Divorce Wars, Children in the Crossfire (also co-prod.), Code of Vengeance, Six Against the Rock, Weekend War, The Great Escape II: The Untold Story, A Deadly Silence, Fire and Rain, Man Against the Mob: The Chinatown Murders, In the Line of Duty: A Cop for the Killing (also co-prod.), In the Line of Duty: Siege at Marion (dir. only), The Nightman (dir., prod. only), Cooperstown (also dir.), For Their Own Good, The Fire Next Time, Broken Trust.

HAIM, COREY
Actor. b. Toronto, Canada, Dec. 23, 1972. Performed in TV commercials at 10; signed as regular on children's show, The Edison Twins.
PICTURES: Firstborn (debut, 1984), Secret Admirer, Silver Bullet, Murphy's Romance, Lucas, The Lost Boys, License to Drive, Watchers, Dream a Little Dream, Fast Getaway, Prayer of the Roller Boys, The Dream Machine, Oh What a Night, Blown Away, The Double-O Kid, National Lampoon's Last Resort, Fast Getaway 2, Tales from the Crypt: Bordello of Blood.
TELEVISION: Movies: A Time to Live, Just One of the Girls. Series: Roomies.

HAINES, RANDA
Director. b. Los Angeles, CA, Feb. 20, 1945. Raised in NYC. Studied acting with Lee Strasberg. e. School of Visual Arts. 1975 accepted into AFI's Directing Workshop for Women. Dir. & co-wrote short film August/September, which led to work as writer for series Family. Appeared in documentary Calling the Shots.
PICTURES: Children of a Lesser God, The Doctor, Wrestling Ernest Hemingway, A Family Thing (co-prod. only).
TELEVISION: Series: Family (writer), Hill Street Blues (dir. of 4 episodes), Alfred Hitchcock Presents (Bang You're Dead), Tales from the Crypt (Judy You're Not Yourself Today). Movie: Something About Amelia. Specials: Under This Sky, The Jilting of Granny Weatherall, Just Pals.

HALE, BARBARA
Actress. b. DeKalb, IL, April 18, 1922. Was married to late actor Bill Williams. Son is actor William Katt. e. Chicago Acad. of Fine Arts. Beauty contest winner, Little Theatre actress. Screen debut, 1943.
PICTURES: Gildersleeve's Bad Day, The Seventh Victim, Higher and Higher, Belle of the Yukon, The Falcon Out West, Falcon in Hollywood, Heavenly Days, West of the Pecos, First Yank in Tokyo, Lady Luck, A Likely Story, Boy with Green Hair, The Clay Pigeon, Window, Jolson Sings Again, And Baby Makes Three, Emergency Wedding, Jackpot, Lorna Doone, First Time, Last of the Comanches, Seminole, Lone Hand, A Lion Is in the Streets, Unchained, Far Horizons, Houston Story, 7th Cavalry, Oklahoman, Slim Carter, Desert Hell, Buckskin, Airport, Soul Soldier, Giant Spider Invasion, Big Wednesday.
TELEVISION: Series: Perry Mason (Emmy Award, 1959). Movies: Perry Mason Returns (1985) and 29 other Perry Mason's incl. The Case of the... Murdered Madam, Avenging Ace, Lady in the Lake, Scandalous Scoundrel, Lethal Lesson, Poisoned Pen, Fatal Fashion, Reckless Romeo.

HALEY, JR., JACK
Executive, Director. b. Los Angeles, CA, Oct.25, 1933. e. Loyola U. Son of late actor Jack Haley. 1959-67 Wolper Prods., 1967-73. sr. v.p. at Wolper before joining MGM. Named dir. of creative affairs. Left in 1974, to join 20th Century-Fox as pres. of TV div. and v.p., TV for 20th-Fox Film Corp. Winner of 2 Peabody Awards, best prod. at Int'l TV Festival at Monte Carlo and 3 Silver Lion Awards at Venice Film Festival. Won Emmy for best dir. in music or variety shows for Movin' On with Nancy. Directed Academy Awards Show in 1970; prod. it in 1974 and 1979. Left Fox 1976 to be indep. prod.
PICTURES: Director: Norwood, The Love Machine, That's Entertainment (also prod, s.p.), Better Late Than Never (prod. only), That's Dancing (also co-prod., s.p.).
TELEVISION: The Incredible World of James Bond, The Legend of Marilyn Monroe, The Supremes, The Hidden World, Movin' with Nancy (Emmy Award, dir., 1968), With Love Sophia, Monte Carlo, Life Goes to War: Hollywood and the Homefront; Heroes

of Rock n' Roll (exec. prod.), 51st Academy Awards (Emmy Award, 1979), Hollywood, the Golden Years (with David Wolper), Ripley's Believe It or Not, The Night They Saved Christmas, Cary Grant: A Celebration (exec. prod.).

HALL, ANTHONY MICHAEL
Actor. b. Boston, MA, Apr. 14, 1968.
PICTURES: Six Pack (debut, 1982), National Lampoon's Vacation, Sixteen Candles, The Breakfast Club, Weird Science, Out of Bounds, Johnny Be Good, Edward Scissorhands, A Gnome Named Norm, Into the Sun, Hail Caesar (also dir.), Six Degrees of Separation, Me and the Mob.
TELEVISION: Series: Saturday Night Live (1985-86). Mini-Series: Texas. Movies: Rascals and Robbers: The Secret Adventures of Tom Sawyer and Huck Finn, Running Out, A Bucket of Blood. Guest: NYPD Blue, Tales from the Crypt, Boys and Girls.

HALL, ARSENIO
Actor, Comedian. b. Cleveland, OH. Feb. 12, 1959. e. Kent State U. Became interested in magic at 7, which later led to own local TV special, The Magic of Christmas. Switched from advertising career to stand-up comedy, 1979. Discovered at Chicago nightclub by singer Nancy Wilson.
PICTURES: Amazon Women on the Moon (debut, 1987), Coming to America, Harlem Nights, Bopha! (exec. prod. only), Blankman.
TELEVISION: Series: The 1/2 Hour Comedy Hour (1983, co-host), Thicke of the Night, Motown Revue, The Late Show (1987, host), The Arsenio Hall Show, The Party Machine With Nia Peeples (prod. only).

HALL, CONRAD
Cinematographer. b. Papeete, Tahiti, June 21, 1926. Worked as camera operator with Robert Surtees, Ted McCord, Ernest Haller; moved to TV as director of photography before feature films.
PICTURES: Wild Seed, The Saboteur–Code Name: Morituri, Harper, The Professionals, Rogue's Gallery, Incubus, Divorce American Style, In Cold Blood, Cool Hand Luke, Hell in the Pacific, Butch Cassidy and the Sundance Kid (Academy Award, 1969), Tell Them Willie Boy Is Here, The Happy Ending, Fat City, Electra Glide in Blue, The Day of the Locust, Smile, Marathon Man, Black Widow, Tequila Sunrise, Class Action, Jennifer Eight, Searching for Bobby Fischer, Love Affair.
TELEVISION: Movie: It Happened One Christmas, Stoney Burke. Series: Outer Limits.

HALL, KURT C.
Executive. b. Burlington, VT. e. Univ. of VT. Served as dir. of financial reporting, dir. of finance, and v.p. & treas. of UA Entertainment before becoming v.p. & treas. of United Artists Theatre Circuit, 1990-91. Named exec. v.p. and CFO of United Artists Theatre Circuit, Inc.

HALL, HUNTZ (HENRY)
Actor. b. Boston, MA, Aug 15, 1920. In 1937 appeared in stage and screen production Dead End.
PICTURES: Dead End (debut, 1937), Crime School, Angels with Dirty Faces, They Made Me a Criminal, Hell's Kitchen, Muggs Rides Again, Live Wires, A Walk in the Sun, Jinx Money, Smuggler's Cove, Fighting Fools, Blues Busters, Bowery Battalion, Ghost Chasers, Crazy Over Horses, Let's Go Navy, Here Come the Marines, Hold That Line, Feudin' Fools, No Holds Barred, Private Eyes, Paris Playboys, Bowery Boys Meet the Monsters, Clipped Wings, Jungle Gents, Bowery to Bagdad, High Society, Spy Chasers, Jail Busters, Dig That Uranium, Up in Smoke, Second Fiddle to a Steel Guitar, Gentle Giant, The Phynx, Herbie Rides Again, The Manchu Eagle Murder Caper Mystery, Won Ton Ton the Dog Who Saved Hollywood, Valentino, Gas Pump Girls, The Escape Artist, Cyclone.
TELEVISION: Series: The Chicago Teddy Bears. Movie: Escape. Guest: Barefoot in the Park, Diff'rent Strokes, Night Heat.

HALL, MONTY; O.C.
Actor. b. Winnipeg, Manitoba, Canada, Aug. 25, 1925. e. U. of Manitoba, B.S. Host of Let's Make a Deal, 1964-86. International chmn., Variety Clubs International.

HALLSTROM, LASSE
Director. b. Stockholm, Sweden, 1946. m. actress Lena Olin. As teenager made 16mm film which was eventually screened on Swedish tv. Began professional career filming and editing inserts for Swedish TV. Directed program Shall We Dance? for Danish TV, followed by TV prod. on The Love Seeker, dir. of program Shall We Got to My or to Your Place or Each Go Home Alone?.
PICTURES: A Love and His Lass (debut, 1974), ABBA: The Movie, Father-to-Be, The Rooster, Happy We, The Children of Bullerby Village, More About the Children of Bullerby Village, My Life as a Dog (also co-s.p.); Acad. Award noms. for dir. & s.p.), Once Around (U.S. debut, 1991), What's Eating Gilbert Grape (also co-exec. prod.), Something to Talk About.

HALMI, ROBERT SR.
Producer. b. Budapest, Hungary, Jan 22, 1924. Originally writer-photographer under contract to Life Magazine.
PICTURES: Created documentaries for U.N. Features include: Hugo the Hippo, Visit to a Chief's Son, The One and Only, Brady's Escape, Cheetah, Mr. and Mrs. Bridge.
TELEVISION: Bold Journey (dir.-cin.), American Sportsman, The Oriental Sportsman, The Flying Doctor, The Outdoorsman, Julius Boros Series, Rexford, Who Needs Elephants, Calloway's Climb, Oberndorf Revisited, True Position, Wilson's Reward, Nurse, Buckley Sails, A Private Battle, My Old Man, Mr. Griffin and Me, When the Circus Came to Town, Best of Friends, Bush Doctor, Peking Encounter, Svengali, China Rose, Cook and Peary-The Race to the Pole, Terrible Joe Moran, Nairobi Affair, The Night They Saved Christmas, Spies, Lies and Naked Thighs, exec. prod.: The Prize Pulitzer, Paradise, Bridesmaids, Face to Face, Margaret Bourke-White, The Incident, Josephine Baker Story, The Secret, An American Story, Call of the Wild, Blind Spot, Incident in a Small Town, Spoils of War, The Yearling, A Promise Kept: The Oksana Baiul Story, A Mother's Gift, Scarlett, Reunion, My Brother's Keeper, White Dwarf, Secrets, Bye Bye Birdie, Kidnapped, Gulliver's Travels (Emmy Award, 1996), Captains Courageous, Dead Man's Walk.

HAMADY, RON
Producer. b. Flint, MI, June 16, 1947. e. U. of California, B.A. 1971. Co-founder of The Crystal Jukebox, record productions, music management and music publishing co. Produced 12 hit albums for Decca Records of England and London Records, U.S. Entered m.p. industry in 1975, producing Train Ride to Hollywood for Taylor-Laughlin dist. Co.
PICTURES: Fade to Black, Surf II, And God Created Woman (1987), Out Cold, Don't Tell Her It's Me.

HAMEL, VERONICA
Actress. b. Philadelphia, PA, Nov. 20, 1943. e. Temple U. Moved to NY and began a modelling career with Eileen Ford Agency. Off B'way debut: The Big Knife. Acted in dinner theater prods. Moved to L.A. 1975.
THEATER: B'way: Rumors. Off B'way: The Big Knife, The Ballad of Boris K.
PICTURES: Cannonball, Beyond the Poseidon Adventure, When Time Ran Out, A New Life, Taking Care of Business.
TELEVISION: Movies: The Gathering, Ski Lift to Death, The Gathering II, The Hustler of Muscle Beach, Valley of the Dolls, Sessions, Twist of Fate, She Said No, Stop at Nothing, Deadly Medicine (also co-exec. prod.), Baby Snatcher (also co-exec. prod.), The Disappearance of Nora, The Conviction of Kitty Dodds, Shadow of Obsession, A Child's Cry for Help, Intensive Care, Secrets, Here Come the Munsters, Blink of an Eye, Brother's Keeper. Mini-Series: 79 Park Avenue, Kane & Abel. Series: Hill Street Blues. Guest: Kojak, Rockford Files, Bob Newhart Show, Switch.

HAMILL, MARK
Actor. b. Oakland, CA, Sept. 25, 1951. While studying acting at LA City Col. made prof. debut in episode of The Bill Cosby Show, 1970. Featured in CD-ROM interactive game Wing Commander III.
THEATER: NY: The Elephant Man (B'way debut), Amadeus (also Natl. tour), Harrigan 'n' Hart, Room Service (off-B'way), The Nerd.
PICTURES: Star Wars (debut, 1977), Wizards (voice), Corvette Summer, The Empire Strikes Back, The Big Red One, The Night the Lights Went Out in Georgia, Britannia Hospital, Return of the Jedi, Slipstream, Midnight Ride, Black Magic Woman, Sleepwalkers (cameo), Time Runner, The Guyver, Batman: Mask of the Phantasm (voice), Village of the Damned.
TELEVISION: Series: General Hospital, The Texas Wheelers, Batman (voice). Movies: Sarah T.-Portrait of a Teenage Alcoholic, Eric, Delancey Street: The Crisis Within, Mallory: Circumstantial Evidence, The City, Earth Angel, Body Bags, Hollyrock-a-Bye Baby (voice). Guest: Room 222, The Partridge Family, Headmaster, Medical Center, Owen Marshall, The FBI, Streets of San Francisco, One Day at a Time, Manhunter, Hooperman, Alfred Hitchcock Presents, Amazing Stories, The Flash, seaQuest DSV. Specials: Get High on Yourself, Night of 100 Stars.

HAMILTON, GEORGE
Actor. b. Memphis, TN, Aug. 12, 1939. e. grammar, Hawthorne, CA; military sch., Gulfport, MS, N.Y. Hacker Prep Sch., FL, Palm Beach H.S. Won best actor award in Florida, high sch. contest.
PICTURES: Crime and Punishment USA (debut, 1959), Home From the Hill, All the Fine Young Cannibals, Where the Boys Are, Angel Baby, By Love Possessed, A Thunder of Drums, Light in the Piazza, Two Weeks in Another Town, Act One, The Victors, Looking for Love, Your Cheatin' Heart, Viva Maria, That Man George, Doctor You've Got to Be Kidding!, Jack of Diamonds, A Time for Killing, The Power, Togetherness, Evel Knievel (also co-p, The Man Who Loved Cat Dancing, Once Is Not Enough, The Happy Hooker Goes to Washington, Love at First Bite (also co-

exec. prod.), Sextette, From Hell to Victory, Zorro the Gay Blade (also co-prod.), The Godfather Part III, Doc Hollywood, Once Upon a Crime.
TELEVISION: Mini-Series: Roots. Movies: Two Fathers' Justice, Monte Carlo, Poker Alice, Caution: Murder Can Be Hazardous to Your Health, The House on Sycamore Street, Two Fathers: Justice for the Innocent, Danielle Steel's Vanished. Series: The Survivors, Paris 7000, Dynasty, Spies, The George and Alana Show (also prod.). Guest: Rin Tin Tin, The Donna Reed Show. Special: The Veil.

HAMILTON, GUY
Director. b. Paris, France, Sept. 24, 1922. Ent. m.p. industry 1939 as apprentice at Victorine Studio, Nice; Royal Navy, 1940-45, in England asst. dir., Fallen Idol, Third Man, Outcast of the Islands, African Queen.
PICTURES: The Ringer, The Intruder, An Inspector Calls, Colditz Story, Manuela, The Devil's Disciple, A Touch of Larceny, The Best of Enemies, The Party's Over, Man in the Middle, Goldfinger, Funeral in Berlin, Battle of Britain, Diamonds Are Forever, Live and Let Die, The Man with the Golden Gun, Force Ten from Navarone, The Mirror Crack'd, Evil Under the Sun, Remo Williams.

HAMILTON, LINDA
Actress. b. Salisbury, MD, Sept. 26, 1956. Appeared on NY stage in Looice and Richard III.
PICTURES: Tag: The Assassination Game, Children of the Corn, The Stone Boy, The Terminator, Black Moon Rising, King Kong Lives!, Mr. Destiny, Terminator 2: Judgment Day, Silent Fall, The Shadow Conspiracy.
TELEVISION: Series: Secrets of Midland Heights, King's Crossing, Beauty and the Beast. Movies: Reunion, Rape and Marriage-The Rideout Case, Country Gold, Secrets of a Mother and Daughter, Secret Weapons, Club Med, Go Toward the Light, A Mother's Prayer. Guest: Hill Street Blues, Murder She Wrote.

HAMLIN, HARRY
Actor. b. Pasadena, CA, Oct. 30, 1951. e. U. of California, Yale U., 1974 in theatre, psychology. Awarded IT&T Fulbright Grant, 1977. Joined American Conservatory Theatre, San Francisco, for two years' study before joining McCarter Theatre, Princeton (Hamlet, Faustus in Hell.). B'way debut Awake and Sing! (1984).
PICTURES: Movie Movie (debut, 1978), King of the Mountain, Clash of the Titans, Making Love, Blue Skies Again, Maxie, Save Me.
TELEVISION: Mini-Series: Studs Lonigan, Master of the Game, Space, Favorite Son. Movies: Laguna Heat, Deceptions, Deadly Intentions... Again?, Deliver Them From Evil: The Taking of Alta View, Poisoned By Love: The Kern County Murders, In the Best of Families: Marriage Pride & Madness, Tom Clancy's Op Center, Her Deadly Rival. Series: L.A. Law.

HAMLISCH, MARVIN
Composer. b. New York, NY, June 2, 1944. e. Juilliard. Accompanist and straight man on tour with Groucho Marx 1974-75; debut as concert pianist 1975 with Minn. Orch. Scores of Broadway shows: A Chorus Line (Tony Award); They're Playing Our Song, Smile, The Goodbye Girl. Winner 4 Grammy Awards.
PICTURES: The Swimmer, Take the Money and Run, Bananas, Save the Tiger, Kotch, The Way We Were (2 Acad. Awards for orig. score and title song, 1973), The Sting (Acad. Award for music adapt., 1973), The Spy Who Loved Me, Same Time Next Year, Ice Castles, Chapter Two, Seems Like Old Times, Starting Over, Ordinary People, The Fan, Sophie's Choice, I Ought to Be in Pictures, Romantic Comedy, D.A.R.Y.L., Three Men and a Baby, Little Nikita, The January Man, The Experts, Frankie and Johnny, Open Season.
TELEVISION: Series: Good Morning America (theme), Brooklyn Bridge. Movies: The Entertainer (also prod.), A Streetcar Named Desire, The Two Mrs. Grenvilles, Women & Men: Stories of Seduction, Switched at Birth, Seasons of the Heart.

HAMMOND, PETER
Actor, Writer, Director. b. London, Eng., Nov.15, 1923. e. Harrow Sch. of Art. Stage debut: Landslide, Westminster Theatre. Screen debut: Holiday Camp. Dir./writer, 1959-61, tv plays.
PICTURES: The Huggetts, Helter Skelter, Fools Rush In, The Reluctant Widow, Fly Away Peter, The Adventurers, Operation Disaster, Come Back, Peter, Little Lambs Eat Ivy, Its Never Too Late, The Unknown, Morning Departure, Confession. Dir.: Spring and Port Wine.
TELEVISION: Series: William Tell, Robin Hood, The Buccaneers. Dir.: Avengers, 4 Armchair Theatres, Theatre 625, BBC classic serials Count of Monte Cristo, Three Musketeers, Hereward the Wake, Treasure Island, Lord Raingo, Cold Comfort Farm, The White Rabbit, Out of the Unknown, Follyfoot; Lukes Kingdom, Time to Think, Franklin's Farm, Sea Song, Shades of Greene, Our Mutual Friend, The House that Jack Built, The King of the Castle, The Black Knight, Kilvert's Diary, Turgenev's Liza, Wuthering Heights, Funnyman, Little World of Don Camillo, Rumpole of the Bailey, Bring on the Girls, Hallelujah Mary Plum,

Aubrey Beardsley, The Happy Autumn Fields, The Combination, Tales of the Unexpected, The Glory Hole, The Hard Word, Shades of Darkness-The Maze, The Blue Dress.

HAMNER, EARL
Producer, Writer. b. Schuyler, VA, July 10, 1923. e. U. of Richmond 1940-43, Northwestern U.; U of Cincinnati, Coll. Conservatory of Music, B.F.A., 1958. With WLW, Cincinnati, as radio writer-producer; joined NBC 1949 as writer; (The Georgia Gibbs Show, The Helen O'Connell Show); freelance 1961-71; writer, prod. Lorimar Prods. 1971-86; writer prod. Taft Entertainment 1986-; Pres. Amanda Prods.
PICTURES: Palm Springs Weekend, Spencer's Mountain, The Tamarind Seed, Charlotte's Web (adaptor), Where the Lilies Bloom.
TELEVISION: *Exec. prod.: Series*: The Waltons (creator, co-prod., narrator), Apple's Way (creator), The Young Pioneers (creator), Joshua's World, Falcon Crest, Boone (also creator), Morning Star/Evening Star (also narrator), *Movies*: The Homecoming: A Christmas Story (writer only), You Can't Get There From Here (writer only), A Wedding on Walton's Mountain, Mother's Day on Walton's Mountain, A Day of Thanks on Walton's Mountain (also actor), The Gift of Love--A Christmas Story (also writer).

HAMPSHIRE, SUSAN
O.B.E., 1995. **Actress**. b. London, Eng., May 12, 1941.
THEATER: Expresso Bongo, Follow That Girl, Fairy Tales of New York, Ginger Man, Past Imperfect, She Stoops to Conquer, On Approval, The Sleeping Prince, A Doll's House, Taming of the Shrew, Peter Pan, Romeo & Jeanette, As You Like It, Miss Julie, The Circle, Arms and the Man, Man and Superman, Tribades, An Audience Called Edward, The Crucifer of Blood, Night and Day, The Revolt, House Guest, Blithe Spirit, Married Love, A Little Night Music, The King and I, Noel & Gertie, Relative Values, Susanna Andler, Black Chiffon.
PICTURES: The Three Lives of Thomasina, Night Must Fall, Wonderful Life, Paris Au Mois d'Aout, The Fighting Prince of Donegal, The Trygon Factor, Monte Carlo or Bust, Rogan, David Copperfield, A Room in Paris, Living Free, Time for Loving, Malpertius, Baffled, Neither the Sea nor the Sand, Roses and Green Peppers, David the King, Bang.
TELEVISION: Andromeda, The Forsyte Saga, Vanity Fair, Katy, The First Churchills; An Ideal Husband, The Lady Is a Liar, The Improbable Mr. Clayville, Dr. Jekyll and Mr. Hyde (musical), The Pallisers, Barchester Chronicles, Leaving, Leaving II, Going to Pot (I, II, and III), Don't Tell Father.

HAMPTON, JAMES
Actor. b. Oklahoma City, OK, July 9, 1936. e. N. Texas St. Univ.
PICTURES: Fade In, Soldier Blue, The Man Who Loved Cat Dancing, The Longest Yard, W.W. & The Dixie Dancekings, Hustle, Hawmps!, The Cat from Outer Space, Mackintosh & T.J., The China Syndrome, Hangar 18, Condorman, Teen Wolf, Teen Wolf Too, Police Academy 5, Pump Up the Volume, The Giant of Thunder Mountain.
TELEVISION: *Series*: F Troop, The Doris Day Show, Love—American Style, Mary, Maggie. *Movies*: Attack on Terror: The FBI Versus the Ku Klux Klan, Force Five, The Amazing Howard Hughes, Three on a Date, Thaddeus Rose and Eddie, Stand By Your Man, Through the Magic Pyramid, World War III, The Burning Bed. *Mini-Series*: Centennial.

HANCOCK, JOHN
Director. b. Kansas City, MO, Feb. 12, 1939. e. Harvard. Was musician and theatre director before turning to films. Dir. play A Man's a Man, NY 1962. Artistic dir. San Francisco Actors Workshop 1965-66, Pittsburgh Playhouse 1966-67. Obie for dir. Midsummer Night's Dream, NY 1968. Nominated for AA for short, Sticky My Fingers, Fleet My Feet.
PICTURES: Let's Scare Jessica to Death, Bang the Drum Slowly, Baby Blue Marine, California Dreaming, Weeds (also co-s.p.), Prancer.
TELEVISION: The Twilight Zone (1986), Hill Street Blues.

HAND, BETHLYN J.
Executive. b. Alton, IL. e. U. of Texas. Entered motion picture industry in 1966 as administrative assistant to president of Motion Picture Association of America, Inc. In 1975 became associate director of advertising administration of MPAA. In 1976 became director of advertising administration; in 1979 became; v.p.-west coast activities, board of directors, Los Angeles. S.P.C.A. 1981, appointed by Governor to Calif. Motion Picture Council 1983, elected vice chmn.; California Motion Picture Council. 1990, named sr. v.p. MPAA.

HANDEL, LEO A.
Producer, Director. b. Vienna, Austria, Mar. 7, 1924. e. Univ. of Vienna (Ph.D. economics). Dir. audience research, MGM, 1942-51; organized Meteor Prod., 1951; organized Leo A. Handel Prod., for TV films, 1953; author, Hollywood Looks at Its Audience, also TV plays; pres., Handel Film Corp. Exec. prod. & v.p., Four Crown Prods., Inc. Prod.-writer-dir., feature film, The Case of Patty Smith, 1961; book, A Dog Named Duke, 1965.

TELEVISION: prod. TV series including Everyday Adventures, Magic of the Atom. exec. prod., Phantom Planet, Americana Series. Also produced numerous educational specials and videos.

HANKS, TOM
Actor. b. Concord, CA, July 9, 1956. m. actress Rita Wilson. Traveled around Northern CA. with family before settling in Oakland, CA. e. Chabot Jr. Col., California State U. Began career with Great Lakes Shakespeare Festival, Cleveland (3 seasons) and NY's Riverside Theater (Taming of the Shrew).
PICTURES: He Knows You're Alone (debut, 1980), Splash, Bachelor Party, The Man With One Red Shoe, Volunteers, The Money Pit, Nothing in Common, Every Time We Say Goodbye, Dragnet, Big (Acad. Award nom.), Punchline, The 'Burbs, Turner and Hooch, Joe Versus the Volcano, The Bonfire of the Vanities, Radio Flyer (unbilled), A League of Their Own, Sleepless in Seattle, Philadelphia (Academy Award, 1993; Golden Globe Award), Forrest Gump (Academy Award, 1994; Golden Globe Award), Apollo 13, Toy Story (voice), That Thing You Do! (also dir.).
TELEVISION: *Series*: Bosom Buddies. *Guest*: The Love Boat, Taxi, Happy Days, Family Ties, Saturday Night Live, Tales from the Crypt (None but the Lonely Heart; also dir.), Fallen Angels (I'll Be Waiting; also dir.), The Naked Truth. *Movie*: Rona Jaffe's Mazes and Monsters. *Episode Dir.*: A League of Their Own.

HANNA, WILLIAM
Executive. b. Melrose, NM, July 14, 1910 e. Compton Coll. Studied engineering and journalism. Joined firm in CA as structural engineer; turned to cartooning with Leon Schlessinger's company in Hollywood. In 1937 hired by MGM as director and story man in cartoon dept. There met Joseph R. Barbera and created famous cartoon series Tom & Jerry, continuing to produce it from 1938 to 1957. Left MGM in 1957 to form Hanna-Barbera Productions to make cartoons for TV. Series have included Yogi Bear, Huckleberry Hound, The Flintstones, The Jetsons. Hanna-Barbera became a subsidiary of Taft Broadcasting Co. in 1968 with both men operating studio under long-term agreements with Taft (which became Great American Broadcasting, 1987). Received Governor's Award from Academy of Television Arts & Sciences, 1988.
PICTURES: Hey There It's Yogi Bear, A Man Called Flintstone, Charlotte's Web, C.H.O.M.P.S., Heidi's Song, Once Upon a Forest, The Flintstones (co-exec. prod. of live-action film; also cameo appearance).
TELEVISION: *Series*: The Huckleberry Hound Show (Emmy Award), Quick Draw McGraw, The Flintstones, The Jetsons, Jonny Quest, Top Cat, Scooby-Doo, Smurfs (2 Emmy Awards). *Movies*: I Yabba Dabba Do!, Hollyrock-a-Bye Baby.

HANNAH, DARYL
Actress. b. Chicago, IL, 1960. Niece of cinematographer Haskell Wexler. e. UCLA. Studied ballet with Maria Tallchief. Studied acting with Stella Adler.
PICTURES: The Fury (debut, 1978), The Final Terror, Hard Country, Blade Runner, Summer Lovers, Reckless, Splash, The Pope of Greenwich Village, Clan of the Cave Bear, Legal Eagles, Roxanne, Wall Street, High Spirits, Crimes and Misdemeanors, Steel Magnolias, Crazy People, At Play in the Fields of the Lord, Memoirs of an Invisible Man, Grumpy Old Men, The Little Rascals, The Tie That Binds, Two Much, Grumpier Old Men.
TELEVISION: *Movies*: Paper Dolls, Attack of the 50 Ft. Woman (also co-prod.).

HANNEMANN, WALTER A.
Film editor. b. Atlanta, GA, May 2, 1914. e. USC, 1935. Editorial training, RKO 1936-40; edit. supvr., Universal, 1941-42; consultant 1970-75 national educational media. Bd. of govs., TV Academy (2 terms, 1960 & 1970); bd. of govs., AMPAS. 1983-86; board of dir., Motion Picture Film Editors, 1944-48, 1981-88, past v.p., American Cinema Editors.
PICTURES: Interval, The Revengers, Dream of Kings, Guns of the Magnificent Seven, Krakatoa: East of Java, The Bob Mathias Story, Pay or Die, Al Capone, (Amer. Cinema Editor's Award, 1959), Hell's Five Hours, Armoured Command, Only the Valiant, Time of Your Life, Kiss Tomorrow Goodbye, Blood on the Sun, Guest in the House, Texas Masquerade, Cannon for Cardoba, El Condor, Maurie, Lost in the Stars, Big Mo, Two Minute Warning (Acad. Award nom.) Smokey and the Bandit (Acad. Award nom.), The Other Side of the Mountain-Part II, The Visitor, The Villain, The Nude Bomb, Charlie Chan and the Curse of the Dragon Queen.
TELEVISION: *Series*: Death Valley Days, Reader's Digest, Rosemary Clooney Show, The New Breed, The Fugitive, Twelve O'Clock High, The Invaders, Hawaii Five-O, Streets of San Francisco, Cannon, Barnaby Jones, Caribe. Movies: The Man Who Broke a 1000 Chains, Intimate Strangers, The Abduction of Saint Anne, The Day the Loving Stopped.Han

HANSON, CURTIS
Director, Writer. b. Los Angeles, CA, 1946. Editor of Cinema magazine before becoming screenwriter.

PICTURES: *Writer*: The Silent Partner, White Dog, Never Cry Wolf. *Director*: The Arousers (Sweet Kill), Little Dragons, The Bedroom Window (also s.p.), Bad Influence, The Hand That Rocks the Cradle, The River Wild.
TELEVISION: *Movie*: The Children of Times Square.

HARBACH, WILLIAM O.
Producer. b. Yonkers, NY, Oct. 12, 1919, e. Brown U. Father was lyricst Otto Harbach. Served with U.S. Coast Guard, 1940-45; actor, MGM, 1945-47; broadcast co-ordinator. NBC, 1947-49; stage mgr., 1949-50; dir., NBC, 1950-53
TELEVISION: *Producer*: Tonight, Steve Allen Show, Bing Crosby shows (also dir.), Milton Berle Special, Hollywood Palace, The Julie Andrews Show (Emmy Award, 1973), Shirley MacLaine's Gypsy in My Soul (Emmy Award, 1976), Bob Hope Specials.

HARBERT, TED
Executive. e. Boston Univ. 1976-77, prod. of new dept. at WHDH radio in Boston. Joined ABC, 1977 as feature film coordinator; 1979, named supervisor, feature film and late-night program planning, then assst. to v.p., program planning & scheduling; 1981, became dir. program planning & scheduling; 1984, promoted to v.p. program planning & scheduling; 1987, named v.p. motion pictures and scheduling, ABC Entertainment; 1988, v.p., prime time, ABC Entertainment; 1989, became exec. v.p., Prime Time, ABC Entertainment; 1993, promoted to pres. of ABC Entertainment.

HARDEN, MARCIA GAY
Actress. b. La Jolla, CA, Aug. 14, 1959.
Father was naval captain. Schooled in Athens, Munich, then returned to states attending Univ. of TX, NYU. Stage work in Washington D.C. in Crimes of the Heart, The Miss Firecracker Contest.
THEATER: *Off-B'way*: The Man Who Shot Lincoln (debut, 1989), Those the River Keeps, The Skin of Our Teeth, The Years, Simpatico. *B'way*: Angels in America: Millenium Approaches/ Perestroika (Theatre World Award; Tony nom.)
PICTURES: Miller's Crossing (debut, 1990), Late for Dinner, Used People, Crush, Safe Passage, The Spitfire Grill, The First Wives Club, Spy Hard.
TELEVISION: *Mini-Series*: Sinatra. *Movie*: Fever.

HARDISON, KADEEM
Actor. b. Brooklyn, NY, July 24, 1966. Studied acting with Earl Hyman and at H.B.Studios.
PICTURES: Beat Street (debut, 1984), Rappin', School Daze, I'm Gonna Git You Sucka, Def by Temptation, White Men Can't Jump, Gunmen, Renaissance Man, Panther, Vampire in Brooklyn.
TELEVISION: *Series*: A Different World. *Specials*: The Color of Friendship, Amazing Grace, Don't Touch, Go Tell It on the Mountain. *Movie*: Dream Date. *Guest*: The Cosby Show, Spenser for Hire.

HARE, DAVID
Writer, Director. b. St. Leonards, Sussex, England, June 5, 1947. e. Lancing Coll., Jesus Coll., Cambridge. After leaving univ. in 1968 formed Portable Theatre Company, experimental touring group. Hired by Royal Court Theater as literary manager, 1969. 1970, first full-length play, Slag, prod. at Hampstead Theatre Club. Resident dramatist, Royal Court (1970-71), and Nottingham Playhouse (1973). Assoc. dir., National Theatre. West End debut, Knuckle.
THEATER: Slag, The Great Exhibition, Brassneck, Knuckle, Fanshen, Teeth 'n' Smiles, Plenty, A Map of the World, Pravda, The Bay at Nice, Secret Rapture, Racing Demon, Murmuring Judges, Rules of the Game (new version of Pirandello Play), Brecht's The Absence of War, Skylight, Galileo, Mother Courage.
PICTURES: *Writer*: Plenty, Wetherby (also dir.), Paris by Night (also dir.), Strapless (also dir.), Damage.
TELEVISION: *Writer*: Licking Hitler (also dir.), Dreams of Leaving (also dir.), Saigon: Year of the Cat, Knuckle, Heading Home (also dir.).

HAREWOOD, DORIAN
Actor. b. Dayton, OH, Aug. 6, 1950. m. actress Ann McCurry. e. U. of Cincinnati.
THEATER: Jesus Christ Superstar (road co.), Two Gentlemen of Verona, Miss Moffat, Streamers, Over Here, Don't Call Back (Theatre World Award), The Mighty Gents.
PICTURES: Sparkle (debut, 1976), Gray Lady Down, Looker, Tank, Against All Odds, The Falcon and the Snowman, Full Metal Jacket, Pacific Heights, Solar Crisis, The Pagemaster (voice), Sudden Death.
TELEVISION: *Series*: Strike Force, Trauma Center, Glitter, The Trials of Rosie O'Neill, Viper. *Mini-Series*: Roots: The Next Generations, Amerika. *Movies*: Foster and Laurie, Panic in Echo Park, Siege, An American Christmas Carol, High Ice, Beulah Land, The Ambush Murders, I Desire, The Jesse Owens Story, Guilty of Innocence, God Bless the Child, Kiss Shot, Polly, Polly-Comin' Home!, Getting Up and Going Home, Bermuda Grace, Shattered Image. *Pilot*: Half 'n' Half.

HARGREAVES, JOHN
Executive. b. Freckleton, Lancashire, Eng., July 1921. Joined Gainsborough Pictures 1945. Transferred to Denham Studios 1946 and later Pinewood Studios. Joined Allied Film Makers 1960, then Salamander Film Productions as Bryan Forbes' financial controller and asst. prod. 1965. Joined EMI Film Prods. Ltd. as asst. man. dir. and prod. controller 1969-72. 1983-, U.K. dir. and production executive for Completion Bond Company, Inc. Cal. USA.
PICTURES: Don Quixote (prod.), The Slipper and the Rose (prod. asst.), International Velvet (assoc. prod.), The Awakening (prod. rep.), The Fiendish Plot of Dr. Fu Manchu (post-prod. exec.), Excalibur (prod. rep.), The Year of Living Dangerously, Carrington (financial consultant).

HARKINS, DANIEL E.
Executive, Exhibitor. b. Mesa, AZ, Feb. 6, 1953. e. Arizona State U. Joined Harkins Theatres in 1968. Acquired company in 1975. President and CEO Harkins Amusement Enterprises, Inc. National NATO bd. member. Pres., Arizona Theatre Assoc. V.P., Governor's Film Commission. Recipient of United Motion Picture Assoc. National Showman of the Year award 1976, 1980, 1981. Hollywood Reported Marketing Concept award, 1983. Box Office Showmandizer award, 1976, 1978, and several others.

HARLIN, RENNY
Director. b. Helsinki, Finland, 1958. e. Univ. of Helsinki film school. Formed prod. co. Midnight Sun Pictures. m. actress Geena Davis.
PICTURES: Born American (debut, 1986), Prison, A Nightmare on Elm Street IV: The Dream Master, Die Hard 2, The Adventures of Ford Fairlane, Rambling Rose (prod. only), Cliffhanger, Speechless (co-prod. only), Cutthroat Island (also prod.), The Long Kiss Goodnight.

HARMON, MARK
Actor. b. Burbank, CA, Sept. 2, 1951. Son of actress Elyse Knox and football star Tom Harmon. m. actress Pam Dawber. Brother of actresses Kelly and Kristin Harmon. On stage in Wrestlers, The Wager (both L.A.), Key Exchange (Toronto).
PICTURES: Comes a Horseman, Beyond the Poseidon Adventure, Let's Get Harry, Summer School, The Presidio, Stealing Home, Worth Winning, Till There Was You, Cold Heaven, Wyatt Earp, Magic in the Water, The Last Supper.
TELEVISION: *Series*: Sam, 240-Robert, Flamingo Road, St. Elsewhere, Reasonable Doubts, Charlie Grace. *Movies*: Eleanor and Franklin: The White House Years, Getting Married, Little Mo, Flamingo Road (pilot), The Dream Merchants, Goliath Awaits, Intimate Agony, The Deliberate Stranger, Prince of Bel Air, Sweet Bird of Youth, Dillinger, Fourth Story, Long Road Home, Shadow of a Doubt. *Guest*: Adam-12, Laverne & Shirley, Nancy Drew, Police Story, Moonlighting. *Mini-Series*: Centennial.

HARNELL, STEWART D.
Executive. b. New York, NY, Aug. 18, 1938. e. U. of Miami, UCLA, New School for Social Research. Entertainer with Youth Parade in Coral Gables, FL, 1948-55, performing for handicapped children, Variety Club, etc. as singer, dancer, musician. Had own bands, Teen Aces & Rhythm Rascals, 1950-56; performed on Cactus Jim TV show and Wood & Ivory, 1953-54, WTVJ, Miami. Catskills, Sand Lake, NY, 1954-55. Joined National Screen Service as exec. trainee in 1960 in Chicago; worked as booker & salesman. Transferred to NY home office, 1963; worked in special trailer production. Promoted to asst. gen. sls. mgr., 1964-66; New Orleans branch mgr., 1966-67; Atlanta division mgr., 1967-70. Formed own distribution co., 1970-77 Harnell Independent Productions. Resumed post as gen. sls. mgr. of NSS, New York, 1977-78; In 1986, founded Cinema Concepts, Inc. Chief dealer at Variety Club of Atlanta, Tent 21, 1972, 1976, 1979, 1988, 1989, 1993, 1994. In 1986 formed Cinema Concepts Communications, film-video animation studio in Atlanta. Motion Picture Pioneers Bd. of Directors (1990-97).

HARPER, JESSICA
Actress. b. Chicago, IL, Oct. 10, 1949. m. prod. exec. Thomas E. Rothman. e. Sarah Lawrence Coll. Understudied on Broadway for Hair for one year. Appeared in summer stock and off-B'way shows (Richard Farina: Long Time Coming Longtime Gone, Doctor Selavy's Magic Theatre.)
PICTURES: Taking Off, Phantom of the Paradise, Love and Death, Inserts, Suspiria, The Evictors, Stardust Memories, Shock Treatment, Pennies from Heaven, My Favorite Year, The Imagemaker, Once Again, The Blue Iguana, Big Man on Campus, Mr. Wonderful, Safe.
TELEVISION: *Series*: Little Women, It's Garry Shandling's Show. *Mini-Series*: Studs Lonigan, Aspen (The Innocent and the Damned), When Dreams Come True. *Special*: The Garden Party. *Guest*: Tales From the Darkside, The Equalizer, Trying Times (Bedtime Story), Wiseguy.

HARPER, TESS
Actress. b. Mammoth Springs, AR, 1952. e. Southwest Missouri State Coll., Springfield. Worked in Houston, then Dallas in children's theater, dinner theater, and commercials.

PICTURES: Tender Mercies (debut, 1983), Amityville 3-D, Silkwood, Flashpoint, Crimes of the Heart (Acad. Award nom.), Ishtar, Far North, Her Alibi, Criminal Law, Daddy's Dyin'... Who's Got the Will?, My Heroes Have Always Been Cowboys, The Man in the Moon, My New Gun.
TELEVISION: Mini-Series: Chiefs, Celebrity. Movies: Kentucky Woman, Starflight: The Plane That Couldn't Land, A Summer to Remember, Promises to Keep, Little Girl Lost, Unconquered, In the Line of Duty: Siege at Marion, Willing to Kill: The Texas Cheerleader Story, Death in Small Doses.

HARPER, VALERIE
Actress. b. Suffern, NY. Aug. 22, 1940. e. Hunter Coll, New Sch. for Social Research. Started as dancer in stage shows at Radio City Music Hall. First professional acting in summer stock in Conn.; actress with Second City Chicago 1964-69; Appeared on B'way. in Lil' Abner, Take Me Along, Wildcat, Subways Are for Sleeping, Something Different, Story Theatre, Metamorphoses. Won 3 Emmys for best performance in supporting role in comedy for portrayal of Rhoda on The Mary Tyler Moore Show and 1 for best leading actress on Rhoda. Off B'way, Death Defying Acts (1995-96).
PICTURES: Rock Rock Rock, Lil Abner, Freebie and the Bean, Chapter Two, The Last Married Couple in America, Blame It on Rio.
TELEVISION: Series: The Mary Tyler Show, Rhoda, Valerie, City, The Office. Movies: Thursday's Game, Night Terror, Fun and Games, The Shadow Box, The Day the Loving Stopped, Farrell for the People (pilot), Don't Go to Sleep, An Invasion of Privacy, Execution, Strange Voices, Drop Out Mother, The People Across the Lake, Stolen: One Husband, A Friend To Die For, The Great Mom Swap.

HARRELSON, WOODY
Actor. b. Midland, TX, July 23, 1961. e. Hanover Col. First professional acting job as understudy for B'way production of Biloxi Blues.
THEATER: NY: The Boys Next Door. LA: 2 on 2 (also wrote & prod.), The Zoo Story (also prod.), Brooklyn Laundry.
PICTURES: Wildcats (debut, 1986), Cool Blue, L.A. Story, Doc Hollywood, Ted and Venus, White Men Can't Jump, Indecent Proposal, I'll Do Anything, The Cowboy Way, Natural Born Killers, Money Train, The Sunchaser, Kingpin, The People vs. Larry Flynt.
TELEVISION: Series: Cheers (Emmy Award, 1989). Movies: Bay Coven, Killer Instinct. Special: Mother Goose Rock 'n' Rhyme.

HARRINGTON, CURTIS
Director, Writer. b. Los Angeles, CA, Sept. 17, 1928. e. U. of Southern California, B.A. Exec. asst. to Jerry Wald, 1955-61 Associate producer at 20th Cent. Fox.
PICTURES: Assoc. Prod.: Mardi Gras (also story), Hound Dog Man, Return to Peyton Place, The Stripper. Director: Night Tide (also s.p.), Queen of Blood (Planet of Blood; also s.p.), Games (also co-story), What's the Matter with Helen?, Who Slew Auntie Roo?, The Killing Kind, Ruby, Mata Hari.
TELEVISION: Series episodes: Hotel, Dynasty, The Colby's, Tales of the Unexpected, Twilight Zone, Baretta, Vega$, Glitter, Logan's Run. Movies: How Awful About Allan, The Cat Creature, Killer Bees, The Dead Don't Die, Devil Dog: The Hound of Hell.

HARRINGTON, PAT
Actor. b. New York, NY, Aug. 13, 1929. e. Fordham U. Served USAF as 1st Lt., 1952-54. Time salesman for NBC, 1954-58.
PICTURES: The Wheeler Dealers, Move Over Darling, Easy Come Easy Go, The President's Analyst, 2000 Years Later, The Candidate.
TELEVISION: Series: The Steve Allen Show, The Danny Thomas Show, The Jack Paar Show, Stump the Stars (host), Mr. Deeds Goes to Town, One Day at a Time (Emmy Award, 1984).

HARRIS, BARBARA
Actress. b. Evanston, IL, July 25, 1935. r.n. Sandra Markowitz. e. Wright Junior Coll., Chicago; Goodman Sch. of the Theatre; U. of Chicago. Joined acting troup, The Compass. Founding member, Second City Players, 1960. Came to NY where first role was in Oh Dad Poor Dad Mama's Hung You in the Closet and I'm Feeling So Sad (Theatre World Award), repeating role in film version.
THEATER: Mother Courage and Her Children, Dynamite Tonight, On a Clear Day You Can See Forever, The Apple Tree (Tony Award, 1967), Mahogany.
PICTURES: A Thousand Clowns (debut, 1965), Oh Dad Poor Dad Mama's Hung You in the Closet and I'm Feeling So Sad, Plaza Suite, Who Is Harry Kellerman and Why Is He Saying Those Terrible Things About Me? (Acad. Award nom.), The War Between Men and Women, The Manchu Eagle Murder Caper Mystery, Mixed Company, Nashville, Family Plot, Freaky Friday, Movie Movie, The North Avenue Irregulars, The Seduction of Joe Tynan, Second Hand Hearts, Peggy Sue Got Married, Nice Girls Don't Explode, Dirty Rotten Scoundrels.
TELEVISION: Guest: Alfred Hitchcock Presents, Naked City, The Defenders.

HARRIS, BURTT
Producer, Actor. Began career as actor; later worked with Elia Kazan as prod. asst. and asst. dir. on America America, Splendor in the Grass, and The Arrangement. Worked as second unit dir. and asst. dir. on many films as well as producer and actor.
PICTURES: Associate Producer: Little Murders, The Wiz, Cruising, Gilda Live. Executive Producer: The Verdict, Just Tell Me What You Want,. See No Evil, Hear No Evil, Family Business. Producer: Prince of the City, Daniel, Deathtrap, Garbo Talks, The Glass Menagerie, Q & A. Co-Producer: D.A.R.Y.L. Actor: Splendor in the Grass, Fail Safe, The Taking of Pelham 1-2-3, The Wanderers, The Verdict, Daniel, Garbo Talks, D.A.R.Y.L., Running on Empty, Hudson Hawk, Undertow, A Stranger Among Us.

HARRIS, ED
Actor. b. Tenafly, NJ, Nov. 28, 1950. m. actress Amy Madigan. Played football 2 years at Columbia U. prior to enrolling in acting classes at OK State U. Summer stock. Grad. CA Institute of the Arts, B.F.A, 1975. Worked in West Coast Theater.
THEATER: NY: Fool For Love (Off-B'way debut; Obie Award), Precious Sons (B'way debut; Theatre World Award), Simpatico, Taking Sides. LA: Scar.
PICTURES: Coma (debut, 1978), Borderline, Knightriders, Dream On, Creepshow, The Right Stuff, Under Fire, Swing Shift, Places in the Heart, Alamo Bay, A Flash of Green, Sweet Dreams, Code Name: Emerald, Walker, To Kill a Priest, Jacknife, The Abyss, State of Grace, Glengarry Glen Ross, The Firm, Needful Things, China Moon, Milk Money, Just Cause, Apollo 13, Eye for an Eye, Nixon, The Rock.
TELEVISION: Movies: The Amazing Howard Hughes, The Seekers, The Aliens Are Coming (Alien Force), The Last Innocent Man, Paris Trout, Running Mates, Riders of the Purple Sage. Mini-Series: The Stand.

HARRIS, JAMES B.
Producer, Director, Writer. b. New York, NY, Aug. 3, 1928. e. Juilliard Sch. U.S. film export, 1947; Realart Pictures, 1948; formed Flamingo Films, 1949; formed Harris-Kubrick Productions, 1954. formed James B. Harris Prods., Inc., 1963.
PICTURES: Producer: The Killing, Paths of Glory, Lolita, The Bedford Incident (also dir.), Some Call It Loving (also dir., s.p.), Telefon, Fast-Walking (also dir., s.p.), Cop (also dir., s.p.), Boiling Point (dir., s.p.).

HARRIS, JULIE
Designer. b. London, England. e. Chelsea Arts Sch. Entered industry in 1945 designing for Gainsborough Studios. First film, Holiday Camp.
PICTURES: Greengage Summer, Naked Edge, The War Lover, Fast Lady, Chalk Garden, Psyche 59, A Hard Day's Night, Darling, Help!, The Wrong Box, Casino Royale, Deadfall, Prudence and the Pill, Decline and Fall, Goodbye Mr. Chips, Sherlock Holmes, Follow Me!, Live and Let Die, Rollerball, Slipper and The Rose, Dracula.
TELEVISION: Laura (with Lee Radziwill), Candleshoe, The Sailor's Return, Lost and Found, The Kingfisher, Arch of Triumph, Sign of Four, Hound of the Baskervilles, A Hazard of Hearts, A Perfect Hero.

HARRIS, JULIE
Actress. b. Grosse Pointe, MI, Dec. 2, 1925. e. Yale Drama Sch.
THEATER: Sundown Beach, Playboy of the Western World, Macbeth, Young and the Fair, Magnolia Alley, Monserrat, Member of the Wedding, I Am a Camera (Tony Award, 1952), Colombe, The Lark (Tony Award, 1956), A Shot in the Dark, Marathon 33, Ready When You Are, C.B., Break a Leg, Skyscraper, Voices, And Miss Reardon Drinks a Little, 40 Carats (Tony Award, 1969), The Last of Mrs. Lincoln (Tony Award, 1973), In Praise of Love, The Belle of Amherst (Tony Award, 1973), Driving Miss Daisy (Natl. co.), Lucifer's Child, Lettice & Lovage (tour), The Fiery Furnace (Off-B'way debut, 1993), The Glass Menagerie.
PICTURES: The Member of the Wedding (debut, 1952; Acad. Award nom.), East of Eden, I Am a Camera, The Truth About Women, The Poacher's Daughter, Requiem for a Heavyweight, The Haunting, Harper, You're a Big Boy Now, Reflections in a Golden Eye, The Split, The People Next Door, The Hiding Place, Voyage of the Damned, The Bell Jar, Nutcracker: The Motion Picture (voice), Gorillas in the Mist, Housesitter, The Dark Half, Carried Away.
TELEVISION: Specials: Little Moon of Alban (Emmy Award, 1959), Johnny Belinda, A Doll's House, Ethan Frome, The Good Fairy, The Lark, He Who Gets Slapped, The Heiress, Victoria Regina (Emmy Award, 1962), Pygmalion, Anastasia, The Holy Terror, The Power and The Glory, The Woman He Loved. Movies: The House on Greenapple Road, How Awful About Alan, Home for the Holidays, The Greatest Gift, The Gift, Too Good To Be True, The Christmas Wife, They've Taken Our Children: The Chowchilla Kidnapping, When Love Kills: The Seduction of John Hearn, One Christmas. Series: Thicker Than Water, The Family Holvak, Knots Landing. Mini-Series: Backstairs at the White House, Scarlett.

HARRIS, MEL
Actress. b. Bethlehem, PA, July 12, 1957. r.n. Mary Ellen Harris. e. Columbia. Career as successful model before turning to acting in 1984. NY theatre debut in Empty Hearts, 1992 (Theatre World Award).
PICTURES: Wanted: Dead or Alive, Cameron's Closet, K-9, Raising Cain, Desperate Motive (Distant Cousins), Suture, The Pagemaster.
TELEVISION: *Series*: thirtysomething, Something So Right. *Guest*: M*A*S*H, Alfred Hitchcock Presents, Rags to Riches, Heart of the City, The Wizard. *Movies*: Seduced, Harry's Hong Kong, Cross of Fire, My Brother's Wife, The Burden of Proof, Grass Roots, Child of Rage, With Hostile Intent, Desperate Journey: The Allison Wilcox Story, Ultimate Betrayal, The Spider and the Fly, The Women of Spring Break, Sharon's Secret.

HARRIS, NEIL PATRICK
Actor. b. Albuquerque, NM, June 15, 1973. While attending week-long theatre camp at New Mexico St. Univ. met writer Mark Medoff who suggested him for co-starring role in Clara's Heart.
THEATER: Luck Pluck and Virtue (Off-B'way debut, 1995).
PICTURES: Clara's Heart (debut, 1988), Purple People Eater, Hairspray.
TELEVISION: *Series*: Doogie Howser M.D., Capitol Critters (voice). *Movies*: Too Good to Be True, Home Fires Burning, Cold Sassy Tree, Stranger in the Family, A Family Torn Apart, Snowbound: The Jim and Jennifer Stolpa Story, Not Our Son, My Antonia, The Man in the Attic, Legacy of Sin: The William Coit Story. *Guest*: B. J. Stryker, Carol & Company, Roseanne, Quantum Leap, Murder She Wrote.

HARRIS, RICHARD
Actor. b. Limerick, Ireland, Oct. 1, 1930. Attended London Acad. of Music and Dramatic Arts. Prod.-dir. Winter Journey 1956. Prof. acting debut in Joan Littlewood's prod. of The Quare Fellow, Royal Stratford, 1956. Recorded hit song MacArthur's Park, 1968. Author of novel Honor Bound (1982) and poetry compilation: I in the Membership of My Days (1973).
THEATER: *London*: A View from the Bridge, Man Beast and Virtue, The Ginger Man. *B'way*: Camelot.
PICTURES: Alive and Kicking (debut, 1958), Shake Hands With the Devil, The Wreck of the Mary Deare, A Terrible Beauty (Night Fighters), The Long The Short and The Tall (Jungle Fighters), The Guns of Navarone, Mutiny on the Bounty, This Sporting Life (Acad. Award nom.), Red Desert, Major Dundee, The Heroes of Telemark, The Bible, Hawaii, Caprice, Camelot, The Molly Maguires, A Man Called Horse, Cromwell, The Hero (Bloomfield; also dir., s.p.), Man in the Wilderness, The Deadly Trackers, 99 and 44/100% Dead, Juggernaut, Echoes of a Summer (also co-exec. prod.), Robin and Marian, Return of a Man Called Horse (also co-exec. prod.), The Cassandra Crossing, Gulliver's Travels, Orca, Golden Rendezvous, The Wild Geese, Ravagers, The Last Word, Game for Vultures, Your Ticket Is No Longer Valid, Highpoint, Tarzan the Ape Man, Martin's Day, Triumphs of a Man Called Horse, Mack the Knife, The Field (Acad. Award nom.), Patriot Games, Unforgiven, Wrestling Ernest Hemingway, Silent Tongue, Savage Hearts, Cry the Beloved Country.
TELEVISION: *Specials*: Ricardo, The Iron Harp, The Snow Goose, Camelot. *Movies*: Maigret, The Return.

HARRIS, ROBERT A.
Archivist, Producer. b. New York, NY, Dec. 27, 1945. e. NYU, Sch. of Commerce and Sch. of Arts, 1968. Worked as exec. trainee with 7 Arts assoc., NY while in school, 1960-68; worked in corp. communications, Pepsico, 1970-71; formed Center for Instructional Resources, SUNY Purchase, 1971-73; organized Images Film Archive, dist. of classic theatrical and non theat. films, 1974; pres., Images Video and Film Archive, 1985; formed Davnor Prods., president 1986-present; formed The Film Preserve, Ltd. pres. 1989-. 1975-80: restored Abel Gance films Beethoven, J'Accuse, Lucretia Borgia; 1974-79: worked with Kevin Brownlow to complete restoration of Abel Gance's Napoleon. Partnered with Francis Coppola/Zoetrope Studios to present Napoleon at Radio City Music Hall, 1981 and worldwide tour; 1986-89; reconstruction and restoration of David Lean's Lawrence of Arabia for Columbia Pictures, released 1989; The Grifters (prod.); restoration and reconstruction of Stanley Kubrick's Spartacus for Univ. Pictures, 1991; restoration of George Cukor's My Fair Lady for CBS Video, 1994, restoration in SuperVistaVision 70 of Alfred Hitchcock's Vertigo, 1996.

HARRIS, ROSEMARY
Actress. b. Ashby, Suffolk, Sept. 19, 1930. e. India and England. Early career, nursing; studied Royal Acad. of Dramatic Art, 1951-52.
THEATER: Climate of Eden (NY debut 1952), Seven Year Itch, Confidential Clerk (Paris Festival), and with Bristol Old Vic in The Crucible, Much Ado About Nothing, Merchant of Venice. With Old Vic, 1955-56; U.S. tour, 1956-57; U.S. stage, 1958-63. Chichester Festivals 1962 and 63; Nat'l Theatre 1963-64; You Can't Take It With You, 1965; The Lion in Winter (Tony Award, 1966), 1967, APA Repertory Co., Heartbreak House, The Royal Family, The New York Idea (Obie Award), Pack of Lies, Hay Fever, Lost in Yonkers, An Inspector Calls, A Delicate Balance.
PICTURES: Beau Brummell, The Shiralee, A Flea in Her Ear, The Boys from Brazil, The Ploughman's Lunch, Crossing Delancey, Tom and Viv (Acad. Award nom.), Hamlet.
TELEVISION: *Series*: The Chisholms. *Specials*: Cradle of Willow (debut, 1951), Othello, The Prince and the Pauper, Twelfth Night, Wuthering Heights, Notorious Woman (Emmy Award, 1976), Blithe Spirit, Profiles in Courage, To the Lighthouse, Strange Interlude, Tales From the Hollywood Hills: The Old Reliable. *Mini-Series*: Holocaust (Golden Globe Award), The Chisholms.

HARRIS, TIMOTHY
Writer, Producer. b. Los Angeles, CA, July 21, 1946. e. Charterhouse, 1963-65; Peterhouse Coll., Cambridge, 1966-69, M.A. Honors Degree, Eng. lit. Author of novels, Kronski/McSmash, Kyd For Hire, Goodnight and Goodbye; author of novelizations, Steelyard Blues, Hit, Heatwave, American Gigolo.
PICTURES: Co-writer with Herschel Weingrod: Cheaper to Keep Her, Trading Places (BAFTA nom., orig. s.p.; NAACP Image Awards, best m.p. 1983), Brewster's Millions, My Stepmother is an Alien, Paint It Black, Twins (People's Choice Award, best comedy, 1988), Kindergarten Cop, Pure Luck. Co-Prod.: Falling Down.
TELEVISION: Street of Dreams (based on his novel Goodnight and Goodbye; also exec. prod.).

HARRISON, GEORGE
Singer, Composer, Producer. b. Liverpool, England, Feb. 25, 1943. Former member, The Beatles. Winner of 2 Grammys on own in addition to Beatles' group awards. Founder of Handmade Films.
PICTURES: *Performer*: A Hard Day's Night (debut, 1964), Help!, Yellow Submarine (cameo), Let It Be, The Concert for Bangladesh (also prod.). *Exec. Prod.*: Little Malcolm. *Exec. Prod.* (for Handmade Films): Life of Brian (also cameo), Time Bandits, Monty Python Live at the Hollywood Bowl, The Missionary, Privates on Parade, Scrubbers, Bullshot, A Private Function, Water (also cameo), Mona Lisa, Shanghai Surprise (also songs, cameo), Withnail and I, Five Corners, Bellman and True, The Lonely Passion of Judith Hearne, Track 29, How to Get Ahead in Advertising, Powwow Highway, Checking Out, Cold Dog Soup, Nuns on the Run, The Raggedy Rawney.

HARRISON, GREGORY
Actor, Producer, Director. b. Avalon, Catalina Island, CA, May 31, 1950. Started acting in school plays; then joined Army (1969-71). Studied at Estelle Harman Actors Workshop; later with Lee Strasberg and Stella Adler. Formed Catalina Productions with Franklin Levy, 1981.
THEATER: Child's Play, Carnal Knowledge, Picnic, The Hasty Heart, Love Letters, Festival, Billy Budd, The Subject Was Roses, The Promise, The Music Man, Paper Moon- The Musical.
PICTURES: Jim: the World's Greatest (debut, 1976), Fraternity Row, Razorback, North Shore (also 2nd unit dir.), Voice of a Stranger (also 2nd unit dir.), Cadillac Girls, It's My Party.
TELEVISION: *Series*: Logan's Run, Trapper John M.D. (also dir. 6 episodes), Falcon Crest, The Family Man, True Detectives, New York News. *Guest*: M*A*S*H, Barnaby Jones, Sisters. *Movies* (actor): The Gathering, Enola Gay, Trilogy in Terror, The Best Place To Be, The Women's Room, For Ladies Only (also co-prod.), The Fighter, Seduced (also exec. prod.), Oceans of Fire, Hot Paint, Red River, Dangerous Pursuit, Angel of Death, Bare Essentials, Breaking the Silence, Duplicates, Split Images, Caught in the Act, A Family Torn Apart, Lies of the Heart: The Story of Laurie Kellogg, Robin Cook's Mortal Fear, A Christmas Romance, A Dangerous Affair, Nothing Lasts Forever. *Mini-series*: Centennial, Fresno, 500 Nations (narrator). *Movies* (exec. prod. only): Thursday's Child, Legs, Samson & Delilah, The Tower.

HARROLD, KATHRYN
Actress. b. Tazewell, VA, Aug. 2, 1950. e. Mills Coll. Studied acting at Neighborhood Playhouse in N.Y., also with Uta Hagen. Appeared in Off-Off-B'way. plays for year; then joined experimental theatre group, Section Ten, touring East, performing and teaching at Connecticut Coll. and NYU. Cast in TV daytime serial, The Doctors.
PICTURES: Nightwing (debut, 1979), The Hunter, Modern Romance, The Pursuit of D.B. Cooper, Yes Gorgio, The Sender, Heartbreakers, Into the Night, Raw Deal, Someone to Love, The Companion.
TELEVISION: *Movies*: Son-Rise: A Miracle of Love, Vampire, The Women's Room, Bogie, An Uncommon Love, Women in White, Man Against the Mob, Dead Solid Perfect, Capital News, Rainbow Drive, Deadly Desire, The Companion. *Series*: The Doctors (1976-78), MacGruder and Loud, Bronx Zoo, I'll Fly Away, The Larry Sanders Show.

HARRYHAUSEN, RAY
Special Effects Expert, Producer, Writer. b. Los Angeles, CA, June 29, 1920. e. Los Angeles City Coll. While at coll. made

16mm animated film, Evolution, which got him job as model animator for George Pal's Puppetoons in early '40s. Served in U.S. Signal Corps; then made series of filmed fairy tales with animated puppets for schools and churches. In 1946 worked on Mighty Joe Young as ass't. to Willis O'Brien. Designed and created special visual effects for The Beast from 20,000 Fathoms; then began evolving own model animation system called Dynarama. In 1952 joined forces with prod. Charles H. Schneer, using new process for first time in It Came from Beneath the Sea. Subsequently made many films with Schneer in Dynamation. Received Gordon E. Sawyer Award for Acad. of Motion Picture Arts & Sciences, 1992. Appeared in films Spies Like Us, Beverly Hills Cop III.
PICTURES: Mighty Joe Young, The Beast From 20000 Fathoms, It Came From Beneath the Sea, Earth Vs. the Flying Saucers, Animal World, Twenty Million Miles to Earth, 7th Voyage of Sinbad, The Three Worlds of Gulliver, Mysterious Island, Jason and the Argonauts, First Men in the Moon, One Million Years B.C., The Valley of Gwangi, The Golden Voyage of Sinbad, Sinbad and the Eye of the Tiger (also co-prod.), Clash of the Titans (also co. prod.).

HART, GARRETT S.
Executive. e. Univ. of MA, Amherst; Queens Col/CUNY. 1979, joined Paramount as mngr. then v.p. of research; 1982, became dir. of comedy develp. Served as sr. v.p., research for Lorimar-Telepictures Corp. before joining Universal 1987; 1990, became sr. v.p., current programs. 1993, named pres. of the network tv division of the Paramount Television Group.

HARTLEY, HAL
Director, Writer. b. Long Island, NY, 1959. e. SUNY/Purchase (film). Following graduation made 3 short movies: Kid, The Cartographer's Girlfriend, Dogs. For PBS made the shorts Theory of Achievement, Ambition, Surviving Desire; also NYC 3/94, Opera No. 1. Music videos: The Only Living Boy in New York (Everything But the Girl), From a Motel 6 (Yo La Tengo), Iris.
PICTURES: Director/Writer. The Unbelievable Truth (debut, 1990), Trust, Simple Men, Amateur, Flirt (also actor, editor).

HARTLEY, MARIETTE
Actress. b. New York, NY, June 21, 1940. Student Carnegie Tech. Inst. 1956-57; studied with Eva Le Gallienne. Appeared with Shakespeare Festival, Stratford 1957-60. Co-host Today Show, 1980. Co-host on CBS Morning Show, 1987. Returned to stage in King John (NYSF in Central Park), 1989. Nominated for 6 Emmys for Best Actress. Received 3 Clio Awards, 1979, 1980, and 1981, for acting in commercials. Autobiography: Breaking the Silence.
PICTURES: Ride the High Country (debut, 1962), Drums of Africa, Marnie, Marooned, Barquero, The Return of Count Yorga, Skyjacked, The Magnificent Seven Ride!, Improper Channels, O'Hara's Wife, 1969, Encino Man.
TELEVISION: Series: Peyton Place, The Hero, Good Night Beantown, WIOU. Guest: The Rockford Files, The Incredible Hulk (Emmy Award, 1979), Stone. Movies: Earth II, Sandcastles, Genesis II, Killer Who Wouldn't Die, Last Hurrah, M.A.D.D.: Mothers Against Drunk Drivers, Drop-Out Father, One Terrific Guy, Silence of the Heart, My Two Loves, Murder C.O.D., Diagnosis of Murder, The House on Sycamore Street, Child of Rage, Heaven & Hell: North and South Book III, Falling From the Sky!: Flight 174. Mini-Series: Passion and Paradise. Special: The Halloween That Almost Wasn't.

HARTMAN, LISA
Actress. Houston, TX, June 1, 1956. m. musician Clint Black. Attended NYC's H.S. of Performing Arts prior to becoming a nightclub performer.
PICTURES: Deadly Blessing, Where the Boys Are.
TELEVISION: Series: Tabitha, Knots Landing, High Performance, 2000 Malibu Road. Movies: Murder at the World Series, Valentine Magic on Love Island, Where the Ladies Go, Gridlock, Jacqueline Susann's Valley of the Dolls 1981, Beverly Hills Cowgirl Blues, Full Exposure: The Sex Tapes Scandal, The Operation, The Take, Bare Essentials, Fire: Trapped on the 39th Floor, Not of This World, Red Wind, The Return of Eliot Ness, Without a Kiss Goodbye, Search for Grace, Dazzle, Someone Else's Child, Have You Seen My Son?

HARTMAN, PHIL
Actor. b. Branford, Ontario, Canada, Sept. 24, 1948. Raised in Connecticut and Los Angeles. e. Cal State Northridge (graphic design). Designed album covers before joining improv. comedy group the Groundlings.
PICTURES: Jumpin' Jack Flash, Three Amigos!, Blind Date, Fletch Lives, Quick Change, Coneheads, So I Married an Axe Murderer, Greedy, Houseguest, Sgt. Bilko, Jingle All the Way.
TELEVISION: Series: Six O'Clock Follies, Saturday Night Live, NewsRadio. Pilots: Top Ten, The Natural Snoop.

HARTZ, JIM
TV Newsman, Panelist. b. Tulsa, OK, Feb. 3, 1940. Pre-med student at U. of Tulsa, where worked in spare time as reporter for radio station KRMG. 1963 left studies for career as newsman and joined KOTV in Tulsa. 1964 moved to NBC News in New York, acting as reporter and anchorman. 1974 became co-host of Today Show, joined Barbara Walters.

HARU, SUMI
Executive. Acting pres., Screen Actors Guild.

HARVEY, ANTHONY
Director, Editor. b. London, Eng., June 3, 1931. Royal Acad. of Dramatic Art. Two yrs. as actor. Ent. m.p. ind. 1949 with Crown Film Unit.
PICTURES: Editor: Private's Progress, Brothers-in-Law, Man in a Cocked Hat (Carlton Brown of the F.O.), I'm Alright Jack, The Angry Silence, The Millionairess, Lolita, The L-Shaped Room, Dr. Strangelove, The Spy Who Came In From the Cold, The Whisperers. Director: Dutchman (debut, 1966), The Lion in Winter, They Might Be Giants, Players, The Abdication, Richard's Things, Grace Quigley.
TELEVISION: Movies: The Disappearance of Aimee, Svengali, The Patricia Neal Story, The Glass Menagerie, This Can't Be Love.

HARWOOD, RONALD
Writer. b. Cape Town, South Africa, 1934. e. Royal Acad. of Dramatic Art.
THEATER: The Dresser, Interpreters, J.J. Farr, Another Time, Reflected Glory, Poison Pen, Taking Sides.
PICTURES: Barber of Stamford Hill, Private Potter, High Wind in Jamaica, Arrivederci Baby, Diamonds for Breakfast, Sudden Terror (Eye Witness), One Day in the Life of Ivan Denisovich, Operation Daybreak (Price of Freedom), The Dresser, The Doctor and the Devils, The Browning Version, Cry the Beloved Country.
TELEVISION: The Barber of Stamford Hill, Private Potter, Take a Fellow Like Me, The Lads, Convalescence, Guests of Honor, The Guests. Adapted several of the Tales of the Unexpected, Mandela, Breakthrough at Rykjavik, Countdown to War, All the World's a Stage (series).

HASSANEiN, RICHARD C.
Executive. b. New York, NY, Aug. 13, 1951; e. Staunton Military Acad., 1966-70; American U., 1970-74. Booker/real estate dept. opns., United Artists Theater Circuit, 1974-77; joined United Film Distribution Co., 1977; 1978-88, pres. of UFD. 1988-91 served as pres., producers' rep., foreign & U.S. sls., of Myriad Enterprises. Joined Todd-AO Glen Glenn Studios in 1991 as v.p. of new bus. ventures. 1991 appointed exec. v.p. of Todd-AO Studios East, NY. 1993, elected to bd. of dirs. of Todd-AO Corp. 1995, appointed v.p. of Todd-AO Studios West, Los Angeles; 1996, pres. and COO of Todd-AO Studios West.

HASSANEIN, SALAH M.
Executive. b. Suez, Egypt, May 31, 1921. e. British Sch., Alexandria, Egypt. Nat'l Bank of Egypt, Cairo, 1939-42. Asst. division mgr. Middle East, 20th-Fox, Cairo, Egypt, 1942-44: U.S. armed forces, 1945-47; usher, asst. mgr., Rivoli Theatre, N.Y., 1947-48. Film buyer, booker, oper. v.p. U.A. Eastern Theas., 1948-59; pres. 1960; exec. v.p. U.A. Communications, Inc. 1960; v.p. United Artists Cable Corp., 1963. Exec. v.p., Todd-AO Corp., 1980. President, Warner Bros. International Theaters, 1988. President, Todd AO Corp., 1994.
PICTURES: Exec. prod.: Knightriders, Creepshow, Hello Again, Love or Money.

HASSELHOFF, DAVID
Actor. b. Baltimore, MD, July 17, 1952.
PICTURES: Starcrash, Witchery, W.B. Blue and the Bean.
TELEVISION: Series: The Young and the Restless, Knight Rider, Baywatch, Baywatch Nights. Movies: Griffin and Phoenix, Semi Tough, The Cartier Affair, Bridge Across Time, Perry Mason: The Case of the Lady in the Lake, Baywatch: Panic at Malibu Pier, Knight Rider 2000, Avalanche.

HASTINGS, DON
Actor. b. Brooklyn, NY, Apr. 1, 1934. e. Professional Children's Sch., Lodge H.S. On B'way in I Remember Mama, Summer and Smoke, etc.; Natl. co. of Life With Father; on various radio shows. Also wrote scripts for tv series The Guiding Light.
TELEVISION: Series: Captain Video, The Edge of Night, As the World Turns (also writer).

HATFIELD, HURD
Actor. b. New York, NY, Dec. 7, 1918. e. Morristown prep, Horace Mann, Riverdale Acad., Bard Col., Chekhov Drama Sch., Devonshire, Eng.
THEATER: Lower Depths, Twelfth Night, Cricket on the Hearth, King Lear, Venus Observed, Camino Real, Love's Labor's Lost, Bullfight, Julius Caesar, The Count of Monte Cristo, Son Juan in Hell, Son of Whistler's Mother, Stuttgart.
PICTURES: Dragon Seed (debut, 1944), The Picture of Dorian Gray, Diary of a Chambermaid, The Beginning or the End?, The Unsuspected, The Checkered Coat, Joan of Arc, Chinatown at

Midnight, Destination Murder, Tarzan and the Slave Girl, The Left-Handed Gun, King of Kings, El Cid, Harlow, Mickey One, The Boston Strangler, Von Richtofen and Brown, King David, Crimes of the Heart, Her Alibi.
TELEVISION: *Movies*: Thief, The Norliss Tapes, You Can't Go Home Again, Lies of the Twins. *Mini-Series*: The Word.

HATFIELD, TED
Executive. b. Wilton Junction, IA, Aug. 26, 1936. e. Hot Springs, AR. U.S. Army-NCO Academy, 1954. 1949-67 ABC Paramount Theatres, advanced from usher to district mgr. 1967-70 MGM asst. exploitation dir.; 1970-83, MGM national advertising coordinator; 1983-87, MGM/UA v.p., field operations. 1987-91, MGM/UA v.p., exhibitor relations. 1991-, Sony Pictures Releasing, v.p., exhib. rltns. Member: Motion Picture Pioneers, Western LA Council, Boy Scout Commissioner, Culver City Chamber of Commerce, past v.p./presidents award, Jaycees, Past State v.p., Advertising Federation, past state pres., Culver City Commissioner.

HAUER, RUTGER
Actor. b. Breukelen, Netherlands, Jan. 23, 1944. Stage actor in Amsterdam for six years.
PICTURES: Repelsteeltje (debut, 1973), Turkish Delight, Pusteblume, The Wilby Conspiracy, Keetje Tippel, Het Jaar van de Kreeft, Max Havelaar, Griechische Feigen, Soldier of Orange, Pastorale 1943, Femme Entre Chien et Loup, Mysteries (also co-prod.), Gripsta en de Gier, Spetters, Nighthawks, Chanel Solitaire, Blade Runner, Eureka, The Osterman Weekend, A Breed Apart, Ladyhawke, Flesh and Blood, The Hitcher, Wanted: Dead or Alive, The Legend of the Holy Drinker, Bloodhounds of Broadway, The Blood of Heroes, Blind Fury, Ocean Point, On a Moonlit Night, Past Midnight, Split Second, Buffy the Vampire Slayer, Arctic Blue, Beyond Forgiveness, Surviving the Game, Nostradamus, The Beans of Egypt Maine, Angel of Death.
TELEVISION: *Movies*: Escape from Sobibor, Inside The Third Reich, Deadlock, Blind Side, Voyage, Amelia Earhart: The Final Flight, Fatherland. *Series*: Floris (Netherlands TV). *Mini-Series*: Maketub: The Law of the Desert (Italy).

HAUG, WILLIAM F.
Executive. Pres. and CEO, Motion Picture and Television Fund.

HAUSER, WINGS
Actor. b. Hollywood, CA, 1947. Nickname derived from playing wing back on h.s. football team. Began studying acting in 1975.
PICTURES: First to Fight, Who'll Stop the Rain, Homework, Vice Squad, Deadly Force, Uncommon Valor (assoc. prod., story only), Mutant (Night Shadows), A Soldier's Story, Jo Jo Dancer Your Life is Calling, 3:15, Tough Guys Don't Dance, Nightmare at Noon, The Wind, Hostage, Dead Man Walking, The Carpenter, The Siege of Firebase Gloria, No Safe Haven (also co-s.p.), L.A. Bounty, Bedroom Eyes II, Beastmaster 2: Through the Portal of Time, Watchers 3.
TELEVISION: *Series*: The Young and the Restless, The Last Precinct, Lightning Force, Command 5, Roseanne. *Movies*: Hear No Evil, Ghost Dancing, The Long Hot Summer, Perry Mason: The Case of the Scandalous Scoundrel, Highway Man.

HAUSMAN, MICHAEL
Producer. Former stockbroker and still photographer. Entered film industry as assoc. prod. and prod. mgr. on The Heartbreak Kid and Taking Off. Worked as head of prod. for Robert Stigwood on Saturday Night Fever.
PICTURES: I Never Promised You a Rose Garden, Alambrista!, Heartland, Rich Kids, One-Trick Pony, Ragtime (exec. prod., 1st asst. dir.), The Ballad of Gregorio Cortez, Silkwood, Amadeus (exec. prod.), Places in the Heart (exec. prod.), Desert Bloom, Flight of the Spruce Goose, No Mercy, House of Games, Things Change, Valmont, State of Grace, Homicide, Nobody's Fool.
TELEVISION: Lip Service (exec. prod.).

HAVERS, NIGEL
Actor. b. London, Eng., Nov. 6, 1949. e. Leicester U., trained for stage at Arts Educational Trust. Father, Sir Michael Havers, was Attorney General of Britain. As child played Billy Owen on British radio series, Mrs. Dale's Diary. Records voice overs and books for the blind.
THEATER: Conduct Unbecoming, Richard II, Man and Superman (RSC), Family Voices, Season's Greetings, The Importance of Being Earnest.
PICTURES: Pope Joan (debut, 1972), Full Circle, Who is Killing the Great Chefs of Europe?, Chariots of Fire, A Passage to India, Burke and Wills, The Whistle Blower, Empire of the Sun, Farewell to the King, Clichy Days.
TELEVISION: *Series*: A Horseman Riding By, Don't Wait Up. *Mini-Series*: The Glittering Prizes, Nicholas Nickleby, Pennies From Heaven, Winston Churchill: The Wilderness Years, Nancy Astor, The Little Princess, Death of the Heart, Naked Under Capricorn, Sleepers. *Movies*: The Charmer, Private War of Lucina Smith, Lie Down With Lions, The Burning Season. *Guest*: Thriller, Star Quality: Noel Coward Stories (Bon Voyage), A Question of Guilt, Aspects of Love, Upstairs Downstairs, Edward VII, Liz: The Elizabeth Taylor Story.

HAVOC, JUNE
Actress. r.n. Hovick. b. Seattle, WA, Nov. 8, 1916. Sister was late Gypsy Rose Lee. Made film bow at 2 yrs. old in Hal Roach/Harold Lloyd productions billed as Baby June. Danced with Anna Pavlova troupe, then entered vaudeville in own act. Later, joined Municipal Opera Company, St. Louis, and appeared in Shubert shows. Musical comedy debut: Forbidden Melody (1936). To Hollywood, 1942. Author: Early Havoc (1959), More Havoc (1980).
THEATER: Pal Joey, Sadie Thompson, Mexican Hayride, Dunnigan's Daughter, Dream Girl, Affairs of State, The Skin of Our Teeth, A Midsummer Night's Dream (Stratford, CT. American Shakespeare Fest., 1958), Tour for U.S. Dept. of St., 1961; wrote Marathon 33. The Ryan Girl, The Infernal Machine, The Beaux Strategem, A Warm Peninsula, Dinner at Eight, Habeas Corpus. An Unexpected Evening with June Havoc (one woman show, London 1985), The Gift (tour), Eleemosynary, The Old Lady's Guide to Survival.
PICTURES: Four Jacks and a Jill (debut, 1941), Powder Town, My Sister Eileen, Sing Your Worries Away, Hi Diddle Diddle, Hello Frisco Hello, No Time for Love, Casanova Burlesque, Timber Queen, Sweet and Low Down, Brewster's Millions, Intrigue, Gentleman's Agreement, When My Baby Smiles at Me, The Iron Curtain, The Story of Molly X, Red Hot and Blue, Chicago Deadline, Mother Didn't Tell Me, Once a Thief, Follow the Sun, Lady Possessed, Three for Jamie Dawn, The Private Files of J. Edgar Hoover, Can't Stop the Music, Return to Salem's Lot.
TELEVISION: Anna Christie, The Bear, Cakes and Ale, Daisy Mayme, The Untouchables, Willy, MacMillan & Wife, The Paper Chase, Murder She Wrote. *Series*: More Havoc (1964-65), Search for Tomorrow, General Hospital.

HAWKE, ETHAN
Actor. b. Austin, TX, Nov. 6, 1970. Attended NYU. Studied acting at McCarter Theatre in Princeton, NJ, the British Theatre Assn., Carnegie Mellon U. Stage debut in St. Joan. Co-founder of Malaparte Theatre Co. in NYC. Dir. & wrote short film Straight to One.
THEATER: *NY*: Casanova (Off-B'way debut, 1991), A Joke, The Seagull (B'way debut, 1992), Sophistry, Hesh, The Great Unwashed.
PICTURES: Explorers (debut, 1985), Dead Poets Society, Dad, White Fang, Mystery Date, A Midnight Clear, Waterland, Alive, Rich in Love, Reality Bites, White Fang 2: Myth of the White Wolf (cameo), Quiz Show (cameo), Floundering, Before Sunrise, Search and Destroy.

HAWN, GOLDIE
Actress, Producer. b. Washington, DC, November 21, 1945. Started as professional dancer (performed in Can-Can at the N.Y. World's Fair, 1964), and made TV debut dancing on an Andy Griffith Special.
PICTURES: The One and Only Genuine Original Family Band (debut, 1968), Cactus Flower (Academy Award, best supporting actress, 1969), There's a Girl in My Soup, $ (Dollars), Butterflies Are Free, The Sugarland Express, The Girl From Petrovka, Shampoo, The Duchess and the Dirtwater Fox, Foul Play, Private Benjamin (Acad. Award nom.; also exec. prod.), Seems Like Old Times, Lovers and Liars (Travels With Anita), Best Friends, Swing Shift, Protocol (also exec. prod.), Wildcats (also exec. prod.), Overboard (also exec. prod.), Bird on a Wire, My Blue Heaven (co-exec. prod. only), Deceived, Crisscross (also co-exec. prod.), Housesitter, Death Becomes Her, Something to Talk About (exec. prod. only), The First Wives Club, Everyone Says I Love You.
TELEVISION: *Series*: Good Morning World, Rowan & Martin's Laugh-In (1968-70). *Specials*: The Goldie Hawn Special, Goldie & Liza Together, Goldie and the Kids: Listen to Us.

HAWTHORNE, NIGEL
Actor. b. Coventry, England, Apr. 5, 1929. Extensive career on stage. Ent. TV ind. 1953. Films, 1957. Won 1991 Tony Award for best actor for Shadowlands; Olivier & Evening Standard Awards for The Madness of George III (Natl. Th.).
PICTURES: Young Winston, The Hiding Place, Watership Down (voice), History of the World Part 1, Plague Dogs (voice), Firefox, Gandhi, The Black Cauldron (voice), The Chain, Turtle Diary, Freddie as F.R.O.7 (voice), Demolition Man, The Madness of King George (Acad. Award nom., BAFTA Award), Richard III, Inside, Twelfth Night.
TELEVISION: Mapp and Lucia, The Knowledge, The Miser, The Critic, Barchester Chronicles, Marie Curie, Edward and Mrs. Simpson, Yes Minister, Yes Prime Minister (series), The Oz Trials, Flea-Bites. The Shawl, Relatively Speaking, Late Flowering Lust.

HAYES, ISAAC
Musician, Actor. b. Covington, TN, Aug. 20, 1942. Was session musician with Stax Records in Memphis, eventually working as composer, producer. Debuted with solo album Presenting Isaac Hayes in 1968.
PICTURES: *Music*: Shaft (Academy Award for best song: Theme from Shaft, 1971), Shaft's Big Score. *Actor*: Wattstax,

Save the Children, Three Tough Guys (also music), Truck Turner (also music), Escape From New York, I'm Gonna Git You Sucka, Guilty as Charged, Posse, Robin Hood: Men in Tights, It Could Happen to You, Flipper.
TELEVISION: *Series theme:* The Men.

HAYES, JOHN MICHAEL
Writer. b. Worcester, MA, May 11, 1919. e. U. of Massachusetts, 1941.
PICTURES: Red Ball Express, Thunder Bay, Torch Song, War Arrow, Rear Window, To Catch a Thief, The Trouble with Harry, It's a Dog's Life, The Man Who Knew Too Much, The Matchmaker, Peyton Place, But Not for Me, Butterfield 8, The Children's Hour, Where Love Has Gone, The Chalk Garden, Judith, Nevada Smith.
TELEVISION: Pancho Barnes.

HAYES, PETER LIND
Actor. b. San Francisco, CA, June 25, 1915. m. Mary Healy. Was radio singer, actor, vaudeville, night clubs. Producer, Grace Hayes Lodge Review: on TV show with Mary Healy.
PICTURES: Million Dollar Legs, All Women Have Secrets, These Glamour Girls, Seventeen, Dancing on a Dime, Playmates, Seven Days Leave, The 5000 Fingers of Dr. T., Once You Kiss a Stranger.

HAYS, ROBERT
Actor. b. Bethesda, MD, July 24, 1947. e. Grossmont Coll., San Diego State U. Left school to join San Diego's Old Globe Theatre five years, appearing in such plays as The Glass Menagerie, The Man in the Glass Booth, Richard III.
PICTURES: Airplane! (debut, 1980), Take This Job and Shove It!, Utilities, Airplane II: The Sequel, Trenchcoat, Touched, Scandalous, Cat's Eye, Honeymoon Academy, Hot Chocolate, Homeward Bound: The Incredible Journey, Fifty Fifty, Raw Justice, Hoemward Bound II: Lost in San Francisco.
TELEVISION: *Series:* Angie, Starman, FM, Cutters. *Movies:* Young Pioneers, Young Pioneers' Christmas, Delta County U.S.A., The Initiation of Sarah, The Girl The Gold Watch and Everything, California Gold Rush, The Fall of the House of Usher, The Day the Bubble Burst, Murder by the Book, Running Against Time, Mr. Mom Till You Mow the Lawn, Deadly Invasion: The Killer Bee Nightmare, Danielle Steel's Vanished. *Mini-Series:* Will Rogers: Champion of the People. *Specials:* Mr. Roberts, Partners. *Guest:* Love Boat, Harry O, Laverne and Shirley.

HAYSBERT, DENNIS
Actor. b. San Mateo, CA, June 2.
THEATER: Wedding Band, Yanks-3 Detroit-0 Top of the Seventh, Diplomacy, Othello, On the Death of, All Over Town, Blood Knot, No Place to Be Somebody, Jimmy Shine, The Time of Your Life, Ten Little Indians.
PICTURES: Major League, Navy SEALS, Mr. Baseball, Love Field, Suture, Major League 2, Amanda, Waiting to Exhale.
TELEVISION: *Series:* Code Red, Off the Rack. *Mini-Series:* Queen. *Movies:* A Summer to Remember, Grambling's White Tiger, K-9000. *Specials:* The Upper Room, Hallelujah.

HEADLY, GLENNE
Actress. b. New London, CT, March 13, 1957. e. High Sch. of Performing Arts. Studied at HB Studios. In Chicago joined St. Nicholas New Works Ensemble. Won 3 Joseph Jefferson awards for work with Steppenwolf Ensemble in Say Goodnight Gracie, Miss Firecracker Contest, Balm in Gilead, Coyote Ugly, Loose Ends. Directed Canadian Gothic.
THEATER: *NY:* Balm in Gilead, Arms and the Man, Extremities, The Philanthropist (Theatre World Award).
PICTURES: Four Friends (debut, 1981), Dr. Detroit, Fandango, The Purple Rose of Cairo, Eleni, Making Mr. Right, Nadine, Stars and Bars, Dirty Rotten Scoundrels, Paperhouse, Dick Tracy, Mortal Thoughts, Getting Even With Dad, Mr. Holland's Opus, Sgt. Bilko, 2 Days in the Valley.
TELEVISION: *Movies:* Seize the Day, Grand Isle, And the Band Played On. *Mini-Series:* Lonesome Dove (Emmy nom.).

HEALD, ANTHONY
Actor. b. New Rochelle, NY, Aug. 25, 1944. e. Michigan St. Univ.
THEATER: *B'way:* The Wake of Jamey Foster, The Marriage of Figaro, Anything Goes, A Small Family Business, Love! Valour! Compassion! *Off-B'way:* The Glass Menagerie, The Electra Myth, Inadmissible Evidence, Misalliance (Theatre World Award), The Caretaker, The Fox, The Philanthropist, Henry V, The Foreigner, Digby, Principia Scriptoriae, The Lisbon Traviata, Elliot Loves, Lips Together Teeth Apart, Pygmalion, Later Life, Love! Valour! Compassion! *Regional:* Quartermaine's Terms, J.B., Look Back in Anger, The Rose Tattoo, Bonjour la Bonjour, The Matchmaker.
PICTURES: Silkwood (debut, 1983), Teachers, Outrageous Fortune, Happy New Year, Orphans, Postcards From the Edge, The Silence of the Lambs, The Super, Whispers in the Dark, Searching for Bobby Fisher, The Ballad of Little Jo, The Pelican Brief, The Client, Kiss of Death.

TELEVISION: *Movies:* A Case of Deadly Force, Royce. *Mini-Series:* Fresno. Pilot: After Midnight. *Special:* Abby My Love. *Guest:* Hard Copy, Crime Story, Spenser for Hire, Miami Vice, Tales From the Darkside, Against the Law, Law and Order, Class of '96, Cheers, Murder She Wrote, Under Suspicion.

HEARD, JOHN
Actor. b. Washington, D.C., Mar. 7, 1946. e. Catholic U. Career began at Organic Theatre, starring in Chicago & N.Y. productions of Warp. Other stage roles include Streamers, G.R. Point (Theatre World Award), Othello, Split, The Glass Menagerie, Total Abandon, The Last Yankee.
PICTURES: Between the Lines (debut, 1977), First Love, On the Yard, Head Over Heels (Chilly Scenes of Winter), Heart Beat, Cutter and Bone (Cutter's Way), Cat People, Best Revenge, Violated, Heaven Help Us, Lies, C.H.U.D., Too Scared to Scream, After Hours, The Trip to Bountiful, The Telephone, The Milagro Beanfield War, The Seventh Sign, Big, Betrayed, Beaches, The Package, Home Alone, End of Innocence, Awakenings, Rambling Rose, Deceived, Mindwalk, Radio Flyer, Gladiator, Waterland, Home Alone 2: Lost in New York, In the Line of Fire, Me and Veronica, The Pelican Brief, Before and After.
TELEVISION: *Series:* John Grisham's The Client. *Specials:* The Scarlet Letter, Edgar Allan Poe: Terror of the Soul. *Mini-Series:* Tender Is the Night. *Movies:* Will There Really Be a Morning?, Legs, Out on a Limb, Necessity, Cross of Fire, Dead Ahead: The Exxon Valdez Disaster, There Was a Little Boy, Spoils of War, Because Mommy Works.

HECKART, EILEEN
Actress. b. Columbia, OH, Mar. 29, 1919. e. Ohio State U., American Theatre Wing. m. Jack Yankee. Inducted into Theatre Hall of Fame, 1995. Awards: Foreign Press, and Donaldson, Oscar nom. and Film Daily Citation (Bad Seed), TV Sylvania for the Haven, Variety Poll of N.Y. and Drama Critics (Dark at The Top of the Stairs); Emmy (Save Me a Place at Forest Lawn). Also 5 Tony noms., 5 Emmy noms. Honorary Doctorates from: Ohio St. Univ., Sacred Heart, Niagara Univ.
THEATER: Voice of the Turtle, Brighten the Corner, They Knew What They Wanted, Hilda Crane, Picnic (Theatre World & Outer Critics Circle Awards), The Bad Seed, A View From the Bridge, Family Affair, Pal Joey, Invitation to a March, Everybody Loves Opal, The Dark at the Top of the Stairs, And Things That Go Bump in the Night, You Know I Can't Hear You When the Water's Running, Too True to Be Good, Barefoot in the Park, Butterflies Are Free, Veronica's Room, The Effect of Gamma Rays on Man in the Moon Marigolds, Eleemosynary, The Cemetery Club, Love Letters, Driving Miss Daisy.
PICTURES: Miracle in the Rain (debut, 1956), Somebody Up There Likes Me, The Bad Seed, Bus Stop, Hot Spell, Heller in Pink Tights, My Six Loves, Up the Down Staircase, No Way to Treat a Lady, The Tree, Butterflies Are Free (Academy Award, best supporting actress, 1972), Zandy's Bride, The Hiding Place, Burnt Offerings, Heartbreak Ridge.
TELEVISION: *Series:* The Five Mrs. Buchanans. *Guest:* Kraft, Suspense, Philco Playhouse, The Web, Mary Tyler Moore, Annie McGuire, Love and War (Emmy Award, 1994). *Movies:* The Victim, FBI Story: The FBI Versus Alvin Karpis, Sunshine Christmas, Suddenly Love, White Mama, FDR: The Last Year, The Big Black Pill, Games Mother Never Taught You, Seize the Day, Ultimate Betrayal. *Mini-Series:* Backstairs at the Whitehouse.

HECKERLING, AMY
Director. b. New York, NY, May 7, 1954. e. Art & Design H.S., NYU, (film and TV), American Film Institute. Made shorts (Modern Times, High Finance, Getting It Over With), before turning to features.
PICTURES: Fast Times at Ridgemont High, Johnny Dangerously, Into the Night (actor only), National Lampoon's European Vacation, Look Who's Talking, Look Who's Talking Too, Look Who's Talking 3 (co-exec. prod. only), Clueless.
TELEVISION: George Burns Comedy Hour, Fast Times, They Came From Queens. *Series:* Clueless.

HEDAYA, DAN
Actor. b. Brooklyn, NY. e. Tufts Univ. Taught junior high school for seven yrs. before turning to acting. Joined NY Shakespeare Fest. in 1973.
THEATER: *NY:* Last Days of British Honduras, Golden Boy, Museum, The Basic Training of Pavlo Hummel, Conjuring an Event, Survivors, Henry V.
PICTURES: The Passover Plot (debut, 1976), The Seduction of Joe Tynan, Night of the Juggler, True Confessions, I'm Dancing As Fast As I Can, Endangered Species, The Hunger, The Adventures of Buckaroo Banzai, Blood Simple, Reckless, Tightrope, Commando, Wise Guys, Running Scared, Joe Vs. the Volcano, Pacific Heights, Tune in Tomorrow, The Addams Family, Boiling Point, Benny & Joon, Rookie of the Year, For Love or Money, Mr. Wonderful, Maverick, Search and Destroy, Clueless, The Usual Suspects, To Die For, Marvin's Room, Freeway.
TELEVISION: *Series:* The Tortellis, One of the Boys. *Movies:* The Prince of Central Park, Death Penalty, The Dollmaker,

Courage, Slow Burn, A Smoky Mountain Christmas, Betrayal of Trust, Reluctant Agent, The Whereabouts of Jenny. *Guest*: Hill Street Blues, Cheers, L.A. Law. *Pilots*: The Earthlings, The Flamingo Kid, The Rock. *Special*: Just Like Family, Mama's Boy, Veronica Clare.

HEDLUND, DENNIS
Executive. b. Hedley, TX, Sept. 3, 1946. e. U. of Texas, Austin, B.A., business admin., 1968. Captain U.S. Marine Corp, 1966-72. 1970-74, newscaster and disc jockey, KGNC Amarillo, TX; KOMA Oklahoma City, OK; WTIX New Orleans, LA; WFLA Tampa, FL; 1974-77, nat'l sales mgr., Ampex Corp., NY; 1977-80, v.p., Allied Artists Video Corp., NY; 1980-present, founder and president, Kultur International Films Ltd. 1990, created White Star Films to produce original programs for tv. TELEVISION: Roger Miller: King of the Road, Jackie Mason: An Equal Opportunity Offender, Merle Haggard: A Portrait of a Proud Man, History of Talk Radio.

HEDREN, TIPPI
Actress. r.n. Nathalie Hedren. b. Lafayette, MN, Jan. 18, 1935. Daughter is actress Melanie Griffith. Was hired by Alfred Hitchcock for leading role in The Birds after being spotted on a commercial on the Today Show. Author of The Cats of Shambala. Founder and pres. of The Roar Foundation. Bd. memeber, The Wildlife Safari, The Elsa Wild Animal Appeal, The ASPCA, The American Heart Assoc., etc.
PICTURES: The Birds (debut, 1963), Marnie, A Countess From Hong Kong, The Man and the Albatross, Satan's Harvest, Tiger By the Tail, Mr. Kingstreet's War, The Harrad Experiment, Where the Wind Dies, Roar (also prod.), Deadly Spygames, Foxfire Light, In the Cold of the Night, Pacific Heights, Inevitable Grace, Teresa's Tattoo, Mind Luge, The Devil Inside.
TELEVISION: *Series*: The Bold and the Beautiful. *Guest*: Run for Your Life, The Courtship of Eddie's Father, Alfred Hitchcock Presents (1985), Baby Boom, Hart to Hart, In the Heat of the Night, Hotel, Improv (guest host), Tales From the Darkside, Murder She Wrote. *Movies*: Alfred Hitchcock Presents..., Through the Eyes of a Killer, Shadow of a Doubt, Perry Mason: The Case of the Skin-Deep Scandal, The Birds II: Land's End, Treacherous Beauties, Heroes Die Hard, Return to Green Acres, Kraft Suspense Theatre: The Trains of Silence.

HEFFNER, RICHARD D.
Executive. b. New York, NY, Aug. 5, 1925. e. Columbia U. Instrumental in acquisition of Channel 13 (WNET) as New York's educational tv station; served as its first gen. mngr. Previously had produced and moderated Man of the Year, The Open Mind, etc. for commercial and public TV. Served as dir. of public affairs programs for WNBC-TV in NY. Was also dir. of special projects for CBS TV Network and editorial consultant to CBS, Inc. Editorial Board. Was radio newsman for ABC. Exec. editor of From The Editor's Desk on WPIX-TV in NY. Taught history at U. of California at Berkeley, Sarah Lawrence Coll., Columbia U. and New School for Social Research, NY. Served as American specialist in communications for U.S. Dept. of State in Japan, Soviet Union, Germany, Yugoslavia, Israel, etc. Prof. of Communications and Public Policy at Rutgers U. 1974-94, chmn. of classification and rating admin. rating board. 1994-95, sr. fellow, Freedom Forum Media Studies Center at Columbia Univ.

HEFFRON, RICHARD T.
Director. b. Chicago, Oct. 6, 1930.
PICTURES: Fillmore, Newman's Law, Trackdown, Futureworld, Outlaw Blues, I the Jury, The French Revolution.
TELEVISION: The Morning After, Dick Van Dyke Special, I Will Fight No More Forever, Toma (pilot), Rockford Files (pilot), North and South (mini-series). *Movies*: The California Kid, Young Joe Kennedy, A Rumor of War, A Whale for the Killing, The Mystic Warrior, V: The Final Battle, Anatomy of an Illness, Convicted: A Mother's Story, Guilty of Innocence, Samaritan, Napoleon and Josephine: A Love Story, Broken Angel, Pancho Barnes.

HEIDER, FREDERICK
Producer. b. Milwaukee, WI, Apr. 9, 1917. e. Notre Dame U., Goodman Theatre, Chicago. Actor in Globe Theatre, Orson Welles' Mercury Theatre.
TELEVISION & RADIO: Chesterfield Supper Club, Sammy Kaye's So You Want to Lead a Band, Frankie Carle Show, Jo Stafford Show, Paul Whiteman Goodyear Revue, Billy Daniels Show, Martha Wright Show, Earl Wrightson Show, Club Seven, Mindy Carson Show; Ted Mack Family Hour, Dr. I.Q., Miss America Pageant, Bishop Sheen's Life Is Worth Living, Voice of Firestone, Music for a Summer Night. Music for a Spring Night, The Bell Telephone Hour. Publisher, Television Quarterly, National Academy of Television Arts and Sciences. Became columnist, The Desert Sun, Palm Springs, CA.

HEILMAN, CLAUDE
Executive. b. Cologne, Germany, June 27, 1927. Early career in Europe in prod. and distribution. In U.S. joined Fox in Hollywood and NY; incl. mgmt. of Grauman's Chinese and other Fox the-

aters. Formed Vintage Prods. Inc., United Film Associates Intlo., Inter Road Shows. Currently pres./chief. exec. GEM Communications and Islandia Enterprises.
PICTURES: This Earth Is Mine, Odyssey of Justice Lee, The Adventure of Gulliver, Desamor, Sound General Quarters, Islandia.

HELGENBERGER, MARG
Actress. b. Nebraska. e. Northwestern U. Came to NY where she landed first professional job as regular on daytime serial Ryan's Hope.
PICTURES: After Midnight (debut, 1989), Always, Crooked Hearts, The Cowboy Way, Species.
TELEVISION: *Series*: Ryan's Hope, Shell Game, China Beach (Emmy Award, 1990). *Movies*: Blind Vengeance, Death Dreams, The Hidden Room, Deadline (pilot), The Tommyknockers, When Love Kills: The Seduction of John Hearn, Where Are My Children?, Red Eagle. *Special*: Fallen Angels. *Guest*: Spenser for Hire, thirtysomething, Tales From the Crypt.

HELLER, FRANKLIN
Producer, Director. b. Dover, NJ, Sept. 15, 1911. e. Carnegie Inst. of Technology, B.A., 1934. Actor, 1934-36; stage mgr., Sam Harris-Max Gordon Prods., 1936-44; exec. prod., USO shows N.Y., 1944-45; prod. & dir., Paramount, 1945-47; dir., summer stock, 1947-48; prod. & dir., CBS TV, 1949-54; exec., prod. and dir. Goodson-Todman Prods., 1954-69; exec. prod. Protocol Prods., 1969-72 Literary Representative 1972. Dirs. Guild of America, Nat'l bd. 1965-77; Treas. 1965-69; Sec. 1970-73; Chr. Publications 1966-76. Retired.
TELEVISION: What's My Line?, Beat the Clock, The Front Page, The Web, Danger, To Tell the Truth, I've Got a Secret.

HELLER, PAUL M.
Producer. b. New York, NY, Sept. 25, 1927. e. Hunter Coll., Drexel Inst. of Technology. President, Intrepid Productions. Studied engineering until entry into U.S. Army as member of security agency, special branch of signal corps. Worked as set designer (Westport, East Hampton, Palm Beach) and in live TV and then on theatrical films. Produced the NY Experience and South Street Venture. Debut as film producer, David and Lisa, 1963. From 1964 to 1969 was president of MPO Pictures Inc. Joined Warner Bros. as prod. exec., 1970. Founded the Community Film Workshop Council for the American Film Institute. In 1972 founded Sequoia Pictures, Inc. with Fred Weintraub. Pres. of Paul Heller Prods. Inc. formed in 1978. Founded the Audrey Skirball-Kenis Theatre. Board of Directors, the British Academy of Film and Television - Los Angeles.
PICTURES: David and Lisa, The Eavesdropper, Secret Ceremony, Enter the Dragon, Truck Turner, Golden Needles, Dirty Knight's Work, Outlaw Blues, The Pack, The Promise, First Monday in October, Withnail and I, My Left Foot (exec. prod.), The Lunatic.
TELEVISION: Pygmalion.

HELLMAN, JEROME
Producer. b. New York, NY, Sept. 4, 1928. e. NYU. Joined ad dept. of New York Times then went to William Morris Agency as apprentice. Made asst. in TV dept. Worked as agent for Jaffe Agency. After hiatus in Europe joined Ashley-Steiner Agency (later IFA) where clients included Franklin Schaffner, Sidney Lumet, George Roy Hill, John Frankenheimer. Functioned as TV prod., including Kaiser Aluminum Hour. Left to form own agency, Ziegler, Hellman and Ross. Switched to feature prod. with The World of Henry Orient in 1964.
PICTURES: The World of Henry Orient, A Fine Madness, Midnight Cowboy (Academy Award for Best Picture, 1969), The Day of the Locust, Coming Home, Promises in the Dark (also dir.), The Mosquito Coast.

HELLMAN, MONTE
Director, Editor. b. New York, NY, 1932. e. Stanford Univ., UCLA. Started by working for Roger Corman's company as director, editor, 2nd Unit director. Replaced deceased directors on the films The Greatest, The Awakening. Dialogue Director: St. Valentine's Day Massacre. Acted in The Christian Licorice Store, Someone to Love.
PICTURES: *Director*: The Beast from Haunted Cave, Back Door to Hell, Flight to Fury, Ride in the Whirlwind (also edit., prod.), The Shooting (also edit., prod.), Two-Lane Blacktop (also edit.), Cockfighter, China 9 Liberty 37 (also prod.), Iguana (also s.p., edit.), Silent Night Deadly Night 3 (also story). *Editor*: The Wild Angels, The Long Ride Home, How to Make It, The Killer Elite. *Second Unit Director*: The Last Woman on Earth, Ski Troop Attack, Creature from the Haunted Sea, The Terror. *Exec. Prod.*: Reservoir Dogs.

HELMOND, KATHERINE
Actress. b. Galveston, TX, July 5, 1934. Initial stage work with Houston Playhouse and Margo Jones Theatre, Dallas. Joined APA Theatre, NY, and Trinity Square Rep. Co., RI, Hartford Stage, CT and Phoenix Rep. NY. In 1950s opened summer stock theatre in the Catskills. Taught acting at American Musical &

Dramatic Acad., Brown U. and Carnegie-Mellon U. 1983, accepted into AFI's Directing Workshop for Women. Directed Bankrupt.
THEATER: The Great God Brown, House of Blue Leaves (Clarence Derwent, NY and LA Drama Critics Awards, 1972), Mixed Emotions.
PICTURES: The Hindenberg, Baby Blue Marine, Family Plot, Time Bandits, Brazil, Shadey, Overboard, Lady in White, Inside Monkey Zetterland.
TELEVISION: Series: Soap, Who's The Boss? (also episode dir), Benson (episode dir. only), Coach. Movies: Dr. Max, Larry, Locusts, The Autobiography of Miss Jane Pittman, The Legend of Lizzie Borden, The Family Nobody Wanted, Cage Without a Key, The First 36 Hours of Dr. Durant, James Dean, Wanted: The Sundance Woman, Little Ladies of the Night, Getting Married, Diary of a Teenage Hitchhiker, Scout's Honor, World War III, For Lovers Only, Rosie: The Rosemary Clooney Story, Meeting of the Minds, When Will I Be Loved?, The Perfect Tribute, Deception: A Mother's Secret, Grass Roots, Liz: The Elizabeth Taylor Story. Special: Christmas Snow.

HEMINGWAY, MARIEL
Actress. b. Ketchum, ID, Nov. 22, 1961. Granddaughter of writer Ernest Hemingway. Sister of actress-model Margaux Hemingway.
PICTURES: Lipstick (debut, 1976), Manhattan (Acad. Award nom.), Personal Best, Star 80, The Mean Season, Creator, Superman IV: The Quest for Peace, Sunset, The Suicide Club (also co-prod.), Delirious, Falling From Grace, Naked Gun 33 1/3: The Final Insult, Bad Moon.
TELEVISION: Series: Civil Wars, Central Park West. Movies: I Want to Keep My Baby, Steal the Sky, Into the Badlands, Desperate Rescue: The Cathy Mahone Story. Mini-Series: Amerika. Guest: Tales From the Crypt.

HEMMINGS, DAVID
Actor, Director. b. Guildford, England, Nov.18, 1941. Early career in opera. Ent. m.p. ind. 1956. Former co-partner in Hemdale Company.
THEATER: Adventures in the Skin Trade, Jeeves.
PICTURES: Five Clues to Fortune, Saint Joan, The Heart Within, In the Wake of a Stranger, No Trees in the Street, Men of Tomorrow, The Wind of Change, The Painted Smile (Murder Can Be Deadly), Some People, Play It Cool, Two Left Feet, West 11, Live It Up (Sing and Swing), The System (The Girl-Getters), Be My Guest, Dateline Diamonds, Eye of the Devil, Blow-Up, Camelot, The Charge of the Light Brigade, Only When I Larf, Barbarella, The Long Day's Dying, The Best House in London, Alfred the Great, The Walking Stick, Fragment of Fear, The Love Machine, Unman Wittering and Zigo, Voices, Juggernaut, Running Scared (dir.only), The Squeeze, The Disappearance, Blood Relatives, Crossed Swords, Power Play, Murder by Decree, Just a Gigolo (also dir.), Thirst, Beyond Reasonable Doubt, The Survivor (dir. only), Harlequin, Race to the Yankee Zephyr (dir., prod. only), Man Woman and Child, Prisoners (also exec. prod.), Coup D'Grat (also prod.), The Rainbow, Dark Horse (dir. only).
TELEVISION: Auto Stop, The Big Toe, Out of the Unknown, Beverly Hills Cowgirl Blues, Clouds of Glory, Davy Crockett: Rainbow in the Thunder (also dir.). Director only: Hardball, Magnum PI, A-Team, Airwolf, Murder She Wrote, In the Heat of the Night, Quantum Leap, The Turn of the Screw, Tales From the Crypt, Passport to Murder (movie). Guest: Northern Exposure, The Raven, Ned Blessing.

HEMSLEY, SHERMAN
Actor. b. Philadelphia, PA, Feb. 1, 1938.
THEATER: NY: Purlie.
PICTURES: Love at First Bite, Stewardess School, Ghost Fever, Mr. Nanny.
TELEVISION: Series: All in the Family, The Jeffersons, Amen, Dinosaurs (voice), Goode Behavior. Guest: The Rich Little Show, Love Boat, E/R, 227, Family Matters, Lois & Clark, Fresh Prince of Bel Air, Sister Sister.

HENDERSON, FLORENCE
Actress, Singer. b. Dale, IN, Feb. 14, 1934. e. AADA. Made B'way debut while teenager in musical Wish You Were Here.
THEATER: Oklahoma!, The Great Waltz, Fanny, The Sound of Music, The Girl Who Came to Supper, South Pacific. Tour: Annie Get Your Gun.
PICTURES: Song of Norway, Shakes the Clown, Naked Gun 33 1/3: The Final Insult, The Brady Bunch Movie.
TELEVISION: Series: Sing Along, The Jack Paar Show, Oldsmobile Music Theatre, The Brady Bunch, The Brady Bunch Hour, The Brady Brides, Florence Henderson's Home Cooking, The Bradys. Movies: The Love Boat (pilot), The Brady Girls Get Married, A Very Brady Christmas, Fudge-A-Mania. Guest: Car 54 Where Are You?, Garry Moore Show, Ed Sullivan Show, Medical Center, The Love Boat, Fantasy Island, It's Garry Shandling's Show, Police Squad, many others. Specials: Huck Finn, Little Women, An Evening With Richard Rodgers, etc.

HENDERSON, SKITCH
Music Director. r.n. Lyle Cedric Henderson. b. Birmingham, England, Jan. 27, 1918. e. U. of California. Began as pianist in dance bands, then theatre orchestras, films and radio on West Coast. Accompanist to Judy Garland on tour. Served, USAF, WW II. Music director radio, Bing Crosby. Toured with own dance band, 47-49. Music Director for NBC Network, Steve Allen Show, Tonight Show, Today Show, Street Scene (NY Opera). Guest conductor, symphony orchestras including NY Philharmonic, London Philharmonic. Founder and Music Director, NY Pops Orchestra. Music Director, Florida Orchestra Pops, Virginia Symphony Pops, Louisville Orchestra Pops. Grammy Award for RCA album NY Philharmonic with Leontyne Price and William Warfield, highlights from Porgy and Bess. Instrumental works: Skitch's Blues, Minuet on the Rocks, Skitch in Time, Come Thursday, Curacao. Scores: American Fantasy, Act One (film).

HENNER, MARILU
Actress. b. Chicago, IL, Apr. 6, 1952. e. U. of Chicago. Studied singing and dancing, appearing in musicals in Chicago and on Broadway in Over Here and Pal Joey. Autobiography: By All Means Keep on Moving (1994).
PICTURES: Between the Lines (debut, 1977), Blood Brothers, Hammett, The Man Who Loved Women, Cannonball Run II, Johnny Dangerously, Rustler's Rhapsody, Perfect, L.A. Story, Noises Off, Chasers.
TELEVISION: Series: Taxi, Evening Shade, Marilu. Movies: Dream House, Stark, Love with a Perfect Stranger, Ladykillers, Chains of Gold, Abandoned and Deceived (co-exec. prod. only), Fight for Justice.

HENNING, LINDA KAYE
Actress, Singer. b. Toluca Lake, CA, Sept. 16, 1944. Daughter of prod. Paul Henning. e. Cal State Northridge, UCLA. Member of California Artists Radio Theatre.
THEATER: Gypsy, Applause, Damn Yankees, I Do, I Do, Pajama Game, Sugar, Wonderful Town, Fiddler on the Roof, Sound of Music, Vanities, Born Yesterday, Mary, Mary, Bus Stop, etc.
PICTURE: Bye Bye Birdie.
TELEVISION: Series: Petticoat Junction, Sliders. Guest: Beverly Hillbillies, Happy Days, Mork & Mindy, Double Trouble, Barnaby Jones, The New Gidget, Hunter. Pilots: Kudzu, The Circle, Family. Movie: The Return of the Beverly Hillbillies.

HENNING, PAUL
Producer, Writer. b. Independence, MO, Sept. 16, 1911. e. Kansas City Sch. of Law, grad. 1932. Radio singer and disc jockey. Also acted, ran sound effects, sang, wrote scripts. To Chicago 1937-38, to write for Fibber McGee and Molly. To Hollywood as writer for Rudy Vallee, 1939. Wrote scripts for Burns and Allen 10 years, including transition radio to TV.
PICTURES: Writer: Lover Come Back, Bedtime Story, Dirty Rotten Scoundrels.
TELEVISION: Series (creator, writer, producer): The Bob Cummings Show, The Beverly Hillbillies, Petticoat Junction, Green Acres (exec. prod.)

HENRIKSEN, LANCE
Actor. b. New York, NY, May 5, 1943. Appeared on B'way in The Basic Training of Pavo Hummel, Richard III.
PICTURES: It Ain't Easy (debut, 1972), Dog Day Afternoon, The Next Man, Mansion of the Doomed, Close Encounters of the Third Kind, Damien: Omen II, The Visitor, The Dark End of the Street, Prince of the City, Piranha II: The Spawning, Nightmares, The Right Stuff, Savage Dawn, The Terminator, Jagged Edge, Choke Canyon, Aliens, Near Dark, Deadly Intent, Pumpkinhead, Hit List, The Horror Show, Johnny Handsome, Survival Quest, The Last Samurai, Stone Cold, Comrades in Arms, Delta Heat, Alien³, Jennifer Eight, Excessive Force, The Outfit, Super Mario Bros., Hard Target, Man's Best Friend, No Escape, Color of Night, The Quick and the Dead, Powder.
TELEVISION: Series: Millenium. Guest: Scene of the Crime, Paul Reiser: Out on a Whim, Tales From the Crypt (Cutting Cards). Movies: Return to Earth, Question of Honor, Blood Feud, Reason for Living: The Jill Ireland Story, Wes Craven Presents Mind Ripper.

HENRY, BUCK
Actor, Writer. b. New York, NY, Dec. 9, 1930. r.n. Henry Zuckerman. e. Dartmouth Coll. Acted in Life with Father, (tour, 1948), Fortress of Glass, Bernardine, B'way; 1952-54, U.S. Army; No Time for Sergeants (Nat'l. Co.), The Premise, improvisational theatre, off-B'way.
PICTURES: Actor: The Secret War of Harry Frigg, Is There Sex After Death?, Taking Off, The Man Who Fell to Earth, Old Boyfriends, Gloria, Eating Raoul, Aria, Dark Before Dawn, Rude Awakening, Tune in Tomorrow, Defending Your Life, The Player, The Linguini Incident, Short Cuts, Even Cowgirls Get the Blues, Grumpy Old Men. Writer: Candy, The Owl and the Pussycat, What's Up Doc?, The Day of the Dolphin, Protocol. Actor-Writer: The Troublemaker, The Graduate, Catch-22, To Die For. Actor-Writer-Director: Heaven Can Wait (co-dir.), First Family.

TELEVISION: *Series*: Garry Moore Show (writer), Steve Allen Show (writer, performer), The Bean Show (writer), That Was the Week That Was (writer, performer), Get Smart (co-creator, story editor), Captain Nice (writer, exec. prod.), Alfred Hitchcock Presents (1985, actor, writer), Quark (writer), The New Show (performer, writer), Falcon Crest (actor), Trying Times: Hunger Chic (dir.). *Guest*: Saturday Night Live, Murphy Brown. *Movies*: Keep the Change, Harrison Bergeron. *Special*: Mastergate.

HENRY, JUSTIN
Actor. b. Rye, NY, May 25, 1971. Debut at age 8 in Kramer vs. Kramer, 1979 for which he received an Academy Award nomination.
PICTURES: Kramer vs Kramer, Sixteen Candles, Martin's Day, Sweet Hearts Dance.
TELEVISION: *Movies*: Tiger Town, Andersonville.

HENSON, LISA
Executive. b. 1960. e. Harvard U. Father was performer-puppeteer-director Jim Henson. Joined Warner Bros., 1983, as exec. asst. to head of prod. 1985, named dir. of creative affairs. 1985, promoted to v.p., prod. 1992, became exec. v.p., production. 1993, named pres. of worldwide prod. of Columbia Pictures. 1994, named pres. of Columbia Pictures. Resigned in 1996 to form own production company.

HEPBURN, KATHARINE
Actress. b. Hartford, CT, May 12, 1907. *Author*: The Making of the African Queen (1987), Me: Stories of My Life (1991). Received a record 12 Academy Award nominations for acting.
THEATER: Death Takes a Holiday, The Warrior's Husband, The Lake, The Philadelphia Story, As You Like It, The Millionairess, The Merchant of Venice, The Taming of the Shrew, Measure for Measure, Coco, A Matter of Gravity, West Side Waltz.
PICTURES: A Bill of Divorcement (debut, 1932), Christopher Strong, Morning Glory (Academy Award, 1933). Little Women, Spitfire, The Little Minister, Break of Hearts, Alice Adams, Sylvia Scarlett, Mary of Scotland, A Woman Rebels, Quality Street, Stage Door, Bringing Up Baby, Holiday, The Philadelphia Story, Woman of the Year, Keeper of the Flame, Stage Door Canteen, Dragon Seed, Without Love, Undercurrent, The Sea of Grass, Song of Love, State of the Union, Adam's Rib, The African Queen, Pat and Mike, Summertime, The Iron Petticoat, The Rainmaker, The Desk Set, Suddenly Last Summer, Long Day's Journey Into Night, Guess Who's Coming to Dinner (Academy Award, 1967), The Lion in Winter (Academy Award, 1968), The Madwoman of Chaillot, The Trojan Women, A Delicate Balance, Rooster Cogburn, Olly Olly Oxen Free, On Golden Pond (Academy Award, 1981), Grace Quigley, Love Affair.
TELEVISION: *Movies*: The Glass Menagerie, Love Among the Ruins (Emmy Award, 1975), The Corn Is Green, Mrs. Delafield Wants To Marry, Laura Lansing Slept Here, The Man Upstairs, This Can't Be Love, One Christmas. *Special*: Katharine Hepburn: All About Me (host, co-writer).

HERALD, PETER
Executive. b. Berlin, Germany, Dec. 20, 1930. e. UCLA, B.A. US Gov't. film officer in Europe 8 years. In charge of continental European prod. operation for Walt Disney Prods., 6 years. Supervisory prod. manager, Columbia Pictures, 3 years. Corporate Prod. mgr. Universal 3 years.
PICTURES: *Executive-, Co-, Assoc.-, Line Producer and/or Production Mgr.*: Almost Angels, Magnificent Rebel, Miracle of the White Stallions, Emil and the Detectives, There Was a Crooked Man, Outrageous Fortune, National Lampoon's Class Reunion, Doctor Detroit, D. C. Cab; The Great Waltz, Foul Play, Nightwing, W. W. and the Dixie Dancekings, Mandingo, W. C. Fields and Me, Alex and the Gypsy, Silver Streak, Star Wars, Stick, Married to It, many others.

HEREK, STEPHEN
Director. b. San Antonio, TX, Nov. 10, 1958.
PICTURES: Critters (debut, 1986), Bill & Ted's Excellent Adventure, Don't Tell Mom the Babysitter's Dead, The Mighty Ducks, The Three Musketeers, Mr. Holland's Opus, 101 Dalmatians.

HERMAN, NORMAN
Producer, Director. b. Newark, NJ, Feb. 10, 1924. e. Rutgers U., NYU. Was accountant in California; in 1955 switched to film ind., joining American Int'l Pictures. Headed AIP prod. dept. 4 years, incl. prod., post-prod., labor negotiations, supervising story dept., etc. Pres. of Century Plaza Prods. for 9 yrs. Sr. v.p./staff writer DEG, 1986-9; Pres. No. Carolina Studios, 1989-90.
PICTURES: *Prod. except as noted*: Sierra Stranger, Hot Rod Girl, Hot Rod Rumble, Crime Beneath Seas, Look in any Window (exec. prod. mgr.), Tokyo After Dark (also dir., s.p.), Everybody Loves It (dir.), Mondy Teeno (also dir. co-s.p.), Glory Stompers, Three in the Attic (assoc. prod.), Pretty Boy Floyd, Dunwich Horror, Three in the Cellar, Angel Unchained, Psych-Out, Sadismo (s.p.), Bloody Mama, Bunny O'Hare, Killers Three, Frogs (exec. prod.), Planet of Life (s.p.), Blacula, Dillinger (s.p.), Legend of Hell House, Dirty Mary Crazy Larry, Rolling Thunder, In God We Trust (exec. prod.), Blue Velvet (consultant).

TELEVISION: *Writer*: Robert Taylor Detective, Iron Horse, Invaders, Adam 12, Lancer. *Director-Producer*: Hannibal Cobb, You Are the Judge.

HEROUX, CLAUDE
Producer. b. Montreal, Canada, Jan. 26, 1942. e. U. of Montreal. 1979, prod. v.p., Film Plan Intl., Montreal.
PICTURES: Valerie, L'Initiation, L'Amour Humain, Je t'aime, Echoes of a Summer, Jacques Brel Is Alive and Well and Living in Paris, Breaking Point,Born for Hell, Hog Wild, City of Fire, Dirty Tricks, Gas, Visiting Hours, Videodrome, The Funny Farm, Going Berserk, Of Unknown Origin, Covergirl.
TELEVISION: The Park is Mine, Popeye Doyle.

HERRMANN, EDWARD
Actor. b. Washington, DC, July 21, 1943. Raised in Grosse Pointe, MI. e. Bucknell U. Postgrad. Fulbright scholar, London Acad. Music and Dramatic Art 1968-69. Acted with Dallas Theater Center for 4 years.
THEATER: *NY*: The Basic Training of Pavlo Hummel, Moonchildren, Mrs. Warren's Profession (Tony Award, 1976), Journey's End, The Beach House, The Philadelphia Story, Plenty, Tom and Viv, Julius Caesar, Not About Heroes, Life Sentences. London: A Walk in the Woods. Regional: many prods. with Williamstown Playhouse; Harvey, Twelfth Night, Love Letters, Three Sisters.
PICTURES: Lady Liberty, The Paper Chase, The Day of the Dolphin, The Great Gatsby, The Great Waldo Pepper, The Betsy, Brass Target, Take Down, The North Avenue Irregulars, Harry's War, Reds, Death Valley, A Little Sex, Annie, Mrs. Soffel, The Purple Rose of Cairo, The Man With One Red Shoe, Compromising Positions, The Lost Boys, Overboard, Big Business, Hero (unbilled), Born Yesterday, My Boyfriend's Back, Foreign Student, Richie Rich.
TELEVISION: *Series*: Beacon Hill, Our Century (host). *Guest*: M*A*S*H, St. Elsewhere. *Mini-Series*: Freedom Road. *Movies*: Eleanor and Franklin, Eleanor and Franklin: The White House Years, A Love Affair: The Eleanor and Lou Gehrig Story, Portrait of a Stripper, The Gift of Life, Memorial Day, So Proudly We Hail, Sweet Poison, Fire in the Dark, The Face on the Milk Carton. *Specials*: Sorrows of Gin, The Private History of The Campaign That Failed, Murrow, Dear Liar, Concealed Enemies, The Return of Hickey, The Beginning of the Firm, Last Act is a Solo, The End of a Sentence, A Foreign Field.

HERSHEY, BARBARA
Actress. r.n. Barbara Herzstein. b. Los Angeles, CA, Feb. 5, 1948. e. Hollywood H.S. m. painter Stephen Douglas. Briefly, in the mid-1970's, acted under the name Barbara Seagull.
PICTURES: With Six You Get Eggroll (debut, 1968), Heaven With a Gun, Last Summer, The Liberation of L.B. Jones, The Baby Maker, The Pursuit of Happiness, Dealing, Boxcar Bertha, Angela (Love Comes Quietly), The Crazy World of Julius Vrooder, Diamonds, You and Me, The Last Hard Men, Dirty Knights' Work, The Stunt Man, Americana, Take This Job and Shove It, The Entity, The Right Stuff, The Natural, Hannah and Her Sisters, Hoosiers, Tin Men, Shy People (Cannes Film Fest. Award, 1987), A World Apart (Cannes Film Fest. Award, 1988), The Last Temptation of Christ, Beaches, Tune in Tomorrow, Defenseless, The Public Eye, Falling Down, Swing Kids, Splitting Heirs, A Dangerous Woman, Last of the Dogmen, Portrait of a Lady, The Pallbearer.
TELEVISION: *Series*: The Monroes, From Here to Eternity. *Guest*: Gidget, The Farmer's Daughter, Run for Your Life, The Invaders, Daniel Boone, CBS Playhouse, Chrysler Theatre, Kung Fu, Alfred Hitchcock Presents (1985). *Movies*: Flood, In the Glitter Palace, Just a Little Inconvenience, Sunshine Christmas, Angel on My Shoulder, My Wicked Wicked Ways... The Legend of Errol Flynn, Passion Flower, A Killing in a Small Town (Emmy & Golden Globe Awards, 1990), Paris Trout, Stay the Night. *Mini-Series*: A Man Called Intrepid, Return to Lonesome Dove. *Special*: Working.

HERSKOVITZ, MARSHALL
Producer, Director, Writer. b. Philadelphia, PA, Feb. 23, 1952. e. Brandeis U., BA, 1973; American Film Inst., MFA. 1975. Worked as freelance writer, dir., and prod. on several TV shows. Received Humanitas Award, 1983 and Writers Guild award, 1984.
PICTURE: Jack the Bear (dir.), Legends of the Fall (co-prod.).
TELEVISION: Family (writer, dir.), White Shadow (writer), Special Bulletin (prod., writer, 2 Emmys for writing and dramatic special), thirtysomething (exec. prod., co-writer, dir; 2 Emmy awards for writing and dramatic series, 1988; Also Humanitas Award and Directors Guild Award, 1988 & 1989, Peabody Award, 1989.) Relativity.

HERTZ, WILLIAM
Executive. b. Wishek, ND, Dec. 5, 1923. Began theatre career in 1939 with Minnesota Amusement in Minneapolis; 1946 joined Fox West Coast Theatres; theatre mgr., booking dept.; 1965 appointed Los Angeles first-run district mgr.; promoted to Pacific

Coast Division Mgr., National General Corp., 1967; v.p. Southern Pacific Div. Mgr., National General Theatres, Inc. 1971. Joined Mann Theatres as dir. of marketing, public relations.

HERZOG, WERNER
Director, Producer, Writer. r.n. Werner Stipetic. b. Sachrang, Germany, September 5, 1942. e. U. of Munich, Duquesne U., Pittsburgh. Wrote first s.p. 1957; 1961 worked nights in steel factory to raise money for films; 1966, worked for U.S. National Aeronautics and Space Admin.
PICTURES: Signs of Life (debut, 1968), Even Dwarfs Started Small, Fata Morgana, The Land of Silence and Darkness, Aguirre—Wrath of God, Every Man for Himself and God Against All (The Mysery of Kasper Hauser), Heart of Glass, Stroszek, Nosferatu: The Vampyre (also cameo), Woyzeck, Fitzcarraldo, Where the Green Ants Dream, Cobra Verde, It Isn't Easy Being God, Echoes of a Somber Empire.

HESSEMAN, HOWARD
Actor. b. Salem, OR, Feb. 27, 1940. Started with the San Francisco group, The Committee and worked as a disc jockey in San Francisco in the late 1960s.
PICTURES: Petulia, Billy Jack, Steelyard Blues, Shampoo, The Sunshine Boys, Jackson County Jail, The Big Bus, The Other Side of Midnight, Silent Movie, Honky Tonk Freeway, Private Lessons, Loose Shoes, Doctor Detroit, This is Spinal Tap, Police Academy 2: Their First Assignment, Clue, My Chauffeur, Flight of the Navigator, Heat, Amazon Women on the Moon, Rubin and Ed, Little Miss Millions.
TELEVISION: Series: WKRP in Cincinnati, One Day at a Time, Head of the Class. Guest: Mary Hartman Mary Hartman, Fernwood 2night, George Burns Comedy Week. Movies: Hustling, The Blue Knight (pilot), Tail Gunner Joe, The Amazing Howard Hughes, Tarantulas: The Deadly Cargo, The Ghost on Flight 401, The Comedy Company, More Than Friends, Outside Chance, The Great American Traffic Jam, Victims, One Shoe Makes It Murder, Best Kept Secrets, The Diamond Trap, Call Me Anna, Murder in New Hampshire: The Pamela Smart Story, Quiet Killer, Lethal Exposure.

HESSLER, GORDON
Producer, Director. b. Berlin, Germany, 1930. e. Reading U., England. Dir., vice pres., Fordel Films, Inc., 1950-58; dir., St. John's Story (Edinborough Film Festival), March of Medicine Series, Dr. Albert Lasker Award; story edit., Alfred Hitchcock Presents 1960-62; assoc. prod., dir., Alfred Hitchcock Hour, 1962; prod., Alfred Hitchcock Hour; prod., dir., Universal TV 1964-66.
PICTURES: The Woman Who Wouldn't Die, The Last Shot You Hear, The Oblong Box, Scream and Scream Again, Cry of the Banshee, Murders of the Rue Morgue, Sinbad's Golden Voyage, Medusa, Embassy, Puzzle, Pray for Death, Rage of Honour, The Misfit Brigade, The Girl in a Swing (also s.p.), Out on Bail, Mayeda, Journey of Honor.
TELEVISION: Series: Alfred Hitchcock Presents (1960-62), Alfred Hitchcock Hour, Run for Your Life, Convoy, Bob Hope Chrysler Show, ABC Suspense Movies of the Week, ABC Movies of the Week, Lucas Tanner, Night Stalker, Amy Prentiss, Switch, Kung Fu, Sara, Hawaii Five-O, Blue Knight, Wonder Woman, Master, CHiPs, Tales of the Unexpected, Equilizer. Pilots: Tender Warriors.

HESTON, CHARLTON
Actor. b. Evanston, IL, Oct. 4, 1924. e. Northwestern U. Sch. of Speech. Radio, stage, TV experience. Following coll. served 8 yrs. 11th Air Force, Aleutians. After war, dir. and co-starred with wife at Thomas Wolfe Memorial Theatre, Asheville, NC in State of the Union, Glass Menagerie; member, Katharine Cornell's Co., during first year on Broadway; Anthony and Cleopatra, other Bway. plays, Leaf and Bough, Cockadoodle Doo; Studio One (TV): Macbeth, Taming of the Shrew, Of Human Bondage, Julius Caesar. Pres. Screen Actors Guild 1966-71; Member, Natl. Council on the Arts, 1967-72; Trustee: Los Angeles Center Theater Group, American Film Inst. 1971, chmn. 1981-; Received Jean Hersholt Humanitarian award, 1978. Autobiographies: The Actor's Life (1978), In the Arena (1995).
RECENT THEATER: A Man for All Seasons, The Caine Mutiny (dir., in China).
PICTURES: Dark City (debut, 1950), The Greatest Show on Earth, The Savage, Ruby Gentry, The President's Lady, Pony Express, Arrowhead, Bad for Each Other, The Naked Jungle, The Secret of the Incas, The Far Horizons, Lucy Gallant, The Private War of Major Benson, The Ten Commandments, Three Violent People, Touch of Evil, The Big Country, The Buccaneer, Ben-Hur (Academy Award, 1959), The Wreck of the Mary Deare, El Cid, The Pigeon That Took Rome, 55 Days at Peking, Major Dundee, The Agony and the Ecstasy, The War Lord, The Greatest Story Ever Told, Khartoum, Counterpoint, Planet of the Apes, Will Penny, Number One, Beneath the Planet of the Apes, Julius Caesar, The Hawaiians, The Omega Man, Antony and Cleopatra (also dir.), Skyjacked, Soylent Green, The Three Musketeers, Airport 1975, Earthquake, The Four Musketeers, The Last Hard Men, Midway, Two Minute Warning, Crossed Swords (The Prince and the Pauper), Gray Lady Down,

Mountain Men, The Awakening, Mother Lode (also dir.), Almost an Angel (cameo), Solar Crisis, Wayne's World 2 (cameo), Tombstone, True Lies, In the Mouth of Madness, Alaska, Hamlet.
TELEVISION: Series: The Colbys. Mini-Series: Chiefs. Movies: The Nairobi Affair, The Proud Men, A Man For All Seasons (also dir.), Original Sin, Treasure Island, The Little Kidnappers, The Crucifer of Blood, Crash Landing: The Rescue of Flight 232, The Avenging Angel, Texas (narrator). Special: Charlton Heston Presents the Bible (also writer).

HEYMAN, JOHN
Producer. b. Germany, 1933. e. Oxford U. Started with Independent British Television creating,. writing and producing entertainment and documentary programs. Had 5 top-ten programs 1955-57. Expanded into personal management, forming International Artsists, representing Elizabeth Taylor, Richard Burton, Richard Harris, Shirley Bassey among others. In 1963, formed World Film Services Ltd. to produce packafe and finance films and World Film Sales Ltd., the first major independent film sales co. Co-financed 250 major studio films 1969-91. In 1973, formed Genesis Project. In 1989 formed Island World and Islet. In 1994, formed World Group of Companies Ltd., parent co. to World Production Ltd.
PICTURES: Privilege, Boom!, Secret Ceremony, Twinky, Bloomfield, The Go-Between (Grand Prix, Cannes 1971), Superstars, Hitler: The Last Ten Days, Black Gunn, Divorce His, Divorce Hers, The Hireling (Grand Prix, Cannes 1973), A Doll's House, Daniel, Beyond the Limit, The Dresser, A Passage to India (co-prod.), Martin's Day, Steaming, D.A.R.Y.L.

HEYWOOD, ANNE
Actress. r.n. Violet Pretty. b. Birmingham, England, Dec. 11, 1931. Family tree dates back to Shakespearean actor Thomas Heywood (1570-1641). e. scholarship London Acad. of Dramatic Art and Music. Joined Highbury Theater Players and Birmingham Rep. Starred as Peter Pan, Shakespeare Memorial Theatre, Stratford on Avon.
PICTURES: Lady Godiva Rides Again (debut, 1951; billed as Violet Pretty), Find the Lady, Checkpoint, Doctor at Large, Dangerous Exile, The Depraved, Violent Playground, Floods of Fear, The Heart of a Man, Upstairs and Downstairs, A Terrible Beauty (The Night Fighters), Carthage in Flames, Petticoat Pirates, Stork Talk, Vengeance (The Brain), The Very Edge, 90 Degrees in the Shade, The Fox, Midas Run, The Chairman, The Nun of Monza, I Want What I Want, Trader Horn, Good Luck Miss Wyckoff, Ring of Darkness, What Waits Below.
TELEVISION: Guest: The Equalizer.

HICKEY, WILLIAM
Actor. b. Brooklyn, NY, 1928.
PICTURES: A Hatful of Rain (debut, 1957), Something Wild, Invitation to a Gunfighter, The Producers, The Boston Strangler, Little Big Man, Happy Birthday Wanda June, 92 in the Shade, Mikey and Nicky, The Sentinel, Nunzio, Prizzi's Honor (Acad. Award nom.), Remo Williams: The Adventure Begins, Flanagan, One Crazy Summer, The Name of the Roses, Bright Lights Big City, Da, Pink Cadillac, Puppet Master, Sea of Love, It Had to Be You, National Lampoon's Christmas Vacation, Tales From the Darkside: The Movie, Any Man's Death, Mob Boss, My Blue Heaven, The Nightmare Before Christmas (voice), The Jerky Boys, Major Payne, Forget Paris.

HICKS, CATHERINE
Actress. b. New York NY, Aug. 6, 1951. e. St. Mary's Notre Dame; Cornell U. (2 year classical acting prog.). On B'way. in Tribute, Present Laughter.
PICTURES: Death Valley, Better Late Than Never, Garbo Talks, The Razor's Edge, Fever Pitch, Peggy Sue Got Married, Star Trek IV: The Voyage Home, Like Father Like Son, Child's Play, She's Out of Control, Cognac, Liebestraum.
TELEVISION: Series: Ryan's Hope (1976-8), The Bad News Bears, Tucker's Witch. Movies: Love for Rent, To Race the Wind, Marilyn- the Untold Story, Valley of the Dolls 1981, Happy Endings, Laguna Heat, Spy, Hi Honey I'm Dead, Redwood Curtain. Pilot: The Circle Game.

HIFT, FRED
Executive. b. Vienna, Nov. 27, 1924. e. Vienna, London, Chicago. Early career reporter Chicago Sun and radio work with CBS News, New York; radio desk of NY Times. 1946 joined Boxoffice magazine; 1947 Quigley Publications; 1950 Variety. 1960 began career as publicist on Exodus. 1961 dir. pub., The Longest Day for Darryl Zanuck. 1962 joined Fox in Paris as ad-pub. dir. for Europe. 1964 became dir. European prod. pub. with headquarters London. Formed own pub., p.r. co., Fred Hift Assoc., 1970. 1979, joined Columbia as dir. of eastern adv.-pub operations in N.Y.; 1980, to United Artists as intl. adv./pub. v.p. Left to establish Fred Hift Assoc., intl. mktg. consultant in New York. 1983, joined Almi Pictures as v.p., mktg. 1985, reactivated F.H.A. 1986, returned to freelance journalism. Currently contributes to a variety of magazines and newspapers and also does reports on radio.
d. July 6,1996

HILL, ARTHUR
Actor. b. Melfort, Saskatchewan, Canada, Aug. 1, 1922. e. U. of British Columbia. Moved to England in 1948, spending ten years in varied stage & screen pursuits
THEATER: *B'way*: The Matchmaker, Home of the Brave, The Male Animal, Look Homeward Angel, All the Way Home, Who's Afraid of Virginia Woolf? (Tony Award, 1963), More Stately Mansions.
PICTURES: Miss Pilgrim's Progress, Scarlet Thread, Mr. Drake's Duck, A Day to Remember, Life With the Lyons, The Crowded Day, The Deep Blue Sea, Raising a Riot, The Young Doctors, The Ugly American, In the Cool of the Day, Moment to Moment, Harper, Petulia, The Chairman, Rabbit Run, The Pursuit of Happiness, The Andromeda Strain, The Killer Elite, Futureworld, A Bridge Too Far, A Little Romance, Butch and Sundance: The Early Days, The Champ, Dirty Tricks, Making Love, The Amateur, Something Wicked This Way Comes (narrator), One Magic Christmas.
TELEVISION: *Series*: Owen Marshall: Counselor-At-Law, Hagen, Glitter. *Movies*: The Other Man, Vanished, Ordeal, Owen Marshall: Counselor at Law (pilot; a.k.a. A Pattern of Morality), Death Be Not Proud, Judge Horton and the Scottsboro Boys, Tell Me My Name, The Ordeal of Dr. Mudd, Revenge of the Stepford Wives, The Return of Frank Cannon, Angel Dusted, Tomorrow's Child, Intimate Agony, Prototype, Love Leads the Way, Murder in Space, Churchill and the Generals, The Guardian, Perry Mason: The Case of the Notorious Nun.

HILL, BERNARD
Actor: b. Manchester, Eng., Dec. 17, 1944. Joined amateur dramatic society in Manchester then studied drama at Manchester Art Coll. Joined Liverpool Everyman rep. co. West End debut as John Lennon in John, Paul, George, Ringo... and Burt. Also in Normal Service, Shortlist, Twelfth Night, Macbeth, Cherry Orchard, Gasping, A View From the Bridge.
PICTURES: Gandhi, The Bounty, The Chain, Restless Natives, No Surrender, Bellman and True, Drowning by Numbers, Shirley Valentine, Mountains of the Moon, Double X: The Name of the Game, Skallagrigg, Madagascar Skin, The Ghost and the Darkness.
TELEVISION: I Claudius, Squaring the Circle, John Lennon: A Journey in the Life, New World, St. Luke's Gospel, Boys from the Blackstuff, Burston Rebellion.

HILL, DEBRA
Producer, Director, Writer. b. Philadelphia, PA. Career on feature films started with work as script supvr., asst. dir. and 2nd unit dir. of 13 pictures. Producer's debut with Halloween, 1980, for which also co-wrote script with director John Carpenter.
PICTURES: Halloween (also co-s.p.), The Fog (and co-s.p.), Escape from New York, Halloween II (and co-s.p.), Halloween III: Season of the Witch, The Dead Zone, Clue, Head Office, Adventures in Babysitting, Big Top Pee-wee, Heartbreak Hotel, Gross Anatomy, The Fisher King.
TELEVISION: Adventures in Babysitting (pilot, exec. prod.), Monsters (dir. episodes), Dream On (dir. episodes). *Movies*: El Diablo, Attack of the 50 Ft. Woman. *Rebel Highway Film Series*: Roadracers, Confessions of a Sorority Girl (also co-writer), Dragstrip Girl, Shake Rattle and Roll, The Cool and the Crazy, Runaway Daughters, Motocycle Gang, Drag Strip Girl, Reform School Girl, Jailbreakers (also co-writer), Girls in Prison.

HILL, GEORGE ROY
Director. b. Minneapolis, MN, Dec. 20, 1921. e. Yale U., Trinity Coll., Dublin. Started as actor, Irish theatres and U.S. Margaret Webster's Shakespeare Repertory Co., also off-B'way. Served as Marine pilot in WWII and Korean War. Wrote TV play, My Brother's Keeper, for Kraft Theatre, later rose to director with show.
THEATER: Look Homeward Angel (B'way debut, 1957), The Gang's All Here, Greenwillow, Period of Adjustment, Moon on a Rainbow Shawl (also prod.), Henry Sweet Henry.
PICTURES: Period of Adjustment (debut, 1962), Toys in the Attic, The World of Henry Orient, Hawaii, Thoroughly Modern Millie, Butch Cassidy and the Sundance Kid, Slaughterhouse Five, The Sting (Academy Award, 1973), The Great Waldo Pepper (also prod., story), Slap Shot, A Little Romance (also co-exec. prod.), The World According to Garp (also co-prod., cameo), The Little Drummer Girl, Funny Farm.
TELEVISION: *Writer-Dir.*: A Night to Remember, The Helen Morgan Story, Judgment at Nuremberg, Child of Our Time.

HILL, TERENCE
Actor, Director. r.n. Mario Girotti. b. Venice, March 29, 1939. Debuted as actor under his real name. First attracted attention as actor in Visconti's The Leopard, 1963. Gained fame in European-made westerns. Formed Paloma Films.
PICTURES: *as Mario Girotti*: Vacanze col Gangster (debut, 1951), Hannibal, Carthage in Flames, Joseph and His Brethren, The Wonders of Aladdin, Magdalena, Seven Seas to Calais, The Leopard, Games of Desire, Arizona Wildcat, Rampage at Apache Wells, Flaming Frontier, Whom the Gods Destroy, Blood River; *as Terence Hill*: God Forgives I Don't, Boot Hill, Ace High,

Barbaglia, Anger of the Wind, They Call Me Trinity, The True and the False, Trinity Is Still My Name, Man of the East, Baron Blood, All the Way Boys!, My Name Is Nobody, Crime Busters, Mr. Billion, March or Die, Super Fuzz, Two Super Cops, Don Camillo (also dir.), Renegade Luke (also exec. prod.), Go for It!, Lucky Luke (also dir.), The F(N)ight Before Christmas (also dir.).
TELEVISION: *Series*: Lucky Luke (also dir.)

HILL, WALTER
Director, Writer, Producer. b. Long Beach, CA, Jan. 10, 1942. e. Michigan State U.
PICTURES: Hickey and Boggs (s.p.), The Getaway (1972; s.p.), Thief Who Came to Dinner (s.p.), The Mackintosh Man (s.p.), The Drowning Pool (s.p.), Hard Times (dir., s.p.), The Driver (dir., s.p.), The Warriors (dir., s.p.), Alien (prod.), The Long Riders (dir.), Southern Comfort (dir., s.p.), 48 HRS (dir., s.p.), Streets of Fire (dir., s.p.), Brewster's Millions (dir.), Crossroads (dir.), Blue City (prod., s.p.), Aliens (exec. prod., story), Extreme Prejudice (dir.), Red Heat (dir., s.p., prod.), Johnny Handsome (dir.), Another 48 HRS (dir.), Alien 3 (s.p., prod.), Trespass (dir.), Geronimo: An American Legend (dir., co-prod.), The Getaway (1993; co-s.p.), Tales From the Crypt Presents Demon Knight (co-exec. prod.), Wild Bill (dir., s.p.), Last Man Standing (dir.).
TELEVISION: *Series*: Dog and Cat (creator, writer), Tales From the Crypt (exec. prod.; also dir. & writer of episodes: The Man Who Was Death, Cutting Cards, Deadline: ACE Award).

HILLER, ARTHUR
Director. b. Edmonton, Alberta, Can., Nov. 22, 1923. e. U. of Alberta, U. of Toronto, U. of British Columbia. Worked for Canadian Broadcasting Corp. as dir. of live tv before moving to L.A. Pres. of DGA. 1993, became pres. of AMPAS. Appeared in Beverly Hills Cop III.
PICTURES: The Careless Years (debut, 1957), Miracle of the White Stallions, The Wheeler Dealers, The Americanization of Emily, Promise Her Anything, Penelope, Tobruk, The Tiger Makes Out, Popi, The Out-of-Towners, Love Story, Plaza Suite, The Hospital, Man of La Mancha, The Crazy World of Julius Vrooder (also co-prod.), The Man in the Glass Booth, W. C. Fields and Me, Silver Streak, Nightwing, The In-Laws (also co-prod.), Making Love, Author Author, Romantic Comedy, The Lonely Guy (also prod.), Teachers, Outrageous Fortune, See No Evil Hear No Evil, Taking Care of Business, The Babe, Married to It.
TELEVISION: Matinee Theatre, Playhouse 90, Climax, Alfred Hitchcock Presents, Gunsmoke, Ben Casey, Rte. 66, Naked City, The Dick Powell Show.

HILLER, DAME WENDY
Actress. D.B.E., 1975, O.B.E., 1971, Hon. LLD, Manchester, 1984. b. Bramhall, Cheshire, Eng., Aug. 15, 1912. e. Winceby House Sch., Bexhill. On stage 1930, Manchester Repertory Theatre, England; then on British tour. London debut 1935 in Love On the Dole; to N.Y., same role 1936. m.p. debut in Lancashire Luck, 1937.
THEATER: First Gentleman, Cradle Song, Tess of the D'Urbervilles, Heiress (NY & London), Ann Veronica, Waters of the Moon, Night of the Ball, Old Vic Theatre, Wings of the Dove, Sacred Flame, Battle of Shrivings, Crown Matrimonial, John Gabriel Borkman, Waters of the Moon (revival), Aspern Papers (revival), The Importance of Being Earnest, Driving Miss Daisy.
PICTURES: Lancashire Luck (debut, 1937), Pygmalion, Major Barbara, I Know Where I'm Going, Outcast of the Islands, Single Handed (Sailor of the King), Something of Value, How to Murder a Rich Uncle, Separate Tables (Academy Award, best supporting actress, 1958) Sons and Lovers, Toys in the Attic, A Man For All Seasons, Murder on the Orient Express, Voyage of the Damned, The Cat and the Canary, The Elephant Man, Making Love, The Lonely Passion of Judith Hearne.
TELEVISION: The Curse of King Tut's Tomb, David Copperfield (theatrical in U.K.), Witness for the Prosecution, Anne of Green Gables-The Sequel, Peer Gynt, The Kingfisher, All Passion Spent, A Taste for Death, Ending Up, The Best of Friends, The Countess Alice.

HILLERMAN, JOHN
Actor. b. Denison, TX, Dec. 20, 1932. e. U. of Texas. While in U.S. Air Force joined community theatre group and went to New York after completing military service. Studied at American Theatre Wing, leading to summer stock and off-B'way.
PICTURES: The Last Picture Show, Lawman, The Carey Treatment, What's Up Doc?, Skyjacked, High Plains Drifter, The Outside Man, The Thief Who Came to Dinner, Paper Moon, Blazing Saddles, Chinatown, At Long Last Love, The Nickel Ride, The Day of the Locust, Lucky Lady, Audrey Rose, Sunburn, History of the World Part I, Up the Creek.
TELEVISION: *Series*: Ellery Queen, The Betty White Show, Magnum P.I. (Emmy Award, 1987), The Hogan Family. *Movies*: Sweet Sweet Rachel, The Great Man's Whiskers, The Law, Ellery Queen, The Invasion of Johnson County, Relentless, Kill Me If You Can, A Guide for the Married Woman, Betrayal, Marathon, The Murder That Wouldn't Die, Little Gloria... Happy at Last, Assault and Matrimony, Street of Dreams, Hands of a Murderer. *Mini-Series*: Around the World in 80 Days.

HILLMAN, WILLIAM BRYON
Writer, Director, Producer. b. Chicago, IL, Feb. 3, 1951. e. Oklahoma Military Acad., UCLA. Head of production at Intro-Media Prod.; Fairchild Ent.; Spectro Prod.; Double Eagle Ent. Corp; Excellent Films Inc.; Creative consultant for The Hit 'Em Corp. Presently head of SpectroMedia Ent.
AUTHOR: Novels: Silent Changes, The Combination, The Liar, Additives The Perfect Crime, Why Me, The Loner.
PICTURES: Dir.-Writer: His Name is Joey (also exec. prod.), Tis the Season (also co-prod.), Strangers (also co-prod.), Back on the Street (also co-prod.), Loner (also co-prod.), Fast & Furious, The Master, Lovelines (s.p. only), Double Exposure (also co-prod.), The Passage, Campus, The Photographer (also prod.), The Man From Clover Grove (also co-prod.), Thetus, The Trail Ride (also co-prod.), Betta Betta (also prod.), Ragin' Cajun (also co-prod.).
TELEVISION: Working Together (pilot writer), Disco-Theque Pilot (dir., writer), Everything Will Be Alright (writer), Money (dir., writer), RIPA (writer).

HINES, GREGORY
Actor, Dancer. b. NY, Feb. 14, 1946. Early career as junior member of family dancing act starting at age 2. Nightclub debut at 5 as Hines Kids with brother Maurice (later renamed Hines Brothers as teenagers) and joined by father as Hines, Hines and Dad. B'way debut at 8 in The Girl in Pink Tights. Continued dancing with brother until 1973. Formed and performed with jazz-rock band, Severance. Solo album, Gregory Hines (1988).
THEATER: The Last Minstral Show (closed out of town). B'way: Eubie (Theatre World Award), Comin' Uptown (Tony nom.), Sophisticated Ladies (Tony nom.), Twelfth Night, Jelly's Last Jam (Tony Award, 1992).
PICTURES: History of the World Part 1 (debut, 1981), Wolfen, Deal of the Century, The Muppets Take Manhattan, The Cotton Club (also choreog.), White Nights, Running Scared, Off Limits, Tap (also choreog.), Eve of Destruction, A Rage in Harlem, Renaissance Man, Waiting to Exhale, Mad Dog Time.
TELEVISION: Movies: White Lie, T Bone N Weasel, Dead Air, A Stranger in Town. Guest: The Tonight Show, Motown Returns to the Apollo, Saturday Night Live.

HINGLE, PAT
Actor. b. Miami, FL, July 19, 1924. e. U. of Texas, 1949. Studied at Herbert Berghof Studio, American Theatre Wing, Actor's Studio.
THEATER: End as a Man (N.Y. debut, 1953), The Rainmaker, Festival, Cat on a Hot Tin Roof, Girls of Summer, Dark at the Top of the Stairs, J.B., The Deadly Game, Macbeth and Troilus and Cresida (with American Shakespeare Festival, Stratford, CT), Strange Interlude, Blues for Mr. Charlie, A Girl Could Get Lucky, The Glass Menagerie, The Odd Couple, Johnny No-Trump, The Price, Child's Play, The Selling of the President, That Championship Season, The Lady from the Sea, A Life, Thomas Edison: Reflections of a Genius (one man show).
RADIO: Voice of America.
PICTURES: On the Waterfront (debut, 1954), The Strange One, No Down Payment, Splendor in the Grass, All the Way Home, The Ugly American, Invitation to a Gunfighter, Nevada Smith, Sol Madrid, Hang 'em High, Jigsaw, Norwood, Bloody Mama, WUSA, The Carey Treatment, One Little Indian, Running Wild, Nightmare Honeymoon, The Super Cops, The Gauntlet, When You Comin' Back Red Ryder?, Norma Rae, America: Lost and Found (narrator), Sudden Impact, Running Brave, Going Berserk, The Falcon and the Snowman, Brewster's Millions, Maximum Overdrive, Baby Boom, The Land Before Time (voice), Batman, The Grifters, Batman Returns, Lightning Jack, The Quick and the Dead, Batman Forever, Large As Life.
TELEVISION: Series: Stone. Guest: Gunsmoke, MASH, Blue Skies, Matlock, Twilight Zone, The Untouchables, Trapper John M.D., Murder She Wrote, In the Heat of the Night, Cheers, Wings, American Gothic. Movies: The Ballad of Andy Crocker, A Clear and Present Danger, The City, Sweet Sweet Rachel, If Tomorrow Comes, Trouble Comes to Town, The Last Angry Man, The Secret Life of John Chapman, Escape from Bogen County, Sunshine Christmas, Tarantulas, Elvis, Stone (pilot), Disaster at the Coastliner, Wild Times, Of Mice and Men, Washington Mistress, The Fighter, Stranger on My Land, The Town Bully, Everybody's Baby: The Rescue of Jessica McClure, Not of This World, Gunsmoke: To the Last Man, Citizen Cohn, The Habitation of Dragons, Simple Justice, Against Her Will: The Carrie Buck Story, Truman. Mini-Series: War and Remembrance, The Kennedy's of Massachusetts.

HINKLE, ROBERT
Actor, Producer, Director. b. Brownfield, TX, July 25, 1930. e. Texas Tech. U. Joined Rodeo Cowboys Association, 1950 and rodeoed professionally until 1953 when began acting career in Outlaw Treasure. Pres. Cinema Pictures, Inc.
PICTURES: Actor: Giant, All the Fine Young Cannibals, Hud, The First Texan, Dakota Incident, Gun the Man Down, The Oklahoman, First Traveling Saleslady, No Place to Land, Under Fire, Speed Crazy, The Gunfight at Dodge City, Broken Land, Law in Silver City, Producer-Director: Ole Rex, Born Hunter,

Trauma, Something Can Be Done, Mr. Chat, Stuntman, Jumping Frog Jubilee, Mr. Chat-Mexico Safari, Trail Ride, Virginia City Cent., Texas Today, Texas Long Horns, Kentucky Thoroughbred Racing, Country Music, Guns of a Stranger.
TELEVISION: Prod. & Dir.: Test Pilot, Dial 111, Juvenile Squad, X13 Vertijet, Cellist Extraordinary, Sunday Challenge, The Drifter, Country Music Tribute, World of Horses, Country Music Videos.

HIRD, DAME THORA
Actress. b. Morecambe, Lancashire, Eng., May28, 1911. e. The Nelson Sch., Morecambe.
PICTURES: (Screen debut, 1940) The Black Sheep of Whitehall; Street Corner, Turn the Key Softly, Personal Affair, The Great Game, Storks Don't Talk, Shop Soiled, For Better or Worse; Love Match, One Good Turn, Quatermass Experiment, Simon and Laura, Lost, Sailor Beware, Home and Away, Good Companions, The Entertainer, A Kind of Loving, Term of Trial, Bitter Harvest, Rattle of a Simple Man, Some Will Some Won't, The Nightcomers, Consuming Passions.
TELEVISION: The Winslow Boy, The Bachelor, What Happens to Love, The Witching Hour, So Many Children, The Queen Came By, Albert Hope, All Things Bright and Beautiful, Say Nothing, Meet the Wife, Who's a Good Boy Then? I AM! Dixon of Dock Green, Romeo and Juliet, The First Lady, Ours Is a Nice House, The Foxtrot, Seasons, She Stoops to Conquer, Villa Maroc, When We Are Married, In Loving Memory, Flesh and Blood, Your Songs of Praise Choice, Hallelujah, Happiness, That's the Main Thing, Intensive Care, In Loving Memory, Praise Be, Last of the Summer Wine, The Fall, Cream Cracker Under the Settee (Talking Heads), Perfect Scoundrels, Wide Eyed and Legless... It's a Girl, Pat & Margaret, Thora on the Broad 'n' Narrow... South Bank Show.

HIRSCH, JUDD
Actor. b. New York, NY, March 15, 1935. e. City Coll. of New York. Studied physics but turned to acting; studied at Amer. Acad. of Dramatic Arts., HB Studios. First acting job in 1962 in Crisis in the Old Sawmill in Estes, Colorado; then to Woodstock Playhouse, before returning to N.Y.C.
THEATER: NY: On the Necessity of Being Polygamous, Barefoot in the Park, Scuba Duba, Mystery Play, HotL Baltimore, King of the United States, Prodigal, Knock Knock, Chapter Two, Talley's Folly (Obie Award), I'm Not Rappaport (Tony Award), Conversations With My Father (Tony Award).
PICTURES: Serpico (debut, 1973), King of the Gypsies, Ordinary People (Acad. Award nom.), Without a Trace, The Goodbye People, Teachers, Running on Empty, Independence Day.
TELEVISION: Series: Delvecchio, Taxi (2 Emmy Awards: 1981, 1983), Detective in the House, Dear John. Movies: The Law, Fear on Trial, Legend of Valentino, The Keegans, Sooner or Later, Marriage is Alive and Well, Brotherly Love, First Steps, The Great Escape II: The Untold Story, She Said No, Betrayal of Trust. Special: The Halloween That Almost Wasn't.

HIRSCHFIELD, ALAN J.
Executive. b. Oklahoma City, OK; Oct.10, 1935. e. U. of Oklahoma, B.A.; Harvard Business School, M.B.A. V.P., Allen & Co., 1959-66; Financial v.p. & dir. Warner/7 Arts, 1967-68; v.p. & dir., American Diversified Enterprises, 1969-73; pres. & chief exec. officer, Columbia Pictures Industries, 1973-78; consultant, Warner Communications, 1979, 1980-85, chmn. and chief exec. officer, 20th Century-Fox. Current: Co-CEO Data Broadcasting Corp. Dir., Cantel Inc., Chyron Corp.

HIRSHAN, LEONARD
Theatrical Agent. b. New York, NY, Dec.27, 1927. e. NYU. Joined William Morris Agency as agent trainee, New York, 1951. Agent legit theatre & TV dept. 1952-54. Sr. exec. agent M.P. dept., California office, 1955; sr. v.p., 1983; head of m.p. dept., west coast, 1986; named exec. v.p. and mem. bd. of dir., William Morris Agency, 1989; mem. bd. of dir., Center Theater Group, 1988; bd. governors Cedars-Sinai Hospital in L.A. 1987.

HIRSCHHORN, JOEL
Composer. b. Bronx, NY, Dec. 18, 1937. e. HS for the Performing Arts, Hunter Col.
PICTURES: Songs (with collaborator Al Kasha): The Fat Spy, The Cheyenne Social Club, The Poseidon Adventure (Academy Award for best song: The Morning After, 1972), The Towering Inferno (Academy Award for best song: We May Never Love Like This Again, 1974), Freaky Friday, Pete's Dragon, Hot Lead Cold Feet, The North Avenue Irregulars, All Dogs Go to Heaven, Rescue Me
TELEVISION: Series: Kids Inc., First and Ten, Getting in Touch, The Challengers. Specials: Kingdom Chums, A Precious Moments Christmas, The Magic Paintbrush, Caddie Woodlawn. Movies: Trapped Beneath the Sea, Someone I Touch, Charles Dickens' David Copperfield.

HITZIG, RUPERT
Producer, Director. b. New York, NY, Aug. 15, 1942. e. Harvard. At CBS as doc. writer-producer-director; later moved into dramas and comedy. Alan King's partner in King-Hitzig Prods.

PICTURES: *Prod.*: Electra Glide in Blue, Happy Birthday Gemini, Cattle Annie and Little Britches, Wolfen (also 2nd unit dir.), Jaws 3-D, The Last Dragon, The Squeeze. Dir.: Night Visitor, Backstreet Dreams, The Legend of O.B. Taggart, Last Lives (dir.).
TELEVISION: Much Ado About Nothing, The Wonderful World of Jonathan Winters, Playboy After Dark, How to Pick Up Girls, Return to Earth, Saturday Night Live, Birds of Prey, Date My Dad, Save Our Streets, annual comedy awards, television series and numerous specials.

HOBERMAN, DAVID
Executive. b. 1953. Started career as prod. exec. with TAT Communications for five years. 1982-85, worked as m.p. agent with Writers and Artists Agency and later at Ziegler Associates and ICM. 1985, named v.p. of prod. for Walt Disney Pictures based at studio. 1987, promoted to sr. v.p., prod. 1988, named president, production. 1989, pres. Touchstone Pictures. 1994, appointed head of all motion pictures produced by Walt Disney. Resigned from Disney, 1995, to form Mandeville Films.

HOCK, MORT
Executive. Blaine-Thompson Agency; A. E. Warner Bros., 1948; David Merrick B'way Prod., 1958; asst. adv. mgr., Paramount Pictures Corp., 1960; adv. mgr., United Artists Corp., 1962; dir. adv., UA Corp., 1964; adv. dir., Paramount, 1965; v.p. adv. & public rltns., Paramount, 1968-71; v.p., marketing, Rastar Prods., 1971; exec. v.p., Charles Schlaifer & Co., 1974; sr. v.p. entertainment div., DDB Needham Worldwide, 1983; exec. v.p. DDB, 1994.

HODGE, PATRICIA
Actress. b. Cleethorpes, Lincolnshire, England, Sept. 29, 1946. Studied at London Acad. of Music and Dramatic Arts.
THEATER: Popkiss, Two Gentlemen of Verona, Pippin, The Mitford Girls, Benefactors, Noel and Gertie, Separate Tables, The Prime of Miss Jean Brodie.
PICTURES: The Elephant Man, Betrayal, Sunset, Thieves in the Night, Diamond's Edge.
TELEVISION: The Naked Civil Servant, Rumpole of the Bailey, Edward and Mrs. Simpson, Holding the Fort, Jemima Shore Investigates, Hay Fever, Hotel Du Lac, The Life and Loves of a She-Devil, Exclusive Yarns, Let's Face the Music of..., Inspector Morse, The Shell Seekers, The Secret Life of Ian Fleming, The Heat of the Day, Rich Tea and Sympathy, The Cloning of Joanna May.

HOFFMAN, DUSTIN
b. Los Angeles, CA, Aug. 8, 1937. m. Lisa Hoffman. e. Los Angeles Conservatory of Music, Santa Monica Coll., Pasadena Playhouse, 1958. Worked as an attendant at a psychiatric institution, a demonstrator in Macy's toy dept., and a waiter. First stage role 1960 in Yes Is for a Very Young Man, at Sarah Lawrence Coll. Acted in summer stock, television and dir. at community theatre. Asst. dir. Off-B'way of A View From the Bridge.
THEATER: *Broadway and Off Broadway*: A Cook for Mr. General (bit part, B'way debut), Harry Noon and Night, Journey of the Fifth Horse (Obie Award), Eh? (Vernon Rice & Theatre World Awards), Jimmy Shine, All Over Town (dir. only), Death of a Salesman (Drama Desk Award), The Merchant of Venice (also London).
PICTURES: The Tiger Makes Out (debut, 1967), Madigan's Millions, The Graduate, Midnight Cowboy, John and Mary, Little Big Man, Who Is Harry Kellerman and Why Is He Saying Those Terrible Things About Me?, Straw Dogs, Alfredo Alfredo, Papillon, Lenny, All the President's Men, Marathon Man, Straight Time, Agatha, Kramer vs. Kramer (Academy Award, 1979), Tootsie, Ishtar, Rain Man (Academy Award, 1988), Family Business, Dick Tracy, Billy Bathgate, Hook, Hero, Outbreak, American Buffalo, Sleepers.
TELEVISION: *Specials*: Journey of the Fifth Horse, The Star Wagons, Free to Be You and Me, Bette Midler: Old Red Hair Is Back, Common Threads: Stories from the Quilt (narrator), The Earth Day Special. Movies: The Point (narrator), Death of a Salesman (Emmy Award, 1985). *Guest*: Naked City, The Defenders.

HOFFMAN, JOSEPH
Writer. b. New York, NY, Feb. 20, 1909. e. UCLA. Newspaperman, screen writer, magazine writer. TV prod. Now TV and screen freelance writer.
PICTURES: China Sky, Don't Trust Your Husband, Gung-Ho, And Baby Makes Three, Weekend with Father, Duel at Silver Creek, At Sword's Point, Has Anybody Seen My Gal?, Against All Flags, No Room for the Groom, Lone Hand, Yankee Pasha, Rails into Laramie, Tall Man Riding, Chicago Syndicate, Live a Little, How to Make Love and Like It, Sex and the Single Girl.
TELEVISION: *Producer*: Ford Theatre, Colt 45. *Writer*: Leave It to Beaver, My Three Sons, The Virginian, Love American Style, Bonanza, Patty Duke Show, Family Affair, etc.

HOGAN, HULK
Actor. r.n. Terry Gene Bollea. b. Augusta, GA, Aug. 11, 1953. Former bodyguard then prof. wrestler using names Sterling Golden, Terry Boulder, then finally Hulk Hogan.

PICTURES: Rocky III (debut, 1982), No Holds Barred, Gremlins 2: The New Batch, Suburban Commado, Mr. Nanny, Santa with Muscles.
TELEVISION: *Series*: Hulk Hogan's Rock 'n' Wrestling (voice), Thunder in Paradise (also exec. prod.). *Pilot*: Goldie and the Bears. *Guest*: The A-Team, The Love Boat.

HOGAN, PAUL
Actor, Writer. b. Lightning Ridge, Australia, Oct. 8, 1939. m. actress Linda Kozlowski. Worked as rigger before gaining fame on Australian TV as host of nightly current affairs show (A Current Affair) and The Paul Hogan Show. Shows now syndicated in 26 countries. In U.S. gained attention with commercials for Australian Tourist Commission. 1985, starred in dramatic role on Australian TV in series, Anzacs. Live one-man show, Paul Hogan's America, 1991.
PICTURES: Fatty Finn (debut, 1980), Crocodile Dundee (also co-s.p.), Crocodile Dundee II (also exec. prod., co-s.p.), Almost an Angel (also exec. prod., s.p.), Lightning Jack (also s.p., co-prod.), Flipper.
TELEVISION: Anzacs: The War Down Under.

HOLBROOK, HAL
Actor. b. Cleveland, OH, Feb. 17, 1925. m. actress Dixie Carter. e. Denison U., 1948. Summer stock 1947-53. Gained fame and several awards for performance as Mark Twain on stage in Mark Twain Tonight over a period of years throughout the US and abroad.
THEATER: Mark Twain Tonight (Tony Award, 1966), Do You Know the Milky Way?, Abe Lincoln in Illinois, American Shakespeare Fest., Lincoln Center Repertory (After the Fall, Marco Millions, Incident at Vichy, Tartuffe), The Glass Menagerie, The Apple Tree, I Never Sang For My Father, Man of La Mancha, Does a Tiger Wear a Necktie?, Lake of the Woods, Buried Inside Extra, The Country Girl, King Lear. Regional: Our Town, The Merchant of Venice, Uncle Vanya.
PICTURES: The Group (debut, 1966), Wild in the Streets, The People Next Door, The Great White Hope, They Only Kill Their Masters, Jonathan Livingston Seagull (voice), Magnum Force, The Girl From Petrovka, All the President's Men, Midway, Julia, Rituals (The Creeper), Capricorn One, Natural Enemies, The Fog, The Kidnapping of the President, Creepshow, The Star Chamber, Girls Night Out (The Scaremaker), Wall Street, The Unholy, Fletch Lives, The Firm, Carried Away.
TELEVISION: *Series*: The Bold Ones: The Senator (Emmy Award, 1971), Designing Women, Portrait of America (4 annual ACE Awards, 2 Emmy Awards, 1988, 1989), Evening Shade. Movies: Coronet Blue, The Whole World is Watching, A Clear and Present Danger, Travis Logan, Suddenly Single, Goodbye Raggedy Ann, That Certain Summer, Murder by Natural Causes, Legend of the Golden Gun, When Hell Was in Session, Off the Minnesota Strip, The Killing of Randy Webster, Under Siege, Behind Enemy Lines, Dress Gray, The Fortunate Pilgrim, Three Wishes for Billy Grier, Emma, Queen of the South Seas, Day One, Sorry Wrong Number, A Killing in a Small Town, Bonds of Love, A Perry Mason Mystery: The Case of the Lethal Lifestyle, A Perry Mason Mystery: The Case of the Grimacing Governor, A Perry Mason Mystery: The Case of the Jealous Jokester, She Stood Alone: The Tailhook Scandal. *Specials*: Mark Twain Tonight, Pueblo (Emmy Award, 1974), Sandburg's Lincoln (Emmy Award, 1976), Our Town, Plaza Suite, The Glass Menagerie, The Awakening Land, The Oath: 33 Hours in the Life of God, Omnibus. *Mini-Series*: North and South Books I & II, Celebrity, George Washington, Rockport Christmas.

HOLDRIDGE, LEE
Composer. b. Port-au-Prince, Haiti, March 3, 1944. e. Manhattan School of Music. Music arranger for Neil Diamond, 1969-73, with whom he collaborated on the score for Jonathan Livingston Seagull. Wrote score for B'way musical Into the Light (1986). With Alan Raph wrote score for the Joffrey Ballet's Trinity. One-act opera for L.A. Opera commission: Journey to Cordoba.
PICTURES: Jeremy, Jonathan Livingston Seagull, Forever Young Forever Free, Mustang Country, The Other Side of the Mountain—Part 2, The Pack, Moment By Moment, Oliver's Story, French Postcards, Tilt, American Pop, The Beastmaster, Mr. Mom, Micki and Maude, Splash, Sylvester, 16 Days of Glory, Transylvania 6-5000, The Men's Club, Big Business, Old Gringo, Pastime, Freefall.
TELEVISION: *Series*: One Life to Live, Hec Ramsey, Moonlighting, Beauty and the Beast, Bob. *Movies*: East of Eden, Fly Away Home, The Day the Loving Stopped, For Ladies Only, The Sharks, The Story Lady, Running Out, In Love With an Older Woman, Running Out, Thursday's Child, Wizards and Warriors, The Mississippi, Legs, I Want to Live, Letting Go, Fatal Judgment, The Tenth Man, I'll Take Manhattan, Do You Know the Muffin Man?, Incident at Dark River, A Mother's Courage, In the Arms of a Killer, Face of a Stranger, Deadly Matrimony, Killer Rules, One Against the Wind, Call of the Wild, Torch Song, Barcelona '92: 16 Days of Glory, Jack Reed: Badge of Honor, Incident in a Small Town, The Yearling, Heidi, Texas, Tyson, Buffalo Girls, The Tuskegee Airmen, Nothing Lasts Forever.

HOLLAND, AGNIESZKA
Director, Writer. b. Warsaw, Poland, Nov. 28, 1948. e. FAMU, Prague. m. director Laco Adamik. Studied filmmaking in Czechoslovakia. Worked in Poland with director Andrzej Wajda. Moved to Paris in 1981.
PICTURES: Screen Tests (dir., s.p. episode), Provincial Actors (dir., s.p.), Bez Znieczulenia (s.p.), A Woman Alone (dir., co-s.p.), Danton (co-s.p.), Interrogation (actor) A Love in Germany (co-s.p.), Angry Harvest (dir., co-s.p.), Anna (s.p., story), Les Possedes (co-s.p.), La Amiga (co-s.p.), To Kill a Priest (dir., co-s.p.), Korczak (s.p.), Europa Europa (dir., s.p.), Olivier Olivier (dir., s.p.), The Secret Garden (dir.), Total Eclipse (dir.).
TELEVISION: Evening With Abdon, The Children of Sunday, Something for Something, Lorenzaccio, The Trial, Largo Desolato.

HOLLAND, TOM
Director, Writer. b. Highland, NY, July 11, 1945. e. Northwestern U. Started as actor, working at Bucks County Playhouse in PA and HB Studios in NY. Appeared on daytime serials Love of Life, Love is a Many-Splendored Thing. Turned to commercial prod. while attended UCLA law school, then took up screenwriting.
PICTURES: Writer: The Beast Within, The Class of 1984, Pyscho II (also actor), Scream for Help, Cloak and Dagger. Director: Fright Night (also s.p.), Fatal Beauty, Child's Play (also co-s.p.), The Temp, Thinner.
TELEVISION: Movie: The Stranger Within. Series: Tales From the Crypt (dir. 3 episodes: Love Come Hack to Me-also co-writer, Four-Sided Triangle-also co-writer, King of the Road). Mini-Series: Stephen King's The Langoliers (also writer, actor).

HOLLIMAN, EARL
Actor. b. Delhi, LA, Sept. 11, 1928. e. U. of Southern California, Pasadena Playhouse. Pres., Actors and Others for Animals.
THEATER: Camino Real (Mark Taper Forum), A Streetcar Named Desire (Ahmanson).
PICTURES: Scared Stiff, The Girls of Pleasure Island, Destination Gobi, East of Sumatra, Devil's Canyon, Tennessee Champ, The Bridges at Toko-Ri, Broken Lance, The Big Combo, I Died a Thousand Times, Forbidden Planet, Giant, The Burning Hills, The Rainmaker, Gunfight at the OK Corral, Trooper Hook, Don't Go Near the Water, Hot Spell, The Trap, Last Train From Gun Hill, Visit to a Small Planet, Armored Command, Summer and Smoke, The Sons of Katie Elder, A Covenant With Death, The Power, Anzio, The Biscuit Eater, Good Luck Miss Wyckoff, Sharky's Machine.
TELEVISION: Series: Hotel de Paree, Wide Country, Police Woman, P.S. I Luv You, Delta. Pilot: Twilight Zone. Movies: Tribes, Alias Smith and Jones, Cannon, The Desperate Mission, Trapped, Cry Panic, I Love You... Goodbye, Alexander: The Other Side of Down, The Solitary Man, Where the Ladies Go, Country Gold, Gunsmoke: Return to Dodge, American Harvest, P.S. I Luv You (pilot). Mini-Series: The Thorn Birds. Specials: The Dark Side of the Earth, The Return of Ansel Gibbs.

HOLM, CELESTE
Actress. b. New York, NY, Apr. 29, 1919. e. Univ. Sch. for Girls, Chicago, Francis W. Parker, Chicago, Lyceae Victor Durui (Paris), U. of Chicago, UCLA. p. Theodor Holm and Jean Parke Holm. m. actor Wesley Addy.
THEATER: B'way: Gloriana, The Time of Your Life, 8 O'Clock Tuesday, Another Sun, Return of the Vagabond, My Fair Ladies, Papa Is All, All the Comforts of Home, The Damask Cheek, Oklahoma!, Bloomer Girl, She Stoops to Conquer, Affairs of State, Anna Christie, The King and I, Interlock, Third Best Sport, Invitation to a March, Mame, Candida, Habeas Corpus, The Utter Glory of Morrissey Hall, I Hate Hamlet. Off-B'way: A Month in the Country. Theatre-in-Concert for the U.S. State Department in 8 countries May-July 1966. Regional: Janet Flanner's Paris Was Yesterday. Natl. Tour: Mame (Sarah Siddons Award), Hay Fever, Road to Mecca, Cocktail Hour.
PICTURES: Three Little Girls in Blue (debut, 1946), Carnival in Costa Rica, Gentleman's Agreement (Academy Award, best supporting actress, 1947), Road House, The Snake Pit, Chicken Every Sunday, Come to the Stable (Acad. Award nom.), A Letter to Three Wives (voice), Everybody Does It, Champagne for Caesar, All About Eve (Acad. Award nom.), The Tender Trap, High Society, Bachelor Flat, Doctor You've Got To Be Kidding, Tom Sawyer, Bittersweet Love, The Private Files of J. Edgar Hoover, Three Men and a Baby.
TELEVISION: Specials: A Clearing in the Wood, Play of the Week, Cinderella, Nora's Christmas Gift. Mini-Series: Backstairs at the White House (Emmy nom.). Movies: Underground Man, Death Cruise, Love Boat II, Midnight Lace, The Shady Hill Kidnapping, This Girl for Hire, Murder by the Book, Polly, Polly-Comin' Home! Pilot: Road Show. Series: Honestly Celeste, Who Pays, Nancy, Jessie, Falcon Crest, Christine Cromwell, Loving. Guest: Love Boat, Trapper John M.D., Magnum P.I.
RADIO: People at the U.N., Theatre Guild on the Air, Mystery Theatre.

HOLM, IAN
C.B.E. Actor. b. Ilford, Essex, England, Sept. 12, 1931. r.n. Ian Holm Cuthbert. e. RADA. On British stage in Love Affair, Titus Andronicus, Henry IV, Ondine, Becket, The Homecoming (B'way: Tony Award, 1967), Henry V, Richard III, Romeo and Juliet, The Sea, etc.
PICTURES: The Bofors Gun (debut, 1968), A Midsummer Night's Dream, The Fixer, Oh! What a Lovely War, A Severed Head, Nicholas and Alexandra, Mary Queen of Scots, Young Winston, The Homecoming, Juggernaut, Robin and Marian, Shout at the Devil, March or Die, Alien, Chariots of Fire (Acad. Award nom.), Time Bandits, Return of the Soldier, Greystoke: The Legend of Tarzan Lord of the Apes, Dance With a Stranger, Wetherby, Dreamchild, Brazil, Laughterhouse, Another Woman, Henry V, Hamlet, Kafka, Naked Lunch, The Advocate, Mary Shelley's Frankenstein, The Madness of King George, Big Night, Night Falls On Manhattan, The Fifth Element.
TELEVISION: Mini-Series/Movies: Les Miserables, S.O.S. Titanic, Napoleon, We the Accused, All Quiet on the Western Front, Holocaust, Man in the Iron Mask, Jesus of Nazareth, Thief of Bagdad, Game Set and Match, A Season of Giants, The Borrowers. Specials: The Browning Version, Murder By the Book, Uncle Vanya, Tailor of Gloucester, The Lost Boys, The Last Romantics.

HOMEIER, SKIP
Actor. r.n. George Vincent Homeier. b. Chicago, IL, Oct. 5, 1930. e. UCLA. Started in radio, 1936-43; on B'way stage, Tomorrow the World, 1943-44 which led to film debut in adaptation of same (billed as Skippy Homeier).
PICTURES: Tomorrow the World (debut, 1944), Boys' Ranch, Mickey, Arthur Takes Over, The Big Cat, The Gunfighter, Halls of Montezuma, Fixed Bayonets, Sealed Cargo, Sailor Beware, Has Anybody Seen My Gal?, The Last Posse, The Lone Gun, Beachhead, Black Widow, Dawn at Socorro, Ten Wanted Men, The Road to Denver, At Gunpoint, Cry Vengeance, The Burning Hills, Between Heaven and Hell, Dakota Incident, No Road Back, Stranger at My Door, Thunder Over Arizona, The Tall T, Lure of the Swamp, Decision at Durango, Day of the Badman, Journey Into Darkness, The Punderers of Painted Flats, Commanche Station, Showdown, Bullet for a Badman, Stark Fear, The Ghost and Mr. Chicken, Dead Heat on a Merry-Go-Round, Tiger By the Tail, The Greatest.
TELEVISION: Series: Dan Raven, The Interns. Guest: Playhouse 90, Alcoa Hour, Kraft Theatre, Studio 1, Armstrong Circle Theatre, Alfred Hitchcock. Movies: The Challenge, Two for the Money, Voyage of the Yes, Helter Skelter, Overboard, The Wild Wild West Revisited. Mini-Series: Washington: Behind Closed Doors.

HOOKS, KEVIN
Actor, Director. b. Philadelphia, PA, Sept. 19, 1958. Son of actor-director Robert Hooks.
PICTURES: Sounder, Aaron Loves Angela, A Hero Ain't Nothin' But a Sandwich, Take Down, Innerspace, Strictly Business (also dir.), Passenger 57 (dir. only), Fled.
TELEVISION: Series: The White Shadow, He's the Mayor. Movies: Just an Old Sweet Song, The Greatest Thing That Almost Happened, Friendly Fire, Can You Hear the Laughter?-The Story of Freddie Prinze, Roots: The Gift (dir.), Murder Without Motive: The Edmund Perry Story (dir.). Mini-Series: Backstairs at the White House. Special: Home Sweet Homeless (dir.).

HOOKS, ROBERT
Actor, Director, Producer. b. Washington, D.C., April 18, 1937. Father of actor-director Kevin Hooks. Co-founder and exec. dir. Negro Ensemble Co. NY 1968-present. Founder DC Black Theatre, Washington, D.C. 1973-77. Co-star of TV series NYPD, 1967-69.
THEATER: Tiger Tiger Burning Bright (B'way. debut, 1962), Ballad for Bimshire, The Blacks, Dutchman, Henry V, Happy Ending, Day of Absence, Where's Daddy? (Theatre World Award for last two), Hallelujah, Baby?, Kongi's Harvest, A Soldier's Play (Mark Taper Forum, LA). Co-prod.: with Gerald S. Krone: Song of the Lusitanian Bogey, Daddy Goodness, Ceremonies in Dark Old Men, Day of Absence, The Sty of the Blind Pig, The River Niger, The First Breeze of Summer.
PICTURES: Sweet Love Bitter, Hurry Sundown, The Last of the Mobile Hot-Shots, Trouble Man, Aaron Loves Angela, Airport '77, Fast-Walking, Star Trek III: The Search For Spock, Passenger 57, Posse, Fled.
TELEVISION: Series: N.Y.P.D., Supercarrier. Pilots: The Cliff Dweller, Two for the Money, Down Home. Movies: Carter's Army, Vanished, The Cable Car Murder, Crosscurrent, Trapped, Ceremonies in Dark Old Men, Just an Old Sweet Song, The Killer Who Wouldn't Die, The Courage and the Passion, To Kill a Cop, A Woman Called Moses, Hollow Image, Madame X, The Oklahoma City Dolls, The Sophisticated Gents, Cassie and Co., Starflight-The Plane that Couldn't Land, Feel the Heat, Sister Sister, The Execution.

HOOL, LANCE
Producer, Director. b. Mexico City, Mex., May 11, 1948. e. Univ. of the Americas.
PICTURES: Producer: Cabo Blanco, Ten to Midnight, The Evil That Men Do, Missing in Action (also s.p.), Missing in Action 2

(dir.), Steel Dawn (also dir.), Options, Damned River, Pure Luck, The Air Up There, Gunmen, Road Flower, Flipper, McHale's Navy.
TELEVISION: The Tracker, Born To Run, Cover Girl Murders,. Flashfire.

HOOPER, TOBE
Director. b. Austin, Texas, Jan. 25, 1943. e. Univ. of TX. Began film career making documentary and industrial films and commercials in Texas. Was asst. dir. of U. of Texas film program, continuing filmmaking while working with students. First feature film: documentary Peter Paul & Mary, followed by Eggshells. Directed Billy Idol video Dancing With Myself.
PICTURES: The Texas Chainsaw Massacre (also prod., co-s.p.), Eaten Alive (Death Trap), The Funhouse, Poltergeist, Lifeforce, Invaders from Mars, The Texas Chainsaw Massacre Part 2 (also co-prod., co- music), Spontaneous Combustion, Sleepwalkers (actor only), Night Terrors, The Mangler (also co-s.p.).
TELEVISION: Movie: I'm Dangerous Tonight. Mini-Series: Salem's Lot. Series episodes: Amazing Stories, Freddy's Nightmares (No More Mr. Nice Guy-1st episode), Equalizer (No Place Like Home), Tales from the Crypt (Dead Wait). Pilots: Haunted Lives, Body Bags.

HOPE, BOB
Actor. r.n. Leslie Townes Hope. b. Eltham, England, May 29, 1903. To U.S. at age 4; raised in Cleveland, OH. Became American citizen in 1920. Was amateur boxer before appearing in vaudeville as comedian/song and dance man. Debuted on B'way 1933 in Roberta, followed by stage work in Ziegfeld Follies, Red Hot & Blue. Began film career 1934, appearing in 8 short films made in NY, before going to Hollywood for feature debut, 1938, signing contract with Paramount. Starred on radio, 1938-56; made countless trips overseas to entertain U.S. troops during wartime; lent name to Bob Hope Desert Classic golf tournament. Voted one of top ten Money-Making Stars in M.P. Herald-Fame Poll: 1941-47, 1949-53. Recipient: 5 special Academy Awards (1940, 1944, 1952, 1959, 1965); special Emmy Awards: Trustees Award (1959), Governors Award (1984); Kennedy Center Honors (1985); Presidential Medal of Freedom, and many other awards. Author (or-co-author): They Got Me Covered, I Never Left Home, So This Is Peace, Have Tux Will Travel, I Owe Russia $1,200, Five Women I Love: Obit Hope's Vietnam Story, The Last Christmas Show, The Road to Hollywood: My 40-Year Love Affair With the Movies, Confessions of a Hooker: My Lifelong Love Affair With Golf, Don't Shoot It's Only Me.
PICTURES: The Big Broadcast of 1938 (feature debut, 1938), College Swing, Give Me a Sailor, Thanks for the Memory, Never Say Die, Some Like It Hot, The Cat and the Canary, Road to Singapore, The Ghost Breakers, Road to Zanzibar, Caught in the Draft, Louisiana Purchase, My Favorite Blonde, Road to Morocco, Nothing But the Truth, They Got Me Covered, Star Spangled Rhythm, Let's Face It, Road to Utopia, The Princess and the Pirate, Monsieur Beaucaire, My Favorite Brunette, Where There's Life, Road to Rio, The Paleface, Sorrowful Jones, The Great Lover, Fancy Pants, The Lemon Drop Kid, My Favorite Spy, Son of Paleface, Road to Bali, Off Limits, Scared Stiff (cameo), Here Come the Girls, Casanova's Big Night, The Seven Little Foys, That Certain Feeling, The Iron Petticoat, Beau James, Paris Holiday (also prod., story), Alias Jesse James (also prod.), The Five Pennies (cameo), The Facts of Life, Bachelor in Paradise, The Road to Hong Kong, Call Me Bwana, A Global Affair, I'll Take Sweden, The Oscar (cameo), Boy Did I Get a Wrong Number!, Not With My Wife You Don't (cameo), Eight on the Lam, The Private Navy of Sgt. O'Farrell, How to Commit Marriage, Cancel My Reservation (also exec. prod.), The Muppet Movie (cameo), Spies Like Us (cameo).
TELEVISION: Series: Chesterfield Sound Off Time, Colgate Comedy Hour (rotating host), Bob Hope Presents the Chrysler Theatre (Emmy Award as exec. prod. and host, 1966). Movie: A Masterpiece of Murder. Many specials incl. prod. of Roberta, annual variety shows; also was frequent host of annual Academy Award telecast.

HOPE, HARRY
Producer, Director, Writer. b. May 26, 1926. e. UCLA, Etudes Universitaires Internationales, Ph.D. Entered m.p. industry as special effects man, Republic Studios, 1944; associate producer Star Productions; formed Blue Bird Film Co. Has since produced, directed and written 33 feature films, including Like the Gull, 1967, which won creative classical film award as Asian Film Festival. Founded Western International and directed First Leisure Corp. as exec. v.p. until 1972. From then until present, pres. of Harry Hope Production. Among recent film credits: Smokey and the Judge, Sunset Cove, Doomsday Machine, Death Dimension, Thunderfist, Tarzana, The Mad Butcher, Death Blow, Pop's Oasis.

HOPKINS, SIR ANTHONY
C.B.E.: Actor. b. Port Talbot, South Wales, Dec. 31, 1937. Trained at Royal Acad. of Dramatic Art; Welsh Coll. of Music & Drama. Joined National Theatre, gaining fame on stage in

England, then TV and films. Appeared in short The White Bus. Recordings: Under Milk Wood (1988), Shostakovich Symphony No. 13 Babi Yar (reciting Yevtushenko's poem, 1994). Dir. An Evening With Dylan Thomas, 1993. Received special award at Montreal Film Festival for Career Excellence, 1992; Evening Standard Film Awards Special Award for Body of Work, 1994; BAFTA Britannia Award for Outstanding Contribution to the International Film and TV Industry, 1995.
THEATER: Julius Caesar (debut, 1964), Juno and the Paycock, A Flea in Her Ear, The Three Sisters, Dance of Death, As You Like It, The Architect and the Emperor of Assyria, A Woman Killed With Kindness, Coriolanus, The Taming of the Shrew, Macbeth, Equus (NY, 1974-75; Outer Critics Circle, NY Drama Desk, US Authors & Celebrities Forum Awards), Equus (LA 1977, also dir.; LA Drama Critics Award), The Tempest, Old Times, The Lonely Road, Pravda (Variety Club Stage Actor Award, 1985; British Theatre Association Best Actor, Laurence Olivier & Observer Awards), King Lear, Antony and Cleopatra, M. Butterfly, August (also dir.).
PICTURES: The Lion in Winter (debut, 1967), The Looking Glass War, Hamlet, When Eight Bells Toll, Young Winston, A Doll's House, The Girl from Petrovka, Juggernaut, Audrey Rose, A Bridge Too Far, International Velvet, Magic, The Elephant Man, A Change of Seasons, The Bounty (Variety Club UK Film Actor Award, 1983), 84 Charing Cross Road (Moscow Film Fest. Award, 1987), The Good Father, The Dawning, A Chorus of Disapproval, Desperate Hours, The Silence of the Lambs (Academy Award, Natl. Board of Review, NY Film Critics, Boston Film Critics & BAFTA Awards, 1991), Freejack, One Man's War, Howards End, The Efficiency Expert (Spotswood), Bram Stoker's Dracula, Chaplin, The Remains of the Day (BAFTA, Variety Club UK Film Actor, LA Film Critics, Japan Critics Awards, 1993), The Trial, Shadowlands (Natl. Board of Review & LA Film Critics Award, 1993), The Road to Wellville, Legends of The Fall, The Innocent, August (also dir.), Nixon, Surviving Picasso.
TELEVISION: A Heritage and Its History, Vanya, Hearts and Flowers, Decision to Burn, War & Peace, Cuculus Canorus, Lloyd George, QB VII, Find Me, A Childhood Friend, Possessions, All Creatures Great and Small, The Arcata Promise, Dark Victory, The Lindbergh Kidnapping Case (Emmy Award, 1976), Victory at Entebbe, Kean, Mayflower: The Pilgrim's Adventure, The Bunker (Emmy Award, 1981), Peter and Paul, Othello, Little Eyolf, The Hunchback of Notre Dame, A Married Man, Corridors of Power, Strangers and Brothers, Arch of Triumph, Mussolini and I / Mussolini: The Rise and Fall of Il Duce (ACE Award), Hollywood Wives, Guilty Conscience, Blunt, The Dawning, Across the Lake, Heartland, The Tenth Man, Great Expectations, One Man's War, To Be the Best, A Few Selected Exits, Big Cats.

HOPKINS, BO
Actor. b. Greenwood, SC, Feb. 2, 1942. Studied with Uta Hagen in N.Y. then with Desilu Playhouse training school in Hollywood. Parts in several prods. for that group won him an agent, an audition with director Sam Peckinpah and his first role in latter's The Wild Bunch.
PICTURES: The Wild Bunch (debut, 1969), Monte Walsh, The Moonshine War, The Culpepper Cattle Co., The Getaway, White Lightning, The Man Who Loved Cat Dancing, American Graffiti, The Nickel Ride, The Day of the Locust, Posse, The Killer Elite, A Small Town in Texas, Tentacles, Midnight Express, More American Graffiti, The Fifth Floor, Sweet Sixteen, Night Shadows, Trapper Country, What Comes Around, War, The Bounty Hunter, The Stalker, Nightmare at Noon, The Tenth Man, Big Bad John, Center of the Web, Inside Monkey Zetterland, The Ballad of Little Jo, Cheyenne Warrior, Radioland Murders, Riders in the Storm, The Feminine Touch.
TELEVISION: Series: Doc Elliott, The Rockford Files, Dynasty. Movies: The Runaway Barge, Kansas City Massacre, Charlie's Angels (pilot), The Invasion of Johnson County, Dawn: Portrait of a Teenage Runaway, Thaddeus Rose and Eddie, Crisis in Sun Valley, Plutonium Incident, A Smoky Mountain Christmas, Beggerman Thief, Down the Long Hills, Last Ride of the Dalton Gang, Casino, Rodeo Girl, Ghost Dancing, Blood Ties. Special: Wyatt Earp: Return to Tombstone.

HOPPER, DENNIS
Actor, Director. b. Dodge City, KS, May 17, 1936. e. San Diego, CA, public schools. Author: Out of the Sixties (1988; book of his photographs).
PICTURES: Rebel Without a Cause, I Died a Thousand Times, Giant, The Steel Jungle, The Story of Mankind, Gunfight at the OK Corral, From Hell to Texas, The Young Land, Key Witness, Night Tide, Tarzan and Jane Regained Sort Of, The Sons of Katie Elder, Queen of Blood, Cool Hand Luke, Glory Stompers, The Trip, Panic in the City, Hang 'Em High, True Grit, Easy Rider (also dir., co-s.p.), The Last Movie (also dir., s.p.), Kid Blue, James Dean-The First American Teenager, Bloodbath (The Sky Is Falling), Mad Dog Morgan, Tracks, The American Friend, Couleur Chair, The Sorcerer's Appentices, L'Ordre et la Securite du Monde, Resurrection, Apocalypse Now, Out of the Blue (also dir.), King of the Mountain, Renacida, White Star, Human

Highway, Rumble Fish, The Osterman Weekend, My Science Project, The Texas Chainsaw Massacre Part 2, Hoosiers (Acad. Award nom.), Blue Velvet, Black Widow, River's Edge, Straight to Hell, The Pick Up Artist, O.C. and Stiggs, Riders of the Storm, Blood Red, Colors (dir. only), Flashback, Chattachoochee, The Hot Spot (dir. only), Superstar: The Life and Times of Andy Warhol, The Indian Runner, Hearts of Darkness: A Filmmaker's Apocalypse, Midnight Heat, Eye of the Storm, Boiling Point, Super Mario Bros., True Romance, Red Rock West, Chasers (also dir.), Speed, Search and Destroy, Waterworld, Acts of Love, Basquiat, Carried Away.
TELEVISION: *Movies*: Wild Times, Stark, Paris Trout, Double-crossed, Backtrack (also dir.), Nails, The Heart of Justice, Witch Hunt. *Guest*: Pursuit, Espionage, Medic, Loretta Young Show.

HORN, ALAN
Executive. b. New York, NY, Feb. 28, 1943. e. Union Coll., Harvard Business Sch. 1971, joined Tandem Prods., 1972; named v.p., business affairs, and of sister co., T.A.T. Communications, 1973; 1977, exec. v.p & COO; pres., 1978. In 1983 named chmn. Embassy Communications. 1986 joined 20th Century Fox as pres. COO. Left Fox Sept. 1986. Co-founded Castle Rock Entertainment 1987; Chmn. & CEO after being acquired by Turner Broadcasting System Inc. in 1994.

HORNE, LENA
Singer, Actress. b. Brooklyn, NY, June 30, 1917. Radio with Noble Sissle, Charlie Barnet, other bands. Floor shows at Cotton Club, Cafe Society, Little Troc, etc. Started screen career 1942. Appeared in short subjects Harlem Hotshots, Boogie Woogie Dream. Autobiographies: In Person (1950), Lena (1965) Recipient Kennedy Center Honors for Lifetime contribution to the Arts, 1984. Spingarn Award, NAACP, 1983; Paul Robeson Award, Actors Equity Assn., 1985.
THEATER: Blackbirds, Dance With Your Gods, Jamaica, Pal Joey (L.A. Music Center), Lena Horne: The Lady and Her Music (Tony Award).
PICTURES: The Duke Is Tops (debut, 1938), Panama Hattie, Cabin in the Sky, Stormy Weather, I Dood It, Thousands Cheer, Broadway Rhythm, Swing Fever, Two Girls and a Sailor, Ziegfeld Follies, Till the Clouds Roll By, Words and Music, Duchess of Idaho, Meet Me in Las Vegas, Death of a Gunfighter, The Wiz, That's Entertainment III.
TELEVISION: *Guest*: Music '55, Perry Como Show, Here's to the Ladies, The Flip Wilson Show, Dean Martin Show, Sesame Street, Ed Sullivan Show, Sanford & Sons, Laugh-In, Hollywood Palace, The Cosby Show. *Specials*: The Lena Horne Show (1959), The Frank Sinatra Timex Show, Lena in Concert, Harry and Lena, The Tony & Lena Show, Lena Horne: The Lady and Her Music.

HORNER, JAMES
Composer. b. Los Angeles, CA. e. Royal Col. of Music: London, USC, UCLA. Received Grammy Awards for the song Somewhere Out There (from the film An American Tail), and for instrumental composition from Glory.
PICTURES: The Lady in Red, Battle Beyond the Stars, Humanoids From the Deep, Deadly Blessing, The Hand, Wolfen, The Pursuit of D.B. Cooper, 48 HRS, Star Trek II: The Wrath of Khan, Something Wicked This Way Comes, Krull, Brainstorm, Testament, Gorky Park, The Dresser, Uncommon Valor, The Stone Boy, Star Trek III: The Search for Spock, Heaven Help Us, Cocoon, Volunteers, Journey of Natty Gann, Commando, Aliens, Where the River Runs Black, The Name of the Rose, An American Tail, P.K. and the Kid, Project X, Batteries Not Included, Willow, Red Heat, Vibes, Cocoon: The Return, The Land Before Time, Field of Dreams, Honey I Shrunk the Kids, Dad, Glory, I Love You to Death, Another 48 HRS., Once Around, My Heroes Have Always Been Cowboys, Class Action, The Rocketeer, An American Tail: Fievel Goes West, Thunderheart, Patriot Games, Unlawful Entry, Sneakers, Swing Kids, A Far Off Place, Jack the Bear, Once Upon a Forest, Searching for Bobby Fischer, The Man Without a Face, Bopha!, The Pelican Brief, Clear and Present Danger, Legends of the Fall, Braveheart, Casper, Apollo 13, Jumanji, Courage Under Fire.

HORSLEY, LEE
Actor. b. Muleshoe, TX, May 15, 1955. e. U. of No. Colorado. On stage in Mack and Mabel, West Side Story, Sound of Music, Oklahoma!, Forty Carats.
PICTURE: The Sword and the Sorcerer, Unlawful Passage.
TELEVISION: *Series*: Nero Wolfe, Matt Houston, Guns of Paradise, Bodies of Evidence, Hawkeye. *Mini-series*: Crossings, North and South Book II. *Movies*: The Wild Women of Chastity Gulch, Infidelity, When Dreams Come True, Thirteen at Dinner, Single Women Married Men, The Face of Fear, Danielle Steel's Palomino, French Silk, The Corpse Had a Familiar Face, Home Song. *Documentary*: Western Ranching Culture In Crisis, AThe Forest Wars.

HORTON, PETER
Actor. b. Bellevue, WA, Aug. 20. e. Univ. of CA, Santa Barbara. Stage work includes appearances with Lobero Rep. Co. Theatre in Santa Barbara, Butterflies Are Free in L.A.

PICTURES: Serial, Fade to Black, Split Image, Children of the Corn, Where the River Runs Black, Amazon Women on the Moon (also co-dir.), Sideout, Singles, The Cure (dir. only), The Baby-sitters Club, 2 Days in the Valley.
TELEVISION: *Series*: Seven Brides for Seven Brothers, thirtysomething (also dir., episodes), Class of '96 (consultant, dir., actor). *Pilot*: Sawyer and Finn. *Movies*: She's Dressed to Kill, Miracle on Ice, Freedom, Choices of the Heart, Children of the Dark. *Special*: The Gift. Guest: The White Shadow, St. Elsewhere. *Director*: The Wonder Years, One Too Many (Afterschool Special).

HORTON, ROBERT
Actor. b. Los Angeles, CA, July 29, 1924. e. U. of Miami, UCLA, Yale. With U.S. Coast Guard; many legit. plays; many radio & TV appearances. Star of Broadway musical 110 in the Shade.
PICTURES: A Walk in the Sun, The Tanks Are Coming, Return of the Texan, Pony Soldier, Apache War Smoke, Bright Road, The Story of Three Loves, Code Two, Arena, Prisoner of War, Men of the Fighting Lady, The Green Slime, The Dangerous Days of Kiowa Jones, The Spy Killer, Foreign Exchange.
TELEVISION: *Series*: Kings Row, Wagon Train, A Man Called Shenandoah, As the World Turns. *Movie*: Red River. *Guest*: Alfred Hitchcock Presents, Suspense, Houston Knights, Murder She Wrote.

HOSKINS, BOB
Actor. b. Bury St. Edmunds, Suffolk, England, Oct. 26, 1942. Porter and steeplejack before becoming actor at 25. Veteran of Royal Shakespeare Co. Appeared with Britain's National Theatre (Man Is Man, King Lear, Guys and Dolls, etc.)
PICTURES: The National Health (debut, 1973), Royal Flash, Inserts, Zulu Dawn, The Long Good Friday, Pink Floyd: The Wall, Beyond the Limit, Lassiter, The Cotton Club, Brazil, Sweet Liberty, Mona Lisa (Acad. Award nom.), A Prayer for the Dying, The Lonely Passion of Judith Hearne, Who Framed Roger Rabbit, The Raggedy Rawney (also dir., co-s.p.), Heart Condition, Mermaids, Shattered, The Inner Circle, The Favor the Watch and the Very Big Fish, Hook, Passed Away, Super Mario Bros., The Rainbow, The Secret Agent, Nixon, Balto (voice), Joseph Conrad's The Secret Agent.
TELEVISION: Villains on the High Road (debut, 1972), New Scotland Yard, On the Move, Rock Follies, In the Looking Glass, Napoleon, Flickers, Pennies from Heaven, Othello, Mussolini, The Dunera Boys, World War II: When Lions Roar, The Changeling.

HOUGH, JOHN
Director. b. London, Eng., Nov. 21, 1941. Worked in British film prod. in various capacities; impressed execs. at EMI-MGM Studios, Elstree, London, so was given chance to direct The Avengers series for TV. Began theatrical films with Sudden Terror for prod. Irving Allen, 1971.
PICTURES: Sudden Terror, The Practice, Twins of Evil, Treasure Island, The Legend of Hell House, Dirty Mary Crazy Larry, Escape to Witch Mountain, Return From Witch Mountain, Brass Target, The Watcher in the Woods, The Incubus, Triumphs of a Man Called Horse, Biggles: Adventures in Time, American Gothic, Howling IV—The Original Nightmare.
TELEVISION: A Hazard of Hearts (also co-prod.), The Lady and the Highwayman (also prod.), A Ghost in Monte Carlo (also prod.), Duel of Hearts (also prod.), Distant Scream, Black Carrion, Check-Mate.

HOWARD, ARLISS
Actor. b. Independence, MO, 1955. e. Columbia Col.
THEATER: American Buffalo, Lie of the Mind.
PICTURES: The Prodigal, Sylvester, Door to Door, The Ladies Club, The Lightship, Full Metal Jacket, Plain Clothes, Tequila Sunrise, Men Don't Leave, For the Boys, Ruby, Crisscross, The Sandlot, Wilder Napalm, Natural Born Killers, To Wong Foo—Thanks for Everything—Julie Newmar.
TELEVISION: *Movies*: Hands of a Stranger, I Know My First Name is Steven, Somebody Has to Shoot the Picture, Iran: Days of Crisis, Till Death Us Do Part, Those Secrets, The Infiltrator.

HOWARD, CLINT
Actor. b. Burbank, CA, Apr. 20, 1959. Brother is director Ron Howard; father is actor Rance Howard.
PICTURES: Rock 'n' Roll High School, Evil Speak, Night Shift, Splash, Cocoon, Gung Ho, The Wraith, End of the Line, Freeway, Parenthood, Tango and Cash, Disturbed, Backdraft, The Rocketeer, Far and Away, Carnosaur, The Ice Cream Man, Forget Paris, Apollo 13.
TELEVISION: *Series*: The Baileys of Balboa, Gentle Ben, The Cowboys, Gung Ho. *Movies*: The Red Pony, The Death of Richie, Cotton Candy.

HOWARD, JAMES NEWTON
Composer. Started as keyboard player for Elton John, before composing and producing for such artists as Cher, Diana Ross, Barbra Streisand, Chaka Khan, Randy Newman.

PICTURES: 8 Million Ways to Die, Five Corners, Promised Land, Some Girls, Everybody's All-American, Major League, The Package, Pretty Woman, Coupe de Ville, Flatliners, Three Men and a Little Lady, Dying Young, The Man in the Moon, My Girl, The Prince of Tides, Grand Canyon, Glengarry Glen Ross, Night and the City, Alive, Falling Down, Dave, The Fugitive, The Saint of Fort Washington, Wyatt Earp, Outbreak, Eye for an Eye, Thr Juror, Primal Fear.

HOWARD, KEN
Actor. b. El Centro, CA, March 28, 1944. e. Yale Drama Sch. Left studies to do walk-on in B'way. musical, Promises Promises.
THEATER: Promises Promises, 1776 (Theatre World Award), Child's Play (Tony Award, 1970), Seesaw, 1600 Pennsylvania Avenue, The Norman Conquests, Equus, Rumors, Camping With Henry and Tom.
PICTURES: Tell Me That You Love Me Junie Moon (debut, 1970), Such Good Friends, The Strange Vengeance of Rosalie, 1776, Second Thoughts, Oscar, Clear and Present Danger, The Net.
TELEVISION: Series: Adam's Rib, The Manhunter, The White Shadow, It's Not Easy, The Colbys, Dynasty, Dream Girl U.S.A., What Happened? (host). Guest: Bonanza, Medical Center. Movies: Manhunter, Superdome, Critical List, A Real American Hero, Damien: The Leper Priest, Victims, Rage of Angels, The Trial of George Armstrong Custer, He's Not Your Son, Rage of Angels: The Story Continues, Murder in New Hampshire: The Pamela Smart Story, Memories of Midnight, Hart to Hart Returns, Moment of Truth: To Walk Again, Tom Clancy's Op Center. Specials: Strange Interlude, The Man in the Brown Suit, Mastergate. Mini-Series: The Thorn Birds.

HOWARD, RON
Actor, Director, Producer. b. Duncan, OK, March 1, 1954. e. Univ. of So. Calif. Los Angeles Valley Col. Acting debut as Ronny Howard at age of 2 with parents, Rance and Jean Howard, in The Seven Year Itch at Baltimore's Hilltop Theatre. Two years later traveled to Vienna to appear in first film, The Journey. Brother is actor Clint Howard, also former child actor. Co-Chairman of Imagine Films Entertainment.
PICTURES: Actor: The Journey (debut, 1959), Five Minutes to Live (Door-to-Door Maniac), The Music Man, The Courtship of Eddie's Father, Village of the Giants, The Wild Country, American Graffiti, Happy Mother's Day... Love George (Run Stranger Run), The Spikes Gang, Eat My Dust!, The Shootist, The First Nudie Musical (cameo), Grand Theft Auto (also dir., co-s.p.), More American Graffiti. Director: Grand Theft Auto (dir. debut, 1977; also actor, co-s.p.), Night Shift, Splash, Cocoon, Gung Ho (also exec. prod.), Willow, Parenthood (also co-story), Backdraft, Far and Away (also co-prod., co-story), The Paper, Apollo 13. Exec. Prod.: Leo & Loree, No Man's Land, Vibes, Clean and Sober, Closet Land, Ransom.
TELEVISION: Series: The Andy Griffith Show, The Smith Family, Happy Days, Fonz and the Happy Days Gang (voice for animated series). Guest: Red Skelton Hour, Playhouse 90, Dennis the Menace, Many Loves of Dobie Gillis, Five Fingers, Twilight Zone, Dinah Shore Show, The Fugitive, Dr. Kildare, The Big Valley, I Spy, Danny Kaye Show, Gomer Pyle USMC, The Monroes, Love American Style, Gentle Ben, Gunsmoke; Disney TV films (incl. A Boy Called Nuthin', Smoke). Movies: The Migrants, Locusts, Huckleberry Finn, Act of Love, Bitter Harvest, Fire on the Mountain, Return to Mayberry. Director (Movies): Cotton Candy (also co-writer), Skyward (also co-exec. prod.), Through the Magic Pyramid (also exec. prod.). Co-Exec. Prod. (Movies): When Your Lover Leaves, Into Thin Air, Splash Too. Exec. Prod. (Series): Gung Ho, Parenthood.

HOWARD, SANDY
Producer. b. Aug. 1, 1927. e. Florida So. Coll. Ent. m.p. ind. 1946.
PICTURES: Perils of the Deep, One Step to Hell, Jack of Diamonds, Tarzan and the Trappers, A Man Called Horse, Man in the Wilderness, Together Brothers, Neptune Factor, The Devil's Rain, Sky Riders, The Last Castle, Embryo, Magna I-Beyond the Barrier Reef, The Battle, Island of Dr. Moreau, City on Fire, Death Ship (exec. prod.), Avenging Angel, The Boys Next Door, Street Justice (exec. prod.), Nightstick, Dark Tower (exec. prod.), Truk Lagoon (exec. prod.).

HOWELL, C. THOMAS
Actor. b. Los Angeles, CA, Dec. 7, 1966. m. actress Rae Dawn Chong. Former junior rodeo circuit champion.
PICTURES: E.T.: The Extra Terrestrial (debut, 1982), The Outsiders, Tank, Grandview U.S.A., Red Dawn, Secret Admirer, The Hitcher, Soul Man, A Tiger's Tale, Young Toscanini, Side Out, Far Out Man, The Return of the Musketeers, Kid, Nickel and Dime, Breaking the Rules, First Force, That Night, Tattle Tale, Streetwise, To Protect and Serve, Gettysburg, Jail Bate, Teresa's Tattoo, Power Play, Treacherous, Mad Dogs and Englishmen.
TELEVISION: Series: Little People (only 4 yrs. old), Two Marriages. Movies: It Happened One Christmas, Into the Homeland, Curiosity Kills, Acting on Impulse, Dark Reflection. Guest: Nightmare Classics (Eye of the Panther).

HOWELLS, URSULA
Actress. b. Sept. 17, 1922. e. St. Paul's Sch., London. Stage debut, 1939, at Dundee Repertory with Bird in Hand followed by several plays inc. Springtime for Henry in N.Y., 1951; m.p. debut in Flesh and Blood, 1950; TV debut in Case of the Frightened Lady for BBC, 1948.
PICTURES: Lolly Madonna XXX, Catch My Soul, Hardcore, Escape from New York, Vice Squad, Total Exposure, Twist of Fate.
TELEVISION: The Small Back Room, A Woman Comes Home, For Services Rendered, Mine Own Executioner, The Cocktail Party.

HUBLEY, SEASON
Actress. b. New York, NY, Mar. 14, 1951. Studied acting with Herbert Berghoff.
THEATER: LA: Heat, Triplet Collection, Rhythm of Torn Stars.
PICTURES: The Oracle (Horse's Mouth), Track the Man Down, They Can't Hang Me, Keep It Clean, Long Arm (Third Key), Death and The Sky Above, Mumsy Nanny Sonny and Girly, Crossplot.
TELEVISION: Series: Kung Fu, Family, All My Children, Pilots: Lond and Davis in New York, Blues Skies, The City. Movies/Specials: She Lives, The Healers, SST—Death Flight, Loose Change, Elvis, Mrs. R's Daughter, Three Wishes of Billy Grier, Under the Influence, Christmas Eve, Shakedown on Sunset Strip, Unspeakable Acts, Child of the Night, Steel Justice, Key to Rebecca, All I Could See From Where I Stood, Stepfather III, Caribbean Mystery, Black Carrion, Vestige of Honor. Guest: The Partridge Family, The Rookies, Kojak, Twilight Zone, Alfred Hitchcock Presents, Twilight Zone, Hitchhiker.

HUDDLESTON, DAVID
Actor, Producer. b. Vinton, VA, Sept. 17, 1930. e. American Acad. of Dramatic Arts. Son is actor Michael Huddleston.
THEATER: A Man for All Seasons, Front Page, Everybody Loves Opal, Ten Little Indians, Silk Stockings, Fanny, Guys and Dolls, The Music Man, Desert Song, Mame. Broadway: The First, Death of a Salesman.
PICTURES: All the Way Home (debut, 1963), A Lovely Way to Die, Slaves, Norwood, Rio Lobo, Fools, Parade, Bad Company, Blazing Saddles, McQ, The World's Greatest Lover, Capricorn One, Gorp, Smokey and the Bandit II, The Act, Santa Claus, Frantic, Life With Mikey, Cultivating Charlie. Something to Talk About (unbilled).
TELEVISION: Series: Tenafly, Petrocelli, The Kallikaks, Hizzoner. Movies: Sarge: The Badge or the Cross, The Priest Killer, Suddenly Single, The Homecoming, Brian's Song, Tenafly (pilot), Brock's Last Case, Hawkins on Murder, Heatwave, The Gun and the Pulpit, The Oregon Trail, Shark Kill, Sherlock Holmes in New York, Kate Bliss and the Ticker Tape Kid, Oklahoma City Dolls, Family Reunion, Computeride, M.A.D.D.: Mothers Against Drunk Drivers, Finnegan Begin Again, Family Reunion, Spot Marks the X, The Tracker, Margaret Bourke-White, In a Child's Name. Mini-Series: Once an Eagle.

HUDSON, ERNIE
Actor. b. Benton Harbor, MI, Dec. 17, 1945. e. Wayne St. Univ., Yale Sch. of Drama. Former Actors Ensemble Theater while in Detroit. Professional stage debut in L.A. production of Daddy Goodness.
PICTURES: Leadbelly (debut, 1976), The Main Event, The Jazz Singer, Penitentiary II, Spacehunter: Adventures in the Forbidden Zone, Going Berserk, Ghostbusters, The Joy of Sex, Weeds, Leviathan, Ghostbusters II, The Hand That Rocks the Cradle, Sugar Hill, No Escape, The Crow, The Cowboy Way, Airheads, Speechless, The Basketball Diaries, Congo, The Substitute.
TELEVISION: Series: Highcliffe Manor, The Last Precinct, Broken Badges. Mini-Series: Roots: The Next Generations, Wild Palms. Movies: White Mama, Dirty Dozen: The Fatal Mission, Love on the Run. Guest: Fantasy Island, Little House on the Praire, One Day at a Time, Diff'rent Strokes, St. Elsewhere.

HUDSON, HUGH
Producer, Director. b. England. e. Eton. Began career as head of casting dept. with ad agency in London; left for Paris to work as editor for small film co. Returned to London to form Cammell-Hudson-Brownjohn Film Co., production house., turning out award-winning documentaries (Tortoise and Hare, A is for Apple). 1970, joined Ridley Scott to make TV commercials. 1975, formed Hudson Films to produce.
PICTURES: Director: Chariots of Fire, Greystoke: The Legend of Tarzan Lord of the Apes (also prod.), Revolution, Lost Angels.

HUGH KELLY, DANIEL
Actor. b. Hoboken, NJ, Aug. 10, 1949. Began acting with the National Players touring U.S. in such plays as Henry IV Part 1, Charlie's Aunt, School for Wives.
THEATER: Arena Stage (DC): An Enemy of the People, Once in a Lifetime, Long Day's Journey Into Night. Actors Theatre (Louisville): Much Ado About Nothing, The Best Man, The Taming of the Shrew, The Rainmaker. Off-B'way: Hunchback of

Notre Dame, Miss Margarita's Way, Juno's Swans, Fishing, Short-Changed Revue. *B'way*: Born Yesterday, Cat on a Hot Tin Roof.
PICTURES: Cujo, Nowhere to Hide, Someone to Watch Over Me, The Good Son, Bad Company.
TELEVISION: *Series*: Chicago Story, Hardcastle and McCormick. *Movies*: Nutcracker, Thin Ice, Murder Ink, Night of Courage, Citizen Cohn, Moment of Truth: A Mother's Deception, A Child's Cry for Help, The Tuskegee Airmen.

HUGHES, BARNARD
Actor. b. Bedford Hills, NY, July 16, 1915. Winner of Emmy for role as Judge in Lou Grant series (1978) and Tony Award for Da (1978). Inducted into Theatre Hall of Fame (1993).
PICTURES: Midnight Cowboy, Where's Poppa?, Cold Turkey, The Pursuit of Happiness, The Hospital, Rage, Sisters, Deadhead Miles, Oh God!, First Monday in October, Tron, Best Friends, Maxie, Where Are the Children?, The Lost Boys, Da, Doc Hollywood, Sister Act 2: Back in the Habit, The Fantasticks.
TELEVISION: *Series*: Doc, Mr. Merlin, The Cavanaughs, Blossom. *Movies*: Guilty or Innocent, The Sam Sheppard Murder Case, See How She Runs, The Caryl Chessman Story, Tell Me My Name, Look Homeward, Angel, Father Brown: Detective, Nova, Homeward Bound, The Sky's No Limit, A Caribbean Mystery, Night of Courage, A Hobo's Christmas, Day One, Home Fires Burning, Guts and Glory: The Rise and Fall of Oliver North, The Incident, Miracle Child, Trick of the Eye, Past the Bleachers. *Guest*: Homicide, The Marshal.

HUGHES, JOHN
Writer, Director, Producer. b. Detroit, MI, Feb. 18, 1950. e. Univ. of AZ. Editor of National Lampoon before writing film script of National Lampoon's Class Reunion (1982). Made directorial debut with Sixteen Candles in 1984 which also wrote. In 1985 entered into deal with Paramount Pictures to write, direct and produce films with his own production unit, The John Hughes Co.
PICTURES: *Writer*: National Lampoon's Class Reunion, National Lampoon's Vacation, Mr. Mom, Nate and Hayes, Sixteen Candles (also dir.), The Breakfast Club (also dir., co-prod.), National Lampoon's European Vacation, Weird Science (also dir.), Pretty in Pink (also co-exec. prod.), 101 Dalmations. *Writer/Prod.*: Ferris Bueller's Day Off (also dir.), Some Kind of Wonderful, Planes Trains & Automobiles (also dir.), She's Having a Baby (also dir.), The Great Outdoors (exec. prod., s.p.), Uncle Buck (also dir.), National Lampoon's Christmas Vacation, Home Alone, Career Opportunities (exec. prod., co-s.p.), Only the Lonely (co-prod. only), Dutch, Curly Sue (also dir.), Home Alone 2: Lost in New York, Dennis the Menace, Baby's Day Out, Miracle on 34th Street.

HUGHES, KATHLEEN
Actress. r.n. Betty von Gerkan; b. Hollywood, CA, Nov. 14, 1928. e. Los Angeles City Coll., UCLA. m. Stanley Rubin, producer, mother of 4, Michael played Baby Matthew on Peyton Place. Studied drama; under contract, 20th-Fox, 1948-51; starred in Seven Year Itch 1954, La Jolla Playhouse; signed by UI, 1952. Theatre includes You Can't Take It With You, An Evening With Tennessee Williams, The Bar Off Melrose.
PICTURES: Road House, Mother is a Freshman, Mr. Belvedere Goes to College, Take Care of My Little Girl, It Happens Every Spring, When Willie Comes Marching Home, My Blue Heaven, Mister 880, No Way Out, I'll See You in My Dreams, They Neighbor's Wife, For Men Only (The Tall Lie), Sally and Saint Anne, Golden Blade, It Came From Outer Space, Dawn at Socorro, Glass Web, Cult of the Cobra, Three Bad Sisters, Promise Her Anything, The President's Analyst, The Take, Pete and Tillie, Ironweed, The Couch Trip, Revenge.
TELEVISION: *Guest*: Bob Cummings Show, Hitchcock, 77 Sunset Strip, G.E. Theatre, Bachelor Father, Frank Sinatra Show, Ed Wynn Show, Alan Young Show, The Tall Man, Danta, Tightrope, Markham, I Dream of Jeannie, Peyton Place, Gomer Pyle, Kismet, Ghost and Mrs. Muir, Bracken's World, The Survivors, Julia, Here's Lucy, To Rome with Love, The Interns, The Man and the City, Mission Impossible, The Bold Ones, Lucas Tanner, Marcus Welby, Barnaby Jones, Medical Center, M.A.S.H., General Hospital, Quincy, Finder of Lost Loves, The Young and the Restless. *Movies*: Babe, Forbidden Love, The Spell, Portrait of an Escort, Capitol, Mirror, Mirror, And Your Name is Jonah.

HUGHES, KEN
Director, Writer. b. Liverpool, Eng., 1922. Ent. ind. as sound engineer with BBC, 1940; Doc. films, Army training films. Wrote book and lyrics for stage musical Oscar. Member: Assn. Cine Technicians, Writers' Guild of Great Britain.
AUTHOR: High Wray, The Long Echo, An Enemy of the State. Scripts: The Matarese Circle, Tussy is Me, The Queen's Own, RatsHallo Berlin.
PICTURES: *Dir./Writer*: Wide Boy, The House Across the Lake, Black 13 (dir. only), The Brain Machine, Case of the Red Monkey, Confession (The Deadliest Sin), Timeslip (The Atomic Man), Joe Macbeth, Wicked as They Come, The Long Haul,

Jazz Boat, In the Nick, The Trials of Oscar Wilde, The Small World of Sammy Lee, Of Human Bondage (dir. only), Arrivederci Baby (also prod.), Casino Royale (co-dir.), Chitty Chitty Bang Bang, Cromwell, The Internecine Project, Alfie Darling (Oh Alfie!), Sextette (dir. only), Night School.
TELEVISION: Eddie (Emmy Award for writing, 1959), Sammy (Brit. Acad. Award). *Serials*: Solo for Canary, Enemy of the State. *Series*: Lenin 1917 (The Fall of Eagles), The Haunting, The Voice, Oil Strike North, Colditz, Churchill (BBC).
AWARDS: Golden Globe, Emmy, British TV Acad. Award (Script Writer of Year), Avorias Festival Merit Award, British Writer's Guild Award, British Critics Award (best serial).

HUGHES, WENDY
Actress. b. Melbourne, Australia. Studied acting at National Institute of Dramatic Art, Sydney.
PICTURES: Sidecar Racers, High Rolling, Newsfront, My Brilliant Career, Kostas, Touch and Go, Hoodwink, Lonely Hearts, Careful He Might Hear You, My First Wife, An Indecent Obsession, Happy New Year, Warm Nights on a Slow Moving Train, Boundaries of the Heart, Luigi's Ladies (also co-s.p.), Wild Orchid II, Princess Caraboo.
TELEVISION: Amerika, Coralie Landsdowne Says No, Can't Get Started, The Heist, A Woman Named Jackie, Homicide: Life on the Street.

HUIZENGA, HARRY WAYNE
Entrepreneur, Entertainment Executive. b. Evergreen Park, IL, Dec 29, 1939. e. Calvin College, 1957-58. m. Martha Jean Pike, Apr. 17, 1972. Vice chmn., pres., chief operating officer Waste Mgmt. Inc., Oak Brook, IL, 1968-84; prin. Huizenga Holdings, Inc., Ft. Lauderdale, FL, 1984–; chmn., chief exec. officer Blockbuster Entertainment Corp., Ft. Lauderdale, 1987-1995; owner Florida Marlins, Miami, 1992–; co-owner Miami Dolphins, Joe Robbie Stadium. Mem. Florida Victory Com., 1988-89, Team Repub. Nat. com., Washington, 1988-90. Recipient Entrepenour of Yr. award Wharton Sch. U. Pa., 1989, Excalibur award Bus. Leader of Yr. News/Sun Sentinel, 1990, Silver Medallion Brotherhood award Broward Region Nat. Conf. Christians and Jews, 1990, Laureates award Jr. Achievement Broward and Palm Beach Counties, 1990, Jim Murphy Humanitarian Award The Emerald Soc., 1990, Entrepreneur of Yr. award Disting. Panel Judges Fla., 1990, Man of Yr. Billboard/Time Mag., 1990, Man of Yr. Juvenile Diabetes Found., 1990, Florida Free Enterpriser of Yr. award Fla. Coun. on Econ. Edn., 1990, commendation for youth restricted video State of Fla. Office of Gov., 1989, Hon. Mem. Appreciation award Bond Club Ft. Lauderdale, 1989, honored with endowed teaching chair Broward Community Coll., 1990. Mem. Lauderdale Yacht Club, Tournament Players Club, Coral Ridge Country Club, Fisher Island Club, Ocean Reef Club, Cat Cay Yacht Club, Linville Ridge Country Club. Avocations: golf, collecting antique cars. Office: 200 S. Andrews Ave., Ft. Lauderdale, FL 33301.

HULCE, TOM
Actor. b. White Water, WI, Dec. 6, 1953. e. NC School of the Arts. Understudied and then co-starred in Equus on Broadway. Directorial stage debut Sleep Around Town. Appeared in IMAX film Wings of Courage. Recipient of Emmy Award, 1996.
THEATER: A Memory of Two Mondays, Julius Caesar, Candida, The Sea Gull, The Rise and Rise of Daniel Rocket, Eastern Standard, A Few Good Men (Tony nom.), Hamlet.
PICTURES: September 30, 1955 (debut, 1978), National Lampoon's Animal House, Those Lips Those Eyes, Amadeus (Acad. Award nom.), Echo Park, Slamdance, Dominick and Eugene, Parenthood, Shadowman, The Inner Circle, Fearless, Mary Shelley's Frankenstein, The Hunchback of Notre Dame (voice).
TELEVISION: *Specials*: Emily Emily, The Rise and Rise of Daniel Rocket, Song of Myself, Forget-Me-Not Lane, Tall Tales and Legends (John Henry). *Mini-Series*: The Adams Chronicles. *Movies*: Murder in Mississippi, Black Rainbow.

HUNNICUT, GAYLE
Actress. b. Fort Worth, TX, February 6, 1943. e. UCLA, B.A., with honors, theater arts & English major. Early career, community theatres in Los Angeles.
THEATER: The Ride Across Lake Constance, Twelfth Night, The Tempest, Dog Days, The Admirable Crichton, A Woman of No Importance, Hedda Gabler, Peter Pan, Macbeth, Uncle Vanya, The Philadelphia Story, Miss Firecracker Contest, Exit The King, The Doctor's Dilemma, So Long on Lonely Street, The Big Knife, Edith Wharton at Home, The Little Foxes, Dangerous Corner.
PICTURES: The Wild Angels (debut, 1966), P.J., Eye of the Cat, Marlowe, Fragment of Fear, The Freelance, Voices, Running Scared, Legend of Hell House, Scorpio, L'Homme Sans Visage, The Spiral Staircase, The Sell Out, Strange Shadows in an Empty Room, Once in Paris, One Take Two, Fantomas, Privilege, Sherlock Holmes, Target, Dream Lover, Turnaround, Silence Like Glass.
TELEVISION: *Series*: Dallas (1989-91). *Movies*: The Smugglers, The Million Dollar Face, The Return of the Man From U.N.C.L.E., The First Olympics: Athens 1896. *Specials*: Man and Boy, The

Golden Bowl, The Ambassadors, The Ripening Seed, Fall of Eagles, The Switch, Humboldt's Gift, The Life and Death of Dylan Thomas, Return of the Saint, The Lady Killers, Savage in the Orient, Strong Medicine. *Mini-Series*: A Man Called Intrepid, The Martian Chronicles, Dream West. *Guest*: Taxi.

HUNT, HELEN
Actress. b. Los Angeles, CA, June 15, 1963. Daughter of director Gordon Hunt.
THEATER: Been Taken, Our Town, The Taming of the Shrew, Methusalem.
PICTURES: Rollercoaster, Girls Just Want to Have Fun, Peggy Sue Got Married, Project X, Miles From Home, Trancers, Stealing Home, Next of Kin, The Waterdance, Only You, Bob Roberts, Mr. Saturday Night, Kiss of Death, Twister.
TELEVISION: *Series*: Swiss Family Robinson, Amy Prentiss, The Fitzpatricks, It Takes Two, Mad About You (Emmy Award, 1996). *Movies*: Pioneer Woman, All Together Now, Death Scream, The Spell, Transplant, Angel Dusted, Child Bride of Short Creek, The Miracle of Kathy Miller, Quarterback Princess, Bill: On His Own, Sweet Revenge, Incident at Dark River, Into the Badlands, Murder in New Hampshire: The Pamela Smart Story, In the Company of Darkness. Specials: Weekend, Land of Little Rain. *Special*: Sexual Healing. *Guest*: St. Elsewhere, Family, Mary Tyler Moore Show, The Hitchhiker.

HUNT, LINDA
Actress. b. Morristown, NJ, Apr. 2, 1945. e. Interlochen Arts Acad., MI, and Chicago's Goodman Theatre & Sch. of Drama. Narrated documentary Ecological Design: Inventing the Future.
THEATER: Long Wharf (New Haven):Hamlet, The Rose Tattoo, Ah Wilderness. *NY*: Mother Courage, End of the World (Tony nom.), A Metamorphosis in Miniature (Obie Award), Top Girls (Obie Award), Aunt Dan and Lemon, The Cherry Orchard. *Regional*: The Three Sisters.
PICTURES: Popeye (debut, 1980) The Year of Living Dangerously (Academy Award, best supporting actress, 1983), The Bostonians, Dune, Silverado, Eleni, Waiting for the Moon, She-Devil, Kindergarten Cop, If Looks Could Kill, Rain Without Thunder, Twenty Bucks, Younger and Younger, Ready to Wear (Pret-a-Porter), Pocahontas (voice).
TELEVISION: *Series*: Space Rangers. *Movie*: The Room Upstairs. *Specials*: Ah Wilderness, The Room. *Guest*: Fame.

HUNT, MARSHA
Actress. b. Chicago, IL, Oct. 17, 1917.
THEATER: *B'way*: Joy to the World, Devils Disciple, Legend of Sarah, Borned in Texas, Tunnel of Love, The Paisley Convertible.
PICTURES: The Virginia Judge (debut, 1935), College Holiday, Easy to Take, Blossoms in the Dust, Panama Hattie, Joe Smith American, These Glamour Girls, Winter Carnival, Irene, Pride and Prejudice, Flight Command, The Affairs of Martha, Kid Glove Killer, Seven Sweethearts, Cheers for Miss Bishop, Trial of Mary Dugan, Thousands Cheer, The Human Comedy, None Shall Escape, Lost Angel, Cry Havoc, Bride by Mistake, Music for Millions, Valley of Decision, A Letter for Evie, Smash-Up, Carnegie Hall, The Inside Story, Raw Deal, Jigsaw, Take One False Step, Actors and Sin, Happy Time, No Place to Hide, Back from the Dead, Bombers B-52, Blue Denim, The Plunderers, Johnny Got His Gun.
TELEVISION: *Series*: Peck's Bad Girl. *Guest*: Philco, Studio One, Ford Theatre, Show of Shows, G.E. Theatre, Climax, Hitchcock, The Defenders, Twilight Zone, Cains Hundred, Gunsmoke, The Breaking Point, Outer Limits, Profiles in Courage, Ben Casey, Accidental Family, Run For Your Life, My Three Sons, The Outsiders, Name of the Game, Univ.'s 120, Ironside, Marcus Welby, M.D., Police Story, The Young Lawyers, Harry-O, The Mississippi, Hot Pursuit, Shadow Chaser, Matlock, Murder She Wrote, Star Trek: The Next Generation.

HUNT, PETER
Director, Editor. b. London, Eng., March 11, 1928. e. Romford, England and Rome, Italy, London Sch. of Music. Actor Angin Rep. Entered film as camera asst. documentary, later asst film editor documentary, then asst editor features, London Films.
PICTURES: *Editor*: Hill in Korea, Admirable Crichton, Cry From the Streets, Greengage Summer (Loss of Innocence), Ferry to Hong Kong, H.M.S. Defiant (Damn the Defiant). *Supervising editor/2nd Unit Director*: Dr. No, Call Me Bwana, From Russia With Love, Goldfinger, The Ipcress File, Thunderball, You Only Live Twice. *Assoc. Prod.*: Chitty Chitty Bang Bang. *Director*: On Her Majesty's Secret Service, Gullivers Travels, Gold, Shout at the Devil, Death Hunt, Wild Geese II, Hyper Sapien, Assassination.
TELEVISION: *Director: Series*: The Persuaders, Shirley's World, The Pencil, Smart Alec Kill (Philip Marlowe). *Movies*: The Beasts Are in the Streets, Eye of a Witness. *Mini-Series*: Last Days of Pompeii.

HUNT, PETER H.
Director. b. Pasadena, CA, Dec. 16, 1938. e. Hotchkiss, Yale U., Yale Drama Sch. m. actress Barbette Tweed. Director for Williamston Theatre since 1957. Lighting designer on B'way. (1963-69) Awards: Tony, Ace, Peabody (twice), N.Y. Drama Critics, London Drama Critics, Edgar Allan Poe, Christopher.

THEATER: 1776 (London & B'way.), Georgy (B'way.), Scratch (B'way.), Goodtime Charley (B'way.), Give 'Em Hell Harry, Magnificent Yankee (Kennedy Center). *Tours*: Bully, Three Penny Opera, Sherlock Holmes, Bus Stop.
PICTURES: 1776, Give 'Em Hell Harry.
TELEVISION: *Specials*: Adventures of Huckleberry Finn, Life on the Mississippi, A Private History of a Campaign That Failed, A New Start, Mysterious Stranger, Sherlock Holmes (cable), Bus Stop (cable). *Movies*: Flying High, Rendezvous Motel, When She Was Bad, Skeezer, The Parade, Sins of the Past, It Came Upon the Midnight Clear, Charley Hannah, Danielle Steel's Secrets, Sworn to Vengeance. *Pilots*: Adam's Rib, Hello Mother Goodbye, Ivan the Terrible, Quark, Mixed Nuts, Wilder and Wilder, The Main Event, Nuts and Bolts, The Good Witch of Laurel Canyon, Masquerade, Stir Crazy, The Wizard of Elm Street, Travelling Man, My Africa.

HUNT, WILLIE
Executive Producer. b. Van Nuys, CA, Oct. 1, 1941. e. Utah State U., B.A., 1963. m. writer Tim Considine. Started in industry as secretary at Warner Bros., 1965; named exec. secty. to Ted Ashley, WB, 1969; story analyst, WB, 1974; story editor, WB, 1975; named West Coast story editor for WB, 1978; joined MGM in 1979 as v.p., motion picture development. Moved to United Artists as v.p.-prod., 1982. 1983 sr. v.p. of prod. at Rastar Prods.; 1984, indep. prod., Tri-Star; 1986, sr. v.p., Freddie Fields Prods. 1988: Loverboy (co-prod.) 1989, sr. v.p. Considine Prods. 1993, partner, Creative Entertainment Group.

HUNTER, HOLLY
Actress. b. Conyers, GA. March 20, 1958. e. studied acting, Carnegie-Mellon Univ. Appeared Off-B'way in Battery (1981) and Weekend Near Madison. Appeared in 5 Beth Henley plays: The Miss Firecracker Contest (Off-B'way), as a replacement in Crimes of the Heart (B'way) The Wake of Jamey Foster (B'way), Lucky Spot (Williamstown Theater Festival), and Control Freaks (L.A.; also co-prod.). Also: A Lie of the Mind (L.A.).
PICTURES: The Burning (debut, 1981), Swing Shift, Raising Arizona, Broadcast News (NY Film Critics, LA Film Critics and Natl. Board of Review Awards, Acad. Award nom., 1987), End of the Line, Miss Firecracker, Animal Behavior, Always, Once Around, The Firm (Acad. Award nom.), The Piano (Academy Award, Cannes Film Fest., LA Film Critics, NY Film Critics, Natl. Board of Review, Natl. Society of Film Critics & Golden Globe Awards, 1993), Home for the Holidays, Copycat, Crash.
TELEVISION: *Movies*: Svengali, An Uncommon Love, With Intent to Kill, A Gathering of Old Men, Roe vs. Wade (Emmy Award, 1989), Crazy in Love, The Positively True Adventures of the Alleged Texas Cheerleader-Murdering Mom (Emmy Award, 1993). *Guest*: Fame (pilot).

HUNTER, KIM
Actress. r.n. Janet Cole. b. Detroit, MI, Nov. 12, 1922. e. public schools. d. Donald and Grace Mabel (Lind) Cole. Studied acting with Charmine Lantaff Camine, 1938-40, Actors Studio; First stage appearance, 1939; played in stock, 1940-42; Broadway debut in A Streetcar Named Desire, 1947; frequent appearances in summer stock and repertory theater, 1940-; appeared Am. Shakespeare Festival, Stratford, CT, 1961. Autobiography-cookbook: Loose in the Kitchen (1975).
THEATER: *NY*: Darkness at Noon, The Chase, The Children's Hour (revival), The Tender Trap, Write Me a Murder, Weekend, The Penny Wars, The Women, The Cherry Orchard, To Grandmother's House We Go, When We Dead Awaken, Territorial Rites, Man and Superman, A Murder of Crows, Eye of the Beholder, All The Way Home. *Tours*: Two Blind Mice, They Knew What They Wanted, And Miss Reardon Drinks a Little, In Praise of Love, The Gin Game. *Regional*: The Glass Menagerie, The Lion in Winter, The Chalk Garden, Elizabeth the Queen, Semmelweiss, The Belle of Amherst, The Little Foxes, Another Part of the Forest, Ghosts, Death of a Salesman, Cat on a Hot Tin Roof, Life With Father, Sabrina Fair, Faulkner's Bicycle, Antique Pink, The Belle of Amherst, Painting Churches, A Delicate Balance, Jokers, Remembrance, The Gin Game, A Murder of Crows, Watch on the Rhine, Suddenly Last Summer, A Smaller Place, Open Window, The Cocktail Hour, The Belle of Amherst, Love Letters, Do Not Go Gentle.
PICTURES: The Seventh Victim (debut, 1943), Tender Comrade, When Strangers Marry (Betrayed), You Came Along, Stairway to Heaven (A Matter of Life and Death), A Canterbury Tale, A Streetcar Named Desire (Academy Award, best supporting actress, 1951), Anything Can Happen, Deadline: U.S.A., The Young Stranger, Bermuda Affair, Storm Center, Money Women and Guns, Lilith, Planet of the Apes, The Swimmer, Beneath the Planet of the Apes, Escape from the Planet of the Apes, Dark August, The Kindred, Two Evil Eyes.
TELEVISION: Made TV debut on Actors Studio Program, 1948. *Series*: The Edge of Night (1979-80). *Specials*: Requiem for a Heavyweight, The Comedian (both on Playhouse 90); Give Us Barabbas, Stubby Pringle's Christmas, Project: U.F.O., Three Sovereigns for Sarah, Vivien Leigh: Scarlett and Beyond, Martin Luther King: The Dream and the Drum, Hurricane Andrew Project. *Guest*: Love American Style, Columbo, Cannon, Night

Gallery, Mission Impossible, Marcus Welby, Hec Ramsey, Griff, Police Story, Ironside, Medical Center, Baretta, Gibbsville, The Oregon Trail, Scene of the Crime, Hunter, Murder She Wrote, Class of '96, Mad About You, L.A. Law. Movies: Dial Hot Line, In Search of America, The Magician (pilot), Unwed Father, Born Innocent, Bad Ronald, Ellery Queen (Too Many Suspects), The Dark Side of Innocence, The Golden Gate Murders, F.D.R.: The Last Year, Skokie, Private Sessions, Drop-Out Mother, Cross of Fire, Bloodlines: Murder in the Family. *Mini-Series:* Once an Eagle, Backstairs at the White House.

HUNTER, ROSS
Producer. r.n. Martin Fuss. b. Cleveland, OH, May 6, 1926. e. Western Reserve U., M.A. Was school teacher before becoming actor at Columbia Pictures; returned to school teaching; stage prod. & dir.; m.p. dialogue dir.; assoc. prod. Universal-International, 1950-51; prod., U-I, 1951. Moved production Co. from Universal to Columbia, 1971. Moved to Paramount, 1974. Moved to NBC, 1978-82.
PICTURES: *As actor:* Louisiana Hayride, Ever Since Venus, She's a Sweetheart, Out of the Depths, Submarine Below, Hit the Hay, Eve Knew Her Apples, Bandit of Sherwood Forest, Groom Wore Spurs. *As producer:* Take Me to Town, All I Desire, Tumbleweed, Taza Son of Cochise, Magnificent Obsession, Naked Alibi, Yellow Mountain, Captain Lightfoot, One Desire, The Spoilers, All That Heaven Allows, There's Always Tomorrow, Battle Hymn, Tammy and the Bachelor, Interlude, My Man Godfrey, The Restless Years, This Happy Feeling, Stranger in My Arms, Imitation of Life, Pillow Talk, Portrait in Black, Midnight Lace, Back Street, Flower Drum Song, Tammy Tell Me True, If a Man Answers, Tammy and the Doctor, The Thrill of It All, The Chalk Garden, I'd Rather Be Rich, The Art of Love, Madame X, The Pad, Thoroughly Modern Millie, Rosie, Airport, Lost Horizon.
TELEVISION: *Movies:* Lives of Jenny Dolan, The Moneychangers, The Best Place to Be, A Family Upside Down, Suddenly Love.
d. March 10, 1996.

HUNTER, TAB
Actor. r.n. Arthur Gelien. b. New York, NY, July 11, 1931. Served with U.S. Coast Guard. Entered industry in 1948.
PICTURES: The Lawless (debut, 1950), Island of Desire, Gun Belt, Steel Lady, Return to Treasure Island, Track of the Cat, Battle Cry, Sea Chase, The Burning Hills, The Girl He Left Behind, Lafayette Escadrille, Gunman's Walk, Damn Yankees, That Kind of Woman, They Came to Cordura, The Pleasure of His Company, Operation Bikini, The Golden Arrow, Ride the Wild Surf, The Loved One, War Gods of the Deep, Birds Do It, Fickle Finger of Fate, Hostile Guns, The Arousers (Sweet Kill), Life and Times of Judge Roy Bean, Timber Tramp, Won Ton Ton the Dog Who Saved Hollywood, Polyester, Pandemonium, Grease 2, Lust in the Dust (also co-prod.), Cameron's Closet, Grotesque, Out of the Dark, Dark Horse (also story).
TELEVISION: *Movies:* San Francisco International, Katie: Portrait of a Centerfold. *Series:* The Tab Hunter Show, Mary Hartman Mary Hartman.

HUNTER, TIM
Director. e. Harvard, AFI.
PICTURES: Over the Edge (co-s.p.). Dir.: Tex (also s.p.), Sylvester, River's Edge, Paint It Black, The Saint of Fort Washington.
TELEVISION: *Movie:* Lies of the Twins.

HUPPERT, ISABELLE
Actress. b. Paris, France, March 16, 1955. e. Conservatoire National d'Art Dramatique.
PICTURES: Faustine and the Beautiful Summer (Growing Up; debut, 1971), Cesar and Rosalie, Going Places, Rosebud, The Rape of Innocence, The Judge and the Assassin, The Lacemaker, Violette (Cannes Fest. Award, 1977), The Bronte Sisters, Loulou, Heaven's Gate, Coup de Torchon, Every Man for Himself, The True Story of Camille, Wings of the Dove, Deep Water, Entre Nous, The Trout, Cactus, Signed Charlotte, The Bedroom Window, The Possessed, Story of Women (Venice Fest Award, 1988), Milan Noir, Madame Bovary, Revenge of a Woman, Malina, Apres l'Amour (After Love), Amateur, The Separation, A Judgment in Stone.

HURD, GALE ANNE
Producer. b. Los Angeles, CA, Oct. 25, 1955. e. Stanford U., Phi Beta Kappa, 1977. Joined New World Pictures in 1977 as exec. asst. to pres. Roger Corman, then named dir. of advertising and pub. and moved into prod. management capacities on several New World films. Left in 1982 to form own co., Pacific Western Productions. Honored by NATO with special merit award for Aliens. Served as juror, U.S. Film Fest., Utah, 1988 and for 1989 Focus Student Film Awards. Member, Hollywood Women's Political Committee. Board of Trustees, AFI. The Amer. Film Inst. created Gale Anne Hurd production grants for Institute's Directing Workshop for Women. Bd. of dir. The Independent Feature Project/West.

PICTURES: Smokey Bites the Dust (co-prod. with Roger Corman, 1981), The Terminator (Grand Prix, Avoriaz Film Fest., France), Aliens (Hugo Award) Alien Nation (Saturn nom.), The Abyss, Downtown (exec. prod.), Tremors (exec. prod.), Terminator 2 (exec. prod.), The Waterdance, Raising Cain, No Escape, Safe Passage, The Relic, The Ghost and The Darkness.
TELEVISION: *Movies:* Cast a Deadly Spell, Witch Hunt, Sugartime.

HURLOCK, ROGER W.
Pres. Hurlock Cine-World. b. Cambridge, MD, May 30, 1912. e. Baltimore City Coll. Ent. m.p. ind. as publicist, Hippodrome Theatre, Balt.; asst. mgr., Lessor-operator Imperial and Majestic Theatres, Balt., 1931-35; real estate, bldg., farming, Maryland and Alaska, 1936-58; elected bd. mem., Allied Artists, 1958; asst. to pres., 1961-63; chmn. budget comm., 1963; chmn. policy comm., 1964; c.p. exec. comm. member, 1964; v.p., chf. operating officer 1965; chmn. exec. comm., 1966; pres., 1967. pres., Hurlock Cine-World, 1969.

HURT, JOHN
Actor. b. Shirebrook, Derbyshire, Jan. 22, 1940. e. St. Martin's Sch. for Art, London, RADA.
THEATER: The Dwarfs, Little Malcolm and His Struggle Against the Eunuchs, Man and Superman, Belcher's Luck, Ride a Cock Horse, The Caretaker, Romeo and Juliet, Ruffian on the Streets, The Dumb Waiter, Travesties, The Arrest, The Seagull, The London Vertigo, A Month in the Country.
PICTURES: The Wild and the Willing (debut, 1962), This is My Street, A Man for All Seasons, The Sailor from Gibraltar, Before Winter Comes, Sinful Davey, In Search of Gregory, 10 Rillington Place, Mr. Forbush and the Penguins, The Pied Piper, Little Malcolm, The Ghoul, East of Elephant Rock, Disappearance, Midnight Express (Acad. Award nom.) Watership Down (voice), The Lord of the Rings (voice), The Shout, Alien, The Elephant Man (Acad. Award nom.), Heaven's Gate, History of the World Part I, Night Crossing, Partners, The Plague Dogs (voice), The Osterman Weekend, Champions, The Hit, Success Is the Best Revenge, 1984, The Black Cauldron (voice), Jake Speed, From the Hip, Spaceballs, Aria, Vincent (voice), White Mischief, Little Sweetheart, Scandal, Frankenstein Unbound, The Field, King Ralph, Romeo-Juliet, Resident Alien, I Dreamt I Woke Up, Lapse of Memory, Dark at Noon, Monolith, Hans Christian Andersen's Thumbelina (voice), Even Cowgirls Get the Blues, Crime and Punishment, Great Moments in Aviation, Second Best, Rob Roy, Wild Bill, Two Nudes Bathing, Dead Man.
TELEVISION: Playboy of the Western World, A Tragedy of Two Ambitions, Green Julia, Nijinsky, Shades of Green, Ten from the Twenties, The Peddler, The Naked Civil Servant, I Claudius, Spectre, Crime and Punishment, The Storyteller (series host), Deadline, The Jim Henson Hour, The Investigation: Inside a Terrorist Bombing, Six Characters in Search of an Author.

HURT, MARY BETH
Actress. b. Marshalltown, IA, Sept. 26, 1946. m. writer-director Paul Schrader. e. U. of Iowa, NYU Sch. of Arts. Stage debut in 1973 with N.Y. Shakespeare Fest. (More Than You Deserve, Pericles, The Cherry Orchard).
THEATER: As You Like It (Central Park), 2 seasons with Phoenix Theater, Love For Love, Tralawny of the Wells, Secret Service, Boy Meets Girl, Father's Day, Crimes of the Heart, The Misanthrope, Benefactors, The Nest of the Wood Grouse, The Day Room, Othello, A Delicate Balance.
PICTURES: Interiors (debut, 1978), Head Over Heels (Chilly Scenes of Winter), A Change of Seasons, The World According to Garp, D.A.R.Y.L., Compromising Positions, Parents, Slaves of New York, Defenseless, Light Sleeper, My Boyfriend's Back, The Age of Innocence, Six Degrees of Separation, From the Journals of Jean Seberg.
TELEVISION: *Series:* Nick and Hillary. *Movies:* Baby Girl Scott, Shimmer. *Specials:* The Five-Forty-Eight, Secret Service (NET Theatre). *Guest:* Kojak.

HURT, WILLIAM
Actor. b. Washington, DC, Mar. 20, 1950. Lived as child in South Pacific when father was dir. of Trust Territories for U.S. State Dept. e. Tufts as theology major, switched to drama in jr. year, Juilliard. Acted with Oregon Shakespearean Fest. Leading actor with New York's Circle Repertory Company (Theatre World Award), since 1976.
THEATER: *NY:* The Fifth of July, My Life (Obie Award), Ulysses in Traction, The Runner Stumbles, Hamlet, Childe Byron, Beside Herself. *NY Shakespeare Festival:* Henry V, A Midsummer's Night's Dream, Hurlyburly (off-B'way and B'way). *Regional:* Good (S.F.), Ivanov (Yale).
PICTURES: Altered States (debut, 1980), Eyewitness, Body Heat, The Big Chill, Gorky Park, Kiss of the Spider Woman (Academy Award, 1985), Children of a Lesser God, Broadcast News, A Time of Destiny, The Accidental Tourist, I Love You to Death, Alice, The Doctor, Until the End of the World, Mr. Wonderful, The Plague, Trial by Jury, Second Best, Smoke, Jane Eyre, Secrets Shared With a Stranger, Michael.
TELEVISION: *Specials:* Verna: USO Girl, Best of Families, All the Way Home, The Odyssey of John Dos Passos (voice).

HUSSEY, OLIVIA
Actress. b. Buenos Aires, Apr. 17, 1951. Attended Italia Conti Stage School, London. Began acting at age 8.
PICTURES: The Battle of the Villa Fiorita (debut, 1965), Cup Fever, All the Right Noises, Romeo and Juliet, Summertime Killer, Lost Horizon, Black Christmas, Death on the Nile, The Cat and the Canary, Virus, The Man With Bogart's Face, Turkey Shoot, Distortions, The Jeweler's Shop, The Undeclared War, Save Me, Ice Cream Man.
TELEVISION: Movies/Mini-Series: Jesus of Nazareth, The Pirate, The Bastard, Ivanhoe, Last Days of Pompeii, The Corsican Brothers, Psycho IV: The Beginning, Stephen King's IT, Save Me, Quest of the Delta Knights, H-Bomb. Guest: Murder She Wrote.

HUSTON, ANJELICA
Actress. b. Santa Monica, CA, July 8, 1951. Father was late writer-dir.-actor, John Huston. Brother is director Danny Huston. Raised in St. Clerans, Ireland. Studied acting at the Loft Studio and with Peggy Furey, Martin Landau. Appeared in 3-D Disney short Captain Eo.
PICTURES: A Walk With Love and Death (debut, 1969), Sinful Davey, Swashbuckler, The Last Tycoon, The Postman Always Rings Twice, Frances, The Ice Pirates, This is Spinal Tap, Prizzi's Honor (Academy Award, best supporting actress, 1985), Good to Go (Short Fuse), Gardens of Stone, The Dead, A Handful of Dust, Mr. North, Crimes and Misdemeanors, Enemies a Love Story (Acad. Award nom.), The Witches, The Grifters (Acad. Award nom.), The Addams Family, The Player, Manhattan Murder Mystery, Addams Family Values, The Perez Family, The Crossing Guard, Bstard Out of Carolina (also prod.).
TELEVISION: Movies: The Cowboy and the Ballerina, Family Pictures, And the Band Played On, Buffalo Girls. Specials: Faerie Tale Theatre, A Rose for Miss Emily. Mini-Series: Lonesome Dove.

HUSTON, DANNY
Director. b. Rome, Italy, May 14, 1962. Youngest son of director-actor John Huston and actress Zoe Sallis. Brother of actress Anjelica and screenwriter Tony Huston. e. Overseas School, Rome; Intl branch of Milfield School in Exeter, London Film School. A constant visitor to his father's sets throughout the world, he began working on his father's films, beginning in Cuernavaca, Mexico as second-unit dir. on Under the Volcano. Directed TV doc. on Peru and on making of Santa Claus: The Movie; and TV features Bigfoot and Mr. Corbett's Ghost.
PICTURES: Mr. North (debut, 1988), Becoming Colette, The Maddening.

HUTTE, ROBERT E.
Exhibitor. b. Escanaba, MI, Oct. 22, 1917. e. Wisc. Inst. of Technology. Mgr. insp. lab. Iowa Ord. Plant 1940-42, Army Artil. 1942, Entered business as exhibitor in Southern Iowa 1943; then theatre owner and manager there. Elected board of directors, Allied Theatre Owners of Iowa, Nebraska & Missouri 1948, 1950, 1952. Democratic candidate Iowa State Auditor 1960; Pres. Insurance Advisors, Des Moines, IA; pres Leisure Homes, Nursing Homes; pres., Leisure Homes of Texas; pres. Wodon & Romar Prods., Austin, TX 1970-75. Real estate broker & pres Leisure Mor, theatres in West TX; elected board of dir. National Independent Theatre Exhibitors 1979; Pres. Southwestern Indep. Theatre Exhibitors Assn. of TX, OK, AR, LA & NM; 1979 elected pres. Natl. Independent Theatre Exhibitors Assn. 1980-present. Lifetime member, Foundation of Motion Picture Pioneers.

HUTTON, BETTY
Actress. r.n. Betty June Thornburg. b. Battle Creek, MI, Feb. 26, 1921. Sister was singer-actress Marion Hutton. Was vocalist for Vincent Lopez orchestra earning nickname the Blonde Bombshell. Debuted on B'way 1940 in Two for the Show, followed by Panama Hattie. Signed by Paramount in 1941. Returned to stage in Fade Out Fade In, Annie.
PICTURES: The Fleet's In (debut, 1942), Star Spangled Rhythm, Happy Go Lucky, Let's Face It, The Miracle of Morgan's Creek and the Angels Sing, Here Come the Waves, Incendiary Blonde, Duffy's Tavern, The Stork Club, Cross My Heart, The Perils of Pauline, Dream Girl, Red Hot and Blue, Annie Get Your Gun, Let's Dance, Sailor Beware (cameo), The Greatest Show on Earth, Somebody Loves Me, Spring Reunion.
TELEVISION: Series: The Betty Hutton Show (1959-60). Special: Satins and Spurs. Guest: Dinah Shore Chevy Show, Greatest Show on Earth, Burke's Law, Gunsmoke.

HUTTON, BRIAN, G.
Director. b. New York, NY, 1935. Started as bit player in films (incl. Fear Strikes Out, Gunfight at the O.K. Corral) before dir. for tv, then features.
PICTURES: The Wild Seed (debut, 1965), The Pad and How to Use It, Sol Madrid, Where Eagles Dare, Kelly's Heroes, X Y and Zee (Zee & Company), Night Watch, The First Deadly Sin, High Road to China, Hostile Takeover.
TELEVISION: Institute For Revenge.

HUTTON, LAUREN
Actress. r.n. Mary Hutton. b. Charleston, SC, Nov. 17, 1943. e. U. of South Florida, Sophie Newcombe Coll. As model featured on more covers than any other American. Stage debut at LA Public Theatre in Extremities.
PICTURES: Paper Lion (debut, 1968), Pieces of Dreams, Little Fauss and Big Halsy, Rocco Papaleo, The Gambler, Gator, Welcome to L.A., Viva Knievel!, A Wedding, American Gigolo, Paternity, Zorro the Gay Blade, Tout Feu tout Flamme (Hecate), Lassiter, Once Bitten, Flagrant Desire, Malone, Blue Blood, Bulldance (Forbidden Sun), Run For Your Life, Billions, Guilty as Charged, Missing Pieces, My Father the Hero.
TELEVISION: Mini-Series: The Rhinemann Exchange, Sins. Movies: Someone Is Watching Me, Institute for Revenge, Starflight, The Cradle Will Fall, Scandal Sheet, The Return of Mike Hammer, Time Stalker, Monte Carlo, Perfect People, Fear. Series: Paper Dolls, Falcon Crest, Lauren Hutton and... (talk show), Central Park West.

HUTTON, TIMOTHY
Actor. b. Malibu, CA, Aug. 16, 1960. Father was late actor Jim Hutton. Debut in bit part in father's film Never Too Late. Acted in high school plays; toured with father in Harvey during vacation. Directed Cars video Drive (1984).
THEATER: NY: Love Letters (B'way debut, 1989), Prelude to a Kiss, Babylon Gardens.
PICTURES: Never Too Late (debut, 1965), Ordinary People (Academy Award, best supporting actor, 1980; also Golden Globe & LA Film Critics Awards), Taps, Daniel, Iceman, The Falcon and The Snowman, Turk 182, Made in Heaven, A Time of Destiny, Betrayed (cameo), Everybody's All American, Torrents of Spring, Q&A, Strangers, The Temp, The Dark Half, French Kiss, Beautiful Girls, The Substance of Fire.
TELEVISION: Movies: Zuma Beach, Friendly Fire, The Best Place to Be, And Baby Makes Six, Young Love First Love, Father Figure, A Long Way Home, Zelda, The Last Word. Director: Amazing Stories (Grandpa's Ghost).

HUYCK, WILLARD
Writer, Director. e. U. of Southern California. Worked as reader for Larry Gordon, executive at American-International Pictures; named Gordon's asst., working on scene rewrites for AIP films. First screen credit on The Devil's Eight as co-writer with John Milius.
PICTURES: Writer: French Postcards (also dir.), Indiana Jones and the Temple of Doom, Best Defense (also dir.), Howard the Duck (also dir.), Radioland Murders, Mission: Impossible.
TELEVISION: A Father's Homecoming (co-exec. prod., co-s.p.), American River (co-exec. prod., co-s.p.).

HYAMS, JOSEPH
Advertising & Publicity Executive. b. New York, NY, Sept. 21, 1926. e. NYU Ent. industry, 1947. Various publicity posts, 20th Century-Fox, Columbia Pictures, 1947-55; eastern pub. mgr., Figaro Prods., 1955-56; West Coast pub. mgr., Hecht-Hill-Lancaster, 1955-58; pub. adv. dir., Batjac Prods. 1959-60 national adv. & pub. dir., Warner Bros.-7 Arts, 1960. v.p., world-wide pub., Warner Bros., Inc., 1970-87; appointed sr. v.p., special projects, 1987.

HYAMS, PETER
Director, Writer, Cinematographer. b. New York, NY, July 26, 1943. e. Hunter Coll., Syracuse U. Joined CBS news staff N.Y. and made anchor man. Filmed documentary on Vietnam in 1966. Left CBS in 1970 and joined Paramount in Hollywood as writer. Hired by ABC to direct TV features.
PICTURES: Writer: T.R. Baskin (also prod.), Telefon, The Hunter. Exec. Prod.: The Monster Squad. Director: Busting (dir. debut 1974; also s.p.), Our Time (also s.p.), Peeper, Capricorn One (also s.p.), Hanover Street (also s.p.), Outland (also s.p.), The Star Chamber (also s.p.), 2010 (also prod., s.p., photog.), Running Scared (also exec. prod., photog.), The Presidio (also photog.), Narrow Margin (also s.p., photog.), Stay Tuned (also photog.), Timecop (also photog.), Sudden Death (also photg.).
TELEVISION: Movies (dir., writer): The Rolling Man, Goodnight My Love.

HYDE, TOMMY
Executive. r.n. Thomas L. b. Meridian, MS, June 29, 1916. e. Lakeland H.S., grad., 1935. Worked E.J. Sparks Theatres, 1932-41. Florida State Theatres, 1941-42. U.S. Navy, 1942-46. Florida State Theatres, 1946-47; city mgr. (Tallahassee). Talgar Theatres, 1947-58; v.p. and gen. mgr. Kent Theatres, 1958-86; vice-pres. Motion Picture Films, Inc.; pres., NATO of Florida, 1961-62; chmn. bd. 1963-70; 1987-, theatre consultant.

HYER, MARTHA
Actress. b. Fort Worth, TX, Aug. 10, 1924. e. Northwestern U., Pasadena Playhouse.
PICTURES: The Locket (debut, 1946), Thunder Mountain, Born to Kill, Woman on the Beach, The Velvet Touch, Gun Smugglers, The Judge Steps Out, Clay Pigeon, Roughshod, The Rustlers, The Lawless, Outcast of Black Mesa, Salt Lake Raiders, Frisco

Tornado, Geisha Girl, The Kangaroo Kid, The Invisible Mr. Unmei, Wild Stallion, Yukon Gold, Abbott and Costello Go to Mars, So Big, Riders to the Stars, Scarlet Spear, Battle of Rogue River, Lucky Me, Down Three Dark Streets, Sabrina, Cry Vengeance, Wyoming Renegades, Kiss of Fire, Paris Follies of 1956, Francis in the Navy, Red Sundown, Showdown at Abilene, Battle Hymn, Kelly and Me, Mister Cory, The Delicate Delinquent, My Man Godfrey, Paris Holiday, Once Upon a Horse, Houseboat, Some Came Running (Acad. Award nom.), The Big Fisherman, The Best of Everything, Ice Palace, Desire in the Dust, Mistress of the World, The Right Approach, The Last Time I Saw Archie, Girl Named Tamiko, The Man from the Diner's Club, Wives and Lovers, Pyro, The Carpetbaggers, First Men in the Moon, Blood on the Arrow, Bikini Beach, The Sons of Katie Elder, The Chase, Night of the Grizzly, Picture Mommy Dead, War Italian Style, The Happening, Some May Live, Lo Scatenato (Catch as Catch Can), House of 1000 Dolls, Once You Kiss a Stranger, Crossplot, The Tyrant.

HYLER, JOAN
Executive. Pres., Women In Film.

I

IANNUCCI, SALVATORE J.
Executive. b. Brooklyn, NY, Sept. 24, 1927. e. NYU, B.A., 1949; Harvard Law School, J.D., 1952. 2 yrs. legal departments RCA and American Broadcasting Companies, Inc.; 14 yrs. with CBS Television Network: asst. dir. of bus. affairs, dir. of bus. affairs, v.p. of bus. affairs; 2 yrs. v.p. admin. National General Corp.; 2-1/2 yrs. pres. of Capital Records; 4-1/2 yrs. Corp. v.p. and dir. of Entertainment Div. of Playboy Enterprises, Inc.; 4 yrs. partner with Jones, Day Reavis & Pogue in Los Angeles office, handling entertainment legal work; Pres., Filmways Entertainment, and sr. v.p., Filmways, Inc.; exec. v.p., Embassy Communications; COO, Aaron Spelling Prods.; sr. partner Bushkin, Gaims, Gaines, & Jonas; pres. and chief operating officer, Brad Marks International; prod. of features, tv movies and infomercials.

IBBETSON, ARTHUR
Cinematographer. b. England, Sept. 8, 1922.
PICTURES: The Horse's Mouth, The Angry Silence, The League of Gentlemen, Tunes of Glory, Whistle Down the Wind, Lisa (The Inspector), Nine Hours to Rama, I Could Go on Singing, The Chalk Garden, A Countess from Hong Kong, Inspector Clouseau, Where Eagles Dare, The Walking Stick, Anne of the Thousand Days (Acad. Award nom.), The Railway Children, Willy Wonka and the Chocolate Factory, A Doll's House, 11 Harrow House, A Little Night Music, The Medusa Touch, The Prisoner of Zenda, Hopscotch, Nothing Personal (co-cin.), The Bounty, Santa Claus: The Movie.
TELEVISION: Frankenstein: the True Story, Little Lord Fauntleroy (Emmy Award), Brief Encounter, Babes in Toyland, Witness for the Prosecution, Master of the Game.

IBERT, LLOYD
Executive. Began career as mgng. editor, Independent Film Journal. 1973, joined Paramount Pictures pub. dept.; named sr. publicist. 1985, appointed dir., natl. pub. for M.P. Group.

ICE CUBE
Actor, Singer. r.n. O'Shea Jackson. b. Los Angeles, 1969. e. Phoenix Inst. of Tech. Debuted as rap performer with group N.W.A. Solor debut 1990 with album Amerikka's Most Wanted.
PICTURES: Boyz N the Hood (debut, 1991), Trespass, Higher Learning, Friday (also co-s.p., co-exec. prod.), The Glass Shield.

ICE-T
Actor, Singer. r.n. Tracy Morrow. b. Newark, NJ. Raised in Los Angeles. Served 4 yrs. as ranger in U.S. army. Made debut as rap performer with 1982 single The Coldest Rap. Received Grammy Award 1990 for Back on the Block.
PICTURES: Breakin' (debut, 1984), Breakin' 2: Electric Boogaloo, New Jack City, Ricochet, Trespass, Who's the Man?, Surviving the Game, Tank Girl, Johnny Mnemonic.
TELEVISION: Guest: New York Undercover.

IDLE, ERIC
Actor, Writer. b. South Shields, Co. Durham, Eng., March 29, 1943. e. Pembroke Coll., Cambridge, 1962-65. Pres. Cambridge's Footlights appearing at Edinburgh Fest. 1963-64. Member Monty Python's Flying Circus appearing on BBC, 1969-74.
THEATER: Oh What a Lovely War, Monty Python Live at the Hollywood Bowl, Monty Python Live, The Mikado (English Natl. Opera, 1986).
BOOKS: Hello Sailor, The Rutland Dirty Weekend Book, Pass the Bulter; as well as co-author of Monty Python books: Monty Python's Big Red Book, The Brand New Monty Python Book, Monty Python and the Holy Grail, The Complete Works of Shakespeare and Monty Python.

PICTURES: And Now for Something Completely Different (also co-s.p.), Monty Python and the Holy Grail (also co-s.p.), Monty Python's Life of Brian (also co-s.p.), Monty Python Live at the Hollywood Bowl (also co-s.p.), Monty Python's The Meaning of Life (also co-s.p.), Yellowbeard, National Lampoon's European Vacation, Transformers (voice), The Adventures of Baron Munchausen, Nuns on the Run, Too Much Sun, Missing Pieces, Mom & Dad Save the World, Splitting Heirs (also s.p., exec. prod.), Casper.
TELEVISION: Isadora (debut, 1965), The Frost Report (writer), Do Not Adjust Your Set, Monty Python's Flying Circus, Rutland Weekend Television (series), All You Need is Cash (The Rutles), Faerie Tale Theater (The Frog Prince; dir., writer ACE Award, 1982; The Pied Piper), Saturday Night Live, The Mikado, Around the World in 80 Days, Nearly Departed (series).

IGER, ROBERT
Executive. b. New York, NY, 1951. e. Ithaca Col. Joined ABC in 1974 as studio supervisor. 1976 moved to ABC Sports. 1985, named v.p. in charge of program plan. & dev. as well as scheduling and rights acquisitions for all ABC Sports properties. 1987, named v.p. program. for ABC Sports and mgr. & dir. for ABC's Wide World of Sports; 1988, appt. exec. v.p., ABC Network Group. 1989 named pres., ABC Entertainment. 1992 became pres. of ABC TV Network Group.; 1993, sr. v.p. CC/ABC Inc., exec. v.p. of Capital Cities/ABC Inc. Sept., 1994, elected pres. & COO.

IMAMURA, SHOHEI
Director, Producer, Writer. b. Tokyo, Japan, Sept. 15, 1926. e. Waseda U. Joined Shochiku Ofuna Studio 1951 asst. dir., transferred Nikkatsu in 1954 as asst. dir., director Stolen Desire 1958 then 4 more films before refusing to work on any film distasteful to him; and wrote play later made into film directed by him in 1968; later turned to documentaries and from 1976 onward as independent; Ballad of Narayama awarded Golden Palm Prize, Cannes Festival, 1983.
PICTURES: Stolen Carnal Desire, Big Brother, Hogs and Warships, Insect Woman, God's Profound Desire, The Pornographers, A Man Vanishes, Human Evaporation, History of Postwar Japan, Vengeance Is Mine, Eijanaika, The Ballad of Nurayama, Zegen, Black Rain.

IMI, TONY
Cinematographer. b. London, March 27, 1937. Ent. ind. 1959.
PICTURES: The Raging Moon, Dulcima, The Slipper and the Rose, International Velvet, Brass Target, Ffolkes, The Sea Wolves, Night Crossing, Nate and Hayes, Not Quite Jerusalem, Enemy Mine, Empire State, American Roulette, Buster, Options, Wired, Fire Birds, Pretty Hattie's Baby, Shopping.
TELEVISION: Queenie, The Return of Sherlock Holmes, Oceans of Fire, The Last Days of Frank and Jesse James, Reunion at Fairborough, A Christmas Carol, Sakharov, Princess Daisy, John Paul II, Little Gloria–Happy at Last, Inside the Third Reich, Dreams Don't Die, For Ladies Only, Nicholas Nickleby, A Tale of Two Cities, Babycakes, Old Man and the Sea, Fourth Story, The Last to Go, Our Sons, Carolina Skeletons, Child of Rage, Queen, Cobb's Law, For the Love of My Child: The Anissa Ayala Story, Blind Angel, Scarlett, The Sunshine Boys, The Turn of the Screw, Dalva, The Abduction, Desperate Justice.

IMMERMAN, WILLIAM J.
Producer, Attorney, Executive. b. New York, NY, Dec. 29, 1937. e. Univ. Wisconsin, BS, 1959; Stanford Law, J.D., 1963. 1963-65, served as deputy district attorney, LA County. 1965-72, assoc. counsel, v.p.-bus. affairs, American Intl. Pictures. 1972-77, v.p., business affairs, sr. v.p. feature film division 20th Century-Fox. 1977-1979, producer at Warner Bros. 1979-82, founder and chmn. of bd. of Cinema Group Inc. 1978-present, pres. Salem Productions. 1988-94, pres. Distribution Expense Co. 1988-present, pres., ImmKirk Financial Corp. 1988-89, spec. consultant to office of pres., Pathe Communications. 1989-90, vice chmn. Cannon Pictures. 1986-90, dir. Heritage Ent., Inc. 1991-present, v.p. The Crime Channel. 1983-93, of counsel to law firm of Barash and Hill. 1993-present, of Counsel to law firm of Kenoff and Machtinger (LA). 1990-present, Regional Adjudicator (Southwest). Member of AFMA Arbitration Panel. Member of AMPAS. Stage Productions: Berlin to Broadway (LA), The Knife Thrower's Assistant (LA, tour), The Wiz (B'way).
PICTURES: Exec. prod.: Highpoint, Southern Comfort, Hysterical, Mind Games, Take this Job and Shove It, Where the Red Ferns Grows Part II, The St. Tammany Miracle. Prod.: Primal Rage, Nightmare Beach (Welcome to Spring Break).

INGALLS, DON
Producer, Writer. b. Humboldt, NE, July 29, 1928. e. George Washington U., 1948. Columnist, Washington Post; producer-writer, ATV England and Australia; writer-prod., Have Gun Will Travel, also prod. for TV: The Travels of Jamie McPheeters,

The Virginian, Honey West, Serpico, Kingston: Confidential. Exec. story consultant The Sixth Sense; prod.: Fantasy Island, T.J. Hooker, Duel at Shiloh, Smile of the Dragon, In Preparation: Watchers on the Mountain, Hearts & Diamonds. PICTURES: Airport—1975, Who's Got the Body? TELEVISION: *Writer*: Gunsmoke, Have Gun Will Travel, The Bold Ones, Marcus Welby M.D., Mod Squad, Star Trek, Honey West, Bonanza, The Sixth Sense, Then Came Bronson, Police Story, World Premier Movie, Shamus, Flood, Capt. America, The Initiation of Sarah, Blood Sport, and others.

INGELS, MARTY
Actor, Former Comedian, Executive. b. Brooklyn, NY, Mar. 9, 1936. m actress-singer Shirley Jones. U.S. Infantry 1954-58. Ent. show business representing Army, Name That Tune. Stage: Sketchbook revue, Las Vegas. Pres., Celebrity Brokerage, packaging celebrity events and endorsements. Active in community affairs and charity funding. PICTURES: The Ladies Man, Armored Command, The Horizontal Lieutenant, The Busy Body, Wild and Wonderful, A Guide for the Married Man, If It's Tuesday It Must be Belgium, For Singles Only, Instant Karma. TELEVISION: *Series*: I'm Dickens... He's Fenster, The Phyllis Diller Show. *Guest*: Phil Silvers Show, Steve Allen, Jack Paar, Playboy Penthouse, Bell Telephone Hour, Manhunt, Ann Sothern Show, Peter Loves Mary, The Detectives, Joey Bishop Show, Hennessey, Dick Van Dyke Show, Burke's Law, Hollywood Palace, Family, Murder She Wrote.

INGSTER, BORIS
Writer, Director. b. 1913.
PICTURES: Writer: The Last Days of Pompeii, Dancing Pirate, Thin Ice, Happy Landing, Paris Underground, Something for the Birds, Abdullah's Harem, California, Cloak & Dagger, The Amazing Mrs. Holliday. Director: The Judge Steps Out, Southside 1-1000. TELEVISION: Wagon Train, The Alaskans, The Roaring 20's, Travels of Jaimie McPheeters, The Man From U.N.C.L.E.

INSDORF, ANNETTE
Film Professor, Critic, Translator, TV Host. b. Paris, France, July 27, 1950. e. 1963-68 studied music at Juilliard Sch. of Music and performed as singer; Queens Coll. (summa cum laude), B.A. 1972; Yale U., M.A., 1973; Yale U., Ph.D., 1975. 1973: soloist in Leonard Bernstein's Mass (European premiere in Vienna and BBC/WNET TV). 1975-87: professor of film, Yale U. Author of Francois Truffaut (1979; updated 1989), Indelible Shadows: Film and the Holocaust (1983, updated 1989). Since 1979: frequent contributor to NY Times (Arts and Leisure), Los Angeles Times, San Francisco Chronicle, Elle, and Premiere. Named Chevalier dans l'ordre des arts et lettres by French Ministry of Culture, 1986. Since 1987, dir. of Undergrad. Film Studies, Columbia U., and prof. Graduate Film Div. 1990 named chmn. of Film Div. 1987: exec.-prod. Shoeshine (short film nom. for Oscar). 1989: exec. prod., Abrams' Performance Pieces (named best fiction short, Cannes Fest).

IRONS, JEREMY
Actor. b. Isle of Wight, Sept. 19, 1948. m. actress Sinead Cusack. e. Sherborne Sch., Dorset. Stage career began at Marlowe Theatre, Canterbury, where he was student asst. stage manager. Accepted at Bristol Old Vic Theatre Sch. for two-yr. course; then joined Bristol Old Vic Co. In London played in Godspell, Much Ado About Nothing, The Caretaker, Taming of the Shrew, Wild Oats, Rear Column, An Audience Called Edouard, etc. N.Y. stage debut, The Real Thing (Tony Award, 1984). PICTURES: Nijinsky (debut, 1980), The French Lieutenant's Woman, Moonlighting, Betrayal, The Wild Duck, Swann in Love, The Mission, Dead Ringers, A Chorus of Disapproval, Danny the Champion of the World (tv in U.S.), Australia, Reversal of Fortune (Academy Award, 1990), Kafka, Waterland, Damage, M. Butterfly, The House of the Spirits, The Lion King (voice), Die Hard With a Vengeance. TELEVISION: The Pallisers, Notorious Woman, Love for Lydia, Langrishe Go Down, Brideshead Revisited, The Captain's Doll, Autogeddon, Tales From Hollywood, The Dream of a Ridiculous Man.

IRONSIDE, MICHAEL
Actor. b. Toronto, Ontario, Canada, Feb. 12, 1950. e. Ontario Col. of Art.
PICTURES: Scanners, Visiting Hours, Spacehunter: Adventures in the Forbidden Zone, The Falcon and the Snowman, Jo Jo Dancer Your Life Is Calling, Top Gun, Extreme Prejudice, Nowhere to Hide, Hello Mary Lou: Prom Night II, Watchers, Total Recall, McBain, Highlander II: The Quickening, The Vagrant, Fortunes of War, The Killing Man, Free Willy, The Next Karate Kid, Major Payne, The Glass Shield. TELEVISION: *Series*: V, ER, seaQuest DSV. *Movie*: Probable Cause (also co-exec. prod.).

IRVIN, JOHN
Director. b. Cheshire, England, May 7, 1940. In cutting rooms at Rank Organisation before making first film documentary, Gala Day, on grant from British Film Inst.; made other award-winning documentaries before turning to features. PICTURES: The Dogs of War (debut, 1981), Ghost Story, Champions, Turtle Diary, Raw Deal, Hamburger Hill, Next of Kin, Eminent Domain, Widow's Peak, A Month by the Lake. TELEVISION: The Nearly Man, Hard Times, Tinker Tailor Soldier Spy, Robin Hood (foreign theatrical), Crazy Horse.

IRVING, AMY
Actress. b. Palo Alto, CA, Sept. 10, 1953. e. American Conservatory Theatre, London Acad. of Dramatic Art. Daughter of late theatre dir. Jules Irving and actress Priscilla Pointer. m. director Bruno Barreto. THEATER: *NY*: Amadeus, Heartbreak House, Road to Mecca, Broken Glass. *LA*: The Heidi Chronicles. PICTURES: Carrie (debut, 1976), The Fury, Voices, Honeysuckle Rose, The Competition, Yentl (Acad. Award nom.), Micki and Maude, Rumpelstiltskin, Who Framed Roger Rabbit (voice), Crossing Delancey, Show of Force, An American Tail: Fievel Goes West (voice), Benefit of the Doubt, Kleptomania, Acts of Love (also co- exec. prod.), I'm Not Rappaport, Carried Away. TELEVISION: *Movies*: James Dean, James A. Michener's Dynasty, Panache, Anastasia: The Mystery of Anna. *Mini-Series*: Once an Eagle, The Far Pavilions. *Specials*: I'm a Fool, Turn of the Screw, Heartbreak House, Twilight Zone: Rod Serling's Lost Classics: The Theater. *Guest*: The Rookies, Police Woman.

IRWIN, BILL
Actor. b. Santa Monica, CA, April 11, 1950. THEATER: *B'way*: Accidental Death of an Anarchist, 5-6-7-8 Dance, Largely New York, Fool Moon. *Off-B'way*: The Regard of Flight, The Courtroom, Not Quite New York, Waiting for Godot. Regional: Scapin (also dir., adaptation). PICTURES: Popeye (debut, 1980), A New Life, Eight Men Out, My Blue Heaven, Scenes From a Mall, Hot Shots, Stepping Out, Silent Tongue. TELEVISION: *Specials*: The Regard of Flight, Bette Midler—Mondo Beyondo, The Paul Daniels Magic Show (BBC), The Last Mile. *Guest*: Saturday Night Live, Tonight Show, Cosby Show, Northern Exposure.

ISAACS, CHERYL BOONE
Executive. b. Springfield, MA. Entered m.p. industry 1977 as staff publicist for Columbia Pictures. Worked five years after that for Melvin Simon Prods., named v.p. Left to become dir. of adv./pub. for The Ladd Co. 1984, named dir., pub. & promo., West Coast, for Paramount Pictures. Promoted vice pres., publicity, Paramount Pictures in 1986. Promoted to sr. v.p., Worldwide Publicity, Paramount in 1991. Member A.M.P.A.S. Board of Governors since 1988. Promoted to exec. v.p. in 1994.

ISAACS, PHIL
Executive. b. New York, NY, May 20, 1922. e. City Coll. of New York. In U.S. Navy, 1943-46. Joined Paramount Pictures in 1946 as bookers asst., N.Y. exch. Branch mgr. in Washington; then mgr. Rocky Mt. div. In 1966 was Eastern-Southern sls. mgr.; 1967 joined Cinema Center Films as v.p. domestic dist. In 1972 named v.p., marketing, for Tomorrow Entertainment; Joined Avco-Embassy 1975 as v.p., gen. sls. mgr., named exec. v.p., 1977. 1978 joined General Cinema Corp. as v.p. 1980 v.p., gen. sls. mgr., Orion Pictures. 1983, formed Phil Isaacs Co; 1988, v.p., general sales mgr., TWE Theatrical; 1989, appointed pres. Became pres. South Gate Entertainment 1989.

ISRAEL, NEAL
Writer, Director, Producer. m. actress Romy Walthall. PICTURES: Tunnelvision (exec. prod., s.p., actor), Cracking Up (s.p., actor), Americathon (dir., s.p.), Police Academy (s.p.), Bachelor Party (dir., s.p.), Johnny Dangerously (actor), Moving Violations (dir., s.p.), Real Genius (s.p.), It's Alive III (s.p.), Buy and Cell (co-s.p.), Look Who's Talking Too (co-prod., actor), Spurting Blood (exec. prod., s.p.), All I Want for Christmas (co-s.p.), Breaking the Rules (dir.), Surf Ninjas (dir., actor). TELEVISION: Lola Falana Special (writer), Mac Davis Show, Ringo, Marie (prod.), Twilight Theatre (writer, prod.), Man of the People (co-prod.), The Wonder Years (dir.), Hearts of the West (dir.). Movies: The Cover Girl and the Cop (dir.), Woman With a Past (co-exec. prod.), Combat High (dir.), Taking the Heat (co-prod.), Dream Date (prod.), Bonnie and Clyde: The True Story (co-prod.), A Quiet Little Neighborhood (co-prod.), Foster's Field Trip (dir., writer), Family Reunion: A Relative Nightmare (dir., co-writer, co-prod.).

ITAMI, JUZO
Director, Actor. b. Kyoto, Japan, 1933. m. actress Nobuko Miyamoto. Son of Mansaku Itami, pioneering Japanese film

director. After successful stint as commercial artist, became an actor as well as essayist (Listen, Women, a collection of his work). Directing debut The Funeral (1984).
PICTURES: *Actor*: 55 Days at Peking, Lord Jim, I Am a Cat, The Makioka Sisters, The Family Game. *Director*: The Funeral (5 Japanese Acad. Awards), Tampopo, A Taxing Woman (8 Japanese Acad. Awards), A Taxing Woman's Return (dir., s.p.), Sweet Home (exec. prod. only), Tales of a Golden Geisha, The Gangster's Moll.

IVANEK, ZELJKO
Actor. b. Ljubljana, Yugoslavia, Aug. 15, 1957. Came to U.S. with family in 1960 and returned to homeland before settling in Palo Alto, CA, in 1967. Studied at Yale, majoring in theatre studies: graduated in 1978. Also graduate of London Acad. of Music and Dramatic Arts. Regular member of Williamstown Theatre Festival, appearing in Hay Fever, Charley's Aunt, Front Page. B'way debut in The Survivor.
THEATER: *B'way*: The Survivor, Brighton Beach Memoirs, Loot, Two Shakespearean Actors, The Glass Menagerie. *Regional*: Master Harold... and the Boys (Yale Rep. premiere prod.), Hamlet (Guthrie), Ivanov (Yale Rep.). *Off B'way*: Cloud 9, A Map of the World, The Cherry Orchard.
PICTURES: Tex, The Sender, The Soldier, Mass Appeal, Rachel River, School Ties.
TELEVISION: *Movies*: The Sun Also Rises, Echoes in the Darkness, Aftermath: A Test of Love, Our Sons, My Brother's Keeper, Truman. *Special*: All My Sons. *Guest*: Homicide: Life on the Street.

IVANY, PETER
Executive. b. Melbourne, Australia, Aug. 23, 1954. e. Monash U. Melbourne, B.A., M.B.A. Victoria Health Commission as strategic planning analyst, 1978-80. Kodak Australia, estimating and planning analyst, 1980-81. Joined Hoyts Corporation Pty Ltd. in 1981 as cinema mgr., then general mgr., Hoyts Video; general mgr., corporate development, 1986-88. Chairman and CEO Hoyts US Holdings, Inc. 1986 then CEO to present.

IVERS, IRVING N.
Executive. b. Montreal, Canada, Feb. 23, 1939. e. Sir George Williams U. Worked for 10 years in radio and TV in variety of executive capacities in station management before entering film business. Joined Columbia Pictures in 1973, serving as director of mktg. and dir. of adv. 1973-77; named Canadian sls. mgr. 1977-78; v.p. of adv./pub. 1978-80. 1980 joined 20th Century-Fox as sr. v.p. of adv./pub./promo.; exec. v.p., worldwide adv., pub., promo. 1980-83; pres., worldwide mkt., MGM/UA/Entertainment Co., 1983-86. 1986 to Warner Bros. as v.p., intl. adv./pub. 1991 to Astral Commun., Toronto as pres. of Astral Films and Astral Video.

IVEY, JUDITH
Actress. b. El Paso, TX, Sept. 4, 1951. m. ind. prod., Tim Braine. e. Illinois State U. Stage debut in The Sea in Chicago, 1974.
THEATER: Bedroom Farce, The Goodbye People, Oh Coward!, Design for Living, Piaf, Romeo and Juliet, Pastorale, Two Small Bodies, Steaming (Tony & Drama Desk Awards), Second Lady (off-B'way work she helped develop), Hurlyburly (Tony & Drama Desk Awards), Precious Sons (Drama Desk nom.), Blithe Spirit, Mrs. Dally Has a Lover, Park Your Car in Harvard Yard (Tony nom.), The Moonshot Tape (Obie Award).
PICTURES: Harry and Son (debut, 1984), The Lonely Guy, The Woman in Red, Compromising Positions, Brighton Beach Memoirs, Hello Again, Sister Sister, Miles from Home, In Country, Everybody Wins, Alice, Love Hurts, There Goes the Neighborhood.
TELEVISION: *Series*: Down Home, Designing Women, The Critic (voice), The Five Mrs. Buchanans. *Movies*: The Shady Hill Kidnapping, Dixie: Changing Habits, We Are the Children, The Long Hot Summer, Jesse and the Bandit Queen, Decoration Day, Her Final Fury: Betty Broderick—The Last Chapter, On Promised Land, Almost Golden: The Jessica Savitch Story. *Special*: Other Mothers (Afterschool Special).

IVORY, JAMES
Director. b. Berkeley, CA, June 7, 1928. e. U. of Oregon, B.F.A., 1951; U. of Southern California, M.A. (cinema) 1956. First film Venice: Theme and Variations (doc. made as M.A. thesis, 1957). Early work: The Sword and the Flute, The Delhi Way. Formed Merchant Ivory Productions with prod. Ismail Merchant and script writer Ruth Prawer Jhabvala. Received D.W. Griffith Lifetime Achievement Award from DGA, 1995.
PICTURES: The Householder, Shakespeare Wallah (also co-s.p.), The Guru (also co-s.p.), Bombay Talkie (also co-s.p.), Savages, The Wild Party, Roseland, The Europeans (also cameo), Quartet, Heat and Dust, The Bostonians, A Room With a View, Maurice (also co-s.p.), Slaves of New York, Mr. and Mrs. Bridge, Howards End, The Remains of the Day, Jefferson in Paris, Surviving Picasso.

TELEVISION: Noon Wine (exec. prod.). Dir: Adventures of a Brown Man in Search of Civilization, Autobiography of a Princess (also released theatrically), Hullabaloo Over George and Bonnie's Pictures, Jane Austen in Manhattan (also released theatrically), The Five Forty Eight.

J

JACKSON, ANNE
Actress. b. Allegheny, PA, Sept. 3, 1926. e. Neighborhood Playhouse, Actors Studio. Married to actor Eli Wallach. Stage debut in The Cherry Orchard, 1944. Autobiography: Early Stages.
THEATER: Major Barbara, Middle of the Night, The Typist and the Tiger, Luv, Waltz of the Toreadors, Twice Around the Park, Summer and Smoke, Nest of the Woodgrouse, Marco Polo Sings a Solo, The Mad Woman of Chaillot, Cafe Crown, Lost in Yonkers, In Persons, The Flowering Peach.
PICTURES: So Young So Bad (debut, 1950), The Journey, Tall Story, The Tiger Makes Out, How to Save a Marriage and Ruin Your Life, The Secret Life of an American Wife, The Angel Levine, Zig Zag, Lovers and Other Strangers, Dirty Dingus Magee, Nasty Habits, The Bell Jar, The Shining, Sam's Son, Funny About Love, Folks!
TELEVISION: *Series*: Everything's Relative. *Special*: 84 Charing Cross Road. *Movies*: The Family Man, A Woman Called Golda, Private Battle, Blinded By the Light, Leave 'em Laughing, Baby M.

JACKSON, BRIAN
Actor, Film & Theatre Producer. b. Bolton, England, 1931. Early career in photography then numerous stage performances incl. Old Vic, Royal Shakespeare. Ent. film/TV industry 1958. Formed Quintus Plays, 1965; formed Brian Jackson Productions 1966; formed Hampden Gurney Studios Ltd. 1970. Co-produced The Others 1967; presented The Button, 1969; co-produced the documentary film Village in Mayfair, 1970; 1971: Formed Brian Jackson Films Ltd.; produced Yesterday, The Red Deer, The Story of Tutankhamen.
THEATER: Mame, Drury Lane, Fallen Angels, In Praise of Love.
PICTURES: Incident in Karandi, Carry On Sergeant, Gorgo, Jack the Ripper, Taste of Fear, Heroes of Telemark, Only the Lonely, The Deadly Females, The Revenge of the Pink Panther, Deceptions, Shadow Chasers.
TELEVISION: Moon Fleet, Private Investigator, Life of Lord Lister, Z Cars, Vendetta, Sherlock Holmes, Mr. Rose, Hardy Heating International, Nearest & Dearest, The Persuaders, The Paradise Makers, The New Avengers, Smugglers Bay, The Tomorrow People, Secret Army, Last Visitor for Hugh Peters, Six Men of Dorset, Commercials: featured as the man from Delmonte for 5 years.

JACKSON, GLENDA
Actress. b. Birkenhead, England, May 9, 1936. Stage debut: Separate Tales (Worthing, Eng. 1957). 1964 joined Peter Brooks' Theatre of Cruelty which led to film debut. Became member of Parliament, 1992.
THEATER: (Eng.): All Kinds of Men, Hammersmith, The Idiot, Alfie. Joined Royal Shakespeare Co in experimental Theatre of Cruelty season. Marat Sade (London, N.Y.), Three Sisters, The Maids, Hedda Gabler, The White Devil, Rose, Strange Interlude (N.Y.), Macbeth (N.Y.), Who's Afraid of Virginia Woolf? (L.A.).
PICTURES: The Persecution and Assassination of Jean-Paul Marat as Performed by the Inmates of the Asylum at Charenton Under the Direction of the Marquis de Sade (debut, 1967), Tell Me Lies, Negatives, Women in Love (Academy Award, 1970), The Music Lovers, Sunday Bloody Sunday, Mary Queen of Scots, The Boy Friend, Triple Echo, The Nelson Affair, A Touch of Class (Academy Award, 1973), The Maids, The Temptress, The Romantic Englishwoman, The Devil is a Woman, Hedda, The Incredible Sarah, Nasty Habits, House Calls, Stevie, The Class of Miss McMichael, Lost and Found, Health, Hopscotch, Giro City, The Return of the Soldier, Turtle Diary, Beyond Therapy, Business as Usual, Salome's Last Dance, The Rainbow, The Visit.
TELEVISION: *Movies*: The Patricia Neal Story, Sakharov. *Mini-Series*: Elizabeth R (2 Emmy Awards, 1972). *Special*: Strange Interlude, A Murder of Quality, The House of Bernarda Alba.

JACKSON, KATE
Actress. b. Birmingham, AL, Oct. 29, 1949. e. U. of Mississippi, Birmingham Southern U. Did summer stock before going to N.Y. to enter American Acad. of Dramatic Arts, appearing in Night Must Fall, The Constant Wife, Little Moon of Alban. Worked as model and became tour guide at NBC. First role on TV in Dark Shadows (series).
PICTURES: Night of Dark Shadows, Limbo, Thunder and Lightning, Dirty Tricks, Making Love, Loverboy.
TELEVISION: *Movies*: Satan's School for Girls, Killer Bees, Death Cruise, Death Scream, Charlie's Angels (pilot), Death at Love House, James at 15 (pilot), Topper, Inmates: A Love

Story, Thin Ice, Listen to Your Heart, The Stranger Within, Quiet Killer, Homewrecker (voice), Adrift, Empty Cradle, Armed and Innocent, Justice in a Small Town. *Series*: Dark Shadows, The Rookies, Charlie's Angels, Scarecrow and Mrs. King, Baby Boom. *Guest*: The Jimmy Stewart Show.

JACKSON, MICHAEL
Singer, Composer. b. Gary, IN, Aug. 29, 1958. Musical recording artist with family group known as Jackson 5: all brothers, Jackie, Jermaine, Tito, Marlon, and Michael. Sister is singer Janet Jackson.
PICTURES: Save the Children, The Wiz, Moonwalker (also exec. prod., story).
TELEVISION: *Series*: The Jacksons (1976-77). *Specials*: Free to Be You and Me, Sandy in Disneyland, Motown on Showtime: Michael Jackson.

JACKSON, MICK
Director. b. Grays, England. e. Bristol Univ. Joined BBC as film editor, following post-grad work in film & tv. Produced and directed many documentaries for the BBC.
PICTURES: Chattahoochee, L.A. Story, The Bodyguard, Clean Slate.
TELEVISION: *Documentaries*: The Ascent of Man, Connections, The Age of Uncertainty. *Movies/Specials*: Threads, The Race for the Double Helix, Yuri Nosenko KGB (HBO), Indictment: The McMartin Trial. *Mini-Series*: A Very British Coup.

JACKSON, PETER
Director. b. New Zealand.
PICTURES: Meet the Feebles, Bad Taste, Dead Alive, Heavenly Creatures, The Frighteners.

JACKSON, SAMUEL L.
Actor. b. 1949. e. Morehouse Col. m. actress LaTanya Richardson. Co-founder, member of the Just Us Theatre Co. in Atlanta.
THEATER: *Negro Ensemble Company*: Home, A Soldier's Story, Sally/Prince, Colored People's Time. *NY Shakespeare Fest*: Mother Courage, Spell No. 7, The Mighty Gents. *Yale Rep*: The Piano Lesson, Two Trains Running. *Seattle Rep*: Fences.
PICTURES: Ragtime (debut, 1981), Eddie Murphy Raw, School Daze, Coming to America, Do the Right Thing, Sea of Love, A Shock to the System, Def by Temptation, Betsy's Wedding, Mo' Better Blues, The Exorcist III, GoodFellas, Mob Justice, Jungle Fever (Cannes Film Fest. & NY Film Critics Awards, 1991), Strictly Business, Juice, White Sands, Patriot Games, Johnny Suede, Jumpin at the Boneyard, Fathers and Sons, National Lampoon's Loaded Weapon 1, Amos & Andrew, Menace II Society, Jurassic Park, True Romance, Hail Caesar, Fresh, The New Age, Pulp Fiction (Acad. Award nom.), Losing Isaiah, Kiss of Death, Die Hard With a Vengeance, Fluke (voice), The Great White Hype, A Time to Kill, The Long Kiss Goodnight.
TELEVISION: *Movies*: Assault at West Point: The Court-Martial of Johnson Whittaker, Against the Wall.

JACOBI, DEREK
O.B.E. Actor. b. London, England, Oct. 22, 1938. e. Cambridge. On stage in Pericles, The Hollow Crown, Hobson's Choice, The Suicide, Breaking the Code (London, NY).
PICTURES: Othello (debut, 1965), Interlude, The Three Sisters, The Day of the Jackal, Blue Blood, The Odessa File, The Medusa Touch, The Human Factor, Enigma, The Secret of NIMH (voice), Little Dorrit, Henry V, Dead Again, Hamlet.
TELEVISION: She Stoops to Conquer, Man of Straw, The Pallisers, I, Claudius, Philby, Burgess and MacLean, Hamlet. Movies: Othello, Three Sisters, Interlude, Charlotte, The Man Who Went Up in Smoke, The Hunchback of Notre Dame, Inside the Third Reich, The Secret Garden, The Tenth Man (Emmy Award). *Series*: Minder, Tales of the Unexpected, Mr. Pye, The Leper of St. Giles.

JACOBS, JOHN
Executive. b. New York, NY. e. Syracuse U.'s Newhouse Communications Sch. Full-service agency background, including 13 years with Grey Advertising agency, where handled Warner Bros. & Warner Home Video accts. Supvr. media on RCA, ABC-TV, Murdoch Publishing, Radio City Musical Hall, etc. Named v.p. & group media dir. for Grey. 1986, left to join Warner Bros. as v.p., media; then sr. v.p. worldwide media.

JACOBS, MICHAEL
Producer, Writer. b. New Brunswick, NJ. Studied at Neighborhood Playhouse in NY. Had first play, Cheaters, prod. on B'way when he was only 22 yrs. old, followed by Getting Along Famously.
PICTURE: Quiz Show.
TELEVISION: *Series (creator/prod.)*: Charles in Charge, No Soap Radio, Together We Stand, Singer and Songs, My Two Dads (also dir.), Dinosaurs, The Torkelsons (Almost Home), Boy Meets World, Where I Live.

JACOBSEN, JOHN M.
Producer, Executive. b. Oslo, Norway, Dec. 27, 1944. Produced number of feature films incl. Pathfinder (Acad. Award nom.), Shipwrecked, Head Above Water. Pres., Norwegian Film and Video Producers Assn.; Pres. AB Svensk Filmindustri Norwegian Operation.

JACOBY, FRANK DAVID
Director, Producer. b. New York, NY, July 15, 1925. e. Hunter Coll., Brooklyn Coll. m. Doris Storm, producer/director educational films, actress. 1949-52, NBC network tv dir.; 1952-56, B.B.D.O., Biow Co., tv prod./dir.; 1956-58 Metropolitan Educational TV Assn., dir. of prod.; 1958-65, United Nation, film prod./dir.; 1965 to present, pres., Jacoby/Storm Prods., Inc., Westport, CT—documentary, industrial, educational films and filmstrips. Clients include Xerox Corp., Random House, Publ., Lippincott Co., IBM, Heublein, G.E., and Pitney Bowes. Winner, Sherwood Award, Peabody Award. Member, Director's Guild of America; winner, Int'l TV & Film Festival, National Educational Film Festival, American Film Festival.

JACOBY, JOSEPH
Producer, Director, Writer. b. Brooklyn, NY, Sept. 22, 1942. e. NYU. Sch. of Arts and Sciences, majoring in m.p. As undergraduate worked part-time as prod. asst. on daytime network TV shows and as puppeteer for Bunin Puppets. 1964 joined Bil Baird Marionettes as full-time puppeteer, working also on Baird film commercials. Made feature m.p. debut as prod.-dir of Shame Shame Everybody Knows Her Name, 1968. Contributing essayist, NY Woman Magazine. Founder/Dir.-Prod., Children's Video Theatre starring The Bil Baird Marionettes.
PICTURES: *Dir./Prod./Writer*: Hurry Up or I'll Be 30, The Great Bank Hoax, Davy Jones' Locker.

JACOBY, SCOTT
Actor. b. Chicago, IL, Nov. 19, 1956.
PICTURES: The Little Girl Who Lives Down the Lane, Love and the Midnight Auto Supply, Our Winning Season, Return to Horror High, To Die For, To Die For II.
TELEVISION: *Movies*: No Place to Run, That Certain Summer (Emmy Award, 1973), The Man Who Could Talk to Kids, Bad Ronald, Smash-Up on Interstate 5, No Other Love, The Diary of Anne Frank. *Mini-Series*: 79 Park Avenue. *Series*: One Life to Live (1973-74). *Guest*: Medical Center, Marcus Welby M.D., The Golden Girls.

JAECKEL, RICHARD
Actor. b. Long Beach, NY, Oct. 10, 1926. e. Hollywood H.S., 1943. Worked as delivery boy in mail room, 20th Century-Fox.
PICTURES: Guadalcanal Diary (debut, 1943), Wing and a Prayer, Jungle Patrol, City Across the River, Battleground, Sands of Iwo Jima, The Gunfighter, Sea Hornet, Hoodlum Empire, My Son John, Come Back Little Sheba, The Big Leaguer, Sea of Lost Ships, Shanghai Story, The Violent Men, Apache Ambush, Attack!, 3:10 to Yuma, The Naked and the Dead, Platinum High School, The Gallant Hours, Town Without Pity, The Young and the Brave, Four for Texas, Town Tamer, The Dirty Dozen, The Devil's Brigade, The Green Slime, Chisum, Sometimes a Great Notion (Acad. Award nom.), Ulzana's Raid, Pat Garrett and Billy the Kid, The Outfit, Chosen Survivors, The Drowning Pool, Part 2—Walking Tall, Grizzly, Mako: The Jaws of Death, Day of the Animals, Twilight's Last Gleaming, Delta Fox, Speedtrap, The Dark, Herbie Goes Bananas, ... All the Marbles, Cold River, Airplane II: The Sequel, Killing Machine, Starman, Black Moon Rising, Delta Force II, Ghetto Blasters, Martial Outlaw.
TELEVISION: *Series*: Frontier Circus, Banyon, Firehouse, Salvage One, At Ease, Spenser for Hire, Supercarrier, Baywatch. *Guest*: U.S. Steel Hour, Elgin Hour, Goodyear Playhouse, Kraft, Producer's Showcase. *Special*: The Petrified Forest. *Movies*: The Deadly Dream, Firehouse, The Red Pony, Partners in Crime, Born Innocent, The Last Day Go West Young Girl, Champions: A Love Story, Salvage, The $5.20 an Hour Dream, Reward, The Awakening of Candra, Dirty Dozen: The Next Mission, Baywatch: Panic at Malibu Pier.

JAFFE, LEO
Executive. b. April 23, 1909. e. NYU. Started at Columbia, 1930; v.p., Columbia Pictures, 1954; 1st v.p., treas., bd. memb.; v.p. & treas., 1958; exec. v.p., Columbia, 1962; pres. Columbia, 1968; pres., Columbia Pictures Industries, Inc, 1970; pres. & CEO, Columbia Pictures Industries, Inc.; chmn. of bd. of dirs. to 1978. Currently chmn. emeritus. Industry honors: Motion Picture Pioneer of the Year, 1972; Acad. of Motion Picture Arts and Sciences Jean Hersholt Humanitarian Award, 1979; NATO Award-Knight of Malta. Gloria Swanson Humanitarian Award, 1984. Chairman, President's Motion Picture Council–Motion Pictures & TV under Pres. Reagan. Dean Madden Award from NYU.

JAFFE, STANLEY R.
Producer. b. New York, NY, July, 31, 1940. Graduate of U. of Pennsylvania Wharton Sch. of Finance. Joined Seven Arts

Associates, 1962; named exec. ass't to pres., 1964; later, head of East Coast TV programming. Produced Goodbye, Columbus, in 1968 for Paramount; then joined that company as exec. v.p., 1969. Named pres. of Paramount in 1970; resigned 1971 to form own prod. unit. Joined Columbia as exec. v.p. of global prod. in 1976, but resigned to be independent producer. Named pres. & COO of Paramount Communications in 1991.
PICTURES: Goodbye Columbus, A New Leaf, Bad Company, Man on a Swing, The Bad News Bears, Kramer vs. Kramer (Academy Award for Best Picture, 1979), Taps, Without a Trace (also dir.). Co-prod.(with Sherry Lansing): Racing with the Moon, Firstborn, Fatal Attraction, The Accused, Black Rain, School Ties.

JAFFE, STEVEN-CHARLES
Producer. b. Brooklyn, NY, 1954. e. U. of Southern California, cinema. First professional job as documentary prod. on John Huston's Fat City. Served as prod. asst. on The Wind and the Lion in Spain. Assoc. prod. on Demon Seed (written by brother Robert); served as location mgr. on Who'll Stop the Rain; assoc. prod. on Time After Time. On tv worked as 2nd unit dir. on The Day After.
PICTURES: Those Lips Those Eyes, Motel Hell (also co-s.p.), Scarab (dir.), Flesh + Blood (2nd unit. dir.), Near Dark, Plain Clothes (exec. prod.), The Fly II, Ghost (exec. prod., 2nd unit dir.), Company Business, Star Trek VI: The Undiscovered Country, Strange Days.

JAGGER, MICK
Singer, Composer, Actor. b. Dartford, Kent, England, July 26, 1943. Lead singer with the Rolling Stones.
PICTURES: The Rolling Stones Rock and Roll Circus, Performance, Ned Kelly, Popcorn, Gimme Shelter, Sympathy for the Devil, Ladies and Gentlemen: The Rolling Stones, The London Rock 'n' Roll Show, Let's Spend the Night Together, At the Max, Freejack.
TELEVISION: Special: The Nightingale (Faerie Tale Theatre).

JAGGS, STEVE
Executive. b. London, England, June 29, 1946. Ent. motion picture industry, 1964. Gained experience in the film production and laboratory areas with Colour Film Service and Universal Laboratories. Joined Agfa-Gevaert Ltd., Motion Picture Division, 1976. Appt. sales manager, 1979; divisional manager, 1989. Joined Rank Organisation, 1992. Appoint. mng. dir. of Pinewood Studios, 1993.

JAGLOM, HENRY
Director, Writer, Editor, Actor. b. London, Eng., Jan. 26, 1943. Studied acting, writing and directing with Lee Strasberg and at Actors Studio. Did off-B'way. shows; went to West Coast where guest-starred in TV series (Gidget, The Flying Nun, etc.). Shot documentary film in Israel during Six Day War. Hired as edit consultant for Easy Rider by producer Bert Schneider. Acted in Psych Out, Drive He Said, The Last Movie, Thousand Plane Raid, Lili Aime Moi, The Other Side of the Wind (Orson Welles' unreleased last film). Wrote and dir. first feature, A Safe Place, in 1971. Created The Women's Film Co. (to prod. and distrib. motion pictures by women filmmakers), and Jagfilms Inc., Rainbow Film Company, and Rainbow Releasing. Presented Academy Award winning documentary Hearts and Minds, 1974.
PICTURES: Dir.-Writer-Prod.-Editor: A Safe Place, Tracks, Sitting Ducks (also actor), National Lampoon Goes to the Movies (co-dir. only), Can She Bake A Cherry Pie?, Always (also actor), Someone To Love (also actor), New Year's Day (also actor), Eating, Venice Venice (also actor), Babyfever, Last Summer in the Hamptons (dir., co-s.p., edit., actor).

JALBERT, JOE JAY
Executive. e. U. of Washington. Was ski captain in school and began film career as technical director on Downhill Racer, 1969, also cinematographer and double for Robert Redford. 1970, produced Impressions of Utah, documentary, with Redford. Won Emmy for cinematography on TV's Peggy Fleming Special. In 1970 formed Jalbert Productions, Inc., to make feature films, TV sports, specials, commercials, etc. Co. has produced Winter Sportscast and 9 official films at Innsbruck Winter Olympics (1976), Lake Placid (1980), Sarajevo (1984). Albertville Winter Olympic Games official film, One Light One World.

JAMES, BRION
Actor. b. Beaumont, CA, Feb. 20, 1945. e. Beaumont h.s., San Diego St. U., 1968. On stage in LA, San Diego, NY, as well as performing stand-up comedy at Comedy Store, The Improv.
THEATER: Long Day's Journey Into Night, Picnic, Basic Training Pavlo Hummell, Mother Courage, George Washington Slept Here, West Side Story, Spec, Lady Windermere's Fan.
PICTURES: Harry and Walter Go to New York (debut, 1976), Treasure of Matecumbe, Bound for Glory, Nickelodeon, Blue

Sunshine, Black Sunday, Corvette Summer, Wholly Moses, The Postman Always Rings Twice, Southern Comfort, The Ballad of Gregorio Cortez, Blade Runner, 48 HRS, A Breed Apart, Silverado, Crimewave, Flesh $PL Blood, Enemy Mine, Armed and Dangerous, Steel Dawn, Dead Man Walking, Cherry 2000, Nightmare at Noon, The Wrong Guys, Red Heat, Red Scorpion, The Horror Show, Mom, Time of the Beast, Tango & Cash, Street Asylum, Savage Land, Another 48 HRS, The Player, Nemesis, Ultimate Desires, Brain Smasher—A Love Story, Nature of the Beast, Time Runner, Wishman, Future Shock, Striking Distance, Pterodactyl Women of Beverly Hills, The Soft Kill, Cyberjack, The Dark, Scanner Cop, Dominion, Cabin Boy, The Companion, Art Deco Detective, F.T.W., Radioland Murders, Steel Frontier, From the Edge, Hong Kong '97. Evil Obsession, Malevolence, Precious Find.
TELEVISION: Movies: Flying High, Mrs. Sundance, Kiss Meets the Phantom of the Park, Trouble in High Timber Country, Killing at Hell's Gate, Hear No Evil, Precious Victims, Rio Diablo, Kenny Rogers as The Gambler: The Adventure Continues, Overkill: The Aileen Wuornos Story, Precious Victims, The Companion, Sketch Artist II: Hands That See, Terminal Virus. Guest: Rockford Files, Hunter, The Young Riders, Cagney & Lacey, Quincy, Little House on the Prairie, Dynasty, Amazing Stories, Tales from the Crypt, A-Team, etc.

JAMES, CLIFTON
Actor. b. Portland, OR, May 29, 1925. e. U. of Oregon. Studied at Actors Studio. Made numerous appearances on stage and TV, as well as theatrical films.
THEATER: NY: B'way: J.B., All the Way Home, The Shadow Box, American Buffalo. Off-B'way: All the King's Men.
PICTURES: On the Waterfront, The Strange One, The Last Mile, Something Wild, Experiment in Terror, David and Lisa, Black Like Me, The Chase, The Happening, Cool Hand Luke, Will Penny, The Reivers, ...tick...tick...tick..., WUSA, The Biscuit Eater, The New Centurions, Kid Blue, Live and Let Die, The Iceman Cometh, Werewolf of Washington, The Last Detail, Bank Shot, Juggernaut, The Man with the Golden Gun, Rancho DeLuxe, Silver Streak, The Bad News Bears in Breaking Training, Superman II, Where Are the Children?, Whoops Apocalypse, Eight Men Out, The Bonfire of the Vanities.
TELEVISION: Series: City of Angels, Lewis and Clark. Movies: Runaway Barge, Friendly Persuasion, The Deadly Tower, Hart to Hart (pilot), Undercover With the KKK, Guyana Tragedy: The Story of Jim Jones, Carolina Skeletons, The John Vernon Story. Mini-Series: Captains and the Kings, Lone Star.

JAMES, DENNIS
Performer. b. Jersey City, NJ, Aug. 24, 1917. e. St. Peter's Coll., Jersey City. Received Doctorate in 1988. Formerly M.C., actor, sports commentator on radio; award winning sports commentator for wrestling, 25 TV first to credit; currently pres., Dennis James Prod. For 47 years has been host of Cerebral Palsy Telethon, having helped raised over 675 million dollars. 1970-present, Natl. Commercial Spokesman for Physicians Mutual Insurance Company of Omaha. Given star on Hollywood Walk of Fame and Palm Springs Walk of Stars.
THEATER: Impossible YEars, Who Was That Lady?, Murder at the Howard Johnson, Two For the Seasaw.
PICTURES: The One and Only, Rocky III, Mr. Universe, The Method.
TELEVISION: Series: Cash and Carry, Prime Time Boxing, The Original Amateur Hour (1948-60), Chance of a Lifetime (host), Two for the Money, Judge for Yourself, The Name's the Same, High Finance, Haggis Baggis, Your First Impression, People Will Talk, The Price Is Right, PDQ, Your All-American College Show, New Price Is Right, Name That Tune. Actor: Kraft Theatre, Dick Powell Theatre, Tycoon, Batman, 77 Sunset Strip.

JAMES, POLLY
Writer. b. Ancon, Canal Zone. e. Smith Coll. Newspaper work, Panama; with trade mag., N.Y.; screenwriter since 1942.
PICTURES: Mrs. Parkington, The Raiders, Redhead from Wyoming, Quantrill's Raiders.

JAMESON, JERRY
Director. b. Hollywood, CA. Started as editorial asst.; then editor and supv. editor for Danny Thomas Prods. Turned to directing.
PICTURES: Dirt Gang, The Bat People, Brute Core, Airport '77, Raise the Titanic.
TELEVISION: Movies: Heatwave!, The Elevator, Hurricane, Terror on the 40th Floor, The Secret Night Caller, The Deadly Tower, The Lives of Jenny Dolan, The Call of the Wild, The Invasion of Johnson County, Superdome, A Fire in the Sky, High Noon--Part II, The Return of Will Kane, Stand By Your Man, Killing at Hell's Gate, Starflight: The Plane That Couldn't Land, Cowboy, This Girl for Hire, Last of the Great Survivors, The Cowboy and the Ballerina, Stormin' Home, One Police Plaza, The Red Spider, Terror on Highway 91, Fire and Rain, Gunsmoke: The Last Ride.

JANKOWSKI, GENE F.
Executive. b. Buffalo, NY, May 21, 1934. e. Canisius Coll., B.S., Michigan State U., M.A. in radio, TV and film. Joined CBS radio network sls, 1961 as acct. exec.; eastern sls. mgr., 1966; moved to CBS-TV as acct. exec. 1969; gen. sls. mgr. WCBS-TV, 1970; dir. sls, 1971; v.p. sls., CBS-TV Stations Divisions, 1973; v.p., finance & planning, 1974; v.p., controller, CBS Inc. 1976; v.p. adm., 1977; exec. v.p. CBS/Broadcast Group, 1977; pres., CBS/Broadcast Group, 1977; chmn. CBS/Broadcast Group, 1988-89; chmn. Jankowski Communications Systems, Inc. 1989-. Member: pres., Intl. Council of National Acad. of Television Arts & Sciences; chmn. & trustee Amer. Film Institute; trustee, Catholic U. of Amer.; director, Georgetown U.; bd. of gov. American Red Cross; vice chmn., business comm. Metropolitan Museum of Art. Member, Library of Congress Film Preservation Board; adjunct prof. telecommunications, Michigan St. U.AWARDS: Received Distinguished Communications Medal from South Baptist Radio & Television Commission; honorary Doctorate of Humanities, Michigan State U.; Humanitarian Award, National Conference of Christians and Jews, etc.

JARMAN, CLAUDE, JR.
Actor. b. Nashville, TN, Sept. 27, 1934. e. MGM Sch. Received special Oscar for The Yearling. Exec. prod. of concert film Fillmore.
PICTURES: The Yearling (debut, 1946), High Barbaree, The Sun Comes Up, Intruder in the Dust, Roughshod, The Outriders, Inside Straight, Rio Grande, Hangman's Knot, Fair Wind to Java, The Great Locomotive Chase.
TELEVISION: Mini-Series: Centennial.

JARMUSCH, JIM
Director, Writer, Composer, Actor. b. Akron, OH, 1953. e. attended Columbia U., went to Paris in senior year. NYU Film Sch., studied with Nicholas Ray and became his teaching asst. Appeared as an actor in Red Italy and Fraulein Berlin. Composed scores for The State of Things and Reverse Angle. Wrote and directed New World using 30 minutes of leftover, unused film from another director. (Won International Critics Prize, Rotterdam Film Festival.) Expanded it into Stranger Than Paradise.
PICTURES: Dir.-Writer: Permanent Vacation (dir. debut, 1980; also prod., music, edit.), Stranger Than Paradise (also edit., Golden Leopard, Locarno Film Festival; Camera d'Or best new director, Cannes), Down by Law, Mystery Train, Night on Earth, Dead Man. Actor: Straight to Hell, Candy Mountain, Mystery Train, Leningrad Cowboys Go America, In the Soup, Tigrero: A Film That Was Never Made.

JARRE, MAURICE
Composer. b. Lyons, France, Sept. 13, 1924. Studied at Paris Cons. Was orchestra conductor for Jean Louis Barrault's theatre company four years. 1951 joined Jean Vilar's nat'l theatre co., composing for plays. Musical dir., French National Theatre for 12 years before scoring films. Also has written ballets (Masques de Femmes, Facheuse Rencontre, The Murdered Poet, Maldroros, The Hunchback of Notre Dame) and served as cond. with Royal Phil. Orch, London, Japan Phil. Orch, Osaka Symph. Orch., Quebec Symp. Orch, Central Orchestra of People's Republic of China.
PICTURES: La Tete contre les Murs (The Keepers; feature debut, 1959), Eyes Without a Face, Crack in the Mirror, The Big Gamble, Sundays and Cybele, The Longest Day, Lawrence of Arabia (Academy Award, 1962), To Die in Madrid, Behold a Pale Horse, The Train, The Collector, Is Paris Burning?, Weekend at Dunkirk, Doctor Zhivago (Academy Award, 1965), The Professionals, Grand Prix, Gambit, The Night of the Generals, Villa Rides!, Five Card Stud, Barbarella, Isadora, The Extraordinary Seaman, The Damned, Topaz, The Only Game in Town, El Condor, Ryan's Daughter, Plaza Suite, Red Sun, Pope Joan, The Life and Times of Judge Roy Bean, The Effect of Gamma Rays on Man-in-the-Moon Marigolds, The Mackintosh Man, Ash Wednesday, Island at the Top of the World, Mandingo, Posse, The Man Who Would Be King, Shout at the Devil, The Last Tycoon, Crossed Swords, Winter Kills, The Magician of Lublin, Resurrection, The American Success Company, The Black Marble, Taps, Firefox, Young Doctors in Love, Don't Cry It's Only Thunder, The Year of Living Dangerously, Dreamscape, A Passage to India (Academy Award, 1984), Top Secret!, Witness (BAFTA Award, 1985), Mad Max Beyond Thunderdome, Solarbabies, The Mosquito Coast, Tai-Pan, No Way Out, Fatal Attraction, Gaby–A True Story, Julia and Julia, Moon Over Parador, Gorillas in the Mist, Wildfire, Distant Thunder, Chances Are, Dead Poets Society (BAFTA Award, 1989), Prancer, Enemies a Love Story, Ghost, After Dark My Sweet, Jacob's Ladder, Almost an Angel, Only the Lonely, Fires Within, School Ties, Shadow of the Wolf, Mr. Jones, Fearless, A Walk in the Clouds (Golden Globe, 1996).

JARRICO, PAUL
Writer, Producer. b. Los Angeles, CA, Jan. 12, 1915. e. USC, 1936.
PICTURES: Prod.: Salt of the Earth. Writer: Beauty for the Asking, The Face Behind the Mask, Tom Dick and Harry

(Acad. Award nom.), Thousands Cheer, Song of Russia, The Search, The White Tower, Not Wanted, The Day the Hot Line Got Hot, Messenger of Death.
TELEVISION: Call to Glory, Fortune Dane, Seaway, The Defenders.

JARROTT, CHARLES
Director. b. London, England, June 16, 1927. Joined British Navy; wartime service in Far East. After military service turned to theatre as asst. stage mgr. with Arts Council touring co. 1949 joined Nottingham Repertory Theatre as stage dir. and juvenile acting lead. 1953 joined new co. formed to tour Canada; was leading man and became resident leading actor for Ottawa Theatre. 1955 moved to Toronto and made TV acting debut opposite Katharine Blake whom he later wed. 1957 dir. debut in TV for Canadian Bdcstg. Co. Became CBC resident dir. Moved to London to direct for Armchair Theatre for ABC-TV. Then became freelance dir., doing stage work, films, TV. Received BAFTA Best Director Award, 1962. Golden Globe Awards, 1969, 1987.
THEATER: The Duel, Galileo, The Basement, Tea Party, The Dutchman, etc.
PICTURES: Time to Remember (debut, 1962), Anne of the Thousand Days, Mary Queen of Scots, Lost Horizon, The Dove, The Littlest Horse Thieves, The Other Side of Midnight, The Last Flight of Noah's Ark, Condorman, The Amateur, The Boy in Blue, Morning Glory (co-s.p. only).
TELEVISION: The Hot Potato Boys, Roll On, Bloomin' Death, Girl in a Birdcage, The Picture of Dorian Gray, Rain, The Rose Affair, Roman Gesture, Silent Song, The Male of the Species, The Young Elizabeth, A Case of Libel, Dr. Jekyll and Mr. Hyde. U.S. Movies/Mini-Series: A Married Man, Poor Little Rich Girl: The Barbara Hutton Story, The Woman He Loved, Till We Meet Again (mini-series), Night of the Fox (mini-series), Lucy & Desi: Before the Laughter, Changes, Yes Virginia There is a Santa Claus, Stranger in the Mirror, Jackie Collins' Lady Boss, Treacherous Beauties, Trade Winds, A Promise Kept: The Oksana Baiul Story (Emmy Award for dir.), At The Midnight Hour.

JASON, RICK
Actor. b. New York, NY, May 21, 1926. e. American Acad. of Dramatic Arts. B'way debut in Now I Lay Me Down To Sleep (Theatre World Award). Has acted in over 400 TV shows, beginning with Live TV (1945) and over 40 feature films.
PICTURES: Sombrero, Saracen Blade, This Is My Love, Lieutenant Wore Skirts, Wayward Bus, Partners, Illegally Yours.
TELEVISION: Series: The Case of the Dangerous Robin, Combat. Mini-Series: Around the World in 80 Days. Movies: The Monk, Who is the Black Dahlia?, The Best Place to Be.

JAYSTON, MICHAEL
Actor. b. Nottingham, England, Oct. 28, 1935. Member of Old Vic theatre Co. & Bristol Old Vic.
PICTURES: A Midsummer Night's Dream, Cromwell, Nicholas and Alexandra, The Public Eye (Follow Me), Alice's Adventures in Wonderland, The Nelson Affair, Tales That Witness Madness, The Homecoming, Craze, The Internecine Project, Dominique, Zulu Dawn.
TELEVISION: She Fell Among Thieves, Tinker Tailor Soldier Spy.

JEFFREYS, ANNE
Actress. b. Goldsboro, NC, Jan. 26. m. actor Robert Sterling. Named by Theatre Arts Magazine as one of the 10 outstanding beauties of the stage. Trained for operatic career. Sang with NY's Municipal Opera Co. while supplementing income as a Powers model. Appeared as Tess Trueheart in Dick Tracy features.
THEATER: B'way: in Street Scene, Kiss Me Kate, Romance, Three Wishes for Jamie, Kismet. Stock: Camelot, King & I, Kismet, Song of Norway, Bells Are Ringing, Marriage Go Round, No Sex Please, We're British, Take Me Along, Carousel, Anniversary Waltz, Do I Hear a Waltz, Ninotchka, Pal Joey, Name of the Game, Destry Rides Again, The Merry Widow, Bitter Sweet, Desert Song, High Button Shoes, Sound of Music.
PICTURES: I Married an Angel, Billy the Kid, Trapped, Joan of Ozark, The Old Homestead, Tarzan's New York Adventure, X Marks the Spot, Yokel Boy, Catterbox, Man from Thunder River, Nevada, Step Lively, Dillinger, Sing Your Way Home, Those Endearing Young Charms, Zombies on Broadway, Dick Tracy Vs. Cueball, Genius at Work, Step By Step, Vacation in Reno, Trail Street, Riffraff, Return of the Bad Men, Boys' Night Out, Panic in the City, Southern Double Cross, Clifford.
TELEVISION: Series: Topper, Love That Jill, Bright Promise, Delphi Bureau, General Hospital, Finder of Lost Loves. Guest: Falcon Crest, Hotel, Murder She Wrote, L.A. Law, Baywatch. Movies: Beggarman Thief, A Message From Holly.

JEFFRIES, LIONEL
Actor, Director. b. Forest Hill, London, England, 1926. e. Queens Elizabeth's Grammar Sch, Wimbone Dorset. Ent. m.p. ind. 1952.
THEATER: Hello, Dolly!, See How They Run, Two Into One, Pygmalion (U.S.), The Wild Duck.

PICTURES: The Black Rider, The Colditz Story, No Smoking, Will Any Gentleman?, Windfall, All for Mary, Bhowani Junction, Eyewitness, Jumping for Joy, Lust for Life, Creeping Unknown (Quatermass Experiment), Baby and the Battleship, Decision Against Time, Doctor at Large, High Terrace, Hour of Decision, Up in the World, Behind the Mask, Blue Murder at St. Trinian's, Dunkirk, Girls at Sea, Law and Disorder, Orders to Kill, Revenge of Frankenstein, Up the Creek, Bobbikins, The Circle (The Vicious Circle), Idol on Parade, Nowhere to Go, The Nun's Story, Jazzboat, Let's Get Married, Trials of Oscar Wilde, Please Turn Over, Tarzan the Magnificent, Two-Way Stretch, Fanny, The Hellions, Life is a Circus, Kill or Cure, Mrs. Gibbons' Boys, Operation Snatch, The Notorious Landlady, The Wrong Arm of the Law, Call Me Bwana, The Crimson Blade, First Men in the Moon, The Long Ships, Murder Ahoy, The Secret of My Success, The Truth About Spring, You Must Be Joking!, Arrivederci Baby!, The Spy With a Cold Nose, Oh Dad Poor Dad, Blast Off! (Rocket to the Moon), Camelot, Chitty Chitty Bang Bang, Sudden Terror, The Railway Children (dir., s.p. only), Lola (Twinky), Who Slew Auntie Roo?, The Amazing Mr. Blunden (dir., s.p. only), Baxter (dir. only), Royal Flash, Wombling Free (voice, also dir., s.p.), The Water Babies (dir. only), The Prisoner of Zenda, Better Late Than Never, A Chorus of Disapproval.
TELEVISION: Father Charlie, Tom Dick and Harriet, Cream in My Coffee, Minder, Danny: the Champion of the World, Jekyll and Hyde, Boon Morse, Ending Up, Look at It This Way, Bed.

JENKINS, DAN
Public Relations Consultant. b. Montclair, NJ, Dec. 5, 1916. e. U. of Virginia. 1938. U.S. Army, 1940-45; major, infantry. P.R. officer, Hq. Eighth Army. Mng. ed., Motion Picture Magazine, 1946-48; editor, Tele-Views Magazine, 1949-50; TV editor, columnist, Hollywood Reporter, 1950-53; Hollywood bureau chief, TV Guide, 1953-63; v.p., exec. dir. TV dept., Rogers, Cowan & Brenner, Inc., 1963-71. Formed Dan Jenkins Public Relations, Inc. 1971. Joined Charles A. Pomerantz Public Relations, Ltd. as v.p., 1975, while retaining own firm. Sr. associate, Porter, Novelli, Assocs., 1981. Mem. bd. trustees, Natl. Academy of TV Arts & Sciences; bd. gov., Hollywood chapter, Natl. Academy of TV Arts & Sciences, 1967-71. Rejoined Rogers & Cowan, 1983, v.p., TV dept. Retired, 1988.

JENKINS, GEORGE
Art Director. b. Baltimore, MD, Nov. 19, 1908. e. U. of Pennsylvania. Hollywood-New York art dir. since 1946; TV pictures for Four Star Playhouse and Revue productions; NBC-TV opera, Carmen; color dir., CBS-TV, 1954; NBC color spec. Annie Get Your Gun, 1957; TV music with Mary Martin, 1959. Professor, Motion Picture Design, UCLA, 1985-88.
THEATER: Mexican Hayride, I Remember Mama, Dark of the Moon, Lost in the Stars, Bell Book and Candle, The Bad Seed, The Happiest Millionaire, Two for the Seesaw, Ice Capades, Song of Norway, Paradise Island, Around the World in 80 Days, Mardi Gras, The Miracle Worker, Critic's Choice, A Thousand Clowns, Jennie, Generation, Wait Until Dark, Only Game in Town, Night Watch, Sly Fox.
PICTURES: The Best Years of Our Lives, The Secret Life of Walter Mitty, A Song Is Born, Rosanna McCoy, The Miracle Worker, Mickey One, Up the Down Staircase, Wait Until Dark, The Subject Was Roses, Klute, 1776, The Paper Chase, The Parallax View, Night Moves, Funny Lady, All the President's Men (Academy Award, 1976), Comes a Horseman, The China Syndrome (Acad. Award nom.), Starting Over, The Postman Always Rings Twice, Rollover, Sophie's Choice, Orphans, See You in the Morning, Presumed Innocent.
TELEVISION: Movie: The Dollmaker.

JENNINGS, PETER
TV News Anchor. b. Toronto, Canada, July 29, 1938. Son of Canadian broadcaster Charles Jennings. e. Carleton U.; Rider Coll. Worked as a bank teller and late night radio host in Canada. Started career as host of Club Thirteen, a Canadian American Bandstand-like dance prog., then as a newsman on CFJR (radio), Ottawa; then with CJOH-TV and CBC. Joined ABC in 1964 as NY corr.; 1965, anchor, Peter Jennings with the News; 1969, overseas assignments for ABC news; 1975, Washington correspondent and anchor for AM America; 1977, chief foreign corr.; 1978, foreign desk anchor, World News Tonight; 1983-, anchor, sr. editor, World News Tonight.

JENS, SALOME
Actress. b. Milwaukee, WI, May 8, 1935. e. Northwestern U. Member Actors Studio.
THEATER: The Disenchanted, Far Country, Night Life, Winter's Tale, Mary Stuart, Antony and Cleopatra, After the Fall, Moon For the Misbegotten, The Balcony.
PICTURES: Angel Baby (debut, 1961), The Fool Killer, Seconds, Me Natalie, Cloud Dancer, Harry's War, Just Between Friends, Coming Out Under Fire (narrator).
TELEVISION: Movies: In the Glitter Palace, Sharon: Portrait of a Mistress, The Golden Moment: An Olympic Love Story, A

Killer in a Family, Playing with Fire, Uncommon Valor. Guest: Mary Hartman, Mary Hartman. Series: Falcon Crest. Mini-Series: From Here to Eternity.

JERGENS, ADELE
Actress. b. Brooklyn, NY, Nov. 26, 1917. Began career in musical shows during summer vacation at 15; won contest, New York's World Fair, as model; appeared on New York stage; night clubs, U.S. and abroad.
PICTURES: A Thousand and One Nights, She Wouldn't Say Yes, The Corpse Came C.O.D., Dwon to Earth, Woman From Tangier, The Fuller Brush Man, The Dark Past, Treasure of Monte Cristo, SLightly French, Edge of Doom, Side Street, Abbott and Costello Meet the Invisible Man, Sugarfoot, Try and Get Me, Show Boat, Somebody Loves Me, Aaron Slick from Punkin' Crick, Overland Pacific, Miami Story, Fireman Save My Child, Big Chase, Strange Lady in Town, The Cobweb, Girls in Prison, The Lonesome Trail, Treasure of Monte Cristo.

JETER, MICHAEL
Actor. b. Lawrenceberg, TN, Aug. 20, 1952.e. Memphis State Univ.
THEATER: Alice, G.R. Point (Theatre World Award), Cloud 9, Greater Tuna, Once in a Lifetime, Zoo Story, Waiting for Godot, Only Kidding, The Boys Next Door, Grand Hotel (Tony Award, 1990).
PICTURES: Hair, Ragtime, Soup for One, Zelig, The Money Pit, Dead-Bang, Tango & Cash, Just Like in the Movies, Miller's Crossing, The Fisher King, Bank Robber, Sister Act 2: Back in the Habit, Drop Zone, Waterworld.
TELEVISION: Series: One Life to Live, Hothouse, Evening Shade (Emmy Award, 1992). Movies: My Old Man, Sentimental Journey, When Love Kills: The Seduction of John Hearn, Gypsy. Mini-Series: From Here to Eternity. Guest: Lou Grant, Designing Women.

JEWISON, NORMAN
Producer, Director. b. Toronto, Canada, July 21, 1926. e. Malvern Collegiate Inst., Toronto, 1940-44; Victoria Coll., U. of Toronto, 1946-50, B.A. Stage and TV actor 1950-52. Director, Canadian Broadcasting Corp 1953-58. Awarded 1988 Acad. of Canadian Cinema and Television Special Achievement Award. Made Companion Order of Canada, 1992.
PICTURES: Director: 40 Pounds of Trouble (debut, 1962), The Thrill of It All, Send Me No Flowers, The Art of Love, The Cincinnati Kid. Director-Producer: The Russians Are Coming the Russians Are Coming (Acad. Award nom. for picture), In the Heat of the Night (dir. only; Acad. Award nom.), The Thomas Crown Affair, Gaily Gaily, Fiddler on the Roof (Acad. Award nom. for dir. & picture), Jesus Christ Superstar (also co-s.p.), Rollerball, F.I.S.T., ... And Justice for All, Best Friends, A Soldier's Story (Acad. Award nom. for picture), Agnes of God, Moonstruck (Acad. Award noms. for dir. & picture), In Country, Other People's Money, Only You, Bogus. Producer: The Landlord, Billy Two Hats, The Dogs of War (exec. prod.), Iceman, The January Man.
TELEVISION: Exec. prod. of 8 episodes of The Judy Garland Show. Prod.-Dir.: Judy Garland specials, The Andy Williams Show. Dir. of Specials: Tonight with Harry Belafonte, The Broadway of Lerner and Loewe.

JHABVALA, RUTH PRAWER
Writer. b. Cologne, Germany, May 7, 1927. Emigrated with her family to England, 1939. e. Hendon County Sch., Queen Mary Coll., London U. (degree in English). m. architect C.S.H. Jhabvala, 1951 and moved to Delhi. Has written most of the screenplays for the films of Ismail Merchant and James Ivory.
AUTHOR: To Whom She Will, Esmond in India, The Nature of Passion, The Householder, Get Ready for Battle, Heat and Dust, In Search of Love and Beauty, Three Continents, Poet and Dancer, Shards of Memory.
PICTURES: The Householder (debut, 1963; based on her novel), Shakespeare Wallah (with Ivory), The Guru (with Ivory), Bombay Talkie (with Ivory), Autobiography of a Princess, Roseland, The Europeans, Jane Austen in Manhattan, Quartet, Heat and Dust (based on her own novel; BAFTA Award), The Bostonians, A Room with a View (Academy Award, 1986), Madame Sousatzka (co.-s.p. with John Schlesinger), Mr. and Mrs. Bridge (NY Film Critics Award), Howards End (Academy Award, 1992), The Remains of the Day, Jefferson in Paris.
TELEVISION: Hullabaloo Over Georgie and Bonnie's Pictures.

JILLIAN, ANN
Actress. b. Cambridge, MA, Jan. 29, 1951. Began career at age 10 in Disney's Babes in Toyland; in film version of Gypsy at age 12. Broadway debut in musical, Sugar Babies, 1979. Formed own company: 9-J Productions, developing TV movies and series.
PICTURES: Babes in Toyland, Gypsy, Mr. Mom, Sammy the Way Out Seal.

TELEVISION: *Series*: Hazel, It's a Living, Jennifer Slept Here, Ann Jillian. *Guest*: Love Boat, Fantasy Island, Twilight Zone, Ben Casey, etc. *Mini-Series*: Ellis Island (Emmy & Golden Globe nom.), Alice in Wonderland, Malibu. *Movies*: Mae West (Emmy & Golden Globe nom.), Death Ride to Osaka, Killer in the Mirror, Convicted: A Mother's Story, Perry Mason: The Case of the Murdered Madam, The Ann Jillian Story (Golden Globe Award; Emmy nom.), Original Sin, This Wife for Hire, Little White Lies, Mario and the Mob, Labor of Love: The Arlette Schweitzer Story, Heart of a Child, The Disappearance of Vonnie, Fast Company, It's Him Or Us, My Son The Match Maker.

JOANOU, PHIL
Director. b. La Canada, CA, Nov. 20, 1961. e. UCLA, USC. Student film The Last Chance Dance won him first professional job directing 2 episodes of tv's Amazing Stories (Santa 85, The Doll).
PICTURES: Three O'Clock High (debut, 1987), U2: Rattle and Hum (also edit., camera operator), State of Grace, Final Analysis, Heaven's Prisoners.
TELEVISION: *Mini-Series*: Wild Palms (co-dir.). *Series*: Fallen Angels (Dead-End for Delia).

JOFFE, CHARLES H.
Executive. b. Brooklyn, NY, July 16, 1929. e. Syracuse U. Joined with Jack Rollins to set up management-production org., clients including Woody Allen, Ted Bessell, Billy Crystal, David Letterman, Tom Poston, Robin Williams.
PICTURES: *Producer*: Don't Drink the Water, Take the Money and Run, Everything You Always Wanted to Know About Sex but Were Afraid To Ask, Love and Death, Annie Hall (Academy Award for Best Picture, 1977), House of God. *Exec. prod.*: Play It Again Sam, Bananas, Sleeper, Manhattan, Interiors, Stardust Memories, Arthur, A Midsummer Nights' Sex Comedy, Zelig, Broadway Danny Rose, The Purple Rose of Cairo, Hannah and Her Sisters, Radio Days, September, Another Woman, New York Stories (Oedipus Wrecks), Crimes and Misdemeanors, Alice, Shadows and Fog, Husbands and Wives, Manhattan Murder Mystery, Bullets Over Broadway.
TELEVISION: Woody Allen specials. Star of the Family, Good Time Harry, Triplecross.

JOFFE, EDWARD
Producer, Director, Writer, Production Consultant. Worked in m.p., theatre, commercial radio and as journalist before ent. TV ind. in Britain as writer/prod with ATV. 1959-61 staff prod. Granada TV. 1962, dir., Traitor's Gate & Traveling Light for Robt Stigwood; prod. dir., numerous series for Grampian TV; 1967, dir. film The Price of a Record—Emmy finalist; 1967-68 films, Columba's Folk & So Many Partings ITV entries in Golden Harp Fest.; 1968, prod., dir. Tony Hancock Down Under in Australia, prod. dir. Up At The Cross; prod. dir. ind. film, Will Ye No' Come Back Again; dir., This Is... Tom Jones; prod. dir., The Golden Shot; 1971, senior production lecturer, Thomson TV College; dir., films for U.S. for London Television Service; Evening Standard Commercials for Thames TV. Co. prod. dir.,ind. film Sound Scene, 1972-8, Contract prod. dir. Thames TV various series: Magpie, Today, Opportunity Knocks, The David Nixon Show, Seven Ages of Man, Problems, Finding Out; 1980 production consultant, CBC-TV; 1978-82, prod. dir. series Writers' Workshop, About Books; 1978, film, Places & Things (British Academy Award nom.) film, Who Do You Think You Are? (British Academy Award nom., ITV's Japan Prize entry, Special Jury Award San Francisco Intl. Film Fest), 1981, Film Images, (British Academy Award nom.; Gold Plaque Chicago Intl. Film Fest.); The Protectors (medal winner Intl. Film & TV Festival, N.Y.). 1982-86: film Rainbow Coloured Disco Dancer. Various Series: Taste of China, Jobs Ltd., Spin-Offs, The Buzz. Doc.: War Games in Italy. 1989-95, devised, prod., dir. Video View for ITV Network; Co-prod. & dir. 2 series Sprockets; dir. Challenge. Dir. Screen Scene Prods, String of Pearls, PLC, String of Pearls 2 PLC. Companies produced mopics Double X, Little Devils - The Birth, To Catch a Yeti, Big Game, Shepherd on the Rock.

JOFFE, ROLAND
Director, Producer. b. London, Eng., Nov. 17, 1945. e. Lycee Francaise, Carmel Col. Manchester U., England. Worked in British theatre with the Young Vic, the National Theatre and the Old Vic. 1973 became youngest director at National Theatre. 1978, moved into directing TV for Granada TV, then Thames and B.B.C. before feature debut in 1984 with The Killing Fields.
PICTURES: *Director*: The Killing Fields (debut, 1984), The Mission, Fat Man and Little Boy (also co-s.p.), City of Joy (also co-prod.), The Scarlett Letter. *Producer*: Made in Bangkok, Super Mario Bros.
TELEVISION: *Documentaries*: Rope, Ann, No Mama No. Plays: The Spongers, Tis Pity She's a Whore, The Legion Hall Bombing, United Kingdom (also co-wrote). *Series*: Coronation Street, Bill Brand, The Stars Look Down.

JOHNS, GLYNIS
Actress. b. Durban, South Africa, Oct. 5, 1923. e. in England. Daughter of Mervyn Johns, actor, and Alys Steele, pianist. On London stage from 1935 (Buckie's Bears, The Children's Hour, A Kiss for Cinderella, Quiet Week-End; Gertie, N.Y. stage, 1952; Major Barbara, N.Y., 1956-57.) Voted one of top ten British Money-making stars in Motion Picture Herald-Pathe poll, 1951-54.
THEATER: Too Good to Be True (NY), The King's Mare, Come as You Are, The Marquise (tour), A Little Night Music (NY; Tony Award), Cause Celebre, Harold and Maude (Canada, Hay Fever (U.K. tour), The Boy Friend (Toronto), The Circle (NY).
PICTURES: South Riding (debut, 1938), Murder in the Family, Prison Without Bars, On the Night of the Fire, Mr. Brigg's Family, Under Your Hat, The Prime Minister, 49th Parallel, Adventures of Tartu, Half-Way House, Perfect Strangers, This Man Is Mine, Frieda, An Ideal Husband, Miranda, Third Time Lucky, Dear Mr. Prohack, State Secret, Flesh and Blood, No Highway in the Sky, Appointment With Venus (Island Rescue), Encore, The Magic Box, The Card (The Promoter), The Sword and the Rose, Rob Roy the Highland Rogue, Personal Affair, The Weak and the Wicked, The Seekers (Land of Fury), The Beachcomber, Mad About Men, Court Jester, Josephine and Men, Loser Takes All, All Mine to Give, Around the World in 80 Days, Another Time Another Place, Shake Hands with the Devil, The Sundowners, The Spider's Web, The Cabinet of Caligari, The Chapman Report, Papa's Delicate Condition, Mary Poppins, Dear Brigitte, Don't Just Stand There, Lock Up Your Daughters, Under Milk Wood, Vault of Horror, Zelly and Me, Nukie, The Ref, While You Were Sleeping.
TELEVISION: *Series*: Glynis, Coming of Age. *Guest*: Dr. Kildare, Roaring Twenties, Naked City, The Defenders, Danny Kaye Show. Also: Noel Coward's Star Quality, Mrs. Amworth, All You Need Is Love, Across a Crowded Room, Little Gloria... Happy at Last, Skagg.

JOHNSON, ARTE
Actor. b. Chicago, IL, Jan. 20, 1934. e. Univ. of IL. To NY in 1950's where he landed role on B'way in Gentlemen Prefer Blondes. Also worked in nightclubs, summer stock, tv commercials. Gained fame on Rowan and Martin's Laugh-In in late 1960's. Much voice work on tv cartoons.
PICTURES: Miracle in the Rain, The Subterraneans, The Third Day, The President's Analyst, Love at First Bite, A Night at the Magic Castle, What Comes Around, Tax Season, Evil Spirits, Munchie, Second Chance, Captiva.
TELEVISION: *Series*: It's Always Jan, Sally, Hennesey, Don't Call Me Charlie, Rowan & Martin's Laugh-In (Emmy Award, 1969), Ben Vereen... Comin' at Ya!, The Gong Show (panelist), Games People Play, Glitter, General Hospital. *Movies*: Twice in a Lifetime, Bud and Lou, If Things Were Different, Detour to Terror, The Love Tapes, Condominium, Making of a Male Model, Alice in Wonderland, Dan Turner--Hollywood Detective.

JOHNSON, BEN
Actor. b. Pawhuska, OK, June 13, 1918. Stunt rider & performer in rodeos, touring country; did stunt work in many films before acting debut.
PICTURES: Three Godfathers, Mighty Joe Young, She Wore a Yellow Ribbon, Wagonmaster, Rio Grande, Wild Stallion, Fort Defiance, Shane, Rebel in Town, War Drums, Slim Carter, Fort Bowie, Ten Who Dared, Tomboy and the Champ, One-Eyed Jacks, Cheyenne Autumn, Major Dundee, The Rare Breed, Will Penny, Hang 'Em High, The Wild Bunch, The Undefeated, Chisum, Something Big, The Last Picture Show (Academy Award, best supporting actor, 1971), Corky, Junior Bonner, The Getaway, Dillinger, The Train Robbers, Kid Blue, The Sugarland Express, Bite the Bullet, Hustle, Breakheart Pass, The Town That Dreaded Sundown, The Greatest, Grayeagle, The Swarm, The Hunter, Terror Train, Soggy Bottom U.S.A., Ruckus, High Country Pursuit, Tex, Champions, Red Dawn, Let's Get Harry, Trespasses, Dark Before Dawn, Cherry 2000, Back to Back, My Heroes Have Always Been Cowboys, Radio Flyer, Angels in the Outfield.
TELEVISION: *Series*: The Monroes. *Movies*: Runaway!, Bloodsport, Dream West, Locusts, The Shadow Riders, Red Pony, The Sacketts, Wild Horses, Wild Times, Stranger on My Land, The Chase, Bonanza: The Return, Bonanza: Under Attack. *Guest*: Alfred Hitchcock Presents (1958), Laramie, Have Gun Will Travel, Bonanza, The Virginian.
(d. April 8, 1996)

JOHNSON, DON
Actor. b. Flatt Creek, MO, Dec. 15, 1949. Worked at ACT (Amer. Conservatory Th.), San Francisco. On stage there in Your Own Thing. In L.A. in Fortune and Men's Eyes. Recording: Heartbeat (1986).
PICTURES: The Magic Garden of Stanley Sweetheart (debut, 1970), Zachariah, The Harrad Experiment, A Boy and His Dog, Return to Macon County, Soggy Bottom USA, Cease Fire, Sweet Hearts Dance, Dead-Bang, The Hot Spot, Harley Davidson and the Marlboro Man, Paradise, Born Yesterday, Guilty as Sin, Tin Cup.

TELEVISION: *Series*: From Here to Eternity, Miami Vice. *Mini-Series*: The Rebels, Beulah Land, The Long Hot Summer. *Movies*: First You Cry, Ski Lift to Death, Katie: Portrait of a Centerfold, Revenge of the Stepford Wives, Amateur Night at the Dixie Bar and Grill, Elvis and the Beauty Queen, The Two Lives of Carol Letner, In Pursuit of Honor. *Special*: Don Johnson's Heartbeat (music video, also exec. prod.). *Guest*: Kung Fu, The Bold Ones, Police Story.

JOHNSON, G. GRIFFITH
Executive. b. New York, NY, Aug. 15, 1912. e. Harvard U., 1934, A.M. 1936, Ph.D. 1938. U.S. Treasury Dept. 1936-39; Dept. of Comm., 1939-40; O.P.A. & predecessor agencies, 1940-46; consulting economist, 1946-47; dir., Econ. Stab. Div., Nat'l. Security Resources Bd., 1948-49; chief econ., U.S. Bur. of Budget, 1949-50; econ. advisor to Econ. Stab. Admin. 1950-52; Exec. v.p. MPEAA, 1965, MPAA, 1971; Asst. Sec'y of State for Economic Affairs, 1962-65; v.p. MPAA, 1953-62. Author of several books & articles.

JOHNSON, J. BOND
Producer, Executive. b. Fort Worth, TX, June 18, 1926. e. Texas Wesleyan Univ., B.S., 1947; Texas Christian U., M.Ed., 1948; Southern Methodist U., B.D., 1952; USC, Ph.D., 1967. Army Air Forces, WWII; public information officer, captain, U.S. Marine Corps, Korean War. Formerly member Marine Corps Reserve, Motion Picture Production Unit, Hollywood. Was Colonel, U.S. Army; now retired. Newspaper reporter, Fort Worth Star-Telegram, 1942-48; pres., West Coast News Service, 1960; pres., exec. prod., Bonjo Prods., Inc., 1960, President, chief executive officer, Cine-Media International, 1975 managing partner, Capra-Johnson Productions, Ltd., 1978.
PICTURES: Sands of Iwo Jima, Retreat Hell, Flying Leathernecks; photographed aerial portions, Jamboree 53, Norfleet, Devil at My Heels, Kingdom of the Spiders, Ordeal at Donner Pass, Place of the Dawn, Lies I Told Myself, Backstretch, Airs Above The Ground, The Jerusalem Concert, The Berkshire Terror, The Seventh Gate.
TELEVISION: *Series*: Creator, story consultant, tech. advisor, Whirlpool. *Exec. producer, creator*. On The Go (TV News-Sports), Coasties, Desert Rangers. *Producer*. Fandango.

JOHNSON, LAMONT
Director, Producer. b. Stockton, CA, Sept. 30, 1922. e. UCLA. 4 time winner of Director's Guild Award for TV work. Directed plays The Egg, Yes Is For a Very Young Man. Dir. two operas, L.A. Philharmonic, 1964; founder, dir., UCLA Professional Theatre Group.
PICTURES: A Covenant With Death (debut, 1967), Kona Coast, The McKenzie Break, A Gunfight, The Groundstar Conspiracy, You'll Like My Mother, The Last American Hero, Visit to a Chief's Son, Lipstick, One on One (also actor), Somebody Killed Her Husband, Cattle Annie and Little Britches, Spacehunter: Adventures in the Forbidden Zone.
TELEVISION: *Series*: The Defenders, Profiles in Courage, Twilight Zone. *Movies/Mini-Series*: Deadlock, My Sweet Charlie, That Certain Summer, The Execution of Pvt. Slovik, Fear on Trial, Off the Minnesota Strip, Crisis at Central High, Escape from Iran, Dangerous Company, Life of the Party: The Story of Beatrice, Ernie Kovacs: Between the Laughter, Wallenberg: A Hero's Story (also co-prod.; Emmy Award, 1985), Unnatural Causes, Gore Vidal's Lincoln (Emmy Award, 1988), The Kennedys of Massachusetts, Voices Within: The Lives of Truddi Chase, Crash Landing: The Rescue of Flight 232, The Broken Chain (also prod.).

JOHNSON, MARK
Producer. b. Washington, DC, Dec. 27, 1945. Moved to Spain at age 7, lived there for eleven years before returning to America. e. Univ. of VA, Univ. of IA. Joined Directors Guild training program receiving first credit on Next Stop Greenwich Village. Worked as prod. asst., then asst. dir. on High Anxiety, Movie Movie, The Brink's Job, and Escape From Alcatraz. Starting with Diner in 1982 served as executive prod. or prod. on all Barry Levinson films. With Levinson formed Baltimore Pictures in 1989.
PICTURES: Diner (exec. prod.). *Producer*: The Natural, Young Sherlock Holmes, Tin Men, Good Morning Vietnam, Rain Man (Academy Award for Best Picture of 1988), Avalon, Kafka (co-exec. prod.), Bugsy (L.A. Film Critics & Golden Globe Awards for Best Picture of 1991), Toys, Sniper, Wilder Napalm, A Perfect World, A Little Princess.

JOHNSON, RICHARD
Actor. b. Upminster, Essex, England, July 30, 1927. Studied at Royal Acad. of Dramatic Art. First stage appearance Opera House, Manchester, then with John Gielgud's repertory season, 1944. Served in Royal Navy 1945-48. Subsequent stage appearances incl. The Madwoman of Chaillot, The Lark. Visited Moscow with Peter Brook's production of Hamlet. Royal Shakespeare Thea.: Stratford, London, 1957-62. Royal Shakespeare Co. 1972-73. National Theatre, 1976-77. Founded United British Artists, 1983.

PICTURES: Captain Horatio Hornblower (debut, 1951), Calling Bulldog Drummond, Scotland Yard Inspector (Lady in the Fog), Saadia, Never So Few, Cairo, The Haunting, 80,000 Suspects, The Pumpkin Eater, The Amorous Adventures of Moll Flanders, Operation Crossbow, Khartoum, The Witch in Love, Deadlier Than the Male, The Rover, Danger Route, A Twist of Sand, Oedipus the King, Lady Hamilton, Some Girls Do, Julius Caesar, The Tyrant, The Beloved, Behind the Door, Hennessy, Night Child, The Cursed Medallion, Aces High, The Last Day of Spring, The Comeback, Zombie, The Monster Club, Screamers, What Waits Below, Lady Jane, Turtle Diary, Foreign Student, Diving In. Producer: Turtle Diary, Castaway, The Lonely Passion of Judith Hearne.
TELEVISION: The Flame is Love, Haywire, The Four Feathers, Portrait of a Rebel: Margaret Sanger, A Man For All Seasons, Voice of the Heart, The Crucifer of Blood, Duel of Hearts. Guest: Wagon Train, Lou Grant, Ironside, Knots Landing, That Girl, MacGyver, Police Story, Route 66, many others. Live TV incl. Lux Video Theatre, Front Row Center, Hallmark Hall of Fame.

JOHNSON, RUSSELL
Actor. b. Ashley, PA, Nov. 10, 1924. e. Girard Coll, Actors Laboratory, L.A. W.W.II, Army Air Corps. Author: Here on Gilligan's Isle (1993).
PICTURES: A Town of the 80's, Stand at Apache Landing, A Distant Trumpet, Ma & Pa Kettle at Waikiki, Rogue Cop, Loan Shark, Seminole, Tumbleweed, Blue Movies, It Came From Outer Space, Many Rivers to Cross, Law and Order, Black Tuesday, This Island Earth, Rock All Night, Attack of the Crab Monsters, The Space Children, For Men Only, The Greatest Story Ever Told, Hitchhike to Hell, MacArthur.
TELEVISION: *Series*: Black Saddle, Gilligan's Island. *Guest*: Studio One, Front Row Center, Playhouse 90, Lux Video Theatre, Mobile One, The Great Adventure Jane Powell Show, Climax, You Are There, Rawhide, Twilight Zone, Gunsmoke, Outer Limits, Cannon, Marcus Welby, That Girl, The FBI, Dallas, Fame, Dynasty, My Two Dads, Bosom Buddies, Buffalo Bill, Vanished, Harry Truman Biography, Truman vs. MacArthur, Knots Landing, Santa Barbara, Roseanne, many others. *Movie*: With a Vengeance.

JOHNSON, VAN
Actor. b. Newport, RI, Aug. 25, 1916. Began in vaudeville; then on N.Y. stage New Faces of 1937, Eight Men of Manhattan, Too Many Girls, Pal Joey. Voted one of the top ten Money Making Stars in Motion Picture Herald-Fame Poll 1945-46. Stage includes The Music Man (London), La Cage aux Folles (NY) and numerous tours.
PICTURES: Too Many Girls (debut, 1940), Murder in the Big House, Somewhere I'll Find You, War Against Mrs. Hadley, Dr. Gillespie's New Assistant, The Human Comedy, Pilot No. 5, Dr. Gillespies's Criminal Case, Guy Named Joe, White Cliffs of Dover, Three Men in White, Two Girls and a Sailor, Thirty Seconds Over Tokyo, Between Two Women, Thrill of Romance, Weekend at the Waldorf, Easy to Wed, No Leave No Love, Till the Clouds Roll By, High Barbaree, Romance of Rosy Ridge, Bride Goes Wild, State of the Union, Command Decision, Mother is a Freshman, In the Good Old Summertime, Scene of the Crime, Battleground, Big Hangover, Duchess of Idaho, Three Guys Named Mike, Grounds for Marriage, Go For Broke, Too Young to Kiss, It's a Big Country, Invitation, When in Rome, Washington Story, Plymouth Adventure, Confidentially Connie, Remains to Be Seen, Easy to Love, Caine Mutiny, Siege at Red River, Men of the Fighting Lady, Brigadoon, Last Time I Saw Paris, End of the Affair, Bottom of the Bottle, Miracle in the Rain, 23 Paces to Baker Street, Slander, Kelly and Me, Action of the Tiger, The Last Blitzkreig, Subway in the Sky, Beyond This Place, Enemy General, Wives and Lovers, Divorce American Style, Yours Mine and Ours, Where Angels Go ... Trouble Follows, Company of Killers, Eagles Over London, The Kidnapping of the President, The Purple Rose of Cairo, Down There in the Jungle, Escape From Paradise, Three Days to a Kill.
TELEVISION: *Special*: Pied Piper of Hamelin. *Mini-Series*: Rich Man Poor Man, Black Beauty. *Movies*: Doomsday Flight, San Francisco International, Call Her Mom, The Girl on the Late Late Show, Superdome. *Guest*: I Love Lucy, G.E. Theatre, Batman, Love American Style, The Love Boat, Murder She Wrote.

JOHNSTON, MARGARET
Actress. b. Sydney, Australia, Aug. 10, 1918. e. Sydney U., Australia; RADA. London stage debut: Murder Without Crime.
THEATER: Ring of Truth, The Masterpiece, Lady Macbeth, Merchant of Venice, Measure for Measure, Othello.
PICTURES: The Prime Minister, The Rake's Progress (The Notorious Gentleman), A Man About the House, Portrait of Clare, The Magic Box, Knave of Hearts, Touch and Go, Burn With Burn (Night of the Eagle), The Nose on My Face, Girl in the Headlines (The Model Murder Case), Life at the Top, The Psychopath, Schizo, Sebastian.

TELEVISION: Always Juliet, Taming of the Shrew, Man with a Load of Mischief, Light of Heart, Autumn Crocus, Androcles and the Lion, Sulky Five, Windmill Near a Frontier, The Shrike, The Out of Towners, Looking for Garrow, The Typewriter, The Glass Menagerie, That's Where the Town's Going, The Vortex.

JOLLEY, STAN
Producer, Director, Production Designer, Art Director. b. New York, NY, May 17, 1926. e. U. of Southern California, col. of architecture. Son of actor I. Stanford Jolley. In Navy in W.W.II. Has acted in capacities listed for many feature films and TV series. One of orig. designers of Disneyland.
PICTURES: Prod./Prod. Designer: Knife for the Ladies. Assoc. Prod./ Prod. Designer: The Good Guys and the Bad Guys. 2nd Unit Dir.: Superman. Prod. Designer: Dutch, The Good Mother, Witness (Acad. Award nom.), Taps, Caddyshack, Cattle Annie and Little Britches, Americathon (also second unit director), The Swarm, Drum, Framed, Dion Brothers, Mixed Company, Walking Tall, Terror in the Wax Museum, Night of the Lepus (also second unit director), War Between Men and Women, Law Man, The Phynx. Art Director: Young Billy Young, Ride Beyond Vengeance, Broken Saber, The Restless Ones, Mail Order Bride, Toby Tyler. Assoc. Prod./Prod. designer & 2nd unit dir.: Happily Ever After.
TELEVISION: Movies (2nd Unit Dir./Prod. Designer): Swiss Family Robinson, Adventures of the Queen, Woman Hunter. Prod. Designer: Abduction of Carrie Swenson, Eagle One, No Man's Land, Last of the Great Survivors, Like Normal People, Rescue From Gilligan's Island, Flood, Voyage of the Yes, The Stranger, Punch & Jody, City Beneath the Sea, Women of San Quentin, The Amazing Mr. Hughes. TV Series: Assoc. Prod./Prod. Designer: Jessie. Art Director: Walt Disney Presents, Pete and Gladys, Gunsmoke, Mr. Ed., Branded, Voyage to the Bottom of the Sea, Land of the Giants, O'Hara, Shane, Acapulco, The Racers. Prod. Designer: Walking Tall, Today's F.B.I., For Love and Honor, Macgyver, Under Fire, Donald in Mathmagic Land, Crisis in the Wetlands (prod./dir.).

JONAS, TONY
Executive. Pres., Warner Bros. Television.

JONES, AMY HOLDEN
Director, Writer. b. Philadelphia, PA, Sept. 17, 1953. m. cinematographer, Michael Chapman. e. Wellesley Coll., B.A., 1974; film and photography courses, Massachusetts Inst. of Technology. Winner, first place, Washington National Student Film Festival, 1973.
PICTURES: Editor: Hollywood Boulevard (debut, 1976), American Boy, Corvette Summer, Second Hand Hearts. Director: Slumber Party Massacre, Love Letters (also s.p.), Mystic Pizza (s.p. only), Maid to Order (also co-s.p.), It Had to Be Steve (also co-s.p.), Rich Man's Wife (also s.p.). Writer: Beethoven, Indecent Proposal, The Getaway.
TELEVISION: Pilot (writer): Jack's Place.

JONES, CHUCK
Producer, Director, Writer, Animator. b. Spokane, WA, Sept. 21, 1912. e. Chouinard Art Inst. Dir., Warner Bros. Animation until 1962 where he created and directed Road Runner & Wile E. Coyote, Pepe le Pew; directed and helped create Bugs Bunny, Porky Pig, Daffy Duck etc. Created Snafu character, U.S. Armed Service. Later headed MGM Animation Dept. Lecturer at many Universities. Establisehd indept. co. Chuck Jones Enterprises. Academy Awards for best animated short subjects: For Scentimental Reasons (1950), The Dot and the Line (1965), best documentary short subject: So Much for So Little (1950). 1989, published Chuck Amuck: The Life and Times of an Animated Cartoonist. 1990, chmn. Chuck Jones Prods.; currently consultant and good-will representative to Warner Bros.
PICTURES: The Phantom Tollbooth, The Bugs Bunny/Road Runner Movie, The Magical World of Chuck Jones; created animated sequences for live-action features Stay Tuned, Mrs. Doubtfire.
TELEVISION: The Bugs Bunny Show (co-prod., writer, dir.). Dir.: How the Grinch Stole Christmas, Horton Hears a Who, Pogo. Producer- Director-Writer: The Cricket in Times Square, A Very Merry Cricket, Yankee Doodle Cricket, Rikki-Tikki-Tavi, The White Seal, Mowgli's Brothers, The Carnival of the Animals, A Connecticut Rabbit in King Arthur's Court, Raggedy Ann and Andy in The Great Santa Claus Caper, The Pumpkin Who Couldn't Smile, Daffy Duck's Thanks-for-Giving Special, Bugs Bunny's Bustin' Out All Over.

JONES, DAVID
Director, Producer. b. Poole, Eng., Feb. 19, 1934. e. Christ's Coll., Cambridge U., B.A., 1954, M.A., 1957. Immigrated to U.S. in 1979. Artistic controller, then assoc. dir., Royal Shakespeare Co., 1964-75; artistic dir, RSC at Aldwych Theatre 1978; artistic dir, Brooklyn Acad. of Music Theatre Co., NY 1979-81; prof. Yale Sch. of Drama, 1981.
THEATER: Sweeney Agonistes (debut, 1961); U.S.: Summerfolk, Loves Labour's Lost, Winter's Tale, Barbarians, Jungle of Cities.
PICTURES: Betrayal, Jacknife, The Trial.

TELEVISION: Prod.: Monitor 1958-64 (BBC series), Play of the Month, The Beaux' Stratagem, Langrishe Go Down, Ice Age. Dir.: Shakespeare series, BBC 1982-83, Devil's Disciple, The Christmas Wife, Sensibility and Sense, Is There Life Out There?

JONES, DEAN
Actor. b. Decatur, AL, Jan. 25, 1931. e. Asbury Coll., Wilmore, KY. Prof. debut as blues singer, New Orleans; U.S. Navy, 1950-54. Author: Under Running Laughter.
PICTURES: Tea and Sympathy (debut, 1956), The Rack, The Opposite Sex, These Wilder Years, The Great American Pastime, Designing Woman, Ten Thousand Bedrooms, Jailhouse Rock, Until They Sail, Imitation General, Torpedo Run, Handle with Care, Night of the Quarter Moon, Never So Few, Under the Yum-Yum Tree, The New Interns, That Darn Cat, Two on a Guillotine, Any Wednesday, The Ugly Dachshund, Monkeys Go Home, Blackbeard's Ghost, The Horse in the Grey Flannel Suit, The Love Bug, $1,000,000 Duck, Snowball Express, Mr. Super Invisible, The Shaggy D.A., Herbie Goes to Monte Carlo, Born Again, Other People's Money, Beethoven, Clear and Present Danger.
TELEVISION: Series: Ensign O'Toole, The Chicago Teddy Bears, What's It All About World?, Herbie the Love Bug, Beethoven (animated; voice). Movies: Guess Who's Sleeping in My Bed?, When Every Day Was the 4th of July, Long Days of Summer, Fire and Rain, The Great Man's Whiskers, Saved By the Bell: Hawaiian Style, The Computer Wore Tennis Shoes. Special: Journey to Mars.
THEATER: There Was a Little Girl, Under the Yum-Yum Tree, Company, Into the Light.

JONES, GEMMA
Actress. b. London, Eng., Dec. 4, 1942. e. Royal Acad. of Dramatic Art.
THEATER: Baal, Alfie, The Cavern, The Pastime of M Robert, Portrait of a Queen, Next of Kin, The Marriage of Figaro, And A Nightingale Sang, reaking the Silence, Howards End, A Midsummer Night's Dream, The Homecoming, Mount Morgan, The Winter's Tale, etc.
PICTURES: The Devils, The Paper House, On the Black Hill, The Devils Feast of July, Sense and Sensibility.
TELEVISION: The Lie, The Way of the World, The Merchant of Venice, The Duchess of Duke Street (series), The Jim Henson Hour, Forget Me Not Lane,Call My Bluff, Dial M For Murder, The Way of the World, Churchill's People, The Cherry Orchard, The Lie, Man In A Sidecar, Shadows of Fear, Crimes of Passion, The Spoils of Poynton, The Duchess of Duke Street, The Importance of Being Earnest, Chelworth, After The Dance, Inspector Morse, The Storyteller, Sevises and Desires, Some Lie Some Die, Wycliffe, The Borrowers, Faith.

JONES, GRACE
Singer, Actress. b. Spanishtown, Jamaica, May 19, 1952. e. Syracuse U. Modelled and appeared in several Italian pictures before career as singer.
PICTURES: Conan the Destroyer, A View to a Kill, Vamp, Straight to Hell, Siesta, Boomerang.

JONES, HENRY
Actor. b. Philadelphia, PA, Aug. 1, 1912. e. St. Joseph's Coll. On stage in Hamlet, Henry IV, Time of Your Life, My Sister Eileen, The Solid Gold Cadillac, Bad Seed, Sunrise at Campobello (Tony Award, 1958), Advise and Consent.
PICTURES: This is the Army, Lady Says No, Taxi, The Bad Seed, The Girl He Left Behind, The Girl Can't Help It, Will Success Spoil Rock Hunter?, 3:10 to Yuma, Vertigo, Cash McCall, The Bramble Bush, Angel Baby, Never Too Late, The Champagne Murders, Stay Away Joe, Project X, Support Your Local Sheriff, Rascal, Angel in My Pocket, Butch Cassidy and the Sundance Kid, Rabbit Run, Dirty Dingus Magee, Skin Game, Support Your Local Gunfighter, Napoleon and Samantha, Pete 'n' Tillie, Tom Sawyer, The Outfit, Nine to Five, Deathtrap, Balboa, Caddo Lake, Nowhere to Run, Dick Tracy, Arachnophobia, The Grifters.
TELEVISION: Series: Honestly Celeste!, Channing, The Girl With Something Extra, Phyllis, Kate Loves a Mystery, Gun Shy, Code Name: Foxfire, I Married Dora. Movies: The Crucible, Something for a Lonely Man, The Movie Murderer, Love Hate Love, Who is the Black Dahlia?, Tail Gunner Joe, CaliforniaGold Rush, The Leftovers, Grass Roots. Guest: Lost in Space, We'll Get By, B.J. and the Bear, Falcon Crest.

JONES, JAMES EARL
Actor. b. Arkabutla, MS, Jan. 17, 1931. e. U. of Michigan. Son of actor Robert Earl Jones. Awarded Hon. Doctor of Fine Arts (Yale, Princeton); Medal for Spoken Language (Amer. Acad. and Inst. of Arts and Letter; Hon. Doctor of Humane Letters (Columbia Coll. & U. of Mich.).
THEATER: Moon on a Rainbow Shawl (Theatre World Award), The Cool World, Othello, Paul Robeson, Les Blancs, The Great White Hope (Tony Award, 1969), The Iceman Cometh, Of Mice and Men, A Lesson from Aloes, Master Harold ... and the Boys, Fences (Tony Award, 1986).

189

PICTURES: Dr. Strangelove, or: How I Learned to Stop Worrying and Love the Bomb (debut, 1964), The Comedians, King: A Filmed Record ... Montgomery to Memphis, End of the Road, The Great White Hope (Acad. Award nom.), Malcolm X (narrator), The Man, Claudine, Deadly Hero, Swashbuckler, The Bingo Long Travelling All-Stars and Motor Kings, The River Niger, The Greatest, Star Wars (voice), Exorcist II: The Heretic, The Last Remake of Beau Geste, A Piece of the Action, The Bushido Blade, The Empire Strikes Back (voice), Conan the Barbarian, Blood Tide (The Red Tide), Return of the Jedi (voice), City Limits, My Little Girl, Soul Man, Allan Quartermain and the Lost City of Gold, Gardens of Stone, Matewan, Pinocchio and the Emperor of the Night (voice), Coming to America, Three Fugitives, Field of Dreams, Best of the Best, The Hunt for Red October, Grim Prairie Tales, The Ambulance, True Identity, Convicts, Patriot Games, Sneakers, Sommersby, The Sandlot, The Meteor Man, Naked Gun 33 1/3: The Final Insult, Clean Slate, The Lion King (voice), Clear and Present Danger, Jefferson in Paris, Judge Dredd (voice), Cry the Beloved Country, Lone Star, A Family Thing.
TELEVISION: Series: As the World Turns, The Guiding Light, Paris, Me and Mom, Gabriel's Fire (Emmy Award, 1991), Pros & Cons, Under One Roof. Movies: The UFO Incident, Jesus of Nazareth, The Greatest Thing That Almost Happened, Guyana Tragedy—The Story of Jim Jones, Golden Moment: An Olympic Love Story, Philby, Burgess and MacLean, The Atlanta Child Murders, The Vegas Strip War, By Dawn's Early Light, Heat Wave (Emmy Award, 1991), Last Flight Out, The Last Elephant, Percy & Thunder, The Vernon Johns Story, Confessions: Two Faces of Evil. Mini-Series: Roots: The Next Generations. Specials: King Lear, Soldier Boy, Mathnet, Bailey's Bridge, Third and Oak: The Pool Hall, Teach 109, Hallelujah. Host: Black Omnibus, Vegetable Soup, Summer Show, Long Ago and Far Away.

JONES, JEFFREY
Actor. b. Buffalo, NY, Sept. 28, 1947. e. Lawrence U., Wisconsin. While pre-med student, performed in 1967 prod. of Hobson's Choice when was invited by Sir Tyrone Guthrie to join Guthrie Theatre in Minneapolis. After short time in South America, studied at London Acad. of Music and Dramatic Arts before joining Stratford Theater in Ontario. 1973-74 worked with Vancouver touring children's theater co. Playhouse Holiday. Moved to N.Y. where performed on stage.
THEATER: The Elephant Man (B'way debut), Trelawney of the Wells, Secret Service, Boy Meets Girl, Cloud Nine, Comedy of Errors, The Tempest, The Death of Von Richtoven, London Suite.
PICTURES: The Revolutionary, The Soldier, Easy Money, Amadeus, Transylvania 6-5000, Ferris Bueller's Day Off, Howard the Duck, The Hanoi Hilton, Beetlejuice, Without a Clue, Who Is Harry Crumb?, Valmont, The Hunt for Red October, Over Her Dead Body, Mom and Dad Save the World, Stay Tuned, Out on a Limb, Heaven and Earth (unbilled), Ed Wood, Houseguest, The Pest.
TELEVISION: Mini-Series: George Washington: The Forging of a Nation, Fresno. Movies: Kenny Rogers as The Gambler III—The Legend Continues, The Avenging Angel. Guest: Amazing Stories, Twilight Zone, Remington Steele. Series: The People Next Door.

JONES, JENNIFER
Actress. r.n. Phyllis Isley. b. Tulsa, OK, Mar. 2, 1919. e. Northwestern U., American Acad. of Dramatic Arts. Daughter of Phil R., Flora Mae (Suber) Isley, exhib. m. industrialist Norton Simon. Son is actor Robert Walker Jr. Toured with parents stock company as child; in summer stock in East; little theat. East & West. Began screen career as Phyllis Isley. Pres., Norton Simon Museum.
PICTURES: Dick Tracy's G-Men (debut, 1939), The New Frontier, The Song of Bernadette (Academy Award, 1943; first film billed as Jennifer Jones), Since You Went Away, Love Letters, Cluny Brown, Duel in the Sun, Portrait of Jennie, We Were Strangers, Madame Bovary, Carrie, Wild Heart (Gone to Earth), Ruby Gentry, Indiscretion of an American Wife (Terminal Station), Beat the Devil, Love Is a Many-Splendored Thing, Good Morning Miss Dove, The Man in the Gray Flannel Suit, The Barretts of Wimpole Street, A Farewell to Arms, Tender Is the Night, The Idol, Angel Angel Down We Go (Cult of the Damned), The Towering Inferno.

JONES, KATHY
Executive. b. Aug. 27, 1949. Began career as acct. exec. for m.p. clients, Stan Levinson assoc., Dallas. Joined Paramount Pictures in 1977 as sr. publicist in field marketing then exec. dir., field mktg. Left to join Time-Life Films as v.p., domestic mktg., for m.p. div. Returned to Paramount 1981 as v.p., domestic pub. & promo. 1984, appt. sr. v.p., domestic pub. & promo. for Motion Picture Group, Paramount. Formed m.p. consultancy with Buffy Shutt, 1987. 1989, appt. exec. v.p., marketing, Columbia Pictures. 1991, appt. exec. v.p. marketing, TriStar Pictures.

JONES, QUINCY
Producer, Composer, Arranger, Recording Artist. b. Chicago, IL, March 14, 1933. e. Seattle U., Berklee Sch. Music, Boston Conservatory. Trumpeter and arranger for Lionel Hampton's orch. 1950-53, played with Dizzy Gillespie, Count Basie and arranged for orchs., singers-Frank Sinatra, Sarah Vaughn, Peggy Lee, Dinah Washington and led own orch. for European tours, and recordings. Prod. recordings for Michael Jackson, Tevin Campbell, Barbra Streisand, Donna Summer. Music dir. and v.p., Mercury Records 1961-64 before scoring films. Prod. & arranged We Are the World recording. Owns own Qwest Records record company. Received Jean Hersholt Humanitarian Award, 1995.
PICTURES: The Pawnbroker, Mirage, The Slender Thread, Made in Paris, Walk Don't Run, Banning, The Deadly Affair, In the Heat of the Night, In Cold Blood (Acad. Award nom.), Enter Laughing, A Dandy in Aspic, For Love of Ivy, The Hell With Heroes, The Split, Up Your Teddy Bear, Jocelyn, McKenna's Gold, The Italian Job, Bob & Carol & Ted & Alice, The Lost Man, Cactus Flower, John and Mary, The Last of the Mobile Hotshots, The Out-of-Towners, They Call Me Mister Tibbs, Brother John, $ (Dollars), The Anderson Tapes, Yao of the Jungle, The Hot Rock, The New Centurions, Come Back Charleston Blue, The Getaway, The Wiz (also cameo), The Color Purple (also co-prod.; Acad. Award nom.), Listen Up.
TELEVISION: Mini-Series: Roots (Emmy, 1977). Special: An American Reunion (exec. prod.). Series: Fresh Prince of Bel Air.

JONES, SAM J.
Actor. b. Chicago, IL, Aug. 12, 1954.
PICTURES: "10," Flash Gordon, My Chauffeur, Silent Assassins, White Fire, One Man Force, Double Trouble, Driving Force, From the Edge, Vegas Vice.
TELEVISION: Series: Code Red, The Highwayman. Movies: The Incredible Journey of Dr. Meg Laurel, Stunts Unlimited, Code Red (pilot), No Man's Land.

JONES, SHIRLEY
Actress. b. Smithton, PA, March 31, 1934. m. actor-prod. Marty Ingels. Mother of actors Shaun and Patrick Cassidy. Former Miss Pittsburgh. Natl. chair, Leukemia Foundation. Book: Shirley & Marty: An Unlikely Love Story (Wm. Morrow, 1990). Received hon. Doctor of Humane Letters degree from Point Park Col. 1991.
THEATER: Appeared with Pittsburgh Civic Light Opera in Lady in the Dark, Call Me Madam. B'way: South Pacific, Me and Juliet, Maggie Flynn.
PICTURES: Oklahoma! (debut, 1955), Carousel, April Love, Never Steal Anything Small, Bobbikins, Elmer Gantry (Academy Award, best supporting actress, 1960), Pepe, Two Rode Together, The Music Man, The Courtship of Eddie's Father, A Ticklish Affair, Dark Purpose, Bedtime Story, Fluffy, The Secret of My Success, The Happy Ending, The Cheyenne Social Club, Beyond the Poseidon Adventure, Tank, There Were Times Dear.
TELEVISION: Movies: Silent Night Lonely Night, But I Don't Want to Get Married, The Girls of Huntington House, The Family Nobody Wanted, Winner Take All, The Lives of Jenny Dolan, Yesterday's Child, Evening in Byzantium, Who'll Save Our Children, A Last Cry For Help, Children of An Lac, Intimates: A Love Story, Widow. Series: The Partridge Family, Shirley, The Slap Maxwell Story. Guest: McMillan, The Love Boat, Hotel, Murder She Wrote, Empty Nest.

JONES, TERRY
Writer, Actor, Director. b. Colwyn Bay, North Wales, Feb. 1, 1942. Worked with various rep. groups before joining BBC script dept. Was member of Monty Python's Flying Circus.
PICTURES: Actor: And Now for Something Completely Different (also co-s.p.), Monty Python and the Holy Grail (also co-dir., co-s.p.), Monty Python's Life of Brian (also dir., co-s.p.), Monty Python's The Meaning of Life (also co-s.p., dir., music), Labyrinth (s.p. only), Personal Services (dir. only), Erik the Viking (also dir., s.p.).
TELEVISION: Late Night Lineup, The Late Show, A Series of Birds, Do Not Adjust Your Set, The Complete and Utter History of Britain, Monty Python's Flying Circus, Secrets, The Crusades (also dir., writer).

JONES, TOMMY LEE
Actor. b. San Saba, TX, Sept. 15, 1946. Worked in oil fields; graduated Harvard, where earned a degree, cum laude, in English. Broadway debut in A Patriot for Me; appeared on stage in Four in a Garden, Ulysses in Nighttown, Fortune and Men's Eyes.
PICTURES: Love Story (debut, 1970), Eliza's Horoscope, Jackson County Jail, Rolling Thunder, The Betsy, Eyes of Laura Mars, Coal Miner's Daughter, Back Roads, Nate and Hayes, The River Rat, Black Moon Rising, The Big Town, Stormy Monday, The Package, Firebirds, JFK (Acad. Award nom.), Under Siege, House of Cards, The Fugitive (Academy Award, best supporting actor, 1993; LA Film Critics & Golden Globe Awards), Heaven and Earth, Blown Away, The Client, Natural Born Killers, Blue Sky, Cobb, Batman Forever.

TELEVISION: *Movies*: Charlie's Angels (pilot), Smash-Up on Interstate 5, The Amazing Howard Hughes, The Executioner's Song (Emmy Award, 1983), Broken Vows, The Park is Mine, Yuri Nosenko: KGB, Gotham, Stranger on My Land, April Morning, The Good Old Boys (also dir., co-writer). *Mini-Series*: Lonesome Dove. *Specials*: The Rainmaker, Cat on a Hot Tin Roof.

JORDAN, GLENN
Director, Producer, b. San Antonio, TX, April 5, 1936. e. Harvard, B.A.; Yale Drama Sch. Directed plays off-B'way. and on tour.
PICTURES: *Director*: Only When I Laugh, The Buddy System, Mass Appeal.
TELEVISION: *Specials*: Hogan's Goat, Paradise Lost, Benjamin Franklin (prod.; Emmy Award), Eccentricities of a Nightingale, The Oath, The Court Martial of Gen. George Armstrong Custer. *Movies*: Frankenstein, The Picture of Dorian Gray, Shell Game, One of My Wives is Missing, Delta County U.S.A., In the Matter of Karen Ann Quinlan, Sunshine Christmas, Les Miserables, Son Rise: A Miracle of Love, The Family Man, The Women's Room (also prod.), The Princess and the Cabbie, Lois Gibbs and the Love Canal, Heartsounds, Dress Grey, Promise (also prod.; 2 Emmy Awards), Something in Common (also prod.), Echoes in the Darkness (also prod.), Jesse (also prod.), Home Fires Burning (also prod.), Challenger (also prod.), Sarah: Plain and Tall (also prod.), Aftermath: A Test of Love (also prod.), The Boys (also prod.), O Pioneers! (also prod.), Barbarians at the Gate (Emmy Award; also co-exec. prod.), To Dance With the White Dog (also prod.), Jane's House (also prod.), My Brother's Keeper (also prod.), A Streetcar Named Desire (also prod.), Jake's Women (also prod.), After Jimmy (also prod.).

JORDAN, NEIL
Director, Writer. b. Sligo, Ireland, Feb. 25, 1950. e. University Coll, Dublin, B.A., 1972. Novels: The Past, Night in Tunisia, Dream of a Beast.
PICTURES: Traveller (s.p.), The Courier (co-exec. prod.). *Writer*: Angel, The Company of Wolves, Mona Lisa (LA Film Critics Award for s.p., 1986), High Spirits, We're No Angels (dir. only), The Miracle, The Crying Game (Academy Award, WGA & NY Film Critics Awards for s.p., 1992), Interview With the Vampire, Michael Collins.
TELEVISION: Mr. Solomon Wept (BBC), RTE (Ireland), Seduction, Tree, Miracles and Miss Langan.

JOSEPHSON, BARRY
Executive. Pres., of production, Sony Pictures Entertainment, Inc.

JOSEPHSON, ERLAND
Actor, Director, Writer. b. Stockholm, Sweden, June 15, 1923. Acted in over 100 plays in Sweden. Joined Sweden's Royal Dramatic Theatre in 1956 replacing Ingmar Bergman as head of the theater, 1966-76. Closely associated with Bergman, with whom he staged plays in his late teens. Co-authored s.p. The Pleasure Garden and Now About These Women. Also has pub. poetry, six novels, and scripts for stage, screen and radio. American stage debut: The Cherry Orchard, 1988.
PICTURES: It Rains on Our Love, To Joy, Brink of Life, The Magician, Hour of the Wolf, The Passion of Anna, Cries and Whispers, Scenes from a Marriage, Face to Face, Beyond Good and Evil, I'm Afraid, Autumn Sonata, To Forget Venice, One and One (also dir.), The Marmalade Revolution (also dir., s.p.), Montenegro, Sezona Mira u Parizu, Fanny and Alexander, Bella Donna, Nostalgia, House of the Yellow Carpet, After the Rehearsal, Angela's War, Behind the Shutters, A Case of Irresponsibility, Dirty Story, Amarosa, The Flying Devils, Garibaldi, The General, The Last Mazurka, The Sacrifice, Saving Grace, Unbearable Lightness of Being, Hanussen, Meeting Venus, The Ox, Sofie, Ulysses' Gaze.

JOSEPHSON, MARVIN
Executive. b. Atlantic City, NJ, March 6, 1927. e. Cornell U., B.A., 1949; L.L.B. NYU, 1952. Lawyer at CBS Television 1952-55; founded company which today is ICM Holdings Inc. in 1955. ICM Holdings Inc. is the parent company of Intl. Creative Management Inc. and ICM Artists Ltd.

JOSIAH, JR., WALTER J.
Executive. b. New York, NY, Nov. 9, 1933. e. Fordham U., B.S., 1955: Harvard Law School, LL.B., 1962. U.S. Air Force, 1955-58, First Lt. and Pilot. Associate, Simpson Thacher & Bartlett, 1962-67. Legal staff, Paramount Pictures, 1967-69. Asst. resident counsel, 1969; chief resident counsel, 1970 and v.p. & chief resident counsel, 1971-82. ex.-v.p. & general counsel, Motion Picture Association of America, Inc., 1983-93. Professional Associations: Chmn., Committee 307, Authors Rights, 1981-82, Patent, Trademark & Copyright Law Section of the American Bar Assn.; Association of the Bar of the City of NY (Committee on Copyright and Literary Property, 1976-

79, 1982-85, chmn. 1986-89): Copyright Society of the U.S.A.—Member of the Board of Trustees commencing 1981; v.p., from 1988; pres. beginning 1990; member, Motion Picture Academy of Arts and Sciences; Copyright Office Advisory Committee, 1981-82; National Sculpture Society advisor to the president; Advisory Board, Publication: Communications and the Law; Member, President's Club Executive Committee and Annual Fund Council, Fordham U.

JOURDAN, LOUIS
Actor, r.n. Louis Gendre. b. Marseille, France, June 19, 1921. Stage actor prior to m.p. On B'way in The Immoralist, Tonight in Samarkand, On a Clear Day You Can See Forever (Boston, previews), 13 Rue de l'Amour.
PICTURES: Le Corsaire (debut, 1940), Her First Affair, La Boheme, L'Arlesienne, La Belle, Adventure, Felicie Nanteuil, The Paradine Case, Letter from an Unknown Woman, No Minor Vices, Madame Bovary, Bird of Paradise, Anne of the Indies, The Happy Time, Decameron Nights, Three Coins in the Fountain, The Swan, Julie, The Bride is Much Too Beautiful, Dangerous Exile, Gigi, The Best of Everything, Can-Can, Leviathan, Streets of Montmartre, Story of the Count of Monte Cristo, Mathias Sandorf, The VIPs, Made in Paris, To Commit a Murder, A Flea in Her Ear, Young Rebel (Cervantes), The Silver Bears, Double Deal, Swamp Thing, Octopussy, The Return of Swamp Thing, Counterforce, Year of the Comet.
TELEVISION: *Series*: Paris Precinct, Romance Theatre (host). *Mini-Series*: The French Atlantic Affair, Dracula. *Movies*: Run a Crooked Mile, Fear No Evil, Ritual of Evil, The Great American Beauty Contest, The Count of Monte Cristo, The Man in the Iron Mask, The First Olympics-Athens, Beverly Hills Madam. *Guest*: Ford Theatre, The FBI, Name of the Game, Charlie's Angels.

JOY, ROBERT
Actor. b. Montreal, Canada, Aug. 17, 1951. e. Memorial Univ. of Newfoundland; Rhodes Scholar. Acted in regional and off-Broadway theatre. Off-B'way debut The Diary of Anne Frank (1978). Has composed music for stage, radio and film.
THEATER: NY Shakespeare Fest. (Found a Peanut, Lenny and the Heartbreakers, The Death of von Richtofen), Life and Limb, Fables for Friends, Welcome to the Moon, What I Did Last Summer, Lydie Breeze, Romeo and Juliet (La Jolla Playhouse; Drama-Logue Award), Hay Fever (B'way debut), Big River (premiere), The Nerd, Hyde in Hollywood, The Taming of the Shrew, Shimada, Goodnight Desdemona (Good Morning Juliet), Abe Lincoln in Illinois.
PICTURES: Atlantic City, Ragtime, Ticket to Heaven, Threshold, Terminal Choice, Amityville 3-D, Desperately Seeking Susan, Joshua Then and Now, Adventure of Faustus Bidgood (also co-prod. music), Radio Days, Big Shots, The Suicide Club, She's Back!, Millenium, Longtime Companion, Shadows and Fog, The Dark Half, Death Wish 5: The Face of Death, I'll Do Anything, Henry & Verlin, Waterworld, A Modern Affair, Pharoah's Army, Harriet the Spy.
TELEVISION: *Series*: One Life to Live. *Guest*: The Equalizer, Moonlighting, Law and Order, The Marshal, New York Undercover, Wings. *Specials*: The Prodigious Hickey, The Return of Hickey, The Beginning of the Firm, Hyde in Hollywood. *Movies*: Escape from Iran: The Canadian Caper, Gregory K, Woman on the Run: The Lawrencia Bembenek Story.

JURADO, KATY
Actress. r.n. Maria Christina Jurado Garcia. b. Guadalajara, Mexico, Jan. 16, 1927. Appeared in numerous Mexican films beginning in 1943. Also m.p. columnist for Mexican publications.
PICTURES: No Maturas (debut, 1943), El Museo del Crimen, Rosa del Caribe, The Bullfighter and the Lady (U.S. debut, 1951), High Noon, San Antone, Arrowhead, Broken Lance (Acad. Award nom.), The Sword of Granada, The Racers, Trial, Trapeze, Man from Del Rio, Dragoon Wells Massacre, The Badlanders, One Eyed Jacks, Barabbas, Seduction of the South, Target for Killing, Smoky, A Covenant With Death, Stay Away Joe, Bridge in the Jungle, Pat Garrett and Billy the Kid, Once Upon a Scoundrel, The Children of Sanchez, Reasons of State, Under the Volcano.
TELEVISION: *Movies*: Any Second Now, A Little Game, Evita Peron, Lady Blue. *Series*: A.K.A. Pablo.

K

KAGAN, JEREMY
Director, Writer. b. Mt. Vernon, NY, Dec. 14, 1945. e. Harvard; NYU, MFA; student Amer. Film Inst. 1971. Film animator, 1968; multi-media show designer White House Conf. on Youth and Ed. Previously credited as Jeremy Paul Kagan.
PICTURES: Scott Joplin, Heroes, The Big Fix, The Chosen (Montreal World Film Fest. Prize, 1981), The Sting II, The Journey of Natty Gann (Gold Prize, Moscow Film Fest., 1987), Big Man on Campus, By the Sword.

TELEVISION: *Series*: Columbo, The Bold Ones, Chicago Hope (Emmy Award, 1996). *Movies*: Unwed Father, Judge Dee and the Monastery Murders, Katherine (also writer), Courage, Roswell (also co-prod., co-story). *Specials*: My Dad Lives in a Downtown Hotel, Conspiracy: The Trial of the Chicago 8 (also writer; ACE Award, 1988).

KAHN, MADELINE
Actress, Singer. b. Boston, MA., Sept. 29. e. Hofstra U. Broadway bow in New Faces of '68. Trained as opera singer and appeared in La Boheme, Showboat, Two by Two, Candide. Appeared in short film The Dove.
THEATER: Promenade, Two by Two, In the Boom Boom Room, On the Twentieth Century, Born Yesterday, The Sisters Rosensweig (Tony Award, 1993).
PICTURES: What's Up Doc? (debut, 1972), Paper Moon (Acad. Award nom.), From the Mixed-Up Files of Mrs. Basil E. Frankweiler (The Hideaways), Blazing Saddles (Acad. Award nom.), Young Frankenstein, At Long Last Love, The Adventures of Sherlock Holmes' Smarter Brother, Won Ton Ton the Dog Who Saved Hollywood, High Anxiety, The Cheap Detective, The Muppet Movie, Simon, Happy Birthday Gemini, Wholly Moses, First Family, History of the World—Part 1, Yellowbeard, Slapstick of Another Kind, City Heat, Clue, My Little Pony (voice), An American Tail (voice), Betsy's Wedding, Mixed Nuts, Nixon.
TELEVISION: *Series*: Comedy Tonight, Oh Madeline!, Mr. President, New York News. *Specials*: Harvey, The Perfect Guy (afterschool special), Celebrating Gershwin: The Jazz Age, Irving Berlin Gala, Stephen Sondheim Gala. *Movie*: For Richer For Poorer.

KAHN, MILTON
Publicist. b. Brooklyn, NY, May 3, 1934. e. Syracuse U., Ohio U., B.S.J. 1957. Formed Milton Kahn Associates, Inc. in 1958. Represented: Gregory Peck, Joan Crawford, Steve Allen, Glenn Ford, Lee Grant, Herb Alpert, Roger Corman, Robert Aldrich, Arthur Hiller, Chuck Norris, Bob Cousy, Adam Oates, Michael Landon, Dean Hargrove, Bill Conti, etc. and New World Pictures (1970-83), Avco-Embassy, Vista Films, Roger Corman's Concorde (1983-), Electric Shadow Prods.

KAHN, RICHARD
Executive. b. New Rochelle, NY, Aug. 19, 1929. e. Wharton Sch. of Finance and Commerce, U. of Pennsylvania, B.S., 1951; U.S. Navy, 3 yrs.; joined Buchanan & Co., 1954; ent. m.p. ind. as pressbook writer, Columbia Pictures, 1955; exploitation mgr., 1958; natl. coord. adv. and pub., 1963; natl. dir. of adv., pub. and exploitation, 1968; v.p., 1969; 1974 v.p. in chg. of special marketing projects; 1975; moved to MGM as v.p. in chg. of worldwide advertising, publicity and exploitation; 1978, named sr. v.p. in chg. worldwide mktg. & pres., MGM Intl. 1980, elected bd. of govs., Academy of M.P. Arts & Sciences. 1982, named exec. v.p. of adv., pub., promo. for MGM/UA; 1983, formed the Richard Kahn Co., dist. & mktg. consultancy. 1984-88. Faculty mem. Peter Stark m.p. producing prog., USC Sch. of Cinema & TV. Exec. chmn., Film Inf. Council. 1982-95 elected secretary Acad. of Motion Picture Arts & Sciences; elected v.p. 1983-87; elected pres. 1988.

KALB, MARVIN
TV news reporter. e. City Coll. of NY; Harvard, M.A., 1953, Russian Language Sch., Middlebury Coll. Worked for U.S. State Dept., American Embassy, Moscow; CBS News, 1957; writer, reporter-researcher. Where We Stand: reporter-assignment editor; Moscow Bureau Chief, 1960-63; first diplomatic corresp., Washington Bureau, 1963. Chief diplomatic corresp. CBS News and NBC News, moderator Meet the Press; Teacher and lecturer; first dir. Joan Shorenstein Barone Center on the Press, Politics and Public Policy at John F. Kennedy Sch. of Govt. of Harvard U., since 1987. Host of PBS series, Candidates '88. Author: Eastern Exposure, Kissinger, Dragon in the Kremlin, Roots of Involvement, The U.S. in Asia 1784-1971, Candidates '88 (with Hendrik Hertzberg).

KALISH, EDDIE
Executive. b. New York, NY, Apr. 27, 1939. Reporter/reviewer, Variety, 1959-64; sr. publicist, Paramount Pictures, 1964-65; adv./pub./promo dir., Ken Greengras Personal Management, 1965-66; pub. dir., Harold Rand & Co., 1966-67; indept. publicist overseas, 1967-75; rejoined Paramount Pictures in 1975 as dir. of intl. mktg.; later named v.p.; 1978, named v.p., worldwide pub & promo. 1979 appt. sr. v.p., worldwide mktg. 1980 joined United Artists as v.p. domestic mktg.; sr. v.p., adv., pub., promo, for MGM/UA 1981-82; became sr. v.p., worldwide mkt., PSO, 1982-1986. Now pres., Kalish/Davidson Marketing, Inc.

KAMBER, BERNARD M.
Executive. e. U. of Pennsylvania. New England exploitation rep. U.A. 1940; Army service 1941-43; dir. special events dept. U.A., 1943; asst. to Gradwell L. Sears, nat'l distrib. chmn. 6th War Loan Drive; dir. pub. 7th War Loan Drive, 1943-47; dir. pub. & prom. Eagle Lion Classics, 1951; org. Kamber Org.,

pub. rel. rep. for ind. prod. v.p. sales, adv. pub. Ivan Tors Prod. Greene-Rouse Prods. 1953; exec. asst. Hecht-Hill-Lancaster, chg. of N.Y. off., 1957; v.p. Hecht-Hill-Lancaster Companies, 1958; formed Cinex Distr. Corp., 1962; Pres. Cinex and Posfilm, Inc.; 1967, v.p. in chg. sls. Du Art Film Lab. Inc; 1975 joined Technicolor, Inc.

KAMEY, PAUL
b. New York, NY, Aug. 25, 1912. Worked on newspapers including NY Journal American. Ent. m.p. industry 1938; worked for MGM and 20th Century Fox; during war was writer, Office of War information; joined Universal, 1949; eastern pub. mgr., Universal Pictures. 1968. Freelance publicist.

KANE, CAROL
Actress. b. Cleveland, OH, June 18, 1952. e. Professional Children's Sch., NY. Began professional acting career at age 14, touring, then on B'way in The Prime of Miss Jean Brodie.
THEATER: The Tempest, The Effect of Gamma Rays on Man-in-the-Moon Marigolds, Are You Now or Have You Ever Been? Arturo Ui, The Enchanted, The Tempest, Macbeth, Tales of the Vienna Woods, Frankie and Johnny in the Claire de Lune, Control Freaks.
PICTURES: Carnal Knowledge (debut, 1971), Desperate Characters, Wedding in White, The Last Detail, Dog Day Afternoon, Hester Street, Harry and Walter Go to New York, Annie Hall, Valentino, The World's Greatest Lover, The Mafu Cage, The Muppet Movie, When a Stranger Calls, Pandemonium, Norman Loves Rose, Over the Brooklyn Bridge, Racing With the Moon, The Secret Diary of Sigmund Freud, Transylvania 6-5000, Jumpin' Jack Flash, Ishtar, The Princess Bride, Sticky Fingers, License to Drive, Scrooged, Flashback, Joe Vs. the Volcano, My Blue Heaven, The Lemon Sisters, Ted and Venus, In the Soup, Addams Family Values, Even Cowgirls Get the Blues, Big Bully, The Pallbearer, Sunset Park.
TELEVISION: *Series*: Taxi (2 Emmy Awards: 1982, 1983), All Is Forgiven, American Dreamer. *Movies*: An Invasion of Privacy, Burning Rage, Drop Out Mother, Dad the Angel and Me, Freaky Friday. *Specials*: Faerie Tale Theatre, Paul Reiser: Out on a Whim, Tales From the Crypt (Judy, You're Not Yourself Today).

KANE, JOHN
Publicity Manager. b. New York, NY. e. Rutgers, B.A.; NYU, M.A. Publicist, Solters & Roskin, 1976-80. Unit publicist: Fame, Tender Mercies, Prince of the City, 1980-82. 1982-90, Home Box Office, unit publicist, manager. 1991, unit publ. for Ricochet, Arizona Dream.

KANE, STANLEY D.
Judge. b. Minneapolis, MN, Dec. 21, 1907. e. U of MN, B.A. (magna cum laude), 1930;, M.A., 1931; MN Coll. of Law, LL.B., 1940. Instructor, U. of Minnesota, 1930-33. Exec. sec. Allied Theatre Owners of the Northwest, 1933-37; city attorney, 1940-60; exec. v.p. & gen. counsel, North Central Allied Independent Theatre Owners, 1946-63; dist. court judge, then sr. judge, Hennepin County, 1963-90.

KANER, MARK
Executive. Pres. of International Television, Fox, Inc.

KANEW, JEFF
Director.
PICTURES: Black Rodeo (also prod., edit.), Natural Enemies (also s.p., edit.), Eddie Macon's Run (also s.p., edit.), Revenge of the Nerds, Gotcha!, Tough Guys, Troop Beverly Hills, V. I. Warshawski.
TELEVISION: Alfred Hitchcock Presents (1985).

KANIN, FAY
Writer. b. New York, NY, May 9. e. Elmira Coll., U. of Southern California, 1937. m. Michael Kanin, writer. Contrib. fiction to mags., Writers Guild of Amer. pres. screen branch, 1971-73; Acad. Motion Picture Arts & Sciences 1983-88. also bd. mem. of latter. Co-chair, National Center for Film and Video Preservation; Bd. of trustees, Amer. Film Institute; Chair, Natl. Film Preservation Board.
THEATER: Goodbye My Fancy, His and Hers, Rashomon, The High Life, Grind (1985).
PICTURES: My Pal Gus, Rhapsody, The Opposite Sex, Teacher's Pet, Swordsman of Siena, The Right Approach.
TELEVISION: Heat of Anger, Tell Me Where It Hurts (Emmy Award, 1974), Hustling (also co-prod.), Friendly Fire (also co-prod., Emmy Award, San Francisco Film Fest. Award, Peabody Award), Heartsounds (Peabody Award; also co-prod.).

KANIN, GARSON
Director, Writer. b. Rochester, NY, Nov. 24, 1912. e. American Acad. of Dramatic Arts. Was married to actress Ruth Gordon (d: 8/28/85). m. actress Marian Seldes, 1990. Started as musician, actor, appearing in Spring Song, Little Ol' Boy, and others.

Prod. assist. to George Abbott on plays Three Men on a Horse, Brother Rat, Room Service. 1937 joined Samuel Goldwyn's prod. staff; 1938, joined RKO, as prod.-dir. 1942, prod. for U.S. Office of Emergency Management. Joined armed forces, WWII. Documentary director: Fellow Americans, Ring of Steel, Night Shift, The True Glory (co-dir. with Carol Reed; Academy Award, 1945), Salute to France (co-dir. with Jean Renoir). 1989, received Writers Guild Valentine Davies Award with brother Michael. Pres., Authors League of America.
AUTHOR: Remembering Mr. Maugham, Cast of Characters, Tracy and Hepburn, Hollywood, Blow Up a Storm, The Rat Race, A Thousand Summers, One Hell of an Actor, It Takes a Long Time to Become Young, Moviola, Smash, Together Again!, Cordelia.
THEATRE: Writer/Dir.: Born Yesterday, The Smile of the World, The Rat Race, The Live Wire, A Gift of Time, Do Re Mi, Come on Strong, Small War on Murray Hill, The Amazing Adele, The Good Soup, Dreyfus in Rehearsal, Happy Ending, Peccadillo. Dir.: Hitch Your Wagon, Too Many Heroes, The Rugged Path, Years Ago, How I Wonder, The Leading Lady, The Diary of Anne Frank, Into Thin Air, Hole in the Head, Sunday in New York, Funny Girl, I Was Dancing, A Very Rich Woman, We Have Always Lived in the Castle, Idiot's Delight, Ho! Ho! Ho!.
PICTURES: Dir.: A Man to Remember, Next Time I Marry, The Great Man Votes, Bachelor Mother, Tom Dick & Harry, My Favorite Wife, They Knew What They Wanted. Dir./Writer: Where It's At, Some Kind of a Nut. Writer: From This Day Forward, A Double Life, Adam's Rib, The Marrying Kind, Pat and Mike, It Should Happen To You, The Rat Race.
TELEVISION: Movie: Hardhat and Legs (co-writer). Series: Mr. Broadway.

KANTER, HAL
Writer, Director, Producer. b. Savannah, GA, Dec. 18, 1918. On B'way contributor to Hellzapoppin. Then began writing radio dramas before mil. service, WW II. Served as combat corresp. Armed Forces Radio; writer, Paramount, 1951-54; dir., RKO, 1956; writer, prod. for Lucille Ball Prods., 1979-80. Savannah Prods., 1982-86. Received Writers Guild Paddy Chayefsky Laurel Award, 1989. Writer (radio): Danny Kaye Show, Amos 'n Andy, Bing Crosby Show, Jack Paar, Beulah. Winner 3 Emmy Awards for writing, 1954, 1991, 1992. Member: bd. of dir., WGAW; bd. of govs. AMPAS; v.p. Writers Guild Foundation.
PICTURES: Writer: My Favorite Spy, Off Limits, Road to Bali, Casanova's Big Night, About Mrs. Leslie, Money from Home, Artists and Models, The Rose Tattoo, I Married a Woman (dir. only), Loving You (also dir.), Mardi Gras, Once Upon a Horse (also dir., prod.), Blue Hawaii, Pocketful of Miracles, Bachelor in Paradise, Move Over Darling, Dear Brigitte.
TELEVISION: Writer: Ed Wynn Show, George Gobel Show (also creator, prod.), Kraft Music Hall (also dir., prod.; 1958-59), Chrysler Theatre (also prod., dir.; 1966-67), Julia (also dir., prod., creator), Jimmy Stewart Show (also prod., dir., creator), All In The Family (exec. prod.: 1975-76), Chico & The Man (spv. prod., 1976-77), You Can't Take It With You. Specials (writer): AFI Life Achievement Awards for Henry Fonda & Alfred Hitchcock, 26 Annual Academy Awards.

KANTER, JAY
Executive. b. Chicago, IL, Dec. 12, 1926. Entered industry with MCA, Inc., where was v.p. Left after more than 20 yrs. to become indep. prod., then pres. of First Artists Production Co., Ltd. 1975 joined 20th-Fox as v.p. prod.; 1976, named sr. v.p., worldwide prod. Named v.p., The Ladd Co., 1979. Joined MGM/UA Entertainment Co. as pres., worldwide prod., Motion Picture Division, 1984. 1985, named pres., worldwide prod., UA Corp.; then pres., production MGM Pictures Inc.; 1989, named chmn. of prod. of Pathe Entertainment Co. 1991, became COO & chmn. of prod., MGM-Pathe Commun. Co. (MGM Communi-cations, 1992). 1994-95, MGM consultant. March, 1995, independent prod.

KANTOR, IGO
Producer, Film Editor. b. Vienna, Austria, Aug. 18, 1930. e. UCLA, A.A. 1950; B.S., 1952; M.S., 1954. Foreign corres., Portugal magazine, FLAMA, 1949-57; music supvr., Screen Gems, Columbia 1954-63; post-prod. supvr., film ed., features, TV; assoc. prod., 1963-64; prod., exec., International Entertainment Corp., 1965. pres., Synchrofilm, Inc., post-production co. and Duque Films, Inc., production co. 1968-74. 1975-present, produced and edited films. 1982, pres., Laurelwood Prods; 1988, pres. Major Arts Corp.
PICTURES: Assoc. Producer: Bye Bye Birdie, Under the Yum Yum Tree, Gidget Goes to Rome, A House Is Not a Home, Pattern for Murder, Willy. Producer: Assault on Agathon (also edit.), FTA, Dixie Dynamite (assoc. prod., edit.), Kingdom of the Spiders (also edit., music spvr.), The Dark (assoc. prod.), Good Luck Miss Wyckoff (prod. spvr.), Hardly Working, Kill and Kill Again, Mutant, Shaker Run, Act of Piracy, They Call Me Bruce Levy.

TELEVISION: From Hawaii with Love (1984), The Grand Tour, It's a Wonderful World (prod.-dir.), Nosotros Golden Eagle Awards (prod.), United We Stand (pre-Olympic special), Legends of the West With Jack Palance, Mom U.S.A., A Desperate Affair, Holiday Classics Cartoons (special).

KAPLAN, GABRIEL
Actor, Comedian. b. Brooklyn, NY, March 31, 1945. After high school worked as bellboy at Lakewood, NJ hotel, spending free time studying comedians doing routines. Put together a comedy act, landing engagements in small clubs and coffee houses all over U.S. Made several appearances on Tonight Show, Merv Griffin Show, Mike Douglas Show, etc. Has played Las Vegas clubs.
PICTURES: Fast Break, Tulips, Nobody's Perfekt.
TELEVISION: Series: Welcome Back Kotter, Gabriel Kaplan Presents the Future Stars, Lewis and Clark. Movie: Love Boat (pilot).

KAPLAN, JONATHAN
Director, Writer. b. Paris, Nov. 25, 1947. Son of composer Sol Kaplan. e. U. of Chicago, B.A.; NYU, M.F.A. Made short film Stanley Stanley. Member of tech. staff Fillmore East, NY 1969-71. New World Pictures' Roger Corman post-grad. sch. of filmmaking, Hollywood, 1971-73. As actor on B'way in Dark at the Top of the Stairs. Appeared in films: Cannonball, Hollywood Boulevard.
PICTURES: Director: Night Call Nurses, Student Teachers, The Slams, Truck Turner, White Line Fever (also co-s.p.), Mr. Billion, Over the Edge, Heart Like a Wheel, Project X, The Accused, Immediate Family, Unlawful Entry, Love Field, Bad Girls.
TELEVISION: Movies: The 11th Victim, The Hustler of Muscle Beach, The Gentleman Bandit, Girls of the White Orchid.

KAPOOR, SHASHI
Actor. b. Calcutta, India, Mar. 18, 1938. Son of late Prithviraj Kapoor, Indian film and stage actor. As child worked in Prithvi Theatre and in brother, Raj's films. Toured with father's co. at 18 and joined the Kendals' Shakespeareana Co. in India. Starred in over 200 Indian films as well as several Merchant-Ivory Prods.
PICTURES: Pretty Polly, Siddhartha, The Householder, Bombay Talkie, Shakespeare Wallah, Heat and Dust, USTAV (Festival of Love, also prod.), The New Delhi Times, Sammy and Rosie Get Laid, The Deceivers, Nomads, Ajuba.

KARDISH, LAURENCE
Curator, Dept. of Film, Museum of Modern Art. b. Ottawa, Ontario, Canada, Jan. 5, 1945. e. Carlton U. Ottawa, Canada, 1966, Honors B.A. in philosophy; Columbia U., Sch. of the Arts, 1968, M.F.A. in film, radio, and television. 1965-66: Canadian Film Inst., programmer for National Film Theatre, Ottawa; researched a history of Canadian filmmaking. 1965: founded first film society in Canada to exhibit Amer. avant-garde films (Carleton U. Cine Club); directed summer seminar on film, Carleton U., 1966. 1966-68: New American Cinema Group, Inc., NY, worked for the Film-Makers' Distribution Center. 1968: joined Dept. of Film, MOMA; made curator 1984. Since 1968 involved with Cineprobe prog. Since 1972 participated in selection of films for New Directors/New Films series; dir. exhibitions of surveys of national cinemas (Senegal, Scandinavia, French-speaking Canada) and retrospectives of ind. Amer. filmmakers (includ. Rudolph Burkhardt, Stan Brakhage, Shirley Clarke), The Lubitsch Touch, Columbia Pictures, Warner Bros., MGM, Universal, RKO, and directors. 1980: toured Europe with prog. of indep. Amer. films. Author: Reel Plastic Magic (1972); also essays and monographs. Dir.feature Slow Run (1968). On jury for Channel 13's Indep. Focus series and on Board of Advisors, Collective for Living Cinema, NY. 1982-82: bd. of dirs. of National Alliance of Media Arts Centers; 1987-89: on Jerome Foundation panel. 1986 on Camera d'Or jury, Cannes Film Fest.

KARLIN, FRED
Composer, Conductor. b. Chicago, IL, June 16, 1936. e. Amherst Coll., B.A. Composer and arranger for Benny Goodman. Won Academy Award for Best Song for For All We Know (from Lovers and Other Strangers) and Emmy for original music in The Autobiography of Miss Jane Pittman. 4 Acad. Award noms., 11 Emmy Award noms.; Image Award for score to Minstrel Man. Author: On the Track: A Guide to Contemporary Film Scoring (with Rayburn Wright), Listening to Movies. Creator and instructor of the ASCAP/Fred Karlin Film Scoring Workshop, since 1988.
PICTURES: Up the Down Staircase, Yours Mine and Ours, The Sterile Cuckoo (including music for song, Come Saturday Morning; Acad. Award nom.), The Stalking Moon, Westworld, Futureworld, Lovers and Other Strangers, Leadbelly, Loving Couples.
TELEVISION: The Autobiography of Miss Jane Pittman, The Awakening Land, The Plutonium Incident, Minstrel Man, Sophia Loren—Her Own Story, Green Eyes, Strangers: The

Story of a Mother and Daughter, Calamity Jane, Ike: the War Years, Inside the Third Reich, Hollywood—The Gift of Laughter, Homeward Bound, Dream West, Hostage Flight, A Place to Call Home, Robert Kennedy and His Times, Dadah is Death, Bridge to Silence, The Secret, Film Music Masters: Jerry Goldsmith (prod. and dir.), Film Music Masters: Elmer Bernstein (prod. and dir.).

KARLIN, MYRON D.
Executive. b. Revere, MA, Sept. 21, 1918. e. UCLA. Joined m.p. business in 1946 as gen. mgr. for MGM in Ecuador. Two yrs. later assigned same spot for MGM in Venezuela. 1952-53 was gen. sales mgr. for MGM in Germany, after which managing dir. in Argentina, returning to Germany as mgr. dir. in 1956. Named mgn. dir. for United Artists in Italy. 1960-68 was pres. of Brunswick Int'l., while also serving as advisor to World Health Organization and UNESCO. 1969 was European mgr. for MGM and mgn. dir. in Italy. Joined Warner Bros. Int'l. in 1970 as v.p. of European dist. 1972 appt. v.p. in chg. of int'l. operations for WB; 1977, appt. pres., WB Intl. & exec. v.p., Warner Bros., Inc; 1985, named exec. v.p., intl. affairs, WB, Inc. Now pres. & COO, Motion Picture Export Assn. July, 1994, sr. consultant, Motion Picture assoc.

KARP, ALLEN
Executive. b. Toronto, Ontario, Canada, Sept. 18, 1940. e. Univ. of Toronto, bachelor of law degree, 1964; called to Ontario bar in 1966; masters of business law degree 1975, from Osgoode Hall Law School, York Univ. Served as buiness lawyer and senior legal advisor, becoming dir. of Odeon Theatre Film circuit, 1977. 1986, named sr. exec. v.p. of Cineplex Odeon Corp. 1988, became pres. North American Theatres Division; 1989, pres. & COO; 1990, elected pres. & CEO.

KARRAS, ALEX
Actor. b. Gary, IN, July 15, 1935. e. Univ. of Iowa. As football player with Iowa State U., picked for All Amer. team. Received Outland Trophy, 1957. Former professional football player with Detroit Lions, 1968-64, and 1964-71. Sportswriter, Detroit Free Press, 1972-73. Also worked as prof. wrestler, salesman, steel worker and lecturer. m. actress Susan Clark. With her formed Georgian Bay Prods., 1979. Books: Even Big Guys Cry (with Herb Gluck, 1977), Alex Karras: My Life in Football Television and Movies (1979), Tuesday Night Football (1991).
PICTURES: Paper Lion (as himself; debut, 1968), Blazing Saddles, FM, Win Place or Steal, Jacob Two-Two Meets the Hooded Fang, When Time Ran Out, Nobody's Perfekt, Porky's, Victor/Victoria, Against All Odds.
TELEVISION: Commentator and host: Monday Night Football (1974-76). Mini-Series: Centennial. Movies: Hardcase, The 500-Pound Jerk, Babe, Mulligan's Stew, Mad Bull, Jimmy B. & Andre (also exec. prod.), Alcatraz: The Whole Shocking Story, Word of Honor (also exec. prod.), Maid in America (also exec. prod.), Fudge-a-Mania, Tracy Takes On.... Series: Webster (also co-prod.).

KARTOZIAN, WILLIAM F.
Executive. b. San Francisco, CA, July 27, 1938. e. Stanford U., 1960; Harvard Law Sch., 1963. Deputy Attorney General State of CA, 1963-64; assoc. in law firm of Lillick, McHose Wheat Adams & Charles, San Francisco, 1964-65; corp. counsel and dir., Natl. Convenience Stores, Houston, 1965-67; v.p. and corp. counsel, UA Theatre Circuit, 1967-75; owner, Festival Enterprises, Inc., 1970-86; chmn. San Francisco Theatre Employers Assoc., 1973-76; Theatre Assoc. of CA, Inc., dir. 1972-86, v.p. 1974-75, pres. 1975-79, chmn. of bd. 1979-81; member, State of CA Industrial Welfare Comm. Amusement and Recreation Industries Wage Board, 1975-76; Natl Assoc. of Theatre Owners: 1976-86, v.p. 1980-86, president 1988-present. Owner, Regency Enterprises, Inc., 1986-present; chmn. of bd., Lakeside Inn & Casino, Stateline, NV 1985-present. Member: Calif. Film Commission, 1988-present.

KASDAN, LAWRENCE
Writer, Director, Producer. b. West Virginia, Jan. 14, 1949. e. U. of Michigan. Clio award-winning advertising copywriter, Detroit and LA before becoming screen writer. Became director with Body Heat (1981).
PICTURES: The Empire Strikes Back (co-s.p.), Raiders of the Lost Ark (co-s.p.), Continental Divide (s.p.), Body Heat (dir., s.p.), Return of the Jedi (co-s.p.), The Big Chill (dir., co-s.p., co- exec. prod.), Into the Night (actor), Silverado (dir., co-s.p., prod.), Cross My Heart (prod.), The Accidental Tourist (dir., co-prod., co-s.p.), Immediate Family (exec. prod.), I Love You to Death (dir., actor), Grand Canyon (dir., co-prod., co-s.p., actor), Jumpin at the Boneyard (exec. prod.), The Bodyguard (s.p., co-prod.), Wyatt Earp (dir., co-prod., co-s.p.), French Kiss (dir.).

KASLOFF, STEVE
Writer. b. New York, NY, Nov. 13, 1952. e. Pratt Institute, 1974, cum laude. Writer/supvr., Young & Rubicam, 1974-76;

writer/sprv., Ally & Gargano, 1976; writer/supvr., Marsteller Inc., 1976-79; writer/creative supvr., Scali, McCabe, Sloves, 1979-82. hired as youngest v.p., Columbia Pictures, 1982; promoted to sr. v.p., creative dir., Columbia, 1983. Sr. v.p. creative dir., 20th Century Fox, 1992. Member, WGA. Winner of numerous Clio and Key Arts Awards and over 200 others for creative work (trailers, TV commercials, posters, etc.) on such films as Tootsie, Ghostbusters, Total Recall, Home Alone, Dances With Wolves, Terminator 2, Home Alone 2, Last Action Hero, Jurassic Park, Schindler's List, Dumb and Dumber, etc. Has directed stage productions, commercials & special teaser trailers. Screen-writing/Production deal with Columbia Pictures, 1988; 20th Century Fox Films, 1993-present.

KASSAR, MARIO
Executive, Producer. b. Lebanon, Oct. 10, 1951. At age of 18 formed own foreign distribution co. Kassar Films International, specializing in sale, dist. and exhibition of films in Asia and Europe. In 1976 became partners with Andrew Vajna who had own dist. co., forming Carolco. First prod. First Blood, followed by Rambo: First Blood Part II. Became sole chmn. of Carolco in 1989. Formed own production co. in 1996.
PICTURES: Exec. Prod.: Angel Heart, Extreme Prejudice, Rambo III, Red Heat, Iron Eagle II, Deep Star Six, Johnny Handsome, Mountains of the Moon, Total Recall, Air America, Jacob's Ladder, L.A. Story, The Doors, Terminator 2: Judgment Day, Rambling Rose, Basic Instinct, Universal Soldier, Light Sleeper, Chaplin, Cliffhanger, Stargate, Showgirls.

KASTNER, ELLIOTT
Producer. b. New York, NY, Jan. 7, 1933. e. U. of Miami, Columbia U. Was agent then v.p. with MCA, before becoming indep. prod., financing and personally producing 65 feature films in 25 yrs. Based in London, NY & LA.
PICTURES: Harper, Kaleidoscope, The Bobo, Sweet November, Sol Madrid, Michael Kohlaas, Laughter in the Dark, Night of the Following Day, Where Eagles Dare, A Severed Head, Tam Lin, The Walking Stick, X Y and Zee (Zee & Company), The Nightcomers, Big Truck and Poor Clare, Face to the Wind, Fear Is the Key, The Long Goodbye, Cops and Robbers, Jeremy, 11 Harrowhouse, Spot, Rancho Deluxe, 92 in the Shade, Farewell My Lovely, Russian Roulette, Breakheart Pass, The Missouri Breaks, Swashbuckler, Equus, A Little Night Music, The Medusa Touch, The Big Sleep, Absolution, Goldengirl, Yesterday's Hero, ffolkes, The First Deadly Sin, Death Valley, Man Woman and Child, Garbo Talks, Oxford Blues, Nomads, Heat, Angel Heart, Jack's Back, The Blob, White of the Eye, Zombie High, Never on Tuesday, Homeboy, A Chorus of Disapproval, The Last Party.
TELEVISION: Movie: Frank and Jesse.

KATLEMAN, HARRIS L.
Executive. b. Omaha, NB, Aug. 19, 1928. e. UCLA. Joined MCA in 1949; 1952 transferred to NY as head of TV Packaging Dept. Left to join Goodson-Todman Prods. in 1955, where named v.p., 1956; exec. v.p., 1958; sr. exec. v.p., 1968. Was directly responsible for all programs prod. in L.A., including The Rebel, Branded, The Richard Boone Show, and Don Rickles Show, on which was exec. prod. Joined M-G-M in 1972 as v.p. of MGM-TV; promoted following year to pres., MGM-TV and sr. v.p. of MGM, Inc. Resigned as pres., MGM-TV, 1977. Formed Bennett/ Katleman Productions under contract to Columbia Pictures. Exec. prod.: From Here to Eternity, Salvage 1; 1980, named bd. chmn. 20th-Fox Television. Appointed pres. & CEO, Twentieth TV, 1982. Oversaw prod. of final years of M*A*S*H, as well as Mr. Belvedere, The Fall Guy, Trapper John M.D., L.A. Law, Hooperman, Anything But Love, Tracey Ullman Show, Alien Nation, The Simpsons, In Living Color. Resigned, 1992. Formed Shadow Hill Prods. under contract to Twentieth TV. Joined Mark Goodson Prods., 1993, as COO.

KATSELAS, MILTON GEORGE
Director, Writer, Teacher, Painter. b. Pittsburgh, PA, Feb. 22, 1933. e. drama dept., Carnegie Inst. of Technology (now Carnegie-Mellon U.). Acting teacher-owner, Beverly Hills Playhouse. Has exhibited paintings in several major solo exhibitions. Awards: 3 time recipient of the L.A. Drama Critics Circle Award, Drama Logue Best Director Award, NAACP and Tony Nominations for Best Director.
THEATER: B'way: The Rose Tattoo, Butterflies are Free, Camino Real. Off-B'way: Call Me By My Rightful Name, The Zoo Story.
PICTURES: Butterflies Are Free, 40 Carats, Report to the Commissioner, When You Comin' Back Red Ryder?
TELEVISION: Movies: The Rules of Marriage, Strangers—The Story of a Mother and Daughter.

KATT, WILLIAM
Actor. b. Los Angeles, CA, Feb. 16, 1955. Son of actors Barbara Hale and Bill Williams. e. Orange Coast Coll. Majored in music, playing piano and guitar. Acted with South Coast

Repertory Theatre, later working in productions at the Ahmanson and Mark Taper Theatres in L.A. Phoenix Rep (N.Y.): Bonjour La Bonjour. Regional: Sarah and Abraham, Days of Wine and Roses.
PICTURES: Carrie (debut, 1976), First Love, Big Wednesday, Butch and Sundance: The Early Days, Baby, Rising Storm, House, White Ghost, Wedding Band, Naked Obsession, Double X: The Name of the Game, House IV: Home Deadly Home, Desperate Motive (Distant Cousins), Tollbooth, The Paperboy, Stranger by Night.
TELEVISION: *Series*: The Greatest American Hero, Top of the Hill, Good Sports. *Movies*: Night Chase, The Daughters of Joshua Cabe, Can Ellen Be Saved?, Perry Mason Returns and several Perry Mason follow-ups (Case of the... Murdered Madam, Avenging Ace, Scandalous Scoundrel, Lady in the Lake, Notorious Nun, Shooting Star, Lost Love, Sinister Spirit), Swim Suit, Problem Child 3: Junior in Love, Piranha. *Specials*: Pippin, The Rainmaker.

KATZ, GLORIA
Producer, Writer. e. UCLA. Film Sch. Joined Universal Pictures as editor, cutting educational films. Later joined forces with Willard Huyck, whom she had met at U.C.L.A. Pair signed by Francis Ford Coppola to write and direct for his newly created company, American Zoetrope.
PICTURES: *Writer*: American Graffiti, Lucky Lady, French Postcards (also prod.), Indiana Jones and the Temple of Doom, Howard the Duck (also prod.), Radioland Murders.
TELEVISION: *Co-Producer, Co-Writer*: A Father's Homecoming, Mothers Daughters and Lovers.

KATZ, JAMES C.
Producer, Executive. b. New York, NY, March 17, 1939. e. Ohio St. U. Started in publicity dept. of United Artists, 1963, eventually serving as v.p. of publicity for UA, 1966-68. Publicity co-ord. on film Khartoum, 1964. To London, 1968 as unit publicist for The Charge of the Light Brigade, Joanna. Prod. & dir. for C.I.C. special shorts and documentaries. 1973-78, prod./dir. commercials for own company in London. 1980, pres. Universal Classics Dept.; 1984, v.p. prod, Universal Pictures. With Robert A. Harris worked on restoration of Spartacus, My Fair Lady.
PICTURES: Three Sisters (co-prod.), Lust in the Dust (exec. prod.), Nobody's Fool (prod.), Scenes From the Class Struggle in Beverly Hills (prod.).

KATZ, MARTY
Producer. b. Landsburg, West Germany, Sept. 2, 1947. e. UCLA, U. of Maryland. Served in Vietnam War as U.S. Army first lieut.; awarded Bronze Star as combat pictorial unit director. 1971, dir. of film prod., ABC Circle Films; 1976, exec. v.p., prod., Quinn Martin Prods; 1978-80, producer and consultant, Paramount Pictures' 1981-85, independent producer (Lost in America, Heart Like a Wheel). 1985, joined Walt Disney Prods. as sr. v.p., motion picture & TV prod. Named exec. v.p. motion picture and TV production, 1988-92. 1992-present, prod. Marty Katz Prods./Walt Disney Studios. Producer of Mr. Wrong.

KATZ, NORMAN B.
Executive. b. Scranton, PA, Aug. 23, 1919. e. Columbia U. In U.S. Army 1941-46 as intelligence officer, airborne forces. Entered m.p. industry in 1947 with Discina Films, Paris, France, as prod. asst. Named exec. asst. to head of prod. in 1948. 1950 named v.p. Discina Int'l. Films and in 1952 exec. v.p. 1954 joined Associated Artists Prods. as foreign mgr.; named dir. of foreign operation in 1958. 1959 became dir. of foreign operations for United Artists Associated. 1961 joined 7 Arts Associated Corp. as v.p. in chg. of foreign optns.; 1964, named exec. v.p., 7 Arts Prods. Int'l.; 1967, exec. v.p. Warner Bros.-7 Arts Int'l. 1969 appt. exec. v.p. & CEO WB Intl. & bd. mem. of WB Inc. 1974 named sr. v.p. int'l. div. of American Film Theatre. Pres. of Cinema Arts Assoc. Corp. 1979, exec. v.p. and bd. member, American Communications Industries and pres., CEO of ACI subsidiary, American Cinema; 1983, pres., The Norkat Co. Also, bd. chmn., CEO, American Film Mktg. Assoc., 1985-87; chmn. Amer. Film Export Assn. 1988-92.

KATZENBERG, JEFFREY
Executive. b. 1950. Entered motion picture industry in 1975 as asst. to Paramount Pictures chmn. and CEO Barry Diller in NY. In 1977, became exec. dir. of mktg.; later same year moved to west coast as v.p. of programming for Paramount TV. Promoted to v.p., feature production for Paramount Pictures 1978; 2 years later assumed role of sr. v.p. prod. of m.p. div; 1982, pres. of prod., m.p. and TV, Paramount Pictures. Left to join The Walt Disney Company, 1984; chairman of The Walt Disney Studios, 1984-94. With Steven Spielberg and David Geffen formed Dreamworks entertainment company, 1995.

KAUFMAN, HAL
Creative director, TV Writer, Producer. b. New York, NY, Dec. 16, 1924. e. U. of TX, 1943-44; U. of MI, 1944-47. Started

career as petroleum geologist, Western Geophysical Co., 1947-48; TV writer-prod-dir., KDYL-TV, Salt Lake City, 1948-49; prog. dir., WLAV-TV, Grand Rapids, 1949-51; prod. mgr., WOOD-TV, Grand Rapids, 1951-54; TV writer-prod., Leo Burnett Company, Chicago, 1954-56; TV writer-prod., Gordon Best Company, Chicago, 1957-58; with Needham Louis & Brorby Inc.: 1959, sr. writer, TV/Radio creative dept.; 1962, v.p., asst. copy dir.; 1963, dir., tv, radio prod.; 1964, dir., broadcast design, production; assoc. creat. dir., asst. exec. v.p., Needham, Harper & Steers, Inc.; 1965; creat. dir. L.A., 1966; sr. v.p. and mem. bd. of dir., 1966. 1969, creative & marketing consultant in Beverly Hills. 1970, exec. v.p., principle, Kaufman, Lansky Inc., Beverly Hills and San Diego; 1974 editor and publisher Z Magazine; program dir., Z Channel, Theta Cable TV. 1979, sr. v.p./adv. & p.r. & asst. to pres. & bd. chmn., World Airways, Inc. 1982, v.p., creative dir., Admarketing, Inc., Los Angeles. 1985, mktg. & adv. consultant copy dir., Teleflora, Inc.; pres. Hal Kaufman Inc., mktg. & adv. consultant; pres. Brochures on Video, library division, creators and prods. of promotional videos, distribs. religious videos to libraries; pres. Pious Publications, prods. and distribs. of religious videos. Member, Directors Guild of America, SAG, AFTRA. 1974.

KAUFMAN, LEONARD B.
Producer, Writer, Director. b. Newark, NJ, Aug. 31, 1927. e. NYU. In W.W.II served with Army Special Services writing and directing camp shows. Nat'l magazine writer, 1945-48; radio writer, including Errol Flynn Show, 1948-50; radio and TV writer, 1950-52. Headed own public relations firm: Kaufman, Schwartz, and Associates, 1952-64. Joined Ivan Tors Films as writer-prod., 1964. Films Corp., 1958.
PICTURES: Clarence the Cross-eyed Lion, Birds Do It (story).
TELEVISION: Daktari, Ivan Tors' Jambo, O'Hara U.S. Treasury (pilot feature and series). Producer: Hawaii-Five O, The New Sea Hunt, Scruples (mini-series), The Hawaiian (pilot), Writer: Knightrider, Dukes of Hazzard, Hawaii-Five O, Wet Heat (pilot), Hawaiian Heat, Island Sons (movie).

KAUFMAN, LLOYD
Executive. e. Yale Univ., 1969. From 1974-present, pres. of Troma, Inc.
PICTURES: The Girl Who Returned (prod., dir., s.p.), Cry Uncle (prod. mgr.), Joe (prod. asst.), Sugar Cookie (exec. prod., s.p.), Silent Night Bloody Night (assoc. prod.), Battle of Love's Return (dir., prod., s.p., actor), Big Gus What's the Fuss (dir., prod.), Sweet Savior (prod. mgr.), Mother's Day (assoc. prod.), Rocky (pre-prod. spvr.), Slow Dancing in the Big City (prod. spvr.), The Final Countdown (assoc. prod.), Squeeze Play (dir., prod.), Waitress (Co-dir., prod.), Stuck on You (co-dir., co-prod., co-s.p.), The First Turn-On (co-dir., co-prod.), Screamplay (exec. prod.), When Nature Calls (assoc. prod.), The Toxic Avenger (co-dir., co-prod., co-s.p., story), Blood Hook (exec. prod.), Girl School Screams (exec. prod.), Class of Nuke 'Em High (co-dir., co-prod.), Lust for Freedom (exec. prod.), Monster in the Closet (exec. prod.), Troma's War (Co-dir., co-prod., co-s.p., story), Toxic Avenger Part II (co-dir., co-prod., co-s.p., story), Fortress of Amerikkka (prod.), Toxic Avenger III: The Last Temptation of Toxie (co-dir., co-s.p., co-prod.), Class of Nuke 'Em High Part II: Subhumanoid Meltdown (co-s.p., co-prod., story), Sgt. Kabukiman N.Y.P.D. (co-dir., co-prod., co-s.p.), The Good the Bad and the Subhumanoid (co-dir., co-prod., co-story).

KAUFMAN, PHILIP
Writer, Director, Producer. b. Chicago, IL, Oct. 23, 1936. e. U. of Chicago, Harvard Law Sch. Was teacher in Italy and Greece before turning to film medium.
PICTURES: *Co-Writer*: The Outlaw Josey Wales, Raiders of the Lost Ark. *Director*: Goldstein (co-dir., co-s.p., co-prod.), Fearless Frank (also s.p., prod.), The Great Northfield Minnesota Raid (also s.p., prod.), The White Dawn, Invasion of the Body Snatchers, The Wanderers (also co-s.p.), The Right Stuff (also s.p.), The Unbearable Lightness of Being (also co-s.p.), Henry & June (also co-s.p.), Rising Sun (also co-s.p.).

KAUFMAN, VICTOR
Executive. b. New York, NY, June 21, 1943. e. Queens Coll.; NYU Sch. of Law, J.D., 1967. Taught criminal law at UCLA before joining Wall St. law firm, Simpson Thacher & Bartlett. Joined Columbia Pictures as asst. general counsel, 1974. Named chief counsel, 1975; then made vice chmn. Columbia Pictures. Later exec. v.p. Columbia Pictures Industries and vice chmn. Columbia Pictures motion picture div. when conceived a new studio as a joint venture between Coca-Cola, Time Inc.'s Home Box Office and CBS, Inc. forming Tri-Star Pictures. Named chmn. and CEO Tri-Star, 1983. When Columbia Pictures and Tri-Star merged in late 1987, became pres. and CEO of new entity, Columbia Pictures Entertainment. In June 1988, dropped title of chmn. of Tri-Star. 1993 became head of Savoy Pictures.

KAUFMANN, CHRISTINE
Actress. b. Lansdorf, Graz, Austria, Jan. 11, 1945. e. school in Munich, Germany. Film debut as a dancer. Salto Mortale at 7 yrs of age.
PICTURES: Rosenrosli (Little Rosie), Schweigende Engel (Silent Angel), Maedchen in Uniform, Winter Vacation, The Last Days of Pompeii, Red Lips, Taras Bulba (U.S debut), Town Without Pity, Murder in the Rue Morgue, Bagdad Cafe, Der Geschichtenerzahler.

KAURISMAKI, AKI
Director, Writer. b. Finland, April 4, 1957. Brother is filmmaker Mika Kaurismaki. First film credit was acting and writing his brother's The Liar in 1980. Directed short subjects: Rocky VI, Thru the Wire, Those Were the Days, These Boots. Served as writer on brother's features: Jackpot 2, The Worthless (also actor), The Clan: The Tale of the Frogs, Rosso.
PICTURES: Director: The Saimaa Gesture (co-dir., with Mika), Crime and Punishment, Calamari Union, Shadows in Paradise, Hamlet Goes Business, Ariel, Leningrad Cowboys Go America, The Match Factory Girl, I Hired a Contract Killer, La Vie de Boheme (The Bohemian Life), Leningrad Cowboys Meet Moses (also s.p., prod., edit.), Take Care of Your Scarf Tatiana (also s.p., prod., edit.).

KAVNER, JULIE
Actress. b. Los Angeles, CA, Sept. 7, 1951. e. San Diego State U. Professional debut as Brenda Morgenstern on TV's Rhoda, 1974.
THEATER: Particular Friendships (Off-B'way), Two for the Seesaw (Jupiter, FLA), It Had to Be You (Canada).
PICTURES: National Lampoon Goes to the Movies, Bad Medicine, Hannah and Her Sisters, Radio Days, Surrender, New York Stories (Oedipus Wrecks), Awakenings, Alice, This Is My Life, Shadows and Fog, I'll Do Anything, Forget Paris.
TELEVISION: Series: Rhoda (Emmy Award, 1978), The Tracey Ullman Show, The Simpsons (voice). Special: The Girl Who Couldn't Lose (Afternoon Playbreak). Movies: Katherine, No Other Love, The Revenge of the Stepford Wives, Don't Drink the Water. Pilot: A Fine Romance. Guest: Lou Grant, Petrocelli, Taxi.

KAYLOR, ROBERT
Director. b. Plains, MT, Aug. 1, 1934. e. Art Center Sch. of Design. Received awards at Cannes, San Francisco and Dallas Film Festivals, Guggenheim Fellow, Amer. Film Inst.
PICTURES: Derby, Carny, Nobody's Perfect.

KAZAN, ELIA
Director. b. Constantinople, Turkey, Sept. 7, 1909. e. Williams Coll., Yale Dramatic Sch. With Group Theatre as apprentice & stage mgr.; on stage, 1934-41; plays include: Waiting for Lefty, Golden Boy, Gentle People, Five-Alarm, Lilliom. Author (novels): The Arrangement, The Assassins, The Understudy, Acts of Love, The Anatolian, A Life (autobiography, 1988), Beyond the Aegean (1994).
THEATER: Director: Skin of Our Teeth, All My Sons, Streetcar Named Desire, Death of a Salesman, Cat on a Hot Tin Roof (co-dir.), One Touch of Venus, Harriet, Jocobowsky and the Colonel, Tea and Sympathy, Dark at the Top of the Stairs, J.B., Sweet Bird of Youth, Lincoln Center Repertory Theatre (co-dir., prod.), After The Fall, But For Whom Charlie.
PICTURES: Actor: City for Conquest, Blues in the Night. Director: A Tree Grows in Brooklyn (debut, 1945), Boomerang!, The Sea of Grass, Gentleman's Agreement (Academy Award, 1947), Pinky, Panic in the Streets, A Streetcar Named Desire, Viva Zapata!, Man on a Tightrope, On the Waterfront (Academy Award, 1954). Producer/Director: East of Eden, Baby Doll, A Face in the Crowd, Wild River, Splendor in the Grass, America America (also s.p.), The Arrangement (also s.p.), The Visitors, The Last Tycoon.

KAZAN, LAINIE
Singer, Actress. b. New York, NY, May 15, 1942. e. Hofstra U.
PICTURES: Dayton's Devils, Lady in Cement, Romance of a Horse Thief, One from the Heart, My Favorite Year, Lust in the Dust, The Delta Force, The Journey of Natty Gann, Harry and the Hendersons, Beaches, Eternity, 29th Street, I Don't Buy Kisses Anymore, The Cemetery Club.
TELEVISION: Series: The Dean Martin Summer Show, Tough Cookies, Karen's Song. Pilot: Family Business, The Lainie Kazan Show. Movies: A Love Affair: The Eleanor and Lou Gehrig Story, A Cry for Love, Sunset Limousine, The Jerk Too, Obsessive Love, Prince for a Day. Guest: Too Close for Comfort, Dick Van Dyke Show, Beverly Hills 90210, Tales From the Crypt, Faerie Tale Theatre (Pinocchio), Hotel, Johnny Carson Show, Dean Martin, Merv Griffin, Joan Rivers, Amazing Stories, Pat Sajak Show, The Famous Teddy Z, Murder She Wrote.

KAZANJIAN, HOWARD G.
Producer. b. Pasadena, CA, July 26, 1943. e. U. of Southern California Film Sch.; DGA Training Program. Exec. Prod.: The Making of Raiders of the Lost Ark.

PICTURES: Asst. Dir.: Camelot, Finian's Rainbow, The Wild Bunch, The Arrangement, The Front Page, The Hindenberg, Family Plot. Assoc. Prod.: Rollercoaster. Producer: More American Graffiti, Raiders of the Lost Ark, Return of the Jedi, Demolition Man.

KAZURINSKY, TIM
Actor, Writer. b. Johnstown, PA, March 3, 1950. Raised in Australia. Worked as copywriter for Chicago ad agency. Took acting class at Second City and quit job to become actor and head writer for Second City Comedy Troupe. Co-starred with John Candy in CTV/NBC's series Big City Comedy, 1980. Joined cast of Saturday Night Live as writer-actor 1981-84.
PICTURES: Actor: My Bodyguard, Somewhere in Time, Continental Divide, Neighbors, Police Academy II: Their First Assignment, Police Academy III: Back in Training, About Last Night (also co-s.p.), Police Academy IV: Citizens on Patrol, For Keeps (s.p. only), Road to Ruin (also s.p.), Hot to Trot, Wedding Band, A Billion for Boris, Shakes the Clown, Plump Fiction.
TELEVISION: Movies: This Wife for Hire, Dinner at Eight.

KEACH, STACY
Actor, Director, Producer. b. Savannah, GA, June 2, 1942. Brother is actor James Keach. Began professional acting career in Joseph Papp's 1964 Central Park prod. of Hamlet.
THEATER: Long Day's Journey into Night (Obie Award), Macbird (Drama Desk & Obie Awards), Indians (Drama Desk Award & Tony nom.), Hamlet, Deathtrap, Hughie, Barnum, Cyrano de Bergerac, Peer Gynt, Henry IV Parts I & II, Idiot's Delight, Solitary Confinement, Richard III, The Kentucky Cycle (Helen Hayes Award), Steiglitz Loves O'Keefe.
PICTURES: The Heart Is a Lonely Hunter (debut, 1968), End of the Road, The Traveling Executioner, Brewster McCloud, Doc, The New Centurions, Fat City, Watched!, The Life and Times of Judge Roy Bean, Luther, The Gravy Train, The Killer Inside Me, Conduct Unbecoming, Street People, The Squeeze, The Duellists (narrator), Slave of the Cannibal God, The Great Battle, Gray Lady Down, Up in Smoke, The Ninth Configuration (Twinkle Twinkle Killer Kane), The Long Riders (also exec. prod., co-s.p.), Nice Dreams, Road Games, Butterfly, That Championship Season, Class of 1999, False Identity, Milena, Raw Justice, Batman: Mask of the Phantasm (voice), New Crime City, Escape from L.A., Prey of the Jaguar.
TELEVISION: Series: Caribe, Mickey Spillane's Mike Hammer, Case Closed (host). Movies: All the Kind Strangers, Caribe, The Blue and the Gray, Princess Daisy, Murder Me Murder You, More Than Murder, Wait Until Dark, Mistral's Daughter, Hemingway, Mickey Spillane's Mike Hammer: Murder Takes All, The Forgotten, Mission of the Shark, Revenge on the Highway, Rio Diablo, Body Bags, Against Their Will: Women in Prison, Texas, Amanda & the Alien. Director: Incident at Vichy, Six Characters in Search of an Author.

KEACH, SR., STACY
Executive. b. Chicago, IL, May 29, 1914. Father of actors, Stacy and James. e. Northwestern U., B.S. & M.A. Was instructor in theatre arts at Northwestern and Armstrong Coll. and dir. at Pasadena Playhouse before entering industry. For 4-1/2 yrs. was under contract at Universal Pictures; 3 yrs. at RKO; had own prod. on NBC, CBS. In 1946 began producing and directing industrial stage presentations for Union Oil Co. and from then on became full-time prod. of m.p. and stage industrial shows. In 1946 formed Stacy Keach Productions, of which he is pres. In addition to directing, producing and writing occasionally appears as actor in films (Cobb, etc.). Played Clarence Birds Eye on TV commercials as well as other commercials. Voiceovers/ spokesman for many major American Cos. Autobiography: Stacy Keach, Go Home! (1996). Received Man of the Year Award from Pasadena Playhouse Alumni in 1995. Recipient of the Diamond Circle Award from the Pacific Pioneers Broadcasters Assoc., 1996.

KEATON, DIANE
Actress, Director. r.n. Diane Hall. b. Santa Ana, CA, Jan. 5, 1946. e. Santa Ana Coll. Appeared in summer stock and studied at Neighborhood Playhouse in N.Y. Made prof. debut in B'way prod. of Hair (1968); then co-starred with Woody Allen in Play It Again Sam, repeating role for film version. Off-B'way: The Primary English Class. Author: photography books: Reservations (co-ed.), Still Life. Directed 1982 short What Does Dorrie Want?
PICTURES: Lovers and Other Strangers (debut, 1970), The Godfather, Play It Again Sam, Sleeper, The Godfather Part II, Love and Death, I Will I Will... for Now, Harry and Walter Go to New York, Annie Hall (Academy Award, 1977), Looking for Mr. Goodbar, Interiors, Manhattan, Reds, Shoot the Moon, The Little Drummer Girl, Mrs. Soffel, Crimes of the Heart, Radio Days, Heaven (dir. only), Baby Boom, The Good Mother, The Lemon Sisters (also prod.), The Godfather Part III, Father of the Bride, Manhattan Murder Mystery, Look Who's Talking Now (voice), Unstrung Heroes (dir. only), Father of the Bride 2, Marvin's Room, The First Wives Club.

TELEVISION: *Movies*: Running Mates, Amelia Earhart: The Final Flight. *Guest*: Love American Style, The FBI, Mannix. *Director*: The Girl With the Crazy Brother, Twin Peaks, Wildflower (movie).

KEATON, MICHAEL
Actor. r.n. Michael Douglas. b. Coraopolis, PA, Sept. 5, 1951. Speech major, Kent State U, 2 years. Drove cab and ice-cream truck, worked for PBS station in Pittsburgh and appeared in regional theatre prods. while performing in local coffeehouses. Became memb. of improvisational troupe Jerry Vale. Moved to L.A. where honed craft at Comedy Store and Second City Improv. Workshops as stand-up comic.
PICTURES: Night Shift (debut, 1982), Mr. Mom, Johnny Dangerously, Gung Ho, Touch and Go, The Squeeze, Beetlejuice, Clean and Sober, The Dream Team, Batman, Pacific Heights, One Good Cop, Batman Returns, Much Ado About Nothing, My Life, The Paper, Speechless, Multiplicity.
TELEVISION: *Series*: All's Fair, Mary, The Mary Tyler Moore Hour, Working Stiffs, Report to Murphy. *Movie*: Roosevelt and Truman.

KEEL, HOWARD
Actor. r.n. Harold Keel. b. Gillespie, IL, April 13, 1919. e. high school, Fallbrook, CA. Began career following George Walker scholarship award for singing, L.A.; appeared in plays, Pasadena Auditorium, concerts; won awards, Mississippi Valley and Chicago Musical Festivals. Stage debut: Carousel, 1945; followed by London prod. of Oklahoma! which led to contract with MGM.
THEATER: Carousel, Oklahoma!, Saratoga, No Strings, The Ambassador, Man of La Mancha.
PICTURES: The Small Voice (debut, 1948), Annie Get Your Gun, Pagan Love Song, Three Guys Named Mike, Show Boat, Texas Carnival, Callaway Went Thataway, Lovely to Look At, Desperate Search, I Love Melvin (cameo), Ride Vaquero!, Fast Company, Kiss Me Kate, Calamity Jane, Rose Marie, Seven Brides for Seven Brothers, Deep in My Heart, Jupiter's Darling, Kismet, Floods of Fear, The Big Fisherman, Armored Command, The Day of the Triffids, The Man From Button Willow (voice), Waco, Red Tomahawk, The War Wagon, Arizona Bushwhackers, That's Entertainment III.
TELEVISION: *Series*: Dallas. *Movie*: Hart to Hart: Home Is Where the Hart Is. *Guest*: Zane Grey Theatre, Bell Telephone Hour, Tales of Wells Fargo, Death Valley Days, Here's Lucy, Sonny and Cher, The Love Boat, etc. *Specials*: A Toast to Jerome Kern, Roberta, Music of Richard Rodgers.

KEESHAN, BOB
Performer. b. Lynbrook, NY, June 27, 1927. e. Fordham U. As network page boy became assistant to Howdy Doody's Bob Smith and originated role of Clarabelle the Clown; created children's programs Time for Fun, Tinker's Workshop, Mister Mayor, Captain Kangaroo (1955-85).

KEITEL, HARVEY
Actor. b. Brooklyn, NY, May 13, 1939. Served in U.S. Marine Corps. Studied with Frank Corsaro, Lee Strasberg, Stella Adler. Member of the Actors' Studio. Debuted in Martin Scorsese's student film Who's That Knocking at My Door?
THEATER: *NY*: Up to Thursday, Death of a Salesman, Hurlyburly, A Lie of the Mind.
PICTURES: Who's That Knocking at My Door? (debut, 1968), Mean Streets, Alice Doesn't Live Here Anymore, That's the Way of the World, Taxi Driver, Mother Jugs and Speed, Buffalo Bill and the Indians or: Sitting Bull's History Lesson, Welcome to L.A., The Duellists, Fingers, Blue Collar, Eagle's Wing, Deathwatch, Saturn 3, Bad Timing, The Border, Exposed, La Nuit de Varennes, Corrupt, Falling in Love, Knight of the Dragon (Star Knight), Camorra, Off Beat, Wise Guys, The Men's Club, The Investigation (The Inquiry), The Pick-Up Artist, The Last Temptation of Christ, The January Man, The Two Jakes, Mortal Thoughts, Thelma & Louise, Two Evil Eyes (The Black Cat), Bugsy (Acad. Award nom.), Sister Act, Reservoir Dogs (also co-prod.), Bad Lieutenant, Point of No Return, Rising Sun, The Piano, Dangerous Game, The Young Americans, Monkey Trouble, Pulp Fiction, Imaginary Crimes, Somebody to Love, Smoke, Clockers, Blue in the Face, Ulysses' Gaze, From Dusk Till Dawn, Head Above Water, Somebody to Love.
TELEVISION: *Movie*: The Virginia Hill Story. *Special*: This Ain't Bebop (Amer. Playhouse).

KEITH, BRIAN
Actor. r.n. Robert Brian Keith. b. Bayonne, NJ, Nov. 14, 1921. Father was actor Robert Keith. U.S. Marines, 1942-45; worked in stock co., radio shows, comm. films for TV; on B'way in Mr. Roberts, Darkness at Noon.
PICTURES: Arrowhead (debut, 1953), Jivaro, Alaska Seas, Bamboo Prison, Violent Men, Tight Spot, Five Against the House, Nightfall, Storm Center, Run of the Arrow, Chicago Confidential, Hell Canyon Outlaws, Dino, Appointment With a Shadow, Desert Hell, Fort Dobbs, Sierra Baron, Villa!, Violent

Road, The Young Philadelphians, Ten Who Dared, The Deadly Companions, The Parent Trap, Moon Pilot, Savage Sam, The Pleasure Seekers, The Raiders, A Tiger Walks, Those Calloways, The Hallelujah Trail, The Rare Breed, Nevada Smith, The Russians Are Coming the Russians Are Coming, Way Way Out, Reflections in a Golden Eye, With Six You Get Egg Roll, Krakatoa: East of Java, Gaily Gaily, Suppose They Gave a War and Nobody Came, The McKenzie Break, Scandalous John, Something Big, The Yakuza, The Wind and the Lion, Joe Panther, Nickelodeon, Hooper, Meteor, Mountain Men, Charlie Chan and the Curse of the Dragon Queen, Sharky's Machine, Death Before Dishonor, Young Guns, After the Rain, Welcome Home.
TELEVISION: Numerous dramas on Studio One, Suspense, Philco Playhouse, etc. *Series*: Crusader, The Westerner, Family Affair, The Little People (The Brian Keith Show), Archer, Hardcastle and McCormick, Pursuit of Happiness, Heartland, Walter & Emily. *Mini-Series*: Centennial, The Chisholms, Great Escapes: Secrets of Lake Success. *Movies*: Second Chance, The Quest, The Loneliest Runner, In the Matter of Karen Ann Quinlan, The Seekers, Moviola: The Silent Lovers, World War III, Cry for the Strangers, The Alamo: 13 Days to Glory, Perry Mason: The Case of the Lethal Lesson, Lady in a Corner, The Gambler Returns: Luck of the Draw, The Return of Hunter.

KEITH, DAVID
Actor, Director. b. Knoxville, TN, May 8, 1954. e. U. of Tennessee, B.A., speech and theater. Appearance at Good-speed Opera House in musical led to role in CBS sitcom pilot, Co-Ed Fever.
PICTURES: The Rose (debut, 1979), The Great Santini, Brubaker, Back Roads, Take This Job and Shove It, An Officer and a Gentleman, Independence Day, The Lords of Discipline, Firestarter, The Curse (dir. only), White of the Eye, The Further Adventures of Tennessee Buck (also dir.), Heartbreak Hotel, The Two Jakes, Off and Running, Desperate Motive (Distant Cousins), Caged Fear, Raw Justice, Temptation, Major League 2, Liar's Edge, Till the End of the Night, Born Wild, Gold Diggers: The Secret of Bear Mountain, Deadly Sins, The Indian in the Cupboard, A Family Thing, Invasion of Privacy, Judge & Jury, Red Blooded American Girl.
TELEVISION: *Series*: Co-ed Fever, Flesh 'N' Blood, Strangers, High Incident. *Movies*: Are You in the House Alone?, Friendly Fire, Gulag, Whose Child Is This?: The War for Baby Jessica, XXX's & OOO's (pilot), James Michener's Texas, If Looks Could Kill: From the Files of America's Most Wanted. *Mini-Series*: If Tomorrow Comes, Golden Moment: An Olympic Love Story, Guts and Glory: The Rise and Fall of Oliver North. *Guest*: Happy Days, Runaways.

KEITH, PENELOPE
O.B.E. Actress. b. Sutton, Surrey, Eng., 1939. London stage debut, The Wars of the Roses (RSC, 1964). Extensive theater work including The Norman Conquests, Donkey's Years, The Apple Cart, Hobson's Choice, Captain Brassbound's Conversion, Hay Fever.
PICTURES: Think Dirty (Every Home Should Have One), Take a Girl Like You, Penny Gold, Priest of Love.
TELEVISION: *Series*: Kate, The Good Life, To the Manor Born, Executive Stress. *Movies-Specials*: Private Lives, The Norman Conquests, Donkey's Years.

KELLER, MARTHE
Actress. b. Basel, Switzerland, 1945. e. Stanislavsky Sch., Munich. Joined a Heidelberg repertory group and Schiller Rep. in Berlin. Started acting in France and attracted attention of U.S. directors after appearing in Claude Lelouch's And Now My Love. Has acted in over 50 plays in French, German, Eng. & Italian.
PICTURES: Funeral in Berlin (debut, 1967), The Devil by the Tail, Give Her the Moon, La Vieille Fille, The Loser, Elle Court (Love in the Suburbs), And Now My Love, Down the Ancient Staircase, Le Guepier, Marathon Man, Black Sunday, Bobby Deerfield, Fedora, The Formula, Les Uns et les Autres, The Amateur, Wagner, Femmes de Personne, Joan Lui, I Come on Monday, Dark Eyes, Rouge Basier, The Artisan, Una Vittoria, Lapse of Memory, Mon Amie Max, According to Pereira.
TELEVISION: The Charterhouse of Parma, The Nightmare Years.

KELLERMAN, SALLY
Actress. b. Long Beach, CA, June 2, 1936. m. Jonathan Krane. e. Hollywood H.S. Studied acting in N.Y. at the Actors Studio and in Hollywood with Jeff Corey. Recorded album Roll With the Feeling. Has done voice-overs for many commercials.
THEATRE: Women Behind Bars, Holiday.
PICTURES: Reform School Girl (debut, 1959), Hands of a Stranger, The Third Day, The Boston Strangler, The April Fools, M*A*S*H (Acad. Award nom.), Brewster McCloud, Last of the Red Hot Lovers, Lost Horizon, Slither, Reflection of Fear, Rafferty and the Gold Dust Twins, The Big Bus,

Welcome to L.A., The Mouse and His Child (voice), Magee and the Lady, A Little Romance, Serial, Head On (Fatal Attraction), Foxes, Loving Couples, Moving Violations, Lethal (KGB: The Secret War), Back to School, That's Life!, Meatballs III, Three For the Road, Someone to Love, You Can't Hurry Love, Paramedics (voice), All's Fair, Limit Up, The Secret of the Ice Cave, The Player, Doppelganger, Happily Ever After (voice), Younger and Younger, Ready to Wear (Pret-a-Porter). TELEVISION: Mini-Series: Centennial. Movies: For Lovers Only, Dempsey, Secret Weapons, September Gun, Drop Dead Gorgeous, Boris and Natasha (also assoc. prod.). Specials: Big Blonde, Verna: USO Girl, Elena, Faerie Tale Theatre, Dr. Paradise. Guest: Mannix, It Takes a Thief, Chrysler Theatre.

KELLEY, DeFOREST
Actor. b. Atlanta, GA, Jan. 20, 1920. e. Decatur Boys' H.S.
PICTURES: Fear in the Night (debut, 1947), Variety Girl, Canon City, The Men, House of Bamboo, Taxi, Illegal, The Man in the Gray Flannel Suit, Tension at Table Rock, Gunfight at the O.K. Corral, Raintree County, The Law and Jake Wade, Warlock, Where Love Has Gone, Marriage on the Rocks, Apache Uprising, Night of the Lepus, Star Trek: The Motion Picture, Star Trek II: The Wrath of Khan, Star Trek III: The Search for Spock, Star Trek IV: The Voyage Home, Star Trek V: The Final Frontier, Star Trek VI: The Undiscovered Country. TELEVISION: Series: Star Trek. Guest: Gunsmoke, The Lineup, Matinee Theatre, The Web, Playhouse 90, Bonanza, Bat Masterson, The Deputy, Perry Mason, The Virginian, Room 222.

KELLEY, SHEILA
Actress. b. Philadelphia,. PA, 1964.
PICTURES: Wish You Were Here, Some Girls, Breaking In, Staying Together, Mortal Passions, Where the Heart Is, Soapdish, Pure Luck, Singles, Passion Fish, Wild Blade. TELEVISION: Series: L.A. Law, Sisters. Movie: The Secretary.

KELLOGG, PHILIP M.
Executive. b. March 17, 1912, Provo, WA. e. UCLA. Special feature writer for Hearst papers and magazines, 1933-34; MGM story dept., production dept., Irving Thalberg unit, 1934-35; Warner Bros. film editor, 1935-41; Berg-Allenberg Agency, 1941-50; U.S. Naval Reserve officer, 1941-46; William Morris Agency, 1950-present, co-head of m.p. dept., dir. WMA, Ltd., London.

KELLY, FRANK
Executive. Was assoc. prod. of AM Los Angeles, then exec. prod./program dir. for KABC-TV prior to joining Paramount. 1983, named v.p. programming for Paramount domestic tv division; 1985, promoted to sr. v.p. 1989, became exec. v.p. programming. 1995, named pres. of creative affairs for domestic tv division of Paramount Television Group.

KELLY, GENE
Actor, Director, Dancer, Choreographer. b. Pittsburgh, PA, Aug. 23, 1912. e. Pennsylvania State U., U. of Pittsburgh. Bricklayer, concrete mixer, soda clerk, dance instructor before going on B'way stage. Special Academy Award for advancing dance films, 1951. Received American Film Institute Life Achievement Award, 1985; Kennedy Center Honors, 1982.
THEATER: Actor: Leave It to Me, One for the Money, The Time of Your Life, Pal Joey. Choreographer: The Time of Your Life, Best Foot Forward, Billy Rose's Diamond Horsehoe. Director: Flower Drum Song.
PICTURES: For Me and My Gal (debut, 1942), Pilot No. 5, Du Barry Was a Lady, Thousands Cheer, The Cross of Lorraine, Cover Girl (also choreog.), Christmas Holiday, Anchors Aweigh (Acad. Award nom.; also choreog.), Ziegfeld Follies, Living in a Big Way (also choreog.), The Pirate (also co-chore-og.), The Three Musketeers, Words and Music, Take Me Out to the Ball Game (also co-choreog.), On the Town (also co-dir., choreog.), Black Hand, Summer Stock, An American in Paris (also choreog.), It's a Big Country, Singin' in the Rain (also co-dir., co-choreog.), The Devil Makes Three, Love Is Better Than Ever (cameo), Brigadoon (also choreog.), Crest of the Wave (Seagulls Over Sorrento), Deep in My Heart, It's Always Fair Weather (also co-dir., choreog.), Invitation to the Dance (also dir., s.p., choreog.), The Happy Road (also dir., prod.), Les Girls, Marjorie Morningstar, The Tunnel of Love (dir. only), Inherit the Wind, Let's Make Love, Gigot (dir. only), What a Way to Go!, A Guide for the Married Man (dir. only), The Young Girls of Rochefort, Hello Dolly! (dir. only), The Cheyenne Social Club (dir., prod. only), 40 Carats, That's Entertainment, That's Entertainment Part 2 (also dir.), Viva Knievel!, Xanadu, That's Dancing, That's Entertainment III.
TELEVISION: Series: Going My Way, The Funny Side. Specials: Salute to Baseball, Dancing Is a Man's Game (Omnibus), The Gene Kelly Pontiac Show, The Gene Kelly Show, The Julie Andrews Show, Gene Kelly in New York New York, Jack and the Beanstalk (also prod., dir.; Emmy Award as prod., 1967), Hollywood Stars of Tomorrow, Gene Kelly's

Welcome to L.A., The Mouse and His Child (voice), Magee Wonderful World of Girls, The Changing Scene, Magnavox Presents Frank Sinatra, Dick Cavett's Backlot USA, The Dorothy Hamill Special, America Salutes Richard Rodgers: The Sound of His Music, Cinderella at the Palace, Oscar's Best Actors, The Stars Salute Israel at 30, The Movie Palaces, Christmas at the Movies, others. Mini-Series: North and South, Sins. Guest: Ed Sullivan Show, $64000 Question, Mary Tyler Moore Hour, Password, The Love Boat.
(d. February 2, 1996)

KELLY, MOIRA
Actress. b. 1969. e. Marymount Col. In addition to acting also trained as violinist, operatic soprano.
PICTURES: The Boy Who Cried Bitch (debut, 1991), Billy Bathgate, The Cutting Edge, Twin Peaks: Fire Walk With Me, Chaplin, With Honors, The Lion King (voice), Little Odessa, The Tie That Binds.
TELEVISION: Movies: Love Lies and Murder, Daybreak.

KELSEY, LINDA
Actress. b. Minneapolis, MN, July 28, 1946. e. U. of Minnesota, B.A.
TELEVISION: Series: Lou Grant, Day by Day, Sessions. Movies: The Picture of Dorian Gray, Something for Joey; Eleanor and Franklin: The White House Years, The Last of Mrs. Lincoln, A Perfect Match, Attack on Fear, His Mistress, Nutcracker, Baby Girl Scott, A Place to Be Loved, A Family Torn Apart, If Someone Had Known. Special: Home Sweet Homeless. Mini-Series: Captains and the Kings.

KEMENY, JOHN
Producer. b. Budapest, Hungary. Producer for National Film Board of Canada, 1957-69. Formed International Cinemedia Center, Ltd. in 1969 in Montreal, as partner.
PICTURES: The Apprenticeship of Duddy Kravitz, White Line Fever, Shadow of the Hawk, Ice Castles, Atlantic City, Bay Boy, The Wraith, Quest for Fire (co-prod.), Nowhere to Hide (exec. prod.), Iron Eagle II, Gate II.
TELEVISION: Murderers Among Us: The Simon Wiesenthal Story (co-prod.), Josephine Baker.

KEMP, JEREMY
Actor. b. Chesterfield, England, Feb. 3, 1935. e. Abbottsholme Sch., Central Sch. of Speech and Drama. Service with Gordon Highlanders. Early career on stage incl. Old Vic Theatre Company, 1959-61. Recent theatre: Celebration, Incident at Vichy, Spoiled, The Caretaker. National Theatre, 1979-80.
PICTURES: Cleopatra (debut, 1963), Dr. Terror's House of Horrors, Face of a Stanger, Operation Crossbow (The Great Spy Mission), Cast a Giant Shadow, The Blue Max, Assignment K, Twist of Sand, The Strange Affair, Darling Lili, The Games, Sudden Terror (Eye Witness), Pope Joan, The Bellstone Fox, The Blockhouse, The Seven Percent Solution, East of Elephant Rock, Queen of Diamonds, A Bridge Too Far, The Thoroughbreds (Treasure Seekers), Leopard in the Snow, Caravans, The Prisoner of Zenda, The Return of the Soldier, Top Secret!, When the Whales Came, Angels and Insects.
TELEVISION: Z Cars, The Lovers of Florence, The Last Reunion, Colditz, Brassneck, Rhinemann Exchange, Lisa, Goodbye, Henry VIII, St. Joan, The Winter's Tale, Unity, The Contract, Sadat, King Lear, Sherlock Holmes, George Washington, Peter the Great, The Winds of War, War and Remembrance, Slip-Up (The Great Paper Chase), Cop-out, Summers Lease, Prisoner of Honor, Duel of Hearts, Star Trek: The Next Generation (guest).

KEMPER, VICTOR J.
Cinematographer. b. Newark, NJ, April 14, 1927. e. Seton Hall, B.S./Engineer. Channel 13, Newark 1949-54; Tech. supervisor EUE Screen Gems NY 1954-56; v.p. engineering General TV Network. Pres. VJK Prods.
PICTURES: Husbands, The Magic Garden of Stanley Sweetheart, They Might Be Giants, Who is Harry Kellerman?, The Hospital, The Candidate, Last of the Red Hot Lovers, Shamus, The Friends of Eddie Coyle, Gordon's War, The Hideaways, The Gambler, The Reincarnation of Peter Proud, Dog Day Afternoon, Stay Hungry, The Last Tycoon, Mikey and Nicky, Slapshot, Audrey Rose, Oh God!, The One and Only, Coma, Eyes of Laura Mars, Magic, Night of the Juggler, And Justice for All, The Jerk, The Final Countdown, Xanadu, The Four Seasons, Chu Chu and the Philly Flash, Partner, Author! Author!, National Lampoon's Vacation, Mr. Mom, The Lonely Guy, Cloak and Dagger, Secret Admirer, Pee-wee's Big Adventure, Clue, Bobo, Hot to Trot, Cohen and Tate, See No Evil, Hear No Evil, Crazy People, FX2, Another You, Married to It, Beethoven, Tommy Boy, Eddie.

KENNEDY, BURT
Director, Writer. b. Muskegon, MI, Sept. 3, 1922. e. Ravenna H.S. U.S. Army 1942-46; awarded Silver Star, Bronze Star and Purple Heart with Oak Leaf Cluster. Began as writer of TV and film scripts, and was writer, producer and director of Combat series and many TV and theatrical westerns.

PICTURES: *Writer:* Seven Men From Now, Gun the Man Down, Man in the Vault, the Tall T, Fort Dobbs, Ride Lonesome, Yellostone Kelly, Comanche Station, Six Black Horses, Stary Away Joe, The Littlest Horse Thiefs, White Hunter Black Heart. *Director:* The Canadians (debut, 1961; also s.p.), Mail Order Bride (also s.p.), The Rounders (also s.p.), The Money Trap, Return of the Seven, The War Wagon, Welcome to Hard Times (also s.p.), Support Your Local Sheriff, The Good Guys and the Bad Guys, Young Billy Young (also s.p.), Dirty Dingus Magee, Support Your Local Gunfighter (also exec. prod.), Hannie Caulder (also s.p. as Z.X. Jones), The Deserter, The Train Robbers (also s.p.), The Killer Inside Me, Wolf Lake (also s.p.), The Trouble with Spies (also prod., s.p.), Big Bad John (also s.p.), Suburban Commando.
TELEVISION: *Series:* Combat (prod., writer) The Rounders (also writer), How the West Was Won, The Yellow Rose, Simon & Simon, Magnum P.I. *Mini-Series:* The Rhinemann Exchange. *Movies:* Shoot out in a One-Dog Town, Side kicks (also prod.), All the Kind Strangers, Kate Bliss and the Ticker Tape Kid, The Wild Wild West Revisted, The Concrete Cowboys, More Wild Wild West, The Alamo-Thirteen Days to Glory, Down the Long Hills, Once Upon a Texas Train (also prod., writer), Where the Hell's That Gold?!!? (also prod., writer).

KENNEDY, GEORGE
Actor. b. New York, NY, Feb. 18, 1925. At 2 acted in touring co. of Bringing Up Father. At 7, disc jockey with his own radio show for children. Served in Army during WWII, earning two Bronze Stars and combat and service ribbons. In Army 16 years, became Capt. and Armed Forces Radio and TV officer. 1957, opened first Army Information Office, N.Y. Served as technical advisor to Phil Silvers's Sergeant Bilko TV series. Began acting in 1959 when discharged from Army.
PICTURES: The Little Shepard of Kingdom Come (debut, 1961), Lonely Are the Brave, The Man From the Diner's Club, Charade, Strait- Jacket, Island of the Blue Dolphins, McHale's Navy, Hush... Hush... Sweet Charlotte, Mirage, In Harm's Way, The Sons of Katie Elder, The Flight of the Phoenix, Shenandoah, Hurry Sundown, The Dirty Dozen, Cool Hand Luke (Academy Award, best supporting actor, 1967), The Ballad of Josie, The Pink Jungle, Bandolero!, The Boston Strangler, The Legend of Lylah Claire, Guns of the Magnificent Seven, Gaily Gaily, The Good Guys and the Bad Guys, Airport, ... tick ... tick ... tick ..., Zigzag, Dirty Dingus Magee, Fool's Parade, Lost Horizon, Cahill: U.S. Marshal, Thunderbolt and Lightfoot, Airport 1975, Earthquake, The Human Factor, The Eiger Sanction, Airport '77, Ningen no Shomei (Proof of the Man), Mean Dog Blues, Death on the Nile, Brass Target, The Concorde—Airport '79, Death Ship, The Double McGuffin, Steel, Virus, Just Before Dawn, Modern Romance, A Rare Breed, Search and Destroy, Wacko, The Jupiter Menace, Bolero, Chattanooga Choo Choo, Hit and Run, Savage Dawn, The Delta Force, Radioactive Dreams, Creepshow 2, Born to Race, Demonwarp, Counterforce, Nightmare at Noon, Private Roads, Uninvited, The Terror Within, The Naked Gun: From the Files of Police Squad, Esmeralda Bay, Ministry of Vengeance, Brain Dead, Hangfire, The Naked Gun 2 1/2: The Smell of Fear, Driving Me Crazy, Distant Justice, Naked Gun 33 1/3: The Final Insult.
TELEVISION: *Series:* The Blue Knight, Sarge, Counterattack: Crime in America, Dallas. *Guest:* Sugarfoot, Cheyenne. *Movies:* See How They Run, Sarge: The Badge or the Cross, Priest Killer, A Great American Tragedy, Deliver Us From Evil, A Cry in the Wilderness, The Blue Knight, The Archer: Fugitive from the Empire, Jesse Owens Story, Liberty, International Airport, Kenny Rogers as the Gambler III, The Gunfighters, What Price Victory, Good Cops Bad Cops, Final Shot: The Hank Gathers Story. *Mini-Series:* Backstairs at the White House.

KENNEDY, JOSEPH W.
Executive. a.k.a. Scott Kennedy. b. New York, NY, Feb. 11, 1934. e. La Salle, NYU. Started as office boy at NBC in 1950, before studying acting in NY. Appeared on TV in The Defenders and The Naked City, in film Advise and Consent. Host of Scott Kennedy Luncheon radio show in 1964. Joined United Artists in Boston in 1967 as salesman. UA Chicago sls. mgr. 1969-72; Jacksonville branch mgr. 1972-78; southern div. mgr. 1978-79. 1980 named v.p. & asst. gen. sls. mgr. responsible for UA eastern sls. territories. 1983 joined Tri-Star Pictures as v.p. southern div. mgr. Dallas.

KENNEDY, KATHLEEN
Producer. b. 1954. Raised in Weaverville and Redding in No. Calif. e. San Diego State U. Early TV experience on KCST, San Diego, working as camera operator, video editor, floor director and news production coordinator. Produced talk show, You're On. Left to enter m.p. industry as prod. asst. on Steven Spielberg's 1941. Founding member and pres. of Amblin Entertainment. 1992, with husband and partner Frank Marshall formed the Kennedy/Marshall Company.

PICTURES: Raiders of the Lost Ark (prod. assoc.), Poltergeist (assoc. prod.), E.T.: The Extra-Terrestrial (prod.), Twilight Zone: The Movie (co-assoc. prod.), Indiana Jones and the Temple of Doom (assoc. prod.). *Exec. prod.* (with Frank Marshall): Gremlins, The Goonies, Back to the Future, The Color Purple (prod.), Young Sherlock Holmes (co-prod.), An American Tail, Innerspace, Empire of the Sun, Batteries Not Included, Who Framed Roger Rabbit, The Land Before Time, Indiana Jones and the Last Crusade, (prod. exec.), Dad, Always (prod.), Joe Versus the Volcano, Gremlins II, Hook (co-prod.), Noises Off, Alive, A Far Off Place, Jurassic Park, Milk Money, The Bridges of Madison County, Congo, The Indian in the Cupboard, Twister. *Exec. Prod:* Schindler's List, A Dangerous Woman, The Flintstones, Lost World.
TELEVISION: Amazing Stories (spv. prod.), You're On (prod.), Roger Rabbit & the Secrets of Toontown (exec. prod.).

KENNEY, H. WESLEY
Producer, Director. b. Dayton, OH, Jan. 3, 1926. e. Carnegie Inst. of Tech. Guest Instructor, UCLA; guest lecturer, Televisia: Mexico City.
THEATER: *Dir.* Ten Little Indians (Advent Th., L.A.), The Best Christmas Pageant Ever, Love Letters (WV State Theatre), Shadowlands (Tracey Roberts Theatre).
TELEVISION: *Series:* All in the Family (dir.), The Jefferson (pilot dir.), Days of Our Lives (exec. prod. 1979-81), Ladies Man (dir.), Filthy Rich (dir.), Flo (dir.), The Young and the Restless (exec. prod. 1981-86), General Hospital (exec. prod. 1986-89). Dir. Sopa Break. Infomercials (dir.): Elements of Beauty, Merle Norman Experience,

KENSIT, PATSY
Actress. b. London, England, Mar. 4, 1968. Made film debut at the age of 4 in The Great Gatsby. Later appeared in commercials directed by Tony Scott and Adrian Lyne.
PICTURES: The Great Gatsby (debut, 1974), Alfie Darling, The Blue Bird, Hanover Street, Absolute Beginners, Lethal Weapon 2, A Chorus of Disapproval, Chicago Joe and the Showgirl, Timebomb, Twenty-One, Blue Tornado, Blame It on the Bellboy, Beltenebros, Kleptomania, The Turn of the Screw, Bitter Harvest, Angels and Insects, Grace of My Heart.
TELEVISION: *BBC:* Great Expectations, Silas Marner, Tycoon: The Story of a Woman, Adam Bede. *U.S.:* The Corsican Brothers, Fall from Grace, Love and Betrayal: The Mia Farrow Story.

KENT, JEAN
Actress. r.n. Joan Summerfield. b. London, England, June 29, 1921. e. Marist Coll., Peekham, London. First stage appearance at 3; at age 10 played in parents' act; chorus girl at Windmill Theatre, London, 1935; 2 yrs. repertory before debuting on screen under real name.
PICTURES: The Rocks of Valpre (High Treason; debut, 1934), It's That Man Again (first film as Jean Kent, 1943), Fanny by Gaslight (Man of Evil), Champagne Charlie, 2000 Women, Madonna of the Seven Moons, The Wicked Lady, The Rake's Progress (The Notorious Gentleman), Caravan, The Magic Bow, The Man Within (The Smugglers), Good Time Girl, Bond Street, Sleeping Car to Trieste, Trottie True (Gay Lady), Her Favorite Husband, The Woman in Question, The Browning Version, The Big Frame (The Lost Hours), Before I Wake (Shadow of Fear), The Prince and the Showgirl, Bonjour Tristesse, Grip of the Strangler (The Haunted Strangler), Beyond This Place (Web of Evidence), Please Turn Over, Bluebeard's Ten Honeymoons, Shout at the Devil, The Saving of Aunt Esther.
TELEVISION: A Call on the Widow, The Lovebird, The Morning Star, November Voyage, Love Her to Death, The Lion and the Mouse, The Web, Sir Francis Drake series, Yvette, Emergency Ward 10, County Policy, Coach 7, Smile on the Face of the Tiger, No Hiding Place, Kipling, This Man Craig, The Killers, Vanity Fair, A Night with Mrs. Da Tanka, United serial. The Family of Fred, After Dark, Thicker than Water series, The Young Doctors, Brother and Sister, Up Pompei, Steptoe and Son, Doctor at Large, Family at War, K is for Killing, Night School, Tycoon series, Crossroads (series), Lyttons Diary, Lovejoy (series), Missing Persons, After Henry (series), Shrinks (series).

KENT, JOHN B.
Theatre executive, Attorney. b. Jacksonville, FL, Sept. 5, 1939. e. Yale U., U. of FL, Law Sch., NYU grad. sch. of law (LL.M. in taxation, 1964). Partner in Kent Ridge & Crawford, P.A.; pres. & dir, Kent Investments, Inc. 1977-; dir., v.p. & gen. counsel, Kent Theatres, Inc. 1970-; dir. & v.p., Kent Enterprises, Inc. 1961-; dir. & v.p. Kent Cinemas Inc. 1993-. Was pres. of Kent Theatres Inc. 1967-70; resigned to devote full time to law practice. NATO dir. 1972 and Presidents' Advisory Cabinet, 1979-; v.p./dir. NATO of FL, 1968-. Member of Rotary Club ofJacksonville, Fla. Bar Ass'n., American Bar Ass'n.

KENYON, CURTIS
Writer. b. New York, NY, March 12, 1914.
PICTURES: Woman Who Dared, Lloyds of London, Wake Up and Live, Love and Hisses, She Knew All the Answers, Twin

Beds, Seven Days' Leave, Thanks for Everything, Bathing Beauty, Fabulous Dorseys, Tulsa, Two Flags West, Mr. Ricco. TELEVISION: Cavalcade of America, Fireside Theatre, Schlitz Playhouse, U.S. Steel Hour, 20th Century-Fox Hour. Series: Hawaii 5-O.

KERASOTES, GEORGE G.
Exhibitor. b. Springfield, IL. e. U. of IL, 1929-33; Lincoln Coll. of Law 1935-37. Past pres. & chmn., Kerasotes Theatres, 1935-85; Pres. & chmn., George Kersotes Corp. & GKC Theatres, Inc., 1984-96.Past pres. Theatre Owners of Illinois. Past pres. & chmn. Kerasotes Theatres, 1935-85. Past pres., Theatre Owners of America, 1959-60. Chmn. of board of TOA 1960-62; chmn. ACE Toll TV com.; bd. mem. NATO; treas., bd. of dirs., memebr, exec. comm., chmn., insurance comm. Director, St. Anthony's Hellenic Church, Hellenic Golf Classic. Director, Will Rogers Hospitals; Director, Pioneers. Robert W. Selig ShoWester of the Year, NATO, Las Vegas, 1992.

KERKORIAN, KIRK
Executive. b. Fresno, CA, June 6, 1917. e. Los Angeles public schools. Served as capt., transport command, RAF, 1942-44. Commercial air line pilot from 1940; founder Los Angeles Air Service (later Trans Intl. Airlines Corp.), 1948; Intl. Leisure Corp., 1968; controlling stockholder, Western Airlines, 1970; chief exec. officer, MGM, Inc., 1973-74; chmn. exec. com., vice-chmn. bd., 1974-1978. Stepped down from exec. positions while retaining financial interest in MGM/UA. Repurchased MGM in the summer of 1996.

KERNER, JORDAN
Producer. e. Stanford U, A.B. Political Science & Communications; U.C. Berkely, J.D.-M.B.A.. Bgean career in entertainment working for CBS affiliate KPIX-TV. Joined law firm of Ball, Hunt, Brown & Baerwitz. Talent & Program Negotiator for CBS. Worked for Universal Pictures & QM Prods., 1978-81. Joined ABC Entertainment as dir., Dramatic Series Develop-ment. Promoted to v.p., 1983. While at ABC, placed Moonlight-ing, MacGyver, Dynasty, Spencer for Hire, Call To Glory. Founded the Avnet/Kerner Co. in 1986 with Jordan Kerner. Currently dir., Allied Communications, Inc. Member, bd. of dirs., The Starbright Foundation, The Chrysalis Foundation. Member, President's Advisory Council for the City of Hope, Sen. Dianne Feinstein's California Cabinet, Planned Parenthood, Earth Communications Office, A.M.P.A.S., A.F.I. Former gov., Academy of Television Arts & Sciences. Founder and former co-chmn., Committee for the Arts of the Beverly Hills Bar Asoc. Founder, COMM/ENT, the Journal of Communications & Entertainment Law.
PICTURES: Less Than Zero, Funny About Love, The Mighty Ducks, Fried Green Tomatoes, The War, The Three Musketeers, When A Man Loves A Woman, D2: The Mighty Ducks, D3: The Mighty Ducks, George of the Jungle, Miami Rhapsody (exec. prod.), Up Close and Personal, Swiss Family Robinson, Dinner For Two at the El Cortez, To Live For, Friday Night Lights, Blaze of Glory, sequel to Fried Green Tomatoes (as yet, untitled), Mila 18.
TELEVISION: The Switch, For Their Own Good, Side By Side, My First Love, Do You Know the Muffin Man, The Nightman, Backfield in Motion, Heat Wave, Breaking Point.

KERNS, JOANNA
Actress. b. San Francisco, CA, Feb. 12, 1953. r.n. Joanna de Varona. Former gymnast, became dancer, appeared on tv commercials. Sister is Olympic swimmer and tv commentator Donna de Varona. NY stage: Ulysses in Nighttown.
PICTURES: Coma, Cross My Heart, Street Justice, An American Summer.
TELEVISION: Series: The Four Seasons, Growing Pains (also wrote one episode). Guest: Three's Company, Magnum P.I., Hill Street Blues, Hunter, etc. Movies: The Million Dollar Rip-Off, Marriage Is Alive and Well, Mother's Day on Walton's Mountain, A Wedding on Walton's Mountain, A Day of Thanks on Walton's Mountain, The Return of Marcus Welby M.D., A Bunny's Tale, The Rape of Richard Beck, Stormin' Home, Mistress, Those She Left Behind, Like Mother Like Daughter, The Preppie Murder, Blind Faith, Captive, The Nightman, Not in My Family, The Man With 3 Wives, Shameful Secrets, No Dessert Dad 'Til You Mow the Lawn, Robin Cook's Mortal Fear, See Jane Run, Whose Daughter Is She?

KERR, DEBORAH
Actress. b. Helensburgh, Scotland, Sept. 30, 1921; e. Phyllis Smale Ballet Sch. On stage 1939 in repertory before Brit. screen career began the following year. Voted Star of Tomorrow by Motion Picture Herald-Fame Poll, 1942. Voted one of top ten British money-making stars in Motion Picture Herald-Fame Poll, 1947. B'way debut in Tea and Sympathy, 1953. Received special Academy Award, 1994.
PICTURES: Major Barbara (debut, 1940), Love on the Dole, Penn of Pennsylvania, Hatter's Castle, The Day Will Dawn (The Avengers), The Life and Death of Colonel Blimp, Perfect Strangers (Vacation From Marriage), I See a Dark Stranger

(The Adventuress), Black Narcissus (Acad. Award nom.), The Hucksters (U.S. debut), If Winter Comes, Edward My Son, Please Believe Me, King Solomon's Mines, Quo Vadis, The Prisoner of Zenda, Thunder in the East, Dream Wife, Julius Caesar, Young Bess, From Here to Eternity (Acad. Award nom.), End of the Affair, The King and I (Acad. Award nom.), The Proud and the Profane, Tea and Sympathy, Heaven Knows Mr. Allison (Acad. Award nom.), An Affair to Remember, Bonjour Tristesse, Separate Tables (Acad. Award nom.), The Journey, Count Your Blessings, Beloved Infidel, The Sundowners (Acad. Award nom.), The Grass Is Greener, The Innocents, The Naked Edge, The Chalk Garden, The Night of the Iguana, Marriage On the Rocks, Casino Royale, Eye of the Devil, Prudence and the Pill, The Gypsy Moths, The Arrangement, The Assam Garden.
TELEVISION: Movies: A Woman of Substance, Reunion at Fairborough, Hold the Dream, Witness for the Prosecution.

KERR, FRASER
Actor. b. Glasgow, Scotland, Feb. 25, 1931. Early career in repertory. Tours of Canada and America. Ent. TV 1956. Series incl. Emergency Ward 10, Dixon of Deck Green, Murder Bag. Many Shakespeare plays. Radio: BBC Drama Rep. Co., 39 Steps, The Ringer, The Bible, What Every Woman Knows, The Ruling Class.
THEATER & TELEVISION: Night Must Fall, Never a Cross Word, The Inside Man, On the Buses, Dr. Finlay's Casebook, Wicked Woman, Madelaine July, Doctor in the House, Counterstrike, Waggoner's Walk, Juno and the Paycock, Aquarius, Erv, Upstairs and Downstairs, Cover to Cover, Janine, Robert the Bruce, Caliph of Bagdad, Watch it, Sailor!, The Fosters, Weekend World, Doctor at Sea, Dads Army, Algernon Blackwood, Waiting for Sheila, Weekend Show, Mind Your Language, Yes, Minister, Dick Emery Show, Bottle Boys, The Hard Man, Brigadoon, Hair of the Dog.
PICTURES: What a Whopper, Carry on Regardless, Way of McEagle, Thomasina, Theatre of Death, Tom, Dick and Harriet, Granny Gets the Point, Nothing but the Night, The Lord of the Rings, Kidnapped, The Derelict, Bloomfield, Ace of Diamonds, Andy Robson, It's a Deal!, Howard's Way, One Step Beyond, The Trawler.
RECORD PRODUCER: Tales of Shakespeare Series, The Casket Letters of Mary Queen of Scots.

KERSHNER, IRVIN
Director. b. Philadelphia, PA, April 29, 1923. e. Tyler Sch. of Fine Arts of Temple U., 1946; Art Center Sch., U. of Southern California. Designer, photography, adv., documentary, architectural; doc. filmmaker, U.S.I.S., Middle East, 1950-52; dir., cameraman, TV doc., Confidential File, 1953-55; dir.-prod.-writer, Ophite Prod. Appeared as actor in film The Last Temptation of Christ.
PICTURES: Stakeout on Dope Street (debut, 1958; also co-s.p.), The Young Captives, The Hoodlum Priest, A Face in the Rain, The Luck of Ginger Coffey, A Fine Madness, The Flim-Flam Man, Loving, Up the Sandbox, S*P*Y*S, The Return of a Man Called Horse, Eyes of Laura Mars, The Empire Strikes Back, Never Say Never Again, Robocop 2.
TELEVISION: Series: The Rebel, Naked City, numerous pilots and other nat'l. shows. Movies: Raid on Entebbe (theatrical in Europe), The Traveling Man. Pilot: seaQuest dsv.

KERWIN, BRIAN
Actor. b. Chicago, IL, Oct. 25, 1949. e. USC.
THEATRE: NY: Emily (Theatre World Award), Lips Together Teeth Apart, Raised in Captivity. LA: Strange Snow (LA Drama Critics Award), Who's Afraid of Virginia Woolf?, A Loss of Roses, Torch Song Trilogy.
PICTURES: Hometown USA (debut, 1979), Nickel Mountain, Murphy's Romance, King Kong Lives, Torch Song Trilogy, S.P.O.O.K.S., Hard Promises, Love Field, Gold Diggers: The Secret of Bear Mountain, Getting Away With Murder, Jack.
TELEVISION: Series: The Young and the Restless (1976-77), The Misadventures of Sheriff Lobo, Angel Falls. Mini-Series: The Chisholms, The Blue and the Gray, Bluegrass. Movies: A Real American Hero, Power, Miss All-American Beauty, Intimate Agony, Wet Gold, The Greatest Thing That Almost Happened, Challenger, Switched at Birth, Against Her Will: An Incident in Baltimore, Abandoned and Deceived, It Came From Outer Space, Sins of Silence. Special: Natica Jackson (Tales of the Hollywood Hills). Guest: St. Elsewhere, The Love Boat, B.J. and the Bear, Roseanne, Murder She Wrote, Simon & Simon, Highway to Heaven.

KEYES, EVELYN
Actress. b. Port Arthur, TX, Nov. 20, 1919. e. high school. Began career as a dancer in night clubs.
AUTHOR: Novel: I Am a Billboard (1971). Autobiographies: Scarlett O'Hara's Younger Sister (1977), I'll Think About That Tomorrow (1991).
PICTURES: Artists and Models (debut, 1937), The Buccaneer, Men With Wings, Artists and Models Abroad, Sons of the Legion, Dangerous to Know, Paris Honeymoon,

Union Pacific, Sudden Money, Gone with the Wind, Slightly Honorable, Before I Hang, Beyond Sacramento, The Lady in Question, The Face Behind the Mask, Here Comes Mr. Jordan, Ladies in Retirement, The Adventures of Martin Eden, Flight Lieutenant, There's Something About a Soldier, Dangerous Blondes, The Desperadoes, Nine Girls, Strange Affair, A Thousand and One Nights, The Jolson Story, Renegades, The Thrill of Brazil, The Mating of Millie, Johnny O'Clock, Enchantment, Mrs. Mike, Mr. Soft Touch, The Killer That Stalked New York, Smuggler's Island, The Iron Man, The Prowler, One Big Affair, Shoot First, 99 River Street, Hell's Half Acre, It Happend in Paris, Top of the World, The Seven Year Itch, Around the World in 80 Days, Across 110th Street, Return to Salem's Lot, Wicked Stepmother.
TELEVISION: Guest: Murder She Wrote.

KEYLOUN, MARK
Actor. b. Dec. 20, 1960. e. Georgetown U. Worked in New York theatre.
PICTURES: Those Lips Those Eyes, Sudden Impact, Forty-Deuce, Mike's Murder.
TELEVISION: Evergreen, War Stories: The Mine.

KIDD, MICHAEL
Choreographer, Dancer, Actor. r.n. Milton Greenwald. b. Brooklyn, NY, Aug. 12, 1919. e. CCNY. Studied dance at School of the American Ballet. Was dancer with Lincoln Kirstein's Ballet Caravan, Eugene Loring's Dance Players, Ballet Theatre. Became stage choreographer starting in 1945.
THEATER: B'way (choreographer): Finian's Rainbow (Tony Award, 1947), Love Life, Arms and the Girl, Guys and Dolls (Tony Award, 1951), Can-Can (Tony Award, 1954), Li'l Abner (Tony Award, 1957; also dir., prod.), Destry Rides Again (Tony Award, 1960; also dir.), Wildcat (also dir., co-prod.), Subways Are for Sleeping (also dir.), Here's Love, Ben Franklin in Paris, Skyscraper, The Rothschilds (also dir.). B'way (dir.): Cyrano, Good News, Pal Joey, The Music Man, The Goodbye Girl.
PICTURES: Choreographer: Where's Charley?, The Band Wagon, Knock on Wood, Seven Brides for Seven Brothers, Guys and Dolls, Merry Andrew (also dir.), Li'l Abner, Star!, Hello Dolly!, Movie Movie (also actor). Actor: It's Always Fair Weather, Smile, Skin Deep.
TELEVISION: Specials (choreographer): Baryshnikov in Hollywood, Academy Awards. Movie (actor): For the Love of It.

KIDDER, MARGOT
Actress. r.n. Margaret Kidder. b. Yellowknife, Canada, Oct. 17, 1948.
PICTURES: The Best Damned Fiddler From Calabogie to Kaladar (debut, 1968), Gaily Gaily, Quackser Fortune Has a Cousin in the Bronx, Sisters, A Quiet Day in Belfast, The Gravy Train, Black Christmas, The Great Waldo Pepper, 92 in the Shade, The Reincarnation of Peter Proud, Superman, Mr. Mike's Mondo Video, The Amityville Horror, Willie and Phil, Superman II, Heartaches, Shoot the Sun Down, Some Kind of Hero, Trenchcoat, Superman III, Little Treasure, GoBots (voice), Superman IV: The Quest for Peace, Miss Right, Mob Story, White Room, Crime and Punishment.
TELEVISION: Series: Nichols, Shell Game. Movies: Suddenly Single, The Bounty Man, Honky Tonk, Louisiana, The Glitter Dome, Picking Up the Pieces, Vanishing Act, Body of Evidence, To Catch a Killer, One Woman's Courage, Bloodknot. Specials: Bus Stop, Pygmalion. Guest: Murder She Wrote. Director: White People, Love 40.

KIDMAN, NICOLE
Actress. b. Hawaii, June 20, 1967. m. actor Tom Cruise. Raised in Australia. Made acting debut at 14 in Australian film Bush Christmas. On Australian stage in Steel Magnolias (Sydney Theatre Critics Award for Best Newcomer).
PICTURES: Bush Christmas (debut, 1982), BMZ Bandits, Windrider, Dead Calm, Emerald City, Days of Thunder, Billy Bathgate, Far and Away, Flirting, Malice, My Life, Batman Forever, To Die For (Golden Globe, 1996), Portrait of a Lady.
TELEVISION: Mini-Series (Australia): Five-Mile Creek, Vietnam, Bangkok Hilton.

KIDRON, BEEBAN
Director. b. London, England. e. National Film School. Made co-dir. debut (with Amanda Richardson) with documentary Carry Greenham Home (Chicago Film Fest. Hugo Award, 1983).
PICTURES: Antonia and Jane, Used People, Great Moments in Aviation, To Wong Foo—Thanks for Everything—Julie Newmar.
TELEVISION: The Global Gamble, Vroom, Oranges Are Not the Only Fruit.

KIEL, RICHARD
Actor. b. Detroit, MI, Sept. 13, 1939. Former nightclub bouncer.
PICTURES: The Phantom Planet (debut, 1961), Eegah!, House of the Damned, The Magic Sword, Roustabout, The Human Duplicators, Las Vegas Hillbillies, A Man Called

Dagger, Skidoo, The Longest Yard, Flash and the Firecat, Silver Streak, The Spy Who Loved Me, Force 10 from Navarone, They Went Thataway and Thataway, Moonraker, The Humanoid, So Fine, Hysterical, Cannonball Run II, Pale Rider, Think Big, The Giant of Thunder Mountain (also co-s.p., co-exec. prod.).
TELEVISION: Series: The Barbary Coast, Van Dyke & Company. Movies: Now You See It Now You Don't, The Barbary Coast (pilot).

KIERZEK, TERRY
Executive. b. Chicago, IL, Feb. 15, 1951. e. U. of Il. Joined Paramount Pictures Domestic Distrib., as booker in Chicago, 1974. Promoted to Sales in 1976, Dallas, TX. Named branch mgr., Dallas/OK City, 1978. V.P., Eastern Division in Washington, D.C., 1982-84. V.P., Southern Division, Dallas, TX., 1984-86. V.P., Western Division, Los Angeles, 1986-89. Orion Pictures v.p., Western Division, 1990-92. Joined National Film Service in 1993 as v.p., sales & mktg. Named exec. v.p., 1995. Appointed pres., National Film Service in 1996.

KIESLOWSKI, KRZYSZTOF
Director. b. Warsaw, Poland, June 27, 1941. Studied at Lodz Film School. Autobiography: Kieslowski on Kieslowksi.
PICTURES: Picture, Workers, First Love, Personnel, Biography, Scar, Politics, Hospital, Calm, Seen by the Night Porter, Station, Anator/Camera Buff, Talking Heads, A Short Day's Work, No End, Blind Chance, A Short Film About Killing/Thou Shalt Not Kill, A Short Film About Life, City Life (Seven Days a Week episode), The Double Life of Veronique, Blue, White, Red.
(d. March 13, 1996)

KILEY, RICHARD
Actor. b. Chicago, IL, Mar. 31, 1922. e. Loyola U. Started prof. career on radio in Jack Armstrong, Tom Mix, Ma Perkins, etc.
THEATER: A Streetcar Named Desire (tour), Misalliance, Kismet, Time Limit, Redhead (Tony Award, 1959), No Strings, Man of LaMancha (Tony Award, 1966), Her First Roman, The Incomparable Max, Voices, Absurd Person Singular, All My Sons.
PICTURES: The Mob (debut, 1951), The Sniper, Eight Iron Men, Pick-Up on South Street, Blackboard Jungle, The Phenix City Story, Spanish Affair, Pendulum, The Little Prince, Looking for Mr. Goodbar, Endless Love, Howard the Duck (voice), Jurassic Park (voice), Phenomenon.
TELEVISION: Series: A Year in the Life (Emmy Award, 1988). Mini-Series: The Thorn Birds (Emmy Award, 1983), George Washington, If Tomorrow Comes, A.D. Movies: Night Gallery, Incident in San Francisco, Murder Once Removed, Jigsaw, Friendly Persuasion, The Macahans, Angel on My Shoulder, Golden Gate, Isabel's Choice, Pray TV, The Bad Seed, Do You Remember Love?, My First Love, The Final Days, Gunsmoke: The Last Apache, Separate But Equal, Absolute Strangers, The Cosby Mysteries, A Passion for Justice: The Hazel Brannon Smith Story, Secrets. Specials: Mastergate, 30 Years of National Geographic Specials (narrator). Guest: Picket Fences (Emmy Award, 1994).

KILMER, VAL
Actor. b. Los Angeles, CA, Dec. 31, 1959. e. Hollywood Professional Sch., Juilliard, NY. Appeared in IMAX film Wings of Courage.
THEATRE: NY: Electra and Orestes, How It All Began (also co- writer), Henry IV Part One, Slab Boys (B'way debut), 'Tis Pity She's a Whore. Also: As You Like It (Gutherie MN), Hamlet (Colorado Shakespeare Fest.).
PICTURES: Top Secret! (debut, 1984), Real Genius, Top Gun, Willow, Kill Me Again, The Doors, Thunderheart, True Romance, The Real McCoy, Tombstone, Batman Forever, Heat, The Island of Dr. Moreau, The Ghost and the Darkness, The Saint.
TELEVISION: Movies: Murders in the Rue Morgue, The Man Who Broke 1000 Chains, Gore Vidal's Billy the Kid.

KIMBLEY, DENNIS
Executive. Early career in Kodak Testing Dept. responsible for quality control motion picture films. Joined Marketing Division 1966. Chairman BKSTS FILM 75 and FILM 79 Conference Committee. President BKSTS 1976-78. Governor, London International Film School, 1983. Bd. member, British Board of Film Classification; dir. of Children's Film Unit.

KIMBROUGH, CHARLES
Actor. b. St. Paul, MN, May 23, 1936. e. Indiana U., Yale U.
THEATER: NY: All in Love (debut, 1961), Cop-Out (B'way debut, 1969), Company (Tony nom.), Candide, Love for Love, The Rules of the Game, Secret Service, Mr. Happiness, Same Time Next Year, Drinks Before Dinner, The Dining Room, Sunday in the Park With George, Hay Fever. Several prods. with Milwaukee Rep. Theatre (1966-73).

PICTURES: The Front (debut, 1976), The Seduction of Joe Tynan, Starting Over, It's My Turn, Switching Channels, The Good Mother, The Hunchback of Notre Dame (voice). TELEVISION: Series: Murphy Brown (Emmy nom.). Movies: For Ladies Only, A Doctor's Story, Weekend War, Cast the First Stone. Pilot: The Recovery Room. Special: Sunday in the Park With George.

KING, ALAN
Actor, Producer. r.n. Irwin Alan Kingberg. b. Brooklyn, NY, Dec. 26, 1927. Started as musician, stand-up comedian in Catskills, then nightclubs. Author: Anybody Who Owns His Own Home Deserves It, Help I'm a Prisoner in a Chinese Bakery.
THEATER: The Impossible Years, The Investigation, Dinner at Eight, The Lion in Winter, Something Different.
PICTURES: Actor: Hit the Deck (debut, 1955), Miracle in the Rain, The Girl He Left Behind, The Helen Morgan Story, On the Fiddle (Operation Snafu), Bye Bye Braverman, The Anderson Tapes, Just Tell Me What You Want, Prince of the City (cameo), Author! Author!, I the Jury, Lovesick, Cat's Eye, You Talkin' to Me?, Memories of Me (also co-prod.), Enemies a Love Story, The Bonfire of the Vanities, Night and the City, Casino. Producer: Happy Birthday Gemini, Cattle Annie and Little Britches (co-prod.), Wolfen (exec. prod.).
TELEVISION: Guest/Host: The Tonight Show, Kraft Music Hall. Prod-star NBC-TV specials: Comedy is King, On Location: An Evening With Alan King at Carnegie Hall, etc. Mini-Series: Seventh Avenue. Movies: Return to Earth (co-exec. prod. only), How to Pick Up Girls (also exec. prod.), Pleasure Palace, Dad the Angel and Me, The Infiltrator. Host: Alan King: Inside the Comic Mind (Comedy Central).

KING, ANDREA
Actress. r.n. Georgette Barry. b. Paris, France, Feb. 1, 1919. e. Edgewood H.S., Greenwich, CT. m. N.H. Willis, attorney. Started career on NY stage, following high school; in Growing Pains & Fly Away Home, Boy Meets Girl, Angel Street (Boston); Life with Father (Chicago); signed by Warner, 1943. Screen debut as Georgette McKee in The Ramparts We Watch, 1940.
PICTURES: Hotel Berlin, God is My Co-Pilot, The Very Thought of You, The Man I Love, The Beast With Five Fingers, Shadow of a Woman, Roughly Speaking, My Wild Irish Rose, Ride the Pink Horse, Mr. Peabody and the Mermaid, Song of Surrender, Southside 1-10001, I Was a Shoplifter, Dial 1119, The Lemon Drop Kid, Mark of the Renegade, World in His Arms, Red Planet Mars, Darby's Rangers, Band of Angels, Daddy's Gone A-Hunting, The Linguini Incident, The Color of Evening.
TELEVISION: Movie: Prescription Murder. Specials: Dream Girl, Officer and the Lady, Witness for the Prosecution. Guest: Fireside Theatre, Maya.

KING, LARRY
Talk Show Host, Writer. b. Brooklyn, NY, Nov. 19, 1933. Started as disc jockey on various Miami radio stations from 1958-64. Became host of radio talk show, broadcast from Miami before moving to Arlington, VA, in 1978. Show has run since then on Mutual Broadcasting System. Host of CNN tv talk show since 1985, Larry King Live. Starred in tv special Larry King Extra. Columnist for Miami Beach Sun-Reporter, Sporting News, USA Today. Appeared in films Ghostbusters, Eddie and the Cruisers II: Eddie Lives, The Exorcist III.
AUTHOR: Larry King by Larry King, Tell It to the King, Mr. King You're Having a Heart Attack, Tell Me More, How to Talk to Anyone Anytime Anywhere: The Secrets of Good Conversation.

KING, PERRY
Actor. b. Alliance, OH, Apr. 30, 1948. e. Yale. Studied with John Houseman at Juilliard. B'way debut 1990 in A Few Good Men.
PICTURES: Slaughterhouse-Five (debut, 1972), The Possession of Joel Delaney, The Lords of Flatbush, Mandingo, The Wild Party, Lipstick, Andy Warhol's Bad, The Choirboys, A Different Story, Search and Destroy (Striking Back), Class of 1984, Killing Hour (The Clairvoyant), Switch, A Cry in the Night.
TELEVISION: Series: The Quest, Riptide, Almost Home, The Trouble With Larry. Guest: Medical Center, Hawaii Five-O, Apple's Way, Cannon. Mini-Series: Aspen, The Last Convertible, Captain and the Kings. Movies: Foster and Laurie, The Cracker Factory, Love's Savage Fury, City in Fear, Inmates: A Love Story, Golden Gate, Helen Keller: The Miracle Continues, Stranded, Perfect People, Shakedown on Sunset Strip, The Man Who Lived at the Ritz, Disaster at Silo 7, The Prize Pulitzer, Danielle Steel's Kaleidoscope, Only One Survived, Something to Live For, Sidney Sheldon's A Stranger in the Mirror, Jericho Fever, Good King Wenceslas, She Led Two Lives. Pilot: Half 'n' Half.

KING, PETER
Executive, Barrister-at-law. b. London, England, Mar. 22, 1928. e. Marlborough, Oxford U. (MA, honors). Bd., Shipman

& King Cinemas Ltd., 1956; borough councillor, 1959-61; chmn., London & Home counties branch, CEA, 1962-63; pres., CEA, 1964; mang. dir. Shipman & King Cinemas Ltd., 1959-68; chmn. & mang. dir. Paramount Pictures (U.K.) Ltd. Britain, 1968-70; mang. dir., EMI Cinemas and Leisure Ltd. 1970-74; chmn. & mang. dir. King Publications/pub. Screen Intl., 1974-89; pres., Screen Intl., 1989-90; chmn. & mang. dir., Rex Publications Ltd., 1990-; pub., Majesty, 1990-; pub. Preview.

KING, STEPHEN
Writer. b. Portland, ME, Sept. 21, 1947. e. Univ. of Maine at Orono (B.S.). Best-selling novelist specializing in thrillers many of which have been adapted to film by others. Movie adaptations: Carrie, The Shining, The Dead Zone, Christine, Cujo, Children of the Corn, Firestarter, Cat's Eye, Stand By Me (The Body), The Running Man, Pet Sematary, Misery, Apt Pupil, The Lawnmower Man, The Dark Half, Needful Things, The Shawshank Redemption, The Mangler, Dolores Claiborne. TV adaptations: Salem's Lot, IT, Sometimes They Come Back, The Tommyknockers, The Langoliers.
PICTURES: Knightriders (actor), Creepshow (s.p., actor), Children of the Corn (s.p.), Silver Bullet (s.p.), Maximum Overdrive (dir., s.p., actor), Creepshow II (actor), Pet Sematary (s.p., actor), Sleepwalkers (s.p., actor).
TELEVISION: Series: Golden Years (creator, writer). Mini-Series: The Stand (writer, actor), The Langoliers (actor).

KING, ZALMAN
Actor, Director, Writer. b. Trenton, NJ, 1941. r.n. Zalman King Lefkowitz. m. writer Patricia Knop.
PICTURES: Actor: The Ski Bum, You've Got to Walk It Like You Talk It or You'll Lose the Beat, Neither by Day Nor Night, Some Call It Loving, Trip with the Teacher, Sammy Somebody, The Passover Plot, Blue Sunshine, Tell Me a Riddle, Galaxy of Terror. Exec. Prod.: Roadie (also co-story), Endangered Species, Siesta. Prod./Writer: 9 1/2 Weeks. Director-Writer: Wildfire, Two Moon Junction, Wild Orchid, Wild Orchid II: Two Shades of Blue, Delta of Venus.
TELEVISION: Series: The Young Lawyers, Red Shoe Diaries (exec. prod., creator, dir. episodes). Guest: Alfred Hitchcock Presents, Land of the Giants, Gunsmoke, Adam 12, Charlie's Angels, etc. Movies: The Dangerous Days of Kiowa Jones, Stranger on the Run, The Young Lawyers (pilot), The Intruders, Smile Jenny You're Dead, Like Normal People, Lake Consequence (co-prod., co-writer).

KINGMAN, DONG
Fine Artist. b. Oakland, CA, Mar. 31, 1911. e. Hong Kong 1916-1920. 1928, mem. motion picture co., Hong Kong branch; 1935; began to exhibit as fine artist in San Francisco; promotional, advertising or main title artwork for following films: World of Suzie Wong, Flower Drum Song, 55 Days of Peking, Circus World, King Rat, The Desperados, The Sand Pebbles, Lost Horizon. 1966-67, created 12 paintings for Universal Studio Tour for posters and promotion; 1968, cover painting for souvenir program for Ringling Bros.,Barnum and Bailey Circus; treasurer for Living Artist Production since 1954; Exec. V.P. 22nd-Century Films, Inc. since 1968, Prod. & dir. short, Hongkong Dong. Also short subject film Dong Kingman, filmed and directed by James Wong Howe. 1993 Chinese-American Arts Council exhibition of all motion picture work. 1996, created official poster for Olympic Games.

KINGSLEY, BEN
Actor. r.n. Krishna Banji. b. Snaiton, Yorkshire, England, Dec. 31, 1943. Started career with Salford Players, amateur co. in Manchester. Turned pro in 1966 and appeared on London stage at a Chichester Festival Theatre. 1967, joined Royal Shakespeare Co., appearing in A Midsummer Night's Dream, Tempest, Measure for Measure, Merry Wives of Windsor, Volpone, Cherry Orchard, Hamlet, Othello, Judgement. On NY stage in Kean. Played Squeers in Nicholas Nickleby in 1980 in London.
PICTURES: Fear Is the Key (debut, 1972), Gandhi (Academy Award, 1982), Betrayal, Turtle Diary, Harem, Maurice, Testimony, Pascali's Island, Without a Clue, Bugsy (Acad. Award nom.), Sneakers, Dave, Searching for Bobby Fisher (Innocent Moves), Schindler's List, Death and the Maiden, Species, Twelfth Night.
TELEVISION: Movies/Specials: Silas Marner, Kean, Oxbridge Blues, Camille, Murderers Among Us: The Simon Wiesenthal Story, Joseph, Moses.

KINGSLEY, WALTER
Executive. b New York, NY, Oct. 20, 1923. e. Phillips Acad., Andover; Amherst Coll., B.A., 1947. Charter member Big Brothers of Los Angeles. WCOP, Boston, 1948-50; Ziv Television Programs, Inc., 1950-58; pres., Independent Television Corp. (ITC), 1958-62; member bd. dir Big Brothers of Amer.; pres. Kingsley Co., 1962-66; exec. v.p. Wolper Prods. Metromedia Prods. Corp., 1966-72; faculty, Inter-Racial Council of Business Opportunity, N.Y.; 1972-82, pres.,

Kingsley Company, Commercial Real Estate; 1983-present, special consultant, American Film Inst.; bd. mem.: Big Brothers/Big Sisters of America; Big Brothers of Greater Los Angeles.

KINOY, ERNEST
Writer. Started career in radio writing sci. fic. programs (X Minus One, Dimension X). Wrote for nearly all early dramatic shows, including Studio One, Philco Playhouse, Playhouse 90.
PICTURES: Brother John, Buck and the Preacher, Leadbelly, White Water Summer (co-s.p.).
TELEVISION: The Defenders (Emmy Award, 1964), Naked City, Dr. Kildare, Jacob and Joseph, David the King, Roots I & II, Victory at Entebbe, Skokie, Murrow, The President's Plane is Missing, Stones for Ibarra, Gore Vidal's Lincoln, The Fatal Shore.

KINSKI, NASTASSJA
Actress. r.n. Nastassja Nakszynski. b. Berlin, Germany, Jan. 24, 1960. m. prod and talent agent, Ibrahim Moussa. Daughter of late actor Klaus Kinski.
PICTURE: Falsche Bewegung (The Wrong Move; debut, 1975), To the Devil a Daughter, Passion Flower Hotel, Stay as You Are, Tess, One From the Heart, Cat People, For Your Love Only, Exposed, The Moon in the Gutter, Unfaithfully Yours, The Hotel New Hampshire, Maria's Lovers, Paris Texas, Revolution, Symphony of Love, Harem, Malady of Love, Silent Night, Torrents of Spring, On a Moonlit Night, Magdalene, The Secret, Night Sun, Faraway So Close!, Crackerjack, Terminal Velocity, The Blonde.

KIRBY, BRUNO
Actor. b. New York, NY, Apr. 28, 1949. Also acted as B. Kirby Jr., and Bruce Kirby Jr. Father is actor Bruce Kirby. On B'way 1991 in Lost in Yonkers.
PICTURES: The Harrad Experiment (debut, 1973), Cinderella Liberty, Superdad, The Godfather Part 2, Baby Blue Marine, Between the Lines, Almost Summer, Where the Buffalo Roam, Borderline, Modern Romance, This Is Spinal Tap, Birdy, Flesh + Blood, Tin Men, Good Morning Vietnam, Bert Rigby You're a Fool, When Harry Met Sally ..., We're No Angels, The Freshman, City Slickers, Hoffa (unbilled), Golden Gate, The Basketball Diaries, Donnie Brasco.
TELEVISION: Series: The Super. Movies: All My Darling Daughters, A Summer Without Boys, Some Kind of Miracle, Million Dollar Infield. Specials: Run Don't Walk (Afterschool Special), The Trap, Mastergate. Guest: Room 222, Columbo, Kojak, Emergency, It's Garry Shandling's Show, Tales From the Crypt, The Larry Sanders Show, Fallen Angels (I'll Be Waiting).

KIRK (BUSH), PHYLLIS
Actress. r.n. Phyllis Kirkegaard. b. Syracuse, NY, Sept. 18, 1926. Perfume repr. model, Conover Agcy.; B'way debut in My Name Is Aquilon followed by Point of No Return. Worked as interviewer-host on all three major networks Executive with ICPR and Stone Associates. Joined CBS News in Los Angeles, 1978; 1988 named v.p. media relations Stone/Hallinan Associates.
PICTURES: Our Very Own (debut, 1950), A Life of Her Own, Two Weeks with Love, Mrs. O'Malley and Mr. Malone, Three Guys Named Mike, About Face, The Iron Mistress, Thunder Over the Plains, House of Wax, Crime Wave, River Beat, Canyon Crossroads, Johnny Concho, Back From Eternity, City After Midnight, The Sad Sack.
TELEVISION: Series: The Red Buttons Show, The Thin Man.

KIRKLAND, SALLY
Actress. b. NY, NY, Oct. 31, 1944. e. Actors Studio, studied acting with Uta Hagen and Lee Strasberg. Achieved notoriety in the 1960s for on-stage nudity (Sweet Eros, Futz), for work in experimental off-off B'way theater and as part of Andy Warhol's inner circle. Appeared as featured actress in over 25 films and countless avant-garde shows, before winning acclaim (and Acad. Award nom.) as the star of Anna (1987). 1983 founded Sally Kirkland Acting Workshop, a traveling transcendental meditation, yoga and theatrical seminar. Formed Artists Alliance Prods. with Mark and David Buntzman, 1988.
THEATER: The Love Nest, Futz, Tom Paine, Sweet Eros, Witness, One Night Stand of a Noisy Passenger, The Justice Box, Where Has Tommy Flowers Gone?, In the Boom Boom Room (L.A., Drama-Logue's best actress award, 1981), Largo Desolato.
PICTURES: The Thirteen Most Beautiful Woman (1964), Blue, Futz!, Coming Apart, Going Home, The Young Nurses, The Way We Were, Cinderella Liberty, The Sting, Candy Stripe Nurses, Big Bad Mama, Bite the Bullet, Crazy Mama, Breakheart Pass, A Star is Born, Pipe Dreams, Hometown U.S.A., Private Benjamin, The Incredible Shrinking Woman, Human Highway, Love Letters, Fatal Games, Talking Walls, Anna, Melanie Rose (High Stakes), Crack in the Mirror (White

Hot), Paint It Black, Cold Feet, Best of the Best, Revenge, Bullseye, Two Evil Eyes, JFK, In the Heat of Passion, The Player, Blast 'Em, Primary Motive, Double Threat, Forever, Cheatin' Hearts (also co-exec. prod.).
TELEVISION: Movies: Kansas City Massacre, Death Scream, Stonestreet: Who Killed the Centerfold Model?, Georgia Peaches, Heat Wave, The Haunted. Double Jeopardy, The Woman Who Loved Elvis, Double Deception. Specials: Willow B—Women in Prison, Summer, Largo Desolato. Series: Falcon Crest. Guest: Roseanne.

KIRKWOOD, GENE
Producer. Company: Kanter-Kirkwood Entertainment.
PICTURES: Rocky, New York New York (assoc. prod.), Comes a Horseman, Uncle Joe Shannon, The Idolmaker, A Night in Heaven, Gorky Park, The Keep, The Pope of Greenwich Village, Ironweed, UHF (co-prod.).

KITT, EARTHA
Actress, Singer. b. Columbia, SC, Jan. 26, 1928. Professional career started as dancer in Katherine Dunham group; toured U.S., Mexico & Europe with group, then opened night club in Paris; in Orson Welles stage prod. of Faust (European tour); N.Y. night clubs before B'way debut in New Faces of 1952. Author: Thursday's Child, A Tart Is Not a Sweet, Alone with Me, Confessions of a Sex Kitten.
THEATRE: NY: New Faces of 1952, Shinbone Alley, Mrs. Patterson, The Skin of Our Teeth, The Owl and the Pussycat, Timbuktu.
PICTURES: New Faces (debut, 1954), The Mark of the Hawk (Accused), St. Louis Blues, Anna Lucasta, Saint of Devil's Island, Synanon, Uncle Tom's Cabin, Up the Chastity Belt, Friday Foster, The Last Resort, The Serpent Warriors, The Pink Chiquitas (voice), Master of Dragonard Hill, Erik the Viking, Ernest Scared Stupid, Boomerang, Fatal Instinct.
TELEVISION: Movies: Lt. Schuster's Wife, To Kill a Cop. Guest: Batman (as Catwoman), I Spy, Miami Vice.

KLEES, ROBERT E.
Executive. b. New York, NY, Feb. 21, 1927. e. Duke U., 1947-51. Univ. of CA Graduate Sch. of Mgt., 1973-75. U.S. Navy, 1944-46; Union Carbide Corp., 1951-57; Beckman Instruments Inc., 1957-69; International Biophysics Corp, 1969-73; sr. v.p., mktg., Deluxe Laboratories Inc., div. of 20th Century Fox, 1975-83. Retired member of AMPAS, ACE, AFI, ASC, SMPTE.

KLEIN, ALLEN
Producer. b. New Jersey, Dec. 18, 1931. e. Upsala. Pres. ABKCO Films, a division of ABKCO Music & Records, Inc.
PICTURES: Force of Impulse, Pity Me Not, Charlie is My Darling, Stranger in Town, Sympathy for the Devil, Mrs. Brown You've Got a Lovely Daughter, The Stranger Returns, The Silent Stranger, Come Together, Pearl & The Pole, Let It Be, Gimme Shelter, El Topo, Blind Man, The Concert for Bangladesh, The Holy Mountain, The Greek Tycoon, Personal Best, It Had to Be You, The Rolling Stones Rock and Roll Circus.

KLEIN, HAROLD J.
Executive. b. New York, NY, e. U. of West Virginia, New York Law Sch. Reviewer, sales staff. Showman's Trade Review; booker, Brandt Theatres; booker, later vice-pres., gen. mgr.; JJ Theatres, 1941-59; account exec., exec. v.p., dir. of world-wide sales, ABC Films, Inc., N.Y., Pres., Klein Film Assn.; exec. v.p., Plitt Theatres, Inc. to Nov. 1985; pres., H.J.K. Film Associates, also acting consultant to P.E.G. (Plitt Entertainment Gp.). Retired.

KLEIN, MALCOLM C.
Executive. b. Los Angeles, CA, Nov. 22, 1927. e. UCLA, grad., 1948; U. of Denver. Prod. dir. management, KLAC-TV (KCOP), L.A., 1948-52; acct. exec., KABC-TV, 1952-56; asst. gen. sales mgr., KABC-TV, 1956-59; exec. v.p. gen. mgr., NTA Broadcasting, N.Y., 1959; v.p., gen. mgr., RKO-General-KHJ-TV, 1960; joined National General Corp. 1968, v.p. creative services and marketing. Pres. National General TV Prods., Inc. Pres. NGC Broadcasting Corp.; 1971, pres. Filmways TV Presentations; 1972, pres. Malcolm C. Klein & Assoc. mgmt. & mktg. consultants; 1973 gen'l. exec. Sterling Recreation Org. & Gen'l Mgr. Broadcast Division; pres., American Song Festival 1976; memb. of faculty, UCLA, USC. Exec. v.p., Telease Inc. & American Subscription Television; 1981, sr. v.p., mng. dir., STAR-TV (subscription TV); 1982, sr. v.p., InterAmerican Satellite TV Network. 1983: Pres. Malcolm C. Klein & Assoc., management consultant. exec. dir. programming, Interactive Network. V.p., bus. development, Interactive Network Inc.

KLEIN, ROBERT
Actor, Comedian. b. New York, NY, Feb. 8, 1942. e. Alfred U, Yale Drama School. Was member of Chicago's Second City comedy group. Comedy albums: Child of the '50s (Grammy nom.), Mind Over Matter, New Teeth, Let's Not Make Love.

THEATRE: *NY*: The Apple Tree, Morning Noon and Night, New Faces of 1968, They're Playing Our Song (Tony Award nom.), The Sisters Rosensweig.
PICTURES: The Landlord, The Owl and the Pussycat, Rivals, The Bell Jar, Hooper, Nobody's Perfekt, The Last Unicorn (voice), Tales from the Darkside—The Movie, Radioland Murders, Mixed Nuts, Jeffrey.
TELEVISION: *Series*: Comedy Tonight, Robert Klein Time, TV's Bloopers and Practical Jokes, Sisters. *Movies*: Your Place or Mine, Poison Ivy, This Wife for Hire. *Guest*: The Tonight Show, ABC Comedy Special, George Burns Comedy Week, Twilight Zone, Late Night With David Letterman. Also appeared in HBO comedy specials.

KLEINER, HARRY
Writer, Producer. b. Philadelphia, PA, Sept. 10, 1916. e. Temple U., B.S.; Yale U., M.F.A.
PICTURES: Fallen Angel, The Street With No Name, Red Skies of Mountain, Kangaroo, Miss Sadie Thompson, Salome, Carmen Jones, The Violent Men, The Garment Jungle (also prod.), Cry Tough (also prod.), The Rabbit Trap (prod. only), Ice Palace, Fever in the Blood, Fantastic Voyage, Bullitt, Le Mans, Extreme Prejudice, Red Heat.
TELEVISION: *Writer*: Rosenberg Trial.

KLEISER, RANDAL
Director, Producer. b. Lebanon, PA, July 20, 1946. e. U. of Southern California. For Disney Theme Parks dir. 70mm 3-D film Honey I Shrunk the Audience.
PICTURES: Street People (s.p.). *Director*: Grease, The Blue Lagoon, Summer Lovers (also s.p.), Grandview U.S.A., Flight of the Navigator, North Shore (exec. prod., co-story only), Big Top Pee-Wee, Getting it Right (also co-prod.), White Fang, Return to the Blue Lagoon (exec. prod. only), Honey I Blew Up the Kid, It's My Party.
TELEVISION: *Movies*: All Together Now, Dawn: Portrait of a Teenage Runaway, The Boy in the Plastic Bubble, The Gathering. *Series*: Marcus Welby, M.D., The Rookies, Starsky and Hutch, Family.

KLINE, FRED W.
Publicist. b. Oakland, CA, May 17, 1918. e. U. of California, Berkeley. M.P. pub. rel. since 1934; pres. & owner The Fred Kline Agency; pres. Kline Communications Corp.; Kline Communications Corp.; Fred W. Kline Prod., Inc.; Capitol News Service, Sacramento; L.A. News Bureau; Capitol Radio News Service, Inc.; Advisor, Calif. Film Commission. Member, Regional Filming Task Force Committee, Los Angeles City Council.

KLINE, KEVIN
Actor. b. St. Louis, MO, Oct. 24, 1947. m. actress Phoebe Cates. e. Indiana U. Studied at Juilliard Theater Center (1968-72), and became founding member of John Houseman's The Acting Company, touring in classics, incl. The School for Scandal, She Stoops to Conquer, The Lower Depths, The Way of the World.
THEATER: Understudied Raul Julia in Lincoln Center's The Threepenny Opera; The Three Sisters (B'way debut, 1973), On the Twentieth Century (Tony Award, 1978), Loose Ends, The Pirates of Penzance (Tony Award, 1981), Richard III, Henry V (Central Park), Arms and the Man, Hamlet, Much Ado About Nothing, Hamlet (1990, also dir.), Measure for Measure.
PICTURES: Sophie's Choice (debut, 1982), The Pirates of Penzance, The Big Chill, Silverado, Violets Are Blue, Cry Freedom, A Fish Called Wanda (Academy Award for Best Supporting Actor, 1988), The January Man, I Love You to Death, Soapdish, Grand Canyon, Consenting Adults, Chaplin, Dave, George Balanchine's The Nutcracker (narrator), Princess Caraboo, French Kiss, Fierce Creatures, The Hunchback of Notre Dame (voice), The Ice Storm.
TELEVISION: *Series*: Search For Tomorrow (1976-77). *Specials*: The Time of Your Life, Hamlet (also co-dir.).

KLINGER, TONY
Producer, Director, Writer, Educator. b. London, 1950. Entered m.p. industry, 1966. In addition to continuing work in m.p. industry, currently lecturing on Film & TV at Bournemouth & Poole College of Art & Design Film School.
PICTURES: The Kids are Alright, Extremes, The Butterfly Ball, Mr. J, The Festival Game, Rock of Ages, Promo Man, Rachel's Man, Gold, Shout at the Devil (assoc. prod.), Electric Sound Sandwich, Deep Purple Rises Over Japan, Riding High (co-prod.).
TELEVISION: *Series*: You Can, Starsigns, Make the Grade (exec. prod.), Make Your Mark, Angles on Horseback.

KLUGMAN, JACK
Actor. b. Philadelphia, PA, April 27, 1922. e. Carnegie Tech. Much tv work in 1950's incl. Captain Video, Tom Corbett—Space Cadet, U.S. Steel Hour, Kraft Television Theatre, Playhouse 90.

THEATRE: *B'way*: Saint Joan, Stevedore, Mister Roberts, Gypsy, I'm Not Rappaport, Three Men on a Horse. *Tour/Stock*: The Odd Couple.
PICTURES: Timetable (debut, 1956), Twelve Angry Men, Cry Terror, The Scarface Mob, Days of Wine and Roses, I Could Go on Singing, The Yellow Canary, Act One, Hail Mafia, The Detective, The Split, Goodbye Columbus, Who Says I Can't Ride a Rainbow?, Two Minute Warning.
TELEVISION: *Series*: The Greatest Gift (daytime serial; 1954-55), Harris Against the World, The Odd Couple (2 Emmy Awards: 1971, 1973), Quincy M.E., You Again? *Guest*: The Defenders (Emmy Award, 1964), The Twilight Zone, The FBI, Ben Casey, 90 Bristol Court. *Movies*: Fame Is the Name of the Game, Poor Devil, The Underground Man, One of My Wives Is Missing, The Odd Couple: Together Again, Parallel Lives. *Mini-Series*: Around the World in 80 Days.

KNIGHT, SHIRLEY
Actress. b. Goessell, KS, July 5, 1936. e. Lake Forest Coll., D.F.A., 1978. Won 1976 Tony Award for Kennedy's Children; Joseph Jefferson Award for Landscape of the Body, 1977; New Jersey Drama Critics Awards for A Streetcar Named Desire, 1979.
PICTURES: Five Gates to Hell (debut, 1959), Ice Palace, The Dark at the Top of the Stairs (Acad. Award nom.) The Couch, Sweet Bird of Youth (Acad. Award nom.), House of Women, Flight from Ashiya, The Group, Dutchman (Venice Film Fest. Award), Petulia, The Counterfeit Killer, The Rain People, Juggernaut, Secrets, Beyond the Poseidon Adventure, Endless Love, The Sender, Prisoners, Color of Night, Stuart Saves His Family, Diabolique, Somebody if Waiting, The Man Who Counted.
TELEVISION: *Movies*: The Outsider, Shadow Over Elveron, Friendly Persuasion, Medical Story, Return to Earth, 21 Hours at Munich, The Defection of Simas Kudirka, Champions: A Love Story, Playing for Time (Emmy nom.), Billionaire Boys Club, Bump in the Night, Shadow of a Doubt, To Save a Child, When Love Kills: The Seduction of John Hearn, A Mother's Revenge, Baby Brokers, The Yarn Princess, A Part of the Family, Children of the Dust, Indictment: The McMartin Trial (Emmy Award, 1995; Golden Glove Award, 1996), Ties That Bind, The Haunting of Patricia Johnson. *Specials*: The Country Girl, The Lie. *Guest*: The Equalizer (Emmy nom.), thirtysomething (Emmy Award), Law and Order (Emmy nom.), NYPD Blue (Emmy Award, 1995), Cybill, Outer Limits Tribute.

KNOTTS, DON
Actor. b. Morgantown, WV, July 21, 1924. e. WV U., U. of AZ. Drafted into U.S. Army where became part of show called Stars and Gripes, teamed with comedian Mickey Shaughnessy. After schooling resumed was offered teaching fellowship but went to New York to try acting instead. Started out in radio show Bobby Benson and the B Bar B's. Appeared on TV, leading to role in No Time for Sergeants on B'way; appeared in film version.
PICTURES: No Time for Sergeants (debut, 1958), Wake Me When It's Over, The Last Time I Saw Archie, It's a Mad Mad Mad Mad World, Move Over Darling, The Incredible Mr. Limpet, The Ghost and Mr. Chicken, The Reluctant Astronaut, The Shakiest Gun in the West, The Love God?, How to Frame a Figg (also co-story), The Apple Dumpling Gang, No Deposit No Return, Gus, Herbie Goes to Monte Carlo, Hot Lead and Cold Feet, The Apple Dumpling Gang Rides Again, The Prize Fighter, Ther Private Eyes, Cannonball Run II, Pinocchio and the Emperor of the Night (voice), Big Bully.
TELEVISION: *Series*: Search for Tomorrow (1953-55), The Steve Allen Show, The Andy Griffith Show (5 Emmy Awards: 1961, 1962, 1963, 1966, 1967), The Don Knotts Show, Three's Company, What a Country, Matlock. *Movies*: I Love a Mystery, Return to Mayberry.

KOCH, HOWARD W.
Producer, Director. b. New York, NY, Apr. 11, 1916. Runner on Wall St. Began film career in Universal's contracts and playdate dept. in NY; asst. cutter, 20th-Fox; asst. dir., 20th-Fox, Eagle Lion, MGM; 2nd unit dir., freelance; In 1953, joined Aubrey Schenck Prod. forming Bel Air Prods., made films for U.A.; 1961-64, prod. Frank Sinatra Enterprises; v.p., chg. prod., Paramount Pictures Corp., 1964-66, Past pres. of the Academy of Motion Picture Arts and Sciences, 1977-79. 1977, elected to the National Board of Directors Guild of America for two year term. 1980 honored by NATO as prod. of year. 1985 Silver Medallion Award of Honor, Motion Picture Television Fund. Produced eight Academy Award shows, 1982-1983. Has had a 24 year relationship with Paramount as exec., prod., and dir. 1990, received Jean Hersholt Humanitarian Award, honored by Amer. Society of Cinematographers. 1991: Frank Capra Award from Directors Guild, Motion Picture Showmanship Award from the Publicists Guild; 1995: David O. Selznick Lifetime Achievement Award from the Producers Guild.
PICTURES: *Executive Producer*: Sergeants 3, The Manchurian Candidate, Come Blow Your Horn, X-15, Robin and the 7 Hoods, None But the Brave, The President's

Analyst, For Those Who Think Young, Dragonslayer. *Producer*: War Paint, Beachhead, Yellow Tomahawk, Desert Sands, Fort Yuma, Frontier Scout, Ghost Town, Broken Star, Crimes Against Joe, Three Bad Sisters, Emergency Hospital, Rebel in Town, The Black Sheep, Pharaoh's Curse, Tomahawk Trail, Revolt at Fort Laramie, War Drums, Voodoo Island, Hellbound, The Dalton Girls, The Odd Couple, On a Clear Day You Can See Forever, Plaza Suite, Star Spangled Girl, Last of the Red Hot Lovers, Jacqueline Susann's Once Is Not Enough, Some Kind of Hero, Airplane II: The Sequel, Collision Course. A Howard W. Koch *Production*: A New Leaf, Airplane!, Ghost. Director: Jungle Heat, Shield for Murder, Big House USA, Fort Bowie, Violent Road, Untamed Youth, Born Reckless, Frankenstein 1970, Andy Hardy Comes Home, The Last Mile, Girl in Black Stockings, Badge 373 (also prod.).
TELEVISION: *Director*: Miami Undercover, The Untouchables, Maverick, Cheyenne, Hawaiian Eye. *Mini-Series*: *Prod.*: The Pirate, Hollywood Wives, Crossings. *Movie*: The Odd Couple: Together Again (prod.). *Specials*: *Prod.*: Ol' Blue Eyes Is Back, Oscar's Best Actors (also dir.), Oscar's Best Movies (also dir.), Who Loves Ya Baby, On the Road with Bing (also dir.), The Stars Salute the Olympics.

KOCH, HOWARD W., JR.
Producer. b. Los Angeles, CA, Dec. 14, 1945. Was asst. dir. and in other industry posts before turning to production. Pres. & exec. off., Rastar (Peggy Sue Got Married, The Secret of My Success, Nothing in Common, Violets Are Blue, Amazing Chuck and Grace prod. under presidency); 1987, set up own prod. co. at De Laurentiis Entertainment Group. Oct. 1987: named president of the De Laurentiis Entertainment Group, Resigned April 1988 to produce independently.
PICTURES: Heaven Can Wait, The Other Side of Midnight, The Frisco Kid (exec. prod.). *Co-prod./prod.*: The Idolmaker, Gorky Park, Honky Tonk Freeway, The Keep, A Night in Heaven, The Pope of Greenwich Village, Rooftops, The Long Walk Home, Necessary Roughness, Wayne's World, The Temp, Sliver, Wayne's World 2, Losing Isaiah, Virtuosity, Primal Fear.

KOCH, JOANNE
Executive Director, The Film Society of Lincoln Center. b. NY, NY, Oct. 7, 1929. e. Goddard College, B.A. political science, 1950. Dept. of Film, Museum of Modern Art, as circulation asst., film researcher, motion picture stills archivist, 1950. Early 1960s, technical dir., film dept. MOMA, supervised the implementation of MOMA's film preservation program. 1967, asst. to publisher of Grove Press, active in preparation of Grove's case in I Am Curious Yellow censorship trial. Joined film div., Grove, first in distribution then as tech. dir. and prod. coord. 1971 joined Film Society of Lincoln Center as prog. dir. of Movies-in-the-Parks. 1971 made admin. dir. Exec. dir. of N.Y. Film Festival, Film Comment magazine, Film-in-Education, New Directors/New Films, annual Film Society Tribute and Walter Reade Theater at Lincoln Center.

KOENEKAMP, FRED J.
Cinematographer. b. Los Angeles, CA, Nov. 11, 1922. Father was special effects cinematographer Hans F. Koenekamp. Member of American Society of Cinematographers.
PICTURES: Doctor You've Got to Be Kidding, Sol Madrid, Stay Away Joe, Live a Little Love a Little, Heaven With a Gun, The Great Bank Robbery, Patton (Acad. Award nom.), Beyond the Valley of the Dolls, Flap, Skin Game, Billy Jack, Happy Birthday Wanda June, Stand Up and Be Counted, Kansas City Bomber, The Magnificent Seven Ride, Rage, Harry in Your Pocket, Papillon, Uptown Saturday Night, The Towering Inferno (Academy Award, 1974), The Wild McCullochs, Doc Savage, Posse, Embryo, Fun With Dick and Jane, The Other Side of Midnight, Islands in the Streams (Acad. Award nom.), The Bad News Bears in Breaking Training, The Dominic Principle, White Line Fever, The Swarm, The Champ, The Hunter, First Family, First Monday in October, Carbon Copy, Yes Giorgio, It Came From Hollywood, Two of a Kind, The Adventures of Buckaroo Banzai: Across the 8th Dimension, Stewardess School, Listen to Me, Welcome Home, Flight of the Intruder.
TELEVISION: *Movies*: Disaster on the Coastline, Tales of the Gold Monkey, Money on the Side, Return of the Man from U.N.C.L.E., Summer Fantasies, Whiz Kids, Flight 90— Disaster on the Potomac, Obsessive Love, City Killer, Las Vegas Strip War, A Touch of Scandal, Not My Kid, Hard Time on Planet Earth (pilot), Return of the Shaggy Dog, Foreign Exchange, Splash Too, Hard Times, many others. *Series*: The Man From U.N.C.L.E. (Emmy nom.)

KOENIG, WALTER
Actor, Writer. b. Chicago, IL, Sept. 14, 1936. e. Grinnell Coll. (IA), U. of California. Performed in summer stock; after college enrolled at Neighborhood Playhouse, N.Y.; first acting job in TV's Day in Court. *Books*: Chekov's Enterprise, Buck Alice and the Actor Robot. Creator and writer of comic book series Raver.

PICTURES: Strange Lovers, The Deadly Honeymoon, Star Trek—The Motion Picture, Star Trek II: The Wrath of Khan, Star Trek III: The Search for Spock, Star Trek IV: the Voyage Home, Star Trek V: the Final Frontier, Moontrap, Star Trek VI: The Undiscovered Country, Star Trek: Generations.
TELEVISION: *Series*: Star Trek. *Guest*: Colombo, Medical Center, Ironside, Mannix, Alfred Hitchcock Presents, Mr. Novak, Ben Casey, The Untouchables, Combat, Babylon V. *Movies*: The Questor Tapes, Goodbye Raggedy Ann. *Writer*: Family, The Class of '65, The Powers of Matthew Starr.

KOHN, HOWARD EDWARD, II
Executive. b. McKeesport, PA, Oct. 25, 1920. e. NYU. National dir. of adv., publicity, roadshow dept., United Artists; indep. prod., Hidden Fear, 1957; pres. Lioni-Warren-Kohn, Inc., 1958; national roadshow dir., Columbia Pictures, Porgy and Bess, 1959; World wide co-ordinator, national co-ordinator adv. & pub. for El Cid, 1961; named world wide co-ordinator adv., pub. all Samuel Bronston Productions, 1962; pres., Starpower Inc., 1968; exec. v.p., Avanti Films, 1970; v.p Avariac Prods., 1971; pres., Blossom Films, 1973. Elected member of ASCAP, 1975. Pres., Avanti Associates, 1976. Pres. Channel Television Prods., Inc., 1985; pres. Search Television Prods. 1988. Pres. Avanti Music Co. 1991. Exec. v.p., Petard TV and Video Prods.

KOHNER, PANCHO
Producer. b. Los Angeles, CA, Jan. 7, 1939. e. U. of Southern California, U. of Mexico, Sorbonne.
PICTURES: The Bridge in the Jungle (also dir., s.p.), The Lie, Victoria (also s.p.), Mr. Sycamore (also dir., s.p.), St. Ives, The White Buffalo, Love and Bullets, Why Would I Lie?, 10 to Midnight, The Evil That Men Do, Murphy's Law, Assassination, Death Wish IV, Messenger of Death, Kinjite.

KOHNER, SUSAN
Actress. b. Los Angeles, CA. Nov. 11, 1936. m. designer & author John Weitz. Sons Paul and Christopher Weitz are screenwriters. Mother, Lupita Tovar, was one of Mexico's leading film actresses. Father was talent rep. Paul Kohner. e. U. of California, 1954-55. Received Golden Globe Awards, 1959 and 1960. Retired from acting in 1964. Co-chair, Juilliard Council, Juilliard Sch. NY.
THEATER: Love Me Little, He Who Gets Slapped, A Quiet Place, Rose Tatoo, Bus Stop, St. Joan, Sunday in New York, Take Her She's Mine, Pullman Car, Hiawatha, as well as summer stock.
PICTURES: To Hell and Back (debut, 1955), The Last Wagon, Trooper Hook, Dino, Imitation of Life (Acad. Award nom.), The Big Fisherman, The Gene Krupa Story, All the Fine Young Cannibals, By Love Possessed, Freud.
TELEVISION: Alcoa Hour, Schlitz Playhouse, Four Star Theatre, Matinee Theatre, Climax, Suspicion, Playhouse 90, Route 66, Dick Powell Theatre.

KONCHALOVSKY, ANDREI
Director, Writer. a.k.a. Mikhalkov Konchalovski. b. Moscow, Soviet Union, Aug. 20, 1937. Great grandfather: painter Sourikov; grandfather: painter Konchalovski; father is a writer; mother poet Natalia Konchalovskaia; brother is director Nikita Mikhalkov. e. as pianist Moscow Conservatoire, 1947-57; State Film Sch. (VGIK) under Mikhail Romm (1964). Dir. debut with 1961 short film The Boy and the Pigeon. Worked as scriptwriter during 1960s especially with Andrei Tarkovsky. 1962: asst. to Tarkovsky on Ivan's Childhood. In 1980, moved to US. In 1991, moved back to Russia.
THEATRE/OPERA: The Seagull (Theatre de L'Odeon, Paris), Eugene Onegin (La Scala, Milan), La Pique Dame (La Scala, Milan & Bastille Opera, Pairs).
PICTURES: *Writer*: The Steamroller and the Violin, Andrey Rublev, Tashkent City of Bread, The Song of Manshuk, The End of Chieftain. *Director*: The First Teacher (feature debut, 1965), Asya's Happiness, A Nest of Gentlefolk, Uncle Vanya, Romance for Lovers, Siberiade (Cannes Film Fest. Award, 1979), Maria's Lovers, Runaway Train, Duet for One, Shy People (also co-s.p.), Tango and Cash, Homer and Eddie, Ryaba, My Chicken (writer, dir.), The Inner Circle (also co-s.p.).
TELEVISION: Split Cherry Terry (short).

KONIGSBERG, FRANK
Executive. b. Kew Gardens, NY, March 10, 1933. e. Yale, Yale Law Sch. Worked as lawyer at CBS for six years; moved to NBC 1960-65 in legal dept. as dir. prog. and talent administration. Left to package TV special for Artists Agency Rep. (later AFA) in Los Angeles; sr. v.p. of West Coast office seven years. Executive producer of many TV series, pilots, variety specials and made-for-TV movies. Formed own Konigsberg Company. Theatrical film debut as prod., Joy of Sex (1984).
TELEVISION: *Movies* (all exec. prod.): Pearl, Ellis Island, Bing Crosby: His Life and Legend, Dummy, Before and After, Guyana Tragedy, A Christmas Without Snow, The Pride of Jesse Hallam, Hard Case, Divorce Wars, Coming Out of the

Ice, Onassis: The Richest Man in the World, Where the Hell's That Gold?!!?, Senior Prom, Babycakes. *Series* (exec. prod.): It's Not Easy, Breaking Away, Dorothy.

KOPELSON, ARNOLD
Producer, Financier, Intl. Distributor. b. New York, NY, Feb. 14, 1935. e. New York Law Sch., J.D., 1959; NYU, B.S. 1956. Has executive-produced, produced, packaged, developed or distributed with partner, Anne Kopelson over 100 films. Handled intl. dist. of Twice in a Lifetime, Salvador, Warlock, Triumph of the Spirit and prod. Platoon. Chmn. Arnold Kopelson Prods., Co-chmn. Inter-Ocean Film Sales, Ltd. Named NATO/ShoWest Producer of the Year, 1994.
PICTURES: *Exec. Prod.*: The Legacy, Lost and Found, Night of the Juggler, Dirty Tricks, Final Assignment, Gimme an "F", Fire Birds, Warlock. *Producer*: Foolin' Around, Platoon (Academy Award for Best Picture, 1986), Triumph of the Spirit, Out for Justice, Falling Down, The Fugitive (Acad. Award nom.), Outbreak, Seven, Eraser.
TELEVISION: *Movie*: Past Tense.

KOPPEL, TED
TV News Correspondent, Anchor, Host. b. Lancashire, England, Feb. 8, 1940. To U.S. in 1953; became citizen, 1963. e. Syracuse U, Stanford U. Started as writer and news correspondent for WMCA radio in NYC. Joined ABC News in New York, 1963, serving as correspondent in Vietnam, 1967, 1969-71; Miami Bureau chief, 1968; Hong Kong Bureau chief, 1969-71; diplomatic correspondent, 1971-76, 1977-79. Anchor of NBC Saturday Night News, 1976-77. Host of Nightline, beginning in 1980. Author: The Wit and Wisdom of Adlai Stevenson, In the National Interest.
TELEVISION: *Series*: ABC News (1971-80), ABC Saturday Night News (1975-77); Nightline (1980-), 20/20 (1986). Host/anchor/writer of many ABC news specials.

KORMAN, HARVEY
Actor, Director. b. Chicago, IL, Feb. 15, 1927. e. Wright Junior Coll. Began dramatic studies at Chicago's Goodman Sch. of Drama at the Arts Inst. Acted in small roles in Broadway plays and did TV commercials until break came as comedian for Danny Kaye Show on TV. Staged comedy sketches for Steve Allen variety series in 1967. Became Carol Burnett's leading man on her show 1967-77. Directed two episodes of The New Dick Van Dyke Show.
PICTURES: Living Venus (debut, 1961), Gypsy, Lord Love a Duck, The Last of the Secret Agents?, The Man Called Flintstone (voice), Three Bites of the Apple, Don't Just Stand There, The April Fools, Blazing Saddles, Huckleberry Finn, High Anxiety, Americathon, Herbie Goes Bananas, First Family, History of the World Part I, Trail of the Pink Panther, Curse of the Pink Panther, The Longshot, Munchie, The Flintstones (voice), Radioland Murders, Dracula: Dead and Loving It.
TELEVISION: *Series*: The Danny Kaye Show, The Carol Burnett Show (4 Emmy Awards: 1969, 1971, 1972, 1974), The Tim Conway Show, Mama's Family, Leo and Liz in Beverly Hills, The Nutt House. *Movies*: Three's a Crowd, Suddenly Single, The Love Boat (pilot), Bud and Lou, The Invisible Woman, Carpool, Crash Course, Based on an Untrue Story. *Special*: The Carol Burnett Show: A Reunion (also co-exec. prod.).

KORMAN, LEWIS J.
Executive. b. 1945. Partner, Kaye, Scholer, Fierman, Hays & Handler 1978; founding partner, Gelberg & Abrams where pioneered dev. of public limited partnerships, Delphi Partners, to help finance Columbia Pictures' and Tri-Star Pictures' films. 1986, became consultant to Tri-Star involved in negotiations that led to acquisition of Loews Theatre Corp. that year. Joined Tri-Star, 1987, as sr. exec. v.p. 1988 appt. to additional post of COO and named dir. of Columbia Pictures Entertainment Inc.; 1989 also became chmn, Motion Picture Group. 1990, resigned his positions after Columbia sale to Sony. Co-founder, pres. & COO of Savoy Pictures Ent., Inc., 1992.

KORTY, JOHN
Director, Producer, Writer, Animator. b. Lafayette, IN, June 22, 1936. e. Antioch Coll, B.A. 1959. President, Korty Films. Documentary: Who Are the DeBolts? And Where Did They Get Nineteen Kids? (Academy Award: 1977; Emmy & DGA Awards: 1978-79). Short Films: The Language of Faces (AFSC, 1961), Imogen Cunningham: Photographer (AFI grant, 1970), The Music School. Animation: Breaking the Habit (Oscar nom.), Twice Upon a Time.
PICTURES: Crazy Quilt (1966), Funnyman, Riverrun, Alex and the Gypsy, Oliver's Story, Twice Upon a Time.
TELEVISION: *Movies*: The People, Go Ask Alice, Class of '63, The Autobiography of Miss Jane Pittman (Emmy & DGA Awards, 1974), Farewell to Manzanar (Humanitas, Christopher Awards), Forever, A Christmas Without Snow (also writer, prod.), The Haunting Passion, Second Sight: A

Love Story, The Ewok Adventure, Resting Place, Baby Girl Scott, Eye on the Sparrow, Winnie, Cast the First Stone, A Son's Promise, Line of Fire: The Morris Dees Story, Long Road Home, Deadly Matrimony, They, Getting Out, Redwood Curtain.

KOTCHEFF, TED
Director. r.n. William Theodore Kotcheff. b. Toronto, Canada, Apr. 7, 1931. Ent. TV ind. 1952. After five years with Canadian Broadcasting Corp. joined ABC-TV in London, 1957.
THEATER: *London*: Progress the Park, Play with a Tiger, Luv, Maggie May, The Au Pair Man, Have You Any Dirty Washing, Mother Dear?
PICTURES: Tiara Tahiti (debut, 1963), Life at the Top, Two Gentlemen Sharing, Wake in Fright, Outback, Billy Two Hats, The Apprenticeship of Duddy Kravitz, Fun with Dick and Jane, Who Is Killing the Great Chefs of Europe?, North Dallas Forty (also co-s.p.), First Blood, Split Image (also prod.), Uncommon Valor (also exec. prod.), Joshua Then and Now, The Check is in the Mail (prod. only), Switching Channels, Winter People, Weekend at Bernie's (also actor), Folks!, The Shooter.
TELEVISION: *Specials*: Of Mice and Men, Desperate Hours, The Human Voice.

KOTEAS, ELIAS
Actor. b. Montreal, Quebec, Canada, 1961. e. AADA.
PICTURES: One Magic Christmas, Some Kind of Wonderful, Gardens of Stone, Tucker: The Man and His Dream, Full Moon in Blue Water, Malarek, Blood Red, Friends Lovers and Lunatics, Teenage Mutant Ninja Turtles, Backstreet Dreams, Desperate Hours, Look Who's Talking Too, Almost an Angel, The Adjuster, Teenage Mutant Ninja Turtles III, Chain of Desire, Camilla, Exotica, The Prophecy.

KOTTO, YAPHET
Actor. b. New York, NY, Nov. 15, 1937. Has many stage credits, including starring roles on Broadway in The Great White Hope, The Zulu and the Zayda. Off-B'way: Blood Knot, Black Monday, In White America, A Good Place To Raise a Boy.
PICTURES: The Limit (also prod.), 4 for Texas, Nothing But a Man, 5 Card Stud, Thomas Crown Affair, The Liberation of L. B. Jones, Man and Boy, Across 110th Street, Bone, Live and Let Die, Truck Turner, Report to the Commissioner, Sharks' Treasure, Friday Foster, Drum, Monkey Hustle, Blue Collar, Alien, Brubaker, Fighting Back, Star Chamber, Eye of the Tiger, Warning Sign, Prettykill, The Running Man, Midnight Run, Nightmare of the Devil (also prod., dir.), Terminal Entry, Jigsaw, A Whisper to a Scream, Tripwire, Ministry of Vengeance, Hangfire, Freddy's Dead, Almost Blue, Intent to Kill, The Puppet Masters, Two If By Sea.
TELEVISION: *Series*: Homicide. *Movies*: Night Chase, Raid on Entebbe, Rage, Playing With Fire, The Park Is Mine, Women of San Quentin, Badge of the Assassin, Harem, Desperado, Perry Mason: The Case of the Scandalous Scoundrel, Prime Target, After the Shock, Chrome Soldiers, It's Nothing Personal, Extreme Justice, The American Clock, The Corpse Had a Familiar Face, Deadline for Murder: From the Files of Edna Buchanan. *Guest*: Alfred Hitchcock Presents.

KOVACS, LASZLO
Cinematographer. b. Hungary, May 14, 1933. Came to U.S. 1957; naturalized 1963. e. Acad. Drama and M.P. Arts, Budapest, MA 1956.
PICTURES: Hell's Angels on Wheels, Hell's Bloody Devils, Psych Out, The Savage Seven, Targets, A Man Called Dagger, Single Room Furnished, Easy Rider, That Cold Day in the Park, Getting Straight, Alex in Wonderland, Five Easy Pieces, The Last Movie, Marriage of a Young Stockbroker, The King of Marvin Gardens, Pocket Money, What's Up Doc?, Steelyard Blues, Paper Moon, Slither, A Reflection of Fear, Huckleberry Finn, For Pete's Sake, Freebie and the Bean, Shampoo, At Long Last Love, Baby Blue Marine, Nickelodeon, Close Encounters of the Third Kind (addl. photog. only), Harry and Walter Go to New York, New York New York, F.I.S.T., The Last Waltz, Paradise Alley, Butch and Sundance: The Early Days, The Runner Stumbles, Heart Beat, Inside Moves, The Legend of the Lone Ranger, Frances, The Toy, Crackers, Ghostbusters, Mask, Legal Eagles, Little Nikita, Say Anything, Shattered, Radio Flyer, Life With Mikey, Deception, The Next Karate Kid, The Scout, Free Willy 2: The Adventure Home, Copycat, Multiplicity.

KOZAK, HARLEY JANE
Actress. b. Wilkes-Barre, PA, Jan. 28, 1957. e. NYU's School of the Arts. Member of Nebraska Repertory Theatre.
PICTURES: House on Sorority Row, Clean and Sober, When Harry Met Sally..., Parenthood, Sideout, Arachnophobia, Necessary Roughness, The Taking of Beverly Hills, All I Want for Christmas, The Favor, Magic in the Water.
TELEVISION: *Series*: The Guiding Light, Santa Barbara, Texas, Harts of the West, Bringing Up Jack. *Guest*: L.A. Law, Highway to Heaven. *Movies*: So Proudly We Hail, The Amy Fisher Story, The Android Affair.

KOZLOWSKI, LINDA
Actress. b. 1956. m. actor Paul Hogan. Began professional
acting career soon after graduating from Juilliard Sch., N.Y.,
1981. Stage debut in How It All Began at the Public Theatre.
In regional theatre appeared in Requiem, Translations, Make
and Break, as well as on Broadway and on tour with Dustin
Hoffman in Death of a Salesman and the TV adaptation.
PICTURES: Crocodile Dundee, Crocodile Dundee II, Pass the
Ammo, Helena, Almost an Angel, The Neighbor, Village of the
Damned.
TELEVISION: Mini-Series: Favorite Son.

KRABBE, JEROEN
Actor. b. Amsterdam, The Netherlands, Dec. 5, 1944. Trained
for stage at De Toneelschool, Acad. of Dramatic Art,
Amsterdam, 1965. Also studied at painting at Acad. of Fine
Arts, grad. 1981. Founded touring theater co. in the
Netherlands and translated plays into Dutch. Also costume
designer. As a painter, work has been widely exhibited (one-
man show at Francis Kyle Galleries, London). Author: The
Economy Cookbook. Dir. debut, new stage adaptation of The
Diary of Anne Frank, 1985 in Amsterdam.
PICTURES: Soldier of Orange, A Flight of Rainbirds, Spetters,
The Fourth Man, Turtle Diary, Jumpin' Jack Flash, No Mercy,
The Living Daylights, Shadow of Victory, A World Apart,
Crossing Delancey, Shadowman, Scandal, The Punisher,
Melancholia, Till There Was You, Kafka, The Prince of Tides,
For a Lost Soldier, The Fugitive, King of the Hill, Immortal
Beloved, Farinelli, Blood of a Poet.
TELEVISION: Danton's Death (debut, 1966), William of
Orange, World War III. Movies: One for the Dancer, Family of
Spies, After the War, Secret Weapon, Robin Hood (theatrical
in Europe), Murder East Murder West, Dynasty: The Reunion,
Stalin.

KRAMER, LARRY
Writer, Producer. b. Bridgeport, CT, June 25, 1935. e. Yale U.,
B.A. 1957. Ent. m.p. ind. 1958. Story edit. Columbia Pictures,
N.Y. London 1960-65. Asst. to David Picker and Herb Jaffe,
UA, 1965. Assoc. prod. and additional dialogue Here We Go
Round the Mulberry Bush, 1968. Writ. prod. Women in Love
(Acad. Award nom. for s.p., 1970). Lost Horizon, 1973 (s.p.).
Novel: Faggots (1978). Theater: The Normal Heart (NY
Shakespeare Festival and throughout the world), Just Say No,
The Destiny of Me. Cofounder: Gay Men's Health Crisis, Inc.
(community AIDS org.). Founder: ACT UP: AIDS Coalition to
Unleash Power (AIDS activist and protest org.). Book of
Essays: Reports from the Holocaust: The Story of an AIDS
Activist (St. Martin's Press, 1995).

KRAMER, SIDNEY
Sales executive. b. New York, NY, Oct. 25, 1911. e. New York
Law Sch., LL.B., City Coll. of New York. Gen. sales mgr., RKO
Pathe, June 1953; dir. and v.p. Cellofilm Corp. 1941-56; foreign
sales mgr., RKO Radio, 1954-59; v.p. Cinemiracle Intl. 1960-
61; v.p. T.P.E.A., 1960-61; foreign sls. mgr., Cinerama, Inc.,
1962-65; exec. Commonwealth Theatres, Puerto Rico, Inc.,
1965-68; exec. v.p Cobian Jr. Enterprises Inc. 1968; m.p. consultant, exhibition, dist., foreign and Caribbean area, 1968-70;
pres. Coqui Int'l Inc.; 1970-80; v.p. of UAPR, Inc., Puerto Rico,
U.A. Communications, Inc. 1981-91. Retired.

KRAMER, STANLEY E.
Producer, Director. b. New York, NY, Sept. 29, 1913. e. NYU,
B.Sc., 1933. Entered m.p. ind. via backlot jobs; with MGM
research dept.; film cutter 3 yrs.; film ed.; m.p. & radio writer;
served in U.S Signal Corps, 1st Lt. during WWII. Recipient of
Irving G. Thalberg Award, 1961.
PICTURES: Assoc. Prod.: So Ends Our Night, The Moon and
Sixpence. Producer: So This Is New York, Champion, Home of
the Brave, The Men, Cyrano de Bergerac, Death of a
Salesman, High Noon, My Six Convicts, The Sniper, The Four
Poster, The Happy Time, Eight Iron Men, The 5000 Fingers of
Dr. T, The Wild One, The Juggler, Caine Mutiny, Pressure
Point, A Child Is Waiting, Invitation to a Gunfighter. Director-
Producer: Not as a Stranger (dir. debut, 1955), The Pride and
the Passion, The Defiant Ones, On the Beach, Inherit the
Wind, Judgment at Nuremberg, It's a Mad Mad Mad Mad
World, Ship of Fools, Guess Who's Coming to Dinner, The
Secret of Santa Vittoria, R.P.M., Bless the Beasts and
Children, Oklahoma Crude, The Domino Principle, The
Runner Stumbles.
TELEVISION: Guess Who's Coming to Dinner? (pilot).

KRANE, JONATHAN
Executive. b. 1952. m. actress Sally Kellerman. e. St. Johns
Coll. grad. with honors, 1972; Yale Law Sch., 1976. Joined
Blake Edwards Entertainment in 1981, becoming pres.
Formed talent management co. Management Company
Entertainment Group representing clients such as John
Travolta, Sally Kellerman, Kathryn Harrold, Sandra Bernhard,
Howie Mandel, Drew Barrymore, others. Began producing
vehicles for clients and transformed co. into production, distri-

bution, management and finance co. Chairman and chief
exec. officer, Management Company Entertainment Group
(MCEG).
PICTURES: Exec. prod./prod.: Boardwalk, Honeymoon, Fly
Away Home, The Man Who Loved Women, Micki & Maude, A
Fine Mess, That's Life, The Chocolate War, The Experts, Fatal
Charm, Boris and Natasha, Look Who's Talking, Chud II: Bud
the Chud, Without You I'm Nothing (prod.), Look Who's Talking
Too, Convicts, Cold Heaven, Breaking the Rules, Look Who's
Talking Now.
TELEVISION: Prod.: Howie Mandel Life at Carnegie Hall,
Howie Mandel: The North American Watusi Tour.

KRANTZ, STEVE
Executive. b. New York, NY, May 20, 1923. m. novelist Judith
Krantz. e. Columbia U., B.A. Dir. progs., NBC, New York, 1953;
dir. prog. dev., Screen Gems, N.Y., 1955; v.p., gen. mgr.
Screen Gems, Canada, 1958; dir. int. sls., 1960; formed Steve
Krantz Productions, Inc. 1964.
PICTURES: Producer: Fritz the Cat, Heavy Traffic, The Nine
Lives of Fritz the Cat, Cooley High, Ruby, Which Way Is Up?,
Jennifer. Swap Meet (also writer).
TELEVISION: Series: Steve Allen Show, Kate Smith Show,
Hazel, Dennis the Menace, Winston Churchill—The Valiant
Years, Marvel Super Heroes, Rocket Robin Hood. Mini-series:
Princess Daisy, Sins, Mistral's Daughter, I'll Take Manhattan.
Movies: Dadah is Death (exec. prod.), Till We Meet Again,
Deadly Medicine, Deadly Matrimony, Torch Song, Jack Reed:
Badge of Honor, House of Secrets, Children of the Dark,
Dazzle.

KREIMAN, ROBERT T.
Executive. b. Kenosha, WI, Sept. 16, 1924. Served WWII,
Capt Army Corps of Engineers-ETO. e. Stanford U.; U. of WI.
Dir., sales training, mgr., audio visual sales, Bell & Howell Co.,
1949-58; v.p., Argus Cameras, Inc., 1958-61; v.p., gen. mgr.,
Commercial & Educ. Div., Technicolor 1961-69, v.p. gen. mgr.,
The Suburban Companies; 1969-71, pres. & CEO, Deluxe
General, Inc. pres. & dir. of Movietonews, Inc.; bd. chmn. Keith
Cole Photograph, Inc. 1972-78; bd. chmn., pres. & CEO, Pace
International Corp., 1969-; past pres. of UCLA. Executive
Program Ass'n. Fellow SMPTE, Member M.P. Academy; TV
Academy; assoc. mem., American Society of
Cinematographers.

KRESS, HAROLD F.
Film Editor, Director. b. Pittsburgh, PA, June 26, 1913. e.
UCLA. Film ed., Command Decision, Madame Curie, Mrs.
Miniver, The Yearling; crime shorts; 5-reel Army documentary
short, Ward Care for Psychotic Patients. Member: Acad. of
M.P. Arts and Sciences, Screen Directors Guild, Film Editors
Guild.
PICTURES: Director: Painted Hills, No Questions Asked,
Apache War Smoke. Editor: Ride Vaquero, Saadia, Rose
Marie, Valley of the Kings, The Cobweb, The Prodigal, I'll Cry
Tomorrow, The Teahouse of the August Moon, Silk Stockings,
Until They Sail, Merry Andrew, Imitation General, The World
the Flesh and the Devil, Count Your Blessings, Home from the
Hill, How the West Was Won (Academy Award, 1963), The
Greatest Story Ever Told, Walk Don't Run, Alvarez Kelly, The
Poseidon Adventure, The Iceman Cometh, 99 and 44/100%
Dead, The Towering Inferno (Academy Award, 1974).

KREUGER, KURT
Actor. b. St. Moritz, Switzerland, July 23, 1917. e. U. of
Lausanne, Polytechnic. London. Came to U.S. 1937, partner in
travel bureau: acted in Wharf Theat. group. Cape Cod, 1939;
Broadway debut in Candle in the Wind with Helen Hayes,
1941.
PICTURES: The Moon Is Down, Edge of Darkness, The
Strange Death of Adolph Hitler, Sahara, Mademoiselle Fifi,
None Shall Escape, Escape in the Desert, Hotel Berlin, Paris
Underground, The Spider, Dark Corner, Unfaithfully Yours,
Spy Hunt, Fear, The Enemy Below, Legion of the Doomed,
What Did You Do in the War Daddy?, The St. Valentine's Day
Massacre.

KRIER, JOHN N.
Executive. b. Rock Island, IL. e. Augustana Coll. Joined A. H.
Blank Theatres, Grad. Publix Theatres Manager Training Sch.,
1930: managed theatres in Illinois, Iowa, Nebraska; joined
Intermountain Theatres, Salt Lake City, 1937: appointed
Purchasing Head, 1946: buyer-booker, 1952: v.p., gen. mgr.,
1955: appt. v.p. gen mgr. ABC Theas., Arizona, 1968: appt. v.p.
gen'l mgr. director Film Buying ABC Theatres of California &
ABC Intermountain Theatres, Feb. 1972. Became consultant
ABC Southern Theatres, 1974. Joined Exhibitors Relations
Inc. as partner, 1978. Elected pres., 1982. Became owner,
1988.

KRIGE, ALICE
Actress. b. Upington, South Africa. Moved to London at 22
and studied at School of Speech and Drama. Professional

debut on British TV: The Happy Autumn Fields. In London prod. of Forever Yours, Maylou. West End debut, Arms and the Man, 1981. Two seasons with Royal Shakespeare Co. at Stratford and London (The Tempest, King Lear, The Taming of the Shrew, Cyrano de Bergerac, Bond's Lear.), Venice Preserved.
PICTURES: Chariots of Fire (debut, 1981), Ghost Story, King David, Barfly, Haunted Summer, See You in the Morning, S.P.O.O.K.S., Sleepwalkers, Habitat, Institute Benjamenta, Amanda.
TELEVISION: Movies: Wallenberg: A Hero's Story, Dream West, A Tale of Two Cities, Second Serve, Baja Oklahoma, Max and Helen, Iran: Days of Crisis, Ladykiller, Judgment Day: The John List Story, Double Deception, Jack Reed: Badge of Honor, Scarlet & Black, Sharpes Honour, Summer, Devil's Advocate, Donor Unknown, Joseph. Mini-Series: Ellis Island.

KRISTOFFERSON, KRIS
Actor, Singer. b. Brownsville, TX, June 22, 1936. e. Pomona Coll., Oxford U. (Rhodes Scholar). Joined U.S. Army briefly and taught English literature at West Point. Started writing songs (country music), hits have included Me and Bobby McGee, Why Me, Lord, Sunday Mornin' Comin' Down, etc.
PICTURES: The Last Movie (debut, 1971), Cisco Pike, Pat Garrett and Billy the Kid, Blume in Love, Bring Me the Head of Alfredo Garcia, Alice Doesn't Live Here Anymore, Vigilante Force, The Sailor Who Fell from Grace with the Sea, A Star Is Born, Semi-Tough, Convoy, Heaven's Gate, Rollover, Flashpoint, Songwriter, Trouble in Mind, Big Top Pee-wee, Millennium, Welcome Home, Original Intent, Night of the Cyclone, Sandino, No Place to Hide, Cheatin' Hearts, Lone Star.
TELEVISION: Movies/Mini-Series: Freedom Road, The Lost Honor of Kathryn Beck, The Last Days of Frank and Jesse James, Blood and Orchids, Stagecoach, The Tracker, Dead or Alive, Pair of Aces, Another Pair of Aces, Miracle in the Wilderness, Christmas in Connecticut, Troubleshooters: Trapped Beneath the Earth, Big Dreams & Broken Hearts: The Dottie West Story, Tad. Mini-Series: Amerika.

KRONICK, WILLIAM
Writer, Director. b. Amsterdam, NY. e. Columbia Coll., A.B. U.S. Navy photography; wrote, dir. featurette, A Bowl of Cherries.
PICTURES: Nights in White Satin (s.p.), Horowitz in Dublin (dir., s.p.), Flash Gordon and King Kong (2nd unit dir.).
TELEVISION: Documentaries: Wrote, dir., prod.: The Ultimate Stuntman: a Tribute to Dar Robinson, To the Ends of the Earth, Mysteries of the Great Pyramid; George Plimpton Specials; National Geographic, Ripley's Believe It or Not, The World's Greatest Stunts. Prod.: In Search of... Series. Dir.: (movie) The 500 Pound Jerk.

KRUEGER, RONALD P.
Executive. b. St. Louis, MO, Oct. 19, 1940. e. Westminister Coll., 1961. Began working in theatres as a teenager. Assumed presidency Wehrenberg Theatres, 1963. Member: NATO, bd. member, regional v.p.; American Film Inst.; advisory bd. mbr., Salvation Army; Motion Picture Pioneers; Demolay Legion of Honor; bd. trustees, Westminster Col. at Fulton, MO; Divan mbr. Moolah Temple Shrine; past Master Tuscan Lodge 360 AF & AM; Scottish Rite 32 KCCH.

KRUGER, HARDY
Actor, Writer. b. Berlin, Germany, April 12, 1928. Ent. m.p. ind. 1943; on stage since 1945. Starred in approx. 25 German films). Has published 8 books, novels, travelogues, etc.
PICTURES: The One That Got Away, Bachelor of Hearts, The Rest Is Silence (German film of Hamlet), Blind Date, Taxi Pour Tobrouk, Sundays and Cybele, Hatari! (U.S. debut, 1963), Le Gros Coup, Les Pianos Mecaniques (The Uninhibited), Le Chant du Monde, Flight of the Phoenix, The Defector, La Grande Sauterelle, Le Franciscain de Bourges, The Nun of Monza, The Secret of Santa Vittoria, The Battle of Neretva, The Red Tent, Night Hair Child, Death of a Stranger, Barry Lyndon, Paper Tiger, Un Solitaire, Potato Fritz, A Bridge Too Far, L'Autopsie d'un Monstre, The Wild Geese, Society Limited, Wrong Is Right, The Inside Man.
TELEVISION: Mini-Series: War and Remembrance. Series: Globetrotter (writer, prod; 1986).

KUBRICK, STANLEY
Director, Producer, Writer. b. Bronx, NY, July 26, 1928. e. Taft H.S. Staff photog. Look magazine; dir., edit., cinematog. of short documentaries Day of the Fight, Flying Padre; dir., cinematog. of documentary The Seafarers. Received Luchino Visconti Award in Italy for contribution to the cinema, 1988.
PICTURES: Director: Fear and Desire (also prod., co-s.p., photog., edit.), Killer's Kiss (also co-prod., co-s.p., story, photog., edit.), The Killing (also s.p.), Paths of Glory (also co-s.p.), Spartacus, Lolita. Director-Producer-Writer: Dr. Strangelove, or: How I Learned to Stop Worrying and Love the Bomb, 2001: A Space Odyssey (also special photog. effects design. & dir.; Academy Award for special effects, 1968), A Clockwork Orange, Barry Lyndon, The Shining, Full Metal Jacket.

KUHN, THOMAS G.
Executive/Executive Producer. e. Northwestern U., B.A.; USC, M.B.A. KNBC-TV sales; NBC business affairs; dir. live night time progs. Warner Bros. TV, v.p. prod.; exec. prod., TV, Alice, The Awakening Land, Torn Between Two Lovers, The Jayne Mansfield Story, Long Way Home. Pres., RCA Video Prods.; pres., Lightyear Ent., 1987. Exec. prod.: Aria, The Return of Swamp Thing, Heaven, The Lemon Sisters, Stories to Remember. With partner Fred Weintraub: The JFK Assassination: The Jim Garrison Tapes, Trouble Bound, Gypsy Eyes, Backstreet Justice, Guinevere, Triplecross, Young Ivanhoe, Young Connecticut Yankee, Undertow, Playboy's Really Naked Truth.

KULIK, SEYMOUR (BUZZ)
Producer, Director. b. New York, NY, 1923. Joined CBS-TV as prod.-dir., 1956; 1964: v.p. chg. West Coast Prods., Bob Banner Associates Inc., 1965; 1967 Prod-Dir. with Paramount Studios.
PICTURES: The Explosive Generation, The Yellow Canary, Warning Shot (also prod.), Villa Rides, Riot, To Find a Man, Shamus, The Hunter.
TELEVISION: Series: Lux Video Theatre, Kraft Theatre, You Are There, Climax, Playhouse 90, The Defenders, Dr. Kildare, Twilight Zone, Dick Powell Playhouse, Kentucky Jones (exec. prod.). Movies: Vanished, Owen Marshall—Counsellor at Law (A Pattern of Morality), Brian's Song (DGA Award), Incident on a Dark Street, Pioneer Woman, Remember When, Bad Ronald, Cage Without a Key, Matt Helm, Babe, The Lindbergh Kidnapping Case, Never Con a Killer, Kill Me If You Can, Ziegfeld: The Man and His Women, From Here to Eternity, Rage of Angels, George Washington (also sprv. prod.), Kane and Abel, Her Secret Life, Women of Valor, Too Young the Hero, Around the World in 80 Days, Jackie Collins' Lucky/Chances, Miles From Nowhere.

KURALT, CHARLES
TV News Correspondent, Author. b. Wilmington, NC, Sept. 10, 1934. e. U. of North Carolina. Reporter-columnist for Charlotte News until joining CBS News as writer in 1957. Promoted to news assignment desk in 1958. Became first host of CBS News series, Eyewitness, in 1960. Named CBS News chief Latin American correspondent (based in Rio de Janeiro) in 1961 Appt. CBS News chief west coast correspondent in 1963; transferred to New York, 1964. Has worked on CBS Reports, CBS News Specials, and On the Road series for CBS Evening News (Emmy Award, 1969). Host of CBS News Sunday Morning, 1979-94. Retired from CBS News, May 1994. Author: To the Top of the World (1968), Dateline America (1979), On the Road with Charles Kuralt (1985), A Life on the Road (1990), Charles Kuralt's America (1995).

KUREISHI, HANIF
Writer. b. South London, Eng., Dec. 5, 1956. e. King's Coll. (philosophy). At 18, first play presented at Royal Court Theatre where he ushered before becoming writer in residence. Early in career, wrote pornography as Antonia French. Stage and TV plays include: The Mother Country, Outskirts, Borderline and adaptations (Mother Courage). The Rainbow Sign, With Your Tongue Down My Throat (novella) and short stories have been pub. Anglo-Pakistani writer's first s.p. My Beautiful Laundrette earned Acad. Award nom., 1986 and began creative relationship with dir. Stephen Frears.
PICTURES: My Beautiful Laundrette, Sammy and Rosie Get Laid, London Kills Me (also dir.).

KURI, EMILE
Set Decorator. b. Cuernavaca, Mex., June 11, 1907. e. Chaminade Coll., 1924-27. Career began with 50 Hopalong Cassidy episodes for Harry Sherman. Under contract to Selznick Intl., Liberty Films, and Walt Disney Prods.; supv. all film and tv sets, and all decor for both Disneyland and Disney World.
PICTURES: 71 films incl.: The Silver Queen (Acad. Award nom.), I'll Be Seeing You, Spellbound, It's a Wonderful Life, Duel in the Sun, Paradine Case, The Heiress (Academy Award, 1949), Fancy Pants, A Place in the Sun, Carrie (Acad. Award nom.), The War of the Worlds, Shane, The Actress, Executive Suite (Acad. Award nom.), 20,000 Leagues Under the Sea (Academy Award, 1954), Old Yeller, The Absent-Minded Professor (Acad. Award nom.), The Parent Trap, Mary Poppins (Acad. Award nom.), Bedknobs & Broomsticks (Acad. Award nom.).
TELEVISION: 15 seasons of The Wonderful World of Disney (Emmy Award, 1963), The Academy Awards (1960-70).

KURI, JOHN A.
Producer, Writer. b. Los Angeles, CA, Feb. 16, 1945. Son of set decorator and Disneyland co-designer, Emile Kuri. Began

13 yr. employment with Disney at age 16 in construction and maintenance at Disneyland. Progressed through mgmt. in Park Operations. 1969 transferred to Disney Studios in set decorating. 1973 became art director. 1975 at 20th Century Fox as exec. asst. to prod. Irwin Allen. 1976, formed own co., wrote and prod. both television and motion picture projects. 1979 thru 1982 developed and prod. television in partnership with Ron Howard. 1988 thru 1990 as pres. of Sheffield Ent. developed master broadcasting plan for KCMY TV, Sacramento, CA. Published works: Determined to Live: An American Epic, Remember Wes.
PICTURES: Captive Hearts (prod., co-s.p. 2nd unit dir., co-lyrics.) Set decorator: Apple Dumpling Gang, Leadbelly, Report to the Commissioner, Castaway Cowboy, Superdad, Mad Mad Movie Makers.
TELEVISION: One More Mountain (prod., writer, 2nd unit dir.; Christopher Award, 1994), Conagher (prod.; Western Heritage Award from Cowboy Hall of Fame), O'Hara (co-creator of series), Airwolf (2nd unit prod., dir.), Skyward (prod., 2nd unit dir.; Golden Halo Award), Skyward Christmas (prod., 2nd unit dir.), Through the Magic Pyramid (assoc. prod., art dir.). Art dir.: The Plutonium Incident, Scared Straight Another Story, Young Love First Love, Marriage is Alive and Well, Little Shots, The Red Pony (and set decorator, Emmy nom., 1973). Set decorator: Michael O'Hara IV, The Mouse Factory (22 episodes).

KUROSAWA, AKIRA
Director, Writer. b. Japan. March 23, 1910. e. Attended Tokyo Acad. of Fine Arts, 1928. Asst. dir. to Kajiro Yamamoto, Photo-Chemical Laboratories (PCL Studios, later renamed Toho Films), 1936-43. Became dir., 1943. Founded Kurosawa Prods., 1960; Dir. Yonki Kai Prods., 1971. Autobiography: Something Like An Autobiography (1982).
PICTURES: Director/Writer: Sanshiro Sugata (debut, 1943), The Most Beautiful, The Men Who Tread on the Tiger's Tail, Sanshiro Sugata Part 2, No Regrets for Our Youth, Those Who Make Tomorrow (co- dir.), One Wonderful Sunday, Drunken Angel, The Quiet Duel, Stray Dog, Scandal, Rashomon, The Idiot, Ikiru, The Seven Samurai, I Live in Fear, The Lower Depths (also co-prod.), Throne of Blood (also co-prod.), The Bad Sleep Well (also co-prod.), The Hidden Fortress (also co-prod.), Yojimbo (also exec. prod.), Sanjuro (also exec. prod.), High and Low (also exec. prod.), Red Beard (also exec. prod.), Dodes 'Ka-Den (also co-prod.), Dersu Uzala, Kagemusha (also co-prod.), Ran, Runaway Train (adapt. from orig. s.p. only), Akira Kurosawa's Dreams, Rhapsody in August.

KURTZ, GARY
Producer, Director. b. Los Angeles, CA, July 27, 1940. e. USC Cinema Sch. Began prof. career during college. Has worked as cameraman, soundman, editor, prod. supervisor and asst. dir. on documentaries and features. Worked on many low budget features for Roger Corman including: The Terror, Beach Ball, Track of the Vampire, Planet of Blood, The Shooting, Ride in the Whirlwind. Drafted into Marines. Spent 2 yrs. in photo field as cameraman, editor and still photo.
PICTURES: The Hostage (prod. spvr., ed.), Two-Lane Blacktop (line prod.), Chandler (line prod.), American Graffiti (co.-prod.); Star Wars (prod.), The Empire Strikes Back (prod.), The Dark Crystal (prod., 2nd unit dir.), Return to Oz (exec. prod.), Slipstream (prod.).

KURTZ, SWOOSIE
Actress. b. Omaha, NE, Sept. 6, 1944. e. Studied at U. Southern Calif., London Acad. of Music and Dramatic Art.
THEATER: A History of the American Film (Drama Desk Award), A Wilderness (Tony nom.), Who's Afraid of Virginia Woolf? (with Mike Nichols and Elaine May), The Effect of Gamma Rays on Man-in-the Moon Marigolds, Fifth of July (Tony, Outer Critics Circle & Drama Desk Awards), House of Blue Leaves (Tony and Obie Awards), Uncommon Women and Others (Obie & Drama Desk Awards), Hunting Cockroaches (Drama League nom.), Six Degrees of Separation, Lips Together Teeth Apart.
PICTURES: Slap Shot, First Love, Oliver's Story, The World According to Garp, Against All Odds, Wildcats, True Stories, Vice Versa, Bright Lights Big City, Dangerous Liaisons, Stanley and Iris, A Shock to the System, Reality Bites, Storybook, Citizen Ruth, Emma, Citizen Ruth.
TELEVISION: Series: As the World Turns (1971), Mary, Love Sidney (Emmy noms.), Sisters (Emmy & SAG noms). Movies: Walking Through the Fire, Marriage Is Alive and Well, Mating Season, A Caribbean Mystery, Guilty Conscience, A Time to Live, Baja Oklahoma (Golden Globe nom.), The Image (Emmy & Cable ACE noms.), Terror on Track 9, The Positively True Adventures of the Alleged Texas Cheerleader-Murdering Mom, And the Band Played On (Emmy & Cable Ace noms.), One Christmas, Betrayed: A Story of Three Women, A Promise to Carolyn. Specials: Uncommon Women, Fifth of July, House of Blue Leaves, The Visit (Trying Times). Guest: Kojak, Carol & Company (Emmy Award, 1990).

KURYS, DIANE
Director, Writer. b. Lyons, France, Dec. 3, 1948. In 1970 joined Jean-Louis Barrault's theatre group, acted for 8 years on stage, television and film. Adapted and translated staged plays. 1977, wrote screenplay for Dibolo Menthe (Peppermint Soda) which she also directed and co-prod. Film won Prix Louis Deluc, Best Picture. Co-prod. Alexandre Arcady's Coup de Sirocco and Le Grand Pardon.
PICTURES: Dir./Writer: Peppermint Soda (also co-prod.), Cocktail Molotov, Entre Nous, A Man in Love, C'est la vie.

KUSTURICA, EMIR
Director. b. Sarajevo, Yugoslavia, 1955. e. FAMU.
PICTURES: Do You Remember Dolly Bell? (debut, 1981; Golden Lion Award at Venice Film Fest.), When Father Was Away on Business (Golden Palme at Cannes Film Fest., 1985), Time of the Gypsies (also co-s.p.), Arizona Dream, Underground (Golden Palme at Cannes Film Fest., 1995).

KWAN, NANCY
Actress. b. Hong Kong, May 19, 1939. Trained as dancer at British Royal Ballet.
PICTURES: The World of Suzie Wong (debut, 1960), Flower Drum Song, The Main Attraction, Tamahine, Fate Is the Hunter, The Wild Affair, Honeymoon Hotel, Arrivederci Baby, Lt. Robin Crusoe USN, The Corrupt Ones, Nobody's Perfect, The Wrecking Crew, The Girl Who Knew Too Much, The McMasters, Girl From Peking, Supercock, The Pacific Connection, Project: Kill, Night Creature, Streets of Hong Kong, Angkor, Walking the Edge, Night Children, Cold Dog Soup, Dragon: The Bruce Lee Story.
TELEVISION: Movies: The Last Ninja, Blade in Hong Kong, Miracle Landing.

KWIT, NATHANIEL TROY, JR.
Executive. b. New York, NY, May 29, 1941. e. Cornell U., B.A.; NYU, M.B.A. 1964-68, American Broadcasting Co., Inc., exec. asst. to pres. of ABC Films. 1968-71, National Screen Service Corp., New York branch mgr., asst. genl. sls. mgr. 1971, founder, CEO Audience Marketing, Inc., later acquired by Viacom International as operating subsidiary. 1974 named v.p. marketing services, Warner Bros., Inc. 1979, named v.p. in charge video and special markets division, United Artists Corp.; 1981, named sr. v.p. in chg. UA television, video, special market div. Following acquisition of UA Corp. by MGM in 1981 promoted to pres., dist. & mktg. for MGM/UA Entertainment Co. 1983, pres. & CEO, United Satellite Communications, direct broadcast TV co. 1986, founder, pres. Palladium Entertainment, Inc.

L

LACHMAN, ED
Cinematographer. b. 1948. Son of a Morristown, NJ movie theater owner. e. Ohio U., BFA. Filmed documentaries Ornette: Made in America, Strippers, Huie's Sermon. Assisted Sven Nykvist on King of the Gypsies, Hurricane; Vittorio Storaro on Luna; Robby Muller on The American Friend and They All Laughed. Co-director of photography on Werner Herzog's La Soufriere and Stroszek and Wim Wenders' Lightning Over Water and A Tokyo Story.
PICTURES: Scalpel, Union City, Say Amen Somebody, Little Wars, Split Cherry Tree, Strippers, The Little Sister, Insignificance (American sequences) Desperately Seeking Susan, True Stories, Making Mr. Right, Chuck Berry: Hail Hail Rock 'n' Roll, Less Than Zero, El Dia Que Me Quieras, Mississippi Masala, Light Sleeper, London Kills Me, My New Gun, My Family/Mi Familia.
TELEVISION: Get Your Kicks on Route 66 (dir., cinematogra-phy, American Playhouse.), A Gathering of Old Men, Backtrack.

LACK, ANDREW
Executive. b. New York, NY, May 16, 1947. e. Sorbonne, Boston Univ. School of Fine Arts (BFA). Starting in 1976, worked at CBS as prod. for Who's Who, 60 Minutes, CBS Reports. 1981, named sr. prod. of CBS Reports and CBS News correspondent, 1983 became exec. prod. Exec. prod. and creator of Face to Face with Connie Chung, West 57th, Crossroads,, Our Times With Bill Moyers. Exec. prod. of Street Stories, specials The 20th Anniversary of Watergate, Malcolm X. 1993, appointed pres. of NBC News.

LADD, JR., ALAN
Executive. b. Los Angeles, CA, Oct. 22, 1937. Son of late actor Alan Ladd. Motion picture agent, Creative Management Associates, 1963-69. M.p. producer, 1969-73. Joined 20th Century-Fox in 1973 in chg. of creative affairs in feature div. Promoted to v.p., prod., 1974. 1975 named sr. v.p. for world-wide prod.; 1976, promoted to pres. of 20th Century-Fox Pictures. Resigned & formed The Ladd Co., 1979. 1985 appt. pres. & COO, MGM/UA Entertainment Film Corp; appointed

chairman of board, CEO Metro-Goldwyn-Mayer Pictures Inc., 1986; resigned 1988; 1989 named co-chmn. Pathe Communications Corp. and chmn., CEO, Pathe Entertainment. Chmn., & CEO, MGM-Pathe Ent., 1989-92. Chmn & CEO MGM-Pathe Commun. Co., 1991-92. Co-chmn. & Co-CEO, MGM, 1992-93. Founded Ladd Pictures. PICTURES: *Prod.*: Walking Stick, A Severed Head, Tam Lin, Villian, Zee and Co. *Exec. prod.*: Fear Is the Key, Nightcomers, Vice Versa, The Brady Bunch Movie, Braveheart (Academy Award).

LADD, CHERYL
Actress. r.n. Cheryl Stoppelmoor. b. Huron, S.D., July 12, 1951. Joined professional Music Shop Band while in high school; after graduation toured with group ending up in Los Angeles. Cast as voice of Melody character in animated Josie and the Pussycats. Studied acting with Milton Katselas. Did TV commercials, small parts in TV. Film debut 1972 in Jamaica Reef (aka Evil in the Deep, unreleased).
PICTURES: Purple Hearts, Now and Forever, Millennium, Lisa, Poison Ivy.
TELEVISION: *Series*: The Ken Berry "Wow" Show, Charlie's Angels, One West Waikiki. *Specials*: Ben Vereen... His Roots, General Electric's All-Star Anniversary, John Denver and the Ladies; The Cheryl Ladd Special, Looking Back: Souvenirs, Scenes From a Special. *Guest*: Police Woman, Happy Days, Switch, etc. *Movies*: Satan's School for Girls, When She Was Bad, Grace Kelly Story, Romance on the Orient Express, A Death in California, Crossings, Deadly Care, Bluegrass, Kentucky Woman, Jekyll & Hyde, The Fulfillment of Mary Gray, The Girl Who Came Between Them, Crash: The Mystery of Flight 1501, Danielle Steel's Changes, Locked Up: A Mother's Rage, Dead Before Dawn, Broken Promises: Taking Emily Back, Dancing With Danger.

LADD, DAVID ALAN
Actor, Producer, Motion Picture Executive. b. Los Angeles, CA, Feb. 5, 1947. e. USC. Son of late actor Alan Ladd. On stage in The Glass Menagerie. Exec. v.p. motion picture prod. at Pathe Entertainment and Metro-Goldwyn-Mayer.
PICTURES: *Actor*: The Big Land, The Proud Rebel (Golden Globe Award), The Sad Horse, A Dog of Flanders, Raymie, Misty, R.P.M., Catlow, Deathline (Raw Meat), The Klansman, The Day of the Locust, Wild Geese. Producer: The Serpent and the Rainbow.
TELEVISION: *Guest*: Zane Gray Theatre, Wagon Train, Pursuit, Ben Casey, Gunsmoke, Love American Style (pilot), Kojak, Emergency, Tom Sawyer, Bonanza, Quest, Police Story, Medical Story, etc. *Producer*: When She Was Bad, ABC Variety specials.

LADD, DIANE
Actress. b. Meridian, MS, Nov. 29. r.n. Diane Rose Lanier. Daughter is actress Laura Dern. e. St. Aloysius Acad.; trained for stage at Actors Studio with Frank Corsaro in N.Y. Worked as model and as Copacabana nightclub dancer. At 18 in touring co. of Hatful of Rain. NY debut: Orpheus Descending.
THEATER: Carry Me Back to Morningside Heights, One Night Stands of a Noisy Passenger. The Wall, The Goddess, The Fantastiks, Women Speak, Texas Trilogy; Lu Ann Hampton Laverty, Love Letters.
PICTURES: Wild Angels (debut, 1966), Rebel Rousers, The Reivers, Macho Callahan, WUSA, White Lightning, Chinatown, Alice Doesn't Live Here Anymore (Acad. Award nom.), Embryo, All Night Long, Sweetwater, Something Wicked This Way Comes, Black Widow, Plain Clothes, National Lampoon's Christmas Vacation, Wild at Heart (Acad. Award nom.), A Kiss Before Dying, Rambling Rose (Acad. Award nom.), The Cemetery Club, Forever, Carnosaur, Hold Me Thrill Me Kiss Me, Father Hood.
TELEVISION: *Movies*: The Devil's Daughter, Black Beauty, Thaddeus Rose and Eddie, Willa, Guyana Tragedy, Desperate Lives, Grace Kelly, Crime of Innocence, Bluegrass, Rock Hudson, The Lookalike, Shadow of a Doubt, Hush Little Baby, Mrs. Munck (also dir., writer). *Guest*: Hazel, Gunsmoke, City of Angels, The Love Boat, Dr. Quinn Medicine Woman (pilot). *Series*: The Secret Storm, Alice (Golden Globe Award). *Special*: The Gift.

LAFFERTY, PERRY
Executive. b. Davenport, IA, Oct. 3, 1920. e. Yale U. With CBS-TV as v.p., programs, Hollywood, 1965-76. Sr. v.p., programs and talent, west coast, for NBC Entertainment, 1979-85.
TELEVISION: Maybe Baby (exec. prod.), Murder C.O.D. (exec. prod.), An Early Frost (prod.).

LaGRAVENESE, RICHARD
Writer. b. Brooklyn, NY, 1960.
PICTURES: Rude Awakening, The Fisher King (Acad. Award nom.), The Ref (also prod.), A Little Princess, The Bridges of Madison County, Unstrung Heroes.

LAHTI, CHRISTINE
Actress. b. Birmingham, MI, April 4, 1950. m. dir. Thomas Schlamme. e. U. of Michigan. Trained for stage at Herbert Berghof Studios with Uta Hagen. TV commercials. As a mime, performed with Edinburgh Scotland's Travis Theatre. N.Y. stage debut in The Woods, 1978.
THEATER: The Zinger, Hooter (Playwrights Horizon), Loose Ends, Division St., The Woods (Theatre World Award), Scenes and Revelations, Present Laughter, The Lucky Spot, Summer and Smoke (LA), The Heidi Chronicles, Three Hotels.
PICTURES: ...And Justice For All (debut, 1979), Whose Life Is It Anyway?, Ladies and Gentlemen the Fabulous Stains, Swing Shift (Acad. Award nom.), Just Between Friends, Housekeeping, Stacking, Running on Empty, Miss Firecracker (cameo), Gross Anatomy, Funny About Love, The Doctor, Leaving Normal, Hideaway, Pie in the Sky, A Weekend in the Country, Lieberman In Love (short; Academy Award).
TELEVISION: *Series*: Chicago Hope. *Movies*: Dr. Scorpion, The Last Tenant, The Henderson Monster, The Executioner's Song, Love Lives On, Single Bars Single Women, No Place Like Home, Crazy From the Heart, The Fear Inside, The Good Fight, The Four Diamonds. *Mini-Series*: Amerika.

LAI, FRANCIS
Composer. b. France, April 26, 1932.
PICTURES: A Man and a Woman, I'll Never Forget What's 'is Name, The Bobo, Three Into Two Won't Go, Hello Goodbye, Hannibal Brooks, The Games, Mayerling, House of Cards, Rider on the Rain, Love Story (Academy Award, 1970), Le Petit Matin, Another Man, Another Chance, Wanted: Babysitter, Bilitis, The Good and the Bad, Widow's Nest, Cat and Mouse, The Body of My Enemy, Emmanuelle 2; The Forbidden Room, International Velvet, Oliver's Story, Passion Flower Hotel, Robert and Robert, The Small Timers, By the Blood Brothers, Beyond the Reef, Bolero, A Second Chance, Edith and Marcel, My New Partner, Marie, A Man and a Woman: 20 Years Later, Bernadette, Itinerary of a Spoiled Child., Der Aten (The Spirit), La Belle Histoire.
TELEVISION: The Berlin Affair, The Sex Symbol, Sins.

LAKE, RICKI
Actress. b. New York, NY, Sept. 21, 1968. e. Manhattan's Professional Children's School. Won role in Hairspray while attending Ithaca Col. Theatre in LA: A Girl's Guide to Chaos.
PICTURES: Hairspray (debut, 1988), Working Girl, Cookie, Cry-Baby, Last Exit to Brooklyn, Where the Day Takes You, Inside Monkey Zetterland, Skinner, Cabin Boy, Serial Mom, Mrs. Winterbourne.
TELEVISION: *Series*: China Beach, Ricki Lake (synd. talk show). *Movies*: Babycakes, The Chase, Based on an Untrue Story.

LAMARR, HEDY
Actress. r.n. Hedwig Kiesler. b. Vienna, Austria, Nov. 9, 1915. Started in films as script girl, bit player before gaining fame for role in 1933 Czech prod. Ecstasy. To Hollywood, 1938. Autobiography: Ecstasy and Me (1966).
PICTURES: Ecstasy, Algiers (U.S. debut, 1938), Lady of the Tropics, I Take This Woman, Boom Town, Comrade X, Come Live With Me, Ziegfeld Girl, H. M. Pulham Esq., Tortilla Flat, Crossroads, White Cargo, The Heavenly Body, The Conspirators, Experiment Perilous, Her Highness and the Bellboy, The Strange Woman, Dishonored Lady, Let's Live a Little, Samson and Delilah, A Lady Without a Passport, Copper Canyon, My Favorite Spy, Love of 3 Queens, The Story of Mankind, The Female Animal.

LAMAS, LORENZO
Actor. b. Los Angeles, CA, Jan. 20, 1958. e. Santa Monica City Coll. Son of the late actor Fernando Lamas and actress Arlene Dahl. Studied at Tony Barr's Film Actors Workshop (Burbank Studios). Appeared on commercials for Diet Coke, BVD, Coors (Hispanic).
PICTURES: Grease, Tilt, Take Down, Body Rock, Snakeater, Night of the Warrior, Snakeater II, Final Impact, Snakeater III: His Law, Killing Streets, CIA Code Name: Alexa, CIA: Target Alexa, The Swordsman, Bounty Tracker, Final Round, C.I.A.: Target Alexa II, Bad Blood.
TELEVISION: *Series*: California Fever, Secrets of Midland Heights, Falcon Crest, Dancin' to the Hits (host), Renegade. *Guest*: The Love Boat, Switch, Sword of Justice, The Hitchhiker, Dear John. *Movies*: Detour to Terror, CIA: Code Name Alexa.

LAMBERT, CHRISTOPHER (also CHRISTOPHE)
Actor, Producer. b. New York , NY, Mar. 29, 1957; reared in Geneva; parents French. Studied at Paris Conservatoire Drama Academy.
PICTURES: La Bar du Telephone (debut, 1981), Putain d'Historie d'Amour, Legitime Violence, Greystoke: The Legend of Tarzan Lord of the Apes, Love Songs, Subway (Cesar Award), Highlander, I Love You, The Sicilian, Love Dream, To Kill a Priest, Un Plan d'Enfer, Why Me?, Highlander 2: The Quickening, Priceless Beauty, Knight Moves, Fortress, Gunmen, Road Flower, Highlander III: The Sorcerer, The Hunted, Nine Months (exec. prod. only), Mortal Kombat, North Star (also exec. prod.), When Saturday Comes (exec. prod. only).

LAMBERT, MARY
Director. b. Arkansas. e. attended U. of Denver, Rhode Island Sch. of Design where began making short films. Worked in variety of prod. jobs before moving to Los Angeles and directing TV commercials and music videos (includ. Madonna's Material Girl, Like a Virgin, Like a Prayer, others for Sting, Janet Jackson and Mick Jagger).
PICTURES: Siesta, Pet Sematary, Pet Sematary 2.
TELEVISION: Movie: Dragstrip Girl.

LAMBERT, VERITY
Producer. b. London, England, Nov. 27. Ent. TV 1961; prod. Dr. Who, Adam Adamant Lives, Detective, Somerset Maugham (all BBC series). Since 1971: (series), Budgie, Between The Wars. 1974: Appt. controller of Drama, Thames Television. 1979: Chief exec. Euston Films. 1983: Director of Production Thorn EMI Films Ltd. Relinquished her position as controller of Drama Thames Television and retained position as chief exec., Euston Films. Became indep. prod. developing projects for film and TV incl. BBC. Founded own company, Cinema Verity Ltd., 1985.
PICTURES: Link, Morons from Outer Space, Restless Natives, Dreamchild, Not for Publication, Clockwise, A Cry in the Dark.
TELEVISION: May to December, The Boys from the Bush, Sleepers, GBH, So Haunt Me, Comics, Coasting, Sam Saturday, Running Late, Class Act, She's Out, Heavy Weather.

LAMOUR, DOROTHY
Actress. r.n. Mary Leta Dorothy LaPorte. b. New Orleans, LA, Dec. 10, 1914. e. Spencer's Business Sch. Miss New Orleans 1931. Sang with bands before being signed to contract by Paramount Pictures. Had two radio shows, Sealtest Variety Hour & Chase and Sanborn Hour. Autobiography: My Side of the Road (1980).
PICTURES: The Jungle Princess (debut, 1936), Swing High Swing Low, High Wide and Handsome, Last Train From Madrid, Thrill of a Lifetime, The Hurricane, Big Broadcast of 1938, Her Jungle Love, Tropic Holiday, Spawn of the North, St. Louis Blues, Man About Town, Disputed Passage, Johnny Apollo, Typhoon, Road to Singapore, Moon Over Burma, Chad Hanna, Road to Zanzibar, Caught in the Draft, Aloma of the South Seas, The Fleet's In, Beyond the Blue Horizon, Road to Morocco, Star Spangled Rhythm, They Got Me Covered, Dixie, Riding High, And the Angels Sing, Rainbow Island, A Medal for Benny, Duffy's Tavern, Masquerade in Mexico, Road to Utopia, My Favorite Brunette, Road to Rio, Wild Harvest, Variety Girl, On Our Merry Way, Lulu Belle, The Girl From Manhattan, The Lucky Stiff, Slightly French, Manhandled, Here Comes the Groom (cameo), The Greatest Show on Earth, Road to Bali, The Road to Hong Kong, Donovan's Reef, Pajama Party, The Phynx (cameo), Won Ton Ton the Dog Who Saved Hollywood (cameo), Creepshow 2.
TELEVISION: Movie: Death at Love House. Guest: Murder She Wrote, I Spy, Marcus Welby, Love Boat, Crazy Like a Fox, Remington Steele, Damon Runyon Theatre, Hart to Hart. Specials: Bob Hope Specials, Entertaining the Troops, Remembering Bing, many others.
(d. September 22, 1996)

LANDAU, MARTIN
Actor. b. Brooklyn, NY, June 20, 1930. e. Pratt Inst., Art Students League, Was cartoon and staff artist on NY Daily News; studied at Actors Studio. Daughter is actress Juliet Landau. Recipient: Lifetime Achievement Awards from Houston Film Fest. and Charleston Film Fest.
THEATER: Middle of the Night, Uncle Vanya, Stalag 17, Wedding Breakfast, First Love, The Goat Song.
PICTURES: Pork Chop Hill (debut, 1959), North by Northwest, The Gazebo, Stagecoach to Dancer's Rock, Cleopatra, The Hallelujah Trail, The Greatest Story Ever Told, Decision at Midnight, Alien Attack, Nevada Smith, They Call Me Mister Tibbs, Situation Normal But All Fouled Up, A Town Called Hell, Black Gunn, Strange Shadows in an Empty Room, Meteor, Destination Moonbase Alpha, Without Warning, Trial By Terror, Cosmic Princess, Journey Through the Black Sun, The Last Word, The Return (The Alien's Return), Alone in the Dark, The Being, Access Code, Treasure Island, Run ... If You Can, Death Blow, W.A.R.: Women Against Rape, Sweet Revenge, Cyclone, Real Bullets, Empire State, Delta Fever, Tucker: The Man and His Dream (Acad. Award nom.), Crimes and Misdemeanors (Golden Globe Award, Acad. Award nom.), Paint It Black, Firehead, Tipperary, The Color of Evening, Mistress, Eye of the Stranger, Sliver, Intersection, Time Is Money, Ed Wood (Academy Award, best supporting actor, 1994; also Golden Globe, SAG, American Comedy, NY Film Critics, LA Film Critics, Natl. Society of Film Critics, Boston Film Critics, Chicago Film Critics & Texas Film Critics Awards), City Hall, Pinocchio.
TELEVISION: Series: Mission Impossible (1966-69; 3 Emmy noms., Golden Globe Award), Space 1999. Movies: Welcome Home Johnny Bristol, Savage, The Death of Ocean View Park,

Harlem Globetrotters on Gilligan's Island, Fall of the House of Usher, Max and Helen (ACE Award nom.), The Neon Empire, By Dawn's Early Light (ACE Award nom.), Something to Live For: The Alison Gertz Story, Legacy of Lies (ACE Award), 12:01, Joseph. Numerous guest appearances.

LANDES, MICHAEL
Executive. b. Bronx, NY, Feb. 4, 1939. e. Fairleigh Dickinson, B.A., 1961; Rutgers, J.D., 1964; NYU, L.L.M., 1965. 17 years of corporate law and financing experience as sr. partner in law firm of Hahn and Hessen. Co-chairman of The ALMI Group formed, 1978. Co-chmn. & CEO of Almi Pictures Inc. formed, 1982. 1986, Almi sold its 97-screen RKO Century Warner Theatre chain to Cineplex Odeon. 1986, purchased Video Shack Inc. assets and formed RKO Warner Video, Inc.; Chmn since inception. 1988, became chairman, Damon Creations, Inc. which merged with Enro Holding Corp. and Enro Shirt Co. into Damon Creations. Sold Damon, 1988. Chmn./CEO, RKO Warner Intl. Ltd. a video franchisor and chmn./CEO of The Lexington Group Ltd., org. 1990. Member: World Presidents Organization (WPO); Chief Executives Organization (CEO); Association for a Better New York; bd. of dirs. Motion Picture Pioneers; Academy of Motion Picture Arts and Sciences; bd. of dirs. Periwinkle Theatre Productions. Produced more than ten pictures throughout his career.

LANDIS, JOHN
Director, Producer, Writer, Actor. b. Chicago, IL, Aug. 3, 1950. Raised in Los Angeles. Started in mailroom at 20th Century-Fox, then worked in Europe as prod. asst. and stuntman before making first low-budget film, Schlock.
PICTURES: Director: Schlock (also actor, writer), The Kentucky Fried Movie (also actor), National Lampoon's Animal House, The Blues Brothers (also co-s.p.), An American Werewolf in London (also s.p., actor), Trading Places, Twilight Zone—The Movie (sequence dir., also s.p., co-prod.), Into the Night (also actor), Spies Like Us, Clue (co-exec. prod., co-story only), Three Amigos!, Amazon Women on the Moon (sequence dir.; also co-exec. prod.), Coming to America, Oscar, Innocent Blood, Beverly Hills Cop III, The Stupids. Actor: Battle for the Planet of the Apes, Death Race 2000, 1941, The Muppets Take Manhattan, Spontaneous Combustion, Darkman, Diva Las Vegas, Sleepwalkers, Venice/Venice, The Silence of the Hams.
TELEVISION: Series: Dream On (exec. prod., dir., actor), Topper (exec. prod., dir.), Weird Science (exec. prod.), Sliders (exec. prod.), Campus Cops (exec. prod.). Movie: Psycho IV (actor), The Stand (actor). Videos: Thriller, Black or White (both for Michael Jackson). Specials: B.B. King Into the Night, Disneyland's 35th Anniversary Celebration.

LANDRES, PAUL
Director. b. New York, NY, Aug. 21, 1912. e. UCLA. Started as asst. film editor at Universal 1931. Editor 1937 to 1949 of many feature films. Director of feature films and TV since 1949. Under directorial contract to Warner Bros. 1961-62. Director of 22 feature films for theatrical release.
PICTURES: Oregon Passage, A Modern Marriage, Mark of the Vampire, Navy Bound, The Curse of Dracula, Miracle of the Hills, 54 Washington Street, Son of a Gunfighter, etc.
TELEVISION: Series: Bonanza, Daktari, The Rifleman, 77 Sunset Strip, Maverick Hawaiian Eye, The Plainsman, Readers Digest, Topper, Wyatt Earp, Blondie.

LANDSBURG, ALAN
Executive, Producer, Writer. b. New York, NY, May 10, 1933. e. NYU. Producer for NBC News Dept., 1951-59; producer-writer, CBS, 1959-60; exec. prod., Wolper Productions/Metromedia Producers Corp., 1961-70; chairman, The Alan Landsburg Company, 1970-present.
PICTURES: Co-exec. prod.: Jaws 3-D, Porky's II: The Next Day.
TELEVISION: Exec. prod.: Biography, National Geographic Specials (1965-70): The Undersea World of Jacques Cousteau; In Search of..., That's Incredible. Movies: Adam, Fear on Trial, Parent Trap II, Adam: His Song Continues, The George McKenna Story, Long Gone, Strange Voices, Bluegrass, A Place at the Table, Too Young the Hero, A Stoning in Fulham County, High Risk, Destined to Live, Quiet Victory: The Charlie Wedemeyer Story, The Ryan White Story, Unspeakable Acts (co-exec. prod., writer), A Mother's Right: The Elizabeth Morgan Story (writer), The Hunter (writer).

LANE, DIANE
Actress. b. New York, NY, Jan. 2, 1965. Acted in stage classics (Medea, Electra, As You Like It) at La Mama Experimental Theatre Club, NY. Addtl. stage: The Cherry Orchard, Agamemnon, Runaways, Twelfth Night.
PICTURES: A Little Romance (debut, 1979), Touched by Love, National Lampoon Goes to the Movies, Cattle Annie and Little Britches, Six Pack, Ladies and Gentlemen the Fabulous Stains, The Outsiders, Rumble Fish, Streets of Fire, The Cotton Club, The Big Town, Lady Beware, Priceless Beauty, Vital Signs, My New Gun, Chaplin, Knight Moves, Indian Summer, Judge Dredd, Wild Bill, Mad Dog Time, Jack.

TELEVISION: *Movies*: Child Bride of Short Creek, Miss All-American Beauty, Descending Angel, Oldest Living Confederate Widow Tells All. *Special*: Edith Wharton's Summer. *Guest*: Fallen Angels (Murder Obliquely). *Mini-Series*: Lonesome Dove.

LANE, NATHAN
Actor. r.n. Joseph Lane. b. Jersey City, NJ, Feb. 3, 1956. Received 1992 Obie Award for Sustained Excellence in Off-B'way Theatre.
THEATER: *B'way*: Present Laughter (Drama Desk nom.), Merlin, The Wind in the Willows, Some Americans Abroad, On Borrowed Time, Guys & Dolls (Drama Desk & Outer Critics Circle Awards; Tony nom.), Laughter on the 23rd Floor, Love! Valour! Compassion! (Drama Desk, Outer Critics Circle and Obie Awards; also Off-B'way), A Funny Thing Happened On The Way To The Forum (Tony Award). *Off-B'way*: A Midsummer Night's Dream, Measure for Measure, The Merry Wives of Windsor, She Stoops to Conquer, Claptrap, The Common Pursuit (Dramalogue Award), In a Pig's Valise, The Film Society, Uncounted Blessings, Hidden in This Picture, Love, The Lisbon Traviata (also L.A.; Drama Desk, Lucille Lortel, LA Drama Critics Circle & Dramalogue Awards), Bad Habits, Lips Together Teeth Apart (also L.A.).
PICTURES: Ironweed (debut, 1987), Joe Vs. the Volcano, The Lemon Sisters, He Said She Said, Frankie and Johnny, Life With Mikey, Addams Family Values, The Lion King (voice of Timon), Jeffrey (American Comedy Award nom.), The Birdcage.
TELEVISION: *Series*: One of the Boys. *Guest*: The Days and Nights of Molly Dodd, Miami Vice, Frasier (Emmy nom.). *Movie*: Hallmark Hall of Fame's The Boys Next Door. *Specials*: Alice in Wonderland, The Last Mile, Co-host 1995 Tony Awards, 1995 Kennedy Center Honors.

LANG, CHARLES
Cinematographer. b. Bluff, UT, March 27, 1902. e. Lincoln H.S., Los Angeles; U. of Southern California. Entered m.p. ind. with Paramount Film Laboratory, then asst. cameraman; dir. of photography, Paramount, 1929-52; then freelance.
PICTURES: Innocents of Paris, The Devil and the Deep, A Farewell to Arms (Academy Award, 1933), She Done Him Wrong, Death Takes a Holiday, Lives of a Bengal Lancer, Souls at Sea, Tovarich, Spawn of the North, Midnight, Arise My Love, The Shepherd of the Hills, The Uninvited, Blue Skies, The Ghost and Mrs. Muir, A Foreign Affair, Miss Tatlock's Millions, Fancy Pants, September Affair, Ace in the Hole, Sudden Fear, The Big Heat, It Should Happen to You, Sabrina, Phffft!, Queen Bee, The Man from Laramie, The Rainmaker, The Solid Gold Cadillac, Gunfight at the O.K. Corral, A Farewell to Arms (1957), Wild Is the Wind, The Matchmaker, Some Like It Hot, The Magnificent Seven, Strangers When We Meet, The Facts of Life, One-Eyed Jacks, Summer and Smoke, Charade, Father Goose, Inside Daisy Clover, How to Steal a Million, Hotel, The Flim Flam Man, Wait Until Dark, The Stalking Moon, Cactus Flower, Bob & Carol & Ted & Alice, The Love Machine, Doctors' Wives, Butterflies Are Free, 40 Carats.

LANG, JENNINGS
Executive. b. New York, NY, May 28, 1915. e. St. John's U. Law Sch. m. actress-singer Monica Lewis. Went into law practice in 1937 with Seligsburg and Lewis, m.p. law specialists. 1938 to Hollywood as 2nd asst. dir. at Grand National Studios. Opened own office as actor's agent; first client, comedian Hugh Herbert. 1940 joined Jaffe Agency; made partner and v.p. in 1942. Was pres. 1948-50, resigned to join MCA. Worked in all phases of MCA operations; 1952 made v.p. of MCA TV Ltd., and bd. mem. Involved with prod. and sales of TV prods. from inception of Revue (now Universal City Studios) in 1950. Organized Revue's New Projects Dept., creator and exec. in chg. of prog. dev. Involved with creation and sales of such series as Wagon Train, The Robert Cummings Show, Bachelor Father, Wells Fargo, Mike Hammer. Supvr. of Universal's World Premiere films. Made exec. prod. at MCA (Universal) for motion pictures.
PICTURES: *Exec. prod.*: Coogan's Bluff, Winning, Tell Them Willie Boy Is Here, Puzzle of a Downfall Child, The Beguiled, They Might Be Giants, Act of the Heart, Play Misty for Me, Slaughterhouse 5, Joe Kidd, The Great Northfield Minneosta Raid, Pete 'n Tillie, High Plains Drifter, Charley Varrick, Breezy, Earthquake, Airport 1975, The Front Page, The Great Waldo Pepper, The Eiger Sanction, The Hindenburg, Airport '77. *Producer*: Swashbuckler, Rollercoaster, House Calls, Nunzio, The Concorde—Airport' 79, Little Miss Marker, The Nude Bomb, The Sting II, Stick.
(d. May 29, 1996)

LANG, OTTO
Producer, Director. b. Tesanj, Austria (now Yugoslavia), Jan. 21, 1908. e. Salzburg, Austria. Four Academy Award nominations for Cinemascope Specials, Twentieth Century-Fox Film Corp.

PICTURES: *Dir.*: Search for Paradise. *Prod.*: Call Northside 777, Five Fingers, White Witch Doctor. *Assoc. prod*: Tora! Tora! Tora!
TELEVISION: Man from U.N.C.L.E., Daktari, Iron Horse, Cheyenne, Dick Powell Show, Zane Gray Theatre, Ann Sothern Show, Rifleman, Bat Masterson, Seahunt, The Deputy, Surfside 6, Hawaiian Eye. Prod. Twentieth Century Fox Hour. *Dir.*: Man and the Challenge, Aquanauts, World of Giants, The Legend of Cortez, Beethoven: Ordeal and Triumph, Saga of Western Man.

LANG, STEPHEN
Actor. b. Queens, NY, July 11, 1952. e. Swarthmore Col. Professional debut 1974 at Washington D.C.'s Folger Theatre.
THEATER: *NY*: Rosencrantz and Guildenstern Are Dead, Henry V, Bloomsday on Broadway, The Shadow of a Gun, Saint Joan, Hamlet, Johnny on the Spot, Death of a Salesman, Barbarians, The Winter's Tale, A Few Good Men, The Speed of Darkness.
PICTURES: Twice in a Lifetime (debut, 1985), Band of the Hand, Manhunter, Project X, Last Exit to Brooklyn, The Hard Way, Another You, Guilty As Sin, Gettysburg, Tombstone, Tall Tale, The Amazing Panda Adventure, The Shadow Conspiracy, An Occasional Hell.
TELEVISION: *Series*: Crime Story. *Movies*: King of America, Death of a Salesman, Stone Pillow, Babe Ruth, Taking Back My Life: The Nancy Ziegenmeyer Story, Darkness Before Dawn, Murder Between Friends, A Season of Hope, The Possession of Michael D., The Phantoms, Strangers *Specials*: Anyone for Tennyson?, The Mother. *Guest*: Tribeca.

LANGE, HOPE
Actress. b. Redding Ridge, CT, Nov. 28, 1936. e. Reed Coll., Portland, OR; Barmore Jr. Coll., N.Y. Parents: John Lange, musician and Minnette Buddecke Lange, actress. Prof. stage debut in The Patriots on Broadway
THEATER: The Hot Corner (understudy), Same Time Next Year, The Supporting Cast.
PICTURES: Bus Stop (debut, 1956), The True Story of Jesse James, Peyton Place (Acad. Award nom.), The Young Lions, In Love and War, The Best of Everything, Wild in the Country, Pocketful of Miracles, Love Is a Ball, Jigsaw, Death Wish, I Am the Cheese, The Prodigal, A Nightmare on Elm Street Part 2, Blue Velvet, Tune in Tomorrow, Clear and Present Danger, Just Cause.
TELEVISION: *Series*: The Ghost and Mrs. Muir (2 Emmy Awards: 1969, 1970), The New Dick Van Dyke Show, Knight and Dave. *Movies*: Crowhaven Farm, That Certain Summer (Emmy nom.), The 500 Pound Jerk, I Love You— Goodbye, Fer-de-Lance, The Secret Night Caller, Love Boat II, Like Normal People, The Day Christ Died, Beulah Land, Pleasure Palace, Private Sessions, Dead Before Dawn, Cooperstown. *Special*: A Family Tree (Trying Times). *Mini-Series*: The Henry Ford Story: Man and the Machine, Message from Nam. *Guest*: Murder She Wrote.

LANGE, JESSICA
Actress. b. Cloquet, MN, Apr. 20, 1949. e. U. of Minnesota. Left to study mime 2 years under Etienne Decroux in Paris. Dancer, Opera Comique, Paris; model with Wilhelmina, NY. Worked in experimental theatre in New York. Broadway debut 1992 in A Streetcar Named Desire (Theatre World Award).
PICTURES: King Kong (debut, 1976), All That Jazz, How to Beat the High Cost of Living, The Postman Always Rings Twice, Frances, Tootsie (Academy Award, best supporting actress, 1982), Country (also co-prod.), Sweet Dreams, Crimes of the Heart, Far North, Everybody's All-American, Music Box, Men Don't Leave, Cape Fear, Night and the City, Blue Sky (Academy Award, 1994), Losing Isaiah, Rob Roy.
TELEVISION: *Special*: Cat on a Hot Tin Roof. *Movies*: O Pioneers!, A Streetcar Named Desire (Golden Globe, 1996).

LANGELLA, FRANK
Actor. b. Bayonne, NJ, Jan. 1, 1938. Studied acting at Syracuse U.; later in regional repertory, summer stock, and On- and Off- B'way. Joined Lincoln Ctr. Rep. Co., 1963.
THEATER: *NY*: The Immoralist (Off-B'way debut, 1963), Benito Cereno, The Old Glory (Obie Award), Good Day (Obie Award), The White Devil (Obie Award), Long Day's Journey Into Night, Yerma, Seascape (B'way debut, 1975; Tony Award), Dracula, A Cry of Players, Cyrano de Bergerac, The Tooth of the Crime, Ring Around the Moon, Amadeus, Passion, Design for Living, Sherlock's Last Case, The Tempest, Booth. *L.A.*: The Devils, Les Liaisons Dangereuses, My Fair Lady, Scenes From an Execution.
PICTURES: Diary of a Mad Housewife (debut, 1970), The Twelve Chairs, The Deadly Trap, The Wrath of God, Dracula, Those Lips Those Eyes, Sphinx, The Men's Club, Masters of the Universe, And God Created Woman, True Identity, 1492: Conquest of Paradise, Body of Evidence, Dave, Brainscan, Junior, Bad Company, Cutthroat Island, Eddie.
TELEVISION: *Specials*: Benito Cereno, The Good Day, The Ambassador, The Sea Gull, The American Woman: Portrait in

Courage, Eccentricities of a Nightingale, Sherlock Holmes, Fortitude (Kurt Vonnegut's Monkey House). *Movies*: The Mark of Zorro, Liberty, Doomsday Gun.

LANGFORD, FRANCES
Singer, Actress. b. Lakeland, FL, April 4, 1913. e. Southern Coll. Stage experience in vaudeville, nightclubs, national radio programs.
PICTURES: Every Night at Eight, Collegiate, Broadway Melody of 1936, Palm Springs, Born to Dance, The Hit Parade, Hollywood Hotel, Dreaming Out Loud, Too Many Girls, The Hit Parade of 1941, All-American Coed, Mississippi Gambler, Yankee Doodle Dandy, Cowboy in Manhattan, This Is the Army, Never a Dull Moment, Career Girl, The Girl Rush, Dixie Jamboree, Radio Stars on Parade, Bamboo Blonde, Make Mine Laughs, People Are Funny, Deputy Marshall, Purple Heart Diary, The Glenn Miller Story.

LANGNER, PHILIP
Producer, b. New York, NY, Aug. 24, 1926. e. Yale U. President of The Theatre Guild and Theatre Guild Films, Inc. Producer the Westport Country Playhouse 1947-53. Joined The Theatre Guild 1954.
THEATER: The Matchmaker, Bells Are Ringing, The Tunnel of Love, Sunrise at Campobello, A Majority of One, The Unsinkable Molly Brown, A Passage to India, Seidman and Son, The Royal Hunt of the Sun, The Homecoming, Absurd Person Singular, Golda.
PICTURES: *Producer*: The Pawnbroker, Slaves, Born to Win. Associate Prod.: Judgment at Nuremberg, A Child Is Waiting.

LANSBURY, ANGELA
Actress. b. London, England, Oct. 16, 1925. Brothers are producers Bruce and Edgar Lansbury. e. South Hampstead Sch. for Girls, England; Acad. of Music, London; Feagin Dramatic Sch., N.Y. Mother was actress Moyna Macgill. To NY 1940 to study drama. Signed to contract by MGM, 1944. Exercise and lifestyle video: Positive Moves, 1988. *Book*: Positive Moves, 1990.
THEATER: *B'way*: Hotel Paradiso (NY debut, 1957), A Taste of Honey, Anyone Can Whistle, Mame (Tony Award, 1966), Dear World (Tony Award, 1969), Prettybelle (closed out of town), All Over, Gypsy (Tony Award, 1975), Hamlet, The King and I, Sweeney Todd: The Demon Barber of Fleet Street (Tony Award, 1979), A Little Family Business, Mame (1983 revival).
PICTURES: Gaslight (debut, 1944; Acad. Award nom.), National Velvet, The Picture of Dorian Gray (Acad. Award nom.), The Harvey Girls, The Hoodlum Saint, The Private Affairs of Bel Ami, Till the Clouds Roll By, If Winter Comes, Tenth Avenue Angel, State of the Union, The Three Musketeers, The Red Danube, Samson and Delilah, Kind Lady, Mutiny, Remains to Be Seen, The Purple Mask, A Lawless Street, The Court Jester, Please Murder Me, The Key Man (A Life at Stake), The Long Hot Summer, The Reluctant Debutante, The Summer of the 17th Doll (Season of Passion), The Dark at the Top of the Stairs, A Breath of Scandal, Blue Hawaii, All Fall Down, The Manchurian Candidate (Acad. Award nom.), In the Cool of the Day, The World of Henry Orient, Dear Heart, The Greatest Story Ever Told, Harlow, The Amorous Adventures of Moll Flanders, Mister Buddwing, Something for Everyone, Bedknobs and Broomsticks, Death on the Nile, The Lady Vanishes, The Mirror Crack'd, The Last Unicorn (voice), The Pirates of Penzance, The Company of Wolves, Beauty and the Beast (voice).
TELEVISION: *Special*: Sweeney Todd. *Movies*: Little Gloria... Happy at Last, The Gift of Love: A Christmas Story, The First Olympics: Athens 1896, A Talent for Murder, Lace, Rage of Angels: The Story Continues, Shootdown, The Shell Seekers, The Love She Sought, Mrs. 'arris Goes to Paris. *Series*: Pantomime Quiz, Murder She Wrote (also exec. prod.). *Guest*: Robert Montgomery Presents, Four Star Playhouse, Studio 57, Playhouse 90.

LANSBURY, BRUCE
Executive. b. London, England, Jan. 12, 1930. Brother of Angela and twin Edgar. e. UCLA. Mother was actress Moyna Macgill. Writer, prod. KABC-TV, Los Angeles, 1957-59; joined CBS-TV, 1959, was ass't dir., program dev., Hollywood, director for daytime and nighttime programs, and v.p., programs, New York; 1964-66, indep. prod., Broadway stage; 1966-69 producer, Wild Wild West, CBS series; 1969-72, prod. Mission: Impossible, Paramount Movies of Week; now v.p., creative affairs, Para-mount TV.
TELEVISION: Great Adventure (series; prod.), Wings of the Water (exec. prod.), Murder She Wrote.

LANSBURY, EDGAR
Producer, Director, Designer. b. London, England, Jan. 12, 1930. e. UCLA. Brother of Angela and Bruce Lansbury. Started career as scenic designer and art director. 1955-60, art dir., CBS; 1962-63, exec. art dir. prod. for WNDT-TV, educational sta.; THEATER: *Producer–B'way*: The Subject Was Roses, Promenade, Waiting for Godot, Long Day's Journey

into Night, Gypsy, The Night That Made America Famous, American Buffalo, Amphigorey: The Musical, Any Given Day, etc. Director on stage: Without Apologies, Advice From a Caterpillar, The Country Club.
PICTURES: *Producer*: The Subject Was Roses, Godspell, The Wild Party, Squirm, Blue Sunshine, He Knows You're Alone, The Clairvoyant.
TELEVISION: The Defenders (art. dir.), Summer Girl (exec. prod.), Wings of the Water (exec. prod.), A Stranger Waits.

LANSING, SHERRY
Executive. b. Chicago, IL, July 31, 1944. e. Northwestern U. m. director William Friedkin. Taught math and English in L.A. city high schools, 1966-69. Acted in films (Loving, Rio Lobo) and numerous TV shows. Story editor for Wagner Intl. Prod. Co., 1972-74. Talent Associates, in chg. West Coast development (all projects), 1974-75. Appt. MGM story editor, 1975. In 1977, named MGM v.p. of creative affairs; Nov., 1977, appointed vice pres., production, at Columbia Pictures. January, 1980, appointed pres., Twentieth Century-Fox Productions. Resigned 1982 to form new production co. with Stanley R. Jaffe: Jaffe—Lansing Prods. Appointed chmn. and CEO, Paramount Motion Picture Group, 1992.
PICTURES: *Co-prod.*: Racing with the Moon, Firstborn, Fatal Attraction, The Accused, Black Rain, School Ties, Indecent Proposal (prod.).
TELEVISION: When the Time Comes (exec. prod.), Mistress.

LaPAGLIA, ANTHONY
Actor. b. Adelaide, Australia, 1959. Former teacher, moved to U.S. in 1984. Made Off-B'way debut in Bouncers, followed by On the Open Road. *B'way*: The Rose Tattoo (Theatre World Award).
PICTURES: Slaves of New York (debut, 1989), Dangerous Obsession (Mortal Sins), Betsy's Wedding, He Said/She Said, One Good Cop, 29th Street, Whispers in the Dark, Innocent Blood, So I Married an Axe Murderer, The Client, The Custodian, Mixed Nuts, Bulletproof Heart, Lucky Break, Empire Records, Nowhere Man, The Funeral, Brilliant Lies.
TELEVISION: *Movies*: Criminal Justice, Keeper of the City, Black Magic, Past Tense, Nitti: The Enforcer. *Series*: Murder One.

LARDNER, RING W., JR.
Writer. b. Chicago, IL, Aug. 19, 1915. p. writer-humorist Ring W. and Ellis A. e. Phillips Andover Acad, Princeton U. Was reporter on New York Daily Mirror. Publ. writer, Selznick International. 1947, member of "Hollywood 10." In collab. with Ian Hunter conceived and wrote under pseudonyms many episodes in 5 TV series while blacklisted. Uncredited writer of such films as A Breath of Scandal, The Cardinal. 1989, received Writers Guild Laurel Award. Author of novels: The Ecstacy of Owen Muir, All For Love, and memoir, The Lardners My Family Remembered. Also collab. on B'way musical Foxy. 1992, WGA Ian McLellan Hunter Memorial Award for Lifetime Achievement.
PICTURES: Woman of the Year (Academy Award, 1942), The Cross of Lorraine, Tomorrow the World, Forever Amber, Forbidden Street, Four Days Leave, Cloak and Dagger, The Cincinnati Kid, M*A*S*H (Academy Award, 1970), Lady Liberty, The Greatest.

LARKIN, JAMES J.
Executive. b. Brooklyn, NY, Nov. 2, 1925. e. Columbia U., 1947-52. U.S. Air Force, 1943-46; BOAC rep. to entertainment ind., 1948-60; pres., Transportation Counselors Inc., 1960-62; pres., Larkin Associates, Inc., 1962-65; exec. Radio N.Y. Worldwide, 1965-68; v.p. Grolier Educational Corp., 1968-69; v.p. Visual Informational Systems, 1969-73; pres., Business TV Services, Inc., 1973; exec. prod., Madhouse Brigade, 1977-79; prod.-writer, All Those Beautiful Girls, 1979-80.

LARROQUETTE, JOHN
Actor. b. New Orleans, LA., Nov. 25, 1947. Disc jockey on FM radio during 1960s and early 70s. Acted on L.A. stage from 1973 (The Crucible, Enter Laughing, Endgame). Prof. debut, TV series Doctor's Hospital, 1976-78. Was narrator for film Texas Chainsaw Massacre.
PICTURES: Altered States, Heart Beat, Green Ice, Stripes, Cat People, Hysterical, Twilight Zone—The Movie, Choose Me, Meatballs Part II, Star Trek III: The Search for Spock, Summer Rental, Blind Date, Second Sight, Madhouse, Tune in Tomorrow, Richie Rich.
TELEVISION: *Series*: Doctor's Hospital, Baa Baa Black Sheep, Night Court (4 Emmy Awards, 1985-88), The John Larroquette Show. *Movies*: Bare Essence, The Last Ninja, Hot Paint, Convicted, One Special Victory (also co-exec. prod.).

LASSALLY, WALTER
Cinematographer. b. Berlin, Germany, Dec. 18, 1926. Entered indust. as clapper-boy at Riverside Studios. During 1950s allied himself with Britain's Free Cinema filmmakers working for Lindsay Anderson, Gavin Lambert, Tony Richardson and Karel Reisz.

PICTURES: A Girl in Black (feature debut, 1956), Beat Girl, A Taste of Honey, Electra, The Loneliness of the Long Distance Runner, Tom Jones, Zorba the Greek (Academy Award, 1964), The Day the Fish Came Out, Joanna, Oedipus the King, The Adding Machine, Three Into Two Won't Go, Something for Everyone, Twinky (Lola), Savages, Happy Mother's Day... Love George, To Kill a Clown, The Wild Party, Pleasantville, The Great Bank Hoax, The Woman Across the Way, Hullabaloo Over George and Bonnie's Pictures, Something Short of Paradise, The Blood of Hussain, Angel of Iron, Memoirs of a Survivor, Too Far to Go, Heat and Dust, Private School, The Bostonians, The Deceivers, Fragments of Isabella, The Perfect Murder, Ballad of the Sad Cafe, The Little Dolphins.
TELEVISION: Mrs. Delafield Wants to Marry, The Man Upstairs.

LASSER, LOUISE
Actress. b. New York, NY, April 11, 1939. e. Brandeis U., New School for Social Research. Appeared on stage before theatrical film debut in 1965 with What's New Pussycat? Won first Clio Award for best actress in a commercial.
THEATER: I Can Get it For You Wholesale, The Third Ear, Henry Sweet Henry, Lime Green/Khaki Blue, The Chinese, Marie & Bruce, A Coupla White Chicks Sitting Around Talking.
PICTURES: What's Up Tiger Lily? (voice), Take the Money and Run, Bananas, Such Good Friends, Everything You Always Wanted to Know About Sex, Slither, Simon, In God We Trust, Stardust Memories, Crimewave, Nightmare at Shadow Woods (Blood Rage), Surrender, Sing, Rude Awakening, Modern Love, Frankenhooker, The Night We Never Met.
TELEVISION: Series: Mary Hartman Mary Hartman, It's a Living. Movies: Coffee Tea or Me?, Isn't It Shocking?, Just Me and You (also writer), For Ladies Only. Guest: Bob Newhart Show, Mary Tyler Moor Show, Taxi, St. Elsewhere, Empty Nest, many others. Special: The Lie.

LASZLO, ANDREW
Cinematographer. b. Papa, Hungary, Jan. 12, 1926. To U.S. in 1947, working as cameraman on tv before turning to feature films.
PICTURES: One Potato Two Potato, You're a Big Boy Now, The Night They Raided Minskys, Popi, The Out of Towners, Lovers and Other Strangers, The Owl and the Pussycat, Jennifer on My Mind, To Find a Man, The Effect of Gamma Rays on Man-in-the-Moon Marigolds, Class of '44, Countdown at Kusini, Thieves, Somebody Killed Her Husband, The Warriors, The Funhouse, Southern Comfort, I the Jury, First Blood, Streets of Fire, Thief of Hearts, Remo Williams: The Adventure Begins, Poltergeist II, Innerspace, Star Trek V: The Final Frontier, Ghost Dad, Newsies.
TELEVISION: Documentaries: High Adventure with Lowell Thomas, The Twentieth Century. Series: The Phil Silvers Show, Joe and Mabel, Mama, Brenner, Naked City, The Nurses, Doctors and Nurses, Coronet Blue. Specials: New York New York, The Beatles at Shea Stadium, Ed Sullivan Specials. Movies and feature pilots: The Happeners, The Cliffdwellers, Daphne, Teacher Teacher, Blue Water Gold, The Man Without a Country, The Unwanted, Spanner's Key, Thin Ice, Love is Forever. Mini-series: Washington Behind Closed Doors, The Dain Curse, Top of the Hill, Shogun, and numerous commericals.

LATSIS, PETER C.
Publicist. b. Chicago, IL, Mar. 9, 1919. e. Wright Jr. Coll., Chicago. Newspaper reporter, Chicago Herald-American, 1942-45; Army, 1943; joined Fox West Coast Theatres, Los Angeles, in theatre operations 1945; adv.-pub. dept. 1946; asst. dir. adv.-pub. 1955; press rep. National Theatres, 1958; press relations dir., National General Corp., 1963; home office special field pub. repr., American International Pictures, 1973; Filmways Pictures, 1980-82; Recipient of Publicists Guild's Robert Yeager Award, 1983. Member, Motion Picture Pioneers. Unit rep., Executive Bd. of Publicists Guild of America, 1993-95.

LATTANZI, MATT
Actor. m. actress-singer Olivia Newton-John.
PICTURES: Xanadu (1980), Rich and Famous, Grease 2, My Tutor, That's Life!, Roxanne, Blueberry Hill, Catch Me If You Can, Diving In.
TELEVISION: Series: Paradise Beach.

LATTUADA, ALBERTO
Director. b. Milan, Italy, 1914. Son of Felice Lattuada, musician, opera composer, and writer of scores of many of son's films. Studied architecture; founded the periodical Cominare. Later founded Italian Film Library of which he still pres. Also, pres., Cinema D'Essay, First screen work as scriptwriter and asst. dir. of two films, 1940.
PICTURES: Mill on the Po, Anna, The Overcoat, La Lupa, Love in the City, White Sister, Flesh Will Surrender, Without Pity, The She Wolf, Tempest, The Unexpected, Mafioso, The Mandrake, Matchless, The Betrayal, The Steppe, Oh Serafina, Stay as You Are.

LAUGHLIN, TOM
Actor, Producer, Director, Writer. b. Minneapolis, MN, 1938. e. U. of Indiana, U. of Minnesota where had athletic scholarships. m. actress Delores Taylor. Travelled around world, studying in Italy with Dr. Maria Montessori. Established, ran a Montessori school in Santa Monica for several yrs. Worked his way to Hollwood, where acted in bit parts until stardom came in Born Losers in 1967. Produced and starred in Billy Jack and The Trial of Billy Jack, also writing s.p. with wife under pseudonym Frank Christina. Heads own prod. co., Billy Jack Enterprises.
PICTURES: Actor: Tea and Sympathy, South Pacific, Gidget, Tall Story, The Slime People. Actor-Dir.-Prod.-Writer: The Proper Time, The Young Sinner, Born Losers, Billy Jack, The Trial of Billy Jack, The Master Gunfighter, Billy Jack Goes to Washington.

LAUNER, DALE
Writer. b. Cleveland, OH. E. Cal State Northridge. Son of actor John S. Launer.
PICTURES: Ruthless People, Blind Date, Dirty Rotten Scoundrels, My Cousin Vinny, Love Potion #9 (also dir.).

LAURENTS, ARTHUR
Writer, Director. b. New York, NY, July 14, 1917. e. Cornell U., B.A., 1937. First Professional writing as radio script writer in 1939. In Army 1941-45. Member of the Council of the Dramatists Guild; Theatre Hall of Fame.
THEATER: Author: Home of the Brave (Sidney Howard Award), Heartsong, The Bird Cage, The Time of the Cuckoo, A Clearing in the Woods, Invitation to a March, West Side Story, Gypsy, Hallelujah, Baby! (Tony Award), Scream, The Enclave, Running Time, Jolson Sings Again, The Radical Mystique. Director: Invitation to a March, I Can Get It for You Wholesale, La Cage aux Folles (Tony Award), Birds of Paradise. Author-Director: Anyone Can Whistle, Do I Hear a Waltz?, The Madwoman of Central Park West, Gypsy (revival), Nick and Nora.
PICTURES: Writer: The Snake Pit, Rope, Caught, Anna Lucasta, Anastasia, Bonjour Tristesse, The Way We Were (from his own novel), The Turning Point (also co-prod.; Golden Globe, Writer's Guild Award).

LAURIA, DAN
Actor. b. Brooklyn, NY, April 12, 1947. e. So Conn. St. Col., Univ. of Conn. Served in U.S. Marine Corps., 1970\-73.
PICTURES: Without a Trace, Stakeout, Another Stakeout, Excessive Force II: Force on Force.
TELEVISION: Series: Love of Life, One Life to Live, Hooperman, The Wonder Years. Movies: Johnny Brass, Johnny Bull, Doing Life, At Mother's Request, Angel in Green, David, Howard Beach: Making the Case for Murder, The Big One: The Great Los Angeles Earthquake, Overexposed, Dead and Alive, From the Files of Joseph Wambaugh: A Jury of One, In the Line of Duty: Ambush in Waco, In the Line of Duty: Hunt for Justice. Guest: Growing Pains, Mike Hammer, Moonlighting, Hill Street Blues. Special: Between Mother and Daughter.

LAURIE, PIPER
Actress. r.n. Rosetta Jacobs. b. Detroit, MI, Jan. 22, 1932. e. Los Angeles H.S. Acted in school plays, signed by U.I. in 1949.
THEATER: The Glass Menagerie (revival), Marco Polo Sings a Solo, The Innocents, Biography, Rosemary, The Alligators, The Last Flapper (tour), The Destiny of Me.
PICTURES: Louisa (debut, 1950), The Milkman, Francis Goes to the Races, The Prince Who Was a Thief, Son of Ali Baba, Has Anybody Seen My Gal, No Room for the Groom, Mississippi Gambler, Golden Blade, Dangerous Mission, Johnny Dark, Dawn at Socorro, Smoke Signal, Ain't Misbehavin', Kelly and Me, Until They Sail, The Hustler (Acad. Award nom.), Carrie (Acad. Award nom.), Ruby, The Boss's Son, Tim, Return to Oz, Children of a Lesser God (Acad. Award nom.), Distortions, Appointment with Death, Tiger Warsaw, Dream a Little Dream, Mother Mother, Other People's Money, Storyville, Rich in Love, Trauma, Wrestling Ernest Hemingway, The Crossing Guard, The Grass Harp.
TELEVISION: Specials: Days of Wine and Roses (Emmy nom.), The Road That Led Afar (Emmy nom.), The Deaf Heart (Emmy nom.), The Secret Life of Margaret Sanger. Movies: In the Matter of Karen Ann Quinlan, Rainbow, Skag, The Bunker (Emmy nom.), Mae West, Love Mary, Toughlove, Promise (Emmy Award, 1987), Go To the Light, Rising Son, Poisoned By Love: The Kern County Murders, Lies and Lullabies, Shadows of Desire, Fighting for My Daughter. Series: Skag, Twin Peaks (Golden Globe Award, Emmy nom.). Mini-Series: The Thorn Birds (Emmy nom.), Tender is the Night. Guest: St. Elsewhere (Emmy nom.)

LAUTER, ED
Actor. b. Long Beach, NY, Oct. 30, 1940.
PICTURES: The New Centurions, Hickey & Boggs, The Last

American Hero, Executive Action, Lolly Madonna XXX, The Longest Yard, French Connection II, Breakheart Pass, Family Plot, King Kong, The Chicken Chronicles, Magic, The Amateur, Death Hunt, Timerider, The Big Score, Eureka, Lassiter, Cujo, Finders Keepers, Death Wish 3, Girls Just Want to Have Fun, Youngblood, 3:15, Raw Deal, Chief Zabu, Revenge of the Nerds II, Gleaming the Cube, Fat Man and Little Boy, Tennessee Waltz, School Ties, Wagons East!, Trial by Jury, Girl in the Cadillac.
TELEVISION: *Series*: B.J. and the Bear. *Movies*: Class of '63, The Migrants, The Godchild, Satan's Triangle, A Shadow in the Streets, Last Hours Before Morning, The Clone Master, The Jericho Mile, Love's Savage Fury, Undercover with the KKK, The Boy Who Drank Too Much, Guyana Tragedy—The Story of Jim Jones, AlcatrazThe Whole Shocking Story, In the Custody of Strangers, Rooster, The Seduction of Gina, Three Wishes of Billy Grier, The Last Days of Patton, The Thanksgiving Promise, Calendar Girl Cop Killer?: The Bambi Bembenek Story, Extreme Justice.

LAVEN, ARNOLD
Director, Producer. b. Chicago, IL, Feb. 23, 1922.
PICTURES: Without Warning (debut, 1952), Vice Squad, Down Three Dark Streets, The Rack, The Monster That Challenged the World, Slaughter on Tenth Ave., Anna Lucasta, Geronimo (also prod.), The Glory Guys (also co-prod.), Clambake (co-prod. only), Rough Night in Jericho, Sam Whiskey (also co-prod.).
TELEVISION: Part creator and director TV pilots: The Rifleman, Robert Taylor's Detectives, The Plainsmen.

LAVIN, LINDA
Actress. b. Portland, ME, Oct. 15, 1937. e. Coll. of William & Mary. First professional job in chorus of Camden County (N.J.) Music Circus. Worked in plays both off and on Broadway before turning to TV, where guest-starred on such series as Family, Rhoda, Alice and Harry O.
THEATER: Oh Kay! (Off-B'way debut, 1960), A Family Affair (B'way debut), Revues: Wet Paint (Theatre World Award), The Game Is Up, The Mad Show, member acting co.: Eugene O'Neil Playwright's Unit, 1968; It's a Bird It's a Plane... It's Superman, Something Different, Little Murders (Outer Critics Circle & Sat. Review Awards), Cop Out, The Last of the Red Hot Lovers (Tony nom.), Story Theatre, Dynamite Tonight, Broadway Bound (Tony, Drama Desk, Outer Critics Circle & Helen Hayes Awards), Gypsy, The Sisters Rosensweig, Death Defying Acts.
PICTURES: The Muppets Take Manhattan, See You in the Morning, I Want to Go Home.
TELEVISION: *Series*: Barney Miller, Alice (2 Golden Globe Awards; 2 Emmy noms.), Room for Two (also co-exec. prod.). *Movies*: The Morning After, Like Mom and Me, The $5.20 an Hour Dream, A Matter of Life and Death (also exec. prod. & developed), Another Woman's Child, A Place to Call Home (also exec. prod. & developed), Lena: My Hundred Children.

LAW, JOHN PHILLIP
Actor. b. Hollywood, CA, Sept. 7, 1937. e. Neighborhood Playhouse. B'way debut in Coming on Strong. Appeared at Lincoln Center in After the Fall, Marco Millions, The Changeling, and Tartuffe. Has made more than 50 films in more than 20 countries world wide.
PICTURES: High Infidelity, Three Nights of Love, The Russians Are Coming The Russians Are Coming The Russians Are Coming (U.S. debut), Hurry Sundown, Barbarella, Danger Diabolik, The Sergeant, Death Rides a Horse, Skidoo, Diary of a Telephone Operator, Von Richtofen and Brown, The Hawaiians, Michael Strogoff, The Love Machine, The Last Movie, The Golden Voyage of Sinbad, Stardust, Open Season, Your God My Hell, The Spiral Staircase, Dr. Justice, African Rage, Whisper in the Dark, Portrait of an Assassin, The Crystal Man, Death in November, Ring of Darkness, The Cassandra Crossing, Der Schimmelreiter, Attack Force Z, Tarzan the Ape Man, Night Train to Terror, The Tin Man, Rainy Day Friends (L.A. Bad), No Time to Die, American Commandos (Mr. Salvage), Johann Strauss, The Moon Under the Trees, Moon in Scorpio, Striker (Combat Force), The Overthrow, Mutiny in Space, Thunder Warrior III, A Case of Honor, Blood Delirium, Alienator, L.A. Heat, Gorilla, The Guest, Alaska Stories, Angel Eyes, Shining Blood, Marilyn Behind Bars, Day of the Pig, The Mountain of the Lord, Europa Mission.
TELEVISION: *Series*: The Young and the Restless (1989). *Movie*: The Best Place to Be, A Great Love Story (It.), Experiences (It.), The Fourth Man (Austrian), Little Women of Today (It.). *Guest*: The Love Boat, Murder She Wrote.

LAW, LINDSAY
Producer. e. NYU School of the Arts. Producer of specials for Warner Bros. Television, head of drama for WNET/New York and prod. for Theatre in America before becoming exec. prod. of American Playhouse. Advisory Board of Independent Feature Project/West, Sundance Film Festival.

PICTURES: *Exec. prod.*: On Valentine's Day, Smooth Talk, Native Son, In a Shallow Grave, Stand and Deliver, The Thin Blue Line, El Norte, The Wizard of Loneliness, Signs of Life, Bloodhounds of Broadway, Big Time, Eat a Bowl of Tea, Longtime Companion, Thousand Pieces of Gold, Straight Out of Brooklyn, Daughters of the Dust, Thank You and Goodnight, All the Vermeers in New York, Brother's Keeper, Ethan Frome, The Music of Chance, Golden Gate, I Shot Andy Warhol.
TELEVISION: *Prod.*: The Girls in Their Summer Dresses, The Time of Your Life, You Can't Take It With You, The Good Doctor, The Most Happy Fella, The Eccentricities of a Nightingale, Cyrano de Bergerac (assoc. prod.). *Prod. for American Playhouse*: Working, for Colored Girls Who Have Considered Suicide/When the Rainbow Is Enuf, Private Contentment, *Exec. prod.*: Concealed Enemies (Emmy Award, 1984), Land of Little Rain, Ask Me Again, The Diaries of Adam and Eve, A Walk in the Woods, Fires in the Mirror.

LAWRENCE, BARBARA
Actress. b. Carnegie, OK, Feb. 24, 1930. e. UCLA. Mother Berenice Lawrence. Child model; successful screen try-out, 1944; screen debut in Billy Rose Diamond Horse Shoe (1945).
PICTURES: Margie, Captain from Castile, You Were Meant for Me, Give My Regards to Broadway, Street with No Name, Unfaithfully Yours, Letter to Three Wives, Mother Is a Freshman, Thieves Highway, Two Tickets to Broadway, Here Come the Nelsons, The Star, Arena, Paris Model, Her 12 Men, Oklahoma, Man with the Gun, Joe Dakota, Kronos.

LAWRENCE, JOEY
Actor. b. Montgomery, PA, Apr. 20, 1976. e. USC.
PICTURES: Summer Rental, Oliver and Company (voice), Pulse, Radioland Murders.
TELEVISION: *Series*: Gimme a Break, Blossom, Brotherly Love. *Pilots*: Scamps, Little Shots. *Specials*: Andy Williams and the NBC Kids, Don't Touch, Alvin Goes Back to School, Umbrella Jack, Adventures in Babysitting, Disney's Countdown to Kids' Day, All That, Blossom in Paris, Kids' Choice Awards (host), etc. *Movies*: Chains of Gold, Prince for a Day.

LAWRENCE, MARC
Actor. r.n. Max Goldsmith. b. New York, NY, Feb. 17, 1914. e. City Coll. of New York. On stage in The Tree (Eva La Galliene Rep. Theatre.), Sour Mountain, Waiting for Lefty, Golden Boy, View From the Bridge.
PICTURES: White Woman, Little Big Shot, Dr. Socrates, Road Gang, San Quentin, The Ox Bow Incident, I Am the Law, While New York Sleeps, Dillinger, Flame of Barbary Coast, Club Havana, Don't Fence Me In, The Virginian, Life with Blondie, Yankee Fakir, Captain from Castile, I Walk Alone, Calamity Jane and Sam Bass, The Asphalt Jungle, Hurricane Island, My Favorite Spy, Girls Marked Danger, Helen of Troy, Johnny Cool, Nightmare in the Sun, Savage Pampas, Johnny Tiger, Custer of the West, Nightmare in the Sun (dir. co- prod., co-story only), Krakatoa East of Java, The Kremlin Letter, Fraser: The Sensuous Lion, The Man With the Golden Gun, Marathon Man, A Piece of the Action, Foul Play, Goin' Cocoanuts, Hot Stuff, Night Train to Terror, The Big Easy, Ruby, Newsies, Marilyn I Love You.

LAWRENCE, MARTIN
Actor, Comedian. b. Frankfurt, Germany, 1965. Started as stand-up comic in Washington D.C.
PICTURES: Do the Right Thing (debut, 1989), House Party, Talkin' Dirty After Dark, House Party 2, Boomerang, You So Crazy (also exec. prod.), Bad Boys.
TELEVISION: *Series*: What's Happening Now?, Kid 'n' Play (voice), Russell Simmons' Def Comedy Jam (host, prod. consultant), Martin (also creator, co-exec. prod.). *Pilots*: Hammer Slammer & Slade, A Little Bit Strange. *Guest*: Stand Up Spotlight, Yo! MTV Laffs, An Evening at the Improv.

LAWRENCE, STEVE
Actor. b. New York, NY, July 8, 1935. m. singer Eydie Gorme. Singer in nightclubs and on TV.
THEATER: What Makes Sammy Run?, Golden Rainbow.
PICTURES: Stand Up and Be Counted, The Blues Brothers, The Lonely Guy.
TELEVISION: *Specials*: Steve and Eydie Celebrate Irving Berlin (also co-exec. prod.; Emmy Award, 1979), many specials. *Series*: Tonight, The Steve Lawrence-Eydie Gorme Show (1958), The Steve Lawrence Show (1965), Foul-Ups Bleeps and Blunders (host). *Guest*: Police Story, Murder, She Wrote. *Movie*: Alice in Wonderland.

LAWRENCE, VICKI
Actress. b. Inglewood, CA, March 26, 1949. Singer and recording artist appearing with Young Americans (1965-67). Gained fame on The Carol Burnett Show as comedienne (1967-78), winning Emmy Award in 1976. Gold record for The Night the Lights Went Out in Georgia (1972). Author: Vicki!: The True Life Adventures of Miss Fireball (Simon & Schuster, 1995).

TELEVISION: *Movies*: Having Babies, Hart to Hart: Old Friends Never Die. *Series*: Carol Burnett Show, Jimmie Rodgers Show, Mama's Family. *Host*: Win Lose or Draw (1987-88), Vicki! (synd. talk show).

LAWSON, SARAH
Actress. b. London, Eng., Aug. 6, 1928. e. Heron's Ghyll Sch., Sussex. Stage debut in Everyman (Edinburgh Festival) 1947.
PICTURES: The Browning Version (debut, 1951), The Night Won't Talk, Street Corner, Street Corner (Both Sides of the Law), Three Steps in the Dark, Meet Mr. Malcolm, You Know What Sailors Are, Blue Peter (Navy Heroes), It's Never Too Late, Links of Justice, Three Crooked Men, The Solitary Child, Night Without Pity, On the Run, The World Ten Times Over, Island of the Burning Doomed, The Devil's Bride (The Devil Rides Out), Battle of Britain, The Stud, The Dawning (prod.).
TELEVISION: Face to Face, River Line, Whole Truth, Lady From the Sea, Mrs. Moonlight, Silver Card, An Ideal Husband, Love and Money, Rendezvous, Invisible Man, Saber Buccaneers, White Hunter, Flying Doctor, On the Night of the Murder, Haven in Sunset, The Odd Man, Zero 1 (series), The Innocent Ceremony, Department S, The Marrying Kind, The Expert, The Persuaders, Trial, Starcast, The Midsummer of Colonel Blossum, Callen, Crime of Passion, Full House, Father Brown, Within These Walls These Walls Series, The Standard, The Purple Twilight, The Professionals, Bergerac, Cuffy, Lovejoy.

LAYBOURNE, GERALDINE
Executive. e. Vassar College, B.A.; U. Penn, M.S. Joined Nickelodeon in 1980. Was vice chmn., MTV Networks; pres., Nickelodeon/Nick at Nite. Bd. member Viacom exec. committee. Left Nickelodeon to join ABC as pres., Disney/ABC Cable Network. Inducted into Broadcast and Cable Hall of Fame, 1996.

LAZARUS, PAUL N.
Executive. b. Brooklyn, NY, March 31, 1913. e. Cornell U., B.A., 1933. In U.S. Army, W.W. II. Entered m.p. ind. 1933 as gen. asst., press book dept., Warner Bros.; pres., AMPA, 1939-40. Joined Buchanan & Co., 1942 as m.p. account exec. To United Artists 1943 as dir. adv. & pub. Named asst. to pres., 1948; joined Columbia exec. staff, New York, 1950; elected v.p. Columbia, 1954-62; exec. v.p. Samuel Bronston Prods., 1962-64; v.p., chg. Motion Pictures, Subscription Television Inc., 1964; exec. officer and partner, Landau Releasing Organization, 1964-65; exec. v.p., member bd. of dir., Nat'l Screen Serv. Corp., 1965-75; lecturer and consultant, Film Studies Program, U. of CA at Santa Barbara, 1975-. Consultant to Kenya Film Corp., Nairobi, 1983. Director, Santa Barbara Intl. Film Festival, 1986-87. Chief of Staff, Santa Barbara Writers' Conference, 1976-. Vice-chmn. Santa Barbara County Film Council, 1989-92.

LAZARUS, PAUL N. III
Executive. b. New York, NY, May 25, 1938. e. Williams Coll., BA.; Yale Law Sch, L.L.B. Third generation film exec. Began career with Palomar Pictures Int'l. as exec. v.p.; joined ABC Pictures Corp. as v.p. in chg. of creative affairs. Mng. dir., CRM Productions, maker of educational films; v.p. for motion pictures. Marble Arch Productions; 1983, v.p. in chg. of prod., Home Box Office. 1985, Film Commissioner, New Mexico; 1987, Dir. of Film Program, U of Miami.
PICTURES: *Prod.:* Extreme Close-Up, Westworld, Futureworld, Capricorn One, Hanover Street, Barbarosa, Doubles.

LAZENBY, GEORGE
Actor. b. Gouburn, Australia, Sept. 5, 1939. Appeared in Australian and British tv commericals before being chosen to star as James Bond.
PICTURES: On Her Majesty's Secret Service (debut, 1969), Universal Soldier, Who Saw Her Die?, The Dragon Flies, Stoner, The Man From Hong Kong, The Kentucky Fried Movie, Death Dimension, The Falcon's Ultimatum, Saint Jack, L'ultimo Harem, Never Too Young to Die, Hell Hunters, Gettysburg.
TELEVISION: Is Anybody There?, Cover Girls, The Newman Shame, The Return of the Man From U.N.C.L.E.

LEACHMAN, CLORIS
Actress. b. Des Moines, IA, April 30, 1926. e. Northwestern U. Broadway stage, television, motion pictures.
PICTURES: Kiss Me Deadly (debut, 1955), The Rack, The Chapman Report, Butch Cassidy and the Sundance Kid, Lovers and Other Strangers, The People Next Door, W.U.S.A., The Steagle, The Last Picture Show (Academy Award, best supporting actress, 1971), Dillinger, Charlie and the Angel, Happy Mother's Day... Love George, Daisy Miller, Young Frankenstein, Crazy Mama, High Anxiety, The Mouse and His Child (voice), The North Avenue Irregulars, The Muppet Movie, Scavenger Hunt, Foolin' Around, Yesterday, Herbie Goes Bananas, History of the World—Part I, My Little Pony

(voice), Shadow Play, Walk Like a Man, Hansel and Gretel, Prancer, Texasville, Love Hurts, My Boyfriend's Back, The Beverly Hillbillies, A Troll in Central park (voice), Now and Then.
TELEVISION: *Series*: Hold It Please, Charlie Wild: Private Detective, Bob and Ray, Lassie, Mary Tyler Moore Show (Emmy Awards 1974, 1975), Phyllis (Golden Globe Award), The Facts of Life, The Nutt House, Walter & Emily. *Movies*: Silent Night Lonely Night, Suddenly Single, Haunts of the Very Rich, A Brand New Life (Emmy Award, 1973), Crime Club, Dying Room Only, The Migrants, Hitchhike!, Thursday's Game, Death Sentence, Someone I Touched, A Girl Named Sooner, Death Scream, The New Original Wonder Woman, The Love Boat (pilot), It Happened One Christmas, Long Journey Back, Willa, Mrs. R's Daughter, S.O.S. Titanic, The Acorn People, Advice to the Lovelorn, Miss All-American Beauty, Dixie: Changing Habits, Demon Murder Case, Ernie Kovacs: Between the Laughter, Deadly Intentions, Love Is Never Silent, Wedding Bell Blues, Danielle Steel's Fine Things, In Broad Daylight, A Little Piece of Heaven, Fade to Black, Without a Kiss Goodbye, Miracle Child, Double Double Toil and Trouble, Between Love and Honor. *Specials*: Oldest Living Graduate, Of Thee I Sing, Breakfast With Les and Bess, Screen Actors Guild 50th Anniversary Celebration (Emmy Award, 1984). *Guest*: Twilight Zone, Untouchables, Big Valley, That Girl, Marcus Welby, Night Gallery, Cher (Emmy Award, 1975), Love Boat.

LEAR, NORMAN
Producer, Director, Writer. b. New Haven, CT, July 27, 1922. e. Emerson Coll. In public relations 1945-49. Began in TV as co-writer of weekly one-hour variety show, The Ford Star Revue in 1950. Followed as writer for Dean Martin and Jerry Lewis on the Colgate Comedy Hour and for the Martha Raye and George Gobel TV shows. With partner, Bud Yorkin, created and produced such specials as Another Evening with Fred Astaire, Henry Fonda and the Family, An Evening with Carol Channing, and The Many Sides of Don Rickles. In 1965 their company, Tandem Productions, also produced the original Andy Williams Show. Moved into motion pictures in 1963, writing and producing Come Blow Your Horn. Formed Act III Communications, 1987.
PICTURES: Come Blow Your Horn (co-prod., s.p.), Never Too Late (prod.), Divorce-American Style (prod., s.p.), The Night They Raided Minsky's (co.-prod., co-s.p.), Start the Revolution Without Me (exec. prod.), Cold Turkey (dir., s.p., prod.), The Princess Bride (exec. prod.), Fried Green Tomatoes (co-exec. prod.).
TELEVISION: *Creator-dir.*: TV Guide Award Show (1962), Henry Fonda and the Family (1963), Andy Williams Specials, Robert Young and the Family. Exec. prod. and creator or developer: All in the Family (3 Emmy Awards), Maude, Good Times, Sanford and Son, The Jeffersons, Mary Hartman Mary Hartman, One Day at a Time, All's Fair, A Year at the Top, All that Glitters, Fernwood 2 Night, The Baxters, Palmerstown, I Love Liberty, Heartsounds, Sunday Dinner, The Powers That Be, 704 Hauser.

LEARNED, MICHAEL
Actress. b. Washington, DC, Apr. 9, 1939. Studied ballet and dramatics in school. Many stage credits include Under Milkwood, The Three Sisters, A God Slept Here, The Sisters Rosensweig, etc.; resident performances with Shakespeare festivals in Canada, Stratford, CT, and San Diego, CA. Gained fame on hit TV series, The Waltons, as the mother, Olivia.
PICTURES: Touched by Love, Shanghai Shadows (narrator), Power, Dragon: The Bruce Lee Story.
TELEVISION: *Series*: The Waltons (3 Emmy Awards: 1973, 1974, 1976), Nurse (Emmy Award, 1982), Hothouse, Living Dolls. *Guest*: Gunsmoke, Police Story, St. Elsewhere, Murder She Wrote, Who's the Boss?. *Movies*: Hurricane, It Couldn't Happen to a Nicer Guy, Widow, Little Mo, Nurse (pilot), Off the Minnesota Strip, A Christmas Without Snow, Mother's Day on Walton Mountain, The Parade, A Deadly Business, Mercy or Murder?, Roots: The Gift, Gunsmoke: The Last Apache, Aftermath: A Test of Love, Keeping Secrets, A Walton Thanksgiving Reunion, A Walton Wedding. *Specials*: All My Sons, Picnic.

LEARY, DENIS
Actor. b. 1957. e. Emerson Coll., Boston. Performed with the New Voices Theater Company, Charlestown Working Theater. Debuted one-man stand-up show No Cure for Cancer at Edinburgh Intl. Arts Fest., then later in London, Off-B'way, and cable tv. Appeared in and dir. short film for Showtime, Thy Neighbor's Wife.
PICTURES: Strictly Business (debut), National Lampoon's Loaded Weapon 1, The Sandlot, Who's the Man?, Gunmen, Demolition Man, Judgment Night, The Ref, Operation Dumbo Drop, The Neon Bible, Two If by Sea (also co-s.p.).

LEAUD, JEAN-PIERRE
Actor. b. Paris, France, May 5, 1944. Parents were screenwriter Pierre Leaud and actress Jacqueline Pierreux. At 14

chosen to play Antoine Doinel in Truffaut's The 400 Blows and subsequent autobiographical films Love at 20, Stolen Kisses, Bed and Board, Love on the Run. Also closely identified with major films by Jean-Luc Godard.
PICTURES: The 400 Blows, The Testament of Orpheus, Love at Twenty, Masculine-Feminine, Made in USA, Le Depart, La Chinoise, Weekend, Stolen Kisses, Le Gai Savoir, Pigsty, The Oldest Profession, Bed and Board, Two English Girls, Last Tango in Paris, Day for Night, Lola's Lolos, Love on the Run, Rebelote, Detective, Just a Movie, Seen by... 20 Years After, Treasure Island, The Grandeur and Decadence of a Small-Time Filmmaker, With All Hands, Time to Aim, Jane B, par Agnes V.; 36 Fillete, La Femme de Paille (The Straw Woman), The Color of the Wind, Femme de Papier, Bunker Palace Hotel, Treasure Island, I Hired a Contract Killer, Paris at Dawn, The Birth of Love.

LEDER, HERBERT JAY
Writer, Director, Producer, b. New York, NY, Aug. 15, 1922. e. B.A., Ph.D. Play Doctor on Broadway; Director TV dept., Benton and Bowles Adv. chg. all T.V. & Film production, 13 yrs. Sponsored Films: Child Molester, Bank Robber, Shoplifter, Untouchables.
PICTURES: *Writer*: Fiend Without a Face, Pretty Boy Floyd (also dir., co-prod.), Nine Miles to Noon (also dir., co-prod.), Aquarius Mission, Love Keeps No Score of Wrongs, The Frozen Dead (also dir., prod.), It (also dir., prod.), Candyman (also dir.), The Winners, The Way It Is, The Cool Crazies.

LEDERER, RICHARD
Executive. b. New York, NY, Sept. 22, 1916. e. U. of Virginia, B.S., 1938. Freelance writer, 1939-41; U.S. Army. Cryptanalyst, Signal Intell. Serv 1941-45; Adv. copywriter, Columbia Pictures, 1946-50; Adv. copywriter, Warner Bros., 1950-53; copy chief, Warner Bros., 1950-53; copy chief, Warner Bros., 1953-57; Asst. Nat'l Adv. mgr., Warner Bros. studios, 1957-59; Prod., theatrical, TV. Warner Bros. studios, 1959-60; Dir. of adv., publicity, Warner Bros. Pictures, 1960; v.p. Warner Bros. Pictures, 1963. V.P. production, Warner Bros. Studio, 1969-70; indep. prod. to 1971, when returned to WB as adv.-pub., v.p. Independent producer. 1980: Hollywood Knights. Joined Orion Pictures as v.p., adv. Resigned, 1984.

LEE, ANNA
Actress. M.B.E. r.n. Joan Boniface Winnifrith. b. Kent, England, Jan. 2, 1913. e. Central School of Speech Training and Dramatic Art, Royal Albert Hall. With London Repertory Theatre; toured in the Constant Nymph and Jane Eyre. In 1930s known as Britain's Glamour Girl. 1939 came to US to star in My Life With Caroline. Entertained troops with U.S.O. during WWII. 1950 moved to N.Y. to appear in live TV.
PICTURES: Ebb Tide (debut, 1932), Yes Mr. Brown, Say It With Music, Mayfair Girl, King's Cup, Chelsea Life, Mannequin, Faces, The Bermondsey Kid, Lucky Loser, The Camels Are Coming, Rolling in Money, Heat Wave, Passing of the Third Floor Back, First a Girl, The Man Who Changed His Mind, O.H.M.S. (You're in the Army Now), King Solomon's Mines, Non-Stop New York, The Four Just Men (The Secret Four), Return to Yesterday, Young Man's Fancy, Seven Sinners, My Life With Caroline, How Green Was My Valley, Flying Tigers, The Commandos Strike at Dawn, Hangmen Also Die, Flesh and Fantasy, Forever and a Day, Summer Storm, Abroad With Two Yanks, Bedlam, G.I. War Brides, High Conquest, The Ghost and Mrs. Muir, Best Man Wins, Fort Apache, Prison Warden, Wyoming Mail, Boots Malone, Daniel Boone—Trail Blazer, Gideon of Scotland Yard, The Last Hurrah, The Horse Soldiers, Jet Over the Atlantic, This Eath Is Mine, The Big Night, The Crimson Kimono, Jack the Giant Killer, Two Rode Together, The Man Who Shot Liberty Valance, What Ever Happend to Baby Jane?, The Prize, The Unsinkable Molly Brown, For Those Who Think Young, The Sound of Music, Torn Curtain, Seven Women, Picture Mommy Dead, In Like Flint, Star!, Clash.
TELEVISION: Guest on many major television shows from 1950-77. *Series*: General Hospital (1978-present). *Movies*: Eleanor and Franklin, The Night Rider, The Beasts are Loose, Scruples.

LEE, CHRISTOPHER
Actor. b. London, England, May 27, 1922. e. Wellington Coll. Served RAF 1940-46. Ent. m.p. ind. 1947. *Autobiography*: Tall, Dark and Gruesome (1977).
PICTURES: include: Corridor of Mirrors (debut, 1947), One Night With You, A Song for Tomorrow, Scott of the Antarctic, Hamlet, The Gay Lady, Capt. Horatio Hornblower, Valley of the Eagles, The Crimson Pirate, Babes in Bagdad, Moulin Rouge, Innocents of Paris, That Lady, The Warriors, Cockleshell Heroes, Storm Over the Nile, Port Afrique, Private's Progress, Beyond Mombasa, Battle of the River Plate, Night Ambush, She Played With Fire, The Traitors, Curse of Frankenstein, Bitter Victory, Truth About Women, Tale of Two Cities, Dracula, Man Who Could Cheat Death, The Mummy, Too Hot to Handle, Beat Girl, City of the Dead

(Horror Hotel), Two Faces of Dr. Jekyll, The Terror of the Tongs, The Hands of Orlac, Taste of Fear, The Devil's Daffodil, Pirates of Blood River, Devil's Agent, Red Orchid, Valley of Fear, Katharsis, Faust '63, The Virgin of Nuremberg, The Whip and the Body, Carmilla, The Devil Ship Pirates, The Gorgon, The Sign of Satan, The House of Blood, Dr. Terror's House of Horrors, She, The Skull, The Mask of Fu Manchu, Dracula, Prince of Darkness, Rasputin, Theatre of Death, Circus of Fear, The Brides of Fu Manchu, Five Golden Dragons, Vengeance of Fu Manchu, Night of the Big Heat, The Pendulum, The Face of Eve, The Devil Rides Out, The Blood of Fu Manchu, The Crimson Altar, Dracula Has Risen from the Grave, The Oblong Box, De Sade 70, Scream and Scream Again, The Magic Christian, Julius Caesar, One More Time, Count Dracula, Bloody Judge, Taste the Blood of Dracula, The Private Life of Sherlock Holmes, El Umbragolo, Scars of Dracula, The House That Dripped Blood, I Monster, Hannie Caulder, Dracula A.D. 1972, Horror Express, Death Line (Raw Meat), Nothing But the Night (also co-exec. prod.), The Creeping Flesh, The Wicker Man, Poor Devil, Dark Places, Satanic Rites of Dracula, Eulalie Quitte les Champs, The Three Musketeers, Earthbound, The Man with the Golden Gun, The Four Musketeers, Killer Force, Diagnosis—Murder, Whispering Death, The Keeper, To the Devil a Daughter, Dracula and Son, Airport '77, Starship Invasions (Alien Encounters), The End of the World, Return from Witch Mountain, Caravans, The Passage, Arabian Adventure, Jaguar Lives, Circle of Iron (The Silent Flute), 1941, Bear Island, Serial, The Salamander, An Eye for an Eye, Safari 3000, House of Long Shadows, The Return of Captain Invincible, The Rosebud Beach Hotel, Roadtrip, Dark Mission, The Howling II: Your Sister is a Werewolf, Olympus Force, Jocks, Murder Story, Mio In the Land of Faraway, The Girl, The Return of the Musketeers, Honeymoon Academy, The French Revolution, Gremlins 2: The New Batch, Curse III: Blood Sacrifice, The Rainbow Thief, L'Avaro, Jackpot, Double Vision, Shogun Mayeda, Special Class, Journey of Honor, Cybereden, Funny Man, Police Academy: Mission to Moscow, A Feast at Midnight, The Stupids, Sorellina.
TELEVISION: The Disputation, Metier du Seigneur, Movies: Poor Devil, Harold Robbins' The Pirate, Captain America II, Once a Spy, Charles and Diana: A Royal Love Story, Far Pavilions, Shaka Zulu, Goliath Awaits, Massarati and the Brain, Around the World in 80 Days, Treasure Island, Young Indiana Jones, The Care of Time, Sherlock Holmes & the Leading Lady, Sherlock Holmes and the Incident at Victoria Falls, Death Train, The Tomorrow People, Tales of Mystery & Imagination, Moses, Ivanhoe.

LEE, JASON SCOTT
Actor. b. Los Angeles, CA, 1966. Raised in Hawaii. e. Fullerton Col., Organge County, CA.
PICTURES: Born in East L.A. (debut, 1987), Back to the Future II, Map of the Human Heart, Dragon: The Bruce Lee Story, Rapa Nui, Rudyard Kipling's The Jungle Book.
TELEVISION: *Movie*: Vestige of Honor. *Special*: American Eyes.

LEE, JOIE
Actress. b. 1968. e. Sarah Lawrence Col. Brother is director-writer Spike Lee. On NY stage in Mulebone. Appeared in short film Coffee and Cigarettes Part Two. Has also been billed as Joy Lee, Joie Susannah Lee.
PICTURES: She's Gotta Have It (debut, 1986), School Daze, Do the Right Thing, Bail Jumper, Mo' Better Blues, A Kiss Before Dying, Fathers and Sons, Crooklyn (also story, co-s.p.), assoc. prod.), Losing Isaiah.

LEE, MICHELE
Actress. b. Los Angeles, CA, June 24, 1942. On Broadway in How to Succeed in Business Without Really Trying, Seesaw.
PICTURES: How to Succeed in Business Without Really Trying, The Love Bug, The Comic.
TELEVISION: *Series*: Knots Landing (also dir. several episodes). *Movies*: Dark Victory, Bud and Lou, Letter to Three Wives, Single Women Married Men (also exec. prod.), The Fatal Image, My Son Johnny, Broadway Bound, When No One Would Listen (also exec. prod.), Big Dreams & Broken Hearts: The Dottie West Story (also exec. prod.).

LEE, PEGGY
Singer, Actress. r.n. Norma Egstrom. b. Jamestown, ND, May 26, 1920. Began career as night club vocalist in Fargo; became& radio singer, WDAY, then with bandleader Sev Olsen in Minneapolis, Will Osborne, Benny Goodman. Collabolrated with Dave Barbour on such songs as Manana, It's a Good Day, What More Can a Woman Do?, Fever, Johnny Guitar, So What's New. Also leading recording artist. PICTURES: Stage Door Canteen, Mr. Music, The Jazz Singer, Pete Kelly's Blues (Acad. Award nom.), Lady and the Tramp (voices, co- compser).
TELEVISION: *Series*: TV's Top Tunes, Songs for Sale. *Guest*: Jimmy Durante, Dean Martin, Ed Sullivan, many others.

LEE, SPIKE
Director, Producer, Writer, Actor. b. Atlanta, GA, Mar. 20, 1957. r.n. Shelton Jackson Lee. Son of jazz bass musician, composer Bill Lee. Sister is actress Joie Lee. e. Morehouse Coll B.A., Mass Comm., MFA NYU Film Sch. Completed 2 student features and hour-long thesis: Joe's Bed-Stuy Barbershop: We Cut Heads which won student Acad. Award from Acad. M.P. Arts & Sciences. Wrote, prod., dir., co-starred in indep. feature, She's Gotta Have It, budgeted at $175,000. Appeared in films Lonely in America, Hoop Dreams. Author of five books on his films. Director of numerous tv commercials for Nike, Levi's, ESPN and others. Director of over 35 music videos for Michael Jackson, Stevie Wonder, Miles Davis, and others.
PICTURES: Joe's Bed-Stuy Barbershop: We Cut Heads (co-prod., dir., s.p., editor). Dir.-Prod.-Writer-Actor. She's Gotta Have It (LA Film Critics Award for best new director, 1986), School Daze, Do the Right Thing (LA Film Critics Awards for best picture & director, 1989), Mo' Better Blues, Jungle Fever, Malcolm X, Crooklyn, Clockers, Girl 6, Get On the Bus. Executive Producer: Drop Squad also actor), New Jersey Drive, Tales From the Hood.
TELEVISION: Guest: The Debbie Allen's Special, Spike & Co. Do It A Capella.

LEEDS, MARTIN N.
Film-TV Executive. b. New York, NY, Apr. 6, 1916. e. NYU, B.S., 1936; J.D.; 1938. Admitted NY Bar, 1938, CA Bar, 1948; dir. ind. rltns. Wabash Appliance Corp., 1943-44; ind. bus. rltns. cons. Davis & Gilbert, 1944-45; dir. ind. rltns. Flying Tiger Lines, 1947; dir. bus. affairs CBS TV div., 1947-53; exec. v.p. Desilu Productions, Inc., 1953-60; v.p. Motion Picture Center Studios, Inc.: memb. Industry comm. War Manpower Comm., 1943; chmn. Comm. to form Television Code of Ethics: U.S. Army 1941. Exec. v.p. in chg. of West Coast oper. & member of bd. of dir. Talent Associates—Paramount Ltd., Hollywood, 1962; TV production consultant; exec. v.p., Electronovision Prods. Inc., 1964; TV prod. & MP prod. consultant, 1965; pres., CEO, memb. of bd., Beverly Hills Studios, Inc., 1969; sr. v.p., American Film Theatre, 1973; 1975, motion picture and TV attorney & consultant.

LEEWOOD, JACK
Producer. b. New York, NY. May 20, 1913. e. Upsala Coll., Newark U., NYU. 1926-31 with Gottesman-Stern circuit as usher, asst. and relief mgr.; 1931-43 Stanley-Warner, mgr. of Ritz, Capitol and Hollywood theatres 1943-47. Joined Warner Bros. field forces in Denver-Salt Lake; Seattle-Portland, 1947-48. Dir. pub. & adv. Screen Guild Prod.; 1948-52, Lippert Productions; prod. exec., 1953-56, Allied Artists; 1957-62 prod. 20th Cent. Fox; 1965-68, prod., Universal; 1976-78. Affiliated Theatre S.F. & HTN.; 1978-83. Hamner Prod.
PICTURES: Holiday Rhythm, Gunfire, Hi-Jacked, Roaring City, Danger Zone, Lost Continent, F.B.I. Girl, Pier 23, Train to Tombstone, I Shot Billy the Kid, Bandit Queen, Motor Patrol, Savage Drums, Three Desperate Men, Border Rangers, Western Pacific Agent, Thundering Jets, Lone Texan, Little Savage, Alligator People, 13 Fighting Men, Young Jesse James, Swingin' Along, We'll Bury You, 20,000 Eyes, Thunder Island, The Plainsman.
TELEVISION: Longest 100 Miles, Escape to Mindanao, Dallas Cowboys Cheerleaders, When Hell Was in Session, Fugitive Family, Dallas Cowboys Cheerleaders II, Million Dollar Face, Portrait of a Showgirl, Margin For Murder, Anatomy of an Illness, Malibu.

LEFFERTS, GEORGE
Producer, Writer, Director. b. Paterson, NJ. e. Univ. of MI. Dir., numerous award-winning TV series, films. Exec. prod.= Time-Life films p./writer, Movie of the Week (NBC) Biog: Who's Who in America, Who's Who in the World. Exec. prod., Bing Crosby Productions, prod., NBC 10 yrs, Independent. Exec. prod. David Wolper prods. 4 Emmy Awards, 2 Golden Globe Awards, 2 New England Journalism Awards, 1 Cine Golden Eagle Award.
THEATER: Hey Everybody.
PICTURES: The Stake, Mean Dog Blues, The Living End, The Boat, The Teenager.
TELEVISION: Specials: Teacher Teacher (Emmy Award, 1969), Benjamin Franklin (Emmy Award, 1975), Purex Specials for Women (Emmy Award, Producer's Guild Award; writer, prod. dir.), Our Group (writer), Jean Seberg Story. Series: Breaking Point (exec. prod.), The Bill Cosby Show, Studio One, Kraft Theatre, Chrysler Theatre, Sinatra Show, Lights Out, Alcoa, The Bold Ones, One Life to Live (WGA Award), Ryan's Hope (prod.). Movies: The Harness, She's Dressed to Kill, The Night They Took Miss Beautiful, Smithsonian Institution Specials (exec. prod.).

LEGRAND, MICHEL JEAN
Composer, Conductor. b. France, Feb. 24, 1932. Son of well-known arranger, composer and pianist, Raymond Legrand. At 11 Michel, a child prodigy, entered Paris Cons. and graduated

nine years later with top honors in composition and as solo pianist. In late fifties turned to composing for films and has composed, orchestrated and conducted scores of more than 140 films.
PICTURES: Lola, Eva, Vivre Sa Vie, La Baie des Anges, The Umbrellas of Cherbourg, Banda a Part, Une Femme Mariee, Une Femme est une Femme, The Young Girls of Rochefort, Ice Station Zebra, The Thomas Crown Affair (Academy Award for best song: The Windmills of Your Mind, 1968), Pieces of Dreams, The Happy Ending, Picasso Summer, Wuthering Heights, The Go-Between, Summer of '42 (Academy Award, 1971), Lady Sings the Blues, The Nelson Affair, Breezy, The Three Musketeers, Sheila Levine, Gable and Lombard, Ode to Billy Joe, The Savage, The Other Side of Midnight, The Fabulous Adventures of the Legendary Baron Munchausen, The Roads of the South, The Hunter, The Mountain Men, Atlantic City, Falling in Love Again, Best Friends, A Love in Germany, Never Say Never Again, Yentl (Academy Award, 1983), Hell Train, Micki and Maude, Secret Places, Spirale, Parking, Switching Channels, Three Seats for the 26th Cinq jours en juin (dir. debut, s.p., music), Dingo, The Pickle, Ready to Wear (Pret-a-Porter).
TELEVISION: Movies: Brian's Song, The Jesse Owens Story, A Woman Called Golda, As Summers Die, Crossings, Sins, Promises to Keep, Not a Penny More Not a Penny Less, The Burning Shore.

LE GROS, JAMES
Actor. b. Minneapolis, MN, Apr. 27, 1962.
THEATER: The Cherry Orchard, Galileo, Ceremony of Innocence, Table Settings, Curse of the Starving Class, American Buffalo, Bits and Bytes, Becoming Memories, Slab Boys.
PICTURES: Solarbabies, Near Dark, Fatal Beauty, Phantasm II, Drugstore Cowboy, Point Break, Blood & Concrete, The Rapture, Where the Day Takes You, Singles, My New Gun, Bad Girls, Floundering, Mrs. Parker and the Vicious Circle, Destiny Turns on the Radio, Panther, Safe, Living in Oblivion, Infinity, The Low Life, Boys, The Destiny of Marty Fine.
TELEVISION: Movie: Gun Crazy.

LEGUIZAMO, JOHN
Actor. b. Bogota, Colombia, July 22, 1964. Moved to Queens, NY at age 5. e. NYU. Appeared in award-winning student film Five Out of Six, while in school. Studied acting with Lee Strasberg and Wynn Handman. Made professional debut on Miami Vice on tv.
THEATER: A Midsummer Night's Dream, La Puta Vida, Parting Gestures, Mambo Mouth (also writer; Obie & Outer Critics Circle Awards), Spic-O-Rama (also writer; Drama Desk & Theatre World Awards).
PICTURES: Casualties of War, Revenge, Die Hard 2, Gentile Alouette, Street Hunter, Out for Justice, Hangin' With the Homeboys, Regarding Henry, Whispers in the Dark, Super Mario Bros., Night Owl, Carlito's Way, A Pyromaniac's Love Story, To Wong Foo—Thanks for Everything—Julie Newmar, Executive Decision, Spawn, Romeo and Juliet, The Pest.
TELEVISION: Series: House of Buggin'. Specials: Talent Pool Comedy Special (ACE Award), Mambo Mouth (also writer); Spic-O-Rama (also writer; 3 Cable ACE Awards).

LEHMAN, ERNEST
Writer, Producer, Director. b. New York, NY, 1923. e. City Coll. of New York. Began career as free-lance journalist and magazine fiction writer. First pub. books, The Comedian, The Sweet Smell of Success. First hardcover novel, The French Atlantic Affair followed by Farewell Performance, and first non-fiction book, Screening Sickness. Pres., WGAW, 1983-85.1987, 1988, 1990: Acad. Awards show (co-writer). The Ernest Lehman Collection is archived at the Humanities Research Center, Univ. of TX at Austin, and in part at USC Film Library and Margaret Herrick Library. Co-prod. of musical stage adaptation of Sweet Smell of Success. Laurel Award for Screen Achievement, WGAW, 1973. Five Best Screenplay Awards, WGAW.
PICTURES: Writer: Executive Suite, Sabrina (co-s.p.; Acad. Award nom.), The King and I, Somebody Up There Likes Me, Sweet Smell of Success (co-s.p.; based on his own novelette), North By Northwest (Acad. Award nom.), From the Terrace, West Side Story (Acad. Award nom.), The Prize, The Sound of Music, Who's Afraid of Virginia Woolf? (also prod.; 2 Acad. Award noms. for picture & s.p.), Hello Dolly! (also prod.; Acad. Award nom. for picture), Portnoy's Complaint (also dir., prod.), Family Plot, Black Sunday (co-s.p.).

LEHMANN, MICHAEL
Director. b. San Francisco. e. UCal, Berkeley, Columbia U. Started in industry supervising video systems used in the Francis Ford Coppola films One From the Heart, Rumble Fish, The Outsiders. Dir. short films for Saturday Night Live incl. Ed's Secret Life. Served as exec. prod. on Ed Wood.
PICTURES: Heathers (debut, 1989), Meet the Applegates, Hudson Hawk, Airheads, The Truth About Cats and Dogs.

LEHRER, JIM

News Anchor. b. Wichita, KS, 1934. e. Victoria Col., Univ. of MO. Served in US Marine Corps. 1959-66, reporter for Dallas Morning News, Dallas Times-Herald; 1968 became Times-Herald's city editor before moving into tv as exec. dir. of public affairs, host and editor of news program on KERA-TV in Dallas. To Washington where he became public affairs coord. for PBS, then corresp. for the Natl. Public Affairs Center for Television. 1973 first teamed with Robert MacNeil to cover Senate Watergate hearings. 1975, served as D.C. corresp. for the Robert MacNeil Report on PBS (showed was re-named The MacNeil/Lehrer Report in 1976). 1983, started The MacNeil/Lehrer NewsHour. 1995, became exec. editor and anchor of new version of series The NewsHour With Jim Lehrer.

LEIBMAN, RON

Actor. b. New York, NY, Oct. 11, 1937. m. actress Jessica Walter. e. Ohio Wesleyan U. Joined Actor's Studio in N.Y.; first professional appearance in summer theatre production of A View from the Bridge.
THEATER: The Premise, Dear Me, The Sky Is Falling, We Bombed in New Haven (Theatre World Award), Cop Out, Room Service, I Oughta Be in Pictures, The Deputy, Bicycle Ride to Nevada, Doubles, Rumors, Angels in America: Millenium Approaches (Tony & Drama Desk Awards).
PICTURES: Where's Poppa (debut, 1970), The Hot Rock, Slaughterhouse Five, Your Three Minutes Are Up, Super Cops, Won Ton Ton the Dog Who Saved Hollywood, Norma Rae, Up the Academy, Zorro the Gay Blade, Romantic Comedy, Phar Lap, Rhinestone, Door to Door, Seven Hours to Judgement, Night Falls on Manhattan.
TELEVISION: Series: Kaz (Emmy Award, 1979), Pacific Station, Central Park West. Movies: The Art of Crime, A Question of Guilt, Rivkin: Bounty Hunter, Many Happy Returns, Christmas Eve, Terrorist on Trial: The United States vs. Salim Ajami.

LEIDER, GERALD J.

Producer, Executive. b. Camden, NJ, May 28, 1931. e. Syracuse U., 1953; Bristol U., Eng., 1954, Fulbright Fellowship in drama. m. Susan Trustman. 1955 joined MCA, Inc., N.Y.; 1956-59 theatre producer in NY, London: Shinbone Alley, Garden District, and Sir John Gielgud's Ages of Man. 1960-61; director of special programs, CBS/TV; 1961-62, dir. of program sales, CBS-TV; 1962-69, v.p., tv optns., Ashley Famous Agency, Inc.; 1969-74, pres. Warner Bros. TV, Burbank; 1975-76, exec. v.p. foreign prod. Warner Bros. Pictures, Rome; 1977-82, indept. prod. under Jerry Leider Prods.; 1982-87, pres., ITC Prods., Inc; named pres. and CEO, ITC Entertainment Group, 1987-present.
PICTURES: Wild Horse Hank, The Jazz Singer, Trenchcoat.
TELEVISION: Movies: And I Alone Survived, Willa, The Hostage Tower, The Scarlet and the Black, Secrets of a Married Man, The Haunting Passion, Letting Go, A Time to Live, The Girl Who Spelled Freedom, Unnatural Causes, Poor Little Rich Girl.

LEIGH, JANET

Actress. r.n. Jeanette Helen Morrison. b. Merced, CA, July 6, 1927. Mother of actresses Jamie Lee Curtis and Kelly Curtis. e. Coll. of Pacific, music. Author: There Really Was a Hollywood (autobiography, 1984), Behind the Scenes of Psycho (1995), House of Destiny (novel; 1995).
THEATER: includes: Murder Among Friends, Love Letters (with Van Johnson).
PICTURES: The Romance of Rosy Ridge (debut, 1947), If Winter Comes, Hills of Home, Words and Music, Act of Violence, Little Women, That Forsyte Woman, Red Danube, Doctor and the Girl, Holiday Affair, Two Tickets to Broadway, Strictly Dishonorable, Angels in the Outfield, It's a Big Country, Just This Once, Scaramouche, Fearless Fagan, Naked Spur, Confidentially Connie, Houdini, Walking My Baby Back Home, Prince Valiant, Living It Up, Black Shield of Falworth, Rogue Cop, My Sister Eileen, Pete Kelly's Blues, Safari, Jet Pilot, Touch of Evil, The Vikings, The Perfect Furlough, Who Was That Lady?, Psycho (Acad. Award nom.), Pepe, The Manchurian Candidate, Bye Bye Birdie, Wives and Lovers, Three on a Couch, Harper, An American Dream, Kid Rodelo, Grand Slam, Hello Down There, One Is a Lonely Number, Night of the Lepus, Boardwalk, The Fog, Other Realms.
TELEVISION: Movies: Honeymoon With a Stranger, House on Green Apple Road, The Monk, Deadly Dream, Mirror Mirror, Telethon, Murder at the World Series. Guest: Matt Houston, Starman, Murder She Wrote. Addtl.: Carriage from Britain, Murder in the First, Dear Deductible, Catch Me If You Can, One for My Baby, My Wives, Jane, The Chairman, Death's Head, This Is Maggie Mulligan, Tales of the Unexpected, On the Road.

LEIGH, JENNIFER JASON

Actress. b. Los Angeles, CA, Feb. 5, 1962. r.n. Jennifer Leigh Morrow. Daughter of late actor Vic Morrow and TV writer Barbara Turner. At age 14 debuted in Disney tv movie The Young Runaway. Won L.A. Valley Coll. best actress award for stage prod. The Shadow Box (1979).
PICTURES: Eyes of a Stranger (debut, 1981), Wrong Is Right, Fast Times at Ridgemont High, Easy Money, Grandview U.S.A., The Hitcher, Flesh + Blood, The Men's Club, Undercover, Sister Sister, Heart of Midnight, The Big Picture, Miami Blues (NY Film Critics Award, 1990), Last Exit to Brooklyn (NY Film Critics Award, 1990), Backdraft, Crooked Hearts, Rush, Single White Female, Short Cuts, The Hudsucker Proxy, Mrs. Parker and the Vicious Circle (Natl. Society of Film Critics & Chicago Film Critics Awards, 1994), Dolores Claiborne, Georgia (also co-prod.), Kansas City.
TELEVISION: Movies: The Young Runaway, Angel City, The Killing of Randy Webster, The Best Little Girl in the World, The First Time, Girls of the White Orchid, Buried Alive.

LEIGH, MIKE

Director, Writer. b. Salford, England, Feb. 20, 1943. e. RADA, Camberwell Art Sch., Central Sch. of Arts & Crafts, London Film Sch. m. actress Alison Steadman. Directed 1977 TV drama Abigail's Party. 1987 short: The Short and Curlies. Recipient of 1995 BAFTA Award for Outstanding British Contribution to Cinema.
PICTURES: Bleak Moments, Hard Labour, Nuts in May, The Kiss of Death, Who's Who, Grown-Ups, Home Sweet Home, Meantime, Four Days in July, High Hopes, Life Is Sweet, Naked, Secrets & Lies (Palme d'Or, Cannes 1996).

LEIGH, SUZANNA

Actress. b. Reading, England, 1945. Studied at the Arts Educational Sch. and Webber Douglas Sch. 1965-66, under contract to Hal Wallis and Paramount.
PICTURES: Oscar Wilde, Bomb in High Street, Boeing Boeing, Paradise Hawaiian Style, The Deadly Bees, Deadlier Than the Male, The Lost Continent, Subterfuge, Lust for a Vampire (To Love a Vampire), Beware My Brethren, Son of Dracula.
TELEVISION: Series: Three Stars (France), One on an Island (West Indies). Special: The Plastic People. Guest: The Persuaders.

LEITCH, DONOVAN

Actor. Son of folksinger Donovan. Brother of actress Ione Skye. Acted in jr. high sch. musical then had bit part in PBS show K.I.D.S.
PICTURES: And God Created Women (1988), The Blob, The In Crowd, Cutting Class, Glory, Gas Food Lodging, Dark Horse, I Shot Andy Warhol.
TELEVISION: Movie: For the Very First Time. Guest: Life Goes On.

LELAND, DAVID

Director, Writer, Actor. b. Cambridge, Eng., April 20, 1947. Began as actor at Nottingham Playhouse. Then joined newly formed company at Royal Court Theatre, London. Also appeared in films Time Bandits, The Missionary, and his own Personal Services (Peter Sellers Award for Comedy) and on TV in The Jewel in the Crown. As stage director specialized in complete seasons of new works at the Crucible in Sheffield and London venues. Wrote play Psy-Warriors.
PICTURES: Mona Lisa (co-s.p.), Personal Services (s.p.), Wish You Were Here (dir., s.p.; BAFTA Award for s.p.), Checking Out (dir.), The Big Man (dir.; a.k.a. Crossing the Line).
TELEVISION: Wrote Birth of a Nation, Flying Into the Wind, Rhino, Made in Britain, Beloved Enemy, Ligmalion, Psy-Warriors.

LELOUCH, CLAUDE

Director, Writer, Producer, Cinematographer, Editor. b. Paris, France, Oct. 30, 1937. Began m.p. career with short subjects, 1956; French military service, motion picture department, 1957-60; formed Films 13, 1960; publicity Films and Scopitones, 1961-62.
PICTURES: Le Propre de l'Homme (The Right of Man; debut, 1960; also s.p., prod., actor), L'amour avec des Si (Love With Ifs; also prod., s.p.), La Femme Spectacle (Night Women; also prod., photog.), Une Fille et des Fusils (To Be a Crook; also co-s.p., prod., edit.), Les Grands Moments (also co-prod.), A Man and A Woman (also co-s.p., story, prod., photog., edit.; Academy Awards for Best Foreign Language Film & Original Screenplay, 1966; also Acad. Award nom. for dir.), Live for Life (also co-s.p., co-photog. , edit.), Farm From Vietnam (segment), 13 Jours en France (Grenoble; also co-s.p.), Life Love Death (also co-s.p.), Love Is a Funny Thing (also photog., co-s.p.), The Crook (also co- photog., co-s.p.), Smic Smac Smoc (also prod., s.p., photog., actor), Money Money Money (also s.p., prod., photog.), La Bonne Annee (Happy New Year; also prod., s.p., co-photog.), Visions of Eight (segment: The Losers), And Now My Love (also s.p., prod.), Marriage (also co-s.p.), Cat and Mouse (also s.p.), The Good and Bad (also s.p., photog.), Second Chance (also s.p.,

prod.), Another Man Another Chance (also s.p.), Robert and Robert (also s.p.), Adventure for Two, Bolero (also s.p., prod.), Edith and Marcel (also prod., s.p.), Vive la Vie (also prod., s.p., photog.), Partier Revenir (also prod., co-s.p.), A Man and a Woman: 20 Years Later (also prod., co-s.p.), Bandits (also prod., s.p.), Itinerary of a Spoiled Child (also co-prod., s.p.), There Were Days and Moons (also prod., co-s.p.), Les Miserables. TELEVISION: Moliere (prod. only).

LE MAT, PAUL
Actor. b. Rahway, NJ, Sept. 22, 1945. Studied with Milton Katselas, Herbert Berghof Studio, A.C.T., San Francisco, Mitchel Ryan-Actor's Studio.
PICTURES: American Graffiti (debut, 1973), Aloha Bobby and Rose, Citizens Band (Handle With Care), More American Graffiti, Melvin and Howard, Death Valley, Jimmy the Kid, Strange Invaders, P.K. and the Kid, Rock & Rule (voice), The Hanoi Hilton, Private Investigations, Puppet Master, Easy Wheels, Deuce Coupe, Grave Secrets, Veiled Threats, Wishman, Caroline at Midnight.
TELEVISION: Movies: Firehouse, The Gift of Life, The Night They Saved Christmas, The Burning Bed, Long Time Gone, Secret Witness, On Wings of Eagles, Into the Homeland, In the Line of Duty: Siege at Marion, Woman With a Past, Blind Witness.

LEMBERGER, KENNETH
Executive. Exec. v.p., Sony Pictures Entertainment, Inc.

LEMMON, JACK
Actor. b. Boston, MA. Feb. 8, 1925. r.n. John Uhler Lemmon III. e. Harvard U. m. actress Felicia Farr. Father of actor Chris Lemmon. Stage debut as a child; radio actor on soap operas; stock companies; U.S. Navy, W.W.II; many TV shows. Narrated film Stowaway in the Sky. Appeared in AFI short Wednesday. Albums: A Twist of Lemmon, Jack Lemmon Plays and Sings Music From Some Like It Hot. Recipient: American Film Institute Life Achievement Award (1988), Lincoln Center Tribute (1993).
THEATER: B'way: Room Service (debut, 1953), Face of a Hero, Tribute (also L.A., Denver), Long Day's Journey into Night (also London, Israel, D.C.). Off-B'way: Power of Darkness. L.A.: Idiot's Delight, Juno and the Paycock, A Sense of Humor (also Denver, S.F.). London: Veterans Day.
PICTURES: It Should Happen to You (debut, 1953), Phffft!, Three for the Show, Mister Roberts (Academy Award, best supporting actor, 1955), My Sister Eileen, You Can't Run Away from It, Fire Down Below, Operation Mad Ball, Cowboy, Bell Book and Candle, Some Like It Hot (Acad. Award nom.), It Happened to Jane, The Apartment (Acad. Award nom.), Pepe, The Wackiest Ship in the Army, The Notorious Landlady, Days of Wine and Roses (Acad. Award nom.), Irma La Douce, Under the Yum Yum Tree, Good Neighbor Sam, How to Murder Your Wife, The Great Race, The Fortune Cookie, Luv, The Odd Couple, The April Fools, The Out-of-Towners, Kotch (dir. debut; also cameo), The War Between Men and Women, Avanti!, Save the Tiger (Academy Award, 1973), The Front Page, The Prisoner of Second Avenue, Alex and the Gypsy, Airport '77, The China Syndrome (Cannes Film Fest. Award; Acad. Award nom., 1979), Tribute (Acad. Award nom.), Buddy Buddy, Missing (Cannes Film Fest. Award; Acad. Award nom., 1982), Mass Appeal, Macaroni, That's Life, Dad, JFK, The Player, Glengarry Glen Ross, Short Cuts, Grumpy Old Men, Getting Away With Murder, The Grass Harp, Grumpier Old Men, A Weekend in the Country, Hamlet, My Fellow Americans.
TELEVISION: Series: That Wonderful Guy, Toni Twin Time (host), Ad Libbers, Heaven For Betsy, Alcoa Theatre. Guest on numerous dramatic shows: Studio One, Playhouse 90 (Face of a Hero), Kraft Theatre, The Web, Suspense, etc. Specials: The Day Lincoln Was Shot, 'S Wonderful 'S Marvelous 'S Gershwin, Get Happy, The Entertainer, Long Day's Journey into Night, The Wild West (narrator), A Life in the Theatre. Movies: The Murder of Mary Phagan, For Richer For Poorer. RADIO: Serials: The Brighter Day, Road of Life.

LENO, JAY
Comedian, Actor. r.n. James Leno. b. New Rochelle, NY, April 28, 1950. e. Emerson College, B.A. speech therapy, 1973. Raised in Andover, MA. Worked as Rolls Royce auto mechanic and deliveryman while seeking work as stand-up comedian. Performed in comedy clubs throughout the U.S. and as opening act for Perry Como, Johnny Mathis, John Denver and Tom Jones. Guest on numerous talk shows and specials.
PICTURES: Fun With Dick and Jane, The Silver Bears, American Hot Wax, Americathon, Collision Course, What's Up Hideous Sun Demon? (voice), Dave, We're Back! (voice), Wayne's World 2, Major League 2, The Flintstones.
TELEVISION: Series: The Marilyn McCoo & Billy Davis Jr. Show, The Tonight Show (guest host: 1987-92; host: 1992-; Emmy Award, 1995). Specials: Jay Leno and the American Dream (also prod.), The Jay Leno Show, Our Planet Tonight, Jay Leno's Family Comedy Hour.

LENZ, KAY
Actress. b. Los Angeles, CA, March 4, 1953.
PICTURES: Breezy (debut, 1973), White Line Fever, The Great Scout and Cathouse Thursday, Moving Violation, Mean Dog Blues, The Passage, Fast-Walking, House, Stripped to Kill, Death Wish IV: The Crackdown, Headhunter, Physical Evidence, Fear, Streets, Falling From Grace.
TELEVISION: Series: Reasonable Doubts. Movies: The Weekend Nun, Lisa, Bright and Dark, A Summer Without Boys, Unwed Father, The Underground Man, The FBI Story: The FBI Versus Alvin Karpis, Journey from Darkness, Rich Man, Poor Man, The Initiation of Sarah, The Seeding of Sarah Burns, Sanctuary of Fear, The Hustler of Muscle Beach, Murder by Night, Heart in Hiding, How the West Was Won, Traveling Man, Escape, Hitler's Daughter, Against Their Will: Women in Prison, Trapped in Space, Shame II: The Secret. Guest: Midnight Caller (Emmy Award, 1989), Moonlighting, Hill St. Blues, Hotel, Cannon, McGyver, Cagney & Lacey, McCloud, Riptide, many others. Mini-Series: Rich Man Poor Man—Book II.

LEON, SOL
Executive. b. New York, NY, July 2, 1913. e. NYU, City Coll. of New York, Brooklyn Law Sch., B.B.L., master of law. Exec. v.p., William Morris Agency, L.A.

LEONARD, ROBERT SEAN
Actor. b. Westwood, NJ, Feb. 28, 1969. Raised in Ridgewood, NJ. Started acting at age 12 in local summer stock. Joined NY Shakespeare Festival at 15.
THEATER: Off-B'way: Coming of Age in Soho, Sally's Gone— She Left Her Name, The Beach House, When She Danced, Romeo and Juliet, Good Evening, The Great Unwashed. B'way: Brighton Beach Memoirs, Breaking the Code, The Speed of Darkness, Candida (Tony nom.), Philadelphia Here I Come!, Arcadia. Regional: Biloxi Blues (tour), Rocky and Diego, Long Day's Journey Into Night, King Lear, The Double Inconstancy.
PICTURES: The Manhattan Project (debut, 1986), My Best Friend Is a Vampire, Dead Poets Society, Mr. & Mrs. Bridge, Swing Kids, Married to It, Much Ado About Nothing, The Age of Innocence, Safe Passage, Killer: A Journal of Murder, I Love You—I Love You Not.
TELEVISION: Movies: My Two Loves, Bluffing It. Pilot: The Robert Klein Show.

LEONARD, SHELDON
Actor, Producer. r.n. Sheldon Leonard Bershad. b. New York, NY, Feb. 22, 1907. e. Syracuse U., B.A. Theatre mgr., Publix; N.Y. stage, 10 yrs.; sec., Directors Guild of America. 3 Emmy awards, Sylvania award, 4 TV Director of the Year nominations by D.G.A, Cinematographers Governors Award, D.G.A. Aldrich Award. Inducted into TV Hall of Fame, 1992.
PICTURES: Another Thin Man, Tall, Dark and Handsome, Private Nurse, Buy Me That Town, Week-End in Havana, Tortilla Flat, Rise and Shine, Street of Chance, Lucky Jordan, Hit the Ice, Uncertain Glory, To Have and Have Not, The Falcon in Hollywood, Why Girls Leave Home, Captain Kidd, Froniter Gal, Somewhere in the Night, Her Kind of Man, It's a Wonderful Life, The Gangster, If You Knew Susie, Sinbad the Sailor, My Dream Is Yours, Take One False Step, Iroquois Trail, Behave Yourself, Here Come the Nelsons, Young Man with Ideas, Stop You're Killing Me, Diamond Queen, Money from Home, Guys and Dolls, Pocketful of Miracles, The Brinks Job.
TELEVISION: Series (actor): The Duke, Make Room for Daddy/The Danny Thomas Show (also dir., prod.; Emmy Awards for dir.: 1956, 1961), Big Eddie. Series (exec. prod.): The Andy Griffith Show, The Dick Van Dyke Show, Gomer Pyler USMC, I Spy, My World and Welcome to It (Emmy Award, 1970). Movies: Top Secret (exec. prod., actor), The Islander (exec. prod.), I Spy Returns (co-exec. prod.). Dir.: Damon Runyon, G.E. Theatre, Electric Theatre, Jewelers' Showcase, Jimmy Durante Show.

LERNER, JOSEPH
Producer, Director, Writer. m. Geraldine Lerner. Actor on Broadway; radio actor & dir.; with RKO, Columbia and Republic as dir., dial. dir., writer, 2nd unit dir., test dir.; dir.-writer & head of special productions U.S. Army Signal Corps Photographic Center; writer of commercial and educational films 1946-47; v.p. in chg. of prod. Visual Arts Productions 1947; v.p. in chg. prod. Laurel Films 1949; Girl on the Run, comm. ind. films; dir., prod., writer, many TV commercials, documentaries 1967-73; pres., The Place for Film Making, Inc.; pres., Astracor Associates Ltd.; writer & line prod. for Gold Shield Prods; also lecturer and instructor at NYU, Wm. Patterson Coll., Broward Community Coll. (FL), College at Boca Raton. Member: Eastern Council of the Directors Guild of America.
TELEVISION: Dir./Prod.: Gangbusters, Grand Tour, Three Musketeers, United Nations Case Book. Dir./Prod./Writer: C-Man, Guilty Bystander, Mr. Universe, Daek of the Day, The Fight Never Ends, etc. Prod./Writer: Olympic Cavalcade, King of The Olympics, and many other documentaries.

LERNER, MICHAEL
Actor. b. Brooklyn, NY, June 22, 1941. e. Brooklyn Col., Univ. of CA, Berkeley. Prior to acting was professor of dramatic literature at San Francisco St. Col., 1968-69. Studied acting in London on Fullbright Scholarship. Was member of San Francisco's American Conservatory Theatre. On NY stage in Twelfth Night; L.A. stage in The Women of Trachis, Hurlyburly.
PICTURES: Alex in Wonderland (debut, 1970), The Candidate, Busting, Newman's Law, Hangup (Superdude), St. Ives, The Other Side of Midnight, Outlaw Blues, Goldengirl, Borderline, Coast to Coast, The Baltimore Bullet, The Postman Always Rings Twice, National Lampoon's Class Reunion, Threshold, Strange Invaders, Movers and Shakers, Anguish, Vibes, Eight Men Out, Harlem Nights, Any Man's Death, The Closer, Barton Fink (Acad. Award nom.), Newsies, Amos & Andrew, Blank Check, No Escape, Radioland Murders, The Road to Wellville, Girl in the Cadillac, A Pyromaniac's Love Story.
TELEVISION: Series: Courthouse. Movies: Thief, Marriage Year One, What's a Nice Girl Like You...?, Magic Carpet, Firehouse (pilot), Reflections of Murder, The Rockford Files (pilot), The Death of Sammy (The Dream Makers), A Cry for Help, Starsky and Hutch (pilot), Sarah T: Portrait of a Teenage Alcoholic, Dark Victory, F. Scott Fitzgerald in Hollywood (The Screen Test), Scott Free, Killer on Board, A Love Affair: The Eleanor and Lou Gehrig Story, Vega$ (pilot), Ruby & Oswald, Hart to Hart (pilot), Moviola: This Year's Blonde, Gridlock (The Great American Traffic Jam), Blood Feud, Rita Hayworth: Love Goddess, The Execution, This Child is Mine, Betrayal of Trust (That Secret Sunday), Hands of a Stranger, King of Love, Framed, Omen IV: The Awakening, The Comrades of Summer. Special: The Missiles of October. Guest: Amazing Stories, Macgyver. Pilots: Grandpa Max, The Boys, I Gave at the Office.

LESLIE, ALEEN
Writer. b. Pittsburgh, PA, Feb. 5, 1908. e. Ohio State U. Contributor to magazines; columnist Pittsburgh Press; orig. & wrote radio series A Date with Judy 1941-50. B'way play Slightly Married, 1943; wrote, prod. Date with Judy, TV series; author, The Scent of the Roses, The Windfall.
PICTURES: Doctor Takes a Wife, Affectionately Yours, Henry Aldrich Plays Cupid, Stork Pays Off, Henry Aldrich Gets Glamour, It Comes Up Love, Rosie the Riveter, A Date With Judy, Father Was a Fullback, Father Is a Bachelor.

LESLIE, JOAN
Actress. r.n. Joan Brodell. b. Detroit, MI, January 26, 1925. e. St. Benedicts, Detroit; Our Lady of Lourdes, Toronto; St. Mary's Montreal; Immaculate Heart. H.S., L.A. Child performer on stage as part of The Three Brodels. Became model before going to Hollywood in 1936. Voted Star of Tomorrow, 1946. Now on bd. of dir., St. Anne's Maternity Home, Damon Runyon Foundation.
PICTURES: (as Joan Brodel): Camille (debut, 1937), Men with Wings, Nancy Drew—Reporter, Love Affair, Winter Carnival, Two Thoroughbreds, High School, Young as You Feel, Star Dust, Susan and God, Military Academy, Foreign Correspondent, Laddie. (as Joan Leslie): Thieves Fall Out, The Wagons Roll at Night, High Sierra, The Great Mr. Nobody, Sergeant York, The Hard Way, The Male Animal, Yankee Doodle Dandy, The Sky's the Limit, This Is the Army, Thank Your Lucky Stars, Hollywood Canteen, Rhapsody in Blue, Where Do We Go From Here?, Too Young to Know, Janie Gets Married, Cinderella Jones, Two Guys From Milwaukee, Repeat Performance, Northwest Stampede, Born To Be Bad, The Skipper Surprised His Wife, Man in the Saddle, Hellgate, Toughest Man in Arizona, The Woman They Almost Lynched, Flight Nurse, Hell's Outpost, Jubilee Trail, The Revolt of Mamie Stover.
TELEVISION: Guest: Ford Theatre, G.E. Theatre, Queen for a Day, Simon and Simon, Murder, She Wrote. Movies: Charley Hannah, The Keegans, Turn Back the Clock. Various commercials.

LESTER, MARK
Actor. b. Oxford, England, July 11, 1958. Ent. m.p. ind. 1963.
THEATER: The Murder Game, The Prince and the Pauper 1976.
PICTURES: Allez France (The Counterfeit Constable; debut, 1963), Spaceflight IC-1, Fahrenheit 451, Arrividerci Baby!, Our Mother's House, Oliver!, Run Wild Run Free, Sudden Terror (Eye Witness), Melody, Black Beauty, Who Slew Auntie Roo?, Redneck, Scalawag, Jungle Boy, Crossed Swords (The Prince and the Pauper).
TELEVISION: The Boy Who Stole the Elephants, Graduation Trip, Danza Alla Porto Gli Olmi (Italian Entry Berlin '75), Seen Dimly Before Dawn.

LESTER, MARK LESLIE
Director. b. Cleveland, OH, Nov. 26, 1949. e. U. of California, Northridge, B.A.
PICTURES: Steel Arena (debut, 1973; also co-prod., s.p.), Truck Stop Women (also prod., co-s.p.), Bobbie Jo and the Outlaw (also prod.), Stunts, Roller Boogie, The Funhouse (co-exec. prod. only), The Class of 1984 (also co-exec. prod., co-s.p.), Firestarter, Commando, Armed and Dangerous, Class of 1999 (also prod., story), Showdown in Little Tokyo, Night of the Running Man.
TELEVISION: Gold of the Amazon Women, Extreme Justice.

LESTER, RICHARD
Director. b. Philadelphia, PA, Jan. 19, 1932. e. Univ. of PA. Started as stagehand at tv studio before becoming dir. and music. dir. CBS-TV in Philadelphia, then CBC-TV, Toronto. To England in 1956 where he resumed work as tv dir. TV dir. The Goon Shows. Composed (with Reg. Owen) Sea War Series. Short Film: composer and dir., The Running Jumping and Standing Still Film. Directed sequences for Mondo Teeno/Teenage Rebellion, Superman.
PICTURES: It's Trad Dad (debut, 1962; aka Ring-a-Ding Rhythm; also prod.), The Mouse on the Moon, A Hard Day's Night, The Knack... and How to Get It, Help!, A Funny Thing Happened on the Way to the Forum, How I Won the War (also prod.), Petulia, The Bed-Sitting Room (also co-prod.), The Three Musketeers, Juggernaut, The Four Musketeers, Royal Flash, Robin & Marian (also co-prod.), The Ritz, Butch and Sundance: The Early Days, Cuba, Superman II, Superman III, Finders Keepers (also exec. prod.), The Return of the Musketeers (tv in U.S.), Get Back.

LESTZ, EARL
Executive. Chmn. of the bd., Permanent Charities Committee of the Entertainment Industries.

LETTERMAN, DAVID
Performer, Writer. b. Indianapolis, IN, Apr. 12, 1947. e. Ball State U. Began career as weatherman and talk show host on Indianapolis TV before going to Hollywood. Cameo appearance in film Cabin Boy.
TELEVISION: Series Writer: Good Times, Paul Lynde Comedy Hour. Writer (specials): John Denver Special, Bob Hope Special. Series Performer: The Starland Vocal Band (also writer), Mary (1978), Tonight Show (guest host 1978-82), The David Letterman Show (Daytime Emmy Award for writing, 1981), Late Night with David Letterman (1982-93, on NBC; 4 Emmy Awards for Writing), Late Show With David Letterman (1993-, on CBS). Guest performer: An NBC Family Christmas, The Larry Sanders Show.

LEVIN, GERALD M.
Executive. b. Philadelphia, PA, May 6, 1939. e. Haverford Col., Univ. of PA Law Sch. Attorney, 1963-67. Gen. mgr. & COO of Development Sources Corp., 1969. IBEC rep. in Tehran, Iran, 1971. Joined HBO in 1972 as v.p. of programming, then pres. & CEO, 1973-76; promoted to chmn, 1976. Became v.p. Time Inc., 1975; group v.p., video, 1979; exec. v.p. in 1984; on bd. of dirs., 1983-87. Named vice-chmn, Time Warner, 1989; COO, 1991; pres. & co-CEO of Time Warner, Inc., 1992; chmn. & CEO of Time Warner Inc., 1993.

LEVIN, ROBERT B.
Executive. b. Chicago, IL. e. U. of Illinois. Operated own adv. firm for five years. 1982, named sr. v.p., Needham Harper World Wide Advertising Agency, Chicago. 1985, joined Walt Disney Pictures as sr. v.p., mktg. 1988: Named pres. Buena Vista Pictures marketing.

LEVINE, ALAN J.
Attorney, Executive. b. Los Angeles, CA, Mar. 8, 1947. e. UCLA 1968, J.D. 1971. Partner at Pacht, Ross, Warne, Bernhard & Sears, 1971-78; Shiff, Hirsch & Schreiber, 1978-80; Armstrong, Hirsch & Levine, 1980-89. Named COO of Sony Pictures Entertainment, 1989. Promoted to pres. and CEO. Member CA Bar, L.A. County Bar, A.M.P.A.S., Academy TV Arts & Sciences.

LEVINSON, ART
Producer. Began film career as office boy at Universal Studios where he entered training program and rapidly rose from asst. director to production manager on Harry and Tonto. Assoc. prod.: Breaking Away, Mr. Mom, Teachers.
PICTURES: Assoc. Prod.: Breaking Away, Mr. Mom, Teachers, Stop or My Mom Will Shoot!. Prod.: My Favorite Year, Racing with the Moon, The Money Pit, Mannequin, Little Nikita. Exec. Prod.: My Stepmother Is an Alien, Great Balls of Fire.
TELEVISION: Billionaire Boys Club (assoc. prod.), Curacao (prod.).

LEVINSON, BARRY
Director, Producer, Writer, Actor. b. Baltimore, MD, Apr. 6, 1942. e. American Univ. Wrote and acted in L.A. comedy show leading to work on network tv incl. writing and performing on The Carol Burnett Show. Co-wrote film scripts with Mel Brooks, and then-wife Valerie Curtin. Apppeared as actor in History of the World Part 1, Quiz Show.

PICTURES: *Writer:* Silent Movie (also actor), High Anxiety (also actor), ... And Justice for All (Acad. Award nom.), Inside Moves, Best Friends, Unfaithfully Yours. *Director:* Diner (also s.p.; Acad. Award nom. for s.p.), The Natural, Young Sherlock Holmes, Tin Men (also s.p.), Good Morning Vietnam, Rain Man (also actor; Academy Award for Best Director, 1988), Avalon (also s.p.; WGA Award, Acad. Award nom. for s.p.), Bugsy (Acad. Award nom.), Toys (also co-s.p.), Jimmy Hollywood (also s.p., co-prod.), Disclosure (also co-prod.), Sleepers (also s.p., co-prod.).
TELEVISION: *Series:* The Tim Conway Comedy Hour (writer), The Marty Feldman Comedy Machine (writer), The Carol Burnett Show (writer; Emmy Awards: 1974, 1975), Harry (exec. prod.), Homicide: Life on the Streets (dir., co-exec. prod.; Emmy Award for directing, 1993). *Pilot:* Diner (exec. prod., dir.). *Specials:* Stopwatch 30 Minutes of Investigative Ticking (exec. prod.).

LEVINSON, NORM
Executive. b. New Haven, CT, Mar. 17, 1925. Started theatre business as usher for Loew's Theatres, 1940. U.S. Army, 1943-46. Returned Loew's Theatres managerial positions New Haven and Hartford, CT. MGM press representative, Minneapolis, Jacksonville, Atlanta, Dallas. General Manager, Trans-Texas Theatres, Dallas. President, Academy Theatres, Inc., Dallas. Promoted World Championship Boxing, Dallas and Johannesburg, South Africa. Executive Vice President, Cobb Theatres, Birmingham, Alabama; v.p.; world-wide mktg.; Artists Releasing Corp., Encino, CA.; head film buyer, Chakeres Theatres, Ohio & Kentucky.

LEVY, BERNARD
Executive. b. Boca Raton, FL. e. Brooklyn Law Sch., L.L.B. Legal staff of Superintendent of Insurance of the state of New York in the rehabilitation and liquidation of guaranteed title and mortgage companies, 1934-36; private practice of law, 1936-46; legal staff, Paramount Pictures, Inc., 1946-50; legal staff, United Paramount Theatres, 1950-51; exec. asst. to Edward L. Hyman, v.p., ABC, Inc., in chg. of theatre administration, north, 1951-62; apptd. exec. liaison officer for southern motion picture theatres, ABC, Inc., 1962-64; exec. liaison officer, m.p. theas., ABC, Inc., 1965-72; v.p., ABC Theatre Division, 1973. Retired, 1976.

LEVY, BUD
Executive. b. Jackson Heights, NY, April 3, 1928. e. NYU. Member: Variety Clubs Int'l., M.P. Pioneers, President's Advisory Board-NATO; director: NATO, TOP, CATO. Elected pres., Trans-Lux Corp., 1980. Pres. Trans Lux Theatres, (a subsidiary of Cinamerica Theatres, later Crown Theatres). Will Rogers Memorial Fund, Chmn., Cara Committee for NATO; chmn. ShowEast; v.p. NATO; dir. Motion Picture Pioneers.

LEVY, DAVID
Executive, Producer, Writer. b. Philadelphia, PA, Jan. 2. e. Wharton Sch., U. of PA, B.S. in Eco., M.B.A., as v.p. & assoc. dir., Young & Rubicam. Inc., 1938-59, acquisitions for clients include: People's Choice, Kate Smith Hour, Wagon Train, Four Star Playhouse, What's My Line, Father Knows Best, Goodyear Playhouse, Life of Riley, Gunsmoke, Arthur Godfrey's Talent Scouts, I Married Joan, The Web, Treasury Men in Action, Person to Person, Maverick, etc. Prod. We the People, Manhattan at Midnight. Writer: Kate Smith radio series, Manhattan at Midnight, Reunion, Robert Montgomery Presents, Grand Central Station, CBS Radio Workshop, Alcoa/Goodyear. With War Finance div. of U.S. Treasury Dept. on detached duty from U.S. Navy, 1944-46. Was v.p. in chg. of network TV progs. & talent, NBC, 1959-61. Acquisitions for network include: Sing-a-Long With Mitch, Peter Pan, Bonanza, Dr. Kildare, Bob Newhart Show, Thriller, Car 54 Where Are You?, Loretta Young Show, Sunday Showcase, Alfred Hitchcock Presents, Dick Powell Show, Saturday Night at the Movies, Hazel, Klondike, Victory at Sea, Joey Bishop Show, Shirley Temple Show, etc. Created: Bat Masterson, The Addams Family, Americans, Outlaws, Pruitts of Southampton, Sarge, Hollywood Screen Test, Face the Music, etc. Developed: Double Life of Henry Phyffe, Name That Tune, You Asked for It, etc. Assigned as writer, training film section, photographic div., Bureau of Aeronautics, U.S. Navy, 1944. Novels: The Chameleons, The Gods of Foxcroft, Network Jungle, Potomac Jungle, as well as numerous TV plays and short stories. Currently creative consultant to Mark Goodson Prods. Pres., Wilshire Prods. Exec. dir., Caucus for Prods., Writers and Dirs.

LEVY, EUGENE
Actor, Writer, Director. b. Hamilton, Canada, Dec. 17, 1946. e. McMaster U. Acted with coll. ensemble theater. Film debut in Ivan Reitman's Cannibal Girls, 1970, before joining Toronto's Second City troupe which eventually led to his work as writer-performer on Second City Television's various programs, 1977-83. *Canadian theater:* Godspell (1971), The Owl and the Pussycat, Love Times Four.

PICTURES: Cannibal Girls, Running, Heavy Metal (voice), National Lampoon's Vacation, Strange Brew, Going Berserk, Splash, Armed and Dangerous, The Canadian Conspiracy, Club Paradise, Speed Zone, Father of the Bride, Once Upon a Crime (also dir.), Stay Tuned, I Love Trouble, Multiplicity.
TELEVISION: *Series:* Second City TV, SCTV Network 90, SCTV Network (Emmy Award as writer, 1983). *Movies:* Partners in Love, Sodbusters (dir., co-writer, co-exec. prod.), Harrison Bergeron.

LEVY, HERMAN M.
Attorney. b. New Haven, CT, Sept. 27, 1904. e. Yale, B.A., 1927, Yale Law Sch., LL.B., 1929; Phi Beta Kappa, was in legal dept. RCA Photophone; newspaper reporter; admitted to Connecticut bar, 1929. 1939 elected exec. secy. of MPTO of Connecticut. 1943 elected gen. counsel MPTOA. Gen. counsel, Theatre Owners of America, 1947-63. Pres., New Haven County Bar Assn., 1964; legislative agent, CT Assn. of Theatre Owners. Retired as legislative agent, 1981. Received Distinguished Service Award from ShowEast '93. *Author:* More Sinned Against, Natl. Bd. of Review Magazine, 1941. Proving the Death of a Non-Resident Alien, Conn. Bar Journal, 1950; Need for a System of Arbitration M.P. Ind., Arbitration Journal, 1950; reprint of Industry Case Digest, 20th Century-Fox vs. Boehm in the Journal (Screen Producers Guild); Book Review of Antitrust in the Motion Picture Industry, by Michael Conant (Univ. of Calif. Law Review).

LEVY, JULES
Producer. b. Los Angeles, CA, Feb. 12, 1923. e. USC. Started in property dept. of WB, 1941; first m.p. unit Army Air Force, Culver City, CA.
PICTURES: The Vampire, Return of Dracula, Vice Squad, Without Warning, Down Three Dark Streets, Geronimo, The Glory Guys, Clambake, The Scalphunters, Sam Whiskey, The McKenzie Break, The Hunting Party, Kansas City Bomber, The Honkers, McQ, Branningan, White Lightning, Gator, Safari 3000.
TELEVISION: *Series:* The Rifleman, Robert Taylor in The Detectives, Law of the Plainsman, The Big Valley.

LEVY, MICHAEL
Executive. b. Brooklyn, NY. e. Brown U. Started in industry in editorial dept. of trade-paper Variety; held posts in New York with ABC Motion Pictures and with Diener/Hauser/Bates Advertising. Worked for Lawrence Gordon Productions as exec. asst. to Gordon and as story editor. Joined 20th Century Fox in January, 1985, as dir. of creative affairs for studio. 1986, named v.p., production, m.p. div., Fox; appointed sr. v.p. production, 20th Century Fox, 1988; named pres., Silver Pictures, 1989.

LEVY, NORMAN
Executive. b. Bronx, NY, Jan. 3, 1935. e. City Coll. of New York. 1957 joined Universal Pictures, holding various sales positions; 1967, went to National General Pictures, ultimately being named v.p. and exec. asst. to pres.; 1974, Columbia Pictures, v.p., gen. sls. mgr. 1975 named Columbia exec. v.p. in chg. of domestic sls.; 1977, exec. v.p., mktg; 1978. pres., Columbia Pictures Domestic Distribution. 1980 joined 20th-Fox as pres. of Entertainment Group; 1981, vice-chmn., 20th Century-Fox Film Corp. Resigned 1985 to become chmn, ceo, New Century/Vista Film Co. 1991, chmn. and CEO, Creative Film Enterprises.

LEWELLEN, A. WAYNE
Executive. b. Dallas, TX, Feb. 16, 1944. e. U. of Texas. Joined Paramount Pictures 1973 as brch. mgr., Dallas-Oklahoma City territory; 1978, v.p. Southern div.; 1984, exec. v.p., gen. sls. mngr.; 1986, pres. domestic distrib.; 1993, pres. M.P. distrib.

LEWIS, ARTHUR
Producer, Director, Writer. b. New York, NY, Sept. 15, 1918. e. USC, Yale U. Began career as writer and assoc. prod. on the Jones Family TV series. Five years in U.S. Army; returned to screenwriting before producing Three Wishes for Jamie on Broadway and producing and directing Guys and Dolls in London's West End. In mid-60s and 70s produced over 25 plays with Bernard Delfont in the West End of London.
PICTURES: *Producer:* Loot, Baxter, The Killer Elite, Brass Target.
TELEVISION: Brenner, The Asphalt Jungle, The Nurses. *Movies:* The Diary of Anne Frank, Splendor in the Grass.

LEWIS, EDWARD
Producer. b. Camden, NJ, Dec. 16, 1922. e. Bucknell U. Began entertainment career as script writer, then co-produced The Admiral Was a Lady and teamed with Marion Parsonnet to bring the Faye Emerson Show to TV. Subsequently prod. first Schlitz Playhouse and China Smith series. Was v.p. of Kirk Douglas' indep. prod. co., where was assoc. prod. and writer-prod. Collaborated with John Frankenheimer on 8 films.

PICTURES: Lizzie (assoc. prod.), The Careless Years (prod., s.p.), Spartacus, The Last Sunset, Lonely Are the Brave, The List of Adrian Messenger, Seconds, Grand Prix, The Fixer (exec. prod.), The Gypsy Moths (exec.), I Walk the Line (exec.), The Horsemen, The Iceman Cometh (exec.), Executive Action, Rhinoceros, Lost in the Stars, Missing (co-prod.), Crackers, The River, Brothers (prod., s.p.).
TELEVISION: Ishi: The Last of His Tribe (exec. prod.), The Thorn Birds (exec. prod.).

LEWIS, GEOFFREY
Actor. b. San Diego, CA, 1935. Father of actress Juliette Lewis, actors Lightfield & Peter Lewis.
PICTURES: Welcome Home Soldier Boys, The Culpepper Cattle Company, Bad Company, High Plains Drifter, Dillinger, Thunderbolt and Lightfoot, Macon County Line, The Great Waldo Pepper, Smile, The Wind and the Lion, Lucky Lady, The Return of a Man Called Horse, Every Which Way But Loose, Tilt, Human Experiments, Tom Horn, Broncho Billy, Heaven's Gate, Any Which Way You Can, Shoot the Sun Down, I the Jury, Ten to Midnight, Night of the Comet, Lust in the Dust, Stitches, Fletch Lives, Out of the Dark, Pink Cadillac, Catch Me If You Can, Disturbed, Double Impact, The Lawnmower Man, Point of No Return, Wishman, The Man Without a Face, Only the Strong, Army of One, Maverick.
TELEVISION: Series: Flo, Gun Shy. Movies: Moon of the Wolf, Honky Tonk, The Great Ice Rip-Off, Attack on Terror: The FBI Versus the Ku Klux Klan, The New Daughters of Joshua Cabe, The Great Houndinis, The Deadly Triangle, The Hunted Lady, When Every Day Was the Fourth of July, The Jericho Mile, Samurai, Salem's Lot, Belle Starr, The Shadow Riders, Life of the Party: The Story of Beatrice, The Return of the Man From U.N.C.L.E., Travis McGee, September Gun, Stormin' Home, Dallas: The Early Years, Day of Reckoning, Gambler V: Playing for Keeps, When the Dark Man Calls, Kansas. Guest: Mannix, Barnaby Jones, Starsky and Hutch, Streets of San Francisco, Police Woman, Little House on the Prairie, Laverne & Shirley, Lou Grant, Magnum P.I., Amazing Stories, Murder She Wrote, Paradise.

LEWIS, HAROLD G.
Executive. b. New York, NY, Sept. 18, 1938. e. Union Coll., 1960, electrical engineer. Joined ATA Trading Corp. in 1960 and has been pres. since 1977. Producer of feature animation. Importer and exporter for theatrical and TV features, documentaries, series, classics. Pres., ATA Trading Corp., and Favorite TV, Inc.

LEWIS, JERRY
Actor, Director, Writer, Producer. r.n. Joseph Levitch. b. Newark, NJ, Mar. 16, 1926. e. Irvington H.S. Parents Danny and Rae Lewis, prof. entertainers. Debut at 5 at a NY Borscht Circuit hotel singing Brother Can You Spare a Dime? 1946 formed comedy-team with Dean Martin at 500 Club, Atlantic City, NJ; then appeared on NBC tv, performed many theatres before being signed by Hal Wallis for m.p. debut. Voted Most Promising Male Star in Television in m.p. Daily's 2nd annual TV poll, 1950. Voted (as team) one of top ten money making stars in m.p. Herald-Fame poll: 1951-56 (including no. 1 position in 1952), voted as solo performer: 1957-59, 1961-64; named best comedy team in m.p. Daily's 16th annual radio poll, 1951-53. 1956 formed Jerry Lewis Prods. Inc., functioning as prod., dir., writer & star. National Chairman & bd. member, Muscular Dystrophy Association. Full professor USC; taught grad. film dir. Book: The Total Filmmaker (1971) based on classroom lectures. Autobiography: Jerry Lewis In Person (1982).
THEATER: Hellzapoppin (regional), Damn Yankees (B'way debut, 1995).
PICTURES: My Friend Irma (debut, 1949), My Friend Irma Goes West, At War With the Army, That's My Boy, Sailor Beware, Jumping Jacks, Scared Stiff, The Stooge, Road to Bali (cameo), The Caddy, Money From Home, Living It Up, Three Ring Circus, You're Never Too Young, Artists and Models, Pardners, Hollywood or Bust, The Delicate Delinquent (also prod.), The Sad Sack, Rock-a-Bye Baby, The Geisha Boy (also prod.), Don't Give Up the Ship, Li'l Abner (cameo), Visit to a Small Planet, Cinderfella (also prod.), The Bellboy (also dir., prod., s.p.), The Ladies Man (also dir., prod., co-s.p.), The Errand Boy (also dir., co-s.p.), It's Only Money, The Nutty Professor (also dir., co-s.p.), Who's Minding the Store?, It's a Mad Mad Mad Mad World (cameo), The Patsy (also dir., co-s.p.), The Disorderly Orderly, Boeing-Boeing, The Family Jewels (also dir., prod., co-s.p.), Three on a Couch (also dir., prod.), Way... Way Out, The Big Mouth (also dir., prod., co-s.p.), Don't Raise the Bridge Lower the River, Hook Line and Sinker (also prod.), Which Way to the Front? (also dir., prod.), One More Time (dir. only), The Day the Clown Cried (also dir., co-s.p.), Hardly Working (also dir., co-s.p.), The King of Comedy, Smorgasbord (Cracking Up; also dir., co-s.p.), Slapstick of Another Kind, Cookie, Mr. Saturday Night (cameo), Arizona Dream, Funny Bones.
TELEVISION: Movie: Fight for Life. Series: Colgate Comedy Hour, The Jerry Lewis Show (1963), The Jerry Lewis Show (1967-69). Guest: Wiseguy (5 episodes).

LEWIS, JOSEPH H.
Director. b. New York, NY, Apr. 6, 1907. e. DeWitt Clinton H.S. Camera boy, MGM; then asst. film ed. in chge. film ed., Republic; dir. in chge. 2nd units; debuted as dir. at Universal; served in U.S. Signal Corps., WW II. Dir. musical numbers for The Jolson Story.
PICTURES: Navy Spy (co-dir. with Crane Wilbur; debut, 1937), Courage of the West, Singing Outlaw, The Spy Ring, Border Wolves, The Last Stand, Two-Fisted Rangers, The Return of Wild Bill, That Gang of Mine, The Invisible Ghost, Pride of the Bowery, Arizona Cyclone, Bombs Over Burma, The Silver Bullet, Secrets of a Co-Ed, The Boss of Hangtown Mesa, The Mad Doctor of Market Street, Minstrel Man, The Falcon in San Francisco, My Name is Julia Ross, So Dark the Night, The Swordsman, The Return of October, The Undercover Man, Gun Crazy, A Lady Without Passport, Retreat Hell!, Desperate Search, Cry of the Hunted, The Big Combo, A Lawless Street, The Seventh Cavalry, The Halliday Brand, Terror in a Texas Town.
TELEVISION: Series: The Rifleman, The Big Valley.

LEWIS, JULIETTE
Actress. b. California, June 21, 1973. Father is actor Geoffrey Lewis.
PICTURES: My Stepmother Is an Alien (debut, 1988), Meet the Hollowheads, National Lampoon's Christmas Vacation, Crooked Hearts, Cape Fear (Acad. Award nom.), Husbands and Wives, That Night, Kalifornia, What's Eating Gilbert Grape, Romeo Is Bleeding, Natural Born Killers, Mixed Nuts, The Basketball Diaries, Strange Days, From Dusk Till Dawn, The Evening Star.
TELEVISION: Series: Homefires, I Married Dora, A Family for Joe. Movie: Too Young to Die?

LEWIS, MICHAEL J.
Composer. b. Wales, 1939. First film score 1969, The Mad Woman of Chaillot, won Ivor Novello Award for best film score. 1973: first Broadway musical, Cyrano, Grammy nomination '74, Caesar and Cleopatra (T.V. '76), The Lion the Witch and the Wardrobe (Emmy, 1979).
PICTURES: The Man Who Haunted Himself, Julius Caesar, Upon This Rock, Unman Wittering and Zigo, Running Scared, Baxter, Theatre of Blood, 11 Harrowhouse, 92 in the Shade, Russian Roulette, The Stick-Up, The Medusa Touch, The Legacy, The Passage, The Unseen, ffolkes, Sphinx, Yes Giorgio, The Hound of the Baskervilles, On the Third Day, The Naked Face.

LEWIS, RICHARD
Comedian, Actor. b. Brooklyn, NY, June 29, 1949. e. Ohio St. Univ. (marketing degree). Was copywriter for adv. agency before becoming stand-up comic performing in nightclubs in NYC, Las Vegas, 1971.
PICTURES: The Wrong Guys (debut, 1988), That's Adequate, Once Upon a Crime, Robin Hood: Men in Tights, Wagons East!, Leaving Las Vegas, Drunks.
TELEVISION: Series: Harry, Anything But Love. Specials: Richard Lewis: I'm in Pain, Richard Lewis: I'm Exhausted, Richard Lewis: I'm Doomed, Living Against the Odds (also writer). Pilot: King of the Building.

LIBERMAN, FRANK P.
Publicist, b. New York, NY, May 29, 1917. e. Cheshire Acad., CT, 1934; Lafayette Coll., Easton, PA, B.A. 1938. m. Patricia Harris, casting dir. Worked as copy boy, N.Y. Daily News, 1938-39. Began career as publicist at Warner Bros., home office as messenger, 1939, promoted to pressbooks dept., transferred to Warner's Chicago office as field exploitation man. U.S. Signal Corps, 1941, public relations officer, Army Pictorial Service, on temporary duty with War Dept., Bureau of Public Relations in Pentagon. Discharged as Capt., 1946. Rejoined Warner Bros. on coast 2 years, 1947, est. own public relations office, 1947. Owner, Frank Liberman and Associates, Inc.

LIBERTINI, RICHARD
Actor. b. Cambridge, MA, May 21. Original member of Second City troupe in Chicago. With MacIntyre Dixon appeared as the Stewed Prunes in cabaret performances.
THEATER: Three by Three (1961), Plays for Bleecker Street, The Cat's Pajamas, The Mad Show, Bad Habits. Solo: The White House Murder Case, Don't Drink the Water, Paul Sill's Story Theatre, Ovid's Metamorphoses, The Primary English Class, Neopolitan Ghosts, Love's Labour's Lost, As You Like It.
PICTURES: The Night They Raided Minsky's, Don't Drink the Water, Catch-22, The Out-of-Towners, Lovers and Other Strangers, Lady Liberty, Fire Sale, Days of Heaven, The In-Laws, Popeye, Sharky's Machine, Soup for One, Best Friends, Deal of the Century, Going Berserk, Unfaithfully Yours, All of Me, Fletch, Big Trouble, Betrayed, Fletch Lives, Animal Behavior. Duck Tales: The Movie (voice), Lemon Sisters, Awakenings, The Bonfire of the Vanities, Cultivating Charlie, Nell.

TELEVISION: *Series*: Story Theatre, The Melba Moore-Clifton Davis Show, Soap, Family Man, The Fanelli Boys, Pacific Station. *Guest*: George Burns Comedy Week, Barney Miller, Bob Newhart. *Pilots*: Calling Dr. Storm, M.D., Fair Game. *Movies*: Three on a Date, Extreme Close-Up. *Specials*: Let's Celebrate, The Fourth Wise Man, Fame (Hallmark Hall of Fame), The Trial of Bernhard Goetz, Equal Justice, Murder She Wrote, Law and Order, L.A. Law.

LICCARDI, VINCENT G.
Executive. b. Brooklyn, NY. Started as messenger at Universal Pictures, asst. adv. mgr. on Around the World in 80 Days, asst. to exec. coord. of sales & Adv. on Spartacus; National Dir. of Adv. & Publ., Continental; Nat. Dir. Adv. & Publ., Braintree Prod., adv. pub. mgr. Allied Artists, ad. mgr. Paramount, National Dir. Adv.-Pub., UMC Pictures, Screenwriter, Playboy to Priest, The Rivals, The Rivals-Part II, The Greatest Disaster of All Time, The Lady on the 9:40, All That Heaven Allows, All Mine to Love, Twice Over, Lightly!, Mr. Jim.

LIEBERFARB, WARREN N.
Executive. e. Wharton Sch. of Commerce and Finance, U. of PA, B.S., economics; U. of Michigan. Started career in industry at Paramount Pictures as dir. of mktg. and exec. asst. to Stanley Jaffe, then pres. Later joined 20th-Fox as v.p., special market dist. (cable, pay-TV, non-theatrical). Joined Warner Bros. as v.p., exec. asst. to Ted Ashley, bd. chmn.; later named v.p., intl. adv.-pub. In 1979 joined Lorimar as v.p., of Lorimar Productions, Inc., the parent company, based in New York. Promoted to sr. v.p. 1982, named v.p. mktg., Warner Home Video; named pres., 1984.

LIEBERMAN, HAL
Executive. Pres. of production, Universal Pictures.

LIEBERMAN, ROBERT
Director, Producer. b. Buffalo, NY, July 16, 1947. e. Univ. of Buffalo. m. actress Marilu Henner. Moved to LA, became editor for Desort-Fisher commercial production house, which led to dir. tv ad spots. Formed own commercial company, Harmony Pictures.
PICTURES: Table for Five, All I Want for Christmas, Fire in the Sky.
TELEVISION: *Movies*: Fighting Back: The Story of Rocky Blier, Will: G. Gordon Liddy, To Save a Child (also exec. prod.). *Series*: thirtysomething, Dream Street (pilot), The Young Riders (pilot), Gabriel's Fire (also exec. prod.), Pros and Cons (exec. consultant), Under Suspicion (also exec. prod.), Medicine Ball (also exec. prod.).

LIEBERSON, SANFORD
Producer. b. Los Angeles, CA, 1936. Early career with William Morris Agency. 1961-62, agent in Rome for Grade Org. Returned to LA as Founding Member CMA agency then exec. in charge of European operations. 1979, named pres. of 20th-Fox Productions, which company he joined in 1977 as v.p. European production. Previously an independent producer forming Good Times. With David Putnam formed Visual Programming Systems to produce, acquire and consult in the Home Video area for CBS, Phillips, Time/Life, etc. As v.p. intl. prod. at Fox, spv. intl. release of such films as Star Wars, 1900, Alien, Chariots of Fire, Nine to Five, Quest for Fire. V.P. Intl. prod. for The Ladd Company. Outland, Body Heat, Blade Runner, The Right Stuff, Police Academy, etc. Chief of prod. at Goldcrest Harvest: Dance With a Stranger, Room With a View, Absolute Beginners, etc. Pres. intl. prod. MGM spv. Russia House, Thelma & Louise, Liebestraum, Not Without My Daughter, Criss Cross, etc. Currently head of prod. at the Natl. Film and Television School of Great Britain.
PICTURES: *Producer*: Melody, Pied Piper, Radio Wonderful, James Dean: First American Teenager, Bugsy Malone, Slade in Flame, Final Programme, Stardust, That'll Be the Day, Brother Can You Spare a Dime, Swastika, Double Headed Eagle, All This and World War II, Mahler, Lisztomania, Jabberwocky, Rita Sue and Bob Too, Stars and Bars, The Mighty Quinn.
TELEVISION: *Movie*: Frank & Jessie (exec. prod.).

LIGHT, JUDITH
Actress. b. Trenton, NJ, Feb. 9. e. Carnegie-Mellon Univ. (BFA). Toured with USO in prod. of Guys and Dolls during college. Acted with Milwaukee and Seattle rep. companies. Made B'way debut in 1975 prod. of A Doll's House with Liv Ullmann. Other stage work: A Streetcar Named Desire, As You Like It, Richard III. Landed role of Karen Wolek on daytime serial One Life to Live in 1977.
TELEVISION: *Series*: One Life to Live (2 Emmy Awards), Who's the Boss?, Phenom. *Movies*: Intimate Agony, Dangerous Affection, The Ryan White Story, My Boyfriend's Back, In Defense of a Married Man, Wife Mother Murderer, Men Don't Tell, Betrayal of Trust, Against Their Will: Women in Prison, Lady Killer, A Husband, A Wife And A Lover. *Guest*: St. Elsewhere, Family Ties, Remington Steele.

LIGHTMAN, M. A.
Exhibitor. b. Nashville, TN, Apr. 21, 1915. e. Southwestern U., Vanderbilt U., 1936, B.A. Bd. chmn. Malco Theatres, Inc., Memphis, Tenn.

LINDBLOM, GUNNEL
Actress, Director. b. Gothenburg, Sweden, 1931. Discovered by Ingmar Bergman while studying at drama school of Gothenburg Municipal Theatre, 1950-53; she moved to Malmo, where he was director of the local Municipal Theatre. Under Bergman's direction she played in Easter, Peer Gynt, Faust, etc. between 1954-59. Later appeared in many Bergman films. Since 1968 has been on staff of Stockholm's Royal Dramatic Theatre, assisting Bergman and then beginning to direct on her own. Made film debut as director with Summer Paradise in 1977.
PICTURES: *Actress*: Love, Girl in the Rain, Song of the Scarlet Flower, The Seventh Seal, Wild Strawberries, The Virgin Spring, Winter Light, The Silence, My Love Is a Rose, Rapture, Loving Couples, Hunger, Woman of Darkness, The Girls, The Father, Brother Carl, Scenes From a Marriage, Misfire, Bakom Jalusin. *Director*: Summer Paradise (also co-s.p.), Sally and Freedom, Summer Nights on Planet Earth (also s.p.).

LINDEN, HAL
Actor. b. Bronx, NY, March 20, 1931. e. City Coll. of New York. Began career as saxophone player and singer, playing with bands of Sammy Kaye, Bobby Sherwood, etc. Drafted and performed in revues for Special Services. After discharge enrolled at N.Y.'s American Theatre Wing; appeared on B'way in Bells Are Ringing, replacing Sydney Chaplin.
THEATER: Wildcat, Something More, Subways Are for Sleeping, Ilya Darling, The Apple Tree, The Education of H*Y*M*A*N K*A*P*L*A*N, On a Clear Day You Can See Forever, Three Men on a Horse, The Pajama Game, The Rothschilds (Tony Award, 1971), I'm Not Rappaport, Unfinished Stories, The Sisters Rosensweig.
PICTURES: Bells Are Ringing, When You Comin' Back Red Ryder?, A New Life.
TELEVISION: *Series*: Animals Animals Animals (host), Barney Miller, Blacke's Magic, F.Y.I. (Emmy Awards, 1983, 1984), Jack's Place, The Boys Are Back. *Specials*: I Do! I Do!, The Best of Everything. *Movies*: Mr. Inside/Mr. Outside, The Love Boat (pilot), How to Break Up a Happy Divorce, Father Figure, Starflight: The Plane That Couldn't Land, The Other Woman, My Wicked Wicked Ways: The Legend of Errol Flynn, The O'Connors, Dream Breakers, The Colony.

LINDHEIM, RICHARD D.
Executive. e. Univ. of Redlands, USC. Started as wrtier/prod. for KNBC in LA. NBC 1969, to NBC as administrator of program testing; 1974, v.p., NBC program research; then v.p. current drama progs. NBC. 1979, joined Universal TV as prod.; 1981, appointed to v.p. of current programming, then sr. v.p. series programming; 1987, named exec. v.p., creative affairs. 1992, became exec. v.p. of Paramount Television Group.

LINDO, DELROY
Actor. b. London, England, Nov. 18, 1952. Received NAACP Image Awards for film Malcolm X and play A Raisin in the Sun.
THEATER: *B'way*: Joe Turner's Come and Gone (Tony nom.), Master Harold and the Boys. *Off-B'way*: District Line, As You Like It, Romeo and Juliet, Spell #7, The Heliotrope Bouquet. *Regional*: Othello, Mrs. Ever's Boys, Cobb, A Raisin in the Sun, My Mark My Name, Union Boys, Macbeth, Black Branch, Home.
PICTURES: The Blood of Heroes (Salute to the Jugger; debut, 1990), Mountains of the Moon, Perfect Witness, The Hard Way, Bright Angel, Malcolm X, Bound by Honor, Mr. Jones, Behanzin, Crooklyn, Congo, Clockers, Get Shorty, Feeling Minnesota, Broken Arrow, Ransom.
TELEVISION: *Guest*: Going to Extremes, Against the Law, Hawk, Beauty and the Beast.

LINDSAY, ROBERT
Actor. b. Ilkeston, Derbyshire, Eng., Dec. 13, 1949. e. GLadstone Boys School, Ilkeston, Royal Acad. of Dramatic Art. With Manchester's Royal Exchange Theatre Co. (Hamlet, The Cherry Orchard, The Lower Depths). Also in Godspell, The Three Musketeers, Me and My Girl, (London—Olivier Award, NY—Tony, Theatre World & Drama Desk Awards, 1987), Becket (Olivier & Variety Club Awards), Cyrano de Bergerac.
PICTURES: That'll Be the Day (debut, 1974), Bert Rigby You're a Fool, Strike It Rich, Fierce Creatures.
TELEVISION: *Series*: Citizen Smith, Give Us A Break. *Mini-series*: Confessional. *Specials*: King Lear, G.B.H. (BAFTA Award), Genghis Cohn, Jake's Progress.

LINDSAY-HOGG, MICHAEL
Director. b. England, 1940. Mother is actress Geraldine Fitzgerald.
PICTURES: Let It Be, Nasty Habits, The Object of Beauty (also s.p.), Frankie Starlight.
TELEVISION: Brideshead Revisted (co-dir.), Master Harold ... and the Boys, As Is.

LINK, WILLIAM
Writer, Producer. b. Philadelphia, PA, Dec. 15, 1933. e. U. of Pennsylvania, B.S., 1956. With partner, late Richard Levinson, wrote and created numerous TV series and movies, specializing in detective-mystery genre. *Books:* Fineman, Stay Tuned: An Inside Look at the Making of Prime-Time Television, Off Camera. *Stage incl.:* Prescription Murder, Guilty Conscience, Merlin.
PICTURES: The Hindenberg, Rollercoaster.
TELEVISION: *Series writer-creator:* Mannix, Ellery Queen, Tenafly, Columbo (Emmy Award as writer, 1972), Murder She Wrote. *Movies* writer-prod.: That Certain Summer, My Sweet Charlie (Emmy Award as writer, 1970), The Judge and Jake Wyler, Savage (exec. prod., writer), The Execution of Private Slovik, The Gun, A Cry for Help (prod. only), The Storyteller, Murder by Natural Causes, Stone, Crisis at Central High, Rehearsal For Murder (also exec. prod.), Take Your Best Shot, Prototype (also exec. prod.), The Guardian (also exec. prod.), Guilty Conscience (also exec. prod.), Vanishing Act (also exec. prod.), The United States Vs. Salim Ajami, The Boys (also co-exec. prod.).

LINKLATER, RICHARD
Director, Writer, Producer. b. Houston, TX, 1961. Founded Austin Film Society, serving as artistic director. Filmed several super 8 films incl. feature It's Impossible to Learn to Plow by Reading Books.
PICTURES: *Director/Writer:* Slacker (also prod.), Dazed and Confused (also co-prod.), Before Sunrise.

LINKLETTER, ART
Emcee, Producer, Author. b. Moose Jaw, Saskatchewan, Canada, July 17, 1912. Raised in San Diego. e. San Diego State Coll. Radio prg. mgr., San Diego Exposition, 1935; radio pgm. mgr. S.F. World's Fair, 1937-39; freelance radio announcer and m.c. 1939-42; m.c. series People Are Funny starting in 1942. Author: The Secret World of Kids, 1959; Kids Say the Darndest Things, 1957; Linkletter Down Under, 1969; Yes You Can, 1979; Old Age Is Not For Sissies, 1988; Cavalcade of the Golden West; Cavalcade of America. Recorded albums: Howls, Boners & Shockers and We Love You, Call Collect (Grammy Award winner, 1966).
PICTURES: People Are Funny, Champagne for Caesar, The Snow Queen.
TELEVISION: *Series:* Art Linkletter's House Party, Life With Linkletter, People Are Funny (emcee), The Art Linkletter Show (emcee), Hollywood Talent Scouts. *Specials:* Inside Salute to Baseball (exec. prod., host), Art Linkletter's Secret World of Kids (host), Ford Startime, Young Man With A Band. *Movies:* Sane Grey Theatre, G.E. Theatre.

LINN-BAKER, MARK
Actor, Director. b. St. Louis, MO, June 17, 1954. e. Yale Univ., Yale Sch. of Drama (M.F.A., 1979). Founding memb. American Repertory Th. in Cambridge, MA; founding prod./dir. NY Stage & Film Co. in NYC & Poughkeepsie. Co-founder of True Pictures, 1990.
THEATER: *B'way:* Doonesbury, Laughter on the 23rd Floor, A Funny Thing Happened On The Way To The Forum.
PICTURES: Manhattan (bit), The End of August, My Favorite Year, Me and Him (voice only), Noises Off, Me and Veronica (co-prod. only).
TELEVISION: *Series:* Comedy Zone, Perfect Strangers, Hangin' With Mr. Cooper (dir. only). *Movies:* Wedding Bell Blues, Bare Essentials. *Specials:* Doonesbury (voice of Kirby), The Ghost Writer (Amer. Playhouse), The Whole Shebang. *Director:* episodes of Family Matters, Family Man, Going Places.

LINSON, ART
Producer, Director. b. Chicago, IL, 1942. e. UCLA; LLD. UCLA, 1967. Was rock music manager with record prod. Lou Adler and ran own record co., Spin Dizzy records before turning to film production. Debuted as director also with Where the Buffalo Roam.
PICTURES: Rafferty and the Gold Dust Twins (co.-prod.), Car Wash, American Hot Wax (also co-s.p.), Where the Buffalo Roam (also dir.), Melvin and Howard, Fast Times at Ridgemont High (co-prod.), The Wild Life (also dir.), The Untouchables (prod.), Scrooged (prod.), Casualties of War (prod.), We're No Angels (prod.), Dick Tracy (exec. prod.), Singles, Point of No Return, This Boy's Life (prod.).

LIOTTA, RAY
Actor. b. Newark, NJ, Dec. 18, 1955. e. Univ. of Miami. First prof. job on tv commercial, followed by continuing role on daytime serial, Another World.
PICTURES: The Lonely Lady (debut, 1983), Something Wild, Dominick and Eugene, Field of Dreams, GoodFellas, Article 99, Unlawful Entry, No Escape, Corrina Corrina, Operation Dumbo Drop, Unforgettable, Turbulence.
TELEVISION: *Series:* Another World, Casablanca, Our Family Honor. *Movies:* Harhat and Legs, Crazy Times, Women and Men 2: In Love There Are No Rules (Domestic Dilemma).

LIPPERT, ROBERT L., JR.
Producer, Exhibitor. b. Alameda, CA, Feb. 28, 1928. e. St Mary's Coll., 1946; all conference football 1947. Career began in theatre exhibition. Entered m.p. production in 1951. Film editor of 45 "b" features. Produced 9 pictures for Lippert Features and 20th Century Fox Films. Returned in 1966 to theatre exhibition. Became pres. of Affiliated, Lippert, Transcontinental theatrs (180 theatres nation-wide). Semi-retired as of 1994.

LIPSTONE, HOWARD H.
Executive, Producer. b. Chicago, IL, Apr. 28, 1928. e. UCLA. USC. Ass't to gen. mgr. at KLTA, 1950-55; program dir. at KABC-TV, 1955-65; exec. ass't to pres. at Selmur Prods., ABC subsidiary, 1965-69. Ivan Tors Films & Studios as exec. v.p., 1969-70; pres., Alan Landsburg Prods., 1970-1985; The Landsburg Co., 1985-. Co-exec. prod.: The Outer Space Connection, The Bermuda Triangle, Mysteries, The White Lions, Jaws 3-D.
TELEVISION: *Exec. in charge of prod.:* The Savage Bees, Ruby and Oswald, The Triangle Factory Fire Scandal, Strange Voices, A Place at the Table, Kate & Allie, Gimme a Break, A Stoning in Fulham County, The Ryan White Story, Quiet Victory, Unspeakable Acts, In Defense of a Married Man, Triumph of the Heart, Nightmare in Columbia County, A Mother's Right, The Elizabeth Morgan Story, The diamond Fleece, Terror in the Night, If Someone Had Known.

LIPTON, PEGGY
Actress. b. New York, NY, Aug. 30, 1947. Former model. Co-wrote song L.A. is My Lady (recorded by Frank Sinatra). Recorded album Peggy Lipton.
PICTURES: The Purple People Eater, Kinjite (Forbidden Subjects), Twin Peaks: Fire Walk With Me.
TELEVISION: *Series:* The John Forsythe Show, The Mod Squad (Golden Globe Award, 1971), Twin Peaks, Angel Falls. *Movies:* The Return of the Mod Squad, Addicted to His Love, Fatal Charm, The Spider and the Fly, Deadly Vows.

LISI, VIRNA
Actress. r.n. Virna Pieralisi. b. Ancona, Italy, Nov. 8, 1936.
PICTURES: Desiderio e Sole, Violenza sul Lago, The Doll That Took the Town, Luna Nova, Vendicatta, La Rossa, Caterina Sforza, Il Mondo dei Miracoli, Duel of the Titans, Eva, Don't Tempt the Devil, The Black Tulip, The Shortest Day, How To Murder Your Wife, Casanova 70, The Possessed, A Virgin for a Prince, Kiss the Other Sheik, The Birds the Bees and the Italians, Made in Italy, La Bambole (The Dolls), Not With My Wife You Don't, Assault on a Queen, The 25th Hour, Anyone Can Play, The Girl and the General, Arabella, Better a Widow, The Girl Who Couldn't Say No, The Christmas Tree, The Secret of Santa Vittoria, If It's Tuesday This Must Be Belgium, Roma Bene, The Statue, Bluebeard, The Serpent, Ernesto, I Love N.Y., I Ragazzi di Via Panisperna, Beyond Good and Evil, Merry Christmas Happy New Year, Miss Right, Queen Margot (Cannes Film Fest. Award, 1994).
TELEVISION: *US:* Christopher Columbus.

LITHGOW, JOHN
Actor. b. Rochester, NY, Oct. 19, 1945. Father was prod. of Shakespeare Fests. in midwest. e. Harvard. Fulbright fellowship to study at London Acad. of Music and Dramatic Art. Interned in London with Royal Shakespeare Co. and Royal Court Theatre.
THEATER: *NY:* The Changing Room (Tony & Drama Desk Awards, 1973), My Fat Friend, Trelawney of the Wells, Comedians, Anna Christie, A Memory of Two Mondays, Once in a Lifetime, Spokesong, Bedroom Farce, Salt Lake City Skyline, Division Street (also LA), Kaufman at Large (also dir., writer), Beyond Therapy, Requiem for a Heavyweight (Drama Desk Award), The Front Page, M Butterfly. *Regional:* The Beggar's Opera, Pygmalion, Of Mice and Men, Troilus and Cressida, The Roar of the Greasepaint, What Price Glory?, The Lady's Not for Burning, Who's Afraid of Virginia Woolf? (LA Drama Critics Circle Award).
PICTURES: Dealing or The Berkeley-to-Boston Forty-Brick Lost-Bag Blues (debut, 1972), Obsession, The Big Fix, Rich Kids, All That Jazz, Blow Out, I'm Dancing as Fast as I Can, The World According to Garp (Acad. Award nom.), Twilight Zone—The Movie, Terms of Endearment (Acad. Award nom.), Footloose, The Adventures of Buckaroo Banzai: Across the Eighth Dimension, 2010, Santa Claus, The Manhattan Project, Mesmerized, Harry and the Hendersons, Distant Thunder, Out Cold, Memphis Belle, Ricochet, At Play in the Fields of the Lord, Raising Cain, Cliffhanger, The Pelican Brief, A Good Man in Africa, Princess Caraboo, Silent Fall, Hollow Point.
TELEVISION: *Series:* Third Rock From the Sun (Emmy Award, 1996). *Guest:* Amazing Stories (Emmy Award, 1987), Saturday Night Live. *Movies:* Mom The Wolfman and Me, Not in Front of the Children, The Day After, The Glitter Dome, Resting Place, Baby Girl Scott, The Traveling Man, The Last Elephant (Ivory Hunters), The Boys, The Wrong Man, Love Cheat and Steal, World War II: When Lions Roared, Redwood

Curtain, The Tuskegee Airmen. *Specials*: The Country Girl (TV debut, 1973), Secret Service, Big Blonde, The Oldest Living Graduate, Goldilocks and the Three Bears (Faerie Tale Theatre).

LITTLE, RICH
Actor. b. Ottawa, Canada, Nov. 26, 1938. Started as radio disc jockey, talk show host in Canada; then impressionist in night clubs.
PICTURES: Dirty Tricks, Happy Hour, Bebe's Kids (voice).
TELEVISION: *Series*: Love on a Rooftop, The John Davidson Show, ABC Comedy Hour (The Kopycats), The Julie Andrews Hour, The Rich Little Show, The New You Asked For It (host). *Specials*: The Rich Little Show, Rich Little's Christmas Carol (also writer), Rich Little's Washington Follies, The Rich Little Specials (HBO), Rich Little's Robin Hood, Come Laugh With Me, Night of 42 Stars, The Christmas Raccoons, Rich Little and Friends in New Orleans, etc.

LITTLEFIELD, WARREN
Executive. b. Montclair, NJ. e. American Univ. in DC, School of Government and Public Admin.; Hobart Col. (psych. degree). 1975-79, Westfall Prods., developing prime-time specials and movies before being promoted to v.p., develop. & prod. 1979, served as WB TV dir., comedy develop. Joined NBC 1979, as mngr. comedy develop. 1981, v.p. current comedy programs at NBC. 1985, sr. v.p. series specials & variety progs., NBC Entertainment; 1987, exec. v.p., Prime-Time progs. NBC Entertainment. 1990, named pres. NBC Entertainment.

LITTMAN, LYNNE
Director, Producer. b. New York, NY, June 26. e. Sarah Lawrence. B.A., 1962; Student the Sorbonne 1960-61. Researcher for CBS News 1965; assoc. prod. Natl. Educational TV 1964-68; dir. NIMH film series on drug abuse UCLA Media Center 1970; prod., dir. documentary films, news and pub. affairs series KCET Community TV, So. Calif. 1971-77; dir. WNET non-fiction film, Once a Daughter 1979; exec. v.p., movies-for-TV, ABC, 1980-81; Received Ford Fdn. Grant 1978 and numerous awards. Acad. Award film tribute to women, 1993.
PICTURES: In the Matter of Kenneth (doc.), Wanted-Operadoras (doc.), Till Death Do Us Part (doc.), Number Our Days (doc. short; Academy Award 1977), Testament (co-prod., dir.), In Her Own Time.

LITTO, GEORGE
Producer. b. Philadelphia, PA. e. Temple U. Joined William Morris Agency in New York and then became indep. literary agent. Opened own office in Hollywood, then. Packaged film and TV productions, including M*A*S*H, Hang 'Em High, Hawaii Five-O for TV prior to entering indep. prod.; 1981-82, chmn. bd. & CEO, Filmways; 1983-85 indep. prod. 20th Century Fox.
PICTURES: Thieves Like Us (exec. prod.), Drive-In (exec. prod.), Obsession (prod.), Over the Edge (prod.), Dressed To Kill (prod.). Blow Out (prod.), Kansas (prod.), Night Game (prod.).

LITVINOFF, SI
Producer, Executive. b. New York, NY, April 5. e. Adelphi Coll., A.B.; NYU Sch. of Law, LL.B. Theatrical lawyer, personal and business manager in New York until 1967 when left firm of Barovick, Konecky & Litvinoff to produce plays and films. June, 1987: sr. v.p. for production and dev., Hawkeye Entertainment, Inc.
THEATER: Leonard Bernstein's Theatre Songs, Cry of the Raindrop, Girl of the Golden West, Little Malcolm and His Struggle Against the Eunuchs, I and Albert (London).
PICTURES: The Queen, All the Right Noises, Walkabout, A Clockwork Orange (exec. prod.), Glastonbury Fayre (exec. in chg. prod.), The Man Who Fell to Earth (exec. prod.)
TELEVISION: *Exec. prod.*: 15th Annual Saturn Awards, Doobie Brothers Retrospective, Listen to the Music 1989.

LIVINGSTON, JAY
Composer, Lyricist. b. McDonald, PA, March 28, 1915. e. U. of PA, 1937, UCLA, 1964-65. Army, WWII. Accompanist and arranger for various NBC singers and singing groups 1940-42, NY; author music and special material for Olsen & Johnson, including various editions of Hellzapoppin', and Sons O'Fun; began composing m.p. songs, 1944. Under contract to Paramount, 1945-55; then freelanced. Cameo appearance in Sunset Boulevard. Writer of songs and special material for Bob Hope starting in 1945. Has written songs for over 100 pictures. Elected to Songwriters Hall of Fame, 1975. Received star on Hollywood Blvd. Walk of Fame, 1995.
SONGS INCLUDE: G'bye Now, Stuff Like That There, To Each His Own, Golden Earrings, Silver Bells, Buttons and Bows (Academy Award, 1949), Mona Lisa (Academy Award, 1951), Que Sera Sera/Whatever Will Be Will Be (Academy Award, 1957), Tammy (Acad. Award nom.), Almost In Your Arms

(Acad. Award nom.), Dear Heart, (Acad. Award nom.), Wish Me a Rainbow, In the Arms of Love, Never Let Me Go, As I Love You, All the Time, Maybe September.
THEATER: *B'way*: Oh Captain!, Let It Ride, Sugar Babies (2 songs).
PICTURES: Monsieur Beaucaire, My Favorite Brunette, The Paleface, My Friend Irma, Sorrowful Jones, My Friend Irma Goes West, Streets of Laredo, Isn't It Romantic?, Fancy Pants, Here Comes the Groom, The Lemon-Drop Kid, Son of Paleface, The Stars Are Singing, Here Come the Girls, Somebody Loves Me, Aaron Slick from Punkin' Crick, Red Garters, The Man Who Knew Too Much, Houseboat, Tammy and the Bachelor, Dear Heart, The Night of the Grizzly, This Property Is Condemned, The Oscar, Never Too Late, Harlow, What Did You Do in the War Daddy?, Wait Until Dark.
TELEVISION: Series themes: Bonanza, Mister Ed.

LLOYD, CHRISTOPHER
Actor. b. Stamford, CT, Oct. 22, 1938. Studied at Neighborhood Playhouse, NY.
THEATER: *NY*: Kaspar (Drama Desk & Obie Awards, 1973), Happy End, Red White and Maddox. Regional: The Father, Hot L Baltimore, The Possessed, A Midsummer Night's Dream.
PICTURES: One Flew Over the Cuckoo's Nest (debut, 1975), Goin' South, Butch and Sundance: The Early Days, The Onion Field, The Lady in Red, Schizoid, The Black Marble, The Postman Always Rings Twice, The Legend of the Lone Ranger, National Lampoon Goes to the Movies, Mr. Mom, To Be or Not to Be, Star Trek III: The Search for Spock, The Adventures of Buckaroo Banzai Across the Eighth Dimension, Joy of Sex, Back to the Future, Clue, Legend of the White Horse, Miracles, Walk Like a Man, Who Framed Roger Rabbit, Track 29, Eight Men Out, The Dream Team, Back to the Future Part II, Why Me?, Back to the Future Part III, Duck Tales: The Movie (voice), White Dragon, Suburban Commando, The Addams Family, Dennis the Menace, Twenty Bucks, Addams Family Values, Angels in the Outfield, Camp Nowhere, Radioland Murders, The Pagemaster, Things to Do in Denver When You're Dead, Cadillac Ranch.
TELEVISION: *Series*: Taxi (Emmy Awards: 1982, 1983), Back to the Future (voice for animated series), Deadly Games. *Specials*: Pilgrim Farewell, The Penny Elf, Tales From Hollywood Hills: Pat Hobby—Teamed With Genius, In Search of Dr. Seuss. *Movies*: Lacy and the Mississippi Queen, The Word, Stunt Seven, Money on the Side, September Gun, The Cowboy and the Ballerina, T Bone N Weasel, Dead Ahead: The Exxon Valdez Disaster. *Guest*: Barney Miller, Best of the West, Cheers, Amazing Stories, Avonlea (Emmy Award, 1992).

LLOYD, EMILY
Actress. b. North London, Eng., Sept. 29, 1970. r.n. Emily Lloyd Pack. Father is stage actor Roger Lloyd Pack; mother worked as Harold Pinter's secretary. Father's agent recommended that she audition for screenwriter David Leland's directorial debut Wish You Were Here when she was 15.
PICTURES: Wish You Were Here (Natl. Society of Film Critics & London Evening Standard Awards, 1987; BAFTA nom.), Cookie, In Country, Chicago Joe and the Showgirl, Scorchers, A River Runs Through It, Under the Hula Moon, When Saturday Comes.

LLOYD, EUAN
Producer. b. Rugby, Warwick, England, Dec. 6, 1923. e. Rugby. Entered m.p. ind. in 1939 as theatre manager, then pub. dir.; dir. of Publ. Rank, 1946; joined Associated British-Pathe, in same capacity; 1952 asst. to prod., Warwick Film Prod. Ltd. v.p. Highroad Productions, 1962-64. Rep. Europe Goldwyn's Porgy & Bess 1959.
PICTURES: April in Portugal, Heart of Variety, Invitation to Monte Carlo, The Secret Ways, Genghis Khan, Poppy Is Also a Flower, Murderer's Row, Shalako, Catlow, The Man Called Noon, Paper Tiger, The Wild Geese, The Sea Wolves, Who Dares Wins, Wild Geese II, The Final Option.

LLOYD, NORMAN
Actor, Producer, Director. b. Jersey City, NJ, Nov. 8, 1914. e. NYU, 1932. Acted on B'way in: Noah, Liberty Jones, Everywhere I Roam, 1935-44; in various stock companies. Joined Orson Welles and John Houseman in the original company of Mercury Theatre, NY, 1937-38. Prod. asst. on films Arch of Triumph, The Red Pony. Produced film Up Above the World.
THEATER: Village Green, King Lear, The Cocktail Party, The Lady's Not for Burning, Madame Will You Walk, The Golden Apple, Major Barbara, The Will & Bart Show, Quiet City. With La Jolla Playhouse (1948-55).
PICTURES: *Actor*: Saboteur, Spellbound, The Southerner, A Walk in the Sun, A Letter for Evie, The Unseen, Green Years, The Beginning or The End, Limelight, Young Widow, No Minor Vices, The Black Book, Scene of the Crime, Calamity Jane and Sam Bass, Buccaneer's Girl, The Flame and the Arrow,

He Ran All the Way, The Light Touch, Audrey Rose, FM, The Nude Bomb, Jaws of Satan, Dead Poets Society, Journey of Honor (Shogun Mayeda), The Age of Innocence.
TELEVISION: *Assoc. prod./exec. prod.*: The Alfred Hitchcock Show. *Prod.-Dir.*: The Alfred Hitchcock Hour, The Name of the Game, Hollywood Television Theater, Tales of the Unexpected, Omnibus (dir. of The Lincoln Films, 1952). *Actor*: St. Elsewhere (series). *Movies* (prod.-dir.): The Smugglers, Companions in Nightmare, What's a Nice Girl Like You (prod.), The Bravos (prod.), Amityville: The Evil Escapes.

LOACH, KEN
Director, Writer. b. Nuneaton, England, June 17, 1936. e. Oxford (studied law). Served in Royal Air Force; then became actor. Began dir. career on British tv in early 1960's.
PICTURES: Poor Cow (debut, 1968; also co-s.p.), Kes (also co-s.p.), Family Life, Black Jack (also co-s.p.), Looks and Smiles (also co- s.p.), Fatherland (Singing the Blues in Red), Hidden Agenda, Riff- Raff, Raining Stones, Land and Freedom.
TELEVISION: Diary of a Young Man, 3 Clear Sundays, The End of Arthur's Marriage, Up the Junction, Coming Out Party, Cathy Come Home, In Two Minds, The Golden Vision, The Big Flame, In Black and White, After a Lifetime, The Rank and the File, Days of Hope, The Price of Coal, Auditions: The Gamekeeper, A Question of Leadership, Which Side Are You On.

LOBELL, MICHAEL
Producer. b. Brooklyn, NY, May 7, 1941. e. Michigan State U. on athletic baseball scholarship. Worked briefly in garment indust. Entered film industry in 1974 by buying Danish distribution rights to The Apprenticeship of Duddy Kravitz. Formed Lobell/ Bergman Prods. with Andrew Bergman.
PICTURES: Dreamer, Windows, So Fine, The Journey of Natty Gann, Chances are, The Freshman, White Fang, Honeymoon in Vegas, Undercover Blues, Little Big League, It Could Happen to You, Striptease.

Lo BIANCO, TONY
Actor. b. New York, NY. Oct. 19, 1936. Performed on N.Y. stage as well as in films and TV. Former artistic dir. Triangle Theatre, NY.
THEATER: Yanks 3—Detroit 0—Top of the Seventh (Obie Award), The Office, The Rose Tattoo, A View From the Bridge (Outer Critics Circle Award), The Royal Hunt of the Sun, Hizzoner, Other People's Money (tour).
PICTURES: The Honeymoon Killers (debut, 1970), The French Connection, The Seven Ups, Demon (God Told Me To), F.I.S.T., Bloodbrothers, Separate Ways, City Heat, Too Scared to Scream (dir. only), Mean Frankie and Crazy Tony, La Romana, City of Hope, The Spiders Web, Boiling Point, The Ascent, The Last Home Run (dir. only), The Juror.
TELEVISION: *Series*: Love of Life, Jessie, Palace Guard. *Guest*: Police Story. *Movies/Mini-Series*: Mr. Inside Mr. Outside, The Story of Joseph and Jacob, Magee and the Lady (She'll Be Sweet), Jesus of Nazareth, Hidden Faces, Legend of the Black Hand, Lady Blue, Marco Polo, Welcome Home Bobby, Blood Ties, A Last Cry for Help, Marciano, Another Woman's Child, The Last Tenant, Goldenrod, Shadow in the Streets, Eugene O'Neill's A Glory of Ghosts, Police Story: The Freeway Killings, The Ann Jillian Story, Body of Evidence, Off Duty, True Blue, Perry Mason: The Case of the Poisoned Pen, Malcolm Takes a Shot, In the Shadow of a Killer, Stormy Weathers, Teamster Boss: The Jackie Presser Story, The First Circle, The Maharajah's Daughter, Tyson. *Specials*: Hizzoner (Emmy Award), A Glory of Ghosts. *Director*: Police Story, Kaz, Cliffhangers, When the Whistle Blows, The Duke.

LOCKE, SONDRA
Actress, Director. b. Shelbyville, TN, May 28, 1947.
PICTURES: The Heart Is a Lonely Hunter (debut, 1968; Acad. Award nom.), Cover Me Babe, Willard, A Reflection of Fear, The Second Coming of Suzanne, Death Game (The Seducers), The Outlaw Josey Wales, The Gauntlet, Every Which Way But Loose, Bronco Billy, Any Which Way You Can, Sudden Impact, Ratboy (also dir.), Impulse (dir. only).
TELEVISION: *Movies*: Friendships, Secrets and Lies, Rosie: The Rosemary Clooney Story. *Guest*: Amazing Stories. *Director*: Death in Small Doses (movie).

LOCKHART, JUNE
Actress. b. New York, NY, June 25, 1925. p. actors, Gene and Kathleen Lockhart. B'way debut For Love or Money, 1947.
PICTURES: A Christmas Carol (debut, 1938), All This and Heaven Too, Adam Had Four Sons, Sergeant York, Miss Annie Rooney, Forever and a Day, White Cliffs of Dover, Meet Me in St. Louis, Son of Lassie, Keep Your Powder Dry, Easy to Wed, She-Wolf of London, Bury Me Dead, The Yearling, T-Men, It's a Joke Son, Time Limit, Butterfly, Deadly Games, Strange Invaders, Troll, Rented Lips, The Big Picture, Dead Women in Lingerie, Tis the Season, Sleep With Me.
TELEVISION: *Series*: Who Said That? (panelist), Lassie, Lost in Space, Petticoat Junction, General Hospital. *Movies*: But I

Don't Want to Get Married, The Bait, Who is the Black Dahlia?, Curse of the Black Widow, The Gift of Love, Walking Through the Fire, The Night They Saved Christmas, Perfect People, A Whisper Kills, Danger Island. *Mini-Series*: Loose Change.

LOCKLEAR, HEATHER
Actress. b. Los Angeles, CA, Sept. 25, 1961. e. UCLA. Appeared in commercials while in college.
PICTURES: Firestarter (debut, 1984), The Return of Swamp Thing, The Big Slice, Illusions, Wayne's World 2, The First Wives Club.
TELEVISION: *Series*: Dynasty, T.J. Hooker, Fright Night Videos (host), Going Places, Melrose Place. *Movies*: Return of the Beverly Hillbillies, Twirl, City Killer, Blood Sport, Rich Men Single Women, Jury Duty: The Comedy, Her Wicked Ways, Dynasty: The Reunion, Body Language, Highway Heartbreaker, Fade to Black, Texas Justice. *Specials*: Battle of the Network Stars, Hollywood Starr, TV Guide 40th Anniversary Special (host). *Guest*: Fantasy Island, The Fall Guy, Matt Houston, Hotel, The Love Boat.

LOCKWOOD, GARY
Actor. r.n. John Gary Yusolfsky. b. Van Nuys, CA, Feb. 21, 1937. Began in Hollywood as stuntman.
PICTURES: Tall Story, Splendor in the Grass, Wild in the Country, The Magic Sword, It Happened at the World's Fair, Firecreek, 2001: A Space Odyssey, They Came to Rob Las Vegas, Model Shop, The Body, R.P.M., Stand Up and Be Counted, The Wild Pair, Night of the Scarecrow.
TELEVISION: *Series*: Follow the Sun, The Lieutenant. *Movies*: Earth II, Manhunter, The FBI Story: The FBI Versus Alvin Karpus—Public Enemy, The Ghost of Flight 401, The Incredible Journey of Dr. Meg Laurel, Top of the Hill, The Girl The Gold Watch & Dynamite, Emergency Room.

LOCKWOOD, ROGER
Executive. b. Middletown, CT, June 7, 1936. e. Ohio Wesleyan U. Sports writer for Akron Beacon Journal, 1960-62. On executive staff of Lockwood & Gordon Theatres; exec. v.p. SBC Theatres, 1969-73. 1974 asst. to exec. v.p., General Cinema Corp. 1975 formed Lockwood/Friedman Theatres, buying-booking and exhibition organization. Pres., Theatre Owners of New England, 1971-72; pres., Young NATO 1965-67; bd. of dir. NATO, 1962-1968. Board of dir. Tone, 1968-present; pres., Jimmy Fund, present; 1979-80, Variety Club of New England, pres. Director, Dana-Farber Cancer Institute, 1983-present. 1988, formed Lockwood/McKinnon Company Inc. operating theatres and Taco Bell Restaurants.

LOEKS, BARRIE LAWSON
Executive. b. Pittsburgh, PA. e. Univ. of MI, Univ. of MI Law Sch., 1979. Began career as associate in Grand Rapids, MI, law firm of Warner Norcross & Judd before serving for 7 yrs. as v.p. and gen. counsel of Jack Loeks Theatres; promoted to pres. of Loeks Michigan Theatre and Loeks-Star joint venture, 1988; Nov. 1992 named co-chmn., with husband Jim Loeks, of Sony Theatres, a Sony Retail Entertainment Co.

LOEKS, JIM
Executive. b. Grand Rapids, MI. e. Univ. of MI. Started as gen. mgr. of John Ball Concessions Inc, becoming chmn. of bd. and owner, 1976-91. 1978, elected v.p. of Jack Loeks Theatres Inc.; named pres. of chain in 1983. 1988, became chmn. & co-owner of Loeks Michigan Theatres Inc., also gen. partner & operating agent of Loeks-Star joint venture with Sony Pictures Entertainment. Nov., 1992 named co-chmn., with wife Barrie Lawson Loeks, of Sony Theatres.

LOEKS, JOHN D. Jr.
Executive. b. E. Grand Rapids, MI, Feb 24, 1945. e. Wheaton Coll., B.A. 1967; Wayne State U., J.D. 1970. Began own law practice in 1970 until 1990. President, Showspan Inc., 1982-present. President, Jack Loeks Theatres Inc., 1990-present. Chmn., Ansable Institute of Environmental Studies; 1988-present, bd. member, Intervaristy Christian Fellowship; 1992-present, bd. of dirs., NATO.

LOESCH, MARGARET
Executive. e. U. of S. MS, B.A; grad. work at U. of New Orleans. President, Fox Children's Network.

LOGAN, JEFF
Exhibitor. b. Mitchell, SD, Dec. 29, 1950. e. Dakota Wesleyan U. & U. of SD. Started working in family's Roxy Theatre at 9 yrs. old. Worked as announcer on KORN radio, 1969-70. Announcer, reporter & photgrapher, KUSD-TV, 1970-71. Relief anchor, KXON-TV, 1972-78. Took over management of family theatre. Built co. into present circuit, Logan Luxury Theatres. Member, bd. of trustess, Dakota Wesleyan U., 1990-present; bd. of trustees, Queen of Peace Hospital, 1991-present. V.P., Variety Club of SD, 1994-96. Dir., NATO/North Central, 1980-90. V.P., VSDA of SD, 1989-present.

LOGGIA, ROBERT
Actor. b. New York, NY, Jan. 3, 1930. e. U. of Missouri, B.A. journalism, 1951. Studied with Stella Adler and at The Actors Studio. Broadway debut, The Man with the Golden Arm, 1955. THEATER: Toys in the Attic, The Three Sisters, In the Boom Boom Room, Wedding Band.
PICTURES: Somebody Up There Likes Me (debut, 1956), The Garment Jungle, Cop Hater, The Lost Missile, Cattle King, The Greatest Story Ever Told, Che, First Love, Speed Trap, Revenge of the Pink Panther, The Ninth Configuration (Twinkle Twinkle Killer Kane), S.O.B., An Officer and a Gentleman, Trail of the Pink Panther, Psycho II, Curse of the Pink Panther, Scarface, Prizzi's Honor, Jagged Edge (Acad. Award nom.), Armed and Dangerous, That's Life, Over the Top, Hot Pursuit, The Believers, Gaby: A True Story, Big, Oliver & Company (voice), Relentless, S.P.O.O.K.S. (Code Name: Chaos), Triumph of the Spirit, Opportunity Knocks, The Marrying Man, Necessary Roughness, Gladiator, Innocent Blood, The Last Tattoo, Bad Girls, I Love Trouble, Man With a Gun, Independence Day, Lost Highway.
TELEVISION: Series: T.H.E. Cat, Emerald Point N.A.S., Mancuso FBI, Sunday Dinner. Specials: Miss Julie, The Nine Lives of Elfego Baca, Conspiracy: The Trial of the Chicago 8, Merry Christmas Baby. Movies: Mallory: Circumstantial Evidence, Street Killing, Scott Free, Raid on Entebbe, No Other Love, Casino, A Woman Called Golda, A Touch of Scandal, Streets of Justice, Intrigue, Dream Breakers (The O'Connors), Afterburn, Lifepod, Nurses on the Line: The Crash of Flight 7, White Mile, Jake Lassiter: Justice on the Bayou, Between Love and Honor, Mercy Mission: The Rescue of Flight 771, Right to Remain Silent. Mini-Series: Arthur Hailey's The Moneychangers, Echoes in the Darkness, Favorite Son, Wild Palms.

LOLLOBRIGIDA, GINA
Actress. b. Subiaco, Italy, July 4, 1927. e. Acad. of Fine Arts, Rome. Film debut (Italy) L'aguila nera, 1946. Published several volumes of her photography incl. Italia Mia, The Wonder of Innocence.
PICTURES: Pagliacci, The City Defends Itself, The White Line, Fanfan the Tulip, Times Gone By, Beat the Devil, Crossed Swords, The Great Game, Beauties of the Night, Wayward Wife, Bread Love and Dreams, Bread Love and Jealousy, Young Caruso, World's Most Beautiful Woman, Trapeze, Hunchback of Notre Dame, Solomon and Sheba, Never So Few, The Unfaithfuls, Fast and Sexy, Where the Hot Wind Blows, Go Naked in the World, Come September, Imperial Venus, Woman of Straw, That Splendid November, Hotel Paradiso, Buona Sera Mrs. Campbell, Plucked, The Private Navy of Sgt. O'Farrell, Bad Man's River, King Queen Knave, The Lonely Woman, Bambole.
TELEVISION: Movie: Deceptions. Series: Falcon Crest.

LOMITA, SOLOMON
Executive. b. New York, NY, April 23, 1937. Started industry career with United Artists Corp. as follows: adm., intl. dept., 1962; asst., intl. sales, same year. 1963, asst. intl. print mgr.; 1965, intl., print mgr. 1973 appt. dir. of film services. 1981, v.p., film services. 1985 named v.p., post-prod., Orion Pictures; 1989-92; then sr. v.p. post-prod.

LONDON, BARRY
Executive. Joined Paramount Pictures 1971 in L.A. branch office as booker; later salesman. 1973, sls. mgr., Kansas City-St. Louis; 1974, branch mgr. Transferred to San Francisco, first as branch mgr.; later as district mgr. 1977, eastern div. mgr. in Washington, DC, 1978-81, western div. mgr. 1981, named v.p., gen. sls. mgr. 1983, advanced to sr. v.p., domestic dis-trib.1984, named pres., domestic div., for Motion Picture Group of Paramount; 1985, named pres., marketing and domestic distrib.; 1988, named pres. worldwide distrib., Motion Picture Group.

LONDON, JASON
Actor. b. San Diego, CA, 1973. Twin brother of actor Jeremy London. Raised in Oklahoma and Texas. Appeared in Aerosmith video Amazing.
PICTURES: The Man in the Moon (debut, 1991), December, Dazed and Confused, Safe Passage, To Wong Foo—Thanks for Everything—Julie Newmar, My Generation.
TELEVISION: Movie: A Matter of Justice. Guest: I'll Fly Away, Tales From the Crypt.

LONDON, JERRY
Director. b. Los Angeles, CA, Jan 21, 1937. Apprentice film editor, Desilu Prods., 1955; film ed., Daniel Boone, 1962; staged plays in local theater workshops; editor, assoc. prod., then dir. Hogan's Heroes. Formed Jerry London Prods., 1984.
PICTURE: Rent-a-Cop (feature debut, 1988).
TELEVISION: Series: Mary Tyler Moore Show, Love American Style, The Bob Newhart Show, Marcus Welby, M.D., Kojak, The Six Million Dollar Man, Police Story, Rockford Files. Mini-series: Wheels, Shogun (DGA, best dir., special award),

Chiefs (also sprv. prod.), Ellis Island (also sprv. prod.), If Tomorrow Comes, A Long Way From Home. Movies: Killdozer, McNaughton's Daughter, Cover Girls, Evening in Byzantium, Women in White, Father Figure, The Chicago Story, The Ordeal of Bill Carney (also prod.), The Gift of Life (also prod.), The Scarlet and the Black, Arthur Hailey's Hotel (also prod.), With Intent to Kill (exec. prod. only), Dark Mansions, Manhunt For Claude Dallas, Harry's Hong Kong, Family Sins (exec. prod. only), Macgruder and Loud (also prod.), Dadah Is Death (also prod.), Kiss Shot (also exec. prod.), The Haunting of Sarah Hardy (also exec. prod.), Vestige of Honor, A Season of Giants, Victim of Love, Grass Roots, Calendar Girl Cop Killer?: The Bambi Bembenek Story (also prod.), A Twist of the Knife, Labor of Love: The Arlette Schweitzer Story, A Mother's Gift.

LONDON, JULIE
Singer, Actress. r.n. Julie Peck. b. Santa Rosa, CA, Sept. 26, 1926. Launched as actress by agent Sue Carol (wife of Alan Ladd) who arranged screen test, followed by contract for 6 films. As singer has appeared in nightclubs and recorded.
PICTURES: Nabonga (Jungle Woman; debut, 1944), On Stage Everybody, Billy Rose's Diamond Horseshoe, Night in Paradise, The Red House, Tap Roots, Task Force, Return of the Frontiersman, The Fat Man, Fighting Chance, The Great Man, The Girl Can't Help It, Crime Against Joe, Drango, Saddle the Wind, Man of the West, Voice in the Mirror, A Question of Adultery, The Wonderful Country, Night of the Quarter Moon, The Third Voice, The George Raft Story.
TELEVISION: Series: Emergency. Guest: Perry Como Show, Steve Allen Show, Ed Sullivan Show. Movie: Emergency (pilot).

LONDON, MILTON H.
Executive. b. Detroit, MI, Jan. 12, 1916. e. U. of Michigan, B.A., 1937. Wayne U. Law Sch., 1938. U.S. Army 1943-46. Invented Ticograph system of positive admissions control for theatres, 1950; pres. Theatre Control Corp., 1950-62; secy-treas. Co-op. Theas. of Michigan Inc., 1956-63; exec. comm., Council of M.P. Organizations, 1957-66; dir. M.P. Investors, 1960-67; exec. dir. Allied States Assoc. of M.P. Exhib., 1961-66; exec. dir. National Assoc. of Theatre Owners, 1966-69; pres., NATO of Michigan, 1954-74; Chief Barker, Variety Club of Detroit, Tent No. 5. 1975-76; Life Patron and Lifeliner, Variety Clubs International; trustee, Variety Club Charity for Children; chmn., Variety Club Myoelectric Center; dir., Motion Picture Pioneers; dir., Will Rogers Inst.; trustee, Detroit Inst. for Children; pres., Metropolitan Adv. Co.; Intl. ambassador, Variety Clubs Int'l; Detroit News 1991 Michiganian of the Year.

LONE, JOHN
Actor. b. Hong Kong. Studied at Chin Ciu Academy of the Peking Opera in Hong Kong, Moved to LA where he studied acting at Pasadena's American Acad. of Dramatic Art, becoming member of the East-West Players.
THEATER: NY: F.O.B., The Dance and the Railroad (Obie Awards for both plays), Paper Angels (dir.), Sound and Beauty (also dir.).
PICTURES: Iceman (debut, 1984), Year of the Dragon, The Last Emperor, The Moderns, Echoes of Paradise, Shadow of China, Shanghai 1920, M. Butterfly, The Shadow, The Hunted.
TELEVISION: The Dance and the Railroad, Paper Angels (dir.).

LONG, SHELLEY
Actress. b. Ft. Wayne, IN, Aug. 23, 1949. e. Northwestern U. Was co-host, assoc. prod. of local tv show Sorting It Out.
PICTURES: A Small Circle of Friends (debut, 1980), Caveman, Night Shift, Losin' It, Irreconcilable Differences, The Money Pit, Outrageous Fortune, Hello Again, Troop Beverly Hills, Don't Tell Her It's Me, Frozen Assets, The Brady Bunch Movie, A Very Brady Sequel.
TELEVISION: Series: Cheers (Emmy Award, 1983), Good Advice. Movies: The Cracker Factory, Princess and the Cabbie, Promise of Love, Voices Within: The Lives of Truddi Chase, Fatal Memories, A Message From Holly, The Women of Spring Break, Freaky Friday. Special: Basic Values: Sex Shock & Censorship in the '90's.

LONGSTREET, STEPHEN
Writer, Painter. b. New York, NY, April 18, 1907. e. Rutgers U.; Parsons Coll.; Rand Sch., London, B.A. Humorist, cartoonist (New Yorker, Collier's, etc.) 1930-37; ed. Free World Theatre, radio plays; edit. film critic, Saturday Review of Literature, 1940, U.S. at War, Time 1942-43. On staff UCLA. Elected pres. Los Angeles Art Assoc. 1970. 1973, joined USC as prof. Film and book critic for Readers' Syndicate starting in 1970.
AUTHOR: Decade, Last Man Around the World, Chico Goes to the Wars, Pedlocks, Lion at Morning, Promoters, Sometimes I Wonder (with Hoagy Carmichael), Wind at My Back (with Pat O'Brien), Goodness Had Nothing to Do With It (with Mae West), The Young Men of Paris, The Wilder Shore, War Cries on Horseback, Yoshiwara, Geishas and Courtesans, Canvas

Falcons, Men and Planes of World War I, We All Went to Paris. Chicago 1860-1919 (show business & society), Divorcing (a novel), The General (novel), All Star Cast (Hollywood), The Queen Bees, Our Father's House, Storyville to Harlem, Dictionary of Jazz, Dreams that Swallowed the World: The Movies, Jazz Solos (poems & images), My Three Nobel Prizes, Life With Faulkner/Hemingway/Lewis.
THEATER: High Button Shoes (book, revived in Jerome Robbins' Broadway, 1989).
PICTURES: The Gay Sisters, Golden Touch, Stallion Road, The Jolson Story, Silver River, Helen Morgan Story, The First Traveling Saleslady, Untamed Youth, The Crime, Uncle Harry, Rider on a Dead Horse, The Imposter.
TELEVISION: Casey Jones (series), Clipper Ship (Playhouse 90), Man Called X, The Sea, Press & Clergy, Viewpoint, Boy in the Model T, John Kennedy Young Man From Boston, Blue and the Grey.

LONSDALE, PAMELA
Producer and Executive Producer for Children's drama, Thames TV for 15 years. Now freelance. Prod. short feature film, Exploits at West Poley (for CFTF), Prod.: News at Twelve (Central TV comedy series). Exec. prod. for E.B.U.'s world drama exchange for 2 years. Winner British Acad. Award for Rainbow, 1975.

LORD, JACK
Actor, Writer, Artist, Director, Producer. r.n. John Ryan. b. New York, NY, Dec. 30, 1930. e. NYU. (Chancellor Chase scholarship), B.S., Fine Arts, 1954. Studied at Sanford Meisner's Neighborhood Playhouse and with Lee Strasberg at the Actors Studio. Made film debut 1949 under his real name. Artist, represented in various museums worldwide. Received Fame Award as new male actor, 1963. Awards: St. Gauden's Artist Award, G. Washington Honor Medal from Freedom Foundation at Valley Forge, Veterans Admin., Administrator's Award, East-West Center Distinguished Service Award. Author: Jack Lord's Hawaii...A Trip Through the Last Eden, 1971. Pres., Lord and Lady Enterprises, Inc. Appeared in Williamsburg documentary Story of a Patriot.
THEATER: B'way: Traveling Lady (Theatre World Award, 1959), Cat on a Hot Tin Roof.
PICTURES: The Red Menace (debut, 1949), Project X, Cry Murder, The Tattooed Stranger, The Court Martial of Billy Mitchell, Tip on a Dead Jockey, God's Little Acre, Man of the West, The Hangman, True Story of Lynn Stuart, Walk Like a Dragon, Dr. No, Ride to Hangman's Tree, The Counterfeit Killer, The Name of the Game Is Kill.
TELEVISION: Series: Stoney Burke (1962-63), Hawaii Five-O (1968-79; also dir. episodes), creator of Tramp Ship, McAdoo, Yankee Trader, The Hunter TV series. Guest: Man Against Crime (debut), Playhouse 90, Goodyear Playhouse, Studio One, U.S. Steel. Have Gun Will Travel (pilot), Untouchables, Naked City, Rawhide, Bonanza, The Americans, Route 66, Gunsmoke, Stagecoach West, Dr. Kildare, Greatest Show on Earth, Combat, Chrysler Theatre, 12 O'Clock High, The Loner, Laredo, The FBI, The Invaders, The Fugitive, The Virginian, Man from U.N.C.L.E., High Chaparral, Ironside. Movie: Doomsday Flight. Director: Death with Father, How to Steal a Masterpiece, Honor Is an Unmarked Grave, The Bells Toll at Noon, Top of the World, Why Won't Linda Die, Who Says Cops Don't Cry; episodes of Hawaii Five-O. Special: M Station: Hawaii (creator, dir., exec. prod.).

LOREN, SOPHIA
Actress. b. Rome, Italy, Sept. 20, 1934. e. Naples. m. producer Carlo Ponti. Autobiography: Sophia: Living and Loving (with A.E. Hotchner, 1979).
PICTURES: Africa Beneath the Seas, Village of the Bells, Good People's Sunday, Neapolitan Carousel, Day in the District Court, Pilgrim of Love, Aida, Two Nights with Cleopatra, Our Times, Attila, Scourge of God, Gold of Naples, Too Bad She's Bad, Scandal in Sorrento, Miller's Beautiful Wife, Lucky to Be a Woman, Boy on a Dolphin (U.S. debut, 1957), The Pride and the Passion, Legend of the Lost, Desire Under the Elms, The Key, Houseboat, The Black Orchid, That Kind of Woman, Heller in Pink Tights, It Started in Naples, A Breath of Scandal, The Millionairess, Two Women (Academy Award, 1961), El Cid, Boccaccio 70, Madame Sans-Gene, Five Miles to Midnight, The Condemned of Altona, Yesterday Today and Tomorrow, The Fall of the Roman Empire, Marriage Italian Style, Operation Crossbow, Lady L, Judith, Arabesque, A Countess from Hong Kong, More than a Miracle, Ghosts—Italian Style, Sunflower, The Priest's Wife, Lady Liberty, White Sister, Man of La Mancha, The Voyage, The Verdict (Jury of One), The Cassandra Crossing, A Special Day, Angela, Brass Target, Firepower, Blood Feud (Revenge), Ready to Wear (Pret-a-Porter), Grumpier Old Men.
TELEVISION: Movies/Specials: Brief Encounter, Sophia Loren—Her Own Story, Softly Softly, Rivals of Sherlock Holmes, Fantasy Island, Aurora, Courage, Mario Puzo's The Fortunate Pilgrim.

LOUDON, DOROTHY
Actress. b. Boston, MA, Sept. 17, 1933.
THEATER: B'way: Nowhere to Go But Up (Theatre World Award), The Fig Leaves Are Falling, Sweet Potato, Three Men on a Horse, The Women, Annie (Tony Award, 1977), Ballroom, Sweeney Todd, West Side Waltz, Noises Off, Jerry's Girls, Comedy Tonight. Off-B'way: The Matchmaker. Regional: Driving Miss Daisy, Love Letters.
PICTURE: Garbo Talks.
TELEVISION: Series: It's a Business?, Laugh Line, The Garry Moore Show, Dorothy, The Thorns (sang opening song). Specials: Many appearances on the Tony Awards; also Carnegie Hall Salutes Stephen Sondheim.

LOUGHLIN, LORI
Actress. b. Long Island, NY, July 28, 1964. Started modeling at age 7 for catalogues, then tv commercials. First professional acting job at 18 as regular on daytime serial The Edge of Night.
THEATER: Grease.
PICTURES: Amityville 3-D (debut, 1983), The New Kids, Secret Admirer, Back to the Beach, The Night Before.
TELEVISION: Series: The Edge of Night, Full House, Hudson Street. Movies: North Beach and Rawhide, Brotherhood of Justice, A Place to Call Home, Doing Time on Maple Drive, A Stranger in the Mirror, Empty Cradle, One of Her Own, Abandoned and Deceived.

LOUIS-DREYFUS, JULIA
Actress. b. New York, NY, Jan. 13, 1961. e. Northwestern Univ. Member of Second City comedy troupe which resulted in casting on Saturday Night Live.
PICTURES: Troll (debut, 1986), Hannah and Her Sisters, Soul Man, National Lampoon's Christmas Vacation, Jack the Bear, North.
TELEVISION: Series: Saturday Night Live (1982-85), Day by Day, Seinfeld (Emmy Award, 1996). Specials: The Art of Being Nick, Spy Magazine's Hit List (host), Sesame Street's All-Star 25th Birthday.

LOUISE, TINA
Actress. r.n. Tina Blacker. b. New York, NY, Feb. 11. e. Miami U., N.Y. Neighborhood Playhouse, Actors Studio.
THEATER: Two's Company, The Fifth Season, John Murray Anderson's Almanac, Li'l Abner, Fade Out Fade In, Come Back to the 5 and Dime Jimmy Dean Jimmy Dean.
PICTURES: God's Little Acre (debut), The Trap, The Hangman, Day of the Outlaw, The Warrior Empress, Siege of Syracuse, Armored Command, For Those Who Think Young, The Wrecking Crew, The Good Guys and the Bad Guys, How to Commit Marriage, The Happy Ending, The Stepford Wives, Mean Dog Blues, Dogsday, Hellriders, Evils of the Night, O.C. and Stiggs, Dixie Lanes, The Pool, Johnny Suede.
TELEVISION: Series: Jan Murray Time, Gilligan's Island, Dallas, Rituals. Guest: Mannix, Ironside, Kung Fu, Police Story, Kojak, Roseanne. Movies: But I Don't Want to Get Married, A Call to Danger, Death Scream, Look What's Happened to Rosemary's Baby, Nightmare in Badham County, SST—Death Flight, Friendships Secrets and Lies, The Day the Women Got Even, Advice to the Lovelorn, The Woman Who Cried Murder.

LOVITZ, JON
Actor, Comedian. b. Tarzana, CA, July 21, 1957. e. U. of California at Irvine. Studied acting at Film Actors Workshop. Took classes at the Groundlings, L.A. comedy improvisation studio, 1982. Performed with Groundling's Sunday Company, before joining main company in Chick Hazzard: Olympic Trials. Developed comedy character of pathological liar which he later performed when he became regular member of Saturday Night Live in 1985.
PICTURES: The Last Resort, Ratboy, Jumpin' Jack Flash, Three Amigos, Big, My Stepmother Is an Alien, The Brave Little Toaster (voice), Mr. Destiny, An American Tail: Fievel Goes West (voice), A League of Their Own, Mom and Dad Save the World, National Lampoon's Loaded Weapon 1, Coneheads, City Slickers II: The Legend of Curly's Gold, North, Trapped in Paradise, The Great White Hype, High School High.
TELEVISION: Series: Foley Square, Saturday Night Live (1985-90), The Critic (voice). Special: The Please Watch the Jon Lovitz Special. Guest: The Paper Chase.

LOWE, CHAD
Actor. b. Dayton, OH, Jan. 15, 1968. Brother is actor Rob Lowe. Stage debut in L.A. production of Blue Denim. On NY stage in Grotesque Love Songs.
PICTURES: Oxford Blues (debut, 1984), Apprentice to Murder, True Blood, Nobody's Perfect, Highway to Hell.
TELEVISION: Movies: Silence of the Heart, There Must Be a Pony, April Morning, So Proudly We Hail, An Inconvenient Woman, Captive, Candles in the Dark, Fighting for My Daughter. Series: Spencer, Life Goes On (Emmy Award, 1993). Special: No Means No (Emmy nom.).

LOWE, PHILIP L.
Executive. b. Brookline, MA, Apr. 17, 1917. e. Harvard. Army 1943-46. Checker, Loew's 1937-39; treasurer, Theatre Candy Co., 1941-58; Pres., ITT Sheraton Corp., 1969-70; Principal, Philip L. Lowe and Assoc.

LOWE, PHILIP M.
Executive. b. New Rochelle, NY, May 9, 1944. e. Deerfield Acad., Harvard Coll., cum laude in psychology, 1966; Columbia Business Sch., 1968. Work experience includes major marketing positions at General Foods, Gillette, Gray Advertising, and Estee Lauder Cosmetics before co-founding Cinema Centers Corp. and Theatre Management Services in Boston. Pres. of Lowe Group of Companies (cable television, broadcasting, hotels, real estate and management consulting). Past pres. and chmn. of the bd; National Association of Concessionaires (NAC); past director, National Association of Theater Owners (NATO). Professor of Marketing, Bentley Coll., Waltham, MA.; Contributing Editor; The Movie Business Book, Prentice-Hall, Inc. 1983.

LOWE, ROB
Actor. b. Charlottesville, VA, Mar. 17, 1964. Raised in Dayton, OH. Started acting as child appearing in commercials, local tv spots, summer stock. Family moved to Malibu when he was 12 yrs. old. Job in Coca Cola commercial was followed by role on series A New Kind of Family. Made B'way debut 1992 in A Little Hotel on the Side. Brother is actor Chad Lowe.
PICTURES: The Outsiders (debut, 1983), Class, The Hotel New Hampshire, Oxford Blues, St. Elmo's Fire, Youngblood, About Last Night..., Square Dance, Masquerade, Illegally Yours, Bad Influence, Stroke of Midnight (If the Shoe Fits), The Dark Backward, Wayne's World, The Finest Hour, Tommy Boy, Mulholland Falls.
TELEVISION: Series: A New Kind of Family. Movies: Thursday's Child, Frank and Jesse (also co-prod.), First Degree. Mini-Series: Stephen King's The Stand. Specials: A Matter of Time, Schoolboy Father, Suddenly Last Summer.

LOWRY, DICK
Director. b. Oklahoma City, OK. e. U. of Oklahoma. Commercial photographer before being accepted by AFI. Dir. short film The Drought.
PICTURE: Smokey and the Bandit Part 3.
TELEVISION: Mini-Series: Dream West. Movies: OHMS, Kenny Rogers as the Gambler, The Jayne Mansfield Story, Angel Dusted, Coward of the County, A Few Days in Weasel Creek, Rascals and Robbers: The Secret Adventures of Tom Sawyer and Huck Finn, Missing Children—A Mother's Story, Living Proof: The Hank Williams Jr. Story, Kenny Rogers as the Gambler—The Adventure Continues (also prod.), Off Sides (Pigs Vs. Freaks), Wet Gold, The Toughest Man in the World, Murder with Mirrors, American Harvest, Kenny Rogers as The Gambler III (also co-exec. prod.), Case Closed, In the Line of Duty: The FBI Murders, Unconquered (also prod.), Howard Beach: Making the Case For Murder, Miracle Landing (also prod.), Archie: To Riverdale and Back, In the Line of Duty: A Cop for the Killing (also prod.), In the Line of Duty: Manhunt in the Dakotas (also prod.), A Woman Scorned: The Betty Broderick Story (also co-prod.), In the Line of Duty: Ambush in Waco (also prod.), In the Line of Duty: The Price of Vengeance, One More Mountain, A Horse for Danny, In The Line of Duty: Hunt for Justice (also prod.), Forgotten Sins, Project Alf, In The Line of Duty: Smoke Jumpers (also prod.).

LOWRY, HUNT
Producer. b. Oklahoma City, OK, Aug. 21, 1954. e. Rollins Coll., & Wake Forest. Abandoned plans to study medicine to enter film-making industry; first job for New World Pictures where he met Jon Davison, with whom was later to co-produce. Next made TV commercials as prod. asst. and then producer. Left to go freelance as commercials producer. 1980, appt. assoc. prod. to Davison on Airplane!
PICTURES: Humanoids from the Deep, Get Crazy, Top Secret!, Revenge, Career Opportunities, Only the Lonely, Last of the Mohicans, Striking Distance, My Life, First Knight, A Time to Kill.
TELEVISION: Movies (exec. prod.): Rascals and Robbers: The Secret Adventures of Tom Sawyer and Huckleberry Finn, Baja Oklahoma. Movies (prod.): His Mistress, Surviving, Wild Horses. Mini-Series: Dream West (prod.).

LUBCKE, HARRY R.
Registered Patent Agent. b. Alameda, CA, Aug. 25, 1905. e. U. of California, B.S., 1929. Holds numerous U.S. and foreign patents on television. In 1931: station W6XAO went on air on what is now television Channel No. 2 to become first station of kind in nation. Built Mt. Lee studios 1941 housing then largest TV stage. Pioneered present television standard of 525 line (Aug., 1940). 1942, television programs to promote war bond sale. 1942-46 dir. war research for which certificates of commendation were received from Army & Navy.

LUCAS, GEORGE
Producer, Director, Writer. b. Modesto, CA, May 14, 1944. e. USC, cinema. Made short film called THX-1138 and won National Student Film Festival Grand Prize, 1967. Signed contract with WB. Ass't. to Francis Ford Coppola on The Rain People, during which Lucas made 2-hr. documentary on filming of that feature entitled Filmmaker. Appeared as actor in film Beverly Hills Cop III. Novel: Shadow Moon (1995). Pres., Lucas Films, Industrial Light & Magic.
PICTURES: Director/Writer: THX-1138, American Graffiti, Star Wars. Executive Producer: More American Graffiti, The Empire Strikes Back (also story), Raiders of the Lost Ark (also co-story), Return of the Jedi (also co-s.p., story), Twice Upon a Time, Indiana Jones and the Temple of Doom (also story), Mishima, Labyrinth, Howard the Duck, Willow (also story), Tucker: The Man and His Dream, The Land Before Time, Indiana Jones and the Last Crusade (also co-story), Radioland Murders (also story).
TELEVISION: Exec. Prod.: The Ewok Adventure (movie), Ewoks: The Battle for Endor (movie); The Young Indiana Jones Chronicles (series).

LUCCHESI, GARY
Executive. b. San Francisco, CA, 1955. e. UCLA. Entered industry as a trainee with the William Morris Agency, 1977. Joined Tri-Star, 1983, as vice pres. of production, became sr. vice pres., 1985. Joined Paramount Pictures as exec. vice pres., April 1987; pres. of motion picture production division, 1987-92. Pres. of the Really Useful Film Company, Inc., 1994-present.
PICTURES: Producer: Jennifer Eight, Three Wishes, Virtuosity, Primal Fear.

LUCCI, SUSAN
Actress. b. Scarsdale, NY, Feb. 23, 1948. e. Marymount Col. Was semifinalist in NY State Miss Universe Pageant. First professional job as "color girl" for CBS, sitting for cameras as new lighting system for color tv was developed. Had bit parts in films Me Natalie and Goodbye Columbus. Performed on 1983 album Love in the Afternoon.
PICTURES: Daddy You Kill Me, Young Doctors in Love (cameo).
TELEVISION: Series: All My Children (1970-). Movies: Invitation to Hell, Mafia Princess, Anastasia: The Story of Anna, Haunted By Her Past, Lady Mobster, The Bride in Black, The Woman Who Sinned, Double Edge, Between Love and Hate, French Silk, Seduced and Betrayed.

LUCKINBILL, LAURENCE
Actor. b. Fort Smith, AR, Nov. 21, 1934. m. actress Lucie Arnaz. e. U. of Arkansas, Catholic U. of America.
THEATER: NY: A Man for All Seasons, Arms and the Man, The Boys in the Band, Alpha Beta, The Shadow Box, Poor Murderer, Chapter Two, Past Tense.
PICTURES: The Boys in the Band, Such Good Friends, The Promise, Not for Publication, Cocktail, Messenger of Death, Star Trek V: The Final Frontier.
TELEVISION: Series: The Secret Storm, Where the Heart Is, The Delphi Bureau. Movies: The Delphi Bureau (pilot), Death Sentence, Panic on the 5:22, Winner Take All, The Lindbergh Kidnapping Case, The Mating Season, To Heal a Nation. Mini-Series: Ike. Specials: Lyndon Johnson (one-man show), Voices and Visions (narrator), The 5:48, Lucy & Desi: A Home Movie (co-exec. prod., co-dir., writer).

LUDDY, TOM
Producer. e. U. of California at Berkeley where he operated student film societies and rep. cinemas. Entered industry via Brandon Films. 1972, prog. dir. and curator of Pacific Film Archives. 1979, joined Zoetrope Studios as dir. of special projects where dev. and supervised revival of Gance's Napoleon and Our Hitler—A Film From Germany. Coordinated Koyaanis-qatsi, Every Man For Himself, Passion. A founder, Telluride Film Fest. Served on selection comm., N.Y. and pres. San Francisco Film Fest.
PICTURES: Mishima (co-prod.), Tough Guys Don't Dance (co-exec. prod.), Barfly, King Lear (assoc. prod.), Manifesto (exec. prod.), Powwaqatsi (assoc. prod.), Wait Until Spring Bandini, Wind, The Secret Garden (co-prod.).

LUDWIG, IRVING H.
Executive. b. Nov. 3. Rivoli Theatre, N.Y., mgr., theatre oper.; Rugoff and Becker, 1938-39; opened first modern art type theatre, Greenwich Village, 1940. With Walt Disney Prod. in charge of theatre oper. on Fantasia, 1940-41; buyer-booker, Rugoff and Becker, 1942-45; film sales admin., Walt Disney Prod. home office, 1945-53; v.p. and domestic sales mgr., Buena Vista Dist. Co., 1953; pres. sales & mktg., 1959-80. Member of bd. of dirs., Will Rogers Memorial Fund, Foundation of M.P. Pioneers; Motion Picture Club; Academy of M.P. Arts & Sciences.

LUEDTKE, KURT
Writer. b. Grand Rapids, MI, Sept. 29, 1938. e. Brown U., B.A., 1961. Reporter Grand Rapids Press 1961-62. Miami Herald, 1963-65; Detroit Free Press (reporter, asst. photography dir., asst. mgr. ed., asst. exec. ed., exec. ed. 1965-78.).
PICTURES: Absence of Malice, Out of Africa (Academy Award, 1985), Walls.

LUFT, LORNA
Actress, Singer. b. Hollywood, CA, Nov. 21, 1952. Daughter of actress-singer Judy Garland and producer Sid Luft. Has sung in nightclubs. Appeared on 1990 recording of Girl Crazy.
THEATER: *NY*: Judy Garland at Home at the Palace, Promises Promises, Snoopy, Extremities. *Tours*: They're Playing Our Song, Grease, Little Shop of Horrors, Jerry Herman's Broadway, The Unsinkable Molly Brown, Guys and Dolls.
PICTURES: I Could Go on Singing (extra, unbilled), Grease 2, Where the Boys Are.
TELEVISION: *Series*: Trapper John. *Movie*: Fear Stalk. *Guest*: Twilight Zone, Hooperman, Murder She Wrote, Tales from the Dark Side, The Cosby Show.

LUKE, PETER
Writer, Director. b. England, Aug. 12, 1919. *Autobiography*: Sisyphus & Reilly.
THEATER: Hadrian VII, Bloomsbury.
TELEVISION: *Writer*: Small Fish Are Sweet, Pigs Ear with Flowers, Roll on Bloomin' Death, A Man on Her Back (with William Sansom), Devil a Monk Won't Be, Anach 'Cuan (also dir.), Black Sound—Deep Song (also dir.).

LUMET, SIDNEY
Director. b. Philadelphia, PA, June 25, 1924. e. Professional Children's Sch.; Columbia U. Child actor in plays: Dead End, George Washington Slept Here, My Heart's in the Highlands, and films: One Third of a Nation. U.S. Armed Forces, WWII, 1942-46; dir. summer stock, 1947-49; taught acting, H.S. of Prof. Arts. Assoc. dir. CBS, 1950, dir. 1951. Appeared in documentary Listen Up: The Lives of Quincy Jones. Author: Making Movies (Alfred A. Knopf, 1995).
PICTURES: 12 Angry Men (debut, 1957), Stage Struck, That Kind of Woman, The Fugitive Kind, A View From the Bridge, Long Day's Journey Into Night, Fail-Safe, The Pawnbroker, The Hill, The Group, The Deadly Affair (also prod.), Bye Bye Braverman (also prod.), The Sea Gull (also prod.), The Appointment, The Last of the Mobile Hotshots (also prod.), King: A Filmed Record ... Montgomery to Memphis (co-dir., prod.), The Anderson Tapes, Child's Play, The Offence, Serpico, Lovin' Molly, Murder on the Orient Express, Dog Day Afternoon, Network, Equus, The Wiz, Just Tell Me What You Want (also co-prod.), Prince of the City (also co-s.p.), Deathtrap, The Verdict, Daniel (also co-exec. prod.), Garbo Talks, Power, The Morning After, Running on Empty, Family Business, Q & A (also s.p.), A Stranger Among Us, Guilty As Sin, Night Falls On Manhattan (also s.p.).
TELEVISION: *Series episodes*: Mama, Danger, You Are There, Omnibus, Best of Broadway, Alcoa, Goodyear Playhouse, Kraft Television Theatre (Mooney's Kid Don't Cry, The Last of My Gold Watches, This Property is Condemned), Playhouse 90, Play of the Week (The Dybbuk, Rashomon, The Iceman Cometh—Emmy Award). *Specials*: The Sacco and Vanzetti Story, John Brown's Raid, Cry Vengeance.

LUNDGREN, DOLPH
Actor. b. Stockholm, Sweden, Nov. 3, 1959. e. Washington State U., won Fulbright to Massachusetts Inst. of Technology, Royal Inst. of Technology, Stockholm, M.S.C. Was doorman at Limelight disco in NY while studying acting. Full Contact Karate champion. Made workout video, Maximum Potential. On stage in Another Octopus.
PICTURES: A View to a Kill, Rocky IV, Masters of the Universe, Red Scorpion, The Punisher, I Come in Peace, Cover-Up, Showdown in Little Tokyo, Universal Soldier, Army of One, Pentathlon, Men of War, Johnny Mnemonic, The Shooter, The Algonquin Goodbye

LUPONE, PATTI
Actress. b. Northport, NY, Apr. 21, 1949. e. Juilliard.
THEATER: School for Scandal, Three Sisters, The Beggars Opera, The Robber Bridegroom, Meaure for Measure, Edward II, The Water Engine, Working, Evita (Tony Award, 1980), Oliver!, Anything Goes, Les Miserables (London), Sunset Boulevard (London), Master Class.
PICTURES: 1941, Fighting Back, Witness, Wise Guys, Driving Miss Daisy, Family Prayers.
TELEVISION: *Series*: Life Goes On. *Movies*: LBJ: The Early Years, The Water Engine.

LYDON, JAMES
Actor. b. Harrington Park, NJ, May 30, 1923; e. St. Johns Mil. Sch. On N.Y. stage in Prologue to Glory, Sing Out the News. For 20th Century Fox tv was assoc. prod. of series Anna and the King, Roll Out. Prod./Writer/Dir. of special The Incredible 20th Century. Dir. for Universal TV: 6 Million Dollar Man, Simon & Simon, Beggarman Thief.
PICTURES: *Actor*: Back Door to Heaven (debut, 1939), Two Thoroughbreds, Racing Luck, Tom Brown's Schooldays, Little Men, Naval Academy, Bowery Boy, Henry Aldrich for President, Cadets on Parade, The Mad Martindales, Star Spangled Rhythm, Henry Aldrich— Editor, Henry Aldrich Gets Glamour, Henry Aldrich Swings It, Henry Aldrich Haunts a House, Henry Aldrich Plays Cupid, Aerial Gunner, Henry Aldrich—Boy Scout, My Best Gal, The Town Went Wild, Henry Aldrich's Little Secret, When the Lights Go on Again, Out of the Night, Twice Blessed, The Affairs of Geraldine, Life With Father, Cynthia, Sweet Genevieve, The Time of Your Life, Out of the Storm, Joan of Arc, An Old-Fashioned Girl, Bad Boy, Miss Mink of 1949, Tucson, Gasoline Alley, Tarnished, When Willie Comes Marching Home, Destination Big House, Hot Rod, September Affair, The Magnificent Yankee, Island in the Sky, The Desperado, Battle Stations, Chain of Evidence, The Hypnotic Eye, I Passed for White, The Last Time I Saw Archie, Brainstorm, Death of a Gunfighter, Scandalous John, Bonnie's Kids, Vigilante Force. Assoc. Prod.: My Blood Runs Cold, An American Dream, A Covenant With Death, First to Fight, The Cool Ones, Chubasco, Countdown, Assignment to Kill, The Learning Tree.
TELEVISION: *Guest*: Frontier Circus (also assoc. prod.). *Co-ordin. Prod.*: Wagon Train, Alfred Hitchcock Hour. *Assoc. Prod.*: McHale's Navy, 77 Sunset Strip, Mr. Roberts. *Series* (actor): So This Is Hollywood, The First Hundred Years, Love That Jill. Movies: Ellery Queen, The New Daughters of Joshua Cabe, Peter Lundy and the Medicine Hat Stallion.

LYLES, A. C.
Producer. b. Jacksonville, FL. May 17, 1918. e. Andrew Jackson H.S. Paramount Publix's Florida Theatre, 1928; interviewed Hollywood celebrities, Jacksonville Journal, 1932; mail boy, Paramount Studios, Hollywood, 1937; publicity dept., 1938; hd. of adv., publ. dept. Pine-Thomas unit at Paramount, 1940; assoc. prod., The Mountain. President, A. C. Lyles Productions, Inc. (Paramount Pictures).
PICTURES: Short Cut to Hell, Raymie, The Young and the Brave, Law of the Lawless, Stage to Thunder Rock, Young Fury, Black Spurs, Hostile Guns, Arizona Bushwackers, Town Tamer, Apache Uprising, Johnny Reno, Waco, Red Tomahawk, Fort Utah, Buckskin, Rogue's Gallery, Night of the Lepus, The Last Day, Flight to Holocaust.
TELEVISION: Rawhide (series; assoc. prod.), A Christmas for Boomer, Here's Boomer (series), Dear Mr. President, Conversations With the Presidents.

LYNCH, DAVID
Director, Writer. b. Missoula, MT, Jan. 20, 1946. e. Pennsylvania Acad. of Fine Arts, where received an independent filmmaker grant from America Film Institute. Made 16mm film, The Grandmother. Accepted by Center for Advanced Film Studies in Los Angeles, 1970. Wrote and directed Eraserhead (with partial AFI financing). Acted in films Zelly & Me, Nadja (also exec. prod.).
PICTURES: *Director-Writer*: Eraserhead (also prod., edit., prod.-design, f/x), The Elephant Man, Dune, Blue Velvet, Wild at Heart, Twin Peaks: Fire Walk With Me (also co-exec. prod., actor), Crumb (presenter).
TELEVISION: *Series*: Twin Peaks (dir., exec. prod., writer), On the Air (exec. prod., dir., writer). *Special*: Hotel Room (co-dir., co-exec. prod.).

LYNCH, KELLY
Actress. b. Minneapolis, MN, 1959. Former model.
PICTURES: Osa, Bright Lights Big City, Cocktail, Road House, Warm Summer Rain, Drugstore Cowboy, Desperate Hours, Curly Sue, For Better and For Worse, Three of Hearts, Imaginary Crimes, The Beans of Egypt Maine, Virtuosity, White Man's Burden.
TELEVISION: *Guest*: Miami Vice, The Equalizer, Spenser for Hire, The Hitcher, The Edge (Black Pudding). *Movie*: Something in Common. *Pilot*: San Berdoo.

LYNCH, PAUL M.
Director.
PICTURES: Hard Part Begins, Blood and Guts, Prom Night, Cross Country, Flying, Blindside, Bullies.
TELEVISION: *Series*: Voyagers, Blacke's Magic, Murder She Wrote, In the Heat of the Night, Tour of Duty, Beauty and the Beast, Twilight Zone (1987), Moonlighting, Star Trek: The Next Generation, Dark Shadows, Tour of Duty, Top Cops, Mike Hammer, Hooperman, Bronx Zoo. *Movies*: Cameo By Night, Going to the Chapel, She Knows Too Much, Murder by Night, Drop Dead Gorgeous.

LYNCH, RICHARD
Actor. b. Brooklyn, NY, Feb. 12. Made B'way debut in The Devils, both on and off B'way. Also in Live Like Pigs, The Orphan, The Basic Training of Pavlo Hummel, The Lady From the Sea, Arturo-Ui, Lion in Winter.
PICTURES: Scarecrow (debut, 1973), The Seven Ups, The Delta Fox, The Premonition, Steel, The Formula, The Sword and the Sorcerer, Savage Dawn, Invasion U.S.A., Cut and Run, Night Force, The Barbarians, Little Nikita, Bad Dreams, Melanie Rose (High Stakes), Spirit, Aftershock, Return to Justice, One Man Force, The Forbidden Dance, October 32nd, Alligator II: The Mutation, Double Threat, H.P. Lovecraft's Necromonicon, Scanner Cop, Crime & Punishment.

TELEVISION: *Series*: Battlestar Gallactica, The Phoenix. *Movies*: Starsky and Hutch (pilot), Roger & Harry: The Mitera Target, Good Against Evil, Dog and Cat, Vampire, Alcatraz—The Whole Shocking Story, Sizzle, White Water Rebels, The Last Ninja.

LYNDON, VICTOR
Producer, Writer. b. London. e. St. Paul's. Ent. m.p. ind. 1942 as asst. dir., Gainsborough Pictures. Novel: Bermuda Blue (1984).
PICTURES: *Prod. mgr.*: The African Queen. *Assoc. Prod.*: Dr. Strangelove, Darling, 2001: A Space Odyssey. *Prod.*: Spare The Rod, Station Six—Sahara, The Optimists.

LYNE, ADRIAN
Director. b. Peterborough, England, March 4, 1941. Started as director of commercials.
PICTURES: Foxes, Flashdance, Nine 1/2 Weeks, Fatal Attraction, Jacob's Ladder, Indecent Proposal.

LYNLEY, CAROL
Actress. b. New York, NY, Feb. 13, 1942. Was model as teenager.
PICTURES: The Light in the Forest (debut, 1958), Holiday for Lovers, Blue Denim, Hound-Dog Man, Return to Peyton Place, The Last Sunset, The Stripper, Under the Yum-Yum Tree, The Cardinal, The Pleasure Seekers, Shock Treatment, Harlow, Bunny Lake Is Missing, The Shuttered Room, Danger Route, Once You Kiss a Stranger, The Maltese Bippy, Norwood, Beware the Blob!, The Poseidon Adventure, Cotter, The Four Deuces, The Washington Affair, The Cat and the Canary, The Shape of Things to Come, Vigilante, Dark Tower, Blackout, Howling VI: The Freaks.
TELEVISION: *Series*: The Immortal. *Movies*: Shadow on the Land, The Smugglers, The Immortal, Weekend of Terror, The Cable Car Murder, The Night Stalker, The Elevator, Death Stalk, Willow B, Women in Prison, Flood, Fantasy Island, Having Babies II, Cops and Robin, The Beasts Are on the Streets.

LYNN, ANN
Actress. b. London, England, 1934. Ent. films and TV, 1958.
PICTURES: Johnny You're Wanted (debut, 1955), Moment of Indiscretion, Naked Fury, Piccadilly Third Stop, The Wind of Change, Strip Tease Murder, Strongroom, Flame in the Streets, HMS Defiant (Damn the Defiant), The Party's Over, Doctor in Distress, The Black Torment, The System (The Girl Getters), A Shot in the Dark, The Uncle, Four in the Morning, Separation, I'll Never Forget What's 'is Name, Baby Love, Hitler—The Last Ten Days, Screamtime.
TELEVISION: *Specials/Movies*: After The Show, All Summer Long, Trump Card, Man at the Top, The Expert, Hine, The Intruders, Too Far, King Lear, The Zoo Gang, Morning Tide, Estuary, Who Pays the Ferryman, The Professionals, Zeticula, Westway, The Perfect House, Minder, To the Sound of Guns, Crown Court, Just Good Friends, Starting Out, Paradise Park. *Series*: The Cheaters, The Other Side of the Underneath.

LYNN, JONATHAN
Director, Writer, Actor. b. Bath, England, Apr. 3, 1943. Was artistic dir. of Cambridge Theatre Company, 1976-81; Company Director of Natl. Theatre, 1987. Playwright: Pig of the Month. Books: A Proper Man, The Complete Yes Minister, Mayday. Appeared as actor in Into the Night, Three Men and a Little Lady.
PICTURES: The Internecine Project (s.p.). *Director*: Clue (also s.p.), Nuns on the Run (also s.p.), My Cousin Vinny, The Distinguished Gentleman, Greedy (also actor), Sgt. Bilko.
TELEVISION: Doctor on the Go, My Name is Harry Worth, My Brother's Keeper, Yes Minister, Yes Prime Minister.

LYNTON, MICHAEL
Executive. Pres., Hollywood Pictures.

LYON, FRANCIS D. "PETE"
Director, Editor. b. Bowbells, ND, July 29, 1905. e. Hollywood H.S., UCLA. WWII: writer, prod., dir., OWI; assoc. with training, exploitation and information films. Maj. U.S. Army Signal Corps. Author: Twists of Fate: An Oscar Winner's International Career.
PICTURES: *Editor*: Things to Come (co-edit.), Knight Without Armour, Rembrandt, Intermezzo, Adam Had Four Sons, The Great Profile, Four Sons, Daytime Wife, Body and Soul (Academy Award, 1947), He Ran All the Way. *Director*: Crazylegs, The Bob Mathias Story (Christopher Award), The Great Locomotive Chase, Cult of the Cobra, The Oklahoman, Gunsight Ridge, Bailout at 43,000, Escort West, Cinerama South Seas Adventure (co-dir.), The Young and the Brave, Destination Inner Space, The Money Jungle, The Girl Who Knew Too Much. *Producer*: Tiger by the Tail.
TELEVISION: *Series*: Laramie, Perry Mason, Zane Grey Theatre, Bus Stop, M. Squad, Wells Fargo, Kraft Suspense Theatre, Death Valley Days, Follow the Sun, etc.

LYON, SUE
Actress. b. Davenport, IA, July 10, 1946. e. Hollywood Prof. Sch.
PICTURES: Lolita (debut, 1962), The Night of the Iguana, Seven Women, Tony Rome, The Flim Flam Man, Evel Knievel, Crash, End of the World, Alligator, Invisible Strangler.
TELEVISION: *Movies*: But I Don't Want to Get Married!, Smash-Up on Interstate 5, Don't Push—I'll Charge When I'm Ready.

LYONS, STUART
Producer. b. Manchester, England, Dec. 27, 1928. e. Manchester U. Ent. m.p. ind. 1955. Asst. dir. TV series 1955-56. Casting dir. Associated British, 1956-60. Freelance cast. dir., 1960-63. Joined 20th Century-Fox Productions as cast. dir., 1963. Appt. director 20th Century-Fox Productions Ltd., 1967, man. dir. 1968. 1971 left Fox on closure Europe prod., to resume indep. prod. London Prod. Rep. for Neue Constantin Film, Munich: Salt on Our Skin, House of the Spirits.
PICTURES: *Casting Director*: Those Magnificent Men in Their Flying Machines, Cleopatra, The Long Ships, Guns at Batasi, High Wind in Jamaica, The Blue Max, many others. *Producer*: The Slipper and the Rose, Meetings with Remarkable Men, Danses Sacrees, Turnaround. *Prod. Consultant*: Eleni, The Witches, A Dangerous Life, Delta Force II, State of Grace, Captive in the Land (as rep. of Completion Bond Co.). *Prod. Spvr.*: Death Train.

M

MAC ARTHUR, JAMES
Actor. b. Los Angeles, CA, Dec. 8, 1937. e. Harvard. p. actress Helen Hayes, writer Charles MacArthur. Stage debut, summer stock; The Corn Is Green, Life with Father.
PICTURES: The Young Stranger (debut, 1957), The Light in the Forest, Third Man on the Mountain, Kidnapped, Swiss Family Robinson, The Interns, Spencer's Mountain, Cry of Battle, The Truth About Spring, The Battle of the Bulge, The Bedford Incident, Ride Beyond Vengeance, The Love-Ins, Hang 'em High, The Angry Breed.
TELEVISION: *Series*: Hawaii Five-O. *Movies*: Alcatraz—The Whole Shocking Story, The Night the Bridge Fell Down. *Special*: Willie and the Yank (Mosby's Marauders).

MACCHIO, RALPH
Actor. b. Long Island, NY, Nov. 4, 1962. Started in TV commercials at age 16 before winning role in series Eight Is Enough. Broadway debut in Cuba and His Teddy Bear, 1986; Off-B'way in Only Kidding.
PICTURES: Up the Academy (debut, 1980), The Outsiders, The Karate Kid, Teachers, Crossroads, The Karate Kid Part II, Distant Thunder, The Karate Kid Part III, Too Much Sun, My Cousin Vinny, Naked in New York.
TELEVISION: *Series*: Eight Is Enough. *Movies*: Journey to Survival, Dangerous Company, The Three Wishes of Billy Grier, The Last P.O.W.?: The Bobby Garwood Story.

MAC CORKINDALE, SIMON
Actor, Producer, Director, Writer. b. Isle-of-Ely, England, Feb. 2, 1952. m. actress Susan George. On stage in Dark Lady of the Sonnets, Pygmalion, French Without Tears, etc.
PICTURES: *Actor*: Death on the Nile, Quatermass Conclusion, Caboblanco, Robbers of the Sacred Mountain, The Sword and the Sorcerer, Jaws 3-D, The Riddle of the Sands, Sincerely Violet. *Producer*: Stealing Heaven, That Summer of White Roses (also co-s.p.), The House That Mary Bought (also dir., co-s.p.).
TELEVISION: *Specials*: I Claudius, Romeo and Juliet, Quatermass. *Movies*: The Manions of America, Falcon's Gold, Jesus of Nazareth, Twist of Fate, Obsessive Love, No Greater Love, At The Midnight Hour, A Family of Cops. *Mini-Series*: Pursuit, The Way to Dusty Death. *Series*: Manimal, Falcon Crest, Counterstrike.

MAC DOWELL, ANDIE
Actress. b. Gaffney, SC, Apr. 21, 1958. r.n. Rose Anderson MacDowell. Started as model for Elite Agency in NY appearing for L'Ordeal Cosmetics, The Gap, Calvin Klein.
PICTURES: Greystoke: The Legend of Tarzan Lord of the Apes (debut, 1984), St. Elmo's Fire, Sex Lies and Videotape (L.A. Film Critics Award, 1989), Green Card, The Object of Beauty, Hudson Hawk, The Player, Groundhog Day, Short Cuts, Deception, Four Weddings and a Funeral, Bad Girls, Unstrung Heroes, Michael, Multiplicity.
TELEVISION: *Movie*: Women and Men 2: In Love There Are No Rules (Domestic Dilemma). *Mini-Series* (Italy): Sahara's Secret.

MAC GRAW, ALI
Actress. b. Pound Ridge, NY, Apr. 1, 1939. e. Wellesley Coll. Son is actor Josh Evans. Editorial asst. Harper's Bazaar Mag.; asst. to photographer Melvin Sokolsky. Was top fashion model. *Author*: Moving Pictures (autobiography, 1991), Yoga Mind & Body (1995).

PICTURES: A Lovely Way to Die (debut, 1968). Goodbye Columbus, Love Story (Acad. Award nom.), The Getaway, Convoy, Players, Just Tell Me What You Want, Natural Causes. TELEVISION: *Mini-Series*: The Winds of War. *Movies*: China Rose, Survive the Savage Sea, Gunsmoke: The Long Ride. *Series*: Dynasty.

MAC LACHLAN, KYLE
Actor. b. Yakima, WA, Feb. 22, 1959. e. Univ. of WA. Acted in high school and college, then in summer stock. Joined Oregon Shakespeare Festival (Romeo and Juliet, Julius Caesar, Henry V). Cast as lead in Dune by director David Lynch in a nationwide search.
THEATRE: *NY*: Palace of Amateurs (Off-B'way).
PICTURES: Dune (debut, 1984), Blue Velvet, The Hidden, Don't Tell Her It's Me, The Doors, Twin Peaks: Fire Walk With Me, Where the Day Takes You, Rich in Love, The Trial, The Flintstones, Showgirls, Trigger Effect, Mad Dog Time.
TELEVISION: *Series*: Twin Peaks. *Guest*: Tales From the Crypt (Carrion Death). *Movies*: Dream Breakers, Against the Wall, Roswell.

MAC LAINE, SHIRLEY
Actress. b. Richmond, VA, April 24, 1934. r.n. Shirley MacLean Beaty. Brother is actor-prod. Warren Beatty. e. Washington and Lee H.S., Arlington, VA. Started as dancer; on B'way as understudy for Carol Haney in The Pajama Game, which resulted in contract with film prod. Hal Wallis. Producer, writer and co- director of Oscar-nominated film documentary: The Other Half of The Sky: A China Memoir. Returned to stage in Gypsy in My Soul, Shirley MacLaine on Broadway. Videos: Shirley MacLaine's Inner Workout, Relaxing Within.
AUTHOR: Don't Fall off the Mountain, You Can Get There from Here, Out on a Limb, Dancing in the Light, It's All In the Playing, Going Within, Dance While You Can, My Lucky Stars. *Editor*: McGovern: The Man and His Beliefs (1972).
PICTURES: The Trouble With Harry (debut, 1955), Artists and Models, Around the World in 80 Days, Hot Spell, The Matchmaker, The Sheepman, Some Came Running (Acad. Award nom.), Ask Any Girl, Career, Can-Can, The Apartment (Acad. Award nom.), Ocean's Eleven (cameo), All in a Night's Work, Two Loves, My Geisha, The Children's Hour, Two for the Seesaw, Irma La Douce (Acad. Award nom.), What a Way to Go!, John Goldfarb Please Come Home, The Yellow Rolls Royce, Gambit, Woman Times Seven, The Bliss of Mrs. Blossom, Sweet Charity, Two Mules for Sister Sara, Desperate Characters, The Possession of Joel Delaney, The Turning Point (Acad. Award nom.), Being There, Loving Couples, A Change of Seasons, Terms of Endearment (Academy Award, 1983), Cannonball Run II, Madame Sousatzka, Steel Magnolias, Postcards From the Edge, Waiting for the Light, Defending Your Life (cameo), Used People, Wrestling Ernest Hemingway, Guarding Tess, Mrs. Winterbourne, The Celluloid Closet, Evening Star.
TELEVISION: *Series*: Shirley's World. Variety *Specials*: The Other Half of the Sky: A China Memoir (also prod., co-writer), If They Could See Me Now, Where Do We Go From Here?, Shirley MacLaine at the Lido, Every Little Movement (Emmy Award for co-writing, 1980), Illusions, The Shirley MacLaine Show. *Movies*: Out on a Limb (also co-writer), The West Side Waltz.

MACLEOD, GAVIN
Actor. b. Mt. Kisco, NY, Feb. 28, 1931. e. Ithaca Coll.
PICTURES: I Want to Live, Compulsion, Operation Petticoat, McHale's Navy, McHale's Navy Joins the Air Force, The Sand Pebbles, Deathwatch, The Party, Kelly's Heroes.
TELEVISION: *Series*: McHale's Navy, The Mary Tyler Moore Show, The Love Boat. *Movies*: The Intruders, Only with Married Men, Ransom for Alice, Murder Can Hurt You, Student Exchange, The Love Boat: The Valentine Voyage. *Mini-Series*: Scruples. *Specials*: Last Act Is a Solo, If I Die Before I Wake.

MAC NAUGHTON, ROBERT
Actor. b. New York, NY, Dec. 19, 1966. Entered entertainment industry in 1979. Member Circle Rep. Co., N.Y.
THEATER: Critic's Choice, A Thousand Clowns, Camelot, The Diviners, The Adventures of Huckleberry Finn, Henry V, Tobacco Road, Master Harold... and the Boys, Tomorrow's Monday, Talley and Son.
PICTURES: E.T.: The Extra-Terrestrial, I Am the Cheese.
TELEVISION: *Movies*: Angel City, A Place to Call Home. *Specials*: Big Bend Country, The Electric Grandmother, Hear My Cry.

MAC NICOL PETER
Actor. b. Dallas, TX. e. U. of Minnesota.
THEATER: Manhattan Theatre Club: Crimes of the Heart. NY Shakespeare Fest: Found a Peanut, Rum and Coke, Twelfth Night, Richard II, Romeo & Juliet. Regional theatre includes Guthrie, Alaska Rep., Long Wharf, Dallas Theatre Center, Trinity Rep. B'way: Crimes of the Heart (Theatre World Award), The Nerd, Black Comedy/White Liars.

PICTURES: Dragonslayer (debut, 1981), Sophie's Choice, Heat, Ghostbusters II, American Blue Note, Hard Promises, Housesitter, Addams Family Values, Radioland Murders, Dracula: Dead and Loving It.
TELEVISION: *Movies*: Johnny Bull, By Dawn's Early Light, Roswell. *Guest*: Faerie Tale Theatre, Days and Nights of Molly Dodd, Cheers. *Series*: Powers That Be, Chicago Hope.

MACY, WILLIAM H.
Actor. b. Miami, FL, Mar. 13, 1950. e. Goddard Col.
THEATER: *NY*: The Man in 605 (debut, 1980), Twelfth Night, Beaurecrat, A Call From the East, The Dining Room, Speakeasy, Wild Life, Flirtations, Baby With the Bathwater, The Nice and the Nasty, Bodies Rest and Motion, Oh Hell!, Life During Wartime, Mr. Gogol and Mr. Preen, Oleanna, Our Town (B'way).
PICTURES: Without a Trace, The Last Dragon, Radio Days, House of Games, Things Change, Homicide, Shadows and Fog, Benny and Joon, Searching for Bobby Fischer, The Client, Oleanna, Murder in the First, Mr. Holland's Opus, Down Periscope, Fargo, Ghosts of Mississippi.
TELEVISION: *Series*: Chicago Hope. *Movies*: The Murder of Mary Phagan, Texan, A Murderous Affair, The Water Engine, Heart of Justice, A Private Matter. *Guest*: ER, Law and Order.

MADDEN, BILL
Executive. b. New York, NY, March 1, 1915. e. Boston U. Joined Metro-Goldwyn-Mayer as office boy, 1930; student salesman, 1938; asst. Eastern div. sales mgr., 1939; U.S. Navy, 1942-46; Boston sales rep., MGM, 1947-53; Philadelphia branch mgr., 1954-59; Midwest div. sales mgr., 1960-68; roadshow sales mgr., 1969; v.p.; gen. sales mgr., 1969-74, MGM; corp., v.p. & gen. sls. mgr., MGM, 1974; retired from MGM, 1975; 1976-present, exec. consultant to motion picture industry; lecturer and instructor at UCLA. Member: AMPAS, Motion Picture Associates, American Film Institute. Motion Picture Pioneers.

MADDEN, DAVID
Executive, Producer, Director. b. Chicago, IL, July 25, 1955. e. Harvard U., 1976; UCLA, M.A., 1978. Joined 20th Century-Fox in 1978 as story analyst. Named story editor, 1980; exec. story editor, 1982. Appt. v.p., creative affairs for 20th-Fox Prods., 1983; v.p., prod., 20th Century-Fox Prods; 1984, v.p., production, Paramount Pictures. Joined Interscope Commun., 1987, as prod.
PICTURES: *Producer*: Renegades, Blind Fury (exec. prod.), The First Power, Eve of Destruction, Jersey Girls, The Hand That Rocks the Cradle, Holy Matrimony, Operation Dumbo Drop, The Tie That Binds.
TELEVISION: *Movies*: A Part of the Family (dir., writer), Body Language (co-exec. prod.).

MADIGAN, AMY
Actress. b. Chicago, IL, Sept. 11, 1951. m. actor Ed Harris. For 10 years traveled country performing in bars and clubs with band. Then studied at Lee Strasberg Inst., L.A. NY Stage: The Lucky Spot (Theatre World Award), A Streetcar Named Desire.
PICTURES: Love Child (debut, 1982), Love Letters, Streets of Fire, Places in the Heart, Alamo Bay, Twice in a Lifetime (Acad. Award nom.), Nowhere To Hide, The Prince of Pennsylvania, Field of Dreams, Uncle Buck, The Dark Half, Female Perversions.
TELEVISION: *Special*: The Laundromat. *Movies*: Crazy Times, The Ambush Murders, Victims, Travis McGee, The Day After, Roe vs. Wade, Lucky Day, And Then There Was One, Riders of the Purple Sage.

MADONNA
Singer, Actress. r.n. Madonna Louise Veronica Ciccone. b. Pontiac, MI, Aug. 16, 1958. e. U. of Michigan. Gained fame as rock & recording star before professional acting debut in Desperately Seeking Susan, 1985. NY stage debut: Speed-the-Plow, 1988. Author: Sex (1992).
PICTURES: A Certain Sacrifice (debut, 1983), Vision Quest, Desperately Seeking Susan, Shanghai Surprise, Who's That Girl?, Bloodhounds of Broadway, Dick Tracy, Truth or Dare (also exec. prod.), Shadows and Fog, A League of Their Own, Body of Evidence, Dangerous Game, Blue in the Face, Four Rooms, Girl 6, Evita.

MADSEN, MICHAEL
Actor. b. Chicago, IL, Sept. 25, 1958. Sister is actress Virginia Madsen. Started acting with Chicago's Steppenwolf Theatre appearing in such plays as Of Mice and Men, A Streetcar Named Desire. On B'way in A Streetcar Named Desire (1992).
PICTURES: WarGames (debut, 1983), Racing With the Moon, The Natural, The Killing Time, Shadows in the Storm, Blood Red, Kill Me Again, The End of Innocence, The Doors, Thelma & Louise, Straight Talk, Inside Edge, Reservoir Dogs, Trouble Bound, House in the Hills, Free Willy, Money for Nothing, Fixing the Shadow, The Getaway, Beyond the Law, Dead Connection, Wyatt Earp, Man With a Gun, Species, Free Willy 2: The Adventure Home, Mulholland Falls, Donnie Brasco.
TELEVISION: *Movies*: Our Family Honor, Montana, Baby Snatcher. *Pilot*: Diner.

MADSEN, VIRGINIA
Actress. b. Chicago, IL, Sept. 11, 1963. Mother is Emmy-winning Chicago filmmaker; brother is actor Michael Madsen. Studied with Chicago acting coach Ted Liss. Prof. debut, PBS, A Matter of Principle. Received Avoriaz & Saturn Awards for Best Actress for Candyman.
PICTURES: Class (debut, 1983), Electric Dreams, Dune, Creator, Fire With Fire, Modern Girls, Zombie High, Slam Dance, Mr. North, Hot to Trot, Heart of Dixie, The Hot Spot, Highlander 2: The Quickening, Candyman, Becoming Colette, Caroline at Midnight, Blue Tiger, The Prophecy.
TELEVISION: Movies: Mussolini: The Untold Story, The Hearst and Davies Affair, Long Gone, Gotham, Third Degree Burn, Ironclads, Victim of Love, Love Kills, Linda, A Murderous Affair: The Carolyn Warmus Story, Bitter Revenge. Guest: The Hitchhiker.

MAGNOLI, ALBERT
Director, Writer, Editor.
PICTURES: Jazz (dir., editor, s.p.), Reckless (edit.), Purple Rain (dir., edit., s.p.), American Anthem (dir. only).
TELEVISION: Movie: Born to Run.

MAGNUSON, ANN
Actress, Writer, Performance Artist. b. Charleston, WV, Jan. 4, 1956. e. Denison U. Intern at Ensemble Studio Theatre when she came to NY in 1978. Ran Club 57, an East Village club, 1979. Has performed Off-B'way, in East Village clubs, downtown art spaces, on college campuses since 1980, and at Whitney Museum, Soguestu Hall (Tokyo), Walker Art Ctr. (Minn.), Lincoln Center, Serious Fun Festival, Joseph Papp's Public Theatre. Also performed with band Bongwater. Debut as solo recording artist on Geffen Records with The Luv Show, 1995.
PICTURES: Vortex, The Hunger, Perfect Strangers, Desperately Seeking Susan, Making Mr. Right, A Night in the Life of Jimmy Reardon, Sleepwalk, Mondo New York, Tequila Sunrise, Checking Out, Heavy Petting, Love at Large, Cabin Boy, Clear and Present Danger, Tank Girl, Before and After.
TELEVISION: Night Flight, Made for TV, Alive from Off Center (co-host), Vandemonium, Table ci Ciro's (Tales From the Hollywood Hills), The Hidden Room, The Adventures of Pete and Pete. Series: Anything But Love, The John Laroquette Show.

MAHARIS, GEORGE
Actor. b. Astoria, NY, Sept. 1, 1928. Studied at The Actors Studio.
PICTURES: Exodus (debut, 1960), Quick Before It Melts, Sylvia, The Satan Bug, A Covenant With Death, The Happening, The Desperadoes, Last Day of the War, The Land Raiders, The Sword and the Sorcerer, Doppelganger.
TELEVISION: Series: Search for Tomorrow, Route 66, Most Deadly Game. Guest: Naked City. Movies: Escape to Mindanao, The Monk, The Victim, Murder on Flight 502, Look What's Happened to Rosemary's Baby, SST—Death Flight, Return to Fantasy Island, Crash, A Small Rebellion. Mini-Series: Rich Man Poor Man. Special: A Death of Princes.

MAHONEY, JOHN
Actor. b. Manchester, Eng., June 20, 1940. Mem. of Stratford Children's Theatre from age 10\-13. Moved to U.S. at 19, taught Eng. at Western Illinois U. Then freelance ed. of medical manuscripts; assoc. ed., Quality Review Bulletin. At 35 quit medical book editing to become an actor. Studied acting, Chicago's St. Nicholas Theatre. Prof. debut, The Water Engine, 1977. Joined Steppenwolf Theatre Co., 1979. (The Hothouse, Taking Steps, Death of a Salesman).
THEATER: Orphans (Theatre World Award), The House of Blue Leaves (Tony and Clarence Derwent Awards), The Subject Was Roses.
PICTURES: Mission Hill, Code of Silence, The Manhattan Project, Streets of Gold, Tin Men, Suspect, Moonstruck, Frantic, Betrayed, Eight Men Out, Say Anything, Love Hurts, The Russia House, Barton Fink, Article 99, In the Line of Fire, Striking Distance, Reality Bites, The Hudsucker Proxy, The American President, Primal Fear.
TELEVISION: Series: Lady Blue, H.E.L.P., The Human Factor, Frasier. Movies: The Killing Floor, Chicago Story, First Steps, Listen to Your Heart, Dance of the Phoenix, First Steps, Trapped in Silence, Favorite Son, The Image, Dinner at Eight, The 10 Million Dollar Getaway, The Secret Passion of Robert Clayton, Unnatural Pursuits. Special: The House of Blue Leaves.

MAJORS, LEE
Actor. r.n. Lee Yeary. b. Wyandotte, MI, April 23, 1939. Star athlete in high school; turned down offer from St. Louis Cardinals in final year at Eastern Kentucky State Coll. to pursue acting career. In L.A. got job as playground supervisor for park dept. while studying acting at MGM Studio. Debuted in films 1964 under his real name.
PICTURES: Strait-Jacket (debut, 1964), Will Penny, The Liberation of L. B. Jones, The Norsemen, Killer Fish, Steel, Agency, The Last Chase, Scrooged, Keaton's Cop.

TELEVISION: Series: The Big Valley, The Men From Shiloh, Owen Marshall-Counselor at Law, The Six Million Dollar Man, The Fall Guy, Tour of Duty, Raven. Pilot: Road Show (also exec. prod.). Movies: The Ballad of Andy Crocker, Weekend of Terror, The Gary Francis Powers Story, The Cowboy and the Ballerina, A Rocky Mountain Christmas, The Return of the Six Million Dollar Man and the Bionic Woman, Danger Down Under (exec. prod., actor), The Bionic Showdown: the Six Million Dollar Man and the Bionic Woman, Fire!, Trapped on the 37th Floor, The Cover Girl Murders, Bionic Ever After?

MAKEPEACE, CHRIS
Actor. b. Montreal, Canada, April 22, 1964. e. Jarvis Collegiate Institute. Trained for stage at Second City Workshop.
PICTURES: Meatballs (debut, 1979), My Bodyguard, The Last Chase, The Oasis, The Falcon and the Snowman, Vamp, Captive Hearts, Aloha Summer.
TELEVISION: Movies: The Terry Fox Story, The Mysterious Stranger, Mazes and Monsters, The Undergrads. Series: Going Great (host, 1982-84), Why On Earth?

MAKO
Actor. r.n. Makoto Iwamatsu. b. Kobe, Japan, Dec. 10, 1933. e. Pratt Inst.
THEATER: NY: Pacific Overtures (Tony nom.), Shimada. Regional: Rashomon.
PICTURES: The Ugly Dachshund, The Sand Pebbles (Acad. Award nom.), The Private Navy of Sgt. O'Farrell, The Great Bank Robbery, The Hawaiians, The Island at the Top of the World, Prisoners, The Killer Elite, The Big Brawl, The Bushido Blade, Under the Rainbow, An Eye for an Eye, Conan the Barbarian, The House Where Evil Dwells, Testament, Conan the Destroyer, Armed Response, P.O.W. The Escape, Silent Assassins, The Wash, Tucker: The Man and His Dream, An Unremarkable Life, Taking Care of Business, Pacific Heights, The Perfect Weapon, Sidekicks, Robocop 3, Rising Sun, Cultivating Charlie, A Dangerous Place, Highlander III: The Sorcerer.
TELEVISION: Series: Hawaiian Heat. Movies: The Challenge, If Tomorrow Comes, The Streets of San Francisco (pilot), Judge Dee and the Monastery Murders, Farewell to Manzanar, When Hell Was in Session, The Last Ninja, Girls of the White Orchid. Guest: McHale's Navy, Ensign O'Toole, 77 Sunset Strip, I Spy, F Troop, Hawaii Five-O.

MALDEN, KARL
Actor. r.n. Mladen Sekulovich. b. Gary, IN, Mar. 22, 1914. e. Art Inst. of Chicago 1933-36; Goodman Theatre Sch. Elected pres., Acad. of Motion Picture Arts & Sciences, 1989.
THEATER: B'way: Golden Boy, Key Largo, Flight to West, Missouri Legend, Uncle Harry, Counterattack, Truckline Cafe, All My Sons, Streetcar Named Desire, Desperate Hours, Desire Under the Elms, The Egghead.
PICTURES: They Knew What They Wanted (debut, 1940), Winged Victory, 13 Rue Madeleine, Boomerang!, Kiss of Death, The Gunfighter, Where the Sidewalk Ends, Halls of Montezuma, A Streetcar Named Desire (Academy Award, best supporting actor, 1951), The Sellout, Diplomatic Courier, Operation Secret, Ruby Gentry, I Confess, Take the High Ground, Phantom of the Rue Morgue, On the Waterfront (Acad. Award nom.), Baby Doll, Bombers B-52, Time Limit (dir. only), Fear Strikes Out, The Hanging Tree, One Eyed Jacks, Pollyanna, The Great Impostor, Parrish, All Fall Down, Birdman of Alcatraz, Gypsy, How the West Was Won, Come Fly With Me, Cheyenne Autumn, Dead Ringer, The Cincinnati Kid, Nevada Smith, Murderer's Row, Hotel, Blue, The Adventures of Bullwhip Griffin, Billion Dollar Brain, Hot Millions, Patton, Cat O'Nine Tails, Wild Rovers, Summertime Killer, Beyond the Poseidon Adventure, Meteor, The Sting II, Twilight Time, Billy Galvin, Nuts.
TELEVISION: Series: Streets of San Francisco, Skag. Movies: Captains Courageous, Word of Honor, With Intent to Kill, Alice in Wonderland, Fatal Vision (Emmy Award, 1985), My Father My Son, The Hijacking of the Achille Lauro, Call Me Anna, Absolute Strangers, Back to the Streets of San Francisco.

MALIN, AMIR JACOB
Executive. b. Tel-Aviv, Israel, Mar. 22, 1954. e. Brandeis U., 1972-76; Boston U. Sch. of Law, 1976-79. Staff atty., WGBH-TV, Boston, 1979-81; pres. and co-CEO, Cinecom Entertainment Group Inc., 1982-92. Films acquired and distributed include Come Back to the Five and Dime Jimmy Dean Jimmy Dean, Metropolis, The Brother from Another Planet, Stop Making Sense, Coca-Cola Kid, A Room with a View, Swimming to Cambodia, Matewan, A Man in Love, Maurice, Miles From Home. Partner, October Films, Inc. Films acquired and distrib.: Life Is Sweet, Adam's Rib, The Living End, Tous les Matins du Monde (All the Mornings of the World), Ruby in Paradise, A Heart in Winter, Bad Behavior, Kika, Cronos, The Cement Garden, The Last Seduction, Search & Destroy, The Funeral, Breaking the Waves, Girlstown.
PICTURES: Exec. prod.: Swimming to Cambodia, Matewan, Miles From Home, Scenes from the Class Struggle in Beverly Hills, The Handmaid's Tale, Tune in Tomorrow.

MALKOVICH, JOHN
Actor, Producer, Director. b. Christopher, IL, Dec. 9, 1953. e. Illinois State U. Founding member Steppenwolf Ensemble in Chicago with group of college friends, 1976. Starred in Say Goodnight Gracie and True West (Obie Award) which then was brought to New York. NY Stage work includes Death of Salesman, Burn This, States of Shock. Director: Balm in Gilead, Arms and the Man, The Caretaker, Libra (also writer).
PICTURES: Places in the Heart (Acad. Award nom.), The Killing Fields, Eleni, Making Mr. Right, The Glass Menagerie, Empire of the Sun, Miles From Home, Dangerous Liaisons, The Accidental Tourist (co-exec. prod. only), The Sheltering Sky, Queens Logic, The Object of Beauty, Shadows and Fog, Of Mice and Men, Jennifer Eight, Alive, In the Line of Fire (Acad. Award nom.), The Convent, Beyond the Clouds, Mary Reilly, Mulholland Falls, Portrait of a Lady.
TELEVISION: Special: Rocket to the Moon. Movies: Word of Honor, American Dream, Death of a Salesman (Emmy Award, 1986), Heart of Darkness.

MALLE, LOUIS
Director, Producer, Writer. b. Thumeries, France, Oct. 30, 1932. m. actress Candice Bergen. e. Sorbonne (Pol. Science). Studied filmmaking at Institut des Hautes Etudes Cinematographiques 1951-53. Started in film industry as assistant to Robert Bresson and cameraman to oceanographer Jacques Cousteau, 1954-55 then corres. for French TV in Algeria, Vietnam and Thailand 1962-64. Became internationally known with Les Amants (The Lovers) in 1958. Has also acted in films (A Very Private Affair, A Very Curious Girl, Milky Way, La Vie de Boheme).
PICTURES: Silent World (co-dir., photog. with J. Y. Cousteau), A Conedmned Man Escapes (prod. asst. to Bresson), Mon Oncle (photog. only). Director: Elevator to the Gallows (also s.p.), The Lovers (also s.p.), Calcutta (doc.; also s.p., photog., actor), Zazie in the Metro (also s.p.), A Very Private Affair (also s.p., actor), Vive Le Tour (doc.; also s.p., photog., actor), The Fire Within (also s.p.), Viva Maria (also prod., s.p.), The Thief of Paris (also prod., s.p.), Spirits of the Dead (co-dir.), Phantom India (doc.; also photog.), Murmur of the Heart (also s.p.; Acad. Award nom. for best s.p.), Humain Trop Humain (doc.; also prod., photog.), Place de la Republique (doc.; also prod., photog.), Lacombe Lucien (also prod., s.p.), Black Moon (also s.p.), Pretty Baby (also prod., story), Atlantic City (Acad. Award nom.), My Dinner With Andre, Crackers, Alamo Bay (also prod.), Au Revoir Les Enfants (Goodbye Children; also s.p., prod.; Golden Lion Award, Venice Film Fest., 1987), May Fools (Milou en Mai; also co-s.p.), Damage (also prod.), Vanya on 42nd Street.
TELEVISION: Documentaries: God's Country, And the Pursuit of Happiness.
(d. November 23, 1995)

MALMUTH, BRUCE
Director, Actor. b. Brooklyn, NY, Feb. 4, 1937. e. City Coll. of New York, Brooklyn Coll. Grad. studies in film, Columbia U. and U. of Southern California. Acted in and dir. college productions. Moved to California and obtained job as page at NBC. In Army assigned to special services as director; reassigned to New York. Upon release began 10-year Clio-winning career as dir. of TV commercials. Debut as director of features with Nighthawks, 1981. Founder, Los Angeles Aspiring Actors and Directors Workshop. Theatre incl.: Two Guys Second Wind (writer, dir., prod.), Thanksgiving Cries (writer, dir.).
PICTURES: Director: Nighthawks, The Man Who Wasn't There, Where Are the Children? (also actor), Hard to Kill, Pentathalon (also actor). Actor: The Karate Kid (also Part II), For Keeps?, Happy New Year, Lean on Me.
TELEVISION: Baseballs or Switchblades? (prod., writer, dir., Emmy Award), A Boy's Dream, Twilight Zone, Beauty and the Beast, Heartbreak Winner.

MALONE, DOROTHY
Actress. b. Chicago, IL, Jan. 30, 1925. e. Southern Methodist U., USC, AADA. Started as RKO starlet, 1943. Stage work incl. Little Me, Practice to Deceive.
PICTURES: The Big Sleep, Night and Day, One Sunday Afternoon, Two Guys From Texas, The Nevadan, The Bushwackers, Jack Slade, The Killer That Stalked New York, Scared Stiff, Torpedo Alley, The Lone Gun, Pushover, Security Risk, Private Hell 36, The Fast and the Furious, Young at Heart, Battle Cry, Sincerely Yours, Artists and Models, At Gunpoint, Five Guns West, Tall Man Riding, Pillars of the Sky, Tension at Table Rock, Written on the Wind (Academy Award, best supporting actress, 1956), Man of a Thousand Faces, Quantez, The Tarnished Angels, Tip on a Dead Jockey, Too Much Toon Soon, Warlock, The Last Voyage, The Last Sunset, Beach Party, Fate is the Hunter (unbilled), Abduction, Golden Rendezvous, Good Luck Miss Wyckoff, Winter Kills, The Day Time Ended, The Being, Basic Instinct, Beverly Hills.
TELEVISION: Series: Peyton Place. Guest: Dick Powell Theatre, Loretta Young Show (twice hosted), Philip Morris Playhouse, Dr. Kildare, Bob Hope Show, Jack Benny Show, The Untouchables, Phyllis Diller Show, Ken Murray's Blackouts, Death Valley Days.

Movies: The Pigeon, Little Ladies of the Night, Murder in Peyton Place, Katie: Portrait of a Centerfold, Condominium, Peyton Place: The Next Generation. Mini-Series: Rich Man Poor Man. Specials: Gertrude Stein Story, The Family That Prays Together.

MALONE, JOHN C.
Executive. b. Milford, CT, Mar. 7, 1941. e. Yale U. Pres. & CEO of Telecommunications Inc., 1973-present. With National Cable Television Association as: dir., 1974-77; treasurer, 1977-78; dir., 1980-94. Dir. of TCI; on bd. of dirs. for Turner Bordacasting, Cable Television Laboratories Inc. BET, Discovery.

MAMET, DAVID
Writer, Director. b. Chicago, IL, Nov. 30, 1947. e. Goddard Coll. Artist-in-residence, Goddard Coll. 1971-73. Artistic dir. St. Nicholas Theatre Co., Chicago, 1973-75. Co-founder Dinglefest Theatre; assoc. artistic dir., Goodman Theatre, Chicago. Appeared as actor in film Black Widow. Novel: The Village (1994).
THEATER: Lakefront, The Woods, American Buffalo, Sexual Perversity in Chicago, Duck Variations, Edmond, A Life in the Theatre, The Water Engine, Prairie du Chien, Glengarry Glen Ross (Pulitzer Prize, Tony Award, 1984), Speed-the-Plow, Sketches of War (benefit for homeless Vietnam Veterans), Oleanna, An Interview (Death Defying Acts), The Cryptogram.
PICTURES: Writer: The Postman Always Rings Twice, The Verdict, The Untouchables, House of Games (also dir.), Things Change (also dir.), We're No Angels, Homicide (also dir.), Hoffa, Vanya on 42nd Street (adaptation), Oleanna (also dir.).
TELEVISION: Lip Service (exec. prod.), Hill Street Blues, A Life in the Theatre, Texan.

MANASSE, GEORGE
Producer. b. Florence, Italy, Jan. 1, 1938. e. U. of North Carolina.
PICTURES: Prod.: Who Killed Mary What's 'er Name?, Squirm, Blue Sunshine, He Knows You're Alone. Prod. Mgr.: Greetings, Joe, Fury on Wheels, Slow Dancing in the Big City, Tribute, Porky's II: The Next Day, Neighbors, Death Wish III, Torch Song Trilogy, Indecent Proposal, Coneheads, Lassie, Die Hard With a Vengeance, Eraser.
TELEVISION: Line Prod.: Series: American Playwright's Theatre (Arts & Ent.) The Saint in Manhattan (pilot), Movie: The Killing Floor, Vengeance: The Story of Tony Cimo. Prod. Mgr.: Series: St. Elsewhere, Annie McGuire. Movies: Sanctuary of Fear, Mr. Griffith and Me, Peking Encounter, When the Circus Came to Town, Murder, Inc. Muggable Mary, Running Out, Dropout Father, He's Hired, She's Fired, Intimate Strangers, Drop Out Mother, Vengeance: The Story of Tony Cimo, The Saint in Manhattan, The Diamond Trap, The Prize Pulitzer (also suprv. prod.), Orpheus Descending (also suprv. prod.), John and Yoko, Marilyn and Me, The Woman Who Sinned.

MANCIA, ADRIENNE
Curator, Dept. of Film, Museum of Modern Art. b. New York, NY. e. U. of Wisconsin. B.A.; Columbia U., M.A. Worked in film distribution industry in New York prior to joining Dept. of Film & Video, Museum of Modern Art, 1964; responsible for film exhibition since 1965. 1977, appointed curator. Restructured Museums' Auditorium Exhibition Prog., creating a balance between classic cinema and contemporary work. Initiated innovative programs such as Cineprobe and New Documentaries (formerly What's Happening?) Served on numerous int'l film juries. Co-founder New Directors/New Films. Chevalier de l'Ordre des Arts et des Lettres (France), 1985). Ufficiale dell Ordine al Merito della Repubblica Italiana, 1988.

MANCUSO, FRANK G.
Executive. b. Buffalo, NY, July 25, 1933. e. State U. of New York. Film buyer and operations supvr. for Basil Enterprises, theatre circuit, 1958-62. Joined Paramount as booker in Buffalo branch, 1962. Named sls. repr. for branch in 1964 and branch mgr. in 1967. 1970 appt. v.p./gen. sls. mgr., Paramount Pictures Canada, Ltd., becoming pres. in 1972. 1976 relocated with Paramount in U.S. as western div. mgr. in LA. 1977, appt. gen. sls. mgr. of NY, office; two months later promoted to v.p. domestic distribution; 1979, named exec. v.p., distrib. & mktg. 1983 made pres. of entire Paramount Motion Picture Group. 1984, appointed chmn. and CEO, Paramount Pictures; resigned 1991. Named Motion Picture Pioneers Man of the Year, 1987. Member of Board: AMPAS, M.P. Assoc. of America, Will Rogers Memorial Fund, Variety Clubs Intl., Sundance Institute, Amer. Film Institute, Museum of Broadcasting, Motion Picture Pioneers. Appointed Chmn. & CEO of MGM, 1993.

MANCUSO, FRANK, JR.
Producer. b. Buffalo, NY, Oct. 9, 1958. Son of Frank G. Mancuso. e. Upsala Coll. Began with industry at age 14, booking short subjects in Canadian theatres. Worked in gross receipts dept. in Paramount corporate offices in New York and later with paralegal div. Initial prod. work as location asst. for Urban Cowboy in Houston, TX. Served as assoc. prod. of Friday the 13th Part II and prod. of Friday the 13th Part III in 3-D.

PICTURES: Off the Wall, The Man Who Wasn't There, April Fool's Day, Friday the 13th, Part IV: The Final Chapter; Friday the 13th—A New Beginning (exec. prod.), Friday the 13th, Part VII (exec. prod.); Back to the Beach; Permanent Record, Internal Affairs, He Said/She Said, Species, Fled.
TELEVISION: Friday the 13th: The Series (exec. prod.).

MANDEL, BABALOO
Writer. r.n. Marc Mandel. b. 1949. Started as comedy writer for Joan Rivers, among others. First teamed with Lowell Ganz on script for 1982 film Night Shift.
PICTURES: Night Shift, Splash (Acad. Award nom.; also actor), Spies Like Us, Gung Ho, Vibes, Parenthood, City Slickers, A League of Their Own, Mr. Saturday Night (also cameo), Greedy, City Slickers II: The Legend of Curly's Gold, Forget Paris, Multiplicity.
TELEVISION: Series co-writer: Laverne and Shirley, Busting Loose, Take Five (also co-creator). Series co-exec. prod.: Gung Ho, Knight and Daye, Parenthood.

MANDEL, LORING
Writer. b. Chicago, IL, May 5, 1928. e. U. of Wisconsin, B.S. 1949. Long career writing scripts for TV, dating back to 1955 when penned Shakedown Cruise. Governor, Natl. Acad. of TV Arts & Sciences 1964-68; Pres. Writers Guild of America East 1975-77; Natl. Chmn. 1977-79.
PICTURES: Countdown, Promises in the Dark, The Little Drummer Girl.
TELEVISION: Do Not Go Gentle Into That Good Night (Emmy, 1967), Breaking Up, Project Immortality (Sylvania Award, 1959), A House His Own, Trial of Chaplain Jensen, The Raider, etc.

MANDEL, ROBERT
Director. e. Columbia Univ.
PICTURES: Night at O'Rears (also prod.), Independence Day, F/X, Touch and Go, Big Shots, School Ties, The Substitute.
TELEVISION: Hard Time on Planet Earth.

MANDELL, ABE
Executive. b. Oct. 4, 1922. e. U. of Cincinnati. Entered broadcasting as actor on Cincinnati radio station prior to W.W.II. Served U.S. Army in Southwest Pacific, 1942-45. Formed indep. motion picture distribution co. in the Far East. Company, which became the largest indep. motion picture dist. in the Far East, also operated and owned motion picture theaters throughout the Phillipines and Indonesia, 1946-56; network-regional sales exec., Ziv Television, 1956-58; dir. foreign operations, Independent Television Corporation, 1958; v.p.-foreign oper., 1960; v.p.-sales and adm., 1961; exec. v.p., 1962; pres. 1965. 1976 corporate name changed from Independent Television Corp. to ITC Entertainment, Inc. President to 1983 of ITC Entertainment; with Robert Mandell heads New Frontier Prods.

MANDOKI, LUIS
Director. b. Mexico City, Mexico. e. San Francisco Art Institute, London Intl. Film School, London College's School of Film. Dir. short film Silent Music which won Intl. Amateur Film Fest. Award at 1976 Cannes Film Fest. Back in Mexico dir. shorts and documentaries for the Instituto Nacional Indignista Concaine, Centro de Produccionde Cortometraje. Won Ariel
PICTURES: Motel (debut, 1982), Gaby--A True Story, White Palace, Born Yesterday, When a Man Loves a Woman.

MANES, FRITZ
Producer. b. Oakland, CA, Apr. 22, 1936. e. U.C., Berkeley, B.A. UCLA, 1956. Armed Service: 1951-54. U.S. Marines, Korea, Purple Heart. TV ad. exec. and stuntman before becoming exec. prod. on films for Clint Eastwood. Has formed own production co., Sundancer Prods. Membership, DGA, SAG.
PICTURES: in various capacities: The Outlaw Josey Wales, The Enforcer. Assoc. prod.: The Gauntlet, Every Which Way But Loose, Escape From Alcatraz, Bronco Billy. Prod.: Any Which Way You Can (also 2nd asst. dir.), Firefox (exec. prod.), Honky Tonk Man (exec. prod.), Tightrope (prod.), Sudden Impact (exec. prod.), City Heat (prod.), Pale Rider (exec. prod.), Ratboy (exec. prod.), Heartbreak Ridge (exec. prod., prod. mgr.), James Dean.

MANKIEWICZ, DON M.
Writer. b. Berlin, Germany, Jan. 20, 1922. p. Herman J. Mankiewicz. e. Columbia, B.A., 1942; Columbia Law Sch. Served in U.S. Army, 1942-46; reporter, New Yorker magazine, 1946-48; author of novels See How They Run, Trial, It Only Hurts a Minute; magazine articles, short stories. President, Producers Guild of America, 1987; on Board of Directors, Writers Guild of America, 1992.
PICTURES: Trial, I Want to Live, (Acad. Award nom.), The Chapman Report, The Black Bird.
TELEVISION: Studio One, On Trial, One Step Beyond, Playhouse 90, Profiles in Courage. Exec. story consultant: Hart to Hart, Simon & Simon, Crazy Like a Fox, Adderly. Pilots: Ironside, Marcus Welby M.D., Sarge, Lanigan's Rabbi (collab.), Rosetti and Ryan (collab.).

MANKIEWICZ, TOM
Writer, Director. b. Los Angeles, CA, June 1, 1942. e. Yale U.
PICTURES: Writer: The Sweet Ride (debut), Diamonds Are Forever, Live and Let Die, The Man with the Golden Gun, Mother Jugs and Speed (also prod.), The Cassandra Crossing, The Eagle Has Landed, Ladyhawke. Exec. Prod.: Hot Pursuit. Creative consultant: Superman, Superman II. Director: Dragnet (also s.p.), Delirious.
TELEVISION: Pilot: Hart to Hart (writer, dir.). Movie: Taking the Heat (dir.). Episode: Tales of the Crypt (dir.)

MANKOWITZ, WOLF
Writer, Producer. b. London, Nov. 7, 1924. Was journalist before ent. m.p. industry in 1952.
THEATRE: Expresso Bongo (from his story), Make Me An Offer, Belle, Pickwick, Passion Flower Hotel, Casanova's Last Stand, etc.
PICTURES: Make Me an Offer, A Kid for Two Farthings, The Bespoke Overcoat, Expresso Bongo, The Millionairess, The Long and the Short and the Tall, The Day the Earth Caught Fire, Waltz of the Toreadors, Where the Spies Are, Casino Royale (co-writer), The Assassination Bureau, Bloomfield, Black Beauty, Treasure Island, The Hebrew Lesson, The Hireling, Almonds and Raisins.
TELEVISION: The Killing Stones, A Cure for Tin Ear, The Battersea Miracle, Series: Conflict, Dickens of London.

MANN, ABBY
Writer. b. Philadelphia, PA, 1927. e. NYU. First gained fame on TV writing for Robert Montgomery Theatre, Playhouse 90, Studio One, Alcoa, Goodyear Theatre. Acad. Award for film adaptation of own teleplay Judgment at Nuremberg into theatrical film.
PICTURES: Judgment at Nuremberg, A Child Is Waiting, The Condemned of Altona, Ship of Fools (Academy Award nom.), The Detective, Report to the Commissioner.
TELEVISION: Series: Kojak (creator), Skag, Medical Story. Movies: The Marcus-Nelson Murders (Emmy Award, 1973; also exec. prod.), Medical Story (also exec. prod.), The Atlanta Child Murders, King (Emmy nom.), Murderers Among Us: The Simon Wiesenthal Story (Emmy Award, 1989; co-writer, co-exec. prod.), Teamster Boss: The Jackie Presser Story (also co-exec. prod.), Indictment: The McMartin Trial (also co-exec. prod.; Emmy Award, 1995, Golden Globe Award).

MANN, DELBERT
Director, Producer. b. Lawrence, KS, Jan. 30, 1920. e. Vanderbilt U., Yale U. U.S. Air Force, 1942-45. Stage mgr., summer stock, dir. Columbia, S.C. Town Theatre, 1947-49. Asst. dir., NBC-TV, 1949; dir., NBC-TV, 1949-55. Past pres., Directors Guild of America.
THEATER: A Quiet Place, Speaking of Murder, Zelda, The Glass Menagerie, The Memoirs of Abraham Lincoln; opera: Wuthering Heights (NY City Center).
PICTURES: Marty (Academy Award, 1955), The Bachelor Party, Desire Under the Elms, Separate Tables, Middle of the Night, The Dark at the Top of the Stairs, The Outsider, Lover Come Back, That Touch of Mink, A Gathering of Eagles, Dear Heart, Quick Before It Melts (also prod.), Mister Buddwing (also prod.), Fitzwilly, The Pink Jungle, Kidnapped, Birch Interval, Night Crossing.
TELEVISION: Philco-Goodyear TV Playhouse, Producer's Showcase, Omnibus, Playwrights '56, Playhouse 90, Ford Star Jubilee, Lights Out, Mary Kay and Johnny, The Little Show, Masterpiece Theatre, Ford Startime. Movies/Specials: Heidi, David Copperfield, No Place to Run, She Waits (also prod.), Jane Eyre, The Man Without a Country, A Girl Named Sooner, Francis Gary Powers: The True Story of the U-2 Spy Incident, Tell Me My Name, Breaking Up, Home to Stay, Love's Dark Ride, Thou Shalt Not Commit Adultery, All Quiet on the Western Front, Torn Between Two Lovers, To Find My Son, All the Way Home, The Member of the Wedding, The Gift of Love, Bronte, Love Leads the Way, A Death in California, The Last Days of Patton, The Ted Kennedy, Jr. Story, April Morning (also co-prod.), Ironclads, Against Her Will: An Incident in Baltimore (also prod.), Incident in a Small Town (also prod.), Lily in Winter.

MANN, MICHAEL
Director, Writer, Producer. b. Chicago, IL, Feb. 5, 1943. e. U. of Wisconsin, London Film Sch. Directed shorts, commercials and documentaries in England. Returned to U.S. in 1972. Wrote for prime-time TV (episodes of Starsky and Hutch, Police Story, created Vegas).
PICTURES: Exec. Prod.: Band of the Hand. Director-Writer: Thief (also exec. prod.), The Keep, Manhunter, The Last of the Mohicans (also co-prod.), Heat (also s.p.).
TELEVISION: The Jericho Mile (writer, dir.; DGA Award, Emmy Award for writing, 1980), Miami Vice (exec. prod.), Crime Story (exec. prod.), L.A. Takedown (dir., writer, exec. prod.). Mini-Series: Drug Wars: The Camarena Story (exec. prod.; Emmy Award, 1990), Drug Wars: The Cocaine Cartel (exec. prod.).

MANNING, MICHELLE
Executive. Exec. v.p., Production Division, Viacom, Inc.

MANOFF, DINAH
Actress. b. New York, NY, January 25, 1958. e. CalArts. Daughter of actress-director Lee Grant and late writer Arnold Manoff. Prof. debut in PBS prod., The Great Cherub Knitwear Strike. Guest starred on Welcome Back Kotter.
THEATER: I Ought to Be in Pictures (Tony & Theatre World Awards, 1980), Gifted Children, Leader of the Pack, Alfred and Victoria: A Life (L.A. Theatre Center), Kingdom of Earth (TheatreWest).
PICTURES: Grease (debut, 1978), Ordinary People, I Ought to Be in Pictures, Child's Play, Staying Together, Bloodhounds of Broadway, Welcome Home Roxy Carmichael.
TELEVISION: Series: Soap, Empty Nest. Movies: Raid on Entebbe, Night Terror, The Possessed, For Ladies Only, A Matter of Sex, The Seduction of Gina, Flight No. 90: Disaster on the Potomac, Classified Love, Crossing the Mob, Backfire, Babies, Maid for Each Other (also co-exec. prod., co-story). Mini-Series: Celebrity.

MANSON, ARTHUR
Executive. b. Brooklyn, NY, Feb. 21, 1928. e. City Coll. of New York, grad. Inst. Film Technique, 1945. Editor, American Traveler, U.S. Army, 1946. Advance agent, co. mgr., Henry V, U.S., 1948-50; producer's publ. rep., Stanley Kramer Distributing Corp., Samuel Goldwyn Productions, 1951-52, dir. of adv. and publ., MGM Pictures of Canada, Ltd., 1952-53; publ. and adv. rep., Cinerama widescreen process, 1953-58; dir. worldwide ad-pub Cinerama 1958-60; adv. mgr., Columbia Pictures, 1961-62; nat'l dir. of adv., publi., Dino De Laurentiis, 1962-64; exec. asst. to v.p. adv. & pub., 20th Century-Fox, 1964-67; v.p., adv. & pub. Cinerama. Inc., and Cinerama Releasing Corp.; 1967-74; exec. v.p., sales & marketing, BCP, service of Cox Broadcasting Corp., 1974-75; v.p. worldwide marketing Warner Bros., 1976. 1977 formed own company, Cinemax Mkt. & Dist. Corp. and is pres. Chmn., NY events committee, AMPAS.

MANTEGNA, JOE
Actor. b. Chicago, IL, Nov. 13, 1947. e. Morton Jr. Coll., Goodman Sch. of Drama, 1967-69. Member: The Organic Theatre Company, Chicago (The Wonderful Ice Cream Suit, Cops, and 2 European tours with ensemble). Later member of Goodman Theater where he began long creative assoc. with playwright-dir. David Mamet (A Life in the Theatre, The Disappearance of the Jews). In national co. of Hair, Godspell, Lenny. B'way debut: Working. Narrated documentaries Crack U.S.A. and Death on the Job.
THEATER: Bleacher Bums (also conceived and co-author), Leonardo (L.A., co-author), Glengarry Glen Ross (Tony Award), Speed-the-Plow.
PICTURES: Who Stole My Wheels? (Towing), Second Thoughts, Compromising Positions, The Money Pit, Off Beat, Three Amigos, Critical Condition, House of Games, Weeds, Suspect, Things Change (Venice Film Fest. Award, 1988), Wait Until Spring Bandini, Alice, The Godfather Part III, Queens Logic, Homicide, Bugsy, Body of Evidence, Family Prayers, Searching for Bobby Fisher, Baby's Day Out, Airheads, For Better or Worse, Forget Paris, Up Close and Personal, Eye for an Eye, Thinner, Albino Alligator.
TELEVISION: Series: Comedy Zone. Guest: Soap, Bosom Buddies, Archie Bunker's Place, Magnum P.I., Open All Night, Fallen Angels (The Quiet Room). Special: Bleacher Bums (Emmy Award). Movies: Elvis, Comrades of Summer, The Water Engine, State of Emergency, Above Suspicion.

MANULIS, MARTIN
Producer, Director. b. New York, NY, May 30, 1915. e. Columbia Col., B.A. 1935. Lt. USN, 1941-45. Head of prod. John C. Wilson, 1941-49; mgr. dir., Westport Country Playhouse, 1945-50; dir. B'way plays; staff prod. & dir. CBS-TV, 1951-58; head prod. 20th-Fox Television. Now pres., Martin Manulis Prods. Ltd. 1987, artistic dir., Ahmanson Theatre, L.A.
THEATER: B'way/and on tour: Private Lives, Made in Heaven, The Philadelphia Story, Pride's Crossing, Laura, The Men We Marry, The Hasty Heart, The Show Off.
PICTURES: Producer: Days of Wine and Roses, Dear Heart, Luv, Duffy, The Out-of-Towners.
TELEVISION: Suspense, Studio One, Climax, Best of Broadway, Playhouse 90. Mini-Series: Chiefs, Space, The Day Christ Died, Grass Roots.

MARA, ADELE
Actress. r.n. Adelaida Delgado; b. Dearborn, MI, April 28, 1923. m. writer-prod. Roy Huggins. Singer, dancer with Xavier Cugat orchestra.
PICTURES: Navy Blues (feature debut, 1941), Shut My Big Mouth, Blondie Goes to College, Alias Boston Blackie, You Were Never Lovelier, Lucky Legs, Vengeance of the West, Reveille With Beverly, Riders of the Northwest Mounted, The Magnificent Rogue, Passkey to Danger, Traffic in Crime, Exposed, The Trespasser, Blackmail, Campus Honeymoon, Twilight on the Rio

Grande, Robin Hood of Texas, Nighttime in Nevada, The Gallant Legion, Sands of Iwo Jima, Wake of the Red Witch, Rock Island Trail, California Passage, The Avengers, The Sea Hornet, Count The Hours, The Black Whip, Back from Eternity, Curse of the Faceless Man, The Big Circus.
TELEVISION: Series: Cool Million. Mini-Series: Wheels.

MARAIS, JEAN
Actor. b. Cherbourg, France, Dec. 11, 1913. e. Coll. St. Germain, Lycee Janson de Sailly, Lycee Condorcet. Painter; photog; stage actor; French Air Army; m.p. debut in Pavillon Brule.
PICTURES: Carmen, Eternal Return, Beauty and the Beast, Ruy Blas, Les Parents Terribles, Secret of Mayerling, Souvenir, Orpheus, Eagle with Two Heads, Inside a Girl's Dormitory, Royal Affairs in Versailles, Paris Does Strange Things, Le Capitan, Le Bossu, La Princesse de Cleves, Le Capitaine Fracasse, Honorable Stanilleu, Agent Secret, Patute, Fantomas, Le Gentleman de Cocody, Stealing Beauty.

MARCHAND, NANCY
Actress. b. Buffalo, NY, June 19, 1928. m. actor-dir. Paul Sparer. e. Carnegie Tech. Stage debut The Late George Apley (1946).
THEATER: The Taming of the Shrew (B'way debut, 1951), The Balcony (Obie Award, 1960), Morning's at Seven (Drama Desk & Outer Critics Circle Awards), Sister Mary Ignatius Explains It All to You, Taken in Marriage, The Plough and the Stars, Awake and Sing, The Cocktail Hour (Obie Award, 1990), The End of the Day, Black Comedy/White Liars. Was an original mem of APA-Phoenix Theater.
PICTURES: The Bachelor Party (debut, 1957), Ladybug Ladybug, Me Natalie, Tell Me That You Love Me Junie Moon, The Hospital, The Bostonians, From the Hip, The Naked Gun: From the Files of Police Squad, Jefferson in Paris, Sabrina.
TELEVISION: Specials: Little Women, Marty, Kiss Kiss Dahlings, many others. Series: Beacon Hill, Adams Chronicles, Love of Life, Search for Tomorrow, Lou Grant (4 Emmy Awards: 1978, 1980, 1981, 1982). Movies: Some Kind of Miracle, Willa, Once Upon a Family, Killjoy, The Golden Moment—An Olympic Love Story, Sparkling Cyanide. Mini-Series: North and South Book II.

MARCOVICCI, ANDREA
Actress, Singer. b. New York, NY, Nov. 18, 1948. e. Bennett Col. Studied acting with Herbert Berghof. Acted on NY stage in The Wedding of Iphigenia, The Ambassadors, Nefertiti, Hamlet, Any Given Day. Frequent performer in night clubs.
PICTURES: The Front (debut, 1976), The Concorde: Airport 1979, The Hand, Spacehunter: Adventures in the Forbidden Zone, Kings and Desperate Men, The Stuff, Someone to Love, White Dragon, Jack the Bear.
TELEVISION: Series: Love Is a Many-Splendored Thing, Berrenger's, Trapper John M.D. Movies: Cry Rape!, Smile Jenny You're Dead, Some Kind of Miracle, A Vacation in Hell, Packin' It In, Sprague, Velvet, The Canterville Ghost, The Water Engine.

MARCUS, MICHAEL E.
Executive. b. Pittsburgh, PA, June 5, 1945. e. Penn State, 1963-67. Moved to LA where he started in industry in mailroom of General Artists Corp. Promoted to agent when co. merged with Creative Management Assocs. 1972 joined Bart/Levy Agency; 1980, became full partner and co-owner of Kohner/Levy/Marcus Agency. 1981, became sr. agent at Creative Artists Agency. 1993, named pres. & COO of MGM Pictures.

MARCUS, MORT
Executive. Pres., Buena Vista Television Production.

MARENSTEIN, HAROLD
Executive. b. New York, NY, Nov. 30, 1916. e. City Coll. of New York, 1937. Shipping, picture checking service, Warner Bros., 1935-45; booking, Loew's Inc., 1945-48; booking, contracts, Selznick Rel. Org., 1948-51; contracts, Paramount, 1951-52; asst. sls. gr., International Rel. Org., 1952; asst. sls. mgr., Janus Films, 1961-64; sls. exec., Rizzoli Films, 1965; 1967, nat'l. sales dir., Continental Dist.; gen. sales mgr., Cinemation Industries, 1968; v.p.-sales, dir., Cinemation Industries, 1971; 1976, gen. sls. mgr., General National Films; 1980, gen. sls. mgr., Lima Productions. Now retired.

MARENZI, GARY
Executive. Pres., MGM/UA Communications Group.

MARGOLIN, STUART
Actor, Director, Writer. b. Davenport, IA, Jan. 31, 1940. Wrote play Sad Choices which was produced Off-B'way when he was only 20.
PICTURES: The Gamblers, Kelly's Heroes, Limbo, Death Wish, The Big Bus, Futureworld, Days of Heaven, S.O.B., Class, Running Hot, A Fine Mess, Paramedics (dir. only), Iron Eagle II, Bye Bye Blues, Guilty By Suspicion.
TELEVISION: Series: Occasional Wife, Love American Style, Nichols, The Rockford Files (Emmy Awards, 1979, 1980), Bret Maverick, Mr. Smith. Guest: Hey Landlord, He & She, The

Monkees, M*A*S*H, Gunsmoke, The Mary Tyler Moore Show (also dir.), Rhoda, Magnum P.I., Hill Street Blues. *Movies*: The Intruders, The Ballad of Andy Crocker (writer, associate prod. only), A Summer Without Boys (voice), The Rockford Files (pilot), The California Kid, This is the West That Was, Lanigan's Rabbi, Perilous Voyage, A Killer in the Family, Three of a Kind, To Grandmother's House We Go, How the West Was Fun (dir. only), The Rockford Files: I Still Love L.A, The Rockford Files: A Blessing in Disguise. *Director*: Suddenly Love, A Shining Season, The Long Summer of George Adams, Double Double Toil and Trouble.

MARGULIES, STAN
Producer. b. New York, NY, Dec. 14, 1920. e. De Witt Clinton H.S., NYU, B.S., June, 1940. Army Air Force, May, 1942; p.r., Air Force and the Infantry, wrote service magazines, newspapers including Yank; spec. feature writer & asst. Sunday editor, Salt Lake City Tribune; publicist, RKO Studios, Hollywood, March, 1947; continued publicity work at CBS-Radio, 20th Century-Fox, Walt Disney Productions. Bryna Films, 1955; became vice-pres., 1958; also served exec. prod., TV series, Tales of the Vikings; prod. asst., Spartacus.
PICTURES: 40 Pounds of Trouble, Those Magnificent Men in Their Flying Machines, Don't Just Stand There, The Pink Jungle, If It's Tuesday This Must Be Belgium, I Love My Wife, Willy Wonka and the Chocolate Factory, One Is a Lonely Number, Visions of Eight.
TELEVISION: *Movies*: The 500 Pound Jerk, She Lives, The Morning After, Unwed Father, Men of the Dragon, I Will Fight No More Forever, Roots (Emmy Award, 1977), Roots: The Next Generations (Emmy Award, 1979), Moviola, Agatha Christie's Murder Is Easy, The Thorn Birds, Agatha Christie's A Caribbean Mystery, A Killer in the Family, Sparkling Cyanide, The Mystic Warrior, A Bunny's Tale, Out on a Limb, Broken Angel, Crossing to Freedom, Separate But Equal (Emmy Award, 1991).

MARILL, ALVIN H.
Writer. b. Brockton, MA, Jan. 10, 1934. e. Boston U., 1955. Director music programming, writer/prod., WNAC, Boston 1961-65; dir. music prog., WRFM, NY 1966-67; publicity writer, RCA Records 1967-72; sr. writer/editor, RCA Direct Marketing 1972-80; partner, TLK Direct Marketing 1977-80; mgr., A & R Administration, RCA Direct Marketing 1980-83; exec. editor, CBS TV (1984-88); editor, Carol Publ. Group (1988-94); v.p., Sandal Enterprises (1994-present). Television editor, Films in Review 1973-84. Writer/researcher: The Great Singers (record/tape collections). Jury member: 1983 Locarno Film Fest. Television Movie Hall of Fame.
AUTHOR: Samuel Goldwyn Presents, Robert Mitchum on the Screen, The Films of Anthony Quinn, The Films of Sidney Poitier, Katharine Hepburn: A Pictorial Study, Boris Karloff—A Pictorial Biography, Errol Flynn—A Pictorial Biography, The Complete Films of Edward G. Robinson, More Theatre: Stage to Screen to Television, Movies Made for Television 1964-96, The Films of Tyrone Power; Editor: Moe Howard & The 3 Stooges, The Films of Tommy Lee Jones, The Ultimate John Wayne Trivia Book. Assoc. editor: Leonard Maltin's Movie & Video Guide.

MARIN, CHEECH (RICHARD)
Actor, Writer. b. Los Angeles, CA, July 13, 1946. e. California State U, B.S. Teamed with Tommy Chong in improvisational group, City Works (Vancouver). Comedy recordings include Sleeping Beauty, Cheech and Chong Big Bama, Los Cochinos, The Wedding Album (Grammy Award), Get Out of My Room.
PICTURES: Up in Smoke (also co-s.p.), Cheech and Chong's Next Movie (also co-s.p.), Cheech and Chong's Nice Dreams (also co-s.p.), Things Are Tough All Over (also co-s.p.), It Came from Hollywood, Still Smokin' (also co-s.p.), Yellowbeard, Cheech and Chong's The Corsican Brothers (also co-s.p.), After Hours, Echo Park, Born in East L.A. (also s.p., dir.), Fatal Beauty, Oliver & Company (voice), Troop Beverly Hills (cameo), Ghostbusters II (cameo), Rude Awakening, Far Out Man, The Shrimp on the Barbie, FernGully... The Last Rainforest (voice), A Million to Juan, The Lion King (voice), Desperado, From Dusk Till Dawn, The Great White Hype, Tin Cup.
TELEVISION: *Series*: The Golden Palace, Nash Bridges. *Movie*: The Cisco Kid. *Specials*: Get Out of My Room (also dir., songs), Charlie Barnett—Terms of Enrollment.

MARK, LAURENCE M.
Producer, Executive. b. New York, NY. e. Wesleyan U., B.A.; NYU, M.A. Started career as trainee and publicist for United Artists; also asst. to producer on Lenny, Smile, etc. Joined Paramount Pictures as mktg./prod. liaison dir. and then exec. dir., pub. for m.p. division in NY. Named v.p., prod./mktg. at Paramount Studio; 1980, v.p., west coast mktg.; 1982 promoted to post as v.p., prod. 1984 (projects incl. Trading Places, Terms of Endearment, Falling in Love, Lady Jane); joined 20th Century-Fox as exec. v.p., prod. (projects incl. The Fly, Broadcast News); 1986, established Laurence Mark Productions at Fox; 1989 moved headquarters to Walt Disney Studios.
THEATER: Brooklyn Laundry (L.A.).

PICTURES: Black Widow (exec. prod.), Working Girl (exec. prod.), My Stepmother is an Alien (exec. prod.), Cookie (prod.), Mr. Destiny (exec. prod.), True Colors (prod.), One Good Cop (prod.), The Adventures of Huck Finn (prod.), Gunmen (prod.), Sister Act 2: Back in the Habit (exec. prod.), Cutthroat Island (prod.), Tom & Huck (prod.), Jerry Maguire (prod.), Romy & Michele's High School Reunion (prod.), Tom and Huck.
TELEVISION: Sweet Bird of Youth (exec. prod.).

MARKHAM, MONTE
Actor. b. Manatee, FL, June 21, 1938. e. U. of Georgia. Military service in Coast Guard after which joined resident theatre co. at Stephens College, MO, where he also taught acting. Joined Actor's Workshop Theatre, San Francisco, for three years. Made TV debut in Mission: Impossible episode. June, 1992 formed Perpetual Motion Films with Adam Friedman.
THEATER: B'way: Irene (Theatre World Award), Same Time Next Year.
PICTURES: Hour of the Gun, Guns of the Magnificent Seven, One Is a Lonely Number, Midway, Airport '77, Ginger in the Morning, Off the Wall, Jake Speed, Hot Pursuit, Defense Play (also dir.), Neon City (also dir.), At First Sight.
TELEVISION: *Series*: The Second Hundred Years, Mr. Deeds Goes to Town, The New Perry Mason, Dallas, Rituals, Baywatch (also dir. episodes), Melrose Place, Campus Cops. *Movies*: Death Takes a Holiday, The Astronaut, Visions, Hustling, Ellery Queen, Relentless, Drop-Out Father, Hotline, Baywatch: Panic at Malibu Pier. *Host-narrator-prod.-dir.*: Air Combat, Combat at Sea, Master of War, Epic Biographies, The Great Ships.

MARKLE, PETER
Director. b. Danville, PA, Sept. 24, 1946.
PICTURES: The Personals (also s.p., photog.), Hot Dog ... The Movie, Youngblood (also co-story, s.p.), Bat-21, Wagons East!
TELEVISION: *Movies*: Desperate, Nightbreaker, Breaking Point, El Diablo, Through the Eyes of a Killer, Jake Lassiter: Justice on the Bayou, White Dwarf.

MARKOWITZ, ROBERT
Director. b. Irvington, NJ, Feb. 7, 1935. e. Boston Univ. Mostly on TV before theatrical debut with Voices, 1979.
TELEVISION: *Movies*: Children of the Night, Phantom of the Opera, The Deadliest Season, The Storyteller, Kojak: The Belarus File, My Mother's Secret Life, Pray TV, A Long Way Home, Alex: The Life of a Child, Adam: His Song Continues, The Wall, A Cry for Help: The Tracey Thurman Story, Too Young to Die, A Dangerous Life, Decoration Day, Love Lies and Murder, Afterburn, Overexposed, Murder in the Heartland, Because Mommy Works, The Tuskegee Airmen. *Special*: Twilight Zone: Rod Serling's Lost Classics.

MARKS, ALFRED
O.B.E. Actor-Comedian. b. London, 1921. TV, own series, Alfred Marks Time with wife, comedienne Paddie O'Neil.
PICTURES: Desert Mice, There Was a Crooked Man, Weekend with Lulu, The Frightened City, She'll Have to Go, Scream and Scream Again, Our Miss Fred, Valentino, Sleeps Six.
TELEVISION: Blanding's Castle, Hobson's Choice, Paris 1900, The Memorandum.

MARKS, ARTHUR
Producer, Director, Writer, Film Executive. b. Los Angeles, CA, Aug. 2, 1927. At 19 began work at MGM Studios as production messenger. Became asst. dir. in 1950, youngest dir. member of Directors Guild of Amer., 1957. President and board member of Arthur Prod., Inc.
PICTURES: Togetherness (prod., dir., s.p.), Class of '74 (dir., s.p.), Bonnie's Kids (dir., s.p.), Roommates (dir., s.p.), Detroit 9000 (prod., dir.), The Centerfold Girls (prod., dir.), A Woman For All Men (dir.), Wonder Woman (exec. prod.), The Candy Snatchers (exec. prod.), Bucktown (dir.), Friday Foster (prod., dir.), J.D.'s Revenge (prod., dir.), Monkey Hustle (prod., dir.). Writer: Empress of the China Seas, Gold Stars, Mean Intentions, Hot Times, Starfire, There's A Killer in Philly.
TELEVISION: *Series*: Perry Mason series (1961-66; prod., also dir. of over 100 episodes; writer-dir. of numerous TV shows including: I Spy, Mannix, Starsky & Hutch, Dukes of Hazzard, Young Daniel Boone, My Friend Tony.

MARKS, RICHARD E.
Executive. e. UCLA, UCLA Sch. of Law. 1978-82, v.p., legal & business affairs for Ziegler/Diskant Literary Agency. Joined Paramount Pictures 1984 as sr. atty. for Network TV Div., as project atty. for Family Ties, Cheers, etc. 1985, named sr. atty. for M.P. Group for Children The Golden Child, Beverly Hills Cop II, etc.; 1987 joined Weintraub Entertainment Group as v.p. business affairs, m.p. div. 1990, counsel for Disney projects such as The Rocketeer, Beauty and the Beast. 1991, joined Media Home Entertainment as sr. v.p. in charge of all business and legal affairs. 1994, joined the Kushner-Locke Company as sr. v.p., business affairs for feature division.

MARS, KENNETH
Actor. b. Chicago, IL, 1936.
PICTURES: The Producers, Butch Cassidy and the Sundance Kid, Desperate Characters, What's Up Doc?, The Parallax View, Young Frankenstein, Night Moves, The Apple Dumpling Gang Rides Again, Full Moon High, Yellowbeard, Protocol, Prince Jack, Beer, Fletch, Radio Days, For Keeps?, Illegally Yours, Rented Lips, Police Academy 6: City Under Siege, The Little Mermaid (voice), Shadows and Fog, We're Back (voice).
TELEVISION: Series: He & She, The Don Knotts Show, Sha Na Na, The Carol Burnett Show (1979). Guest: The Facts of Life. Movies: Second Chance, Guess Who's Sleeping in My Bed?, Someone I Touched, The New Original Wonder Woman, Before and After, The Rules of Marriage, Get Smart Again.

MARSH, JEAN
Actress, Writer. b. London, Eng., July 1, 1934. NY stage debut in Much Ado About Nothing, 1959. As a child appeared in films: Tales of Hoffman; as principal dancer in Where's Charley. Co-creator, co-author and starred as Rose, in Upstairs, Downstairs.
THEATER: B'way: Travesties, The Importance of Being Earnest, Too True to Be Good, My Fat Friend, Whose Life Is It Anyway?, Blithe Spirit.
PICTURES: Cleopatra, Unearthly Stranger, The Limbo Line, Frenzy, Dark Places, The Eagle Has Landed, The Changeling, Return to Oz, Willow.
TELEVISION: Upstairs Downstairs (Emmy Award, 1975), Nine to Five, The Grover Monster, A State Dinner with Queen Elizabeth II, Mad About the Boy: Noel Coward—A Celebration, Habeas Corpus, Uncle Vanya, Twelfth Night, Pygmalion, On the Rocks Theatre, The Corsican Brothers, Master of the Game, Danny, the Champion of the World, Act of Will, A Connecticut Yankee in King Arthur's Court.

MARSHALL, ALAN
Producer. b. London, Eng., Aug. 12, 1938. Co-founder Alan Parker Film Company, 1970. Formerly film editor. Received Michael Balcon Award, British Acad., Outstanding Contribution to Cinema, 1985.
PICTURES: Bugsy Malone, Midnight Express, Fame, Shoot the Moon, Pink Floyd: The Wall, Another Country (Cannes Film Fest. Award, 1984), Birdy (Special Jury Award, Cannes Film Fest., 1985), Angel Heart, Homeboy, Jacob's Ladder, Basic Instinct, Cliffhanger, Showgirls.
TELEVISION: No Hard Feelings, Our Cissy, Footsteps.

MARSHALL, E. G.
Actor. r.n. Everett G. Marshall. b. Owatonna, MN, June 18, 1910. e. Univ. of MN. Acting debut with Oxford Players, 1933.
THEATER: B'way: Jason, Jacobowsky and the Colonel, Skin of Our Teeth, Iceman Cometh, Woman Bites Dog, The Survivors, The Gambler, The Crucible, The Little Foxes.
PICTURES: The House on 92nd Street (debut, 1945), 13 Rue Madeleine, Call Northside 77, The Caine Mutiny, Pushover, Bamboo Prison, Broken Lance, The Silver Chalice, The Left Hand of God, The Scarlet Hour, The Mountain, 12 Angry Men, The Bachelor Party, Man on Fire, The Buccaneer, The Journey, Compulsion, Cash McCall, Town Without Pity, The Chase, The Bridge at Remagen, Tora! Tora! Tora!, The Pursuit of Happiness, Billy Jack Goes to Washington, Interiors, Superman II, Creepshow, Power, My Chauffeur, La Gran Fiesta, National Lampoon's Christmas Vacation, Two Evil Eyes (The Black Cat), Consenting Adults, Nixon.
TELEVISION: Series: The Defenders (2 Emmy Awards: 1962, 1963), The Bold Ones (The New Doctors), Chicago Hope. Movies: Collision Course, The Winter of Our Discontent, Under Siege, At Mother's Request, Emma, Queen of the South Seas, The Hijacking of the Achille Lauro, Ironclads, Stephen King's The Tommyknockers, Oldest Living Confederate Widow Tells All.

MARSHALL, FRANK
Producer, Director. b. 1954. Raised in Newport Beach, CA. Worked on first feature film in 1967 while still a student at UCLA. Protege of Peter Bogdanovich, working on his production crew and as asst. on Targets, location manager on The Last Picture Show, What's Up Doc?, assoc. prod. on Paper Moon, Daisy Miller, Nickelodeon, etc. Line producer on Orson Welles' The Other Side of the Wind (unreleased) and Martin Scorsese's The Last Waltz. Worked with Walter Hill on The Driver (assoc. prod.) and The Warriors (exec. prod.). Began collaboration with Steven Spielberg as prod. for Raiders of the Lost Ark. 1992, with wife and partner Kathleen Kennedy formed the Kennedy/Marshall Company.
PICTURES: Raiders of the Lost Ark (prod.), Poltergeist (prod.), E.T.: The Extra-Terrestrial (prod. suprv.). Exec. Producer: Twilight Zone—The Movie, Indiana Jones and the Temple of Doom, Fandango, Gremlins, The Goonies, Back to the Future (prod. also 2nd unit dir.), The Color Purple (prod.), Young Sherlock Holmes, An American Tail, Innerspace, The Money Pit (prod.), Empire of the Sun (prod.), Who Framed Roger Rabbit (prod., 2nd unit dir.), The Land Before Time, Indiana

Jones and the Last Crusade, Dad, Back to the Future Part II, Always (prod.), Joe Versus the Volcano, Back to the Future Part III, Gremlins II, Arachnophobia (also dir.), Cape Fear, An American Tail: Fievel Goes West, Hook (co-prod.), Noises Off (prod.), Alive (also dir.), Swing Kids, A Far Off Place, We're Back, Milk Money, Congo (also dir.), The Indian in the Cupboard.
TELEVISION: Amazing Stories (series exec. prod.), Roger Rabbit and the Secrets of Toontown (exec. prod.), Alive: The Miracle of the Andes (exec. prod.).

MARSHALL, GARRY
Producer, Director, Writer, Actor. b. New York, NY, Nov. 13, 1934. r.n. Garry Marscharelli. Sister is director-actress Penny Marshall. e. Northwestern U. Copy boy and reporter for NY Daily News while writing comedy material for Phil Foster, Joey Bishop. Was drummer in his own jazz band and successful stand-up comedian and playwright. Turned Neil Simon's play The Odd Couple into long running TV series (1970). Partner with Jerry Belson many years. Playwright: The Roast (with Belson, 1980), Wrong Turn at Lungfish (with Lowell Ganz, 1992; also dir., actor). Autobiography: Wake Me When It's Funny (1995).
PICTURES: Writer-Producer: How Sweet It Is, The Grasshopper. Director: Young Doctors in Love (also exec. prod.), The Flamingo Kid (also co-s.p.), Nothing in Common, Overboard, Beaches, Pretty Woman, Frankie and Johnny (also co-prod.), Exit to Eden. Actor: Psych-Out, Lost in America, Jumpin' Jack Flash, Soapdish, A League of Their Own, Hocus Pocus, Dear God.
TELEVISION: Series Writer: Jack Paar Show, Joey Bishop Show, Danny Thomas Show, Lucy, Dick Van Dyke Show, I Spy. Series creator/exec. prod./writer: Hey Landlord (also dir.), The Odd Couple, The Little People (The Brian Keith Show), Happy Days, Laverne & Shirley, Makin' It (creator only), Angie. Series exec. prod./writer: Blansky's Beauties (also dir.), Who's Watching the Kids?, Mork and Mindy (also dir.), Joanie Loves Chachi. Series exec. prod.: The New Odd Couple, Nothing in Common. Series actor: The Ugliest Girl in Town, A League of Their Own. Movie: Evil Roy Slade (co-prod., co-writer). Special: The Last Shot (actor).

MARSHALL, PENNY
Actress, Director. b. New York, NY, Oct. 15, 1942. Father: industrial filmmaker and Laverne and Shirley prod., Tony Marscharelli. Brother is producer-director Garry Marshall. Daughter is actress Tracy Reiner. Dropped out of U. of New Mexico to teach dancing. Acted in summer stock and competed on The Original Amateur Hour before going to Hollywood to make TV debut in The Danny Thomas Hour (1967-68).
PICTURES: Actress: How Sweet It Is, The Savage Seven, The Grasshopper, 1941, Movers and Shakers, The Hard Way, Hocus Pocus. Director: Jumpin' Jack Flash (debut, 1986), Big, Awakenings, A League of Their Own, Renaissance Man, The Preacher's Wife. Exec. Prod.: Calendar Girl.
TELEVISION: Series: The Bob Newhart Show, The Odd Couple, Friends and Lovers, Laverne and Shirley. Guest: Danny Thomas Hour, The Super, Happy Days, Saturday Night Live, Comedy Zone, Chico and the Man. Movies: The Feminist and the Fuzz, Evil Roy Slade, The Couple Takes a Wife, The Crooked Hearts, Love Thy Neighbor, Let's Switch, More Than Friends, Challenge of a Lifetime, The Odd Couple: Together Again. Specials: Lily for President, The Laverne and Shirley Reunion. Series Director: Laverne and Shirley, Working Stiffs, Tracey Ullman Show, A League of Their Own.

MARSHALL, PETER
Actor, TV Show Host. r.n. Pierre La Cock. b. Clarksburg, WV, March 30. Sister is actress Joanne Dru. Began career as NBC page in N.Y. Teamed with the late Tommy Noonan in comedy act for nightclubs, guesting on Ed Sullivan Show and other variety shows. In 1950, made Las Vegas stage debut and since has been headliner there and in Reno and Lake Tahoe. New York stage, in B'way musical Skyscraper. On London stage in H.M.S. Pinafore, Bye Bye Birdie. In La Cage aux Folles (national company and B'way), 42nd St. (Atlantic City), Rumors (natl. co.).
PICTURES: The Rookie, Swingin' Along (Double Trouble), Ensign Pulver, The Cavern, Americathon, Annie.
TELEVISION: Host: Two of the Most (local N.Y. show), The Hollywood Squares, NBC Action Playhouse, The Peter Marshall Variety Show, Mrs. America Pageant, Mrs. World; many guest appearances.

MARTEL, GENE
Producer, Director. b. New York, NY, June 19, 1906. e. City Coll. of New York , U. of Alabama, Sorbonne, Paris. Newspaperman, New York and Birmingham, AL; dancer, actor, choreographer, director Broadway; prod. dir., many documentaries; films for State Dept., others; dir. for Paramount Pictures. Joined Princess Pictures 1952 to make films in Europe; formed own co., Martel Productions Inc., 1956.
PICTURES: Check-mate, Double-Barrelled Miracle, The Lie, Double Profile, Sergeant and the Spy, Black Forest, Eight Witnesses, Fire One, Phantom Caravan, Doorway to Suspicion, Diplomatic Passport, Immediate Disaster.

MARTIN, ANDREA
Actress. b. Portland, ME, Jan. 15, 1947.
THEATRE: *NY:* My Favorite Year (Tony Award & Theatre World Award), The Merry Wives of Windsor.
PICTURES: Cannibal Girls, Soup for One, Club Paradise, Rude Awakening, Worth Winning, Too Much Sun, Stepping Out, All I Want for Christmas, Ted and Venus,. Bogus.
TELEVISION: *Series:* Second City TV, SCTV Network 90 (2 Emmy Awards for writing), The Martin Short Show. *Special:* In Search of Dr. Seuss. *Movie:* Harrison Bergeron.

MARTIN, DEAN
Actor, Singer. r.n. Dino Crocetti. b. Steubenville, OH, June 7, 1917. e. Steubenville H.S. Was amateur prizefighter; worked at odd jobs, mill hand, gasoline attendant, prior to singing career. Joined comedian Jerry Lewis at 500 Club, Atlantic City, NJ, as straight man-singer, 1946; as team played many theatres, night clubs until 1956. Voted (with Jerry Lewis) one of the top ten Money-Making Stars in Motion Picture Herald-Fame poll, 1951, 1953-55; number One, 1952; solo: 1967, 1968.
PICTURES: My Friend Irma (debut, 1949), My Friend Irma Goes West, At War With the Army, That's My Boy, Sailor Beware, Jumping Jacks, The Stooge, The Caddy, Road to Bali (cameo), Scared Stiff, Money from Home, Living It Up, Three Ring Circus, You're Never Too Young, Artists and Models, Pardners, Hollywood or Bust, Ten Thousand Bedrooms, The Young Lions, Some Came Running, Rio Bravo, Career, Who Was That Lady?, Bells Are Ringing, Ocean's Eleven, Pepe, All in a Night's Work, Ada, The Road to Hong Kong (cameo), Sergeants 3, Who's Got the Action?, Toys in the Attic, Come Blow Your Horn (cameo), Who's Been Sleeping in My Bed?, Four for Texas, What a Way to Go!, Robin and the Seven Hoods, Kiss Me Stupid!, The Sons of Katie Elder, Marriage on the Rocks, The Silencers, Texas Across the River, Murderers' Row, The Ambushers, Rough Night in Jericho, Bandolero, Five Card Stud, How to Save a Marriage and Ruin Your Life, The Wrecking Crew, Airport, Something Big, Showdown, Mr. Ricco, The Cannonball Run, Cannonball Run II.
TELEVISION: *Series:* The Colgate Comedy Hour, The Dean Martin Show (1965-74), Half Nelson. *Guest:* Club Oasis, Danny Thomas Show, Rawhide, Lucy Show, Carol Burnett, Sheriff Lobo, many others.
(d. December 25, 1995)

MARTIN, DEWEY
Actor. b. Katemcy, TX, Dec. 8, 1923. e. U. of Georgia. U.S. Navy, WWII. In stock before film debut in 1949.
PICTURES: Knock on Any Door, Kansas Raiders, The Thing, The Big Sky, Tennessee Champ, Prisoner of War, Men of the Fighting Lady, Land of the Pharaohs, Desperate Hours, The Proud and Profane, 10,000 Bedrooms, Battle Ground, The Longest Day, Savage Sam, Seven Alone.
TELEVISION: G.E. Theatre, U.S. Steel, Playhouse 90, Playwrights 56, Daniel Boone, Doc Holliday, Wheeler and Murdoch, Outer Limits, Twilight Zone.

MARTIN, EDWIN DENNIS
Executive. b. Columbus, GA, Jan. 30, 1920. e. U. of Georgia, B.S., 1940. Past pres., Martin Theatre Cos.; past pres., TOA, International, past pres., Variety. Retired.

MARTIN, GARY
Executive. b. Aug, 14, 1944. V.P. of production, Columbia Pictures, 1984-86; exec. v.p., production, 1986-88. Named pres. of production admin., 1988. Member, AMPAS, D.G.A.

MARTIN, MILLICENT
Actress, Singer. b. Romford, Eng., June 8, 1934. Toured U.S. in The Boy Friend, 1954-57.
THEATER: Expresso Bongo, The Crooked Mile, Our Man Crichton, Tonight at 8:30, The Beggar's Opera, Puss 'n Boots, Aladdin, Peter Pan, The Card, Absurd Person Singular, Aladdin, Side by Side by Sondheim, King of Hearts, Move Over Mrs. Markham, Noises Off, One Into Two, 42nd Street (N.Y. & L.A.), The Cemetery Club, Shirley Valentine, The Boyfriend, Noel, Follies.
TELEVISION: *Series:* The Picadilly Palace, From a Bird's Eye View, Mainly Millicent, Millie, Dowtown. Also: Harry Moorings, Kiss Me Kate, London Palladium Color Show, Tom Jones, Englebert Humperdinck show, That Was the Week That Was, LA Law, Max Headroom, Newhart, Murphy Brown.
PICTURES: Libel, The Horsemasters (tv in U.S.), The Girl on the Boat, Nothing But the Best, Those Magnificent Men in Their Flying Machines, Alfie, Stop the World I Want To Get Off, Invasion Quartet.

MARTIN, PAMELA SUE
Actress. b. Westport, CT, Jan. 15, 1953. Did modelling and TV commercials before entering films.
PICTURES: To Find a Man, The Poseidon Adventure, Buster and Billie, Our Time, The Lady in Red, Torchlight (also assoc. prod. & s.p.), Flicks, A Cry in the Wild.
TELEVISION: *Series:* Nancy Drew Mysteries, Hardy Boys Mysteries, Dynasty, The Star Games (host). *Movies:* The Girls of Huntington House, The Gun and the Pulpit, Human Feelings, Bay Coven.

MARTIN, STEVE
Actor, Writer. b. Waco, TX, Aug. 14, 1945. e. Long Beach Col., UCLA. Raised in Southern California. Worked at Disneyland, teaching himself juggling, magic and the banjo. Became writer for various TV comedy shows, incl. Smothers Brothers Comedy Hour (Emmy Award for writing, 1968-69), Glen Campbell Show, Sonny & Cher. Co-writer for special Van Dyke and Company. Wrote and starred in Acad. Award nominated short The Absent-Minded Waiter. *Author:* Cruel Shoes (1980). *Albums:* Let's Get Small (Grammy Award, 1977), A Wild and Crazy Guy (Grammy Award, 1978), Comedy Is Not Pretty, The Steve Martin Brothers. Gold Record for single King Tut.
THEATER: *Actor:* Waiting for Godot (Off-B'way debut, 1988). *Author:* Picasso at the Lapin Agile (regional, 1993), WASP (Off-B'way).
PICTURES: Sgt. Pepper's Lonely Hearts Club Band (debut, 1978), The Kids Are Alright, The Muppet Movie, The Jerk (also co-s.p.), Pennies From Heaven, Dead Men Don't Wear Plaid (also co-s.p.), The Man With Two Brains (also co-s.p.), The Lonely Guy, All of Me (NY Film Critics & Natl. Board of Review Awards, 1984), Movers and Shakers, Three Amigos! (also co-s.p., exec. prod.), Little Shop of Horrors, Roxanne (also s.p., exec. prod.; Natl. Society of Film Critics & L.A. Film Critics Awards for actor, WGA Award for adapt. s.p., 1987), Planes Trains & Automobiles, Dirty Rotten Scoundrels, Parenthood, My Blue Heaven, L.A. Story (also s.p., co-exec. prod.), Father of the Bride, Grand Canyon, Housesitter, Leap of Faith, A Simple Twist of Fate (also s.p., exec. prod.), Mixed Nuts, Father of the Bride 2, Sgt. Bilko.
TELEVISION: *Series:* Andy Williams Presents Ray Stevens, The Ken Berry "WOW" Show, Half the George Kirby Comedy Hour, The Sonny and Cher Comedy Hour, The Smothers Brothers Show (1975), The Johnny Cash Show. *Guest:* The Tonight Show, Cher, The Carol Burnett Show, Saturday Night Live, The Muppet Show, Steve Allen Comedy Hour. *Specials:* HBO On Location: Steve Martin, Steve Martin—A Wild and Crazy Guy, Comedy Is Not Pretty, All Commercials: A Steve Martin Special, Steve Martin's Best Show Ever, The Winds of Whoopie, Texas 150--A Celebration, The Smothers Brothers Comedy Hour 20th Reunion, Learned Pigs and Fireproof Women. *Producer:* Domestic Life (series). *Pilot:* Leo & Liz in Beverly Hills (writer, creator, co-prod., dir.). *Movies:* The Jerk Too (exec. prod. only), And the Band Played On.

MARTIN, TONY
Singer, Musician, Actor. b. Oakland, CA, Dec. 25, 1913. r.n. Alvin Morris. e. Oakland H.S., St. Mary's Coll. m. actress-dancer Cyd Charisse. Sang, played saxophone & clarinet in high school band, engaged by nearby theatres for vaudeville; with Five Red Peppers, jazz group at 14 yrs.; two yrs. later with band, Palace Hotel, San Francisco; radio debut Walter Winchell program, 1932; joined Tom Gerund's band, World's Fair Chicago, 1933; played night clubs. First starring radio show, Tune Up Time (singer & emcee); on Burns and Allen program; own show for Texaco, Carnation Contented Hour. Recordings: Begin the Beguine, Intermezzo, The Last Time I Saw Paris, I'll See You in My Dreams, Domino, September Song, For Every Man There's a Woman.
PICTURES: Pigskin Parade (debut, 1936), Banjo on My Knee, Sing Baby Sing, Follow the Fleet, Back to Nature, The Holy Terror, Sing and Be Happy, You Can't Have Everything, Life Begins in College, Ali Baba Goes to Town, Sally Irene and Mary, Kentucky Moonshine, Thanks for Everything, Up the River, Winner Take All, Music in My Heart, Ziegfeld Girl, The Big Store, Till the Clouds Roll By, Casbah, Two Tickets to Broadway, Here Come the Girls, Easy to Love, Deep in My Heart, Hit the Deck, Quincannon—Frontier Scout, Let's Be Happy, Dear Mr. Wonderful.

MASLANSKY, PAUL
Producer. b. New York, NY, Nov. 23, 1933. e. Washington and Lee U., 1954. Moved to Europe performing as jazz musician in Paris, 1959-60. Entered film business with documentary, Letter from Paris. Asst. to prods. Charles Shneer and Irving Allan in England, Italy and Yugoslavia, 1961-62. In charge of physical prod. in Europe for UA, 1965-67.
PICTURES: Castle of the Living Dead, Revenge of the Blood Beast, Sudden Terror (Eye Witness), Raw Meat, Deathline, Sister of Satan, Big Truck, Poor Claire, Deathline, Sugar Hill (also dir.), Race With the Devil, Hard Times, The Blue Bird, Circle of Iron, Damnation Alley (co-prod.), When You Comin' Back Red Ryder (co-prod.), Hot Stuff, The Villain, Scavenger Hunt, The Salamander, Ruckus, Love Child, Police Academy, Police Academy 2: Their First Assignment, Return to Oz, Police Academy 3: Back in Training, Police Academy 4: Citizens on Patrol, Police Academy 5: Assignment Miami Beach, For Better or Worse (exec. prod.), Police Academy 6: City Under Siege, Ski Patrol (exec. prod.), Honeymoon Academy (exec. prod.). The Russia House, Cop and a Half, Police Academy: Mission to Moscow, Fluke.
TELEVISION: *Movie:* The Gun and the Pulpit. *Mini-Series:* King.

MASON, JACKIE
Comedian, Actor. b. Sheboygan, WI June 9, 1934. e. City College. Was a rabbi before becoming stand-up comedian. Records include The World According to Me! Has lectureship in his name at Oxford Univ. in England.
THEATER: Enter Solly Gold (1965), A Teaspoon Every Four Hours (Amer. National Theatre & Academy Theatre), Sex-a-Poppin (revue, prod. only), The World According to Me! (one-man show, special Tony Award, 1987), Jackie Mason: Brand New, Politically Incorrect.
PICTURES: Operation Delilah (debut, 1966), The Stoolie (also prod.), The Jerk, History of the World Part I, Caddyshack II.
TELEVISION: Guest: Steve Allen, Ed Sullivan, Jack Paar, Garry Moore, Perry Como and Merv Griffin Shows. Johnny Carson, Arsenio Hall, Evening at the Improv, Late Night with David Letterman. Series: Chicken Soup, Jackie Mason (synd.). Specials: Jack Paar is Alive and Well!, The World According to Me! (ACE Award), Jackie Mason on Broadway (Emmy Award for Writing).

MASON, JOHN DUDLEY
Executive. b. Ashland, KY, Oct 29, 1949. e. Amherst Coll., B.A., cum laude, 1971; Claremont Graduate Sch. and University Center, M.A., 1973; Amos Tuck Sch. of Business Administration, Dartmouth Coll., M.B.A., 1978. Program officer, National Endowment for the Humanities, 1972-76; analyst (1978-79), asst. mgr. (1979-80), mgr. (1980) strategic planning, Consolidated Rail Corp.; Consultant, Frito-Lay, Division, PepsiCo (1980-82); mgr, corporate planning, Dun & Bradstreet Corp. (1982-86); finance director, anti-piracy (1986-90), v.p. finance, anti-piracy (1990-92), Motion Picture Association of America, Inc. Chmn, New Century Artists' Mgmt., 1990-present. Chmn., Finance Comm. and mem., bd. of dir. Association de Gestion Int'l. Collective des Oeuvres Audiovisuelles (AGICOA) 1987-88. Director, Instituto Venezolano de Representacion Cinematografica (INVERECI), Caracas, Venezuela (1988-92). Director: Foundation for the Protection of Film & Video Works (FVWP), Taipei, Taiwan (1987-92). Dir. sec. Korean Federation Against Copyright Theft, 1990-92; Dir., Japan & Intl. M.P. Copyright Assn., Tokyo, 1990-92; Trustee and Treasurer, Design Industries Foundation for AIDS, 1990-1994.

MASON, KENNETH M.
Executive. b. Rochester, NY; Sept. 21, 1917. e. Washington and Jefferson Coll. (BA, 1938); U. of Rochester, graduate work; Dr. of Laws (H), Washington & Jefferson Coll., 1989. Began career with Eastman Kodak Co. in Kodak Park cine processing dept. in 1935; transferred following year to film dev. dept., Kodak Research Lab. Later joined film planning dept., remaining there until entering U.S. Navy in 1943. Returned to Kodak in 1946 as staff engineer in Kodak Office motion picture film dept. 1950 appt. mgr. of Midwest Division, of M.P. Film Dept.; became gen. mgr., Midwest Division, m.p. products sales dept. in 1963; named sls. mgr. of NYC region in 1965; appt. regional sls. mgr., Pacific Southern Region, Hollywood, in 1970; 1974 appt. mgr., product programs and research, Motion Picture and Audiovisual Markets Division, Kodak Office; 1974 named gen. mgr. of that division. Elected asst. v.p. of co., 1974, then v.p., 1978. Retired 1982. Former chmn., Inter-Society Committee for the Enhancement of Theatrical Presentation. Member, Trustee emeritus, Board of Trustees of Washington and Jefferson Coll. (and former chmn); past pres. of Society of Motion Picture & Television Engineers and honorary member; honorary fellow of British Kinematograph Sound & Television Society; mem. of University Film & Video Assn., Motion Picture Academy, American Society of Cinematographers. Board of dir.: Univ. Film & Video Foundation.

MASON, MARSHA
Actress. b. St. Louis. April 3, 1942. e. Webster Coll. Came to N.Y. to continue dramatic studies and embark on theatre career. Member of American Conservatory Theatre, San Francisco.
THEATER: The Deer Park, Cactus Flower, The Indian Wants the Bronx, Happy Birthday Wanda June, Private Lives, You Can't Take It With You, Cyrano de Bergerac, A Doll's House, The Crucible, The Good Doctor, Old Times, The Big Love, Lake No Bottom. Dir.: Juno's Swans.
PICTURES: Hot Rod Hullabaloo (debut, 1966), Blume in Love, Cinderella Liberty (Acad. Award nom.), Audrey Rose, The Goodbye Girl (Acad. Award nom.), The Cheap Detective, Promises in the Dark, Chapter Two (Acad. Award nom.), Only When I Laugh (Acad. Award nom.), Max Dugan Returns, Heartbreak Ridge, Stella, Drop Dead Fred, I Love Trouble, Nick of Time, 2 Days in the Valley.
TELEVISION: Series: Love of Life, Sibs. Specials: Brewsie and Willie, The Good Doctor, Cyrano de Bergerac. Movies: Lois Gibbs and the Love Canal, Surviving, Trapped in Silence, The Image, Dinner at Eight, Broken Trust. Dir.: Little Miss Perfect.

MASON, PAMELA
Actress, Writer. b. Westgate. England. Mar. 10, 1918. Stage debut, 1936, The Luck of the Devil, London; also playwright (in collab. with James Mason: Flying Blind, Made in Heaven),

AUTHOR: This Little Hand, A Lady Possessed, The Blinds Are Down, Ignoramus, Marriage Is the First Step Toward Divorce, The Female Pleasure Hunt. Columnist for Movieline Magazine.
PICTURES: I Met a Murderer, They Were Sisters, The Upturned Glass, Pandora and the Flying Dutchman, Lady Possessed, Everything You Always Wanted to Know About Sex.
TELEVISION: Series (synd): The Pamela Mason Show, The Weaker Sex?.

MASSEN, OSA
Actress. b. Denmark, Copenhagen. Jan. 13, 1916.
PICTURES: Honeymoon in Bali, Honeymoon for Three, A Woman's Face, Accent on Love, You'll Never Get Rich, The Devil Pays Off, Iceland, Jack London, Cry of the Werewolf, Tokyo Rose, Strange Journey, Night Unto Night, Deadline at Dawn, Gentleman Misbehaves, Rocketship XM, Outcasts of the City.

MASSEY, ANNA
Actress. b. Sussex, England, Aug. 11, 1937. Daughter of late actor Raymond Massey. Brother is actor Daniel Massey. On London stage in The Reluctant Debutante (debut, 1958), The Prime of Jean Brodie, Slag, The Importance of Being Earnest, Spoiled, Doctor's Delimma, School for Scandal, With National Theatre, 1989.
PICTURES: Gideon of Scotland Yard, Peeping Tom, Bunny Lake Is Missing, DeSade, The Looking Glass War, David Copperfield (TV in U.S.), Frenzy, A Doll's House, Vault of Horror, A Little Romance, Sweet William, Another Country, The Chain, Five Days One Summer, Foreign Body, Mountains of the Moon, La Couleur du Vent, The Tall Guy, Killing Dad, Impromptu, Haunted.
TELEVISION: Remember the Germans, Wicked Woman, The Corn Is Green, Sakharov, Hotel Du Lac (BAFTA Award), A Hazard of Hearts, Around the World in 80 Days, Tears in the Rain, The Man from the Pru.

MASSEY, DANIEL
Actor. b. London, Eng., Oct. 10, 1933. e. Eaton and King's Colleges, Cambridge U. Father was late actor Raymond Massey. Sister is actress Anna Massey. On B'way in She Loves Me, Gigi. Recent London theatre incl. Follies, The Devil's Disciple.
PICTURES: In Which We Serve (debut, 1942), Girls at Sea, Upstairs and Downstairs, The Queen's Guard, Go to Blazes, The Entertainer, Operation Bullshine (Girls in Arms), The Amorous Adventures of Moll Flanders, The Jokers, Star! (Acad. Award nom.), Fragment of Fear, Mary Queen of Scots, Vault of Horror, The Incredible Sarah, The Devil's Advocate, Warlords of Atlantis, Bad Timing: A Sensual Obsession, The Cat and the Canary, Victory, Scandal, In the Name of the Father.
TELEVISION: Series: The Roads to Freedom. Mini-series: The Golden Bowl. Movies/Specials: Aren't We All (debut, 1958), Love with a Perfect Stranger, Intimate Contact, Inspector Morse, Look of Love, Bye Bye Columbus, Stalin, GBH.

MASTERS, BEN
Actor. b. Corvallis, OR, May 6, 1947. e. Univ. of Oregon.
THEATER: The Cherry Orchard, Waltz of the Toreadors, Plenty, Captain Brassbound's Conversion, The Boys in the Band, Eden Court, What the Butler Saw, The White Whore and the Bit Player, Key Exchange.
PICTURES: Mandingo, All That Jazz, Key Exchange, Dream Lover, Making Mr. Right.
TELEVISION: Series: Heartbeat. Guest: Barnaby Jones, Kojack. Movies: One of Our Own, The Shadow Box, The Neighborhood, Illusions, The Deliberate Stranger, Street of Dreams, Cruel Doubt, Running Mates, A Twist of the Knife, A Time to Heal, Lady Killer. Mini-Series: Loose Change, Celebrity, Noble House.

MASTERSON, MARY STUART
Actress. b. Los Angeles, CA, June 28, 1966. Daughter of writer-director-actor Peter Masterson and actress Carlin Glynn. e. Goddard Col. Made film debut at age 8 in The Stepford Wives (1975), which featured her father. Spent summer at Stage Door Manor in Catskills; two summers at Sundance Inst. Studied acting with Gary Swanson. Member of the Actor's Studio. Off-off B'way debut in Been Taken. Off-B'way debut in Lily Dale followed by The Lucky Spot (Manhattan Theatre Club). Regional: Moonlight and Valentines, Three Sisters.
PICTURES: The Stepford Wives (debut, 1975), Heaven Help Us, At Close Range, My Little Girl, Some Kind of Wonderful, Gardens of Stone, Mr. North, Chances Are, Immediate Family (Natl. Board of Review Award, 1989), Funny About Love, Fried Green Tomatoes, Mad at the Moon, Married to It, Benny & Joon, Bad Girls, Radioland Murders, Heaven's Prisoners, Bed of Roses.
TELEVISION: Movie: Love Lives On. Guest: Amazing Stories (Go to the Head of the Class).

MASTERSON, PETER
Actor, Writer, Director. r.n. Carlos Bee Masterson, Jr. b. Houston, TX, June 1, 1934. m. actress Carlin Glynn. Daughter is actress Mary Stuart Masterson. e. Rice U., Houston, BA. 1957. NY stage debut, Call Me By My Rightful Name, 1961.

THEATER: Marathon '33, Blues for Mr. Charlie, The Trial of Lee Harvey Oswald, The Great White Hope, That Championship Season, The Poison Tree, The Best Little Whorehouse in Texas (co-author, dir.), The Last of the Knucklemen (dir.).
PICTURES: Actor: Ambush Bay (debut, 1965), Counterpoint, In the Heat of the Night, Tomorrow, The Exorcist, Man on a Swing, The Stepford Wives, Gardens of Stone. Writer: The Best Little Whore House in Texas. Director: The Trip to Bountiful, Full Moon in Blue Water, Blood Red, Night Game, Convicts.
TELEVISION: Camera Three, Pueblo; The Quinns; A Question of Guilt.

MASTORAKIS, NICO
Writer, Director, Producer. b. Athens, Greece, 1941. Writer of novels and screenplays, including Fire Below Zero, and Keepers of the Secret (co-author). Pres. Omega Entertainment Ltd. since 1978.
PICTURES: Writer/dir./prod.: The Time Traveller, Blind Date, Sky High, The Zero Boys, The Wind, Terminal Exposure, Nightmare at Noon, Glitch, Ninja Academy, Hired to Kill, In the Cool of the Night, At Random. Prod.: The Greek Tycoon, Red Tide, Grandmother's House, Darkroom, Bloodstone (prod., co-s.p.).

MASTRANTONIO, MARY ELIZABETH
Actress. b. Oak Park, IL, Nov. 17, 1958. e. U. of Illinois 1976-78 where she trained for opera. m. director Pat O'Connor. Worked as singer & dancer for summer at Opryland Theme Park in Nashville. Came to NY as understudy and vacation replacement as Maria in West Side Story revival.
THEATER: NY: Copperfield (1981), Oh Brother, Amadeus, Sunday in the Park With George (Playwright's Horizons), The Human Comedy, Henry V, The Marriage of Figaro, Measure for Measure, The Knife, Twelfth Night.
PICTURES: Scarface (debut, 1983), The Color of Money (Acad. Award nom.), Slamdance, The January Man, The Abyss, Fools of Fortune, Class Action, Robin Hood: Prince of Thieves, White Sands, Consenting Adults, A Day to Remember, Three Wishes, Two Bits.
TELEVISION: Mini-Series: Mussolini: The Untold Story. Special: Uncle Vanya (BBC).

MASTROIANNI, MARCELLO
Actor. b. Fontana Liri, Italy, Sept. 28, 1924. e. U. of Rome theatrical company. Draftsman in Rome, 1940-43. WWII, drew military maps until captured by Nazis and escaped. Theatrical debut in Rome in Angelica, 1948. Formed indep. prod. co., Master Films, 1966.
THEATER: Death of a Salesman, Streetcar Named Desire, Ciao Rudy.
PICTURES: I Miserabili (debut, 1947), Too Bad She's Bad, A Dog's Life, Three Girls from Rome, The Miller's Beautiful Wife, Fever to Live, The Ladykillers of Rome, Love a La Carte, Days of Love, White Nights, Big Deal on Madonna Street, Where the Hot Wind Blows, The Tailor's Maid, Most Wonderful Moment, Bell Antonio, La Dolce Vita, Divorce Italian Style, Ghosts of Rome, La Notte, A Very Private Affair, The Organizer, 8 1/2, Yesterday Today and Tomorrow, Marriage Italian Style, Casanova '70, The 10th Victim, The Poppy Is Also a Flower, Shoot Loud Louder... I Don't Understand, The Stranger, Ghosts Italian Style (cameo), Kiss the Other Shiek, The Man With the Balloons, A Place for Lovers, Leo the Last, Diamonds for Breakfast, Sunflower, The Pizza Triangle, The Priest's Wife, Fellini's Roma (cameo), It Only Happens to Others, What?, The Grande Bouffe, Massacre in Rome, Down the Ancient Stairs, The Sunday Woman, The Gangster's Doll, The Divine Nymph, A Special Day, Lunatics and Lovers, One Way or Another, Ladies and Gentlemen Good Night, Wifemistress, Bye Bye Monkey, Stay as You Are, Blood Feud, Neapolitan Mystery, City of Women, The Terrace, Ghost of Love, The Skin, Beyond the Door, Gabriella, La Nuit de Varennes, The General of the Dead Army, Piera's Story, Henry IV, The Last Horror Film (cameo), Macaroni, Ginger and Fred, Intervista, Dark Eyes, Miss Arizona, Traffic Jam, The Two Lives of Martia Pascal, Splendor, What Time Is It?, Everybody's Fine, Toward Evening, The Suspended Step of the Stork, A Fine Romance, Used People, The Beekeeper, The Children Thief, 1-2-3 Sun, I Don't Want to Talk About It, Pret-a-Porter (Ready to Wear), A Hundred and One Nights, According to Pereira, Beyond the Clouds, Three Lives and Only One Death.

MASUR, RICHARD
Actor. b. New York, NY, Nov. 20, 1948. Directed Oscar-nominated short, Love Struck, 1987.
THEATRE: B'way: The Changing Room.
PICTURES: Whiffs (debut, 1975), Bittersweet Love, Semi-Tough, Who'll Stop the Rain, Hanover Street, Scavenger Hunt, Heaven's Gate, I'm Dancing as Fast as I Can, The Thing, Timerider, Risky Business, Under Fire, Nightmares, The Mean Season, My Science Project, Head Office, Heartburn, The Believers, Walker, Rent-a-Cop, Shoot to Kill, License to Drive, Far from Home, Flashback, Going Under, My Girl, Encino Man, The Man Without a Face, Six Degrees of Separation, My Girl 2, Forget Paris, Multiplicity.

TELEVISION: Series: Hot L Baltimore, One Day at a Time, Empire. Mini-Series: East of Eden. Movies: Having Babies, Betrayal, Mr. Horn, Walking Through the Fire, Fallen Angel, Money on the Side, An Invasion of Privacy, The Demon Murder Case, Adam, John Steinbeck's The Winter of Our Discontent, Flight #90: Disaster on the Potomac, The Burning Bed, Obsessed With a Married Woman, Wild Horses, Embassy, Adam: His Song Continues, Roses Are for the Rich, Cast the First Stone, When the Bough Breaks, Settle the Score, Always Remember I Love You, Stephen King's IT, The Story Lady, And the Band Played On, Search for Grace, My Brother's Keeper, The Face on the Milk Carton, Hiroshima. Director: Torn Between Two Fathers (After School Special).

MATHESON, TIM
Actor. b. Los Angeles, CA, Dec. 31, 1947. e. California State U. Debut on TV at age 12 in Window on Main Street. At 19, contract player for Universal. 1985, turned to direction: St. Elsewhere episode and music videos. Set up own production co. at Burbank Studios 1985; acted off-B'way in True West. With partner Daniel Grodnick bought National Lampoon from founder Matty Simons, becoming exec. officer and chmn. 1989; resigned in 1991. Co-prod. film Blind Fury.
PICTURES: Divorce American Style (debut, 1967), Yours Mine and Ours, How to Commit Marriage, Magnum Force, Almost Summer, National Lampoon's Animal House, Dreamer, The Apple Dumpling Gang Rides Again, 1941, House of God, A Little Sex, To Be or Not To Be, Up the Creek, Impulse, Fletch, Speed Zone, Drop Dead Fred, Solar Crisis, Black Sheep.
TELEVISION: Movies: Owen Marshall: Counselor-at-Law, Lock Stock and Barrel, Hitched, Remember When, The Last Day, The Runaway Barge, The Quest, Mary White, Listen to Your Heart, Obsessed with a Married Woman, Blind Justice, Warm Hearts Cold Feet, Bay Coven, The Littlest Victims, Little White Lies, Buried Alive, Joshua's Heart, Stephen King's Sometimes They Come Back, The Woman Who Sinned, Quicksand: No Escape, Relentless: Mind of a Killer, Trial & Error, Dying to Love You, A Kiss to Die For, Robin Cook's Harmful Intent, Target of Suspicion, Breach of Conduct (dir., co-exec. prod. only), While Justice Sleeps, Fast Company. Series: Window on Main Street, Jonny Quest (voice), The Virginian, Bonanza, The Quest, Tucker's Witch, Just in Time (also co-exec. prod.), Charlie Hoover. Pilot: Nikki & Alexander. Special: Bus Stop.

MATHIS, SAMANTHA
Actress. b. New York, NY, 1971. Mother is actress Bibi Besch; grandmother was actress Gusti Huber. Began acting as teen landing role in tv pilot Aaron's Way at age 16.
PICTURES: The Bulldance (debut, 1988 in Yugoslav film), Pump Up the Volume, This Is My Life, FernGully ... The Last Rainforest (voice), Super Mario Bros., The Music of Chance, The Thing Called Love, Little Women, Jack and Sarah, How to Make an American Quilt, The American President, Broken Arrow.
TELEVISION: Series: Knightwatch. Movies: Cold Sassy Tree, To My Daughter, 83 Hours 'Til Dawn.

MATLIN, MARLEE
Actress. b. Morton Grove, IL, Aug. 24, 1965. e. John Hersey H.S., Chicago, public school with special education program for deaf; William Rainey Harper Coll., majoring in criminal justice. Performed at Children's Theatre of the Deaf in Des Plaines at age 8, playing many leading roles. As adult appeared in only one stage show. Theatrical film debut in Children of a Lesser God. Production company, Solo One Productions.
PICTURES: Children of a Lesser God (debut, 1986; Academy Award, Golden Globe), Walker, The Player, The Linguini Incident, Hear No Evil, It's My Party, Snitch.
TELEVISION: Series: Reasonable Doubts, The Outer Limits, Picket Fences. Movies: Bridge to Silence, Against Her Will: The Carrie Buck Story. Specials: Face the Hate, Meaning of Life, Free to Laugh, Creative Spirit, The Big Help, People In Motion (host). Guest: Sesame Street, Adventures in Wonderland, Picket Fences (Emmy Award nom.), Seinfeld (Emmy Award nom.).

MATTHAU, CHARLES
Director. b. New York, NY, Dec. 10, 1964. Son of actor Walter Matthau. e. U. of Southern California Film School. While at USC wrote and dir. The Duck Film, a silent comedy short (Golden Seal Award, London Amateur Film Fest. and C.I.N.E. Eagle Award.) Also dir. short, I Was a Teenage Fundraiser. President, The Matthau Company, organized 1989.
PICTURES: Doin' Time on Planet Earth. (nom. Saturn Award, best dir., Acad. of Science Fiction.), The Grass Harp (dir., prod.)
TELEVISION: Movie: Mrs. Lambert Remembers Love (dir., prod.; Golden Eagle, Golden Medal & Houston Fest. Grand & Angel Awards).

MATTHAU, WALTER
Actor. b. New York, NY, Oct. 1, 1920. Served in Air Force WWII. Studied journalism at Columbia U. and acting at New Sch. for Social Research's dramatic workshop, 1946, then acted in summer stock.

THEATER: *B'way*: Anne of the Thousand Days (debut, 1948), Will Success Spoil Rock Hunter?, Once More With Feeling, Once There Was a Russian, A Shot in the Dark (Tony Award, 1962), The Odd Couple (Tony Award, 1965). LA: Juno and the Paycock.
PICTURES: The Kentuckian (debut, 1955), The Indian Fighter, Bigger Than Life, A Face in the Crowd, Slaughter on Tenth Avenue, King Creole, The Voice in the Mirror, Ride a Crooked Trial, Onionhead, Strangers When We Meet, The Gangster Story (also dir.), Lonely Are the Brave, Who's Got the Action?, Island of Love, Charade, Ensign Pulver, Fail Safe, Goodbye Charlie, Mirage, The Fortune Cookie (Academy Award, best supporting actor, 1966), A Guide for the Married Man, The Odd Couple, The Secret Life of an American Wife, Candy, Cactus Flower, Hello Dolly!, A New Leaf, Plaza Suite, Kotch (Acad. Award nom.), Pete n' Tillie, Charley Varrick, The Laughing Policeman, Earthquake, The Taking of Pelham One Two Three, The Front Page, The Sunshine Boys (Acad. Award nom.), The Bad News Bears, Casey's Shadow, House Calls, California Suite, Little Miss Marker (also exec. prod.), Hopscotch, First Monday in October, Buddy Buddy, I Ought to Be in Pictures, The Survivors, Movers and Shakers, Pirates, The Couch Trip, Il Piccolo Diavolo (The Little Devil), JFK, Dennis the Menace, Grumpy Old Men, I.Q., The Grass Harp, I'm Not Rappaport, Grumpier Old Men.
TELEVISION: Many appearances 1952-65 on Philco-Goodyear Playhouse, Studio One, Playhouse 90, Kraft Theatre, Awake and Sing, Insight. *Series*: Tallahassee 7000 (1961). *Movies*: The Incident, Mrs. Lambert Remembers Love, Against Her Will: An Incident in Baltimore, Incident in a Small Town. *Special*: The Stingiest Man in Town (voice).

MATURE, VICTOR
Actor. b. Louisville, KY, Jan. 29, 1913. Acted with Pasadena Playhouse before film debut. On B'way in Lady in the Dark; served with U.S. Coast Guard, WWII.
PICTURES: The Housekeeper's Daughter (debut, 1939), One Million B.C., Captain Caution, No No Nanette, I Wake Up Screaming, Shanghai Gesture, Song of the Islands, My Gal Sal, Footlight Serenade, Seven Days Leave, My Darling Clementine, Moss Rose, Kiss of Death, Fury at Furnace Creek, Cry of the City, Red Hot and Blue, Easy Living, Samson and Delilah, Wabash Avenue, I'll Get By (cameo), Stella, Gambling House, Las Vegas Story, Androcles and the Lion, Million Dollar Mermaid, Something for the Birds, Glory Brigade, Affair with a Stranger, The Robe, Veils of Bagdad, Dangerous Mission, Betrayed, Demetrius & the Gladiators, The Egyptian, Chief Crazy Horse, Violent Saturday, Last Frontier, The Sharkfighters, Safari, Zarak, The Long Haul, Pickup Alley, China Doll, Tank Force, The Bandit of Zhobe, Escort West, Big Circus, Timbuktu, Hannibal, The Tartars, After the Fox, Head, Every Little Crook and Nanny, Won Ton Ton the Dog Who Saved Hollywood, Firepower, The Screamer.
TELEVISION: *Movie*: Samson and Delilah.

MAURA, CARMEN
Actress. b. Madrid, Spain, Sept. 15, 1945. e. Madrid's Catholic Inst. Daughter of ophthalmologist; faced family disapproval and custody battle when she became an actress. After working as cabaret entertainer, translator (has degree in French) and occasional voiceover dubber, met aspiring director Pedro Almodovar when they were cast in stage prod. of Sartre's Dirty Hands and starred in several of his films. Hosted weekly Spanish tv talk show Esta Noche.
PICTURES: El Hombre Oculto (debut, 1970), El Love Feroz, The Petition, Paper Tigers, Que Hace una Chica Como tu en un Sitio Como Este?, Pepi Luci Bom ... And Other Girls on the Heap (1980), El Cid Cabreador, Dark Habits, What Have I Done to Deserve This?, Extramuros, Se Infiel y No Mires Con Quien, Matador, Law of Desire, Women on the Verge of a Nervous Breakdown, Baton Rouge, Ay Carmela!, Between Heaven and Earth, The Anonymous Queen, Shadows in a Conflict, Louis the Child King, How to Be Miserable and Enjoy It, The Flowers of My Secret.

MAUREY, NICOLE
Actress. b. France, Dec. 20, 1926. Studied dancing; French films include Blondine, Pamela, Le Cavalier Noir, Journal D'Un Cure De Campagne, Les Compagnes de la Nuit; many television and stage appearances in France; U.S. film debut in Little Boy Lost (1953).
PICTURES: Little Boy Lost, The Secret of the Incas, The Bold and the Brave, The Weapon, The Constant Husband, The Scapegoat, Me and the Colonel, The Jayhawkers, House of the Seven Hawks, High Time, Day of the Triffids, Why Bother to Knock?, The Very Edge.
TELEVISION: *U.S.* and *U.K.*: Tomorrow We Will Love, Casablanca, The Billion Franc Mystery, Champion House, I Thought They Died Years Ago.

MAXWELL, LOIS
Actress. r.n. Lois Hooker. b. Canada, 1927. Started in U.S. films in late 1940's before working in Italy then Britain. Has done numerous Canadian films for tv.

PICTURES: That Hagen Girl, The Decision of Christopher Blake, The Big Punch, The Dark Past, Kazan, Domani e troppa Tardi (Tomorrow Is Too Late), La Grande Speranza (The Great Hope), Aida, Passport to Treason, Satellite in the Sky, Time Without Pity, Lolita, Dr. No, Come Fly With Me, The Haunting, From Russia With Love, Goldfinger, Thunderball, Operation Kid Brother, You Only Live Twice, On Her Majesty's Secret Service, Adventure in Rainbow Country, The Adventurers, Diamonds Are Forever, Live and Let Die, The Man With the Golden Gun, The Spy Who Loved Me, Moonraker, Mr. Patman, For Your Eyes Only, Octopussy, A View to a Kill, Martha Ruth and Eddie.

MAXWELL, RONALD F.
Director, Writer, Producer. b. Jan. 5, 1947. e. NYU Coll. of Arts & Sciences; NYU Sch. of the Arts, Inst. of Film & Television Graduate Sch., M.F.A., 1970. Producer-Director for PBS Theater-in-America (1974-78).
PICTURES: *Director*: The Guest, Little Darlings, The Night the Lights Went Out in Georgia, Kidco, Gettysburg (also co-s.p.).
TELEVISION: *Director*: Sea Marks (also prod.), Verna: USO Girl (also prod.), Parent Trap II.

MAY, ELAINE
Actress, Director, Writer. b. Philadelphia, PA, April 21, 1932. Daughter is actress Jeannie Berlin. Father was prod.-dir. Jack Berlin whose travelling theater she acted with from age 6 to 10. Repertory theatre in Chicago, 1954; comedy team with Mike Nichols starting in 1955. Appeared with improvisational theater group, The Compass, Chicago. Co-starred in An Evening with Mike Nichols and Elaine May.
THEATRE: *Playwright*: A Matter of Position, Not Enough Rope, Hot Line, Better Point of Valour, Mr. Gogol & Mr. Preen, Hotline (Death Defying Acts).
PICTURES: Luv (actress), Enter Laughing (actress), A New Leaf (actress, dir., s.p.), Such Good Friends (s.p. as Esther Dale), The Heartbreak Kid (dir.), Mikey and Nicky (dir., s.p.), Heaven Can Wait (co-s.p.), California Suite (actress), Ishtar (dir., s.p.), In the Spirit (actress), The Birdcage (s.p.).
TELEVISION: *Series regular*: Keep Talking (1958-59). *Guest*: Jack Paar, Omnibus, Dinah Shore Show, Perry Como, Laugh Lines.

MAYER, GERALD
Producer, Director. b. Montreal, Canada, 1919. Father was Jerry G. Mayer, mgr. MGM studio. e. Stanford U., journalism; corresp. for San Francisco Examiner; pres. Sigma Delta Chi, prof. journalism soc. Navy lieut., amphibious forces, WWII. Entered m.p. ind. in prod. dept. MGM studios; first dir. assignment Dial 1119 (1950).
PICTURES: Dial 1119, Inside Straight, The Sellout, Holiday for Sinners, Bright Road (Christopher Award for direction), The Marauders, African Drumbeat, The Man Inside (Canadian).
TELEVISION: Canadian Broadcasting Corp. (prod./dir., TV drama), prod. The Swiss Family Robinson (British-Canadian-West German TV series). Director for U.S. TV: One Last Ride (mini-series), Airwolf, Night Heat, Lou Grant, Eight Is Enough, Quincy, Logan's Run, Mannix, Mission Impossible, Police Surgeon, Cimarron Strip, Peyton Place, Judd for the Defense, Bonanza, The Fugitive, Chrysler Thea., Ben Casey, Slattery's People, Profiles in Courage, The Defenders, Gunsmoke, etc.

MAYER, MICHAEL F.
Attorney, Executive. b. White Plains, NY, Sept. 8, 1917. e. Harvard Coll., B.S., 1939; Yale Law Sch., L.L.B., 1942. Armed Forces 1942-46, Air Medal (1945). V.P., Kingsley International Pictures Corp., 1954-62. Exec. dir. and gen. counsel, Independent Film Importers and Distributors of America Inc. (IFIDA), 1959-67. Special Counsel, French Society of Authors, Composers and Publishers, 1961-72; British Performing Rights Society, 1962-67. Author: Foreign Films on American Screens (1966), Divorce and Annulment (1967), What You Should Know About Libel and Slander (1968), Rights of Privacy (1972), The Film Industries (1973, revised ed. pub. in 1978). Teacher of courses on Business Problems in Film, New School (1971-82). Secty. of Film Society of Lincoln Center, Inc. (1972-88).

MAYER, ROGER LAURANCE
Executive. b. New York, NY, Apr. 21, 1926. e. Yale U., B.A. 1948; Yale Law Sch., L.L.B. and J.D. 1951. In 1952 was practicing attorney; joined Columbia Pictures that year as atty. and named general studio exec., 1957. Left in 1961 to join MGM Studio as asst. gen. mgr. With MGM as follows: v.p., operations, 1964; v.p., administration, 1975-84. Also exec. v.p., MGM Laboratories, 1974-83. Named pres., MGM Laboratories and sr. v.p., studio admin.; MGM Entertainment Co. 1983-86; joined Turner Entertainment Co. as pres. and COO, 1986-present. Member of Los Angeles County Bar Assn., Calif. Bar Assn., Los Angeles Copyright Society, bd of dirs., Acad. of Motion Picture Arts & Sciences. Trustee, chmn. Motion Picture & TV Fund, bd. of dirs., Permanent Charities Fund.

MAYO, VIRGINIA
Actress. r.n. Virginia Jones. b. St. Louis, MO, Nov. 30, 1920. e. St. Louis dramatic school. With Billy Rose's Diamond Horseshoe; then N.Y. stage, Banjo Eyes.

PICTURES: Jack London (debut, 1943), Up in Arms, The Princess and the Pirate, Wonder Man, The Kid from Brooklyn, The Best Years of Our Lives, The Secret Life of Walter Mitty, Out of the Blue, A Song Is Born, Smart Girls Don't Talk, The Girl from Jones Beach, Flaxy Martin, Colorado Territory, Always Leave Them Laughing, White Heat, Red Light, Backfire, The Flame and the Arrow, West Point Story, Along the Great Divide, Captain Horatio Hornblower, Painting the Clouds with Sunshine, Starlift, She's Working Her Way Through College, Iron Mistress, She's Back on Broadway, South Sea Woman, Devil's Canyon, King Richard and the Crusaders, The Silver Chalice, Pearl of the South Pacific, Great Day in the Morning, The Proud Ones, Congo Crossing, The Big Land, The Story of Mankind, The Tall Stranger, Fort Dobbs, Westbound, Jet Over the Atlantic, Young Fury, Fort Utah, Castle of Evil, Won Ton Ton the Dog Who Saved Hollywood, French Quarter, Evil Spirits, Seven Days Ashore.

MAYRON, MELANIE
Actress, Director. b. Philadelphia, PA, Oct. 20, 1952. e. American Academy of Dramatic Arts, 1972. Debut Godspell (tour), NY stage debut: The Goodbye People, 1979. Gethsemane Springs, (Mark Taper Forum, 1976), Crossing Delancey, (1986, Jewish Rep. Theatre, NY). With Catlin Adams, co-prod., co-wrote short, Little Shiny Shoes.
PICTURES: Actress: Harry and Tonto (debut, 1974), Gable and Lombard, Car Wash, The Great Smokey Roadblock, You Light Up My Life, Girl Friends (Locarno Film Fest. Award) Heartbeeps, Missing, The Boss' Wife, Sticky Fingers (also co-s.p., co-prod), Checking Out, My Blue Heaven. Director: The Babysitters Club.
TELEVISION: Series: thirtysomething (Emmy Award, 1989). Movies: Playing For Time, Will There Really Be a Morning?, Hustling, The Best Little Girl in the World, Wallenberg: A Hero's Story, Ordeal in the Arctic, Other Women's Children. Guest: Rhoda. Specials: Lily Tomlin: Sold Out, Cinder Ella: A Modern Fairy Tale, Wanted: The Perfect Guy. Director: Tribeca: Stepping Back (also writer), thirtysomething, Sirens, Moon Over Miami, Winnetka Road, Freaky Friday (movie).

MAYSLES, ALBERT
Director, Cinematographer. b. Boston, MA, Nov. 1926. e. Syracuse (B.A.), Boston U, M.A. Taught psychology there for 3 years. With late brother David (1932-87) pioneer in direct cinema documentary filmmaking, using a hand-held synchronous sound camera, no narration, to capture the drama of daily life, without need to invent stories. Entered filmmaking photographing Primary with D.A. Pennebaker, Richard Leacock and Robert Drew, 1960. Formed Maysles Films, Inc. 1962, making non-fiction feature films, commercials and corp. films.
PICTURES: Showman (1962), Salesman, What's Happening! The Beatles in the U.S.A., Meet Marlon Brando, Gimme Shelter, Christo's Valley Curtain, Grey Gardens, Running Fence, Vladimir Horowitz: The Last Romantic, Ozawa, Islands, Horowitz Plays Mozart, Fellow Passengers, Christo in Paris, Soldiers of Music: Rostropovitch Returns to Russia, Baroque Duet, Umbrellas.
TELEVISION: Vladimir Horowitz: The Last Romantic (Emmy Award, 1987), Soldiers of Music: Rostopovich Returns to Russia (Emmy Award, 1991). Sports Illustrated: The Making of the Swimsuit Issue (co-dir.), Abortion: Desperate Choices.

MAZURSKY, PAUL
Producer, Director, Writer, Actor. b. Brooklyn, NY, April 25, 1930. e. Brooklyn Coll. Started acting in 1951 Off-B'way (Hello Out There, The Seagull, Major Barbara, Death of a Salesman, He Who Gets Slapped), TV and films. Was nightclub comic 1954-1960 and directed plays. Began association with Larry Tucker by producing, directing, writing and performing in Second City, semi-improvisational revue. For four years they wrote the Danny Kaye TV show and created and wrote the Monkees series. First theatrical film I Love You Alice B. Toklas, 1968, which he wrote and exec. produced with Tucker. Exec. prod. of film Taking Care of Business.
PICTURES: Dir.-Writer: Bob and Carol and Ted and Alice, Dir.-Prod.-Writer-Actor: Alex in Wonderland, Blume in Love, Harry and Tonto, Next Stop Greenwich Village (dir., prod., s.p. only), An Unmarried Woman, Willie and Phil, Tempest, Moscow on the Hudson, Down and Out in Beverly Hills, Moon Over Parador, Enemies: a Love Story, Scenes From a Mall, The Pickle, Faithful. Actor: Fear and Desire, Blackboard Jungle, Deathwatch, A Star Is Born, A Man a Woman and a Bank, History of the World Part 1, Into the Night, Punchline, Scenes From the Class Struggle in Beverly Hills, Man Trouble, Carlito's Way, Love Affair, Miami Rhapsody, 2 Days in the Valley.

MAZZELLO, JOSEPH
Actor. b. Rhineback, NY, Sept. 21, 1983. Made acting debut at age 5 in tv movie Unspeakable Acts.
PICTURES: Presumed Innocent (debut, 1990), Radio Flyer, Jurassic Park, Shadowlands, The River Wild, The Cure, Three Wishes.
TELEVISION: Movies: Unspeakable Acts, Desperate Choices: To Save My Child, A Father for Charlie.

McBRIDE, JIM
Director, Writer. b. New York, NY, Sept. 16, 1941. e. NYU. m. costume designer Tracy Tynan. Began in underground film scene in New York. First film: David Holzman's Diary, 1967, which won grand prize at Mannheim and Pesaro Film Festivals, and was named to the Library of Congress' list of important American films designated for preservation in 1991. Appeared as actor in film Last Embrace.
PICTURES: Director: David Holzman's Diary (also prod.), My Girlfriend's Wedding (also actor, s.p.), Glen and Randa (also s.p.), Hot Times (also s.p., actor), Breathless (also co-s.p.), The Big Easy, Great Balls of Fire (also co-s.p.), Uncovered (also co-s.p.).
TELEVISION: Series: The Wonder Years (3 episodes), Twilight Zone (The Once and Future King, 1986). Movies: Blood Ties, The Wrong Man, Field of Blood, Pronto. Special: Fallen Angels (Fearless).

McCALL, JOAN
Writer, Actress. b. Grahn, KY. e. Berea Coll. Staff writer for Days of Our Lives, Another World, As the World Turns, under the pen name Joan Pommer; also Search for Tomorrow, Capitol, Santa Barbara, Divorce Court. Starred on B'way in Barefoot in the Park, The Star Spangled Girl, A Race of Hairy Men, and road companies of Barefoot in the Park, Any Wednesday, Star Spangled Girl, and Don't Drink the Water, Los Angeles co. of Jimmy Shine.
PICTURES: Grizzly, Act of Vengeance, The Devil Times Five. Screenwriter: Predator, Between Two Worlds, Timelapse, Heart Like a Wheel.

McCALLUM, DAVID
Actor. b. Glasgow, Scotland, Sept. 19, 1933. Early career in rep. theatres and dir. plays for Army. Entered industry in 1953.
PICTURES: The Secret Place (debut, 1957), Hell Drivers, Robbery Under Arms, Violent Playground, A Night to Remember, The Long and the Short and the Tall, Carolina, Jungle Street, Billy Budd, Freud, The Great Escape, The Greatest Story Ever Told, To Trap a Spy, The Spy With My Face, Around the World Under the Sea, One Spy Too Many, Three Bites of the Apple, Sol Madrid, Mosquito Squadron, The Kingfisher Caper, Dogs, King Solomon's Treasure, The Watcher in the Woods, Terminal Choice, The Wind, The Haunting of Morella, Hear My Song, Dirty Weekend, Healer.
TELEVISION: Series: The Man From U.N.C.L.E., Colditz (BBC, 1972-74), The Invisible Man, Sapphire and Steel (BBC), Trainer (BBC). Guest: Hitchcock, Murder She Wrote. Movies: Teacher Teacher, Hauser's Memory, Frankenstein: The True Story, Behind Enemy Lines, Freedom Fighters, She Waits, The Man Who Lived at the Ritz, The Return of Sam McCloud, Mother Love (BBC), Shattered Image.

McCAMBRIDGE, MERCEDES
Actress. b. Joliet, IL, March 17, 1918. e. Mundelein Coll., Chicago, B.A. Did some radio work while in college; opposite Orson Welles two seasons, on Ford Theatre, other air shows; New York stage in: Hope for the Best, (1945); Place of Our Own, Twilight Bar, Woman Bites Dog, The Young and Fair, Lost in Yonkers. Starred on own radio show, 1952. Member of National Inst. Alcohol Abuse and Alcoholism, Washington. Autobiography: The Two of Us.
PICTURES: All the King's Men (debut, 1949; Academy Award, best supporting actress), Lightning Strikes Twice, Inside Straight, The Scarf, Johnny Guitar, Giant, A Farewell to Arms, Touch of Evil (unbilled), Suddenly Last Summer, Cimarron, Angel Baby, 99 Women, Like a Crow on a June Bug (Sixteen), The Exorcist (voice), Thieves, The Concorde—Airport '79, Echoes.
TELEVISION: Series: One Man's Family, Wire Service; also numerous guest appearances. Movies: Killer By Night, Two For the Money, The Girls of Huntington House, The President's Plane Is Missing, Who Is the Black Dahlia?, The Sacketts.

McCARTHY, ANDREW
Actor. b. Westfield, NJ, Nov. 29, 1962. Raised in Bernardsville, NJ. e. NYU. While at college won role in film Class. Studied acting at Circle-in-the-Square.
THEATER: B'way: The Boys of Winter. Off B'way: Bodies Rest and Motion, Life Under Water, Neptune's Hips, Mariens Kammer.
PICTURES: Class (debut, 1983), Heaven Help Us, St. Elmo's Fire, Pretty in Pink, Mannequin, Waiting for the Moon, Less Than Zero, Kansas, Fresh Horses, Weekend at Bernie's, Quiet Days in Clichy, Dr. M (Club Extinction), Year of the Gun, Only You, Weekend at Bernie's 2, The Joy Luck Club, Getting In (Student Body), Night of the Running Man, Mrs. Parker & the Vicious Circle, Dream Man, Dead Funny, Mulholland Falls, Things I Never Told You.
TELEVISION: Movie: The Courtyard. Specials: Dear Lola, Common Pursuit. Guest: Amazing Stories (Grandpa's Ghost), Tales From the Crypt (Loved to Death).

McCARTHY, KEVIN
Actor. b. Seattle, WA, Feb. 15, 1914. Sister was late author Mary McCarthy. e. U. of Minnesota. Acted in sch. plays, stock; B'way debut in Abe Lincoln in Illinois. Served in U.S. Army.
THEATER: B'way: Flight to West, Winged Victory, Truckline Cafe, Joan of Lorraine, The Survivors, Death of a Salesman (London), Anna Christie, The Deep Blue Sea, Red Roses For Me, A Warm Body, Something About a Soldier, Love's Labour's Lost, Advise and Consent, The Day The Money Stopped, Two For the Seesaw, Cactus Flower, Alone Together, The Three Sisters, Happy Birthday Wanda June.
PICTURES: Death of a Salesman (debut, 1951; Acad. Award nom.), Drive a Crooked Road, The Gambler From Natchez, Stranger on Horseback, Annapolis Story, Nightmare, Invasion of the Body Snatchers, The Misfits, 40 Pounds of Trouble, A Gathering of Eagles, The Prize, The Best Man, An Affair of the Skin, Mirage, A Big Hand for the Little Lady, Three Sisters, Hotel, The Hell With Heroes, If He Hollers Let Him Go, Revenge in El Paso, Ace High, Kansas City Bomber, Alien Thunder (Dan Candy's Law), Order to Kill, Buffalo Bill and the Indians, Piranha, Invasion of the Body Snatchers (1978, cameo), Hero at Large, Those Lips Those Eyes, The Howling, My Tutor, Twilight Zone—The Movie, Hostage, Innerspace, UHF, Fast Food, Dark Tower, Love or Money, The Sleeping Car, Eve of Destruction, Final Approach, The Distinguished Gentleman, Matinee, Greedy, Just Cause, Steal Big Steal Little.
TELEVISION: Active on TV since 1949. Movies: U.M.C., A Great American Tragedy, Exo-Man, Mary Jane Harper Cried Last Night, Flamingo Road, Portrait of an Escort, Rosie: The Story of Rosemary Clooney, Making of a Male Model, Invitation to Hell, Deadly Intentions, The Midnight Hour, A Masterpiece of Murder, Poor Little Rich Girl: The Barbara Hutton Story, The Long Journey Home, Once Upon a Texas Train, In the Heat of the Night, Channel 99, The Rose and the Jackal, Dead on the Money, Duplicates, The Sister-in-Law. Mini-series: Passion and Paradise. Series: The Colbys, The Survivors, Flamingo Road, Amanda's, Second Start. Guest: Dynasty. Pilot: Second Stage.

McCARTNEY PAUL
Singer, Musician. r.n. James Paul McCartney. b. Liverpool, England, June 18, 1942. Formerly with The Beatles, Wings.
PICTURES: Performer: A Hard Day's Night, (debut, 1964; also songs) Help! (also songs), Yellow Submarine (cameo; also songs), Let It Be (also songs; Academy Award for best original song score, 1970), Rockshow (concert film), Give My Regards to Broad Street (also s.p., songs), Eat the Rich (cameo), Get Back (concert film) Songs for films: Live and Let Die (title song; Acad. Award nom.), Oh Heavenly Dog, Spies Like Us. Scores: The Family Way, Beyond the Limit.
TELEVISION: Specials: James Paul McCartney, Sgt. Pepper: It Was 20 Years Ago Today, Put It There, Paul McCartney Live in the New World, The Beatles Anthology.

McCLANAHAN, RUE
Actress. b. Healdton, OK, Feb. 21. e. U. of Tulsa (B.A. cum laude). Member: Actors Studio, NYC.
THEATER: On B'way in Sticks and Bones, Jimmy Shine, California Suite. Off-B'way: Who's Happy Now? (Obie Award, 1970), After Play. Vienna: Lettice and Lovage. London: Harvey.
PICTURES: Five Minutes to Love, Hollywood After Dark, How to Succeed With Girls, They Might Be Giants, The People Next Door, The Pursuit of Happiness, Modern Love, This World Then The Fireworks, Dear God, Starship Troopers.
TELEVISION: Series: Maude, Mama's Family, The Golden Girls (Emmy Award, 1987), The Golden Palace, Apple Pie, Balckbird Hall. Movies: Having Babies III, Sgt. Matlovich Vs. the U.S. Air Force, Rainbow, Topper, The Great American Traffic Jam, Word of Honor, The Day the Bubble Burst, The Little Match Girl, Liberace, Take My Daughters Please, Let Me Hear You Whisper, To the Heroes, After the Shock, Children of the Bride, To My Daughter, The Dreamer of Oz, Baby of the Bride, Mother of the Bride (also co-exec. prod.), A Burning Passion: The Margaret Mitchell Story, Innocent Victims, A Christmas Love. Specials: The Wickedest Witch, The Man in the Brown Suit, Nunsense 2: The Sequel. Mini-Series: Message From Nam.

McCLORY, SEÁN
Actor. b. Dublin, Ireland, March 8, 1924. e. Jesuit Coll., Nat'l U. at Galway (medical sch.). With Gaelic Theatre, Galway; Abbey Theatre, Dublin. Brought to U.S. in 1946 under contract to RKO Pictures, then Warners, then Batjac (John Wayne's co.). Prod. and dir. numerous plays, member of the Directors Guild of America and author of drama, Moment of Truth; Pax: The Benedictions in China. Editor: The Jester: The Masques Club 50th Anniv. Mng. Editor: A.N.T.A. News (2 yrs.) For past 4 years starred in 40 ninety-minute radio dramas for California Artists Radio Theatre and written some 90 min. shows for National Public Radio.
THEATER: Shining Hour, Juno and the Paycock, Anna Christie, Escape to Autumn, King of Friday's Men, Lady's Not for Burning, Billy Budd, Dial M for Murder, The Winslow Boy, Shadow of a Gunman (Dramalogue Award), Saint Joan, The Importance of Being Earnest, many others.

PICTURES: Roughshod, Beyond Glory, The Daughter of Rosie O'Grady, Anne of the Indies, Storm Warning, Lorna Doone, What Price Glory?, The Quiet Man, Rogue's March, Plunder of the Sun, Island in the Sky, Them, Ring of Fear, Man in the Attic, The Long Grey Lane, Diane, I Cover the Underworld, The King's Thief, Moonfleet, Guns of Fort Petticoat, Valley of the Dragons, Cheyenne Autumn, Follow Me Boys, The Gnome-Mobile, Bandolero, Day of the Wolves, Roller Boogie, In Search of Historic Jesus, My Chauffeur, The Dead.
TELEVISION: Series: The Californians (also dir. episodes), Kate McShane, Bring 'Em Back Alive, General Hospital. Mini-Series: The Captains and the Kings, Once an Eagle. Movies: Kate McShane (pilot), The New Daughters of Joshua Cabe, Young Harry Houdini. Guest: Matinee Theatre, Climax, Lost in Space, My Three Sons, Suspense, The Untouchables, Hitchcock, Thriller, Beverly Hillbillies, Bonanza, Gunsmoke, Mannix, Little House on the Prairie, Perry Mason, S.W.A.T., Fish, Columbo, How the West Was Won, Fantasy Island, Battlestar Galactica, Trapper John M.D., Blue Knight, Falcon Crest, Simon and Simon, Murder She Wrote.

McCLUGGAGE, KERRY
Executive. b. 1955. e. USC, Harvard U. 1978, programming asst. at Universal; 1979, dir. of current srs. programming; 1980, became v.p., Universal TV. 1982, sr. v.p. creative affairs. Served as v.p. of production, Universal Pictures and supv. prod. on series Miami Vice. 1987-1991, pres. of Universal Television. 1991, joined Paramount as pres. of the Television Group. 1992, named chmn. of the Television Group of Paramount Pictures.

McCLURE, MARC
Actor. b. San Mateo, CA, Mar. 31, 1957.
PICTURES: Freaky Friday, Coming Home, I Wanna Hold Your Hand, Superman, Superman II, Superman III, Superman IV: The Quest for Peace, Amazon Women on the Moon, Perfect Match, Chances Are, After Midnight, Back to the Future Part III, Grim Prairie Tales, The Vagrant, Apollo 13, Sleepstalker.
TELEVISION: Series: California Fever. Movies: James at 15, Little White Lies. Guest: The Commish.

McCLURG, EDIE
Actress. b. Kansas City, MO, July 23, 1951. e. Syracuse Univ. Newswriter and documentary producer for National Public Radio affiliate, KCUR-FM. Joined the Pitschel Players in LA in 1975; then became member of the Groundlings Improv Comedy Revue.
PICTURES: Carrie (debut, 1976), Cheech and Chong's Next Movie, Oh God Book II, Secret of NIMH (voice), Pandemonium, Cracking Up, Eating Raoul, Mr. Mom, The Corsican Brothers, Ferris Bueller's Day Off, Back to School, The Longshot, Planes Trains and Automobiles, She's Having a Baby, Elvira: Mistress of the Dark, The Little Mermaid (voice), Curly Sue, A River Runs Through It, Stepmonster, Airborne, Natural Born Killers, Under the Hula Moon.
TELEVISION: Series: Tony Orlando and Dawn, The Kallikaks, The Big Show, Harper Valley PTA, No Soap Radio, Madame's Place, Small Wonder, Toegther We Stand, Valerie (The Hogan Family), Drexell's Class, Life with Louie, Martin Mull's White POlitics in America. Specials: Cinderella (Faerie Tale Theatre), The Pee-wee Herman Show, Martin Mull's History of White People in America, Once Upon a Brothers Grimm, The Chevy Chase Show, A Home Run for Love. Guest: WKRP in Cincinnati, The Richard Pryor Show, The Jeffersons, Trapper John M.D., Alice, Diff'rent Strokes, The Incredible Hulk, Madame's Place, Picket Fences. Movies: Bill on His Own, Crash Course, Dance 'til Dawn, Menu for Murder. Voice Characterizations: The Snorks, The 13 Ghosts of Scooby Doo, The New Jetsons, Casper, Problem Child, Bobby's World of Monsters.

McCORMICK, PAT
Writer, Actor. b. July 17, 1934. Served as comedy writer for such performers as Jonathan Winters, Phyllis Diller.
PICTURES: Actor: Buffalo Bill and the Indians, Smokey and the Bandit, A Wedding, Hot Stuff, Scavenger Hunt, Smokey and the Bandit 2, History of the World Part 1, Under the Rainbow (also co-s.p.), Smokey and the Bandit 3, Bombs Away, Rented Lips, Scrooged, Beverly Hills Vamp.
TELEVISION: Series (as writer): Jack Paar Show, Tonight Show, etc. Series (as actor): The Don Rickles Show, The New Bill Cosby Show, Gun Shy. Movies (as actor): Mr. Horn, Rooster, The Jerk Too.

McCOWEN, ALEC
Actor. b. Tunbridge Wells, England, May 26, 1925. e. Royal Acad. of Dramatic Art. On stage in London in Hadrian the Seventh, among others. On B'way in Antony and Cleopatra, After the Rain, The Philanthropist, The Misanthrope, Equus, Someone Who'll Watch Over Me, etc.
PICTURES: The Cruel Sea, The Divided Heart, The Deep Blue Sea, The Good Companions, The Third Key (The Long Arm),

Time Without Pity, Town on Trial, The Doctor's Dilemma, A Night to Remember, The One That Got Away, Silent Enemy, The Loneliness of the Long Distance Runner, In the Cool of the Day, The Devil's Own (The Witches), The Hawaiians, Frenzy, Travels with My Aunt, Stevie, Hanover Street, Never Say Never Again, The Assam Garden, Personal Services, Cry Freedom, Henry V, The Age of Innocence.

McCRANE, PAUL
Actor. b. Philadelphia, PA, Jan. 19, 1961. Stage debut at age 16 in NY Shakespeare Fest. prod. of Landscape of the Body.
THEATER: NY: Dispatches, Runaway, Split, The House of Blue Leaves, The Palace of Amateurs, Hooters, The Hostage, Curse of an Aching Heart
PICTURES: Rocky II (debut, 1979), Fame (also songwriter), The Hotel New Hampshire, Purple Hearts, Robocop, The Blob, The Shawshank Redemption.
TELEVISION: Series: Cop Rock.

McDERMOTT, DYLAN
Actor. b. Connecticut, Oct. 26, 1961. Raised in New York City. e. Fordham U., studied acting at Neighborhood Playhouse with Sanford Meisner.
THEATER: The Seagull, Golden Boy, The Glass Menagerie, Biloxi Blues (B'way), Floating Rhoda and the Glue Man.
PICTURES: Hamburger Hill, The Blue Iguana, Twister, Steel Magnolias, Where Sleeping Dogs Lie, Hardware, In the Line of Fire, The Cowboy Way, Miracle on 34th Street, Destiny Turns on the Radio, Home for the Holidays.
TELEVISION: Movies: The Neon Empire, Into the Badlands, The Fear Inside.

McDONNELL, MARY
Actress. b. Ithaca, NY, 1952.
THEATER: NY: Buried Child, Savage in Limbo, All Night Long, Black Angel, A Weekend Near Madison, Three Ways Home, Still Life, The Heidi Chronicles. Regional: National Athems, A Doll's House, A Midsummer Night's Dream, The Three Sisters.
PICTURES: Matewan, Tiger Warsaw, Dances With Wolves (Acad. Award nom.), Golden Globe Award), Grand Canyon, Sneakers, Passion Fish (Acad. Award nom.), Blue Chips, Mariette in Ecstasy, Independence Day.
TELEVISION: Series: E/R, High Society. Movies: Money on the Side, Courage, The American Clock. Special: O Pioneers!

McDORMAND, FRANCES
Actress. b. Illinois, 1958. Daughter of a Disciples of Christ preacher, traveled Bible Belt with family settling in PA at 8. e. Yale Drama School. Regional theater includes Twelfth Night, Mrs. Warren's Profession, The Three Sisters, All My Sons. Two seasons with O'Neill Playwrights Conference.
THEATER: Awake and Sing, Painting Churches, On the Verge, A Streetcar Named Desire (Tony nom.), The Sisters Rosensweig, The Swan.
PICTURES: Blood Simple, Raising Arizona, Mississippi Burning (Acad. Award nom.), Chattahoochee, Dark Man, Miller's Crossing (unbilled), Hidden Agenda, The Butcher's Wife, Passed Away, Short Cuts, Beyond Rangoon, Fargo, Lone Star, Primal Fear, Palookaville.
TELEVISION: Series: Leg Work. Guest: Twilight Zone, Spenser: For Hire, Hill St. Blues. Movies: Crazy in Love, The Good Old Boys.

McDOWALL, BETTY
Actress. b. Sydney, Australia. e. Mt. Bernard Convent, N. Sydney. Early career radio, stage in Australia; ent. BBC TV, 1952; since in West End plays, many TV and radio plays and films. Radio plays include: Anna Christie, The Little Foxes, Another Part of the Forest, The Archers.
THEATER: Age of Consent, Ghost Train, The Kidders, The Dark Halo, Period of Adjustment, Rule of Three, Signpost to Murder, Hippolytus, The Winslow Boy, Woman in a Dressing Gown, As Long as It's Warm, Caprice—in a Pink Palazzo, Sweet Bird of Youth, There Was an Old Woman, What the Butler Saw, Two Dozen Red Roses, A Boston Story, The Man Most Likely To..., Sleeping Partner.
PICTURES: Timelock, She Didn't Say No, Jack the Ripper, The Shiralee, Jackpot, Dead Lucky, Spare the Rod, Golliwog, Echo of Diana, First Men in the Moon, Ballad in Blue, The Liquidators, Willy Wagtails by Moonlight, The Omen.
TELEVISION: Mid-Level and Glorification of Al Toolum, The Black Judge, Phone Call for Matthew Quade, Thunder on the Snowy, Shadow of Guilt, Traveling Lady, Torment, Biography, Notes for a Love Song, Esther's Altar, The Corridor People, The Braden Beat, The Douglas Fairbanks, Ivanhoe, The Foreign Legion, Fabian of the Yard, Four Just Men, Flying Doctor, No Hiding Place, Z' Cars, Days of Vengeance, Flower of Evil, Outbreak of Murder, Call Me Sam, The Prisoner, Public Eye, The Forgotten Door, All Out for Kangaroo Valley, Barry Humphries Scandals, Castle Haven, Albert and Victoria, Follyfoot, The Man Who Came to Dinner, Anne of Avoniea, Little Lord Fauntleroy, The Bass Player and the Blond (4 plays), The Gingerbread Lady. Series: Boyd Q.C.

McDOWALL, RODDY
Actor. b. London, England, Sept. 17, 1928. e. St. Joseph's, London. First appeared in British film Murder in the Family at age of 9. In 1940, was signed by 20th Century-Fox. Voted Star of Tomorrow, 1944. Named Screen Actors Guild representative on National Film Preservation Bd., 1989. Published four volumes of his photography: Double Exposure (& II, III, IV).
THEATER: B'way: Misalliance, Escapade, Doctor's Dilemma, No Time for Sergeants, Good as Gold, Compulsion, Handful of Fire, Look After Lulu, The Fighting Cock (Tony Award, 1960), Camelot, The Astrakhan Coat.
PICTURES: Murder in the Family (debut, 1938), I See Ice, John Halifax Gentleman, Convict 99, Scruffy, Yellow Sands, Hey Hey USA, Poison Pen, The Outsider, Dead Man's Shoes, Just Williams, His Brother's Keeper, Saloon Bar, You Will Remember, This England, Man Hunt (U.S. debut, 1941), How Green Was My Valley, Confirm or Deny, Son of Fury, On the Sunny Side, The Pied Piper, My Friend Flicka, Lassie Come Home, White Cliffs of Dover, The Keys of the Kingdom, Thunderhead Son of Flicka, Molly and Me, Holiday in Mexico, Macbeth, Rocky, Kidnapped, Tuna Clipper, Black Midnight, Killer Shark, Everybody's Dancin', Big Timber, Steel Fist, The Subterraneans, Midnight Lace, The Longest Day, Cleopatra, Shock Treatment, The Greatest Story Ever Told, That Darn Cat, The Loved One, The Third Day, Inside Daisy Clover, Lord Love a Duck, The Defector, It, The Adventures of Bullwhip Griffin, The Cool Ones, Planet of the Apes, Five Card Stud, Hello Down There, Midas Run, Angel Angel Down We Go (Cult of the Damned), Pretty Maids All in a Row, Escape from the Planet of the Apes, Bedknobs and Broomsticks, Corky (unbilled), Conquest of the Planet of the Apes, The Devil's Widow (Tam Lin; dir. only), Life and Times of Judge Roy Bean, The Poseidon Adventure, The Legend of Hell House, Arnold, Battle for the Planet of the Apes, Dirty Mary Crazy Larry, Funny Lady, Mean Johnny Barrows, Embryo, Sixth and Main, Rabbit Test, Laserblast, The Cat from Outer Space, Circle of Iron, Scavenger Hunt, The Black Hole (voice), Charlie Chan and the Curse of the Dragon Queen, Evil Under the Sun, Class of 1984, Fright Night, GoBots: Battle of the Rock Lords (voice), Dead of Winter, Overboard (also exec. prod.), Doin' Time on Planet Earth, The Big Picture, Destroyer, Fright Night Part 2, Cutting Class, Shakma, Going Under, The Color of Evening, Double Trouble, The Naked Target, Mirror Mirror 2, Angel 4: Undercover, Last Summer in the Hamptons, The Grass Harp.
TELEVISION: Series: Planet of the Apes, Fantastic Journey, Tales of the Gold Monkey, Bridges to Cross. Specials: Stratford Shakespeare Festival, Heart of Darkness, He's for Me, Not Without Honor (Emmy Award, 1961), The Fatal Mistake, Camilla (Nightmare Classics). Movies: Night Gallery, Terror in the Sky, A Taste of Evil, What's a Nice Girl Like You...?, Miracle on 34th Street, The Elevator, Flood, Thief of Baghdad, The Immigrants, The Martian Chronicles, Hart to Hart (pilot), The Memory of Eva Ryker, Million Dollar Face, Mae West, This Girl for Hire, The Zany Adventures of Robin Hood, Alice in Wonderland, Earth Angel, An Inconvenient Woman, Deadly Game, The Sands of Time, Heads, Hart to Hart: Home Is Where the Hart Is. Mini-Series: The Rhinemann Exchange, Hollywood Wives, Around the World in 80 Days. Guest: Goodyear TV Playhouse, Ponds Theatre, Oldsmobile Music Theatre, Campbell Soundstage, Batman, The Invaders, Love American Style, Carol Burnett Show, George Burns Comedy Week, Love Boat, Matlock, Murder She Wrote, many others.

McDOWELL, MALCOLM
Actor. b. Leeds, England, June 13, 1943. Was spearholder for the Royal Shakespeare Co. in season of 1965-66 when turned to TV and then to films. NY stage: Look Back in Anger (also on video), In Celebration, Another Time. LA stage: Hunting Cockroaches.
PICTURES: Poor Cow (debut, 1967), If..., Figures in a Landscape, The Raging Moon (Long Ago Tomorrow), A Clockwork Orange, O Lucky Man!, Royal Flash, Voyage of the Damned, Aces High, The Passage, Time After Time, Caligula, Cat People, Britannia Hospital, Blue Thunder, Cross Creek, Get Crazy, Sunset, Buy and Cell, The Caller, Class of 1999, Disturbed, In the Eye of the Snake, Moon 44, The Maestro, Schweitzer (The Light in the Jungle), Assassin of the Tsar, The Player, Happily Ever After (voice), Chain of Desire, East Wind, Night Train to Venice, Bopha!, Milk Money, Star Trek: Generations, Tank Girl, Kids of the Round Table, Where Truth Lies.
TELEVISION: Series: Pearl. Guest: Faerie Tale Theatre (Little Red Riding Hood), Tales fromt the Crypt (Reluctant Vampire). Movies: Arthur the King, Gulag, Monte Carlo, Seasons of the Heart, The Man Who Wouldn't Die.

McELWAINE, GUY
Executive. b. Culver City, CA, June 29, 1936. Started career in pub. dept. of MGM, 1955; 1959, joined m.p. div. of Rogers and Cowen; 1964, formed own public relations firm; then joined CMA. Left to become sr. exec. v.p. in chg. worldwide m.p. production, Warner Bros., 1975. 1977 became sr. exec. v.p. in chg. worldwide m.p. activities and pres. of intl. film mktg. at Intl. Creative Management (ICM), formerly CMA. 1981, named pres.

and CEO, Rastar Films. Left in 1982 to become pres., Columbia Pictures; given additional title of CEO, 1983. 1985 named chmn. and on board of Columbia Pictures Industries. Resigned, 1986. Joined Weintraub Entertainment Group as exec. v.p. and chmn., m.p. div. 1987-89; returned to ICM, 1989 as vice chmn.

McEVEETY, BERNARD
Director. Father was pioneer as unit mgr. at New York's Edison Studios; Brothers dir. Vincent and writer Joseph. Began career in 1953 at Paramount where he was asst. dir. for 6 yrs. Dir. debut on TV series, The Rebel.
PICTURES: Ride Beyond Vengeance, Brotherhood of Satan, Napoleon and Samantha, One Little Indian, The Bears and I.
TELEVISION: Numerous episodes on Bonanza, Gunsmoke, Combat and Cimarron Strip (also prod.), Centennial, Roughnecks, The Machans.

McEVEETY, VINCENT
Director. Brother is dir. Bernard McEveety. Joined Hal Roach Studios in 1954 as second asst. dir. Then to Republic for The Last Command. First Disney assignments: Davy Crockett shows and Mickey Mouse Club. Moved to Desilu as first asst. dir. on The Untouchables; made assoc. prod. with option to direct. Did segments of many series, including 34 Gunsmoke episodes.
PICTURES: Firecreek (debut, 1968), $1,000,000 Duck, The Biscuit Eater, Charley and the Angel, Superdad, The Strongest Man in the World, Gus, Treasure of Matecumbe, Herbie Goes to Monte Carlo, The Apple Dumpling Gang Rides Again, Herbie Goes Bananas, Amy.
TELEVISION: Blood Sport, Wonder Woman, High Flying Spy, Ask Max, Gunsmoke: Return to Dodge, Murder She Wrote, Simon and Simon (26 episodes), Columbo: Rest in Peace Mrs. Columbo.

McGAVIN, DARREN
Actor. b. Spokane, WA, May 7, 1922. e. Coll. of the Pacific. Studied acting at Neighborhood Playhouse, Actors Studio. Landed bit roles in films starting in 1945.
THEATER: Death of a Salesman, My Three Angels, The Rainmaker, The Lovers, The King and I, Dinner at Eight (revival), Captain Brassbound's Conversion (LA), The Night Hank Williams Died, Greetings.
PICTURES: A Song to Remember (debut, 1945), Kiss and Tell, Counter-Attack, She Wouldn't Say Yes, Fear, Queen for a Day, Summertime, The Man With the Golden Arm, The Court Martial of Billy Mitchell, Beau James, The Delicate Delinquent, The Case Against Brooklyn, Bullet for a Badman, The Great Sioux Massacre, Ride the High Wind, Mission Mars, Mrs. Polifax—Spy, Happy Mother's Day... Love George (Run Stranger Run; dir. only), No Deposit No Return, Airport '77, Hot Lead and Cold Feet, Zero to Sixty, Firebird 2015 A.D., A Christmas Story, The Natural, Turk 182, Raw Deal, From the Hip, Dead Heat, Blood and Concrete: A Love Story, Billy Madison.
TELEVISION: Series: Crime Photographer, Mike Hammer, Riverboat, The Outsider, Kolchak: The Night Stalker, Small & Frye. Movies: The Outsider (pilot), The Challenge, The Challengers, Berlin Affair, Tribes, Banyon, The Death of Me Yet, Night Stalker, Something Evil, The Rookies, Say Goodbye Maggie Cole, The Night Strangler, The Six Million Dollar Man (pilot), Brink's: The Great Robbery, Law and Order, The Users, Love for Rent, Waikiki, Return of Marcus Welby M.D., My Wicked Wicked Ways, Inherit the Wind, The Diamond Trap, By Dawn's Early Light, The American Clock, Danielle Steel's A Perfect Stranger, Derby. Specials: Unclaimed Fortunes (host), Clara (ACE Award), Mastergate, Miracles and Ohter Wonders (host), The Secret Discovery of Noah's Ark (host). Mini-Series: Ike, The Martian Chronicles, Around the World in 80 Days. Guest: Goodyear TV Playhouse, Alfred Hitchcock Presents, Route 66, U.S. Steel Hour, The Defenders, Love American Style, The Name of the Game, Owen Marshall, Police Story, The Love Boat, Murphy Brown (Emmy Award, 1990), many others.

McGILLIS, KELLY
Actress. b. Newport Beach, CA, July 9, 1957. Studied acting at Pacific Conservatory of Performing Arts in Santa Maria, CA; Juilliard. While at latter, won role in film Reuben Reuben.
THEATER: D.C. Stage: The Merchant of Venice, Twelfth Night, Measure for Measure, Much Ado About Nothing. NY Stage: Hedda Gabler.
PICTURES: Reuben Reuben (debut, 1983), Witness, Top Gun, Once We Were Dreamers (Promised Land), Made in Heaven, The House on Carroll Street, The Accused, Winter People, Cat Chaser, Before and After Death, The Babe, North.
TELEVISION: Movies: Sweet Revenge, Private Sessions, Grand Isle (also prod.), Bonds of Love, In the Best of Families: Marriage Pride & Madness. Special: Out of Ireland (narrator).

McGINLEY, JOHN C.
Actor. b. New York, NY, Aug. 3, 1959. e. NYU (M.F.A.), 1984.
THEATRE: NY: Danny and the Deep Blue Sea, The Ballad of Soapy Smith, Jesse and the Games, Requiem for a Heavyweight, Love as We Know It, Talk Radio, Florida Crackers, Breast Men.

PICTURES: Sweet Liberty, Platoon, Wall Street, Shakedown, Talk Radio, Lost Angels, Fat Man and Little Boy, Born on the Fourth of July, Point Break, Highlander 2: The Quickening, Article 99, Little Noises, A Midnight Clear, Fathers and Sons, Hear No Evil, Watch It (also co-prod.), Car 54 Where Are You?, On Deadly Ground, Surviving the Game, Suffrin' Bastards (also co-s.p.), Wagons East!, Born to Be Wild, Captive (co-prod. only), Seven, Nixon, Johns, The Rock.
TELEVISION: Movies: Clinton & Nadine, Cruel Doubt, The Last Outlaw, The Return of Hunter. Guest: Frasier.

McGOOHAN, PATRICK
Actor, Director. b. New York, Mar. 19, 1928. Early career in repertory in Britain. London stage 1954 in Serious Charge; 1955, Orson Welles' Moby Dick. On B'way in Pack of Lies (1987).
PICTURES: The Dam Busters (debut, 1954), I Am a Camera, The Dark Avenger (The Warriors), Passage Home, Zarak, High Tide at Noon, Hell Drivers, The Gypsy and the Gentleman, Nor the Moon by Night (Elephant Gun), Two Living One Dead, All Night Long, Life for Ruth (Walk in the Shadow), The Quare Fellow, The Three Lives of Thomasina, Dr. Syn: Alias the Scarecrow (U.S. tv as: The Scarecrow of Romney Marsh), Ice Station Zebra, The Moonshine War, Mary—Queen of Scots, Catch My Soul (dir. only), Un Genio due Campari e un Pollo (The Genius), Porgi d'altra Guancia (Nobody's the Greatest), Silver Streak, Brass Target, Escape From Alcatraz, Scanners, Kings and Desperate Men, Finding Katie, Baby: Secret of the Lost Legend, Braveheart, The Phantom, A Time to Kill.
TELEVISION: Series: Danger Man (also dir. episodes), Secret Agent, The Prisoner (also creator, prod.), Rafferty. Movies/Specials: The Hard Way, Jamaica Inn, Of Pure Blood, The Man in the Iron Mask, Three Sovereigns for Sarah. Guest: Columbo (Emmy Awards: 1975, 1990; also dir. episodes).

McGOVERN, ELIZABETH
Actress. b. Evanston, IL, July 18, 1961. Family moved to Southern California when she was 10. Acted in high school in North Hollywood; performance in prod. of the Skin of Our Teeth won her agency represenation. Studied at American Conservatory Theatre, San Francisco and Juilliard Sch. of Dramatic Art. Open audition for Ordinary People resulted in her film debut. Appeared in IMAX film Wings of Courage.
THEATER: NY: To Be Young Gifted and Black (1981, debut), My Sister in This House (Theatre World, Obie Awards), Painting Churches, The Hitch-Hiker, A Map of the World, Aunt Dan and Lemon (L.A.), Two Gentlemen of Verona, A Midsummer Night's Dream (NY Shakespeare Fest.), Love Letters, Twelfth Night (Boston), Major Barbara (Alaska), Ring Aroung the Moon (D.C.), Maids of Honor, The Three Sisters, As You Like It.
PICTURES: Ordinary People (debut, 1980), Ragtime (Acad. Award nom.), Lovesick, Racing with the Moon, Once Upon a Time in America, Native Son, The Bedroom Window, She's Having a Baby, Johnny Handsome, The Handmaid's Tale, A Shock to the System, Tune in Tomorrow, King of the Hill, Me and Veronica, The Favor.
TELEVISION: Series: If Not for You. Movies: Women and Men: Stories of Seduction (The Man in the Brooks Brothers Shirt), Broken Trust. Specials: Ashenden, Tales From Hollywood, The Changeling (BBC).

McGRATH, JUDY
Executive. e. Cedar Crest Coll. President, MTV. Began at MTV as on-air promotions writer. Created Unplugged, MTV Books, MTV Online.

McGRATH, THOMAS J.
Producer, Attorney, Writer, Lecturer. b. New York, NY, Oct. 8, 1932. e. Washington Square Coll. of NYU, B.A., 1956; NYU Sch. of Law, LL.B., 1960. Served in Korea with U.S. Army, 1953-54. Has practiced law in N.Y. from 1960 to date. Became indep. prod. with Deadly Hero in 1976; Author, Carryover Basis Under The 1976 Tax Reform Act, published in 1977. Cobntributing author, Estate and Gift Tax After ERTA, 1982. Lecturer and writer: American Law Institute 1976-81; Practicing Law Institute, 1976-present. Dir., New York Philharmonic; Oloffson Corp.; East Food Development Corp. Trustee: American Austrian Foundation; Tanzania Wildlife Fund.

McGREGOR, CHARLES
Executive. b. Jersey City, NJ, April 1, 1927. e. NYU. 1958-69, co-founder, pres. and CEO, Banner Films, Inc. (World Wide TV Distribution); 1955-58, salesman and div. mgr., Flamingo Films (domestic TV Dist.); Professional mgr. ABC Music Publishing. 1951-53: Prod. and partner Telco Prods. and GM Productions (prods. of network and local shows). 1969-77: exec. v.p. in chg. of worldwide dist., WB-TV; 1977-89, pres. WB-TV Distribution. 1989, named exec. v.p., corp. projects, WB.

McGUIRE, DOROTHY
Actress. b. Omaha, NE, June 14, 1919. e. Ladywood convent, Indianapolis; Pine Manor, Wellesley, MA. Acting debut as teenager at Omaha Community Playhouse. Following summer

stock and radio work, made B'way debut in 1938 as Martha Scott's understudy in Our Town. Came to Hollywood to repeat stage role in film version of Claudia.
THEATER: Our Town, My Dear Children, Swinging the Dream, Claudia, Legend of Lovers, Winesberg Ohio, Night of the Iguana (1976), Cause Celebre, Another Part of the Forest, I Never Sang for My Father.
PICTURES: Claudia (debut, 1943), A Tree Grows in Brooklyn, The Enchanted Cottage, The Spiral Staircase, Claudia and David, Till the End of Time, Gentleman's Agreement (Acad. Award nom.), Mother Didn't Tell Me, Mister 880, Callaway Went Thataway, I Want You, Invitation, Make Haste to Live, Three Coins in the Fountain, Trial, Friendly Persuasion, Old Yeller, The Remarkable Mr. Pennypacker, This Earth Is Mine, A Summer Place, The Dark at the Top of the Stairs, Swiss Family Robinson, Susan Slade, Summer Magic, The Greatest Story Ever Told, Flight of the Doves, Jonathan Livingston Seagull (voice).
TELEVISION: Series: Little Women. Movies: She Waits, The Runaways, Little Women, The Incredible Journey of Dr. Meg Laurel, Ghost Dancing, Amos, Between the Darkness and the Dawn, Caroline? Mini-Series: Rich Man Poor Man. Specials: The Philadelphia Story, To Each His Own, Another Part of the Forest, I Never Sang for My Father. Guest: The Love Boat, The Young & the Restless, Highway to Heaven, Fantasy Island, St. Elsewhere.

McGURK, CHRIS
Executive. Pres., The Walt Disney Motion Pictures Group.

McHATTIE, STEPHEN
Actor. b. Antigonish, Nova Scotia, Canada, Feb. 3, e. Acadia U. Trained for stage at American Acad. of Dramatic Arts.
THEATER: NY: The American Dream (debut, 1968), Pictures in the Hallway, Twelfth Night, Mourning Becomes Electra, The Iceman Cometh, Alive and Well in Argentina, The Winter Dancers, Casualties, The Three Sisters, The Misanthrope, Heartbreak House, Mensch Meier, Haven, Search and Destroy.
PICTURES: Von Richthofen and Brown (debut, 1970), The People Next Door, The Ultimate Warrior, Moving Violation, Tomorrow Never Comes, Death Valley, Best Revenge, Belizaire the Cajun, Salvation!, Call Me, Sticky Fingers, Caribe, Bloodhounds on Broadway, Erik, The Dark, Geronimo: An American Legend, Beverly Hills Cop III, Art Deco Detective.
TELEVISION: Series: Highcliffe Manor, Mariah, Scene of the Crime. Mini-series: Centennial. Movies: Search for the Gods, James Dean, Look What's Happened to Rosemary's Baby, Mary and Joseph: A Story of Faith, Roughnecks, Terror on Track 9, Jonathan Stone: Threat of Innocence, Deadlocked: Escape From Zone 14, Convict Cowboy.

McKEAN, MICHAEL
Actor, Writer. b. NYC, Oct. 17, 1947. e. NYU. Featured on L.A. radio show, The Credibility Gap.
THEATRE: Accomplice (Theatre World Award).
PICTURES: 1941, Used Cars, Young Doctors in Love, This is Spinal Tap (also co-s.p., co-wrote songs), D.A.R.Y.L., Clue, Jumpin' Jack Flash, Light of Day, Planes Trains and Automobiles, Short Circuit 2, Earth Girls Are Easy, The Big Picture (also co-s.p.), Hider in the House, Flashback, Book of Love, True Identity, Memoirs of an Invisible Man, Man Trouble, Coneheads, Airheads, Radioland Murders, Across the Moon, The Brady Bunch Movie, Edie and Pen, Jack.
TELEVISION: Series: Laverne & Shirley, Grand, Sessions, Saturday Night Live, Dream On. Movies: More Than Friends, Classified Love, Murder in High Places, MacShayne: The Final Roll of the Dice. Specials: Spinal Tap Reunion, The Laverne and Shirley Reunion.

McKELLEN, SIR IAN
Actor. b. Burnley, England, May 25, 1939. e. Cambridge. C.B.E. 1979, Knighted 1991.
THEATRE: London: A Scent of Flowers (debut, 1964), Trelawny of the Wells, A Lily in Little India, The Man of Destiny, Black Comedy, Dr. Faustus, Henceforward, Bent, Uncle Vanya, Hamlet, Macbeth, Romeo & Juliet, Richard III. B'way: The Promise, Amadeus (Tony Award, 1981), Ian McKellen Acting Shakespeare, Wild Honey (also London), Richard III (Brooklyn), A Knight Out. Assoc. Dir. Nat'l Theatre. Prof. of Contemporary Theatre, Oxford Univ., 1991.
PICTURES: Alfred the Great, Thank You All Very Much, A Touch of Love, Priest of Love, The Keep, Plenty, Zina, Scandal, Last Action Hero, The Ballad of Little Jo, Six Degrees of Separation, The Shadow, Jack & Sarah, Restoration, Thin Ice, Richard III (also co-s.p.), Apt Pupil.
TELEVISION: Hamlet, David Copperfield, The Scarlet Pimpernel, Macbeth, Ian McKellen Acting Shakespeare, Every Good Boy Deserves Favor, Loving Walter, Windmills of the Gods, Macbeth, Othello, Countdown to War, And the Band Played On, Mister Shaw's Missing Millions, Tales of the City, Cold Comfort Farm, Rasputin.

McKEON, DOUG
Actor. b. Pompton Plains, NJ, June 10, 1966.
THEATRE: Dandelion Wine, Truckload, Brighton Beach Memoirs, Death of a Buick, The Big Day.

PICTURES: Uncle Joe Shannon, On Golden Pond, Night Crossing, Mischief, Turnaround, Where the Red Fern Grows Part 2, The Empty Mirror.
TELEVISION: Series: Edge of Night, Big Shamus Little Shamus, Little Niagra. Mini-Series: Centennial. Movies: Tell Me My Name, Daddy I Don't Like It Like This, The Comeback Kid, An Innocent Love, Desperate Lives, At Mother's Request, Silent Eye, Heart of a Champion: The Ray Mancini Story, Breaking Home Ties, Without Consent.

McKEON, NANCY
Actress. b. Westbury, NY, Apr. 4, 1966.
PICTURE: Where the Day Takes You.
TELEVISION: Series: Stone, The Facts of Life, Can't Hurry Love. Movies: A Question of Love, The Facts of Life Goes to Paris, High School U.S.A., This Child Is Mine, Poison Ivy, Firefighter (also co-exec. prod.), The Facts of Life Down Under, Strange Voices (also co-exec. prod.), A Cry for Help: The Tracey Thurman Story, A Mother's Gift. Specials: Schoolboy Father, Scruffy (voice), Please Don't Hit Me Mom, Candid Kids (co-host).

McKERN, LEO
Actor. r.n. Reginald McKern. b. Sydney, New South Wales, Australia, Mar. 16, 1920.
THEATER: She Stoops to Conquer, Hamlet, Merry Wives of Windsor, Cat on a Hot Tin Roof, A Man for All Seasons, Boswell for the Defence, Hobson's Choice.
PICTURES: Murder in the Cathedral, All For Mary, X the Unknown, Time Without Pity, A Tale of Two Cities, The Mouse That Roared, Yesterday's Enemy, Scent of Mystery, Jazz Boat, Mr. Topaze (I Like Money), The Day the Earth Caught Fire, Lisa (The Inspector), Doctor in Distress, A Jolly Bad Fellow, King and Country, Agent 8 3/4 (Hot Enough for June), Help!, The Amorous Adventures of Moll Flanders, A Man for All Seasons, Assignment K, Decline and Fall of a Bird Watcher, The Shoes of the Fisherman, Ryan's Daughter, Massacre in Rome, The Adventure of Sherlock Holmes' Smarter Brother, The Omen, Candleshoe, Damien: Omen II, The Last Tasmanian, The Blue Lagoon, The French Lieutenant's Woman, Ladyhawke, The Chain, Traveling North (Australian Film Award), Dave and Dad on Our Selection.
TELEVISION: King Lear, Murder with Mirrors, House on Garibaldi Street, Reilly: Ace of Spies, Rumpole of the Bailey, The Master Builder, The Last Romantics, A Foreign Field, Good King Wenceslas.

McLAGLEN, ANDREW V.
Director. b. London, Eng., July 28, 1920. Son of late actor Victor McLaglen. e. U. of Virginia, 1939-40. Asst. m.p. dir., 1944-54.
PICTURES: Gun the Man Down (debut, 1956), Man in the Vault, The Abductors, Freckles, The Little Shepherd of Kingdom Come, McLintock!, Shenandoah, The Rare Breed, The Way West, Monkeys Go Home!, The Ballad of Josie, The Devil's Brigade, Bandolero, Hellfighters, The Undefeated, Chisum, Fool's Parade (also prod.), Something Big (also prod.), One More Train to Rob, Cahill: U.S. Marshal, Mitchell, The Last Hard Men, The Wild Geese, Breakthrough (Sergeant Steiner), ffolkes (North Sea Hijack), The Sea Wolves, Sahara, Return to the River Kwai, Eye of the Widow.
TELEVISION: Series: Gunsmoke, Have Gun—Will Travel, Perry Mason, Rawhide, The Lineup, The Lieutenant. Movies: Log of the Black Pearl, Stowaway to the Moon, Banjo Hackett: Roamin' Free, Murder at the World Series, Louis L'Amour's The Shadow Riders, Travis McGee, The Dirty Dozen: The Next Mission. Mini-Series: The Blue and the Gray, On Wings of Eagles.

McLERIE, ALLYN ANN
Actress. b. Grand Mere, Quebec, Canada, Dec. 1, 1926. e. Prof. childrens school. m. actor-singer George Gaynes. e. high school, N.Y. Dancer since 15 in many B'way shows.
THEATER: One Touch of Venus, On the Town, Finian's Rainbow, Where's Charley?, Miss Liberty, Time Limit, South Pacific, Night of the Iguana, Julius Caesar, West Side Story, My Fair Lady, The Beast in Me, To Dorothy a Son.
PICTURES: Words and Music (debut 1948), Where's Charley?, Desert Song, Calamity Jane, Phantom of the Rue Morgue, Battle Cry, They Shoot Horses Don't They?, Monte Walsh, The Cowboys, Jeremiah Johnson, The Magnificent Seven Ride, The Way We Were, Cinderella Liberty, All the President's Men.
TELEVISION: Series: Tony Randall Show, Punky Brewster, Days and Nights of Molly Dodd. Mini-Series: The Thorn Birds, Beulah Land. Specials: Oldest Living Graduate, The Entertainer, Return Engagement, Shadow of a Gunman. Guest: WKRP in Cincinnati, Barney Miller, St. Elsewhere, Hart to Hart, Love Boat, Dynasty.

McMAHON, ED
Performer. b. Detroit, MI, March 6, 1923. e. Boston Coll.; Catholic U. of America, B.A., 1949. U.S. Marines, 1942-53. First job on TV was as the clown on Big Top, 1950-51. First joined Johnny Carson as his sidekick on daytime quiz show Who Do You Trust? in 1958.
THEATRE: stock; B'way: Impossible Years.

PICTURES: The Incident, Slaughter's Big Rip-Off, Fun with Dick and Jane, The Last Remake of Beau Geste (cameo), Butterfly, Full Moon High, Love Affair.
TELEVISION: Series: Big Top, Who Do You Trust?, The Tonight Show (1962-92), Missing Links (emcee), Snap Judgment (emcee), The Kraft Music Hall (host, 1968), Concentration (emcee), NBC Adventure Theatre (host), Whodunnit? (emcee), Star Search (host), TV's Bloopers and Practical Jokes (host). Movies: Star Marker, The Great American Traffic Jam (Gridlock), The Kid From Left Field. Specials: Macy's Thanksgiving Day Parade (host), Jerry Lewis Labor Day Telethon (co-host).

McMAHON, JOHN J.
Executive. b. Chicago, IL, 1932. e. Northwestern U. Served with U.S. Army in Korea, beginning career on WGN-TV, Chicago; associated with ZIV-United Artists TV Productions during 1950s; joined ABC in 1958; v.p. & gen. mgr. WXYTZ-TV, Detroit, then KABC-TV, Los Angeles, 1968; v.p., ABC, 1968-72; joined NBC in 1972 as v.p., programs, west coast, NBC-TV; president, Hollywood Radio & Television Society; board member, Permanent Charities Committee. 1980, named pres. of Carson Prods. (Johnny Carson's prod. co.).
TELEVISION: If It's Tuesday It Still Must Be Belgium (exec. prod.), My Father My Son (exec. prod.).

McMARTIN, JOHN
Actor. Warsaw, IN, e. Columbia U. Off-B'way debut: Little Mary Sunshine (1959: Theatre World Award).
THEATER: The Conquering Hero, Blood Sweat and Stanley Poole, Children from Their Games, A Rainy Day in Newark, Pleasures and Palaces (Detroit), Sweet Charity (Tony nom.), Follies, The Great God Brown (Drama Desk Award), Sondheim: A Musical Tribute, Forget-Me-Not-Lane (Mark Taper Forum), The Visit, Chemin de Fer, The Rules of the Game, A Little Family Business, Passion (Mark Taper), Solomon's Child, Julius Caesar, A Little Night Music (Ahmanson), Love for Love, Happy New Year, Don Juan (Drama Desk Award, Tony nom.), Artist Descending a Staircase, Henry IV (Kennedy Ctr.), Custer (Kennedy Ctr.), Money & Friends (L.A.), Show Boat (Tony nom.).
PICTURES: A Thousand Clowns, What's So Bad About Feeling Good?, Sweet Charity, All The President's Men, Thieves, Brubaker, Blow Out, Pennies From Heaven, Dream Lover, Legal Eagles, Native Son, Who's That Girl, A Shock to the System.
TELEVISION: Series: Falcon Crest, Beauty and the Beast. Guest: Cheers, Mary Tyler Moore Show, Murder She Wrote, Magnum P.I., The Golden Girls, Empty Nest, Law and Order, others. American Playhouse Specials: Edith Wharton Story, Rules of the Game, The Greatest Man in the World, Private Contentment, The Fatal Weakness, Concealed Enemies. Movies: Ritual of Evil, Fear on Trial, The Defection of Simas Kudirka, The Last Ninja, Murrow, Day One, Roots: The Gift, Separate But Equal, Citizen Cohn.

McNAMARA, WILLIAM
Actor. b. Dallas, TX, 1965. e. Columbia U. Joined Act I theatre group at Williamstown Theatre Festival, 1986; studied acting at Lee Strasberg Institute.
PICTURES: The Beat (debut, 1988), Stealing Home, Dream a Little Dream, Stella, Texasville, Terror at the Opera, Aspen Extreme, Surviving the Game, Chasers, Storybook, Girl in the Cadillac, Copycat.
TELEVISION: Series: Island Son. Specials: Soldier Boys (Afterschool Special), Secret of the Sahara, The Edge (Indian Poker), It's Only Rock 'n' Roll (Afterschool Special). Movies: Wildflower (ACE Award nom.), Doing Time on Maple Drive, Honor Thy Mother, Sworn to Vengeance, Radio Inside, Liz: The Elizabeth Taylor Story. Pilot: The Wyatts.

McNAUGHTON, JOHN
Director. b. Chicago, IL, Jan. 13, 1950.
PICTURES: Henry: Portrait of a Serial Killer, The Borrower, Sex Drugs Rock & Roll, Mad Dog and Glory, Normal Life.

McNICHOL, KRISTY
Actress. b. Los Angeles, CA, Sept. 11, 1962. Brother is actor Jimmy McNichol. Made debut at age of 7 performing in commercials. Given regular role in Apple's Way; began appearing on such series as Love American Style and The Bionic Woman. Attracted attention of Spelling-Goldberg Productions, who cast her as Buddy Lawrence in Family series, 1976-80.
PICTURES: The End (debut, 1978), Little Darlings, The Night the Lights Went Out in Georgia, Only When I Laugh, White Dog, The Pirate Movie, Just the Way You Are, Dream Lover, You Can't Hurry Love, Two Moon Junction, The Forgotten One.
TELEVISION: Series: Apple's Way, Family (2 Emmy Awards: 1977, 1979), Empty Nest. Movies: The Love Boat II, Like Mom Like Me, Summer of My German Soldier, My Old Man, Blinded by the Light, Love Mary, Women of Valor, Children of the Bride, Mother of the Bride (also co-exec. prod.).

McRANEY, GERALD
Actor. b. Collins, MS, Aug. 19, 1948. m. actress Delta Burke. e. U. of Mississippi. Left school to become surveyor in oil fields

after which joined acting company in New Orleans. Studied acting with Jeff Corey; landed guest role on TV series, Night Gallery.
PICTURES: Night of Bloody Horror, Keep Off My Grass, The Neverending Story, American Justice.
TELEVISION: Series: Simon & Simon, Major Dad (also exec. prod.), Home of the Brave. Guest: The Incredible Hulk, The Rockford Files, The Dukes of Hazzard, Eight Is Enough, How the West Was Won, Hawaii Five-O, Barnaby Jones, Gunsmoke, Designing Women. Movies: Roots II, The Jordan Chance, Women in White, Trial of Chaplain Jenson, The Law, The Haunting Passion, A Hobo's Christmas, Where the Hell's That Gold?!!?, The People Across the Lake, Dark of the Moon, Murder By Moonlight, Blind Vengeance, Vestige of Honor, Love and Curses... and All That Jazz (also dir., co-exec. prod.), Fatal Friendship, Scattered Dreams: The Kathryn Messenger Story, Armed and Innocent, Motorcycle Gang, Deadly Vows, Someone She Knows, Not Our Son, Simon & Simon: In Trouble Again, The Stranger Beside Me, Nothing Lasts Forever. Special: Fast Forward.

McSHANE, IAN
Actor. b. Blackburn, England, Sept. 29, 1942. e. RADA. Stage work includes The House of Fred Ginger, The Easter Man, The Glass Menagerie (England). NY: The Promise. LA: Inadmissible Evidence, Betrayal.
PICTURES: The Wild and the Willing (debut, 1962), The Pleasure Girls, Gypsy Girl (Sky West and Crooked), If It's Tuesday This Must Be Belgium, The Battle of Britain, Freelance, Pussycat Pussycat I Love You, The Devil's Widow (Tam-Lin), Villain, Sitting Target, The Left Hand of Gemini, The Last of Sheila, Ransom, Journey Into Fear, The Fifth Musketeer, Yesterday's Hero, Cheaper to Keep Her, Exposed, Torchlight, Ordeal By Innocence, Too Scared to Scream.
TELEVISION: Wuthering Heights, The Pirate, Disraeli, The Letter, Marco Polo, Bare Essence, Grace Kelly, Evergreen, A.D., The Murders in the Rue Morgue, Grand Larceny, War and Remembrance, Chain Letter (pilot), The Great Escape II: the Untold Story, The Young Charlie Chaplin, Lovejoy (also II), Sauce For Goose, Dick Francis Mysteries (Blood Sport), Perry Mason: The Case of the Desperate Deception, Columbo: Rest in Peace Mrs. Columbo.

McTIERNAN, JOHN
Director. b. Albany, NY, Jan. 8, 1951. e. Juilliard (acting), SUNY/Old Westbury (filmmaking). m. prod. Donna Dubrow. First effort was film The Demon's Daughter, unreleased to date. Appeared in film Death of a Soldier.
PICTURES: Nomads (also s.p.), Predator, Die Hard, The Hunt for Red October, Medicine Man, Last Action Hero (also co-prod.), Die Hard With a Vengeance.

MEADOWS, JAYNE
Actress. b. Wu Chang, China, Sept. 27, 1924. m. performer Steve Allen. Sister of deceased actress Audrey Meadows. Parents were Episcopal missionaries. Came to U.S. in early 1930's. Studied acting with Stella Adler, Lee Strasberg, David Craig. Made B'way debut in 1941 in Spring Again.
THEATRE: NY: Spring Again, Another Love Story, Kiss Them for Me, The Gazebo, Once in a Lifetime (revival), Many Happy Returns, etc. Regional: Love Letters, Lost in Yonkers, The Fourposter, Cinderella, Tonight at 8:30, Powerful Women in History (1 woman show).
PICTURES: Undercurrent (debut, 1946), Dark Delusion, Lady in the Lake, Song of the Thin Man, Luck of the Irish, Enchantment, David and Bathsheba, The Fat Man, College Confidential, Da Capo (Finland), Norman Is That You?, City Slickers (voice), The Player, City Slickers II: The Legend of Curly's Gold (voice), Casino.
TELEVISION: Series: I've Got a Secret, The Steve Allen Show, Art Linkletter Show, Steve Allen Comedy Hour, Medical Center, Steve Allen's Laugh Back, Meeting of Minds, It's Not Easy, High Society. Movies: Now You See It Now You Don't, James Dean, Sex and the Married Woman, The Gossip Columnist, Miss All-American Beauty, The Ratings Game, Alice in Wonderland, A Masterpiece of Murder, Parent Trap Hawaiian Honeymoon. Guest: Robert Montgomery Presents, The Web, Ann Sothern Show, Love American Style, Here's Lucy, The Paper Chase, Fantasy Island, The Love Boat, St. Elsewhere, Sisters, Murder She Wrote, many others.

MEANEY, COLM
Actor. b. Ireland. Started acting as a teen, appearing at Gate Theatre in Dublin in play, The Hostage. Studied at Abbey Theatre then joined London's 7-84 Theatre Co., Half Moon Theatre Co., Belt and Braces touring co. On NY stage in Breaking the Code. Also acted with Great Lakes Fest. in Cleveland, OH, in Nicholas Nickelby.
PICTURES: The Dead, Dick Tracy, Die Hard 2, Come See the Paradise, The Commitments, The Last of the Mohicans, Under Siege, Far and Away, Into the West, The Snapper (Golden Globe nom.), The Road to Wellville, The Englishman Who Went Up a Hill But Came Down a Mountain, The Van, Last of the High Kings.
TELEVISION: Series: Star Trek: The Next Generation, Deep Space Nine. Mini-Series: Scarlett.

MEANEY, DONALD V.
Executive. b. Newark, NJ. e. Rutgers U. Sch. of Journalism. Worked as reporter for Plainfield (NJ) Courier-News, Newark Evening News. Became news director of radio station WCTC in New Brunswick, NJ; later for WNJR, Newark. Joined NBC in 1952 as news writer; two years later became nat'l TV news editor. Promoted to mgr., national news, 1960 and mrg., special news programs, 1961. Appt. dir. of news programs 1962 and gen. mgr., NBC News, 1965; v.p., news programming, NBC, 1967; v.p. news, Washington, 1974; mng. dir., affiliate & intl. liaison, 1979; sr. mng. editor, intl. liaison, 1984; retired from NBC, 1985. Now on faculty of American U. Sch. of Communications.

MEARA, ANNE
Actress, Writer. b. Brooklyn, NY Sept. 20, 1929. m. actor-writer Jerry Stiller. Son is actor-director Ben Stiller; daughter is actress Amy Stiller. e. Herbert Berghof Studio, 1953-54. Apprenticed in summer stock on Long Island and Woodstock NY, 1950-53. Acted with NY Shakespeare Fest. 1957 and 1988 (Romeo and Juliet). With husband joined St. Louis improv. theater The Compass, 1959 and Chicago's Medium Rare. They formed comedy act in 1962 appearing (34 times) on The Ed Sullivan Show and making the nightclub and comedy club circuit incl. The Village Gate, The Blue Angel, The Establishment. Formed own prod. company, writing, prod. and recording award-winning radio and TV commercials. With husband co-hosted and wrote video, So You Want to Be an Actor?
THEATER: A Month in the Country, Maedchen in Uniform, Ulysses in Nightown, The House of Blue Leaves, Spookhouse, Bosoms and Neglect, Eastern Standard, Anna Christie (Tony nom.), After-Play (also author).
PICTURES: The Out-of-Towners, Lovers and Other Strangers, Nasty Habits, The Boys From Brazil, Fame, The Perils of P.K., The Longshot, My Little Girl, Awakenings, Highway to Hell, Reality Bites, Heavyweights, Kiss of Death, An Open Window, The Daytrippers.
TELEVISION: Guest on numerous TV game and talk shows and variety shows. Series: The Greatest Gift (1954 soap opera), The Paul Lynde Show, The Corner Bar, Take Five with Stiller and Meara (1977-78; synd.), Kate McShane, Rhoda, Archie Bunker's Place, ALF (also writer), All My Children. Movies: Kate McShane (pilot), The Other Woman. Specials: The Sunset Gang, Avenue Z Afternoon.

MECHANIC, BILL
Executive. b. Detroit, MI. e. Michigan State U., B.A.; U. of Southern California, Ph.D. in film pending. Entered industry 1978 as dir. of programming for SelecTV; promoted to v.p., 1980. Joined Paramount 1982; 1984, to Disney as v.p., pay TV sls. 1985, named sr. v.p., video, of new Walt Disney video div.; 1987, named president, int'l theatrical distribution and worldwide video, Walt Disney. Became pres. 20th Century Fox, 1993.

MEDAK, PETER
Director. b. Budapest, Hungary, Dec. 23, 1940. Appeared in film Beverly Hills Cop III.
THEATRE: Miss Julie. Operas: Salome, La Voix Humaine, Rigoletto.
PICTURES: Negatives, A Day in the Death of Joe Egg, The Ruling Class, Ghost in the Noonday Sun, The Odd Job, The Changeling, Zorro the Gay Blade, The Men's Club, The Krays, Let Him Have It, Romeo Is Bleeding, Pontiac Moon.
TELEVISION: Third Girl from the Left, The Babysitter, The Dark Secret of Black Bayou, Mistress of Paradise, Cry for the Stranger, Faerie Tale Theatre, Twilight Zone, Nabokov, Crime Story, Mount Royal, La Voix Humaine, Tales From the Crypt, Homicide, The Kindred, Falls Road.

MEDAVOY, MIKE
Executive. b. Shanghai, China, Jan. 21, 1941. Lived in China until 1947 when family moved to Chile. Came to U.S. in 1957. e. UCLA, grad. 1963 with honors in history. Started working in mail room at Universal Studios and became a casting director, then went to work for Bill Robinson as an agent trainee. Two years later joined GAC and CMA where he was a v.p. in the motion picture dept. 1971 joined IFA as v.p. in charge of motion picture dept. Represented American and foreign creative talents, incl. Jane Fonda, Donald Sutherland, Michelangelo Antonioni, Jean-Louis Trintignant, Karel Reisz, Steven Spielberg, Robert Aldrich, George Cukor, John Milius, Terry Malick, Raquel Welch, Gene Wilder and Jeanne Moreau. While at IFA was involved in packaging The Sting, Young Frankenstein, Jaws and others, before joining United Artists Corp. in 1974, as sr. v.p. in chg. of West Coast prod. While at UA, was responsible for One Flew Over the Cuckoo's Nest, Annie Hall and Rocky among others. 1978 named exec. v.p., Orion Pictures Co. where he was responsible for Platoon, Amadeus, Dances With Wolves and Silence of the Lambs. (In 1982 Orion team took over Filmways, Inc.). 1990, appointed chairman Tri-Star Pictures, & member Columbia Pictures Board of Directors. Resigned in 1994. Became chmn. and CEO of Phoenix Pictures in 1995. Co-chmn., St. Petersburg Film Festival, 1994. Chmn. of the Jury, Tokyo Film Festival, 1994. Member of Filmex board; board of trustees, UCLA

Foundation; advisory board, College for Intl. Strategic Affairs at UCLA; steering committee of Royce 270, UCLA; visiting committee, Boston Museum of Fine Arts; advisory bd., Tel Aviv U.; bd., Museum of Science & Industry; Co-Chmn.: Olympic Sports Federation, Music Center Unified Fund Campaign; bd. of governors, Sundance Inst.

MEDOFF, MARK
Writer. e. U. of Miami, Stanford U. Honorary doctor of humane letters, Gallaudet Univ. Prof. & dramatist in residence, New Mexico St. Univ. Novel: Dreams of Long Lasting.
THEATER: When You Comin' Back Red Ryder? (Obie Award), Children of a Lesser God (Tony Award), The Wager, Kringle's Window.
PICTURES: Off Beat, Children of a Lesser God, Clara's Heart, City of Joy, Homage (also prod.).
TELEVISION: Movie: Apology.

MEDWIN, MICHAEL
Actor, Writer, Producer. b. London, England, 1923. e. Institut Fischer, Switzerland. Stage debut 1940; m.p. acting debut in Root of All Evil, 1946. Acted with National Theatre 1977-78.
THEATRE: Spring and Port Wine, Joe Egg, Forget-me-not Lane, Chez Nous, Alpha Beta, Another Country, Crystal Clear, Interpreters, Orpheus, Noises Off.
PICTURES: Actor: My Sister and I, Mrs. Christopher, Gay One, Children of Chance, Operation Diamond, Black Memory, Just William's Luck, Ideal Husband, Picadilly Incident, Night Beat, Courtney's of Curzon Street, Call of the Blood, Anna Karenina, William Comes to Town, Woman Hater, Look Before You Love, Forbidden, For Them That Trespass, Queen of Spades, Trottie True, Boys in Brown, Trio, Long Dark Hall, Curtain Up, Street Corner (Both Sides of the Law), I Only Asked, Carry on Nurse, Wind Cannot Read, Heart of a Man, Crooks Anonymous, It's All Happening, Night Must Fall, I've Gotta Horse, 24 Hours To Kill, Scrooge, The Jigsaw Man. Prod.: Charlie Bubbles, If..., Spring and Port Wine, O Lucky Man! Gumshoe, Law and Disorder, Memoirs of a Survivor, Diamond's Edge.
TELEVISION: Granada's Army Game, Shoestring, The Love of Mike, Three Live Wires.

MELCHIOR, IB
Director, Writer. b. Copenhagen, Denmark, Sept. 17, 1917. Son of late singer Lauritz Melchior. e. Coll., Stenhus, Denmark, 1936; U. of Copenhagen, 1937. Actor. stage mgr., English Players, 1937-38; co-dir. 1938; actor in 21 stage prod. in Europe and U.S. on radio; set designer; stage man. dept., Radio City Music Hall, 1941-42; U.S. Military Intelligence, 1942-45; writer, dir., m.p. shorts for TV, 1947-48; TV actor, 1949-50; assoc. dir., CBS-TV, 1950; assoc. prod., G-L Enterprises, 1952-53; dir., Perry Como Show, 1951-54; dir. March of Medicine, 1955-56. Documentary writ. & prod., received Top Award by Nat'l. Comm. for Films for Safety, 1960. Golden Scroll Award, Acad. of Science Fiction, Best Writing, 1976; Hamlet Award, Shakespeare Society of America, excellence in playwriting, Hour of Vengeance, 1982.
AUTHOR: Order of Battle, Sleeper Agent, The Haigerloch Project, The Watchdogs of Abaddon, The Marcus Device, The Tombstone Cipher, Eva, V-3, Code Name: Grand Guignol, Steps & Stairways, Quest, Order of Battle: Hitler's Werewolves, Case by Case.
PICTURES: Writer: When Hell Broke Loose, Live Fast—Die Young, The Angry Red Planet (also dir.), The Case of Patty Smith (assoc. prod.), Reptilicus, Journey to the Seventh Planet, Robinson Crusoe on Mars, The Time Travellers (also dir.), Ambush Bay, Planet of the Vampires, Death Race 2000.

MELEDANDRI, CHRIS
Executive. Pres., Fox Family Films.

MELNICK, DANIEL
Executive. b. New York, NY, April 21, 1934. e. NYU. 1952-54, prod. The Children's Theatre at Circle in the Sq., NY. In 1954 was (youngest) staff prod. for CBS-TV; then exec. prod., East Side West Side and N.Y.P.D. Joined ABC-TV as v.p. in chg. of programming. Partner in Talent Associates. Joined MGM as v.p. in chg. of prod.; in 1974 named sr. v.p. & worldwide head of prod.; 1977 in charge of worldwide production, Columbia Pictures; named pres., 1978. Resigned to form independent production co., IndieProd. Company.
PICTURES: Prod.: Straw Dogs, That's Entertainment (exec. prod.), That's Entertainment Part 2, All That Jazz (exec. prod.), Altered States (exec. prod.), First Family, Making Love, Unfaithfully Yours (exec. prod.), Footloose (exec. prod.), Quicksilver, Roxanne, Punchline, Mountains of the Moon, Total Recall, Air America, L.A. Story.
TELEVISION: Specials: Death of a Salesman (prod.; Emmy Award, 1967), The Ages of Man (prod.; Emmy Award, 1966). Exec. prod.: East Side/West Side, N.Y.P.D., Get Smart, Chain Letter (pilot, exec. prod.). Movie: Get Smart Again! (exec. prod.).

MELNIKER, BENJAMIN
Producer, Attorney. b. Bayonne, NJ. e. Brooklyn Coll., LL.B., Fordham Law Sch. Loew's Theatres usher; private law practice;

employed by Legal Department MGM, v.p. & gen. counsel, 1954-69; exec. v.p., 1968-70; resigned from MGM, 1971; also member MGM bd. of dirs. and mem. MGM exec. com.; adjunct assoc. prof., NY Law Sch., 1976-77; prod. & exec. prod. motion pictures, 1974-86; former m.p. chmn. Anti-Defamation League, B'nai Brith; Mem. Amer., NY State bar assns., Bar Assn. of City NY, AMPAS.
PICTURES: Mitchell, Shoot, Winter Kills, Swamp Thing, Batman (exec. prod.), The Return of the Swamp Thing (prod.), Batman Returns, Batman: Mask of the Phantasm (prod.), Batman Forever (exec. prod.), Batman & Robin (exec. prod.).
TELEVISION: Three Sovereigns for Sarah, Television's Greatest Bits, Where On Earth Is Carmen Sandiego (exec. prod., Emmy Award), Little Orphan Annie's Very Animated Christmas (exec. prod.), Swamp Thing (exec. prod.), Harmful Intent (exec. prod.), Fish Police (exec. prod.), Dinosaucers (exec. prod.).

MELVIN, MURRAY
Actor. b. London, England, 1932. On stage with Theatre Workshop.
PICTURES: The Criminal (debut, 1960), A Taste of Honey, HMS Defiant (Damn the Defiant), Sparrows Can't Sing, The Ceremony, Alfie, Kaleidoscope, Smashing Time, The Fixer, Start the Revolution Without Me, A Day in the Death of Joe Egg, The Devils, The Boy Friend, Ghost in the Noonday Sun, Barry Lyndon, The Bawdy Adventures of Tom Jones, Joseph Andrews, Comrades, Testimony, Little Dorrit, The Krays, Let Him Have It, Princess Caraboo.
TELEVISION: Little World of Don Camilllo, The Soldiers Tale, A Christmas Carol, This Office Life, Bulman, William Tell, Stuff of Madness, Sunday Pursuit, The Memorandum, The Stone of Montezuma, Surprises, England My England, The Village.

MENGES, CHRIS
Cinematographer, Director. b. Kington, Eng., Sept. 15, 1940.
PICTURES: Cinematographer: Kes, Gumshoe, The Empire Strikes Back (second unit), Local Hero, Comfort and Joy, The Killing Fields (Acad. Award, 1984), Marie, The Mission (Acad. Award, 1986), Singing the Blues in Red, Shy People, High Season. Director: A World Apart, Crisscross, Second Best.
TELEVISION: World in Action, Opium Warlords, Opium Trail, East 103rd Street, etc.

MENKEN, ALAN
Composer. b. New York, NY, July 22, 1949. Raised in New Rochelle, NY. e. NYU. Began composing and performing at Lehman Engel Musical Theatre Workshop at BMI, where he met future partner, lyricist Howard Ashman. With Ashman made Off-B'way debut in 1979 with score of God Bless You Mr. Rosewater. Wrote music for workshop Battle of the Giants, and music and lyrics for Manhattan Theatre Club Prod. of Real Life Funnies. With Ashman wrote 1982 Off-B'way hit Little Shop of Horrors. Other theatre credits include: The Apprenticeship of Duddy Kravitz, Diamonds, Personals, Let Freedom Sing, Weird Romance, Beauty and the Beast, A Christmas Carol. Grammy Awards: The Little Mermaid (2), Beauty and the Beast (3), Aladdin (4), Pocahontas (1).
PICTURES: Little Shop of Horrors (Acad. Award. for song Mean Green Mother From Outer Space), The Little Mermaid (2 Academy Awards: best song, Under the Sea, and music score, 1989), Rocky V (song), Beauty and the Beast (2 Academy Awards: best song, title song, and music score, 1991), Newsies, Aladdin (2 Academy Awards: for song, A Whole New World, and music score, 1992), Home Alone 2: Lost in New York (song), Life With Mikey, Pocahontas (Academy Awards for Best Score & Best Original Song), The Hunchback of Notre Dame.
TELEVISION: Special: Lincoln. Movie: Polly (song).

MERCHANT, ISMAIL
Producer, Director. b. Bombay, India, Dec. 25, 1936. e. St. Xavier's Coll., Bombay; NYU, M.A. business admin. Formed Merchant Ivory Prods., 1961 with James Ivory. First film, The Creation of Women (theatrical short, 1961, nom. for Acad. Award). Published 3 cookbooks: Ismail Merchant's Indian Cuisine, Ismail Merchant's Passionate Meals, Ismail Merchant's Florence; and book Hullabaloo in Old Jeypore: The Making of The Deceivers (1989).
PICTURES: Producer: The Householder, Shakespeare Wallah, The Guru, Bombay Talkie, Savages, Autobiography of a Princess, The Wild Party, Roseland, Hullabaloo Over Georgie and Bonnie's Pictures, The Europeans, Jane Austen in Manhattan, Quartet, Heat and Dust, The Bostonians, A Room With a View, Maurice, My Little Girl (exec. prod.), The Deceivers, Slaves of New York, The Perfect Murder (exec. prod.), Mr. and Mrs. Bridge, Ballad of the Sad Cafe, Howards End (BAFTA Award), The Remains of the Day, In Custody (dir. debut), Jefferson in Paris (also cameo), Feast of July (exec. prod.), The Proprietor.
TELEVISION: Director: Mahatma and the Mad Boy, Courtesans of Bombay.

MEREDITH, BURGESS
Actor. b. Cleveland, OH, Nov. 16, 1907. e. Amherst Coll., M.A. (hon.). m. Kaja Sundsten. Served as Capt. U.S. Army Air Corps, WWII. Stage debut, 1929, Civic Repertory Co., NY. Autobiography: So Far So Good (1994).
THEATER: Little Ol' Boy, She Loves Me Not, The Star Wagon, Winterset, High Tor, The Remarkable Mr. Pennypacker, James Joyce's Women (dir.), etc.
PICTURES: Winterset (debut, 1936), There Goes the Groom, Spring Madness, Idiot's Delight, Of Mice and Men, Castle on the Hudson, Second Chorus, San Francisco Docks, That Uncertain Feeling, Tom Dick and Harry, Street of Chance, The Story of G.I. Joe, Diary of a Chambermaid (also s.p., co-prod.), Magnificent Doll, On Our Merry Way (also prod.), Mine Own Executioner, Jigsaw, The Man on the Eiffel Tower (also dir.), The Gay Adventure, Joe Butterfly, Advise and Consent, The Cardinal, In Harm's Way, A Big Hand for the Little Lady, Madame X, Batman, Crazy Quilt (narrator), Hurry Sundown, Torture Garden, Stay Away Joe, Skidoo, Mackenna's Gold, Hard Contract, The Reivers (narrator), There Was a Crooked Man, Clay Pigeon, Such Good Friends, A Fan's Notes, The Man, Golden Needles, The Day of the Locust (Acad. Award nom.), 92 in the Shade, The Hindenburg, Burnt Offerings, Rocky (Acad. Award nom.), The Sentinel, Golden Rendezvous, The Manitou, Foul Play, Magic, The Great Bank Hoax, Rocky II, Final Assignment, When Time Ran Out, Clash of the Titans, True Confessions, The Last Chase, Rocky III, Twilight Zone: The Movie (narrator), Broken Rainbow (voice), Santa Claus, King Lear, Hot to Trot (voice), Full Moon in Blue Water, State of Grace, Rocky V, Odd Ball Hall, Grumpy Old Men, Camp Nowhere, Across the Moon, Tall Tale, Grumpier Old Men.
TELEVISION: Movies: Lock Stock and Barrel, Getting Away From It All, The Last Hurrah, Johnny We Hardly Knew Ye, Tail Gunner Joe (Emmy Award, 1977), Probe, Outrage!, Wet Gold, Night of the Hunter. Series: Mr. Novak, Batman (frequent guest), Search, Those Amazing Animals (host), Gloria. Specials: Faerie Tale Theatre (Thumbelina), From Sea to Shining Sea, The Wickedest Witch, Mastergate. Guest: G.E. Theatre, Studio One, DuPont Show of the Month, The Twilight Zone, Ben Casey, Wild Wild West, Night Gallery, Love American Style, CHiPs, In the Heat of the Night.

MERRICK, DAVID
Producer. r.n. David Margulois. b. Hong Kong, Nov. 27, 1912. e. Washington U.; St. Louis U. L.L.B.
THEATER: B'way: Fanny, The Matchmaker, Look Back in Anger, The Entertainer, Jamaica, The World of Suzie Wong, La Plume de Ma Tante, Epitaph for George Dillon, Destry Rides Again, Gypsy, Take Me Along, Irma La Douce, A Taste of Honey, Becket (Tony Award, 1961), Do Re Mi, Carnival, Sunday in New York, Ross, Subways Are For Sleeping, I Can Get It for You Wholesale, Stop the World—I Want to Get Off, Tchin Tchin, Oliver!, Luther, 110 in the Shade, Arturo Ui, Hello Dolly! (Tony Award, 1964), Oh What a Lovely War, Pickwick, The Roar of the Greasepaint—The Smell of the Crowd, Inadmissible Evidence, Cactus Flower, Marat/Sade (Tony Award, 1966), Philadelphia Here I Come, Don't Drink the Water, I Do! I Do!, How Now Dow Jones, The Happy Time, Rosencrantz and Guildenstern Are Dead (Tony Award, 1968), 40 Carats, Promises, Promises, Play It Again Sam, Child's Play, Four in a Garden, A Midsummer Night's Dream, Sugar, Out Cry, Mack and Mabel, Travesties, Very Good Eddie, Private Lives, 42nd Street (Tony Award, 1981), Oh Kay!.
PICTURES: Child's Play (debut, 1972), The Great Gatsby, Semi-Tough, Rough Cut.

MERRILL, DINA
Actress. r.n. Nedenia Hutton. b. New York, NY, Dec. 29, 1928. Fashion model, 1944-46. A co-owner and vice-chmn., RKO Pictures, m.p. and TV prod. co.
THEATER: Regional: My Sister Eileen, Major Barbara, Misalliance, Othello, Twelfth Night, Loved, Surprise. Off-B'way: Importance of Being Earnest, Smile of the Cardboard Man, Suddenly Last Summer. B'way: Angel Street, Are You Now or Have You Ever Been?, On Your Toes.
PICTURES: The Desk Set (debut, 1957), A Nice Little Bank That Should Be Robbed, Don't Give Up the Ship, Operation Petticoat, The Sundowners, Butterfield 8, Twenty Plus Two, The Young Savages, The Courtship of Eddie's Father, I'll Take Sweden, Running Wild, The Meal (Deadly Encounter), The Greatest, A Wedding, Just Tell Me What You Want, Twisted, Caddyshack II, True Colors, The Player, Open Season, The Point of Betrayal.
TELEVISION: Debut: Kate Smith Show 1956. Guest: Four Star Theatre, Playwrights `56, Climax!, Playhouse 90, Westinghouse Presents, The Investigators, Checkmate, The Rogues, Bob Hope Presents, To Tell the Truth, The Doctors, The Name of the Game, Hotel, Hawaii Five-O, Murder She Wrote, Something Wilder. Series: Hot Pursuit. Mini-Series: Roots: The Next Generations. Movies: The Sunshine Patriot, Seven in Darkness, The Lonely Profession, Mr. & Mrs. Bo Jo Jones, Family Flight, The Letters, Kingston: The Power Play, The Tenth Month, Repeat Performance, Turn Back the Clock, Fear, Brass Ring, Anne to the Infinite, Not in My Family.

MERSON, MARC
Producer. b. New York, NY, Sept. 9, 1931. e. Swarthmore Coll. Entered Navy in 1953; assigned as publicist to Admiral's Staff of Sixth Fleet Command in the Mediterranean. Upon discharge joined trade paper Show Business as feature editor. Joined CBS-TV as asst. to casting director. Left after 3 yrs. to work for Ely Landau as casting dir., packager and sometime producer of The Play of the Week on TV. Returned to CBS for 3-yr. stint doing specials and live programs. Left to organize Brownstone Productions as indep. prod. Partner with Alan Alda in Helix Productions to package and produce TV shows.
PICTURES: The Heart Is a Lonely Hunter, People Soup (short), Leadbelly, Doc Hollywood (exec. prod.).
TELEVISION: Series: Kaz, We'll Get By, Off the Rack, Jessica Novak, Waverly Wonders, Stage 67, Androcles and the Lion, Dummler and Son (pilot), The David Frost Revue (synd. series), We'll Get By. Movie: Rules of Marriage (spr. prod.).

MESSICK, DON
Actor. b. Buffalo, NY, Sept. 7, 1926. e. Nanticoke H.S., Maryland; Ramsay Street Sch. of Acting, Baltimore; American Theatre Wing, NY. Began performing as ventriloquist at age 13 in rural Maryland. Own radio show at 15 in Salisbury, MD (WBOC) for two years, writing and portraying all the characters in a one-man weekly comedy show. Worked in Hanna-Barbera cartoons since company began in 1957, voicing Ruff in their first series on NBC, 1958. Voices: Boo Boo Bear and Ranger Smith on Yogi Bear Show, Astro on The Jetsons, Scooby Doo and Scrappy Doo on Scooby Doo series, Papa Smurf and Azrael on Smurfs, Droopy on Droopy & Dripple, Dr. Benton Quest on Jonny Quest (all Hanna-Barbera Prods.); Hamton J. Pig on Tiny Toon Adventures (WB). Has done numerous national commercials.

MESTRES, RICARDO A. III
Executive. b. New York, NY, Jan. 23, 1958. e. Harvard U., A.B. 1980. Gained filmmaking experience during summers as prod. asst. on TV features. Joined Paramount Pictures as creative exec. 1981. Promoted to exec. dir. of production in 1982 and to v.p., prod. in 1984. Named v.p. of prod., Walt Disney Pictures, 1985. Promoted to sr. v.p., prod.,1986-88. Named pres. production, Touchstone Pictures, 1988-89. In 1989, became pres., Hollywood Pictures. Resigned, 1994. Co-founder Great Oaks Entertainment with John Hughes, 1995-present. Member, AMPAS.
PICTURES: Prod.: Jack, 101 Dalmatians, Flubber, Reach the Rock.

METCALF, LAURIE
Actress. b. Edwardsville, IL, June 16, 1955. e. Illinois St. Univ. One of the original members of the Steppenwolf Theatre Company. On B'way in My Thing of Love.
THEATRE: Chicago: True West, Fifth of July. NY: Balm in Gilead (Obie & Theatre World Awards). LA: Wrong Turn at Lungfish.
PICTURES: Desperately Seeking Susan (debut, 1985), Making Mr. Right, Candy Mountain, Stars and Bars, Miles From Home, Uncle Buck, Internal Affairs, Pacific Heights, JFK, Mistress, A Dangerous Woman, Blink, Leaving Las Vegas, Dear God.
TELEVISION: Series: Roseanne (3 Emmy Awards: 1992-4). Movie: The Execution of Raymond Graham.

METZLER, JIM
Actor. b. Oneonta, NY, June 23, 1951. e. Dartmouth Coll.
PICTURES: Four Friends, Tex, River's Edge, Hot to Trot, Sundown: The Vampire in Retreat, 976-EVIL, Old Gringo, Circuitry Man, Delusion, One False Move, Waxwork II: Lost in Time, A Weekend with Barbara und Ingrid, Gypsy Eyes, C.I.A. Trackdown, Plughead Rewired: Circuitry Man II, Children of the Corn III: Urban Harvest, Cadillac Ranch, A Gun A Car A Blonde.
TELEVISION: Series: Cutter to Houston, The Best Times. Mini-Series: North and South, North and South Book II, On Wings of Eagles. Movies: Do You Remember Love, Princess Daisy, Christmas Star, The Alamo: 13 Days to Glory, The Little Match Girl, Murder By Night, Crash: The Mystery of Flight 1501, Love Kills, French Silk, The Gulf.

MEYER, BARRY M.
Executive. b. New York, NY, Nov. 28, 1943. With ABC-TV in legal and business affairs depts. before joining Warner Bros. TV in 1971 as dir. of business affairs. 1972, named v.p. of business affairs for Warner TV arm; promoted to exec. v.p. of div. 1978. 1984, named exec. v.p. of Warner Bros., Inc. 1994, named COO.

MEYER, NICHOLAS
Director, Writer. b. New York, NY, Dec. 24, 1945. e. U. of Iowa. Was unit publicist for Love Story, 1969. Story ed. Warner Bros. 1970-71.
AUTHOR: The Love Story Story, The Seven Percent Solution, Target Practice, The West End Horror, Black Orchid, Confession of a Homing Pigeon, The Canary Trainer.

PICTURES: The Seven Percent Solution (s.p.), Time After Time (s.p., dir.), Star Trek II: The Wrath of Khan (dir.), Volunteers (dir.), The Deceivers (dir.), Company Business (dir., s.p.) Star Trek VI: The Undiscovered Country (dir., co-s.p.), Sommersby (co-s.p.).
TELEVISION: Movies: Judge Dee (writer), The Night That Panicked America (writer), The Day After (dir.).

MEYER, RON
Executive. b. 1945. Served in US Marine Corps. 1985, co-founded, with Mike Ovitz, Creative Artists talent agency, eventually serving as pres. 1995, appointed pres. & COO of MCA.

MEYER, RUSS
Producer, Director. b. Oakland, CA, March 21, 1922. In 1942 joined Army Signal Corps, learned m.p. photography and shot combat newsreels. Worked as photographer for Playboy Magazine. Pres., RM Films Intl. Inc. 3 vol. autobiography: A Clean Breast: The Life and Loves of Russ Meyer.
PICTURES: The Immoral Mr. Teas, Eve and the Handyman, Erotica, Wild Gals of the Naked West, Heavenly Bodies, Lorna, Motor Psycho, Fanny Hill, Mudhoney, Mondo Topless, Faster Pussycat Kill Kill, Finders Keepers Lovers Weepers, Goodmorning and Goodbye, Common Law Cabin, Vixen, Cherry Harry & Raquel, Beyond the Valley of the Dolls, The Seven Minutes, Black Snake, Supervixens, Up, Beneath the Valley of the Ultra Vixens, Amazon Women on the Moon (actor).

MEYERS, NANCY
Writer, Producer. b. Philadelphia, PA. e. American U., D.C. Began as story editor for Ray Stark. First teamed with Charles Shyer to write screenplay for Private Benjamin.
PICTURES: Writer/Producer. Private Benjamin (Acad. Award nom., Writers Guild Annual Award), Irreconcilable Differences, Baby Boom, Father of the Bride, I Love Trouble, Father of the Bride II.

MEYERS, ROBERT
Executive. b. Mount Vernon, NY, Oct. 3, 1934. e. NYU. Entered m.p. industry as exec. trainee in domestic div. of Columbia Pictures, 1956; sales and adv. 1956-60; transferred to sales dept. Columbia Pictures Int'l, NY: posts there included supervisor of int'l roadshows and exec. assistant. to continental mgr. Joined National General Pictures as v.p.-foreign sales, 1969. Created JAD Films International Inc. in Feb. 1974 for independent selling and packaging of films around the world. September, 1977, joined Lorimar Productions Inc. as sr. v.p. of Lorimar Distribution Intl. Became pres. in 1978. Joined Filmways Pictures in 1980, named pres. & COO. Pres. of American Film Mktg. Assn.; 1982, formed new co., R.M. Films International. Rejoined Lorimar 1985. as pres., Lorimar Motion Pictures, int'l distribution. 1988-92, pres., Orion Pictures Int'l. 1993-94, pres., Odyssey Entertainment. In 1995, joined Village Roadshow International as pres.

MICHAELS, JOEL B.
Producer. b. Buffalo, NY, Oct. 24, 1938. Studied acting with Stella Adler. Many co-prods. with Garth Drabinsky, Cineplex Corp. Pres. of Cineplex Odeon, 1986-90.
PICTURES: The Peace Killers, Your Three Minutes Are Up (prod. spvr.), Student Teachers (prod. spvr.), The Prisoners (assoc. prod.), Lepke (assoc. prod.), The Four Deuces (asso. prod.), Bittersweet Love, The Silent Partner, The Changeling, Tribute, The Amateur, Losin' It (exec. prod.), The Philadelphia Experiment, Three of Hearts (exec. prod.), Cutthroat Island (co-prod.).

MICHAELS, LORNE
Writer, Producer. b. Toronto, Canada, Nov. 17, 1944. e. U. of Toronto, 1966. CEO, Broadway Video, since 1979. Named Broadcaster of the Year by the International Radio and Television Society, 1992.
THEATER: Gilda Radner Live From New York (prod., dir.).
PICTURES: Producer. Gilda Live (also co-s.p.), Nothing Lasts Forever, Three Amigos (also co-s.p.), Wayne's World, Coneheads, Wayne's World 2, Lassie, Tommy Boy, Stuart Saves His Family, Black Sheep.
TELEVISION: Series: Rowan and Martin's Laugh-In (writer, 1968-69), Saturday Night Live (creator, prod., writer: 1975-80, 4 Emmy Awards; 1985-), The New Show (prod.), The Kids in the Hall (series co-prod.), Late Night With Conan O'Brien (exec. prod.). Specials: Lily Tomlin Specials (writer, prod.: 1972-75, 2 Emmy Awards), Perry Como (writer, prod., 1974), Flip Wilson (writer, prod.), Beach Boys (writer, prod.), The Paul Simon Special (writer, prod., Emmy Award, 1978), The Rutles: All You Need Is Cash (writer, prod.), Steve Martin's Best Show Ever (prod.), Simon and Garfunkel: The Concert in the Park (exec. prod.), The Coneheads (exec. prod.), 1988 Emmy Awards (prod.), Coca-Cola Presents Live: The Hard Rock, On Location: Kids in the Hall (exec. prod.), The Rolling Stones: Steel Wheels Concert (exec. prod.), Paul Simon: Born at the Right Time in Central Park (exec. prod.).

MICHAELS, RICHARD
Director. b. Brooklyn, NY, Feb. 15, 1936. e. Cornell U. Script supervisor 1955-64 and associate producer before starting directing career in 1968 with Bewitched (54 episodes; also assoc. prod.).
PICTURES: How Come Nobody's On Our Side?, Blue Skies Again.
TELEVISION: Series: Love American Style, The Odd Couple, Delvecchio, Ellery Queen, Room 222. Movies: Once an Eagle (mini-series), Charlie Cobb, Having Babies II, Leave Yesterday Behind, My Husband Is Missing, ... And Your Name Is Jonah (winner, Christopher Award), Once Upon a Family, The Plutonium Incident, Scared Straight, Another Story (Scott Newman Drug Abuse Prevention Award), Homeward Bound (Banff Intl. TV Fest. Special Jury Award & Christopher Award), Berlin Tunnel 21, The Children Nobody Wanted, One Cooks, The Other Doesn't, Jessie (pilot), Silence of the Heart, Heart of a Champion: The Ray Mancini Story, Rockabye, Kay O'Brien (pilot), Leg Work (pilot), Red River (movie), Indiscreet, Love and Betrayal, Her Wicked Ways, Leona Helmsley: The Queen of Mean, Triumph of the Heart: The Ricky Bell Story, Backfield in Motion, Miss America: Behind the Crown, Father and Scout. Mini-series: Sadat, I'll Take Manhattan.

MICHEL, WERNER
Executive. e. U. of Berlin, U. of Paris, Ph.D., Sorbonne, 1931. Radio writer, dir., co-author two Broadway revues, 1938, 1940. Broadcast dir., Voice of America, 1942-46. Prod. & dir., CBS, 1946-48; asst. prog. dir., CBS, 1948-50. Prod. Ford TV Theatre, 1950-52 Prod. DuMont TV network, 1952-55. Dir. Electronicam TV-Film Prod., 1955-56. Prod. of Edge of Night, Procter and Gamble, 1956-57. V.P. & dir., TV-radio dept., Reach, McClinton Advertising, Inc., 1957-62. Consultant, TV Programming & Comm'l-Prod., N.W. Ayer & Son Inc. V.P. & dir., TV dept., SSCB Advertising, 1963. Program exec. at ABC-TV Hollywood, 1975. Sr. v.p. of creative affairs, MGM-TV, 1977. Exec. v.p., Wrather Entertainment Intl., 1979. Returned to MGM-TV as sr. v.p., creative affairs, 1980-82. COO, Guber-Peters TV, 1982-84. Sr. v.p., corporate TV dept., Kenyon & Eckhart, & NY, 1984-86. Currently sr. v.p., sr. partner of TV dept., Bozell, Inc. NY.

MICHELL, KEITH
Actor. b. Adelaide, Australia, Dec. 1, 1926. Early career as art teacher, radio actor; toured Australia with Stratford Shakespearean Co. 1952-53; Stratford Memorial Theatre 1954-55, Old Vic Theatre 1956-57. Served as Artistic Director, Chichester Festival Theatre, touring Australia.
THEATER: Irma la Douce, Art of Seduction, The First 400 Years, Robert & Elizabeth, Kain, The King's Mare, Man of La Mancha, Abelard & Heloise, Hamlet, Crucifer of Blood, On the Twentieth Century, Pete McGynty, Captain Beaky Christmas Show, On the Rocks, The Tempest, Amadeus, La Cage aux Folles, Portraits, The Bacarat Scandal, Henry VIII, Aspects of Love, Scrooge, Brazilian Blue, Caesar & Cleopatra.
PICTURES: True as a Turtle, Dangerous Exile, Gypsy and the Gentleman, The Hellfire Club, All Night Long, Seven Seas to Calais, Prudence and the Pill, House of Cards, Henry VIII and his Six Wives, Moments, The Deceivers.
TELEVISION: U.K.: Pygmalion, Act of Violence, Mayerling Affair, Wuthering Heights, The Bergonzi Hand, Ring Round The Moon, Spread of the Eagle, The Shifting Heart, Loyalties, Julius Caesar, Antony and Cleopatra, Kain, The Ideal Husband, The Six Wives of Henry VIII (series), Dear Love, Captain Beaky & His Band, Captain Beaky, Volume 2, The Gondoliers, The Pirates of Penzance, Ruddigore. U.S.: Story of the Marlboroughs, Jacob and Joseph, Story of David, The Tenth Month, The Day Christ Died, The Miracle, Murder She Wrote. Australia: Series: My Brother Tom, Captain James Cook.

MIDLER, BETTE
Actress, Singer. b. Honolulu, HI, Dec. 1, 1945. e. U. of Hawaii. Studied acting at Berghof Studios. Appeared on B'way in Fiddler on the Roof, Salvation; also in Tommy with Seattle Opera Co., 1971. Gained fame as singer-comic in nightclubs and cabarets. Has toured extensively with own stage shows: The Divine Miss M, Clams on the Half-Shell, Divine Madness, Art of Bust, Experience the Divine. Grammy Awards: The Divine Miss M, The Rose, Blueberry Pie (from In Harmony), Wind Beneath My Wings. Author: A View From a Broad, The Saga of Baby Divine. Special Tony Award, 1973.
PICTURES: Hawaii (debut, 1966), The Rose (Acad. Award nom.; 2 Golden Globe Awards), Divine Madness, Jinxed, Down and Out in Beverly Hills, Ruthless People, Outrageous Fortune, Big Business, Oliver & Company (voice), Beaches (also co-prod.), Stella, Scenes from a Mall, For the Boys (Acad. Award nom., Golden Globe Award; also co-prod.), Hocus Pocus, Get Shorty, First Wives Club.
TELEVISION: Specials: The Fabulous Bette Midler Show, Ol' Red Hair is Back (Emmy Award), Divine Madness (also co-writer), Art or Bust (also prod., co-writer), Bette Midler's Mondo Beyondo (also creator, co-writer), Mud Will Be Flung Tonight. Movie: Gypsy. Guest: Cher, The Tonight Show (Emmy Award, 1992).
RECORDINGS: The Divine Miss M, Bette Midler, Songs for the

New Depression, Live at Last, The Rose, Thighs and Whispers, Divine Madness, No Frills, Mud Will Be Flung Tonight, Beaches, Some People's Lives, For the Boys, Experience the Divine, Bette of Roses.

MIFUNE, TOSHIRO
Actor. b. Tsingtao, China, April 1, 1920. e. Japanese schools. Served five years Japanese army. Joined Toho Studio 1946.
PICTURES: Snow Trail, Drunken Angel, Eagle of Pacific, Seven Samurai, I Live in Fear, Legend of Musashi, Throne of Blood, Riksha Man, Three Treasures, Last Gunfight, I Bombed Pearl Harbor, Rose in Mud, Rashomon, Yojimbo, Animus Trujano, Kiska, Red Beard, High and Low, Judo Saga, Grand Prix, Rebellion, Tunnel to the Sun, The Lost World of Sinbad, Admiral Yamamoto, Hell in the Pacific, Under the Banner of the Samurai, Red Sun, Paper Tiger, Midway, Winter Kills, 1941, The Challenge, Inchon, The Bushido Blade, Princess from the Moon, The Death of a Master, Journey of Honor, Shadow of the Wolf, Picture Bride.
TELEVISION: US: Shogun.

MIGDEN, CHESTER L.
Executive. b. New York, NY, May 21, 1921; e. City Coll. of New York, B.A., 1941, Columbia U., J.D., 1947. Member New York Bar. Attorney for National Labor Relations Board 1947-51. Exec of Screen Actors Guild 1952-81. Nat'l exec. dir., 1973-81. Exec. dir., Assn. of Talent Agents, 1982-94.

MIKELL, GEORGE
Actor. b. Lithuania. In Australia 1950-56 acting with Old Vic Co. Ent. films 1955. TV 1957. To England 1957.
THEATER: Five Finger Exercise, Altona, The Millionairess, Love from a Stranger, Portrait of a Queen, Farewell, Judas, Flare Path.
PICTURES: The Guns of Navarone, The Password Is Courage, The Great Escape, Deadline for Diamonds, Where The Spies Are, The Spy Who Came in From the Cold, I Predoni Del Sahara (Italy), Sabina (Israel), The Double Man, Attack on the Iron Coast, Zeppelin, Young Winston, Scorpio, The Tamarind Seed, Sweeney Two, The Sea Wolves, Victory, Emerald, Kommissar Zufall (Germany).
TELEVISION: Counsel at Law, Six Eyes on a Stranger, The Mask of a Clown, Green Grows the Grass, Opportunity Taken, OSS Series, Espinage, The Danger Man, Strange Report, The Survivors, The Adventurer, Colditz, The Hanged Man, Quiller, Martin Hartwell, Flambards, Sweeney, The Secret Army, Sherlock Holmes, When the Boat Comes In, Brack Report, Bergerac, The Brief, Glass Babies (Australia), Hannay, Night of the Fox (mini-series), Secrets (Australia), Stark (Australia).

MILCHAN, ARNON
Producer. b. Israel, Dec. 6, 1944. Began producing and financing films in Israel. Also producer of stage plays including: Ipi Tombi, It's So Nice to be Civilized, and Amadeus in Paris starring Roman Polanski. Appeared in film Can She Bake a Cherry Pie?
PICTURES: Black Joy, The Medusa Touch, Dizengoff 99, The King of Comedy, Once Upon a Time in America (also actor), Brazil, Stripper (exec. prod.), Legend, Man on Fire, Who's Harry Crumb?, The War of the Roses, Big Man on Campus, Pretty Woman, Q & A, Guilty by Suspicion, JFK (exec. prod.), The Mambo Kings, Memoirs of an Invisible Man (exec. prod.), The Power of One, Under Siege, Sommersby, Falling Down (exec. prod.), Made in America, Free Willy (exec. prod.), That Night, Striking Distance, George Balanchine's The Nutcracker (exec. prod.), Six Degrees of Separation, Heaven and Earth, The Client, The New Age, Second Best, Boys on the Side, Copycat (co-prod.), Under Siege 2: Dark Territory, Free Willy 2: The Adventure Home, Heat, Bogus, Tin Cup (exec. prod.), A Time to Kill.
TELEVISION: Mini-Series: Masada. Series: John Grisham's The Client (exec. prod.)

MILES, CHRISTOPHER
Director. b. London, England, April 19, 1939. e. I.D.H.E.C., 1962. Sister is actress Sarah Miles. Studied film in Paris at the Institut des Hautes Etudes Cinematographiques.
PICTURES: The Six-Sided Triangle, Up Jumped a Swagman, The Virgin and the Gypsy, Time for Loving, The Maids (also co-s.p.), That Lucky Touch, Alternative 3 (also co-s.p.), Priest of Love (also prod.), The Marathon (also co-s.p.), Aphrodisias (also co-s.p.), Some Stones of No Value (also co-s.p.), Love In The Ancient World (also s.p.).

MILES, SARAH
Actress. b. Ingatestone, Eng., Dec. 31, 1941. e. RADA. Was married to late writer Robert Bolt. Brother is actor Christopher Miles. Appeared in short film Six-Sided Triangle.
THEATER: Dazzling, World War 2 1/2, Kelly's Eye, Vivat! Vivat Regina!
PICTURES: Term of Trial (debut, 1962), The Servant, The Ceremony, Those Magnificent Men in Their Flying Machines, I Was Happy Here (Time Lost and Time Remembered), Blow-Up,

Ryan's Daughter (Acad. Award nom.), Lady Caroline Lamb, The Man Who Loved Cat Dancing, The Hireling, Bride to Be (Pepita Jimenez), The Sailor Who Fell From Grace With the Sea, The Big Sleep, Priest of Love, Venom, Ordeal by Innocence, Steaming, Hope and Glory, White Mischief, The Silent Touch.
TELEVISION: Loving Walter (Walter and June), James Michener's Dynasty, Great Expectations, Harem, Queenie, A Ghost in Monte Carlo, Dandelion Dead, Ring Round the Moon, The Rehearsal.

MILES, SYLVIA
Actress. b. New York, NY, Sept. 9, 1934. Attended Pratt Inst., NYC. e. Washington Irving H.S., Actors Studio, Dramatic Workshop of the New School.
THEATER: Rosebloom, The Iceman Cometh, The Balcony, The Riot Act, Vieux Carre, Before Breakfast, The Night of the Iguana, Tea with Mommy and Jack, Ruthless.
PICTURES: Murder Inc. (debut, 1960), Parrish, Pie in the Sky, Violent Midnight, Terror in the City, Midnight Cowboy (Acad. Award nom.), The Last Movie, Who Killed Mary Whats'ername?, Heat, 92 in the Shade, Farewell My Lovely (Acad. Award nom.), The Great Scout and Cathouse Thursday, The Sentinel, Shalimar (Deadly Thief), Zero to Sixty, The Funhouse, Evil Under the Sun, No Big Deal, Critical Condition, Sleeping Beauty, Wall Street, Crossing Delancey, Spike of Bensonhurst, She-Devil, Denise Calls Up.
TELEVISION: Series: All My Children. Guest: Miami Vice, The Equalizer, Tonight Show, etc.

MILES, VERA
Actress. r.n. Vera Ralston. b. Boise City, OK, Aug. 23, 1929. e. public schools, Pratt and Wichita, KS.
PICTURES: Two Tickets to Broadway (debut, 1951), For Men Only, Rose Bowl Story, Charge at Feather River, So Big, Pride of the Blue Grass, Tarzan's Hidden Jungle, Wichita, The Searchers, 23 Paces to Baker Street, Autumn Leaves, Wrong Man, Beau James, Web of Evidence, FBI Story, Touch of Larceny, Five Branded Women, Psycho, Back Street, The Man Who Shot Liberty Valance, A Tiger Walks, Those Calloways, Follow Me Boys!, The Spirit Is Willing, Gentle Giant, Sergeant Ryker, Kona Coast, It Takes All Kinds, Hellfighters, Mission Batangas, The Wild Country, Molly and Lawless John, One Little Indian, The Castaway Cowboy, Twilight's Last Gleaming, Thoroughbred, Run for the Roses, Brainwaves, Psycho II, The Initiation, Into the Night.
TELEVISION: Movies: The Hanged Man, In Search of America, Cannon (pilot), Owen Marshall: Counselor at Law (pilot), A Howling in the Woods, Jigsaw, A Great American Tragedy, Baffled!, Runaway!, Live Again Die Again, Underground Man, The Strange and Deadly Occurence, NcNaughton's Daughter, Judge Horton and the Scottsboro Boys, Smash-up on Interstate 5, Fire!, And I Alone Survived, Roughnecks, Our Family Business, Rona Jaffe's Mazes and Monsters, Travis McGee, Helen Keller: The Miracle Continues, The Hijacking of the Achille Lauro. Guest: Climax, Pepsi Cola Playhouse, Schlitz Playhouse, Ford Theatre.

MILGRAM, HANK
Theatre Executive. b. Philadelphia, PA, April 20, 1926. e. U. of PA, Wharton Sch. Exec. v.p., Milgram Theatres. Variety Club Board member, past president and chairman of the board of Variety Club of Philadelphia; past Variety Club Intl. v.p.; President's council. Served for 12 yrs. as bd. member, Hahneman Univ. until 1993.

MILIUS, JOHN
Writer, Director. b. St. Louis, MO. April 11, 1944. e. Los Angeles City Coll., U. of Southern California (cinema course). While at latter, won National Student Film Festival Award. Started career as ass't. to Lawrence Gordon at AIP. Began writing screenplays, then became director with Dillinger (1973). Appeared in documentary, Hearts of Darkness.
PICTURES: The Devil's Eight (co-s.p.), Evel Knievel (co-s.p.), The Life and Times of Judge Roy Bean (s.p.), Jeremiah Johnson (co-s.p.), Deadhead Miles (actor), Dillinger (dir. debut, 1973; also s.p.), Magnum Force (co-s.p.), The Wind and the Lion (dir., s.p.), Big Wednesday (dir., co-s.p., actor), Hardcore (exec. prod.), Apocalypse Now (s.p.), 1941 (exec. prod., co-story), Used Cars (co-exec. prod.), Conan the Barbarian (dir., co-s.p.), Uncommon Valor (co-prod.), Red Dawn (dir., co-s.p.), Extreme Prejudice (story), Farewell to the King (dir., s.p.), Flight of the Intruder (dir., co-s.p), Geronimo: An American Legend (co-s.p. story), Clear and Present Danger (co-s.p.).

MILKIS, EDWARD
Producer. b. Los Angeles, CA, July 16, 1931. e. U. of Southern California. Began career as asst. editor, ABC-TV, 1952; Disney, 1954; MGM, 1957; editor, MGM, 1960-65; assoc. prod., Star Trek, 1966-69; exec. in chg. post-prod., Paramount, 1969-72; formed Miller-Milkis Prods., 1972; Miller-Milkis-Boyett, 1979. Now heads Edward K. Milkis Prods.
PICTURES: Silver Streak, Foul Play, The Best Little Whorehouse in Texas.
TELEVISION: Petrocelli, Bosom Buddies (exec. prod.), Happy Days, Laverne and Shirley, Feel the Heat.

MILLAR, STUART
Producer, Director. b. New York, NY, 1929. e. Stanford U.; Sorbonne, Paris. Ent. industry working for Motion Picture Branch, State Dept., Germany. documentaries, Army Signal Corps, Long Island, Germany; journalist, International News Service, San Francisco; assoc. prod.-dir., The Desperate Hours; assoc. prod.-dir., Friendly Persuasion.
PICTURES: Producer: The Young Stranger, Stage Struck, Birdman of Alcatraz, I Could Go On Singing, The Young Doctors, Stolen Hours, The Best Man, Paper Lion, Little Big Man, When The Legends Die (also dir.), Rooster Cogburn (dir. only), Shoot the Moon (co-exec. prod.).
TELEVISION: Producer: Isabel's Choice, Vital Signs (also dir.), Killer Instinct, Dream Breaker (also dir.), Lady in a Corner.

MILLER, ANN
Actress. r.n. Lucille Ann Collier. b. Houston, TX, Apr. 12, 1923. e. Albert Sidney Johnson H.S., Houston; Lawler Prof. Sch., Hollywood. Studied dance as child; played West Coast vaudeville theatres. Autobiography: Miller's High Life (1974), Tapping Into the Force.
THEATER: George White's Scandals, Mame, Sugar Babies.
PICTURES: Anne of Green Gables (debut, 1934), The Good Fairy, Devil on Horseback, New Faces of 1937, Life of the Party, Stage Door, Radio City Revels, Having Wonderful Time, Room Service, You Can't Take It with You, Tarnished Angel, Too Many Girls, Hit Parade of 1941, Melody Ranch, Time Out for Rhythm, Go West Young Lady, True to the Army, Priorities on Parade, Reveille with Beverly, What's Buzzin' Cousin?, Jam Session, Hey Rookie, Carolina Blues, Eadie Was a Lady, Eve Knew Her Apples, Thrill of Brazil, Easter Parade, The Kissing Bandit, On the Town, Watch the Birdie, Texas Carnival, Two Tickets to Broadway, Lovely To Look At, Small Town Girl, Kiss Me Kate, Deep in My Heart, Hit the Deck, The Opposite Sex, The Great American Pastime, Won Ton Ton the Dog Who Saved Hollywood, That's Entertainment III.
TELEVISION: Specials: Dames at Sea, Disney-MGM Special. Guest: Love American Style, The Love Boat.

MILLER, ARTHUR
Writer. b. New York, NY, Oct. 17, 1915. e. U. of Michigan. Plays include All My Sons, Death of a Salesman (Pulitzer Prize, 1949), The Crucible (Tony Award), A View from the Bridge, After the Fall, Incident at Vichy, The Price, Up From Paradise, Situation Normal, The American Clock, I Can't Remember Anything, Some Kind of Love Story, Clara, Broken Glass. Novel: Focus. Novella: Homely Girl. Autobiography: Time-bends (1987).
PICTURES: Film versions of plays: All My Sons, Death of a Salesman, The Crucible, A View From the Bridge. Original s.p.: The Misfits, Everybody Wins, The Crucible.
TELEVISION: Death of a Salesman (Emmy Award, 1967), Fame, After The Fall, Playing for Time (Emmy Award, 1981).

MILLER, BARRY
Actor. b. Los Angeles, CA, Feb. 6, 1958. New York stage debut, My Mother My Father and Me, 1980.
THEATER: Forty Deuce, The Tempest, Biloxi Blues (Tony, Theatre World, Outer Critics Circle and Drama Desk Awards, 1985), Crazy He Calls Me.
PICTURES: Lepke (debut, 1975), Saturday Night Fever, Voices, Fame, The Chosen, The Journey of Natty Gann, Peggy Sue Got Married, The Sicilian, The Last Temptation of Christ, Love at Large, The Pickle, Love Affair.
TELEVISION: Specials: The Roommate, Conspiracy: The Trial of the Chicago Eight. Series: Joe and Sons, Szysznyk, Equal Justice. Guest: The Bill Cosby Show. Movies: Brock's Last Case, Having Babies, The Death of Richie.

MILLER, CHERYL
Actress. b. Sherman Oaks, CA, Feb. 4, 1942. e. UCLA, Los Angeles Conservatory of Music.
PICTURES: Casanova Brown, Marriage is a Private Affair, Unconquered, Cheaper by the Dozen, Fourteen Hours, Mr. 880, Executive Suite, The Next Voice You Hear, The Matchmaker, Blue Denim, North by Northwest, The Parent Trap, The Monkey's Uncle, Clarence the Cross-Eyed Lion, The Initiation, Doctor Death, Mr. too Little.
TELEVISION: Series: Daktari, Bright Promise. Guest: Perry Mason, Bachelor Father, Flipper, Donna Reed, Leave It to Beaver, Farmer's Daughter, Wonderful World of Color, Moutain Man, Dobie Gillis, Bright Promise, Love American Style, Emergency, Cade's County. Movie: Gemini Man.

MILLER, DENNIS
Comedian, Actor. b. Pittsburgh, PA, Nov. 3, 1953. e. Point Park Coll., (journalism degree). Began as stand-up comic in local clubs, then moved to NY appearing at Catch a Rising Star and the Comic Strip. Back in Pittsburgh wrote essays for PM Magazine and hosted Saturday-morning series for teens, Punchline. Recording: The Off-White Album.
PICTURES: Madhouse, Disclosure, The Net, Tales From the Crypt: Bordello of Blood.

TELEVISION: *Series*: Saturday Night Live (1985-91), The Dennis Miller Show (talk), Dennis Miller Live (also writer; Emmy Award for writing, 1996). *Specials* (also exec. prod./writer): Mr. Miller Goes to Washington, Dennis Miller: Black and White, They Shoot HBO Specials Don't They?, MTV Video Awards (host, 1996), Dennis Miller: Citizen Arcane (also exec. prod./writer; Emmy Award, 1996).

MILLER, DENNIS
Executive. Exec. v.p., Sony Pictures Entertainment, Inc.

MILLER, DICK (RICHARD)
Actor, Writer. b. New York, NY, Dec. 25, 1928. e. City Coll. of New York, Columbia U. Grad. NYU. Theater Sch. of Dramatic Arts. Commercial artist, psychologist (Bellevue Mental Hygiene Clinic, Queens General Hosp. Psychiatric dept.) Served in U.S. Navy, WWII. Boxing champ, U.S. Navy. Semi-pro football. Broadway stage, radio disc jockey, The Dick Miller Show, WMCA, WOR-TV. Over 500 live shows. Did first live night talk show with Bobby Sherwood, Midnight Snack, CBS, 1950. Wrote, produced and directed radio and TV shows in NY in early 1950s. Wrote screenplays; T.N.T. Jackson, Which Way to the Front, Four Rode Out and others. Has appeared on many major TV series and was a regular on Fame (3 years) and The Flash.
PICTURES: Has appeared in over 150 features, including: Apache Woman, Oklahoma Woman, It Conquered the World, The Undead, Not of This Earth, The Gunslinger, War of the Satellites, Naked Paradise, Rock All Night, Sorority Girl, Carnival Rock, A Bucket of Blood, Little Shop of Horrors, Atlas, Capture That Capsule, Premature Burial, X—The Man With the X Ray Eyes, The Terror, Beach Ball, Ski Party, Wild Wild Winter, Wild Angels, Hell's Angels on Wheels, The Trip, St. Valentine's Day Masacre, A Time for Killing, The Dirty Dozen, Targets, The Legend of Lilah Clare, Wild Racers, Target Harry, Which Way to the Front (also co-s.p.), Night Call Nurses, The Grissom Gang, Ulzana's Raid, Executive Action, The Slams, Student Nurses, Big Bad Mama, Truck Turner, Capone, T.N.T. Jackson, The Fortune, White Line Fever, Crazy Mama, Moving Violation, Hustle, Cannonball, Vigilante Force, New York New York, Mr. Billion, Hollywood Boulevard, Grand Theft Auto, I Wanna Hold Your Hand, Piranha, Corvette Summer, Rock 'n' Roll High School, Lady in Red, Dr. Heckle and Mr. Hype, The Happy Hooker Goes Hollywood, Used Cars, The Howling, Heartbeeps, White Dog, Get Crazy, Lies, Heart Like a Wheel, All the Right Moves, Twilight Zone: The Movie, National Lampoon Goes to the Movies, Space Raiders, Swing Shift, Gremlins, The Terminator, Explorers, After Hours, Night of the Creeps, Project X, Armed Response, Chopping Mall, Amazon Women on the Moon, Innerspace, Angel III, The 'Burbs, Under the Boardwalk, Far From Home, Mob Boss, Gremlins 2: The New Batch, Unlawful Entry, Amityville 1992: It's About Time, Motorama, Matinee, Batman: Mask of the Phantasm (voice), Mona Must Die, Number One Fan, Tales From the Crypt Presents Demon Knight.

MILLER, (DR.) GEORGE
Director, Producer. b. Chinchilla, Queensland, Australia, 1945. Practiced medicine in Sydney; quit to work on films with Byron Kennedy, who became longtime partner until his death in 1983. Early work: Violence in the Cinema Part One (short: dir., s.p.), Frieze—An Underground Film (doc.: editor only), Devil in Evening Dress (doc.: dir., s.p.). First worldwide success with Mad Max.
PICTURES: Mad Max (dir., s.p.), Chain Reaction (assoc. prod.), The Road Warrior (dir., co-s.p.), Twilight Zone—The Movie (dir. segment), Mad Max Beyond Thunderdome (co-dir., prod., co-s.p.), The Witches of Eastwick (dir.), The Year My Voice Broke (exec. prod.), Dead Calm (exec. prod.), Flirting (exec. prod.), Lorenzo's Oil (dir., co-s.p., co-prod.), Babe (co-prod.).
TELEVISION: The Dismissal (mini-series; exec. prod., co-writer & dir. of first episode). Prod.: Bodyline, The Cowra Breakout. Exec. Prod.: Vietnam (mini-series), Dirtwater Dynasty, Sports Crazy.

MILLER, GEORGE
Director. b. Australia.
PICTURES: In Search of Anna (asst. dir.), The Man from Snowy River, The Aviator, The Never Ending Story II, Over the Hill, Frozen Assets, Gross Misconduct, Andre.
TELEVISION: Cash and Company, Against the Wind, The Last Outlaw, All the Rivers Run.

MILLER, JAMES R.
Executive. Began m.p. industry career in 1971 in legal dept. of United Artists (N.Y.). Left to go with Paramount Pictures in legal dept.; then moved to Columbia in 1977 as sr. counsel; later assoc. gen. counsel. In 1979, named Warner Bros. v.p., studio business affairs; 1984, v.p. in chg. world-wide business affairs; 1987, sr. v.p.; 1989, exec. v.p. business and acquisition.

MILLER, JP
Writer. b. San Antonio, TX, Dec. 18, 1919. e. Rice U., 1937-41; Yale Drama Sch., 1946-47. U.S. Navy, Lieut., 1941-46; pub. poetry, short stories. Author of novels The Race for Home, Liv, The Skook.

THEATER: Days of Wine and Roses, The People Next Door, Privacy.
PICTURES: The Rabbit Trap, (story, s.p.) Days of Wine and Roses (story, s.p.) The Young Savages (co-author, s.p.) Behold a Pale Horse (s.p.) The People Next Door (story, s.p.).
TELEVISION: Philco TV Playhouse: Hide and Seek, Old Tasslefoot, The Rabbit Trap, The Pardon-me Boy; Playhouse 90, Days of Wine and Roses, CBS Playhouse, The People Next Door (Emmy Award, 1969), The Unwanted, The Lindbergh Kidnapping Case, Helter Skelter, Gauguin the Savage, I Know My First Name is Steven (story, co-s.p.).

MILLER, JASON
Writer, Actor. b. Scranton, PA, April 22, 1939. Entered regional playwriting contest during high school in Scranton, PA and since has moved back and forth between acting and writing. Wrote Nobody Hears a Broken Dream, That Championship Season (NY Drama Critics & Tony Awards, Pulitzer Prize, 1973). Acted on stage in Juno and the Paycock, Long Day's Journey Into Night.
PICTURES: *Actor*: The Exorcist (Acad. Award nom.), The Nickel Ride, The Ninth Configuration (Twinkle Twinkle Killer Kane), Monsignor, Toy Soldiers, Light of Day, The Exorcist III, Rudy. *Director-Writer*: That Championship Season.
TELEVISION: *Movies*: A Home of Our Own, F. Scott Fitzgerald in Hollywood, Vampire, The Henderson Monster, Marilyn: The Untold Story, The Best Little Girl in the World, Deadly Care, A Mother's Courage: The Mary Thomas Story. *Mini-Series*: The Dain Curse.

MILLER, MAX B.
Executive. b. Los Angeles, Feb. 23, 1937. Father, Max Otto Miller, producer silent features and shorts. Great grandfather was Brigham Young. e. Los Angeles Valley Coll., UCLA, Sherwood Oaks Coll. Writer of articles on cinema for American Cinematographer and other publications. Owns and manages Fotos Intl., entertainment photo agency with offices in 46 countries. Recipient of Golden Globe Award in 1976 for Youthquake, documentary feature. Also director of Films International (prod., Shoot Los Angeles) and pres. of MBM Prod., Inc. Active member of Hollywood Foreign Press Assn. (from 1974-82 bd member; twice chmn.), Independent Feature Project, Acad. of TV Arts & Sciences, L.A. Int'l, Film Exhibition, Soc. of M.P. & TV Engineers, Film Forum, Amer. Cinemateque.

MILLER, PENELOPE ANN
Actress. b. Los Angeles, CA, Jan. 13, 1964. Daughter of actor-filmmaker Mark Miller and journalist-yoga instructor Bea Ammidown. e. studied acting with Herbert Berghof.
THEATER: *NY*: The People From Work (1984), Biloxi Blues (B'way and LA), Moonchildren, Our Town (Tony nom.), On the Waterfront.
PICTURES: Adventures in Babysitting (1987, debut), Biloxi Blues, Big Top Pee-Wee, Miles From Home, Dead-Bang, Downtown, The Freshman, Awakenings, Kindergarten Cop, Other People's Money, Year of the Comet, The Gun in Betty Lou's Handbag, Chaplin, Carlito's Way, The Shadow, The Relic.
TELEVISION: *Series*: The Guiding Light, As the World Turns, The Popcorn Kid. *Guest*: Tales From the Darkside, Miami Vice, St. Elsewhere, Family Ties, The Facts of Life. *Specials*: Tales From the Hollywood Hills: The Closed Set, Our Town. *Movie*: Witchhunt.

MILLER, ROBERT ELLIS
Director. b. New York, NY, July 18, 1932. e. Harvard U. Worked on Broadway and TV before feature film debut with Any Wednesday (1966).
PICTURES: Any Wednesday (debut, 1966), Sweet November, The Heart Is a Lonely Hunter, The Buttercup Chain, The Big Truck, The Girl from Petrovka, The Baltimore Bullet, Reuben Reuben, Brenda Starr, Hawks, Bed and Breakfast.
TELEVISION: The Voice of Charlie Pont, The Other Lover, Madame X, Just an Old Sweet Song, Her Life as a Man, Ishi: Last of His Tribe, Intimate Strangers, Killer Rules, Point Man (pilot), A Walton Wedding.

MILLS, DONNA
Actress. b. Chicago, IL, Dec. 11, 1945. e. U. of Illinois. Left school to pursue career in theatre, beginning as dancer with stage companies around Chicago and touring. In NY became regular on soap opera, The Secret Storm. On B'way in Don't Drink the Water.
PICTURES: The Incident (debut, 1968), Play Misty for Me.
TELEVISION: *Series*: Love Is a Many Splendored Thing, The Good Life, Knots Landing. *Guest*: Lancer, Dan August. *Movies/Mini-Series*: Haunts of the Very Rich, Rolling Man, Night of Terror, The Bait, Live Again Die Again, Who is the Black Dahlia?, Beyond the Bermuda Triangle, Look What's Happened to Rosemary's Baby, Smash-Up on Interstate 5, Fire!, Curse of the Black Widow, The Hunted Lady, Superdome, Doctors' Private Lives, Hanging by a Thread, Waikiki, Bare Essence, He's Not Your Son, Woman on the Run, Outback Bound, The Lady Forgets, Intimate Encounters (also exec. prod.), The World's Oldest Living Bridesmaid (also exec. prod.), Runaway Father

(also co-exec. prod.), False Arrest, In My Daughter's Name (also co-exec. prod.), The President's Child, Barbara Taylor Bradford's Remember, My Name Is Kate (also exec. prod.), Dangerous Intentions, Element of Truth (exec. prod.), Stepford Husbands.

MILLS, HAYLEY
Actress. b. London, Eng., April 18, 1946. Father is actor John Mills. Sister is actress Juliet Mills. e. Elmhurst Boarding Sch., Surrey, and actress Alpine Vidamanette, Switz. Made m.p. debut in Tiger Bay 1959 with father; then signed Disney contract 1960. Received special Academy Award for her role in Pollyanna.
THEATER: The Wild Duck, Peter Pan, Trelawney of the Wells, The Three Sisters, A Touch of Spring, The Importance of Being Earnest, Rebecca, The Summer Party, Hush & Hide, My Fat Friend, Tally's Folly, Dial M for Murder, The Secretary Bird, Toys in the Attic, The Kidnap Game, The King and I (Australian tour), Fallen Angels (U.K., Australia, New Zealand), Dead and Guilty.
PICTURES: Tiger Bay (debut, 1959), Pollyanna, The Parent Trap, Whistle Down the Wind, In Search of the Castaways, Summer Magic, The Chalk Garden, The Moonspinners, That Darn Cat, The Truth About Spring, Sky West and Crooked (Gypsy Girl), The Trouble With Angels, The Family Way, A Matter of Innocence (Pretty Polly), Twisted Nerve, Take a Girl Like You, Mr. Forbush and the Penguins (Cry of the Penguins), Endless Night, Deadly Strangers, Silhouettes, What Changed Charley Farthing, The Kingfisher Caper, Appointment with Death, After Midnight, A Troll in Central Park (voice).
TELEVISION: The Flame Trees of Thika (mini-series), Parent Trap (Parts II, III, IV, V), Amazing Stories, Illusion of Life, Good Morning Miss Bliss (series), Murder She Wrote, Back Home (series), Tales of the Unexpected, Deadly Strangers, Only a Scream Away, Walk of Life.

MILLS, SIR JOHN
Actor, Producer. b. Suffolk, England, February 22, 1908, m. Mary Hayley Bell. Father of actresses Hayley and Juliet Mills. Worked as clerk before becoming actor. One of top ten money-making Brit. stars in Motion Picture Herald-Fame Poll, 1945, 1947, 1949-50, 1954, 1956-58. Knighted, 1977. Recipient special award 1988, British Academy of Film and Television Arts. Autobiography: Up in the Clouds Gentlemen Please (1981).
THEATER: London: Good Companions, Great Expectations, Separate Tables, Goodbye Mr. Chips, Little Lies (also Toronto), The Petition, Pygmalion (NY), An Evening With John Mills.
PICTURES: The Midshipmaid (debut, 1932), Britannia of Billingsgate, The Ghost Camera, The River Wolves, A Political Party, The Lash, Those Were the Days, Blind Justice, Doctor's Orders, Regal Cavalcade, Born for Glory, Car of Dreams, Charing Cross Road, First Offence, Nine Days a Queen, OHMS (You're in the Army Now), The Green Cockatoo (Four Dark Hours), Goodbye Mr. Chips, Old Bill and Son, Cottage to Let, The Black Sheep of Whitehall, The Big Blockade, The Young Mr. Pitt, In Which We Serve, We Dive at Dawn, This Happy Breed, Waterloo Road, The Way to the Stars, Great Expectations, So Well Remembered, The October Man, Scott of the Antarctic, The History of Mr. Polly, The Rocking Horse Winner (also prod.), Morning Departure (Operation Disaster), Mr. Denning Drives North, The Gentle Gunman, The Long Memory, Hobson's Choice, The End of the Affair, The Colditz Story, Above Us the Waves, Escapade, It's Great to Be Young, War and Peace, Around the World in 80 Days, Baby and the Battleship, Town on Trial, Vicious Circle, I Was Monty's Double, Dunkirk, Ice Cold in Alex, Summer of the 17th Doll (Season of Passion), Tiger Bay, Tunes of Glory, The Singer Not the Song, Swiss Family Robinson, Flame in the Streets, Tiara Tahiti, The Valiant, The Chalk Garden, The Truth About Spring, Operation Crossbow (The Great Spy Mission), King Rat, The Wrong Box, Sky West and Crooked (Gypsy Girl; dir., prod. only), The Family Way, Africa—Texas Style, Chuka, Emma Hamilton, La Morte non ha Sesso (A Black Veil For Lisa), Oh! What a Lovely War, Run Wild Run Free, Ryan's Daughter (Academy Award, best supporting actor, 1970), A Black Veil for Lisa, Adam's Woman, Dulcima, Oklahoma Crude, Young Winston, Lady Caroline Lamb, The Human Factor, Trial By Combat (Dirty Knight's Work), The Devil's Advocate, The Big Sleep, Zulu Dawn, The 39 Steps, Gandhi, Sahara, Who's That Girl, When the Wind Blows (voice), Deadly Advice.
TELEVISION: Masks of Death, Murder with Mirrors, Woman of Substance, Hold the Dream, Edge of the Wind, When the Wind Blows, Around the World in 80 Days, The Lady and the Highwayman, The True Story of Spit MacPhee, A Tale of Two Cities, Ending Up, Frankenstein, The Big Freeze.

MILLS, JULIET
Actress. b. London, England, Nov. 21, 1941. m. actor Maxwell Caulfield. Father is actor John Mills. Sister is actress Hayley Mills. Made stage debut at 14 in Alice Through the Looking Glass. Also toured with Fallen Angels with sister; 1995, The Cherry Orchard, in Canada. Also in 1995, The Molière Comedies and Time of My Life.
PICTURES: So Well Remembered, The History of Mr. Polly, No My Darling Daughter, Twice Round the Daffodils, Nurse on Wheels, Carry on Jack, The Rare Breed, Oh! What a Lovely War, Avanti!, Beyond the Door, The Man With the Green Cross, Primevals.
TELEVISION: Series: Nanny and the Professor. Movies: Wings of Fire, The Challengers, Letters from Three Lovers, Alexander: The Other Side of Dawn, The Cracker Factory, Barnaby and Me (Australia), Columbo: No Time to Die, A Stranger in the Mirror. Mini-Series: QB VII (Emmy Award, 1975), Once an Eagle. Guest: Hotel, Dynasty, The Love Boat. Special: She Stoops to Conquer.

MILNER, MARTIN
Actor. b. Detroit, MI, Dec. 28, 1931. e. USC. Army 1952-54, directed 20 training films.
PICTURES: Life With Father (debut, 1947), Sands of Iwo Jima, The Halls of Montezuma, Our Very Own, Operation Pacific, I Want You, The Captive City, Battle Zone, Mr. Roberts, Pete Kelly's Blues, On the Threshold of Space, Gunfight at the O.K. Corral, Sweet Smell of Success, Marjorie Morningstar, Too Much Too Soon, Compulsion, 13 Ghosts, Valley of the Dolls.
TELEVISION: Series: The Stu Erwin Show, The Life of Riley, Route 66, Adam-12, Swiss Family Robinson. Movies: Emergency!, Runaway!, Hurricane, Swiss Family Robinson (pilot), Flood, SST—Death Flight, Black Beauty, Little Mo, Crisis in Mid-Air, The Seekers, The Ordeal of Bill Carney. Mini-Series: The Last Convertible.

MIMIEUX, YVETTE
Actress. b. Los Angeles, CA, Jan. 8, 1942. e. Vine Street Sch., Le Conte Jr. H.S., Los Angeles, Los Ninos Heroes de Chapultepec, Mexico City, Hollywood H.S., CA. Appeared with a theatrical group, Theatre Events; Concerts: Persephone, Oakland Orchestra, 1965, N.Y. Philharmonic, Lincoln Center, L.A. Philharmonic, Hollywood Bowl.
THEATER: I Am a Camera (1963), The Owl and the Pussycat.
PICTURES: Platinum High School (debut, 1960), The Time Machine, Where the Boys Are, The Four Horsemen of the Apocalypse, Light in the Piazza, The Wonderful World of the Brothers Grimm, Diamond Head, Toys in the Attic, Joy in the Morning, The Reward, Monkeys Go Home, The Caper of the Golden Bulls, Dark of the Sun, The Picasso Summer, Three in the Attic, The Delta Factor, Skyjacked, The Neptune Factor, Journey Into Fear, Jackson County Jail, The Black Hole, Mystique (Circle of Power), Lady Boss.
TELEVISION: Series: The Most Deadly Game, Berrenger's. Movies: Death Takes A Holiday, Black Noon, Hit Lady (also writer), The Legend of Valentino, Snowbeast, Ransom for Alice, Devil Dog: The Hound of Hell, Outside Chance, Disaster on the Coastliner, Forbidden Love, Night Partners, Obsessive Love (also co-prod., co-writer), Perry Mason: The Case of the Desperate Deception.

MINER, STEVE
Director. b. Chicago, IL, June 18, 1951. e. Dean Junior Col. Began career as prod. asst. on Last House on the Left (1970). Launched a NY-based editorial service, and dir., prod., edited sport, educational and indust. films.
PICTURES: Here Come the Tigers! (co-prod.), Manny's Orphans (co-prod., s.p.), Friday the 13th (assoc. prod.). Director: Friday the 13th Part 2 (also prod.), Friday the 13th Part 3, Soul Man, House, Warlock (also prod.), Wild Hearts Can't Be Broken, Forever Young, My Father the Hero, Big Bully.
TELEVISION: Series: The Wonder Years (sprv. prod., dir., DGA Award for pilot). Pilots: B-Men, Elvis, Laurie Hill, Against the Grain.

MINNELLI, LIZA
Actress, Singer. b. Los Angeles, CA, Mar. 12, 1946. p. actress-singer Judy Garland & dir. Vincente Minnelli. e. attended sch. in CA, Switzerland, and the Sorbonne. Left to tour as lead in The Diary of Anne Frank, The Fantastiks, Carnival and The Pajama Game. In concert with mother, London Palladium 1964. In concert Carnegie Hall, 1979, 1987, 1993. Film debut as child in mother's film In the Good Old Summertime (1949). Recordings incl. Liza with a Z, The Singer, Live at the Winter Garden, Tropical Nights, Live at Carnegie Hall, Liza Minnelli at Carnegie Hall, Results, Live at Radio City Music Hall, The Day After That.
THEATER: Best Foot Forward (off-B'way debut, 1963, Theatre World Award), Flora The Red Menace (Tony Award, 1965), Liza at the Winter Garden (special Tony Award, 1974), Chicago, The Act (Tony Award, 1978), Are You Now or Have You Ever Been?, The Rink (Tony nom.).
PICTURES: In the Good Old Summertime, Journey Back to Oz (voice; 1964, released in U.S. in 1974), Charlie Bubbles, The Sterile Cuckoo (Acad. Award nom.), Tell Me That You Love Me Junie Moon, Cabaret (Academy Award; also British Acad. & Golden Globe Awards, 1972), That's Entertainment!, Lucky Lady, Silent Movie, A Matter of Time, New York New York, Arthur, The Muppets Take Manhattan, That's Dancing!, Rent-a-Cop, Arthur 2 on the Rocks, Stepping Out.
TELEVISION: Specials: Judy and Liza at the London Palladium, The Dangerous Christmas of Red Riding Hood, Liza, Liza with a Z (Emmy Award, 1972). Goldie and Liza Together, Baryshnikov

on Broadway, Liza in London, Faerie Tale Theater (Princess and the Pea), A Triple Play: Sam Found Out, Frank Sammy and Liza: The Ultimate Event, Liza Minnelli Live From Radio City Music Hall. *Movies*: A Time to Live (Golden Globe Award), Parallel Lives, The West Side Waltz.

MIOU-MIOU
Actress r.n. Sylvette Herry. b. Paris, France, Feb. 22, 1950. First job as apprentice in upholstery workshop. In 1968, helped to create Montparnasse cafe-theatre, Cafe de la Gare, with comedian Coluche. Returned to stage in Marguerite Duras' La Musica, 1985.
PICTURES: La Cavale (debut, 1971), Themroc, Quelques Messieurs Trop Tranquilles, Elle Court, Elle Court La Banlieue, Les Granges Brulees, The Mad Adventures of Rabbi Jacob, Going Places, Un Genie Deux Associes une Cloche, D'Amour et D'Eau Fraiche, Victory March, F... comme Fairbanks, On Aura Tout Vu, Jonah Who Will Be 25 in the Year 2000, Dites-lui Que Je l'aime, Les Routes du Sud, Le Grand Embouteillage, Memoirs of a French Whore, Au Revoir...a Lundi, La Femme Flic (Lady Cop), Est-ce Bien Raisonnable?, La Geule du Loup, Josepha, Guy De Maupassant, Coup de Foudre (Entre Nous), Canicule, Le Vol du Sphinx, Blanche et Marie, Menage, The Revolving Doors, La Lectrice, Milou in May, La Totale, Le Bal des Casse-Pieds, Tango, Montparnasse-Pondichery, Germinal.

MIRISCH, DAVID
Executive. b. Gettysburg, PA, July 24, 1935. e. Ripon Coll. United Artists Corp., 1960-63; former exec. with Braverman-Mirisch adv. public rel. firm.

MIRISCH, MARVIN E.
Executive. b. New York, NY, March 19, 1918. e. CCNY, B.A., 1940. Print dept., contract dept., asst. booker, NY exch.; head booker, Grand National Pictures, Inc., 1936-40; officer, gen. mgr. vending concession operation 800 theatres, Midwest, Theatres Candy Co., Inc., Milwaukee, Wisc., 1941-52; exec., corporate officer in chg., indep. producer negotiations, other management functions, Allied Artists Pictures, Inc., 1953-57; chmn. of bd., CEO in chg. of all business affairs, admin. & financing, distr. liaison, The Mirisch Company, Inc., 1957 to present. Member of Board of Governors and former v.p., AMPAS. Member Motion Pictures Pioneers. Past president of AMPAS Foundation.
PICTURES: *Exec. prod.*: Dracula, Romantic Comedy.

MIRISCH, WALTER
Producer. b. New York, NY, Nov. 8, 1921. e. U. of Wisconsin, B.A., 1942; Harvard Grad. Sch. of Business Admin., 1943. In m.p. indust. with Skouras Theatres Corp., 1938-40; Oriental Theatre Corp., 1940-42. 1945 with Monogram/Allied Artists; apptd. exec. prod. Allied Artists, 1951 (spv. such films as The Big Combo, The Phoenix City Story, Invasion of the Body Snatchers, Friendly Persuasion, Love in the Afternoon); established The Mirisch Company, supervising such films as Some Like It Hot, The Horse Soldiers, The Apartment, West Side Story, Irma La Douce, The Great Escape, The Pink Panther, A Shot in the Dark, The Fortune Cookie, The Russians Are Coming the Russians Are Coming, Fiddler on the Roof; 1960-61 Pres. of Screen Prod. Guild; 1962, mem. bd. dir., MPAA; bd. Gvnrs., AMPAS, 1964, 1972; 1967, pres., Center Thea. Group of L.A.; named pres. and exec. head of prod., The Mirisch Corporation, 1969; pres., Permanent Charities Committee 1962-63; pres., AMPAS, 1973-77. Recipient: Irving Thalberg Award 1978, Jean Hersholt Humanitarian Award 1984, Honorary Doctor of Humanities, Univ. of WI 1989, UCLA Medal 1989.
PICTURES: *Producer or Exec. Producer.* Fall Guy, I Wouldn't Be in Your Shoes, Bomba on Panther Island, Bomba the Jungle Boy, Bomba and the Hidden City, County Fair, The Lost Volcano, Cavalry Scout, Elephant Stampede, Flight to Mars, The Lion Hunters, Rodeo, African Treasure, Wild Stallion, The Rose Bowl Story, Flat Top, Bomba and the Jungle Girl, Hiawatha, Safari Drums, The Maze, The Golden Idol, Killer Leopard, The Warriors, Annapolis Story, Lord of the Jungle, Wichita, The First Texan, The Oklahoman, The Tall Stranger, Fort Massacre, Man of the West, Cast a Long Shadow, Gunfight at Dodge City, The Man in the Net, The Magnificent Seven, By Love Possessed, Two for the Seesaw, Toys in the Attic, In the Heat of the Night (Academy Award for Best Picture, 1967), Sinful Davey, Some Kind of a Nut, Halls of Anger, The Hawaiians, They Call Me Mister Tibbs, The Organization, Scorpio, Mr. Majestyk, Midway, Gray Lady Down, Same Time Next Year, The Prisoner of Zenda, Dracula, Romantic Comedy.
TELEVISION: *Movies* (exec. prod.): Desperado, Return of Desperado, Desperado: Avalanche at Devil's Ridge, Desperado: The Outlaw Wars, Desperado: Badlands Justice, Troubleshooters: Trapped Beneath the Earth, Lily In Winter, A Case for Life.

MIRREN, HELEN
Actress. b. London, England, 1946.
THEATER: Troilus and Cressida, 2 Gentlemen of Verona, Hamlet, Miss Julie, Macbeth, Teeth 'n' Smiles, The Seagull, Bed Before Yesterday, Henry VI, Measure for Measure, The Duchess

of Malfi, Faith Healer, Antony and Cleopatra, Roaring Girl, Extremities, Madame Bovary, Two Way Mirror, Sex Please We're Italian!, Woman in Mind (LA), A Month in the Country (also B'way).
PICTURES: A Midsummer's Night Dream (debut, 1968), Age of Consent, Savage Messiah, O Lucky Man!, Hamlet, Caligula, Hussy, The Fiendish Plot of Dr. Fu Manchu, Excalibur, The Long Good Friday, Cal, 2010, White Nights, Heavenly Pursuits, The Mosquito Coast, Pascali's Island, When the Whales Came, The Cook The Thief His Wife and Her Lover, The Comfort of Strangers, Where Angels Fear to Tread, Dr. Bethune, The Gift, The Hawk, Prince of Jutland, The Madness of King George (Acad. Award nom.; Cannes Film Fest. Award), Losing Chase, Some Mother's Son.
TELEVISION: Miss Julie, The Applecart, The Little Minister, The Changeling, Blue Remembered Hills, As You Like It, A Midsummer Night's Dream, Mrs. Reinhart, After the Party, Cymbeline, Coming Through, Cause Celebre, Red King White Knight, Prime Suspect (BAFTA Award), Prime Suspect 2, Prime Suspect 3 (Emmy Award, 1996).

MISCHER, DON
Producer, Director. b. San Antonio, TX, March 5, 1941. e. U. of TX, B.A. 1963, M.A. 1965. Pres., Don Mischer Productions. Founded Don Mischer Productions, 1978. Recipient of 11 Emmy Awards.
TELEVISION: *Producer.* Opening and closing ceremonies of the 1996 Centennial Olympics Games, Michael Jackson's Super Bowl XXVII Halftime Show, The Kennedy Center Honors (Emmy Awards, 1981, 1987, 1994, 1996), Tony Awards (3 yrs; Emmy Awards, 1987, 1989), Carnegie Hall 100th Anniversary, Gregory Hines Tap Dance in America, Opening of EuroDisney, The Muppets Celebrate Jim Henson, AFI Salutes to Billy Wilder and Gene Kelly, Irving Berlin's 100th Birthday (Emmy Award, 1988), Baryshnikov by Tharp, Motown 25: Yesterday Today Forever (Emmy Award, 1983), Motown Returns to the Apollo (Emmy Award, 1985), Grand Reopening of Carnegie Hall specials with Goldie Hawn, Liza Minnelli, Bob Hope, Robin Williams, Pointer Sisters. Also: The Great American Dream Machine, Donohue and Kids: Project Peacock (Emmy Award, 1981), The Presidential Inaugural, 6 Barbara Walters Specials, Ain't Misbehavin', It's Garry Shandling's Show.

MITCHUM, ROBERT
Actor. b. Bridgeport, CT, Aug. 6, 1917. Joined Long Beach Players Guild; appeared in Hopalong Cassidy series with William Boyd; in Westerns 8 yrs.
PICTURES: Hoppy Serves a Writ (debut, 1943), The Leather Burners, Border Patrol, Follow the Band, Colt Comrades, The Human Comedy, We've Never Been Licked, Beyond the Last Frontier, Bar 20, Doughboys in Ireland, Corvette K-225, Aerial Gunner, The Lone Star Trail, False Colors, The Dancing Masters, Riders of the Deadline, Cry Havoc, Gung Ho, Johnny Doesn't Live Here Anymore, When Strangers Marry, The Girl Rush, Thirty Seconds Over Tokyo, Nevada, West of the Pecos, The Story of G.I. Joe (Acad. Award nom.), Undercurrent, Locket, Till the End of Time, Pursued, Desire Me, Crossfire, Out of the Past, Rachel and the Stranger, Blood on the Moon, The Red Pony, The Big Steal, Holiday Affair, Where Danger Lives, My Forbidden Past, His Kind of Woman, The Racket, Macao, One Minute to Zero, The Lusty Men, Angel Face, White Witch Doctor, Second Chance, She Couldn't Say No, River of No Return, Track of the Cat, Night of the Hunter, Not as a Stranger, Man with the Gun, Foreign Intrigue, Bandido, Heaven Knows Mr. Allison, Fire Down Below, The Enemy Below, Thunder Road (also exec. prod., story, wrote song), The Hunters, The Angry Hills, The Wonderful Country (also exec. prod.), Home from the Hill, A Terrible Beauty (Night Fighters), The Grass is Greener, The Sundowners, The Last Time I Saw Archie, Cape Fear (1962), The Longest Day, Two for the Seesaw, The List of Adrian Messenger, Rampage, Man in the Middle, What a Way to Go!, Mr. Moses, The Way West, El Dorado, Villa Rides, Anzio, Five Card Stud, Secret Ceremony, Young Billy Young, The Good Guys and the Bad Guys, Ryan's Daughter, Going Home, The Wrath of God, The Friends of Eddie Coyle, The Yakuza, Farewell My Lovely, Midway, The Last Tycoon, The Amsterdam Kill, The Big Sleep, Breakthrough, Matilda, Nightkill, Agency (Mind Games), That Championship Season, Maria's Lovers, The Ambassador, Mr. North, Scrooged, Midnight Ride, Presumed Dangerous, Cape Fear (1991), Woman of Desire, Tombstone (voice), Dead Man.
TELEVISION: *Series*: A Family for Joe, African Skies. *Mini-Series*: The Winds of War, North and South, War and Remembrance. *Movies*: One Shoe Makes It Murder, A Killer in the Family, The Hearst and Davies Affair, Reunion at Fairborough, Promises to Keep, Thompson's Last Run, Brotherhood of the Rose, Jake Spanner: Private Eye, A Family for Joe (pilot).

MOCIUK, YAR W.
Executive. b. Ukraine, Jan. 26, 1927. e. CCNY; World U.; Peoples U. of Americas, Puerto Rico. Expert in field of m.p. care and repair; holds U.S. patent for method and apparatus for

treating m.p. film. Has also been film producer and director. Founder and pres. of CM Films Service, Inc. until 1973. Now chmn. of bd. and pres. of Filmtreat International Corp. Member: M.P. & TV Engineers; Univ. Film Assn. Pres., Ukrainian Cinema Assn. of America.

MODINE, MATTHEW
Actor. b. Loma Linda, CA, March 22, 1959. Raised in Utah. Studied acting with Stella Adler. Stage work incl. Our Town, Tea and Sympathy, The Brick and the Rose.
PICTURES: Baby It's You (debut, 1983), Private School, Streamers, The Hotel New Hampshire, Mrs. Soffel, Birdy, Vision Quest, Full Metal Jacket, Orphans, Married to the Mob, La Partita (The Gamble), Gross Anatomy, Pacific Heights, Memphis Belle, Wind, Equinox, Short Cuts, The Browning Version, Bye Bye Love, Fluke, Cutthroat Island.
TELEVISION: Movies: And the Band Played On, Jacob. Specials: Amy and the Angel, Eugene O'Neill: Journey Into Greatness. Series: Texas (daytime serial).

MOFFAT, DONALD
Actor. b. Plymouth, England, Dec. 26, 1930. Studied acting Royal Academy of Dramatic Art, 1952-54. London stage debut Macbeth, 1954. With Old Vic before Broadway debut in Under Milkwood, 1957. Worked with APA-Phoenix Theatre Co. and as actor and dir. of numerous B'way and regional productions.
THEATER: The Bald Soprano, Jack, Ivanov, Much Ado About Nothing, The Tumbler, Duel of Angels, A Passage to India, The Affair, The Taming of the Shrew, The Caretaker, Man and Superman, War and Peace, You Can't Take It With You, Right You Are... If You Think You Are, School for Scandal, The Wild Duck, The Cherry Orchard, Cock-a-Doodle Dandy, Hamlet, Chemin de Fer, Father's Day, Forget-Me-Not-Lane, Terra Nova, The Kitchen, Waiting for Godot, Painting Churches, Play Memory, Passion Play, The Iceman Cometh, Uncommon Ground, Love Letters, As You Like It, The Heiress.
PICTURES: Pursuit of the Graf Spee (The Battle of the River Plate; debut, 1957), Rachel Rachel, The Trial of the Catonsville Nine, R.P.M., The Great Northfield Minnesota Raid, Showdown, The Terminal Man, Earthquake, Land of No Return (Snowman), Promises in the Dark, Health, On the Nickel, Popeye, The Thing, The Right Stuff, Alamo Bay, The Best of Times, Monster in the Closet, The Unbearable Lightness of Being, Far North, Music Box, The Bonfire of the Vanities, Class Action, Regarding Henry, Housesitter, Clear and Present Danger, Trapped in Paradise.
TELEVISION: Series: The New Land, Logan's Run. Guest: Camera Three (1958), You Can't Have Everything (U.S. Steel Hour), Murder, She Wrote, Dallas. Specials: Forget-Me-Not Lane, Tartuffe, Waiting for Godot. Movies: Devil and Miss Sarah, Call of the Wild, Eleanor and Franklin: The White House Years, Exo-Man, Mary White, Sergeant Matlovich vs. the U.S. Air Force, The Word, The Gift of Love, Strangers: The Story of a Mother and Daughter, Ebony Ivory and Jade, Mrs. R's Daughter, The Long Days of Summer, Jacqueline Bouvier Kennedy, Who Will Love My Children?, Through Naked Eyes, License to Kill, Cross of Fire, A Son's Promise, Kaleidoscope, The Great Pretender, Babe Ruth, Columbo: No Time to Die, Teamster Boss: The Jackie Presser Story, Majority Rule, Love Cheat and Steal, Is There Life Out There? Mini-Series: Tales of the City.

MOGER, STANLEY H.
Executive. b. Boston, MA, Nov. 13, 1936. e. Colby Coll., Waterville, ME, B.A., 1958. Announcer/TV personality/WVDA and WORL (Boston) 1953-54; WGHM (Skowhegan) 1955-56; WTWO-TV (Bangor) 1955; WMHB (Waterville) 1956-57; WTVL (Waterville) 1957-58; unit pub. dir., Jaguar Prods., 1958-59; US Army reserve, 1958-64, with calls to active duty in 1958-59, 1961-62. Account exec., NBC Films/California National Productions, Chicago 1959-60; asst. sales mgr., Midwest, RCA/NBC Medical Radio System, 1960; acct. exec. Hollingbery Co., Chicago, 1960-63; and NY 1963-66; acct. exec., Storer TV Sales, 1966-69; co-founded SFM, 1969. 1978, named pres., SFM Entertainment which was responsible for the revival of Walt Disney's Mickey Mouse Club, The Adventures of Rin-Tin-Tin; Mobil Showcase Network, SFM Holiday Network. Pres., SFM Entertainment, Exec. Vice Pres., SFM Media Corp. Exec. prod.: Television-Annual, 1978-79: Your New Day with Vidal Sassoon, The Origins Game, Believe You Can and You Can, Walt Disney Presents Sport Goofy (series), The World of Tomorrow, March of Time ... on the March (England), Sports Pros and Cons, Unclaimed Fortunes, Sea World Summer Night Magic, America's Dance Honors, Allen & Rossi's 25th Anniversary Special, Paris '89 Celebration, U.S. Sports Academy Awards, K-Nite Color Radio, Into the Night With Brad Garrett (ABC-TV).

MOKAE, ZAKES
Actor. b. Johanesburg, South Africa, Aug. 5, 1935. e. RADA. Came to US in 1969. Has appeared in many plays written by Athol Fugard incl. Master Harold...and the Boys, Blood Knot.
PICTURES: The Comedians, The Island, Roar, Cry Freedom, The Serpent and the Rainbow, A Dry White Season, Gross Anatomy, Dad, A Rage in Harlem, The Doctor, Body Parts, Dust Devil, Outbreak, Waterworld, Vampire in Brooklyn.

TELEVISION: Special: Master Harold... and the Boys. Movies: One in a Million: The Ron LeFlore Story, Parker Kane, Percy & Thunder, Slaughter of the Innocents, Rise & Walk: The Dennis Byrd Story.

MOLEN, GERALD R.
Producer. Unit prod. mngr. on The Postman Always Rings Twice, Tootsie, Let's Spend the Night Together, A Soldier's Story, The Color Purple. Assoc. prod. on Batteries Not Included. Co-prod. on Rain Man. Joined Amblin Entertainment to oversee prod. of feature film projects.
PICTURES: Exec. Producer: Bright Lights Big City, Days of Thunder, A Far Off Place, The Flintstones, The Little Rascals, Little Giants, Casper, To Wong Foo Thanks for Everything Julie Newmar, Twister. Producer: Hook, Jurassic Park, Schindler's List (Academy Award for Best Picture, 1993).

MOLINA, ALFRED
Actor. b. London, Eng., May 24, 1953. e. Guildhall Sch. of Music and Drama. Began acting with the National Youth Theatre. Worked as stand-up comic for street theatre group. Joined Royal Shakespeare Co., 1977.
THEATER: Frozen Assets, The Steve Biko Inquest, Dingo, Bandits, Taming of the Shrew, Happy End, Serious Money, Speed-the-Plow, Accidental Death of an Anarchist (Plays and Players' Most Promising New Actor Award), The Night of the Iguana, Molly Sweeney (off-B'way).
PICTURES: Raiders of the Lost Ark (debut, 1981), Meantime, Number One, Ladyhawke, Eleni, Water, Letter to Brezhnev, Prick Up Your Ears, Manifesto, Not Without My Daughter, Enchanted April, American Friends, The Trial, When Pigs Fly, Cabin Boy, White Fang 2: Myth of the White Wolf, Maverick, Hideaway, The Perez Family, The Steal, Species, Before and After, Dead Man, Scorpion Spring, Anna Karenina.
TELEVISION: The Losers, Anyone for Dennis, Joni Jones, Cats' Eyes, Blat, Casualty, Virtuoso, Apocolyptic Butterflies, The Accountant, Drowning in the Shallow End, El C.I.D., Ashenden, Hancock, A Polish Practice, Year in Provence, Requiem Apache, Nervous Energy.

MOLL, RICHARD
Actor. b. Pasadena, CA, Jan. 13, 1943.
PICTURES: Caveman, The Sword and the Sorcerer, Metal-storm: The Destruction of Jared-Syn, The Dungeonmaster, House, Wicked Stepmother, Think Big, Driving Me Crazy, National Lampoon's Loaded Weapon 1, Sidekicks, The Flintstones, Storybook, Galaxis, The Glass Cage, The Secret Agent Club, The Perils of Being Walter Wood.
TELEVISION: Series: Night Court. Movies: The Jericho Mile, The Archer: Fugitive from the Empire, Combat High, Dream Date, Class Cruise, Summertime Switch, The Ransom of Red Chief. Specials: Reach for the Sun, The Last Halloween, Words Up! Guest: Remington Steele, Facts of Life, Sledge Hammer, My Two Dads, Highlander, Weird Science, Married...With Children.

MONASH, PAUL
Producer, Writer. b. New York, NY, June 14, 1917. e. U. of WI, Columbia U. Was in U.S. Army Signal Corps and Merchant Marine; newspaper reporter, high school teacher, and civilian employee of U.S. gov't. in Europe. Wrote two novels: How Brave We Live, The Ambassadors. Entered industry writing TV scripts for Playhouse 90, Studio One, Theatre Guild of the Air, Climax, etc. Authored two-part teleplay which launched The Untouchables. 1958 won Emmy award for The Lonely Wizard (Schlitz Playhouse of Stars), dramatization of life of German-born electrical inventor Charles Steinmetz. Made m.p. debut as exec. prod. of Butch Cassidy and the Sundance Kid, 1969.
PICTURES: Exec. Prod.: Butch Cassidy and the Sundance Kid. Producer: Slaughterhouse-Five, The Friends of Eddie Coyle (also s.p.), The Front Page, Carrie, Big Trouble in Little China.
TELEVISION: Series: Peyton Place (exec. prod.). Movies (exec. prod.): The Trial of Chaplain Jensen, The Day the Loving Stopped, Child Bride of Short Creek, Killer Rules (writer), Stalin (writer), Kingfish: A Story of Huey P. Long (writer).

MONICELLI, MARIO
Director. b. Rome, Italy, May 15, 1915. Ent. m.p. industry in pro-duction; later co-authored, collab., comedies.
PICTURES: The Tailor's Maid (also s.p.), Big Deal on Madonna Street (also s.p.), The Great War, The Passionate Thief, Boccaccio '70 (dir. segment; cut for U.S. release), The Organizer (also s.p.), Casanova '70 (also s.p.), Girl With a Pistol, The Queens, Lady Liberty (Mortadella), Romanzo Popolare (also s.p.), My Friends, Caro Michele, Signore e Signori Buonanotte (also s.p.), The New Monsters, Hurricane Rosy, Sono Fotogencio, Lovers and Liars (Travels With Anita; also s.p.), Il Marchese del Grillo (also s.p.), Amici Miei Atto (All My Friends 2; also s.p.), Bertolo Bertoldino e Cacasenna (also s.p.), The Two Lives of Mattia Pascal (also s.p.), Let's Hope It's a Girl (also s.p.), The Rogues (also co-s.p.), The Obscure Illness (also s.p.), Looking for Paradise.

MONKHOUSE, BOB
Comedian, Writer. b. Beckenham, Kent, England, June 1, 1928. e. Dulwich Coll. Debut 1948 while serving in RAF, own radio comedy series 1949-83 (winters), own TV series, BBC 1952-56, ITV 1956-83, BBC 1983-90, ITV 1990-. Major cabaret attraction. Voted Comedian of the Year, 1987. After-Dinner Speaker of the Year, 1989.
THEATER: The Boys from Syracuse, Come Blow Your Horn; The Gulls, several West End revues.
PICTURES: Carry On Sergeant, Weekend with Lulu, Dentist in the Chair, She'll Have to Go, The Bliss of Mrs. Blossom
TELEVISION: *Series*: What's My Line?; Who Do You Trust?, Mad Movies, Quick on the Draw, Bob Monkhouse Comedy Hour, The Golden Shot, Celebrity Squares, I'm Bob He's Dickie!, Family Fortunes, Bob Monkhouse Tonight (1983-86), Bob's Full House (1984-90), Bob Says Opportunity Knocks (1987-89), $64,000 Question (1990-ongoing).

MONKS, JOHN, JR.
Writer, Actor, Producer, Director. b. Brooklyn, NY, June 25, 1910. e. Virginia Military Inst., A.B. Actor, stock, B'way, radio, m.p. U.S. Marines, 1942; commissioned Major, 1945. Co-author of Brother Rat. Wrote book A Ribbon and a Star.
PICTURES: *Writer*: Brother Rat, Brother Rat and a Baby, Strike Up the Band, The House on 92nd Street, 13 Rue Madeleine, Wild Harvest, Dial 1119, The West Point Story, People Against O'Hara, Where's Charley, So This Is Love, Knock on Any Door, No Man Is an Island.
TELEVISION: Climax (The Gioconda Smile, A Box of Chocolates), 20th Century-Fox Hour (Miracle on 34th St.), Gen. Electric Theatre: (Emily), CBS Special: High Tor, SWAT. *Creator serial*: Paradise Bay.

MONTAGNE, EDWARD J.
Producer, Director. b. Brooklyn, NY, May 20, 1912. e. Loyola U., Univ. of Notre Dame. RKO Pathe, 1942; U.S. Army, 1942-46; prod. many cos. after army. Exec. prod. of film-CBS-N.Y. Prod. & head of programming, Wm. Esty Adv. Co., 1950; Program consultant, William Esty Co.; v.p. Universal TV prod. & dir.
PICTURES: Tattooed Stranger, The Man with My Face, McHale's Navy, McHale's Navy Joins the Air Force, P.J., The Reluctant Astronaut, Angel in My Pocket.
TELEVISION: Man Against Crime, Cavalier Theatre, The Vaughn Monroe Show, The Hunter, I Spy, McHale's Navy, Phil Silvers Show. TV *Movies*: Ellery Queen: A Very Missing Person, Short Walk to Daylight, Hurricane, Terror on the 40th Floor, Francis Gary Powers, Million Dollar Ripoff, Crash of Flight 401, High Noon—Part 2.

MONTALBAN, RICARDO
Actor. b. Mexico City, Mex., Nov. 25, 1920. Appeared in Mexican pictures 1941-45. On B'way in Her Cardboard Lover with Tallulah Bankhead. Later in Jamaica, The King and I, Don Juan in Hell. Autobiography: A Life in Two Worlds (1980).
PICTURES: Fiesta (U.S. debut, 1947), On an Island With You, The Kissing Bandit, Neptune's Daughter, Battleground, Border Incident, Mystery Street, Right Cross, Two Weeks with Love, Across the Wide Missouri, Mark of the Renegade, My Man and I, Sombrero, Latin Lovers, The Saracen Blade, The Courtesans of Babylon (Queen of Babylon), Sombra Verde, A Life in the Balance, Untouched, The Son of the Sheik, Three for Jamie Dawn, Sayonara, Let No Man Write My Epitaph, The Black Buccaneer, Hemingway's Adventures of a Young Man, The Reluctant Saint, Love Is a Ball, Cheyenne Autumn, The Money Trap, Madame X, The Singing Nun, Sol Madrid, Blue, Sweet Charity, The Deserter, Escape From the Planet of the Apes, Conquest of the Planet of the Apes, The Train Robbers, Joe Panther, Won Ton Ton the Dog Who Saved Hollywood, Star Trek II: The Wrath of Khan, Cannonball Run II, The Naked Gun: From the Files of Police Squad.
TELEVISION: *Series*: Fantasy Island, The Colbys, Heaven Help Us. *Guest*: How the West Was Won Part II (Emmy Award, 1978). *Movies*: The Longest Hundred Miles, The Pigeon, Black Water Gold, The Aquarians, Sarge: The Badge or the Cross, Face of Fear, Desperate Mission, Fireball Foreward, Wonder Woman, The Mark of Zorro, McNaughton's Daughter, Fantasy Island (pilot), Captains Courageous, Return to Fantasy Island.

MONTGOMERY, GEORGE
Actor. r.n. George Montgomery Letz. b. Brady, MT, Aug. 29, 1916. e. U. of MT. Armed Services, WWII. Was champion heavyweight boxer. Debuted in films as extra, stuntman, then bit player billed as George Letz.
PICTURES: Singing Vagabond (debut, 1935), Cisco Kid and the Lady, Star Dust, Young People, Charter Pilot, Jennie, Cowboy and the Blonde, Accent on Love, Riders of the Purple Sage, Last of the Duanes, Cadet Girl, Roxie Hart, Ten Gentlemen from West Point, Orchestra Wives, China Girl, Brasher Doubloon, Three Little Girls in Blue, Lulu Belle, Belle Starr's Daughter, Girl From Manhattan, Sword of Monte Cristo, Texas Rangers, Indian Uprising, Cripple Creek, Pathfinder, Jack McCall Desperado, Fort Ti, Gun Belt, Battle of Rogue River, The Lone Gun, Masterson of Kansas, Seminole Uprising, Robbers' Roost, Too

Many Crooks, Stallion Trail, The Steel Claw, Watusi, Samar, Hallucination Generation, Hostile Guns, Ransom in Blood.
TELEVISION: *Series*: Cimarron City.

MOODY, RON
Actor. r.n. Ronald Moodnick. b. London, England, Jan. 8, 1924. e. London Sch. of Economics. *Novels*: The Devil You Don't, Very Very Slightly Imperfect, Off The Cuff, The Amazon Box.
THEATER: *London*: Intimacy at Eight (debut, 1952), For Adults Only, Candide, Oliver! (also NY revival: Theatre World Award), Joey Joey (Bristol; also writer, composer, lyricist), Peter Pan, Hamlet, The Clandestine Marriage, The Showman (also writer), Sherlock Holmes—The Musical. *Author*: Saturnalia, Move Along Sideways.
PICTURES: Davy (debut, 1958), Follow a Star, Make Mine Mink, Five Golden Hours, The Mouse on the Moon, A Pair of Briefs, Summer Holiday, Ladies Who Do, Murder Most Foul, San Ferry Ann, The Sandwich Man, Oliver! (Acad. Award nom.), The Twelve Chairs, Flight of the Doves, Dogpound Shuffle, Dominique, Unidentified Flying Oddball, Wrong Is Right, Where Is Parsifal?, A Kid in King Arthur's Court.
TELEVISION: *Series*: Nobody's Perfect, Tales of the Gold Monkey. *Mini-Series*: The Word. *Movies*: David Copperfield (theatrical in U.K.), Dial M for Murder (U.S.), The Caucasian Chalk Circle, Hideaway. *Specials*: Portrait of Petulia, Bing Crosby's Merrie Olde Christmas, Winter's Tale, Othello, Other Side of London, Baden Powell, Lights Camera Action, Last of the Summer Wine.

MOONJEAN, HANK
Producer, Director. Began as asst. dir. at MGM. Later turned to producing.
PICTURES: *Assoc. Prod.*: The Great Gatsby, WUSA, The Secret Life of An American Wife, Child's Play, Welcome to Hard Times, The Singing Nun. *Exec. Prod.*: The Fortune, The End. *Producer*: Hooper, Smokey and the Bandit II, The Incredible Shrinking Woman, Paternity, Sharky's Machine, Stroker Ace, Stealing Home, Dangerous Liaisons.

MOORE, CONSTANCE
Actress. b. Sioux City, IA, Jan. 18, 1922. Sang on radio: Lockheed program, Jurgen's Show. Screen debut 1938. TV shows, nightclubs. N.Y. Stage: The Boys from Syracuse, By Jupiter, Annie Get Your Gun, Bells Are Ringing, Affairs of State.
PICTURES: Prison Break, A Letter of Introduction, You Can't Cheat an Honest Man, I Wanted Wings, Take a Letter Darling, Show Business, Atlantic City, Delightfully Dangerous, Earl Carroll Vanities, In Old Sacramento, Hit Parade of 1947, Spree.

MOORE, DEMI
Actress. b. Roswell, NM, Nov. 11, 1962. r.n. Demi Guynes. m. actor Bruce Willis. Began modeling at age 16. *Off-B'way debut*: The Early Girl, 1987 (Theatre World Award).
PICTURES: Choices (debut, 1981), Parasite, Young Doctors in Love, Blame It on Rio, No Small Affair, St. Elmo's Fire, About Last Night, One Crazy Summer, Wisdom, The Seventh Sign, We're No Angels, Ghost, Nothing But Trouble, Mortal Thoughts (also co-prod.), The Butcher's Wife, A Few Good Men, Indecent Proposal, Disclosure, The Scarlett Letter, Now and Then (also co-prod.), The Juror, The Hunchback of Notre Dame, Striptease.
TELEVISION: *Series*: General Hospital. *Guest*: Kaz, Vega$, Moonlighting, Tales from the Crypt (Dead Right). *Specials*: Bedrooms, The New Homeowner's Guide to Happiness. *Movies*: If These Walls Could Speak.

MOORE, DICKIE
Actor. b. Los Angeles, CA, Sept. 12, 1925. m. actress Jane Powell. Began picture career when only 11 months old, playing John Barrymore as a baby in The Beloved Rogue. Appeared in numerous radio, television and stage prods. in NY and L.A. and over 100 films; appeared in several Our Gang shorts. Co-author and star, RKO short subject, The Boy and the Eagle (Acad. Award nom.). *Author*: Opportunities in Acting, Twinkle Twinkle Little Star (But Don't Have Sex or Take the Car), 1984. Now public relations executive.
PICTURES: Passion Flower, The Squaw Man, Manhattan Parade, Million Dollar Legs, Blonde Venus, So Big, Gabriel Over the White House, Oliver Twist, Cradle Song, This Side of Heaven, Upper World, Little Men, Peter Ibbetson, So Red the Rose, The Story of Louis Pasteur, The Life of Emile Zola, The Arkansas Traveler, The Under-Pup, The Blue Bird, A Dispatch From Reuters, Sergeant York, Adventures of Martin Eden, Miss Annie Rooney, Heaven Can Wait, The Happy Land, The Eve of St. Mark, Youth Runs Wild, Out of the Past, Killer Shark, 16 Fathoms Deep, Eight Iron Men, The Member of the Wedding.

MOORE, DUDLEY
Actor, Writer, Musician. b. Dagenham, Essex, Eng., April 19, 1935. e. Oxford, graduating in 1958. Toured British Isles with jazz group before joining Peter Cook, Jonathan Miller and Alan Bennett in creating hit revue, Beyond the Fringe, in U.K. and N.Y. Appeared later with Peter Cook on B'way in Good Evening. Composed film scores: Inadmissible Evidence, Staircase.

PICTURES: The Wrong Box (debut, 1966), Bedazzled (also composer), 30 is a Dangerous Age Cynthia (also co-s.p., composer), Monte Carlo or Bust (Those Daring Young Men in Their Jaunty Jalopies), The Bed Sitting Room, Alice's Adventures in Wonderland, The Hound of the Baskervilles, Foul Play, "10", Wholly Moses, Arthur (Acad. Award nom.), Six Weeks, Lovesick, Romantic Comedy, Unfaithfully Yours, Best Defense, Micki and Maude, Santa Claus, Like Father Like Son, Arthur 2 On the Rocks (also exec. prod.), The Adventures of Milo and Otis (narrator), Crazy People, Blame It on the Bellboy, The Pickle, A Weekend in the Country.
TELEVISION: Series: Dudley, Daddy's Girls. Movie: Parallel Lives.

MOORE, ELLIS
Consultant. b. New York, NY, May 12, 1924. e. Washington and Lee U., 1941-43. Newspaperman in AK, TN, 1946-52. Joined NBC 1952; mgr. of bus. pub., 1953; dir., press dept., 1954; dir., press & publicity, 1959; vice-pres., 1961; pub. rel. dept., Standard Oil Co. (N.J.), 1963-66; v.p. press relations, ABC-TV Network, 1966-68; v.p. public relations ABC-TV Network, 1968-70; v.p. public relations, ABC, 1970, v.p. public relations, ABC, Inc., 1972; v.p. corporate relations, ABC, Inc., 1979; v.p., public affairs, ABC, Inc., 1982-85. P.R. consultant, 1985. Retired, 1992.

MOORE, JULIANNE
Actress. b. 1961. e. Boston Univ. Sch. for the Arts.
THEATRE: Off-B'way: Serious Money, Ice Cream/Hot Fudge, The Road to Nirvana, Hamlet, The Father.
PICTURES: Tales From the Darkside (debut, 1990), The Hand That Rocks the Cradle, Body of Evidence, Benny & Joon, The Fugitive, Short Cuts, Vanya on 42nd Street, Roommates, Safe, Nine Months, Assassins, Surviving Picasso.
TELEVISION: Series: As the World Turns (Emmy Award). Movies: I'll Take Manhattan, The Last to Go, Cast a Deadly Spell.

MOORE, KIERON
Actor. r.n. Kieron O'Hanrahan. b. Skibereen, Co. Cork, Eire, 1925. e. St. Mary's Coll., Dublin. Stage debut, 1945 in Desert Rats; appeared in Red Roses For Me. Debuted in films under his real name.
PICTURES: The Voice Within (debut, 1945), A Man About the House (1st billing as Kieron Moore), Anna Karenina, Mine Own Executioner, Saints and Sinners, The Naked Heart, Honeymoon Deferred, Ten Tall Men, David and Bathsheba, Man Trap (Woman in Hiding), Conflict of Wings (Fuss Over Feathers), The Green Scarf, Blue Peter, Satellite in the Sky, The Steel Bayonet, Three Sundays to Live, The Key, The Angry Hills, Darby O'Gill and the Little People, The Day They Robbed the Bank of England, League of Gentlemen, The Siege of Sidney Street, Faces of Evil, Lion of Sparta, I Thank a Fool, Double Twist, The Day of the Triffids, The Thin Red Line, The Main Attraction, Crack in the World, Son of a Gunfighter, Never Love a Savage, Arabesque, Run Like a Thief, Custer of the West. Director: The Progress of Peoples, The Parched Land.

MOORE, MARY TYLER
Actress. b. Brooklyn. NY, Dec. 29, 1936. Began as professional dancer and got first break as teenager in commercials (notably the elf in Hotpoint appliance ads); then small roles in series Bachelor Father, Steve Canyon, and finally as the switchboard oper. in series Richard Diamond Private Detective (though only her legs were seen). Chairman of Bd., MTM Enterprises, Inc, which she founded with then-husband Grant Tinker.
THEATER: B'way: Breakfast at Tiffany's (debut), Whose Life Is It Anyway? (special Tony Award, 1980), Sweet Sue.
PICTURES: X-15 (debut, 1961), Thoroughly Modern Millie, Don't Just Stand There, What's So Bad About Feeling Good?, Change of Habit, Ordinary People (Acad. Award nom.), Six Weeks, Just Between Friends, Flirting With Disaster.
TELEVISION: Series: Richard Diamond—Private Detective, The Dick Van Dyke Show (2 Emmy Awards: 1964, 1966), The Mary Tyler Moore Show (1970-77; 4 Emmy Awards: 1973, 1974 (2), 1976), Mary (1978), The Mary Tyler Moore Hour (1979), Mary (1985-86), Annie McGuire, New York News. Guest: Bachelor Father, Steve Canyon, 77 Sunset Strip, Hawaiian Eye, Love American Style, Rhoda. Movies: Run a Crooked Mile, First You Cry, Heartsounds, Finnegan Begin Again, Gore Vidal's Lincoln, The Last Best Year, Thanksgiving Day, Stolen Babies (Emmy Award, 1993). Specials: Dick Van Dyke and the Other Woman, How to Survive the 70's, How to Raise a Drugfree Child.

MOORE, MICHAEL
Director, Writer. b. Davison, MI, 1954. e. Univ. of MI. Was editor of The Michigan Voice and Mother Jones magazine, commentator on radio show All Things Considered, before gaining fame with first film Roger & Me. Established Center for Alternative Media to support indept. filmmakers.
PICTURES: Dir./Prod./Writer/Actor: Roger & Me (debut, 1989), Canadian Bacon.
TELEVISION: Series: TV Nation (dir., exec. prod., writer, host). Special: Pets and Meat: The Return to Flint.

MOORE, ROGER
Actor. b. London, England, Oct. 14, 1927. e. art school, London; Royal Acad. of Dramatic Art. Had bit parts in British films Vacation From Marriage, Caesar and Cleopatra, Piccadilly Incident, Gay Lady. Appointed Special Ambassador for UNICEF, 1991.
THEATER: Mr. Roberts, I Capture the Castle, Little Hut, others. B'way: A Pin to See the Peepshow.
PICTURES: The Last Time I Saw Paris, Interrupted Melody, The King's Thief, Diane, The Miracle, Gold of the Seven Saints, The Sins of Rachel Cade, Rape of the Sabines, Crossplot, The Man Who Haunted Himself, Live and Let Die, Gold, The Man With the Golden Gun, That Lucky Touch, Street People, Shout at the Devil, The Spy Who Loved Me, The Wild Geese, Escape To Athena, Moonraker, ffolkes (North Sea Hijack), The Sea Wolves, Sunday Lovers, For Your Eyes Only, The Cannonball Run, Octopussy, The Curse of the Pink Panther, The Naked Face, A View to a Kill, The Magic Snowman (voice), Fire Ice and Dynamite, Bed and Breakfast, Bullseye!, The Quest.
TELEVISION: Series: The Alaskans, Maverick, The Saint, The Persuaders. Movies: Sherlock Holmes in New York, The Man Who Wouldn't Die (also co-exec. prod.).

MOORE, TERRY
Actress. r.n. Helen Koford. b. Los Angeles, CA, Jan. 7, 1929. Mother was Luella Bickmore, actress. Photographer's model as a child; acted on radio; with Pasadena Playhouse 1940. Voted Star of Tomorrow: 1958. Author: The Beauty and the Billionaire (1984). Formed Moore/Rivers Productions, 1988 with partnermanager Jerry Rivers. Has also acted as Helen Koford, Judy Ford, and Jan Ford.
PICTURES: Maryland (debut as Helen Koford, 1940), The Howards of Virginia, On the Sunny Side (billed as Judy Ford), A-Haunting We Hill Go, My Gal Sal, True to Life, Date With Destiny, Gaslight, Since You Went Away, Son of Lassie, Sweet and Low Down, Shadowed, Summer Holiday, Devil on Wheels, The Return of October (1st billing as Terry Moore), Mighty Joe Young, The Great Ruppert, He's a Cockeyed Wonder, Gambling House, The Barefoot Mailman, Two of a Kind, Sunny Side of the Street, Come Back Little Sheba (Acad. Award nom.), Man on a Tightrope, Beneath the 12-Mile Reef, King of the Khyber Rifles, Daddy Long Legs, Shack Out on 101, Postmark for Danger (Portrait of Alison), Between Heaven and Hell, Peyton Place, Bernardine, A Private's Affair, Cast a Long Shadow, Why Must I Die?, Platinum High School, City of Fear, Black Spurs, Town Tamer, Waco, A Man Called Dagger, Daredevil, Death Dimension (Black Eliminator), Double Exposure, Hellhole, W.A.R., Beverly Hills Brats (also co-prod., co-story).
TELEVISION: Series: Empire. Movies: Quarantined, Smash-Up on Interstate 5, Jake Spanner: Private Eye.

MOORE, THOMAS W.
Executive. e. U. of Missouri. Naval aviator, USNR, 1940-45. Adv. dept., The Star, Meridian, MS; v.p. adv. mgr., Forest Lawn Memorial Park; account exec., CBS-TV Film Sales, Los Angeles; gen. sales mgr., CBS-TV Film Sales, 1956; v.p. in chg. programming & talent, 1958; pres., ABC-TV Network, 1962; chmn. bd., Ticketron, 1968; pres., Tomorrow Entertainment, Inc. 1971; chmn., 1981.

MORALES, ESAI
Actor. b. Brooklyn, NY, 1963. e. NY's High School for the Performing Arts. NY stage debut at age 17 in NY Shakespeare Fest. prod. of The Tempest, 1981.
THEATRE: Short Eyes, Tamer of Horses, El Mermano, Salome.
PICTURES: Forty Deuce (debut, 1982), Bad Boys, L.A. Bad, Rainy Day Friends, La Bamba, The Principal, Bloodhounds of Broadway, Naked Tango, Amazon, Freejack, In the Army Now, Rapa Nui, My Family/Mi Familia, Scorpion Spring.
TELEVISION: Mini-Series: On Wings of Eagles. Movies: The Burning Season, Deadlocked: Escape From Zone 14. Special: The Great Love Experiment. Guest: The Equalizer, Miami Vice.

MORANIS, RICK
Actor, Writer. b. Toronto, Canada, Apr. 18, 1954. Began career as part-time radio engineer while still in high school. Hosted own comedy show on radio then performed in Toronto cabarets and nightclubs and on TV. Joined satirical TV series SCTV during its 3rd season on CBC, for which he won Emmy for writing when broadcast in U.S. Created characters of the McKenzie Brothers with Dave Thomas and won Grammy nom. for McKenzie Brothers album. With Thomas co-wrote, co-directed and starred in film debut Strange Brew, 1983. Supplied voice for cartoon series Rick Moranis in Gravedale High.
PICTURES: Strange Brew (debut, 1983; also co-dir., co-s.p.), Streets of Fire, Ghostbusters, The Wild Life, Brewster's Millions, Head Office, Club Paradise, Little Shop of Horrors, Spaceballs, Ghostbusters II, Honey I Shrunk the Kids, Parenthood, My Blue Heaven, L.A. Story, Honey I Blew Up the Kid, Splitting Heirs, The Flintstones, Little Giants, Big Bully.

MOREAU, JEANNE
Actress. b. Paris, France, Jan. 23, 1928. e. Nat'l Conservatory of Dramatic Art. Stage debut with Comedie Francaise, acting there

until 1952 when she joined the Theatre Nationale Populaire. Directorial debut: La Lumiere (film), 1976. Recipient of 1995 BAFTA Film Craft Fellowship Award.
THEATER: A Month in the Country, La Machine Infernale, Pygmalion, Cat on a Hot Tin Roof.
PICTURES: The She-Wolves, Elevator to the Scaffold, The Lovers, Le Dialogue Des Carmelites, Les Liaisons Dangereuses, Moderato Cantabile, La Notte, Jules and Jim, A Woman Is a Woman, Eva, The Trial, Bay of Angels, The Victors, Le Feu Follet, Diary of a Chambermaid, The Yellow Rolls-Royce, The Train, Mata Hari, Viva Maria, Mademoiselle, Chimes at Midnight, Sailor From Gibraltar, The Bride Wore Black, The Immortal Story, Great Catherine, Monte Walsh, Alex in Wonderland, The Little Theatre of Jean Renoir, Louise, The Last Tycoon, French Provincial, La Lumiere (also dir., s.p.), Mr. Klein, The Adolescent (dir., s.p. only), Palin Sud, Querelle, The Trout, Le Miracule, La Femme Nikita, The Suspended Step of the Stork, La Femme Farde, Until the End of the World, Alberto Express, The Lover (voice), Map of the Human Heart, Anna Karamazova, The Summer House, See You Tomorrow, My Name Is Victor, The Old Lady Who Walks in the Sea, Beyond the Clouds, I Love You I Love You Not, The Proprietor.
TELEVISION: A Foreign Field (BBC).

MORENO, RITA
Actress. r.n. Rosa Dolores Alvario. b. Humacao, Puerto Rico, Dec. 11, 1931. Spanish dancer since childhood; night club entertainer. Has won all 4 major show business awards: Oscar, Tony, 2 Emmys and Grammy (for Best Recording for Children: The Electric Company, 1972).
THEATER: Skydrift (debut, 1945), The Sign in Sidney Brustein's Window, Gantry, Last of the Red Hot Lovers, The National Health (Long Wharf, CT), The Ritz (Tony Award, 1975), Wally's Cafe, The Odd Couple (female version).
PICTURES: So Young So Bad (debut, 1950, as Rosita Moreno), Pagan Love Song, The Toast of New Orleans, Singin' in the Rain, The Ring, Cattle Town, Ma and Pa Kettle on Vacation, Latin Lovers, Fort Vengeance, Jivaro, El Alamein, Yellow Tomahawk, Garden of Evil, Untamed, Seven Cities of Gold, Lieutenant Wore Skirts, The King and I, The Vagabond King, The Deerslayer, This Rebel Breed, Summer and Smoke, West Side Story (Academy Award, best supporting actress, 1961), Cry of Battle, The Night of the Following Day, Marlowe, Popi, Carnal Knowledge, The Ritz, The Boss' Son, Happy Birthday Gemini, The Four Seasons, Life in the Food Chain (Age Isn't Everything), The Italian Movie, Blackout, I Like It Like That, Angus.
TELEVISION: Series: The Electric Company, Nine to Five, B.L. Styker, Top of the Heap, The Cosby Mysteries. Movies: Evita Peron, Anatomy of a Seduction, Portrait of a Showgirl. Guest: The Muppet Show (Emmy Award, 1977), The Rockford Files (Emmy Award, 1978). Special: Tales From the Hollywood Hills: The Golden Land.

MORGAN, ANDRE
Producer. b. Morocco, 1952. e. U. of Kansas. Golden Harvest Films 1972-84, Producer. Exec. v.p., Golden Communications 1976-84. Formed Ruddy-Morgan Organization with Albert S. Ruddy, 1984.
PICTURES: Enter the Dragon, The Amsterdam Kill, The Boys in Company C, Cannonball Run II, High Road to China, Lassiter, Farewell to the King, Speed Zone, Impulse, Ladybugs, Bad Girls, The Scout, Heaven's Prisoners.
TELEVISION: Series: Walker Texas Ranger. Movies: Miracle in the Wilderness, Staying Afloat.

MORGAN, HARRY
Actor. r.n. Harry Bratsburg. b. Detroit, MI, Apr. 10, 1915. e. U. of Chicago. Previously acted as Henry Morgan.
THEATER: Gentle People, My Heart's in the Highlands, Thunder Rock, Night Music, Night Before Christmas.
PICTURES: To the Shores of Tripoli (debut, 1942), The Loves of Edgar Allen Poe, Crash Dive, Orchestra Wives, The Ox-Bow Incident, Happy Land, Wing and a Prayer, A Bell for Adano, Dragonwyck, From This Day Forward, The Gangster, All My Sons, The Big Clock, Moonrise, Yellow Sky, Madame Bovary, The Saxon Charm, Dark City, Appointment with Danger, The Highwayman, When I Grow Up, The Well, The Blue Veil, Bend of the River, Scandal Sheet, My Six Convicts, Boots Malone, High Noon, What Price Glory, Stop You're Killing Me, Arena, Torch Song, Thunder Bay, The Glenn Miller Story, About Mrs. Leslie, Forty-Niners, The Far Country, Not as a Stranger, Backlash, Strategic Air Command, The Teahouse of the August Moon, Inherit the Wind, The Mountain Road, How the West Was Won, John Goldfarb Please Come Home, What Did You Do in the War Daddy?, Frankie and Johnny, The Flim Flam Man, Support Your Local Sheriff, Viva Max!, The Barefoot Executive, Support Your Local Gunfighter, Scandalous John, Snowball Express, Charlie and the Angel, The Apple Dumpling Gang, The Greatest, The Shootist, The Cat From Outer Space, The Apple Dumpling Gang Rides Again, Dragnet.

TELEVISION: Series: December Bride, Pete and Gladys, The Richard Boone Show, Kentucky Jones, Dragnet, The D.A., Hec Ramsey, M*A*S*H (Emmy Award, 1980), After M*A*S*H, Blacke's Magic, You Can't Take It With You. Movies: Dragnet (pilot), But I Don't Want to Get Married!, The Feminist and the Fuzz, Ellery Queen: Don't Look Behind You, Hec Ramsey (pilot), Sidekicks, The Last Day (narrator), Exo-Man, The Magnificent Magnet of Santa Mesa, Maneaters Are Loose!, Murder at the Mardi Gras, The Bastard, Kate Bliss and the Ticker Tape Kid, The Wild Wild West Revisited, Better Late Than Never, Roughnecks, Scout's Honor, More Wild Wild West, Rivkin: Bounty Hunter, Agatha Christie's Sparkling Cyanide, The Incident, Against Her Will: An Incident in Baltimore, Incident in a Small Town. Mini-Series: Backstairs at the White House, Roots: The Next Generations.

MORGAN, MICHELE
Actress. r.n. Simone Roussel. b. Paris, France, Feb. 29, 1920. e. Dieppe, dramatic school, Paris. Won starring role at 17 opposite Charles Boyer in Gribouille (The Lady in Question). Made several pictures abroad; to U.S. 1941. Recent theatre includes Les Monstres Sacres. Autobiography: With Those Eyes (1977).
PICTURES: Gribouille, Port of Shadows, Joan of Paris (U.S. debut, 1942), The Heart of a Nation, Two Tickets to London, Higher and Higher, Passage to Marseilles, The Chase, La Symphonie Pastorale, The Fallen Idol, Fabiola, Souvenir, The Naked Heart (Maria Chapdelaine), The Moment of Truth, Daughters of Destiny, The Proud and the Beautiful, Napoleon, Grand Maneuver, Marguerite de la Nuit, Marie Antoinette, There's Always a Price Tag, The Mirror Has Two Faces, Maxime, Love on the Riviera, Three Faces of Sin, Crime Does Not Pay, Landru (Bluebeard), Web of Fear, Lost Command, Benjamin, Cat and Mouse, Robert et Robert, A Man and a Woman: 20 Years Later, Everybody's Fine.

MORIARTY, CATHY
Actress. b. Bronx, NY, Nov. 29, 1960. Raised in Yonkers, NY.
PICTURES: Raging Bull (debut, 1980; Acad. Award nom.), Neighbors, White of the Eye, Burndown, Kindergarten Cop, Soapdish, The Mambo Kings, The Gun in Betty Lou's Handbag, Matinee, Another Stakeout, Me and the Kid, Pontiac Moon, Forget Paris, Casper, Foxfire, Opposite Corners.
TELEVISION: Series: Bless This House. Movie: Another Midnight Run. Guest: Tales from the Crypt (ACE Award).

MORIARTY, MICHAEL
Actor. b. Detroit, MI, April 5, 1941. e. Dartmouth. Studied at London Acad. of Music and Dramatic Arts. Appeared with New York Shakespeare Festival, Charles Street Playhouse (Boston), Alley Theatre (Houston) and Tyrone Guthrie Theatre (Minneapolis). B'way debut in The Trial of the Catonsville Nine.
THEATER: Find Your Way Home (Tony & Theatre World Awards, 1974), Richard III, Long Day's Journey Into Night, Henry V, GR Point, Whose Life Is It Anyway (Kennedy Center), The Ballad of Dexter Creed, Uncle Vanya, The Caine Mutiny Court-Martial, My Fair Lady.
PICTURES: Glory Boy (debut, 1971), Hickey and Boggs, Bang the Drum Slowly, The Last Detail, Shoot It Black Shoot It Blue, Report to the Commissioner, Who'll Stop the Rain, Q, Blood Link, Odd Birds, Pale Rider, The Stuff, Troll, The Hanoi Hilton, It's Alive III: Island of the Alive, Return to Salem's Lot, Dark Tower, Full Fathom Five, The Secret of the Ice Cave, Courage Under Fire.
TELEVISION: Series: Law and Order. Movies: A Summer Without Boys, The Glass Menagerie (Emmy Award, 1974), The Deadliest Season, The Winds of Kitty Hawk, Too Far to Go (also distributed theatrically), Windmills of the Gods, Frank Nitti: The Enforcer, Tailspin: Behind the Korean Airline Tragedy, Born Too Soon, Children of the Dust. Mini-Series: Holocaust (Emmy Award, 1978). Guest: The Equalizer.

MORITA, NORIYUKI "PAT"
Actor. b. Isleton, CA, June 28, 1932. Began show business career as comedian in nightclubs for such stars as Ella Fitzgerald, Johnny Mathis, Diana Ross and the Supremes, Glen Campbell, etc. Worked in saloons, coffee houses, and dinner theatres before becoming headliner in Las Vegas showrooms, Playboy Clubs, Carnegie Hall, etc. Guest on most TV talk, variety shows and series: M*A*S*H, Love Boat, Magnum, P.I. etc.
PICTURES: Thoroughly Modern Millie, Every Little Crook and Nanny, Cancel My Reservation, Where Does It Hurt?, Midway, When Time Ran Out, Full Moon High, Savannah Smiles, Jimmy the Kid, The Karate Kid (Acad. Award nom.), Night Patrol, Slapstick of Another Kind, The Karate Kid Part II, Captive Hearts, Collision Course, The Karate Kid Part III, Do Or Die, Lena's Holiday, Honeymoon in Vegas, Miracle Beach, Even Cowgirls Get the Blues, The Next Karate Kid, American Ninja 5.
TELEVISION: Series: The Queen and I, Sanford and Son, Happy Days, Mr. T and Tina, Blansky's Beauties, Ohara, The Karate Kid (voice for animated series). Movies: Evil Roy Slade, A Very Missing Person, Brock's Last Case, Punch and Jody, Farewell to Manzanar, Human Feelings, For the Love of It, The Vegas Strip Wars, Amos, Babes in Toyland, Hiroshima: Out of the Ashes, Greyhounds, Hart to Hart: Secrets of the Hart.

MORITZ, MILTON I
Executive. b. Pittsburgh, PA, Apr. 27, 1933. e. Woodbury Coll., grad. 1955. Owned, operated theatres in L.A., 1953-55; U.S. Navy 1955-57; American International Pictures asst. gen. sls. mgr., 1957; nat'l. dir. of adv. and publ. 1958; v.p. and bd. mem. of American International Pictures, 1967; pres. of Variety Club of So. Cal, Tent 25, 1975-76; 1975, named sr. v.p.; in 1980, formed own co., The Milton I. Moritz Co., Inc., Inc., mktg. & dist. consultant. 1987-94, joined Pacific Theatres as v.p. in chg. of adv., p.r. & promotions. 1995, reactived the Milton I. Morvitz Co., Inc.

MORRICONE, ENNIO
Composer, Arranger. b. Rome, Italy, Nov. 10, 1928. Studied with Goffredo Petrassi at the Acad. of Santa Cecilia in Rome. Began career composing chamber music and symphonies as well as music for radio, TV and theater. Wrote for popular performers including Gianni Morandi. Early film scores for light comedies. Gained recognition for assoc. with Italian westerns of Sergio Leone (under name of Dan Davio).
PICTURES: Il Federal (1961, debut), A Fistful of Dollars, The Good the Bad and the Ugly, El Greco, Fists in the Pocket, Battle of Algiers, Matchless, Theorem, Once Upon a Time in the West, Investigation of a Citizen, Fraulein Doktor, Burn, The Bird with the Crystal Plumage, Cat O'Nine Tails, The Red Tent, Four Flies in Grey Velvet, The Decameron, The Black Belly of the Tarantula, Bluebeard, The Serpent, Blood in the Streets, Eye of the Cat, The Human Factor, Murder on the Bridge, Sunday Woman, The Inheritance, Partner, Orca, Exorcist II: The Heretic, 1900, Days of Heaven, La Cage aux Folles, Bloodline, Stay as You Are, The Humanoid, The Meadow, A Time to Die, Travels With Anita (Lovers and Liars), When You Comin' Back Red Ryder?, Almost Human, La Cage aux Folles II, The Island, Tragedy of a Ridiculous Man, Windows, Butterfly, So Fine, White Dog, Copkiller, Nana, The Thing, Treasure of the Four Crowns, Sahara, Once Upon a Time in America, Thieves After Dark, The Cage, La Cage aux Folles III, The Forester's Sons, The Red Sonja, Repentier, The Mission, The Venetian Woman, The Untouchables, Quartiere (Neighborhood), Rampage, Frantic, A Time of Destiny, Casualties of War, Cinema Paradiso, State of Grace, Hamlet, Bugsy, City of Joy, The Bachelor, In the Line of Fire, Wolf, Love Affair, Disclosure.
TELEVISION: U.S.: Marco Polo, Moses—The Lawgiver, Scarlet and the Black, C.A.T. Squad, The Endless Game, Octopus 4, Abraham.

MORRIS, ERROL
Director, Writer. b. Hewlett, NY, 1948. e. Univ. of WI, Univ. of CA/Berkeley.
PICTURES: Gates of Heaven, Vernon Florida, The Thin Blue Line, A Brief History of Time, The Dark Wind.

MORRIS, GARRETT
Actor. b. New Orleans, LA, Feb. 1, 1937. e. Dillard Univ., Julliard Sch. of Music, Manhattan Sch. of Music. Was singer and arranger for Harry Belafonte Folk Singers and B'way actor before achieving fame as original cast member of Saturday Night Live.
THEATER: Porgy and Bess, I'm Solomon, Show Boat, Hallelujah Baby!, The Basic Training of Pavlo Hummel, Finian's Rainbow, The Great White Hope, Ain't Supposed to Die a Natural Death, The Unvarnished Truth.
PICTURES: Where's Poppa? (debut, 1970), The Anderson Tapes, Cooley High, Car Wash, How to Beat the High Cost of Living, The Census Taker, The Stuff, Critical Condition, The Underachievers, Dance to Win, Motorama.
TELEVISION: Series: Roll Out, Saturday Night Live (1975-80), It's Your Move, Hunter, Martin, Cleghorne! Movies: The Invisible Woman, Maid for Each Other, Black Scorpion. Guest: Scarecrow and Mrs. King, Love Boat, Married With Children, Murder She Wrote, The Jeffersons.

MORRIS, HOWARD
Actor, Director, Writer. b. New York, NY, Sept. 4, 1919. e. NYU. U.S. Army, 4 yrs.
THEATER: Hamlet, Call Me Mister, John Loves Mary, Gentlemen Prefer Blondes, Finian's Rainbow.
PICTURES: Director: Who's Minding the Mint?, With Six You Get Egg Roll, Don't Drink the Water, Goin' Cocoanuts. Actor: Boys' Night Out, 40 Pounds of Trouble, The Nutty Professor, Fluffy, Way... Way Out, High Anxiety, History of the World Part 1, Splash, Transylvania Twist, Life Stinks.
TELEVISION: Series: Your Show of Shows (also writer), Caesar's Hour. Movies: The Munster's Revenge, Portrait of a Showgirl, Return to Mayberry. Voices: Jetsons, Flintstones, Mr. Magoo. Producer: The Corner Bar. Director: Dick Van Dyke Show, Get Smart, Andy Griffith Show (also frequent guest); also many commericals.

MORRIS, JOHN
Composer, Conductor, Arranger. b. Elizabeth, NJ, Oct. 18, 1926. e. student Juilliard Sch. Music 1946-48, U. of Washington, 1947, New Sch. Social Research 1946-49. Member: ASCAP, Acad. of M.P. Arts & Sciences, American Federation of Musicians.

THEATER: Composer. B'way: My Mother My Father and Me, A Doll's House, Camino Real, A Time For Singing (musical), Take One Step, Young Andy Jackson, 15 Shakespeare plays for NY Shakespeare Fest. & Amer. Shakespeare Fest, Stratford CT. Musical supervisor, conductor, dance music arranger: Mack and Mabel, Much Ado About Nothing, Bells Are Ringing, Bye Bye Birdie and 23 other B'way musicals. Off-B'way: Hair.
PICTURES: The Producers, The Twelve Chairs, Blazing Saddles (Acad. Award nom.), Bank Shot, Young Frankenstein, The Adventure of Sherlock Holmes' Smarter Brother, Silent Movie, The Last Remake of Beau Geste, The World's Greatest Lover, High Anxiety, The In-Laws, In God We Trust, The Elephant Man (Acad. Award nom.), History of the World Part 1, Table for Five, Yellowbeard, To Be or Not to Be, The Woman in Red, Johnny Dangerously, The Doctor and the Devils, Clue, Haunted Honeymoon, Dirty Dancing, Spaceballs, Ironweed, The Wash, Second Sight, Stella, Life Stinks.
TELEVISION: Composer: Fresno, Katherine Anne Porter, Ghost Dancing, The Firm, The Mating Season, Splendor in the Grass, The Electric Grandmother, The Scarlet Letter, Georgia O'Keeffe, The Adams Chronicles, The Franken Project, The Tap Dance Kid (Emmy Award, 1986), Make Believe Marriage, The Desperate Hours, The Skirts of Happy Chance, Infancy and Childhood, The Fig Tree, The Little Match Girl, Favorite Son, The Last Best Year, The Last to Go, The Sunset Gang, Our Sons, When Lions Roared, Scarlett. Themes: ABC After School Special, Making Things Grow, The French Chef, Coach. Musical sprv., conductor, arranger Specials: Anne Bancroft Special (Emmy Award), S'Wonderful S'Marvelous S'Gershwin (Emmy Award), Hallmark Christmas specials.
RECORDINGS: Wildcat, All-American, Bells Are Ringing, First Impressions, Bye Bye Birdie, Kwamina, Baker Street, Rodgers and Hart, George Gershwin Vols. 1 & 2, Jerome Kern, Lyrics of Ira Gershwin, Cole Porter, others.

MORRIS, OSWALD
Cinematographer. b. London, Eng., Nov. 22, 1915. Left school at 16 to work for two years as camera dept. helper at studios. Was lensman for cameraman Ronald Neame who gave Morris first job as cameraman; in 1949, when Neame directed The Golden Salamander, he made Morris dir. of photography.
PICTURES: The Golden Salamander, The Card, The Man Who Never Was, Moulin Rouge, Beat the Devil, Moby Dick, Heaven Knows Mr. Allison, A Farewell to Arms, The Roots of Heaven, The Key, The Guns of Navarone, Lolita, Term of Trial, Of Human Bondage, The Pumpkin Eater (BFA Award, 1964), Mister Moses, The Hill (BFA Award, 1965), The Spy Who Came in from the Cold, Life at the Top, Stop the World- -I Want to Get Off, The Taming of the Shrew, Reflections in a Golden Eye, Oliver!, Gooodbye Mr. Chips, Scrooge, Fiddler on the Roof (Academy Award, 1971), Sleuth, Lady Caroline Lamb, The Mackintosh Man, The Odessa File, The Man Who Would Be King, The Seven Per Cent Solution, Equus, The Wiz, Just Tell Me What You Want, The Great Muppet Caper, The Dark Crystal.
TELEVISION: Dracula (1974).

MORRISSEY, PAUL
Writer, Director, Photographer. b. New York, NY, 1938. e. Fordham U. 2nd lt. in Army. A writer, cameraman and director in independent film prod. prior to becoming Andy Warhol's mgr. in all areas except painting. Discovered and managed The Velvet Underground and Nico. Founded Intreview magazine. Story, casting, dir. & photog. for Warhol's Chelsea Girls, Four Stars, Bike Boy, I A Man, Lonesome Cowboys, Blue Movie, and San Diego Surf.
PICTURES: writer/photog./edit.: Flesh, Trash, Heat, L'Amour, Women in Revolt. writer/dir.: Andy Warhol's Frankenstein, Andy Warhol's Dracula, The Hound of the Baskervilles, Forty Deuce, Mixed Blood, Beethoven's Nephew, Spike of Bensonhurst.

MORROW, ROB
Actor. b. New Rochelle, NY, Sept. 21, 1962.
THEATRE: NY: The Substance of Fire, Aven'U Boys, The Chosen, Scandal (workshop), Soulful Scream of a Chosen Son, The Boys of Winter, Slam, Third Secret.
PICTURES: Private Resort, Quiz Show, The Last Dance, Mother.
TELEVISION: Series: Tattinger's, Northern Exposure. Guest: Spenser: For Hire, Everything's Relative, Fame.

MORSE, DAVID
Actor. b. Beverly, MA, Oct. 11, 1953.
THEATRE: B'way: On the Waterfront.
PICTURES: Inside Moves, Desperate Hours, The Indian Runner, The Good Son, The Getaway, The Crossing Guard, Twelve Monkeys, The Rock.
TELEVISION: Series: St. Elsewhere, Big Wave Dave's. Movies: Shattered Vows, When Dreams Come True, Prototype, Downpayment on Murder, Six Against the Rock, Winnie, Brotherhood of the Rose, Cross of Fire, A Cry in the Wild: The Taking of Peggy Ann, Dead Ahead: The Exxon Valdez Disaster, Miracle on Interstate 880, Tecumseh: The Last Warrior. Mini-Series: Stephen King's The Langoliers. Guest: Nurse. Special: A Place at the Table.

MORSE, ROBERT
Actor. b. Newton, MA, May 18, 1931. Served U.S. Navy. Studied with American Theatre Wing, New York. Following radio work, appeared on B'way stage in The Matchmaker, 1956.
THEATER: *B'way:* The Matchmaker, Say Darling (Theatre World Award), Take Me Along, How to Succeed in Business Without Really Trying (Tony Award, 1962), Sugar, So Long 174th Street, Tru (Tony Award, 1990).
PICTURES: The Proud and the Profane (debut, 1956), The Matchmaker, The Cardinal, Honeymoon Hotel, Quick Before It Melts, The Loved One, Oh Dad Poor Dad Mama's Hung You in the Closet and I'm Feeling So Sad, How to Succeed in Business Without Really Trying, A Guide for the Married Man, Where Were You When the Lights Went Out?, The Boatniks, Hunk, The Emperor's New Clothes.
TELEVISION: *Series:* The Secret Storm (1954), That's Life. *Specials:* The Stingiest Man in Town (voice), Kennedy Center Tonight—Broadway to Washington, Tru (Emmy Award, 1993). *Movie:* The Calendar Girl Murders. *Mini-Series:* Wild Palms. *Guest:* Masquerade, Alfred Hitchcock Presents, Naked City, Love American Style, Twilight Zone, Murder She Wrote.

MORTON, ARTHUR
Composer, Arranger. b. Duluth, MN, Aug. 8, 1908. e. U. of MN, 1929.
PICTURES: Night Life of the Gods, Princess O'Hara, Riding on Air, Fit for a King, Turnabout, Walking Hills, The Nevadan, Rogues of Sherwood Forest, Father is a Bachelor, Never Trust a Gambler, Harlem Globetrotters, Big Heat, Pushover, He Laughed Last. Orchesrtal Arrangements: Laura, From Here to Eternity, Jolson Story, Salome, Born Yesterday, The Long Gray Line, Man from Laramine, My Sister Eileen, Picnic, Strangers When We Meet, That Touch of Mink, Diamond Head, Toys in the Attic, Von Ryan's Express, In Harm's Way, What a Way to Go, The New Interns, Our Man Flint, Planet of the Apes, Patton, Tora Tora Tora, Papillon, Chinatown, Capone's Run, The Omen, MacArthur, The Boys from Brazil, Magic, Superman, Alien, Star Trek: The Motion Picture, Poltergeist, First Blood, Gremlins, Rambo: First Blood Part II, Hoosiers, The 'Burbs, Star Trek V: The Final Frontier, Total Recall, Medicine Man, Gladiator, Mr. Baseball, Forever Young, The Vanishing, Rudy, Angie, The Shadow, The River Wild, many others.
TELEVISION: Black Saddle, Laramie, Bus Stop, Follow the Sun, My Three Sons, Peyton Place, Medical Center, Daniel Boone, Lancers, National Geographic, Say Goodbye, How to Stay Alive, Hooray For Hollywood, The Waltons, Apple's Way, Masada, Medical Story.

MORTON, JOE
Actor. b. New York, NY, Oct. 18, 1947. e. Hofstra U.
THEATRE: *NY:* Hair, Raisin (Theatre World Award), Oh Brother, Honky Tonk Nights, A Midsummer Night's Dream, King John, Cheapside, Electra, A Winter's Tale, Oedipus Rex, Julius Caesar, The Tempest. Director: Heliotrope Bouquet.
PICTURES: ...And Justice for All, The Brother From Another Planet, Trouble in Mind, Zelly and Me, The Good Mother, Tap, Terminator 2: Judgment Day, City of Hope, Of Mice and Men, Forever Young, The Inkwell, Speed, The Walking Dead, Lone Star, Executive Decision.
TELEVISION: *Series:* Grady, Equal Justice, Tribeca (also dir.), Under One Roof, New York News. *Movies:* The Challenger, Terrorist on Trial: The United States vs. Salim Ajami, Howard Beach: Making a Case for Murder, Death Penalty, Legacy of Lies, In the Shadow of Evil. *Special:* The File of Jill Hatch. *Guest:* A Different World, Hawk, Homicide: Life on the Street.

MOSES, CHARLES ALEXANDER
Executive, Writer, Producer. b. Chicago, IL, March 1, 1923. e. Aeronautical U., Northwestern U., Englewood Eve. Jr. Coll.; Antioch U. Field adv-promo exec., United Artists, unit publicist for over 30 films; exec., Screen Gems; European adv-publ. supry., Paris, United Artists; adv-pub dir., Bel Air Prod., U.S. adv-pub dir., Associates & Aldrich Co.; adv-pub dir., Sinatra Enterprises; assoc. studio publ. dir., Universal Studios; adv-pub rep., Universal Studios from Paris for Europe; exec-in-chg NY domestic & foreign adv-publ. dept., Universal; adv-pub superv., Orion Pictures Co. Started own firm, Charles A. Moses Co., adv-marketing-pub. rel., acc'ts included United Artists, Columbia Picts., 20th Century-Fox, UA-TV, Cinemation Industries, Hemdale Leisure Corp., American Internat'l Picts., Filmways, etc. Orig. story: Frankenstein 1970. Prod.: Radio Free Europe, Munich, Goldblatt radio, TV shows (WGN); Writer-prod-dir.; documentaries: Carson Prod., Mason City. Past pres., The Publicists Guild of America (IATSE, Local 818).

MOSK, RICHARD M.
Executive. b. Los Angeles, CA, May 18, 1939. e. Stanford U, Harvard Law School. Admitted to California Bar, 1964. Principal in firm of Sanders Barnet Goldman Simons & Mosk, a prof. corp. Named chmn. of the movie industry's voluntary rating system, the Classification & Rating Administration, June 1994.

MOSLEY, ROGER E.
Actor. b. Los Angeles, CA. Planned career in broadcasting but turned to acting, first appearing in small roles on TV in: Night Gallery, Baretta, Kojak, Cannon, Switch.
PICTURES: The New Centurions (debut, 1972), Hit Man, Terminal Island, Stay Hungry, Leadbelly, The Greatest, Semi-Tough, Steel, Heart Condition, Unlawful Entry.
TELEVISION: *Series:* Magnum P.I., You Take the Kids. *Guest:* Baretta, Kojak, Cannon, Switch. *Movies:* Cruise Into Terror, I Know Why the Caged Bird Sings, The Jericho Mile, Attica. *Mini-Series:* Roots: The Next Generations.

MOSS, FRANK L.
Writer, Producer. b. New York, NY, Aug. 25, 1913. e. Duke U., Columbia U. Reporter, drama & film critic, N.Y. U.S. Army Air Force, 1942-46. Instructor, UCLA, 1985-86 on advanced screenplay writing. 1987-88, private tutoring on screenplay and TV writing. For military made 22 Air Force training films, 17 documentaries. Author: The Hack.
THEATER: *Author:* Glamour Girl, Call To Arms (collab), So Goes the Nation (collab), Some People's Children, American Pastoral, City on a Hill.
PICTURES: To Have and Have Not, The Unvanquished, Whiphand, Caribbean, Sangaree, Papago Wells, The Half Breed, Sweetheart of Sigma Chi.
TELEVISION: *Writer:* Telephone Hour, Four Star Playhouse, Winston Churchill's Valiant Years, Route 66, Wagon Train, Laramie, Wild Wild West, The Texan, G.E. Theater, Wire Service, U.S. Marshall, M-Squad, Stoney Burke, Tales of the Texas Rangers, T.V. Reader's Digest, Sheriff of Cochise, Whirlybirds, Line-Up, Wyatt Earp, Rin Tin Tin, Walter Winchell File, Daniel Boone, Man Who Never Was, Felony Squad, Richard Diamond, Lassie, Like the Rich People, Hired Mother, Shenandoah, Counterspy, White Hunter, Hondo, Northwest Mounted Police, Casey Jones, Cowboy in Africa. *Pilots:* Outer Limits, Grand Jury, The Texam, Bush Pilot, Lafitte, Cortez. *Prod./Story Ed.:* Screen Televideo, Sovereign Prod., Wire Service, T.V. Reader's Digest, Wyatt Earp.

MOSS, IRWIN
Executive. e. Syracuse U., Harvard Law Sch. Member NY State Bar. Began industry career as director of package negotiations for CBS-TV; 1970-80, exec. v.p. & natl. head of business affairs for I.C.M.; 1978-80, sr. v.p., NBC Entertainment; 1980, pres., Marble Arch TV. 1982, joined Paramount Pictures as sr. v.p. for motion picture div. 1984, exec. v.p., L. Taffner Ltd.

MOSTEL, JOSH
Actor, Director. b. New York, NY, Dec. 21, 1946. Father was late actor Zero Mostel. m. producer Peggy Rajski. e. Brandeis U., B.A. 1970. Part of The Proposition, a Boston improvisational comedy group. Stage debut, The Homecoming (Provincetown Playhouse, MA).
THEATER: *Actor:* Unlikely Heroes, The Proposition, An American Millionaire, A Texas Trilogy, Gemini, Men in the Kitchen, The Dog Play, The Boys Next Door, A Perfect Diamond, Threepenny Opera, My Favorite Year, The Flowering Peach. *Director:* Ferocious Kisses, Love As We Know It, Misconceptions, Red Diaper Baby.
PICTURES: Going Home (debut, 1971), The King of Marvin Gardens, Jesus Christ Superstar, Harry and Tonto, Deadly Hero, Fighting Back, Sophie's Choice, Star 80, Almost You, The Brother from Another Planet, Windy City, Compromising Positions, The Money Pit, Stoogemania, Radio Days, Matewan, Wall Street, Heavy Petting, Animal Behavior, City Slickers, Naked Tango, Little Man Tate, City of Hope, Searching for Bobby Fischer, The Chase, City Slickers II: The Legend of Curly's Gold, Billy Madison, The Basketball Diaries, The Maddening.
TELEVISION: *Series:* Delta House, At Ease, Murphy's Law. *Mini-Series:* Seventh Avenue. *Special:* The Boy Who Loved Trolls (PBS). *Co-writer:* Media Probes: The Language Show.

MOUND, FRED
Executive. b. St. Louis, MO, April 10, 1932. e. St. Louis U., Quincy Coll. 1946-52, assoc. with father, Charles Mound, at Park Theatre in Valley Park, Mo.; 1952-53, Universal Pictures (St. Louis); 1953, booker, UA, St. Louis; 1955 promoted to salesman in Kansas City; 1957, salesman, St. Louis; 1962, Indianapolis branch mgr. 1967 named UA regional mgr., Dallas and in 1970 became S.W. div. mgr; 1976-77, asst. sls. mgr. for Southern, N.W. and S.W. div. operating out of Dallas. 1977 appt. v.p., asst. gen. sls. mgr. of UA; 1978, appt. v.p. gen sls. mgr. for AFD Pictures in Los Angeles; 1981, v.p. asst. gen. sls. mgr. for Universal; 1984, sr. v.p., gen. sls. mgr., Universal Pictures Distribution; named exec. v.p. 1988. Foundation of Motion Picture Pioneers v.p., 1989. Appointed pres. Universal distrib., 1990.

MOUNT, THOM
Executive. b. Durham, NC, May 26, 1948. e. Bard Coll.; CA Institute of the Arts, MFA. Started career with Roger Corman and as asst. to prod., Danny Selznick at MGM. Moved to Universal under prod. exec. Ned Tanen. At 26, named pres. and

head of prod. at Universal. During 8-year tenure, was responsible for dev. and prod. of more than 140 films (including Smokey and the Bandit, Animal House, others).
THEATER: Open Admissions (co-prod.), Death and the Maiden.
PICTURES: Pirates (exec. prod.), My Man Adam, Can't Buy Me Love, Frantic, Bull Durham (co-prod.), Stealing Home, Tequila Sunrise, Roger Corman's Frankenstein Unbound, The Indian Runner (exec. prod.), Death and the Maiden.
TELEVISION: Son of the Morning Star, Open Admissions.

MOYERS, BILL
TV Correspondent. b. Hugo, OK, June 5, 1934. e. U. of Texas; Southwestern Baptist Theological Sem. Aide to Lyndon B. Johnson; assoc. dir., Peace Corps, 1961-2, and deputy dir., 1963. Spec. asst. to Pres. Johnson, 1963-65 and press secty., 1965-67. Editor and chief corr., CBS Reports. Bill Moyers Journal on PBS. Established Public Affairs TV, Inc., 1986.

MUDD, ROGER
Newscaster. b. Washington, DC, Feb. 9, 1928. e. Washington & Lee U., U. of North Carolina. Reporter for Richmond News-Leader, 1953; news. dir., WRNL, 1954; WTOP, Washington, 1956; joined CBS News 1961 as Congressional correspondent (2 Emmy Awards). 1977, Natl. Aff. corr.; 1978, corr., CBS Reports; 1980-87: NBC News as chief Washington corr., chief political corr., co-anchor; 1987 joined The MacNeil/Lehrer News Hour as special correspondent; essayist, and chief congressional correspondent. 1992 became contributing correspondent.

MUELLER-STAHL, ARMIN
Actor. b. Tilsit, East Prussia, Dec. 17, 1930. Moved to West Germany in 1980. e. Berlin Conservatory. Studied violin before turning to acting. Author: Verordneter Sonntag (Lost Sunday), Drehtage.
PICTURES: Naked Among the Wolves, The Third, Jacob the Liar, The Flight, Lite Trap, Lola, Wings of Night, Veronika Voss, A Cop's Sunday, A Love in Germany, Thousand Eyes, Trauma, Colonel Redl, L'Homme blesse, God Doesn't Believe in Us Anymore, Angry Harvest, The Blind Director, Following the Fuhrer, Momo, The Jungle Mission, Lethal Obsession, Midnight Cop, Music Box, Das Spinnenetz, Just for Kicks, Avalon, Bronstein's Children, Kafka, The Power of One, Night on Earth, Utz, The House of the Spirits, Holy Matrimony, The Last Good Time, A Pyromaniac's Love Story, Taxandria, Shine, Theodore Rex.
TELEVISION: Mini-Series: Amerika.

MUHL, EDWARD E.
Executive, Producer. b. Richmond, IN, Feb. 17, 1907. Gen. mgr., Universal 1948-53; v.p., studio in charge of prod. 1953-68. Consultant, Alcor Prods., Ft. Smith, AR, 1985-90. Co-author, consultant, s.p., Soldier: Other Side of Glory, 1991-92.

MUIR, E. ROGER
Producer. b. Canada, Dec. 16, 1918. e. U. of Minnesota. Partner Minn. Advertising Services Co.; Photographer, Great Northern Railway; motion picture producer Army Signal corps; NBC TV producer, Howdy Doody; exec. producer, Concentration. Now pres. Nicholson-Muir Prods. TV program packager, U.S. Spin-Off, Pay Cards, Canada Pay Cards, Headline Hunters, Definition, Celebrity Dominoes; co-creator Newlywed Game, exec. prod. I Am Joe's Heart, I Am Joe's Lung, I Am Joe's Spine, I Am Joe's Stomach, The New Howdy Doody Show, Supermates, Second Honeymoon, Groaner, Generation Jury, Shopping Game, Guess What, I Am Joe's Kidney, I Am Joe's Liver, It's Howdy Doody Time: A 40 Year Celebration. Retired 1993.

MULDAUR, DIANA
Actress. b. New York, NY, Aug. 19, 1943. e. Sweet Briar Coll. Began on New York stage then turned to films and TV, appearing on numerous major network shows.
PICTURES: The Swimmer (debut, 1968), Number One, The Lawyer, One More Train to Rob, The Other, McQ, Chosen Survivors, Beyond Reason.
TELEVISION: Series: The Secret Storm, The Survivors, McCloud, Born Free, The Tony Randall Show, Hizzoner, Fitz and Bones, A Year in the Life, L.A. Law, Star Trek: The Next Generation. Movies: McCloud: Who Killed Miss U.S.A.?, Call to Danger, Ordeal, Planet Earth, Charlie's Angels (pilot), Pine Canyon is Burning, Deadly Triangle, Black Beauty, To Kill a Cop, Maneaters Are Loose!, The Word, The Miracle Worker, The Return of Frank Cannon, Terror at Alcatraz, The Return of Sam McCloud.

MULGREW, KATE
Actress. b. Dubuque, IA, April 29, 1955. e. NYU. Stage work includes stints with American Shakespeare Festival, NY Shakespeare Festival, Seattle Rep. Theatre, Mark Taper Forum (LA). B'way: Black Comedy.
PICTURES: Lovespell, A Stranger Is Watching, Remo Williams: The Adventure Begins, Throw Momma from the Train, Camp Nowhere.

TELEVISION: Series: Ryan's Hope (1975-77), Kate Columbo (Kate Loves a Mystery), Heartbeat, Man of the People, Star Trek: Voyager. Movies: The Word, Jennifer: A Woman's Story, A Time for Miracles, The Manions of America, Roses Are for the Rich, Roots: The Gift, Danielle Steel's Daddy, Fatal Friendship, For Love and Glory.

MULHERN, MATT
Actor. b. Philadelphia, PA, July 21, 1960. e. Rutgers Univ.
THEATRE: NY: Biloxi Blues, Wasted, The Night Hank Williams Died.
PICTURES: One Crazy Summer, Extreme Prejudice, Biloxi Blues, Junior.
TELEVISION: Series: Major Dad. Movie: Gunsmoke: To the Last Man, Terror in the Night, A Burning Passion: The Margaret Mitchell Story.

MULHOLLAND, ROBERT E.
Executive. b. 1933. e. Northwestern U. Joined NBC News as newswriter in Chicago in 1962. 1964 made midwestern field producer for Huntley-Brinkley Report. 1964 moved to London as European producer for NBC News; 1965, named Washington producer of Huntley-Brinkley Report. Transferred to L.A. in 1967 to be director of news, west coast. Named exec. prod. of NBC Nightly News. 1973 appt. v.p., NBC news.; 1974 exec. v.p. of NBC News. 1977 appt. pres. of NBC Television Network; also elected to board of directors; 1981, pres. & CEO. Resigned, 1984. Dir. Television Info. Office, NYC 1985-87. Prof. Northwestern U. 1988-.

MULL, MARTIN
Actor. b. Chicago, IL, Aug. 18, 1943. e. Rhode Island Sch. of Design. Started as humorist, making recordings for Warner Bros., Capricorn, ABC Records, etc.
PICTURES: FM (debut, 1978), My Bodyguard, Serial, Take This Job and Shove It, Flicks, Mr. Mom, Bad Manners, Clue, O.C. and Stiggs, Home Is Where the Hart Is, Rented Lips (also s.p., exec. prod.), Cutting Class, Ski Patrol, Far Out Man, Think Big, Ted and Venus, The Player, Miracle Beach, Mrs. Doubtfire, Mr. Write, Edie and Pen.
TELEVISION: Series: Mary Hartman Mary Hartman, Fernwood 2-Night, America 2-Night, Domestic Life, His and Hers, Roseanne, The Jackie Thomas Show, Family Dog (voice). Specials: The History of White People in America (also prod.), Candid Camera Christmas Special (1987), Portrait of a White Marriage, The Whole Shebang. Movies: Sunset Limousine, California Girls, The Day My Parents Ran Away, How the West Was Fun.

MULLER, ROBBY
Cinematographer. b. Netherlands, April 4, 1940. e. Dutch Film Acad. Asst. cameraman in Holland before moving to Germany where he shot 9 films for Wim Wenders.
PICTURES: Kings of the Road, Alice in the Cities, Wrong Move, The American Friend, Saint Jack, Honeysuckle Rose, They All Laughed, Body Rock, Repo Man, Paris Texas, To Live and Die in L.A., THe Longshot, Down By Law, Tricheurs, The Believers, Barfly, Il Piccolo Diavolo (The Little Devil), Mystery Train, Korczak, Until the End of the World, Mad Dog and Glory.

MULLIGAN, RICHARD
Actor. b. New York, NY Nov. 13, 1932.
THEATER: Nobody Loves an Albatross, All the Way Home, Never Too Late, Mating Dance, Hogan's Goat, Thieves, etc.
PICTURES: Love With the Proper Stranger (debut, 1963), One Potato Two Potato, The Group, The undefeated, Little Big Man, Irish Whiskey Rebeliion, From the Mixed-Up Files of Mrs. Basil E. Frankweiler, The Big Bus, Scavenger Hunt, S.O.B., Trail of the Pink Panther, Meatballs Part II, Teachers, Micki and Maude, Doin' Time, The Heavenly Kid, A Fine Mess, Quicksilver, Oliver & Company (voice).
TELEVISION: Movies: Having Babies III, Malibu, Jealousy, Poler Alice, Gore Vidal's Lincoln, Guess Who's Coming for Christmas? Series: The Hero, Diana, Soap (Emmy Award, 1980), Reggie, Empty Nest (Emmy Award, 1989)

MULLIGAN, ROBERT
Director. b. Bronx, NY. Aug. 23, 1925. e. Fordham U. Served in Navy during WWII. After working as copyboy for NY Times joined CBS in mailroom. Eventually became TV director before moving into features.
PICTURES: Fear Strikes Out (debut, 1957), The Rat Race, The Great Imposter, Come September, The Spiral Road, To Kill a Mockingbird, Love With the Proper Stranger, Baby the Rain Must Fall, Inside Daisy Clover, Up the Down Staircase, The Stalking Moon, The Pursuit of Happiness, Summer of `42, The Other, The Nickel Ride, Bloodbrothers, Same Time Next Year, Kiss Me Goodbye, Clara's Heart, The Man in the Moon.
TELEVISION: The Moon and the Sixpence (Emmy Award, 1960), Billy Budd, Ah Wilderness, A Tale of Two Cities, The Bridge of San Luis Rey, Playhouse 90, Philco-Goodyear, Suspense, Studio One, Hallmark Hall of Fame.

MULRONEY, DERMOT
Actor. b. Alexandria, VA, Oct. 31, 1963. e. Northwestern Univ.
PICTURES: Sunset, Young Guns, Survival Quest, Staying Together, Longtime Companion, Career Opportunities, Bright Angel, Where the Day Takes You, Samantha, Point of No Return, The Thing Called Love, Silent Tongue, Bad Girls, Angels in the Outfield, There Goes My Baby, Living in Oblivion, Copycat, How to Make an American Quilt, Kansas City, Trigger Effect.
TELEVISION: Movies: Sin of Innocence, Daddy, Unconquered, Long Gone, The Heart of Justice, Family Pictures, The Last Outlaw. Special: Toma: The Drug Knot.

MUMY, BILL
Actor. r.n. Charles William Mumy Jr. b. El Centro, CA, Feb. 1, 1954. Began acting as Billy Mumy at age 6. Played with band America in 1970's, also with bands Bill Mumy & The Igloos, and The Jenerators. Has made 8 albums with Barnes & Barnes. With actor Miguel Ferrer, wrote comic books Comet Man and Trip to the Acid Dog. Has also written stories for Star Trek, The Hulk, and Spiderman comic books, and Lost in Space comic published by Innovation. Wrote music for Disney's Adventures in Wonderland series (Emmy nom.)
PICTURES: Tammy Tell Me True, Palm Springs Weekend, A Ticklish Affair, A Child is Waiting, Dear Brigitte, Rascal, Bless the Beasts and Children, Papillon, Twilight Zone—The Movie, Hard to Hold, Captain America, Double Trouble.
TELEVISION: Series: Lost in Space, Sunshine. Movies: Sunshine, The Rockford Files (pilot), Sunshine Christmas. Guest: The Twilight Zone, Alfred Hitchcock Presents, Bewitched, The Virginian, I Dream of Jeannie, The Adventures of Ozzie and Harriet, Ben Casey, The Red Skelton Show, Lancer, Here Come the Brides, Riverboat, Have Gun Will Travel, Matlock, Me and Mom, The Flash, Superboy, Babylon 5. Pilots: The Two of Us, Archie, Space Family Robinson. Host: Inside Space (SciFi Channel).

MURDOCH, RUPERT
Executive. b. Australia, March 11, 1931. Son of Sir Keith Murdoch, head of The Melbourne Herald and leading figure in Australian journalism. e. Oxford U., England. Spent two years on Fleet St. before returning home to take over family paper, The Adelaide News. Acquired more Australian papers and in 1969, expanded to Britain, buying The News of the World. Moved to U.S. in 1973, buying San Antonio Express and News. Conglomerate in 1985 included New York Post, New York Magazine, The Star, The Times of London, The Boston Herald, The Chicago Sun-Times along with TV stations, book publishing companies, airline, oil and gas companies, etc. 1985, made deal to buy 20th Century-Fox Film Corp. from owner Martin Davis. Sold the NY Post, 1988 to conform with FCC regulations. Purchased Triangle Publications 1988 (including TV Guide).

MURPHY, BEN
Actor. b. Jonesboro, AR, March 6, 1942. e. U. of Illinois. Degree in drama from Pasadena Playhouse. Acted in campus productions and toured in summer stock. Film debut with small role in The Graduate, 1967.
PICTURES: Yours Mine and Ours, The Thousand Plane Raid, Sidecar Racers, Time Walker.
TELEVISION: Series: The Name of the Game, Alias Smith and Jones, Griff, Gemini Man, The Chisholms, Lottery!, Berrenger's, The Dirty Dozen. Movies: The Letters, Wild Bill Hickock, Bridger, Heat Wave, Runaway, This Is the West That Was, Gemini Man, Hospital Fire, The Cradle Will Fall, Stark: Mirror Image. Mini-Series: The Winds of War.

MURPHY, EDDIE
Actor. b. Brooklyn, NY, Apr. 3, 1961. e. Roosevelt High Sch. Wrote and performed own comedy routines at youth centers and local bars at age 15. Worked on comedy club circuit; at 19 joined TV's Saturday Night Live as writer and performer. Recordings: Eddie Murphy, Eddie Murphy: Comedian, How Could It Be?, Love's Alright. Voted Top-Money Making Star of 1988 on Quigley Poll, NATO/ShoWest Star of the Decade, for 1980's.
PICTURES: 48 HRS. (debut, 1982), Trading Places, Best Defense, Beverly Hills Cop, The Golden Child, Beverly Hills Cop II, Eddie Murphy Raw (also s.p., exec. prod.), Coming to America (also story), Harlem Nights (also dir., s.p., exec. prod.), Another 48 HRS., Boomerang (also story), The Distinguished Gentleman, Beverly Hills Cop III, Vampire in Brooklyn (also co-prod.), The Nutty Professor (also co-exec. prod.).
TELEVISION: Series: Saturday Night Live (1981-84). Pilots (exec. prod.): What's Alan Watching? (also cameo), Coming to America. Movie (exec. prod.): The Kid Who Loved Christmas.

MURPHY, LAWRENCE P.
Executive. Exec. v.p. of strategic planning & development, The Walt Disney Company.

MURPHY, MICHAEL
Actor. b. Los Angeles, CA, May 5, 1938. e. U. of Arizona. m. actress Wendy Crewson. Taught English and Drama in L.A. city school system, 1962-64. N.Y. stage debut as director of Rat's Nest, 1978.

PICTURES: Double Trouble (debut, 1967), Countdown, The Legend of Lylah Clare, The Arrangement, That Cold Day in the Park, M*A*S*H, Count Yorga: Vampire, Brewster McCloud, McCabe and Mrs. Miller, What's Up Doc?, The Thief Who Came to Dinner, Phase IV, Nashville, The Front, An Unmarried Woman, The Great Bank Hoax, The Class of Miss MacMichael, Manhattan, The Year of Living Dangerously, Strange Behavior, Cloak and Dagger, Salvador, Mesmerized, Shocker, Folks!, Batman Returns, Clean Slate, Bad Company, Kansas City.
TELEVISION: Series: Two Marriages, Hard Copy. Guest: Saints and Sinners, Ben Casey, Dr. Kildare, Bonanza, Combat. Movies: The Autobiography of Miss Jane Pittman, The Caine Mutiny Court-Martial, Tailspin: Behind the Korean Airlines Tragedy. Specials: John Cheever's Oh Youth and Beauty, Tanner '88.

MURPHY, THOMAS S.
Executive. e. Cornell Univ (B.S.M.E.), Harvard U. Grad. Sch. of Bus. Admin. (M.B.A.). Joined Capital Cities at its inception in 1954. Named a dir. in 1957, then pres. in 1964. Chmn. & CEO of Capital Cities, 1966-90. Company named Capital Cities/ABC Inc. in 1986 after acquistion of American Broadcasting Companies Inc. 1990-94, chmn. of bd. Resumed position of chmn. & CEO in Feb., 1994.

MURRAY, BARBARA
Actress. b. London, England, Sept. 27, 1929. Stage debut in Variety, 1946.
PICTURES: Badger's Green (debut, 1948), Passport to Pimlico, Don't Ever Leave Me, Boys in Brown, Poets Pub, Tony Draws a Horse, Dark Man, Frightened Man, Mystery Junction, Another Man's Poison, Hot Ice, Street Corner (Both Sides of the Law), Meet Mr. Lucifer, Doctor at Large, Campbell's Kingdom, A Cry from the Streets, Girls in Arms, A Dandy in Aspic, Tales From the Crypt.
TELEVISION: Series: The Power Game, The Bretts.

MURRAY, BILL
Actor. b. Wilmette, IL, Sept. 21, 1950. e. attended Regis Coll. Was pre-med student; left to join brother, Brian Doyle-Murray, in Second City the Chicago improvisational troupe. Appeared with brother on radio in National Lampoon Radio Hour, and in off-B'way revue, National Lampoon Show. Also on radio provided voice of Johnny Storm the Human Torch on Marvel Comics' Fantastic Four. Hired by ABC for Saturday Night Live with Howard Cosell; then by NBC for Saturday Night Live, 1977.
PICTURES: Jungle Burger (debut, 1975), Meatballs, Mr. Mike's Mondo Video, Where the Buffalo Roam, Loose Shoes (Coming Attractions), Caddyshack, Stripes, Tootsie, Ghostbusters, The Razor's Edge (also co-s.p.), Nothing Lasts Forever, Little Shop of Horrors, Scrooged, Ghostbusters II, Quick Change (also co-dir., co-prod.), What About Bob?, Groundhog Day, Mad Dog and Glory, Ed Wood, Space Jam, Larger Than Life, Kingpin.
TELEVISION: Series: Saturday Night Live (1977-80; also writer; Emmy Award for writing 1977). Pilot: The TV TV Show. Movie: All You Need Is Cash. Specials: It's Not Easy Being Me—The Rodney Dangerfield Show, Steve Martin's Best Show Ever, Second City—25 Years in Revue.

MURRAY, DON
Actor, Director, Writer. b. Hollywood, CA, July 31, 1929. e. AADA. Mother was a Ziegfeld Girl, father was dance dir. for Fox Studio.
THEATER: B'way: Insect Comedy, The Rose Tattoo, The Skin of Our Teeth, The Hot Corner, Smith (musical), The Norman Conquests, Same Time Next Year. National tours: California Suite, Chicago.
PICTURES: Bus Stop (debut, 1956; Acad. Award nom.), The Bachelor Party, A Hatful of Rain, From Hell to Texas, These Thousand Hills, Shake Hands With the Devil, One Foot in Hell, The Hoodlum Priest (also co-prod., co-s.p. as Don Deer), Advise and Consent, Escape From East Berlin, One Man's Way, Baby the Rain Must Fall, Kid Rodelo, The Plainsman, Sweet Love Bitter, The Viking Queen, Childish Things (Confession of Tom Harris; also prod., co-s.p.), The Cross and the Switchblade (dir., co-s.p. only), Happy Birthday Wanda June, Conquest of the Planet of the Apes, Cotter, Call Me by My Rightful Name (also prod., co-s.p.), Deadly Hero, Damien (dir., s.p. only), Endless Love, I Am the Cheese, Radioactive Dreams, Peggy Sue Got Married, Scorpion, Made in Heaven, Ghosts Can't Do It.
TELEVISION: Series: Made in America (panelist), The Outcasts, Knots Landing, Brand New Life, Sons and Daughters. Movies: The Borgia Stick, Daughter of the Mind, The Intruders, The Girl on the Late Late Show, The Sex Symbol, A Girl Named Sooner, Rainbow, Crisis in Mid-Air, If Things Were Different, The Boy Who Drank to Much, Fugitive Family, Return of the Rebels, Thursday's Child, Quarterback Princess, License to Kill, A Touch of Scandal, Something in Common, Stillwatch, The Stepford Children, Mistress, Brand New Life. Specials: For I Have Loved Strangers (also writer), Hasty Heart, Billy Budd, Winterset, Alas Babylon, Justin Morgan Had a Horse, My Dad Isn't Crazy Is He?, Montana Crossroads (Emmy nom.).

MURRAY, JAN
Comedian, Actor. b. Bronx, NY, Oct. 4, 1917. Started as comedian, nightclub performer, continuing on radio, tv.
THEATER: A Funny Thing Happened on the Way to the Forum, Guys and Dolls, Silk Stockings, Bye Bye Birdie, A Thousand Clowns, Come Blow Your Horn, The Odd Couple, Make a Million, Don't Drink the Water, Critic's Choice, You Know I Can't Hear You When the Water Is Running.
PICTURES: Who Killed Teddy Bear? (debut, 1965), Tarzan and the Great River, The Busy Body, A Man Called Dagger, Which Way to the Front?, History of the World Part I, Fear City.
TELEVISION: Series (emcee/host): Songs for Sale, Go Lucky, Sing It Again, Blind Date, Dollar a Second (also creator, prod.), Jan Murray Time, Treasure Hunt (also creator, prod.), Charge Account (also creator, prod.), Chain Letter. Guest: Zane Grey Theatre, Dr., Kildare, Burke's Law, The Lucy Show, Love American Style, Mannix, Ellery Queen, Hardcastle and McCormick. Movies: Roll Freddy Roll, Banjo Hackett: Roamin' Free, The Dream Merchants.

MUSANTE, TONY
Actor. b. Bridgeport, CT, June 30. e. Oberlin Coll. B.A. Directed local theatre, then appeared off-Broadway, in regional theater, and on Dupont Show of the Month (Ride With Terror).
THEATER: B'way: The Lady From Dubuque, P.S. Your Cat Is Dead, 27 Wagons Full of Cotton, Memory of Two Mondays. Off-B'way: Grand Magic, Cassatt, A Gun Play, Benito Cereno, L'Histoire du Soldat, Match-Play, The Zoo Story, The Pinter Plays (The Collection), Kiss Mama, The Balcony, Snow Orchid, The Flip Side, Frankie and Johnny in the Claire de Lune. Regional: The Big Knife, A Streetcar Named Desire, The Taming of the Shrew, Widows, The Archbishop's Ceiling, Dancing in the Endzone, Two Brothers, Souvenir, APA Shakespeare Rep., Wait Until Dark, Anthony Rose, Mount Allegro, Double Play, Falling Man, Breaking Legs, Love Letters, others. Regional: The Sisters, Italian Funerals and Other Festive Occasions.
PICTURES: Once a Thief, The Incident, The Detective, The Mercenary, The Bird with the Crystal Plumage, The Grissom Gang, The Last Run, Anonymous Venetian, Collector's Item, The Repenter, The Pisciotta Case, Goodbye and Amen, Break Up, Nocturne, The Pope of Greenwich Village, One Night at Dinner, Appointment in Trieste, Devil's Hill.
TELEVISION: Series: Toma. Guest: Chrysler Theatre, Alfred Hitchcock Hour, N.Y.P.D., The Fugitive, Trials of O'Brien, Police Story, Medical Story, Thomas Gottschallk's Late Night TV. Movies: Rearview Mirror, The Court Martial of Lt. William Calley, Desperate Miles, The Quality of Mercy, Nowhere to Hide, My Husband is Missing, The Story of Esther, High Ice, Last Waltz on a Tightrope, Weekend (Amer. Playhouse), Nutcracker: Money Madness & Murder, Breaking Up Is Hard To Do, The Baron.

MYERS, JULIAN F.
Public Relations Executive. b. Detroit, MI, Feb. 22, 1918. e. Wayne U., 1935-37, USC, 1937-39. Distribution, Loew's Detroit, 1941-42; asst. story editor, idea man, Columbia, 1942-46; publicist, 20th Century-Fox, 1948-62; public relations, Julian F. Myers, Inc., 1962; pres., Myers Studios, Inc., 1966; pres., New Horizons Broadcasting Corp., 1968-69; sr. publicist American Intl. Pictures, 1970-80. Pres., Hollywood Press Club; former member Variety Club; Academy of Motion Pictures Arts & Sciences; Board of Governors Film Industry Workshops, Inc. 1977, 1979, western v.p.; Publicists Guild; Recipient of Publicists Guild's Robert Yeager Award. First male member Hollywood Women's Press Club. Co-founder HANDS (Hollywood Answering Needs of Disaster Survivors). Member, M.P. Pioneers. Winner, 1980 Publicists Guild Les Mason Award. Instructor in publicity, UCLA, 1979-present, and at Loyola Marymount U, 1991-present. Filmways Pictures, pub. dept., 1980-81. Exec. v.p., worldwide m.p. and TV pub./mktg., Hanson & Schwam Public Relations 1981-91. Author of Myersystem and Myerscope guides. Member: USC Cinema & TV Alumni Assn., West Coast P.R. Will Rogers Inst., Acad TV Arts Sciences; p.r. co-ord. committee Academy of Motion Picture Arts & Sciences. Bd. of Dirs., Show Biz Expo. Publicist, Prods. Guild of America. Pres. Julian Myers Public Relations, nominated MoPic Showmanship of the Year, Publicists Guild of America, 1993.

MYERS, PETER S.
Executive. b. Toronto, Ont., Canada, May 13, 1923. e. U. of Toronto. Toronto branch mgr., 20th Century-Fox, 1948; mng. dir., Canada, 1951; gen. sales mgr. in charge of domestic distrib., US & Canada, 1968; sr. v.p., 20th-Fox Ent.; pres., 20th-Fox Classics 1983; pres., Hemdale Releasing Company, 1986; pres. & CEO, Four Seasons Entertainment, 1989.

MYERS, STANLEY
Composer. b. London, England, 1939.
PICTURES: Kaleidoscope (debut, 1966), Ulysses, No Way to Treat a Lady, Michael Kohlhaas, Otley, Two Gentlemen Sharing, Take a Girl Like You, Tropic of Cancer, The Walking Stick, Long Ago Tomorrow, A Severed Head, Tam Lin, King Queen Knave, Sitting Target, Summer Lightning, X Y & Zee, The Blockhouse, The Apprenticeship of Duddy Kravitz, Caravan to Vaccares,

Little Malcolm, The Wilby Conspiracy, Coup de Grace, The Greek Tycoon, The Deer Hunter, The Class of Miss MacMichael, A Portrait of the Artist as a Young Man, The Secret Policeman's Other Ball, Yesterday's Hero, Watcher in the Woods, Absolution, The Incubus, Lady Chatterly's Lover, Eureka, Moonlighting, Blind Date, Beyond the Limit, The Next One, Success is the Best Revenge, The Chain, Dreamchild, Insignificance, The Lightship, The Wind, Castaway, My Beautiful Laundrette, Prick Up Your Ears, Wish You Were Here, The Second Victory, Taffin, Track 29, Stars and Bars, Trading Hearts, Sammy and Rosie Get Laid, Scenes From the Class Struggle in Beverly Hills, Torrents of Spring.
TELEVISION: Series (U.K.): Widows (parts 1 & 2), Nancy Astor, Diana. Series (U.S.): The Martian Chronicles, Florence Nightingale. Movies: Strong Medicine, Smart Money, Baja Oklahoma, Monte Carlo.

MYERSON, BERNARD
Executive. b. New York, NY, March 25, 1918. Entered m.p. ind. with Fabian Theatres, 1938-63; last position as exec. v.p.; joined Loew's Theatres as v.p., 1963; exec. v.p. and board member, Loew's Corp.; pres. Loew's Theatres, 1971. Chmn. & pres., Loews Theatre Management Corp., 1985, presently retired. Member of Executive Committee Greater N.Y. Chapter, National Foundation of March of Dimes; Honorary chmn., bd. mem., & former pres., Will Rogers Memorial Fund; exec. comm., bd., National Assn. Theatre Owners; past member & former pres., Motion Picture Pioneers; treas. Variety Intl.; member bd. of dirs., Burke Rehabilitation Center; member, N.Y.S. Governor's Council on M.P. & T.V. Development; vice-chmn., adv. bd. of Tisch Sch. of Arts, NYU.

N

NABORS, JIM
Actor. b. Sylacauga, AL, June 12, 1932. Discovered performing in an L.A. nightclub in early 1960's by Andy Griffith, who asked him to appear on his series. Developed a second career as a singer. Between 1966-72 had 12 albums on best selling charts.
PICTURES: The Best Little Whorehouse in Texas, Stroker Ace, Cannonball Run II.
TELEVISION: Series: The Andy Griffith Show, Gomer Pyle USMC, The Jim Nabors Hour, The Lost Saucer, The Jim Nabors Show (synd. talk show). Movie: Return to Mayberry.

NADER, GEORGE
Actor. b. Pasadena, CA, Oct. 19, 1921. e. Occidental Coll., B.A.; Pasadena Playhouse, B.T.A. Served in U.S. Navy. Wrote novel: Chrome (Putnam).
PICTURES: Monsoon (debut, 1953), Memory of Love, Robot Monster, Rustlers on Horseback, Overland Telegraph, Carnival Story, Miss Robin Crusoe, Sins of Jezebel, Phone Call from a Stranger, Four Guns to the Border, Six Bridges to Cross, Lady Godiva, The Second Greatest Sex, Away All Boats, Appointment With a Shadow, Congo Crossing, The Unguarded Moment, Four Girls in Town, Man Afraid, The Female Animal, Flood Tide, Joe Butterfly, Nowhere to Go, The Secret Mark of D'Artagnan, The Great Space Adventure, Zigzag, The Human Duplicators, House of a Thousand Dolls, The Million Eyes of Sumuru, Alarm on 83rd Street, Murder at Midnight, Count-Down for Manhattan, Dynamite in Green Silk, The Check and an Icy Smile, Murder Club from Brooklyn, Death in Red Jaguar, End Station of the Damned, Beyond Atlantis.
TELEVISION: Series: Ellery Queen, Man and the Challenge, Shannon. Guest: Letter to Loretta, Fireside Theatre, Chevron Theatre, Alfred Hitchcock, Andy Griffith Show, etc. Movie: Nakia.

NAIFY, MARSHALL
Executive. Chairman, Todd-AO/Glenn Studios.

NAIFY, ROBERT
Executive. b. Sacramento, CA. e. Attended Stanford U. Worked for United California Theatres starting in 1946 in various capacities including: theatre manager, purchasing agent, film buyer, general manager and president. 1963 became exec. v.p. United Artists Communications; 1971 became pres. & CEO until 1987. Currently president, Todd-AO Corporation.

NAIR, MIRA
Director, Producer. b. Bhubaneswar, India, 1957. e. Irish Catholic Missionary School in India, Delhi U., Harvard U. A course in documentary filmmaking at Harvard led to directing 4 non-fiction films including India Cabaret (1985) and Children of Desired Sex.
PICTURES: Director-Producer: Salaam Bombay! (Cannes Film Fest. Camera d'Or/Prix du Publique; Acad. Award nom.), Mississippi Masala (also s.p.), The Perez Family.

NALLE, BILLY
Theatre Concert Organist, Composer. b. Fort Myers, FL, Apr. 24, 1921. Postgrad, Juilliard Sch. Over 5,000 major tele-

casts from NY; now artist emeritus, Wichita Theatre Organization, Inc. RCA, Telarc, Reader's Digest & WTO Records Artist. Now residing in Fort Myers, FL.

NAMATH, JOE
Actor. b. Beaver Falls, PA, May 31, 1943. e. U. of Alabama. Former professional football star.
PICTURES: Norwood (debut, 1970), C.C. & Company (Chrome Hearts), The Last Rebel, Avalanche Express, Chattanooga Choo Choo, Going Under.
TELEVISION: Series: The Waverly Wonders. Host: Monday Night Football (1985). Movie: Marriage Is Alive and Well. Guest: Here's Lucy, The Brady Bunch, The Love Boat, Kate and Allie.

NARDINO, GARY
Executive. b. Garfield, NJ, Aug. 26, 1935. e. Seton Hall U. Awarded honorary degree of Doctor of Laws. Entered industry in 1959 as agent, representing Lorimar Prods. and Talent Associates, among others. Named sr. v.p. of ICM's New York TV dept; then v.p. of William Morris Agency, heading N.Y. TV dept. Pres. of Paramount TV Production Division, 1977-83. Pres. of Gary Nardino Prods., Inc., formed 1983, to dev. and produce theatrical features and TV programming; 1988-90, chmn. & CEO, Orion Television Entertainment.
PICTURES: Star Trek III: The Search for Spock (exec. prod.), Fire with Fire (prod.).
TELEVISION: Exec. prod.: Brothers, At Your Service, Joanna.

NARIZZANO, SILVIO
Producer, Director. b. Montreal, Canada, Feb. 8, 1927. e. U. of Bishop's, Lennoxville, Quebec, B.A. Was active as actor-director in Canadian theatre before going to England for TV and theatrical film work.
PICTURES: Director: Under Ten Flags (co-dir.), Die! Die! My Darling! (Fanatic), Georgy Girl, Blue, Loot, Redneck (also prod.), The Sky Is Falling, Why Shoot the Teacher?, The Class of Miss MacMichael, Choices, Double Play. Producer: Negatives, Fadeout.
TELEVISION: Come Back Little Sheba, Staying On, Young Shoulders, Miss Marple (series).

NASH, N. RICHARD
Writer. b. Philadelphia, PA, June 8, 1913.
AUTHOR: Cry Macho, East Wind, Rain, The Last Magic, Aphrodite's Cave, Radiance, Behold the Man, The Wildwood.
THEATER: B'way: Second Best Bed, The Young and Fair, See the Jaguar, The Rainmaker, Girls of Summer, Handful of Fire, Wildcat, 110 in the Shade, Fire, The Happy Time, Echoes, Wildfire, The Torch, Magic, The Bluebird of Happiness, The Loss of D-Natural, Breaking the Tie, Come As You Are, Everybody Smile, Life Anonymous, The Green Clown.
PICTURES: Nora Prentiss, Welcome Stranger, The Vicious Years, The Rainmaker, Dear Wife, Porgy and Bess, Sainted Sisters, Dragonfly.
TELEVISION: Many TV plays for Television Playhouse, U.S. Steel, General Electric.

NAUGHTON, DAVID
Actor, Singer. b. Hartford, CT, Feb. 13, 1951. Brother is actor James Naughton. e. U. of Pennsylvania, B.A. Studied at London Acad. of Music and Dramatic Arts. Numerous TV commercials, including music for Dr. Pepper. On B'way in Hamlet, Da, Poor Little Lambs.
PICTURES: Midnight Madness (debut, 1980), An American Werewolf in London, Separate Ways, Hot Dog... The Movie, Not for Publication, The Boy in Blue, Separate Vacations, Kidnapped, Quite By Chance, Beanstalk, The Sleeping Car, Overexposed, Wild Cactus, Desert Steel, Ice Cream Man, Midnight Madness, The Boy In Blue.
TELEVISION: Series: Making It, At Ease, My Sister Sam, Temporary Insanity, The Belles of Bleeker St., Those Two. Movies: I Desire, Getting Physical, Goddess of Love. Guest: Twilight Zone, Murder She Wrote.

NAUGHTON, JAMES
Actor. b. Middletown, CT, Dec. 6, 1945. Father of actor Greg Naughton. e. Brown U., A.B., 1967; Yale U., M.F.A., drama, 1970.
THEATER: NY: I Love My Wife (B'way debut, 1977), Long Day's Journey Into Night (Theatre World, Drama Desk and New York Critics Circle Awards, 1971), Whose Life Is It Anyway?, Losing Time, Drinks Before Dinner, City of Angels (Tony & Drama Desk Awards, 1990), Four Baboons Adoring the Sun. Regional: Who's Afraid of Virginia Woolf? (Long Wharf), The Glass Menagerie (Long Wharf), Hamlet (Long Wharf), Julius Caesar (Amer. Shakespeare Festival), 8 seasons at Williamstown Theatre Festival.
PICTURES: The Paper Chase (debut, 1973), Second Wind, A Stranger is Watching, Cat's Eye, The Glass Menagerie, The Good Mother, First Kid.
TELEVISION: Special: Look Homeward Angel (1972). Series: Faraday and Company, Planet of the Apes, Making the Grade, Trauma Center, Raising Miranda, The Cosby Mysteries. Movies: F. Scott Fitzgerald and the Last of the Belles, The Last

36 Hours of Dr. Durant, The Bunker, My Body My Child, Parole, The Last of the Great Survivors, Between Darkness and the Dawn, Sin of Innocence, Traveling Man, Antigone, The Cosby Mysteries (pilot), The Birds II: Land's End, Cagney & Lacey: The Return, Cagney & Lacey: Together Again, Raising Caines.

NEAL, PATRICIA
Actress. b. Packard, KY, Jan. 20, 1926. e. Northwestern U. Worker as doctor's asst., cashier, hostess, model, jewelry store clerk prior to prof. career as actress. In summer stock before B'way debut in The Voice of the Turtle, 1946. Autobiography: As I Am (with Richard DeNeut, 1988).
THEATER: NY: The Voice of the Turtle, Another Part of the Forest (Tony, Donaldson & Drama Critic Awards), The Children's Hour, Roomful of Roses, The Miracle Worker. England: Suddenly Last Summer.
PICTURES: John Loves Mary (debut 1949), The Fountainhead, It's a Great Feeling, The Hasty Heart, Bright Leaf, Three Secrets, The Breaking Point, Raton Pass, Operation Pacific, The Day the Earth Stood Still, Weekend With Father, Diplomatic Courier, Washington Story, Something for the Birds, Stranger from Venus (Immediate Disaster), Your Woman, A Face in the Crowd, Breakfast at Tiffany's, Hud (Academy Award, BFA Award, 1963), Psyche '59, In Harm's Way (BFA Award, 1965), The Subject Was Roses (Acad. Award nom.), The Night Digger, Baxter, Happy Mother's Day Love George (Run Stranger Run), "B" Must Die, The Passage, Ghost Story, An Unremarkable Life.
TELEVISION: Movies: The Homecoming, Things in Their Season, Eric, Tail Gunner Joe, A Love Affair: The Eleanor and Lou Gehrig Story, The Bastard, All Quiet on the Western Front, Shattered Vows, Love Leads the Way, Caroline?, A Mother's Right: The Elizabeth Morgan Story, Heidi. Guest: Little House on the Prairie, Murder She Wrote. BBC: Days & Nights of Beebee Finstermaker, The Country Girl, Clash By Night, The Royal Family.

NEAME, RONALD
Cinematographer, Producer, Director. b. Hendon, Eng. April 23, 1911. e. U. Coll. Sch., London. p. Elwin Neame, London photog., & Ivy Close, m.p. actress. Entered m.p. ind. 1928; asst. cameraman on first full-length Brit. sound film, Blackmail, dir. by Alfred Hitchcock, 1929; became chief cameraman & lighting expert, 1934; in 1945 joint assoc. prod., Noel Coward Prods.
PICTURES: Cinematographer: Girls Will Be Boys (co-cine.), Happy (co-cine.), Elizabeth of England, Honours Easy (co-cine.), Invitation to the Waltz (co-cine.), Joy Ride, Music Hath Charms, The Crimes of Stephen Hawke, The Improper Dutchess, A Star Fell From Heaven, Against the Tide, Brief Ecstasy, Feather Your Nest, Keep Fit, Weekend Millionaire, Gaunt Stranger, The Phantom Strikes, The Crime of Peter Frame, Dangerous Secrets, I See Ice (co-cine.), Penny Paradise, Who Goes Next? Cheers Boys Cheer, Sweeney Todd: The Demon Barber of Fleet Street, Let's Be Famous, Trouble Brewing, The Ware Case, It's In the Air (co-cine.), Let George Do It, Return to Yesterday, Saloon Bar, Just Men, Major Barbara, A Yank in the R.A.F. (Brit. flying sequence), One of Our Aircraft is Missing, In Which We Serve, This Happy Breed, Blithe Spirit, Brief Encounter, Great Expectations (also co-s.p.), Oliver Twist (also co-s.p.), A Young Man's Fancy, Passionate Friends. Director: Take My Life, Golden Salamander (also co-s.p.), The Card (The Promoter; also prod.), Man With a Million (The Million Pound Note), The Man Who Never Was, The Seventh Sin, Windom's Way, The Horse's Mouth, Tunes of Glory, Escape from Zahrain, I Could Go on Singing, The Chalk Garden, Mister Moses, Gambit, A Man Could Get Killed (co-dir.), Prudence and the Pill (co-dir.), The Prime of Miss Jean Brodie, Scrooge, The Poseidon Adventure, The Odessa File, Meteor, Hopscotch, First Monday in October, Foreign Body, The Magic Balloon.

NEEDHAM, HAL
Director, Writer. b. Memphis, TN, March 6, 1931. e. Student public schools. Served with Paratroopers, U.S. Army 1951-54. Founder Stunts Unlimited, Los Angeles, 1970; stuntman Stunts Unlimited, 1956-65; dir. and stunt coordinator second unit, 1965-75. Chmn. of bd., Camera Platforms International, Inc. 1985. Owner Budweiser Rocket Car (fastest car in the world). Member Screen Actors Guild, AFTRA, Writers Guild of America, Directors Guild of America.
PICTURES: Dir.: Smokey and the Bandit (debut, 1977; also co-story), Hooper, The Villain, Smokey and the Bandit II, The Cannonball Run, Megaforce (also co-s.p.), Stroker Ace (also co-s.p.), Cannonball Run II (also co-s.p.), RAD, Body Slam.
TELEVISION: Series: Hal Needham's Wild World of Stunts (synd. series; also writer, star). Movie: Death Car on the Freeway. Pilot: Stunts Unlimited (pilot). Episode: B.L. Stryker.

NEESON, LIAM
Actor. b. Ballymena, Northern Ireland, June 7, 1952. m. actress Natasha Richardson. Former amateur boxer. Was driving

a fork lift truck for a brewery when he joined the Lyric Player's Theatre in Belfast. Made prof. debut in The Risen (1976) and stayed with rep. co. 2 years. Moved to Dublin as freelance actor before joining the Abbey Theatre.
THEATER: The Informer (Dublin Theatre Fest.), Translations (National Theatre, London). NY theatre debut 1992 in Anna Christie (Theatre World Award).
PICTURES: Excalibur (debut, 1981), Krull, The Bounty, Lamb, The Innocent, The Mission, Duet For One, A Prayer for the Dying, Suspect, Satisfaction, The Dead Pool, The Good Mother, High Spirits, Next of Kin, Dark Man, Crossing the Line (The Big Man), Shining Through, Under Suspicion, Husbands and Wives, Leap of Faith, Ethan Frome, Deception, Schindler's List (Acad. Award nom.), Nell, Rob Roy, Before and After, Michael Collins.
TELEVISION: Merlin and the Sword, Across the Water (BBC), Ellis Island, A Woman of Substance, Sweet As You Are.

NEILL, SAM
Actor. b. Northern Ireland, Sept. 14, 1947. Raised in New Zealand. e. U. of Canterbury. In repertory before joining N.Z. National Film Unit, acting and directing documentaries and shorts. 1992, awarded the O.B.E. for his services to acting. Co-directed, co-wrote and appeared in New Zealand documentary Cinema of Unease: A Personal Journey by Sam Neill.
PICTURES: Sleeping Dogs (debut, 1977), The Journalist, My Brilliant Career, Just Out of Reach, Attack Force Z, The Final Conflict, Possession, Enigma, Le Sang des Autres, Robbery Under Arms, Plenty, For Love Alone, The Good Wife, A Cry in the Dark (Australian Film Inst. Award), Dead Calm, The French Revolution, The Hunt for Red October, Until the End of the World, Hostage, Memoirs of an Invisible Man, Death in Brunswick, Jurassic Park, The Piano, Sirens, Rudyard Kipling's The Jungle Book, In the Mouth of Madness, Country Life, Restoration, Victory.
TELEVISION: The Sullivans, Young Ramsay, Lucinda Brayford, The Country Girls. Mini-Series: Kane and Abel, Reilly Ace of Spies, Amerika. Movies: From a Far Country: Pope John Paul II, Ivanhoe, The Blood of Others, Arthur Hailey's Strong Medicine, Leap of Faith, Fever, One Against the Wind, The Sinking of the Rainbow Warrior, Family Pictures.

NELLIGAN, KATE
Actress. b. London, Ontario, Canada, March 16, 1951.
THEATER: Barefoot in the Park, A Streetcar Named Desire, Playboy of the Western World, Private Lives, Plenty, Serious Money, Spoils of War, Bad Habits.
PICTURES: The Romantic Englishwoman (debut, 1975), Dracula, Mr. Patman, Eye of the Needle, Without a Trace, The Mystery of Henry Moore, Eleni, Frankie and Johnny (BAFTA Award), The Prince of Tides (Acad. Award nom.), Shadows and Fog, Fatal Instinct, Wolf, Margaret's Museum, How to Make an American Quilt, Up Close and Personal.
TELEVISION: Movies/Specials: The Onedin Line, The Lady of the Camelias, Therese Raquin, Count of Monte Cristo, Victims, Kojak: The Price of Justice, Love and Hate: The Story of Colin and Joann Thatcher, Three Hotels, Terror Strikes the Class Reunion, Diamond Fleece, Liar Liar, Shattered Trust: The Shari Karney Story, Spoils of War, Million Dollar Babies.

NELSON, BARRY
Actor. r.n. Robert Neilson. b. Oakland, CA, Apr. 16, 1920. e. U. of California. London stage in No Time for Sergeants, 1957.
THEATER: B'way: Light Up the Sky, The Rat Race, The Moon Is Blue, Mary Mary, Cactus Flower, Everything in the Garden, Seascape, The Norman Conquests, The Act, 42nd Street.
PICTURES: Shadow of the Thin Man, Johnny Eager, Dr. Kildare's Victory, Rio Rita, Eyes in the Night, Bataan, The Human Comedy, A Guy Named Joe, Winged Victory, The Beginning or the End, Undercover Maisie, The Man With My Face, The First Traveling Saleslady, Mary Mary, Airport, Pete 'n' Tillie, The Shining, Island Claws.
TELEVISION: Series: The Hunter, My Favorite Husband. Mini-Series: Washington: Behind Closed Doors. Movies: The Borgia Stick, Seven in Darkness, Climb an Angry Mountain. Guest: Suspense, Alfred Hitchcock Presents, Longstreet, Taxi, Magnum P.I., Murder She Wrote.

NELSON, CRAIG T.
Actor. b. Spokane, WA, April 4, 1946. Began career as writer/performer on Lohman and Barkley Show in Los Angeles. Teamed with Barry Levinson as a comedy writer. Wrote for Tim Conway Show, Alan King TV special; guest appearances on talk shows and Mary Tyler Moore Show. Produced series of 52 half-hour films on American artists, American Still. Returned to L.A. in 1978 and acting career.
PICTURES: And Justice for All (debut, 1979), Where the Buffalo Roam, Private Benjamin, Stir Crazy, The Formula, Poltergeist, Man Woman and Child, All the Right Moves, The Osterman Weekend, Silkwood, The Killing Fields, Poltergeist II, Red Riding Hood, Action Jackson, Rachel River, Me and Him, Troop Beverly Hills, Turner & Hooch, I'm Not Rappaport, Ghosts of Mississippi.

TELEVISION: Series: Call to Glory, Coach (Emmy Award, 1992).Guest: Wonder Woman, Charlie's Angels, How the West Was Won. Movies: Diary of a Teenage Hitchhiker, Rage, Promise of Love, Inmates: A Love Story, Chicago Story, Paper Dolls, Alex: The Life of a Child, The Ted Kennedy Jr. Story, Murderers Among Us: The Simon Wiesenthal Story, Extreme Close-Up, The Josephine Baker Story, The Switch, The Fire Next Time, Ride With the Wind (also co-writer), Probable Cause, Take Me Home Again. Mini-Series: Drug Wars: The Camarena Story.

NELSON, DAVID
Actor. b. New York, NY, Oct. 24, 1936. e. Hollywood H.S., U. of Southern California. Son of Ozzie Nelson and Harriet Hilliard Nelson; brother of late Rick Nelson.
PICTURES: Here Comes the Nelsons, Peyton Place, The Remarkable Mr. Pennypacker, Day of the Outlaw, The Big Circus, "30", The Big Show, No Drums No Bugles, Cry-Baby. Director: A Rare Breed, The Last Plane Out.
TELEVISION: Series: The Adventures of Ozzie and Harriet (also dir. episodes). Movies: Smash-Up on Interstate 5, High School U.S.A. Guest: Hondo, The Love Boat. Dir.: Easy To Be Free (special), OK Crackerby (series).

NELSON, GENE
Dancer, Actor, Director, Choreographer. r.n. Gene Berg. b. Seattle, WA, March 24, 1920. e. Santa Monica, CA, H.S. Began dancing and ice skating in school; joined Sonja Henie Hollywood Ice Revue, featured in It Happens on Ice in NY; served in WWII. Joined Hollywood group prod. stage musical, Lend an Ear; to Warner for Daughter of Rosie O'Grady (1950). Prof. of Theatre Arts at San Francisco State U. School of Creative Arts, 1989-90.
THEATER: B'way: Actor: Lend an Ear, Follies, The Music Music, Good News. Director: Follies, Elephant Man, Oklahoma!, Stepping Out.
PICTURES: Actor: This Is the Army (debut, 1943), I Wonder Who's Kissing Her Now, Gentleman's Agreement, Apartment For Peggy, The Daughter of Rosie O'Grady, Tea for Two, Starlift, The West Point Story, Lullaby of Broadway, Painting the Clouds With Sunshine, She's Working Her Way Through College, She's Back on Broadway, Three Sailors and a Girl, Crime Wave, So This Is Paris, Oklahoma!, The Way Out (Dial 999), The Atomic Man (Timeslip), 20,000 Eyes, The Purple Hills, Thunder Island, S.O.B. Director: The Hand of Death, Hootenany Hoot, Your Cheatin' Heart, Kissin' Cousins, Harum Scarum, The Cool Ones (also s.p.).
TELEVISION: Series Director: Mod Squad, I Dream of Jeannie, FBI, 12 O'Clock High, Hawaii Five-O, Farmer's Daughter, Donna Reed Show, Burke's Law, Felony Squad, Laredo, The Rifleman, The Wackiest Ship, Iron Horse, FBI, The Rookies, Quincy, Operation Petticoat. Movies (Director): Wake Me When the War is Over (also co-prod.), The Letters. Movies (Actor): Family Flight, A Brand New Life.

NELSON, JUDD
Actor. b. Portland, ME, Nov. 28, 1959. e. Haverford/Bryn Mawr Coll. Studied acting at Stella Adler Conservatory. NY theatre includes Carnal Knowledge.
PICTURES: Making the Grade (debut, 1984), Fandango, The Breakfast Club, St. Elmo's Fire, Blue City, Transformers (voice), From the Hip, Relentless, Far Out Man, New Jack City, The Dark Backward, Primary Motive, Entangled, Conflict of Interest, Caroline at Midnight, Hail Caesar, Every Breath (also s.p.), Flinch, Circumstances Unknown, Blackwater Trail.
TELEVISION: Series: Suddenly Susan. Guest: Moonlighting. Movies: Billionaire Boys Club, Hiroshima: Out of the Ashes, Conflict of Interest, Blindfold: Acts of Obsession.

NELSON, LORI
Actress. r.n. Dixie Kay Nelson. b. Santa Fe, NM, Aug. 15, 1933. e. Canoga Park H.S. Started as child actress, photographer's model before film debut in 1952.
THEATER: The Pleasure of His Company, Who Was That Lady I Saw You With, Affairs of Mildred Wilde, Sweet Bird of Youth, Picnic, 'Night Mother.
PICTURES: Ma and Pa Kettle at the Fair (debut, 1952), Bend of the River, Francis Goes to West Point, All I Desire, All-American, Walking My Baby Back Home, Tumbleweed, Underwater, Destry, Revenge of the Creature, I Died a Thousand Times, Sincerely Yours, Mohawk, Day the World Ended, Pardners, Hot Rod Girl, Ma and Pa Kettle at Waikiki, Gambling Man, Untamed Youth.
TELEVISION: Series: How to Marry a Millionaire. Guest: Wagon Train, Laramie, Family Affair, The Texan, Wanted Dead or Alive, Sam Spade, G.E. Theatre, Riverboat, Sugarfoot, The Young and the Restless, Climax, The Millionaire, Wells Fargo, etc. Special: The Pied Piper of Hamelin.

NELSON, TRACY
Actress, Singer, Dancer. b. Santa Monica, CA, Oct., 1963. e. Bard Coll. Daughter of late singer-actor Rick Nelson. Sister of singers Matthew & Gunnar Nelson. Studied acting in England.
THEATER: Grease (Nat'l touring co. & B'way).

PICTURES: Yours Mine and Outs (debut, 1968), Maria's Lovers, Down and Out in Beverly Hills, Chapters.
TELEVISION: *Series*: Square Pegs, Glitter, Father Dowling Mysteries, A League of Their Own, Melrose Place, The Man from Snowy River. *Movies*: Katie's Secret, Tonight's the Night, If It's Tuesday It Still Must Be Belgium, Fatal Confessions, For Hope, In the Shadiow of Evil, Pleasures, Highway Heartbreaker, Ray Alexander: Murder in Mind, Ray Alexander: A Taste for Justice, No Child of Mine. *Guest*: The Adventures of Ozzie and Harriet, Hotel, Family Ties, The Love Boat.

NELSON, WILLIE
Composer, Singer, Actor. b. Abbott, TX, April 30, 1933. Worked as salesman, announcer, host of country music shows on local Texas stations; bass player with Ray Price's band. Started writing songs in the 60's; performing in the 70's.
PICTURES: The Electric Horseman (debut, 1979), Honeysuckle Rose, Thief, Barbarosa, Hell's Angels Forever, Songwriter, Red-Headed Stranger (also prod.), Walking After Midnight.
TELEVISION: *Movies*: The Last Days of Frank and Jesse James, Stagecoach, Coming Out of the Ice, Baja Oklahoma, Once Upon a Texas Train, Where the Hell's That Gold?!!?, Pair of Aces, Another Pair of Aces, Wild Texas Wind, Big Dreams & Broken Hearts: The Dottie West Story. *Special*: Willie Nelson—Texas Style (also prod.).

NEMEC, CORIN
Actor. r.n. Joseph Charles Nemec IV. b. Little Rock, AR, Nov. 5, 1971. Began acting in commercials at age 13.
PICTURES: Tucker: The Man and His Dream, Solar Crisis, Drop Zone, Operation Dumbo Drop.
TELEVISION: *Series*: Parker Lewis Can't Lose. *Movies*: I Know My First Name is Steven (Emmy nom.), For the Very First Time, My Son Johnny, The Lifeforce Experiment. *Mini-Series*: The Stand. *Pilot*: What's Alan Watching? *Guest*: Webster, Sidekicks.

NERO, FRANCO
Actor. r.n. Franceso Sparanero. b. Parma, Italy, Nov. 23, 1942. e. Univ. La Bocconi, Milan.
PICTURES: Celestina (Made at Your Service; debut, 1964), The Deadly Diaphanoids, I Knew Her Well, Wild Wild Planet, The Third Eyes, The Bible, The Tramplers, Django, The Avenger (Texas Addio), Hired Killer, The Brute and the Beast, Mafia, Camelot, L'uomo l'Orgoglio la Vendetta, Island of Crime, The Mercenary, The Day of the Owl, A Quiet Place in the Country, The Battle of Neretva, Detective Belli, Sardinia: Ramsom, Companeros, Tristana, The Virgin and the Gypsy, Drop Out!, Confessions of a Police Commissioner, Killer From Yuma, Redneck, The Monk, The Vacation, Pope Joan, Deaf Smith and Johnny Ears, The Fifth Day of Peace, The Aquarian, High Crime, Blood Brothers (I Guappi), Cry Onion, The Anonymous Avenger, Challenge to White Fang, Death Drive, Violent Breed, Submission, The Last Days of Mussolini, Force Ten From Navarone, The Man With Bogart's Face, The Visitor, Shark Hunter, Blue-Eyed Bandit, Danzig Roses, Day of the Cobra, The Falcon, The Salamander, Sahara Cross, Enter the Ninja, Mexico in Flames, Querelle, Wagner, Sweet Country, The Girl, Garibaldi the General, Race to Danger, Marathon, Django Strikes Again, Top Line, Silent Night, Young Toscanini, The Betrothed, The Magistrate, Heart of Victory, The Repenter, The Forester's Sons, Die Hard 2, Brothers and Sisters, Crimson Down, Oro, Deep Blue, The Lucona Affair, Babylon Complot, A Breath of Life, Jonathan of the Bears, Conflict of Interest, The Dragon's Ring, Talk of Angels, The Innocent Sleep, The King and Me.
TELEVISION: *Mini-series*: The Last Days of Pompeii. *Movies*: The Legend of Valentino, 21 Hours at Munich, The Pirate, Young Catherine.

NESMITH, MICHAEL
Musician, Producer. b. Houston, TX, Dec. 30, 1942. Original member of The Monkees, later became producer of videos and films. Chmn. & CEO Pacific Arts Publishing video company. Won Grammy award for music video Elephant Parts. Exec. prod. & performer in video Dr. Duck's Super Secret All-Purpose Sauce.
PICTURES: *Actor*: Head, Burglar (cameo). *Exec. Prod.*: Timerider (also co-s.p.), Repo Man, Square Dance, Tapeheads.
TELEVISION: *Series*: The Monkees, Michael Nesmith in Television Parts (also prod.). *Special*: 33-1/3 Revolutions Per Monkee.

NETTER, DOUGLAS
Executive, Producer. b. Seattle, WA. 1955-57, gen. mgr. Todd A.O.; 1958-60, Sam Goldwyn Productions; 1961-67, formed own co. representing producers; 1968-69, Jalem Productions; 1969-75, exec. v.p. MGM. Films: Mr. Ricco (prod.), The Wild Geese (co-prod.).
TELEVISION: Louis L'Amour's The Sacketts (prod.), The Buffalo Soldiers (exec. prod.), Wild Times (prod.), Roughnecks (exec. prod.), Cherokee Trail (exec. prod.), Five Mile Creek (exec. prod.; Australian based TV series for Disney Channel), Captain Power and the Soldiers of the Future (exec. prod.), Stealth F22 (exec. prod.), Babylon 5 (exec. prod.).

NETTLETON, LOIS
Actress. b. Oak Park, IL, 1931. e. Studied at Goodman Theatre, Chicago and Actors Studio. Replaced Kim Hunter in Darkness at Noon on B'way. Emmy Award: Performer Best Daytime Drama Spec., The American Woman: Portraits in Courage (1977). Also Emmy: Religious Program, Insight (1983).
THEATER: Cat on a Hot Tin Roof, Silent Night, Lonely Night, God and Kate Murphy, The Wayward Stork, The Rainmaker, A Streetcar Named Desire.
PICTURES: A Face in the Crowd (debut, 1957), Period of Adjustment, Come Fly with Me, Mail Order Bride, Valley of Mystery, Bamboo Saucer, The Good Guys and the Bad Guys, Dirty Dingus Magee, The Sidelong Glances of a Pigeon Kicker, The Honkers, The Man in the Glass Booth, Echoes of a Summer, Deadly Blessing, Butterfly, Soggy Bottom U.S.A., The Best Little Whorehouse in Texas.
TELEVISION: *Series*: Accidental Family, You Can't Take It With You. *Guest*: Medical Center, Barnaby Jones, Alfred Hitchcock, All That Glitters, In the Heat of the Night. *Movies*: Any Second Now, Weekend of Terror, The Forgotten Man, Terror in the Sky, Women in Chains, Fear on Trial, Tourist, Brass, Manhunt for Claude Dallas. *Mini-Series*: Washington: Behind Closed Doors, Centennial. *Specials*: Rendezvous, Meet Me in St. Louis, Traveler's Rest.

NEUFELD, MACE
Producer. b. New York, NY, July 13, 1928. e. Yale Col. Started as professional photographer, before becoming prod. asst. at Dumont Television Network. Wrote musical material for performers incl. Sammy Davis Jr., Dorothy Loudon, Ritz Brothers, etc., and theme for Heckle and Jeckle animated series. In 1951, formed independent TV prod. and personal mgmt. co. For TV produced programs for Dick Van Dyke, Elaine May and Mike Nichols. Formed independent production co. with Nichols and Buck Henry. In 1980, created Neufeld-Davis Prods. with Marvin Davis. Formed Neufeld/Rehme Prods. with Robert G. Rehme in 1989. On B'way, prod. Flying Karamazov Brothers show. Voted Producer of the Year by NATO/ShoWest, 1992.
PICTURES: The Omen, Damien: Omen II, The Frisco Kid, The Funhouse, The Aviator, Transylvania 6-5000, No Way Out, The Hunt for Red October, Flight of the Intruder, Necessary Roughness, Patriot Games, Gettysburg, Beverly Hills Cop III, Clear and Present Danger.
TELEVISION: *Movies/Miniseries*: East of Eden, Angel on My Shoulder, American Dream, Cagney and Lacey (pilot), A Death in California. *Specials*: The Magic Planet, The Flying Karamazov Brothers.

NEUWIRTH, BEBE
Actress. b. Newark, NJ, Dec. 31. e. Juilliard. Started as chorus dancer.
THEATER: *NY*: Little Me, Dancin', Upstairs at O'Neal, The Road to Hollywood, Sweet Charity (Tony Award, 1986), Showing Off, Damn Yankees. *Tour*: A Chorus Line. Regional: Just So, Kicks (also choreog.), Chicago. *London*: Kiss of the Spider Woman.
PICTURES: Say Anything... (debut, 1989), Green Card, Bugsy, Paint Job, Malice, Jumanji, All Dogs Go to Heaven (voice), The Associate.
TELEVISION: *Series*: Cheers (2 Emmy Awards). *Movies*: Without Her Consent, Unspeakable Acts. *Mini-Series*: Wild Palms. *Guest*: Frasier.

NEWELL, MIKE
Director. b. St. Albans, England, 1942. e. Cambridge U. Took directorial training course at Granada Television.
PICTURES: The Awakening (debut, 1980), Bad Blood, Dance With a Stranger, The Good Father, Amazing Grace and Chuck, Common Ground, Enchanted April, Into the West, Four Weddings and a Funeral, An Awfully Big Adventure, Donnie Brasco.
TELEVISION: Baa Baa Black Sheep, Silver Wedding, Jill and Jack, Ready When You Are Mr. McGill, Lost Your Tongue, Mr. & Mrs. Bureaucrat, Just Your Luck, The Man in the Iron Mask, The Gift of Friendship, Destiny, Tales Out of School, Birth of a Nation, Blood Feud.

NEWHART, BOB
Actor, Comedian. b. Chicago, IL, Sept. 5, 1929. e. Loyola U. In Army 2 yrs., then law school; left to become copywriter and accountant. Acted with theatrical stock co. in Oak Park; hired for TV man-in-street show in Chicago. Recorded hit comedy album for Warner Bros., The Button-Down Mind of Bob Newhart (Grammy Award, 1960), followed by two more successful albums. Did series of nightclub engagements and then acquired own TV variety series in 1961. Grand Marshall: Tournament of Roses Parde, 1991. Inducted into TV Hall of Fame, 1993.

PICTURES: Hell Is for Heroes (debut, 1962), Hot Millions, Catch-22, On a Clear Day You Can See Forever, Cold Turkey, The Rescuers (voice), Little Miss Marker, First Family, The Rescuers Down Under (voice).
TELEVISION: *Series*: The Bob Newhart Show (1961-62, variety), The Entertainers, The Bob Newhart Show (1972-78, sitcom), Newhart, Bob. *Movies*: Thursday's Game, Marathon, The Entertainers.

NEWLAND, JOHN
Actor, Director. b. Cincinnati, OH, Nov. 23, 1917. Began as a singer-dancer in vaudeville and on B'way; many TV appearances, especially as host of One Step Beyond. Actor, dir., Robert Montgomery Show, My Lover, My Son. Turned to fulltime dir. and prod. in the 1960's.
PICTURES: Bulldog Drummond, That Night, The Violators, The Spy With My Face, Hush-a-Bye Murder, Purgatory.
TELEVISION: *Series*: One Man's Family, Robert Montgomery Presents, Alcoa Presents: One Step Beyond (host), The Next Step Beyond (host, prod.). *Guest*: Philco TV Playhouse, Eye Witness, Schlitz Playhouse of Stars, Loretta Young Show, Thriller. *Director*: Star Trek, Route 66, Dr. Kildare, Man from U.N.C.L.E.

NEWLEY, ANTHONY
Actor, Writer, Composer, Singer. b. Hackney, Eng., Sept. 24, 1931. Recipient of Male Singer of the Year Award, Las Vegas, 1972; Elected to Songwriters Hall of Fame, 1989. Gold records for composing Goldfinger, Candy Man, What Kind of Fool Am I?
THEATER: *West End stage*: Cranks (also dir., writer), Stop The World—I Want to Get Off (also composer with Leslie Bricusse, dir., writer; also NY), The Roar of the Greasepaint—The Smell of the Crowd (also composer with Bricusse, writer, dir.; also NY), The Good Old Bad Old Days (also composer with Bricusse, writer, dir.), Royalty Follies (also dir., writer), The World's Not Entirely to Blame, It's a Funny Old World We Live In. *Regional*: Chaplin, Once Upon a Song. *British tour*: Scrooge (1992-95).
PICTURES: Adventures of Dusty Bates (debut, 1946), Little Ballerina, The Guinea Pig, Vice Versa, Oliver Twist, Vote for Huggett, Don't Ever Leave Me, A Boy a Girl and a Bike, Golden Salamander, Madeleine, Highly Dangerous, Those People Next Door, Top of the Form, The Weak and the Wicked, Up to His Neck, Blue Peter, The Cockleshell Heroes, Battle of the River Plate, Above Us the Waves, Port Afrique, The Last Man to Hang, Fire Down Below, How to Murder a Rich Uncle, Good Companions, X the Unknown, High Flight, No Time to Die (Tank Force), The Man Inside, The Bandit of Zhobe, The Lady Is a Square, Idle on Parade, Killers of Kilimanjaro, Let's Get Married, Jazz Boat, In the Nick, The Small World of Sammy Lee, Play It Cool, Stop the World I Want to Get Off (songs only), Doctor Dolittle, Sweet November, Can Hieronymus Merkin Ever Forget Mercy Humppe and Find True Happiness? (also dir., s.p., songs), Willie Wonka and the Chocolate Factory (songs only), Summertree (dir. only), Mr. Quilp (also music), It Seemed Like a Good Idea at the Time, The Garbage Pail Kids Movie.
TELEVISION: *Specials*: Sunday Night Palladium, Saturday Spectaculars, Anthony Newley Special (London). *Guest*: The Johnny Darling Show, Hollywood Squares, Merv Griffin Show, The Tonight Show, Limited Partners, Fame, Magnum P.I., Alfred Hitchcock Theatre, Murder She Wrote, Simon & Simon. *Movies*: Malibu, Alice in Wonderland, Blade in Hong Kong, Stagecoach, Coins in a Fountain, Polly Comin' Home, Boris and Natasha, Anna Lee: Dupe. *Series* (BBC): Sammy, The Strange World of Gurney Slade, The Anthony Newley Show (1972).

NEWMAN, ALFRED S.
Executive. b. Brooklyn, NY, Nov. 16. e. NYU. Public relations work for Equitable Life Insurance, Trans World Airlines prior to joining Columbia Pictures in 1968 as writer in publicity dept.; named New York publicity mgr., 1970; national publicity mgr., 1972; joined MGM as East adv.-pub. dir., 1972; named director of adv., pub. and promotion, 1974; named v.p., worldwide adv., pub., promo., 1978; v.p., pub.-promo., MGM/UA, 1981. With 20th Century-Fox as v.p. adv.-pub.-promo. for TV & corporate, 1984-85; joined Rogers & Cowan as sr. v.p. & head of corporate entertainment, 1985; named exec. v.p., 1987; Oct. 1988 named pres. and CEO. Sterling Entertainment Co. and exec. v.p. worldwide marketing of parent co. MCEG; formed Newman & Associates, 1989; joined Hill and Knowl Entertainment as founding mng. dir., 1990. Re-opened Newman and Assocs., 1991.

NEWMAN, BARRY
Actor. b. Boston, MA, Nov. 7, 1938. e. Brandeis U.
PICTURES: Pretty Boy Floyd (debut, 1960), The Moving Finger, The Lawyer, Vanishing Point, The Salzburg Connection, Fear is the Key, City on Fire, Amy.
TELEVISION: *Series*: Petrocelli, Nightingales. *Movies*: Night Games, Sex and the Married Woman, King Crab, Fantasies, Having It All, Second Sight: A Love Story, Fatal Vision, My Two Loves, The Mirror Crack'd (BBC).

NEWMAN, DAVID
Composer. b. Los Angeles, CA, Mar. 11, 1954. e. USC (masters degree). Son of late composer Alfred Newman. Cousin of composer Randy Newman. Music director at Robert Redford's Sundance Institute.
PICTURES: Critters, Vendetta, The Kindred, My Demon Lover, Malone, Dragnet, Throw Momma from the Train, Pass the Ammo, Bill & Ted's Excellent Adventure, Disorganized Crime, The Brave Little Toaster, Heathers, Little Monsters, Gross Anatomy, The War of the Roses, Madhouse, Fire Birds, The Freshman, DuckTales: The Movie, Mr. Destiny, Meet the Applegates, The Marrying Man, Talent for the Game, Don't Tell Mom the Babysitter's Dead, Bill & Ted's Bogus Journey, Rover Dangerfield, Paradise, Other People's Money, The Runestone, The Mighty Ducks, Hoffa, The Sandlot, Coneheads, The Air Up There, My Father the Hero, The Flintstones, The Cowboy Way, Tommy Boy, Operation Dumbo Drop, The Phantom, Mathilda, The Nutty Professor.

NEWMAN, DAVID
Writer. b. New York, NY, Feb. 4, 1937. e. U. of Michigan, M.S., 1959. Was writer-editor at Esquire Magazine where he met Robert Benton, an art director, and formed writing partnership. All early credits co-written with Benton; later ones with Leslie Newman and others.
THEATER: It's a Bird... It's a Plane... It's Superman (libretto), Oh! Calcutta (one sketch).
PICTURES: Bonnie and Clyde, There Was a Crooked Man, What's Up Doc?, Bad Company, Superman, Superman II, Jinxed, Still of the Night (co-story), Superman III, Sheena, Santa Claus, Moonwalker.

NEWMAN, EDWIN
News Correspondent. b. New York, NY, Jan. 25, 1919. Joined NBC News in 1952, based in N.Y. since 1961. Reports news on NBC-TV and often assigned to anchor instant specials. Has been substitute host on Today, appeared on Meet the Press and has reported NBC News documentaries. Series host: Edwin Newman Reporting, The Nation's Future, What's Happening to America, Comment, Speaking Freely, Television (PBS series).

NEWMAN, JOSEPH M.
Producer, Director, Writer. b. Logan, UT, Aug. 7, 1909. Started as office boy MGM, 1925; jobs in production dept. to 1931; asst. to George Hill, Ernst Lubitsch, etc., 1931-37; asstd. in organization of MGM British studios 1937; dir. short subjects 1938; dir. Crime Does Not Pay series 1938-42; Major in U.S. Army Signal Corps 1942-46; dir. 32 Army Pictorial Service Pictures. TV work includes Alfred Hitchcock Presents, Twilight Zone, Romance, SDG Masons.
PICTURES: Northwest Rangers, Abandoned, Jungle Patrol, Great Dan Pitch, 711 Ocean Drive, Lucky Nick Cain, The Guy Who Came Back, Love Nest, Red Skies of Montana, Outcasts of Poker Flat, Pony Soldier, Dangerous Crossing, Human Jungle, Kiss of Fire, This Island Earth, Flight to Hong Kong, Fort Massacre, The Big Circus, Tarzan the Ape Man, King of the Roaring Twenties, Twenty Plus Two, The George Raft Story, Thunder of Drums.

NEWMAN, LARAINE
Actress. b. Los Angeles, CA, Mar. 2, 1952. Founding member of comedy troupe the Groundlings.
THEATER: *B'way*: Fifth of July.
PICTURES: Tunnelvision (debut, 1976), American Hot Wax, Wholly Moses!, Stardust Memories (unbilled), Perfect, Sesame Street Presents Follow That Bird (voice), Invaders from Mars, Problem Child 2, Witchboard II, Coneheads, The Flintstones.
TELEVISION: *Series*: Manhattan Transfer, Saturday Night Live. *Guest*: George Burns Comedy Week, St. Elsewhere, Laverne & Shirley, Alfred Hitchcock Presents, Amazing Stories, Faerie Tale Theatre (The Little Mermaid), Twilight Zone, Dream On, Likely Suspects. *Specials*: Steve Martin's Best Show Ever, The Lily Tomlin Special, Bob Ray Jane Laraine & Gilda. *Movies*: Her Life as a Man, This Wife for Hire.

NEWMAN, NANETTE
Actress, Writer. b. Northampton, Eng., 1936. m. prod.-dir.-writer Bryan Forbes. Ent. films in 1946 and TV in 1951.
AUTHOR: God Bless Love, That Dog, Reflections, The Root Children, Amy Rainbow, Pigalev, Archie, Christmas Cookbook, Summer Cookbook, Small Beginnings, Bad Baby, Entertaining with Nanette Newman and Her Daughters, Charlie the Noisy Caterpillar, Sharing, The Pig Who Never Was, ABC, 123, Cooking for Friends, Spider the Horrible Cat, There's a Bear in the Bath, Karmic Mothers (Teleplay), There's a Bear in the Classroom, The Importance of Being Ernest the Earwig, Take 3 Cooks.
PICTURES: The Personal Affair, The League of Gentlemen, The Rebel, Twice Around the Daffodils, The L-Shaped Room, The Wrong Arm of the Law, Of Human Bondage, Seance on a Wet Afternoon, The Wrong Box, The Whisperers, Deadfall,

The Madwoman of Chaillot, Captain Nemo and the Underwater City, The Raging Moon (Long Ago Tomorrow), The Stepford Wives, It's a 2'2" Above the Ground World (The Love Ban), Man at the Top, International Velvet, The Endless Game.
TELEVISION: The Glorious Days, The Wedding Veil, Broken Honeymoon, At Home, Trial by Candlelight, Diary of Samuel Pepys, Faces in the Dark, Balzac (BBC), Fun Food Factory, TV series, Stay with Me Till Morning, Let There Be Love (series), West Country Tales, Jessie, Late Expectations (series).

NEWMAN, PAUL
Actor, Director, Producer. b. Cleveland, OH, Jan. 26, 1925. m. actress Joanne Woodward. e. Kenyon Coll., Yale Sch. of Drama, The Actors Studio. Formed First Artists Prod. Co., Ltd. 1969 with Sidney Poitier, Steve McQueen and Barbra Streisand. Appeared in documentaries: King: A Filmed Record... Memphis to Montgomery, Hello Actors Studio. Recipient of special Academy Award, 1986; Jean Hersholt Humanitarian Award, 1994.
THEATER: B'way: Picnic, The Desperate Hours, Sweet Bird of Youth, Baby Want a Kiss.
PICTURES: The Silver Chalice (debut, 1954), The Rack, Somebody Up There Likes Me, The Helen Morgan Story, Until They Sail, The Long Hot Summer, The Left-Handed Gun, Cat on a Hot Tin Roof, Rally 'Round the Flag Boys!, The Young Philadelphians, From the Terrace, Exodus, The Hustler, Paris Blues, Sweet Bird of Youth, Hemingway's Adventures of a Young Man, Hud, A New Kind of Love, The Prize, What a Way to Go!, The Outrage, Harper, Lady L, Torn Curtain, Hombre, Cool Hand Luke, The Secret War of Harry Frigg, Rachel Rachel (dir. prod. only), Winning, Butch Cassidy and the Sundance Kid, WUSA (also prod.), Sometimes a Great Notion (also dir.), Pocket Money, The Life and Times of Judge Roy Bean, The Effect of Gamma Rays on Man-in-the-Moon Marigolds (dir., prod. only), The Mackintosh Man, The Sting, The Towering Inferno, The Drowning Pool, Buffalo Bill and the Indians or Sitting Bull's History Lesson, Silent Movie, Slap Shot, Quintet, When Time Ran Out..., Fort Apache the Bronx, Absence of Malice, The Verdict, Harry and Son (also dir., co-s.p., co-prod.), The Color of Money (Academy Award, 1986), The Glass Menagerie (dir. only), Fat Man & Little Boy, Blaze, Mr. and Mrs. Bridge, The Hudsucker Proxy, Nobody's Fool.
TELEVISION: Guest (on 1950's anthology series): The Web (Bell of Damon, One for the Road), Goodyear TV Playhouse (Guilty is the Stranger), Danger (Knife in the Dark), Appointment With Adventure (Five in Judgment), Philco TV Playhouse (Death of Billy the Kid), Producers Showcase (Our Town), Kaiser Aluminum Hour (The Army Game, Rag Jungle), U.S. Steel Hour (Bang the Drum Slowly), Playhouse 90 (The 80-Yard Run). Movie (dir. only): The Shadow Box.

NEWMAN, RANDY
Composer, Singer. b. Los Angeles, CA, Nov. 28, 1943. Nephew of musicians Lionel and Alfred Newman. Studied music at UCLA. Debut album: Randy Newman Creates Something New Under the Sun. Songs include Short People, I Think It's Gonna Rain Today, I Love L.A. Was music director on film Performance. Began writing songs and scores for films in 1971 with The Pursuit of Happiness. Composed opera, Faust.
PICTURES: Pursuit of Happiness, Cold Turkey, Ragtime, The Natural, Three Amigos (also co-wrote s.p.), Parenthood, Avalon, Awakenings, The Paper, Maverick, James and the Giant Peach, The Quest.

NEWMAN, SYDNEY
Producer, Writer. O. C., F.R.S.A., F.R.T.S. for Canadian Film Development Corp. b. Toronto, Canada, Apr. 1, 1917. Studied painting, drawing, commercial art at Central Tech. Sch. To Hollywood in 1938. Joined National Film Board of Canada under John Grierson. Prod. over 300 shorts. Later became exec. prod. all Canadian government cinema films, 1947-52; Canadian Broadcasting Corp., 1952, as dir. outside broadcasts, features and documentaries. Later became drama sup. and prod. General Motors Theatre. Joined ABC-TV in England, 1958 as sup. of drama and prod. of Armchair Theatre: Head of Drama Group, TV, BBC, 1963. Commissioned and prod. first TV plays by Arthur Hailey, Harold Pinter, Mordecai Richler, Alun Owen, Angus Wilson, Peter Luke. Devised, created Dr. Who (1962) and The Avengers (1959). Fellow of Society of Film & TV Arts, 1968; Fellow of Royal Television Society, 1990. Prod. Associated British Pictures. SFTA award 1968; Zeta award, Writers Guild, Gt. Btn., 1970. 1970, special advisor, ch. dir., Broadcast Programmes branch, Canadian Radio & TV Commission, Ottawa. 1970, appt. Canadian Govt. Film Commissioner and chmn., National Film Board of Canada; Trustee, National Arts Centre, Ottawa; bd. mem., Canadian Broadcasting Corporation, Canadian Film Development Corp. Recognition Award from S.M.P.T.E. (USA), Canadian Picture Pioneers Special Award. Special Advisor on Film to the Secretary of State for Canada, 1975-77; pres., Sydney Newman

Enterprises. 1981, made officer of the Order of Canada. Left Canadian Film Develop. Corp. 1983. At present Creative Consultant to film & tv producers.

NEWMAR, JULIE
Actress. r.n. Julie Newmeyer. b. Hollywood, CA, Aug. 16, 1933. e. UCLA. Studied acting with Lee Strasberg at the Actor's Studio. Holds patent for special panty hose design. Appeared in George Michael video Too Funky.
THEATER: NY: Silk Stockings, Li'l Abner, The Marriage-Go-Round (Tony Award, 1959). Other: In the Boom Boom Room (L.A.), Damn Yankees, Irma La Douce, Guys and Dolls, Dames at Sea, Stop the World, The Women.
PICTURES: Just for You (debut, 1952), Seven Brides for Seven Brothers, The Rookie, Li'l Abner, The Marriage-Go-Round, For Love or Money, McKenna's Gold, The Maltese Bippy, Hysterical, Streetwalkin', Body Beat, Nudity Required, Ghosts Can't Do It, Oblivion, To Wong Foo—Thanks for Everything—Julie Newmar.
TELEVISION: Series: My Living Doll, Batman (frequent guest; as Catwoman). Movies: McCloud: Who Killed Miss U.S.A.?, The Feminist and the Fuzz, A Very Missing Person, Terraces. Guest: Omnibus, Route 66, Jonathan Winters Show, Beverly Hillbillies, The Monkees, Love American Style, Love Boat, Half Nelson, Fantasy Island, Hart to Hart, Buck Rogers.

NEWTON-JOHN, OLIVIA
Actress, Singer. b. Cambridge, Eng. Sept. 26, 1948. m. actor Matt Lattanzi. Brought up in Melbourne, Australia, where won first talent contest at 15, winning trip to England. Stayed there 2 yrs. performing as part of duo with Australian girl singer Pat Carroll (Farrar) in cabarets and on TV. Started recording; several hit records. Became a regular guest on TV series, It's Cliff Richard. Gained world-wide prominence as singer, winning several Grammys and other music awards. 1983 opened Koala Blue, U.S. Clothing Stores featuring Australian style clothes and goods.
PICTURES: Tomorrow (debut, 1970), Grease, Xanadu, Two of a Kind.
TELEVISION: Specials: Olivia Newton-John: Let's Get Physical, Standing Room Only: Olivia Newton-John, Olivia Newton-John in Australia, Christmas in Washington. Movies: A Mom for Christmas, A Christmas Romance.

NEY, RICHARD
Actor, Writer, Producer, Financier. b. New York, NY, Nov. 12, 1917. e. Columbia U., B.A., 1940. Acted in RCA TV demonstration, New York World's Fair; on stage in Life with Father. Was Naval Officer in WWII. Financial advisor consultant, Richard Ney and Associates; financial advisor, lecturer; author, The Wall Street Jungle, The Wall Street Gang, Making it in the Market.
PICTURES: Mrs. Miniver, The War Against Mrs. Hadley, The Late George Apley, Ivy, Joan of Arc, The Fan, Secret of St. Ives, Lovable Cheat, Babes in Bagdad, Miss Italia, Sergeant and The Spy, Midnight Lace, The Premature Burial.

NGOR, HAING S.
Actor. b. Cambodia, 1947. Started as doctor in Cambodia, serving as medical officer in the Cambodian Army. Escaped to Thailand following four years in captivity under the Khmer Rouge, then immigrated to U.S. in 1980, resuming career as doctor before being picked for debut role in The Killing Fields. Subject of documentaries: A Man Without a Country, Beyond the Killing Field. Autobiography: A Cambodia Odyssey (1987).
PICTURES: The Killing Fields (debut, 1984; Academy Award, best supporting actor; also BAFTA & Golden Globe Awards), Iron Triangle, Vietnam Texas, Ambition, My Life, Heaven and Earth, Fortunes of War.
TELEVISION: Movies: In Love and War, Last Flight Out. Series: Vanishing Son. Guest: Hotel, China Beach, Miami Vice, Highway to Heaven. Special: Vietnam War Story (The Last Outpost), The Doctors Wilde.
(d. March 3, 1996)

NICHOLAS, DENISE
Actress, Writer. b. Detroit, MI, July 12, 1945. e. Univ. of MI., USC. Short story published in Essence Magazine.
THEATER: Productions with The Free Southern Theatre, The Negro Ensemble Company, Cross Roads Theatre Co., New Federal Theatre incl. Daddy Goodness, Ceremonies in Dark Old Men, Dame Lorraine, Summer of the 17th Doll, Poetry Show, Their Eyes Were Watching God. Author. Buses (prod. at Crossroads theatre, New Brunswick, NJ).
PICTURES: Blacula, The Soul of Nigger Charley, Mr. Ricco, Let's Do It Again, A Piece of the Action, Capricorn One, Marvin and Tige, Ghost Dad.
TELEVISION: Series: Room 222, Baby I'm Back, In the Heat of the Night (also wrote 6 episodes). Movies: Five Desperate Women, The Sophisticated Gents, On Thin Ice, Mother's Day, Ring of Passion, Return to the Valley of the Dolls, In the Heat of the Night: By Duty Bound. Guest: NYPD, The FBI, Night Gallery, Love American Style, Police Story, The Love Boat, The Paper Chase, Magnum P.I., Benson, The Cosby Show, A Different World, many others.

271

NICHOLS, MIKE
Director, Producer, Performer. r.n. Michael Igor Peschkowsky. b. Berlin, Germany, Nov. 6, 1931. m. news correspondent Diane Sawyer. e. U. of Chicago. Member of Compass Players; later teamed with Elaine May in night clubs.
THEATER: *Director*: Barefoot in the Park (Tony Award), The Knack, Luv (Tony Award), The Odd Couple, The Apple Tree, The Little Foxes, Plaza Suite (Tony Award), Uncle Vanya, The Prisoner of 2nd Avenue (Tony Award), Streamers, Comedians, The Gin Game, Drinks Before Dinner, Annie (prod. only; Tony Award), The Real Thing (2 Tony Awards), Hurlyburly, Social Security, Waiting for Godot, Elliot Loves, Death and the Maiden.
PICTURES: *Director*: Who's Afraid of Virginia Woolf? (debut, 1966), The Graduate (Academy Award, 1967), Catch-22, Carnal Knowledge, The Day of the Dolphin, The Fortune, Gilda Live, Silkwood (also co-prod.), The Longshot (exec. prod. only), Heartburn, Biloxi Blues, Working Girl, Postcards From the Edge, Regarding Henry, The Remains of the Day (co-prod. only), Wolf, The Birdcage.
TELEVISION: *Specials*: B'way, An Evening with Mike Nichols and Elaine May. *Exec. prod.*: Family, The Thorns.

NICHOLS, NICHELLE
Actress. b. Robbins, IL, 1936. Started singing and dancing with Duke Ellington and his band at age 16. Was appointee to the bd. of dirs. of the National Space Institute in the 1970's; recruited women and minority astronauts for Space Shuttle Program. Received NASA's distinguished Public Service Award. Member of the bd. of govs. of the National Space Society. One of the original founders of KWANZA Foundation. Awarded star on Hollywood Walk of Fame (1992). *Autobiography*: Beyond (1994). Novels: Saturn's Child (1995), Saturna's Quest (1996).
THEATER: Horowitz and Mrs. Washington, Reflections (one woman show). Nominated for Sarah Siddons Award for performances in Kicks and Company, The Blacks.
PICTURES: Porgy and Bess, Mr. Buddwing, Made in Paris, Truck Turner, Star Trek: The Motion Picture, Star Trek II: The Wrath of Khan, Star Trek III: The Search for Spock, Star Trek IV: The Voyage Home, The Supernaturals, Star Trek V: The Final Frontier, Star Trek VI: The Undiscovered Country.
TELEVISION: *Series*: Star Trek. *Guest*: The Lieutenant, Tarzan. *Special*: Antony and Cleopatra.

NICHOLSON, JACK
Actor, Producer, Director, Writer. b. Neptune, NJ, April 22, 1937. Began career in cartoon department of MGM. Made acting debut in Hollywood stage production of Tea and Sympathy. Made directing debut with Drive, He Said (1971). Has received 10 Academy Award nominations for acting. Recipient of American Film Institute's Life Achievement Award, 1994.
PICTURES: Cry Baby Killer (debut, 1958), Too Soon to Love, Little Shop of Horrors, Studs Lonigan, The Wild Ride, The Broken Land, The Raven, The Terror, Thunder Island (co-s.p. only), Back Door to Hell, Flight to Fury (also s.p.), Ensign Pulver, Ride in the Whirlwind (also co-prod., s.p.), The Shooting (also co-prod.), The St. Valentine's Day Massacre, Rebel Rousers, Hell's Angels on Wheels, The Trip (s.p. only), Head (also co-prod., co-s.p.), Psych-Out, Easy Rider, On a Clear Day You Can See Forever, Five Easy Pieces, Carnal Knowledge, Drive He Said (dir., co-prod., co-s.p. only), A Safe Place, The King of Marvin Gardens, The Last Detail, Chinatown, Tommy, The Passenger, The Fortune, One Flew Over the Cuckoo's Nest (Academy Award, 1975), The Missouri Breaks, The Last Tycoon, Goin' South (also dir.), The Shining, The Postman Always Rings Twice, Reds, The Border, Terms of Endearment (Academy Award, best supporting actor, 1983), Prizzi's Honor, Heartburn, The Witches of Eastwick, Broadcast News, Ironweed, Batman, The Two Jakes (also dir.), Man Trouble, A Few Good Men, Hoffa, Wolf, The Crossing Guard, Mars Attacks!, The Evening Star.
TELEVISION: *Guest*: Tales of Wells Fargo, Cheyenne, Hawaiian Eye, Dr. Kildare, Andy Griffith Show, Guns of Will Sonnett.

NICHOLSON, WILLIAM
Writer. b. England, 1948. e. Cambridge U. Was graduate trainee at BBC, becoming prod./dir./writer of over 40 documentaries.
THEATER: Shadowlands, Map of the Heart.
PICTURES: Sarafina!, Shadowlands (Acad. Award nom.), Nell, First Knight.
TELEVISION: *Exec. Prod.*: Everyman, Global Report, Lovelaw. *Writer*: Martin Luther, New World, Life Story, The Vision, Sweet as You Are, The March.

NICKSAY, DAVID
Executive, Producer. e. Mass., Hampshire Coll. Entered industry through Directors Guild of America's training program, apprenticing on Rich Man Poor Man and rising to second asst. dir. on Oh, God. Producer of many TV projects and theatrical films with Edgar Scherick prod. co. In 1986, joined

Paramount Pictures as v.p., prod., for M.P. Group. Assoc. prod., prod. mgr.: I'm Dancing as Fast as I Can. Became sr. v.p., prod. Paramount, M.P. Group, 1987; resigned 1989 to become pres. and head of prod. at Morgan Creek Prods. Mem. of bd.
PICTURES: *Prod.*: Mrs. Soffel, Lucas, Up Close and Personal. *Sprv. prod.*: Big Top Pee-Wee, Summer School, Coming to America, The Untouchables, Scrooged, Star Trek V: The Final Frontier, Major League, Were No Angels, Harlem Nights, The Two Jakes, White Sands, Stay Tuned.
TELEVISION: Call to Glory (pilot), Little Gloria Happy at Last.

NICOL, ALEX
Actor, Director. b. Ossining, NY, Jan. 20, 1919. e. Fagin Sch. of Dramatic Arts, Actor's Studio. U.S. Cavalry.
THEATER: Forward the Heart, Sundown Beach, Hamlet, Richard II, South Pacific, Mr. Roberts, Cat on a Hot Tin Roof.
PICTURES: The Sleeping City, Tomahawk, Target Unknown, Air Cadet, Raging Tide, Meet Danny Wilson, Red Ball Express, Because of You, Redhead From Wyoming, Lone Hand, Law and Order, Champ for a Day, Black Glove, Heat Wave, About Mrs. Leslie, Dawn at Socorro, Strategic Air Command, Man from Laramie, Great Day in the Morning, The Gilded Cage, Sincerely Yours, Five Branded Women, Via Margutta, Under 10 Flags, Gunfighters at Casa Grande, The Screaming Skull (dir.), Then There Were Three (dir.), The Brutal Land, Bloody Mama, Homer, Point of Terror (dir.), The Night God Screamed, A-P-E.

NIELSEN, LESLIE
Actor. b. Regina, Sask., Canada, Feb. 11, 1926. e. Victoria H.S., Edmonton. Disc jockey, announcer for Canadian radio station; studied at Lorne Greene's Acad. of Radio Arts, Toronto and at Neighborhood Playhouse; N.Y. radio actor summer stock. Toured country in one-man show, Darrow, 1979. *Author:* The Naked Truth (1993), Leslie Nielsen's Stupid Little Golf Book (1995).
PICTURES: Ransom (debut, 1956), Forbidden Planet, The Vagabond King, The Opposite Sex, Hot Summer Night, Tammy and the Bachelor, The Sheepman, Night Train To Paris, Harlow, Dark Intruder, Beau Geste, The Plainsman, Gunfight in Abilene, The Reluctant Astronaut, Rosie!, Counterpoint, Dayton's Devils, How to Commit Marriage, Change of Mind, Four Rode Out, The Resurrection of Zachary Wheeler, The Poseidon Adventure, And Millions Will Die, Day of the Animals, Viva Knievel!, The Amsterdam Kill, City on Fire, Airplane!, Prom Night, The Creature Wasn't Nice, Wrong Is Right, Creepshow, The Patriot, Soul Man, Nightstick, Nuts, Home Is Where the Hart Is, The Naked Gun: From the Files of Police Squad!, Dangerous Curves, Repossessed, The Naked Gun 2 1/2: The Smell of Fear, All I Want for Christmas, Surf Ninjas, Naked Gun 33 1/3: The Final Insult, Dracula: Dead and Loving It, Spy Hard (also co-exec. prod.).
TELEVISION: *Series*: The New Breed, Peyton Place, The Protectors, Bracken's World, The Explorers (host), Police Squad, Shaping Up. *Guest*: Studio One, Kraft, Philco Playhouse, Robert Montgomery Presents, Pulitzer Prize Playhouse, Suspense, Danger, Justice, Man Behind the Badge, Ben Casey, Walt Disney (Swamp Fox), Wild Wild West, The Virginian, The Loner. *Special*: Death of a Salesman. *Movies*: See How They Run, Shadow Over Elveron, Hawaii Five-O (pilot), Companions in Nightmare, Trial Run, Deadlock, Night Slaves, The Aquarians, Hauser's Memory, Incident in San Francisco, They Call It Murder, Snatched, The Letters, The Return of Charlie Chan (Happiness Is a Warm Clue), Can Ellen Be Saved?, Brink's: The Great Robbery, Little Mo, Institute for Revenge, OHMS, The Night the Bridge Fell Down, Cave-In!, Reckless Disregard, Blade in Hong Kong, Fatal Confession: A Father Dowling Mystery, Chance of a Lifetime. *Mini-Series*: Backstairs at the White House.

NIMOY, LEONARD
Actor, Director. b. Boston, MA, Mar. 26, 1931. e. Boston Col. Joined Pasadena Playhouse. Along with active career in films, TV and stage, has been writer and photographer. Author of three books on photography and poetry, as well as autobiography, I Am Not Spock. Has also been speaker on college lecture circuit. Created comic book Primortals.
THEATER: Full Circle, Equus, Sherlock Holmes, Vincent (also dir., one-man show), Love Letters.
PICTURES: Queen for a Day, Rhubarb, Francis Goes to West Point, Them!, Satan's Satellites (edited from serial Zombies of the Stratosphere), The Brain Eaters, The Balcony, Catlow, Invasion of the Body Snatchers, Star Trek—The Motion Picture, Star Trek II: The Wrath of Khan, Star Trek III: The Search for Spock (also dir.), Transformers: The Movie (voice), Star Trek IV: The Voyage Home (also. dir., co-story), Three Men and a Baby (dir. only), The Good Mother (dir. only), Star Trek V: The Final Frontier, Funny About Love (dir. only), Star Trek VI: The Undiscovered Country (also exec. prod., co-story), Holy Matrimony (dir. only), The Pagemaster (voice).
TELEVISION: *Series*: Star Trek, Mission: Impossible, In Search Of... (host), Outer Limits. *Movies*: Assault on the Wayne, Baffled, The Alpha Caper, The Missing Are Deadly,

The Sun Also Rises, A Woman Called Golda, Never Forget (also co-prod.), Bonanza: Under Attack. *Mini-Series*: Marco Polo. *Guest*: Bonanza, Twilight Zone, Perry Mason, Laramie, Wagon Train, Man From U.N.C.L.E., The Virginian, Get Smart, Night Gallery, Columbo, T.J. Hooker, Star Trek: The Next Generation. *Special*: Seapower: A Global Journey (narrator). *Episode Dir.*: Deadly Games.

NIVEN, DAVID, JR.
Executive. b. London, England, Dec. 15, 1942. e. Univ. of Grenoble; London Sch. of Economics. Joined William Morris Agency in Beverly Hills in 1963. Transferred same yr. to New York; over next five yrs. worked for agency's European offices in Rome, Madrid and London. 1968-72, Columbia Pictures' U.K. office as v.p. of production; 1972-76, mng. dir. and v.p. of Paramount Pictures in U.K. 1976 became indep. prod. West Coast corresp. & interviewer for Inside Edition. Appeared as actor in films Lisa, Cool Surface, and on tv series, America's Most Wanted. 1993, became chmn. of R.A.D.D. (Recording-Artists Against Drunk Driving)
PICTURES: *Producer*: The Eagle Has Landed, Escape to Athena, Monsignor, Better Late Than Never, Kidco, That's Dancing!, Pyscho Cop II, Girl With the Hungry Eyes, Cool Surface (also actor), Blue Flame.
TELEVISION: The Night They Saved Christmas (exec. prod., s.p.), Cary Grant: A Celebration, Minnelli on Minnelli, The Wonderful Wizard of Oz. Panelist: To Tell the Truth (1991-92).

NIX, WILLIAM PATTERSON
Executive. b. Philadelphia, PA, April 10, 1948. e. Georgetown U., A.B., 1970; Antioch, M.A., 1971; Hofstra U. Sch. of Law, J.D., 1976; NYU Sch. of Law, LL.M., 1979. Formerly, v.p., Cartier, Frankfurt, Garbus, Klein & Selz, P.C., Entertainment & Media co. V.P. bus. affairs, NBA Properties Inc., NY. Prior to that, was sr. v.p. of both the Motion Picture Association of America and Motion Picture Export Assoc. of America. Chmn. of MPAA committee on copyright and literary property matters, and COO of film industry's intellectual property protection division (1976-91). Lifetime member, AMPAS.

NIXON, AGNES
Writer, Producer. b. Nashville, TN, Dec. 10, 1927. e. Northwestern Sch. of Speech, Catholic U. Landed 1st job writing radio serial dialogue (Woman in White, 1948-51), three days after graduating from college. Became a freelance writer for TV dramatic series. Guest writer, New York Times 1968-72, and TV Guide. Trustee, Television Conference Inst., 1979-82. Received National Acad. of Television Arts & Sciences' Trustee Award, 1981; Junior Diabetic Assn. Super Achiever Award, 1982; Communicator Award for American Women in Radio and Television, 1984. Gold Plate Award, American Acad. Achievement, 1993; inducted into TV Hall of Fame, 1993. Popular Culture Lifetime Achievement Award, 1995; Public Service Award, Johns Hopkins Hospital, 1995. Member, Int'l Radio & TV Society; Nat'l Acad. of TV Arts & Sciences; bd. of Harvard Foundation; The Friars Club.
TELEVISION: *Series writer*: Studio One, Philco Playhouse, Robert Montgomery Presents, Somerset Maugham Theatre, Armstrong Circle Theatre, Hallmark Hall of Fame, My True Story, Cameo Theatre, Search For Tomorrow, As The World Turns, Guiding Light, Another World. *Series creator-producer*: One Life to Live, All My Children, Loving. *Mini-Series*: The Manions of America.

NIXON, CYNTHIA
Actress. b. New York, NY, April 9, 1966. e. Barnard Coll. Started stage career at age 14.
THEATER: *B'way*: The Philadelphia Story (Theatre World Award), Hurlyburly, The Real Thing, The Heidi Chronicles, Angels in America: Millenium Aproaches/Perestroika, Indiscretions. *Off-B'way*: Moonchildren, Romeo and Juliet, The Balcony Scene, Servy N Bernice 4-Ever, On the Bum, The Illusion, The Scarlet Letter.
PICTURES: Little Darlings (debut, 1980), Tattoo, Prince of the City, I Am the Cheese, Amadeus, The Manhattan Project, Let It Ride, Addams Family Values, The Pelican Brief, Baby's Day Out, Marvin's Room.
TELEVISION: *Movies*: The Murder of Mary Phagan, The Love She Sought, Love Lies and Murder, Face of a Stranger. *Specials*: The Fifth of July, Kiss Kiss Dahlings, Tanner '88. *Guest*: The Equalizer, Gideon Oliver, Murder She Wrote.

NOBLE, PETER
Writer, Producer, Actor, TV personality. b. London, Eng., June 18; e. Hugh Myddelton Sch., Latymer Sch. Author several books on m.p. ind.; writer/host movie radio prog. for B.B.C. & Luxembourg (Film Time, Movie-Go-Round, Peter Noble's Picture Parade). Formed Peter Noble Productions, 1953; edit. Screen International, 1975; edit. Screen International Film & TV Yearbook, 1974. London Columnist for the Hollywood Reporter, 1967-75. Radio Show, 1989-90. Editor: British Film Year Book. AUTHOR: biographies of Bette Davis, Erich Von Stroheim, Ivor Novello, Orson Welles; I Know That Face, The Negro in Films.

PICTURES: Runaway Bus (prod. assoc.), To Dorothy a Son (asst. prod.), Fun at St. Fanny's (co-prod, s.p.), Three Girls in Paris (s.p.), Lost (assoc. prod.), Captain Banner (s.p.), Strange Inheritance (prod.).
TELEVISION: Find the Link, Other Screen, Film Fanfare, Movie Memories, Yakity Yak, Startime, Thank Your Lucky Stars, Juke Box, Jury, Simon Dee Show, Star Parade, Show Business, Who's Whose, Movie Magazine, The Big Noise, The Name Game, Line Up, Tea Break, Today, Anything You Can Do, Looks Familiar, Two's Company, Sounds Familiar, Electric Picture Show, Gossip, This Is Britain (cable series), Cannes Film Festival (cable), Kilroy, Good Afternoon New York (U.S.), Loose Ends, The Pete Murray Show, Cinema 2, Where Are They Now?, The Golden Gong (TV film), Elstree—The British Hollywood, Saturday Night at the Movies (series). Prod. consult.: On The Braden Beat, The Frost Program, Dee Time, Simon Dee Show, Movie Quiz (series), Musical Time Machine BBC2 series,
RADIO: BBC Star Sound, Radio Luxembourg, Film Focus, Newsnight, Looks Familiar Nationwide, Hotel TV Network, The Time of Your Life, Channel 4 News, Nationwide, The Colour Supplement (series);

NOIRET, PHILIPPE
Actor. b. Lille, France, Oct. 1, 1930. e. Centre Dramatique de l'Ouest. Company member of Theatre National Populaire 1951-63; nightclub entertainer before film debut in Agnes Varda's short, La Pointe Court. B'way debut Lorenzaccio (1958).
PICTURES: Gigi (debut, 1948), Olivia, Agence Matrimoniale, La Pointe Courte, Ravissante, Zazie dans le Metro, The Billionaire, Crime Does Not Pay, Therese Desqueyroux, Cyrano and D'Artagnan, None But the Lonely Spy, Death Where Is Thy Victory?, Monsieur, Les Copains, Lady L, La Vie de Chateau, Tender Scoundrel, The Night of the Generals, Woman Times Seven, The Assassination Bureau, Mr. Freedom, Justine, Topaz, Clerambard, Give Her the Moon, A Room in Paris, Murphy's War, A Time for Loving, Five-Leaf Clover, The Assassination, Sweet Deception, Poil de Carotte, The French Conspiracy, The Serpent, The Day of the Jackel, La Grande Bouffe, Let Joy Reign Supreme, The Old Gun, The Judge and the Assassin, A Woman at Her Window, Purple Taxi, Dear Inspector, Due Pezzi di Pane, Who Is Killing the Great Chefs of Europe?, Death Watch, Street of the Crane's Foot, A Week's Vacation, Heads or Tails, Three Brothers, Kill Birgitt Haas, Coup de Torchon, L'Etoile du Nord, Amici, Miei, Atto 2, L'Africain, A Friend of Vincents, Le Grand Carnival, Fort Saganne, Les Ripoux, Souvenirs, Next Summer, The Gold-Rimmed Glasses, No Downing Allowed, My New Partner, 'Round Midnight, Let's Hope It's a Girl, The 4th Power, The Thrill of Genius, The Secret Wife, Twist Again in Moscow, Masks, The Family Chouans!, IL Frullo del Passero, Young Toscanini, The Return of the Musketeers, Moments of Love, Cinema Paradiso, Life and Nothing But, Palermo Connection, My New Partner 2, Uranus, I Don't Kiss, The Two of Us, Especially on Sunday, The Postman, Grosse Fatigue.

NOLTE, NICK
Actor. b. Omaha, NB, Feb. 8, 1941. Attended 5 colleges in 4 yrs. on football scholarships, including Pasadena City Coll. and Phoenix City Coll. Joined Actors Inner Circle at Phoenix and appeared in Orpheus Descending, After the Fall, Requiem For a Nun. Did stock in Colorado. In 1968, joined Old Log Theatre in Minneapolis and after 3 yrs. left for New York, appearing at Cafe La Mama. Went to L.A. and did plays The Last Pad and Picnic, as well as several guest spots on TV series before big break in mini-series, Rich Man Poor Man as Tom Jordache.
PICTURES: Return to Macon County (debut, 1975), The Deep, Who'll Stop the Rain, North Dallas Forty, Heart Beat, Cannery Row, 48 HRS., Under Fire, Teachers, Grace Quigley, Down and Out in Beverly Hills, Extreme Prejudice, Weeds, Three Fugitives, New York Stories (Life Lessons), Farewell to the King, Everybody Wins, Q&A, Another 48 HRS, Cape Fear, The Prince of Tides (Golden Globe Award, Acad. Award nom.), The Player, Lorenzo's Oil, I'll Do Anything, Blue Chips, I Love Trouble, Jefferson in Paris, Mulholland Falls, Nightwatch, Mother Night.
TELEVISION: *Mini-Series*: Rich Man Poor Man. *Movies*: Winter Kill (pilot), The California Kid, Death Sentence, The Runaway Barge. *Guest*: Medical Center, Streets of San Francisco, The Rookies.

NOONAN, TOM
Actor, Writer. b. Greenwich, CT, Apr. 12, 1951. e. Yale.
THEATER: Buried Child (Off-B'way debut, 1978), Invitational Farmyard, The Breakers, Five of Us, Spookhouse, What Happened Was (also writer), Wifey (also writer).
PICTURES: Heaven's Gate, Wolfen, Eddie Macon's Run, Easy Money, The Man With One Red Shoe, F/X, Manhunter, The Monster Squad, Mystery Train, Robocop 2, Last Action Hero, What Happened Was (also dir., s.p.).

NORMAN, BARRY
Writer/presenter. b. London. Early career as show business editor London Daily Mail; humorous columnist for The Guardian. Entered TV as writer, presenter FILM 1972-81 and 1983-93. 1982, presenter Omnibus. Writer/host: The Hollywood Greats and Talking Pictures. Radio work incl.: Going Places, The News Quiz, Breakaway, The Chip Shop.
AUTHOR: The Hollywood Greats, Movie Greats, Film Greats, Talking Pictures, 100 Best Films of the Century. Novels: A Series of Defeats, Have a Nice Day, Sticky Wicket, The Bird Dog Tapes.

NORRIS, CHUCK
Actor. r.n. Carlos Ray. b. Ryan, OK, Mar. 10, 1940. World middle weight karate champion 1968-74. Owner of LA karate schools which led to film career.
PICTURES: The Wrecking Crew (debut, 1969), Slaughter in San Francisco, Return of the Dragon, The Student Teachers, Breaker! Breaker!, Good Guys Wear Black, Game of Death, A Force of One, The Octagon, An Eye for an Eye, Silent Rage, Forced Vengeance, Lone Wolf McQuade, Missing in Action, Missing in Action 2, Code of Silence, Invasion U.S.A. (also co-s.p.), Delta Force, Firewalker, Braddock: Missing in Action III (also co-s.p.), Hero and the Terror, Delta Force II, The Hitman, Sidekicks (also co-exec. prod.), Hellbound, Top Dog.
TELEVISION: Series: Chuck Norris's Karate Kommandos (animated series, voice), Walker: Texas Ranger (also co-exec. prod.). Special: The Ultimate Stuntman: A Tribute to Dar Robinson (host), Wind in the Wire.

NORTH, SHEREE
Actress. r.n. Dawn Bethel. b. Los Angeles, CA, Jan. 17, 1933. e. Hollywood H.S. Amateur dancer with USO at 11; prof. debut at 13; many TV appearances
THEATER: B'way: Hazel Flagg (Drama Desk Award, Critics' Award), I Can Get It For You Wholesale. Other: Madwoman of Chaillot, ... And to My Daughter, Stepping Out, California Dogfight, 6 Rms. Riv Vue, Turnstyle, Thursday Is a Good Night, Dutchman, Private Lives, Irma La Douce, Bye Bye Birdie, Your Own Thing, Can-Can, Two for the Seesaw, Breaking Up the Act, etc. Also directed and produced several productions.
PICTURES: Excuse My Dust, Here Come the Girls, Living It Up, How to Be Very Very Popular, The Lieutenant Wore Skirts, The Best Things in Life Are Free, Way to the Gold, No Down Payment, In Love and War, Mardi Gras, Destination Inner Space, Madigan, The Gypsy Moths, The Trouble With Girls, Lawman, The Organization, Charley Varick, The Outfit, Breakout, The Shootist, Telefon, Rabbit Test, Telefon, Cold Dog Soup, Defenseless.
TELEVISION: Series: Big Eddie, I'm a Big Girl Now, Bay City Blues. Guest: Hawaii 5-0, Kojak, Family, Archie Bunker's Place, Murder She Wrote, Golden Girls, Matlock, Seinfeld, Hunter, Magnum P.I., many others. Movies: Then Came Bronson (pilot), Vanished, Rolling Man, Trouble Comes to Town, Snatched, Maneater, Key West, Winter Kill, A Shadow in the Streets, Most Wanted, The Night They Took Miss Beautiful, A Real American Hero, Amateur Night at the Dixie Bar and Grill, Women in White, Portrait of a Stripper, Marilyn: The Untold Story, Legs, Scorned and Swindled, Jake Spanner—Private Eye, Dead on the Money.

NOSSECK, NOEL
Director, Producer. b. Los Angeles, CA, Dec. 10, 1943. Began as editor with David Wolper Prods; made documentaries; turned to features.
PICTURES: Director: Best Friends (also prod.), Youngblood, Dreamer, King of the Mountain.
TELEVISION: Movies: Return of the Rebels, The First Time, Night Partners, Summer Fantasies, Different Affair, Stark, A Mirror Image, Roman Holiday, Full Exposure: The Sex Tapes Scandal, Follow Your Heart, Opposites Attract, A Mother's Justice, Without a Kiss Goodbye, Born Too Soon, French Silk, Sister in Law, Down Out and Dangerous. Pilots: Aaron's Way, Half 'n Half, Fair Game, Heaven Help Us.

NOURI, MICHAEL
Actor. b. Washington, DC, Dec. 9, 1945. e. Avon Old Farms, Rollins Coll., Emerson Coll. Studied for theatre with Larry Moss and Lee Strasberg. New York stage debut in Forty Carats, 1969.
THEATER: Forty Carats, Victor/Victoria.
PICTURES: Goodbye Columbus (debut, 1969), Flashdance, Gobots (voice), The Imagemaker, The Hidden, Chameleon, Fatal Sky, Total Exposure, Black Ice, Fortunes of War, To the Limit.
TELEVISION: Series: Beacon Hill, Search for Tomorrow, The Curse of Dracula, The Gangster Chronicles, Bay City Blues, Downtown, Love and War. Movies: Contract on Cherry Street, Fun and Games, Secrets of a Mother and Daughter, Sprague, Between Two Women, Rage of Angels: The Story Continues, Quiet Victory: the Charlie Wedemeyer Story, Shattered Dreams, Danielle Steel's Changes, In the Arms of a

Killer, Psychic, Exclusive, The Sands of Time, The Hidden 2, Eyes of Terror, Between Love and Honor. Mini-Series: The Last Convertible.

NOVAK, KIM
Actress. r.n. Marilyn Novak. b. Chicago, IL, Feb. 13, 1933. e. Wright Junior Coll., Los Angeles City Coll. Started as model, named World's Favorite Actress, Brussels World's Fair.
PICTURES: The French Line (debut, 1954), Pushover, Phffft!, Five Against the House, Son of Sinbad, Picnic, The Man with the Golden Arm, The Eddy Duchin Story, Jeanne Eagles, Pal Joey, Vertigo, Bell Book and Candle, Middle of the Night, Pepe, Strangers When We Meet, The Notorious Landlady, Boys' Night Out, Of Human Bondage, Kiss Me Stupid, The Amorous Adventures of Moll Flanders, The Legend of Lylah Clare, The Great Bank Robbery, Tales That Witness Madness, The White Buffalo, The Mirror Crack'd, Just a Gigolo, The Children, Liebestraum.
TELEVISION: Series: Falcon Crest. Guest: Alfred Hitchcock Presents (1985). Movies: Third Girl From the Left, Satan's Triangle, Malibu.

NOVELLO, DON
Writer, Comedian, Actor. b. Ashtabula, OH, Jan. 1, 1943. e. U. of Dayton, B.A., 1964. Best known as Father Guido Sarducci on Saturday Night Live. Was advertising copy writer before writing and performing on The Smothers Brothers Comedy Hour (1975). Writer for Van Dyke and Company, and writer-performer on Saturday Night Live 1978-80. Producer: SCTV Comedy Network (1982) and performer-writer on B'way in Gilda Radner—Live From New York (1979), as well as filmed version (Gilda Live!). Recordings: Live at St. Douglas Convent, Breakfast in Heaven. Author: The Lazlo Letters: The Amazing Real-Life Actual Correspondence of Lazlo Toth, American!, The Blade, Citizen Lazlo.
PICTURES: Gilda Live!, Head Office, Tucker: The Man and His Dream, New York Stories (Life Without Zoe), The Godfather Part III, Casper (cameo), One Night Stand, Jack.
TELEVISION: Cable specials: Fr. Guido Sarducci Goes to College, The Vatican Inquirer—The Pope Tour.

NOYCE, PHILIP
Director. b. Griffith, New South Wales, Australia, Apr. 27, 1950. Began making films at school and university. Made first short film at age 15, Better to Reign in Hell. In 1980, became part-time mgr., Sydney Filmmaker's Co-operative and in 1973 was selected for Australian Nat'l Film School in Sydney, for year-long training prog. which resulted in shorts, Good Afternoon, Caravan Park, Castor and Pollux, God Knows Why But It Works, and 60-minute film Backroads.
PICTURES: Backroads (also prod., s.p.), Newsfront (also s.p.; Australian Acad. Awards for best dir. & s.p., 1978), Heatwave (also co-s.p.), Echoes of Paradise, Dead Calm, Blind Fury, Patriot Games, Sliver (also cameo), Clear and Present Danger.
TELEVISION: Mini-Series: Dismissal, Cowra Breakout. Episodes: The Hitchhiker, Nightmare Cafe.

NUNN, BILL
Actor. b. Pittsburgh, PA. Teamed with friend Al Cooper as member of comedy team Nunn and Cooper in nightclubs, 1980-83. On stage with various theatrical companies including the Alliance, the Academy, Theatrical Oufit, Just Us Theatre.
THEATER: T-Bone and Weasel, Split Second, Home, A Lesson From Aloes, A Soldier's Play, Macbeth, The River Niger, Fences.
PICTURES: School Daze, Do the Right Thing, Def by Temptation, Cadillac Man, Mo' Better Blues, New Jack City, Regarding Henry, Sister Act, National Lampoon's Loaded Weapon 1, The Last Seduction, Canadian Bacon, Things to Do in Denver When You're Dead.
TELEVISION: Movie: The Littlest Victims. Specials: Native Strangers, Dangerous Heart, War Stories, A Yankee in King Arthur's Court. Guest: Fallen Angels.

NYKVIST, SVEN
Cinematographer. b. Moheda, Sweden, Dec. 3, 1922. e. Stockholm Photog. Sch. Asst. cameraman 1941-44. Became internationally known by photographing most of Ingmar Bergman's pictures. Recipient of American Society of Cinematographers Life Achievement Award, 1996.
PICTURES: Sawdust and Tinsel, The Virgin Spring, Winter Light, Karin Mansdotter, The Silence, Loving Couples, Persona, Hour of the Wolf, Cries and Whispers (Academy Award, 1973), The Dove, Black Moon, Scenes from a Marriage, The Magic Flute, Face to Face, One Day in the Life of Ivan Denisovich, The Tenant, The Serpents' Egg, Pretty Baby, Autumn Sonata, King of the Gypsies, Hurricane, Starting Over, Willie and Phil, From the Life of the Marionettes, The Postman Always Rings Twice, Cannery Row, Fanny and Alexander (Academy Award, 1983), Swann in Love, The Tragedy of Carmen, After the Rehearsal, Agnes of God, Dream Lover, The Sacrifice, The Unbearable Lightness

of Being, Katinka, Another Woman, New York Stories (Oedipus Wrecks), Crimes and Misdemeanors, The Ox (dir., co-s.p. only), Chaplin, Sleepless in Seattle, What's Eating Gilbert Grape, With Honors, Kirsten Lavrandatter, Only You, Mixed Nuts, Something to Talk About, Confession.
TELEVISION: *Movie:* Nobody's Child.

O'BRIAN, HUGH
Actor. r.n. Hugh C. Krampe. b. Rochester, NY, Apr. 19, 1925. Raised in Chicago. e. Kemper Military Sch., U. of Cincinnati, UCLA. U.S. Marine Corps, where at age 18 he served as youngest drill instructor in Marine Corps history. Actor in stock cos. before film career. Founder, chmn. development: Hugh O'Brian Youth Foundation, 1958; Nat'l Chmn., Cystic Fibrosis Research Foundation 1969-74; Co-founder and pres. Thalians 1955-58; Founder Hugh O'Brian Annual Acting Awards at UCLA, 1962.
THEATER: *B'way:* Destry Rides Again, First Love, Guys and Dolls, Cactus Flower, The Decision. Regional: The Music Man, Rainmaker, Plaza Suite, On 20th Century, Stalag 17, Thousand Clowns, etc.
PICTURES: Young Lovers (debut, 1949), Never Fear, Rocketship X-M, The Return of Jesse James, Vengeance Valley, Fighting Coast Guard, Little Big Horn, On the Loose, The Cimarron Kid, Red Ball Express, The Battle at Apache Pass, Sally and Saint Anne, Son of Ali Baba, The Raiders, The Lawless Breed, Meet Me at the Fair, Seminole, Man from the Alamo, Back to God's Country, The Stand at Apache River, Saskatchewan, Fireman Save My Child, Drums Across the River, Broken Lance, There's No Business Like Show Business, White Feather, The Twinkle in God's Eye, Brass Legend, The Fiend Who Walked the West, Alias Jesse James, Come Fly with Me, Love Has Many Faces, In Harm's Way, Ten Little Indians, Ambush Bay, Africa--Texas Style!, Killer Force, The Shootist, Game of Death, Doin' Time on Planet Earth, Twins.
TELEVISION: *Series:* The Life and Legend of Wyatt Earp, Search. *Specials:* Dial M for Murder, A Punt a Pass and a Prayer, Going Home, Engagement Ring, Invitation to a Gunfighter, Reunion, Chain of Command, It's a Man's World, Wyatt Earp: Return to Tombstone. *Movies:* Wild Women, Harpy, Probe (Search), Murder on Flight 502, Benny & Barney: Las Vegas Undercover, Fantasy Island, Murder at the World Series, Cruise Into Terror, The Seekers, Gunsmoke: The Last Apache, The Gambler Returns: Luck of the Draw.

O'BRIEN, CONAN
Performer, Writer. b. Brookline, MA, Apr. 18, 1963. e. Harvard. Served two years as pres. of Harvard Lampoon before landing work as tv writer for The Simpsons, Saturday Night Live (Emmy Award, 1989). Prod. of pilot Lookwell. Series: Not Necessarily the News, NBC's Late Night With Conan O'Brien (Emmy nom., 1996).

O'BRIEN, MARGARET
Actress. r.n. Angela Maxine O'Brien. Los Angeles, CA, Jan. 15, 1938. Screen debut at 3 in Babes on Broadway (1941). Awarded special Academy Award as best child actress, 1944. Voted one of ten best money-making stars in Motion Picture Herald-Fame Poll 1945-46.
PICTURES: Babes on Broadway (debut, 1941), Journey for Margaret, Dr. Gillespie's Criminal Case, Lost Angel, Thousands Cheer, Madame Curie, Jane Eyre, The Canterville Ghost, Meet Me in St. Louis, Music for Millions, Our Vines Have Tender Grapes, Bad Bascomb, Three Wise Fools, Unfinished Dance, Tenth Avenue Angel, The Big City, The Secret Garden, Little Women, Her First Romance, Two Persons Eyes (Jap.), Agente S3S Operazione Uranio (It.), Glory, Heller in Pink Tights, Anabelle Lee, Diabolic Wedding, Amy, Sunset After Dark.
TELEVISION: *Movies:* Death in Space, Split Second to an Epitaph, Testimony of Two Men. *Guest:* Robert Montgomery Presents, Lux Video Theatre, Playhouse 90, Wagon Train, Studio One, U.S. Steel Hour, Dr. Kildare, Love American Style, Marcus Welby M.D.

O'BRIEN, VIRGINIA
Actress. b. Los Angeles, CA, Apr. 18, 1919. e. North Hollywood h.s. Singer, comedienne with a distinctive dead-pan delivery. On stage in Meet the People. 1990, performed at London Palladium.
PICTURES: Hullabaloo (debut, 1940), The Big Store, Lady Be Good, Ringside Maisie, Ship Ahoy, Panama Hattie, DuBarry Was a Lady, As Thousands Cheer, Meet the People, Two Girls and a Sailor, The Harvey Girls, Ziegfeld Follies, Till Clouds Roll By, The Showoff, Merton of the Movies, Francis in the Navy, Gus.

OBST, LYNDA
Producer. b. New York, NY, Apr. 14, 1950. e. Pomona Col., Columbia Univ. Former editor for New York Times Magazine,

1976-79; then exec. at Polygram Pictures, 1979-81; Geffen Films, 1981-83, co-prod. at Paramount, 1983-85; prod. for Walt Disney, 1986, before moving over to Columbia. Co-Author: Dirty Dreams (with Carol Wolper).
PICTURES: Flashdance (assoc. prod.). *Producer:* Adventures in Babysitting, Heartbreak Hotel, The Fisher King, This Is My Life. *Exec. Prod.:* Sleepless in Seattle.

O'CONNELL, JACK
Producer, Director, Writer. b. Boston, MA. e. Princeton U., Harvard Business Sch. After being a creative group head in all media and doing 500 tv commercials entered feature films working with Fellini on La Dolce Vita, then asst. dir. to Antonioni on L'Avventura.
PICTURES: *Writer/Prod./Dir.:* Greenwich Village Story, Revolution, Christa (aka Swedish Flygirls), Up the Girls Means Three Cheers for Them All, The Hippie Revolution.

O'CONNOR, CARROLL
Actor. b. New York, NY, Aug. 2, 1924. e. University Coll., Dublin; U. of Montana. Three years with Dublin's Gate Theatre, then N.Y.
THEATER: *NY:* Ulysses in Nighttown, Playboy of the Western World, The Big Knife, Brothers (also dir.), Home Front. Author: Ladies of Hanover Tower.
PICTURES: A Fever in the Blood (debut, 1961), Parrish, By Love Possessed, Lad: A Dog, Belle Sommers, Lonely Are the Brave, Cleopatra, In Harm's Way, What Did You Do in the War Daddy?, Hawaii, Not With My Wife You Don't, Warning Shot, Point Blank, Waterhole No. 3, The Devil's Brigade, For Love of Ivy, Death of a Gunfighter, Marlowe, Kelly's Heroes, Doctors' Wives, Law and Disorder.
TELEVISION: *Series:* All in the Family (4 Emmy Awards: 1972, 1977, 1978, 1979; later retitled Archie Bunker's Place), In the Heat of the Night (Emmy Award, 1989). *Guest:* U.S. Steel Hour, Armstrong Circle Theatre, Kraft Theatre, The Untouchables, Dr. Kildare, East Side/West Side, Gunsmoke, Wild Wild West, Party of Five, Mad About You, etc. *Special:* Of Thee I Sing. *Movies:* Fear No Evil, The Last Hurrah (also writer), Brass, Convicted, The Father Clements Story, In the Heat of the Night: A Matter of Justice (also co-exec. prod.), In the Heat of the Night: Who Was Geli Bendl? (also co-exec. prod.), In the Heat of the Night: By Duty Bound (also co-exec. prod.), In the Heat of the Night: Grow Old With Me (also co-exec. prod.).

O'CONNOR, DONALD
Actor. b. Chicago, IL, Aug. 28, 1925. In vaudeville with family and Sons o' Fun (Syracuse, N.Y.) before screen debut 1938 in Sing You Sinners; return to vaudeville 1940-41, then resumed screen career with What's Cookin'?, 1942. Entered armed services, 1943. Voted Star of Tomorrow, 1943; best TV performer by M.P. Daily poll, 1953.
PICTURES: Sing You Sinners (debut, 1938), Sons of the Legion, Men With Wings, Tom Sawyer—Private Detective, Unmarried, Death of a Champion, Million Dollar Legs, Night Work, On Your Toes, Beau Geste, Private Buckaroo, Give Out Sisters, Get Hep to Love, When Johnny Comes Marching Home, Strictly in the Groove, It Comes Up Love, Mr. Big, Top Man, Chip Off the Old Block, Patrick the Great, Follow the Boys, The Merry Monahans, Bowery to Broadway, This Is the Life, Something in the Wind, Are You With It?, Feudin' Fussin' and-a-Fightin', Yes Sir That's My Baby, Francis, Curtain Call at Cactus Creek, The Milkman, Double Crossbones, Francis Goes to the Races, Singin' in the Rain, Francis Goes to West Point, I Love Melvin, Call Me Madam, Francis Covers the Big Town, Walking My Baby Back Home, Francis Joins the WACS, There's No Business Like Show Business, Francis in the Navy, Anything Goes, The Buster Keaton Story, Cry for Happy, The Wonders of Aladdin, That Funny Feeling, That's Entertainment, Ragtime, Pandemonium, A Time to Remember, Toys.
TELEVISION: *Series:* The Colgate Comedy Hour (host: 1951-54; Emmy Award, 1954), The Donald O'Connor Texaco Show (1954-55), The Donald O'Connor Show (synd., 1968). *Movies:* Alice in Wonderland, Bandit and the Silver Angel. *Guest:* Dinah Shore, Hollywood Palace, Carol Burnett, Julie Andrews, Ellery Queen, The Love Boat, Highway to Heaven, Tales From the Crypt. *Specials:* The Red Mill, Hollywood Melody, Olympus 7-0000.

O'CONNOR, GLYNNIS
Actress. b. New York, NY, Nov. 19, 1955. Daughter of ABC News prod. Daniel O'Connor and actress Lenka Peterson. e. State U., NY at Purchase. Stage includes Domestic Issues (Circle Rep., NY, 1983), The Taming of the Shrew (Great Lakes Shakespeare Fest.), The Seagull (Mirror Rep.).
PICTURES: Jeremy (debut, 1973), Baby Blue Marine, Ode to Billy Joe, Kid Vengeance, California Dreaming, Those Lips Those Eyes, Night Crossing, Melanie, Johnny Dangerously.
TELEVISION: *Series:* Sons and Daughters. *Mini-series:* Black Beauty. *Movies:* The Chisholms, Someone I Touched, All Together Now, The Boy in the Plastic Bubble, Little Mo, My

Kidnapper, My Love, The Fighter, Love Leads the Way, Why Me?, Sins of the Father, The Deliberate Stranger, To Heal a Nation, Death in Small Doses, Past the Bleachers.

O'CONNOR, KEVIN J.
Actor. b. 1964. e. DePaul Univ.'s Goodman Sch. of Drama. On stage in Colorado Catechism (NY), El Salvador (Chicago).
PICTURES: One More Saturday Night, Peggy Sue Got Married, Candy Mountain, The Moderns, Signs of Life, Steel Magnolias, Love at Large, F/X 2, Hero, Equinox, No Escape, Color of Night, Virtuosity, Lord of Illusions, Canadian Bacon.
TELEVISION: Movie: The Caine Mutiny Court Martial. Special: Tanner 88. Guest: Birdland.

O'CONNOR, PAT
Director. b. Ardmore, Ireland, 1943. After working in London at odd jobs (putting corks in wine bottles, paving roads), came to U.S. e. UCLA, B.A. Studied film and TV at Ryerson Institute in Toronto. 1970, trainee prod., dir. with Radio Telefis Eireann. 1970-78 prod. and dir. over 45 TV features and current affairs documentaries. (The Four Roads, The Shankhill, Kiltyclogher, One of Ourselves, Night in Ginitia). A Ballroom of Romance won BAFTA Award (1981).
PICTURES: Cal (debut, 1984), A Month in the Country, Stars and Bars, The January Man, Fools of Fortune, Circle of Friends, Sacred Hearts.
TELEVISION: Movie: Zelda.

O'DONNELL, CHRIS
Actor. b. Winetka, IL, 1970.
PICTURES: Men Don't Leave (debut, 1990), Fried Green Tomatoes, School Ties, Scent of a Woman, The Three Musketeers, Blue Sky, Circle of Friends, Mad Love, Batman Forever, The Chamber, In Love and War.

O'DONNELL, ROSIE
Actress. b. Commack, NY, 1961. e. Dickinson Col., Boston Univ. Stand-up comic first gaining attention on series Star Search.
THEATER: Grease! (B'way debut, 1994).
PICTURES: A League of Their Own, Sleepless in Seattle, Another Stakeout, Car 54 Where are You?, I'll Do Anything, The Flintstones, Exit to Eden, Now and Then, Beautiful Girls, Harriet the Spy.
TELEVISION: Series: Gimme a Break, Stand-Up Spotlight (host, exec. prod.), Stand by Your Man, The Rosie O'Donnell Show (host).

O'HARA, CATHERINE
Actress, Writer, Director. b. Toronto, Canada, Mar. 4, 1954. Professional debut in 1974 with Toronto's Second City. Co-founder of SCTV in 1976 (Emmy and Canadian Nellie Awards for writing).
PICTURES: Nothing Personal, Rock & Rule (voice), After Hours, Heartburn, Beetlejuice, Dick Tracy, Betsy's Wedding, Home Alone, Little Vegas, There Goes the Neighborhood, Home Alone 2: Lost in New York, The Nightmare Before Christmas (voice), The Paper, Wyatt Earp, A Simple Twist of Fate, Tall Tale, Last of the High Kings.
TELEVISION: Series: SCTV, Steve Allen Comedy Hour, SCTV Network 90. Guest: Trying Times (Get a Job), Comic Relief, Dream On (also dir.).

O'HARA, GERRY
Director, Writer. b. Boston-Lincs, England 1924. e. St. Mary's Catholic Sch., Boston. Junior Reporter Boston Guardian. Entered industry in 1942 with documentaries and propaganda subjects.
PICTURES: Director: That Kind of Girl (debut, 1963), Game for Three Lovers, Pleasure Girls (also s.p.), Maroc 7, Love in Amsterdam, All the Right Noises (also s.p.), Leopard in the Snow, The Bitch, Fanny Hill, The Mummy Lives (also co-s.p.). Writer: Ten Little Indians, Havoc in Chase County, Phantom of the Opera, De Sade's Nightmare, Sherlock Holmes and the Affair in Transylvania, Catherine the Great.
TELEVISION: The Avengers, Man in a Suitcase, Journey into the Unknown, The Professionals (story editor, writer), Special Squad (story consultant), Cats Eyes (exec. story editor), Operation Julie (writer; mini-series), Sherlock Holmes & The Leading Lady, Sherlock Holmes & The Incident at Victoria Falls (co-writer).

O'HARA, MAUREEN
Actress. r.n. Maureen FitzSimons. b. Dublin. Aug. 17, 1921. Abbey Sch. of Acting. Won numerous prizes for elocution. Under contract to Erich Pommer-Charles Laughton. Co-starred, Abbey & Repertory Theatre.
PICTURES: Kicking the Moon Around (debut, 1938), My Irish Molly, Jamaica Inn, The Hunchback of Notre Dame, A Bill of Divorcement, Dance Girl Dance, They Met in Argentina, How Green Was My Valley, To the Shores of Tripoli, Ten Gentlemen From West Point, The Black Swan, The Immortal Sergeant, This Land Is Mine, The Fallen Sparrow, Buffalo Bill, The Spanish Main, Sentimental Journey, Do You Love Me?, Miracle on 34th Street, Sinbad the Sailor, The Homestretch, The Foxes of Harrow, Sitting Pretty, Woman's Secret, Forbidden Street, Father Was a Fullback, Bagdad, Comanche Territory, Tripoli, Rio Grande, At Sword's Point, Flame of Araby, The Quiet Man, Kangaroo, Against All Flags, The Redhead From Wyoming, War Arrow, Fire Over Africa, The Magnificent Matador, Lady Godiva, Long Gray Line, Lisbon, Everything But the Truth, Wings of Eagles, Our Man in Havana, The Parent Trap, The Deadly Companions, Mr. Hobbs Takes a Vacation, McLintock!, Spencer's Mountain, The Battle of the Villa Fiorita, The Rare Breed, How Do I Love Thee?, Big Jake, Only the Lonely.
TELEVISION: Movie: The Red Pony, The Christmas Box. Specials: Mrs. Miniver, Scarlet Pimpernel, Spellbound, High Button Shoes, Who's Afraid of Mother Goose.

O'HERLIHY, DAN
Actor. b. Wexford, Ireland, May 1, 1919. e. National U. of Ireland (Bachelor of Architecture). Actor with Abbey Theatre, Dublin Gate, Longford Prod.; announcer on Radio Eireann; on Broadway in The Ivy Green.
PICTURES: Odd Man Out (debut, 1946), Kidnapped, Larceny, Macbeth, Iroquois Trail, The Blue Veil, The Desert Fox, The Highwayman, Soldiers Three, At Swords Point, Invasion U.S.A., Operation Secret, Actors and Sin, Sword of Venus, The Adventures of Robinson Crusoe (Acad. Award nom.), The Black Shield of Falworth, Bengal Brigade, The Purple Mask, The Virgin Queen, City After Midnight, Home Before Dark, Imitation of Life, The Young Land, Night Fighters (A Terrible Beauty), One Foot in Hell, The Cabinet of Caligari, Fail-Safe, The Big Cube, 100 Rifles, Waterloo, The Carey Treatment, The Tamarind Seed, MacArthur, Halloween III: The Season of the Witch, The Last Starfighter, The Whoopee Boys, Robocop, The Dead, Robocop 2.
TELEVISION: Series: The Travels of Jamie McPheeters, The Long Hot Summer, Hunter's Moon, Whiz Kids, Man Called Sloane, Twin Peaks. Mini-series: QB VII, Jennie: Lady Randolph Churchill, Nancy Astor. Movies: The People, Deadly Game, Woman on the Run, Good Against Evil, Love Cheat and Steal. Guest: The Equalizer, L.A. Law, Murder She Wrote, Ray Bradbury Theatre, Father Dowling. BBC: Colditz, The Secret Servant, Artemis, The Last Day, Jennie, Nancy Astor.

OHLMEYER, DONALD W., JR.
Executive, Producer, Director. b. New Orleans, LA, Feb. 3, 1945. e. U. of Notre Dame, B.A. (Communications), 1967. Producer and director at both ABC and NBC. Formed Ohlmeyer Communications Company, 1982 (diversified prod. and dist. of entertainment and sports prog.). Assoc. dir., ABC Sports, NY 1967-70; director, ABC Sports, 1971-72 (dir. 1972 Olympic Games); prod.: ABC Sports, NY 1972-77 (prod. and dir. 1976 Winter and Summer Olympics; prod. ABC's Monday Night Football, 1972-76); exec. prod.: NBC Sports, NY 1977-82 (exec. prod., 1980 Olympics, The World Series, The Super Bowl). Special Bulletin (exec. prod.), John Denver's Christmas in Aspen (exec. prod.). Chmn. and CEO, Ohlmeyer Communications Co., LA, 1982-present. 1993, named pres. NBC West Coast. Recipient of 14 Emmy Awards, Humanitas Prize, Award for Excellence, National Film Board. Member, Directors Guild of America.
TELEVISION: Specials: Heroes of Desert Storm (dir.), Disney's Christmas on Ice (dir.), Crimes of the Century (prod.). Series: Lifestories (dir./exec. prod.), Fast Copy (prod.). Movies: Cold Sassy Tree (exec. prod.), Crazy in Love (exec. prod.), Right to Die (exec. prod.).

O'KEEFE, MICHAEL
Actor. b. Larchmont, NY, April 24, 1955. e. NYU, AADA. m. singer Bonnie Raitt. Co-founder, Colonnades Theatre Lab, NY. THEATER: B'way: Mass Appeal (Theatre World Award), Fifth of July. Off-B'way: Killdere (NYSF), Moliere in Spite of Himself, Christmas on Mars, Short Eyes. Regional: Streamers, A Few Good Men (tour).
PICTURES: Gray Lady Down (debut, 1978), The Great Santini (Acad. Award nom.), Caddyshack, Split Image, Nate and Hayes, Finders Keepers, The Slugger's Wife, Ironweed, Out of the Rain, Me and Veronica, Nina Takes a Lover, Three Lovers, Edie and Pen, Ghosts of Mississippi.
TELEVISION: Series: Against the Law, Roseanne. Movies: The Lindbergh Kidnapping Case, Friendly Persuasion, Panache, The Dark Secret of Harvest Home, A Rumor of War, Unholy Matrimony, Bridge to Silence, Disaster at Silo 7, Too Young to Die?, In the Best Interest of the Child, Fear, Incident at Deception Ridge, The People Next Door.

OLDKNOW, WIILIAM H.
Executive. b. Atlanta, GA, Sept. 3, 1924. e. U.S.C. Served in USNR from 1943-46. Pres., Sero Amusement Co., 1947-present (drive-in theatres, shopping centers, and commercial real-estate). Sole proprietor, Starlight Drive-in Theatre, Atlanta, GA. Chmn. and pres., De Anza Land & Leisure Corp.

OLDMAN, GARY
Actor. b. New Cross, South London, Eng., March 21, 1958. Won scholarship to Rose Bruford Drama College (B.A. Theatre Arts) after studying with Greenwich Young People's Theatre. Acted with Theatre Royal, York and joined touring theatre co. Then in 1980 appeared with Glasgow Citizens Theatre in Massacre at Paris, Chinchilla, Desperado Corner, A Waste of Time (also touring Europe and South America). Received Evening Standard Film Award for Best Newcomer for Sid and Nancy, 1986.
THEATER: *London*: Minnesota Moon, Summit Conference, Rat in the Skull, Women Beware Women, The War Plays, Real Dreams, The Desert Air, Serious Money (Royal Shakespeare Co.), The Pope's Wedding (Time Out's Fringe Award, best newcomer 1985-86; British Theatre Assc. Drama Mag. Award, Best Actor 1985).
PICTURES: Sid and Nancy (debut, 1986), Prick Up Your Ears, Track 29, We Think the World of You, Criminal Law, Chattahoochee, State of Grace, Rosencrantz and Guildenstern Are Dead, Exile, Before and After Death, JFK, Bram Stoker's Dracula, True Romance, Romeo Is Bleeding, The Professional, Immortal Beloved, Murder in the First, Dead Presidents, The Scarlet Letter, Basquiat.
TELEVISION: Remembrance, Meantime, Honest Decent and True, Rat in the Skull, The Firm, Heading Home, Fallen Angels.

OLIN, KEN
Actor, Director. b. Chicago, IL, July 30, 1954. e. Univ. of PA. m. actress Patricia Wettig. Studied acting with Warren Robertson and Stella Adler. Made Off-B'way debut in Taxi Tales, 1978.
PICTURES: Ghost Story, Queen's Logic, White Fang 2: Myth of the White Wolf (dir.).
TELEVISION: *Series*: The Bay City Blues, Hill Street Blues, Falcon Crest, thirtysomething (also dir.). *Movies* (actor): Women at West Point, Flight 90: Disaster on the Potomac, There Must Be a Pony, Tonight's the Night, Cop Killer, A Stoning in Fulham County, Goodnight Sweet Wife: A Murder in Boston, Telling Secrets, Nothing But the Truth. *Movies (director)*: The Broken Cord, Doing Time on Maple Drive, In Pursuit of Honor. *Guest*: Murder She Wrote, Hotel, The Hitchhiker.

OLIN, LENA
Actress. b. Stockholm, Sweden, 1955. Member of the Royal Dramatic Theatre in Stockholm. Daughter of actor-director Stig Olin. m. director Lasse Hallstrom.
THEATER: *NY*: Miss Julie.
PICTURES: The Adventures of Picasso, Karleken, Fanny and Alexander, Grasanklingar, After the Rehearsal, A Matter of Life and Death, Friends, The Unbearable Lightness of Being, S/Y Joy (Gladjen), Enemies a Love Story (Acad. Award nom.), Havana, Mr. Jones, Romeo Is Bleeding, The Night and the Moment, Night Falls on Manhattan.

OLMI, ERMANNO
Director, Writer, Producer, Editor. b. Bergamo, Italy, July 24, 1931. e. Accademia d'Arte Drammatica, Milan. Worked as a clerk for an electric company Edisonvolta 1949-52, until 1952 when he began directing theatrical and cinematic activities sponsored by co. 1952-61, directed or supervised over 40 short 16mm and 35mm documentary films. 1959 first feature film, semi-doc. Time Stood Still. With other friends and Tullio Kezich formed prod. co., 22 December S.P.A., 1961. 1982, Helped found Hypothesis Cinema, a sch. for aspiring dirs.
PICTURES: *Director/Writer*: Time Stood Still (debut, 1959), The Sound of Trumpets, The Fiances (also prod.), And There Came a Man (A Man Named John), One Fine Day (also edit.), The Tree of the Wood Clogs (Cannes Film Fest. Award, 1978; also photog., edit.), Camminacammina (also photog., edit., design), Milano '83 (also photog., edit.), Long Live the Lady (also co-photog., edit.), Legend of the Holy Drinker (also edit.), Il Segreto Del Bosco Vecchio. Documenatries: Artigiani Veneti, Lungo Il Fiume.
TELEVISION: The Scavengers (also photog.), During the Summer (also photog., edit.), The Circumstance (also photog., edit.).

OLMOS, EDWARD JAMES
Actor. b. East Los Angeles, CA, February 24, 1947. e. East Los Angeles City Coll., CA State U. m. actress Lorraine Bracco. Started as rock singer with group Eddie James and the Pacific Ocean. By the early 1970s acted in small roles on Kojak and Hawaii Five-O. 1978 starred in Luis Valdez's musical drama Zoot Suit at Mark Taper Forum (L.A. Drama Critics Circle Award, 1978), later on B'way (Theatre World Award, Tony nom.), and in film version. Formed YOY Productions with director Robert Young. Numerous awards for humanitarian work.
PICTURES: Aloha Bobby and Rose (debut, 1975), Alambrista!, Virus, Wolfen, Zoot Suit, Blade Runner, The Ballad of Gregorio Cortez (also assoc. prod., composer and musical adaptor), Saving Grace, Stand and Deliver (Acad.

Award nom.; also co-prod.), Triumph of the Spirit, Talent for the Game, American Me (also dir., co-prod.), A Million to Juan, Mirage, My Family/Mi Familia, Roosters, Caught.
TELEVISION: *Movies*: Evening in Byzantium, 300 Miles for Stephanie, Menendez: A Killing in Beverly Hills, The Burning Season. *Specials*: Sequin, Y.E.S. Inc. *Series*: Miami Vice (Golden Globe & Emmy Awards, 1985; also dir. episodes). *Mini-series*: Mario Puzo's The Fortunate Pilgrim.

O'LOUGHLIN, GERALD STUART
Actor. b. New York, NY, Dec. 23, 1921. e. Blair Acad., Lafayette Col., U. of Rochester, Neighborhood Playhouse. U.S. Marine, WWII.
THEATER: *B'way*: Streetcar (ANTA series), Shadow of a Gunman, Dark at the Top of the Stairs, A Touch of the Poet, Cook for Mr. General, One Flew Over the Cuckoo's Nest, Calculated Risk, Lovers and Other Strangers. *Off-B'way*: Who'll Save the Plowboy (Obie Award), Harry Noon and Night, Machinal.
PICTURES: Lovers and Lollipops, Cop Hater, A Hatful of Rain, Ensign Pulver, A Fine Madness, In Cold Blood, Ice Station Zebra, Desperate Characters, The Organization, The Valachi Papers, Twilight's Last Gleaming, Frances, Crimes of Passion, City Heat, Quicksilver.
TELEVISION: *Movies*: The D.A.: Murder One, Murder at the World Series, Something for Joey, A Love Affair: The Eleanor and Lou Gehrig Story, Crash, Detour to Terror, Pleasure Palace, A Matter of Life and Death, Under Siege, Perry Mason: The Case of the Notorious Nun, Child's Cry, In the Arms of a Killer. *Mini-Series*: Wheels, Roots: The Next Generations, Blind Ambition, Women in White, The Blue and the Gray. *Series*: The Storefront Lawyers (Men at Law), The Rookies, Automan, Our House. *Guest*: Alcoa Premiere, Philco-Goodyear, Suspense, The Defenders, Ben Casey, Dr. Kildare, 12 O'Clock High, Going My Way, Naked City, Gunsmoke, Green Hornet, Mission Impossible, Mannix, Judd For The Defense, Hawaii 5-0, Cannon, Room 222, Charlie's Angels, M*A*S*H, Trapper John M.D., Fame, T.J. Hooker, Murder She Wrote, Highway to Heaven, Dirty Dancing, many others.

OLSON, DALE C.
Executive. b. Fargo, ND, Feb. 20, 1934. e. Portland State Coll., OR. Owner, Dale C. Olson & Associates; formerly sn. v.p. & pres., m.p. div., Rogers & Cowan public relations. Journalist on Oregonian newspaper, West Coast editor, Boxoffice Magazine, 1958-60; critic and reporter, Daily Variety, 1960-66; dir. of publ., Mirisch Corp., 1966-68; Rogers & Cowan, 1968-85. Past pres., Hollywood Press Club, awarded Bob Yaeger and Les Mason award by Publicists Guild; v.p. Diamond Circle, City of Hope; delegate for U.S. to Manila International Film Festival. Chmn. public relations. coordin. committee & member nat'l bd. of trustees, A.M.P.A.S., 1989-91. Chmn. Western Council, Actors Fund of America, 1991. On Nat'l Bd. of Trustees, 1992-present.

OLSON, JAMES
Actor. b. Evanston, IL, Oct. 8, 1930. e. Northwestern U.
THEATER: *NY*: The Young and the Beautiful, Romulus, The Chinese Prime Minister, J.B., Slapstick Tragedy, Three Sisters, Sin of Pat Muldoon, Winter's Tale, Of Love Remembered, Twelve Dreams.
PICTURES: The Sharkfighters, The Strange One, Rachel Rachel, Moon Zero Two, The Andromeda Strain, The Groundstar Conspiracy, The Mafu Cage, Ragtime, Amityville II: The Possession, Commando, Rachel River.
TELEVISION: *Movies*: Paper Man, Incident on a Dark Street, Manhunter, A Tree Grows in Brooklyn, The Sex Symbol, The Family Nobody Wanted, Someone I Touched, Man on the Outside, Strange New World, Law and Order, The Spell, Moviola: The Silent Years, Cave-In!, The Parade. *Specials*: Missiles of October, Vince Lombardi Story, Court-Martial of Geoge Armstrong Custer.

OLSON, NANCY
Actress. b. Milwaukee, WI, July 14, 1929. e. U. of Wisconsin, UCLA. No prof. experience prior to films.
PICTURES: Canadian Pacific (debut, 1949), Sunset Boulevard (Acad. Award nom.), Union Station, Mr. Music, Submarine Command, Force of Arms, Big Jim McLain, So Big, The Boy From Oklahoma, Battle Cry, Pollyanna, The Absent-Minded Professor, Son of Flubber, Smith!, Snowball Express, Airport 1975, Making Love.
TELEVISION: *Series*: Kingston: Confidential, Paper Dolls. *Special*: High Tor.

O'NEAL, RON
Actor. b. Utica, NY, Sept. 1, 1937. e. Ohio State U. Spent 9 yrs. at Karamu House in Cleveland (inter-racial theatre) from 1957 to 1966, acting in 40 plays. 1967-68 spent in N.Y. teaching acting in Harlem. Appeared in all-black revue 1968, The Best of Broadway, then in summer stock. Acted off-B'way in American Pastorale and The Mummer's Play. 1970 joined the

Public Theatre. Break came with No Place To Be Somebody, which won him the Obie, Clarence Derwent, Drama Desk and Theatre World Awards.
THEATER: Tiny Alice, The Dream of Monkey Mountain.
PICTURES: Move (debut, 1970), The Organization, Super Fly, Super Fly TNT (also dir., co-story), The Master Gunfighter, Brothers, A Force of One, When a Stranger Calls, The Final Countdown, St. Helens, Red Dawn, Mercenary Fighters, Hero and the Terror, Up Against the Wall (also dir.), Death House.
TELEVISION: Series: Bring 'em Back Alive, The Equalizer. Mini-Series: North and South. Movies: Freedom Road, Brave New World, Guyana Tragedy: The Story of Jim Jones, Sophisticated Gents, Playing with Fire, North Beach and Rawhide, As Summers Die.

O'NEAL, RYAN
Actor. r.n. Patrick Ryan O'Neal. b. Los Angeles, CA, April 20, 1941. Parents, screenwriter-novelist, Charles O'Neal, and actress Patricia Callaghan. Daughter is actress Tatum O'Neal; son is actor Griffin O'Neal. Boxer, L.A. Golden Gloves, 1956-57. Began career as stand-in, stunt man, then actor in Tales of the Vikings series, in Germany, 1959; freelanced in Hollywood.
PICTURES: The Big Bounce (debut, 1969), The Games, Love Story (Acad. Award nom.), Wild Rovers, What's Up Doc?, Paper Moon, The Thief Who Came to Dinner, Barry Lyndon, Nickelodeon, A Bridge Too Far, The Driver, Oliver's Story, The Main Event, So Fine, Green Ice, Partners, Irreconcilable Differences, Fever Pitch, Tough Guys Don't Dance, Chances Are, Faithful.
TELEVISION: Series: Empire, Peyton Place, Good Sports. Movies: Love Hate Love, Small Sacrifices, The Man Upstairs. Special: Liza Minnelli: A Triple Play. Guest: Dobie Gillis, Bachelor Father, Leave It to Beaver, My Three Sons, Perry Mason, The Larry Sanders Show. Pilot: 1775.

O'NEAL, TATUM
Actress. b. Los Angeles, CA, Nov. 5, 1963. Daughter of actors Ryan O'Neal and Joanna Moore. NY stage debut 1992 in A Terrible Beauty, followed by Adroscoggin Fugue.
PICTURES: Paper Moon (debut, 1973; Academy Award, best supporting actress), The Bad News Bears, Nickelodeon, International Velvet, Little Darlings, Circle of Two, Certain Fury, Little Noises.
TELEVISION: Movie: Woman on the Run: The Lawrencia Bembenek Story. Special: 15 and Getting Straight. Guest: Cher, Faerie Tale Theatre (Goldilocks and the Three Bears).

O'NEIL, THOMAS F.
Executive. b. Kansas City, MO, Apr. 18, 1915. e. Holy Cross Coll., 1933-37. Employed by General Tire and Rubber Co., 1937-41; U.S. Coast Guard, 1941-46; v.p., dir., Yankee Network, Boston, 1948-51; pres. chmn. of bd. RKO General, Inc., 1952. Arranged purchase RKO Radio by General Teleradio, Inc. from Howard Hughes, July, 1955; chairman of the Board, RKO General, Inc., dir., General Tire & Rubber Co.

O'NEILL, ED
Actor. b. Youngstown, OH, Apr. 12, 1946. e. Ohio Univ., Youngstown State. Taught social studies in Youngstown prior to becoming an actor. Made NY stage debut Off-Off-B'way in Requiem for a Heavyweight at SoHo Rep. Theatre. B'way debut in Knockout.
PICTURES: Deliverance, Cruising, The Dogs of War, Disorganized Crime, K-9, The Adventures of Ford Fairlane, Sibling Rivalry, Dutch, Wayne's World, Wayne's World 2, Blue Chips, Little Giants.
TELEVISION: Series: Married... With Children. Pilot: Farrell for the People. Movies: When Your Lover Leaves, The Day the Women Got Even, Popeye Doyle, A Winner Never Quits, Right to Die, Police School, The Whereabouts of Jenny, W.E.I.R.D. World.

O'NEILL, JENNIFER
Actress. b. Rio de Janeiro, Brazil, Feb. 20, 1949. e. Dalton Sch. Model before entering films. Spokeswoman: CoverGirl cosmetics. Pres., Point of View Productions and Management.
PICTURES: Rio Lobo, Summer of '42, Such Good Friends, The Carey Treatment, Glass Houses, Lady Ice, The Reincarnation of Peter Proud, Whiffs, Caravans, The Psychic, The Innocent, A Force of One, Cloud Dancer, Steel, Scanners, Committed, I Love N.Y., Love is Like That, Invasion of Privacy, The Gentle People.
TELEVISION: Series: Bare Essence, Cover Up. Movies: Love's Savage Fury, The Other Victim, Chase, Perry Mason: The Case of the Shooting Star, The Red Spider, Glory Days, Full Exposure: The Sex Tapes Scandal, Personals, Perfect Family, The Cover Girl Murders, Jonathan Stone: Threat of Innocence. Mini-Series: A.D.

ONTKEAN, MICHAEL
Actor. b. Vancouver, British Columbia, Canada, Jan. 24, 1946. e. U. of New Hampshire. Son of Leonard and Muriel Cooper Ontkean, actors. Acting debut at 4 with father's rep. theater. Child actor with Stratford Shakespeare Fest., CBC and Natl Film Bd. Attended coll. 4 years on hockey scholarship. Has performed with Public Theatre, NY, Williamstown Theatre Fest., Mark Taper Lab, The Kitchen, Soho.
PICTURES: The Peace Killers (debut, 1971), Pick Up on 101, Necromancy, Hot Summer Week, Slap Shot, Voices, Willie and Phil, Making Love, Just the Way You Are, The Allnighter, Maid to Order, Clara's Heart, Street Justice, Cold Front, Bye Bye Blues, Postcards From the Edge, Bayou Boy, The Toy Factory, Summer, Access All Areas, Le Sang des Autres, Cutting Loose, Square Deal, Rapture.
TELEVISION: Series: The Rookies, Twin Peaks. Movies: The Rookies (pilot), The Blood of Others, Kids Don't Tell, The Right of the People, Twin Peaks (pilot), Defense of a Married Man, In a Child's Name, Legacy of Lies, Whose Child Is This? The War for Baby Jessica, Vendetta 2: The New Mafia, Danielle Steel's Family Album, The Man Next Door, Man From the South.

OPHULS, MARCEL
Director, Writer. r.n. Hans Marcel Oppenheimer. b. Frankfurt-am-Main, Germany, Nov. 1, 1927. Son of German director Max Ophuls. e. Occidental Coll., U. of California, Berkeley, Sorbonne (philosophy). Family moved to France, 1932, then to Hollywood, 1941. Military service with Occupation forces in Japan, 1946; performed with theater unit, Tokyo. 1951 began working in French film industry as asst. dir., using name Marcel Wall. Asst. dir. on Moulin Rouge, Act of Love, Marianne de ma Jeunesse, Lola Montes. 1956-59, radio and TV story ed., West Germany. Later worked for French TV as reporter and dir. news mag. features. Dir. & wrote short film Henri Matisse. 1968 doc. dir. for German TV. 1975-78 staff prod. CBS News, then ABC News. MacArthur Fellowship 1991. Member of AMPAS.
PICTURES: Director/Writer: Love at 20 (dir. segment), Banana Peel, Fire at Will, Munich or Peace in Our Time, The Sorrow and the Pity (also prod.; Natl. Soc. of Film Critics, NY Film Critics & Prix de Dinard Awards, 1970), The Harvest at Mai Lai, A Sense of Loss, The Memory of Justice, Hotel Terminus--The Life and Times of Klaus Barbie (also prod.; Academy Award, Berlin Peace Prize, Cannes Jury Prize, 1988), The Troubles We've Seen (also prod., Intl. Film Critics Prize, 1994).
TELEVISION: America Revisited, Two Whole Days, November Days.

OPOTOWSKY, STAN
Executive. b. New Orleans, LA, Apr. 13, 1923. e. Tulane U. Served in U.S. Marine Corps as combat corr. and later joined United Press, working in New Orleans, Denver, and New York. Published own weekly newspaper in Mississippi before returning to N.Y. to join New York Post as mgr. editor and traveling natl. corr. Is also cinematographer and film editor. Joined ABC News as TV assignment editor; named asst. assignment mgr. 1974 named dir. of operations for ABC News TV Documentaries. 1975 named dir. of TV News Coverage, ABC News.
TELEVISION: Author: The Big Picture, The Longs of Louisiana, The Kennedy Government, Men Behind Bars.

O'QUINN, TERRY
Actor. b. Michigan.
THEATER: B'way: Foxfire, Curse of an Aching Heart. Off-B'way: Richard III, Groves of Academy, Total Abandon. Regional: Streamers, Measure for Measure, The Front Page.
PICTURES: Heaven's Gate, Without a Trace, All the Right Moves, Places in the Heart, Mrs. Soffel, Mischief, Silver Bullet, SpaceCamp, The Stepfather, Black Widow, Young Guns, Pin, Stepfather 2, Blind Fury, The Rocketeer, Prisoners of the Sun, Company Business, The Cutting Edge, Amityville: A New Generation, Tombstone, Lipstick Camera.
TELEVISION: Movies: FDR: The Final Year, Prisoner Without a Name Cell Without a Number, Right to Kill, Unfinished Business, An Early Frost, Stranger on My Land, Women of Valor, When the Time Comes, Perry Mason: The Case of the Desperate Deception, Son of the Morning Star, The Last to Go, Deliver Them From Evil: The Taking of Alta View, Trial: The Price of Passion, Sexual Advances, Wild Card, The Good Fight, Born Too Soon, Visions of Murder, Heart of a Child, Don't Talk to Strangers, Justice in a Small Town, A Friend to Die For, Ray Alexander: A Menu for Murder.

ORBACH, JERRY
Actor. b. Bronx, NY, Oct. 20, 1935. e. U. of Illinois, Northwestern U. Trained for stage with Herbert Berghof and Lee Strasberg. N.Y. stage debut in Threepenny Opera, 1955.
THEATER: The Fantasticks (original cast, 1960), Carnival, The Cradle Will Rock, Guys and Dolls, Scuba Duba, Promises Promises (Tony Award, 1969), 6 Rms Riv Vu, Chicago, 42nd Street.
PICTURES: Cop Hater, Mad Dog Coll, John Goldfarb Please Come Home, The Gang That Couldn't Shoot Straight, A Fan's Notes, Foreplay (The President's Woman), The Sentinel,

Underground Aces, Prince of the City, Brewster's Millions, F/X, The Imagemaker, Dirty Dancing, Someone to Watch Over Me, Crimes and Misdemeanors, Last Exit to Brooklyn, I Love N.Y., A Gnome Named Norm, California Casanova, Dead Women in Lingerie, Out for Justice, Toy Soldiers (unbilled), Delusion, Delirious, Beauty and the Beast (voice), Straight Talk, Universal Soldier, Mr. Saturday Night, The Cemetery Club.
TELEVISION: *Series:* The Law and Harry McGraw, Law and Order. *Guest:* Shari Lewis Show, Jack Paar, Bob Hope Presents, Love American Style, Murder She Wrote, Kojak, Golden Girls, Hunter. *Movies:* An Invasion of Privacy, Out on a Limb, Love Among Thieves, In Defense of a Married Man, Broadway Bound, Quiet Killer. *Mini-Series:* Dream West.

ORMOND, JULIA
Actress. b. England, 1965. Studied acting at Webber Douglas Acad., London.
THEATER: The Rehearsal, Wuthering Heights, Arms and the Man, The Crucible, Faith Hope and Charity (London Drama Critics Award, 1989).
PICTURES: The Baby of Macon, Nostradamus, Legends of the Fall, First Knight, Captives, Sabrina.
TELEVISION: *Mini-Series:* Traffik. *Movies:* Young Catherine, Stalin.

ORTEGA, KENN
Director, Choreographer. b. Palo Alto, CA. e. American Conserv. Theatre, Canada Coll. Started acting at age 13. Earned several scholarships to dance academies in San Francisco area. Regional theatre roles in Oliver, Hair, The Last Sweet Days of Isaac, before staging shows for rock band The Tubes. First major tv job choreographing Cher special. Directed/choreographed concerts and/or music videos for such performers as Michael Jackson, Kiss, Elton John, Cher, Rod Stewart, Diana Ross, Madonna, Billy Joel, Oingo Boingo, Miami Sound Machine, Pointer Sisters, Toto. Artistic dir. and choreographer, 1996 Centennial Olympic Games opening and closing ceremonies.
PICTURES: *Director/Choreographer:* Newsies, Hocus Pocus. *Choreographer:* The Rose (asst. to Toni Basil), Xanadu, One From the Heart, St. Elmo's Fire, Pretty in Pink, Ferris Bueller's Day Off, Dirty Dancing, Salsa (also assoc. prod.), Shag, To Wong Foo—Thanks for Everything–Julie Newmar.
TELEVISION: *Series:* Dirty Dancing (dir., choreog.), Hull High (dir., co-exec. prod., choreog.) Choreographed many specials including American Music Awards, Academy Awards, NAACP Awards, music specials starring Cher, Olivia Newton-John, Neil Diamond, Smokey Robinson, etc. *Director:* Second Noah.

O'SHEA, MILO
Actor. b. Dublin, Ireland, June 2, 1926. Member of Dublin Gate Theatre Co., 1944, before screen career.
THEATER: *NY:* Staircase, Dear World, The Comedians, A Touch of the Poet, Waiting For Godot (Brooklyn Acad. of Music), Mass Appeal, My Fair Lady, Corpse!, Meet Me in St. Louis, Remembrance (Off-B'way), Philadelphia Here I Come!, Alive Alive Oh! (alo co-writer), Mrs. Warren's Profession. *London:* Treasure Hunt, Glory Be, Hans Andersen, Corpse, Can-Can.
PICTURES: Carry on Cabby, Never Put It in Writing, Ulysses, Romeo and Juliet, Barbarella, The Adding Machine, The Angel Levine, Paddy, Sacco and Vanzetti, Loot, Theatre of Blood, Digby: The Biggest Dog in the World, It's Not the Size That Counts, Arabian Adventure, The Pilot, The Verdict, The Purple Rose of Cairo, The Dream Team, Opportunity Knocks, Only the Lonely, The Playboys, Rooney, Never Put It In Writing.
TELEVISION: *Series:* Once a Hero, Frasier. *Mini-Series:* QB VII, Ellis Island, The Best of Families. *Movies/Specials:* Two By Forsythe, Peter Lundy and the Medicine Hat Stallion, Portrait of a Rebel: Margaret Sanger, And No One Could Save Her, A Times for Miracles, Broken Vows, Angel in Green, Murder in the Heartland. *Guest:* The Golden Girls, Cheers, Who's the Boss, Beauty and the Beast, St. Elsewhere.

OSHIMA, NAGISA
Director, Writer. b. Kyoto, Japan, March 31, 1932. e. U. of Kyoto (law), 1954. Joined Shochiku Ofuna Studios in 1954 as asst. dir.; 1956 wrote film criticism and became editor-in-chief of film revue Eiga hihyo; 1959 promoted to director. 1962-65 worked exclusively in TV; 1962-64 made documentaries in Korea and Vietnam; 1975 formed Oshima Prods. 1976, his book of Realm of the Senses seized by police. With editor, prosecuted for obscenity, acquitted. Pres. of Directors Guild of Japan, 1980-present.
PICTURES: *Dir./Writer.* A Town of Love and Hope (debut, 1959), Cruel Story of Youth, The Sun's Burial, Night and Fog in Japan, The Catch (dir. only), The Christian Rebel, A Child's First Adventure, I'm Here Bellett, The Pleasures of the Flesh, Violence at Noon (dir. only), Band of Ninja (also co-prod.), Sing a Song of Sex (also co- prod.), Japanese Summer: Double Suicide (also co-prod.), Death By Hanging, Three

Resurrected Drunkards (A Sinner in Paradise), Diary of a Shinjuku Thief, Boy (dir. only), He Died After the War, The Ceremony, Dear Summer Sister, In the Realm of the Senses, Phantom Love, Empire of Passion (Phantom Love; also co-prod.), Merry Christmas Mr. Lawrence, Max My Love.

OSMOND, DONNY
Singer, TV Host. b. Ogden, UT, Dec. 9, 1957. Seventh of 9 children, he was fifth member of family to become professional singer. (Four brothers: Alan, Wayne, Merrill and Jay, were original members of Osmond Bros., who originally sang barbershop quartet.) Made debut at 4 on Andy Williams Show. Has had 12 gold albums. Was co-host with sister of Donny & Marie on TV.
THEATER: Little Johnny Jones, Joseph and the Amazing Technicolor Dreamcoat.
PICTURE: Goin' Coconuts.
TELEVISION: *Series:* The Andy Williams Show, Donny and Marie. *Movie:* The Wild Women of Chastity Gulch. *Guest:* The Jerry Lewis Show, Here's Lucy, The Love Boat.

OSMOND, MARIE
Singer, TV Host. b. Ogden, UT, Oct. 13, 1959. Began career at age of 3 on Andy Williams Show. Her first album, Paper Roses went gold. Appeared with brother Donny in feature film Goin' Coconuts.
TELEVISION: *Series:* Donny and Marie, Marie, Ripley's Believe It or Not (co-host), Maybe This Time. *Movies:* Gift of Love, I Married Wyatt Earp, Side By Side.

O'STEEN, SAM
Editor, Director. b. Nov. 6, 1923. Entered m.p. industry 1956 as asst. to editor George Tomassini on The Wrong Man. Became full editor in 1963 on Youngblood Hawke. Directorial debut with TV film A Brand New Life, 1972.
PICTURES: Youngblood Hawke, Kisses for My President, Robin and the 7 Hoods, Marriage on the Rocks, None But the Brave, Who's Afraid of Virginia Woolf?, Cool Hand Luke, The Graduate, Rosemary's Baby, The Sterile Cuckoo (spv. edit.), Catch-22, Carnal Knowledge, Portnoy's Complaint, The Day of the Dolphin, Chinatown, Sparkle (dir.), Straight Time, Hurricane, Amityville II: The Possession, Silkwood, Heartburn, Nadine, Biloxi Blues, Frantic, Working Girl, A Dry White Season (co-edit.), Postcards from the Edge, Regarding Henry, Wolf.
TELEVISION: *Director:* A Brand New Life, I Love You Goodbye, Queen of the Stardust Ballroom (DGA Award), High Risk, Look What's Happened to Rosemary's Baby, The Best Little Girl in the World, Kids Don't Tell.

O'SULLIVAN, KEVIN P.
Executive. b. New York, NY, April 13, 1928. e. Queens Coll., Flushing, NY. Associated with television 40 yrs., initially as a talent; later as businessman. Won first prize in Arthur Godfrey Talent Scouts competition in 1948. 1950-55 professional singer, actor on TV, in theatre, night clubs. 1955-57 on radio-TV promotion staff, Ronson Corp. 1958-61, salesman, Television Programs of America. 1961-67 dir. of program services, Harrington, Righter and Parsons. 1967 joined ABC Films, domestic sales div. as v.p. & gen. sales mgr. 1969 named v.p., gen. mgr. then pres., ABC Films, Inc.; 1970 made pres., ABC Int'l. TV, while retaining position as pres., ABC Films. 1973 became pres., COO, Worldvision Enterprises, Inc., co. formed to succeed ABC Films when FCC stopped networks from TV program dist. Elected chmn. & CEO, Worldvision, 1982. Named pres., Great American Broadcasting Group, 1987. Resigned, 1988. Named pres., Kenmare Prods. Inc., 1988.

O'SULLIVAN, MAUREEN
Actress. b. Boyle, Ireland, May 17, 1911. Daughter is actress Mia Farrow. e. convents in Dublin, London; finishing sch., Paris. Discovered by dir. Frank Borzage; came to Hollywood in 1930 under contract to Fox.
THEATER: Never Too Late, The Front Page, No Sex Please, We're British, Mornings at Seven; regional theatre.
PICTURES: Song of My Heart (debut, 1930), Just Imagine, The Princess and the Plumber, A Connecticut Yankee, Skyline, The Big Shot, Tarzan the Ape Man, The Silver Lining, Skyscraper Souls, Strange Interlude, Payment Deferred, Tugboat Annie, Stage Mother, The Barretts of Wimpole Street, The Thin Man, Tarzan and His Mate, Hide-Out, David Copperfield, West Point of the Air, The Flame Within, Woman Wanted, Anna Karenina, Cardinal Richelieu, The Bishop Misbehaves, Tarzan Escapes, The Voice of Bugle Ann, The Devil Doll, A Day at the Races, The Emperor's Candlesticks, Between Two Women, My Dear Miss Aldrich, A Yank at Oxford, Hold That Kiss, Port of Seven Seas, The Crowd Roars, Spring Madness, Let Us Live, Tarzan Finds a Son, Sporting Blood, Pride and Prejudice, Maisie Was a Lady, Tarzan's Secret Treasure, Tarzan's New York Adventure, The Big Clock, Where Danger Lives, Bonzo Goes to College, All I Desire, Mission Over Korea, Duffy of San Quentin, The Steel

Cage, The Tall T, Wild Heritage, Never Too Late, The Phynx, Too Scared to Scream, Hannah and Her Sisters, Peggy Sue Got Married, Stranded.
TELEVISION: *Movies*: The Crooked Hearts, The Great Houdinis, With Murder in Mind, The Habitation of Dragons, Hart to Hart: Home is Where the Hart Is. *Guest*: Pros & Cons, many others. *Special*: Good Old Boy (Wonderworks).

O'TOOLE, ANNETTE
Actress. b. Houston, TX, April 1, 1953. e. UCLA.
PICTURES: Smile (debut, 1975), One on One, King of the Gypsies, Foolin' Around, Cat People, 48 HRS, Superman III, Cross My Heart, Love at Large, Andre (voice), Imaginary Crimes.
TELEVISION: *Movies*: The Girl Most Likely To..., The Entertainer, The War Between the Tates, Love For Rent, Stand By Your Man, Copacabana, Arthur Hailey's Strong Medicine, Broken Vows, Stephen King's IT, The Dreamer of Oz, White Lies, Kiss of a Killer, Love Matters, A Mother's Revenge, My Brother's Keeper. *Mini-Series*: The Kennedys of Massachusetts. *Specials*: Vanities, Best Legs in the Eighth Grade, Secret World of the Very Young, Unpublished Letters, On Hope.

O'TOOLE, PETER
Actor. b. Connemara, Ireland, Aug. 2, 1932. Studied at Royal Acad. of Dramatic Art. Early career with Bristol Old Vic. Partner with Jules Buck, Keep Films, Ltd. Autobiography: Loitering With Intent (1993).
THEATER: *London*: Major Barbara, Oh My Papa, The Long the Short and the Tall, Baal, Hamlet, Ride a Cock Horse, Macbeth, Man and Superman, Jeffrey Bernard is Unwell, Our Song. 1960, with the Stratford-on-Avon Company (The Taming of the Shrew, Merchant of Venice, etc). *Dublin*: Arms and the Man, Waiting for Godot. *Toronto*: Present Laughter, Uncle Vanya. B'way debut 1987: Pygmalion.
PICTURES: Kidnapped (debut, 1959), The Savage Innocents, The Day They Robbed the Bank of England, Lawrence of Arabia, Becket, Lord Jim, What's New Pussycat?, The Bible, How to Steal a Million, The Night of the Generals, Casino Royale (cameo), Great Catherine, The Lion in Winter, Goodbye Mr. Chips, Brotherly Love (Country Dance), Murphy's War, Under Milk Wood, The Ruling Class, Man of La Mancha, Rosebud, Man Friday, Foxtrot, Caligula, Power Play, Zulu Dawn, The Stunt Man, My Favorite Year, Supergirl, Creator, Club Paradise, The Last Emperor, High Spirits, On a Moonlit Night, Helena, Wings of Fame, The Nutcracker Prince (voice), The Rainbow Thief, Isabelle Eberhardt, King Ralph, Rebecca's Daughters, The Seventh Coin.
TELEVISION: *Movies*: Rogue Male (BBC), Svengali, Kim, Crossing to Freedom, Heaven & Hell: North and South Book III. *Specials*: Present Laughter, Pygmalion, The Dark Angel. *Series*: Strumpet City (BBC). *Mini-Series*: Masada.

OTWELL, RONNIE RAY
Theatre Executive. b. Carrollton, GA, Aug. 13, 1929. e. Georgia Inst. of Technology. Entered industry as mgr., Bremen Theatre, GA, 1950; dir. pub.; adv., Martin Theatres, Columbus, GA, 1950-63; v.p.; dir. Martin Theatres of Ga., Inc., 1963, Martin Theatres of Ala., Inc., 1963; dir. Martin Theatres of Columbus, 1963; sr. v.p., Martin Theatres Companies, 1971.

OVERALL, PARK
Actress. b. Nashville, TN, March 15, 1957. Attended British boarding school, earned teaching degree, before turning to acting.
THEATER: *NY*: Biloxi Blues, Wild Blue, Only You, Loose Ends, Something About Baseball, Marathon '88.
PICTURES: Body Passion, Biloxi Blues, Mississippi Burning, Talk Radio (voice), Lost Angels, Kindergarten Cop, The Vanishing, House of Cards, Undercover Blues.
TELEVISION: *Series*: Empty Nest. *Movies*: Luck of the Draw: The Gambler Returns, Overkill: The Aileen Wuornos Story, Precious Victims, The Good Old Boys. *Pilot*: The Line.

OVITZ, MICHAEL
Talent Agent, Executive. b. Chicago, IL, Dec. 14, 1946. e. UCLA, 1968. Started as trainee at William Morris Agency before becoming agent, 1969-75. Co-founder of Creative Artists Agency, 1975; became chmn. and chief stock holder. 1995 named pres. The Walt Disney Company.

OWEN, BILL
Actor. r.n. Bill Rowbotham. b. Acton, Eng., Mar. 14, 1914.
PICTURES: The Way to the Stars (debut, 1945), School for Secrets, Daybreak, Dancing With Crime, Easy Money, When the Bough Breaks, My Brother's Keeper, Martha, Parlor Trick, The Roundabout, Trottie True, Once a Jolly Swagman, A Day to Remember, You See What I Mean, Square Ring, Rainbow Jacket, Ship That Died of Shame, Not so Dusty, Davy, Carve Her Name with Pride, Carry on Sergeant, Carry on Nurse, Night Apart, Shakedown, Hell Fire Club, Carry on Regardless, Carry on Cabby!, Secret of Blood Island, Georgy Girl,

Headline Hunters, O Lucky Man!, Kadoyng, In Celebration, When The Screaming Stopped, Comeback, Laughter House.
TELEVISION: *Series*: Last of the Summer Wine.

OWENSBY, EARL
Producer, Actor. b. North Carolina, 1935. Set up his own studio in Shelby, NC. Built new studio in Gaffney, SC, 1985.
PICTURES: Challenge, Dark Sunday, Buckstone County Prison, Frank Challenge—Manhunter, Death Driver, Wolfman, Seabo, Day of Judgment, Living Legend, Lady Grey, Rottweiler, Last Game, Hyperspace, Hit the Road Running, Rutherford County Line.

OXENBERG, CATHERINE
Actress. b. NY, NY, Sept. 21, 1961. Daughter of the exiled Princess Elizabeth of Yugoslavia, raised among intl. jet set with Richard Burton acting as her tutor. Modeled before making TV debut in The Royal Romance of Charles and Diana (1982).
PICTURES: The Lair of the White Worm, The Return of the Musketeers.
TELEVISION: *Series*: Dynasty, Acapulco H.E.A.T. *Movies*: The Royal Romance of Charles and Diana, Roman Holiday, Swimsuit, Trenchcoat in Paradise, Ring of Scorpio, K-9000, Charles & Diana: Unhappily Ever After, Rubdown, Treacherous Beauties.

OZ, FRANK
Puppeteer, Director, Performer. b. Hereford, Eng., May 25, 1944. r.n. Frank Oznowicz. Gained fame as creator and performer of various characters on Sesame Street and the Muppet Show (Fozzie Bear, Miss Piggy, Animal, Cookie Monster, Grover and Bert). V.P., Jim Henson Prods.
PICTURES: *Performer*: The Muppet Movie, The Blues Brothers, The Empire Strikes Back, The Great Muppet Caper (also prod.), An American Werewolf in London, The Dark Crystal (also co-dir.), Return of the Jedi, Trading Places, The Muppets Take Manhattan (also dir., co-s.p.), Spies Like Us, Labyrinth, Innocent Blood, The Muppet Christmas Carol (also exec. prod.), Muppet Treasure Island (voice). *Director only*: Little Shop of Horrors, Dirty Rotten Scoundrels, What About Bob?, Housesitter, The Indian in the Cupboard.
TELEVISION: *Series*: Sesame Street (3 Emmy Awards), The Muppet Show (Emmy Award, 1978), Saturday Night Live; various variety shows.

P

PAAR, JACK
Actor. b. Canton, OH, May 1, 1918. Radio announcer in Cleveland, Buffalo; served in U.S. Armed Forces, WWII; entertained in Pacific zone with 28th Special Service Div. On radio with own show, then quiz show Take It or Leave It. First host of The Tonight Show; various specials.
AUTHOR: I Kid You Not, My Sabre Is Bent, Three on a Toothbrush, P.S. Jack Paar.
PICTURES: Variety Time (debut, 1948), Easy Living, Walk Softly Stranger, Footlight Varieties, Love Nest, Down Among the Sheltering Palms.
TELEVISION: *Series*: Up to Paar (emcee, 1952), Bank on the Stars (emcee, 1953), The Jack Paar Show (1954), The Morning Show (1954), The Tonight Show (retitled The Jack Paar Show: 1957-62), The Jack Paar Program (1962-65), ABC Late Night (1973). *Specials*: Jack Paar Diary, Jack Paar Remembers, Jack Paar Is Alive and Well (also prod.), He Kids You Not.

PACINO, AL
Actor. b. New York, NY, Apr. 25, 1940. e. High Sch. for the Performing Arts, NY; Actors Studio, 1966; HB Studios, NY. Gained attention as stage actor initially at Charles Playhouse, Boston (Why Is a Crooked Letter, The Peace Creeps, Arturo Ui). Served as artistic dir. (with Ellen Burstyn), Actors Studio (1982-84).
THEATER: *NY*: The Indian Wants the Bronx (Obie Award), Does a Tiger Wear a Necktie? (Tony & Theatre World Awards, 1969), The Local Stigmatic, Camino Real, The Connection, Hello Out There, Tiger at the Gates, The Basic Training of Pavlo Hummel (Tony Award, 1977), Richard III, American Buffalo, Julius Caesar, Chinese Coffee, Salome, Hughie (also dir.).
PICTURES: Me Natalie (debut, 1969), The Panic in Needle Park, The Godfather, Scarecrow, Serpico, The Godfather Part II, Dog Day Afternoon, Bobby Deerfield, ... And Justice for All, Cruising, Author! Author!, Scarface, Revolution, Sea of Love, Dick Tracy, The Godfather Part III, Frankie and Johnny, Glengarry Glen Ross, Scent of a Woman (Academy Award, 1992), Carlito's Way, A Day to Remember, City Hall, Heat, Two Bits, Looking for Richard (also dir.), Donnie Brasco.

PACULA, JOANNA
Actress. b. Tomszowau, Poland, Jan. 2, 1957. Member of Polish National Theatre School. Model in Poland, France, then U.S. where she moved in early 1980's.

PICTURES: Gorky Park, Not Quite Paradise, Death Before Dishonor, The Kiss, Sweet Lies, Options, Marked for Death, Husbands and Lovers, Tombstone.
TELEVISION: *Series*: E.A.R.T.H. Force. *Movies*: Escape From Sobribor, Breaking Point, Not Like Us.

PAGE, ANTHONY
Director. b. Bangalore, India, Sept. 21, 1935. e. Oxford. Stage work includes Inadmissible Evidence, Waiting for Godot, A Patriot for Me, Look Back in Anger, Uncle Vanya, Mrs. Warren's Profession, Alpha Beta, Heartbreak House, Absolute Hell, etc.
PICTURES: Inadmissible Evidence (debut, 1968), Alpha Beta, I Never Promised You a Rose Garden, Absolution, The Lady Vanishes.
TELEVISION: *Specials*: Pueblo, The Missiles of October, The Parachute, Sheppey. *Movies*: Collision Course, F. Scott Fitzgerald in Hollywood, FDR—The Last Year, The Patricia Neal Story, Bill, Johnny Belinda, Grace Kelly, Bill—On His Own, Murder: By Reason of Insanity, Forbidden, Monte Carlo, Second Serve, Pack of Lies, Scandal in a Small Town, The Nightmare Years, Chernobyl: The Final Warning, Absolute Hell, Guests of the Emperor, Middlemarch.

PAGE, PATTI
Performer, Recording Artist. r.n. Clara Ann Fowler. b. Claremore, OK, Nov. 8, 1927. e. U. of Tulsa. Staff performer, radio stat. KTUL, Tulsa; Top recording star of the 1950's and 60's (The Tennessee Waltz, Cross Over the Bridge, How Much is That Doggie in the Window?, etc.). Appeared on CBS radio show. Author of Once Upon a Dream.
PICTURES: Elmer Gantry (debut, 1960), Dondi, Boys' Night Out.
TELEVISION: *Series host*: Music Hall, Scott Music Hall, The Patti Page Show, The Big Record, The Patti Page Olds Show. *Guest*: Appointment With Adventure, U.S. Steel Hour, Bachelor Father, etc.

PAGET, DEBRA
Actress. r.n. Debrahlee Griffin. b. Denver, CO, Aug. 19, 1933. e. Hollywood Prof. Sch. , also studied drama & dancing privately. Stage debut in Merry Wives of Windsor, 1946; in Jeanne D'Arc little theatre prod.
PICTURES: Cry of the City (debut, 1948), It Happens Every Spring, House of Strangers, Broken Arrow, Fourteen Hours, Bird of Paradise, Anne of the Indies, Belles on Their Toes, Les Miserables, Stars & Stripes Forever, Prince Valiant, Demetrius & the Gladiators, Princess of the Nile, Gambler from Natchez, White Feather, Seven Angry Men, Last Hunt, The Ten Commandments, Love Me Tender, The River's Edge, Omar Khayyam, From the Earth to the Moon, Why Must I Die?, Cleopatra's Daughter, Journey to the Lost City, The Most Dangerous Man Alive, Tales of Terror, The Haunted Palace.
TELEVISION: *Guest*: Steve Allen, Colgate Comedy Hour, Climax, Wagon Train, Rawhide, etc.

PAGETT, NICOLA
Actress. b. Cairo, Egypt, June 15, 1945. r.n. Nicola Scott. e. Royal Acad. of Dramatic Art. Appeared with Citizen's Rep. Theatre, Glasgow.
THEATER: Cornelia (debut, 1964, Worthing, U.K.), A Boston Story (London debut, 1968), A Midsummer Night's Dream, Widowers' Houses, The Misanthrope, A Voyage 'Round My Father, The Ride Across Lake Constance, Ghosts, The Seagull, Hamlet, The Marriage of Figaro, A Family and a Fortune, Gaslight, Yahoo, Old Times (L.A.).
PICTURES: Anne of the Thousand Days, There's a Girl in My Soup, Operation Daybreak, Oliver's Story, Privates on Parade.
TELEVISION: *Series*: Upstairs Downstairs. *Movies*: Frankenstein: The True Story, The Sweeney, Aren't We All, A Woman of Substance (mini-series), Anna Karenina.

PAIGE, JANIS
Actress r.n. Donna Mae Jaden. b. Tacoma, WA, Sept. 16, 1923. Sang with Tacoma Opera Co. Star of Tomorrow, 1947. Album: Let's Fall in Love. Owns and operates Ipanema, Janeiro, Rio-Cali, and Dindi Music Cos.
THEATER: Pajama Game, Remains to Be Seen, Here's Love, Mame, Alone Together.
PICTURES: Hollywood Canteen (debut, 1944), Of Human Bondage, Two Gals and a Guy, The Time the Place and the Girl, Two Guys from Milwaukee, Her Kind of Man, Cheyenne, Love and Learn, Always Together, Wallflower, Winter Meeting, One Sunday Afternoon, Romance on the High Seas, House Across the Street, The Younger Brothers, Mr. Universe, Fugitive Lady, Two Guys and a Gal, Silk Stockings, Please Don't Eat the Daisies, Bachelor in Paradise, The Caretakers, Welcome to Hard Times, The Dark Road (It.), Follow the Boys (Fr.).
TELEVISION: *Special*: Roberta (1958 and 1969). *Series*: It's Always Jan, Lanigan's Rabbi, Gun Shy, Baby Makes Five, Trapper John M.D, Capitol, General Hospital, Santa Barbara. *Guest*: Plymouth Playhouse, Alcoa Premiere, Columbo,

Banacek, Flamingo Road, St. Elsewhere. *Movies*: The Turning Point of Jim Malloy, Return of Joe Forrester, Lanigan's Rabbi (pilot), Valentine Magic on Love Island, Angel on My Shoulder, The Other Woman, No Man's Land.

PAINE, CHARLES F.
Executive. b. Cushing, TX, Dec. 23, 1920. e. Stephen F. Austin U. Pres. Tercar Theatre Company; pres., NATO of Texas, 1972-73. NATO board member, 1973 to present; Motion Picture Pioneers member; Variety Club of Texas member.

PAKULA, ALAN J.
Producer, Director. b. New York, NY, April 7, 1928. e. Yale U., B.A., 1948. Worked in Leland Hayward's office; asst. administrator, Warner Bros. cartoon dept, Prod. apprentice, MGM, 1950; prod. asst., Paramount 1951; prod. Paramount, 1955. Own prod. co., Pakula-Mulligan Prod. Stage prod. and m.p. dir. prod. 1988 received Eastman Award for Continued Excellence in M.P. Won London Film Critics Award for best director for Klute.
THEATER: Comes a Day, Laurette, There Must Be a Pony.
PICTURES: *Producer*: Fear Strikes Out, To Kill a Mockingbird, Love With the Proper Stranger, Baby the Rain Must Fall, Inside Daisy Clover, Up the Down Staircase, The Stalking Moon. *Director*: The Sterile Cuckoo, Klute (also prod.), Love and Pain and the Whole Damn Thing (also prod.), The Parallax View (also prod.), All the President's Men (NY Film Critics Award, 1976), Comes a Horseman, Starting Over (also prod.), Rollover, Sophie's Choice (also prod., s.p.), Dream Lover (also prod.), Orphans (also prod.), See You in the Morning (also prod., s.p.), Presumed Innocent, Consenting Adults (also prod.), The Pelican Brief (also prod., co-s.p.).

PALANCE, JACK
Actor. b. Lattimer, PA, Feb. 18, 1920. e. U. of North Carolina. Professional fighter; U.S. Air Corps.
THEATER: The Big Two, Temporary Island, The Vigil, A Streetcar Named Desire, Darkness at Head.
PICTURES: Panic in the Streets (debut, 1950), Halls of Montezuma, Sudden Fear (Acad. Award nom.), Shane (Acad. Award nom.), Flight to Tangier, Arrowhead, Second Chance, Man in the Attic, Sign of the Pagan, Silver Chalice, Kiss of Fire, Big Knife, I Died a Thousand Times, Attack!, Lonely Man, House of Numbers, The Man Inside, Ten Seconds to Hell, Battle of Austerliz, Sword of the Conqueror, The Mongols, Barabbas, Warriors Five, Contempt, Once a Thief, The Professionals, Torture Garden, Kill a Dragon, The Mercenary, Deadly Sanctuary, They Came to Rob Las Vegas, The Desperados, Che, Legion of the Damned, A Bullet for Rommel, The McMasters, Monte Walsh, Companeros, The Horsemen, Chato's Land, Oklahoma Crude, Craze, The Four Deuces, The Great Adventure, The Sensuous Nurse, Portrait of a Hitman, One Man Jury, Angel's Brigade, The Shape of Things to Come, Cocaine Cowboys, Hawk the Slayer, Without Warning, Alone in the Dark, Gor, Bagdad Cafe, Young Guns, Outlaw of Gor, Batman, Tango and Cash, City Slickers (Academy Award, best supporting actor, 1991), Solar Crisis, Cops and Robbersons, City Slickers II: The Legend of Curly's Gold, The Swan Princess (voice).
TELEVISION: *Specials*: Requiem for a Heavyweight (Emmy Award, 1957), Dr. Jekyll and Mr. Hyde, Twilight Zone: Rod Serling's Lost Classics: Where the Dead Are. *Movies*: Dracula, The Godchild, The Hatfields and the McCoys, Bronk (pilot), Last Ride of the Dalton Gang, The Ivory Ape, Golden Moment: An Olympic Love Story, Keep the Change, Buffalo Girls. *Series*: The Greatest Show on Earth, Bronk, Ripley's Believe It or Not (host).

PALCY, EUZHAN
Director. b. Martinique, 1957. e. Earned a degree in French lit., Sorbonne and a film degree from Vaugirard School in Paris. Began career working as TV writer and dir. in Martinique. Also made 2 children's records. In Paris worked as film editor, screenwriter and dir. of shorts. She received grant from French gov. to make 1st feature Sugar Cane Alley which cost $800,000 and won Silver Lion Prize at Venice Film Fest., 1983.
PICTURES: Sugar Cane Alley, A Dry White Season (also co-s.p.).

PALIN, MICHAEL
Actor, Writer. b. Sheffield, Yorkshire, England, May 5, 1943. e. Oxford. Performed there in The Birthday Party and in revue Hang Your Head Down and Die (also in West End prod., 1964). At Oxford met Terry Jones, began writing comedy together, incl. TV series The Frost Report. Became member of Monty Python's Flying Circus. On stage with troupe both in London and on B'way.
PICTURES: And Now for Something Completely Different (also co-s.p.), Monty Python and the Holy Grail (also co-s.p.), Jabberwocky, Life of Brian (also co-s.p.), Time Bandits, The Secret Policeman's Other Ball, Monty Python Live at the

Hollywood Bowl (also co-s.p.), The Missionary (also co-prod., s.p.), Monty Python's The Meaning of Life (also co-music, co-s.p.), A Private Function, Brazil, A Fish Called Wanda, American Friends (also co-s.p.), Fierce Creatures, The Wind In The Willows (voice).
TELEVISION: Do Not Adjust Your Set, The Frost Report, Monty Python's Flying Circus, Marty Feldman Comedy Machine, How To Irritate People, Pythons in Deutschland, Secrets, Ripping Yarns, Around the World in 80 Days, GBH, Pole to Pole.

PALMER, BETSY
Actress. b. East Chicago, IN, Nov. 1, 1929. e. DePaul U. Studied at Neighborhood Playhouse, HB Studio with Uta Hagen. On Broadway in The Grand Prize, South Pacific, Affair of Honor, Cactus Flower, Roar Like a Dove, Eccentricities of a Nightingale, Same Time Next Year and many regional prods.
PICTURES: Mister Roberts, The Long Gray Line, Queen Bee, The Tin Star, The Last Angry Man, Friday the 13th, Friday the 13th Part 2.
TELEVISION: All major live shows such as Studio One, U.S. Steel Hour, Kraft Theatre. Series: Masquerade Party (panelist), What's It For? (panelist), I've Got a Secret (panelist, 11 years), No. 96 (series), Candid Camera (host), The Today Show (host), Wifeline (host). Guest: As the World Turns, Murder She Wrote, Out of This World, Charles in Charge, Knots Landing, Newhart, Love Boat. Movies: Isabel's Choice, Windmills of the Gods, Goddess of Love, Still Not Quite Human, Columbo: Death Hits the Jackpot.

PALMER, GREGG
Actor. r.n. Palmer Lee. b. San Francisco, CA, Jan. 25, 1927. e. U. of Utah. U.S. Air Force, 1945-46; radio announcer, disc jockey; then to Hollywood.
PICTURES: Cimarron Kid, Battle at Apache Pass, Son of Ali Baba, Red Ball Express, Francis Goes to West Point, Sally and St. Anne, The Raiders, Back at the Front, Redhead From Wyoming, Column South, Veils of Bagdad, Golden Blade, The All American, Taza Son of Cochise, Magnificent Obsession, Playgirl, To Hell and Back, Creature Walks Among Us, Hilda Crane, Zombies of Mora Tau, Revolt of Fort Laramie, Rebel Set, Thundering Jets, Forty Pounds of Trouble, Night Hunt, The Undefeated, Chisum, Rio Lobo, Big Jake, Providenza (It.), Ci Risiamo Vero Providenza (It-Sp), The Shootist, The Man With Bogart's Face, Scream.
TELEVISION: Series: Run Buddy Run. Guest appearances incl: Wagon Train, Loretta Young, Wyatt Earp, Have Gun Will Travel, Sea Hunt, Roaring 20's, Mannix, The High Chaparral, Cannon, Baretta, Gunsmoke, etc. Movies: Mongo's Back in Town, Go West Young Girl, Hostage Heart, How the West Was Won, True Grit, Beggarman Thief, The Blue and the Gray (mini-series).

PALMER, PATRICK
Producer. b. Los Angeles, CA, Dec. 28, 1936. Began career with 10-year apprenticeship at Mirisch Company, involved in making of West Side Story, Seven Days in May, The Fortune Cookie, etc. 1966, began association with Norman Jewison, serving as assoc. prod. on The Landlord, Fiddler on the Roof, Jesus Christ Superstar, Rollerball, etc. 1972, prod., with Jewison, Billy Two Hats; exec. prod. on The Dogs of War.
PICTURES: Co-prod.: And Justice for All, Best Friends, Iceman, A Soldier's Story, Agnes of God, Children of a Lesser God, Moonstruck, Stanley & Iris, Mermaids, Paradise.

PALMINTERI, CHAZZ
Actor, Writer. b. Bronx, NY, May 15, 1951. e. Bronx Comm. Coll. NY stage in The Guys in the Truck (B'way), The King's Men, 22 Years, The Flatbush Faithful, A Bronx Tale (which he also wrote).
PICTURES: The Last Dragon (debut, 1985), Oscar, Innocent Blood, There Goes the Neighborhood, A Bronx Tale (also s.p.), Bullets Over Broadway (Acad. Award nom.), The Perez Family, The Usual Suspects, Faithful (also s.p.), Jade, Mulholland Falls, Diabolique.
TELEVISION: Movie: The Last Word.

PALTROW, BRUCE
Director, Producer, Writer. b. New York, NY, Nov. 26, 1943. e. Tulane U., B.F.A. m. actress Blythe Danner. Daughter is actress Gwyneth Paltrow. Has also produced stage plays.
PICTURE: A Little Sex (co-prod., dir.).
TELEVISION: Movies: Shirts and Skins (co-prod., writer), Ed McBain's 87th Precinct (dir.). Series: The White Shadow (creat. dir.), St. Elsewhere (exec. prod.-dir.), Tattinger's (exec. prod., dir., co-writer), Nick & Hillary (exec. prod.).

PALTROW, GWYNETH
Actress. b. Los Angeles, CA. p. actress Blythe Danner, prod. Bruce Paltrow. Family moved to NY when she was 11.
THEATER: Williamstown: Picnic, The Adventures of Huck Finn, Sweet Bye and Bye, The Seagull.
PICTURES: Shout (debut, 1991), Hook, Malice, Flesh and Bone, Mrs. Parker and the Vicious Circle, Jefferson in Paris, Moonlight and Valentino, Seven, The Pallbearer, Sydney, Emma.
TELEVISION: Movie: Cruel Doubt.

PANAMA, CHARLES A. (CHUCK)
Publicist, b. Chicago, IL, Feb. 2, 1925. e. Northwestern U., Beloit Coll., UCLA. Publicist, Los Angeles Jr. Chamber of Commerce; So. Calif. sports ed., Los Angeles bureau, INS; publicist, 20th Century-Fox Studios; adv.-pub. dir., Arcola Pics.; opened L.A. office, John Springer Associates; v.p. Jerry Pam & Assoc.; account exec., Rogers, Cowan & Brenner, Inc.; dir. m.p. div., Jim Mahoney & Assoc.; v.p. Guttman & Pam, Ltd.; asst. pub. dir., Twentieth T.V. Owner, pres. Chuck Panama P.R.; winner 1990 Les Mason Award and 1993 Robert Yeager Award 1993, Publicists Guild of America.

PANAMA, NORMAN
Writer, Producer, Director. b. Chicago, IL, Apr. 12, 1914. Co-authored The Glass Bed (novel), and plays: A Talent for Murder, The Bats of Portobello.
PICTURES: Co-Writer: My Favorite Blonde, Happy Go Lucky, Star-Spangled Rhythm, Thank Your Lucky Stars, And the Angels Sing, Duffy's Tavern, Road to Utopia (Acad. Award nom.), Our Hearts Were Growing Up, Monsieur Beaucaire, It Had to Be You, Mr. Blandings Builds His Dream House, Return of October, White Christmas, Li'l Abner, The Facts of Life. Co-Dir./Co-Writer (with Melvin Frank): The Reformer and the Redhead, Strictly Dishonorable, Callaway Went Thataway, Above and Beyond, Knock on Wood (Acad. Award nom. for s.p.), The Court Jester. Dir./Writer: The Road to Hong Kong, Not With My Wife You Don't, How to Commit Marriage, I Will I Will... for Now.
TELEVISION: Dir.: Barnaby and Me, The Stewardesses, Li'l Abner, Mrs. Katz and Katz (pilot), How Come You Never See Dr. Jekyll and Mr. Hyde Together?, Coffee Tea or Me.

PANKIN, STUART
Actor. b. Philadelphia, PA, Apr. 8, 1946. e. Dickinson Coll., Columbia U. Stage debut 1968 in The War of the Roses.
THEATER: NY: Timon of Athens, Tale of Cymbeline, Mary Stuart, The Crucible, Twelfth Night, Glorious Age, Wings, Gorky, Joseph and the Amazing Technicolor Dreamcoat, Three Sisters, The Inspector General.
PICTURES: Scavenger Hunt, Hangar 18, The Hollywood Knights, An Eye for an Eye, Earthbound, Irreconcilable Differences, The Dirt Bike Kid, Fatal Attraction, Love at Stake, Second Sight, That's Adequate, Arachnophobia, Mannequin 2 on the Move, The Vagrant, I Love Trouble, The Silence of the Hams, Squanto: A Warrior's Tale, Congo.
TELEVISION: Series: The San Pedro Beach Bums, No Soap Radio, Not Necessarily the News (ACE Award), Nearly Departed, Dinosaurs (voice). Movies: Valentine Magic on Love Island, Father & Scout, Down Out and Dangerous. Pilots: Car Wash, Wonderful World of Philip Malley. Guest: Night Court, Crazy Like a Fox, Golden Girls, Stingray, Family Ties, It's Garry Shandling's Show, Hooperman, Barney Miller. Special: Stuart Pankin (also co-exec. prod., co-writer).

PANTOLIANO, JOE
Actor. b. Jersey City, NJ, Sept. 12, 1954.
THEATER: NY: The Kitchen, The Off Season, The Death Star, Visions of Kerouac. Regional: One Flew Over the Cuckoo's Nest, Skaters, Brothers, Italian American Reconciliation (Dramalogue Award), Orphans (Dramalogue Award, Drama Critic Circle nomination), Pvt. Wars.
PICTURES: The Idolmaker, Monsignor, Risky Business, Eddie and the Cruisers, The Mean Season, The Goonies, Running Scared, La Bamba, The Squeeze, Amazon Women on the Moon, Empire of the Sun, The In Crowd, Midnight Run, Downtown, The Last of the Finest, Short Time, Zandalee, Used People, Three of Hearts, Goin' to Mexico, The Fugitive, Calendar Girl, Me and the Kid, Teresa's Tattoo, Baby's Day Out, Bad Boys, Congo, Steal Big Steal Little, Bound, The Immortals.
TELEVISION: Series: Free Country, The Fanelli Boys. Mini-Series: Robert F. Kennedy: His Life and Times, From Here to Eternity. Guest: Tales from the Crypt (ACE Award nomination), Amazing Stories, L.A. Law, The Hitchhiker. Movies: More Than Friends, Alcatraz: The Whole Shocking Story, Nightbreaker, Destination America, El Diablo, One Special Victory, Through the Eyes of a Killer, The Last (also co-assoc. prod.).

PAPAS, IRENE
Actress. b. Chiliomodion, Greece, Sept. 3, 1926. Entered dramatic school at 12. At 16 sang and danced in variety shows before debuting in Greek films, 1950. 1958 appeared with Greek Popular Theatre in Athens. Received Salonika Film Fest. Awards for the films Antigone, Electra.
THEATER: The Idiot, Journey's End, The Merchant of Venice, Inherit the Wind, That Summer, That Fall, Iphigenia in Aulis.
PICTURES: Lost Angels (debut, 1950), Dead City, The Unfaithful, Atilla the Hun, Theodora the Slave Empress, Whirlpool, Tribute to a Bad Man, Antigone, The Guns of Navarone, Electra, The Moon-Spinners, Zorba the Greek, We Still Kill the Old Way, The Desperate Ones, The Brotherhood, Anne of the Thousand Days, Z, A Dream of Kings, The Trojan Women, Roma Bene, Bambina, Mohammed: Messenger of

God, Iphigenia, Bloodline, (Christ Stopped at) Eboli, Lion of the Desert, Erendira, Into the Night, The Assisi Underground, Sweet Country, High Season, Chronicle of a Death Foretold, Island, Drums of Fire, Banquet, Zoe, Up Down and Sideways. TELEVISION: Moses the Lawgiver.

PARE, MICHAEL
Actor. b. Brooklyn, NY, Oct. 9, 1959. e. Culinary Inst. of America, Hyde Park, NY. Worked as chef and model before being discovered by ABC talent agent.
PICTURES: Eddie and the Cruisers (debut, 1983), Streets of Fire, The Philadelphia Experiment, Under Cover (Aust.), Space Rage, Instant Justice, The Women's Club, World Gone Wild, Eddie and the Cruisers II: Eddie Lives, Moon 44, Dragon Fight, Concrete War, The Closer, Into the Sun, Midnight Heat, First Light, Point of Impact, Village of the Damned, Bad Moon.
TELEVISION: Series: The Greatest American Hero, Houston Knights. Movie: Crazy Times.

PARISH, JAMES ROBERT
Film Historian, Executive. b. Cambridge, MA, Apr. 21, 1944. e. U. of PA (BBA, Phi Beta Kappa); U. of PA Law School (LLB). Member of NY Bar. Founder Entertainment Copyright Research Co., Inc. 1968-69, film reporter, Motion Picture Daily, weekly Variety. 1969-70, entertainment publicist, Harold Rand & Co. (NY). Currently marketing consultant in direct marketing industry, contributor to arts sections of major national newspapers and entertainment trade papers, series editor of show business books and author of over 85 books on the entertainment industry including: Hollywood's Great Musicals, Prostitution in Hollywood Films, Ghosts & Angels in Hollywood Films, Hollywood Songsters, Prison Pictures From Hollywood, Hollywood Baby Boomers, The Great Detective Pictures, The Great Cop Pictures, The Great Science Fiction Pictures II, Complete Actors TV Credits (1948-88), The Great Combat Pictures, Black Action Pictures From Hollywood, The Great Detective Pictures, The Great Western Pictures II: The Great Gangster Pictures II: The Great Spy Pictures II, Actors TV Credits, The Best of MGM, The Forties Gals, The Great American Movies Book, Hollywood Happiness, The Funsters, Hollywood on Hollywood, The Hollywood Beauties, Elvis!, The Great Science Fiction Pictures, The Child Stars, The Jeannette MacDonald Story, Great Movie Heroes, Liza!, The RKO Gals, Vincent Price Unmasked, The George Raft File, The Emmy Awards, Hollywood Death Book, Gays & Lesbians in Mainstream Cinema, Hollywood Celebrity Death Book (updated), Let's Talk: America's Favorite TV Talk Show Hosts, Today's Black Hollywood, Pirates and Seafaring Swashbucklers.

PARKER, ALAN
Director, Writer. b. Islington, London, England, Feb. 14, 1944. Worked way up in advertising industry from mail room to top writer and director of nearly 500 TV commercials between 1969-78.
PICTURES: Melody (s.p., 1968). Director: No Hard Feelings (also s.p.), Our Cissy (also s.p.), Footsteps (also s.p.), Bugsy Malone (also s.p.; Brit. Acad. Award for best s.p.), Midnight Express (Brit. Acad. Award), Fame, Shoot the Moon, Pink Floyd—The Wall, Birdy, Angel Heart, Mississippi Burning, Come and See the Paradise (also s.p.), The Commitments (also cameo; BAFTA Award for best dir., 1991), The Road to Wellville (also s.p., co-prod.), Evita.
TELEVISION: The Evacuees (Brit. Acad. Award).

PARKER, COREY
Actor. b. New York, NY, July 8, 1965. e. NYU.
THEATER: NY: Meeting the Winter Bike Rider (Off-B'way debut, 1984), Been Taken, The Bloodletters, The Semi-Formal.
PICTURES: Scream for Help (debut, 1984), Friday the 13th Part V: A New Beginning, Something Special, Nine 1/2 Weeks, Biloxi Blues, How I Got Into College, Big Man on Campus, White Palace.
TELEVISION: Series: Eddie Dodd, Blue Skies. Movies: Courage, At Mother's Request, Liz: The Elizabeth Taylor Story, A Mother's Prayer. Specials: Don't Touch, Teen Father, The Lost Language of Cranes. Pilot: Sons of Gunz. Guest: The Bronx Zoo, thirtysomething.

PARKER, ELEANOR
Actress. b. Cedarville, OH, June 26, 1922. In Cleveland play group; in summer stock Martha's Vineyard; at Pasadena Community Playhouse.
PICTURES: They Died With Their Boots On (debut, 1941), Buses Roar, Mysterious Doctor, Mission to Moscow, Between Two Worlds, The Very Thought of You, Crime By Night, Hollywood Canteen, Last Ride, Pride of the Marines, Never Say Goodbye, Of Human Bondage, Escape Me Never, Woman in White, Voice of the Turtle, It's a Great Feeling, Chain Lightning, Caged (Acad. Award nom.), Three Secrets, Valentino, Millionaire for Christy, Detective Story (Acad. Award nom.), Scaramouche, Above and Beyond, Escape from Fort

Bravo, Naked Jungle, Valley of the Kings, Many Rivers to Cross, Interrupted Melody (Acad. Award nom.), Man with the Golden Arm, King and Four Queens, Lizzie, Seventh Sin, A Hole in the Head, Home from the Hill, Return to Peyton Place, Madison Avenue, Panic Button, The Sound of Music, The Oscar, An American Dream, Warning Shot, Tiger and the Pussycat, Eye of the Cat, Sunburn.
TELEVISION: Series: Bracken's World. Movies: Maybe I'll Come Home in the Spring, Vanished, Home for the Holidays, The Great American Beauty Contest, Fantasy Island (pilot), The Bastard, She's Dressed to Kill, Once Upon a Spy, Madame X, Dead on the Money. Pilot: Guess Who's Coming to Dinner. Special: Hans Brinker. Guest: Buick Electra Playhouse, Kraft Suspense Theatre, The Man from U.N.C.L.E., Vega$, Hawaii 5-0, The Love Boat, Hotel, Murder She Wrote, etc.

PARKER, FESS
Actor. b. Fort Worth, TX, Aug. 16, 1924. e. USC. U.S. Navy, 1943-46; national co., Mr. Roberts, 1951.
PICTURES: Untamed Frontier (debut, 1952), No Room for the Groom, Springfield Rifle, Thunder Over the Plains, Island in the Sky, The Kid From Left Field, Take Me to Town, Them!, Battle Cry, Davy Crockett—King of the Wild Frontier (from Disney TV show), Davy Crockett and the River Pirates (from TV show), The Great Locomotive Chase, Westward Ho! the Wagons, Old Yeller, The Light in the Forest, The Hangman, Alias Jesse James (cameo), The Jayhawkers, Hell Is for Heroes, Smoky.
TELEVISION: Series: Mr. Smith Goes to Washington, Daniel Boone. Guest: Jonathan Winters, Walt Disney presents (Davy Crockett), Playhouse 90 (Turn Left at Mount Everest), Ed Sullivan, Danny Kaye Show, Phyllis Diller, Joey Bishop, Dean Martin, Red Skelton, Glen Campbell, Andy Williams, Vicki Lawrence. Movie: Climb an Angry Mountain.

PARKER, JAMESON
Actor. b. Baltimore, MD, Nov. 18, 1947. e. Beloit Coll. Professional stage debut in Washington Theatre Club production, Caligula. Acted with Arena Stage in DC; worked in dinner theatres and summer stock. Moved to N.Y., working in TV commercials and acted in play, Equus (Coconut Grove Playhouse).
PICTURES: The Bell Jar (debut, 1979), A Small Circle of Friends, White Dog, American Justice (also prod.), Prince of Darkness, Curse of the Crystal Eye.
TELEVISION: Series: Somerset, One Life to Live, Simon and Simon. Movies: Women at West Point, Anatomy of a Seduction, The Gathering Part II, The Promise of Love, Callie and Son, A Caribbean Mystery, Who Is Julia?, Spy, She Says She's Innocent, Dead Before Dawn, Simon & Simon: In Trouble Again.

PARKER, MARY-LOUISE
Actress. b. Ft. Jackson, SC, Aug. 2, 1964. e. Bard Coll. 1990, received Clarence Derwent Award for her work in the theatre.
THEATER: B'way: Prelude to a Kiss (Theatre World Award). Off-B'way: Hayfever, The Girl in Pink, Babylon Gardens, Throwing Your Voice, Four Dogs and a Bone. Regional: The Importance of Being Earnest, Up in Saratoga, The Miser, Hay Fever, The Night of the Iguana, The Age of Pie.
PICTURES: Signs of Life (debut, 1989), Longtime Companion, Grand Canyon, Fried Green Tomatoes, Mr. Wonderful, Naked in New York, The Client, Bullets Over Broadway, Boys on the Side, Reckless, Portrait of a Lady.
TELEVISION: Movies: Too Young the Hero, A Place for Annie.

PARKER, SARAH JESSICA
Actress. b. Nelsonville, OH, Mar. 25, 1965. Was dancer with Cincinnati Ballet and American Ballet Theatre. Professional debut at age 8 in TV special The Little Match Girl.
THEATER: NY: The Innocents, By Strouse, Annie (title role for 2 yrs.), To Gillian on her 37th Birthday, The Heidi Chronicles, The Substance of Fire, Sylvia, How To Succeed In Business Without Really Trying, once Upon A Mattress.
PICTURES: Rich Kids (debut, 1979), Somewhere Tomorrow, Footloose, Firstborn, Girls Just Want to Have Fun, Flight of the Navigator, L.A. Story, Honeymoon in Vegas, Hocus Pocus, Striking Distance, Ed Wood, Miami Rhapsody, If Lucy Fell, The Substance of Fire, First Wives Club, Extreme Measures, Mars Attacks!.
TELEVISION: Series: Square Pegs, A Year in the Life, Equal Justice. Specials: The Almost Royal Family, Life Under Water. Movies: My Body My Child, Going for the Gold: The Bill Johnson Story, A Year in the Life, The Room Upstairs, Dadah Is Death, Twist of Fate, The Ryan White Story, In the Best Interest of the Children, The Sunshine Boys.

PARKER, SUZY
Actress. r.n. Cecelia Parker. b. San Antonio, TX, Oct. 28, 1933. m. actor Bradford Dillman. e. schools in NY, FL. Began career at 17 as fashion model; becoming the highest paid fashion model and cover girl in U.S.; went to Paris under contract

283

to fashion magazine; film debut as model in Funny Face (1957); signed by 20th-Fox prod. chief Buddy Adler for part opposite Cary Grant in Kiss Them for Me.
PICTURES: Funny Face, Kiss Them For Me, Ten North Frederick, The Best of Everything, Circle of Deception, The Interns, Flight From Ashiya, Chamber of Horrors.

PARKES, WALTER F.
Producer, Writer. b. Bakersfield, CA. e. Yale, Stanford Univ. 1978 prod. & dir. documentary The California Reich which was nominated for Acad. Award.
PICTURES: WarGames (s.p.; Acad. Award nom.). Producer: Volunteers, Project X, True Believer, Awakenings (Acad. Award nom.), Sneakers (also co-s.p.).
TELEVISION: Series: Eddie Dodd (prod., writer). Pilot: Birdland (prod., writer).

PARKINS, BARBARA
Actress. b. Vancouver, British Columbia, Canada, May 22, 1943.
PICTURES: Valley of the Dolls, The Kremlin Letter, The Mephisto Waltz, Puppet on a Chain, Asylum, Shout at the Devil, Bear Island, Breakfast in Paris.
TELEVISION: Series: Peyton Place, Scene of the Crime. Mini-Series: Captains and the Kings. Movies: A Taste of Evil, Snatched, Law of the Land, Testimony of Two Men, Young Joe: The Forgotten Kennedy, Ziegfield: The Man and His Women, The Critical List, The Manions of America, Uncommon Valor, To Catch a King, Calendar Girl Murders, Peyton Place: The Next Generation, Jennie: Lady Randolph Churchill. Guest: G.E. Theatre, My Three Sons, Dr. Kildare, Gibbsville, Hotel, The Love Boat, Murder She Wrote. Special: Jennie.

PARKS, GORDON
Director, Writer, Photographer, Composer, Poet, Photojournalist. b. Fort Scott, KS, Nov. 30, 1912. From the age of 15 worked as piano player, bus boy, dining car waiter and prof. basketball player in MN before taking up photography in late 1930's. Awarded 1st Julius Rosenwald Fellowship in photog., 1942. Worked with Roy Stryker at Farm Security Admin., WWII Office of War Info. correspondent. Photo-journalist, Life Mag., 1949-68, editorial dir. (and founder): Essence Magazine 1970-73. Film debut 1961 with doc. Flavio (dir. and writer), followed by Diary of a Harlem Family (doc.; Emmy Award). Winner of numerous awards including NAACP's Spingarn Medal and Kansas Governor's Medal of Honor, Nat'l Medal of Arts, 1988. Recipient of 23 honorary degrees in lit., fine arts, humane letters. Member of NAACP, AMPAS, PEN American Center, AFI, etc.
AUTHOR: The Learning Tree, A Choice of Weapons, A Poet and His Camera, Whispers of Intimate Things, In Love, Born Black, Moments Without Proper Names, Flavio, To Smile in Autumn, Shannon, Voices in the Mirror.
PICTURES: The Learning Tree (Library of Congress Nat'l Film Registry Classics honor, 1989), Shaft, Shaft's Big Score, Super Cops, Leadbelly.
TELEVISION: The Odyssey of Solomon Northup, Moments Without Proper Names, Martin.

PARKS, MICHAEL
Actor. b. Corona, CA, April 4, 1938.
PICTURES: Wild Seed (debut, 1964), Bus Riley's Back in Town, The Bible, The Idol, The Happening, The Last Hard Men, Sidewinder One, ffolkes, Hard Country, Savannah Smiles, Spiker, Club Life, The Return of Josey Wales (also dir.), Spiker, Arizona Heat, Nightmare Beach, Prime Suspect, The Hitman, Storyville, Death Wish 5: The Face of Death, Stranger by Night.
TELEVISION: Series: Then Came Bronson, The Colbys, Twin Peaks. Movies: Can Ellen Be Saved?, Savage Bees, Chase, Dangerous Affection, Gore Vidal's Billy the Kid, The China Lake Murders, Hart to Hart: Secrets of the Hart.

PARRETTI, GIANCARLO
Executive. b. Orvieto, Italy, Oct. 23, 1941. Hotelier in Sicily in the late 1970's. Managing dir. of Naples newspaper Diario, until 1981. 1987, purchased Cannon Group, renaming it Pathe Communications. 1990, company acquired MGM/UA, Communications. Resigned 1991.

PARSONS, ESTELLE
Actress. b. Marblehead, MA, Nov. 20, 1927. e. Connecticut Coll. for Women, Bachelor's degree in political science. Attended Boston U. Law Sch. Helped harvest crops in England with the Women's Land Army. Was active in politics; worked for the Committee for the Nation's Health in Wash. and the Republican Finance Committee in Boston. Was elected to public office in Marblehead, Mass. Joined NBC-TV's Today Show as prod. asst.; then writer, feature producer and commentator. Appeared in two Julius Monk revues, Jerry Herman's Nightcap.
THEATER: Happy Hunting, Whoop Up, Beg Borrow or Steal, Mrs. Dally Has a Lover (Theater World Award), Next Time I'll Sing to You (Obie Award), In the Summer House (Obie

Award), Ready When You Are C.B., Malcolm, The Seven Descents of Myrtle, ...And Miss Reardon Drinks a Little, The Norman Conquests, Ladies of the Alamo, Miss Margarida's Way, Pirates of Penzance, The Unguided Missile, Threepenny Opera, Lincoln Center Repertory Theatre, Mahagonny, Forgiving Typhoid Mary, Shimada, The Shadow Box, Twice Removed.
PICTURES: Ladybug Ladybug (debut, 1963), Bonnie and Clyde (Academy Award, best supporting actress, 1967), Rachel Rachel (Acad. Award nom.), Don't Drink the Water, Watermelon Man, I Walk the Line, I Never Sang for My Father, Two People, For Pete's Sake, Foreplay (The President's Woman), Dick Tracy. The Lemon Sisters, Boys on the Side, That Darn Cat, Looking for Richard.
TELEVISION: Mini-Series: Backstairs at the White House. Special: The Front Page. Guest: All in the Family, Roseanne. Movies: Terror on the Beach, The Gun and the Pulpit, The UFO Incident, The Gentleman Bandit, Open Admissions, A Private Matter, The American Clock.

PARTON, DOLLY
Singer, Composer, Actress. b. Sevierville, TN, Jan. 19, 1946. Gained fame as country music singer, composer and radio and TV personality. Co-partner with Sandy Gallin, Sandollar Prods. Author: My Life and Other Unfinished Business (autobiography), Coat of Many Colors.
PICTURES: Nine to Five (debut, 1980; also wrote & sang title song), The Best Little Whorehouse in Texas (also wrote addtl. songs), Rhinestone (also songs), Steel Magnolias, Straight Talk (also songs), The Beverly Hillbillies.
TELEVISION: Series: Dolly (1976), Dolly (1987-88). Guest: Porter Wagoner Show, Cass Walker program, Bill Anderson Show, Wilbur Bros. Show. Specials: Kenny Dolly & Willie: Something Inside So Strong, A Tennessee Mountain Thanksgiving. Movies: A Smoky Mountain Christmas (also songs), Wild Texas Wind (also co-writer, co-prod.), Big Dreams & Broken Hearts: The Dottie West Story.

PASDAR, ADRIAN
Actor. b. Pittsfield, MA. E. Univ. of Central FL. Studied acting with People's Light and Theatre Co., Lee Strasberg Institute.
THEATER: Regional: The Glass Menagerie, Shadow Box, Hotters, Sorry Wrong Number, Cold Foot, Monkey's Paw.
PICTURES: Top Gun (debut, 1986), Streets of Gold, Solarbabies, Near Dark, Made in USA, Cookie, Vital Signs, Torn Apart, Just Like a Woman, The Pompatus of Love.
TELEVISION: Series: Profit. Movies: The Lost Capone, A Mother's Gift. Special: Big Time.

PASETTA, MARTY
Producer-Director. b. June 16, 1932. e. U. Santa Clara.
TELEVISION: AFI Salutes to Fred Astaire, John Huston, Lillian Gish, Alfred Hitchcock and Jimmy Stewart, Gene Kelly Special, Elvis Aloha From Hawaii, Oscar (17), Emmy (2) and Grammy (8) Award Shows, A Country Christmas (1978-81), The Monte Carlo Show, Texaco Star Theatre-Opening Night, Burnett Discovers Domingo, Disneyland's 30th Anniversary Celebration, 15 Years of Cerebral Palsy Telethons, A Night at the Moulin Rouge, Soap Opera Awards, An All-Star Celebration Honoring Martin Luther King, Disneyland's Summer Vacation Party, Disney's Captain EO Grand Opening, 15th Anniversary of Disney World; Beach Boys... 25 Years Together, Super Night at the Superbowl, 20th Anniversary of Caesars Palace, Paris by Night with George Burns, I Call You Friend Papal Spacebridge '87, Walt Disney World's Celebrity Circus, Las Vegas: An All-Star 75th Anniversary, Julio Iglesias—Sold Out, The Ice Capades with Kirk Cameron, American All-Star Tribute Honoring Elizabeth Taylor.

PASSER, IVAN
Director, Writer. b. Prague, Czechoslovakia, July 10, 1933. e. Film Faculty of Acad. of Musical Arts, Prague. 1961, asst. dir. to Milos Forman on Audition which led to scripting for Forman. 1969, moved to U.S., worked in NY as longshoreman while studying Eng. U.S. dir. debut: Born to Win, 1971.
PICTURES: Writer: Loves of a Blonde, A Boring Afternoon, Fireman's Ball. Director: Intimate Lighting (also s.p.), Born to Win, Law and Disorder, Crime and Passion, The Silver Bears, Cutter and Bone, Creator, Haunted Summer.
TELEVISION: U.S.: Faerie Tale Theatre. Movies: Fourth Story, Stalin, While Justice Sleeps, Kidnapped.

PASTER, GARY M.
Executive. b. St. Louis, MO, July 4, 1943. e. U. of MO, B.A.; UCLA, USC Graduate Sch. of Business. 1970, joined Burbank Studios as asst. to pres., treas.; 1976 v.p., admin. and chmn. of the exec. comm.; 1977 pres. Member: AMPAS, LA Film Dev. Council, Hollywood Radio & T.V. Society, Acad. of Television Arts and Sciences. Advisory bd., Kaufman Astoria Studios, N.Y.

PATINKIN, MANDY
Actor. b. Chicago, IL, Nov. 30, 1952. r.n. Mandel Patinkin. e. U. of Kansas, Juilliard Sch. (Drama Div.; 1972-74). m. actress

Kathryn Grody. In regional theatre before coming to New York where played with Shakespeare Festival Public Theater (Trelawny of the Wells, Hamlet, Rebel Women). Recordings: Mandy Patinkin, Dress Casual, Experiment.
THEATER: Savages, The Shadow Box (B'way debut), Evita (Tony Award, 1980), Henry IV, Part I (Central Park), Sunday in the Park With George (Tony nom.), The Knife, Follies in Concert, A Winter's Tale, Mandy Patinkin: Dress Casual (solo concert), The Secret Garden, Falsettos.
PICTURES: The Big Fix (debut, 1978), Last Embrace, French Postcards, Night of the Juggler, Ragtime, Daniel, Yentl, Maxie, The Princess Bride, The House on Carroll Street, Alien Nation, Dick Tracy, True Colors, Impromptu, The Doctor, The Music of Chance, Life With Mikey (cameo), Squanto: A Warrior's Tale.
TELEVISION: Series: Chicago Hope (Emmy Award, 1995). Guest: That Thing on ABC, That 2nd Thing on ABC, Taxi, Sparrow, Streets of Gold, Midnight Special. Movie: Charleston.

PATRIC, JASON
Actor. b. Queens, NY, June 17, 1966. Son of playwright-actor Jason Miller. Grandson of performer Jackie Gleason. Began professional career with Vermont's Champlain Shakespeare Festival.
THEATER: NY: Out of Gas on Lovers' Leap.
PICTURES: Solarbabies (debut, 1986), The Lost Boys, The Beast, Denial, After Dark My Sweet, Roger Corman's Frankenstein Unbound, Rush, Geronimo: An American Legend, The Journey of August King, Sleepers.
TELEVISION: Movie: Tough Love. Special: Teach 109.

PATRICK, C.L.
Theatre Executive. b. Honaker, VA, Dec. 6, 1918. Former pres. of Fuqua Industries which owned Martin Theatres and Gulf States Theatres. Prior to this was pres. and chairman of Martin Theatres. Presently chairman of board Carmike Cinemas, Inc.; v.p. Variety International; director, Will Rogers Institute; Motion Picture Pioneer of 1976; Recipient of: Sherrill Corwin Award, 1984; Salah Hassanein Humanitarian Award, ShowEast '88; Show South's Exhibitor of the Decade Award, 1990.

PATRICK, MICHAEL W.
Executive. b. Columbus, GA, May 17, 1950. e. Columbus Coll., B.S., 1972. Pres., CEO, Carmike Cinemas. 1989, assumed additional post of chief exec. Board of dir., Columbus Bank and Trust Co. Member: exec. comm., Will Rogers Institute; Variety Int'l; Motion Picture Pioneers.

PATTON, WILL
Actor. b. Charleston, SC, June 14, 1954. e. NC School of the Arts, 1975.
THEATER: NY: Tourists and Refugees #2 (La Mama E.T.C.), Obie Award), Fool For Love (Obie Award), Goose and Tomtom (Public Theatre), A Lie of the Mind.
PICTURES: King Blank, Silkwood, Variety, Desperately Seeking Susan, After Hours, Chinese Boxes, Belizaire the Cajun, No Way Out, Stars and Bars, Wildfire, Signs of Life, Everybody Wins, A Shock to the System, The Rapture, Cold Heaven, In the Soup, The Paint Job, Romeo Is Bleeding, Natural Causes, Midnight Edition, Tollbooth, The Client, The Puppet Masters, Copycat, Johns.
TELEVISION: Movies: Kent State, Dillinger, A Gathering of Old Men, The Deadly Desire, In the Deep Woods, A Child Lost Forever, Taking the Heat, Judicial Consent. Series: Ryan's Hope, Search For Tomorrow.

PAULEY, JANE
TV Host, Journalist. b. Indianapolis, IN, Oct. 31, 1950. m. Doonesbury creator Garry Trudeau. e. Indiana U. Involved in Indiana state politics before joining WISH-TV, Indianapolis, as reporter. Co-anchored midday news reports and anchored weekend news reports. Co-anchor of nightly news at WMAQ-TV, NBC station in Chicago. Joined Today Show in October, 1976, as featured regular, prior to which had made guest appearances on that program; co-host until 1990. Began own series Real Life With Jane Pauley in 1991.

PAVAN, MARISA
Actress, r.n. Marisa Pierangeli. b. Cagliari, Sardinia, Italy, June 19, 1932. e. Torquato Tasso Coll. Twin sister of late actress Pier Angeli. Came to U.S. 1950.
PICTURES: What Price Glory? (debut, 1952), Down Three Dark Streets, Drum Beat, The Rose Tattoo (Acad. Award nom.), Diane, The Man in the Gray Flannel Suit, The Midnight Story, John Paul Jones, Solomon and Sheba, A Slightly Pregnant Man.

PAVLIK, JOHN M.
Executive. b. Melrose, IA, Dec. 3, 1939. e. U. of Minnesota, B.A., 1963. Reporter, Racine (WI) Journal-Times, San Bernardino (CA) Sun-Telegram, 1963-66; writer, News Bureau, Pacific Telephone, Los Angeles, 1966-68; asst. dir. of

publ. rltns., Association of Motion Picture and Television Producers, 1968-72; dir. of publ. rltns., 1972-78; v.p., 1978-79; exec. admin., Academy of Motion Picture Arts and Sciences, 1979-82; exec. dir., M.P. & TV Fund, 1982-88; consultant, 1988-89; dir. of endowment dev., Academy Foundation, 1989-present; member, bd. of dir., Permanent Charities Comm. of the Entertainment Industries, 1979-84; member, bd. of dir., Hollywood Chamber of Commerce, 1979-85; v.p., Los Angeles Film Dev. Committee, 1977-78, member, exec. council, 1974-85; special consultant, California Motion Picture Council, 1974-79; member, advisory board, Assn. of Film Commissioners int'l, 1988-present.

PAXTON, BILL
Actor. b. Fort Worth, TX, May 17, 1955. e. NYU. First professional job as set dresser for film Big Bad Mamma. Studied acting in NYC with Stella Adler. Dir. short films Fish Heads, Scoop (also s.p.)
PICTURES: Stripes, The Lords of Discipline, Mortuary, Streets of Fire, Impulse, The Terminator, Weird Science, Commando, Aliens, Near Dark, Pass the Ammo, Slipstream, Next of Kin, Back to Back, Brain Dead, The Last of the Finest, Navy SEALS, Predator 2, The Dark Backward, One False Move, The Vagrant, Trespass, Indian Summer, Boxing Helena, Future Shock, Monolith, Tombstone, True Lies, Apollo 13, The Last Supper, Twister, The Evening Star.
TELEVISION: Mini-Series: Fresno. Movies: Deadly Lessons, The Atlanta Child Murders, An Early Frost, Frank and Jesse. Guest: Miami Vice.

PAY, WILLIAM
UK Manager Quigley Publishing Co., Inc. b. London, England. Joined London office Quigley Publications. Served in RAF, 1941-46; rejoined Quigley; dir. Burnup Service Ltd., 1951; London news ed., Quigley Pub., 1955; dir., Quigley Pub. Ltd., 1961; appt. mgr. dir., 1963; mgr. dir., Burnup Company. Appt. Sec. British Kinematograph Sound & TV Society. Conference Co-ordinator biennial Intern. Film & TV Technology Conferences in U.K., 1975-87.

PAYMER, DAVID
Actor. b. Long Island, NY, Aug. 30, 1954. e. Univ. of Mich. First professional job with natl. company of Grease, which he later appeared in on B'way. Has also taught acting at UCLA and the Film Actor's Workshop, performed stand-up comedy and served as staff writer on The New Leave It to Beaver Show.
PICTURES: The In-Laws (debut, 1979), Airplane II: The Sequel, Best Defense, Irreconcilable Differences, Perfect, Howard the Duck, City Slickers, Crazy People, City Slickers, Mr. Saturday Night (Acad. Award nom.), Searching for Bobby Fischer, Heart and Souls, City Slickers II: The Legend of Curly's Gold, Quiz Show, City Hall, The American President, Unforgettable, Nixon.
TELEVISION: Series: The Commish. Movies: Grace Kelly, Pleasure, Cagney & Lacey: The Return, Cagney & Lacey: Together Again. Guest: Cagney & Lacey, The Paper Chase, Taxi, Cheers, L.A. Law, Hill Street Blues, Moonlighting, Murphy Brown. Special: In Search of Dr. Seuss.

PAYNTER, ROBERT
Cinematographer. b. London, England, Mar. 12, 1928. e. Mercer Sch. First job in industry at 15 years as camera trainee with Government Film Dept.
PICTURES: Hannibal Brooks (debut, 1969), The Games, Lawman, The Nightcomers, Chato's Land, The Mechanic, Scorpio, The Big Sleep, Superman, Firepower, The Final Conflict, Superman II, An American Werewolf in London, Superman III, Trading Places, The Muppets Take Manhattan, Into the Night, National Lampoon's European Vacation, Spies Like Us, Little Shop of Horrors, When the Whales Came, Strike It Rich, Get Back.

PAYS, AMANDA
Actress. b. Berkshire, England, June 6, 1959. m. actor Corbin Bernsen. Began as a model. Studied French, art and pottery at Hammersmith Polytechnic. Acting debut: Cold Room (HBO).
PICTURES: Oxford Blues, The Kindred, Off Limits, Leviathan, Exposure, Solitaire for Two.
TELEVISION: Series: Max Headroom, The Flash. Mini-Series: A.D. Movies: 13 at Dinner, The Pretenders, Parker Kane, Dead on the Money, The Thorn Birds: The Lost Years.

PAYSON, MARTIN D.
Executive. b. Brooklyn, NY, Jan. 4, 1936. e. Cornell U., NYU Sch. of Law, LLB, 1961. Practiced law privately before joining Warner Communications, Inc. as v.p. 1970. Later named exec. v.p., gen. counsel. 1987, appt. to 3-member office of pres., WCI. Was vice chmn. Time Warner Inc., until Dec. 1992. Retired.

PEAKER, E. J.
Actress, Singer, Dancer. r.n. Edra Jeanne Peaker. b. Tulsa, OK, Feb. 22. e. U. of New Mexico, U. of Vienna, Austria. Stage debut Bye, Bye Birdie

PICTURES: Hello Dolly! (debut, 1969), All American Boy, Private Roads, The Four Deuces, Graduation Day, Fire in the Night, I Can't Lose, Out of This World.
TELEVISION: *Series*: That's Life. *Guest*: The Flying Nun, That Girl, Love American Style, Odd Couple, Police Woman, Rockford Files, Get Christie Love, Houston Knights, Hunter, Quincy, Charlie's Angels, Six Million Dollar Man. *Movies*: Three's a Crowd, Getting Away From It All, Broken Promises (assoc. prod., writer).

PEARCE, CHRISTOPHER
Producer. b. Dursley, Eng, Nov. 19, 1943. Entered industry as gen. mgr. American Zoetrope. From 1982 to 1985 served as exec. in chg. of prod. for Cannon Films Inc. overseeing prod. on 150 films incl. That Championship Season, Runaway Train, Fool For Love and Barfly. 1987 became sr. v.p. and COO Cannon Group. Has since become pres. & CEO Cannon Pictures. TV movie: Coming Out of the Ice.

PEARCE, RICHARD
Director, Cinematographer. b. San Diego, CA, Jan. 25, 1943. e. Yale U., B.A. degree in Eng. lit., 1965. New School for Social Research, M.A., degree in political economics. Worked with Don Pennebaker and Richard Leacock on documentaries. Photographed Emile de Antonio's America Is Hard to See. In 1970 went to Chile where he dir., photographed and edited Campamento, an award-winning documentary.
PICTURES: As photographer (Academy Award winning documentaries): Woodstock, Marjoe, Interviews With My Lai Veterans, Hearts and Minds. *Director*: Heartland (debut, 1979), Threshold, Country, No Mercy, The Long Walk Home, Leap of Faith, A Family Thing.
TELEVISION: The Gardener's Son, Siege, No Other Love, Sessions, Dead Man Out, The Final Days.

PECK, GREGORY
Actor, Producer. r.n. Eldred Gregory Peck. b. La Jolla, CA, April 5, 1916. e. U. of California; Neighborhood Playhouse Sch. of Dramatics. Father of actors Tony and Cecilia Peck. On dramatic stage (The Doctor's Dilemma, The Male Animal, Once in a Lifetime, The Play's the Thing, You Can't Take It With You, The Morning Star, The Willow and I, Sons and Soldiers, etc.). Voted one of ten best Money-Making Stars Motion Picture Herald-Fame Poll, 1947, 1952. Co-prod. and starred in Big Country, for his company, Anthony Productions; prod. the Trial of the Catonsville Nine, The Dove (St. George Productions). Pres., Acad. M.P. Arts and Sciences, 1967-70. Founding mem., bd. mem. and chmn. American Film Inst. Recipient, Jean Hersholt Humanitarian Award, 1986. AFI Life Achievement Award, 1989. Voice of Florenz Ziegfeld in 1991 B'way musical The Will Rogers Follies.
PICTURES: Days of Glory (debut, 1944), The Keys of the Kingdom, The Valley of Decision, Spellbound, The Yearling, Duel in the Sun, The Macomber Affair, Gentleman's Agreement, The Paradine Case, Yellow Sky, The Great Sinner, Twelve O'Clock High, The Gunfighter, Only the Valiant, David and Bathsheba, Captain Horatio Hornblower, The World in His Arms, The Snows of Kilimanjaro, Roman Holiday, Night People, Man With a Million, The Purple Plain, The Man in the Gray Flannel Suit, Moby Dick, Designing Woman, The Bravados, The Big Country (also co-prod.), Pork Chop Hill (also prod.), Beloved Infidel, On the Beach, Guns of Navarone, To Kill a Mockingbird (Academy Award, 1962), Cape Fear (also prod.), How the West Was Won, Captain Newman M.D., Behold a Pale Horse (also prod.), John F. Kennedy: Years of Lightning—Day of Drums (narrator), Mirage, Arabesque, MacKenna's Gold, Stalking Moon, The Chairman, Marooned, I Walk the Line, Shootout, Billy Two Hats, The Omen, MacArthur (also prod.), The Boys from Brazil (also prod.), The Sea Wolves (also prod.), Amazing Grace and Chuck, Old Gringo, Other People's Money, Cape Fear (1991).
TELEVISION: *Mini-series*: The Blue and the Gray. *Movies*: The Scarlet and the Black (also prod.), The Portrait. *Special*: We the People 200: The Constitutional Gala, The First 50 Years.

PEDAS, JIM
Executive. b. Youngstown, OH. e. Thiel College. Opened Circle Theatre in Washington, D.C. in 1957 with brother Ted. 1984 formed Circle Releasing, serving as Secretary/Treasurer; Circle Films, serving as v.p. See Ted Pedas entry.

PEDAS, TED
Executive. b. Farrell, PA, May 6, 1931. e. Youngstown St. Univ., Wharton Sch. of Business at Univ. of Pa., Geo. Washington Univ. 1957, with brother Jim, opened Circle Theatre in Washington D.C. one of the first repertory houses. Circle/Showcase group of m.p. theatres expanded to over 80 quality screens before being sold in 1988. 1973-78, served on board of Cinema 5 in NY. 1984, Circle Releasing formed to distribute films with Ted serving as president. Releases include Blood Simple, The Navigator and the Killer. Circle Films has produced the Coen Brothers' Raising Arizona, Miller's Crossing, Barton Fink and Caught.

PEERCE, LARRY
Director. b. Bronx, NY. Father was late singer Jan Peerce.
PICTURES: One Potato Two Potato, The Big T.N.T. Show, The Incident, Goodbye Columbus, The Sporting Club, A Separate Peace, Ash Wednesday, The Other Side of the Mountain, Two Minute Warning, The Other Side of the Mountain—Part II, The Bell Jar (also exec. prod.), Why Would I Lie?, Love Child, Hard to Hold, Wired.
TELEVISION: *Movies*: A Stranger Who Looks Like Me, Love Lives On, I Take These Men, The Fifth Missile, Prison for Children, Queenie, Elvis and Me, The Neon Empire, The Court-Martial of Jackie Robinson, Child of Rage, Poisoned by Love: The Kern County Murders, Heaven & Hell: North and South Book III, A Burning Passion: The Margaret Mitchell Story, In Pursuit of Honor (co-exec. prod. only).

PENA, ELIZABETH
Actress. b. Cuba, Sept. 23, 1961. Moved to New York City in 1969 where she attended NY High School for Performing Arts. Off-B'way in Blood Wedding, Antigone, Romeo & Juliet, Act One & Only, Italian American Reconciliation.
PICTURES: El Super, Times Square, They All Laughed, Fat Chance, Crossover Dreams, Down and Out in Beverly Hills, La Bamba, Batteries Not Included, Vibes, Blue Steel, Jacob's Ladder, The Waterdance, Across the Moon, Free Willy 2: The Adventure Home, Fair Game, Dead Funny, Lone Star.
TELEVISION: *Series*: Tough Cookies, I Married Dora, Shannon's Deal. *Movies*: Fugitive Among Us, Roommates.

PENDLETON, AUSTIN
Actor. b. Warren, OH, Mar. 27, 1940. e. Yale Univ. Started acting with Williamstown Theatre Festival. Teaches acting at the Herbert Berghof Studio. Named artistic dir. of NY's Circle Rep. Theatre, 1995.
THEATER: *Actor*: Oh Dad Poor Dad Mama's Hung You in the Closet and I'm Feeling So Sad, Fiddler on the Roof, The Little Foxes, The Last Sweet Days of Isaac (NY Drama Critics & Outer Critics Circle Awards), Educating Rita, Doubles, The Sorrows of Frederick, Grand Hotel, Hamlet, Sophistry. *Director*: The Runner Stumbles, Say Goodnight Gracie, John Gabriel Borkman, The Little Foxes. *Author*: Booth, Uncle Bob.
PICTURES: Skidoo (debut, 1968), Catch-22, What's Up Doc?, Every Little Crook and Nanny, The Thief Who Came to Dinner, The Front Page, The Great Smokey Roadblock (The Last of the Cowboys), The Muppet Movie, Starting Over, Simon, First Family, My Man Adam, Off Beat, Short Circuit, Hello Again, Mr. & Mrs. Bridge, The Ballad of the Sad Cafe, True Identity, My Cousin Vinny, Charlie's Ear, Rain Without Thunder, My Boyfriend's Back, Searching for Bobby Fischer, Mr. Nanny, Greedy, Guarding Tess, Dangerous Minds, Two Much, Home for the Holidays, Sgt. Bilko.
TELEVISION: *Movie*: Don't Drink the Water. *Guest*: Miami Vice, The Equalizer.

PENN, ARTHUR
Director. b. Philadelphia, PA, Sept. 27, 1922. e. Black Mountain Coll., Asheville, NC; U. of Perugia, U. of Florence in Italy. Began as TV dir. in 1953, twice winner of Sylvania Award. Appeared in 1994 film Naked in New York.
THEATER: Two for the Seesaw, Miracle Worker (Tony Award, 1960), Toys in the Attic, All the Way Home, Golden Boy, Wait Until Dark, Sly Fox, Monday After the Miracle, Hunting Cockroaches.
PICTURES: The Left-Handed Gun (debut, 1958), The Miracle Worker (Acad. Award nom.), Mickey One (also prod.), The Chase, Bonnie and Clyde (Acad. Award nom.), Alice's Restaurant (Acad. Award nom.; also co-s.p.), Little Big Man, Visions of Eight (dir. segment: The Highest), Night Moves, The Missouri Breaks, Four Friends (also co-prod.), Target, Dead of Winter, Penn and Teller Get Killed (also prod.), Inside.
TELEVISION: *Movie*: The Portrait.

PENN, CHRISTOPHER
Actor. b. Malibu, CA. Son of director Leo Penn and actress Eileen Ryan. Brother of actor Sean Penn and musician Michael Penn. Studied acting with Peggy Feury.
PICTURES: Rumble Fish (debut, 1983), All the Right Moves, Footloose, The Wild Life, Pale Rider, At Close Range, Made in USA, Return From the River Kwai, Best of the Best, Mobsters, Leather Jackets, Reservoir Dogs, Best of the Best 2, The Pickle, The Music of Chance, True Romance, Short Cuts, Josh and S.A.M., Beethoven's 2nd, Imaginary Crimes, First of the Northstar, Under the Hula Moon, To Wong Foo—Thanks for Everything-Julie Newmar, Sacred Cargo, Mulholland Falls, The Boys Club, The Funeral.
TELEVISION: *Guest*: Magnun P.I., The Young Riders, North Beach, Rawhide, Chicago Hope.

PENN, SEAN
Actor, Director, Writer. b. Burbank, CA, Aug. 17, 1960. Son of actor-director Leo Penn and actress Eileen Ryan. Brother of actor Christopher Penn and musician Michael Penn. m. actress Robin Wright. e. Santa Monica H.S. Served as apprentice

for two years at Group Repertory Theatre, L.A. Acted in Earthworms, Heartland, The Girl on the Via Flaminia, etc. First prof appearance as guest star on TV's Barnaby Jones. On B'way in Heartland, Slab Boys. Also Hurlyburly (Westwood Playhouse, LA).
PICTURES: *Actor*: Taps (debut, 1981), Fast Times at Ridgemont High, Bad Boys, Crackers, Racing with the Moon, The Falcon and the Snowman, At Close Range, Shanghai Surprise, Colors, Judgment in Berlin, Casualties of War, We're No Angels, State of Grace, Carlito's Way, Dead Man Walking.
Dir./Writer: The Indian Runner, The Crossing Guard (also co-prod.).
TELEVISION: *Movie*: The Killing of Randy Webster. *Guest*: Barnaby Jones. *Special*: Dear America (reader).

PENNEBAKER, D.A.
Director. b. Evanston, IL, July 15, 1925. r.n. Donn Alan Pennebaker. e. Yale U. Studied engineering, set up own electronics firm. Worked in advertising, before writing and directing documentaries, as well as experimental films. 1958 joined Richard Leacock, Willard Van Dyke and Shirley Clarke in equipment-sharing film co-op, Filmakers. 1960 joined Robert Drew operating our Life with Leacock, Albert Maysles and others. Set up Leacock Pennebaker with Leacock and made several films that were blown up from 16mm to 35mm and released in theatres. Currently works with co-dir. and wife Chris Hegedus and son Frazer Pennebaker, continuing to film unscripted dramas of real events in cinema verite style. Dir. music videos for Suzanne Vega, Victoria Williams, Branford Marsalis, Randy Newman, etc.
PICTURES: Daybreak Express (1956), Opening in Moscow, Primary, David, Jane, Crisis, The Chair, On the Pole, Mr. Pearson, Don't Look Back, Monterey Pop, Beyond the Law, One P.M., Sweet Toronto, Maidstone, Ziggy Stardust and the Spiders From Mars, On the Pole, Town Bloody Hall, The Energy War, Dance Black America, Rockaby, Delorean, Happy Come Home, Depeche Mode, The Music Tells You, The War Room.

PEPLOE, MARK
Writer. b. Kenya. Sister is writer Clare Peploe. Raise in England and Italy. e. Magdalen Col., Oxford. Became researcher for documentary dept. of the BBC; then worked as research, writer and dir. for series Creative Persons.
PICTURES: The Pied Piper, The Passenger, The Babysitter, High Season, The Last Emperor (Academy Award, 1987), The Sheltering Sky, Afraid of the Dark (also dir.), Little Buddha.

PERAKOS, SPERIE P.
Executive. b. New Britain, CT, Nov. 12, 1915. e. Cheshire Acad., Yale U., Harvard Law Sch. Student mgr., Stanley-Warner Theatres, 1939-40; Perakos Theatres 1940 to present; Capt., U.S.A. Intelligence with 35 inf. division. Fellow, Pierson Coll., Yale, 1946-present; Yale Alumni Bd., 1949 to present; Yale Alumni Film Bd. 1952 to 1980; member Alumni Council for Yale Drama Sch.; past pres. Yale Club of New Britain, Conn.; dir. of Films & Filmings Seminars, Pierson Coll., Yale; prod. Antigone, 1962; pres. Norma Film Prod., Inc., 1962 to present. Past pres. and chmn. Yale's Peabody Museum Associates. Pres., Perakos Theatres, Conn. Theatre Circuit, Inc. Member, Exec. Board of Natl' Assn. of Theatre Owners, C.A.R.A.

PERENCHIO, ANDREW J.
Executive. b. Fresno, CA, Dec. 20, 1930. e. U. of California. Vice pres., Music Corp. of America, 1958-62; General Artists Corp., 1962-64; pres., owner, Chartwell Artists, Ltd., theatrical agency, Los Angeles, 1964; pres. & CEO, Tandem Productions, Inc., and TAT Communications Co., 1973-83, then became principal with Norman Lear in Embassy Communications. Held post of pres. & CEO of Embassy Pictures.

PEREZ, ROSIE
Actress. b. Brooklyn, 1964. Attended sch. in L.A. where she became a dancer on Soul Train; then choreographer for music videos and stage shows for such performers as Bobby Brown, The Boys, Diana Ross, LL Cool J, etc. Acting debut in Do the Right Thing.
PICTURES: Do the Right Thing (also choreog.; debut, 1989), White Men Can't Jump, Night on Earth, Untamed Heart, Fearless (Acad. Award nom.), It Could Happen to You, Somebody to Love, A Brother's Kiss.
TELEVISION: *Movie*: Criminal Justice. *Series*: In Living Color (choreographer). *Specials*: Rosie Perez Presents Society's Ride (exec. prod.), In a New Light: Sex Unplugged (co-host).

PERKINS, ELIZABETH
Actress. b. Forest Hills, Queens, NY, Nov. 18, 1960. Grew up in Vermont. After high school moved to Chicago to study at Goodman School of Drama. Two months after moving to NY in 1984, landed a role in the national touring co. of Brighton Beach Memoirs, later performing part on Broadway. Acted with Playwright's Horizon, NY Ensemble Theater, Shakespeare in the Park and Steppenwolf Theatre Co. Appeared in short film Teach 109.
PICTURES: About Last Night... (debut, 1986), From the Hip, Big, Sweet Hearts Dance, Love at Large, Avalon, Enid Is Sleeping (Over Her Dead Body), He Said She Said, The Doctor, Indian Summer, The Flintstones, Miracle on 34th Street, Moonlight and Valentino.
TELEVISION: *Movie*: For Their Own Good.

PERKINS, MILLIE
Actress. b. Passaic, NJ, May 12, 1938. Was model when chosen by dir. George Stevens for starring role in The Diary of Anne Frank.
PICTURES: The Diary of Anne Frank (debut, 1959), Wild in the Country, Dulcinea, Ensign Pulver, Ride in the Whirlwind, The Shooting, Wild in the Streets, Cockfighter, Lady Cocoa, The Witch Who Came From the Sea, Table for Five, At Close Range, Jake Speed, Slam Dance, Wall Street, Two Moon Junction, The Pistol, Bodily Harm.
TELEVISION: *Series*: Knots Landing, Elvis. *Guest*: thirtysomething, Murder She Wrote, Our House, Jessie, Hart to Hart, Glitter, Wagon Train. *Movies*: A.D., The Thanksgiving Promise, Penalty Phase, Anatomy of an Illness, Shattered Vows, License to Kill, Strange Voices, Broken Angel, Best Intentions, The Other Love, Haunting Passion, A Gun in the House, Model Mother, Macbeth (cable tv), Call Me Anna, 72 Hours, Murder of Innocence. *Guest*: U.S. Steel Hour, Breaking Point.

PERKINS, ROWLAND
Executive. Vice-President, Creative Services, William Morris Agency, 1952–75. Founding President, Creative Artists Agency, 1975–95. Established The Rowland Perkins Company (a.k.a. Double Eagle Entertainment) in 1994 to develop and produce feature, network and cable films; television series and sepcials; Broadway shows; etc.

PERLMAN, RHEA
Actress. b. Brooklyn, NY, March 31, 1948. e. Hunter Coll. m. actor-dir. Danny DeVito. Co-founder Colonnades Theatre Lab., NY and New Street prod. co with Danny DeVito.
PICTURES: Love Child, My Little Pony (voice), Enid is Sleeping (Over Her Dead Body), Ted & Venus, Class Act, There Goes the Neighborhood, Canadian Bacon, Sunset Park, Matilda.
TELEVISION: *Series*: Cheers (4 Emmy Awards: 1984, 1985, 1986, 1989), Pearl (co-exec. prod.). *Movies*: I Want to Keep My Baby!, Stalk the Wild Child, Having Babies II, Intimate Strangers, Mary Jane Harper Cried Last Night, Like Normal People, Drop-out Father, The Ratings Game, Dangerous Affection, A Family Again, To Grandmother's House We Go, A Place to Be Loved, Spoils of War. *Specials*: Funny You Don't Look 200, Two Daddies (voice), The Last Halloween.

PERLMAN, RON
Actor. b. New York, NY, April 13, 1950. While in high school, part of comedy team that played clubs. e. City U. of NY, U. of Minnesota, M.F.A. Joined Classic Stage Company, NY, for 2 years.
THEATER: *NY*: The Architect and the Emperor of Assyria (also toured Europe), American Heroes, The Resistible Rise of Arturo Ui, Tiebele and Her Demon, La Tragedie de Carmen, A Few Good Men.
PICTURES: Quest for Fire, The Ice Pirates, The Name of the Rose, Sleepwalkers, The Adventures of Huck Finn, Double Exposure, Romeo Is Bleeding, Crime and Punishment, Cronos, Fluke, The City of Lost Children, The Last Summer, The Island of Dr. Moreau.
TELEVISION: *Series*: Beauty and the Beast. *Movies*: A Stoning in Fulham County, Blind Man's Bluff, Original Sins.

PERLMUTTER, DAVID M.
Producer. b. Toronto, Canada, 1934. e. U. of Toronto. Pres., Quadrant Films Ltd.
PICTURES: The Neptune Factor, Sunday in the Country, It Seemed Like a Good Idea at the Time, Love at First Sight, Find the Lady, Blood and Guts, The Third Walker, Two Solitudes, Fast Company, Double Negative, Nothing Personal, Misdeal, Love.

PERMUT, DAVID A.
Producer. b. New York, NY, Mar. 23, 1954. In 1974, became pres., Diversified Artists Intl.; 1975, pres., Theatre Television Corp.; 1979, formed Permut Presentations, Inc., of which is pres. Production deals with Columbia Pictures (1979), Lorimar Productions (1981), Universal (1985), United Artists (1986), and New Line Cinema (1991).
PICTURES: Give 'Em Hell Harry, Fighting Back (exec. prod.), Blind Date, Richard Pryor—Live in Concert (exec. prod.), Dragnet, The Marrying Man, 29th Street, Captain Ron, Consenting Adults, The Temp, Three of Hearts, Surviving the Game, Trapped in Paradise, Eddie, Face Off.

TELEVISION: Mistress (sprv. prod.), Love Leads the Way (exec. prod.), Triumph of the Heart: The Ricky Bell Story (prod.), Breaking the Silence (prod.).

PERREAU, GIGI
Actress. r.n. Ghislaine Perreau. b. Los Angeles, CA, Feb. 6, 1941. e. Immaculate Heart H.S. & College. Many stage and TV guest appearances. Now teaching and directing. Among first 50 stars to be honored with star on Hollywood Walk of Fame.
PICTURES: Madame Currie (debut, 1943), Abigail, Dear Heart, Dark Waters, San Diego I Love You, Two Girls and a Sailor, The Master Race, The Seventh Cross, Mr. Skeffington, Yoland and the Thief, Voice of the Whistler, God Is My Co-Pilot, To Each His Own, Alias Mr. Twilight, High Barbaree, Song of Love, Green Dolphin Street, Family Honeymoon, Enchantment, Sainted Sisters, Roseanna McCoy, Song of Surrender, My Foolish Heart, Shadow on the Wall, For Heaven's Sake, Never a Dull Moment, Reunion in Reno, The Lady Pays Off, Weekend with Father, Has Anybody Seen My Gal, Bonzo Goes to College, There's Always Tomorrow, The Man in the Gray Flannel Suit, Dance With Me Henry, Wild Heritage, The Cool and the Crazy, Girls' Town, Tammy Tell Me True, Look in Any Window, Journey to the Center of Time, Hell on Wheels.
TELEVISION: Series: The Betty Hutton Show, Follow the Sun.

PERRINE, VALERIE
Actress. b. Galveston, TX, Sept. 3 1943. e. U. of Arizona. Was showgirl in Las Vegas before discovered by agent Robert Walker who got her contract with Universal Pictures.
PICTURES: Slaughterhouse 5 (debut, 1972), The Last American Hero, Lenny (NY Film Critics & Cannes Film Fest. Awards; Acad. Award nom.), W. C. Fields & Me, Mr. Billion, Superman, The Magician of Lublin, The Electric Horseman, Can't Stop the Music, Superman II, Agency, The Border, Water, Maid to Order, Reflections in a Dark Sky, Bright Angel, Boiling Point, Girl in the Cadillac, The Break.
TELEVISION: Movies: The Couple Takes a Wife, Ziegfeld: The Man and His Women, Marian Rose White, Malibu, When Your Lover Leaves, Sweet Bird of Youth, Un Casa a Roma, The Burning Shore. Series: Leo and Liz in Beverly Hills. Special: Steambath.

PERRY, LUKE
Actor. b. Fredricktown, OH, Oct. 11, 1966. r.n. Coy Luther Perry III. To LA then NY as teen to become actor, landing role on daytime serial Loving.
PICTURES: Terminal Bliss (debut, 1992), Scorchers, Buffy the Vampire Slayer, At Home With the Webbers (cameo), 8 Seconds, From the Edge, Christmas Vacation, Normal Life.
TELEVISION: Series: Loving, Another World, Beverly Hills 90210.

PERRY, SIMON
Producer, Writer. b. Farnham, Eng., Aug. 5, 1943. e. Cambridge Univ., 1965. Ent. ind. 1974. Early career in stage and television production. Prod. mini-budget feature Knots; prod. dir. Eclipse. Served on bureau staff of Variety. Ran the National Film Development Fund for two years. 1982 set up Umbrella Films to produce Another Time Another Place, Loose Connections, Nineteen Eighty Four, Hotel Du Paradis, Nanou, White Mischief, The Playboys, Innocent Lies. Chief exec. of British Screen Finance since 1991.

PERSKY, LESTER
Executive. b. New York, NY, July 6, 1927. e. Brooklyn Coll. Officer in U.S. Merchant Marine, 1946-48. Founder and pres. of own adv. agency, 1951-1964. Theatrical stage producer, 1966-69. 1973 creative director and co-owner Persky Bright Org. (owner-financier of numerous motion pictures for private investment group). Films: Last Detail, Golden Voyage of Sinbad, For Pete's Sake, California Split, The Man Who Would Be King, The Front, Shampoo, Hard Times, Taxi Driver, Missouri Breaks, Funny Lady, Gator, Bound for Glory, Sinbad and the Eye of the Tiger. Lester Persky Productions, Inc.
PICTURES: Producer: Fortune and Men's Eyes, Equus, Hair, Yanks.
TELEVISION: Mini-Series: Poor Little Rich Girl (Golden Globe Award, 1987), A Woman Named Jackie (Emmy Award, 1992), Liz: The Elizabeth Taylor Story.

PERSOFF, NEHEMIAH
Actor. b. Jerusalem, Israel, Aug. 2, 1919. e. Hebrew Technical Inst., 1934-37. Electrician, 1937-39; signal maint., N.Y. subway, 1939-41. Studied acting with Stella Adler and the Actors Studio. L.A. Critics Award 1971 for Sholem-Sholem Alecheim, and The Dybbuk. Has had exhibitions of his watercolor paintings in California, Florida.
THEATER: Sundown Beach, Galileo, Richard III, King Lear, Peter Pan, Peer Gynt, Tiger At the Gates, Colombe, Flahooly, Montserrat, Only in America. Tour: Fiddler on the Roof, Man of La Mancha, Oliver, Death of a Salesman (Stratford, Ont.), Peter Pan, I'm Not Rappaport, Sholem Aleichem (Drama Log & Bay Area Critics Circle Awards).

PICTURES: On the Waterfront, The Wild Party, The Harder They Fall, The Wrong Man, Men in War, This Angry Age, The Badlanders, Never Steal Anything Small, Al Capone, Some Like It Hot, Green Mansions, The Big Show, The Comancheros, The Hook, A Global Affair, Fate Is the Hunter, The Greatest Story Ever Told, The Power, The Money Jungle, Panic in the City, Mafia, The People Next Door, Mrs. Pollifax—Spy, Red Sky at Morning, Psychic Killer, Voyage of the Damned, In Search of Historic Jesus, Yentl, An American Tail (voice), The Last Temptation of Christ, Testament, Twins, The Dispossessed, An American Tail: Fievel Goes West (voice).
TELEVISION: Guest: Playhouse 90, Philco-Goodyear Show, Kraft, For Whom the Bells Tolls (Sylvania Award, 1958), Producers Showcase, Danger, You Are There, Untouchables, Route 66, Naked City, Wagon Train, Rawhide, Gunsmoke, Thriller, Hitchcock, Bus Stop, Five Fingers, Mr. Lucky, The Wild Wild West, I Spy, Columbo, Barney Miller, L.A. Law, Star Trek, Law and Order, Reasonable Doubts. Movies: Sadat, Adderly, The French Atlantic Affair.

PESCI, JOE
Actor. b. Newark, NJ, Feb. 9, 1943. Raised in Belleville, NJ. First show business job as child on TV's Star Time Kids. Worked as mason's laborer, restaurant owner, prior to becoming actor.
PICTURES: Death Collector, Raging Bull, I'm Dancing as Fast as I Can, Dear Mr. Wonderful (Ruby's Dream), Easy Money, Eureka, Once Upon a Time in America, Man on Fire, Moonwalker, Lethal Weapon 2, Betsy's Wedding, Goodfellas (Academy Award, best supporting actor, 1990), Home Alone, The Super, JFK, My Cousin Vinny, Tuti Dentro, Lethal Weapon 3, The Public Eye, Home Alone 2: Lost in New York, A Bronx Tale, Jimmy Hollywood, With Honors, Casino.
TELEVISION: Series: Half Nelson. Movies: Half Nelson (pilot), Backtrack. Guest: Tales From the Crypt (Split Personality).

PETERS, BERNADETTE
Actress. r.n. Bernadette Lazzara. b. New York, NY, Feb. 28, 1948. e. Quintano Sch. for Young Professionals, NY. Professional debut at age 5 on TV's Horn & Hardart Children's Hour, followed by Juvenile Jury and Name That Tune. Stage debut with N.Y. City Center production of The Most Happy Fella (1959).
THEATER: Gypsy (1961), This is Goggle, Riverwind, The Penny Friend, Curley McDimple, Johnny No-Trump, George M! (Theatre World Award), Dames at Sea (Drama Desk Award), La Strada, W.C. & Me, On the Town (1971 revival), Tartuffe, Mack and Mabel, Sally and Marsha, Sunday in the Park With George, Song and Dance (Tony, Drama Desk & Drama League Awards), Into the Woods, The Goodbye Girl.
PICTURES: Ace Eli and Rodger of the Skies (debut, 1973), The Longest Yard, W.C. Fields & Me, Vigilante Force, Silent Movie, The Jerk, Tulips, Pennies from Heaven, Heartbeeps, Annie, Slaves of New York, Pink Cadillac, Alice, Impromptu.
TELEVISION: Series: All's Fair. Mini-Series: The Martian Chronicles. Specials: George M, They Said It with Music, Party at Annapolis, Rich Thin and Beautiful (host), Faerie Tale Theatre, The Last Mile. Pilot: The Owl and the Pussycat. Movies: The Islander, David, Fall from Grace, The Last Best Year.

PETERS, BROCK
Actor. r.n. Brock Fisher. b. Harlem, NY, July 2, 1927. e. CCNY, U. of Chicago. Had numerous featured roles on and off B'way. in road and stock cos., nightclubs, TV. Toured with DePaur Infantry Chorus as bass soloist, 1947-50. Appeared in short film From These Roots.
THEATER: Porgy and Bess (debut, 1943), Anna Lucasta, My Darlin' Aida, Mister Johnson, King of the Dark Chamber, Othello, Kwamina, The Great White Hope (tour), Lost in the Stars, Driving Miss Daisy (Natl. Co.).
PICTURES: Carmen Jones (debut, 1954), Porgy and Bess, To Kill a Mockingbird, Heavens Above, The L-Shaped Room, The Pawnbroker, Major Dundee, The Incident, P.J., The Daring Game, Ace High, The MacMasters, Black Girl, Soylent Green, Slaughter's Big Rip-off, Lost in the Stars, Million Dollar Dixie Deliverance, Framed, Two-Minute Warning, Star Trek IV: The Voyage Home, Star Trek VI: The Undiscovered Country, Alligator II: The Mutation, The Importance of Being Earnest.
TELEVISION: Arthur Godfrey's Talent Scouts (debut, 1953), Series: The Young and the Restless. Guest: Eleventh Hour, It Takes a Thief, Mannix, Mod Squad. Mini-series: Seventh Avenue, Black Beauty, Roots: The Next Generations. Movies: Welcome Home Johnny Bristol, SST: Death Flight, The Incredible Journey of Doctor Meg Laurel, The Adventures of Huckleberry Finn, Agatha Christie's Caribbean Mystery, To Heal a Nation, Broken Angel, The Big One: The Great Los Angeles Earthquake, Highway Heartbreakers, The Secret. Specials: Challenge of the Go Bots (voice), Living the Dream: A Tribute to Dr. Martin Luther King. Co-prod.: This Far By Faith.

PETERS, JON
Producer. b. Van Nuys, CA, 1947. Started hair-styling business; built it into multimillion-dollar firm before turning film

producer. Formed Jon Peters Organization. 1980, joined with Peter Guber and Neil Bogart to form The Boardwalk Co. (dissolved 1981). Later Guber-Peters-Barris Company. 1989, became co-chairman of Columbia Pictures. Resigned, 1991.
PICTURES: A Star Is Born, Eyes of Laura Mars, The Main Event, Die Laughing, Caddyshack. *Co-Prod./Co-Exec. Prod. with Peter Guber:* An American Werewolf in London, Missing, Six Weeks, Flashdance, D.C. Cab, Vision Quest, Legend of Billie Jean, Clue, The Color Purple, Head Office, The Clan of the Cave Bear, Youngblood, The Witches of Eastwick, Innerspace, Who's That Girl, Gorillas in the Mist, Caddyshack II, Rain Man, Batman, Tango and Cash, The Bonfire of the Vanities, Batman Returns, This Boy's Life, With Honors, Money Train.
TELEVISION: *Movies:* Bay Coven (co-exec. prod.), Nightmare at Bitter Creek (exec. prod.).

PETERSEN, PAUL
Actor. b. Glendale, CA, Sept. 23, 1945. e. Valley Coll. Original Disney Mouseketeer (TV). Recorded hit songs She Can't Find Her Keys, and My Dad in 1962. In the late 1960's turned to writing beginning with a Marcus Welby script followed by paperback novels in 1970's. Author of book about Disney empire, Walt Mickey and Me (1977), and co-author of It's a Wonderful Life Trivia Book (1992). President and founder of A Minor Consideration, a support foundation for former kid actors with a current membership of 150 movie, tv and sports stars spanning the past 70 years.
PICTURES: Houseboat, This Could Be the Night, The Happiest Millionaire, Journey to Shiloh, A Time for Killing.
TELEVISION: *Series:* The Donna Reed Show. *Guest:* Playhouse 90, Lux Video Theatre, GE Theatre, The Virginian, Ford Theatre, Valentine's Day, Shindig. *Movies:* Something for a Lonely Man, Gidget Grows Up, Scout's Honor.

PETERSEN, WILLIAM
Actor. b. Chicago, IL, 1953. e. Idaho State U. Active in Chicago theatre; helped to found Ix, an ensemble acting group now called the Remains Theatre. Acted in Moby Dick, In the Belly of the Beast, A Streetcar Named Desire, etc. 1986, formed company with prod. Cynthia Chvatal called High Horse Prods.
THEATER: *NY:* Night of the Iguana.
PICTURES: To Live and Die in L.A., Manhunter, Amazing Grace and Chuck, Cousins, Young Guns II, Hard Promises (also co-prod.), Passed Away, Fear.
TELEVISION: *Movies:* Long Gone (HBO), Keep the Change (also co-prod.), Curacao. *Mini-Series:* The Kennedys of Massachusetts, Return to Lonesome Dove, The Beast.

PETERSEN, WOLFGANG
Director, Writer. b. Emden, Germany, Mar. 14, 1941. Career as asst. stage director at Ernst Deutsch Theatre in Hamburg before entering 4 year program at the German Film & TV Academy wher he directed for television and later theatrical films.
PICTURES: One of Us Two, Black and White Like Day and Night (also s.p.), The Consequence (also s.p.), Das Boot (The Boat; also s.p.; Acad. Award nom. for dir.), The Neverending Story (also s.p.), Enemy Mine, Shattered (also s.p., co-prod.), In the Line of Fire (also co-exec.prod.), Outbreak (also co-prod.).
TELEVISION: I Will Kill You Wolf (dir. debut 1970), Tatort (series), Smog (Prix Futura Award, 1975), For Your Love Only (also released theatrically), Scene of the Crime (series).

PETERSON, S. DEAN
Executive. b. Toronto, Canada, December 18, 1923. e. Victoria Coll., U. of Toronto. WWII service RCNVR; 1946 TV newsreel cameraman NBC; founded own co. in 1947; incorporated Dordean Realty Limited to acquire new studios 1959; formed Peterson Productions Limited in 1957 to make TV commercials and sponsored theatrical shorts; formed Studio City Limited in 1965 to produce TV series and features acquiring an additional studio complex and backlot in Kleinberg, Ontario; 1972 formed SDP Communications Ltd. to package M.P. and TV; 1970 incorporated Intermedia Financial Services Limited to provide specialized financing and consultation to companies in M.P. and TV. industries. Past-President Canadian Film and Television Production Assn., mbr. Variety Club, Tent 28; Canadian Society of Cinematographers; Directors Guild of America, Directors Guild of Canada, SMPTE.

PETERSON, RICHARD W.
Executive. b. Denver, CO, June 15, 1949. e. Col. Sch. of Broadcasting, Harper Coll. Joined Kennedy Theatres, Chicago, 1966. 1968 went with Great States Theatres (now Cineplex Odeon), Chicago. Was city mgr. of Crocker and Grove Theatres, Elgin, IL. 1973 joined American Automated Theatres, Oklahoma City, as dir. of adv., pub. Promoted to dir. of U.S. theatre operations. Worked for American International Pictures, Dallas, TX. Then moved to Dal Art Film Exchange

and B & B Theatres as general mgr.; 1987 took over 7 screens from McLendon and formed own co., Peterson Theatres, Inc, now operating 17 screens.

PETIT, HENRI-DOMINIQUE
Executive. b. Baden-Baden, Germany. e. Ecole Superieure de Physique et Chimie de Paris, Univ. of Paris. Joined Kodak 1975 as asst. mgr. of the Purchasing Division, Kodak Pathe, France. 1980, asst., then mgr. of Kodak Pathe Photofinishing Lab (1981). 1984, became bus. mgr. Business Information Systems and Corporate Accounts, Kodak Pathe. 1987, named bus. mgr. of Photofinishing Systems Division. 1989, appointed gen. mgr. and v.p. Motion Picture and Television Imaging, Europe/Africa/Middle East Region. Dec., 1990, named v.p and gen. mgr. Motion Picture and Television Imaging.

PETRIE, DANIEL
Director. b. Glace Bay, Nova Scotia, Nov. 26, 1920. e. St. Francis Xavier U., Nova Scotia; Columbia U., MA, 1945; post-grad. Northwestern U. Broadway actor 1945-46. TV director from 1950. Son Daniel Petrie Jr. is a screenwriter; son Donald Petrie is a director.
THEATER: Shadow of My Enemy, Who'll Save the Plowboy?, Mornin' Sun, Monopoly, The Cherry Orchard, Volpone, A Lesson from Aloes.
PICTURES: The Bramble Bush (debut, 1960), A Raisin in the Sun, The Main Attraction, Stolen Hours, The Idol, The Spy With a Cold Nose, The Neptune Factor, Buster and Billie, Lifeguard, The Betsy, Resurrection, Fort Apache The Bronx, Six Pack, The Bay Boy (also s.p.; Genie Award), Square Dance (also prod.), Rocket Gibraltar, Cocoon: The Return, Lassie.
TELEVISION: *Movies:* Silent Night Lonely Night, A Howling in the Woods, A Stranger in Town, Moon of the Wolf, Trouble Comes to Town, Mousey, Returning Home, Eleanor and Franklin (Emmy Award, 1976), Sybil, Eleanor and Franklin: The White House Years (Emmy Award, 1977), Harry Truman, Plain Speaking (Emmy nom.), The Dollmaker (Emmy nom.), The Execution of Raymond Graham (Emmy nom.), Half a Lifetime, My Name is Bill W. (also prod.; Emmy nom.), Mark Twain and Me (also prod., Emmy Award), A Town Torn Apart (also prod., Emmy nom.), Kissinger and Nixon.

PETRIE, DONALD
Director. b. New York, NY. Son of dir. Daniel Petrie. Moved to LA as teenager, becoming tv actor. Attended American Film Inst. dir. program, where he made short film The Expert. Was then hired to dir. Mister Magic esisode of Amazing Stories.
PICTURES: Mystic Pizza (debut, 1988), Opportunity Knocks, Grumpy Old Men, The Favor, Richie Rich, The Associate.
TELEVISION: *Series episodes:* MacGyver, The Equalizer, L.A. Law. *Special:* Have You Tried Talking to Patty?

PETROU, DAVID MICHAEL
Writer, Producer, Public Relations Executive. b. Washington, DC, Nov. 3, 1949. e. U. of Maryland, B.A.; Georgetown U., M.A. Publicity assoc., Psychiatric Institutes of America, Washington, DC, 1971; assoc. dir. of publicity & film liaison, Random House, 1974; guest lecturer, screen writing & film production, The American University Consortium, Washington, DC, spring, 1980; Woodrow Wilson Fellowship, 1971. Entered industry in 1975. Joined Salkind Organization in chg. of literary projects. Worked in numerous production capacities on Crossed Swords, Superman, Superman II. 1977, exec. in chg. of literary development, Salkind. Wrote Crossed Swords (1978) and The Making of Superman. Co-authored screenplay, Shoot to Kill. 1978-79, promotional dev. on Time after Time for Warner Bros.; 1980-83, dir., special projects Joseph Kennedy Foundation. 1983-84, sr. edit. for entertainment, Regardie's Magazine; 1984-86, sr. exec., p.r. div., Abramson Associates; 1986-88, sr. v.p., Eisner, Held & Petrou, Inc., p.r. agency; 1988-present, pres. & COO, Eisner Petrou & Associates Inc. Baltimore-Wash., marketing communications agency. 1992, named chmn. of American Film Institute's Second Decade Council.

PETTET, JOANNA
Actress. b. London, England, Nov. 16, 1944. Raised in Canada. Studied acting at Neighborhood Playhouse in NY.
PICTURES: The Group (debut, 1966), The Night of the Generals, Casino Royale, Robbery, Blue, The Best House in London, Welcome to Arrow Beach (Tender Flesh), The Evil, An Eye for an Eye, Double Exposure, Sweet Country, Terror in Paradise.
TELEVISION: *Series:* Knots Landing. *Mini-Series:* Captains and the Kings. *Movies:* Footsteps, The Delphi Bureau, The Weekend Nun, Pioneer Woman, A Cry in the Wilderness, The Desperate Miles, The Hancocks, The Dark Side of Innocence, Sex and the Married Woman, Cry of the Innocent, The Return of Frank Cannon.

PETTY, LORI
Actress. b. Chattanooga, TN, 1965. Worked as graphic artist before turning to acting.

PICTURES: Cadillac Man, Point Break, A League of Their Own, Free Willy, Poetic Justice, In the Army Now, Tank Girl, The Glass Shield.
TELEVISION: *Series*: The Thorns, Booker, Lush Life.

PEYSER, JOHN
Producer, Director. b. New York, NY, Aug. 10, 1916. e. Colgate U., 1938. In TV ind. since 1939, with Psychological Warfare Div., ETO., W.W.II; pres. Peyser/Vance Productions, Woodland Hills, CA.
PICTURES: The Open Door, Kashmiri Run, Four Rode Out, Massacre Harbor.
TELEVISION: *Director*: Hawaii Five-O, Mannix, Movin On, Swiss Family Robinson, Bronk, Combat, Untouchables, Rat Patrol, Honeymoon with a Stranger.

PFEIFFER, MICHELLE
Actress. b. Santa Ana, CA, Apr. 29, 1957. Sister of actress Deedee Pfeiffer. While attending jr. coll. and working as super-market checkout clerk, won Miss Orange County beauty contest. Began taking acting classes in L.A. Stage debut in L.A. prod. of A Playground in the Fall. NY Theatre debut 1989 in Twelfth Night (Central Park).
PICTURES: The Hollywood Nights (debut, 1980), Falling in Love Again, Charlie Chan and the Curse of the Dragon Queen, Grease 2, Scarface, Into the Night, Ladyhawke, Sweet Liberty, The Witches of Eastwick, Amazon Women on the Moon, Married to the Mob, Tequila Sunrise, Dangerous Liaisons (Acad. Award nom.), The Fabulous Baker Boys (NY, LA & & Natl. Society of Film Critics Awards; Acad. Award nom.), The Russia House, Frankie and Johnny, Batman Returns, Love Field (Acad. Award nom.), The Age of Innocence, Wolf, Dangerous Minds, Up Close and Personal, To Gillian On Her 37th Birthday.
TELEVISION: *Series*: Delta House, B.A.D. Cats. *Movies*: The Solitary Man, Callie and Son, Splendor in the Grass, The Children Nobody Wanted. *Specials*: One Too Many, Tales from the Hollywood Hills (Natica Jackson). *Guest*: Fantasy Island.

PHILLIPS, JULIA
Producer. b. Brooklyn, NY, April 7, 1944. e. Mt. Holyoke Coll. Production asst. at McCall's Magazine; later became textbook copywriter for Macmillan; story editor, Paramount; creative exec., First Artists Prods., NY. In 1970 with former husband, Michael Phillips and actor Tony Bill formed Bill/Phillips Productions to develop film projects. Author of You'll Never Eat Lunch in This Town Again (Random House, 1991).
PICTURES: Steelyard Blues, The Sting (Academy Award for Best Picture, 1973), Taxi Driver, The Big Bus, Close Encounters of the Third Kind, The Beat (co-prod.).

PHILLIPS, LESLIE
Actor, Producer. b. London, England, April 20, 1924. Early career as child actor. Ent. m.p. ind. 1935.
PICTURES: A Lassie From Lancashire (debut, 1935), The Citadel, Rhythm Serenade, Train of Events, The Woman With No Name (Her Paneled Door), Pool of London, The Galloping Major, Breaking the Sound Barrier, The Fake, The Limping Man, Time Bomb (Terror on a Train), The Price of Greed, Value for Money, The Gamma People, As Long as They're Happy, The Big Money, Brothers in Law, The Barretts of Wimpole Street, Just My Luck, Les Girls, The Smallest Show on Earth, High Flight, I Was Monte's Double, The Man Who Liked Funerals, The Angry Hills, Carry on Nurse, Ferdinand of Naples, This Other Eden, Carry on Teacher, Please Turn Over, The Navy Lark, Doctor in Love, Watch Your Stern, No Kidding (Beware of Children), Carry on Constable, Inn for Trouble, Raising the Wind, In the Doghouse, Very Important Persons, Crooks Anonymous, The Longest Day, The Fast Lady, Father Came Too, Doctor in Clover, You Must Be Joking, Maroc 7, Some Will Some Won't, Doctor in Trouble, The Magnificent 7 Deadly Sins, Not Now Darling, Don't Just Lie There Say Something!, Spanish Fly, Not Now Comrade, Out of Africa, Empire of the Sun, Scandal, Mountains of the Moon, King Ralph, Carry on Columbus, August, Caught In The Act.
TELEVISION: Our Man at St. Marks, Impasse, The Gong Game, Time and Motion Man, Reluctant Debutante, A Very Fine Line, The Suit, The Culture Vultures (series), Edward Woodward Show, Casanova 74 (series), Redundant—or the Wife's Revenge, You'll Never See Me Again, Mr. Palfrey of Westminister, Monte Carlo, Rumpole, Summers Lease, Chancer, Comic Strip, Who Bombed Birmingham, Life After Life, Thacker, Chancer II, The Oz Trial, Lovejoy, Boon, The Changeling, Bermuda Grace, Royal Celebration, Honey for Tea, House of Windsor, Two Golden Balls, Love on a Branch Line, Vanity Dies Hard, Edgar Wallace (Germany), Canterville Ghost, Woof, The Bill, The Pale Horse.

PHILLIPS, LOU DIAMOND
Actor. b. Philippines, Feb. 17, 1962. Raised in Corpus Christi, TX. e. U. of Texas, Arlington (BFA drama). Studied film technique with Adam Roarke, becoming asst. dir./instructor with the Film Actor's Lab, 1983-86. Regional theater includes: A

Hatful of Rain, Whose Life Is It Anyway?, P.S. Your Cat Is Dead, The Lady's Not for Burning, Doctor Faustus, Hamlet.
THEATER: *NY*: The King and I (Bdwy. debut, Tony nom.)
PICTURES: Angel Alley, Interface, Trespasses (also co-s.p.), Harley, La Bamba, Stand and Deliver, Young Guns, Dakota (also assoc. prod.), Disorganized Crime, Renegades, The First Power, A Show of Force, Young Guns II, Ambition (also s.p.), The Dark Wind, Shadow of the Wolf, Dangerous Touch (also dir.), Teresa's Tattoo, Sioux City (also dir.), Undertow, Boulevard, Courage Under Fire.
TELEVISION: *Movies*: Time Bomb, The Three Kings, Extreme Justice, The Wharf Rat. *Specials*: Avenue Z Afternoon, Wind in the Wire. *Guest*: Dallas, Miami Vice.

PHILLIPS, MICHAEL
Producer. b. Brooklyn, NY, June 29, 1943. e. Dartmouth Coll., B.A., 1965. NYU, Law Sch. J.D., 1968. Indep. m.p. prod. 1971.
PICTURES: Steelyard Blues, The Sting (Academy Award for Best Picture, 1973), Taxi Driver (Golden Palm Award at Cannes), The Big Bus, Close Encounters of the Third Kind, Heartbeeps, Cannery Row, The Flamingo Kid, Don't Tell Mom the Babysitter's Dead, Mom and Dad Save the World, Eyes of an Angel, The Companion.
TELEVISION: *Movie*: Jane's House.

PHILLIPS, MICHELLE
Actress. b. Long Beach, CA, June 4, 1944. r.n. Holly Michelle Gilliam. Daughter is actress-singer Chynna Phillips. Former member of The Mamas and the Papas. Co-wrote hit single California Dreamin'. Author: California Dreamin': The Story of The Mamas and The Papas (1986).
PICTURES: Monterey Pop, The Last Movie, Dillinger, Valentino, Sidney Sheldon's Bloodline, The Man With Bogart's Face, Savage Harvest, American Anthem, Let It Ride, Scissors, Army of One, Keep on Running.
TELEVISION: *Series*: Hotel, Knots Landing, Second Chances. *Mini-Series*: Aspen, The French Atlantic Affair. *Movies*: The Death Squad, The California Kid, The Users, Moonlight, Mickey Spillane's Mike Hammer: Murder Me Murder You, Secrets of a Married Man, Stark: Mirror Image, Assault and Matrimony, Trenchcoat in Paradise, Rubdown, Paint Me a Murder, Covenant. *Guest*: Owen Marshall, Matt Houston, The Fall Guy, Murder She Wrote, T.J. Hooker, Hotel, Fantasy Island, Love Boat, Burke's Law, Robin's Hood, Lois & Clark, Herman's Head, many others.

PHILLIPS, SIAN
Actress. b. Bettws, Wales. e. Univ. of Wales. Studied acting at RADA. London stage debut 1957 in title role in Hedda.
THEATER: Saint Joan, The Three Sisters, Taming of the Shrew, Duchess of Malfi, Lizard on the Rock, Gentle Jack, The Night of the Iguana, Ride a Cock Horse, Man and Superman, The Burglar, The Cardinal of Spain, Alpah Beta, Spinechiller, A Woman of No Importance, You Never Can Tell, Dear Liar, Pal Joey, Major Barbara, Gigi, Paris Match, Ghosts, Marlene, Painting Churches, Vanilla, Ghosts (Artist of the Year nom.), Marlene, many others. B'way debut 1994 in An Inspector Calls.
PICTURES: Becket, Young Cassidy, Laughter in the Dark, Goodbye Mr. Chips (NY Film Critics & Critics Circle Awards, 1969), Murphy's War, Under Milk Wood, Nijinsky, Clash of the Titans, Dune, The Doctor and the Devils, Valmont, The Age of Innocence, A Painful Case, House of America.
TELEVISION: *Mini-Series*: Shoulder to Shoulder, How Green Was My Valley (BAFTA Award), I Claudius (BAFTA & Royal TV Society Awards), Crime and Punishment, Tinker Tailor Soldier Spy, Vanity Fair. *Movies*: A Painful Case, Ewoks: The Battle for Endor, The Two Mrs. Grenvilles, Out of Time, Dark River. *Specials*: Off to Philadelphia in the Morning, Sean O'Casey, How Many Miles to Babylon?, Lady Windermere's Fan, Language and Landscape, Heartbreak House, Don Juan in Hell, Summer Silence, Shadow of the Noose, Snow Spider, The Quiet Man, The Sex Game, A Mind To Kill, Ivanhoe, Chestnut Soldier (BAFTA nom.).

PIALAT, MAURICE
Director, Writer. b. Cunlhat, Puy de Dome, France, Aug. 21, 1925. Worked as a painter and sometime actor before turning to film in 1952. Made a number of short films including L'Amour Existe (award winner Venice Film Fest., 1960). Worked in television before feature debut in 1967.
PICTURES: *Dir./Writer*: L'Enfance Nue (Naked Childhood; Prix Jean Vigo Award), We Will Not Grow Old Together, La Gueule Ouverte (also prod.), Passe ton Bac d'Abord (Graduate First), Loulou, A Nos Amours (also actor; Prix Louis Delluc Award), Police, Under Satan's Sun (also actor; Golden Palm Award, Cannes Festival), Van Gogh, Le Garcu.
TELEVISION: Janine, Maitre Galip, La Maison des Bois.

PICARDO, ROBERT
Actor. b. Philadelphia, PA, Oct. 27, 1953. e. Yale. Studied acting at Circle in the Square Theater School.
THEATER: *NY*: Sexual Perversity in Chicago, Gemini, Tribute.

PICTURES: The Howling, Star 80, Oh God You Devil, Explorers, Legend, Back to School, Munchies, Innerspace, Amazon Women on the Moon, Jack's Back, Dead Heat, The 'Burbs, 976-EVIL, Loverboy, Total Recall, Gremlins II, Samantha, Motorama, Matinee, Wagons East!
TELEVISION: *Series:* China Beach, The Wonder Years, Star Trek: Voyager. *Movies:* The Dream Merchants, The Violation of Sarah McDavid, Lois Gibbs and the Love Canal, Dixie: Changing Habits, The Other Woman, Runaway Daughters, White Mile.

PICCOLI, MICHEL
Actor. b. Paris, France, Dec. 27, 1925. r.n. Jacques Piccoli. Since his film debut in The Sorcerer in 1945 has had impressive career on the French stage and in films working for major French dirs. Renoir, Bunuel, Melville, Resnais, Clouzot, Godard as well as Hitchcock. Until 1957 was mgr. of Theatre Babylone in Paris. Formed prod. co. Films 66. Produced: Themroc (1972); La Faille; Les Enfants Gates.
PICTURES: The Sorcerer, Le Point du Jour, French Can Can, The Witches of Salem, Le Bal des Espiona, Gina, Le Doulos, Contempt, Diary of a Chambermaid, Lady L, La Guerre Est Finie, The Young Girls of Rochefort, Un Homme de Trop, Belle de Jour, La Chamade, Dillinger Is Dead, L'Invasion, The Milky Way, Topaz, The Things of Life, Ten Days' Wonder, The Discreet Charm of the Bourgeoisie, Themroc, Wedding in Blood, La Grande Bouffe, The Last Woman, Leonor, 7 Deaths by Prescription, The Weak Spot, F For Fairbanks, Mado, Todo Modo, Rene the Cane, Spoiled Children, Strauberg Is Here, The Fire's Share, Little Girl in Blue Velvet, The Savage State, The Sugar, The Bit Between the Teeth, La Divorcement, Leap into the Void, The Price for Survival, Atlantic City, The Prodigal Daughter, Beyond the Door, The Eyes The Mouth, Passion, A Room in Town, Will the High Salaried Workers Please Raise Their Hands!!!, The General of the Dead Army, La Passante, The Prize of Peril, Adieu Bonaparte, Dangerous Moves, Danger in the House, Long Live Life!, Success Is the Best Revenge, The Sailor 512, Departure, Return, Mon Beau-Frere a Tue Ma Soeur, The Nonentity, The Prude, Bad Blood, Undiscovered Country, Blanc de Chine, Le Peuple Singe (narrator), The French Revolution, May Fools, La Belle Noiseuse, The Children Thief, Archipelago, Punctured Life, Martha and I, Traveling Companion.

PICERNI, PAUL
Actor. b. New York, NY, Dec. 1, 1922. e. Loyola U., Los Angeles. U.S. Air Force 1943-46; head of drama dept. Mt. St. Mary's Coll., 1949-50.
PICTURES: Saddle Tramp, Breakthrough, Operation Pacific, The Tanks Are Coming, Force of Arms, I Was a Communist for the FBI, Mara Maru, Operation Secret, The Desert Song, She's Back on Broadway, House of Wax, The System, Shanghai Story, To Hell and Back, Bobby Ware Is Missing, Miracle in the Rain, Omar Khayyam, The Brothers Rico, Marjorie Morningstar, The Young Philadelphians, Strangers When We Meet, The Young Marrieds, The Scarface Mob, The Scalphunters, Che!, Airport, Kotch, Beyond the Poseidon Adventure.
TELEVISION: *Series:* The Untouchables. *Guest:* Philco Playhouse, Climax, Lux, Loretta Young Show, Desilu, Kojak, Mannix, Police Story, Lucy Special, Quincy, Alice, Trapper John M.D., Vegas, Fall Guy, Capitol, Hardcastle and McCormick, Matt Houston, Simon and Simon.

PICKER, DAVID V.
Executive. b. New York, NY, May 14, 1931. e. Dartmouth Coll., B.A., 1953. Father Eugene Picker, exec. Loew's Theatres. Ent. industry in 1956 as adv. pub. & exploitation liaison with sls. dept., United Artists Corp.; exec. v.p. U.A. Records; asst. to Max Youngstein, v.p.; v.p. U.A.; first v.p. UA; pres. 1969. Resigned 1973 to form own production co. 1976 joined Paramount Pictures as pres. of m.p. div.; v.p., Lorimar Productions; independent; 1987, pres. & COO, Columbia Pictures. Resigned.
PICTURES: Juggernaut, Lenny, Smile, Royal Flash, Won Ton Ton the Dog Who Saved Hollywood, The One and Only, Oliver's Story, Bloodline (prod.), The Jerk (prod.), Dead Men Don't Wear Plaid (prod.), The Man with Two Brains, Beat Street (prod.), The Appointments of Dennis Jennings (short, prod.), Stella (exec. prod.), Traces of Red, Leap of Faith, Matinee, The Saint of Fort Washington, The Crucible.

PICKMAN, JEROME
Executive. b. New York, NY, Aug. 24, 1916. e. St. John's U.; Brooklyn Law Sch. of St. Lawrence U., LL.B. Reporter N.Y. newspapers; U.S. Army World War II; Ad-pub exec. 20th-Fox, 1945-46; v.p., dir., adv. & pub., later v.p. domestic gen. sls. mgr., Paramount Pictures; sr. sls. exec. Columbia Pictures; pres. Motion Picture Div. of Walter Reade Org.; pres., Levitt-Pickman Film Corp.; sr. v.p., domestic distribution, Lorimar Productions; pres., Pickman Film Corp., Cineworld Enterprises Corp.; pres. Scotti Bros. Pictures Distribution, 1986. Consultant, various entertainment entities, legal and financial individuals and organizations.

PIERCE, DAVID HYDE
Actor. b. Albany, NY, Apr. 3, 1959. e. Yale U.
PICTURES: The Terminator, Moving Violations, Bright Lights Big City, Crossing Delancey, Rocket Gibraltar, The Fisher King, Little Man Tate, Sleepless in Seattle, Addams Family Values, Wolf, Nixon.
TELEVISION: *Series:* The Powers That Be, Frasier (Emmy Award, 1995; Emmy nom., 1996). *Guest:* Dream On, Crime Story, Spenser: For Hire, The OUter Limits.
THEATER: *Off-B'way:* Summer, That's It Folks, Donuts, Hamlet, The Moderati, The Cherry Orchard, Zero Positive, Much About Nothing, Elliot Loves. *B'way:* Beyond Therapy, The Heidi Chronicles. *Regional:* work with Long Wharf, Guthrie, Goodman, Doolittle Theatres.

PIERCE, FREDERICK S.
Executive. b. New York, NY, April 8, 1933. e. Bernard Baruch Sch. of B.A., City Coll. of New York. Served with U.S. Combat Engineers in Korean War. Associated with Benj. Harrow & Son, CAP, before joining ABC in 1956. Served as analyst in TV research dep.; prom. to supvr. of audience measurements, 1957, named mgr. next year. 1961 made dir. of research; 1962 dir. of research, sales dev. Named dir. of sales planning, sales devel. 1962; elec. v.p., 1964 and made nat. dir. of sales for TV. 1968 named v.p., planning; 1970 named asst. to pres.; 1972, named v.p. in chg. ABC TV planning and devel. and asst. to pres. ABC TV, 1973. Named sr. v.p., ABC TV, 1974. Elected pres., ABC Television Division, 1974. Pres. & COO, ABC, Inc., 1983. Formed Frederick Pierce Co. and also Pierce/Silverman Co. with Fred Silverman, 1989.

PIERSON, FRANK
Producer, Director, Writer. b. Chappaqua, NY, May 12, 1925. e. Harvard U. Was correspondent for Time magazine before entering show business as story editor of TV series, Have Gun, Will Travel. Later served as both producer and director for show. Developed a number of properties for Screen Gems before writing theatrical screenplays.
PICTURES: *Writer:* Cat Ballou, The Happening, Cool Hand Luke, The Anderson Tapes, Dog Day Afternoon (Academy Award, 1975), In Country, Presumed Innocent. *Director-Writer:* The Looking Glass War, A Star Is Born, King of the Gypsies.
TELEVISION: *Series:* Nichols (prod.), Alfred Hitchcock Presents (1985; dir.). *Movies:* The Neon Ceiling (dir.), Haywire (co-writer), Somebody Has to Shoot the Picture (dir.; ACE Award, 1990), Citizen Cohn (dir.), Lakota Woman: Siege at Wounded Knee (dir.), Truman.

PIGOTT-SMITH, TIM
Actor. b. Rugby, England, May 13, 1946. e. U. of Bristol, B.A., Bristol Old Vic Theatre Sch., 1969. Acted with Bristol Old Vic, Royal Shakespeare Co. Artistic Director of Compass Theatre, 1989-93.
THEATER: *Actor:* As You Like It, Major Barbara, Hamlet, School for Scandal, Sherlock Holmes (B'way debut, 1974), Benefactors, Entertaining Strangers, The Winter's Tale, Antony and Cleopatra, Cymbeline, The Tempest, Jane Eyre, The Picture of Dorian Gray, Retreat. *Director:* Company, Royal Hunt of the Sun, Playing the Wife, Hamlet, The Letter, Retreat, Mary Stuart.
PICTURES: Aces High (debut, 1975), Man in a Fog, Sweet William, Richard's Things, Joseph Andrews, Clash of the Titans, Lucky Village, Victory, State of Emergency, The Remains of the Day.
TELEVISION: Dr. Who (debut, 1970). *Mini-series:* Winston Churchill: The Wilderness Years, The Jewel in the Crown. *Movies:* Eustace and Hilda, The Lost Boys, I Remember Nelson, Measure for Measure, Henry IV, Day Christ Died, The Hunchback of Notre Dame, Fame Is the Spur, Glittering Prizes, Dead Man's Folly, The Case of Sherlock Holmes (host), Life Story, Hannah, The True Adventures of Christopher Columbus, The Chief, Bullion Boys, The Shadowy Third, Calcutta Chronicles.

PIKE, CORNELIA M.
Executive. b. Holyoke, MA, 1933. e. Boston U. Sch. of Commun., BS Magna Cum Laude. Asst. Promotion & Publicity Dir. WNAC/WNAC-TV 1954-56, Boston, MA. Women's Director/On-air personality: WKNE Keene, NH 1957-60; WSMN Nashua, NH 1963-67; WHOB, Nashua, NH 1967-68. Mngr. Trade Winds Interior Design, Boston, MA 1979-81. Sls. Mngr./VP Pike Productions, Inc. 1981 to present. Company produces and markets trailers to exhibitors in U.S., UK, Germany, Australia and New Zealand. Alpha Epsilon Rho, Natl. Bdcstg. Soc. 1st VP, Variety Club of New England. Bd. dirs., Variety Club of New England. Life Patron, Variety Clubs International.

PIKE, JOHN S.
Executive. b. Cleveland, OH, Oct. 26, 1946. e. Univ. of Miami. Joined Paramount Pictures as v.p., video programming; promoted to sr. v.p., video prog. 1984, named sr. v.p., current net-

work programming; 1985, promoted to exec. v.p., Paramount Network TV. Appt. pres., Network TV and Intl. co-production, 1991.

PINCHOT, BRONSON
Actor. b. New York, NY, May 20, 1959. e. Yale U. Grew up in Pasadena. Studied acting at Yale. On NY stage in Poor Little Lambs, Zoya's Apartment.
PICTURES: Risky Business (debut, 1983), Beverly Hills Cop, The Flamingo Kid, Hot Resort, After Hours, Second Sight, Blame It on the Bellboy, True Romance, Beverly Hills Cop III, It's My Party, Courage Under Fire.
TELEVISION: Series: Sara, Perfect Strangers, The Trouble With Larry. Movie: Jury Duty—The Comedy. Mini-Series: Stephen King's The Langoliers.

PINSKER, ALLEN
Executive. b. New York, NY, Jan. 23, 1930. e. NYU. Mgr., Hempstead Theatre, 1950. 1954 joined Island Theatre Circuit as booker-buyer; named head buyer 1958. 1968 joined United Artists Eastern Theatres as film buyer; head buyer, 1969, v.p., 1970. Named v.p. United Artists Theatre Circuit, 1972. 1973 named UAET exec. v.p., member bd., 1974. Appt. pres. & COO, UA Communications, Inc., theatre division, 1987. 1987, named pres. and CEO, United Artists Theatre Circuit, Inc. and exec. v.p., United Artists Communications, Inc.; 1988, became member, bd. dir. United Artists Comm. Inc.

PINTER, HAROLD
Writer, Director, Actor. b. London, England, Oct. 10, 1930. Began career as actor then turned to writing and direction.
THEATER: The Dumb Waiter, Slight Ache, The Room, The Birthday Party, The Caretaker, The Homecoming, The Collection, Landscape, Silence, Old Times, No Man's Land, The Hothouse, Betrayal, One for the Road, Mountain Language, Party Time, Moonlight.
PICTURES: Writer: The Caretaker (The Guest), The Servant (also actor), The Pumpkin Eater, The Quiller Memorandum, Accident (also actor), The Birthday Party, The Go-Between, The Homecoming, Butley (dir. only), The Last Tycoon, The French Lieutenant's Woman, Betrayal, Turtle Diary (also actor), The Handmaid's Tale, Reunion, The Comfort of Strangers, The Trial.
TELEVISION: A Night Out, Night School, The Lover, Tea Party, The Basement, Langrishe Go Down, Heat of the Day.

PISANO, A. ROBERT
Executive. e. San Jose St. Univ., Boalt Hall School of Law at Univ. of CA, Berkeley. Was partner at law firm of O'Melveny & Myers prior to entering m.p. industry. 1985-91, exec. v.p. of Paramount Pictures serving as gen. counsel, member of office of chmn.; 1993, named exec. v.p. of MGM responsible for all business and legal affairs and labor relations.

PISCOPO, JOE
Actor, Comedian. b. Passaic, NJ, June 17, 1951. Stage appearances in regional and dinner theaters in South and Northeast. Worked as stand-up comic at the Improvisation and the Comic Strip clubs, NY 1976-80. Author: The Piscopo Tapes. Television debut as regular on Saturday Night Live, 1980.
PICTURES: American Tickler or the Winner of 10 Academy Awards (1976), King Kong, Johnny Dangerously, Wise Guys, Dead Heat, Sidekicks.
TELEVISION: Series: Saturday Night Live (1980-84). Guest: Comic Relief. Special: The Joe Piscopo Special (HBO). Movie: Huck and the King of Hearts.

PISIER, MARIE-FRANCE
Actress. b. Indochina, May 10, 1944. Began appearing in French films at age 17. Returned to school at Univ. of Paris for degrees in law and political science; continued to work in films.
PICTURES: Qui ose nous Accuser? (debut, 1961), Love at Twenty (Truffaut episode), La Mort d'un Tueur, Les Yeux cernes, Trans-Europe Express, Stolen Kisses, Celine and Julie Go Boating, French Provincial, Cousin Cousine, Serail, Barocco, The Other Side of Midnight, Love on the Run, Les Apprentis Sourciers, The Bronte Sisters, French Postcards, La Banquiere, Chanel Solitaire, Der Zauberberg (The Magic Mountain), Miss Right, Hot Touch, The Prize of Peril, The Silent Ocean, L'Ami de Vincent, Les Nanas, Parking, Blue Note, Why is My Mother in My Bed?
TELEVISION: U.S.: French Atlantic Affair, Scruples.

PITT, BRAD
Actor. b. Shawnee, OK, Dec. 18, 1963. r.n. William Bradley Pitt. Raised in Springfield, MO. Studied journalism at Univ. of MO at Columbia. Moved to L.A. to attend art school, instead studying acting with Roy London. Appeared in short film Contact.
PICTURES: Cutting Class (debut, 1989), Happy Together, Across the Tracks, Thelma & Louise, Cool World, Johnny

Suede, A River Runs Through It, Kalifornia, True Romance, The Favor, Interview With the Vampire. Legends of the Fall, Seven, Twelve Monkeys (Golden Globe, 1996), Sleepers, Devil's Own.
TELEVISION: Series: Another World, Glory Days. Movies: A Stoning in Fulham County, Too Young to Die, The Image. Guest: Dallas, Growing Pains, Head of the Class, Tales From the Crypt.

PIVEN, JEREMY
Actor. b. New York, NY. Raised in Chicago where parents ran Piven Theater Workshop. e. Drake Univ. Studied acting at Eugene O'Neill Theater Center, Natl. Theater of Great Britain, NYU. Eventually joined Chicago's Second City comedy troupe. Co-founded Chicago's New Criminals Theatre Company, 1988.
THEATER: Fear & Loathing in Las Vegas, Peacekeeper, Methusalen, Knuckle, Macbeth.
PICTURES: Lucas, One Crazy Summer, Say Anything, White Palace, The Grifters, Pay Dirt, The Player, Bob Roberts, Singles, Judgment Night, Twenty Bucks, Car 54 Where Are You?, Twogether, PCU, Miami Rhapsody, Dr. Jekyll and Ms. Hyde, Heat.
TELEVISION: Series: Carol and Company, The Larry Sanders Show, Pride and Joy. Pilots: Heads Will Roll, Ready or Not.

PLACE, MARY KAY
Actress, Writer. b. Tulsa, OK, Sept. 23, 1947. e. U. of Tulsa. Worked in production jobs and as Tim Conway's asst. for his TV show also as sect. for Norman Lear on Maude before starting to write for TV series (Mary Tyler Moore Show, Phyllis, Maude, M*A*S*H, etc.).
PICTURES: Bound For Glory (debut, 1976), New York New York, More American Graffiti, Starting Over, Private Benjamin, Modern Problems, Waltz Across Texas, The Big Chill, Smooth Talk, A New Life, Bright Angel, Captain Ron, Samantha, Teresa's Tattoo, Manny and Lo, Precious, Citizen Ruth.
TELEVISION: Series: Mary Hartman Mary Hartman (Emmy Award, 1977). Guest: All in the Family, Mary Tyler Moore Show, Fernwood 2-Night, Tonight Show, Saturday Night Live (host), thirtysomething. Movies: The Girl Who Spelled Freedom, Act of Love, For Love or Money, Out on the Edge, Just My Imagination, Telling Secrets, In the Line of Duty: The Pride of Vengeance. Specials: John Denver Special, Martin Mull's History of White People in America I & II, Portrait of a White Marriage, The Gift, Tales of the City, Leslie's Folly.

PLATT, OLIVER
Actor. b. 1962. Raised in Asia, Africa and Washington DC. e. Tufts Univ.
THEATER: Off-B'way: The Tempest, Moon Over Miami, Sparks in the Park, Urban Blight, Ubu, Elliot Loves.
PICTURES: Married to the Mob (debut, 1988), Working Girl, Crusoe, Flatliners, Postcards From the Edge, Beethoven, Diggstown, The Temp, Indecent Proposal, Benny & Joon, The Three Musketeers, Tall Tale, Funny Bones, Executive Decision, A Time to Kill.
TELEVISION: Movie: The Infiltrator.

PLESHETTE, SUZANNE
Actress. b. New York, NY, Jan. 31, 1937. e. H.S. for the Performing Arts, Finch Coll., Syracuse U. Broadway debut, Compulsion.
THEATER: The Cold Wind and the Warm, The Golden Fleecing, The Miracle Worker, Compulsion, Two for the Seesaw, Special Occasions.
PICTURES: The Geisha Boy (debut, 1958), Rome Adventure, 40 Pounds of Trouble, The Birds, Wall of Noise, A Distant Trumpet, Fate Is the Hunter, Youngblood Hawke, A Rage to Live, The Ugly Dachshund, Nevada Smith, Mister Buddwing, The Adventures of Bullwhip Griffin, Blackbeard's Ghost, The Power, If It's Tuesday This Must Be Belgium, Suppose They Gave a War and Nobody Came, Target Harry (How to Make It), Support Your Local Gunfighter, The Shaggy D.A., Hot Stuff, Oh God! Book II.
TELEVISION: Series: The Bob Newhart Show, Suzanne Pleshette Is Maggie Briggs, Bridges to Cross, Nightingales, The Boys Are Back. Movies: Wings of Fire, Along Came a Spider, Hunters Are for Killing, River of Gold, In Broad Daylight, Law and Order, Richie Brockelman: Missing 24 Hours, Kate Bliss and the Ticker Tape Kid, Flesh and Blood, For Love or Money, Fantasies, If Things Were Different, Help Wanted—Male, Dixie Changing Habits, Starmaker, One Cooks, The Other Doesn't, Legend of Valentino, Kojak The Belarus File, A Stranger Waits, Alone in the Neon Jungle, Leona Helmsley: The Queen of Mean, Battling for Baby, A Twist of the Knife.

PLESKOW, ERIC
Executive. b., Vienna, Austria, April 24, 1924. Served as film officer, U.S. War dept., 1946-48; entered industry in 1948 as asst. gen. mgr., Motion Picture Export Association, Germany; 1950-51, continental rep. for Sol Lesser Prods.; joined United

Artists in 1951 as Far East Sales Mgr.; named mgr., S. Africa, 1952; mgr., Germany, 1953-58; exec. asst. to continental mgr., 1958-59; asst. continental mgr., 1959-60; continental mgr., 1960-62; v.p. in charge of foreign distrib., 1962; exec. v.p. & CEO, Jan., 1973; pres. & CEO, Oct. , 1973. Resigned in 1978 to become pres. and CEO of Orion Pictures Co.; 1982, became pres. & CEO, Orion Pictures Corp; appointed chmn. of bd. 1991. Resigned 1992. Partner, Pleskow/Spikings Partnership, Beverly Hills, 1992-present. Prod., Beyond Rangoon.

PLIMPTON, MARTHA
Actress. b. New York, NY, Nov. 16, 1970. Daughter of actors Shelley Plimpton and Keith Carradine. Acting debut in film workshop of Elizabeth Swados's musical Runaways. At 11 gained recognition as model in Richard Avedon's commercials for Calvin Klein jeans. Also on stage in The Hagadah, Pericles, The Heidi Chronicles, Robbers, subUrbia, The Great Unwashed.
PICTURES: Rollover (debut 1981, in bit role), The River Rat, The Goonies, The Mosquito Coast, Shy People, Stars and Bars, Running on Empty, Another Woman, Parenthood, Stanley and Iris, Silence Like Glass, Samantha, Inside Monkey Zetterland, Josh and S.A.M., My Life's in Turnaround, Mrs. Parker and the Vicious Circle, The Beans of Egypt Maine, Last Summer in the Hamptons, Beautiful Girls, I Shot Andy Warhol, I'm Not Rappaport.
TELEVISION: Movies: Daybreak, Chantilly Lace.

PLOWRIGHT, JOAN
C.B.E. Actress. b. Scunthrope, Brigg, Lincolnshire, Eng., Oct. 28, 1929. m. late actor, Lord Laurence Olivier. Trained for stage at Laban Art of Movement Studio, 1949-50; Old Vic Theatre Sch. 1950-52; with Michel St. Denis, Glen Byam Shaw and George Devine. London stage debut The Duenna, 1954. Broadway debut The Entertainer, 1958. Won Tony Award in 1961 for A Taste of Honey. With Bristol Old Vic Rep., Royal Court, National Theatre in numerous classics and contemporary plays.
RECENT THEATER: Saturday Sunday Monday, The Seagull, The Bed Before Yesterday, Filumena, Enjoy, Who's Afraid of Virginia Woolf?, Cavell, The Cherry Orchard, The Way of the World, Mrs. Warren's Profession, Time and the Conways, If We Are Women.
PICTURES: Moby Dick (debut, 1956), Time Without Pity, The Entertainer, Uncle Vanya, Three Sisters, Equus, Brimstone and Treacle, Britannia Hospital, Wagner (tv in U.S.), Revolution, The Dressmaker, Drowning By Numbers, I Love You to Death, Avalon, Enchanted April (Acad. Award nom.), Last Action Hero, Dennis the Menace, A Pin for the Butterfly, The Summer House, Widow's Peak, A Pyromaniac's Love Story, Hotel Sorrento, The Scarlett Letter, Jane Eyre, Mr. Wrong, Surviving Picasso, 101 Dalmatians.
TELEVISION: Odd Man In, Secret Agent, School for Scandal, The Diary of Anne Frank, Twelfth Night, Merchant of Venice, Daphne Laureola, Saturday Sunday Monday, The Divider, Conquest of the South Pole, A Nightingale Sang, House of Bernarda Alba, Stalin, On Promised Land, A Place for Annie, The Return of the Native. Pilot: Driving Miss Daisy (U.S.).

PLUMMER, AMANDA
Actress. b. New York, NY, March 23, 1957. e. Middlebury Coll. Daughter of actors Christopher Plummer and Tammy Grimes.
THEATER: Artichokes, A Month in the Country, A Taste of Honey (Theatre World Award), Agnes of God (Tony Award, 1982), The Glass Menagerie, A Lie of the Mind, Life Under Water, You Never Can Tell, Pygmalion, The Milk Train Doesn't Stop Here Anymore.
PICTURES: Cattle Annie and Little Britches (debut, 1981), The World According to Garp, Daniel, The Hotel New Hampshire, Static, The Courtship, Made in Heaven, Prisoners of Inertia, Joe Versus the Volcano, California Casanova, The Fisher King, Freejack, So I Married an Axe Murderer, Needful Things, Nostradamus, Pulp Fiction, Pax, Butterfly Kiss, The Propechy, Drunks, Freeway.
TELEVISION: Movies: The Dollmaker, The Unforgivable Secret, Riders to the Sea, Miss Rose White (Emmy Award, 1992), The Sands of Time, Last Light, Whose Child Is This? The War for Baby Jessica. Guest: Outer Limits (Emmy Award, 1996). Specials: Gryphon, The Courtship. Pilot: True Blue.

PLUMMER, CHRISTOPHER
Actor. b. Toronto, Canada, Dec. 13, 1927. Daughter is actress Amanda Plummer. Stage & radio career began in Canada (French & English).
THEATER: toured U.S. in The Constant Wife; B'way debut in The Starcross Story, 1953. B'way: The Dark is Light Enough, Home Is the Hero, J.B., The Lark, The Good Doctor, Cyrano (Tony Award, 1974), Othello (Tony nom.), Macbeth, No Man's Land. London: leading actor, Royal Shakespeare Theatre, 1961-62; Becket (Evening Standard Award), Natl. Theatre, 1969-70. Canada: leading actor, Stratford Festival (6 yrs.).

PICTURES: Stage Struck (debut, 1958), Wind Across the Everglades, The Fall of the Roman Empire, The Sound of Music, Inside Daisy Clover, The Night of the Generals, Triple Cross, Oedipus the King, The High Commissioner (Nobody Runs Forever), The Battle of Britain, The Royal Hunt of the Sun, Lock Up Your Daughters, Waterloo, The Pyx, The Return of the Pink Panther, Conduct Unbecoming, The Man Who Would Be King, The Spiral Staircase, Aces High, Assassination at Sarajevo (The Day That Shook the World), The Assignment, The Disappearance, International Velvet, Murder by Decree, The Silent Partner, Hanover Street, Starcrash, RIEL, Highpoint, Somewhere in Time, Eyewitness, Being Different (narrator), The Amateur, Dreamscape, Ordeal by Innocence, Lily in Love, The Boy in Blue, The Boss' Wife, An American Tail (voice), Dragnet, Souvenir, Light Years (voice), Nosferatu in Venice, I Love N.Y., Shadow Dancing, Mindfield, Kingsgate, Red-Blooded American Girl, Where the Heart Is, Don't Tell Mom the Babysitter's Dead, Star Trek VI: The Undiscovered Country, Firehead, Rock-a-Doodle (voice), Money, Liar's Edge, Impolite, Malcolm X, Wolf, Dolores Claiborne, Twelve Monkeys.
TELEVISION: Series: Counterstrike. Movies/Specials: Hamlet at Elsinore (Emmy nom.), Don Juan in Hell (BBC), Little Moon of Alban, Prince and the Pauper, Jesus of Nazareth, Steiglitz and O'Keefe, Oedipus Rex, Omnibus, After the Fall, The Moneychangers (Emmy Award, 1977), Desperate Voyage, The Shadow Box, When the Circus Came to Town, Dial M for Murder, Little Gloria—Happy at Last, The Scarlet and the Black, The Thorn Birds, The Velveteen Rabbit, Crossings, A Hazard of Hearts, A Ghost in Monte Carlo, Young Catherine, Danielle Steel's Secrets, Stranger in the Mirror, Liar's Edge, Madeline (narrator; Emmy Award, 1994), Harrison Bergeron.

PODELL, ALBERT N.
Attorney. b. New York, NY, Feb. 25, 1937. e. Cornell U., U. of Chicago, NYU Sch. of Law. Non-fiction editor, Playboy magazine, 1959-60; dir. of photog. and m.p. reviewer Argosy magazine, 1961-64; Author: Who Needs a Road? (Bobbs-Merrill, 1967), mng. edit., The Players Magazine, 1965-66; account exec. on 20th Century-Fox at Diener, Hauser, Greenthal, 1966-68; national advertising mgr., Cinema Center Films, 1969; account supervisor and creative dir. on Columbia Pictures at Charles Schlaifer, 1969-72; creator & dir. of Annual Motion Picture Advertising Awards sponsored by Cinema Lodge, B'nai B'rith. Attorney specializing in litigation, matrimonial law, rep. of performers (1976-present). Pres., 1990-95 Jean Cocteau Rep. Th. Chmn. of Trustees; 1980-90, Assn. for Development of Dramatic Arts. Pres., Far Above Films. Dir. & writer: A Class Above, The Class on the Cutting Edge, Lift the Chorus.

PODHORZER, MUNIO
Executive. b. Berlin, Germany, Sept. 18, 1911. e. Jahn-Realgymnasium, U. of Berlin Medical Sch. U.S. Army, 1943-47; pres. United Film Enterprises, Inc.; formerly secy.-treas. 86th St. Casino Theatre, N.Y.; former v.p. Atlantic Pictures Corp.; former pres. Casino Films, Inc.; former pres. Film Development Corp.; former rep. Export-Union of the German Film Ind.; former U.S. rep. Franco-London Film, Paris; former pres., Venus Productions Corp.; former U.S. rep. Atlas Int'l Film GmbH, Munich; former U.S. rep. Bavaria Atelier Gesellschaft U.S.; past rep. Israfilm Ltd., Tel-Aviv; past rep. Tigon British Film Prod., London; past rep. Elias Querejeta, P.C., Madrid; past rep. Equiluz Films, Madrid; past rep. Airport Cine, Haiti; Les Films Du Capricorne, Paris; Schongerfilm, German; Profilmes, Spain; Ligno, Spain; Films D'Alma, France; Intra Films, Italy. Member: Variety Club, Cinema Lodge, B'nai B'rith, Past Board of Governors IFIDA; past pres. CID Agents Assoc. Former gen. foreign sales mgr., theatrical division of National Telefilm Associates; past rep. Barcino Films, S.A. Spain; Eagle Films Ltd., UK; Les Films Jacques Leitienne, France; Nero Film Classics, USA; Schongerfilm, Germany; Profilmes, S.A. Spain; VIP Ltd., Israel. Presently representing Atlas Film & AV, Germany; KFM Films, Inc. U.S.A.; Compagnie France Film, Canada; Cia. Iberoamerican de TV, S.A. Spain; Israel. Co-chmn., entertainment div., United Jewish Appeal, Federation of Jewish Philanthropies, 1981-83.

PODHORZER, NATHAN
Executive. b. Brody, Poland, Nov. 27, 1919. e. City Coll. of New York, Rutgers U., U. of Southern California. U.S. Army, 1942-46; documentary film prod., Israel, 1946-57; CEO, United Film Enterprises, Inc.

POE, STEPHEN
Executive. Began career as lawyer with Rutan & Tucker; 1976, joined 20th Century-Fox as prod. counsel; later v.p., business affairs. Turned to producing in 1982, first in association with Frank Mancuso Jr. Productions. 1986, acted as consultant and indep. prod. counsel for United Artists Pictures. 1987, joined CBS/Fox Video as sr. v.p. of acquisitions and programming.

POITIER, SIDNEY
Actor, Director. b. Miami, FL, Feb. 20, 1927. Raised in the
Bahamas. m. actress Joanna Shimkus. e. Miami, FL. On stage
with Amer. Negro Theatre in Days of Our Youth. Appeared in
Army Signal Corps documentary From Whence Cometh My
Help. Formed First Artists Prod. Co. Ltd., 1969, with Paul
Newman and Barbra Streisand. Autobiography: This Life
(1980). Recipient 1992 AFI Life Achievement Award.
THEATER: Strivers Road, You Can't Take It With You, Anna
Lucasta (B'way debut, 1948), Lysistrata, Freight, A Raisin in the
Sun.
PICTURES: No Way Out (debut 1950), Cry the Beloved Country,
Red Ball Express, Go Man Go, Blackboard Jungle, Goodbye My
Lady, Edge of the City, Something of Value, Band of Angels, Mark
of the Hawk, The Defiant Ones, Virgin Island, Porgy and Bess, All
the Young Men, A Raisin in the Sun, Paris Blues, Pressure Point,
Lilies of the Field (Academy Award, 1963), The Long Ships, The
Greatest Story Ever Told, The Bedford Incident, The Slender
Thread, A Patch of Blue, Duel at Diablo, To Sir With Love, In the
Heat of the Night, Guess Who's Coming to Dinner, For Love of Ivy,
The Lost Man, They Call Me Mister Tibbs, Brother John, The
Organization, Buck and the Preacher (also dir.), A Warm
December (also dir.), Uptown Saturday Night (also dir.), The Wilby
Conspiracy, Let's Do It Again (also dir.), A Piece of the Action
(also dir.), Stir Crazy (dir. only), Hanky Panky (dir. only), Fast
Forward (dir. only), Shoot To Kill, Little Nikita, Ghost Dad (dir.
only), Sneakers.
TELEVISION: Movies: Separate But Equal, Children of the
Dust, To Sir With Love II. Guest: Philco TV Playhouse, ABC
Stage '67.

POLANSKI, ROMAN
Director, Writer. b. Paris, France, Aug. 18, 1933. m. actress
Emmanuelle Seigner. Lived in Poland from age of three. Early
career, art school in Cracow; Polish Natl. Film Acad., Lodz 1954-
59. Radio Actor 1945-47; on stage 1947-53; asst. dir., Kamera film
prod. group 1959-61. Co-founder Cadre Films, 1964. Wrote, dir.
and acted in short films: Two Men and a Wardrobe, When Angels
Fall, The Fat and the Lean, Mammals. On stage as actor in
Amadeus (and dir., Warsaw & Paris), Metamorphosis (Paris,
1988). Autobiography: Roman (1984).
PICTURES: Dir./Writer: Knife in the Water (feature debut,
1962), Repulsion, Cul-de-Sac, The Fearless Vampire Killers
or: Pardon Me But Your Teeth Are in My Neck (also actor),
Rosemary's Baby, A Day at the Beach (s.p. only), Weekend of
a Champion (prod. only), Macbeth (also prod.), What? (a.k.a.
Che?; also actor), Chinatown (dir. & actor only), The Tenant
(also actor), Tess, Pirates, Frantic, Bitter Moon, Death and the
Maiden. Actor only: The Generation, The Magic Christian,
Andy Warhol's Dracula, Back in the U.S.S.R., A Pure
Formality, Grosse Fatigue.

POLEDOURIS, BASIL
Composer. b. Kansas City, MO, Aug. 21, 1945. e. Long Beach
St. Univ., USC. While at USC composed music for short films
by John Milius and Randal Kleiser. Became first American
Film Institute intern.
PICTURES: Big Wednesday, Tintorera, Dolphin, The Blue
Lagoon, Conan the Barbarian, Summer Lovers, House of God,
Conan the Destroyer, Making the Grade, Red Dawn, Protocol,
Flesh and Blood, Iron Eagle, Robocop, No Man's Land, Cherry
2000, Spellbinder, Split Decisions, Farewell to the King, Wired,
The Hunt for Red October, Quigley Down Under, Flight of the
Intruder, White Fang, Return to the Blue Lagoon, Harley Davidson
& the Marlboro Man, Wind, Hot Shots Part Deux, Free Willy,
Robocop 3, On Deadly Ground, Serial Mom, Lassie, The Jungle
Book, Under Siege 2: Dark Territory, Free Willy 2: The Adventure
Home, It's My Party, Celtic Pride.
TELEVISION: Mini-Series: Amerika, Lonesome Dove (Emmy
Award, 1989). Movies: Congratulations It's a Boy, A Whale for
the Killing, Fire on the Mountain, Amazons, Single Women
Single Bars, Prison for Children, Misfits of Science, Island
Sons, Intrigue, L.A. Takedown, Nasty Boys, Ned Blessing,
Lone Justice, Danielle Steel's Zoya.

POLL, MARTIN H.
Producer. b. New York, NY, Nov. 24, 1926. e. Wharton Sch., U.
of Pennsylvania. Pres. Gold Medal Studios (1956-61).
PICTURES: A Face in the Crowd, Middle of the Night, The
Goddess, Butterfield 8, Love Is a Ball, Sylvia, The Lion in
Winter, The Appointment, The Magic Garden of Stanley
Sweetheart, The Man Who Loved Cat Dancing, Night Watch,
Love and Death (exec. prod.); The Man Who Would Be King,
The Sailor Who Fell From Grace with the Sea, Somebody
Killed Her Husband, Nighthawks, Gimme an F, Haunted
Summer, My Heroes Have Always Been Cowboys.
TELEVISION: Series: Car 54 Where Are You? Movies: Arthur
the King, Stunt Seven. Mini-Series: A Town Called Alice, The
Dain Curse, Diana: Her True Story.

POLLACK, SYDNEY
Director, Producer. b. South Bend, IN, July 1, 1934. m. Claire
Griswold. e. Neighborhood Playhouse. Assistant to Sanford

Meisner at Neighborhood Playhouse. Appeared as actor on
B'way in A Stone for Danny Fisher, The Dark is Light Enough.
Dir. debut in 1960. Dir. play at UCLA, P.S. 193. Prepared the
American version of The Leopard.
TELEVISION: As actor. Playhouse 90 (several segments),
Shotgun Slade. Dir.: Ben Casey (15 episodes), The Game
(Bob Hope-Chrysler Theatre; Emmy Award), Two is the
Number. Co-prod. (movie): A Private Matter. Exec. prod.
(series): Fallen Angels.
PICTURES: Director. The Slender Thread (debut, 1965), This
Property Is Condemned, The Scalphunters, Castle Keep,
They Shoot Horses Don't They? (also prod.), Jeremiah
Johnson, The Way We Were (also prod.), The Yakuza (also
prod.), Three Days of the Condor, Bobby Deerfield (also
prod.), The Electric Horseman, Asence of Malice (also prod.),
Tootsie (also prod., actor), Out of Africa (also prod.; Academy
Awards for Best Picture & Director, 1985), Havana (also
prod.), The Firm, Sabrina (also prod.). Producer: Songwriter,
Bright Lights Big City, The Fabulous Baker Boys, Presumed
Innocent. Exec. Producer: Honeysuckle Rose, White Palace,
King Ralph, Dead Again, Leaving Normal, Searching for
Bobby Fischer, Flesh and Bone, Sense and Sensibility. Actor:
War Hunt, The Player, Death Becomes Her, Husbands and
Wives.

POLLAK, KEVIN
Actor. b. San Francisco, CA, Oct. 30, 1958. Started doing
stand-up comedy in the San Francisco Bay area, then contin-
ued in L.A. clubs.
PICTURES: Million Dollar Mystery (debut, 1987), Willow,
Avalon, L.A. Story, Another You, Ricochet, A Few Good Men,
The Opposite Sex and How to Live With Them, Indian
Summer, Wayne's World 2, Grumpy Old Men, Reality Bites,
Clean Slate, Miami Rhapsody, The Usual Suspects, Canadian
Bacon, Casino, Nowhere Man, Chameleon, House Arrest,
Grumpier Old Men, That Thing You Do!.
TELEVISION: Series: Coming of Age, Morton and Hayes.
Specials: One Night Stand (also prod., writer), Stop With the
Kicking (also prod., writer), The Seven Deadly Sins (also
writer, dir.).

POLLAN, TRACY
Actress. b. New York, NY, June 22, 1960. m. actor Michael J.
Fox.
THEATER: B'way: Jake's Women.
PICTURES: Promised Land, Bright Lights Big City, A Stranger
Among Us.
TELEVISION: Series: Family Ties. Movies: For Lovers Only,
Sessions, Trackdown: Finding the Goodbar Killer, A Good
Sport, Dying to Love You, Children of the Dark.

POLLARD, MICHAEL J.
Actor. r.n. Michael J. Pollack. b. Passaic, NJ, May 30, 1939. e.
Montclair Academy, Actors Studio.
THEATER: Comes a Day, Loss of Roses, Enter Laughing, Bye
Bye Birdie, Leda Had a Little Swan, Our Town.
PICTURES: Adventures of a Young Man (debut, 1962), The
Stripper, Summer Magic, The Russians Are Coming, The
Russians Are Coming, The Wild Angels, Caprice, Enter
Laughing, Bonnie and Clyde (Acad. Award nom.), Jigsaw,
Hannibal Brooks, Little Fauss and Big Halsy, The Legend of
Frenchie King (Petroleum Girls), Dirty Little Billy, Between the
Lines, Melvin and Howard, Heated Vengeance, America, The
Patriot, The American Way (Riders of the Storm), Roxanne,
Scrooged, Fast Food, Season of Fear, Next of Kin, Tango and
Cash, Night Visitor, Sleepaway Camp 3, Why Me?, Dick Tracy, I
Come in Peace, Joey Takes a Cab, The Art of Dying, Another You,
Enid Is Sleeping (Over Her Dead Body), Split Second, The Arrival,
Heartstopper, Arizona Dream, Motorama, Skeeter.
TELEVISION: Series: Leo and Liz in Beverly Hills. Guest:
Alfred Hitchcock Presents (Anniversary Gift), Going My Way,
Route 66, Here's Lucy, Mr. Novak, Honey West, I Spy, Lost in
Space, Dobie Gillis, Get Christie Love, Star Trek, Simon &
Simon, The Fall Guy, Gunsmoke, Guns of Paradise, The
Young Riders, Nasty Boys. Movies: The Smugglers, Stuck
With Each Other, Working Trash.

POLLEXFEN, JACK
Producer, Director, Writer. b. San Diego, CA, June 10, 1918. e.
Los Angeles City Coll. Newspaperman, magazine writer, play-
wright: prod. for RKO, United Artists, Columbia, Allied Artists.
PICTURES: Son of Sinbad, At Swords Point, Secret of
Convict Lake, Desert Hawk, Lady in the Iron Mask, Dragon's
Gold, Problem Girls, Captive Women, Captain Kidd and the
Slave Girl, Neanderthal Man, Captain John Smith and
Pocahontas, Return to Treasure Island, Sword of Venus,
Daughter of Dr. Jekyll, Monstrosity, Son of Dr. Jekyll, Mr. Big,
Man from Planet X, Indestructible Man, Port Sinister, Treasure
of Monte Cristo, Bulldog Drummond, Grey City.

POLLOCK, DALE
Producer. b. Cleveland, OH, May 18, 1950. e. Brandeis U.,
B.A. anthropology, San Jose State, M.S., mass communication.

Began journalistic career in Santa Cruz in early '70s, serving as reporter and film critic for Daily Variety, 1977-80. Joined Los Angeles Times as film writer, winning paper's Award for Sustained Excellence in 1984. 1985 left to take post with The Geffen Film Co. as executive in chg. creative development. Joined A&M Films as v.p. in chg. prod., 1986. Became pres., 1989. Author: Skywalking (about George Lucas). PICTURES: The Beast (exec. prod.), The Mighty Quinn (exec. prod.). Producer: House of Cards, Worth Winning, Blaze, Crooked Hearts, A Midnight Clear, A Home of Our Own, S.F.W., Mrs. Winterbourne.

POLLOCK, THOMAS
Executive. b. 1943. In 1971, after 3 years as business mgr. for American Film Institute's film marketing wing, formed law firm Pollock Bloom, and Dekom with young filmmakers such as George Lucas and Matthew Robbins as clients. Served as chmn. Filmex, 1973-81. 1986, named chmn. MCA's Universal motion picture group., now vice chmn., MCA, Inc.

POLONSKY, ABRAHAM
Writer, Director. b. New York, NY, Dec. 5, 1910. e. CCNY, B.A.; Columbia Law Sch. Taught at City Coll. 1932 until war. Blacklisted from 1951-66.
AUTHOR: The Enemy Sea, The Discoverers, The World Above, The Season of Fear, Zenia's Way.
PICTURES: Writer: Golden Earrings, Body and Soul (also story), Force of Evil (also dir.), I Can Get It for You Wholesale, Odds Against Tomorrow, Madigan, Tell Them Willie Boy is Here (also dir.), Romance of a Horse Thief, Avalanche Express, Monsignor.

PONTECORVO, GILLO
Director. b. Pisa, Italy, Nov. 19, 1919. Younger brother of Prof. Bruno Pontecorvo, Harwell scientist who defected in 1950. Former photo-journalist. Worked as asst. dir., directed documentary shorts before feature debut in 1957.
PICTURES: Die Windrose (Giovanna episode), La Grande Strada Azzurra (The Long Blue Road; also co-s.p.), Kapo (also co-s.p.), The Battle of Algiers (also story; Acad. Award noms. as dir. & writer), Queimada! (Burn; also co-story), Ogro (The Tunnel; also co-s.p.).

PONTI, CARLO
Producer. b. Milan, Italy, Dec. 11, 1913. m. actress Sophia Loren. e. U. of Milan, 1934. Prod. first picture in Milan, Little Old World; prod. Lux Film Rome; prod. first of a series of famous Toto pictures, Toto Housefunting.
PICTURES: A Dog's Life, The Knight Has Arrived, Musolino, The Outlaw, Romanticism, Sensuality, The White Slave, Europe 1951, Toto in Color, The Three Corsairs, The Gold of Naples, Ulysses, The Woman of the River, An American of Rome, Attila, La Strada, War and Peace, The Last Lover, The Black Orchid, That Kind of Woman, A Breath of Scandal, Heller in Pink Tights, Two Women, Boccaccio '70, Bluebeard, The Condemned of Altona, Marriage Italian Style, Casanova '70, Operation Crossbow, Doctor Zhivago, Lady L, Blow Up, More Than a Miracle, The Girl and the General, Sunflower, The Best House in London, Zabriskie Point, The Priest's Wife, Lady Liberty, White Sister, What?, Andy Warhol's Frankenstein, The Passenger, The Cassandra Crossing, A Special Day, Saturday Sunday Monday.
TELEVISION: Mario Puzo's The Fortunate Pilgrim (exec. prod.).

POOLE, FRANK S.
Executive. b. London, England, Oct. 11, 1913. e. Dulwich Coll., 1925-31. Ent. m.p. ind. 1931. Early career with Pathe Pictures, Twickenham Film Distributors, until joining 20th Century Fox as London branch office supervisor 1939. War service 1940-46. Rejoined Fox 1946-53; appt. Leed Branch mgr. 1954-59; supv. 1959-61; asst. sls. mgr., 1961 until joined Rank Film Distrib. as asst. sls. mgr. 1962; appt. sls. mgr. 1965, and to board as dir. of sls.; appt. gen. mgr. 1968; jnt. mng. dir. 1969; appt. mng. dir. 1970; appt. dir. Rank Overseas Film Dist. Ltd., 1972; appt. co-chmn Fox-Rank Distributors Ltd., 1972; appt. vice-chmn. Rank Film Distributors Ltd. 1977; 1975, elected to Committee of Cinema & TV Veterans; 1978, retired from Rank Organisation. Appt. chmn., Appeal Tribunal for the Film Industry, chmn., Grebelands Mgt. Committee & to exec. council of CTBF; 1979; assoc. Geoff Reeve & Associates. 1980, chmn. & mng. dir., Omandry Intl. Ltd. 1982 appointed film consultant U.K./Europe to the Alberta Government. Pres., Cinema & TV Veterans 1990-92.

POP, IGGY
Musician, Actor. b. MI, April 21, 1947. r.n. James Osterberg. Has recorded 16 albums with band the Stooges and solo.
PICTURES: Actor: Cry Baby, Hardware (voice only), Dead Man, The Crow: City of Angels. Songs: Rock 'N' Rule.

POPE OSBORNE, MARY
Executive. Pres., Author's Guild, Inc.

PORTER, DON
Actor. b. Miami, OK, Sept. 24, 1912. e. Oregon Inst. of Tech. Wide theatre work; then m.p. roles. U.S. Army, 3 yrs.

THEATER: The Best Man, Any Wednesday, Generation, Plaza Suite, The Price, How To Succeed in Business Without Really Trying, Harvey.
PICTURES: The Racket, The Savage, 711 Ocean Drive, Because You're Mine, Our Miss Brooks, Bachelor in Paradise, Youngblood Hawke, The Candidate, 40 Carats, Mame, White Line Fever.
TELEVISION: Series: Private Secretary, Ann Sothern Show, Gidget. Guest: Bionic Woman, Hawaii Five-O, Switch, Love Boat, Three's Company, The President's Mistress, The Murder That Wouldn't Die, The Last Song, Dallas, Old Money.

POST, TED
Producer, Director. b. Brooklyn, NY, March 31, 1918. Dir. many stage plays; dir. CBS-TV Repertoire Thea.; Producer-dir., NBC-TV Coney Island of the Mind. Directed Everyone Can Make Music.
TELEVISION: Series: Studio One, Ford Theatre, Playhouse of Stars, Alcoa Theatre, Gunsmoke, Rawhide, Twilight Zone, Wagon Train, Combat, Peyton Place, Alcoa, Defenders, Route 66, Baretta, Columbo. Movies: Night Slaves, Dr. Cook's Garden, Yuma, Five Desperate Women, Do Not Fold Spindle or Mutilate, The Bravos, Sandcastles, Girls in the Office, Diary of a Hitchhiker, Stagecoach. Pilots: Cagney & Lacey, Beyond Westworld, Steve Canyon, Perry Mason. Mini-series: Rich Man, Poor Man II (episode 3).
PICTURES: The Peacemaker (debut, 1956), The Legend of Tom Dooley, Hang 'em High, Beneath The Planet of the Apes, The Baby, The Harrad Experiment, Magnum Force, Whiffs, Good Guys Wear Black, Go Tell the Spartans, Nightkill, The Human Shield.

POSTER, STEVEN
Cinematographer. A.S.C. b. Chicago, IL, Mar. 1, 1944. e. L.A. Art Center Coll. Started as commercial cinematographer before moving into feature films. 2nd unit work includes: Close Encounters of the Third Kind, Blade Runner. 2nd v.p., American Society of Cinematographers.
PICTURES: Blood Beach, Dead and Buried, Spring Break, Strange Brew, Testament, The New Kids, The Heavenly Kid, Blue City, The Boy Who Could Fly, Aloha Summer, Someone to Watch Over Me, Big Top Pee-wee, Next of Kin, Opportunity Knocks, Rocky V, Life Stinks, The Cemetery Club.
TELEVISION: Movies: The Grass is Always Greener, The Cradle Will Fall, I'll Take Manhattan, Class of '65, Courage, Shanghai La Plaza, Roswell.

POSTLETHWAITE, PETE
Actor. b. Lancashire, England. Feb. 16, 1946.
THEATER: RSC: Every Man and His Humour, A Midsummer Night's Dream, MacBeth, King Lear, The Taming of the Shrew.
PICTURES: The Duellists, A Private Function, Distant Voices Still Lives, The Dressmaker, To Kill a Priest, Hamlet, Alien[3], The Last of the Mohicans, Waterland, In the Name of the Father (Acad. Award nom.), Anchoress, The Usual Suspects, James and the Giant Peach (voice), Dragonheart, When Saturday Comes.
TELEVISION: The Muscle Market, A Child From the South, Treasure Island (theatrical in U.K.), Martin Chuzzlewit.

POSTON, TOM
Actor. b. Columbus, OH, Oct. 17, 1927. Made B'way debut 1947 in Cyrano de Bergerac.
PICTURES: City That Never Sleeps (debut, 1953), Zotz!, The Old Dark House, Soldier in the Rain, Cold Turkey, The Happy Hooker, Rabbit Test, Up the Academy, Carbon Copy.
TELEVISION: Movies: The Girl The Gold Watch and Everything, Save the Dog!, A Quiet Little Neighborhood A Perfect Little Murder. Series: The Steve Allen Show (Emmy Award, 1959), Pantomime Quiz, To Tell the Truth, On the Rocks, We've Got Each Other, Mork and Mindy, Newhart, Grace Under Fire. Guest: Goodyear Playhouse, Phil Silvers Show, Password, The Defenders, Fame, The Love Boat, Dream On, etc.

POTTS, ANNIE
Actress. b. Nashville, TN, Oct. 28, 1952. e. Stephens Coll., MO, BFA. Amateur stage debut at 12 in Heidi. Then in summer stock; on road in Charley's Aunt, 1976. Serves on auxilliary bd. of MADD (Mothers Against Drunk Driving). Ambassador for Women for the Amer. Arthritis Fdn.
PICTURES: Corvette Summer (debut, 1978), King of the Gypsies, Heartaches, Ghostbusters, Crimes of Passion, Pretty in Pink, Jumpin' Jack Flash, Pass the Ammo, Who's Harry Crumb?, Ghostbusters II, Texasville, Breaking the Rules, Toy Story (voice).
TELEVISION: Movies: Black Market Baby, Flatbed Annie and Sweetie Pie, Cowboy, It Came Upon the Midnight Clear, Why Me?, Her Deadly Rival. Series: Goodtime Girls, Designing Women, Love & War, Dangerous Minds. Guest: Remington Steele, Magnum P.I., Twilight Zone.

POUND, LESLIE
Executive. b. London, Eng., Nov. 3, 1926. Entered industry in 1943 as reporter on British trade paper, The Cinema. Now,

Screen International. Following military service in India and Singapore returned to work for that publication until 1952 when joined Paramount pub. office in London on the The Greatest Show on Earth. Named dir. of adv./pub. in U.K. for Paramount. 1958, retained Paramount position when Cinema Int'l Corp. was formed. 1977, joined Lew Grade in ITC Entertainment as worldwide dir. of pub./adv. 1977, int'l pub. chief for Embassy Pictures in Los Angeles. 1982, named Paramount Pictures v.p., int'l mktg. for motion picture div., N.Y. 1983. Relocated to L.A. with mktg. div. as sr. v.p. Returned to London, 1993 as sr. v.p. International markets for Paramount Pictures.

POWELL, JANE
Actress, Singer. r.n. Suzanne Burce. b. Portland, OR, Apr. 1, 1929. m. pub. relations exec. Dick Moore. Had own radio program over KOIN, Portland; singer on nat'l networks; Star of Tomorrow, 1948. Autobiography: The Girl Next Door ... and How She Grew (1988). Video: Jane Powell's Fight Back With Fitness.
THEATER: Irene (B'way, 1974). After-Play (off-B'way, 1996). Toured nationally with South Pacific, Peter Pan, My Fair Lady, The Unsinkable Molly Brown, I Do I Do, Same Time Next Year, Chapter Two.
PICTURES: Song of the Open Road (debut, 1944), Delightfully Dangerous, Holiday in Mexico, Three Daring Daughters, A Date With Judy, Luxury Liner, Nancy Goes to Rio, Two Weeks With Love, Royal Wedding, Rich Young and Pretty, Small Town Girl, Three Sailors and a Girl, Seven Brides for Seven Brothers, Athena, Deep in My Heart, Hit the Deck, The Girl Most Likely, The Female Animal, Enchanted Island.
TELEVISION: Specials: Ruggles of Red Gap, Give My Regards to Broadway, Meet Me in St. Louis, Jane Powell Show. Series: Alcoa Theatre, Loving, As the World Turns. Guest: The Love Boat, Growing Pains, Murder She Wrote, others. Movies: The Letters, Mayday at 40,000 Feet. Host: The Movie Musicals (PBS).

POWELL, ROBERT
Actor. b. Salford, England, June 1, 1944. e. Manchester U. Stage work includes Tovarich.
PICTURES: Robbery (debut, 1967), Far From the Madding Crowd, Joanna, The Italian Job, Walk a Crooked Path, Secrets, Running Scared, Asylum, The Asphyx (Horror of Death), Mahler, Tommy, Oltre il Bene e il Male (Beyond Good and Evil), Cocktails for Three, The Thirty-Nine Steps, The Dilessi Affair, Harlequin (Dark Forces), Jane Austin in Manhattan, The Survivor, Imperative (Venice Film Fest. Award), The Jigsaw Man, What Waits Below, D'Annunio and I Down There in the Jungle, Romeo-Juliet (voice), The Sign of Command, Once on Chunuk Bar.
TELEVISION: Series: Doomwatch, Hannay, The First Circle. Mini-Series: Jesus of Nazareth. Movies/Specials: Shelley, Jude the Obscure, Mrs. Warren's Profession, Mr. Rolls & Mr. Royce, Looking for Clancy, The Four Feathers, The Hunchback of Notre Dame, Pygmalion, Frankenstein, Shaka Zulu, Merlin of the Crystal Cave, The Golden Years.

POWERS, MALA
Actress. r.n. Mary Ellen Powers. b. San Francisco, CA, Dec. 20, 1931. p. George and Dell Powers, latter, dramatic coach. e. Studied acting with Michael Chekhov. e. UCLA. Pasadena Playhouse in For Keeps, 1946, followed by Distant Isle; Actor's Lab, Hollywood; did considerable radio, theatre and tv work. Writer, narrator Children's Story, and Dial A Story (1979). Author: Follow the Star (1980), Follow the Year (1984). Teaches Michael Chekhov technique of acting.
PICTURES: Tough as They Come (debut, 1942), Outrage, Edge of Doom, Cyrano de Bergerac, Rose of Cimarron, City Beneath the Sea, City That Never Sleeps, Geraldine, The Yellow Mountain, Rage at Dawn, Bengazi, Tammy and the Bachelor, The Storm Rider, Death in Small Doses, The Colossus of New York, Sierra Baron, The Unknown Terror, Man on the Prowl, Flight of the Lost Balloon, Rogue's Gallery, Doomsday, Daddy's Gone-A-Hunting, Six Tickets to Hell.
TELEVISION: Series: Hazel, The Man and the City. Guest: Daniel Boone.

POWERS, C. F. (MIKE) JR.
Executive. b. San Francisco, CA, March 6, 1923. e. Park Coll., MO, Columbia U., N.Y., graduated U. of Oregon. Entered film business with P.R.C. in Portland, OR, 1947. Became Eagle Lion branch mgr. in Portland, 1950, and then United Artists. Moved to Seattle, WA as branch mgr. of 20th Century Fox, 1960. Was then western division mgr. for 20th Century Fox until 1967, then western division mgr. for Cinerama until 1973. Became exec. v.p., head film buyer for Robert L. Lippert Theatres, Transcontinental Theatres and Affiliated Theatres until 1978. Western div. mgr. Orion Pictures, 1982-4. Mike Powers Ent. (a buying and booking combine and indept. film distrib.). 1984-86 Western district mgr. Embassy Pictures. Became western division mgr. for Filmways Pictures. Past president of Catholic Entertainment Guild of Northern Calif.; past pres. of Variety Club Tent 32, San Francisco. Currently m.p. consultant to U.S. Federal Govt.

POWERS, STEFANIE
Actress. r.n. Stefania Federkiewicz. b. Hollywood, CA, Nov. 2, 1942. After graduation from Hollywood High signed by Columbia Studios.
PICTURES: Tammy Tell Me True (debut, 1962), Experiment in Terror, The Young Sinner, The Interns, If a Man Answers, McClintock!, Palm Springs Weekend, The New Interns, Love Has Many Faces, Die Die My Darling (Fanatic), Stagecoach, Warning Shot, The Boatniks, Crescendo, The Magnificent 7 Ride, Herbie Rides Again, Gone With the West, It Seemed Like a Good Idea at the Time, Escape to Athena, Invisible Stranger (The Astral Factor).
TELEVISION: Series: The Girl From U.N.C.L.E., Feather and Father Gang, Hart to Hart. Mini-series: Washington: Behind Closed Doors, Hollywood Wives. Movies: Five Desperate Women, Paper Man, Sweet Sweet Rachel, Hardcase, No Place to Run, Shootout in a One-Dog Town, Skyway to Death, Sky Heist, Return to Earth, Family Secrets (also prod.), A Death in Canaan, Nowhere to Run, Mistral's Daughter, Deceptions, At Mother's Request, Beryl Markham: A Shadow on the Sun (also co-prod.), She Was Marked for Murder, Love and Betrayal, When Will I Be Loved?, The Burden of Proof, Survive the Night, Hart to Hart Returns (also co-prod.), Hart to Hart: Home is Where the Hart Is, Hart to Hart: Crimes of the Hart (also co-prod.), Hart to Hart: Old Friends Never Die, The Good Ride, Good King Wenceslas, Hart to Hart: Secrets of the Hart, Hart to Hart: Til Death Do Us Hart.

PRENTISS, PAULA
Actress. r.n. Paula Ragusa. b. San Antonio, TX, March 4, 1939. m. actor-director Richard Benjamin. e. Northwestern U., Bachelor degree in drama, 1959. On stage in As You Like It, Arf!, The Norman Conquests, Love Letters, Secrets, Demons (Amer. Rep. Theatre, Cambridge, MA).
PICTURES: Where the Boys Are (debut, 1960), The Honeymoon Machine, Bachelor in Paradise, The Horizontal Lieutenant, Follow the Boys, Man's Favorite Sport?, The World of Henry Orient, Looking for Love, In Harm's Way, What's New Pussycat?, Catch-22, Move, Born to Win, Last of the Red Hot Lovers, Crazy Joe, The Parallax View, The Stepford Wives, The Black Marble, Saturday the 14th, Buddy Buddy, Mrs. Winterbourne.
TELEVISION: Series: He & She, Burke's Law. Movies: The Couple Takes a Wife, Having Babies II, No Room to Run (Australian), Friendships Secrets and Lies, Top of the Hill, Packin' It In, M.A.D.D.: Mothers Against Drunk Drivers.

PRESLE, MICHELINE
Actress. r.n. Micheline Chassagne. b. Paris, France, Aug. 22, 1922. e. Raymond Rouleau Dram. Sch. m.p. debut in Je Chante; on stage in Colinette. Am. Stram Gram, Spectacle des Allies; to U.S., 1945; Flea in Her Ear, Magic Circus, Who's Afraid of Virginia Woolf? (tour), Gigi, Nuit de Valognes, Boomerang, Adriana Mont, etc.
PICTURES: Jeunes Filles en Detresse, L'Histoire de Rire, La Nuit Fantastique, Felicie Nanteuil, Seul Amour, Faibalas, Boule de Suif, Jeux Sont Faix, Diable au Corps, Under My Skin, Some Kind of News, An American Guerilla in the Philippines, Adventures of Captain Fabian, Sins of Pompeii, House of Ricordi, Archipelago of Love, Thieves After Dark, Le Chien, At the Top of the Stairs, Le Jour de Rois. Fine Weather, But Storms Due Towards Evening, Confidences, Alouette, Je te plumerai, I Want to Go Home.
TELEVISION: The Blood of Others.

PRESLEY, PRISCILLA
Actress. b. Brooklyn, NY, May 24, 1945. Raised in Connecticut. e. Wiesbaden, West Germany where met and married Elvis Presley (1967-73). Studied acting with Milton Katselas, dance at Steven Peck Theatre Art School and karate at Chuck Norris Karate School. Formed a business, Bis and Beau, marketing exclusive dress designs. Became TV spokesperson for beauty products.
PICTURES: The Naked Gun: From the Files of Police Squad! (debut, 1988), The Adventures of Ford Fairlane, The Naked Gun 2 1/2: The Smell of Fear, Naked Gun 33 1/3: The Final Insult.
TELEVISION: Series: Those Amazing Animals (host, 1980-81), Dallas. Movies: Love is Forever, Elvis and Me (prod. only).

PRESSMAN, EDWARD R.
Producer. b. New York, NY. e. Fieldston Sch.; grad., Stanford U.; studied at London Sch. of Economics. Began career with film short, Girl, in collaboration with director Paul Williams in London. They formed Pressman-Williams Enterprises.
PICTURES: Prod.: Out of It, The Revolutionary, Dealing: or the Berkeley to Boston Forty Brick, Lost Bag Blues, Sisters, Badlands, Phantom of the Paradise, Despair (exec. prod.), Paradise Alley (exec. prod.), Old Boyfriends, Heartbeat (exec. prod.), The Hand, Conan the Barbarian (exec. prod.), Das Boot (exec. prod.), The Pirates of Penzance (exec. prod.), Crimewave (exec. prod.), Plenty (exec. prod.), Half Moon Street (exec. prod.), True Stories (exec. prod.), Good Morning

Babylon (exec. prod.), Masters of the Universe, Walker (exec. prod.), Wall Street, Cherry 2000 (exec. prod.), Paris By Night (exec. prod.), Talk Radio, Martians Go Home (exec. prod.), Blue Steel, Reversal of Fortune, To Sleep with Anger (exec. prod.), Waiting for the Light (exec. prod.), Homicide, Year of the Gun, Iron Maze (co-exec. prod.), Storyville, Bad Lieutenant, Hoffa, Dream Lover (exec. prod.), The Crow, Street Fighter, Judge Dredd (exec. prod.), City Hall, The Island of Dr. Moreau.

PRESSMAN, LAWRENCE
Actor. b. Cynthiana, KY, July 10, 1939. e. Kentucky Northwestern U. On B'way in Man in the Glass Booth, Play It Again, Sam, etc.
PICTURES: The Man in the Glass Booth, The Crazy World of Julius Vrooder, Hellstrom Chronicle, Shaft, Making It, Walk Proud, Nine to Five, Some Kind of Hero, The Hanoi Hilton, The Waterdance.
TELEVISION: Series: Mulligan's Stew, Doogie Howser M.D., Law and Order, N.Y.P.D. Blue. Movies: Cannon, The Snoop Sisters, The Marcus-Nelson Murder, Winter Kill, The First 36 Hours of Dr. Durant, Rich Man, Poor Man, Man from Atlantis, The Trial of Lee Harvey Oswald, The Gathering, Like Mom, Like Me, Blind Ambition, Little Girl Lost, Breaking Point, White Hot: The Mysterious Murder of Thelma Todd.

PRESSMAN, MICHAEL
Director, Producer. b. New York, NY, July 1, 1950. e. California Inst. of Arts. Comes from show business family; was actor in college.
PICTURES: Director: The Great Texas Dynamite Chase, The Bad News Bears Breaking Training, Boulevard Nights, Those Lips Those Eyes (also prod.), Some Kind of Hero, Doctor Detroit, Teenage Mutant Ninja Turtles II: The Secret of the Ooze, To Gillian On Her 37th Birthday.
TELEVISION: Movies: Like Mom, Like Me, The Imposter, The Christmas Gift, Final Jeopardy, Private Sessions, Haunted by Her Past, To Heal a Nation, Shootdown, The Revenge of Al Capone, Incident at Dark River, Man Against the Mob (also co-prod.), Joshua's Heart, Quicksand: No Escape.

PRESTON, FRANCES W.
Executive. Joined Broadcast Music Inc. in 1958. Pres. & CEO BMI, 1986-present.

PRESTON, KELLY
Actress. b. Honolulu, HI, Oct. 13, 1962. e. UCLA, USC. m. actor John Travolta.
PICTURES: Metalstorm: The Destruction of Jared-Syn (debut, 1983), Christine, Mischief, Secret Admirer, SpaceCamp, 52 Pick-Up, Amazon Women on the Moon, A Tiger's Tale, Love at Stake, Spellbinder, Twins, The Experts, Run, Only You, Love Is a Gun, Cheyenne Warrior, Waiting to Exhale, From Dusk Till Dawn, Citizen Ruth, Jerry Maguire.
TELEVISION: Series: For Love and Honor, Capitol. Movies: The Perfect Bride, The American Clock, Mrs. Munck. Guest: Quincy, Blue Thunder, Riptide.

PREVIN, ANDRE
Composer, Conductor. b. Berlin, Germany, Apr. 6, 1929. Composed and conducted over 50 m.p. scores. Music director, Pittsburgh Symphony Orchestra, & conductor emeritus of London Symphony Orchestra. Music Director, Royal Philharmonic Orch., 1985-89. Guest conductor of most major symphony orchestras in U.S. and Europe. Music dir., Pittsburgh Symphony 1972-81. Conductor, London Symphony, 1968-78. Conductor Emeritus London Symphony, 1992-present. Received Knighthood of British Empire in 1996.
PICTURES: Three Little Words, Cause for Alarm, It's Always Fair Weather, Bad Day at Black Rock, Invitation to the Dance, Catered Affair, Designing Woman, Silk Stockings, Gigi (Academy Award, 1958), Porgy and Bess (Academy Award, 1959), The Subterraneans, Bells Are Ringing, Pepe, Elmer Gantry, The Four Horsemen of the Apocalypse, One Two Three, Two for the Seesaw, Long Day's Journey Into Night, Irma LaDouce (Academy Award, 1963), My Fair Lady (Academy Award, 1964), Goodbye Charlie, Inside Daisy Clover, The Fortune Cookie, Thoroughly Modern Millie, Valley of the Dolls, Paint Your Wagon, The Music Lovers, Jesus Christ Superstar, Rollerball, One Trick Pony.

PRICE, FRANK
Executive. b. Decatur, IL, May 17, 1930. e. Michigan State U. following naval service. Joined CBS in N.Y. in 1951 as story editor and writer. Moved to Hollywood in 1953, serving as story editor first at Columbia and then NBC (Matinee Theatre). In 1958 joined Universal as an assoc. prod. and writer. In 1961 named exec. prod. of The Virginian TV series. Appt. exec. prod. of Ironside; later did It Takes a Thief and several World Premiere movies. 1964 named v.p. of Universal TV; 1971, sr. v.p.; 1974, pres. Also v.p., MCA, Inc. 1978 left to join Columbia as pres. of new company unit, Columbia Pictures Productions. In 1979 named chmn. & CEO of Columbia Pictures. In 1983

joined Universal: named chmn., motion picture group, pres. of Universal Pictures, and v.p. of MCA. In 1987 formed Price Entertainment Inc. as chmn. & CEO to produce movies and create TV shows for dist. through Columbia Pictures Entertainment. 1990, integrated Price Entertainment Inc., into Columbia and was named chairman. Resigned, 1991. Prod. tv movie The Tuskegee Airmen.

PRICE, RICHARD
Writer. b. Bronx, NY, Oct. 12, 1949. e. Cornell Univ., Columbia Univ.
AUTHOR: The Wanderers, Bloodbrothers, Ladies' Man, The Breaks, Clockers.
PICTURES: Cameos: The Wanderers, The Paper. Writer: The Color of Money (Acad. Award nom.; also cameo), Streets of Gold, New York Stories (Life Lessons; also cameo), Sea of Love, Night and the City (also cameo), Mad Dog and Glory (also exec. prod., cameo), Ethan Frome (exec. prod. only), Mad Dog and Glory (also exec. prod., cameo), Kiss of Death (also cameo), Clockers.

PRIES, RALPH W.
Executive. b. Atlanta, GA, August 31, 1919. Graduated Georgia Inst. of Technology. V.P., MEDIQ, Inc.; pres. MEDIQ/PRN Life Support Services, Inc.; past pres., Odgen Food Service Corp.; exec. comm. and bd., Firstrust Savings Bank and chmn. of audit comm.; past chmn. of St. Christopher's Hospital for Children, Moss Rehabilitation Hospital, United Hospital Corp., Philadelphia Heart Instit. Former intl pres., Variety Clubs Intl.; previously on bd. of Hahnemann U. and Hosp., chmn. of bd. Likoff Cardiovascular Instit., pres. Main Line Reform Temple, Wynnewood, PA.

PRIESTLEY, JASON
Actor. b. Vancouver, Canada, Aug. 28, 1969. First screen appearance as baby in 1969 film That Cold Day in the Park, in which his mother had bit part. Child actor in many Canadian TV commercials. First major U.S. acting job in 1986 TV movie Nobody's Child. Moved to L.A. in 1987. Theatre includes The Addict, The Breakfast Club.
TELEVISION: Series: Sister Kate, Beverly Hills 90210 (also co-prod.). Movies: Stacie (Canada), Nobody's Child, Teen Angel & Teen Angel Returns (Disney TV). Guest: Danger Bay (Canada), MacGyver, 21 Jump Street, Adventures of Beans Baxter, Quantum Leap.
PICTURES: The Boy Who Could Fly, Nowhere to Run, Watchers, Calendar Girl, Tombstone, Coldblooded.

PRIMUS, BARRY
Actor. b. New York, NY, Feb. 16, 1938. e. Bennington Coll., City Coll. of NY.
THEATER: Henry and the Duke, The Nervous Set, Henry IV, Parts I and II, Creating the World, Teibele and the Demon, Lincoln Center Rep. (The Changling, After the Fall).
PICTURES: The Brotherhood, Puzzle of a Downfall Child, Been Down So Long It Looks Like Up to Me, Von Richtofen and Brown, Boxcar Bertha, The Gravy Train, New York New York, Avalanche, Autopsy, The Rose, Heartland, Night Games, Absence of Malice, The River, Down and Out in Beverly Hills, Jake Speed, SpaceCamp, Talking Walls, The Stranger, Big Business, Cannibal Women in the Avocado Jungle of Death, Torn Apart, Guilty by Suspicion, Mistress (dir., s.p. only), Night and the City.
TELEVISION: Series: Cagney and Lacey. Mini-Series: Washington Behind Closed Doors. Movies: Big Rose, Roger & Harry: The Mitera Target, Portrait of a Showgirl, Paper Dolls, I Want to Live, Heart of Steel, Brotherly Love, The Women of Spring Break. Guest: Law and Order.

PRINCE
Singer, Actor. r.n. Prince Rogers Nelson. b. Minneapolis, MN, June 7, 1958. Rock star and recording artist.
PICTURES: Purple Rain (also wrote songs; Acad. Award for best orig. song score, 1984). Under the Cherry Moon (also dir., s.p., songs), Sign O' the Times (also dir., songs), Batman (songs only), Graffiti Bridge (also dir., s.p., songs).

PRINCE, HAROLD
Director. b. New York, NY, Jan. 30, 1928. e. U. of Pennsylvania. Worked as stage mgr. for George Abbott on three shows, later co-produced, produced and/or directed the following: The Pajama Game (Tony Award), Damn Yankees (Tony Award), New Girl In Town, West Side Story, A Swim in the Sea, Fiorello! (Tony Award, Pulitzer Prize), Tenderloin, A Call on Kurpin, Take Her She's Mine, A Funny Thing Happened on the Way to the Forum (Tony Award), She Loves Me, The Matchmaker (revival), Fiddler on the Roof, Poor Bitos, Baker Street, Flora, The Red Menace, Superman, Cabaret (Tony Award), Zorba, Company, Follies, The Great God Brown, The Visit, Love for Love (the last three all revivals), A Little Night Music (Tony Award), Candide (Tony Award), Pacific Overtures, Side by Side by Sondheim, Some of My Best Friends, On the Twentieth Century, Evita (also London), Sweeney Todd (Tony Award 1979; also London),

Merrily We Roll Along, A Doll's Life, Play Memory, End of the World, Diamonds, Grind, Roza, Cabaret (revival), Phantom of the Opera (Tony Award, 1988; also London), Grandchild of Kings (dir. & adapt.), Kiss of the Spider Woman (Tony Award, 1993), Show Boat (Tony Award, 1995); and also directed the operas Ashmadei, Silverlake, Sweeney Todd, Candide and Don Giovanni for N.Y. City Opera, Girl of Golden West for Chicago Lyric Opera Co. and San Francisco Opera; Willie Stark for Houston Grand Opera; Madama Butterfly for Chicago Lyric Opera and Turandot for Vienna State Opera and Faust for Metropolitan Opera.
AUTHOR: Contradictions: Notes on Twenty-Six Years in the Theatre (1974).
PICTURES: Co-producer: The Pajama Game, Damn Yankees. Director: Something for Everyone, A Little Night Music.

PRINCE, WILLIAM
Actor. b. Nichols, NY, Jan. 26, 1913. With Maurice Evans, actor, 2 yrs., radio announcer. On N.Y. stage, Ah, Wilderness; m.p. debut in 1943. Many TV credits.
THEATER: Guest in the House, Across the Board on Tomorrow Morning, The Eve of St. Mark, John Loves Mary, As You Like It, I Am a Camera, Forward the Heart, Affair of Honor, Third Best Sport, The Highest Tree, Venus at Large, Strange Interlude, The Ballad of the Sad Cafe, Mercy Street.
PICTURES: Destination Tokyo, Cinderella Jones, The Very Thought of You, Roughly Speaking, Objective Burma, Pillow to Post, Carnegie Hall, Dead Reckoning, Lust for Gold, Cyrano de Bergerac, Secret of Treasure Mountain, Macabre, Sacco and Vanzetti, The Heartbreak Kid, The Stepford Wives, Family Plot, Network, Rollercoaster, The Gauntlet, The Cat from Outer Space, The Promise, Bronco Billy, Love & Money, Kiss Me Goodbye, Movers and Shakers, Fever Pitch, Spies Like Us, Nuts, Vice Versa, Spontaneous Combustion, The Taking of Beverly Hills, The Paper.
TELEVISION: Series: The Mask, Justice, The American Girls. Mini-Series: Aspen, George Washington, War and Remembrance. Movies: Key West, Night Games, Murder 1 Dancer O, Found Money, The Portrait.

PRINCIPAL, VICTORIA
Actress. b. Fukuoka, Japan, Jan 3, 1950. Father was in U.S. air force. Went to New York to become model; studied acting privately with Jean Scott at Royal Acad. of Dramatic Art in London before moving to Hollywood. Worked as talent agent in the mid-1970's.
PICTURES: The Life and Times of Judge Roy Bean (debut, 1972), The Naked Ape, Earthquake, I Will I Will... for Now, Vigilante Force.
TELEVISION: Series: Dallas. Guest: Fantasy Island (pilot), Love Story, Love American Style, Greatest Heroes of the Bible. Movies: The Night They Stole Miss Beautiful, The Pleasure Palace, Last Hours Before Morning, Not Just Another Affair, Mistress, Naked Lie (also exec. prod.), Blind Witness (also exec. prod.), Sparks: The Price of Passion (also exec. prod.), Don't Touch My Daughter (also exec. prod.), The Burden of Proof, Seduction: Three Tales From the Inner Sanctum (also co-exec. prod.), Midnight's Child (exec. prod. only), Beyond Obsession, River of Rage: The Taking of Maggie Keene, Dancing in the Dark, The Abduction.

PRINE, ANDREW
Actor. b. Jennings, FL, Feb. 14, 1936. e. U. of Miami. m. actress Heather Lowe. Mem. Actors Studio. On stage in Look Homeward, Angel, A Distant Bell, Mrs. Patterson, Borak. Ahmanson Theatre, LA: Long Day's Journey into Night, The Caine Mutiny. South Coast Rep.: Goodbye Freddy.
PICTURES: The Miracle Worker, Advance to the Rear, Texas Across the River, Bandolero!, The Devil's Brigade, This Savage Land, Generation, Chisum, Riding Tall, Simon: King of the Witches, Barn of the Naked Dead (Terror Circus), One Little Indian, The Centerfold Girls, Grizzly, The Town That Dreaded Sundown, Winds of Autumn, High Flying Lowe, The Evil, Amityville II: The Possession, Playing with Fire, Eliminators, Chill Factor, The Big One, Life on the Edge, Double Exposure, Gettysburg, Inferno, Dark Dancer, Gathering Evidence, Without Evidence.
TELEVISION: Series: The Wide Country, The Road West, W.E.B., Dallas, Room for Two, Weird Science. Movies: And the Children Shall Lead, Roughing It, Callie & Son, The Deputies, Another Part of the Forest, Night Slaves, Split Second to an Epitaph, Along Came a Spider, Night Slaves, Wonder Woman, Law of the Land, Tail Gunner Joe, Last of the Mohicans, A Small Killing, Mind over Murder, M-Station Hawaii, Christmas Miracle in Caulfield, Young Abe Lincoln, U.S.A., Donner Pass: The Road to Survival, Mission of the Shark, Scattered Dreams: The Kathryn Messenger Story, The Avenging Angel. Mini-Series: V: The Final Battle.

PROCHNOW, JURGEN
Actor. b. Berlin, Germany, 1941. Studied acting at the Folkswangschule. In provincial theatre before making tv debut on the series Harbour at the Rhine River, 1970.

PICTURES: Zoff (debut, 1971), Zartlchket der Wolfe, The Lost Honor of Katharina Blum, The Consequence, Einer von uns Beiden, Das Boot (The Boat; Berlin Film Fest. Award), The Keep, Dune, Der Bulle und das Madchen, Killing Cars, Terminus, Beverly Hills Cop II, Devil's Paradise, The Seventh Sign, A Dry White Season, The Fourth War, The Man Inside, Twin Peaks: Fire Walk With Me, Body of Evidence, In the Mouth of Madness, Judge Dredd.
TELEVISION: Forbidden, Murder by Reason of Insanity, Danielle Steel's Jewels, The Lucona Affair, Love Is Forever, Robin Hood, The Fire Next Time.

PROSKY, ROBERT
Actor. b. Philadelphia, PA, Dec. 13, 1930. Won TV amateur talent search contest, leading to scholarship with American Theatre Wing. 23-year veteran with Washington's Arena stage. Taught acting and appeared in over 150 plays
THEATER: Death of a Salesman, Galileo, The Caucasian Chalk Circle, You Can't Take it With You, Our Town, The Price (Helen Hayes Award). B'way: Moonchildren, A View from the Bridge, Pale Horse Pale Rider, Arms and the Man, Glengarry Glen Ross (Tony nom.), A Walk in the Woods (Tony nom.). Off-B'way: Camping With Henry and Tom. Tours incl.: Our Town, Inherit the Wind, A Walk in the Woods (Soviet Union), After the Fall (Hong Kong).
PICTURES: Thief, Hanky Panky, Monsignor, The Lords of Discipline, Christine, The Keep, The Natural, Outrageous Fortune, Big Shots, Broadcast News, The Great Outdoors, Things Change, Loose Cannons, Gremlins II: The New Batch, Funny About Love, Green Card, Life in the Food Chain (Age Isn't Everything), Far and Away, Hoffa, Last Action Hero, Rudy, Mrs. Doubtfire, Miracle on 34th Street, The Scarlet Letter, Dead Man Walking.
TELEVISION: Series: Hill Street Blues, Lifestories (host). Movies: World War III, The Ordeal of Bill Carny, Lou Grant, The Adams Chronicles, Old Dogs, Into Thin Air, The Murder of Mary Phagan, Home Fires Burning, From the Dead of Night, Heist, Dangerous Pursuit, Johnny Ryan, Against the Mob, A Green Journey, The Love She Sought, Double Edge, Life on the High Wire, Teamster Boss: The Jackie Presser Story. Guest: Coach.

PROVINE, DOROTHY
Actress. b. Deadwood, SD, Jan. 20, 1937. e. U. of Washington. Retired from films in 1969.
PICTURES: The Bonnie Parker Story (debut, 1958), Live Fast Die Young, Riot in Juvenile Prison, The 30 Foot Bride of Candy Rock, Wall of Noise, It's a Mad Mad Mad Mad World, Good Neighbor Sam, The Great Race, That Darn Cat, One Spy Too Many, Kiss the Girls and Make Them Die, Who's Minding the Mint?, Never a Dull Moment.
TELEVISION: Series: The Alaskans, The Roaring 20's. Movie: The Sound of Anger.

PRYCE, JONATHAN
Actor. b. North Wales, June 1, 1947. e. Royal Acad. of Dramatic Art. Actor and artistic dir. of Liverpool Everyman Theatre Co.
THEATER: London: Comedians, Taming of the Shrew, Antony and Cleopatra, Tally's Folly, Hamlet (Olivier Award), Macbeth, The Seagull, Uncle Vanya, Miss Saigon (Olivier & Variety Club Awards), Oliver! NY: Comedians (Tony & Theatre World Awards, 1977), Accidental Death of an Anarchist, Miss Saigon (Tony & Drama Desk Awards, 1991).
PICTURES: Voyage of the Damned (debut, 1976), Breaking Glass, Loophole, The Ploughman's Lunch, Something Wicked This Way Comes, The Doctor and the Devils, Brazil, Haunted Honeymoon, Jumpin' Jack Flash, Man on Fire, Consuming Passions, The Adventures of Baron Munchausen, The Rachel Papers, Freddie as F.R.O. 7 (voice), Glengarry Glen Ross, The Age of Innocence, A Business Affair, Great Moments in Aviation, A Troll in Central Park (voice), Deadly Advice, Shopping, Carrington (Cannes Film Fest. Award, 1995), Evita.
TELEVISION: Comedians, Playthings, Partisans, For Tea on Sunday, Timon of Athens, Praying Mantis, Murder Is Easy, Daft as a Brush, Martin Luther Heretic, The Caretaker, Glad Day, The Man From the Pru, Roger Doesn't Live Here Anymore, Selling Hitler, Whose Line is It Anyway?, Mr. Wroes Virgins, Barbarians at the Gate, Thicker Than Water.

PRYOR, RICHARD
Actor. b. Peoria, IL, Dec. 1, 1940. At age 7 played drums with professionals. Made NY debut as standup comic in 1963, leading to appearances on TV (Johnny Carson, Merv Griffin, Ed Sullivan). Co-wrote TV scripts for Lily Tomlin (Emmy Award, 1974) and Flip Wilson. Won Grammy Awards for albums That Nigger's Crazy, Is It Something I Said?, Bicentennial Nigger. Autobiography: Pryor Convictions and Other Life Sentences (1995).
PICTURES: The Busy Body (debut, 1967), The Green Berets, Wild in the Streets, The Phynx, You've Got to Walk It Like You Talk It Or You'll Lose That Beat, Dynamite Chicken, Lady Sings the Blues, Hit!, Wattstax, The Mack, Some Call It

Loving, Blazing Saddles (co-s.p. only), Uptown Saturday Night, Adios Amigo, The Bingo Long Traveling All-Stars and Motor Kings, Car Wash, Silver Streak, Greased Lightning, Which Way Is Up?, Blue Collar, The Wiz, California Suite, Richard Pryor—Live in Concert (also prod., s.p.), The Muppet Movie, Richard Pryor Is Back Live in Concert (also s.p.), Wholly Moses, In God We Trust, Stir Crazy, Bustin' Loose (also co-prod., co-s.p.), Richard Pryor Live on the Sunset Strip (also prod., s.p.), Some Kind of Hero, The Toy, Superman III, Richard Pryor Here and Now (also dir., s.p.), Brewster's Millions, Jo Jo Dancer Your Life Is Calling (also dir., prod., s.p.), Critical Condition, Moving, See No Evil Hear No Evil, Harlem Nights, Another You.
TELEVISION: Series: The Richard Pryor Show (1977), Pryor's Place. Guest: Wild Wild West, The Partridge Family, The Mod Squad, Chicago Hope. Movies: The Young Lawyers, Carter's Army.

PRYOR, THOMAS M.
Journalist. b. New York, NY, May 22, 1912. Joined NY Times, 1929; m.p. dept. 1931 as reporter, asst. film critic; Hollywood bureau chief, corres., NY Times, 1951-59; editor, Daily Variety, 1959-88; 1988-90. Consultant to Variety & Daily Variety. 1990, retired.

PTAK, JOHN
Agent. b. San Diego, CA. Graduated UCLA film department, 1968. Theatre mgr. and booker for Walter Reade Organization and Laemmle Theatres, 1966-1969. Admin. exec. at American Film Institute's Center for Advanced Studies, 1969\-1971. International Famous Agency (ICM), 1971-1975, William Morris Agency, 1976-91, Creative Artists Agency, 1991-. Represents motion picture and television talent.

PULLMAN, BILL
Actor. b. Hornell, NY, Dec. 17, 1953. e. SUNY at Oneonta, Univ. of Mass. at Amherst.
THEATER: NY: Dramathon '84, Curse of the Starving Class. LA: All My Sons, Barabbas, Nanawatai, Demon Wine, Control Freaks.
PICTURES: Ruthless People (debut, 1986), Spaceballs, The Serpent and the Rainbow, Rocket Gibraltar, The Accidental Tourist, Cold Feet, Brain Dead, Sibling Rivalry, Bright Angel, Going Under, Newsies, A League of Their Own, Singles, Nervous Ticks, Sommersby, Sleepless in Seattle, Malice, Mr. Jones, The Favor, Wyatt Earp, While You Were Sleeping, Casper, Mr. Wrong, Independence Day.
TELEVISION: Movies: Home Fires Burning, Crazy in Love, The Last Seduction (also released theatrically).

PURCELL, PATRICK B.
Executive. b. Dublin, Ireland, Mar. 16, 1943. e. Fordham U., M.B.A., 1973. In pub. & acct., England, 1969-69; acct., Associated Hosp. Service, N.Y., 1968-70; joined Paramount Pictures, 1970; v.p., fin., 1980-83; exec. v.p. chief fin. & admin. officer 1983-.

PURDOM, EDMUND
Actor. b. Welwyn Garden City, England, Dec. 19, 1924. e. St. Ignatius Coll., London. Played leads, character roles for Northampton Rep. Co., Kettering Rep., two seasons at Stratford-On-Avon; London stage in Way Things Go, Malade Imaginaire, Romeo and Juliet, played in Caesar and Cleopatra, Antony and Cleopatra, London and N.Y.
PICTURES: Titanic (debut, 1953), Julius Caesar, The Student Prince, The Egyptian, Athena, The Prodigal, The King's Thief, Strange Intruder, Trapped in Tangiers, The Cossacks, Herod the Great, The Loves of Salambo, Malaga (Moment of Danger), The Last of the Vikings, Nights of Rasputin, Lafayette, White Slave Ship, Queen of the Nile, Suleiman the Conqueror, The Comedy Man, The Beauty Jungle (Contest Girl), Last Ride to Santa Cruz, The Charge of the 7th, The Yellow Rolls Royce, Man With the Golden Mask, The Black Corsair, The Satanists, Evil Fingers, Frankenstein's Castle of Freaks, Night Child, Cursed Medallion, Mister Scarface, The New Godfathers, L'altra Donna, Ator the Fighting Eagle, Pieces, Don't Open Till Christmas (also dir.), After the Fall of New York, The Assissi Underground, Killer vs. Killer, Appointment in Trieste.
TELEVISION: Mini-Series: The Winds of War, The Scarlet and the Black. Movie: Sophia Loren: Her Own Story.

PURL, LINDA
Actress. b. Greenwich, CT, Sept. 2, 1955. Moved to Japan at age 2. Appeared in Japanese theatre, TV. e. Toho Geino Academy. Back to US in 1971. On stage in The Baby Dance (New Haven, NYC), Hedda Gabler, The Real Thing (Mark Taper), The Merchant of Venice (Old Globe Theatre), Romeo & Juliet, Doll's House.
PICTURES: Jory, Crazy Mama, W.C. Fields & Me, Leo and Loree, The High Country, Visiting Hours, Viper, Natural Causes.
TELEVISION: Series: The Secret Storm, Beacon Hill, Happy Days, Matlock, Under Cover, Young Pioneers, Robin's Hoods.

Movies: Eleanor and Franklin, Little Ladies of the Night, Testimony of Two Men, A Last Cry for Help, Women at West Point, Like Normal People, The Flame is Love, The Night the City Screamed, The Adventures of Nellie Bly, The Last Days of Pompeii, The Manions of America, Addicted to His Love, Spies Lies and Naked Thighs, Before the Storm, Spy Games, Danielle Steel's Secrets, Body Language, Accidental Meeting, Incident at Deception Ridge.

PUTTNAM, SIR DAVID
CBE: Hon. LL.D Bristol 1983; Hon. D. Litt, Leicester 1986. Hon. Litt. D., Leeds 1992. Knighted, 1995. Producer. b. London, England 1941. e. Michenden Sch. In advertising before joining VPS/Goodtimes Prod. Co. Dir. of Britain's National Film Finance Corp. (1980-85); Also served on Cinema Films Council and governing council of the British Acad. of Film & Television Arts. Officier dans L'Ordre des Arts et des Lettres, 1986. Chmn. National Film and Television Sch., 1988. Past Pres., Council for the Protection of Rural England; Fellow, Royal Soc. of Arts; Fellow, Royal Geographical Soc., Hon. Fellow, The Chartered Society of Designers. appt. Chmn. & CEO, Columbia Pictures. Resigned 1987. Received Eastman 2nd Century Award, 1988. 1988 formed a joint venture for his Enigma Productions Ltd. with Warner Bros., Fujisankei Comm. Gp. of Japan, British Satellite Broadcasting & Country Nat West to prod. 4 films. Appt. chmn. ITEL intl. TV dist. agency, 1989. Dir., Anglia Television Group and Survival Anglia. Dir., Chrysalis Group, PLC. V.P., BAFTA. Member, U.K. Arts Lottery Board. Founding pres., Atelier du Cinema Europeen. Member, European Commission's 'Think Tank' for audio-visual policy.
PICTURES: Melody, The Pied Piper, That'll Be The Day, Stardust, Mahler, Bugsy Malone, The Duellists, Midnight Express, Foxes, Chariots of Fire (Academy Award for Best Picture, 1981), Local Hero, Cal, The Killing Fields, The Mission, Defence of the Realm, Memphis Belle, Meeting Venus, Being Human, War of the Buttons, Le Confessional. Co-produced documentaries: Swastika, James Dean—The First American Teenager, Double-Headed Eagle, Brother Can You Spare a Dime?
TELEVISION: P'Tang Yang Kipperbang, Experience Preferred, Secrets, Those Glory Glory Days, Sharma and Beyond, Winter Flight, Josephine Baker, Without Warning: The James Brady Story, A Dangerous Man: Lawrence After Arabia, The Burning Season.

Q

QUAID, DENNIS
Actor. b. Houston, TX Apr. 9, 1954. Brother is actor Randy Quaid. m. actress Meg Ryan. e. U. of Houston. Appeared in Houston stage productions before leaving for Hollywood. On N.Y. stage with his brother in True West, 1984. Performer with rock band The Electrics; wrote songs for films The Night the Lights Went Out in Georgia, Tough Enough, The Big Easy. Formed Summers/Quaid Productions with producer Cathleen Summers, 1989.
PICTURES: Crazy Mama (debut, 1975), I Never Promised You a Rose Garden, September 30, 1955, Our Winning Season, Seniors, G.O.R.P., Breaking Away, The Long Riders, All Night Long, Caveman, The Night the Lights Went Out in Georgia, Tough Enough, Jaws 3-D, The Right Stuff, Dreamscape, Enemy Mine, The Big Easy, Innerspace, Suspect, D.O.A., Everybody's All-American, Great Balls of Fire, Postcards From the Edge, Come See the Paradise, Wilder Napalm, Undercover Blues, Flesh & Bone, Wyatt Earp, Hideaway (co-prod. only), Something to Talk About, Dragonheart.
TELEVISION: Movies: Are You in the House Alone?, Amateur Night at the Dixie Bar and Grill, Bill, Johnny Belinda, Bill: On His Own.

QUAID, RANDY
Actor. b. Houston, TX, Oct. 1, 1950. Brother is actor Dennis Quaid. Discovered by Peter Bogdanovich while still jr. at Drama Dept. at U. of Houston and cast in his Targets and The Last Picture Show, 1971. Off-B'way debut: True West (1983).
PICTURES: Targets (debut, 1968), The Last Picture Show, What's Up Doc?, Paper Moon, Lolly-Madonna XXX, The Last Detail (Acad. Award nom.), The Apprenticeship of Duddy Kravitz, Breakout, The Missouri Breaks, Bound for Glory, The Choirboys, Midnight Express, Three Warriors, Foxes, The Long Riders, Heartbeeps, National Lampoon's Vacation, The Wild Life, The Slugger's Wife, Fool for Love, The Wraith, Sweet Country, No Man's Land, Moving, Caddyshack II, Parents, Bloodhounds of Broadway, Out Cold, National Lampoon's Christmas Vacation, Martians Go Home!, Days of Thunder, Quick Change, Cold Dog Soup, Texasville, Freaked, The Paper, Major League 2, Bye Bye Love, The Last Dance, Independence Day, Kingpin.
TELEVISION: Movies: Getting Away From It All, The Great Niagara, The Last Ride of the Dalton Gang, To Race the Wind, Guyana Tragedy: The Story of Jim Jones, Of Mice and Men,

Inside the Third Reich, Cowboy, A Streetcar Named Desire, LBJ: The Early Years, Dead Solid Perfect, Evil in Clear River, Frankenstein, Roommates, Next Door, Ed McBain's 87th Precinct. *Series:* Saturday Night Live (1985-86), Davis Rules. *Special:* Dear America (reader).

QUIGLEY, MARTIN, JR.
Educator, Writer. b. Chicago, IL, Nov. 24, 1917. e. A.B. Georgetown U.; M.A., Ed. D., Columbia U. M.P. Herald, Oct. 1939; spcl. ed. rep., M.P. Herald & M.P. Daily, May, 1941; wartime work in U.S., England, Eire & Italy, Dec. 1941-Oct. 1945; assoc. ed., Quigley Pub., Oct. 1945; ed. M.P. Herald, July, 1949; also edit. dir. of all Quigley Pub., 1956; pres. Quigley Pub. Co., 1964; author, Great Gaels, 1944, Roman Notes, 1946, Magic Shadows—The Story of the Origin of Motion Pictures, 1948; Gov't. Relations of Five Universities, 1975; Peace Without Hiroshima, 1991; First Century of Film, 1995. Editor, New Screen Techniques, 1953; m.p. tech. section, Encyclopaedia Brit., 1956; co-author, Catholic Action in Practice, 1963. Co-author: Films in America, 1929-69, 1970. Pres., QWS, Inc., educational consultants, 1975-81. Adjunct professor of higher education, Baruch College Univ. City of New York 1977-1989; Teachers College, Columbia Univ., 1990. Village of Larchmont, N.Y., trustee, 1977-79; mayor, 1980-84. Board of trustees, American Bible Society, 1984-; Religious Education Ass'n., treasurer, 1975-80 & chairperson, 1981-84; Laymen's Nat'l. Bible Association, chmn. education committee, 1983-93; Will Rogers Institute, chmn. Health education committee, 1980-; Director, William J. Donovan Memorial Foundation, 1995-.

QUIGLEY, WILLIAM J.
Executive. b. New York, NY, July 6, 1951. e. Wesleyan U., B.A., 1973; Columbia U., M.S., 1983. From 1973 to 1974 was advt. circulation mgr. for Quigley Publishing Co. Taught school in Kenya in 1974; returned to U.S. to join Grey Advt. as media planner. 1975 joined Walter Reade Organization as asst. film buyer; promoted to head film buyer in 1977. Named v.p., 1982. In 1986 joined Vestron, Inc. as sr. v.p. to establish Vestron Pictures. Named pres., Vestron Pictures, 1987-89. In 1990 joined Fair Lanes Entertainment, Inc. as v.p. mktg. 1993, joined United Artists Theatre as sr. v.p., marketing & new business.
PICTURES: *Exec. prod.:* Steel Dawn, The Dead, Salome's Last Dance, The Unholy, Waxwork, Burning Secret, The Lair of the White Worm, Paint It Black, The Rainbow, Twister.

QUINLAN, KATHLEEN
Actress. b. Pasadena, CA, Nov. 19, 1954. Played small role in film, One Is a Lonely Number, while in high school.
THEATER: Taken in Marriage (NY Public Theatre; Theatre World Award), Uncommon Women and Others, Accent on Youth (Long Wharf, CT), Les Liaisons Dangereuses.
PICTURES: One Is a Lonely Number (debut, 1972), American Graffiti, Lifeguard, Airport '77, I Never Promised You a Rose Garden, The Promise, The Runner Stumbles, Sunday Lovers, Hanky Panky, Independence Day, Twilight Zone—The Movie, The Last Winter, Warning Sign, Wild Thing, Man Outside, Sunset, Clara's Heart, The Doors, Trial by Jury, Apollo 13.
TELEVISION: *Movies:* Can Ellen Be Saved?, Lucas Tanner (pilot), Where Have All the People Gone?, The Missing Are Deadly, The Abduction of St. Anne, Turning Point of Jim Malloy, Little Ladies of the Night, She's in the Army Now, When She Says No, Blackout, Children of the Night, Dreams Lost Dreams Found, Trapped, The Operation, Strays, An American Story, Stolen Babies, Last Light, Perfect Alibi.

QUINN, AIDAN
Actor. b. Chicago, IL, March 8, 1959. Raised in Rockwell, IL, also spent time in Ireland as a boy and following high sch. graduation. Returned to Chicago at 19, worked as tar roofer before debuting on Chicago stage in The Man in 605, followed by Scheherazade, The Irish Hebrew Lesson, Hamlet.
THEATER: Fool for Love (off-B'way debut), A Lie of the Mind, A Streetcar Named Desire (Theatre World Award).
PICTURES: Reckless (debut, 1984), Desperately Seeking Susan, The Mission, Stakeout, Crusoe, The Handmaid's Tale, The Lemon Sisters, Avalon, At Play in the Fields of the Lord, The Playboys, Benny & Joon, Blink, Mary Shelley's Frankenstein, Legends of the Fall, The Stars Fell on Henrietta, Haunted, Looking for Richard, Michael Collins.
TELEVISION: *Special:* All My Sons. *Movies:* An Early Frost, Perfect Witness, Lies of the Twins, A Private Matter.

QUINN, ANTHONY
Actor. b. Chihuahua, Mexico, Apr. 21, 1915. Came to U.S. as child. Brief stage work before bit roles in films. Autobiographies: The Original Sin (1972), One Man Tango (1995).
THEATER: *B'way:* A Streetcar Named Desire, Beckett, Zorba.
PICTURES: Parole (debut, 1936), Daughter of Shanghai, Last Train From Madrid, Partners in Crime, The Plainsman, Swing High Swing Low, Waikiki Wedding, The Buccaneer (1938),

Bulldog Drummond in Africa, Dangerous to Know, Hunted Men, King of Alcatraz, Tip-Off Girls, Island of Lost Men, King of Chinatown, Television Spy, Union Pacific, City for Conquest, Emergency Squad, Ghost Breakers, Parole Fixer, Road to Singapore, Blood and Sand, Bullets for O'Hara, Knockout, Manpower, The Perfect Snob, Texas Rangers Ride Again, They Died With Their Boots On, Thieves Fall Out, The Black Swan, Larceny Inc., Road to Morocco, Guadalcanal Diary, The Ox-Bow Incident, Buffalo Bill, Irish Eyes Are Smiling, Roger Touhy Gangster, Ladies of Washington, China Sky, Back to Bataan, Where Do We Go From Here?, California, Imperfect Lady, Sinbad the Sailor, Black Gold, Tycoon, The Brave Bulls, Mask of the Avenger, Viva Zapata! (Academy Award for Best Supporting Actor, 1952), The Brigand, The World in His Arms, Against All Flags, Ride Vaquero, City Beneath the Sea, Seminole, Blowing Wild, East of Sumatra, Long Wait, Magnificent Matador, Ulysses, Naked Street, Seven Cities of Gold, La Strada, Attila the Hun, Lust for Life (Academy Award for Best Supporting Actor, 1956), Wild Party, Man from Del Rio, The Hunchback of Notre Dame, Ride Back, The River's Edge, Wild is the Wind, The Buccaneer (1958; dir. only), Hot Spell, Black Orchid, Last Train From Gun Hill, Warlock, Portrait in Black, Heller in Pink Tights, Savage Innocents, The Guns of Navarone, Barabbas, Requiem for a Heavyweight, Lawrence of Arabia, Behold a Pale Horse, The Visit, Zorba the Greek (also assoc. prod.), High Wind in Jamaica, Marco the Magnificent, Lost Command, The 25th Hour, The Happening, Guns for San Sebastian, The Rover, The Magus, Shoes of the Fisherman, The Secret of Santa Vittoria, A Dream of Kings, A Walk in the Spring Rain, R.P.M., Flap, Across 110th Street (also exec. prod.), Deaf Smith and Johnny Ears, The Don Is Dead, The Destructors, The Inheritance, The Con Artists, Mohammad: Messenger of God, The Greek Tycoon, Caravans, The Passage, Lion of the Desert, High Risk, The Salamander, A Man of Passion, Stradivarius, Revenge, Ghosts Can't Do It, A Star for Two, Only the Lonely, Jungle Fever, Mobsters, Last Action Hero, Somebody to Love, A Walk in the Clouds.
TELEVISION: Much dramatic work in the early 1950s. *Series:* The City, American Playwrights Theater (host). *Movies:* Jesus of Nazareth, Treasure Island (Italian TV), Onassis: The Richest Man in the World, The Old Man and the Sea, This Can't Be Love, Hercules and the Amazon Women, Hercules and the Lost Kingdom, Hercules and the Circle of Fire, Gotti.

R

RABE, DAVID WILLIAM
Writer. b. Dubuque, IA, March 10, 1940. m. actress Jill Clayburgh. e. Loras Coll.
THEATER: The Basic Training of Pavlo Hummel (Obie Award, 1971), Sticks and Bones (Tony Award, 1971), The Orphan, In the Boom Boom Room, Streamers, Hurlyburly, Those the River Keeps.
PICTURES: I'm Dancing As Fast As I Can (also exec. prod.), Streamers, Casualties of War, State of Grace.
TELEVISION: *Special:* Sticks and Bones.

RABINOVITZ, JASON
Executive. b. Boston, MA, e. Harvard Coll., B.A. where elected to Phi Beta Kappa. Following WWII service as military intelligence captain with paratroops, took M.B.A. at Harvard Business Sch., 1948. Started in industry in 1949 as asst. to secty.-treas., United Paramount Theatres. Asst. controller, ABC, 1953; adm. v.p., ABC-TV, 1956; joined MGM as asst. treas., 1957; named MGM-TV gen. mgr., director of business & financial affairs, 1958; treas. & chief financial officer, MGM, Inc., 1963; financial v.p. & chief financial officer, 1967. 1971 named exec. v.p., American Film Theatre, 1974-75. Rejoined MGM as v.p./exec. asst. to the pres., 1976. Elected v.p. finance, 1979; promoted to sr. v.p., finance & corporate admin., MGM Film Co. & UA Prods. Resigned, 1984. Now film & TV consultant and indep. producer. Dir., Pacific Rim Entertainment, 1993-95.

RADIN, PAUL
Producer. b. New York, NY, Sept. 15, 1913. e. NYU. After college went in adv. Became v.p. in chg. of m.p. div. of Buchanan & Co. During WWII posted in Middle East as film chief for Office of War Information for that area. On return to U.S. assigned by Buchanan to ad campaign for Howard Hughes' The Outlaw. Turned to talent mgr., joining the Sam Jaffe Agency. Then joined Ashley-Famous Agency. Became exec. prod. for Yul Brynner's indep. prod. co. based in Switzerland, with whom made such films as The Journey, Once More with Feeling, Surprise Package.
PICTURES: Born Free, Living Free, Phase IV, The Blue Bird, The Ghost and the Darkness.
TELEVISION: The Incredible Journey of Dr. Meg Laurel, The Ordeal of Dr. Mudd, Crime of Innocence. *Series:* Born Free, The Wizard.

RADNITZ, ROBERT B.
Producer. b. Great Neck, NY, Aug. 9, 1924. e. U. of VA. Taught 2 years at U. of VA, then became reader for Harold Clurman; wrote several RKO This Is America scripts, then to Broadway where co-prod. The Frogs of Spring; prod. The Young and the Beautiful; to Hollywood working at United Artists, then as story consultant to Buddy Adler, head of prod., 20th Century-Fox, 1957-58. V.P., Producer Guild of America, 1982, 1984, 1985; bd. member, Producers Branch, AMPAS, last 4 yrs. First producer with retrospective at Museum of Modern Art, and first producer honored by joint resolution of both houses of Congress for his work, 1973. Pres. Robert B. Radnitz Productions, Ltd.
PICTURES: *Producer:* A Dog of Flanders (debut, 1960; first U.S. film to win Golden Lion Award at Venice Film Fest.), Misty, Island of the Blue Dolphins, and Now Miguel, My Side of the Mountain, The Little Ark, Sounder (Acad. Award nom.), Where the Lilies Bloom, Birch Interval, Sounder 2, A Hero Ain't Nothin' But a Sandwich, Cross Creek.
TELEVISION: Mary White (Emmy & Christopher Awards), Never Forget (ACE Award nom.).

RAFELSON, BOB
Producer, Director, Writer. b. New York, NY, Feb. 21, 1933. e. Dartmouth, B.A. (philosophy). Left NY in teens to ride in rodeos in AZ. Worked on cruise ship, then played drums and bass with jazz combos in Acapulco. 1953 won Frost Natl. Playwriting competition. Dir. his award-winning play at Hanover Experimental Theatre, N.H. After Army Service did program promotion for a radio station, was advisor for Shochiku Films, Japan, then hired by David Susskind to read scripts for Talent Assocs. Writer-assoc. prod., DuPont Show of the Month and Play of the Week (also script sprv.). Joined Screen Gems in California, developing program ideas for Jackie Cooper, then head of TV prod. arm of Columbia. Later formed BBS Productions with Burt Schneider and Steve Blauner. Appeared as actor in 1985 film Always.
PICTURES: *Co-Prod.* only: Easy Rider, The Last Picture Show, Drive He Said. *Director:* Head (debut, 1968; also co-prod., co-s.p.), Five Easy Pieces (also co-prod., co-story; Acad. Award noms. for picture & writing), The King of Marvin Gardens (also prod., co-s.p), Stay Hungry (also co-prod., co-s.p.), The Postman Always Rings Twice (also co-prod.), Black Widow, Mountains of the Moon (also co-s.p.), Man Trouble.
TELEVISION: *Series:* The Monkees (1966-68, creator, writer, dir.; Emmy Award, 1967), Adapted 34 prods., Play of the Week. *Dir. music video:* All Night Long, with Lionel Ritchie.

RAFFERTY, FRANCES
Actress. b. Sioux City, IA, June 26, 1922. e. U. of California, premedical student UCLA. TV series, December Bride, Pete and Gladys.
PICTURES: Seven Sweethearts, Private Miss Jones, Girl Crazy, War Against Mrs. Hadley, Thousands Cheer, Dragon Seed, Honest Thief, Mrs. Parkington, Barbary Coast Gent, Hidden Eye, Abbott and Costello in Hollywood, Adventures of Don Coyote, Money Madness, Lady at Midnight, Old Fashioned Girl, Rodeo, Shanghai Story, Wings of Chance.

RAFFIN, DEBORAH
Actress. b. Los Angeles, CA, March 13, 1953. m. producer Michael Viner. Mother is actress Trudy Marshall. e. Valley Coll. Was active fashion model before turning to acting when discovered by Ted Witzer. Author: Sharing Christmas (Vols. I & II). Debut in 40 Carats (1973). Publisher Dove Books On Tape. Head of Dove Films, prod. co.
PICTURES: 40 Carats (debut, 1973), The Dove, Once Is Not Enough, God Told Me To (Demon), Assault on Paradise (Maniac!), The Sentinel, Touched by Love, Dance of the Dwarfs (Jungle Heat), Death Wish 3, Claudia, Scanners II, Morning Glory (also co-s.p.).
TELEVISION: *Series:* Foul Play. *Movies:* A Nightmare in Badham County, Ski Lift to Death, How to Pick Up Girls, Willa, Mind Over Murder, Haywire, For the Love of It, Killing at Hell's Gate, For Lovers Only, Running Out, Sparkling Cyanide, Threesome, The Sands of Time, A Perry Mason Mystery: The Case of the Grimacing Governor. *Mini-Series:* The Last Convertible, James Clavell's Noble House, Windmills of the Gods (also co-prod.). *Guest:* B.L. Stryker.

RAGLAND, ROBERT OLIVER
Composer. b. Chicago, IL, July 3, 1931. e. Northwestern U., American Conservatory of Music, Vienna Acad. of Music. Professional pianist at Chicago nightclubs. In U.S. Navy; on discharge joined Dorsey Bros. Orchestra as arranger. On sls. staff at NBC-TV, Chicago. 1970, moved to Hollywood to become composer for movies; has scored 67 feature films plus many TV movies and series segments. Has also written some 45 original songs.
PICTURES: The Touch of Melissa, The Yin and Yang of Mr. Go, The Thing with Two Heads, Project: Kill, Abby, Seven Alone, The Eyes of Dr. Chaney, Return to Macon County, The Daring Dobermans, Shark's Treasure, Grizzly, Pony Express Rider,

Mansion of the Doomed, Mountain Family Robinson, Only Once in a Lifetime, Jaguar Lives, The Glove, Lovely But Deadly, "Q", The Day of the Assassin, A Time To Die, The Winged Serpent, Trial by Terror, The Guardian, Ten to Midnight, Dirty Rebel, Hysterical, Brainwaves, Where's Willie?, The Supernaturals, Nightstick, Messenger of Death, The Fifth Monkey, No Place to Hide, The Buffalo Soldiers, The Raffle, Morty, Crime and Punishment.
TELEVISION: Photoplay's Stars of Tomorrow, Wonder Woman, Barnaby Jones, Streets of San Francisco, High Ice, The Girl on the Edge of Town, The Guardian, etc.

RAILSBACK, STEVE
Actor. b. Dallas, TX, 1948. Studied with Lee Strasberg. On stage in Orpheus Descending, This Property Is Condemned, Cherry Orchard, Skin of Our Teeth, etc.
PICTURES: The Visitors, Cockfighter, Angela, The Stunt Man, Deadly Games, Turkey Shoot, The Golden Seal, Torchlight, Lifeforce, Armed and Dangerous, Blue Monkey, The Wind, Distortions, Deadly Intent, Alligator II: The Mutation, After-Shock, Private Wars, Forever, Calendar Girl, Nukie, Save Me.
TELEVISION: *Movies:* Helter Skelter, Good Cops Bad Cops, The Forgotten, Spearfield's Daughter, Sunstroke, Bonds of Love, Separated by Murder. *Mini-Series:* From Here to Eternity.

RAIMI, SAM
Director, Writer, Producer, Actor. b. Royal Oak, MI, Oct. 23, 1959. e. Michigan St. Univ. Formed Renaissance Pictures, Inc.
PICTURES: *Dir./Writer:* The Evil Dead, Crimewave, Evil Dead II, Darkman, Army of Darkness, The Quick and the Dead (dir. only). *Co-Producer:* Hard Target, Timecop. *Actor:* Spies Like Us, Thou Shalt Not Kill... Except, Maniac Cop, Miller's Crossing, Innocent Blood, Indian Summer, Intruder, The Hudsucker Proxy (also co-writer), The Flintstones.
TELEVISION: *Movies:* Journey to the Center of the Earth (actor), Mantis (prod., writer), Body Bags (actor), The Stand (actor). *Series:* American Gothic (exec. prod.).

RAJSKI, PEGGY
Producer. b. Stevens Point, WI. e. Univ. of Wisconsin. m. actor Josh Mostel. Began film career as prod. manager on John Sayles film Lianna, before becoming producer. Prod. of Bruce Springsteen music videos, incld. Glory Days which won American Video Award. Received 1994 Academy Award for short film Trevor.
PICTURES: The Brother From Another Planet, Matewan, Eight Men Out, The Grifters, Little Man Tate, Used People, Home for the Holidays.

RAKSIN, DAVID
Composer. b. Philadelphia, PA, Aug. 4, 1912. e. U. of Pennsylvania, studied music with Isadore Freed and Arnold Schoenberg. Composer for films, ballet, dramatic and musical comedy, stage, radio and TV, symphony orchestra and chamber ensembles. Arranger of music of Chaplin film, Modern Times; pres. Composers and Lyricists Guild of America, 1962-70; animated films include Madeline and The Unicorn in the Garden (UPA). Professor of Music and Urban Semester, U. of Southern California. Coolidge Commission from the Library of Congress: Oedipus Memneitai (Oedipus Remembers) for bass/baritone, 6-part chorus and chamber orchestra premiered there under dir. of composer, Oct. 1986. Pres., Society for the Preservation of Film Music, 1992. Recipient of ASCAP Golden Score Award for Career Achievement, 1992. Elected to ASCAP bd. of dirs., 1995.
PICTURES: Laura, Secret Life of Walter Mitty, Smoky, Force of Evil, Across the Wide Missouri, Carrie, Bad and the Beautiful, Apache, Suddenly, Big Combo, Jubal, Hilda Crane, Separate Tables, Al Capone, Night Tide, Too-Late Blues, Best of the Bolshoi (music for visual interludes), Two Weeks in Another Town, The Redeemer, Invitation to a Gunfighter, Sylvia, A Big Hand for the Little Lady, Will Penny, Glass Houses, What's the Matter With Helen?
TELEVISION: *Series:* Five Fingers, Life With Father, Father of the Bride, Ben Casey, Breaking Point. *Specials:* Journey, Tender is the Night, Prayer of the Ages, Report from America, The Olympics (CBC), The Day After, Lady in a Corner.

RALPH, SHERYL LEE
Actress. b. Waterbury, CT, Dec. 30, 1956. e. Rutgers U. Studied with Negro Ensemble Company in NYC.
THEATER: *NY:* Reggae, Dreamgirls. *LA:* Identical Twins From Baltimore.
PICTURES: A Piece of the Action (debut, 1977), Oliver and Company (voice), The Mighty Quinn, Skin Deep, To Sleep With Anger, Mistress, The Distinguished Gentleman, Sister Act 2: Back in the Habit, The Flintstones, White Man's Burden, Bogus.
TELEVISION: *Series:* Code Name: Foxfire, Search for Tomorrow, It's a Living, Designing Women, George. *Movies:* The Neighborhood, Sister Margaret and the Saturday Night Ladies, Luck of the Draw: The Gambler Returns, No Child of Mine. *Specials:* Happy Birthday Hollywood, Voices That Care, Story of a People: The Black Road to Hollywood (host).

RAMIS, HAROLD
Writer, Director, Actor, Producer. b. Chicago, IL, Nov. 21, 1944. e. Washington U., St. Louis. Assoc. ed. Playboy Mag. 1968-70; writer, actor, Second City, Chicago 1970-73; National Lampoon Radio Show, 1974-75.
PICTURES: National Lampoon's Animal House (co-s.p.), Meatballs (co-s.p.), Caddyshack (co-s.p., dir.), Stripes (co-s.p., actor), Heavy Metal (voice), National Lampoon's Vacation (dir.), Ghostbusters (co-s.p., actor), Back to School (co-s.p., exec. prod.), Club Paradise (co-s.p., dir.), Armed and Dangerous (exec. prod., co-s.p.), Baby Boom (actor), Caddyshack II (co-s.p.), Stealing Home (actor), Ghostbusters II (co-s.p., actor), Rover Dangerfield (co-story), Groundhog Day (dir., co-s.p., co-prod., actor), Airheads (actor), Love Affair (actor), Stuart Saves His Family (dir.), Multiplicity (dir., co-prod.).
TELEVISION: Series: SCTV (head writer, performer, 1976-78), Rodney Dangerfield Show (head writer, prod.). Special: Will Rogers—Look Back and Laugh (exec. prod.).

RAMPLING, CHARLOTTE
Actress. b. Sturmer, England, Feb. 5, 1946. e. Jeanne D'Arc Academie pour Jeune Filles, Versailles; St. Hilda's, Bushey, England.
PICTURES: The Knack... and How to Get It (debut, 1965), Rotten to the Core, Georgy Girl, The Long Duel, Sequestro di Persona (Island of Crime), The Damned, Target: Harry (How to Make It), Three, The Ski Bum, Corky, Addio Fratello Crrudele (Tis Pity She's a Whore), Asylum, The Night Porter, Giordano Bruno, Zardoz, Caravan to Vaccares, La Chair de L'orchidee, Farewell My Lovely, Foxtrot (The Other Side of Paradise), Yuppi-Du, Orca, Purple Taxi, Stardust Memories, The Verdict, Viva La Vie, Tristesse et Beaute, On ne Meurt que deux Fois (He Died With His Eyes Open), Angel Heart, Mascara, D.O.A., Max My Love, Rebus, Paris By Night, Helmut Newton: Frames from the Edge (doc.), Hammers Over the Anvil, Time is Money, Invasion of Privacy, Asphalt Tango.
TELEVISION: BBC Series: The Six Wives of Henry VIII, The Superlative Seven, The Avengers. Movies: Sherlock Holmes in New York, Mystery of Cader Iscom, The Fantasists, What's in it for Henry, Zinotchka, Infidelities, La Femme Abandonnee, Radetzky March, Murder In Mind, Samson Le Maqnifique, La Dernière Fête.

RAND, HAROLD
Executive. b. New York, NY, Aug. 25, 1928. e. Long Island U., B.S., 1948-50; CCNY, 1945-46. U.S. Army 1946-48; ent. m.p. ind. 1950, pub. dept. 20th-Fox; variety of posts incl. writer, trade press, newspaper contact; joined Walt Disney's Buena Vista pub. mgr., 1957; pub. mgr. Paramount Pictures, 1959; formed own pub. rel. firm, 1961; dir. of pub. Embassy Picture Corp. 1962; dir. of world prdn. 20th Century Fox 1962; resigned 1963; dir. of adv. & pub., Landau Co., 1963; dir. world pub., Embassy Pictures, 1964; est. Harold Rand & Co., Inc., 1966, pres. of p.r. & mktg. firm. Appt. mktg., dir., Kaufman Astoria Studios, 1984; elected v.p., 1985.

RANDALL, TONY
Actor. r.n. Leonard Rosenberg. b. Tulsa, OK, Feb. 26, 1920. e. Northwestern U. Prof. N.Y. debut as actor in Circle of Chalk; U.S. Army 1942-46; radio actor on many shows. Founder/Artistic Director of National Actors Theatre in NYC, 1991.
THEATER: Candida, The Corn is Green, Antony & Cleopatra, Caesar & Cleopatra, Inherit the Wind, Oh Men! Oh Women!, Oh Captain, The Sea Gull, The Master Builder, M. Butterfly, A Little Hotel on the Side, Three Men on a Horse, The Government Inspector, The Odd Couple (tour).
PICTURES: Oh Men! Oh Women! (debut, 1957), Will Success Spoil Rock Hunter?, No Down Payment, The Mating Game, Pillow Talk, The Adventures of Huckleberry Finn, Let's Make Love, Lover Come Back, Boys' Night Out, Island of Love, The Brass Bottle, 7 Faces of Dr. Lao, Send Me No Flowers, Fluffy, The Alphabet Murders, Bang Bang You're Dead, Hello Down There, Everything You Always Wanted to Know About Sex* But Were Afraid to Ask, Scavenger Hunt, Foolin' Around, The King of Comedy, My Little Pony (voice), It Had to Be You, That's Adequate, Gremlins 2: The New Batch (voice), Fatal Instinct.
TELEVISION: Series: One Man's Family, Mr. Peepers, The Odd Couple (Emmy Award, 1975), The Tony Randall Show, Love Sidney. Guest: TV Playhouse, Max Liebman Spectaculars, Sid Caesar, Dinah Shore, Playhouse 90, Walt Disney World Celebrity Circus. Movies: Kate Bliss and the Ticker Tape Kid, Sidney Shorr: A Girl's Best Friend, Off Sides, Hitler's SS: Portrait in Evil, Sunday Drive, Save the Dog!, The Odd Couple: Together Again.

RANSOHOFF, MARTIN
Executive. b. New Orleans, LA, 1927. e. Colgate U., 1949. Adv., Young & Rubicam, 1948-49; slsmn, writer, dir., Gravel Films, 1951; formed own co., Filmways, 1952; industrial films, commercials; formed Filmways TV Prods., Filmways, Inc.,

Filmways of Calif.; bd. chmn. Filmways, Inc. Resigned from Filmways in 1972 and formed own independent motion picture and television production company.
PICTURES: Boys' Night Out, The Wheeler Dealers, The Americanization of Emily, The Loved One, The Sandpiper, The Cincinnati Kid, The Fearless Vampire Killers, Don't Make Waves, Ice Station Zebra, Castle Keep, Hamlet (exec. prod.), Catch-22, The Moonshine War, King Lear, See No Evil, 10 Rillington Place, Fuzz, Save The Tiger, The White Dawn, Silver Streak (exec. prod.), Nightwing, The Wanderers, The Mountain Men, A Change of Seasons, American Pop, Hanky Panky, Class, Jagged Edge, The Big Town, Switching Channels, Physical Evidence, Welcome Home, Guilty as Sin.
TELEVISION: Series: Mister Ed, The Beverly Hillbillies, Petticoat Junction, Green Acres, The Addams Family.

RAPAPORT, MICHAEL
Actor. b. New York, NY, 1970. Started as stand-up comic appearing at Improv in LA before becoming actor.
PICTURES: Zebrahead, Point of No Return, Poetic Justice, Money for Nothing, True Romance, The Scout, Higher Learning, The Basketball Diaries, Kiss of Death, Mighty Aphrodite, The Pallbearer, A Brother's Kiss.

RAPHAEL, FREDERIC
Writer. b. Chicago, IL, Aug. 14, 1931. e. Charterhouse, St. John's Coll., Cambridge.
AUTHOR: The Earlsdon Way, The Limits of Love, A Wild Surmise, The Graduate Wife, The Trouble With England, Lindmann, Orchestra and Beginners, Like Men Betrayed, Who Were You With Last Night?, April June and November, Richard's Things, California Time, The Glittering Prizes, Sleeps Six & Other Stories, Oxbridge Blues & Other Stories, Heaven & Earth, Think of England and other stories, After the War, A Double Life, The Latin Lover and other stories, Old Scores. Biographies: Somerset Maugham and His World, Byron. Translations: (with Kenneth McLeish), Poems of Catullus The Oresteia. Essays: Cracks in the Ice, Of Gods and Men.
THEATER: From the Greek (1979), An Early Life.
PICTURES: Nothing But the Best, Darling (Academy Award, 1965), Two for the Road, Far from the Madding Crowd, A Severed Head, Daisy Miller, Richard's Things.
TELEVISION: The Glittering Prizes (Royal TV Society Writer Award 1976), Rogue Male, School Play, Something's Wrong, Best of Friends, Richard's Things, Oxbridge Blues (ACE Award, best writer), After the War, Byrow, The Man in the Brooks Brothers Shirt (also dir.; ACE Award best picture).

RAPHEL, DAVID
Executive. b. Boulogne-Seine, France, Jan. 9, 1925. e. university in France. Entered m.p. ind. as asst. to sales mgr. in France, 20th-Fox, 1950-51; asst. mgr. in Italy, 1951-54; mgr. in Holland, 1954-57; asst. to European mgr. in Paris, 1957-59; European mgr. for TV activities in Paris, 1959-61; Continental mgr. in Paris, 1961-64, transferred to NY as v.p. in chg. of intl. sales, 1964; named pres., 20th Century-Fox International, 1973. 1975, also appointed sr. v.p., worldwide marketing, feature film division, for 20th-Fox, (L.A.). 1976, joined ICM, appointed dir. general of ICM (Europe) headquartered in Paris. 1979 elected pres. ICM (L.A.) 1980, formed Cambridge Film Group Ltd.

RAPPER, IRVING
Director. b. London, Eng., Jan. 16, 1904. Stage prod. London: Five Star Final, Grand Hotel. NY: The Animal Kingdom, The Firebird, The Late Christopher Bean.
PICTURES: Shining Victory (debut, 1941), One Foot in Heaven, The Gay Sisters, Now Voyager, The Adventures of Mark Twain, Rhapsody in Blue, The Corn Is Green, Deception, The Voice of the Turtle, Anna Lucasta, The Glass Menagerie, Another Man's Poison, Forever Female, Bad for Each Other, The Brave One, Strange Intruder, Marjorie Morningstar, The Miracle, Joseph and His Brethren, Pontius Pilate, The Christine Jorgensen Story, Born Again, Justus.

RAPPOPORT, GERALD J.
Executive, Film Producer. b. New York, NY, Aug. 25, 1925. e. NYU. U.S. Marine Corps. Pres., Major Artists Representatives Corp., 1954-58; dir. of Coast Sound Services, Hollywood; 1959-61, pres., International Film Exchange Ltd.; 1960-91, CEO of IFEX Int'l; 1991-94, pres. CIFEX Corporation.

RASHAD, PHYLICIA
Actress-singer. b. Houston, TX, June 19, 1948. m. sportscaster Ahmad Rashad. Sister of Debbie Allen. e. Howard U., B.F.A., magna cum laude, 1970. NY School of Ballet. Acted under maiden name of Phylicia Ayers-Allen. Recording, Josephine Superstar (1979). Conceived (with Michael Peters) and appeared in revue Phylicia Rashad & Co. in 1989 in Las Vegas.
THEATER: Ain't Supposed to Die a Natural Death, The Duplex, The Cherry Orchard, The Wiz, Weep Not For Me, Zooman and the Sign, In an Upstate Motel, Zora, Dreamgirls, Sons and Fathers of Sons, Puppetplay, A Raisin in the Sun, Into the Woods, Jelly's Last Jam.

PICTURE: Once Upon A Time...When We Were Colored.
TELEVISION: *Series*: One Life to Live, The Cosby Show (People's Choice Award, NAACP Image Award, Emmy nom.), Cosby. *Movies*: Uncle Tom's Cabin, False Witness, Polly, Polly—Comin' Home!, Jailbirds, David's Mother, The Possession of Michael D. *Specials*: Nell Carter—Never Too Old to Dream, Superstars and Their Moms, Our Kids and the Best of Everything, The Debbie Allen Special, Hallelujah.

RATHER, DAN
News Correspondent, Anchor. b. Wharton, TX, Oct. 31, 1931. e. Sam Houston State Teachers Coll., BA journalism, 1953. Instructor there for 1 year. Graduate e.: U. of Houston Law School, S. Texas School of Law. Worked for UPI and Houston Chronicle. Radio: KSAM, Huntsville, KTRH, Houston. Joined CBS News in 1962 as chief of southwest bureau in Dallas. Transferred to overseas burs. (including chief of London Bureau 1965-66), then Vietnam before returning as White House corr. 1966. White House Correspondent, 1964-74. Covered top news events, from Democratic and Republican national conventions to President Nixon's trip to Europe (1970) and to Peking and Moscow (1972). Anchored CBS Reports, 1974-75. Presently co-editor of 60 minutes (since 1975) and anchors Dan Rather Reporting on CBS Radio Network (since 1977). Anchor for 48 Hours, 1988. Winner of numerous awards, including 5 Emmys. Anchorman on CBS-TV Evening News, 1981-. Books: The Palace Guard (1974); The Camera Never Blinks (1977); I Remember (1991); The Camera Never Blinks Twice (1994); Mark Sullivan's Our Times (editor, 1995).

RAUCHER, HERMAN
Writer. b. Apr. 13, 1928. e. NYU. Author of novels Watermelon Man, Summer of '42 and Ode to Billy Joe, adapted to films by him. Other novels inc. A Glimpse of Tiger, There Should Have Been Castles, Maynard's House.
PICTURES: Sweet November, Can Hieronymous Merkin Ever Forget Mercy Humppe and Find True Happiness?, Watermelon Man, Summer of '42, Class of '44, Ode to Billy Joe, The Other Side of Midnight.
TELEVISION: Studio One, Alcoa Hour, Goodyear Playhouse, Matinee Theatre, Remember When? (movie).

RAVETCH, IRVING
Writer, Producer. b. Newark, NJ, Nov. 14, 1920. e. UCLA. m. Harriet Frank, with whom he often collaborated.
PICTURES: *Writer*: Living in a Big Way, The Outriders, Vengeance Valley, Ten Wanted Men, The Long Hot Summer, The Sound and the Fury, Home from the Hill, The Dark at the Top of the Stairs, Hud (also co-prod.), Hombre (also co-prod.), The Reivers (also prod.), House of Cards (as James P. Bonner), The Cowboys, Conrack, Norma Rae, Murphy's Romance, Stanley and Iris.

RAYBURN, GENE
Performer, b. Christopher, IL, Dec. 22, 1917. e. Knox Coll., Galesburg, IL. NBC guide; with many radio stations in Baltimore, Philadelphia, NY; US Army Air Force, 1942-45; Rayburn and Finch Show, WNEW, NY, 1945-52; Gene Rayburn Show, NBC radio; TV shows: Many appearances as host-humorist on game shows, variety shows, drama shows. Also acted in summer stock; AFTRA, past pres. NY local; trustee on H&R Board for over 25 years.
THEATER: *B'way*: Bye Bye Birdie, Come Blow Your Horn.
TELEVISION: *Series*: The Name's the Same, Tonight (second banana), Make the Connection, The Steve Allen Show, The Steve Lawrence-Eydie Gorme Show (announcer), The Match Game, Dough Re Mi, The Sky's the Limit, Choose Up Sides, Tic Tac Dough, Play Your Hunch, Snap Judgment, Amateur's Guide to Love. *Guest*: The Love Boat, Fantasy Island.

RAYMOND, PAULA
Actress. r.n. Paula Ramona Wright, b. San Francisco, CA., Nov. 23, 1925. e. San Francisco Jr. Coll. 1942. Started career in little theatre groups, concerts, recitals, San Francisco; lead-ing stage roles in Ah! Wilderness, Peter Pan, etc.; also sang lead coloratura rules in Madame Butterfly, Aidia, Rigoletto, Faust, etc.; ballerina with S.F. Opera Ballet; classical pianist; model, Meade-Maddick Photographers.
PICTURES: Racing Luck (debut, 1948), Rusty Leads the Way, Blondie's Secret, East Side West Side, Challenge of the Range, Adam's Rib, Devil's Doorway, Sons of New Mexico, Duchess of Idaho, Crisis, Grounds For Marriage, Inside Straight, The Tall Target, Texas Carnival, The Sellout, Bandits of Corsica, City That Never Sleeps, The Beast from 20,000 Fathoms, The Human Jungle, King Richard & the Crusaders, The Gun That Won the West, Hand of Death, The Flight That Disappeared, The Spy With My Face, Blood of Dracula's Castle, Five Bloody Graves.
TELEVISION: *Guest*: Perry Mason, 77 Sunset Strip, Wyatt Earp, Man from U.N.C.L.E., Maverick, The Untouchables, Bachelor Father, Bat Masterson, Temple Houston, Peter Gunn, many others.

RAYNOR, LYNN S.
Producer, Production Executive. b. Chicago, IL, Feb. 11, 1940. Produced West Coast premiere of The Balcony by Genet, The Crawling Arnold Review by Feiffer. Joined Television Enterprises, 1965; Commonwealth United, 1968 as business affairs exec. later prod. spvr. 1972 opened London branch of the Vidtronics Co. 1974, formed Paragon Entertainment & RAH Records. 1980-95, prod. of TV Movies and Mini-Series. Prod. & editor of 12 minute tv vignettes, A Hall of Fame Story.
PICTURE: Freejack.
TELEVISION: *Special*: Waiting for Godot. *Movies*: Marilyn: The Untold Story, The Execution, A Winner Never Quits, On Wings of Eagles, Stranger in My Bed, Hands of a Stranger, The High Price of Passion, The Kennedys of Massachusetts, Common Ground, Face of Love, The Rape of Doctor Willis, Quiet Killer, Love Honor & Obey: The Last Mafia Marriage, Tony & Nancy: The Inside Story, Tecumseh: The Last Warrior. *Series*: Camp Wilderness. *Pilot*: Murphy's Law.

REA, STEPHEN
Actor. b. Belfast, Northern Ireland, Oct. 31, 1948. e. Queens Univ. (BA in English Lit.). Started acting at Abbey Theatre in Dublin. Formed the Field Day Theatre Co. in 1980 in Londonderry, acting in or directing most of their productions. Also acted with Royal Natl. Theatre.
THEATER: Playboy of the Western World, Comedians, High Society, Endgame, Freedom of the City, Someone Who'll Watch Over Me (also B'way; Theatre World Award, Tony nom.).
PICTURES: Danny Boy (Angel), Loose Connections, The Company of Wolves, The Doctor and the Devils, The House, Life Is Sweet, The Crying Game (Acad. Award nom.), Bad Behavior, Angie, Princess Caraboo, Ready to Wear (Pret-a-Porter), Between the Devil and the Deep Blue Sea, Interview With A Vampire, All Men Are Mortal, Michael Collins, Last of the High Kings.
TELEVISION: Shadow of a Gunman, Fugitive, I Didn't Know You Cared, Professional Foul, The Seagull, Out of Town Boys, Calbe Williams, Joyce in June, The House, Four Days in July, Shergar, Scout, Lost Belongings, The Big Gamble, Not With a Bang, Saint Oscar, Hedda Gabler, Citizen X, Crime of the Century.

REAGAN, RONALD
Actor, Politician. b. Tampico, IL, Feb. 6, 1911. e. high school, Eureka Coll. m. former actress Nancy Davis. Wrote weekly sports column for a Des Moines, IA newspaper; broadcast sporting events. Signed as actor by Warner Bros. in 1937. In WWII 1942-45, capt., USAAF. Actor until 1966. Served as Governor, California, 1967-74. Businessman and rancher. Elected President of the United States, 1980. Re-elected, 1984. Autobiography: Where's the Rest of Me? (1965).
PICTURES: Love Is On the Air (debut, 1937), Hollywood Hotel, Sergeant Murphy, Swing Your Lady, Brother Rat, Going Places, Accidents Will Happen, Cowboy from Brooklyn, Boy Meets Girl, Girls on Probation, Dark Victory, Naughty but Nice, Hell's Kitchen, Code of the Secret Service, Smashing the Money Ring, Angels Wash Their Faces, Brother Rat and a Baby, Murder in the Air, Tugboat Annie Sails Again, Knute Rockne—All American, Santa Fe Trail, Angel From Texas, Nine Lives Are Not Enough, The Bad Man, International Squadron, Million Dollar Baby, Kings Row, Juke Girl, Desperate Journey, This Is the Army, Stallion Road, That Hagen Girl, The Voice of the Turtle, Night Unto Night, John Loves Mary, The Girl From Jones Beach, It's a Great Feeling (cameo), The Hasty Heart, Louisa, Storm Warning, The Last Outpost, Bedtime for Bonzo, Hong Kong, She's Working Her Way Through College, The Winning Team, Tropic Zone, Law & Order, Prisoner of War, Cattle Queen of Montana, Tennessee's Partner, Hellcats of the Navy, The Young Doctors (narrator), The Killers.
TELEVISION: *Series*: The Orchid Award (emcee), General Electric Theater (host, frequent star), Death Valley Days (host). *Guest*: Ford Theratre, Schlitz Playhouse of Stars, Lux Video Theatre, Startime.

REARDON, BARRY
Executive. b. Hartford, CT, Mar. 8, 1931. e. Holy Cross Col., Trinity Col. Began industry career with Paramount Pictures; named v.p.; left to join General Cinema Theatres Corp. as sr. v.p. Now with Warner Bros. as pres. of domestic distribution co.

REASON, REX
Actor. b. Berlin, Germany, Nov. 30, 1928. e. Hoover H.S., Glendale, CA. Worked at various jobs; studied dramatics at Pasadena Playhouse.
PICTURES: Storm Over Tibet, Salome, Mission Over Korea, Taza Son of Cochise, This Island Earth, Smoke Signal, Lady Godiva, Kiss of Fire, Creature Walks Among Us, Raw Edge, The Rawhide Trail, Under Fire, Thundering Jets, The Sad Horse, Yankee Pasha, Band of Angels, Miracle of the Hills.
TELEVISION: *Series*: Man Without a Gun, Roaring Twenties.

REDDY, HELEN
Singer. b. Melbourne, Australia, Oct. 25, 1942. Parents were producer-writer-actor Max Reddy and actress Stella Lamond. e. in Australia. Began career at age four as singer and had appeared in hundreds of stage and radio roles with parents by age of 15. Came to New York in 1966, subsequently played nightclubs, appeared on TV. First single hit record: I Don't Know How To Love Him (Capitol). Grammy Award, 1973, as best female singer of year for I Am Woman. Most Played Artist by the music operators of America: American Music Award 1974; Los Angeles Times Woman of the Year (1975); No. 1 Female Vocalist in 1975 and 1976; Record World, Cash Box and Billboard; named one of the Most Exciting Women in the World by International Bachelor's Society, 1976. Heads prod. co. Helen Reddy, Inc.
THEATER: B'way: Blood Brothers.
PICTURES: Airport 1975 (debut), Pete's Dragon.
TELEVISION: Series: The Helen Reddy Show (Summer, 1973), Permanent host of Midnight Special. Appearances: David Frost Show, Flip Wilson Show, Mike Douglas Show, Tonight Show, Mac Davis Show, Merv Griffin Show (guest host), Sesame Street, Live in Australia (host, 1988); Muppet Show, Home for Easter.

REDFORD, ROBERT
Actor, Director, Producer. b. Santa Monica, CA, Aug. 18, 1937. r.n. Charles Robert Redford. Attended U. of Colorado; left to travel in Europe, 1957. Attended Pratt Inst. and American Acad. of Dramatic Arts. Founded Sundance Film Institute, Park City, Utah, workshop for young filmmakers.
THEATER: B'way: Tall Story (walk on), The Highest Tree, Sunday in New York (Theatre World Award), Barefoot in the Park.
PICTURES: Actor: War Hunt (debut, 1962), Situation Hopeless But Not Serious, Inside Daisy Clover, The Chase, This Property Is Condemned, Barefoot in the Park, Downhill Racer (also exec. prod.), Butch Cassidy and the Sundance Kid, Tell Them Willie Boy is Here, Little Fauss and Big Halsy, The Hot Rock, The Candidate (also co-exec. prod.), Jeremiah Johnson, The Way We Were, The Sting (Acad. Award nom.), The Great Gatsby, The Great Waldo Pepper, Three Days of the Condor, All The President's Men (also exec. prod.), A Bridge Too Far, The Electric Horseman, Brubaker, The Natural, Out of Africa, Legal Eagles, Havana, Sneakers, Indecent Proposal, Up Close and Personal. Exec. Producer: Promised Land, Some Girls, Yosemite: The Fate of Heaven (also narrator), The Dark Wind, Incident at Oglala (also narrator), Strawberry & Chocolate (presenter). Director: Ordinary People (Academy Award, 1980), The Milagro Beanfield War (also co-prod.), A River Runs Through It (also prod., narrator), Quiz Show (also prod.; NY Film Critics Award for Best Picture; Acad. Award noms. for picture & dir.).
TELEVISION: Guest: Maverick, Playhouse 90, Play of the Week (The Iceman Cometh), Alfred Hitchcock Presents, Route 66, Twilight Zone, Dr. Kildare, The Untouchables, The Virginian, The Defenders.

REDGRAVE, CORIN
Actor. b. London, England, July 16, 1939. e. Cambridge. p. late Sir Michael Redgrave and Rachel Kempson. Brother of Vanessa and Lynn Redgrave.
THEATER: On stage with England Stage Co.: A Midsummer Night's Dream, Chips with Everything. RSC: Lady Windermere's Fan, Julius Caesar, Comedy of Errors, Antony and Cleopatra. Young Vic: Rosmersholm.
PICTURES: A Man for All Seasons, The Deadly Affair, Charge of the Light Brigade, The Magus, Oh What a Lovely War, When Eight Bells Toll, Serail, Excalibur, Eureka, Between Wars, The Fool, In the Name of the Father, Four Weddings and a Funeral, Persuasion.
TELEVISION: I Berlioz, Measure for Measure, Persuasion, Henry IV, Circle of Deceit.

REDGRAVE, LYNN
Actress. b. London, England, Mar. 8, 1943. Sister of Vanessa and Corin Redgrave. p. late Sir Michael Redgrave and Rachel Kempson. m. dir.-actor-manager John Clark. Ent. m.p. and TV industries, 1962.
THEATER: NY: Black Comedy (B'way debut), My Fat Friend (1974), Mrs. Warren's Profession, Knock Knock, Misalliance, St. Joan, Twelfth Night (Amer. Shakespeare Fest), Sister Mary Ignatius Explains It All For You, Aren't We All?, Sweet Sue, A Little Hotel on the Side, The Master Builder, Shakespeare for My Father (also writer). LA: Les Liaisons Dangereuses.
PICTURES: Tom Jones (debut, 1963), Girl With Green Eyes, Georgy Girl (Acad. Award nom.), The Deadly Affair, Smashing Time, The Virgin Soldiers, Last of the Mobile Hot-Shots, Los Guerilleros (Killer From Yuma), Viva la Muerta—Tua! (Don't Turn the Other Cheek), Every Little Crook and Nanny, Everything You Always Wanted to Know About Sex* But Were Afraid to Ask, The National Health, The Happy Hooker, The Big Bus, Sunday Lovers, Morgan Stewart's Coming Home, Midnight, Getting It Right, Shine.

TELEVISION: BBC: Pretty Polly, Ain't Afraid to Dance, The End of the Tunnel, I Am Osango, What's Wrong with Humpty Dumpty, Egg On the Face of the Tiger, Blank Pages, A Midsummer Night's Dream, Pygmalion, William, Vienna 1900, Daft as a Brush, Not For Women Only, Calling the Shots. United States: Co-host: A.M. America. Movies: Turn of the Screw, Sooner or Later, Beggarman Thief, Gauguin the Savage, Seduction of Miss Leona, Rehearsal for Murder, The Bad Seed, My Two Loves, Jury Duty: The Comedy, What Ever Happened to Baby Jane? Mini-Series: Centennial. Series: House Calls, Teachers Only, Chicken Soup. Guest: The Muppet Show, Walking on Air, Candid Camera Christmas Special, Woman Alone, Tales From the Hollywood Hills: The Old Reliable, Death of a Son.

REDGRAVE, VANESSA
O.B.E. Actress. b. London, England, Jan. 30, 1937. p. Sir Michael Redgrave and Rachel Kempson. Sister of Lynn and Corin Redgrave. Mother of actresses Joely and Natasha Richardson. Early career with Royal Shakespeare Company. Appeared in documentary Tonight Let's All Make Love in London. Autobiography, 1994.
THEATER: Daniel Deronda, Cato Street, The Threepenny Opera, Twelfth Night, As You Like It, The Taming of the Shrew, Cymbeline, The Sea Gull, The Prime of Miss Jean Brodie, Antony & Cleopatra, Design for Living, Macbeth, Lady from the Sea, The Aspern Papers, Ghosts, Anthony and Cleopatra, Tomorrow Was War, A Touch of the Poet, Orpheus Descending, Madhouse in Goa, The Three Sisters, When She Danced, Maybe, Heartbreak House, Vita & Virginia.
PICTURES: Behind the Mask (debut, 1958), Morgan!: A Suitable Case for Treatment (Acad. Award nom.), A Man for All Seasons, Blow-Up, The Sailor From Gibraltar, Red and Blue, Camelot, The Charge of the Light Brigade, Isadora (Acad. Award nom.), Oh! What a Lovely War, The Sea Gull, A Quiet Place in the Country, Drop Out, The Trojan Women, La Vacanza, The Devils, Mary—Queen of Scots (Acad. Award nom.), Murder on the Orient Express, Out of Season, The Seven Percent Solution, Julia (Academy Award, best supporting actress, 1977), Agatha, Yanks, Bear Island, The Bostonians (Acad. Award nom.), Steaming, Wetherby, Prick Up Your Ears, Consuming Passions, Comrades, The Ballad of the Sad Cafe, Romeo-Juliet (voice), Howards End (Acad. Award nom.), Breath of Life, Sparrow, The House of the Spirits, Crime and Punishment, Mother's Boys, Great Moments in Aviation, Little Odessa, A Month by the Lake.
TELEVISION: Movies/Specials: A Farewell to Arms, Katherine Mansfield, Playing for Time (Emmy Award, 1981), My Body My Child, Wagner (theatrical in Europe), Three Sovereigns for Sarah, Peter the Great, Second Serve, A Man For All Seasons, Orpheus Descending, Young Catherine, What Ever Happened to Baby Jane?, They, Down Came a Blackbird. Guest: Faerie Tale Theatre (Snow White and the 7 Dwarfs).

REDSTONE, EDWARD S.
Exhibitor. b. Boston, MA, May 8, 1928. e. Colgate U., B.A., 1949; Harvard Grad. Sch. of Bus. Admin., M.B.A., 1952. v.p., treas., Northeast Drive-In Theatre Corp.; v.p.; Theatre Owners of New England, 1962; chmn., advis. coms., mem. bd. dirs., TOA; gen. conven. chmn., joint convention TOA & NAC, 1962; pres. National Assn. of Concessionaires, 1963; chief barker. Variety Club of New England, 1963; pres., Theatre Owners of New England; gen. chmn., 35th annual reg. convention.

REDSTONE, SUMNER MURRAY
Entertainment Corporation Executive, Lawyer; b. Boston, MA, May 27, 1923. e. Harvard, B.A., 1944, LL.B., 1947. Served to 1st Lt. AUS, 1943-45. Admitted to MA Bar 1947; U.S. Ct. Appeals 1st Circuit 1948, 8th Circuit 1950, 9th Circuit 1948; D.C. 1951; U.S. Supreme Ct. 1952; law sec. U.S. Ct. Appeals for 9th Circuit 1947-48; instr. U. San Francisco Law Sch. and Labor Management Sch., 1947; special asst. to U.S. Atty. General, 1948-51; partner firm Ford Bergson Adams Borkland & Redstone, Washington, D.C. 1951-54; exec. v.p. Northeast Drive-In Theatre Corp., 1954-68; pres. Northeast Theatre Corp.; chmn. bd., pres. & CEO, National Amusements, Inc.; chmn. bd., Viacom Int'l, Inc., 1987; asst. pres. Theatre Owners of America, 1960-63; pres. 1964-65; bd. chmn, National Assoc. of Theatre Owners, 1965-66. Member: Presidential Advisory Committee John F. Kennedy Center for the Performing Arts; chmn. Jimmy Fund, Boston 1960; chmn., met. div. Combined Jewish Philanthropies 1963; sponsor Boston Museum of Science; Trustee Children's Cancer Research Foundation; Art Lending Library; bd. of dirs. of TV Acad. of Arts and Sciences Fund; bd. dirs. Boston Arts Festival; v.p., exec. committee Will Rogers Memorial Fund; bd. overseers Dana Farber Cancer Institute; corp. New England Medical Center; Motion Picture Pioneers; bd. mem. John F. Kennedy Library Foundation; 1984-85; 1985-86 State Crusade Chairman American Cancer Society; Board of Overseers Boston Museum of Fine Arts; Professor, Boston U. Law Sch. 1982-83, 1985-86; Boston Latin School's Graduate of the Year, 1989; Acquired Viacom in 1987 which purchased

Paramount Communications in 1993. Member of exec. committe of the National Assoc. of Theatre Owners. Member, exec. bd., Combined Jewish Philanthropies. Judge on Kennedy Library Foundation. Founding trustee, American Cancer Society.
AWARDS: (Entertainment related) include: Communicator of the Year B'nai B'rith Communications, Cinema Lodge 1980; Man of the Year, Entertainment Industries div.; UJA-Federation, NY, 1988; Variety of New England Humanitarian Award, 1989; Motion Picture Pioneers Pioneer of the Year, 1991; Golden Plate Award American Acad. Achievement 32nd Annual Salute to Excellence Program; 1994, Man of the Year Award from MIPCOM, the Int'l Film and Programme Market for TV Video Cable and Satellite; 1995, Variety Club International Humanitarian Award; Hall of Fame Award, Broadcast & Cable Magazine, 1995.

REED, OLIVER
Actor. b. Wimbledon, England, Feb. 13, 1938. Nephew of late British dir. Sir Carol Reed. Dropped out of school in teens and worked as bouncer, boxer, taxi driver before first break on BBC-TV series The Golden Spur. Film debut as extra in Value for Money.
PICTURES: Value for Money (debut, 1955), Hello London, The Square Peg, The Captain's Table, Beat Girl (Wild for Kicks), The League of Gentlemen, The Angry Silence, The Two Faces of Dr. Jekyll (House of Fright), Sword of Sherwood Forest, His and Hers, No Love for Johnnie, The Bulldog Breed, The Rebel (Call Me Genius), Curse of the Werewolf, The Pirates of Blood River, Captain Clegg (Night Creatures), These Are the Damned, The Party's Over, The Scarlet Blade, Paranoic, The System (The Girl-Getters), The Brigand of Kandahar, The Trap, The Jokers, The Shuttered Room, I'll Never Forget What's 'is Name, Oliver!, The Assassination Bureau, Hannibal Brooks, Women in Love, Take a Girl Like You, The Lady in the Car with Glasses and a Gun, The Hunting Party, The Devils, Z.P.G., Sitting Target, Triple Echo, One Russian Summer, Dirty Weekend, Revolver (Blood in the Streets), Blue Blood, The Three Musketeers, Tommy, The Four Musketeers, Lisztomania (cameo), Ten Little Indians, Royal Flash, Sell Out, Blood in the Streets, Burnt Offerings, The Great Scout and Cathouse Thursday, Assault on Paradise (Ransom), Tomorrow Never Comes, Crossed Swords (The Prince and the Pauper), The Big Sleep, The Class of Miss MacMichael, Touch of the Sun, Dr. Heckyl & Mr. Hype, The Brood, Lion of the Desert, Condorman, Venom, The Great Question, Spasms, The Sting II, 99 Women, Two of a Kind, Black Arrow, Gor, Captive, Castaway, Dragonard, Fair Trade, The Return of the Musketeers, Hold My Hand I'm Dying, Fire With Fire, The Misfit Brigade, Rage to Kill, Skeleton Coast, Damnation Express, Captive Rage, The Adventures of Baron Munchausen, The Fall of the House of Usher, Master of Dragonard Hill, Outlaws, The Pit and the Pendulum, Panama, Severed Ties, Funny Bones.
TELEVISION: The Lady and the Highwayman, Treasure Island, A Ghost in Monte Carlo, Prisoner of Honor, Army, Return to Lonesome Dove.

REED, PAMELA
Actress. b. Tacoma, WA, Apr. 2, 1953. Ran day-care center and worked with Head Start children before studying drama at U. of Washington. Worked on Trans-Alaska pipeline. Off-Broadway showcases.
THEATER: Curse of the Starving Class (Off-B'way debut, 1978), All's Well That Ends Well (Central Park), Getting Out (Drama Desk Award), Aunt Dan and Lemon, Fools, The November People (Broadway debut), Sorrows of Stephen, Mrs. Warren's Profession, Getting Through the Night, Best Little Whorehouse in Texas, Fen, Standing on My Knees, Elektra.
PICTURES: The Long Riders (debut, 1980), Melvin and Howard, Eyewitness, Young Doctors in Love, The Right Stuff, The Goodbye People, The Best of Times, Clan of the Cave Bear, Rachel River, Chattahoochee, Cadillac Man, Kindergarten Cop, Passed Away, Bob Roberts, Junior.
TELEVISION: Series: The Andros Targets (TV debut, 1977), Grand, Family Album, The Home Court. Movies: Inmates—A Love Story, I Want To Live, Heart of Steel, Scandal Sheet, Caroline?, Woman With a Past, Born Too Soon, Deadly Whispers, The Man Next Door. Special: Tanner '88. Mini-Series: Hemingway. Guest: L.A. Law, The Simpsons (voice).

REES, ROGER
Actor. b. Aberystwyth, Wales, May 5, 1944. e. Camberwell Sch. of Art, Slade Sch. of Fine Art. Stage debut Hindle Wakes (Wimbledon, U.K., 1964). With Royal Shakespeare Co. from 1967. Starred in the title role The Adventures of Nicholas Nickleby (London and NY, Tony Award), also on stage in Hapgood (London, L.A.), Indiscretions (NY). Off-B'way in The End of the Day. Assoc. dir. Bristol Old Vic Theatre Co., 1986-present. Playwright with Eric Elice of Double Double and Elephant Manse.
PICTURES: Star 80 (debut, 1983), Keine Storung Bitte, Mountains of the Moon, If Looks Could Kill, Stop! Or My Mom Will Shoot, Robin Hood: Men in Tights, Sudden Manhattan.

TELEVISION: Movies: A Christmas Carol (released theatrically in Europe), Place of Peace, Under Western Eyes, Bouquet of Barbed Wire, Saigon: The Year of the Cat, Imaginary Friends, The Adventures of Nicolas Nickleby, The Comedy of Errors, Macbeth, The Voysey Inheritance, The Ebony Tower, The Finding, The Return of Sam McCloud, Charles & Diana: Unhappily Ever After, The Tower, The Possession of Michael D. Series: Cheers, Singles, M.A.N.T.I.S.

REESE, DELLA
Actress, Singer. b. Detroit, MI, July 6, 1932. r.n. Deloreese Patricia Early. e. Wayne St. Univ. As teen toured with Mahalia Jackson. Began recording in 1950's. Hit songs include Don't You Know.
PICTURES: Let's Rock!, Psychic Killer, Harlem Nights, The Distinguished Gentleman, A Thin Line Between Love and Hate.
TELEVISION: Series: The Della Reese Show, Chico and the Man, It Takes Two, Charlie & Company, The Royal Family, Touched by an Angel. Guest: The Ed Sullivan Show, Sanford and Son, The Rookies, McCloud, Welcome Back Kotter, The Love Boat, Night Court, The A-Team. Movies: The Voyage of the Yes, Twice in a Lifetime, The Return of Joe Forrester, Nightmare in Badham County. Mini-Series: Roots: The Next Generations.

REEVE, CHRISTOPHER
Actor. b. New York, NY, Sept. 25, 1952. e. Cornell U., B.A.; graduate work at Juilliard. Stage debut at McCarter Theatre in Princeton at age 9. B'way debut with Katharine Hepburn in A Matter of Gravity.
THEATER: NY: A Matter of Gravity, My Life, Fifth of July, The Marriage of Figaro, A Winter's Tale, Love Letters. LA: Summer and Smoke. Williamstown: The Front Page, Mesmer, Richard Corey, Royal Family, The Seagull, The Greeks, Holiday, Camino Real, John Brown's Body, Death Takes a Holiday, The Guardsman. Regional: The Irregular Verb to Love, Beggar's Opera, Troilus and Cressida, The Love Cure. London debut: The Aspern Papers.
PICTURES: Gray Lady Down (debut, 1978), Superman, Somewhere in Time, Superman II, Deathtrap, Monsignor, Superman III, The Bostonians, The Aviator, Street Smart, Superman IV: The Quest for Peace (also co-story), Switching Channels, Noises Off, Morning Glory, The Remains of the Day, Above Suspicion, Speechless, Village of the Damned.
TELEVISION: Series: Love of Life. Mini-Series: Kidnapped. Movies: Anna Karenina, The Great Escape II: The Untold Story, The Rose and the Jackal, Bump in the Night, Death Dreams, Mortal Sins, Nightmare in the Daylight, The Sea Wolf, Black Fox. Specials: Faerie Tale Theatre (Sleeping Beauty), The Last Ferry Home, Earth and the American Dream. Guest: Tales From the Crypt.

REEVES, KEANU
Actor. b. Beirut, Lebanon, Sept. 2, 1964. Lived in Australia and NY before family settled in Toronto. e. studied at Toronto's High School for the Performing Arts, then continued training at Second City Workshop. Made Coca-Cola commercial at 16. At 18 studied at Hedgerow Theatre in PA for summer. Professional debut on Hanging In, CBC local Toronto TV show. Toronto stage debut in Wolf Boy; later on stage in Romeo and Juliet, Hamlet.
PICTURES: Youngblood (debut, 1986), River's Edge, The Night Before, Permanent Record, The Prince of Pennsylvania, Dangerous Liaisons, Bill and Ted's Excellent Adventure, Parenthood, I Love You to Death, Tune in Tomorrow, Point Break, Bill and Ted's Bogus Journey, My Own Private Idaho, Bram Stoker's Dracula, Much Ado About Nothing, Freaked (cameo), Even Cowgirls Get the Blues, Little Buddha, Speed, Johnny Mnemonic, A Walk in the Clouds, Chain Reaction, Feeling Minnesota.
TELEVISION: Movies: Act of Vengeance, Under the Influence, Brotherhood of Justice, Babes In Toyland. Specials: I Wish I Were Eighteen Again, Life Under Water. Guest: The Tracey Ullman Show.

REEVES, STEVE
Actor. b. Glasgow, MT, Jan. 21, 1926. Delivered newspapers before winning body building titles Mr. Pacific, Mr. America, Mr. World, Mr. Universe. On stage in Kismet, The Vamp, Wish You Were Here.
PICTURES: Athena (debut, 1954), The Hidden Face, Jail Bait, Hercules, Hercules Unchained, Goliath and the Barbarians, The White Warrior, The Giant of Marathon, Morgan the Pirate, Thief of Baghdad, The Last Days of Pompeii, Duel of the Titans, The Trojan Horse, The Avenger (The Last Glories of Troy), The Slave (Son of Spartacus), The Shortest Day, Sandokan the Great, A Long Ride From Hell.

REHME, ROBERT G.
Executive. b. Cincinnati, OH, May 5, 1935. e. U. of Cincinnati. 1953, mgr., RKO Theatres, Inc., Cincinnati; 1961, adv. mgr., Cincinnati Theatre Co.; 1966, dir. of field adv., United Artists Pictures; 1969, named dir. of pub. and field adv./promotion,

Paramount Pictures; 1972, pres., BR Theatres and v.p., April Fools Films, gen. mgr. Tri-State Theatre Service; 1976, v.p. & gen. sls. mgr., New World Pictures; 1978, joined Avco Embassy Pictures as sr. v.p. & COO, then named exec. v.p.; 1979, named pres., Avco Embassy Pictures, Inc.; 1981, joined Universal Pictures as pres. of distrib. & marketing; 1982, named pres. of Universal Pictures; 1983, joined New World Pictures as co-chmn. & CEO; elected pres., Academy Foundation, 1988; pres. Foundation of Motion Picture Pioneers, 1989; 1st v.p., AMPAS; 1989, partner, Neufeld/Rehme prods. at Paramount; 1992, pres. of Academy of Motion Picture Arts & Sciences.
PICTURES: Patriot Games, Necessary Roughness, Gettysburg, Beverly Hills Cop III, Clear and Present Danger.

REID, BERYL
O.B.E. Actress. b. Hereford, England, June 17, 1920. Career in radio before London stage debut in revue, After the Show, 1951. Also on stage in The Killing of Sister George (London, NY, Tony Award), Spring Awakening, Campiello, Born in the Gardens, etc.
PICTURES: The Belles of St. Trinian's, The Extra Day, Trial and Error (The Dock Brief), Two-Way Stretch, Inspector Clouseau, Star!, The Killing of Sister George, The Assassination Bureau, Entertaining Mr. Sloane, The Beast in the Cellar, Dr. Phibes Rises Again, Psychomania, Father Dear Father, No Sex Please We're British, Joseph Andrews, Carry on Emmanuelle, Yellowbeard, The Doctor and the Devils, Didn't You Kill My Brother?
TELEVISION: Series: Educating Archie (BBC, 1952-56), Beryl Reid Says Good Evening, The Secret Diary of Adrian Mole. Mini-Series: Tinker Tailor Soldier Spy, Smiley's People. Movie: Duel of Hearts. Numerous specials.

REID, TIM
Actor. b. Norfolk, CA, Dec. 19, 1944. m. actress Daphne Maxwell. Started as half of comedy team of Tim and Tom in 1969, before becoming solo stand-up comedian. Published photo/poetry collection As I Find It, 1982.
PICTURES: Dead Bang, The Fourth War, Once Upon A Time...When We Were Colored.
TELEVISION: Series: Easy Does It... Starring Frankie Avalon, The Marilyn McCoo and Billy Davis Jr. Show, The Richard Pryor Show, WKRP in Cincinnati, Teachers Only, Simon and Simon, Frank's Place (also co-exec. prod.), Snoops (also co-exec. prod.). Guest: That's My Mama, Rhoda, What's Happening, Matlock. Movies: Perry Mason: The Case of the Silenced Singer, Stephen King's IT, Race to Freedom: The Underground Railroad (also co-exec. prod.), Simon & Simon: In Trouble Again. Special: Mastergate.

REILLY, CHARLES NELSON
Actor, Director. b. New York, NY, Jan. 13. 1931. e. U. of CT. On Broadway mostly in comedy roles before turning to TV and films. Recently directed stage plays.
THEATER: As actor: Bye Bye Birdie (debut), How to Succeed in Business Without Really Trying (Tony Award, 1962), Hello Dolly!, Skyscraper, God's Favorite. Acted in 22 off-B'way plays. Founded musical comedy dept. HB Studios. Conceived and dir.: The Belle of Amherst, Paul Robeson, The Nerd (dir.). Resident dir.: Burt Reynolds' Jupiter Theatre.
PICTURES: A Face in the Crowd, Two Tickets to Paris, The Tiger Makes Out, Cannonball Run II, Body Slam, All Dogs Go to Heaven (voice), Rock-a-Doodle (voice), A Troll in Central Park (voice).
TELEVISION: Series: The Steve Lawrence Show, The Ghost and Mrs. Muir, Dean Martin Presents The Golddiggers, Liddsville, Arnie, It Pays to Be Ignorant (1973-74), Match Game P.M., Sweethearts (game show host). Guest: Tonight Show (guest host), Dean Martin Show. Movies: Call Her Mom, The Three Kings, Bandit, Bandit Goes Country. Special: Wind in the Wire.

REILLY, MICHAEL
Executive. Pres., Variety Clubs International.

REINAUER, RICHARD
Executive. b. Chicago, IL, April 28, 1926. e. U. of Illinois, grad. 1952. Prod., dir., freelance, 1952-59; bus. mgr., asst. prod., Showcase Theatre Evanston, 1952; prod., dir., NBC, Chicago, 1953-55; film dir., Kling Studios, 1956; broadcast supvis. Foote Cone & Belding, 1956-59; dir., radio, TV & m.p., American Medical Assoc., 1959-64; pres., Communications Counselors, 1963-64; exec. dir., TV Arts & Sciences Foundation, 1964; pres., Acad. of TV Arts & Sciences, Chicago Chapter, 1970-72; assoc. prod. & asst. dir. Wild Kingdom & asst. to pres., Don Meier Prods., 1965-1988. Member: Illinois Nature Preserve Commission. Lifetime member: Acad. of TV Arts & Sciences, Pres. Pinewood Prods. Film Co. Communications consultant and advisor.

REINER, CARL
Actor, Director, Writer, Producer. b. New York, NY, March 20, 1922. Son is actor-director-writer Rob Reiner. Comedian on B'way: Call Me Mr., Inside U.S.A., Alive and Kicking. Author (novels): Enter Laughing, All Kinds of Love, Continue Laughing. Playwright: Something Different.
PICTURES: Actor only: Happy Anniversary, Gidget Goes Hawaiian, It's a Mad Mad Mad Mad World, The Russians Are Coming the Russians Are Coming, Don't Worry We'll Think of a Title, A Guide for the Married Man, Generation, The End, The Spirit of '76. Writer-Actor: The Gazebo, The Thrill of It All (also co-prod.), The Art of Love. Director: Enter Laughing (also co-s.p.), The Comic (also s.p., actor), Where's Poppa?, Oh God! (also actor), The One and Only, The Jerk (also actor), Dead Men Don't Wear Plaid (also co-s.p., actor), The Man With Two Brains (also co-s.p.), All of Me, Summer Rental, Summer School (also actor), Bert Rigby You're a Fool (also s.p.), Sibling Rivalry, Fatal Instinct (also actor).
TELEVISION: Series: The Fashion Story, The Fifty-Fourth Street Revue, Eddie Condon's Floor Show, Your Show of Shows (also writer), Droodles (panelist), Caesar's Hour (also writer; 2 Emmy Awards for supporting actor, 1956, 1957), Sid Caesar Invites You, Keep Talking, Dinah Shore Chevy Show (writer), Take a Good Look (panelist), The Dick Van Dyke Show (also creator-prod.-dir.-writer; 5 Emmy Awards: writing: 1962, 1963, 1964, producing: 1965, 1966), Art Linkletter Show, The Celebrity Game (host), The New Dick Van Dyke Show (creator-prod.-writer), Good Heavens (also exec. prod.), Sunday Best (host). Movies: Medical Story, Skokie. Guest: Comedy Spot, Judy Garland Show, Burke's Law, That Girl, Night Gallery, Faerie Tale Theatre (Pinocchio), It's Garry Shandling's Show, Mad About You (Emmy Award, 1995). Special: The Sid Caesar-Imogene Coca-Carl Reiner-Howard Morris Special (Emmy Award for writing, 1967).
RECORDINGS: Carl Reiner and Mel Brooks, The 2000 Year Old Man, The 2001 Year Old Man, 2013 Year Old Man, Continue Laughing, A Connecticut Yankee in King Arthur's Court, Miracle on 34th Street, Jack and the Beanstalk, Aesop's Fables.

REINER, ROB
Actor, Director, Writer. b. New York, NY, March 6, 1947. Father is actor-writer-director-producer Carl Reiner. Worked as actor with regional theatres and improvisational comedy troupes. Wrote for the Smothers Brothers Comedy Hour. Breakthrough as actor came in 1971 when signed by Norman Lear for All in the Family. Directorial debut with This Is Spinal Tap, 1984. Co-founder of Castle Rock Entertainment.
PICTURES: Actor: Enter Laughing, Halls of Anger, Where's Poppa?, Summertree, Fire Sale, Throw Momma From the Train, Postcards From the Edge, The Spirit of '76, Sleepless in Seattle, Bullets Over Broadway, Mixed Nuts, Bye Bye Love. Director: This is Spinal Tap (also actor, co-s.p.), The Sure Thing, Stand by Me, The Princess Bride. Dir./Co-Prod.: When Harry Met Sally..., Misery, A Few Good Men (Acad. Award nom. for best picture; DGA nom.), North, The American President, Ghosts of Mississippi.
TELEVISION: Series: All in the Family (2 Emmy Awards: 1974, 1978), Free Country (also co-writer), Morton & Hayes (also co-creator, co-exec. prod.). Movies: Thursday's Game, More Than Friends (also co-writer, co-exec. prod.), Million Dollar Infield (also co-prod., co-writer). Guest: Gomer Pyle, Batman, Beverly Hillbillies, Room 222, Partridge Family, Odd Couple, It's Garry Shandling's Show. Special: But... Seriously (exec. prod.).

REINHOLD, JUDGE
Actor. b. Wilmington, DE, May 21, 1957. r.n. Edward Ernest Reinhold Jr. e. Mary Washington Coll., North Carolina Sch. of Arts. Acted in regional theatres including Burt Reynolds dinner theater in FL before signed to TV contract at Paramount.
PICTURES: Running Scared (debut, 1979), Stripes, Pandemonium, Fast Times at Ridgemont High, Lords of Discipline, Roadhouse 66, Gremlins, Beverly Hills Cop, Head Office, Off Beat, Ruthless People, Beverly Hills Cop II, Vice Versa, Rosalie Goes Shopping, Daddy's Dyin', Enid is Sleeping (Over Her Dead Body), Zandalee, Near Misses, Baby on Board, Bank Robber, Beverly Hills Cop III, The Santa Clause.
TELEVISION: Series: Secret Service Guy. Movies: Survival of Dana, A Matter of Sex, Promised a Miracle, Black Magic, Four Eyes and Six-Guns, Dad the Angel and Me, As Good as Dead, The Wharf Rat. Guest: Seinfeld. Specials: A Step Too Slow, The Willmar Eight, The Parallax Garden.

REISENBACH, SANFORD E.
Executive. e. NYU. Associated with Grey Advertising for 20 years; exec. v.p. and pres. of Grey's leisure/entertainment division in N.Y. In August, 1979, joined Warner Bros. as exec. v.p. in chg. of worldwide adv. & pub.; named pres., worldwide adv. & pub., 1985. Appt. exec. v.p. of marketing and planning, Warner Bros. Inc., 1988.

REISER, PAUL
Actor. b. New York, NY, Mar. 30, 1957. e. SUNY/Binghamton. Started performing as a stand-up comic in such clubs as Catch a Rising Star, the Improv, and the Comic Strip. Author: Couplehood (1994).

PICTURES: Diner (debut, 1982), Beverly Hills Cop, Aliens, Beverly Hills Cop II, Cross My Heart, Crazy People, The Marrying Man, Mr. Write, Bye Bye Love.
TELEVISION: Series: My Two Dads, Mad About You. Special: Paul Reiser—Out on a Whim. Guest: The Tonight Show, Late Night With David Letterman. Movies: Sunset Limousine, The Tower. Pilots: Diner, Just Married.

REISNER, ALLEN
Director. b. New York, NY.
PICTURES: The Day They Gave the Babies Away, St. Louis Blues, All Mine to Give.
TELEVISION: Movies/Specials: Captain and the Kings, Mary Jane Harper Cried Last Night, Your Money or Your Wife, To Die in Paris, The Clift, Skag, They're Playing Our Song, The Gentleman From Seventh Avenue, Escape of Pierre Mendes-France, Deliverance of Sister Cecelia, The Sound of Silence. Series: Murder She Wrote, Twilight Zone, Hardcastle & McCormick, Airwolf, The Mississippi, Hawaii Five-O, Blacke's Magic, Law and Harry McGraw, Playhouse 90, Studio One, Climax, United States Steel Hour, Suspense, Danger, etc.

REISS, JEFFREY C.
Executive. b. Brooklyn, NY, April 14, 1942. e. Washington U., St. Louis, B.A., 1963. Consultant at NYU and Manhattanville Coll. and instructor at Brooklyn Coll. before entering industry. Agent in literary dept. for General Artists Corp., 1966. Supervised development in NY of Tandem Prods. for Norman Lear, 1968. Produced off-B'way plays 1968-70. Dir. of program acquistion devel. for Cartridge TV, Inc. (mfg. of first home video cassette players-recorders), 1970-73. Joined ABC Entertainment as director of network feature films, 1973-75. Founder and pres., Showtime Pay TV Network, 1976-80. Co-founder, pres. & CEO, Cable Health Network, 1981-83. 1983, named vice chmn. & CEO, Lifetime Cable Network following Cable Health Network merger with Daytime. Chmn. of the board, pres. & CEO, Reiss Media Enterprises, Inc. 1984. Founder & chmn. of board, Request Television (pay-per-view svc.), 1985.

REISS, STUART A.
Set Decorator. b. Chicago, IL, July 15, 1921. e. L.A. High Sch., 1939. Property man, 20th-Fox, 1939-42; U.S. Army Air Corps, 1942-45; joined 20th-Fox as set decorator in 1945. Worked on over 30 tv shows and over 100 motion pictures, receiving 6 Academy Award noms. and 2 Oscars.
PICTURES: Titanic, How to Marry a Millionaire, Hell and High Water, There's No Business Like Show Business, Soldier of Fortune, The Seven Year Itch, Man in the Grey Flannel Suit, Teen Age Rebel, The Diary of Anne Frank (Academy Award, 1959), What a Way to Go, Fantastic Voyage (Academy Award, 1966), Doctor Doolittle, Oh God!, The Swarm, Beyond the Poseidon Adventure, Carbon Copy, All the Marbles, The Man Who Loved Women, Micki and Maude, A Fine Mess.

REITMAN, IVAN
Director, Producer. b. Komarmo, Czechoslovakia, Oct. 26, 1946. Moved to Canada at age 4. e. McMaster U. Attended National Film Board's Summer Institute directing three short films including Orientation (1968) which received theatrical distribution. Produced Canadian TV show in 1970s with Dan Aykroyd as announcer.
THEATER: Prod.: The National Lampoon Show, The Magic Show, Merlin (also dir.).
PICTURES: Dir./Prod.: Foxy Lady (debut, 1971; also edit., music), Cannibal Girls, Meatballs (dir. only), Stripes, Ghostbusters, Legal Eagles (also co-story), Twins, Ghostbusters II, Kindergarten Cop, Dave, Junior. Prod. only: Columbus of Sex, They Came From Within (Shivers), Death Weekend (The House By the Lake), Rabid (co-exec. prod.), Blackout, National Lampoon's Animal House, Heavy Metal, Spacehunter: Adventures in the Forbidden Zone (exec. prod.), Big Shots (exec. prod.), Casual Sex? (exec. prod.), Feds (exec. prod.), Stop! Or My Mom Will Shoot, Beethoven (exec. prod.), Beethoven's 2nd (exec. prod.).
TELEVISION: Series: Delta House.

RELPH, MICHAEL
Producer, Director, Writer, Designer. 1942, became art dir. Ealing Studios then assoc. prod. to Michael Balcon on The Captive Heart, Frieda, Kind Hearts and Coronets, Saraband (also designed: Oscar nom.). 1948 appt. producer and formed prod/dir. partnership Basil Dearden (until 1972). 1971-76, Governor, Brit. Film Institute. Chairman BFI Prod. Board. Chairman Film Prod. Assoc. of G.B.; member Films Council.
PICTURES: For Ealing: The Blue Lamp (BFA Award, 1950), I Believe in You, The Gentle Gunman, The Square Ring, The Rainbow Jacket, Out of the Clouds, The Ship That Died of Shame, Davy, The Smallest Show on Earth (for Brit. Lion), Violent Playground (for Rank), Rockets Galore (Island Fling), Sapphire (BFA Award, 1959). 1960 Founder Dir. Allied Film Makers: Prod. The League of Gentlemen, Man in the Moon (co-s.p.), Victim, Life For Ruth (Walk in the Shadow). Also pro-

duced: Secret Partner, All Night Long, The Mind Benders, A Place To Go (s.p.), Woman of Straw (co-s.p.), Masquerade (co-s.p.), The Assassination Bureau (prod., s.p., designer), The Man Who Haunted Himself (prod., co-s.p.). 1978, exec. in chg. prod., Kendon Films, Ltd. Exec. prod., Scum, 1982. Co-prod., An Unsuitable Job for a Woman. 1984, exec. prod.: Treasure Houses of Britain; TV series, prod., Heavenly Pursuits, 1985-86; Gospel According to Vic (U.S.). Prod. Consultant: Torrents of Spring.

RELPH, SIMON
Producer. b. London, Eng., April 13, 1940. Entered industry 1961.
PICTURES: Reds (exec. prod.), The Return of the Soldier, Privates on Parade, The Ploughman's Lunch, Secret Places, Laughterhouse (exec. prod.), Wetherby, Comrades, Enchanted April (exec. prod.), Damage (coprod.), The Secret Rapture, Camilla, Look Me In The Eye, Blue Juice, The Slab Boys.

RELYEA, ROBERT E.
Producer, Executive. b. Santa Monica, CA, May 3, 1930. e. UCLA, B.S., 1952. In Army 1953-55. Entered industry in 1955; asst. dir. on The Magnificent Seven and West Side Story; assoc. prod. and 2nd unit dir. on The Great Escape; partnered with Steve McQueen as exec. prod. on Bullitt and The Reivers. 1979-82, exec. v.p. with Melvin Simon Prods. Served as exec. v.p. in chg. world wide prod., Keith Barish Prods. 1983-85. Served as sr. v.p. prod., Lorimar Prods. 1985-90. Named sr. v.p. features prod. management, Paramount Pictures Motion Picture Gp., 1989.
PICTURES: Exec. Prod.: Bullitt, The Reivers, Day of the Dolphin. Prod.: Love at First Bite, My Bodyguard, Porky's.

REMAR, JAMES
Actor. b. Boston, MA, Dec. 31, 1953. Studied acting at NY's Neighborhood Playhouse and with Stella Adler. Appeared on NY stage in Yo-Yo, Early Dark, Bent, California Dog Fight.
PICTURES: On the Yard (debut, 1979), The Warriors, Cruising, The Long Riders, Windwalker, Partners, 48 HRS, The Cotton Club, The Clan of the Cave Bear, Band of the Hand, Quiet Cool, Rent-a-Cop, The Dream Team, Drugstore Cowboy, Tales from the Darkside, Silence Like Glass, White Fang, Fatal Instinct, Blink, Renaissance Man, Miracle on 34th Street, Boys on the Side, Session Man (Academy Award, Best Action Short, 1991), Across the Moon, Judge Dredd (unbilled), The Quest, The Phantom, Robo-Warriors, Tale From The Darkside: The Movie, WIld Bill, Exquisite Tenderness, The Phantom.
TELEVISION: Movies: The Mystic Warrior, Desperado, Deadlock, Brotherhood of the Gun, Fatal Charm, Indecency. Guest: Hill Street Blues, Miami Vice, The Equalizer, The Hitchhiker, Tales From The Crypt.

REMBUSCH, MICHAEL J.
Executive. b. Indianapolis, IN, April 8, 1950. e. Ball State U. Son of Trueman T. Rembusch. Began working for father's circuit, Syndicate Theatres, Inc., in 1967. From 1970-80, managed various theatres in circuit. 1980-85, v.p., operations. 1985-90, acquired Heaston circuit (Indianapolis). Became pres., Syndicate Theatres, Inc. 1987-90, chmn, Indiana Film Commission. 1992 to present, pres., Theatre Owners of Indiana.

REMBUSCH, TRUEMAN T.
Exhibitor. b. Shelbyville, IN, July 27, 1909. f. Frank J. Rembusch, pioneer exhibitor. Inventor & manufacturer Glass Mirror Screen. e. U. of Notre Dame Sch. of Commerce, 1928. m. Mary Agnes Finneran. Ent. m.p. ind., 1928, servicing sound equip., father's circuit; became mgr., 1932; elect. bd. of dir., Allied Theatre Owners of Ind., 1936-45, pres. 1944-51, 1952-53; dir. chmn. Allied TV Committee, 1945-50; pres. Allied States Assn., 1950-51; 1952, named by Allied as one of tri-umvirate heading COMPO; 1953, named by Gov. of Indiana as dir. State Fair Board; elected chmn. Joint Com. on Toll TV, 1954; currently pres. Syndicate Theatres, Inc., Franklin, Ind; member, Notre Dame Club of Indianapolis (Man of Yr., 1950); BPOE, 4th Degree K of C, Meridian Hills Country Club, Marco Island Country Club. American Radio Relay League (amateur & commerce, licenses); OX5 Aviation Pioneers; awarded patent, recording 7 counting device, 1951; dir. Theatre Owners of Indiana; dir. to NATO; dir. NATO member ad hoc comm; 1972 chair., NATO Statistical Committee; 1976, NITE Award service to Independent Exhibition.

REMSEN, BERT
Actor. b. Glen Cove, NY, Feb. 25, 1925. e. Ithaca Coll.
PICTURES: Pork Chop Hill, Kid Galahad, Moon Pilot, Brewster McCloud, Thieves Like us, Baby Blue Marine, McCabe and Mrs. Miller, Sweet Hostage, California Split, Nashville, Tarantulas, Buffalo Bill and the Indians, A Wedding, The Rose, Uncle Joe Shannon, Carny, Borderline, Second Hand Hearts, Joni, Inside Moves, Looking to Get Out, I

Sting II, Lies, Independence Day, Code of Silence, Stand Alone, Eye of the Tiger, South of Reno, Remote Control, Vietnam Texas, Miss Firecracker, Daddy's Dyin'...Who's Got the Will?, Dick Tracy, Only the Lonely, Evil Spirits, The Player, The Bodyguard, Jack the Bear, Army of One, Maverick.
TELEVISION: *Series*: Gibbsville, It's a Living, Dallas. *Movies*: Who Is Julia?, The Awakening Land, Burning Rage, Crazy Times, Hobson's Choice, If Tomorrow Comes, Love For Rent, Mothers Against Drunk Driving, Little Ladies of the Night, Memorial Day, Maid for Each Other, There Was a Little Boy, In the Shadows Someone's Watching, Rise and Walk: The Dennis Byrd Story. *Guest*: Matlock, Jake and the Fatman. *Mini-Series*: Space.

RENO, JEAN
Actor. b. Casablanca, Morocco. To France in early 1970's to serve in French military. Began acting in Paris with theatre workshop, then established his own travelling acting company.
PICTURES: Claire de Femme, Le Dernier Combat, Subway, Signes Exterieurs de Richesse, Notre Histoire, I Love You, The Big Blue, La Femme Nikita, L'homme au Masque d'Or, L'Operation Corned Beef, Loulou Graffiti, The Professional (Leon), French Kiss, The Visitors (also s.p.), Beyond the Clouds.

RESNAIS, ALAIN
Director. b. Cannes, France, June 3, 1922. Began career as asst. dir. to Nicole Vedres on compilation of film for Paris 1900. During '50s worked as asst. editor and editor; experimented with making his own 16mm films. Directed or co-dir. several short films: Van Gogh, Gauguin, Guernica, The Statues Also Die, Night and Fog, etc.
PICTURES: Hiroshima Mon Amour (feature debut, 1959), Last Year at Marienbad, Muriel, La Guerre Est Finie (The War Is Over), Je t'Aime Je t'Aime (also co-s.p.), Stavisky, Providence, Mon Oncle d'Amerique, Life Is a Bed of Roses, L'Amour a Mort (Love Unto Death), Melo (also s.p.), I Want to Go Home, No Smoking.

RESNICK, JOEL H.
Executive. b. New York, NY, April 28, 1936. e. U. of PA, B.A., 1958; NY Law Sch. 1961, admitted to NY State Bar. 1962 received Masters of Law degree in taxation; 1961-66 served as associate with NY law firm, Phillips Nizer Benjamin Krim & Ballon; Was in-house counsel to United Artists Corp. 1967, joined UA as spec. asst. to the sr. v.p. & gen. mgr.; 1970, moved to American Multi-Cinema, Inc., Kansas City, as asst. to pres.; 1972, named v.p. in chg. development; 1976, promoted to v.p. in chg. film development; 1977, named exec. v.p.; 1983, elected exec. v.p. & dir., AMC Entertainment; 1984, appt. to office of pres. as chmn. & CEO, film mktg.; 1986, resigned to join Orion Pictures Distribution Corp. as pres.; has served as co-chmn. NATO trade practices comm. since 1979. 1982 elected pres., NATO; 1984, became chmn. NATO bd.; 1989, v.p. Foundation of Motion Picture Pioneers; 1990, resigned from Orion; pres., GKC Theatres, Springfield, IL, 1991-92; Cinemark Theatres, Intl. Development, 1994-.

REUBENS, PAUL (PEE-WEE HERMAN)
Actor, Writer. r.n. Paul Rubenfeld. Professional name Paul Reubens. b. Peekskill, NY, Aug. 27, 1952. Raised in Sarasota, FL. e. Boston U., California Inst. of the Arts (1976). Pee-wee character made debut, 1978 at Groundlings, improvisational theater, Los Angeles followed by The Pee-wee Herman Show, a live show which gave 5 months of sold-out performances at the L.A. rock club, Roxy, and was later taped for HBO special. Guest appearances on Late Night With David Letterman, The Gong Show, 227, Tonight Show, Mork & Mindy, Joan Rivers' The Late Show, and The Dating Game.
PICTURES: Midnight Madness, The Blues Brothers, Cheech & Chong's Next Movie, Cheech and Chong's Nice Dreams, Pandemonium, Meatballs Part II, Pee-wee's Big Adventure (also co-s.p.), Flight of the Navigator (voice), Back to the Beach, Big Top Pee-wee (also co-s.p., co-prod.), Batman Returns, Buffy the Vampire Slayer, Tim Burton's The Nightmare Before Christmas (voice), Dunston Checks In, Matilda.
TELEVISION: *Series*: Pee-wee's Playhouse (also creator, co-dir., co-writer, exec. prod.; 12 Emmy Awards). *Specials*: Pinocchio (Faerie Tale Theatre), Pee-wee Herman Show, Pee-wee's Playhouse Christmas Special (also exec. prod., co-dir. co-writer). *Guest*: Murphy Brown.

REVILL, CLIVE
Actor. r.n. Selsby. b. Wellington, New Zealand, Apr. 18, 1930. e. Rongotai Coll., Victoria U.
THEATER: Irma La Douce, The Mikado, Oliver, Marat/Sade, Jew of Malta, Sherry, Chichester Season, The Incomparable Max, Sherlock Holmes, Lolita, Pirates of Penzance, Mystery of Edwin Drood, My Fair Lady, Bandido.
PICTURES: Reach for the Sky, The Headless Ghost, Bunny Lake Is Missing, Once Upon a Tractor, Modesty Blaise, A Fine Madness, Kaleidoscope, The Double Man, Fathom, Italian

Secret Service, Nobody Runs Forever, Shoes of the Fisherman, Assassination Bureau, The Private Life of Sherlock Holmes, The Buttercup Chain, A Severed Head, Boulevard de Rhum, Avanti!, Escape to the Sun, Ghost in the Noonday Sun, The Legend of Hell House, The Little Prince, The Black Windmill, One of Our Dinosaurs Is Missing, Galileo, Matilda, Zorro the Gay Blade, Transformers (voice), Rumpelstiltskin, The Emperor's New Clothes, Mack the Knife, CHUD II: Bud the Chud, Frog Prince, Let Him Have It, Robin Hood: Men in Tights, Crime and Punishment, Arabian Knight (voice), The Wacky Adventures of Dr. Boris and Nurse Shirley, Dracula—Dead and Loving It!
TELEVISION: Chicken Soup with Barley, Volpone, Bam Pow Zapp, Candida, Platonov, A Bit of Vision, Mill Hill, The Piano Player, Hopcroft in Europe, A Sprig of Broome, Ben Franklin in Paris, Pinocchio, The Great Houdini, Show Business Hall of Fame, Feather and Father, Winner Take All, The New Avengers, Licking Hitler, Columbo, Centennial, A Man Called Sloane, Nobody's Perfect, Marya, Moviola, Diary of Anne Frank, Mikado, The Sorcerer, Wizards & Warriors, George Washington, Murder She Wrote, Faerie Tale Theatre, Twilight Zone, Newhart, Hunter, Star Trek, The Sea Wolf, Babylon 5, Fortune Hunter, The Preston Episodes (series), Murphy Brown.

REYNOLDS, BURT
Actor, Director. b. Waycross, GA, Feb. 11, 1936. Former Florida State U. football star; TV and film stunt performer. Won fame as actor on TV in series Riverboat. Founded the Burt Reynolds Dinner Theater in Jupiter, FL, 1979. *Autobiography*: My Life (1994).
THEATER: Mister Roberts (NY City Center), Look We've Come Through (B'way debut, 1956), The Rainmaker.
PICTURES: Angel Baby (debut, 1961), Armored Command, Operation CIA, Navajo Joe, Fade In, Impasse, Shark, Sam Whiskey, 100 Rifles, Skullduggery, Fuzz, Deliverance, Everything You Always Wanted To Know About Sex, Shamus, White Lightning, The Man Who Loved Cat Dancing, The Longest Yard, W.W. & The Dixie Dancekings, At Long Last Love, Hustle, Lucky Lady, Gator (also dir.), Silent Movie, Nickelodeon, Smokey and the Bandit, Semi-Tough, The End (also dir.), Hooper, Starting Over, Rough Cut, Smokey and the Bandit II, Cannonball Run, Paternity, Sharky's Machine (also dir.), The Best Little Whorehouse in Texas, Best Friends, Stroker Ace, Smokey and the Bandit III (cameo), The Man Who Loved Women, Cannonball Run II, City Heat, Stick (also dir.), Uphill All the Way (cameo), Heat, Malone, Rent-a-Cop, Switching Channels, Physical Evidence, Breaking In, All Dogs Go to Heaven (voice), Modern Love, The Player (cameo), Cop and a Half, The Maddening, Devil Inside, Meet Wally Sparks, Striptease, Mad Dog Time, Citizen Ruth.
TELEVISION: *Series*: Riverboat, Gunsmoke, Hawk, Dan August, Out of This World (voice), B.L. Stryker (also co-exec. prod.), Evening Shade (Emmy Award, 1991). *Movies*: Hunters Are for Killing, Run Simon Run, The Man Upstairs (co-exec. prod. only), The Man From Left Field (also dir.). *Host*: The Story of Hollywood. *Special*: Wind in the Wire. *Dir.*: Alfred Hitchcock Presents (1985).

REYNOLDS, DEBBIE
Actress. r.n. Mary Frances Reynolds. b. El Paso, TX, April 1, 1932. Daughter is actress Carrie Fisher. e. Burbank & John Burroughs H.S., Burbank, CA. With Burbank Youth Symphony during h.s.; beauty contest winner (Miss Burbank) 1948; signed by Warner Bros.; on stage in Personal Appearances, Blis-Hayden Theater. Voted Star of Tomorrow, 1952. *Autobiography*: Debbie: My Life (1988).
THEATER: B'way: Irene, Woman of the Year.
PICTURES: June Bride (debut, 1948), The Daughter of Rosie O'Grady, Three Little Words, Two Weeks With Love, Mr. Imperium, Singin' in the Rain, Skirts Ahoy, I Love Melvin, Give a Girl a Break, The Affairs of Dobie Gillis, Susan Slept Here, Athena, Hit the Deck, The Tender Trap, The Catered Affair, Bundle of Joy, Tammy and the Bachelor, This Happy Feeling, The Mating Game, Say One for Me, It Started with a Kiss, The Gazebo, The Rat Race, Pepe (cameo), The Pleasure of His Company, The Second Time Around, How the West Was Won, My Six Loves, Mary Mary, Goodbye Charlie, The Unsinkable Molly Brown (Acad. Award nom.), The Singing Nun, Divorce American Style, How Sweet It Is, What's the Matter with Helen?, Charlotte's Web (voice), That's Entertainment!, The Bodyguard (cameo), Heaven and Earth, That's Entertainment III, Mother.
TELEVISION: *Series*: The Debbie Reynolds Show, Aloha Paradise. *Movies*: Sadie and Son, Perry Mason: The Case of the Musical Murders, Battling for Baby. *Special*: Jack Paar Is Alive and Well.

REYNOLDS, GENE
Executive, Producer. b. Cleveland, OH, April 4, 1925. Acted from 1936-55. Executive producer of Room 222, Anna and the King, Karen. Producer of M*A*S*H, 1972-76. Currently pres., Director's Guild of America, Inc.

REYNOLDS, KEVIN
Director, Writer. b. 1950. e. Texas Marine Acad., Trinity Univ., Baylor Univ. (law degree), USC film school. Student film Proof led to offer to do expanded feature version subsequently retitled Fandango.
PICTURES: Red Dawn (co-s.p.). *Director:* Fandango (dir. debut, 1985; also s.p.), The Beast, Robin Hood: Prince of Thieves, Rapa Nui (also s.p.), Waterworld.

REYNOLDS, MARJORIE
Actress. r.n. Marjorie Goodspeed. b. Buhl, ID, Aug. 12, 1921. On screen as child actor in silent films. Resumed career during talkies billed as Marjorie Moore, then Reynolds, starting in 1937.
PICTURES: Scaramouche (debut, 1923), Revelation, College Humor (as Marjorie Moore), Wine Women and Song, Big Broadcast of 1936, Collegiate, College Holiday (1st billing as Marjorie Reynolds), Murder in Greenwich Village, Champagne Waltz, Western Trails, Mr. Wong in Chinatown, Sky Patrol, Enemy Agent, Robin Hood of the Precos, Dude Cowboy, Cyclone on Horseback, Up in the Air, The Great Swindle, Tillie the Toiler, Top Sergeant Mulligan, Holiday Inn, Star-Spangled Rhythm, Dixie, Ministry of Fear, Up in Mabel's Room, Three Is a Family, Duffy's Tavern, Bring on the Girls, Monsieur Beaucaire, Meet Me on Broadway, The Time of Their Lives, Heaven Only Knows, Bad Men of Tombstone, That Midnight Kiss, The Great Jewel Robbery, Customs Agent, Rookie Fireman, The Home Town Story, His Kind of Woman, No Holds Barred, Models Inc. (Call Girl), Mobs Inc., Juke Box Rhythm, The Silent Witness, ... All the Marbles.
TELEVISION: *Series:* The Life of Riley.

REYNOLDS, SHELDON
Writer, Producer, Director. b. Philadelphia, PA, 1923. e. NYU. Radio-TV writer; programs include My Silent Partner, Robert Q. Lewis Show, We the People, Danger, Adventures of Sherlock Holmes (prod., dir., writer), Dick and the Duchess (prod., dir., writer), Foreign Intrigue (dir., prod., writer). TV Special: Sophia Loren's Rome (dir., writer). Movies: Foreign Intrigue (dir., prod., s.p.), Assignment to Kill (dir., s.p.).

REYNOLDS, STUART
Producer. b. Chicago, IL, March 22, 1907. e. Chicago law schools. Adv. exec., Lord and Thomas, BBDO. General Mills; sales exec. Don Lee-Mutual; formed Stuart Reynolds Prod., TV films. Now motion picture & TV program consultant.
TELEVISION: General Electric Theatre, Cavalcade of America, Your Jeweler's Showcase, Wild Bill Hickok. Producer and worldwide distributor of educational/training films; Eye of the Beholder.

RHAMES, VING
Actor. e. Juilliard Sch. of Drama.
THEATER: *B'way:* The Boys of Winter. *Off-B'way:* Map of the World, Short Eyes, Richard III, Ascension Day. *Europe:* Ajax.
PICTURES: Patty Hearst, Casualties of War, Jacob's Ladder, The Long Walk Home, Flight of the Intruder, Homicide, The People Under the Stairs, Stop! Or My Mom Will Shoot, Bound by Honor, Dave, The Saint of Fort Washington, Pulp Fiction, Drop Squad, Kiss of Death, Mission: Impossible, Striptease, Rosewood.
TELEVISION: *Series:* Another World. *Movie:* The Iran Project. *Special:* Go Tell It on the Mountain. *Guest:* Miami Vice, Spenser: For Hire, Tour of Duty, Crime Story.

RHODES, CYNTHIA
Actress, Dancer. b. Nashville, TN, Nov. 21, 1956. m. singer Richard Marx. Appeared on many TV specials, inc. Opryland USA, Music Hall America.
PICTURES: Xanadu, One From the Heart, Flashdance, Staying Alive, Runaway, Dirty Dancing, Curse of the Crystal Eye.

RHYS-DAVIES, JOHN
Actor. b. Salisbury, England, 1944. Grew up in Wales and East Africa. Began acting at Truro School in Cornwall at 15. e. U. of East Anglia where he founded school's dramatic society. Worked as teacher before studying at Royal Academy of Dramatic Art, 1969. Appeared in 23 Shakespearean plays.
PICTURES: The Black Windmill, Sphinx, Raiders of the Lost Ark, Victor/Victoria, Sahara, Sword of the Valiant, Best Revenge, King Solomon's Mines, In the Shadow of Kilimanjaro, Firewalker, The Living Daylights, Waxwork, Rising Storm, Indiana Jones and the Last Crusade, Young Toscanini, Journey of Honor, Unnameable II, The Seventh Coin, The Great White Hype.
TELEVISION: *Mini-series:* Shogun, James Clavell's Noble House, Riley, Ace of Spies, I, Claudius, War and Remembrance. *Movies:* The Little Match Girl, Sadat, Kim, The Naked Civil Servant, The Trial of the Incredible Hulk, Goddess of Love, The Gifted One, Great Expectations, Desperado, Secret Weapon, Before the Storm, Spy Games, Perry Mason: The Case of the Fatal Framing. *Series:* Under Cover, The Untouchables, Archaeology, Sliders.

RICCI, CHRISTINA
Actress. b. Santa Monica, CA, 1980. Raised in Long Island, NY, and Montclair, NJ. Started professional acting career in commercials.
PICTURES: Mermaids (debut, 1990), The Hard Way, The Addams Family, The Cemetery Club, Addams Family Values, Casper, Gold Diggers: The Secret of Bear Mountain, Now and Then, Last of the High Kings, The Ice Storm.

RICH, JOHN
Producer, Director. b. Rockaway Beach, NY, e. U. of Michigan, B.A., Phi Beta Kappa, 1948; M.A. 1949; Sesquicentennial Award, 1967; bd. of dir., Screen Dir. Guild of America, 1954-1960; v.p. 1958-1960, Founder-Trustee, Producers-Directors Pension Plan, chmn. of bd. 1965, 1968, 1970; treasurer, Directors Guild of America, 1966-67; v.p. 1967-72. Awards: Directors Guild Award, Most Outstanding Directorial Achievement, 1971. Christopher award: Henry Fonda as Clarence Darrow, 1975. NAACP Image Award, 1974; 2 Golden Globe Awards: All in the Family, 1972-73. DGA Robert B. Aldrich Award for 1992.
PICTURES: *Director:* Wives and Lovers, The New Interns, Roustabout, Boeing-Boeing, Easy Come Easy Go.
TELEVISION: *Director:* Academy Awards, The Dick Van Dyke Show, All in the Family (also prod.), Mr. Sunshine, Dear John, MacGyver.

RICH, LEE
Producer, Executive. b. Cleveland, OH, Dec. 10, 1926. e. Ohio U. Adv. exec.; resigned as sr. v.p., Benton & Bowles, to become producer for Mirisch-Rich TV, 1965 (Rat Patrol, Hey Landlord). Resigned 1967 to join Leo Burnett Agency. Left to form Lorimar Productions in 1969 and served as pres. until 1986 when left to join MGM/UA Communications as chmn. & CEO. Resigned 1988; signed 3-year deal with Warner Bros. setting up Lee Rich Prods. there. Twice named Television Showman of the Year by Publishers' Guild of Amer.
PICTURES: *Producer:* The Sporting Club, Just Cause, The Amazing Panda Adventure, Big Bully. *Executive Producer:* The Man, The Choirboys, Who Is Killing the Great Chefs of Europe?, The Big Red One, Hard to Kill, Innocent Blood, Passenger 57.
TELEVISION: *Exec. Prod.: Series:* The Waltons (Emmy Award, 1973), Dallas, Knots Landing, Against the Grain. *Mini-series:* The Blue Knight, Helter Skelter, Studs Lonigan. *Movies:* Do Not Fold Spindle or Mutilate, The Homecoming: A Christmas Story, The Crooked Hearts, Pursuit, The Girls of Huntington House, Dying Room Only, Don't Be Afraid of the Dark, A Dream for Christmas, The Stranger Within, Bad Ronald, The Runaway Barge, Runaways, Returning Home, Eric, Conspiracy of Terror, Widow, Green Eyes, Killer on Board, Desperate Women, Long Journey Back, Mary and Joseph: A Story of Faith, Mr. Horn, Some Kind of Miracle, Young Love, First Love, A Man Called Intrepid, Flamingo Road, Marriage Is Alive and Well, A Perfect Match, Reward, Skag, Killjoy, A Matter of Life and Death, Our Family Business, Mother's Day on Walton's Mountain, This is Kate Bennett, Two of a Kind, A Wedding on Walton's Mountain, A Day of Thanks on Walton's Mountain, Secret of Midland Heights, Face of Fear, Killer Rules.

RICHARD, SIR CLIFF
O.B.E. Singer, Actor. r.n. Harry Webb. b. India, Oct. 14, 1940. Ent. show business 1958 in TV series Oh Boy. Other TV includes Sunday Night at the London Palladium, several Cliff Richard Shows; top British Singer, 1960-71. Voted top box-office star of Great Britain, 1962-63, 1963-64. Twice rep. U.K. in Eurovision Song Contest. Innumerable platinum, gold and silver discs. 1989 became first UK artist to release 100 singles; voted top male vocalist of the 80's by UK Indept. TV viewers. Has made numerous videos. Knighted, 1995.
THEATER: Aladdin, Five Finger Exercise, The Potting Shed, Time.
PICTURES: Serious Charge (debut, 1959), Expresso Bongo, The Young Ones (Wonderful to Be Young), Summer Holiday, Wonderful Life (Swingers' Paradise), Finder's Keepers, Two a Penny, Take Me High (Hot Property).

RICHARDS, BEAH
Actress. b. Vicksburg, MS. e. Dillard U. On B'way in The Miracle Worker, A Raisin in the Sun, The Amen Corner (Theatre World Award), etc.
PICTURES: Take a Giant Step, The Miracle Worker, Gone Are the Days, In the Heat of the Night, Hurry Sundown, Guess Who's Coming to Dinner, The Great White Hope, Mahogany, Homer and Eddie, Drugstore Cowboy.
TELEVISION: *Series:* The Bill Cosby Show (1970), Sanford and Son, Frank's Place (Emmy Award, 1988), Hearts Afire. *Movies:* Footsteps, Outrage, A Dream for Christmas, Just an Old Sweet Song, Ring of Passion, Roots II—The Next Generation, A Christmas Without Snow, One Special Victory, Out of Darkness.

RICHARDS, DICK
Director, Producer, Writer. b. New York, NY, July 9, 1934. In U.S. Army as photo-journalist; work appeared in Life, Look, Time, Esquire, etc. Won over 100 int'l. awards, for commercials and photographic art work.
PICTURES: Director: The Culpepper Cattle Co. (also story), Rafferty and the Gold Dust Twins, Farewell My Lovely, March or Die (also co- prod., co-story), Death Valley, Tootsie (co-prod. only), Man Woman and Child, Heat.

RICHARDS, MICHAEL
Actor. b. Culver City, July 14, 1950. e. California Inst. of Arts. Work as stand-up comedian led to appearances on tv including regular stint on series Fridays. Acted on stage with San Diego Rep. Co.
THEATER: LA: The American Clock, Wild Oats.
PICTURES: Young Doctors in Love, Transylvania 6-5000, Whoops Apocalypse, UHF, Problem Child, Coneheads, So I Married an Axe Murderer, Airheads, Unstrung Heroes.
TELEVISION: Series: Fridays, Marblehead Manor, Seinfeld (2 Emmy Awards: 1993, 1994).

RICHARDSON, JOELY
Actress. b. London, Eng., January 9, 1965. Daughter of actress Vanessa Redgrave and director Tony Richardson, sister of actress Natasha Richardson. e. Lycee, St. Paul's Girl's School, London; Pinellas Park H.S. (Florida), The Thacher Sch. (Ojai, CA), Royal Acad. of Dramatic Art. London stage: Steel Magnolias, Beauty and the Beast (Old Vic); also at Liverpool Playhouse, RSC.
PICTURES: Wetherby (debut, 1985 with mother), Drowning By Numbers, About That Strange Girl, King Ralph, Shining Through, Rebecca's Daughters, I'll Do Anything, Sister My Sister, Hollow Reed, Lochness, 101 Dalmations.
TELEVISION: Body Contact, Behaving Badly, Available Light, Heading Home, Lady Chatterly.

RICHARDSON, MIRANDA
Actress. b. Southport, England, 1958. Studied acting at the drama program at Bristol's Old Vic Theatre School. Began acting on stage, 1979. Appeared in Moving, at the Queen's Theatre and continued in All My Sons, Who's Afraid of Virginia Woolf?, The Life of Einstein in provincial theatres. Also A Lie of the Mind (London), The Changeling, Mountain Language.
PICTURES: Dance With a Stranger (debut, 1985), The Innocent, Empire of the Sun, Eat the Rich, Twisted Obsession, The Bachelor, Enchanted April, The Crying Game, Damage (BAFTA Award; Acad. Award nom.), Tom and Viv, Century, The Night and the Moment, Kansas City, The Evening Star.
TELEVISION: The Hard Word, Sorrel and Son, A Woman of Substance, After Pilkington, Underworld, Death of the Heart, The Black Adder (series), Die Kinder (mini-series), Sweet as You Are (Royal TV Society Award), Fatherland (Golden Globe Award).

RICHARDSON, NATASHA
Actress. b. London, Eng., May 11, 1963. m. actor Liam Neeson. Daughter of actress Vanessa Redgrave and director Tony Richardson; sister is actress Joely Richardson. e. Central Sch. of Speech and Drama. Appeared at the Leeds Playhouse in On the Razzle, Top Girls, Charley's Aunt. Performed A Midsummer Night's Dream and Hamlet with the Young Vic. 1985 starred with mother in The Seagull (London), also starred in the musical High Society. Won London Theatre Critics Most Promising Newcomer award, 1986. NY stage debut 1992 in Anna Christie.
PICTURES: Every Picture Tells a Story (debut, 1984). Gothic, A Month in the Country, Patty Hearst, Fat Man and Little Boy, The Handmaid's Tale, The Comfort of Strangers, The Favor the Watch and the Very Big Fish, Past Midnight, Widow's Peak, Nell.
TELEVISION: Ellis Island (mini-series), In a Secret State, The Copper Beeches (epis. of Sherlock Holmes), Ghosts, Suddenly Last Summer, Hostages, Zelda.

RICHARDSON, PATRICIA
Actress. b. Bethesda, MD, Feb. 23, 1951. e. Southern Methodist Univ.
THEATER: NY: Gypsy, Loose Ends, The Wake of Jamie Foster, The Collected Works of Billy the Kid, The Frequency, Vanities, The Miss Firecracker Contest, The Coroner's Plot, Fables for Friends. Regional: The Killing of Sister George, King Lear, The Philadelphia Story, Fifth of July, About Face.
PICTURES: Gas, C.H.U.D., You Better Watch Out, Lost Angels, In Country.
TELEVISION: Series: Double Trouble, Eisenhower and Lutz, FM, Home Improvement, Storytime (PBS). Movies: Hands of a Stranger, Parent Trap III. Guest: Love Sidney, Kate and Allie, The Cosby Show, Quantum Leap.

RICHMAN, PETER MARK
Actor. b. Philadelphia, PA, April 16, 1927. e. Philadelphia Coll. of Pharmacy & Science with Bachelor of Science Degree in Pharmacy. Previously acted as Mark Richman. Member of Actors Studio since 1954.

THEATER: B'way: End as a Man, Masquerade, A Hatful of Rain, The Zoo Story. Regional: Blithe Spirit, The Night of the Iguana, 12 Angry Men, Babes in Toyland, Funny Girl, The Best Man, Equus, The Rainmaker, 4 Faces (also author; Drama-Logue Best Performance Award, 1995).
PICTURES: Friendly Persuasion, The Strange One, The Black Orchid, Dark Intruder, Agent for H.A.R.M., For Singles Only, Friday 13th Part VIII—Jason Takes Manahattan, The Naked Gun 2 1/2: The Smell of Fear, Judgment Day (Manila).
TELEVISION: Series: Longstreet, Dynasty, Cain's Hundred, My Secret Summer (Berlin). Movies: House on Greenapple Road, Yuma, Mallory: Circumstantial Evidence, The Islander, Dempsey, Blind Ambition, City Killer, Bonanza: The Next Generation. Guest: Three's Company, Murder She Wrote, Star Trek: The Next Generation, Matlock, Beverly Hills 90210, and over 500 guest roles.

RICHMOND, TED
Producer. b. Norfolk, VA, June 10, 1912. e. MIT. Entered m.p. ind. as publicity dir., RKO Theatres; later mgr. Albany dist.; publ. dir. Fabian circuit, NY, Paramount upper NY state theats.; Grand Nat'l Pictures. Author Grand Nat'l series Trigger Pal, Six Gun Rhythm. Formed T. H. Richmond Prods., Inc., 1941. Formed Copa Prod. with Tyrone Power, 1954. Formed Ted Richmond Prod. Inc. for MGM release, 1959. Reactivated Copa Prod. Ltd., England, 1960.
PICTURES: Hit the Hay, The Milkman, Kansas Raiders, Shakedown, Smuggler's Island, Strange Door, Cimarron Kid, Bronco Buster, Has Anybody Seen My Gal, No Room for the Groom, Weekend with Father, The Mississippi Gambler, Desert Legion, Column South, Bonzo Goes to College, Forbidden, Walking My Baby Back Home, Francis Joins the Wacs, Bengal Brigade, Count Three and Pray, Nightfall, Abandon Ship, Solomon and Sheba, Charlemagne, Bachelor in Paradise, Advance to the Rear, Pancho Villa, Return of the 7, Red Sun, Papillon (exec. prod.), The Fifth Musketeer.

RICHTER, W. D.
Writer, Director. b. New Britain, CT, Dec. 7, 1945. e. Dartmouth Coll., B.A.; U. of Southern California Film Sch., grad. study.
PICTURES: Writer: Slither, Peeper, Nickelodeon, Invasion of the Body Snatchers, Dracula, Brubaker, All Night Long, Big Trouble in Little China, Needful Things, Home for the Holidays. Prod.-Dir.: Adventures of Buckaroo Banzai Across the Eighth Dimension, Late for Dinner.

RICKERT, JOHN F.
Executive. b. Kansas City, MO, Oct. 29, 1924. e. USC. Joined Universal Pictures in 1951; left in 1957 to start independent productions. 1960-68 handled indep. roadshow distribution (4-walling). 1969 formed Cineworld Corporation, natl. dist. co., of which he is pres. 1975-76 did tax shelter financing for 13 films. Currently involved in distribution, production packaging and intl. co-production as pres. of Coproducers Corp.

RICKLES, DON
Actor, Comedian. b. New York, NY, May 8, 1926. e. AADA.
PICTURES: Run Silent Run Deep, Rabbit Trap, The Rat Race, X: The Man With the X-Ray Eyes, Muscle Beach Party, Bikini Beach, Beach Blanket Bingo, Enter Laughing, The Money Jungle, Where It's At, Kelly's Heroes, Keaton's Cop, Innocent Blood, Casino, Toy Story (voice).
TELEVISION: Series: The Don Rickles Show (1968), The Don Rickles Show (1972), C.P.O. Sharkey, Foul-Ups Bleeps and Blunders, Daddy Dearest. Movie: For the Love of It. Guest: The Big Show, F Troop, Laugh-In, Kraft Music Hall, Dean Martin's Celebrity Roasts, Tales From the Crypt, many others.

RICKMAN, ALAN
Actor. b. London, England. Began as graphic designer before studying acting at RADA. Joined the Royal Shakespeare Co. where he starred in Les Liaisons Dangereuses; received Tony Award nomination for 1987 NY production.
THEATER: Commitments, The Last Elephant, The Grass Widow, Lucky Chance, The Seagull, As You Like It, Troilus and Cressida, Tango At the End of Winter, Hamlet.
PICTURES: Die Hard (debut, 1988), The January Man, Quigley Down Under, Closet Land, Truly Madly Deeply, Robin Hood: Prince of Thieves (BAFTA Award, 1991), Close My Eyes, Bob Roberts, Mesmer, An Awfully Big Adventure, Sense and Sensibility, Rasputin, Michael Collins.
TELEVISION: Series: The Barchester Chronicles (BBC). Specials: Smiley's People, Romeo and Juliet, Bonnie Prince Charley, Girls on Top. Guest: Fallen Angels (Murder Obliquely). Movie: Rasputin (Emmy Award, 1996).

RICOTTA, FRANK
Executive. Pres., Technicolor, Inc., Association of Cimena & Video Laboratories, Inc.

RIEGERT, PETER
Actor. b. New York, NY, Apr. 11, 1947. e. U. of Buffalo, B.A. Brief stints as 8th grade English teacher, social worker, and

aide de camp to politician Bella Abzug 1970, before turned actor, off-off B'way. Appeared with improvisational comedy group War Babies. Film debut in short, A Director Talks About His Film.
THEATER: Dance with Me (B'way debut), Minnie's Boys (as Chico Marx), Sexual Perversity in Chicago, Isn't it Romantic?, La Brea Tarpits, A Rosen By Any Other Name, The Nerd, Mountain Language/The Birthday Party, The Road to Nirvana.
PICTURES: National Lampoon's Animal House, Americathon, Head Over Heels, National Lampoon Goes to the Movies, Local Hero, City Girl, A Man in Love, Le Grand Carnaval, The Stranger, Crossing Delancey, That's Adequate, The Passport, A Shock to the System, The Object of Beauty, Beyond the Ocean, Oscar, The Runestone, Passed Away, Utz, The Mask, White Man's Burden, Coldblooded, Pie in the Sky.
TELEVISION: Specials: Concealed Enemies, The Hit List, W. Eugene Smith: Photography Made Difficult. Mini-Series: Ellis Island. Movies: News at Eleven, Barbarians at the Gate, Gypsy, The Infiltrator, Element of Truth. Series: The Middle Ages.

RIFKIN, RON
Actor. b. New York, NY, Oct. 31, 1939. e. NYU.
PICTURES: The Devil's 8 (debut, 1969), Flareup, Silent Running, The Sunshine Boys, The Big Fix, The Sting II, Husbands and Wives, Manhattan Murder Mystery, Wolf, Last Summer in the Hamptons, The Substance of Fire.
TELEVISION: Series: Adam's Rib, When Things Were Rotten, Husbands Wives & Lovers, One Day at a Time, Falcon Crest. Mini-Series: The Winds of War.
THEATER: B'way: Come Blow Your Horn, The Goodbye People, The Tenth Man. Off-B'way: Rosebloom, The Art of Dining, Temple, The Substance of Fire.

RIGG, DIANA
C.B.E. (1987). Actress. b. Doncaster, England, July 20, 1938. With the Royal Shakespeare Co. at Aldwych Theatre, 1962-64. Recent London stage: Follies, Medea (also B'way).
PICTURES: A Midsummer's Night Dream (debut, 1968), The Assassination Bureau, On Her Majesty's Secret Service, Julius Caesar, The Hospital, Theatre of Blood, A Little Night Music, The Great Muppet Caper, Evil Under the Sun, Snow White, A Good Man in Africa.
TELEVISION: Series: The Avengers, Diana, Mystery (host). Movies: In This House of Brede, Witness for the Prosecution, A Hazard of Hearts, Mother Love, Mrs. 'arris Goes to Paris, Running Delilah, Genghis Cohn, Danielle Steel's Zoya, The Haunting of Helen Walker. Specials: King Lear, Bleak House.

RINGWALD, MOLLY
Actress. b. Sacramento, CA, Feb. 16, 1968. Daughter of jazz musician Bob Ringwald; began performing at age 4 with his Great Pacific Jazz Band at 6 and recorded album, Molly Sings. Professional debut at 5 in stage play, The Glass Harp. Appeared in bit on TV's New Mickey Mouse Club, a West Coast stage production of Annie and in TV series, The Facts of Life, Off-B'way debut: Lily Dale (Theatre World Award, 1986).
PICTURES: Tempest (debut, 1982), P.K. and the Kid, Spacehunter: Adventures in the Forbidden Zone, Sixteen Candles, The Breakfast Club, Pretty in Pink, The Pick-Up Artist, For Keeps?, King Lear, Fresh Horses, Strike It Rich, Betsy's Wedding, Face the Music, Bastard Brood.
TELEVISION: Series: The Facts of Life, Townies. Movies: Packin' It In, Surviving, Women and Men: Stories of Seduction (Dust Before Fireworks), Something to Live For: The Alison Gertz Story. Mini-Series: The Stand.

RISHER, SARA
Executive. Chairperson of production, New Line Productions, Inc.

RISSIEN, EDWARD L.
Executive. b. Des Moines, IA. e. Grinnell Coll., Stanford U., B.A., 1949. Army Air Force, WWII. B'way stage, mgr., 1950-53; v.p., Mark Stevens. Prods., 1954-56; prod., v.p., Four Star, 1958-60; prog. exec., ABC-TV, 1960-62; v.p., Bing Crosby Prods., 1963-66; v.p., Filmways TV Prods.; assoc. prod., Columbia, 1968-69; indept. prod., 1970; prod., WB, 1971; exec. v.p., Playboy Prods., 1972-80; consultant & indept. prod., 1981-82; sr. consultant, cable, Playboy Prods., 1982-85; pres., Playboy Programs, 1985-88; bd. of dirs.: Heritage Entertainment, Inc. 1985-88; indept. prod., 1989-present. Theatre producer in London: The School of Night.
PICTURES: Snow Job (prod.), Castle Keep (prod. exec.), The Crazy World of Julius Vrooder (prod.), Saint Jack (exec. prod.).
TELEVISION: Movies (exec. prod.): Minstrel Man, A Whale for the Killing, The Death of Ocean View Park, Big Bob Johnson, The Great Niagara, Third Girl from the Left, A Summer Without Boys.

RISSNER, DANTON
Executive. b. Brooklyn, NY, March 27, 1940. e. Florida So. Col. Began as agent with Ashley Famous (later Intl. Famous), 1967-69. 1969 joined Warner Bros. as v.p., chg. European prod.;

1970, moved to United Artists as v.p., chg. European prod.; 1973, named v.p. in chg. East Coast & European prod. for UA; 1975- 78, v.p. in chg. of world-wide prod.; 1981, exec. v.p., 20th Century-Fox.; 1984, joined UA as sr. v.p., motion pictures.
PICTURES: Prod.: Up the Academy, A Summer Story.
TELEVISION: Backfire (prod.).

RITCHIE, MICHAEL
Director. b. Waukesha, WI, Nov. 28, 1938. e. Harvard U. where he directed first production of Arthur Kopit's play, Oh Dad Poor Dad Mama's Hung You in the Closet and I'm Feeling So Sad. Professional career began as ass't. to Robert Saudek on Ford Foundation's Omnibus TV series. Later became assoc. prod. and then dir. on Saudek's Profiles in Courage series; dir. assignments on tv series. Appeared as actor in film Innocent Blood.
PICTURES: Downhill Racer (debut, 1969), Prime Cut, The Candidate, Smile (also prod., lyricist), The Bad News Bears, Semi-Tough, An Almost Perfect Affair (also co-s.p.), The Island, Divine Madness (also prod.), The Survivors, Fletch, Wildcats, The Golden Child, The Couch Trip, Fletch Lives, Diggstown, Cops and Robbersons, The Scout, The Fantasticks.
TELEVISION: Series: Profiles in Courage (also prod.), The Man from U.N.C.L.E., Run for Your Life, Dr. Kildare, The Big Valley, Felony Squad, The Outsider (pilot), The Sound of Anger. Movie: The Positively True Adventures of the Alleged Texas Cheerleader-Murdering Mom.

RITTER, JOHN
Actor. b. Burbank, CA, Sept. 17, 1948. Father was late Tex Ritter, country-western star. Attended Hollywood H.S. Began acting at USC in 1968. Appeared with college cast at Edinburgh Festival; later with Eva Marie Saint in Desire Under the Elms.
PICTURES: The Barefoot Executive (debut, 1971), Scandalous John, The Other, The Stone Killer, Nickelodeon, Americathon, Hero at Large, Wholly Moses, They All Laughed, Real Men, Skin Deep, Problem Child, Problem Child II, Noises Off, Stay Tuned, North, Slingblade.
TELEVISION: Movies: The Night That Panicked America, Leave Yesterday Behind, The Comeback Kid, Pray TV, In Love With an Older Woman, Sunset Limousine, Love Thy Neighbor, Letting Go, Unnatural Causes, A Smoky Mountain Christmas, The Last Fling, Prison for Children, Tricks of the Trade, My Brother's Wife, Stephen King's IT, The Dreamer of Oz, The Summer My Father Grew Up, Danielle Steel's Heartbeat, The Only Way Out, Gramps, The Colony, Unforgivable. Series: The Waltons, Three's Company (Emmy Award, 1984), Three's a Crowd, Hooper-man, Have Faith (exec. prod.), Anything But Love (exec. prod., also guest), Fish Police (voice), Hearts Afire.

RIVERA, CHITA
Actress, Dancer. b. Washington, DC, Jan. 23, 1933. r.n. Concita del Rivero. Trained for stage at American School of Ballet.
THEATER: Call Me Madam (1952), Guys and Dolls, Can-Can, Shoestring Revue, Seventh Heaven, Mr. Wonderful, Shinbone Alley, West Side Story, Bye Bye Birdie, Bajour, Sondheim: A Musical Tribute, Chicago, Hey Look Me Over, Merlin, The Rink (Tony Award, 1984), Jerry's Girls, Kiss of the Spider Woman (Tony Award, 1993).
PICTURE: Sweet Charity (1969).
TELEVISION: Series: The New Dick Van Dyke Show. Specials: Kennedy Center Tonight—Broadway to Washington!, Pippin, Toller Cranston's Strawberry Ice, TV Academy Hall of Fame, 1985. Movies: The Marcus-Nelson Murders, Mayflower Madam.

RIVERA, GERALDO
Journalist. b. New York, NY, July 4, 1943. e. U. of Arizona, Brooklyn Law Sch., 1969, Columbia Sch. of Journalism. Started legal career 1st as lawyer with Harlem Assertion of Rights Community Action for Legal Services 1968-70. Switched to journalism, joined WABC-TV, New York, 1970. Made several TV documentaries on such subjects as institutions for retarded, drug addiction, migrant workers, etc. Chmn., One-to-One Foundation. Winner 3 national and 4 local Emmys, George Peabody Award, 2 Robert F. Kennedy Awards. Appeared in film The Bonfire of the Vanities.
TELEVISION: Series: Geraldo Rivera: Good Morning America (contributor), Good Night America, 20/20, Gerald Show, Now It Can Be Told. Specials: The Mystery of Al Capone's Vault, American Vice: The Doping of a Nation, Innocence Lost: The Erosion of American Childhood, Sons of Scarface: The New Mafia, Murder: Live From Death Row, Devil Worship: Exposing Satan's Underground. Movie: Perry Mason: The Case of the Reckless Romeo.

RIVERS, JOAN
Actress, Writer, Director. r.n. Joan Molinsky. b. New York, NY, June 8, 1933. e. Barnard Coll. (Phi Beta Kappa). Formerly

fashion coordinator for Bond clothing stores. Performed comedy act in nightclubs, then with Second City 1961-62; TV debut: Johnny Carson Show, 1965; nat'l syndicated columnist, Chicago Tribune 1973-76; Hadassah Woman of the Year, 1983; Jimmy Award for Best Comedian 1981; Chair., National Cystic Fibrosis Foundation. 1978 created TV series Husbands Wives and Lovers.
AUTHOR: Having a Baby Can Be a Scream (1974), Can We Talk? (1983), The Life and Hard Times of Heidi Abramowitz (1984), Enter Talking (1986), Still Talking (1990).
THEATER: B'way: Fun City (also co-writer), Broadway Bound, Sally Marr... and Her Escorts (also co-writer).
PICTURES: The Swimmer, Rabbit Test (also dir., s.p.), The Muppets Take Manhattan, Spaceballs (voice), Serial Mom.
TELEVISION: Series: The Tonight Show (regular substitute guest host: 1983-86), The Late Show (host), The New Hollywood Squares, The Joan Rivers Show (morning talk show). Movies: How to Murder a Millionaire, Tears and Laughter: The Joan and Melissa Rivers Story.

ROBARDS, JASON
Actor. b. Chicago, IL, July 26, 1922. Served in Navy during WWII. Studied acting at Acad. of Dramatic Arts. Began with Children's World Theatre (1947), then stock radio parts, asst. stage mgr. and actor in Stalag 17, The Chase, D'Oyly Carte Opera Co., Stratford Ontario Shakespeare Fest. American Gothic, Circle in the Square.
THEATER: The Iceman Cometh (Obie Award, 1956), Long Day's Journey into Night (Theatre World Award), The Disenchanted (Tony Award, 1959), Toys in the Attic, Big Fish Little Fish, A Thousand Clowns, After the Fall, But for Whom Charlie, Hughie, The Devils, We Bombed in New Haven, The Country Girl, A Moon for the Misbegotten, Long Day's Journey Into Night (Brooklyn Acad. of Music, 1975; B'way, 1988), A Touch of the Poet, O'Neill and Carlotta, You Can't Take It With You, Ah Wilderness, A Month of Sundays, Established Price (Long Wharf), Love Letters, Park Your Car in Harvard Yard, No Man's Land.
PICTURES: The Journey (debut, 1959), By Love Possessed, Tender Is the Night, Long Day's Journey Into Night, Act One, A Thousand Clowns, A Big Hand for the Little Lady, Any Wednesday, Divorce American Style, The St. Valentine's Day Massacre, Hour of the Gun, The Night They Raided Minsky's, (Loves of) Isadora, Once Upon a Time in the West, Operation Snafu, The Ballad of Cable Hogue, Tora! Tora! Tora!, Fools, Julius Caesar, Johnny Got His Gun, Murders in the Rue Morgue, The War Between Men and Women, Pat Garrett and Billy the Kid, A Boy and His Dog, Mr. Sycamore, All the President's Men (Academy Award, best supporting actor, 1976), Julia (Academy Award, best supporting actor, 1977), Comes a Horseman, Hurricane, Raise the Titanic!, Caboblanco, Melvin and Howard, Legend of the Lone Ranger, Burden of Dreams, Max Dugan Returns, Something Wicked This Way Comes, Square Dance, Bright Lights Big City, The Good Mother, Dream a Little Dream, Parenthood, Quick Change, Reunion, Storyville, The Adventures of Huck Finn, The Trial, Philadelphia, The Paper, Little Big League, Crimson Tide.
TELEVISION: Specials: Abe Lincoln in Illinois, The Iceman Cometh, A Doll's House, Noon Wine, Belle of 14th Street, The House Without a Christmas Tree, For Whom the Bell Tolls, You Can't Take It With You, Hughie. Mini-Series: Washington: Behind Closed Doors. Movies: A Christmas to Remember, Haywire, F.D.R.: The Last Year, The Atlanta Child Murders, The Day After, Sakharov, Johnny Bull, The Long Hot Summer, Laguna Heat, Norman Rockwell's Breaking Home Ties, Inherit the Wind (Emmy Award, 1988), The Christmas Wife, The Perfect Tribute, Chernobyl: The Final Warning, An Inconvenient Woman, Black Rainbow, Mark Twain & Me, Heidi, The Enemy Within, My Antonia. Guest: Studio One, Philco Playhouse, Hallmark.

ROBARDS, SAM
Actor. b. New York, NY, December 16. m. actress Suzy Amis. Son of actors Jason Robards and Lauren Bacall. e. National Theater Institute and studied with Uta Hagen at H.B. Studios.
THEATER: Off-B'way: Album, Flux, Taking Steps, Moonchildren. Kennedy Center: Idiot's Delight and regional theater.
PICTURES: Tempest, Not Quite Paradise, Fandango, Bright Lights Big City, Bird, Casualties of War, The Ballad of Little Jo, Mrs. Parker and the Vicious Circle.
TELEVISION: Series: Movin' Right Along (PBS), TV 101, Get a Life! Movies: Jacobo Timerman: Prisoner Without a Name Cell Without a Number, Into Thin Air, Pancho Barnes.

ROBBINS, MATTHEW
Writer, Director. e. U. of Southern California Sch. of Cinema. Wrote early scripts in collaboration with Hal Barwood, Robbins branching out into directing also with Corvette Summer in 1978.
PICTURES: Writer: The Sugarland Express, The Bingo Long Traveling All-Stars and Motor Kings, Corvette Summer (also dir.), Dragonslayer (also dir.), Warning Sign, Batteries Not Included (also dir.), Bingo (dir. only).

ROBBINS, RICHARD
Composer. b. Boston, MA, Dec. 4, 1940. Bachelor of Music and Graduate Studies at New England Conservatory of Music. Received Frank Huntington Beebe Fellowship to Austria where he studied musicology, chamber music. Later became dir. of Mannes College of Music Preparatory School, N.Y. Has worked closely with James Ivory and Ismail Merchant. Also dir. doc. films Sweet Sounds, Street Musicians of Bombay.
Awards: Best Score, Venice Film Festival for Maurice; Best Score, BFI Anthony Asquith Award for A Room With a View. Acad. Award nom. for Howards End.
PICTURES: The Europeans (supr. score), Jane Austen in Manhattan, Quartet, Heat and Dust, The Bostonians, A Room with a View, Maurice, Sweet Lorraine, My Little Girl, Slaves of New York, Mr. & Mrs. Bridge, The Ballad of the Sad Cafe, Howards End, The Remains of the Day, Jefferson in Paris.
TELEVISION: Love and Other Sorrows.

ROBBINS, TIM
Actor, Director. b. West Covina, CA, Oct. 16, 1958. Son of Greenwich Village folksinger, worked as actor while in high school. e. NYU. Transferred to UCLA theatre program appearing in guest roles on tv. 1981, co-founder and artistic dir., The Actors Gang, in L.A.; dir. them in and co-authored Alagazam: After the Dog Wars, Violence: The Misadventures of Spike Spangle—Farmer, Carnage: A Comedy (also prod. in NY).
PICTURES: Toy Soldiers (debut, 1984), No Small Affair, Fraternity Vacation, The Sure Thing, Top Gun, Howard the Duck, Five Corners, Bull Durham, Tapeheads, Miss Firecracker, Twister (cameo), Erik the Viking, Cadillac Man, Jacob's Ladder, Jungle Fever, The Player (Cannes Film Fest. Award, 1992), Bob Roberts (also dir., s.p., co-wrote songs), Short Cuts, The Hudsucker Proxy, The Shawshank Redemption, Ready to Wear (Pret-a-Porter), I.Q., Dead Man Walking (dir.).
TELEVISION: Movies: Quarterback Princess, Malice in Wonderland. Guest: Hardcastle and McCormick, St. Elsewhere, Hill Street Blues.

ROBERTS, CURTIS
Producer. b. Dover, England. e. Cambridge U. Child actor. England, Germany; numerous pictures for Rank Org.; prod. England, on Broadway in Gertie, Island Visit; co-prod. on Broadway, Horses in Midstream, Golden Apple, Tonight or Never; tour and NY The Journey. Recipient: Lawrence J. Quirk Photoplay Award 1990. Now pres., CGC Films, Munich.
AUTHOR: History of Summer Theatre, The History of Vaudeville, Other Side of the Coin, History of Music (Popular) 1900-70, History of English Music Halls, Latta, Then There Were Some, I Live to Love, Gabor the Merrier, I Live to Love II.
THEATER: Tours: Blithe Spirit, Showboat, Kiss Me Kate, Generation, The Camel Bell, Farewell Party, Twentieth Century, Great Sebastians, Goodbye Charlie, Time of the Cuckoo, Under Papa's Picture, Everybody's Gal, Divorce Me Darling, Gingerbread Lady, September Song, Same Time Next Year, Funny Girl, Pal Joey, South Pacific, It Girl, Fanny, Breaking Up the Act, Good, Good Friends, Together, I Remember Mama.
PICTURES: An Actress in Love, La Die, Hypocrite, Jet Over the Atlantic, The Vixen, Farewell Party, Polly's Return, Rain Before Seven, Halloween, Malaga, My Dear Children, Norma, The Lion's Consort, Whispers, Golden Idol, London Belongs To Me.
TELEVISION: Rendezvous, Deadly Species, Top Secret, The Ilona Massey Show, When In Rome, Ethan Frome, Black Chiffon, Illusion in Java (mini-series), Diamonds Don't Brun (mini-series).

ROBERTS, ERIC
Actor. b. Biloxi, MS, April 18, 1956. Father founded Actors and Writers Workshop in Atlanta, 1963. Sister is actress Julia Roberts. Began appearing in stage prods. at age 5. Studied in London at Royal Acad. of Dramatic Art, 1973-74. Returned to U.S. to study at American Acad. of Dramatic Arts. Stage debut in Rebel Women.
THEATER: Mass Appeal, The Glass Menagerie (Hartford Stage Co.), A Streetcar Named Desire (Princeton's McCarter Theater), Alms for the Middle Class (Long Wharf), Burn This (B'way debut; Theatre World Award).
PICTURES: King of the Gypsies (debut, 1978), Raggedy Man, Star 80, The Pope of Greenwich Village, The Coca Cola Kid, Runaway Train (Acad. Award nom.), Nobody's Fool, Rude Awakening, Blood Red, Best of the Best, The Ambulance, Lonely Hearts, Final Analysis, Best of the Best 2, By the Sword, Freefall, Babyfever, Love Is a Gun, The Specialist, Nature of the Beast, The Grave, Heaven's Prisoners, It's My Party, From the Edge, The Immortals, The Grave, Power 98, The Cable Guy, American Strays.
TELEVISION: Series: Another World. Specials: Paul's Case, Miss Lonelyhearts, Dear America (reader). Movies: To Heal a Nation, The Lost Capone, Descending Angel, Vendetta: Secrets of a Mafia Bride, Fugitive Among Us, Love Honor & Obey: The Last Mafia Marriage, Voyage, Love Cheat and Steal, Dark Angel.

ROBERTS, JULIA
Actress. b. Smyrna, GA, Oct. 28, 1967. r.n. Julie Roberts. Brother is actor Eric Roberts. Parents ran theater workshop in Atlanta. Moved to NY to study acting; modeled for the Click Agency before making prof. debut in brother's film Blood Red.
PICTURES: Blood Red (debut, 1986), Satisfaction, Mystic Pizza, Steel Magnolias (Acad. Award nom.), Pretty Woman (Acad. Award nom.), Flatliners, Sleeping With the Enemy, Dying Young, Hook, The Player, The Pelican Brief, I Love Trouble, Ready to Wear (Pret-a-Porter), Something to Talk About, Mary Reilly, Michael Collins, Everyone Says I Love You.
TELEVISION: Movie: Baja Oklahoma. Guest: Crime Story, Friends.

ROBERTS, PERNELL
Actor. b. Waycross, GA, May 18, 1930. e. U. of Maryland. Left college to begin working with summer stock companies, joining Arena Stage in Washington, DC in 1950. 1952 began appearing off-B'way (where he won a Drama Desk Award for Macbeth, 1957); made B'way debut in 1958 in Tonight in Samarkand.
PICTURES: Desire Under the Elms (debut, 1958), The Sheepman, Ride Lonesome, The Errand Boy (cameo), Four Rode Out, The Magic of Lassie.
TELEVISION: Series: Bonanza, Trapper John M.D., FBI: The Untold Stories (host). Movies: The Silent Gun, San Francisco International, The Bravos, Adventures of Nick Carter, Assignment: Munich, Dead Man on the Run, The Deadly Tower, The Lives of Jenny Dolan, Charlie Cobb: Nice Night for a Hanging, The Immigrants, The Night Rider, Hot Rod, High Noon Part II: The Return of Will Kane, Incident at Crestridge, Desperado, Perry Mason: The Case of the Sudden Death Payoff, Perry Mason: The Case of the All-Star Assassin, Donor. Mini-Series: Captains and the Kings, Centennial, Around the World in 80 Days.

ROBERTS, TONY
Actor. b. New York, NY, Oct. 22, 1939. e. Northwestern U.
THEATER: B'way: How Now Dow Jones, Don't Drink the Water, Play It Again Sam, Promises Promises, Barefoot in the Park, Absurd Person Singular, Sugar, Murder at the Howard Johnson's, They're Playing Our Song, Doubles, Arsenic and Old Lace, Jerome Robbins' Broadway, The Seagull, The Sisters Rosensweig, Victor/Victoria. Off-B'way: The Cradle Will Rock, The Good Parts, Four Dogs and a Bone. NY City Opera: Brigadoon, South Pacific. Dir: One of the All-Time Greats (Off-B'way).
PICTURES: Million Dollar Duck, Star Spangled Girl, Play It Again Sam, Serpico, The Taking of Pelham One Two Three, Lovers Like Us (Le Sauvage), Annie Hall, Just Tell Me What You Want, Stardust Memories, A Midsummer Night's Sex Comedy, Amityville 3-D, Key Exchange, Hannah and Her Sisters, Radio Days, 18 Again, Popcorn, Switch.
TELEVISION: Series: Rosetti and Ryan, The Four Seasons, The Lucie Arnaz Show, The Thorns. Movies: The Lindbergh Kidnapping Case, Girls in the Office, If Things Were Different, Seize the Day, Messiah on Mott Street, A Question of Honor, A Different Affair, Our Sons, Not in My Family, The American Clock, A Perry Mason Mystery: The Case of the Jealous Jokester. Guest: The Defenders, Phyllis, Storefront Lawyers, MacMillan, Trapper John M.D., Love American Style, Love Boat, Hotel.

ROBERTS, WILLIAM
Writer, Producer. b. Los Angeles, CA. e. U. of Southern California.
PICTURES: The Mating Game, The Magnificent Seven, The Wonderful World of the Brothers Grimm, Come Fly With Me, The Devil's Brigade, The Bridge At Remagen, One More Train to Rob, Red Sun, The Last American Hero, Posse, Ten to Midnight.
TELEVISION: Donna Reed Show (creator).

ROBERTSON, CLIFF
Actor, Writer, Director. b. La Jolla, CA, Sept. 9, 1925.
THEATER: Mr. Roberts, Late Love, The Lady and the Tiger, Ghosts of 87 (one-man show). B'way: The Wisteria Tree, Orpheus Descending (Theatre World Award), Love Letters.
PICTURES: Picnic (debut, 1955), Autumn Leaves, The Girl Most Likely, The Naked and the Dead, Gidget, Battle of the Coral Sea, As the Sea Rages, All in a Night's Work, Underworld USA, The Big Show, The Interns, My Six Loves, PT 109, Sunday in New York, The Best Man, 633 Squadron, Love Has Many Faces, Masquerade, Up From the Beach, The Honey Pot, The Devil's Brigade (also wrote), Charly (Academy Award, 1968), Too Late the Hero, J.W. Coop (also dir.), The Great Northfield Minnesota Raid, Ace Eli and Rodger of the Skies, Man on a Swing, Out of Season, Three Days of the Condor, Shoot, Obsession, Dominique, Fraternity Row (narrator), Class, Brainstorm, Star 80, Shaker Run, Malone, Wild Hearts Can't Be Broken, Wind, Renaissance Man, Dazzle, The Sunset Boys, Escape From L.A.

TELEVISION: Series: Falcon Crest. Guest: Philco-Goodyear, Studio One, Robert Montgomery Presents, The Game (Emmy Award, 1966), Batman. Movies: Man Without a Country, My Father's House, Washington: Behind Closed Doors, Dreams of Gold, Key to Rebecca, Henry Ford—The Man and the Machine, Dead Reckoning, Dazzle, The Last Best Days, Assignment Berlin. Special: Days of Wine and Roses (Playhouse 90). Also spokesman for AT&T.

ROBERTSON, DALE
Actor, Producer. r.n. Dayle Robertson. b. Harrah, OK, July 14, 1923. e. Oklahoma Military Coll. Prof. prizefighter; U.S. Army, 1942-45. Film debut as bit player. Voted Star of Tomorrow, M.P. Herald Fame Poll, 1951.
PICTURES: The Boy With Green Hair (debut, 1948), Flamingo Road, Fighting Man of the Plains, Caribou Trail, Two Flags West, Call Me Mister, Take Care of My Little Girl, Golden Girl, Lydia Bailey, Return of the Texan, The Outcasts of Poker Flat, O. Henry's Full House, The Farmer Takes a Wife, Devil's Canyon, The Silver Whip, City of Bad Men, The Gambler from Natchez, Sitting Bull, Son of Sinbad, Day of Fury, Dakota Incident, Hell Canyon Outlaws, Fast and Sexy, Law of the Lawless, Blood on the Arrow, Coast of Skeletons, The One-Eyed Soldier.
TELEVISION: Series: Tales of Wells Fargo, The Iron Horse, Death Valley Days, Dynasty, Dallas, J.J. Starbuck. Movies: Scalplock, Melvin Purvis: G-Man, Kansas City Massacre, Last Ride of the Dalton Gang. Guest: The Love Boat, Matt Houston, Murder She Wrote.

ROBERTSON, TIMOTHY B.
Executive. e. Univ of VA, Gordon-Conwell Thelogical Seminary, Columbia Univ. Manager of WXNE-TV in Boston, 1980-82; supervisor of Christian Broadcasting Network's tv facility; 1982-90, in charge of Middle East Television after purchase by CBN. Became President & CEO of International Family Entertainment Inc., holdings include The Family Channel, Cable Health Club, The Family Channel in the UK, MTM Entertainment Inc.

ROBINSON, BRUCE
Actor, Director, Writer. b. Kent, England, 1946. e. Central School of Speech and Drama. As actor appeared in 12 films but began writing novels and screenplays long before he gave up acting in 1975.
PICTURES: Actor: Romeo and Juliet (debut), The Story of Adele H. (last film as actor). Writer: The Killing Fields (Acad. Award nom.), Fat Man and Little Boy. Director-Writer: Withnail and I, How to Get Ahead in Advertising, Jennifer Eight.

ROBINSON, JAMES G.
Executive, Producer. e. Univ. of Maryland. Was prof. photographer and business entrepreneur prior to entering m.p. industry as co-prod. of The Stone Boy, and exec. prod. of Where the River Runs Black, Streets of Gold. Founded Morgan Creek Prods. in 1988, Morgan Creek Intl. in 1989, Morgan Creek Music Group in 1990, Morgan Creek Theatres and Morgan Creek International Theatres in 1992. Chairman and CEO of Morgan Creek.
PICTURES: Exec. Prod. for Morgan Creek: Young Guns, Skin Deep, Renegades, Enemies a Love Story, Nightbreed, Coupe de Ville, Young Guns II, The Exorcist III, Pacific Heights, Robin Hood: Prince of Thieves, Freejack, White Sands, The Last of the Mohicans, True Romance. Prod. for Morgan Creek: Stay Tuned, The Crush, Ace Ventura: Pet Detective, Major League II, Chasers, Trial by Jury, Silent Fall, Imaginary Crimes, A Walk in the Clouds, Big Bully, Ace Ventura: When Nature Calls, Two If By Sea.

ROBINSON, PHIL ALDEN
Director, Writer. b. Long Beach, NY, Mar. 1, 1950. e. Union Coll., Schenectady. Write and directed training films for Air Force, before writing two episodes for series Trapper John M.D.
PICTURES: Rhinestone (co-s.p.), All of Me (s.p., assoc. prod.). Dir./Writer: In the Mood, Field of Dreams, Sneakers.
TELEVISION: Series: Trapper John M.D. (writer), The George Burns Comedy Week (dir.)

ROCCO, ALEX
Actor. b. Cambridge, MA, Feb. 29, 1936.
PICTURES: Motor Psycho, St. Valentine's Day Massacre, Blood Mania, The Godfather, Slither, Detroit 9000, Friends of Eddie Coyle, The Outside Man, Stanley, Freebie and the Bean, Three the Hard Way, Rafferty and the Gold Dust Twins, Hearts of the West, Fire Sale, House Calls, Rabbit Test, Voices, Herbie Goes Bananas, The Stunt Man, Nobody's Perfekt, The Entity, Cannonball Run II, Stick, Gotcha!, P.K. and the Kid, Return to Horror High, Dream a Little Dream, Wired, The Pope Must Die.
TELEVISION: Series: Three for the Road, The Famous Teddy Z (Emmy Award, 1990), Sibs, The George Carlin Show. Movies: Hustling, The Blue Knight, A Question of Guilt, The

Grass is Always Greener Over the Septic Tank, Badge of the Assassin, Rock 'n' Roll Mom, The First Time, A Quiet Little Neighborhood A Perfect Little Murder, An Inconvenient Woman, Boris & Natasha, Love Honor & Obey: The Last Mafia Marriage, Robin Cook's Harmful Intent. *Mini-Series*: 79 Park Avenue.

RODDAM, FRANC
Director. b. Stockton, England, Apr. 29, 1946. Studied at London Film Sch. Spent two years as adv. copywriter/prod. with Ogilvy, Benson, Mather before joining BBC as documentary filmmaker. Founder of Union Pictures 1991.
PICTURES: Quadrophenia (also co-s.p.), The Lords of Discipline, Rain Forest (s.p. only), The Bride, Aria (sequence), War Party (also co-exec. prod.), K2.
TELEVISION: *Director*: The Family, Mini, Dummy. *Creator*: Aufwiedersehen Pet, Making Out, Masterchief, Harry.

RODRIGUEZ, ROBERT
Director, Writer, Producer, Editor. e. Univ. of TX. While in college created comic strip Los Hooligans. Made several short films including Bedhead which won several festival awards.
PICTURES: *Director/Writer:* El Mariachi (feature debut, 1993; also co-prod., story, photog., editor, sound), Desperado (also prod., editor), Four Rooms (segment), From Dusk Till Dawn (dir.).
TELEVISION: *Movie (dir./writer):* Roadracers.

ROEG, NICOLAS
Director, Cameraman. b. London, England. Aug. 15, 1928. m. actress Theresa Russell. Entered film industry through cutting rooms of MGM's British Studios, dubbing French films into English. Moved into prod. as clapper boy and part of photographer Freddie Young's crew at Marylebone Studios London, 1947. Next became camera operator (Trials of Oscar Wilde, The Sundowners). Had first experience as cameraman on TV series (Police Dog and Ghost Squad). Debut as director on Performance, co-directed with Donald Cammell. First solo dir. film, Walkabout.
PICTURES: *Cameraman*: The Miniver Story, The Trial of Oscar Wilde, The Sundowners, Lawrence of Arabia, Jazz Boat, Information Received, The Great Van Robbery. *Dir. of Photography*: The Caretaker, Dr. Crippen, Nothing But the Best, Masque of the Red Death, A Funny Thing Happened on the Way to the Forum, Fahrenheit 451, Far from the Madding Crowd, The Girl-Getters, Petulia. *Director-Cameraman*: Performance (co.-dir.), Walkabout. *Director*: Don't Look Now, The Man Who Fell To Earth, Bad Timing, Eureka, Insignificance, Castaway, Aria (sequence, also co-s.p.), Track 29, The Witches, Without You I'm Nothing (exec. prod. only), Cold Heaven.
TELEVISION: *Movies*: Sweet Bird of Youth, Heart of Darkness.

ROËVES, MAURICE
Actor, Director, Writer. b. Sunderland, England, Mar. 19, 1937. Ent. industry, 1964. Played Macduff to Alec Guinness's Macbeth, London stage. Early films: Ulysses, Oh! What a Lovely War, Young Winston, The Eagle Has Landed, Who Dares Wins. Dir. many stage plays.
THEATER: The Killing of Michael Malloy (Best Leading Actor Award, 1994).
PICTURES: Hidden Agenda, Last of the Mohicans, Judge Dredd.
TELEVISION: In *USA* and *UK* incl.: Scobie (series), The Gambler, Allergy, Magnum P.I., Remington Steele, Escape to Victoria, Inside the Third Reich, Journal of Bridgitte Hitler, Tutti Frutti, Unreported Incident, Bookie, North & South Part II, 919 Fifth Ave., Moses (mini-series).

ROGERS, CHARLES (BUDDY)
Actor. b. Olathe, KS, Aug. 13, 1904. e. U. of Kansas, and was trained for screen in Paramount Picture Sch. In armed services WWII. 1945 named v.p. & treas. Comet Prods., Inc. Assoc. prod. Sleep My Love, 1950, pres. PRB, Inc., prod. radio, video shows.
PICTURES: Fascinating Youth, So's Your Old Man, Wings, My Best Girl, Get Your Man, Abie's Irish Rose, The Lawyer's Secret, Road to Reno, Working Girls, This Reckless Age, Best of Enemies, Take a Chance, Dance Band, Old Man Rhythm, One in a Million, Let's Make a Night of It, This Way Please, Golden Hoofs, Mexican Spitfire's Baby, Sing for Your Supper, Mexican Spitfire at Sea, Mexican Spitfire Sees a Ghost, Don't Trust Your Husband, The Parson and the Outlaw, many others.

ROGERS, FRED
Television Host, Producer. b. Latrobe, PA, March 20, 1928. e. Rollins Coll., B.A., music composition, 1951; Pittsburgh Theol. Seminary, M. Div. 1962. 1951 served as asst. prod. of NBC-TV's The Voice of Firestone and NBC-TV Opera Theatre. Later promoted to network floor dir., supervising Your Lucky Strike Hit Parade, Kate Smith Hour, etc. 1953, joined WQED-TV in Pittsburgh, educational TV station, to handle programming. 1954 started Children's Corner series, writing, producing and per-

forming; it ran 7 years. 1963 was ordained minister of Presbyterian Church, dedicated to working with children and families through media. Same year introduced Mister Rogers on Canadian Broadcasting Corp. of 15-min. daily program. Ran for one year—was similar in content to present half-hour program, Mister Rogers' Neighborhood. 1964 programs were incorporated into larger, half-hour format on ABC affiliate in Pittsburgh. 1966, 100 programs acquired by Eastern Educational Network, broadcast in Pittsburgh, and seen for first time in other cities (and on some cable services) with underwriting by Sears & Roebuck Foundation. Mister Rogers' Neighborhood in its present format began on Feb. 19, 1968 on NET (now PBS). Program now carried over 300 PBS stations. Author of numerous fiction books for children and non-fiction books for adults; and albums and videos released by Family Communication. Also prod. 20 part PBS series Old Friends New Friends, interview/documentary format for adults, 1978-9. Produced Fred Rogers' Heroes (adult special for PBS). Recipient of 2 Emmy Awards, 2 Peabody Awards and over 25 honorary degrees from colleges and universities.

ROGERS, KENNY
Singer, Actor, Songwriter. b. Crockett, TX, Aug. 21, 1938. Country and western singer. Member Bobby Doyle Trio, Christy Minstrels, 1966-67; The First Edition 1967-76. On screen in Six Pack (1982).
TELEVISION: *Series*: McShane (NBC Friday Night Mystery). *Movies*: The Dream Makers, Kenny Rogers as The Gambler, Coward of the County, Kenny Rogers as the Gambler: The Adventure Continues, Wild Horses; Kenny Rogers as The Gambler Part III: The Legend Continues, Christmas in America, The Gambler Returns: Luck of the Draw, Real West, Rio Diablo, MacShayne: The Final Roll of the Dice, Gambler IV: Playing for Keeps, Big Dreams & Broken Hearts: The Dottie West Story. *Specials*: Kenny, Dolly & Willie: Something Inside So Strong, and numerous others. *Guest*: Dr. Quinn, Medicine Woman.

ROGERS, LAWRENCE H., II
Executive. b. Trenton, NJ, Sept. 6, 1921. e. Princeton U. 1942, U.S. Army, 1942-1946; with WSAZ, Huntington, WV, as radio & tv. v.p. & gen. mgr., 1949-55; WSAZ, Inc., pres., 1955-59; Taft Broadcasting Co., v.p., 1959-63; Taft Broadcasting Co., pres., 1963-76; cert., Harvard Business Sch., 1963; vice chmn., Hanna-Barbera Prods., LA, and Cinemobile Systems, Hollywood. Director: Cine Artists International, Hollywood; Theater Development Fund, NY. Author: Orlando Shoot-Out, 1990.

ROGERS, MIMI
Actress. b. Coral Gables, FL, Jan. 27, 1956.
PICTURES: Blue Skies Again (debut, 1983), Gung Ho, Street Smart, Someone to Watch Over Me, The Mighty Quinn, Hider in the House, Desperate Hours, The Doors, The Rapture, The Palermo Connection, The Player, White Sands, Dark Horse, Monkey Trouble, Far From Home: The Adventures of Yellow Dog, Bulletproof Heart, Reflections in the Dark, The Mirror Has Two Faces.
TELEVISION: *Series*: The Rousters, Paper Dolls. *Episodes*: Magnum, P.I., Hart to Hart, Quincy, M.E., Hill Street Blues, Tales From the Crypt. *Movies*: Divorce Wars, Hear No Evil, You Ruined My Life, Fourth Story, Deadlock, Ladykiller, Bloodlines: Murder in the Family, A Kiss to Die For.

ROGERS, PETER
Executive. b. Rochester, Eng., Feb. 20, 1916. e. Kings Sch., Rochester. Journalist and in theatre and BBC; joined G. W. H. Productions 1941 as script writer; with Gainsborough Studios; asst. scenario ed. to Muriel Box; assoc. prod.; personal asst. to Sydney Box 1949.
PICTURES: Dear Murderer, Holiday Camp, When the Bough Breaks, Here Come the Huggetts, Huggetts Abroad, Vote for Huggett, It's Not Cricket, Marry Me, Don't Ever Leave Me, Appointment with Venus (Island Rescue), The Clouded Yellow, The Dog and the Diamonds (Children's Film Found), Up to His Neck, You Know What Sailors Are, Cash on Delivery, To Dorothy A Son, Gay Dog, Circus Friends, Passionate Stranger, After the Ball, Time Lock, My Friend Charles, Chain of Events, Carry on Sergeant, Flying Scott, Cat Girl, Solitary Child, Carry On Teacher, Carry On Nurse, Carry On Constable, Please Turn Over, Watch Your Stern, The Tommy Steele Story, The Duke Wore Jeans, No Kidding, Carry On Regardless, Raising the Wind, Twice Around the Daffodils, Carry on Cruising, The Iron Maiden, Nurse on Wheels, Carry on Cabby, This Is My Street, Carry On Jack, Carry on Spying, Carry on Cleo, The Big Job, Carry on Cowboy, Carry on Screaming, Don't Lose Your Head, Follow that Camel, Carry on Doctor, Carry on Up the Khyber, Carry on Camping, Carry on Assault, Carry on Henry, Quest, Revenge, Carry on At Your Convenience, All Coppers Are..., Carry on Matron, Carry on Abroad, Bless This House, Carry on Girls, Carry on Dick, Carry on Behind, Carry on England, The Best of Carry On, Carry on Emmanuelle, Carry on Columbus.
TELEVISION: Ivanhoe (series), Carry on Laughing, Carry on Laughing, What a Carry On, Laugh With the Carry On's.

ROGERS, ROY
Actor. r.n. Leonard Slye. b. Cincinnati, OH Nov. 5, 1911. m. actress-singer Dale Evans. Radio singer. Changed named to Dick Wesson and formed singing group Sons of the Pioneers, with which he made his film debut. Voted No. 1 Money-Making Western Star in M.P. Herald-Fame, 1943-54 inclusive; also voted one of ten best money-making stars in 1945, 1946. Acting & prod. TV films, 1952 with wife, Dale Evans; one-hour spectaculars, Chevy Show, 1959-60; contracted for several TV specials and for nationwide appearances with Roy Rogers touring show in Canada & U.S., 1962; state fairs, rodeos since 1962; TV series; Happy Trails with Roy and Dale (cable). Star of 86 feature films and 104 TV episodes.
PICTURES: Way Up Thar (debut, 1935, as Dick Wesson), Rhythm on the Range, Under Western Stars (1st billing as Roy Rogers), The Old Barn Dance, Billy the Kid Returns, Come On Rangers, Rough Riders, Round-Up, Frontier, Pony Express, Southward Ho!, In Old Caliente, Wall Street Cowboy, Heart of the Golden West, Sunset Serenade, Pals of the Golden West, Son of Paleface, Alias Jesse James (cameo), MacIntosh and T.J.
TELEVISION: *Series*: The Roy Rogers Show, The Roy Rogers & Dale Evans Show.

ROGERS, THOMAS C.
Executive. e. Columbia Law School, Wesleyan Univ. 1981-86, sr. counsel, U.S. House of Representatives Subcommittee on Telecommunications, Consumer Protection and Finance; Joined NBC in 1987 as v.p., policy and planning and business development. 1988 became pres. of NBC Cable and Business Development. 1992, also named exec. v.p. of NBC.

ROGERS, WAYNE
Actor. b. Birmingham, AL, April 7, 1933. e. Princeton U.
PICTURES: Odds Against Tomorrow (debut, 1959), The Glory Guys, Chamber of Horrors, Cool Hand Luke, WUSA, Pocket Money, Once in Paris, The Gig, The Killing Time, Ghosts of Mississippi.
TELEVISION: *Series*: Edge of Night, Stagecoach West, M*A*S*H, City of the Angels, House Calls, High Risk (host). *Movies*: Attack on Terror: The FBI Versus the Ku Klux Klan, Making Babies II, It Happened One Christmas, The Top of the Hill, Chiefs, He's Fired She's Hired, The Lady from Yesterday, American Harvest, Drop-Out Mother, One Terrific Guy, Bluegrass, Passion and Paradise, Miracle Landing, The Goodbye Bird. *Mini-Series*: Chiefs. *Exec. prod.*: Perfect Witness, Age-Old Friends.

ROHRBECK, JOHN H.
Executive. e. Univ. of WA. 1967, account exec. for NBC Spot Sales in San Francisco, then NY. 1969-78, with KNBC-TV in mngmt. and sales, became station manager in 1976. 1978-84, v.p. & gen. mngr. WRC-TV in Washington DC. Became pres. & gen. mngr. of KNBC-TV in 1984. Named pres. of NBC Television Stations, 1991. Also in charge of network's daytime programming 1992-95.

ROHMER, ERIC
Director. Writer. r.n. Jean Maurice Scherer. b. Nancy, France, April 4, 1920. Professor of literature. Film critic for La Gazette du Cinema and its successor Cahiers du Cinema which he edited, 1957-63. With Claude Chabrol wrote book on Alfred Hitchcock as a Catholic moralist, 1957. 1959 directorial debut, Le Signe du Lion. 1962 began a series of 6 Moral Tales; from 1980 with The Aviator's Wife began another series of 7 films called Comedies and Proverbs. Staged Catherine de Heilbronn in Nanterre, 1979.
PICTURES: *Short films*: Presentation ou Charlotte et Son Steack (1961), La Boulangere de Monceau, Veronique et Son Cancre, Nadja a Paris, Place de L'etoile, Une Etudiante d'aujourd'hui, Fermiere a Montfaucon. *Feature films* (dir. & s.p.): Le Signe du Lion (The Sign of Leo; debut, 1959), La Carriere de Suzanne, Six in Paris (episode), La Collectionneuse, My Night at Maude's, Claire's Knee, Chloe in the Afternoon, The Marquise of O, Perceval, The Aviator's Wife, Le Beau Mariage, Pauline at the Beach, Full Moon in Paris, Summer, Boyfriends and Girlfriends, Four Adventures of Reinette and Mirabelle (also prod.), A Tale of Springtime, A Tale of Winter.
TELEVISION: Carl Dreyer, Le Celluloid et le Marbre, Ville Nouvelle, Catherine de Heilbronn. Between 1964-69 directed series of documentaries for French TV: Les Cabinets et Physique du XVIII siecle, Les Metamorphoses du Paysage Industriel, Don Quichotte, Edgar Poe, Pascal, Louis Lumiere, etc.

ROIZMAN, OWEN
Cinematographer. b. Brooklyn, NY, Sept. 22, 1936. e. Gettysburg Col.
PICTURES: The French Connection, The Gang That Couldn't Shoot Straight, Play It Again Sam, The Heartbreak Kid, The Exorcist, The Taking of Pelham 1-2-3, The Stepford Wives, Independence, Three Days of the Condor, The Return of the Man Called Horse, Network, Straight Time, Sgt. Pepper's Lonely Hearts Club Band, The Electric Horseman, The Black

Marble, True Confessions, Absence of Malice, Taps, Tootsie, Vision Quest, I Love You to Death, Havana, The Addams Family, Grand Canyon, Wyatt Earp, French Kiss.

ROLLE, ESTHER
Actress. b. Pompano Beach, FL, Nov. 8, 1922. e. New School for Social Research. An original member of Negro Ensemble Co. in NY. Has appeared both off and on B'way (in The Blacks, Amen Corner, Blues for Mister Charlie, Don't Play Us Cheap, Member of the Wedding) and in several TV series.
PICTURES: Nothing But a Man, Cleopatra Jones, P.K. and the Kid, The Mighty Quinn, Driving Miss Daisy, House of Cards, How to Make an American Quilt.
TELEVISION: *Guest*: N.Y.P.D., Like It Is, Darkroom, The Winners, The Grand Baby. *Series*: One Life to Live, Maude, Good Times. *Movies*: I Know Why the Caged Bird Sings, Summer of My German Soldier (Emmy Award, 1979), A Raisin in the Sun, Age-Old Friends, The Kid Who Loved Christmas, To Dance With the White Dog. *Mini-Series*: Scarlett.

ROLLINS, HOWARD
Actor. b. Baltimore, MD, Oct. 17, 1950. e. Towson State Coll.
THEATER: *NY*: We Interrupt This Program, Traps, Streamers, The Mighty Gents, Medal of Honor Rag, G.R. Point. *Other stage* (London): I'm Not Rappaport, Othello (Statford, Ontario).
PICTURES: Ragtime (debut, 1981; Acad. Award nom.), The House of God, A Soldier's Story, On the Block, Drunks.
TELEVISION: *Series*: Our Street (PBS 1969-73), All My Children, Wildside, In the Heat of the Night. *Mini-series*: King, Roots: The Next Generation. *Movies*: My Old Man, Doctor's Story, He's Fired, She's Hired, The Boy King, The Children of Times Square. Johnnie Mae Gibson: FBI, With Murder in Mind. *Specials*: Eliza: Our Story, Dear America: Letters Home From Vietnam (reader).

ROLLINS, JACK
Producer. b. 1914. Co-founder of talent management firm Rollins, Joffe, Mora and Brezner Inc. handling careers of Woody Allen, Nichols and May, Robin Williams, Robert Klein, David Letterman, Dick Cavett, Billy Crystal.
PICTURES: Co-prod./exec. prod. with Charles Joffe: Take the Money and Run, Bananas, Everything You Always Wanted to Know About Sex, Sleeper, Love and Death, The Front, Annie Hall (Academy Award for Best Picture, 1977), Interiors, Manhattan, Stardust Memories, Zelig, Broadway Danny Rose (also actor), The Purple Rose of Cairo, Hannah and Her Sisters, Radio Days, September, Another Woman, New York Stories (Oedipus Wrecks), Crimes and Misdemeanors, Alice, Shadows and Fog, Husbands and Wives, Manhattan Murder Mystery, Bullets Over Broadway.
TELEVISION: *Prod./exec. prod.*: The Dick Cavett Show, Late Night With David Letterman.

ROMAN, LAWRENCE
Writer. b. Jersey City, NJ, May 30, 1921. e. UCLA, 1943.
THEATER: *Author*: Under the Yum Yum Tree, P.S. I Love You, Alone Together, Buying Out, Crystal, Crystal Chandelier (prod. in Stockbridge, Mass), Coulda Woulda Shoulda (prod. in Berlin, Germany), Moving Mountains (prod. in Berlin as Grapes and Raisins).
PICTURES: Drums Across the River, Vice Squad, Naked Alibi, One Desire, Man from Bitter Ridge, Kiss Before Dying, Slaughter on Tenth Avenue, Under the Yum Yum Tree, The Swinger, Paper Lion, Red Sun, A Warm December, McQ.
TELEVISION: *Movies*: Anatomy of an Illness, Badge of the Assassin, Three Wishes for Jamie, Final Verdict, The Ernest Green Story (Peabody Award).

ROMAN, RUTH
Actress. b. Boston, MA, Dec. 23, 1924. p. professionals. e. Girls H.S., Boston; Bishop Lee Dramatic Sch. Started career with little theatre groups: New Eng. Repertory Co., Elizabeth Peabody Players. Chicago Theatre includes Night of the Iguana, Two for the Season (Sarah Siddons Award). Screen debut in Universal serial, Queen of the Jungle.
PICTURES: Good Sam, Belle Starr's Daughter, The Window, Champion, Barricade, Beyond the Forest, Always Leave Them Laughing, Colt .45, Three Secrets, Dallas, Strangers on a Train, Tomorrow is Another Day, Invitation, Lightning Strikes Twice, Starlift, Mara Maru, Young Man With Ideas, Blowing Wild, Far Country, Shanghai Story, Tanganyika, Down Three Dark Streets, Joe Macbeth, Bottom of the Bottle, Great Day in the Morning, Rebel in Town, Five Steps to Danger, Bitter Victory, Desert Desperadoes, Look in Any Window, Miracle of the Cowards (Spanish), Love Has Many Faces, Impulse, The Killing Kind, The Baby, Day of the Animals, Echoes.
TELEVISION: *Series*: The Long Hot Summer, Knots Landing. *Guest*: Naked City, Route 66, The Defenders, Breaking Point, Eleventh Hour, Producers Showcase, Dr. Kildare, Murder She Wrote, Cannon, Ironside. *Movies*: The Old Man Who Cried Wolf, Incident in San Francisco, Go Ask Alice, Punch and Jody, The Sacketts.

ROMERO, GEORGE A.
Director, Writer, Editor. b. New York, NY, 1940. e. Carnegie-Mellon Univ.
PICTURES: *Dir./Writer/Cameraman*: Night of the Living Dead (debut, 1968), There's Always Vanilla (The Affair), The Crazies (Code Name: Trixie), Jack's Wife (Hungry Wives; also edit.). *Director-Writer*: Martin (also edit., actor), Dawn of the Dead (dir. only), Knightriders, Creepshow (dir., co-edit. only), Day of the Dead (also edit.), Monkey Shines, Night of the Living Dead (s.p., co-exec. prod. only), Two Evil Eyes (The Facts in the Case of M. Valdemar), The Dark Half (also exec. prod.).
TELEVISION: Tales from the Dark Side (exec. prod., writer).

ROOKER, MICHAEL
Actor. b. Jasper, AL, 1955. e. Goodman School of Drama. Studied Japanese martial art of Aikido prior to establishing himself in Chicago theatre, where he appeared in Union Boys, The Crack Walker and Moon Children.
PICTURES: Streets of Fire (debut, 1984), Light of Day, Rent-a-Cop, Eight Men Out, Mississippi Burning, Sea of Love, Music Box, Henry: Portrait of a Serial Killer, Days of Thunder, JFK, The Dark Half, Cliffhanger, Tombstone, The Hard Truth, Mallrats, The Trigger Effect, Rosewood.
TELEVISION: *Movies*: Afterburn, Johnny & Clyde.

ROONEY, ANDREW A
Writer, Producer. b. Albany, NY, Jan. 14, 1919. e. Colgate U. Started career as writer at MGM 1946-7, then for Arthur Godfrey, Garry Moore, Sam Levenson, Victor Borge; wrote and produced documentaries, including Black History: Lost Stolen or Strayed (Emmy Award, 1969), An Essay on War, An Essay on Bridges, In Praise of New York City, Mr. Rooney Goes to Washington, etc. Regularly appears on 60 Minutes (CBS). Newspaper columnist for Tribune Syndicate, 1979-current.

ROONEY, MICKEY
Actor. r.n. Joe Yule, Jr. b. Brooklyn, NY, Sept. 23, 1920. Son of Joe Yule & Nell Carter, vaudeville performers. U.S. Army, WWII. In vaudeville as child with parents and others before m.p. debut and after; from age of 5 to 12 (1926-33) created screen version of Fontaine Fox newspaper comic character Mickey McGuire in series of short subjects (also billed as Mickey McGuire). Adopted name of Mickey Rooney, returned to vaudeville, then resumed screen career in features. Special Academy Award 1940 for Andy Hardy characterization; voted among first ten Money-Making Stars in M.P. Herald-Fame Poll: 1938-43. Autobiographies: i.e. (1965), Life is Too Short (1991). Novel: The Search for Sonny Skies (1994). Received honorary Academy Award, 1983.
THEATER: *B'way*: Sugar Babies, The Will Rogers Follies. *Regional*: W.C., Lend Me a Tenor.
PICTURES: Orchids and Ermine (feature debut, 1927), Emma, The Beast of the City, Sin's Pay Day, High Speed, Officer Thirteen, Fast Companions, My Pal the King, The Big Cage, The Life of Jimmy Dolan, The Big Chance, Broadway to Hollywood, The World Changes, The Chief, Beloved, I Like It That Way, Love Birds, Half a Sinner, The Lost Jungle, Manhattan Melodrama, Upperworld, Hide-Out, Chained, Blind Date, Death on the Diamond, The County Chairman, Reckless, The Healer, A Midsummer Night's Dream, Ah Wilderness, Riff-Raff, Little Lord Fauntleroy, The Devil is a Sissy, Down the Stretch, Captains Courageous, Slave Ship, A Family Affair, Hoosier Schoolboy, Live Love and Learn, Thoroughbreds Don't Cry, You're Only Young Once, Love is a Headache, Judge Hardy's Children, Hold That Kiss, Lord Jeff, Love Finds Andy Hardy, Boys Town, Stablemates, Out West With the Hardys, The Adventures of Huckleberry Finn, The Hardys Ride High, Andy Hardy Gets Spring Fever, Babes in Arms (Acad. Award nom.), Judge Hardy and Son, Young Tom Edison, Andy Hardy Meets Debutante, Strike Up the Band, Andy Hardy's Private Secretary, Men of Boy's Town, Life Begins for Andy Hardy, Babes on Broadway, The Courtship of Andy Hardy, A Yank at Eton, Andy Hardy's Double Life, The Human Comedy (Acad. Award nom.), Girl Crazy, Thousands Cheer, Andy Hardy's Blonde Trouble, National Velvet, Love Laughs at Andy Hardy, Killer McCoy, Summer Holiday, Words and Music, The Big Wheel, Quicksand, He's a Cockeyed Wonder, The Fireball, My Outlaw Brother, The Strip, Sound Off, All Ashore, Off Limits, A Slight Case of Larceny, Drive a Crooked Road, The Atomic Kid (also prod.), The Bridges at Toko-Ri, The Twinkle in God's Eye, Francis in the Haunted House, The Bold and the Brave (Acad. Award nom.), Magnificent Roughnecks, Operation Mad Ball, Baby Face Nelson, Andy Hardy Comes Home, A Nice Little Bank That Should Be Robbed, The Last Mile, The Big Operator, Platinum High School, The Private Lives of Adam and Eve (also co-dir.), Breakfast at Tiffany's, King of the Roaring Twenties, Requiem for a Heavyweight, Everything's Ducky, It's a Mad Mad Mad Mad World, Secret Invasion, 24 Hours to Kill, The Devil in Love, Ambush Bay, How to Stuff a Wild Bikini, The Extraordinary Seaman, Skidoo, The Comic, 80 Steps to Jonah, The Cockeyed Cowboys of Calico County, Hollywood

Blue, B.J. Lang Presents (The Manipulator), Richard, Pulp, The Godmothers (also s.p., music), Ace of Hearts, Thunder County, That's Entertainment, Journey Back to Oz (voice), From Hong Kong With Love, Rachel's Man, Find the Lady, The Domino Principle, Pete's Dragon, The Magic of Lassie, The Black Stallion (Acad. Award nom.), Arabian Adventure, The Fox and the Hound (voice), The Emperor of Peru, The Black Stallion Returns, The Care Bears Movie (voice), Lightning the White Stallion, Erik the Viking, My Heroes Have Always Been Cowboys, Sweet Justice, The Legend of Wolf Mountain, Little Nemo (voice), Silent Night Deadly Night 5: The Toymaker, The Milky Life (La Vida Lactea), Revenge of the Red Baron, That's Entertainment III.
TELEVISION: *Series*: Hey Mickey, One of the Boys, The Black Stallion. *Many specials including*: Playhouse 90, Pinocchio, Eddie, Somebody's Waiting, The Dick Powell Theater. *Movies*: Evil Roy Slade, My Kidnapper My Love, Leave 'Em Laughing, Bill (Emmy Award, 1982), Senior Trip, Bill: On His Own, It Came Upon the Midnight Clear, Bluegrass, Home for Christmas, The Gambler Returns: Luck of the Draw. *Many guest appearances including*: The Golden Girls, The Judy Garland Show, Naked City, Wagon Train, Twilight Zone, The Lucy Show, Hollywood Squares, Night Gallery, The Love Boat.

ROOS, FRED
Producer. b. Santa Monica, CA, May 22, 1934. e. UCLA, B.A. Directed documentary films for Armed Forces Radio and Television Network. Worked briefly as agent for MCA and story editor for Robert Lippert Productions. Worked as casting dir. in 1960s and served as casting dir. on The Godfather, beginning longtime association with filmmakers Francis Coppola and George Lucas.
PICTURES: The Conversation, The Godfather Part II, Apocalypse Now, The Black Stallion, The Escape Artist (exec. prod.), The Black Stallion Returns, Hammett, One From the Heart, The Outsiders, Rumble Fish, The Cotton Club, One Magic Christmas, Seven Minutes in Heaven, Peggy Sue Got Married (special consultant), Barfly, Gardens of Stone (co-exec. prod.), Tucker: The Man and His Dream, New York Stories (Life Without Zoe), Wait Until Spring Bandini, The Godfather Part III, Hearts of Darkness: A Filmmaker's Apocalypse (exec. prod.), The Secret Garden, Radioland Murders, Jack (spec. consultant).
TELEVISION: *Series*: The Outsiders (exec. prod.). *Movie*: Montana.

ROSE, ALEX
Producer. r.n. Alexandra Rose. b. Jan. 20, 1946. e. U. of WI, BS. Started in m.p. distribution with Medford Films. Later became asst. sls. mgr. for New World Pictures.
PICTURES: *Co-prod.*: Drive-In, I Wanna Hold Your Hand, Big Wednesday, Norma Rae, Nothing in Common (solo prod.), Overboard (co-prod.), Quigley Down Under, Frankie and Johnny.
TELEVISION: Nothing in Common (co-exec. prod. with Garry Marshall), *Pilots*: Norma Rae, Just Us Kids.

ROSE, CHARLIE
Talk Show Host. b. Henderson, NC, Jan. 5, 1942. e. Duke Univ. (history, law). Was exec. prod. for Bill Moyers' Journal, 1975.
TELEVISION: *Series* (host/anchor): A.M. Chicago, The Charlie Rose Show (NBC, 1979, 1981), CBS News Nightwatch, E.D.J. Entertainment Daily Journal (Personalities), Charlie Rose (synd; also exec. prod., editor). *Specials*: Public Debate With Charlie Rose, In Concert at the United Nations (host).

ROSE, REGINALD
Writer, b. New York, NY, Dec. 10, 1920. e. City Coll. of New York. Worked as clerk, publicist, Warner Bros.; adv. acct. exec., copy chief; U.S. Air Force, WWII; first TV play, Bus to Nowhere, 1951; since then numerous TV plays, Studio One, Playhouse 90. Creator of The Defenders, other programs.
PICTURES: Crime in the Streets, 12 Angry Men, Dino, Man of the West, The Man in the Net, Baxter, Somebody Killed Her Husband, The Wild Geese, The Sea Wolves, Whose Life Is It Anyway?, Wild Geese II, The Final Option.
TELEVISION: Dear Friends, Thunder on Sycamore Street, Tragedy in a Temporary Town, My Two Loves, The Rules of Marriage, Studs Lonigan, Escape from Sobibor.

ROSE, STEPHEN
Executive. Entered m.p. industry in 1964 with Columbia Pictures; named adv. dir. 1970 joined Cinema V Distributing, Inc. as dir. of adv.; left in 1971 to take post at Cinemation Industries, where was named v.p. and bd. member. 1975 joined Paramount Pictures as dir. of adv.; promoted to v.p./adv. 1979 formed Barrich Prods. with Gordon Weaver. 1982, rejoined Paramount as v.p., mktg; 1983, named v.p. of mktg. for Paramount; sr. v.p., mktg., 1983. Resigned in 1984 to form Barrich Marketing with Gordon Weaver.

ROSEANNE
Actress. b. Salt Lake City, UT, Nov. 3, 1952. Started performing in bars; prod. showcase for women performers, Take Back the Mike at U. of Boulder. 1983 won Denver Laff-Off. Moved to Los Angeles where performed at The Comedy Store, and showcased on TV special Funny and The Tonight Show. Has previously performed under the names Roseanne Barr, Roseanne Arnold. *Autobiographies:* My Life as a Woman (1989), My Lives (1994).
PICTURES: She-Devil (debut, 1989), Look Who's Talking Too (voice), Freddy's Dead, Even Cowgirls Get the Blues, Blue in the Face.
TELEVISION: *Series:* Roseanne (also co-exec. prod.); Peabody & Golden Globe Awards for Best Series; Emmy Award for Best Actress, 1993), The Jackie Thomas Show (co-exec. prod, guest), Tom (co-exec. prod.). *Specials:* Fast Copy, Rodney Dangerfield—It's Not Easy Bein' Me, Live From Minneapolis: Roseanne, Roseanne Arnold: Live From Trump Castle. *Movies:* Backfield in Motion, The Woman Who Loved Elvis (also co-exec. prod.).

ROSEN, ROBERT L.
Producer. b. Palm Springs, CA, Jan. 7, 1937. e. U. of Southern Calif.
PICTURES: French Connection II, Black Sunday, Prophecy, Going Ape, The Challenge, Courage (also dir.), Porky's Revenge, World Gone Wild, Dead-Bang (exec. prod.). *Exec. in chg. of prod.:* Little Big Man, Le Mans, The Reivers, Rio Lobo, Big Jake, Scrooge, Fourth War (Line Producer).
TELEVISION: Gilligan's Island, Hawaii Five-O, Have Gun Will Travel.

ROSENBERG, FRANK P.
Producer, Writer. b. New York, NY, Nov. 22, 1913. e. Columbia U., NYU. Joined Columbia 1929; writer m.p. novelizations & radio dramatizations; 1933, conceived and wrote script for first-ever ship-to-shore CBS network broadcast for Lady for a Day; exploit, mgr., 1941; apptd. national dir. adv., publicity, exploitation, Columbia Pictures, 1944. Pub. dir. M.P. Victory Loan, 1945; dir. pub. Columbia Pictures Studios, Hollywood, 1946. Resigned 1947 to enter production.
PICTURES: Man-Eater of Kumaon, Where the Sidewalk Ends (co-adapt.), The Secret of Convict Lake, Return of the Texan, The Farmer Takes a Wife, King of the Khyber Rifles, Illegal, Miracle in the Rain, The Girl He Left Behind, One-Eyed Jacks, Critic's Choice, Madigan, The Steagle (exec. prod.), The Reincarnation of Peter Proud, Gray Lady Down.
TELEVISION: Exec. prod. and prod. for Schlitz Playhouse programs during 1957-58; prod., The Troubleshooters; exec. prod., Arrest and Trial, 1963-64; exec. prod. Kraft Suspense Theatre, 1964-65; v.p. MCA Universal 1964-69; co-exec. prod., CBS tv movie Family of Strangers, 1993.

ROSENBERG, GRANT E.
Executive. b. San Francisco, CA, 1952. e. Univ. of Cal. at Davis. Started career in research dept., NBC; 1977, joined Paramount in research and later in development; 1984, v.p., dramatic dev.; then sr. v.p., dev., for TV group, Paramount. 1985, named sr. v.p., network TV for Walt Disney Pictures; 1988, named pres., Lee Rich Productions, TV div., and exec. prod. of Molloy TV series. 1990, writer, prod., Paramount TV. Series: MacGyver (writer), Star Trek: The Next Generation (writer), Time Trax (exec. co-prod., creator), Lois & Clark (writer, prod.). Writer, prod. for Warner Bros. TV.

ROSENBERG, RICHARD K.
Executive, Attorney. b. Paterson, NJ, Apr. 4, 1942. e. Indiana Univ. Corporation & intl. entertainment attorney for major corps. and celebrities. Formed RKR Entertainment Group in 1977 with subsidiaries RKR Releasing, RKR Artists and RKR Productions. Subsequently consolidated into RKR Pictures Inc. Author: Negotiating Motion Picture Contracts. Films include Alice Sweet Alice (Holy Terror), Hell's Angels Forever, Mother Lode, Best Revenge, The Wild Duck, Primary Motive, Fatal Past, Dutchman's Creek.

ROSENBERG, RICK
Producer. b. Los Angeles, CA. e. Los Angeles City Coll., UCLA. Started career in mail room of Columbia Pictures, then asst. to prod. Jerry Bresler on Major Dundee and Love Has Many Faces. Asst. to Col. v.p., Arthur Kramer. Was assoc. prod. on The Reivers and in 1970 prod. first feature, Adam at Six A.M., with Bob Christiansen, with whom co-prod. all credits listed below.
PICTURES: Adam at Six A.M., Hide in Plain Sight.
TELEVISION: Suddenly Single, The Glass House, A Brand New Life, The Man Who Could Talk to Kids, The Autobiography of Miss Jane Pittman, I Love You... Goodbye, Queen of the Stardust Ballroom, Born Innocent, A Death in Canaan, Strangers, Robert Kennedy and His Times, Kids Don't Tell, As Summers Die, Gore Vidal's Lincoln, Red Earth White Earth, Heist, A House of Secrets and Lies, The Last Hit, Heart of Darkness, Tad, Kingfish: A Story of Huey P. Long, Redwood Curtain.

ROSENBERG, STUART
Director, Producer. b. New York, NY, Aug. 11, 1927. e. NYU.
PICTURES: Murder, Inc. (co-dir.; debut, 1960), Question 7, Cool Hand Luke, The April Fools, Move (also co-exec. prod.), WUSA (also co-exec. prod.), Pocket Money, The Laughing Policeman (also prod.), The Drowning Pool, Voyage of the Damned, The Amityville Horror, Love and Bullets, Brubaker, The Pope of Greenwich Village, Let's Get Harry (under pseudonym Allan Smithee), My Heroes Have Always Been Cowboys.
TELEVISION: Numerous episodes of such series as The Untouchables, Naked City, The Defenders (Emmy Award, 1963), Espionage, Chrysler Theatre, Twilight Zone, Alfred Hitchcock Theater.

ROSENFELT, FRANK E.
Executive. b. Peabody, MA, Nov. 15, 1921. e. Cornell U., B.S.; Cornell Law Sch., L.L.B. Served as atty. for RKO Radio Pictures, before joining MGM in 1955 as member of legal dept. Appt. secty. in 1966. Named v.p., gen. counsel in 1969 and pres. in 1973. 1974-81, CEO, bd. chmn. & CEO, MGM; now vice chmn., MGM/UA Communications Co. Member: Bd. of Governors, Academy of M.P. Arts & Sciences for 9 years. Retired from MGM/UA in Aug. 1990, now consultant to MGM-Pathe Commun. Co.

ROSENFELT, SCOTT
Producer, Director. b. Easton, PA, Dec. 20, 1955. e. NYU.
PICTURES: *Producer:* Teen Wolf, Extremities, Russkies, Mystic Pizza, Big Man on Campus (co-prod.), Home Alone, Family Prayers (dir.).

ROSENFIELD, JONAS, JR.
Executive. b. Dallas, TX, June 29, 1915. e. U. of Miami, A.B. In U.S. Navy, WWII. Warner Bros. advertising copy dept., 1936-40; adv. mgr. Walt Disney, 1941; a founder & pres. N.Y. Screen Publicists Guild; adv. mngr. & dir., 20th Cent.-Fox, 1941-1950; v.p. Italian Films Export, 1950-55; v.p. in chg. adv. pub. expl. Columbia Pictures, 1955-63; v.p. worldwide adv., publ. and promotion, 20th Century-Fox, 1963-77; film mktg. consultant, 1977-78; lecturer in mktg., USC, 1978-79; v.p. in chg. of worldwide mktg., Melvin Simon Prods., 1979-1981; Filmways Pictures as exec. v.p., worldwide adv./pub., promo. 1982; lecturer adjunct, USC Sch. of Cinema & TV, 1982-84; pres. American Film Marketing Association, 1983 to present.

ROSENMAN, HOWARD
Producer. b. Brooklyn, NY, Feb. 1, 1945. e. Brooklyn Col. Asst. to Sir Michael Benthall on B'way show; prod., Benton & Bowles Agency; ABC-TV; RSO Prods. Co-pres., Sandollar Prods.; currently pres. Brillstein-Grey Motion Pictures.
PICTURES: Sparkle, The Main Event, Resurrection, Lost Angels, Gross Anatomy, True Identity, Father of the Bride, Shining Through, Straight Talk, A Stranger Among Us, Buffy the Vampire Slayer.
TELEVISION: *Movies:* Isn't It Shocking? Altogether Now, Death Scream, Virginia Hill, Killer Bees. *Specials:* Common Threads: Stories from the Quilt (co-exec. prod.), Tidy Endings.

ROSENMAN, LEONARD
Composer. b. New York, NY, Sept. 7, 1924.
PICTURES: East of Eden, Cobweb, Rebel Without a Cause, Edge of the City, The Savage Eye, The Chapman Report, Fantastic Voyage, Hellfighters, Beneath the Planet of the Apes, Barry Lyndon (Academy Award, 1975), Birch Interval, Race With the Devil, Bound For Glory (Academy Award, 1976), A Man Called Horse, The Car, September 30, 1955, The Enemy of the People, The Lord of the Rings, Promises in the Dark, Prophecy, Hide in Plain Sight, The Jazz Singer, Making Love, Miss Lonely Hearts, Cross Creek, Heart of the Stag, Star Trek IV: The Voyage Home, Robocop 2, Ambition.
TELEVISION: *Movies/Mini-Series:* Sybil (Emmy Award), Friendly Fire (Emmy Award), City in Fear, Murder in Texas, Vanished, The Wall, Miss Lonelyhearts, Celebrity, The Return of Marcus Welby MD, Heartsounds, First Steps, Promised a Miracle, Keeper of the City.

ROSENSTEIN, GERTRUDE
Director. b. New York, NY. e. Barnard Coll., B.A.; Neighborhood Playhouse. exec. asst. to George Balanchine & Lincoln Kirstein, N.Y.C. Ballet. Assoc. with Gian Carlo Menotti, Festival of Two Worlds, Spoleto, Italy. Member of Emmy Awards committee. TV staff dir., NBC. Now freelance director, news programs, election coverage, music and dance programs, commercials. Governor, NY Television Academy.
TELEVISION: *Assoc. dir.:* NBC Opera, Emmy Awards, Kennedy Memorial Mass. *Dir.:* Concentration.

ROSENTHAL, BUD
Executive. b. Brooklyn, NY, Mar. 21, 1934. e. Brooklyn Coll., B.A., 1954, NYU. US Army, 1954-56; college correspondent, NY Times; ent. m.p. ind. as assoc. editor, Independent Film

Journal, 1957-59; joined Columbia Pictures publicity dept. as trade paper contact and news writer, 1959; newspaper and syndicate contact 1960; natl. publicity mngr., Columbia Pictures Corp., 1962-67; publ. dir., Anderson Tapes, Such Good Friends, The Blue Bird; story edit. and casting dir., Sigma Prods., 1972-75; associate prod., Broadway play, Full Circle, 1973; Warner Bros. project coordinator, Superman, Superman II, Superman III; project coordinator, Time Warner Presents The Earth Day Special, Warner Bros. Studios Rededication, Celebration of Tradition, 1990.
PICTURES: Something for Everyone (asst. prod.), Rosebud (assoc. prod.). Int'l mktg. co-ord. on films: Ghostbusters, Labyrinth, Batman, Boyz 'N the Hood, Addams Family, Batman Returns, A Few Good Men, Last Action Hero.

ROSENTHAL, JANE
Executive. b. Denver, CO. e. NYU. 1976-84, dir. of film for TV at CBS; 1984-87, v.p. prod. Disney; 1987-88, v.p. of TV & Mini-Series, Warners TV; 1988-93, exec. v.p., Tribeca Prods.; 1993-present, pres. of Tribeca Prods.; 1992-93, exec. prod. of series Tribeca. Producer of films Faithful, Marvin's Room.

ROSENTHAL, RICK
Director. b. New York, NY, June 15, 1949. e. Harvard, B.A. cum laude, 1971. Launched career as filmmaker-in-residence with New Hampshire TV Network. Moved to Los Angeles to study at American Film Institute where filmed Moonface, 1973.
PICTURES: Halloween II (debut, 1981), Bad Boys, American Dreamer, Russkies, Distant Thunder.
TELEVISION: Movies: Fire on the Mountain, Code of Vengeance, Secrets of Midland Heights, Nasty Boys, Devlin. Series: Life Goes On.

ROSENZWEIG, BARNEY
Producer. b. Los Angeles, CA, Dec. 23, 1937. e. USC, 1959. m. actress Sharon Gless.
PICTURES: Morituri (assoc. prod.), Do Not Disturb (assoc. prod.), Caprice (assoc. prod.), Who Fears the Devil (prod.).
TELEVISION: Prod.: Daniel Boone (series), Men of the Dragon, One of My Wives Is Missing, Charlie's Angels (series), Angel on My Shoulder, American Dream (pilot), John Steinbeck's East of Eden (mini-series; Golden Globe Award). Exec. prod.: Modesty Blasie (pilot), This Girl for Hire (movie), Cagney and Lacey (series; 2 Emmy Awards: 1985, 1986), The Trials of Rosie O'Neill (series), Christy (movie, series), Cagney & Lacey: The Return (movie), Cagney & Lacey: Together Again (movie), Cagney & Lacey: The View Through the Glass Ceiling (movie), Cagney & Lacey: True Convictions (movie).

ROSS, DIANA
Singer, Actress. b. Detroit, MI, Mar. 26, 1944. Formed musical group at age 14 with two friends, Mary Wilson and Florence Ballard. In 1960 they auditioned for Berry Gordy, head of Motown Record Corp. and were hired to sing backgrounds on records for Motown acts. After completing high school, the trio was named the Supremes and went on tour with Motor Town Revue. Over period of 10 yrs. Supremes had 15 consecutive hit records and once had five consecutive records in the number one spot on charts. In 1969 Diana Ross went on her own, appearing on TV and in nightclubs. Memoirs: Secrets of a Sparrow (1993).
PICTURES: Lady Sings the Blues (debut as actress, 1972; Acad. Award nom.), Mahogany, The Wiz.
TELEVISION: Movie: Out of Darkness (also co-exec. prod.). Specials: Diana! (also exec. prod. & writer), Motown 25: Yesterday Today Forever, Motown Returns to the Apollo, Diana's World Tour.

ROSS, HERBERT
Director. b. New York, NY, May 13, 1927. m. Lee Radziwill. e. studied dance with Doris Humphrey, Helene Platova, Caird Leslie. Trained for stage with Herbert Berghof, 1946-50. As B'way dancer in Laffing Room Only, Beggars Holiday, Bloomer Girl, Look Ma I'm Dancing, Inside U.S.A., and with the American Ballet Theatre. Resident choreographer 1958-59 ABT for Caprichos, Concerto in D, The Maids, Tristan, Thief Who Loved a Ghost. Ent. m.p. ind. as choreographer for Carmen Jones, The Young Ones, Summer Holiday (also dir. musical sequences), Inside Daisy Clover, Dr. Doolittle, Funny Girl (also dir. musical numbers). Exec. prod. on film Soapdish.
THEATER/OPERA: B'way Choreographer-Director: A Tree Grows in Brooklyn, The Gay Life, I Can Get It For You Wholesale, Tovarich, Anyone Can Whistle, Do I Hear a Waltz, On a Clear Day You Can See Forever, The Apple Tree, Finian's Rainbow, Wonderful Town. Dir.: Chapter Two, I Ought To Be in Pictures, Follies in Concert, Anyone Can Whistle (fundraiser for GMHC; Grammy nom.), La Bohème (L.A. & Dallas).
PICTURES: Goodbye Mr. Chips (debut, 1969), The Owl and the Pussycat, T.R. Baskin, Play It Again Sam, The Last of Sheila (also prod.), Funny Lady, The Sunshine Boys, The Seven Percent Solution (also prod.), The Turning Point (also prod.), The Goodbye Girl, California Suite, Nijinsky (also

prod.), Pennies from Heaven (also prod.), I Ought to Be in Pictures (also prod.), Max Dugan Returns (also prod.), Footloose, Protocol (also prod.), The Secret of My Success (also prod.), Dancers (also prod.), Steel Magnolias, My Blue Heaven (also prod.), True Colors (also prod.), Undercover Blues (also exec. prod.), Boys on the Side (also prod.).
TELEVISION: Choreographer: Series: Milton Berle Show (1952-57), Martha Raye Show, Bell Telephone Hour (also prod., dir.). Specials: Wonderful Town (also dir.), Meet Me in St. Louis, Jerome Kern Special, Bea Lillie and Cyril Ritchard Show (dir.), The Fantastiks, The Fred Astaire Special (1963, dir.).

ROSS, KATHARINE
Actress. b. Los Angeles, CA, Jan. 29, 1943. m. actor Sam Elliott. e. Santa Rosa Coll. Joined the San Francisco Workshop, appeared in The Devil's Disciple, The Balcony. TV debut, 1962 in Sam Benedict segment.
PICTURES: Shenandoah (debut, 1965), Mister Buddwing, The Singing Nun, Games, The Graduate (Golden Globe Award, Acad. Award nom.), Hellfighters, Butch Cassidy and the Sundance Kid, Tell Them Willie Boy is Here, Fools, Get to Know Your Rabbit, They Only Kill Their Masters, The Stepford Wives, Voyage of the Damned, The Betsy, The Swarm, The Legacy, The Final Countdown, Wrong Is Right, Daddy's Deadly Darling, Red-Headed Stranger.
TELEVISION: Movies: The Longest Hundred Miles, Wanted: The Sundance Woman, Murder by Natural Causes, Rodeo Girl, Murder in Texas, Marian Rose White, Shadow Riders, Travis McGee, Secrets of a Mother and Daughter, Conagher (also co-script). Guest: Ben Casey, The Bob Hope-Chrysler Theatre, The Virginian, Wagon Train, Kraft Mystery Theatre, The Lieutenant, The Road West. Series: The Colbys.

ROSS, KENNETH
Writer. b. London, Sept. 16, 1941. Entered m.p. industry 1970.
THEATER: The Raft, Under The Skin, Mr. Kilt & The Great I Am.
PICTURES: Brother Sun Sister Moon, Slag, The Reckless Years (also orig. story), Abelard & Heloise, The Day of the Jackal (So. Cal. M.P. Council Award; nom. for Writers' Guild, SFTA, and Golden Globes), The Devil's Lieutenant, The Odessa File (nom. for Writers' Guild Award), Quest (also orig. story), Black Sunday (Edgar Allen Poe Award, Mystery Writers of America, 1977), The Fourth War, Epiphany (also orig. story).
TELEVISION: The Roundelay, The Messenger.

ROSSELLINI, ISABELLA
Actress. b. Rome, Italy, June 18, 1952. Daughter of actress Ingrid Bergman and director Roberto Rossellini. Came to America in 1972. Worked as translator for Italian News Bureau. Taught Italian at New Sch. for Social Research. Worked 3 years on second unit assignments for journalist Gianni Mina and as NY corresp. for Ital. TV series, The Other Sunday. Model for Vogue, Harper's Bazaar, Italian Elle, Lancome Cosmetics.
PICTURES: A Matter of Time (debut 1976; with her mother), The Meadow, Il Pap'Occhio, White Nights, Blue Velvet, Tough Guys Don't Dance, Siesta, Red Riding Hood, Zelly and Me, Cousins, Les Dames Galantes, The Siege of Venice, Wild at Heart, Death Becomes Her, The Pickle, Fearless, Wyatt Earp, Immortal Beloved, The Innocent, Big Night.
TELEVISION: Movies: The Last Elephant, Lies of the Twins, The Crime of the Century. Guest: The Tracey Ullman Show. Specials: The Gift, Fallen Angels (The Frightening Frammis). Guest: Tales From the Crypt (You Murderer).

ROSSO, LEWIS, T.
Executive. b. Hoboken, NJ, Feb. 3, 1909. Ent. m.p. ind. 1930; prod. & mgt. for Consolidated Film Ind., 1930-44; Republic producer, 1944-50; prod. mgr., 1950-55; asst. sec'y & asst. treas., 1959; exec. asst. to exec. prod. mgr., 20th Century-Fox Films, 1960; plant mgr., Samuel Goldwyn Studios, 1961-71; exec. admin. asst. plant mgr., The Burbank Studios, 1972-88.

ROSSOVICH, RICK
Actor. b. Palo Alto, CA, August 28, 1957. e. Calif. St. Univ. Sacramento (art history). Studied acting with coach Vincent Chase.
PICTURES: The Lords of Discipline (debut, 1983), Losin' It, Streets of Fire, The Terminator, Fast Forward, Warning Sign, Top Gun, Let's Get Harry, The Morning After, Roxanne, Paint It Black, The Witching Hour, Spellbinder, Navy SEALS, Cognac, Tropical Heat, New Crime City.
TELEVISION: Series: MacGruder and Loud, Sons and Daughters, ER. Guest: Tales from the Crypt (The Switch). Special: 14 Going On 30. Movies: Deadly Lessons, The Gambler Returns: Luck of the Draw, Black Scorpion.

ROTH, BOBBY
Director, Writer, Producer.
PICTURES: The Boss' Son, Circle of Power, Independence Day, Heartbreakers.

TELEVISION: *Episodes*: Miami Vice, The Insiders, Crime Story. *Movies*: Tonight's the Night, The Man Who Fell to Earth, Dead Solid Perfect (dir., co-s.p.), Baja Oklahoma (dir., co-s.p.), The Man Inside.

ROTH, JOE
Executive, Producer, Director. b. New York, NY, 1948. Began career working as prod. assistant on commercials and feature films in San Francisco. Also ran the lights for improv group Pitchel Players. Moved with them to Los Angeles, and produced their shows incl. the $250,000 film Tunnelvision. 1987 co-founder of independent film prod. co. Morgan Creek Productions. 1989 left to become chairman of newly-formed Fox Film Corp., the theatrical film unit of 20th Century Fox Film Corp. Also named head of News Corp. unit. Resigned from Fox, 1993. Pres. & founder, Caravan Pictures, 1993. 1994, became chmn. Walt Disney Motion Pictures Group.
PICTURES: *Producer*: Tunnelvision, Cracking Up, Americathon, Our Winning Season, The Final Terror, The Stone Boy, Where the River Runs Black, Bachelor Party, Off Beat, Streets of Gold (also dir. debut), Tall Tale, Angels in the Outfield. *Exec. prod.*: Revenge of the Nerds II: Nerds in Paradise (also dir.), Young Guns, Dead Ringers, Skin Deep, Major League, Renegades, Enemies a Love Story, Pacific Heights, The Three Musketeers, Angie, I Love Trouble, Angels in the Outfield, A Low Down Dirty Shame, Houseguest, Tall Tale, While You Were Sleeping. *Dir.*: Coupe de Ville.

ROTH, PAUL A.
Executive. b. Asheville, NC, March 28, 1930. e. U. of North Carolina, A.B. political science, 1948-51; George Washington U. Law Sch., 1951-52. U.S. Army 1952-55. Dist. Mgr. Valley Enterprises, Inc. 1955-56; v.p. Roth Enterprises, Inc. 1956-65; pres. Roth Enterprises, Inc. 1965-present; pres., Valley Lanes Inc. 1975-present; v.p., CAPA Ltd. 1976-present; pres., Carolina Cinema Corp., 1980-present; pres., Thrashers Ocean Fries, 1987-present; dir. Riggs Bank of Maryland, 1984-93; pres. NATO of Virginia 1971-73; chmn. bd. NATO of Virginia, 1973-75; member National NATO Board, 1971-present; exec. comm. NATO of VA & MD, 1965-present; Variety Club Tent 11 Board Member 1959-65; pres. National NATO, 1973-75; chmn. National NATO bd. dir. 1975-77. Chmn., NATO Government Relations Committee, 1988-1996. member Foundation Motion Picture Pioneers, 1973-present; member & advisory committee, Will Rogers Hospital, 1973-present; trustee American Film Institute, 1973-75; Recipient: NATO Mid-Atlantic Exhibitor of the Year (1990), S.M. Hassanein Humanitarian Award at ShowEast (1991), ShoWester Award (1993).

ROTH, RICHARD A.
Producer. b. Beverly Hills, CA, 1943. e. Stanford U. Law Sch. Worked for L.A. law firm before beginning film career as lawyer and literary agent for Ziegler-Ross Agency. In 1970 left to develop s.p. Summer of '42 with Herman Raucher.
PICTURES: Summer of '42, Our Time, The Adventures of Sherlock Holmes' Smarter Brother, Julia, Outland, In Country, Havana.

ROTH, TIM
Actor. b. London, England, 1961. Started acting with various fringe theatre groups such as Glasgow Citizen's Theatre, The Oval House, and the Royal Court. Also on London stage in Metamorphosis.
PICTURES: The Hit, A World Apart, The Cook the Thief His Wife and Her Lover, Vincent & Theo, Rosencrantz and Guildenstern Are Dead, Jumpin at the Boneyard, Reservoir Dogs, Backsliding, Bodies Rest and Motion, Pulp Fiction, Rob Roy (BAFTA Award, 1995), Little Odessa, Captives, Hoodlums, Four Rooms, Everyone Say I Love You.
TELEVISION: *Specials/Movies* (BBC): Meantime, Made in Britain, Metamorphosis, Knuckle, Yellow Backs, King of the Ghetto, The Common Pursuit, Murder in the Heartland (U.S.), Heart of Darkness.

ROTHMAN, THOMAS E.
Executive. b. Baltimore, MD, Nov. 21, 1954. m. actress Jessica Harper. e. Brown U., B.A. 1976; Columbia Law Sch., J.D. 1980. Worked as law clerk with Second Circuit Court of Appeals 1981-82 before becoming partner at entertainment law firm, Frankfurt Garbus Klein & Selz 1982-87; 1987 joined Columbia Pictures as exec. v.p. and asst. to pres., named exec. prod. v.p. Left in 1989 to join Samuel Goldwyn Co. as pres. of worldwide production. Currently pres. of Fox Searchlight Films.
PICTURES: *Co-prod.*: Down By Law, Candy Mountain. *Exec. Prod.*: The Program.

ROTUNNO, GIUSEPPE
Cinematographer. b. Rome, Italy, March 19, 1923. Gained fame as leading cinematographer of Italian films working with Federico Fellini. Later worked in Hollywood.
PICTURES: Tosca, Monte Carlo Story, White Nights, The Naked Maja, On the Beach, Fast and Sexy, The Angel Wore Red, Five Branded Women, Rocco and His Brothers, Boccaccio '70, The Leopard, The Organizer, Juliet of the Spirits, The Bible, Anizo, Candy, Spirits of the Dead, Fellini Satyricon, The Secret of Santa Vittoria, Carnal Knowledge, Fellini's Roma, Man of La Mancha, Amarcord, Love and Anarchy, Fellini's Casanova, All Screwed Up, End of the World in Our Usual Bed in a Night Full of Rain, Orchestra Rehearsal, All That Jazz, City of Women, Popeye, Rollover, Five Days One Summer, And the Ship Sails On, American Dreamer, Desire, Nothing Left to Do But Cry, The Red Sonja, Hotel Colonial, Julia and Julia, Rent-a-Cop, Rebus, Haunted Summer, The Adventures of Baron Munchausen, Regarding Henry, Once Upon a Crime, Wolf, The Night the Moment, Sabrina, La Sindrome di Stendhal.
TELEVISION: The Scarlet and the Black.

ROUNDTREE, RICHARD
Actor. b. New Rochelle, NY, July 9, 1942. e. Southern Illinos U. Former model, Ebony Magazine Fashion Fair; joined workshop of Negro Ensemble Company, appeared in Kongi's Harvest, Man Better Man, Mau Mau Room; played lead role in Philadelphia road company of The Great White Hope before film debut.
PICTURES: What Do You Say to a Naked Lady? (debut, 1970), Shaft, Embassy, Charley One-Eye, Shaft's Big Score, Embassy, Shaft in Africa, Earthquake, Man Friday, Portrait of a Hitman, Escape to Athena, Game for Vultures, An Eye for an Eye, Inchon, Q (The Winged Serpent), One Down Two to Go, The Big Score, Young Warriors, Killpoint, City Heat, Opposing Force, Jocks, Maniac Cop, Homer and Eddie, Angel III: The Final Chapter, The Party Line, Getting Even, American Cops, The Banker, Night Visitor, Crack House, Bad Jim, Lost Memories, Body of Influence, Deadly Rivals, Amityville: A New Generation, Gypsy Angels, Mind Twister, Seven, Once Upon A Time...When We Were Colored.
TELEVISION: *Series*: Shaft, Outlaws, Cop Files (host). *Movies*: Firehouse, The Fifth Missile, Christmas in Connecticut, Bonanza: The Return, Shadows of Desire, Bonanza: Under Attack. *Mini-Series*: Roots, A.D.

ROURKE, MICKEY
Actor. b. Schenectady, NY, Sept. 1956. Moved to Miami as a boy. Fought as an amateur boxer 4 years in Miami. Studied acting with Sandra Seacat while working as a nightclub bouncer, a sidewalk pretzel vendor and other odd jobs. Moved to LA, 1978. Debut: TV movie City in Fear (1978).
PICTURES: 1941 (debut, 1979), Fade to Black, Heaven's Gate, Body Heat, Diner (Natl. Society of Film Critics Award, 1982), Rumblefish, Eureka, The Pope of Greenwich Village, Year of the Dragon, 9-1/2 Weeks, Angel Heart, A Prayer for the Dying, Barfly, Homeboy (also wrote orig. story), Francesco, Johnny Handsome, Wild Orchid, Desperate Hours, Harley Davidson and the Marlboro Man, White Sands, F.T.W., Fall Time.
TELEVISION: *Movies*: City in Fear, Rape and Marriage: The Rideout Case, Act of Love, The Last Outlaw.

ROUSSELOT, PHILIPPE
Cinematographer. b. Meurthe-et-Moselle, France, 1945. e. Vaugirard Film Sch., Paris. Worked as camera assistant to Nestor Almendros on My Night at Maud's, Claire's Knee, Love in the Afternoon.
PICTURES: The Guinea Pig Couple, Adom ou le sang d'Abel, Paradiso, Pauline et l'ordinateur, Peppermint Soda, For Clemence, Cocktail Molotov, La Provinciale, A Girl From Lorraine, Diva (Cesar, Natl. Society of Film Critics, and Moscow Awards), The Jaws of the Wolf, The Moon in the Gutter, Thieves After Dark, The Emerald Forest, Therese (Cesar Award), Hope and Glory, Dangerous Liaisons, The Bear, We're No Angels, Too Beautiful for You, Henry and June, A River Runs Through It (Academy Award, 1992), Sommersby, Interview With the Vampire, Queen Margot.

ROWE, ROY
Exhibitor. b. Burgaw, May 29, 1905. e. U. of NC. Eng. instructor, private bus. coll., 1926-29; Publix Sch. for Mgrs., NY, 1930-31; mgr. theatres, Spartanburg, SC; Greensboro & Raleigh, NC; Warner Theatre, Pittsburgh, PA, 1931-34; city mgr. for Warner Theatres, Washington, PA, 1934-35; opened own theatres in NC 1935; member NC Senate, 1937, 1941, 1945, 1949, 1957, 1965; 1935-75, House of Rep., 1943; Major, Civil Air Patrol, WWII; pres. Carolina Aero Club, 1943-44; chmn. NC Aeronautics Comm., 1941-49; dir. Theatre Owners No. & So. Carolina 1943-45; pres., Theatre Owners of SC & NC 1944-45; pres., Assn. of Governing Boards of State Univs., 1964; Rowe Insurance Agency, 1967-69; Mem. Exec. Bd., U. of NC Trustees, 1969. Principal Clerk, NC Senate 1969-75. Owner-operator Rowe Amusement Co., Burgaw, NC. Retired.

ROWLAND, ROY
Director. b. New York, NY, Dec. 31, 1902. e. U. of Southern California, law. Script clerk; asst. dir.; asst. to late W. S. Van Dyke on Tarzan pictures; dir. of shorts, ``How to'' Benchley series; Crime Does Not Pay series; Pete Smith Specialties.

PICTURES: Think First, Stranger in Town, Lost Angel, Our Vines Have Tender Grapes, Tenth Avenue Angel, Night Patrol, Ski Soldier, Boys' Ranch, Romance of Rosy Ridge, Killer McCoy, Scene of the Crime, Outriders, Excuse My Dust, Two Weeks With Love, Bugles in the Afternoon, The 5000 Fingers of Dr. T, Affair with a Stranger, The Moonlighter, Witness to Murder, Rogue Cop, Many Rivers to Cross, Hit the Deck, Meet Me in Las Vegas, Slander, Somewhere I'll Find Him, Gun Glory, The Seven Hills of Rome, The Girl Hunters, Gunfighters of Casa Grande, They Called Him Gringo, Tiger of the Seven Seas, Thunder Over the Indian Ocean.

ROWLANDS, GENA
Actress. r.n. Virginia Cathryn Rowlands. b. Cambria, WI, June 19, 1934. e. U. of Wisconsin. Son is actor Nicholas Cassavetes. Came to New York to attend American Acad. of Dramatic Arts, where she met and married John Cassavetes. Made B'way debut as understudy and then succeeded to role of The Girl in The Seven Year Itch. Launched as star with part in The Middle of the Night, which she played 18 mos.
PICTURES: The High Cost of Loving (debut, 1958), Lonely Are the Brave, The Spiral Road, A Child Is Waiting, Tony Rome, Faces, Machine Gun McCain, Minnie and Moskowitz, A Woman Under the Influence (Acad. Award nom.), Two Minute Warning, The Brink's Job, Opening Night, Gloria (Acad. Award nom.), Tempest, Love Streams, Light of Day, Another Woman, Once Around, Ted and Venus, Night on Earth, The Neon Bible, Something to Talk About, Unhook The Stars.
TELEVISION: Movies: A Question of Love, Strangers: The Story of a Mother & Daughter, Thursday's Child, An Early Frost, The Betty Ford Story (Emmy Award, 1987), Montana, Face of a Stranger (Emmy Award, 1992), Crazy in Love, Silent Cries, Parallel Lives. Guest: The Philco TV Playhouse, Studio One, Alfred Hitchcock Presents, Dr. Kildare, Bonanza, The Kraft Mystery Theatre, Columbo. Series: Top Secret USA, 87th Precinct, Peyton Place.

ROWLEY, JOHN H.
Executive. b. San Angelo, TX, Oct. 6, 1917. e. U. of TX, 1935-39. Past pres., NATO of Texas; past Int'l Chief barker, Variety Clubs Int'l; past pres., TOA. Currently exec. dir. NATO of TX.

RUBEN, JOSEPH
Director. b. Briarcliff, NY, 1951. e. U. of Michigan, majoring in theater and film; Brandeis U., B.A. Interest in film began in high sch. Bought a Super-8 camera and filmed his first movie, a teenage love story. First feature, The Sister-in-Law, a low budget feature which he wrote and dir. in 1975.
PICTURES: Dir./Writer: The Sister-in-Law (also prod.), The Pom-Pom Girls (also prod.), Joy Ride, Our Winning Season. Dir.: G.O.R.P., Dreamscape (also co-s.p.), The Stepfather, True Believer, Sleeping With the Enemy, The Good Son, Money Train.
TELEVISION: Breaking Away (pilot), Eddie Dodd.

RUBIN, STANLEY
Producer, Writer. b. New York, NY, Oct. 8, 1917; ed. UCLA, 1933-37. Phi Beta Kappa. Writer for radio, magazines, pictures, 1937-41; U.S. Army Air Force, 1942-45; writer, prod., owner, Your Show Time, Story Theatre TV series; winner of 1st Emmy awarded to filmed series: The Necklace, 1949. Producer, RKO, 20th-Fox, U.I., MGM, Paramount, Rastar.
PICTURES: The Narrow Margin, My Pal Gus, Destination Gobi, River of No Return, Destry, Francis in the Navy, Behind the High Wall, Rawhide Years, The Girl Most Likely, Promise Her Anything, The President's Analyst, Revenge, White Hunter Black Heart (co-prod.).
TELEVISION: G.E. Theatre, Ghost and Mrs. Muir, Bracken's World, The Man and the City, Executive Suite. Movies: Babe (co-prod.; Golden Globe Award), And Your Name is Jonah, Don't Look Back: The Story of Satchel Page (Image Award), Escape From Iran: The Canadian Caper (exec. prod.).

RUBINEK, SAUL
Actor. b. Fohrenwold, Germany, July 2, 1948. Family moved to Canada when he was a baby. Acting debut at age 8 with local theatre groups. Founding member of the Toronto Free Stage Theatre.
PICTURES: Nothing Personal, Highpoint, Agency, Death Ship, Ticket to Heaven, Soup for One, Young Doctors in Love, By Design, Against All Odds, Martin's Day, Sweet Liberty, Taking Care, Wall Street, Obsessed, The Outside Chance of Maximillian Glick, The Bonfire of the Vanities, Man Trouble, Unforgiven, The Quarrel, True Romance, Undercover Blues, Death Wish V, Getting Even With Dad, I Love Trouble, Open Season, Nixon.
TELEVISION: Concealed Enemies, The Terry Fox Story, Clown White, Interrogation in Budapest, Woman on the Run, And the Band Played On, The Android Affair.

RUBINSTEIN, JOHN
Actor, Composer, Director. b. Los Angeles, CA, December 8, 1946. Son of concert pianist Arthur Rubinstein and dancer-writer Aniela Rubinstein. e. UCLA.

THEATER: Pippin (NY debut, 1972; Theatre World Award), Picture (Mark Taper, LA), Children of a Lesser God (Tony Award, Drama Desk, L.A. Drama Critics Awards, 1980), Fools, The Caine Mutiny Court-Martial, M. Butterfly, Kiss of the Spider Woman. Director: The Rover, Les Liaisons Dangereuses, Phantasie, Nightingale, The Old Boy.
PICTURES: Journey to Shiloh (debut, 1968), The Trouble With Girls, Getting Straight, The Wild Pack, Zachariah, The Car, The Boys From Brazil, In Search of Historic Jesus, Daniel, Someone to Watch Over Me, Another Stakeout, Mercy.
TELEVISION: Series: Family, Crazy Like a Fox. Guest: The Virginian, Ironside, Dragnet, Room 222, The Psychiatrist, The Mary Tyler Moore Show, Cannon, The Mod Squad, Nichols, Hawaii Five-O, Barnaby Jones, Policewoman, Barbary Coast, The Rookies, The Streets of San Francisco, Harry O, Vegas, The Class of '65, Movin' On, Stop the Presses, Wonder Woman, Lou Grant, Fantasy Island, The Quest, Quincy, Trapper John M.D., The Love Boat, Father Dowling, The Paper Chase, Murder She Wrote. Special: Triple Play—Sam Found Out. Movies: The Marriage Proposal, God Bless the Children, A Howling in the Woods, Something Evil, All Together Now, The Gift of the Magi, Roots: The Next Generations, Just Make Me an Offer, The French Atlantic Affair, Corey: For the People, Happily Ever After, Moviola, Skokie, The Mr. and Ms. Mysteries, Killjoy, Freedom to Speak, Someone's Killing the High Fashion Models; I Take These Men, M.A.D.D.: Mothers Against Drunk Driving, Liberace, Voices Within: The Lives of Truddi Chase, In My Daughter's Name, The American Clock. Director: A Matter of Conscience, Summer Stories: The Mall.
SCORES: Films: Paddy, Jeremiah Johnson, The Candidate, Kid Blue, The Killer Inside Me. Television: All Together Now, Emily, Emily, Stalk the Wild Child, Champions: A Love Story, To Race the Wind, The Ordeal of Patty Hearst, Amber Waves, Johnny Belinda, Secrets of a Mother and Daughter, Choices of the Heart, The Dollmaker, Family (Emmy nom.), The Fitzpatricks, The Mackenzies of Paradise Cove, The New Land, For Heaven's Sake, The Lazarus Syndrome, The City Killer, China Beach.

RUBINSTEIN, RICHARD P.
Producer, Executive. b. New York, NY, June 15, 1947. e. American U. B.S. 1969, Columbia U. MBA 1971. Pres. & CEO, New Amsterdam Entertainment, Inc.
PICTURES: Martin, Dawn Of The Dead, Knightriders, Creepshow, Day Of The Dead, Creepshow 2, Pet Sematary, Tales From the Darkside: The Movie.
TELEVISION: Exec. Prod.: Series: Tales From the Darkside, Monsters, Stephen King's Golden Years. Mini-Series: Stephen King's The Stand. Movies: The Vernon Johns Story, Precious Victims.

RUDDY, ALBERT S.
Producer. b. Montreal, Canada, March 28, 1934. e. U. of Southern California, B.S. in design, Sch. of Architecture, 1956. Exec. prod. of 1991 TV movie Miracle in the Wilderness.
PICTURES: The Wild Seed, Little Fauss & Big Halsey, Making It, The Godfather, The Longest Yard, Coonskin, Matilda, The Cannonball Run, Megaforce, Lassiter, Cannonball Run II, Farewell to the King, Paramedics, Speed Zone, Impulse, Ladybugs, Bad Girls, The Scout, Heaven's Prisoners.
TELEVISION: Series: Walker—Texas Ranger. Movies: Miracle in the Wilderness, Staying Afloat.

RUDIE, EVELYN
Actress, Singer, Songwriter. r.n. Evelyn Rudie Bernauer. b. Hollywood, Calif. March 28. e. Hollywood H.S., UCLA. At 19, after childstar career in TV and films, stage debut at Gallery Theatre in Hollywood as songwriter, musical dir., choreographer and star performer: Ostrogoths and King of the Schnorrers. Currently producer, artistic dir., Santa Monica Playhouse; founder of own repertoire co. Received Emmy Nomination for first TV leading role, Eloise, Playhouse 90, 1956. Filmdom's Famous Fives critics award, 1958. Star on Hollywood's Walk of Fame.
PICTURES: Daddy Long Legs (debut, 1955). The Wings of Eagles, Gift of Love, Bye Bye Birdie.
TELEVISION: Hostess with the Mostess, Playhouse 90, Dinah Shore, Red Skelton Show, George Gobel Show, Omnibus, Matinee Theatre, Hitchcock Presents, Gale Storm Show, Jack Paar, Wagon Train, G.E. Theatre, 77 Sunset Strip, etc.

RUDIN, SCOTT
Executive. b. New York, NY, July 14, 1958. Began career as prod. asst. on B'way for producers Kermit Bloomgarden, Robert Whitehead; then casting director. 1984, became producer for 20th Century Fox; named exec. v.p. prod.; 1986, appt. pres. prod., 20th-Fox. Resigned 1987 becoming independent producer.
PICTURES: Prod.: I'm Dancing as Fast as I Can, Reckless, Mrs. Soffel, Flatliners (exec. prod.), Pacific Heights, Regarding Henry, Little Man Tate, The Addams Family, White Sands, Sister Act, Jennifer Eight, Life With Mikey, The Firm,

Searching for Bobby Fisher, Addams Family Values, Sister Act 2: Back in the Habit, Nobody's Fool, I.Q., Clueless, Sabrina, Up Close and Personal, Marvin's Room.
TELEVISION: Little Gloria... Happy at Last (exec. prod.).

RUDNER, RITA
Actress, Writer. b. Miami, FL, 1956. m. producer Martin Bergman. Was stage dancer then stand-up comic. Author: Naked Beneath My Clothing: Tales of a Revealing Nature, Rita Rudner's Guide to Men.
THEATER: Annie (B'way), Promises Promises, Follies, Mack and Mabel.
PICTURES: The Wrong Guys (debut, 1988), Gleaming the Cube, That's Adequate, Peter's Friends (also co-s.p.), A Weekend in the Country (also s.p.).
TELEVISION: Series: George Schlatter's Funny People (co-host). Specials: Women of the Night, One Night Stand: Rita Rudner, Rita Rudner: Born to Be Mild, The Rita Rudner Comedy Specials (also writer), Comic Relief, Rita Rudner: Married Without Children.

RUDOLPH, ALAN
Director, Writer. b. Los Angeles, CA, Dec. 18, 1943. Son of Oscar Rudolph, TV director of '50s and '60s. Made his screen debut in his father's The Rocket Man (1954). Began in industry doing odd jobs in Hollywood studios. 1969 accepted by Directors Guild assistant director's training program. Worked with Robert Altman as asst. dir. on California Split, The Long Goodbye and Nashville and co-writer on Buffalo Bill and the Indians.
PICTURES: Director: Welcome to L.A. (debut, 1977; also s.p.), Remember My Name (also s.p.), Roadie (also story), Endangered Species (also co-s.p.), Return Engagement, Songwriter, Choose Me (also s.p.), Trouble in Mind (also s.p.), Made in Heaven, The Moderns (also co-s.p.), Love at Large (also s.p.), Mortal Thoughts, The Player (actor only), Equinox (also s.p.), Mrs. Parker and the Vicious Circle (also co-s.p.).

RUEHL, MERCEDES
Actress. b. Queens, NY, 1950. Raised in Silver Spring, MD. e. College of New Rochelle, B.A. English lit. Worked for years in regional theater, mostly in classics.
THEATER: B'way: I'm Not Rappaport, Lost in Yonkers (Tony Award, 1991), The Shadow Box, The Rose Tattoo. Off-B'way: American Notes, The Marriage of Bette and Boo (Obie Award), Coming of Age in Soho, Other People's Money.
PICTURES: The Warriors (debut, 1979), Four Friends, Heartburn, Radio Days, 84 Charing Cross Road, The Secret of My Success, Leader of the Band, Big, Married to the Mob, Slaves of New York, Crazy People, Another You, The Fisher King (Academy Award, best supporting actress, 1991), Lost in Yonkers, Last Action Hero.
TELEVISION: Movie: Indictment: The McMartin Trial. Series: Frasier. Pilot: Late Bloomer. Guest: Our Family Honor. Special: On Hope.

RUGOLO, PETE
Composer, Arranger. b. Sicily, Italy, Dec. 25, 1915. To U.S., 1919. e. San Francisco State Coll., Mills Coll., Oakland. Armed Forces, 1942-46; pianist, arr. for many orch. including Stan Kenton. Conductor and arrang. for Nat King Cole, Peggy Lee, Harry Belafonte, many others. Received 3 Emmy Awards.
PICTURES: The Strip, Skirts Ahoy, Glory Alley, Latin Lovers, Easy to Love, Jack the Ripper, Foxtrot, Buddy Buddy, Chu Chu and the Philly Flash.
TELEVISION: Richard Diamond, The Thin Man, Thriller, The Fugitive, Run for Your Life, The Bold Ones, Leave It to Beaver, more than 25 movies.

RUIZ-ANCHIA, JUAN
Cinematographer. b. Bilbao, Spain. e. Escuela Official de Cinematografica, 1972. Worked on such Spanish prods. as 19/19, Cornica del Alba, Odd and Even, Soldier of Metal. Moved to L.A. Granted 2 yr. fellowship at American Film Inst. from which he graduated in 1981. First U.S. prod. was Reborn, 1982.
PICTURES: The Stone Boy, That Was Then This Is Now, Maria's Lovers, At Close Range, Where the River Runs Black, House of Games, Surrender, The Seventh Sign, Things Change, Lost Angels, The Last of the Finest, Dying Young, Naked Tango, Liebstraum, Glengarry Glen Ross, A Far Off Place, Mr. Jones, The Jungle Book, Two Bits.

RULE, JANICE
Actress. b. Cincinnati, OH, Aug. 15, 1931. e. Wheaton & Glenbard H.S., Glen Ellyn, IL. Received Phd in Clinical & Research Psychoanalysis, 1983. Dancer 4 yrs. in Chicago & New York nightclubs; stage experience in It's Great To Be Alive, as understudy of Bambi Lynn.
THEATER: Miss Liberty, Picnic (B'way debut, 1953), The Happiest Girl in the World.
PICTURES: Goodbye My Fancy (debut, 1951), Starlift, Holiday for Sinners, Rogue's March, A Woman's Devotion, Gun for a Coward, Bell Book and Candle, The Subterraneans,

Invitation to a Gunfighter, The Chase, Alvarez Kelly, Welcome to Hard Times, The Swimmer, The Ambushers, Doctors' Wives, Gumshoe, Kid Blue, 3 Women, Missing, Rainy Day Friends, American Flyers.
TELEVISION: Movies: Shadow on the Land, Trial Run, The Devil and Miss Sarah, The Word.

RUSH, BARBARA
Actress. b. Denver, CO, Jan. 4, 1927. e. U. of California. First stage appearance at age of ten, Loberto Theatre, Santa Barbara, CA, in fantasy, Golden Ball; won acting award in college for characterization of Birdie (The Little Foxes); scholarship, Pasadena Playhouse Theatre Arts Coll.
THEATER: A Woman of Independent Means, 40 Carats, Same Time Next Year, Steel Magnolias.
PICTURES: Molly (debut, 1950), The First Legion, Quebec, When Worlds Collide, Flaming Feather, Prince of Pirates, It Came From Outer Space, Taza—Son of Cochise, The Magnificent Obsession, The Black Shield of Falworth, Captain Lightfoot, Kiss of Fire, World in My Corner, Bigger Than Life, Flight to Hong Kong, Oh Men! Oh Women!, No Down Payment, The Young Lions, Harry Black and the Tiger, The Young Philadelphians, The Bramble Bush, Strangers When We Meet, Come Blow Your Horn, Robin and the 7 Hoods, Hombre, The Man, Superdad, Can't Stop the Music, Summer Lovers.
TELEVISION: Series: Saints and Sinners, Peyton Place, The New Dick Van Dyke Show, Flamingo Road. Movies: Suddenly Single, Cutter, Eyes of Charles Sand, Moon of the Wolf, Crime Club, The Last Day, Death on the Freeway, The Seekers, Flamingo Road (pilot), The Night the Bridge Fell Down.

RUSH, HERMAN
Executive. b. Philadelphia, PA, June 20, 1929. e. Temple U., Sales mgr., Official Films Inc., 1952-57. Headed Flamingo Telefilms, Inc. 1957-60; 1960-71, pres., tv div. of Creative Mgt. Assoc.; pres., Herman Rush Assoc. Inc., 1971-77; 1977-78 chmn. bd., Rush-Flaherty Agency, Inc.; 1970 headed Marble Arch TV; 1980 named pres., Columbia TV; 1984, pres. of newly formed Columbia Pictures TV Group; 1986, chmn. of newly formed Coca-Cola Telecommunications, Inc.; 1988, chmn., Rush Entertainment Group; 1989, became creative consultant for CBN Producers Group; 1992, Katz/Rush Ent., partner; co-founder, dir. of Transactional Media, Informercial and Transactional Program Production Co.; 1993-94 exec. prod., Willard Scott's New Original Amateur Hour; 1994-95, exec. prod. Susan Powter Show; exec. prod. of The Montel Williams Show.

RUSH, RICHARD
Director, Producer, Writer. b. New York, NY, 1930.
PICTURES: Director: Too Soon To Love (also prod., s.p.), Of Love and Desire (also prod., s.p.), A Man Called Dagger, Fickle Finger of Fate, Thunder Alley, Hell's Angels on Wheels, Psych-Out (also s.p.), Savage Seven, Getting Straight (also prod.), Freebie and the Bean (also prod.), The Stunt Man (also prod., s.p.; Acad. Award nom. for best dir., s.p.), Air America (co-s.p.), Color of Night.

RUSSELL, CHUCK
Director. Asst. dir., and line prod. on many low-budget films for Roger Corman and Sunn Classics, including Death Race 2000.
PICTURES: Dreamscape (co-s.p., line prod.), Back to School (prod.), Nightmare on Elm Street III (dir., co-s.p.), The Blob (dir., co-s.p.), The Mask, Eraser.

RUSSELL, JANE
Actress. r.n. Ernestine Jane Russell. b. Bemidji, MN, June 21, 1921. e. Max Reinhardt's Theatrical Workshop & Mme. Ouspenskaya. Photographer's model.
PICTURES: The Outlaw (debut, 1943), Young Widow, The Paleface, His Kind of Woman, Double Dynamite, Macao, Son of Paleface, Montana Belle, Las Vegas Story, Road to Bali (cameo), Gentlemen Prefer Blondes, The French Line, Underwater, Gentlemen Marry Brunettes, Foxfire, Tall Men, Hot Blood, The Revolt of Mamie Stover, The Fuzzy Pink Nightgown, Fate Is the Hunter, Waco, Johnny Reno, Born Losers, Darker Than Amber.
TELEVISION: Series: Yellow Rose.

RUSSELL, KEN
Director, Producer, Writer. b. Southampton, England, July 3, 1927. e. Walthamstow Art Sch. Early career as dancer, actor, stills photographer, TV documentary film-maker. Ent. TV ind. 1959. Made 33 documentaries for BBC-TV. Also made numerous pop videos.
PICTURES: French Dressing, Billion Dollar Brain, Women in Love, The Music Lovers (also prod.), The Devils (also prod., s.p.), The Boy Friend (also prod., s.p.), Savage Messiah (also prod.), Mahler (also s.p.), Tommy (also prod., s.p.), Lisztomania (also s.p.), Valentino, Altered States, Crimes of Passion, Gothic, Aria (sequence), Salome's Last Dance (also

s.p., actor), The Lair of the White Worm (also prod., s.p.), The Rainbow (also prod., co-s.p.), The Russia House (actor only), Whore (also s.p.), Mindbender.
TELEVISION: The Secret Life of Sir Arnold Box, Lady Chatterly's Lover, Portrait of a Soviet Composer, Elgar, A House in Bayswater, Always on Sunday, The Debussy Film, Isadora Duncan, Dantes Inferno, Song of Summer—Delius, Dance of the Seven Veils. HBO: Dust Before Fireworks, Prisoner of Honor.

RUSSELL, KURT
Actor. b. Springfield, MA, March 17, 1951. Son of former baseball player-turned-actor Bing Russell (deputy sheriff on Bonanza). At 12 got lead in tv series The Travels of Jamie McPheeters (1963-64). Starred as child in many Disney shows and films. Professional baseball player 1971-73. Host, Kurt Russell Celebrity Shoot Out, 4-day hunting tournament.
PICTURES: It Happened at the World's Fair (debut, 1963), Follow Me Boys, The One and Only Genuine Original Family Band, The Horse in the Grey Flannel Suit, The Computer Wore Tennis Shoes, The Barefoot Executive, Fools' Parade, Now You See Him Now You Don't, Charley and the Angel, Superdad, The Strongest Man in the World, Used Cars, Escape from New York, The Fox and The Hound (voice), The Thing, Silkwood, Swing Shift, The Mean Season, The Best of Times, Big Trouble in Little China, Overboard, Tequila Sunrise, Winter People, Tango and Cash, Backdraft, Unlawful Entry, Captain Ron, Tombstone, StarGate, Executive Decision, Escape From L.A.
TELEVISION: Series: The Travels of Jamie McPheeters, The New Land, The Quest. Movies: Search for the Gods, The Deadly Tower, The Quest (pilot), Christmas Miracle in Caulfield U.S.A., Elvis, Amber Waves. Guest: The Fugitive, Daniel Boone, Gilligan's Island, Lost in Space, The F.B.I., Love American Style, Gunsmoke, Hawaii Five-O.

RUSSELL, THERESA
Actress. r.n. Theresa Paup. b. San Diego, CA, Mar. 20, 1957. m. dir.-cinematographer Nicolas Roeg. e. Burbank H.S. Began modeling career at 12. Studied at Actors' Studio in Hollywood.
PICTURES: The Last Tycoon (debut, 1976), Straight Time, Bad Timing/A Sensual Obsession, Eureka, The Razor's Edge, Insignificance, Black Widow, Aria, Track 29, Physical Evidence, Impulse, Whore, Kafka, Cold Heaven, The Grotesque.
TELEVISION: Mini-Series: Blind Ambition. Movie: Thicker Than Water.

RUSSO, JAMES
Actor. b. New York, NY, Apr. 23, 1953. e. NYU, where he wrote and starred in prize-winning short film Candy Store.
THEATER: to Andromeda, Deathwatch, Marat/Sade, Extremities (Theatre World Award).
PICTURES: A Strange Is Watching (debut, 1982), Fast Times at Ridgemont High, Vortex, Exposed, Once Upon a Time in America, Beverly Hills Cop, The Cotton Club, Extremities, China Girl, The Blue Iguana, Freeway, We're No Angels, State of Grace, A Kiss Before Dying, My Own Private Idaho, Cold Heaven, Dangerous Game, Bad Girls, Donnie Brasco.
TELEVISION: Movie: The Secretary.

RUSSO, RENE
Actress. b. California, 1955. Raised in Burbank. Worked as top fashion model for Eileen Ford Agency prior to acting.
PICTURES: Major League (debut, 1989), Mr. Destiny, One Good Cop, Freejack, Lethal Weapon 3, In the Line of Fire, Outbreak, Get Shorty, Tin Cup, Ransom.
TELEVISION: Series: Sable.

RUTHERFORD, ANN
Actress. b. Toronto, Canada, Nov. 2, 1920. Trained by mother (cousin of Richard Mansfield); with parents in stock as child; later on Los Angeles radio programs. Screen debut, 1935.
PICTURES: Waterfront Lady (debut, 1935), Judge Hardy's Children, Of Human Hearts, A Christmas Carol, You're Only Young Once, Dramatic School, Love Finds Andy Hardy, Out West With the Hardys, The Hardys Ride High, Four Girls in White, Dancing Co-Ed, Andy Hardy Gets Spring Fever, Gone With the Wind, These Glamour Girls, Judge Hardy and Son, Wyoming, Pride and Prejudice, The Ghost Comes Home, Andy Hardy Meets Debutante, Washington Melodrama, Life Begins for Andy Hardy, Badlands of Dakota, Andy Hardy's Private Secretary, Whistling in the Dark, Orchestra Wives, The Courtship of Andy Hardy, Whistling in Dixie, Andy Hardy's Double Life, This Time for Keeps, Happy Land, Whistling in Brooklyn, Bermuda Mystery, Two O'Clock Courage, Bedside Manner, The Madonna's Secret, Murder in the Music Hall, Inside Job, The Secret Life of Walter Mitty, Operation Haylift, Adventures of Don Juan, They Only Kill Their Masters, Won Ton the Dog Who Saved Hollywood.

RYAN, ARTHUR N.
Executive. Joined Paramount in N.Y. in 1967 as asst. treas; later made dir. of admin. and business affairs, exec. asst. to

Robert Evans and asst. scty. 1970 appt. v.p.-prod. adm. 1975 named sr. v.p. handling all prod. operations for Paramount's m.p. and TV divisions; 1976, asst. to the chmn. & CEO; chmn. & pres. Magicam, Inc.; chmn. Fortune General Corp.; chmn. Paramount Communications; co-chmn. of scholarship comm. of AMPAS; trustee of Univ. Film Study Center in Boston; joined Technicolor in 1976 as pres., COO & dir.; vice chmn., 1983-85; chmn. & CEO, 1985-; chmn. Technicolor Audio-Visual Systems International, Inc.; dir. Technicolor S.P.A.; dir. Technicolor, Film Intl.; and chmn. of exec. committee, Technicolor Graphics Services, Inc.; dir. Technicolor, Inc.; chmn., Technicolor Fotografica, S.A.; chmn. Technicolor Film Intl. Service Company, Inc.; dir. & deputy chmn. Technicolor Ltd.; chmn. & dir., The Vidtronics Company, Inc.; chmn. & CEO, Compact Video, Inc., 1984-; dir, Four Star Int'l., 1983-; dir., MacAndrews & Forbes, Inc. 1985-; Permanent charities committee of the Entertainment Industry; Hollywood Canteen Foundations. Vice-chmn. & dir., Calif. Inst. of Arts. Trustee: Motion Picture & Television Fund. 1985 named chmn., Technicolor.

RYAN, JOHN
Actor. b. New York, NY, July 30, 1936. e. City Coll. of NY.
THEATER: NY: Duet for Three, Sgt. Musgrave's Dance, Yerma, Nobody Hears a Broken Drum, The Love Suicide at Schofield Barracks, The Silent Partner, Twelve Angry Men, Medea.
PICTURES: The Tiger Makes Out (debut, 1967), A Lovely Way to Die, What's So Bad About Feeling Good?, Five Easy Pieces, The King of Marvin Gardens, The Legend of Nigger Charley, Cops and Robbers, Dillinger, Shamus, It's Alive, The Missouri Breaks, Futureworld, It Lives Again, The Last Flight of Noah's Ark, On the Nickel, The Postman Always Rings Twice, The Escape Artist, Breathless, The Right Stuff, The Cotton Club, Runaway Train, Avenging Force, Death Wish 4: The Crackdown, Delta Force II, Fatal Beauty, Three O'Clock High, Rent-a-Cop, Paramedics, City of Shadows, Best of the Best, White Sands, Hoffa, Star Time, Young Goodman Brown, Batman: Mask of the Phantasm (voice), Tall Tale, Bound.
TELEVISION: Series: Archer. Guest: M*A*S*H, Kojak, Starsky & Hutch, Matt Helm, Matt Houston, Miami Vice. Movies: Target Risk, Death Scream, Kill Me If You Can, A Killing Affair, Houston: The Legend of Texas, Blood River, Shooting Stars.

RYAN, MEG
Actress. b. Bethel, CT, Nov. 19, 1961. e. NYU. m. actor Dennis Quaid. Supported herself, while studying journalism at NYU, by making commercials. Auditioned for and won first prof. role as Candice Bergen's daughter in film Rich and Famous.
PICTURES: Rich and Famous (debut, 1981), Amityville 3-D, Top Gun, Armed and Dangerous, Innerspace, Promised Land, D.O.A., The Presidio, When Harry Met Sally, Joe Versus the Volcano, The Doors, Prelude to a Kiss, Sleepless in Seattle, Flesh & Bone, When a Man Loves a Woman, I.Q., French Kiss, Restoration, Courage Under Fire.
TELEVISION: Series: One of the Boys, As the World Turns (1982-84), Wild Side (Disney TV).

RYAN, MITCHELL
Actor. b. Louisville, KY, Jan. 11, 1928. Entered acting following service in Navy during Korean War. Was New York stage actor working off-B'way for Ted Mann and Joseph Papp; on B'way in Wait Until Dark. Member of Arena Stage group in Washington.
PICTURES: Monte Walsh, The Hunting Party, My Old Man's Place, High Plains Drifter, The Friends of Eddie Coyle, ElectraGlide in Blue, Magnum Force, Labyrinth, Winter People.
TELEVISION: Series: Chase, Executive Suite, Having Babies, The Chisholms, Dark Shadows, High Performance, King Crossings. Movies: Angel City, The Five of Me, Death of a Centerfold—The Dorothy Stratten Story, Uncommon Valor, Medea, Kenny Rogers as the Gambler—The Adventure Continues, Robert Kennedy & His Times, Fatal Vision, Favorite Son, The Ryan White Story, Margaret Bourke-White.

RYDELL, MARK
Director, Producer, Actor. b. March 23, 1934. e. Juilliard Sch. of Music. Studied acting with Sanford Meisner of NY Neighborhood Playhouse. Became member of Actors Studio. Was leading actor for six years on daytime CBS serial, As The World Turns. Made Broadway debut in Seagulls over Sorrento and film bow in Crime in the Streets. Went to Hollywood as TV director (Ben Casey, I Spy, Gunsmoke, etc.). Partner with Sydney Pollack in Sanford Prods., film, TV prod. co. Formed own production co., Concourse Productions.
PICTURES: Director: The Fox (debut, 1968), The Reivers, The Cowboys (also prod.), Cinderella Liberty (also prod.), Harry and Walter Go To New York, The Rose, On Golden Pond, The River, Man in the Moon (prod. only), For the Boys (also exec. prod.), Intersection (also co-prod.). Actor: Crime in the Streets, The Long Goodbye, Punchline, Havana.

RYDER, WINONA
Actress. b. Winona, MN, Oct. 29, 1971. r.n. Winona Horowitz. Grew up in San Francisco. At 7, moved with family to Northern

CA commune. At 13 discovered by talent scout during a performance at San Francisco's American Conservatory theatre, where she was studying, and given screen test.
PICTURES: Lucas (debut, 1986), Square Dance, Beetlejuice, 1969, Heathers, Great Balls of Fire, Welcome Home Roxy Carmichael, Edward Scissorhands, Mermaids, Night on Earth, Bram Stoker's Dracula, The Age of Innocence (Golden Globe Award; Acad. Award nom.), Reality Bites, The House of the Spirits, Little Women (Acad. Award nom.), How to Make an American Quilt, Boys, Looking for Richard, The Crucible.

S

SACKHEIM, WILLIAM B.
Producer, Writer. b. Gloversville, NY, Oct. 31, 1921. e. UCLA.
PICTURES: The Art of Love, The In-Laws (co-prod.), The Competition, First Blood (co-s.p.), The Survivors (prod.), No Small Affair (prod.), The Hard Way (prod.), Pacific Heights (prod.), White Sands (prod.).
TELEVISION: The Law (Emmy Award, 1975), Gideon Oliver (series, exec. prod.), Almost Grown (exec. prod.), The Antagonists (exec. prod.), The Human Factor (exec. prod.).

SACKS, SAMUEL
Attorney, Agent. b. New York, NY, March 29, 1908. e. CCNY, St. John's Law Sch., LL.B., 1930. Admitted Calif. Bar, 1943; priv. law practice, NY 1931-42; attorney, William Morris Agency, Inc., 1942; head of west coast TV business affairs, 1948-75; bd. of dir., Alliance of Television Film Producers, 1956-60; LA Copyright Society Treasurer, Beverly Hills Bar Assn., LA Bar Assn., American Bar Assn.; Academy of TV Arts & Sciences; Hollywood Radio & TV Society; counsel, entertainment field, Simon & Sheridan, 1975-89, Los Angeles Citizens' Olympic Committee; arbitrator for Screen Actors Guild, Assn. of Talent Agents and American Arbitration Assn.; bd. of dirs., Friars Club, 1991-95; Counsel for the Caucus for Producers, Writers & Directors, 1975-95.

SADLER, WILLIAM
Actor. b. Buffalo, NY, Apr. 13, 1950. e. SUNY, Cornell U. Made stage debut in title role in Hamlet for Colorado Shakespeare Fest. Also acted with La Jolla Playhouse, Yale Rep.
THEATER: NY: Ivanov (Off-B'way debut, 1975), Limbo Tales (Obie Award), Chinese Viewing Pavilion, Lennon, Necessary Ends, Hannah, Biloxi Blues (B'way debut, 1985; Clarence Derwent & Dramalogue Awards). Regional: Journey's End, A Mad World My Masters, Romeo and Juliet, Night Must Fall, etc.
PICTURES: Hanky Panky, Off Beat, Project X, K-9, Hard to Kill, Die Hard 2, The Hot Spot, Bill & Ted's Bogus Journey, Rush, Trespass, Freaked, The Shawshank Redemption, Tales From the Crypt Presents Demon Knight, Solo.
TELEVISION: Series: Private Eye. Movies: The Great Walendas, Charlie and the Great Balloon Race, Face of Fear, The Last to Go, Bermuda Grace. Guest: Hooperman, Roseanne, Dear John, Gideon Oliver, The Equalizer, In the Heat of the Night, Tales From the Crypt, Murphy Brown.

SAFER, MORLEY
News Correspondent. b. Toronto, Ont., 1931. e. U. of Western Ontario. Started as corresp. and prod. with Canadian Broadcasting Corp. Joined CBS News London Bureau 1964, chief of Saigon Bureau, 1965. Chief of CBS London bureau 1967-70. Joined 60 Minutes as co-editor in Dec., 1970.

SAFFLE, M. W. "BUD"
Executive. b. Spokane, WA, June 29, 1923. e. U. of Washington. In service 1943-46. Started in m.p. business as booker, 1948. Entire career with Saffle Theatre Service as buyer-booker; named pres. in 1970. Also pres. of Grays Harbor Theatres, Inc., operating theatres in Aberdeen, WA. Also operates drive-in in Centralia, WA. On bd. of NATO of WA for 15 yrs; pres. of same for 2 terms and secty.-treas. 6 yrs. Elected to National NATO bd. in 1972. Founder of Variety Tent 46, serving as chief barker three times.

SAGANSKY, JEFF
Executive. b. 1953. Joined CBS 1976 in bdcst. finance; 1977, NBC, assoc. in pgm. development.; 1977, mgr. film pgms.; 1978, dir. dramatic dev.; 1978, v.p., dev. David Gerber Co.; 1981, returned to NBC as series dev. v.p.; 1983, sr. v.p. series programming; 1985, joined Tri-Star Pictures as pres. of production; 1989 promoted to president of Tri-Star, later that year joined CBS as entertainment division president. Resigned, 1994.

SAGEBRECHT, MARIANNE
Actress. b. Starnberg, Germany, Aug. 27, 1945. In 1977 conceived revue Opera Curiosa, followed by stage role in Adele Spitzeder.
PICTURES: Die Schaukel (debut, 1983), Sugarbaby, Crazy Boys, Bagdad Cafe, Moon Over Parador, The War of the

Roses, Rosalie Goes Shopping, The Milky Life (La Vida Lactea), Dust Devil, Mona Must Die, Martha and I, Erotique, All Men Are Mortal.
TELEVISION: Movies: Herr Kischott, Eine Mutter Kampft un Ihren Sohn, My Lord.

SAGET, BOB
Actor. b. Philadelphia, PA, May 17, 1956. Started as stand-up comedian.
PICTURE: Critical Condition.
TELEVISION: Series: Full House, America's Funniest Home Videos (host). Movie: Father and Scout (also co-exec. prod.).

SAINT, EVA MARIE
Actress. b. Newark, NJ, July 4, 1924. e. Bowling Green State U., Ohio, Actors Studio. Radio, tv actress; on Broadway in Trip to Bountiful before film debut.
THEATER: Trip to Bountiful, The Rainmaker, Desire Under the Elms, The Lincoln Mask, Summer and Smoke, Candida, Winesburg Ohio, First Monday in October, Duet for One, The Country Girl, Death of a Salesman, Love Letters, The Fatal Weakness, On The Divide.
PICTURES: On the Waterfront (debut, 1954; Academy Award, best supporting actress), That Certain Feeling, Raintree County, Hatful of Rain, North by Northwest, Exodus, All Fall Down, 36 Hours, The Sandpiper, The Russians Are Coming the Russians Are Coming, Grand Prix, The Stalking Moon, Loving, Cancel My Reservation, Nothing in Common, Mariette in Ecstasy.
TELEVISION: Movies: Carol for Another Christmas, The Macahans, A Christmas to Remember, When Hell Was in Session, Fatal Weakness, Curse of King Tut's Tomb, Best Little Girl in the World, Splendor in the Grass, Malibu, Jane Doe, Love Leads the Way, Fatal Vision, The Last Days of Patton, A Year in the Life, Norman Rockwell's Breaking Ties, I'll Be Home for Christmas, Voyage of Terror: The Achille Lauro Affair, People Like Us (Emmy Award, 1991), Danielle Steel's Palomino, Kiss of a Killer, My Antonia, After Jimmy. Series: Campus Hoopla, One Man's Family, Moonlighting. Special: Our Town, First Woman President, Primary Colors: The Story of Corita.

SAINT JAMES, SUSAN
Actress. b. Los Angeles, CA, Aug. 14, 1946. r.n. Susan Miller. e. Connecticut Coll. for Women. Was model for 2 years; then signed to contract by Universal Pictures.
TELEVISION: Series: The Name of the Game (Emmy Award, 1969), McMillan & Wife, Kate and Allie. Movies: Fame Is the Name of the Game, Alias Smith and Jones, Once Upon a Dead Man, Magic Carpet, Scott Free, Night Cries, Desperate Women, The Girls in the Office, Sex and the Single Parent, S.O.S. Titanic, The Kid from Nowhere, I Take These Men. Special: A Very Special Christmas Party.
PICTURES: P.J., Where Angels Go... Trouble Follows, What's So Bad About Feeling Good?, Jigsaw, Outlaw Blues, Love at First Bite, How to Beat the High Cost of Living, Carbon Copy, Don't Cry It's Only Thunder.

ST. JOHN, JILL
Actress. r.n. Jill Oppenheim. b. Los Angeles, CA, Aug. 19, 1940. m. actor Robert Wagner. On radio series One Man's family. Television debut, A Christmas Carol, 1948.
PICTURES: Summer Love, The Remarkable Mr. Pennypacker, Holiday for Lovers, The Lost World, The Roman Spring of Mrs. Stone, Tender Is the Night, Come Blow Your Horn, Who's Minding the Store?, Who's Been Sleeping in My Bed?, Honeymoon Hotel, The Liquidator, The Oscar, Banning, Tony Rome, Eight on the Lam, The King's Pirate, Diamonds Are Forever, Sitting Target, The Concrete Jungle, The Act, The Player.
TELEVISION: Series: Emerald Point. Movies: Fame Is the Name of the Game, How I Spent My Summer Vacation, The Spy Killer, Foreign Exchange, Brenda Starr, Telethon, Hart to Hart (pilot), Rooster. Guest: Dupont Theatre, Fireside Theatre, Batman, The Love Boat. Mini-Series: Around the World in 80 Days.

SAJAK, PAT
TV Host. b. Chicago, IL, Oct. 26, 1946. e. Columbia Coll., Chicago. Broadcasting career began as newscaster for Chicago radio station. 1968 drafted into Army, where served 4 years as disc jockey for Armed Forces Radio in Saigon, Vietnam. Moved to Nashville, where continued radio career while also working as weatherman and host of public affairs prog. for local TV station. 1977 moved to LA to become nightly weatherman on KNBC. Took over as host of daytime edition of Wheel of Fortune and later the syndicated nighttime edition (4 Emmy nom.). 1989, The Pat Sajak Show.
PICTURE: Airplane II: The Sequel.
TELEVISION: Host: The Thanksgiving Day Parade, The Rose Parade.

SAKS, GENE
Director, Actor. b. New York, NY, Nov. 8, 1921. e. Cornell U. Attended dramatic workshop, New School for Social

Research. Active in off-Broadway in 1948-49, forming cooperative theatre group at Cherry Lane Theatre. Joined Actor's Studio, followed by touring and stock. Also appeared in live TV dramas (Philco Playhouse, Producer's Showcase). Directed many Broadway plays before turning to film direction with Barefoot in the Park (1967) President of SSDC.
THEATER: *B'way: Director:* Enter Laughing, Nobody Loves an Albatross, Generation, Half a Sixpence, Mame, A Mother's Kisses, Sheep on the Runway, How the Other Half Loves, Same Time Next Year, California Suite, I Love My Wife (Tony Award), Brighton Beach Memoirs (Tony Award), Biloxi Blues (Tony Award), The Odd Couple (1985), Broadway Bound, Rumors, Lost in Yonkers, Jake's Women. *Actor:* Middle of the Night, Howie, The Tenth Man, A Shot in the Dark, A Thousand Clowns.
PICTURES: *Director:* Barefoot in the Park, The Odd Couple, Cactus Flower, Last of the Red Hot Lovers, Mame, Brighton Beach Memoirs, A Fine Romance. *Actor:* A Thousand Clowns, Prisoner of Second Avenue, The One and Only, Lovesick, The Goodbye People, Nobody's Fool, I.Q.

SALANT, RICHARD S.
Executive. b. New York, NY, Apr. 14, 1914. e. Harvard Coll. A.B., 1931-35; Harvard Law Sch., 1935-38. Atty. Gen.'s Com. on Admin. Procedure, 1939-41; Office of Solicitor Gen., U.S. Dept. of Justice, 1941-43; U.S. Naval Res., 1943-46; assoc., Roseman, Goldmark, Colin & Kave, 1946-48; then partner, 1948-51; pres. CBS news div., 1961-64; v.p. special asst. to pres. CBS, Inc., 1951-61, 1964-66; pres., CBS news div., 1966; mem. bd. of dir., CBS, Inc. 1964-69; vice chmn., NBC bd., 1979-81; sr. adviser, 1981-83; pres. CEO, National News Council, 1983-84. Retired.

SALDANA, THERESA
Actress. b. Brooklyn, NY, Aug. 20, 1954. Following attack by stalker founded advocacy group Victims for Victims. *Author:* Beyond Survival, 1986.
PICTURES: Nunzio, I Wanna Hold Your Hand, Defiance, Raging Bull, Double Revenge, Angel Town.
TELEVISION: *Series:* The Commish. *Movies:* Sophia Loren: Her Own Story, Victims for Victims: The Theresa Saldana Story, Confessions of a Crime.

SALEH, ANGELIKA T.
Executive. Chmn., Angelika Films, Inc.

SALES, SOUPY
Comedian. r.n. Milton Hines. b. Franklinton, NC, Jan. 8, 1926. Was radio DJ before debuting with his own children show in Detroit, 1953. Program was picked up by ABC in 1955. Continued to perform on radio over the years.
PICTURES: Birds Do It, And God Spoke.
TELEVISION: *Series:* Soupy Sales (1955), Lunch With Soupy Sales, The Soupy Sales Show (1962), The Soupy Sales Show (1965-67), What's My Line (panelist), The Soupy Sales Show (1978-79), Sha Na Na. *Guest:* The Rebel, The Real McCoys, Route 66, The Beverly Hillbillies, Love American Style, The Love Boat, Wings.

SALHANY, LUCIE
Executive. Formerly chairman of Fox Broadcasting Co. Currently pres. & CEO, United Paramount Network.

SALKIND, ALEXANDER
Producer. b. Danzig/Gdansk, of Russian extraction, June 2, 1921. Grew up in Berlin where father, Miguel, produced films. Went to Cuba with father to assist him in film production. First solo venture a Buster Keaton comedy, 1945. Returned to Europe where made many pictures in Spain, Italy, France and Hungary. PICTURES: *Prod.:* Austerlitz, The Trial, Kill! Kill! Kill! (with Ilya Salkind), Bluebeard. *Exec. prod.:* The Light at the Edge of the World, The Three Musketeers, The Four Musketeers, The Prince and the Pauper, Superman, Supergirl, Santa Claus: The Movie, Christopher Columbus: The Discovery.
TELEVISION: Superboy.

SALKIND, ILYA
Producer. b. Mexico City, 1947. e. U. of London. Father is producer, Alexander Salkind. First film job as production runner on The Life of Cervantes for father. Was assoc. prod. on Light at the Edge of the World.
PICTURES: The Three Musketeers, The Four Musketeers, Superman, Superman II (exec. prod.), Supergirl (exec. prod.), Superman III (exec. prod.), Christopher Columbus: The Discovery.
TELEVISION: Superboy (exec. prod.).

SALKOW, SIDNEY
Director, Writer. b. New York, NY, June 16, 1911. e. City Coll. of New York, B.A.; Harvard Law Sch. Master of Fine Arts, USC. Stage dir. & prod. asst. number N.Y. dram. prods. (Dir. Bloodstream, Black Tower, etc.) and mgr. summer theatre.

From 1933 variously dialogue dir., assoc. dir., writer & dir. numerous pictures Paramount, Universal, Republic, Columbia, etc.; dir. number of pictures in Lone Wolf series (for Columbia), Tillie the Toiler, Flight Lieutenant, etc. In armed service, WWII. Head of film dept., CSUN, emeritus prof.
PICTURES: Millie's Daughter, Bulldog Drummond at Bay, Admiral Was a Lady, Fugitive Lady, Golden Hawk, Scarlet Angel, Pathfinder, Prince of Pirates, Jack McCall Desperado, Raiders of the 7 Seas, Sitting Bull, Robbers' Roost, Shadow of the Eagle, Las Vegas Shakedown, Toughest Man Alive, Chicago Confidential, Iron Sheriff, Great Sioux Massacre, Martin Eden.
TELEVISION: *Created, prod. dir.:* This Is Alice series for Desilu, Lassie, Fury, Wells Fargo series. Headed prod. for FF Prod. in Rome, 1967-71.

SALOMON, MIKAEL
Cinematographer. b. Copenhagen, Denmark, Feb. 24, 1945.
PICTURES: *Europe:* The Dreamers, Z.P.G., Three From Haparanda, The Five, Me and My Kid Brothers, The Owlfarm Brothers, Five on the Run, Magic in Town, 24 Hours With Ilse, Why?, Bedside Freeway, My Sister's Children Goes Astray, Around the World, Tumult, Welcome to the Club, Violets Are Blue, Tintomare, Tell It Like It Is Boys, Cop, Elvis Elvis, Hearts Are Trump, The Marksman, The Flying Devils, Peter von Scholten, The Baron, Once a Cop..., Early Spring, The Wolf at the Door. *U.S.:* Zelly and Me, Torch Song Trilogy, Stealing Heaven, The Abyss (Acad. Award nom.), Always, Arachnophobia, Backdraft, Far and Away, A Far Off Place (dir. only), Congo (2nd unit dir.), Judge Dredd (trailer dir.).
TELEVISION: *Movie:* The Man Who Broke 1,000 Chains (ACE Award). *Series:* Space Rangers (dir.). Also commercials for Mitsubishi, Nescafe, Converse, Mazda, etc.

SALZBURG, JOSEPH S.
Producer, Editor. b. New York, NY, July 27, 1917. Film librarian, then rose to v.p. in chg. of prod., Pictorial Films, 1935-42; civilian chief film ed. U.S. Army Signal Corps Photo Center, 1942-44; U.S. Army Air Forces, 1944-46; prod. mgr., Pictorial Films, 1946-50; prod. mgr. Associated Artists Prod., then M.P. for TV, 1950-51; org. m.p. prod. & edit. service for theatrical, non-theatrical & TV films 1951-56; prod. mgr., dir. of films oper., official Films. 1956-59; prod. sup. tech. dir. Lynn Romero Prod. features and TV; assoc. prod. Lynn Romero Prod. TV series, Counterthrust 1959-60; v.p., sec'y, B.L. Coleman Assoc., Inc. & Newspix, Inc. 1961; pres. National Production Assoc., Inc. 1960-1962, chief of production, UPI Newsfilm, 1963-66. Prod./account exec. Fred A. Niles Comm. Center, 1966. Appt. v.p., F.A. Niles Communications Centers Inc., N.Y., 1969. 1979 appointed in addition exec. producer & gen. mgr., F. A. Niles Communication centers Inc., N.Y. studio. 1989, elected mem. bd. dir., Florida Motion Pictures & Television Assn., Palm Beach area chap.; 1989 professor m.p. & TV prod. course at Palm Beach Comm. Coll.: Breaking into TV and Movie Making in South Florida.

SAMMS, EMMA
Actress. b. London, England, Aug. 28, 1960. Former fashion model. Has worked as commercial photographer for such magazines as Ritz, Metro, and Architectural Digest. Co-founder of charitable org. the Starlight Foundation.
PICTURES: Arabian Adventure (debut, 1979), The Shrimp on the Barbie, Delirious.
TELEVISION: *Series:* General Hospital, Dynasty, The Colbys. *Movies:* Goliath Awaits, Agatha Christie's Murder in Three Acts, The Lady and the Highwayman, A Connecticut Yankee in King Arthur's Court, Bejeweled, Shadow of a Stranger, Robin Cook's Harmful Intent, Treacherous Beauties. *Guest:* Hotel, The New Mike Hammer, Murder She Wrote, Newhart, My Two Dads.

SAMPSON, LEONARD E.
Exhibitor. b. New York, NY, Oct. 9, 1918. e. City Coll. of New York, B.B.A., 1939. Entered m.p. industry as stagehand helper and usher, Skouras Park Plaza, Bronx 1932-36; asst. mgr. Gramercy Park, 1937-38; mgr., 5th Avenue Playhouse, 1939-41; mgr., Ascot Bronx, 1941-42. In Army 1942-46. On return entered into partnership with cousin Robert C. Spodick in Lincoln, a New Haven art house. Organized Nutmeg Theatres in 1952 in assn. with Norman Bialek, operating 6 art and conventional theatres in Conn., mainly in Westport and Norwalk. Sold Nutmeg in 1968 to Robert Smerling (became Loews Theatres, now Sony Theatres). Built Groton, CT, Cinemas I & II in 1970 and Norwich, CT, Cinema I & II, 1976 and acquired Village Cinemas I, II & III, Mystic, in association with Spodick and William Rosen. Operated as Gemini Theatre Circuit. Acquired Westerly Cinema I, II & III, 1982. Sold Gemini Theatre Circuit to Hoyts Theatres, 1987. Retains partnership with Spodick in New Haven's York Sq., until 1996 when he became an inactive partner due to illness.

SAMUELSON, DAVID W.
F.R.P.S., F.B.K.S., B.S.C.: Executive. b. London, England, July 6, 1924. Son of early producer G.B. Samuelson. Joined

ind. 1941 with British Movietone News. Later film cameraman, 1947. Left Movietone 1960 to join family company, Samuelson Film Service Ltd. Dir., Samuelson Group Plc, 1958-84. Past president British Kinematograph Sound & TV Soc., Past Chmn, British Board of Film Classification, London Intl. Film Sch. Author: Hands On Manual for Cinematographer, Motion Picture Camera and Lighting Equipment, Motion Picture Camera Techniques, Motion Picture Camera Data, Samuelson Manual of Cinematography, Panaflex User's Manual and Cinematographers Computer Program. Currently consultant on technology film making, author, lecturer. Won Acad. Award for Engineering, 1980 and Acad. Award for Tech. Achievement, 1987.

SAMUELSON, PETER GEORGE WYLIE
Producer. b. London, England, October 16, 1951. e. Cambridge U., M.A., English literature. Early career as interpreter, production assistant, then prod. mgr. 1975, Return of the Pink Panther. 1979-85, exec. v.p., Interscope Communications, Inc. 1982-present, Intl. Pres., Starlight Foundation. 1986-present, pres., Film Associates, Inc. 1985-90 chmn., Samuelson Group. 1990-present, partner, Samuelson Prods. of Los Angeles and London.
PICTURES: Speed Merchants, High Velocity, One by One, Return of the Pink Panther, Santa Fe, A Man a Woman and a Bank, Revenge of the Nerds, Turk 182, Tom and Viv, Playmaker, The Gathering.

SAMUELSON, SIR SYDNEY
C.B.E., B.S.C., Hon. F.B.K.S., Executive. b. London, England, Dec. 7, 1925. e. Irene Avenue Council Sch., Lancing, Sussex. Early career as cinema projectionist, 1939-42; Gaumont British News, 1942-43; Royal Air Force, 1943-47; asst. cameraman, cameraman, director/cameraman until 1960; founded Samuelson Film Service, 1954; Trustee and chmn. board of management, British Acad. of Film and Television Arts (chmn. of Council 1973-76). Member (Pres. 1983-86; Trustee: 1982-89) Cinema and Television Benevolent Fund. Member of Executive, Cinema & Television Veterans (pres. 1980-81); assoc. member, American Society of Cinematographers. Hon. Tech. Adviser, Royal Naval Film Corp. Hon. member, Guild of British Camera Technicians, 1986 (now BECTU); Member, British Society of Cinematographers (governor, 1969-79; 1st vice pres., 1976-77), Hon. Mem. for Life, Assn. of Cinema & Television Technicians, 1990. Appointed first British Film Commissioner by U.K. government, 1991. Recipient of two British Academy Awards: Michael Balcon (1985), Fellowship (1993). Received knighthood for services to British Film Industry, 1995. Lifetime Honorary Fellowship, British Kinematograph, Sound & Television Society, 1995.

SANDA, DOMINIQUE
Actress. b. Paris, France, March 11, 1951. r.n. Dominique Varaigne. e. Saint Vincent de Paul, Paris. Was a popular model for women's magazines when cast by Robert Bresson as the tragic heroine in his Dostoyevsky adaptation Un Femme Douce (1968).
THEATER: Madame Klein, Les Liaisons Dangereuses, Un Mari Ideal, Carte Blanche de Dominique Sanda.
PICTURES: Un Femme Douce, First Love, The Conformist, The Garden of the Finzi-Contini, La Notte Dei Fiori, Sans Mobile Apparent, Impossible Object, Steppenwolf, Conversation Piece, 1900, L'Heritage, Le Berceau de Cristal, Damnation Alley, Au Dela du Bien et du Mal, Beyond Good and Evil, The Song of Roland, Utopia, The Navire Night, Travels on the Sly, Caboblanco, A Room in Town, Dust of the Empire, The Way to Bresson, The Sailor 512, Corps et Biens, Les Mendiants, On a Moonlit Night, Warrior and Prisoners, Je Ne Vous Derangerai Plus, Moi La Pire De Toutes, Le Voyage, Emile Rosen, Henri Le Vert.
TELEVISION: The Sealed Train, La Naissance Du Jour, Il Decimo Clandestino, Voglia Di Vivere, Achille Lauro, Warburg, Comme Par Hazard, Non Siamo Soli, Albert Savarus, Der Lange Weg des Lukas B, The Lucona Affair, Nobody's Children, Brennendes Herz, Joseph.

SANDERS, JAY O.
Actor. b. Austin, TX, Apr. 16, 1953. e. SUNY/Purchase. First professional theatre experience with NY Shakespeare-in-the-Park prods. of Henry V and Measure for Measure. Appeared in Abel's Sister for England's Royal Court Theatre.
THEATER: NY: Loose Ends, The Caine Mutiny Court-Martial, Buried Child, In Trousers, Geniuses, The Incredibly Famous Willy Powers, Heaven on Earth, Girls Girls Girls, King John, Saint Joan, Three Birds Alighting on a Field.
PICTURES: Starting Over (debut, 1979), Hanky Panky, Eddie Macon's Run, Cross Creek, Tucker: The Man and His Dream, The Prince of Pennsylvania, Glory, Just Like in the Movies, Mr. Destiny, V.I. Warshawski, Defenseless, Meeting Venus, JFK, Angels in the Outfield, Kiss of Death, Down Came a Blackbird, The Big Green.
TELEVISION: Series: Aftermath, Crime Story. Movies: The Day Christ Died, Living Proof: The Hank Williams Jr. Story, A Doctor's Story, Cold Sassy Tree, Hostages, State of Emergency, Nobody's Children. Special: The Revolt of Mother. Guest: Roseanne, The Young Riders, Spenser: For Hire, A

Man Called Hawk, Kate and Allie, Miami Vice, Northern Exposure, NY Undercover.

SANDERS, TERRY BARRETT
Producer, Director, Writer. b. New York, NY, Dec. 20, 1931. e. UCLA, 1951; Co-prod., photographed, A Time Out of War, 1954. Academy Award best two-reel subject, and won first prize Venice Film Festival, etc.; co-wrote The Day Lincoln Was Shot, CBS-TV; s.p. The Naked and the Dead; prod. Crime and Punishment—USA., prod., co-dir. War Hunt; prod. and dir. Portrait of Zubin Mehta for U.S.I.A. Assoc. dean, Film Sch., California Inst. of the Arts. Prod.-Dir.: Four Stones for Kanemitsu (Acad. Award nom.). Prod.-Dir.-Writer: Rose Kennedy: A Life to Remember (Acad. Award nom.) Professor, UCLA. Pres., American Film Foundation.
PICTURES: Maya Lin: A Strong Clear Vision (prod., Academy Award), Never Give Up: The 20th Century Odyssey of Herbert Zipper (prod., dir., Academy Award nom.).
TELEVISION: Prod./dir.: Hollywood and the Stars, The Legend of Marilyn Monroe, National Geographic Society specials, The Kids from Fame, Film Bios Kennedy Center Honors, Slow Fires, Lillian Gish: The Actor's Life for Me (Emmy Award).

SANDRICH, JAY
Director. b. Los Angeles, CA, Feb. 24, 1932. e. UCLA.
TELEVISION: Special: The Lily Tomlin Show (DGA Award, 1975). Movies: The Crooked Hearts, What Are Best Friends For?, For Richer For Poorer. Series: The Mary Tyler Moore Show (Emmy Awards: 1971, 1973), Soap, Phyllis (pilot), Tony Randall Show (pilot), Bob Newhart Show (pilot), Benson (pilot), Golden Girls (pilot), Empty Nest (pilot), The Cosby Show (Emmy Awards: 1985, 1986; DGA Award 1985).
PICTURE: Seems Like Old Times.

SANDS, JULIAN
Actor. b. Yorkshire, Eng. 1958. e. Central School of Speech and Drama, London 1979. Formed small theater co. that played in schools and youth clubs. Professional debut in Derek Jarman's short, Broken English and one-line part in Privates on Parade. Then opposite Anthony Hopkins in British TV series A Married Man (1981).
PICTURES: Privates on Parade (debut, 1982), Oxford Blues, The Killing Fields, After Darkness, The Doctor and the Devils, A Room with a View, Gothic, Siesta, Vibes, Wherever You Are, Manika: The Girl Who Lived Twice, Arachnophobia, Warlock, Night Sun, Impromptu, Naked Lunch, Wicked, Husbands and Lovers, Tale of a Vampire, Boxing Helena, Warlock: The Armageddon, Black Water, The Browning Version, Leaving Las Vegas.
TELEVISION: Series: A Married Man. Movies: Romance on the Orient Express, Harem, The Room, Murder By Moonlight, Grand Isle, Crazy in Love, Witch Hunt, The Great Elephant Escape.

SANDS, TOMMY
Singer. b. Chicago, IL, Aug. 27, 1937. e. Schools there and Houston, TX, Greenwood, LA. Father, Benny Sands, concert pianist. Started career as guitar player, singer when 5, at KWKH station, Shreveport. One of pioneers of rock music. First manager was Col. Tom Parker. Acting debut: Kraft TV show The Singin' Idol; recording contract won him million record sales of Teen Age Crush.
PICTURES: Sing Boy Sing, Mardi Gras, Love in a Goldfish Bowl, Babes in Toyland, The Longest Day, Ensign Pulver, None But the Brave, The Violent Ones.

SANFORD, ISABEL
Actress. b. New York, NY, Aug. 29, 1929. e. Textile H.S., Evander Childs H.S. Began acting in elementary school and continued through high school. Joined American Negro Theatre in the 1930's (then The Star Players) which disbanded in W.W.II. Later associated with YWCA project and off-B'way plays. B'way debut in The Amen Corner.
PICTURES: Guess Who's Coming to Dinner, The Young Runaways, Pendulum, The Comic, Stand Up and Be Counted, The New Centurions, Love at First Bite, South Beach, Original Gangstas.
TELEVISION: Series: All in the Family, The Jeffersons (Emmy Award, 1981). Movie: The Great Man's Whiskers. Guest: Fresh Prince of Bel Air, Roseanne, Hangin' With Mr. Cooper, Living Single, In the House, Fresh Prince of Bel Air, Lois & Clark, Cybill.

SAN GIACOMO, LAURA
Actress. b. New Jersey, 1962. e. Carnegie Melon Univ. m. actor Cameron Dye. Appeared Off-B'way in North Shore Fish, Beirut, The Love Talker, Italian American Reconciliation, Wrong Turn at Lungfish, Three Sisters.
PICTURES: Sex Lies and Videotape (debut, 1989), Pretty Woman, Vital Signs, Quigley Down Under, Once Around, Under Suspicion, Where the Day Takes You, Nina Takes a Lover, Stuart Saves His Family.
TELEVISION: Series: Just Shoot Me. Movie: For Their Own Good. Mini-Series: Stephen King's The Stand.

SANSOM, LESTER A.
Producer. b. Salt Lake City, UT, Apr. 24, 1910. e. U. of Utah. Radio singer under name of Jack Allen, 1930; ent. m.p. ind. in editorial dept., Fox Film Corp., 1931; served in U.S. Navy as head of film library, Washington, DC, 1942-45; head of edit. dept. & post-prod., Allied Artists, from 1953; assoc. prod. Skabenga; prod., co-writer, Battle Flame; assoc. prod. Hell to Eternity, exec. prod. The Thin Red Line, prod. Crack in the World; prod. Bikini Paradise, Battle of the Bulge, Custer of the West, Co-prod., Krakatoa—East of Java; exec. prod. 12+1.

SAPERSTEIN, DAVID
Writer, Director. b. Brooklyn, NY. e. Bronx H.S. of Science, CCNY, Film Institute, Chemical Engineering. 1960-80 wrote, prod. and dir. documentary films, TV commercials. Also wrote lyrics and managed rhythm and blues and rock 'n roll groups. Assoc. Professor NYU Graduate Film & TV. Has directed various music videos.Wrote libretto and lyrics for Blue PLanet Blue, Clowns and Cocoon: The Musical.
AUTHOR: Cocoon, Killing Affair, Metamorphosis, Red Devil, Funerama.
PICTURES: Cocoon (story), Killing Affair (dir., s.p.), Personal Choice (dir., s.p.), Fatal Reunion (s.p.), Queen of America (s.p.), Torch, Sara Deri, Hearts & Diamonds, Vets, Do Not Disturb, Point of Honor, Snatched, Jack in the Box, Schoolhouse, Roberto: The Roberto Clemente Story, Roamers, Joshua's Golden Band, Beyond the Stars (dir., s.p.), Bab's Labs (s.p.), Fighting Back (s.p.).
TELEVISION: The Vintage Years (pilot), Dance of the Athletes (dir., writer), Rodeo—A Matter of Style (dir., writer), Mama Sings, The Corky Project, OB/GYN (pilot).

SAPERSTEIN, HENRY G.
Executive. b. Chicago, IL, June 2, 1918. e. U. of Chicago. Theatre owner, Chicago, 1943-45; pres. Television Personalities, Inc., 1955-67, Mister Magoo, Dick Tracy, TV shows, 1960-62; 1960-67 Glen Films, Inc.; prod., All-Star Golf, 1958-62; prod. Championship Bowling, 1958-60; prod. Ding Dong School, 1959-60; pres. owner, UPA Pictures, Inc. Prod.: Mr. Magoo, Dick Tracy cartoon series, Mr. Magoo's Christmas Carol, T.N.T. Show, Turnon, Tune In Drop Out. Pres. Screen Entertainment Co., Benedict Pictures Corp., United Prod. of America; pres. H. G. Saperstein & Associates. Producer: The Vaudeville Thing, Tchaikovsky Competition, Gerald McBoing Boing Show.
PICTURES: Producer. Gay Purr-ee, What's Up Tiger Lily?, T-A-M-I, Swan Lake, Monster Zero, War of the Gargantuas, Hell in the Pacific.

SARA, MIA
Actress. b. Brooklyn, NY, 1968. Started doing TV commercials; landed role in soap opera, All My Children.
PICTURES: Legend (debut, 1986), Ferris Bueller's Day Off, The Long Lost Friend, Apprentice to Murder, A Row of Crows, Imagination, Any Man's Death, Shadows in the Storm, A Stranger Among Us, By the Sword, Timecop, The Pompatus of Love, The Maddening, Undertow, Bullet to Beijing, Black Day Blue Night.
TELEVISION: Movies: Queenie, Till We Meet Again, Daughter of Darkness, Blindsided, Call of the Wild, The Set Up. Special: Big Time. Guest: Alfred Hitchcock Presents.

SARAFIAN, RICHARD C.
Director. b. New York, NY. April 28, 1935. Studied medicine and law before entering film industry with director Robert Altman making industrial documentaries.
TELEVISION: Gunsmoke, Bonanza, Guns of Will Sonnet, I Spy Wild, Wild West; Maverick, Twilight Zone, Gangster Chronicles. Movies: Shadow on the Land, Disaster on the Coastline, Splendor in the Grass, A Killing Affair, Liberty, Golden Moment—An Olympic Love Story. As Actor: Foley Square (series).
PICTURES: Andy (debut, 1965), Run Wild Run Free, Ballad of a Badman, Fragment of Fear, Man in the Wilderness, Vanishing Point, Lolly Madonna XXX, The Man Who Loved Cat Dancing, The Next Man (also prod.), Sunburn, The Bear, Songwriter (actor only), Street Justice (also actor), Crisis 2050, Truk Lagoon.

SARANDON, CHRIS
Actor. b. Beckley, WV, July 24, 1942. e. U. of West Virginia. Mem. Catholic U.'s National Players touring U.S. in Shakespeare and Moliere. Acted with Washington, D.C. improvisational theater co. and Long Wharf. B'way debut, The Rothschilds.
THEATER: Two Gentlemen of Verona, Censored Scenes from King Kong, Marco Polo Sings a Solo, The Devil's Disciple, The Soldier's Tale, The Woods, Nick & Nora.
PICTURES: Dog Day Afternoon (debut, 1975; Acad. Award nom.), Lipstick, The Sentinel, Cuba, The Osterman Weekend, Protocol, Fright Night, Collision Course, The Princess Bride, Child's Play, Slaves of New York, Forced March, Whispers, The Resurrected, Dark Tide, The Nightmare Before Christmas (voice), Just Cause, Tales From the Crypt: Bordello of Blood, Edie and Pen.

TELEVISION: Series: The Guiding Light. Movies: Thursday's Game, You Can't Go Home Again, The Day Christ Died, A Tale of Two Cities, This Child Is Mine, Broken Promises, Liberty, Mayflower Madam, Tailspin: Behind the Korean Airliner Tragedy, The Stranger Within, A Murderous Affair: The Carolyn Warmus Story, David's Mother, When the Dark Man Calls.

SARANDON, SUSAN
Actress. r.n. Susan Tomaling. b. New York, NY, Oct. 4, 1946. e. Catholic U. Raised in Metuchen, New Jersey. Returned to New York to pursue acting, first signing with Ford Model Agency.
THEATER: NY: An Evening with Richard Nixon and..., A Coupla White Chicks Sitting Around Talking, Extremities.
PICTURES: Joe (debut, 1970), Lady Liberty, Lovin' Molly, The Front Page, The Great Waldo Pepper, The Rocky Horror Picture Show, Dragonfly (One Summer Love), Checkered Flag or Crash, The Last of the Cowboys (The Great Smokey Roadblock; also co-prod.), The Other Side of Midnight, Pretty Baby, King of the Gypsies, Something Short of Paradise, Loving Couples, Atlantic City (Acad. Award nom.), Tempest, The Hunger, The Buddy System, Compromising Positions, The Witches of Eastwick, Bull Durham, Sweet Hearts Dance, The January Man, A Dry White Season, Through the Wire (narrator), White Palace, Thelma & Louise (Acad. Award nom.), The Player, Light Sleeper, Bob Roberts, Lorenzo's Oil (Acad. Award nom.), The Client (Acad. Award nom.), Little Women, Safe Passage, The Celluloid Closet, Dead Man Walking (Academy Award), James and the Giant Peach (voice).
TELEVISION: Series: Search For Tomorrow. Guest: Calucci's Dept, Owen Marshall: Counsellor at Law. Specials: Rimers of Eldritch, June Moon, Who Am I This Time?, One Woman One Vote (narrator). Mini-Series: A.D. Movies: F. Scott Fitzgerald & the Last of the Belles, Mussolini: Decline and Fall of Il Duce, Women of Valor.

SARGENT ALVIN
Writer. b. Philadelphia, PA, Apr. 12, 1927. Began career as writer for TV, then turned to theatrical films.
PICTURES: Gambit (co-s.p.), The Stalking Moon, The Sterile Cuckoo, I Walk the Line, The Effect of Gamma Rays on Man-in-the-Moon Marigolds, Paper Moon (Acad. Award nom.), Love and Pain (and the Whole Damn Thing), Julia (Academy Award, 1977), Bobby Deerfield, Straight Time (co-s.p.), Ordinary People (Academy Award, 1980), Nuts (co-s.p.), Dominick and Eugene (co-s.p.), White Palace (co-s.p.), What About Bob? (co-story), Other People's Money, Hero (co-story), Bogus.
TELEVISION: Movies: Footsteps, The Impatient Heart. Series: The Naked City, Route 66, Ben Casey, Alfred Hitchcock Presents, The Nurses, Mr. Novak, Empire.

SARGENT, JOSEPH
Director. r.n. Giuseppe Danielle Sargente. b. Jersey City, NJ, July 25, 1925. e. studied theatre, New Sch. for Social Research 1946-49.
PICTURES: One Spy Too Many, The Hell With Heroes, Colossus: The Forbin Project, White Lightning, The Taking of Pelham One Two Three, MacArthur, Goldengirl, Coast to Coast, Nightmares, Jaws—The Revenge (also prod.).
TELEVISION: Special: The Spy in the Green Hat. Mini-series: The Manions of America, James Mitchener's Space. Movies: The Sunshine Patriot, The Immortal (pilot), The Man, Tribes, The Marcus-Nelson Murders (Emmy Award, 1973), Maybe I'll Come Home in the Spring (also prod.), The Man Who Died Twice, The Night That Panicked America, Sunshine (also prod.), Friendly Persuasion, Amber Waves, Hustling, Freedom, Tomorrow's Child, Memorial Day, Terrible Joe Moran, Choices of the Heart (also prod.), Space, Love Is Never Silent (Emmy Award, 1986), Passion Flower, Of Pure Blood, There Must Be a Pony, The Karen Carpenter Story, Day One, The Incident, Caroline? (Emmy Award, 1990), The Last Elephant, Never Forget, Miss Rose White (Emmy Award, 1992), Somebody's Daughter (also prod.), Skylark (also prod.), Abraham, World War II: When Lions Roared, My Antonia.

SARLUI, ED
Executive. b. Amsterdam, The Netherlands, Nov. 10, 1925. Owner, Peruvian Films, S.A.; pres., Radio Films of Peru, S.A.; pres. Bryant Films Educatoriana, S.A.; partner, United Producers de Colombia Ltd.; pres. Royal Film N.V.; pres., United Producers de Centroamerica, S.A.; pres. United Producers de Mexico, S.A.; pres., United Producers Int'l, Inc., Continental Motion Pictures, Inc. 1988, formed Cinema Corp. of America with Moshe Diamant and Elliott Kastner. Co-chmn. Epic Prods. Inc.
PICTURES: Exec. prod.: Full Moon in Blue Water, High Spirits, Teen Witch, Courage Mountain, Night Game.

SARNOFF, ROBERT W.
Executive. b. New York, NY, July 2, 1918. e. Harvard U., B.A., 1939; Columbia Law Sch. 1940. In office of Coordinator of

Info., Wash., DC, Aug. 1941; the U.S. Navy, Mar. 1942; asst. to publisher, Gardner Cowles, Jr., 1945; mem. of staff Look Mag., 1946, with NBC, 1948-65; pres., 1955-58; chmn. bd., 1958; bd. of dir. RCA, 1957; chmn bd. CEO, NBC, 1958-65; pres. RCA, 1966; CEO, 1968; bd. chmn., 1970-75; member, TV Pioneers, 1957; pres., 1952-53; International Radio & TV Society, Broadcasters Committee for Radio Free Europe, Am Home Products, Inc.; dir., of Business Committee for the Arts; chmn, past pres. council, Acad. of TV Arts & Sciences; formerly v.p. & bd. of dir., Acad. of TV Arts & Sciences Foundation.

SARNOFF, THOMAS W.
Executive. b. New York, NY, Feb. 23, 1927. e. Phillips Acad., Andover, MA, 1939-43, Princeton U., 1943-45, Stanford U. grad. 1948, B.S. in E.E.; Grad Sch. of Bus. Admin. 1948-49. Sgt., U.S. Army Signal Corps, 1945-46; prod. & sales, ABC-TV, Hollywood, 1949-50; prod. dept. MGM, 1951-52; asst. to dir. of finance and oper., NBC, 1952-54; dir. of prod. and bus. affairs, 1954-57; v.p., prod. and bus. affairs, 1957-60; v.p. adm. west coast, 1960-62; v.p. west coast, 1962; exec. v.p. 1965-77; bd. of dir., NBC prods 1961-77; bd of dir Hope Enterprises 1960-75; dir. NABCAT, Inc. 1967-75; dir. Valley County Cable TV, Inc. 1969-75; Pres. NBC Entertainment Corp. 1972-77; pres. Sarnoff International Enterprises, Inc. 1977-81; pres., Sarnoff Entertainment Corp., 1981-; pres., Venturetainment Corp. 1986-; past pres. Research Foundation at St. Joseph Hospital of Burbank; past pres. Permanent Charities of the Entertainment Ind.; past ch. bd. of trustees, National Acad. of TV Arts and Sciences. Pres. Acad. of TV Arts & Sciences Foundation 1990-.

SARRAZIN, MICHAEL
Actor. r.n. Jacques Michel Andre Sarrazin. b. Quebec, Canada, May 22, 1940. Began acting at 17 on CBC TV; signed by Universal, 1965.
PICTURES: Gunfight in Abilene (debut, 1967), The Flim-Flam Man, The Sweet Ride, Journey to Shiloh, A Man Called Gannon, Eye of the Cat, In Search of Gregory, They Shoot Horses Don't They?, The Pursuit of Happiness, Sometimes a Great Notion, Believe in Me, The Groundstar Conspiracy, Harry in Your Pocket, For Pete's Sake, The Reincarnation of Peter Proud, The Loves and Times of Scaramouche, The Gumball Rally, Caravans, Double Negative, The Seduction, Fighting Back, Joshua Then and Now, Captive Hearts, Mascara, Keeping Track, Malarek, Lena's Holiday, Bullet to Beijing.
TELEVISION: Movies: The Doomsday Flight, Frankenstein: The True Story, Beulah Land, Passion and Paradise. Guest: Chrysler Theatre, The Virginian, World Premiere.

SAUL, OSCAR
Writer. b. Brooklyn, NY, Dec. 26, 1912. e. Brooklyn Coll. 1932. Co-author play, Medicine Show; m.p. ed., U.S. Public Health Svce; numerous radio and TV plays. Wrote novel The Dark Side of Love.
PICTURES: Once Upon a Time, Strange Affair, Road House, Lady Gambles, Once More My Darling, Woman in Hiding, Secret of Convict Lake, A Streetcar Named Desire, Thunder on the Hill, Affair in Trinidad, Let's Do It Again (prod.), Helen Morgan Story, Joker is Wild, The Naked Maja, The Second Time Around, Major Dundee, The Silencers, Man and Boy.
TELEVISION: A Streetcar Name Desire, many others.

SAUNDERS, DAVID
Executive. Pres., Triumph Films, Inc.

SAUNDERS, WILLIAM
Executive. b. London, England, Jan. 4, 1923. e. left Upton House Central Sch. at 16. Served in British Eighth Army, 1941-47. Entered industry in 1947 as salesman with 20th Century Fox Film Co. in London; sales mgr., Anglo-Amalgamated Film Co., London, 1951-61; with Motion Picture Producers Assoc. of Amer. as sales dir. in Lagos, Nigeria, dist. Amer. feature films to West African countries, 1962-64; joined 20th Century Fox TV Intl., Paris as v.p. European TV sales, 1964-83; 20th Century TV Intl., Los Angeles as sr. v.p., 1983; named exec. v.p. 1987 and pres., 1988. Retired.

SAURA, CARLOS
Director. b. Huesca, Spain, January 4, 1932. e. educated as engineer. Worked as professional photographer from 1949. Studied at Instituto de Investigaciones y Experiencias Cinematograficos, Madrid, 1952-57 where he then taught from 1957-64 until being dismissed for political reasons. 1957-58 dir. shorts La tarde del domingo and Cuenca.
PICTURES: Director/Writer: Los Golfos (The Urchins), Lament for a Bandit, La Caza (The Hunt), Peppermint Frappe, Stress es Tres Tres, La Madriguera (The Honeycomb), The Garden of Delights, Anna and the Wolves, Cousin Angelica (Cannes Fest. jury prize, 1974), Cria! (Cannes Fest. jury prize, 1976), Elisa Vide Mia, Los ojos Vendados (Blindfold), Mama Turns 100, Hurry Hurry (Golden Bear, Berlin Fest., 1981),

Blood Wedding, Dulces Horas (Sweet Hours), Antonieta, Carmen, Los Zancos (The Stilts), El Amor Brujo (Love the Magician), El Dorado, The Dark Night, Ay Carmela!

SAVAGE, DAVID
Executive Producer, Advertising Executive, b. New York, NY, March 17, 1929. e. Rochester Inst. of Technology. In research development & testing div., Eastman Kodak Co., 2 yrs.; adv. mgr. asst. nat'l sales mgr., Official Films; org., film dept. mgr. WCBS-TV; dir. of film procurement, CBS; mgr. of film procurement, NBC; mgr. planning, merchandising, Recorded Tape Dept., RCA Records; promo. mgr., special products mktg. RCA Records Div.; program and marketing chmn. RCA SelectaVision group; v.p., operations, Wunderman, Rilotto, & Kline, 1970; pres., Response Industries, Inc., (direct response adv. agency), 1973 which became affiliate of McCann Erickson, and was sr. v.p. of McCann Erickson Pres., Mattel Direct Marketing, 1982; v.p. and man. dir., Foote Cene Belding, subsid. Knipp-Taylor USA, 1985.

SAVAGE, FRED
Actor. b. Highland Park, IL, July 9, 1976. e. Stanford Univ. While in kindergarten auditioned for commercial at local community center. Didn't get the job but called back by same dir. for two more tests. Chosen for Pac-Man vitamin ad which led to 27 on-camera TV commercials and 36 voice-over radio spots.
PICTURES: The Boy Who Could Fly, The Princess Bride, Vice Versa, Little Monsters, The Wizard.
TELEVISION: Series: Morningstar/Eveningstar, The Wonder Years. Movies: Convicted: A Mother's Story, Run Till You Fall, When You Remember Me, Christmas on Division Street, No One Would Tell. Special: Runaway Ralph. Guest: The Twilight Zone.

SAVAGE, JOHN
Actor. r.n. John Youngs. b. Old Bethpage, Long Island, NY, Aug. 25, 1949. Studied at American Acad. of Dramatic Arts. In Manhattan organized Children's Theatre Group which performed in public housing. Won Drama Desk Award for performance in One Flew Over the Cuckoo's Nest (Chicago & LA).
THEATER: Fiddler on the Roof, Ari, Siamese Connections, The Hostage, American Buffalo, Of Mice and Men.
PICTURES: Bad Company (debut, 1972), Steelyard Blues, The Killing Kind, The Sister in Law (also composed score), The Deer Hunter, Hair, The Onion Field, Inside Moves, Cattle Annie and Little Britches, The Amateur, Brady's Escape, Maria's Lovers, Salvador, Beauty and the Beast, Hotel Colonial, Soldier's Revenge, The Beat, Caribe, Do the Right Thing, Point of View, Any Man's Death, The Godfather Part III, Hunting, Primary Motive, My Forgotten Man, C.I.A. II: Target Alexa, Red Scorpion 2, Killing Obsession, Carnosaur 2, From the Edge, The Dangerous, Centurion Force, The Crossing Guard, White Squall, Where Truth Lies, American Strays.
TELEVISION: Series: Gibbsville. Movies: All the Kind Strangers, Eric (also wrote and performed songs), The Turning Point of Jim Malloy, Coming Out of the Ice, The Tender Age (The Little Sister), Silent Witness, The Nairobi Affair, Desperate, The Burning Shore, Daybreak, Shattered Image, Tom Clancy's Op Center. Special: Date Rape (Afterschool Special). Guest: Birdland, X Files, The Outer Limits.

SAVOCA, NANCY
Director. e. NYU film sch. m. prod.-writer Richard Guay. While in school directed and wrote short films Renata and Bad Timing. Received Haig P. Manoogian Award for filmmaking at 1984 NYU Student Film Festival. Made feature debut with True Love which won Grand Jury Prize at 1989 United States Film Festival.
PICTURES: True Love (also co-s.p.), Dogfight, Household Saints (also co-s.p.).

SAWYER, DIANE
News Correspondent, Anchor. b. Glasgow, KY, Dec. 22, 1945. m. director Mike Nichols. e. Wellesley Coll. Studied law before deciding on career in TV. Former Junior Miss winner and weather reporter on a Louisville TV station before arriving in Washington, 1970. Worked for Nixon Administration in press office from 1970-74; assisted Nixon in writing memoirs, 1975-78. Joined CBS News as reporter in Washington bureau in 1978; named correspondent in 1980. Served as CBS State Dept. correspondent 1980-81. Joined Charles Kuralt as co-anchor of the weekday editions of CBS Morning News in 1981; 1984-89 correspondent on 60 Minutes; 1989, signed by ABC News as co-anchor of Primetime Live news prog. with Sam Donaldson. 1994, co-anchor of Turning Point.

SAXON, JOHN
Actor. r.n. Carmine Orrico. b. Brooklyn, NY, Aug. 5, 1936.
PICTURES: Running Wild (debut, 1955), The Unguarded Moment, Rock Pretty Baby, Summer Love, The Reluctant Debutante, This Happy Feeling, The Restless Years, The Big

Fisherman, Cry Tough, Portrait in Black, The Unforgiven, The Plunderers, Posse from Hell, Mr. Hobbs Takes a Vacation, War Hunt, Evil Eye, The Cardinal, The Ravagers, The Cavern, The Appaloosa, Queen of Blood, Night Caller From Outer Space, For Singles Only, Death of a Gunfighter, Company of Killers, Joe Kidd, Enter The Dragon, Black Christmas, Mitchell, The Swiss Conspiracy, Strange Shadows in an Empty Room, Moonshine County Express, Shalimar, The Bees, The Glove, The Electric Horseman, Battle Beyond the Stars, Beyond Evil, Blood Beach, Cannibal in the Streets, Wrong Is Right, The Big Score, Nightmare on Elm Street, Prisioners of the Lost Universe, Fever Pitch, Nightmare on Elm Street 3: Dream Warriors, Criminal Act, Death House (also dir.), My Mom's a Werewolf, Aftershock, Blood Salvage, Hellmaster, Crossing the Line, Maximum Force, No Escape No Return, Jonathan of the Bears, Killing Obsession, Beverly Hills Cop III, Wes Craven's New Nightmare.
TELEVISION: *Series*: The Bold Ones (The New Doctors), Falcon Crest. *Movies*: The Doomsday Flight, Winchester 73, Istanbul Express, The Intruders, Snatched, Linda, Can Ellen Be Saved?, Planet Earth, Crossfire, Strange New World, Raid on Entebbe, The Immigrants, Golden Gate, Rooster, Prisoners of the Lost Universe, Payoff, Blackmail, Genghis Khan, Liz: The Elizabeth Taylor Story.

SAYLES, JOHN
Writer, Director, Editor, Actor. b. Schnectady, NY, Sept. 28, 1950. e. Williams Coll., B.S. psychology, 1972. Wrote two novels: Pride of the Bimbos, 1975 and Union Dues, 1978; also The Anarchist's Convention, collection of short stories and Thinking in Pictures: The Making of the Movie Matewan (1987). Wrote and directed plays off-B'way (New Hope for the Dead, Turnbuckle). Directed Bruce Springsteen music videos (Born in the U.S.A., I'm on Fire, Glory Days). Recipient of MacArthur Foundation Grant for genius.
PICTURES: Piranha (s.p., co-story, actor), Lady in Red (s.p.), Battle Beyond the Stars (story, s.p.), Return of the Secaucus Seven (dir., s.p., actor, edit.), Alligator (s.p., story), The Howling (co-s.p., actor), The Challenge (co-s.p.), Lianna (dir., s.p., actor, edit.), Baby It's You (dir., s.p.), The Brother from Another Planet (dir., s.p., edit., actor), Enormous Changes at the Last Minute (co-s.p.), The Clan of the Cave Bear (s.p.), Hard Choices (actor), Something Wild (actor), Wild Thing (s.p.), Matewan (dir., s.p., actor), Eight Men Out (dir., s.p., actor), Breaking In (s.p.), Little Vegas (actor), City of Hope (dir., s.p., edit., actor), Straight Talk (actor), Malcolm X (actor), Passion Fish (dir., s.p., edit.), Matinee (actor), My Life's in Turnaround (actor), The Secret of Roan Inish (dir., s.p., edit.), Lone Star (dir., s.p.).
TELEVISION: *Movies*: A Perfect Match, Unnatural Causes (actor, writer), Shannon's Deal (writer, creative consult.). *Special*: Mountain View (Alive From Off Center).

SCACCHI, GRETA
Actress. b. Milan, Italy, Feb. 18, 1960. e. England and Australia. Acted in Bristol Old Vic Theatre in England.
PICTURES: Das Zweiter Gesicht, Heat and Dust, The Coca Cola Kid, Burke & Wills, Defence of the Realm, A Man in Love, Good Morning Babylon, White Mischief, Paura e Amore (Fear and Love), Woman in the Moon, Presumed Innocent, Fires Within, Shattered, The Player, Turtle Beach, Desire, The Browning Version, Jefferson in Paris, Country Life, Cosi.
TELEVISION: *Mini-Series*: Waterfront (Australia). *Movies*: Ebony Tower, Dr. Fischer of Geneva, Camille, Rasputin (Emmy Award, 1996).

SCARWID, DIANA
Actress. b. Savannah, GA. e. St. Vincent's Acad. (Savannah), American Acad. of Dramatic Arts, Pace U., 1975. Member of National Shakespeare Conservatory (Woodstock, NY) and worked in regional theatres before moving to Hollywood 1976.
PICTURES: Pretty Baby (debut, 1978), Honeysuckle Rose, Inside Moves (Acad. Award nom.), Mommie Dearest, Rumble Fish, Strange Invaders, Silkwood, The Ladies Club, Psycho III, Extremities, Heat, Brenda Starr, Gold Diggers: The Secret of Bear Mountain, The Cure, The Neon Bible, Bastard Out of Carolina.
TELEVISION: *Mini-Series*: Studs Lonigan. *Movies*: In the Glitter Palace, The Possessed, Forever, Battered, Guyana Tragedy: The Story of Jim Jones, Desperate Lives, Thou Shalt Not Kill, A Bunny's Tale, After the Promise, Night of the Hunter, Simple Justice, Labor of Love: The Arlette Schweitzer Story, JFK: Reckless Youth, Truman. *Series*: The Outer Limits.

SCHAEFER, CARL
Media Consultant, Publicist, b. Cleveland, OH, Sept. 2, 1908. e. UCLA. Contr. to mag., including Vanity Fair, Hollywood Citizen-News, 1931-35; Warner Bros., 1935.; Huesped de Honor, Mexico, 1943; OSS WWII, 1944-45; Int'l Comt. AMPS, chmn. 1966-67; Italian Order of Merit, 1957; Chevalier de l'ordre de la Couronne, Belgium, 1963. Pres., Foreign Trade Assn. of Southern Calif., 1954; chmn. of bd., 1955; British-American C. of C., Dir., 1962; Chevalier French

Legion d'Honneur, 1955; Comm. Hollywood Museum; dir., intl. relations, Warner Bros. Seven Arts Int'l Corp., 1960; formed own firm, Carl Schaefer Enterprises, 1971. Dir. pub. rel., British-American Chamber of Commerce, 1971; dir. pub. rel. for Iota Intl. Pictures, 1971; dir. pub. rel. Lyric Films Intl., 1971; bureau chief (Hollywood) Movie/TV Marketing, 1971; man. dir., Intl. Festival Advisory Council, 1971; dir. pub. rel. & adv. Francis Lederer Enterprises Inc. (American National Acad. of Performing Arts, and Canoga Mission Gallery) 1974; West Coast rep. Angelika Films of N.Y. 1974, Hwd. rep Korwitz/Geiger Products. 1975-; Hwd. corresp. Movie News, S'pore, & Femina, Hong Kong, 1974-; member Westn. Publications Assn. 1975-; field rep. Birch Records 1975; Hollywood rep Antena Magazine, Buenos Aires; dir. pub. rel., Style Magazine. Coordinator Hollywood Reporter Annual Key Art Awards; coordinator Hollywood Reporter Annual Marketing Concept Awards; exec. comm. & historian ShoWest; Mem: National Panel of Consumer Arbitrators, 1985; Hollywood Corr., Gold Coast Times of Australia, 1986-87. Winner 1990 Key Art Award. Member: AMPAS, awarded certif. of Appreciation, 1962; charter member, Publicists Guild of America; pres. Pacific Intercollegiate Press Assn., while UCLA Daily Bruin Editor, 1930-31. Poetry anthologies, 1995-96, National Library of Poetry.

SCHAEFER, GEORGE
Director, Producer. b. Wallingford, CT, Dec. 16, 1920. e. Lafayette Coll., Yale Drama Sch. 1986, joined UCLA as chairman, Theatre Film TV; later assoc. Dean, now Emeritus Professor.
THEATRE: B'way:The Linden Tree; Man and Superman; Body Beautiful, Last of Mrs. Lincoln, G.I. Hamlet, Mixed Couples, The Heiress (revival), Idiot's Delight (revival), Teahouse of the August Moon, Write Me a Murder.
PICTURES: Pendulum, Generation, Doctors' Wives, Once Upon a Scoundrel, Macbeth, An Enemy of the People.
TELEVISION: *Director*: Hamlet, One Touch of Venus, The Corn Is Green, The Good Fairy, The Little Foxes, Little Moon of Alban (Emmy Award, 1959), Harvey, Macbeth (Emmy Award, 1961), The Magnificent Yankee (Emmy Award, 1965), Kiss Me Kate, Elizabeth the Queen (Emmy Award, 1968), A War of Children (Emmy Award, 1973), Pygmalion, F. Scott Fitzgerald, Blind Ambition, First You Cry, Our Town, Sandburg's Lincoln, The People vs. Jean Harris, A Piano for Mrs. Cimino, The Deadly Game, Children in the Crossfire, Right of Way, Stone Pillow, Mrs. Delafield Wants to Marry, Laura Lansing Slept Here, Let Me Hear You Whisper, The Man Upstairs.

SCHAFFEL, ROBERT
Producer. b. Washington, DC, March 2, 1944. Partner with Jon Voight in Voight-Schaffel Prods. Now heads Robert Schaffel Prods.
PICTURES: Gordon's War, Sunnyside, Lookin' to Get Out, Table for Five, American Anthem, Distant Thunder, Jacknife, Diggstown.

SCHATZBERG, JERRY
Director. b. New York, NY, June 26, 1927. e. student U. of Miami, 1947-48. Early career in photography as asst. to Bill Helburn 1954-56. Freelance still photographer and TV commercials dir. 1956-69. Contrib. photographs to several mags. incl. Life.
PICTURES: Puzzle of a Downfall Child (debut, 1970), The Panic in Needle Park, Scarecrow, Sweet Revenge (also prod.), The Seduction of Joe Tynan, Honeysuckle Rose, Misunderstood, No Small Affair, Street Smart, Reunion.
TELEVISION: *Movie*: Clinton and Nadine.

SCHEIDER, ROY
Actor. b. Orange, NJ, Nov. 10, 1932. e. Franklin and Marshall Coll. where he twice won the Theresa Helburn Acting Award. First professional acting in 1961 NY Shakespeare Festival prod. of Romeo and Juliet. Became member of Lincoln Center Repertory Co. and acted with Boston Arts Festival, American Shakespeare Festival, Arena Stage (Wash., DC) and American Repertory Co. Appeared in documentary In Our Hands.
THEATER: Richard III, Stephen D, Sergeant Musgrave's Dance, The Alchemist, Betrayal.
PICTURES: Curse of the Living Corpse (debut, 1964), Paper Lion, Star!, Stiletto, Loving, Puzzle of a Downfall Child, Klute, The French Connection (Acad. Award nom.), The Outside Man, The French Conspiracy, The Seven Ups, Sheila Levine is Dead and Living in New York, Jaws, Marathon Man, Sorcerer, Jaws 2, Last Embrace, All That Jazz (Acad. Award nom.), Still of the Night, Blue Thunder, 2010, Mishima (narrator), The Men's Club, 52 Pickup, Cohen and Tate, Listen to Me, Night Game, The Fourth War, The Russia House, Naked Lunch, Romeo Is Bleeding, Covert Assassin.
TELEVISION: *Movies*: Assignment Munich, Jacobo Timerman: Prisoner Without a Name Cell Without a Number, Tiger Town, Somebody Has to Shoot the Picture, Wild Justice. *Series*: seaQuest DSV. *Guest*: Hallmark Hall of Fame, Studio One, N.Y.P.D. *Special*: Portrait of the Soviet Union (host).

SCHEINMAN, ANDREW
Producer. b. 1948. e. Univ. of VA, law degree. Professional tennis player before entering film business as producer of three Charlton Heston films. Became one of 5 founding partners of Castle Rock Entertainment.
PICTURES: *Prod/Exec. Prod.*: The Mountain Man, The Awakening, Modern Romance, Mother Lode, The Sure Thing, Stand By Me, The Princess Bride, When Harry Met Sally..., Misery, A Few Good Men, North (also co-s.p.). *Director*: Little Big League.
TELEVISION: *Series*: Seinfeld (exec. prod.)

SCHELL, MARIA
Actress. b. Vienna, Austria, Jan. 5, 1926. Brother is actor Maximilian Schell. Made debut as teenager in Swiss film, Steinbruch (Quarry). Subsequently appeared in many British and American films.
PICTURES: Quarry (debut, 1941), Angel with the Trumpet, The Affairs of Dr. Holl, The Magic Box, Angelika, So Little Time, The Heart of the Matter, Der Traumende Mund (Dreaming Lips), The Last Bridge (Cannes Film Fest. Award, 1954), Angelika, The Rats, Napoleon, Gervaise (Venice Film Fest. Award, 1956), Liebe (Love), Rose Bernd, Le Notti Bianche (White Nights), Une Vie (End of Desire), The Brothers Karamazov, The Hanging Tree, Der Schinderhanners (Duel in the Forest), As the Sea Rages, Cimarron, The Mark, Only a Woman, La Assassin connait la Musique, Rendevzous in Trieste, Who Has Seen the Wind?, 99 Women, Devil By the Tail, Night of the Blood Monster, Lust in the Sun, The Odessa File, Voyage of the Damned, Folies Bourgeoises (The Twist), Superman, Just a Gigolo, 1919.
TELEVISION: *U.S.*: Heidi, Christmas Lilies of the Field, Inside the Third Reich, Martian Chronicles, Samson and Delilah.

SCHELL, MAXIMILIAN
Actor, Director. b. Vienna, Dec. 8, 1930. Sister is actress Maria Schell. e. Switzerland. Stage debut 1952. B'way debut in Interlock.
PICTURES: Children Mother and the General (debut, 1955), The Young Lions (U.S. debut, 1958), Judgment at Nuremberg (Academy Award, 1961), Five Finger Exercise, The Reluctant Saint, The Condemned of Altona, Topkapi, Return from the Ashes, The Deadly Affair, Counterpoint, The Desperate Ones, The Castle (also prod.), Krakatoa—East of Java, Simon Bolivar, First Love (also dir., co-s.p., co-prod.), Trotta (co-s.p.), Pope Joan, Paulina 1880, The Pedestrian (also dir., prod., s.p.), The Odessa File, The Man in the Glass Booth, End of the Game (also dir., co-prod., co-s.p.), St. Ives, The Day That Shook the World, A Bridge Too Far, Cross of Iron, Julia, Players, Avalanche Express, Together?, The Black Hole, Tales From the Vienna Woods (also prod., s.p.), The Chosen, Les Iles, Morgen in Alabama, Marlene (dir., s.p., interviewer), The Rose Garden, The Freshman, Labyrinth, An American Place, A Far Off Place, Little Odessa.
TELEVISION: Judgment at Nuremberg (Playhouse 90), The Fifth Column, The Diary of Anne Frank, Turn The Key Deftly, Phantom of the Opera, Heidi, The Assisi Underground, Peter the Great (mini-series), Young Catherine, Stalin, Miss Rose White, Candles in the Dark (also dir.).

SCHENCK, AUBREY
Producer. b. Brooklyn, NY, Aug. 26, 1908. e. Cornell U., NYU. With law firm of O'Brien, Driscoll & Raftery; buyer & attorney for Natl. Theatres, 1936; prod for 20th Century-Fox 1945; exec. prod. Eagle Lion 1946; contract prod. Universal Internatl. 1948; Aubrey Schenck Productions, Inc.
PICTURES: Shock, Johnny Comes Flying Home, Strange Triangle, Repeat Performance, T-Men, Mickey, It's a Joke Son, Trapped, Port of New York, Wyoming Man, Undercover Girl, Fat Man, Target Unknown; formed own co. to prod. War Paint, Beachhead. Also: Yellow Tomahawk, Shield for Murder, Big House, U.S.A., Crime Against Joe, Emergency Hospital, Ghost Town, Broken Star, Rebels in Town, Pharaoh's Curse, Three Bad Sisters, Fort Yuma, Desert Sands, Quincannon, Frontier Scout, Black Sleep, Hot Cars, War Drums, Voodoo Island, Revolt at Fort Laramie, Tomahawk Trail, Untamed Youth, Girl in Black Stockings, Bop Girl Goes Calypso, Up Periscope, Violent Road, Reckless, Frankenstein 1970, Wild Harvest, Robinson Crusoe On Mars, Don't Worry, Ambush Bay, Kill a Dragon, Impasse, More Dead Than Alive, Barquero, Daughters of Satan.
TELEVISION: Miami Undercover, series.

SCHEPISI, FRED
Producer, Director, Writer. b. Melbourne, Australia, Dec. 26, 1939. e. Assumption Col., Marist Bros. Juniorate, Marcellin Col. Assessed student films at Melbourne's Swinburne Inst. of Tech.; worked on gov. sponsored experimental Film Fund; made TV commercials. Founded The Film House prod. co. Dir. short film The Party.
PICTURES: *Director*: Libido (co-dir.), The Devil's Playground (also prod., s.p.), The Chant of Jimmie Blacksmith (also prod., s.p.), Barbarosa, Iceman, Plenty, Roxanne, A Cry in the Dark

(also co-s.p.; Australian Film Inst. Award for best dir. & s.p.). *Dir./Prod.*: The Russia House, Mr. Baseball, Six Degrees of Separation, I.Q.

SCHERICK, EDGAR J
Executive, Producer. b. New York, NY, Oct. 16, 1924. e. Harvard U.; elected to Phi Beta Kappa. Asst. dir. of radio and TV; assoc. media dir. and dir. of sports special events, Dancer-Fitzgerald-Sample ad agency, NY during 1950s. Introduced Wide World of Sports on TV through his co., Sports Programs, Inc. Was v.p. in chg. of network programming at ABC-TV. Pres. of Palomar Pictures Int'l. Now independent producer.
PICTURES: For Love of Ivy, The Birthday Party, Take the Money and Run, They Shoot Horses Don't They?, The Killing of Sister George, Ring of Bright Water, Jenny, Sleuth, The Heartbreak Kid, Law and Disorder, The Stepford Wives, I Never Promised You a Rose Garden, The Taking of Pelham One Two Three, American Success Company, I'm Dancing As Fast As I Can, Shoot the Moon, White Dog, He Makes Me Feel Like Dancin' (Academy Award, 1983), Reckless, Mrs. Soffel.
TELEVISION: The Man Who Wanted to Live Forever, The Silence, Circle of Children, Raid on Entebbe, Panic in Echo Park, Zuma Beach, An American Christmas Carol, The Seduction of Miss Leona, Revenge of the Stepford Wives, Hitler's SS, The High Price of Passion, The Stepford Children, Unholy Matrimony, Little Gloria... Happy at Last, On Wings of Eagles, Hands of a Stranger, Home Fires, He Makes Me Feel Like Dancin' (Emmy Award, 1983), Stranger on My Land (exec. prod.), Amy and the Band Played On, The Kennedys of Massachusetts, Satin's Touch (exec. prod.), Phantom of the Opera, The Secret Life of Ian Fleming, Tyson.

SCHIAVELLI, VINCENT
Actor. b. Brooklyn, NY. e. NYU. On Stage in Hunting Cockroaches, Alphabetical Order, Angel City.
PICTURES: One Flew Over the Cuckoo' Nest, American Pop (voice), Chu Chu and the Philly Flash, Night Shift, Fast Times at Ridgemont High, The Adventures of Buckaroo Banzai Across the 8th Dimension, Amadeus, Cold Feet, Valmont, Homer and Eddie, Ghost, Waiting for the Light, Another You, Ted & Venus, Batman Returns, 3 Ninjas Knuckle Up, A Little Princess, Lord of Illusions.
TELEVISION: *Series*: The Corner Bar, Fast Times. *Movies*: Escape to Witch Mountain, The Whipping Boy.

SCHIFRIN, LALO
Composer, b. Buenos Aires, Argentina, June 21, 1932. Father was conductor of Teatro Colon in B.A. for 30 years. Schifrin studied with Juan Carlos Paz in Arg. and later Paris Cons. Returned to homeland and wrote for stage, modern dance, TV. Became interested in jazz and joined Dizzie Gillespie's band in 1962 as pianist and composer. Settled in L.A. Pres. Young Musicians Fed. Music; dir. and conductor, Paris Philharmonic 1987.
PICTURES: Rhino!, The Cincinnati Kid, The Liquidator, Once a Thief, Venetian Affair, Murderer's Row, Blindfold, Joy House, Cool Hand Luke, The President's Analyst, Sol Madrid, Where Angels Go--Trouble Follows, Coogan's Bluff, Hell in the Pacific, Bullitt, Beguiled, The Fox, The Brotherhood, Eye of the Cat, Kelly's Heroes, Hellstrom Chronicles, THX 1138, Dirty Harry, Joe Kidd, Prime Cut, Enter the Dragon, Charley Varrick, Magnum Force, Man on a Swing, The Four Musketeers, The Eagle Has Landed, Voyage of the Damned, Rollercoaster, Telefon, Nunzio, The Cat from Outer Space, The Manitou, Boulevard Nights, The Concorde: Airport '79, Love and Bullets, Serial, The Big Brawl, Brubaker, Escape to Athena, The Amityville Horror, The Nude Bomb, The Competition, When Time Ran Out, Caveman, Buddy, Buddy, The Seduction, A Stranger Is Watching, Amityville II: The Possession, The Sting II, The Osterman Weekend, Sudden Impact, The Mean Season, The New Kids, Doctor Detroit, Tank, The Silence at Bethany, The Fourth Protocol, The Dead Pool, Berlin Blues (also songs), Return From the River Kwai, Naked Tango, F/X 2, The Beverly Hillbillies, Scorpion Spring.
TELEVISION: Mission Impossible (theme), Mannix (theme), Petrocelli (theme), Hollywood Wives, A.D., Private Sessions, Foster and Laurie, Medical Center, Petrocelli, Starsky and Hutch, Earth Star Voyager, Princess Daisy, Falcon's Gold, Kung Fu: The Movie, Original Sin, The Neon Empire, Shakedown on Sunset Strip, Little White Lies, Face to Face, El Quixote, Danger Theatre (theme).

SCHILLER, FRED
Playwright, Screen & TV Writer. b. Vienna, Austria, Jan. 6, 1924. e. Columbia Univ. (B.A.). Awarded: New York Literary Prize for McCall magazine story Ten Men and a Prayer. Member of Dramatists' Guild and Writer's Guild of America. Formerly chief corresp. European Newspaper Feature Services. Honored by the U. of Wyoming and the American Heritage Center for literary achievements with a special Fred Schiller Collection for their library. Awarded the Honor Silver Cross by Austrian Govt., for literary achievements and for furthering cultural relations between Austria and U.S.

THEATER: Come On Up (U.S. key citiies , London), Anything Can Happen (London), Demandez Vicky (Paris), Finder Please Return (L.A., San Francisco, Madrid, Vienna), Finder Bitte Melden (Berlin, Baden-Baden, Vienna), The Love Trap.
TELEVISION: Wrote some 53 TV plays incl. The Inca of Perusalem, Demandez Vicky! for Paris and Finder Bitte Melden! for Austria.

SCHILLER, LAWRENCE J.
Producer, Director. b. New York, NY, Dec. 28, 1936. Photojournalist with Life Magazine & Saturday Evening Post, 1958-70; collaborated on numerous books including three by Norman Mailer: The Executioner's Song, Marilyn, and The Faith of Graffiti; also Muhammad Ali (with Wilfrid Sheed), Minamata (with Eugene Smith).
PICTURES: The Man Who Skied Down Everest (editorial concept & direction), Butch Cassidy & the Sundance Kid (conceived and executed special still montages & titles); The American Dreamer (prod., dir.).
TELEVISION: Prod.: Hey I'm Alive (also dir.), The Trial of Lee Harvey Oswald, The Winds of Kitty Hawk, Marilyn, The Untold Story, An Act of Love, Child Bride of Short Creek, The Executioner's Song (also dir.), Peter the Great, Margaret Bourke-White (also dir.).

SCHINE, G. DAVID
Executive. b. Gloversville, NY, Sept. 11, 1927. e. Harvard U., Pres., gen. mgr. Schine Hotels 1950-63. Film exhibitor until 1966 in New York, Ohio, Kentucky, Maryland, Delaware, and West Virginia. Exec. prod. of French Connection, 1971. Writer, prod., dir. of That's Action!, 1977. Chief Exec. officer of Schine Productions (production) and Epic Productions (distribution), Visual Sciences, Inc., High Resolution Sciences, Inc., and Studio Television Services, Inc.

SCHLAIFER, CHARLES
Executive. b. Omaha, NB, July 1, 1909. Reporter Daily News, World-Herald (Omaha). 1930 appt. adv. mngr. Paramount theatres, then Publix theatres in Omaha; then mngr. of Tri-State circuit, NE, Iowa; 1936-42 mng. dir. United Artists Theatres, San Francisco; adviser, nat'l adv., United Artists prods.; 1942 appt. adv. mgr. 20th Cent.-Fox; 1944, named asst. dir. adv., publicity, & exploitation; 1945-49, v.p. & dir. of advertising, pub., exploitation and radio; 1949, resigned to establish own adv. agency becoming pres., Charles Schlaifer & Co., Inc.; chmn. advertising advisory council, MPAA; revised m.p. adv. code; permanent chmn. first MPAA public relations committee.

SCHLATTER, GEORGE
Producer, Director, Writer. b. Birmingham, AL, Dec. 31, 1932. m. former actress Jolene Brand. e. Pepperdine U. on football scholarship. First industry job was MCA agent in band and act dept. Then gen. mgr. and show producer Ciro's nightclub (where he met Dick Martin and Dan Rowan). Produced shows at Frontier Hotel and Silver Slipper, Las Vegas. Sang 2 seasons St. Louis Municipal Opera Co.
TELEVISION: Created: Laugh-In, Real People (3 Emmys, 27 nominations). Specials with: Goldie Hawn, Robin Williams, Shirley MacLaine, Doris Day, John Denver, Frank Sinatra, Jackie Gleason, Danny Thomas, Bob Hope, Milton Berle, Danny Kaye, George Burns, Dinah Shore, Lucille Ball, Goldie & Liza Together, Salute to Lady Liberty, Las Vegas 75th Anniversary, Speak Up America, Real Kids, Best of Times, Look At Us, Shape of Things, Magic or Miracle, Grammy Awards (first 5 years: also writer), series with Dinah Shore, Judy Garland, Bill Cosby, Steve Lawrence; also ABC American Comedy Awards (3 years), George Schlatter's Comedy Club, George Schlatter's Funny People, Beverly Hills 75th Anniversary, Humor and the Presidency, Frank Liza & Sammy... The Ultimate Event, Comedy Hall of Fame, She TV (series), Sinatra's 75th Birthday, The Best Is Yet to Come, Muhammad Ali's 50th Birthday, Welcome Home America, Laugh-In 25th Anniversary Reunion.

SCHLESINGER, JOHN
Director, Producer. b. London, England, Feb. 16, 1926. e. Oxford U., BBC dir. 1958-60: Wrote and dir. Terminus for British Transport Films (Golden Lion, best doc., Venice); The Class. Some episodes The Valiant Years series. Appeared as actor in films: Sailor of the King (1953), Pursuit of the Graf Spee, Brothers in Law, The Divided Heart, The Last Man to Hang, Fifty Years of Action (DGA doc.). Assoc. dir., National Theatre, London 1973-89. Recipient of 1995 BAFTA Fellowship.
THEATER: No Why (RSC), Timon of Athens (RSC), Days in the Trees (RSC), I and Albert, Heartbreak House (NT), Julius Caesar (NT), True West (NT).
PICTURES: A Kind of Loving (Berlin Golden Bear Award, 1961), Billy Liar, Darling (NY Film Critics Award), Far From the Madding Crowd, Midnight Cowboy (Academy Award, 1969), Sunday Bloody Sunday, Visions of Eight (sequence), The Day of the Locust, Marathon Man, Yanks, Honky Tonk Freeway,

The Falcon and the Snowman (also co-prod.), The Believers (also co-prod.), Madame Sousatzka (also co-s.p.), Pacific Heights (also cameo), The Innocent, Eye for an Eye.
TELEVISION: Separate Tables, An Englishman Abroad (BAFTA Award), The Lost Language of Cranes (actor only), A Question of Attribution (BAFTA Award), Cold Comfort Farm.
OPERA: Les Contes d'Hoffmann (Royal Opera House 1981; SWET award), Der Rosenkavalier, Un Ballo in Maschera (Salzburg Fest., 1989).

SCHLONDORFF, VOLKER
Director. b. Wiesbaden, Germany, March 31, 1939. m. dir.-actress Margarethe von Trotta. Studied in France, acquiring degree in political science in Paris. Studied at French Intl. Film Sch. (IDHEC) before becoming asst. to Jean-Pierre Melville, Alain Resnais, and Louis Malle.
PICTURES: Young Torless (debut, 1966; also s.p.), A Degree of Murder (also s.p.), Michael Kohlhass, Baal, The Sudden Fortune of the Poor People of Kombach, Die Moral der Ruth Halbfass, A Free Woman, The Lost Honor of Katharina Blum (also s.p.), Coup de Grace, The Tin Drum (also s.p.), Valeska Gert (also s.p.), Circle of Deceit, Swann in Love (also s.p.), The Handmaid's Tale, Voyager (also co-s.p.).
TELEVISION: Death of a Salesman, A Gathering of Old Men.

SCHLOSSBERG, JULIAN
Producer, Distributor, Director, Radio TV Host. b. New York, NY, Jan. 26, 1942. e. N.Y. Joined ABC-TV network 1964 as asst. acct. rep.; named acct. rep. 1965; 1966, joined Walter Reade Organization as asst. v.p. chg. of TV; 1969, moved to WRO Theatre Div.; 1970, joined faculty of School of Visual Arts; 1971 named v.p. of WRO Theatres; 1976, joined Paramount Pictures as v.p. in charge of feature film acquisition. Since 1978 pres. & owner of Castle Hill Productions; 1974, prod. & moderated An Evening with Joseph E. Levine at Town Hall, N.Y.; 1974-1980, host of radio show Movie Talk on WMCA (N.Y.), WMEX (Boston), WICE (Providence); 1982-83 host of syndicated TV show, Julian Schlossbergs' Movie Talk; producers' rep. for Elia Kazan, Dustin Hoffman, Elaine May, George C. Scott. Responsible for restored version of Orson Welles' Othello, re-released in 1992.
THEATER: It Had To Be You, An Evening with Nichols and May, Rainbow Room N.Y., Mr. Gogol and Mr. Preen, Damn Yankees, Death Defying Acts.
PICTURES: Going Hollywood: The War Years, Hollywood Uncensored, Hollywood Ghost Stories, No Nukes, Going Hollywood: The 30's, 10 From Your Show of Shows, In the Spirit, Bad Girls, Widow's Peak.
TELEVISION: Steve Allen's Golden Age of Comedy; All the Best, Steve Allen, Sex & Justice: The Anita Hill/Clarence Thomas Hearings, Slapstick Too, Elia Kazan: A Director's Journey.

SCHLOSSER, HERBERT S.
Executive. b. Atlantic City, NJ, April 21, 1926. e. Princeton U., Yale Law Sch. Joined law firm of Phillips, Nizer, Benjamin, Krim & Ballon, 1954; attorney, California National Productions (subsidiary of National Broadcasting Company) 1957; v.p. & gen. mgr., 1960; joined NBC-TV as director, talent & program admin., 1961; v.p., talent & program admin., 1962; v.p. programs, west coast, 1966-72; exec. v.p., NBC-TV, 1972; pres., 1973; pres. & COO, 1974-76; pres. & CEO, 1977-78; exec. v.p. RCA, 1978-85; sr. advisor, broadcasting & entertainment, Wertheim Schroder & Co., 1986.

SCHMIDT, WOLF
Producer, Distributor. b. Freiburg/Br., Germany, June 30, 1937. Came to U.S. 1962 as freelance journalist. Started producing in 1969, distributing independently since 1972. Now pres. Big Bearing Licensing Corp.
PICTURES: Prod./Exec. Prod.: Ski Fever, Stamping Ground, Young Hannah, Things Fall Apart, The Passover Plot, Run for the Roses, Ghost Fever, Defense Play, Riding the Edge, The Fourth War, Neon City, Extreme Justice, Silent Hunter.

SCHMOELLER, DAVID
Writer, Director. b. Louisville, KY, Dec. 8, 1947. e. Universidad de Las Americas, 1967-69, studied film and theater under Luis Bunuel and Alejandro Jodorowsky; U. of TX, B.A., M.A., 1969-74. Wrote and directed 7 short films while studying at college; won 27 intl. awards. In Hollywood spent 6 months working as intern to Peter Hyams on film, Capricorn One. Now heads own co., The Schmoeller Corp.
AUTHOR: The Seduction.
PICTURES: Tourist Trap (debut as dir.), The Seduction (dir., s.p.), Crawlspace (dir., s.p.). Writer: The Day Time Ended, The Peeper, Last Chance Romance, Thrill Palace, Warriors of the Wind (Eng. adaptation), Ghost Town (story). Director: Catacombs, Puppet Master, The Arrival, Netherworld, Catch the Wind (also s.p.).
TELEVISION: James at 15 (writer), Kid Flicks (cable; writer, prod.), Silk Stalkings (dir.), Renegades (dir.).

SCHNEER, CHARLES H.
Producer, b. Norfolk, VA, May 5, 1920. e. Columbia Coll. pres., Morningside Prods. Inc. & Pictures Corp.; 1956. Founded Andor Films 1974. Chmn, Acad. of MP Arts & Sciences, London Screening Committee.
PICTURES: Prod.: The 3 Worlds of Gulliver, The 7th Voyage of Sinbad, I Aim at the Stars, Face of a Fugitive, Good Day for a Hanging, Battle of the Coral Sea, Tarawa Beachhead, Mysterious Island, Jason and the Argonauts, First Men In The Moon, Half A Sixpence, Land Raiders, Valley of Gwangi, The Executioner, The Golden Voyage of Sinbad, Sinbad & The Eye of the Tiger, Clash of the Titans.

SCHNEIDER, DICK
Producer, Director. b. Cazadero, CA, Mar. 7. e. Univ. of the Pacific, Stockton, CA. US Navy, WWII. Has received 9 Emmy Awards.
TELEVISION: Dough Re Mi, Wide Wide World, Colgate Comedy Hour, Beatrice Lillie, Jackie Gleason, Henry Morgan Show, Kate Smith Show, Big Story, Treasury Men in Action, Doorway to Danger, Today Show, Home, Tonight Show, General Mills Circus, Princess Margaret's Wedding, Paris Summit Conference, Eleanor Roosevelt Specials, Something Special 61, At This Very Moment, Inauguration, Gemini, Papal Mass for all networks at Yankee Stadium, Orange Bowl, Jr. Miss Pageant, College Queen (Emmy Award), New Communication, Big Sur, Dream House, Who What or Where, Stars and Stripes, Post Parade, Salute to Sir Lew, NBC Star Salute, Rose Parade, UCP Telethons, Macy's Parade, People's Choice, Jeopardy, Photo Finish.

SCHNEIDER, JOHN
Actor. b. Mount Kisco, NY, Apr. 8, 1954. Active in drama club in high school in Atlanta. Worked as fashion model and played guitar singing own compositions in various Atlanta clubs. Active in local community theatre. Summer stock in New Hampshire. B'way debut 1991 in Grand Hotel.
PICTURES: Smokey and the Bandit, Million Dollar Dixie Deliverance, Eddie Macon's Run, The Curse, Cocaine Wars, Speed Zone, Ministry of Vengeance.
TELEVISION: Series: Dukes of Hazzard, Grand Slam, Second Chances, Heaven Help Us. Specials: John Schneider—Back Home, Wild Jack. Movies: Dream House, Happy Endings, Stagecoach, Christmas Comes to Willow Creek, Outback Bound, Gus Brown and Midnight Brewster, Highway Heartbreaker, Desperate Journey: The Allison Wilcox Story, Texas.

SCHNEIDER, PETER
Executive. President of feature animation, Walt Disney Pictures and Touchstone Pictures.

SCHNEIER, FREDERICK
Executive. b. New York, NY, May 31, 1927; e. NYU, 1951, bus. admin.; NYU Grad. Sch., M.B.A., 1953. Dir. sls. planning, Mutual Broadcasting System, 1947-53; media research dir., RKO Teleradio, 1953-55; RKO Teleradio Advisory Comm., 1955-56; exec. staff RKO Teleradio & dir., marketing services, 1956-58; exec. vice-pres., Showcorporation, 1958-71; v.p. TV programming, RKO General, 1972-1973; v.p., Hemdale Leisure Corp., 1973-79; Viacom Enterprises v.p., feature films, 1979; sr. v.p., program acquisitions & motion pictures, 1980-83; sr. v.p., acquisitions, Showtime/The Movie Channel, 1983-85; sr. v.p. program acquisitions, program enterprises, 1985-87; exec. v.p., programming; 1987-89; pres. & CEO, Viacom Pictures Inc., 1989-92; pres. & CEO, FSA Film Enterprises.

SCHOEFFLING, MICHAEL
Actor. b. Philadelphia, PA. e. Temple Univ.
PICTURES: Sixteen Candles (debut, 1984), Vision Quest, Sylvester, Bellizaire the Cajun, Let's Get Harry, Slaves of New York, Longtime Companion, Mermaids, Wild Hearts Can't Be Broken.

SCHOENFELD, LESTER
Executive. b. Brooklyn, NY, Dec. 6, 1916. e. CCNY, 1934-38. Asst. mgr., Randforce Amusement, 1936-38; mgr., Rugoff & Becker circuit, 1938-47; mgr., Golden & Ambassador Theatres, 1948; print & sales dept., Film Classics, 1948-50; chg. of theatrical, non-theatrical & TV dist., Brit. Info. Serv.; est. Lester A. Schoenfeld Films, 1958; Schoenfeld Films Distributing Corp., 1960.

SCHORR, DANIEL
Radio, Television News Correspondent. b. New York, NY, Aug. 31, 1916. e. City Coll. of New York. Started with various news services and newspapers. Joined CBS in 1953 as Washington correspondent; 1955, reopened CBS bureau in Moscow; 1958-60, roving assignment; 1960-1966, chief German Bureau; 1966-76, Washington Bureau; 1979, Public Radio and TV; 1980, sr. Washington correspondent for Cable News Network; 1985, sr. news analyst, National Public Radio.

SCHRADER, PAUL
Writer, Director. b. Grand Rapids, MI, July 22, 1946. m. actress Mary Beth Hurt. e. Calvin Coll. (theology & philosophy); Columbia U., UCLA, M.A., cinema. Served as film critic for L.A. Free Press and Cinema 1970-72. Former professor at Columbia U.
PICTURES: The Yakuza (co-s.p.), Taxi Driver (s.p.), Rolling Thunder (s.p.), Obsession (s.p.), Blue Collar (co-s.p., dir.). Hardcore (s.p., dir.), Old Boyfriends (co-s.p., exec. prod.), American Gigolo (s.p., dir.), Raging Bull (co-s.p.), Cat People (dir.), Mishima (s.p., dir.), The Mosquito Coast (s.p.), Light of Day (dir., s.p.), The Last Temptation of Christ (s.p.), Patty Hearst (dir.), The Comfort of Strangers (dir.), Light Sleeper (dir., s.p.), City Hall (co-s.p.).
TELEVISION: Movie: Witch Hunt (dir.).

SCHRODER, RICK
Actor. b. Staten Island, NY, April 13, 1970. Started modelling while only four months; did many TV commercials before theatrical film debut in The Champ, at age eight.
PICTURES: The Champ, The Last Flight of Noah's Ark, The Earthling, Apt Pupil, Across the Tracks, There Goes My Baby, Crimson Tide.
TELEVISION: Series: Silver Spoons. Movies: Little Lord Fauntleroy, Something So Right, Two Kinds of Love, A Reason to Live, Too Young the Hero, Terror on Highway 91, Out on the Edge, A Son's Promise, The Stranger Within, Blood River, My Son Johnny, Miles From Nowhere, Call of the Wild, To My Daughter with Love, Texas. Mini-Series: Lonesome Dove, Return to Lonesome Dove.

SCHROEDER, BARBET
Producer, Director. b. Teheran, Iran, Aug. 26, 1941. Critic for Cahiers du Cinema and L'Air de Paris, 1958-63. 1963: asst. to Jean-Luc Godard on Les Carabiniers. 1964: formed own prod. co. Les Films du Losange. As actor only: Paris vu par, La Boulangere de Monceau Roberte, Celline and Julie Go Boating, Beverly Hills Cop III, La Reine Margot.
PICTURES: Producer: La Boulangere de Monceau (26 mins.), La Carriere de Suzanne (52 mins.), Mediterrannee, Paris Vu Par, La Collectionneuse, Tu Imagines Robinson, My Night at Maud's, Claire's Knee, Chloe in the Afternoon, Out One (co-prod.), The Mother and the Whore (co-prod.), Celine and Julie Go Boating, Flocons D'Or, The Marquise of O, Roulette Chinoise (co-prod.), The American Friend (co-prod.), Le Passe-Montagne, The Rites of Death, Perceval Le Gallois, Le Navire Night, Le Pont du Nord, Mauvaise Conduite, Une Sale Historie. Director & Producer: More (1969), Sing-Sing (doc.), La Vallee, General Idi Amin Dada (doc.), Maitresse, Koko a Talking Gorilla (doc.), Charles Bukowski Tapes (doc.), Tricheurs, Barfly, Reversal of Fortune, Single White Female, Kiss of Death, Before and After (also prod.).

SCHUCK, JOHN
Actor. b. Boston, MA, Feb. 4, 1940. e. Denison (BA). Cabaret act: An Evening With John Schuck.
THEATER: B'way: Annie. Off-B'way: The Streets of NY, The Shrike. London: The Caine Mutiny. Regional incl. Long Day's Journey Into Night, As You Like It.
PICTURES: M*A*S*H, The Moonshine War, Brewster McCloud, McCabe and Mrs. Miller, Hammersmith Is Out, Blade, Thieves Like Us, Butch and Sundance: The Early Days, Just You and Me Kid, Earthbound, Finders Keepers, Star Trek VI: The Voyage Home, Outrageous Fortune, The New Adventures of Pippi Longstocking, My Mom's a Werewolf, Second Sight, Dick Tracy, Star Trek IV: The Undiscovered Country, Holy Matrimony, Pontiac Moon, Tales From the Crypt Presents Demon Knight.
TELEVISION: Series: McMillan and Wife, Holmes and Yoyo, Turnabout, The New Odd Couple, The Munsters Today. Mini-Series: Roots. Movies: Once Upon a Dead Man, Hunter, Till Death Us Do Part. Guest: Murder She Wrote, Time Trax, Deep Space Nine, many others.

SCHULBERG, BUDD WILSON
Writer. b. New York, NY, Mar. 27, 1914. son of B. P. Schulberg, prod. e. Dartmouth Coll. Publicist, Paramount Pictures, 1931; writer for screen from 1932. Armed services WWII. Syndicated newspaper columnist: The Schulberg Report.
AUTHOR: Novels: What Makes Sammy Run?, The Disenchanted, The Harder They Fall, On the Waterfront, Some Faces in the Crowd, Everything That Moves, Sanctuary V, Love Action Laughter and Other Sad Tales. Non-fiction books: Writers in America, Moving Pictures: Memories of a Hollywood Prince, Swan Watch, Loser and Still Champion: Muhammad Ali, Sparring With Hemingway and Other Legends of the Fight Game. Short stories: Some Faces In the Crowd, Love, Action, Laughter and Other Sad Tales
THEATER: The Disenchanted (with Harvey Breit, 1958), What Makes Sammy Run? (book for musical), On the Waterfront (with Stan Silverman).
PICTURES: A Star is Born (additional dial.), Nothing Sacred (add. dial.), Little Orphan Annie (co-s.p.), Winter Carnival (co-s.p. with F. Scott Fitzgerald), Weekend for Three (orig. and co-

s.p.), City Without Men (co-story), Government Girl (adapt.). Original s.p.: On the Waterfront (Academy Award, & Writers Guild Award, 1954), A Face in The Crowd, Wind Across the Everglades, Joe Louis: For All Time (doc., Cine Golden Eagle Award, 1985).
TELEVISION: *Teleplays*: What Makes Sammy Run?, Paso Doble, The Pharmacist's Mate, Memory In White, The Legend That Walks Lives A Man, A Question of Honor, A Table at Ciro's.

SCHULMAN, JOHN A.
Executive. b. Washington, D.C., June 13, 1946. e. Yale U., 1968; law degree from Boalt Hall, U. of California, Berkeley, 1972. Founding partner in Beverly Hills law firm, Weissmann, Wolff, Bergman, Coleman & Schulman in 1981 after nine years with firm of Kaplan, Livingston, Goodwin, Berkowitz & Selvin. Joined Warner Bros. 1984 as v.p. & gen. counsel; 1989 sr. v.p. and gen. counsel; 1991, exec. v.p. and gen. counsel.

SCHULTZ, DWIGHT
Actor. b. Baltimore, MD, Nov. 24, 1947. e. Towson St. Univ. Acted with Williamstown Theatre Fest. prior to NY stage work, incl. The Crucifer of Blood, The Water Engine, Night and Day.
PICTURES: The Fan, Alone in the Dark, Fat Man and Little Boy, The Long Walk Home, The Temp.
TELEVISION: *Series*: The A-Team, Star Trek: The Next Generation. *Movies*: Child of Rage, When Your Lover Leaves, Perry Mason: The Case of the Sinister Spirit, Perry Mason: The Case of the Musical Murder, A Woman With a Past, The Last Wish, A Killer Among Us, Victim of Love: The Shannon Mohr Story, Menendez: A Killing in Beverly Hills.

SCHULTZ, MICHAEL
Director, Producer. b. Milwaukee, WI, Nov. 10, 1938. e. U. of Wisconsin, Marquette U.
THEATER: The Song of the Lusitainian Bogey, Kongi's Harvest, Does a Tiger Wear a Necktie?, Operation Sidewinder, What the Winesellers Buy, The Cherry Orchard, Mulebone, Dream on Monkey Mountain.
PICTURES: *Director*: Together for Days, Honeybaby Honeybaby, Cooley High, Car Wash, Greased Lightning, Which Way Is Up?, Sgt. Pepper's Lonely Hearts Club Band, Scavenger Hunt, Carbon Copy, The Last Dragon, Krush Groove (also prod.), Disorderlies (also co-prod.), Livin' Large.
TELEVISION: *Specials*: To Be Young Gifted and Black, Ceremonies in Dark Old Men, For Us the Living, Fade Out: The Erosion of Black Images in the Media (documentary), Hollywood Follies, Travels With Father. *Series*: The Young Indiana Jones Chronicles, Picket Fences, Chicago Hope, Sisters. *Pilot*: Shock Treatment. *Movies*: Benny's Place, The Jerk Too, Timestalkers, Rock 'n' Roll Mom, Tarzan in Manhattan, Jury Duty, Dayo.

SCHUMACHER, JOEL
Director, Writer. b. New York, NY, Aug. 29, 1939. Worked as design and display artist for Henri Bendel dept. store NY while attending Parson's Sch. of Design. As fashion designer opened own boutique, Paraphernalia. Joined Revlon as designer of clothing and packaging before entering m.p. indus. as costume designer on Play It As It Lays, Sleeper, The Last of Sheila, Blume in Love, Prisoner of 2nd Avenue, Interiors.
PICTURES: *Writer*: Car Wash, Sparkle, The Wiz. *Director*: The Incredible Shrinking Woman (debut, 1981), D.C. Cab (also s.p.), St. Elmo's Fire (also s.p.), The Lost Boys, Cousins, Flatliners, Dying Young, Falling Down, The Client, Batman Forever, A Time to Kill, Batman & Robin.
TELEVISION: *Director*: *Movies*: The Virginia Hill Story (also writer), Amateur Night at the Dixie Bar & Grill (also writer). *Music video*: Devil Inside for rock group INXS (dir.). *Series*: 2000 Malibu Drive. *Exec. Prod.*: Slow Burn.

SCHWAB, SHELLY
Executive. Station mgr., WAGA-TV, Atlanta; various sls. & mgr. posts with CBS. Joined MCA, 1978, becoming exec. v.p., MCA-TV. 1986, appt. pres., MCA TV Enterprises, 1989 appt. pres. MCA TV.

SCHWARTZ, BERNARD
Producer. Brought to Hollywood by the late Howard Hughes to watch his film interests; Schwartz teamed with atty. Greg Bautzer to package movie deals for clients. Re-cut number of Buster Keaton's silent movies into documentary anthologies (The Golden Age of Comedy, When Comedy Was King, etc.). Subsequently made TV series, One Step Beyond, followed by The Wackiest Ship in the Army, Miss Teen International specials, etc. Named pres. Joseph M. Schenck Enterprises, for which he made Journey to the Center of the Earth, Eye of the Cat, A Cold Wind in August, I Passed for White, The Shattered Room, Trackdown. Presently partnered with Alan Silverman.
PICTURES: Coal Miner's Daughter (prod.), Road Games (exec. prod.) Psycho II (exec. prod.), St. Elmo's Fire (co-exec. prod.).
TELEVISION: Elvis and Me (co-exec. prod.).

SCHWARY, RONALD L.
Producer. b. Oregon, May 23, 1944. e. U. of Southern California. Started as movie extra before becoming asst. dir.; served as assoc. prod. on The Electric Horseman.
PICTURES: Ordinary People (Academy Award for Best Picture, 1980), Absence of Malice, Tootsie, A Soldier's Story, Batteries Not Included, Havana, Scent of a Woman, Cops and Robbersons, Sabrina.
TELEVISION: Tour of Duty.

SCHWARZENEGGER, ARNOLD
Actor. b. Graz, Austria, July 30, 1947. m. NBC reporter Maria Shriver. e. U. Wisconsin, B.A. Bodybuilding Titles: Junior Mr. Europe (at age 18), Mr. Universe (3 time winner), Mr. Olympia (7 times), Mr. Europe, Mr. World. Special Olympics weightlifting Coach (1989), Prison Weightlifting Rehabilitation Prog. Awards: Sportsman of the Year (1977, Assn. Physical Fitness Ctrs.), Golden Globe (best newcomer, 1977), ShoWest '85 Intl. Star., ShoWest Career Achievement Award, NATO Male Star of Yr. (1987).
AUTHOR: Arnold: The Education of a Bodybuilder, Arnold's Bodyshaping for Women, Arnold's Bodybuilding for Men, The Encyclopedia of Modern Bodybuilding, Arnold's Fitness for Kids (3 Vols.).
PICTURES: Hercules in New York (a.k.a. Hercules Goes Bananas; debut, 1970; billed as Arnold Strong), The Long Goodbye, Stay Hungry, Pumping Iron, The Villain, Scavenger Hunt, Conan the Barbarian, Conan the Destroyer, The Terminator, Red Sonja, Commando, Raw Deal, Predator, The Running Man, Red Heat, Twins, Total Recall, Kindergarten Cop, Terminator 2: Judgment Day, Beretta's Island (cameo), Dave (cameo), Last Action Hero (also exec. prod.), True Lies, Junior, Eraser, Jingle All the.Way, Batman and Robin.
TELEVISION: *Movie*: The Jayne Mansfield Story. *Special*: A Very Special Christmas Party (host). *Guest*: Streets of San Francisco. *Director*: Tales from the Crypt (The Switch), Christmas in Connecticut (movie).

SCHYGULLA, HANNA
Actress. b. Kattowitz, Germany, Dec. 25, 1943. Worked with Rainer Werner Fassbinder in Munich's Action Theater; a founder of the ``anti-theatre'' group. Made film debut in 1968 short Der Brautigam die Komodiantin und der Zuhalter (The Bridegroom, the Comedienne and the Pimp).
PICTURES: Love Is Colder Than Death (feature debut, 1969), Gods of the Plague, Beware of a Holy Whore, The Merchant of Four Seasons, The Bitter Tears of Petra Von Kant, House by the Sea, Jail Bait, Effi Briest, The Marriage of Maria Braun, Berlin Alexanderplatz, Lili Marleen, The Night of Varennes, Passion, A Labor of Love, A Love in Germany, The Delta Force, The Future Is a Woman, Forever Lulu, Miss Arizona, The Summer of Ms. Forbes, Dead Again.
TELEVISION: *U.S.*: Rio das Mortes, Peter the Great, Barnum, Casanova.

SCIORRA, ANNABELLA
Actress. b. New York, NY, 1964. As teen studied acting at HB Studio; then AADA. Founded The Brass Ring Theatre Co. Won role of Sophia Loren's daughter in mini-series Fortunate Pilgrim.
THEATER: Orpheus Descending, Bus Stop, Three Sisters, Snow Angel, Cries and Shouts, Trip Back Down, Love and Junk, Stay With Me, Those the River Keeps.
PICTURES: True Love (debut, 1989), Internal Affairs, Cadillac Man, Reversal of Fortune, The Hard Way, Jungle Fever, The Hand That Rocks the Cradle, Whispers in the Dark, The Night We Never Met, Mr. Wonderful, Romeo is Bleeding, The Cure, The Addiction, The Innocent Sleep, The Funeral.
TELEVISION: *Mini-Series*: The Fortunate Pilgrim. *Movie*: Prison Stories: Women on the Inside.

SCOFIELD, PAUL
Actor. b. Hurstpierpoint, England, Jan. 21, 1922. Started acting at age 14.
THEATER: ADventure Story, Ring Round the Moon, Richard II, The Way of the World, Venice Preserved, Time Remembered, Hamlet, Power and the Glory, Family Reunion, Espresso Bongo, A Man For All Seasons (also B'way: Tony Award, 1962), Coriolanus, Don Armando, King Lear, Timon, Staircase, The Government Inspector, Hotel In Amsterdam, Uncle Vanya, The Captain of Kopernik, Rules of the Game, Savages, The Tempest, Volpone, The Family, Amadeus, Othello, Don Quixote, A Midsummer Night's Dream, I'm Not Rappaport, Heart-break House.
PICTURES: That Lady (debut, 1955), Carve Her Name With Pride, The Train, A Man for All Seasons (Academy Award, 1966), Tell Me Lies, King Lear, Bartleby, Scorpio, A Delicate Balance, 1919, When the Whales Came, Henry V, Hamlet, Utz, Quiz Show, London (narrator), The Crucible.
TELEVISION: *Movies*: Anna Karenina, The Attic: The Hiding of Anne Frank. *Specials*: The Male of the Species (Emmy Award, 1969), The Ambassadors, The Potting Shed, Martin Chuzzlewit, Little Riders, The Crucible.

SCOGGINS, TRACY
Actress. b. Galveston, TX, Nov. 13, 1959. Studied acting at H.B. Studies, Wynn Handman Studios. Appeared on stage in L.A. in The Sicilian Bachelor.
PICTURES: Some Kind of Hero, Toy Soldier, In Dangerous Company, The Gumshoe Kid, Watchers II, Time Bomb, Silhouette, Ultimate Desires, Alien Intruder, Demonic Toys, Dead On.
TELEVISION: Series: Renegades, Hawaiian Heat, The Colbys, Lois & Clark: The New Adventures of Superman. Movies: Twirl, Jury Duty, Dan Turner: Hollywood Detective, Jake Lassiter: Justice on the Bayou. Pilots: The Naturals, High Life, Unauthorized Biographies. Guest: Hotel, Crazy Like a Fox, Dallas, Magnum P.I., The Fall Guy, Mike Hammer, The Heights.

SCOLA, ETTORE
Director, Writer. b. Trevico, Italy, May 10, 1931. e. U. of Rome. Began career in 1947 as journalist; 1950, wrote for radio shows. Then made first film as script writer 1954; debut as director-writer, 1964. Has written 50 other scripts for other directors.
PICTURES: Dir/Writer: Let's Talk about Women (debut, 1964), La Congiuntura, Thrilling (segment: Il Vittimista), The Devil in Love, Will Your Heroes Find Their Friends Who Disappeared so Mysteriously in Africa?, Inspector Pepe, The Pizza Triangle, Rocco Papaleo, The Greatest Evening of My Life, We All Loved Each Other So Much, Down and Dirty, Signore e Signori Buonanotte (segment), A Special Day, Viva Italia! (segment), The Terrace, Passion d'Amore, La Nuit de Varennes, Le Bal, Macaroni, The Family, Splendor, What Time is It?, Le Capitain Fracassa, Mario Maria and Mario, Romanzo di un Giovane Povero

SCOLARI, PETER
Actor. b. New Rochelle, NY, Sept. 12, 1954.
PICTURES: The Rosebud Beach Hotel, Corporate Affairs, Ticks, Camp Nowhere, That Thing You Do!.
TELEVISION: Series: Goodtime Girls, Bosom Buddies, Baby Makes Five, Newhart, Family Album, Dweebs. Movies: Carpool, Amazon, Fatal Confession, The Ryan White Story. Guest: Remington Steele, The Love Boat, Family Ties, The New Mike Hammer, Trying Times (Death and Taxes), Fallen Angels (I'll Be Waiting).

SCORSESE, MARTIN
Writer, Director, Editor, Actor. b. New York, NY, Nov. 17, 1942. Began career while film arts student at NYU, doing shorts What's A Nice Girl Like You Doing in a Place Like This? (dir., s.p.), It's Not Just You Murray and The Big Shave. Other short films: Street Scenes, Italianamerican, American Boy, Mirror Mirror, Somewhere Down the Crazy River. Dir. 2 commercials for Armani. Currently campaigning for the preservation and restoration of historic films.
THEATER: The Act.
PICTURES: Editor: Woodstock, Medicine Ball Caravan, Unholy Rollers, Elvis on Tour. Producer: The Grifters, Mad Dog and Glory, Naked in New York (exec. prod.), Clockers. Actor: Cannonball, 'Round Midnight, Akira Kurosawa's Dreams, Guilty by Suspicion, Quiz Show, Search and Destroy (also co-exec. prod.). Director: Who's That Knocking at My Door? (also s.p., assoc. prod., actor), Boxcar Bertha (also actor), Mean Streets (also co-s.p., actor), Alice Doesn't Live Here Anymore, Taxi Driver (also actor), New York New York, The Last Waltz (also cameo), Raging Bull, The King of Comedy (also actor), After Hours (also cameo), The Color of Money, The Last Temptation of Christ, New York Stories (Life Lessons; also cameo), GoodFellas (also co-s.p.), Cape Fear, The Age of Innocence (also co-s.p., cameo), Casino (also co-s.p.).
TELEVISION: Series episode: Amazing Stories (dir.). Special: A Personal Journey With Martin Scorsese Through American Movies (dir. writer).

SCOTT, CAMPBELL
Actor. b. New York, NY, July 19, 1962. e. Lawrence Univ. Son of George C. Scott and Colleen Dewhurst. Studied with Geraldine Page and Stella Adler.
THEATER: NY: The Last Outpost, The Real Thing, Copperhead, The Queen and the Rebels, Hay Fever, A Man For All Seasons, Long Day's Journey Into Night, Measure for Measure, Pericles, On the Bum. Regional: Romeo and Juliet, Our Town, Gilette, School for Wives, Hamlet.
PICTURES: Five Corners (debut, 1988), From Hollywood to Deadwood, Longtime Companion, The Sheltering Sky, Dying Young, Dead Again, Singles, Mrs. Parker and the Vicious Circle, The Innocent, The Daytrippers, Big Night (also co-dir.).
TELEVISION: Mini-Series: The Kennedys of Massachusetts. Guest: Family Ties, L.A. Law. Movie: The Perfect Tribute.

SCOTT, GEORGE C.
Actor, Director. b. Wise, VA, Oct. 18, 1927. m. actress Trish VanDevere. Son is actor Campbell Scott. Served 4 years Marine Corps. e. U. of Missouri, appeared in varsity productions, summer stock, Shakespeare.

THEATER: Off-B'way: Richard III (Theatre World Award), As You Like It, Children of Darkness, General Seeger, Merchant of Venice, Desire Under the Elms, Antony and Cleopatra, Wrong Turn at Lungfish (also L.A.), Inherit the Wind (Tony nom.). B'way: Comes a Day, The Andersonville Trial, The Wall, The Little Foxes, Plaza Suite, Uncle Vanya, All God's Chillun Got Wings (dir.), Death of a Salesman (also dir.), Sly Fox, Present Laughter (also dir.), The Boys in Autumn, On Borrowed Time (also dir.).
PICTURES: The Hanging Tree (debut, 1959), Anatomy of a Murder, The Hustler, The List of Adrian Messenger, Dr. Strangelove: Or How I Learned to Stop Worrying and Love the Bomb, The Yellow Rolls Royce, The Bible, Not With My Wife You Don't, The Flim-Flam Man, Petulia, This Savage Land, Patton (Academy Award, 1970), They Might Be Giants, The Last Run, The Hospital, The New Centurions, Rage (also dir.), Oklahoma Crude, The Day of the Dolphin, Bank Shot, The Savage Is Loose (also dir., prod.), The Hindenburg, Islands in the Stream, Crossed Swords, Movie Movie, Hardcore, The Changeling, The Formula, Taps, Firestarter, The Exorcist III, The Rescuers Down Under (voice), Malice, Angus.
TELEVISION: Series: East Side West Side, Mr. President, Traps. Movies: Jane Eyre, Fear on Trial, Oliver Twist, China Rose, A Christmas Carol, Choices, The Last Days of Patton, The Murders in the Rue Morgue, Pals, The Ryan White Story, Descending Angel, Finding the Way Home, Curacao, The Whipping Boy, In the Heat of the Night: A Matter of Justice, Tyson. Mini-Series: Mussolini--The Untold Story. Guest: DuPont Show of the Month, Playhouse 90, Hallmark Hall of Fame, Kraft Theatre, Omnibus, Armstrong Theatre, Play of the Week, NBC Sunday Showcase, Dow Hour of Great Mysteries, Esso Theatre. Specials: Power and the Glory, The Brass Bottle, The Savage Land, The Crucible, The Price (Emmy Award, 1971), Beauty and the Beast, The Andersonville Trial (dir.).

SCOTT, MARTHA
Actress. b. Jamesport, MO, September 22, 1914. e. U. of Michigan. In little theatres over U.S.; summer stock NY; on radio with Orson Welles; Broadway debut Our Town (1938), film debut in film adaptation of same. Became theater producer in 1968 with Henry Fonda and Alfred De Liagre at Kennedy Center and on B'way (Time of Your Life, First Monday in October).
THEATER: Our Town, Soldier's Wife, The Voice of the Turtle, The Number, The Male Animal, The Remarkable Mr. Pennypacker, Forty-Second Cousin, The Crucible.
PICTURES: Our Town (debut, 1940; Acad. Award nom.), The Howards of Virginia, Cheers for Miss Bishop, They Dare Not Love, One Foot in Heaven, In Old Oklahoma (The War of the Wildcats), Hi Diddle Diddle, So Well Remembered, Strange Bargain, When I Grow Up, The Desperate Hours, The Ten Commandments, Eighteen and Anxious, Sayonara, Ben-Hur, Charlotte's Web (voice), Airport 1975, The Turning Point, Doin' Time on Planet Earth.
TELEVISION: Movies: The Devil's Daughter, Thursday's Game, The Abduction of Saint Anne, Medical Story, Charleston, Father Figure, Summer Girl, Adam, Adam: His Song Continues, Love and Betrayal, Daughter of the Streets. Mini-Series: The Word, Beulah Land. Guest: Murder She Wrote, Hotel, A Girl's Life (pilot).

SCOTT, RIDLEY
Director, Producer. b. South Shields, Northumberland, Eng., Nov. 30, 1937. Brother is director Tony Scott. e. Royal College of Art, London. Joined newly formed Film Sch. First film: Boy on Bicycle (short). Won design scholarship in NY. Returned to London and joined BBC as set designer (Z-Cars, The Informer series). Directed almost 3,000 commercials in 18 years. Formed Percy Main Prods. Also mng. dir. of Ridley Scott Assocs.Exec. Prod. film Monkey Trouble, prod. of The Browning Version.
PICTURES: Director: The Duellists (debut, 1978), Alien, Blade Runner, Legend, Someone to Watch Over Me (also exec. prod.), Black Rain, Thelma & Louise (also prod.), 1492: Conquest of Paradise (also prod.), White Squall (also exec. prod.).

SCOTT, TONY
Director. b. Newcastle, England. Began career in TV commercials, being partnered with his brother Ridley in prod. co. Winner of numerous Clios, Gold & Silver Lions, and other awards. Entered m.p. industry 1972, directing half-hr. film, One of the Missing, for British Film Inst. and Loving Memory, 1-hr. feature for Albert Finney.
PICTURES: The Hunger (debut, 1983), Top Gun, Beverly Hills Cop II, Revenge, Days of Thunder, The Last Boy Scout, True Romance, Crimson Tide, The Fan.

SCOTT-THOMAS, KRISTIN
Actress. b. England. Lived in France since 18. e. Central School of Speech and Drama, London and Ecole Nationale

des Arts et Technique de Theatre in Paris. Stage debut in La Lune Declinante Sur 4 Ou 5 Personnes Qui Danse. Other theater work in Paris.
PICTURES: Djomel et Juliette, L'Agent Troube, La Meridienne, Under the Cherry Moon, A Handful of Dust, Force Majeure, Bille en tete, The Bachelor, Four Weddings and a Funeral, Bitter Moon, An Unforgettable Summer, The Confessional, Angels and Insects, The Pompatus of Love, Les Milles, Richard III.
TELEVISION: L'Ami D'Enfance de Maigret, Blockhaus, Chameleon/La Tricheuse (Aust.), Sentimental Journey (Germany), The Tenth Man, Endless Game, Framed, Body & Soul, Look at It This Way.

SCULLY, JOE
Talent Executive, Casting Director, Producer, Writer. b. Kearny, NJ, March 1, 1926. e. Goodman Memorial Theatre of the Art Inst. of Chicago, 1946. m. Penelope Gillette. Acted until 1951. CBS-TV, NY. Casting Dir., Danger, You Are There, Omnibus, The Web, 1951-56. Wrote The Little Woman for CBS Danger Anthology Series, 1954. 1956-60, CBS-TV, Associate Prod., Studio One, Dupont Show of the Month, Playhouse 90; 1962-64, Writer for CBS Repertoire Workshop anthology series; 1963-64, CBS Stations div. KNXT, prod., Repertoire Workshop; 1965-70 casting dir., 20th Century-Fox Films; 1970-74, indept. casting dir.; 1974-75 Universal TV, casting dir. Member, AMPAS since 1975; NBC-TV Manager, Casting & Talent; 1978, re-established Joe Scully Casting, indept. service to the industry. Founding member, CSA, 1982; 1983, casting dir., Walt Disney Pictures. 1991 published story in Emmy Magazine: Have You Ever... You Know? Conducted AMPAS Seminar, 'The Casting Process in Motion Pictures.'
PICTURES: Hello Dolly, In Like Flint, Valley of the Dolls, Planet of the Apes, The Flim-Flam Man, Sounder, Lady Sings the Blues, Play It as It Lays, The Stone Killer, Parallax View, Lifeguard, Man in the Glass Booth, Middle Age Crazy, Death Wish II, Frankenweenie (short), North of Chiang Mai, Chained in Paradiso (video).
TELEVISION: Series: Peyton Place, Bonanza, Room 222, Nichols, Snoop Sisters, Columbo, Switch, McMillan & Wife, Tales of the Unexpected, Gone Are the Days (Disney Channel). Pilots: Julia, The Ghost and Mrs. Muir, The Bill Cosby Show. Movies: Thief, Missiles of October, Gone Are the Days, Earth II. Australian: Flair (mini-series), Ebb Tide (movie).

SEAGAL, STEVEN
Actor, Director, Producer, Writer. b. Lansing, MI, April 10, 1952. Became skilled at martial arts at an early age, studying Aikido. Lived in Japan for 15 yrs. where he opened a martial arts academy. Opened similar academy upon his return to U.S. in Los Angeles. Was martial arts choreographer/coordinator on film The Challenge.
PICTURES: Above the Law (debut, 1988; also co-prod., co-story), Hard to Kill, Marked for Death (also co-prod.), Out for Justice (also co-prod.), Under Siege (also co-prod.), On Deadly Ground (also dir., co-prod.). Under Siege 2: Dark Territory (also co- prod.), Executive Decision, The Glimmer Man.

SEAGROVE, JENNY
Actress. b. Kuala Lumpur, Malaysia. e. Bristol Old Vic. Theatre Sch. Stage debut 1979. Early TV: The Brack Report, The Woman in White, Diana. Recent stage: Jane Eyre, King Lear, Present Laughter, The Miracle Worker, Dead Guilty.
PICTURES: Moonlighting, Local Hero, Nate and Hayes, Appointment With Death, A Chorus of Disapproval, The Guardian, Bullseye!, Miss Beatty's Children.
TELEVISION: A Woman of Substance, Hold The Dream, In Like Flynn, Killer, Lucy Walker, Magic Moments, Some Other Spring, The Betrothed, Deadly Game, The Sign of Four, The Incident at Victoria Falls, A Shocking Accident.

SECOMBE, SIR HARRY
C.B.E.: Singer, Comedian, Actor. b. Swansea, Wales, Sept. 8, 1921. Awarded, C.B.E., 1963. Awarded Knight Bachelor, 1991. AUTHOR: Twice Brightly, Goon for Lunch, Katy and the Nurgla, Welsh Fargo, Goon Abroad, The Harry Secombe Diet Book, Harry Secombe's Highway, The Highway Companion. Autobiography: Arias and Raspberries.
THEATER: London: Pickwick (also NY), The Four Musketeers, The Plumber's Progress, Pickwick (revival: Chichester Fest., Sadlers Wells Theatre, natl. tour, 1993-95).
PICTURES: Hocus Pocus (debut, 1948), Helter Skelter, London Entertains, Penny Points to Paradise, Forces' Sweetheart, Down Among the Z Men, Svengali, Davy, Jet Storm, Oliver!, The Bed Sitting Room, Song of Norway, Rhubarb, Doctor in Trouble, The Magnificent Seven Deadly Sins, Sunstruck.
TELEVISION: Numerous appearances, incl. own series: Secombe and Friends, The Harry Secombe Show, Secombe with Music. Also special version, Pickwick. Presenter of Tyne Tees TV's Highway 1983-93; Presenter of BBC-TV Songs of Praise, 1995-96.

SEDGWICK, KYRA
Actress. b. New York, NY, Aug. 19, 1965. e. USC. m. actor Kevin Bacon.
THEATER: NY: Time Was, Dakota's Belly Wyoming, Ah Wilderness (Theatre World Award), Maids of Honor. LA: Oleanna.
PICTURES: War and Love, Tai-Pan, Kansas, Born on the Fourth of July, Mr. & Mrs. Bridge, Pyrates, Singles, Heart & Souls, Murder in the First, Something to Talk About, The Low Life, Losing Chase, Phenomenon.
TELEVISION: Movies: The Man Who Broke 1000 Chains, Women & Men II (In Love There Are No Rules), Miss Rose White, Family Pictures. Series: Another World. Guest: Amazing Stories. Specials: Cinder Ella: A Modern Fairy Tale, The Wide Net, Lemon Sky.

SEGAL, GEORGE
Actor. b. New York, NY, Feb. 13, 1934. e. Columbia U., B.A., 1955. Worked as janitor, ticket-taker, soft-drink salesman, usher and under-study at NY's Circle in the Square theatre. Acting debut: Downtown Theatre's revival of Don Juan. Formed a nightclub singing act with Patricia Scott. Record album of ragtime songs and banjo music: The Yama Yama Man. Dir. debut: Bucks County Playhouse prod. Scuba Duba.
THEATER: The Iceman Cometh (1956 revival), Antony and Cleopatra N.Y. Shakespeare Festival, Leave It to Jane, The Premise (satiric improv revue), Gideon, Rattle of a Simple Man, The Knack, Requiem for a Heavyweight, The Fourth Wall (regional).
PICTURES: The Young Doctors (debut, 1961), The Longest Day, Act One, The New Interns, Invitation to a Gunfighter, Ship of Fools, King Rat, Lost Command, Who's Afraid of Virginia Woolf? (Acad. Award nom.), The Quiller Memorandum, The St. Valentine's Day Massacre, Bye Bye Braverman, No Way to Treat a Lady, The Southern Star, The Bridge at Remagen, The Girl Who Couldn't Say No, Loving, The Owl and the Pussycat, Where's Poppa?, Born to Win, The Hot Rock, A Touch of Class, Blume in Love, The Terminal Man, California Split, Russian Roulette, The Black Bird, The Duchess and the Dirtwater Fox, Fun with Dick and Jane, Rollercoaster, Who Is Killing the Great Chefs of Europe?, Lost and Found, The Last Married Couple in America, Carbon Copy, Killing 'em Softly, Stick, All's Fair, Look Who's Talking, The Clearing, For the Boys, Look Who's Talking Now, Army of One, Direct Hit, Deep Down, Flirting With Disaster, The Cable Guy, The Feminine Touch, The Mirror Has Two Faces.
TELEVISION: Series: Take Five, Murphy's Law, High Tide. Specials: Death of a Salesman, Of Mice and Men, The Desperate Hours. Guest: The Nurses, Naked City, Alfred Hitchcock Presents. Movies: Trackdown: Finding the Goodbar Killer, The Cold Room, The Zany Adventures of Robin Hood, Not My Kid, Many Happy Returns, Endless Game, Taking the Heat, Following Her Heart.

SEGAL, MAURICE
Publicist. b. New York, NY, July 22, 1921. e. CCNY, 1937-41. Entered m.p. ind., adv. dept., 20th Fox, 1941-42; U.S. Army 1942-46; feature writer, publ. dept., 20th Fox, 1946; asst. to dir., adv., publ., Century Circuit, 1947; press book dept., Paramount, 1949; trade press rep. 1950; trade press rep. RKO Radio, 1952; resigned to join Richard Condon-Kay Norton, publicists, 1953; adv., pub. dept., U-I. 1954; asst. pub. mgr., United Artists 1957; Hollywood publ. coordinator, 1958; exec. in chg. of M.P. press dept., Universal City Studios, 1966; West Coast adv.-publ. dir., National Gen. Pictures, 1971; pres., Maurice E. Segal Co., 1974; dir., West Coast operations, Charles Schlaifer & Co., 1976; v.p., Max Youngstein Enterprises, 1979; exec. v.p., Taft Intl. Pictures, 1980; pres. Maurice E. Segal Co., 1982; pres. The Segal Company, 1987.

SEIDELMAN, ARTHUR ALLAN
Director, Producer, Writer. b. New York, NY, October 11. e. Whittier Coll., B.A.; UCLA, M.A. Former staff member, Repertory Theatre of Lincoln Center and Phoenix Theatre, NY.
THEATER: Dir.: LA: The Sisters, Gypsy Princess, the Beautiful People, Five Finger Exercise, The Purification, etc. Dir.: NY: Awakening of Spring, Hamp, Ceremony of Innocence, The Justice Box, Billy, Vieux Carre, The World of My America, Awake and Sing, The Four Seasons, Inherit the Wind, The Most Happy Fella, as well as numerous regional prods. and national tours.
PICTURES: Hercules in New York, Children of Rage (dir., s.p.), Echoes, The Caller, Rescue Me.
TELEVISION: Director: Family, Magnum, P.I., Murder She Wrote, Hill Street Blues, Trapper John M.D., Paper Chase, Knots Landing, Bay City Blues, Capitol News, WIOU, L.A. Law, FBI: The Untold Stories, Sweet Justice, Heaven Help Us, Amazing Grace. Movies: Which Mother is Mine? A Special Gift, Schoolboy Father, A Matter of Time, I Think I'm Having a Baby, Sin of Innocence, Kate's Secret, Ceremony of Innocence, Poker Alice, The People Across the Lake, Addicted to His Love, Kate's Secret, A Friendship in Vienna, A Place at the Table, An Enemy Among Us, Glory Years, Strange

Voices, A Taste of Honey, Look Away, False Witness, The Kid Who Loved Christmas, Body Language, Trapped in Space, Dying to Remember, Wing and a Prayer, Harvest of Fire, I Love Liberty..

SEIDELMAN, SUSAN
Director. b. near Philadelphia, PA, Dec.11, 1952. e. Drexel Univ. B.A. Worked at a UHF television station in Phila., NYU film school M.F.A. Debut: 28-min. student film And You Act Like One Too. Then dir. Deficit (short, funded by AFI), and Yours Truly, Andrea G. Stern.
PICTURES: Smithereens (dir., prod., co-s.p.; 1st Amer. indep. feature accepted into competition at Cannes Film Fest., 1982), Desperately Seeking Susan, Making Mr. Right, Cookie (also exec. prod.), She-Devil, The Dutch Master (short, Academy Award nom.).
TELEVISION: Confessions of a Suburban Girl (BBC; also writer, actress), The Barefoot Executive.

SEINFELD, JERRY
Comedian, Actor. b. Brooklyn, NY, Apr. 29, 1954. e. Queens Col. Stand-up comic; guested on such shows as The Tonight Show, Late Night With David Letterman. Received American Comedy Award for funniest male comedy stand-up, 1988. Author: Seinlanguage (1993).
TELEVISION: Series: Benson, Seinfeld (also co-creator, writer). Pilot: The Seinfeld Chronicles. Specials: Jerry Seinfeld—Stand-Up Confidental (also writer), Abott and Costello Meet Jerry Seinfeld (host).

SELBY, DAVID
Actor. b. Morgantown, WV. Feb. 5, 1941. e. West Virginia U. Acted in outdoor dramas in home state and did regional theatre elsewhere. Was asst. instructor in lit. at Southern Illinois U.
PICTURES: Night of Dark Shadows, Up the Sandbox, Super Cops, Rich Kids, Raise the Titanic, Rich and Famous, Dying Young, Intersection, Headless Body in Topless Bar.
TELEVISION: Series: Dark Shadows, Flamingo Road, Falcon Crest. Mini-Series: Washington: Behind Closed Doors. Movies: Telethon, The Night Rider, Love for Rent, Doctor Franken, King of the Olympics: The Lives and Loves of Avery Brundage, Grave Secrets: The Legacy of Hilltop Drive, Lady Boss. Guest: Kojak, Doogie Howser M.D.

SELF, WILLIAM
Producer. b. Dayton, OH, June 21, 1921. e. U. of Chicago, 1943. Prod.-dir., Schlitz Playhouse of Stars, 1952-56; prod., The Frank Sinatra Show, 1957; exec. prod., CBS-TV, The Twilight Zone, Hotel De Paree; 1960-61 exec. prod., 20th Century-Fox TV: Hong Kong, Adventures in Paradise, Bus Stop, Follow The Sun, Margie; v.p. in chg. of prod., 20th Century-Fox TV, 1962; exec. v.p., 1964; pres., Fox TV 1969; v.p. 20th Century Fox Film Corp., 1969; pres. of William Self Productions, Inc., partner, Frankovich/Self Productions; 1975; v.p., programs, Hollywood CBS TV Network, 1976; 1977, v.p. motion pictures for tv and miniseries, CBS TV; 1982, pres., CBS Theatrical Films; 1985, pres., William Self Prods. in association with CBS Prods; 1990, pres. Self Productions, Inc.
TELEVISION: Movies (exec. prod.): The Tenth Man (also prod.), Sarah Plain & Tall, Skylark.

SELIG, ROBERT WILLIAM
Exhibitor. b. Cripple Creek, CO, Feb., 1910. e. U. of Denver, 1932, B.A.; doctorate, 1959. 1932 joined advertising sales div., 20th Century Fox, Denver. Founding mem. Theatre Owners of Amer. and NATO. Consultant, Pacific Theatres. Lifetime Trustee, U. of Denver. Member Kappa Sigma, Omicron Delta Kappa, Beta Gamma Sigma; Nat'l Methodist Church Foundation; Past Pres., Theatre Association of California and CEO NATO of CA; board of directors Los Angeles Chamber of Commerce; founder NATO/ShoWest Conventions. Received NATO Sherrill C. Corwin Award, 1989.

SELLECCA, CONNIE
Actress. b. Bronx, NY, May 25, 1955. m. anchor-host John Tesh.
TELEVISION: Series: Flying High, Beyond Westworld, The Greatest American Hero, Hotel, P.S. I Luv U, Second Chances. Movies: The Bermuda Depths (debut, 1978), Flying High (pilot), Captain America II, She's Dressed to Kill, The Last Fling, International Airport, Downpayment on Murder, Brotherhood of the Rose, Turn Back the Clock, Miracle Landing, People Like Us, A House of Secrets and Lies (also co-exec. prod.), Passport to Murder, She Led Two Lives, A Dangerous Affair. Specials: The Celebrity Football Classic, Celebrity Challenge of the Sexes, Circus of the Stars.

SELLECK, TOM
Actor. b. Detroit, MI, Jan. 29, 1945. e. U. of Southern California. Grew up in Southern California, appearing in several commercials before being signed to 20th Century Fox. First acting job was on tv series Lancer.

PICTURES: Myra Breckenridge (debut, 1970), Midway, The Washington Affair, Coma, High Road to China, Lassiter, Runaway, Three Men and a Baby, Her Alibi, An Innocent Man, Quigley Down Under, Three Men and a Little Lady, Folks!, Christopher Columbus: The Discovery, Mr. Baseball.
TELEVISION: Series: Magnum P.I. (Emmy Award, 1984; also Golden Globe & People's Choice Awards). Movies: Most Wanted, Superdome, Returning Home, The Sacketts, The Concrete Cowboys, Divorce Wars, Louis L'Amour's The Shadow Riders, Broken Trust, Ruby Jean and Joe. Exec. prod.: Magnum P.I., B.L. Stryker (series), Revealing Evidence, The Silver Fox. Guest: The Young and the Restless, The Rockford Files, Friends

SELTZER, DAVID
Writer, Director. b. Highland Park, IL, 1940. m. flutist Eugenia Zukerman. e. Northwestern U. School for Film and Television. Moved to NY where worked on TV game show I've Got a Secret. Made short My Trip to New York. 1966 moved to LA to write for David Wolper's Incredible World of Animals. Then dir. and prod. Wolper documentaries. Worked as ghostwriter on film Willy Wonka and the Chocolate Factory.
PICTURES: Writer: The Hellstrom Chronicle, One Is a Lonely Number, The Omen, Damien: The Omen Part II, The Other Side of the Mountain, Six Weeks, Table for Five, Lucas (also dir.), Punchline (also dir.), Bird on a Wire, Shining Through (also dir., co-exec. prod.).
TELEVISION: National Geographic Specials (prod., dir., writer), William Holden in Unconquered Worlds (prod., dir., writer), The Underworld of Jacques Cousteau. Movies (writer): The Story of Eric, Green Eyes, My Father's House, Larry.

SELTZER, WALTER
Executive. b. Philadelphia, PA, Nov. 7, 1914. e. U. of PA. Publicity Asst. for Warner Bros. Theatres, Philadelphia; Fox West Coast Theatres; with MGM 1936-39; Warner Bros., 1939-40; Columbia, 1940-41. Enlisted U.S. Marine Corp., 1941-44. Publ. dir., Hal Wallis, 1945-54; v.p. in chg. adv & pub., Hecht-Lancaster Orgn., 1954-56; assoc. prod., The Boss; partner, Glass-Seltzer, pub. rel. firm; v.p. & exec. prod, Pennebaker Production; 1982, v.p., M.P. & TV Fund; pres., WSP Inc. Bd. of trustees, v.p. 1980-87 of Motion Picture and TV Fund.
PICTURES: One-Eyed Jacks, Shake Hands With the Devil, Paris Blues, The Naked Edge, Man in the Middle, Wild Seed, War Lord, Beau Geste, Will Penny, Number One, Darker Than Amber, The Omega Man, Skyjacked, Soylent Green, The Cay, The Last Hard Men.

SEMEL, TERRY
Executive. b. New York, NY, Feb. 24, 1943. e. Long Island Univ., B.S. Accounting 1964. Warner Bros. sales trainee 1966. Branch mgr., Cleveland, Los Angeles. V.P. Domestic sls. mgr. for CBS, 1971-73. Buena Vista as v.p., gen. sls. mgr., 1973-5. 1975 went to Warner Bros. as pres. domestic sls. 1978 named exec. v.p. and COO WB Inc. Named pres., Warner Bros. & COO, 1980. Named Pioneer of the Year by Foundation of Motion Picture Pioneers, 1990.

SEMLER, DEAN
Cinematographer. b. Australia. Served as 2nd unit dir. and cameraman on the mini-series Lonesome Dove, Son of the Morningstar.
PICTURES: The Earthling, The Coca Cola Kid, The Road Warrior, Kitty and the Bagman, Razorback, Mad Max Beyond Thunderdome, The Coca-Cola Kid, Going Sane, The Lighthorsemen, Cocktail, Young Guns, Farewell to the King, K-9, Dead Calm, Impulse, Young Guns II, Dances With Wolves (Academy Award, 1990), City Slickers, The Power of One, Super Mario Bros., Last Action Hero, The Three Musketeers, The Cowboy Way, Waterworld.

SEMPLE, LORENZO, JR.
Writer.
THEATER: The Golden Fleecing (filmed as The Honeymoon Machine).
PICTURES: Fathom, Pretty Poison, Daddy's Gone A-Hunting (co-s.p.), The Sporting Club, The Marriage of a Young Stockbroker, Papillon (co-s.p.), Super Cops, The Parallax View (co-s.p.), The Drowning Pool (co-s.p.), Three Days of the Condor (co-s.p.), King Kong, Hurricane (and exec. prod.), Flash Gordon, Never Say Never Again, Sheena (co-s.p.), Never Too Young to Die.
TELEVISION: Series: Batman (1966). Movie: Rearview Mirror.

SENDREY, ALBERT
Music Composer, Arranger, Conductor. b. Chicago, IL, Dec. 26, 1921. e. Trinity Coll. Music, London, USC, Paris, & Leipzig Conservatories. Composer, arr., orch. for many plays, films and TV. On stage was pianist/conductor for Lauritz Melchior, Kathryn Grayson, Ray Bolger, Danny Kaye, Tony Martin, Buddy Ebsen. Numerous B'way productions, including Mary Martin's Peter Pan, Ginger Roger's Pink Jungle and Yul Brynner's Penelope.

PICTURES: *Orchestrations*: The Yearling, Three Musketeers, Father's Little Dividend, Duchess of Idaho, Royal Wedding, Easy to Love, Great Caruso, An American in Paris, Brigadoon, Guys and Dolls, Meet Me in Las Vegas, High Society, Raintree County, Ride the High Country, Hallelujah Trail, The Hook, The Comancheros, Nevada Smith, The Oscar, Thoroughly Modern Millie, Hello Down There, Private Navy of Sgt. O'Farrell, Bad Day at Black Rock (with Andre Previn), Undercurrent, Sea of GRass (with H. Stothart).
TELEVISION: *Comp. music*: Laramie, Wagon Train, Ben Casey, Wolper Documentaries, Americans Abroad, J. F. Kennedy Anthology, Young Man from Boston, High Chaparral, The Monroes, Ken Murray's Hollywood.

SERGENT, HERB
Executive. Pres., Writer Guild of America East, Inc.

SERNA, ASSUMPTA
Actress. b. Barcelona, Spain, Sept. 16, 1957. Abandoned plans to be a lawyer, making stage debut 1978 with anti-Franco theatre company.
PICTURES: Sweet Hours (debut, 1980), The Hunting Ground, Crime of Cuenca, Revolt of the Birds, Circle of Passions, Tin Soldier, Secret Garden, Extramuros, The Old Music, Lola, Matador, Ballad of Dogs, Lucky Ravi, La Brute, La Nuite de L'Ocean, What Belongs to Caesar, Neon Man, Wild Orchid, I the Worst of All, Rossini Rossini, Adelaide, Chain of Desire, Cracked Nut, Fencing Master, Green Henry, Nostradamus, Shortcut to Paradise, Belle al Bar, The Shooter.
TELEVISION: Valentina, First Brigade, Falcon Crest, Fur Elise, Drug Wars, Revolver, Sharpe, Day of Reckoning, Les Derniers Jours de la Victime.

SEYMOUR, JANE
Actress. r.n. Joyce Frankenberg. b. Hillingdon, England, Feb. 15, 1951. Dancer with London Festival Ballet at 13. On B'way in Amadeus (1980). British Repetory including Canterbury, Harrogate, Sussex, Windsor.
PICTURES: Oh! What a Lovely War (debut, 1968), The Only Way, Young Winston, Live and Let Die, Sinbad and the Eye of the Tiger, Battlestar Galactica, Oh Heavenly Dog, Somewhere in Time, Lassiter, Head Office, The Tunnel, The French Revolution, Keys to Freedom.
TELEVISION: *Series*: The Onedine Line, Dr. Quinn: Medicine Woman (Golden Globe, 1996). *Movies/Mini-Series*: Frankenstein: The True Story, Captains and the Kings, Benny and Barney: Las Vegas Undercover, Seventh Avenue, Killer on Board, The Four Feathers, The Awakening Land, Love's Dark Ride, Dallas Cowboys Cheerleaders, Our Mutual Friend, East of Eden, The Scarlet Pimpernal, Phantom of the Opera, The Haunting Passion, Dark Mirror, The Sun Also Rises, Obsessed with a Married Woman, Jamaica Inn, Crossings, War and Remembrance, The Woman He Loved, Onassis: The Richest Man in the World (Emmy Award, 1988), Jack the Ripper, Angel of Death, I Remember You, Memories of Midnight, Are You Lonesome Tonight?, Matters of the Heart, Sunstroke (also exec. prod.), Heidi, Praying Mantis (also co-exec. prod.), A Passion for Justice: The Hazel Brannon Smith Story (also co-exec. prod.). *Host*: The Heart of Healing.

SHABER, DAVID
Screenwriter. b. Cleveland, OH. e. Western Reserve U., Yale U., Taught at Allegheny Coll. and Smith Coll. in speech and drama dept. Prof. of screenwriting Columbia Univ. Film School. Contributor to Cosmopolitan, Life, Esquire; had several short stories in O'Henry prize collections. Also wrote dramas (Shake Hands with the Clown, The Youngest Shall Ask, Bunker Reveries, etc.). First screenplay was Such Good Friends for Otto Preminger.
PICTURES: The Last Embrace, The Warriors, Those Lips, Those Eyes, Night Hawks, Rollover, The Hunt for Red October (uncredited), Flight of the Intruder.

SHAFER, MARTIN
Executive. Pres., Castle Rock Pictures, a division of Castle Rock Entertainment.

SHAGAN, STEVE
Writer. b. New York, NY. Oct. 25, 1927. Apprenticed in little theatres, film lab chores, stagehand jobs. Wrote, produced and directed film short, One Every Second; moved to Hollywood in 1959. Was IATSE technician, working as grip, stagehand, electrician to pave for film writing. Also did freelance advertising and publicity; produced Tarzan TV show. In 1968 began writing and producing two-hour films for TV.
AUTHOR: Save the Tiger, City of Angels, The Formula, The Circle, The Discovery, Vendetta, Pillars of Fire, A Cast of Thousands.
PICTURES: *Writer*: Save the Tiger (also prod.; Acad. Award nom., WGA Award, 1973), W.W. and the Dixie Dancekings (exec. prod.), Hustle, Voyage of the Damned (co.-s.p.; Acad. Award nom.), Nightwing (co-s.p.), The Formula (also prod.), The Sicilian, Primal Fear (co-s.p.).

TELEVISION: *Writer-producer*: River of Mystery, Spanish Portrait, Sole Survivor, A Step Out of Line, House on Garibaldi Street (exec. prod.), John Gotti.

SHAIMAN, MARC
Composer, Arranger. b. Newark, NJ, Oct. 22, 1959. Moved to NY at 16 where he met Bette Milder; was arranger and lyricists for her stage shows and the album Thighs & Whispers. Wrote music for Saturday Night Live, musical material for Billy Crytsal for the Academy Awards. Prod. and arranger for several Harry Connick, Jr. albums. Appeared on stage in Harlem Nocturne.
PICTURES: Divine Madness (music dir., arranger), The Cotton Club (music sprv., arranger), Broadcast News (cameo), Big Business (music sprv., arranger), Beaches (arranger), When Harry Met Sally... (music sprv.), Misery (music), Scenes From a Mall (music, adapt., cameo), City Slickers (music), Hot Shots (cameo), For the Boys (music sprv., arranger, co-composer), The Addams Family (music, cameo, co-wrote song "Mamuschka"), Sister Act (music, adapt.), Mr. Saturday Night (music, cameo), A Few Good Men (music), Life With Mikey (music sprv.), Sleepless in Seattle (musical sprv., co-wrote song "With a Wink and a Smile"), Hocus Pocus (music prod.), Heart and Souls (music, cameo), For Love or Money (co-composer), Addams Family Values (music), Sister Act 2: Back in the Habit (music, adaptations), That's Entertainment III (music sprv.), City Slickers II: The Legend of Curly's Gold (music), North (music, cameo), Speechless, Stuart Saves His Family, Forget Paris.

SHALIT, GENE
Critic. b. New York, NY, 1932. e. U. of Illinois. Started as freelance writer; joined NBC Radio Network, working on Monitor, 1968. Has been book and film critic, sports and general columnist. Since 1973 has been featured regular on NBC Today Show. Edits newsletter Shalit's Sampler.

SHANDLING, GARRY
Actor, Comedian, Writer, Producer. b. Chicago, IL, Nov. 29, 1949. e. Univ. of AZ. Moved to LA where he became writer for such sitcoms as Sandford & Son, Welcome Back Kotter, Three's Company. Became stand-up comedian in nightclubs which led to appearances on The Tonight Show.
PICTURES: The Night We Never Met (debut, 1993), Love Affair, Mixed Nuts.
TELEVISION: *Series*: It's Garry Shandling's Show (also exec. prod., writer; ACE Awards for Best Series & Actor), The Larry Sanders Show (also co-exec. prod., co-creator, co-writer). *Specials*: Garry Shandling—Alone in Las Vegas (also writer, prod.), It's Garry Shandling's Show—25th Anniversary Special (also exec. prod., writer), Grammy Awards (host), Garry Shandling: Stand-Up (also writer). Guest: Tonight Show (also frequent guest host), Late Night With David Letterman.

SHANLEY, JOHN PATRICK
Writer, Director. b. New York, NY, 1950. e. NYU. Cameo appearance in 1988 film Crossing Delancey. Dir. and wrote short I am Angry.
THEATER: *Writer*: Rockaway, Welcome to the Moon, Danny and the Deep Blue Sea, Savage in Limbo, Dreamer Examines His Pillow. *Writer-Dir.*: Italian-American Reconciliation, Beggars in the House of Plenty, Four Dogs and a Bone.
PICTURES: *Writer*: Moonstruck (Academy Award & Writers Guild Award, 1987), Five Corners (also assoc. prod.), The January Man, Joe Versus the Volcano (also dir.), Alive, We're Back!, Congo.

SHAPIRO, ROBERT W.
Producer. b. Brooklyn, NY, March 1, 1938. e. USC. Joined William Morris Agency, Inc., 1958; dir. and head of motion picture dept., William Morris Agency (UK) Ltd., 1969; mng. dir., 1970; 1974 v.p., head int'l. m.p. dept.; 1977 joined Warner Bros. as exec. v.p. in chg. of worldwide production; 1981, named WB pres., theatrical production div. Resigned 1983 to produce films.
PICTURES: Pee-Wee's Big Adventure, Empire of the Sun (exec. prod.), Arthur 2 On the Rocks, There Goes My Baby, Dr. Jekyll and Ms. Hyde.
TELEVISION: *Movie*: The Summer My Father Grew Up.

SHARE, MICHAEL
Executive. Began career with Paramount Pictures 1974 as booker in Indianapolis; 1975-76 appt. salesman; 1976-77 sls. mgr. in Philadelphia; 1977, Cincinnati branch mgr.; 1980, Chicago branch mgr.; 1985, promoted to v.p., eastern div., Paramount.

SHARIF, OMAR
Actor. r.n. Michel Shahoub. b. Alexandria, Egypt, April 10, 1932. e. Victoria Coll., Cairo; pres. of College Dramatic Society. Starred in 21 Egyptian (billed as Omar el Cherif or Omar Cherif) and two French films prior to English-language debut in Lawrence of Arabia. Left Egypt 1964. Champion contract bridge player. 1983 made rare stage appearance in The Sleeping Prince (Chichester, then West End).

PICTURES: The Blazing Sun (debut, 1954), Our Happy Days, La Chatelane du Liban, Goha, The Mameluks, Lawrence of Arabia (Acad. Award nom.), The Fall of the Roman Empire, Behold a Pale Horse, Marco the Magnificent, Genghis Khan, The Yellow Rolls-Royce, Doctor Zhivago, The Poppy Is Also a Flower, The Night of the Generals, More Than a Miracle, Funny Girl, Mackenna's Gold, The Appointment, Mayerling, Che!, The Last Valley, The Horsemen, The Burglars, The Right to Love (Brainwashed), The Tamarind Seed, The Mysterious Island of Captain Nemo, Juggernaut, Funny Lady, Crime and Passion, The Pink Panther Strikes Again (cameo), Ashanti, Bloodline, The Baltimore Bullet, Oh Heavenly Dog, Green Ice, Chanel Solitaire, Top Secret!, The Possessed, Paradise Calling, The Blue Pyramids, Keys to Freedom, Novice, Mountains of the Moon, Michelangelo and Me, Drums of Fire, Le Guignol, The Puppet, The Rainbow Thief, Journey of Love, Mother, 588 Rue Paradis.
TELEVISION: S*H*E, Pleasure Palace, The Far Pavilions, Peter the Great, Harem, Anastasia, Grand Larceny, Omar Sharif Returns to Egypt, The Mysteries of the Pyramids Live (host), Memories of Midnight, Mrs. 'arris Goes to Paris, Lie Down with Lions.

SHARP, ALAN
Writer. b. Glasgow, Scotland.
PICTURES: The Hired Hand, Ulzana's Raid, Billy Two Hats, Night Moves, The Osterman Weekend, Little Treasure (also dir.), Freeway, Cat Chaser (co-s.p.).
TELEVISION: Coming Out of the Ice.

SHATNER, WILLIAM
Actor. b. Montreal, Quebec, Mar. 22, 1931. e. McGill U. Toured Canada in various stock, repertory companies before U.S. tv debut in 1956. Author: TekWar, TekLords, TekLab, Tek Vengeance, TekSecret, Believe, Star Trek Memories (co-author with Chris Kreski), Star Trek Movie Memories (co-author with Kreski), The Return, Man O'War.
THEATER: NY: Tamburlaine the Great, The World of Susie Wong (Theatre World Award), A Shot in the Dark, L'Idiote.
PICTURES: The Brothers Karamazov (debut, 1958), Judgment at Nuremberg, The Explosive Generation, The Intruder, The Outrage, Incubus, White Comanche, Impulse, Big Bad Mama, The Devil's Rain, Kingdom of the Spiders, Land of No Return, Star Trek—The Motion Picture, The Kidnapping of the President, Visiting Hours, Star Trek II: The Wrath of Khan, Airplane II: The Sequel, Star Trek III: The Search for Spock, Star Trek IV: The Voyage Home, Star Trek V: The Final Frontier (also dir., orig. story), Bill & Ted's Bogus Journey (cameo), Star Trek VI: The Undiscovered Country, National Lampoon's Loaded Weapon 1, Star Trek: Generations.
TELEVISION: Series: For the People, Star Trek, Barbary Coast, T.J. Hooker, Rescue 911 (host), TekWar: The Series (also dir., co-exec. prod.). Movies: Sole Survivor, Vanished, Owen Marshall: Counselor at Law (pilot), The People, The Hound of the Baskervilles, Incident on a Dark Street, Go Ask Alice, The Horror at 37000 Feet, Pioneer Woman, Indict and Convict, Pray for the Wildcats, Barbary Coast (pilot), Perilous Voyage, The Bastard, Little Women, Crash, Disaster on the Coastliner, The Baby Sitter, Secrets of a Married Man, North Beach and Rawhide, Broken Angel, Family of Strangers, Columbo: Butterfly in Shades of Grey, TekWar (also dir., co-exec. prod.), TekLab, TekWar: TekJustice, Janek: A Silent Betrayal. Special: The Andersonville Trial, TekPower, TekMoney, Ashes of Money. Mini-Series: Testimony of Two Men.

SHAVELSON, MELVILLE
Writer, Director. b. Brooklyn, NY, April 1, 1917. e. Cornell U., 1937, A.B. Radio writer: We The People, Bicycle Party, 1937, Bob Hope Show, 1938-43, then screen writer; apptd. prod., Warner Bros., 1951. Conceived for TV: Make Room for Daddy, My World and Welcome To It. Author: book, How To Make a Jewish Movie, Lualda, The Great Houdinis, The Eleventh Commandment, Ike, Don't Shoot It's Only Me. Pres., Writers Guild of America, West, 1969-71, 1979-81, 1985-87; Pres., Writers Guild Foundation 1978-96.
PICTURES: Writer: The Princess and the Pirate, Wonder Man, The Kid From Brooklyn, Sorrowful Jones, It's a Great Feeling, The Daughter of Rosie O'Grady, Always Leave Them Laughing, Where There's Life, On Moonlight Bay, Double Dynamite, I'll See You in My Dreams, Room for One More (The Easy Way), April in Paris, Trouble Along the Way, Living It Up. Director-Writer: The Seven Little Foys (dir. debut, 1955), Beau James, Houseboat, It Started in Naples, The Five Pennies, On the Double, The Pigeon That Took Rome (also prod.), A New Kind of Love (also prod.), Cast a Giant Shadow (also prod.), Yours Mine and Ours, The War Between Men and Women, Mixed Company.
TELEVISION: Movies: The Legend of Valentino, The Great Houdinis, Ike, The Other Woman, Deceptions. Specials: Academy Awards, 1988, 1990 (writer).

SHAVER, HELEN
Actress. b. St. Thomas, Ontario, Canada, Feb. 24, 1951. e. Banff Sch. of Fine Arts, Alberta. Worked on stage and screen in Canada before coming to Los Angeles 1978.
THEATER: Tamara, Are You Lookin'? Ghost on Fire, A Doll's House, The Master Builder, The Hostage, Jake's Women (B'way debut; Theatre World Award).
PICTURES: Christina, Shoot, Starship Invasions, Outrageous!, High-Ballin', The Amityville Horror, In Praise of Older Women, Who Has Seen the Wind, Gas, Harry Tracy, The Osterman Weekend, Best Defense, Desert Hearts, The Color of Money, The Believers, The Land Before Time (voice), Walking After Midnight, Innocent Victim (Tree of Hands), Zebrahead, That Night, Dr. Bethune, Morning Glory, Change of Heart, Open Season, Born to Be Wild.
TELEVISION: Series: United States, Jessica Novak, WIOU. Movies: Lovey: Circle of Children II, Between Two Brothers, Many Happy Returns, The Park is Mine, Countdown To Looking Glass, No Blame, B.L. Stryker: The Dancer's Touch, Pair of Aces, Columbo: Rest in Peace Mrs. Columbo, Survive the Night, Poisoned By Love: The Kern County Murders, Trial & Error, The Forget-Me-Not Murders, Ride With the Wind, Without Consent, Janek: A Silent Betrayal. Guest: Ray Bradbury Theatre, Amazing Stories.

SHAW, MICHAEL M. (JOHN)
Executive. b. Ashland, KY, Jan. 10, 1945. e. Eastern KY Univ., Univ. of KY, Univ of MS. 1968-69, asst. booker, 20th Century Fox, Denver; 1969, head booker, Fox; 1970, salesman, Paramount Pictures, S.F.; 1970-71, head booker, sales Paramount L.A.; 1971-73, booker, Commonwealth Theatres; 1973, booker, McLendon theatres, Dallas; 1973-78, div. mngr. Mulberry Square Prods., Dallas; 1978-79, branch mngr. Filmways Pictures, Dallas; 1980-82, owner, Sequoyah Cinema Svc., Denver; 1983-87, head film buyer, Presidio Theatres, Austin; 1987-88, head film buyer, Santikos Theatres, San Antonio; 1988-present, pres./CEO, Film Bookiung Office Corp., Movieline Int'l, Dallas. Member: Motion Picture Pioneers, Variety Club.

SHAW, STAN
Actor. b. Chicago, IL, July 14, 1952. On stage received NAACP Image Award for West Coast premiere of Home, 1982.
PICTURES: The Bingo Long Travelling All-Stars and Motor Kings, Rocky, The Boys in Company C, The Great Santini, Tough Enough, Runaway, The Monster Squad, Harlem Nights, Fried Green Tomatoes, Body of Evidence, Rising Sun, Houseugest, Cutthroat Island, Daylight.
TELEVISION: Series: The Mississippi. Mini-Series: Roots: The Next Generations. Movies: Call to Glory, Maximum Security, The Gladiator, The Billionaire Boys Club, The Three Kings, The Court-Martial of Jackie Robinson, Lifepod. Guest: Starsky and Hutch, Wiseguy, Murder She Wrote, Hill Street Blues, Matlock.

SHAWN, WALLACE
Playwright, Actor. b. New York, NY, Nov. 12, 1943. Son of former New Yorker editor William Shawn. e. Harvard; Oxford U. Taught English in India on a Fulbright scholarship 1965-66. English, Latin and drama teacher, NY 1968-70.
THEATER: Writer: Our Late Night (1975, Obie Award), The Mandrake (translation, also actor), A Thought in Three Parts, Marie and Bruce, The Hotel Play, Aunt Dan and Lemon (also actor), The Fever (Obie Award, 1991; also actor). Opera: The Music Teacher (with Allen Shawn). Actor: The Master and Margarita, Chinchilla, Wifey.
PICTURES: Manhattan (debut, 1979), Starting Over, All That Jazz, Strong Medicine, Simon, Atlantic City, My Dinner With Andre (also co-s.p.), A Little Sex, Lovesick, The First Time, Deal of the Century, Strange Invaders, Saigon—Year of the Cat, Crackers, The Hotel New Hampshire, The Bostonians, Micki and Maude, Heaven Help Us, Head Office, The Bedroom Window, Radio Days, Prick Up Your Ears, Nice Girls Don't Explode, The Princess Bride, The Moderns, She's Out of Control, Scenes From the Class Struggle in Beverly Hills, We're No Angels, Shadows and Fog, Mom and Dad Save the World, Nickel and Dime, The Cemetery Club, Un-Becoming Age, The Meteor Man, Vanya on 42nd Street, Mrs. Parker and the Vicious Circle, A Goofy Movie (voice), Clueless, Canadian Bacon, Toy Story (voice), The Wife, House Arrest, All Dogs Go to Heaven II (voice).

SHAYE, ROBERT
Executive. b. Detroit, MI, Mar. 4, 1939. e. U. of Michigan, B.B.A.; Columbia U. Law. At 15 wrote, prod. dir. training film for father's supermarket staff. Later won first prize in Society of Cinematologists' Rosenthal Competition (best m.p. by American dir. under 25). Wrote, prod., dir., edited short films, trailers and TV commercials, including award-winning shorts, Image and On Fighting Witches (prod., dir.). Founded New Line Cinema 1967. Chmn. & CEO, New Line Cinema.
PICTURES: Prod./exec. prod.: Stunts, XTRO, Alone in the Dark, The First Time, Polyester, Critters, Quiet Cool, My Demon Lover, A Nightmare on Elm Street (also parts

2,3,4,5,6), The Hidden, Stranded, Critters 2, Hairspray, Heart Condition, Book of Love (dir.), Wes Craven's New Nightmare (also actor).
TELEVISION: Freddy's Nightmare: the Series (exec. prod.).

SHEA, JOHN
Actor. b. Conway, NH, April 14, 1949. Raised in MA. e. Bates Coll., ME, B.A. 1970; Yale Drama School, M.F.A. 1973. Worked as asst. dir. Chelsea Theater; taught part-time at Pratt Inst.
THEATER: Yentl (debut 1975, Off-B'way and B'way; Theatre World Award), Sorrows of Stephen, Long Day's Journey Into Night (Joseph Jefferson Award nom.), The Master and Margarita, Romeo and Juliet (Circle in the Sq.), American Days (Drama Desk Award), The Dining Room, End of the World (B'way), The Normal Heart (London, 1987), Animal Kingdom, Rosmersholm (La Mama), Impossible Spy (China's Golden Panda Award).
PICTURES: Hussy, Missing, Windy City (Best Actor Montreal Film Festival), A New Life, Unsettled Land, Honeymoon, Stealing Home, Freejack, Honey I Blew Up the Kid, A Weekend in the Country.
TELEVISION: Series: WIOU, Lois and Clark. Movies: The Nativity, Family Reunion, Coast to Coast (BBC), Hitler's S.S.: Portrait in Evil, A Case of Deadly Force, The Impossible Spy, Magic Moments, Baby M (Emmy Award), Do You Know the Muffin Man, Small Sacrifices, Notorious, Ladykiller, Justice in a Small Town, See Jane Run, Forgotten Sins. Mini-Series: The Last Convertible, Kennedy. Special: Leslie's Folly.

SHEAFF, DONALD J.
Executive. b. Oct. 23, 1925. e. U.of California at L.A., 1948; Pierce Coll., 1957. Served 4 yrs. during W.W.II in Navy Air Corps in South Pacific. 1946, joined Technicolor Motion Picture Div. in supervisory capacity; 1957, lab. supervisor, Lookout Mountain Air Force Station, handling Top Secret film for Air Force and Atomic Energy Commission; est. and org. the installation of Vandenberg Air Force Base Lab. facilities, which Technicolor designed; 1961 joined Panacolor Corp.; 1963, joined Pacific Title and Art Studio in charge of color control for special effects and titles; returned to Technicolor Corp. app't. Plant Mgr. of TV div., 1966; v.p. & gen. mngr. of the TV div., 1973; appt v.p. & gen. mgr., Motion Picture Division, 1976; mgr., special visual effects, Universal City Studios. Member: SMPTE, Nat'l Academy of Television Arts & Sciences. Has conducted scientific seminars for SMPTE.

SHEARER, HARRY
Writer, Actor. b. Los Angeles, CA, Dec. 23, 1943. e. UCLA (pol. science); grad. work in urban gov., Harvard. At 7 appeared on The Jack Benny Show. Worked as freelance journalist for Newsweek, L.A. Times and publ. articles in New West, L.A. Magazine and Film Comment. Also taught h.s. Eng. and social studies and worked in CA State Legislature in Sacramento. Founding mem. The Credibility Gap, co-wrote, co-prod. and performed on comedy group's albums (A Great Gift Idea, The Bronze Age of Radio). Co-wrote, co-prod. Albert Brooks' album A Star is Bought. Performed with group Spinal Tap. Host of Le Show, L.A. radio prog. Writer-cast mem. Saturday Night Live (1979-80 & 1984-85).
THEATER: Accomplice (Pasadena Playhouse).
PICTURES: Actor: Abbott and Costello Go to Mars (debut, as child, 1953), Cracking Up, Real Life (also co-s.p.), Animalympics (voice), The Fish That Saved Pittsburgh, Serial, One-Trick Pony, The Right Stuff, This is Spinal Tap (also co-s.p.), Plain Clothes, My Stepmother is an Alien (voice), Oscar, Pure Luck, Blood & Concrete, The Fisher King, A League of Their Own, Wayne's World 2, I'll Do Anything, Speechless.
TELEVISION: Series: Fernwood 2-Night (creative consultant), The Simpsons (voice), Harry Shearer's News Quiz. Specials: Likely Stories, It's Just TV, Paul Shaffer: Viva Shaf Vegas, Comedy Hour, Portrait of a White Marriage (also dir.), The Magic of Live, Spinal Tap Reunion (also co-writer).

SHEEDY, ALLY
Actress. r.n. Alexandra Sheedy. b. New York, NY, June 13, 1962. e. USC. m. actor David Lansbury. Daughter of literary agent Charlotte Sheedy. As child performed with American Ballet Theatre. At age 12 wrote children's book, She Was Nice to Mice; later wrote pieces for NY Times, Village Voice, Ms. Published book of poetry: Yesterday I Saw the Sun. Began acting in TV commercials at 15. Chicago Theatre in Wrong Turn at Lungfish; NY stage debut in Advice from a Caterpillar.
PICTURES: Bad Boys (debut, 1983), WarGames, Oxford Blues, The Breakfast Club, St. Elmo's Fire, Twice in a Lifetime, Blue City, Short Circuit, Maid to Order, Heart of Dixie, Betsy's Wedding, Only the Lonely, Home Alone 2: Lost in New York (cameo), Tattletale, The Pickle, Man's Best Friend, One Night Stand.
TELEVISION: Movies: The Best Little Girl in the World, The Violation of Sarah McDavid, The Day the Loving Stopped, Splendor in the Grass, Deadly Lessons, We Are the Children, Fear, The Lost Capone, Lethal Exposure, Chantilly Lace, Ultimate Betrayal, Parallel Lives, The Haunting of Seacliff Inn, The Tin Soldier. Guest: Hill Street Blues, St. Elsewhere.

SHEEN, CHARLIE
Actor. r.n. Carlos Irwin Estevez. b. Los Angeles, Sept. 3, 1965. Father is actor Martin Sheen. Brother of actors Emilio, Ramon and Renee Estevez. Made debut as extra in TV movie, The Execution of Private Slovik (starring father) and as extra in Apocalypse Now (also starring father).
PICTURES: Grizzly II—The Predator, Red Dawn, The Boys Next Door, Lucas, Ferris Bueller's Day Off, The Wraith, Platoon, Wisdom, Three for the Road, No Man's Land, Wall Street, Never on Tuesday, Young Guns, Eight Men Out, Major League, Beverly Hills Brats, Courage Mountain, Navy Seals, Men at Work, The Rookie, Cadence, Hot Shots!, National Lampoon's Loaded Weapon 1 (cameo), Hot Shots Part Deux!, DeadFall, The Three Musketeers, The Chase (also co-exec. prod.), Major League 2, Beyond the Law, Terminal Velocity, The Shadow Conspiracy, All Dogs Go to Heaven II (voice), The Arrival.
TELEVISION: Movies: Silence of the Heart, Backtrack.

SHEEN, MARTIN
Actor. r.n. Ramon Estevez. b. Dayton, OH, Aug. 3, 1940. Father of actors Emilio Estevez, Charlie Sheen, Ramon Estevez and Renee Estevez. Wrote play (as Ramon G. Estevez) Down the Morning Line (prod. Public Theatre, 1969). Emmy Award as dir., exec. prod. Babies Having Babies (1986).
THEATER: The Connection (debut, 1959 with the Living Theater), Women of Trachis, Many Loves, In the Jungle of Cities, Never Live Over a Pretzel Factory, The Subject Was Roses, The Wicked Crooks, Hamlet, Romeo and Juliet, Hello Goodbye, The Happiness Cage, Death of a Salesman (with George C. Scott), Julius Caesar, The Crucible.
PICTURES: The Incident (debut, 1967), The Subject Was Roses, Catch-22, No Drums No Bugles, Rage, Pickup on 101, Badlands, The Legend of Earl Durrand, The Cassandra Crossing, The Little Girl Who Lives Down the Lane, Apocalypse Now, Eagle's Wing, The Final Countdown, Loophole, Gandhi, That Championship Season, Enigma, Man Woman and Child, The Dead Zone, Firestarter, The Believers, Siesta, Wall Street, Walking After Midnight, Da (also co-exec. prod.), Judgment in Berlin (also exec. prod.), Beverly Hills Brats, Cold Front, Beyond the Stars, The Maid, Cadence (also dir.), JFK (narrator), Hear No Evil, Hot Shots Part Deux (cameo), Gettysburg, Trigger Fast, Hits!, Fortunes of War, Sacred Cargo, The Break, Dillinger & Capone, Captain Nuke and the Bomber Boys, Ghost Brigade, The Cradle Will Rock, Dead Presidents, Dorothy Day, Gospa, The American President, The War At Home.
TELEVISION: Series: As the World Turns. Movies: Then Came Bronson, Mongo's Back in Town, Welcome Home Johnny Bristol, That Certain Summer, Letters for Three Lovers, Pursuit, Catholics, Message to My Daughter, The Execution of Private Slovik, The California Kid, The Missiles of October, The Story of Pretty Boy Floyd, Sweet Hostage, The Guardian, The Last Survivors, Blind Ambition, The Long Road Home (Emmy Award, 1981), In the Custody of Strangers, Choices of the Heart, The Atlanta Child Murders, Consenting Adult, Shattered Spirits, News at Eleven, Out of the Darkness, Samaritan, Conspiracy: The Trial of the Chicago 8, No Means No (exec. prod. only), Nightbreaker (also exec. prod.), Guilty Until Proven Innocent, The Water Engine (voice), The Last P.O.W.?: The Bobby Garwood Story, A Matter of Justice, One of Her Own, Roswell. Mini-Series: Kennedy, Queen. Guest: Tales From the Crypt, Murphy Brown (Emmy Award, 1994). Narrator: Eyewitness (PBS).

SHEFFER, CRAIG
Actor. b. York, PA, 1960. e. East Stroudsberg Univ., PA. Started career in tv commercials; in soap opera, One Life to Live. On NY stage in Fresh Horses, G.R. Point, Torch Song Trilogy (B'way & Off-B'way). Starred in IMAX film Wings of Courage.
PICTURES: That Was Then This Is Now (debut, 1985), Fire with Fire, Some Kind of Wonderful, Voyage of the Rock Aliens, Split Decisions, Nightbreed, Instant Karma (also exec. prod.), Blue Desert, Eye of the Storm, A River Runs Through It, Fire in the Sky, The Program, Sleep With Me, Roadflower, The Grave, Head Above Water.
TELEVISION: Series: The Hamptons. Movies: Babycakes, In Pursuit of Honor, The Desperate Trail.

SHEFFIELD, JOHN
Actor. b. Pasadena, CA, April 11, 1931. e. UCLA. Stage debut at 7 in On Borrowed Time. Created screen role of Tarzan's son in Tarzan Finds a Son, followed by 7 other entries in Tarzan series, and role of Bomba in Bomba series.
PICTURES: Babes in Arms, Tarzan Finds a Son, Lucky Cisco Kid, Little Orvie, Knute Rockne—All-American, Million Dollar Baby, Tarzan's Secret Treasure, Tarzan's New York Adventure, Tarzan Triumphs, Tarzan's Desert Mystery, Tarzan and the Amazons, Tarzan and the Leopard Woman, Tarzan and the Huntress, Roughly Speaking, Bomba the Jungle Boy, Bomba on Panther Island, Lost Volcano, Bomba and the Hidden City,

The Lion Huntress, Bomba and the Elephant Stampede, African Treasure, Bomba and the Jungle Girl, Safari Drums, The Golden Idol, Killer Leopard, Lord of the Jungle. TELEVISION: *Series*: Bantu the Zebra Boy.

SHEINBERG, SIDNEY JAY
Executive. b. Corpus Christi, TX, Jan. 14, 1935. e. Columbia Coll., A.B. 1955; LL.B., 1958. Admitted to Calif. bar, 1958; assoc. in law U. of California Sch. of Law, Los Angeles, 1958-59; joined MCA, Inc, 1959; pres., TV div., 1971-74; exec. v.p., parent co., 1969-73. Named MCA pres. & chief oper. off., 1973. Resigned from position 1995 to form company The Bubble Factory to produce films for MCA.

SHELDON, DAVID
Producer, Director, Writer. b. New York, NY. e. Yale U. Sch. of Drama, M.F.A.; Principia Coll., B.A.; Actors Studio, directors unit. 1972-74 was exec. at American Int'l Pictures supervising development and production of 18 films include: Futureworld, Walking Tall, Dillinger, Sisters, Macon County Line, Reincarnation of Peter Proud, Slaughter, Dr. Phibes. *Prod./Dir.*, The Gateway Playhouse in NY where dir. over 50 plays and musicals. Started the Sheldon/Post Company in 1991 with Ira Post. *Exec. prod./writer* of Secret of a Small Town. Currently working with Orion on three tv series; with Kushner-Locke and the Larry Thompson Organization on movies; and with Merv Griffin Ent.
PICTURES: *Producer-Writer*: Grizzly, Sheba Baby, The Evil, Project: Kill. *Producer*: Just Before Dawn, Abby, Day of the Animals, The Manitou. *Director*: Lovely But Deadly. *Writer*: The Predator.

SHELDON, JAMES
Director. r.n. Schleifer. b. New York, NY. Nov. 12. e. U. of NC. Page boy, NBC; announcer-writer-dir., NBC Internat'l Div.; staff dir., ABC radio; staff prod. dir., Young & Rubicam; free lance prod. dir. of many programs live tape and film, N.Y. and Hollywood.
TELEVISION: *Series* (prod./ dir.): Mr. Peepers, Armstrong Circle Theatre, Robert Montgomery Presents, Schlitz Playhouse, West Point, Zane Grey Theatre, The Millionaire, Desilu Playhouse, Perry Mason, Twilight Zone, Route 66, Naked City, The Virginian, Alfred Hitchcock Presents, Fugitive, Espionage, Defenders, Nurses, Bing Crosby Show, Family Affair, Wonderful World of Disney, Man From UNCLE, Felony Squad, That Girl, Ironside, My World and Welcome To It, To Rome With Love, Owen Marshall, Room 222, Apple's Way, Love American Style, McMillan and Wife, Sanford and Son, Ellery Queen, Rich Man, Poor Man II, Family, MASH, Switch, Loveboat, Sheriff Lobo, Knots Landing, The Waltons, 240-Robert, Nurse, Dukes of Hazard, Todays F.B.I., McLain's Law, 7 Brides for 7 Brothers, Lottery, Partners in Crime, Jessie, Santa Barbara, Half Nelson, Stir Crazy, The Equalizer, Sledge Hammer, Cagney & Lacey. *Movies*: Gidget Grows Up, With This Ring, The Gossip Columnist.

SHELDON, SIDNEY
Writer, Director, Producer, Novelist. b. Chicago, IL, Feb. 11, 1917. e. Northwestern U.
AUTHOR: The Naked Face, The Other Side of Midnight, A Stranger in the Mirror, Bloodline, Rage of Angels, Master of the Game, If Tomorrow Comes, Windmills of the Gods, The Sands of Time, Memories of Midnight, The Doomsday Conspiracy, The Stars Shine Down, Nothing Lasts Forever, Morning Noon & Night.
THEATER: Redhead (Tony Award, 1959). Alice in Arms, Jackpot, Dream With Music, Merry Widow (revision), Roman Candle.
PICTURES: *Writer*: The Bachelor and the Bobbysoxer (Academy Award, 1947), Easter Parade, Annie Get Your Gun, Three Guys Named Mike, Dream Wife (also dir.), Remains to Be Seen, You're Never Too Young, Pardners, The Buster Keaton Story (also prod., dir.), The Birds and the Bees, Gambling Daughters, Dangerous Lady, Bill Rose's Jumbo. *Novels made into films*: The Naked Face, The Other Side of Midnight, Bloodline.
TELEVISION: *Series*: Patty Duke Show (creator), I Dream of Jeannie (creator, prod.), Nancy (creator, prod.), Hart to Hart (creator). *Novels made into Mini-Series/Movies*: Rage of Angels, Master of the Game, Windmills of the Gods, If Tomorrow Comes, Memories of Midnight, The Sands of Time, Stranger in the Mirror, Nothing Lasts Forever.

SHELLEY, CAROLE
Actress. b. London, England, Aug. 16, 1939. e. Arts Educational Sch., RADA.
THEATER: *NY*: The Odd Couple (debut, 1965), The Astrakhan Coat, Loot, Sweet Potato, Little Murders, Hay Fever, Absurd Person Singular (Tony nom.), The Norman Conquests, The Elephant Man (Tony Award, 1979), Twelve Dreams (Obie Award), The Misanthrope, Noises Off, Stepping Out (Tony nom.), What the Butler Saw, The Miser, Maggie and Misha, The Destiny of Me, Later Life, London Suite, Show Boat.

London: Simon and Laura (debut, 1955), New Cranks, Boeing-Boeing, Mary Mary, Lettice and Lovage. Also appearances with Shaw Festival, Stratford Fest., Amer. Shakespeare Fest., etc.
PICTURES: Give Us this Day (debut, 1949), Cure for Love, It's Great to Be Young, Carry on Regardless, Carry on Cabby, The Odd Couple, The Boston Strangler, The Aristocats (voice), Robin Hood (voice), The Super, Little Noises, Quiz Show, The Road to Wellville.
TELEVISION: *Series*: The Odd Couple. *Specials*: Coconut Downs, Gabby, A Salute to Noel Coward. *Movie*: Devlin. *Guest*: Brian Rix, Dickie Henderson Show, The Avengers.

SHELTON, RON
Writer, Director, Producer. b. Whittier, CA, Sept. 15, 1945. e. Westmont Coll., Santa Barbara, CA, 1967; U of Arizona, Tucson, AZ, 1974. For 5 years played second base for Baltimore Orioles farm team. Cleaned bars and dressed mannequins to support his art: painting and sculpture. A script he wrote, A Player to Be Named Later (which he later filmed himself as Bull Durham), attracted attention of dir. Roger Spottiswoode who directed his first two scripts.
PICTURES: The Pursuit of D. B. Cooper (assoc. prod.), Open Season (exec. prod.). *Writer*: Under Fire (also 2nd unit dir.), The Best of Times (also 2nd unit dir.), Bull Durham (also dir.), Blaze (also dir.), White Men Can't Jump (also dir.), Blue Chips (also co-exec. prod.), Cobb (also dir.), The Great White Hype (co-s.p.), Tin Cup (also prod., s.p.).

SHENSON, WALTER
Producer. b. San Francisco, CA. e. Stanford U., Calif.; Ent. m.p. ind. 1941; studio exec., writing, prod., prom. shorts, trailers, Columbia; sup. publ., expl., London, Columbia European production, 1955.
PICTURES: *Prod.*: The Mouse That Roared, A Matter of Who, The Mouse on the Moon, A Hard Day's Night, Help!, 30 Is a Dangerous Age Cynthia, Don't Raise the Bridge Lower the River, A Talent for Loving, Welcome to the Club (also dir.), The Chicken Chronicles, Reuben Reuben, Echo Park, Ruby Jean and Joe.

SHEPARD, SAM
Writer, Actor. r.n. Samuel Shepard Rogers. b. Fort Sheridan, IL, Nov. 5, 1943. Raised in California, Montana and South Dakota. Worked as stable hand, sheep shearer, orange picker in CA, a car wrecker in MA and musician with rock group Holy Modal Rounders. Lived near San Francisco, where, in addition to writing, ran a drama workshop at the U. of California at Davis. Recipient of Brandeis U. Creative Arts Citation, 1976, and American Acad. of Arts and Letters Award, 1975.
THEATER: *Playwright*: Icarus' Mother, Red Cross (triple bill—Obie Award, 1966), La Turista (Obie Award, 1967), Forensic and the Navigators, Melodrama Play, Tooth of Crime (Obie Award, 1973), Back Dog Beast Bait, Operation Sidewinder, 4-H Club, The Unseen Hand, Mad Dog Blues, Shaved Splits, Rock Garden, Curse of the Starving Class (Obie Award, 1978), Buried Child (Obie Award & Pulitzer Prize, 1979), True West, Fool For Love, A Lie of the Mind, Simpatico.
PICTURES: *Actor*: Renaldo and Clara (debut, 1978), Days of Heaven, Resurrection, Raggedy Man, Frances, The Right Stuff (Acad. Award nom.), Country, Fool for Love, Crimes of the Heart, Baby Boom, Steel Magnolias, Bright Angel, Defenseless, Voyager, Thunderheart, The Pelican Brief, Safe Passage. *Writer*: Me and My Brother (co-s.p.), Zabriskie Point (co-s.p.), Oh Calcutta! (contributor), Renaldo and Clara (co-s.p.), Paris Texas, Fool for Love, Far North (also dir.), Silent Tongue (also dir.).
TELEVISION: *Special*: Fourteen Hundred Thousand Blue Bitch (BBC). *Movie*: The Good Old Boys.

SHEPHERD, CYBILL
Actress, Singer. b. Memphis, TN, Feb. 18, 1950. e. Hunter Coll., NYU, USC. Was fashion model (won Model of the Year title, 1968) before acting debut in 1971. Debut record album, Cybill Does It... To Cole Porter, 1974, followed by Stan Getz: Mad About the Boy, Vanilla, Somewhere Down the Road.
PICTURES: The Last Picture Show (debut, 1971), The Heartbreak Kid, Daisy Miller, At Long Last Love, Taxi Driver, Special Delivery, Silver Bears, The Lady Vanishes, The Return, Chances Are, Texasville, Alice, Once Upon a Crime, Married to It.
TELEVISION: *Series*: The Yellow Rose, Moonlighting, Cybill (also co-exec. prod.); Golden Globe, 1996). *Movies*: A Guide for the Married Woman, Secrets of a Married Man, Seduced, The Long Hot Summer, Which Way Home, Memphis (also co-writer, co-exec. prod.), Stormy Weathers, Telling Secrets, There Was a Little Boy, Baby Brokers, For the Love of My Daughter, While Justice Sleeps, The Last Word.

SHEPHERD, RICHARD
Producer. b. Kansas City, MO, June 4, 1927. e. Stanford U. In U.S. Naval Reserve, 1944-45. Entered entertainment field as exec. with MCA, 1948, functioning in radio, TV, and m.p. fields

until 1956, with time out for U.S. Army, 1950-52. 1956 became head of talent for Columbia Pictures. 1962 joined CMA talent agency on its founding, becoming exec. v.p. in chg. of m.p. div.; 1972-74, exec. v.p. for prod. Warner Bros.; 1974 became indept. prod.; 1976 named MGM sr. vp. & worldwide head of theatrical prod. 1985 to present, partner in The Artists Agency.
PICTURES: Twelve Angry Men, The Hanging Tree, The Fugitive Kind, Breakfast at Tiffany's, Alex and the Gypsy, Robin and Marian, Volunteers, The Hunger.

SHER, LOUIS K.
Executive. b. Columbus, OH, Feb. 25, 1914. e. Ohio State U., 1933. Exec., Stone's Grills Co., 1934-37; owned & operated, Sher Vending Co., 1937-43. U.S. Army, 1943-46. V.p., Sons Bars & Grills, 1947-54; org. & pres. Art Theatre Guild, 1954; opened art theatres for first time in many cities, org. opera film series, film classic series and similar motion picture activities in many cities; org., Film Festival at Antioch Coll., 1960; pioneer in fighting obscenity laws in Ohio; operates 4 theatres in midwest and western states. Co-producer of the musical broadway production Shenandoah and American Dance Machine. Produced film, Deathmask.

SHERAK, THOMAS
Executive. b. Brooklyn, NY June 22, 1945. e. New York Community Coll., mktg. degree. 1967-69, US Army, Specialist E5 Sgt.; 1970, began career in m.p. industry, Paramount Pictures sls. dept.; 1974, R/C Theatres, booking dept.; 1977, joined General Cinema Theatres as district film buyer; 1978, promoted to v.p.; films; 1982, promoted to v.p. head film buyer; 1983, joined 20th Century Fox as pres., domestic dist. & mktg.; 1985, pres., domestic dist.; 1986, president, domestic dist. & marketing. 1990-present, exec. v.p., 20th Century Fox.

SHERIDAN, JAMEY
Actor. b. Pasadena, CA, July 12, 1951. e. Univ. of CA, Santa Barbara.
THEATER: Off-B'way: Just a Little Bit Less Than Normal, The Arbor, One Wedding Two Rooms Three Friends. B'way: The Man Who Came to Dinner, Hamlet, Biloxi Blues, All My Sons (Tony nom.), Long Day's Journey Into Night, Ah Wilderness, The Shadow Box. Regional: Major Barbara, Loose Ends, Deathtrap, Homesteaders.
PICTURES: Jumpin' Jack Flash (debut, 1986), The House on Carroll Street, Distant Thunder, Stanley & Iris, Quick Change, Talent for the Game, All I Want for Christmas, A Stranger Among Us, Whispers in the Dark, White Squall.
TELEVISION: Series: Shannon's Deal, Chicago Hope. Movies: One Police Plaza, Shannon's Deal (pilot), A Mother's Courage: The Mary Thomas Story, Murder in High Places, My Breast, Spring Awakening, Killer Rules. Mini-Series: The Stand. Guest: The Doctors, Another World, St. Elsewhere, Spenser: For Hire, Picket Fences, The Equalizer.

SHERIDAN, JIM
Director, Writer. b. Dublin, Ireland, 1949. e. Univ Col. in Dublin, NYU Inst. of Films & TV. Started as director-writer at Lyric Theatre in Belfast and Abbey Theatre in Dublin; also at Project Arts Theatre (1976-80), NY Irish Arts Center (1982-87) as artistic director. Founded Children's Theatre Company in Dublin.
PICTURES: Dir.-Writer: My Left Foot, The Field, Into the West (s.p. only), In the Name of the Father.
THEATER: Writer: Mobile Homes, Spike in the First World War (Edinburgh Festival Fringe Award for best play, 1983).

SHERIDAN, NICOLLETTE
Actress. b. Worthing, Sussex, England, Nov. 21, 1963. Moved to LA in 1973. Became model in NYC before turning to acting.
PICTURES: The Sure Thing (debut, 1985), Noises Off, Spy Hard.
TELEVISION: Series: Paper Dolls, Knots Landing. Movies: Dark Mansions, Agatha Christie's Dead Man's Folly, Jackie Collins' Lucky/Chances, Deceptions, A Time to Heal, Shadows of Desire, Robin Cook's Virus.

SHERMAN, RICHARD M.
Composer, Lyricist, Screenwriter. b. New York, NY, June 12, 1928. e. Bard Coll., B.A., 1949. Info. & Educ. Br., U.S. Army, 1953-55. Songwriter, composer, Walt Disney Prods 1960-71, then freelance. With partner-brother Robert has won, 9 Acad. Award nom., 2 Grammys, 17 gold and platinum albums, 1st Prize, Moscow Film Fest. (for Tom Sawyer) and a star on Hollywood Walk of Fame. Have written over 500 pub. and recorded songs. Also wrote score for B'way musical Over Here (1974) and songs for Disney Theme Parks.
SONGS: Things I Might Have Been, Tall Paul, Christmas in New Orleans, Mad Passionate Love, Midnight Oil, The Ugly Bug Ball, You're Sixteen, That Darn Cat, The Wonderful Thing About Tiggers, It's a Small World, A Spoonful of Sugar, Supercalifragilistic, Feed the Birds, Let's Go Fly a Kite, Age of Not Believing, When You're Loved, Pineapple Princess, Let's Get Together, Maggie's Theme, Chim Chim Cheree (Academy

Award, 1964), Chitty Chitty Bang Bang, Hushabye Mountain, Winnie the Pooh, Fortuosity, Slipper and the Rose Waltz, many others. Comedy Album: Smash Flops.
PICTURES: Nightmare, The Cruel Tower, The Absent Minded Professor, The Parent Trap, Big Red, In Search of the Castaways, Moon Pilot, Bon Voyage, Legend of Lobo, Summer Magic, Miracle of the White Stallions, The Sword in the Stone, The Misadventures of Merlin Jones, Mary Poppins (2 Academy Awards for song & score, 1964), Those Calloways, The Monkey's Uncle, That Darn Cat, Follow Me Boys!, Winnie the Pooh, Monkeys Go Home!, Chitty Chitty Bang Bang, The Gnome-Mobile, The Jungle Book, The Happiest Millionaire, The One and Only Genuine Original Family Band, The Aristocats, Bedknobs & Broomsticks, Snoopy Come Home, Charlotte's Web, Beverly Hills Cop III, The Mighty Kong. Songs & S.P.: Tom Sawyer, The Slipper and the Rose, The Magic of Lassie, Huckleberry Finn, Little Nemo: Adventures in Slumberland.
TELEVISION: Wonderful World of Color, Bell Telephone Hour, Welcome to Pooh Corner, The Enchanted Musical Playhouse, The Timberwood Tales, Goldilocks, Harry Anderson's Sideshow.

SHERMAN, ROBERT B.
Composer, Lyricist, Screenwriter. b. New York, NY, Dec. 19, 1925. e. Bard Coll., B.A., 1949. U.S. Army, WWII, 1943-45 (purple heart). Songwriter, 1952-60; pres., Music World Corp.; 1958; songwriter, composer, Walt Disney, 1971, then freelance. Hon. Phd., Lincoln Col, 1990. With partner-brother Richard Sherman, has won, 9 Acad. Award nom., 2 Grammys, 17 gold and platinum albums, 1st Prize, Moscow Film Fest. (for Tom Sawyer) and a star on Hollywood Walk of Fame. Have written over 500 pub. and recorded songs. Also wrote score for B'way musical Over Here (1974) and songs for Disney Theme Parks. (see Richard M. Sherman for co-writing credits.)

SHERMAN, SAMUEL M.
Producer, Director, Writer. b. New York, NY. e. CCNY, B.A. Entered m.p. ind. as writer, cameraman, film ed., neg. & sound cutter; nat'l mag. ed., Westerns Magazine 1959; pres., Signature Films; prod., dir., TV pilot, The Three Mesquiteers, 1960; prod., Pulse Pounding Perils, 1961; helped create, ed., dir., Screen Thrills Illustrated; exec. prod., Screen Thrills; v.p., Golden Age Films, 1962; prod., Joe Franklin's Silent Screen, 1963; NY rep., Victor Adamson Prods.; NY rep., Tal prods., Hlywd.; adv. & pub. Hemisphere Pictures; prod., writer, Chaplin's Art of Comedy, The Strongman; prod., Hollywood's Greatest Stuntman; story adapt., Fiend With the Electronic Brain; tech. consul., Hal Roach Studios, Music from the Land; 1968, NY rep. East West Pict. of Hollywood. 1968, N.Y. rep., Al Adamson Prods. of Hollywood; Ed.-in-chief, bk., The Strongman; pres., Independent-International Pictures Corp. (and tv div.); pres., Producers Commercial Productions, Inc. Chmn. of Creditors' Committee, Allied Artists Television Corp.; pres., Technovision Inc.; pres., Super Video, Inc.
PICTURES: Assoc. prod.: Horror of the Blood Monsters, Blood of Ghastly Horror. Prod., s.p.: Brain of Blood. Prod. supervisor: Dracula vs. Frankenstein. Exec. prod.: Angels, Wild Women, The Naughty Stewardesses (prod., s.p.), Girls For Rent, The Dynamite Brothers, Blazing Stewardesses (prod., s.p.), Cinderella 2000, Team-Mates (also story), Raiders of the Living Dead (dir., s.p.).

SHERMAN, VINCENT
Director. b. Vienna, GA, July 16, 1906. e. Oglethorpe U. B.A. Writer, actor, dialogue dir., then prod. dir.
PICTURES: The Return of Doctor X (debut, 1939), Saturday's Children, The Man Who Talked Too Much, Underground, Flight from Destiny, The Hard Way, All Through the Night, Old Acquaintance, In Our Time, Mr. Skeffington, Pillow to Post, Janie Gets Married, Nora Prentiss, The Unfaithful, Adventures of Don Juan, The Hasty Heart, The Damned Don't Cry, Harriet Craig, Goodbye My Fancy, Lone Star, Affair in Trinidad, Difendo il mio Amore, The Garment Jungle, The Naked Earth, The Young Philadelphians, Ice Palace, A Fever in the Blood, The Second Time Around, Cervantes (The Young Rebel).
TELEVISION: 35 episodes of Medical Center, Westside Medical, Baretta, Waltons, Doctors Hospital, Trapper John, Movies: The Last Hurrah, Women at West Point, The Yeagers (pilot), Bogey, The Dream Merchants, Trouble in High Timber Country, High Hopes—The Capra Years.

SHERRIN, NED
Producer, Director, Writer. b. Low Ham, Somerset, England, Feb. 18, 1931. Early career writing plays and musical plays. Prod., dir., ATV Birmingham, 1955-57; prod., Midlands Affairs, Paper Talk, etc. Joined BBC-TV 1957 and produced many TV talk programs. Novels: (with Caryl Brahms) Cindy-Ella or I Gotta Shoe (also prod. as stage play), Rappell 1910, Benbow Was His Name.
AUTHOR: Autobiography: A Small Thing Like a Earthquake. Anthology: Cutting Edge Theatrical Anecdotes. 1995. edit. of Oxford Dictionary of Humorous Quotations. Novel: Scratch an Actor. Diaries: Serrin's Year: 1995.

PICTURES: *Prod.*: The Virgin Soldiers (with Leslie Gilliat), Every Home Should Have One, Up Pompeii, Girl Stroke Boy (co-author with Caryl Brahms), Up the Chastity Belt, Rentadick, The Garnet Saga, Up the Front, The National Health, The Cobblers of Umbridge (dir. with Ian Wilson). *Actor*: Orlando.
TELEVISION: *England: Prod.*: Ask Me Another, Henry Hall Show, Laugh Line, Parasol. *Assoc. prod.*: Tonight series, Little Beggars. *Prod., creator*: That Was The Week That Was. *Prod., dir.*: Benbow Was His Name (co-author), Take a Sapphire (co-author), The Long Garden Party, The Long Cocktail Party. ABC of Britain revue, Not So Much a Programme—More a Way of Life. Appearances inc.: Your Witness, Quiz of The Week, Terra Firma, Who Said That, The Rather Reassuring Programme, Song by Song, Loose Ends Radio 4.

SHERWOOD, MADELEINE
Actress. b. Montreal, Canada, Nov. 13, 1922. e. Yale Drama Sch. Trained with Montreal Rep. and Actors Studio. Has dir. prods. at Actors Studio and regional theaters, as well as 2 AFI films Goodnight Sweet Prince and Sunday.
THEATER: The Crucible, Sweet Bird of Youth, Cat on a Hot Tin Roof, Invitation to a March, The Garden of Sweets, Camelot, Hey You, Light Man!, Brecht on Brecht, Night of the Iguana, Arturo Ui, Do I Hear a Waltz?, Inadmissible Evidence, All Over, Older People, Getting Out, The Suicide, Eclipse, Miss Edwina.
PICTURES: Baby Doll, Cat on a Hot Tin Roof, Parrish, Sweet Bird of Youth, The 91st Day, Hurry Sundown, Pendulum, Wicked Wicked, The Changeling, Resurrection, Teachers, An Unremarkable Life, Silence Like Glass.
TELEVISION: *Series*: The Flying Nun. *Mini-Series*: Rich Man Poor Man. *Movies*: The Manhunter, Nobody's Child, Palace Guard; many guest appearances.

SHIELDS, BROOKE
Actress. b. New York, NY, May 31, 1965. e. Princeton U. Honors in French Lit. Discovered at age 11 months by photographer Francesco Scavullo to pose in Ivory Soap ads.
THEATER: *Off-B'way*: The Eden Cinema; *B'way debut* 1994 in Grease! (Theatre World Award).
PICTURES: Alice Sweet Alice (Holy Terror/Communion; debut 1977), Pretty Baby, King of the Gypsies, Tilt, Wanda Nevada, Just You and Me Kid, The Blue Lagoon, Endless Love, Sahara, The Muppets Take Manhattan (cameo), Speed Zone (cameo), Back Street Dreams, Brenda Starr, An American Love (It.), The Seventh Floor, Freeway.
TELEVISION: *Movies*: The Prince of Central Park, Wet Gold, The Diamond Trap, I Can Make You Love Me: The Stalking of Laura Black; Nothing Lasts Forever; numerous specials. *Guest*: Friends. *Series*: Suddenly Susan.

SHIELDS, WILLIAM A.
Executive. b. New York, NY, 1946. e. El Camino Coll., California State Coll. at LA. Entered the motion picture industry in 1966 with Pacific Theatres, then MGM sales dept., L.A. and Denver, 1970; New World Pictures, 1972; 20th Century-Fox, Washington, 1973; NY district manager, 20th Century-Fox, 1973-75; joined Mann Theatres Corp. of California as head booker in 1975; gen. sls. mgr., Far West Films, 1977-79; joined Avco Embassy as Western div. mgr., promoted to asst. gen. sls. mgr., 1980; promoted to v.p.-gen. sls. mgr., 1981; 1983 joined New World Pictures as exec. v.p., worldwide mktg. & acquisitions; promoted to pres., worldwide sls. & mktg., 1985; 1987, pres. CEO, New World Intl.; 1989, joined Trans Atlantic Pictures as pres., CEO when company purchased assets of New World's feature film division. Sold ownership in Trans Atlantic and formed G.E.L. Prod. & Distrib., 1992. Exec. prod. Au Pair (1991); exec. in charge of prod. Death Ring (1992). Exec. prod. of Uninvited. Past chmn, American Film Mktg. Assn. (1987-91). Presently chmn. American Film Export Assn.

SHIFF, RICHARD
Executive. b. New York, NY, Mar. 3, 1942. e. Queens College, B.A., M.A., Brooklyn Col., P.D. Joined Warner Bros. as sales analyst, 1977. 1979 named dist. coordinator; 1980, asst. dir. sls. admin. 1982, promoted to post, dir. sls. admin. 1987, v.p., theatrical sls. operations.

SHIRE, DAVID
Composer. b. Buffalo, NY, July 3, 1937. m. actress Didi Conn. e. Yale U., 1959, B.A. Composer of theater scores: The Sap of Life, Urban Blight, Starting Here Starting Now, Baby, Closer Than Ever, Big. Emmy noms. Raid on Entebbe, The Defection of Simas Kudirka, Do You Remember Love? and The Kennedys of Massachusetts. Grammy Awards for Saturday Night Fever.
PICTURES: One More Train to Rob, Summertree, Drive, He Said; Skin Game, To Find a Man, Showdown, Two People, Steelyard Blues (adapt.), Class of '44, The Conversation, The Taking of Pelham 1-2-3, The Fortune, Farewell My Lovely, The Hindenberg, All the President's Men, The Big Bus, Harry and

Walter Go to New York, Saturday Night Fever (adapt. & add. music), Straight Time, The Promise (Acad. Award nom.), Old Boyfriends, Norma Rae (Academy Award for best song, It Goes Like It Goes, 1979), Only When I Laugh, The Night the Lights Went Out in Georgia, Paternity, The World According to Garp, Max Dugan Returns, Oh God You Devil, 2010, Fast Break, Return to Oz, Short Circuit, 'night Mother, Vice Versa, Monkey Shines, Bed and Breakfast, One Night Stand.
TELEVISION: *Series themes*: Sarge, McCloud, The Practice, Sirota's Court, Joe & Sons, Lucas Tanner, Alice, Tales of the Unexpected, Brewster Place, Room for Two. *Movies*: Priest Killer, McCloud, Harpy, Three Faces of Love, Killer Bees, Tell Me Where It Hurts, The Defection of Simus Kudirka, Three for the Road, Amelia Earhart, Something for Joey, Raid on Entebbe, The Storyteller, Promise, Mayflower Madam, Echoes in the Darkness, Jesse, God Bless the Child, Common Ground, The Clinic, Convicted, The Women of Brewster Place, I Know My First Name is Steven, The Kennedys of Massachusetts (mini-series), The Great Los Angeles Earthquake, The Boys, Sarah: Plain and Tall, Always Remember I Love You, Paris Trout, Four Eyes, Broadway Bound, Bed of Lies, Last Wish, Alison, Habitation of Dragons, Lily in Winter, Reunion, Serving in Silence, My Brother's Keeper, My Antonia, The Heidi Chronicles, The Man Who Wouldn't Die, Tecumseh: The Last Warrior, Almost Golden: The Jessica Savitch Story, many others.

SHIRE, TALIA
Actress. r.n. Talia Coppola. b. New York, NY, April 25, 1946. Raised on road by her father, arranger-conductor Carmine Coppola, who toured with Broadway musicals. After 2 yrs. at Yale Sch. of Drama she moved to L.A. where appeared in many theatrical productions. Brother is dir. Francis Ford Coppola. Started in films as Talia Coppola.
PICTURES: The Wild Racers, The Dunwich Horror, Gas-s-s-s, The Christian Licorice Store, The Outside Man, The Godfather, The Godfather Part II (Acad. Award nom.), Rocky (Acad. Award nom.), Old Boyfriends, Prophecy, Rocky II, Windows, Rocky III, Rocky IV, RAD, Lionheart (co-prod.), New York Stories (Life Without Zoe), Rocky V, The Godfather III, Bed and Breakfast, Cold Heaven, DeadFall, One Night Stand (dir. only).
TELEVISION: *Mini-Series*: Rich Man Poor Man. *Movies*: Foster and Laurie, Kill Me If You Can, Daddy I Don't Like It Like This, For Richer For Poorer, Chantilly Lace. *Special*: Please God I'm Only 17.

SHIVAS, MARK
Producer. e. Oxford.
PICTURES: *Producer*: Richard's Things, Moonlighting, A Private Function, The Witches. *Exec. Prod.*: Bad Blood, Truly Madly Deeply, Enchanted April, The Grass Arena, Memento Mori, The Snapper, Priest, An Awfully Big Adventure, Jude, The Van, Small Faces.
TELEVISION: Presenter of Cinema. *Producer*: The Six Wives of Henry VIII, Casanova, The Edwardians, The Evacuees, The Glittering Prizes, Abide With Me, Rogue Male, 84 Charing Cross Road, The Three Hostages, She Fell Among Thieves, Professional Foul, Telford's Change, On Giant's Shoulders, The Price, What If it's Raining?, The Story Teller. Now head of Films, BBC.

SHORE, HOWARD
Composer, Musician. Began career as musical director for Saturday Night Live.
PICTURES: Scanners, Videodrome, The Brood, The Fly, After Hours, Heaven, Belizaire the Cajun, Nadine, Moving, Big, Dead Ringers, The Lemon Sisters, An Innocent Man, Postcards From the Edge (musical numbers sprv.), The Silence of the Lambs, A Kiss Before Dying, Naked Lunch, Prelude to a Kiss, Single White Female, Sliver, Guilty as Sin, M. Butterfly, Mrs. Doubtfire, Philadelphia, Ed Wood, The Truth About Cats & Dogs, Striptease.
TELEVISION: Coca-Cola Presents Live: The Hard Rock.

SHORE, PAULY
Actor. b. Los Angeles, CA, 1968. Son of comedian Sammy Shore and nightclub owner Mitzi Shore. Worked as stand-up comedian at mother's club, The Comedy Store.
PICTURES: For Keeps? (debut, 1988), 18 Again!, Lost Angels, Phantom of the Mall, Wedding Band, Encino Man, Class Act, Son-in-Law, In the Army Now, Jury Duty, Bio-Dome.
TELEVISION: *Series*: Totally Pauly, Totally Different Pauly. *Special*: Pauly Does Dallas. *Movie*: Home By Midnight. *Guest*: 21 Jump Street, Married... with Children.

SHORT, MARTIN
Actor, Comedian, Writer. b. Toronto, Can., Mar. 26, 1950. e. McMaster U. Trained as social worker but instead performed on stage in Godspell as well as in revues and cabarets in Toronto, 1973-78, including a stint as a member of the Toronto unit of the Second City comedy troupe, 1977-78. Created

such characters as Ed Grimley, Jackie Rogers Jr. B'way debut 1993 in The Goodbye Girl (Theatre World Award; Tony nom.).
PICTURES: Lost and Found, The Outsider, Three Amigos!, Innerspace, Cross My Heart, Three Fugitives, The Big Picture, Pure Luck, Father of the Bride, Captain Ron, Clifford, The Pebble and the Penguin (voice), Father of the Bride Part 2, An Indian in the City, Mars Attacks!.
TELEVISION: Series: The Associates, I'm a Big Girl Now, SCTV Network (Emmy Award for writing, 1983), Saturday Night Live (1985- 86), The Completely Mental Misadventures of Ed Grimley (cartoon series), The Martin Short Show (also exec. prod., writer). Specials: All's Well That Ends Well, Really Weird Tales, Martin Short's Concert for the North Americas (SHO), Martin Short Goes Hollywood (HBO), The Show Formerly Known as the Martin Short Show (also exec. prod., co-writer). Movies: The Family Man, Sunset Limousine, Money for Nothing (BBC).

SHORT, THOMAS C.
Executive. International pres., International Alliance of Theatrical Stage Employees & Moving Picture Machine Operators of the U.S. and Canada (AFL-CIO-CLC).

SHOWALTER, MAX
Actor, Composer. r.n. Casey Adams. b. Caldwell, KS, June 2, 1917. e. Caldwell H.S.; Pasadena Playhouse. Composed background music for films: Vicki, Return of Jack Slade, B'way Harrigan 'n Hart (composer), Touch of the Child (lyricist-composer). Recordings incl. The Brementown Musicians, The Gold Dog (as narrator, composer, pianist and singer). On bd. of trustees: Eugene O'Neill Theatre Center, Natl. Theatre of the Deaf, Ivorytown Playhouse, Shoreline Alliance for the Arts. Gov's Bd.: Commission for the Arts.
THEATER: B'way: Knights of Song, Very Warm for May, My Sister Eileen, Showboat, Lend a Hand, Make Mine Manhattan, Lend an Ear, Hello Dolly!, The Grass Harp.
PICTURES: Always Leave Them Laughing (debut, 1949), With a Song in My Heart, What Price Glory?, My Wife's Best Friend, Niagara, Destination Gobi, Dangerous Crossing, Vicki, Night People, Naked Alibi, The Indestructible Man, The Return of Jack Slade, Never Say Goodbye, Bus Stop, Dragoon Wells Massacre, Down Three Dark Streets, Designing Woman, Female Animal, The Monster That Challenged the World, Voice In the Mirror, The Naked and the Dead, It Happened to Jane, Elmer Gantry, Return to Peyton Place, Summer and Smoke, The Music Man, Bon Voyage, My Six Loves, Move Over Darling, Sex and the Single Girl, Fate Is the Hunter, How to Murder Your Wife, Lord Love a Duck, A Talent for Loving, The Moonshine War, The Anderson Tapes, 10, Racing with the Moon, Sixteen Candles.

SHUE, ELISABETH
Actress. b. South Orange, NJ, Oct. 6, 1963. e. Harvard. Brother is actor Andrew Shue.
PICTURES: The Karate Kid (debut, 1984), Adventures in Babysitting, Link, Cocktail, Back to the Future Part II, Back to the Future Part III, The Marrying Man, Soapdish, Twenty Bucks, The Underneath, Leaving Las Vegas (Chicago Film Critics Award; Nat'l Film Critics Award), Trigger Effect.
TELEVISION: Series: Call to Glory. Movies: Charles and Diana, Double Switch, Hale the Hero, Blind Justice, Radio Inside.

SHULER-DONNER, LAUREN
Producer. b. Cleveland, OH. B.S. in film & bdcstg., Boston U. Began filmmaking career as ed. of educational films then camera-woman in TV; assoc. prod., story editor, creative affairs exec.; TV movie: Amateur Night at the Dixie Bar and Grill (prod.). Assoc. prod. on film Thank God It's Friday. Cameo in film Maverick.
PICTURES: Mr. Mom, Ladyhawke, St. Elmo's Fire, Pretty in Pink, Three Fugitives, The Favor, Radio Flyer, Dave, Free Willy, Free Willy 2: The Adventure Home, Assassins.

SHULL, RICHARD B.
Actor. b. Evanston, IL, Feb. 24, 1929. e. State U. of Iowa. B.A. drama, 1950., Kemper Mil. Sch. AA Humanities, 1986. U.S. Army, 1953. Armed Forces Korea Network. 1953-56, exec. asst. prod. Gordon W. Pollock Prods.; 1954-56 stage mgr. Hyde Park Playhouse; other prod. jobs and freelance stage mgr. and dir. 1950-70. NY stage debut in Wake Up Darling (1956), also in Minnie's Boys, Goodtime Charley (Tony nom.; Drama Desk nom.), The Marriage of Bette and Boo (Obie Award), One of the All-Time Greats, Ain't Broadway Grand, Victor Victoria.
PICTURES: The Anderson Tapes (debut, 1971), B.S. I Love You, Such Good Friends, Hail to the Chief, Slither, Sssss, Cockfighter, The Fortune, The Black Bird, Hearts of the West, The Big Bus, The Pack, Dreamer, Wholly Moses, Heartbeeps, Spring Break, Lovesick, Unfaithfully Yours, Splash, Garbo Talks, Tune in Tomorrow, Housesitter, For Love or Money, Trapped in Paradise, Cafe Society.

TELEVISION: Series: Diana, Holmes & Yoyo. Guest: Your Hit Parade (1950), Rockford Files, Good Times, Love American Style, Hart to Hart, Lou Grant. Movies: Ziegfeld: A Man and His Women, Studs Lonigan, Will There Really Be a Morning? The Boy Who Loved Trolls, Keeping the Faith, Seize the Day.

SHURPIN, SOL
Executive. b. New York, NY, Feb. 22, 1914. e. Pace Inst., 1936. Law stenog., 1932-33; Joe Hornstein, Inc., 1933-41; National Theatre Supply, 1941-48; purchased interest in Raytone Screen Corp., became v.p., 1948; pres., Raytone, 1952; pres., Technikote Corp., which succeeded Raytone Screen, 1956-present; sole owner, Technikote Corp., 1962.

SHUTT, BUFFY
Executive. e. Sarah Lawrence Col. Joined Paramount 1973 as sect. with N.Y. pub. staff; 1975, natl. mag. contact. 1978, named dir. of pub.; later exec. dir. of pub. Promoted 1980 to v.p., pub. & promo. Resigned to join Time-Life Films as v.p. of East coast prod; returned to Paramount in 1981 as sr. v.p. & asst. to pres. of Motion Picture Group. 1984, appt. exec. v.p.-mktg. for M.P. Group, Paramount. 1985, appoint. pres. of mktg. 1986, resigned. Formed Shutt-Jones Communications, 1987, marketing consultancy with Kathy Jones. 1989, appt. marketing pres., Columbia Pictures & Tri-Star Pictures. 1991, mktg. pres. of TriStar.

SHYER, CHARLES
Director, Writer. b. Los Angeles, CA. e. UCLA. Was asst. dir. and prod. mgr. before becoming head writer for tv series The Odd Couple. First teamed with Nancy Meyers on Private Benjamin.
PICTURES: Writer: Smokey and the Bandit, House Calls, Goin' South, Private Benjamin (Acad. Award nom.; also prod.). Director-Writer: Irreconcilable Differences, Baby Boom, Father of the Bride, I Love Trouble, Father of the Bride Part II.

SIDARIS, ANDY
Producer, Director, Writer. b. Chicago, IL, Feb. 20, 1932. e. Southern Methodist U., B.A., radio-TV. Began television career in 1950 in Dallas, TX as a director at station WFAA-TV; now pres., The Sidaris Company. Won 8 Emmy Awards.
PICTURES: Dir.: Stacey, The Racing Scene, M*A*S*H (football sequences), Seven (also prod.). Dir.-Writer: Malibu Express (also prod.), Hard Ticket to Hawaii, Picasso Trigger, Savage Beach, Guns, Do or Die, Hard Hunted, Fit to Kill. Exec. Prod.: Enemy Gold, The Dallas Connection.
TELEVISION: Dir.: The Racers/Mario Andretti/Joe Leonard/Al Unser, ABC's Championship Auto Racing, ABC's NCAA Game of the Week, 1968 Summer Olympics: 1968 (Mexico City), 1972 (Munich), 1976 (Montreal), 1984 (L.A.), Winter Olympics: 1964 (Innsbruck), 1968 (Grenoble), 1976 (Innsbruck), 1980 (Lake Placid), 1988 (Calgary), Wide World of Sports, The Racers/Craig and Lee Breedlove, The Burt Reynolds Late Show, Kojak episode, Nancy Drew episodes.

SIDNEY, GEORGE
Director, Producer. b. New York, NY, Oct. 4, 1916. Son of L. K. Sidney, veteran showman and v.p. MGM, and Hazel Mooney, actress. From 1932 at MGM as test, second unit and short subjects dir. Won Academy Awards for shorts: Quicker 'n a Wink (Pete Smith speciality), Of Pups and Puzzles (Passing Parade). In 1941 made feature dir. debut, MGM. Pres., Director's Guild of America, 16 yrs; spec. presidential assignment to Atomic Energy Commission and U.S. Air Force; 1961-66, pres., Hanna-Barbera Productions; Doctorate of Science Hanneman Medical University and Hospital. Member ASCAP. Pres., Directors, Inc., since 1969; v.p., Directors Foundation; v.p., D.W. Griffith Foundation; life mem., ACTT (England) and DGA. Directed U.N. special, Who Has Seen the Wind? Awarded Gold Medal for service to D.G.A. 1959, Doctorate from Collegio Barcelona 1989, Life Membership in D.G.A.
PICTURES: Free and Easy (debut, 1941), Pacific Rendezvous, Pilot No. 5, Thousands Cheer, Bathing Beauty, Anchors Aweigh, The Harvey Girls, Holiday in Mexico, Cass Timberlane, The Three Musketeers, Key to the City, Annie Get Your Gun, Show Boat, Scaramouche, Young Bess, Kiss Me Kate, Jupiter's Darling, The Eddy Duchin Story, Jeanne Eagels (also prod.), Pal Joey, Who Was That Lady? (also prod.), Pepe (also prod.), Bye Bye Birdie, A Ticklish Affair, Viva Las Vegas (also co-prod.), The Swinger (also prod.), Half a Sixpence (also co-prod.).

SIDNEY, SYLVIA
Actress. b. New York, NY, Aug. 8, 1910. r.n. Sophia Kosow. e. Theatre Guild Sch. Prof. stage debut at age 16. NY debut 1927.
THEATER: Nice Women, Crossroads, Bad Girl, The Gentle People, Auntie Mame, Joan of Lorraine, Angel Street, Enter Laughing, Vieux Carre.
PICTURES: Broadway Nights (debut, 1927), Thru Different Eyes, City Streets, Ladies of the Big House, Confessions of a Co-Ed, An American Tragedy, Street Scene, The Miracle Man,

Merrily We Go to Hell, Make Me a Star (cameo), Madame Butterfly, Pick-Up, Jennie Gerhardt, Good Dame, Thirty Day Princess, Behold My Wife, Accent on Youth, Mary Burns—Fugitive, The Trail of the Lonesome Pine, Fury, Sabotage (A Woman Alone), You Only Live Once, Dead End, You and Me, One Third of a Nation, The Wagons Roll at Night, Blood on the Sun, Mr. Ace, The Searching Wind, Love From a Stranger, Les Miserables, Violent Saturday, Behind the High Wall, Summer Wishes Winter Dreams (Acad. Award nom.), Gold Told Me To (Demons), I Never Promised You a Rose Garden, Damien: Omen II, Corrupt, Hammett, Beetlejuice, Used People, Mars Attacks!.
TELEVISION: *Movies*: Do Not Fold Spindle or Mutilate, Death at Love House, Raid on Entebbe, The Gossip Columnist, FDR—The Last Year, The Shadow Box, A Small Killing, Come Along With Me, Having It All, Finnegan Begin Again, An Early Frost, Pals. *Specials*: Andre's Mother, The Witching of Ben Wagner. *Guest*: thirtysomething.

SIEMASZKO, CASEY
Actor. b. Chicago, IL, March 17, 1961. r.n. Kazimierz Siemaszko. e. Goodman Theatre School of Drama, Chicago.
PICTURES: Class (debut, 1983), Secret Admirer, Back to the Future, Stand By Me, Gardens of Stone, Three O'Clock High, Biloxi Blues, Young Guns, Breaking In, Back to the Future Part II, Of Mice and Men, Teresa's Tattoo, My Life's in Turnaround, Milk Money, The Phantom.
TELEVISION: *Movie*: Miracle of the Heart: A Boys Town Story.

SIGHVATSSON, SIGURJON (JONI)
Producer. b. Reykjavik, Iceland, June 15, 1952. e. Iceland Community Col, Univ. of Iceland. Came to U.S. in 1978. Also attended USC. Was film and music video prod. for Blue-Ice Prods. Founder and chairperson with Steve Golin of Propaganda Films.
PICTURE: *Assoc. Producer*: Hard Rock Zombies, American Drive-In. *Producer*: Private Investigations, The Blue Iguana, Kill Me Again, Fear Anxiety and Depression, Daddy's Dyin'... Who's Got the Will?, Wild at Heart, Truth or Dare, Ruby, A Stranger Among Us, Candyman, Kalifornia, Red Rock West, S.F.W., Lord of Illusions, Canadian Bacon.
TELEVISION: *Movie*: Memphis. *Specials*: Rock the Vote, Education First, Tales of the City. *Series*: Twin Peaks.

SIKKING, JAMES B.
Actor. b. Los Angeles, CA, March 5, 1934. e. UCLA, B.A. Theatre includes Waltz of the Toreadors, Plaza Suite, Damn Yankees, The Big Knife.
PICTURES: The Magnificent Seven, Von Ryan's Express, Chandler, The New Centurions, The Electric Horseman, Capricorn One, Ordinary People, Outland, The Star Chamber, Up the Creek, Star Trek III—The Search for Spock, Morons from Outer Space, Soul Man, Narrow Margin, Final Approach.
TELEVISION: *Series*: General Hospital, Turnabout, Hill Street Blues. Doogie Howser, M.D. *Movies*: The Jesse Owens Story, First Steps, Bay Coven, Brotherhood of the Rose, Too Good to be True, Desperado: Badlands Justice, Doing Time on Maple Drive, Jake Lassiter: Justice on the Bayou, In Pursuit of Honor, Tyson. *Mini-Series*: Around the World in 80 Days. *Specials*: Tales from the Hollywood Hills (Golden Gate), Ollie Hopnoodle's Haven of Bliss.

SILLIPHANT, STIRLING
Executive, Writer. b. Detroit, MI, Jan. 16, 1918. e. USC, B.A., 1938. On pub. staff, Walt Disney Productions, Burbank 1938-41; 1941-42, exploit. & pub., Hal Horne Org. for 20th Century-Fox in NY & other key cities; 1942-43, asst. to Spyros P. Skouras. U.S. Navy, WWII. 1946, with 20th-Fox; in chg. special events and promotions, 1949; appt. Eastern pub. mgr. 1951.
PICTURES: *Prod.*: The Joe Louis Story, Shaft's Big Score (exec. prod.). *Writer*: Five Against the House (also co-prod.), The Nightfall, The Lineup, Village of the Damned, The Slender Thread, In the Heat of the Night (Academy Award, 1967), Charly, Marlowe, A Walk in the Spring Rain, The Liberation of L.B. Jones, Murphy's War, The New Centurions, The Poseidon Adventure, Shaft in Africa, The Towering Inferno, The Killer Elite, The Enforcer, Telefon, The Swarm, Circle of Iron, When Time Ran Out, Over the Top, Catch the Heat (also co-exec. prod.), The Grass Harp.
TELEVISION: *Series*: The Naked City, Route 66, Space, Golden Gate, Fly Away Home (also prod.). *Movies/Mini-Series*: Mussolini—The Untold Story, Pearl (also exec. prod.), Salem's Lot (exec. prod.), Welcome to Paradise (also exec. prod.), Travis McGee, The Three Kings (also prod.), Brotherhood of the Rose (exec. prod.), Day of Reckoning. (d. April 26, 1996)

SILVA, HENRY
Actor. b. Brooklyn, NY, 1928. Studied acting with Group Theatre, Actors Studio.
PICTURES: Viva Zapata!, Crowded Paradise, A Hatful of Rain, The Law and Jake Wade, The Bravados, Green Mansions, Cinderfella, Ocean's Eleven, Sergeants 3, The

Manchurian Candidate, A Gathering of Eagles, Johnny Cool, The Secret Invasion, Hail Mafia, The Return of Mr. Moto, The Reward, The Hills Ran Red, The Plainsman, Matchless, Never a Dull Moment, The Animals, Man and Boy, The Italian Connection, The Kidnap of Mary Lou, Shoot, Thirst, Buck Rogers in the 25th Century, Love and Bullets, Virus, Alligator, Sharky's Machine, Wrong Is Right, Megaforce, Cannonball Run II, Lust in the Dust, Code of Silence, Alan Quartermain and the Lost City of Gold, Amazon Women on the Moon, Above the Law, Bulletproof, Dick Tracy, Fists of Steel, Trained to Kill, Possessed by the Night.
TELEVISION: *Movies*: Black Noon, Drive Hard Drive Fast, Contract on Cherry Street, Happy. *Series*: Buck Rogers in the 25th Century.

SILVER, CASEY
Executive. Pres., Universal Pictures, Inc.

SILVER, JOAN MICKLIN
Writer, Director. b. Omaha, NB, May 24, 1935. m. producer Raphael Silver. Daughter is dir. Marisa Silver. e. Sarah Lawrence Coll. Began career as writer for educational films. Original s.p., Limbo, purchased by Universal Pictures. In 1972 Learning Corp. of Am. commissioned her to write and direct a 30-min. film, The Immigrant Experience. Also wrote and directed two children's films for same co; dir. & wrote short film Bernice Bobs Her Hair. First feature was Hester Street, which she wrote and directed.
THEATER: *Director*: Album, Maybe I'm Doing It Wrong, A ... My Name is Alice, A ... My Name is Still Alice (co-conceived & co-dir. with Julianne Boyd).
PICTURES: *Director*: Hester Street (also s.p.), Between the Lines, On the Yard (prod.), Head Over Heels (also s.p.; retitled Chilly Scenes of Winter), Crossing Delancey, Loverboy, Big Girls Don't Cry... They Get Even.
TELEVISION: Finnegan Begin Again (dir.), The Nightingale: Faerie Tale Theatre (writer), Parole Board (Prison Stories: Women on the Inside), A Private Matter (dir.).

SILVER, JOEL
Producer. b. South Orange, NJ, July 14, 1952. e. NYU. Made first film, a short called Ten Pin Alley; moved to Los Angeles with job as asst. to Lawrence Gordon. Named pres., Lawrence Gordon Prods.; developed with Gordon and produced and marketed Hooper, The End, The Driver, The Warriors (also assoc. prod.). At Universal Pictures as prod. v.p.; supervising Smokey and the Bandit II. Honored 1990 as NATO/ShoWest's Producer of the Year. Appeared in 1988 film Who Framed Roger Rabbit.
PICTURES: Xanadu (co-prod.), Jekyll & Hyde ... Together Again (exec. prod.), 48 HRS., Streets of Fire, Brewster's Millions, Weird Science, Commando, Jumpin' Jack Flash, Lethal Weapon, Predator, Action Jackson, Die Hard, Road House, Lethal Weapon 2, The Adventures of Ford Fairlane, Die Hard 2, Predator 2, Hudson Hawk, Ricochet, The Last Boy Scout, Lethal Weapon 3, Demoliton Man, The Hudsucker Proxy, Richie Rich, Tales From the Crypt Presents Demon Knight (co-exec. prod.), Fair Game, Assassins, Executive Decision.
TELEVISION: Tales from the Crypt (exec. prod. & prod.; also dir. episode), Two Fisted Tales, Parker Can, W.E.I.R.D. World (co-exec. prod.).

SILVER, LEON J.
Executive. b. Boston, MA, March 25, 1918. e. USC, 1935-39. Independent prod. of short subjects, 1939; story analyst, Paramount, 1940, film writer, U.S. Army Pictorial Service, 1941-45; freelance writer, 1946; film writer. prod., U.S. Public Health Service, 1946-51; asst. chief, foreign film prod., U.S. Dept. of State, 1951-54; acting chief, domestic film prod., U.S. Information Agency, 1955; division chief, Worldwide Documentary Film & Television Product, U.S. Information Agency, 1968; 1978-79, sr. advisor U.S. film production. Coordinator of TV & film, all Fed Govt. Agencies Private Industry under Exec. Office, pres. of U.S. 1980. Resigned, 1980. Now TV network writer-producer-novelist.

SILVER, MARISA
Director. b. New York, NY, April 23, 1960. Daughter of director Joan Micklin Silver and prod.-dir. Raphael Silver. e. Harvard U. where she directed short Dexter T. and edited doc. Light Coming Through: a Portrait of Maud Morgan.
PICTURES: Old Enough, Permanent Record, Vital Signs, He Said/She Said (co-dir.).
TELEVISION: *Co-dir.*: A Community of Praise (an episode of PBS series Middletown, 1982).

SILVER, RAPHAEL D.
Producer. b. Cleveland, OH, 1930. e. Harvard Coll. and Harvard Graduate Sch. of Business Adm. Is pres. of Middex Devel. Corp. 1973 formed Midwest Film Productions to produce Hester Street, written and directed by Joan Micklin Silver. Also distributed film independently. Also produced

Between the Lines. Exec. prod. of Crossing Delancey. Directed On the Yard and a Walk on the Moon. Currently pres. Silverfilm Prods. Inc.

SILVER, RON
Actor, Director. b. New York, NY, July 2, 1946. e. U. of Buffalo, St. John's U., Taiwan, M.A. Trained for stage at Herbert Berghof Studios and Actors Studio. N.Y. stage debut in Kasper and Public Insult, 1971. Elected pres. of Actors Equity Assn., 1991.
THEATER: El Grande de Coca Cola, Lotta, More Than You Deserve, Angel City (Mark Taper, LA), Hurlyburly, Social Security, Hunting Cockroaches, Speed-the-Plow (Tony & Drama Desk Award), Gorilla (Chicago, Jefferson Award nom.; N.YU. & L.A., Dramalogue Award), Friends, And, Broken Glass.
PICTURES: Tunnelvision, Welcome to L.A., Semi-Tough, Silent Rage, Best Friends, The Entity, Lovesick, Silkwood, Garbo Talks, Oh God! You Devil, Goodbye People, Eat and Run, Enemies A Love Story, Blue Steel, Reversal of Fortune, Mr. Saturday Night, Married to It, Timecop, Danger Zone, Deadly Takeover, Girl 6, The Arrival.
TELEVISION: Series: Mac Davis Show, Rhoda, Dear Detective, The Stockard Channing Show, Baker's Dozen, Chicago Hope. Movies: The Return of the World's Greatest Detective, Murder at the Mardi Gras, Betrayal, Word of Honor, Billionaire Boys Club, Fellow Traveler, Forgotten Prisoners: The Amnesty Files, Live Wire, Blindside, Lifepod (also dir.), Almost Golden: The Jessica Savitch Story, Billionaire Boys Club (Emmy nom.). Mini-Series: A Woman of Independent Means. Guest: Trying Times (Drive He Said), Hill Street Blues. Special: Loyalty and Betrayal: The Story of the American Mob (narrator).

SILVERMAN, FRED
Producer. b. New York, NY, Sept., 1937. e. Syracuse U., Ohio State U., master's in TV and theatre arts. Joined WGN-TV, indep. sta. in Chicago. Came to NY for exec. post at WPIX-TV, where stayed only six weeks. CBS-TV hired him as dir. of daytime programs. Named v.p., programs 1970. 1975 left CBS to become pres., ABC Entertainment. 1978, named pres. and CEO of NBC. Now Pres., Fred Silverman Company, Los Angeles.
TELEVISION: Prod./exec. prod.: Series: Perry Mason Movies, Matlock, In the Heat of the Night, Jake and the Fatman, Father Dowling Mysteries, Dick Van Dyke Mystery Movies. Movies: In the Heat of the Night: A Matter of Justice, Gramps, Diagnosis Murder, My Very Best Friend, Journey to Mars, Bonechillers & Bedtime Stories.

SILVERMAN, JONATHAN
Actor. b. Los Angeles, CA, Aug. 5, 1966. e. USC, NYU.
THEATER: NY: Brighton Beach Memoirs, Biloxi Blues, Broadway Bound. LA: The Illusion (Dramalogue Award), Pay or Play (Dramalogue Award), Sticks and Stones (Dramalogue Award).
PICTURES: Brighton Beach Memoirs (debut, 1986), Caddyshack II, Stealing Home, Weekend at Bernie's, Class Action, Breaking the Rules, Life in the Food Chain (Age Isn't Everything), Little Sister, Weekend at Bernie's II, Little Big League, Teresa's Tattoo, French Exit, At First Sight.
TELEVISION: Series: Gimme a Break, The Single Guy. Movies: Challenge of a Lifetime, Traveling Man, For Richer For Poorer, Broadway Bound, 12:01, Sketch Artist II: Hands That See.

SILVERSTEIN, ELLIOT
Director. b. Boston, MA, Aug. 3, 1927. e. Boston Coll., Yale U. Started career on television.
PICTURES: Belle Sommers (debut, 1962), Cat Ballou, The Happening, A Man Called Horse, Deadly Honeymoon, The Car (also co-prod.).
TELEVISION: Movies: Betrayed by Innocence, Night of Courage, Fight for Life, Rich Men Single Women. Series: Tales From the Crypt.

SILVERSTEIN, MAURICE
Executive. b. Syracuse, NY, March 1, 1912. Booker, salesman, MGM domestic dep't; International Dep't, MGM; supervisor Southeast Asia Hdqts. Singapore, MGM, 1938-42; OWI chief, film distribution for Europe, hdqts. London, during WWII; asst. sales supervisor, Far East, MGM; regional director, Latin America, 1947; liaison exec. to handle independent productions MGM, 1956; v.p., MGM International, 1957; first v.p., 1958; pres., MGM International, 1963; v.p., parent company, Metro-Goldwyn-Mayer Inc. in charge of foreign production, 1970; Silverstein Int'l Corp., pres.

SILVERSTONE, ALICIA
Actress. b. California, 1977. Made stage debut at Met Theater in Los Angeles in Carol's Eve. Starred in three Aerosmith videos including Cryin'. Formed own production co., First Kiss Prods.

PICTURES: The Crush (debut, 1993), The Babysitter, True Crime, Le Nouveau Monde, Hideaway, Clueless, Excess Baggage (also prod.).
TELEVISION: Movies: Torch Song, Shattered Dreams, The Cool and the Crazy. Guest: The Wonder Years.

SIMMONS, ANTHONY
Director, Writer. b. London, England. e. Grad. from the LSE with LL.B. Practiced briefly as a barrister before entering the industry as writer/director of documentaries, then commercials and feature films. Awards: Grand Prix (shorts), Venice, Grand Prix, Locarno; 2 Int. Emmys, various Intl. Awards for commercials. Publications: The Optimists of Nine Elms, A Little Space for Issie Brown.
PICTURES: Sunday By the Sea, Bow Bells, Time Without Pity (co- prod.), Four in the Morning, The Optimists, Black Joy, Little Sweetheart, Poison Candy.
TELEVISION: On Giant's Shoulders, Supergran and the Magic Ray, Harry Carpenter Never Said It Was Like This, Life After Death, Day After the Fair, Inspector Morse, Van de Valk, Inspector Frost, The Good Guys, 99-1.

SIMMONS, JEAN
Actress. b. London, England, Jan. 31, 1929. e. Aida Foster Sch., London. Screen debut 1944 at age 14. Voted one of top ten British money-making stars in M.P. Herald-Fame Poll, 1950-51. London stage: A Little Night Music. Awards: Cannes Film Festival Homage 1988, Italian Outstanding Film Achievement Award 1989, French Govt. Commandeur de L'Ordre des Arts des Lettres. 1990.
PICTURES: Give Us the Moon (debut, 1944), Mr. Emmanuel, Meet Sexton Blake, Kiss the Bride Goodbye, Sports Day, Caesar and Cleopatra, Way to the Stars, Great Expectations, Hungry Hill, Black Narcissus, Uncle Silas, The Women In the Hall, Hamlet (Acad. Award nom.), Blue Lagoon, Adam and Evelyne, Trio, So Long at the Fair, Cage of Gold, The Clouded Yellow, Androcles and the Lion (U.S. film debut, 1953), Angel Face, Young Bess, Affair with a Stranger, The Actress, The Robe, She Couldn't Say No, A Bullet Is Waiting, The Egyptian, Desiree, Footsteps in the Fog, Guys and Dolls, Hilda Crane, This Could be the Night, Until They Sail, The Big Country, Home Before Dark, This Earth Is Mine, Elmer Gantry, Spartacus, The Grass Is Greener, All the Way Home, Life at the Top, Mister Buddwing, Rough Night in Jericho, Divorce American Style, The Happy Ending (Acad. Award nom.), Say Hello to Yesterday, Mr. Sycamore, Dominique, Going Undercover, The Dawning, How to Make an American Quilt.
TELEVISION: Movies & Specials: Heidi, Beggarman Thief, The Easter Promise, The Home Front, Golden Gate, Jacqueline Susann's Valley of the Dolls 1981, A Small Killing, Inherit the Wind, Great Expectations, Sensibility and Sense, The Laker Girls, Perry Mason: The Case of Lost Love, People Like Us, December Flower. Mini-Series: The Dain Curse, The Thorn Birds (Emmy Award, 1983), North and South Book II. Series: Dark Shadows (1991).

SIMMONS, MATTY
Producer. b. Oct. 3. As bd. chmn., National Lampoon, Inc. produced National Lampoon Radio Hour, National Lampoon Lemmings, National Lampoon Show. Resigned from National Lampoon Inc. 1989. Now heads Matty Simmons Productions.
PICTURES: National Lampoon's Animal House, National Lampoon's Vacation, National Lampoon Goes to the Movies, National Lampoon's Class Reunion, National Lampoon's European Vacation, National Lampoon's Christmas Vacation (exec. prod.).
TELEVISION: National Lampoon's Disco Beavers, National Lampoon's Class of '86 (exec. prod.), Delta House.

SIMON, MELVIN
Executive. b. New York, NY, Oct. 21, 1926. e. City Coll.of New York, B.B.A., 1949; graduate work at Indiana U. Law Sch. Owner and operator, in partnership with two brothers, of over 110 shopping centers in U.S. 1978 formed Melvin Simon Productions, privately owned corp., to finance films. Dissolved Co. in 1983.
PICTURES: Exec. Prod.: Dominique, Love at First Bite, When a Stranger Calls, The Runner Stumbles, Scavenger Hunt, Cloud Dancer, The Stunt Man, My Bodyguard, Zorro the Gay Blade, Chu Chu and the Philly Flash, Porky's, Porky's II—The Next Day, Uforia, Wolf Lake, Porky's Revenge.

SIMON, NEIL
Playwright, Screenwriter, Producer. b. Bronx, NY, July 4, 1927. e. NYU. U.S. Army Air Force, 1945-46. Wrote comedy for radio with brother, Danny, (Robert Q. Lewis Show and for Goodman Ace), also TV scripts for Sid Caesar, Red Buttons, Jackie Gleason, Phil Silvers, Garry Moore, Tallulah Bankhead Show. With Danny contributed to B'way revues Catch a Star (1955), and New Faces of 1956. Adapted most of own plays to screen.
THEATER: Playwright: Come Blow Your Horn, Little Me, Barefoot in the Park, The Odd Couple (Tony Award, 1965), Sweet Charity, The Star Spangled Girl, Plaza Suite, Promises

Promises, Last of the Red Hot Lovers, The Gingerbread Lady, The Prisoner of Second Avenue, The Sunshine Boys, The Good Doctor, God's Favorite, California Suite, Chapter Two, They're Playing Our Song, I Ought to Be in Pictures, Fools, Little Me (revised version), Brighton Beach Memoirs, Biloxi Blues (Tony Award, 1985), The Odd Couple (female version), Broadway Bound, Rumors, Lost in Yonkers (Pulitzer Prize, Tony Award, 1991), Jake's Women, The Goodbye Girl (musical), Laughter on the 23rd Floor, London Suite (Off-B'way).
PICTURES: After the Fox, Barefoot in the Park (also assoc. prod.), The Odd Couple, The Out-of-Towners, Plaza Suite, Last of the Red Hot Lovers, The Heartbreak Kid, The Prisoner of Second Avenue, The Sunshine Boys, Murder by Death, The Goodbye Girl, The Cheap Detective, California Suite, Chapter Two, Seems Like Old Times, Only When I Laugh (also co-prod.), I Ought to Be in Pictures (also co-prod.), Max Dugan Returns (also co-prod.), The Lonely Guy (adaptation), The Slugger's Wife, Brighton Beach Memoirs, Biloxi Blues (also co-prod.), The Marrying Man, Lost in Yonkers.
TELEVISION: *Specials*: The Trouble With People, Plaza Suite. *Movie*: Broadway Bound, Jake's Women.

SIMON, PAUL
Singer, Composer, Actor. b. Newark, NJ, Oct. 13, 1941. e. Queens Coll., BA; postgrad. Brooklyn Law Sch. Teamed with Art Garfunkel in 1964, writing and performing own songs; they parted in 1970. Reunited for concert in New York, 1982, which was televised on HBO. Songs: With Garfunkel incl.: Mrs. Robinson (Grammy Award), The Boxer, Bridge Over Troubled Water (Grammy Award).
PICTURES: The Graduate (songs), Annie Hall (actor), One Trick Pony (s.p., actor, composer)
TELEVISION: *Specials*: The Fred Astaire Show, The Paul Simon Special (Emmy Award), Home Box Office Presents Paul Simon, Graceland: The African Concert, Mother Goose Rock 'n' Rhyme, Paul Simon's Concert in the Park. *Guest*: Sesame Street.
ALBUMS: with Garfunkel: Wednesday Morning 3 a.m., Sounds of Silence, Parsley, Sage, Rosemary and Thyme, The Graduate (Grammy Award), Bookends, Bridge Over Troubled Water (Grammy Award), Simon & Garfunkel's Greatest Hits, Concert in the Park. *Solo*: Paul Simon, There Goes Rhymin' Simon, Live Rhymin', Still Crazy After All These Years (Grammy Award), Greatest Hits, One Trick Pony, Hearts and Bones, Graceland (Grammy Award), Negotiations and Love Songs, The Rhythm of the Saints, Paul Simon's Concert in the Park.

SIMON, SIMONE
Actress. b. April 23, 1911, Marseilles, France. Played in many films in Europe, among them Les Beaux Jours, La Bete Humaine, and Lac aux Dames. On stage in Toi C'est Moi, and others.
PICTURES: Girl's Domitory (U.S. debut, 1936), Ladies in Love, Seventh Heaven, All That Money Can Buy, Cat People, Tahiti Honey, Johnny Doesn't Live Here Any More, The Curse of the Cat People, Mademoiselle Fifi, Petrus, Temptation Harbor, La Ronde, Olivia (Pit of Loneliness), Le Plaisir (House of Pleasure), Double Destin, The Extra Day, La Femme en Bleu.

SIMPSON, DON
Producer. b. Anchorage, AL, Oct. 29, 1945. e. U. of Oregon, Phi Beta Kappa. Began career in industry as acct. exec. with Jack Woodel Agency, San Francisco, where supervised mktg. of Warner Bros. films. Recruited by WB in 1971 as mktg. exec. specializing in youth market; oversaw Woodstock, A Clockwork Orange, Billy Jack, etc. Co-writer on low-budget films, Aloha, Bobby and Rose and Cannonball. Joined Paramount as prod. exec. 1975; promoted 1977 to v.p., prod. Named sr. v.p. of prod., 1980; pres. of worldwide prod., 1981. Formed Don Simpson/Jerry Bruckheimer Prods. 1983, entering into exclusive deal with Paramount to develop and produce for m.p. and TV divisions. Company moved to Walt Disney in early 1990's.
PICTURES: *Co-writer*: Aloha Bobby and Rose, Cannonball. *Producer*: Flashdance, Thief of Hearts, Beverly Hills Cop, Top Gun, Beverly Hills Cop II, Days of Thunder, The Ref, Bad Boys, Dangerous Minds.
(d. January 19, 1996)

SIMPSON, GARRY
Producer, Director, Executive. b. Camden, MI, Feb. 16, 1914. e. Stanford U. Major shows with NBC-TV: Jimmy Durante Show, Armstrong Circle Theatre, Campbell Soundstage, Comedy Hour, Ford Festival, Chevrolet Tele-Theater, Ed Wynn Show, The World of Mr. Sweeney, Philco TV Playhouse, Wide Wide World, Ballet Theatre. Dir. of programming, Vermont State PBS Network and writer-prod. of documentary films. Awards: Peabody, NY Film & TV Fest., Chicago Film Fest., & 3 Emmys.

SIMPSON, O.J.
Actor. b. San Francisco, CA, July 9, 1947. r.n. Orenthal James Simpson. e. U. of Southern California. Was star collegiate and professional football player and winner of Heisman Trophy. Began sportscasting in 1969.
PICTURES: The Klansman (debut, 1974), The Towering Inferno, Killer Force, The Cassandra Crossing, Capricorn One, Firepower, Hambone & Hillie, The Naked Gun: From the Files of Police Squad, The Naked Gun 2 1/2: The Smell of Fear, Naked Gun 33 1/3: The Final Insult.
TELEVISION: *Mini-Series*: Roots. *Movies*: A Killing Affair, Goldie and the Boxer (also exec. prod.), Detour to Terror (also exec. prod.), Goldie and the Boxer Go to Hollywood (also exec. prod.), Cocaine and Blue Eyes (also exec. prod.), Student Exchange. Prod.: High Five (pilot), Superbowl Saturday Night (host & co-prod.). *Series*: First and Ten (HBO), NFL Live (co-host).

SIMS, JOAN
Actress. b. Laindon, England, May 9, 1930. e. Trained at RADA. Early career in repertory and West End Theatre.
PICTURES: Dry Rot, Off the Record, No Time for Tears, Just My Luck, The Naked Truth, The Captain's Table, Passport to Shame, Emergency Ward 10, Most of the Carry On' films, Doctor in Love, Watch Your Stern, Twice Round the Daffodils, The Iron Maiden, Nurse on Wheels, Doctor in Clover, Doctor in Trouble, The Garnett Saga, Not Now Darling, Don't Just Lie There Say Something, Love Among the Ruins, One of Our Dinosaurs Is Missing, Till Death Us Do Part, The Way of the World, Deceptions, The Fool, My Good Friend, As Time Goes By, The Canterville Ghost.
TELEVISION: Over 100 shows incl. Stanley Baxter Show, Dick Emery Show, Carry on Shows, Love Among the Ruins, Born and Bred, Worzel Gummidge, Ladykillers, Crown Court, Cockles, Fairly Secret Army, Tickle on the Tum, Miss Marple: A Murder Is Announced, Hay Fever, In Loving Memory, Drummonds, Farrington of the F.O., Dr. Who, On the Up (3 series), Boys From the Bush, Simon & the Witch, Children's TV, Boys From the Bush, Tender Loving Care, Canterville Ghost, My Good Friend, Smokescreen, As Time Goes By, Just William, Henrietta Wainthrop Investigates.

SINATRA, FRANK
Actor, Singer. b. Hoboken, NJ, Dec. 12, 1915. Sportswriter; then singer on radio various NY stations; joined Harry James orchestra, later Tommy Dorsey. Children: singer-actress Nancy Sinatra, singer-conductor Frank Sinatra Jr., producer Tina Sinatra. On screen as a band vocalist in Las Vegas Nights, Ship Ahoy, Reveille with Beverly. Special Academy Award 1945 for acting in The House I Live In, short subject on tolerance. Received Jean Hersholt Humanitarian Award, 1971.
PICTURES: Las Vegas Nights (debut, 1941), Ship Ahoy, Reveille With Beverly, Higher and Higher (acting debut, 1943), Step Lively, Anchors Aweigh, Till the Clouds Roll By, It Happened in Brooklyn, The Miracle of the Bells, The Kissing Bandit, Take Me Out to the Ball Game, On the Town, Double Dynamite, Meet Danny Wilson, From Here to Eternity (Academy Award, best supporting actor, 1953), Suddenly, Young at Heart, Not as a Stranger, The Tender Trap, Guys and Dolls, The Man With the Golden Arm, Meet Me in Las Vegas (cameo), Johnny Concho (also prod.), High Society, Around the World in 80 Days, The Pride and the Passion, The Joker Is Wild, Pal Joey, Kings Go Forth, Some Came Running, A Hole in the Head, Never So Few, Can-Can, Ocean's Eleven, Pepe (cameo), The Devil at 4 O'Clock, Sergeants 3 (also prod.), The Road to Hong Kong (cameo), The Manchurian Candidate, Come Blow Your Horn, The List of Adrian Messenger, 4 for Texas, Robin and the 7 Hoods (also prod.), None But the Brave (also dir., prod.), Von Ryan's Express, Marriage on the Rocks, Cast a Giant Shadow, The Oscar (cameo), Assault on a Queen, The Naked Runner, Tony Rome, The Detective, Lady in Cement, Dirty Dingus Magee, That's Entertainment!, The First Deadly Sin (also exec. prod.), Cannonball Run II (cameo), Listen Up: The Lives of Quincy Jones.
TELEVISION: *Series*: The Frank Sinatra Show (1950-52; 1957-58); numerous specials, and guest appearances, incl. Club Oasis, Anything Goes (1954), Hollywood Palace, Our Town (1955), Frank Sinatra: A Man and His Music (Emmy Award, 1965), Francis Albert Sinatra Does His Thing, Ol' Blue Eyes Is Back, Magnum P.I., Frank Liza & Sammy: The Ultimate Event, Sinatra: Concert for the Americas. *Movies*: Contract on Cherry Street, Young at Heart.

SINBAD
Actor. r.n. David Adkins. b. Benton Harbor, MI, Nov. 10, 1956. e. Univ. of Denver. Served in Air Force before becoming stand-up comic. Career was subsquently launched by appearances on tv series Star Search.
PICTURES: Necessary Roughness (debut, 1991), Coneheads, The Meteor Man, Houseguest, First Kid (also co-exec. prod.), Jingle All the Way, Homeward Bound II: Lost in San Francisco, First Kid, Jingle All the Way.
TELEVISION: *Series*: The Redd Foxx Show, A Different World, It's Showtime at the Apollo (host), The Sinbad Show (also exec. prod.). *Specials*: Sinbad: Brain Damaged, Afros and Bellbottoms, Take No Prisoners, Sinbad and Friends All the Way Live... Almost (also writer), Aliens for Breakfast. *Guest*: The Cosby Show, Saturday Night Live.

SINCLAIR, MADGE
Actress. b. Kingston, Jamaica, April 28, 1938. e. Shortwood Women's College. Worked in Jamaica as a teacher and in the insurance business before moving to NY. Chairwoman, Madge Walters Sinclair Inc., Caribbean Child Life Foundation. Awards: NAACP Image Award, 1981 and 1983, best actress in dramatic series, Trapper John M.D.; Drama-Logue Critics Award, 1986, Boseman & Lena; Mother of the Year Award, 1984. L.A. area Emmy Award, Look Away. Member: bd. of dir., Lost Angeles Theatre Center.
THEATER: Kumaliza (NYSF, debut, 1969), Iphigenia (NYSF, NY and with Young Vic, London), Mod Donna, Ti-Jean and His Brothers, Blood, Division Street (Mark Taper Forum), Boesman & Lena (LA Theatre Center), Tartuffe (L.A. Theatre Center), Stars in the Morning (LATC), Piano (LATC), Jacques and His Master (LATC), Trinity (New Federal Theatre).
PICTURES: Conrack (debut, 1974), Cornbread Earl & Me, Leadbelly, I Will I Will... For Now, Convoy, Uncle Joe Shannon, Star Trek IV: The Voyage Home, Coming to America, The Lion King (voice).
TELEVISION: Series: Grandpa Goes to Washington, Trapper John M.D., O'Hara, Gabriel's Fire (Emmy Award, 1991; revamped as Pros & Cons), Me and the Boys. Guest: Madigan, Medical Center, The Waltons, Joe Forester, Doctor's Hospital, Executive Suite, Medical Story, Serpico, The White Shadow, All in the Family, Homeroom, Midnight Caller, Roseanne. Mini-Series: Roots, The Orchid House (Britain), Queen. Movies: I Love, You, Goodbye, One in a Million: The Ron LeFlore Story, I Know Why the Caged Bird Sings, High Ice, Jimmy B and Andre, Guyana Tragedy: The Story of Jim Jones, Victims, Look Away: The Emancipation of Mary Todd Lincoln, Divided We Stand, Jonathan: The Boy Nobody Wanted, The Man With 3 Wives. Special: A Century of Women.

SINDEN, DONALD
Actor. b. Plymouth, England, Oct. 9, 1923. Stage debut 1942 in fit-up shows; London stage includes There's a Girl in My Soup, The Relapse, Not Now Darling, King Lear, Othello, Present Laughter, Uncle Vanya, The School for Scandal, Two Into One, The Scarlet Pimpernel, Oscar Wilde, Major Barbara, Out of Order, Venus Observed, She Stoops to Conquer, Hamlet, That Good Night. B'way: London Assurance, Habeas Corpus. TV debut 1948.
PICTURES: Portrait From Life (The Girl in the Painting; debut, 1948), The Cruel Sea, Mogambo, A Day to Remember, You Know What Sailors Are, Doctor in the House, The Beachcomber, Mad About Men, An Alligator Named Daisy, Black Tent, Eyewitness, Tiger in the Smoke, Doctor at Large, Rockets Galore (Mad Little Island), The Captain's Table, Operation Bullshine, Your Money or Your Wife, The Siege of Sydney Street, Twice Around the Daffodils, Mix Me a Person, Decline and Fall, Villain, Rentadick, The Island at the Top of the World, That Lucky Touch, The Children, The Canterville Ghost.
TELEVISION: Bullet in the Ballet, Road to Rome, Dinner With the Family, Odd Man In, Love from Italy, The Frog, The Glove, The Mystery of Edwin Drood, The Happy Ones, The Comedy of Errors, The Wars of the Roses, The Red House, Blackmail, A Bachelor Gray, Our Man at St. Marks (3 series), The Wind in the Tall Paper Chimney, A Woman Above Reproach, Call My Bluff, Relatively Speaking, Father Dear Father, The 19th Hole, Seven Days in the Life of Andrew Pelham (serial), The Assyrian Rejuvenator, The Organization (serial), The Confederacy of Wives, Tell It to the Chancellor, The Rivals, Two's Company (4 series), All's Well That Ends Well, Never the Twain (11 series), Cuts.

SINGER, LORI
Actress. b. Corpus Christi, TX, Nov. 6, 1962. Brother is actor Marc Singer; father was symphony conductor Jacques Singer. Concert cellist while in teens. Won starring role in TV series Fame (1981).
PICTURES: Footloose (debut, 1984), The Falcon and The Snowman, The Man with One Red Shoe, Trouble in Mind, Summer Heat, Made in U.S.A., Warlock, Equinox, Sunset Grill, Short Cuts, F.T.W.
TELEVISION: Series: Fame, VR5. Movies: Born Beautiful, Storm and Sorrow. Special: Sensibility and Sense.

SINGER, MARC
Actor. b. Vancouver, B.C., Canada, Jan. 29. Brother of actress Lori Singer. Son of symphony conductor Jacques Singer. Trained in summer stock and regional theatre.
PICTURES: Go Tell the Spartans, If You Could See What I Hear, The Beastmaster, Born to Race, A Man Called Sarge, Watchers II, Body Chemistry, Dead Space, In the Cold of the Night, Beastmaster 2, Sweet Justice, The Berlin Conspiracy, Alien Intruder, Beastmaster 3.
TELEVISION: Series: The Contender, V, Dallas. Mini-Series: 79 Park Avenue, Roots: The Next Generation. Movies: Things in Their Season, Journey from Darkness, Something for Joey, Never Con a Killer, Sergeant Matlovich vs. the U.S. Air Force,

The Two Worlds of Jennie Logan, For Ladies Only, Paper Dolls, V, Her Life as a Man, V—The Final Battle, Deadly Game, The Sea Wolf.

SINGLETON, JOHN
Director, Writer. b. Los Angeles, CA, Jan. 6, 1968. Entered USC's Filmic Writing Program, where he received a Robert Riskin Writing Award and two Jack Nicholson Writing Awards. With debut feature Boyz N the Hood (1991) he became the first African-American and youngest person ever to be nominated for an Academy Award for Best Director. Appeared in film Beverly Hills Cop III.
PICTURES: Director-Writer: Boyz N the Hood (Acad. Award noms. for dir. & s.p.), Poetic Justice (also co-prod.), Higher Learning (also co-prod.), Rosewood.

SINGLETON, PENNY
Actress. r.n. Dorothy McNulty. b. Philadelphia, PA, September 15, 1908. e. Columbia U. First Broadway success came as top comedienne in Good News., exec. pres. AGVA.
PICTURES: Outside of Paradise, Swing Your Lady, Men Are Such Fools, Boy Meets Girl, Mr. Chump, Mad Miss Manton, Garden of the Moon, Secrets of an Actress, Hard to Get, 28 films in Blondie series (from Blondie, 1938, to Blondie's Hero, 1950), Rocket Busters, Go West Young Lady, Footlight Glamor, Young Widow, The Best Man, Jetsons: The Movie (voice).
TELEVISION: Series: The Jetsons (voice).

SINISE, GARY
Actor, Director. b. 1955. Co-founder and artistic dir. of Chicago's Steppenwolf Theatre Company, 1974.
THEATER: NY: Balm in Gilead, True West, The Caretaker, The Grapes of Wrath. Chicago: Of Mice and Men, Getting Out. Director: True West (Obie Award), Orphans, Buried Child.
PICTURES: Miles From Home (dir. only), A Midnight Clear, Of Mice and Men (also dir., co-prod.), Jack the Bear, Forrest Gump (Acad. Award nom.), The Quick and the Dead, Apollo 13, Albino Alligator, Ransom.
TELEVISION: Mini-Series: The Stand. Movies: Family Secrets, My Name is Bill W, The Final Days, Truman (Golden Globe Award). Director: Crime Story, thirtysomething, China Beach.

SIODMAK, CURT
Director, Writer. b. Dresden, Germany, Aug. 10, 1902. e. U. of Zurich. Engineer, newspaper reporter, writer in Berlin; novelist, including F.P.1 Does Not Answer, adapt. 1932 for Ufa. Originals and screenplays in France and England including France (Le Bal), Transatlantic Tunnel, GB.
PICTURES: Writer: Her Jungle Love (co-story), The Invisible Man Returns, Black Friday, The Ape, Aloma of the South Sea (co-story), The Wolf Man, Invisible Agent, Frankenstein Meets the Wolf Man, I Walked With a Zombie, Son of Dracula (co-story), The Mantrap, House of Frankenstein (story), The Climax, Shady Lady, The Beast with Five Fingers, Berlin Express (story), Tarzan's Magic Fountain, Four Days Leave, Bride of the Gorilla (also dir.), The Magnetic Monster (also dir.), Curucu—Beast of the Amazon (also dir.), Love Slaves of the Amazon (also dir., prod.), Riders to the Stars, Creature with the Atom Brain, Earth vs. the Flying Saucers.

SIZEMORE, TOM
Actor. b. Detroit, MI. e. Wayne St. Univ., Temple Univ.Stage incl. The Land of the Astronauts in NYC and D.C.
PICTURES: Lock Up, Rude Awakening, Penn and Teller Get Killed, Born on the Fourth of July, Blue Steel, Flight of the Intruder, Guilty by Suspicion, Harley Davidson and the Marlboro Man, A Matter of Degrees, Passenger 57, Watch It, Heart and Souls, True Romance, Striking Distance, Wyatt Earp, Natural Born Killers, Devil in a Blue Dress, Strange Days, Heat.

SKASE, CHRISTOPHER
Executive. b. Australia, 1946. Began career as reporter for Fairfax publication, Australian Financial Review. In 1970s set up investment company with about $20,000. Revived Australian TV Seven network in Melbourne and then in U.S. bought Hal Roach Studios and TV based prod.-dist. Robert Halmi which he merged into Qintex Entertainment. Qintex Entertainment produced TV mini-series Lonesome Dove.

SKELTON, RED
Actor, Comedian. r.n. Richard Skelton. b. Vincennes, IN, July 18, 1913. Joined medicine show at age 10; later in show boat stock, minstrel shows, vaudeville, burlesque, circus. On radio from 1936. Best Comedian, Best Comedy Writing. Received ATAS Governor's Award in 1986. Composer of music, writer of short stories and painter. Received Gorgas Gold Medal, 1995.
PICTURES: Having Wonderful Time (debut, 1939), Flight Command, Lady Be Good, The People vs. Dr. Kildare, Dr. Kildare's Wedding Day, Whistling in the Dark, Whistling in Dixie, Ship Ahoy, Maisie Gets Her Man, Panama Hattie, Du Barry Was a Lady, Thousands Cheer, I Dood It, Whistling in

Brooklyn, Bathing Beauty, Ziegfeld Follies, Merton of the Movies, The Fuller Brush Man, A Southern Yankee, Neptune's Daughter, The Yellow Cab Man, Three Little Words, The Fuller Brush Girl (cameo), Duchess of Idaho (cameo), Watch the Birdie, Excuse My Dust, Texas Carnival, Lovely to Look At, The Clown, Half a Hero, The Great Diamond Robbery, Susan Slept Here (cameo), Around the World in 80 Days (cameo), Public Pigeon No. 1, Ocean's Eleven (cameo), Those Magnificent Men in Their Flying Machines.
TELEVISION: *Series*: The Red Skelton Show (1951-71; Emmy Awards as Best Comedian: 1951; as writer: 1961).

SKERRITT, TOM
Actor. b. Detroit, MI, Aug. 25, 1933. e. Wayne State U., UCLA. Model for Guess? jeans ads.
PICTURES: War Hunt (debut, 1962), One Man's Way, Those Calloways, M*A*S*H, Wild Rovers, Fuzz, Run Joe Run, Big Bad Mama, Thieves Like Us, The Devil's Rain, La Madonna, The Turning Point, Up in Smoke, Ice Castles, Alien, Savage Harvest, The Silence of the North, A Dangerous Summer (The Burning Man), Fighting Back, The Dead Zone, Top Gun, Opposing Force (Hell Camp), SpaceCamp, Wisdom, Maid to Order, The Big Town, Poltergeist III, Steel Magnolias, Big Man on Campus, Honor Bound, The Rookie, Wild Orchid II: Two Shades of Blue, Poison Ivy, Singles, A River Runs Through It, Knight Moves.
TELEVISION: *Series*: Ryan's Four, Cheers, Picket Fences (Emmy Award, 1993). *Movies*: The Bird Men, The Last Day, Maneaters Are Loose!, The Calendar Girl Murders, Miles to Go, Parent Trap II, A Touch of Scandal, Poker Alice, Moving Target, Nightmare at Bitter Creek, The Heist, Red King White Knight, The China Lake Murders, Child of the Night, In Sickness and in Health, Getting Up and Going Home. *Director*: A Question of Sex (Afterschool Special), Picket Fences (3 episodes).

SKLAR, MARTY
Executive. Pres., Walt Disney Imagineering.

SKOLIMOWSKI, JERZY
Director, Writer. b. Lodz, Poland, May 5, 1938. e. Warsaw U., State Superior Film Sch., Lodz, Poland. Scriptwriter for Wajda's Innocent Sorcerers (also actor), Polanski's Knife in the Water and Lomnicki's Poslizg. Author: Somewhere Close to Oneself, Somebody Got Drowned.
PICTURES: *Director-Writer*: Identification Marks—None (also actor, edit., art dir.), Walkover (also actor, edit.), Barrier, The Departure, Hands Up (also actor), Dialogue, The Adventures of Gerard, Deep End, King Queen Knave (dir. only), The Shout, Circle of Deceit (actor only), Moonlighting (also prod., actor), Success Is the Best Revenge, The Lightship, White Nights (actor), Big Shots (actor), Torrents of Spring (actor), 30 Door Key (also co-s.p., prod.), The Hollow Men (prod.).

SKYE, IONE
Actress. b. London, Eng., Sept. 4, 1971. r.n. Ione Skye Leitch. Daughter of folksinger Donovan (Leitch) and sister of actor Donovan Leitch. m. singer-actor Adam Horovitz. Raised in San Francisco, Connecticut, Los Angeles. Fashion photo of her in magazine led to audition for film River's Edge.
PICTURES: River's Edge (debut, 1987 as Ione Skye Leitch), Stranded, A Night in the Life of Jimmy Reardon, Say Anything..., The Rachel Papers, Mindwalk, The Color of Evening, Wayne's World, Gas Food Lodging, Samantha, Guncrazy, Four Rooms, Dream for an Insomniac.
TELEVISION: *Series*: Covington Cross. *Movies*: Napoleon and Josephine, Girls in Prison. *Specials*: It's Called the Sugar Plum, Nightmare Classics (Carmilla).

SLATER, CHRISTIAN
Actor. b. New York, NY, Aug. 18, 1969. Mother is NY casting dir. Mary Jo Slater; father Los Angeles stage actor Michael Hawkins. Made prof. debut at 9 in The Music Man starring Dick Van Dyke, natl. tour, then on B'way Also on B'way in Macbeth, A Christmas Carol, David Copperfield and Merlin. Off-B'way in Landscape of the Body, Between Daylight and Boonville, Somewhere's Better. Also summer theatre. Directed 1992 L.A. prod. of The Laughter Epidemic.
PICTURES: The Legend of Billie Jean (debut, 1985), Twisted, The Name of the Rose, Tucker: The Man and His Dream, Gleaming the Cube, Heathers, The Wizard, Tales from the Dark Side: The Movie, Beyond the Stars (Personal Choice), Young Guns II, Pump Up the Volume, Robin Hood: Prince of Thieves, Mobsters, Star Trek VI: The Undiscovered Country (cameo), Kuffs, FernGully... The Last Rainforest (voice), Where the Day Takes You, Untamed Heart, True Romance, Jimmy Hollywood, Interview With the Vampire, Murder in the First, Broken Arrow, Bed of Roses.
TELEVISION: *Soap operas*: One Life to Live, Ryan's Hope. *Specials*: Sherlock Holmes, Pardon Me for Living, The Haunted Mansion Mystery, Cry Wolf, The Edge (Professional Man). *Movies*: Living Proof: The Hank Williams Jr. Story, Desperate For Love.

SLATER, HELEN
Actress. b. New York, NY, Dec. 19, 1963. *Off-B'way*: Responsible Parties, Almost Romance.
PICTURES: Supergirl (debut, 1984), The Legend of Billie Jean, Ruthless People, The Secret of My Success, Sticky Fingers, Happy Together, City Slickers, A House in the Hills, Betrayal of the Dove, Lassie, The Steal.
TELEVISION: *Series*: Capital News. *Movies*: 12:01, Chantilly Lace, Parallel Lives.

SLATZER, ROBERT FRANKLIN
Writer, Director, Producer. b. Marion, OH, April 4, 1927. e. Ohio State U., UCLA, 1947. Radio news commentator sportscaster, wrote radio serials; adv. dir., Brush-Moore Newspapers; feature writer, Scripps-Howard Newspapers; adv. exec., The Columbus Dispatch; syn. columnist, NY Journal-American; wrote guest columns for Dorothy Kilgallen; author of western short stories and novels; wrote, dir., prod. industrial films, docs., sports specials and commercials; 1949-51, writer for Grand National Studios Prods, Monogram Pictures, Republic Studios, Eagle-Lion Films; 1951, publicist, Hope Enterprises; pub. dir., Paramount Pictures; 1952, personal mgr. to Marilyn Monroe, Ken Maynard, James Craig, Gail Russell and other stars; 1953, story editor and assoc. prod., Joe Palooka Productions; 1953-54, staff writer Universal Studios, RKO Radio Pictures, MGM, Columbia and Paramount; 1958, formed Robert F. Slatzer Productions; 1960, exec. in chg. of prod., Jaguar Pictures Corp.; 1963-65, pres., Slatzer Oil & Gas Co.; 1966-67, bd. dir., United Mining & Milling Corp.; 1970-74, exec., Columbia Pictures Corp.; 1974, resumed producing and financing features and television films; 1976, honored as Fellow, Mark Twain Inst.
AUTHOR: *Novels*: Desert Empire, Rose of the Range, Rio, Rawhide Range, The Cowboy and the Heiress, Daphne, Campaign Girl, Scarlet, The Dance Studio Hucksters, Born to be Wild, Single Room Furnished, The West is Still Wild, Gusher, The Young Wildcats. *Biographies*: The Life and Curious Death of Marilyn Monroe, The Life and Legend of Ken Maynard, Who Killed Thelma Todd?, The Duke of Thieves, Bing Crosby—The Hollow Man, Duke: The Life and Times of John Wayne, The Marilyn Files.
PICTURES: White Gold, The Obsessed, Mike and the Heiress, Under Texas Skies, They Came To Kill, Trail of the Mounties, Jungle Goddess, Montana Desperado, Pride of the Blue, Green Grass of Wyoming, The Naked Jungle, Warpaint, Broken Lance, Elephant Walk, South of Death Valley, The Big Gusher, Arctic Flight, The Hellcats, Bigfoot, John Wayne's No Substitute for Victory', Joniko-Eskimo Boy, Operation North Slope, Claws, Don't Go West, Mulefeathers, The Unfinished, Single Room Furnished, Viva Zapata, Inchon.
TELEVISION: The Great Outdoors, Adventures of White Arrow, Let's Go Boating, The Joe Palooka Story, Amos & Andy, I Am the Law, Files of Jeffrey Jones, Fireside Theatre, The Unser Story, Year of Opportunity, The Big Ones, Ken Maynard's West, Where are They Now?, The Groovy Seven, The Untouchables, The Detectives, Wild Wild West, Wagon Train, Playhouse 90, Highway Patrol, David Frost Special, Today Show, ABC News, 20/20, Inside Edition, The Reporters, Current Affair, The Geraldo Show, Hard Copy, Larry King Show, Marilyn and Me, The Marilyn Files.

SLAVIN, GEORGE
Writer. b. Newark, NJ, Mar. 2, 1916. e. Bucknell U., drama, Yale U. Has written over 300 TV episodes & pilots. WGA TV Award. Collected works at U. Wyoming. Received Stanford U, Maxwell Anderson Playwriting Award.
PICTURES: Intrigue, Woman on Pier 13, The Nevadan, Mystery Submarine, Peggy, Red Mountain, City of Bad Men, Weekend with Father, Thunder Bay, Rocket Man, Smoke Signal, Uranium Boom, Desert Sands, The Halliday Brand, Son of Robin Hood, Big House USA, Fighting Stallions.

SLOAN, JOHN R.
Producer. e. Merchiston Castle School, Edinburg, 1932-39; asst. dir. and prod. man Warners, London, Hollywood; 1939-46, Army.
PICTURES: Sea Devils, The End of the Affair, Port Afrique, Abandon Ship, The Safecracker, Beyond this Place, The Killers of Kilimanjaro, Johnny Nobody, The Reluctant Saint, The Running Man, The Last Command, To Sir With Love, Fragment of Fear, Dad's Army, Lord Jim, No Sex Please, We're British, The Odessa File, Force 10 From Navarone, The Children's Story.

SLOCOMBE, DOUGLAS
Cinematographer. b. England, Feb. 10, 1913. Former journalist. Filmed the invasion of Poland and Holland. Under contract to Ealing Studios 17 years.
PICTURES: Dead of Night, The Captive Heart, Hue and Cry, The Loves of Joanna Godden, It Always Rains on Sunday, Saraband for Dead Lovers, Kind Hearts and Coronets, Cage of Gold, The Lavender Hill Mob, Mandy, The Man in the White Suit, The Titfield Thunderbolt, Man in the Sky, Ludwig II,

Lease on Life, The Smallest Show on Earth, Tread Softly, Stranger, Circus of Horrors, The Young Ones, The Mark, The L-Shaped Room, Freud, The Servant (BAFTA Award), Guns at Batashi, A High Wind in Jamaica, The Blue Max, Promise Her Anything, The Vampire Killers, Fathom, Robbery, Boom, The Lion in Winter, The Italian Job, The Music Lovers, Murphy's War, The Buttercup Chain, Travels With My Aunt (Acad. Award nom.), Jesus Christ Superstar, The Great Gatsby, Rollerball, Hedda, The Sailor Who Fell From Grace With the Sea, Nasty Habits, Julia (Acad. Award nom.), Close Encounters of the Third Kind (co-photog.), Caravans, Lost and Found, The Lady Vanishes, Nijinsky, Raiders of the Lost Ark (Acad. Award nom.), The Pirates of Penzance, Never Say Never Again, Indiana Jones and the Temple of Doom, Water, Lady Jane, Indiana Jones and the Last Crusade.
TELEVISION: Movie: Love Among the Ruins.

SMART, JEAN
Actress. b. Seattle, WA, Sept. 13, 1951. e. Univ. of WA. Member of Oregon Shakespeare Fest, 1975-77; also with Hartford Stage Co., Pittsburgh Public Theatre Co., Intiman Theatre Co.
THEATER: *Regional*: Equus, Much Ado About Nothing, A Moon for the Misbegotten, Terra Nova, Cat's Play, Saint Joan, A History of the American Film, Last Summer at Bluefish Cove (LA Drama Critics Circle, Dramalogue & LA Drama Desk Awards), Mrs. California, Strange Snow. *NY*: Last Summer at Bluefish Cove, Piaf (B'way debut, 1981).
PICTURES: Flashpoint (debut, 1984), Protocol, Fire With Fire, Project X, Mistress, Homeward Bound: The Incredible Journey.
TELEVISION: *Series*: Reggie, Teachers Only, Designing Women, High Society. *Movies*: Single Bars Single Women, A Fight for Jenny, A Seduction in Travis County, A Stranger in Town (also co-prod.), The Yarn Princess, The Yearling, A Stranger in Town. *Specials*: Piaf, Maximum Security, Royal Match, A Palce at the Table.

SMITH, CHARLES MARTIN
Actor, Director. b. Los Angeles, CA, Oct. 30, 1953. e. California State U. Father is animation artist Frank Smith.
PICTURES: The Culpepper Cattle Company (debut, 1972), Fuzz, The Spikes Gang, American Graffiti, Pat Garrett and Billy the Kid, Rafferty and the Gold Dust Twins, No Deposit No Return, The Hazing, The Buddy Holly Story, More American Graffiti, Herbie Goes Bananas, Never Cry Wolf (also co-wrote narration), Starman, Trick or Treat (also dir.), The Untouchables, The Experts, The Hot Spot, Deep Cover, Fifty-Fifty (also dir.), I Love Trouble, Perfect Alibi, Speechless, He Ain't Heavy.
TELEVISION: *Series*: Speed Buggy (voice). *Guest*: The Brady Bunch, Monte Nash, Baretta, Streets of San Francisco, Petrocelli, The Rookies, Grizzly Adams, Twilight Zone, Ray Bradbury Theatre, Outer Limits, L.A. Law, Picket Fences, Northern Exposure, Tales From the Crypt. *Movies*: Go Ask Alice, Law of the Land, Cotton Candy, Boris and Natasha (also dir.), And the Band Played On, Roswell. *Special*: Partners. *Mini-Series*: Streets of Laredo.

SMITH, DAVID R.
Archivist. b. Pasadena, CA, Oct. 13, 1940. e. Pasadena City Coll., A.A., 1960; U. of California, Berkeley, B.A. 1962, MLS 1963. Writer of numerous historical articles. Worked as librarian at Library of Congress, 1963-65 and as reference librarian, UCLA 1965-70 before becoming archivist for The Walt Disney Co. 1970-present. Exec. dir., The Manuscript Society, 1980-; member, Society of CA Archivists, Intl. Animated Film Society (ASIFA), Fellow of the Manuscript Society, 1993. Received service award, ASIFA, and award of distinction, Manuscript Soc, 1983. Co-Author: The Ultimate Disney Trivia Book (1992), Book 2 (1994), Disney A to Z: The Official Encyclopedia (1996).

SMITH, HOWARD K.
News commentator. b. Ferriday, LA, May 12, 1914. e. Tulane U., 1936; Heidelberg U., Germany; Oxford U., Rhodes scholarship. United Press, London, 1939; United Press Bureau, Copenhagen; United Press, Berlin, 1940; joined CBS News, Berlin corr., 1941. Reported on occupied Europe from Switzerland to 1944; covered Nuremberg trials, 1946; ret. to U.S., moderator, commentator or reporter, CBS Reports, Face the Nation, Eyewitness to History, The Great Challenge, numerous news specials (Emmy Award, 1960 for The Population Explosion). Sunday night news analysis. CBS News Washington corr., 1957; chief corr. & mgr., Washington Bureau, 1961; joined, ABC News, Jan. 1962. News and comment, ABC news. Anchorman and commentator, ABC Evening News. Author: Last Train from Berlin, 1942, The State of Europe, 1949. Washington, D.C.—The Story of Our Nation's Capital, 1967.

SMITH, HY
Executive. b. New York, NY, June 3, 1934. e. Baruch Sch., CCNY, B.B.A. Joined Paramount Pictures 1967, foreign ad.-pub coordinator; 1969, joined United Artists as foreign ad.-pub mgr.; named intl. ad.-pub dir., 1970; named v.p., intl. adv.-pub. 1976; v.p. worldwide adv., publ. & promo., 1978; 1981, named first v.p., adv./pub./promo; 1982, joined Rastar Films as v.p., intl. project director for Annie; 1983, joined United Intl. Pictures as sr. v.p., adv/pub based in London. 1984, named sr. v.p., mktg. 1995, promoted to exec. v.p., mktg.

SMITH, JACLYN
Actress. b. Houston, TX, Oct. 26, 1947. Started acting while in high school and studied drama and psychology at Trinity U. in San Antonio. Appeared in many commercials as model.
PICTURES: The Adventurers, Bootleggers, Nightkill, Deja Vu.
TELEVISION: *Series*: Charlie's Angels, Christine Cromwell. *Guest*: McCloud, Get Christy Love, The Rookies. *Movies*: Probe (Switch), Charlie's Angels (pilot), Escape From Bogen County, The Users, Jacqueline Bouvier Kennedy, Rage of Angels, The Night They Saved Christmas, Sentimental Journey, Florence Nightingale, Rage of Angels: The Story Continues, Windmills of the Gods, The Bourne Identity, Settle the Score, Danielle Steel's Kaleidoscope, Lies Before Kisses, The Rape of Dr. Willis, In the Arms of a Killer, Nightmare in the Daylight, Love Can Be Murder, Cries Unheard: The Donna Yalich Story, Danielle Steel's Family Album.

SMITH, JAN
Exexcutive. Vice President, Disney Publishing & Mouseworks.

SMITH, JOSEPH P.
Executive. b. Brooklyn, NY, March 28, 1921. e. Columbia U. Started career Wall Street; joined RKO Radio Pictures, served in sales and managerial posts; exec. v.p., Lippert Productions, Hollywood; v.p., Telepictures, Inc.; formed and pres., Cinema-Vue Corp.; pres., Pathe Pictures, Inc., Pathe News, Inc.

SMITH, KURTWOOD
Actor. b. New Lisbon, WI, July 3, 1943. e. B.A. San Jose (1966), M.F.A. Stanford (1969). Starred in Oscar-nominated short 12:01 P.M.
THEATER: Plymouth Rock, The Price, Faces by Chekhov, Familiar Faces, Enemy of the People, The Debutante Ball (all in Calif.), The Lucky Spot (Williamston), Signature (Poughkeepsie), Hamlet, Taming of the Shrew, and over 20 other Shakespeare productions in CA.
PICTURES: Roadie (debut, 1980), Zoot Suit, Going Berserk, Staying Alive, Flashpoint, Robocop, Rambo III, True Believer, Dead Poets Society, Heart of Dixie, Quick Change, Oscar, Company Business, Star Trek VI: The Undiscovered Country, Shadows and Fog, The Crush, Heart and Souls, Fortress, Boxing Helena, Under Siege 2: Dark Territory, Last of the Dogmen, To Die For, Broken Arrow, A Time to Kill, Citizen Ruth, Precious.
TELEVISION: *Series*: The Renegades, The New Adventures of Beans Baxter, Big Wave Dave's. *Movies*: Murder in Texas, Missing Pieces, The Midnight Hour, International Airport, Deadly Messages, The Christmas Gift, Doorways, While Justice Sleeps. *Mini-Series*: North and South Book II, The Nightmare Years (Ace Award nom.). *Guest*: Stir Crazy, Stingray, Newhart, 21 Jump Street, It's Garry Shandling's Show, The Famous Teddy Z, Picket Fences.

SMITH, LANE
Actor. b. Memphis, TN, Apr. 29.
THEATER: *NY*: Visions of Kerouac, Brechtesgarten, Glengarry Glen Ross (Drama Desk Award).
PICTURES: Network, Honeysuckle Rose, Prince of the City, Frances, Purple Hearts, Red Dawn, Places in the Heart, Weeds, Prison, Race for Glory, Air America, My Cousin Vinny, The Mighty Ducks, The Distinguished Gentleman, Son-in-Law, The Scout.
TELEVISION: *Series*: V, Kay O'Brien, Good Sports, Good and Evil. *Mini-Series*: Chiefs. *Movies*: A Death in Canaan, Crash, The Solitary Man, Disaster on the Coastliner, City in Fear, Gideon's Trumpet, A Rumor of War, The Georgia Peaches, Mark I Love You, Dark Night of the Scarecrow, Prime Suspect, Thou Shalt Not Kill, Special Bulletin, Something About Amelia, Dress Gray, The Final Days, False Arrest, Duplicates. *Specials*: Displaced Person, Member of the Wedding.

SMITH, DAME MAGGIE
D.B.E. C.B.E. Actress. b. Ilford, England, Dec. 28, 1934. Early career Oxford Playhouse. With the Old Vic 1959-60. Also with Stratford Ontario Shakespeare Fest. 1975-78, & 1980. Received C.B.E. 1970; D.B.E., 1990.
THEATER: Twelfth Night (debut, 1952), Cakes and Ale, New Faces of 1956 (NY debut, as comedienne), Share My Lettuce, The Stepmother, What Every Woman Knows, Rhinoceros, The Rehearsal, The Private Ear, The Public Eye, Mary Mary, The Recruiting Officer, Othello, The Master Builder, Hay Fever, Much Ado About Nothing, Black Comedy, Miss Julie, Trelawney of the Wells, The Beaux Stratagem, The Three Sisters, Hedda Gabler, Design for Living (L.A.), Private Lives (London & NY), Slap, Peter Pan, As You Like It, Macbeth,

Night and Day (London & NY), Virginia, Way of the World, Lettice and Lovage (London & NY, Tony Award), The Importance of Being Earnest, Three Tall Women.
PICTURES: Nowhere to Go (debut, 1958), Go to Blazes, The V.I.P.s, The Pumpkin Eater, Young Cassidy, Othello, The Honey Pot, Hot Millions, The Prime of Miss Jean Brodie (Academy Award, BAFTA Award, 1969), Oh! What a Lovely War, Travels With My Aunt, Love and Pain and the Whole Damn Thing, Murder by Death, Death on the Nile, California Suite (Academy Award, best supporting actress, 1978), Clash of the Titans, Quartet, Evil Under the Sun, The Missionary, Better Late Than Never, A Private Function (BAFTA Award, 1985), Lily in Love, A Room with a View, The Lonely Passion of Judith Hearne, Romeo-Juliet (voice), Hook, Sister Act, The Secret Garden, Sister Act 2: Back in the Habit, Richard III.
TELEVISION: Much Ado About Nothing, Man and Superman, On Approval, Home and Beauty, Mrs. Silly, Bed Among the Lentils, Memento Mori, Suddenly Last Summer.

SMITH, ROGER
Actor, Producer. b. South Gate, CA, Dec. 18, 1932. m. actress-performer Ann Margret. e. U. of Arizona. Started career at age 7, one of the Meglin Kiddies, appearing at the Mayan Theater, Wilshire, Ebell. Sings, composes, American folk songs. Producer: Ann-Margret cabaret and theater shows.
PICTURES: No Time to Be Young, Crash Landing, Operation Madball, Man of a Thousand Faces, Never Steal Anything Small, Auntie Mame, Rogues Gallery.
TELEVISION: The Horace Heidt Show, Ted Mack Original Amateur Hour, 77 Sunset Strip (series), writer, ABC-TV.

SMITH, WILL
Actor, Singer. b. Philadelphia, PA, Sept. 25, 1968. Teamed with musician Jeff Townes as rap duo D.J. Jazzy Jeff & the Fresh Prince. Albums: Rock the House, He's the DJ I'm the Rapper, And in This Corner, Homebase. Recipient of 2 Grammy Awards.
PICTURES: Where the Day Takes You (debut, 1992), Made in America, Six Degress of Separation, Bad Boys, Independence Day, Men in Black.
TELEVISION: Series: Fresh Prince of Bel Air (also co-exec. prod.).

SMITH, WILLIAM
Actor. b. Columbia, MO, May 24, 1932. e. Syracuse, U., BA; UCLA, MA.
PICTURES: Darker Than Amber, C.C. and Company, The Losers, Run, Angel, Run, Blood and Guts, Seven, Fast Company, No Knife, Twilight's Last Gleaming, The Frisco Kid, Any Which Way You Can, Rumble Fish, Red Dawn, Eye of the Tiger, Commando Squad, Moon in Scorpio, Hell Comes to Frogtown, Maniac Cop, Red Nights, Nam, B.O.R.N., Action U.S.A., Deadly Breed, Evil Altar, Jungle Assault, L.A. Vice, Slow Burn, Terror in Beverly Hills, Hell on the Battleground, Forgotten Heroes, Instant Karma, Empire of Ash, Emperor of the Bronx.
TELEVISION: Mini-Series: Rich Man Poor Man. Series: Laredo, Rich Man Poor Man: Book II. Series: Laredo, Rich Man Poor Man: Book II, Hawaii 5-0, Wildside. Movies: The Over-the-Hill Gang, Crowhaven Farm, The Rockford Files (pilot), The Sex Symbol, Death Among Friends, Manhunter, The Rebels, Wild Times, The Jerk Too.

SMITROVICH, BILL
Actor. b. Bridgeport, CT, May 16, 1947. e. Univ. of Bridgeport, Smith Col. Studied acting at Actors and Directors Lab.
THEATER: B'way: The American Clock. Off-B'way: Never Say Die, Frankie and Johnny in the Claire de Lune, Seks. Regional: Requeim for a Heavyweight, Food from Trash, Of Mice and Men, The Love Suicide at Schofield Barracks.
PICTURES: A Little Sex, Without a Trace, Splash, Maria's Lovers, Key Exchange, Silver Bullet, Band of the Hand, Manhunter, A Killing Affair, Her Alibi, Renegades, Crazy People, Bodily Harm.
TELEVISION: Series: Crime Story, Life Goes On. Guest: Miami Vice. Movies: Born Beautiful, Muggable Mary, Gregory K, Labor of Love: The Arlette Schweitzer Story, Children of the Dark, Texas Justice.

SMITS, JIMMY
Actor. b. New York, NY, July 9, 1955. e. Brooklyn Coll., B.A.; Cornell U., M.F.A. Worked as community organizer before acting with NY Shakespeare Fest. Public Theater.
THEATER: Hamlet (NY Shakespeare Fest., 1983), Little Victories, Buck, The Ballad of Soapy Smith, Death and the Maiden.
PICTURES: Running Scared (debut, 1986), The Believers, Old Gringo, Vital Signs, Fires Within, Switch, Gross Misconduct, My Family/Mi Familia.
TELEVISION: Series: L.A. Law (Emmy Award, 1990), NYPD Blue (Golden Globe, 1996). Pilot: Miami Vice. Movies: Rockabye, The Highwayman, Dangerous Affection, Glitz, The Broken Cord, The Tommyknockers, The Cisco Kid, Solomon

and Sheba, The Last Word. Specials: The Other Side of the Border (narrator), Happily Ever After Fairy Tales: Cinderella, Hispanic Americans: The New Frontier (host).

SMOTHERS BROTHERS
Comedians, Singers.
SMOTHERS, DICK: b. New York, NY, Nov. 20, 1939. e. San Jose State College. Films: The Silver Bears (debut, 1978), Casino.
SMOTHERS, TOM: b. New York, NY, Feb. 2, 1937. e. San Jose State College. In films Get to Know Your Rabbit, The Silver Bears, There Goes the Bride, Serial, Pandemonium.
Began career as coffeehouse folk singers with a bit of comic banter mixed in. After success at some of hipper West Coast clubs, appeared on Jack Paar's Tonight Show, The Jack Benny Show and as regulars on Steve Allen's show, 1961. 1962-65 had a series of popular albums. After starring in a situation comedy show, they hosted their own variety program. On B'way in musical I Love My Wife. Both appeared in film Speed Zone.
TELEVISION: Series: The Steve Allen Show (1961), The Smothers Brothers Show (1965-66), The Smothers Brothers Comedy Hour (1967-69), The Smothers Brothers Show (1970), The Smothers Brothers Show (1975), Fitz and Bones, The Smothers Brothers Comedy Hour. Specials: The Smothers Brothers Reunion.

SNELL, PETER R. E.
Producer. b. Nov. 17, 1941. Entered industry 1967. Appt. head of prod. and man. dir. British Lion 1973. Joined Robert Stigwood group 1975. Returned to indep. prod., 1978; Hennessy. Appt. chief exec., Britannic Film & Television Ltd. 1985, purchased British Lion Film Prods., Ltd. from Thorn/EMI 1986-87. 1988: chmn. and chief executive British Lion.
PICTURES: Prod.: Winters Tale, Some May Live, A Month in the Country, Carnaby 68, Subterfuge, Julius Caesar, Goodbye Gemini, Antony and Cleopatra, The Wicker Man, Hennessy, Bear Island, Mother Lode, Lady Jane, Turtle Diary, A Prayer for the Dying.
TELEVISION: Exec. Prod.: A Man For All Seasons, Tears in the Rain, Treasure Island, The Crucifer of Blood. Prod.: Death Train, Nightwatch.

SNIDER, STACEY
Exeutive. President of production, TriStar Pictures (A Sony Pictures Entertainment Co., Inc.).

SNIPES, WESLEY
Actor. b. Bronx, NY, July 31, 1962. e. SUNY/Purchase. Performed with puppet theatre group called Struttin Street Stuff before landing NY stage work. Appeared in Michael Jackson video Bad.
PICTURES: Wildcats (debut, 1986), Streets of Gold, Critical Condition, Major League, Mo' Better Blues, King of New York, New Jack City, Jungle Fever, White Men Can't Jump, The Waterdance, Passenger 57, Boiling Point, Rising Sun, Demolition Man, Sugar Hill, Drop Zone, To Wong Foo—Thanks for Everything—Julie Newmar, Money Train, Waiting to Exhale, The Fan.
TELEVISION: Series: H.E.L.P. Special: Vietnam War Stories (ACE Award, 1989). Guest: Miami Vice.
THEATER: B'way: The Boys of Winter, Death and the King's Horsemen, Execution of Justice.

SNODGRESS, CARRIE
Actress. b. Chicago, IL, Oct 27, 1945. e. Northern Illinois U. and M.A. degree from the Goodman Theatre. Plays include All Way Home, Oh What a Lovely War, Caesar and Cleopatra and Tartuffe (Sarah Siddons Award, 1966), The Price, Vanities, The Curse of the Starving Class.
PICTURES: Rabbit Run (debut, 1970), Diary of a Mad Housewife (Acad. Award nom.), The Fury, The Attic, Homework, Trick or Treats, A Night in Heaven, Pale Rider, Rainy Day Friends, Murphy's Law, Blueberry Hill, The Chill Factor, Nowhere to Run, Across the Tracks, The Ballad of Little Jo, 8 Seconds, Blue Sky, White Man's Burden.
TELEVISION: Movies: The Whole World Is Watching, Silent Night Lonely Night, The Impatient Heart, Love's Dark Ride, Fast Friends, The Solitary Man, Nadia, The Rose and the Jackal, Woman With a Past, Rise & Walk: The Dennis Byrd Story. Guest: The Outsider, The Virginian, Judd for the Defense, Medical Center, Marcus Welby, M.D.

SNOW, MARK
Composer. b. Brooklyn, NY, 1946. e. Juilliard School of Music, 1968. As co-founder and member of New York Rock 'n' Roll Ensemble, appeared in the Boston Pops, at Carnegie Hall concerts and on the college circuit in the 1960s and 1970s.
PICTURES: Skateboard, Something Short of Paradise, High Risk, Jake Speed, Born to Be Wild.
TELEVISION: Series: The Rookies, Starsky and Hutch, The Gemini Man, Family, The San Pedro Beach Bums, The Love Boat, The Next Step Beyond, Vega$, Hart to Hart, When the

Whistle Blows, Dynasty, Falcon Crest, Strike Force, Cagney and Lacey, T.J. Hooker, The Family Tree, Lottery!, Double Trouble, Crazy Like a Fox, Hometown, The X-Files. *Mini-series*: Blood and Orchids. *Movies*: The Boy in the Plastic Bubble, Overboard, The Return of the Mod Squad, Angel City, Games Mother Never Taught You, John Steinbeck's Winter of Our Discontent, Packin' It In, I Married a Centerfold, Something About Amelia, Challenge of a Lifetime, California Girls, I Dream of Jeannie: Fifteen Years Later, Not My Kid, The Lady From Yesterday, Beverly Hills Cowgirl Blues, Acceptable Risks, News at Eleven, The Girl Who Spelled Freedom (Emmy nom.), Murder By the Book, A Hobo's Christmas, The Father Clements Story, Still Crazy Like a Fox, Cracked Up, Roman Holiday, Pals, Murder Ordained, Louis L'Amour's Down the Long Hills, The Saint, The Return of Ben Casey, Bluegrass, Alone in the Neon Jungle, Those She Left Behind, Stuck With Each Other, Settle the Score, Archie: To Riverdale and Back Again, Child of the Night, Dead Reckoning, Follow Your Heart, The Girl Who Came Between Them, The Little Kidnappers, Miracle Landing, When He's Not a Stranger, Opposites Attract, Crash: The Mystery of Flight 1501, In the Line of Duty: The Marla Hanson Story, A Woman Scorned: The Betty Broderick Story, Highway Heartbreaker, Deliver Them From Evil: The Taking of Alta View, An American Story, Telling Secrets, The Man With 3 Wives, Born Too Soon, In the Line of Duty: Ambush in Waco, Precious Victims, Scattered Dreams: The Kathryn Messenger Story, In the Line of Duty: The Price of Vengeance, Murder Between Friends, Moment of Truth: Cradle of Conspiracy, Substitute Wife, Down Out and Dangerous. *Specials*: Day-to-Day Affairs, Vietnam War Story.

SNYDER, BRUCE M.
Executive. b. New York, NY, July 1, 1946. e. Queens Coll. Began entertainment career with Paramount Pictures as a booker in San Francisco, 1968-69. Paramount sales, NY 1969-76. Became eastern div. mgr., 20th century Fox, 1976-80. New York sales mgr., American Cinema Releasing, 1980-82. Eastern div. mgr., Embassy Pictures, 1982-83. Eastern div. mgr., TriStar Pictures, 1984-85. General sales mgr., 20th Century Fox, 1985-89. Pres., domestic distribution, 20th Century Fox, 1989-present.

SNYDER, TOM
Newscaster, Host. b. Milwaukee, WI, May 12, 1936. e. Marquette U. First job in news dept. of WRIT, Milwaukee. Subsequently with WSAV-TV, Savannah; WAII-TV, Atlanta; KTLA-TV, Los Angeles; and KYW-TV, Philadelphia, before moving to KNBC in L.A. in 1970 as anchorman for weeknight newscast. Named host of NBC-TV's Tomorrow program in 1973 (Emmy Award), moved to NY in 1974, as anchorman of one-hour segment of NewsCenter 4. 1975, inaugurated the NBC News Update, one-minute weeknight prime time news spot. Host for Tomorrow talk show, Tom Snyder Show (ABC Radio), The Late Late Show With Tom Snyder.

SOADY, WILLIAM C.
Executive. b. Toronto, Canada, Oct. 7, 1943. Career with Universal Pictures started in 1970 when named Toronto branch mgr.; promoted to v.p. & gen. sls. mgr. of Universal Film (Canada) in 1971. Promoted to v.p. & gen. sls. mgr., Universal Pictures, 1981, in NY relocating to L.A. later that year. 1983 named pres. of Universal Pictures Distribution, new domestic dist. div. of Universal; resigned, 1988. Named exec. v.p. distrib., Tri-Star Pictures, 1988; pres. of distrib. , 1992.

SOAMES, RICHARD
Executive. b. London, England, June 6, 1936. Joined Film Finances Ltd. 1972; Appt. director Film Finances Ltd., 1977: Appt. man. dir. 1979. Appt. pres. Film Finances Canada Ltd. 1982: Appt. pres., Film Finances Inc. Also formed Doric Prods, Inc. PICTURES: The Boss's Wife, The Principal, Honey I Shrunk the Kids, Tap.

SODERBERGH, STEVEN
Director, Writer, Editor. b. Atlanta, GA, Jan. 14, 1963. First major professional job was directing concert film for rock group Yes for Grammy-nominated video, 1986. PICTURES: Director-Editor. Sex Lies and Videotape (debut, 1989; also s.p.; Cannes Fest. Palme d'Or Award; Acad. Award nom. for s.p.), Kafka, King of the Hill (also s.p.), Suture (exec. prod. only), The Underneath (also s.p.), Schizopolis (alos actor). TELEVISION: Series: Fallen Angels (The Quiet Room).

SOKOLOW, DIANE
Executive. b. New York, NY. e. Temple U. m. Mel Sokolow. 1975, v.p., East Coast operations, for Lorimar; with Warner Bros. 1977-81; served as v.p. of East Coast production. Left to form The Sokolow Co. with husband, Mel, to produce films. 1982, returned to WB as v.p., East Coast prod. 1984, joined Motown Prods. as exec. v.p.; producer, MGM-UA 1986-87. Currently co-pres. Sokolow Co. with Mel Sokolow. PICTURE: My Son's Brother (co-prod.).

TELEVISION: *Exec. Prod.*: Miles from Nowhere, Trial: The Price of Passion, Lady Against the Odds, Fallen Champ, Silent Cries.

SOLO, ROBERT H.
Producer. b. Waterbury, CT, Dec. 4, 1932. e. U. of Connecticut, BA. Early career as agent with Ashley-Famous; later production as exec. asst. to Jack Warner and Walter MacEwen at Warner Bros. 1971, named WB v.p., foreign production 1974, named exec. v.p., prod. at Burbank Studio. Now indep. prod. PICTURES: Scrooge, The Devils (co-prod.), Invasion of the Body Snatchers, The Awakening, I the Jury, Bad Boys, Colors, Above the Law (exec. prod.), Winter People, Blue Sky, Car 54 Where Are You?, Body Snatchers.

SOLT, ANDREW W.
Producer, Writer, Director. b. London, Eng. December 13, 1947. e. UCLA. PICTURES: Imagine: John Lennon, This is Elvis, It Came From Hollywood. TELEVISION: Honeymooners' Reunion, The Muppets... A Celebration of 30 Years, Cousteau's Mississippi, Happy Birthday Donald Duck, America Censored, Remembering Marilyn, Great Moments in Disney Animation, ET & Friends, Disney's DTV, Heroes of Rock 'n Roll, Bob Hope's Christmas Tours, Disney Goes To The Oscars, Cousteau: Oasis In Space (series), Cousteau: Odyssey, Best of the Ed Sullivan Show (4 specials), The History of Rock 'n' Roll, Sesame Street's 25th Birthday Special, Grammy's Greatest Moments, TV Guide's 40th Anniversary Special, 25x5: The Continuing Adventures of the Rolling Stones, Andy Griffith Show Reunion, Cousteau: Search for Atlantis I&II, All My Children 25th Anniversary Special, Hunt for Amazing Treasure, Great Moments in Disney Animation.

SOMERS, SUZANNE
Actress. r.n. Suzanne Mahoney. b. San Bruno, CA, Oct. 16, 1946. e. Lone Mountain Sch., San Francisco Coll. for Women. Pursued modeling career; worked as regular on Mantrap, syndicated talk show. Did summer stock and theatrical films. *Author*: Touch Me Again, Keeping Secrets, Some People Live More Than Others, Wednesday's Children: Adult Survivors of Abuse Speak Out. PICTURES: Bullitt (debut, 1968), Daddy's Gone A-Hunting, Fools, American Graffiti, Magnum Force, Yesterday's Hero, Nothing Personal, Serial Mom. TELEVISION: *Series*: Three's Company, She's the Sheriff, Step by Step, The Suzanne Somers Show (talk). *Guest*: One Day at a Time, Lotsa Luck, The Rockford Files, Starsky & Hutch, The Rich Little Show, Battle of the Network Stars, Love Boat. *Movies*: Sky Heist, It Happened at Lakewood Manor (Ants), Happily Ever After, Zuma Beach, Rich Men Single Women, Keeping Secrets (also exec. prod.), Exclusive (also co-exec. prod), Seduced by Evil. *Mini-Series*: Hollywood Wives. *Specials*: Us Against the World, Suzanne, Suzanne Somers Presents: Showtime's Triple Crown of Comedy, Disney's Totally Minnie.

SOMMER, ELKE
Actress. r.n. Elke Schletz. b. Berlin, Germany, Nov. 5, 1940. Entered films in Germany, 1958. PICTURES: Das Totenschiff (debut, 1958), Lampenfieber, The Day It Rained, Heaven and Cupid, Love the Italian Way, Why Bother to Knock? (English-language debut, 1961), Daniela by Night, Violent Ecstasy, Auf Wiedersehen, Cafe Oriental, Bahia de Palma, The Victors, Island of Desire, The Prize, Frontier Hellcat, Le Bamboie (The Dolls), A Shot in the Dark, The Art of Love, The Money Trap, The Corrupt Ones, The Oscar, Boy Did I Get a Wrong Number, The Venetian Affair, Deadlier Than the Male, The Wicked Dreams of Paula Schultz, The Invincible Six, They Came to Rob Las Vegas, The Wrecking Crew, Baron Blood, Zeppelin, Percy, It's Not the Size That Counts (Percy's Progress), Ten Little Indians, The Swiss Conspiracy, Carry on Behind, House of Exorcism (Lisa and the Devil), Das Netz, The Astral Factor (Invisible Strangler), Thoroughbreds, I Miss You—Hugs and Kisses, The Prisoner of Zenda, A Nightingale Sang in Berkeley Square, The Double McGuffin, Exit Sunset Blvd., The Man in Pyjamas, Lily in Love, Death Stone, Himmelsheim, Neat and Tidy, Severed Ties. TELEVISION: *Movies*: Probe, Stunt Seven, The Top of the Hill, Inside the Third Reich, Jenny's War, Anastasia: The Mystery of Anya. *Mini-Series*: Peter the Great.

SOMMER, JOSEF
Actor. b. Greifswald, Germany, June 26, 1934. Raised in North Carolina. e. Carnegie-Mellon U. Studied at American Shakespeare Festival in Stratford, CT, 1962-64. US Army, 1958-60. NY stage debut in Othello, 1970. PICTURES: Dirty Harry (debut, 1971), Man on a Swing, The Front, Close Encounters of the Third Kind, Oliver's Story, Hide in Plain Sight, Absence of Malice, Reds, Rollover, Hanky Panky, Still of the Night, Sophie's Choice (narrator),

Independence Day, Silkwood, Iceman, Witness, D.A.R.Y.L., Target, The Rosary Murders, Chances Are, Dracula's Widow, Forced March, Bloodhounds of Broadway, Shadows and Fog, The Mighty Ducks, Malice, Cultivating Charlie, Nobody's Fool, Strange Days.
TELEVISION: *Series*: Hothouse, Under Cover. *Specials*: Morning Becomes Electra, The Scarlet Letter, Saigon. *Movies*: Too Far to Go, Doctor Franken, The Henderson Monster, Sparkling Cyanide, The Betty Ford Story, A Special Friendship, Bridge to Silence, The Bionic Showdown: The Six Million Dollar Man and the Bionic Woman, Money Power Murder, Spy Games, An American Story, Citizen Cohn, Hostages, The Enemy Within, Don't Drink the Water, The Minutes, Kansas, Letter to My Killer. *Mini-Series*: The Kennedys of Massachusetts, A Woman Named Jackie.

SONDHEIM, STEPHEN
Composer, Lyricist. b. New York, NY, March 22, 1930. e. Williams Coll. Writer for Topper TV series, 1953. Wrote incidental music for The Girls of Summer (1956), Invitation to a March (1961), Twigs (1971). Winner of 6 Grammy Awards: Cast Albums 1970, 1973, 1979, 1984, 1988 and song of the year 1975. Named Visiting Prof. of Contemporary Theater, Oxford U. 1990.
THEATER: *Lyrics only:* West Side Story, Gypsy, Do I Hear a Waltz? *Music and lyrics*: A Funny Thing Happened on the Way to the Forum, Anyone Can Whistle, Company (Tony Award, 1971), Follies (Tony Award, 1972), A Little Night Music (Tony Award, 1973), The Frogs, Candide (new lyrics for revival), Pacific Overtures, Sweeney Todd, (Tony Award, 1979), Merrily We Roll Along, Sunday in the Park with George (Pulitzer Prize, 1985), Into the Woods (Tony Award, 1988), Assassins, Passion (Tony Award, 1994). Theater anthologies of his songs: Side By Side By Sondheim; Marry Me a Little, You're Gonna Love Tomorrow, Putting It Together.*Play*: The Doctor Is In.
PICTURES: West Side Story (lyrics), Gypsy (lyrics), A Funny Thing Happened on the Way to the Forum (music, lyrics), The Last of Sheila (s.p.), Stavisky (score), A Little Night Music (music, lyrics), Reds (score), Dick Tracy (music, lyrics; Academy Award for best song: Sooner or Later, 1990).
TELEVISION: *Special*: Evening Primrose (music, lyrics; ABC Stage '67).

SONNENFELD, BARRY
Director, Cinematographer. b. 1953. Received Emmy Award for photography on series Out of Step.
PICTURES: *Cinematographer:* Blood Simple (debut, 1984), Compromising Positions, Raising Arizona, Three O'Clock High, Throw Momma From the Train, Big, When Harry Met Sally..., Miller's Crossing, Misery. *Director:* The Addams Family (debut, 1991), For Love or Money (also co-prod.), Addams Family Values (also cameo), Get Shorty (also exec. prod.).

SORVINO, PAUL
Actor. b. New York, NY, 1939. Daughter is actress Mira Sorvino.
THEATER: Bajour, An American Millionaire, The Mating Dance, King Lear, That Championship Season, Marlon Brando Sat Right Here.
PICTURES: Where's Poppa? (debut, 1970), The Panic in Needle Park, Made for Each Other, A Touch of Class, The Day of the Dolphin, The Gambler, Shoot It Black Shoot It Blue, I Will I Will... For Now, Oh God, Bloodbrothers, Slow Dancing in the Big City, The Brink's Job, Lost and Found, Cruising, Reds, I The Jury, That Championship Season, Off the Wall, Very Close Quarters, Turk 182, The Stuff, A Fine Mess, Vasectomy, Dick Tracy, GoodFellas, The Rocketeer, Life in the Food Chain (Age Isn't Everything), The Firm, Nixon, Romeo and Juliet.
TELEVISION: *Series*: We'll Get By, Bert D'Angelo: Superstar, The Oldest Rookie, Law and Order. *Mini-Series*: Seventh Avenue, Chiefs. *Movies*: Tell Me Where It Hurts, It Couldn't Happen to a Nicer Guy, Dummy, A Question of Honor, My Mother's Secret Life, With Intent to Kill, Surviving, Don't Touch My Daughter, The Case of the Wicked Wives, Parallel Lives, Without Consent. *Guest*: Moonlighting, Murder She Wrote. *Special*: The Last Mile.

SOTHERN, ANN
Actress. r.n. Harriet Lake. b. Valley City, ND, Jan. 22, 1909. e. Washington U. p. Annette Yde-Lake, opera singer. In m.p. since 1927. Star of 10 Maisie movies in series from 1939-47. Has recently become noted painter.
PICTURES: Broadway Nights (debut in bit part, 1927), Hearts in Exile, The Show of Shows, Hold Everything, Whoopee, Doughboys, Broadway Through a Keyhole, Let's Fall in Love, Melody in Spring, The Party's Over, The Hellcat, Blind Date, Kid Millions, Folies Bergere, Eight Bells, Hooray for Love, The Girl Friend, Grand Exit, You May Be Late, Hell Ship Morgan, Don't Gamble With Love, My American Wife, Walking on Air, The Smartest Girl in Town, Dangerous Number, Fifty Roads to Town, There Goes My Girl, Super Sleuth, Danger: Love at

Work, There Goes the Groom, She's Got Everything, Trade Winds, Hotel For Women, Maisie (and subsequent series of 9 other films), Fast and Furious, Joe and Ethel Turp Call on the President, Brother Orchid, Dulcy, Lady Be Good, Panama Hattie, Cry Havoc, Thousands Cheer, Three Hearts for Julia, April Showers, Words and Music, The Judge Steps Out, A Letter to Three Wives, Shadow on the Wall, Nancy Goes to Rio, The Blue Gardenia, Lady in a Cage, The Best Man, Sylvia, Chubasco, The Killing Kind, Golden Needles, Crazy Mama, The Manitou, The Little Dragons, The Whales of August (Acad. Award. nom).
TELEVISION: *Series*: Private Secretary, The Ann Sothern Show, My Mother The Car (voice of the car). *Movies*: The Outsider, Congratulations It's a Boy, A Death of Innocence, The Weekend Nun, The Great Man's Whiskers, A Letter to Three Wives. *Mini-Series*: Captains and the Kings.

SOUL, DAVID
Actor. r.n. David Solberg. b. Chicago, IL, Aug. 28, 1943.
PICTURES: Johnny Got His Gun, Magnum Force, Dog Pound Shuffle, The Hanoi Hilton, Appointment with Death, Pentathalon.
TELEVISION: *Series*: Here Come the Brides, Owen Marshall-Counselor at Law, Starsky and Hutch, Casablanca, Yellow Rose, Unsub. *Movies*: The Disappearance of Flight 412, Starsky and Hutch (pilot), Little Ladies of the Night, Salem's Lot, Swan Song (also co-prod.), Rage, Homeward Bound, The Manions of America, World War III, Through Naked Eyes, The Fifth Missile, Harry's Hong Kong, In the Line of Duty: The FBI Murders, Prime Target, So Proudly We Hail, Bride in Black, A Cry in the Wild, The Taking of Peggy Ann, Perry Mason: The Case of the Fatal Framing, Grave Secrets: The Legacy of Hilltop Drive.

SPACEK, SISSY
Actress. r.n. Mary Elizabeth Spacek. b. Quitman, TX, Dec. 25, 1949. m. director Jack Fisk. Cousin of actor Rip Torn. Attended acting classes in New York under Lee Strasberg. Had bit role in Andy Warhol's Trash. Worked as set decorator on films Death Game, Phantom of the Paradise.
PICTURES: Prime Cut (debut, 1972), Ginger in the Morning, Badlands, Carrie, Welcome to L.A., 3 Women, Heart Beat, Coal Miner's Daughter (Academy Award, 1980), Raggedy Man, Missing, The Man With Two Brains (voice), The River, Marie, Violets Are Blue, 'night Mother, Crimes of the Heart, The Long Walk Home, JFK, Hard Promises, Trading Mom, The Grass Harp.
TELEVISION: *Movies*: The Girls of Huntington House, The Migrants, Katherine, A Private Matter, The Good Old Boys, If These Walls Could Speak. *Special*: Verna: USO Girl. *Guest*: The Rookies, The Waltons.

SPACEY, KEVIN
Actor. b. South Orange, NJ, July 26, 1959. Raised in southern CA. e. L.A. Valley Coll., appearing in stage productions as well as stand-up comedy clubs, before attending Juilliard Sch. of Drama. Has appeared in numerous regional and repertory productions including Kennedy Center (The Seagull), Williamstown Theatre Fest. and Seattle Rep. Theatre, and with New York Shakespeare Fest.
THEATER: Henry IV Part I, The Robbers, Barbarians, Ghosts, Hurlyburly, Long Day's Journey into Night, National Anthems, Lost in Yonkers (Tony Award, 1991), Playland.
PICTURES: Heartburn (debut, 1986), Rocket Gibraltar, Working Girl, See No Evil Hear No Evil, Dad, A Show of Force, Henry and June, Glengarry Glen Ross, Consenting Adults, Iron Will, The Ref, Outbreak, Swimming With Sharks (also co-prod.), The Usual Suspects (Academy Award, Chicago Film Critics Award), Seven, Albino Alligator (dir.), A Time to Kill, Looking for Richard.
TELEVISION: *Specials*: Long Day's Journey into Night, Darrow. *Movies*: The Murder of Mary Phagan, Fall from Grace, When You Remember Me, Doomsday Gun. *Series*: Wiseguy, Tribeca. *Guest*: L.A. Law.

SPADE, DAVID
Actor. b. Birmingham, MI. Raised in Scottsdale, AZ. Performed stand-up comedy in clubs and colleges which led to debut on Saturday Night Live in 1990.
PICTURES: Light Sleeper (debut, 1982), Coneheads, Reality Bites, PCU, Tommy Boy, Black Sheep.
TELEVISION: *Series*: Saturday Night Live.

SPADER, JAMES
Actor. b. Boston, MA, Feb. 7, 1960. e. Phillips Academy. Studied acting at Michael Chekhov Studio.
PICTURES: Endless Love (debut, 1981), The New Kids, Tuff Turf, Pretty in Pink, Mannequin, Baby Boom, Less Than Zero, Wall Street, Jack's Back, The Rachel Papers, Sex Lies and Videotape (Cannes Fest. Award, 1989), Bad Influence, White Palace, True Colors, Storyville, Bob Roberts, The Music of Chance, Dream Lover, Wolf, Stargate, 2 Days in the Valley.

TELEVISION: *Series*: The Family Tree. *Movies*: Cocaine: One Man's Seduction, A Killer in the Family, Starcrossed, Family Secrets. *Pilot*: Diner.

SPANO, VINCENT
Actor. b. New York, NY, Oct. 18, 1962. While attending Stuyvesant H.S. made stage debut at 14 in The Shadow Box (Long Wharf and B'way).
THEATER: The Shadow Box, Balm in Gilead.
PICTURES: Over the Edge (debut, 1979), The Double McGuffin, The Black Stallion Returns, Baby It's You, Rumblefish, Alphabet City, Maria's Lovers, Creator, Good Morning Babylon, And God Created Woman, 1753: Venetian Red, High Frequency (Aquarium), Oscar, City of Hope, Alive, Indian Summer, The Ascent, The Tie That Binds.
TELEVISION: *Series*: Search for Tomorrow. *Movies*: The Gentleman Bandit, Senior Trip, Blood Ties, Afterburn.

SPEARS, JR., HAROLD T.
Executive. b. Atlanta, GA, June 21, 1929. e. U. of Georgia, 1951. With Floyd Theatres, Lakeland, FL, since 1953; now pres. Pres., Sun South Theatres, Inc., 1996.

SPECKTOR, FREDERICK
Executive. b. Los Angeles, CA, April 24, 1933. e. USC, UCLA. M.P. agent, Ashley Famous Agency, 1962-64; Artists Agency Corp., 1964-68; exec. M.P. dept., William Morris Agency, 1968-78; exec. Creative Artists Agency, 1978-present. Trustees Council, Education First, bd. of dirs., Amer. Jewish Committee. Bd. of dirs. for the ACLU and Center for Gun-Violence Prevention.

SPELLING, AARON
Executive. b. Dallas, TX, Apr. 22, 1928. Daughter is actress Tori Spelling. Was actor/writer before becoming producer at Four Star in 1957. Producer of series and tv movies: 1967, formed Thomas/Spelling Productions; 1969, formed his own co., Aaron Spelling Productions; 1972, partnered with Leonard Goldberg; then producer on his own company banner. and over 111 movies for television.
PICTURES: Mr. Mom (exec. prod.), Surrender, Three O'Clock High (exec. prod.), Cross My Heart (co-exec. prod.), Satisfaction (co-prod.), Loose Cannons, Soapdish.
TELEVISION: *Series*: The Mod Squad, The Rookies, Charlie's Angels, Fantasy Island, Starsky and Hutch, Hart to Hart, T.J. Hooker, Family, The Love Boat, Vega$, Dynasty, Matt Houston, Hotel, The Colbys, Life with Lucy, Nightingales, HeartBeat, Beverly Hills 90210, The Heights, Melrose Place, The Round Table, Winnetka Road, 7th Heaven. *Movies* (exec. prod./prod.): The Over-the-Hill Gang, Wake When the War Is Over, The Monk, The Pigeon, The Ballad of Andy Crocker, Say Goodbye Maggie Cole, Rolling Man, Shooting Stars, Dark Mirror, Making of a Male Model, The Three Kings, Nightingales, Day One (Emmy Award, 1989), Rich Men Single Women, The Love Boat: The Valentine Voyage, Jailbirds, Back to the Streets of San Francisco, Grass Roots, Terror on Track 9, A Stranger in the Mirror, and The Band Played On (Emmy Award, 1994), Jane's House, Green Dolphin Beat, many others.

SPENGLER, PIERRE
Producer. b. Paris, France, 1947. Went on stage at 15; returned to language studies at Alliance Franccaise. Entered film industry as production runner and office boy. Teamed for first time with friend Ilya Salkind on The Light at the Edge of the World, produced by Alexander Salkind.
PICTURES: Bluebeard, The Three Musketeers, The Four Musketeers, Crossed Swords, Superman, Superman II, Superman III, Santa Claus: The Movie, The Return of the Musketeers (tv in U.S.).

SPHEERIS, PENELOPE
Director. b. New Orleans, LA, 1945. e. UCLA. Film Sch., MFA.
PICTURES: Real Life (prod. only). Director: The Decline of Western Civilization (also prod., s.p.), Suburbia (also s.p.), The Boys Next Door, Summer Camp Nightmare (s.p. only), Hollywood Vice Squad, Dudes, The Decline of Western Civilization-Part II: The Metal Years, Wedding Band (actress only), Wayne's World, The Beverly Hillbillies, The Little Rascals, Black Sheep.
TELEVISION: Saturday Night Live (prod. only), Danger Theatre (co-creator, dir., co-writer). Movie: Prison Stories: Women on the Inside (New Chicks).

SPIEGEL, LARRY
Producer, Writer, Director. b. Brooklyn, NY. e. Ohio U. With CBS-TV; Benton & Bowles; Wells, Rich, Green; BBDO. Now heads Appledown Films, Inc.
PICTURES: Hail (s.p.), Book of Numbers (s.p.), Death Game (prod.), Stunts (prod.), Spree (dir., s.p.), Phobia (prod.), Remo Williams: The Adventure Begins (prod.), Dove Against Death (prod.), The Sunchaser (prod.).
TELEVISION: *ABC Afterschool Specials*, Bear That Slept Through Christmas (writer), Never Fool With A Gypsy Ikon (writer), Planet of The Apes (animated; writer), Jan Stephenson Golf Video (prod.), Remo Williams (pilot ABC; prod.).

SPIELBERG, STEVEN
Director, Producer. b. Cincinnati, OH, Dec. 18, 1947. e. California State Coll. m. actress Kate Capshaw. Made home movies as child; completed first film with story and actors at 12 yrs. old in Phoenix. At 13 won film contest for 40-min. war movie, Escape to Nowhere. At 16 made 140-min. film, Firelight. At California State Coll. made five films. First professional work, Amblin', 20 min. short which led to signing contract with Universal Pictures at age 20. Formed own co. Amblin Entertainment, headquartered at Universal Studios. Received Irving G. Thalberg Memorial Award, 1987; American Film Institute Life Achievement Award, 1995. Partnered with David Geffen and Jeffrey Katzenberg formed film company DreamWorks, 1995.
PICTURES: *Director*: The Sugarland Express (debut, 1974; also story), Jaws, Close Encounters of The Third Kind (also s.p.; Acad. Award nom. for dir.), 1941, Raiders of the Lost Ark (Acad. Award nom.), E.T. The Extra-Terrestrial (also co-prod.; Acad. Award noms. for dir. & picture), Twilight Zone—The Movie (sequence dir.; also exec. prod.), Indiana Jones and the Temple of Doom, The Color Purple (also co-prod.; Acad. Award nom. for picture), Empire of the Sun (also co-prod.), Indiana Jones and the Last Crusade, Always (also co-prod.), Hook, Jurassic Park, Schindler's List (also co-prod.; Academy Awards for Best Director & Picture, 1993; DGA, Golden Globe & Natl. Society of Film Critics Awards for director; NY Film Critics, LA Film Critics, Natl. Board of Review. Natl. Society of Film Critics & Golden Globe Awards for picture), The Lost World. *Co-exec. prod.*: I Wanna Hold Your Hand, Used Cars, Continental Divide (exec. prod.), Poltergeist (co-prod., co-s.p.), Gremlins (also cameo), The Goonies (also story), Back to the Future, Young Sherlock Holmes, The Money Pit, An American Tail, Innerspace, Batteries Not Included, Who Framed Roger Rabbit, The Land Before Time, Dad, Back to the Future Part II, Joe Versus the Volcano, Back to the Future Part III, Gremlins 2: The New Batch, Arachnophobia, Cape Fear, An American Tail: Fievel Goes West (co-prod.), We're Back!: A Dinosaur's Story, The Flintstones, The Little Rascals, Casper (co-prod.), The Bridges of Madison County (co-prod.). *Actor only*: The Blues Brothers, Listen Up: The Lives of Quincy Jones.
TELEVISION: *Series* episodes (dir.): Columbo, Owen Marshall: Counsellor-at-Law, The Pyschiatrist. *Movies* (dir.): Night Gallery (episode dir.), Duel, Something Evil, Savage. *Exec. prod.*: Amazing Stories (series; also dir. of 2 episodes), Tiny Toon Adventures (series; Emmy Award, 1991), Class of '61 (movie), Family Dog (series), seaQuest DSV (series), Pinky and the Brain (series).

SPIKINGS, BARRY
Executive. b. Boston, England, Nov. 23, 1939. Ent. m.p. ind. 1973. Joint man. dir. British Lion Films Ltd., 1975. Appt. jnt. man. dir. EMI Films Ltd., 1977. 1979, appt. chmn. & chief exec., EMI Film & Theatre Corp.; chmn. & chief exec, EMI Films, Ltd., chmn. EMI Cinemas, Ltd.; chmn., Elstree Studios, Ltd.; chmn. EMI-TV Programs, Inc., 1980; appt. chmn. chief exec., EMI Films Group, 1982; 1985 Barry Spikings Productions Inc. (U.S.A.); 1985 became director Galactic Films Inc. (with Lord Anthony Rufus Issacs); 1986, acquired Embassy Home Entertainment from Coca Cola Co., renamed Nelson Entertainment Inc., appointed pres. and COO. 1992, Pleskow/Spikings Partnership, film prod. and distrib. partnership with Eric Pleskow.
PICTURES: *Prod.*: Conduct Unbecoming, The Man Who Fell to Earth, The Deer Hunter, Texasville, Beyond Rangoon. *Exec. prod.*: Convoy.

SPINER, BRENT
Actor. b. Houston, TX. Recorded solo album Ol' Yellow Eyes I Back.
THEATER: *NY*: The Seagull, The Three Musketeers, Sunday in the Park With George, Big River.
PICTURES: Stardust Memories, Rent Control, The Miss Firecracker Contest, Corrina Corrina, Star Trek: Generations, Independence Day, Phenomenon, Star Trek: First Contact.
TELEVISION: *Series*: Star Trek: The Next Generation (also dir. episode).

SPINETTI, VICTOR
Actor. b. South Wales, Sept. 2, 1933. e. Monmouth School. Entered industry in 1955. Appeared on Broadway in Oh! What a Lovely War winning 1965 Tony and Theatre World Awards.
THEATER: *London*: Expresso Bongo, Candide, Make Me an Offer, Oh What a Lovely War (also B'way), The Odd Couple, Cat Among the Pigeons, etc.
PICTURES: A Hard Day's Night, The Wild Affair, Help!, The Taming of the Shrew, The Biggest Bundle of Them All, Can Hieronymous Merkin Ever Forget Mercy Humppe and Find True Happiness?, Under Milk Wood, The Little Prince, The Return of the Pink Panther, Under the Cherry Moon, The Krays, The Princess and the Goblin (voice).
TELEVISION: The Magical Mystery Tour, Vincent Van Gogh, Paradise Club, The Attic.

SPIRA, STEVEN S.
Executive. b. New York, NY, Mar. 25, 1955. e. City Coll. of New
York; Benjamin Cardozo Sch. of Law. Associated 10 years with
N.Y. law firm, Monasch Chazen & Stream. 1984, joined 20th
Century Fox as sr. counsel; 1985, to Warner Bros. Now WB sr.
v.p., theatrical business affairs.

SPODICK, ROBERT C.
Exhibitor. b. New York, NY, Dec. 3, 1919. e. CCNY, 1940; ent.
NYC m.p. ind. as errand boy Skouras Park Plaza, Bronx 1932-
33; reel boy, asst. mgr., Loew's Theatres; mgr., Little Carnegie
and other art theatres; exploitation man, United Artists.
Acquired Lincoln, New Haven art house in 1945 in partnership
with cousin Leonard E. Sampson; developed Nutmeg Theatre
circuit, which was sold in 1968 to Robert Smerling. Beginning
in 1970, built Groton, CT., Cinemas I and II; Norwich Cinemas
I and II, Mystic Village Cinemas I, II and III, and Westerley
Triple Cinemas in RI as Gemini Cinema Circuit in partnership
with Sampson and William Rosen. Gemini sold to Interstate
Theatres, 1986. With Sampson presently operates York
Square I & II and The New Lincoln in New Haven. Pres., Allied
of CT, 1962-64; Pres. NATO of Conn. 1968-73. Past Chmn.
Exec. Comm., CT Ass'n of Theatre Owners, and still active
member of Board of Directors in 1994.

SPOTTISWOODE, ROGER
Director. b. England. Film editor of TV commercials and doc-
umentaries before turning to direction.
PICTURES: Editor: Straw Dogs, The Getaway, Pat Garrett and
Billy the Kid, Hard Times, The Gambler; Who'll Stop the Rain?
(assoc. prod.), Baby: Secret of the Lost Legend (exec. prod.).
Director: Terror Train (debut, 1980), The Pursuit of D.B.
Cooper, Under Fire, The Best of Times, Shoot to Kill, Turner &
Hooch, Air America, Stop Or My Mom Will Shoot.
TELEVISION: Movies: The Renegades, The Last Innocent
Man, Third Degree Burn, And the Band Played On, Hiroshima.
Special: Time Flies When You're Alive.

SPRADLIN, G.D.
Actor. b. Daylight Township, Garvin County, OK, Aug. 31,
1920. e. Univ. of Oklahoma-doctor of Juris Prudence (1948).
Started career as lawyer, became Independent Oil Producer.
Active in local politics before turning to acting. Joined
Oklahoma Repertory Theatre in 1964.
PICTURES: Will Penny (debut, 1968), Number One, Zabriskie
Point, Monte Walsh, Tora! Tora! Tora!, The Hunting Party, The
Godfather Part II, MacArthur, One on One, North Dallas Forty,
Apocalypse Now, The Formula, Wrong Is Right, The Lords of
Discipline, Tank, The War of the Roses, Clifford, Ed Wood,
Canadian Bacon.
TELEVISION: Series: Rich Man Poor Man Book II. Mini-
Series: Space, Dream West, Nutcracker: Money Madness and
Murder, Robert Kennedy and His Times, War and
Remembrance. Movies: Dial Hot Line, Sam Hill: Who Killed
the Mysterious Mr. Foster?, Oregon Trail, Maneaters Are
Loose!, And I Alone Survived, Jayne Mansfield Story, Resting
Place, Shoot First: A Cop's Vengeance, Telling Secrets.

SPRINGER, PAUL D.
Executive. e. Brooklyn Law Sch. Served as assoc. for NY law
firm, Johnson and Tannebaum. Later with legal dept. of
Columbia Pictures. 1970, joined Paramount Pictures N.Y.
legal dept. 1970; promoted to v.p. Theatrical Distrib. Counsel,
1979; promoted to sr. v.p., chief resident counsel, 1987; promoted to sr. v.p., asst. general counsel responsible for all legal
functions for Paramount's distribution and marketing depts.
Mem., NY and California Bars.

SPRINGFIELD, RICK
Actor, Singer, Songwriter. b. Sydney, Australia, Aug. 23,
1949.
PICTURES: Battlestar Galactica, Hard to Hold (act., addl.
music).
TELEVISION: Series: General Hospital, Human Target, High
Tide. Specials: An Evening at the Improv, Countdown '81.
Movies: Nick Knight, Dead Reckoning, In the Shadows
Someone's Watching.

STACK, ROBERT
Actor. b. Los Angeles, CA, Jan. 13, 1919. e. U. of Southern
California. In U.S. Armed Forces (Navy), W.W.II. Studied act-
ing at Henry Duffy School of Theatre 6 mo. then signed a con-
tract with Universal. National skeet champion at age 16.
Autobiography: Straight Shooting (1980).
PICTURES: First Love (debut, 1939), When the Daltons Rode,
The Mortal Storm, A Little Bit of Heaven, Nice Girl?, Badlands
of Dakota, To Be or Not To Be, Eagle Squadron, Men of Texas,
Fighter Squadron, A Date With Judy, Miss Tatlock's Millions,
Mr. Music, The Bullfighter and the Lady, My Outlaw Brother,
Bwana Devil, War Paint, Conquest of Cochise, Sabre Jet, The
Iron Glove, The High and the Mighty, House of Bamboo, Good
Morning Miss Dove, Great Day in the Morning, Written on the
Wind (Acad. Award nom.), The Gift of Love, The Tarnished

Angels, John Paul Jones, The Last Voyage, The Caretakers, Is
Paris Burning?, The Corrupt Ones, Action Man, Story of a
Woman, A Second Wind, 1941, Airplane!, Uncommon Valor,
Big Trouble, Transformers (voice), Plain Clothes, Caddyshack
II, Dangerous Curves, Joe Versus the Volcano.
TELEVISION: Series: The Untouchables (Emmy Award,
1960), The Name of the Game, Most Wanted, Strike Force,
Unsolved Mysteries (host), Final Appeal (host). Guest:
Playhouse 90 (Panic Button). Movies: The Strange and Deadly
Occurance, Adventures of the Queen, Murder on Flight 502,
Most Wanted (pilot), Undercover With the KKK (narrator),
Midas Valley, Perry Mason: The Case of the Sinister Spirit,
The Return of Eliot Ness. Mini-Series: George Washington,
Hollywood Wives.

STAHL, AL
Executive. b. July 3, 1916. Syndicated newspaper cartoonist;
asst. animator, Max Fleischer; prod. first animated TV cartoon show; pres., Animated Prod., prod. live and animated
commercials; member of bd. NTFC. Developed and built first
animation camera and stand, 1950. Designed and produced
opening animation for The Honeymooners, The Electric
Company, Saturday Night Live. Produced over 5,000 tv spots.
Prod. 50 min. documentary War and Pieces for U.S. Army
Commandy of War in the Gulf, 1991.

STAHL, NICK
Actor. b. Dallas, TX, 1980. Started acting at age 4.
PICTURES: The Man Without a Face (debut, 1993), Safe
Passage, Tall Tale.
TELEVISION: Movies: Stranger at My Door, Woman With a
Past, Incident in a Small Town.

STALLONE, SYLVESTER
Actor, Writer, Director. b. New York, NY, July 6, 1946. After
high school taught at American Coll. of Switzerland instructing
children of career diplomats, young royalty, etc. Returned to
U.S. in 1967 and studied drama at U. of Miami, 1969. Came to
New York to seek acting career, taking part-time jobs, includ-
ing usher for Walter Reade Theatres. Then turned to writing,
selling several TV scripts.
PICTURES: Party at Kitty and Studs (debut, 1970), Bananas,
Rebel (A Man Called Rainbo), The Lords of Flatbush (also co-
s.p.), The Prisoner of 2nd Avenue, Capone, Death Race 2000,
Farewell My Lovely, Cannonball, Rocky (also s.p.; Acad.
Award noms. for actor & s.p.), F.I.S.T. (also co-s.p.), Paradise
Alley (also s.p., dir.), Rocky II (also s.p., dir.), Nighthawks,
Victory, Rocky III (also s.p., dir.), First Blood (also co-s.p.),
Staying Alive (cameo; also dir., prod., co-s.p.), Rhinestone
(also co-s.p.), Rambo: First Blood Part II (also co-s.p.), Rocky
IV (also dir., s.p.), Cobra (also s.p.), Over the Top (also co-
s.p.), Rambo III (also co-s.p.), Lock Up, Tango and Cash,
Rocky V (also s.p.), Oscar, Stop Or My Mom Will Shoot,
Cliffhanger (also co-s.p.), Demolition Man, The Specialist,
Judge Dredd, Assassins, Daylight.
TELEVISION: Guest: Kojak, Police Story, Dream On.

STAMOS, JOHN
Actor. b. Cypress, CA, Aug. 19, 1963. Landed role of Blackie
Parrish on daytime serial General Hospital in 1982. Has
toured with his own band John Stamos and the Bad Boyz.
THEATER: B'way: How to Succeed in Business Without Really
Trying.
PICTURES: Never Too Young to Die, Born to Ride.
TELEVISION: Series: General Hospital, Dreams, You Again?,
Full House. Movies: Daughter of the Streets, Captive, The
Disappearance of Christina, Fatal Vows: The Alexandra
O'Hara Story.

STAMP, TERENCE
Actor. b. London, England, July 23, 1938. Stage experience
including Alfie on Broadway. Recent stage: Dracula, The Lady
from the Sea, Airborne Symphony. Autobiography: Coming
Attractions (1988).
PICTURES: Billy Budd (debut 1962; Acad. Award nom.), Term
of Trial, The Collector (Cannes Film Fest. Award, 1965),
Modesty Blaise, Far from the Madding Crowd, Poor Cow,
Blue, Teorema, Spirits of the Dead, The Mind of Mr. Soames,
A Season in Hell, Hu-Man, The Divine Nymph, Strip-Tease,
Superman, Meetings with Remarkable Men, Together?,
Superman II, Monster Island, Death in the Vatican, The Hit,
The Company of Wolves, Link, Legal Eagles, The Sicilian,
Wall Street, Young Guns, Alien Nation, Stranger in the House
(also dir., co-s.p.), Genuine Risk, Beltenebros, The Real
McCoy, The Adventures of Priscilla--Queen of the Desert,
Mindbender.
TELEVISION: Movie: The Thief of Bagdad.

STANFILL, DENNIS C.
Executive. b. Centerville, TN, April 1, 1927. e. Lawrenceburg
H.S.; U.S. Naval Acad., B.S., 1949; Oxford U. (Rhodes
Scholar), M.A., 1953; U. of South Carolina, L.H.D. (hon.).

Corporate finance specialist, Lehman Brothers 1959-65; v.p. finance, Times Mirror Company, Los Angeles, 1965-69; exec. v.p. finance, 20th Century-Fox Film Corp., 1969-71, pres., 1971, chmn. bd./CEO, 1971-81; pres., Stanfill, Bowen & Co., venture capital firm, 1981-90; chmn. bd./CEO, AME, Inc., 1990-92; co-chmn. bd./co-CEO, MGM, 1992-93. Sr. advisor to Credit Lyonnais, 1993-95. Private Investments, 1995-.

STANG, ARNOLD
Performer, b. Chelsea, MA, Sept. 28, 1927. Radio, 1935-50; on B'way, in five plays and in m.p. and short subjects; guest appearances on TV shows. Much voice-over cartoon work. Starred in 36 shorts.
TELEVISION: *Series*: School House, Henry Morgan Show, Doc Corkle, Top Cat (voice), Broadside. *Guest*: Captain Video, Milton Berle, Danny Thomas, Perry Como, Ed Sullivan, Red Skelton, Frank Sinatra, Wagon Train, Jack Benny, Johnny Carson, December Bride, Playhouse 90, Batman, Bonanza, Bob Hope, Danny Kaye, Jackie Gleason, Emergency, Feeling Good, Chico & the Man, Super Jaws & Catfish, Busting Loose, Flying High, Robert Klein Specials, Tales from the Dark Side, True Blue, Cosby Show.
PICTURES: Seven Days Leave, My Sister Eileen, Let's Go Steady, They Got Me Covered, So This is New York, Double for Della, Return of Marco Polo, Spirit of '76, The Man with the Golden Arm, Dondi, The Wonderful World of the Brothers Grimm, It's a Mad Mad Mad Mad World, Pinocchio in Outer Space (voice), Alakazam the Great (voice), Hello Down There, Skidoo, The Aristocats (voice), Raggedy Ann & Andy (voice), Gang That Couldn't Shoot Straight, That's Life, Hercules in New York, Ghost Dad, Dennis the Menace, At The Cottonwood.

STANLEY, KIM
Actress. r.n. Patricia Reid. b. Tularosa, NM, Feb. 11, 1925. e. U. of NM. Began stage acting in college and later in stock. Worked as model in NY while training with Elia Kazan and Lee Strasberg at Actors Studio. In late 1960s and 1970s taught drama, Coll. of Santa Fe, NM.
THEATER: The Dog, Beneath the Skin (NY debut, 1948), Him, Yes Is For a Very Young Man, Montserrat, The House of Bernarda Alba, The Chase, Picnic (NY Drama Critics Award, 1953), The Traveling Lady, The Great Dreamer, Bus Stop, A Clearing in the Woods, A Touch of the Poet, A Far Country, Natural Affection, The Three Sisters.
PICTURES: The Goddess (debut, 1958), Seance on a Wet Afternoon (Acad. Award nom.), The Three Sisters, Frances (Acad. Award nom.), The Right Stuff.
TELEVISION: *Specials*: Clash by Night, The Travelling Lady, Cat on a Hot Tin Roof (Emmy Award, 1985). *Movie*: U.M.C. *Guest*: Ben Casey (A Cardinal Act of Mercy; Emmy Award, 1963).

STANTON, HARRY DEAN
Actor. b. West Irvine, KY, July 14, 1926. Acting debut at Pasadena Playhouse. Billed in early film appearances as Dean Stanton.
PICTURES: Revolt at Fort Laramie (debut, 1957), Tomahawk Trail, The Proud Rebel, Pork Chop Hill, The Adventures of Huckleberry Finn, A Dog's Best Friend, Hero's Island, The Man From the Diner's Club, Ride in the Whirlwind, The Hostage, A Time for Killing, Rebel Rousers, Cool Hand Luke, Day of the Evil Gun, The Miniskirt Mob, Kelly's Heroes, Cisco Pike, Two-Lane Blacktop, Face to the Wind (Cry for Me Billy), Pat Garrett and Billy the Kid, Dillinger, Where the Lilies Bloom, Cockfighter, Zandy's Bride, The Godfather Part II, Rafferty and the Gold Dust Twins, Rancho Deluxe, Farewell My Lovely, 92 in the Shade, Win Place or Steal, The Missouri Breaks, Straight Time, Renaldo and Clara, Alien, The Rose, Wise Blood, Death Watch, The Black Marble, Private Benjamin, Escape From New York, One From the Heart, Young Doctors in Love, Christine, Repo Man, Red Dawn, The Bear, Paris Texas, The Care Bears Movie (voice), One Magic Christmas, Fool for Love, UFOria, Pretty in Pink, Slamdance, Stars and Bars, Mr. North, The Last Temptation of Christ, Dream a Little Dream, Twister, The Fourth War, Stranger in the House, Wild at Heart, Man Trouble, Twin Peaks: Fire Walk With Me, Blue Tiger, Never Talk to Strangers, Down Periscope.
TELEVISION: *Movies*: Flatbed Annie & Sweetpie: Lady Truckers, I Want to Live, Payoff, Hostages, Against the Wall. *Special*: Hotel Room (Tricks).

STAPLETON, JEAN
Actress. r.n. Jeanne Murray. b. New York, NY. e. Wadleigh H.S. Summer stock in NH, ME, MA, and PA. Broadway debut in In the Summer House (1954). President, Advisory bd., Women's Research and Education Instit. (Wash., D.C.); bd.: Eleanor Roosevelt Val-kill, Hyde Park; trustee: Actors Fund of America.
THEATER: Harvey, Damn Yankees, Bells Are Ringing, Juno, Rhinoceros, Funny Girl, Arsenic and Old Lace (B'way and tour), Mountain Language/The Birthday Party (Obie Award), The Learned Ladies, Bon Appetit, The Roads to Home, Night

Seasons, Morning's at Seven, You Can't Take It With You, The Show-Off, The Mystery of Edwin Drood (natl. tour). and extensive regional work at the Totem Pole Playhouse, Fayetteville, PA, Pocono Playhouse, Mountain Home Pa; Peterborough Playhouse, N.H. and others. Operatic debut with Baltimore Opera Co. in Candide, then The Italian Lesson and Bon Appetit. Starred in San Jose Civic Light Opera Co.'s Sweeney Todd.
PICTURES: Damn Yankees (debut, 1958), Bells Are Ringing, Something Wild, Up the Down Staircase, Cold Turkey, Klute, The Buddy System, Michael.
TELEVISION: *Series*: All in the Family (3 Emmy Awards: 1971, 1972, 1978), Bagdad Cafe, Mrs. Piggle-Wiggle. *Movies*: Tail Gunner Joe, Aunt Mary, Angel Dusted, Isabel's Choice, Eleanor: First Lady of the World (Emmy nom.), A Matter of Sex, Dead Man's Folly, Fire in the Dark, The Habitation of Dragons, Ghost Mom. *Specials*: You Can't Take It With You, Grown-Ups (ACE nom.), Jack and the Beanstalk and Cinderella (Faerie Tale Theatre), Something's Afoot, Let Me Hear You Whisper, Mother Goose Rock 'n' Rhyme, Parallax Garden.

STAPLETON, MAUREEN
Actress. b. Troy, NY, June 21, 1925. e. Siena Col. Worked as a model and waitress while studying acting with Herbert Berghof in NY. Became member of Actors Studio. Broadway debut, 1946, in The Playboy of the Western World. *Autobiography*: A Hell of a Life (1995).
THEATER: *NY*: Antony and Cleopatra, Detective Story, The Bird Cage, The Rose Tattoo (Tony Award, 1951), The Emperor's Clothes, The Crucible, Richard III, The Seagull, 27 Wagons Full of Cotton, Orpheus Descending, The Cold Wind and the Warm, Toys in the Attic, The Glass Menagerie (1965 & 1975), Plaza Suite, Norman Is That You?, The Gingerbread Lady (Tony Award, 1971), The Country Girl, The Secret Affairs of Mildred Wild, The Gin Game, The Little Foxes. *LA*: Juno and the Paycock.
PICTURES: Lonelyhearts (debut, 1958; Acad. Award nom.), The Fugitive Kind, A View From the Bridge, Bye Bye Birdie, Airport (Acad. Award nom.), Plaza Suite, Interiors (Acad. Award nom.), Lost and Found, The Runner Stumbles, The Fan, On the Right Track, Reds (Academy Award, best supporting actress, 1981), Johnny Dangerously, The Cosmic Eye (voice), Cocoon, The Money Pit, Heartburn, Sweet Lorraine, Made in Heaven, Nuts, Doin' Time on Planet Earth (cameo), Cocoon: The Return, Passed Away, Trading Mom, The Last Good Time.
TELEVISION: *Series*: What Happened? (panelist, 1952), The Thorns. *Specials*: For Whom the Bell Tolls, Among the Paths to Eden (Emmy Award, 1968).*Movies*: Tell Me Where It Hurts, Queen of the Stardust Ballroom, Cat on a Hot Tin Roof, The Gathering, Letters From Frank, The Gathering Part II, The Electric Grandmother, Little Gloria--Happy at Last, Family Secrets, Sentimental Journey, Private Sessions, Liberace: Behind the Music, Last Wish, Miss Rose White.

STARGER, MARTIN
Producer, Executive. b. New York, NY, May 8, 1932. e. CCNY. Served in U.S. Army Signal Corp., where prod. training films. Joined BBDO, starting in TV prod. dept.; later made v.p. & assoc. dir. of TV. Joined ABC in 1966, as v.p. of programs, ABC-TV, East Coast. 1968, promoted to v.p. and natl prog. dir; 1969 named v.p. in chg. progr.; named pres., ABC Entertainment, 1972; 1975 formed & became pres. of Marstar Productions Inc., M.P. & TV prod. co.; 1978 formed Marble Arch Productions, of which he was pres. Formed Rule/Starger Co. with Elton Rule, 1988.
PICTURES: *Exec. prod./Producer*: Nashville, The Domino Principle, Movie/Movie, The Muppet Movie, Raise the Titanic, Saturn 3, The Great Muppet Caper, Hard Country, The Legend of the Lone Ranger, On Golden Pond, Sophie's Choice, Barbarosa, Mask.
TELEVISION: Friendly Fire (Emmy Award, 1979), Escape from Sobibor, Consenting Adult, Earth Star Voyager, Marcus Welby M.D., A Holiday Affair, The Return of Marcus Welby M.D., The Elephant Man, All Quiet on the Western Front.

STARK, RAY
Producer. e. Rutgers U. Began career after WWII as agent handling Red Ryder radio scripts, and later literary works for such writers as Costain, Marquand and Hecht. Publicity writer, Warner Bros. Joined Famous Artists Agency, where he represented such personalities as Marilyn Monroe, Kirk Douglas and Richard Burton; in 1957, resigned exec. position to form Seven Arts Prods. with Eliot Hyman, serving as exec. v.p. and head of production until 1966, when he left to take on personal production projects. Founded Rastar Prods. and Ray Stark Prods. Received Irving Thalberg Award from Acad. of M.P. Arts and Sciences 1980. TV production: Barbarians at the Gate.
PICTURES: The World of Susie Wong, The Night of the Iguana, This Property Is Condemned, Oh Dad Poor Dad Mama's Hung You in the Closet and I'm Feeling So Sad,

Reflections in a Golden Eye, Funny Girl, The Owl and the Pussycat, Fat City, The Way We Were, Summer Wishes Winter Dreams, For Pete's Sake, Funny Lady, The Sunshine Boys, Robin and Marian, Murder by Death, The Goodbye Girl, Casey's Shadow, The Cheap Detective, California Suite, The Electric Horseman, Chapter Two, Seems Like Old Times, Annie, The Slugger's Wife, Nothing in Common, Brighton Beach Memoirs, Biloxi Blues, Steel Magnolias, Revenge, Lost in Yonkers.

STARR, MIKE
Actor. b. Queens, NY. e. Hofstra Univ. Theatre debut with Manhattan Punchline.
THEATER: NY: Requiem for a Heavyweight, The Guys in the Truck, Map of the World, Vesper's Ever.
PICTURES: Bushido Blade, Cruising, The Natural, The Last Dragon, Cat's Eye, The Money Pit, Violets Are Blue, Off-Beat, Collision Course, Five Corners, Funny Farm, Lean on Me, Blue Steel, Uncle Buck, Last Exit to Brooklyn, Miller's Crossing, GoodFellas, Billy Bathgate, Freejack, The Bodyguard, Mac, Mad Dog and Glory, Son of the Pink Panther, Cabin Boy, On Deadly Ground, The Hudsucker Proxy, Blown Away, Baby's Day Out, Trial by Jury, Ed Wood, Radioland Murders, Dumb & Dumber, A Pyromaniac's Love Story, Clockers, Two If By Sea.
TELEVISION: Series: Hardball. Movies: The Frank Nitti Story, Hot Paint, Stone Pillow. Guest: Kojak, Hawk, The Equalizer, Crime Story, Spenser: For Hire.

STARR, RINGO
O.B.E. Singer, Musician, Songwriter, Actor. r.n. Richard Starkey. b. Liverpool, England, July 7, 1940. m. actress Barbara Bach. Former member of The Beatles.
PICTURES: A Hard Day's Night (debut, 1964), Help!, Yellow Submarine (cameo), Candy, The Magic Christian, Let It Be, 200 Motels, Blindman, The Concert for Bangladesh, Lisztomania, The Last Waltz, Sextette, The Kids Are Alright, Caveman, Give My Regards to Broad Street, Water (cameo), Walking After Midnight.
TELEVISION: Movies: Princess Daisy, Alice in Wonderland. Series: Shining Time Station.

STEADMAN, ALISON
Actress. b. Liverpool, England, Aug. 26, 1946. m. director Mike Leigh. Studied acting with East 15 Acting School.
THEATER: The Prime of Miss Jean Brodie, Hamlet, Wholesome Glory, The Pope's Wedding, The Anchor, The King, Abigail's Party, Joking Apart, Unlce Vanya, The Rise and Fall of Little Voice, Othello, The Plotters of Cabbage Patch Corner.
PICTURES: Kipperbang (debut, 1982), Champions, Number One, A Private Function, Clockwise, Stormy Monday, The Misadventures of Mr. Wilt, Shirley Valentine, Life Is Sweet, Blame It on the Bellboy.
TELEVISION: Virtuoso, The Singing Detective, The Finding, Hard Labour, Nuts in May, Throught the Night, Pasmore.

STEEL, DAWN
Executive. b. New York, NY, Aug. 19, 1946. m. producer Charles Roven. e. marketing student, Boston U. 1964-65, NYU 1966-67; sportswriter, Major League Baseball Digest and NFL/NY 1968-69; 1969-75, editor of Penthouse Magazine; Pres. Oh Dawn! merchandising co. 1979-80, v.p. merchandising Paramount Pictures; 1978-79, merchandising consult., Playboy NYC; 1980-83, v.p. prod. Paramount Pictures. Joined Columbia Pictures 1987 as president (first woman studio pres.), resigned 1990. Formed Steel Pictures for the Walt Disney Co., 1990. Prod. for Disney: Honey I Blew Up the Kid, Cool Runnings, Sister Act 2. Prod. for New Line: Angus. Recipient of Crystal Award (1989). Author: They Can Kill You... But They Can't Eat You (1993). Member: AMPAS, Amer. Film Inst. (bd. 1988-90), NOW Legal Defense Fund; 1993-present, member of dean's advisory bd. at UCLA Sch. of Theatre, Film & TV.

STEELE, BARBARA
Actress. b. Trenton Wirrall, England, Dec. 29, 1937. Studied to be painter prior to joining rep. cos. in 1957.
PICTURES: Bachelor of Hearts (debut, 1958), Sapphire, Your Money or Your Wife, Black Sunday, The Pit and the Pendulum, Revenge of the Mercenaries, The Horrible Dr. Hitchcock, 8 1/2, Danse Macabre (Castle of Blood), The Ghost, The Hours of Love, White Voices, Nightmare Castle, The Maniacs, Terror Creatures From the Grave, The She Beast, Young Torless, Crimson Cult, They Came From Within, Caged Heat, I Never Promised You a Rose Garden, Piranha, Pretty Baby, The Silent Scream.

STEELE, TOMMY
Performer. r.n. Tommy Hicks. b. London, Dec. 17, 1936. Early career Merchant Navy. 1956 first gained fame as successful pop singer. First TV and film appearances, 1957. Composed and sang title song for The Shiralee.

THEATER: Half a Sixpence, Hans Andersen, Singin' in the Rain, Some Like It Hot.
PICTURES: Kill Me Tomorrow (debut, 1957), The Tommy Steele Story (Rock Around the World), The Duke Wore Jeans, Tommy the Toreador, Light Up the Sky, It's All Happening (The Dream Maker), The Happiest Millionaire, Half a Sixpence, Finian's Rainbow, Where's Jack?
TELEVISION: Tommy Steele Spectaculars, Richard Whittington Esquire (Rediffusion), Ed Sullivan Show, Gene Kelly in NY NY, Perry Como Show, Twelfth Night, The Tommy Steele Hour, Tommy Steele in Search of Charlie Chaplin, Tommy Steele and a Show, Quincy's Quest.

STEENBURGEN, MARY
Actress. b. Newport, AR, Feb. 8, 1953. Graduated from Neighborhood Playhouse. Received honorary doctorate degrees from Univ. of Ark. at Little Rock and Hendrix Col. in Conway, AR. On B'way stage 1993 in Candida.
PICTURES: Goin' South (debut, 1978), Time After Time, Melvin and Howard (Academy Award, best supporting actress, 1980), Ragtime, A Midsummer Night's Sex Comedy, Cross Creek, Romantic Comedy, One Magic Christmas, Dead of Winter, End of the Line (also exec. prod.), The Whales of August, Miss Firecracker, Parenthood, Back to the Future Part III, The Long Walk Home (narrator), The Butcher's Wife, What's Eating Gilbert Grape, Philadelphia, Clifford, It Runs in the Family (My Summer Story), Pontiac Moon, My Family/Mi Familia, Powder, The Grass Harp, Nixon.
TELEVISION: Series: Ink (also co-exec. prod.). Mini-Series: Tender Is the Night. Specials: Faerie Tale Theatre (Little Red Riding Hood), The Gift. Movie: The Attic: The Hiding of Anne Frank. Series: Back to the Future (voice for animated series), Ink.

STEIGER, ROD
Actor. b. Westhampton, NY, Apr. 14, 1925. e. Westside H.S., Newark, NJ. Served in U.S. Navy, then employed in Civil Service; studied acting at N.Y. Theatre Wing Dramatic Workshop Actors' Studio; numerous TV plays; on Broadway in ANTA prod. of Night Music.
PICTURES: Teresa (debut, 1951), On the Waterfront, The Big Knife, Oklahoma!, The Court Martial of Billy Mitchell, Jubal, The Harder They Fall, Back From Eternity, Run of the Arrow, The Unholy Wife, Across the Bridge, Cry Terror, Al Capone, Seven Thieves, The Mark, World in My Pocket, 13 West Street, Convicts 4, The Longest Day, Hands Over the City, Time of Indifference, The Pawnbroker, The Loved One, Dr. Zhivago, And There Came a Man (A Man Called John), In the Heat of the Night (Academy Award, 1967), The Girl and the General, No Way to Treat a Lady, The Sergeant, The Illustrated Man, Three Into Two Won't Go, Waterloo, Happy Birthday Wanda June, Duck You Sucker! (A Fistful of Dynamite), The Heroes, Lolly Madonna XXX, Lucky Luciano, Mussolini: Dead or Alive (The Last Days of Mussolini), Hennessey, Dirty Hands, W.C. Fields and Me, Wolf Lake, F.I.S.T., Breakthrough (Sgt. Steiner), The Amityville Horror, Love and Bullets, Klondike Fever, The Lucky Star, Lion of the Desert, Cattle Annie and Little Britches, The Chosen, The Magic Mountain, Portrait of a Hitman (Jim Buck), The Naked Face, The Kindred, Catch the Heat, American Gothic, The January Man, Men of Respect, The Ballad of the Sad Cafe, Midnight Murders, Guilty as Charged, That Summer of White Roses, The Player, The Neighbor, The Last Tattoo, Black Water, The Specialist, Mars Attacks!.
TELEVISION: Many appearances in 1950s live TV including Marty. Movies: Jesus of Nazareth, Cook & Perry: The Race to the Pole, Sword of Gideon, Desperado: Avalanche at Devil's Ridge, Passion and Paradise, In the Line of Duty: Manhunt in the Dakotas, Sinatra, Tom Clancy's Op Center, Choices of the Heart: The Margaret Sanger Story, In Pursuit of Honor, Columbo: Strange Bedfellows. Mini-Series: Hollywood Wives. Special: Tales of the City.

STEINBERG, DAVID
Actor, Writer, Director. b. Winnipeg, Canada, Aug. 9, 1942. e. U. of Chicago; Hebrew Theological Coll. Member Second City troupe; comedian at comedy clubs: Mr. Kelly's Hungry i, Bitter End. Starred in London and B'way stage prods. B'way includes Little Murders, Carry Me Back to Morningside Heights.
PICTURES: Actor: The End, Something Short of Paradise. Director: Paternity, Going Berserk (also co.-s.p.).
TELEVISION: Series: Music Scene (writer, co-host), Tonight Show (guest host), David Steinberg Show. Special: Second City: 25 Years in Revue. Director: Newhart, The Popcorn Kid, Golden Girls, One Big Family, Faerie Tale Theatre, Richard Belzer Special, Baby on Board, Annie McGuire, Seinfeld, Mad About You, Evening Shade, Designing Women, and many commercials.

STEINBERG, HERB
b. New York, NY, July 3, 1921. e. City Coll. of New York, 1937-41. Capt. U.S. Army, 1942-46; pub. PRC, 1946, Eagle Lion,

1946-49, Paramount 1949; pub. mgr. 1951; expl. mgr., 1954; studio adv. & pub. dir., 1958; exec. chg. of spec. proj., press dept., Universal City Studio, 1963; v.p., Universal Studio Tours, 1971; 1974 v.p., MCA Recreation Services. Appt. to California Tourism Commission, Calif. Tourism Hall of Fame, 1984; consultant, MCA, Inc., 1987; bd. trustees, Motion Picture & TV Fund, 1987; bd. of trustees Hollywood Canteen Foundation, 1988; Communications dir. Alliance of Motion Picture & Television Producers.

STEINMAN, MONTE
Executive. b. New York, NY, May 18, 1955. e. Wharton Sch. of Univ. of PA. Joined Paramount Pictures 1980 as sr. financial analyst. Series of promotions followed, culminating in appt. as dir. of financial planning of Gulf & Western's Entertainment and Communications Group, 1984. 1985, named exec. dir., financial planning. 1990, joined Viacom Intl., as mgr. financial planning. 1993, dir. financial planning, MTV Networks. 1994, v.p. finance at MTV Networks.

STEMBLER, JOHN H.
Executive. b. Miami, FL, Feb. 18, 1913. e. U. of FL Law Sch., 1937. Asst. U.S. att., South. dist. of FL, 1941; U.S. Air Force, 1941-45; pres. Georgia Theatre Co., 1957; named chmn., 1983; NATO member exec. comm. and past pres.; Major Gen. USAF (Ret); past bd. chmn., National Bank of Georgia.

STEMBLER, WILLIAM J.
Executive. b. Atlanta, GA, Nov. 29, 1946. e. Westminster Sch., 1964; U. of FL, 1968; U. of GA Law Sch., 1971. 1st. lt. U.S. Army, 1971; capt., U.S. Army Reserve; resigned 1976. Enforcement atty., SEC, Atlanta office, 1972-73; joined Georgia Theatre Co., 1973; pres. 1983-86; joined United Artists Communications, Inc., 1986, as v.p.; Incorporated Value Cinemas 1988 and Georgia Theatre Co. II in 1991 as its chmn. & pres. Bd. of dir., & vice chmn., NATO; member, NATO OF GA & past-pres., 1983-85; Rotary Club of Atlanta, pres. 1991-92.

STEPHENS, ROBERT
Actor. b. Bristol, England, July 14, 1931. e. Esme Church School, Bradford. Made his stage debut at age 13; joined the Royal Court Company in 1956. Son is actor Toby Stephens.
THEATER: London: The Crucible, The Good Woman of Setzuan, The Country Wife, The Entertainer, Look After Lulu, The Wrong Side of the Park, Saint Joan, The Recruiting Officer, Royal Hunt of the Sun, The Beaux Stratagem, Armstrong's Last Goodnight, Apropos of Falling Sleet (also dir.), Murderer, Private Lives, King Lear. NY: Epitaph for George Dillon, Sherlock Holmes.
PICTURES: Circle of Deception (debut, 1961), A Taste of Honey, Pirates of Tortuga, Lisa (The Inspector), The Small World of Sammy Lee, Cleopatra, Morgan!, Romeo and Juliet, The Prime of Miss Jean Brodie, The Private Life of Sherlock Holmes, The Asphyx, Travels With My Aunt, Luther, The Duellists, The Shout, Empire of the Sun, Testimony, High Season, Wonderland (The Fruit Machine), Henry V, The Bonfire of the Vanities, The Pope Must Die, Afraid of the Dark, Chaplin, Searching for Bobby Fisher, The Secret Rapture, Century.
TELEVISION: Vienna 1900 (series), Parnell and O'Shea, Gangsters, Softly Softly, The Holocaust (series, Vienna), Eustace and Hilda, Voyage of Charles Darwin, Kean, Office Story, Friends in Space Society, Suez, Hesther for Example, The Executioner, Eden End, Year of the French, Box of Delights (series), By the Sword Divided, Hells Bells (series), War and Remembrance, Window Sir, Lizzies Pictures (series), Fortunes of War (series), Inspector Morse, Radical Chambers, Adam Bede.

STERLING, JAN
Actress. r.n. Jane Sterling Adriance. b. New Yor, NY, April 3, 1923. e. private tutors; Fay Compton Sch. of Dramatic Art, London. N.Y. stage debut: Bachelor Born.
THEATER: Panama Hattie, Present Laughter, John Loves Mary, Two Blind Mice, Front Page, Over 21, Born Yesterday, The November People.
PICTURES: Johnny Belinda (debut, 1948), Appointment with Danger, Mystery Street, Caged, Union Station, The Skipper Surprised His Wife, The Big Carnival (Ace in the Hole), The Mating Season, Rhubarb, Flesh and Fury, Sky Full of Moon, Pony Express, The Vanquished, Split Second, Alaska Seas, The High and the Mighty (Acad. Award nom.), Return From the Sea, Human Jungle, Women's Prison, Female on the Beach, Man with the Gun, 1984, The Harder They Fall, Slaughter on Tenth Avenue, Kathy O', The Female Animal, High School Confidential, Love in a Goldfish Bowl, The Incident, The Angry Breed, The Minx, First Monday in October.
TELEVISION: Series: You're in the Picture (panelist, 1961), Made in America, The Guiding Light (1969-70). Mini-Series: Backstairs at the White House. Movies: Having Babies, Dangerous Company, My Kidnapper My Love.

STERLING, ROBERT
Actor. r.n. William Sterling Hart. b. Newcastle, PA, Nov. 13, 1917. e. U. of Pittsburgh. m. Anne Jeffreys, actress. Daughter is actress Tisha Sterling. Fountain pen salesman, day laborer, clerk, industrial branch credit mgr., clothing salesman on West Coast; served as pilot-instructor U.S. Army Corps. 3 yrs.
PICTURES: The Amazing Mr. Williams (debut, 1939), Blondie Brings Up Baby, Blondie Meets the Boss, Only Angels Have Wings, Manhattan Heartbeat, Yesterday's Heroes, Gay Caballero, Penalty, I'll Wait for You, Get-Away, Ringside Maisie, Two-Faced Woman, Dr. Kildare's Victory, Johnny Eager, This Time for Keeps, Somewhere I'll Find You, Secret Heart, Roughshod, Bunco Squad, Sundowners, Show Boat, Column South, Voyage to the Bottom of the Sea, Return to Peyton Place, A Global Affair.
TELEVISION: Series: Topper, Love That Jill, Ichabod and Me.
Movies: Letters from Three Lovers, Beggarman, Thief.

STERN, DANIEL
Actor, Director. b. Bethesda, MD, Aug. 28, 1957. e. H.B. Studios. Appeared in 1984 short film Frankenweenie.
PICTURES: Breaking Away (debut, 1979), Starting Over, A Small Circle of Friends, Stardust Memories, It's My Turn, One-Trick Pony, Honky Tonk Freeway, I'm Dancing As Fast As I Can, Diner, Blue Thunder, Get Crazy, C.H.U.D., Key Exchange, The Boss' Wife, Hannah and Her Sisters, Born in East L.A., D.O.A., The Milagro Beanfield War, Leviathan, Little Monsters, Friends Lovers and Lunatics, Coupe de Ville, My Blue Heaven, Home Alone, City Slickers, Home Alone 2: Lost in New York, Rookie of the Year (also dir.), City Slickers II: The Legend of Curly's Gold, Bushwhacked (also exec. prod.), Celtic Pride.
TELEVISION: Movies: Samson and Delilah, Weekend War, The Court-Martial of Jackie Robinson. Series: Hometown, The Wonder Years (narrator; also episode dir.).

STERN, EDDIE
Film buyer. b. New York, NY, Jan. 13, 1917. e. Columbia Sch. of Journalism. Head film buyer and booker, specializing in art theatres, for Rugoff and Becker, NY; Captain, USAF; joined Wometco Ent. in 1952 as asst. to film buyer; v.p. motion picture theatre film buying and booking, Wometco Enterprises, Inc. Retired from Wometco 1985. Now handling film buying and booking for Theatres of Nassau, Ltd.

STERN, EZRA E.
Attorney. b. New York, NY, Mar. 22, 1908. e. Southwestern U. 1930, LL.B. pres., Wilshire Bar Assn. Former legal counsel for So. Calif. Theatre Owners Assn. Member: Calif. State Bar; member, Int'l Variety Clubs; former chief barker, Variety Club So. Calif. Tent 25; pres., Variety Int'l Boys' Club; board of dir., Los Angeles Metropolitan Recreation & Youth Services Council; bd. of trustees, Welfare Planning Council, Los Angeles Region; former mem. Los Angeles Area Council, Boys' Club of America; pres., Variety International Boys' Club 1976-77 and 1979-80. Member bd., Will Rogers Inst., M.P. Pioneers. 1984, honored by Variety Boys and Girls Club as founder of youth recreational facility.

STERN, STEWART
Writer. b. New York, NY, Mar. 22, 1922. e. Ethical Culture Sch., 1927-40; U. of Iowa, 1940-43. Rifle Squad Leader, S/Sgt. 106th Inf. Div., 1943-45; actor, asst. stage mgr., The French Touch, B'way, 1945-46; dialogue dir. Eagle-Lion Studios, 1946-48. 1948 to date: screenwriter.
TELEVISION: Crip, And Crown Thy Good, Thunder of Silence, Heart of Darkness, A Christmas to Remember, Sybil (Emmy Award, 1977).
PICTURES: Teresa, Rebel Without a Cause, The Rack, The James Dean Story, The Outsider, The Ugly American, Rachel Rachel, The Last Movie, Summer Wishes Winter Dreams.

STERNHAGEN, FRANCES
Actress. b. Washington, DC, Jan. 13, 1930. e. Vassar Coll., drama dept.; Perry-Mansfield School of Theatre. Studied with Sanford Meisner at Neighborhood Playhouse, NY. Was teacher at Milton Acad. in MA. Acted with Arena Stage, Washington, DC, 1953-54.
THEATER: Thieves Carnival (off-B'way debut, 1955), The Skin of Our Teeth, The Carefree Tree, The Admirable Bashville, Ulysses in Night Town, Viva Madison Avenue!, Red Eye of Love, Misalliance, Great Day in the Morning, The Right Honorable Gentleman, The Displaced Person, The Cocktail Party, Cock-a-Doodle Dandy, Playboy of the Western World, The Sign in Sidney Brustein's Window, Enemies, The Good Doctor (Tony Award, 1974), Equus, Angel, On Golden Pond, The Father, Grownups, Summer, You Can't Take It With You, Home Front, Driving Miss Daisy, Remembrance, A Perfect Ganesh, The Heiress (Tony Award, 1995).
PICTURES: Up the Down Staircase (debut, 1967), The Tiger Makes Out, The Hospital, Two People, Fedora, Starting Over, Outland, Independence Day, Romantic Comedy, Bright Lights Big City, See You in the Morning, Communion, Sibling Rivalry, Misery, Doc Hollywood, Raising Cain.

TELEVISION: *Series*: Love of Life, Doctors, Golden Years, Under One Roof, The Road Home. *Movies*: Who'll Save Our Children?, Mother and Daughter: The Loving War, Prototype, Follow Your Heart, She Woke Up, Labor of Love: The Arlette Schweitzer Story, Reunion. *Guest*: Cheers, Tales From the Crypt, Outer Limits.

STEUER, ROBERT B.
Executive. b. New Orleans, LA, Nov. 18, 1937. e. U. of Illinois, & 1955-57; Tulane U., 1957-59, B.B.A. Booker-Southern D.I. circuit, New Orleans, 1959; assoc., prod., Poor White Trash; 1960; v.p. Cinema Dist. America, 1961; co-prod., Flesh Eaters, Common Law Wife, Flack Black Pussy Cat; partner, gen. mgr., radio station WTVF, Mobile, 1963; dir. special projects, American Intl. Pictures, 1967; so. div. sls. mgr., AIP, 1971; v.p. asst. gen. sls. mgr., AIP, 1974; partner, United Producers Organization, producing Screamers, 1977; v.p., sls., Ely Landau Org., 1979; v.p., gen. sls. mgr., Film Ventures Intl., 1981; exec. v.p. world-wide mktg., 1983; pres., FVI, 1986-89. 1987, exec. v.p. world-wide mktg. Film Ventures Intl; 1987-88 exec. prod. Operation: Take No Prisoners, Most Dangerous Women Alive, Tunnels, Criminal Act, Au Pair; 1989 sales consultant, 20th Century Fox, 1990-present, prods. rep.; When the Wales Came, China Cry, Twogether, Sweet and Short, Taxi to Soweto, and worldwide mktg., distrib. and sls. consultant to entertainment industry. Films incl. Bound and Gagged: A Love Story, Skin Art, Yankee Zulu.

STEVENS, ANDREW
Actor, Director, Writer, Producer. b. Memphis, TN, June 10, 1955. Mother is actress Stella Stevens. e. Antioch U., L.A., B.A. (psychology). L.A. stage includes Journey's End, Mass Appeal, Leader of the Pack, Billy Budd (also prod.), P.S. Your Cat is Dead, Bouncers (L.A. Drama Circle Critics Award). Pres., CEO Royal Oaks Entertainment Intl. Film Distributors.
PICTURES: *Actor*: Shampoo, Day of the Animals, Massacre at Central High, Las Vegas Lady, Vigilante Force, The Boys in Company C, The Fury, Death Hunt, The Seduction, Ten to Midnight, Scared Stiff, Tusks, Fine Gold, Deadly Innocents, Down the Drain, Eyewitness to Murder, The Ranch, The Terror Within, Blood Chase, Counterforce, The Terror Within II (also dir., s.p.), Red Blooded American Girl, Night Eyes (also s.p., prod.), Munchie, Double Threat, Night Eyes II (also s.p., prod.), Deadly Rivals, Night Eyes III (also s.p., dir.), Body Chemistry III (also prod.), Scorned (also dir.), Illicit Dreams (also dir.), Victim of Desire (prod. only), The Skateboard Kid 2 (also dir.), Body Chemistry 4 (prod. only), Hard Bounty (prod. only), Grid Runners (prod. only), Munchie Strikes Back. Producers: Victim of Desire, Body Chemistry 4, Starhunter, Cyber Zone, Masseuse, Virtual Desire, Alone in the Woods, Invisible Mom, Innocence Betrayed, Illicit Dreams 2, Over the Wire, Terminal Rush, Flash Frame (also dir.)
TELEVISION: *Series*: Oregon Trail, Code Red, Emerald Point N.A.S., Dallas. *Mini-Series*: Hollywood Wives, Once an Eagle. *Movies*: Beggarman Thief, The Rebels, The Bastard, The Last Survivors, The Oregon Trail, Secrets, Topper (also prod.), Women at Westpoint, Code Red, Miracle on Ice, Journey's End, Forbidden Love, Murder in Malibu (Columbo). *Special*: Werewolf of Woodstock. *Guest*: Adam-12, Apple's Way, The Quest, Police Story, Shazam, Hotel, Westside Medical, Murder She Wrote, Love Boat. *Director*: Swamp Thing (3 episodes), Silk Stalkings (2 episodes), General Hospital (3 eps), Walker—Texas Ranger, Marker.

STEVENS, CONNIE
Actress. r.n. Concetta Ann Ingolia. b. Brooklyn, NY, August 8, 1938. e. Sacred Heart Acad., Hollywood Professional Sch. Began career as winner of several talent contests in Hollywood; prof. debut, Hollywood Repertory Theatre's prod. Finian's Rainbow; B'way in Star Spangled Girl (Theatre World Award); recordings include: Kookie Kookie Lend Me Your Comb, 16 Reasons, What Did You Wanna Make Me Cry For, From Me to You, They're Jealous of Me, A Girl Never Knows.
PICTURES: Eighteen and Anxious (debut, 1957), Young and Dangerous, Dragstrip Riot, Rock-a-Bye Baby, The Party Crashers, Parrish, Susan Slade, Palm Springs Weekend, Two on a Guillotine, Never Too Late, Way ... Way Out, The Grissom Gang, The Last Generation, Scorchy, Sgt. Pepper's Lonely Hearts Club Band (cameo), Grease 2, Back to the Beach, Tapeheads, Love Is All There Is.
TELEVISION: *Movies*: Mister Jerico, Call Her Mom, Playmates, Every Man Needs One, The Sex Symbol, Love's Savage Fury, Scruples, Bring Me the Head of Dobie Gillis, Race with Destiny: The James Dean Story. *Series*: Hawaiian Eye, Wendy and Me, Kraft Music Halls Presents The Des O'Connor Show, Starting from Scratch.

STEVENS, CRAIG
Actor. r.n. Gail Shikles. b. Liberty, MO, July 8, 1918. Was married to late actress Alexis Smith. e. U. of Kansas. Played in coll. dramatics.
PICTURES: Affectionately Yours (debut, 1941), Law of the Tropics, Dive Bomber, Steel Against the Sky, Secret Enemies, Spy Ship, The Hidden Hand, Hollywood Canteen, Since You

Went Away, The Doughgirls, God Is My Co-Pilot, Roughly Speaking, Too Young to Know, Humoresque, The Man I Love, That Way With Women, Love and Learn, Night Unto Night, The Lady Takes a Sailor, Where the Sidewalk Ends, Blues Busters, The Lady From Texas, Drums in the Deep South, Phone Call from a Stranger, Murder Without Tears, Abbott and Costello Meet Dr. Jekyll Mr. Hyde, The French Line, Duel on the Mississippi, The Deadly Mantis, Buchanan Rides Alone, Gunn, S.O.B., La Truite (The Trout).
TELEVISION: *Guest*: Lux Video Theatre, Four Star Playhouse, Loretta Young Show, Schlitz Playhouse, Dinah Shore, Ernie Ford Shows, Chevy Show, Summer on Ice, The Millionaire, The Bold Ones. *Series*: Peter Gunn (1958-61), Man of the World (ATV England), Mr. Broadway, The Invisible Man, Dallas. *Movies*: The Killer Bees; The Cabot Connection, The Home Front, Supercarrier, Marcus Welby, M.D.-A Holiday Affair. *Mini-Series*: Rich Man Poor Man.
THEATER: Here's Love, King of Hearts, Plain and Fancy, Critics Choice, Mary Mary, Cactus Flower (natl. co.), My Fair Lady.

STEVENS, FISHER
Actor. b. Chicago, IL, Nov. 27, 1963. e. NYU. Artistic Director of Naked Angels Theatre Co. in NYC.
THEATER: *NY*: Torch Song Trilogy (Off-B'way & B'way), Brighton Beach Memoirs, A Perfect Ganesh, Carousel.
PICTURES: The Burning, Baby It's You, The Brother From Another Planet, The Flamingo Kid, My Science Project, Short Circuit, The Boss's Wife, Short Circuit 2, Point of View, Reversal of Fortune, The Marrying Man, Mystery Date, Bob Roberts, Hero, When the Party's Over, Super Mario Bros., Nina Takes a Lover, Only You, Hackers, Cold Fever.
TELEVISION: *Series*: Key West. *Guest*: Columbo. *Special*: It's Called the Sugar Plum.

STEVENS, GEORGE, JR.
Director, Writer, Producer. b. Los Angeles, CA, Apr. 3, 1932. Son of late director George Stevens. e. Occidental Coll., 1949-53, B.A. 1st Lieut. U.S. Air Force; TV dir., Alfred Hitchcock Presents, Peter Gunn, 1957-61; prod. asst. Giant Productions, 1953-54; prod. asst. Mark VII, Ltd., 1956-57; dir. M.P. Service, U.S. Information Agency 1962-67; chmn., U.S. deleg. to Film Festivals at Cannes (1962, 1964), Venice (1962, 1963), Moscow (1963); Founding director, American Film Institute, 1967-79; co-chmn., American Film Institute, 1979 to present.
PICTURES: The Diary of Anne Frank (assoc. prod.), The Greatest Story Ever Told (assoc. prod.), John F. Kennedy: Years of Lightning Day of Drums (prod.), America at the Movies (prod.), George Stevens: A Filmmaker's Journey (dir., s.p., prod.); 1988 WGA Award for TV broadcast).
TELEVISION: *Specials*: American Film Institute's Salutes (exec. prod./writer, 1973-; received 1975 Emmy Award as exec. prod. of The American Film Institue Salute to James Cagney), The Stars Salute America's Greatest Movies (exec. prod.), The Kennedy Center Honors (prod./writer, 1978-; Emmy Awards: 1984, 1986, 1989), America Entertains Vice Premier Deng (prod./writer), Christmas in Washington, (exec. prod./writer, 1982-), Movies: The Murder of Mary Phagan (co-writer, prod., 1988; Emmy Award for prod.; also Christopher & Peabody Awards), Separate But Equal (dir., writer, co-exec. prod.; Emmy Award for exec. prod.; also Christopher Award, Ohio State Award, Paul Selvin Award by the Writers Guild of America), George Stevens: D-Day to Berlin, The Kennedy Center Honors (co. prod., co-writer; Emmy Award, 1996).

STEVENS, STELLA
Actress, Director. b. Yazoo City, MS, Oct. 1, 1937. r.n. Estelle Eggleston. Mother of actor Andrew Stevens. e. Attended Memphis State U. Modeled in Memphis when she was discovered by talent scouts. Was briefly a term contract actress at 20th Century-Fox, later under exclusive contract to Paramount, then Columbia. *Director*: The American Heroine (feature length doc.), The Ranch (feature comedy).
PICTURES: Say One For Me (debut, 1959), The Blue Angel, Li'l Abner, Man Trap, Girls! Girls! Girls!, Too Late Blues, The Nutty Professor, The Courtship of Eddie's Father, Advance to the Rear, Synanon, The Secret of My Success, The Silencers, Rage, Where Angels Go Trouble Follows, How to Save a Marriage and Ruin Your Life, Sol Madrid, The Mad Room, The Ballad of Cable Hogue, A Town Called Hell, Slaughter, Stand Up & Be Counted, The Poseidon Adventure, Arnold, Cleopatra Jones and the Casino of Gold, Las Vegas Lady, Nickelodeon, The Manitou, Wacko, Chained Heat, The Longshot, Monster in the Closet, Down the Drain, Last Call, The Terror Within II, Eye of the Stranger, The Guest, Exiled in America, The Nutty Nut, Hard Drive, Molly & Gina, Body Chemistry 3: Point of Seduction, Illicit Dreams, The Granny.
TELEVISION: *Series*: Ben Casey, Flamingo Road, Santa Barbara. *Guest*: Bob Hope Bing Crosby Special, Frontier Circus, Johnny Ringo, Alfred Hitchcock, Love Boat, Highway to Heaven, Murder She Wrote, Martin Mull's White America, A Table at Ciros, In the Heat of the Night, Hotel, Night Court, Newhart, Dangerous Curves, The Commish, Burke's Law.

Movies: In Broad Daylight, Climb an Angry Mountain, Linda, The Day The Earth Moved, Honky Tonk, New Original Wonder Woman (pilot), Kiss Me Kill Me, Wanted the Sundance Woman, Charlie Cobb (pilot), The Night They Took Miss Beautiful, Murder in Peyton Place, The Jordan Chance, Cruise into Terror, New Love Boat (pilot), Friendship Secrets and Lies, Hart to Hart (pilot), The French Atlantic Affair, The Pendragon Affair (Eddie Capra Mystery pilot), Make Me an Offer, Children of Divorce, Twirl, Amazons, Women of San Quentin, No Man's Land, A Masterpiece of Murder, Fatal Confessions (Father Dowling pilot), Man Against The Mob, Jake Spanner: Private Eye. *Special*: Attack of the 5'2" Woman.

STEVENSON, CYNTHIA
Actress. b. Oakland, CA, Aug. 2, 1963. Raised in Washington, Vancouver.
THEATER: Ladies Room.
PICTURES: The Player, The Gun in Betty Lou's Handbag, Watch It, Forget Paris, Home for the Holidays.
TELEVISION: *Series*: My Talk Show, Bob, Hope and Gloria.

STEVENSON, JULIET
Actress. b. England, Oct. 30, 1956. e. RADA.
THEATER: Other Worlds, Measure for Measure, Breaking the Silence, Troilus and Cressida, As You Like It, Les Liaisons Dangereuses, Yerma, Hedda Gabler, On the Verge, Burn This, Death and the Maiden, Scenes From an Execution (LA), The Duchess of Malfi.
PICTURES: Drowning by Numbers (debut, 1988), Ladder of Swords, Truly Madly Deeply, The Trial, The Secret Rapture, Emma.
TELEVISION: The Mallens (TV debut), Maybury, Bazaar and Rummage, Life Story, Stanley, Out of Love, Antigone, Oedipus at Colonus, Living With Dinosaurs, Amy, The March, A Doll's House, The Politician's Wife.

STEVENSON, PARKER
Actor. b. Philadelphia, PA, June 4, 1952. e. Princeton U. m. actress Kirstie Alley. Began professional acting career by starring in film, A Separate Peace, while high school senior, having attracted attention through work on TV commercials.
PICTURES: A Separate Peace (debut, 1972), Our Time, Lifeguard, Stroker Ace, Stitches, Official Denial.
TELEVISION: *Series*: Hardy Boys Mysteries, Falcon Crest, Probe, Baywatch, Melrose Place. *Guest*: The Streets of San Francisco, Gunsmoke. *Mini-Series*: North & South Book II, All the Rivers Run. *Movies*: This House Possessed, Shooting Stars, That Secret Sunday, Baywatch: Panic at Malibu Pier, The Cover Girl and the Cop, Are You Lonesome Tonight?, Nighttide, Shadow of a Stranger, Official Denial, Not of This Earth.

STEWART, DOUGLAS DAY
Writer, Director.
PICTURES: *Writer*: The Blue Lagoon, An Officer and a Gentleman. *Director-Writer*: Thief of Hearts, Listen to Me.
TELEVISION: *Writer*: Boy in the Plastic Bubble, The Man Who Could Talk to Kids, Murder or Mercy.

STEWART, JAMES
Actor. b. Indiana, PA, May 20, 1908. e. Mercersburg Acad.; Princeton U. With Falmouth Stock Co., Cape Cod; on NY stage in Goodbye Again; stage mgr. for Camille with Jane Cowl (Boston). In films since 1935; joined U.S. Air Force 1942, commissioned 1944. Retired as Brig. Gen. Voted one of top ten money-making stars, M.P. Herald-Fame poll, 1950, 1952, 1954, 1957; No. 1 Money-Making Star, 1955. 1968, Screen Actors Guild Award. Mem.: Bd. of Trustees, Princeton U. Trustee, Claremont Coll.; exec. bd. of Los Angeles Council of Boy Scouts of America; bd. of dirs., Project Hope. Honorary Academy Award, 1984. Author: Jimmy Stewart and His Poems (1989).
THEATER: Spring in Autumn, All Good Americans, Yellow Jack, Journey at Night, Harvey.
PICTURES: Murder Man (debut, 1935), Rose Marie, Wife vs. Secretary, Next Time We Love, Small Town Girl, Speed, The Gorgeous Hussy, Born to Dance, After the Thin Man, Seventh Heaven, The Last Gangster, Navy Blue and Gold, Of Human Hearts, You Can't Take It With You, Vivacious Lady, The Shopworn Angel, Made For Each Other, Ice Follies of 1939, Mr. Smith Goes to Washington (Acad. Award nom.), It's A Wonderful World, Destry Rides Again, The Shop Around the Corner, The Mortal Storm, No Time For Comedy, The Philadelphia Story (Academy Award, 1940), Come Live With Me, Pot O'Gold, Ziegfeld Girl, It's a Wonderful Life (Acad. Award nom.), Magic Town, Call Northside 777, On Our Merry Way (A Miracle Can Happen), Rope, You Gotta Stay Happy, The Stratton Story, Malaya, Winchester 73, Broken Arrow, Harvey (Acad. Award nom.), The Jackpot, No Highway in the Sky, The Greatest Show on Earth, Carbine Williams, Bend of the River, The Naked Spur, Thunder Bay, The Glenn Miller Story, Rear Window, The Far Country, Strategic Air Command, The Man From Laramie, The Man Who Knew Too Much, The

Spirit of St. Louis, Night Passage, Vertigo, Bell Book and Candle, Anatomy of a Murder (Acad. Award nom.), The FBI Story, The Mountain Road, X-15 (narrator), Two Rode Together, The Man Who Shot Liberty Valance, Mr. Hobbs Takes a Vacation, How the West Was Won, Take Her She's Mine, Cheyenne Autumn, Dear Brigitte, Shenandoah, The Flight of the Phoenix, The Rare Breed, Firecreek, Bandolero, The Cheyenne Social Club, Fool's Parade, That's Entertainment, The Shootist, Airport '77, The Big Sleep, The Magic of Lassie, Africa Mongotari (A Tale of Africa), An American Tail: Fievel Goes West (voice).
TELEVISION: *Series*: The Jimmy Stewart Show (1971-72), Hawkins (1973-74). *Movies*: Hawkins on Murder, Right of Way. *Special*: The Windmill, The Town With a Past, Let's Take a Trip, Flashing Spikes, Mr. Kreuger's Christmas.

STEWART, JAMES L.
Executive. e. U. of Southern California, B.A. in cinema-TV and M.B.A. in finance. Worked for two years in sales for CBS Radio Network-West Coast. Spent four years with MGM in promotion and marketing. With Walt Disney Prods. for 12 years, functioning in marketing, management and administrative activities; named v.p.-corp. relations & admin. asst. to pres. 1978 joined in formation of Aurora Pictures, as exec. v.p., secty., & COO.
PICTURES: *Exec. prod.*: Why Would I Lie?, The Secret of NIMH, Eddie and the Cruisers, Heart Like a Wheel, East of the Sun, West of the Moon, Maxie.

STEWART, MARILYN
Marketing & Public Relations Executive. b. New York, NY. e. Hunter Coll. Entered ind. as scty. then asst. to MGM dir. of adv. Left to become prom.-pub. dir. for Verve/Folkways Records; duties also included ar and talent scouting. In 1966 joined 20th-Fox as radio/tv pub. coordinator. In 1969 went to Para. Pictures as mag. pub. coordinator; 1970 named worldwide dir. of pub. for Para., including creation of overall mkt. concepts, becoming 1st woman to be appt. to that position at major co. Campaigns included Love Story and The Godfather. 1972 opened own consulting office specializing in m.p. marketing and p.r. Headquarters in NY; repr. in L.A. Has represented The Lords of Flatbush, Bang the Drum Slowly, The Kids Are Alright, Autumn Sonata, The Tin Drum, A Cry in the Dark, The Russia House, Filmex, Michael Moriarty, Arthur Hiller, Fred Schepisi, Volker Schlondorff, Hemdale Pictures, Lucasfilm.

STEWART, PATRICK
Actor. b. Mirfield, England, July 13, 1940. Trained at Bristol Old Vic Theatre School. Made professional stage debut 1959 in Treasure Island with Lincoln Rep. Co. at the Theatre Royal in Lincoln.
THEATER: *NY*: A Midsummer Night's Dream, A Christmas Carol, The Tempest. Numerous London theatre credits incl.: The Investigation, Henry V, The Caretaker, Body and Soul, Who's Afraid of Virginia Woolf?, Yonadab. Associate artist with Royal Shakespeare Co. since 1967; many appearances with them incl. Antony and Cleopatra for which he received the Olivier Award for Best Supporting Actor in 1979.
PICTURES: Hennessey, Hedda, Excalibur, The Plague Dogs (voice), Races, Dune, Lifeforce, Code Name: Emerald, Wild Geese II, The Doctor and the Devils, Lady Jane, L.A. Story, Robin Hood: Men in Tights, Gunmen, Star Trek: Generations, The Pagemaster (voice), Liberation (narrator), Jeffrey, Star Trek: First Contact.
TELEVISION: *Series*: Eleventh Hour (BBC), Maybury (BBC), Star Trek: The Next Generation (U.S.). *Mini-Series*: I Claudius, Smiley's People. *Movies*: Little Lord Fauntleroy, Pope John Paul II, Death Train. *Special*: In Search of Dr. Seuss. *BBC Specials*: Oedipus Rex, Miss Julie, Hamlet, The Devil's Disciple, Fall of Eagles, The Artist's Story, Love Girl and the Innocent, Conrad, A Walk With Destiny, Alfred the Great, The Madness, When the Actors Come, Tolstoy: A Question of Faith, The Anatomist, The Mozart Inquest.

STIERS, DAVID OGDEN
Actor. b. Peoria, IL, Oct. 31, 1942. Guest conductor: 50 American orchestras incl. Chicago, San Diego, Dallas, Utah, and Chamber Orchestra of Baltimore. Resident conductor of Yaquina Chamber Orchestra in Oregon.
THEATER: *NY*: The Magic Show, Ulysses in Nighttown, The Three Sisters, Beggar's Opera, Measure for Measure.
PICTURES: Drive He Said, THX 1138, Oh God!, The Cheap Detective, Magic, Harry's War, The Man With One Red Shoe, Better Off Dead, Creator, Another Woman, The Accidental Tourist, Doc Hollywood, Beauty and the Beast (voice), Shadows and Fog, Iron Will, Bad Company, Pocahontas (voice), Steal Big Steal Little, Mighty Aphrodite, Meet Wally Sparks, The Hunchback of Notre Dame (voice).
TELEVISION: *Series*: Doc, M*A*S*H. *Movies*: Charlie's Angels (pilot), A Circle of Children, A Love Affair: The Eleanor and Lou Gehrig Story, Sgt. Matlovich Vs. the U.S. Air Force, Breaking Up is Hard to Do, Damien: The Leper Priest, The Day the Bubble Burst, Anatomy of an Illness, The First Olympics: Athens 1896, The Bad Seed, 5 Perry Mason Movies

(Shooting Star, Lost Love, Sinister Spirit, Avenging Ace, Lady in the Lake), Mrs. Delafield Wants to Marry, The Alamo: 13 Days to Glory, The Kissing Place, Final Notice, The Final Days, How to Murder a Millionaire, Wife Mother Murderer, The Last of His Tribe, Without a Kiss Goodbye. *Specials:* The Oldest Living Graduate, The Innocents Abroad, Mastergate. *Mini-Series:* North and South (also Book II).

STILLER, BEN
Actor, Director. b. New York, NY, 1966. Son of performers Jerry Stiller and Anne Meara. e. UCLA. Made short film parody of The Color of Money, called The Hustler of Money which landed him work on Saturday Night Live. Acting debut in 1985 B'way revival of The House of Blue Leaves.
PICTURES: Hot Pursuit, Empire of the Sun, Fresh Horses, Next of Kin, That's Adequate, Stella, Highway to Hell, Reality Bites (also dir.), Heavyweights, Get Shorty, Flirting With Disaster, The Cable Guy (also dir.).
TELEVISION: *Series:* Saturday Night Live (also writer), The Ben Stiller Show (also creator, dir., writer; Emmy Award as writer). *Specials:* House of Blue Leaves, Colin Quinn Back in Brooklyn (dir., writer). *Movie:* Working Trash.

STILLER, JERRY
Actor. b. New York, NY, June 8, 1929. m. actress Anne Meara. Son is actor Ben Stiller. With partner Meara gained recognition as comedy team in nightclubs, theatres and on tv, most notably The Ed Sullivan Show.
THEATER: *B'way:* The Ritz, Passione, Hurlyburly, Three Men on a Horse, What's Wrong With This Picture?
PICTURES: The Taking of Pelham One Two Three, Airport 1975, The Ritz, Nasty Habits, Those Lips Those Eyes, In Our Hands, Hot Pursuit, Nadine, Hairspray, That's Adequate, Little Vegas, Highway to Hell, The Pickle, Heavyweights.
TELEVISION: *Movies:* Madame X, The Other Woman, Seize the Day. Series: The Paul Lynde Show, Joe and Sons, Take Five With Stiller and Meara (synd), Tattingers, Seinfeld. *Guest:* L.A. Law, In the Heat of the Night, Homicide.

STING
Musician, Actor. r.n. Gordon Matthew Sumner. b. Newcastle-Upon-Tyne, England, Oct. 2, 1951. e. Warwick U. A schoolteacher before helping form rock group, The Police as songwriter, singer and bass player. Broadway debut: Threepenny Opera, 1989.
PICTURES: Quadrophenia, Radio On, The Great Rock 'n' Roll Swindle, The Secret Policeman's Other Ball, Brimstone and Treacle, Dune, The Bride, Plenty, Bring on the Night, Julia and Julia, Stormy Monday, The Adventures of Baron Munchausen, Resident Alien, The Music Tells You, The Grotesque.

STOCKWELL, DEAN
Actor. b. Hollywood, CA, Mar. 5, 1935. p. Harry and Betty Veronica Stockwell. Brother is actor Guy Stockwell. e. Long Island public schools and Martin Milmore, Boston. On stage in Theatre Guild prod. Innocent Voyage. Appeared on radio in Death Valley Days and Dr. Christian. Named in 1949 M.P. Herald-Fame Stars of Tomorrow poll; 1976 retired to Santa Monica as a licensed real estate broker but soon returned to acting.
PICTURES: Anchors Aweigh (debut, 1945), The Valley of Decision, Abbott and Costello in Hollywood, The Green Years, Home Sweet Homicide, The Mighty McGurk, The Arnelo Affair, The Romance of Rosy Ridge, Song of the Thin Man, Gentleman's Agreement, Deep Waters, The Boy With Green Hair, Down to the Sea in Ships, The Secret Garden, The Happy Years, Kim, Stars in My Crown, Kim, Cattle Drive, Gun for a Coward, The Careless Years, Compulsion, Sons and Lovers, Long Day's Journey Into Night, Rapture, Psych-Out, The Dunwich Horror, The Last Movie, The Loners, The Werewolf of Washington, Win Place or Steal (The Big Payoff), Won Ton Ton The Dog Who Saved Hollywood, Stick Fighter (South Pacific Connection), Tracks, She Came to the Valley, Alsino and the Condor, Sandino, Human Highway (also co-dir., s.p.), Wrong Is Right, To Kill a Stranger, Paris Texas, Dune, The Legend of Billie Jean, To Live and Die in L.A., Blue Velvet, Gardens of Stone, Beverly Hills Cop II, Banzai Runner, The Blue Iguana, Tucker: The Man and His Dream, Married to the Mob (Acad. Award nom.), Palais Royale, Limit Up, Buying Time, Time Guardian, The Player, Chasers, Mr. Wrong.
TELEVISION: *Series:* Quantum Leap. *Guest:* Miami Vice, Hart to Hart, Simon and Simon, The A-Team, Wagon Train, Twilight Zone, Playhouse 90, Bonanza, Hallmark Hall of Fame, Hunter, Police Story, Greatest Show on Earth. *Movies:* Paper Man, The Failing of Raymond, The Adventures of Nick Carter, The Return of Joe Forrester, Three for the Road, A Killing Affair, Born to Be Sold, Sweet Smell of Death (U.K.), The Gambler III: The Legend Continues, Son of the Morning Star, Backtrack, Shame, Fatal Memories, Bonanza: The Return, In the Line of Duty: The Price of Vengeance, Justice in a Small Town, The Innocent, Madonna: Innocence Lost, Deadline for Murder: From the Files of Edna Buchanan, Stephen King's The Langoliers. *Pilot:* Caught in the Act.

STODDARD, BRANDON
Executive. b. Brideport, CT, March 31, 1937. e. Yale U., Columbia Law Sch. Was program ass't. at Batton, Barton, Durstine and Osborn before joining Grey Advertising, where was successively, program operations supvr., dir. daytime programming, v.p. in chg. of TV, radio programming. Joined ABC in 1970; named v.p. daytime programs for ABC Entertainment, 1972; v.p. children's programs, 1973. Named v.p., motion pictures for TV, 1974; 1976 named v.p., dramatic programs and m.p. for TV; 1979, named pres., ABC Motion Pictures; 1985 appt. pres., ABC Entertainment. Resigned 1989 to head ABC Prods. unit to create and prod. series and movies for ABC and other networks.

STOLNITZ, ART
Executive. b. Rochester, NY, March 13, 1928. e. U. of Tennessee, LL.B., 1952. U.S. Navy Air Force. Legal dept., William Morris Agency, 1953, dir. business affairs, ZIV, 1959; dir. new program development, ZIV-United Artists, 1960; literary agent, MCA, 1961; dir. business affairs, Selmur Productions, Selmur Pictures, 1963; v.p. ABC Pictures, 1969; v.p. Metromedia Producers Corporation, 1970, executive v.p. Metromedia Producers Corporation; 1975 exec. v.p. and prod. Charles Fries Prods. 1976, prod. Edgar J. Scherick Productions; 1976-77 prod., Grizzly Adams (TV); 1977; v.p. business affairs, Warner Bros.-TV; 1980, sr. v.p., business affairs; 1990, exec. v.p. business & financial affairs, Lorimar; 1993, exec. v.p. business and financial affairs, Warner Bros. TV.

STOLOFF, VICTOR
Producer, Writer, Director, Editor. b. March 17, 1913. e. French Law U. Ac. Fines Arts. Prod. dir. writer of award winning documentaries (Warner Bros. release); Prod. dir. writer first U.S. film made in Italy, When in Rome; contract writer, dir. to Sidney Buchman, Columbia.
PICTURES: *Writer:* Volcano, The Sinner, Shark Reef, Journey Around the World. Of Love and Desire (also prod.), Intimacy (also prod., dir.), The Washington Affair (prod., dir.), The 300 Year Weekend (also dir.).
TELEVISION: Ford Theatre, Lloyd Bridges series, National Velvet, High Adventure with Lowell Thomas, *Prod.:* Hawaii Five-O. *Created* Woman of Russia (dir., writer), Audience (exec. prod., dir.).

STOLTZ, ERIC
Actor. b. Los Angeles, CA, 1961. Moved to American Samoa at age 3; family returned to California when he was 8. Spent 2 years at U. of Southern California in theatre arts; left to study with Stella Adler and later William Traylor and Peggy Feury. Stage work with an American rep. co. in Scotland in Tobacco Road, You're a Good Man Charlie Brown, Working. Off-B'way: The Widow Claire, The American Plan, Down the Road. Broadway debut Our Town (1988, Theatre World Award, Tony nom. & Drama Desk nom.), followed by Two Shakespearean Actors.
PICTURES: Fast Times at Ridgemont High (debut, 1982), Surf II, Running Hot, The Wild Life, The New Kids, Mask, Code Name: Emerald, Some Kind of Wonderful, Lionheart, Sister Sister, Haunted Summer, Manifesto, The Fly II, Say Anything, Memphis Belle, The Waterdance, Singles (cameo), Bodies Rest & Motion (also co-prod.), Naked in New York, Killing Zoe, Sleep With Me (also prod.), Pulp Fiction, Little Women, Rob Roy, Fluke, The Prophecy, Kicking and Screaming, Grace of My Heart, 2 Days in the Valley, Inside.
TELEVISION: *Movies:* The Grass Is Always Greener Over the Septic Tank, The Seekers, The Violation of Sarah McDavid, Paper Dolls, Thursday's Child, A Killer in the Family, Money, The Heart of Justice, Foreign Affairs, Roommates. *Specials:* Things Are Looking Up, Sensibility and Sense, Our Town. *Guest:* Mad About You.

STONE, ANDREW L.
Director, Producer, Writer. b. Oakland, CA, July 16, 1902. e. U. of CA. Ent. ind. 1918 at Universal San Francisco exch.; later author, prod., dir. series of pictures for Paramount; prod., dir. for Sono-Art; 1932-36 org. and oper. Race Night company. Formed Andrew Stone Prods., 1943. Co-prod. with wife Virginia beginning in 1958.
PICTURES: *Dir.:* Dreary House (debut, 1928; also prod.), Hell's Headquarters, The Girl Said No (also prod., story), Stolen Heaven (also prod., story), Say It in French (also prod.), The Great Victor Herbert (also prod., co-story), There's Magic in Music (also prod., co-story), Stormy Weather, Hi Diddle Diddle (also prod.), Sensations of 1945 (also prod., co-s.p.), Bedside Manner (also prod.), The Bachelor's Daughters (also prod., s.p.), Fun on a Weekend (also prod., s.p.), Highway 301 (also s.p.), Confidence Girl (also prod., story, s.p.), The Steel Trap (also story, s.p.), Blueprint for Murder (also story, s.p.), The Night Holds Terror (also prod., story), Julie (also s.p.). *Dir./Co-Prod./Writer:* Cry Terror, The Decks Ran Red, The Last Voyage, Ring of Fire, The Password Is Courage, Never Put It in Writing, The Secret of My Success, Song of Norway, The Great Waltz.

STONE, AUBRY
Executive. b. Charlotte, NC, Jan. 14, 1964. e. U. of NC-Chapel Hill. Joined Consolidated Theatres Inc. in 1987. Helped to found a new motion picyire exhibition business, consolidated Theatres/The Stone Group, 1990. V.P., Consolidates Theatres/The Stone Group, 1990-95. Assumed role of v.p./general mgr. in 1996. Bd. of dirs., NATO of NC & SC, 1991-present. Bd of dirs., National NATO, 1995-present; vice chmn., Programs & Services Committee, National NATO.

STONE, BURTON
Executive. b. Feb. 16, 1928; e. Florida Southern Coll. Was film ed., Hollywood Film Co. 1953-61; serv. mgr., sales mgr. and gen. mgr., Consolidated Film Inds., 1953-61; nat'l sales mgr., Movielab, 1961-63; pres., Allservice Film Laboratories, 1963-64; v.p. Technicolor, Inc., 1964-70. Pres., Precision Film Labs., 1965-76. Pres., Deluxe Laboratories, Inc., a wholly-owned subsidiary of 20th Century Fox, 1976-91. 1991, pres. Deluxe color, a sub of the Rank Org. Member: Board of directors, Will Rogers Foundation and Motion Picture Pioneers; member Acad. of Motion Picture Arts & Sciences, American Society of Cinematographers; awarded fellowship in Society of Motion Picture & Television Engineers; past pres., Association of Cinema & Video Laboratories; awarded fellowship in British Kinematograph, Sound & Television Society.

STONE, DEE WALLACE
Actress. r.n. Deanna Bowers. b. Kansas City, MO, Dec. 14, 1948. m. actor Christopher Stone. e. U. of Kansas, theater and education. Taught high school English. Came to NY to audition for Hal Prince and spent 2 years working in commercials and industrial shows. First break in Police Story episode.
PICTURES: The Stepford Wives (debut, 1975), The Hills Have Eyes, 10, The Howling, E.T. the Extra-Terrestrial, Jimmy the Kid, Cujo, Critters, Secret Admirer, Club Life, Shadow Play, The White Dragon, Alligator II: The Mutation, Popcorn, Rescue Me, Frighteners.
TELEVISION: Series: Together We Stand, Lassie, High Sierra Search and Rescue. Movies: The Sky's No Limit, Young Love First Love, The Secret War of Jackie's Girls, Child Bride of Short Creek, The Five of Me, A Whale for the Killing, Skeezer, Wait Til Your Mother Gets Home, Happy, I Take These Men, Hostage Flight, Sin of Innocence, Addicted to His Love, Stranger on My Land. Terror in the Sky, The Christmas Visitor, I'm Dangerous Tonight, Prophet of Evil: The Ervil LeBaron Story, Witness to the Execution, Search and Rescue, Moment of Truth: Cradle of Conspiracy, Huck and the King of Hearts. Guest: CHiPs.

STONE, MARIANNE
Actress. b. London, England. Studied Royal Acad. of Dramatic Art, West End debut in The Kingmaker, 1946.
PICTURES: Brighton Rock, Seven Days to Noon, The Clouded Yellow, Wrong Arm of the Law, Heavens Above, Stolen Hours, Nothing But the Best, Curse of the Mummy's Tomb, Hysteria, The Beauty Jungle, A Hard Day's Night, Rattle of a Simple Man, Echo of Diana, Act of Murder, Catch Us If You Can, You Must Be Joking, The Countess from Hong Kong, The Wrong Box, To Sir With Love, The Bliss of Mrs. Blossom, Here We Go Round the Mulberry Bush, Carry on Doctor, The Twisted Nerve, The Best House in London, Oh! What a Lovely War; The Raging Moon, There's a Girl in My Soup, All the Right Noises, Assault, Carry On at Your Convenience, All Coppers Are..., Carry on Girls, Penny Gold, The Vault of Horror, Percy's Progress, Confessions of a Window Cleaner, Carry on Dick, That Lucky Touch, Sarah, Carry on Behind, Confessions from a Holiday Camp, The Chiffy Kids, What's Up Superdoc?; The Class of Miss McMichael, The Human Factor, Dangerous Davies, Funny Money, Terry on the Fence, Carry on Laughing.
TELEVISION: Maigret, Bootsie and Snudge, Jimmy Edwards Show, Wayne and Schuster Show, Roy Hudd Show, Harry Worth Show, Steptoe and Son, Informer, Love Story, Father Dear Father, Bless This House, The Man Outside, Crown Court, Public Eye, Miss Nightingale, She, Little Lord Fauntleroy/The Secret Army (2 series), Shillingbury Tale, The Bright Side (series), Tickets for the Titanic (series), The Balance of Nature, Always, Hammer House of Mystery & Suspense, The Nineteenth Hole.

STONE, OLIVER
Director, Writer. b. New York, NY, Sept. 15, 1946. e. Yale U., NYU, B.F.A., 1971. Teacher in Cholon, Vietnam 1965-66. U.S. Infantry specialist 4th Class. 1967-68 in Vietnam (Purple Heart, Bronze Star with Oak Leaf Cluster honors).
PICTURES: Sugar Cookies (assoc. prod.), Seizure (dir., s.p., co-editor, 1974), Midnight Express (s.p.: Academy Award, 1978), The Hand (dir., s.p., cameo), Conan the Barbarian (co-s.p.), Scarface (s.p.), Year of the Dragon (co-s.p.), Salvador (dir., co-s.p., co-prod.), 8 Million Ways to Die (co-s.p.), Platoon (dir., s.p., cameo; Academy Award & DGA Award for Best Director, 1986), Wall Street (dir., co-s.p., cameo), Talk Radio (dir., co-s.p.), Born on the Fourth of July (dir., co-s.p., cameo;

Academy Award & DGA Award for Best Director, 1989), Blue Steel (co-prod.), Reversal of Fortune (co-prod.), The Doors (dir., co-s.p., cameo), Iron Maze (co-exec. prod.), JFK (dir., co-prod., co-s.p.), South Central (co-exec. prod.), Zebrahead (co-exec. prod.), Dave (actor), The Joy Luck Club (co-exec. prod.), Heaven and Earth (dir., co-prod., s.p.), Natural Born Killers (dir., co-prod., co-s.p.), The New Age (exec. prod.), Nixon (dir., co-s.p., co-prod.; Chicago Film Critics Award), Killer: A Journal of Murder (co-exec. prod.), The People vs. Larry Flynt (prod.).
TELEVISION: Mini-Series: Wild Palms (co-exec. prod.). Movie: Indictment: The McMartin Trial (co-exec. prod.).

STONE, PETER
Writer. b. Los Angeles, CA, Feb. 27, 1930. Son of film prod. John Stone and screenwriter Hilda Hess Stone. e. Bard Col., B.A. 1951; Yale U., M.F.A., 1953. Won Mystery Writers of America Award for Charade, Christopher Award for 1776.
THEATER: Kean, Skyscraper, 1776 (Tony and NY Drama Critics Circle Awards, 1969), Two By Two, Sugar, Full Circle, Woman of the Year (Tony Award, 1981), My One and Only, Grand Hotel, Will Rogers Follies (Tony, Grammy and NY Drama Critics Circle Awards, 1991).
PICTURES: Charade, Father Goose (Academy Award, 1964), Mirage, Arabesque, The Secret War of Harry Frigg, Jigsaw, Sweet Charity, Skin Game, The Taking of Pelham One Two Three, 1776, The Silver Bears, Who Is Killing the Great Chefs of Europe?, Why Would I Lie?, Just Cause.
TELEVISION: Studio One, Brenner, Witness, Asphalt Jungle, The Defenders (Emmy Award, 1962). Androcles and the Lion, Adam's Rib (series), Ivan the Terrible (series), Baby on Board, Grand Larceny.

STONE, SHARON
Actress. b. Meadville, PA, March 10, 1958. e. Edinboro St. Univ. Started as model, appearing in several TV commercials.
PICTURES: Stardust Memories (debut, 1980), Deadly Blessing, Bolero, Irreconcilable Differences, King Soloman's Mines, Allan Quartermain and the Lost City of Gold, Cold Steel, Police Academy 4: Citizens on Patrol, Action Jackson, Above the Law, Blood and Sand, Beyond the Stars (Personal Choice), Total Recall, He Said/She Said, Scissors, Year of the Gun, Basic Instinct, Diary of a Hit Man, Where Sleeping Dogs Lie, Sliver, Last Action Hero (cameo), Intersection, The Specialist, The Quick and the Dead (also co- prod.), Casino (Golden Globe Award), The Last Dance, Diabolique.
TELEVISION: Series: Bay City Blues. Mini-Series: War and Remembrance. Movies: Not Just Another Affair, The Calendar Girl Murders, The Vegas Strip Wars, Tears in the Rain. Pilots: Mr. & Mrs. Ryan, Badlands 2005. Guest: T.J. Hooker, Magnu P.I., Roseanne.

STOPPARD, TOM
Writer, Director. b. Zlin, Czechoslovakia, July 3, 1937. r.n. Tomas Straussler. Playwright whose works include Rosencrantz and Guildenstern Are Dead, Jumpers, Travesties, The Real Thing, Hapgood, Arcadia.
PICTURES: The Romantic Englishwoman, Despair, The Human Factor, Squaring the Circle, Brazil, Empire of the Sun, The Russia House, Rosencrantz and Guildenstern Are Dead (also dir.), Billy Bathgate.

STORARO, VITTORIO
Cinematographer. b. Rome, Italy, June 24, 1940. Trained at Rome's Centro Sperimentale Cinematografia and began filming short films. His work as Bernardo Bertolucci's regular cinematographer won him an international reputation and award-winning work in Europe and America, including 3 Academy Awards.
PICTURES: Giovinezza Giovinezza (Youthful Youthful), The Conformist, The Spider's Stratagem, 'Tis Pity She's a Whore, Last Tango in Paris, Giordano Bruno, 1900, Submission, Agatha, Apocalypse Now (Academy Award, 1979), Luna, Reds (Academy Award, 1981), One From the Heart, Wagner, Ladyhawke, Captain Eo, Ishtar, The Last Emperor (Academy Award, 1987), Tucker: The Man and His Dream, New York Stories (Life Without Zoe), Dick Tracy, The Sheltering Sky, Tosca, Little Buddha, Roma! Imago Urbis, Flamenco, Taxi.

STOREY, FREDERICK
Executive. b. Columbus, GA, Nov. 12, 1909. e. Georgia Tech. Adv. staff Atlanta Journal, 1933-38; adv. staff C. P. Clark Adv. Agcy., 1938; partner 1940; U.S. Navy, 1941-46; staff Georgia Theatre Co., 1946; v.p. 1947-52. Founded Storey Theatres Inc., Atlanta, GA; 1952, now bd. chmn. emeritus (formerly pres.) of Georgia State Theatres; dir. numerous theatre cos.; v.p. dir., Motion Picture Theatre Owners of Georgia, Dist. Alumnus award, Georgia Tech, 1979.

STORKE, WILLIAM F.
Producer. b. Rochester, NY, Aug. 12, 1927. e. UCLA, B.A. 1948. In Navy, WWII. First position with NBC Hollywood guest relations staff, 1948. Moved to continuity acceptance dept. as

comm. editor. Prom. to asst. mgr, comm. spvr. before joining NBC West Coast sales dept., 1953. Transferred to N.Y. as prog. acct. exec., 1955; named administrator, participating prog. sales, 1957. Named dir., participating program sales, 1959. Named dir., program adm., NBC-TV, 1964; then elected v.p., program adm.; 1967 named v.p., programs, East Coast; 1968, appt. v.p., special programs, NBC-TV Network; 1979, pres., Claridge Group, Ltd.; exec. v.p. Entertainment Partners, Inc., N.Y., 1982-. Pres., Storke Enterprises Inc. 1988-.
TELEVISION: *Producer*: Oliver Twist, To Catch A King, A Christmas Carol, The Last Days of Patton, A Special Friendship, The Ted Kennedy Jr. Story, Buck James (series, exec. prod.), Old Man and the Sea, Hands of a Murderer (Sherlock Holmes).

STORM, GALE
Actress. r.n. Josephine Cottle. b. Bloomington, TX, April 5, 1922. Won Gateway to Hollywood talent contest while still in high school, in 1939. Also launched successful recording career. *Autobiography*: I Ain't Down Yet (1981).
PICTURES: Tom Brown's Schooldays (debut, 1939), Smart Alecks, Foreign Agent, Nearly Eighteen, Where Are Your Children?, Revenge of the Zombies, The Right to Live, Sunbonnet Sue, Swing Parade of 1946, It Happened on Fifth Avenue, The Dude Goes West, Stampede, The Kid From Texas, Abandoned, Between Midnight and Dawn, Underworld Story, Curtain Call at Cactus Creek, Al Jennings of Oklahoma, Texas Rangers, Woman of the North Country.
TELEVISION: *Series*: My Little Margie, Oh Susanna.

STOSSEL, JOHN
News Correspondent. b. 1947. e. Princeton U. Started as producer-reporter with KGW-TV in Portland, OR. Joined WCBS-TV in New York as investigative reporter and consumer editor, winning 15 local Emmy Awards. 1981 joined ABC-TV, appearing on Good Morning America and 20/20 as consumer editor. Also provides twice-weekly consumer reports on ABC Radio Information Network. Author: Shopping Smart (1982).

STOWE, MADELEINE
Actress. b. Los Angeles, CA, Aug. 18, 1958. e. USC. m. actor Brian Benben. Began acting at the Solari Theatre in Beverly Hills where she appeared in The Tenth Man.
PICTURES: Stakeout (debut, 1987), Tropical Snow, Worth Winning, Revenge, The Two Jakes, Closet Land, China Moon, Unlawful Entry, The Last of the Mohicans, Another Stakeout, Short Cuts, Blink, Bad Girls, Twelve Monkeys.
TELEVISION: *Series*: The Gangster Chronicles. *Movies*: The Nativity, The Deerslayer, Amazons, Blood and Orchids. *Mini-Series*: Beulah Land.

STRAIGHT, BEATRICE
Actress. b. Old Westbury, NY, Aug. 2, 1914. Trained in classics; won Tony award early in career for best actress in Arthur Miller's The Crucible.
THEATER: *NY*: King Lear, Twelfth Night, The Possessed, Land of Fame, Eastward in Eden, The Heiress (B'way & on tour), The Crucible (Tony Award), Phedra, Everything in the Garden, Ghosts, All My Sons. *Regional*: A Streetcar Named Desire, The Lion in Winter, Old Times.
PICTURES: Phone Call from a Stranger (debut, 1952), Patterns, The Nun's Story, Garden Party, Network (Academy Award, best supporting actress, 1976), The Promise, Bloodline, The Formula, Endless Love, Poltergeist, Two of a Kind, Power.
TELEVISION: *Series*: Beacon Hill, King's Crossing, Jack and Mike. *Mini-Series*: The Dain Curse, Robert Kennedy and His Times. *Specials*: The Borrowers, Faerie Tale Theatre (The Princess and the Pea). *Movies*: Killer on Board, Under Siege, Run Till You Fall, Chiller, People Like Us.

STRASBERG, SUSAN
Actress. b. New York, NY, May 22, 1938. e. NY. p. late Lee Strasberg, stage dir. & dir. of Actors Studio, and Paula Miller, actress. Off-B'way stage debut in Maya; followed by The Duchess and the Smugs, Romeo and Juliet, The Diary of Anne Frank (B'way; Theatre World Award), Time Remembered, Zeffirelli's Lady of the Camillias, Shadow of a Gunman, Agnes of God (tour). Author: Bittersweet. Also teaches acting.
PICTURES: The Cobweb (debut, 1955), Picnic, Stage Struck, Scream of Fear, Adventures of a Young Man, The High Bright Sun (McGuire Go Home!), The Trip, Psych-Out, Chubasco, The Name of the Game Is Kill, The Brotherhood, So Evil My Sister, Legend of Hillbilly John, And Millions Will Die, Rollercoaster, The Manitou, In Praise of Older Women, Sweet 16, The Delta Force, Bloody Birthday, Prime Suspect, The Runnin' Kind, Schweitzer, The Cherry Orchard.
TELEVISION: *Movies*: Marcus Welby M.D. (A Matter of Humanities), Hauser's Memory, Mr. & Mrs. Bo Jo Jones, SST-Death Flight, Beggarman, Thief, The Immigrants, Toma (pilot), Frankenstein, Rona Jaffe's Mazes and Monsters. *Series*: The Marriage, Toma. *Guest*: Murder She Wrote, Cagney and Lacy.

STRATHAIRN, DAVID
Actor. b. San Francisco, CA, 1949. e. Williams Col.
THEATER: Einstein and the Polar Bear, Blue Plate Special, Fen, I'm Not Rappaport, Salonika, A Lie of the Mind, The Birthday Party, Danton's Death, Mountain Language, L'Atelier, A Moon for the Misbegotten, Temptation.
PICTURES: Return of the Secaucus 7, Lovesick, Silkwood, Iceman, The Brother from Another Planet, When Nature Calls, Enormous Changes at the Last Minute, At Close Range, Matewan, Stars and Bars, Dominick and Eugene, Call Me, Eight Men Out, The Feud, Memphis Belle, City of Hope, Big Girls Don't Cry... They Get Even, A League of Their Own, Bob Roberts, Sneakers, Passion Fish, Lost in Yonkers, The Firm, A Dangerous Woman, The River Wild, Losing Isaiah, Dolores Claiborne, Mother Night.
TELEVISION: *Series*: The Days and Nights of Molly Dodd. *Movies*: Day One, Son of the Morning Star, Heat Wave, Judgment, Without Warning: The James Brady Story, O Pioneers!, The American Clock. *Guest*: Miami Vice, The Equalizer.

STRAUSS, PETER
Actor. b. Croton-on-Hudson, NY., Feb. 20, 1947. e. Northwestern U. Spotted at N.U. by talent agent and sent to Hollywood. On stage at Mark Taper Theatre in Dance Next Door, The Dirty Man.
PICTURES: Hail Hero! (debut, 1969), Soldier Blue, The Trial of the Catonsville Nine, The Last Tycoon, Spacehunter: Adventures in the Forbidden Zone, Nick of Time.
TELEVISION: *Series*: Moloney. *Movies*: The Man Without a Country, Attack on Terror: The FBI Versus the Ku Klux Klan, Young Joe: The Forgotten Kennedy, The Jericho Mile (Emmy Award, 1979), Angel on My Shoulder, Heart of Steel, Under Siege, A Whale for the Killing, Penalty Phase, Proud Men, Brotherhood of the Rose, Peter Gunn, 83 Hours Till Dawn, Flight of Black Angel, Fugitive Among Us, Trial: The Price of Passion, Men Don't Tell, Thicker Than Blood: The Larry McLinden Story, The Yearling, Reunion, Texas Justice. *Mini-Series*: Rich Man Poor Man, Masada, Kane & Abel, Tender Is The Night.

STRAUSS, PETER E.
Executive. b. Oct. 7, 1940. e. Oberlin Coll., London Sch. of Economics, Columbia U. Sch. of Law, L.L.B., 1965. Vice pres., University Dormitory Dev. Co., 1965-68; v.p., Allart Cinema 16, 1968-69; v.p. prod., Allied Artists Pictures Corp., 1970; 1978-80, exec. v.p. Rastar Films; left to become independent as pres., Panache Prods., 1980-86. 1987, pres. & CEO of The Movie Group.
PICTURE: *Producer*: Best of the Best, Cadence, By the Sword, Best of the Best II, Best of the Best III.

STREEP, MERYL
Actress. r.n. Mary Louise Streep. b. Summit, NJ, June 22, 1949. e. Vassar. Acted for a season with traveling theater co. in VT. Awarded scholarship to Yale Drama School, 1972. N.Y. stage debut: Trelawny of the Wells (1975) with New York Shakespeare Fest. Appeared in 1984 documentary In Our Hands.
THEATER: *Off-B'way*: 27 Wagons Full of Cotton (Theatre World Award), A Memory of Two Mondays, Secret Service, Henry V, (NY Shakespeare Fest.), Measure for Measure (NYSF), The Cherry Orchard, Happy End (B'way debut, 1977), The Taming of the Shrew (NYSF), Taken in Marriage, Alice in Concert, Isn't It Romantic?
PICTURES: Julia (debut, 1977), The Deer Hunter, Manhattan, The Seduction of Joe Tynan, Kramer vs. Kramer (Academy Award, best supporting actress, 1979), The French Lieutenant's Woman, Still of the Night, Sophie's Choice (Academy Award, 1982), Silkwood, Falling in Love, Plenty, Out of Africa, Heartburn, Ironweed, A Cry in the Dark, She-Devil, Postcards From the Edge, Defending Your Life, Death Becomes Her, The House of the Spirits, The River Wild, The Bridges of Madison County, Before and After, Marvin's Room.
TELEVISION: *Mini-Series*: Holocaust (Emmy Award, 1978). *Movie*: The Deadliest Season. *Specials* (PBS): Secret Service, Uncommon Women and Others, Age 7 in America (host).

STREISAND, BARBRA
Singer, Actress, Director, Producer. b. New York, NY, April 24, 1942. e. Erasmus H.S., Brooklyn. Son is actor Jason Gould. Appeared as singer in NY night clubs. NY stage debut: Another Evening with Harry Stoones (1961), followed by Pins and Needles. On Broadway in I Can Get It For You Wholesale, Funny Girl. Performed song Prisoner for 1978 film Eyes of Laura Mars. Appeared in 1990 documentary Listen Up.
PICTURES: Funny Girl (debut; Academy Award, 1968), Hello Dolly!, On a Clear Day You Can See Forever, The Owl and the Pussycat, Up the Sandbox, The Way We Were (Acad. Award nom.), For Pete's Sake, Funny Lady, A Star Is Born (also co-composer, exec. prod.; Academy Award for best song: Evergreen, 1976), The Main Event (also co-prod.), All Night Long, Yentl (also dir., prod., co- s.p.), Nuts

(also prod., co-composer), The Prince of Tides (also dir., co-prod.; Acad. Award nom. for picture), The Mirror Has Two Faces (also dir.).
TELEVISION: *Specials*: My Name Is Barbra (Emmy Award, 1965), Color Me Barbra, The Belle of 14th Street, A Happening in Central Park, Barbra Streisand... And Other Musical Instruments, Putting It Together, One Voice, Barbra Streisand: The Concert (also co-prod.; 2 Emmy Awards, 1995). *Movie*: Serving in Silence: The Margarethe Cammermeyer Story (co-exec. prod. only). *Guest*: Ed Sullivan, Merv Griffin, Judy Garland Show, Saturday Night Live, Late Show With David Letterman.

STRICK, WESLEY
Writer. b. New York, NY, Feb. 11, 1954. e. UC at Berkeley, 1975. Was rock critic for magazines Rolling Stone, Cream, Circus.
PICTURES: True Believer, Arachnophobia, Cape Fear, Final Analysis, Batman Returns, Wolf, The Tie That Binds (dir.), The Saint (s.p.).
TELEVISION: *Series*: Eddie Dodd (pilot).

STRICKLAND, GAIL
Actress. b. Birmingham, AL, May 18. e. Florida St. Univ. NY Theatre includes Status Quo Vadis, I Won't Dance.
TELEVISION: *Series*: The Insiders, What a Country, Heartbeat. *Movies*: Ellery Queen, My Father's House, The Dark Side of Innocence, The Gathering, A Love Affair: The Eleanor and Lou Gehrig Story, The President's Mistress, Ski Lift to Death, Letters from Frank, King Crab, Rape and Marriage: The Rideout Case, A Matter of Life and Death, My Body My Child, Eleanor: First Lady of the World, Life of the Party: The Story of Beatrice, Starlight: The Plane That Couldn't Land, The Burden of Proof, Silent Cries, Spies, Barbara Taylor Bradford's Remember, A Mother's Prayer.
PICTURES: The Drowning Pool, Bittersweet Love, Bound for Glory, One on One, Who'll Stop the Rain, Norma Rae, Lies, Oxford Blues, Protocol, The Man in the Moon, Three of Hearts, When a Man Loves a Woman.

STRICKLYN, RAY
Actor. b. Houston, TX, October 8, 1928. e. U. of Houston. Official U.S. representative at Edinburgh Int'l Festival (1988); and Israel Intl. Festival (1989).
THEATER: The Climate of Eden (B'way debut; Theatre World Award). Tour: Stalag 17. Off-B'way: The Grass Harp, Confessions of a Nightingale (also LA, tour; LA Drama Critics, LA Weekly, Dramalogue, Oscar Wilde Awards). LA: Vieux Carre, Compulsion, The Caretaker, Naomi Court, Bus Stop.
PICTURES: The Proud and the Profane, Crime in the Streets, Somebody Up There Likes Me, The Catered Affair, The Last Wagon, Return of Dracula, 10 North Frederick, The Remarkable Mr. Pennypacker, The Big Fisherman, Young Jesse James, The Plunderers, The Lost World, Track of Thunder, Arizona Raiders, Dogpound Shuffle.
TELEVISION: *Movies*: Jealousy, Danielle Steel's Secrets, Hart to Hart Returns.

STRINGER, HOWARD
Executive. b. Cardiff, Wales. Feb. 19, 1942. e. Oxford U., B.A., M.A., modern history/international relations. Received Army Commendation Medal for meritorious achievement for service in Vietnam (1965-67). Joined CBS, 1965, at WCBS-TV, NY, rising from assoc. prod., prod. to exec. prod. of documentary broadcasts. Served as prod., dir. and writer of CBS Reports: The Palestinians (Overseas Press Club of America, Writers Guild Awards, 1974); The Rockefellers (Emmy Award, 1973). Won 9 Emmy Awards as exec. prod., prod., writer or dir: CBS Reports: The Boston Goes to China; CBS Reports: The Defense of the United States; CBS Evening News with Dan Rather: The Beirut Bombing; The Countdown Against Cancer; The Black Family. Exec. prod., CBS Reports; exec. prod., CBS Evening News with Dan Rather, 1981-84. Appointed exec. vice pres., CBS News Division, 1984; pres., CBS News, 1986; pres., CBS/Broadcast Group, 1988.

STRITCH, ELAINE
Actress. b. Detroit, MI, Feb. 2, 1926. e. studied acting with Erwin Piscator at the New Sch. for Social Research. Major career on stage. B'way debut 1946 in Loco.
THEATER: NY: Made in Heaven, Angel in the Wings, Call Me Madam, Pal Joey, On Your Toes, Bus Stop, Goldilocks, Sail Away, Who's Afraid of Virginia Woolf?, Wonderful Town, Company, Show Boat, A Delicate Balance (Tony Award nom.). *London*: Gingerbread Lady, Small Craft Warnings, Company.
PICTURES: The Scarlet Hour (debut, 1955), Three Violent People, A Farewell to Arms, The Perfect Furlough, Who Killed Teddy Bear?, Sidelong Glances of a Pigeon Kicker, The Spiral Staircase, Providence, September, Cocoon: The Return, Cadillac Man.
TELEVISION: *Series*: Growing Paynes (1948), Pantomine Quiz (regular, 1953-55, 1958), My Sister Eileen, The Trials of O'Brien, Two's Company (London), Nobody's Perfect (London;

also adapt.) The Ellen Burstyn Show. *Specials*: Company: the Making of the Album, Kennedy Center Tonight, Follies in Concert, Sensibility and Sense. Movies: The Secret Life of Archie's Wife, An Inconvenient Woman, Chance of a Lifetime. *Guest*: Law & Order (Emmy Award, 1993).

STROCK, HERBERT L.
Producer, Writer, Director, Film editor. b. Boston, MA, Jan. 13, 1918. e. USC, A.B., M.A. in cinema. Prof. of cinema, USC, 1941. Started career, publicity leg man, Jimmy Fidler, Hollywood columnist; editorial dept., MGM, 1941-47; pres., IMPPRO, Inc., 1955-59; assoc. prod.-supv. film ed., U.A.; director: AIP, Warner Bros. independent, Phoenix Films. Pres., Herbert L. Strock Prods. Lecturer at American Film Institute.
PICTURES: Storm Over Tibet, Magnetic Monster, Riders to the Stars, The Glass Wall. *Director*: Gog, Battle Taxi, Donovan's Brain, Rider on a Dead Horse, Devil's Messenger, Brother on the Run, One Hour of Hell, Witches Brew, Blood of Dracula, I Was a Teenage Frankenstein, The Crawling Hand; Soul Brothers Die Hard, Monstroids. *Writer-film editor*, Hurray for Betty Boop (cartoon). *Sound Effects editor* on Katy Caterpillar (cartoon feature). Editor: Night Screams, Detour. *Post-prod. spvr.*: King Kung Fu, Sidewalk Motel. *Co-director*: Deadly Presence. *Editor*: Snooze You Lose, Gramma's Gold, Distance, Fish Outta Water. *Prod/edit.*: The Visitors, Statistically Speaking.
TELEVISION: Highway Patrol, Harbor Command, Men of Annapolis, I Led Three Lives, The Veil, Dragnet, 77 Sunset Strip, Maverick, Cheyenne, Bronco, Sugarfoot, Colt 45, Science Fiction Thea., Seahunt, Corliss Archer, Bonanza, Hallmark Hall of Fame, The Small Miracle, Hans Brinker, The Inventing of America (specials); What Will We Say to a Hungry World (telethon), They Search for Survival (special), Flipper (series). *Documentaries*: Atlantis, Legends, UFO Journals, UFO Syndrome, Legend of the Lochness Monster, China-Mao to Now, El-Papa—Journey to Tibet. *Editor*: Peace Corps' Partnership in Health. *L.A. Dept. of Water & Power*: Water You Can Trust. Olympic Comm. Your Olympic Legacy—AAF.

STROLLER, LOUIS A.
Producer. b. Brooklyn, NY, April 3, 1942. e. Nicholas Coll. of Business Admin., BBA, 1963. Entered film business in 1963 doing a variety of jobs in local NY studios, and TV commercials. Unit manager on The Producers. Moved to L.A. in 1970s. First asst. dir. Charley, Take the Money and Run, Lovers and Other Strangers, They Might Be Giants, Man on a Swing, 92 in the Shade. Prod. mgr.: Mortadella, Sisters, Sweet Revenge, The Eyes of Laura Mars, Telefon. *Assoc. prod.*: Badlands, Carrie. The Seduction of Joe Tynan.
PICTURES: *Exec. prod. or prod.*: Simon, The Four Seasons, Venom, Eddie Macon's Run, Scarface, Sweet Liberty, Real Men, A New Life, Sea of Love, Betsy's Wedding, Back in the U.S.S.R., The Real McCoy, Carlito's Way, The Shadow, The Rock, Nothing to Lose.
TELEVISION: Half a Lifetime (exec. prod.; nom. 4 ACE Awards), Blue Ice.

STRONG, JOHN
Producer, Director, Writer, Actor. b. New York, NY, Dec. 3. e. U. of Miami, Cornell U., B.S., architectural engineering. Began acting in small role in film Duel in the Sun; on B'way in Annie Get Your Gun and understudy for James Dean in Immoralist. Appeared in many radio and TV serials, regular on Captain Video and the Video Ranger, later under contract as actor to Universal and Warner Bros. Member, Writers Guild America West, Directors Guild of America, Producers Guild of America, Dramatists Guild. Pres., Cinevent Corp.
PICTURES: Perilous Journey (exec. prod., s.p.), Eddie & the Cruisers (sprv. prod.), Heart Like a Wheel (sprv. prod.), For Your Eyes Only (s.p.), The Earthling (prod.), The Mountain Men (actor, prod.), Savage Streets (prod.), Steel Justice (prod.), Knights of the City (prod.), Garbage Pail Kids (sprv. prod.), Cop (sprv. prod.), Wild Thing (sprv. prod.), Summer Heat (sprv. prod.), Teen Wolf II (sprv. prod.), Atlantic Entertainment (sprv. prod.), Show of Force (prod., s.p.), Prime Directive (prod., s.p.), Sinapore Sling (prod., s.p.), Willie Sutton Story (prod.), Bandit Queen (prod.), Fatal Charm (exec. prod.), Colors of Love (prod.), Black Ice (dir., s.p.).
TELEVISION: The John Strong Show (host, exec. prod.), The Nurse (special, writer), McCloud (prod., writer), The Thrill of the Fall (prod.), Search (prod., writer, 2nd unit dir.), Outer Limits (exec. chg. prod.), Name of the Game (exec. chg. prod.), I Spy (writer), Love American Style (writer), All in the Family (writer), Changes (prod., dir., writer), Charlie's Angels (writer), Hawaii Five O' (writer).

STROUD, DON
Actor. b. Honolulu, Hawaii, Sept. 1, 1943. e. Kaimuki h.s. Was surfing champion, ranked 4th in the world.
PICTURES: Games, Madigan, Journey to Shiloh, What's So Bad About Feeling Good?, Coogan's Bluff, Bloody Mama, Explosion, Angel Unchained, Tick Tick Tick, Von Richtofen and Brown, Joe Kidd, Slaughter's Big Rip-Off, Scalawag,

Murph the Surf, The Killer Inside Me, The House by the Lake, The Choirboys, The Buddy Holly Story, The Amityville Horror, The Night the Lights Went Out in Georgia, Search and Destroy, Sweet Sixteen, Armed and Dangerous, Licence to Kill, Down the Drain, The Divine Enforcer, King of the Kickboxers, Cartel, Mob Boss, Street Wars, Frogtown, Deady Avenger, Danger Sign, Carnosaur II, Of Unknown Origin, Sudden Death, Dillinger and Capone, Twisted Justice, Two to Tango, Ghost Ship, Precious Find, Wild America.
TELEVISION: *Series*: Kate Loves a Mystery, Mike Hammer, The New Gidget, Dragnet. *Movies*: Split Second to an Epitaph, Something for a Lonely Man, DA: Conspiracy to Kill, Deadly Dream, Daughters of Joshua Cabe, Rolling Man, The Elevator, Return of Joe Forrester, High Risk, Katie: Portrait of a Centerfold, Out on a Limb, I Want to Live, Manhunters, Murder Me Murder You, The Alien Within, Sawbones, Barefoot in Paradise. *Special:* Hatful of Rain. *Guest:* Murder She Wrote, Quantum Leap, The FBI, Gunsmoke, Baywatch, Starsky and Hutch, The Mod Squad, Marcus Welby, Babylon 5, Walker: Texas Ranger, many others.

STRUTHERS, SALLY
Actress. b. Portland, OR, July 28, 1947. First tv appearance was as dancer on a Herb Alpert special. Appeared on Broadway stage in Wally's Cafe.
PICTURES: The Phynx, Five Easy Pieces, The Getaway.
TELEVISION: *Series*: The Summer Smothers (1970), The Tim Conway Comedy Hour, All in the Family (Emmy Awards: 1972, 1979), Pebbles and Bamm-Bamm (voice), Flintstones Comedy Hour (voice), Gloria, 9 to 5, Dinosaurs (voice). *Movies*: The Great Houdinis, Aloha Means Goodbye, Hey I'm Alive, Intimate Strangers, My Husband is Missing, And Your Name is Jonah, A Gun in the House, A Deadly Silence, In the Best Interests of the Children.

STUBBS, IMOGEN
Actress. b. Newcastle-upon-Tyne, 1961. Brought up in West London on sailing barge on the Thames. Grandmother was playwright Esther McCracken. e. Exeter Coll. First class degree at Oxford U. in English. Joined Oxford U. Dramatic Society appearing in revues and at Edinburgh Festival in play called Poison. Trained for stage at Royal Acad. of Dramatic Art. Prof. stage debut in Cabaret and The Boyfriend, in Ipswich. Acted with Royal Shakespeare Co. in The Two Noble Kinsmen, The Rover (promising newcomer critics award), Richard II, Othello, Heartbreak House, St. Joan, Uncle Vanya.
PICTURES: Privileged, A Summer Story, Nanou, Erik the Viking, True Colors, A Pin for the Butterfly, Sandra C'est la Vie, Jack & Sarah, Sense and Sensibility, Twelfth Night.
TELEVISION: The Browning Version, Deadline, The Rainbow, Fellow Traveller, After the Dance, Relatively Speaking, Othello, Anna Lee.

STULBERG, GORDON
Executive. b. Toronto, Canada, Dec. 17, 1927. e. U. of Toronto, B.A., Cornell Law Sch., LL.B. Was assoc. & member, Pacht, Ross, Warne & Bernhard; ent. m.p. ind. as exec. asst. to v.p., Columbia Pictures Corp., 1956-60; v.p. & chief studio admin. off., 1960-67; pres. of Cinema Center Films (div. of CBS) 1967-71; pres. 20th Century-Fox, 1971-75; 1980, named pres. & COO, PolyGram Pictures. Member of NY, Calif. bars, Chairman, American Interactive Media (Polygram subsidiary).

SUGAR, LARRY
Executive. b. Phoenix, AZ, May 26, 1945. m. Bonnie Sugar. e. Cheshire Acad., 1962; CSUN, B.A., 1967; U. of Southern Calif., J.D., 1971. Writer and co-author, Calif. Primary Reading Program, 1967-68. Joined Warner Bros. as dir., legal and corp. affairs, 1971-74; 20th Century Fox legal staff, 1974-77; co-owner with Bonnie Sugar, Serendipity Prods., 1977-81; named pres., intl., Lorimar Prods. 1981-84; exec. v.p., distribution, CBS 1984-85; exec. v.p. worldwide distribution, Weintraub Entertainment Group 1987-89; formed Sugar Entertainment, chmn., 1989-1991; pres. intl., Republic Pictures, Inc. 1991-93; pres. Larry Sugar Entertainment, 1993-.
PICTURES: *Exec. prod.*: Slapstick, Steel Dawn, Options, Damned River, Fatal Sky, Graveyard Shift, Shattered, Dark Horse, Family Prayers, The Plague, Boxing Helena. *Prod.*: With Deadly Intent, Annie O, Robin of Locksley.

SUGARMAN, BURT
Producer. b. Beverly Hills, CA, Jan. 4. e. U. of Southern California. Chmn. & CEO, GIANT GROUP, LTD., diversified co. traded on NYSE.
PICTURES: Kiss Me Goodbye, Extremities, Children of a Lesser God, Crimes of the Heart.
TELEVISION: Midnight Special, Switched on Symphony, The Mancini Generation, Johnny Mann's Stand Up and Cheer, etc.

SULLIVAN, REV. PATRICK J.
S.J., S.T.D.: Provost. Graduate Center at Tarrytown, Fordham U. b. New York, NY, March 25, 1920. e. Regis H.S.; Georgetown U., A.B., 1943; Woodstock Coll., M.A., 1944;

Fordham U., 1945-47; S.T.L. Weston Coll., 1947-51; S.T.D. Gregorian U. (Rome), 1952-54. Prof. of Theology, Woodstock Coll., 1954-57; Consultor, Pontifical Commission for Social Communications, 1968-82; Exec. Dir., U.S. Catholic Conference, Film & Broadcasting Office, 1965-80; Fordham Univ. Grad Sch. of Business, Assoc. Dean 1982-83, Dean 1983-85.

SUNSHINE, ROBERT HOWARD
Publisher. b. Brooklyn, NY, Jan. 17, 1946. e. U. of RI; Brooklyn Law Sch., 1971. Admitted to NY State Bar, 1971. President of Pubsun Corp., owner of The Film Journal. Publisher of The Film Journal. Exec. dir., Theatre Equipment Association, 1979-present; sec. and exec. dir. Foundation of the Motion Picture Pioneers, 1975-present; exec. dir., Natl. Assoc. of Theatre Owners of NY State, 1985-present; Producer of Variety Telethon, 1985-present; coordinator and producer, Show East Convention; coordinator and prod., Cinema Expo Intl., Amsterdam, Holland; coordinator, m.p. CineAsia, Singapore.

SURTEES, BRUCE
Cinematographer. b. Los Angeles, CA, July 23, 1937. Son of cinematographer Robert L. Surtees.
PICTURES: The Beguiled, Play Misty for Me, Dirty Harry, The Great Northfield Minnesota Raid, Conquest of the Planet of the Apes, Joe Kidd, The Outfit, High Plains Drifter, Blume in Love, Lenny (Acad. Award nom.), Night Moves, Leadbelly, The Outlaw Josey Wales, The Shootist, Three Warriors, Sparkle, Big Wednesday, Movie Movie (segment: Baxter's Beauties of 1933), Dreamer, Escape from Alcatraz, Ladies and Gentlemen the Fabulous Stains, White Dog, Firefox, Inchon, Honkytonk Man, Bad Boys, Risky Business, Sudden Impact, Tightrope, Beverly Hills Cop, Pale Rider, Psycho III, Out of Bounds, Ratboy, Back to the Beach, License to Drive, Men Don't Leave, Run, The Super, The Crush, That Night. Corrina Corrina, The Stars Fell on Henrietta, The Substitute.

SUSCHITZKY, PETER
Cinematographer. Spent long time in Latin America as documentary cinematographer. Later made commercials in France, England and U.S. First feature was It Happened Here, 1962.
PICTURES: Over 30 features including: A Midsummer Night's Dream, Charlie Bubbles, Leo the Last, Privilege, That'll Be the Day, Lisztomania, The Rocky Horror Picture Show, All Creatures Great and Small (TV in U.S.), Valentino, The Empire Strikes Back, Krull, Falling in Love, In Extremis, Dead Ringers, Where the Heart Is, Naked Lunch, The Public Eye, The Vanishing, M. Butterfly, Immortal Beloved, Crash, Mars Attacks.

SUTHERLAND, DONALD
Actor. b. St. John, New Brunswick, Canada, July 17, 1935. Son is actor Kiefer Sutherland. e. U. of Toronto, B.A., 1956. At 14 became a radio announcer and disc jockey. Worked in a mine in Finland. Theatre includes: The Male Animal (debut), The Tempest (Hart House Theatre, U. of Toronto), Two years at London Acad. of Music and Dramatic Art. Spent a year and a half with the Perth Repertory Theatre in Scotland, then repertory at Nottingham, Chesterfield, Bromley and Sheffield.
THEATER: August for the People (London debut), On a Clear Day You Can See Canterbury, The Shewing Up of Blanco Posnet, The Spoon River Anthology, Lolita (B'way debut, 1981).
PICTURES: Castle of the Living Dead (debut, 1964), The World Ten Times Over, Dr. Terror's House of Horrors, Die Die My Darling (Fanatic), The Bedford Incident, Promise Her Anything, The Dirty Dozen, Billion Dollar Brain, Sebastian, Oedipus the King, Interlude, Joanna, The Split, M*A*S*H, Start the Revolution Without Me, Act of the Heart, Kelly's Heroes, Alex in Wonderland, Little Murders, Klute, Johnny Got His Gun, F.T.A. (also co-prod., co-dir., co-s.p.), Steelyard Blues (also exec. prod.), Lady Ice, Alien Thunder (Dan Candy's Law), Don't Look Now, S*P*Y*S, The Day of the Locust, End of the Game (cameo), Fellini's Casanova, The Eagle Has Landed, 1900, The Disappearance, The Kentucky Fried Movie, National Lampoon's Animal House, Invasion of the Body Snatchers, The Great Train Robbery, Murder by Decree, Bear Island, A Man a Woman and a Bank, Nothing Personal, Ordinary People, Blood Relatives, Gas, Eye of the Needle, Threshold, Max Dugan Returns, Crackers, Ordeal by Innocence, Heaven Help Us, Revolution, Wolf at the Door, The Rosary Murders, The Trouble With Spies, Apprentice to Murder, Lost Angels, Lock Up, A Dry White Season, Eminent Domain, Backdraft, Buster's Bedroom, JFK, Scream of Stone, Buffy the Vampire Slayer, Shadow of the Wolf, Benefit of the Doubt, Dr. Bethune (Bethune: The Making of a Hero), Younger and Younger, Six Degrees of Separation, Robert A. Heinlein's The Puppet Masters, Disclosure, Outbreak, Hollow Point, The Shadow Conspiracy, A Time to Kill.
TELEVISION: *Specials*: (British) Marching to the Sea, The Death of Bessie Smith, Hamlet at Elsinore, Gideon's Way, The Champions, Bethune (Canada), Give Me Your Answer True,

The Prize (narrator), People of the Forest: The Chimps of Gombe (narrator). *Guest*: The Saint, The Avengers. *Movies*: The Sunshine Patriot, The Winter of Our Discontent, Quicksand: No Escape, The Railway Station Man, The Lifeforce Experiment, Oldest Living Confederate Widow Tells All, Citizen X (Emmy Award, 1995; Golden Globe Award 1995). *Series*: Great Books (narrator).

SUTHERLAND, KIEFER
Actor. b. London, England, CA, Dec. 18, 1966. Son of actor Donald Sutherland and actress Shirley Douglas. Moved to Los Angeles at age 4, then to Toronto at 8. Debut with L.A. Odyssey Theater at age 9 in Throne of Straw. Worked in local Toronto theater workshops before landing starring role in The Bay Boy (1984) for which he won Canadian Genie Award.
PICTURES: Max Dugan Returns (debut, 1983), The Bay Boy, At Close Range, Stand By Me, Crazy Moon, The Lost Boys, The Killing Time, Promised Land, Bright Lights Big City, Young Guns, 1969, Renegades, Flashback, Chicago Joe and the Showgirl, Flatliners, Young Guns II, The Nutcracker Prince (voice), Article 99, Twin Peaks: Fire Walk With Me, A Few Good Men, The Vanishing, The Three Musketeers, The Cowboy Way, Teresa's Tattoo, Eye for an Eye, Freeway, A Time To Kill.
TELEVISION: *Movies*: Trapped in Silence, Brotherhood of Justice, Last Light (also dir.), Dark Reflection (co-exec. prod. only). *Guest*: Amazing Stories (The Mission).

SUTTON, JAMES T.
Executive. b. California, Sept. 13. e. Columbia U. Film inspector, U.S. government; overseas m.p. service, WW II; co-owner, gen. mgr., Hal Davis Studios; hd. TV commercial div., Allan Sandler Films; Academy Art Pictures; pres., chmn. of bd., exec. prod., Royal Russian Studios, Inc., western hemisphere div.; pres. exec. prod. Gold Lion Prods., Inc.; pres. exec. prod. James T. Sutton-John L. Carpenter Prods.; pres., exec. dir., Airax Corp.; pres. of Skyax (div. of Airax).

SUZMAN, JANET
Actress. b. Johannesburg, South Africa, Feb. 9, 1939. e. Kingsmead Coll., U. of Witwaterstrand. Trained at L.A.M.D.A. London stage debut in The Comedy of Errors. *Recent theater*: Another Time, Hippolytos, The Sisters Rosensweig. *Director*: Othello for Market Theatre and Channel 4 (TV), Death of a Salesman, A Dream of People, The Deep Blue Sea.
PICTURES: Nicholas and Alexandra (Acad. Award nom.), A Day in the Death of Joe Egg, The Black Windmill, Nijinsky, Priest of Love, The Draughtsman's Contract, And the Ship Sails On, A Dry White Season, Nuns on the Run, Leon the Pig Farmer.
TELEVISION: *Specials/Movies*: The Three Sisters, Hedda Gabler, The House on Garibaldi Street, The Zany Adventures of Robin Hood, Miss Nightingale, Macbeth, Mountbatten—Last Viceroy of India (series), The Singing Detective (series), Clayhanger (series), The Miser, Revolutionary Witness, Saint Joan, Twelfth Night, Master Class on Shakespearean Comedy, Inspector Morse, The Ruth Rendell Mysteries.

SVENSON, BO
Actor. b. Goteborg, Sweden, Feb. 13, 1941. e. UCLA, 1970-74. U.S. Marine Corps 1959-65.
PICTURES: Maurie (debut, 1973), The Great Waldo Pepper, Part 2: Walking Tall, Breaking Point, Special Delivery, Portrait of a Hitman, Final Chapter: Walking Tall, Our Man in Mecca, The Inglorious Bastard, North Dallas Forty, Virus, Night Warning, Thunder Warrior, Deadly Impact, Wizards of the Lost Kingdom, The Manhunt, The Delta Force, Choke Canyon, Heartbreak Ridge, War Bus 2, Silent Hero, Thunder Warrior II, White Phantom, Deep Space, Justice Done, The Train, Soda Cracker, Curse II: The Bite, Captain Henkel, Running Combat, Steel Frontier.
TELEVISION: *Series*: Here Come the Brides, Walking Tall. *Movies*: The Bravos, Frankenstein, You'll Never See Me Again, Hitched, Target Risk, Snowbeast, Gold of the Amazon Women, Jealousy.

SWAIM, BOB
Director, Writer. b. Evanston, IL, Nov. 2, 1943. e. Calif. State U, B.A.; L'Ecole Nationale de la Cinematographie, Paris, BTS 1969. American director who has often worked in France. Began career making shorts: Le Journal de M Bonnafous, Self Portrait of a Pornographer, Vivre les Jacques. Received Cesar award French Acad. M.P., 1982; Chevalier des Arts et des Lettres 1985.
PICTURES: La Nuit de Saint-Germain-des-Pres (1977), La Balance, Half Moon Street, Masquerade, Atlantide, Da Costa, Parfum de Meurte, Femme de Passions.

SWANSON, DENNIS
Executive. e. Univ. of IL. B.A. in journalism, 1961, M.S. in communications/political science, 1966. 1966-67, news prod. & assignment mngr. for WGN radio & tv in Chicago; 1968-70, assign. edit. & field prod. for NBC news at WMAQ TV in Chicago; 1971-74, sportscaster and prod. WMAQ; worked for TVN in Chicago and served as company's NY dir. of news division; 1976, became exec. prod. of KABC-TV in LA; 1981, appointed station mngr. KABC-TV; 1983, v.p. & gen. mngr. WLS-TV, Chicago; 1985, named pres. of ABC Owned TV Stations; 1986, became pres. of ABC Sports; 1990, pres., ABC Daytime and ABC Children's Programming.

SWANSON, KRISTY
Actress. b. Mission Viejo, CA, 1969. Signed with modeling agency at age 9, appearing in over 30 commercials. Acting debut at 13 on Disney series Dreamfinders.
PICTURES: Pretty in Pink, Ferris Bueller's Day Off, Deadly Friend, Flowers in the Attic, Diving In, Mannequin Two on the Move, Hot Shots, Highway to Hell, Buffy the Vampire Slayer, The Program, The Chase, Getting In (Student Body), Higher Learning, The Phantom.
TELEVISION: *Series*: Dreamfinders, Knots Landing, Nightingales. *Movies*: Miracle of the Heart: A Boys Town Story, Not Quite Human.

SWAYZE, PATRICK
Actor, Dancer. b. Houston, TX. Aug. 18, 1952. e. San Jacinto Col. m. actress-dancer Lisa Niemi. Son of choreographer Patsy Swayze (Urban Cowboy). Brother is actor Don Swayze. Began as dancer appearing in Disney on Parade on tour as Prince Charming. Songwriter and singer with 6 bands. Studied dance at Harkness and Joffrey Ballet Schs. On B'way as dancer in Goodtime Charley, Grease. Co-author of play Without a Word.
PICTURES: Skatetown USA (debut, 1979), The Outsiders, Uncommon Valor, Red Dawn, Grandview USA (also choreographer), Youngblood, Dirty Dancing (also co-wrote and sang She's Like the Wind), Steel Dawn, Tiger Warsaw, Road House, Next of Kin, Ghost, Point Break, City of Joy, Father Hood, Tall Tale, To Wong Foo—Thanks for Everything—Julie Newmar, Three Wishes.
TELEVISION: *Mini-Series*: North and South—Books I and II. *Movies*: The Comeback Kid, Return of the Rebels, The Renegades (pilot), Off Sides. *Series*: Renegades. *Guest*: M*A*S*H, Amazing Stories.

SWEENEY, D.B.
Actor. r.n. Daniel Bernard Sweeney. b. Shoreham, NY, 1961. e. NYU, 1984 B.F.A.
THEATER: *NY*: The Caine Mutiny Court-Martial (B'way), The Seagull: The Hamptons: 1990, Distant Fires (L.A.), among others.
PICTURES: Power (debut, 1986), Fire With Fire, Gardens of Stone, No Man's Land, Eight Men Out, Memphis Belle, Blue Desert, Sons, Leather Jackets, Heaven Is a Playground, The Cutting Edge, A Day in October, Hear No Evil, Fire in the Sky, Roommates.
TELEVISION: *Series*: Strange Luck. *Mini-Series*: Lonesome Dove. *Movies*: Out of the Darkness, Miss Rose White.

SWERLING, JO
Writer. b. Russia, Apr. 8, 1897. Newspaper & mag. writer; author vaude. sketches; co-author plays, The Kibitzer, Guys and Dolls (Tony Award, 1951).
PICTURES: The Kibitzer, Platinum Blonde, Washington Merry-Go-Round, Dirigible, Man's Castle, Whole Town's Talking, No Greater Glory, Pennies from Heaven, Double Wedding, Made for Each Other, The Westerner, Confirm or Deny, Blood and Sand, Pride of the Yankees, Lady Takes a Chance, Crash Dive, Lifeboat, Leave Her to Heaven, Thunder in the East.
TELEVISION: The Lord Don't Play Favorites.

SWERLING, JO, JR.
Executive, Producer. b. Los Angeles, CA, June 18, 1931. e. UCLA, 1948-51; California Maritime Acad., 1951-54. Son of writer Jo Swerling. Active duty US Navy 1954-56. Joined Revue Prods./Universal Television, 1957-81, as prod. coordinator, assoc. prod., prod., assoc. exec. prod., exec. prod., writer, director, actor; currently sr. v.p. and supervising prod., The Cannell Studios.
TELEVISION: *Series*: Kraft Suspense Theater (prod.), Run for Your Life (prod., writer, Emmy, nom.), The Rockford Files (prod., writer), Cool Million (prod.), Alias Smith & Jones (assoc. exec. prod.), Baretta (prod., Emmy nom.), City of Angels (exec. prod.), Toma (exec. prod.), Jigsaw (prod.), The Bold Ones (prod., writer), Lawyers (prod., writer). *Mini-series*: Captains and the Kings (prod., Emmy nom.), Aspen (prod.), The Last Convertible (exec. prod., dir.). *Movies* (prod.): This Is the West That Was, The Whole World Is Watching, The Invasion of Johnson County, The Outsider, Do You Take This Stranger, Burn the Town Down, The Three-Thousand Mile Chase, How to Steal an Airplane. *Supervising prod.*, Stephen J. Cannell Productions: The Greatest American Hero, Quest, The A-Team, Hardcastle & McCormick, Riptide, The Last Precinct, Hunter, Stingray, Wiseguy, 21 Jump Street, J.J. Starbuck, Sonny Spoon, The Rousters, Unsub, Booker, Top of the Hill, Broken Badges, Dead End Brattigan, The Hat Squad, Traps, Profit.

SWIFT, LELA
Director.
TELEVISION: Studio One, Suspense, The Web, Justice, DuPont Show of the Week, Purex Specials For Women (Emmy Award) Dark Shadows, Norman Corwin Presents, ABC Late Night 90 min. Specials, ABC Daytime 90 min. Play Break, Ryan's Hope (Emmy Awards: 1977, 1979, 1980; Montior Awards: 1985, 1989), The Rope (A & E).

SWINK, ROBERT E.
Film Editor. b. Rocky Ford, CO, June 3, 1918. Joined editorial dept., RKO Radio, 1936; appt. film ed., 1941. In U.S. Army Signal Corps, 1944-45; supv. editor, Fox studio. Edited numerous productions.
PICTURES: Detective Story, Carrie, Roman Holiday, Desperate Hours, Friendly Persuasion, The Big Country, The Diary of Anne Frank, The Young Doctors, The Children's Hour, The Best Man, The Collector, How to Steal a Million, The Flim Flam Man, Funny Girl, The Liberation of L.B. Jones, The Cowboys, Skyjacked, Lady Ice, Papillion, Three the Hard Way, Rooster Cogburn, Midway, Islands in the Stream, Gray Lady Down, The Boys From Brazil, The In-Laws, Going in Style, Sphinx, Welcome Home.

SWIT, LORETTA
Actress. b. Passaic, NJ, Nov. 4, 1939. Stage debut in Any Wednesday. Toured in Mame for year. Arrived in Hollywood in 1971 and began TV career.
THEATER: Same Time Next Year, The Mystery of Edwin Drood (B'way), Shirley Valentine (Sarah Siddons Award).
PICTURES: Stand Up and Be Counted (debut, 1972), Freebie and the Bean, Race with the Devil, S.O.B., Beer, Whoops Apocalypse, Lords of Tanglewood.
TELEVISION: Series: M*A*S*H (Emmy Awards, 1980, 1982; also Genii, Silver Satellite & People's Choice Awards), Those Incredible Animals (host). Guest: Perry Como Show, Mac Davis, Dolly Parton, Bobby Vinton, etc. Movies: Hostage Heart, Shirts/Skins, The Last Day, Coffeeville, Valentine, Mirror Mirror, Friendships Secrets and Lies, Cagney & Lacey, Games Mother Never Taught You, Friendships Secrets & Lies, First Affair, The Execution, Dreams of Gold: The Mel Fisher Story, Hell Hath No Fury, A Killer Among Friends. Specials: 14 Going on 30, Best Christmas Pageant Ever, Texaco Salute to Broadway, It's a Bird It's a Plane It's Superman, Miracle at Moreaux, My Dad Can't Be Crazy Can He?, A Matter of Principal.

SWOPE, HERBERT BAYARD, JR.
Director, Producer, Commentator. b. New York, NY. e. Horace Mann Sch., Princeton U. U.S. Navy, 1941-46; joined CBS-TV as remote unit dir., 1946 directing many firsts in sportscasting; winner, Variety Show Management Award for sports coverage & citation by Amer. TV Society, 1948; joined NBC as dir., 1949; prod. dir., 1951; winner, 1952 Sylvania TV Award Outstanding Achievement in Dir. Technique; became exec. prod., NBC-TV in charge of Wide Wide World; film prod., 20th Century-Fox; 1960-62, exec. prod. 20th-Fox TV; 1970-72 exec. at N.Y. Off-Track Betting Corp. 1973-74; v.p., Walter Reade Organization, Inc.; 1975-76 producer-host, This Was TV, Growth of a Giant; 1976 to present commentator-interviewer, Swope's Scope, (radio—WSBR-AM)); Critic's Views (TV: WTVJ, Ch. 5); Column: Now and Then (Palm Beach Pictorial).
THEATER: Dir./Co-Prod.: Step on a Crack, Fragile Fox, Fair Game for Lovers.
PICTURES: Producer: Hilda Crane, Three Brave Men, True Story of Jesse James, The Bravados, The Fiend Who Walked the West.
TELEVISION: Prod/Dir.: Lights Out, The Clock, The Black Robe, Robert Montgomery Presents, Arsenic and Old Lace, Climax, Many Loves of Dobie Gillis, Five Fingers.

SYKES, ERIC
O.B.E.: Writer, Comedian, Actor. b. Oldham, England, 1923. Early career as actor; 1948 wrote first three series, BBC's Educating Archie TV comedy series for Frankie Howerd, Max Bygraves, Harry Secombe. BBC panel show member. Sykes Versus TV, The Frankie Howerd Series. Longterm contract with ATV 1956. Own BBC series 1958-78, Sykes and A... Specials: Silent Movies for TV, The Plank (also dir. & s.p.), If You Go Down Into the Woods Today, Rhubarb, It's Your Move, Mr. H Is Late, 19th Hole, The Big Freeze.
THEATER: Big Bad Mouse (tour: 1966-9 in America, Rhodesia, Australia, Canada), One Man Show (1982), Time and Time Again, Run for Your Wife, Two Into One, The 19th Hole, several pantomimes.
PICTURES: Watch Your Stern, Very Important Person, Invasion Quartet, Village of Daughters, Kill or Cure, Heavens Above, The Bargee, One Way Pendulum, Those Magnificent Men in Their Flying Machines, Rotten to the Core, The Liquidator, The Spy With The Cold Nose, Shalako, Monte Carlo or Bust, Theatre of Blood, Boys in Blue, Gabrielle and the Doodleman, Absolute Beginners, Splitting Heirs.

SYLBERT, ANTHEA
Executive. b. New York, NY, Oct. 6, 1939. e. Barnard Coll., B.A.; Parsons Sch. of Design, M.A. Early career in costume design with range of B'way (The Real Thing), off-B'way and m.p. credits (Rosemary's Baby, F.I.S.T., Shampoo, The Fortune, A New Leaf, The Heartbreak Kid. Two A.A. nominations for costume designs for Julia and Chinatown. Joined Warner Bros. in 1977, as v.p., special projects, acting as liaison between creative execs., prod. dept., and creative talent producing films for company. 1978, named v.p., prod. (projects included One Trick Pony, Personal Best, etc.). 1980 appointed v.p. prod., for United Artists, working on Jinxed, Still of the Night, Yentl, etc. 1982 became indept. prod. in partnership with Goldie Hawn (Hawn/Sylbert Movie Co.) producing Swing Shift, Protocol, Wildcats, Overboard, My Blue Heaven, Deceived, Crisscross, Something to Talk About. TV Movie: Truman.

SYMES, JOHN
Executive. e. Univ. of CA at Berkeley. Started at Paramount in tech. opts. dept. of Paramount's domestic tv distrib. div., then became mngr. of videotape opts., dir. of opts. Became sr. v.p. current programs for Paramount Network tv, then exec. v.p. crative affairs for same. Jan. 1994, became pres. of MGM Worldwide TV.

SYMS, SYLVIA
Actress. b. London, Dec. 3, 1934. e. Convent and Grammar Sch.
PICTURES: My Teenage Daughter (debut, 1956), No Time For Tears, The Birthday Present, Woman in a Dressing Gown, Ice Cold in Alex (Desert Attack), The Moonraker, Bachelor of Hearts, No Trees in the Street, Ferry to Hong Kong, Expresso Bongo, Conspiracy of Hearts, The Virgins of Rome, The World of Suzie Wong, Flame in the Streets, Victim, The Quare Fellow, The Punch and Judy Man, The World Ten Times Over, East of Sudan, Operation Crossbow, The Big Job, Hostile Witness, Danger Route, Run Wild Run Free, The Desperados, Asylum, The Tamarind Seed, Give Us Tomorrow, There Goes the Bride, Absolute Beginners, A Chorus of Disapproval, Shirley Valentine, Shining Through, Dirty Weekend.
TELEVISION: The Human Jungle (series), Something to Declare, The Saint (series), The Baron (series), Bat Out of Hell, Department in Terror, Friends and Romans, Strange Report, Half-hour Story, The Root of All Evil, The Bridesmaid, Clutterbuck, Movie Quiz, My Good Woman, Looks Familiar, Love and Marriage, The Truth About Verity, I'm Bob, He's Dickie, Blankety Blank, The Story of Nancy Astor, Give Us a Clue, Sykes, Crown Court, A Murder Is Announced, Murder at Lynch Cross, Rockcliffes Follies, Dr. Who, Countdown, Ruth Rendell Mystery, May to December, Intimate Contact, Thatcher the Final Days, Natural Lies, Mulberry, Peak Practice, Half the Picture, Original Sin.

SZABO, ISTVAN
Director. b. Budapest, Hungary, Feb. 18, 1938. e. Academy of Theatre and Film Art, Budapest, 1961. Debut Koncert (short, diploma film) 1961. Short films: Variations on a Theme, You, Piety, Why I Love It, City Map. Appeared in film Tusztortenet (Stand Off).
PICTURES: Age of Illusions (feature debut, 1964), Father, A Film About Love, 25 Fireman's Street, Premiere, Tales of Budapest, The Hungarians, Confidence (Silver Bear Award, Berlin Fest.), The Green Bird, Mephisto (Hungarian Film Critics Award; Academy Award, Best Foreign Film, 1982), Colonel Redl, Hanussen (also co-s.p.), Opera Europa, Meeting Venus.

SZWARC, JEANNOT
Director. b. Paris, France, Nov. 21, 1939.
PICTURES: Extreme Close-Up, Bug, Jaws II, Somewhere in Time, Enigma, Supergirl, Santa Claus, Honor Bound.
TELEVISION: Series: Ironside, To Catch a Thief, Kojak, Columbo, Night Gallery, Crime Club, True Life Stories, Twilight Zone (1986). Movies: Night of Terror, The Weekend Nun, The Devil's Daughter, You'll Never See Me Again, The Small Miracle, Lisa: Bright and Dark, A Summer Without Boys, Crime Club, Code Name: Diamond Head, Murders in the Rue Morgue, The Rockford Files: A Blessing in Disguise.

T

MR. T
Actor. r.n. Lawrence Tero. b. Chicago, IL, May 21, 1953. Professional bodyguard when hired by Sylvester Stallone in 1980 to play prizefighter in Rocky III.
PICTURES: Penitentiary II, Rocky III, D.C. Cab, Freaked.
TELEVISION: Series: The A Team, T & T. Movie: The Toughest Man in the World. Guest: Silver Spoons.

TAFFNER DONALD L.
Executive. b. New York, NY. e. St. Johns U. William Morris Agency, 1950-59; Paramount Pictures. 1959-63; D. L. Taffner Ltd., 1963-present.
TELEVISION: Prod.: Three's Company, Too Close For Comfort.

TAGAWA, CARY-HIROYUKI
Actor.
PICTURES: The Last Emperor, Spellbinder, Licence to Kill, The Last Warrior, Kickboxer 2, Showdown in Little Tokyo, American Me, Nemesis, Rising Sun, Picture Bride, Mortal Kombat, The Phantom.
TELEVISION: Movies: Mission of the Shark, Not of This World, Vestige of Honor, Murder in Paradise.

TAIT, CATHERINE
Executive. Exec. dir., The Independent Feature Project.

TAKEI, GEORGE
Actor. b. Los Angeles, CA, April 20, 1937. e. U. of California, UCLA. Professional debut in Playhouse 90 production while training at Desilu Workshop in Hollywood. Gained fame as Sulu in Star Trek TV series. Author: Mirror Friend Mirror Foe (novel), To the Stars (autobiography; 1994).
PICTURES: Ice Palace, A Majority of One, Hell to Eternity, PT 109, Red Line 7000, An American Dream, Walk Don't Run, The Green Berets, Star Trek: The Motion Picture, Star Trek II: The Wrath of Khan, Star Trek III: The Search for Spock, Star Trek IV: The Voyage Home, Star Trek V: The Final Frontier, Return From the River Kwai, Prisoners of the Sun, Star Trek VI: The Undiscovered Country, Live by the Fist, Oblivion.
TELEVISION: Series: Star Trek. Movies: Kissinger and Nixon, Space Cases, Star Trek Voyager. Guest: Perry Mason, Alcoa Premiere, Mr. Novak, The Wackiest Ship in the Army, I Spy, Magnum PI, Trapper John M.D., Miami Vice, Murder She Wrote, McGyver, Hawaiian Eye, Californian, Hawaii 5-O, My Three Sons, John Forsythe Show, Death Valley Days, Theatre in America, Game Night, Kung Fu: The Legend Continues.

TAMBLYN, RUSS
Actor b. Los Angeles, CA, Dec. 30, 1934. e. No. Hollywood H.S. West Coast radio shows; on stage with little theater group; song-and-dance act in Los Angeles clubs, veterans hospitals.
PICTURES: The Boy with Green Hair, Reign of Terror, Samson and Delilah, Gun Crazy, Kid from Cleveland, The Vicious Years, Captain Carey U.S.A., Father of the Bride, As Young As You Feel, Father's Little Dividend, Cave of Outlaws, Winning Team, Retreat Hell, Take the High Ground, Seven Brides for Seven Brothers, Deep in My Heart, Many Rivers to Cross, Hit the Deck, Last Hunt, Fastest Gun Alive, The Young Guns, Don't Go Near the Water, Peyton Place (Acad. Award nom.), High School Confidential, Tom Thumb, Cimarron, West Side Story, Wonderful World of the Brothers Grimm, How the West Was Won, Follow the Boys, The Haunting, Long Ships, Son of a Gunfighter, War of the Gargantuas, Scream Free, Dracula Vs. Frankenstein, Satan's Sadists, The Female Bunch, The Last Movie, Win Place or Steal, Murder Gang, Human Highway, Aftershock, Commando Squad, Cyclone, Necromancer, B.O.R.N., Phantom Empire, Bloodscream, Wizards of the Demon Sword, Desert Steel, Cabin Boy, Attack of the 60 Ft. Centerfold.
TELEVISION: Series: Twin Peaks. Guest: The Walter Winchell Show, ABC's Wide World of Entertainment, The Ed Sullivan Show, Gunsmoke, Name of the Game, Tarzan, Rags to Riches, Channing, Iron Horse, Perry Como Show, Love American Style, Grizzly Adams, Fame, Running Mates, Greatest Show on Earth, Burke's Law, Cade's County, The Quest, Quantum Leap, Babylon 5, Invisible Mom.

TAMBOR, JEFFREY
Actor. b. San Francisco, CA, July 8, 1944. e. San Francisco St. (BA), Wayne St. (MA). Acted with Seattle Rep., Actors Theatre of Louisville, Loeb Drama Ctr. (Harvard), Milwaukee Rep. Theatre, Acad. Festival Theatre (Chicago), Old Globe Theatre in San Diego, South Coast Rep. Theatre. B'way in Measure for Measure, Sly Fox.
PICTURES: And Justice for All, Saturday the 14th, Mr. Mom, The Man Who Wasn't There, No Small Affair, Three O'Clock High, Lisa, City Slickers, Life Stinks, Pastime, Article 99, Brenda Starr, Crossing the Bridge, At Home with the Webbers, Face Dancer, Under Pressure, A House in the Hills, Radioland Murders, Heavyweights, Big Bully, Learning Curves.
TELEVISION: Series: The Ropers, Hill Street Blues, 9 to 5, Mr. Sunshine, Max Headroom, Studio 5-B, American Dreamer, The Larry Sanders Show. Movies: Alcatraz: The Whole Shocking Story, A Gun in the House, The Star Maker, Take Your Best Shot, Cocaine: One Man's Seduction, Sadat, The Awakening of Candra, The Three Wishes of Billy Grier, The Burden of Proof, Honey Let's Kill the Neighbors, The

Countdown Has Begun. Mini-Series: Robert Kennedy & His Times. Guest: Three's Company, M*A*S*H, Barney Miller, Tales From the Crypt, The Golden Globe, Empty Nest, Doogie Howser M.D., Equal Justice, Murder She Wrote.

TANEN, NED
Executive. b. Los Angeles, CA, 1931. e. UCLA, law degree. Joined MCA, Inc. 1954; appt. v.p. in 1968. Brought Uni Records, since absorbed by MCA Records, to best-seller status with such artists as Neil Diamond, Elton John, Olivia Newton-John. First became active in theatrical film prod. in 1972. 1975 began overseeing feature prod. for Universal. 1976 named pres. of Universal Theatrical Motion Pictures, established as div. of Universal City Studios. Left in 1982 to become independent producer. 1985, joined Paramount Pictures as pres. of Motion Picture Group. Resigned 1988 to continue as sr. advisor at Paramount. Producer: Guarding Tess, Cops and Robbersons.

TANKERSLEY, ROBERT K.
Executive. b. Decatur, IL, July 31, 1927. In U.S. Navy, 1945-46; Marine Corps, 1949-55. With Natl. Theatre Supply as salesman in Denver 13 yrs. 1959-87, pres. Western Service & Supply, Denver, theatre equip. co.; 1960-87, mgr., Tankersley Enterprises theatre equip. Also was CEO of Theatre Operators, Inc., Bozeman, Mont. Member: Theatre Equipment Assn. (past pres.), National NATO Presidents Advisory Council; Rocky Mt. Motion Picture Assn. (past pres.), SMPTE, Motion Picture Pioneers, past chief barker, Variety Club Tent #37. Colorado, Wyoming NATO (past pres.) chmn.-elect Exhibitors West.

TAPLIN, JONATHAN
Producer. b. Cleveland, OH, July 18, 1947. e. Princeton U.
PICTURES: Mean Streets, The Last Waltz, Carny (exec. prod.), Grandview U.S.A. (co-exec. prod.), Under Fire, Baby, My Science Project, Until the End of the World, K2, To Die For (exec. prod.), Rough Magic (exec. prod.).
TELEVISION: Series: Shelly Duvall's Faerie Tale Theatre (6 episodes), 1968: The 25th Anniversary, The Native Americans, The Prize.

TAPS, JONIE
Producer. Executive. Columbia Studio. Member of Friars Club, Hillcrest Country Club.
PICTURES: Produced: When You're Smiling, Sunny Side of Street, Sound Off, Rainbow Round My Shoulder, All Ashore, Cruisin' Down the River, Drive a Crooked Road, Three for the Show, Bring Your Smile Along, He Laughed Last, Shadow on the Window.

TARADASH, DANIEL
Writer, Director. b. Louisville, KY, Jan. 29, 1913. e. Harvard Coll., B.A., 1933; Harvard Law Sch., LL.B., 1936. Passed NY Bar, 1937; won nationwide playwriting contest, 1938; U.S. Army WWII. Pres. Screen Writers Branch, WGA, 1955-56; v.p.; Writers Guild of America, West 1956-59; mem. Writers Guild Council, 1954-65; mem., bd. of govnrs. Motion Picture Acad. Arts & Sciences, 1964-74, 1990-93; v.p. 1968-70 and pres. 1970-73. Trustee, Producers-Writers Guild Pension plan 1960-73. chmn., 1965. Mem. Bd. of Trustees of American Film Institute 1967-69. WGA's Valentine Davies Award, 1971. Pres., Academy M.P. Arts & Sciences, 1970-73, mem. bd. trustees, Entertainment Hall of Fame Foundation. Mem., Public Media General Programs panel for the National Foundation for the Arts, 1975-85, 1992; Pres. Writers Guild of America, West, 1977-79. Natl. chmn., Writers Guild of America, 1979-81. WGA's Morgan Cox Award, 1988. WGA's Edmund H. North Founders Award 1991. Festival to present Taradash Screenwriting Award 1992-; USC retrospective and tribute, 1992. Writer of TV special Bogie. Recipient of the Writers Guild of America West Laurel Award, 1996.
PICTURES: Golden Boy, A Little Bit of Heaven, Knock on Any Door, Rancho Notorious, Don't Bother to Knock, From Here to Eternity (Academy Award 1953), Desiree, Storm Center (also dir., co-story), Picnic, Bell Book and Candle, The Saboteur Code Name—Morituri, Hawaii, Castle Keep, Doctors' Wives, The Other Side of Midnight.

TARANTINO, QUENTIN
Writer, Director, Actor, Producer. b. Knoxville, TN, March 27, 1963. Graduate of Sundance Institute Director's Workshop and Lab. With producer Lawrence Bender, formed production co. A Band Apart.
PICTURES: Past Midnight (assoc. prod., co-s.p.), Reservoir Dogs (dir., s.p., actor), True Romance (s.p.), Killing Zoe (co-exec. prod.), Natural Born Killers (story), Sleep With Me (actor), Pulp Fiction (dir., s.p., co-story, actor; Cannes Film Fest. Award for Best Film; LA Film Critics, NY Film Critics, Natl. Soc. of Film Critics, Chicago Film Critics & Independent Spirit Awards for s.p.; Academy Award & Golden Globe for s.p.; Natl. Bd. of Review Award for dir., 1994), Destiny Turns on the Radio (actor), Somebody to Love (actor),

Desperado (actor), Four Rooms (co-s.p., co-exec. prod.), From Dusk Till Dawn (s.p., actor, co-exec. prod.), Girl 6 (actor), Curdled (exec. prod.).
TELEVISION: *Guest*: The Golden Girls, All-American Girl. *Dir*: E/R (1 episode).

TARNOFF, JOHN B.
Producer. b. New York, NY, Mar. 3, 1952. e. UCLA, motion pictures & TV, 1973-74; Amherst Coll., B.A., 1969-73. Named field exec. with Taylor-Laughlin Distribution (company arm of Billy Jack Enterprises) 1974; left in 1975 to be literary agent with Bart/Levy, Inc.; later with Michael Levy & Associates, Paul Kohner/Michael Levy Agency; Headed TV dept., Kohner/Levy, 1979. Joined MGM as production exec., 1979; v.p., development, 1979-80; sr. v.p. production & devel., 1981-82; exec. v.p., Kings Road Prods., 1983-84; v.p., prod., Orion Pictures Corp., 1985; exec. prod., Out of Bounds, Columbia Pictures, 1986; v.p., prod., De Laurentiis Entertainment Group, 1987. Head of production, DeLaurentiis Entertainment, Australia, 1987-88. Exec. v.p. production, Village Roadshow Pictures, 1988-. *Exec. Prod.*: The Delinquents, Blood Oath.

TARSES, JAMIE
Executive. b. Pittsburgh, PA. e. Williams Coll. Worked as a casting director for Lorimar Productions. Joined NBC in Sept. 1987 as mgr., creative affairs for NBC Productions. In Dec. 1987, named mgr., current comedy programs, NBC Entertainment and was NBC's program exec. for such series as Cheers, Amen and A Different World. In 1988, named manager of comedy development. In 1995, promoted to s.v.p., primetime series. In June of 1996, joined ABC Entertainment as President.

TARSES, JAY
Producer, Writer, Actor. b. Baltimore, MD, July 3, 1939. e. U. of Washington, degree in theater. Wrote and acted with little-theater co. in Pittsburgh, drove a truck in NY for Allen Funt's Candid Camera and worked in advertising and promotion for Armstrong Cork Co. in Lancaster, PA where he met Tom Patchett. Formed Patchett and Tarses, stand-up comedy team that played coffeehouse circuit in the late 1960s. Later two-some became TV writing team and joined writing staff of Carol Burnett Show winning Emmy in 1972.
PICTURES: *Co-s.p. with Patchett*: Up the Academy, The Great Muppet Caper, The Muppets Take Manhattan.
TELEVISION: As actor: *Series*: Make Your Own Kind of Music, Open All Night, The Days and Nights of Molly Dodd. *Specials*: Arthur Godfrey's Portable Electric Medicine Show, The Duck Factory. With Tom Patchett: The Bob Newhart Show (exec. prod., writer), The Tony Randell Show (creator, exec. prod., writer), We've Got Each Other (creator, exec. prod.), Mary (prod.), Open All Night (creator, prod., writer), Buffalo Bill (exec. prod., writer). *Solo*: The Days and Nights of Molly Dodd (creator, prod., writer), The "Slap" Maxwell Story (creator, prod., writer), Public Morals. *Pilots*: The Chopped Liver Brothers (exec. prod., writer), The Faculty (exec. prod., dir., writer).

TARTIKOFF, BRANDON
Executive. b. New York, NY, Jan. 13, 1949. e. Yale U. Started TV career in 1971 in promo. dept. of ABC affiliates in New Haven, CT Joined promo. staff at ABC affiliate in Chicago. In 1976 went to New York, with ABC-TV as mgr., dramatic development; moved to NBC Entertainment in Sept., 1977, as dir., comedy programs. In 1978 appt. v.p., programs, West Coast, NBC Entertainment; 1980, named pres. of that division. Pres. NBC Entertainment since 1980. Also heads own prod. co., NBC Productions. 1990, appointed chairman of NBC Entertainment Group. 1991, appointed chmn. of Paramount Pictures. Resigned from Paramount, Oct. 1992. Became chmn. of New World Entertainment, 1994. *Co-exec. prod. tv movie* Tom Clancy's Op Center.
PICTURES: Square Dance, Satisfaction.

TAVERNIER, BERTRAND
Director, Writer. b. Lyon, France, April 25, 1941. After 2 yrs. of law study, quit to become film critic for Cahiers du Cinema and Cinema 60. Asst. to dir. Jean-Pierre Melville on Leon Morin Priest (1961), also worked as film publicist. Wrote film scripts and a book on the Western and a history of American cinema. Partner for 6 yrs. with Pierre Rissient in film promotion company, during which time he studied all aspects of filmmaking. 1963: directed episode of Les Baisers. Pres., Lumiere Inst., Lyon. Book: 50 Years of American Cinema, Qu'est ce Qu'on Attend?, Amis Americains.
PICTURES: *Director-Co-writer*: The Clockmaker (L'Horloger de Saint-Paul), Let Joy Reign Supreme (Que La Fête Commence), The Judge and the Assassin (Le Judge et l'Assassin), Spoiled Children (also co-prod.), Deathwatch. *Dir./Co-Writer/Prod.*: A Week's Vacation, Clean Slate (Coup de Torchon; 11 César nom.), Mississippi Blues (co-dir. with Robert Parrish), A Sunday in the Country (Un Dimanche a la Campagne; Best Direction Cannes, New york Critics Prize), 'Round Midnight, Beatrice (dir. co-prod. only), Life and Nothing But, Daddy Nostalgia, The Undeclared War (co-dir. with Patrick Rutman), L627, La Fille de D'Artagnan, L'Appat.
TELEVISION: Phillippe Soupault, October Country (co-dir. with Robert Parrish), Lyon, le regard interieur.

TAVIANI, PAOLO and VITTORIO
Directors, Writers. b. San Miniato, Pisa, Italy, (Paolo: Nov. 8, 1931; Vittorio: Sept. 20, 1929); e. Univ. of Pisa (Paolo: liberal arts; Vittorio: law). The two brothers always work in collaboration from script preparation through shooting and editing. 1950: With Valentino Orsini ran cine-club at Pisa. 1954: In collab. with Caesare Zavattini directed short about Nazi massacre at San Miniato. 1954-59: with Orsini made series of short documentaries (Curatorne e Montanara; Carlo Pisacane; Ville della Brianza; Lavatori della pietra; Pitori in cita; I Pazzi della domenica; Moravia, Cabunara). Worked as assistant to Rosellini, Luciano Emmer and Raymond Pellegrini. 1960: collaborated on an episode of Italy Is Not a Poor Country.
PICTURES (all by both): A Man for Burning (debut, 1962; co-dir. with Valentino Orsini), Matrimonial Outlaws (co-dir. with Orsini), The Subversives, Under the Sign of Scorpio, Saint Michael Had a Rooster, Allonsanfan, Padre Padrone (Cannes Film Fest.: Grand Prix & Critics International Prize, 1977), The Meadow, The Night of the Shooting Stars (1981, Best Director Award, Natl. Society of Film Critics; Special Jury Prize, Cannes), Kaos, Good Morning Babylon, The Sun Also Shines at Night, Fiorile.

TAYLOR, DELORES
Actress, Writer, Producer. b. Winner, SD, Sept. 27, 1939. e. U. of South Dakota, studying commercial art. m. Tom Laughlin. First TV experience was heading art dept. at RCA wholesale center in Milwaukee. Established first Montessori School in U.S. in Santa Monica for several yrs., with husband. Made feature film debut as actress in Billy Jack in 1971. Wrote s.p. with husband for that and sequels, The Trial of Billy Jack, Billy Jack Goes to Washington, under pseudonym Teresa Christina.
PICTURES: *Exec. Prod., Writer*: Proper Time, Young Sinners, Born Losers, The Master Gunfighter. *Exec. Prod., Writer, Actress*: Billy Jack, Trial of Billy Jack, Billy Jack Goes to Washington, Return of Billy Jack.

TAYLOR, DON
Actor, Director. b. Freeport, PA, Dec. 13, 1920. e. Pennsylvania State U. Appeared in Army Air Corps' Winged Victory on stage & screen.
PICTURES: *Actor*: The Human Comedy, Girl Crazy, Thousands Cheer, Swing Shift Maisie, Salute to the Marines, Winged Victory, The Red Dragon, Song of the Thin Man, The Naked City, For the Love of Mary, Battleground, Ambush, Father of the Bride, Target Unknown, Father's Little Dividend, Submarine Command, Flying Leathernecks, The Blue Veil, Japanese War Bride, Stalag 17, The Girls of Pleasure Island, Destination Gobi, Johnny Dark, Men of Sherwood Forest, I'll Cry Tomorrow, The Bold and the Brave, Lost Slaves of the Amazon, Ride the High Iron, The Savage Guns. *Director*: Everything's Ducky (debut, 1961), Ride the Wild Surf, Jack of Diamonds, Five Man Army, Escape From the Planet of the Apes, Tom Sawyer, Echoes of a Summer, The Great Scout and Cathouse Thursday, The Island of Dr. Moreau, Damien—Omen II, The Final Countdown.
TELEVISION: *Movies* (director): Something for a Lonely Man, Wild Women, Heat of Anger, Night Games, Honky Tonk, The Manhunter, Circle of Children, The Gift, The Promise of Love, Broken Promise, Red Flag: The Ultimate Game, Drop Out Father, Listen to Your Heart, September Gun, My Wicked Wicked Ways: The Legend of Errol Flynn, Secret Weapons, Going for the Gold: The Bill Johnson Story, Classified Love, Ghost of a Chance, The Diamond Trap.

TAYLOR, ELIZABETH
Actress. b. London, Eng., Feb. 27, 1932. e. Bryon House, London. When 3 years old danced before Princess Elizabeth, Margaret Rose. Came to U.S. at outbreak of WWII. *Author*: World Enough and Time (with Richard Burton; 1964), Elizabeth Taylor (1965), Elizabeth Takes Off (1988). Initiated Ben Gurion U.—Elizabeth Taylor Fund for Children of the Negev, 1982. Co-founded American Foundation for AIDS Research, 1985. Named Comdr. Arts & Letters (France) 1985, Legion of Honor, 1987. Established the Elizabeth Taylor AIDS Foundation in 1991. Developed various perfume products: Elizabeth Taylor's Passion, Passion Body Riches, Passion for Men, White Diamonds, Diamonds and Emeralds, Diamonds and Sapphires, Diamond and Rubies; 1993 launched Elizabeth Taylor Fashion Jewelry Collection. Recipient of AFI Life Achievement Award (1993), Jean Hersholt Humanitarian Award (1993).
THEATER: *B'way*: The Little Foxes (also London), Private Lives.

PICTURES: There's One Born Every Minute (debut, 1942), Lassie Come Home, Jane Eyre, White Cliffs of Dover, National Velvet, Courage of Lassie, Life with Father, Cynthia, A Date With Judy, Julia Misbehaves, Little Women, Conspirator, The Big Hangover, Father of the Bride, Father's Little Dividend, A Place in the Sun, Callaway Went Thataway (cameo), Love Is Better Than Ever, Ivanhoe, The Girl Who Had Everything, Rhapsody, Elephant Walk, Beau Brummel, The Last Time I Saw Paris, Giant, Raintree County, Cat on a Hot Tin Roof, Suddenly Last Summer, Scent of Mystery (cameo), Butterfield 8 (Academy Award, 1960), Cleopatra, The V.I.P.s, The Sandpiper, Who's Afraid of Virginia Woolf? (Academy Award, 1966), The Taming of the Shrew, Doctor Faustus, Reflections in a Golden Eye, The Comedians, Boom!, Secret Ceremony, The Only Game in Town, X Y and Zee (Zee and Company), Under Milk Wood, Hammersmith Is Out, Night Watch, Ash Wednesday, That's Entertainment!, The Driver's Seat, The Blue Bird, A Little Night Music, Winter Kills (cameo), The Mirror Crack'd, Genocide (narrator), Young Toscanini, The Flintstones.
TELEVISION: Movies: Divorce His/Divorce Hers, Victory at Entebbe, Return Engagement, Between Friends, Malice in Wonderland, There Must Be a Pony, Poker Alice, Sweet Bird of Youth. Mini-Series: North and South. Guest: Here's Lucy (1970 with Richard Burton), General Hospital (1981), All My Children (1983), Hotel. Specials: Elizabeth Taylor in London, America's All-Star Salute to Elizabeth Taylor.

TAYLOR, LILI
Actress. b. Chicago, 1967.
THEATER: NY: What Did He See, Aven U Boys. Regional: Mud, The Love Talker, Fun. Director: Collateral Damage.
PICTURES: Mystic Pizza (debut, 1988), Say Anything, Born on the Fourth of July, Bright Angel, Dogfight, Watch It, Household Saints, Short Cuts, Rudy, Arizona Dream, Mrs. Parker and the Vicious Circle, Ready to Wear (Pret-a-Porter), The Addiction, Cold Fever, Four Rooms, Things I Never Told You, I Shot Andy Warhol, Girl's Town, Ransom.

TAYLOR, MESHACH
Actor. b. Boston, MA, Apr. 11. e. Florida A & M Univ. Hosted Chicago TV show Black Life.
THEATER: Streamers, Sizwe Banzi is Dead, The Island, Native Son, Wonderful Ice Cream Suit, Bloody Bess, Sirens of Titan, Night Feast, Huckleberry Finn, Cops.
PICTURES: Damien: Omen II, The Howling, The Beast Within, Explorers, Warning Sign, One More Saturday Night, From the Hip, Mannequin, The Allnighter, House of Games, Welcome to Oblivion, Mannequin 2 on the Move, Class Act.
TELEVISION: Series: Buffalo Bill, Designing Women, Dave's World. Guest: Lou Grant, Barney Miller, Melba, Golden Girls, M*A*S*H, The White Shadow, What's Happening Now, ALF. Movies: An Innocent Man, How to Murder a Millionaire, Double Double Toil and Trouble, Virtual Seduction. Specials: Huckleberry Finn, The Rec Room.

TAYLOR, RENEE
Actress, Writer. b. New York, NY, March 19, 1935. Wife of actor Joseph Bologna, with whom she collaborates in writing. Their B'way plays include Lovers and Other Strangers, It Had to Be You. Stage actress: One of the All-Time Greats.
PICTURES: Actress: The Errand Boy, The Detective, The Producers, A New Leaf, Lovers and Other Strangers (also s.p.), Made for Each Other (also s.p.), Last of the Red Hot Lovers, Lovesick, It Had to Be You (also co-dir., co-s.p.), That's Adequate, White Palace, End of Innocence, Delirious, All I Want for Christmas, Forever.
TELEVISION: Writer: Acts of Love... and Other Comedies (Emmy Award, 1973), Paradise, Calucci's Department, The American Dream Machine, Bedrooms (Writers Guild Award, 1984), etc. Actress: Series regular: The Jack Paar Show, Mary Hartman Mary Hartman, Daddy Dearest, The Nanny. Movie: Woman of the Year (also co-writer).

TAYLOR, ROD
Actor. b. Sydney, Australia, Jan. 11, 1930. e. East Sydney Fine Arts Coll. Started out as artist then turned to acting on stage. Formed own company, Rodler, Inc., for TV-film production.
PICTURES: The Sturt Expedition (debut, 1951), King of the Coral Sea, Long John Silver, Top Gun, The Virgin Queen, Hell on Frisco Bay, World Without End, The Rack, Giant, The Catered Affair, Raintree County, Step Down to Terror, Separate Tables, Ask Any Girl, The Time Machine, Seven Seas to Calais, 101 Dalmatians (voice), The Birds, A Gathering of Eagles, The V.I.P.s, Sunday in New York, Fate is the Hunter, 36 Hours, Young Cassidy, Do Not Disturb, The Glass Bottom Boat, The Liquidator, Hotel, Chuka (also prod.), Dark of the Sun, High Commissioner (Nobody Runs Forever), The Hell with Heroes, Zabriskie Point, Darker Than Amber, The Man Who Had Power Over Women, The Heroes, The Train Robbers, Trader Horn, The Deadly Trackers, Hell River, Blondy, Picture Show Man, A Time To Die, On the Run, Close Enemy, Open Season, Point Deception.

TELEVISION: Movies: Powerkeg, Family Flight, The Oregon Trail, Cry of the Innocent, Jacqueline Bouvier Kennedy, Charles and Diana: A Royal Love Story, Outlaws, Danielle Steel's Palomino, Grass Roots. Series: Hong Kong, Bearcats, Masquerade, The Oregon Trail, Outlaws, Falcon Crest.

TAYLOR, RONNIE
Director of Photography. b. London, England, 1924. Ent. m.p. ind. 1941 at Gainsborough Studios
PICTURES: Tommy, The Silent Flute, Circle of Iron, Savage Harvest, Gandhi, High Road to China, The Hound of the Baskervilles, The Champions, Master of the Game (UK shoot), A Chorus Line, Foreign Body, Cry Freedom, Opera (Italy), The Experts, Sea of Love, Popcorn, The Rainbow Thief, Jewels, Age of Treason, The Steal, The Good King.

TAYLOR, JOHN RUSSELL
Writer, Critic. b. Dover, England, June 19, 1935. e. Cambridge U., B.A., 1956. Editor: Times Educational Supplement, London, 1959-60; film critic, The Times, London, 1962-73; art critic, 1978-; editor, Films and Filming, 1983-; prof., division of Cinema, USC, 1972-78. Member: London Film and TV Press Guild, London Critics Circle, NY Society of Cinematologists.
BOOKS: Joseph L. Mankiewicz: An Index, The Angry Theatre, Anatomy of a Television Play, Cinema Eye Cinema Ear, Shakespeare: A Celebration (cont.), New English Dramatists 8 (ed. & intr.), The Hollywood Musical, The Second Wave: Hollywood Dramatists for the 70s, Masterworks of the British Cinema, Directors and Directions: Peter Shaffer, Hitch, Cukor's Hollywood, Impressionism, Strangers in Paradise, Ingrid Bergman, Alec Guinness: A Celebration, Vivien Leigh, Hollywood 1940s, Portraits of the British Cinema.

TAYLOR-YOUNG, LEIGH
Actress. b. Washington, DC, Jan. 25, 1945. e. Northwestern U. B'way debut 1966 in Three Bags Full. Additional stage: The Beckett Plays (Off-B'way, LA), Knives, Sleeping Dogs.
PICTURES: I Love You Alice B. Toklas (debut, 1968), The Games, The Big Bounce, The Adventurers, The Buttercup Chain, The Horsemen, The Gang That Couldn't Shoot Straight, Soylent Green, Can't Stop the Music, Looker, Secret Admirer, Jagged Edge, Honeymoon Academy, Accidents.
TELEVISION: Series: Peyton Place, The Devlin Connection, The Hamptons, Dallas, Picket Fences (Emmy Award, 1994). Movies: Marathon, Napoleon and Josephine: A Love Story, Perry Mason: The Case of the Sinister Spirit, Who Gets the Friends, Bonnie and McCloud, Moment of Truth: Murder or Memory? Guest: Civil Wars, The Young Riders, Alfred Hitchcock Presents, Spenser for Hire, Evening Shade. Pilots: Ghostwriter, Houston Knights.

TEAGUE, LEWIS
Director. b. 1941. e. NYU. Editor and/or 2nd unit dir. on such films as Cockfighter, Crazy Mama, Death Race 2000, Avalanche, Fast Charlie: The Moonbeam Rider, The Big Red One.
PICTURES: Dirty O'Neil (co-dir.), Lady in Red (also editor), Alligator, Fighting Back, Cujo, Cat's Eye, The Jewel of the Nile, Collision Course, Navy SEALS.
TELEVISION: Series episodes: Alfred Hitchcock Presents, Daredevils, Shannon's Deal. Movies: T Bone N Weasel, Tom Clancy's Op Center.

TELLER, IRA
Executive. b. New York, NY, July 3, 1940. e. City Coll. of New York, & 1957-61; NYU Graduate Sch. of Arts, 1961-62. Publicist, Pressbook Dept., 20th Century Fox., 1961-62; asst. to adv. mgr., Embassy Pictures Corp., 1962-63; asst. adv. mgr., Columbia Pictures Corp., 1963; adv. mgr., Columbia Pictures Corp., 1964, 1964-65; asst. to chmn. of bd., Diener, Hauser, Greenthal Agy., 1966; adv. mgr., 20th Century-Fox, 1966-67; 1967, adv. dir. 20th Cent.-Fox.; dir. of adv., Nat'l General Pictures Corp., 1969; eastern dir., adv.-pub., 1972; national dir., adv-pub., 1973; Bryanston Distributors, Inc. v.p. adv.-pub., 1974; Cine Artists Pictures Corp. v.p. adv-pub., 1975; Lorimar Productions, v.p., adv.-marketing, 1976-77; 1977-present, pres. Ira Teller and Company, Inc.; This Is It, exec. prod.

TEMPLE, JULIEN
Director. b. London, England, Nov. 26, 1953. e. Cambridge, London's National Film School. Dir. many rock videos.
PICTURES: The Great Rock 'n' Roll Swindle (debut, 1979), The Secret Policeman's Other Ball, Undercover (also s.p.), Running Out of Luck (also s.p.), Absolute Beginners, Aria (segment: Rigoletto), Earth Girls Are Easy, Rolling Stones: At the Max (creative consultant).

TEMPLE (BLACK), SHIRLEY
Actress, Diplomat. b. Santa Monica, CA, April 23, 1928. In 1932 screen debut, Red Haired Alibi. In 1933 To the Last Man; then leading figure in series of Educational shorts called Baby

Burlesque and Frolics of Youth, until breakthrough role in Stand Up and Cheer, 1934, which resulted in career as child and teen star. Voted one of ten best Money-Making Stars in Motion Picture Herald-Fame Poll, 1934-39. As an adult, turned her attention to government and international issues. Republican candidate for U.S. House of Representatives, 1967. Rep. to 24th General Assembly of U.N. (1969-70). Special asst. to chmn., President's Council on the Environment (1970-72). U.S. Ambassador to Ghana (1974-76). Chief of Protocol, White House (1976-77); member of U.S. delegation on African Refugee problems, Geneva, 1981; 1987 made 1st honorary U.S. Foreign Service Rep. for State Dept.; 1989, appt. Ambassador to Czechoslovakia. *Autobiography*: Child Star (1988).
PICTURES: The Red-Haired Alibi (feature debut, 1932), To the Last Man, Out All Night, Mandalay, Carolina, Stand Up and Cheer, Baby Take a Bow, Now and Forever, Bright Eyes, Now I'll Tell, Change of Heart, Little Miss Marker, The Little Colonel, Our Little Girl, Curly Top, The Littlest Rebel, Captain January, Poor Little Rich Girl, Dimples, Stowaway, Wee Willie Winkle, Heidi, Rebecca of Sunnybrook Farm, Little Miss Broadway, Just Around the Corner, Little Princess, Susannah of the Mounties, The Blue Bird, Young People, Kathleen, Miss Annie Rooney. Since You Went Away, I'll Be Seeing You, Kiss and Tell, That Hagen Girl, Honeymoon, Bachelor and the Bobby-Soxer, Fort Apache, Mr. Belvedere Goes to College, Adventure in Baltimore, Story of Seabiscuit, Kiss for Corliss.
TELEVISION: *Series*: Shirley Temple's Storybook (host, performer).

TENNANT, VICTORIA
Actress. b. London, England, Sept. 30, 1953. e. Central Sch. of Speech & Drama. Daughter of ballerina Irina Baronova and talent agent Cecil Tennant.
THEATER: Love Letters (Steppenwolf), Getting Married (NY).
PICTURES: The Ragman's Daughter, Horror Planet (Inseminoid), Strangers Kiss, All of Me, The Holocraft Covenant, Best Seller, Flowers in the Attic, Fool's Mate, The Handmaid's Tale, L.A. Story, Whispers, The Plague.
TELEVISION: *Mini-Series*: Voice of the Heart, Winds of War, Chiefs, War and Remembrance, Act of Will, The Man from Snowy River. *Movies*: Maigret, Dempsey, Under Siege.

TESICH, STEVE
Writer. b. Titovo, Utice, Yugoslavia, Sept. 29, 1942. e. Indiana U., Columbia U. Came to U.S. at age 14. While doing graduate work in Russian literature at Columbia left to begin writing. Taken up by American Place Theatre which did his play, The Carpenters, in 1970.
THEATER: Division Street, Square One, The Speed of Darkness, and On the Open Road.
PICTURES: Breaking Away (Academy Award, 1979), Eyewitness, Four Friends, The World According to Garp, American Flyers, Eleni.
(d. July 1, 1996)

TETZLAFF, TED
Director. b. Los Angeles, CA, June 3, 1903. Joined camera dept. Fox Studios, became first cameraman; dir., 1940; served in U.S. Air Corps as a Major, WWII.
PICTURES: *Cameraman*: Enchanted Cottage, Notorious. *Dir.*: World Premiere, Riffraff, Fighting Father Dunne, Window, Johnny Allegro, Dangerous Profession, Gambling House, White Tower, Under the Gun, Treasure of Lost Canyon, Terror on a Train, Son of Sinbad, Seven Wonders of the World, The Young Land.

TEWKESBURY, JOAN
Writer, Director. b. Redlands, CA, April 8, 1936. e. USC. Student American Sch. Dance 1947-54. Was ostrich and understudy in Mary Martin's Peter Pan. Directed and choreographed Theatre prods. in L.A., London, Edinburgh Festival, Scotland. Taught dance and theory, American Sch. of Dance 1959-64; taught in theatre arts depts. of two universities: USC, Immaculate Heart. Became script supvr. for Robert Altman on McCabe & Mrs. Miller. *Off-B'way*: Cowboy Jack Street (writer, dir.). Teacher in film dept. UCLA. Sundance advisor, 1992-93; directors lab-writers lab. American Musical Theatre Festival in Philadelphia: Chippy (dir.).
PICTURES: Thieves Like Us (co.-s.p.), Nashville, (s.p.), Old Boyfriends (dir.), Hampstead Center (doc. of Anna Freud, writer, dir.), A Night in Heaven (s.p.), The Player (actress).
TELEVISION: *Series*: Alfred Hitchcock Presents (dir., writer), Elysian Fields (pilot; dir., writer, exec. prod.), Almost Grown (dir.), Shannon's Deal (dir., writer). *Movies*: The Acorn People (dir., s.p.), The Tenth Month (dir., s.p.), Cold Sassy Tree (dir., s.p.), Sudie and Simpson (dir.), Wild Texas Wind (dir.), The Stranger (writer, dir.), On Promised Land (dir.).

THALHIMER, JR., MORTON G.
Former Theatre Executive. b. Richmond, VA, June 27, 1924. e. Dartmouth Coll., 1948, B.A.; U. of Virginia, 1959. Naval aviator in WWII. Joined Century Theatres as trainee 1948;

Jamestown Amusement, 1949-50. Past pres. Neighborhood Theatre, Inc. 1967-86. Charter member of Theatre Owners of America; past member and v.p. of NATO, served on finance comm. and Trade Practice comm. bd. member and past president of NATO of VA, 1973-75. Mem. Variety Club Int'l., Tent 11; patron life member, Variety Club of Israel, Tent 51.

THAXTER, PHYLLIS
Actress. b. Portland, ME, Nov. 20, 1919. e. St. Genevieve Sch., Montreal. Daughter is actress Skye Aubrey.
PICTURES: Thirty Seconds Over Tokyo (debut, 1944), Bewitched, Weekend at the Waldorf, Sea of Grass, Living in a Big Way, Tenth Avenue Angel, Sign of the Ram, Blood on the Moon, Act of Violence, No Man of Her Own, The Breaking Point, Fort Worth, Jim Thorpe_All American, Come Fill the Cup, She's Working Her Way Through College, Springfield Rifle, Operation Secret, Women's Prison, Man Afraid, The World of Henry Orient, Superman.
TELEVISION: *Movies*: Incident in San Francisco, The Longest Night, Three Sovereigns for Sarah. *Mini-Series*: Once an Eagle. *Guest*: Wagon Train, Alfred Hitchcock, Twilight Zone, Purex Specials For Women, Playhouse 90, The Fugitive, The Defenders, Murder She Wrote.

THEODORAKIS, MIKIS
Composer. b. Greece, 1925.
PICTURES: Eva, Night Ambush, Shadow of the Cat, Phaedra, Five Miles to Midnight, Zorba the Greek, The Day the Fish Came Out, The Trojan Women, State of Siege, Serpico, Iphigenia.

THEWLIS, DAVID
Actor. b. Blackpool, England, 1962. e. Guildhall School of Music and Drama, The Barbicon, London. First prof. job in breakfast food commercial.
PICTURES: Little Dorrit, Resurrected, Life Is Sweet, Afraid of the Dark, Damage, The Trial, Naked (Cannes Film Fest., NY Film Critics & Natl. Soc. of Film Critics Awards, 1993), Black Beauty, Restoration, Total Eclipse, Dragonheart, James and the Giant Peach (voice), The Island of Dr. Moreau.
TELEVISION: Only Fools and Horses, The Singing Detective, Filipino Dreamgirls, Prime Suspect, Dandelion Dead.

THIGPEN, LYNNE
Actress, Singer. b. Joliet, IL, Dec. 22, 1948.
THEATER: *NY*: Godspell, The Magic Show, But Never Jam Today, Tintypes, And I Ain't Finished Yet, Full Hookup, Balm in Gilead, A Month of Sundays, Fences, Boesman & Lena.
PICTURES: Godspell (debut, 1973), The Warriors, Tootsie, Streets of Fire, Sweet Liberty, Hello Again, Running on Empty, Lean on Me, Impulse, Article 99, Bob Roberts, The Paper, Naked in New York, Blankman, Just Cause.
TELEVISION: *Series*: Love Sidney, The News is the News, FM, All My Children, Where in the World is Carmen Sandiego? *Pilot*: Pottsville. *Guest*: The Equalizer, Gimme a Break, L.A. Law, Days and Nights of Molly Dodd, Roseanne, Frank's Place, The Cosby Show, Dear John, thirtysomething, Preston Episodes. *Movies*: Fear Stalk, Separate But Equal, A Mother's Instinct, Boys Next Door, Cagney & Lacey. *Pilot*: For the People, Those Two.

THINNES, ROY
Actor. b. Chicago, IL, April 6, 1938. Made tv debut as teen on DuPont Theatre, 1957.
PICTURES: Journey to the Far Side of the Sun, Charlie One-Eye, Airport 75, The Hindenburg, Rush Week.
TELEVISION: *Series*: General Hospital (1963-65), The Long Hot Summer, The Invaders, The Psychiatrist, From Here to Eternity, One Life to Live, Falcon Crest, Dark Shadows. *Movies*: The Other Man, The Psychiatrist: God Bless the Children, Black Noon, The Horror at 37000 Feet, The Norliss Tales, Satan's School for Girls, Death Race, The Manhunter, Secrets, Code Name: Diamond Head, Sizzle, The Return of the Mod Squad, Freedom, Dark Holiday, Blue Bayou, The Hand in the Glove, An Inconvenient Woman, Lady Against the Odds, Stormy Weathers. *Mini-Series*: From Here to Eternity, Scruples.

THOMAS, BETTY
Director, Actress. b. St. Louis, MO, July 27, 1949. e. Ohio U, Chicago Art Inst., Roosevelt U. Former member of Chicago's Second City improv group.
PICTURES: *Actress*: Tunnelvision, Chesty Anderson—U.S. Navy, Loose Shoes, Used Cars, Homework, Troop Beverly Hills, Jackson County Jail. *Director*: Only You, The Brady Bunch Movie.
TELEVISION: *Series*: Hill Street Blues (Emmy Award, 1985). *Movies*: Outside Chance, Nashville Grab, When Your Lover Leaves, Prison for Children. Director (series): Doogie Howser M.D., Dream On (Emmy Award, 1993), Hooperman, Mancusco FBI, Arresting Behavior, Couples. *Movie*: My Breast.

THOMAS, DAVE
Actor, Writer, Director. b. St. Catherines, Ontario, Canada, May 20, 1949. e. McMaster Univ.
PICTURES: Stripes (debut, 1981), Strange Bew (also co-dir., co-s.p.), My Man Adam, Sesame Street Presents Follow That Bird, Love at Stake, Nightflyers, Moving, The Experts (dir. only), Cold Sweat, Coneheads.
TELEVISION: Series (actor/writer): Second City TV, SCTV Network The New Show, The Dave Thomas Comedy Show (also exec. prod., dir.), Maniac Mansion, Grace Under Fire (actor only). Movies: Home to Stay, Just Me and You, The Canadian Conspiracy, Boris and Natasha, Ghost Mom (writer). Pilot: From Cleveland. Specials: Twilight Theatre, Martin Short Concert for the North, Dave Thomas: The Incredible Time Travels of Henry Osgood (also dir., exec. prod., writer), Andrea Martin: Together Again, Inside America's Totally Unsolved Lifestyles (also exec. prod., writer).

THOMAS, HARRY E.
Exhibitor. b. Monroe, LA, May 22, 1920. e. Louisiana State U., 1938-41. Psychological Branch of Army Air Force, 1942-46. Past pres., secy., and treas. of NATO of MS. Dir. of Design & Const. & Sec. Gulf State Theatres Inc. Retired 1978.

THOMAS, HENRY
Actor. b. San Antonio, TX, Sept. 8, 1971. Made film debut at the age of 9 in Raggedy Man, 1981. On stage in Artichoke, The Guardsman.
PICTURES: Raggedy Man (debut, 1981), E.T. The Extra-Terrestrial, Misunderstood, Cloak and Dagger, The Quest, Murder One, Valmont, Fire in the Sky, Legends of the Fall.
TELEVISION: Movies: Psycho IV: The Beginning, A Taste for Killing, Curse of the Starving Class, Indictment: The McMartin Trial. Special: The Steeler and the Pittsburgh Kid.

THOMAS, JAY
Actor. b. New Orleans, LA, July 12, 1948. Started as stand-up comedian before pursuing acting career in NY. Appeared on NY stage with Playwrights Horizons and Off-B'way in Isn't It Romantic? Also morning disc jockey on L.A. radio station KPWR-FM.
PICTURES: C.H.U.D., The Gig, Straight Talk, Mr. Holland's Opus.
TELEVISION: Series: Mork & Mindy, Cheers, Married People, Love & War. Guest: Murphy Brown (Emmy Award, 1991).

THOMAS, JEREMY
Producer. b. London, Eng., July 26, 1949. e. Millfield School. Son of dir. Ralph Thomas (Doctor comedies) and nephew of dir. Gerald Thomas (Carry On... comedies). Entered industry 1969. Worked as film edit. on Brother Can You Spare a Dime, 1974. Received Evening Standard Special Award for Outstanding Contribution to Cinema in 1990, BAFTA's Michael Balcon Award in 1991. Appointed chmn. of British Film Institute, 1992.
PICTURES: Mad Dog Morgan, The Shout, The Great Rock 'n' Roll Swindle, Bad Timing: A Sensual Obsession, Eureka, Merry Christmas Mr. Lawrence, The Hit, Insignificance, The Last Emperor (Academy Award, 1987), Everybody Wins, The Sheltering Sky, Let Him Have It (exec. prod.), Naked Lunch, Little Buddha.

THOMAS, LEO J.
Executive. b. Grand Rapids, MN. e. Univ. of MI, Univ. of IL. Started as research chemist in 1961 at Color Photog. Division of the Kodak Research Labs. 1967-70, head of Color Physics and Engingeering Lab; 1970-72, asst. head of Color Photog. Division; 1972-74, tech. asst. to dir. of the Research Labs; 1974, appointed sec. of Technical Affairs Committe. 1977, named dir. of Research Laboratories; later that year became v.p. of the company; 1978 elected sr. v.p. 1984, appointed gen. mgr. Life Sciences. 1988, v.p. Sterling Drug; 1989, gen. mgr. of Health Group; 1989, v.p. of Health Group; 1991, pres. of Imaging Group; 1994, exec. v.p. Eastman Kodak Company.

THOMAS, MARLO
Actress. b. Detroit, MI, Nov. 21, 1938. Daughter of late Danny Thomas. m. Phil Donahue. Brother is TV producer Tony Thomas. e. U. of Southern California. Started career with small TV roles, summer stock. Appeared in London stage prod. of Barefoot in the Park. Most Promising Newcomer Awards from both Fame and Photoplay for series That Girl. Conceived book, record and TV special Free to Be You and Me (Emmy Award, 1974).
THEATER: NY: Thieves, Social Security, The Shadow Box.Regional: Six Degrees of Separation.
PICTURES: Jenny, Thieves, In the Spirit.
TELEVISION: Series: The Joey Bishop Show, That Girl. Specials: Acts of Love and Other Comedies, Free To Be You and Me (also prod.; Emmy Award, 1974), The Body Human: Facts for Girls (Emmy Award, 1981), Love Sex... and Marriage (also exec. prod.), Free to Be a Family (host, exec. prod.;

Emmy Award, 1989). Movies: It Happened One Christmas (also co-prod.), The Lost Honor of Kathryn Beck (also exec. prod.), Consenting Adult, Nobody's Child (Emmy Award, 1986), Leap of Faith (co-exec. prod. only), Held Hostage: The Sis and Jerry Levin Story, Ultimate Betrayal, Reunion (also co-exec. prod.). Guest: Dobie Gillis, Zane Grey Theatre, Thriller.

THOMAS, PHILIP MICHAEL
Actor. b. Columbus, OH, May 26, 1949. e. Oakwood Coll.
PICTURES: Black Fist, Sparkle, Death Drug, The Wizard of Speed and Time.
TELEVISION: Series: Miami Vice. Movies: Toma, The Beasts Are on the Streets, This Man Stands Alone, Valentine, A Fight for Jenny, False Witness. Special: Disney's Totally Minnie, The Debbie Allen Special.

THOMAS, RALPH
Director. b. Hull, Yorkshire, England, Aug. 10, 1915. e. Tellisford Coll., Clifton and University Coll., London. Journalist in early career, entered m.p. ind. 1932 as film ed.; service with 9th Lancers, 1939-45; then film director.
PICTURES: Helter Skelter, Once Upon a Dream, Traveller's Joy, The Clouded Yellow, Appointment With Venus (Island Rescue), The Assassin (The Venetian Bird), A Day to Remember, Doctor in the House, Mad about Men, Above Us the Waves, Doctor at Sea, The Iron Petticoat, Checkpoint, Doctor at Large, Campbell's Kingdom, A Tale of Two Cities, The Wind Cannot Read, The 39 Steps, Upstairs and Downstairs, Conspiracy of Hearts, Doctor in Love, No Love for Johnnie, No My Darling Daughter, A Pair of Briefs, The Wild and the Willing, Doctor in Distress, Hot Enough for June (Agent 8 3/4), The High Bright Sun (McGuire Go Home!), Doctor in Clover, Deadlier Than the Male, Nobody Runs Forever (The High Commissioner), Some Girls Do, Doctor in Trouble, Percy, Quest for Love, The Love Ban, Percy's Progress (It's Not the Size That Counts), A Nightingale Sang in Berkeley Square, Pop Pirates.

THOMAS, RICHARD
Actor. b. New York, NY, June 13, 1951. e. Columbia U. Made TV debut at age 7 on Hallmark Hall of Fame special The Christmas Tree. That same year appeard on Brodawy in Sunrise at Campobello.
THEATER: Sunrise at Campobello, Everything in the Garden, Fifth of July, The Front Page, Love Letters, Square One, The Lisbon Traviata, Danton's Death, Richard II, Richard III.
PICTURES: Winning (debut, 1969), Last Summer, Red Sky at Morning, The Todd Killings, You'll Like My Mother, September 30, 1955, Battle Beyond the Stars.
TELEVISION: Series: One Two Three Go, As the World Turns, The Waltons (Emmy Award, 1973). Guest: Great Ghost Tales, Bonanza, Love American Style, Medical Center, Marcus Welby M.D., The F.B.I., Tales From the Crypt (Mute Witness to Murder), The Outer Limits. Movies: Homecoming, The Red Badge of Courage, The Silence, Getting Married, No Other Love, All Quiet on the Western Front, To Find My Son, Berlin Tunnel 21, Johnny Belinda, Living Proof: The Hank Williams Jr. Story, Hobson's Choice, The Master of Ballantrae, Final Jeopardy, Glory Glory, Go To the Light, Common Ground, Stephen King's IT, Mission of the Shark, Yes Virginia There Is a Santa Claus, Crash Landing: The Rescue of Flight 232, I Can Make You Love Me: The Stalking of Laura Black, Precious Victims, Linda, A Walton Thanksgiving Reunion, Death in Small Doses, A Walton Wedding, Down Out and Dangerous. Specials: A Doll's House, Give Us Barabbas, HMS Pinafore, Barefoot in the Park, Fifth of July, Andre's Mother.

THOMAS, ROBERT G.
Producer, Director. b. Glen Ridge, NJ, July 21, 1943. e. U. of Bridgeport, Fairleigh Dickinson U. Prod. educational radio programs, 1962, WPKN-FM. Asst. stage mgr. Meadowbrook Dinner Theatre, 1963; 1964, began career as TV cameraman for NY stations. Worked both full-time and freelance for major TV and video tape studios. 1968, started Bob Thomas Productions, producing business/sales films and TV commercials. Has 8 awards from natl. film festivals; nominated for 5 Emmys for TV series called The Jersey Side he produced for WOR-TV. Inventor of Futurevision 2000 multi-imaging video system for conventions and exhibits and museums (American Museum of Natural History: Hall of Human Biology to be shown over 15 years). Inventor and pres. of Video Mail Marketing Inc., low cost, light weight paper board video cassettes for the direct mail video marketing industry. Shorts: Valley Forge with Bob Hope, New Jersey—200 Years, Road-Eo '77.
TELEVISION: The Jersey Side (talk/entertainment), Jersey People (weekly talk/entertainment prog.), Movies '89 (synd. film preview series).

THOMAS, ROBERT J. (BOB)
Columnist, Associated Press, Hollywood. b. San Diego, CA, Jan. 26, 1922. p. George H. Thomas, publicist. e. UCLA.

Joined Associated Press staff, Los Angeles, 1943; corr. Fresno, 1944; Hollywood since 1944. Writer mag. articles; appearances, radio; orig. story Big Mike.
AUTHOR: The Art of Animation, King Cohn, Thalberg, Selznick, Winchell—Secret Boss of California, The Heart of Hollywood, Howard—The Amazing Mr. Hughes, Weekend '33, Marlon—Portrait of the Rebel as an Artist, Walt Disney—An American Original, Bud and Lou—The Abbott and Costello Story, The Road to Hollywood (with Bob Hope), The One and Only Bing, Joan Crawford, Golden Boy: The Secret Life of William Holden, Astaire: The Man the Dancer, I Got Rhythm—The Ethel Merman Story, Liberace, Clown Prince of Hollywood (Jack L. Warner), Disney's Art of Animation.

THOMOPOULOS, ANTHONY D.
Executive. b. Mt. Vernon, NY, Feb. 7, 1938. e. Georgetown U. Began career in broadcasting at NBC, 1959, starting as mail-room clerk and moving to radio division in prod. & admin. Shortly named to post in int'l division sales, involved with programming for stations and in dev. TV systems for other nations. Joined Four Star Entertainment Corp. as dir. of foreign sales, 1964; named v.p., 1965; exec. v.p., 1969; 1970 joined RCA SelectaVision Div. as dir. of programming; 1971 joined Tomorrow Entertainment as v.p.; 1973 joined ABC as v.p., prime-time programs in N.Y.; 1974, named v.p., primetime TV creative operations, ABC Entertainment; 1975 named v.p. of special programs, ABC Entertainment; 1976 made v.p., ABC-TV, assisting pres. Frederick S. Pierce in supervising all activities of the division; 1978 named pres. of ABC Entertainment; 1983 promoted to pres., ABC Broadcast Group in chg. all TV & radio operations; 1986-88, pres. & COO, United Artists Corp.; independent prod. with Columbia, 1989.

THOMPSON, CAROLINE
Writer. b. Washington, DC, Apr. 23, 1956. e. Amherst Col., Harvard. Started as free-lance journalist. Wrote novel First Born, which led to screenwriting.
PICTURES: Edward Scissorhands (also assoc. prod.), The Addams Family, Homeward Bound: The Incredible Journey, The Secret Garden (also assoc. prod.), The Nightmare Before Christmas, Black Beauty (also dir.).

THOMPSON, EMMA
Actress. b. London, England, Apr. 15, 1959. e. Cambridge Univ. Daughter of actors Eric Thompson and Phyllida Law. Acted with the Footlights at the Edinburgh Fringe. At Cambridge co-wrote, co-produced, co-directed and co-starred in school's first all-female revue Woman's Hour, as well as solo show Short Vehicle.
THEATER: London: Me and My Girl, Look Back in Anger. Renaissance Theatre Company (World Tour): A Midsummer Night's Dream, King Lear.
PICTURES: Henry V, The Tall Guy, Impromptu, Dead Again, Howards End (Academy Award, BAFTA, NY Film Critics, LA Film Critics, Golden Globe, Nat'l Society of Film Critics & Nat'l Board of Review Awards for Best Actress of 1992), Peter's Friends, Much Ado About Nothing, The Remains of the Day (Acad. Award nom.), In the Name of the Father (Academy Award nom.), My Father the Hero (unbilled), Junior, Carrington, Sense and Sensibility (also s.p.; BAFTA Award, 1995; Academy Award, 1996; Writers Guild Award, 1996; Golden Globe Award, 1996).
TELEVISION: Series: Thompson (also writer). Mini-Series: Tutti Frutti, Fortunes of War (BAFTA Best Actress award). Specials: The Emma Thompson Special, The Winslow Boy, Look Back in Anger, Knuckle, The Blue Boy. Guest: Cheers.

THOMPSON, FRED (DALTON)
Actor. b. Sheffield, AL, Aug. 19, 1942. Raised in TN. e. Memphis St. U, Vanderbilt U, studying law. Was Federal prosecutor before going to DC to serve as minority counsel on the Senate Select Committe on Presidential Campaign Activies, which involved investigation of the Watergate scandal. Hired to serve as consultant on film Marie, then was asked to play himself in the movie, resulting in acting career. 1994 elected to U.S. senate as Republican representative from Tennessee.
Author: At That Point in Time (1975).
PICTURES: Marie (debut, 1985), No Way Out, Feds, Fat Man and Little Boy, The Hunt for Red October, Days of Thunder, Die Hard 2, Flight of the Intruder, Class Action, Necessary Roughness, Curly Sue, Cape Fear, Thunderheart, White Sands, Aces: Iron Eagle III, Born Yesterday, In the Line of Fire, Baby's Day Out.
TELEVISION: Movies: Bed of Lies, Keep the Change, Stay the Night, Day-O, Barbarians at the Gate.

THOMPSON, J. LEE
Director, Writer, Producer. b. Bristol, England, 1914. On Brit. stage as actor with Nottingham Rep. Co.; Playwright: Murder Without Crime, Cousin Simon, Curious Dr. Robson (collab.) Thousands of Summers, Human Touch. To films, 1934 as actor, then writer, before turning to directing.

PICTURES: Writer: The Middle Watch, For Them That Trespass. Director: Murder Without Crime (dir. debut, 1950; also story, s.p.), The Yellow Balloon (also s.p.), The Weak and the Wicked (also co-s.p.), For Better or Worse (also s.p.), As Long as They're Happy, An Alligator Named Daisy, Yield to the Night, The Good Companions (also co-prod.), Woman in the Dressing Gown (also co-prod.), Ice Cold in Alex (Desert Attack), No Trees in the Street (also co-exec. prod.), Northwest Frontier (Flame Over India), Tiger Bay, I Aim at the Stars, The Guns of Navarone, Cape Fear, Taras Bulba, Kings of the Sun, What a Way to Go!, John Goldfarb Please Come Home (also co-exec. prod.), Return From the Ashes (also prod.), Eye of the Devil, Mackenna's Gold, Before Winter Comes, The Chairman, Country Dance (Brotherly Love), Conquest of the Planet of the Apes, Battle for the Planet of the Apes, Huckleberry Finn, The Reincarnation of Peter Proud, St. Ives, The White Buffalo, The Greek Tycoon, The Passage, Caboblanco, Happy Birthday to Me, 10 to Midnight, The Evil That Men Do, The Ambassador, King Solomon's Mines, Murphy's Law, Firewalker, Death Wish IV: The Crackdown, Messenger of Death, Kinjite.
TELEVISION: A Great American Tragedy, The Blue Knight, Widow.

THOMPSON, JACK
Actor. r.n. John Payne. b. Sydney, Australia, Aug. 31, 1940. e. Queensland U. Joined drama workshop at school; first part was in TV soap opera as continuing character. 1988, appt. to bd. of Australian Film Finance Corp. Formed Pan Film Enterprises.
PICTURES: The Savage Wild, Outback (Wake in Fright), Libido, Petersen, A Sunday Too Far Away, Caddie, Scobie Malone, Mad Dog Morgan, The Chant of Jimmie Blacksmith, The Journalist, Breaker Morant, The Earthling, The Club, The Man From Snowy River, Bad Blood, Merry Christmas Mr. Lawrence, Flesh + Blood, Burke & Willis, Ground Zero, Waterfront, Turtle Beach, Wind, A Far Off Place, Deception, The Sum of Us, The Last Dance.
TELEVISION: The Last Frontier, A Woman Called Golda, Waterfront, The Letter, Beryl Markham: A Shadow on the Sun, Paradise, Last Frontier, Wreck of the Stinson, A Woman of Independent Means.

THOMPSON, LEA
Actress. b. Rochester, MN, May 31, 1961. m. director Howard Deutch. Danced professionally since age of 14; won scholarship to Pennsylvania Ballet Co., American Ballet Theatre, San Francisco Ballet. Gave up that career for acting, appearing in several commercials for Burger King. L.A. stage: Bus Stop, The Illusion.
PICTURES: Jaws 3-D (debut, 1983), All the Right Moves, Red Dawn, The Wild Life, Back to the Future, SpaceCamp, Howard the Duck, Some Kind of Wonderful, Casual Sex?, Going Undercover, The Wizard of Loneliness, Back to the Future Part II, Back to the Future Part III, Article 99, Dennis the Menace, The Beverly Hillbillies, The Little Rascals.
TELEVISION: Series: Caroline in the City. Movies: Nightbreaker, Montana, Stolen Babies, The Substitute Wife, The Unspoken Truth. Guest: Tales From the Crypt.

THOMPSON, SADA
Actress. b. Des Moines, IA, Sept. 27, 1929. e. Carnegie Inst. of Technology, Pittsburgh. First N.Y. stage appearance in Under Milk Wood. B'way incl. The Effect of Gamma Rays (Obie, Drama Desk, Variety Poll), Twigs (Tony Award, 1972), Saturday, Sunday, Monday. Recent theater: Real Estate, Any Given Day.
PICTURES: Pursuit of Happiness, Desperate Characters.
TELEVISION: Specials: Sandburg's Lincoln, Our Town, The Skin of Our Teeth, Andre's Mother, Painting Churches. Movies: The Entertainer, Princess Daisy, My Two Loves, Fatal Confession: A Father Dowling Mystery, Home Fires Burning, Fear Stalk, Indictment: The McMartin Trial. Series: Family (Emmy Award, 1978). Mini-Series: Queen.

THULIN, INGRID
Actress, Director. b. Solleftea, Sweden, Jan. 27, 1929. m. Harry Schein. Made acting debut at 18 at the Municipal Theatre in Norrkoping. Studied at Stockholm's Royal Dramatic Theatre. Worked with Malmo and Stockholm repertory. Appeared on Swedish stage in nearly 50 plays including Gigi, Peer Gynt, Two for the Seesaw, Twelfth Night, Miss Julie. Has directed plays and films in Stockholm. N.Y. stage debut, 1967: Of Love Remembered. Author: Somebody I Knew (1993).
PICTURES: Where the Wind Blows, Love Will Conqueror, Jack of Hearts, Foreign Intrigue, Wild Strawberries, Brink of Life (Cannes Film Fest. Award), The Magician, The Judge, The Four Horsemen of the Apocalypse, Winter Light, The Silence, Games of Desire, Return From the Ashes, La Guerre est Finie, Night Games, Adelaide, Hour of the Wolf, I a Virgin, The Ritual, The Damned, Cries and Whispers, A Handful of Love, La Cage, Moses, Madame Kitty, The Cassandra Crossing, Broken Sky, At the Rehearsal, Control, House of Smiles, Rabbit Face.

371

THURMAN, UMA
Actress. b. Boston, MA, Apr. 29, 1970. Named after a Hindu deity. Raised in Woodstock, NY and Amherst, MA where father taught Asian studies. Father's work took family to India where they lived three years. e. Professional Children's School, NY. Worked as model while still in high school.
PICTURES: Kiss Daddy Good Night (debut, 1988), Johnny Be Good, Dangerous Liaisons, The Adventures of Baron Munchausen, Where the Heart Is, Henry and June, Final Analysis, Jennifer Eight, Mad Dog and Glory, Even Cowgirls Get the Blues, Pulp Fiction (Acad. Award nom.), A Month by the Lake, The Truth About Cats and Dogs, Beautiful Girls, Batman and Robin.
TELEVISION: Movie: Robin Hood.

THURSTON, DONALD A.
Executive. b. Gloucester, MA, April 2, 1905. Chairman of the board, Broadcast Music, Inc.

TICOTIN, RACHEL
Actress. b. Bronx, NY, Nov. 1, 1958. Began career as dancer with the Ballet Hispanico of New York, before becoming a production assist. on such films as The Wanderers, Dressed to Kill and Raging Bull.
PICTURES: King of the Gypsies, Fort Apache: The Bronx, Critical Condition, Total Recall, One Good Cop, FX2, Falling Down, Natural Born Killers, Don Juan DeMarco, Steal Big Steal Little.
TELEVISION: Series: For Love and Honor, Ohara, Crime and Punishment. Movies: Love Mary, Rockabye, When the Bough Breaks, Spies Lies and Naked Thighs, Prison Stories: Women on the Inside, Keep the Change, From the Files of Joseph Wambaugh: A Jury of One, Thicker Than Blood: The Larry McLinden Story, Deconstructing Sarah.

TIERNEY, LAWRENCE
Actor. b. Brooklyn, NY, Mar. 15, 1919. Brother of actor Scott Brady. e. Manhattan Coll. Track athlete (natl. championship Cross Country Team, N.Y. Athletic Club). Stage actor before screen debut 1943.
PICTURES: The Ghost Ship (debut, 1943), Government Girl, Gildersleeve on Broadway, The Falcon Out West, Youth Runs Wild, Back to Bataan, Dillinger, Mama Loves Papa, Those Endearing Young Charms, Badman's Territory, Step By Step, San Quentin, The Devil Thumbs a Ride, Born to Kill, Bodyguard, Kill or Be Killed, Shakedown, The Hoodlum, The Bushwhackers, Best of the Bad Men, The Greatest Show on Earth, The Steel Cage, Female Jungle, Singing in the Dark, A Child Is Waiting, Custer of the West, Such Good Friends, Abduction, Andy Warhol's Bad, The Kirlian Witness, Never Pick Up a Stranger (Bloodrage), Gloria, Arthur, Rosemary's Killer, Midnight, Prizzi's Honor, Stephen King's Silver Bullet, Murphy's Law, Tough Guys Don't Dance, The Offspring (From a Whisper to a Scream), The Horror Show, Wizards of the Demon Sword, Why Me?, City of Hope, The Runestone, Reservoir Dogs, A Kiss Goodnight, Junior.
TELEVISION: Movies: Terrible Joe Moran, Dillinger. Guest: Hill Street Blues, Star Trek: The Next Generation, Tales From the Dark Side, Hunter.

TIFFIN, PAMELA
Actress. r.n. Pamela Wonso. b. Oklahoma City, OK, Oct. 13, 1942. e. Hunter Coll., Columbia U., Loyola U, Rome Center. Studied acting with Stella Adler and Harold Clurman. Started modeling as a teenager.
THEATER: Dinner at Eight (Theatre World Award), Uncle Vanya.
PICTURES: Summer and Smoke (debut, 1961), One Two Three, State Fair, Come Fly with Me, For Those Who Think Young, The Lively Set, The Pleasure Seekers, Kiss the Other Sheik, The Hallelujah Trail, Harper, Paranoia, Viva Max!, The Godson, Giornata Nera per l'Ariete, Deaf Smith and Johnny Ears, Puntto e a Capo, Evil Fingers.

TIGHE, KEVIN
Actor. b. Los Angeles, CA, Aug. 13, 1944. e. Cal. State, B.A. in psychology; USC M.F.A. in performing arts. Served in U.S. Army, 1967-69. Received N.E.A. Director's Fellowship, Seattle Rep. Theatre, 1988-89.
PICTURES: The Graduate (debut, 1967), Matewan, Eight Men Out, K-9, Lost Angels, Road House, Another 48 HRS, Bright Angel, City of Hope, Newsies, School Ties, A Man in Uniform (Genie Award), Geronimo: An American Legend, What's Eating Gilbert Grape, Scorpion Spring, Jade, Race the Sun.
TELEVISION: Series: Emergency, Murder One. Guest: Tales From the Crypt (Cutting Cards). Movies: Better Off Dead, Betrayal of Trust, The Avenging Angel.

TILLY, JENNIFER
Actress. b. Harbour City, CA, 1958. Sister is actress Meg Tilly.
THEATER: One Shoe Off (Off-B'way debut, 1993; Theatre World Award).
PICTURES: No Small Affair, Moving Violations, Inside Out, He's My Girl, Johnny Be Good, Rented Lips, High Spirits, Far From Home, Let It Ride, The Fabulous Baker Boys, Made in

America, The Getaway, Bullets Over Broadway (Acad. Award nom.), Man With a Gun, Embrace of the Vampire, House Arrest, The Pompatus of Love, Bound, Bird of Prey, Edie and Pen, American Strays.
TELEVISION: Series: Shaping Up. Movie: Heads.

TILLY, MEG
Actress. b. Long Beach, CA, Feb. 14, 1960. Sister is actress Jennifer Tilly. Began acting and dancing in community theatrical prods. while in high school. To New York at 16; appeared on TV in Hill Street Blues. Author: Singing Songs (1994).
PICTURES: Fame (debut, 1980), Tex, Psycho II, One Dark Night, The Big Chill, Impulse, Agnes of God (Acad. Award nom.), Off Beat, Masquerade, The Girl in a Swing, Valmont, The Two Jakes, Leaving Normal, Body Snatchers, Sleep with Me.
TELEVISION: Series: Winnetka Road. Specials: The Trouble With Grandpa, Camilla (Nightmare Classics). Movies: In the Best Interest of the Child, Trick of the Eye. Guest: Fallen Angels (Dead-End for Delia).

TINKER, GRANT A.
Executive. b. Stamford, CT., Jan. 11, 1926. e. Dartmouth Coll., 1947. Joined NBC radio prog. dept. 1949. In 1954 with McCann-Erickson ad agency, TV dept. In 1958, Benton & Bowles Ad Agency, TV dept.; 1961-66 with NBC, v.p., programs, West Coast; v.p. in chg. of programming, NY, 1966-67; joined Universal Television as v.p., 1968-69; 20th-Fox, v.p., 1969-70. Became pres. MTM Enterprises, Inc. 1970. Named NBC bd. chmn. & CEO, 1981-86. Received ATAS Governor's Award in 1987. Formed indep. prod. co. G.T.G. Entertainment, 1988.

TISCH, LAURENCE A.
Executive. b. Brooklyn, NY, March 5, 1923. e. NYU, 1941; U. of Pennsylvania Wharton Sch., 1942; Harvard Law Sch., 1946. Pres. Tisch Hotels, Inc., 1950-59; pres. Americana Hotel, Inc., Miami Beach, 1956-59; Chmn. of bd. and co-chief executive officer of Loews Corp since 1960. Also chmn. of bd. of CNA Financial Corp since 1947. President and chief executive officer and chmn. of board, CBS since 1986.

TISCH, PRESTON ROBERT
Executive. b. Brooklyn, NY, April 29, 1926. e. Bucknell U., Lewisberg, PA, 1943-44; U. of Michigan, B.A., 1948. Pres. Loew's Corporation. Postmaster General of the U.S. 1986-1988. March, 1988 returned to Loews Corp. as president and co-chief executive. Elected member of bd. CBS Inc. 1988, 1994, position changed to co-chmn. & co-CEO of Loews Corp.

TISCH, STEVE
Producer. b. Lakewood, NJ, 1949. e. Tufts U. Son of Preston Tisch. Worked during school breaks for John Avildsen and Fred Weintraub. Signed upon graduation as exec. asst. to Peter Guber, then prod. head at Columbia Pictures. Entered producer ranks with Outlaw Blues, 1977, collaborating with Jon Avnet with whom formed Tisch/Avnet Prods. Alliance with Phoenix Entertainment 1988.
PICTURES: Outlaw Blues, Almost Summer, Coast to Coast, Risky Business, Deal of the Century, Soul Man, Big Business, Hot to Trot, Heart of Dixie, Heart Condition, Bad Influence, Forrest Gump (Academy Award for Best Picture, 1994), Corrina Corrina, The Long Kiss Goodnight (exec. prod.), Dear God, Wild America (exec. prod.).
TELEVISION: Homeward Bound, No Other Love, Prime Suspect, Something So Right, Calendar Girl Murders, The Burning Bed (exec. prod.), Call to Glory (series), Triple Cross, Silence of the Heart, In Love and War (sole prod.), Evil in Clear River, Dirty Dancing (series), Out on the Edge (exec. prod.), Judgment (exec. prod.), Lies of the Heart, The Vidiots (pilot), Victim of Love, Keep the Change, Afterburn (exec. prod.), Freshman Dorm (pilot & series), The People Next Door.

TOBACK, JAMES
Writer, Producer, Director. b. New York, NY, Nov. 23, 1944. e. Harvard U. Taught literature at City Coll. of New York; contributed articles and criticism to Harper's, Esquire, Commentary, etc. Wrote book Jim, on actor-athlete Jim Brown (1971). First screenplay, The Gambler, filmed in 1974.
PICTURES: Writer: The Gambler, Fingers (also dir.), Love and Money (also dir., prod.), Exposed (also dir.), The Pick-Up Artist (also dir.), The Big Bang (also dir., actor), Alice (actor), Bugsy (also actor).

TOBOLOWSKY, STEPHEN
Actor. b. Dallas, TX, May 30, 1951. e. Southern Methodist Univ.
THEATER: Actor: Whose Life Is It Anyway?, Crimes of the Heart, Godspell, Three Sisters, The Glass Menagerie, Barabass, The Wake of Jamey Foster, The Wild Duck, No Scratch, The Miss Firecracker Contest, The Importance of Being Earnest, Purlie, Whispers in the Wind. Director: The

Miss Firecracker Contest, The Lucky Spot, The Bridgehead (Dramalogue Award), The Secret Rapture (Dramalogue Award), Our Town, The Debutante Ball.
PICTURES: Swing Shift, True Stories (co-s.p.), Nobody's Fool, Spaceballs, Mississippi Burning, Checking Out, Two Idiots in Hollywood (dir. & s.p.), Great Balls of Fire!, In Country, Breaking In, Bird on a Wire, Funny About Love, Welcome Home Roxy Carmichael, The Grifters, Thelma & Louise, Memoirs of an Invisible Man, Basic Instinct, Roadside Prophets, Single White Female, Sneakers, Where the Day Takes You, Sneakers, Hero, Groundhog Day, The Pickle, Calendar Girl, Josh and S.A.M., My Father the Hero, Radioland Murders, Murder in the First, Dr. Jekyll and Ms. Hyde, Power 98.
TELEVISION: Movies: Last Flight Out, Marla Hanson Story, Perry Mason: The Case of the Maligned Mobster, Tagget, Deadlock, Deadly Medicine, When Love Kills: The Seduction of John Hearn. Series: Against the Grain, Blue Skies, A Whole New Ballgame, Dweebs. Guest: Crazy Like a Fox, Designing Women, L.A. Law, Days and Nights of Molly Dodd, Seinfeld, Picket Fences, Chicago Hope, Hearts of the West, Baby Talk, Knots Landing, Falcon Crest.

TODD, BEVERLY
Actress, Director, Producer. b. Chicago, IL, July 11, 1953.
THEATER: NY: Carry Me Back to Morningside Heights, Black Visions. Producer: A Laugh a Tear: The Story of Black Humor in America, A Tribute to Ella Fitzgerald. Director: I Need a Man.
PICTURES: The Lost Man, They Call Me Mister Tibbs!, Brother John, Vice Squad, Homework, The Ladies Club, Happy Hour, Baby Boom, Moving, Clara's Heart, Lean on Me, The Class of '61.
TELEVISION: Series: Love of Life, Having Babies, The Redd Foxx Show. Mini-Series: Roots. Movies: Deadlock, The Ghost of Flight 401, Having Babies II, The Jericho Mile, Don't Look Back, A Touch of Scandal, A Different Affair. Guest: Magnum P.I., The Robert Guillaume Show, Falcon Crest, Quincy M.E., Hill Street Blues, Family, Benson, Lou Grant, A Different World. Special: Don't Hit Me Mom (Afterschool Special).

TODD, RICHARD
O.B.E. Actor. b. Dublin, Ireland, June 11, 1919. e. Shrewsbury. In repertory, 1937; founder-member, Dundee Repertory Theatre, 1939; distinguished war service, 1939-46; Dundee Repertory, 1946-48; screen debut, 1948; For Them That Trespass, 1948. 1970 Founder-Director Triumph Theatre Productions. Published autobiography, 1986, Volume II, 1989. Awarded O.B.E., 1993.
THEATER: An Ideal Husband, Dear Octopus. Co-founder, Triumph Theatre Prods., Ltd. plays since 1970: Roar Like a Dove, Grass Is Greener, The Marquise (U.S.). Sleuth (England and Australia). Murder by Numbers, The Hollow Crown (with RSC), Equus. On Approval, Quadrille, This Happy Breed, The Business of Murder (London), Intent to Kill, The Woman in Black, Beyond Reasonable Doubt, Sweet Revenge, Brideshead Revisted.
PICTURES: For Them That Trespass (debut, 1948), The Hasty Heart, Interrupted Journey, Stage Fright, Portrait of Clare, Lightning Strikes Twice (U.S.), Flesh and Blood, Story of Robin Hood, 24 Hours of a Woman's Life, The Venetian Bird, Sword and the Rose, Rob Roy, Les Secrets d'Alcove (Fr.), A Man Called Peter (U.S.), The Virgin Queen (U.S.), Dam Busters, D-Day the Sixth of June (U.S.), Marie Antoinette (Fr.), Yangtse Incident, Saint Joan, Chase a Crooked Shadow, The Naked Earth, Intent to Kill, Danger Within, Never Let Go, The Long the Short and the Tall, Don't Bother to Knock (also exec. prod.), The Hellions, The Longest Day, Crime Does Not Pay (Fr.), The Boys, The Very Edge, Death Drums Along the River, Battle of the Villa Fiorita, Operation Crossbow, Coast of Skeletons, The Love-Ins, Subterfuge, Dorian Gray, Asylum, The Sky is Falling, Number One of the Secret Service, The Big Sleep, House of the Long Shadows.
TELEVISION: Wuthering Heights, Carrington V.C., The Brighton Mesmerists, Beautiful Lies, The Boy Dominic, Murder She Wrote, Virtual Murder.

TOKOFSKY, JERRY H.
Executive. b. New York, NY, Apr. 14, 1936. e. NYU, B.S., journalism, 1956; New York Law, 1959. Entered William Morris Agency while at NYU 1953, working in night club dept. to live TV. Moved to Beverly Hills office, 1959. Entered m.p. div. WMA, 1960. Joined Columbia Pictures, as prod. v.p., 1963-70. Joined Paramount Pictures 1970 as prod. v.p. To MGM as prod. v.p., 1971. Now producer & exec. v.p., Zupnik Enterprises, Inc.
PICTURES: Producer: Where's Poppa, Born to Win, Paternity, Dreamscape, Fear City, Wildfire, Glengarry Glen Ross.

TOLKAN, JAMES
Actor. b. Calumet, MI, June 20, 1931. e. Univ. of Iowa. Trained with Stella Adler.
THEATER: NY: Abe Lincoln in Illinois, Once in a Lifetime, Three Sisters, The Cannibals, Mary Stuart, The Silent Partner, 42 Seconds from Broadway, Full Circle, Macbeth, Dream of a Blacklisted Actor, Jungle of Cities, Wings.

PICTURES: Stiletto, They Might Be Giants, The Friends of Eddie Coyle, Serpico, Love and Death, The Amityville Horror, Wolfen, Prince of the City, Author! Author!, Hanky Panky, Nightmares (voice), WarGames, Iceman, The River, Turk 182!, Flanagan, Back to the Future, Off Beat, Top Gun, Armed and Dangerous, Masters of the Universe, Made in Heaven, Viper, Split Decisions, True Blood, Second Sight, Back to the Future Part II, Family Business, Opportunity Knocks, Back to the Future Part III, Dick Tracy, Hangfire, Problem Child 2, Driving Me Crazy, Boiling Point.
TELEVISION: Series: Mary, The Hat Squad, Cobra. Movies: Little Spies, Leap of Faith, Weekend War, The Case of the Hillside Stranglers, Sketch Artist, Beyond Betrayal, Sketch Artist II: Hands That See. Guest: Remington Steele, Miami Vice, The Equalizer, Tales From the Crypt.

TOLKIN, MICHAEL
Writer, Director, Producer. b. New York, NY, Oct. 17, 1950. e. Middlebury Col, VT. Started as writer for LA Times, Village Voice, before becoming story editor on tv series Delta House. Novels: The Player (1988), Among the Dead (1992).
PICTURES: Writer: Gleaming the Cube, The Rapture (also dir.), The Player (also co-prod.; actor; WGA Award, Acad. Award nom.), Deep Cover (also story), The New Age (also dir.).
TELEVISION: Movie: The Burning Season (co-writer).

TOMEI, MARISA
Actress. b. Brooklyn, NY, Dec. 4, 1964. e. Boston U.
THEATER: Beirut (L.A.). NY: Daughters (Theatre World Award), The Comedy of Errors, What the Butler Saw, Slavs!
PICTURES: The Flamingo Kid (debut, 1984), Playing for Keeps, Oscar, Zandalee, My Cousin Vinny (Academy Award, best supporting actress, 1992), Chaplin, Untamed Heart, Equinox, The Paper, Only You, The Perez Family, Four Rooms, A Brother's Kiss, Unhook the Stars.
TELEVISION: Series: As the World Turns, A Different World. Guest: Seinfeld. Movie: Parker Kane.

TOMLIN, LILY
Actress. r.n. Mary Jean Tomlin. b. Detroit, MI, Sept. 1, 1939. e. Wayne State U. (studied pre-med). Studied mime with Paul Curtis. Started inventing characters for comedy sketches in college, used them in cafe and night club dates in Detroit. 1965 went to NY performing skits on coffee-house circuit, landed job on The Garry Moore Show. Moved to L.A. where she appeared on The Music Scene. 1969, first appeared on Laugh-In TV series, gaining national attention with such characters as telephone operator Ernestine and child Edith Ann.
THEATER: Appearing Nitely (special Tony Award, 1977), The Search for Signs of Intelligent Life in the Universe (1985, on B'way and on tour; Tony Award).
PICTURES: Nashville (debut, 1975; NY Film Critics Award; Acad Award nom.), The Late Show, Moment by Moment, Nine to Five, The Incredible Shrinking Woman, All of Me, Big Business, The Search for Signs of Intelligent Life in the Universe, Shadows and Fog, The Player, Short Cuts, The Beverly Hillbillies, Blue in the Face, Getting Away With Murder, The Celluloid Closet (narrator), Flirting With Disaster.
TELEVISION: Series: The Music Scene (host, 1969), Rowan and Martin's Laugh-In (1969-73), Magic School Bus (voice for animated series), Murphy Brown. Specials: Lily (Emmy Award as writer, 1974), Lily Tomlin (Emmy Award as writer, 1976), The Paul Simon Special (Emmy Award as writer, 1978), Lily—Sold Out (also exec. prod.; Emmy Award as exec. prod., 1981), The Muppets Go to the Movies, Lily for President?, Live—and in Person, Funny You Don't Look 200, Free to Be... a Family, Edith Ann: A Few Pieces of the Puzzle (voice, exec. prod.), Edith Ann: Homeless Go Home (voice, exec. prod.). Movie: And the Band Played On. Guest: Homicide.
RECORDS: This Is a Recording (Grammy Award, 1971), Modern Scream, And That's the Truth, Lily Tomlin On Stage.

TOPOL
Actor. b. Tel-Aviv, Israel, Sept. 9, 1935. r.n. Chaim Topol.
THEATER: Fiddler on the Roof (London, 1967, 1994-95 also U.K. tour; NY 1989: Tony nom.; Canada & Japan tour) Chicester Fest. Theatre: Caucasian Chalk Circle, Romanov and Juliet, Othello, View From the Bridge.
PICTURES: Sallah, Cast a Giant Shadow, Before Winter Comes, A Talent for Loving, Fiddler on the Roof (Acad. Award nom.), Follow Me (The Public Eye), Galileo, Flash Gordon, For Your Eyes Only, Ervinka, A Dime Novel.
TELEVISION: Movies: House on Garibaldi Street, Queenie. Mini-Series: The Winds of War, War and Remembrance. Series (BBC): It's Topol, Topol's Israel.

TORME, MEL
Singer, Actor. b. Chicago, IL, Sept. 13, 1925. Singing debut at age of 4; won radio audition 1933; on radio; composed song Lament to Love; with Chico Marx's orchestra as drummer, arranger & vocalist 1942; served in U.S. Army, WWII; org. vocal group Meltones; many recordings; night club and con-

cert appearances. *Author*: The Other Side of the Rainbow: With Judy Garland on the Dawn Patrol (1970), It Wasn't All Velvet (1988), My Singing Teachers: Reflections on Singing Popular Music (1994).
PICTURES: Higher and Higher (debut, 1943), Pardon My Rhythm, Let's Go Steady, Janie Gets Married, Junior Miss, Night and Day, Good News, Words and Music, Duchess of Idaho, The Big Operator, Girls Town, Walk Like a Dragon, The Patsy, A Man Called Adam, The Land of No Return (Snowman), Daffy Duck's Quackbusters (voice), The Naked Gun 2 1/2: The Smell of Fear.
TELEVISION: Series: TV's Top Tunes, The Judy Garland Show (musical advisor, frequent guest), It Was a Very Good Year (host). Movie: Pray TV. *Guest*: Night Court.

TORN, RIP
Actor. r.n. Elmore Torn, Jr. b. Temple, TX, Feb. 6, 1931. e. Texas A & M U., U. of TX. Served in army. Signed as under-study for lead in Cat on a Hot Tin Roof on Broadway.
THEATER: Orpheus Descending, Sweet Bird of Youth (Theatre World Award), Daughter of Silence, Macbeth, Desire Under the Elms, Strange Interlude, Blues For Mr. Charlie, The Kitchen, The Deer Park (Obie Award), The Beard, The Cuban Thing, Dream of a Blacklisted Actor, The Dance of Death, Anna Christie.
PICTURES: Baby Doll (debut, 1956), A Face in the Crowd, Time Limit, Pork Chop Hill, King of Kings, Hero's Island, Sweet Bird of Youth, Critic's Choice, The Cincinnati Kid, One Spy Too Many, You're a Big Boy Now, Beach Red, Sol Madrid, Beyond the Law, Coming Apart, Tropic of Cancer, Maidstone, Slaughter, Payday, Crazy Joe, Birch Interval, The Man Who Fell to Earth, Nasty Habits, The Private Files of J. Edgar Hoover, Coma, The Seduction of Joe Tynan, Heartland, One Trick Pony, First Family, A Stranger is Watching, The Beastmaster, Jinxed, Airplane II: The Sequel, Cross Creek (Acad. Award nom.), Misunderstood, Songwriter, Flashpoint, City Heat, Summer Rental, Beer, Extreme Prejudice, Nadine, The Telephone (also dir.), Cold Feet, Hit List, Blind Curve, The Hunt for Red October, Defending Your Life, Silence Like Glass, Beautiful Dreamers, Hard Promises, Robocop 3, Dolly Dearest, Where the Rivers Flow North, Canadian Bacon, How to Make an American Quilt, Down Periscope.
TELEVISION: Series: The Larry Sanders Show (Emmy Awatd, 1996). Movies: The President's Plane Is Missing, Attack on Terror: The FBI vs. the Ku Klux Klan, Betrayal, Steel Cowboy, A Shining Season, Sophia Loren—Her Own Story, Rape and Marriage—The Rideout Case, Laguna Heat, When She Says No, The Execution, The Atlanta Child Murders, Manhunt for Claude Dallas, J. Edgar Hoover, The King of Love, April Morning, Sweet Bird of Youth, Pair of Aces, By Dawn's Early Light, Another Pair of Aces, My Son Johnny, Death Hits the Jackpot, T Bone N Weasel, A Mother's Right: The Elizabeth Morgan Story, Dead Ahead: The Exxon Valdez Disaster, She Stood Alone: The Tailhook Scandal, Letter to My Killer. Mini-Series: Blind Ambition, The Blue and the Gray, Heaven & Hell: North and South Book III, Heart of a Child.

TORNATORE, GIUSEPPE
Director. b. Bagheria, Sicily, Italy, 1956. Made directorial debut at age 16 with short film Il Carretto. 1978- 85, served as pres. of the CLTC filmmaking cooperative.
PICTURES: The Professor (debut, 1986), Cinema Paradiso, Everybody's Fine, The Blue Dog (segment), Especially on Sunday (segment), A Pure Formality.
TELEVISION: Portrait of a Thief, Metting With Francesco Rosi, Sicilian Writers and Films, Il Diario di Guttuso, Ethnic Minorities in Sicily (Salerno Film Fest. Prize), A Hundred Days in Palermo (also writer, 2nd unit dir.).

TOTTER, AUDREY
Actress. b. Joliet, IL, Dec. 20, 1918. In many stage plays. On radio 1939-44.
THEATER: Copperhead, Stage Door, Late Christopher Bean, My Sister Eileen.
PICTURES: Main Street After Dark (debut, 1944), Her Highness and the Bellboy, Dangerous Partners, The Sailor Takes a Wife, Adventure, The Hidden Eye, The Secret Heart, The Postman Always Rings Twice, Cockeyed Miracle, Lady in the Lake, Beginning or the End, Unsuspected, High Wall, The Saxon Charm, Alias Nick Beal, Any Number Can Play, Tension, The Set-Up, Under the Gun, The Blue Veil, Sellout, F.B.I. Girl, Assignment-Paris, My Pal Gus, Woman They Almost Lynched, Cruisin' Down the River, Man in the Dark, Mission Over Korea, Champ for a Day, Massacre Canyon, Women's Prison, A Bullet for Joey, Vanishing American, Ghost Diver, Jet Attack, Man or Gun, The Carpetbaggers, Harlow, Chubasco, The Apple Dumpling Gang Rides Again.
TELEVISION: Series: Cimarron City, Our Man Higgins, Medical Center (1972-76). Movies: The Outsider, U.M.C., The Nativity, The Great Cash Giveaway, City Killer. Guest: Murder, She Wrote.

TOWERS, CONSTANCE
Actress. b. Whitefish, MT, May 20, 1934. m. John Gavin, actor and former U.S. Ambassador to Mexico. e. Juilliard Sch. of Music. Stage work on Broadway and tour.
THEATER: B'way: Ari, Anya, Engagement Baby, The King and I (1977-79 opp. Yul Brynner). Regional: Steel Magnolias, Follies.
PICTURES: Horse Soldiers, Sergeant Rutledge, Fate Is the Hunter, Shock Corridor, Naked Kiss, Sylvester, Fast Forward, Nutty Nut, The Next Karate Kid, The Relic.
TELEVISION: Series: Love Is a Many Splendored Thing, VTV, Capitol, 2000 Malibu Road. Mini-Series: On Wings of Eagles, Sands of Time. Guest: Home Show, The Loner, Murder, She Wrote, Hour Mag, MacGyver, Designing Women, Midnight Caller, Matlock, Baywatch, Prince of Bel Air, Thunder in Paradise, L.A. Law, Civil Wars, Frasier, Robin's Nest, Caroline In the City, The Young & the Restless.

TOWERS, HARRY ALAN
Executive, Producer. b. London, England, 1920.
PICTURES: Sanders of the River (also s.p.), Code Seven Victim Five (also s.p.), City of Fear, Mozambique, Coast of Skeletons, Sandy the Seal, 24 Hours to Kill, The Face of Fu Manchu, Ten Little Indians, Marrakesh, Circus of Fear, The Brides of Fu Manchu, Sumuru, Five Golden Dragons, The Vengeance of Fu Manchu, Jules Verne's Rocket to the Moon, House of a Thousand Dolls, The Face of Eve, Blood of Fu Manchu, 99 Women, Girl From Rio, Marquis de Sade's Justine, Castle of Fu Manchu, Venus in Furs, Philosophy in the Boudoir, Eugenie, Dorian Gray, Count Dracula, The Bloody Judge. Black Beauty, Night Hair Child, The Call of the Wild, Treasure Island, White Fang, Death in Persepolis, Ten Little Indians, End of Innocence, Black Cobra, Black Velvet—White Silk, Night of The High Tide, King Solomon's Treasure, Shape of Things to Come, Klondike Fever, Fanny Hill, Frank and I, Black Venus, Christmas, Black Arrow, Pompeii, Love Circles, Lightning—The White Stallion, Gor, Outlaw of Gor, Dragonard, Skeleton Coast, Master of Dragonard Hill, Nam, Fire With Fire, Jekyll and Hyde, River of Death, Cobra Strike, The Howling IV: The Original Nightmare, Skeleton Coast, Edge of Sanity, Ten Little Indians, Platoon Leader, Captive Rage, American Ninja III: Blood Hunt, The Fall of the House of Usher, Edgar Allan Poe's Buried Alive, Phantom of the Opera, Oddball Hall, Terror of Manhattan, The Lost World, Return to the Lost World, Black Museum, Golden Years of Sherlock Holmes, The Mangler, Midnight in St. Petersburg, Bullet to Beijing (The Return of Harry Palmer), Cry the Beloved Country, China Bill, She, Stanley & Livingstone, The Zodiac Conspiracy.

TOWNE, ROBERT
Writer, Director, Producer. b. Los Angeles, CA, 1936. Raised in San Pedro. Was member of Warren Beatty's production staff on Bonnie and Clyde and contributed to that screenplay. Also uncredited, wrote Pacino-Brando garden scene in The Godfather; script doctor on Marathon Man, The Missouri Breaks and others.
PICTURES: Writer: The Last Woman on Earth (as Edward Wain), The Tomb of Ligeia, Villa Rides, The Last Detail, Chinatown (Academy Award, 1974), Shampoo (co-s.p.), The Yazuka (co-s.p.), Personal Best (also dir., prod.), Greystoke: The Legend of Tarzan (s.p., uncredited), Tequila Sunrise (also dir.), Days of Thunder, The Two Jakes, The Firm (co-s.p.), Love Affair (co-s.p.), Mission: Impossible (co-s.p.).

TOWNSEND, ROBERT
Actor, Producer, Director, Writer. b. Chicago, IL, Feb. 6, 1957. e.Illinois State U., Hunter Coll. Veteran of Experimental Black Actors Guild and Second City. TV commercials; stand-up comedy at NY Improvisation; taped Evening at the Improv.
PICTURES: Actor: Cooley High (debut, 1974), Willie and Phil, Streets of Fire, A Soldier's Story, American Flyers, Odd Jobs, Ratboy, Hollywood Shuffle (also prod., dir., co-s.p.), Eddie Murphy Raw (dir. only), The Mighty Quinn, That's Adequate, The Five Heartbeats (also dir., exec. prod., co-s.p.), The Meteor Man (also dir., s.p., co-prod.).
TELEVISION: Series: Another Page (PBS series), Townsend Television, The Parent 'Hood (also co-creator, co-exec. prod.). Specials: Robert Townsend and His Partners in Crime, Take No Prisoners: Robert Townsend and His Partners in Crime II (HBO). Movies: Women at West Point, Senior Trip!, In Love With an Older Woman.

TRAMBUKIS, WILLIAM J.
Executive. b. Providence, R.I., July 26, 1926. e. Mt. Pleasant Bus. Col. Began career as usher with Loew's in Providence, RI, 1941. Served 1943-46 with Navy Seabees. Recipient of Quigley Awards. Managed/supervised Loew's Theatres in several New England cities, Harrisburg, PA, Syracuse, Rochester, Buffalo, NY, Washington, DC, Richmond, Norfolk, VA, Toronto, Canada, Atlanta, GA. Appt. Loew's NorthEastern Division mgr. 1964, Loew's gen. mgr. 1975: v.p. in 1976; sr. v.p., 1985. Retired, 1987.

TRAVANTI, DANIEL J.
Actor. b. Kenosha, WI, March 7, 1940. e. U. of Wisconsin (B.A.), Loyola Marymount Univ. (M.A.), Yale Sch. of Drama. Woodrow Wilson fellow, 1961. Formerly acted as Dan Travanty. On stage in Twigs, Othello, I Never Sang for My Father, Only Kidding, The Taming of the Shrew, Les Liaisons Dangereuses, A Touch of the Poet, Antony & Cleopatra.
PICTURES: St. Ives, Midnight Crossing, Millenium, Megaville, Weep No More My Lady, Just Cause, Siao Yu, Who Killed Teddy Bear.
TELEVISION: Series: General Hospital, Hill Street Blues (Emmy Awards, 1981, 1982; Golden Globe Award, 1981), Missing Persons. Movies: The Love War, Adam, Aurora, Murrow, Adam: His Song Continues, I Never Sang for My Father, Fellow Traveler, Howard Beach: Making the Case for Murder, Tagget, Eyes of a Witness, The Christmas Stallion, In the Shadows Someone's Watching, My Name is Kate, Wasp Woman, A Case of Libel, To Sir With Love II.

TRAVIS, NANCY
Actress. b. New York, NY, Sept. 21, 1961. Raised in Baltimore, MD, and Farmingham, MA. e. NYU. Attended Circle-in-the-Square Theatre school. Acted with NY Amer. Jewish Theatre before landing role in touring prod. of Brighton Beach Memoirs.
THEATER: NY: It's Hard to Be a Jew, The Signal Season of Dummy Hoy, I'm Not Rappaport (B'way). Tour: Brighton Beach Memoirs. La Jolla Playhouse: My Children My Africa, Three Sisters.
PICTURES: Three Men and a Baby (debut, 1987), Married to the Mob, Eight Men Out, Internal Affairs, Loose Cannons, Air America, Three Men and a Little Lady, Passed Away, Chaplin, The Vanishing, So I Married an Axe Murderer, Greedy, Destiny Turns on the Radio, Fluke, Bogus.
TELEVISION: Series: Almost Perfect. Movies: Malice in Wonderland, Harem, I'll Be Home for Christmas, Body Language. Special: High School Narc (ABC Afterschool Special).

TRAVOLTA, JOHN
Actor. b. Englewood, NJ, Feb. 18, 1954. m. actress Kelly Preston. First stage role in Who Will Save the Plowboy? Did off-B'way prod. of Rain; then on Broadway in Grease (also on tour for 10 months), Over Here (with the Andrew Sisters).
PICTURES: The Devil's Rain (debut, 1975), Carrie, Saturday Night Fever (Acad. Award nom.), Grease, Moment by Moment, Urban Cowboy, Blow Out, Staying Alive, Two of a Kind, Perfect, The Experts, Look Who's Talking, Look Who's Talking Too, Shout, Eyes of an Angel, Look Who's Talking Now, Pulp Fiction (Acad. Award nom.), White Man's Burden, Get Shorty (Golden Globe winner), Broken Arrow, Phenomenon, Michael.
TELEVISION: Series: Welcome Back Kotter. Movies: The Boy in the Plastic Bubble, Chains of Gold, Boris & Natasha (cameo). Special: The Dumb Waiter. Guest: Emergency, Owen Marshall--Counselor at Law, The Rookies, Medical Center.

TREBOT, JEAN-PIERRE
Executive. Exec. dir., The Friars Club.

TREMAYNE, LES
Actor. b. London, England, Apr. 16, 1913. e. Northwestern U., Chicago Art Inst., Columbia U., UCLA. First professional appearance in British mp., 1916, with mother; stock, little theatres, vaudeville, 1925-40; entered radio field, 1930. Blue ribbon award for best perf. of the month for A Man Called Peter; dir. Hollywood Rep. Theatre, 1957; pres. Hollywood Actors' Council, 1951-58; chmn. Actors Div. workshop com. Acad. TV Arts & Sciences; Mem.: The Workshop Comm. of the Hollywood M.P. & TV Museum Comm. One of 17 founding members, Pacific Pioneer Broadcasters; Life member, Actor's Fund; charter/founding mem. AFTRA, Chicago local. (delegate to most conventions since 1938). mem. Local, L.A, and Natl. AFTRA bds.
THEATER: Woman in My House, Errand of Mercy, You Are There, One Man's Family, Heartbeat Theatre, The First Nighter (lead 7 yrs.); on Broadway in Heads or Tails, Detective Story.
PICTURES: The Racket, Blue Veil, Francis Goes to West Point, It Grows on Trees, I Love Melvin, Under the Red Sea, Dream Wife, War of the Worlds, Susan Slept Here, Lieutenant Wore Skirts, Unguarded Moment, Everything But the Truth, Monolith Monsters, Perfect Furlough, North by Northwest, Say One for Me, The Gallant Hours, The Angry Red Planet, The Story of Ruth, The Fortune Cookie, Daffy Duck's Movie: Fantastic Island (voice), Starchaser (voice).
TELEVISION: Lux Video Theatre, 20th Century-Fox Hour, Navy Log, One Man's Family, Meet Mille, The Millionaire, The Whistler, Truth or Consequences, NBC Matinee, The Girl, O'Henry series, Rin Tin Tin, Bachelor Father, The Texan, Adventures of Ellery Queen, Court of Last Resort, Rifleman, State Trooper, Rescue 8, June Allyson-Dupont Show, Wagon Train, M Squad, Hitchcock Presents, Mr. Ed., Perry Mason.

TREVOR, CLAIRE
Actress. b. New York, NY, Mar. 8, 1910. e. American Acad. of Dramatic Arts; Columbia U. On Broadway in Party's Over, Whistling in the Dark, Big Two. On radio in Big Town for 4 yrs.
PICTURES: Life in the Raw (debut, 1933), The Last Trail, Mad Game, Jimmy and Sally, Hold That Girl, Baby Take a Bow, Elinore Norton, Wild Gold, Dante's Inferno, Spring Tonic, Navy Wife, Black Sheep, Human Cargo, My Marriage, The Song and Dance Man, To Mary—With Love, 15 Maiden Lane, Career Woman, Star for a Night, One Mile From Heaven, Time Out for Romance, Second Honeymoon, Big Town Girl, Dead End (Acad. Award nom.), King of Gamblers, The Amazing Dr. Clitterhouse, Walking Down Broadway, Valley of the Giants, Two of a Kind, I Stole a Million, Stagecoach, Allegheny Uprising, Dark Command, Texas, Honky Tonk, Street of Chance, The Adventures of Martin Eden, Crossroads, Woman of the Town, The Desperadoes, Good Luck Mr. Yates, Murder My Sweet, Johnny Angel, Crack-Up, The Bachelor's Daughters, Born to Kill, Raw Deal, The Babe Ruth Story, The Velvet Touch, Key Largo (Academy Award, best supporting actress, 1948), The Lucky Stiff, Borderline, Best of the Bad Men, Hard Fast and Beautiful, Hoodlum Empire, My Man and I, Stop You're Killing Me, The Stranger Wore a Gun, The High and the Mighty (Acad. Award nom.), Man Without a Star, Lucy Gallant, The Mountain, Marjorie Morningstar, Two Weeks in Another Town, The Stripper, How to Murder Your Wife, The Capetown Affair, Kiss Me Goodbye.
TELEVISION: Specials/Movies: If You Knew Elizabeth, Dodsworth (Emmy Award, 1957), No Sad Songs for Me, Ladies in Retirement, Breaking Home Ties. Guest: Alfred Hitchcock Presents, The Untouchables, Love Boat, Murder She Wrote.

TREXLER, CHARLES B.
Exhibitor. b. Wadesboro, NC, Feb. 8, 1916. 1937-48 was practicing CPA except for 2 yrs. in U.S. Army in WWII. Joined Stewart & Everett Theatres in 1948 as controller. 1953 named gen. mgr.; 1954, exec. v.p., treas.; 1962 named pres.; 1983, named bd. chmn.; former bd. chmn., NATO of North and South Carolina; v.p. & bd. mem., National NATO.

TRIKONIS, GUS
Director. b. New York, NY. Started career in chorus of West Side Story on B'way. Turned to directing, making low-budget weekenders (films shot in 12 days only on weekends).
PICTURES: Moonshine County Express, The Evil, Touched by Love, Take This Job and Shove It.
TELEVISION: Movies: The Darker Side of Terror, She's Dressed To Kill, Flamingo Road (pilot), Elvis and the Beauty Queen, Twirl, Miss All-American Beauty, Dempsey, First Affair, Malice in Wonderland, Love on the Run, Open Admissions, The Great Pretender. Mini-Series: The Last Convertible (co-dir.). Episode: Twilight Zone (1985).

TRINTIGNANT, JEAN-LOUIS
Actor. b. Aix-en-Provence, France, Dec. 11, 1930. m. Nadine Marquand, director. Theatre debut: 1951, To Each According to His Hunger. Then Mary Stuart, Macbeth (at the Comedie de Saint-Etienne). 1955 screen debut.
PICTURES: Si Tous Les Gars du Monde, La Loi des Rues, And God Created Woman, Club de Femmes, Les Liaisons Dangereuses, L'Estate Violente, Austerlitz, La Millieme Fenetre, Pleins Feux sur L'Assasin, Coeur Battant, L'Atlantide, The Game of Truth, Horace 62, Les Sept Peches Capitaux (7 Capital Sins), Le Combat dans L'Ile, The Easy Life, Il Successo, Nutty Naughty Chateau, Les Pas Perdus, La Bonne Occase, Mata-Hari, Meurtre a L'Italienne, La Longue Marche, Un Jour a Paris, Is Paris Burning?, The Sleeping Car Murders, A Man and a Woman, Enigma, Safari Diamants, Trans-Europ-Express, Mon Amour, Mon Amour, Un Homme a Abattre, La Morte Ha Fatto L'Uovo, Les Biches, Grand Silence, Z, Ma Nuit Chez Maud (My Night at Maud's), The Conformist, The Crook, Without Apparent Motive, The Outside Man, The French Conspiracy, Simon the Swiss, Agression, Les Violons du Bal, The Sunday Woman, Under Fire, La Nuit de Varennes, Long Live Life!, Next Summer, Departure, Return, The Man With the Silver Eyes, Femme Je Personne, Confidentially Yours, A Man and a Woman: 20 Years Later, La Vallee Fantome; Rendezvous, Bunker Palace Hotel, Three Colors: Red, The City of Lost Children, Fiesta.

TRIPP, STEVEN L.
Executive. b. Worthington, MN, Sept. 29, 1958. e. St. Cloud Community Coll. Managed local hometown theatres from 1978-82, then promoted to operation mgr., Tentelino Enterprises Circuit. Became general mgr. after Tentelino was purchased by Lakes & Rivers Cinemas in 1989. 1994-present, general mgr. and film buyer.

TRIPPLEHORN, JEANNE
Actress. b. Tulsa, OK, 1964. e. Julliard Sch. of Drama. On stage at NY's Public Theatre in The Big Funk, 'Tis Pity She's a Whore.
PICTURES: Basic Instinct (debut, 1992), The Night We Never Met, The Firm, Waterworld.
TELEVISION: Movie: The Perfect Tribute.

TRUMBULL, DOUGLAS
Cinematographer, Director, Writer. b. Los Angeles, CA, Apr. 8, 1942. Inventor Showscan Film process. Did Special Effects for Universal Studios attraction Back to the Future: The Ride; Luxor Live, Theatre of Time, In Search of the Obelisk. Director: Showscan short films New Magic, Let's Go, Big Ball, Leonardo's Dream, Night of the Dreams, Chevy Collector. Vice chmn., The Imax Corp.; pres. & CEO, Ridefilm Corp.; pres., Entertainment Design Workshop.
PICTURES: 2001: A Space Odyssey, Silent Running (also dir.), The Andromeda Strain, Close Encounters of the Third Kind, Star Trek: The Motion Picture, Blade Runner, Brainstorm (also dir., prod.).

TUBB, BARRY
Actor. b. Snyder, TX, 1963. Former rodeo star. Studied acting at Amer. Conservatory Theatre in SF.
THEATER: Sweet Sue (B'way), The Authentic Life of Billy the Kid.
PICTURES: Mask, The Legend of Billie Jean, Top Gun, Valentino Returns, Warm Summer Rain, Guilty By Suspicion.
TELEVISION: Series: Bay City Blues. Guest: Hill Street Blues. Movies: Consenting Adult, The Billionaire Boys Club, Without Her Consent. Mini-Series: Lonesome Dove, Return to Lonesome Dove.

TUCCI, STANLEY
Actor. b. Peekskill, NY. e. SUNY.
THEATER: B'way: The Misanthrope, Brighton Beach Memoirs, The Iceman Cometh. Moon Over Miami, Scapin, Dalliance, Balm in Gilead.
PICTURES: Who's That Girl, Monkey Shines, Slaves of New York, Fear Anxiety and Depression, The Feud, Quick Change, Men of Respect, Billy Bathgate, Beethoven, Prelude to a Kiss, The Public Eye, In the Soup, Undercover Blues, The Pelican Brief, It Should Happen to You, Mrs. Parker and the Vicious Circle, Kiss of Death, A Modern Affair, Big Night (also co-dir.).
TELEVISION: Series: The Street, Wiseguy, Murder One. Guest: Miami Vice, The Equalizer, thirtysomething, Equal Justice.

TUCKER, MELVILLE
Executive. b. New York, NY, Mar. 4, 1916. e. Princeton U. Asst. purchasing agent Consolidated Laboratories, N.Y., 1934-36; sound effects & picture ed., Republic Productions, Inc. 1936-8; then asst. production mgr. & first asst. dir., 1938-42; served in U.S. Army 1942-46; asst. prod. Republic 1946; assoc. producer, 1947-52; prod., Universal 1952-54; prod. exec. v.p., Universal, 1955-70; production exec. U-I, 1954-71; became prod.Verdon Prods., 1971.
PICTURES: Prod.: The Missourians, Thunder in God's Country, Rodeo King and the Senorita, Utah Wagon Train, Drums Across the River, Black Shield of Falworth, A Warm December, Uptown Saturday Night, Let's Do It Again, A Piece of the Action. Exec. prod.: Stir Crazy, Hanky Panky, Fast Forward.

TUCKER, MICHAEL
Actor. b. Baltimore, MD, Feb. 6, 1944. m. actress Jill Eikenberry. e. Carnegie Tech. Drama Sch. Worked in regional theater (Long Wharf, Washington's Arena Stage, Milwaukee Rep.) and with the NY Shakespeare Festival in Trelawney of the Wells, Comedy of Errors, Measure for Measure, The Merry Wives of Windsor. Also prod. revival of El Grande de Coca Cola (1986).
THEATER: Moonchildren, Modigliani, The Goodbye People, The Rivals, Mother Courage, Waiting for Godot, Oh What a Lovely War, I'm Not Rappaport (American Place Theatre).
PICTURES: A Night Full of Rain (debut, 1977), An Unmarried Woman, Eyes of Laura Mars, Diner, The Goodbye People, The Purple Rose of Cairo, Radio Days, Tin Men, Checking Out, For Love or Money, D2: The Mighty Ducks.
TELEVISION: Series: L.A. Law. Movies: Concealed Enemies, Vampire, Assault and Matrimony, Day One, Spy, Too Young to Die?, Casey's Gift: For Love of a Child, The Secret Life of Archie's Wife, In the Nick of Time, A Town Torn Apart. Specials: Love Sex... and Marriage, A Family Again, On Hope. Guest: Hill Street Blues.

TUCKERMAN, DAVID R.
Executive. b. Perth Amboy, NJ, Nov. 9, 1946. e. Monmouth Coll., F.L.U. 1967-70; B.S.B.A. Entered industry with A.I.T. Theatres, 1967; gen. mgr., Music Makers Theatres, 1973; v.p., Leigh Group, MMT, head film buyer, 1976; sr. v.p., MMT, 1980; Loews Film Buyer, 1986; Loews (now Sony) v.p. film, 1993. Member: SMPTE, Variety Int., MPBC, AFI, Motion Picture Pioneers.

TUGGLE, RICHARD
Director, Writer. b. Coral Gables, FL, Aug. 8, 1948. e. U. Virginia, B.A. 1970. Wrote screenplays before directorial debut with Tightrope, 1984.
PICTURES: Escape from Alcatraz (s.p.), Tightrope (dir., s.p.), Out of Bounds (dir.).

TUNE, TOMMY
Actor, Director, Choreographer, Dancer. b. Wichita Falls, TX, Feb. 28, 1939. e. Univ of Texas at Austin. Began professional career dancing in chorus of B'way shows (Baker Street, A Joyful Noise, How Now Dow Jones, etc.). Recipient of 9 Tony Awards.
THEATER: Performer: Seesaw, My One and Only, Bye Bye Birdie (tour), Tommy Tune Tonite! (B'way & tour). Director and/or choreographer: The Club, Cloud 9, The Best Little Whorehouse in Texas, Nine, A Day in Hollywood/A Night in the Ukraine, Stepping Out, My One and Only, Grand Hotel, The Will Rogers Follies.
PICTURES: Hello Dolly!, The Boy Friend.
TELEVISION: Series: Dean Martin Presents the Goldiggers; also numerous specials and Tony Award Shows.

TURMAN, LAWRENCE
Producer. b. Los Angeles, CA, Nov. 28, 1926. e. UCLA. In textile business 5 years, then joined Kurt Frings Agency; left in 1960 to form Millar-Turman Prods.
PICTURES: Prod.: The Young Doctors, I Could Go on Singing, The Best Man. Formed own prod. co., Lawrence Turman, Inc., to make The Flim-Flam Man, The Graduate, Pretty Poison (exec. prod.), The Great White Hope, The Marriage of a Young Stockbroker (also dir.), The Nickel Ride (exec. prod.), The Drowning Pool, First Love, Heroes, Walk Proud, Tribute, Caveman, The Thing, Second Thoughts (also dir.), Mass Appeal, The Mean Season, Short Circuit, Running Scared, Short Circuit 2, Full Moon in Blue Water, Gleaming the Cube, The Getaway, The River Wild.
TELEVISION: Co-prod. with David Foster: The Gift of Love, News at Eleven, Between Two Brothers. Prod.: The Morning After, She Lives, Unwed Father. Co-exec. prod.: Jesse.

TURNER, FREDERICK
Executive. b. London, England. Ent. m.p. ind. 1946. Early career with Eagle-Lion before transferring to Rank Overseas Film Distributors, then Rank Film Distributors. Became financial controller and appt. managing director 1981. Currently responsible for Film Investments and Distribution, UK and Overseas, covering all media.

TURNER, JANINE
Actress. r.n. Janine Gauntt. b. Lincoln, NE, Dec. 6, 1962. Raised in Texas. Studied dance, joined Forth Worth Ballet. Started modeling at age 15 in NYC, enrolled in Professional Children's School. First major acting job was on series Dallas. On stage in Full Moon and High Tide in the Ladies Room.
PICTURES: Young Doctors in Love, Knights of the City, Tai-Pan, Monkey Shines, Steel Magnolias, The Ambulance, Cliffhanger.
TELEVISION: Series: Behind the Screen, General Hospital (1982-83), Northern Exposure. Guest: The Love Boat, The A-Team, Mike Hammer.

TURNER, KATHLEEN
Actress. b. Springfield, MO, June 19, 1954. e. U. of Maryland, SMSU.
THEATER: B'way: Gemini, Cat on a Hot Tin Roof (Theatre World Award), Indiscretions. Regional: Camille (Long Wharf), A Midsummer Night's Dream (DC), Toyer (DC).
PICTURES: Body Heat (debut, 1981), The Man With Two Brains, Romancing the Stone, Crimes of Passion, A Breed Apart, Prizzi's Honor, The Jewel of the Nile, Peggy Sue Got Married (Acad. Award nom.), Julia and Julia, Switching Channels, Who Framed Roger Rabbit (voice), The Accidental Tourist, The War of the Roses, V.I. Warshawski, House of Cards, Undercover Blues, Serial Mom, Naked in New York, Moonlight & Valentino.
TELEVISION: Series: The Doctors. Movie: Friends at Last. Special: Dear America: Letters Home From Vietnam (reader). Director: Leslie's Folly.

TURNER, TED (ROBERT EDWARD)
Executive. b. Cincinnati, OH., Nov. 19, 1938. e. Brown U. m. actress Jane Fonda. Began career in Savannah in family's outdoor adv. business, selling space on billboards. Inherited co. in 1963 and in 1970 entered broadcasting with purchase of a failing TV station in Atlanta which he turned into WTBS, a "superstation" which in 1994 reached 95% of U.S. homes equipped with cable. 1980, established CNN a 24-hr. cable news service. Purchased MGM film library. Co-owner of two professional sports teams in Atlanta: Braves (baseball) and Hawks (basketball). Started Headline News, 1982; CNN International 1985; Turner Network Television 1988; Sportsouth, 1990; Cartoon Network in 1992; Turner Classic Movies, 1994; CNNfn Financial Network, 1995.

TURNER, TINA
Singer, Actress. r.n. Annie Mae Bullock. b. Brownsville, TX, Nov. 26, 1939. Previously married to Ike Turner and appeared with him on road in Ike and Tina Turner Revue. Many hit records. Autobiography: I Tina.

PICTURES: Gimme Shelter, Taking Off, Soul to Soul, Tommy, Sound of the City, Mad Max Beyond Thunderdome, What's Love Got to Do With It (vocals), Last Action Hero.
TELEVISION: *Special*: Tina—Live From Rio.

TURTURRO, JOHN
Actor. b. Brooklyn, NY, Feb. 28, 1957. e. SUNY/New Paltz; Yale Drama School, 1983. m. actress Katherine Borowitz. Worked in regional theater and off-B'way.
THEATER: Danny and the Deep Blue Sea (Obie & Theatre World Awards, 1985), Men Without Dates, Tooth of the Crime, La Puta Viva, Chaos and Hard Times, The Bald Soprano, Of Mice and Men, The Resistible Rise of Arturo Ui, Death of a Salesman (B'way debut, 1984).
PICTURES: Raging Bull (debut, 1980), Exterminator II, The Flamingo Kid, Desperately Seeking Susan, To Live and Die in L.A., Hannah and Her Sisters, Gung Ho, Off Beat, The Color of Money, The Sicilian, Five Corners, Do the Right Thing, Mo' Better Blues, State of Grace, Miller's Crossing, Men of Respect, Jungle Fever, Barton Fink (Cannes Film Fest. Award), Brain Donors, Mac (also dir., co-s.p.), Fearless, Being Human, Quiz Show, Search and Destroy, Clockers, Unstrung Heroes, Girl 6, Grace of My Heart.
TELEVISION: *Mini-Series*: The Fortunate Pilgrim. *Movie*: Backtrack.

TUSHINGHAM, RITA
Actress. b. Liverpool, England, March 14, 1942. Student at Liverpool Playhouse.
THEATER: The Giveaway, Lorna and Ted, Mistress of Novices, The Undiscovered Country, Mysteries.
PICTURES: A Taste of Honey (debut, 1961; BFA Award), The Leather Boys, A Place to Go, Girl With Green Eyes, The Knack... and How to Get It, Doctor Zhivago, The Trap, Smashing Time, Diamonds for Breakfast, The Guru, The Bed Sitting Room, Straight on Till Morning, The Case of Laura C., Where Do You Go From Here?, Situation, Instant Coffee, The Human Factor, Rachel's Man, The Slum Boy, The Black Journal, Bread Butter and Jam, Mysteries, Felix Krull, Spaghetti Thing, Dream to Believe, Flying, Seeing Red, The Housekeeper, Resurrected, Dante and Beatrice in Liverpool, Hard Days Hard Nights, Paper Marriage, Desert Lunch, An Awfully Big Adventure, The Boy From Mercury.
TELEVISION: *U.S.*: Green Eyes, Bread, Sunday Pursuit, Gutt Ein Journalist, Hamburg Poison.

TUTIN, DOROTHY
Actress. b. London, Eng., Apr. 8, 1930. e. St. Catherine's Sch. Bramley, Guildford (Surrey). Stage debut in The Thistle & the Rose, 1949.
THEATER: Much Ado About Nothing, The Living Room, I Am a Camera, The Lark, Wild Duck, Juliet, Ophelia, Viola, Portia, Cressida, Rosalind, The Devils, Once More With Feeling, The Cherry Orchard, Victoria Regina-Portrait of a Queen, Old Times, Peter Pan, What Every Woman Knows, Month in the Country, Macbeth, Antony and Cleopatra, Undiscovered Country, Reflections, After the Lions, Ballerina, A Kind of Alaska, Are You Sitting Comfortably?, Chalk Garden, Brighton Beach Memoirs, Thursday's Ladies, The Browning Version, A Little Night Music, Henry VIII, Party Time, The Seagull, Getting Married.
PICTURES: The Importance of Being Earnest, The Beggar's Opera, A Tale of Two Cities, Cromwell, Savage Messiah, The Shooting Party, Murder with Mirrors, Great Moments in Aviation, The Great Kandinsky.
TELEVISION: Living Room, Victoria Regina, Invitation to a Voyage, Antigone, Colombe, Carrington V.C., The Hollow Crown, Scent of Fear, From Chekhov With Love, Anne Boleyn in The Six Wives of Henry VIII, Flotsam and Jetsam, Mother & Son, South Riding, Willow Cabins, Ghosts, Sister Dora, The Double Dealer, The Combination, La Ronde, Tales of the Unexpected, 10 Downing Street, Life After Death, King Lear, Landscape, The Father, The Demon Lover, Robin Hood, All Creatures Great and Small, A Kind of Alaska, The Bill, Lease of Death, Anglo-Saxon Attitudes, Body and Soul, Jake's Progress, Indian Summer.

TWAINE, MICHAEL
Actor, Director. b. New York, NY, Nov. 1, 1939. e. Ohio State U. Served U.S. Army. While studying with Lee Strasberg, worked as private detective, school teacher. Made stage debut City Center, 1956, in Mr. Roberts. Became village coffee house and club comedian 1968 to 1972.
PICTURES: Marriage Italian Style (voice), American Soap, Blood Bath, F.I.S.T., Cheap Shots, Platoon (voice), Billy Bathgate (voice).
TELEVISION: The Silent Drum, Starsky & Hutch, Wonder Woman, Streets of San Francisco, Soap, Lou Grant, Diff'rent Strokes, Nurse, Stalk the Wild Child, The Courage and the Passion, Eischied, America's Most Wanted, Beyond the Universe.

TWIGGY
Actress. r.n. Leslie Hornby. b. London, England, Sept. 19, 1949. m. actor Leigh Lawson. At 17 regarded as world's lead-

ing high fashion model. Made m.p. debut in The Boy Friend, 1971. Starred in many London West End Shows, including Cinderella and Captain Beaky Presents. 1983: on Broadway in musical, My One and Only.
PICTURES: The Boyfriend (debut, 1971), W, There Goes the Bride, The Blues Brothers, The Doctor and the Devils, Club Paradise, Madame Sousatzka, Istanbul.
TELEVISION: *Series*: Twiggy, Twiggy and Friends, Juke Box (U.S.), Princesses (U.S.). *Specials*: Pygmalion, Sun Child, Young Charlie Chaplin. *Movies*: The Diamond Trap, Body Bags.

TYLER, LIV
Actress. b. July, 1977. Daughter of musician Steven Tyler. Began as a model at age 14.
PICTURES: Silent Fall (debut), Empire Records, Heavy, Stealing Beauty, That Thing You Do!, Inventing the Abbotts.

TYRRELL, SUSAN
Actress. b. San Francisco, CA, 1946. Made first prof. appearance with Art Carney in summer theatre tour prod. of Time Out for Ginger. Worked in off-B'way prods. and as waitress in coffee house before attracting attention in Lincoln Center Repertory Co. prods. of A Cry of Players, The Time of Your Life, Camino Real.
THEATER: The Knack, Futz, Father's Day, A Coupla White Chicks Sitting Around Talking, The Rotten Life.
PICTURES: Shoot Out (debut, 1971), The Steagle, Been Down So Long It Looks Like Up to Me, Shoot Out, Fat City (Acad. Award nom.), Catch My Soul, Zandy's Bride, The Killer Inside Me, Islands in the Stream, Andy Warhol's Bad, I Never Promised You a Rose Garden, Another Man Another Chance, September 30, 1955, Racquet, Loose Shoes, Forbidden Zone, Subway Riders, Night Warning, Fast-Walking, Liar's Moon, Tales of Ordinary Madness, Fire and Ice (voice), Angel, The Killers, Avenging Angel, Flesh and Blood, The Chipmunk Adventure (voice), The Offspring, Big Top Pee-Wee, Tapeheads, The Underachievers, Far From Home, Cry-Baby, Motorama, Powder.
TELEVISION: *Series*: Open All Night. *Movies*: Lady of the House, Midnight Lace, Jealousy, Thompson's Last Run, Poker Alice, The Christmas Star, Windmills of the Gods. *Mini-Series*: If Tomorrow Comes.

TYSON, CICELY
Actress. b. New York, NY, Dec. 19, 1933. e. NYU. Studied at Actor's Studio. Former secretary and model. Co-founder, Dance Theatre of Harlem.
THEATER: The Blacks, Moon on a Rainbow Shawl, Tiger Tiger Burning Bright, The Corn Is Green.
PICTURES: A Man Called Adam (debut, 1966), The Comedians, The Heart Is a Lonely Hunter, Sounder (Acad. Award nom.), The Blue Bird, The River Niger, A Hero Ain't Nothin' But a Sandwich, The Concorde—Airport '79, Bustin' Loose, Fried Green Tomatoes, The Grass Harp.
TELEVISION: *Series*: East Side West Side, The Guiding Light, Sweet Justice. *Movies*: Marriage: Year One, The Autobiography of Miss Jane Pittman (Emmy Award, 1974), Just An Old Sweet Song, Wilma, A Woman Called Moses, The Marva Collins Story, Benny's Place, Playing with Fire, Acceptable Risks, Samaritan: The Mitch Snyder Story, The Women of Brewster Place, Heat Wave, The Kid Who Loved Christmas, Duplicates, When No One Would Listen, House of Secrets, Oldest Living Confederate Widow Tells All (Emmy Award, 1994). *Guest*: B.L. Stryker. *Special*: Without Borders (host). *Mini-Series*: Roots. *Pilot*: Clippers.

U

UGGAMS, LESLIE
Singer. b. New York, NY, May 25, 1943. e. Professional Children's Sch., grad., 1960. Juilliard Sch. of Music. Beg. singing career age 5. TV debut as Ethel Waters' niece on Beulah. Also on Johnny Olsen's TV kids at age 7, Your Show of Shows as singer, 1953; Recording artist for Columbia Records, Atlantic, Motown Wrote The Leslie Uggams Beauty Book (1962).
THEATER: Hallelujah Baby (Tony & Theatre World Awards, 1968), Her First Roman, Blues in the Night, Jerry's Girls, Anything Goes (natl. co. & Bdwy), Stringbean (Dallas), Into the Woods (Long Beach, CA).
PICTURES: Two Weeks in Another Town, Poor Pretty Eddie, Black Girl, Heartbreak Motel, Skyjacked, Sugar Hill.
TELEVISION: *Series*: Sing Along With Mitch, The Leslie Uggams Show (1969), Fantasy (Emmy Award, 1984). *Guest*: Beulah (1949), Kids and Company, Milton Berle Show, Name That Tune, Jack Paar Show, Garry Moore. *Mini-Series*: Roots, Backstairs at the White House. *Movie*: Sizzle. *Specials*: The Book of Lists (co-host). Fantasy (Emmy Award, 1983, host), I Love Men, 'S Wonderful, 'S Marvelous, 'S Gershwin, Sinatra and Friends, Placido Domingo Steppin' Out With the Ladies, Jerry Herman Tribute, Rooms for Improvement.
RADIO: Peter Lind Hayes-Mary Healy Show, Milton Berle, Arthur Godfrey, Star Time.

ULLMAN, TRACEY
Actress, Comedian, Singer. b. Hackbridge, England, Dec. 29, 1959. m. British TV prod. Allan McKeown. e. won a performance sch. scholarship at 12. Attended the Italia Conti School for 4 years. Soon after appeared on British TV and onstage in Grease and The Rocky Horror Picture Show. Also performed in improvisational play Four in a Million (1981) at the Royal Court Theatre, London (London Theatre Critics Award). Recorded gold-selling album You Broke My Heart in Seventeen Places. Appeared in music video They Don't Know. U.S. TV debut, The Tracey Ullman Show (debuted April, 1987).
THEATRE: NY: The Taming of the Shrew, The Big Love.
PICTURES: Give My Regards to Broad Street, Plenty, Jumpin' Jack Flash, I Love You to Death, Happily Ever After (voice), Robin Hood: Men in Tights, Household Saints, Bullets Over Broadway, Ready to Wear (Pret-a-Porter).
TELEVISION: Series: Three of a Kind (BBC), The Tracey Ullman Show (Emmy Awards, 1989, 1990), Tracey Takes On.... Specials: The Best of the Tracey Ullman Show (Emmy Award, 1990), Tracey Ullman: Takes on New York (Emmy Award, 1994), Tracey Ullman—A Class Act. Guest: Love & War (Emmy Award, 1993).

ULLMANN, LIV
Actress. b. Tokyo, Japan, of Norwegian parents, Dec. 16, 1939. Accompanied parents to Canada when WWII began and later returned to Norway. Was catapulted to fame in a succession of Swedish films directed by Ingmar Bergman. Author: Changing, Choices. Ambassador for UNICEF since 1980. Youngest person to date to receive the Order of St. Olav from the King of Norway. Recipient of 11 honorary doctorates.
THEATER: U.S.: A Doll's House, Anna Christie, I Remember Mama (musical), Ghosts, Old Times.
PICTURES: Fjols til Fjells (debut, 1957), The Wayward Girl, Tonny, Kort ar Sommaren, De Kalte Ham Skarven, Persona, Hour of the Wolf, Shame, The Passion of Anna, The Night Visitor, Cold Sweat, The Emigrants, Pope Joan, Cries and Whispers, Lost Horizon, Forty Carats, The New Land, Scenes From a Marriage, Zandy's Bride, The Abdication, Leonor, Face to Face, Couleur Chair, A Bridge Too Far, The Serpent's Egg, Autumn Sonata, Players (cameo), Richard's Things, The Wild Duck, Bay Boy, Dangerous Moves, Let's Hope It's a Girl, Gaby—A True Story. Moscow Adieu (Donatello Award, 1987), A Time of Indifference, La Amiga, The Rose Garden, Mindwalk, The Ox, The Long Shadow, Sophie (dir., co-s.p. only), Kristin Lavrandsdatter (dir., s.p. only).
TELEVISION: Lady From the Sea, Jacobo Timerman: Prisoner Without a Name Cell Without a Number.

UNDERWOOD, BLAIR
Actor. b. Tacoma, WA, Aug. 25, 1964. e. Carnegie-Mellon Univ. NY stage: Measure for Measure.
PICTURES: Krush Groove, Posse, Just Cause, Set It Off, The Eighth Day.
TELEVISION: Series: One Life to Live, Downtown, L.A. Law, High Incident. Movies: The Cover Girl and the Cop, Heat Wave, Murder in Mississippi, Father & Son: Dangerous Relations (also assoc. prod.), Soul of the Game, Mistrial. Guest: Scarecrow and Mrs. King, The Cosby Show, Knight Rider, 21 Jump Street.

UNDERWOOD, RON
Director. b. Glendale, CA, Nov. 6, 1953. e. USC, American Film Institute.
PICTURES: Tremors (also co-story), City Slickers, Heart and Souls, Speechless.
TELEVISION: The Mouse and the Motorcycle (Peabody Award), Runaway Ralph (Emmy nom.).

UNGER, ANTHONY B.
Executive, Producer. b. New York, NY, Oct. 19, 1940. e. Duke U., USC. Prod. ass't Third Man, TV series, 1961. v.p. Unger Productions, Inc., 1964; v.p. Landau-Unger Co., Inc., 1965; v.p. Commonwealth United Entertainment in London, 1968; pres., Unger Prods. Inc., 1978-present.
PICTURES: The Desperate Ones. The Madwoman of Chaillot. The Battle of Neretva, The Magic Christian, Julius Caesar, The Devil's Widow, Don't Look Now, Force Ten From Navarone, The Unseen, Silent Rage.

UNGER, STEPHEN A.
Executive. b. New York, NY, May 31, 1946. e. NYU, Grad. Film and Television Instit. Started as independent prod. and dist. of theatrical and TV films. 1978, joined Universal Pictures Intl. Sales as foreign sls. mgr.; named v.p. Universal Theatrical Motion Pictures in 1979, responsible for licensing theatrical or TV features not handled by U.I.P. in territories outside U.S. & Canada and worldwide acquisitions; 1980 joined CBS Theatrical Films as intl. v.p., sls.; 1982-88, pres., Unger Intl. Distributors, Inc.; 1988 joined Korn/Ferry Intl. as exec. v.p., worldwide entertainment div. Promoted to mng. dir., 1989-91. Joined Spencer Stuart Exec. Search Consultants as mng. dir., Worldwide Ent. Div. 1991.

URICH, ROBERT
Actor. b. Toronto, OH, Dec. 19, 1946. e. Florida State U., B.A., radio and TV communications; Michigan State U., M.A. Communications Mgmt. Appeared in university plays. Was sales account executive at WGN Radio, Chicago, before turning to stage acting (Ivanhoe Theatre, Chicago).
PICTURES: Magnum Force, Endangered Species, The Ice Pirates, Turk 182.
TELEVISION: Series: Bob & Carol & Ted & Alice, S.W.A.T., Soap, Tabitha, Vega$, Gavilan, Spenser For Hire, American Dreamer, Crossroads, National Geographic Explorers (host), It Had to Be You, Lazarus Man. Guest: The FBI, Gunsmoke, Kung Fu, Marcus Welby MD, The Love Boat. Movies: Killdozer, Vega$ (pilot), Leave Yesterday Behind, When She Was Bad, Fighting Back, Killing at Hell's Gate, Take Your Best Shot, Princess Daisy, Invitation to Hell, His Mistress, Scandal Sheet, Young Again, April Morning, The Comeback, She Knows Too Much, Murder By Night, Night Walk, Blind Faith, Spooner, A Quiet Little Neighborhood A Perfect Little Murder, Stranger at My Door, And Then She Was Gone, Survive the Savage Sea, Blind Man's Bluff (also co-prod.), Double Edge, Revolver, Deadly Relations, Spenser: Ceremony (also co-exec. prod.), Spenser: Pale Kings and Princes (also co-exec. prod.), Danielle Steel's A Perfect Stranger, Spenser: The Judas Goat, A Horse for Danny, She Stood Alone: The Tailhook Scandal. Mini-Series: Mistral's Daughter, Amerika, Lonesome Dove.

URMAN, MARK
Executive. b. New York, NY, Nov. 24, 1952. e. Union Coll., 1973; NYU, cinema, 1973-74. m. story analyst Deborah Davis 1973, apprentice publicist, Universal Pictures; 1973-82, United Artists intl. dept. as assoc. publicist, sr. publicist and ultimately asst. to v.p. worldwide ad-pub.; 1982-84, dir., publicity and marketing, Triumph Films (Columbia/Gaumont); 1985-86, exec. dir. East Coast pub., Columbia Pictures; 1986-89, v.p. East Coast pub., Columbia Pictures. Joined Dennis Davidson Associates as v.p., 1989; promoted to sr.v.p., 1991. Member: Motion Picture Academy.

URQUHART, ROBERT
Actor, Writer. b. Scotland, October 16, 1922. e. George Heriots, Edinburgh. Served in Merchant Navy 1938-45; stage debut, Park Theatre, Glasgow; screen debut: You're Only Young Twice, 1951.
PICTURES: Isn't Life Wonderful, The House Of The Arrow, Knights of the Round Table, Happy Ever After (Tonight's the Night), Golden Ivory, The Dark Avenger, You Can't Escape, Yangtse Incident, Curse of Frankenstein, Dunkirk, The Trouble with Eve, Danger Tomorrow, Foxhole in Cairo, Murder in Mind, The Bulldog Greed, 55 Days At Peking, The Break, Murder at the Gallup, The Syndicate, The Limbo Line, The Looking Glass War, Brotherly Love (Country Dance), Playing Away, Restless Natives, Sharma and Beyond, P'Tang Bang Clipper Bang, Kitchen Toto, Testimony.
TELEVISION: Tamer Tamed, Infinite Shoeblack, Morning Departure, The Human Touch, The Iron Harp, Sleeping Clergyman, The Naked Lady, For Services Rendered, The Bright One, Jango, Murder Swamp, She Died Young, Plane Makers (series), Reporter, Inheritors (series); Mr. Goodall (series), The Nearly Man, The Button Man, Happy Returns, Endless-Aimless, Bleak House, The Queens Arms, Shostakovich. Writer: House of Lies, End of the Tether, Landfall, The Touch of a Dead Hand.

USLAN, MICHAEL E.
Producer, Writer. b. Bayonne, NJ, June 2, 1951. e. Indiana U., A.B., M.S., J.D. Wrote 12 books, including Dick Clark's 1st 25 Years of Rock 'n' Roll; 1976-80 atty. with United Artists; writer of syndicated comic strip Terry and the Pirates; produced with Benjamin Melniker.
PICTURES: Swamp Thing (prod.), The Return of Swamp Thing, Batman (exec. prod.), Batman Returns (exec. prod.), Batman: The Animated Movie (prod.), Batman Forever (exec. prod), Batman & Robin (exec. prod.).
TELEVISION: Three Sovereigns for Sarah (exec. prod.), Dinosaucers (exec. prod., creator, writer), Swamp Thing (exec. prod. for both live-action and animated series), Fish Police (exec. prod.), South Korea cultural segments NBC Summer Olympics 1988 (exec. prod.), Television's Greatest Bits (prod., creator, writer), 1st National Trivia Quiz (prod., writer), Where in the World Is Carmen Sandiego? (animated, exec. prod.; Emmy Award), Robin Cook's Harmful Intent (exec. prod.), Little Orphan Annie's Very Animated Christmas (exec. prod., writer); remakes of The Kiss, The Sneeze, The Great Train Robbery, The Barbershop, Streetcar Chivalry, Smashing a Jersey Mosquito (prod., dir.).

USTINOV, SIR PETER
Actor, Writer, Director. b. London, Eng., Apr. 16, 1921. e. Westminster Sch. In Brit. Army, W.W.II. On Brit. stage from 1937. Screen debut 1941 in Brit. picture Mein Kampf, My Crimes. Awards: 3 Emmy Awards (Specials: Life of Samuel

Johnson, Barefoot in Athens, A Storm in Summer); Grammy Award for Peter and the Wolf; NY Critics Award and Donaldson Award for best foreign play (The Love of Four Colonels); British Critics Award (Romanoff and Juliet). Chancellor, Durham Univ., 1992. Received Britannia Award from BAFTA, 1992; Critics Circle Award, 1993; German Cultural Award, 1994; German Bambi, 1994; Rudolph Valentino Award, 1995.
THEATER: Romanoff and Juliet, N.Y., London; and 17 other plays. Dir., acted, Photo Finish; wrote, Life In My Hands, The Unknown Soldier and His Wife, Half Way Up The Tree, King Lear, Beethoven's Tenth, An Evening With Peter Ustinov.
PICTURES: Actor: The Goose Steps Out, One of Our Aircraft Is Missing, The Way Ahead (co-s.p.), School for Secrets (wrote, dir. & co-prod. only), Vice Versa (dir., s.p. only), Private Angelo (also adapt., dir., co-prod.), Odette, Quo Vadis (Acad. Award nom.), The Magic Box, Hotel Sahara, The Egyptian, Beau Brummell, We're No Angels, Lola Montez, The Spies, The Man Who Wagged His Tail, School for Scoundrels (adapt. only), The Sundowners, Spartacus (Academy Award, best supporting actor, 1960), Romanoff and Juliet (also prod., s.p.), Billy Budd (also prod., dir., s.p.), Topkapi (Academy Award, best supporting actor, 1964), John Goldfarb Please Come Home, Lady L. (also dir., s.p.), The Comedians, Blackbeard's Ghost, Hot Millions, Viva Max, Hammersmith Is Out (also dir.), Robin Hood (voice), One of Our Dinosaurs Is Missing, Logan's Run, Treasure of Matecumbe, Purple Taxi, The Last Remake of Beau Geste, Doppio Delitto, Death on the Nile, Ashanti, Charlie Chan and the Curse of the Dragon Queen, Grendel Grendel Grendel (voice), The Great Muppet Caper, Evil Under the Sun, Memed My Hawk (also dir., s.p.), Appointment with Death, Lorenzo's Oil, The Phoenix and the Magic Carpet.
RECENT TV: The Well Tempered Bach, 13 at Dinner, Deadman's Folly, Peter Ustinov's Russia, World Challenge, Murder in Three Acts, The Secret Identity of Jack the Ripper (host), Around the World in 80 Days, The Mozart Mystique, Ustinov on the Orient Express, Ustinov Meets Pavarotti, Inside the Vatican, The Old Curiosity Shop, Haydn Gala, An Evening With Sir Peter Ustinov, Paths of the Gods.

V

VACCARO, BRENDA
Actress. b. Brooklyn, NY, Nov. 18, 1939. e. Thomas Jefferson H.S., Dallas; studied two yrs. at Neighborhood Playhouse in N.Y. Was waitress and model before landing first B'way role in Everybody Loves Opal. Toured in Tunnel of Love and returned to N.Y. for role in The Affair.
THEATER: Everybody Loves Opal (Theatre World Award), Tunnel of Love (tour), The Affair, Children From Their Games, Cactus Flower (Tony Award, 1965), The Natural Look, How Now Dow Jones (Tony nom.), The Goodbye People (Tony nom.), Father's Day, The Odd Couple, Jake's Women.
PICTURES: Where It's At (debut, 1969), Midnight Cowboy, I Love My Wife, Summertree, Going Home, Once Is Not Enough (Acad. Award nom., Golden Globe Award), Airport '77, House by the Lake (Death Weekend), Capricorn One, Fast Charlie the Moonbeam Rider, The First Deadly Sin, Zorro the Gay Blade, Supergirl, Water, Cookie, Heart of Midnight, Masque of the Red Death, Ten Little Indians, Lethal Games, Love Affair.
TELEVISION: Series: Sara, Dear Detective, Paper Dolls. Guest: The F.B.I., The Name of the Game, The Helen Reddy Show, The Shape of Things (Emmy Award, 1974), The Golden Girls, Columbo, Murder She Wrote, Flesh & Blood, Golden Girls (Emmy nom.), Civil Wars, Red Shoe Diaries, Friends. Movies: Travis Logan D.A., What's a Nice Girl Like You...?, Honor Thy Father, Sunshine, The Big Ripoff, Guyana Tragedy, The Pride of Jesse Hallam, The Star Maker, A Long Way Home, Deceptions, Julius and Ethel Rosenberg: Stolen: One Husband, Red Shoes Diaries, Following Her Heart.

VADIM, ROGER
Director, Writer. b. Paris, Jan. 26, 1928. r.n. Roger Vadim Plemiannikow. m. actress Marie-Christine Barrault. Appeared in films Rich and Famous, Into the Night.
PICTURES: Futures Vedettes (s.p.). Writer-Director: And God Created Woman, No Sun in Venice, The Night Heaven Fell, Les Liaisons Dangereuses, Blood and Roses, Please Not Now!, Seven Capital Sins (Pride segment), Love on a Pillow, Vice and Virtue (also prod.), Nutty Naughty Chateau, La Ronde (Circle of Love), The Game is Over (also prod.), Spirits of the Dead (Metzengerstein segment), Barbarella, Pretty Maids All in a Row, Helle, Ms. Don Juan, Night Games, Hot Touch, Surprise Party, Come Back, And God Created Woman (1988), The Mad Lover.
TELEVISION: Beauty and the Beast (Faerie Tale Theatre).

VAJNA, ANDREW
Executive. b. Budapest, Hungary, Aug. 1, 1944. e. UCLA. Launched career with purchase of m.p. theaters in Far East.

Founded Panasia Film Ltd. in Hong Kong. Exhibitor and dist. of feature films since 1970. Formed Carolco Service, Inc. (foreign sls. org.), with Mario Kassar 1976. Founder and Pres., American Film Mkt. Assn., 1982. Resigned from Carolco, 1989; formed independent production co., Cinergi Prods., 1989.
PICTURES: Exec. Prod.: The Deadly China Doll, The Silent Partner, The Changeling, Victory, The Amateur, First Blood, Superstition, Rambo: First Blood Part II, Angel Heart, Extreme Prejudice, Rambo III, Red Heat, Iron Eagle II, Deepstar Six, Johnny Handsome, Music Box, Mountains of the Moon, Total Recall, Air America, Narrow Margin, Jacob's Ladder, Medicine Man, Tombstone, Renaissance Man, Color of Night, Die Hard With a Vengeance, Judge Dredd, The Scarlet Letter, The Shadow Conspiracy, Nixon.

VALE, EUGENE
Writer. b. April 11, 1916. e. Zurich, Switzerland. m. Evelyn Wahl. Story and s.p., The Second Face, The Shattered Dream, 1954 SWG award nom.; best written telefilm; The Dark Wave. 1957, m.p. academy award nominations.
PICTURES: A Global Affair, Francis of Assisi, The Bridge of San Luis Rey, A Family Scandal, The Thirteenth Apostle, Hold the Split Second.
TELEVISION: Four Star Playhouse, Fireside Theatre, 20th Century Fox Hour, Schlitz Playhouse, Hollywood Opening Night, NBC, Crusader, Lux Video Theatre, Danger, CBS, Chevron Theatre, Douglas Fairbanks, Pepsi Cola Playhouse, Waterfront, Christophers, Cavalcade of America, Hallmark Hall of Fame.
AUTHOR: The Technique of Screen & Television Writing, The Thirteenth Apostle, Chaos Below Heaven, Passion Play, Some State of Affairs.

VALENTI, JACK J.
Executive. b. Sept. 5, 1921. e. U. of Houston, B.A., 1946; Harvard U., M.B.A., bus. admin., 1948. Air force pilot in European theatre, W.W.II; adv. and pub. rel. exec. in Houston; special asst. and advisor to Pres. Lyndon B. Johnson, 1963-66, elected pres., Motion Picture Association of America, MPEA and AMPTP, since June, 1966. Named Motion Picture Pioneer of the Year, 1988.

VALENTINE, KAREN
Actress. b. Sebastopol, CA, May 25, 1947.
PICTURES: Forever Young Forever Free, Hot Lead and Cold Feet, The North Avenue Irregulars.
TELEVISION: Series: Room 222 (Emmy Award, 1970), Karen, Our Time (host). Guest: My Friend Tony, Hollywood Squares, Laugh-In, The Bold Ones, Sonny and Cher, Mike Hammer, Murder, She Wrote. Movies: Gidget Grows Up, The Daughters of Joshua Cabe, Coffee Tea or Me?, The Girl Who Came Gift-Wrapped, The Love Boat (pilot), Having Babies, Murder at the World Series, Return to Fantasy Island, Go West Young Girl, Muggable Mary: Street Cop, Money on the Side, Skeezer, Illusions, Jane Doe, Children in the Crossfire, He's Fired She's Hired, A Fighting Choice, Perfect People. Special: The Emancipation of Lizzie Stern (Afterschool Special).

VALLI, ALIDA
Actress. r.n. Alida von Altenburger. b. Pola, Italy, May 31, 1921. e. M.P. Acad., Rome (dramatics); m. Oscar de Mejo, pianist-composer. In Italian m.p.; won Venice Film Festival Award in Piccolo Mondo Antico (Little Old World); to U.S. in 1947, billed simply as Valli.
PICTURES: Vita Ricomincia, Giovanna; The Paradine Case, The Miracle of the Bells, The Third Man, Walk Softly Stranger, The White Tower, Lovers of Toledo, We the Women, Senso, The Stranger's Hand, The Outcry, The Night Heaven Fell, This Angry Age (The Sea Wall), The Horror Chamber of Dr. Faustus, The Long Absence, The Happy Thieves, The Castilian, Ophelia, Oedipus Rex, The Spider's Stratagem, Tender Dracula, La Jeu de Solitaire, The Cassandra Crossing, Suspiria, 1900, The Tempter, Luna, Inferno, Le Jupon Rouge, A Notre Regrettable Epoux, A Month by the Lake.

VALLONE, RAF
Actor. b. Turin, Italy, Feb. 17, 1916. e. U. of Turin. Former newspaper writer. Directed operas Norma, La Traviata, Adrianna in NY, San Francisco and Houston.
PICTURES: Bitter Rice (debut, 1949), Vendetta, Under the Olive Tree, Anna, Path of Hope, White Line, Rome 11 O'Clock, Strange Deception, Anita Garibaldi, Daughters of Destiny, Teresa Raquin, Riviera, The Secret Invasion. Two Women, El Cid, Phaedra, A View From the Bridge, The Cardinal, Harlow, Nevada Smith, Kiss the Girls and Make Them Die, The Desperate Ones, The Secret Invasion, The Italian Job, The Kremlin Letter, Cannon for Cordoba, A Gunfight, Summertime Killer, Rosebud, The Human Factor, That Lucky Touch, The Other Side of Midnight, The Devil's Advocate, The Greek Tycoon, An Almost Perfect Affair, A Time to Die, Lion of the Desert, The Godfather Part III.

TELEVISION: Fame (Hallmark Hall of Fame), Honor Thy Father, Catholics, The Scarlet and the Black, Christopher Columbus, Goya.

VAN ARK, JOAN
Actress. b. New York, NY. m. NBC news reporter John Marshall. e. Yale U of Drama. Began career in touring co., then on Broadway and in London in Barefoot in the Park. Also appeared on B'way with the APA-Phoenix Rep. Co. in the 1970s. As a runner has competed in 12 marathons, incl. Boston Marathon. On TV also created voices for animated series Spiderwoman, Thundarr and Dingbat, Dumb and Dumber, Santo Bugito and the Creeps and special Cyrano de Bergerac. Estee Lauder spokesperson.
THEATER: School for Wives (Tony Award nom.; Theatre World Award), The Rules of the Game (Theatre World Award). L.A.: Cyrano de Bergerac, Ring Around the Moon, Chemin de Fer, As You Like It (L.A. Drama Critics Award). Williamstown Theatre Fest.: Night of the Iguana, The Legend of Oedipus, Little Night Music. Off-B'way & L.A.: Love Letters, Three Tall Women.
PICTURES: Frogs, Dedication Day (dir. only).
TELEVISION: Series: Temperatures Rising, We've Got Each Other, Dallas, Knots Landing. Guest: The F.B.I., The Girl with Something Extra, Quark, Dallas, Quincy, Rockford Files, Rhoda. Co-host: Miss USA and Miss Universe Pageants, Battle of the Network Stars, Macy's Thanksgiving Parade, Tournament of Roses Parade. Movies: The Judge and Jake Wyler, Big Rose, Testimony of Two Men, Shell Game, The Last Dinosaur, Red Flag—The Ultimate Game, Glitter, Shakedown on the Sunset Strip, My First Love, Always Remember I Love You, The Grand Central Murders, Tainted Blood, In the Shadows Someone's Watching (also co-exec. prod.), Moment of Truth: A Mother's Deception, When the Dark Man Calls. Special: Boys Will Be Boys (also dir.).

VANCE, COURTNEY B.
Actor. b. Detroit, MI, Mar. 12, 1960. e. Harvard (B.A.), Yale Drama Sch. (M.A.).
THEATER: B'way: Fences (Theatre World & Clarence Derwent Awards; Tony nom.), Six Degrees of Separation (Tony nom.). Off-B'way: My Children My Africa (Obie Award), Romeo and Juliet, Temptation. Regional: A Lesson From Aloes, Rosencrantz and Guildenstern Are Dead, Hamlet, Butterfly, Jazz Wives Jazz Lives, Geronimo Jones.
PICTURES: Hamburger Hill, The Hunt for Red October, The Adventures of Huck Finn, Holy Matrimony, Panther, Dangerous Moves, The Last Supper, The Preacher's Wife.
TELEVISION: Movies: Percy and Thunder, Race to Freedom, Tuskegee Airmen, The Affair, Black Tuesday.

VAN DAMME, JEAN-CLAUDE
Actor. b. Brussels, Belgium, Apr. 1, 1961. r.n. Jean-Claude Van Varenberg. Former European karate champion, began studying martial arts at 11 yrs. old. Won the European Professional Karate Association's middleweight championship. As teen established the California Gym in Brussels; also worked as a model before coming to U.S. in 1981. Resumed career teaching martial arts before landing first film role.
PICTURES: No Retreat No Surrender, Bloodsport, Black Eagle, Cyborg, Kickboxer (also co-story), Death Warrant, Lionheart (also co-s.p., story), Double Impact (also co-prod., co-s.p., co-story, fight choreog.), Universal Soldier, Nowhere to Run, Last Action Hero (cameo), Hard Target, Timecop, Street Fighter, Sudden Death, The Quest (also dir. & story), Maximum Risk.

VAN DEVERE, TRISH
Actress. b. Englewood Cliffs, NJ, March 9, 1945. e. Ohio Wesleyan U. m. actor George C. Scott. On B'way in Sly Fox, Tricks of the Trade, etc.
PICTURES: The Landlord (debut, 1970), Where's Poppa?, The Last Run, One Is a Lonely Number, Harry in Your Pocket, The Day of the Dolphin, The Savage Is Loose, Movie Movie, The Changeling, The Hearse, Uphill All the Way, Hollywood Vice Squad, Messenger of Death.
TELEVISION: Movies: Stalk the Wild Child, Beauty and the Beast, Sharon: Portrait of a Mistress, Mayflower—The Pilgrim's Adventure, All God's Children, Haunted, Curacao.

VAN DOREN, MAMIE
Actress. r.n. Joan Lucille Olander. b. Rowena, SD, Feb. 6, 1933. e. Los Angeles H.S. Secy. law firm, L.A.; prof. debut as singer with Ted Fio Rita orch.; debuted in films as Joan Olander.
THEATER: Stock: Once in a Lifetime, Boy Meets Girl, Come Back Little Sheba.
PICTURES: His Kind of Woman (debut, 1951), Forbidden, The All-American, Yankee Pasha, Francis Joins the WACs, Ain't Misbehavin', The Second Greatest Sex, Running Wild, Star in the Dust, Untamed Youth, The Girl in Black Stockings, Teacher's Pet, Guns Girls and Gangsters, High School

Confidential, The Beat Generation, The Big Operator, Born Reckless, Girls' Town, The Private Lives of Adam and Eve, Sex Kittens Go to College, College Confidential, Vice Raid, The Sheriff Was a Lady, The Candidate, Three Nuts in Search of a Bolt, The Navy vs. the Night Monsters, Las Vegas Hillbillies, You've Got to Be Smart, Voyage to the Planet of the Prehistoric Women, The Arizona Kid, Boarding School (Free Ride).

VAN DYKE, DICK
Actor. b. West Plains, MO, Dec., 13, 1925. Brother is actor Jerry Van Dyke. Son is actor Barry Van Dyke. Served in USAF, WWII. After discharge from service, opened advertising agency in Danville, IL. Teamed with friend in nightclub act called Eric and Van, The Merry Mutes, for 4 yrs. toured country doing a routine in which they pantomimed and lip-synched to records. 1953 hosted local TV show in Atlanta, then New Orleans. 1955 to NY as host of CBS Morning show.
THEATER: NY: The Girls Against the Boys (Theatre World Award), Bye Bye Birdie (Tony Award, 1961), The Music Man (revival).
PICTURES: Bye Bye Birdie (debut, 1963), What a Way to Go!, Mary Poppins, The Art of Love, Lt. Robin Crusoe USN, Divorce American Style, Fitzwilly, Chitty Chitty Bang Bang, Some Kind of a Nut, The Comic, Cold Turkey, The Runner Stumbles, Dick Tracy.
TELEVISION: Series: The Morning Show (host), CBS Cartoon Theatre (host), The Chevy Showroom, Pantomime Quiz, Laugh Line (emcee), The Dick Van Dyke Show (3 Emmy Awards: 1964, 1965, 1966), The New Dick Van Dyke Show, Van Dyke and Company (Emmy Award, 1977), The Carol Burnett Show, The Van Dyke Show, Diagnosis Murder. Movies: The Morning After, Drop-Out Father, Found Money, The Country Girl, Ghost of a Chance, Keys to the Kingdom, Daughters of Privilege, Diagnosis of Murder, The House on Sycamore Street, A Twist of the Knife. Pilot: Harry's Battles. Specials: The Dick Van Dyke Special, Dick Van Dyke and the Other Woman, Julie and Dick in Covent Garden, The Confessions of Dick Van Dyke, CBS Library: The Wrong Way Kid (Emmy Award, 1984), The Town Santa Forgot (narrator).

VAN DYKE, JERRY
Actor. b. Danville, IL, July 27, 1931. Brother is actor Dick Van Dyke. Served in U.S. Air Force before becoming standup comic, banjo player in nightclubs. Guested on The Dick Van Dyke Show, playing Van Dyke's brother.
PICTURES: The Courtship of Eddie's Father (debut, 1963), McLintock!, Palm Springs Weekend, Love and Kisses, Angel in My Pocket, W.A.R.: Women Against Rape.
TELEVISION: Series: Picture This, The Judy Garland Show, My Mother the Car, Accidental Family, Headmaster, 13 Queens Boulevard, Coach. Mini-Series: Fresno. Movie: To Grandmother's House We Go. Pilots: My Boy Googie, You're Only Young Twice.

VANGELIS
Composer, Conductor. Full name: Vangelis Papathanassiou. b. Greece, March 23, 1943. Began composing as child, performing own compositions at 6. Left Greece for Paris by late 1960s. Composed and recorded his symphonic poem Faire que Ton Reve Soit Plus Long que la Nuit, and album Terra. Collaborated with filmmaker Frederic Rossif for whom composed La Cantique des Creatures. Moved to London then to Greece in 1989. Formed band Formynx in Greece; then Aphrodite's Child in Paris.
PICTURES: Chariots of Fire (Academy Award, 1981), Antarctica, Missing, Blade Runner, The Year of Living Dangerously, The Bounty, Wonders of Life, Wild and Beautiful, Nosferatu in Venice, Francesco, 1492: Conquest of Paradise, Bitter Moon.

VANOCUR, SANDER
News Commentator. b. Cleveland, OH, Jan. 8, 1928. e. Northwestern U. Began career as journalist on London staff of Manchester Guardian 1954-5; City staff, NY Times 1956-57. Joined NBC in 1957, hosting First Tuesday series. Resigned in 1971 to be correspondent of the National Public Affairs Center for PBS. TV Critic for Washington Post, 1975-7. In 1977 joined ABC News as v.p., special reporting units 1977-80. Chief overview corr. ABC news, 1980-81; sr. corr. 1981-present. Anchor: Business World.

VAN PALLANDT, NINA
Actress. b. Copenhagen, Denmark, July 15, 1932. e. USC. Returned to Denmark where she was married to Baron Frederik Van Pallandt with whom she appeared as folk singer throughout Europe, as well as making 3 films with him; went on world tour together before divorcing. Has appeared in New York as singer.
PICTURES: The Long Goodbye, Assault on Agathon, A Wedding, Quintet, American Gigolo, Cloud Dancer, Cutter and Bone, Asi Como Habian Sido, The Sword and the Sorcerer, Jungle Warriors, Time Out, O.C. and Stiggs.
TELEVISION: Movie: Guilty or Innocent: The Sam Shepherd Murder Case.

VAN PATTEN, DICK
Actor. b. New York, NY, Dec. 9, 1928. Sister is actress Joyce Van Patten. Father of actors James and Vincent Van Patten. Began career as child actor with B'way debut at 7 yrs., playing son of Melvyn Douglas in Tapestry in Gray.
THEATER: The Lady Who Came to Stay, O Mistress Mine, On Borrowed Time, Ah, Wilderness, Watch on the Rhine, The Skin of Our Teeth, Kiss and Tell, Mister Roberts, Thieves.
PICTURES: Reg'lar Fellers (debut, 1941), Psychomania, Charly, Zachariah, Making It, Joe Kidd, Soylent Green, Dirty Little Billy, Westworld, Superdad, The Strongest Man in the World, Gus, Treasure of Matecumbe, The Shaggy D.A., Freaky Friday, High Anxiety, Spaceballs, The New Adventures of Pippi Longstocking, Robin Hood: Men in Tights, A Dangerous Place.
TELEVISION: Series: Mama, The Partners, The New Dick Van Dyke Show, When Things Were Rotten, Eight Is Enough, WIOU. Guest: Arnie, The Rookies, Cannon, Banyon, The Little People, The Streets of San Francisco, Hotel, Growing Pains, Love Boat, Murder She Wrote. Specials: Jay Leno's Family Comedy Hour, A Mouse A Mystery and Me, 14 Going On 30. Movies: Hec Ramsey (pilot), The Crooked Hearts, The Love Boat (pilot), With This Ring, Diary of a Hitchhiker, Eight Is Enough Reunion, Going to the Chapel, An Eight Is Enough Wedding, Jake Spanner—Private Eye, The Odd Couple: Together Again, The Gift of Love.

VAN PATTEN, JOYCE
Actress. b. New York, NY, March 9, 1935. Brother is actor Dick Van Patten. Mother of actress Talia Balsam.
THEATER: NY: Spoon River Anthology, Same Time Next Year, The Supporting Cast, The Seagull, I Ought to Be in Pictures, Brighton Beach Memoirs, Murder at the Howard Johnson's, Rumors, Jake's Women.
PICTURES: Reg'lar Fellers (debut, 1941), Fourteen Hours, The Goddess, I Love You Alice B. Toklas, Making It, Something Big, Thumb Tripping, The Manchu Eagle Murder Caper Mystery, Mame, The Bad News Bears, Mikey and Nicky, The Falcon and the Snowman, St. Elmo's Fire, Billy Galvin, Blind Date, Trust Me, Monkey Shines.
TELEVISION: Series: The Danny Kaye Show, The Good Guys, The Don Rickles Show, Mary Tyler Moore Hour, Unhappily Ever After. Guest: Brooklyn Bridge. Movies: But I Don't Want to Get Married!, Winter Kill, The Stranger Within, Let's Switch, Winner Take All, To Kill a Cop, Murder at the Mardi Gras, The Comedy Company, Eleanor: First Lady of the World, Another Woman's Child, The Demon Murder Case, In Defense of Kids, Malice in Wonderland, Under the Influence, The Haunted, Maid for Each Other. Mini-Series: The Martian Chronicles. Special: Bus Stop.

VAN PEEBLES, MARIO
Actor, Director, Producer, Writer. b. Mexico D.F., Mexico, Jan. 15, 1957. Father is filmmaker Melvin Van Peebles. e. Columbia U., B.A. economics, 1980. Studied acting with Stella Adler 1983. Served as budget analyst for NY Mayor Ed Koch and later worked as a Ford model. Directed music videos for Kid Creole and the Coconuts, Nighttrain (also prod., cameo) and for film Identity Crisis. Appeared as child in father's film Sweet Sweetback's Baadasssss Song. Dir., prod., wrote and starred in short, Juliet. Exec. prod. of soundtracks for Posse and Gunmen.
THEATER: Waltz of the Stork (B'way debut, 1984), Take Me Along, The Legend of Deadwood Dick, Champeen, Friday the 13th.
PICTURES: The Cotton Club, Delivery Boys, Exterminator II, 3:15, Rappin' (also wrote and performed 5 songs), South Bronx Heroes, Heartbreak Ridge (also songs), Last Resort, Jaws: the Revenge, Hot Shot, Identity Crisis (also s.p.), New Jack City (also dir.), Posse (also dir.), Gunmen, Highlander: The Sorcerer, Panther (also dir., prod.), Jaws IV: The Revenge, Solo.
TELEVISION: Series: Sonny Spoon. Guest: L.A. Law, One Life to Live, The Cosby Show, The Pat Sajack Show (guest host), In Living Color, Living Single. Movies: The Cable Car Murder, Sophisticated Gents, Children of the Night (Bronze Halo Award), The Facts of Life Down Under, The Child Saver, Blue Bayou, Triumph of the Heart: The Ricky Bell Story, Stompin' at the Savoy, In the Line of Duty: Street War, Crosscurrents; Cable Car Murder, Full Eclipse. Specials: American Masters: A Glory of Ghosts (Emperor Jones, All God's Chillun), Third & Oak: The Pool Hall (Strangers: Leave, Gang In Blue, Riot. Director: Sonny Spoon, 21 Jump Street, Top of the Hill, Wise Guy, Malcolm Takes a Shot (DGA nom.), Gabriel's Fire, Missing Persons.

VAN PEEBLES, MELVIN
Producer, Director, Writer, Composer, Editor, Actor. b. Chicago, IL, Aug. 21, 1932. e. Ohio Wesleyan U., 1953. Father of actor Mario Van Peebles. Was portrait painter in Mexico, cable car driver in San Francisco; journalist in Paris and (in 1970s) options trader on Wall Street. Dir. Funky Beat music video.

AUTHOR: Books: The Big Heart, A Bear for the FBI, Le Chinois de XIV, La Permission (Story of a Three Day Pass) La Fete a Harlem, The True American, Sweet Sweetback's Baadassss Song, Just an Old Sweet Song, Bold Money, No Identity Crisis (co-author with Mario Van Peebles), Panther.
THEATER: B'way (writer, prod., dir.): Ain't Supposed to Die a Natural Death, Don't Play Us Cheap, Waltz of the Stork (also actor). Off-B'way: Champeen, Waltz of the Stork, Kickin the Science.
PICTURES: The Story of a Three-Day Pass (dir., s.p., music), Watermelon Man (dir., music), Sweet Sweetback's Baadasssss Song (prod., dir., s.p., edit., music, actor), Don't Play Us Cheap (prod., dir., s.p., edit., music), Greased Lightning (co-s.p.), America (actor), O.C. and Stiggs (actor), Jaws: The Revenge (actor), Identity Crisis (prod., dir., co-edit., actor), True Identity (actor), Boomerang (actor), Posse (actor), Last Action Hero (actor), Terminal Velocity (actor), Fist of the North Star (actor), Panther (s.p., actor, prod., co-edit.).
TELEVISION: Writer: Down Home, Just an Old Sweet Song, The Day They Came to Arrest the Book (Emmy Award). Actor: Taking Care of Terrific, Sophisticated Gents, Sonny Spoons (series). Director: Nipsey Russell at Harrah's, Vroom Vroom Vroom (also writer; German tv).
ALBUMS: Composer: Brer Soul, Watermelon Man, Sweet Sweetback's Baadasssss Song, As Serious as a Heart Attack, Don't Play Us Cheap, Ain't Suppose to Die a Natural Death, What the #*!% You Mean I Can't Sing, Ghetto Gothic.

VAN PRAAG, WILLIAM
Executive, Producer, Director, Writer, Editor, Advertising Consultant. b. New York, NY, Sept. 13, 1924. e. CREI, Columbia U. U.S. Army, 1942. Paramount, 1945; Brandt Bros. Prods., 1946; NBC, 1947; v.p. Television Features, 1948; devlpd. vidicon system in m.p. prod.; 1949; Started, pres., Van Praag Prod. Inc. 1951; formed Ernst-Van Praag, Inc. 1971, a communications and marketing counseling firm (NY, Brussels, Tokyo); pres., International Film, TV and A-V Producers Assn. 1969; creator of Van-O-Vision. Winner of commercial, short subject and feature theatrical awards. Author of Color Your Picture, Primer of Creative Editing, and Van Praag's Magic Eye. Past pres., Film Producer's Assn, mem. DGA, SAG, 771 IATSE, National Academy of TV Arts and Sciences, International Radio and TV Executive Society and Soc. of MP and TV Engineers.

VAN SANT, GUS
Director, Writer. b. Louisville, KY, 1952. Raised in Darien, CT, then moved to Oregon at age 17. e. Rhode Island Sch. of Design, where he studied painting. Went to L.A. in 1976, becoming prod. asst. to dir. Ken Shapiro. Made first low-budget film, Alice in Hollywood, which was never released. Later made commercials for NY ad agency before returning to film-making.
PICTURES: Mala Noche, Drugstore Cowboy (Natl. Soc. of Film Critics Awards for best dir. & s.p.; NY Film Critics & L.A. Film Critics Award for s.p.), My Own Private Idaho, Even Cowgirls Get the Blues, To Die For.

VARNEY, JIM
Actor. b. Lexington, KY, June 15, 1949. Studied acting at the Barter Theatre. Performed as stand-up comedian in NY and LA. Appeared in dinner theatre productions of Death of a Salesman, Camelot, Guys and Dolls, etc. During 1970's starred as Sgt. Glory in long running series of TV commercials. Became famous with character of Ernest P. Worrell in TV commercials beginning in 1980.
PICTURES: Ernest Goes to Camp, Ernest Saves Christmas, Fast Food, Ernest Goes to Jail, Ernest Scared Stupid, Wilder Napalm, The Beverly Hillbillies, Ernest Rides Again, Ernest Goes to School, Toy Story (voice).
TELEVISION: Series: The Johnny Cash Show (1976), Operation Petticoat, Pink Lady, Tom T.'s Pop Goes the Country, The Rousters, Hey Vern It's Ernest (Emmy Award, 1989). Guest: Fernwood 2-Night, Alice, America 2-Nite. Pilot: Operation Petticoat.

VAUGHN, ROBERT
Actor. b. New York, NY, Nov. 22, 1932. e. L.A. State coll., B.S. and M.A. Theatre Arts 1956; USC, Ph.D. Communications, 1970. Gained fame as Napoleon Solo in The Man From U.N.C.L.E. tv series. Author: Only Victims, 1972.
PICTURES: The Ten Commandments (debut, 1956), Hell's Crossroads, No Time to Be Young, Teenage Caveman, Unwed Mother, Good Day for a Hanging, The Young Philadelphians (Acad. Award nom.), The Magnificent Seven, The Big Show, The Caretakers, To Trap a Spy, The Spy With My Face, One Spy Too Many, The Glass Bottom Boat (cameo), The Venetian Affair, How to Steal the World, Bullitt, The Bridge at Remagen, If It's Tuesday This Must Be Belgium (cameo), The Mind of Mr. Soames, Julius Caesar, The Statue, Clay Pigeon, The Towering Inferno, The Babysitter, Lucifer Complex, Demon Seed (voice), Starship Invasions, Brass Target, Good Luck Miss Wycoff, Hangar 18, Sweet Dirty Tony, Battle Beyond the

Stars, Virus, S.O.B., Superman III, Black Moon Rising, The Delta Force, Rampage, Nightstick, Hour of the Assassin, Skeleton Coast, River of Death, Captive Rage, Nobody's Perfect, Fair Trade, Edgar Allan Poe's Buried Alive, That's Adequate, Blind Vision, C.H.U.D. II: Bud the Chud, Transylvania Twist, Going Under, Twilight Blue, Joe's Apartment.
TELEVISION: Series: The Lieutenant, The Man From U.N.C.L.E., The Protectors, Emerald Point N.A.S., The A-Team, Danger Theatre, As the World Turns. Mini-Series: Captains and the Kings, Washington: Behind Closed Doors (Emmy Award, 1978), Centennial, Backstairs at the White House, The Blue and the Gray, Evergreen. Movies: The Woman Hunter, Kiss Me Kill Me, The Islander, The Rebels, Mirror Mirror, Doctor Franken, The Gossip Columnist, City in Fear, Fantasies, The Day the Bubble Burst, A Question of Honor, Inside the Third Reich, Intimate Agony, The Return of the Man From U.N.C.L.E., International Airport, Murrow, Prince of Bel Air, Desperado, Perry Mason: The Case of the Defiant Daughter, Dark Avenger, Dancing in the Dark. BBC: One of Our Spies is Missing, The Spy in the Green Hat, The Karate Killers.

VELDE, JAMES R.
Executive. b. Bloomington, IL, Nov. 1, 1913. e. Illinois Wesleyan U. Entered m.p. ind. as night shipper Paramount ex. Detroit, 1934; then city salesman, office mgr. until joining Army, 1943, rejoining same ex. upon dischge., 1946; to Paramount, Washington as Baltimore city salesman, same yr.; br. mgr. Selznick Rel. Org. Pittsburgh, 1948; salesman Eagle-Lion Classics, Pittsburgh, 1949; br. mgr. ELC, Des Moines, 1949; br. mgr., ELC, Detroit, 1950; west coast dist. mgr., United Artists, April, 1951; Western div. mgr. UA, 1952; gen. sales mgr., 1956; v.p.; 1958; dir., UA, 1968; sr. v.p., 1972. Retired, 1977. Worked with Ray Stark as advisor, 1978-83.

VEL JOHNSON, REGINALD
Actor. b. Queens, NY, Aug. 16, 1952. e. Long Island Inst. of Music and Arts, NYU.
THEATER: NY: But Never Jam Today, Inacent Black, World of Ben Caldwell, Staggerlee.
PICTURES: Wolfen (debut, 1981), Ghostbusters, The Cotton Club, Remo Williams, Armed and Dangerous, Crocodile Dundee, Die Hard, Turner & Hooch, Die Hard 2, Posse.
TELEVISION: Series: Perfect Strangers, Family Matters. Movies: Quiet Victory: The Charlie Wedemeyer Story, The Bride in Black, Jury Duty: The Comedy, Grass Roots, One of Her Own.

VENORA, DIANE
Actress. b. Hartford, CT, 1952. e. Juilliard Sch. (BFA degree). Member of Juilliard's Acting Company, Circle Repertory Co. and the Ensemble Studio Theatre.
THEATER: A Midsummer Night's Dream, Hamlet (New York Shakespeare Festival), Uncle Vanya (at La Mama), Messiah (Manhattan Theatre Club), Penguin Toquet, Tomorrow's Monday (Circle Rep), Largo Desolato, School for Scandal, The Seagull, A Man for All Seasons (Paramount Theatre Co.), Peer Gynt (Williamstown Fest.), The Winter's Tale, Hamlet (NYSF).
PICTURES: All That Jazz, Wolfen, Terminal Choice, The Cotton Club, F/X, Ironweed, Bird (NY Film Critics Award, 1988; Golden Globe nom.), Heat, Three Wishes, Surviving Picasso, The Subsitute, Romeo and Juliet.
TELEVISION: Mini-Series: A.D. Movie: Cook and Peary: The Race to the Pole. Specials: Getting There, Rehearsing Hamlet, Hamlet. Guest: Law and Order. Series: Thunder Alley, Chicago Hope.

VERDON, GWEN
Actress, Dancer, Choreographer. b. Culver City, CA, Jan. 13, 1925. Married to late dir.-choreographer Bob Fosse. Studied dancing with her mother, E. Belcher, Carmelita Marrachi, and Jack Cole.
THEATER: Bonanza Bound!, Magdalena (asst. choreographer to Jack Cole), Alive and Kicking, Can-Can (Donaldson & Tony Awards, 1954), Damn Yankees (Tony Award, 1956), New Girl in Town (Tony Award, 1958), Redhead (Tony Award, 1959), Sweet Charity, Children! Children!, Milliken's Breakfast Show, Damn Yankees (revival Westbury), Chicago, Dancin' (asst. choreographer, prod. sprv. road co.), Sing Happy (tribute to Kander and Ebb), Parade of Stars Playing the Palace (Actors' Fund benefit), Night of 100 Stars II (1985).
PICTURES: On the Riviera (debut, 1951), David and Bathsheba, The Mississippi Gambler, Meet Me After the Show, The Merry Widow, The I Don't Care Girl, Farmer Takes a Wife, Damn Yankees, The Cotton Club, Cocoon, Nadine, Cocoon: The Return, Alice, Marvin's Room.
TELEVISION: Movies: Legs, The Jerk Too, Oldest Living Confederate Widow Tells All. Special: Steam Heat. Guest: M*A*S*H, Fame, All My Children, Magnum P.I., The Equalizer, All is Forgiven, Dear John, Dream On, Homicide, many others.

VEREEN, BEN
Singer, Dancer, Actor. b. Miami, FL, Oct. 10, 1946. e. High School of Performing Arts.
THEATER: NY: Hair, Sweet Charity, Jesus Christ Superstar (Theatre World Award, 1973), Pippin (Tony Award, 1973), Grind.
PICTURES: Sweet Charity, Gasss, Funny Lady, All That Jazz, The Zoo Gang, Buy and Cell, Friend to Friend, Once Upon a Forest (voice).
TELEVISION: Movies: Louis Armstrong—Chicago Style, The Jesse Owens Story, Lost in London, Intruders. Mini-Series: Roots, Ellis Island, A.D.. Series: Ben Vereen... Comin' at Ya, Ten Speed and Brown Shoe, Webster, Zoobilee Zoo, You Write the Songs (host), J.J. Starbuck, Silk Stalkings. Specials: Ben Vereen—His Roots, Uptown— A Tribute to the Apollo Theatre.

VERHOEVEN, PAUL
Director. b. Amsterdam, The Netherlands, July 18, 1938. e. U. of Leiden, Ph.D., (mathematics and physics) where he began making films.
PICTURES: Business Is Business, Turkish Delight, Keetje Tippel (Cathy Tippel), Soldier of Orange, Spetters, The Fourth Man, Flesh + Blood, Robocop, Total Recall, Basic Instinct, Showgirls, Starship Troopers.

VERNON, ANNE
Actress. r.n. Edith Antoinette Alexandrine Vignaud. b. Paris, Jan. 7, 1924. e. Ecole des Beaux Arts, Paris. Worked for French designer; screen debut in French films; toured with French theatre group; first starring role, Le Mannequin Assassine 1948. Wrote French cookbooks. Was subject of 1980 French TV film detailing her paintings, Les Peintres Enchanteurs.
PICTURES: Edouar et Caroline, Terror on a Train, Ainsi Finit La Nuit, A Warning to Wantons, Patto Col Diavolo, A Tale of Five Cities, Shakedown, Song of Paris, The Umbrellas of Cherbourg, General Della Rovere, La Rue L'Estrapade, Love Lottery, Therese and Isabelle.

VERNON, JOHN
Actor. b. Montreal, Canada, Feb. 24, 1932. r.n. Adolphus Raymondus Vernon Agopowicz. e. Banff Sch. of Fine Arts, Royal Acad. of Dramatic Art. Worked on London stage and radio. First film work as voice of Big Brother in 1984 (1956). Daughter is actress Kate Vernon.
PICTURES: 1984 (voice; debut, 1956), Nobody Waved Goodbye, Point Blank, Justine, Topaz, Tell Them Willie Boy is Here, One More Train to Rob, Dirty Harry, Fear Is the Key, Charley Varrick, W (I Want Her Dead), The Black Windmill, Brannigan, Sweet Movie, The Outlaw Josey Wales, Angela, A Special Day, The Uncanny, Golden Rendezvous, National Lampoon's Animal House, It Rained All Night the Day I Left, Crunch, Fantastica, Herbie Goes Bananas, Heavy Metal (voice), Airplane II: The Sequel, Chained Heat, Curtains, Savage Streets, Jungle Warriors, Fraternity Vacation, Doin' Time, Double Exposure (Terminal Exposure), Ernest Goes to Camp, Blue Monkey, Nightstick, Border Heat, Deadly Stranger, Dixie Lanes, Killer Klowns From Outer Space, Bail-Out, I'm Gonna Git You Sucka, Office Party, War Bus Commando, Mob Story, The Naked Truth.
TELEVISION: Series: Tugboat Annie (Canadian tv), Wojeck (Canadian tv), Delta House, Hail to the Chief. Movies: Trial Run, Escape, Cool Million, Hunter, The Questor Tapes, Mousey, The Virginia Hill Story, The Imposter, Swiss Family Robinson, The Barbary Coast, Matt Helm, Mary Jane Harper Cried Last Night, The Sacketts, The Blood of Others, Two Men (Can.), The Woman Who Sinned, The Fire Next Time, The Forget-Me-Not Murders. Mini-Series: The Blue and the Gray, Louisiana (Fr.). Pilots: B-Men, War of the Worlds. Guest: Tarzan, Kung Fu, Faerie Tale Theatre (Little Red Riding Hood), The Greatest American Hero, Fall Guy, Alfred Hitchcock Presents, Knight Rider, Tales From the Crypt, etc.

VERONA, STEPHEN
Director, Producer, Writer. b. Illinois, Sept. 11, 1940. e. Sch. of Visual Arts. Directed and wrote some 300 commercials (over 50 award-winners) before turning to feature films in 1972, which he wrote as well. Also dir. award-winning short subjects (featuring Barbra Streisand, The Beatles, Simon and Garfunkle and The Lovin' Spoonful). Also prod., dir. of Angela Lansbury's Positive Moves video. Is an artist whose works have been exhibited at numerous CA and NY galleries. Dir. Acad. Award nom. short subject, The Rehearsal, 1971.
PICTURES: Director: The Lords of Flatbush (prod., co-dir., co-s.p.), Pipe Dreams (also prod., s.p.), Boardwalk (also co-s.p.), Talking Walls (also s.p.).
TELEVISION: Class of 1966 (prod. designer, ani. dir.), Diff'rent Strokes, The Music People, Sesame Street, Take a Giant Step, Double Exposure, Flatbush Avenue (pilot, prod., co-s.p.).

VETTER, RICHARD
Executive. b. San Diego, CA, Feb. 24, 1928. e. Pepperdine Coll., B.A., 1950; San Diego State Coll., M.A., 1953; UCLA,

Ph.D., 1959. U.S. Navy: aerial phot., 1946-48, reserve instr., San Diego County Schools, 1951-54; asst. prof., audio-vis. commun., U.C.L.A., 1960-63. Inventor, co-dev., Dimension 150 Widescreen Process. 1957-63: formed D-150 Inc., 1963; exec. v.p. mem.: SMPTE, Technical & Scientific Awards Committee, AMPAS.

VICTOR, JAMES
Actor. r.n. Lincoln Rafael Peralta Diaz. b. Santiago, Dominican Republic, July 27, 1939. e. Haaren H.S., N.Y. Studied at Actors Studio West. On stage in Bullfight, Ceremony for an Assassinated Blackman, Latina, The Man in the Glass Booth, The M.C. (1985 Drama-Logue Critics, and Cesar best actor awards), I Gave You a Calendar (1983 Drama-Logue Critics Award), I Don't Have To Show You No Stinking Badges (1986 Drama-Logue Critics Award), The Rooster and the Egg. Member of Academy of Mo. Pic. Arts & Sciences, Actors Branch. Recipient of Cleo Award, 1975, for Mug Shot; L.A. Drama-Logue Critics Award, 1980, for Latina; Golden Eagle Award, 1981, for consistent outstanding performances in motion pictures.
PICTURES: Fuzz, Rolling Thunder, Boulevard Nights, Defiance, Losin' It, Borderline; Stand and Deliver.
TELEVISION: Series: Viva Valdez, Condo, I Married Dora, Angelica Mi Vida, The New Zorro, Murder She Wrote. Many appearances on specials. Movies: Robert Kennedy and His Times, Twin Detectives, Remington Steel, The Streets of L.A., I Desire, Second Serve, Grand Slam, Gunfighter's Moon. Mini-Series: Streets of Laredo.

VIGODA, ABE
Actor. b. New York, NYUU, Feb. 24, 1921.
PICTURES: The Godfather, The Don Is Dead, Newman's Law, The Cheap Detective, Vasectomy - A Delicate Matter, Plain Clothes, Look Who's Talking, Prancer, Joe vs. the Volcano, Sugar Hill, Jury Duty.
TELEVISION: Series: Dark Shadow, Barney Miller, Fish, One Life to Live. Movies: The Devil's Daughter, Tomaa, Having Babies, How to Pick Up Girls, Death Car on the Freeway. Guest: Mannix, Kojak, The Rookies, B.J. and the Bear, B.K. Stryker.

VINCENT, JR., FRANCIS T
Executive. b. Waterbury, CT, May 29, 1938. e. Williams Coll. B.A., 1960; Yale Law Sch. LL.B., 1963. Bar, CT 1963; NY, 1964; D.C. 1969. 1969-78, partner in law firm of Caplin & Drysdale, specializing in corporate banking and securities matters; 1978, assoc. dir. of, Division of Corporation Finance of Securities & Exchange Commission; exec. v.p. of the Coca-Cola Company and pres. & CEO of its entertainment business sector. Also chmn. & CEO of Columbia Pictures Industries, Inc.; appt. pres. CEO, 1978; mem. bd. of dir. of The Coca-Cola Bottling Co. of NY. 1987-88; rejoined law firm of Caplin & Drysdale, Washington, D.C., 1988. Trustee of Williams Coll. & The Hotchkiss Sch.

VINCENT, JAN-MICHAEL
Actor. b. Denver, CO, July 15, 1945. e. Ventura City (CA) Coll. as art major. Joined National Guard. Discovered by agent Dick Clayton. Hired by Robert Conrad to appear in his film, Los Bandidos. Signed to 6-mo. contract by Universal, for which made U.S. debut in Journey to Shiloh. Then did pilot TV movie for 20th-Fox based on Hardy Boys series of book. Originally called self Michael Vincent; changed after The Undefeated.
PICTURES: Los Bandidos (debut, 1967), Journey to Shiloh, The Undefeated, Going Home, The Mechanic, The World's Greatest Athlete, Buster and Billie, Bite the Bullet, White Line Fever, Baby Blue Marine, Vigilante Force, Shadow of the Hawk, Damnation Alley, Big Wednesday, Hooper, Defiance, Hard Country, The Return, The Last Plane Out, Born in East L.A., Enemy Territory, Hit List, Deadly Embrace, Demonstone, Hangfire, Raw Nerve, Alienator, Haunting Fear, Gold of the Samurai, The Divine Enforcer, Beyond the Call of Duty, Sins of Desire, Hidden Obsession, Xtro II, Deadly Avenger, Midnight Witness, Ice Cream Man, Abducted II: The Reunion.
TELEVISION: Series: Dangerous Island (Banana Splits Hour), The Survivors, Airwolf. Movies: Tribes, The Catcher, Sandcastles, Deliver Us From Evil, Six Against the Rock, Tarzan in Manhattan. Mini-Series: The Winds of War. Guest: Lassie, Bonanza.

VINCENT, KATHARINE
Actress. r.n. Ella Vincenti. b. St. Louis, MO, May 28, 1918.
THEATER: B'way: Love or Bust, Could She Tell?, Banners of 1939, Czarina Smith.
PICTURES: Peptipa's Waltz, Error in Her Ways, Stars and Stripes on Tour, Sink Deep, The Hungry, Voodoo Village, Welcome to Genoa, Unknown Betrayal, The Hooker, Study by M. Atget.
TELEVISION: The Untouchables, Moses the Lawgiver, Dolce Far Niente (mini-series, Roma).

VINER, MICHAEL
Producer, Writer. b. 1945. m. actress Deborah Raffin. e. Harvard U., Georgetown U. Served as aide to Robert

Kennedy; was legman for political columnist Jack Anderson. Settled in Hollywood, where worked for prod. Aaron Rosenberg, first as prod. asst. on three Frank Sinatra films; then asst. prod. on Joaquin Murietta. In music industry was record producer, manager, executive, eventually heading own division, at MGM. Debut as writer-producer in 1976 with TV special, Special of the Stars. Theatrical film debut as prod.-co-writer of Touched by Love, 1980. Television: Windmills of the Gods (exec. prod.). Exec. Prod.: Rainbow Drive; Prod.: Memories of Midnight. President: Dove Audio.

VITALE, RUTH
Executive. e. Tufts U., B.A.; Boston U., M.S. Prior to motion picture career, worked in advertising and media. Senior v.p., Vestron Pictures then s.v.p. of feature production at United Artists and management at Constantin Film Development before joining New Line. Joined New Line as exec. v.p. of worldwide acquisitions. Currently pres., Fine Line Features, a wholly owned division of New Line Cinema.

VITTI, MONICA
Actress. r.n. Maria Luisa Ceciarelli. b. Rome, Italy, Nov. 3, 1933. Started acting in plays as teen, studying at Rome's Natl. Acad. of Dramatic Arts.
PICTURES: Ridere Ridere Ridere (debut, 1955), Smart Girls, L'Avventura, La Notte, L'Eclipse, Dragees du Poivre (Sweet and Sour), Three Fables of Love, The Nutty Naughty Chateau, Alta Infidelitata (High Infidelity), The Red Desert, Le Bambole (The Dolls), Il Disco Volante, Le Fate (The Queens), Modesty Blaise, The Chastity Belt (On My Way to the Crusades I Met a Girl Who...), Girl with a Pistol, La Femme Ecarlate, The Pizza Triangle, The Pacifist, Teresa la Ladra, Tosca, The Phantom of Liberty, Midnight Pleasures, My Loves, Duck in Orange Sauce, An Almost Perfect Affair, The Mystery of Oberwald, Tigers in Lipstick, The Flirt (also s.p.), When Veronica Calls, Secret Scandal (also dir., co- s.p.).

VOGEL, DAVID E.
Executive. President of Walt Disney Pictures.

VOIGHT, JON
Actor. b. Yonkers, NY. Dec. 29, 1938. e. Archbishop Stepinac H.S., White Plains, NY; Catholic U. of Amer., D.C. (B.F.A.) 1960; studied acting at the Neighborhood Playhouse and in private classes with Stanford Meisner, four yrs.
THEATER: B'way: The Sound of Music (debut, 1959), That Summer That Fall (Theatre World Award), The Seagull. Off-B'way: A View From the Bridge (1964 revival). Regional: Romeo & Juliet, A Streetcar Named Desire, Hamlet.
PICTURES: Hour of the Gun (debut, 1967), Fearless Frank, Midnight Cowboy, Out of It, Catch-22, The Revolutionary, Deliverance, All-American Boy, Conrack, The Odessa File, End of the Game, Coming Home (Academy Award, 1978), The Champ, Lookin' To Get Out (also co-s.p., prod.), Table for Five (also prod.), Runaway Train, Desert Bloom, Eternity, Heat, Rosewood.
TELEVISION: Movies: Chernobyl: The Final Warning, The Last of His Tribe, The Tin Soldier (also dir.), Convict Cowboy. Mini-Series: Return to Lonesome Dove. Special: The Dwarf (Public Broadcast Lab). Guest: Gunsmoke, Naked City, The Defenders, Coronet Blue, NYPD.

VON DER ESCH, LEIGH
Executive. President of the Utah Film Office, Association of Film Commissioners International.

VON SYDOW, MAX
Actor. b. Lund, Sweden, April 10, 1929. m. Keratin Olin, actress, 1951. Theatrical debut in a Cathedral Sch. of Lund prod. of The Nobel Prize. Served in the Swedish Quartermaster Corps two yrs. Studied at Royal Dramatic Theatre Sch. in Stockholm. Tour in municipal theatres. Has appeared on stage in Stockholm, London (The Tempest, 1988), Paris and Helsinki in Faust, The Legend and The Misanthrope. 1954 won Sweden's Royal Foundation Cultural Award. Appeared on B'way in Duet for One.
PICTURES: Bara en Mor (Only a Mother; debut, 1949), Miss Julie, Ingen Mans Kvinna, Ratten att Alska, The Seventh Seal, Prasten i Uddarbo, Wild Strawberries, Brink of Life, Spion 503, The Face, The Magician, The Virgin Spring, Brollopsdagen, Through a Glass Darkly, Nils Holgerssons Underbara Resa, Alskarinnen, Winter Light, 4x4, The Greatest Story Ever Told (English-language debut, 1965), The Reward, Hawaii, The Quiller Memorandum, Hour of the Wolf, Here Is Your Life, Svarta Palmkronor, Shame, Made in Sweden, The Kremlin Letter, The Passion of Anna, The Night Visitor, The Touch, The Emigrants, Appelbriget, I Hausbandet, Embassy, The New Land, The Exorcist, Steppenwolf, Egg! Egg!, Illustrious Corpses, Three Days of the Condor, The Ultimate Warrior, Foxtrot (The Other Side of Paradise), Cuore di Cane, Voyage of the Damned, Les Desert des Tartares, Exorcist II: The Heretic, March or Die, Black Journal, Brass Target, Gran Bolitto, Hurricane, Deathwatch, Venetian Lies, Flash Gordon,

Victory, She Dances Alone (voice), Conan the Barbarian, Flight of the Eagle, Strange Brew, Never Say Never Again, Target Eagle, Dreamscape, Dune, Code Name: Emerald, Hannah and Her Sisters, Duet for One, The Second Victory, The Wolf at the Door, Pelle the Conqueror (Acad. Award nom.), Katinka (dir.), Cellini: A Violent Life, Awakenings, A Kiss Before Dying, Until the End of the World, Zentropa (narrator), The Bachelor, The Best Intentions, The Ox, Father, Grandfather's Journey, Needful Things, The Silent Touch, Time Is Money, The Atlantic (narrator), Judge Dredd.
TELEVISION: *Movies/Mini-Series*: Samson and Delilah, Christopher Columbus, Kojak: The Belarus File, Brotherhood of the Rose, Hiroshima: Out of the Ashes, Red King White Knight, Radetzky March, Citizen X.

VON TROTTA, MARGARETHE
Director, Writer. b. Berlin, Germany, Feb. 21, 1942. e. Studied German and Latin literature in Munich and Paris. Studied acting in Munich and began career as actress. 1970 began collaborating on Schlondorff's films as well as acting in them.
PICTURES: *Actress*: Schrage Vogel, Brandstifter, Gotter der Pest, Baal, Der Amerikanische Soldat, The Sudden Wealth of the Poor People of Kombach (also co-s.p.), Die Moral der Ruth Halbfass, Strohfeuer (Free Woman; also co-s.p.), Desaster, Ubernachtung in Tirol, Coup de Grace (also co-s.p.). *Dir./ Co-s.p.*: The Lost Honor of Katharina Blum (co-dir., co-s.p., with Schlondorff), The Second Awakening of Christa Klages, Sisters or the Balance of Happiness, Marianne and Julianne, Heller Wahn (Sheer Madness), Rosa Luxemburg, Paura e Amore (Three Sisters), The African Woman, The Long Silence, The Promise (Years of the Wall).

VON ZERNECK, FRANK
Producer. b. New York, NY, Nov. 3, 1940. e. Hofstra Coll., 1962. Has produced plays in New York, Los Angeles and on national tour. Partner, von Zerneck/Sertner Films. Devised Portrait film genre for TV movies: Portrait of a Stripper, Portrait of a Mistress, Portrait of a Centerfold, etc. Past chmn. of California Theatre Council; former officer of League of Resident theatres; member of League of New York Theatres & Producers; Producers Guild of America; chmn's council, the Caucus for Producers, Writers and Directors; Board of Directors, Allied Communications, Inc. Museum of Radio & Television in NYC, Hollywood Television & Radio Society, Acad. of TV Arts & Sciences, Natl. Acad. of Cable Programming. Received American Film Institute Charles Fries Producer of the Year Award.
PICTURE: God's Lonely Man.
TELEVISION: 21 Hours at Munich, Dress Gray, Miracle on Ice, Combat High, Queenie, In the Custody of Strangers, The First Time, Baby Sister, Policewoman Centerfold, Obsessive Love, Invitation to Hell, Romance on the Orient Express, Hostage Flight. *Exec. prod.*: The Proud Men, Man Against the Mob, To Heal a Nation, Lady Mobster, Maybe Baby, Full Exposure: the Sex Tapes Scandal, Gore Vidal's Billy the Kid, Too Young to Die, The Great Los Angeles Earthquake, The Court-Martial of Jackie Robinson, White Hot: The Mysterious Murder of Thelma Todd, Survive the Savage Sea, Opposites Attract, Menu for Murder, Battling for Baby, Woman With a Past, Jackie Collins' Lady Boss, Danger Island, The Broken Chain, Beyond Suspicion, French Silk, The Corpse Had a Familiar Face, Robin Cook's Mortal Fear, Take Me Home Again, The Other Woman, Seduced and Betrayed, Robin Cook's Virus, The West Side Waltz, Crazy Horse, Robin Cook's Terminal, She Said No, Terror In the Family, My Son Is Innocent, Tornado!, Broder Music.

W

WADLEIGH, MICHAEL
Director. b. Akron, OH, Sept. 24, 1941. e. Ohio State U., B.S., B.A., M.A., Columbia Medical Sch.
PICTURES: Woodstock (dir.), Wolfen (dir., co-s.p.), Out of Order, The Village at the End of the Universe (dir., s.p.).

WAGGONER, LYLE
Actor. b. Kansas City, KS, April 13, 1935. e. Washington U., St. Louis. Was salesman before becoming actor with road co. prod. of Li'l Abner. Formed own sales-promo co. to finance trip to CA for acting career in 1965. Did commercials, then signed by 20th-Fox for new-talent school.
PICTURES: Love Me Deadly, Journey to the Center of Time, Catalina Caper, Surf II, Murder Weapon, Dead Women in Lingerie, Gypsy Angels.
TELEVISION: *Series*: The Carol Burnett Show, The Jimmie Rodgers Show, It's Your Bet (host), Wonder Woman. *Movies*: Letters from Three Lovers, The New Original Wonder Woman, The Love Boat II, The Gossip Columnist, Gridlock.

WAGNER, JANE
Writer, Director, Producer. b. Morristown, TN, Feb. 2, 1935. e. attended Sch. of Visual Arts, NY. Worked as designer for Kimberly Clark, created Teach Me Read Me sheets for Fieldcrest.

THEATER: *B'way*: Appearing Nitely (dir., co-writer), The Search for Signs of Intelligent Life in the Universe (dir., writer; NY Drama Desk Award & Special NY Drama Critics Award), both starring Lily Tomlin.
PICTURES: Moment by Moment (s.p., dir.), The Incredible Shrinking Woman (s.p., exec. prod.), The Search for Signs of Intelligent Life in the Universe (s.p., exec. prod.).
TELEVISION: *Specials*: J.T. (writer; Peabody Award), Lily (prod., co-writer; Emmy & WGA Awards, 1974), Lily Tomlin (prod., writer; Emmy Award for writing, 1976), People (prod., writer), Lily—Sold Out (exec. prod., co-writer; Emmy Award for producing, 1981), Lily for President? (exec. prod., co-writer), The Edith Ann Show (writer, exec. prod.).

WAGNER, LINDSAY
Actress. b. Los Angeles, CA, June 22, 1949. Appeared in school plays in Portland, OR; studied singing and worked professionally with rock group. In 1968 went to L.A. Signed to Universal contract in 1971.
PICTURES: Two People, The Paper Chase, Second Wind, Nighthawks, High Risk, Martin's Day, Ricochet.
TELEVISION: *Series*: The Bionic Woman (Emmy Award, 1977), Jessie, Peaceable Kingdom. *Guest*: The F.B.I., Owen Marshall: Counselor at Law, Night Gallery, The Bold Ones, Marcus Welby M.D., The Six Million Dollar Man. *Movies*: The Rockford Files (pilot), The Incredible Journey of Dr. Meg Laurel, The Two Worlds of Jennie Logan, Callie and Son, Memories Never Die, I Want to Live, Princess Daisy, Two Kinds of Love, Passions, This Child Is Mine, Child's Cry, Convicted, Young Again, Stranger in My Bed, The Return of the Six Million Dollar Man and the Bionic Woman, Student Exchange, Evil in Clear River, The Taking of Flight 847, Nightmare at Bitter Creek, From the Dead of Night, The Bionic Showdown: The Six-Million Dollar Man and the Bionic Woman, Shattered Dreams, Babies, Fire in the Dark, She Woke Up, Treacherous Crossing, To Be the Best, A Message From Holly, Nurses on the Line: The Crash of Flight 7, Danielle Steel's Once in a Lifetime, Bionic Ever After?, Fighting for My Daughter.

WAGNER, RAYMOND JAMES
Producer. b. College Point, NY, Nov. 3, 1925. e. Middlebury Coll., Williams Coll. Joined Young & Rubicam, Inc., as radio-TV commercial head in Hollywood, 1950-59. Head of pilot development, Universal Studios, 1960-65. V.p. of production (features) for MGM, 1972-79. Presently independent producer.
PICTURES: *Prod.*: Petulia, Loving (exec. prod.), Code of Silence, Rent-a-Cop, Hero and the Terror, Turner and Hooch, Run, Fifty Fifty.

WAGNER, ROBERT
Actor. b. Detroit, MI, Feb. 10, 1930. e. Saint Monica's H.S. m. actress Jill St. John. Signed to contract with 20th Century-Fox, 1950.
PICTURES: The Happy Years (debut, 1950), The Halls of Montezuma, The Frogmen, Let It Legal, With a Song in My Heart, What Price Glory?, Stars and Stripes Forever, The Silver Whip, Titanic, Beneath the 12-Mile Reef, Prince Valiant, Broken Lance, White Feather, A Kiss Before Dying, The Mountain, Between Heaven and Hell, The True Story of Jesse James, Stopover Tokyo, The Hunters, In Love and War, Say One for Me, All the Fine Young Cannibals, Sail a Crooked Ship, The Longest Day, The War Lover, The Condemned of Altona, The Pink Panther, Harper, Banning, The Biggest Bundle of Them All, Don't Just Stand There, Winning, The Towering Inferno, Midway, The Concorde—Airport '79, Trail of the Pink Panther, Curse of the Pink Panther, I Am the Cheese, Delirious, The Player, Dragon: The Bruce Lee Story.
TELEVISION: *Series*: It Takes A Thief, Colditz (UK), Switch, Hart to Hart, Lime Street. *Movies*: How I Spent My Summer Vacation, City Beneath the Sea, The Cable Car Murder, Killer by Night, Madame Sin (also exec. prod.), Streets of San Francisco (pilot), The Affair, The Abduction of St. Anne, Switch (pilot), Death at Love House, Cat on a Hot Tin Roof, The Critical List, Hart to Hart (pilot), To Catch a King, There Must Be a Pony, Love Among Thieves, Windmills of the Gods, Indiscreet, This Gun for Hire, False Arrest, Daniel Steel's Jewels, Deep Trouble, Hart to Hart Returns (also co-exec. prod.), Hart to Hart: Home is Where the Hart Is, Hart to Hart: Crimes of the Hart, Hart to Hart: Old Friends Never Die, Parallel Lives, Hart to Hart: Secrets of the Heart. *Mini-Series*: Pearl, Around the World in 80 Days, Heaven & Hell: North and South Book III.

WAHL, KEN
Actor. b. Chicago, IL, Feb. 14, 1953. No acting experience when cast in The Wanderers in 1978.
PICTURES: The Wanderers (debut, 1979), Fort Apache The Bronx, Race to the Yankee Zephyr, Jinxed, The Soldier, Purple Hearts, The Omega Syndrome, The Taking of Beverly Hills (also co-exec. prod.), The Favor, Back in the U.S.A.
TELEVISION: *Movies*: The Dirty Dozen: The Next Mission, The Gladiator, Search for Grace, Wise Guy. *Series*: Double Dare, Wiseguy.

WAITE, RALPH
Actor. b. White Plains, NY, June 22, 1929. e. Bucknell U., Yale U. Social worker, publicity director, assistant editor and minister before turning to acting. Founder of the Los Angeles Actors Theatre.
THEATER: *B'way*: Hogan's Goat, The Watering Place, Trial of Lee Harvey Oswald. *Off-B'way*: The Destiny of Me, The Young Man From Atlanta. *Regional*: Hometown Heroes.
PICTURES: Cool Hand Luke, A Lovely Way to Die, Last Summer, Five Easy Pieces, Lawman, The Grissom Gang, The Sporting Club, The Pursuit of Happiness, Chato's Land, The Magnificent Seven Ride, Trouble Man, Kid Blue, The Stone Killer, On the Nickel (also dir., prod., s.p.), Crash and Burn, The Bodyguard, Cliffhanger, Sioux City, Homeward Bound II: Lost in San Francisco.
TELEVISION: *Series*: The Waltons, The Mississippi. *Movies*: The Secret Life of John Chapman, The Borgia Stick, Red Alert, Ohms, Angel City, The Gentleman Bandit, A Wedding on Waltons Mountain, Mother's Day on Waltons Mountain, A Day for Thanks on Waltons Mountain, A Good Sport, Crime of Innocence, Red Earth White Earth, A Walton Thanksgiving Reunion, Sin and Redemption, A Season of Hope, A Walton Wedding. *Mini-Series*: Roots.

WAITE, RIC
Cinematographer. b. Sheboygan, WI, July 10, 1933. e. Univ. of CO. Photographed more than 40 movies-of-the-week for TV, 1979-83.
PICTURES: The Other Side of the Mountain (debut, 1975), Defiance, On the Nickel, The Long Riders, The Border, Tex, 48 Hrs., Class, Uncommon Valor, Footloose, Red Dawn, Volunteers, Summer Rental, Brewster's Millions, Cobra, Adventures in Babysitting, The Great Outdoors, Marked for Death, Out for Justice, Rapid Fire, On Deadly Ground.
TELEVISION: Captains and the Kings (Emmy Award, 1977), Tail Gunner Joe (Emmy nom.), Huey P. Long (Emmy nom.), Revenge of the Stepford Wives, Baby Comes Home.

WAITS, TOM
Singer, Composer, Actor. b. Pomona, CA, Dec. 7, 1949. Recorded numerous albums and received Acad. Award nom. for his song score of One from the Heart. Composed songs for On the Nickel, Streetwise, Paradise Alley, Wolfen, American Heart, Dead Man Walking, Night on Earth (score). Featured songs in Smoke and Things to Do in Denver When You're Dead. Has starred in Chicago's Steppenwolf Theatre Co.'s Frank's Wild Years (also co-wrote, wrote the music) and Los Angeles Theatre Co.'s Demon Wine. Wrote songs and music for opera The Black Rider (1990). Co-wrote songs and music for opera Alice by Robert Wilson. Received Grammy Award for album, Blue Machine, 1992.
PICTURES: *As actor*: Paradise Alley, Poetry in Motion, The Outsiders, Rumble Fish, The Cotton Club, Down by Law (also music), Ironweed, Candy Mountain, Big Time (also co-s.p.), Cold Feet, Bearskin, On a Moonlit Night (music only), The Two Jakes, Queens Logic, The Fisher King, At Play in the Fields of the Lord, Bram Stoker's Dracula, Short Cuts.

WAJDA, ANDRZEJ
Director, Writer. b. Suwalki, Poland, March 6, 1926. e. Fine Arts Academy, Krakow, Poland, 1945-48; High School of Cinematography, Lodz, Poland, 1950-52. 1940-43, worked as asst. in restoration of Polish war paintings. 1942, joined Polish gov. in exile's A.K. (Home Army Resistance) against German occupation. 1950-52, directed shorts (While You Sleep; The Bad Boy, The Pottery of Ilzecka) as part of film school degree; 1954, asst. dir. to Aleksander Ford on 5 Boys from Barska Street. 1981, concentrated on theatrical projects in Poland and film prods. with non-Polish studios. 1983, gov. dissolved his Studio X film prod. group. 1984, gov. demanded Wajda's resignation as head of filmmakers' assoc. in order to continue org.'s existence. 1989, appt. artistic dir. of Teatr Powszechny, official Warsaw theater. Also leader of the Cultural Comm. of the Citizen's Committee. 1989, elected senator. Short films: While You Sleep, The Bad Boy, The Pottery of Ilza, I Go to the Sun.
PICTURES: *Dir.-Writer*: A Generation (debut, 1957), Kanal, Ashes and Diamonds, Lotna, Innocent Sorcerers, Samson, Siberian Lady Macbeth (Fury Is a Woman), Love at 20 (Warsaw Poland episode), Ashes, Gates to Paradise, Everything for Sale, Hunting Flies, Landscape After the Battle, The Wedding, Promised Land, Shadow Line, Man of Marble, Without Anesthetic, The Girls From Wilko, The Orchestra Conductor, Man of Iron (Golden Palm Award, Cannes, 1981), Danton, A Love in Germany, Chronicle of Love Affairs, The Possessed, Korczak.
TELEVISION: Roly-Poly, The Birch Wood, Pilate and the Others, The Dead Class, November Night, Crime and Punishment.

WALD, MALVIN
Writer, Producer. b. New York, NY, Aug. 8, 1917. e. Brooklyn Coll., B.A., J.D. Woodland U. Coll. of Law; grad. work Columbia U., NYU, USC. Newspaper reporter and editor, publicist, social worker, radio actor. Screenplays and original stories for Columbia, 20th-Fox, UA, MGM, WB; U.S. Air Force; tech. sgt., wrote 30 doc. films for film unit; exec. prod., 20th Century Fox tv doc. unit, 1963-64; writer-prod. U.S.I.A., 1964-65; writer-prod., Ivan Tors Films, 1965-69; prof., USC Sch. of Cinema, Television, 1956-96; bd. of dir., Writer's Guild of America; 1983-85, Trustee, Writers Guild Foundation, edit. bd. WGA Journal, 1996; editorial bd., Creative Screenwriting, 1996; Acad. of Motion Picture Arts and Sciences, co-author of book, Three Major Screenplays. Contributor to books, American Screenwriters, Close-Ups, Henry Miller: A Book of Tributes, Tales From the Casting Couch. Published s.p., Naked City. Consultant, Natl. Endowment for Humanities and Corp. for Public Broadcasting. Visiting professor, Southern Illinois Univ., Univ of PA. Pre-selection judge, Focus writing awards. Media & prod. consultant, Apache Mountain Spirit (PBS); playwright, ANTA-West, Actors Alley, Rep. Theatre. Co-author, L.A. Press Club 40th Anniversary Show, 1987. Mag. articles published in Film Comment, Journal of Popular Film & TV, Journal of Writers Guild of America, American Heritage, Creative Screenwriting, Directors Guild Magazine, Hollywood: Then and Now, Writers Digest, 1991-. Shorts: An Answer, Employees Only (Acad. Award nom.), Boy Who Owned a Melephant (Venice Children's Film Fest. gold medal), Unarmed in Africa, The Policeman, James Weldon Johnson, Me an Alcoholic?, Problem Solving, Managerial Control, UFO—Fact or Fiction? Was admitted to Producers Guild Hall of Fame, 1996.
PICTURES: The Naked City (Acad. Award nom., best story), Behind Locked Doors, The Dark Past, Ten Gentlemen from West Point, The Powers Girl, Two in a Taxi, Undercover Man, Outrage, On the Loose, Battle Taxi, Man on Fire, Al Capone, Venus in Furs, In Search of Historic Jesus, Legend of Sleepy Hollow, Mysteries From Beyond Earth.
TELEVISION: Many credits including Playhouse 90, Marilyn Monroe, Hollywood: The Golden Years, The Rafer Johnson Story, D-Day, Project: Man in Space, Tales of Hans Christian Andersen, John F. Kennedy, Biography of A Rookie, Alcoa-Goodyear Hour, Climax, Shirley Temple Storybook, Life of Riley, Peter Gunn, Perry Mason, Dobie Gillis, Combat, Moonport (U.S.I.A.; prod., writer), Daktari, (assoc. prod.) Primus, California Tomorrow (prod.), Mod Squad, Untamed World, Around the World of Mike Todd, The Billie Jean King Show, Life and Times of Grizzly Adams, Mark Twain's America, Greatest Heroes of the Bible, Littlest Hobo., Rich Little's You Asked For It, Hugh Hefner's Bunny Memories.

WALKEN, CHRISTOPHER
Actor. b. Astoria, NY, Mar. 31, 1943. Began career in off-B'way play J.B. billed as Ronnie Walken. Appeared in Madonna video Bad Girl.
THEATER: *NY*: Best Foot Forward (Clarence Derwent Award), Kid Champion (Obie Award), High Spirits (B'way debut, 1964), The Lion in Winter (Clarence Derwent Award). The Rose Tattoo (Theatre World Award), Hurlyburly (B'way), Him (also author). NY Shakespeare Festival: Coriolanus, Othello.
PICTURES: The Anderson Tapes (debut, 1971), The Happiness Cage, Next Stop Greenwich Village, The Sentinel, Annie Hall, Roseland, The Deer Hunter (Academy Award, best supporting actor, 1978), Last Embrace, Heaven's Gate, The Dogs of War, Shoot the Sun Down, Pennies from Heaven, Brainstorm, The Dead Zone, A View to a Kill, At Close Range, Deadline, The Milagro Beanfield War, Biloxi Blues, Puss in Boots, Homeboy, Communion, King of New York, The Comfort of Strangers, McBain, All-American Murder, Batman Returns, Mistress, Le Grand Pardon, Day of Atonement, True Romance, Wayne's World 2, A Business Affair, Pulp Fiction, Search and Destroy, The Prophecy, The Addiction, Wild Side, Things to Do in Denver When You're Dead, Nick of Time, The Funeral, Last Man Standing.
TELEVISION: *Movies*: Sarah: Plain and Tall, Skylark, Scam. *Special*: Who Am I This Time? *Guest*: Saturday Night Live.

WALKER, E. CARDON
Executive. b. Rexburg, ID, Jan. 9, 1916. e. UCLA, B.A. 1938. Four years officer, U.S. Navy. Started with Walt Disney Productions 1938; camera, story, unit director short subjects, budget control. Headed adv. & pub 1950. 1956, v.p. in chg. of adv. & sales. 1960 member bd. of dir. & exec. comm. 1965 v.p., mkt. 1967 exec. v.p. operations. 1968, exec. v.p. and chief operating officer; pres., 1971; 1976 pres. and chief executive officer; 1980, named bd. chmn. & chief executive officer; 1983-84, chmn. of exec. committee. Remains a board member.

WALKER, KATHRYN
Actress. b. Philadelphia, PA, Jan. 9. m. singer-songwriter James Taylor. e. Wells Coll., Harvard. Studied acting at London Acad. of Music and Dramatic Art on Fulbright Fellowship. Stage roles include part in Private Lives with Elizabeth Taylor and Richard Burton, and Wild Honey with Ian McKellen.
PICTURES: Slap Shot, Rich Kids, Neighbors, D.A.R.Y.L., Dangerous Game, Emma and Elvis.

TELEVISION: *Series*: Beacon Hill. *Movies*: The Winds of Kitty Hawk, Too Far to Go, FDR: The Last Year, A Whale for the Killing, Family Reunion, Special Bulletin, The Murder of Mary Phagan. *Mini-Series*: The Adams Chronicles (Emmy Award, 1976).

WALLACE, MIKE
TV Commentator, Interviewer. b. Brookline, MA, May 9, 1918. e. U. of Michigan, 1939. Night Beat, WABD, N.Y., 1956; The Mike Wallace Interview, ABC, 1956-58; newspaper col., Mike Wallace Asks, N.Y. Post, 1957-58; News Beat, WNTA-TV, 1959-61; The Mike Wallace Interview, WNTA-TV, 1959-61; Biography, 1962; correspondent, CBS News, 1963, CBS Radio; Personal Closeup, Mike Wallace at Large; Co-editor, 60 Minutes (Emmy Awards, 1971, 1972, 1973), CBS News, Host, 20th Century, 1994.

WALLACH, ELI
Actor. b. Brooklyn, NY, Dec. 7, 1915. m. actress Anne Jackson. e. U. of TX. Capt. in Medical Admin. Corps during WWII. After college acting, appeared in summer stock. Charter member of the Actors Studio.
THEATER: Skydrift (B'way debut, 1945), Antony & Cleopatra, The Rose Tattoo (Tony Award, 1951), Mademoiselle Colombe, Camino Real, The Teahouse of August Moon (also London), Major Barbara, Rhinoceros, Luv, Twice Around the Park, Cafe Crown, The Price, In Persons (Off-B'way), The Flowering Peach.
PICTURES: Baby Doll (debut, 1956; BFA Award), The Line Up, The Magnificent Seven, Seven Thieves, The Misfits, Hemingway's Adventures of A Young Man, How the West Was Won, The Victors, Act One, The Moonspinners, Kisses for My President, Lord Jim, Genghis Khan, How to Steal a Million, The Good the Bad and the Ugly, The Tiger Makes Out, How to Save a Marriage and Ruin Your Life, MacKenna's Gold, A Lovely Way to Die, Ace High, The Brain, Zigzag, The People Next Door, The Angle Levine, The Adventures of Gerard, Romance of a Horse Thief, Cinderella Liberty, Crazy Joe, Stateline Motel, Don't Turn the Other Cheek, The Sentinel, Nasty Habits, The Deep, The Domino Principle, Girlfriends, Movie Movie, Circle of Iron, Firepower, Winter Kills, The Hunter, The Salamander, Sam's Son, Tough Guys, Nuts, Funny, The Two Jakes, The Godfather Part III, Article 99, Mistress, Night and the City, Two Much, The Associate.
TELEVISION: *Series*: Our Family Honor. *Guest*: Studio One, Philco Playhouse, Playhouse 90, The Poppy Is Also a Flower (Emmy Award, 1967), Law & Order. *Movies*: Cold Night's Death, Indict and Convict, Seventh Avenue, The Pirate, Fugitive Family, Pride of Jesse Halam, Skokie, The Wall, Anatomy of an Illness, Murder: By Reason of Insanity, Something in Common, Executioner's Song, Christopher Columbus, Embassy, The Impossible Spy, Vendetta: Secrets of a Mafia Bride, Legacy of Lies, Teamster Boss: The Jackie Presser Story, Vendetta 2: The New Mafia.

WALLACH, GEORGE
Producer, Writer, Director. b. New York, NY, Sept. 25, 1918. e. SUNY-Westbury. Actor in theater & radio 1936-45; U.S. Navy 1942-45; supvr. radio-TV Div. of American Theatrical Wing 1946-48; dir., WNEW, 1946-48; prod./dir., Wendy Barrie Show, 1948-49; prod.-dir. for WNBC-WNBT, 1950; dir., news, spec. events WNBT-WNBC, 1951-52; prod. mgr., NBC Film Div. 1953-56, appt. TV officer, U.S.I.A., 1957. Film-TV officer American Embassy, Bonn, Germany, 1961. Film-TV officer American Embassy; Tehran, Iran, 1965-66; MoPix Prod. Officer, JUSPAO, American Embassy, Saigon, 1966; prod.-dir.-wr., Greece Today, 1967-68. Exec. prod.-dir., George Wallach Productions, spec. doc., travel, and industrial films, chairman, Film-TV Dept., N.Y. Institute of Photography, 1968-75; Prof. film-TV-radio, Brooklyn Coll., 1975-80; dir., special projects, Directors Guild of America 1978-88; presently international representative for Denver Film Festival, U.S. Contact for Moscow Film Festival, U.S. prod. for A Native of Beijing in NY, a series of 20 1 hr. programs for Beijing TV.
PICTURES: It Happened in Havana, Bwana Devil (assoc. prod., prod. mgr.).
TELEVISION: *NBC producer*: Inner Sanctum, The Falcon, His Honor Homer Bell, Watch the World. *Dir.*: Wanted.

WALSH, DYLAN
Actor. Raised in Africa, Indonesia, India, Washington D.C. e. Univ. of VA. On D.C. stage with Arena Stage and Studio Theatre, Heritage Rep. Co. Appearing in A Midsummer Night's Dream, Curse of the Starving Class, Romeo & Juliet, Death of a Salesman.
PICTURES: Where the Heart Is, Betsy's Wedding, Arctic Blue, Nobody's Fool, Congo, Eden.
TELEVISION: *Series*: Gabriel's Fire. *Guest*: Kate and Allie. *Movies*: Telling Secrets, Radio Inside.

WALSH, J.T.
Actor. b. San Francisco, CA. Did not begin acting until age 30, when he quit job in sales to join off-B'way theater co.

THEATER: Glengarry Glen Ross (Drama Desk Award), Rose, Last Licks, Richard III, Macbeth, Half a Lifetime, The American Clock.
PICTURES: Eddie Macon's Run, Hard Choices, Power, Hannah and Her Sisters, Tin Men, House of Games, Good Morning Vietnam, Things Change, Tequila Sunrise, Wired, The Big Picture, Dad, Crazy People, Why Me?, Narrow Margin, Misery, The Grifters, The Russia House, Backdraft, Defenseless, True Identity, Iron Maze, A Few Good Men, Hoffa, Sniper, National Lampoon's Loaded Weapon 1, Red Rock West, Needful Things, Morning Glory, Blue Chips, The Client, Miracle on 34th Street, Outbreak, The Low Life, Nixon, Executive Decision, The Babysitter, Black Day Blue Night.
TELEVISION: *Movies*: Little Gloria: Happy at Last, Jacobo Timerman: Prisoner Without a Name Cell Without a Number, Right to Kill, Tough Cookies, Windmills of the Gods, In the Shadow of a Killer, The American Clock, The Last Seduction, Against Their Will: Women in Prison, Crime of the Century. *Special*: Partners.

WALSH, M. EMMET
Actor. r.n. Michael Emmet Walsh. b. Ogdensburg, NY, Mar. 22, 1935. e. Clarkson Col. (B.B.A., 1958), Academy of Dramatic Arts (1959-61).
THEATER: *B'way*: Does the Tiger Wear a Necktie?, That Championship Season. *Off-B'way*: The Old Glory, The Outside Man, Death of the Well Loved Boy, Shepherds of the Shelf, Three From Column 'A', Are You Now or Have You Ever Been; also summer stock and regional theatre (Hometown Heroes).
PICTURES: Midnight Cowboy, Stiletto, Alice's Restaurant, End of the Road, Loving, The Traveling Executioner, Little Big Man, Cold Turkey, They Might Be Giants, Escape from the Planet of the Apes, Get to Know Your Rabbit, What's Up Doc?, Kid Blue, Serpico, The Gambler, The Prisoner of 2nd Avenue, At Long Last Love, Mikey and Nicky, Nickelodeon, Bound for Glory, Airport '77, Slap Shot, Straight Time, The Fish That Saved Pittsburgh, The Jerk, Brubaker, Raise the Titanic, Ordinary People, Back Roads, Reds, Cannery Row, The Escape Artist, Blade Runner, Fast-Walking, Silkwood, Scandalous, (Raw) Courage, The Pope of Greenwich Village, Grandview USA, Missing in Action, Blood Simple, Fletch, The Best of Times, Wildcats, Critters, Back to School, Raising Arizona, Harry and the Hendersons, No Man's Land, The Milagro Beanfield War, Sunset, Clean and Sober, Sundown: The Vampire in Retreat, The Mighty Quinn, Red Scorpion, Thunderground, War Party, Catch Me If You Can, Chattahoochee, Narrow Margin, White Sands, Killer Image, Equinox, The Naked Truth, The Music of Chance, Bitter Harvest, Wilder Napalm, Cops and Robbersons, Dead Badge, Probable Cause, The Child, Camp Nowhere, The Glass Shield, Panther, Free Willy 2: The Adventure Home, Criminal Hearts, Portraits of Innocence, Albino Alligator, The Killing Jar, A Time to Kill, Romeo & Juliet.
TELEVISION: *Series*: The Sandy Duncan Show, Dear Detective, Unsub. *Movies*: Sarah T.—Portrait of a Teenage Alcoholic, Crime Club, Invasion of Johnson County, Red Alert, Superdome, A Question of Guilt, No Other Love, The Gift, Skag, City in Fear, High Noon Part II, Hellinger's Law, Night Partners, The Deliberate Stranger, Resting Place, Broken Vows, Hero in the Family, The Abduction of Kari Swenson, Murder Ordained, Brotherhood of the Rose, Love and Lies, Fourth Story, Wild Card, Four Eyes and Six-Guns, From the Mixed-Up Files of Mrs. Basil E. Frankweiler. *Mini-Series*: The French-Atlantic Affair, East of Eden. *Guest*: Julia, Amy Prentiss, The Jimmy Stewart Show, Bonanza, All in the Family, Rockford Files, Baretta, The Waltons, Nichols, Starsky & Hutch, Amazing Stories, Twilight Zone, The Flash, Jackie Thomas Show, Tales From the Crypt, Home Improvement, The Outer Limits, Home Improvement, many others. *Pilot*: Silver Fox.

WALSTON, RAY
Actor. b. New Orleans, LA, Nov. 2, 1918. Stage debut in Houston, 1936. To NY where he appeared on stage in South Pacific, The Front Page, Me and Juliet, Damn Yankees (Tony Award, 1956).
PICTURES: Kiss Them For Me (debut, 1957), South Pacific, Damn Yankees, Say One for Me, Tall Story, The Apartment, Portrait in Black, Convicts Four, Wives and Lovers, Who's Minding the Store?, Kiss Me Stupid, Caprice, Paint Your Wagon, The Sting, Silver Streak, The Happy Hooker Goes to Washington, Popeye, Galaxy of Terror, Fast Times at Ridgemont High, O'Hara's Wife, Private School, Johnny Dangerously, RAD, From the Hip, O.C. and Stiggs, A Man of Passion, Blood Relations, Saturday the 14th Strikes Back, Paramedics, Ski Patrol, Blood Salvage, Popcorn, The Player, Of Mice and Men, House Arrest.
TELEVISION: *Series*: My Favorite Martian, Stop Susan Williams (Cliffhangers), Silver Spoons, Fast Times, Picket Fences (Emmy Awards, 1995 & 1996). *Guest*: You Are There, Producers Showcase, There Shall Be No Night, Studio One, Playhouse 90, Oh Madeline, Crash Course. *Movies*: Institute for Revenge, The Kid With the Broken Halo, The Fall of the

House of Usher, This Girl for Hire, The Jerk Too, Amos, Red River, I Know My First Name Is Steven, One Special Victory. *Mini-Series*: Stephen King's The Stand.

WALTER, JESSICA
Actress. b. Brooklyn, NY, Jan. 31, 1944. m. actor Ron Leibman. e. H.S. of the Performing Arts. Studied at Bucks County Playhouse and Neighborhood Playhouse. Many TV performances plus lead in series, For the People. Broadway debut in Advise and Consent, 1961. Also, Photo Finish (Clarence Derwent Award), Night Life, A Severed Head, Rumors.
PICTURES: Lilith (debut, 1964), The Group, Grand Prix, Bye Bye Braverman, Number One, Play Misty for Me, Goldengirl, Going Ape, Spring Fever, The Flamingo Kid, Tapeheads, Ghost in the Machine.
TELEVISION: *Series*: For the People, Love of Life, Amy Prentiss (Emmy Award, 1975), Bare Essence, Aaron's Way, Dinosaurs (voice), The Round Table. *Movies*: The Immortal (pilot), Three's a Crowd, They Call It Murder, Women in Chains, Home for the Holidays, Hurricane, Having Babies, Victory at Entebbe, Black Market Baby, Wild and Wooly, Dr. Strange, Secrets of Three Hungry Wives, Vampire, She's Dressed to Kill, Miracle on Ice, Scruples, Thursday's Child, The Return of Marcus Welby M.D., The Execution, Killer in the Mirror, Leave of Absence. *Mini-Series*: Wheels.

WALTER, TRACEY
Actor. b. Jersey City, NJ, Nov. 25.
PICTURES: Goin' South, Blue Collar, Hardcore, The Hunter, The Hand, Raggedy Man, Honkytonk Man, Timerider, Rumble Fish, Conan the Destroyer, Repo Man, At Close Range, Something Wild, Malone, Mortuary Academy, Married to the Mob, Under the Boardwalk, Out of the Dark, Batman, Homer and Eddie, Young Guns II, The Two Jakes, Pacific Heights, The Silence of the Lambs, City Slickers, Delusion, Amos and Andrew, Philadelphia, Mona Must Die, Destiny Turns on the Radio, Wild America, Road to Ruin, Dorothy Day, Junior, Amanda, Larger Than Life, Matilda.
TELEVISION: *Series*: Best of the West, On the Air. *Movies*: Ride With the Wind, In the Line of Duty: Kidnapped, Buffalo Girls, Bill On His Own, Mad Bull, Out of this World.

WALTERS, BARBARA
Broadcast Journalist. b. Boston, MA, Sept. 25, 1931. Daughter of Latin Quarter nightclub impressario Lou Walters. e. Sarah Lawrence Coll. Began working in TV after graduation. Joined The Today Show in 1961 as writer-researcher, making occasional on-camera appearances. In 1963, became full-time on camera. In April, 1974, named permanent co-host. Also hosted own synd. prog., Not for Women Only. In 1976, joined ABC-TV Evening News, (host, 1976-78), correspondent World News Tonight (1978); corresp. 20/20 (1979-present). Host of The Barbara Walters Specials (1979-present). Author: How to Talk with Practically Anybody About Practically Anything (1970). Recipient of numerous awards including Emmy, Media, Peabody. Named one of women most admired by American People in 1982 & -84 Gallup Polls. Inducted into the Television Academy Hall of Fame, 1990. 1994, co-anchor of Turning Point.

WALTERS, JULIE
Actress. b. Birmingham, England, Feb. 22, 1950. Trained for 2 years to be a nurse before studying drama at Manchester Polytechnic, followed by year at Granada's Stables Theatre. Joined Everyman Theatre, Liverpool. Also toured Dockland pubs with songs, dance and imitations.
THEATER: Breezeblock Park, Funny Perculiar, The Glad Hand, Good Fun, Educating Rita, Jumpers, Fool for Love, When I Was a Girl I Used to Scream and Shout, Frankie and Johnnie in the Claire de Lune, Macbeth, Having a Ball, The Rose Tattoo, Jumpers, Fool for Love, When I Was a Girl I Used to Scream and Shout, Frankie and Johnny.
PICTURES: Educating Rita (debut, 1983; Acad. Award nom.), She'll Be Wearing Pink Pyjamas, Car Trouble, Personal Services, Prick Up Your Ears, Buster, Mack the Knife, Killing Dad, Stepping Out, Wide Eyed and Legless, The Summer House, The Wedding Gift, Just Like a Woman, Sister My Sister.
TELEVISION: Unfair Exchanges, Talent, Nearly a Happy Ending, Family Man, Happy Since I Met You, The Secret Diary of Adrian Mole (series), Wood and Walters (series), Say Something Happened, Intensive Care, The Boys from the Black Stuff, Talking Heads, Victoria Wood As Seen on TV (series & special), The Birthday Party, Her Big Chance, Nearly a Happy Ending, Julie Walters & Friends (special), GBH (series), The All-Day Breakfast Show (special).

WANG, WAYNE
Director. b. Hong Kong, 1949. m. actress Cora Miao. e. came to U.S. to study photography at College of Arts and Crafts, Oakland, CA. With a Master's Degree in film and television, returned to Hong Kong. Worked on TV comedy series. First

dir. work, as asst. dir. for Chinese sequences of Golden Needle. First film was A Man, A Woman and a Killer. Won grant from AFI and National Endowment for the Arts, used to finance Chan is Missing (1982) which cost $22,000.
PICTURES: Chan is Missing (also s.p., editor, prod.), Dim Sum: A Little Bit of Heart (also prod., story), Slam Dance, Eat a Bowl of Tea, Life is Cheap... But Toilet Paper is Expensive (also exec. prod., story), The Joy Luck Club, Smoke, Blue in the Face (also co-s.p.).

WARD, DAVID S.
Writer, Director. b. Providence, RI, Oct. 24, 1947. Raised in Cleveland. e. Pomona Col. (BA), UCLA (MFA).
PICTURES: *Writer*: Steelyard Blues, The Sting (Academy Award, 1973), Cannery Row (also dir.), The Sting II, The Milagro Beanfield War (co-s.p.), Major League (also dir.), King Ralph (also dir.), Sleepless in Seattle (co-s.p.; Acad. Award nom.), The Program (also dir.), Major League 2 (dir., co-s.p.). *Director*: Major League II, Down Periscope.

WARD, FRED
Actor. b. San Diego, CA, 1943. Raised in Louisiana and Texas. Studied at Herbert Berghof Studio. Moved to Rome to work in experimental theatre. Returned to U.S. to appear on San Fransico stage with Sam Shepard's Magic Theatre in Inacoma and Angel City. Additional stage work in The Glass Menagerie, One Flew Over the Cuckoo's Nest, Domino Courts, Simpatico.
PICTURES: Escape From Alcatraz (debut, 1979), Tilt, Carny, Southern Comfort, Timerider, The Right Stuff, Silkwood, Uncommon Valor, Swing Shift, Uforia, Secret Admirer, Remo Williams: The Adventure Begins, Off Limits, Big Business, The Prince of Pennsylvania, Tremors, Miami Blues (also co-exec. prod.), Henry and June, Thunderheart, The Player, Bob Roberts, The Dark Wind, Equinox, Short Cuts, Naked Gun 33 1/3: The Final Insult, Two Small Bodies, The Blue Villa, Chain Reaction.
TELEVISION: *Movies*: Belle Starr, Noon Wine, Florida Straits, Cast a Deadly Spell, Backtrack, Four Eyes and Six-Guns. *Special*: Noon Wine (Amer. Playhouse).

WARD, RACHEL
Actress. b. London, 1957. m. actor Bryan Brown. Top fashion and TV commercial model before becoming actress. Studied acting with Stella Adler and Robert Modica. On stage in Sydney in A Doll's House, Hopping to Byzantium.
PICTURES: Night School (debut, 1981), The Final Terror, Sharky's Machine, Dead Men Don't Wear Plaid, Against All Odds, The Good Wife, Hotel Colonial, How to Get Ahead in Advertising, After Dark My Sweet, Christopher Columbus: The Discovery, Wide Sargasso Sea, The Ascent.
TELEVISION: *Mini-Series*: The Thorn Birds, Shadow of the Cobra (U.K.). *Movies*: Christmas Lillies of the Field, Fortress, And the Sea Will Tell, Black Magic, Double Jeopardy.

WARD, SELA
Actress. b. Meridian, MS, July 11, 1956.
PICTURES: The Man Who Loved Women, Rustler's Rhapsody, Nothing in Common, Steel Justice, Hello Again, The Fugitive.
TELEVISION: *Series*: Emerald Point N.A.S., Sisters (Emmy Award, 1994). *Movie*: Almost Golden: The Jessica Savitch Story.

WARD, SIMON
Actor. b. London, England, Oct. 19, 1941. Ent. ind. 1964.
PICTURES: If... (debut, 1969), Frankenstein Must Be Destroyed, I Start Counting, Quest for Love, Young Winston, Hitler—The Last Ten Days, The Three Musketeers, The Four Musketeers, Deadly Strangers. Aces High, Children of Rage, Battle Flag, The Chosen, Dominique, Zulu Dawn, La Sabina, The Monster Club, L'Etincelle, Supergirl, Leave All Fair, Double X, Wuthering Heights.
TELEVISION: Spoiled, Chips with Everything, The Corsican Brothers, All Creatures Great and Small, Dracula, Valley Forge, The Last Giraffe (Raising Daisy Rothschild), Around the World in 80 Days.

WARD, VINCENT
Director, Writer. b. New Zealand, 1956. e. llam Sch. of Art. At 21 dir. & co-wrote short film A State of Siege (Hugo Award, Chicago Film Fest.)
PICTURES: In Spring One Plants Alone (Silver Hugo, Chicago Film Fest.), Vigil (Grand Prix Awards, Madrid & Prades Film Fests), The Navigator (Australian Film Awards for Best Picture & Director), Alien[3] (story only), Map of the Human Heart.

WARDEN, JACK
Actor. b. Newark, NJ, Sept. 18, 1920. r.n. Jack Warden Lebzelter. Started with Margo Jones theatre in Dallas (rep. co.).
THEATER: *B'way*: Golden Boy, Sing Me No Lullaby, Very Special Baby, Cages (Obie Award), A View from the Bridge,

The Man in the Glass Booth, The Body Beautiful. *Repertory*: Twelfth Night, She Stoops to Conquer, The Importance of Being Earnest, Summer and Smoke, The Taming of the Shrew, etc.
PICTURES: You're in the Navy Now (U.S.S. Teakettle; debut, 1951), The Frogmen, The Man With My Face, Red Ball Express, From Here to Eternity, Edge of the City, 12 Angry Men, The Bachelor Party, Darby's Rangers, Run Silent Run Deep, The Sound and the Fury, That Kind of Woman, Wake Men When It's Over, Escape From Zahrain, Donovan's Reef, The Thin Red Line, Blindfold, Bye Bye Braverman, The Sporting Club, Summertree, Who Is Harry Kellerman?, Welcome to the Club, Billy Two Hats, The Man Who Loved Cat Dancing, The Apprenticeship of Duddy Kravitz, Shampoo (Acad. Award nom.), All the President's Men, The White Buffalo, Heaven Can Wait (Acad. Award nom.), Death on the Nile, The Champ, Dreamer, Beyond the Poseidon Adventure, And Justice for All, Being There, Used Cars, The Great Muppet Caper, Chu Chu and the Philly Flash, Carbon Copy, So Fine, The Verdict, Crackers, The Aviator, September, The Presidio, Everybody Wins, Problem Child, Problem Child 2, Passed Away, Night and the City, Toys, Guilty As Sin, Bullets Over Broadway, While You Were Sleeping, Things to Do in Denver When You're Dead, Mighty Aphrodite, Ed.
TELEVISION: *Series*: Mr. Peepers, Norby, The Asphalt Jungle, The Wackiest Ship in the Army, N.Y.P.D., Jigsaw John, The Bad News Bears, Crazy Like a Fox. *Guest*: Philco Goodyear Producer's Showcase, Kraft. *Movies*: The Face of Fear, Brian's Song (Emmy Award, 1972), What's a Nice Girl Like You...?, Man on a String, Lt. Schuster's Wife, Remember When, The Godchild, Journey From Darkness, They Only Come Out at Night, Raid on Entebbe, Topper, A Private Battle, Hobson's Choice, Helen Keller: The Miracle Continues, Hoover vs. The Kennedys, The Three Kings, Dead Solid Perfect, Judgment, Problem Child 3: Junior in Love. *Mini-Series*: Robert Kennedy and His Times, A.D.

WARNER, DAVID
Actor. b. Manchester, England, July 29, 1941. e. Royal Acad. of Dramatic Art. Made London stage debut in Tony Richardson's version of A Midsummer Night's Dream (1962). Four seasons with Royal Shakespeare Co. Theater includes Afore Night Comes, The Tempest, The Wars of the Roses, The Government Inspector, Twelfth Night, I Claudius.
PICTURES: Tom Jones (debut, 1963), Morgan!, The Deadly Affair, A King's Story (voice), Work Is a Four Letter Word, A Midsummer's Night Dream, The Bofors Gun, The Fixer, The Seagull, Michael Kolhaas, The Ballad of Cable Hogue, Perfect Friday, Straw Dogs, A Doll's House, From Beyond the Grave, Little Malcolm (and His Struggle Against the Eunuch), Mr. Quilp, The Omen, Providence, The Disappearance, Cross of Iron, Silver Bears, Nightwing, The Concorde—Airport '79, Time After Time, The 39 Steps, The Island, The French Lieutenant's Woman, Time Bandits, Tron, The Man With Two Brains, The Company of Wolves, Hansel and Gretel, My Best Friend Is a Vampire, Waxworks, Mr. North, Silent Night, Office Party, Hanna's War, Pulse Pounders, Keys to Freedom, Star Trek V: The Final Frontier, S.P.O.O.K.S., Tripwire, Mortal Passions, Teenage Mutant Ninja Turtles II: The Secret of the Ooze, Star Trek VI: The Undiscovered Country, Blue Tornado, Drive, Unnameable II, Dark at Noon, In the Mouth of Madness.
TELEVISION: *Movies*: S.O.S. Titantic, Desperado, A Christmas Carol, Hitler's SS—Portrait in Evil, Perry Mason: The Case of the Poisoned Pen, The Secret Life of Ian Fleming, Cast a Deadly Spell, The House on Sycamore Street, Perry Mason: The Case of the Skin-Deep Scandal, John Carpenter Presents Body Bags, Danielle Steel's Zoya. *Mini-Series*: Holocaust, Masada (Emmy Award, 1981), Marco Polo, Wild Palms. *Specials*: Love's Labour's Lost, Uncle Vanya.

WARNER, JULIE
Actress. b. New York, NY. e. Brown Univ., B.A. in Theatre Arts.
PICTURES: Doc Hollywood (debut, 1991), Mr. Saturday Night, Indian Summer, The Puppet Masters, Tommy Boy.
TELEVISION: *Series*: Pride and Joy. *Guest*: Star Trek: The Next Generation, 21 Jump Street, The Outsiders.

WARNER, MALCOLM-JAMAL
Actor. b. Jersey City, NJ, Aug. 18, 1970. Raised in Los Angeles. Was 13 years old when signed to play Bill Cosby's son on The Cosby Show.
THEATER: Three Ways Home (off-B'way debut, 1988).
PICTURE: Drop Zone (debut, 1994).
TELEVISION: *Series*: The Cosby Show (also dir. episode), Here and Now, Magic School Bus (voice), Malcolm & Eddie. *Movies*: The Father Clements Story, Mother's Day, Tyson. *Special*: Kids Killing Kids (host).

WARNER, GENE
Executive. b. Denver, CO, Aug. 12, 1916. Pres. of Excelsior Prods., prod. co. specializing in special effects and animation. Has headed 2 other cos. of similar nature over past 20 years, functioning at various times as prod., dir., studio prod. head

and writer. Producer-director of following shorts: The Tool Box, Suzy Snowflake, Santa and the Three Dwarfs, Land of the Midnight Sun and these documentaries/training films: Mariner I, Mariner III, Apollo, U.S. Navy titles. Special effects on theatrical features incl: Black Sunday, tom thumb, The Time Machine (Academy Award, 1960), The Wonderful World of the Brothers Grimm, 7 Faces of Dr. Lao, The Power, Legend of Hillybilly John. TV series include: The Man from Atlantis, Land of the Lost, Star Trek, Outer Limits, Twilight Zone, Mission Impossible. *TV Movie*: Satan's School for Girls.

WARREN, JENNIFER
Actress, Producer. b. New York, NY, Aug. 12, 1941. e. U. of Wisconsin, Madison, B.A. Graduate work at Wesleyan U. Studied acting with Uta Hagen at HB Studios. As part of AFI Women's Directing Workshop, directed Point of Departure, short film which received Cine Golden Eagle and Aspen Film Festival awards. Formed Tiger Rose Productions, indep. film-TV prod. co., 1988. Exec. prod., You Don't Have to Die (Acad. Award, doc. short, 1989). Director: The Beans of Egypt Maine (1994). Recipient of 2 Spirit Awards.
THEATER: Scuba Duba (off-B'way debut, 1967), 6 RMS RIV VU (Theatre World Award), Harvey, P.S., Your Cat Is Dead, B'way: Saint Joan, Volpone, Henry V (Guthrie Theatre).
PICTURES: Night Moves (debut, 1975), Slapshot, Another Man Another Chance, Ice Castles, Fatal Beauty.
TELEVISION: *Series*: Paper Dolls. *Pilots*: Double Dare, Knights of the Kitchen Table. *Movies*: Kojak. *Movies*: Banjo Hackett: Roamin' Free, Shark Kill, First You Cry, Steel Cowboy, Champions: A Love Story, Angel City, The Choice, The Intruder Within, Freedom, Paper Dolls (pilot), Confessions of a Married Man, Amazons, Full Exposure: The Sex Tape Scandal. *Mini-Series*: Celebrity.

WARREN, LESLEY ANN
Actress. b. New York, NY, Aug. 16, 1946. Studied acting under Lee Strasberg. Big break came in Rodgers and Hammerstein's 1964 tv prod. of Cinderella, where she was seen by Disney scout. Broadway debut in 110 in the Shade (1963, Theatre World Award), followed by Drat! The Cat! Appeared in Aerosmith video Janie's Got a Gun.
PICTURES: The Happiest Millionaire (debut, 1967), The One and Only Genuine Original Family Band, Pickup on 101, Harry and Walter Go to New York, Victor/Victoria (Acad. Award nom.), A Night in Heaven, Songwriter (Golden Globe nom.), Choose Me, Race to the Yankee Zephyr, Clue, Burglar, Cop, Worth Winning, Life Stinks, Pure Country, Color of Night, Bird of Prey, Natural Enemy, The First Man, 79 Park Avenue (Golden Globe winner).
TELEVISION: *Series*: Mission: Impossible. *Mini-Series*: 79 Park Avenue, Pearl, Evergreen, Family of Spies, Joseph. *Movies*: Seven in Darkness, Love Hate Love, Assignment Munich, The Daughters of Joshua Cabe, The Letters, The Legend of Valentino, Betrayal, Portrait of a Stripper, Beulah Land, Portrait of a Showgirl, A Fight for Jenny, Apology, Baja Oklahoma (Ace Award nom.), A Seduction in Travis County, In Sickness and Health, Willing to Kill: The Texas Cheerleader Story, A Mother's Revenge, Family of Spies (Emmy nom.), Murderous Intent, 27 Wagons Full of Cotton. *Specials*: The Saga of Sonora, It's a Bird It's a Plane It's Superman, A Special Eddie Rabbit, The Dancing Princess, 27 Wagons Full of Cotton (Ace Award nom.), Willie Nelson: Big Six-O.

WARRICK, RUTH
Actress. b. St. Joseph, MO, June 29, 1916. Started as radio singer. Autobiography: The Confessions of Phoebe Tyler (1980).
PICTURES: Citizen Kane (debut, 1941), Obliging Young Lady, The Corsican Brothers, Journey Into Fear, Forever and a Day, Perilous Holiday, The Iron Major, Secret Command, Mr. Winkle Goes to War, Guest in the House, China Sky, Song of the South, Driftwood, Daisy Kenyon, Arch of Triumph, The Great Dan Patch, Make Believe Ballroom, Three Husbands, Let's Dance, One Too Many, Roogie's Bump, Ride Beyond Vengeance, The Great Bank Robbery, Deathmask, The Returning.
TELEVISION: *Movie*: Peyton Place—The Next Generation. *Series*: Peyton Place, All My Children. *Guest*: Studio One, Robert Montgomery Presents, Lux Star Playhouse. *Special*: Sometimes I Don't Love My Mother.

WARZEL, PETER C.
Executive. b. Buffalo, NY, May 31, 1952. e. Univ. of Rochester, Canisius Col. Joined Tele-Communications Inc., 1982, also serving as v.p. of industrial relations at Community Tele-Communications Inc., a TCI subsidiary. 1988, became sr. v.p. of United Artists Entertainment Co.; 1990, promoted to pres. & CEO of United Artists Theatre Circuit. 1992, was party to management buy-out of UATC as pres. & COO.

WASHBURN, DERIC
Writer. b. Buffalo, NY. e.Harvard U., English lit. Has written number of plays, including The Love Nest and Ginger Anne.
PICTURES: Silent Running (co-s.p.), The Deer Hunter (co-s.p.), The Border, Extreme Prejudice.

WASHINGTON, DENZEL
Actor. b. Mt. Vernon, NY, Dec. 28, 1954. e. Fordham U., B.A., journalism. Studied acting with American Conservatory Theatre, San Francisco.
THEATER: When the Chickens Come Home to Roost (Audelco Award), Coriolanus, Spell #7, The Mighty Gents, Ceremonies in Dark Old Men, A Soldier's Play, Checkmates, Richard III.
PICTURES: Carbon Copy (debut, 1981), A Soldier's Story, Power, Cry Freedom (Acad. Award nom.), The Mighty Quinn, For Queen and Country, Glory (Academy Award, best supporting actor, 1989; Golden Globe Award), Heart Condition, Mo' Better Blues, Ricochet, Mississippi Masala, Malcolm X (NY Film Critics Award; Acad. Award nom.), Much Ado About Nothing, Philadelphia, The Pelican Brief, Crimson Tide, Virtuosity, Devil in a Blue Dress, Courage Under Fire, The Preacher's Wife.
TELEVISION: Movies: Wilma, Flesh and Blood, License to Kill, The George McKenna Story. Series: St. Elsewhere.

WASSERMAN, DALE
Writer, Producer. b. Rhinelander, WI, Nov. 2, 1917. Stage: lighting designer, dir., prod.; dir. for. attractions, S. Hurok; began writing, 1954. Founding member & trustee of O'Neill Theatre Centre; artistic dir. Midwest Playwrights Laboratory; member, Acad. M.P. Arts & Sciences; awards include Emmy, Tony, Critics Circle (Broadway), Outer Circle; Writers Guild.
PICTURES: Cleopatra, The Vikings, The Sea and the Shadow, Quick Before It Melts, Mister Buddwing, A Walk with Love and Death, Man of La Mancha.
TELEVISION: The Fog, The Citadel, The Power and the Glory, Engineer of Death, The Lincoln Murder Case, I Don Quixote, Elisha and the Long Knives, and others.PLAYS: Livin' the Life, 998, One Flew Over the Cuckoo's Nest, The Pencil of God, Man of La Mancha, Play With Fire, Shakespeare and the Indians, Mountain High, Western Star, Green.

WASSERMAN, LEW
Executive. b. Cleveland, OH, March 15, 1913. National dir. advertising and pub., Music Corporation of Amer. 1936-38; v.p. 1938-39; v.p. motion picture div. 1940; Chairman of the bd., Chief Executive Officer, MCA, Inc., Universal City, CA. Named chairman emeritus of MCA in 1995. Received Jean Hersholt Humanitarian Award, 1973; awarded Presidential Medal of Freedom, 1995.

WASSON, CRAIG
Actor. b. Ontario, OR, March 15, 1954. Also musician/songwriter.
THEATER: Godspell, All God's Chillun Got Wings, Death of a Salesman (also wrote incidental music), Jock, Children of Eden, M. Butterfly, Skin of Our Teeth, The Sisters (Pasadena Playhouse), etc. Wrote incidental music for prod. of The Glass Menagerie.
PICTURES: Rollercoaster, The Boys in Company C (also wrote and performed song Here I Am), Go Tell the Spartans, The Outsider, Carny, Schizoid, Ghost Story, Four Friends, Second Thoughts (also wrote and performed music), Body Double, The Men's Club, A Nightmare on Elm Street 3, The Trackers, Midnight Fear, Malcolm X, Bum Rap (also wrote and performed music).
TELEVISION: Series: Phyllis (also wrote and performed orig. songs), Skag, One Life to Live, The Tomorrow Man. Guest: M*A*S*H, Baa Baa Black Sheep, Rockford Files, Hart to Hart, L.A. Law, Kung Fu: The Legend Continues, Dr. Quinn Medicine Woman, Murder She Wrote. Movies: The Silence, Mrs. R's Daughter, Skag, Thornwell, Why Me?, Strapped, Trapped in Space, The Calvin Mire Story, The Becky Bell Story, The Sister in Law. Specials: A More Perfect Union, Innocents Abroad.

WATANABE, GEDDE
Actor. b. Ogden, UT, June 26. Trained for stage at American Conservatory Theatre, San Francisco. Appeared with N.Y. Shakespeare Fest. Shakespeare in the Park series and with Pan Asian Repertory Theatre, N.Y.
THEATER: Pacific Overtures (debut, as Tree Boy, B'way and on tour, 1976), Bullet Headed Birds, Poor Little Lambs, Dispatches, Music Lesson, Good Person.
PICTURES: Sixteen Candles (debut, 1984), Gremlins, Volunteers, Gung Ho, Vamp, UHF, Boys on the Side.
TELEVISION: Series: Gung Ho. Movie: Miss America: Behind the Crown.

WATERHOUSE, KEITH
Writer. b. Leeds, England, Feb. 6, 1929. Early career as journalist, novelist. Author of There is a Happy Land, Billy Liar, Jubb, The Bucket Shop. Ent. m.p. ind. 1960.
PICTURES: Writer (with Willis Hall): Whistle Down the Wind, A Kind of Loving, Billy Liar, Man in the Middle, Pretty Polly, Lock Up Your Daughters, The Valiant, West Eleven.
TELEVISION: Series: Inside George Webley, Queenie's Castle, Budgie, Billy Liar, There is a Happy Land, Charters and Caldicott.

WATERS, JOHN
Director, Writer. b. Baltimore, MD, Apr. 22, 1946. First short film Hag in a Black Leather Jacket (1964) shot in Baltimore, as are most of his films. Other shorts include Roman Candles, Eat Your Makeup. Feature debut, Mondo Trasho. Appeared as actor in films Something Wild, Homer and Eddie. On tv in Homicide: Life on the Streets.
PICTURES: Director/Writer: Mondo Trasho (also prod., photo., edit.), Multiple Maniacs (also prod., editor, sound), Pink Flamingos (also prod., photo., edit.), Female Trouble (also photo., prod.), Desperate Living (also prod.), Polyester (also prod.), Hairspray (also co-prod., actor), Cry-Baby, Serial Mom.

WATERSTON, SAM
Actor. b. Cambridge, MA, Nov. 15, 1940. e. Yale U. Spent jr. year at Sorbonne in Paris as part of the Amer. Actors' Workshop run by American dir. John Berry. Broadway debut in Oh Dad Poor Dad ... (1963). Film debut, The Plastic Dome of Norma Jean (made 1965; unreleased). TV debut Pound (Camera Three). Has worked in New York Shakespeare Festival prods. since As You Like It (1963).
THEATER: N.Y. Shakespeare Festival: As You Like It, Ergo, Henry IV (Part I & II), Cymbeline, Hamlet, Much Ado About Nothing, The Tempest. Off-B'way: The Knack, La Turista, Waiting for Godot, The Three Sisters. B'way: The Paisley Convertible, Halfway Up the Tree, Indian, Hay Fever, The Trial of Cantonsville Nine, A Meeting by the River, Much Ado About Nothing (Drama Desk and Obie Awards), A Doll's House, Lunch Hour, Benefactors, A Walk in the Woods, Abe Lincoln in Illinois.
PICTURES: Fitzwilly, Three, Generation, Cover Me Babe, Mahoney's Estate, Who Killed Mary What's 'er Name?, Savages, The Great Gatsby, Journey Into Fear, Rancho Deluxe, Sweet Revenge, Capricorn One, Interiors, Eagle's Wing, Sweet William, Hopscotch, Heaven's Gate, The Killing Fields, Warning Sign, Hannah and Her Sisters, Just Between Friends, A Certain Desire, The Devil's Paradise, September, Welcome Home, Crimes and Misdemeanors, The Man in the Moon, Mindwalk, A Captive in the Land, Serial Mom, The Journey of August King (also co-prod.), The Shadow Conspiracy.
TELEVISION: Specials: Pound, Robert Lowell, The Good Lieutenant, Much Ado About Nothing, Oppenheimer, A Walk in the Woods. Movies: The Glass Menagerie, Reflections of Murder, Friendly Fire, Games Mother Never Taught You, In Defense of Kids, Dempsey, Finnegan Begin Again, Love Lives On, The Fifth Missile, The Room Upstairs, Terrorist on Trial: The United States vs. Salim Ajami, Gore Vidal's Lincoln, Lantern Hill, The Shell Seekers, Assault at West Point: The Court-Martial of Johnson Whittaker, David's Mother, The Enemy Within. Mini-Series: The Nightmare Years, The Civil War (voice). Series: Q.E.D., I'll Fly Away. Guest: Amazing Stories.

WATKIN, DAVID
Director of Photography. b. Margate, Eng., March 23, 1925. Entered British documentary industry in Jan., 1948. With British Transport Films as asst. cameraman, 1950 -55; as cameraman, 1955 -61. Feature film debut The Knack beginning long creative relationship with director Richard Lester.
PICTURES: The Knack... and How to Get It (debut, 1965), Help!, Marat/Sade, How I Won the War, The Charge of the Light Brigade, The Bed-Sitting Room, Catch-22, The Devils, The Boyfriend, The Homecoming, A Delicate Balance, The Three Musketeers, The Four Musketeers, Mahogany, To the Devil a Daughter, Robin and Marian, Joseph Andrews, Hanover Street, Cuba, That Summer, Endless Love, Chariots of Fire, Yentl, The Hotel New Hampshire, Return to Oz, White Nights, Out of Africa (Academy Award, 1985), Moonstruck, Sky Bandits, Masquerade, The Good Mother, Last Rites, Journey to the Center of the Earth, Memphis Belle, Hamlet, The Object of Beauty, Used People, This Boy's Life, Bopha!, Milk Money.

WAX, MORTON DENNIS
Public Relations Executive. b. New York, NY, March 13, 1932. e. Brooklyn Coll., 1952. President of Morton Dennis Wax & Assoc., Inc., p.r. and marketing firm servicing int'l creative marketplace, established 1956. Contrib. writer to Box Office Magazine, Film Journal. Recent articles: Creativity (Advertising Age), Rolling Stone's Marketing Through Music, Words & Music, Campaign Magazine, Songwriters Guild of America National Edition. As sect. of VPA, conceptualized int'l Monitor Award, an annual event, currently under auspices of ITS. Public relations counsel to London Int'l Advertising Awards. Member of The Public Relations Society of America, Nat'l Academy of TV Arts & Sciences, Nat'l Acadrmy of Recording Arts & Sciences, Publishers Publicity Association. Morton Dennis Wax & Assocs. in NY was awarded the first EPM Entertainment Marketing Cause Event Award for creating, developing and promoting a nat'l fund raising campaign to combat homelessness, called Brother Can You Spare a Dime Day.

WAYANS, DAMON
Actor, Writer, Producer. b. New York, NY, 1960. Brother is comedian-actor Keenen Ivory Wayans. Started as stand up comedian.
PICTURES: Beverly Hills Cop (debut, 1984), Hollywood Shuffle, Roxanne, Colors, Punchline, I'm Gonna Git You Sucka, Earth Girls Are Easy, Look Who's Talking Too (voice), The Last Boy Scout, Mo' Money (also s.p., co-exec. prod.), Last Action Hero (cameo), Blankman (also co-s.p., exec. prod.), Major Payne (also co-s.p., co-exec. prod.), The Great White Hype, Bulletproof.
TELEVISION: Series: Saturday Night Live (1985 -6), In Living Color (also writer). Special: The Last Stand? (HBO).

WAYANS, KEENEN IVORY
Actor, Director, Writer. b. NYC, June 8, 1958. e. Tuskegee Inst. Began as stand-up comic at The Improv in NYC and L.A. Brother is comedian-actor Damon Wayans.
PICTURES: Star 80 (debut, 1983), Hollywood Shuffle (also co-s.p.), Eddie Murphy Raw (co-prod., co-s.p. only), I'm Gonna Git You Sucka (also dir., s.p.), The Five Heartbeats (co-s.p. only), A Low Down Dirty Shame (also dir., s.p.), The Glimmer Man.
TELEVISION: Series: For Love and Honor, In Living Color (also exec. prod. & writer; Emmy Award 1990). Guest: Benson, Cheers, CHiPS, A Different World. Special: Partners in Crime (also co-writer).

WAYLAND, LEN
Actor. b. California, Dec. 28. e. Junior Coll., Modesto, CA. Wrote, prod. weekly radio series 1939-41, KPAS, KTRB, Calif. Service, radar navigator, 1941-45; theatre, Tobacco Road, 1946; 1973, formed Len Wayland Prods. for prod. of theatrical pictures and TV series. 1976-77: prod./dir.: Don't Let It Bother You. 1978, prod., dir., You're not there yet, for own co.
THEATER: A Streetcar Named Desire (B'way, tour), Heaven Can Wait, My Name Is Legion, Love of Four Colonels, Stalag 17, A Man For All Seasons.
TELEVISION: A Time to Live (serial), First Love, Armstrong Circle Theatre, Justice, Sgt. Bilko, Kraft Theatre; Dr. Weaver, From These Roots. Profiles in Courage, Dr. Kildare, Gunsmoke, Slattery's People, Ben Casey, A Noise in the World, Love Is a Many Splendored Thing; Dragnet, Outsider; Ironside, Name of the Game, The Bold Ones, Daniel Boone, The Virginian, Project U.F.O., Sam (series), The Blue and the Gray, Hunter, A-Team, Dallas, Amy on the Lips, Generations (serial).

WAYNE, JOEL
Executive. Began career with Grey Advertising; in 17 years won many awards (60 Clios, 25 N.Y. Art Director Club Awards, etc.). Was exec. v.p. & creative dir. of agency when left in 1979 to join Warner Bros. as v.p., creative adv. 1987, named sr. v.p., worldwide creative adv., then exec. v.p. worldwide creative adv. & publicity.

WAYNE, MICHAEL A.
Executive. r.n. Michael A. Morrison. b. Los Angeles, CA, Nov. 23, 1934. Father was late actor John Wayne. e. Loyola H.S.; Loyola U., B.B.A. Asst. dir., various companies, 1955-56; asst. dir., Revue Prods., 1956-57; pres. Batjac Prods. and Romina Prods., 1961.
PICTURES: Asst. to producer: China Doll, Escort West, The Alamo (asst. to prod.). Prod.: McLintock!, Cast Giant Shadow (co- prod.), The Green Berets, Chisum (exec. prod.), Big Jake, The Train Robbers, Cahill: U.S. Marshal, McQ (exec. prod.), Brannigan (exec. prod.).

WAYNE, PATRICK
Actor. b. Los Angeles, July 15, 1939. e. Loyola U, 1961, BS in biology. Father was late actor John Wayne. Made film debut at age 11 in Rio Grande with father.
PICTURES: The Long Gray Line, Mister Roberts, The Searchers, The Alamo, The Comancheros, McClintock, Donovan's Reef, Cheyenne Autumn, Shenandoah, An Eye for an Eye, The Green Berets, The Deserter, Big Jake, The Gatling Gun, Beyond Atlantis, The Bears and I, Mustang Country, Sinbad and the Eye of the Tiger, The People Time Forgot, Rustler's Rhapsody, Young Guns, Her Alibi, Blind Vengeance, Chill Factor.
TELEVISION: Series: The Rounders, Shirley. Movies: Sole Survivor, Yesterday's Child, Flight to Holocaust, The Last Hurrah, Three on a Date. Guest: Frank's Place.

WEATHERS, CARL
Actor. b. New Orleans, LA, Jan. 14, 1948. e. San Diego State Univ.
PICTURES: Bucktown (debut, 1975), Friday Foster, Rocky, Close Encounters of the Third Kind, Semi-Tough, Force Ten From Navarone, Rocky II, Death Hunt, Rocky III, Rocky IV, Predator, Action Jackson, Hurricane Smith, Happy Gilmore.
TELEVISION: Series: Fortune Dane, Tour of Duty, Street Justice, In the Heat of the Night. Movies: The Hostage Heart, The Bermuda Depths, Breaker, Dangerous Passion, In the Heat of the Night: A Matter of Justice, In the Heat of the Night: Who Was Geli Bendl?, In the Heat of the Night: By Duty Bound, Tom Clancy's Op Center, In the Heat of the Night: Grow Old With Me, The Defiant Ones. Director: Silk Stalkings (2 episodes), Renegade (1 episode).

WEAVER, DENNIS
Actor, Director. b. Joplin, MO, June 4, 1925. e. U. of Oklahoma, B.A., fine arts, 1948.
PICTURES: Horizons West (debut, 1952), The Raiders, The Redhead From Wyoming, The Lawless Breed, Mississippi Gambler, Law and Order, It Happens Every Thursday, Column South, The Man From the Alamo, The Golden Blade, The Nebraskan, War Arrow, Dangerous Mission, Dragnet, Ten Wanted Men, The Bridges at Toko-Ri, Seven Angry Men, Chief Crazy Horse, Storm Fear, Touch of Evil, The Gallant Hours, Duel at Diablo, Way... Way Out, Gentle Giant, Mission Batangas, A Man Called Sledge, What's the Matter With Helen?, Walking After Midnight.
TELEVISION: Series: Gunsmoke (Emmy Award, 1959), Kentucky Jones, Gentle Ben, McCloud, Stone, Emerald Point NAS, Buck James, Lonesome Dove. Movies: McCloud: Who Killed Miss USA?, The Forgotten Man, Duel, Rolling Man, Female Artillery, The Great Man's Whiskers, Terror on the Beach, Intimate Strangers, The Islander, Ishi: The Last of His Tribe, The Ordeal of Patty Hearst, Stone (pilot), Amber Waves, The Ordeal of Dr. Mudd, The Day the Loving Stopped, Don't Go to Sleep, Cocaine: One Man's Seduction, Bluffing It, Disaster at Silo 7, The Return of Sam McCloud (also co-exec. prod.), Greyhounds. Mini-Series: Centennial, Pearl. Special: Mastergate.

WEAVER, FRITZ
Actor. b. Pittsburgh, PA, Jan. 19, 1926. e. U. of Chicago.
THEATER: The Chalk Garden (Theatre World Award), Miss Lonelyhearts, All American, A Shot in the Dark, Baker Street, Child's Play (Tony, 1970), The Price, The Crucible, The Professional, etc.
PICTURES: Fail Safe (debut, 1964), The Guns of August (narrator), The Maltese Bippy, A Walk in the Spring Rain, Company of Killers, The Day of the Dolphin, Marathon Man, Demon Seed, Black Sunday, The Big Fix, Jaws of Satan, Creepshow, Power.
TELEVISION: Movies: The Borgia Stick, Berlin Affair, Heat of Anger, The Snoop Sisters, Hunter, The Legend of Lizzie Borden, Captains Courageous, The Hearst and Davies Affair, A Death in California, My Name is Bill W, Ironclads, Citizen Cohn, Blind Spot. Mini-Series: Holocaust, The Martian Chronicles, Dream West, I'll Take Manhattan.

WEAVER, SIGOURNEY
Actress. r.n. Susan Weaver. b. New York, NY, Oct. 8, 1949. e. Stanford U., Yale U. Daughter of Sylvester (Pat) Weaver, former NBC pres. Mother, actress Elizabeth Inglis (one-time contract player for Warner Bros.). After college formed working partnership with fellow student Christopher Durang for off-B'way improv. productions. First professional appearance on stage in 1974 in The Constant Wife with Ingrid Bergman. Formed Goat Cay Prods.
THEATER: Off-Off-B'way: The Nature and Purpose of the Universe. Off-B'way: Titanic/Das Lusitania Songspiel (also co-writer), Gemini, Marco Polo Sings a Solo, New Jerusalem, The Merchant of Venice, Beyond Therapy. B'way: Hurlyburly.
PICTURES: Madman (Israeli; debut, 1976), Annie Hall, Alien, Eyewitness, The Year of Living Dangerously, Deal of the Century, Ghostbusters, One Woman or Two, Aliens (Acad. Award nom.), Half Moon Street, Gorillas in the Mist (Acad. Award nom.), Working Girl (Acad. Award nom.), Ghostbusters II, Alien 3 (also co-prod.), 1492: Conquest of Paradise, Dave, Death and the Maiden, Jeffrey, Copycat, The Ice Storm.
TELEVISION: Series: The Best of Families (PBS), Somerset. Special: The Sorrows of Gin.

WEAVER, SYLVESTER L., JR.
Executive. b. Los Angeles, CA, Dec. 21, 1908. e. Dartmouth Coll. Daughter is actress Sigourney Weaver. CBS, Don Lee Network, 1932-35; Young & Rubicam adv. agency, 1935-38; adv. mgr., American Tobacco Co., 1938-47; v.p. Young & Rubicam, 1947-49; joined NBC as v.p., chg. TV, 1949; appt'd v.p. chg. NBC Radio & TV networks, 1952; vice-chmn. bd., NBC, 1953; pres., NBC, 1953; bd. chmn., 1955; as head of NBC during TV's formative years, Weaver is credited as the father of TV talk/service program, founding both Tonight and Today shows, also innovated the rotating multi-star anthology series, the Wide Wide World series and concept of TV "special;" Own firm, 430 Park Avenue, N.Y., 1956; chmn. of bd. McCann-Erickson Corp. (Intl.), 1959; pres., Subscription TV, Inc. Comm. Consultant in Los Angeles, CA and President, Weaver Productions, Inc. On magazine series Television: Inside and Out (1981-82). Author: The Best Seat in the House (1994). Awards: Emmy Trustees' and Governor's Award (1967) and Governor's Award (1983), TV Hall of Fame (1984), NAB Hall of Fame (1986), Dartmouth Lifetime Achievement Award, 1993.

WEBB, CHLOE
Actress. b. New York, NY. e. Boston Conservatory of Music and Drama. On stage with Boston Shakespeare Co., Goodman Theatre in Chicago and Mark Taper Forum, L.A., improv. groups Imagination Theatre Co., Paul Sills Theatre.
THEATER: Forbidden Broadway (Off-B'way and L.A.), Addiction, Family Album, The Model Apartment (LA Critics Circle & Dramalogue Awards), House of Blue Leaves (Dramlogue Award), School Talk, A Midsummer Night's Dream.
PICTURES: Sid and Nancy (debut, 1986; Natl. Society of Film Critics Award), Twins, Heart Condition, The Belly of an Architect, Queens Logic, A Dangerous Woman, Love Affair.
TELEVISION: Series: Thicke of the Night. Special: Who Am I This Time? Movies: Lucky Day, Silent Cries. Mini-Series: Tales of the City. Guest: Remington Steele, China Beach (pilot).

WEBER, STEVEN
Actor. e. Purchase Col. Acted with Mirror Rep. Co. Off-B'way.
THEATER: NY: Paradise Lost, The Real Thing (B'way debut, 1985), Something About Baseball. Regional: Made in Bangkok, Come Back Little Sheba, Naked at the Coast, Death of a Salesman.
PICTURES: The Flamingo Kid, Flanagan, Hamburger Hill, Les Anges, Single White Female, The Temp, Jeffrey, Dracula: Dead and Loving It.
TELEVISION: Series: Wings. Mini-Series: The Kennedys of Massachusetts. Movies: In the Company of Darkness, In the Line of Duty: The Undercover Murders, Deception: A Mother's Secret, Betrayed by Love. Special: Pudd'nhead Wilson.

WEDGEWORTH, ANN
Actress. b. Abilene, TX, Jan. 21, 1935. e. U. of Texas. On stage in Thieves, Blues for Mr. Charlie, Chapter Two (Tony Award, 1978), etc.
PICTURES: Andy, Bang the Drum Slowly, Scarecrow, The Catamount Killing, Law and Disorder, Dragonfly (One Summer Love), Birch Interval, Thieves, Handle With Care, No Small Affair, Sweet Dreams, The Men's Club, Made in Heaven, A Tiger's Tale, Far North, Miss Firecracker, Steel Magnolias, Green Card, Love and a .45.
TELEVISION: Series: The Edge of Night, Another World, Somerset, Three's Company, Filthy Rich, Evening Shade. Movies: The War Between the Tates, Bogie, Elvis and the Beauty Queen, Killjoy, Right to Kill?, A Stranger Waits, Cooperstown, A Burning Passion: The Margaret Mitchell Story. Pilot: Harlan & Merleen.

WEILER, GERALD E.
Producer. b. Mannheim, Germany, May 8, 1928. e. Harvard, 1946-48; Columbia, B.S., 1949-51; New York U. Grad. Sch., 1951-53. Writer, WHN, N.Y. writer, sports ed., news ed., Telenews Prod., Inc., 1948-52; asst. to prod., Richard de Rochemont, Vavin, Inc., 1952; U.S. Army, 1953-55; v.p., Vavin Inc. 1955-73; President, Weiler Communications Inc. 1973. Winner, NY "Lotto" Lottery, 1988; retired 1989.

WEILL, CLAUDIA
Director. b. New York, NY 1947. e. Radcliffe, B.A., 1969. Teacher of acting, Cornish Institute, 1983; guest lecturer on film directing, NYU and Columbia U. Winner of Donatello Award, best director, 1979; Mademoiselle Woman of the Year, 1974; AFI Independent Filmmakers Grant, 1973. Worked as prod. asst. on doc., Revolution.
THEATER: An Evening for Merlin Finch (debut, 1975, Williamstown), Stillife, Found a Peanut, The Longest Walk.
PICTURES: Doc. shorts: This Is the Home of Mrs. Levant Grahame, Roaches' Serenade, Joyce at 34. Director: The Other Half of the Sky—A China Memoir (also photog., edit.), Girlfriends (also prod., story), It's My Turn.
TELEVISION: The 51st State, Sesame Street, Joyce at 34, The Great Love Experiment, thirtysomething. Movie: A Child Lost Forever.

WEINBLATT, MIKE
Executive. b. Perth Amboy, NJ, June 10, 1929. e. Syracuse U. Served in Army as counter-intelligence agent, mostly in Japan, 1952-53. Joined NBC in 1957; has headed two major TV network functions—talent/program admin. & sls.; joined network business affairs dept. in 1958 as mgr., business affairs, facilities operations; rose to post of director, pricing & financial services before moving to sales in 1962, as mgr., participating program sales; named v.p., eastern sales, NBC-TV, 1968; named v.p., talent & program admin., 1968; promoted to v.p. sales, 1973; 1975 named sr. v.p., sales; later became exec. v.p.; appointed exec. v.p. & gen. mgr. of NBC TV network, 1977; appointed Pres., NBC Entertainment, 1978; 1980, joined Showtime/Movie Channel as pres. & COO; 1984, pres., Multi Media Entertainment; 1990, chmn. Weinblatt Communications Co. Inc. 1991, mng. dir. Interequity Capital Corp.

WEINGROD, HERSCHEL
Writer, Producer. b. Milwaukee, WI, Oct. 30, 1947. e. U. of Wisconsin, 1965-69; London Film Sch., 1969-71.

PICTURES: Co-writer with Timothy Harris: Cheaper to Keep Her, Trading Places (BAFTA nom.), Brewster's Millions, My Stepmother Is An Alien, Paint It Black, Twins, Kindergarten Cop, Pure Luck, Falling Down (prod. only), Space Jam (co-s.p.).
TELEVISION: Street of Dreams (exec. prod.).

WEINSTEIN, BOB
Executive. With brother Harvey founded distribution company Miramax Films in 1979. Company branched into feature production in 1989 with film Scandal. Serves as Miramax co-chairman.
PICTURES: Light Years (Bob: prod., Harvey: dir. of U.S. version). Co-Executive Producers: Scandal, The Lemon Sisters, Hardware, A Rage in Harlem, The Miracle, Crossing the Line, The Night We Never Met, Benefit of the Doubt, True Romance, Into the West, Mother's Boys, Pulp Fiction, Ready to Wear (Pret-a-Porter), The Englishman Who Went Up a Hill But Came Down a Mountain, Smoke, The Crossing Guard, The Journey of August King, Last of the High Kings.

WEINSTEIN, HARVEY
Executive. With brother Bob founded distribution company Miramax Films in 1979. Company branched into feature production in 1989 with film Scandal. Serves as Miramax co-chairman. (For list of films see Bob Weinstein).

WEINSTEIN, PAULA
Producer. b. Nov. 19, 1945. e. Columbia U. Daughter of late prod. Hannah Weinstein. Raised in Europe. Partnered with Gareth Wigan in WW Productions at Warner Brothers. Started as theatrical agent with William Morris and ICM. With Warner Brothers, 1976-78 as production v.p.; left to go to 20th Century-Fox in same capacity; named Fox sr. v.p., worldwide prod; 1980, appointed v.p., prod., the Ladd Company; 1981, joined United Artists as pres., m.p. div.; 1983, began own prod. company at Columbia Pictures, also serving as a consultant for Columbia; 1987, joined MGM as exec. consultant; With late husband Mark Rosenberg formed Spring Creek Prods.
PICTURES: Prod.: A Dry White Season, The Fabulous Baker Boys, Fearless, Flesh and Bone, With Honors, Something to Talk About.
TELEVISION: TV Movies: The Rose and the Jackal, Citizen Cohn, Truman (Emmy Award, 1996).

WEINTRAUB, FRED
Executive, Producer. b. Bronx, NY, April 27, 1928. e. U. of PA, Wharton Sch. of Bus. Owner of The Bitter End Coffeehouse to 1971. Personal management, Campus Coffee House Entertain-ment Circuit; TV Production Hootenanny, Popendipity; syndicated TV show host: From The Bitter End; motion picture prod.; v.p., creative services, Warner Bros. 1969; exec. in chg. Woodstock; prod. motion pictures, Weintraub-Heller Productions, 1974; then Fred Weintraub Productions, which became Weintraub/Kuhn Prods. in 1990.
PICTURES: Enter the Dragon, Rage, Black Belt Jones, Truck Turner, Golden Needles, Animal Stars, Hot Potato, The Ultimate Warrior, Dirty Knights Work, Those Cuckoo Crazy Animals, Crash, Outlaw Blues, The Pack, The Promise, Tom Horn, Battle Creek Brawl, Force Five, High Road to China, Out of Control, Gymkata, Princess Academy, Born to Ride.
TELEVISION: My Father My Son (prod.), Triplecross. Produced: Trouble Bound, Dead Wrong, documentaries: JFK Assassination, The Bruce Lee Story.

WEINTRAUB, JERRY
Producer. b. New York, NY, Sept. 26, 1937. m. former singer Jayne Morgan. Sole owner and chmn. of Management Three, representing entertainment personalities, including John Denver, John Davidson, Frank Sinatra, Neil Diamond, etc. Also involved with Intercontinental Broadcasting Systems, Inc. (cable programming) and Jerry Weintraub/Armand Hammer Prods. (production co.). 1985, named United Artists Corp. chmn. Resigned, 1986. 1987: formed Weintraub Entertainment Group.
PICTURES: Nashville, Oh God!, Cruising, All Night Long, Diner, The Karate Kid, The Karate Kid Part II, The Karate Kid Part III, Pure Country, The Firm (actor), The Next Karate Kid, The Specialist.

WEINTRAUB, SY
Executive. b. New York, NY, 1923. e. U. of Missouri, B.A., journalism, 1947; graduate of American Theater Wing. Started career in 1949 forming with associates a TV syndication co., Flamingo Films, Inc., which merged with Associated Artists to form Motion Pictures for Television, Inc., largest syndicator at that time. Originated Superman and Grand Ol' Opry series for TV. 1958, bought Sol Lesser Prods., owners of film rights for Tarzan, and began producing and distributing Tarzan films through Banner Productions, Inc. Also formerly chmn. of bd. of Panavision, Inc.; bd. mem. and pres. of National General Television Corp., and pres. of KMGM-TV in Minneapolis. In 1978, named chmn. of Columbia Pictures Industries' new Film Entertainment Group, also joining office of the chief executive of CPI.

WEIR, PETER
Director, Writer. b. Sydney, Australia, Aug. 21, 1944. e. attended Scots Coll. and Sydney U. Briefly worked selling real estate, traveled to Eng. 1965. Entered Australian TV industry as stagehand 1967 while prod. amateur revues. *Dir. shorts*: Count Vim's Last Exercise, The Life and Times of Reverend Buck Shotte, Homeside, Incredible Floridas, What Ever Happened to Green Valley? 1967-73.
PICTURES: *Director*: Three to Go (debut, 1970; segment: Michael), The Cars That Ate Paris (also s.p., co-story; a.k.a. The Cars That Eat People), Picnic at Hanging Rock, The Last Wave (also s.p.), The Plumber (also s.p.; tv in Australia). Gallipoli (also story), The Year of Living Dangerously (also co-s.p.), Witness, The Mosquito Coast, Dead Poets Society, Green Card (also prod., s.p.), Fearless.

WEIS, DON
Director, Writer, Producer. b. Milwaukee, WI, May 13, 1922. e. USC. Started as dialogue dir. on such films as Body and Soul, The Red Pony, Champion, Home of the Brave, The Men.
PICTURES: Bannerline (debut, 1951), It's a Big Country (segment), Just This Once, You for Me, I Love Melvin, Remains to Be Seen, A Slight Case of Larceny, Half a Hero, The Affairs of Dobie Gillis, The Adventures of Haji Baba, Ride the High Iron, The Gene Krupa Story, Critic's Choice, Looking for Love, Pajama Party, Billie (also prod.), The King's Pirate, Did You Hear the One About the Traveling Saleslady?, Zero to Sixty.
TELEVISION: Dear Phoebe, The Longest Hundred Miles, It Takes a Thief, Ironside, M*A*S*H., Happy Days, Planet of the Apes, Bronk, Petrocelli, The Magician, Mannix, Night Stalker, Barbary Coast, Courtship of Eddie's Father, Starsky & Hutch, Hawaii Five-O, Chips, Charlie's Angels, Love Boat, Fantasy Island, Remington Steele, Hill St. Blues, Murphy's Law.

WEISS, STEVEN ALAN
Executive. b. Glendale, CA, Oct. 19, 1944. e. Los Angeles City Coll., A.A., 1964; USC, B.S., 1966; Northwestern U., B.S., 1967; LaSalle Extension U., J.D., 1970. U.S. Navy-San Diego, Great Lakes, Vallejo & Treasure Island, 1966-67; shipyard liaison officer, Pearl Harbor Naval Shipyard, U.S. Navy, 1970; gen. mgr., Adrian Weiss Prods., 1970-74; organized Weiss Global Enterprises with Adrian Weiss 1974 for production, acquisition & distribution of films. Purchased with Tom J. Corradine and Adrian Weiss from the Benedict E. Bogeaus Estate nine features, 1974. Secty./treas. of Film Investment Corp. & Weiss Global Enterprises. (Cos. own, control or have dist. rights to over 300 features, many TV series, documentaries, etc.). Member of the Nat'l Assn. of TV Program Executive Int'l, National Cable TV Assn., American Film Institute.

WEISSMAN, MURRAY
Executive. b. New York, NY, Dec. 23. e. U. of Southern California. Asst. dir. of press info., CBS, 1960-66; mgr., TV press dept., Universal Studio, 1966-68; executive in charge of m.p. press dept., Universal Studios & asst. secy., Universal Pictures, 1968-76; marketing exec., Columbia Pictures, 1976-77; vice pres. of advertising & publicity, Lorimar Productions, 1977; vice pres., ICPR Public Relations Company, 1978-81; now principal, Weissman/Angellotti.

WEISWASSER, STEPHEN A.
Executive. e. Wayne St. Univ., John Hopkins Univ., Harvard Law School. Partner at Wilmer Cutler & Pickering law firm until he joined Capital Cities/ABC in 1986 as sr. v.p. Aug. 1993 became pres. of Capital Cities/ABC Multimedia Group until Oct. 1995. Nov. 1995, became pres. & CEO of Americast.

WEITZNER, DAVID
Executive. b. New York, NY, Nov. 13, 1938. e. Michigan State U. Entered industry in 1960 as member Columbia Pictures adv. dep't; later with Donahue and Coe as ass't exec. and Loew's Theatres adv. dep't; later with Embassy Pictures, adv. mgr.; dir. of adv. and exploitation for Palomar Pictures Corp.; v.p. in charge of adv., pub., and exploitation for ABC Pictures Corp.; v.p., entertainment/leisure div., Grey Advertising; v.p., worldwide adv., 20th Century Fox; exec. v.p. adv./pub./promo., Universal Pictures; exec. v.p., mktg. & dist., Embassy Pictures; 1985, joined 20th Century-Fox Films as pres. of mktg. 1987, pres., mktg., Weintraub Entertainment Group; 1988 joined MCA/Universal as pres. worldwide marketing, MCA Recreation Services.

WELCH, RAQUEL
Actress. r.n. Raquel Tejada. b. Chicago, IL, Sept. 5, 1940. e. La Jolla H.S. Theatre arts scholarship San Diego State Coll. Worked as model before landing bit parts in films. Broadway debut, Woman of the Year, 1981.
PICTURES: A House Is Not a Home (debut, 1964), Roustabout, Do Not Disturb, A Swingin' Summer, Fantastic Voyage, Shoot Loud Louder... I Don't Understand, One Million Years B.C., Fathom, The Oldest Profession, Bedazzled, The Biggest Bundle of Them All, Le Fate (The Queens),

Bandolero, Lady in Cement, 100 Rifles, Flare Up, The Magic Christian, Myra Breckinridge, Restless, Hannie Caulder, Kansas City Bomber, Fuzz, Bluebeard, The Last of Sheila, The Three Musketeers, The Four Musketeers, The Wild Party, Mother Jugs and Speed, Crossed Swords, L'Animal, Naked Gun 33 1/3: The Final Insult.
TELEVISION: *Specials*: Really Raquel, Raquel. *Movies*: The Legend of Walks Far Woman, Right to Die, Scandal in a Small Town, Trouble in Paradise, Tainted Blood, Judith Krantz's Torch Song, Hollyrock-a-Bye Baby (voice). *Guest*: Cher, The Muppet Show, Saturday Night Live.

WELD, TUESDAY
Actress. r.n. Susan Weld. b. New York, NY, Aug. 27, 1943. m. violinist Pinchas Zuckerman. e. Hollywood Professional Sch. Began modeling at 4 yrs.
PICTURES: Rock Rock Rock (debut, 1956), Rally 'Round the Flag Boys! The Five Pennies, Because They're Young, High Time, Sex Kittens Go to College, The Private Lives of Adam and Eve, Return to Peyton Place, Wild in the Country, Bachelor Flat, Soldier in the Rain, I'll Take Sweden, The Cincinnati Kid, Lord Love a Duck, Pretty Poison, I Walk the Line, A Safe Place, Play It As It Lays, Looking for Mr. Goodbar (Acad. Award nom.), Who'll Stop the Rain, Serial, Thief, Author! Author!, Once Upon a Time in America, Heartbreak Hotel, Falling Down.
TELEVISION: *Series*: The Many Loves of Dobie Gillis (1959-60). *Movies*: Reflections of Murder, F. Scott Fitzgerald in Hollywood, A Question of Guilt, Mother and Daughter: The Loving War, Madame X, The Winter of Our Discontent, Scorned and Swindled, Something in Common, Circle of Violence. *Special*: The Rainmaker.

WELLER, PETER
Actor. b. Stevens Point, WI, June 24, 1947. Acting since 10 years old. e. North Texas State U. Studied at American Acad. of Dramatic Arts with Uta Hagen. Member, Actor's Studio.
THEATER: Sticks and Bones (moved up from understudy, B'way debut), Full Circle, Summer Brave, Macbeth, The Wool-Gatherer, Rebel Women, Streamers, The Woods, Serenading Louie, Daddy Wolf.
PICTURES: Butch and Sundance: The Early Years (debut, 1979), Just Tell Me What You Want, Shoot the Moon, Of Unknown Origin, The Adventures of Buckaroo Banzai Across the 8th Dimension, Firstborn, Robocop, Shakedown, A Killing Affair, Leviathan, The Tunnel, Robocop 2, Cat Chaser, Naked Lunch, Fifty Fifty, Sunset Grill, The New Age, Screamers, Mighty Aphrodite, Beyond the Clouds.
TELEVISION: *Movies*: The Man Without a Country, The Silence, Kentucky Woman, Two Kinds of Love, Apology, Women & Men: Stories of Seduction (Dust Before Fireworks), Rainbow Drive, The Substitute Wife, The Road to Ruin, Decoy. *Guest*: Lou Grant, Exit 10. *Special*: Partners (also dir., co-writer).

WENDERS, WIM
Director, Writer. b. Dusseldorf, Germany, August 14, 1945. Studied film 1967-70 at Filmhochschule in Munich. Worked as film critic 1968-70 for Filmkritik and Die Suddeutsche Zeitung. 1967 made first short films (Schauplatze) and three others before first feature, Summer in the City.
PICTURES: *Director-Writer*: Summer in the City (debut, 1970; also prod., actor), The Scarlet Letter, The Goalie's Anxiety at the Penalty Kick, Alice in the Cities, Wrong Move (dir. only), Kings of the Road (also prod.), The American Friend, Lightning Over Water (also actor), Chambre 66 (dir., actor), Hammett (dir. only), The State of Things, Paris Texas (dir. only), I Played It for You (dir., actor only), Tokyo-Ga (also edit.), Wings of Desire (also prod.), Notebooks on Cities and Clothes (also photog.), Until the End of the World, Faraway So Close! (also prod.), Lisbon Story, Beyond the Clouds (co-dir. & co-s.p. with Michelangelo Antonioni) *Actor only*: Long Shot, King Kong's Faust, Helsinki Napoli All Night Long, Motion and Emotion.

WENDKOS, PAUL
Director. b. Philadelphia, PA, Sept. 20, 1926. e. Temple U., Columbia, the New School.
PICTURES: The Burglar, Tarawa Beachhead, Gidget, Face of a Fugitive, Battle of the Coral Sea, Because They're Young, Angel Baby, Gidget Goes to Rome, Miles to Terror, Guns of the Magnificent Seven, Cannon for Cordova, The Mephisto Waltz, Special Delivery.
TELEVISION: Hawaii 5-0 (pilot), Fear No Evil, The Brotherhood of the Bell, Travis Logan D.A., A Tattered Web, A Little Game, A Death of Innocence, The Delphi Bureau, Haunts of the Very Rich, Footsteps, The Strangers in 7-A, Honor Thy Father, Terror on the Beach, The Underground Man, The Legend of Lizzie Borden, Death Among Friends, The Death of Ritchie, Secrets, Good Against Evil, Harold Robbins' 79 Park Avenue, A Woman Called Moses, The Ordeal of Patty Hearst, Act of Violence, Ordeal of Doctor Mudd, A Cry for Love, The Five of Me, Golden Gate, Farrell for

the People, Cocaine: One Man's Seduction, Intimate Agony, The Awakening of Candra, Celebrity, Scorned and Swindled, The Execution, The Bad Seed, Picking Up the Pieces, Rage of Angels: The Story Continues, Sister Margaret and the Saturday Night Ladies, Six Against the Rock, Right to Die, The Taking of Flight 847: The Uli Derickson Story, The Great Escape II: The Untold Story (co-dir.), From the Dead of Night, Cross of Fire, Blind Faith, Good Cops Bad Cops, The Chase, White Hot: The Murder of Thelma Todd, Guilty Until Proven Innocent, The Trail, Bloodlines.

WENDT, GEORGE
Actor. b. Chicago, IL, Oct. 17, 1948. e. Rockhurst Col. Joined Second City's acting troupe in 1973. Appeared in NBC pilot Nothing but Comedy.
PICTURES: My Bodyguard, Somewhere in Time, Airplane II: The Sequel, Jekyll & Hyde Together Again, The Woman in Red, Dreamscape, Thief of Hearts, No Small Affair, Fletch, House, Gung Ho, Plain Clothes, Guilty by Suspicion, Forever Young, The Little Rascals, Man of the House.
TELEVISION: *Series*: Making the Grade, Cheers, The George Wendt Show. *Guest*: Alice, Soap, Taxi, Hart to Hart, Saturday Night Live, Seinfeld. *Movies*: Oblomov (BBC), The Ratings Game, Hostage for a Day, Columbo: Strange Bedfellows, Shame II: The Secret, Bye Bye Birdie.

WERNER, PETER
Producer, Director. b. New York, NY, Jan. 17, 1947. e. Dartmouth Coll., AFI. Received Academy Award for short subject, In the Region of Ice, 1976.
PICTURES: Don't Cry It's Only Thunder, No Man's Land.
TELEVISION: *Director*: Battered, William Faulkner's Barnburning, Moonlighting (Emmy & D.G.A. nom.), Aunt Mary, Women in Song, Outlaws (pilot), LBJ: The Early Years. Men (exec. prod., dir.; Emmy nom.), The Image (Ace Award), Hiroshima: Out of the Ashes (D.G.A. nom.), D.E.A. (pilot), Ned Blessing (pilot), Middle Ages (co-exec. prod.), Substitute Wife, The Four Diamonds, The Unspoken Truth, Almost Golden: The Jessica Savitch Story (D.G.A. nom.), Nash Bridges (pilot), For the Love of Zachary.

WERTHEIMER, THOMAS
Executive. b. 1938. e. Princeton U., B.A. 1960; Columbia U., LLB, 1963. V.p. business affairs subs. ABC 1964-72; joined MCA Inc, 1972; v.p. Universal TV dir.; corp. v.p. 1974 -83; exec. v.p. 1983-; chmn., MCA Television and Home Entertainment Groups.

WERTMULLER, LINA
Director, Writer. b. Rome, Italy, Aug. 14, 1928. m. sculptor-set designer Enrico Job. e. Acad. of Theatre, Rome, 1951. Began working in theatre in 1951; Prod.-dir. avant-garde plays in Italy 1951-52; member puppet troupe 1952-62; actress, stage mgr., set designer, publicity writer, for theater, radio & TV, 1952-62. Began film career as asst. to Fellini on 8 1/2 in 1962. Following year wrote and directed first film, The Lizards. Had big TV success with series called Gian Burasca and then returned to theatre for a time. 1988, named Special Commissioner of Centro Sperimentale di Cinematografia. Was the first woman to be nominated for an Academy Award for Best Director (Seven Beauties, 1976).
PICTURES: *Director-Writer*. The Lizards (dir. debut, 1963), Let's Talk About Men, The Seduction of Mimi (Cannes Film Fest Award, 1972), Love and Anarchy, All Screwed Up, Swept Away... By an Unusual Destiny in the Blue Sea of August, Seven Beauties (Acad. Award noms. for dir. & s.p., 1976), The End of the World in Our Usual Bed in a Night Full of Rain, Blood Feud, A Joke of Destiny (Lying in Wait Around the Corner Like a Bandit), A Complex Plot About Women, Sotto Sotto (Softly Softly), Summer Night With Greek Profile Almond Eyes and a Scent of Basil, The Tenth One in Hiding, On a Moonlit Night, Saturday Sunday Monday, Ciao Professore!
TELEVISION: Rita the Mosquito, Il Decimo Clandestino (Cannes Fest. Award).

WEST, ADAM
Actor. b. Walla Walla, WA, Sept. 19, 1929. r.n. William West Anderson. e. Whitman Col. (B.A.), Stanford Univ. Appeared in interactive short film Ride for Your Life, and CD-ROM title The Golden Nugget.
PICTURES: The Young Philadelphians, Geronimo, Soldier in the Rain, Tammy and the Doctor, Robinson Crusoe on Mars, The Outlaws Is Coming!, Mara of the Wilderness, Batman, The Girl Who Knew Too Much, Marriage of a Young Stockbroker, The Specialist, Hell River, Hooper, The Happy Hooker Goes to Hollywood, Blonde Ambition, One Dark Night, Young Lady Chatterly, Hell Raiders, Zombie Nightmare, Doin' Time on Planet Earth, Mad About You, John Travis: Solar Survivor, Maxim Xul, Night of the Kickfighter, The New Age, Not This Part of the World, Bigger Than Watermelon, An American Vampire Story.
TELEVISION: *Series*: The Detectives, Batman, The Last Precinct, Danger Theatre, The Clinic. *Movies*: The Eyes of Charles Sands, For the Love of It, I Take These Men, Nevada

Smith, Poor Devil, The Last Precinct. *Guest*: Hawaiian Eye, 77 Sunset Strip, Bonanza, The Outer Limits, Petticoat Junction, Bewitched, The Big Valley, Love American Style, Night Gallery, Mannix, Alice, Murder She Wrote, Hope and Gloria, Lois and Clark, Burke's Law, The Simpsons (voice), The Critic (voice), Batman (animated series; voice), Politically Incorrect, Weird Science, Rugrats (voice), Animaniacs (voice). *Pilots*: Lookwell, 1775, Reel Life, Doc Holliday, Burnett, Johnny Cinderella, Alexander the Great.

WEST, TIMOTHY
Actor. b. Yorkshire, England, Oct. 20, 1934. m. actress Prunella Scales. e. John Lyon Sch. Harow. Ent. ind. 1960. Began acting 1956 after two years as recording engineer. Worked in regional repertory, London's West End and for Royal Shakespeare Company. Dec., 1979 appointed artistic controller of Old Vic. Has directed extensively in the theatre.
PICTURES: Twisted Nerve, The Looking Glass War, Nicholas and Alexandra, The Day of the Jackal, Hedda, Joseph Andrews, The Devil's Advocate, Agatha, The Thirty Nine Steps, Rough Cut, Cry Freedom, Consuming Passions.
TELEVISION: Edward VII, Hard Times, Crime and Punishment, Henry VIII, Churchill and the Generals, Brass, The Monocled Mutineer, The Good Doctor Bodkin Adams, What the Butler Saw, Harry's Kingdom, The Train, When We Are Married, Breakthrough at Reykjavik, Strife, A Shadow on the Sun, The Contractor, Blore, m.p., Survival of the Fittest, Oliver Twist, Why Lockerbie, Framed, Smokescreen, Eleven Men Against Eleven, Cuts, The Place of the Dead.

WESTON, JAY
Producer. b. New York, NY, March 9, 1929. e. New York U. Operated own pub. agency before moving into film prod. In 1965 launched Weston Production; sold orig. s.p., The War Horses, to Embassy Pictures; acquired and marketed other properties. Became prod. story exec. for Palomar-ABC Pictures in 1967.
THEATER: Does a Tiger Wear a Necktie? (co-prod.).
PICTURES: For Love of Ivy (co-prod.), Lady Sings the Blues (co-prod.), W.C. Fields and Me, Chu Chu and the Philly Flash, Night of the Juggler, Buddy Buddy.
TELEVISION: Laguna Heat (exec. prod.).

WETTIG, PATRICIA
Actress. b. Cincinnati, OH, Dec. 4, 1951. m. actor Ken Olin. e. Temple Univ. Studied at Neighborhood Playhouse. Began acting career with NY's Circle Repertory Company appearing in The Wool Gatherer, The Diviners and A Tale Told. Other theatre work includes The Dining Room, Talking With (LA), Threads, Innocent Thoughts, My Mother Said I Never Should.
PICTURES: Guilty by Suspicion, City Slickers, Veronica & Me, City Slickers II: The Legend of Curly's Gold.
TELEVISION: *Series*: St. Elsewhere, thirtysomething (2 Emmy Awards), Courthouse. *Movies*: Silent Motive, Taking Back My Life: The Nancy Ziegenmeyer Story, Parallel Lives, Nothing But the Truth, Kansas. *Mini-Series*: Stephen King's The Langoliers.

WEXLER, HASKELL
Cinematographer, Director. b. Chicago, Feb. 6, 1922. Photographed educational and industrial films before features. Documentaries as cinematographer include: The Living City, The Savage Eye, T. for Tumbleweed, Stakeout on Dope Street, Brazil—A Report on Torture, Interviews With Mai Lai Veterans, Interview—Chile's President Allende, Introduction to the Enemy. Elected by AMPAS to Bd. of Governors, Cinematographers Branch. 1991, elected by AMPAS to bd. of govs., Cinematographers Branch; 1993, received lifetime achievement award from American Society of Cinematographers.
PICTURES: Studs Lonigan, Five Bold Women, The Hoodlum Priest, Angel Baby, A Face in the Rain, America America, The Best Man, The Bus (also dir., prod.), The Loved One (also co-prod.), Who's Afraid of Virginia Woolf? (Academy Award, 1966), In the Heat of the Night, The Thomas Crown Affair, Medium Cool (also dir., co-prod., s.p.), Trial of Catonsville Nine, American Graffiti, One Flew Over the Cuckoo's Nest, Bound for Glory (Academy Award, 1976), Coming Home, Days of Heaven (addit. photog.), No Nukes (also co-dir.), Second Hand Hearts, Richard Pryor: Live on the Sunset Strip, Lookin' to Get Out, The Man Who Loved Women, Matewan (Oscar nom.), Colors, Latino (dir., writer only), Three Fugitives, Blaze (Oscar nom.), Through the Wire, Other People's Money, Rolling Stones at the MAX, The Babe, The Secret of Roan Inish, Canadian Bacon, Mulholland Falls, Rich Man's Wife, IMAX: Mexico, Stakeout on Dope Street.

WHALEY, FRANK
Actor. b. Syracuse, NY, July 20, 1963. e. SUNY, Albany. With his brother formed rock band the Niagaras. Member of Malaparte Theatre Co. in NY.
THEATER: *NY*: Tigers Wild (debut, 1986), Face Divided, The Indian Wants the Bronx, The Years, Good Evening, Hesh, The Great Unwashed.

PICTURES: Ironweed (debut, 1987), Field of Dreams, Little Monsters, Born on the Fourth of July, The Freshman, Cold Dog Soup, The Doors, Career Opportunities, JFK, Back in the U.S.S.R., A Midnight Clear, Hoffa, Swing Kids, Pulp Fiction, I.Q., Swimming With Sharks, Homage, Cafe Society, Broken Arrow.
TELEVISION: Specials: Soldier Boys, Seasonal Differences. Movies: Unconquered, Flying Blind, Fatal Deception: Mrs. Lee Harvey Oswald, To Dance With the White Dog, The Desperate Trail. Pilot: Flipside. Guest: Spenser: For Hire, The Equalizer.

WHALLEY-KILMER, JOANNE
Actress. b. Manchester, England, Aug. 25, 1964. Began stage career while in teens including season of Edward Bond plays at Royal Court Theatre (Olivier Award nom.) and The Three Sisters, The Lulu Plays. NY: What the Butler Saw (Theatre World Award).
PICTURES: Dance with a Stranger, No Surrender, The Good Father, Willow, To Kill a Priest, Scandal, Kill Me Again, Navy SEALS, Crossing the Line, Shattered, Storyville, Mother's Boys, The Secret Rapture, Trial by Jury, A Good Man in Africa.
TELEVISION: The Singing Detective, A Quiet Life, Edge of Darkness, A Christmas Carol, Save Your Kisses, Will You Love Me Tomorrow, Scarlett.

WHEATON, WIL
Actor. r.n. Richard William Wheaton III. b. Burbank, CA, July 29, 1972. Began acting in commercials at age 7. Graduated L.A. Professional H.S., June, 1990.
PICTURES: The Secret of NIMH (voice), The Buddy System, Hambone and Hillie, The Last Starfighter, Stand by Me, The Curse, Toy Soldiers, December, The Liars' Club, Pie in the Sky.
TELEVISION: Series: Star Trek: The Next Generation. Pilots: Long Time Gone, 13 Thirteenth Avenue, The Man Who Fell to Earth. Movies: A Long Way Home (debut, 1981), The Defiant Ones, Young Harry Houdini, The Last Prostitute. Specials: The Shooting, My Dad Can't Be Crazy Can He?, Lifestories (A Deadly Secret). Guest: St. Elsewhere, Family Ties, Tales From the Crypt, Outer Limits.

WHITAKER, FOREST
Actor, Director. b. Longview, TX, July 15, 1961. Raised in Los Angeles. e. Pomona Col., studying music; USC, studying opera and drama. Prof. debut in prod. of The Beggar's Opera.
THEATER: Swan, Romeo and Juliet, Hamlet, Ring Around the Moon, Craig's Wife, Whose Life Is It Anyway?, The Greeks (all at Drama Studio London); School Talk (LA), Patchwork Shakespeare (CA Youth Theatre), The Beggar's Opera, Jesus Christ Superstar. Dir.: Look Back in Anger, Drums Across the Realm.
PICTURES: Tag: The Assassination Game (debut, 1982), Fast Times at Ridgemont High, Vision Quest, The Color of Money, Platoon, Stakeout, Good Morning Vietnam, Bloodsport, Bird (Cannes Film Fest. Award, 1988), Johnny Handsome, Downtown, Rage in Harlem (also co-prod.), Article 99, Diary of a Hit Man, Consenting Adults, The Crying Game, Bank Robber, Body Snatchers, Blown Away, Jason's Lyric, Ready to Wear (Pret-a-Porter), Smoke, Species, Waiting to Exhale (dir.only), Phenomenon.
TELEVISION: Movies: Hands of a Stranger, Criminal Justice, Last Light, Strapped (dir. only), Lush Life, The Enemy Within. Guest: Amazing Stories, Hill Street Blues, Cagney and Lacey, Trapper John M.D., The Fall Guy, Different Strokes. Mini-Series: North and South Parts I & II.

WHITE, BETTY
Actress. b. Oak Park, IL, Jan. 17, 1924. Graduated from Beverly Hills H.S. Performed on radio beginning in early 1940's on such shows as Blondie, The Great Gildersleeve, This Is Your FBI. Became local L.A. tv personality in early 1950's prior to starring in her first series to be seen nationwide, Life With Elizabeth, in 1953. Was married to late tv host Allen Ludden. Autobiography: Here We Go Again: My Life in Television (1995).
PICTURE: Advise and Consent.
TELEVISION: Series: Life With Elizabeth, Make the Connection (panelist), Date With the Angels, The Betty White Show (1958), The Jack Paar Show, The Pet Set, The Mary Tyler Moore Show (2 Emmy Awards: 1975, 1976), Match Game P.M. (panelist), Liar's Club (panelist), The Betty White Show (1977-78), Just Men (host; Emmy Award, 1983), Mama's Family, The Golden Girls (Emmy Award, 1986), The Golden Palace, Bob, Maybe This Time. Movies: Vanished, With This Ring, The Best Place to Be, Before and After, The Gossip Columnist, Chance of a Lifetime. Host: Macy's Thanksgiving Parade for 10 yrs, Tournament of Roses Parade (20 yrs.). Guest: The Millionaire, U.S. Steel Hour, Petticoat Junction, The Odd Couple, Sonny and Cher, The Love Boat, Hotel, Matlock, The John Laroquette Show (Emmy Award, 1996), many others.

WHITE, JESSE
Actor. r.n. Jesse Weidenfeld. b. Buffalo, NY, Jan. 3, 1918. e. Akron, OH H.S. Did odd jobs, then salesman; radio, vaude-ville, burlesque, nightclubs and little theatre work; Broadway

stage debut in Moon is Down, 1942; other shows include Harvey, Born Yesterday, etc. Played Maytag repairman on long-running tv commercial 1967-89.
PICTURES: Harvey (debut, 1950), Death of a Salesman, Callaway Went Thataway, Million Dollar Mermaid, Witness to Murder, Forever Female, Not as a Stranger, The Bad Seed, Back from Eternity, Designing Woman, Marjorie Morningstar, The Rise and Fall of Legs Diamond, A Fever in the Blood, Sail a Crooked Ship, It's Only Money, The Yellow Canary, It's a Mad Mad Mad Mad World, Looking For Love, A House Is Not a Home, Dear Brigitte, The Reluctant Astronaut, Bless the Beasts and Children, The Cat from Outer Space, Monster in the Closet, Matinee.
TELEVISION: Series: Private Secretary, The Danny Thomas Show, The Ann Sothern Show.

WHITE, LEONARD
Executive. Chairman & CEO, Orion Pictures Corporation.

WHITE, ROY B.
Executive, Exhibitor. b. Cincinnati, OH, July 30, 1926. e. U. of Cincinnati. Flight engineer, U.S. Air Force during WWII; sales department of 20th Century-Fox, 1949-52; began in exhibition, 1952; past pres., Mid-States Theatres; chmn. R. M. White Management, Inc.; past president, National Association of Theatre Owners, past Chairman of the Board, NATO, Board of Trustees—American Film Inst.; bd.of dirs. NATO of Ohio, Motion Picture Pioneers Foundation; Will Rogers Hospital, Nat'l. Endowment for Arts.

WHITELAW, BILLIE
C.B.E., D.Litt.: Actress. b. Coventry, England, June 6, 1932. Acted on radio and television since childhood. Winner of the TV Actress of the Year and 1972, Guild Award, Best Actress, 1960. British Acad. Award 1969; U.S. National Society of Film Critics Award best supp. actress, 1968. Evening News, Best Film Actress, 1977; best actress Sony Radio Radio Award 1987, 1989. 1988 Evening Standard Award for best Actress.
THEATER: England Our England (revue), Progress to the Park, A Touch of the Poet, Othello; 3 yrs. with Natl. Theatre of Great Britain; Trelawney of the Wells, After Haggerty, Not I, Alphabetical Order, Footfalls, Molly, The Greeks, Happy Days, Passion Play, Rockaby (also in N.Y. and Adelaide Festival), Tales from Hollywood, Who's Afraid of Virginia Woolf?
PICTURES: The Fake (debut, 1953), Companions in Crime, The Sleeping Tiger, Room in the House, Small Hotel, Miracle in Soho, Gideon of Scotland Yard, Carve Her Name With Pride, Bobbikins, Mania, Hell Is a City, Make Mine Mink, No Love for Johnnie, Mr. Topaze (I Like Money), Payroll, The Devil's Agent, The Comedy Man, Charlies Bubbles, The Adding Machine, Twisted Nerve, Start the Revolution Without Me, Leo the Last, Eagle in a Cage, Gumshoe, Frenzy, Night Watch, The Omen, Leopard in the Snow, The Water Babies, An Unsuitable Job for a Woman, The Dark Crystal (voice), Tangier, Slayground, Shadey, The Chain, Murder Elite, Maurice, The Dressmaker, Joyriders, The Krays, Freddie as F.R.O.7 (voice), Deadly Advice.
TELEVISION: Over 100 leading roles including: No Trains to Lime Street, Lady of the Camelias, Resurrection, Beyond the Horizon, Anna Christie, You and Me, A World of Time, Dr. Jekyll and Mr. Hyde, Poet Game, Sextet (8 plays for BBC), Wessex Tales, The Fifty Pound Note, Supernatural (2 plays), Four plays by Samuel Beckett, Eustace and Hilda, The Oresteia of Aeschylus, The Haunted Man, Private Schultz, Jamaica Inn, Happy Days, Camille, Imaginary Friends, The Secret Garden, The Picnic, A Tale of Two Cities, The Fifteen Streets, Three Beckett plays, Lorna Doone, Duel of Love, A Murder of Quality, The Cloning of Joanna May, The Entertainer, Firm Friends, Skallagrigg.

WHITEMORE, HUGH
Writer. b. England, 1936. Studied acting at Royal Acad. of Dramatic Art. Has since written for television, film, theatre.
THEATER: Stevie, Pack of Lies, Breaking the Code, The Best of Friends, It's Ralph.
PICTURES: All Neat in Black Stockings, All Creatures Great and Small, Stevie, The Return of the Soldier, 84 Charing Cross Road, Utz, Jane Eyre.
TELEVISION: Cider With Rosie (Writers' Guild Award 1971), Elizabeth R (Emmy Award, 1971), Country Matters (Writers' Guild Award, 1972), Dummy (RAT—Prix Italia, 1979), Rebecca, All For Love, A Dedicated Man, Down at the Hydro, A Bit of Singing and Dancing, Concealed Enemies (Emmy & Neil Simon Awards, 1984), Pack of Lies, The Final Days, The Best of Friends, The Turn of the Screw.

WHITMAN, STUART
Actor. b. San Francisco, CA., Feb. 1, 1928. Army Corp. of Engineers (1945-1948), at Fort Lewis, WA; while in army, competed as light heavyweight boxer. Studied drama under G.I. Bill at Ben Bard Drama Sch. and L.A. City Coll. Performed in Heaven Can Wait and became member of Michael Chekhov Stage Society and Arthur Kennedy Group. Entered films in early 1950's. TV debut on 26 episodes of Highway Patrol.

PICTURES: When Worlds Collide, The Day The Earth Stood Still, Rhapsody, Seven Men From Now, War Drums, Johnny Trouble, Darby's Rangers, Ten North Frederick, The Decks Ran Red, China Doll, The Sound and the Fury, These Thousand Hills, Hound Dog Man, The Story of Ruth, Murder Inc., Francis of Assisi, The Fiercest Heart, The Mark (Acad. Award nom.), The Comancheros, Convicts 4, The Longest Day, The Day and the Hour (Fr./It.), Shock Treatment, Rio Conchos, Those Magnificent Men In Their Flying Machines, Sands of the Kalahari, Signpost to Murder, An American Dream, The Invincible Six, The Last Escape, Captain Apache (US/Sp.), Night Of The Lepus, Welcome To Arrow Beach (Tender Flesh), Crazy Mama, Call Him Mr. Shatter, Assault on Paradise (Maniac/Ransom), Mean Johnny Barrows, Las Vegas Lady, Eaten Alive!, Tony Saitta/Tough Tony (It.), Strange Shadows In An Empty Room, Ruby, The White Buffalo; Delta Fox, Thoroughbred (Run for the Roses), Oil (It. as Red Adair), La Murjer de la Tierra Caliente (Sp./It.); Guyana: Cult of the Damned, Cuba Crossing, Jamaican Gold, The Monster Club, Demonoid, Butterfly, Treasure of The Amazon, John Travis: Solar Survivor, Deadly Reactor, Moving Target, Mob Boss, Private Wars, Trail by Jury, Improper Conduct, Land of Milk and Honey.
TELEVISION: Series: Cimarron Strip, Shaunessy (pilot). Guest: The Crowd Pleaser (Alcoa-Goodyear), Highway Patrol, Dr. Christian, Hangman's Noose (Zane Grey), Walker Texas Ranger, Adventures of Brisco County Jr., Time Trax, Courthouse. Mini-Series: The Last Convertible, Hemingway. Movies: The Man Who Wanted to Live Forever, City Beneath the Sea, Revenge, The Woman Hunter, The Man Who Died Twice, Cat Creature, Go West Young Girl, The Pirate, Women in White, The Seekers, Condominium, Stillwatch, Once Upon a Texas Train, Wounded Heart.

WHITMORE, JAMES
Actor. r.n. James Allen Whitmore, Jr. b. White Plains, NY, Oct. 1, 1921. e. Yale U. In Yale Drama Sch. players; co-founder Yale radio station, 1942; U.S. Marine Corps, W.W.II; in USO, in American Wing Theatre school, in stock. Broadway debut in Command Decision, 1947.
THEATER: Give 'em Hell Harry, Will Rogers USA, Almost an Eagle.
PICTURES: The Undercover Man (debut, 1949), Battleground (Acad. Award nom.), The Asphalt Jungle, The Next Voice You Hear, Mrs. O'Malley and Mr. Malone, The Outriders, Please Believe Me, Across the Wide Missouri, It's a Big Country, Because You're Mine, Above and Beyond, The Girl Who Had Everything, All the Brothers Were Valiant, Kiss Me Kate, The Command, Them!, Battle Cry, The McConnell Story, The Last Frontier (Savage Wilderness), Oklahoma!, Crime in the Streets, The Eddie Duchin Story, The Deep Six, Face of Fire, Who Was That Lady?, Black Like Me, Chuka, Waterhole No. 3, Nobody's Perfect, Planet of the Apes, Madigan, The Split, Guns of the Magnificent Seven, Tora! Tora! Tora!, Chato's Land, The Harrad Experiment, Where the Red Fern Grows, Give 'em Hell Harry (Acad. Award nom.), The Serpent's Egg, Bully, The First Deadly Sin, The Adventures of Mark Twain (voice), Nuts, Old Explorers, The Shawshank Redemption.
TELEVISION: Series: The Law and Mr. Jones, My Friend Tony, Temperature's Rising. Movies: The Challenge, If Tomorrow Comes, I Will Fight No More Forever, Rage, Mark I Love You, Glory! Glory!, Sky High. Mini-Series: The Word, Celebrity, Favorite Son. Special: All My Sons.

WHITTON, MARGARET
Actress. b. Baltimore, MD, Nov. 30, 1950. Raised in Haddonfield, NJ. Has written articles for Village Voice, The National.
THEATER: NY: Nourish the Beast (Off-B'way debut, 1973), Another Language, The Art of Dining, Chinchilla, Othello, One Tiger to a Hill, Henry IV Part 1, Don Juan, Steaming, Aunt Dan and Lemon, Ice Cream/Hot Fudge. Regional: Hamlet, Camille, Time and the Conways, The House of Blue Leaves.
PICTURES: National Lampoon Goes to the Movies (debut, 1981), Love Child, The Best of Times, 9-1/2 Weeks, The Secret of My Success, Ironweed, Major League, Little Monsters, Big Girl Don't Cry... They Get Even, The Man Without a Face, Major League 2, Trial by Jury.
TELEVISION: Series: Search for Tomorrow, Hometown, A Fine Romance, Good and Evil. Special: Motherlove. Movies: The Summer My Father Grew Up, Menendez: A Killing in Beverly Hills.

WICKES, MARY
Actress. r.n. Mary Wickenhauser. b. St. Louis, MO. e. Washington U., St. Louis (A.B., D. Arts, Hon.); post-grad, UCLA. Lecturer, seminars on acting in comedy, Coll. of Wm. & Mary, Washington U. at St. Louis, Am. Conserv. Th. in S.F. Debut at Berkshire Playhouse, Stockbridge, MA. Bd. of dir., Med. Aux Center for Health Sciences, UCLA, 1977-1995; L.A. Oncologic Inst., 1987-1995.
THEATER: (B'way) Stage Door, Father Malachy's Miracle, The Man Who Came to Dinner, Jackpot, Hollywood Pinafore, Town House, Park Avenue, Oklahoma! (revival). Stock and regional

theatre at Mark Taper Forum, Ahmanson and Chandler Pavillion (L.A.), Berkshire Playhouse in Stockbridge, Cape Playhouse in Dennis (MA), Amer. Conservatory Theatre (San Francisco), and many others.
PICTURES: The Man Who Came to Dinner (debut, 1941), Now Voyager, Who Done It?, Mayor of 44th Street, How's About It?, Higher and Higher, Happy Land, Rhythm of the Islands, My Kingdom for a Cook, Decision of Christopher Blake, June Bride, Anna Lucasta, Petty Girl, I'll See You in My Dreams, On Moonlight Bay, The Story of Will Rogers, Young Man With Ideas, By the Light of the Silvery Moon, Half a Hero, The Actress, White Christmas, Proud Rebel, Dance With Me Henry, Don't Go Near the Water, It Happened to Jane, Sins of Rachel Cade, Cimarron (1961), The Music Man, Fate is the Hunter, Dear Heart, How to Murder Your Wife, The Trouble With Angels, The Spirit Is Willing, Where Angels Go Trouble Follows, Snowball Express, Touched By Love, Postcards from the Edge, Sister Act, Sister Act 2: Back in the Habit, Little Women, The Hunchback of Notre Dame (voice).
TELEVISION: Series: Halls of Ivy, Mrs. G Goes to College, Dennis the Menace, Doc, Sigmund and the Sea Monsters, Father Dowling Mysteries. Guest: Make Room for Daddy, Lucy Show, M*A*S*H, Wonderworks (The Canterville Ghost), Studio One (Mary Poppins, Miss Hargreaves, The Storm), Highway to Heaven, You Can't Take It With You, Murder She Wrote. Movies: The Monk, Willa.
(d. October 24, 1995)

WIDMARK, RICHARD
Actor. b. Sunrise, MN, Dec. 26, 1914. e. Lake Forest U. Was drama instructor, 1936, before going to NY where he acted on many radio dramas, then stage.
PICTURES: Kiss of Death (debut, 1947), Road House, Street With No Name, Yellow Sky, Down to the Sea in Ships, Slattery's Hurricane, Night and the City, Panic in the Streets, No Way Out, Halls of Montezuma, The Frogmen, Red Skies of Montana, Don't Bother to Knock, O. Henry's Full House, My Pal Gus, Destination Gobi, Pickup on South Street, Take the High Ground, Garden of Evil, Hell & High Water, Broken Lance, Prize of Gold, The Cobweb, Backlash, Run for the Sun, The Last Wagon, Saint Joan, Time Limit, The Law and Jake Wade, The Tunnel of Love, The Trap, Warlock, The Alamo, The Secret Ways, Two Rode Together, Judgment at Nuremberg, How the West Was Won, Flight from Ashiya, The Long Ships, Cheyenne Autumn, The Bedford Incident, Alvarez Kelly, The Way West, Madigan, Death of a Gunfighter, A Talent for Loving, The Moonshine War, When The Legends Die, Murder on the Orient Express, The Sell Out, To the Devil a Daughter, Twilight's Last Gleaming, The Domino Principle, Rollercoaster, Coma, The Swarm, Dinero Maldito, Bear Island, National Lampoon Goes to the Movies, Hanky Panky, Who Dares Wins, The Final Option, Against All Odds, True Colors.
TELEVISION: Series: Madigan. Movies: Vanished, Brock's Last Case, The Last Day, Mr. Horn, All God's Children, A Whale for the Killing, Blackout, A Gathering of Old Men, Once Upon a Texas Train, Cold Sassy Tree. Special: Benjamin Franklin.

WIESEN, BERNARD
Producer, Director, Writer, Executive. b. New York, NY. e. City Coll. of New York, B.A.; Pasadena Playhouse Coll. of Theatre, Master of Theatre Arts; Dramatic Workshop of New School.
THEATER: First Monday in October (B'way, co. prod).
PICTURES: Producer-Director: Fear No More. Asst. Dir.: The King and I, The Left Hand of God, The Rains of Ranchipur, To Catch a Thief, The Trouble with Harry.
TELEVISION: Director: How to Marry a Millionaire, Valentine's Day. Assoc. Producer: Valentine's Day, Three on an Island, Cap'n Ahab, Sally and Sam. Assoc. Prod.: Daniel Boone. Producer/Director: Julia, Co-Producer-Director: The Jimmy Stewart Show. Prod. Exec.: Executive Suite (pilot). Exec. Paramount TV, director of current programming. Writer: Love 4 Love, The Grand Turk.

WIEST, DIANNE
Actress. b. Kansas City, MO, March 28, 1948. e. U. of Maryland. Studied ballet but abandoned it for theatre. Did regional theatre work (Yale Repertory, Arena Stage), per-formed with NY Shakespeare Festival, toured with American Shakespeare Co.
THEATER: Regional: Arena Stage (DC): Heartbreak House, Our Town, The Dybbuk, Inherit the Wind. Yale Rep.: Hedda Gabler, A Doll's House. NY: Ashes (NY debut, 1977, at Public Theatre), Agamemnon, Leave It to Beaver Is Dead, The Art of Dining (Obie & Theatre World Awards), Bonjour La Bonjour, Frankenstein (B'way), Three Sisters, Othello, Beyond Therapy, Other Places, Serenading Louie (Obie Award), After the Fall, Not About Heroes (dir.; also at Williamstown Fest.), Hunting Cockroaches, Square One, In the Summer House, Blue Light.
PICTURES: It's My Turn (debut, 1980), I'm Dancing as Fast as I Can, Independence Day, Footloose, Falling in Love, The Purple Rose of Cairo, Hannah and Her Sisters (Academy

Award, supporting actress, 1986), Radio Days, The Lost Boys, September, Bright Lights Big City, Parenthood (Acad. Award nom.), Cookie, Edward Scissorhands, Little Man Tate, Cops and Robbersons, The Scout, Bullets Over Broadway (Academy Award, best supporting actress, 1994; also Golden Globe, NY Film Critics, LA Film Critics, Natl. Board of Review Awards), Drunks, The Birdcage, The Associate.
TELEVISION: *Specials*: Zalman or the Madness of God, Out of Our Father's House. *Movies*: The Wall, The Face of Rage.

WIGAN, GARETH
Executive. b. London, England, Dec. 2, 1931. e. Oxford. Agent, MCA London; 1957; John Redway & Associates, 1960; co-founder, agent Gregson & Wigan Ltd., 1961; co-founder, agent London Intl., 1968; independent prod., 1970; v.p., creative affairs, 20th Century Fox, 1975; v.p., prod., Fox, 1976; v.p., The Ladd Co., 1979 -83. Company W.W. Prods. Currently exec. production consultant, Columbia Pictures.
PICTURES: Unman Wittering & Zigo, Running Scared.

WIHTOL, ARN S.
Executive. b. Millville, NJ, Sept. 4, 1944. e. San Jose State. Exec. v.p., international sales, Pacific International Enterprises.
PICTURES: *Production Exec., Co-Writer*: Mystery Mansion. Casting, *Controller*: Dream Chasers. *Producer's asst.*: Sacred Ground.

WILBY, JAMES
Actor. b. Rangoon, Burma, Feb. 20, 1958. Lived a nomadic childhood moving from Burma to Ceylon, then Jamaica and finally England. e. Durham U. Trained at Royal Acad. of Dramatic Art where he played Shakespearean roles and landed a part in Oxford Film Foundation's Privileged (1982). West End stage debut Another Country. Also acted in regional theater. 1988: The Common Pursuit.
PICTURES: Privileged (debut, 1982), Dreamchild, Maurice, A Handful of Dust, A Summer Story, Immaculate Conception, Howards End, The Chess Game, Une Partie d'Echec.
TELEVISION: Dutch Girls, A Tale of Two Cities, Mother Love, Tell Me That You Love Me, Adam Bede, Lady Chatterly, You Me and It, Crocodile Shoes.

WILDE, ARTHUR L.
Publicist. b. San Francisco, CA, May 27. S.F. Daily News; Matson Lines; pub. dept., Warner Bros., 1936; photo editor at Columbia Pictures, RKO Pictures, Universal Pictures; dir. exploitation, CBS; pub. dir., Hal Wallis Prod.; pub. dept., Paramount; pub., Hecht-Hill-Lancaster; v.p., Arthur Jacobs, public rel.; Blowitz-Maskell Publicity Agency; pub. dir., C. V. Whitney Pictures; gen. v.p., 1958; owner, pub.-ad. agency, The Arthur L. Wilde Co., 1961-65; freelance publicist, 1965-66; pub. rel. consultant, Marineland of Florida 1965; unit publicity dir., United Artists, National General, Paramount, 1966-69; freelance publicity, 1971; unit publicist, MGM, Paramount, United Artists, 1972-74; staff position; Features Publicity at Paramount Pictures, 1973. Freelance unit publicist again in 1976 at Universal, Paramount and Lorimar Productions. 1978-79, Columbia Pictures & Universal Studios; 1980, Marble Arch. Prods. & Northstar Intl. Productions; 1981, studio pub. mgr. 20th Century-Fox; recently staff unit publicist for 20th-Fox; 1984-89; currently freelance unit publicist for feature films.

WILDER, BILLY
Director, Writer, Producer. r.n. Samuel Wilder. b. Austria, June 22, 1906. Newspaperman in Vienna and Berlin; then author of screen story People on Sunday (debut, 1929) followed by 10 other German films. including Emil and the Detectives (s.p.). Co-dir. French film Mauvaise Graine with Alexander Esway (also story), marking debut as director, 1933. To Hollywood 1934. Head of Film Section, Psych. Warfare Div., U.S. Army, 1945, American Zone, Germany. Recipient: American Film Institute Life Achievement Award, 1987; Irving Thalberg Memorial Award, 1988.
PICTURES: *U.S.: Co-Writer*: Adorable (co-story), Music in the Air, Lottery Lover, Champagne Waltz (co-story), Bluebeard's Eighth Wife, Midnight, Ninotchka, What a Life, Rhythm on the River (co-story), Arise My Love, Ball of Fire, Hold Back the Dawn. *Director/Co-Writer*: The Major and the Minor (U.S. dir. debut, 1942), Five Graves to Cairo, Double Indemnity, The Lost Weekend (Academy Awards for Best Director and Adapted Screenplay, 1945), The Emperor Waltz, A Foreign Affair, Sunset Boulevard (Academy Award for Best Original Story & Screenplay, 1950). *Director-Co-Writer-Producer*: Ace in the Hole (The Big Carnival), Stalag 17, Sabrina, The Seven Year Itch (dir. & co-s.p. only), The Spirit of St. Louis, Love in the Afternoon, Witness for the Prosecution (dir. & co-s.p. only), Some Like It Hot, The Apartment (Academy Awards for Best Picture, Director and Original Story & Screenplay, 1960), One Two Three, Irma La Douce, Kiss Me Stupid, The Fortune Cookie, The Private Life of Sherlock Holmes, Avanti!, The Front Page (dir. & co-s.p. only), Fedora, Buddy Buddy (dir. & co-s.p. only).

WILDER, GENE
Actor, Director, Writer. r.n. Jerry Silberman. b. Milwaukee, WI, June 11, 1935. e. U. of Iowa. Joined Bristol Old Vic company in England, became champion fencer; in NY, worked as chauffeur, fencing instructor, etc. before NY off-B'way debut in Roots. Co-founder of Gilda's Club, a cancer support center in Manhattan.
THEATER: *B'way*: The Complacent Lover, Mother Courage, Luv, One Flew Over the Cuckoo's Nest.
PICTURES: Bonnie and Clyde (debut, 1967), The Producers (Acad. Award nom.), Start the Revolution Without Me, Quackser Fortune Has a Cousin in the Bronx, Willy Wonka and the Chocolate Factory, Everything You Always Wanted to Know About Sex* But Were Afraid to Ask, Rhinoceros, Blazing Saddles, The Little Prince, Young Frankenstein (also co-s.p.), The Adventure of Sherlock Holmes' Smarter Brother (also dir., s.p.), Silver Streak, The World's Greatest Lover (also dir., s.p., prod.), The Frisco Kid, Stir Crazy, Sunday Lovers (also dir. & s.p.; episode: Skippy), Hanky Panky, The Woman in Red (also dir., s.p.), Haunted Honeymoon (also dir., s.p., prod.), See No Evil Hear No Evil (also co-s.p.), Funny About Love, Another You.
TELEVISION: *Series*: Something Wilder. *Specials*: The Man Who Refused to Die, Death of a Salesman (1966), The Scarecrow, Acts of Love—And Other Comedies, Annie and the Hoods, The Trouble With People, Marlo Thomas Special. *Movie*: Thursday's Game.

WILLENBORG, GREGORY H.
Producer. b. Miami, FL, Feb. 18, 1959. e. Geroge Washington U., B.B.A. 1981; UCLA M.B.A. Marketing & Strategic Planning 1983. During grad. school, worked at the political fundraising firm of Lynn, Bryan & Associates. In 1983, he formed Willenborg & Associates, a consulting grp. specializing in marketing and fundraising. Raised 25 million for the Bob Hope Cultural Center in Palm Desert, CA.
TELEVISION: America's Hope Awards (creator), America's Dance Awards (creator), America's Hope Award Honoring Bob Hope, America's All-Star Tribute to Elizabeth Taylor, Ray Charles: 50 Years in Music, An All-Star Tribute to Oprah Winfrey, Jerry Herman's Broadway at the Hollywood Bowl.

WILLIAMS, ANDY
Singer, Performer. b. Wall Lake, IA, Dec. 3, 1927. Sang as teen with brothers, performing on radio in Des Moines, Chicago, and Los Angeles. William Brothers were back up singers on Bing Crosby's hit recording of Swinging on a Star. Andy dubbed singing voice of Lauren Bacall in To Have and Have Not. Went solo after group disbanded in early 1950's.
PICTURES: Something to Sing About, I'd Rather Be Rich.
TELEVISION: *Series*: The College Bowl, Tonight (with Steve Allen; 1954-57), The Andy Williams and June Valli Show, The Chevy Showroom, The Andy Williams Show (1958), The Andy Williams Show (1962-67, 1969-71), The Andy Williams Show (synd.: 1976-77). *Specials*: Love Andy, Kaleidoscope Company, Magic Lantern Show Company, The NBC Kids Search for Santa, The NBC Kids Easter in Rome, many Christmas specials.

WILLIAMS, BERT
Executive, Actor. b. Newark, NJ, April 12, 1922. e. USC. Navy, 1942-45. Summer Stock, 1940-41; world's prof. diving champion, 1945-48; star diver, Larry Crosby, Buster Crabbe, Johnny Weismuller, Dutch Smith Shows, 1945-48; writer, asst. prod., Martin Mooney Prods., PRC, Goldwyn Studios; pres., Bert Prods., Bert Williams Motion Picture Producers and Distributors, Inc. Member, MP Academy of Fine Arts & TV Academy of Arts & Science. Masters Outdoor & Indoor National Diving, 1985-87, 89, 90. 1989 World Masters Diving Champion; 1990 & 1994 World Games Diving Champion.
THEATER: Cat on a Hot Tin Roof, Hamlet, Run From The Hunter, Sugar and Spice, Hope Is a Thing Called Feathers, 69 Below, Tribute.
PICTURES: *Actor*: Fort Apache, Rio Grande, American Bandito, Angel Baby; The Nest of the Cuckoo Birds (also prod., dir.), Around the World Under the Sea, Deathwatch 28 (s.p.), Gambit, No Secret, This Must be the Last Day of Summer, Twenty Eight Watched (dir.), Adventure To Treasure Reef (prod., dir.), Knife Fighters (s.p.). Black Freedom; A Crime of Sex, The Masters (prod., dir.), Crazy Joe, Serpico, Lady Ice, The Klansman, Report to the Commissioner, Tracks, All the President's Men, From Noon Till Three, While Buffalo, Shark Bait (s.p.), The Big Bus, Wanda Nevada, Cuba Crossing, Sunnyside, Cuba, The Last Resort, The All Night Treasure Hunt. Tom Horn, Kill Castro, Midnight Madness, The All-American Hustler, 10 to Midnight, Police Academy 2, One More Werewolf Picture, Silent Scream, Murphy's Law, Cobra, Assassinations, Penitentiary III, Messenger of Death, Death Under the Rock, Innocent Blood, Public Access, Tropic of Desire, Duel at Pueblo Solo, Project Eliminators, No Secret, Usual Suspect.
TELEVISION: Flipper, Sea Hunt, Final Judgment, Project Eliminator, Speargun, Gentle Ben, The Law (pilot) and Police Story (actor), Get Christy Love, General Hospital, Columbo,

Brenner for the People, Mayday 40,000 Feet, Jigsaw John (Blue Knight episode), Police Woman, Chips, Mobil One, Street Killing, East of Eden, Rose for Emily, Brett Maverick, Today's F.B.I., The Judge, Fifth St. Gym (also prod., dir., s.p.; pilot), Helter Skelter, The Green Eyed Bear, The Amazing Howard Hughes, Mike Douglas Show, Johnny Carson Show, Tales from the Dark Side, The Last Car, This Is the Life, Deadly Intentions, Divorce Court, Man Who Broke 1000 Chains, Nightmare Classics (Eye of the Panther), Man from Atlantis, Land's End.

WILLIAMS, BILLY DEE
Actor. b. New York, NY, April 6, 1937. e. National Acad. of Fine Arts and Design. Studied acting with Paul Mann and Sidney Poitier at actor's workshop in Harlem. Was child actor in the Firebrand of Florence with Lotte Lenya; Broadway adult debut in The Cool World in 1961.
THEATER: A Taste of Honey, Hallelujah Baby, I Have a Dream, Fences.
PICTURES: The Last Angry Man (debut, 1959), The Out-of-Towners, The Final Comedown, Lady Sings the Blues, Hit!, The Take, Mahogany, The Bingo Long Travelling All-Stars and Motor Kings, Scott Joplin, The Empire Strikes Back, Nighthawks, Return of the Jedi, Marvin and Tige, Fear City, Number One with a Bullet, Deadly Illusion, Batman, The Pit and the Pendulum, Driving Me Crazy, Giant Steps, Alien Intruder.
TELEVISION: Series: The Guiding Light, Double Dare. Mini-Series: Chiefs. Movies: Carter's Army, Brian's Song, The Glass House, Christmas Lilies of the Field, Children of Divorce, The Hostage Tower, The Imposter, Courage, Oceans of Fire, The Right of the People, Dangerous Passion, The Jacksons: An American Dream, Marked for Murder, Percy & Thunder, Heaven & Hell: North and South Book III, Falling for You. Guest: The F.B.I., The Interns, Mission Impossible, Mod Squad, Dynasty, In Living Color.

WILLIAMS, CARA
Actress. r.n. Bernice Kamiat. b. Brooklyn, NY, June 29, 1925. e. Hollywood Professional Sch. Ent. ind., 20th Century Fox, child actress.
PICTURES: The Happy Land (debut, 1943), Something for the Boys, In the Meantime Darling, Boomerang!, Don Juan Quilligan, Sitting Pretty, The Saxon Charm, Knock on Any Door, The Girl Next Door, Monte Carlo Baby, The Great Diamond Robbery, Meet Me in Las Vegas, The Helen Morgan Story, Never Steal Anything Small, The Defiant Ones (Acad. Award nom.), The Man from the Diners' Club, Doctors' Wives, The White Buffalo.
TELEVISION: Series: Pete and Gladys, The Cara Williams Show, Rhoda. Guest: Alfred Hitchcock Presents, Desilu Playhouse, The Jackie Gleason Show, Henry Fonda Special.

WILLIAMS, CARL W.
Executive. b. Decatur, IL, March 9, 1927. e. Illinois State Normal U., B.S., 1949; UCLA, M.A., 1950. dir. adv. photo., Clark Equipment Co., 1951-54; film dir., WKAR-TV, E. Lansing, MI, 1954-56; Prod., dir., Capital Films, E. Lansing, MI, 1957; dir., A-V Laboratory, U.C.L.A., 1957-63; co-dev. Dimension 150 Widescreen process, 1957; formed D-150 Inc., 1963; Filbert Co., 1970, v.p.; 1977; v.p.; Cinema Equipment Sales of Calif., Inc., 1986; pres. 1992. Member: AMPAS, SMPTE, AFI.

WILLIAMS, CINDY
Actress. b. Van Nuys, CA., Aug. 22, 1947. e. Los Angeles City Coll. Appeared in high school and college plays; first prof. role in Roger Corman's film Gas-s-s-s. Made TV debut in Room 222 and had recurring role.
PICTURES: Gas-s-s-s (debut, 1970), Beware! the Blob, Drive He Said, The Christian Licorice Store, Travels With My Aunt, American Graffiti, The Conversation, Mr. Ricco, The First Nudie Musical, More American Graffiti, UFOria, Rude Awakening, Big Man on Campus, Bingo!, Father of the Bride II (co-prod. only), Meet Wally Sparks.
TELEVISION: Series: The Funny Side, Laverne and Shirley, Normal Life, Getting By. Guest: Barefoot in the Park, My World and Welcome to It, Love American Style, Nanny and the Professor, Getting Together, Lois and Clark. Movies: The Migrants, Helped Wanted: Kids, Save the Dog, Tricks of the Trade, The Leftovers, Perry Mason: The Case of the Poisoned Pen, Menu for Murder (Murder at the PTA Luncheon), Earth Angel, Escape From Terror: The Teresa Stamper Story. Special: The Laverne and Shirley Reunion. Pilot: Steel Magnolias, The Neighbors.

WILLIAMS, CLARENCE, III
Actor. b. New York, NY, Aug. 21, 1939. B'way stage: Slow Dance on the Killing Ground (Tony nom.; Theatre World Award), The Great Indoors, Night and Day.
PICTURES: Rituals, The End, Judgment, Road to Galveston, Purple Rain, 52 Pick-Up, Tough Guys Don't Dance, I'm Gonna Git You Sucka, My Heroes Have Always Been Cowboys, Deep Cover, Dead Fall, Sugar Hill, Tales From the Hood, The Immortals.

TELEVISION: Series: The Mod Squad. Guest: The Nasty Boys, Crazy Love, Miami Vice, Twin Peaks, Uptown Undercover, Cosby Mysteries. Movies: The Return of the Mod Squad, Against the Wall.

WILLIAMS, ELMO
Film Editor, Director, Producer. b. Oklahoma City, OK, Apr. 30, 1913. Film editor 1933-39, with British & Dominion Studio, England. Since then with RKO-Radio as film editor for numerous major productions; mgr., dir., 20th Century Fox Prod. Ltd. v.p., worldwide production, 20th Century-Fox Film 1971. President Ibex Films. Exec. v.p., Gaylord Prods., 1979; promoted to pres., worldwide prods.
PICTURES: High Noon (edit; Academy Award, 1952), Tall Texan (dir., edit.), The Cowboy (prod., dir., edit.), 20,000 Leagues Under the Sea (edit.), Apache Kid (dir.), The Vikings (2nd unit dir., film ed.), The Big Gamble (2nd Unit dir.), The Longest Day (assoc. prod.), Zorba the Greek (exec. prod.), Those Magnificent Men in Their Flying Machines (exec. prod.), The Blue Max (exec. prod.), Tora! Tora! Tora! (prod.), Sidewinder One (edit.), Caravans (edit.), Man Woman and Child (prod.).
TELEVISION: Tales of the Vikings (co-prod., dir.).

WILLIAMS, ESTHER
Actress, Swimmer. b. Los Angeles, CA, Aug. 8, 1923. e. USC. Swimmer at San Francisco World's Fair Aquacade; professional model. Signed to movie contract by MGM. Voted one of Top Ten Money-Making Stars in M.P. Herald-Fame poll, 1950.
PICTURES: Andy Hardy's Double Life (debut, 1942), A Guy Named Joe, Bathing Beauty, Thrill of a Romance, Ziegfeld Follies, The Hoodlum Saint, Easy to Wed, Fiesta, This Time for Keeps, On an Island With You, Take Me Out to the Ball Game, Neptune's Daughter, Pagan Love Song, Duchess of Idaho, Texas Carnival, Callaway Went Thataway (cameo), Skirts Ahoy!, Million Dollar Mermaid, Dangerous When Wet, Easy to Love, Jupiter's Darling, The Unguarded Moment, Raw Wind in Eden, The Big Show, The Magic Fountain, That's Entertainment III.
TELEVISION: Specials: Esther Williams in Cypress Gardens, Live From New York, Esther Williams Aqua Spectacular.

WILLIAMS, JO BETH
Actress. b. Houston, TX, 1953. m. director John Pasquin. e. Brown U. One of Glamour Magazine's top 10 college girls, 1969-70. Acted with rep. companies in Rhode Island, Philadelphia, Boston, Washington, DC, etc. Spent over two years in New York-based daytime serials, Somerset and The Guiding Light.
THEATER: Ladyhouse Blues (1979), A Coupla White Chicks Sitting Around Talking, Gardenia.
PICTURES: Kramer vs. Kramer (debut, 1979), Stir Crazy, The Dogs of War, Poltergeist, Endangered Species, The Big Chill, American Dreamer, Teachers, Desert Bloom, Poltergeist II, Memories of Me, Welcome Home, Switch, Dutch, Stop Or My Mom Will Shoot, Me Myself & I, Wyatt Earp.
TELEVISION: Movies: Fun and Games, The Big Black Pill, Feasting with Panthers, Jabberwocky, The Day After, Adam, Kids Don't Tell, Adam: His Song Continues, Murder Ordained, Baby M, My Name is Bill W, Child of the Night, Bump in the Night (co-exec. prod. only), Victim of Love, Jonathan: The Boy Nobody Wanted, Sex Love and Cold Hard Cash, Chantilly Lace, Final Appeal, Parallel Lives, Voices From Within, A Season of Hope. Series: Fish Police (voice), John Grisham's The Client.

WILLIAMS, JOHN
Composer. b. New York, NY, Feb. 8, 1932. e. UCLA, Juilliard Sch. Worked as session musician in '50s; began career as film composer in late '50s. Considerable experience as musical director and conductor as well as composer. Since 1977 conductor of Boston Pops.
PICTURES: I Passed for White, Because They're Young, The Secret Ways, Bachelor Flat, Diamond Head, Gidget Goes to Rome, The Killers, None But the Brave, John Goldfarb Please Come Home, The Rare Breed, How to Steal a Million, The Plainsman, Not with My Wife You Don't, Penelope, A Guide for the Married Man, Fitzwilly, Valley of the Dolls, Daddy's Gone A-Hunting, Goodbye Mr. Chips (music supvr. & dir.), The Reivers, Fiddler on the Roof (musc. dir.; Academy Award, 1971). The Cowboys, Images, Pete 'n' Tillie, The Poseidon Adventure, Tom Sawyer (musc. supvr.), The Long Goodbye, The Man Who Loved Cat Dancing, The Paper Chase, Cinderella Liberty, Conrack, The Sugarland Express, Earthquake, The Towering Inferno, The Eiger Sanction, Jaws (Academy Award, 1975), Family Plot, The Missouri Breaks, Midway, Black Sunday, Star Wars (Academy Award, 1977), Raggedy Ann & Andy, Close Encounters of the Third Kind, The Fury, Jaws II, Superman, Meteor, Quintet, Dracula, 1941, The Empire Strikes Back, Raiders of the Lost Ark, Heartbeeps, E.T.: The Extra-Terrestrial (Academy Award, 1982), Yes Giorgio, Monsignor, Return of the Jedi, Indiana Jones and the Temple of Doom, The River, SpaceCamp, The

Witches of Eastwick, Empire of the Sun, The Accidental Tourist, Indiana Jones and the Last Crusade, Born on the Fourth of July, Always, Stanley & Iris, Presumed Innocent, Home Alone, Hook, JFK, Far and Away, Home Alone 2: Lost in New York, Jurassic Park, Schindler's List (Academy Award, 1993), Sabrina. TELEVISION: Once Upon a Savage Night, Jane Eyre (Emmy Award), Sergeant Ryker, Heidi (Emmy Award), The Ewok Adventure. *Series themes*: Checkmate, Alcoa Premiere, Wide Country, Lost in Space, The Time Tunnel, NBC News Theme, Amazing Stories.

WILLIAMS, KENNETH S.
Executive. b. Tulsa, OK, Dec. 31, 1955. e. Harvard Coll., B.A. 1978; Columbia U., M.S. 1985. Began as team leader of Chase Manhattan's motion picture lending group 1978-81. Joined Sony Pictures Entertainment in Jan. 1982 as dir. of corporate finance, was promoted to assistant treas. Oct. 1982. He became treas. in Feb. 1984 and named a v.p. in Nov. 1984. Served as pres. & treas. of both Columbia PIctures Industries, Inc. and the Entertainment Business Sector of the Coca-Cola Co. (Sony Pictures previous parent co.), 1986-87. 1987-90, corporate v.p. & treas. of Sony Pictrues Entertainment and was then promoted to s.v.p., Corporate Operations. Was named exec. v.p. of Sony Picture Entertainment in Aug. 1995.

WILLIAMS, PAUL
Actor, Composer. b. Omaha, NE, Sept. 19, 1940. Began career at studios as set painter and stunt parachutist. Bit and character parts in commercials followed. Became song writer, collaborating briefly with Biff Rose and later with Roger Nichols, with whom wrote several best-sellers, including We've Only Just Begun, Rainy Days and Mondays, Just an Old-Fashioned Love Song.
PICTURES: *Actor*: The Loved One (debut, 1965), The Chase, Watermelon Man, Battle for the Planet of the Apes, Phantom of the Paradise (also songs), Smokey and the Bandit, The Cheap Detective, The Muppet Movie (also songs), Stone Cold Dead, Smokey and the Bandit II, Smokey and the Bandit 3, Zombie High, The Chill Factor, The Doors, Solar Crisis (voice), A Million to Juan, Headless Body in Topless Bar. *Songs for Films*: Cinderella Liberty, Bugsy Malone (also vocals), Lifeguard, A Star Is Born (co-composer; Academy Award for best song: Evergreen, 1976), One on One, The End, Agatha, Ishtar, The Muppet Christmas Carol, Headless Body in Topless Bar.
TELEVISION: *Series*: Sugar Time! (songs, music spvr.). *Movies (actor)*: Flight to Holocaust, The Wild Wild West Revisted, Rooster, The Night They Saved Christmas, People Like Us, Hart to Hart Returns.

WILLIAMS, PAUL
Director. b. New York, NY, Nov. 12, 1943. e. Harvard (Phi Beta Kappa, 1965). First gained attention as director of film short, Girl, which won Golden Eagle award, made in collaboration with producer Edward R. Pressman, with whom he formed Pressman-Williams Enterprises which prod. Badlands, Phantom of the Paradise, etc. Now with Fulcrum Productions.
PICTURES: Out of It (also s.p.), The Revolutionary, Dealing: or the Berkeley-to-Boston Forty-Brick Lost-Bag-Blues (also s.p.), Nunzio, Miss Right (also story), The November Men (also actor), Mirage (also actor).

WILLIAMS, RICHARD
Producer, Painter, Film Animator. b. March, 1933, Toronto, Canada. Entered industry in 1955. Founded Richard Williams Animation Ltd. in 1962, having entered films by producing The Little Island (1st Prize, Venice Film Festival) in 1955. His company produces TV commercials for England, America, France and Germany, entertainment shorts and animated films. Designed animated feature titles/sequences for What's New Pussycat?, A Funny Thing Happened On The Way To The Forum, Casino Royale, The Charge of the Light Brigade, A Christmas Carol (Academy Award for best animated short, 1972), Who Framed Roger Rabbit (dir. of animation), Arabian Knight (dir., prod., co-s.p.). Awards: at Festivals at Venice, Edinburgh, Mannheim, Montreal, Trieste, Melbourne, West Germany, New York, Locarno, Vancouver, Philadelphia, Zagreb, Hollywood, Cork, Los Angeles. 1989, Academy Award, BAFTA Award, AMPAS Award, special effects, also Special Achievement Awards for work over 30 years, esp. Roger Rabbit by both BAFTA and AMPAS.

WILLIAMS, ROBIN
Actor, Comedian. b. Chicago, IL, July 21, 1951. e. Claremont Men's Coll. (CA), Coll. of Marin (CA), studying acting at latter. Continued studies at Juilliard with John Houseman in New York augmenting income as a street mime. As San Francisco club performer appeared at Holy City Zoo, Intersection, The Great American Music Hall and The Boardinghouse. In Los Angeles performed as stand-up comedian at The Comedy Store, Improvisation, and The Ice House. First TV appearance on 1977 Richard Pryor series followed by The Great American Laugh Off. Guest on Happy Days as extraterrestrial Mork from Ork, led to own series.

PICTURES: Can I Do It...Til I Need Glasses? (debut, 1977), Popeye, The World According to Garp, The Survivors, Moscow on the Hudson, The Best of Times, Club Paradise, Good Morning Vietnam (Acad. Award nom.), The Adventures of Baron Munchausen, Dead Poets Society (Acad. Award nom.), Cadillac Man, Awakenings, Dead Again, The Fisher King (Acad. Award nom.), Hook, Shakes the Clown, FernGully... The Last Rainforest (voice), Aladdin (voice), Toys, Mrs. Doubtfire (also co-prod.), Being Human, Nine Months, To Wong Foo—Thanks for Everything—Julie Newmar, Jumanji, Birdcage, Jack, Hamlet, Joseph Conrad's The Secret Agent.
TELEVISION: *Series*: The Richard Pryor Show (1977), Laugh-In (1977-78 revival; later aired as series in 1979), Mork and Mindy, Shakespeare: The Animated Tales (host). *Guest*: America Tonight, Ninety Minutes Live, The Alan Hamel Show. *Specials*: An Evening With Robin Williams, E.T. & Friends, Faerie Tale Theatre (The Frog Prince), Carol Carl Whoopi and Robin (Emmy Award, 1987), Free To Be... a Family, Dear America: Letters Home from Vietnam (reader), ABC Presents a Royal Gala (Emmy Award, 1988), In Search of Dr. Seuss. *Movie*: Seize the Day.

WILLIAMS, ROGER
Pianist, Concert, Film, TV Personality. b. Omaha, NE, Oct. 1, 1924. e. Drake U., Idaho State Coll. Hon. Ph.D. Midland and Wagner Colls. Served U.S. Navy WWII. Appeared as guest artist in number of films. Public debut on TV's Arthur Godfrey Talent Scouts and Chance of a Lifetime. Other TV appearances include Ed Sullivan, Hollywood Palace, Kraft Summer Series, Celanese Special. Recorded 75 Albums, Kapp (now MCA) Records, with sales over 15 million albums.

WILLIAMS, TREAT
Actor. r.n. Richard Williams. b. Rowayton, CT, Dec. 1, 1952. e. Franklin and Marshall Coll. Landed role on B'way in musical, Over Here! also played leading role in Grease on B'way.
THEATER: Over Here, Bus Stop (Equity Library Theatre), Once in a Lifetime, The Pirates of Penzance, Some Men Need Help, Oh Hell, Oleanna.
PICTURES: Deadly Hero (debut, 1976), The Ritz, The Eagle Has Landed, Hair, 1941, Why Would I Lie?, Prince of the City, The Pursuit of D. B. Cooper, Once Upon a Time in America, Flashpoint, Smooth Talk, The Men's Club, Dead Heat, Sweet Lies, Heart of Dixie, Night of the Sharks, Russicum, Beyond the Ocean, Where the Rivers Flow North, Hand Gun, Things to Do in Denver When You're Dead, Mulholland Falls, The Phantom.
TELEVISION: *Movies*: Dempsey, A Streetcar Named Desire, J. Edgar Hoover, Echoes in the Darkness, Third Degree Burn, Max and Helen, Final Verdict, Till Death Us Do Part, The Water Engine, Deadly Matrimony, Bonds of Love (also co-exec. prod), Parallel Lives, In the Shadow of Evil. *Mini-Series*: Drug Wars: The Camarena Story. *Specials*: The Little Mermaid (Faerie Tale Theatre), Some Men Need Help, Texan (also dir.), Edgar Allan Poe: Terror of the Soul. *Series*: Eddie Dodd, Good Advice. *Guest*: Tales From the Crypt.

WILLIAMS-JONES, MICHAEL
Executive. b. England, June 3, 1947. Joined United Artists as trainee, 1967; territorial mgr., South Africa, 1969; territorial mgr., Brazil, 1971; territorial mgr., England, 1976; appt. v.p., continental European mgr., 1978; sr. v.p. foreign mgr., 1979; 1982 joined United Intl. Pictures as sr. v.p. intl. sls., based in London. 1984, named pres. UIP motion picture group; 1986, named pres. & CEO. In Dec. 96, retired from UIP to create own production co., Merlin Angelsey U.K. Ltd.

WILLIAMSON, FRED
Actor, Director, Producer, Writer. b. Gary, IN, March 5, 1937. e. Northwestern U. Spent 10 yrs. playing pro football before turning to acting.
PICTURES: M*A*S*H (debut, 1970), Tell Me That You Love Me Junie Moon, The Legend of Nigger Charley, Hammer, Black Caesar, The Soul of Nigger Charley, Hell Up in Harlem, That Man Bolt, Crazy Joe, Three Tough Guys, Black Eye, Three the Hard Way, Boss Nigger, Bucktown, No Way Back (also dir., prod., s.p.), Take a Hard Ride, Adios Amigo, Death Journey (also dir., prod.), Joshua, Blind Rage, Fist of Fear Touch of Death, 1990: The Bronx Warriors, One Down Two to Go (also dir., prod., Vigilante, Warriors of the Wasteland, Deadly Impact, The Big Score (also dir.), The Last Fight (also dir.), Foxtrap (also dir., prod.), Warrior of the Lost World, Deadly Intent, Delta Force, Commando, Taxi Killer (prod.), Hell's Heroes, Three Days to a Kill (also dir., s.p.), Justice Done (also dir.), Soda Cracker (also dir., prod.), South Beach (also dir., prod.), Silent Hunter (also dir.), From Dusk Till Dawn, Original Gangstas (also prod.).
TELEVISION: *Series*: Julia, Monday Night Football, Half Nelson. *Guest*: Police Story, The Rookies, Lou Grant.

WILLIAMSON, NICOL
Actor. b. Hamilton, Scotland, Sept. 14, 1938. Has played many classical roles with Royal Shakespeare Co., including

Macbeth, Malvolio, and Coriolanus. Starred on Broadway in Inadmissible Evidence, Rex (musical debut), Macbeth, I Hate Hamlet. *London*: Jack.
PICTURES: Inadmissible Evidence (debut, 1968), The Bofors Gun, Laughter in the Dark, The Reckoning, Hamlet, The Jerusalem File, The Monk, The Wilby Conspiracy, Robin and Marian, The Seven Percent Solution, The Goodbye Girl (cameo), The Cheap Detective, The Human Factor, Excalibur, Venom, I'm Dancing as Fast as I Can, Return to Oz, Black Widow, The Exorcist III, Apt Pupil, The Advocate.
TELEVISION: *Movies*: Sakharov, Passion Flower. *Mini-Series*: Lord Mountbatten, The Word, Christopher Columbus. *Specials*: Of Mice and Men, Macbeth, I Know What I Meant.

WILLIAMSON, PATRICK
Executive. b. England, Oct. 1929. Joined Columbia Pictures London office 1944—career spanned advertising & publicity responsibilities until 1967 when appt. managing dir. Columbia Great Britain; also mng. dir. on formation of Columbia-Warner; promoted to exec. position in Columbia's home office, NY, 1973, and pres. of intl. optns. 1974; v.p., Coca-Cola Export Corp., 1983; exec. v.p. Columbia Pictures Industries, 1985; director, CPI, 1985; exec. v.p., Coca-Cola Entertainment Business Sector, 1987; promoted to special asst. to pres. & CEO of Coca-Cola Entertainment Business Sector, 1987; served on boards of Tri-Star Pictures, RCA/Columbia Home Video, RCA/Columbia Int'l. Video; 1987, named pres. Triumph Releasing Corp., a unit of Columbia Pictures Entertainment; Consultant to Sony Pictures Entertainment, 1989. 1994, dir. & co-founder, Sports Alliance Intl. TV.

WILLIS, BRUCE
Actor. b. Germany, March 19, 1955. m. actress Demi Moore. Moved to New Jersey when he was 2. After graduating high school, worked at DuPont plant in neighboring town. First entertainment work was as harmonica player in band called Loose Goose. Formed Night Owl Promotions and attended Montclair State Coll. NJ, where he acted in Cat on a Hot Tin Roof. *NY stage debut*: Heaven and Earth. Member of Barbara Contardi's First Amendment Comedy Theatre; supplemented acting work by doing Levi's 501 jeans commercials and as bartender in NY nightclub, Kamikaze. Appeared as extra in film The First Deadly Sin.
THEATER: Fool for Love.
PICTURES: Blind Date, Sunset, Die Hard, In Country, Look Who's Talking (voice), That's Adequate, Die Hard 2, Look Who's Talking Too (voice), The Bonfire of the Vanities, Mortal Thoughts, Hudson Hawk (also co-story), Billy Bathgate, The Last Boy Scout, The Player, Death Becomes Her, National Lampoon's Loaded Weapon 1 (cameo), Striking Distance, North, Color of Night, Pulp Fiction, Nobody's Fool, Die Hard With a Vengeance, Twelve Monkeys, Last Man Standing.
TELEVISION: *Series*: Moonlighting (Emmy Award, 1987). *Guest*: Hart to Hart, Miami Vice, Twilight Zone. *Special*: Bruce Willis: The Return of Bruno (also writer, prod.).

WILLIS, GORDON
Cinematographer. Acted two summers in stock at Gloucester, MA, where also did stage settings and scenery. Photographer in Air Force; then cameraman, making documentaries. In TV did commercials and documentaries.
PICTURES: End of the Road, Loving, The Landlord, The People Next Door, Little Murders, Klute, The Godfather, Bad Company, Up the Sandbox, The Paper Chase, The Parallax View, The Godfather Part II, The Drowning Pool, All the President's Men, Annie Hall, Interiors, September 30, 1955, Comes a Horseman, Manhattan, Stardust Memories, Pennies from Heaven, A Midsummer Night's Sex Comedy, Zelig, Broadway Danny Rose, The Purple Rose of Cairo, Perfect, The Money Pit, The Pick-Up Artist, Bright Lights Big City, Presumed Innocent, The Godfather Part III, Malice. *Director*: Windows (1980; debut).
TELEVISION: *Movie*: The Lost Honor of Kathryn Beck.

WILSON, ELIZABETH
Actress. b. Grand Rapids, MI, April 4, 1921.
THEATER: *B'way*: Picnic (debut, 1953), The Desk Set, The Tunnel of Love, Little Murders, Big Fish Little Fish, Sheep on the Runway, Sticks and Bones (Tony Award, 1972), Uncle Vanya, Morning's at Seven, Ah! Wilderness, The Importance of Being Earnest, You Can't Take It With You, A Delicate Balance. *Off-B'way*: Sheep on the Runway, Token in Marriage (Drama Desk Award), Three Penny Opera, Salonika, Ante Room, Eh?, All's Well That Ends Well. *Tour*: The Cocktail Hour.
PICTURES: Picnic (debut, 1955), Patterns, The Goddess, The Tunnel of Love, Happy Anniversary, A Child is Waiting, The Birds, The Tiger Makes Out, The Graduate, Jenny, Catch-22, Little Murders, Day of the Dolphin, Man on a Swing, The Happy Hooker, The Prisoner of Second Avenue, Nine to Five, The Incredible Shrinking Woman, Grace Quigley, Where Are the Children?, The Believers, Regarding Henry, The Addams Family, Quiz Show, Nobody's Fool.

TELEVISION: *Series*: East Side West Side, Doc, Morningstar/Eveningstar, Delta. *Movies*: Miles to Go Before I Sleep, Once Upon a Family, Million Dollar Infield, Sanctuary of Fear, Morning's at Seven, Nutcracker: Money Madness and Murder (Emmy nom.), Conspiracy of Love, Skylark, In the Best of Families: Marriage Pride & Madness, Bitter Blood, In the Best Families, Spring Awakening, Journey to Mars. *Mini-Series*: Queen, Scarlett. *Specials*: Patterns, Happy Endings, You Can't Take It With You. *Guest*: U.S. Steel Hour, Maude, All in the Family, Love Sidney, Murder She Wrote, The Boys Next Door.

WILSON, FLIP
Performer. r.n. Clerow Wilson. b. Newark, NJ, Dec. 8, 1933. Left school at 16 to join Air Force; played clubs in FL & Bahamas until 1965 when made guest appearance on NBC.
PICTURES: Uptown Saturday Night, Skatetown USA, The Fish That Saved Pittsburgh.
TELEVISION: *Series*: The Flip Wilson Show (Emmy Award for writing, 1971), People Are Funny (1984, host), Charlie & Co. *Guest*: That's Life, Sammy and Company, Love American Style, Here's Lucy, The Six Million Dollar Man, 227, etc. *Specials*: Flip Wilson Special (1969), Clerow Wilson and the Miracle of P.S. 114, Clerow Wilson's Great Escape, Pinocchio, Zora is My Name.

WILSON, HUGH
Producer, Director, Writer. b. Miami, FL, Aug. 21, 1943. e. Univ. of FL., 1965. Gained fame for creating, writing, producing and directing TV series, WKRP in Cincinnati, Frank's Place and The Famous Teddy Z. Feature film dir. debut with Police Academy (1984).
PICTURES: *Writer*: Stroker Ace, Down Periscope. *Director-Writer*: Police Academy, Rustler's Rhapsody, Burglar, Guarding Tess (also voice), Down Persicope (co-s.p.). *Dir.*: The First Wives Club.

WILSON, SCOTT
Actor. b. Atlanta, GA, 1942. Was college athlete on basketball scholarship when injured and had to leave school. Moved to L.A. and enrolled in local acting class.
PICTURES: In the Heat of the Night (debut, 1967), In Cold Blood, The Gypsy Moths, Castle Keep, The Grissom Gang, The New Centurions, Lolly Madonna XXX, The Great Gatsby, Twinkle Twinkle Killer Kane (The Ninth Configuration), The Right Stuff, The Aviator, On the Line, A Year of the Quiet Sun, Blue City, Malone, Johnny Handsome, The Exorcist III, Young Guns II, Femme Fatale, Pure Luck, Flesh and Bone, Geronimo: An American Legend, Tall Tale, Judge Dredd.
TELEVISION: *Movies*: Jesse, Elvis and the Colonel.

WINANS, CHARLES A.
Executive. Exec. dir., National Association of Concessionaires.

WINCER, SIMON
Director. b. Australia. Directed over 200 hours of dramatic programs for Australian TV, including Cash and Company, Tandarra, Ryan, Against the Wind, The Sullivans, etc. Exec. prod. of The Man from Snowy River, then the top-grossing theatrical film in Australia.
PICTURES: Snapshot (The Day After Halloween), Harlequin, Phar Lap, D.A.R.Y.L., The Lighthorsemen (also co.-prod.), Quigley Down Under, Harley Davidson and the Marlboro Man, Free Willy, Lightning Jack (also co-prod.), Operation Dumbo Drop, The Phantom.
TELEVISION: *Movies*: The Last Frontier, Bluegrass, Lonesome Dove (Emmy Award, 1989), The Girl Who Spelled Freedom. *Series*: The Young Indiana Jones Chronicles.

WINCHELL, PAUL
Actor, Ventriloquist. b. New York, NY, Dec. 21, 1922. e. Sch. of Industrial Arts. At 13 won first prize Major Bowes Radio Amateur Hour; signed by Ted Weems; created dummies Jerry Mahoney and Knucklehead Smiff. On radio as host of his own show in 1940's. In the news in 1975 as inventor of an artificial heart.
PICTURES: Stop! Look! and Laugh! (actor), Winnie the Pooh and the Blustery Day (short; voice), The Aristocats (voice), Which Way to the Front? (actor), Winnie the Pooh and Tigger Too (short; voice), The Fox and the Hound (voice).
TELEVISION: *Series*: The Bigelow Show, The Paul Winchell-Jerry Mahoney Spiedel Show (also prod., writer), Jerry Mahoney's Club House (also writer), What's My Name?, Circus Time (ringmaster), Toyland Express (also prod.), The Paul Winchell Show (1957-60), Banana Splits Adventure Hour (voice), Runaround. *Voices for series:* The Wacky Races, Cartoonsville, Dastardly and Mutley, Help It's the Hair Bear Bunch, Goober and the Ghost Chaser, The Oddball Couple, Clue Club, The C.B. Bears, Wheelie and the Chopper, Heathcliff and Marmaduke Show, The Smurfs, Winnie the Pooh Hour, various Dr. Seuss specials, Smurf specials. *Movie*: The Treasure Chest. *Guest*: Pat Boone Show, Polly Bergen Show, The Lineup, Candid Camera, The Beverly Hillbillies, 77 Sunset Strip, Donna Reed Show, Perry Mason, Dick Van Dyke Show, Lucy Show, Love American Style, Brady Bunch, many others.

WINCOTT, MICHAEL
Actor. b. Canada. Studied acting at Juilliard. NY stage incl. Talk Radio, States of Shock.
PICTURES: Wild Horse Hank (debut, 1979), Circle of Two, Ticket to Heaven, Curtains, The Sicilian, Talk Radio, Suffering Bastards, Bloodhounds of Broaway, Born on the Fourth of July, The Doors, Robin Hood: Prince of Thieves, 1492: Conquest of Paradise, The Three Musketeers, Romeo Is Bleeding, The Crow, Panther, Strange Days, Dead Man, Basquiat.
TELEVISION: Movies: Tragedy of Flight 103: The Inside Story. Guest: Miami Vice, Crime Story, The Equalizer. Special: High School Narc.

WINDOM, WILLIAM
Actor. b. New York, NY, Sept. 28, 1923.
PICTURES: To Kill a Mockingbird (debut, 1962), Cattle King, For Love or Money, One Man's Way, The Americanization of Emily, Hour of the Gun, The Detective, The Gypsy Moths, The Angry Breed, Brewster McCloud, Fool's Parade, Escape From the Planet of the Apes, The Mephisto Waltz, The Man, Now You See Him Now You Don't, Echoes of a Summer, Mean Dog Blues, Separate Ways, Last Plane Out, Grandview U.S.A., Prince Jack, Space Rage, Funland, Pinocchio and the Emperor of the Night (voice), Planes Trains and Automobiles, She's Having a Baby, Sommersby, Miracle on 34th Street.
TELEVISION: Series: The Farmer's Daughter, My World and Welcome to It (Emmy Award, 1970), The Girl With Something Extra, Brothers and Sisters, Murder She Wrote, Parenthood. Movies: Prescription: Murder, U.M.C., The House on Greenapple Road, Assault on the Wayne, Escape, A Taste of Evil, Marriage: Year One, The Homecoming, Second Chance, A Great American Tragedy, Pursuit, The Girls of Huntington House, The Day the Earth Moved, The Abduction of St. Anne, Journey from Darkness, Guilty or Innocent: The Sam Sheppard Murder Case, Bridger, Richie Brockelman: Missing 24 Hours, Hunters of the Reef, Portrait of a Rebel: Margaret Sanger, Leave 'Em Laughing, Side Show, Desperate Lives, The Rules of Marriage, Why Me?, Off Sides, Velvet, Surviving, There Must Be a Pony, Dennis the Menace, Chance of a Lifetime, Attack of the 50 Ft. Woman. Mini-Series: Once an Eagle, Seventh Avenue, Blind Ambition. Guest: Robert Montgomery Presents, Ben Casey, Lucy Show, The FBI, Gunsmoke, Partridge Family, That Girl, The Rookies, Streets of San Francisco, Barney Miller, Kojak, Police Woman, Love Boat, St. Elsewhere, Newhart, Night Gallery, Twilight Zone, many others.

WINDSOR, MARIE
Actress. r.n. Emily Marie Bertelsen. b. Marysvale, UT, Dec. 11, 1919. Winner of beauty contests, including Queen of Covered Wagon Days. Worked as telephone girl, dancing teacher. Trained for acting by Maria Ouspenskaya. Won Look Mag. Award, best supporting actress, 1957.
PICTURES: All-American Co-Ed (debut, 1941), Song of the Thin Man, Unfinished Dance, On an Island With You, Three Musketeers, Kissing Bandit, Force of Evil, Oupost in Morocco, Fighting Kentuckian, Beautiful Blonde From Bashful Bend, Frenchie, Dakota Lil, Little Big Horn, Two Dollar Bettor, Hurricane Island, The Narrow Margin, Japanese War Bride, The Jungle, The Sniper, The Tall Texan, The City That Never Sleeps, The Eddie Cantor Story, Trouble Along the Way, Cat Women of the Moon, Hell's Half Acre, The Bounty Hunter, No Man's Woman, Abbott & Costello Meet the Mummy, Swamp Women, Two Gun Lady, The Killing, The Unholy Wife, The Story of Mankind, Girl in Black Stockings, Parson and the Outlaw, Island Woman, Paradise Alley, The Day Mars Invaded Earth, Critics Choice, Mail Order Bride, Bedtime Story, Chamber of Horrors, Support Your Local Gunfighter, The Good Guys and the Bad Guys, One More Train To Rob, Cahill U.S. Marshall, The Outfit, Hearts of the West, Freaky Friday, Lovely But Deadly.
TELEVISION: Series: Supercarrier. Movies: Wild Women, Manhunter, Salem's Lot, J.O.E. and the Colonel.

WINFIELD, PAUL
Actor. b. Los Angeles, CA, May 22, 1940. e. attended U. of Portland 1957-59, Stanford U., L.A. City Coll. and UCLA. Inducted in Black Filmmakers Hall of Fame.
THEATER: Regional work at Dallas Theatre Center (A Lesson From Aloes), Goodman Theatre (Enemy of the People), Stanford Repertory Theatre and Inner City Cultural Center, L.A.; At Lincoln Center in The Latent Heterosexual, and Richard III. B'way: Checkmates, Othello, Merry Wives of Windsor.
PICTURES: The Lost Man (debut, 1969), R.P.M., Brother John, Sounder (Acad. Award nom.), Trouble Man, Gordon's War, Conrack, Huckleberry Finn, Hustle, Twilight's Last Gleaming, The Greatest, Damnation Alley, A Hero Ain't Nothin' But a Sandwich, High Velocity, Carbon Copy, Star Trek II—The Wrath of Khan, White Dog, On the Run, Mike's Murder, The Terminator, Blue City, Death Before Dishonor, Big Shots, The Serpent and the Rainbow, Presumed Innocent, Cliffhanger, Dennis the Menace, Original Gangstas, Mars Attacks!.

WINFREY, OPRAH
TV Talk Show Hostess, Actress, Producer. b. Kosciusko, MS, Jan. 29, 1954. e. Tennessee State U. Started as radio reporter then TV news reporter-anchor in Nashville. Moved to Baltimore in same capacity, later co-hosting successful morning talk show. Left for Chicago to host own show AM Chicago which became top-rated in only a month; expanded to national syndication in 1986. Formed own production co., Harpo Productions, Inc. in 1986 which assumed ownership and prod. of The Oprah Winfrey Show in 1988. Named Broadcaster of the Year by Intl. Radio and TV Soc., 1988. Purchased Chicago movie and TV production facility, 1988; renamed Harpo Studios. National Daytime Emmy Award, 1987, Outstanding Talk/Service Program Host.
PICTURES: The Color Purple (debut, 1985; Acad. Award nom.), Native Son, Throw Momma From the Train (cameo).
TELEVISION: Movies: The Women of Brewster Place (actress, co-exec. prod.), Overexposed (co-prod. only), There Are No Children Here. Series: The Oprah Winfrey Show (many Emmy Awards), Brewster Place (also exec. prod.). Special: Peewee's Playhouse Christmas Special.

WINGER, DEBRA
Actress. b. Cleveland, OH, May 16, 1955. e. California State U. Began career on TV series Wonder Woman.
PICTURES: Slumber Party '57 (debut, 1977), Thank God It's Friday, French Postcards, Urban Cowboy, Cannery Row, An Officer and a Gentleman (Acad. Award nom.), Terms of Endearment (Acad. Award nom.), Mike's Murder, Legal Eagles, Black Widow, Made in Heaven, Betrayed, Everybody Wins, The Sheltering Sky, Leap of Faith, Wilder Napalm, A Dangerous Woman, Shadowlands (Acad. Award nom.), Forget Paris.
TELEVISION: Movie: Special Olympics. Guest: Wonder Woman, James at 16.

WINITSKY, ALEX
Producer. b. New York, NY, Dec. 27, 1924. e. NYU, BS, LLB, JD. In partnership as attorneys in L.A. for 20 years with Arlene Sellers before they turned to financing and later production of films.
PICTURES: Co-prod. with Sellers: End of the Game, The White Dawn, The Seven-Per-Cent Solution, Cross of Iron, Silver Bears, The Lady Vanishes, Cuba, Blue Skies Again, Irreconcilable Differences, Scandalous, Swing Shift, Bad Medicine, Stanley & Iris, Circle of Friends.
TELEVISION: Ford—The Man and the Machine.

WINKLER, HENRY
Actor, Producer, Director. b. New York, NY, Oct. 30, 1945. e. Emerson Coll., Yale Sch. of Drama, MA. Appeared with Yale Repertory Co.; returned to N.Y. to work in radio. Did 30 TV commercials before starring in The Great American Dream Machine and Masquerade on TV. Formed Winkler/Daniel Prod. Co. with Ann Daniel.
PICTURES: Actor: Crazy Joe (debut, 1974), The Lords of Flatbush, Heroes, The One and Only, Night Shift. Exec. Prod: The Sure Thing. Director: Memories of Me, Cop and a Half.
TELEVISION: Series (actor): Happy Days, Monty. Series (prod.): Ryans Four (co-prod.), Mr. Sunshine (co-exec. prod.), MacGyver, A Life Apart. Guest: The Mary Tyler Moore Show, The Bob Newhart Show, The Paul Sand Show, Rhoda, Laverne & Shirley, The Larry Sanders Show. Specials: Henry Winkler Meets William Shakespeare, America Salutes Richard Rodgers, A Family Again (exec. prod.), Two Daddies (voice, exec. prod.). Movies: Katherine, An American Christmas Carol, Absolute Strangers, The Only Way Out, Truman Capote's One Christmas, A Child Is Missing. Director: A Smoky Mountain Christmas (movie), All the Kids Do It (also actor, exec. prod.; Emmy Award as exec. prod., 1985). Exec. prod.: Who Are the DeBolts and Where Did They Get 19 Kids?, Scandal Sheet, When Your Lover Leaves, Starflight, Second Start, Morning Glory (pilot), MacGyver: Lost Treasure of Atlantis, MacGyver: Trail to Doomsday.

WINKLER, IRWIN
Producer, Director. b. New York, NY, May 28, 1934. e. NYU.
PICTURES: Producer: Double Trouble, Blue, The Split, They Shoot Horses Don't They?, The Strawberry Statement, Leo the Last, Believe in Me, The Gang That Couldn't Shoot Straight, The Mechanic, The New Centurions, Up the Sandbox, Busting, S*P*Y*S, The Gambler, Breakout, Peeper,

Rocky (Academy Award for Best Picture, 1976), Nickelodeon, New York New York, Valentino, Comes a Horseman, Uncle Joe Shannon, Rocky II, Raging Bull, True Confessions, Rocky III, Author! Author!, The Right Stuff, Rocky IV, Revolution, 'Round Midnight, Betrayed, Music Box, GoodFellas, Rocky V, The Juror. *Director*: Guilty by Suspicion (also s.p.), Night and the City, The Net (also co-s.p., co-prod.).

WINNER, MICHAEL
Producer, Director, Writer. b. London, Eng., Oct. 30, 1935. e. Cambridge U. Ent. m.p. ind. as columnist, dir., Drummer Films. *Presenter*: Michael Winner's True Crimes. *Actor*: For the Greater Good, Decadence, Calliope, Kenny Everett Show, The Full Wax, Birds of a Feather.
PICTURES: *Writer*: Man With A Gun. *Director-Writer*: Haunted England (also prod.), Shoot to Kill, Swiss Holiday, Climb Up the Wall, Out of the Shadow, Some Like It Cool, Girls Girls Girls, It's Magic, Behave Yourself, The Cool Mikado, You Must Be Joking, West 11 (dir. only). *Director/Producer*: The System (The Girl-Getters), I'll Never Forget What's 'is Name, The Jokers, Hannibal Brooks (also s.p.), The Games, Lawman, The Nightcomers, Chato's Land, The Mechanic (dir. only), Scorpio (also s.p.), The Stone Killer, Death Wish, Won Ton Ton the Dog Who Saved Hollywood, The Sentinel (also s.p.), The Big Sleep (also s.p.), Firepower (also s.p.), Death Wish II, The Wicked Lady (also s.p.), Scream for Help, Death Wish III (dir. only), Appointment With Death (also s.p.), A Chorus of Disapproval (also s.p.), Bullseye (also s.p.), Dirty Weekend (also s.p.).
TELEVISION: *Series*: White Hunter, Dick and the Duchess.

WINNINGHAM, MARE
Actress. b. Phoenix, AZ, May 16, 1959. TV debut at age 16 as a singer on The Gong Show. Debut solo album What Might Be released in 1992.
PICTURES: One-Trick Pony, Threshold, St. Elmo's Fire, Nobody's Fool, Made in Heaven, Shy People, Miracle Mile, Turner and Hooch, Hard Promises, Teresa's Tattoo, Wyatt Earp, The War, Georgia.
TELEVISION: *Mini-Series*: The Thorn Birds, Studs Lonigan. *Movies*: Special Olympics, The Death of Ocean View Park, Amber Waves (Emmy Award), Off the Minnesota Strip, The Women's Room, Freedom, A Few Days in Weasel Creek, Missing Children: A Mother's Story, Helen Keller: The Miracle Continues, Single Bars Single Women, Love Is Never Silent, Who is Julia, A Winner Never Quits, Eye on the Sparrow, God Bless the Child, Love and Lies, Crossing to Freedom, Fatal Exposure, She Stood Alone, Those Secrets, Intruders, Better Off Dead, Betrayed by Love, Letter to My Killer, The Deliverance of Elaine.

WINSTON, STAN
Makeup and Special Effects Artist. b. 1946. e. UofVA. Started in business in 1970 as apprentice to Robert Schiffer at makeup dept. of Walt Disney Studios. Established Stan Winston Studio in Van Nuys, CA.
PICTURES: W.C. Fields and Me, The Wiz, Dead and Buried, Heart Beeps, The Thing, The Entity, Something Wicked This Way Comes, The Terminator, Starman, Invaders From Mars, Aliens (Academy Award for Visual Effects, 1986), Predator, The Monster Squad, Alien Nation, Pumpkinhead (dir. debut), Leviathan, Predator 2, Edward Scissorhands, Terminator 2: Judgment Day (2 Academy Awards: Visual Effects and Makeup, 1991), A Gnome Named Gnorm (dir.), Batman Returns, Jurassic Park (Academy Award for Visual Effects, 1993), Interview With the Vampire, Tank Girl, Congo.
TELEVISION: *Movies*: Gargoyles (Emmy Award for Makeup, 1972), The Autobiography of Miss Jane Pittman (Emmy Award for Makeup, 1974), Roots. *Specials*: Masquerade, Pinocchio, An Evening With Diana Ross.

WINTER, ALEX
Actor. b. London, England, July 17, 1965. e. NYU. At age 4 began studying dance. Played opposite Vincent Price in St. Louis Opera production of Oliver! Co-founder of Stern-Winter Prods. Produced videos for Red Hot Chili Peppers, Human Radio, Ice Cube, etc. Co-directed TV special Hard Rock Cafe Presents: Save the Planet.
THEATER: *B'way*: The King and I (1977 revival), Peter Pan (1979 revival). *Off-B'way*: Close of Play.
PICTURES: Death Wish III, The Lost Boys, Haunted Summer, Bill & Ted's Excellent Adventure, Rosalie Goes Shopping, Bill & Ted's Bogus Journey, Freaked (also co-dir., co-s.p., co-prod.).
TELEVISION: *Movie*: Gaugin the Savage. *Series*: Idiot Box (also co-creator, co-dir., co-writer).

WINTERS, DAVID
Choreographer, Actor, Director. b. London, April 5, 1939. Acted in both Broadway and m.p. version of West Side Story (as A-rab). Directed and acted in number of TV shows. Choreography credits include films Viva Las Vegas, Billie, Send Me No Flowers, Tickle Me, Pajama Party, Girl Happy,

The Swinger, Made in Paris, Easy Come, Easy Go, The Island of Doctor Moreau, Roller Boogie, A Star is Born, Blame It on the Night. Was choreographer for TV series Hullabaloo, Shindig, Donny and Marie Osmond, The Big Show, and Steve Allen Show, and TV specials starring Joey Heatherton, Nancy Sinatra, Diana Ross, Raquel Welch, Ann Margret, Lucille Ball. Pres., A.I.P. Distribution, A.I.P. Productions and A.I.P. Home Video, 1989, formed Pyramid Distributors. Features incl.: Firehead, Raw Nerve, Center of the Web, Double Vision.

WINTERS, DEBORAH
Actress. b. Los Angeles, CA. e. Professional Children's Sch., New York; began studying acting at Stella Adler's with Pearl Pearson. at age 13 and Lee Strasberg at 16. Acting debut at age 5 in TV commercials. Casting dir.: Aloha Summer (asst.), Breakdancers From Mars (assoc. prod., casting dir.), Into the Spider's Web, The Hidden Jungle, Haunted, Broken Spur, Behind the Mask (also assoc. prod.).
PICTURES: Me Natalie, Hail Hero!, The People Next Door, Kotch, Class of '44, Blue Sunshine, The Lamp, The Outing.
TELEVISION: *Special*: Six Characters in Search of an Author. *Guest*: Matt Houston, Medical Center. *Movies*: Lottery, Gemini Man. Tarantulas: The Deadly Cargo, Little Girl Lost, Space City. *Mini-Series*: The Winds of War.

WINTERS, JONATHAN
Actor. b. Dayton, OH, Nov. 11, 1925. e. Kenyon Coll.; Dayton Art Inst., B.F.A. Disc jockey, Dayton and Columbus stations; night club comedian performing at Blue Angel and Ruban Bleu (NY), Black Orchid (Chicago), Flamingo, Sands, Riviera (Las Vegas), then on B'way in John Murray Anderson's Almanac. Author: Mouse Breath, Conformity and Other Social Ills, Winters Tales, Hang Ups (book on his paintings). Recorded 7 comedy albums. Won Grammy Award for "Crank Calls" comedy album, 1996.
PICTURES: Alakazam the Great! (voice), It's a Mad Mad Mad Mad World, The Loved One, The Russians Are Coming The Russians Are Coming, Penelope, Oh Dad Poor Dad Mama's Hung You in the Closet and I'm Feeling So Sad, Eight on the Lam, Viva Max, The Fish That Saved Pittsburgh, The Longshot, Say Yes, Moon Over Parador, The Flintstones, The Shadow, Arabian Knight (voice).
TELEVISION: *Series*: And Here's the Show, NBC Comedy Hour, The Jonathan Winters Show (1956-57), Masquerade Party (panelist), The Andy Williams Show, The Jonathan Winters Show (1967-69), Hot Dog, The Wacky World of Jonathan Winters, Mork and Mindy, Hee Haw, The Smurfs (voice of Papa Smurf), The Completely Mental Misadventures of Ed Grimley (voices), Davis Rules (Emmy Award, 1991), Fish Police (voice). *Guest*: Steve Allen Show, Garry Moore Show, Jack Paar, Omnibus, Twlight Zone, Bob Hope specials, Tonight Show, Hollywood Squares, many others. *Specials*: The Jonathan Winters Special, The Jonathan Winters Show (1964, 1965), Jonathan Winters Presents 200 Years of American Humor, 'Tis the Season to Be Smurfy (voice). *Movies*: Now You See It—Now You Don't, More Wild Wild West.

WINTERS, SHELLEY
Actress. r.n. Shirley Schrift. b. St. Louis, MO, Aug. 18, 1922. e. Wayne U. Clerked in 5 & 10 cent store; in vaudeville, chorus girl in night clubs; NY stage (Conquest, Night Before Christmas, Meet the People, Rosalinda, A Hatful of Rain, Girls of Summer, Minnie's Boys, One Night Stand of a Noisy Passenger. (Off-B'way). *Autobiographies*: Shelley Also Known as Shirley (1981), Shelley II: The Middle of My Century (1989).
PICTURES: What a Woman! (debut, 1943), Nine Girls, Sailor's Holiday, Knickerbocker Holiday, Cover Girl, A Double Life, Cry of the City, Larceny, Take One False Step, Johnny Stool Pigeon, The Great Gatsby, South Sea Sinner, Winchester '73, Frenchie, A Place in the Sun, He Ran All the Way, Behave Yourself, The Raging Tide, Phone Call From a Stranger, Meet Danny Wilson, Untamed Frontier, My Man and I, Tennessee Champ, Executive Suite, Saskatchewan, Playgirl, To Dorothy a Son (Cash on Delivery), Mambo, Night of the Hunter, I Am a Camera, Big Knife, Treasure of Pancho Villa, I Died a Thousand Times, The Diary of Anne Frank (Academy Award, best supporting actress, 1959), Odds Against Tomorrow, Let No Man Write My Epitaph, Young Savages, Lolita, Chapman Report, The Balcony, Wives and Lovers, Time of Indifference, A House Is Not a Home, A Patch of Blue (Academy Award, best supporting actress, 1965), The Greatest Story Ever Told, Harper, Alfie, Enter Laughing, The Scalphunters, Wild in the Streets, Buona Sera Mrs. Campbell, The Mad Room, How Do I Love Thee?, Bloody Mama, Flap, What's the Matter with Helen?, Who Slew Auntie Roo?, The Poseidon Adventure, Cleopatra Jones, Something to Hide, Blume in Love, Diamonds, Journey Into Fear, That Lucky Touch, Next Stop Greenwich Village, The Tenant, Tentacles, Pete's Dragon, King of the Gypsies, The Magician of Lublin, The Visitors, City on Fire, S.O.B., Over the Brooklyn Bridge, Ellie, Witchfire (also assoc. prod.), Deja Vu, Very Close Quarters, The Delta Force, The Order of Things, Purple People Eater, An

Unremarkable Life, Touch of a Stranger, Stepping Out, Weep No More My Lady, The Pickle, The Silence of the Hams, Heavy, Jury Duty, Portrait of a Lady.
TELEVISION: *Special*: Bob Hope Chrysler Theatre: Two Is the Number (Emmy Award, 1964). *Movies*: Revenge, A Death of Innocence, The Adventures of Nick Carter, The Devil's Daughter, Big Rose, The Sex Symbol, The Initiation of Sarah, Elvis, Alice in Wonderland, Mrs. Munck. *Mini-Series*: The French Atlantic Affair.

WINTMAN, MELVIN R.
Theatre Executive, b. Chelsea, MA. e. U. of Massachusetts, Northeastern U., J.D. Major, infantry, AUS, W.W.II. Attorney. Now consultant & dir., General Cinema Corp.; formerly exec. v.p., GCC and pres., GCC Theatres, Inc., Boston. Dir. Will Rogers Memorial Fund. Former pres. Theatre Owners of New England (1969-70); past dir. NATO (1969-70); treas., Nat'l Assoc. of Concessionaires (1960).

WISDOM, NORMAN
O.B.E. Actor, Singer, Comedian. Musical and legit. b. London, Eng., Feb. 4, 1915. Awarded Order of the British Empire (O.B.E.), 1995. Many London West End stage shows including royal command performances. New York Broadway shows include Walking Happy and Not Now Darling.
PICTURES: A Date With a Dream (debut, 1948), Meet Mr. Lucifer, Trouble in Store, One Good Turn, As Long as They're Happy, Man of the Moment, Up in the World, Just My Luck, The Square Peg, Follow a Star, There Was a Crooked Man, The Bulldog Breed, The Girl on the Boat, On the Beat, A Stitch in Time, The Early Bird, Press for Time, The Sandwich Man, The Night They Raided Minsky's, What's Good for the Goose, Double X.
TELEVISION: Androcles and the Lion.

WISE, ROBERT
Director, Producer. b. Winchester, IN, Sept. 10, 1914. e. Franklin Coll., Franklin, IN. Ent. m.p. ind. in cutting dept. RKO, 1933; sound cutter, asst. edit.; film edit., 1938; edited Citizen Kane, Magnificent Ambersons; 1944, became dir.; to 20th Century-Fox, 1949; ass'n. Mirisch Co. independent prod. 1959; assn MGM independent prod., 1962; assn. 20th Century Fox Independent Prod. 1963. Partner, Filmakers Group, The Tripar Group.
PICTURES: Curse of the Cat People (debut as co-dir., 1944), Mademoiselle Fifi, The Body Snatcher, A Game of Death, Criminal Court, Born to Kill, Mystery in Mexico, Blood on the Moon, The Set-Up, Three Secrets, Two Flags West, The House on Telegraph Hill, The Day the Earth Stood Still, The Captive City, Something for the Birds, Destination Gobi, The Desert Rats, So Big, Executive Suite, Helen of Troy, Tribute to a Bad Man, Somebody Up There Likes Me, Until They Sail, This Could Be the Night, Run Silent Run Deep, I Want to Live!, Odds Against Tomorrow (also prod.), West Side Story (co-dir., prod.; Academy Awards for Best Picture & Director, 1961), Two For the Seesaw, The Haunting (also prod), The Sound of Music (also prod.; Academy Awards for Best Picture & Director, 1965), The Sand Pebbles (also prod.), Star! (also prod.), The Andromeda Strain (also prod.), Two People (also prod.), The Hindenburg (also prod.), Audrey Rose, Star Trek: The Motion Picture, Wisdom (exec. prod. only), Rooftops.

WISEMAN, FREDERICK
Documentary Filmmaker, Producer, Director & Editor. b. Boston, MA, Jan. 1, 1930. e. Williams College, B.A., 1951; Yale Law Sch., L.L.B., 1954. Member: MA Bar. Private law practice, Paris, 1956-57. Lecturer-in-Law, Boston U. Law Sch., 1959-61; Russell Sage Fndn. Fellowship, Harvard U., 1961-62; research assoc., Brandeis U., dept. of sociology, 1962-66; visiting lecturer at numerous universities. Author: Psychiatry and Law: Use and Abuse of Psychiatry in a Murder Case (American Journal of Psychiatry, Oct. 1961). Co-author: Implementation (section of report of President's Comm. on Law Enforcement and Administration of Justice). Fellow, Amer. Acad. of Arts & Sciences, 1991; John D. and Catherine T. MacArthur Foundation Fellowship, 1982-87; John Simon Guggenheim Memorial Foundation Fellowship, 1980-81. Films are distributed through his Zipporah Films, located in Cambridge, MA. Awards include 3 Emmys, Peabody Award, Intl. Documentary Assn. Career Achievement Award, 3 Columbia Dupont Awards for Excellence in Broadcast Journalism, among others.
PICTURES: Titicut Follies, High School, Law and Order, Hospital, Basic Training, Essene, Juvenile Court, Primate, Welfare, Meat, Canal Zone, Sinai Field Mission, Manoeuvre, Model, Seraphita's Diary, The Store, Racetrack, Deaf, Blind, Multi-Handicapped, Adjustment and Work, Missile, Near Death, Central Park, Aspen, Zoo, High School II, Ballet, La Comedie Francaise.

WISEMAN, JOSEPH
Actor. b. Montreal, Canada, May 15, 1918.
THEATER: King Lear, Golden Boy, The Diary of Anne Frank,
Uncle Vanya, The Last Analysis, Enemies, Detective Story, Three Sisters, Tenth Man, Incident at Vickey, Marco Williams, Unfinished Stories, many others.
PICTURES: Detective Story (debut, 1951), Viva Zapata, Les Miserables, Champ for a Day, The Silver Chalice, The Prodigal, Three Brave Men, The Garment Jungle, The Unforgiven, Happy Thieves, Dr. No, Bye Bye Braverman, The Counterfeit Killer, The Night They Raided Minsky's, Stiletto, Lawman, The Valachi Papers, The Apprenticeship of Duddy Kravitz, Journey Into Fear, The Betsy, Buck Rogers in the 25th Century, Jaguar Lives.
TELEVISION: *Mini-Series*: QB VII, Masada, Rage of Angels. *Movies*: Pursuit, Murder at the World Series, Seize the Day, Lady Mobster. *Series*: Crime Story.

WITHERS, GOOGIE
Actress. b. Karachi, India, Mar. 12, 1917. Trained as a dancer under Italia Conti, Helena Lehmiski & Buddy Bradley; stage debut Victoria Palace in Windmill Man, 1929. Best Actress Award, Deep Blue Sea, 1954. Began screen career at 18. TV also. Theatrical tours Australia, Sun Award, Best Actress, 1974. Awarded officer of the Order of Australia (A.O.) 1980. U.S. ACE Cable award, best actress for Time After Time, 1988.
THEATER: *Britain*: Winter Journey, Deep Blue Sea, Hamlet, Much Ado About Nothing. *Australia*: Plaza Suite, Relatively Speaking, Beckman Place, Woman in a Dressing Gown, The Constant Wife, First Four Hundred Years, Roar Like a Dove, The Cherry Orchard, An Ideal Husband. *London*: Getting Married, Exit the King. *New York*: The Complaisant Lover. Chichester Festival Theatre and Haymarket, London, in The Circle, The Kingfisher, Importance of Being Earnest, The Cherry Orchard, Dandy Dick, The Kingfisher (Australia and Middle East), Time and the Conways (Chichester), School for Scandal (London), Stardust (UK tour). 1986: The Chalk Garden, Hay Fever, Ring Round the Moon, The Cocktail Hour (UK, Australian tour), High Spirits (Aus. tour), On Golden Pond (UK tour).
PICTURES: Haunted Honeymoon, Jeannie, One of Our Aircraft Is Missing, On Approval, Dead of Night, It Always Rains on Sunday, Miranda, Traveler's Joy, Night and the City, White Corridors, Lady Godiva Rides Again, Derby Day, Devil on Horseback, Safe Harbor, Nickel Queen, Country Life, Shine.
TELEVISION: *Series*: Within These Walls, Time After Time, *Movies*: Hotel Du Lac, Northanger Abbey, Ending Up.

WITHERS, JANE
Actress. b. Atlanta, GA, April 12, 1927. By 1934 attracted attention as child player on screen, after radio appearance in Los Angeles and experimental pictures parts, in 1934 in Fox production Bright Eyes, Ginger; thereafter to 1942 featured or starred in numerous 20th-Fox prod. Voted Money-Making Star M.P. Herald-Fame Poll, 1937, 1938. Starred as Josephine the Plumber in Comet tv commercials. TV Movie: All Together Now.
PICTURES: Handle With Care (debut, 1932), Bright Eyes, Ginger, This Is the Life, The Farmer Takes a Wife, Paddy O'Day, Pepper, Gentle Julia, Little Miss Nobody, Can This Be Dixie?, Wild and Woolly, The Holy Terror, Checkers, Angel's Holiday, Forty-Five Fathers, Always in Trouble, Rascals, Keep Smiling, Arizona Wildcat, Pack Up Your Troubles, Chicken Family Wagon, Boy Friend, Shooting High, High School, Youth Will Be Served, The Girl From Avenue A, Golden Hoofs, A Very Young Lady, Her First Beau, Small Town Deb, Young America, The Mad Martindales, Johnny Doughboy, The North Star, My Best Gal, Faces in the Fog, The Affairs of Geraldine, Danger Street, Giant, The Right Approach, Captain Newman M.D.

WITT, PAUL JUNGER
Producer. b. New York, NY, Mar. 20, 1941. e. Univ. of VA. Was assoc. prod., prod. and dir. for Screen Gems, starting in 1965; prod. for Spelling-Goldberg Prods., 1972; Prod.-exec. prod. for Danny Thomas Prods., 1973. With Tony Thomas became co-founder, exec. prod. of Witt/Thomas Prods., 1975.
PICTURES: Firstborn, Dead Poets Society, Final Analysis, Mixed Nuts.
TELEVISION: *Series*: Here Come the Brides, The Partridge Family, The Rookies, Soap, Benson, It's a Living, I'm a Big Girl Now, It Takes Two, Condo, Hail to the Chief, The Golden Girls (Emmy Awards: 1986, 1987), Beauty and the Beast, Empty Nest, Blossom, Good and Evil, Herman's Head, Nurses, Woops, Golden Palace, The John Larroquette Show, Brotherly Love, Minor Adjustments, Common Law, Pearl. *Movies*: Brian's Song (Emmy Award: 1972), No Place to Run, Home for the Holidays, A Cold Night's Death, The Letters, Blood Sport, Remember When, The Gun and the Pulpit, Satan's Triangle, Griffin and Phoenix, High Risk, Trouble in High Timber Country.

WOLF, DICK
Producer, Writer. b. New York, NY, Dec. 20, 1946. e. Univ. of PA. Started in advertising winning three Clio Awards for excellence.

PICTURES: *Prod./Writer:* Skateboard, Gas, No Man's Land, Masquerade (exec. prod., writer, actor), School Ties (story only).
TELEVISION: *Series (exec. prod.):* Miami Vice (also writer), Gideon Oliver (also writer), Christine Cromwell (also creator), Nasty Boys (also creator, writer), H.E.L.P. (also creator, writer), Law and Order (also creator, writer), Mann and Machine (also writer), The Human Factor, Crime and Punishment (also creator), South Beach (also creator), New York Undercover (also creator), The Wright Verdicts (also creator), FEDS (creator).

WOLF, EMANUEL L.
Executive b. Brooklyn, NY, Mar. 27, 1927. e. Syracuse U., B.A., 1950; Maxwell Sch., Syracuse U., M.A. 1952; Maxwell Scholar in Public Admin.-Economics; Chi Eta Sigma (Econ. Hon.). 1952-55. Management consultant, exec. office of Secretary of Navy & Dept. of Interior, Wash, DC, 1956; pres. E.L. Wolf Assocs., Washington, DC, 1961-65; Kalvex, Inc., treas: 1962, dir.: 1963, pres./chmn. of bd.: 1966; dir. Allied Artists Pictures Corp., 1965; chmn. of bd. Vitabath, Inc., Lexington Instruments, Pharmaceutical Savings Plan, Inc. (also pres.) Syracuse U.; corp. advisory bd., American Committee for the Weizmann Institute of Science (Bd. of Directors); pres. & chmn. of bd., Allied Artists Pictures Corp: 1976: pres., bd. chmn. & CEO, Allied Artists Industries Inc., created by Merger of Allied Artists Pictures Corp., Kalvex Inc. and PSP, Inc. 1985, formed indep. prod. co., Emanuel L. Wolf Prods.; 1986-90, pres. & chmn. of bd., Today Home Entertainment. 1991-present. Emanuel L. Wolf Prods., Inc. Chmn., Allied Artists Entertainment Group. Member, AMPAS.

WOLF, THOMAS HOWARD
TV News Exec. b. New York, NY, April 22, 1916. e. Princeton U., B.A., magna cum laude, 1937. Time & Life Mag. 1937-39; 1937-39 NEA (Scripps-Howard) 1940-46; European mgr., NEA, 1942-46. War correspondent, (ETO, MTO) NBC radio correspondent, Paris, 1944-45; co-owner, pres., Information Prod., Inc. founded 1951; co-owner, chmn. Butterfield & Wolf, Inc. founded 1955; prod. CBS series Tomorrow, 1960; exec. prod., CBS daily live Calendar Show, 1961-62; sr. prod., ABC News Report, 1963; exec. prod., ABC Scope, 1964-66. v.p. dir. of TV Documentaries, 1966; v.p., dir. of TV Public Affairs, 1974; dir. TV Cultural Affairs, 1976. Pres., Wolf Communications, Inc., 1981-; consultant Smithsonian Institution, 1981-88.

WOLFSON, RICHARD
Executive. b. New York, NY, Jan. 7, 1923. e. Harvard Coll., Yale Law Sch., 1945-47, law clerk to Justice Wiley Rutledge, U.S. Supreme Court. Law instructor at NYU Law Sch.; 1952, joined Wometco Ent. as counsel and asst. to pres.; named v.p. and dir. in 1959 and sr. v.p. in 1962; named exec. v.p. and general counsel in 1973; named chmn., exec. comm., 1976; retired from Wometco 1982.

WOLPER, DAVID L.
Producer. b. New York, NY, Jan. 11, 1928. m. Gloria Diane Hill. e. Drake U., U. of Southern California. Treas., Flamingo Films, 1948; merged with Associated Artist to form M.P. for TV, Inc., acting as v.p. in chg. of West Coast oper., 1950; v.p. reactivated Flamingo Films, 1954; also pres. Harris-Wolper Pictures, Inc.; pres. Wolper Prod. 1958: pres. Dawn Prod.; v.p. bd. dir. Metromedia, 1965; pres. Wolper Pictures Ltd. 1967; ch. of bd. Wolper Prod., Inc., 1967; pres. Wolper Pictures, 1968; pres. Wolper Productions, 1970; pres. & chmn. of bd. of dir. The Wolper Organization, Inc., 1971; consultant to Warner Bros. & Warner Communications. Pres., David L. Wolper Prods., Inc. 1977. Received Jean Hersholt Humanitarian Award, 1985; Intl. Documentary Assn. Career Achievement Award, 1988. Also received French Natl. Legion of Honor Medal, Lifetime Achievement Award from Producers Guild, Charles de Gaulle Centennial Medal.
PICTURES: Four Days in November, If It's Tuesday This Must Be Belgium, One Is a Lonely Number, The Hellstrom Chronicle, Willy Wonka and the Chocolate Factory, I Love My Wife, Visions of Eight, Birds Do It Bees Do It, This Is Elvis, The Man Who Saw Tomorrow, Imagine: John Lennon, Murder in the First.
TELEVISION: *Specials:* The Race For Space, The Making of the President (1960, 1964, 1968), National Geographic Society Specials (1965-68, 1971-75), The Rise and Fall of the Third Reich, The Undersea World of Jacques Cousteau (1967-68), George Plimpton specials (1970-72), American Heritage specials (1973-74), Primal Man specials (1973-75), Judgment specials (1974), Smithsonian Specials, Sandburg's Lincoln, The Man Who Saw Tomorrow, Opening & Closing Ceremonies: Olympic Games 1984, Liberty Weekend 1986, A Celebration of Tradition for Warner Bros, Here's Looking at You Warner Bros., Golf—The Greatest Game. *Series:* Story of..., Biography, Hollywood and the Stars, Men in Crisis, The March of Time (1965-66), Appointment With Destiny, Get Christie Love, Chico and the Man, Welcome Back Kotter,

Casablanca, Golf: Heroes of the Game. *Movies:* Say Goodbye, The 500 Pound Jerk, I Will Fight No More Forever, Victory at Entebbe, Agatha Christie's Murder Is Easy, What Price Victory, Roots: The Gift, When You Remember Me, The Betty Ford Story, Dillinger, The Plot to Kill Hitler, Murder in Mississippi, Bed of Lies, The Flood: Who Will Save Our Children?, Fatal Deception: Mrs. Lee Harvey Oswald. *Mini-Series:* Roots (Emmy Award, 1977), Roots: The Next Generations, (Emmy Award, 1979), Moviola (This Year's Blonde, The Scarlett O'Hara War, The Silent Lovers), The Thorn Birds, North & South, North & South Book I: Love & War, North & South Book III: Heaven & Hell, Napoleon & Josephine: A Love Story, Queen, Without Warning.

WONG, VICTOR
Actor. Was reporter in San Francisco's Chinatown, 1968-75, before working on stage at Joseph Papp's Public Theatre.
PICTURES: Dim Sum: A Little Bit of Heart, Year of the Dragon, Big Trouble in Little China, Shanghai Surprise, The Golden Child, Prince of Darkness, The Last Emperor, Eat a Bowl of Tea, Tremors, Life Is Cheap... But Toilet Paper Is Expensive, 3 Ninjas, The Joy Luck Club, The Ice Runner, 3 Ninjas Kick Back, 3 Ninjas Knuckle Up, The Stars Fell on Henrietta.
TELEVISION: *Series:* Search for Tomorrow. *Movies/Specials:* Night Song, Fortune Cookie, Paper Angel, Mild Bunch, Search, China Nights.

WOO, JOHN
Director. b. Guangzhou, China, 1948. e. Matteo Ricci Col, Hong Kong. Started making experimental 16 mm films in 1967. Joined film industry in 1969 as prod. asst. for Cathay Film Co., then asst. dir. 1971 joined Shaw Brothers working as asst. dir. to Zhang Che.
PICTURES: The Young Dragons (debut, 1973), The Dragon Tamers, Countdown in Kung Fu, Princess Chang Ping, From Riches to Rags, Money Crazy, Follow the Star, Last Hurrah for Chivalry, To Hell With the Devil, Laughing Times, Plain Jane to the Rescue, Sunset Warriors (Heroes Shed No Tears), The Time You Need a Friend, Run Tiger Run, A Better Tomorrow, A Better Tomorrow II, Just Heroes, The Killer, Bullet in the Head, Once a Thief, Hard Boiled, Hard Target (U.S. debut, 1993), Broken Arrow.

WOOD, ELIJAH
Actor. b. Cedar Rapids, IA, Jan. 28, 1981. Started in commercial modeling. Landed first acting job in Paula Abdul video Forever Your Girl.
PICTURES: Back to the Future Part II (debut, 1989), Internal Affairs, Avalon, Paradise, Radio Flyer, Forever Young, The Adventures of Huck Finn, The Good Son, North, The War, Flipper, The Ice Storm.
TELEVISION: *Movies:* Child of the Night, Day-O.

WOODARD, ALFRE
Actress. b. Tulsa, OK, Nov. 8, 1953. e. Boston U., B.A. Soon after graduation landed role in Washington, D.C. Arena Stage theater in Horatio, and Saved.
THEATER: A Christmas Carol, Bugs Guns, Leander Stillwell, For Colored Girls Who Have Considered Suicide/When the Rainbow Is Enuf, A Map of the World, A Winter's Tale, Two By South.
PICTURES: Remember My Name, Health, Cross Creek (Acad. Award nom.), Extremities, Scrooged, Miss Firecracker, Grand Canyon, The Gun in Betty Lou's Handbag, Passion Fish, Rich in Love, Heart and Souls, Blue Chips, Crooklyn, How to Make an American Quilt, Primal Fear, Star Trek: First Contact, Follow Me Home.
TELEVISION: *Series:* Tucker's Witch, Sara, St. Elsewhere. *Guest:* Palmerstown USA, What Really Happened to the Class of '65?, Hill Street Blues (Emmy Award, 1984), L.A. Law (Emmy Award, 1987). *Movies:* Freedom Road, Sophisticated Gents, Go Tell It on the Mountain, Sweet Revenge, Unnatural Causes, The Killing Floor, Mandela, A Mother's Courage: The Mary Thomas Story, Blue Bayou, Race to Freedom: The Underground Railroad, The Piano Lesson. *Specials:* For Colored Girls Who Haved Considered Suicide/When the Rainbow Is Enuf, Trial of the Moke, Words by Heart, Aliens for Breakfast.

WOODS, DONALD
Actor. b. Brandon, Manitoba, Canada, Dec. 2, 1906. e. UC Berkeley. Appeared in WB shorts Song of a Nation, and Star in the Night (Oscar winner, 1945).
THEATER: Holiday, Charley's Aunt, Dracula, Strange Interlude, Two for the Seesaw, Rosmersholm, One by One, Soldier, You Can't Take It With You, Twelfth Night, Assassination 1865, Perfect Gentleman, Kansas City Repertory.
PICTURES: A Tale of Two Cities, Story of Louis Pasteur, Anthony Adverse, Forgotten Girls, Love Honor and Oh Baby, I Was a Prisoner on Devil's Island, Watch on the Rhine, Bridge of San Luis Rey, Wonder Man, Roughly Speaking, Barbary Pirate, 13 Ghosts, Kissin' Cousins, Moment to Moment; many other films.

TELEVISION: G.E. Theatre, Wind from the South, Wagon Train, Thrillers, Sunset Strip, Ben Casey, Laramie, The Rebel, The Law and Mr. Jones, The Roaring 20's, Wild Wild West, Bonanza. *Series*: Tammy.

WOODS, JAMES
Actor. b. Vernal UT, Apr. 18, 1947. e. Massachusetts Inst. of Technology (appeared in 36 plays at MIT, Harvard and Theatre Co. of Boston). Left college to pursue acting career in New York.
THEATER: Borstal Boy (B'way debut, 1970), followed by Conduct Unbecoming (off-B'way, Obie Award), Saved, Trial of the Catonsville Nine, Moonchildren (Theatre World Award), Green Julia (off-B'way), Finishing Touches.
PICTURES: The Visitors (debut, 1971), Hickey and Boggs, The Way We Were, The Gambler, Distance, Night Moves, Alex and the Gypsy, The Choirboys, The Onion Field, The Black Marble, Eyewitness, Fast-Walking, Split Image, Videodrome, Against All Odds, Once Upon a Time in America, Cat's Eye, Joshua Then and Now, Salvador (Acad. Award nom.; Indept. Film Project Spirit Award, 1986), Best Seller, Cop (also co-prod.), The Boost, True Believer, Immediate Family, The Hard Way, Straight Talk, Diggstown, Chaplin, The Getaway, The Specialist, For Better or Worse, Casino, Nixon, Killer: A Journal of Murder, Ghosts of Mississippi.
TELEVISION: *Movies*: Footsteps, A Great American Tragedy, Foster and Laurie, F. Scott Fitzgerald in Hollywood, The Disappearance of Aimee, Raid on Entebbe, Billion Dollar Bubble, The Gift of Love, The Incredible Journey of Dr. Meg Laurel, And Your Name Is Jonah, Badge of the Assassin, Promise (Emmy & Golden Globe Awards, 1987), In Love and War, My Name is Bill W. (Emmy Award, 1989), Women & Men: Stories of Seduction (Hills Like White Elephants), The Boys, Citizen Cohn, Jane's House, Next Door, Curse of the Starving Class, Indictment: The McMartin Trial. *Specials*: All the Way Home, Crimes of Passion (host), Wildfire (host), Mobs and Mobsters (host), Fallen Angels. *Mini-series*: Holocaust. *Guest*: Kojak, Rockford Files, Streets of San Francisco, The Rookies, Police Story, Saturday Night Live, Dream On, The Simpsons (voice).

WOODWARD, EDWARD
O.B.E.: Actor, Singer. b. Croydon, England, June 1, 1930. e. Royal Acad. of Dramatic Art. As singer has recorded 11 LPs. 2 Gold Discs. Television Actor of the Year, 1969-70; also Sun Award, Best Actor, 1970-72. Has received 15 national & international awards.
THEATER: With Royal Shakespeare Company, 1958-59; Cyrano, 20 West End plays and musicals, including The Art of Living, The Little Doctor, A Rattle of a Simple Man (West End/B'way), The High Bid, The Male of the Species, High Spirits (B'way musical), The Best Laid Plans, On Approval, The Wolf, Richard III, The Assassin.
PICTURES: Where There's a Will (debut, 1955), Becket, File on the Golden Goose, Incense for the Damned, Young Winston, Sitting Target, Hunted, Wicker Man, Callan, Stand Up Virgin Soldiers, Breaker Morant, The Appointment, The Final Option (Who Dares Wins), Champions, King David, Mister Johnson, Deadly Advice.
TELEVISION: *Series*: Callan, Nice Work, The Equalizer (4 Emmy noms., Golden Globe Award), Over My Dead Body, In Suspicious Cirumstances. *Movies/Specials*: Sword of Honour, Bassplayer and Blonde (mini-series), Saturday, Sunday, Monday, Rod of Iron, The Trial of Lady Chatterly, Wet Job–Callan Special, Churchill: The Wilderness Years, Blunt Instrument, Killer Contract, Arthur the King, Uncle Tom's Cabin, A Christmas Carol, Codename: Kyril, Hunted, The Man in the Brown Suit, Hands of a Murderer, World War II, Suspicious Circumstances, The Shamrock Conspiracy, Common as Muck, Harrison, Gulliver's Travels.

WOODWARD, JOANNE
Actress. b. Thomasville, GA, Feb. 27, 1930. m. Paul Newman. e. Louisiana State U. Studied at Neighborhood Playhouse Dramatic Sch. and the Actors Studio. Appeared in many TV dramatic shows.
THEATER: Picnic, The Lovers, Baby Want a Kiss, Candida, The Glass Menagerie (Williamstown, The Long Wharf), Golden Boy (dir., the Blue Light Theatre Company).
PICTURES: Count Three and Pray (debut, 1955), A Kiss Before Dying, Three Faces of Eve (Academy Award, 1957), No Down Payment, The Long Hot Summer, Rally 'Round the Flag Boys, The Sound and the Fury, The Fugitive Kind, From the Terrace, Paris Blues, The Stripper, A New Kind of Love, Signpost to Murder, A Big Hand for the Little Lady, A Fine Madness, Rachel Rachel (Acad. Award nom.), Winning, WUSA, They Might Be Giants, The Effect of Gamma Rays on Man-in-the-Moon Marigolds, Summer Wishes Winter Dreams (Acad. Award nom.), The Drowning Pool, The End, Harry and Son, The Glass Menagerie, Mr. and Mrs. Bridge (Acad. Award nom.), The Age of Innocence (narrator), Philadelphia.
TELEVISION: *Specials*: Broadway's Dreamers: The Legacy of The Group Theater (host, co-prod.; Emmy Award, 1990), Family Thanksgiving Special (dir. only). *Movies*: Sybil, Come

Back Little Sheba, See How She Runs (Emmy Award, 1978), A Christmas to Remember, The Streets of L.A., The Shadow Box, Crisis at Central High, Passions, Do You Remember Love? (Emmy Award, 1985), Foreign Affairs, Blind Spot (also co-prod.).

WOOLDRIDGE, SUSAN
Actress. b. London, England. e. Central Sch. of Speech & Drama/Ecole/Jacques LeCoq. Paris. Ent. ind. 1971.
THEATER: Macbeth, School for Scandal, Merchant of Venice, The Cherry Orchard, Look Back in Anger, 'night Mother, Map of the Heart.
PICTURES: The Shout, Butley, Loyalties, Hope and Glory, How to Get Ahead in Advertising, Bye Bye Blues, Twenty-One, Afraid of the Dark, Just Like a Woman, Butter.
TELEVISION: The Naked Civil Servant, John McNab, The Racing Game, The Jewel in the Crown, The Last Place on Earth, Hay Fever, Time and the Conways, Dead Man's Folly, The Devil's Disciple, The Dark Room, Pastoralcare, The Small Assassin, A Fine Romance, Ticket to Ride, Changing Step, Pied Piper, Crimestrike, Broke, Miss Pym's Day Out, An Unwanted Woman, The Humming Bird Tree, Inspector Alleyn Mysteries, Tracey Ullman Show, Bad Company, Under the Hammer, All Quiet on the Preston Front, Wycliffe, The Writing Game.

WOOLF, SIR JOHN
Knighted 1975. Producer. b. England, 1913. e. Institut Montana, Switzerland. Awarded U.S. Bronze star for service in WWII. Asst. dir. Army Kinematography, War Office 1944-45; Founder and chmn. Romulus Films Ltd, since 1948. Man dir. since 1967; chmn. since 1982 of British & American Film Holdings Plc; dir. First Leisure Corp. Plc since 1982. Co-founder and exec. dir., Anglia TV Group PLC, 1958-83. Member: Cinematograph Films Council, 1969-79; bd. of gov., Services Sound & Vision Corp (formerly Services Kinema Corp.) 1974-83; exec. council and trustee, Cinema and Television Benevolent Fund; Freeman, City of London, 1982; FRSA 1978. Received special awards for contribution to British film indust. from Cinematograph Exhibitors Assoc. 1969. and Variety Club of GB, 1974.
PICTURES: *Prod. by Romulus Gp.*: The African Queen, Pandora and the Flying Dutchman, Moulin Rouge, Beat the Devil, I Am a Camera, Carrington VC, The Bespoke Overcoat (short; Acad. Award, BAFTA Award), Story of Ester Costello, Room at the Top (BAFTA Award, best film, 1958), Wrong Arm of the Law, The L-Shaped Room, Term of Trial, Life at the Top, Oliver! (Acad. Award, Golden Globe, best film, 1968), Day of the Jackal, The Odessa File.
TELEVISION: *Prod. for Anglia TV incl.*: 100 Tales of the Unexpected, Miss Morrison's Ghosts, The Kingfisher, Edwin, Love Song.

WOPAT, TOM
Actor. b. Lodi, WI, Sept. 9, 1951. e. U. of Wisconsin. Left school to travel for two years with rock group as lead singer and guitarist. Spent two summers at Barn Theater in MI. Came to New York; *Off-B'way* in A Bistro Car on the CNR. *On B'way* in I Love My Wife, City of Angels, Guys and Dolls.
TELEVISION: *Series*: The Dukes of Hazzard, Blue Skies, A Peaceable Kingdom, Cybill. *Movies*: Christmas Comes to Willow Creek, Burning Rage, Just My Imagination.

WORKMAN, CHUCK
Director, Writer, Producer. b. Philadelphia, PA. June 5. e. Rutgers U., B.A.; Cornell U. Pres., International Documentary Assoc. 1987-88; Member: Directors Guild of America, National Board; Bd. mem.: Santa Monica Arts Fdn. Lecturer, U. of Southern California. Pres. Calliope Films, Inc. Winner Clio Award, 1969, 1970. Acad. Award, 1987.
THEATER: Bruno's Ghost (1981, writer, dir.), Diplomacy (writer, dir.), The Man Who Wore White Shoes (writer), Bloomers (writer).
PICTURES: Monday's Child (1967, editor), Traitors of San Angel (editor), The Money (dir., s.p.), Protocol (dir., media sequences), Stoogemania (dir., co-s.p.), Precious Images (Acad. Award, Best Live Action Short, 1986; Gold Hugo Award, Cannes Film Fest., N.Y. Film Fest.), Words (Best Short, Houston Fest., N.Y. Film Fest., 1988), Pieces of Silver, Superstar (dir.-prod.), The First 100 Years (dir., prod.).
DOCUMENTARIES: The Making of the Deep (prod., dir., writer), The Director and the Image (CINE Golden Eagle Award, 1980), The Game, The Best Show in Town (CINE Golden Eagle), And the Winner Is..., The Keeper of the Light.

WORONOV, MARY
Actress. b. Brooklyn, NY, Dec. 8, 1946. e. Cornell. On NY stage in In the Boom Boom Room (Theatre World Award).
PICTURES: The Chelsea Girls, Kemek: It's Controlling Your Mind, Sugar Cookies, Seizure, Cover Girl Models, Death Race 2000, Cannonball, Jackson County Jail, Hollywood Boulevard, Bad Georgia Road, Mr. Billion, The One and Only, The Lady in Red, Rock 'n' Roll High School, National Lampoon Goes to the

Movies, Angel of H.E.A.T., Heartbeeps, Eating Raoul, Get Crazy, Night of the Comet, Hellhole, My Man Adam, Nomads, Movie House Massacre, Chopping Mall, Terrorvision, Black Widow, Scenes From the Class Struggle in Beverly Hills, Let It Ride, Mortuary Academy, Dick Tracy, Watchers II, Warlock, Club Fed, Where Sleeping Dogs Lie, Motorama, Good Girls Don't, Hell-Rollers, Grief.
TELEVISION: *Movies*: In the Glitter Palace, Challenge of a Lifetime, Acting on Impulse.

WORTH, IRENE
Actress. b. Nebraska, June 23, 1916. e. UCLA. Formerly a teacher. B'way debut in The Two Mrs. Carrolls, after which went to London where made her home. Appeared with Old Vic and Royal Shakespeare Co.; returned to U.S. to appear on B'way in the Cocktail Party.
THEATER: Hotel Paradiso, Mary Stuart, The Potting Shed, Toys in the Attic, Tiny Alice (Tony Award, 1965), Sweet Bird of Youth (Tony Award, 1976), Cherry Orchard, Old Times Happy Days, Coriolanus (NY Shakespeare Fest), Lost in Yonkers (Tony Award, 1991).
PICTURES: One Night With You, Secret People, Orders to Kill (British Acad. Award, best actress), The Scapegoat, Seven Seas to Calais, King Lear, Nicholas and Alexander, Rich Kids, Eyewitness, Deathtrap, Fast Forward, Lost in Yonkers.
TELEVISION: The Lady from the Sea, The Duchess of Malfi, The Way of the World, Prince Orestes, Forbidden, The Big Knife, The Shell Seekers.

WORTH, MARVIN
Producer, Writer. b. Brooklyn, NY. Jazz promoter and manager before starting to write special material for Alan King, Buddy Hackett, Joey Bishop, Lenny Bruce and many others.
THEATER: Lenny (prod.).
PICTURES: *Writer*: Boys' Night Out, Three on a Couch, Promise Her Anything. *Producer*: Diabolique, Where's Poppa?, Malcolm X (documentary), Lenny, Fire Sale, The Rose, Up the Academy, Soup for One, Unfaithfully Yours, Rhinestone, Falling in Love, Less Than Zero, Patty Hearst, Running Mates, See No Evil, Hear No Evil, Flashback, Malcolm X.
TELEVISION: Steve Allen Show, Jackie Gleason, Ray Bolger's Washington Square, Chevy Shows, General Motors' 50th Anniversary Show, Milton Berle Show, Colgate Comedy Hour, Martha Raye Show, Polly Bergen Show, Ann Sothern Show, Judy Garland Show, Get Smart, others.

WOWCHUK, HARRY N.
Actor, Writer, Photographer, Producer, Executive. b. Philadelphia, PA. Oct. 16, 1948. e. Santa Monica City Coll., UCLA, theater arts, 1970. Started film career as actor, stunt-driver-photographer. T.V. and commercial credits include: TV Guide, Seal Test, Camel Cigarettes, Miller High Life, American Motors, Camera V, AW Rootbeer. Former exec. v.p. International Cinema, in chg. of prod. and distribution; V.P. J. Newport Film Productions; pres., United West Productions.
PICTURES: The Lost Dutchman, Las Vegas Lady, This Is a Hijack, Tidal Wave, Tunnel Vision, Incredible 2-Headed Transplant, Jud, Bad Charleston Charlie, Some Call It Loving, Summer School Teachers, Five Minutes of Freedom, Pushing Up Daisies, Money-Marbles-Chalk, The Models, Love Swedish Style, Up-Down-Up, Sunday's Child, Soul Brothers, Freedom Riders, Perilous Journey, Claws of Death, Georgia Peaches.

WOWCHUK, NICHOLAS
Executive, Producer, Writer, Editor, Financier. b. Philadelphia, PA. e. St. Basil's Coll., UCLA. Founder-publisher: All-American Athlete Magazine, Sports and Health Digest, The Spectator. Former sports writer: Phila. Evening Public Ledger; Phila. Daily Record; Phila. Inquirer. Founder & bd. chmn.: Mutual Realty Investment Co.; Mutual Mortgage Co., Beverly Hills, CA. President: Mutual General Films, Bev. Hills, CA; Abbey Theatrical Films, NY; Mutual Film Distribution Co.; Mutual Recording & Broadcasting Enterprises.
PICTURES: *Exec. Prod.*: Perilous Journey, The Incredible 2-Headed Transplant, Pushing Up Daisies, Money-Marbles-Chalk, Five Minutes of Freedom, The Campaign, Claws of Death. *Prod.*: Scorpion's Web, Pursuit, Brave Men, Sea of Despair, Cossacks in Battle, The Straight White Line, Tilt, Rooster, To Live... You Gotta Win.

WRAY, FAY
Actress. b. Alberta, Canada, Sept. 15, 1907. On stage in Pilgrimage Play, Hollywood, 1923; m.p. debut in Gasoline Love; thereafter in many m.p. for Paramount to 1930; then in films for various Hollywood and Brit. prod. Autobiography: On the Other Hand (1989).
PICTURES: Streets of Sin, The Wedding March, The Four Feathers, The Texan, Dirigible, Doctor X, The Most Dangerous Game, The Vampire Bat, The Mystery of the Wax Museum, King Kong, The Bowery, Madame Spy, The Affairs of Cellini, The Clairvoyant, They Met in a Taxi, Murder in Greenwich Village, The Jury's Secret, Smashing the Spy Ring, Navy

Secrets, Wildcat Bus, Adam Had Four Sons, Melody for Three, Not a Ladies' Man, Small Town Girl, Treasure of the Golden Condor, Queen Bee, The Cobweb, Hell on Frisco Bay, Crime of Passion, Rock Pretty Baby, Tammy and the Bachelor, Summer Love, Dragstrip Riot.
TELEVISION: *Series*: Pride of the Family. *Movie*: Gideon's Trumpet.

WRIGHT, AMY
Actress. b. Chicago, IL, Apr. 15, 1950. e. Beloit Col. Studied acting with Uta Hagen; 1976, joined Rip Torn's Sanctuary Theatre. B'way in Fifth of July, Noises Off, Mrs. Klein.
PICTURES: Not a Pretty Picture, Girlfriends, The Deer Hunter, Breaking Away, The Amityville Horror, Heartland, Wise Blood, Stardust Memories, Inside Moves, Off Beat, The Telephone, Crossing Delancey, The Accidental Tourist, Miss Firecracker, Daddy's Dyin', Deceived, Love Hurts, Hard Promises, Josh and S.A.M., Tom and Huck.
TELEVISION: *Movies*: Trapped in Silence, Settle the Score, To Dance With the White Dog. *Special*: Largo Desolato. *Pilot*: A Fine Romance.

WRIGHT, ROBERT C.
Executive. b. Rockville Center, NY, April 23, 1943. e. Coll. Holy Cross, B.A. history, 1965; U. of Virginia, LLB 1968. Mem. NY, VA, MA, NJ Bar. 1969, joined General Electric; lawyer in plastics div. Later moved into product & sls. management in plastics div. 1980, moved to Cox Cable as pres. Returned to GE 1983 heading small appliances div.; moved to GE Financial Services & GE Credit Corp. as pres., which posts he held when named head of NBC following purchase of NBC's parent RCA by GE. Pres. and CEO, National Broadcasting Co. (NBC), 1986-.

WRIGHT, ROBIN
Actress. b. Dallas, TX, 1966. m. actor Sean Penn. Was model at age 14 before making acting debut on tv series The Yellow Rose.
PICTURES: Hollywood Vice Squad (debut, 1986), The Princess Bride, Denial, State of Grace, The Playboys, Toys, Forrest Gump, The Crossing Guard, Moll Flanders.
TELEVISION: *Series*: Santa Barbara. *Pilot*: Home.

WRIGHT, TERESA
Actress. b. New York, NY, Oct. 27, 1918. e. Columbia H.S., Maplewood, NJ, 1938.
THEATER: *Tours*: Mary Mary, Tchin-Tchin, The Effect of Gamma Rays on Man-in-the-Moon Marigolds, Noel Coward in Two Keys, The Master Builder. *Regional*: Long Day's Journey into Night, You Can't Take It With You, All The Way Home, Wings. *NY*: Life with Father, Dark at the Top of the Stairs, I Never Sang for My Father, Death of a Salesman, Ah Wilderness!, Morning's at Seven (also London), On Borrowed Time.
PICTURES: The Little Foxes (debut, 1941), Pride of the Yankees, Mrs. Miniver (Academy Award, best supporting actress, 1942), Shadow of a Doubt, Casanova Brown, The Best Years of Our Lives, The Trouble With Women, Pursued, Imperfect Lady, Enchantment, The Capture, The Men, Something to Live For, California Conquest, Steel Trap, Count the Hours, The Actress, Track of the Cat, The Search for Bridey Murphy, Escapade in Japan, The Restless Years, Hail Hero, The Happy Ending, Roseland, Somewhere in Time, The Good Mother.
TELEVISION: *Specials*: The Margaret Bourke-White Story, The Miracle Worker, The Golden Honeymoon, The Fig Tree, A Century of Women. *Movies*: Crawlspace, The Elevator, Flood, Bill—On His Own, Perry Mason: The Case of the Desperate Deception.

WUHL, ROBERT
Actor, Writer. b. Union, NJ, Oct. 9, 1951. e. Univ. of Houston. Worked as stand-up comedian and joke writer. Was story editor on series Police Squad! Appeared in 1988 Academy Award winning short Ray's Male Heterosexual Dance Hall.
PICTURES: The Hollywood Knights (debut, 1980), Flashdance, Good Morning Vietnam, Bull Durham, Batman, Blaze, Wedding Band, Mistress, A Kiss Goodnight, Blue Chips, Cobb, Dr. Jekyll and Ms. Hyde, Open Season (also dir., s.p.).
TELEVISION: *Series*: Arliss. *Pilots*: Rockhopper, Sniff. *Guest*: Tales from the Crypt, Moonlighting, L.A. Law, Falcon Crest. *Specials*: The Big Bang (also dir.), Comic Relief IV, The Earth Day Special, The Real Deal. *Movie*: Percy & Thunder. *Writer*: Police Squad, Sledge Hammer, Grammy Awards (1987-89), Academy Awards (Emmy Award, 1991).

WYATT, JANE
Actress. b. New York, NY, Aug. 12, 1910. e. Miss Chapin's Sch., Barnard Coll. m. Edgar B. Ward. Joined Apprentice Sch., Berkshire Playhouse, Stockbridge, Mass. Understudied in Tradewinds and The Vinegar Tree. Appeared in Give Me Yesterday and the Tadpole. In 1933 succeeded Margaret Sullavan in Dinner at Eight.

THEATER: The Autumn Garden (NY), The Bishop Misbehaves, Conquest, Eveningsong, The Mad Hopes, Hope for the Best, The Joyous Season For Services Rendered, Driving Miss Daisy, Love Letters.
PICTURES: One More River (debut, 1934), Great Expectations, We're Only Human, The Luckiest Girl in the World, Lost Horizon, The Girl From God's Country, Kisses for Breakfast, Hurricane Smith, Weekend for Three, Army Surgeon, The Navy Comes Through, The Kansan, Buckskin Frontier, None But the Lonely Heart, Strange Conquest, The Bachelor's Daughters, Boomerang!, Gentleman's Agreement, Pitfall, No Minor Vices, Bad Boy, Canadian Pacific, Task Force, House By the River, Our Very Own, My Blue Heaven, The Man Who Cheated Himself, Criminal Lawyer, Interlude, Two Little Bears, Never Too Late, Treasure of Matecumbe, Star Trek IV: The Voyage Home.
TELEVISION: Series: Father Knows Best (1954-59; 3 Emmy Awards: 1957, 1958, 1959). Guest: Bob Hope Chrysler Theater, The Virginian, Wagon Train, U.S. Steel Hour, Bell Telephone Hour, Confidential For Women, My Father My Mother, Barefoot in the Park, The Ghost and Mrs. Muir, Here Come the Brides, Love American Style, Fantasy Island, Love Boat. Movies: Katherine, Tom Sawyer, Father Knows Best Reunion, A Love Affair, Amelia Earhart, Superdome, The Nativity, The Millionaire, Missing Children—A Mother's Story, Amityville: The Evil Escapes, Neighbors, Ladies of the Corridor, Star Trek.

WYMAN, JANE
Actress. r.n. Sarah Jane Fulks. b. St. Joseph, MO, Jan. 5, 1917. e. Univ. of MO. Started in show business as radio singer calling herself Jane Durrell. Debuted in films as bit player using her real name. Voted one of top ten money-making stars in M.P. Herald-Fame poll, 1954.
PICTURES: Cain and Mabel, Golddiggers of 1937, My Man Godfrey, King of Burlesque, Smart Blonde, Stage Struck, King and the Chorus Girl, Ready Willing and Able, Slim, The Singing Marine, Public Wedding, Mr. Dodd Takes the Air, The Crowd Roars, Brother Rat, Wide Open Faces, The Spy Ring, He Couldn't Say No, Fools for Scandal, Kid Nightingale, Tail Spin, Private Detective, Kid from Kokomo, Torchy Plays With Dynamite, Brother Rat and a Baby, An Angel From Texas, Gambling on the High Seas, Tugboat Annie Sails Again, My Love Came Back, The Body Disappears, Honeymoon for Three, Bad Men of Missouri, You're in the Army Now, Larceny, Inc., My Favorite Spy, Footlight Serenade, Princess O'Rourke, Doughgirls, Make Your Own Bed, Crime by Night, Hollywood Canteen, Lost Weekend, One More Tomorrow, Night and Day, The Yearling, Cheyenne, Magic Town, Johnny Belinda (Academy Award, 1948), A Kiss in the Dark, The Lady Takes a Sailor, It's a Great Feeling, Stage Fright, The Glass Menagerie, Three Guys Named Mike, Here Comes the Groom, Blue Veil, Starlift, Just for You, Story of Will Rogers, Let's Do It Again, So Big, Magnificent Obsession, Lucy Gallant, All That Heaven Allows, Miracle in the Rain, Holiday for Lovers, Pollyanna, Bon Voyage, How to Commit Marriage.
TELEVISION: Series: Fireside Theatre (The Jane Wyman Show), Summer Playhouse, Falcon Crest. Movies: The Failing of Raymond, The Incredible Journey of Dr. Meg Laurel.

WYMAN, THOMAS H.
Executive. b. 1931. Joined CBS, Inc. in 1980 as pres. & chief exec. Then chmn until 1986. Prior career as chief exec. of Green Giant Co.; became v. chmn. to 1988, of Pillsbury Co. when it acquired Green Giant in 1979.

WYNN, TRACY KEENAN
Writer. b. Hollywood, CA, Feb. 28, 1945. e. UCLA Theatre Arts Dept., BA in film/TV division, 1967. Fourth generation in show business: son of actor Keenan Wynn, grandson of Ed Wynn, great-grandson of Frank Keenan, Irish Shakespearean actor who made B'way debut in 1880.
PICTURES: The Longest Yard, The Drowning Pool (co-s.p.), The Deep (co. s.p.).
TELEVISION: Movies: The Glass House, Tribes (also assoc. prod.: Emmy & WGA Awards, 1971), The Autobiography of Miss Jane Pittman (Emmy Award & WGA Awards, 1974), Hit Lady (dir. only), Quest, Bloody Friday (also co-prod.), Capone in Jail, Carolina Skeletons.

Y

YABLANS, FRANK
Executive. b. Brooklyn, NY, Aug. 27, 1935. Ent. m.p. ind. as Warner Bros. booker, 1957. Warner Bros. salesman in N.Y., Boston, Milwaukee, Chicago, 1957-59. Milwaukee br. mgr. Buena Vista, 1959-66. Midwest sales mgr., Sigma III, 1966. Eastern sales mgr., 1967, sales v.p. 1968. V.P. general sales mgr., Paramount Pic. Corp., 1969; v.p.-dist., 1970; sr. v.p.-mkt., 1970; exec. v.p., 1971; named pres. 1971. 1975, became an indep. prod., his company called, Frank Yablans Presentations Inc. 1983, MGM/UA Entertainment Co. as bd. chmn. & chief oper. off. Held titles of bd. chmn. & CEO with

both MGM and UA Corp when resigned, 1985. Same year teamed with PSO Delphi to form Northstar Entertainment Co.; 1986, non-exclusive deal with Empire Entertainment; 1988, non-exclusive 3-year deal with Columbia Pictures; 1989, pres. Epic Prods., pres., CEO Nova Intl. Films Inc.
PICTURES: Producer: Silver Streak (exec. prod.), The Other Side of Midnight, The Fury, North Dallas Forty (also co-s.p.), Mommie Dearest (also co-s.p.), Monsignor (co.-prod), Star Chamber, Kidco, Buy and Cell, Lisa, Congo (exec. prod.).

YABLANS, IRWIN
Executive. b. Brooklyn, NY, July 25, 1934. Began career in industry at WB in 1956 after two-yr. stint with U.S. Army in Germany. Held m.p. sales posts in Washington, DC, Albany, Detroit, Milwaukee and Portland. In 1962 joined Paramount as L.A. mgr.; in 1964 made western sales mgr. In 1972 entered production as assoc. prod. on Howard W. Koch's Badge 373. Pres. of Compass Intl. Pictures. Exec. v.p., low budget films, Lorimar Productions. Resigned June, 1984. In 1985 named chmn., Orion Pictures Distributing Corp. 1988: named chmn. and CEO of newly formed Epic Pictures.
PICTURES: The Education of Sonny Carson. Exec. prod.: Halloween, Roller Boogie (also story), Fade To Black (also story), Seduction (prod.), Halloween II, Halloween III: Season of the Witch, Parasite, Tank, Hell Night, Prison Arena, Why Me?, Men at Work.

YATES, PETER
Producer, Director. b. Ewshoot, Eng., July 24, 1929. e. Royal Acad. of Dramatic Art. Ent. m.p. ind. as studio mgr. and dubbing asst. with De Lane Lea. Asst. dir.: The Entertainer, The Guns of Navarone, A Taste of Honey, The Roman Spring of Mrs. Stone. Stage dir.: The American Dream, The Death of Bessie Smith, Passing Game, Interpreters. Received Acad. Award noms. for Best Director/Picture (Producer): Breaking Away, The Dresser.
PICTURES: Summer Holiday, One Way Pendulum, Robbery (also co-s.p.), Bullitt, John and Mary, Murphy's War, The Hot Rock, The Friends of Eddie Coyle, For Pete's Sake, Mother Jugs and Speed (also prod.), The Deep, Breaking Away (also prod.), Eyewitness (also prod.), Krull, The Dresser (also prod.), Eleni, Suspect, The House on Carroll Street (also prod.), An Innocent Man, Year of the Comet (also co-prod.), Needful Things (exec. prod. only), Roommates, The Run of the Country (also co-prod.).
TELEVISION: Series: Danger Man (Secret Agent), The Saint.

YELLEN, LINDA
Producer, Director, Writer. b. New York, NY, July 13. e. Barnard Coll., B.A., Columbia U., M.F.A., Ph.D. Also lecturer Barnard Coll., Yale U., asst. professor, City U. of New York. Member: exec. council, DGA.
THEATER: Chantilly Lace (dir., prod., writer), Parallel Lives (dir., prod. writer).
PICTURES: The End of Summer (dir., prod., s.p.), Looking Up (prod., dir.), Prospera, Come Out Come Out, Everybody Wins (prod.).
TELEVISION: Movies: Mayflower: The Pilgrims' Adventure (prod.), Playing for Time (exec. prod.; Emmy, Peabody & Christopher Awards, 1980), Hardhat and Legs (prod.), The Royal Romance of Charles and Diana (exec. prod., co-writer), Prisoner Without a Name Cell Without a Number (prod., dir., co-writer; Peabody & WGA Awards), Liberace: Behind the Music (exec. prod.), Sweet Bird of Youth (exec. prod.), Rebound (dir., co-writer).

YORDAN, PHILIP
Writer. b. Chicago, IL, Apr. 1, 1914. e. U. of Illinois, B.A., Kent Coll. of Law, LL.D. Was attorney, then author, producer, playwright (Anna Lucasta). Began screen writing 1942 with collab. s.p. Syncopation.
PICTURES: Unknown Guest, Johnny Doesn't Live Here, When Strangers Marry, Dillinger (Acad. Award nom.), Whistle Stop, The Chase, Suspense, Anna Lucasta, House of Strangers, Edge of Doom, Detective Story (Acad. Award nom.), Mary Maru, Houdini, Blowing Wild, Man Crazy, Naked Jungle, Johnny Guitar, Broken Lance (Academy Award for story, 1954), Conquest of Space, Man from Laramie, Last Frontier, The Harder They Fall (also prod.), Men In War (also prod.), No Down Payment (also prod.), God's Little Acre (also prod.), The Bravados, The Time Machine, The Day of the Outlaw, Studs Lonigan, King of Kings, El Cid, 55 Days at Peking, Fall of the Roman Empire, Battle of the Bulge, Royal Hunt of the Sun, Brigham, Cataclysm, Night Train to Terror, Satan's Warriors, Cry Wilderness, Bloody Wednesday (also prod.), The Unholy, Dead Girls Don't Dance (also prod.).

YORK, MICHAEL
Actor. r.n. Michael York-Johnson. b. Fulmer, England, March 27, 1942. Early career with Oxford U. Dramatic Society and National Youth Theatre; later Dundee Repertory, National Theatre. Chmn., California Youth Theatre. 1992 Autobiography: Accidentally on Purpose (Simon & Schuster).

THEATER: Any Just Cause, Hamlet, Ring Round the Moon (Los Angeles), Cyrano de Bergerac. *B'way*: Outcry, Bent, The Little Prince and the Aviator, Whisper in the Mind, The Crucible, Someone Who'll Watch Over Me, Nora.
PICTURES: The Taming of the Shrew, Accident, Red and Blue, Smashing Time, Romeo and Juliet, The Strange Affair, The Guru, Alfred the Great, Justine, Something for Everyone, Zeppelin, La Poudre D'Escampette, Cabaret, England Made Me, Lost Horizon, The Three Musketeers, Murder on the Orient Express, The Four Musketeers, Conduct Unbecoming, Logan's Run, Seven Nights in Japan, The Last Remake of Beau Geste, The Island of Dr. Moreau, Fedora, The Riddle of the Sands (also assoc. prod.), Final Assignment, The White Lions, The Weather in the Streets, Success Is the Best Revenge, Dawn, Lethal Obsession (Der Joker), The Return of the Musketeers, Phantom of Death, The Secret of the Sahara, Midnight Cop, The Wanderer, The Long Shadow, Wide Sargasso Sea, Rochade, Discretion Assured, The Shadow of a Kiss, Gospa.
TELEVISION: *Specials*: The Forsyte Saga, Rebel in the Grave, Jesus of Nazareth, True Patriot, Much Ado About Nothing. *Series*: Knots Landing. *Guest*: Seaquest, The Naked Truth, Babylon 5. *Movies*: Great Expectations, A Man Called Intrepid, The Phantom of the Opera, The Master of Ballantrae, Space, For Those I Loved, The Far Country, Dark Mansions, Sword of Gideon, Four Minute Mile, The Lady and the Highwayman, The Heat of the Day, Till We Meet Again, Night of the Fox, A Duel of Love, The Road to Avonlea, Charles Dickens' David Copperfield (voice), Fall from Grace, Tek War: Tek Lab, September, A Young Connecticut Yankee in King Arthur's Court, Not of This Earth, The Out of Towner, Danielle Steel's The Ring. *Host*: The Hunt for Stolen War Treasure, The Magic Paint Brush, Gardens of the World.

YORK, SUSANNAH
Actress. b. London, England, Jan. 9, 1941. Ent. TV 1959. Ent. films in 1960. Wrote two books: In Search of Unicorns and Lark's Castle.
THEATER: A Cheap Bunch of Flowers, Wings of the Dove, Singular Life of Albert Nobbs, Man and Superman, Mrs. Warren's Profession, Peter Pan, The Maids, Private Lives, The Importance of Being Earnest, Hedda Gabler (New York), Agnes of God, The Human Voice, Penthesilea, Fatal Attraction, The Apple Cart, Private Treason, Lyric for a Tango, The Glass Menagerie, A Streetcar Named Desire, September Tide. Produced The Big One, a variety show for peace, 1984.
PICTURES: Tunes of Glory (debut, 1960), There Was a Crooked Man, Greengage Summer (Loss of Innocence), Freud, Tom Jones, The Seventh Dawn, Sands of the Kalahari, Kaleidoscope, A Man for All Seasons, Sebastian, Duffy, The Killing of Sister George, Oh What a Lovely War, The Battle of Britain, Lock Up Your Daughters, They Shoot Horses Don't They? (Acad. Award nom.), Brotherly Love (Country Dance), Zee & Co. (X Y & Zee), Happy Birthday Wanda June, Images, The Maids, Gold, Conduct Unbecoming, That Lucky Touch, Sky Riders, The Silent Partner, Superman, The Shout, Falling in Love Again, The Awakening, Superman II, Loophole, Yellowbeard, Land of Faraway, Superman IV (voice), Prettykill, Bluebeard Bluebeard, A Summer Story, American Roulette, Diamond's Edge, Melancholia.
TELEVISION: The Crucible, The Rebel and the Soldier, The First Gentleman, The Richest Man in the World, Slaughter of St. Teresa's Day, Kiss On A Grass Green Pillow, Fallen Angels, Prince Regent, Second Chance, Betjeman's Briton, We'll Meet Again, Jane Eyre, A Christmas Carol, Star Quality, Macho, Return Journey, After the War, The Man From the Pru, The Haunting of the New, Devices and Desires, Boon, Little Women, Trainer.

YORKIN, BUD
Producer, Director. r.n. Alan Yorkin. b. Washington, PA, Feb. 22, 1926. e. Carnegie Tech., Columbia U. U.S. Navy, 1942-45; Began career in TV in NBC's engineering dept. Moved into prod., first as stage mgr., then assoc. dir. of Colgate Comedy Hour (Martin and Lewis) and dir. of Dinah Shore Show. Formed Tandem Productions with Norman Lear; 1974 formed own production co.
PICTURES: Come Blow Your Horn (dir., co-prod., adapt.), Never Too Late (dir), Divorce American Style (dir.), The Night They Raided Minsky's (exec. prod.), Inspector Clouseau (dir.), Start the Revolution Without Me (prod., dir.), Cold Turkey (exec. prod.), Thief Who Came to Dinner (prod., dir.), Deal of the Century (prod.), Twice in a Lifetime (prod., dir.), Arthur 2 on the Rocks (dir.), Love Hurts (prod., dir.), For the Boys (actor), Intersection (co-prod.).
TELEVISION: *Series director*: Songs at Twilight, Martin & Lewis Show, Abbott and Costello Show, Spike Jones Show, Tony Martin Show (also prod., writer), George Gobel Show, The Ford Show Starring Tennessee Ernie Ford (also prod.). *Specials (dir.)*: An Evening with Fred Astaire (Emmy Award, 1959), Another Evening with Fred Astaire, The Jack Benny Hour Specials (Emmy Award, 1960), Henry Fonda and the Family, We Love You Madly with Duke Ellington, TV Guide

Awards Show, Bobby Darin and Friends, Danny Kaye Special, Where It's At with Dick Cavett, Many Sides of Don Rickles, Robert Young and the Family, owner. *Series co-prod.*: All In The Family, Sanford and Son, Maude, Good Times, What's Happening!, Carter Country, Diff'rent Strokes, Archie Bunker's Place.

YOUNG, ALAN
Actor. r.n. Angus Young. b. North Shield, Northumberland, England, Nov. 19, 1919. First acted as monologist for 13 years in Canada; radio comedian 10 yrs. in Canada and U.S.; served in Canadian Navy as sub-lt. 1942-44; wrote, dir. and acted in comedy broadcasts. Author: Mister Ed and Me (1995).
PICTURES: Margie (debut, 1946), Chicken Every Sunday, Mr. Belvedere Goes to College, Aaron Slick from Punkin Crick, Androcles and the Lion, Gentlemen Marry Brunettes, Tom Thumb, The Time Machine, Baker's Hawk, The Cat from Outer Space, The Great Mouse Detective (voice), Duck Tales: The Movie (voice), Beverly Hills Cop III.
TELEVISION: *Series*: The Alan Young Show (Emmy Award, 1950), Saturday Night Revue, Mr. Ed, Coming of Age. *Movies*: Earth Angel, Hart to Hart: Home is Where the Hart Is.

YOUNG, BURT
Actor, Writer. b. New York, NY, April 30, 1940. Worked at variety of jobs (boxer, trucker, etc.) before turning to acting and joining Actor's Studio. Appeared in off-B'way plays which led to Hollywood career. On B'way in Cuba and His Teddy Bear.
PICTURES: Cinderella Liberty, Chinatown, The Gambler, Murph the Surf, The Killer Elite, Rocky (Acad. Award nom.), Twilight's Last Gleaming, The Choirboys, Convoy, Uncle Joe Shannon (also s.p.), Rocky II, Blood Beach, All the Marbles, Rocky III, Lookin' To Get Out, Amityville II: The Possession, Over the Brooklyn Bridge, Once Upon a Time in America, The Pope of Greenwich Village, Rocky IV, Back to School, Blood Red, Beverly Hills Brats, Last Exit to Brooklyn, Medium Rare, Betsy's Wedding, Wait Until Spring Bandini, Diving In, Backstreet Dreams, Rocky V, Bright Angel, Red American, Club Fed, Excessive Force.
TELEVISION: *Series*: Roomies. *Guest*: M*A*S*H, Baretta, Tales From the Crypt. *Movies*: The Great Niagara, Hustling, Serpico: The Deadly Game, Woman of the Year, Daddy I Don't Like It Like This (also s.p.), Murder Can Hurt You, A Summer to Remember, Double Deception, Vendetta 2: The New Mafia, Columbo: Undercover.

YOUNG, CHRIS
Actor. b. Chambersburg, PA, Apr. 28, 1971. Stage debut in college production of Pippin, followed by On Golden Pond.
PICTURES: The Great Outdoors (debut, 1988), Book of Love, December, The Runestone, Warlock: The Armageddon, PCU, Deep Down.
TELEVISION: *Series*: Max Headroom, Falcon Crest, Live-In, Married People. *Pilot*: Jake's Journey. *Movies*: Dance 'Til Dawn, Breaking the Silence, MacShayne: The Final Roll of the Dice, Runaway Daughters. *Special*: Square One. *Guest*: Crime & Punishment.

YOUNG, FREDDIE
O.B.E. Cinematographer. b. England, 1902. r.n. Frederick Young. Entered British film industry in 1917. Gaumont Studio Shepherd's Bush, London as lab asst. First picture as chief cameraman, 1927 then chief cameraman to Herbert Wilcox British & Dominions Studios Elstree Herts. Army capt. Army Film prod. group directing training films 3 yrs. Invalided out. Signed with MGM British 15 yrs. Also credited as F.A. Young. BAFTA Fellowship 1972, Prix D'Honeur (Lawrence of Arabia) O.B.E. 1970.
PICTURES: Victory 1918, A Peep Behind the Scenes, The Speckled Band, Goodnight Vienna, The Loves of Robert Burns, The King of Paris, White Cargo (first British talkie), Rookery Nook, A Cuckoo in the Nest, Canaries Sometimes Sing, A Night Like This, Plunder, Thark, On Approval, Mischief, Return of the Rat, The Happy Ending, Yes Mr. Brown, This'll Make You Whistle, That's a Good Girl, Nell Gwynne, Peg of Old Drury, The Little Damozel, Bitter Sweet, The Queen's Affair, Sport of Kings, A Warm Corner, The W Plan, Victoria the Great, Sixty Glorious Years, Goodbye Mr. Chips, Nurse Edith Cavell, The 49th Parallel, Contraband, Busman's Honeymoon, The Young Mr. Pitt, Caesar and Cleopatra, Escape, So Well Remembered, Edward My Son, The Conspirator, The Winslow Boy, Calling Bulldog Drummond, Ivanhoe, Knights of the Round Table, Mogambo, Invitation to the Dance, Bhowani Junction, The Barretts of Wimpole Street, The Little Hut, Indiscreet, I Accuse, Inn of the Sixth Happiness, Solomon and Sheba, Betrayed, Island in the Sun, Treasure Island, Lust for Life, Macbeth, Greengage Summer, Lawrence of Arabia (Academy Award, 1962), The Seventh Dawn, Lord Jim, The Deadly Affair, Rotten to the Core, Doctor Zhivago (Academy Award, 1965), You Only Live Twice, The Battle of Britain, Sinful Davey, Ryan's Daughter (Academy Award, 1970), Nicholas and Alexandra, The Asphyx, Luther, The Tamarind Seed, Permission to Kill, The

Blue Bird, Seven Nights in Japan, Stevie, Bloodline, Rough Cut, Richard's Things, Invitation to the Wedding, Sword of the Valiant.
TELEVISION: Great Expectations, The Man in the Iron Mask, Macbeth (Emmy Award, 1960), Ike: The War Years, Arthur's Hollowed Ground (director).

YOUNG, IRWIN
Executive. b. New York, NY. e. Perkiomen Sch., Lehigh U., B.S., 1950. Pres., Du Art Film Laboratories, Inc.

YOUNG, IRWIN W.
Executive. President of the Film Society of Lincoln Center.

YOUNG, KAREN
Actress. b. Pequonnock, NJ, Sept. 29, 1958. Trained at Image Theatre/Studio in NYC.
THEATER: A Lie of the Mind, 3 Acts of Recognition, Five of Us, Mud People.
PICTURES: Deep in the Heart (debut, 1983), Almost You, Birdy, 9-1/2 Weeks, Heat, Jaws the Revenge, Torch Song Trilogy, Criminal Law, Night Game, The Boy Who Cried Bitch, Hoffa, The Wife.
TELEVISION: Movies: The Execution of Raymond Graham, The 10 Million Dollar Getaway, The Summer My Father Grew Up.

YOUNG, LORETTA
Actress. r.n. Gretchen Young. b. Salt Lake City, UT, Jan. 6, 1913. e. Ramona Convent, Alhambra, CA, Immaculate Heart Coll. Hollywood. Family moved to Hollywood when she was 3 yrs. old; began acting as child. After small part in Naughty But Nice, lead in Laugh Clown, Laugh. Played in almost 100 films.
Autobiography: The Things I Had to Learn (1962).
PICTURES: Laugh Clown Laugh (debut, 1928), Loose Ankles, The Squall, Kismet, I Like Your Nerve, The Devil to Pay, Platinum Blonde, The Hatchet Man, Big Business Girl, Life Beings, Zoo in Budapest, Life of Jimmy Dolan, Midnight Mary, Heroes for Sale, The Devil's in Love, She Had to Say Yes, A Man's Castle, The House of Rothschild, Bulldog Drummond Strikes Back, Born to Be Bad, Caravan, The White Parade, Clive of India, Call of the Wild, Shanghai, The Crusades, The Unguarded Hour, Private Number, Ramona, Ladies in Love, Love is News, Cafe Metropolis, Wife Doctor and Nurse, Second Honeymoon, Four Men and a Prayer, Suez, Kentucky, Three Blind Mice, Wife Husband and Friend, The Story of Alexander Graham Bell, Eternally Yours, The Doctor Takes a Wife, He Stayed for Breakfast, Lady from Cheyenne, The Men in Her Life, Bedtime Story, A Night to Remember, China, Ladies Courageous, And Now Tomorrow, Along Came Jones, The Stranger, The Perfect Marriage, The Farmer's Daughter (Academy Award, 1947), The Bishop's Wife, Rachel and the Stranger, The Accused, Mother Is a Freshman, Come to the Stable, Key to the City, Cause for Alarm, Half Angel, Paula, Because of You, It Happens Every Thursday.
TELEVISION: Series: The Loretta Young Show (1953-61; 3 Emmy Awards: 1954, 1956, 1959), The New Loretta Young Show (1962-63). Movies: Christmas Eve, Lady in a Corner.

YOUNG, ROBERT
Actor. b. Chicago, IL, Feb. 22, 1907. Acted at Pasadena Playhouse which led to film roles.
PICTURES: Black Camel (debut, 1931), The Sin of Madelon Claudet, Strange Interlude, The Kid From Spain, Today We Live, Men Must Fight, Hell Below, Tugboat Annie, Saturday's Millions, The Right to Romance, Carolina, Lazy River, The House of Rothchild, Spitfire, Paris Interlude, Whom the Gods Destroy, Death on the Diamond, The Band Plays On, Vagabond Lady, Calm Yourself, Red Salute, Remember Last Night?, West Point of the Air, The Bride Comes Home, It's Love Again, Secret Agent, 3 Wise Guys, The Bride Walks Out, Sworn Enemy, The Longest Night, Stowaway, Dangerous Number, Married Before Breakfast, The Emperor's Candlesticks, I Met Him in Paris, The Bride Wore Red, Navy Blue and Gold, Paradise for Three, Josette, The Toy Wife, Three Comrades, Rich Man Poor Girl, Shining Hour, Bridal Suite, Honolulu, Miracles For Sale, Maisie, Northwest Passage, The Mortal Storm, Florian, Western Union, Sporting Blood, Dr. Kildare's Crisis, The Trial of Mary Dugan, Lady Be Good, Married Bachelor, H.M. Pulham Esq., Joe Smith American, Cairo, Journey for Margaret, Slightly Dangerous, Claudia, Sweet Rosie O'Grady, The Canterville Ghost, The Enchanted Cottage, Those Endearing Young Charms, The Searching Wind, Claudia and David, Lady Luck, They Won't Believe Me, Crossfire, Relentless, Sitting Pretty, Adventure in Baltimore, That Forsyte Woman, Bride for Sale, And Baby Makes Three, The Second Woman, The Half-Breed, Goodbye My Fancy, Secret of the Incas.
TELEVISION: Series: Father Knows Best (2 Emmy Awards: 1956, 1957), Window on Main Street, Marcus Welby M.D. (Emmy Award, 1970). Movies: Marcus Welby M.D. (pilot; a.k.a. A Matter of Humanities), Vanished, All My Darling Daughters, My Darling Daughters' Anniversary, Little Women, The Return of Marcus Welby M.D., Marcus Welby M.D.: A Holiday Affair.

YOUNG, ROBERT M.
Director. b. New York, NY, Nov. 22, 1924. e. Harvard.
PICTURES: Nothing But a Man (prod., co-s.p.), The Plot Against Harry (co-prod., photog.), Short Eyes, Rich Kids, One-Trick Pony, The Ballad of Gregorio Cortez (also s.p. adapt.), Alambrista! (also s.p., photog.), Extremities, Saving Grace, Dominick and Eugene, Triumph of the Spirit, Talent for the Game, American Me (co-prod. only), Children of Fate (exec. dir. & exec. prod. only), Roosters, Caught.
TELEVISION: Specials: Sit-In, Angola—Journey to a War (Peabody Award), The Inferno (Cortile Cascino; also prod., writer, edit.), Anatomy of a Hospital, The Eskimo: Fight for Life (Emmy Award, 1971). Movie: Solomon and Sheba.

YOUNG, SEAN
Actress. b. Louisville, KY, Nov. 20, 1959. r.n. Mary Sean Young. e. Interlochen Arts Acad., MI, studied dance, voice, flute and writing. After graduating, moved to N.Y., worked as receptionist, model for 6 months and signed with ICM. Shortly after signing with ICM debuted in Jane Austen in Manhattan. On L.A. Stage in Stardust.
PICTURES: Jane Austen in Manhattan (debut, 1980), Stripes, Blade Runner, Young Doctors in Love, Dune, Baby: The Secret of the Lost Legend, No Way Out, Wall Street, The Boost, Cousins, Fire Birds, A Kiss Before Dying, Love Crimes, Once Upon a Crime, Hold Me Thrill Me Kiss Me, Forever, Fatal Instinct, Ace Ventura: Pet Detective, Even Cowgirls Get the Blues, Mirage, Dr. Jekyll and Ms. Hyde, The Proprietor.
TELEVISION: Special: Under the Biltmore Clock. Mini-Series: Tender Is the Night. Movies: Blood and Orchids, The Sketch Artist, Blue Ice, Witness to the Execution, Model by Day, Evil Has a Face, Everything to Gain.

YOUNGSTEIN, MAX E.
Executive. b. March 21, 1913. e. Fordham U. Member New York Bar. Motion picture consultant and indep. prod. Member, Producers Guild. Pres., Max E. Youngstein Enterprises. 1940-41, dir. adv. & pub., 20th Century Fox; later dir. studio special svcs.; asst. to pres. 1942-44, US Army Signal Corps. 1945, v.p. & gen. mgr., Stanley Kramer Prods. 1946-48, dir. adv. & pub., Eagle Lion Films; v.p. chg. adv. & pub. & prod. liaison. 1949-50, dir. adv. & pub., Paramount; mem. exec. comm. & v.p. & dir. dist. co. 1951-62, gen. v.p., partner, bd. mem., dir. adv. & pub., United Artists Corp. Formed UA Music Co. Pres., UA Records. 1977, consultant to Bart-Palevsky Prods. Advisor, Golden Harvest Films. Consultant, Rico-Lion. 1979, Shamrock Prods., Rank Film Distributors, Taft Bdcst. Co., Encore Prods., Bobrun Prods., Selkirk Films. 1980, named chmn. & CEO, Taft Int'l. Pictures. 1984, Consultant, Orion, 20th Century-Fox. 1985-86, pres., Great American Pictures. Consultant, H&M Trust, Color Systems Technology, Mickey Rooney Film Prods., Peachtree Prods.
PICTURES: Young Billy Young, Best of Cinerama, Man in the Middle, Fail Safe, The Money Trap, The Dangerous Days of Kiowa Jones, Welcome to Hard Times.

YULIN, HARRIS
Actor. b. Los Angeles, Nov. 5, 1937. On B'way in Watch on the Rhine, A Lesson from Aloes, etc. Founder of the Los Angeles Classic Theatre.
THEATER: The Little Foxes, Who's Afraid of Virginia Woolf?, Becket, The Entertainer, The Doctor's Dilemma, Night of the Iguana, School for Wives, Uncle Vanya, Tempest, Timon of Athens, The Seagull, Next Time I'll Sing to You (NY debut), Look Back in Anger, A Midsummer Night's Dream, King John, Hamlet, Julius Caesar, Tartuffe, Approaching Zanzibar, Henry V, The Visit (B'way), Arms and the Man, It's a Mad Mad World, Arts and Leisure. Dir. credits incl. Baba Goya, The Front Page, The Guardsman, Sheba, The Man Who Came to Dinner, Guns of Carrar, Cuba Si, Candida, Don Juan in Hell, Jitta's Atonement, etc.
PICTURES: End of the Road, Doc, The Midnight Man, Night Moves, Steel, Scarface, The Believers, Fatal Beauty, Candy Mountain, Bad Dreams, Judgement in Berlin, Another Woman, Ghostbusters II, Narrow Margin, Final Analysis, There Goes the Neighborhood, Clear and Present Danger, Stuart Saves His Family, The Baby-sitters Club, Looking for Richard, Multiplicity, Loch Ness.
TELEVISION: Specials/Movies: The Thirteenth Day--The Story of Esther, When Every Day Was the Fourth of July, Missiles of October, Conspiracy: Trial of the Chicago Seven, Last Ride of the Dalton Gang, Robert Kennedy and His Times, Tailspin: Behind the Korean Airlines Tragedy, Face of a Stranger, The Last Hit, Incident at Vichy, How the West Was Won, Truman. Series: WIOU, Frasier.

Z

ZAENTZ, SAUL
Producer. b. Passaic, NJ.
PICTURES: One Flew Over the Cuckoo's Nest (Academy Award for Best Picture, 1975), Three Warriors, The Lord of the

Rings, Amadeus (Academy Award for Best Picture, 1984), The Mosquito Coast (exec. prod.), The Unbearable Lightness of Being, At Play in the Fields of the Lord, The English Patient.

ZAILLIAN, STEVEN
Writer. Director. b. 1953.
PICTURES: The Falcon and the Snowman, Awakenings, Jack the Bear, Searching for Bobby Fischer (also dir.), Schindler's List (Academy Award, 1993; WGA & Golden Globe Awards), Clear and Present Danger (co-s.p.), Primal Fear.

ZANE, BILLY
Actor. b. Chicago, IL, 1966. Sister is actress Lisa Zane. Studied acting at American School in Switzerland. To Hollywood in 1984 landing small role in Back to the Future. On stage in American Music (NY), The Boys in the Backroom (Actors' Gang, Chicago).
PICTURES: Back to the Future (debut, 1985), Critters, Dead Calm, Back to the Future Part II, Megaville, Memphis Belle, Blood & Concrete: A Love Story, Billions, Femme Fatale, Sniper, Posse, Orlando, Flashfire, Tombstone, The Silence of the Hams, Cyborg Agent, Only You, Tales From the Crypt Presents Demon Knight, Reflections in the Dark, Danger Zone, The Phantom.
TELEVISION: Series: Twin Peaks. Movie: Brotherhood of Justice, The Case of the Hillside Stranglers, Lake Consequence, Running Delilah, The Set Up.

ZANUCK, LILI FINI
Producer, Director. b. Leominster, MA, Apr. 2, 1954. e. Northern VA Community Coll. Worked for Carnation Co. in LA prior to entering film business. Joined Zanuck/Brown Company in 1978 working in development and various phases of production; 1984-present, prod. Made directorial debut in 1991 with Rush. Named Producer of the Year (1985) by NATO, along with Richard D. Zanuck and David Brown; Producer of the Year (1989) by Producers Guild of America, with Zanuck.
PICTURES: Cocoon, Cocoon: The Return, Driving Miss Daisy (Academy Award, Golden Globe & Natl. Board of Review Awards for Best Picture 1989), Rush (dir.), Rich in Love, Clean Slate, Wild Bill, Mulholland Falls, The Double.

ZANUCK, RICHARD DARRYL
Executive, b. Los Angeles, CA, Dec 13, 1934. e. Stanford U. 1952-56. Father was exec. Darryl Zanuck. Story dept., 20th Century Fox, 1954; NY pub. dept., 1955; asst. to prod.: Island in the Sun, The Sun Also Rises, The Longest Day; v.p. Darryl F. Zanuck Prods. 1958; first credit as prod. Compulsion (1959); president's prod. rep., 20th Century Fox Studio, 1963; v.p. charge prod., 20th Fox; pres., 20th Fox TV exec. v.p. chge. prod.; 1968 Chmn. of Bd., Television div., 20th Century Fox, 1969 Pres., 20th Century Fox Film Corp. Joined Warner Bros., 1971, as sr. exec. v.p.; resigned 1972 to form Zanuck-Brown Production Company, Universal Pictures. Joined 20th Century-Fox, 1980-83. To Warner Bros., 1983. To MGM Entertainment, 1986. 1988, dissolved 16-year partnership with David Brown. Formed The Zanuck Company, 1989. Recipient: Irving Thalberg Award (1991).
PICTURES: Compulsion, The Chapman Report, Ssssssss, The Sting (Academy Award for Best Picture, 1973), The Sugarland Express, Willie Dynamite, The Black Windmill, The Girl from Petrovka, The Eiger Sanction, Jaws, MacArthur, Jaws 2, The Island, Neighbors, The Verdict, Cocoon, Target, Cocoon: The Return, Driving Miss Daisy (Academy Award for Best Picture, 1989), Rush, Rich in Love, Clean Slate, Wild Bill, Mulholland Falls.

ZEFFIRELLI, FRANCO
Director, Writer. b. Florence, Italy, Feb. 12, 1923. e. Florence Univ. Was stage director before entering film industry. Set designer 1949 -52 for Visconti plays (A Streetcar Named Desire, The Three Sisters). Worked as asst. dir. on La Terra Trema, Bellissima, Senso. Director of operas.
PICTURES: Director-Screenplay: The Taming of the Shrew (also co-prod.), Romeo and Juliet (also exec. prod.), Brother Sun Sister Moon, The Champ (dir. only), Endless Love (dir. only), La Traviata (also prod. design), Otello, Young Toscanini (dir., story), Hamlet, Jane Eyre.
TELEVISION: Mini-Series: Jesus of Nazareth.

ZELNICK, STRAUSS
Executive. b. Boston, MA, June 26, 1957. e. Wesleyan U. B.A., 1979 (Summa Cum Laude); Harvard Grad. School of Business Administration, M.B.A., 1983; Harvard Law School, J.D., 1983 (Cum Laude). 1983-86, v.p., international television sales, Columbia Pictures International Corp. 1988-89, pres. & chief operating officer, Vestron, Inc.; 1989-93, pres. & chief operating officer, Fox Film Corp. Became pres. & CEO of Bertelsman Music Group Entertainment in North America.

ZEMECKIS, ROBERT
Director, Writer. b. Chicago, IL, 1952. m. actress Mary Ellen Trainor. e. U. of Film Awards sponsored by M.P. Academy of

Arts & Sciences, plus 15 intl. honors. Has film editing background, having worked as cutter on TV commercials in Illinois. Also cut films at NBC News, Chicago, as summer job. After schooling went to Universal to observe on set of TV series, McCloud. Wrote script for that series in collab. with Bob Gale. Turned to feature films, directing I Wanna Hold Your Hand and co-writing s.p. with Gale.
PICTURES: Director: I Wanna Hold Your Hand (also co-s.p.), Used Cars (also co-s.p.), Romancing the Stone, Back to the Future (also co-s.p.), Who Framed Roger Rabbit, Back to the Future II (also story), Back to the Future III (also story), Death Becomes Her (also co-prod.), Forrest Gump (Academy Award, Golden Globe & DGA Awards, 1994). Co-Writer: 1941, Trespass. Exec. Prod.: The Public Eye, Tales From the Crypt Presents Demon Knight, Frighteners, Tales From the Crypt Presents Bordello of Blood.
TELEVISION: Amazing Stories, Tales From the Crypt (exec. prod.; also dir., All Through the House, You Murderer).

ZENS, WILL
Producer, Director. b. Milwaukee, WI, June 26, 1920. e. Marquette U., USC, B.A., M.A. Wrote, produced and directed many TV shows. Formed Riviera Productions in 1960 to produce theatrical motion pictures.
PICTURES: Capture That Capsule, The Starfighters, To the Shores of Hell, Road to Nashville, Hell on Wheels, From Nashville with Music, Yankee Station, Help Me ... I'm Possessed!, Hot Summer in Barefoot County, The Fix, Truckin' Man, The Satan Crossing (dir., s.p.), Death on the Carrier, Terror in the Streets.
TELEVISION: Punch & Trudy, Your Police, Aqua Lung Adventures, Teletunes, Sunday Drive.

ZERBE, ANTHONY
Actor. b. Long Beach, CA, May 20, 1936. Studied at Stella Adler Theatre Studio.
THEATER: NY: Solomon's Child, The Little Foxes.
PICTURES: Cool Hand Luke, Will Penny, The Liberation of L.B. Jones, The Molly Maguires, The Call Me Mister Tibbs, Cotton Comes to Harlem, The Omega Man, The Life and Times of Judge Roy Bean, The Strange Vengeance of Rosalie, The Laughing Policeman, Papillon, The Parallax View, Farewell My Lovely, Rooster Cogburn, The Turning Point, Who'll Stop the Rain, The First Deadly Sin, The Dead Zone, Off Beat, Opposing Force, Private Investigation, Steel Dawn, Listen to Me, See No Evil Hear No Evil, Licence to Kill.
TELEVISION: Series: Harry-O (Emmy Award, 1976), The Young Riders. Movies: The Priest Killer, The Hound of the Baskervilles, Snatched, She Lives, The Healers, In the Glitter Palace, KISS Meets the Phantom of the Park, Attica, The Seduction of Miss Leona, Rascals and Robbers: The Secret Adventures of Tom Sawyer and Huck Finn, A Question of Honor, The Return of the Man from U.N.C.L.E., One Police Plaza. Mini-Series: Once an Eagle, Centennial, The Chisholms, George Washington, A.D.

ZIDE, LARRY M.
Executive. b. Flushing, NY, Oct. 16, 1954. 3rd generation in mp. industry. Started 1972 with American Intl. Pictures in sls. & adv.; 1973, named branch sls. mgr., Memphis. 1975, joined Dimension Pictures as print controller; 1978, formed Zica Films Co. serving m.p. industry; 1985, Zica merged with Filmtreat Intl. Corp; named pres., newly formed Filmtreat West Corp.

ZIDE, MICHAEL (MICKEY)
Executive. b. Detroit, MI, May 31, 1932. Joined m.p. industry with American Intl. Pictures as print controller; 1962, promoted to asst. gen. sls. mgr. Named v.p., special projects; 1970; 1972, joined Academy Pictures as v.p. of prod. Later went with Zica Film Co.; 1985, named exec. v.p., Filmtreat West Corp.

ZIEFF, HOWARD
Director. b. Chicago, IL. e. Art Center School in Los Angeles. Started as artist and photographer, working as newsreel photographer for L.A. TV station. Went to N.Y. to do still photography; became top photo artist in advertising. Turned to film direction with Slither.
PICTURES: Slither (debut, 1973), Hearts of the West, House Calls, The Main Event, Private Benjamin, Unfaithfully Yours, The Dream Team, My Girl, My Girl 2.

ZIFKIN, WALTER
Executive. b. July 16, 1936. New York, NY. e. UCLA, A.B., 1958; USC, LL.B., 1961. CBS legal dept., 1961-63; William Morris Agency 1963-present; exec. vice-pres.; 1989 also COO.

ZIMBALIST, EFREM, JR.
Actor. b. New York, NY, Nov. 30, 1923. Son of violinist Efrem Zimbalist and opera singer Alma Gluck. Daughter is actress Stephanie Zimbalist. e. Fay Sch., Southboro, MA; St. Paul's, Concord, NH; Yale. Studied drama, Neighborhood Playhouse. N.Y. Stage debut, The Rugged Path. Shows with American

Repertory Theatre; Henry VIII, Androcles and the Lion, What Every Woman Knows, Yellow Jack, Hedda Gabler, Fallen Angels. Co-prod., The Medium, The Telephone, The Consul. Gave up acting after death of his wife and served as asst. to father, Curtis Inst. of Music for 4 years. Returned to acting, stock co., Hammonton, NJ, 1954.
PICTURES: House of Strangers (debut, 1949), Bombers B-52, Band of Angels, The Deep Six, Violent Road, Girl on the Run, Too Much Too Soon, Home Before Dark, The Crowded Sky, A Fever in the Blood, By Love Possessed, The Chapman Report, The Reward, Harlow, Wait Until Dark, Airport 1975, Elmira, Hot Shots!, Batman: Mask of the Phantasm (voice).
TELEVISION: Series: Concerning Miss Marlowe (daytime serial), 77 Sunset Strip, The FBI, Hotel. Guest: Philco, Goodyear Playhouse, U.S. Steel Hour. Movies: Who Is the Black Dahlia?, A Family Upside Down, Terror Out of the Sky, The Best Place to Be, The Gathering Part II, Baby Sister, Shooting Stars. Host: You Are the Jury, The Tempest. Mini-Series: Scruples.

ZIMBALIST, STEPHANIE
Actress. b. New York, NY, Oct. 8. Father is actor Efrem Zimbalist Jr.; grandparents: violinist Efrem Zimbalist and soprano Alma Gluck; aunt is novelist Marcia Davenport.
THEATER: LA: Festival, The Tempest, American Mosaic, Love Letters, Baby Dance, The Crimson Thread, Ad Wars. Williamstown Theatre Festival: Barbarians, Summer and Smoke, Threepenny Opera. Tours: My One and Only, Carousel. Regional: The Philadelphia Story, The Cherry Orchard, The Baby Dance.
PICTURES: The Magic of Lassie, The Awakening.
TELEVISION: Series: Remington Steele. Mini-Series: Centennial. Movies: Yesterday's Child, In the Matter of Karen Ann Quinlan, The Gathering, The Long Journey Back, Forever, The Triangle Factory Fire Scandal, The Best Place to Be, The Baby Sitter, The Golden Moment—An Olympic Love Story, Elvis and the Beauty Queen, Tomorrow's Child, Love on the Run, A Letter to Three Wives, Celebration Family, The Man in the Brown Suit, Caroline?, Personals, The Killing Mind, The Story Lady, Some Kind of Love, Breaking the Silence, Sexual Advances, Jericho Fever, Incident in a Small Town, Voices From Within, The Great Elephant Escape, Whose Daughter Is She? Stop the World—I Want to Get Off, Dead Ahead.

ZIMMER, HANS
Composer. b. Germany. Member of the Buggles, producing hit song Video Killed the Radio Star. Pioneered use of digital synthesizers with computer technology and traditional orchestras. Establsed Lillie Yard Studio in London. Received Grammy Award for best instrumental arragement with vocals and Golden Globe for best original score for The Lion King.
PICTURES: Burning Secret, A World Apart, Rain Man, Paperhouse, Wonderland, Black Rain, Driving Miss Daisy, Bird on a Wire, Days of Thunder, Pacific Heights, Green Card, Thelma & Louise, Backdraft, Radio Flyer, The Power of One, K-2, A League of Their Own, Toys, Younger and Younger, True Romance, Cool Runnings, I'll Do Anything, The House of the Spirits, Renaissance Man, The Lion King (Academy Award, 1994), Drop Zone, Crimson Tide, Nine Months, Something to Talk About, Beyond Rangoon, Muppet Treasure Island, Broken Arrow.
TELEVISION: Two Deaths.

ZINNEMANN, FRED
Director. b. Vienna, Austria, Apr. 29, 1907. e. Vienna U., law. Studied violin as a boy; after law, studied photographic technique, lighting & mechanics (Paris); asst. cameraman 1 yr. Berlin; came to U.S. 1929; extra in m.p. All Quiet on the Western Front, 1930; asst. to Berthold Viertel, script clerk & asst. to Robert Flaherty, 1931; dir. Mexican documentary The Wave, 1934; short subjects dir., MGM, winning Academy Award for That Mothers Might Live, 1938; feature dir. 1942; winner of first Screen Directors' Award 1948 with The Search. 4 N.Y. Film Critics Awards; 2 Director's Guild Annual Awards; 4 Acad. Awards, 9 Acad. Award noms., 3 Golden Globe Awards. Other awards: U.S. Congressional Life Achievement Award (1987), Gold Medal City of Vienna, Donatello Award (Italy), Order of Arts & Letters (France), Golden Thistle Award (Edinburgh, Scotland), etc. Fellowships: BAFTA and BFI. Director of Acad. Award winning short Benjy (for L.A. Orthopedic Hospital, 1951). 1994, John Huston Award from Artists Rights Foundation, hon. dr. lit. Univ. of Durham (England). Author: My Life in the Movies (Scribner, 1992).
PICTURES: Kid Glove Killer (debut, 1942), Eyes in the Night, The Seventh Cross, Little Mister Jim, My Brother Talks to Horses, The Search, Act of Violence, The Men, Teresa, High Noon (NY Film Critics Award, 1952), The Member of the Wedding, From Here to Eternity (Academy Award, DGA & NY Film Critics Awards, 1953), Oklahoma!, A Hatful of Rain, The Nun's Story (NY Film Critics Award, 1959), The Sundowners (also prod.), Behold a Pale Horse (also prod.), A Man for All Seasons (also prod.; Academy Awards for Best Picture & Director; also DGA & NY Film Critics Awards, 1966), The Day of the Jackal, Julia, Five Days One Summer (also prod.).

ZINNEMANN, TIM
Producer. b. Los Angeles, CA. e. Columbia U. Son of dir. Fred Zinnemann. Began career industry as film editor; then asst. dir. on 20 films. Production mgr. for 5 projects; assoc. prod. on The Cowboys and Smile. Produced Straight Time for Warners with Stanley Beck.
PICTURES: A Small Circle of Friends, The Long Riders, Tex, Impulse, Fandango, Crossroads, The Running Man, Pet Sematary (exec. prod.).
TELEVISION: The Jericho Mile.

ZISKIN, LAURA
Producer. e. USC Cinema School. Worked as game show writer, development prod. before joining Jon Peters' prod. co. where she worked on A Star is Born, Eyes of Laura Mars (assoc. prod.). Formed Fogwood Films with Sally Field. Became pres. of company Fox 2000 Pictures.
PICTURES: Murphy's Romance, No Way Out, D.O.A., The Rescue, Everybody's All American, Pretty Woman (exec. prod.), What About Bob?, The Doctor, Hero (also co-story), To Die For, Courage Under Fire.

ZITO, JOSEPH
Director. b. New York, NY, May 14, 1949. e. City Coll. of New York.
PICTURES: Abduction, The Prowler, Friday the 13th: The Final Chapter, Missing in Action, Invasion U.S.A., Red Scorpion.

ZSIGMOND, VILMOS
Cinematographer. b. Szeged, Hungary, June 16, 1930. e. National Film Sch. Began career photographing Hungarian Revolution of 1956. Later escaped from Hungary with friend Laszlo Kovacs, also a cinematographer. Winner of Academy Award and British Academy Award for cinematography, also several int'l and domestic awards as dir. of TV commercials.
PICTURES: The Time Travelers (1964), The Sadist, The Name of the Game Is Kill, Futz, Picasso Summer, The Monitors, Red Sky at Morning, McCabe and Mrs. Miller, The Hired Hand, The Ski Bum, Images, Deliverance, Scarecrow, The Long Goodbye, Cinderella Liberty, The Sugarland Express, The Girl From Petrovka, Sweet Revenge, Death Riders, Obsession, Close Encounters of the Third Kind (Academy Award, 1977), The Last Waltz, The Deer Hunter (BAFTA Award; Acad. Award nom.), Winter Kills, The Rose, Heaven's Gate, Blow Out, The Border, Jinxed, Table for Five, No Small Affair, The River (Acad. Award nom.), Real Genius, The Witches of Eastwick, Fat Man and Little Boy, The Two Jakes, Journey to Spirit Island, The Bonfire of the Vanities, The Long Shadow (dir.), Sliver, Intersection, Maverick (also actor), The Crossing Guard, Assassins, The Ghost and the Darkness.
TELEVISION: Flesh and Blood, Stalin (Emmy Award, ACE Award, ASC Award).

ZORADI, MARK
Executive. Began working for Disney in 1980, currently pres., Buena Vista International. Distributor of the Year, Cinema Expo International, 1996.

ZUCKER, DAVID
Producer, Director, Writer. b. Milwaukee, WI, Oct. 16, 1947. e. U. of Wisconsin, majoring in film. With brother, Jerry, and friend Jim Abrahams founded the Kentucky Fried Theatre in Madison in 1971 (moved theater to L.A. 1972); later wrote script for film of that name released in 1977.
PICTURES: The Kentucky Fried Movie (co-s.p., actor), Airplane! (co-s.p., co-dir., actor), Top Secret (co-dir., co-s.p., co-exec. prod.), Ruthless People (co-dir.), The Naked Gun: From the Files of Police Squad! (exec. prod., dir., co-s.p.), The Naked Gun 2 1/2: The Smell of Fear (dir., exec. prod., co-s.p., actor), Brain Donors (co-exec. prod.), The Naked Gun 33 1/3: The Final Insult (prod., co-s.p., actor), A Walk in the Clouds (co-prod.).
TELEVISION: Police Squad (series), Our Planet Tonight (special).

ZUCKER, JERRY
Producer, Director. Writer. b. Milwaukee, WI, Mar. 11, 1950. e. U. of Wisconsin, majoring in education. With brother, David, and friend Jim Abrahams founded the Kentucky Fried Theatre in Madison in 1970 and wrote script for film of that name released in 1977.
PICTURES: The Kentucky Fried Movie (co-s.p., actor), Rock 'n' Roll High School (2nd unit dir.), Airplane! (co-dir., co-s.p.), Top Secret (co-dir., co-s.p.), Ruthless People (co-dir.), The Naked Gun (exec. prod., co-s.p.), Ghost (dir.), The Naked Gun 2-1/2 (exec. prod.), Brain Donors (co-exec. prod.), My Life (co-prod.), Naked Gun 33-1/3 (co-exec. prod.), First Knight (dir.), A Walk in the Clouds (co-prod.).
TELEVISION: Series: Police Squad! (co-exec. prod., dir.; co-wrote first episode).

ZUGSMITH, ALBERT
Producer, Director, Writer. b. Atlantic City, NJ, April 24, 1910. e. U. of VA. Pres. Intercontinental Broadcasting Corp.; ed. publ. Atlantic City Daily World; v.p. Smith Davis Corp.; chmn of bd., Continental Telecasting Corp., Television Corp. of America; assoc. ed. American Press; pres. World Printing Co.; exec. CBS; pres. American Pictures Corp.; pres. Famous Players Int'l Corp.
PICTURES: *Producer*: Invasion USA, Top Banana, Female on the Beach, Raw Edge, Written on the Wind, Man in the Shadow, Red Sundown, Star in the Dust, Tarnished Angels, The Incredible Shrinking Man, The Girl in the Kremlin, The Square Jungle, Female on the Beach, Touch of Evil, Captive Women, Sword of Venus, Port Sinister, Paris Model, Slaughter on Tenth Avenue, The Female Animal (also story), High School Confidential, Night of the Quarter Moon, The Beat Generation, The Big Operator, Girls Town, Violated!, Platinum High School, Private Lives of Adam and Eve, Dondi (also dir., s.p.), College Confidential (also dir.), Confessions of an Opium Eater (also dir.), Sex Kitten Go to College (also dir., story), The Great Space Adventure, On Her Bed of Roses, Fanny Hill, The Rapist!, How to Break Into the Movies, Movie Star American Style: or LSA I Love You (dir., story, co- s.p.), The Chinese Room, Street Girl, The President's Girl Friend, The Phantom Gunslinger, Sappho Darling (s.p. only), Menage a Trois, Two Roses and a Goldenrod (dir., s.p. only), The Friendly Neighbors, Why Me God?, Tom Jones Rides Again.

ZUNIGA, DAPHNE
Actress. b. Berkeley, CA, 1962. e. UCLA.
PICTURES: Pranks (debut, 1982), The Dorm That Dripped Blood, The Initiation, Vision Quest, The Sure Thing, Modern Girls, Spaceballs, Last Rites, The Fly II, Gross Anatomy, Staying Together, Eight Hundred Leagues Down the Amazon.
TELEVISION: *Movies*: Quarterback Princess, Stone Pillow, Prey of the Chameleon. *Series*: Melrose Place. *Guest*: Family Ties, Nightmare Classics (Eye of the Panther).

ZWICK, EDWARD
Writer, Producer, Director. b. Chicago, IL, Oct. 8, 1952. e. Harvard U., B.A., 1974; American Film Inst. Center for Advanced Film Studies, M.F.A., 1976. Editor and feature writer, The New Republic and Rolling Stone magazines, 1972-74. Author: Literature and Liberalism (1975). Formed Bedford Falls Production Co. with Special Bulletin collaborator Marshall Herskovitz.
PICTURES: *Director*: About Last Night... (debut, 1986), Glory, Leaving Normal, Legends of the Fall (also co-prod.), Courage Under Fire.
TELEVISION: *Series*: Family (writer, then story editor, dir., prod., Humanitas Prize Award, 1980), thirtysomething (co-exec. prod.; Emmy Award, 1988), Dream Street (exec. prod.). *Movies (dir.)*: Paper Dolls, Having It All, Extreme Close-Up (also co-exec. prod., co-story), Relativity. *Special*: Special Bulletin (dir., co-prod., co-story; 2 Emmy Awards, also DGA, WGA & Humanitas Prize Awards, 1983).

ZWICK, JOEL
Director. b. Brooklyn, NY, Jan. 11, 1942. e. Brooklyn Coll., B.A., M.A.
THEATER: Dance with Me, Cold Storage, Esther, Cafe La Mama.
PICTURE: Second Sight.
TELEVISION: *Series*: Laverne and Shirley, Mork and Mindy, It's a Living, America 2100, Goodtime Girls, Hot W.A.C.S. (also exec. prod.), Little Darlings, Joanie Loves Chachi, The New Odd Couple (also supv. prod.), Webster, Brothers (supv. prod.), Perfect Strangers (also pilot), Full House (also pilot), Getting By (also prod.). *Pilots*: Angie, Bosom Buddies, Struck by Lightning, Family Matters, Adventures in Babysitting, Morning Glory, Star of the Family, Up to No Good, Going Places, Hangin' With Mr. Cooper, Life Happens, On Our Own, Making Out, Nowhere Fast.

OBITUARIES

(OCT. 1, 1995 — SEPT. 30, 1996)

Martin Balsam	2/13/96	Patric Knowles	12/23/95
Saul Bass	4/25/96	Dorothy Lamour	9/22/96
Pandro S. Berman	7/13/96	Jenning Lang	5/29/96
Whit Bissell	3/8/96	Lash Larue	5/24/96
Vivian Blaine	12/9/95	Norm Levinson	9/26/97
Ralph Blane	11/13/96	Viveca Lindfors	10/25/95
Albert "Cubby" Broccoli	6/27/96	Jeffrey Lynn	12/1/96
George Burns	3/1/96	Guy Madison	2/6/96
Rosalind Cash	10/31/95	Louis Malle	11/23/95
Jesse Chinich	1/7/96	Walter Manley	1/20/96
Virginia Christine	7/24/96	Dean Martin	12/25/95
Rene Clement	3/17/96	Edward Dennis Martin	7/4/96
Claudette Colbert	7/30/96	Butterfly McQueen	12/22/95
Winston H. (Tony) Cox	9/21/96	Audrey Meadows	2/3/96
John Craven	11/24/95	Richard Morris	4/28/96
Saul David	6/7/96	Haing S. Ngor	3/3/96
Joanne Dru	9/10/96	David Opatoshu	4/30/96
Paul Eddington	11/4/95	Robert Parrish	12/4/95
Herb Edelman	7/21/96	Jon Pertwee	5/20/96
Vince Edwards	3/11/96	Tommy Rettig	2/13/96
William K. Everson	4/14/96	Jack Rose	10/20/95
Louise Fitch	9/11/96	Joe Seneca	8/15/96
Greer Garson	4/6/96	Stirling Silliphant	4/26/96
Bryant Haliday	7/28/96	Don Simpson	1/19/96
Margaux Hemingway	7/1/96	Terry Southern	10/29/95
Georg Heinemann	8/21/96	Lyle Talbot	3/3/96
Fred Hift	7/6/96	Steve Tesich	7/1/96
Harry Horwitz	9/21/96	Claire Townshend	12/19/95
Ross Hunter	3/10/96	Jamie Uys	1/29/96
Dorothy Jeakins	11/24/95	Jo Van Fleet	6/10/96
Ben Johnson	4/8/96	James R. Velde	7/24/96
Gene Kelly	2/2/96	Jack Weston	5/3/96
Frederick H. Kent	9/22/95	Mary Wickes	10/24/95
Krzystof Kieslowski	3/13/96	Joseph Youngerman	11/22/95

Services

Advertising & Publicity
Services 413

Animation 415

Casting Services 419

Consultants & Technical
Services 420

Costume & Prop Rentals . 420

Editing Services 422

Film & Video Stock 424

Film Preservation
Processing, Repair
& Storage 425

Financial Services 426

Market Research
Services 427

Sound Services 428

Special Effects 429

Stock Shots 433

Studio & Equipment
Services 435

Subtitles & Captions 437

Talent Agencies 437

Theatrical Trailers 440

Advertising & Publicity Services

A.C. COMMUNICATIONS
8489 W. Third St., #1096, Los Angeles, CA 90048. (213) 655-5833. FAX: (213) 655-5849.

AC & R ADVERTISING INC
16 E. 32 St., New York, NY 10016. (212) 685-2500. FAX: (212) 689-2258.
PRESIDENT
Alvin Chereskin

BOB ABRAMS AND ASSOCIATES
2030 Prosser Ave., Los Angeles, CA 90025. (310) 475-7739. FAX: (310) 475-7739.
Bob Abrams

AMMIRATI, PURIS & LINTAS INC.
100 Fifth Ave., New York, NY 10011. (212) 206-0500. FAX: (212) 337-9481.
CHAIRMAN
Ralph Ammirati

AUSTIN/SIMONS & ASSOCS.
P.O. Box 641523, Los Angeles, CA 90064. (310) 478-8900. FAX: (310) 478-8976.

N.W. AYER & PARTNERS
Worldwide Plaza, 825 Eighth Ave., New York, NY 10019-7498. (212) 474-5000. FAX: (212) 474-5400.
CHAIRMAN & CEO
Steve Dworkin
VICE CHAIRMAN
Dominick Rossi

BACKER, SPIELVOGEL, BATES WORLDWIDE INC.
405 Lexington Ave., 8th Fl., New York, NY 10174. (212) 297-7000.

BAKER, WINOKUR, RYDER
405 S. Beverly Dr., 5th fl., Beverly Hills, CA 90212. (310) 277-6200.
250 W. 57 St., #1610, New York, NY 10017. (212) 582-0700.

BBDO WEST
10960 Wilshire Blvd., # 1600, Los Angeles, CA 90024. (310) 444-4500. FAX: (310) 444-7581.

BBDO WORLDWIDE
1285 Avenue of the Americas, New York, NY 10019. (212) 459-5000.
CHAIRMAN
Allen Rosenshine

BENDER, GOLDMAN & HELPER
11500 W. Olympic Blvd., Suite 655, Los Angeles, CA 90064. (310) 473-4147. FAX: (310) 478-4727.
400 Madison Ave., New York NY 10017. (212) 371-0798. FAX: (212) 754-4380.

WALTER F. BENNETT COMMUNICATIONS
13355 Noel Rd., Suite 1815, Dallas, TX 75240. (214) 661-1122. FAX: (214) 980-0640.
PRESIDENT
Ted Dienert
CFO/COO
Benjamin C. Bell

BIEDERMAN, KELLY & SHAFFER INC.
475 Park Ave. South, New York, NY 10016. (212) 213-5500. FAX: (212) 213-4775.
CHAIRMAN
Barry Biederman

MARION BILLINGS PUBLICITY LTD,
250 W. 57 St., #2420, New York, NY 10107. (212) 581-4493.

RALPH BING ADVERTISING CO.
16109 Selva Dr., San Diego, CA 92128. (714) 487-7444.
PRESIDENT
Ralph Bing

MICHELLE BOLTON & ASSOCS.
100 S. Doheny Dr., #420, Los Angeles, CA 90048. (310) 273-4030. FAX: (310) 273-2640.

BOZELL, INC.
40 W. 23 St., New York, NY 10010. (212) 727-5000. FAX: (212) 645-9262.

CEO
Charles D. Peebler, Jr.

BROKAW COMPANY
9255 Sunset Blvd., #804, Los Angeles, CA 90069. (310) 273-2060. FAX: (310) 276-4037.

LEO BURNETT COMPANY, INC.
35 W. Wacker, Chicago, IL 60601. (312) 220-5959. FAX: (312) 220-6566.
CHAIRMAN
Richard Fizdale
CEO
William Lynch

BURSON-MARSTELLER
230 Park Ave. South, New York, NY 10003-1566. (212) 614-4000. FAX: (212) 598-6942.
CHAIRMAN
Harold Burson

CLEIN & WHITE
8584 Melrose Ave., 2nd fl., W. Hollywood, CA 90069. (310) 659-4141. FAX: (213) 659-3995.
33 W. 54th St., New York, NY 10019. (212) 247-4100.

COMMUNICATIONS PLUS INC.
102 Madison Ave. So., New York, NY 10016. (212) 686-9570.

D'ARCY, MASIUS, BENTON & BOWLES
1675 Broadway, New York, NY 10019-5809. (212) 468-3622. FAX: (212) 468-4385.
6500 Wilshire Blvd., Los Angeles, CA 90048. (213) 658-4500.
CEO
Roy J. Bostock
PRESIDENT
Clayton Wilmite

DENNIS DAVIDSON & ASSOCS. INC.
5670 Wilshire Blvd., Suite 700, Los Angeles, CA 90036. (213) 954-5858.
1776 Broadway, New York, NY 10019. (212) 246-0500.

DDB NEEDHAM WORLDWIDE INC.
437 Madison Ave., New York, NY 10022. (212) 415-2000. FAX: (212) 415-3591.
CHAIRMAN/CEO
Keith Reinhard
PRESIDENT, NY
Ken Kaes

SAMANTHA DEAN & ASSOCS.
36 W. 44 St., New York, NY 10036. (212) 391-2675.

DELLA FEMINA, TRAVISANO & PARTNERS
5900 Wilshire Blvd., #1900, Los Angeles, CA 90036. (310) 937-8540.

DENTSU, INC.
4751 Wilshire Blvd., #203, Los Angeles, CA 90010. (213) 939-3452. FAX: (213) 939-3857.

W. B. DONER & CO.
25900 Northwestern Highway, Southfield, MI 48075. (313) 354-9700. FAX: (313) 827-8448.
2305 N. Charles Street, Baltimore, MD 21218. (301) 338-1600.
PRESIDENT/COO
Alan Kalter

DOREMUS & COMPANY
200 Varick St., 11th & 12th fls., New York, NY 10014. (212) 366-3000. FAX: (212) 366-3632.
PRESIDENT
Carl Anderson
EXECUTIVE V.P., WORLDWIDE CREATIVE DIRECTOR
Rebecca Tudor-Foley

LARRY DORN ASSOCS. INC.
5820 Wilshire Blvd., Suite 306, Los Angeles, CA 90036. (213) 935-6266. FAX: (213) 935-9523.
Larry Dorn, Linda Dorn-Wallerstein, Lucy Kohn.

EARL, PALMER & BROWN
1710 East Franklin Street, Richmond, VA 23223. (804) 775-0700.
CHAIRMAN
Bill Bergman

EDELMAN PUBLIC RELATIONS WORLDWIDE
5670 Wilshire Blvd., #1500, Los Angeles, CA 90048. (213) 857-9100. FAX: (213) 857-9117.

EISAMAN, JOHNS & LAWS INC.
5700 Wilshire Blvd., 6th fl., Los Angeles, CA 90036. (213) 932-1234. FAX: (213) 965-6134.

MAX EISEN
234 W. 44 St., New York, NY 10036. (212) 391-1072.

EVANS GROUP
110 Social Hall Ave., Salt Lake City, UT 84111. (801) 364-7452. FAX: (801) 364-7484.
CHAIRMAN/CEO
Donald B. Kraft

FELDMAN PUBLIC RELATIONS
9220 Sunset Blvd., #230, Los Angeles, CA 90069. (310) 859-9062. FAX: (310) 859-9563.

FOOTE, CONE & BELDING COMMUNICATIONS, INC.
101 East Erie Street, Chicago, IL 60611-2897. (312) 751-7000. FAX: (312) 751-3501.
CHAIRMAN & CEO
Bruce Mason

B. D. FOX & FRIENDS, INC. ADVERTISING
1111 Broadway, Santa Monica, CA 90401. (310) 394-7150. FAX: (310) 393-1569.
CEO
Brian D. Fox.

ALBERT FRANK GUENTHER LAW INC.
71 Broadway, New York, NY 10006. (212) 248-5200.
CHAIRMAN
Gary Goldstein
PRESIDENT
James H. Feeney

GS ENTERTAINMENT MARKETING GROUP
8721 Beverly Blvd., Los Angeles, CA 90048. (310) 358-8640. FAX: (310) 289-1854.
Steven Zeller.

GELFOND, GORDON AND ASSOCIATES
11500 Olympic Blvd., Suite 350, Los Angeles, CA 90064. (310) 478-3600. FAX: (213) 477-4825.

GERBER ADVERTISING AGENCY
209 S.W. Oak St., Portland, OR 97204. (503) 221-0100. FAX: (503) 228-7471.
PRESIDENT & CEO
Phil Stevens

GOLIN/HARRIS COMMUNICATIONS
500 N. Michigan Ave., Chicago, IL 60611. (312) 836-7100. FAX: (312) 836-7170.
CHAIRMAN
Alvin Golin
PRESIDENT & CEO
Rich Jerntedt

FRANK GOODMAN
1776 Broadway, New York, NY 10019. (212) 246-4180.

GREY ADVERTISING, INC.
777 Third Ave., New York, NY 10017. (212) 546-2000. FAX: (212) 546-1495.
CHAIRMAN & CEO
Edward H. Meyer

GREY ENTERTAINMENT & MEDIA
875 Third Ave., New York, NY 10022. (212) 303-2400.

GRISWOLD COMMUNICATIONS, INC.
101 Prospect Ave. West, Cleveland, OH 44115. (216) 696-3400. FAX: (216) 696-3405.
CHAIRMAN, PRESIDENT & CEO
Patrick J. Morin

GUTTMAN ASSOCIATES
118 S. Beverly Dr., Suite 201, Beverly Hills, CA 90212. (310) 246-4600. FAX: (310) 246-4601.

HANSON & SCHWAM
2020 Ave. of Stars, Suite 410, Los Angeles, CA 90067. (310) 557-1199. FAX: (310) 557-9090.

HODES, BERNARD, ADV. INC.
555 Madison Ave., New York, NY 10022. (212) 758-2600. FAX: (212) 751-6278.
PRESIDENT & CEO
Bernard S. Hodes

HUTCHINS/YOUNG & RUBICAM
400 Midtown Tower, Rochester, NY 14604. (716) 546-6480.
PRESIDENT & CEO
M.A. Sapos

JACOBS & GERBER INC.
731 N. Fairfax Ave., Los Angeles, CA 90046-7293. (213) 655-4082. FAX: (213) 655-0195.
PRESIDENT & CEO
Albert B. Litewka

HENRY J. KAUFMAN & ASSOCIATES, INC.
2233 Wisconsin Ave. NW, Washington, DC 20007. (202) 333-0700.
CHAIRMAN, PRESIDENT & CEO
Michael G. Carberry

KETCHUM COMMUNICATIONS, INC.
Six PPG Place, Pittsburgh, PA 15222. (412) 456-3500.
PRESIDENT, CHAIRMAN & CEO
Paul Alvarez

LANDIN MEDIA INC.
3033 N. 44 St., #375, Phoenix, AZ 85018-7229. (602) 553-4080. FAX: (602) 553-4090.
PRESIDENT & CEO
Larry L. Cummings

LEE & ASSOCIATES
145 S. Fairfax Ave., Los Angeles, CA 90036. (213) 938-3300. FAX: (213) 938-3305.

LEVINE, SCHNEIDER, PUBLIC RELATIONS CO.
8730 Sunset Blvd., Los Angeles, CA 90069. (310) 659-6400. FAX: (310) 659-1309.

LEWIS & ASSOCIATES
3600 Wilshire Blvd. #200, Los Angeles, CA 90010. (213) 739-1000.

LINTAS: WORLDWIDE
One Dag Hammarskjold Plaza, New York, NY 10017-2203. (212) 605-8000. FAX: (212) 935-2164.
CHAIRMAN & PRESIDENT
Spencer Plavoukos
CHAIRMAN & CEO
Kenneth L. Robbins

LIPPIN GROUP INC.
6100 Wilshire Blvd., #400, Los Angeles, CA 90048. (213) 965-1990. FAX: (213) 965-1993.

MARCUS ADVERTISING INC.
Landmark Center, 25700 Science Park Dr., Cleveland, OH 44122. (216) 292-4700. FAX: (216) 831-6189.
CHAIRMAN & CEO
Donald M. Marcus

THE MARKETING GROUP
1411 Fifth St., #306, Santa Monica, CA 90401. (310) 393-5505. FAX: (310) 393-1716.

MCCANN-ERICKSON
750 Third Ave., New York, NY 10017. (212) 697-6000. FAX: (212) 867-5177.
CHAIRMAN & CEO
Robert L. James
PRESIDENT & COO
John J. Dooner

MELDRUM & FEWSMITH COMMUNICATIONS, INC.
1350 Euclid Ave., Cleveland, OH 44115. (216) 241-2141. FAX: (216) 479-2437.
CHAIRMAN, CEO & CREATIVE DIRECTOR
Chris Perry

MOMENTUM INTERNATIONAL MARKETING
P.O. Box 5889, Sherman Oaks, CA 91413. (818) 752-4500. FAX: (818) 752-4554.

MOROCH & ASSOCIATES
3625 N. Hall St., #1200, Dallas, TX 75219. (214) 520-9700. FAX: (214) 520-6464.
CHAIRMAN
Tom Moroch

JULIAN MYERS PUBLIC RELATIONS
2040 Ave. of the Stars, 4th Fl., Century City, 90067. (213) 557-1525. FAX: (213) 557-0133.

OGILVY & MATHER INC.
309 W. 49 St., New York, NY 10019. (212) 237-4000. FAX: (212) 237-5123.
CHAIRMAN
Charlotte Beers

DALE C. OLSON & ASSOCS.
6310 San Vicente Blvd., #340, Los Angeles, CA 90048. (213) 932-6026. FAX: (213) 932-1989.

PMK INC.
955 Carrillo Dr., Suite 200, Los Angeles, CA 90048. (213) 954-4000. FAX: (213) 954-4011.
1775 Broadway, New York, NY 10019. (212) 582-1111.

POLLACK PR MARKETING GROUP
2049 Century Park E., #2520, Los Angeles, CA 90067. (310)
556-4443. FAX: (310) 556-2350.
President: Noemi Pollock.

PORTER/NOVELLI
12100 Wilshire Blvd., #1800, Los Angeles, CA 90025. (310)
444-7000.

MYRNA POST ASSOCIATES
1650 Broadway, New York, NY10019. (212) 757-5021.

PUBLICITY WEST
2155 Ridgemont Dr., Los Angeles, CA 90046. (213) 654-3816.
(818) 954-1951. FAX: (213) 654-6084.

ROGERS & COWAN
1888 Century Park East, Suite 500, Los Angeles, CA 90067-
1709. (310) 201-8800. FAX: (310) 552-0412.
475 Park Ave. S., 32nd Fl., New York, NY 10016. (212) 779-3500.

**ROSENFELD, SIROWITZ, HUMPHREY & STRAUSS
ADVERTISING**
111 Fifth Ave., New York, NY 10002. (212) 505-0200. FAX:
(212)505-7309.
CO-CHAIRMEN & CEO's
Leonard Sirowitz, Harold Strauss

ROSKIN-FRIEDMAN ASSOCS., INC.
8425 W. 3rd St., #309, Los Angeles, CA 90048. (213) 653-
5411. FAX: (213) 653-5474.
PRESIDENT
Monroe Friedman.
72 Reade St., New York, NY 10007. (212) 385-0005. FAX:
(212) 385-0951.
PRESIDENT
Sheldon Roskin

ROSS ROY COMMUNICATIONS
100 Bloomfield Hills Pkwy., Bloomfield Hills, MI 48304. (313)
433-6000. FAX: (313): (313) 433-6421.
CHAIRMAN, PRESIDENT & CEO
Peter Mills

SAATCHI & SAATCHI ADVERTISING
375 Hudson St., New York, NY 10014-3620. (212) 463-2000.
FAX: (212) 463-9855.
CHAIRMAN & COO
Harvey Hoffenberg
PRESIDENT & COO
Michael Keeshan

**SAATCHI & SAATCHI/THE SAATCHI ENTERTAINMENT
GROUP**
3501 Sepulveda Blvd., Torrance, CA 90505. (310) 214-6000.
FAX: (310) 214-6008.
DIRECTOR
Alfa Tate-O'Neill.

NANCY SELTZER & ASSOCS.
1775 Broadway, New York, NY 10019. (212) 307-0117.

SIMONS MICHELSON ZIEVE INC.
900 Wilshire Dr., Troy, MI 48084-1600. (313) 362-4242. FAX:
(313) 362-2014.
CHAIRMAN
Morton Zieve

SUDLER & HENNESSEY INC.
1633 Broadway, New York, NY 10019. (212) 696-5800. FAX:
(212) 969-5991.
CHAIRMAN, PRESIDENT & CEO
Willliam B. Gibson

TARGET & RESPONSE
420 N. Wabash Ave., Chicago, IL 60610. (312) 573-0500. FAX:
(312) 573-0516.
PRESIDENT/GENERAL MANAGER
Lawrence Levis

TATHAM EURO RSCG
980 N. Michigan Ave., Chicago, IL 60611. (312) 337-4400.
FAX: (312) 337-5930.
CHAIRMAN & CEO
Ralph Rydholm

J. WALTER THOMPSON COMPANY
466 Lexington Ave., New York, NY 10017. (212) 210-7000.
FAX: (212) 210-6889.
CHAIRMAN & CEO
Burt Manning

TIERNEY & PARTNERS
200 S. Broad St., Philadelphia, PA 19102. (215) 790-4100.
FAX: (215) 790-4363.
PRESIDENT & CEO
Brian P. Tierney
S.V.P., MEDIA DIRECTOR
William Melnick

TRACY-LOCKE ADVERTISING INC.
200 Crescent Ct., Dallas, TX 75250. (214) 969-9000.
PRESIDENT & CEO
Michael S. Rawlings

TUCKER WAYNE/LUCKIE & CO.
1100 Peachtree St., N.E., Suite 1800, Atlanta, GA 30309. (404)
347-8700. FAX: (404) 347-8800.
CHAIRMAN & CEO
Knox Massey, Jr.
PRESIDENT
Sidney L. Smith

MORTON D. WAX PUBLIC RELATIONS
1560 Broadway, New York, NY 10019. (212) 302-5360. FAX:
(212) 302-5364. e-mail: 72124.250@compuserve.com
PRESIDENT
Morton D. Wax

WELLS, RICH, GREENE B.D.D.P. COMMUNICATIONS, INC.
9 W. 57 St., New York, NY 10019. (212) 303-5000. FAX: (212)
303-5040.
CHAIRMAN & CEO
Ken Olshan

WORLDWIDE INTELLIGENCE
9437 Santa Monica Blvd., #202, Beverly Hills, CA 90210. (310)
205-2828. FAX: (310) 205-2820.

YOUNG & RUBICAM INC.
285 Madison Ave., New York, NY 10017-6486. (212) 210-3000.
FAX (212) 490-9073.
CHAIRMAN
Alexander S. Kroll
PRESIDENT & CEO
Peter A. Georgescu

ANIMATION

ABRAMS/GENTILE ENTERTAINMENT
244 W. 54th St., 9th Floor, New York, NY 10019. (212) 757-0700.
PRESIDENT
John Gentile

AMBLIMATION
(see Dreamworks)

ANGEL FILMS
967 Highway 40, New Franklin, MO 65274. (573) 698-3900.
PRESIDENT
William H. Hoehne, Jr.

ANIMOTION
501 W. Fayette St., Syracuse, NY 13204. (315) 471-3533. FAX:
(315) 475-1969.
David Hicock, Larry Royer.

ATOMIX
1800 North Vine Street, Suite 310, Hollywood, CA 90028.
(310) 962-4745.
PRESIDENT
Chris Mitchell

BAER ANIMATION COMPANY INC.
3765 Cahuenga Blvd. West, Studio City, CA 91604. (818) 760-
8666. FAX: 818-760-9698.
PRESIDENT
Jane Baer

BAGDASARIAN PRODS.
1192 East Mountain Drive, Montecito, CA 93108. (805) 969-
3349.
CEO
Ross Bagdasarian

BILL MELENDEZ PRODUCTIONS
439 N. Larchmont Ave., Los Angeles, CA 90004. (213) 463-4101.
PRESIDENT
Bill Melendez

BLUE SKY PRODUCTIONS, INC.
100 Executive Boulevard., Ossining, NY 10562. (914) 941-5260.
PRESIDENT
David Brown

BLUR STUDIO, INC.
1130 Abbot Kinney Blvd., Venice, CA 90291. (310) 581-8848.
EXECUTIVE PRODUCER
Cat Chapman

BOBTOWN
2003 Canyon Drive, Hollywood, CA 90068. (213) 462-6116.
PRESIDENT
John Lamb

BOHBOT ENTERTAINMENT
41 Madison Avenue, New York, NY 10010. (212) 213-2700.
PRESIDENT
Allen J. Bohbot

BROADWAY VIDEO DESIGN
1619 Broadway, 4th Floor, New York, NY 10019. (212) 333-0500.
VICE PRESIDENT
Peter Rosnick

BUZZCO ASSOCIATES INC.
33 Bleecker St., New York, NY 10012. (212) 473-8800. FAX: (212) 473-8891. e-mail: BUZZCO@aol.com
Candy Kugel

CALABASH PRODUCTIONS
657 West Ohio, Chicago, IL 60610. (312) 243-3433. FAX: 312-243-6227.
EXEUCTIVE PRODUCER
Monica Kendall

CALICO LTD.
9340 Eton Ave., Chatsworth, CA 91311-5879. (818) 407-5200. FAX: (818) 407-5323.
PRESIDENT & CEO
Tom Burton

THE CALVERT COMPANY
5050 Tujunga Ave., Suite 5, N. Hollywood, CA 91601. (818) 760-8700.
PRESIDENT
Fred Calvert

CELLULOID STUDIOS
2128 15th Street, Denver, CO 80202. (303) 595-3152.
EXECUTIVE PRODUCER
Olivier Katz

CHELSEA ANIMATION COMPANY
3035A W. Cary St., Richmond, VA 23221. (804) 353-0793.
PRESIDENT
John O'Donnell

CHIODO BROTHERS PRODUCTIONS, INC.
425 S. Flower St., Burbank, CA 91502. (818) 842-5656.
PRESIDENT
Stephen Chiodo

CHUCK JONES FILM PRODUCTIONS
4000 Warner Blvd., Bldg. 131, Burbank, CA 91522. (818) 954-2655.
Linda Jones Clough

CHURCHILL MEDIA
6917 Valjean Ave., Van Nuys, CA 91406-4716. (818) 778-1978.
DIRECTOR, PRODUCT DEVELOPMENT
George Holland

CINAR FILMS (U.S.) INC.
9350 Wilshire Blvd., Suite 400, Beverly Hills, CA 90212. (310) 285-7400. e-mail: CinarFilms@aol.com
V.P., DEVELOPMENT & PRODUCTION
Sam Wendel
1055 Rene Levesque Blvd. E., Montreal, Quebec, Canada H2L 4S5. (514) 843-7070. FAX: (514) 843-7080.
PRESIDENT
Ronald A. Weinberg

CINEPIX ANIMATION
900 Broadway, Suite 800, New York, NY 10003. (212) 995-9662. FAX: (212) 475-2284.
V.P., BUSINESS AFFAIRS
John J. Graves

CLASS 6 ENTERTAINMENT
6777 Hollywood Blvd., 7th Floor, Hollywood, CA 90028. (213) 465-0300.

EXECUTIVE PRODUCER
Reuben Frias

COFFEY/BALLANTINE
10202 W. Washington Blvd., SPP 3650, Culver City, CA 90232. (310) 280-6585.
PRESIDENT
Vanessa Coffey, Jim Coffey

COLOSSAL PICTURES
2800 3rd. St., San Francisco, CA 94107. (415) 550-8772.
PRESIDENT
Drew Takahashi

CORNELL/ABOOD
4400 Coldwater Canyon Ave., Suite 100, Studio City, CA 91604. (818) 508-1215.
ASSOCIATE PRODUCER
Karen Inwood

CURIOUS PICTURES
440 Lafayette, New York, NY 10003. (212) 674-1400.
EXECUTIVE PRODUCER
Richard Winkler

D'OCON FILMS
3694 Barham Blvd., Suite F-203, Los Angeles, CA 90068. (213) 878-6648.
MANAGING DIRECTOR
Robert Mitrani

DADDY-O PRODUCTIONS
6051 Alcott Ave., Van Nuys, CA 91401. (818) 782-1930.
Tom McLaughlin

DIC ENTERTAINMENT
202 N. Glen Oaks Blvd., Burbank, CA 91502. (818) 955-5400.
PRESIDENT
Andy Heyward

DREAMWORKS FEATURE ANIMATION
100 Universal City Plaza, Bldg. 601, Universal City, CA 91608. (818) 733-6000.
PRODUCTION CHIEF
Sandy Rabins

DREAMWORKS TELEVISION ANIMATION
(see address above). (818) 733-7500.
PRODUCTION CHIEF
Stephanie Graziano

ENCORE ENTERPRISES
25510 Stanford Ave., Suite 101, Valencia, CA 91355. (805) 295-0675.
PRESIDENT
Bill Hutton

ENOKI FILMS U.S.A., INC.
16501 Venture Blvd., Suite 606, Encino, CA 91436. (818) 907-6503.
Ricki Ames

FILM ROMAN, INC.
12020 Chandler Blvd., Suite 200, North Hollywood, CA 91607. (818) 761-2544.
PRESIDENT
Phil Roman

FLEISCHER STUDIOS, INC.
10160 Cielo Dr., Beverly Hills, CA 90210. (310) 276-7503.
PRESIDENT
Richard Fleischer

FLINT PRODUCTIONS INC.
1015 N. Orlando, Los Angeles, CA 90069. (213) 654-0503. FAX: (213) 848-9637.
Roger Flint

FOX ANIMATION STUDIOS
2747 E. Camelback Rd., Phoenix, AZ 85016. (602) 808-4600.
EXECUTIVE VICE PRESIDENT
Steve Brain

FRED WOLF FILMS
4222 W. Burbank Blvd., Burbank, CA 91505. (818) 846-0611.
PRESIDENT
Fred Wolf

GATEWAYS TO SPACE
5976 W. Las Positas, Suite 122, Pleasanton, CA 94588. (510) 847-2777.
PRESIDENT
Louis Karagochos

GRACIE FILMS
10202 W. Washington Blvd., Sidney Poitier Bldg., #2221, Culver City, CA 90232.
PRESIDENT
Richard Sakai

GREATEST TALES
22477 MacFarlane Dr., Woodland Hills, CA 90024. (310)
446-6000.
PRESIDENT
Fred Ladd

GROUP W PRODUCTIONS
10877 Wilshire Blvd., Los Angeles, CA 90024. (310) 446-6000.
PRESIDENT
Derk Zimmerman

GUNTHER-WAHL PRODUCTIONS
6345 Balboa Blvd., Suite 285, Encino, CA 91316. (818) 776-
9200. FAX: 818-776-9293.
PRESIDENT
Michael Wahl

HALLMARK
1235 Avenue of the Americas, 21st Fl., New York, NY 10019.
(212) 977-9001.
SENIOR VICE PRESIDENT
Joel Denton

HANNA-BARBERA PRODUCTIONS
3400 Cahuenga Blvd., Hollywood, CA 90068. (213) 851-5000.
PRESIDENT
Fred Seibert

HARVEY ENTERTAINMENT
100 Wilshire Blvd., 14th Fl., Santa Monica, CA 90401-1110.
(310) 451-3377. FAX: (310) 458-6995.
PRESIDENT
Jeffrey Montgomery

HEARST ANIMATION PRODUCTIONS
1640 S. Sepulveda Blvd., Los Angeles, CA 90025. (310)
478-1700.
PRESIDENT
Wiliam Miller

HEART OF TEXAS PRODUCTIONS
2600 Dellana Lane, Suite 100, Austin, TX 78746. (512) 329-
8262.
PRESIDENT
Don Smith

JIM HENSON PRODUCTIONS
c/o Raleigh Studios, 5358 Melrose Ave., West Bldg., 3rd
Floor, Hollywood, CA 90038. (213) 960-4096.
PRESIDENT
Brian Henson

HUBLEY STUDIO
2575 Palisade Ave., Riverdale, NY 10463. (718) 543-5958.
Faith Hubley

HYPERION ANIMATION
111 N. Maryland Ave., Suite 200, Glendale, CA 91206. (818)
244-4704.
PRESIDENT
Tom Wilhite

I.N.I ENTERTAINMENT GROUP, INC.
11845 Olympic Blvd., Suite 1145W, Los Angeles, CA 90064.
(310) 479-6755.
CEO
Irv Hollender

ICE TEA PRODUCTIONS
160 E. 38 St., #15-G, New York, NY 10016. (212) 557-8185.
Richard Durkin

IMAGINATION STUDIOS
11684 Ventura Blvd., Suite 144, Studio City, CA 91604. (310)
633-4230.
CEO
Dana Blanchard

THE INK TANK
2 W. 47th St., New York, NY 10036. (212) 869-1630.
EXECUTIVE PRODUCER
Brian O'Connell

ITC
9100 Wilshire Blvd., Suite 600 West, Beverly Hills, CA 90212.
(310) 724-8100.
PRESIDENT
Jules Haimovitz

J.J. SEDELMAIER PRODUCTIONS, INC.
199 Main St., 10th Floor, White Plains, NY 10601. (914) 949-7979.
PRESIDENT
J.J. Sedelmaier

JETLAG PRODUCTIONS
15315 Magnolia Blvd., Suite 310, Sherman Oaks, CA 91403.
(818) 385-3400.
PRESIDENT
Jean Chalopin

JUMBO PICTURES
75 Spring St., 6th Floor, New York, NY 10012. (212) 226-7890.
Jim Jinkins

KLASY-CSUPO, INC.
1258 N. Highland Ave., Hollywood, CA 90038. (213) 463-0145.
PRESIDENT
Terry Thoren

KOOKANOOGA TOONS
12754 Ventura Blvd., Suite D, Studio City, CA 91604. (818)
841-9900.
PRODUCTION MANAGER
Molly Bradford

THE KRISLIN COMPANY
23901 Calabasas Road, Suite 1501, Calabasas, CA 91302.
(818) 222-0555.
PRESIDENT
Walt Kubiak

KURTZ & FRIENDS
2312 W. Olive Ave., Burbank, CA 91506. (818) 841-8188.
PRESIDENT
Bob Kurtz

L.A. ANIMATION
2920 W. Olive Ave., Burbank, CA 91505. (818) 563-2300.
PRESIDENT
Lyn Henderson

JERRY LIEBERMAN PRODUCTIONS
76 Laight Street, New York, NY 10013. (212) 431-3452. FAX:
(212) 941-8976.
Jerry Lieberman

M3D PRODUCTIONS
18520 Arminta Dr., Van Nuys, CA 91406. (818) 785-6662.
PRESIDENT
Marcel Nottea

MARVEL FILMS ANIMATION
1440 S. Sepulveda Blvd., Los Angeles, CA 90025. (310) 444-
8644. FAX: (310) 444-8168.
PRESIDENT
Avi Arad

MATINEE ENTERTAINMENT
345 N. Maple Dr., Suite 285, Beverly Hills, CA 90210. (310)
246-9044. FAX: (310) 246-9066.
PRESIDENT
Michael I. Yanover

MATTHEWS PRODUCTIONS
P.O. Box 74, Cedar Glen, CA 92321. (909) 867-5068.
PRODUCER
John Clark Matthews

MEDIAMAX PRODUCTIONS
9538 Brighton Way, Beverly Hills, CA 90210. (310) 285-0550.
PRESIDENT
Frederick Ittah

METROLIGHT STUDIOS
5724 W. 3rd St., Suite 400, Los Angeles, CA 90036-3078.
(213) 932-0400.
PRESIDENT
James W. Kristoff

MGM ANIMATION
2500 Broadway St., Santa Monica, CA 90404. (310) 449-3795.
GENERAL MANAGER
Don Mirisch

MICHAEL SPORN ANIMATION, INC.
632 Broadway, 4th Floor, New York, NY 10012. (212) 228-3372.
PRESIDENT
Michael Sporn

MIKE YOUNG PRODUCTIONS
20315 Ventura Blvd., Suite B, Woodland Hills, CA 91364. (818)
999-0062.
PRESIDENT
Mike Young

MOON MESA MEDIA
P.O. Box 7848, Northridge, CA 91327. (818) 360-6224.
PRESIDENT
Sheryl Hardy

MORGAN CREEK PRODUCTIONS
4000 Warner Blvd., Bldg. 76, Burbank, CA 91522. (818)
954-4800.
Brian Robinson

MTM ENTERPRISES
12700 Ventura Blvd., Studio City, CA 91604. (818) 755-2400.
PRESIDENT
Tony Thomopolous

417

MTV ANIMATION
15 Columbus Circle, 40th Floor, New York, NY 10023. (212) 373-6710.
VICE PRESIDENT
John Andrews

MUSIVISION
195 E. 85th St., New York, NY 10028. (212) 860-4420.
Fred Kessler

NELVANA COMMUNICATIONS, INC.
4500 Wilshire Blvd., 1st Floor, Los Angeles, CA 90010. (213) 549-4222.
SENIOR VICE PRESIDENT
Toper Taylor

NEST ENTERTAINMENT
333 North Glenoaks Blvd., 3rd Floor, Burbank, CA 91502. (818) 846-9850.
SENIOR VICE PRESIDENT
Don Barrett

NEW WORLD ANIMATION
3340 Ocean Park Blvd., Santa Monica, CA 90405. (310) 444-8113.
PRESIDENT
Rick Unger

NICKELODEON
1440 S. Sepulveda Blvd., Los Angeles, CA 91607. (818) 753-3255.
VICE PRESIDENT
Mary Harrington

OPTICAM INC.
810 Navy St., Santa Monica, CA 90405. (310) 396-4665. FAX: (310) 452-0040.
Nancy Harris

OVATION/ANIMATION
9 Caccamo St., Westport, CT 06880. (203) 227-9346.
Art Petricone

PACIFIC DATA IMAGES
1111 Karlstad Drive, Sunnyvale, CA 94089. (408) 745-6755.
PRESIDENT
Carl Rosendahl

PERENNIAL PICTURES FILM CORP.
2102 E. 52nd St., Indianapolis, IN 46205. (317) 253-1519.
PRESIDENT
Jerry Reynolds

PIXAR ANIMATION STUDIOS
1001 W. Cutting Blvd., Point Richmond, CA 94804. (510) 236-4000.
EXECUTIVE VICE PRESIDENT
Ed Catmull

PLAYLIGHT PICTURES
1401 N. La Brea Ave., Hollywood, CA 90028. (213) 851-2112.
DIRECTOR
Ted Wooley

POLESTAR FILMS
231 W. 29th St., Suite 203, New York, NY 10001. (212) 268-2088.
Don Duga, Irra Verbitsky

PORCHLIGHT ENTERTAINMENT
11828 LaGrange Ave., Los Angeles, CA 90025. (310) 477-8400.
PRESIDENT
Bruce Johnson

QUARTER STAR PRODUCTIONS, INC.
7216 Park Rd., Charlotte, NC 28210. (704) 554-7127.
PRESIDENT
Patrick W. May

RED APPLE FILMS
14011 Ventura Blvd., Sherman Oaks, CA 91423. (818) 906-7299.
Boris Chacham

R/GREENBERG ASSOC. INC.
350 W. 39th St., New York, NY 10018. (212) 946-4000. FAX: (212) 946-4010.
Michael di Girolamo

RHYTHM N'HUES
5404 Jandy Place, Los Angeles, CA 90066. (310) 448-7500.
PRESIDENT
John Hughes

RICH ANIMATION STUDIOS
333 N. Glenoaks Blvd., 3rd Floor, Burbank, CA 91502. (818) 846-0166.
Tom Tobin

RICK REINERT PICTURES, INC.
32107 Lindero Canyon Rd., Suite 224, Westlake Village, CA 91361. (818) 889-8977.
PRESIDENT
Rick Reinert

RUBY-SPEARS PRODUCTIONS
710 S. Victory Blvd., Suite 201, Burbank, CA 91502. (818) 840-1234.
PRESIDENT
Joe Ruby

SABAN ENTERTAINMENT
10960 Wilshire Blvd., Suite 2400, Los Angeles, CA 90024. (310) 235-5100.
PRESIDENT
Haim Saban

7TH LEVEL
900 Allen Ave., Glendale, CA 91201. (818) 547-1955.
V.P., ANIMATION
Dan Kuenster

SHERWOOD ANIMATION
346 N. Kanan Rd., Suite 202, Agura Hills, CA 91304. (818) 879-1668.
David Egbert

SILVERLINE PICTURES
11846 Ventura Blvd., Suite 100, Studio City, CA 91604. (818) 752-3730.
PRESIDENT
Axel Munch

SINGLE FRAME FILMS
437-1/2 N. Genessee Ave., Los Angeles, CA 90036. (213) 655-2664.
Gary Schwartz

SKELLINGTON PRODUCTIONS
375 Seventh St., San Francisco, CA 94103. (415) 864-2846.
PRESIDENT
Henry Selick

SONY PICTURES IMAGEWORKS
10202 W. Washington Blvd., TriStar Bldg., Suite 207, Culver City, CA 90232. (310) 280-7600.
SENIOR VICE PRESIDENT
Bill Birrell

SPUMCO INC.
5625 Melrose Ave., Hollywood, CA 80038. (213) 462-2943.
PRESIDENT
John Kricfalusi

ST PRODUCTIONS
2041 Manning St., Burbank, CA 91505. (818) 846-3939. FAX: (818) 846-2530.

STARTOONS, INC.
P.O. Box 1232, Homewood, IL 60430. (708) 335-3535. FAX: (708) 339-3999.
EXECUTIVE PRODUCER
Christine McLenahan

STREAMLINE PICTURES
2908 Nebraska Ave., Santa Monica, CA 90404. (310) 998-0070.
PRESIDENT
Carl Macek

STRIBLING PRODUCTIONS
6528 Carnellia Ave., N. Hollywood, CA 91606. (818) 509-0748.
PRESIDENT
Mike Stribling

SUNBOW PRODUCTIONS
100 5th Ave., New York, NY 10011. (212) 886-4900. FAX: (212) 366-4242.
PRESIDENT
C.J. Kettler

TANDEM COMMUNICATIONS
9000 Sunset Blvd., Penthouse, Los Angeles, CA 90069. (310) 859-2941.
PRESIDENT
Joseph Perez

TAWEEL-LOOS & CO. ENTERTAINMENT
3965 Carpenter Ave., Studio City, CA 91604. (818) 760-2222.
George Taweel

TMS/KYOKUICHI CORPORATION
15760 Ventura Blvd., Suite 700, Encino, CA 91436. (818) 905-8881.
Andrew Berman

TOEI ANIMATION CO., LTD.
444 W. Ocean Blvd., Suite 1000, Long Beach, CA 90802. (310) 901-2444.
Mary Jo Winchester

TOON MAKERS, INC.
16007 Knapp St., North Hills, CA 91343. (818) 766-2460.
EXECUTIVE PRODUCER
Ricky Solotoff

THE TOONIVERSAL CO.
6324 Variel Ave., Suite 318, Woodland Hills, CA 91367. (818) 884-2374. FAX: 818-884-2259.
PRESIDENT
Igor Meglic

TURNER FEATURE ANIMATION
3330 Cahuenga Blvd., 2nd Floor, Los Angeles, CA 90068. (213) 436-3100.
Michelle Lynskey

UNITED MEDIA
330 Primrose Rd., Suite 310, Burlingame, CA 94010. (415) 342-8284.
DIRECTOR
Lee Mendelson

UNIVERSAL CARTOON STUDIOS
100 Universal City Plaza, Universal City, CA 91608. (818) 777-1000.
PRESIDENT
Jeff Segal

UPA PRODUCTIONS OF AMERICA
14101 Valleyheart Dr., Sherman Oaks, CA 91423. (818) 990-3800.
PRESIDENT
Hank Saperstein

VIDE-U PRODUCTIONS
9976 Westwanda Dr., Beverly Hills, CA 90210. (310) 276-5509. FAX: (310) 276-1183.
Bradley Freeman

WALT DISNEY FEATURE ANIMATION
500 S. Buena Vista Dr., Burbank, CA 91512. (818) 560-8000.
PRESIDENT
Peter Schneider

WALT DISNEY TELEVISION ANIMATION
(see address above)
PRESIDENT
Dean Valentine

WARNER BROS. FEATURE ANIMATION
500 N. Brand St. Glendale, CA 91203-1923. (818) 977-7600.
PRESIDENT
Max Howard

WARNER BROS. TELEVISION ANIMATION
15303 Ventura Blvd., Suite 1200, Sherman Oaks, CA 91403. (818) 977-8700.
PRESIDENT
Jean MacCurdy

WILL VINTON STUDIOS
1400 N. W. 22nd Ave., Portland, OR 97210. (503) 225-1130.
Will Vinton

WORLDWIDE SPORTS
345 North Maple Dr., Suite 285, Beverly Hills, CA 90210. (310) 246-9044.
PRESIDENT
Norman J. Singer

WSE FILMS, INC.
1700 Broadway, Suite 1202, Denver, CO 80290-1201. (303) 831-1275.
PRESIDENT
Norman J. Singer

ZEN ENTERTAINMENT
1323-A 3rd St. Promenade, Santa Monica, CA 90401. (310) 451-1361.
Peter Keefe

CASTING SERVICES

BRAMSON & ASSOC.
7400 Beverly Blvd., Los Angeles, CA 90036. (213) 938-3595. FAX: (213) 938-0852.

THE CASTING COMPANY
7461 Beverly Blvd., PH, Los Angeles, CA 90036-2704. (213) 938-0700.
Janet & Michael Hirshenson

CASTING SOCIETY OF AMERICA
6565 Sunset Blvd., Suite 306, Los Angeles, CA 90028. (213) 463-1925.

CENTRAL CASTING
1700 W. Burbank Blvd., Burbank, CA 91506. (818) 569-5200. FAX: (818) 562-2786.

ENTERTAINMENT PARTNERS
3601 W. Olive Ave., 8th fl., Burbank, CA 91505. (818) 955-6000. FAX: (818) 845-6507.

DANNY GOLDMAN & ASSOCIATES CASTING
1006 N. Cole Ave., Los Angeles, CA 90038. (213) 463-1600. FAX: (213) 463-3139.

MEDIA CASTING
23391 Mulholland Dr., #477, Woodland, CA 91364. (800) 859-8422.

NEW AGE CASTING
7471 Melrose Ave., #23, W. Hollywood, CA 90046-7551. (213) 782-6968.

PAGANO, BIALY, MANWILLER
c/o 20th Century Fox, 10201 W. Pico, Trailer 67, Los Angeles, CA 90035. (213) 871-0051.

PRIME CASTING
7060 Hollywood Blvd., #1025, Hollywood, CA 90028. (213) 962-0377. FAX: (213) 465-1667.

RAINBOW CASTING
12501 Chandler Blvd., #206, N. Hollywood, CA 91607. (818) 752-2278. FAX: (818) 752-6580.
1282 Vallecita Dr., Santa Fe, NM 87501. (505) 268-9315. FAX: (505) 255-9801.
Theresa Neptune

MARY JO SLATER CASTING
2401 Colorado, 3rd Fl., Santa Monica, CA 90404. (310) 449-3695.

RON SMITH RON CELEBRITY LOOK-ALIKES
7060 Hollywood Blvd., #1215, Hollywood, CA 90028. (213) 467-3030. FAX: (213) 467-6720.

LYNN STALMASTER, & ASSOCIATES
5005 Sepulveda Blvd., Suite 600, Los Angeles, CA 90049. (310) 552-0983.

VOICECASTER
1832 W. Burbank Blvd., Burbank, CA 91506-1348. (818) 841-5300. FAX: (818) 841-2085.
MANAGER
Lisa Dyson

Consultants & Technical Services

BENNER MEDICAL
(Medical consultants on set)
601 W. 26 St., New York, NY 10001. (212) 727-9815.

BIGGS-ADAMS
(Union Labor Consultant)
8019 Corbin Ave., Canoga Park, CA 91306. (818) 349-4057.
FAX: (818) 993-8642.

BOOZ, ALLEN & HAMILTON INC.
(Strategy, reorganization for companies)
101 Park Ave., New York, NY 10178. (212) 697-1900.

BROADCAST BUSINESS CONSULTANTS, LTD.
(Talent payment and residuals)
317 Madison Ave., New York, NY 10017. (212) 687-3525. FAX:
949-9143.

PAUL BRONSTON, M.D.
(Medical Adviser)
1 Jib St., #202, Marina Del Rey, CA 90292. (310) 301-9426.

CONSULTANTS FOR TALENT PAYMENT INC.
(Talent payment and residuals)
22 W. 27 St., New York, NY 10001. (212) 696-1100.

COUNCIL OF CONSULTING ORGANIZATIONS
521 Fifth Ave., 35th fl., New York, NY 10175. (212) 697-8262.

DALE SYSTEM INC.
1101 Stewart Ave., Garden City, NY 11530. (516) 794-2800.
FAX: (516) 542-1083.
250 W. 57 St., New York, NY 10107. (212) 586-1320.
PRESIDENT
Harvey M. Yaffe

CURT DECKERT ASSOCS. INC.
(Technical management consultants)

18061 Darmel Pl., Santa Ana, CA 92705. (714) 639-0746.
FAX: (714) 639-0746.

DEWITT MEDIA INC.
(Media consulting, advertising planning and buying)
460 Park Ave. S., 10th Fl., New York, NY 10106. (212) 545-0120.

IMERO FIORENTINO ASSOCIATES
(Lighting consultants)
33 W. 60 St., New York, NY 10023. (212) 246-0600. FAX: (212)
246-6408.
P.R. DIRECTOR
Angela Linsell

NINA FOCH STUDIOS
(Creative consultant)
P.O. Box 1884, Beverly Hills, CA 90213. (310) 553-5805. FAX:
(310) 553-6149.
Maud Valot

MARSHALL/PLUMB RESEARCH ASSOCIATES
(Legal research, script clearances)
4150 Riverside Dr., Suite 209, Burbank, CA 91505. (818) 848-
7071.

MIRIMAR ENTERPRISES
(Script consultants)
P.O. Box 4621, N. Hollywood, CA 91607. (818) 784-4177. FAX:
(818) 990-3439.
Mirk Mirkin

ROSS-GAFFNEY
(Assembling production crews)
21 W. 46 St., New York, NY 10036. (212) 719-2744.

SECOND LINE SEARCH
(Stock footage researchers)
1926 Bdwy., New York, NY 10023. (212) 787-7500.

Costume & Prop Rentals

ABRAHAM RUGS GALLERY
525 N. La Cienega Blvd., Los Angeles, CA 90048. (310) 652-
6520. (800) 222-RUGS.

ADELE'S OF HOLLYWOOD
5034 Hollywood Blvd., Los Angeles, 90027. (213) 663-2231.
FAX: (213) 663-2232.

AGAPE UNIFORM CO.
3606 W. Washington Blvd., Los Angeles, CA 90018. (213) 731-
0621. FAX: (213) 731-0690.

AIM PROMOTIONS
Kaufman Astoria Studios, 34-12 36th St., Astoria, Queens, NY
11106. (718) 729-9288.

ALLAN UNIFORM RENTAL SERVICE INC.
121 E. 24 St., New York, NY 10010. (212) 529-4655.

WALTER ALLEN PLANT RENTALS
4996 Melrose Ave., Los Angeles, CA 90029-3738. (213) 469-
3621.

ALTMAN LUGGAGE
135 Orchard St., New York, NY 10002. (212) 254-7275.

AMERICAN COSTUME CORP.
12980 Raymer St., North Hollywood, CA 91605. (818) 764-
2239. FAX: (213) 765-7614.

ANIMAL MAKERS
2250 Turquoise, Newbury Park, CA 91320. (805) 499-9779.
FAX: (805) 499-3454.

ANIMAL OUTFITS FOR PEOPLE CO.
2255 Broadway, New York, NY 10024. (212) 877-5085.

ANTIQUARIAN TRADERS
9031 W. Olympic Blvd., Beverly Hills, CA 90211. (310) 247-
3900. FAX: (310) 247-8864.

399 Lafayette St., New York NY 10003. (212) 260-1200. FAX:
(212) 529-5320.

ANTIQUE & CLASSIC AUTOS
811 Union St., Brooklyn, NY 11215. (718) 788-3400.
Leonard Shiller

ANTIQUE & CLASSIC CAR RENTALS
611 1/2 W. Vernon Ave., Los Angeles, CA 90037. (213) 232-
7211.

ANTIQUE GUILD
8800 Venice Blvd., Los Angeles, CA 90034. (310) 838-3131.
FAX: (310) 287-2486.

ARENSON OFFICE FURNISHINGS
315 E. 62 St., New York, NY 10021. (212) 838-8880.

ARTS & CRAFTERS INC.
175 Johnson St., Brooklyn, NY 11201. (718) 875-8151.

BEDFELLOWS
12250 Ventura Blvd., Sherman Oaks, CA 91604. (818) 985-
0500. FAX: (818) 985-0617.

THE BRUBAKER GROUP
10560 Dolcedo Way, Los Angeles, CA 90077. (310) 472-4766.

BUENA VISTA STUDIOS
500 S. Buena Vista St., Burbank, CA 91521. (818) 560-1056.

CAL-EAST WIGS
232 S. Beverly Dr., #211, Beverly Hills, CA 90212. (310) 270-
4720.

CAMERA READY CARS
11161 Slater Ave., Fountain Valley, CA 92708. (714) 444-1700.

CARTHAY SET SERVICES
5907 West Pico Blvd., Los Angeles, CA 90038. (213) 938-
2101.

CENTRAL PROPERTIES
514 W. 49 St., 2nd Floor, New York, NY 10019. (212) 265-7767.

CENTRE FIREARMS CO, INC.
10 W. 37 St., New York, NY 10018. (212) 244-4040, (212) 244-4044. FAX: (212) 947-1233.

CINEMAFLOAT
1624 W. Ocean Front, Newport Beach, CA 92663. (714) 675-8888.

CLASSIC CARS LEASING CO.
500 Park Ave., New York, NY 10022. (212) 752-8080.

CLASSIC CAR SUPPLIERS
1905 Sunset Plaza Dr., W. Hollywood, CA 90069. (310) 657-7823.

CONTINENTAL SCENERY
7802 Clybourn Ave., Sun Valley, CA 91352. (818) 768-8075.

COOPER FILM CARS
132 Perry, New York, NY 10014. (212) 929-3909.

COSTUME ARMOUR INC.
2 Mill St., Cornwall, NY 12518. (914) 534-9120.

THE COSTUME PLACE
3117 Hamilton Way, Los Angeles, CA 90029. (213) 661-2597.

COSTUME RENTALS CO.
1149 Vanowen St., North Hollywood, CA 91605. (818) 753-3700. FAX: (818) 753-3737.

ELIZABETH COURTNEY COSTUMES
431 S. Fairfax Ave., 3rd fl., Los Angeles, CA 90036. (213) 937-0184.

CREATIVE COSTUME CO.
330 W. 38 St., New York, NY 10018. (212) 564-5552.

CUSTOM CHARACTERS
621 Thompson Ave., Glendale, CA 91201-2032. (818) 507-5940. FAX: (818) 507-1619.

DARROW'S FUN ANTIQUES
11011 First Ave., New York, NY 10021. (212) 838-0730.

DAVID'S OUTFITTERS, INC.
36 W. 20 St., New York, NY 10011. (212) 691-7388.

WALT DISNEY STUDIOS
500 S. Buena Vista St., Burbank, CA 91521. (818) 560-0044.

DOMSEY INTERNATIONAL SALES CORP.
431 Kent Ave., Brooklyn, NY 11211. (800) 221-RAGS. (718) 384-6000.

DOZAR OFFICE FURNITURE
9937 Jefferson Blvd., Culver City, CA 90232. (310) 559-9292. FAX: (310) 559-9009.

E. C. 2 COSTUMES
4019 Tujunga Ave., Studio City, CA 91604. (818) 506-7695. FAX: (818) 506-077

EASTERN COSTUME
7243 Coldwater Canyon, N. Hollywood, CA 91605. (818) 982-3611. FAX: (818) 503-1913.

EAVES-BROOKS COSTUME CO., INC.
21-07 41st Ave., Long Island City, NY 11101. (718) 729-1010.

ECLECTIC ENCORE PROPERTIES INC.
620 W. 26 St., 4th floor, New York, NY 10001. (212) 645-8880. FAX: (212) 243-6508.
James Gill

ELLIS MERCANTILE CO.
169 N. La Brea Ave., Los Angeles, CA 90036. (213) 933-7334. FAX: (213) 930-1268.

ENVIRION VISION
3074 Whaleneck Dr., Merrick, NY 11566. (516) 378-2250.

EXPENDABLE SUPPLY STORE
7830 N. San Fernando Rd., Sun Valley, CA 91352. (818) 767-5065. (213) 875-2409.

EYES ON MAIN
3110 Main St., #108, Santa Monica, CA 90405. (310) 399-3302. FAX: (310) 399-7682.

FANTASY COSTUMES
4649-1/2 San Fernando Rd., Glendale, CA 91204. (213) 245-7367.

FILMTRIX, INC.
P.O. Box 715, N. Hollywood, CA 91603. (818) 980-3700. FAX: (818) 980-3703. e-mail: FILMTRIX@aol.com
Kevin Pike

LARRY FIORITTO SPECIAL EFFECTS SERVICES
1067 E. Orange Grove, Burbank, CA 91501. (818) 954-9829.

FORMAL TOUCH ANTIQUE TUXEDO SERVICE
842 N. Fairfax Ave., Los Angeles, CA 90046. (213) 658-5553.

GARY GANG STABLES
13801 Gladstone, Sylmar, CA 91342. (818) 362-4648.

PETER GEYER ACTION PROPS & SETS
8235 Lankershim Blvd., Suite G, N. Hollywood, CA 91605. (818) 768-0070.

GLENDALE COSTUMES
746 W. Doran St., Glendale, CA 91203. (818) 244-1161. FAX: (818) 244-8576.

GLOBAL EFFECTS INC.
7119 Laurel Canyon Blvd., Unit 4, N. Hollywood, CA 91605. (818) 503-9273. FAX: (818) 503-9459.

GROSH SCENIC STUDIOS
4114 Sunset Blvd., Los Angeles, CA 90029. (213) 662-1134. FAX: (213) 664-7526.

HAND PROP ROOM, INC.
5700 Venice Blvd., Los Angeles, CA 90019. (213) 931-1534. FAX: (213) 931-2145.

HOLLYWOOD BREAKAWAY
15125-B Califa St., Van Nuys, CA 91411. (818) 781-0621.

HOLLYWOOD CENTRAL PROPS
9171 San Fernando Rd., Sun Valley, CA 91352. (818) 394-4504. FAX: (818) 394-4509.
V.P. & GENERAL MANAGER
Rick Caprarelli

HOLLYWOOD TOYS & COSTUMES
6562 Hollywood Blvd., Hollywood, CA 90028. (213) 465-3119.

HOUSE OF COSTUMES LTD.
166 Jericho Turnpike, Mineola, NY 11501. (516) 294-0170.

HOUSE OF PROPS
1117 Gower St., Hollywood, CA 90038. (213) 463-3166. FAX: (213) 463-8302.

IMAGE ENGINEERING, INC.
736 N. Reese Place, Burbank, CA 91506. (818) 840-1444.
Peter Chesney

IN COSTUME
37 W. 20 St., New York, NY 10011. (212) 255-5502.

INDEPENDENT STUDIO SERVICES
11907 Wicks St., Sun Valley, CA 91352. (818) 764-0840, (818) 768-5711.

INTERNATIONAL COSTUME
1423 Marcellina Ave., Torrance, CA 90501. (310) 320-6392. FAX: (310) 320-3054.

IWASAKI IMAGES OF AMERICA
(food replicas)
20460 Gramercy Pl., Torrance, CA 90501. (310) 328-7121. FAX: (310) 618-0876.

IZQUIERDO STUDIOS
118 W. 22 St., New York, NY 10011. (212) 807-9757.

KREISS COLLECTION
8619 Melrose Ave., Los Angeles, CA 90069-5010. (310) 657-3990.

KUTTNER PROP RENTALS INC.
56 W. 22 St., New York, NY 10010. (212) 242-7969. FAX: (212) 247-1293.
Barbara Guest

L.A. EYEWORKS
7407 Melrose Ave., Los Angeles, CA 90046. (213) 653-8255. FAX: (213) 653-8176.

LILLIAN COSTUME CO. OF L.I. INC.
226 Jericho Turnpike, Mineola, NY 11501. (516) 746-6060.

GENE LONDON STUDIOS
10 Gramercy Park So., New York, NY 10003. (212) 533-4105.

ELIZABETH LUCAS COLLECTION
1021 Montana Ave., Santa Monica, CA 90403. (310) 451-4058.

MERCURY NEON LIGHTING & SIGN UNLIMITED
104 E. 7 St., New York, NY 10009. (212) 473-NEON.

MODERN PROPS
5500 W. Jefferson Blvd., Los Angeles, CA 90016. (213) 934-3000. FAX: (213) 934-3155.

NATIONAL HELICOPTER SERVICE
16800 Roscoe Blvd., Van Nuys, CA 91406. (818) 345-5222.
FAX: (818) 782-0466.
Richard Hart, Helen Kosmala

A NEON SHOP
13026 Saticoy St., Unit 28, No. Hollywood, CA 91605. (818)
764-7181.

NICCOLINI ANTIQUES
19 W. 21 St., New York, NY 10010. (212) 243-2010. (800) 734-9974.

NIGHTS OF NEON
7442 Varna Ave., N. Hollywood, CA 91605. (818) 982-3592.
FAX: (818) 503-1090.

NORCOSTCO, INC.
3606 W. Magnolia Blvd., Burbank, CA 91505. (818) 567-0753.
FAX: (818) 567-1961.
GENERAL MANAGER
Wayne Thorton

OMEGA CINEMA PROPS
5857 Santa Monica, Blvd., Los Angeles, CA 90038. (213) 466-
8201. FAX: (213) 461-3643.

ONE NIGHT AFFAIR GOWN RENTAL
2370 Westwood Blvd., #H, W. Los Angeles, CA 90064-2120.
(310) 474-7808. FAX: (310) 474-6543.

PALACE COSTUME COMPANY
835 N. Fairfax Ave., Los Angeles, CA 90046. (213) 651-5458.
FAX: (213) 658-7133.

PARAMOUNT COSTUME DEPARTMENT
5555 Melrose Ave., Hollywood, CA 90038. (213) 956-5288.
FAX: (213) 956-2342.

PARK PLACE STUDIO
4801 Penn Ave., Pittsburgh, PA 15224. (412) 363-7538. (800)
831-2410. FAX: (412) 363-4318.

PERIOD PROPS
235 W. Olive Ave., Burbank, CA 91502. (818) 848-PROP. (818)
41S-ERVE. FAX: (818) 843-4745.

PICTURE CARS, EAST, INC.
72 Huntington St., Brooklyn, NY 11231. (718) 852-2300.

PROPS DISPLAYS & INTERIORS, INC.
132 W. 18 St., New York, NY 10011. (212) 620-3840. FAX:
(212) 620-5472.

PROPS FOR TODAY
330 W. 34th St. New York, NY 10001. (212) 244-9600. FAX:
(212) 244-1053.

PROP MASTERS, INC.
912 W. Isabel St., Burbank, CA 91506. (818) 846-3915, (818)
846-3957. FAX: (818) 846-1278.

PROP SERVICES WEST INC.
915 N. Citrus Ave., Los Angeles, CA 90038. (213) 461-3371.
FAX: (818) 846-1278.

R/C MODELS
P.O. Box 6026, San Pedro, CA 90734. (310) 833-4700.

ROSCHU
7100 Fair Ave., N. Hollywood, CA 91605. (818) 503-9392.

RUBIE'S COSTUME CO., INC.
120-08 Jamaica Ave., Richmond Hill, Queens, NY 11418. (718)
846-1008.

SJACQUELINE SARTINO
953 N. Edinburgh Ave., Los Angeles, CA 90046. (213) 654-
3326. FAX: (213) 656-6192.

SCENIC HIGHLIGHTS
4640 Sperry St., Los Angeles, CA 90039. (818) 956-3610.
FAX: (818) 956-3616.

SCHOEPFER STUDIOS
138 W. 31 St., New York, NY 10001. (212) 736-6939.

SONY PICTURES STUDIOS WARDROBE
10202 W. Washington Blvd., Culver City, CA 90232. (310) 280-
7260.

STARBUCK STUDIO
162 W. 21 St., New York, NY 10011. (212) 807-7299.

STICKS & STONES
12990 Branford St., Suite M, Arleta, CA 91331. (818) 252-
2088. FAX: (818) 252-2087.
Rob Burman, Jennifer E. McManus

STUDIO PICTURE VEHICLES
5418 Fair Ave., N. Hollywood, CA 91601. (818) 765-1201,
(818) 781-4223. FAX: (818) 506-4789.

THE STUDIO WARDROBE DEPT.
1130 N. Highland, Los Angeles, CA 90038. (818) 781-4267.

TONY'S UNIFORMS
2527 W. Magnolia Blvd., Burbank, CA 91505. (818) 842-
1494.

TRIANGLE SCENERY/DRAPERY/LIGHTING CO.
1215 Bates Ave., Los Angeles, CA 90029. (213) 662-8129.

TUXEDO CENTER
7360 Sunset Blvd., Los Angeles, CA 90046. (213) 874-4200.

20TH CENTURY PROPS
11651 Hart St., N. Hollywood, CA 91605-5802. (818) 759-
1190. FAX: (818) 759-0081.

UNIVERSAL FACILITIES RENTAL
100 Universal City Plaza, #480-3, Universal City, CA 91608.
(818) 777-3000, (800) 892-1979. FAX: (818) 733-1579.

URSULA'S COSTUMES INC.
2516 Wilshire Blvd., Santa Monica, CA 90403. (310) 582-8230.
FAX: (310) 582-8233.

WESTERN COSTUME CO.
11041 Van Owen St., N. Hollywood, CA 91605. (818) 760-0902.

VISUAL SERVICES
40 W. 72 St., New York, NY 10023. (212) 580-9551.

WARNER BROS. STUDIOS
4000 Warner Blvd., Burbank, CA 91522. (818) 954-2923. FAX:
(818) 954-2677.

WAVES
(Antique radios)
32 E. 13 St., New York, NY 10003. (212) 989-9284.

WEAPONS SPECIALISTS LTD.
33 Greene St., 1-W, New York, NY 10013. (212) 941-7696.
(800) 878-7696. FAX: (212) 941-7654.
Rick Washburn

WONDERWORKS
7231 Remmet Ave., #F, Canoga Park, CA 91303. (818) 992-
8811. FAX: (818) 347-4330.

EDITING SERVICES

ABSOLUTE POST
2911 W. Olive Ave., Burbank, CA 91505. (818) 953-4820. FAX:
(818) 845-9179.

ADVENTURE FILM & TAPE
1034 N. Seward St., Hollywood, CA 90038. (213) 460-4557.

ALTER IMAGE
1818 S. Victory Blvd., Glendale, CA 91201. (818) 244-6030.

ANIMATED PRODS., INC.
600 Broadway, New York, NY 10019. (212) 265-2942, (800)
439-1360.

ARCHIVE FILMS, INC.
530 W. 25 St., New York, NY 10001. (212) 620-3955. FAX:
(212) 645-2137.
Eric Rachlis

ASTROFILM SERVICE
932 N. La Brea Ave., Los Angeles, CA 90038. (213) 851-1673.

AVAILABLE LIGHT LTD.
3110 W. Burbank Blvd., Burbank, CA 91505. (818) 842-2109.

AVID TECHNOLOGY
4000 W. Alameda Ave., Suite 400, Burbank, CA 91505. (818)
557-2520. FAX: (818) 557-2558.

JERRY BENDER EDITORIAL SERVICE, INC.
27 E. 39 St., New York, NY 10016. (212) 867-1515.

BEXEL CORP.
801 S. Main St., Burbank, CA 91506. (818) 841-5051.

BIRNS & SAWYER, INC.
1026 N. Highland Ave., Hollywood, CA 90038. (213) 466-8211. FAX: (213) 466-7049.

BIG SKY EDITORIAL
10 E. 40 St., Suite 1201, New York, NY 10016. (212) 683-4004.

BIG TIME PICTURE COMPANY, INC.
12210-1/2 Nebraska Ave., Los Angeles, CA 90025-3620. (310) 207-0921. FAX: (310) 826-0071.

CALIFORNIA COMMUNICATIONS INC.
6900 Santa Monica Blvd., Los Angeles, CA 90038. (213) 466-8511. FAX: (213) 466-8511. e-mail: Sales info@CCIPOST.com
Hope Schenk

CAMERA SERVICE CENTER INC.
625 W. 54 St., New York, NY 10019. (212) 757-0906.

B. CANARICK'S CO., LTD
50 E. 42 St., New York, NY 10017. (212) 972-1015.

CARTER, JOHN, ASSOCS., INC.
300 W. 55 St., #10-V, New York, NY 10019. (212) 541-7006.

MICHAEL CHARLES EDITORIAL
6 E. 45 St., New York, NY 10017. (212) 953-2490.

BOB CHENOWETH
1860 E. N. Hills Dr., La Habra, CA 90631. (310) 691-1652. FAX: (310) 690-8362.

CHRISTY'S EDITORIAL FILM SUPPLY, INC.
135 N. Victory Blvd., Burbank, CA 91502. (818) 845-1755. (213) 849-1148. FAX: (213) 849-2048.

CINE TAPE, INC.
241 E. 51 St., New York, NY 10022. (212) 355-0070.

COMPREHENSIVE SERVICE AV INC.
432 W. 45 St., New York, NY 10036. (212) 586-6161.

CONSOLIDATED FILM INDUSTRIES
959 Seward St., Hollywood, CA 90038. (213) 462-3161, (213) 960-7444. FAX: (213) 460-4885.

CREST NATIONAL FILM & VIDEOTAPE LABS
1000 N. Highland Ave., Hollywood, CA 90038. (213) 466-0624. FAX: (213) 461-8901.

CREW CUTS FILM & TAPE, INC.
25 W. 43 St., New York, NY 10017. (212) 371-4545.

THE CULVER STUDIOS
9336 W. Washington Blvd., Culver City, CA 90230. (310) 202-3396, (310) 836-5537. (310) 202-3272.

CUTTING EDGE ENTERPRISES
432 W. 45 St., New York, NY 10036. (212) 541-9664.

DJM FILMS, INC.
4 E. 46 St., New York, NY 10017. (212) 687-0111.

DAVID DEE'S EVEN TIME, LTD.
62 W. 45 St., New York, NY 10036. (212) 764-4700.

JEFF DELL & PARTNERS
241 E. 51 St., New York, NY 10022. (212) 371-7915. FAX: (212) 935-9539
Jeff Dell

DELTA PRODUCTIONS
3333 Glendale Blvd., Suite 3, Los Angeles, CA 90039. (213) 663-8754. FAX: (213) 663-3460.

DIRECTORS SOUND & EDITORIAL SERVICE
1150 W. Olive Ave., Burbank, CA 91506. (818) 843-0950. FAX: (818) 843-0357.

EAGLE EYE FILM CO.
10825 Burbank Blvd., N. Hollywood, CA 91601. (818) 506-6100. FAX: (818) 506-4313.

EASY EDIT
432 W. 45 St., New York, NY 10036. (212) 541-9664.

ECHO FILM SERVICES, INC.
4119 Burbank Blvd., Burbank, CA 91505. (818) 841-4114. FAX: (818) 841-5038.
Joe Melody, Russ Tinsley

EDIT DECISIONS, LTD.
311 W. 43 St., New York, NY 10036. (212) 757-4742. FAX: (212) 757-5258.
Harvey Kopel

THE EDITING COMPANY
8300 Beverly Blvd., Los Angeles, CA 90048. (213) 653-3570. FAX: (213) 653-8855.

EDITING CONCEPTS
214 E. 50 St., New York, NY 10022. (212) 980-3340.

THE EDITING MACHINE, INC.
630 Ninth Ave., New York, NY 10036. (212) 757-5420.

EDIT POINT POST PRODUCTION SYSTEMS
620 N. Victory Blvd., Burbank, CA 91502. (818) 841-7336. FAX: (818) 841-7378.

FILM CORE
849 N. Seward St., Hollywood, 90038. (213) 464-7303.

FILMSERVICE LABORATORIES, INC.
6325 Santa Monica Blvd., Los Angeles, CA 90038. (213) 464-5141.

FILM VIDEO ARTS INC.
817 Broadway, 2nd floor, New York, NY 10003-4797. (212) 673-9361.

525 POST PRODUCTION
6424 Santa Monica Blvd., Hollywood, CA 90038. (213) 466-3348. FAX: (213) 467-1589.

FOUR MEDIA CO.
2813 W. Alameda Ave., Burbank, CA 91505. (818) 840-7000. (800) 423-2277.

GRENADIER PRODS., INC.
220 E. 23 St., New York, NY 10010. (212) 545-0388.

ALAN GORDON ENTERPRISES, INC.
1430 Cahuenga Blvd., Hollywood, CA 90028. (213) 466-3561. FAX: (213) 871-2193.

HI-TECH RENTALS
2907 W. Olive Ave., Burbank, CA 91505. (213) 469-9000, (800) 954-3000. FAX: (818) 848-0112.
Andrew Bruce Overton

HOLLYWOOD FILM CO.
3294 E. 26th St., Los Angeles, CA 90023. (213) 462-3284. FAX: (213) 263-9665.

ROBERT HOROWITZ FILMS
321 W. 44 St., New York, NY 10036. (212) 397-9380.

J & R FILM CO., INC.
1135 Mansfield Ave., Los Angeles, CA 90038. (213) 467-3107. FAX (213) 466-2201.

J.P.C. VISUALS
11 E. 47 St., New York, NY 10017. (212) 223-0555.

J.R. PRODUCTIONS
738 Cahuenga Blvd., Hollywood, CA 90038. (213) 463-9836.

KESSER POST PRODUCTION
21 S.W. 15 Rd., Miami, FL 33129. (305) 358-7900. FAX: (305) 358-2209.

LASER-PACIFIC MEDIA CORP.
540 N. Hollywood Way, Burbank, CA 91505. (818) 842-0777. FAX: (818) 566-9834.

MAGNASYNC/MOVIELA CORP.
1141 N. Mansfield Ave., Los Angeles, CA 90038. (213) 962-0382.

MAGNO SOUND, INC.
729 Seventh Ave., New York, NY 10019. (212) 302-2505.

MAYSLES FILM INC.
250 W. 54 St., New York, NY 10019. (212) 582-6050.

WILLIAM MOFFIT ASSOCS.
747 N. Lake Ave., #B, Pasadena, CA 91104. (818) 791-2559. FAX: (818) 791-3092.

MONACO LABS & VIDEO
234 Ninth St., San Francisco, CA 94103. (415) 864-5350.

MONTAGE GROUP, LTD.
4116 W. Magnolia Blvd., #103, Burbank, CA 91505. (818) 955-8801. FAX: (818) 355-8808.
1 W. 85th St., New York, NY 10024. (212) 595-0400.
Jim Beaton

MOTION PICTURES ENTERPRISES, INC.
430 W. 45 St., New York, NY 10036. (212) 245-0969.

MOVIE TECH INC.
832 N. Seward St., Hollywood, CA 90038. (213) 467-8491, (213) 467-5423. FAX: (213) 467-8471.

P.A.T. FILM SERVICES
630 Ninth Ave., New York, NY 10036. (212) 247-0900.

PDR PRODUCTIONS, INC.
219 E. 44 St., New York, NY 10017. (212) 986-2020.

PALESTRINI FILM EDITING, INC.
575 Lexington Ave., New York, NY 10022. (212) 752-EDIT.

PARAMOUNT STUDIO GROUP
5555 Melrose Ave., Hollywood 90038. (213) 468-5000.

PELCO EDITORIAL INC.
757 Third Ave., New York, NY 10017. (212) 319-EDIT.

PHANTASMAGORIA PRODS.
111 Eighth Ave., New York, NY 10011. (212) 366-0909.

GLORIA PINEYRO FILM SERVICES CORP.
19 W. 21 St., New York, NY 10010. (212) 627-0707.

POST GROUP
6335 Homewood Ave., Los Angeles, CA 90028. (213) 462-2300.
c/o Walt Disney-MGM Studios, Roy O. Disney Production
Center, Lake Buena Vista, FL 32830. (407) 560-5600.

POST PLUS INC.
3301 Barham Blvd., Los Angeles, CA 90068. (213) 874-7110.

POST TIME
4640 Lankershim Blvd., #600, N. Hollywood, CA 90046. (213)
851-4123. FAX: (213) 851-9959.

PRECISION POST
1641 20th St., Santa Monica, CA 90404. (310) 829-5684. FAX:
(310) 453-9068.

PRODUCTIONS WEST
6311 Romaine St., Suite 4134, Los Angeles, CA 90038. (213)
464-0169. FAX: (213) 461-3841.

REBELEDIT
292 Madison Ave., 26th Floor, New York, NY 10017. (212) 686-
8622.

THE REEL THING, INC
7001 Melrose Ave., Hollywood, CA 90038. (213) 933-5701.
FAX: (213) 933-4908.

RICH ENTERPRISES CORP.
208 W. 30 St., New York, NY 10001. (212) 947-3943.

ROBERT RICHTER PRODS., INC.
330 W. 42 St., New York, NY 10036. (212) 947-1395.

ROSS-GAFFNEY, INC.
21 W. 46 St., New York, NY 10036. (212) 719-2744.

SOUND ONE CORP.
1619 Broadway, 8th floor, New York, NY 10019. (212) 765-4757.

SANDPIPER EDITORIAL SERVICE
298 Fifth Ave., New York, NY 10018. (212) 564-6643.

LEONARD SOUTH PRODS.
4883 Lankershim Blvd., N. Hollywood, CA 91601-2746. (818)
760-8383. FAX: (818) 766-8301.

SPECTRUM ASSOCS. INC.
536 W. 29 St., New York, NY 10001. (212) 563-1680.

SPLICE IS NICE
920 Broadway, New York, NY 10010. (212) 677-6007. FAX:
(212) 473-8164.
Dick Langenbach

STEENBECK INC.
9554 Vasser Ave., Chatsworth, CA 91311-4169. (818) 998-
4033. FAX: (818) 998-6992.
Bob Campos

STONE CUTTERS FILM & VIDEO
123 E. 54 St., #5-C, New York, NY 10022. (212) 421-9404.

SYNCROFILM SERVICES, INC.
72 W. 45 St., New York, NY 10036. (212) 719-2966.

TAKE 5 EDITORIAL SERVICES, INC.
9 E. 38 St., New York, NY 10016. (212) 683-6104.

TAPE HOUSE INC.
216 E. 45 St., New York, NY 10017. (212) 557-4949.

TAPESTRY PRODUCTIONS, LTD.
920 Broadway, New York, NY 10010. (212) 677-6007.

TELEVISION CENTER
6311 Romaine St., Los Angeles, CA 90038. (213) 464-6638.

TODD-AO STUDIOS
Please see listing under Sound, Post Production & Music.

UNIVERSAL FACILITIES RENTAL DIV.
100 Universal City Plaza, Universal City, CA 91608. (818) 777-
3000. FAX: (818) 777-2731. URL: http://www.mca.com/studio

VALKHN FILMS INC.
1650 Broadway, Suite 404, New York, NY 10019. (212) 586-
1603.

GARY WACHTER EDITORIAL, INC.
159 W. 53 St., New York, NY 10019. (212) 399-7770.

WARMFLASH PRODUCTIONS, INC.
630 Ninth Ave., New York, NY 10036. (212) 757-5969.

WARNER BROS. STUDIOS
4000 Warner Blvd., Burbank, CA 91522. (818) 954-6000.

WARNER HOLLYWOOD STUDIOS
1041 N. Formosa Ave., W. Hollywood, CA 90046. (213) 850-2500.

WILDWOOD FILM SERVICE
6855 Santa Monica Blvd., Suite 400, Los Angeles, CA 90038.
(213) 462-6388.

BILLY WILLIAMS ENTERPRISES
216 E. 45 St., New York, NY 10017. (212) 983-3348. FAX:
(212) 983-3349.
Bernadette Quinn

WOLLIN PRODUCTION SERVICES, INC.
666 N. Robertson Blvd., Los Angeles, CA 90069. (310) 659-
0175. FAX: (310) 659-2946.

WORLD CINEVISIONS SERVICES, INC.
321 W. 44 St., New York, NY 10036. (212) 265-4587.

FILM & VIDEO STOCK

**EASTMAN KODAK CO., PROFESSIONAL MOTION
IMAGING DIVISION**
Home Office: 343 State St., Rochester, NY 14608. (716)
724-4000.
6700 Santa Monica Blvd., Hollywood, CA, 90038. (213)
464-6131. FAX: (213) 468-1568.
1901 W. 22nd St., Oakbrook, IL 60521. (312) 654-5300.
360 W. 31st St., New York, NY 10001.

FUJI PHOTO FILM U.S.A., INC.
555 Taxter Rd., Elmsford, NY 10523. (914) 789-8100. (800)
755-3854.

ILFORD PHOTO, INC.
W. 70 Century Rd., Paramus, NJ 07653. (201) 265-6000.

3M AUDIO & VIDEO COLOR SYSTEMS DIVISION
3130 Damon Way, Burbank, CA 91505. (818) 843-5935.
(213) 726-6387. FAX: (213) 727-2142.
6023 S. Garfield Ave., Los Angeles, CA 90040. (213) 726-
6333. FAX: (213) 726-6562.

RESEARCH TECHNOLOGY, INC.
4700 Chase Ave., Lincolnwood, IL 60646. (847) 677-
3000.

STUDIO FILM & TAPE INC.
6674 Santa Monica Blvd., Hollywood, CA 90038. (213) 466-
8101, (800) 824-3130. FAX: (213) 466-6815.
630 Ninth Ave., New York, NY 10036. (212) 977-9330.

Film Preservation, Processing, repair & Storage

ACCUTREAT FILMS, INC.,
630 Ninth Ave., New York, NY 10036. (212) 247-3415.

AFD/PHOTOGRAD FILM COATING LAB
1015 N. Cahuenga Blvd., Hollywood, CA 90038. (213) 469-8141. FAX: (213) 469-1888.

ALLIED FILM & VIDEO SERVICES
1322 W. Belmont Ave., Chicago, IL 60657. (312) 348-0373. FAX: (312) 348-5669.
4 Dallas Communications Complex, 6305 N. O'Connor Rd., #111, Irving, TX 75039. (214) 869-0100.

ALPHA CINE LABORATORY INC.
307 W. 200 South, #4004, Salt Lake City, UT 84101. (801) 363-9465.
1001 Lenora St., Seattle, WA 98121. (206) 682- 8230, (800) 426-7016. FAX: (206) 682-6649.
Roberta Ukura, Bill Scott

AMERICAN ARCHIVES, INC.
2636 North Ontario, Burbank, CA 91504. (818) 558-6995. FAX: (818) 558-7791.

ARCHIVES FOR ADVANCED MEDIA
3205 Burton Ave., Burbank, CA 91504. (818) 848-9766.

ASTRO COLOR LAB
61 W. Erie St., Chicago, IL 60610. (312) 280-5500.

BARTCO CO.
924 N. Formosa, Hollywood, CA 90046. (213) 851- 5411.

BENTON FILM FORWARDING CO.
150 Great Southwest Pkwy., Atlanta, GA 30336. (404) 699-2020. FAX: (404) 699-5588.
Lucy Benton

BONDED FILM STORAGE
550 Main St., Fort Lee, NJ 07024. (201) 944-3700.

BRAMBLES INFORMATION MANAGEMENT
P.O. Box 128, Sun Valley, CA 91352. (800) 310-DATA. FAX: (818) 504-6918.
Reed E. Irvin

BROADCAST STANDARDS, INC.
2044 Cottner Ave., Los Angeles, CA 90025. (310) 312-9060.

CINE MAGNETICS FILM & VIDEO
298 Fifth Ave.,New York, NY 10016. (212) 564-6737.

CINE MOTION PICTURE SERVICE LABORATORIES, INC.
278 Babcock St., Boston, MA 02215. (617) 254-7882.

CINEFILM LABORATORY
2156 Faulkner Rd., N.E., Atlanta, GA 30324. (404) 633-1448, (800) 633-1448. FAX: (404) 633-3867.

CINESITE
1017 N. Las Palmas Ave., Suite 300, Hollywood, CA 90038. (212) 468-4400. FAX: (213) 468-4404.

CONSOLIDATED FILM INDUSTRIES (CFI)
959 N. Seward St., Hollywood, CA 90038. (213) 462-3161.

CONTINENTAL FILM LABS, INC.
1998 NE 150 St., N. Miami, FL 33181. (305) 949-4252, (800) 327-8396. FAX: (305) 949-3242.
Vincent Hogan
7675 Currency Drive, Orlando, FL 33181. (407) 856-8958. FAX: (407) 856-4070.
A. J. Robbins

CREST NATIONAL VIDEO FILM LABS
1141 N. Seward St., Hollywood, CA 90038. (213) 466-0624, (213) 462-6696. FAX: (213) 461-8901.

DELUXE LABORATORIES, INC.
1377 N. Serrano Ave., Hollywood, CA 90027. (213) 462-6171, (800) 2DE-LUXE.

DU ART FILM LABORATORIES
245 W. 55 St., New York, NY 10019. (212) 757-4580.

DELTA PRODUCTIONS
3333 Glendale Blvd., Suite 3, Los Angeles, CA 90039. (213) 663-8754. FAX: (213) 663-3460.

FILM CRAFT LAB., INC.
66 Sibley St., Detroit, MI 48201. (313) 962-2611.

FILM PRESERVE
2 Depot Plaza, #202-B, Bedford Hills, NY 10507. (914) 242-9838. FAX: (914) 242-9854.
Robert A. Harris

FILM TECHNOLOGY COMPANY INC.
726 N. Cole Ave., Hollywood, CA 90038. (213) 464-3456. FAX: (213) 464-7439.

FILMACK STUDIOS
1327 S. Wabash Ave., Chicago, IL 60605. (312) 427-3395, (800) FILMACK. FAX: (312) 427-4866.
Robert Mack

FILMLIFE INC. AMERICAN FILM REPAIR INSTITUTE
P.O. Box 604, Lake Worth, FL 33460. (941) 582-6700. FAX: (941) 582-3535.
Marvin A. Bernard

FILMTREAT INTERNATIONAL CORP.
42-24 Orchard St., Long Island City, NY 11101. (718) 784-4040. FAX: (718) 784-4677.
Y. W. Mociuk, Sam Borodinsky

FILMTREAT WEST CORP.
10810 Cantara St., Sun Valley, CA 91352. (818) 771-5390.

FORDE MOTION PICTURE LABS
306 Fairview Ave. N., Seattle, WA 98109. (206) 682-2510. (800) 682-2510.

FORT LEE FILM STORAGE & SERVICE
1 Mt. Vernon, St., Ridgefield Park, NJ 07660. (201) 440-6200. FAX: (201) 440-5799.
EXECUTIVE VICE PRESIDENT
Patricia Miller

FOTO-KEM FOTO-TRONICS, FILM-VIDEO LAB
2800 W. Olive Ave., Burbank, CA 91505. (818) 846-3101. FAX: (818) 841-2130.

FOTORAMA
1507 N. Cahuenga Blvd., Los Angeles, CA 90028. (213) 469-1578.

FOUR MEDIA COMPANY
2813 W. Alameda Ave., Burbank, CA 91505. (818) 840-7000. FAX: (818) 840-7195.

GUFFANTI FILM LABORATORIES INC.
630 Ninth Ave., New York, NY 10036. (212) 265-5530.

HIGHLAND LABS
840 Battery St., San Francisco, CA 94111. (415) 981-5010.

HOLLYWOOD FILM CO.
826 Seward St., Hollywood, CA 90038. (213) 462-1971, (213) 462-3284. FAX: (213) 263-9665.

HOLLYWOOD FILM & VIDEO INC.
6060 Sunset Blvd., Hollywood, 90028. (213) 464-2181. FAX: (213) 464-0893.

HOLLYWOOD VAULTS, INC.
Vault: 742 N. Seward St., Hollywood, 90038. (213) 461-6464. Office: 1700 Prospect Ave., Santa Barbara, CA 93103. (805) 569-5336. FAX: (805) 569-1657.

FRANK HOLMES LABORATORIES
6609 Santa Monica Blvd., Hollywood, CA 90038. (213) 461-8078.

INTERNATIONAL CINE SERVICES, INC.
920 Allen Ave., Glendale, CA 91201. (818) 242-3839. FAX: (818) 242-1566.

IRON MOUNTAIN RECORDS MANAGEMENT
6190 Boyle Ave., Vernon, CA 90058-3952. (213) 466-9271. FAX: (213) 467-8068.

LAB LINK, INC.
115 W. 45 St.,New York, NY 10036. (212) 302-7373.

LASER-PACIFIC MEDIA CORP.
809 N. Cahuenga Blvd., Hollywood, CA 90038. (213) 462-6266. FAX: (213) 464-3233.

KEN LIEBERMAN LABORATORIES INC.
118 W. 22 St., New York, NY 10011. (212) 633-0500. FAX: (212) 675-0500.
Ken Lieberman

LUCASFILM LTD.
P.O. Box 2009, San Rafael, CA 94912. (415) 662-1800.

MAGNO SOUND INC.
729 Seventh Ave., New York, NY 10019. (212) 302-2505. FAX: (212) 819-1282.

MAGNO VISUALS
115 W. 45 St., New York, NY 10036. (212) 575-5162, (212) 575-5159. FAX: (212) 719-1867.

METRO BUSINESS ARCHIVES
609 W. 51 St., New York, NY 10019. (212) 489-7890.

MILLENNIUM FILM WORK SHOP
66 E. 4 St., New York, NY 10003. (212) 673-0090.

MONACO LABORATORIES, INC.
234 Ninth St., San Francisco, CA 94103. (415) 864-5350.

MOTION PICTURE LABORATORIES, INC.
781 S. Main St., Memphis, TN 38106. (901) 774-4944, (800) 4MP-LMPL.

MULTI-LAB
1633 Maria St., Burbank, CA 91504. (213) 465-9970.

NATIONAL PHOTOGRAPHIC LABORATORIES
1926 W. Gray, Houston, TX 77019. (713) 527-9300. FAX: (713) 528-2584.

NEWELL COLOR LAB
221 N. Westmoreland Ave., Los Angeles, CA 90004. (213) 380-2980.

NEWSFILM & VIDEO LABORATORY, INC.
516 N. Larchmont Blvd., Hollywood, CA 90004. (213) 462-6814.

P.A.T. FILM SERVICES, INC.
630 Ninth Ave., New York, NY 10036. (212) 247-0900.

PACIFIC TITLE ARCHIVES
4800 San Vicente Blvd., Los Angeles, 90019. (213) 938-3711. FAX: (213) 938-6364.
David Weeden
561 Mateo St., Los Angeles, 90013. (213) 617-8650. FAX: (213) 617-7876.
10717 Vanowen St., N. Hollywood, 91605. (818) 760-4223. FAX: (818) 760-1704.
900 Grand Central Ave., Glendale, CA 91201. (818) 547-0090. FAX: (818) 548-7990.
Dan Gentile

PACIFIC TITLE & ART STUDIO
6350 Santa Monica Blvd., Los Angeles, CA 90038. (213) 464-0121.

PRODUCERS COLOR SERVICE
2921 E. Grand Blvd., Detroit, MI 48202. (313) 874-1112.

PRODUCERS FILM CENTER
948 N. Sycamore Ave., Hollywood, 90038. (213) 851-1122.

RGB COLOR LAB
816 N. Highland Ave., Los Angeles, CA 90038. (213) 469-1959.

SINA'S CUSTOM LAB
3136 Wilshire Blvd., Los Angeles, CA 90010. (213) 381-5161.

THE SITE
6918 Tujunga Ave., N. Hollywood, CA 91605. (818) 508-0505. FAX: (818) 508-5581.

SPECTRUM MOTION PICTURE LAB
399 Gundersen Dr., Carol Stream, IL 60188. (708) 665-4242, (800) 345-6522.

SPORTS FILM LAB
361 W. Broadway, South Boston, MA 02127. (617) 268-8388. FAX: (617) 268-8390.

TECHNICOLOR INC.
Professional Film Division, 4050 Lankershim Blvd., North Hollywood, CA 91608. (818) 769-8500.
321 W. 44 St., New York, NY 10036. (212) 582-7310.

TITRA FILM CALIFORNIA INC.
733 Salem St., Glendale, CA 91203. (818) 244-3663. FAX: (818) 244-6205.

TODD-AO/CHACE PRESERVATION SERVICES
201 S. Victory Blvd., Burbank, CA 91502. (818) 842-8346. FAX: (818) 843-8353.
MANAGING PARTNER
Robert Heiber

VALDHERE INC.
3060 Valleywood Dr., Dayton, OH 45429. (513) 293-2191.

VAN CHROMES CORP.
21 W. 46 St., New York, NY 10036. (212) 302-5700.

YALE LABS
1509 N. Gordon St., Los Angeles, CA 90028. (213) 464-6181.

FINANCIAL SERVICES

BANK OF AMERICA
Entertainment Industries Division, 2049 Century Park E., #300, Los Angeles, CA 90067. (310) 785-6050.

BANK OF CALIFORNIA
Entertainment Division, 9401 Wilshire Blvd., Beverly Hills, CA 90212. (310) 273-7200. FAX: (310) 273-9030.

BANK OF NEW YORK
530 Fifth Ave., New York, NY 10036. (212) 852-4099.

BANKERS TRUST
Media Division, 300 S. Grand Ave., Los Angeles, CA 90071. (213) 620-8200. FAX: (213) 620-8484.

BURNHAM COMPANY
474 Sylvan Ave., Englewood Cliffs, NJ 07632. (201) 568-9800, (212) 563-7000. FAX: (201) 568-5599.

CHASE MANHATTAN BANK, N.A.
Media & Communications Component, 1 Chase Manhattan Plaza, 5th floor, New York, NY 10081. (212) 552-2222. 552-4848.

CHEMICAL BANK
1800 Century Park E., #400, Los Angeles, CA 90067. (310) 788-5600.
Entertainment Industries Group, 277 Park Ave., New York, NY 10172. (212) 935-9935.

CITY NATIONAL BANK
Entertainment Division, 400 N. Roxbury Dr., Suite 400, Beverly Hills, CA 90210. (310) 550-5696.

COHEN INSURANCE
225 W. 34th St., New York, NY 10122. (212) 244-8075.

DE WITT STERN GROUP, INC.
420 Lexington Ave., New York, NY 10170. (212) 867-3550.

DELOITTE & TOUCHE
2029 Century Park E., #300, Los Angeles, CA 90067. (213) 551-6705.

FILM CAPITAL CORP.
P.O. Box 2465, Palm Springs, CA 92263-2465. (619) 778-7461. (800) 538-7997.

FILM FINANCES INC.
9000 Sunset Blvd., Suite 1400, Los Angeles, CA 90069. (310) 275-7323. FAX: (310) 275-1706.

FIRST CHARTER BANK
Entertainment Division, 265 N. Beverly Drive, Beverly Hills, CA 90210. (310) 275-2225.

FIRST INTERSTATE BANK OF CALIFORNIA
Entertainment Division, 9601 Wilshire Blvd., Beverly Hills, CA 90210. (310) 285-5768.

FIRST LOS ANGELES BANK
Entertainment Division, 9595 Wilshire Blvd., Beverly Hills, CA 90212. (310) 557-1211.

HILTON FINANCIAL GROUP, INC.
P.O. Box 2026, N. Hollywood, CA 91610-0026. (213) 851-6532. FAX: (213) 851-6532.

LEWIS HORWITZ ORGANIZATION
1840 Century Park East, Los Angeles, CA 90067. (310) 275-7171. FAX: (310) 275-8055.

IMPERIAL BANK
Entertainment Banking, 9777 Wilshire Blvd., Beverly Hills, CA 90212. (310) 338-3139.

INTERNATIONAL FILM GUARANTORS (FIREMAN'S FUNDINSURANCE CO.)
Entertainment Industry Div., 5750 Wilshire Blvd., Los Angeles, CA 90024. (213) 930-1910.

MARATHON NATIONAL BANK
11150 W. Olympia Blvd., W. Los Angeles, CA 90064. (310) 996-9100.

MERCANTILE NATIONAL BANK
1840 Century Park East, Los Angeles, CA 90067. (310) 277-2265.

THE MOTION PICTURE BOND COMPANY
1901 Avenue of the Stars, #2000, Los Angeles, CA 90067. (310) 551-0371. FAX: (310) 551-0518.

D. R. REIFF & ASSOCIATES
41 W. 83 St., New York, NY 10024. (212) 877-1099.

RICHMAR BROKERAGE
310 Northern Blvd., Great Neck, NY 11021. (718) 895-7151. (516) 829-5200.

RUBEN, ALBERT G., & CO.
48 West 25 St., 12 Floor, New York, NY 10010. (212) 627-7400.

UNION BANK
445 S. Figueroa, 15th fl., Los Angeles, CA 90071. (213) 236-5780.

WESTERN SECURITY BANK
Entertainment Division, 4100 W. Alameda Ave., Toluca Lake, CA 91505. (818) 843-0707.

MARKET RESEARCH SERVICES

ASI MARKET RESEARCH, INC.,
101 N. Brand Blvd., #1700, Glendale, CA 91203-2619. (818) 637-5600. FAX: (818) 637-5615.

AMERICAN MARKETING ASSOCIATION
6404 Wilshire Blvd., #1111, Los Angeles, CA 90048. (213) 655-1951. FAX: (213) 655-8627.

BRAMSON & ASSOCIATES
7400 Beverly Blvd., Los Angeles, CA 90036. (213) 938-3595. FAX: (213) 938-0852.

ROBERT A. BRILLIANT, INC.
13245 Riverside Dr., #530, Sherman Oaks, CA 91423. (818) 386-6600. FAX: (818) 990-9007.

CERTIFIED MARKETING SERVICES, INC. (CMS)
Route 9, Kinderhook, NY 12106. (518) 758-6405.

CINEMA CONSULTANTS GROUP
8033 Sunset Blvd., P.O. Box 93, Los Angeles, CA 90046-2427. (213) 650-5807. FAX: (213) 650-2006.
Michael Goldman

CINEMASCORE
8524 Sahara Blvd., P.O. Box 173, Las Vegas, NV 89117. (702) 255-9963.

CONSUMERS PERSPECTIVE
1456 Canfield Ave., Los Angeles, CA 90035. (310) 556-3006. FAX: (310) 556-3002.

DALE SYSTEM INC., THEATRE DIVISION
1101 Stewart Ave., Garden City, NY 11530. (516) 794-2800. FAX: (516) 542-1063.

ENTERTAINMENT DATA, INC.
8350 Wilshire Blvd., #210, Beverly Hills, CA 90210. (213) 658-8300.

EXHIBITOR RELATIONS CO., INC.
116 N. Robertson Blvd., #606, Los Angeles, CA 90048. (310) 657-2005. FAX: (310) 657-7283.

THE GALLUP ORGANIZATION
47 Hulfish St., Princeton, NJ 08542. (609) 924-9600.

HISPANIC ENTERTAINMENT SPECIALIST
3726 Laurel Canyon Blvd., Studio City, CA 91604. (818) 766-9100. FAX: (818) 766-9201.

IMAGE ANALYSTS ALL-MEDIA
P.O. Box 1587, Santa Monica, CA 90406. (310) 458-0503.

INTERNATIONAL RESEARCH & EVALUATION,
21098 IRE Control Ctr., Eagan, MN 55121-0098. (612) 888-9635. FAX: (612) 888-9124.
Rick Kenrick

MCCANN-ERICKSON INC.
6420 Wilshire Blvd., Los Angeles, CA 90048. (213) 655-9420.

MARKET RESEARCH CORP. OF AMERICA
819 S. Wabash, Chicago, IL 60605. (708) 480-9600.
2215 Sanders Road, Northbrook, IL 60062. (708) 480-9600.

MOMENTUM INTERNATIONAL
P.O. Box 5889, Sherman Oaks, CA 91413. (818) 752-4500. FAX: (818) 752-4554.

CHARLES A. MOSES
3211 W. Alameda Ave., Suite A, Burbank, CA 91505-4112. (818) 848-0513. FAX: (818) 848-4977.

A.C. NIELSEN COMPANY
150 N. Martingale Rd., Schaumburg, IL 60173. (708) 605-5000.
731 Wilshire Blvd., #940, Los Angeles, CA 90010. (213) 386-7316. FAX: (213) 386-7317.
299 Park Ave., New York, NY 10171. (212) 708-7500.

OPINION RESEARCH CORP.
P.O. Box 183, Princeton, NJ 08542-0183. (609) 924-5900.

JOAN PEARCE RESEARCH ASSOCS.
8111 Beverly Blvd., #308, Los Angeles, CA 90048. (213) 655-5464. FAX: (213) 655-4770.

PROFESSIONAL RESEARCH ASSOCIATES
913 California Ave., Suite A, Santa Monica, CA 90403. (310) 394-1650.

RADIO TV REPORTS
6255 Sunset Blvd., #1515, Los Angeles, CA 90028. (213) 466-6124.

R. SELTZER ASSOCIATES
15445 Ventura Blvd., #14, Sherman Oaks, CA 91413. (818) 888-8450. FAX: (818) 888-8446.

SINDLINGER & CO., INC.
405 Osborne St., Wallingford, PA 19086. (610) 565-0247.

JANET SNOW & ASSOCIATES
327 Reeves Dr., Beverly Hills, CA 90212. (310) 552-0082.

VIDEO MONITORING SERVICES OF AMERICA
6430 W. Sunset Blvd., #504, Los Angeles, CA 90028. (213) 993-0111.

SOUND SERVICES

A & J RECORDING STUDIOS, INC.
225 W. 57 St., New York, NY 10019. (212) 247-4860.

ADVANTAGE AUDIO
1026 Hollywood Way, Burbank, CA 91505. (818) 566-8555.

JOHN ERIC ALEXANDER MUSIC INC.
9 John Walsh Blvd., Suite 400, Peekskill, NY 10566. (914) 736-2829. FAX: (914) 736-3134.

ASSOCIATED PRODUCTION MUSIC
6255 Sunset Blvd., Suite 820, Hollywood, CA 90028. (213) 461-3211. FAX (213) 461-9102.

AUDIO EFFECTS COMPANY
1600 N. Western Ave., Hollywood 90027. (213) 469-3692.

THE AUDIO DEPARTMENT
119 W. 57 St., New York, NY 10019. (212) 586-3503.

WALLY BURR RECORDING
1126 Hollywood Way, #203, Burbank, CA 91505. (818) 845-0500.

CORELLI-JACOBS RECORDING INC.
25 W. 45 St., New York, NY 10036. (212) 382-0220. FAX: (212) 382-0220.
Andrew Jacobs

CREATIVE MUSICAL SERVICES
13601 Ventura Blvd., #358, Sherman Oaks, CA 91423. (818) 385-1517. FAX: (818) 385-1266.
Dana Ferandelli

DISNEY-MGM STUDIOS
P.O. Box 10200, 1675 Buena Vista Blvd., Lake Buena Vista, FL 32830-0200. (407) 560-7299, (407) 560-5600.

DOLBY LABORATORIES, INC.
100 Potrero Ave., 94103. (415) 558-0200. Telex: 34409.
3375 Barham Blvd., Los Angeles, CA 90068. (213) 845-1880.
1350 Ave. of the Americas, 28th Floor, New York, NY 10019-4703. (212) 767-1700.

FIESTA SOUND
1655 S. Compton Ave., Los Angeles, CA 90021. (213) 748-2057. FAX: (213) 748-5388.
R. G. Robeson

JOHN HILL MUSIC
116 E. 37 St., New York, NY 10016. (212) 683-2273. FAX: (212) 683-2546.
Rosemary Rogers

THE HIT FACTORY, INC.
237 W. 54 St., New York, NY 10019. (212) 664-1000.

INTERLOCK AUDIO POST
6520 Sunset Blvd., Los Angeles, CA, 90028. (213) 469-3986. FAX: (213) 469-8507.
Lisa Pegnato

INTERSOUND, INC.
8746 Sunset Blvd., Los Angeles, CA 90069. (310) 652-3741. FAX: (310) 854-7290.
PRESIDENT
Kent Harrison Hayes

INTERWEAVE ENTERTAINMENT
22723 Berdon St., Woodland Hills, CA 91367. (818) 883-1920. FAX: (818) 883-9650.
VICE PRESIDENT
Lynne Weaver

KILLER MUSIC
3518 Cahuenga Blvd. West, Suite 108, Los Angeles, CA 90068. (213) 850-1966. FAX: (213) 850-3288.
Lori Colantuoni

LITTLE GEMSTONE MUSIC/24 CARAT PRODUCTIONS
P.O. Box 1703, Fort Lee, NJ 07024. (201) 488-8562.
Kevin D. Noel

LOOK INC.
168 5th Ave., New York, NY 10010. (212) 627-3500. FAX: (212) 633-1980.
Joanne Look

LUCASFILM LTD. (SPROCKET SYSTEMS, INC.)
P.O. Box 2009, San Rafael, CA 94912. (415) 662-1800.

LEE MAGID, INC.
P.O. Box 532, Malibu, CA 90265. (213) 463-5998. FAX: (310) 457-8891.

EDDY MANSON PRODUCTIONS, INC.
7245 Hillside Ave., Suite 216, Los Angeles, CA 90046-2329. (213) 874-9318. FAX: (213) 874-9338.

MOVIE TECH STUDIOS
832 N. Seward St., Hollywood, CA 90038. (213) 467-8491. FAX: (213) 467-8471.

NAMRAC MUSIC
15456 Cabrito Road, Van Nuys, CA 91406. (213) 873-7370.

PARAMOUNT RECORDING STUDIOS
6245 Santa Monica Blvd., Hollywood, CA 90038. (213) 465-4000. FAX: (213) 469-1905.

RYDER SOUND SERVICES, INC.
1161 Vine St., Hollywood, CA 90038. (213) 469-3511.

SOUND THINKING MUSIC RESEARCH
1534 N. Moorpark Rd., #333, Thousand Oaks, CA 91360. (805) 495-3306. FAX: (805) 495-3306.
Gary Ginell

SOUTHERN LIBRARY OF RECORDED MUSIC
4621 Cahuenga Blvd., Toluca Lake, CA 91602. (818) 752-1530. FAX: (818) 508-0213.
Roy Kohn

STUDIO M PRODUCTIONS UNLIMITED
4032 Wilshire Blvd., #403, Los Angeles, CA 90010. (213) 389-7372, (888) 389-7372. FAX: (213) 389-3299.
8715 Waikiki Station, Honolulu, HI 96830. (808) 734-3345, (888) 734-3345. FAX: (888) 734-3299.

SOUNDCASTLE RECORDING STUDIO
2840 Rowena Ave., Los Angeles, CA 90039. (213) 665-5201. FAX: (213) 662-4273.
Candace Corn

SUNSET SOUND RECORDERS
6650 Sunset Blvd., Hollywood, CA 90028. (213) 469-1186. FAX: (213) 465-5579.

TODD-AO/EDITWORKS
3399 Peachtree Rd. N.E., Suite 200, Atlanta, GA 303216. (404) 237-9977. FAX: (404) 237-3923.
PRESIDENT
Patrick Furlong

TODD-AO STUDIOS
900 N. Seward St., Hollywood, CA 90038. (213) 962-4000. FAX: (213) 466-2327.
PRESIDENT
Christopher Jenkins
4024 Radford St., Studio City, CA 91604. (818) 760-5069. FAX: (818) 760-5388.
SCORING STAGE MANAGER
Kirsten Smith

TODD-AO STUDIOS EAST
259 W. 54th St., New York, NY 10019. (212) 265-6225. FAX: (212) 247-5206.
PRESIDENT
Stephen Castellano

TODD-AO STUDIOS WEST
3000 Olympic Blvd., Bldg. One, Santa Monica, CA 90404. (310) 315-5000. FAX: (310) 315-5099.
PRESIDENT
Richard Hassanein

TOM THUMB MUSIC/ RUTH WHITE FILMS
Box 34485, Los Angeles, CA 90034. (310) 836-4678.
Ruth White

UNIVERSAL CITY STUDIOS
100 Universal City Plaza, Universal City, CA 91608. (818) 777-1000.

VOICES
16 E. 48 St., New York, NY 10017. (212) 935-9820. FAX: (212) 755-1150.
Richard Leonardi

WARNER BROS. STUDIOS
4000 Warner Blvd., Burbank, CA 91522. (818) 954-6000.
WARNER HOLLYWOOD STUDIOS, 1041 N. Formosa, Los Angeles, CA 90046. (213) 850-2500. FAX: (213) 850-2839.

WAVES SOUND RECORDERS
1956 N. Cahuenga Blvd., Hollywood, CA 90048. (213) 466-6141. FAX: (213) 466-3751.

WESTLAKE AUDIO
7265 Santa Monica Blvd., Los Angeles, CA 90046. (213) 851-9800. FAX: (213) 851-9386.

SID WOLOSHIN INC.
95 Madison Ave., New York, NY 10016. (212) 684-7222. FAX: (212) 689-5084.
Sid Woloshin, Carla Hill

SAUL ZAENTZ COMPANY FILM CENTER
2600 Tenth St., Berkeley, CA 94710. (510) 549-2500, (800) 227-0466. FAX: (510) 486-2015.

ZOUNDS, INC.
123 W. 18 St., New York, NY 10011. (212) 627-7700.

Special Effects

A & A SPECIAL EFFECTS
7021 Hayvenhurst Ave., Van Nuys, CA 91406. (818) 909-6999.

AAFAB ENGINEERING
3112 Hermosa Ave., La Crescenta, CA 91214. (818) 249-9575.

ACCLAIM
12001 Ventura Pl., Suite 300, Studio City, CA 91604. (818) 752-5900. FAX: (818) 752-5917.

ACTION JETS F/X
6312 Hollywood Blvd., Suite 113, Hollywood, CA 90028-6269. (213) 769-4249.

ADVANCED CAMERA SYSTEMS
16117 Cohasset St., Van Nuys, CA 91406-2908. (818) 989-5222. FAX: (818) 994-8405.

ADVANCED FIRE & RESCUE SERVICES
10044 Columbus Ave., Mission Hills, CA 91345. (818) 837-7336. FAX: (818) 830-9221.
Craig Sanford, Mark Pedro.

ALCONE COMPANY, INC
5-49 49th Ave., Long Island City, New York, NY 11011. (718) 361-8373.

ALL EFFECTS COMPANY, INC.
7915 Ajay Dr., Sun Valley, CA 91352. (818) 768-2000. FAX: (818) 768-2312.

DAVID ALLEN PRODUCTIONS
918 W. Oak St., Sun Valley, CA 91506. (818) 845-9270. FAX: (818) 567-4954.
David Allen

ALIAS/WAVEFRONT
11835 W. Olympic Blvd., Suite 350, Los Angeles, CA 90064. (310) 914-1566. FAX: (310) 914-1580. URL: www.aw.sgi.com

ALTERED ANATOMY, INC.
7125 Laurel Canyon Blvd., Suite A, North Hollywood, CA 91605. (818) 765-1192. FAX: (818) 765-5147.

ALTERIAN STUDIOS
1107 S. Mountain Ave., Monrovia, CA 91016. (818) 932-1488. FAX: (818) 932-1494.

AMALGAMATED DYNAMICS
21604 Marilla St., Chatsworth, CA 91311. (818) 882-8638. FAX: (818) 882-7327.

ANATOMORPHEX
8210 Lankershim, Suite 14, North Hollywood, CA 91605. (818) 768-2880. FAX: (818) 768-4808.
Robert Devine, James Clark

HOWARD A. ANDERSON CO.
100 Universal City Plaza, # 504-3, Universal City, CA 19608. (818) 777-2402.

ANIMUS FILMS
2 W. 47 St., New York, NY 10036. (212) 391-8716.

APA STUDIOS
230 W. 10 St., New York, NY 10014. (212) 929-9436.

ART F/X
3575 Caheunga Blvd. W., Suite 560, Los Angeles, CA 90068. (213) 876-9469.

ARTEFFEX
5419 Clean St., North Hollywood, CA 91601. (818) 506-5358. FAX: (818) 506-3171.

AVAILABLE LIGHT, INC.
1125 Flower St., Burbank, CA 91502. (818) 842-2109. FAX: (818) 842-0661.

BALSMEYER & EVERETT
230 W. 17 St., New York, NY 10011. (212) 627-3430.

BIFROST LASERFX
6733 Sale Ave., Wesy Hills, CA 91307. (818) 704-0423. FAX: (818) 704-0423.

BIGGER THAN LIFE INC.
1327 Fayette St., El Cajon, CA 92020. (800) 383-9980. FAX: (619) 449-8299.

BIOVISION
1580 California St., San Francisco, CA 94109. (415) 292-0333. FAX: (415) 292-0344.

BLACKSHEAR COMMUNICATIONS, INC.
6922 Hollywood Blvd., Suite 923, Hollywood, CA 90028. (213) 466-6412. FAX: (213) 466-1557.

BLACKSTONE MAGIK ENTERPRISES, INC.
12800 Puesta Del Sol, Redlands, CA 92373-7408.

BLUR STUDIO, INC.
1130 Abbot Kinney Blvd., Venice, CA 90291. (310) 581-8848. FAX: (310) 581-8850.
Cat Chapman

BODYTECH
13659 Victory Blvd., Suite 145, Van Nuys, CA 91401. (818) 385-0633.

BOSS FILM STUDIOS
13335 Maxella Ave., Marina Del Rey, CA 90292. (310) 823-0433. FAX: (310) 305-8576.

BRANAM ENTERPRISES, INC.
13335 Maxella Ave., Marina Del Rey, CA 90292. (818) 361-5030. FAX: (818) 361-8438.

BROOKLYN MODEL WORKS
60 Washington Ave., Brooklyn, NY 11205. (718) 834-1944. FAX: (718) 596-8934.
John Kuntzsch

THE BRUBAKER GROUP
10560 Dolcedo Way, Los Angeles, CA 90077. (310) 472-4766.

BUENA VISTA IMAGING
500 South Buena Vista St., Burbank, CA 91521-5073. (818) 560-5284. FAX: (818) 842-0532.
ohn Chambers.

BURMAN STUDIOS, INC.
4706 W. Magnolia Blvd., Burbank, CA 91505. (818) 980-6587. FAX: (818) 980-6589.

MICHAEL BURNETT PRODUCTIONS
8952 Glenoaks Blvd., Sun Valley, CA 91352. (818) 768-6103. FAX: (818) 768-6136.

CACIOPPO PRODUCTION DESIGN INC.
928 Broadway, Suite 1204, New York, NY 10010. (212) 777-1828. FAX: 212-777-1847.

CALICO ENTERTAINMENT
9340 Eton Ave., Chatsworth, CA 91311-5879. (818) 407-5200. FAX: (818) 407-5323.
PRESIDENT & CEO
Tom Burton

ADAMS R. CALVERT
17402 Chase St., Northridge, CA 91325. (818) 345-7703. FAX: (818) 365-0882.

CASTLE/BRYANT/JOHNSEN
210 N. Pass Ave., Suite 106, Burbank, CA 91505. (818) 557-7495. FAX: (818) 557-7498.

THE CHARACTER SHOP, INC.
9033 Owensmouth Ave., Canoga Park, CA 91304-1417. (818) 718-0094. FAX: (818) 718-0967.
Rick Lazzarini

CHARLEX, INC.
2 W. 45 St., New York, NY 10036. (212) 719-4600.

CHIODO BROS. PRODUCTIONS, INC.
425 S. Flower St., Burbank, CA 91502. (818) 842-5656. FAX: (818) 848-0891.

CIMMELLI INC.
16 Walter St., Pearl River, NY 10965. (914) 735-2090.

CINEMA ENGINEERING COMPANY
7243 Atoll Ave., Suite A, N. Hollywood, CA 91605-4105. (818) 765-5340. FAX: (818) 765-5349.

CINEMA NETWORK (CINENET)
2235 1st Ave., Suite 111, Simi Valley, CA 93065. (805) 527-0093. FAX: (805) 527-0305.

CINEMA RESEARCH CORP./ DIGITAL RESOLUTION
6860 Lexington Ave., Los Angeles, CA 90038. (213) 460-4111. FAX: (213) 469-4266.
V.P., MARKETING & SALES
Lena Evans

CINEMORPH EFFECTS GROUP
3123 Livonia Ave., Los Angeles, CA 90034. (310) 287-1674.

CINESITE DIGITAL FILM CENTER
1017 N. Las Palmas Ave., Suite 300, Hollywood, CA 90038.
(213) 468-4400. FAX: (213) 468-4404.

CINNABAR
1040 N. Las Palmas Ave., Hollywood, CA 90038. (213) 462-3737. Fax: (213) 462-0515.

COLLINS ENTERTAINMENT CONCEPTS CORP.
P.O. Box 292847, Kettering, OH 45429. (513) 293-0040. FAX: (513) 293-4431.

COMPOSITE IMAGE SYSTEMS
1144 N. Las Palmas Ave., Hollywood, CA 90038. (213) 463-8811.

THE COMPUTER FILM COMPANY
8522 National Blvd., Suite 103, Culver City, CA 92032. (310) 838-3456. FAX: (310) 838-1713.

CREATIVE CHARACTER ENGINEERING
7107 Gerald Ave., Van Nuys, CA 91406. (818) 901-0507. FAX: (818) 901-8417.

CREATIVE EFFECTS, INC.
760 Arroyo Ave., San Fernando, CA 91340-2222. (818) 365-0655. FAX: (818) 365-0651.

CRISWELL PRODUCTIONS
16535 Cualt St., Van Nuys, CA 91406. (818) 781-7739. FAX: (818) 781-7759.

CRUSE AND COMPANY, INC.
7000 Romaine St., Hollywood, CA 90038. (213) 851-8814. FAX: (213) 851-8788.

D'ANDREA PRODUCTIONS INC.
12 W. 37 St., New York, NY 10018. (212) 947-1211.

DAVE'S MARINE SERVICES INC.
1438 W. 14th St., Long Beach, CA 90813. (310) 437-4772. FAX: (310) 503-0848.

DAY SHADES
6859 Leetsdale Dr., Suite 202, Denver, CO 80224. (303) 399-8889. FAX: (303) 399-8881.
Craig T. Jones

DOM DE FILIPPO STUDIO, INC.
207 E. 37 St., New York, NY 10016. (212) 986-5444. FAX: 867-4220.

DE LA MARE ENGINEERING, INC.
1908 1st St., San Fernando, CA 91340-2610. (818) 365-9208. FAX: (818) 365-8775.

DESIGN FX CO.
936 N. Reese Place, Burbank, CA 91506. (818) 840-1444.

DIGISCOPE
6775 Centinela Ave., Stage 17, Culver City, CA 90230. (310) 574-5505. FAX: (310) 574-5509.

DIGITAL DOMAIN
300 Rose Ave., Venice, CA 90291. (310) 314-2800.

DIGITAL MAGIC COMPANY
3000 W. Olympic Blvd., Santa Monica, CA 90404. (310) 315-4720. FAX: (310) 315-4721.

DIRECT EFFECTS
31-00 47th Ave., Long Island City, NY 11101. (718) 706-6133. FAX: (718) 706-8026.
Tim Considine

WALT DISNEY IMAGINEERING
1401 Flower St., P.O. Box 25020, Glendale, CA 91221-5020. (818) 544-6500.

DREAM QUEST IMAGES
2635 Park Center Dr., Simi Valley, CA 93065. (805) 581-2671. FAX: (805) 583-4673.

DREAM THEATER
21345 Lassen Street, Suite 200, Chatsworth, CA 91311. (818) 773-4979. FAX: (818) 773-4970.
Darren Chuckru

DREAMLIGHT IMAGES, INC.
12700 Ventura Blvd., Studio City, CA 90038. (213) 850-1996. FAX: (213) 850-5318.

EASTERN OPTICAL EFFECTS
321 West 44th St., #401, New York, NY 10036. (212) 541-9220.

EDITEL
222 E. 44 St., New York, NY 10017. (212) 867-4600.
729 N. Highland Ave., Hollywood, CA 90038-3437. (213) 931-1821. FAX: (213) 931-7771.

E=MC2 INC.
621 E. Ruberta Ave., Suites 2, 3, 4, Glendale, CA 91201. (818) 243-2424. FAX: (818) 243-5126.
Bob Morgenroth

EFEX SPECIALISTS
43-17 37th St., Long Island City, NY 11101. (718) 937-2417.

EFILM
1146 N. Las Palmas, Hollywood, CA 90038. (213) 463-7041. FAX: (213) 465-7342.

EFFECTIVE ENGINEERING
6727 Flanders Dr., Suite 106, San Diego, CA 92121. (619) 450-1024. FAX: (619) 452-3241. e-mail: mlipsky@effecteng.com
Mark Lipsky

THE EFFECTS HOUSE
111 8th Ave., Suite 914, New York, NY 10011. (212) 924-9150. FAX: (212) 924-9193.

THE EFFECTSMITH
7831 Alabama Ave., Suite 19, Canoga Park, CA 91304. (818) 999-4560. FAX: (818) 999-4560.

ELECTRIC MACHINE ENTERTAINMENT
1930 Purdue Ave., Suite 6, Los Angeles, CA 90025. (310) 330-8841. FAX: (310) 477-1270.
Clive Milton

ELECTROFEX
1146 N. Central, Suite 231, Glendale, CA 91202. (818) 775-3838.

ENCORE VISUAL
702 Arizona Ave., Santa Monica, CA 90401. (310) 656-7663. FAX: (310) 656-7699.
Bob Coleman

ENERGY FILM LIBRARY
12700 Ventura Blvd., 4th flr, Studio City, CA 91604. (818) 508-1444, (800) IMAGERY. FAX: 818-508-1293.
Joan Sargent

EUE/SCREEN GEM PRINTS
222 E. 44 St., New York, NY 10017. (212) 867-4030.

FANTASY II FILM EFFECTS
504 S. Varney St., Burbank, CA 91502. (818) 843-1413. FAX: (818) 848-2824.

RUSS FARBER
19324 Oxnard St., Tarzana, CA 91356-1123. (818) 882-8220. FAX: (818) 708-8113.

FIM TECHNICAL SERVICES/SPECIAL EFFECTS
11118 Ventura Blvd., Studio City, CA 91604. (818) 508-1094.

FILMTRIX, INC.
P.O. Box 715, N. Hollywood, CA 91603. (818) 980-3700. FAX: (818) 980-3703.

FINE ART PRODUCTIONS/ RICHIE SURACI PICTURES
67 Maple St., Newburgh, NY 12550-4034. (914) 542-1585. FAX: (914) 561-5866. e-mail: Richie.Suraci@bbs.mhv.net
URL: http://www.geopages.com/Hollywood/1077

LARRY FIORITTO SPECIAL EFFECTS SERVICES
1067 E. Orange Grove Ave., Burbank, CA 91501. (818) 954-9828. FAX: (818) 954-9828.
Larry Fioritto

4-WARD PRODUCTIONS
2801 Hyperion Ave., Studio 104, Los Angeles, CA 90027. (213) 660-2430. FAX: (213) 660-2445.

F-STOP INC.
120 S. Buena Vista St., Burbank, CA 91505. (818) 843-7867.

FX ZONE
Jamboree Center, 1 Parl Plaza, 6th Floor, Irvine, CA 92714. (714) 852-7375. FAX: (714) 434-2776.
Jeff Miller

JOHN GATI FILM EFFECTS, INC.
6456 83rd Pl., Middle Village, NY 11379. (718) 894-5753.

PETER GEYER ACTION PROPS & SETS
8235 Lankershim Blvd., Suite G, North Hollywood, CA 91605. (818) 768-0070.

GILDERFLUKE & COMPANY
820 Thompson Ave., Suite 35, Glendale, CA 91202. (818) 546-1618. FAX: (818) 546-1619.

GLOBAL EFFECTS INC.
7119 Laurel Canyon Blvd., Unit 4, North Hollywood, CA 91605. (818) 503-9273. FAX: (818) 503-9459.

GLOBUS STUDIOS, INC.
44 W. 24 St., New York, NY 10010. (212) 243-1008.

GLOBAL EFECTS, INC.,
7119 Laurel Canyon Blvd., Unit 4, North Hollywood, CA 91605. (818) 503-39273. FAX: (818) 503-9459.

R/GREENBERG ASSOCIATES
350 W. 39 St., New York, NY 10018. (212) 239-6767.

RICHARD HAAS PHOTO IMAGERY LTD.
P.O. Box 8385, Universal City, CA 91608. (818) 417-2064. FAX: (818) 836-0817.

HANSARD ENTERPRISES INC.
P.O. Box 469, Culver City, CA 90232. (310) 840-5660. FAX: (310) 840-5662.

HBO STUDIO PRODUCTIONS
120-A E. 23rd St., New York, NY 10010. (212) 512-7800. FAX: (212) 512-7951.
Judy Glassman

JIM HENSON'S CREATURE SHOP
2821 Burton Ave., Burbank, CA 91504. (818) 953-3030. FAX: (818) 953-3039.

HFWD VISUAL EFX
6666 Santa Monica Blvd., Hollywood, CA 90038. (213) 962-2225. FAX: (213) 962-2220.

HILL PRODUCTION SERVICE INC.
6902 W. Sunset Blvd., Hollywood, CA 90028. (213) 463-1182. FAX: (213) 463-2862.

HOLLYWOOD DIGITAL
6690 Sunset Blvd., Hollywood, CA 90028. (213) 465-0101. FAX: (213) 469-8055.

HOLOGRAPHIC STUDIOS
240 E. 26 St., New York, NY 10010. (212) 686-9397.

HUNTER GRATZNER INDUSTRIES, INC.
4107 Redwood Ave., Los Angeles, CA 90088. (310) 578-9929. FAX: (310) 578-7370.
Matthew Gratzner, Ian Hunter

ILLUSIONS
21205 Burton Ave., Burbank, CA 91504. (805) 296-0620. FAX: 9815) 296-9621.
Dave Simmons

IMAGE CREATORS INC.
2712 6th St., Santa Monica, CA 90405. (310) 392-3583. FAX: (310) 396-6972.

IMAGE ENGINEERING INC.
736 N. Reese Place, Burbank, CA 91506. (818) 840-1444.

IMAGINE THAT
28064 Avenue, Unti K, Valencia, CA 91355.

INDUSTRIAL F/X PRODUCTIONS INC.
3522 Nobhill Dr., Sherman Oaks, CA 91423. (818) 501-1822. FAX: (818) 501-4526.

INDUSTRIAL LIGHT & MAGIC (ILM)
P.O. Box 2459, San Rafael, CA 94912. (415) 258-2000.

INTERNATIONAL CREATIVE EFFECTS
401 S. Flower St., Burbank, CA 91502. (818) 840-8338. FAX: (818) 840-8023.

INTROVISION INTERNATIONAL
1011 N. Fuller Ave., Hollywood, CA 90046. (213) 851-9262. FAX: (213) 851-1649.

JEX FX
47 Paul Dr., #9, San Rafael, CA 94903. (415) 499-9477. FAX: (415) 499-0911. e-mail: Gary@jexfx.com

STEVE JOHNSON'S X/FX INC.
8010 Wheatland Ave., Unit J, Sun Valley, CA 91352. (818) 504-2177. FAX: (818) 504-2838.

THE JONES EFFECTS STUDIO
26007 Huntington Lane, Suite 9, Santa Clarita, CA 91355-2746. (805) 294-9159. FAX: (805) 294-9689.
Andrew Jones

GENE KRAFT PRODUCTIONS
29 Calvados, Newport Beach, CA 92657. (714) 721-0609.
Gene Kraft

PETER KUNZ CO., INC.
55 Creek Rd., High Falls, NY 12440. (914) 687-0400.

LASER-PACIFIC MEDIA CORP.
540 N. Hollywood Way, Burbank, CA 91505. (818) 842-0777. FAX: (818) 566-9834.
809 N. Cahuenga Blvd., Hollywood, CA 90038. (213) 463-6266.

LAZARUS LIGHTING DESIGN
4718 San Fernando Rd., Glendale, CA 91204-1825. (800) 553-5554. FAX: (818) 956-3233.

ROBERT LEONARD PRODUCTIONS, INC.
P.O. Box 81440, Las Vegas, NV 89180. (702) 877-2449.

DANIEL LEVY
408 E. 13 St., New York, NY 10009. (212) 254-8964.

LEXINGTON SCENERY & PROPS
10443 Arminta St., Sun Valley, CA 91352-4109. (818) 768-5768. FAX: (818) 768-4217.

LIBERTY STUDIOS, INC.
238 E. 26 St., New York, NY 10010. (212) 532-1865.

LINKER SYSTEMS
13612 Onkayha Circle, Irvine, CA 92720-3235. (714) 552-1904. FAX: (714) 552-6985.

LIVE WIRE PRODUCTIONS
28729 S. Western, #209, Rancho Palos Verdes, CA 90275-0800. (310) 831-6227. e-mail: LiveWirefx@aol.com

LOWTECH
11825 Major St., Suite 8, Culver City, CA 90230. (310) 398-7094.

LUCASFILM, LTD.
(see Industrial Light & Magic)

LUMENI PRODUCTIONS, INC.
1632 Flower Street, Glendale, CA 91201-2357. (818) 956-2200. FAX: (818) 956-3298.

MAGICRAFT
5722-A Union Pacific Ave., Commerce, CA 90022. (213) 724-2279.

MAGICAL MEDIA INDUSTRIES, INC. (M.M.I.)
12031 Vose St., North Hollywood, CA 91605. (818) 765-6150.

MAKEUP & EFFECTS LABORATORIES, INC.
7110 Laurel Canyon Blvd., Unit E, N. Hollywood, CA 91605. (818) 982-1483. FAX: (818) 982-5712.

MAKEUP & MONSTERS
18535 Devonshire Rd., Suite 109, Northridge, CA 91343. (818) 407-0197.

TODD MASTERS COMPANY
10312 Norris Ave., Unit D, Arleta, CA 91331. (818) 834-3000.

MATTE WORLD DIGITAL
24 Digital Dr., Suite 6, Novato, CA 94949. (415) 382-1929. FAX: (415) 382-1999. email: info@matteworld.com
Krystyna Demkowicz

PAUL MANTELL STUDIO
16 Yale Ave., Jersey City, NJ 07304. (212) 966-9038.

MCCOURRY & ROBIN, INC.
22647 Ventura Blvd., Suite 240, Woodland Hills, CA 913643. (818) 702-9544. FAX: (818) 386-2113.

MELROSE TITLES & OPTICAL EFFECTS
(213) 469-2070. FAX: (213) 469-7088.

METROLIGHT STUDIOS
5724 W. 3rd St., Suite 400, Los Angeles, CA 90016. (213) 932-3344. FAX: (213) 932-8440.

MILLER IMAGING INTERNATIONAL, INC.
2718 Wilshire Blvd., Santa Monica, CA 90403. (310) 264-4711. FAX: (310) 264-4717.

DAVID MILLER STUDIO
14141 Covello, Van Nuys, CA 91406. (818) 782-5615.

MODUS EFX PRODUCTIONS
11535 Tuxford St., Sun Valley, CA 91352. (818) 771-0016. FAX: (818) 771-0017.

MOHAVE WEAPON SYSTEMS
P.O. Box 3821, Kingman, AZ 86402. (602) 565-3251.

MONSTER MECANIX
4319 Shitset Ave., Suite 3, Studio City, CA 91604.

MOTION ARTISTS, INC.
1400 N. Hayworth Ave., Suite 36, Los Angeles, CA 90046. (213) 851-7737. FAX: (213) 851-7649.

MOVIE TECH STUDIOS
832 N. Seward St., Hollywood, CA 90038. (213) 467-8491. FAX: (213) 467-8471.
Ewing M. "Lucky" Brown

NETWORK ART SERVICE
630 S. Mariposa St., Burbank, CA 91506. (818) 843-5078. FAX: (818) 843-2528.

NOVOCOM
6314 Santa Monica Boulevard, Hollywood, CA 90038. (213) 461-3688.

OBSCURE ARTIFACTS
8217 Lankershim Blvd., Suite 31, N. Hollywood, CA 91605.
(818) 767-8236. FAX: (818) 767-8236.

OCS/FREEZE FRAME/PIXEL MAGIC
10635 Riverside Dr., Toluca Lake, CA 91602. (818) 760-0862.
FAX: (818) 760-0483.
Ray McIntyre Jr., Dave Fiske

ONE UP
1645 N. Vine, Hollywood, CA 90028. (213) 957-9007.

JAMES O'NEIL & ASSOCIATES
725 N. Western Ave., Suite 109, Los Angeles, CA 90029. (213)
464-2995. FAX: (213) 464-2994.
Mandi Tinsley

OPTIC NERVE STUDIOS
9818 Glenoaks Blvd., Sun Valley, CA 91352. (818) 771-1007.
FAX: (818) 771-1009.

OPTICAL HOUSE, INC.
25 W. 45 St., New York, NY 10036. (212) 924-9150.

OWEN MAGIC SUPREME
734 N. McKeever Ave., Azusa, CA 91702. (818) 969-4519.
FAX: (818) 969-4614.

PACIFIC DATA IMAGES
1111 Karlstad Dr., Sunnyvale, CA 94089. (408) 745-6755. FAX:
(408) 745-6746.
3500 W. Olive Ave., Suite 980, Burbank, CA 91505. (818) 953-
7600. FAX: (818) 953-4191.
EXECUTIVE PRODUCER
Brad Lewis

PACIFIC TITLE & ART STUDIO
6350 Santa Monica Blvd., Los Angeles 90038. (213) 464-0121.
938-3711.

PACIFIC TITLE DIGITAL
5055 Wilshire Blvd., Suite 300, Los Angeles, CA 90036. (213)
938-8553. FAX: (213) 938-2836.

PENDLETON SYSTEMS, INC.
3710-A Foothill Blvd., Glendale, CA 91214. (818) 248-8310.
FAX: (818) 353-8428.

PERFORMANCE WORLD SPECIAL EFFECTS
416 S. Victory Blvd., Burbank, CA 91502. (818) 845-2704. FAX:
(818) 846-1145.
PRESIDENT
Jerry Williams

PERPETUAL MOTION PICTURES
24730 Tibbets Avenue, Suite 160, Valencia, CA 91355. (805)
294-0788. FAX: (815) 294-0786.
Richard Malzahn

PINNACLE EFX
2334 Elliot Ave., Seattle, WA 98121. (206) 441-9878. FAX:
(206) 728-2266.
EXECUTIVE PRODUCER
Karen Olcott

PLAYHOUSE PICTURES
1401 N. La Brea Ave., Hollywood, CA 90028-7505. (213) 851-
2112. FAX: (213) 851-2117.

POLAR TECHNOLOGIES USA
11419 Sunrise Gold Circle, Suite 2, Rancho Cordova, CA
95742. (916) 853-1111. FAX: (916) 853-9188.

PYROS PICTURES
1201 Dove St., Suite 550, Newport Beach, CA 92660. (714)
833-0334. FAX: (714) 833-8655.

QUANTEL
28 Thorndale Circle, Darien, CT 06820. (213) 656-3100. FAX:
(203) 656-3459.
Guy Walsingham

R/C MODELS
803 Channel St., San Pedro, CA 90731. (310) 833-4700. FAX:
(310) 833-9167.

RGA/LA
6526 Sunset Blvd., Los Angeles, CA 90028. (213) 957-6868.
FAX: (213) 957-9577.

RANDO PRODUCTIONS
1829 Dana St., Glendale, CA 91201. (818) 552-2900. FAX:
(818) 552-2388.

REEL EFX
5539 Riverton Ave., N. Hollywood, CA 91601. (818) 762-1710.

REELISTIC FX
21318 Hart St., Canoga Park, CA 91303. (818) 346-2484. FAX:
(818) 346-2710.

RHYTHM AND HUES
910 N. Sycamore Ave., Los Angeles, CA 90038. (213) 851-
6500. FAX: (213) 851-5505.

ROARING MOUSE ENTERTAINMENT
1800 Bridgegate St., Suite 204, Westlake Village, CA 91361.
(805) 373-8131. FAX: (805) 373-8133.

SAFARI ANIMATION & EFFECTS
10845 Van Owen St., Unit E, N. Hollywood, CA 91605. (805)
762-5203. FAX: (805) 762-3709.

SCENIC TECHNOLOGIES
4170 W. Harmon Ave., Suite 6, Las Vegas, NV 89103. (702)
876-1451. FAX: (702) 876-2795.
Robert Mealmear

SCHWARTZBERG & COMPANY
12700 Ventura Blvd., 4th Floor, Studio City, CA 91604. (818)
508-1833. FAX: (818) 508-1253.

SCREAMING MAD GEORGE, INC.
11750 Roscoe Blvd., Suite 11, Sun Valley, CA 91352. (818)
767-1631. FAX: (818) 768-3968.

SEE 3
2115 Colorado Ave., Santa Monica, CA 90404. (310) 264-
7970. FAX: (310) 264-7980.

SFX–STARLIGHT EFFECTS
923 N. Louise St., Suite C, Glendale, CA 91207. (818) 246-
5776. FAX: (818) 243-3308.

SIDESHOW PRODUCTIONS
31364 Via Colinas, Suite 106, Westlake Village, CA 90041.
(818) 259-0922.

SINGLE FRAME FILMS
437-1/2 N. Genesee Ave., Los Angeles, CA 90036. (213) 655-
2664.
Gary Schwartz

SLAGLE MINIMOTION, INC.
39 E. Walnut St., Pasadena, CA 91103. (818) 584-4088. FAX:
(818) 584-4099.

SOLDIERS OF LIGHT PRODUCTIONS
P.O. Box 16354, Encino, CA 91416-6354. (818) 345-3866. FAX:
(818) 345-1162.

ELAN SOLTES FX + DESIGN
3025 W. Olympic Blvd., Santa Monica, CA 90404-5001. (310)
315-2175. FAX: (310) 315-2176.

SONY PICTURES IMAGEWORKS
12020 W. Washington Blvd., Culver City, CA 90232. (310) 280-
7600. FAX: (310) 280-2342.

S.O.T.A. FX
7338 Valjean St., Van Nuys, CA 91406. (818) 780-1003. FAX:
(818) 780-4315.

SOUTHBAY MAKEUP FX STUDIOS
429 W. Laurel St., Suite A, Rancho Dominguez, CA 90220.
(310) 762-6057. FAX: (310) 490-0669.

SPECIAL EFFECTS SYSTEMS
26846 Oak Ave., Unit J, Canyon Country, CA 91351-2473.
(805) 251-1333. FAX: (805) 251-6619.

SPECIAL EFFECTS UNLIMITED, INC.
1005 Lillian Way, Los Angeles, CA 90038. (213) 466-3361.
FAX: (213) 466-5712.

SPECTAK PRODUCTIONS INC.
222 N. Sepulveda Blvd., Suite 2000, El Segundo, CA 90245.
(310) 335-2038.

STAGE 18
18 Leonard St., Norwalk, CT 06850. (203) 852-8185. FAX:
(203) 838-3126.

STICKS & STONES
12990 Branford St., Suite M, Arleta, CA 91331. (818) 252-
2088. FAX: (818) 252-2087.
Rob Burman, Jenifer E. McManus

DAVID STIPES PRODUCTIONS, INC.
685 Glenandale Ter., Glendale, CA 91206. (818) 243-1442.

STOKES/KOHNE ASSOCIATES, INC.
742 Cahuenga Blvd., Hollywood, CA 90038. (213) 469-8176.
FAX: (213) 469-0377.

STUDIO PRODUCTIONS
650 N. Bronson Ave., Suite 223, Hollywood, CA 90004. (213)
856-8048. FAX: (213) 461-4202.

SYNCHRONIC STUDIOS, INC.
535 Lipoa Pkwy., Suite 102, Kihei, Maui, HI 96753. (808) 875-
8600. FAX: (808) 875-8700.
Craig Robin

T&T OPTICAL EFFECTS
1619 1/2 S. Victory Blvd., Glendale, CA 91201. (818) 241-7407. FAX: (818) 241-7207.

THE TALKING LASER COMPANY
13248 Maxella Ave., Suite 261, Marina Del Rey, CA 90292-5671. (310) 822-6790. FAX: (310) 821-4010.

TECHNICREATIONS
2328 N. Batavia, Suite 106, Orange, CA 92665. (714) 282-8423. FAX: (714) 282-7853.

T.E.S.T. KREASHENS
26536 Golden Valley Rd., Suite 612, Saugus, CA 91350. (805) 251-6466. FAX: (805) 251-1153.

THIRD DIMENSION EFFECTS
330 N. Screenland Dr., Suite 138, Burbank, CA 91505. (818) 842-5665. FAX: (818) 842-9132.

3-D VIDEO
5240 Medina Rd., Woodland Hills, CA 91364-1913. (818) 592-0999. FAX: (818) 592-0987.

TITLE HOUSE INC.
738 N. Cahuenga Blvd., Los Angeles, CA 90038. (213) 469-8171. FAX: (213) 469-0377.

TODD-AO DIGITAL IMAGES
6601 Romaine St., Hollywood, CA 90038. (213) 962-4141. FAX: (213) 466-7903.
PRESIDENT
Brian Jennings

TRIBAL SCENERY
3216 Vanowen St., Burbank, CA 91505. (818) 558-4045.

TRI-ESS SCIENCES, INC.
1020 W. Chestnut St., Burbank, CA 91506. (818) 848-7838. FAX: (818) 848-3521.
Kim Greenfield

MIKE TRISTANO WEAPONS & SPECIAL EFFECTS
14431 Ventura Blvd., Suite 185, Sherman Oaks, CA 91423. (818) 888-6970. FAX: (818) 888-6447.

TRUE VIRTUAL REALITY
195 Sunset Hill Road, North Conway, NH 03860. (603) 356-7412. FAX: (603) 356-7412.

21ST CENTURY DIGITAL
3007 Washington Blvd., Marina Del Rey, CA 90292. (310) 574-1075.
Guerin "Gary" LaVaraque

TWO HEADED MONSTER
6161 Santa Monica Blvd., Suite 100, Los Angeles, CA 90038. (213) 957-5370. FAX: (213) 957-5371.

ULTIMATE EFFECTS
642 Sonora Ave., Glendale, CA 91201. (818) 547-4743.

VARITEL
3575 Cahuenga Blvd. W., Suite 675, Los Angeles, CA 90068. (213) 850-1165. FAX: (213) 850-6151.

THE VIDEO AGENCY
10900 Ventura Blvd., Studio City, CA 91604. (818) 505-8300. FAX: (818) 505-8370.

VIDEO DIMENSIONS INC.
6922 Hollywood Blvd., Suite 923, Hollywood, CA 90028. (213) 466-6412. FAX: (213) 466-1557.

VIEW STUDIOS INC.
6715 Melrose Ave., Hollywood, CA 90038. (213) 965-1270. FAX: (213) 965-1277.

VIEWPOINT DATA LABS
625 S. State Street, Orem, UT 84058. (801) 229-3000. FAX: (801) 229-3300.

VISIONART
3025 W. Olympic Blvd., Santa Monica, CA 90404. (210) 264-5566. FAX: (310) 264-6660.

VISUAL CONCEPT ENGINEERING
13300 Ralston Ave., Sylmar, CA 91342. (818) 367-9187. FAX: (818) 362-3490.
Peter Kuran

VISUAL IMPULSE PRODUCTIONS
10850 Wilshire Blvd., Suite 380, Los Angeles, CA 90024. (310) 441-2556. FAX: (310) 441-2558.

DON WAYNE MAGIC EFFECTS
10929 Hartsook St., N. Hollywood, CA 91601. (818) 763-3192. FAX: (818) 985-4953.

WILDFIRE ULTRAVIOLET VISUAL EFFECTS
11250 Playa Ct., Culver City, CA 90230-6150. (310) 398-3831. FAX: (310) 398-1871.
Richard Gleen

STAN WINSTON STUDIO
7032 Valjean Ave., Van Nuys, CA 91406. (818) 782-0870.

WONDERWORKS INC.
7231 Remmet Ave., Canoga Park, CA 91303. (818) 992-8811. FAX: (818) 347-4330.

WORKS NEW YORK, INC.
180 Varick St., New York, NY 10014. (212) 229-0741.

WORLDS, INC.
3160 W. Bayshore Rd., Palo Alto, CA 94303. (415) 813-5224. FAX: (415) 859-1130.

WUNDERFILM DESIGN
6690 Sunset Blvd., Hollywood, CA 90028-8116. (213) 466-1941. FAX: (213) 769-6095.

XAOS
600 Townsend St., Suite 271 E, San Francisco, CA 94103. (415) 558-9267. FAX: (415) 558-9160.
Helene Plotkin

Y.L.S. PRODUCTIONS
P.O. Box 34, Los Alamitos, CA 90720. (310) 430-2890. FAX: (310) 596-9563.

KEVIN YAGHER PRODUCTIONS
6615 Valjean Ave., Van Nuys, CA 91406. (818) 374-3210. FAX: 9818) 374-3214.

GENE YOUNG EFFECTS
517 W. Windsor Street, Glendale, CA 91204. (818) 243-8593.

Stock Shots

ACADEMY OF MOTION PICTURE ARTS & SCIENCES LIBRARY
333 S. La Cienega Blvd., Beverly Hills, CA 90211. (310) 247-3020, (310) 247-3000. FAX: (310) 657-5193.

AMERICAN FILM INSTITUTE LIBRARY
2021 N. Western Ave., Los Angeles, 90027. (213) 856-7600.

AMERICAN MUSEUM OF NATURAL HISTORY FILM ARCHIVES
Central Park West at 79th St., New York, NY 10024. (212) 769-5419.

AMERICAN STOCK PHOTOGRAPHY
6255 Sunset Blvd., #716, Los Angeles, CA 90028. (213) 469-3900. FAX: (213) 469-3909.

ARCHIVE FILMS
530 W. 25 St., New York, NY 10001. (212) 620-3955. FAX: (212) 645-2137.
V.P., SALES
Eric Rachlis

ASSOCIATED MEDIA IMAGES, INC.
650 N. Bronson, Suite 300, Los Angeles, 90004. (213) 871-1340. FAX: (213) 469-6048.

BRITANNICA FILMS
425 N. Michigan Ave., Chicago, IL 60611. (312) 347-7400, ext. 6512, (800) 554-9862.

BUDGET FILMS
4590 Santa Monica Blvd., Los Angeles, 90029. (213) 660-0187. FAX: (213) 660-5571.

BUENA VISTA STUDIOS
500 S. Buena Vista St., Burbank, 91521. (818) 560-1270.

CAMEO FILM LIBRARY, INC.
10760 Burbank Blvd., North Hollywood, 91601. (818) 980-8700. FAX: (818) 980-7113.
Steven Vrabel

CHERTOK ASSOCIATES, INC.
100 S. Main St., New City, NY 10956. (914) 639-4238. FAX: (914) 639-4239.

DICK CLARK MEDIA ARCHIVES, INC.
3003 W. Olive Ave., Burbank, CA 91505. (818) 841-3003. FAX: (818) 954-8609.

CLASSIC IMAGES
1041 N. Formosa Ave., W. Hollywood, CA 90046. (213) 850-2980, (800) 949-CLIP. FAX: (213) 850-2981.

CLIP JOINT FOR FILM
833-B N. Hollywood Way, Burbank, CA 91505. (818) 842-2525. FAX: (818) 842-2644.
Ken Kramer

COE FILM ASSOCIATES, INC.
65 E. 96 St.,New York, NY 10128. (212) 831-5355. FAX: (212) 645-0681.

LARRY DORN ASSOCS.
5820 Wilshire Blvd., #306, Los Angeles, 90036. (213) 935-6266. FAX: (213) 935-9523.

ENERGY FILM LIBRARY
12700 Ventura Blvd., Studio City, 91604. (818) 508-1444, (800) IMAGERY. FAX: (818) 508-1293.
Joan Sargent, Rafael Dalmua, Randy Gitsch.

FILE TAPE COMPANY
210 E. Pearson, Chicago, IL 60611. (312) 649-0599.

FILM & VIDEO STOCK SHOTS, INC.
10442 Burbank Blvd., N. Hollywood, CA 91601-2217. (818) 760-2098. FAX: (818) 760-3294. e-mail: stockshot@earthlink.net
URL: http://www.stockshots.com
PRESIDENT
Stephanie Siebart

FILM BANK
425 S. Victory Blvd., Burbank, 91502. (818) 841-9176.

THE FILM PRESERVE
2 Depot Plaza, #202-B, Bedford Hills, NY 10507. (914) 242-9838.

FISH FILMS FOOTAGE WORLD
4548 Van Noord Ave., Studio City, 91604-1013. (818) 905-1071. FAX (818) 905-0301.

GORDY COMPANY MEDIA LIBRARY
6255 Sunset Blvd., #1800, Los Angeles, CA 90028. (213) 856-3500. FAX: (213) 461-9526.

GREAT WAVES FILM LIBRARY
483 Mariposa Dr., Ventura, 93001-2230. (805) 653-2699.

GRINBERG FILM LIBRARIES, INC.
1040 N. McCadden Pl., Hollywood, CA 90038. (213) 464-7491. FAX: (213) 462-5352.
630 Ninth Ave., Suite 1200, New York, NY 10036. (212) 397-6200. FAX: (212) 262-1532.
Rich Sabreen

HALCYON DAYS PRODUCTIONS
1926 Broadway, #302, New York, NY10023. (212) 724-2626.

HOLLYWOOD NEWSREEL SYNDICATE INC.
1622 N. Gower St., Hollywood, 90028. (213) 469-7307. FAX: (213) 469-8251.

THE IMAGE BANK FILM & PHOTOGRAPHY LIBRARY
2400 Broadway, #220, Santa Monica, CA 90404. (310) 264-4850. FAX: (310) 453-1482.
111 Fifth Ave., New York, NY 10003. (212) 529-6793. FAX: (212) 529-8886.

IMAGEWAYS, INC.
412 W. 48 St., New York, NY 10036. (212) 265-1287.

INTERVIDEO INC.
10623 Riverside Dr., Toluca Lake, CA 91602. (818) 843-3633. (818) 569-4000. FAX: 843-6884.

JALBERT PRODUCTIONS, INC.
775 Park Ave., Huntington, NY 11743. (516) 351-5878. FAX: (516) 351-5875.
Carol Randel

KESSER STOCK LIBRARY
21 S.W. 15 Rd., Miami, FL 33129. (305) 358-7900.

KILLIAM SHOWS, INC.
500 Greenwich St., New York, NY 10013. (212) 925-4291.

CLAY LACY AVIATION INC.
7435 Valjean Ave., Van Nuys, 91406. (818) 989-2900. FAX: (818) 909-9537.

LIBRARY OF MOVING IMAGES
6671 Sunset Blvd., #1581, Hollywood, CA 90028. (213) 469-7499. FAX: (213) 469-7559.
Michael Yakaitis

MAC GILLIVRAY FREEMAN FILM & TAPE LIBRARY
P.O. Box 205, Laguna Beach, CA 92652. (714) 494-1055. FAX: (714) 494-2079.

MOONLIGHT PRODUCTIONS
3361 St. Michael Ct., Palo Alto, CA 94306. (415) 961-7440. FAX: (415) 961-7440.

MUSEUM OF MODERN ART FILM LIBRARY
11 W. 53 St., New York, NY 10019. (212) 708-9400.

NBC NEWS ARCHIVES
30 Rockefeller Plaza, New York, NY 10112. (212) 664-3797. FAX: (212) 957-8917. e-mail: ychin@nbc.com
Yuien Chin

NATIONAL GEOGRAPHIC FILM LIBRARY
1600 M St. NW, Washington, DC 20036. (202) 857-7659. FAX: (202) 429-5755.

NEWSREEL ACCESS SYSTEMS, INC.
50 E. 58 St., New York, NY 10155. (212) 826-2800.

PALISADES WILDLIFE LIBRARY
1205 S. Ogden Dr., Los Angeles, 90019. (213) 931-6186.

PARAMOUNT PICTURES STOCK FOOTAGE LIBRARY
5555 Melrose Ave., Hollywood, CA 90038. (213) 956-5510. FAX: (213) 956-1833.

PHOTO-CHUTING ENTERPRISES
12619 Manor Dr., Hawthorne, 90250-4313. (213) 678-0163.
Jean Boenish

PRELINGER ASSOC., INC.
430 W. 14 St., New York, NY 10014. (212) 633-2020.

PRODUCERS LIBRARY SERVICE
1051 N. Cole Ave., Hollywood, 90038. (213) 465-0572. FAX: (213) 465-1671.

PYRAMID MEDIA
2801 Colorado Ave., Santa Monica, 90404. (310) 828-7577. FAX: (310) 453-9083.
Pat Hamada

RETROSPECT FILM ARCHIVE
11693 San Vicente Blvd., #111, Los Angeles, CA 90049. (310) 471-1906. FAX: (310) 471-1430.

RON SAWADE CINEMATOGRAPHY.
P.O. Box 1310, Pismo Beach, CA 93448. (805) 481-0586. FAX: (805) 481-9752.

SECOND LINE SEARCH
1926 Broadway, New York, NY 10023. (212) 787-7500.

THE SOURCE STOCK FOOTAGE
738 N. Constitution Dr., Tucson, AZ 85748. (520) 298-4810. FAX: (520) 290-8831.
LIBRARY MANAGER
Don French

SPECTRAL COMMUNICATIONS
178 S. Victory Blvd., #106, Burbank, CA 91502. (818) 840-0111. FAX: (818) 840-0618.
Michael Povar

SPORTS CINEMATOGRAPHY GROUP
73 Market St., Venice, CA 90291. (310) 785-9100. FAX: (310) 396-7423.

STREAMLINE FILM ARCHIVES
432 Park Ave. S., New York, NY 10016. (212) 696-2616. FAX: (212) 696-0021.
Mark Trust

THE STOCK HOUSE
6922 Hollywood Blvd., Suite 621, Los Angeles, 90028. (213) 461-0061. FAX: (213) 461-2457.

TIMESCAPE IMAGE LIBRARY
12700 Ventura Blvd., 4th fl., Studio City, CA 91604. (818) 508-1444. FAX: (818) 508-1293.

TURNER ENTERTAINMENT CO.
10100 Venice Blvd., Culver City, 90232. (310) 558-7300.

20TH CENTURY FOX
P.O. Box 900, Beverly Hills, CA 90213. (310) 369-1000.

434

UCLA FILM & TELEVISION ARCHIVE
Commercial Services Division, 1015 N. Cahuenga Blvd.,
Hollywood, CA 90038. (213) 466-8559. FAX: (213) 461-6317.
Fonda Burrell

UNIVERSAL STUDIOS FILM LIBRARY
100 Universal City Plaza, Universal City, 91608. (818) 777-
3000. FAX: (818) 733-1579.

THE VIDEO AGENCY
10900 Ventura Blvd., Studio City, CA 91604. (818) 505-8300.
FAX: (818) 505-8370.
PRESIDENT
Jeffrey Goddard

VIDEO TAPE LIBRARY LTD.
1509 N. Crescent Heights Blvd. #2, Los Angeles, 90046. (213)
656-4330. FAX: (213) 656-8746. e-mail: vtl@earthlink.net
URL: http:// www.videotapelibrary.com
Melody St. John, Peggy Shannon

WISH YOU WERE HERE FILM & VIDEO
1455 Royal Blvd., Glendale, CA 91207. (818) 243-7043. FAX:
(818) 241-1720.

WORLDWIDE TELEVISION NEWS
12401 W. Olympic Blvd., Los Angeles, CA 90064. (310) 826-
8133. FAX: (310) 826-6503.

STUDIO & EQUIPMENT SERVICES

ABC TELEVISION CENTER
4151 Prospect Ave., Los Angeles, CA 90027. (213) 557-7777.

ADVENTURE FILM STUDIOS
40-13 104 St., Queens, NY 11368. (718) 478-2639.

APOLLO THEATRE FOUNDATION, INC.
253 W. 125 St., New York, NY 10027. (212) 222-0992. FAX:
(212) 749-2743.
Charlotte Sutton

ATELIER CINEMA VIDEO STAGES
295 W. 4 St., New York, NY 10014. (212) 243-3550.

AVALON STAGES
6918 Tujunga Ave., N. Hollywood, CA 91605. (818) 508-0505.
FAX: (818) 508-5581.

BC STUDIOS
152 W. 25 St., New York, NY 10001. (212) 242-4065.

BIG VALLEY STAGE
7311 Radford Ave., No. Hollywood, CA 91605. (818) 340-1256.

BOKEN SOUND STUDIO
513 W. 54 St., New York, NY 10019. (212) 581-5507.

BREITROSE SELTZER STAGES, INC.
443 W. 18 St., New York, NY 10011. (212) 807-0664.

BROADWAY STUDIOS
25-09 Broadway, Long Island City, NY 11106. (718) 274-9121.

BURBANK MEDIA CENTER
2801 W. Olive Ave., Burbank, CA 91505. (818) 845-3531.

CBS STUDIO CENTER
4024 N. Radford Ave., Studio City, CA 91604. (818) 760-5000.
FAX: (818) 760-5048.

CBS TELEVISION CITY
7800 Beverly Blvd., Los Angeles, CA 90036. (213) 852-2345.

CFI (CONSOLIDATED FILM INDUSTRIES)
959 Seward St., Hollywood, CA 90038. (213) 960-7444. FAX:
(213) 460-4885.

THE CANNELL STUDIOS
7083 Hollywood Blvd., Hollywood, CA 90028. (213) 465-5800.
FAX: (213) 463-4987.

CARMAN PRODUCTIONS INC.
15456 Cabrito Rd., Van Nuys, CA 91406. (818) 787-6436. FAX:
(818) 787-3981.
Tom Skeeter

CAROLCO STUDIOS
1223 N. 23 St., Wilmington, NC 28405. (910) 343-3500.

CARTHAY STUDIOS, INC.
5907 W. Pico Blvd., Los Angeles, CA 90035. (213) 938-2101.
FAX: (213) 936-2769.

CECO INTERNATIONAL CORP.
440 W. 15 St., New York, NY 10011. (212) 206-8280. FAX:
(212) 727-2144.
Jody Baran

CHANDLER TOLUCA LAKE STUDIOS
11405 Chandler Blvd., No. Hollywood, CA 91601. (818) 763-
3650. FAX: (818) 990-4755.

CHAPLIN STAGE
1416 N. La Brea Ave., Hollywood, CA 90028. (213) 856-2682.
FAX: (213) 856-2795.
Bill Taylor

CHARLES RIVER STUDIOS
184 Everett St., Boston, MA 02134. (617) 787-4747.

CINE STUDIO
241 W. 54 St., New York, NY 10019. (212) 581-1916.

CINEMA SERVICES OF LAS VEGAS
4445 South Valley View Blvd., #8, Las Vegas, NV 89103.
(702) 876-4667. FAX: ((702) 876-4542.

CINEWORKS-SUPERSTAGE
1119 N. Hudson Ave., Los Angeles, CA 90038. (213) 464-
0296. FAX: (213) 464-1202.

THE COMPLEX
6476 Santa Monica Blvd., Hollywood, CA 90038. (213) 465-
0383, (213) 464-2124. FAX: (213) 469-5408.

COMTECH VIDEO PRODUCTIONS
770 Lexington Ave., New York, NY 10021. (212) 826-2935.
FAX: (212) 688-4264.
Ellen Zack

THE CULVER STUDIOS
9336 W. Washington Blvd., Culver City, CA 90230. (310) 202-
1234. FAX: (310) 202-3272.
Jack Kindberg

WALT DISNEY STUDIOS
500 S. Buena Vista St., Burbank, CA 91521. (818) 560-5151,
(818) 560-1000. FAX: (818) 560-1930.

WALT DISNEY/MGM STUDIOS
3300 N. Bonnett Creek Rd., Lake Buena Vista, FL 32830.
(407) 560-5353. (407) 560-6188.

DOM DE FILIPPO STUDIO
207 E. 37 St., New York, NY 10016. (212) 986-5444, (212)
867-4220.

EMPIRE BURBANK STUDIOS
1845 Empire Ave., Burbank, CA 91504. (818) 840-1400. FAX:
(818) 567-1062.
Robert Bagley, Don Buccola, Felix Girard

EMPIRE STAGES OF NY
25-19 Borden Ave., Long Island City, NY 11101. (718) 392-
4747.

ERECTER SET, INC.
1150 S. La Brea Ave., Los Angeles, CA 90019. (213) 938-
4762. FAX: (213) 931-9565.

FARKAS FILMS, INC.
385 Third Ave., New York, NY 10016. (212) 679-8212. FAX:
(212) 889-8364. URL: http://www.non-stop.com/farkas
F. E. Robinson

GMT STUDIOS
5751 Buckingham Parkway, Unit C, Culver City, CA 90230.
(310) 649-3733. FAX: (310) 216-0056.

GLENDALE STUDIOS
1239 S. Glendale Ave., Glendale, CA 91205. (818) 502-5300,
(818) 502-5500. FAX: (818) 502-5555.
Steven Makhanian

GLOBUS STUDIOS
44 W. 24 St., New York, NY 10011. (212) 243-1008.

GREAT SOUTHERN STUDIOS
15221 N.E. 21 Ave., N. Miami Beach, FL 33162. (305) 947-
0430.

GROUP W PRODUCTIONS
One Lakeside Plaza, 3801 Barham Blvd., Los Angeles, CA 90068. (213) 850-3800. FAX: (213) 850-3889.

HBO STUDIO PRODS.
120 E. 23 St., New York, NY 10010. (212) 512-7800.

HARPO STUDIOS
1058 W. Washington Blvd., Chicago, IL 60607. (312) 738-3456.

HOLLYWOOD CENTER STUDIOS, INC.
1040 N. Las Palmas Ave., Los Angeles, CA 90038. (213) 860-0000. FAX: (213) 860-8105.

HOLLYWOOD NATIONAL STUDIOS
6605 Eleanor Ave., Los Angeles, CA 90038. (213) 467-6272.

THE HOLLYWOOD STAGE
6650 Santa Monica Blvd., Los Angeles, CA 90038. (213) 466-4393.

HORVATH & ASSOCIATES STUDIOS LTD.
95 Charles St., New York, NY 10014. (212) 741-0300.

INTER VIDEO, INC.
10623 Riverside Dr., Toluca Lake, CA 91602. (818) 843-3633, (818) 569-4000. FAX: (818) 843-6884.

INTERSOUND INC.
8746 Sunset Blvd., Los Angeles, CA 90069. (310) 652-3741. FAX: (310) 854-7290.

KCET STUDIOS
4401 W. Sunset Blvd., Los Angeles, CA 90027. (213) 953-5258, (213) 666-6500. FAX: (213) 953-5496.

KAUFMAN ASTORIA STUDIOS
34-12 36th St., Astoria, NY 11106. (718) 392-5600. FAX: (718) 706-7733.

LIGHTING & PRODUCTION EQUIPMENT, INC.
1700 Marietta Blvd., Atlanta, GA 30318. (404) 352-0464.

MAGNO SOUND INC.
729 Seventh Ave., New York, NY10019. (212) 302-2505.

MELROSE STAGE
1215 Bates Ave., Los Angeles, CA 90029. (213) 660-8466.

MOLE-RICHARDSON CO.
937 N. Sycamore Ave., Los Angeles 90038. (213) 851-0111.

MORO-LANDIS
10960 Ventura Blvd., Studio City, CA 91604. (818) 753-5081. FAX: (818) 752-1689.

MODERN TELECOMMUNICATIONS/MTI
1 Dag Hammarskjold Pl., New York, NY 10017. (212) 355-0510.

MOTHERS FILM STAGE
210 E. 5 St., New York, NY 10003. (212) 529-5097.

MOVIE TECH STUDIOS
832 N. Seward St., Hollywood, CA 90038. (213) 467-8491. FAX: (213) 467-8471.

NBC TELEVISION
3000 W. Alameda Ave., Burbank, CA 91523. (818) 840-4444.

NATIONAL VIDEO CENTER/RECORDING STUDIOS, INC.
460 W. 42 St., New York, NY 10036. (212) 279-2000.

OCCIDENTAL STUDIOS
201 N. Occidental Blvd., Los Angeles, CA 90026. (213) 384-3331. FAX: (213) 384-2684.

PARAMOUNT STUDIO GROUP
5555 Melrose Ave., Los Angeles, CA 90038. (213) 956-5000.

PATCHETT KAUFMAN ENTERTAINMENT
8621 Hayden Place, Culver City, CA 90232. (310) 838-7000.

PRIMALUX VIDEO PRODUCTION, INC.
30 W. 26 St., New York, NY 10010. (212) 206-1402. FAX: (212) 206-1826.
Judy Cashman

RALEIGH STUDIOS
5300 Melrose Ave., Los Angeles, CA 90038. (213) 466-3111. FAX: (213) 871-5600.
Sharon Bode

REN-MAR STUDIOS
846 North Cahuenga Blvd., Los Angeles, CA 90038. (213) 463-0808.

SANTA CLARITA STUDIOS
25135 Anza Dr., Santa Clarita, CA 91355. (805) 294-2000. FAX: (805) 294-2020.

S.I.R. FILM STUDIOS, INC.
3322 La Cienega Pl., Los Angeles, CA 90016. (310) 287-3600. FAX: (310) 287-3608.

SHINBONE ALLEY STAGE
680 Broadway, New York, NY 10012. (212) 420-8463.

SILVERCUP STUDIOS
42-25 21st St., Long Island City, NY 11101. (718) 784-3390, (212) 349-9600.

SONY PICTURES STUDIOS
10202 W. Washington Blvd., Culver City, CA 90232. (310) 280-6926.

SUNSET-GOWER STUDIOS LTD.
1438 N. Gower St., Los Angeles, CA 90028. (213) 467-1001.

TELETECHNIQUES, INC.
1 W. 19 St., New York, NY 10011. (212) 206-1475.

TELEVISION CENTER
6311 Romaine St., Los Angeles, CA 90038. (213) 464-6638.

3-G STAGE CORP.
236 W. 61 St., New York, NY 10023. (212) 247-3130.

TWENTIETH CENTURY FOX STUDIOS
10201 W. Pico Blvd., Los Angeles, CA 90035. (310) 369-1000.

UNITEL VIDEO SERVICES INC.
515 W. 57 St., New York, NY 10019. (212) 265-3600.

UNIVERSAL CITY STUDIOS
100 Universal City Plaza, Universal City, CA 91608. (818) 777-3000.

UNIVERSAL STUDIOS FLORIDA
1000 Universal Studios Plaza, Orlando, FL 32819. (407) 363-8400.

VPS STUDIOS
800 N. Seward St., Hollywood, CA 90038. (213) 469-7244. FAX: (213) 463-7538.

VANCO LIGHTING SERVICES
9561 Satellite Blvd., Orlando, FL 32837. (407) 855-8060. FAX: (407) 855-8059.

VERITAS STUDIOS
527 W. 45 St., New York, NY 10036. (212) 581-2050.

VIDEO PLANNING INC.
250 W. 57 St., New York, NY 10019. (212) 582-5066.

VISUAL IMAGES UNLIMITED
1608 Mayflower, Unit A, Monrovia, CA 91016. (213) 994-6119.
Mark Enzenauer

WTN-WORLDWIDE TV NEWS PRODS.
1995 Broadway, New York, NY 10023. (212) 362-4440. FAX: (212) 446-1269.
MARKETING MANAGER
Earl Adams

WARNER BROS. INC.,
4000 Warner Blvd., Burbank, CA 91522. (818) 954-6000, (818) 954-923. FAX: (818) 954-4213.

WARNER HOLLYWOOD STUDIOS
1041 N. Formosa Ave., W. Hollywood, CA 90046. (213) 850-2837. FAX: (213) 850-2839.

WHITEFIRE THEATRE, THE SOUNDSTAGE RENTAL
13500 Ventura Blvd., Sherman Oaks, CA 91423. (818) 990-2324.

SUBTITLES & CAPTIONS

CAPTION CENTER
610 N. Hollywood Way, #350, Burbank, CA 91505. (818) 562-3344. FAX: (818) 562-3388.
125 Western Ave., Boston, MA 02134. (617) 492-9225. FAX: (617) 582-0590. URL: http://www.wgbh.org/caption
475 Park Ave. S., 10th fl., New York, NY 10016. (212) 223-4930. FAX: (212) 688-2181.

CAPTIONS, INC.
2479 Lanterman Terr., Los Angeles, CA 90039. (213) CAPTION.
2619 Hyperion Ave., Suite A, Los Angeles, CA 90027. (213) 227-8466.

CINETYP, INC.
843 Seward St., Hollywood, CA 90038. (213) 463-8569. FAX: (213) 463-4129.

CREST NATIONAL VIDEOTAPE FILM LABS
1000 N. Highland Ave., Hollywood, CA 90038. (213) 466-0624. 462-6696. FAX: (213) 461-8901.

DEVLIN VIDEO SERVICE
1501 Broadway, Suite 408, New York, NY 10036. (212) 391-1313.

FOREIGN LANGUAGE GRAPHICS
4303 N. Figueroa St., Los Angeles, CA 90065. (213) 224-8417. FAX: (213) 224-8446.

GLOBAL LANGUAGE SERVICES
2027 Las Lunas, Pasadena, CA 91107. (818) 792-0862, (818) 792-0576. FAX: (818) 792-8793.

HOMER AND ASSOCIATES, INC.
Sunset Gower Studios, 1420 N. Beachwood Dr., Hollywood, CA 90028. (213) 462-4710.

INTEX AUDIOVISUALS
9021 Melrose Ave., Suite 205, Los Angeles, CA 90069. (310) 275-9571. FAX: (310) 271-1319.

LINGUATHEQUE OF L.A.
13601 Ventura Blvd., #102, Sherman Oaks, CA 91423. (818) 995-8933. FAX: (818) 995-1228.
Eric Laufer

MASTERWORDS
1512 Eleventh St., #205, Santa Monica, CA 90401-2907. (310) 390-1033. FAX: (310) 394-7954.

NATIONAL CAPTIONING INSTITUTE
1443 Beachwood Dr., Hollywood, CA 90028. (213) 469-7000. FAX: (213) 957-5266.

P.F.M. DUBBING INTERNATIONAL
8306 Wilshire Blvd., Suite 947, Beverly Hills, CA 90211. (310) 936-7577. FAX: (310) 936-1691.

PACIFIC TITLE & ART STUDIO
6350 Santa Monica Blvd., Los Angeles, CA 90038. (213) 938-3711. FAX: (213) 938-6364.

JOY RENCHER'S EDITORIAL SERVICE
738 Cahuenga Blvd., Hollywood, CA 90038. (213) 463-9836. FAX: (213) 469-0377.

SOFTNI CORP/SDI SUBTITLING & DUBBING INTL.
11444 W. Olympic Blvd., 10th fl., Los Angeles, CA 90064. (310) 312- 9558. FAX: (310) 473-6052.

TITLE HOUSE INC.
738 N. Cahuenga Blvd., Los Angeles, CA 90038. (213) 469-8171. FAX: (213) 469-0377.

WORDS IN PICTURES
1028 S. Alfred, Los Angeles, CA 90035. (213) 655-9221. FAX: (213) 655-3350.

TALENT AGENCIES

ABRAMS ARTISTS & ASSOCS.
9200 Sunset Blvd., 11th Floor, Los Angeles, CA 90069. (310) 859-0625. FAX: (310) 276-6193.
420 Madison Ave., Suite 1400, New York, NY 10017. (212) 935-8980.

ABRAMS, RUBALOFF & LAWRENCE., INC.
8075 West 3rd, Suite 303, Los Angeles, CA 90048. (213) 935-1700. FAX: (213) 932-9901.

ACTORS GROUP AGENCY
8730 Sunset Blvd., Suite 220 W., Los Angeles, CA 90069. (310) 657-7113. FAX: (310) 657-1756.
157 W. 57 St., Suite 211, New York, NY 10019. (212) 245-2930. FAX: (212) 245-7096.
Pat House

THE AGENCY
1800 Avenue of the Stars, #400, Los Angeles, CA 90067. (310) 551-3000. FAX: (310) 551-1424.

AGENCY FOR THE PERFORMING ARTS
9000 Sunset Blvd., #1200, Los Angeles, CA 90069. (310) 273-0744. FAX: (310) 888-4242.
888 Seventh Ave., New York, NY10106. (212) 582-1500. FAX: (212) 245-1647.

AIMEE ENTERTAINMENT ASSOCIATION
1500 Ventura Blvd., Sherman Oaks, CA 91403. (818) 783-9115.

ALL-STAR TALENT AGENCY
7834 Alabama Ave., Canoga Park, CA 91304-4905. (818) 346-4313.
AGENT
Robert Allred

ALL TALENT AGENCY
2437 E. Washington Blvd., Pasadena, CA 91104. (818) 797-8202. FAX: (818) 791-5250.

CARLOS ALVARADO AGENCY
8455 Beverly Blvd., Suite 406, Los Angeles, CA 90048-3416. (213) 655-7978.

AMBROSIO/MORTIMER & ASSOCS.
9150 Wilshire Blvd., Suite 175, Beverly Hills, CA 90212. (310) 274-4274. FAX: (310) 274-9642.

AMERICAN-INT'L TALENT
303 W. 42 St., New York, NY 10036. (212) 245-8888. FAX: (212) 245-8926.

AMSEL, EISENSTADT & FRAZIER, INC.
6310 San Vicente Blvd., Suite 407, Los Angeles, CA 90048. (213) 939-1188. FAX: (213) 939-0630.

BEVERLY ANDERSON
1501 Broadway, New York, NY 10036. (212) 944-7773.

THE ARTISTS AGENCY
10000 Santa Monica Blvd., Suite 305, Los Angeles, CA 90067. (310) 277-7779. FAX: (310) 785-9338.

ARTIST NETWORK
8438 Melrose Pl., Los Angeles, CA 90039. (213) 651-4244. FAX: (213) 651-4699.
Debra Hope

ASSOCIATED BOOKING CORP.
1995 Broadway, New York, NY 10023. (212) 874-2400.

RICHARD ASTOR
250 W. 57th St., New York, NY 10107. (212) 581-1970

ATKINS & ASSOCS.
303 S. Crescent Heights Blvd., Los Angeles, CA 90048. (213) 658-1025.

BDP AND ASSOCS.
10637 Burbank Blvd., North Hollywood, 91601. (818) 506-7615.

BADGLEY/CONNOR
9229 Sunset Blvd., #311, Los Angeles, CA 90069. (310) 278-9313. FAX: (310) 278-4128.

BAUMAN, HILLER & ASSOCS.
5757 Wilshire Blvd., PH 5, Los Angeles, CA 90036. (213) 857-6666. FAX: (213) 857-0638.
250 W. 57 St., #2223, New York, NY 10019. 757-0098. FAX: (212) 489-8531.

J. MICHAEL BLOOM & ASSOC.
9255 Sunset Blvd., Suite 710, Los Angeles, CA 90069. (310) 275-6800. FAX: (310) 275-6941.
233 Park Ave. S., New York, NY 10003. (212) 529-6500. FAX: (212) 529-5838.

BENNETT AGENCY
150 S. Barrington Ave., Suite 1, Los Angeles, CA 90049. (310) 471-2251. FAX: (310) 471-2254.

BORINSTEIN ORECK BOGART AGENCY
8271 Melrose Ave., Suite 110, Los Angeles, CA 90046. (213) 658-7500. FAX: (213) 658-8866.

THE BRANDT COMPANY
15250 Ventura Blvd., #720, Sherman Oaks, CA 91403. (818) 783-7747. FAX: (818) 784-6012.
Geoffrey Brandt

KELLY BRESLER & ASSOCIATES
15760 Ventura Blvd., #1730, Encino, CA 91436. (818) 905-1155.

CURTIS BROWN, LTD.
606 N. Larchmont Blvd., #309, Los Angeles, CA 90004. (213) 473-5400.

CNA & ASSOCS.
1801 Avenue of the Stars, #1250, Los Angeles, CA 90067. (310) 556-4343. FAX: (310) 556-4633.

CAMDEN-ITG
822 S. Robertson Blvd., #200, Los Angeles, CA 90035. (310) 289-2700. FAX: (310) 286-2718.

WILLIAM CARROLL AGENCY
139 N. San Fernando Blvd., Suite A, Burbank, CA 91502. (818) 848-9948. FAX: (213) 849-2553.

CAVALERI & ASSOCIATES
405 Riverside Dr., Burbank, CA 91506. (818) 955-9300. FAX: (818) 955-9399.
Ray Cavaleri

CENTURY ARTISTS, LTD.
9744 Wilshire Blvd., Suite 308, Beverly Hills, CA 90212. (310) 273-4366.

THE CHASIN AGENCY
8899 Beverly Blvd., Suite 715, Los Angeles, CA 90048. (310) 278-7505. FAX: (310) 275-6685.

CINEMA TALENT AGENCY
8033 W. Sunset Blvd., #808. Los Angeles, CA 90046. (213) 656-1937. FAX: (213) 654-4678.

CIRCLE TALENT AGENCY
433 N. Camden Dr., #400, Beverly Hills, CA 90210. (310) 285-1585.

COMMERCIALS UNLIMITED, INC.
9601 Wilshire Blvd., #620, Los Angeles, CA 90210. (310) 888-8788. FAX: (310) 888-8712.

CONTEMPORARY ARTISTS LTD.
1427 Third St., #205, Santa Monica, CA 90401. (310) 395-1800.

CORALIE JR. AGENCY
4789 Vineland Ave., #100, N. Hollywood, CA 91602. (818) 766-9501.

THE CRAIG AGENCY
8485 Melrose Pl., Suite E, Los Angeles, CA 90069. (213) 655-0236. FAX: (213) 655-1491.

CREATIVE ARTISTS AGENCY
9830 Wilshire Blvd., Beverly Hills, CA 90212. (310) 288-4545. FAX: (310) 288-4800.

LIL CUMBER ATTRACTIONS AGENCY
6363 Sunset Blvd., Suite 807, Los Angeles, CA 90028. (213) 469-1919. FAX: (213) 469-4883.

CUNNINGHAM, ESCOTT, DIPENE & ASSOC.
10635 Santa Monica Blvd., #130, Los Angeles, CA 90025-4900. (310) 475-2111. FAX: (310) 475-1929.
257 Park Ave. South, Suite 900, New York, NY 10010. (212) 477-1666. FAX: (212) 979-2011.

DADE/SCHULTZ ASSOCS.
11846 Ventura Blvd., #101, Studio City, CA 91604. (818) 760-3100. FAX: (818) 760-1395.

DIAMOND ARTISTS AGENCY, LTD.
215 N. Barrington Ave., Los Angeles, CA 90049. (310) 472-7579. FAX: (310) 472-2687.

ENTERTAINMENT ENTERPRISES
1680 Vine St., Suite 519, Los Angeles, CA 90028. (213) 462-6001. FAX: (213) 462-6003.

FAVORED ARTISTS
122 S. Robertson Blvd., #202, Los Angeles, CA 90048. (310) 247-1040. FAX: (310) 247-1048.

WILLIAM FELBER
2126 Cahuenga Blvd., Los Angeles, CA 90068. (213) 466-7627.

LIANA FIELDS AGENCY
3325 Wilshire Blvd., #749, Los Angeles, CA 90010. (213) 487-3656.

FILM ARTISTS ASSOCIATES
7080 Hollywood Blvd., Suite 704, Los Angeles, CA 90028. (213) 463-1010. FAX: (213) 463-0702.

FIRST ARTISTS AGENCY
10000 Riverside Dr., Suite 10, Toluca Lake, CA 91602. (818) 509-9292. FAX: (818) 509-9295.

FLASHCAST/PETCAST
Centrum Towers, Ground Floor, 3575 Cahuenga Blvd. West, Universal City, CA 90068. (818) 760-7986, (800) 273-9008. FAX: (818) 760-6792.
Chris Adams, Richard Weiner

FLICK EAST-WEST TALENTS INC.
9057 Nemo St., Suite A, W. Hollywood, 90069. (310) 247-1777. FAX: (310) 858-1357.
Carnegie Hall Studio 1110, 881 Seventh Ave., New York, NY 10019. (212) 307-1850.

THE GAGE GROUP
9255 Sunset Blvd., Suite 515, Los Angeles, CA 90069. (310) 859-8777. FAX: (310) 859-8166.
315 W. 57 St., New York, NY 10019. 541-5250.

DALE GARRICK INTL. AGENCY
8831 Sunset Blvd., #402, Los Angeles, CA 90069. (310) 657-2661.

GEDDES AGENCY
1201 Greenacre Ave., Los Angeles, CA 90046-5707. (213) 878-1155. FAX: (213) 878-1150.

DON GERLER TALENT AGENCY
3349 Cahuenga Blvd. West, Suite 1, Los Angeles, CA 90068. (213) 850-7386.

THE GERSH AGENCY
232 N. Canon Dr., Beverly Hills, CA 90210. (310) 274-6611. FAX: (310) 274-3923.
130 W. 42 St., #1804, New York, NY 10036. (212) 997-1818.

GILLA ROOS LTD.
9744 Wilshire Blvd., #203, Beverly Hills, CA 90212. (310) 274-9356. FAX: (310) 274-3604.

GOLD/MARSHAK ASSOCIATES
3500 W. Olive, Suite 1400, Burbank, CA 91505. (818) 972-4300. FAX: (818) 955-6411.

GORFAINE/SCHWARTZ AGENCY
3301 Barham Blvd., #201, Los Angeles, CA 90068. (213) 969-1011. FAX: (213) 969-1022.

GROSSMAN & ASSOCIATES
211 S. Beverly Dr., Suite 206, Beverly Hills, CA 90212. (310) 550-8127.

HAMILBURG AGENCY
292 S. La Cienega, Suite 312, Beverly Hills, CA 90211. (310) 657-1501.

MICHAEL HARTIG
156 Fifth Ave., New York, NY 10010. (212) 929-1772.

BEVERLY HECHT AGENCY
8949 Sunset Blvd., Suite 203, Los Angeles, CA 90069. (310) 278-3544.

HENDERSON/ HOGAN AGENCY
247 S. Beverly Dr., #102, Beverly Hills, CA 90212. (310) 274-7815.
850 Seventh Ave., New York, NY 10019. (212) 765-5190.

IFA TALENT AGENCY
8730 Sunset Blvd., #490, Los Angeles, CA 90069. (310) 659-5522.

INNOVATIVE ARTISTS
1999 Ave. of the Stars, Suite 2850, Los Angeles, CA 90067-6082. (310) 553-5200. FAX: (310) 557-2211.
1776 Broadway, New York, NY 10019. (212) 315-4455. FAX: (212) 315-4455.

INTERNATIONAL CREATIVE MANAGEMENT
8942 Wilshire Blvd., Beverly Hills, CA 90211. (310) 550-4000. FAX: (310) 550-4108.
40 W. 57 St., New York, NY 10019. (212) 556-5600.

INTERNATIONAL TALENT GROUP
9000 Sunset Blvd., Los Angeles, CA 90069. (310) 247-0680.

JAN J. AGENCY
365 W. 34 St., New York, NY 10001. (212) 967-5265.

JORDAN, GILL & DORNBAUM
156 Fifth Ave., #711, New York, NY 10010. (212) 463-8455.

KAPLAN-STAHLER AGENCY
8383 Wilshire Blvd., #923, Beverly Hills, CA 90211. (213) 653-4483. FAX: (213) 653-4506.

KAZARIAN SPENCER & ASSOCS. INC.
11365 Ventura Blvd., #100, Studio City, CA 91604. (818) 769-9111. FAX: (818) 769-9840.

KELMAN/ARLETTA AGENCY
7813 Sunset Blvd., Los Angeles, CA 90046. (213) 851-8822. FAX: (213) 851-4923.

KOHNER AGENCY
9300 Wilshire Blvd., #555, Beverly Hills, CA 90212. (310) 550-1060. FAX: (310) 276-1083.

THE KOPALOFF COMPANY
1800 Avenue of the Stars, #400, Los Angeles, CA 90067. (310) 551-3000. FAX: (310) 277-9513.

THE KRAFT-BENJAMIN AGENCY
8491 Sunset Blvd., Suite 492, Los Angeles, CA 90069. (310) 652-6065. FAX: (310) 652-6146.

LUCY KROLL
390 West End Ave., New York, NY 10024. (212) 877-0627.

L.A. ARTISTS
606 Wilshire Blvd., #416, Santa Monica, CA 90401. (310) 395-9589.

L.A. TALENT
8335 Sunset Blvd., Los Angeles, CA 90069. (213) 656-3722. FAX: (213) 650-4272.

SUSAN LANE MODEL & TALENT
14071 Windsor Pl., Santa Ana, CA 92705. (714) 731-1420. FAX: (714) 731-5223.

LANTZ OFFICE
888 Seventh Ave., #2500, New York, NY 10106. (212) 586-0200.

LIONEL LARNER LTD.
119 W. 57 St., Suite 1412, New York, NY 10019. (212) 246-3105. FAX: (212) 956-2851.

LEVIN AGENCY
9255 Sunset Blvd., #400, W. Hollywood, 90069. (310) 278-0353.

ROBERT LIGHT AGENCY
6404 Wilshire Blvd., Suite 900, Los Angeles, CA 90048. (213) 651-1777. FAX: (213) 651-4933.

LYONS/SHELDON AGENCY
800 S. Robertson Blvd., #46, Los Angeles, CA 90069. (310) 652-8778.

MARGE MCDERMOTT
216 E. 39 St., New York, NY 10016. (212) 889-1583.

SANDRA MARSH MANAGEMENT
9150 Wilshire Blvd., #220, Beverly Hills, CA 90210. (310) 285-0303. FAX: (310) 285-0218.

MARTEL AGENCY
1680 N. Vine St., Suite 203, Los Angeles, CA 90028. (213) 461-5943. FAX: (213) 461-6350.

JOHNNIE MARTINELLI ATTRACTIONS
888 Eighth Ave., New York, NY 10019. (212) 586-0963.

MEDIA ARTISTS GROUP
8383 Wilshire Blvd., Suite 954, Beverly Hills, CA 90211-2408. (213) 658-5050.

MERIDIAN TALENT AGENCY
373 S. Robertson Blvd., Beverly Hills, CA 90211. (310) 652-7799. FAX: (310) 854-3966.
Arthur Braun

WILLIAM MORRIS AGENCY
151 El Camino Dr., Beverly Hills, 90212. (310) 274-7451. FAX: (310) 859-4462.
1350 Ave. of the Americas, New York, NY 10019. (212) 586-5100.

OMNIPROP INC. TALENT AGENCY WEST
10700 Ventura Blvd., 2nd fl., Studio City, 91604 (818) 980-9267. FAX: (818) 980-9371.

OPPENHEIM-CHRISTIE ASSOC.
13 E. 37 St., New York, NY 10016. (212) 213-4330.

FIFI OSCARD AGENCY
24 W. 40 St., New York, NY 10018. (212) 764-1100.

PARADIGM AGENCY
10100 Santa Monica Blvd., 25th fl., Los Angeles, CA 90067. (310) 277-4400.

PORTMAN ORGANZATION
8033 Sunset Blvd., #964, Los Angeles, CA 90046. (213) 871-8544. FAX: (708) 982-9383.

PREMIER TALENT AGENCY
3 E. 54 St., New York, NY 10022. (212) 758-4900. FAX: (212) 755-3251.

PREMIERE ARTISTS AGENCY
8899 Beverly Blvd., #102, Los Angeles, CA 90048. (310) 271-1414. FAX: (310) 205-3981.

PRIVILEGE TALENT AGENCY
8170 Beverly Blvd., Suite 204, Los Angeles, CA 90048. (213) 658-8781.

PROGRESSIVE ARTISTS AGENCY
400 S. Beverly Dr., Suite 216, Beverly Hills, CA 90212. (310) 553-8561.

THE ROBERTS COMPANY
10345 W. Olympic Blvd., PH, Los Angeles, CA 90064. (310) 552-7800. FAX: (310) 552-9324.

MARION ROSENBERG
8428 Melrose Pl., Suite B, Los Angeles, CA 90069. (213) 653-7383. FAX: (213) 653-9268.

THE SANDERS AGENCY LTD.
8831 Sunset Blvd., Suite 304, Los Angeles, CA 90069. (310) 652-1119. FAX: (310) 652-7810.
1204 Broadway, New York, NY 10001. (212) 779-3737.

IRV SCHECTER COMPANY
9300 Wilshire Blvd., #400, Beverly Hills, CA 90212. (310) 278-8070. FAX: (310) 278-6058.

SCHULLER TALENT
276 Fifth Ave., New York, NY 10001. (212) 532-6005.

DON SCHWARTZ & ASSOC.
6922 Hollywood Blvd., #508, Los Angeles, CA 90028. (213) 464-4366. FAX: (213) 464-4661.

SELECTED ARTISTS AGENCY
3900 W. Alameda Blvd., Suite 1700, Burbank, CA 91505. (818) 972-1747.

DAVID SHAPIRA ASSOCIATES, INC.
15301 Ventura Blvd., Suite 345, Sherman Oaks, CA 91403. (818) 906-0322. FAX: (818) 783-2562.

MICHAEL SLESSINGER & ASSOCS.
8730 Sunset Blvd., #220 West, Los Angeles, CA 90069. (310) 657-7113. FAX: (310) 657-1756.

SUSAN SMITH & ASSOCIATES
121 N. San Vicente Blvd., Beverly Hills, CA 90211. (310) 852-4777.

STONE/MANNERS AGENCY
8091 Selma Ave., Los Angeles, CA 90046. (213) 654-7575.

H. N. SWANSON
8523 Sunset Blvd., Los Angeles, CA 90069. (310) 652-5385.

TALENT GROUP INC.
9250 Wilshire Blvd., #208, Beverly Hills, CA 90212. (310) 273-9559. FAX: (310) 273-5147.

TALENT REPS., INC.
20 E. 53 St., New York, NY 10022. (212) 752-1835.

HERB TANNEN & ASSOC.
1800 N. Vine St., Suite 305, Los Angeles, CA 90028. (213) 466-6191. FAX: (213) 466-0863.

TWENTIETH CENTURY ARTISTS
15315 Magnolia Blvd., Suite 429, Sherman Oaks, 91403. (818) 788-5516.

UNITED TALENT AGENCY
9560 Wilshire Blvd., #500, Beverly Hills, CA 90212. (310) 273-6700. FAX: (310) 247-1111.

RUTH WEBB ENTERPRISES, INC.
13834 Magnolia Blvd., Sherman Oaks, CA 91423. (818) 905-7000. FAX: (213) 874-1860.
Scott Stander

BOB WATERS AGENCY
1501 Broadway, #705, New York, NY 10036. (212) 302-8787.

HANNS WOLTERS THEATRICAL AGENCY
10 W. 37 St., New York, NY 10018. (212) 714-0100. FAX: (212) 695-2385.

WRITERS & ARTISTS AGENCY
924 Westwood Blvd., Suite 900, Los Angeles, CA 90024. (310) 824-6300.
19 W. 44 St., #1000, New York, NY 10036. (212) 391-1112.

THEATRICAL TRAILERS

HOWARD A. ANDERSON, CO.
100 Universal City Plaza, #504-3, Universal City, CA 91608. (818) 777-2402. FAX: (818) 733-1118.

AVAILABLE LIGHT LTD.
3110 W. Burbank Blvd., CA 91505. (818) 842-2109. FAX: (818) 842-0661.

BLOOMFILM
7722 W. Sunset Blvd., Los Angeles, CA 90046. (213) 850-5575. FAX: (213) 850-7304.

CINEMA CONCEPTS THEATRE SERVICE COMPANY, INC.
2030 Powers Ferry Rd., Suite 214, Atlanta, GA 30339. (770) 956-7460, (800) SHOWADS. FAX: (770) 956-8358.
URL: http://www.cinemation.com

THE CREATIVE PARTNERSHIP, INC.
7525 Fountain Ave., Hollywood, CA 90046. (213) 850-5551. FAX: (213) 850-0391.

CRUSE & CO.
7000 Romaine St., Hollywood, CA 90038. (213) 851-8814. FAX: (213) 851-8788.

EAST END PRODUCTIONS
513 W. 54 St., New York, NY 10019. (212) 489-1865.

PABLO FERRO & ASSOCIATES
1756 N. Sierra Bonita Ave., Hollywood, CA 90046. (213) 850-6193.

FILMACK STUDIOS
1327 S. Wabash Ave., Chicago, IL 60605. (312) 427-3395. (800) FILMACK. FAX: (312) 427-4866.
Robert Mack

GLASS/SCHOOR FILMS
706 N. Citrus Ave., Los Angeles, CA 90038-3402. (213) 525-1155. FAX: (213) 525-1156.

HOLLYWOOD NEWSREEL SYNDICATE INC.
1622 N. Gower St., Los Angeles, CA 90028. (213) 469-7307. FAX: (213) 469-8251.

HOMER & ASSOCIATES, INC.
1420 N. Beachwood Dr., Hollywood, CA 90028. (213) 462-4710.

JKR PRODUCTIONS, INC.
12140 W. Olympic Blvd., Suite 21, Los Angeles, CA 90064. (310) 826-3666.

KALEIDOSCOPE FILMS INC.
844 N. Seward St., Hollywood, CA 90038. (213) 465-1151. FAX: (213) 871-1376.

LUMENI PRODUCTIONS
1632 Flower St., Glendale, CA 91201-2357. (818) 956-2200. FAX: (818) 956-3298.

NATIONAL SCREEN SERVICE GROUP INC.
2001 S. La Cienega Blvd., Los Angeles, CA 90034. (310) 836-1505.
40 Rockwood Pl., Englewood, NJ 07631. (201) 871-7900.
1800 Baltimore Ave., Kansas City, MO 64108. (816) 842-5893. FAX: (816) 842-4553.
MANAGER
Eric Allen

PIKE PRODUCTIONS, INC.
11 Clarke St., Box 300, Newport, RI 02840. (401) 846-8890. FAX: (401) 847-0070.

QUARTERMOON PRODUCTIONS
12 Morand Lane, Wilton, CT 06897. (203) 762-2663. FAX: (203) 762-0509.
Gary Balionis

JIM RUXIN
12140 W. Olympic Blvd., Suite 21, Los Angeles, CA 90064. (310) 826-3666.

SILVER-GLAZER FILMS INC.
116 S. La Brea Ave., Los Angeles, CA 90036. (213) 935-2200. FAX: (213) 935-2022.

SOUND SERVICES INC.
7155 Santa Monica Blvd., Los Angeles, CA 90046. (213) 874-9344. FAX: (213) 850-7189.
Stuart Bartell

LEONARD SOUTH PRODUCTIONS
4883 Lankershim Blvd., N. Hollywood, CA 91601. (818) 760-8383. FAX: (818) 760-8301.

HERBERT L. STROCK PRODUCTIONS
6311 Romaine Ave., Suite 7113, Los Angeles, CA 90038. (213) 461-1298.
Herbert L. Strock

VIDE-U PRODUCTIONS
9976 Westwanda Dr., Beverly Hills, CA 90210. (310) 276-5509. FAX: (310) 276-1185.

U.S. STATE AND CITY FILM COMMISSIONS

ALABAMA
Michael Boyer
Alabama Film Office
401 Adams Ave.
Montgomery, AL 36130
(800) 633-5898, (205) 242-4195. FAX: (205) 242-2077
URL: http://www.telefilm-south.com/Alabama/Alabama.html

ALASKA
Mary Pignalberi, Coordinator
Alaska Film Office, Frontier Bldg.
3601 "C" St., Suite 700
Anchorage, AK 99503
(907) 269-8137. FAX: (907) 269-8136

ARIZONA
Linda Peterson Warren, Director
Arizona Film Commission
3800 N. Central Ave., Bldg. D
Phoenix, AZ 85012
(602) 280-1380, (800) 523-6695. FAX: (602) 280-1384

City of Phoenix Film Office
Luci Fontanilla Marshall, Program Manager
200 W. Washington, 10th fl.
Phoenix, AZ 85003
(602) 262-4850. FAX: (602) 534-2295

City of Scottsdale
Jan Horne, Film Liaison
3939 Civic Center Blvd.
Scottsdale, AZ 85251
(602) 994-2636. FAX: (602) 994-7780

City of Tucson
Tom B. Hilderband, Executive Director
Tucson Film Office
32 N. Stone Ave., #100
Tucson, AZ 85701
(602) 791-4000, (602) 429-1000. FAX: (602) 791-4963

ARKANSAS
Suzy Lilly, Manager of Film Services
AR Motion Picture Development Office
One State Capitol Mall, Suite 2C-200
Little Rock, AR 72201
(501) 682-7676. FAX: (501) 682-FILM
email: SLILLY@AIDC.STATE.AR.US

CALIFORNIA
Patti Stolkin Archuletta, Director
California Film Commission
6922 Hollywood Blvd., Suite 600
Hollywood, CA 90028
(213) 736-2465, (800) 858-4PIX. FAX: (213) 736-2465

City of Los Angeles
Jonathan Roberts, Director
Motion Picture/Television Division
6922 Hollywood Blvd., Suite 614
Hollywood, CA 90028
(213) 461-8614. FAX: (213) 847-5009

County of Los Angeles
Stephanie Leiner, Director
Entertainment Industry Dvlpmnt. Corp./
Los Angeles Film Office
6922 Hollywood Blvd., Suite 602
Los Angeles, CA 90028
(213) 957-1000. FAX: (213) 463-0613

City of Oakland
Jeanie Rucker
Oakland Film Office
505 14th St., #910
Oakland, CA 94612
(510) 238-2193. FAX: (510) 238-2227

City of San Diego
Cathy Anderson, Film Commissioner
San Diego Film Commission
402 W. Broadway, Suite 1000
San Diego, CA 92101
(619) 234-3456. FAX: (619) 234-0571

City of San Francisco
Robin Eickman, Director
San Francisco Film and Video Arts Commission
401 Van Ness Ave., Rm. 417
San Francisco, CA 94102
(415) 554-6244. FAX: (415) 554-6503

City of San Jose
Joe O'Kane, Executive Director
San Jose Film & Video Commission
333 W. San Carlos St., Suite 1000
San Jose, CA 95110
(408) 295-9600, (800) SAN-JOSE. FAX: (408) 295-3937
email: jokane@sanjose.org, URL: http://www.sanjose.org

Monterey County
Karen Nordstrand, Director
Monterey County Film Commission
P.O. Box 111
Monterey, CA 93942-0111
(408) 646-0910. FAX: (408) 655-9244, email: mryfilm@aol.com
URL: http://mry.infonet.com/MontereyFilmCommission/home.htm

Sonoma County
Sheree Green, Director
Sonoma County Film Liaison Office
5000 Roberts Lake Rd.
Rohnert Park, CA 94928
(707) 584-8100. FAX: (707) 584-8111

COLORADO
Michael Klein, Director
Colorado Motion Picture & TV Commission
1625 Broadway, Suite 1700
Denver, CO 80202
(303) 620-4500, (800) SCO-UTUS. FAX: (303) 620-4545

Boulder County
Shelly Helmerick
Boulder County Film Commission
P.O. Box 73
Boulder, CO 80306
(303) 442-1044, (800) 444-0447. FAX: (303) 938-8837

City of Colorado Springs
Paula Vickerman
Colorado Springs Film Commission
6 N. Teton, Suite 400
Colorado Springs, CO 80903
(719) 578-6943. FAX: (719) 578-6394, email: vickers@usa.net

CONNECTICUT
Bert Brown, Director
Connecticut Film Office
865 Brook St.
Rocky Hill, CT 06067
(860) 258-4339. FAX: (860) 258-4275

DELAWARE
Carol Myers
Delaware Film Office
99 Kings Highway, P.O. Box 1401
Dover, DE 19903
(800) 441-8846, (302) 739-4271. FAX: (302) 739-5749

DISTRICT OF COLUMBIA
Crystal Palmer Brazil, Director
Mayor's Office of TV & Film
717 12th St. NW, 10th fl.
Washington, D.C. 20005
(202) 727-6600. FAX: (202) 727-3787

FLORIDA
John Reitzammer
Florida Entertainment Commission
505 17 St.
Miami Beach, FL 33139
(305) 673-7468. FAX: (305) 673-7168

Fort Lauderdale Area/Broward County
Elizabeth Wentworth, Director
Motion Picture & TV Office
Broward Economic Development Council
200 E. Las Olas Blvd., Suite 1850
Fort Lauderdale, FL 33301
(305) 524-3113. FAX: (305) 524-3167

City of Jacksonville
Todd Roobin
Jacksonville Film & TV Office
128 E. Forsythe St., Suite 505
Jacksonville, FL 32202
(904) 630-2522. FAX: (904) 630-1485

Miami-Dade County
Jeff Peel, Director
Miami-Dade Office of Film, TV & Print
111 Northwest 1st Street, Suite 2510
Miami, FL 33128
(305) 375-3288. FAX: (305) 375-3266

Ocala/Marion County
Sue Sargent-Latham
Community Liaison
Ocala/Marion County Film Commission
Economic Development Council
110 E. Silver Springs Blvd.
Ocala, FL 34470
(904) 629-2757. FAX: (904) 629-1581

Orlando/Central Florida
Katherine Ramsberger, Director
Metro Orlando Film and Television Office
200 E. Robinson St., Suite 600
Orlando, FL 32801-1950
(407) 422-7159. FAX: (407) 843-9514
email: filminfo@film-orlando.org
URL: www.film-orlando.org

Palm Beach County
Chuck Eldred, Film Commission
Palm Beach County Film & Television Commission
1555 Palm Beach Lakes Blvd., Suite 414
West Palm Beach, FL 33401
(407) 233-1000, (800) 745-FILM. FAX: (407) 683-6857
URL: http://www.co.palmbeach.fl.us/film

GEORGIA
Norman Bielowicz, Director
Georgia Film & Videotape Office
285 Peachtree Center Avenue, NW, Suite 1000
Atlanta, GA 30303
(404) 656-3591. FAX: (404) 651-9063
email: Film@itt.state.ga.us
URL: http://www.Georgia-on-my-mind.org

HAWAII
Georgette T. Deemer, Manager
Hawaii Film Office
P.O. Box 2359
Honolulu, HI 96804
(808) 586-2570. FAX: (808) 586-2572

IDAHO
Peg Owens
Film Promotion, Idaho Film Bureau
700 W. State St., 2nd floor
Boise, ID 83720-2700
(208) 334-2470, (800) 942-8338. FAX: (208) 334-2631

ILLINOIS
Ron Ver Kuilen, Director
Illinois Film Office
100 W. Randolph, Suite 3-400
Chicago, IL 60601
(312) 814-3600. FAX: (312) 814-8874

City of Chicago
Richard M. Moskal, Director
Chicago Film Office
One North LaSalle, Suite 2165
Chicago, IL 60602
(312) 744-6415. FAX: (312) 744-1378

INDIANA
Jane Rulon, Director, Indiana Film Office
Indiana Department of Commerce
1 N. Capitol Ave., Suite 700
Indianapolis, IN 46204-2288
(317) 233-8829. FAX: (317) 233-6887
email: idoc70@indyvax.iupui.edu
URL: http://www.a1.com/derringer/filmcomm.html

IOWA
Wendol Jarvis
Iowa Film Office
200 E. Grand Ave.
Des Moines, IA 50309
(515) 242-4726, (800) 779-FILM. FAX: (515) 242-4859

KANSAS
Vicky Henley, Film Commissioner
Kansas Film Commission
700 SW Harrison St., Suite 1300
Topeka, KS 66603-3712
(913) 296-4927. FAX: (913) 296-6988, TTY: (913) 296-3487

KENTUCKY
Russ Slone
Kentucky Film Commission
Capitol Plaza Tower
500 Mero St., 22nd floor
Frankfort, KY 40601
(502) 564-FILM, (800) 345-6591. FAX: (502) 564-7588

LOUISIANA
Ed Lipscomb, III, Director
Louisiana Film Commission
P.O. Box 44320
Baton Rouge, LA 70804-4320
(504) 342-8150. FAX: (504) 342-7988
URL: http://www.doa.state.la.us/crt/filmvid.htm

City of New Orleans
Kimberly Carbo
New Orleans Film and Video Commission
1515 Poydras St.
New Orleans, LA 70112
(504) 565-8104. FAX: (504) 565-0801

MAINE
Lea Girardin, Director
Greg Gadberry, Location Specialist
Maine Film Office
Station 59
Augusta, ME 04333-0059
(207) 287-5703. FAX: (207) 287-8070
URL:http://www.state.me.us/deed/film/mainefilm.htm

MARYLAND
Michael Styer, Director
Maryland Film Office
217 E. Redwood St., 9th floor
Baltimore, MD 21202
(410) 767-6340, (800) 333-6632. FAX: (410) 333-0044

MASSACHUSETTS
Robin Dawson, Director
Massachusetts Film Office
10 Park Plaza, Suite 2310
Boston, MA 02116
(617) 973-8800. FAX: (617) 973-8810

MICHIGAN
Janet Lockwood
Michigan Film Office
201 N. Washington Sq.
Lansing, MI 48913
(517) 373-0638, (800) 477-3456. FAX: (517) 241-0593
email: lockwoodj@state.mi.us
URL: http://www.mjc.state.mi.us/mjc/business/filmoffice/index

MINNESOTA
Randy Adamsick, Kelly Pratt
Minnesota Film Board
401 N. Third St., Suite 460
Minneapolis, MN 55401
(612) 332-6493. FAX: (612) 332-3735

MISSISSIPPI
Ward Emling, Director
Mississippi Film Office
520 George St., P.O. Box 849
Jackson, MS 39205-0849
(601) 359-3297. FAX: (601) 359-5757

City of Columbus
Carolyn Denton, Director
Columbus Film Commission
P.O.Box 789
Columbus, MS 39703
(601) 329-1191, (800) 327-2686. FAX: (601) 329-8969

City of Natchez
Anne Mohon
Natchez Film Commission
P.O. Box 1485, Natchez, MS 39121
(601) 446-6345, (800) 647-6724. FAX: (601) 442-0814

MISSOURI
Kate Arnold-Schuck, Manager
Missouri Film Office
301 West High, Room 770, P.O. Box 118
Jefferson City, MO 65102
(573) 751-9050. FAX: (573) 751-7385
email: katnolds@mail.state.mo.us

MONTANA
Lonie Stimac, Director
Montana Film Office
1424 Ninth Ave.
Helena, MT 59620
(406) 444-3762, (800) 553-4563. FAX: (406) 444-4191
email: montanafilm@travel.mt.gov
URL: http://montanafilm.mt.gov

City of Billings
John Brewer
Billings Film Liaison Office
P.O. Box 31177
Billings, MT 59107
(406) 245-4111, (800) 711-2630. FAX: (406) 245-7333

City of Butte
Connie Kinney, Film Commissioner
Butte Film Liaison Office
2950 Harrison Ave.
Butte, MT 59701
(406) 494-5595

City of Great Falls and Northern Montana
Peggy Gentry
Great Falls Regional Film Liaison
710 First Ave. N.
Great Falls, MT 59401
(406) 761-4434, (800) 735-8535. FAX: (406) 761-6129

NEBRASKA
Laurie J. Richards
Nebraska Film Office
P.O. Box 94666
Lincoln NE 68509-4666
(402) 471-3797, (800) 228-4307. FAX: (402) 471-3026
email: laurier@ded2.ded.state.ne.us

City of Omaha/Douglas County
Julie Ginsberg
Omaha Film Commission
6800 Mercy Rd., Suite 202
Omaha, NE 68106
(402) 444-7736. FAX: (402) 444-4511

NEVADA
Robert Hirsch, Motion Picture Division/C.E.D.
Nevada Economic Development Commission
3770 Howard Hughes Pkwy., Suite 295
Las Vegas, NV 89109
(702) 486-7150, (702) 791-0839 (after hours and holidays)
FAX: (702) 486-7372

NEW HAMPSHIRE
Ann Kennard, Director
New Hampshire Film and Television Bureau
Box 1856, 172 Pembroke Rd.
Concord, NH 03302-1856
(603) 271-2598. FAX: (603) 271-2629

NEW JERSEY
Joseph Friedman
New Jersey Motion Picture and Television Commission
P.O. Box 47023, 153 Halsey St., 5th fl.
Newark, NJ 07101
(201) 648-6279. FAX: (201) 648-7350

NEW MEXICO
Linda Taylor Hutchison, Director
New Mexico Film Commission
1050 Old Pecos Trail
Santa Fe, NM 87503
(505) 827-7365, (800) 545-9871
URL: http://www.edd.state.nm.us

City of Albuquerque
Victoria Dye, Special Projects Manager
Albuquerque Film and Television Commission
Albuquerque Convention & Visitor's Bureau
P.O. Box 26866
Albuquerque, NM 87125
(505) 842-9918, (800) 733-9918. FAX: (505) 247-9101

NEW YORK
Pat Swinney Kaufman, Deputy Commissioner & Director
New York State Governor's Office for Motion Picture &
Television Development
633 Third Ave., 33rd floor
New York, NY 10017
(212) 803-2330. FAX: (212) 803-2339
email: erodgers@empire.state.ny.us

City of New York
Patricia Reed Scott, Commissioner
Mayor's Office of Film, Theatre & Broadcasting
1697 Broadway, 6th fl.
New York, NY 10019
(212) 489-6710. FAX: (212) 307-6237
URL: http://www.ci.nyc.ny.us/htwl/filmcomm.html

Nassau County
Debra Markowitz, Director
Nassau County Film Office
1550 Franklin Ave., Rm. 207
Mineola, NY 11501
(516) 571-4160. FAX: (516) 571-4161

Suffolk County
Thomas Junor, Commissioner
Suffolk County Motion Picture & TV Commission
220 Rabro Dr., Box 6100
Hauppage, NY 11788-0099
(516) 853-4800, (800) 762-GROW. FAX: (516) 853-4888

NORTH CAROLINA
William Arnold, Director
North Carolina Film Commission
430 N. Salisbury St.
Raleigh, NC 27611
(919) 733-9900, (800) 232-9227. FAX: (919) 715-0151

NORTH DAKOTA
North Dakota Film Office
604 E. Blvd., 2nd floor, Liberty Memorial Bldg.
State Capitol
Bismarck, ND 58505
(701) 328-2525, (800) 328-2871. FAX: (701) 328-4878

OHIO
Eve Lapolla, Manager
Ohio Film Bureau
77 S. High St., 29th Floor
Columbus, OH 43266-0101
(614) 466-2284, (800) 848-1300. FAX: (614) 466-6744

City of Cincinnati
Lori Holladay, Executive Director
Greater Cincinnati Film Commission
632 Vine St., Suite 1010
Cincinnati, OH 45202
(513) 784-1744. FAX: (513) 768-8963
email: gcfc@eos.net

OKLAHOMA
Mary Nell Clark, Director
Oklahoma Film Office
440 S. Houston, Suite 4
Tulsa, OK 74127
(800) 766-3456, (918) 581-2660. FAX: (918) 581-2244

OREGON
David Woolson, Executive Director
Oregon Film & Video Office
One World Trade Center
121 S.W. Salmon St., Suite 300A
Portland, OR 97204
(503) 229-5832. FAX: (503) 229-6869
email: shoot@oregonfilm.org

City of Portland
Nancy Blasi
Portland Film & Video Office
1220 S.W. Fifth Ave., Room 211
Portland, OR 97204
(503) 823-3030. FAX: (503) 823-3036

PENNSYLVANIA
Timothy D. Chambers, Director
Pennsylvania Film Office
Department of Commerce
200 N. 3rd St., Suite 901
Harrisburg, PA 17101
(717) 783-3456. FAX: (717) 772-3581

City of Philadelphia
Sharon Pinkenson, Executive Director
Greater Philadelphia Film Office
1600 Arch St., 12th Floor
Philadelphia, PA 19103
(215) 686-2668. FAX: (215) 686-3659
email: sharon@film.org
URL: http://www.film.org

RHODE ISLAND
Richardson Smith, Director
Rhode Island Film & TV Office
7 Jackson Walkway
Providence, RI 02903
(401) 277- 3456. FAX: (401) 277-2102

SOUTH CAROLINA
Isabel Hill, Director
South Carolina Film Office
P.O. Box 7367
Columbia, SC 29202
(803) 737-0490. FAX: (803) 737-3104

SOUTH DAKOTA
Gary Keller, Film Office Coordinator
South Dakota Film Commission
711 E. Wells Ave.
Pierre, SD 57501-3369
(605) 773-3301. FAX: (605) 773-3256
email: garyk@goed.state.sd.us

TENNESSEE
Marsha Blackburn, Executive Director
Tennessee Film, Entertainment & Music Commission
Rachel Jackson Bldg.
320 Sixth Ave. N., 7th floor
Nashville, TN 37243-0790
(615) 741-3456, (800) 251-8594. FAX: (615) 741-5829

Memphis & Shelby County
Linn Sitler, Executive Director
Memphis-Shelby Co. Film/Tape/Music Commission
Beale St. Landing
245 Wagner Pl., Suite 4
Memphis, TN 38103-3815
(901) 527-8300. FAX: (901) 527-8326

TEXAS
Tom Copeland, Executive Director
Texas Film Commission
P.O. Box 13246
Austin, TX 78711
(512) 463-9200. FAX: (512) 463-4114
email: film@governor.texas.gov

City of El Paso
Susie Gaines
El Paso Film Commission
One Civic Center Plaza
El Paso, TX 79901
(915) 534-0698, (800) 351-6024. FAX: (915) 532-2963

City of Houston
Rick Ferguson, Director
Houston Film Commission
801 Congress
Houston, TX 77002
(800) 365-7575, (713) 227-3100 x615
FAX: (713) 223-3816

City of Irving
Ellen Sandoloski Mayers, Director
Irving Texas Film Commission
6309 N. O'Connor Rd., Suite 222
Irving, TX 75039-3510
(214) 869-0303, (800) 247-8464. FAX: (214) 869-4609
email: itfc@airmail.net

Dallas/Fort Worth
Roger Burke
Dallas/Fort Worth Regional Film Commission
P.O. Box 610246
DFW Airport, TX 75261
(214) 621-0400, (800) 234-5699. FAX: (214) 929-0916

UTAH
Leigh von der Esch, Executive Director
Utah Film Commission
324 South State, Suite 500
Salt Lake City, UT 84114
(801) 538-8740, (800) 453-8824. FAX: (801) 538-8886

City of Moab
Bette L. Stanton, Executive Director
Moab To Monument Valley Film Commission
50 East Center, #1
Moab, UT 84532
(801) 259-6388. FAX: (801) 259-6399

Park City
Nancy V. Kolmer, Director
Park City Film Commission
P.O. Box 1630
Park City, UT 84060
(800) 453-1360. FAX: (801) 649-4132, (801) 649-6100

VERMONT
J. Gregory Gerdel, Director
Vermont Film Bureau
Agency of Development and Community Affairs
134 State St.
Montpelier, VT 05601-1471
(802) 828-33847. FAX: (802) 828-3233
email: ggerdel@dca.state.vt.us

VIRGINIA
Rita McClenny, Director
Virginia Film Office
901 E. Byrd St.
Richmond, VA 23219
(804) 371-8204. FAX: (804) 371-8177

WASHINGTON STATE
Christine Lewis, Manager
Washington State Film & Video Office
2001 6th Ave., Suite 2600
Seattle, WA 98121
(206) 464-7148. FAX: (206) 464-7722

WEST VIRGINIA
Mark McNabb, Director
West Virginia Film Office
State Capitol Complex
Building 6, Rm. 525
Charleston, WV 25305
(304) 558-2234. FAX: (304) 558-1189, (800) 982-3386

WISCONSIN
Stanley Solheim
Wisconsin Film Office
Department of Tourism
123 W. Washington Ave.
Madison, WI 53702-0001
(608) FILM-WIS. FAX: (608) 266-3403
email: ssolheim@mail.state.wi.us

WYOMING
Bill D. Lindstrom, Manager
Wyoming Film Office
Wyoming Travel Commission
Interstate 25 at College Dr.
Cheyenne, WY 82002-0660
(800) 458-6657 or (307) 777-7851. FAX: (307) 777-6904
email: blindstr@wyoming.com

City of Jackson Hole
Deborah Supowit, Director/Liaison
Jackson Hole Film Commission
P.O. Box E
Jackson, WY 83001
(307) 733-3316. FAX: (307) 733-5585

PUERTO RICO
Puerto Rico Film Commission
355 F. D. Roosevelt Ave.
Fomento Bldg., Suite 106
San Juan, PR 00918
(787) 758- 4747, ext. 2250-2255. FAX: (787) 756-5706
URL: http://www.prfilm.com/

U.S. VIRGIN ISLANDS
Manny Centeno, Director
Film Promotion Office
78 Contant 1-2-3
St. Thomas U.S. VI 00804
(809) 774-8784, (809) 775-1444. FAX: (809) 774-4390

FEDERAL GOVERNMENT FILM & MEDIA SERVICES

EXECUTIVE DEPARTMENTS

DEPARTMENT OF AGRICULTURE
Video and Teleconference Division
Office of Public Affairs, 1614 South Bldg., USDA, Washington, DC 20250-1300. (202) 720-6072. FAX: (202) 720-5773.
CHIEF OF DIVISION
Larry Quinn

DEPARTMENT OF COMMERCE
Audiovisual Section
Office of Public Affairs, 14th St., Rm. 5521, Washington, DC 20230. (202) 482-3263. FAX: (202) 482-2639.
SECTION CHIEF
Bob Nassiks

International Trade Administration
Office of Service Industries
Information Industries Division, 14th St. and Constitution Ave., Rm. H-1114, Washington, DC 20230. (202) 482-4781. FAX: (202) 482-2669.
SENIOR INTERNATIONAL TRADE SPECIALIST
John Siegmund

National Telecommunications and Information Administration
Main Commerce Bldg., 1401 Constitution Ave., Washington, DC 20230. (202) 482-1840. FAX: (202) 482-1635.
ASST. SECRETARY, COMMUNICATIONS & INFORMATION
Larry Irving

National Technical Information Service
5282 Port Royal Rd., Springfield, VA 22161. (800) 553-6847. FAX: (703) 321-8547.
DIRECTOR
Dr. Donald Johnson

DEPARTMENT OF DEFENSE
Special Assistant (Audiovisual)
Office of the Assistant Secretary of Defense (Public Affairs), The Pentagon, Room 2E789, Washington, DC 20301. (703) 695-2936. FAX: (703) 695-1149.
HEAD OF DIVISION
Philip M. Strub

Broadcast-Pictorial Branch
Office of the Assistant Secretary of Defense (Public Affairs), The Pentagon, Room 2E765, Washington, DC 20301. (703) 695-0168. FAX: (703) 697-3501.
BRANCH CHIEF
Jim Kout

MILITARY SERVICES
Secretary of the Air Force
Office of Public Affairs, Media Division, The Pentagon, Room 5C879, Washington, DC 20330-1000. (703) 697-2769. FAX: (703) 614-7486.
CHIEF OF DIVISION
Lt. Col. Virginia Pribyla.

Secretary of the Army
Media Relations Division, Army Public Affairs, The Pentagon, Room 2E641, Washington, DC 20310-1500, (703) 697-2564. FAX: (703) 657-2159.
CHIEF OF DIVISION
Judith Johnston

Department of the Navy
Chief of Information, Audiovisual Entertainment, The Pentagon, Room 2E352, Washington, DC 20350-1200. (703) 697-4627.
DIRECTOR
Robert Manning

Headquarters, U.S. Marine Corps
Media Branch Public Affairs Division, Code PAM, The Pentagon, Washington, DC 20380. (703) 614-8010. FAX: (703) 697-5362.
CHIEF OF BRANCH
Lt. Col. Pat Messer

DEPARTMENT OF EDUCATION
Office of Public Affairs
Audiovisual Division, 600 Independence Ave. SW, Rm. 2200, Washington, DC 20202. (202) 401-1576. FAX: (202) 401-3130.
AUDIOVISUAL OFFICER
Greg Grayson

Office of Special Education and Rehabilitation Services
600 Independence Ave. SW, Washington, DC 20202. (202) 205-5465. FAX: (202) 205-9252.
BRANCH CHIEF, CAPTIONING
Ernie Hairston

DEPARTMENT OF ENERGY
Office of Public Affairs
Forrestal Bldg.,1000 Independence Ave. SW, CP41, Room IE200, Washington, DC 20585. (202) 586-6250.
DIRECTOR OF INTERNAL COMMUNICATIONS
Chett Gray

DEPARTMENT OF HEALTH AND HUMAN SERVICES
Office of Public Affairs
200 Independence Ave. SW, Room 647D, Washington, DC 20201. (202) 690-7850. FAX: (202) 690-5673.
DIRECTOR OF COMMUNICATIONS
Jackie Nedell

Administration for Children & Family
370 L'Enfant Promenade SW, 7th floor, Washington, DC 20447. (202) 401-9215. FAX: (202) 205-9688.
DIRECTOR
Michael Kharfen

Health Care Financing Administration
200 Independence Ave. SW, Room 314G, Washington, DC 20201. (202) 690-6113. FAX: (202) 690-6262.
ADMINISTRATOR
Bruce Vladeck

Social Security Administration Office of Public Affairs
4200 West High Rise, 6401 Security Blvd., Baltimore, MD 21235. (401) 965-1720. FAX: (401) 965-3903.
DIRECTOR
Joan Wainwrithe

DEPARTMENT OF HOUSING AND URBAN DEVELOPMENT
Office of Public Affairs
HUD Bldg., 451 7th St. SW, Rm. 10132, Washington, DC 20410. (202) 708-0980. FAX: (202) 619-8153.
ASSISTANT SECRETARY
Jon Cowan

DEPARTMENT OF THE INTERIOR
Office of Public Information Audiovisual Programs
1849 C St. NW, Washington, DC 20240. (202) 501-9649. FAX: (202) 208-64116.
MANAGER OF AUDIOVISUAL PROGRAMS
Steve Brooks

DEPARTMENT OF JUSTICE
Audiovisual Services
10th St. & Pennsylvania Ave., Rm. 1313, Washington, DC 20530. (202) 514-4387. FAX: (202) 514-6741.
SUPERVISOR
Joe Keyerleber

DEPARTMENT OF LABOR
Audiovisual and Photographic Services Branch
Audiovisual Division, 200 Constitution Ave. NW, N6311, Washington, DC 20210. (202) 219-7910. FAX: (202) 219-4788.
DIRECTOR
Lionel White
EXECUTIVE PRODUCER
Stan Hankin

DEPARTMENT OF STATE

International Communications and Information Policy
Department of State, Rm. 4826, 2201 C St. NW, Washington, DC 20520. (202) 647-5727. FAX: (202) 647-5957.

DEPUTY ASST. SECRETARY
Ambassador Vonya B. McCann

Office of International Trade Control
Department of State, 1700 N. Lynn St., Rm. 200, Arlington, VA 22209. (703) 875-6644. FAX: (703) 0875-6647.

DIRECTOR OF STAFF
William Lowell

Office of Press Relations
Department of State, Rm. 2109-A, Washington, DC 20520. (202) 647-0874. FAX: (202) 647-0244.

DIRECTOR OF STAFF
John Dinger

DEPARTMENT OF TRANSPORTATION

Federal Highway Administration Audiovisual and Visual Aids
400 7th St. SW, Rm. 4429, HMS51, Washington, DC 20590. (202) 366-0481.

AUDIOVISUAL CHIEF
Colonel Giles

National Highway and Traffic Safety Administration
Public Affairs, Audiovisual Section, 400 7th St. SW, Rm. 5232, Washington, DC 20590. (202) 366-9550. FAX: (202) 366-5962.

PUBLIC AFFAIRS SPECIALIST
Tina Foley

U.S. Coast Guard Motion Picture & Television Liaison Office
11000 Wilshire Blvd., Room 10125, Los Angeles, CA 90024. (310) 235-7817. FAX: (310) 235-7851.

LIAISON OFFICERS
Cmdr. Dwight McGee, CWO Dan Dewell, CWO Lance Jones

U.S. Coast Guard Media Relations Branch
2100 2nd St. SW, Washington, DC 20593. (202) 267-1587. (202) 267-4307.

CHIEF OF DEPARTMENT
Lt. Cmdr. Pat Philbin

U.S. Coast Guard Audiovisual Branch, (202) 267-0923. FAX: (202) 267-4307.

AUDIOVISUAL SPECIALIST
Wayne Paugh

DEPARTMENT OF TREASURY

Office of Public Affairs
1500 Pennsylvania Ave. NW, Rm. 3442, Washington, DC 20220. (202) 622-2960. FAX: (202) 622-2808.

ASSISTANT SECRETARY
Howard Schloss

EXECUTIVE AGENCIES

ENVIRONMENTAL PROTECTION AGENCY

Audiovisual Division
401 M St. SW, North Conference, Washington, DC 20460. (202) 260-6735. FAX: (301) 585-7976.

DIRECTOR
Mawell Jama

FEDERAL COMMUNICATIONS COMMISSION

1919 M St. NW, Washington, DC 20554. (202) 418-0200. FAX: (202) 418-0999.

CHAIRMAN
Reed E. Hunt

COMMISSIONERS
James H. Quello, Andrew C. Barrett, Rachelle B. Chong, Susan Ness

CHIEF JUDGE, OFFICE OF ADMINISTRATIVE LAW JUDGES
Joesph Stirmer

GENERAL COUNSEL
William E. Kennard

MANAGING DIRECTOR
Andrew S. Fishel

CHIEF, MASS MEDIA BUREAU
Roy J. Steward

CHIEF, CABLE SERVICES BUREAU
Meredith Jones

CHIEF, COMMON CARRIER BUREAU
Kthleen M.H. Wallman

CHIEF, COMPLIANCE & INFORMATION BUREAU
Beverly G. Baker

DIRECTOR, OFFICE OF LEGISLATIVE & INT'L GOVERNMENTAL AFFAIRS
Judith L. Harris

Office of Public Affairs (202) 418-0500.

DEPUTY DIRECTOR, PUBLIC AFFAIRS
Maureen Pertino

FEDERAL TRADE COMMISSION

6th St. and Pennsylvania Ave. NW, Washington, DC 20580. (202) 326-2180. FAX: (202) 326-2050.

CHAIRMAN
Robert Pitofsky

LIBRARY OF CONGRESS

Copyright Office
Madison Bldg., Rm. 403, Washington, DC 20540. (202) 707-8350. FAX: (202) 707-8366.

REGISTER OF COPYRIGHTS
Marybeth Peters

Copyright Cataloging Division
Rm. 513. (202) 707-8040. FAX: (202) 707-8049.

CHIEF OF DIVISION
William Collins

Motion Picture, Collections Services,
Madison Bldg., Rm. 338, Washington, DC 20540. (202) 707-5840. FAX: (202) 707-2371.

CHIEF OF DIVISION
David Francis

NATIONAL AERONAUTICS & SPACE ADMINISTRATION

NASA Video Library
Code AP42, Bldg. 423, Johnson Space Center, Houston, TX 77058. (713) 483-2973. FAX: (713) 483-2848.

DIRECTOR
Jody Russel

NATIONAL ARCHIVES AND RECORDS ADMINISTRATION

Motion Picture Sound and Video Branch
7th St. & Pennsylvania Ave. NW, Room 2W, Washington, DC 20408. (202) 501-5449.

BRANCH CHIEF
Jack Saunders

Presidential Libraries Central Office
7th St. & Pennsylvania Ave. NW, Rm. 104, Washington, DC 20408. (202) 501-5700. FAX: (202) 501-5709.

ACTING DIRECTOR
Lewis Bellardo

NATIONAL ENDOWMENT FOR THE ARTS

Creation & Presentation—Media Arts Program
1100 Pennsylvania Ave. NW, Rm. 726, Washington, DC 20506. (202) 682-5452. FAX: (202) 682-5721.

MEDIA ARTS DIRECTOR
Brian O'Doherty

NATIONAL ENDOWMENT FOR THE HUMANITIES

Humanities Projects in Media
1100 Pennsylvania Ave. NW, Rm. 426, Washington, DC 20506. (202) 606-8278. FAX: (202) 606-8557.

PROGRAM OFFICER
James Dougherty

SECURITIES AND EXCHANGE COMMISSION

Division of Corporation Finance
450 5th St. NW, Washington, DC 20549. (202) 942-8088.

Radio, Television, and Telegraph
Rm. 3113. (202) 942-2800. FAX: (202) 942-9525.

ASSISTANT DIRECTOR
H. Christopher Owings

Motion Pictures
Rm. 3134. (202) 942-1800.

ASSISTANT DIRECTOR
James Daly

SMITHSONIAN INSTITUTION

Film Archives
Archives Division, National Air and Space Museum,
Washington, DC 20560. (202) 357-3133. FAX: (202) 786-2835.

FILM ARCHIVIST
Mark Taylor

447

Telecommunications Office
National Museum of American History, Rm. BB40,
Washington, DC 20560. (202) 357-2984. FAX: (202) 357-1565.
DIRECTOR
Paul Johnson

U.S. INFORMATION AGENCY
Television and Film Service
601 D St. NW, Rm. 5000, Washington, DC 20547. (202) 501-7806. FAX: (202) 501-6664.
DIRECTOR
Charles W. Fox

U.S. INTERNATIONAL TRADE COMMISSION
Office of the Secretary
500 E Street, Rm. 112, Washington, DC 20436. (202) 205-2000. FAX: (202) 205-2104.
SECRETARY
Donna R. Koehnke

MILITARY FILM LIAISONS

ARMY CHIEF OF PUBLIC AFFAIRS
11000 Wilshire Blvd., Room 10104, Los Angeles, CA 90024-3688. (310) 235-7621. FAX: (310) 473-8874.

CHIEF OF PUBLIC AFFAIRS
Lt. Col. Alfred Lott
TECHNICAL ADVISOR
Master Sgt. Grant Stombaugh
PUBLIC INFORMATION OFFICER
Kathy Canham Ross

MARINE CORPS PUBLIC AFFAIRS
11000 Wilshire Blvd., Room 10117, Los Angeles, CA 90024. (310) 235-7272. FAX: (310) 235-7274.
OFFICER IN CHARGE
Major N. J. LaLuntas

U. S. AIR FORCE, MOTION PICTURE AND TELEVISION LIAISON OFFICE
11000 Wilshire Blvd., Room 10114, Los Angeles, CA 90024. (310) 235-7522. FAX: (310) 235-7500.
CHIEF, ENTERTAINMENT LIAISON
Charles E. Davis

U. S. COAST GUARD, MOTION PICTURE AND TELEVISION OFFICE
11000 Wilshire Blvd., Los Angeles, CA 90024. (310) 235-7817. FAX: (310) 235-7851.
LIAISON OFFICERS
Cmdr. Dwight McGee, CWO Dan Dewell, CWO Lance Jones

INTERNATIONAL
FESTIVALS & MARKETS

Listed by month. The address and telephone number of Festival Organizers have been provided for your convenience.

JANUARY

Annual Kidfilm Festival, U.S.A. Film Festival
2917 Swiss Ave., Dallas, TX 75205
(214) 821-6300. FAX: (214) 821-6364

Palm Springs International Film Festival
P.O. Box 2930, Palm Springs, CA 92263
(619) 322-2930. FAX: (619) 322-4087

Filmfestival Max Ophuls Prize
Mainzerstrasse 8, 6600 Saarbrucken, Germany
(49-681) 329452. FAX: (49-681) 9051943

Brussels International Film Festival
30 Chausee de Louvain, B-1030 Brussels, Belgium
(2) 2181055. FAX: (2) 2186627

FIPA (Festival International de Programmes Audiovisuel)
Faubourg St. Honore, 75008 Paris, France
(33-1) 45 61 01 66. FAX: (33-1) 40 74 07 96

Fajr International Film Festival
Farhang Cinema, Dr. Shariati Avenue, Gholhak, Tehran 19139
Iran. (21) 2052088. FAX: (21) 267082

Solothurner Filmtage
P.O. Box 1030, CH-4502 Solothurn, Switzerland
(0) 65 233161. FAX: (0) 65 236410

Clermont-Ferrand Short Film Festival
26 rue des Jacobins, 63000 Clermont-Ferrand, France
73 91 65 73. FAX: 73 92 11 93

Rotterdam International Film Festival
P.O. Box 21696, 3001 AR Rotterdam, Netherlands
(10) 411 8080. FAX: (10) 413 5132

Tromso International Film Festival
Georgernes Verft 3, 5011 Bergen, Norway
(55) 322 590. FAX: (55) 323 740

International Film Festival of India
Ministry of Information & Broadcasting, Government of India,
Lok Nayak Bhavan, Khan Market, New Delhi 110003
(11) 461 5963. FAX: (11) 469 4920

CineAsia
Cinema Expo International, 244 W. 49th Street, New York,
NY 10019 (212) 246-6460. FAX: (212) 265-6428

NATPE
2425 Olympic Blvd., Suite 550E, Santa Monica, CA 90404
(310) 453-4440. FAX: (310) 453-5258

Sundance Film Festival
P.O. Box 16450, Salt Lake City, UT 84116 (801) 328-3455.
FAX: (801) 575 5174

FEBRUARY

MILIA
MIDEM Organisation, 179 ave. Victor Hugo, 75016 Paris,
France. (33-1) 44 34 44 44. FAX: (3301) 44 34 44 00

Berlin International Film Festival
Budapesterstrasse 50, 10787 Berlin, Germany
(49-30) 254 890. FAX: (49-30) 2548 9249

Fantasporto (Opporto International Film Festival)
Rua da Constituicao 311, 4200 Potro, Portugal
(2) 550 8990. FAX: (2) 550 8210

Gothenburg Film Festival
Box 7079, 40232 Gothenburg, Sweden
(31) 410 546. FAX: (31) 410 063

Miami Film Festival
444 Brickell Avenue, Miami, FL 33131
(305) 377-3456. FAX: (305) 577-9768

Hungaria Film Week
Magyar Filmunio, Varoslglieti Sasor 38, 1068 Budapest, Hungary
(1) 269 7760. FAX: (1) 268 0070

Monte Carlo Television Festival & Market
Boulevard Louis II, 98000 Monaco
104 060. FAX: 507 014

American Film Market
Ms. Brady Caine, AMFA, 120850 Wilshire Blvd., 9th fl., Los
Angeles, CA 90024. (310) 446-1000. FAX: (310) 446-1600

Brussels Cartoon & Animated Film Festival, Folioscope
rue de la Rhetorique 19, B-1060 Brussels, Belgium
(2) 534 4125. FAX: (2) 534 2279

Portland International Film Festival
Northwest Film Center, 1219 S.W. Park Ave., Portland, OR
97205. (503) 221-1156. FAX: (503) 226-4842

Aspen Shortfest
P.O. Box 8910, Aspen, CO 81611
(910) 925-6882. FAX: (910) 925-1967

MARCH

NATO ShoWest
116 North Robertson, Suite F, Los Angeles, CA 90048
(310) 654-7724. FAX: (310) 657 4758

Santa Barbara International Film Festival
1216 State St., Santa Barbara, CA 93101
(805) 963-0023. FAX: (805) 962-2524

Fribourg Film Festival
rue de Locarno 8, 1700 Fribourg, Switzerland
(37) 222 232. FAX: (37) 227 950

Dublin Film Festival
1 Suffolk Street, Dublin 2, Ireland
(1) 679 2937. FAX: (1) 679 2939

Tampere International Short Film Festival
Box 305, 33101 Tampere, Finland
(31) 213 0034. FAX: (31) 223 0121

Brussels International Festival of Fantasy, Thriller & Science Fiction Films
111 avenue de la Reine, 1210 Brussels, Belgium
(2) 201 1713. FAX: (2) 201 1469

Bergamo Film Meeting
Via Pascoli 3, 24121 Bergamo, Italy
(35) 234011. FAX: (35) 233129

International Women's Film Festival
Maison des Arts, Place Salvador Allende, 94000 Creteil,
France. (1) 49 80 39 98. FAX: (1) 43 99 04 10

Local Heroes International Screen Festival
10022-103 St., Edmonton, Alberta T5J 0X2, Canada
(403) 421-4084. FAX: (403) 425-8090

New Directors/New Films
The Film Society of Lincoln Center, 70 Lincoln Center Plaza,
New York, NY 10023. (212) 875-5610. FAX: (212) 875-5636

San Francisco Asian American International Film Festival
346 Ninth St., San Francisco, CA 94103
(415) 863-0814. FAX: (415) 863-7428

London Lesbian & Gay Film Festival
National Film Theatre, South Bank, Waterloo, London SE1
8XT, England. (171) 815 1323. FAX: (171) 633 0786

Cartagena Film Festival
P.O. Box 1834, Cartagena, Colombia
(5753) 600 966. FAX: (5753) 600 970

APRIL

MIP – TV
MIDEM Organisation, 179 avenue Victor Hugo, 75016 Paris,
France. (33 1) 44 34 44 44. FAX: (33 1) 44 34 44 00

Los Angeles International Animation Celebration
28024 Dorothy Dr., Agoura Hills, CA 91301
(818) 991-2884. FAX: (818) 991-3773

Istanbul International Film Festival
Istiklal Caddest 146, Luvr Apt. Beyoglu, 80070 Istanbul,
Turkey. (212) 293 31 33. FAX: (212) 249 77 71

Hong Kong International Film Festival
Festivals Office, Level 7, Administration Bldg., Hong Kong
Cultural Centre, 10 Salisbury Rd., Tsimshatsui, Kowloon,
Hong Kong. 734 2903. FAX: 366 5206

Singapore International Film Festival
169 Kim Seng Road, Singapore 0923
738 7567. FAX: 738 7578

Black Filmworks
Black Filmmakers Hall of Fame, P.O. Box 28055, Oakland,
CA 94606. (510) 465-0804. FAX: (510) 839-9858

USA Film Festival
2917 Swiss Ave., Dallas, TX 75204
(214) 821 6300. FAX: (214) 821 6364

Chicago Latino Film Festival
600 South Michigan Ave., Chicago, IL 60605
(312) 431-1330. FAX: (312) 360-0629

Worldfest – Houston
P.O. Box 56566, Houston, TX 77256
(713) 965-9955. FAX: (713) 965-9960

Rivertown: Minneapolis/
St. Paul International Film Festival
425 Ontario St. S.E., Minneapolis, MN 55414
(612) 627-4432. FAX: (612) 627-4111

Cape Town International Film Festival
c/o University of Cape Town, Private Bag, Rondebosch 7700,
Cape Town, South Africa. (21) 238 257. FAX: (21) 242 355

International Cinema Week
Via S. Giacomo alla Pignano. 6, 37121 Verona, Italy
(45) 800 6778. FAX: (45) 590 624

International Short Film Festival Oberhausen
Christian-Steger Strasse 10, 46042 Oberhausen, Germany.
(208) 807 008. FAX: (45) 590 624

International Electronic Cinema Festival
P.O. Box 1451, 1820 Montreux, Switzerland
(21) 963 3220. FAX: (21) 963 8851

Baltimore Film Festival
10 Art Museum Drive, Baltimore, MD 21218
(410) 889-1993. FAX: (410) 889-2567

Cleveland International Film Festival
The Cleveland Film Society, 1621 Euclid Ave., Cleveland, OH
44115. (216) 623-0400. FAX: (216) 623-0101

San Francisco International Film Festival
1521 Eddy Street, San Francisco, CA 94115
(415) 929-5000. FAX: (415) 921-5032

Cognac International Film Festival of the Thriller
c/o Promo 2000, 36 rue Perriet, 92200 Neuilly-sur-Seine,
France. 46 40 55 00. FAX: 46 40 55 39

Academic Film Olomuc
Krizkiveskeho 8, 771 47 Olomuc, Czech Republic
(68) 5508 277. FAX: (68) 26 476

Festival of French Cinema
Tel Aviv Cinematheque, 2 Sprintzak St., Tel Aviv, Israel

Lille International Festival of Short & Documentary Films
24-34 rue Washington, 75008 Paris, France

MAY

Cannes Film Festival
99 Boulevard Malesherbes, 75008 Paris, France
(33 1) 45 61 66 00. FAX: (33 1) 45 61 97 60

Philadelphia Festival of World Cinema
Int'l House of Philadelphia, 3701 Chestnut St., Philadelphia,
PA 19104. (215) 895-6593. FAX: (215) 895-6562

Brighton Festival
21-22 Old Steine, Brighton, BN1 1EL, England
(12 73) 713 875. FAX: (12 73) 622 453

Independent Film Days
Filmburo Augsburg, Schroeckstrasse 6, 86152 Augsburg,
Germany. (821) 153 077. FAX: (821) 155 518

Seattle International Film Festival
801 East Pine Street, Seattle, WA 98122
(206) 324-9996. FAX: (206) 324-9998

Ethnogenre Film Festival
184 Dorchester Rd., Rochester, NY 14610
(716) 288-2152. FAX: (716) 288-2156

Prix Danube
Mylneska Dolina, 845 45 Bratislava, Slovakia
(7) 727 448. FAX: (7) 729 440

International Short Film Festival – Kracow
c/o Apollo Film, ul. Pychowicka 7, 30-364 Kracow, Poland
(12) 672 340. FAX: (12) 671 552

Golden Prague International TV Festival
Czechoslovak TV, Kaveci Hory 140 70, Prague 4, Czech
Republic. (2) 6121 2882. FAX: (2) 6121 2891

The Human Rights Watch International Film Festival
485 Fifth Ave., New York, NY 10017
(212) 972-8400. (212) 972-0905

New England Film & Video Festival
Boston Film/Video Foundation, 1126 Boylston St., Boston,
MA 02215. (617) 536-1540. FAX: (617) 536-3576

JUNE

Cinema Expo International
244 West 49th Street, New York, NY 10019
(212) 246-6460. FAX: (212) 265-6428

Sydney Film Festival
Paul Byrnes, P.O. Box 950, Glebe, NSW 2037, Australia
(2) 660 3844. fax: (2) 692 8793

Austrian Film Days
Austrian Film Office, Columbusgasse 2, 1100 Vienna, Austria
(1) 604 0126. FAX: (1) 602 0795

Florida Film Festival
Enzian Theater, 1300 S. Orlando Ave., Maitland, FL 32789
(407) 629-1088. FAX: (407) 629-6870

Melbourne International Film Festival
P.O. Box 2206, Fitzroy Mail Centre, Victoria 3065, Australia
(3) 9417 2011. FAX: (3) 9417 3804

The Montreal International Festival of New
Cinema & Video
3726 Blvd. St. Laurent, Montreal, Quebec H2X 2V8, Canada
(514) 843-4725. FAX: (514) 843-4631

Bellaria Film Festival
Viale Paolo Guidi 108, 47041 Bellaria Igea Marina (RN), Italy
(541) 347 186. FAX: (541) 347 186

Vue Sur Les Docs
3 Square Stalingrad, 13001 Marseille, France
91 84 40 17. FAX: 91 84 38 34

San Francisco Lesbian & Gay Film
Festival and Market
Frameline, 346 Ninth St., San Francisco, CA 94103
(415) 703-8658. FAX: (415) 861-1404

Banff Television Festival
P.O. Box 219, Suite 9000, Banff, Alberta TOL OCO, Canada
(403) 678-9260. FAX: (403) 678-9269

International Advertising Film Festival
c/o 2nd floor, Woolverstone House, 61-62 Berners St., London
W1P 3AE, England. (171) 636 6122. FAX: (171) 636 6086

Munich Film Festival
Kaiserstrasse 39, 80801 Munich, Germany
(89) 381 9040. FAX: (89) 381 90427

London Jewish Film Festival
South Bank, Waterloo, London SE1 8XT, England
(171) 815 1322. FAX: (171) 633 0786

Mystfest (International Mystery Film Festival)
Centro Cultural Polivalente, Piazza Della Repubblica 34, 47033
Catolica (FO), Italy. (541) 967 802. FAX: (541) 967 803.

Donostia Screenings
c/o Euroaim, 210 avenue Winston Churchill, B-1180 Brussels,
Belgium. (2) 346 1500. FAX: (2) 346 3842

La Rochelle International Film Festival
16 rue Saint Sabin, 75011 Paris, France
(1) 48 06 16 66. FAX: (1) 48 06 15 40

Newark Black Film Festival
The Newark Museum Assn., 49 Washington St., P.O. Box 540,
Newark, NJ 07101. (201) 596-6637. FAX: (201) 642-0459

AFI Los Angeles International Film Festival
2021 N. Western Ave., Los Angeles, CA 90027
(213) 856-7707. FAX: (213) 462-4049

Dylan Dog Horror Films
Via M. Buonarotti 38, 20145 Milan, Italy
(2) 4800 2877. FAX: (2) 4801 1937

French American Film Workshop
10 Montee de la Tour, Villeneuve Les Avignon, France
90 25 93 23. FAX: 90 25 93 24

Marketskaya
c/o Seineva Organisation, 10 rue de la Boetie, 75008 Paris,
France. (1) 53 76 16 28. FAX: (1) 45 61 94 27

Midnight Sun Film Festival
Malminkatu 36 B 102, Helsinki, Finland
(0) 685 2242. FAX: (0) 694 5560

Pesaro Film Festival
Via Villefranca 20, 00185 Rome, Italy
(6) 445 6643. FAX: (6) 491 163

Festival of Festivals
10 Kamennoostrovsky Ave., St. Petersburg 197101, Russia
(812) 238 5811. FAX: (812) 232 8881

Troia International Film Festival
Troia, 2902 Setubal Codex, Portugal
(65) 441 21. FAX: (65) 441 23

Norwegian Short Film Festival
Storengveien 8B, N-1342 Jar, Norway
(67) 122 013. FAX: (67) 124 865

JULY

Philafilm
IAMPTP, 215 South Broad St., Philadelphia, PA 19107
(215) 977-2831. FAX: (215) 546-8055

19th Asian American International Film Festival
Asian Cinevision, 32 E. Broadway, New York, NY 10002
(212) 925-8685. FAX: (212) 925-8157

Vevey International Comedy Film Festival
Buureau du Festival du Film de Comedie, La Greneyye,
Grand Place 29, CH-1800 Vevey, Switzerland.
(21) 922 2027. FAX: (21) 922 2024

Auckland International Film Festival
P.O. Box 9544, Wellington, New Zealand
(4) 385 0162. FAX: (4) 801 7304

Cambridge Film Festival
Cambridge Arts Cinema, 8 Market Passage, Cambridge CB2
2PF, England. (1223) 352 001. FAX: (1223) 462 555

Durban International Film Festival
U. of Natal, King George V Ave., Durban 4001, South Africa.
(31) 811 3978. FAX: (31) 261 7107

International Film Festival of Gijon
Paseo de Begona 24, Entreselvo, 33205 Gijon, Spain
(85) 343 735. FAX: (85) 354 152

Jerusalem Film Festival
P.O. Box 8561, Jerusalem, Israel
(2) 724 131. FAX: (2) 733 076

Karlovy Vary Film Festival
Ministry of Culture, Nadace, Valdstejnsska 12, 11811 Prague 1,
Czech Republic. (2) 513 2473. FAX: (2) 530 542

Short & Documentary Film Festival
Farhang Cinema, Dr. Shariati Ave., Gholbak, Tehran 19139,
Iran. 265 086. FAX: 678 155

Taormina International Film Festival
Via Pirandello 31, 98039 Taormina, Italy
(942) 211 42. FAX: (942) 233 48

Hometown Video Festival
Buske Group, 30001 J Street, Sacramento, CA 95816
(916) 441-6277. FAX: (916) 441-7670

Wellington Film Festival
P.O. Box 9544, Te Aro, Wellington, New Zealand
(4) 385 0162. FAX: (4) 801 7304

Wine Country Film Festival
12000 Henro Rd., P.O. Box 303, Glen Ellen, CA 95442
(707) 996-2536. FAX: (707) 996-6964

AUGUST

Montreal World Film Festival
Serge Losique, 1432 de Bleury St., Montreal, Quebec,
Canada H3A 2J1. (514) 848-3883. FAX: (514) 848-3886

Odense International Film Festival
Vindegade 18, DK-5000 Odense C, Denmark
(45) 6613 1372. FAX: (45) 6591 4318

Giffoni International Film Festival
Piazza Umberto 1, 84095 Giffoni Valle Piana (Salerno), Italy
(89) 868 544. FAX: (89) 866 111

Locarno International Film Festival
Via della Posta 6, Cassella Postale, 6600 Locarno, Switzerland
(93) 310 232. FAX: (93) 317 465

Gramado Cinema Festival
Avenida des Hortensias 2029, Cap. 9567, 1000 Gramado,
R.G. Sul, Brazil. (54) 286 2335. FAX: (54) 286 2397

Drambuie Edinburgh Film Festival
88 Lothian Road, Edinburgh EH3 9BZ, Scotland
(131) 228 4051. FAX: (131) 228 5501

Espoo Cine Film Festival
P.O. Box 95, 02101 Espoo, Finland
(0) 466 599. FAX: (0) 466 458

International Animation Festival in Japan-Hiroshima
4-17 Kalo-machi, Naka-ku, Hirshima 730, Japan
(82) 245 0245. FAX: (82) 245 1246

Norwegian International Film Festival
P.O. Box 145, 5501 Haugesund, Norway
(52) 734 430. FAX: (52) 734 420

Brisbane International Film Festival
Level 3, Hoyts Regent Bldg., 167 Queen St. Mall, Brisbane,
Queensland 4000, Australia
(7) 3 220 0333. FAX: (7) 3 220 0400.

Alexandria Film Festival
9 Oraby Street, Cairo, Eqypt
578 0042. FAX: 768 727

Weekly Mail/Guardian Film Festival
P.O. Box 2601245, Excom 2023, South Africa
(11) 331 1712. FAX: (11) 331 3339

SEPTEMBER

Toronto International Film Festival
2 Carlton, Toronto, Ontario M5B 1J3, Canada
(416) 967-7371. FAX: (416) 967-9477

Venice Film Festival (Biennale)
Mostra Internazionale d'Arte Cinematografica, La Biennale,
San Marco, Ca'Giustinian, 30124 Venice, Italy
(41) 521 8860. FAX: (41) 520 0569. Telex: 410685 BLE-VE-1

San Sebastian International Film Festival
Plaza de Okendo s/n, Donostioa-San Sebastian 20080, Spain
(43) 481 212. FAX: (43) 481 212

Festival International de Cinema Figueira da Foz
Partado dos Correios 50407, 1709 Lisbon Codex, Portugal
(1) 346 9556. FAX: (1) 342 0890

Banco Nacional International Film Festival
Rua Voluntarios de Patria 97, Botafogo, Rio de Janeiro
22270, Brazil. (21) 286 8505. FAX: (21) 286 4029

Telluride Film Festival
Box B-1156, 53 South Main St., Suite 212, Hanover, NH
03755. (603) 643-1255. FAX: (603) 643-5938

Deauville Festival of American Films
c/o Promo, 36 rue Perriet, 92200 Neuilly-sur-Seine, France
(1) 46 40 55 00. FAX: (1) 46 40 55 39

Santa Fe de Bogota Festival
Calle 26 No. 4-92, Aparteado Aereo 23398, Santa Fe de
Bogota, Colombia. (1) 282 5196. FAX: (1) 342 2872

International Children's Film Festival
Deutsches Filmmuseum, Schaumainkai 41, 60596 Frankfurt-
am-Main, Germany. (69) 2123 3369. FAX: (69) 2123 7881

Boston Film Festival
333 Victory Rd., Quincy, MA 02171
(617) 471-1778. FAX: (617) 479-0778

Prix Italia
c/o RAI, Viale Mazzini 14, 00195 Rome, Italy
(6) 3751 4996. FAX: (6) 3613 3401

Copenhagen Film Festival
Bulowsvej 50A, DK-1870 Frederiksberg C, Copenhagen,
Denmark. (45) 3537 2507. FAX: (45) 3135 5758

Independent Feature Film Market
104 West 29th St., New York, NY 10011
(212) 465-8200. FAX: (212) 465-8525

International Film Forum "Arsenals"
Marstalulela 14, P.O. Box 626, LV-1047 Riga, Latvia
(2) 221 620. FAX: (2) 882 0445

Haifa International Film Festival
142 Hanassi Ave., Haifa 34633, Israel
(4) 386 246. FAX: (4) 384 327

Netherlands Film Festival
Hoogt 4, 3512 GW Utrecht, Netherlands
(30) 2 322 684. FAX: (30) 2 313 200

Magdeburg International Film Festival
Coquistrasse 18A, D-39104 Magdeburg, Germany
(391) 401 0875. FAX: (391) 48668

America Film Festival
Museumstrasse 31, A-6020 Innsbruck, Austria
(512) 580 723. FAX: (512) 581 762

British Short Film Festival
Room 313, BBC Threshold House, 65-69 Shepherds Bush
Green, London W12 7RJ, England
(181) 743 8000. FAX: (181) 740 8540

Helsinki Film Festival – Love and Anarchy
Unioninkatu 10 A 27, SF-00130 Helsinki, Finland
(0) 629 528. FAX: (0) 631 450

Europacinema Festival
Via Giulia 66, 00186 Rome, Italy
(6) 686 7581. FAX: (6) 688 05417

Atlantic Film Festival
1541 Barrington St., Suite 326, Halifax, Nova Scotia, Canada
(902) 422-3456. FAX: (902) 422-4006

Aspen Filmfest
P.O. Box 8910, Aspen, Colorado
(303) 925-6882. FAX: (303) 925-1967

Ottawa International Animation Festival
2 Daly Ave., Ottaa, Ontario K1N 6E2, Canada
(613) 232-6727. FAX: (613) 232-6315

Hamburg Film Festival
Friedensallee 7, 22765 Hamburg, Germany
(40) 3982 6210. FAX: (40) 3982 6211

Feminale – International Women's Film Festival
Luxemburgerstrasse 72, D-50674 Cologne, Germany
(221) 416 066. FAX: (221) 417 568

Festival International du Film Francophone
175 rue des Brasseurs, 5000 Namur, Belgium
(81) 241 236. FAX: (81) 241 164

Cairo International Children's Film Festival
17 Kasr El Nil St., Cairo, Eqypt
3923 562. FAX: 3938 979

Tokyo International Film Festival
4th Floor, Landic Ginza Bldg. II, 1-6-5 Ginza, Chuo-Ku,
Tokyo 104, Japan. (3) 3563 6305. FAX: (3) 3563 6310

Vancouver International Film Festival
Ste. 410-1008 Homer St., Vancouver B.C. V6B 2X1, Canada
(604) 685 0260. FAX: (604) 688 8221

OCTOBER

ShowEast
NATO ShowEast, 244 W. 49th Street, Suite 200, New York,
NY 10019. (212) 246-6460. FAX: (212) 265-6428

New York Film Festival
Film Society of Lincoln Center, 70 Lincoln Center Plaza, New
York, NY 10023. (212) 875-5610. FAX: (212) 875-5636

MIPCOM
MIDEM Organisation, 179 avenue Victor Hugo, 75016 Paris,
France. (3301) 44 34 44 44. FAX: (3301) 44 34 44 00

MIFED
Mrs. Elena Lloyd, E.A. Fiera Internazionale di Milano, Largo
Dommodossola 1, 20145 Milano, Italy.
(39-2) 48012 912 x 2920. FAX: (39-2) 49977 020

Shots In The Dark
Broadway, 14 Broad Street, Nottingham, NG1 3 AL, England
(115) 952 6600. FAX: (115) 952 6622

Cork Film Festival
Festival Office, Hatfield House, Tobin St., Cork, Ireland
(21) 271 711. FAX: (21) 275 945

Israel Film Festival
IsraFest Foundation, 6404 Wilshire Blvd., Suite 1151, Los
Angeles CA 90048. (213) 966-4166. FAX: (213) 658-6346

Mill Valley Film Festival
38 Miller Ave., Mill Valley CA 94941
(415) 383-5256. FAX: (415) 383-8606

Warsaw Film Festival
P.O. Box 816, 00-950 Warsaw 1, Poland
Tel/FAX: (2) 635 7591

Flanders International Film Festival
Kortrijksesteenweg 1104, B-9051 Ghent, Belgium
(9) 221 8946. FAX: (9) 221 9074

Sitges Fantasy Film Festival
Calle Rossello 257, 3E, 08008 Barcelona, Spain
(3) 415 3938. FAX: (3) 237 6521

Pordenone Silent Film Festival
c/o La Cineteca del Friuli, Via Osoppo 26, 33013 (UD) Italy
(432) 980 458. FAX: (432) 970 542

Nyon – Visions du Reel
Case Postale 2320, CH-1260, Nyon Switzerland
(22) 3 616 060. FAX: (22) 3 617 071

Independent Film Days
Filmburo Augsburg, Schroeckstrasse 6, 86152 Augsburg,
Germany. (821) 153 079. FAX: (821) 349 5218

Margaret Mead Film Festival
American Museum of Natural History, 79th St. & Central Park
West, New York, NY 10024
(212) 769-5305. FAX: (212) 769-5329

Denver International Film Festival
999 18th Street, Denver, CO 80202
(303) 298-8223. FAX: (303) 298-0209

Leeds International Film Festival
19 Wellington Street, Leeds LS1 4DG, England
(113) 247 8389. FAX: (113) 247 8397

Valencia Film Festival
Plaza del Arzobispo, 2 Bajo, 46003 Valencia, Spain
(96) 392 1506. FAX: (96) 391 5156

Birmingham International Film and Television Festival
c/o Central Independent TV, Central House, Broad Street,
Birmingham B1 2JP, England.
(121) 634 4213. FAX: (121) 634 4392

Viennale (Vienna International Film Festival)
Stiftgasse 6, A-1070 Vienna, Austria
(1) 526 5947. FAX: (1) 934 172

International Filmfestival Mannheim – Heidelberg
Collini Center, Galerie, D-68161 Mannheim, Germany
(621) 102 943. FAX: (621) 291 564

Sportel
6040 Boulevard East, Ste. 27C, West New York, NJ 07093.
(201) 869-4022. FAX: (201) 869-4335

Geneva Film Festival
Case Postale 561, CH-1211 Geneva 11, Switzerland
(22) 321 5466. FAX: (22) 321 9862

Hamptons International Film Festival
3 Newtown Mews, East Hampton, NY 11937
(516) 324-4600

Uppsala International Short Film Festival
Box 1746, S-75147, Uppsala, Sweden
(18) 120 025. FAX: (18) 121 350

Norwich Festival of Women Filmmakers
Cinema City, St. Andrews St., Norwich NR2 4AD, England
(16 3) 622 047

Chicago International Film Festival
415 N. Dearborn, Chicago, IL 60610
(312) 644-3400. FAX: (312) 644-0784

Los Angeles International Film Festival
AFI Festivals, 2021 N. Western Ave., Los Angeles, CA 90027
(213) 856-7707. FAX: (213) 462-4049

Montpellier Festival of Mediterranean Cinema
6 rue Vieille-Aguillerie, 34000 Montpellier, France
67 66 36 36. FAX: 67 66 36 37

Sao Paulo International Film Festival
Al. Lorena 937, CJ 303, 01424-001 Sao Paulo, Brazil
(11) 883 5137. FAX: (11) 853 7936

Valladolid International Film Festival
P.O. Box 646, 47080 Valladoli, Spain
(83) 305 700. FAX: (83) 309 835

International Hofer Filmtage
c/o Heinz Badewitz, Lothstrasse 28, 80335 Munich, Germany
(89) 129 7422. FAX: (89) 123 6868

San Juan Cinemafest
P.O. Box 4543, San Juan, Puerto Rico 00902
(809) 721-6125. FAX: (809) 723-6412

Yamagata International Documentary Film Festival
Kitagawa Building, 4th floor, 6-42 Kagurazaka Shinjuku-ku,
Tokyo 162, Japan. (3) 3266 9704. FAX: (3) 3266 9700

NOVEMBER

London Film Festival
London Film Festival, South Bank, London SE1 8XT, England
(717) 815 1322. FAX: (171) 633 0786

Annual SPAA Conference
Southern Cross Hotel, 131 Exhibition St., Melbourne 3001,
Australia. (2) 262 2277. FAX: (2) 262 2323

Film Art Festival
Cankarjec Dom, Presernova 10, 61000 Ljubljana, Slovenia
(61) 125 8121. FAX: (61) 212 492

Fort Lauderdale International Film Festival
2633 East Sunrise Blvd., Fort Lauderdale, FL 33304-3205

Heartland Film Festival
613 N. East Street, Indianapolis, IN 46202
(317) 464-9405. FAX: (317) 635-4201

Nordic Film Days Lubeck
D-23539 Lubeck, Germany
(451) 122 4105. FAX: (451) 122 7197

Northwest Film & Video Festival
Northwest Film Center, 1219 S.W. Park Ave., Portland, OR
97205. (503) 221-1156. FAX: (503) 226-4842

Amiens International Film Festival
36 rue de Noyon, 8000 Amiens, France
22 91 01 44. FAX: 22 92 53 04

British Film Festival
8 Passage Digard, 50100 Cherbourg, France
33 93 38 94. FAX: 33 01 20 78

Hawaii International Film Festival
700 Bishop St., Suite 400, Honolulu, HI 96813
(808) 528-3456. FAX: (808) 528-1410

Children's Film Festival
Filmburo Augsberg, Schroekstr. 6, 86152 Augsberg, Germany
(821) 153 079. FAX: (821) 349 5218

Duisberg Film Week
Am Konig-Heinrich-Platz, D-47049, Guisberg, Germany
(203) 283 4187. FAX: (203) 283 4130

Cinequest (The San Jose Film Festival)
P.O. Box 720040, San Jose, CA 95172
(408) 995-6305. FAX: (408) 277-3862

Sarasota French Film Festival
5555 North Tamiami Trail, Sarasota, FL 34243
(813) 351-9010. FAX: (813) 351-5796

Worldfest – Charleston
P.O. Box 838, Charleston, SC 29401
(713) 965-9955. FAX: (713) 965-9960

New York Exposition of Short Film & Video
New York Expo, 532 La Guardia Place, Box 330, New York,
NY. (212) 505-7742

Puerto Rico International Film Festival
70 Mayaguez St., Ste. B-1 Hato Rey, Puerto Rico 00918
(809) 764-7044. FAX: (809) 763-4997

International Thessaloniki Film Festival
36 Sina Street, GR 10672 Athens, Greece
(1) 361 0418. FAX: (1) 362 1023

Stockholm International Film Festival
P.O. Box 7673, 10395 Stockholm, Sweden
(8) 200 950

Welsh International Film Festival
Unit 8C, Cefn Llan, Aberystwyth, Dyfed SY23 3AH, Wales
(1970) 617 995. FAX: (1970) 617 942

Festival Sinatron Indonesia
Sekretariat Pantap, Kedoya Center, Jl. Perjuangan-Block II
No. 1, Kebon Jeruk, Jakarta 11063, Indonesia
(21) 533 0467. FAX: (21) 533 0467

Junior Dublin Film Festival
Irish Film Centre, 6 Eustace St., Dublin 2, Ireland
(1) 677 7095. FAX: (1) 677 8755

Oulu International Children's Film Festival
Torikatu 8, 90100 Oulu, Finland
(81) 314 1735. FAX: (81) 314 1730

Tyneside European Film Festival
Tyneside Cinema, 10 Pilgrim St., Newcastle-upon-Tyne NE1
6QG, England. (191) 232 8289. FAX: (191) 221 0535

Festival Internazionale Cinema Giovani
Via Monte di Pieta 1, 10120 Torino, Italy
(11) 562 3309. FAX: (11) 562 9796

Raindance Film Showcase & Market
81 Berwick St., London W1V 3PF, England
(171) 437 3991. FAX: (171) 439 2243

Holland Animation Film Festival
Hoogt 4, 3512 GW Utrecht, The Netherlands
(30) 312 216. FAX: (30) 312 940

International Animated Film Festival
Rua 62, No. 251 4501 Espinho Codex, Portugal
(2) 721 611. FAX: (2) 726 015

Festival dei Popoli
Via Castellani 8, 50122 Firenze, Italy
(55) 294 353. FAX: (55) 213 698

Festival International
du Film Juif et Israelien de Montpellier
500 Boulevard d'Antigone, 34000 Montpellier, France
67 15 08 72. FAX: 67 15 08 72

Cairo International Film Festival
17 Kasr El Nir Street, Cairo, Egypt
(3) 392 3962. FAX: (2) 392 3562

The Americas Film Festival
19th & Constitution Ave., NW, Washington DC 20006
(202) 458-6379. FAX: (202) 458-3122

Festival des 3 Continents
19 Passage Pmmeraye, BP-3306, 44033 Nantes Cedex 01,
France. 40 69 74 14. FAX: 40 73 55 22

Taipei Golden Horse Film Festival
Room 7F, No. 45 Chilin Rd., Taipei 104, Taiwan
(2) 567 5861. FAX: (2) 531 8966

DECEMBER

MIP Asia Screenings & Conferences
Reed Midem Organisation, 179 Victor Hugo, 75116 Paris,
France. (1) 44 34 44 44. FAX: (1) 44 34 44 00

Rencontres du Cinema Italien D'Annecy
Banlieu Scene Nationale, 1 rue Jean Jaures-BP 294, 74007
Annecy Cedex, France. 50 33 44 00. FAX: 50 51 82 09

Noir In Festival
Via dei Coronari 44, 00186 Rome, Italy
(6) 683 3844. FAX: (6) 686 7902

International Documentary Filmfestival
Amsterdam (IFDA)
Kleine Gartmenplantsoen 10, 1017 RR Amsterdam, The
Netherlands. (20) 627 3329. FAX: (20) 638 5388

Festival of International Cinema Students
FFICS Secretariat, c/o Tokyo Agency Inc., 4-8-18 Akasaka,
Minato-ku, Tokyo 107, Japan
(3) 3475 3855. FAX: (3) 5411 0382

Essen International Festival of Films
for Children
Baumstrasse 24, D-45128 Essen, Germany
(201) 794 951. FAX: (201) 794 952

TRADE PUBLICATIONS

QUIGLEY PUBLISHING COMPANY
Publishers of International Motion Picture Almanac (Annual), International Television and Video Almanac (Annual) and Quigleys Entertainment Industry Reference CD-ROM. 159 W. 53 St., New York, NY 10019. (212) 247-3100. FAX: (212) 489-0871. email: QUIGLEYPUB@aol.com
PRESIDENT AND PUBLISHER
Martin Quigley
VICE PRESIDENT
Katherine D. Quigley
EDITOR & VICE PRESIDENT
James D. Moser
MANAGING EDITOR
Tracy Stevens
EDITORIAL ASSISTANT
Alicia Ocana

LONDON BUREAU
William Pay, Manager and London Editor. 15 Samuel Rd., Langdon Hills, Basildon, Essex SS16 6E, England. (01 268) 417-055.

CANADIAN BUREAU
Patricia Thompson, Editor. 1430 Yonge St., Suite 214, Toronto, Ont. M4T 1Y6 Canada.

FOREIGN CORRESPONDENTS
GREECE: Rena Velissariou, 32, Kolokotroni Str., Aguia Paraskevi, Attikis, Athens. 153 42, Greece. (65) 67 665.
INDIA: B. D. Garga, 11 Verem Villas, Reis Magos, Bardez, Goa 403114 India. FAX: (91 832) 43433.
PAKISTAN: A.R. Slote, P.O. Box 7426, Karachi, 74400, Pakistan.

INTERNATIONAL MOTION PICTURE ALMANAC
(Annual) 159 W. 53 St., New York, NY 10019. (212) 247-3100. FAX: (212) 489-0871. email: QUIGLEYPUB@aol.com
EDITOR
James D. Moser
MANAGING EDITOR
Tracy Stevens
BRITISH EDITOR
William Pay
CANADIAN EDITOR
Patricia Thompson

INTERNATIONAL TELEVISION & VIDEO ALMANAC
(Annual) 159 W. 53 St., New York, NY 10019. (212) 247-3100. FAX: (212) 489-0871. email: QUIGLEYPUB@aol.com
EDITOR
James D. Moser
MANAGING EDITOR
Tracy Stevens
BRITISH EDITOR
William Pay
CANADIAN EDITOR
Patricia Thompson

QUIGLEY'S ENTERTAINMENT INDUSTRY REFERENCE
(CD-ROM, Annual) 159 W. 53 St., New York, NY 10019. (212) 247-3100. FAX: (212) 489-0871. email: QUIGLEYPUB@aol.com
PUBLISHER
Martin S. Quigley
EDITORS
Tracy Stevens
James D. Moser
EDITOR
BRITISH EDITOR
William Pay
CANADIAN EDITOR
Patricia Thompson

ACADEMY PLAYERS DIRECTORY
(Tri-Annual)
Academy of Motion Picture Arts & Sciences, 8949 Wilshire Blvd., Beverly Hills, CA 90211-1972. (310) 247-3000. FAX: (310) 550-5034.
EDITOR
Keith W. Gonzales

ADVERTISING AGE
(Weekly)
740 N. Rush St., Chicago, IL 60611. (312) 649- 5200. 220 E. 42 St., New York, NY 10017. (212) 210-0100.
CHAIRMAN
Mrs. G. D. Crain
PUBLISHING DIRECTOR
Joe Cappo

PUBLISHER
Ed Erhardt
PRESIDENT & EDITOR-IN-CHIEF
Rance Crain

THE AMERICAN CINEMATOGRAPHER
(Monthly)
Published by American Society of Cinematographers, Inc., P.O. Box 2230, Hollywood, CA 90078. (213) 969-4333. FAX: (213) 876-4973.
EDITOR
Stephen Pizzello
ASSOCIATE EDITOR
David E. Williams
ASSISTANT EDITOR
Andrew O. Thompson
CIRCULATION MANAGER
Saul Molina

AMERICAN PREMIERE MAGAZINE
(Bi-monthly)
8421 Wilshire Blvd., Penthouse, Beverly Hills, CA 90211. (213) 852-0434.
PUBLISHER & EDITOR
Susan Royal
ASSISTANT EDITOR
Dawn Brooks

ANNUAL INDEX TO MOTION PICTURE CREDITS
(Annual compilation of feature film credits)
c/o Academy of Motion Picture Arts and Sciences, 8949 Wilshire Blvd., Beverly Hills, CA 90211. (310) 247-3000. FAX: (310) 859-9619.
EXECUTIVE DIRECTOR
Bruce Davis
EDITOR
Byerly Woodward

AV GUIDE: THE LEARNING MEDIA NEWSLETTER
(Monthly)
380 Northwest Highway, Des Plaines, IL 60016-2282. (847) 298-6622. FAX: (847) 390-0408.
PUBLISHER
H. S. Gillette
EDITOR
Natalie Ferguson
CIRCULATION DIRECTOR
Linda Lambdin

BILLBOARD
(Weekly)
5055 Wilshire Blvd., Los Angeles, CA 90036-4396. (310) 525-2300. FAX: (213) 525-2394.
1515 Broadway, New York, NY 10036. (212) 764-7300. FAX: (212) 536-5358.
49 Music Square W., Nashville, TN 37203. (615) 321-4290. FAX: (615) 327-1575.
806 15 St., NW, Washington, D.C. 20005. (202) 783-3282. FAX: (202) 737-3833.
23 Ridgmount St., 3rd fl., London WC1E 7AH. (01 71) 323-6686. FAX: (01 71) 631-0428.
PRESIDENT & PUBLISHER
Howard Lander
EDITOR-IN-CHIEF
Timothy White
MANAGING EDITOR
Susan Nunziata
ASSOCIATE PUBLISHER, MARKETING & SALES
Gene Smith

BOXOFFICE
6640 Sunset Blvd., #100, Hollywood, CA 90028. (213) 465-1186. FAX: (213) 465-5049. Published by RLD Communications, Inc., 203 N. Wabash Ave., Chicago, IL 60605
PUBLISHER
Robert L. Deitmeier
EDITOR-IN-CHIEF
Ray Greene
NATIONAL AD DIRECTOR
Robert Vale

BROADCASTING & CABLE—THE NEWS WEEKLY OF TELEVISION AND RADIO
(Weekly)
1705 DeSales St., NW, Washington, DC 20036. (202) 659-2340. FAX: (202) 429-0651.
245 W. 17 St., New York, NY 10011. (212) 645-0067. FAX: (212) 337-7028.

5700 Wilshire Blvd., #120, Los Angeles, CA 90036. (213) 549-4100. FAX: (213) 937-4240.
PUBLISHER
Peggy Conlon
SENIOR VICE PRESIDENT & EDITOR
Donald V. West

CELEBRITY SERVICE INTERNATIONAL
Publisher of Celebrity Bulletin (daily).and Celebrity Service International Contact Book (annual).
1780 Broadway, New York, NY 10019. (212) 757-7979. FAX: (212) 397-4626.
8833 Sunset Blvd., Los Angeles, CA 90069. (310) 652-1700. FAX: (310) 652-9244.
EDITOR, CELEBRITY BULLETIN (NY)
Bill Murray
EDITOR, CELEBRITY BULLETIN (LA)
Todd Longwell
EDITORS, CELEBRITY SERVICE INTERNATIONAL CONTACT BOOK
Vicki Bagley, Mark Kerrigan

COMING ATTRACTIONS
(Monthly)
Connell Communications Inc., 86 Elm St., Peterborough, NH 03458. (603) 924-7271. FAX: (603) 924-7013.
PUBLISHER
Kathy Morris

CINEFEX
(Quarterly)
P.O. Box 20027, Riverside, CA 92516.
PUBLISHER
Don Shay
EDITOR
Jody Duncan

COSTUME DESIGNERS GUILD DIRECTORY
(Annual)
c/o Costume Designers Guild, 13949 Ventura Blvd., #309, Sherman Oaks, CA 91423. (818) 905-1557. FAX: (818) 905-1560.

DAILY VARIETY
(Daily)
5700 Wilshire Blvd., Suite 120, Los Angeles, CA 90036. (213) 857-6600. FAX: (213) 857-0494.
SPECIAL EDITIONS EDITOR
Steven Gaydos
MANAGING EDITOR
Jonathan Taylor
NATIONAL SALES MANAGER
Charles Koones
PRODUCTION MANAGER
Bob Butler

EDITOR & PUBLISHER
(Weekly)
11 W. 19 St., New York, NY 10011. (212) 675- 4380. FAX: (212) 929-1259.
PRESIDENT & EDITOR
Robert U. Brown
MANAGING EDITOR
John P. Consoli

ELECTRONIC MEDIA
(Weekly.)
740 N. Rush St., Chicago, IL 60611, (312) 649- 5293. FAX: (312) 649-5465.
VICE PRESIDENT, PUBLISHER & EDITORIAL DIRECTOR
Ron Alridge
EDITOR
P. J. Bednarski

ELECTRONICS
(Monthly)
Penton Publishing, 1100 Superior Ave., Cleveland, OH 44114. (216) 696-7000.
PUBLISHER/EDITOR
Jonah McLeod

ELECTRONICS NOW
(Monthly)
500 Bi-County Blvd., Farmingdale, NY 11735. (516) 293-3000. FAX: (516) 293-3115. url: http://www.gernsback.com
PUBLISHER
Larry Steckler
EDITOR
Carl Laron

FILM & VIDEO MAGAZINE
(Monthly)
Organized 1983. 8455 Beverly Blvd., #508, Los Angeles, CA 90048-3416. (213) 653-8053. FAX: (213) 653-8053.

ASSOCIATE PUBLISHER/EDITOR
Paula Swartz
ASSOCIATE PUBLISHER
Debbie Vodenos
SENIOR EDITOR
Collen O'Mara
ASSOCIATE EDITORS
Cristina Clapp
ASSISTANT EDITOR
Debbie Sweeney
NATIONAL SALES DIRECTOR
Steven Rich

FILM JOURNAL, THE
(Monthly)
244 W. 49 St., Suite 200, New York, NY 10019. (212) 246-6460. FAX: (212) 265-6428.
PUBLISHER-EDITOR
Robert H. Sunshine
ASSOCIATE PUBLISHER
Jimmy Sunshine
MANAGING EDITOR
G. Kevin Lally
ASSOCIATE EDITORS
Ed Kelleher, Mitch Neuhauser
ASSISTANT EDITOR
Glenn Slavin
DIRECTOR OF ADVERTISING/SALES
Jim Merck
WEST COAST EDITOR
Myron Meisel
CIRCULATION MANAGER
Michelle Lederkramer

FILM QUARTERLY
(Quarterly)
University of California Press, 2120 Berkeley Way, Berkeley, CA 94720. (510) 601-9070. FAX: (510) 601-9036.
EDITOR
Ann Martin
Published by University of California Press

FILMS IN REVIEW
P.O. Box 589, New York, NY 10021. (212) 628-1594.
EDITOR
Robin Little

HOLLYWOOD CREATIVE DIRECTORY
(Annual)
3000 Olympic Blvd., Santa Monica, CA 90404. (310) 315-4815. e-mail: hcd@hollyvision.com

THE HOLLYWOOD REPORTER
(Daily)
5055 Wilshire Blvd., Los Angeles, CA 90036. (213) 525-2000, (213) 525-2068 (editorial). FAX: (213) 525-2377 (editorial), (213) 525-2189 (advertising), (213) 957-5766 (special issues).
1515 Broadway, New York, NY, 10036. (212) 536-5344, (212) 536-5325 (editorial). FAX: (212) 536-5345.
PUBLISHER & EDITOR-IN-CHIEF
Robert J. Dowling
EDITOR
Alex Ben Block
MANAGING EDITOR
Glenn Abel
BUREAUS:
806 15th St., N.W., # 421, Washington, DC 20005. (202) 737-2828. FAX: (202) 737-3833.
1515 Broadway, New York, NY, 10036. (212) 536-5344, (212) 536-5325.
23 Ridgmount St., London WC1E 7AH England. (01 71) 323-6686. FAX: (01 71) 323-2314, (01 71) 323-2316.

I.A.T.S.E. OFFICIAL BULLETIN
(Quarterly)
1515 Broadway, Suite 601, New York, NY 10036. (212) 730-1770. FAX: (212) 921-7699.
EDITOR
Michael W. Proscia
ASSISTANT EDITOR
Karen Pizzuto

IN MOTION FILM & VIDEO PRODUCTION MAGAZINE
(Monthly)
Phillips Business Information, 1201 Seven Locks Rd., Suite 300, Potomac, MD 20854. (301) 340-1520.
PUBLISHER
David Durham
EDITOR
Allison Dollar

INTERNATIONAL DOCUMENTARY
1551 S. Robertson Blvd., Suite 201, Los Angeles, CA 90035. (310) 284-8422. FAX: (310) 785-9334.
EDITOR
Diana Rico

INTERNATIONAL PHOTOGRAPHER

(Monthly)
7715 Sunset Blvd., Suite 300, Hollywood, CA 90046. (213) 876-0160.
PUBLISHER
International Photographers Guild
EDITOR-IN-CHIEF
George Spiro Dibie, ASC
EDITOR
Suzanne R. Lezotte

JOURNAL OF THE SYD CASSYD ARCHIVES ACADEMY OF TELEVISION ARTS & SCIENCES/HOLLYWOOD REPORT

(Quarterly)
917 S. Tremaine, Hollywood 90019, CA. (213) 939-2345. Founded 1946.
FOUNDER
Syd Cassyd

MILLIMETER

(A monthly magazine covering the motion picture and television production industries.)
122 E. 42 St., #900, New York, NY 10168. (212) 309-7650. Fax: (212) 867-5893.
5300 Melrose Ave., # 219E, Hollywood, CA 90038. (213) 960-4050. FAX: (213) 960-4059.
PUBLISHER
Sam Kintzer
EDITOR
Bruce Stockler

PACIFIC COAST STUDIO DIRECTORY

(3 times per year)
P.O. Box V, Pine Mountain, CA 93222-4921. (805) 242-2722. FAX: (805) 242-2724.
PUBLISHER
Jack Reitz

PERFORMANCE MAGAZINE

(Weekly)
2049 Century Park E., Suite 1100, Los Angeles, CA 90067. (310) 552-3118. FAX: (310) 286-1990.
PUBLISHER
Don Waitt
L.A. SENIOR EDITOR
Stann Findelle
MANAGING EDITOR
Jane Cohen

PRODUCER'S MASTERGUIDE

(Annual)
60 E. 8th St., 31st Floor, New York, NY 10003. (212) 777-4002. FAX: (212) 777-4101. url: http://www.producers.masterguide. com
PUBLISHER
Shmuel Bension

REEL DIRECTORY, THE

(Annual)
P.O. Box 866, Cotati, CA 94931. (707) 584-8083.
PUBLISHER & EDITOR
Bonnie Carroll

SMPTE JOURNAL (SOCIETY OF MOTION PICTURE AND TELEVISION ENGINEERS)

(Monthly)
595 West Hartsdale Ave., White Plains, NY 10607. (914) 761-1100. FAX: (914) 761-3115.
EDITOR
Jeffrey B. Friedman
DIRECTOR OF MARKETING & COMMUNICATIONS
John Izzo

SCREEN ACTOR/CALL SHEET

(Bi-Monthly)
5757 Wilshire Blvd., Los Angeles, CA 90036. (213) 549-6652. FAX: (213) 549-6656.

SHOOT

(Weekly)
1515 Broadway, New York, NY 10036. (212) 764-7300. FAX: (212) 536-5321.
5055 Wilshire Blvd., Los Angeles, CA 90036. (213) 525-2262. FAX: (213) 525-0275.
Merchandise Mart Plaza, #936, Chicago, IL 60654. (312) 464-8555. FAX: (312) 464-8550.
PUBLISHER
Roberta Griefer
EDITOR
Peter Caranicas

TV GUIDE

(Weekly)
News America Publications, Inc., 100 Matsonford Rd., Radnor, PA 19088. (215) 293-8500.

EDITOR-IN-CHIEF
Steven Reddicliffe
PRESIDENT/CEO
Joseph F. Barletta
PUBLISHER/SENIOR VICE PRESIDENT
Mary G. Berner
MANAGING EDITOR-PROGRAMMING
Elisabeth Bacon
EXECUTIVE EDITOR-NATIONAL EDITORIAL
Barry Golson

TAPE/DISC BUSINESS

(Monthly)
Knowledge Industry Publications, Inc., 701 Westchester Ave., White Plains, NY 10604-3098. (914) 328-9157. FAX: (914) 328-9093.
EDITOR
Patricia Casey
CIRCULATION DIRECTOR
Jeff Hartford

TELEVISION & CABLE FACTBOOK

(Annual)
Warren Publishing, Inc., 2115 Ward Court, N.W., Washington, DC 20037. (202) 872- 9200. FAX: (202) 293-3435.
EDITOR & PUBLISHER
Albert Warren
MANAGING EDITOR
Michael C. Taliaferro
EDITORIAL DIRECTOR
Mary Appel

TELEVISION DIGEST WITH CONSUMER ELECTRONICS

(Weekly)
Warren Publishing, Inc., 2115 Ward Court, N.W., Washington, DC 20037. (202) 872-9200. FAX: (202) 293-3435.
EDITOR & PUBLISHER
Albert Warren
EDITORIAL DIRECTOR
David Lachenbruch
EXECUTIVE EDITOR
Dawson B. Nail
SENIOR EDITOR & EXECUTIVE PUBLISHER
Paul Warren
SENIOR EDITOR & ASSOCIATE PUBLISHER
Daniel Warren

TELEVISION INDEX

40-29 27th St., Long Island City, NY 11101-3869, (718) 937-3990.
EDITOR & PUBLISHER
Jonathan Miller

TELEVISION QUARTERLY

(Quarterly)
National Academy of Television Arts & Sciences, 111 W. 57 St., New York, NY 10019. (212) 586-8424.
EDITOR
Richard Pack
ADVERTISING
Trudy Wilson

VARIETY

(Weekly)
Reed Publishing, Inc., 249 W. 17 St., 4th fl., New York, NY 10011. (212) 645-0067. FAX: (212) 337-6977.
5700 Wilshire Blvd., Suite #120, Los Angeles, CA 90036, (213) 857-6600. FAX: (213) 857-0494.
1483 Chain Bridge Rd., McLean, VA 22101, (703) 448-0510. FAX: (703) 827-8214.
P.O. Box 535, Lake Bluff, IL, 60044, (708) 615-9742, FAX: (708) 615-9743.
33 Champs Elysees, 75008 France. Phone (33-1) 43-55-07-43.
Lungotevere Flaminio 22, Rome 00196. (39-6) 361-3103.
34/35 Newman St., W1P 3PD England, (44-01 71) 637-3663.
Madrid: Phone (34-1) 576-4262.
Sydney, Australia: Phone: (61-2) 372-5577.
CHAIRMAN/CEO
Robert L. Krakoff
VICE PRESIDENT, PUBLISHING OPERATIONS
Gerard A. Byrne
EDITORIAL DIRECTOR
Peter Bart
MANAGING EDITORS
Elizabeth Guider, Jonathan Taylor
EUROPEAN EDITOR
Adam Dawtrey

VARIETY'S ON PRODUCTION

5700 Wilshire Blvd., Suite 120, Los Angeles, CA 90036. (213) 857-6600. FAX: (213) 549-4184.e-mail: onprodmag@aol.com
PUBLISHER
Jerry Brandt

VIDEO
(Consumer magazine covering home theatre, audio, video, and multimedia hardware and software.)
Published by Hachette Filipacchi Magazines, Inc., 1633 Broadway, 45th Floor, New York, NY 10019. (212) 767-6020. FAX: (212) 767-5615. email: VideoMag@aol.com
GROUP PUBLISHER
Tony Catalaro
EDITOR-IN-CHIEF
Bill Wolfe

VIDEO BUSINESS
(Weekly)
Chilton Publications, 825 Seventh Ave., New York, NY 10019. (212) 887-8400.
PUBLISHER
John Gaffney
EDITOR
Bruce Apar
ADVERTISING DIRECTOR
Stacy Kelly
ADVERTISING SALES
Andi Elliott, Linda Buckley

VIDEO STORE MAGAZINE
(Weekly)
201 E. Sandpointe Ave., Ste. 600, Santa Ana, CA 92707. (714) 513-8400, (800) 854-3112. FAX: (714) 513-8403.
PRESIDENT OF PUBLICATIONS
Brian Nairn
GROUP VICE PRESIDENT
Glenn Rogers
PUBLISHER
Don Rosenberg
EDITOR IN CHIEF
Thomas K. Arnold
ASSOCIATE PUBLISHER
Anne Sadler
MARKET RESEARCH DIRECTOR
Judith McCourt

VIDEO SYSTEMS MAGAZINE
(Monthly)
9800 Metcalf Ave., Overland Park, KS 66212-2215. (913) 341-1300. FAX: (913) 967-1898.
PUBLISHER
Dennis Triola
GROUP VICE PRESIDENT
Cameron Bishop
MARKETING DIRECTOR
Tom Brick
AD PRODUCTION COORDINATOR
Pat Eisenman

VIDEO WEEK
(Weekly)
Warren Publishing, Inc. 2115 Ward Court N.W., Washington, DC 20037-1213. (202) 872-9200. FAX: (202) 293-3435.

VIDEOGRAPHY MAGAZINE
(Monthly)
2 Park Ave., Suite 1820, New York, NY 10016. (212) 779-1919. FAX: (212) 213-3484.
PUBLISHER
Paul Gallo
EDITOR
Brian McKernan

WHO'S WHO IN THE MOTION PICTURE INDUSTRY/WHO'S WHO IN TELEVISION
(Semi-Annual)
Packard Publishing, P.O. Box 2187, Beverly Hills, CA 90213. (310) 275-6531. FAX: (818) 501-7392. e-mail: rodpub@aol.com

PUBLISHER & EDITOR
Rodman W. Gregg

GREAT BRITAIN

BROADCAST
(Published weekly).
EMAP Media Ltd., 33-39 Bowling Green Lane, London, EC1R ODA. (01 71) 837 9263. FAX: (01 71) 837 8250.
EDITOR
Mike Jones

EYEPIECE
Journal of the Guild of British Camera Technicians, 5-11 TauntonRoad, Metropolitan Centre, Greenford, Middx., UB6 8UQ. (01 81) 578 9243. FAX: (01 81) 575 5972.
EDITORS
Kerry Anne-Burrows, Charles Hewitt
ADVTG. CONSULTANT
Ron Bowyer

IMAGE TECHNOLOGY
Journal of the British Kinematograph, Sound and Television Society. M6-M14 Victoria House, Vernon Place, London, WC1B 4DF. England. (01 71) 242-8400. FAX: (01 71) 405 3560.
MANAGING EDITOR
John Gainsborough

MOVING PICTURES
(Published weekly) 1 Richmond Mews, London W1V 5AG. (01 71) 287-0070. FAX: (01 71) 287-9637.
EDITORS
Sara Squire
Damon Wise

SCREEN INTERNATIONAL EUROGUIDE
(Annual directory for the motion picture and television industry in Europe).
Published by EMAP Media, 33-39 Bowling Green Lane, London EC1R 0DA, England. (01 71) 837-1212. FAX: (01 71) 278-4003.
EDITOR IN CHIEF
Oscar Moore

TELEVISUAL
(Published monthly).
Centaur Group, St. Giles House, 50 Poland St., London, W1V 4AX. (01 71) 439 4222. FAX: (01 71) 287 0768.
PUBLISHER
Tim Macpherson
EDITOR
Mundy Ellis

CANADA

FILM CANADA YEARBOOK
1430 Yonge St., Suite 214, Toronto, ON, M4T 1Y6. (416) 696-2382. FAX: (416) 696-6496.
EDITOR
Patricia Thompson

FRANCE

LE FILM FRANCAIS
(Weekly French motion picture trade magazine)
103 Blvd. St. Michel, Paris, France, 75005. (143) 29 4090. FAX: (143) 29 1405.
PUBLISHER
Claude Pommereau
EDITOR
Marie-Claude Arbaudie

Motion Picture and television Information Research and Data Analysis Companies

CERTIFIED REPORTS INC. (CRI) EAST
7 Hudson St., Kinderhook NY 12106. (518) 758-6400. FAX:
(518) 758-6451. (Theatre checking open, blind and trailer
checking nationwide.)
CHAIRMAN OF BOARD
Jack J. Spitzer
PRESIDENT
Bill Smith
EXECUTIVE VICE PRESIDENT
Bryan Zweig
VICE PRESIDENT
Frank Falkenhainer
VICE PRESIDENT, ADMINISTRATION & FINANCE
Michael F. Myers

CERTIFIED REPORTS INC. (CRI) WEST
9846 White Oak Ave., Suite 202, Northridge CA 91325. (818)
727- 0929. FAX: (818) 727-7426.
VICE PRESIDENT
Elizabeth Stevens

ENTERTAINMENT DATA INC.
8350 Wilshire Blvd., Suite 210, Beverly Hills CA 90211. (213)
658-8300. BRANCHES: Los Angeles, Washington DC, San
Francisco, New York, Dallas, Chicago, Toronto, Atlanta,
London, Munich.
(Provides daily box-office information for exhibition and distrib-
ution. On-line access to data.)
PRESIDENT
Marcy Polier
SENIOR VICE PRESIDENT
Philip Garfinkle

EXHIBITOR RELATIONS CO., INC.
116 N. Robertson Blvd., Suite 606, Los Angeles CA 90048.
(310) 657-2005. FAX: (310) 657-7283.
PRESIDENT
John N. Krier

THE GALLUP ORGANIZATION
47 Hulfish St., Princeton, NJ 08542. (609) 924-9600.

HANOVER SECURITY REPORTS
952 Manhattan Beach Blvd., Suite 250, Manhattan Beach CA
90266. (310) 545-9891. (800) 634-5560. FAX: (310) 545-7690.
EXECUTIVE VICE PRESIDENT
Nancy Stein

INTERNATIONAL RESEARCH & EVALUATION,
21098 IRE Control Ctr., Eagan, MN 55121-0098. (612) 888-
9635. FAX: (612) 888-9124.
Rick Kenrick

PAUL KAGAN ASSOCIATES, INC.
126 Clock Tower Place, Carmel CA 93923-8734. (408) 624-
1536. FAX: (408) 625-3225. (Research and analysis of entertainment, communications and media industries.)
PRESIDENT
Paul Kagan

KINDERHOOK RESEARCH, INC.
P.O. Box 589, Kinderhook NY 12106. (518) 758-1492. FAX:
(518) 758-9896. (Distributor/ exhibitor open and blind checking.
housekeeping/integrity surveys. industry research.)
PRESIDENT
Andrea Koppel

MARKET RESEARCH CORP. OF AMERICA
819 S. Wabash, Chicago, IL 60605. (708) 480-9600.
2215 Sanders Road, Northbrook, IL 60062. (708) 480-9600.

MCCANN-ERICKSON INC.
6420 Wilshire Blvd., Los Angeles, CA 90048. (213) 655-9420.

A.C. NIELSEN COMPANY
150 N. Martingale Rd., Schaumburg, IL 60173. (708) 605-5000.
731 Wilshire Blvd., #940, Los Angeles, CA 90010. (213) 386-
7316. FAX: (213) 386-7317.
299 Park Ave., New York, NY 10171. (212) 708-7500.

Organizations

ACADEMY OF TELEVISION ARTS AND SCIENCES
(Formed in 1948 to advance the arts and sciences of television. Awards Emmys for nighttime programming and publishes Emmy Magazine.)
5220 Lankershim Blvd., No. Hollywood, CA 91601. (818) 754-2800. FAX: (818) 761-2827. URL: http://www.emmys.org
PRESIDENT
Richard Frank
VICE PRESIDENT
Stu Berg
SECOND VICE PRESIDENT
Jan Scott
V.P., LOS ANGELES
Don Tillman
SECRETARY
Nancy Wiard
TREASURER
Meryl Marshall
EXECUTIVE COMMITTEE
John Agoglla, Vince Gutierrez, Ted Harbert, Mark Allen Itkin, Barry Meyer, Leslie Moonves, Tom Sarnoff, Noreen Stone, Dean Valentine
EXECUTIVE DIRECTOR
James Loper
CFO
Herb Jellinek
DIRECTOR, AWARDS
John Leverence
DIRECTOR, MEMBERSHIP ACTIVITIES
Linda Loe
PUBLIC RELATIONS REPRESENTATIVE
Weissman/Angellotti
BOARD OF GOVERNORS
Jeanene Ambler, Ray Angona, Conrad G. Bachmann, Susan Baerwald, June M. Baldwin, Alan S. Bergmann, James Castle, Rocci Chatfield, Jay Chattaway, Patrick Collins, Jusy Crown, Nelson Davis, Clifford Dektar, James DiPasquale, Maura R. Dunbar, Marian Effinger, Hal Eisner, Alan Fama, Gerald Perry Finnerman, David E. Fluhr, Geriann Geraci, Dan Gingold, Mark Glamack, Richard C. Glouner, Douglas H. Grindstaff, Vince Gutierrez, Michael A. Hoey, Mark Allen Itkin, Paula L. Kaatz, Marvin Kaplan, Theresa Koenig, Richard A. Larson, Alfred E. Lehman, Linda Mancuso, Sheila Manning, Anthony Mazzei, David Michaels, Bill Millar, Deborah Miller, Lee Miller, John Nachreiner, Meryl O'Loughlin, Dorothea G. Petrie, John S. Shaffner, Ame Simon, Susan Simons, Noreen Stone, Mark Teschner, Sherman L. Thompson, Matthew J. Tombers, Patricia Van Ryker

ACTORS' EQUITY ASSOCIATION
(AAAA-AFL-CIO-CLC)
(Organized May 26, 1913. Membership: 38,000.)
165 W. 46 St., New York, NY 10036. (212) 869-8530. FAX: (212) 719-9815.
235 Pine St., #1100, San Francisco, CA 94104.
6430 Sunset Blvd., Hollywood, CA 90028.
203 N. Wabash Ave., Chicago, IL 60601.
PRESIDENT
Ron Silver
FIRST VICE PRESIDENT
Patrick Quinn
SECOND VICE PRESIDENT
Richard Warren Pugh
THIRD V.P. & EASTERN REGIONAL V.P.
Donald Christy
CENTRAL REGIONAL V.P.
Madeleine Fallon
WESTERN REGIONAL V.P.
Carol Swarbrick
EASTERN REGIONAL V.P.
Arne Gundersen
SECRETARY & TREASURER
Conard Fowkes
COUNSEL
Spivak, Lipton, Watanabe, Spivak (NY)
Taylor, Roth, Bush & Geffner (LA)

ADVERTISING COUNCIL, THE
261 Madison Ave., 11th floor, New York, NY 10016-2303. (212) 922-1500. FAX: (212) 922-1676.
740 Rush St., Chicago, IL 60611.
1233 20th St., NW, Suite 500, Washington, DC 20036.
CHAIRMAN & CEO
Philip Guarascio

PRESIDENT
Ruth A. Wooden
EXECUTIVE VICE PRESIDENT
Eva N. Kasten
S.V.P., FINANCIAL DEVELOPMENT
Elinor U. Biggs
DIRECTOR, PUBLIC RELATIONS
Paula A. Veale

ADVERTISING RESEARCH FOUNDATION
641 Lexington Ave., New York, NY 10022. (212) 751- 5656. FAX: (212) 319-5265.
PRESIDENT
Michael J. Naples
S.V.P., MEDIA RESEARCH
Lawrence R. Stoddard
S.V.P., DIRECTOR OF OPERATIONS
James H. Moore

ALLIANCE FOR COMMUNITY MEDIA
666 Eleventh St., NW, Suite 806, Washington, DC 20001-4542. (202) 393-2650. FAX: (202) 393-2653.
EXECUTIVE DIRECTOR
Barry Forbes

ALLIANCE OF MOTION PICTURE AND TELEVISION PRODUCERS
15503 Ventura Blvd., Encino, CA 91436-3140. (818) 995-3600. FAX: (818) 789-7431.
PRESIDENT
J. Nicholas Counter III
S.V.P., LEGAL & BUSINESS AFFAIRS
Carol A. Lombardini
V.P., LEGAL AFFAIRS
Helayne Antler

AMERICAN ADVERTISING FEDERATION
1101 Vermont Ave., NW, Suite 500, Washington, DC 20005. (202) 898-0089. FAX: (202) 898-0159.
PRESIDENT & CEO
Wallace Snyder
V.P., COMMUNICATIONS & CORPORATE DEVELOPMENT
Julie Dolan
DIRECTOR, MEDIA RELATIONS
Jeff Custer

AMERICAN ASSOCIATION OF ADVERTISING AGENCIES
405 Lexington Ave., New York, NY 10174-1801. (212) 682-2500. FAX: (212) 953-5665.
URL: http://www.commercepark.com/AAAA
CHAIRMAN
David Bell, Bozell Worldwide, Inc. (NY)
VICE CHAIRMAN
Ralph W. Rydholm, Tatham EURO RSCG (Chicago)
SECRETARY & TREASURER
Byron Lewis, UniWorld Group, Inc. (NY)
PRESIDENT & CEO
O. Burtch Drake, A.A.A.A., NY
EXECUTIVE V.P., CONSULTING
Harry Paster
SENIOR VICE PRESIDENTS
Marilyn Bockman, Michael D. Donahue, Robert J. Finn, Joyce Harrington, James C. Martucci Jr.
VICE PRESIDENTS
Marsha Appel, Dorothy Forget, Robert Linden, Jacqueline Llewellyn, Jack Mennis, Thomas M. Phelan, Beverly Plyer, Karen Proctor, Joseph Sampang

AMERICAN CINEMA EDITORS
(Organized November 28, 1950. Membership: 400)
1041 N. Formosa Ave., W. Hollywood, CA 90046. (213) 850-2900. FAX: (213) 850-2922.
PRESIDENT
Tom Rolf
VICE PRESIDENT
Bill Gordian
SECRETARY
George Hirely
TREASURER
Jack Tucker

AMERICAN FEDERATION OF MUSICIANS
(AFL-CIO)
(Organized October, 1896. Membership: 150,000.)
1501 Broadway, New York, NY 10036. (212) 869-1330. FAX: (212) 764-6134.

PRESIDENT
Steve Young
VICE PRESIDENT
Tom Lee, 4400 MacArthur Blvd. NW, Washington, DC 20001.
CANADIAN VICE PRESIDENT
Ray Petch, 75 The Donway West, Suite 1010, Don Mills,
Ontario, Canada M3C 2E9.
SECRETARY & TREASURER
Stephen R. Sprague
EXECUTIVE BOARD
Thomas C. Bailey, Ray Hair, Bill Moriarity, Tim Shea, Kenneth
B. Shirk

AMERICAN FEDERATION OF TELEVISION AND RADIO ARTISTS (AAAA-AFL-CIO)

(Organized August, 1937. Membership 72,000)
260 Madison Ave., 7th Fl., New York, NY 10016. (212) 532-
0800.
NATIONAL PRESIDENT
Shelby Scott
FIRST VICE PRESIDENT
Denny Delk
SECOND VICE PRESIDENT
Richard Holter
VICE PRESIDENTS
Susan Boyd, Belva Davis, Bob Edwards, J. R. Horne, Ray
Bradford, Daryl Hogue, Dave Corey.
TREASURER
Lillian Clark
RECORDING SECRETARY
Fred Anderson
NATIONAL REPRESENTATIVES
Louis Santillana, Jr., Jonathan Dunn-Rankin, Stan Farber, John
Armstrong, Mathis L Dunn Jr., Peter Cleaveland, Toni D.
Everett.

AMERICAN GUILD OF MUSICAL ARTISTS (AFL-CIO), BRANCH OF ASSOCIATED ACTORS AND ARTISTES OF AMERICA

(Organized 1936. Membership 5,500)
1727 Broadway, New York, NY 10019-5284. (212) 265-3687.
FAX: (212) 262-9088.
PRESIDENT
Gerald Otte
FIRST VICE PRESIDENT
Michael Byars
SECOND VICE PRESIDENT
Pamela Smith
THIRD VICE PRESIDENT
Eugene Lawrence
FOURTH VICE PRESIDENT
John W. Coleman
FIFTH VICE PRESIDENT
Sandra Darling
TREASURER
William Cason
ADMINISTRATOR FOR DANCE
Alexander Dubae
COUNSEL
Becker, London & Kossow
MEMBERSHIP SUPERVISOR
Carol Caldwell
FINANCIAL SECRETARY
Grace Pedro
DIRECTOR OF PUBLIC RELATIONS
Michael Rubino
CANADA: Christopher Marston, 260 Richmond St. E, Toronto,
Ontario M5A 1P4. (416) 867-9165. CHICAGO: Barbara J.
Hillman, Cornfield & Feldman, 343 S. Dearborn St., 13th Fl.,
Chicago, IL 60604. (312) 922-2800. NEW ENGLAND: Robert
M. Segal, 11 Beacon St., Boston, MA 02108. (617) 742-0208.
NEW ORLEANS: Rosemary Le Boeuf, 4438 St. Peter St., New
Orleans, LA 70119. (504) 486-9410. NORTHWEST: Carolyn C.
Carpp, 11021 NE 123rd Lane, Apt. C114, Kirkland, WA 98034.
(206) 820-2999. PHILADELPHIA: Gail Lopez-Henriquez, 400
Market St., Philadelphia, PA 19106. (215) 925-8400. PITTS-
BURGH: Frank Kerin, 223 Thompson Run, Pittsburgh, PA
15232. (412) 498- 0550. SAN FRANCISCO: Harry Polland,
Donald Tayer, Ann Sebastian, 235 Pine St., Suite 100, San
Francisco, CA 94104. (415) 986-4060. TEXAS: Benny Hopper,
3915 Fairlakes Dr., Dallas, TX 75228. (214) 279-4720. WASH-
INGTON DC: Eleni Kallas, 16600 Shea Lane, Gaithersburg,
MD 20877. (301) 869- 8266.

AMERICAN GUILD OF VARIETY ARTISTS (AAAA AFL-CIO)

(Organized July 14, 1939. Registered Membership: 78,000.
Active Membership: 5,000.)
184 Fifth Ave., New York, NY 10010. (212) 675-1003.
4741 Laurel Canyon Blvd., #208, N. Hollywood, CA 91607.
(818) 508-9984. FAX: (818) 508-3029.
HONORARY FIRST VICE PRESIDENT
Rip Taylor

HONORARY THIRD VICE PRESIDENT
Gloria DeHaven
PRESIDENT
Rod McKuen
SECRETARY & TREASURER
Frances Gaar
REGIONAL VICE PRESIDENTS
Emelise Aleandri, Bobby Brookes, Ron Chisholm, David
Cullen, John Eaden, Bobby Faye, Doris George, Wayne
Hermans, Elaine Jacovini-Gonella, Deedee Knapp-Brody,
Eddie Lane, Tina Marie, Angela Martin, Scott Senatore,
Dorothy Stratton, Susan Streater, Dorothy Zuckerman

AMERICAN HUMANE ASSOCIATION

(Organized 1877. Liaison with the television and motion picture
industry as supervisors of the use of animals in television and
motion picture production.)
63 Inverness Dr., East Englewood, CO 80112. (303) 792-9900.
15503 Ventura Blvd., Encino, CA 91436. (818) 501-0123.
NATIONAL PRESIDENT
Charles Granoski
VICE PRESIDENT
Loretta Kowal
TREASURER
Timothy O'Brien
DIRECTOR, L.A. REGIONAL OFFICE
Betty Denny Smith

AMERICAN SOCIETY OF CINEMATOGRAPHERS, INC.

(Organized 1919. Membership: 286)
1782 N. Orange Dr., Hollywood, CA 90028. (213) 876-5080.
FAX: (213) 882-6391.
PRESIDENT
Victor Kemper
FIRST VICE PRESIDENT
Woody Omens
SECOND VICE PRESIDENT
Steven Poster
THIRD VICE PRESIDENT
Allen Daviau
SECRETARY
John Bailey
TREASURER
Howard A. Anderson, Jr.
SERGEANT AT ARMS
Richard C. Glouner

AMERICAN SOCIETY OF COMPOSERS, AUTHORS AND PUBLISHERS (ASCAP)

(Organized February 13, 1914. Membership: 39,000 Writers,
18,000 Publishers)
One Lincoln Plaza, New York, NY 10023. (212) 621-6000. FAX:
(212) 721-0955.
7920 Sunset Blvd., Hollywood, CA 90046. (213) 883-1000.
FAX: (213) 883-1049.
PRESIDENT AND CHAIRMAN
Marilyn Bergman
VICE PRESIDENTS
Cy Coleman, Jay Morgenstern
SECRETARY
Arthur Hamilton
TREASURER
Arnold Broido
COUNSEL
I. Fred Koenigsberg
COO
John A. LoFrumento
DIRECTOR OF MEMBERSHIP
Todd Brabec, ASCAP, 7920 Sunset Blvd., Los Angeles, CA 90046
SOUTHERN REGIONAL EXECUTIVE DIRECTOR
Connie Bradley, ASCAP, 2 Music Square W., Nashville, TN 37203

ASIAN CINEVISION, INC.

(A not-for-profit organization dedicated to encouraging Asian
and Asian-American media arts)
32 East Broadway, New York, NY 10002. (212) 925- 8685. FAX:
(212) 925-8157.
EXECUTIVE DIRECTOR
Bill J. Gee

ASSOCIATED ACTORS AND ARTISTES OF AMERICA (AAAA-AFL-CIO)

(Organized July 18, 1919. Membership: 90,000)
165 W. 46 St., New York, NY 10036. (212) 869-0358. FAX:
(212) 869-1746.
PRESIDENT
Theodore Bikel
VICE PRESIDENTS
Ken Orsatti, Thomas Jamerson, Bruce York, Rod McKuen,
Seymour Rexite
TREASURER
John Sucke
EXECUTIVE SECRETARY
Alan Eisenberg

ASSOCIATION OF AMERICA'S PUBLIC TELEVISION STATIONS
(Organized 1979. Research, planning and representation for member public television stations throughout the U.S.)
1350 Connecticut Ave. NW, Suite 200, Washington, D.C. 20036. (202) 887-1700. e-mail: info@apts.org
URL: http://www.universe.digex.net/~apts
PRESIDENT
David J. Brugger
BOARD OF TRUSTEES
Ronald Becker, Howard W. Bell, Jr., Richard Bodorff, David J. Brugger, Burnill F. Clark, Susan Farmer, Elsie Garner, Robert F. Larson, Carolyn Bailey Lewis, John L. Maxey II, George L. Miles Jr., Steven Newberry, Maynard Orme, William Reed, Karen Sherrin, Joseph N. Traigle, Jerry Wareham, Viviane Warren, Caroline Whitson

ASSOCIATION OF INDEPENDENT COMMERCIAL PRODUCERS
(Organized 1972.)
P.O. Box 2007, San Francisco, CA 94126-2007. (415) 771-6268. FAX: (415) 861-4212.
PRESIDENT
Tony Hurd, Six Foot Two Productions
PAST PRESIDENT
Marcia Herman McLean, Marcia Can, Inc.
TREASURER
Rachel Leibert, Red Sky Films
SECRETARY
Michelle Dennis, Phoenix Editorial Services
VICE PRESIDENTS
Lori Anderson (Varitel Video), Deborah Giarratana (Pacific Data Images), Shari Hanson (Industrial Light & Magic), Larry Walsh (Hammond Martin Walsh & Smith)
BRANCHES
National—New York. Chicago, Denver, Miami, Atlanta, Dallas, Seattle, Los Angeles.

ASSOCIATION OF INDEPENDENT TELEVISION STATIONS
1320 19th St., Suite 300, Washington, DC 20036. (202) 887-1970. FAX (202) 887-0950.
CHAIRMAN
Kevin O'Brien
PRESIDENT
James B. Hedlund
V.P., LEGAL & LEGISLATIVE AFFAIRS
David L. Donovan
V.P. & GENERAL COUNSEL
James Popham
V.P., FINANCE
Al Petrionio
DIRECTOR, CONGRESSIONAL RELATIONS
Angela Giroux
BOARD OF DIRECTORS
Richard Ballinger, Linda Cochran, Dennis Fitzsimmons, William Frank, Ed Karlik, Mike Liff, James Major, Sharon Maloney, Patrick North, Kevin O'Brien, Roger Ottenbach, David Pulido, Brooke Spectorsky, J. Daniel Sullivan, Ed Trimbele

ASSOCIATION OF INDEPENDENT VIDEO AND FILMMAKERS, INC.
(A national membership organization dedicated to the growth of independent media.Publishes *The Independent Magazine*.)
625 Broadway, New York, NY 10012. (212) 473-3400.
EXECUTIVE DIRECTOR
Ruby Lerner
DIRECTOR OF PROGRAMS & SERVICES
Pamela Calvert
EDITOR
Pat Thompson
MANAGING EDITOR
Michele Shapiro
BOARD OF DIRECTORS
Joe Berlinger, Melissa Burch, Loni Ding, Barbara Hammer, Ruby Lerner, James Klein, Diane Markrow, Meni Matias, Robb Moss, Robert Richter, James Schamus, Norman Wang, Burton Wiess

ASSOCIATION OF NATIONAL ADVERTISERS, INC.
155 E. 44 St., New York, NY 10017. (212) 697-5950. FAX: (212) 661-8057.
CHAIRMAN
Janet Soderstrom (VISA U.S.A.)
VICE CHAIRMAN
Richard Costello (General Electric Company)
PRESIDENT & CEO
John J. Sarsen, Jr.

ASSOCIATION OF TALENT AGENTS
(Organized April, 1937. Official organization of talent agents in Hollywood.)
9255 Sunset Blvd., Suite 318, Los Angeles, CA 90069. (310) 274-0628. FAX: (310) 274-5063. e-mail: agentassoc@aol.com
EXECUTIVE DIRECTOR
Karen Stuart

FIRST VICE PRESIDENT
Sandy Bresler
VICE PRESIDENTS
Sid Craig
T. J. Escott
Sheldon Sroloff
Sonjia Warren Brandon
SECRETARY & TREASURER
Martin Gage

AUTHORS' GUILD, INC.
(Membership: 6,600.)
330 W. 42 St., 20th floor, New York, NY 10036-6902. (212) 563-5904. FAX: (212) 564-8363.
PRESIDENT
Mary Pope Osborne
VICE PRESIDENT
Sidney Offit
SECRETARY
Letty Cottin Pogrebin
TREASURER
Paula J. Giddings
EXECUTIVE DIRECTOR
Robin Davis Miller

AUTHORS LEAGUE OF AMERICA, INC., THE
(Membership: 15,000.)
Authors League, 330 W. 42 St., 20th floor, New York, NY 10036. (212) 564-8350.
PRESIDENT
Garson Kanin
VICE PRESIDENT
Robert Anderson
SECRETARY
Eve Merriam
TREASURER
Gerold Frank
ADMINISTRATOR
Robin Davis Miller

BMI (BROADCAST MUSIC, INC.)
320 W. 57 St., New York, NY 10019. (212) 586-2000. FAX: (212) 582-5972.
8730 Sunset Blvd., 3rd fl. West, Los Angeles, CA 90069. (310) 659-9109.
10 Music Square E., Nashville, TN 37203. (615) 401-2000.
79 Marylebone Rd., London NW1 5HN, England. (44) 171 935-8517.
CHAIRMAN OF THE BOARD
Donald A. Thurston
PRESIDENT & CEO
Frances W. Preston
S.V.P. & GENERAL COUNSEL
Marvin Berenson
S.V.P., FINANCE & ADMINISTRATION & CFO
Fred Willms
S.V.P., PERFORMING RIGHTS, WRITER & PUBLISHER RELATIONS
Del Bryant
V.P., CORPORATE RELATIONS
Robbin Ahrold
S.V.P., INTERNATIONAL
Ekke Schnabel
S.V.P. & SPECIAL COUNSEL
Theodora Zavin
S.V.P., LICENSING
John M. Shaker
V.P., INFORMATION TECHNOLOGY
Bob Barone
V.P. & CONTROLLER
Thomas Curry
V.P., NASHVILLE
Roger Sovine
V.P., WRITER & PUBLISHER RELATIONS, CALIFORNIA
Rick Riccobono
V.P., WRITER & PUBLISHER RELATIONS, NEW YORK
Charles S. Feldman
V.P., GENERAL LICENSING
Tony Annastas
V.P., HUMAN RESOURCES & SECRETARY
Edward W. Chapin
V.P., EUROPEAN WRITER & PUBLISHER RELATIONS
Philip R. Graham
V.P., RESEARCH & INFORMATION
John Marsillo
V.P., TELECOMMUNICATIONS
Larry Sweeney

BROADCAST PIONEERS FOUNDATION
320 W. 57 St., New York, NY 10019. (212) 830-2581.
PRESIDENT
James Delmonico
VICE PRESIDENT
Don Mercer
EXECUTIVE DIRECTOR
Edward J. DeGray

CABLE TELEVISION ADVERTISING BUREAU
757 Third Ave., New York, NY 10017. (212) 751-7770. FAX: (212) 832-3268.
CHAIRMAN
Don Mitzner
PRESIDENT & CEO
Joe Ostrow

CABLE TELEVISION INFORMATION CENTER (CTIC)
(Organized 1972. Provides community governments and consumers with objective information about the cable industry.)
1700 Shaker Church Rd., Olympia, WA 98502. (206) 866-2080.
PRESIDENT
Harold E. Horn

CATHOLIC ACTORS GUILD OF AMERICA
(Organized April, 1914. Membership: 550.)
1501 Broadway, Suite 510, New York, NY 10036. (212) 398-1868.
PRESIDENT
William J. O'Malley
VICE PRESIDENT
Hildegarde
TREASURER
Martin Kiffel

COMMUNICATION COMMISSION OF THE NATIONAL COUNCIL OF THE CHURCHES OF CHRIST IN THE USA
475 Riverside Dr., Room 856, New York, NY 10115. (212) 870-2574. FAX: (212) 870-2152.
CHAIRPERSON
Roger Burgess
DIRECTOR OF COMMUNICATION
Mike Maus
DIRECTOR OF ELECTRONIC MEDIA
David W. Pomeroy

CORPORATION FOR PUBLIC BROADCASTING
901 E St., N.W. Washington, DC 20004. (202) 879-9600. FAX: (202) 783-1019. URL: http://www.cpb.org
PRESIDENT & CEO
Richard W. Carlson
EXECUTIVE VICE PRESIDENT
Robert T. Coonrod
S.V.P., GOVERNMENT RELATIONS & GENERAL COUNSEL
Lillian Fernandez
S.V.P., SYSTEM & STATION DEVELOPMENT
Frederick L. DeMarco
S.V.P., POLICY & PUBLIC AFFAIRS
Michael Schoenfeld
S.V.P., EDUCATION & PROGRAMMING
Carolynn Reid-Wallace
TREASURER
Renee Ingram
CHAIRMAN
Ritajean Butterworth
VICE CHAIR
Alan Sagner
MEMBERS
Honey Alexander, Carolyn Bacon, Diane Blair, Henry Cauthen, Frank Cruz, Alan Sagner, Sheila Tate

DIRECTORS GUILD OF AMERICA, INC. (DGA)
7920 Sunset Blvd., Hollywood, CA 90046. (310) 289-2000. FAX: (213) 289-2029.
110 W. 57 St., New York, NY 10019. (212) 581-0370.
400 N. Michigan Ave., Suite 307, Chicago, IL 60611. (312) 644-5050.
2410 Hollywood Blvd., Hollywood, FL 33020. (305) 927-3338.
PRESIDENT
Gene Reynolds
NATIONAL VICE PRESIDENT
Jane Schimel
EXECUTIVE DIRECTOR
Glenn Gumpel
VICE PRESIDENTS
Larry Auerbach, Robert Butler, Martha Coolidge, Nancy Littlefield, Daniel Petrie, Jack Shea, Max A. Schindler
SECRETARY & TREASURER
Sheldon Leonard

DRAMATISTS GUILD, INC., THE
(Membership: 813 Active, 5,656 Associate, 350 Subscribing)
234 W. 44 St., New York, NY 10036. (212) 398-9366. FAX: (212) 944-0420.
PRESIDENT
Peter Stone
EXECUTIVE DIRECTOR
Richard Garmise
VICE PRESIDENT
Terrence McNally
SECRETARY
Arthur Kopit
TREASURER
Richard Lewine

COUNSEL
Cahill Gordon & Reindel
DIRECTOR OF MEMBERSHIP
Todd Neal

ELECTRONIC INDUSTRIES ASSOCIATION
2500 Wilson Blvd., Arlington, VA 22201. (703) 907-7500. FAX: (703) 907-7501.
CHAIRMAN OF THE BOARD
Clifford H. Tuttle, Pres. & CEO, Aerovox, Inc.
VICE CHAIRMAN
Jerry Kalov, Pres. & CEO, Cobra Electronics
PRESIDENT
Peter F. McCloskey
VICE PRESIDENT PUBLIC AFFAIRS
Mark V. Rosenker
TREASURER
Veronica Haggart, V.P., Motorola

EPISCOPAL ACTORS GUILD OF AMERICA, INC.
(Organized 1926. Membership: 750)
1 E. 29 St., New York, NY 10016. (212) 685-2927.
HONORARY PRESIDENT & PRESIDING BISHOP
The Right Rev. Edmond L. Browning
HONORARY PRESIDENT & BISHOP OF NEW YORK
The Right Reverend Richard F. Grein
PRESIDENT
Barnard Hughes
VICE PRESIDENTS
Rev. Norman J. Catir, Jr., Warden of the Guild. Joan Fontaine, Peter Harris, Joan Warren, Edward Crimmins, Cliff Robertson.
RECORDING SECRETARY
Tom Ferriter
TREASURER
Alvin Lum

INSTITUTE OF ELECTRICAL AND ELECTRONICS ENGINEERS, INC.
345 E. 47 St., New York, NY 10017-2394. (212) 705-7900.
PRESIDENT
Wallace S. Read
GENERAL MANAGER
Daniel J. Senese
EXECUTIVE DIRECTOR
T. W. Hissey

INTERACTIVE TELEVISION ASSOCIATION
1030 Fifteenth St. NW, Suite 1053, Washington, DC 20005 (202) 408-0008. FAX: (202) 408-0111.
PRESIDENT
Andrew L. Sernovitz
EXECUTIVE VICE PRESIDENT
Peter C. Waldheim
MEMBERSHIP
Yasha M. Harari
MEMBER SERVICES
Mathew I. Laurencelle
RESEARCH AND PUBLICATIONS
Philip R. Strohi

INTERNATIONAL ALLIANCE OF THEATRICAL STAGE EMPLOYEES & MOVING PICTURE MACHINE OPERATORS OF THE U.S. AND CANADA (AFL-CIO, CLC)
(Organized nationally, July 17, 1893; internationally, October 1, 1902. The Alliance comprises approximately 800 local unions covering the United States, Canada and Hawaii.)
1515 Broadway, Suite 601, New York, NY 10036-5741. (212) 730-1770. FAX: (212) 921-7699.
INTERNATIONAL PRESIDENT
Thomas C. Short
GENERAL SECRETARY-TREASURER
Michael W. Proscia
FIRST VICE PRESIDENT
John J. Nolan
SECOND VICE PRESIDENT
John J. Ryan
THIRD VICE PRESIDENT
Edward C. Powell
FOURTH VICE PRESIDENT
Nick Long
FIFTH VICE PRESIDENT
Daniel J. Kerins
SIXTH VICE PRESIDENT
Rudy N. Napoleone
SEVENTH VICE PRESIDENT
Carmine A. Palazzo
EIGHTH VICE PRESIDENT
Jean Fox
NINTH VICE PRESIDENT
Ben F. Lowe
TENTH VICE PRESIDENT
Timothy Magee
ELEVENTH VICE PRESIDENT
James Wood

463

STUDIO MECHANICS, LOCAL 479 (IATSE) ATLANTA
P.O. Box 78757, Atlanta, GA 30357. (404) 607-7773. FAX:
(404) 367-0240.
SECRETARY
Suzanne L. Carter

STUDIO MECHANICS, LOCAL 812 (IATSE) DETROIT
20017 Van Dyke, Detroit, MI 48234. (313) 368-0825. FAX:
(313) 368-1151.
SECRETARY
Timothy F. Magee

STUDIO MECHANICS, LOCAL 480 (IATSE) SANTA FE
P.O. Box 8481, Albuquerque, NM 87198-0481. (505) 265-1500.
FAX: (505) 266-7155.
SECRETARY
Ryan Blank

STUDIO MECHANICS, LOCAL 209 (IATSE) OHIO
1468 West 9th St., Room 435, Cleveland, OH 44113. (216)
621-9537.FAX: (216) 621-3518.
SECRETARY
Peter Lambros

STUDIO MECHANICS, LOCAL 484 (IATSE) TEXAS
440 Louisiana, Suite 480, Houston, TX 77002. (713) 229-8357.
FAX: (713) 229-8138.
SECRETARY
Janelle V. Flanagan

TELEVISION BROADCASTING STUDIO
EMPLOYEES, LOCAL 794 (IATSE), NEW YORK
P.O. Box 154, Lenox Hill Sta., New York, NY 10021. (516) 724-
4815. FAX: (516) 724-4815.
SECRETARY
Cerena Gourdine

THEATRICAL WARDROBE ATTENDANTS,
LOCAL 769 (IATSE), CHICAGO
1220 Hawkins Ct., Bartlett, IL 60103. (708) 289-4568. FAX:
(708) 289-4568.
SECRETARY
Cheryl Ryba

THEATRICAL WARDROBE ATTENDANTS,
LOCAL 768 (IATSE), LOS ANGELES
13949 Ventura Blvd., Suite 307, Sherman Oaks, CA 91423.
(818) 789-8735. FAX: (818) 905-6297.
SECRETARY
Mary Seward

THEATRICAL WARDROBE UNION, LOCAL 764 (IATSE),
NEW YORK
151 W. 46 St., 8th fl., New York, NY 10036. (212) 221-1717.
FAX: (212) 302-2324.
SECRETARY
James Roberts

INTERNATIONAL COUNCIL OF THE NATIONAL ACADEMY
OF TELEVISION ARTS AND SCIENCES
(Awards the International Emmy in recognition of excellence in
television programs produced and broadcast outside the U.S.)
142 W. 57 St., 16th fl., New York, NY 10019. (212) 489-6969.
FAX: (212) 489-6557. e-mail: intcouncil@aol.com
URL: http://www.intlemmys.org
PRESIDENT
Tom Rogers
CHAIRMAN
Kay Koplovitz
VICE CHAIRMAN (Int'l)
Robert Phillis
VICE CHAIRMAN (US)
Larry Gershman
EXECUTIVE DIRECTOR
Arthur F. Kane
GENERAL MANAGER
Linda Alexander

INTERNATIONAL RADIO AND TELEVISION SOCIETY
FOUNDATION
420 Lexington Ave. Suite 1714, New York, NY 10170-0101.
(212) 867-6650. FAX: (212) 867-6653.
PRESIDENT
Stephen A. Weiswasser
VICE PRESIDENT & GENERAL COUNSEL
Ellen Shaw Agress
VICE PRESIDENTS
Timothy M. McAuliff, Douglas W. McCormick, Joe Quinlan,
Diane Seaman
SECRETARY
Jack Higgins
TREASURER
James M. McKenna
EXECUTIVE DIRECTOR
Joyce M. Tudryn

MOTION PICTURE AND TELEVISION FUND
23388 Mulholland Drive, Woodland Hills, CA 91364. (818) 876-
1888.
Bob Hope Health Center, 335 N. LaBrea Ave., Los Angeles,
CA 90036. (213) 634-3850.
Toluca Lake Health Center, 4323 Riverside Dr., Burbank, CA
91505, (818) 556-2700.
Westside Health Center, 1950 Sawtelle Blvd., Suite 130, Los
Angeles, CA 90025. (310) 996-9355.
Samuel Goldwyn Foundation Children's Center, 2114 Pontius
Ave., Los Angeles, CA 90025, (310) 445-8993.
CHAIRMAN
Roger H. Davis
VICE CHAIRMAN
Chester L. Migden, Frank I. Davis, Janet Leigh Brandt,
Marshall Wortman
TREASURER
Roger L. Mayer
SECRETARY
Irma Kalish
PRESIDENT/CEO
William F. Haug
V.P., PROFESSIONAL SERVICES
Timothy M. Lefevre, M.D.
CFO
Frank Guarrera

THE MUSEUM OF TELEVISION & RADIO
(Formerly the Museum of Broadcasting. Founded in 1976, the
museum houses a permanent collection of over 60,000 televi-
sion and radio programs and commercials.)
25 W. 52 St., New York, NY 10019. (212) 621-6600. FAX: (212)
621-6700.
CHAIRMAN
Frank A. Bennack
PRESIDENT
Robert M. Batscha

NATIONAL ACADEMY OF TELEVISION ARTS AND
SCIENCES, THE
(Organized 1947. Awards Emmys for daytime programming.
Publishers of Television Quarterly.)
National Office: 111 W. 57 St., New York, NY 10019. (212) 586-
8424. FAX: (212) 246-8129.
CHAIRMAN OF THE BOARD
David Louie
PRESIDENT
John Cannon
VICE CHAIRMAN
Malachy Wienges
VICE PRESIDENT
Thea Flaum
NATIONAL AWARDS DIRECTOR
Trudy Wilson
CHAPTER SERVICES DIRECTOR
Nick Nicholson
PUBLIC RELATIONS
Robert F. Blake, Robert H. Christie
MEMBERSHIP INFORMATION
Michael Grigaliunas
EDITOR OF TELEVISION QUARTERLY
Richard Pack

NATIONAL ASSOCIATION OF BROADCASTERS
(Organized 1922.)
1771 N St., N.W., Washington, DC 20036-2891. (202) 429-
5300. (202) 429-5406.
CHAIRMAN, TELEVISION
Ralph W. Babbard
VICE-CHAIRMAN
James A. Babb, Jr.
JOINT BOARD OF DIRECTORS CHAIRMAN
Philip A. Jones
PRESIDENT
Edward O. Fritts
S.V.P., TELEVISION
Charles Sherman
TELEVISION BOARD OF DIRECTORS
James G. Babb Jr., L. Martin Brantly, Elizabeth Murphy
Burns, John Conomikes, W. Don Cornwell, Richard Cotton,
Nick Evans Jr., Michael Finkelstein, Dennis J. FitzSimons,
Martin D. Franks, Ralph W. Gabbard, John Hayes, Philip A.
Jones, Amy McCombs, Howard W. Meagle Jr., Thomas A.
Oakley, Preston Padden, Clyde Payne, Bill Pitts, G. William
Ryan, Patricia C. Smullin, Bill Sullivan, Nick Trigony, John P.
Zanotti

NATPE (NATIONAL ASSOCIATION OF TELEVISION
PROGRAM EXECUTIVES)
2425 Olympic Blvd., #550-E, Santa Monica, CA 90404. (310)
453-4440. FAX: (310) 453-5258.
PRESIDENT & COO
Bruce Johansen

CHAIRMAN & CEO
Jane Adair
S.V.P., MARKETING
Ron Gold
S.V.P., CONFERENCES & SPECIAL EVENTS
Nick Orfanopoulos
V.P., CREATIVE SERVICES
Beth Braen
V.P., FINANCE
Jon Dobkin

NATIONAL CABLE TELEVISION ASSOCIATION
(Organized 1951. Trade association that lobbies for cable tele-
vision interest.)
1724 Massachusetts Ave. NW, Washington, DC 20036. (202)
775-3550.
PRESIDENT & CEO
Decker Anstrom
EXECUTIVE VICE PRESIDENT
June E. Travis
V.P., SCIENCE & TECHNOLOGY
Wendell Bailey
V.P., LAW & REGULATORY POLICY PROJECTS
Daniel L. Brenner
V.P., ASSOCIATION AFFAIRS
Jadz Janucik
DEPUTY V.P., GOVERNMENT RELATIONS
Pamela Turner
V.P., INDUSTRY AFFAIRS
Barbara York
V.P., RESEARCH & POLICY ANALYSIS
Cynthia Brumfield
BOARD OF DIRECTORS
CHAIRMAN & PRESIDENT
R.E. "Ted" Turner
VICE CHAIRMAN
Amos B. Hostetter, Jr.
MEMBERS OF THE BOARD
Barry L. Babcock, Peter R. Barton, Jeffrey D. Bennis, Jeffrey L.
Bewkes, Matthew C. Balnk, Steven Bornstein, William J.
Bresnan, Peter P. Brubaker, Michael C. Burrus, Scott D.
Chambers, Joseph J. Collins, F. Steven Crawford, Nickolas
Davatzes, James L. Dolan, Frank M. Drendel, John M. Egan,
John D. Evans, Joseph S. Gans III, John W. Goddard, Leo J.
Hindery Jr., Glenn R. Jones, Marvin L. Jones, Kay Koplovitz,
Jerry D. Lindauer, Jeffrey A. Marcus, Thomas O. Might, Robert
Miron, James A. Monroe, John J. Rigas, Timothy B. Robertson,
Paul F. Schonewolf, Michael S. Wilner, John O. Wynne

NATIONAL MUSIC PUBLISHERS' ASSOCIATION, INC.
711 Third Ave., 8th floor, New York, NY 10017. (212) 370-5330.
PRESIDENT AND CEO
Edward P. Murphy
VICE PRESIDENT
Ralph Peer II
TREASURER
Stanley Mills

NEW YORK WOMEN IN FILM & TELEVISION
(Organized in 1977.)
274 Madison Ave., Suite 1202, New York, NY 10016-0701.
(212) 679-0870. FAX: (212) 679-0899.
PRESIDENT
Harlene Freezer
V.P., DEVELOPMENT
Sandra Colony
V.P., PROGRAMMING
Lisa Hackett Stafford
V.P., SPECIAL EVENTS
Karen L. King
SECRETARY
Barbara Goodman
TREASURER
Debra Kozee
BOARD OF DIRECTORS
Marsha Brooks, Kathy Demerit, Alma Derricks, Marlene
Freezer, Barbara Goodman, Linda Kahn, Debra Kozee, Karen
King, Valerie Light, Susan Margolin, Wanda McGill, Eileen
Newman, Marquita Pool-Eckert, Marcie Setlow, Dana Thrush,
Vivian Treves, Charlette Van Doren, Ellen Zalk.
LEGAL COUNSEL
Marsha Brooks
EXECUTIVE DIRECTOR
Raquel R. Levin
CHAPTERS
Atlanta, Baltimore, Boston, Chicago, Dallas, Denver, Los
Angeles, Orlando, Savannah, Seattle, Washington, D.C.,
Jamaica, London, Melbourne, Montreal, Paris, Sydney, Toronto,
Vancouver

PERMANENT CHARITIES COMMITTEE OF THE
ENTERTAINMENT INDUSTRIES
(Supports community-wide charities.)
11132 Ventura Blvd., Suite 401, Studio City, CA 91604-3156.
(818) 760-7722. FAX: (818) 760-7898.

CHAIRMAN OF THE BOARD
Earl Lestz
PRESIDENT & CEO
Lisa Paulsen
FIRST VICE PRESIDENT
Harry J. Floyd
SECOND VICE PRESIDENT
Roger L. Mayer
SECRETARY
T. J. Baptie
TREASURER
Robert S. Colbert, CPA
V.P., ADMINISTRATION
Marilyn Augustine
V.P., COMMUNICATIONS & CORPORATE RELATIONS
Danielle M. Guttman

PRODUCER-WRITERS GUILD OF AMERICA
PENSION PLAN
1015 N. Hollywood Way, Burbank, CA 91505. (818) 846-1015,
(800) 227-7863. FAX: (818) 566-8445.
CHAIRMAN
David Karp
VICE-CHAIRMAN
Richard Mittleman
SECRETARY
Bernard Gehan
VICE SECRETARY
Helayne Antler

SESAC INC.
(A music licensing organization.)
55 Music Square East, Nashville, TN 37203. (800) 826-9996.
CHAIRMEN
Freddie Gershon, Stephen Swid, Ira Smith
PRESIDENT & COO
Bill Velez

SCREEN ACTORS GUILD (AAAA-AFL-CIO)
(Organized July 1933. Membership: 88,000.)
5757 Wilshire Blvd., Los Angeles, CA 90036. (213) 465-4600.
FAX: (213) 856-6603.
PRESIDENT
Richard Masur
VICE PRESIDENT
Sumi Haru
THIRD VICE PRESIDENT
Paul Hecht
FOURTH VICE PRESIDENT
Mel Boudrot
FIFTH VICE PRESIDENT
Mary Seibel
SIXTH VICE PRESIDENT
Scott DeVenney
TREASURER
F.J. O'Neil
NATIONAL EXECUTIVE DIRECTOR
Ken Orsatti
ASSOCIATE NATIONAL EXECUTIVE DIRECTOR
John McGuire
DIRECTOR, COMMUNICATIONS
Katherine Moore
COUNSEL
Leo Geffner
DIRECTOR, FINANCE
Gerald Wilson
DIRECTOR OF ADMINSTRATION
Clinta Dayton
DISTRICT OFFICES
ARIZONA: John McGuire, 1616 East Indian School Rd., Suite
330, Phoenix, AZ 85016. (602) 265-2712. MASSACHUSETTS:
11 Beacon St., Rm. 512, Boston, MA 02108. (617) 742-2688.
ILLINOIS: 75 E. Wacker Dr., 14th Fl., Chicago, IL 60601. (312)
372-8081. COLORADO: 950 South Cherry Street, Suite 502,
Denver, CO 80222. (303) 757-6226. DALLAS: 6060 N. Central
Expressway, #302, LB 604, Dallas, TX 75206. (214) 363-8300.
MICHIGAN: 28690 Southfield Rd., #290 A&B, Lathrup Village,
MI 48076. (810) 559-9450. FLORIDA: 7300 N. Kendall Dr.,
#620, Miami, FL 33145. (305) 444-7677. GEORGIA: 455 E.
Paces Ferry Rd., NE, #334, Atlanta, GA 30305. (404) 239-
0131. HAWAII: 949 Kapiolani Boulevard, Suite 105, Honolulu,
HI 96814. (808) 596-0388. HOUSTON: 2650 Fountainview,
Suite 326, Houston, TX 77057. (713) 972-1806. NEW YORK:
1515 Broadway, 44th Floor, New York, NY 10036. (212) 944-
1030. PENNSYLVANIA: 230 South Broad Street, 10th Floor,
Philadelphia, PA 19102. (215) 545-3150. SAN DIEGO: 7827
Convoy Court, #400, San Diego, CA 92111. (619) 278-7695.
SAN FRANCISCO: 235 Pine St., 11th fl., San Francisco, CA
94104. (415) 391-7510. TENNESSEE: P.O. Box 121087,
Nashville, TN 37212. (615) 327-2958. WASHINGTON DC/BAL-
TIMORE: 5480 Wisconsin Avenue, Suite 201, Chevy Chase,
MD 20815. (301) 657-2560.

SOCIETY OF MOTION PICTURE AND TELEVISION ENGINEERS

(Organized 1916. Membership: 9,700.)
595 W. Hartsdale Ave., White Plains, NY 10607-1824. (914) 761-1100. FAX: (914) 761-3115.
PRESIDENT
Stanley N. Baron
PAST PRESIDENT
Irwin Young
EXECUTIVE VICE PRESIDENT
David L. George
V.P., ENGINEERING
Kenneth P. Davies
V.P., EDITORIAL
Peter A. Dare
V.P., FINANCE
Charles H. Jablonski
V.P., CONFERENCE
Edward P. Hobson II
SECRETARY/TREASURER
Richard L. Thomas
EXECUTIVE DIRECTOR
Lynette Robinson
DIRECTOR, MARKETING
John Izzo, Jr.

THE SONGWRITERS GUILD OF AMERICA

1500 Harbor Blvd., Weehawken, NJ 07087-6732. (201) 867-7603. FAX: (201) 867-7335.
1560 Broadway, Room 1306, New York, NY 10036. (212) 768-7902. FAX: (212) 768-9048.
6430 Sunset Blvd., Suite 1011, Hollywood, CA 90028. (213) 462-1108. FAX: (213) 462-5430.
1222 16th Avenue South, Suite 25, Nashville, TN 37212. (615) 329-1782. FAX: (615) 329-2623.
PRESIDENT
George David Weiss
EXECUTIVE DIRECTOR
Lewis M. Bachman

STATION REPRESENTATIVES ASSOCIATION, INC.

230 Park Ave., New York, NY 10017. (212) 687-2484. FAX: (212) 972-4372.
PRESIDENT
Tom Olson
V.P., TV
Jack Oken
SECRETARY
George Pine
TREASURER
Carl Butrum
MANAGING DIRECTOR
Jerry Feniger

TELEVISION BUREAU OF ADVERTISING

(Organized 1954.)
850 Third Ave., 10th floor, New York, NY 10022. (212) 486-1111. FAX: (212) 935-5631.
PRESIDENT
Ave Butensky
CHAIRMAN OF THE BOARD
Barry Baker
TREASURER
Jack Oken
CHAIRMAN EX-OFFICIO
Jack Sander
S.V.P., STRATEGIC PLANNING
Joseph C. Tirinato
S.V.P., MARKETING
Thomas A. Conway
V.P., RESEARCH
Harold Simpson

THEATRE AUTHORITY, INC.

(Organized May 21, 1934.)
16 E. 42 St., Suite 202, New York, NY 10017-6907. (212) 682-4215. FAX: (212) 682-8407.
EXECUTIVE DIRECTOR
Helen Leahy
PRESIDENT
Jane Powell
FIRST VICE PRESIDENT
John H. Sucke

SECOND VICE PRESIDENT
Terry Walker
THIRD VICE PRESIDENT
Robert J. Bruyr
FOURTH VICE PRESIDENT
Rod McKuen
RECORDING SECRETARY
Thomas H. Jamerson
TREASURER
Joan Greenspan
REPRESENTATIVE
Francis Garr
ADVISORY COMMITTEE
Julie Andrews, Harry Belafonte, Theodore Bikel, Joey Bishop, Ellen Burstyn, Billy Davis Jr., Patty Duke, Richard Dysart, Barbara Feldon, Joan Fontaine, John Forsythe, Robert Goulet, Charlton Heston, Jerome Hines, Bob Hope, Barnard Hughes, Jack Jones, Alan King, Werner Klemperer, Angela Lansbury, Jerry Lewis, Patti Lupone, Marilyn McCoo, Ed McMahon, Estelle Parsons, Gregory Peck, Jane Powell, Tony Randall, Lou Rawls, Debbie Reynolds, Tony Roberts, Frank Sinatra, Barbra Streisand, Nancy Wilson

UNITED NATIONS—MEDIA DIVISION

United Nations, New York, NY 10017. (212) 963-6945. FAX: (212) 963-0765.
DIRECTOR, MEDIA DIVISION
Francois Giuliani

UNITED STATES CATHOLIC CONFERENCE, DEPARTMENT OF COMMUNICATIONS, OFFICE FOR FILM & BROADCASTING

1011 First Ave., Suite #1300, New York, NY 10022. (212) 644-1880. FAX: (212) 644-1886.
DIRECTOR, OFFICE FOR FILM & BROADCASTING
Henry Herx

WOMEN IN COMMUNICATIONS, INC.

(Organized 1909.)
10605 Judicial Dr., #A-4, Fairfax, VA 22030. (703) 359-9000. FAX: (703) 359-0603.
PRESIDENT
Carol Fenstermacher
BRANCHES
187 chapters

WOMEN IN FILM

(Organized 1973.)
6464 Sunset Blvd., #530, Hollywood, CA 90028. (213) 463-6040. FAX: (213) 463-0963.
PRESIDENT EMERITUS—FOUNDER
Tichi Wilkerson-Kassel
PRESIDENT
Joan Hyler
EXECUTIVE DIRECTOR
Harriet Silverman

WRITERS GUILD OF AMERICA

NATIONAL CHAIRMAN
Edward Adler

WRITERS GUILD OF AMERICA, EAST, INC.

555 W. 57 St., New York, NY 10019. (212) 767-7800. FAX: (212) 582-1909.
PRESIDENT
Herb Sargent
VICE PRESIDENT
Claire Labine
SECRETARY & TREASURER
Jane C. Bollinger
EXECUTIVE DIRECTOR
Mona Mangan

WRITERS GUILD OF AMERICA, WEST, INC.

7000 W. Third St., Los Angeles, CA 90048. (310) 550-1000. FAX: (310) 550-8185.
PRESIDENT
Brad Radnitz
VICE PRESIDENT
Dan Petrie, Jr.
SECRETARY & TREASURER
John Wells
EXECUTIVE DIRECTOR
Brian Walton

EMMY AWARDS

PRIMETIME AWARDS

OUTSTANDING COMEDY SERIES
Frasier, Executive Producers: Peter Casey, David Angell, David Lee, Christopher Lloyd, Vic Rauseo, Linda Morris; Co-Executive Producer: Steven Levitan; Producers: Maggie Randell, Chuck Ranberg, Anne Flett-Giordano; Co-Producers: Joe Keenan, Jack Burditt, Mary Fukuto. Directors: James Burrows, Kelsey Grammer, Gordon Hunt, David Lee, Philip Charles MacKenzie, Jeff Melman. Created by David Angell, Peter Casey and David Lee. NBC—Grub Street Prods. in association with Paramount.

OUTSTANDING DRAMA SERIES
ER, Executive Producers: John Wells, Michael Crichton. Co-Executive Producers: Carol Flint, Mimi Leder, Lydia Woodward. Producer: Christopher Chulack; Supervising Producer: Paul Manning. Co-Producer: Wendy Spence. Directors: Christopher Chulack, Mimi Leder, Felix Alcala, Donna Deitch, Anthony Edwards, Lance Gentile, Lesli Glatter, Barnet Kellman, Eric Laneuville, Dean Parisot, Whitney Ransack, Richard Thorpe, Thomas Schlamme. Created by Michael Crichton. NBC—Constant C Productions/Amblin Television in association with Warner Bros. Television.

OUTSTANDING MINISERIES
Gulliver's Travels, Executive Producers: Robert Halmi Sr., Brian Henson. Producer: Duncan Kenworthy. Teleplay: Simon Moore based on the novel by Jonathan Swift. Director: Charles Sturridge. NBC—RHI Entertainment, Inc. and Channel Four Television presentation from Jim Henson Productions.

OUTSTANDING MADE FOR TELEVISION MOVIE
Truman, Executive Producers: Paula Weinstein, Anthea Sylbert. Producer: Doro Bachrach. Screenplay: Tom Rickman based on the book by David McCullough. Director: Frank Pierson. HBO—A Spring Creek Production.

OUTSTANDING VARIETY, MUSIC OR COMEDY SPECIAL
Dennis Miller: Citizen Arcane, Executive Producers: Dennis Miller, John Moffit, Pat Tourk Lee. Supervising Producer: Nancy Kushner. Written by: Dennis Miller. Director: Jim Yukich. HBO—Happy Family Productions.

OUTSTANDING VARIETY, MUSIC OR COMEDY SERIES
The Kennedy Center Honors, Producers: George Stevens, Jr., Don Mischner. Written by: George Stevens, Jr., Bob Shrum, Sara Lukinson, John Frook. Director: Louis J. Horvitz. CBS—Kennedy Center Television Productions.

OUTSTANDING LEAD ACTRESS IN A COMEDY SERIES
Helen Hunt, "Mad About You," NBC

OUTSTANDING LEAD ACTOR IN A COMEDY SERIES
John Lithgow, "Third Rock From the Sun," NBC

OUTSTANDING LEAD ACTRESS IN A DRAMA SERIES
Kathy Baker, "Picket Fences," CBS

OUTSTANDING LEAD ACTOR IN A DRAMA SERIES
Mandy Patinkin, "Chicago Hope," CBS

OUTSTANDING LEAD ACTOR IN A MINISERIES OR SPECIAL
Alan Rickman, "Rasputin," HBO

OUTSTANDING LEAD ACTRESS IN A MINISERIES OR SPECIAL
Helen Mirren, "Prime Suspect" PBS

OUTSTANDING SUPPORTING ACTRESS IN A COMEDY SERIES
Julie Louis-Dreyfus, "Seinfeld," NBC

OUTSTANDING SUPPORTING ACTOR IN A COMEDY SERIES
Rip Torn, "The Larry Sanders Show," HBO

OUTSTANDING SUPPORTING ACTRESS IN A DRAMA SERIES
Tyne Daly, "Christy," CBS

OUTSTANDING SUPPORTING ACTOR IN A DRAMA SERIES
Ray Walston, "Picket Fences," CBS

OUTSTANDING SUPPORTING ACTOR IN A MINISERIES OR A SPECIAL
Tom Hulce, "The Heidi Chronicles," HBO.

OUTSTANDING SUPPORTING ACTRESS IN A MINISERIES OR SPECIAL (TIE)
Greta Scacchi, "Rasputin," HBO.

OUTSTANDING GUEST ACTRESS IN A COMEDY SERIES
Betty White, "The John Larroquette Show," ("Here We Go Again"), NBC.

OUTSTANDING GUEST ACTOR IN A COMEDY SERIES
Tim Conway, "Coach," ("The Gardener"), ABC

OUTSTANDING GUEST ACTRESS IN A DRAMA SERIES
Amanda Plummer, "The Outer Limits" ("A Stitch In Time"), Showtime.

OUTSTANDING GUEST ACTOR IN A DRAMA SERIES
Peter Boyle, "The X-Files" ("Clyde Bruckman's Final Repose"), FOX.

OUTSTANDING INDIVIDUAL ACHIEVEMENT IN DIRECTING IN A DRAMA SERIES
Jeremy Kagan, "Chicago Hope" ("Leave of Absence"), CBS.

OUTSTANDING INDIVIDUAL ACHIEVEMENT IN DIRECTING IN A COMEDY SERIES
Michael Lembeck, "Friends" ("The One After the Superbowl"), NBC.

OUTSTANDING INDIVIDUAL ACHIEVEMENT IN DIRECTING FOR A MINISERIES OR A SPECIAL
John Frankenheimer, "Andersonville," TNT.

OUTSTANDING INDIVIDUAL ACHIEVEMENT IN DIRECTING IN A VARIETY OR MUSIC PROGRAM
Louis Horvitz, "The Kennedy Center Honors," CBS.

OUTSTANDING INDIVIDUAL ACHIEVEMENT IN WRITING IN A COMEDY SERIES
Joe Keenan, Christopher Lloyd, Rob Greenburg, Jack Burditt, Chuck Ranberg, Amme Flett-Giordano, Linda Morris, Vic Rauseo, "Frasier," ("Moon Dance"), NBC.

OUTSTANDING INDIVIDUAL ACHIEVEMENT IN WRITING IN A DRAMA SERIES
Darin Morgan, "The X-Files" ("Clyde Brickman's Final Repose"), FOX.

OUTSTANDING INDIVIDUAL ACHIEVEMENT IN WRITING IN A MINISERIES OR A SPECIAL
Simon Moore, "Gulliver's Travels," NBC.

OUTSTANDING INDIVIDUAL ACHIEVEMENT IN WRITING IN A VARIETY OR MUSIC PROGRAM
Dennis Miller, Eddie Feldman, David Feldman, Mike Gandolfi, Tom Hertz, Leah Krinsky, Rick Overton, "Dennis Miller Live," HBO.

OUTSTANDING ANIMATED PROGRAM (FOR PROGRAMMING ONE HOUR OR LESS)
A Pinky and the Brain Christmas Special, Executive Producer: Steven Spielberg, Senior Producer: Tom Ruegger, Producer/Writer: Peter Hastings, Producer/Director: Rusty Mills. WB—Warner Bros. Television Animation in association with Amblin Entertainment.

OUTSTANDING CULTURAL PROGRAM
Itzhak Perlman: In the Fiddler's House, ("Great Performances"), Executive Producer: Jac Venza. Executive Producers/Co-Directors: Glenn DuBose, James Arntz. Coordinating Producer: Bill Murphy. Producer/Writer: Sara Lukinson. Co-Director: Don Lenzer. Performer: Itzhak Perlman. PBS—Thirteen/WNET.

OUTSTANDING INDIVIDUAL ACHIEVEMENT IN COSTUME DESIGN FOR A SERIES
Carolyn Griffel, "Remember WENN," ("Hillary Booth Registered Nurse), AMC—The Entertainment Group/Turtleback Prods. in association with American Movie Classics.

OUTSTANDING INDIVIDUAL ACHIEVEMENT IN COSTUME DESIGN FOR A MINISERIES OR A SPECIAL
Dinah Collin, "Pride and Prejudice" (Part 1), A&E—A&E/BBC co-production.

OUTSTANDING INDIVIDUAL ACHIEVEMENT IN COSTUMING FOR A SERIES
Leslie Simmons Potts, Marion Kirk, Daniel Grant North, "Cybill" ("Where's Zoey"), CBS—Carsey-Werner Co. in association with Jay Daniel Prods. and River Siren Prods.

OUTSTANDING INDIVIDUAL ACHIEVEMENT IN COSTUME DESIGN FOR A VARIETY OR MUSIC PROGRAM
Jane Ruhm, "The Best of Tracey Takes On," HBO—A Takes on Productions Inc. production in association with Witzend Prods.

OUTSTANDING INDIVIDUAL ACHIEVEMENT IN GRAPHIC DESIGN AND TITLE SEQUENCES
James Castle, Bruce Bryant, Carol Johnsen, (main title designers), "Caroline in the City", NBC—Barron-Pennette Prods., Three Sisters Entertainment in association with CBS Entertainment.

OUTSTANDING INDIVIDUAL ACHIEVEMENT IN MAKEUP FOR A SERIES
Michael Westmore, Greg Nelson, Scott Wheeler, Tina Kalliongis-Hoffman, Mark Shostrum, Gil Mosko, Ellis Burman, Steve Weber, Brad Look, (makeup artists), "Star Trek: Voyager" ("Threshold"), UPN—Star Trek in association with Paramount Pictures.

OUTSTANDING INDIVIDUAL ACHIEVEMENT IN MAKEUP FOR A MINISERIES OR A SPECIAL
Patricia Green (key makeup artist), **Kevin Haney** (effects makeup artist), "Kissinger and Nixon," TNT—A Paragon Entertainment Corp. Prod. in association with Daniel H. Blatt Prods., Lionel Chetwynd Prods., and Dreyfuss/James Prods.

OUTSTANDING INDIVIDUAL ACHIEVEMENT IN HAIR-STYLING FOR A SERIES
Karl Wesson (key hairstylist), **Kelly Kline** (hairstylist to Ms. Seymour), **Deborah Dobson, Laura Lee Grubich, Virgina Grobeson, Christine Lee** (hairstylists), "Dr. Quinn, Medicine Woman," ("When A Child Is Born"), CBS—CBS Entertainment Prods./the Sullivan Co.

OUTSTANDING INDIVIDUAL ACHIEVEMENT IN HAIRSTYLING FOR A MINISERIES OR A SPECIAL
Aileen Seaton (hair designer), "Gulliver's Travels," (Part 1), NBC—RHI Entertainment Inc. and Channel Four Television present from Jim Henson Prods.

OUTSTANDING INDIVIDUAL ACHIEVEMENT IN CASTING FOR A SERIES
Debi Manwiller (casting director), "Chicago Hope," CBS—David E. Kelley Prods. in association with 20th Century Fox Television.

OUSTANDING INDIVIDUAL ACHIEVEMENT IN CASTING FOR A MINISERIES OR A SPECIAL (TIE)
Mary Colquhoun (casting), "Truman," HBO—A Spring Creek Production.
Robi Reed-Humes (casting director), "Tuskegee Airmen," HBO—A Price Entertainment Production.

OUTSTANDING INDIVIDUAL ACHIEVEMENT IN SOUND EDITING FOR A SERIES
Thierry Couturier (sound supervisor), **Maciek Malish, Chris Reeves, Michael Goodman, Marty Stein** (dialogue editors), **Debby Ruby-Winsberg** (ADR editor), **Susan Welsh, Michael Kimball, Rick Hinson, Ira Leslie** (effects editors), **Jeff Charbonneau** (music editor), **Kitty Malone, Joe Sabella** (Foley artists), "The X-Files," ("Nisei"), FOX—Ten Thirteen Prods. in assocation with 20th Television.

OUTSTANDING INDIVIDUAL ACHIEVEMENT IN SOUND EDITING FOR A MINISERIES OR A SPECIAL
G. Michael Graham, M.P.S.E. (supervising sound editor), **Joseph Melody** (co-supervising sound editor), **Anton Holden, Bob Costanza, Tim Terusa, Mike Dickeson, Mark Steele, Darren Wright, Mike Lyle, Gary Macheel, John Adams, Rick Steele, Mark Friedgen, Bill Bell** (sound editors), **Kristi Johns** (ADR editor), **Stan Jones, Mark Haynes** (music editors), **Jill Schachne, Tim Chilton** (Foley editors), "Tuskegee Airmen," HBO—A Price Entertainment Production.

OUTSTANDING INDIVIDUAL ACHIEVEMENT IN SOUND MIXING FOR A DRAMA SERIES
Michael Williamson (production mixer), **David West, Nello Tori, Doug Turner** (re-recording mixers), "The X-Files," ("Nisei"), FOX—Ten Thirteen Prods. in assocation with 20th Television.

OUTSTANDING INDIVIDUAL ACHIEVEMENT IN SOUND MIXING FOR A VARIETY OR MUSIC SERIES OR A SPECIAL
Richard Lewzet (production mixer), **Ken Hahn** (recording mixer), "Music for the Movies: The Hollywood Sound," PBS—Alternate Currents, Les Films d'Ici, NHK & La Spet/Arte in association with Thirteen/WNET.

OUTSTANDING INDIVIDUAL ACHIEVEMENT IN SOUND MIXING FOR A COMEDY SERIES OR A SPECIAL
Dana Mark McClure (production mixer), **Thomas Ruth, C.A.S., David M. Wishaar, C.A.S., Robert Douglass** (re-recording mixers), "Frasier," ("Kisses Sweeter Than Wine"), NBC—Grub Street Prods. in association with Paramount.

OUTSTANDING INDIVIDUAL ACHIEVEMENT IN SOUND MIXING FOR A DRAMA MINISERIES OR A SPECIAL
Richard Birnbaum, C.A.S. (production mixer), **Sam Black, C.A.S., David Fluhr, C.A.S., John Asman, C.A.S.** (re-recording mixers), "Harvest of Fire," CBS—Sofronski Prods. in association with Hallmark Hall of Fame Productions, Inc.

OUTSTANDING INDIVIDUAL ACHIEVEMENT IN MUSIC COMPOSITION FOR A SERIES
Hummie Mann, "Picture Windows" ("Language of the Heart"), Showtime—Yorktown Prods. in association with Skyvision.

OUTSTANDING INDIVIDUAL ACHIEVEMENT IN MUSIC COMPOSITION FOR A MINISERIES OR A SPECIAL
Ernest Troost, "The Canterville Ghost, " ABC—Anasazi Prods. in association with Signboard Hill.

OUTSTANDING INDIVIDUAL ACHIEVEMENT IN MAIN TITLE THEME MUSIC
Mike Post, "Murder One," ABC—Steven Bochco Prods.

OUTSTANDING INDIVIDUAL ACHIEVEMENT IN MUSIC DIRECTION
Glen Roven, "Sinatra: 80 Years My Way," ABC—George Schlatter Prods.

OUTSTANDING INDIVIDUAL ACHIEVEMENT IN ART DIRECTION FOR A VARIETY OR MUSIC PROGRAM
Val Strazovec (production designer), **Jim Dultz** (art director), **Jenny Wilkinson** (set director), "Muppets Tonight," (with special guest star Tony Bennet), ABC—Jim Henson Prods.

OUTSTANDING INDIVIDUAL ACHIEVEMENT IN ART DIRECTION FOR A SERIES
Paul Eads (production designer), **Mondy Roffman** (art director), **Mary Ann Biddle** (set decorator), "Murder One," ("Chapter One"), ABC—Steven Bochcho Prods.

OUTSTANDING INDIVIDUAL ACHIEVEMENT IN ART DIRECTION FOR A MINISERIES OR A SPECIAL
Roger Hall (production designer), **John Fenner** (supervising art director), **Alan Tomkins** (U.K. art director), **Frederic Evard** (Portugal art director), **Rosalind Shingleton** (set decorator), "Gulliver's Travels," (Part 1), NBC—RHI Entertainment Inc. and Channel Four Television presentation from Jim Henson Prods.

OUTSTANDING INDIVIDUAL ACHIEVEMENT IN EDITING FOR A SERIES—SINGLE-CAMERA PRODUCTION
Jon Koslowsky, A.C.E., "JAG," (Pilot), NBC—Belisarius Prods. in association with NBC Prods. and Paramount.

OUTSTANDING INDIVIDUAL ACHIEVEMENT IN EDITING FOR A SERIES—MULTI-CAMERA PRODUCTION
Ron Volk, "Frasier," ("The Show Where Diane Comes Back"), NBC—Grub Street Orids, in association with Paramount.

OUTSTANDING INDIVIDUAL ACHIEVEMENT IN EDITING FOR A MINISERIES OR A SPECIAL — SINGLE-CAMERA PRODUCTION
David Beatty, "Tuskegee Airmen," HBO—Price Entertainment Prods.

OUTSTANDING INDIVIDUAL ACHIEVEMENT IN EDITING FOR A MINISERIES OR A SPECIAL—MULTI-CAMERA PRODUCTION
Mark West, "20 Years of Comedy on HBO," HBO—An HBO Production.

OUTSTANDING INDIVIDUAL ACHIEVEMENT IN CINEMATOGRAPHY FOR A SERIES
John Bartley, C.S.C, "The X-Files" ("Grotesque"), FOX—Ten Thirteen Prods. in assocation with 20th Television.

OUTSTANDING INDIVIDUAL ACHIEVEMENT IN CINEMATOGRAPHY FOR A MINISERIES OR A SPECIAL
Elmer Ragaly, "Rasputin," HBO—A Rysher/Citadel Entertainment production.

OUTSTANDING INDIVIDUAL ACHIEVEMENT IN LIGHTING DIRECTION (ELECTRONIC) FOR A COMEDY SERIES
Donald A. Morgan (director of photography), "Home Improvement" ("Room Without Wind"), ABC—Wind Dancer Production Group in assocation with Touchstone Television.

OUTSTANDING INDIVIDUAL ACHIEVEMENT IN LIGHTING DIRECTION (ELECTRONIC) FOR A DRAMA SERIES, VARIETY PROGRAM, MINI SERIES OR SPECIAL

Greg Bunton (lighting designer), "The 68th Annual Academy Awards," CBS—a production of the Academy of Motion Picture Arts and Sciences.

OUTSTANDING TECHNICAL DIRECTION/CAMERA/VIDEO FOR A SERIES

Michael Stramisky (technical director), **Les Atkinson, Hank Geving, Dave Levisohn, Wayne Orr, Rob Palmer, John Slagle, Kurt Tonnessen** (electronic camera), **Bill Gardhouse, Jr., Lance Gardhouse** (senior video), "The Tonight Show With Jay Leno," (no. 914), NBC—Bog Dogs Prods. in association with NBC Studios Inc.

OUTSTANDING INDIVIDUAL ACHIEVEMENT IN TECHNICAL DIRECTION/CAMERA/VIDEO FOR A MINISERIES OR A SPECIAL

John Field (technical director), **Ted Ashton** (electronic camera), **David Eastwood, Larry Heider, David Levisohn, Bill Philbin, David Plakos, Hector Ramirez, Ron Sheldon** (electronic camera), **Kris Wilson** (ENG electronic camera), **Thomas Teimpidis, Keith Winikoff** (senior video), "Sinatra: 80 Years My Way," ABC—George Schlatter Prods.

OUTSTANDING INDIVIDUAL ACHIEVEMENT IN CHOREOGRAPHY

Anita Mann, Charonne Mose, "1995 Miss America Pageant," NBC—Jeff Margolis Prods. in association with the Miss America Organization.

OUTSTANDING INFORMATIONAL SPECIAL

Surivors of the Holocaust, Executive Producer: Pat Mitchell. Senior Producer: Vivian Schiller. Producers: June BEallor, James Moll. Director: Alan Holzman. TBS—A co-production of Turner Original Prods. and Survivors of the Shoah Visual History Foundation.

OUTSTANDING INFORMATIONAL SERIES

Time Life's Lost Civilizations, Executive Producer: Joel Westbrook. Producer: Jason Williams. Producer/Director/Writer: Robert Gardner. Coordinating Producer: William Morgan. Writer: Ed Fields. Host: Sam Waterston. NBC—Time Life Video & Television.

OUTSTANDING INFORMATIONAL PROGRAMMING (TIE)

The Private LIfe of Plants, Camera: Tim Shepherd, Richard Kirby, Richard Ganiclift, Neil Brom,hall, Gavin Thurston, Michael Pitts. TBS—A co-production of BBC and Turner Original Prods. **Surivors of the Holocaust**, Editor/Director: Alan Holzman. TBS—A co-production of Turner Original Prods. and Survivors of the Shoah Visual History Foundation.

OUTSTANDING CHILDREN'S PROGRAM

Peter and the Wolf, Executive Producer: George Daugherty. Co-executive producer: David Wong. Producers: Linda Jones Clough, Adrian Workman. Director: Allan Holzman. ABC—IF/X Prods. in association with BMG Entertainment International.

DAYTIME PROGRAMMING

OUTSTANDING DRAMA SERIES

General Hospital, Executive Producer: Wendy Riche. ABC.

OUTSTANDING GAME/AUDIENCE PARTICIPATION SHOW

The Price Is Right, Executive Producer: Bob Barker. CBS.

OUTSTANDING PRE=SCHOOL CHILDREN"S SERIES

Sesame Street, Executive Producer: Michael Loman. PBS.

OUTSTANDING CHILDREN'S SPECIAL

Stand Up (CBS Schoolbreak Special), Producer: Eda Godel Hallinan. CBS.

OUTSTANDING ANIMATED CHILDREN'S PROGRAM

Animaniacs, Executive Producer: Steven Spielberg. WB.

OUTSTANDING TALK SHOW

The Oprah Winfrey Show, Executive Producer: Dianne Atkinson Hudson. Syndicated.

OUTSTANDING LEAD ACTRESS IN A DRAMA SERIES

Erika Slezak, One Life to Live. ABC.

OUTSTANDING LEAD ACTOR IN A DRAMA SERIES

Charles Keating, Another World, ABC.

OUTSTANDING SUPPORTING ACTRESS IN A DRAMA SERIES

Anna Holbrook, Another World. ABC.

OUTSTANDING SUPPORTING ACTOR IN A DRAMA SERIES

Jerry Van Dorn, Guiding Light. CBS.

OUTSTANDING YOUNGER ACTRESS IN A DRAMA SERIES

Kimberly McCullough, General Hospital. ABC.

OUTSTANDING YOUNGER ACTOR IN A DRAMA SERIES

Kevin Mambo, Guiding Light. CBS.

OUTSTANDING PERFORMER IN A CHILDREN'S SERIES

Shari Lewis, Lamb Chop's Play Along. PBS.

OUSTANDING TALK SHOW HOST

Montel Williams, The Montel Williams Show. Syndicated.

OUSTANDING DRAMA SERIES DIRECTING TEAM

Heather Hull, Frank Pacelli, Mike Denney, Kathryn Foster (Directors), **Betty Rothenberg, Sally McDonald, Dan Brumett, Robbin Masick Phillips** (Associate Directors), **Randall Hill, Don Jacob, Bob Welsh** (Stage Managers), The Young and the Restless. CBS.

OUSTANDING DRAMA SERIES WRITING TEAM

Agnes Nixon, Lorraine Broderick, Megam McTavish, Hal Corley, Frederick Johnson, Gail Lawrence, Jeff Beldner, Kern L. Lewis, Elizabeth Smith, Michelle Patrick, Bettina F. Bradbury, Judith Donato, Kathleen Klein, Ralph Wakefield, Pete T. Rich, (Writers), All My Children. ABC.

National & International Awards

Golden Globe Awards

BEST SERIES—DRAMA
Party of Five, Keyser Lippman Prods./Columbia Pictures TV. Fox.
BEST ACTRESS IN A DRAMA SERIES
Jane Seymour, "Dr. Quinn Medicine Woman."
BEST ACTOR IN A DRAMA SERIES
Jimmy Smits, "NYPD Blue."
BEST SERIES—MUSICAL OR COMEDY
Cybill, YBYL in association with Jay Daniel, Chuck Lorre, River Siren and Carsey Warner. CBS.
BEST ACTRESS IN A MUSICAL OR COMEDY SERIES
Cybill Shepherd, "Cybill."
BEST ACTOR IN A MUSICAL OR COMEDY SERIES
Kelsey Grammer, "Frasier."
BEST MINISERIES OR TELEFILM
Indictment: The McMartin Trial, HBO Pictures/Ixtlan Prods./Abby Mann Prods./Breakheart Films. HBO.
BEST ACTRESS IN A MINISERIES OR TELEFILM
Jessica Lange, "A Streetcar Named Desire."
BEST ACTOR IN A MINISERIES OR TELEFILM
Gary Sinise, "Truman."
BEST SUPPORTING ACTRESS IN A SERIES, MINISERIES OR TELEFILM
Shirley Knight, "Indictment: The McMartin Trial."
BEST SUPPORTING ACTOR IN A SERIES, MINISERIES OR TELEFILM
Donald Sutherland, "Citizen X."

Directors Guild of America Awards

BEST COMEDY SERIES
Gordon Hunt, "The Alan Brady Show," Mad About You, TriStar. NBC.
BEST DRAMATIC SERIES
Christopher Chulack, "Hell and High Water," ER, Constant c Prods. & Amblin TV in association with Warner Bros. TV. NBC.
BEST DRAMATIC SPECIAL
Mick Jackson, "Indictment" The McMartin Trial," HBO Pictures.
BEST MUSICAL OR VARIETY PROGRAM
Matthew Diamond, "Some Enchanted Evening," Celebrating Oscar Hammerstein II, Great Performances, WNET-13. PBS.
BEST DAYTIME DRAMA SERIES
William Ludel, Alan Pultz, "General Hospital (#8248)," Capital Cities/ABC Inc. ABC.
HONOREE LIFE ACHIEVEMENT IN SPORTS
Tony Verna.
HONOREE LIFE ACHIEVEMENT IN NEWS
Arthur Bloom.

Writers Guild of America Awards

BEST ORIGINAL LONG FORM
ER (pilot), Written by Michael Crichton. Warner Bros. Television Productions. NBC.
BEST ADAPTED LONG FORM
Citizen X, Teleplay by Chris Gerolmo based upon the book "The Killer Department" by Robert Cullen. HBO Films, Inc. HBO.
BEST EPISODIC DRAMA
"Love's Labor Lost" (ER), Written by Lance A. Gentile. Warner Bros. Television Productions. NBC.
BEST EPISODIC COMEDY
"The Matchmaker" (Frasier), Written by Joe Keenan. Network Television Division, Paramount Pictures. NBC.
BEST VARIETY, MUSICAL AWARD, TRIBUTE, SPECIAL EVENT
Dennis Miller Live, Show #8, Writing supervised by Eddie Feldmann; Jeff Cesario, Ed Driscoll, David Feldman, Gergory Greenberg, Dennis Miller, Kevin Rooney, (writers). Happy Family Productions. HBO.
BEST DAYTIME SERIAL
General Hospital, Written by Clare Labine, Matthew Labine, Eleanor Mancusi, Meg Bennett, Ralph Ellis, Michele Val Jean, Stephanie Braxton, Karen Harris, Lewis Arlt, Judith Pinsker. ABC.

BEST CHILDREN'S SCRIPT
Stand Up (CBS Schoolbreak Special), Written by Gordon Rayfield. CBS.
BEST DOCUMENTARY—CURRENT EVENTS
The Human Quest: The Nature of Human Nature, Episode 1, Written by Roger Bingham and Carl Byker. PBS.
BEST DOCUMENTARY—OTHER THAN CURRENT EVENTS
The American Experience: The Way West, Written by Ric Burns. PBS.
BEST TELEVISION SPOT NEWS SCRIPT
48 Hours: No Place to Hide, Written by Greg Kandra. CBS.

British Academy of Film and Television Arts (BAFTA) Awards

BEST SINGLE DRAMA
Persuasion, Fiona Finley, Roger Michell, Nick Dear.
BEST DRAMA SERIES
Cracker, Hilary Bevan Jones.
BEST DRAMA SERIAL
The Politician's Wife, Jenny Edwards, Jeanna Polley, Neal Weisman, Graham Theakston, Paula Milne.
BEST FACTUAL SERIES
The Death of Yugoslavia, Norma Percy.
BEST LIGHT ENTERTAINMENT (PROGRAM OR SERIES)
The Mrs Merton Show, Peter Kessler, Pati Marr, Dominic Brigstocke.
BEST COMEDY (PROGRAM OR SERIES)
Father Ted, Geoffrey Perkins, Declan Lowney, Graham Linehan,. Arthur Matthews.
THE HUW WELDON AWARD FOR BEST ARTS PROGRAM OR SERIES
The Children of the Revolution, John Wyver, David Hinton.
BEST FACTUAL CHILDREN'S PROGRAM
Short Change, Roy Milani.
BEST FICTION/ENTERTAINMENT CHILDREN'S PROGRAM
Coping with Christmas, Sue Nott, Dan Zeff, Peter Corey.
THE FLAHERTY DOCUMENTARY AWARD
The Betrayed (True Stories), Clive Gordon.
BEST ACTRESS
Jennifer Ehle, "Pride and Prejudice."
BEST ACTOR
Robbie Coltrane, "Cracker."
BEST LIGHT ENTERTAINMENT PERFORMANCE
Rory Bremner, "Rory Bremner—Who Else?"
BEST COMEDY PERFORMANCE
Martin Clunes, "Men Behaving Badly."
BEST NEWS COVERAGE
C4 News Coverage of War Crimes in the Former Yugoslavia, Production Team (ITN for C4).
BEST SPORTS/EVENTS COVERAGE IN REAL TIME
VE Day Coverage, Peter Hylton Cleaver, Neil Eccles, Philip S. Gilbert and Team.
BEST TALK SHOW
Panorama Interview with H.R.H. The Princess of Wales, Martin Bashir, Mike Robinson.
BEST FOREIGN TELEVISION PROGRAM
ER, Warner Bros. Television Prods.
THE RICHARD DIMBLEBY AWARD
Jeremy Paxman, for the year's most important personal contribution on the screen in Factual Television.
THE DENNIS POTTER AWARD
Roy Clark.
THE LEW GRADE AWARD FOR A SIGNIFICANT AND POPULAR TELEVISION PROGRAM.
The Antiques Roadshow.
THE ALAN CLARKE AWARD
Roy Battersby, for outstanding contribution to television.
THE TELEVISION AWARD FOR ORIGINALITY
Aardman Animation.
THE SPECIAL AWARD
Camera Team Survival.
THE LLOYD'S BANK PEOPLE'S VOTE FOR FAVOURITE TV PROGRAM
The X Files.

TELEVISION MOVIES & MINISERIES

1990—1996

TELEVISION MOVIES & MINISERIES

(OCTOBER 1, 1995—SEPTEMBER 30, 1996)

The Abduction
A Lifetime Original Movie from Lifetime Entertainment. Shown on July 7, 1996.
Cast: Victoria Principal.

The Affair
HBO Showcase, BBC and the Smithson Film Co. Executive Producer: Harry Belafonte. Producers: John Smithson, David Thompson. Director: Paul Seed. Shown on HBO October 14, 1995.
Cast: Courtney B. Vance, Kerry Fox, Leland Gantt, Beatie Edney, Ciraran Hinds, Ned Beatty.

Alien Avengers
A Concorde New Horizons and Showtime Inc. film in the Roger Corman Presents series. Executive Producer: Roger Corman. Producer: Michael Amato. Director: Lev L. Spiro. Shown on Showtime August 17, 1996.
Cast: Christopher Brown, Shanna Reed, George Wendt, Anastasia Sakelaris, Steven Burrows, Dan Martin.

Alien Nation: Millennium
National Studios Inc. in association with Kenneth Johnson Productions for Twentieth Television. Executive Producer: Kenneth Johnson. Producer: Paul Kurta. Director: Kenneth Johnson. Shown on Fox January 2, 1996.
Cast: Gary Graham, Eric Pierpoint, Michele Scarabelli, Terri Treas, Sean Six, Lauren Woodland.

Alistair MacLean's Night Watch
British Lion Prods., Jadran Film and USA Pictures. Producer: Peter Snell. Co-producer: Mike Mihalic. Director-Writer: David S. Jackson. Shown on USA October 4, 1995.
Cast: Pierce Brosnan, Alexandra Paul, William Devane, Michael J. Shannon, Lim Kay Siu, Irene Ng.

All She Ever Wanted
ABC Productions. Shown on ABC April 14, 1996.
Cast: Marcia Cross, James Marshall, Leila Kenzie, CCH Pounder.

Almost Golden: The Jessica Savitch Story
Sofronski Prods. and ABC Prods. Executive Producer: Bernard Sofronski. Producer: Adam Haight. Director: Peter Werner. Shown on Lifetime September 4, 1995.
Cast: Sela Ward, Ron Silver, Judith Ivey, Jeffrey DeMunn, William Converse-Roberts, Sean McCann.

America's Dream: Long Black Song
HBO in association with Carrie Prods. Executive Producers, series: Danny Glover, Carolyn McDonald. Producer: David Knoller. Director: Kevin Rodney Sullivan. Based on the short story by Richard Wright. Shown on HBO January 17, 1996.
Cast: Danny Glover, Tate Donovan, Tina Lifford, Daniel Tucker Kamin.

America's Dream: The Reunion
Executive Producers, series: Danny Glover, Carolyn McDonald. Producer: David Knoller. Director: Paris Barclay. Based on the short story by Maya Angelou. Shown on HBO January 17, 1996.
Cast: Bennet Guillory, Carl Lumbly, Susanna Thompson, Lorraine Toussaint, Summer Ross Jefferson.

America's Dream: The Boy Who Painted Christ Black
Executive Producers, series: Danny Glover, Carolyn McDonald. Producer: David Knoller. Director: Bill Duke. Based on the short story by John Henrick Clarke. Shown on HBO January 17, 1996.
Cast: Wesley Snipes, Norman D. Golden II, Jasmine Guy, Rae'ven A'lyia Kelly.

Andersonville
TNT Prods. in association with Gideon Prods. Executive Producers: Ethel Winant, John Frankenheimer. Writer-Producer: David W. Rintels. Director: John Frankenheimer. Shown on TNT March 3 & 4, 1996.

Angel Flight Down
C.S.P. Films, Carla Singer Productions. Director: Charles Wilkinson. Shown on ABC April 29, 1996.

Cast: Patricia Kalember, David Charvet, Christopher Atkins, Garwin Sanford, Gary Graham.

Annie: A Royal Adventure
Director: Ian Toynton. Shown on ABC November 18, 1995.
Cast: Ashley Johnson, Emily Ann Lloyd, Camilla Bell, George Hearn, Joan Collins.

The Babysitter's Seduction
A Hearst Entertainment Production.Director: David Burton Morris. Shown on NBC January 22, 1996.
Cast: Keri Russel, Stephen Collins, Phylicia Rashad.

The Barefoot Executive
ZM Prods. in association with Walt Disney Television. Executive Producers: George Zaloom, Les Mayfield, Scott Immergut. Producers: Joan Van Horn, Irwin Marcus. Director: Susan Seidelman. Shown on ABC November 11, 1995.
Cast: Jason London, Eddie Albert, Michael March, Terri Ivens, Jay Mohr, Ann Magnuson, Shannon O'Hurley, Yvonne De Carlo.

Beastmaster III: The Eyes of Braxus
Shown on WB May 27, 1996.
Cast: Marc Singer, Casper Van Dien, David Warner, Tony Todd, Lesley-Anne Down.

Bermuda Triangle
BBK Prods., Katie Face Prods., McPherson/Bradley Prods. and TriStar TV. Executive Producers: Stephen McPherson, Elizabeth Bradley, Tony Danza. Producers: Pierre De Lespinois, Boris Malden. Director: Ian Toynton. Shown on ABC April 4, 1996.
Cast: Lisa Jakub, David Gallagher, Susanna Thompson, Sam Behrens, Jerry Hardin.

Beyond the Call
Chris/Rose Productions in association with Barnstorm Films. Executive Producers: Bob Christiansen, Rick Rosenberg. Producer: Helen Bartlett. Director-Producer: Tony Bill. Shown on Showtime June 23, 1996.
Cast: Sissy Spacek, David Strathairn, Arliss Howard, Janet Wright, Lindsay Murrell, Les Carlson, Ken James, Christina Collins.

Bloodhounds
CNM Entertainment in association with Wilshire Court Productions. Executive Producer-Writer: Pablo F. Fenjves. Producer: Bob Roe. Director: Michael Katleman. Shown on USA Network April 3, 1996.
Cast: Corbin Bernsen, Christine Harnos, Kirk Baltz, Markus Flanagan, Gina Mastrogiacomo.

Blue River
Signboard Hill Productions. Executive Producer: Richard Welsh. Producer: Brent Shields. Director: Larry Elikann. Shown on Fox November 21, 1995.
Cast: Jerry O'Connell, Nick Stahl, Susan Dey, Sam Elliott, Jean Marie Barnwell, Rebecca Rogers, Patarick Renna.

Born Free: A New Adventure
ABC Productions. Shown on ABC April 27, 1996.
Cast: Jonathan Brandis, Ariana Richards, Lea Moreno, Chris Noth.

The Boys Next Door
Hallmark Hall of Fame Prods. Executive Producer: Richard Welsh. Producer-Director: John Erman. Shown on CBS February 4, 1996.
Cast: Tony Goldwyn, Michael Jeter, Nathan Lane, Robert Sean Leonard, Lynne Thigpen, Courtney B. Vance, Mare Winningham, Jenny Robertson, Elizabeth Wilson.

Brothers on the Frontier
Shown on ABC April 6, 1996.
Cast: Joey Lawrence, Matthew Lawrence, Andrew Lawrence.

A Brother's Promise: The Dan Jansen Story
Director: Bill Corcoran. Shown on CBS February 14, 1996.
Cast: Matt Keeslar, Jayne Brook, Christina Cox.

Butterbox Babies
Sullivan Entertainment in association with CBC; Executive
Producers: Kevin Sullivan, Trudy Grant; Producer: Kevin
Sullivan; Director: Don McBrearty. Shown on A&E Aug. 9,
1996.
*Cast: Susan Clark, Peter McNeill, Michael Riley, Catherine
Fitch, Nicholas Campbell, Cedric Smith.*

Bye Bye Birdie
RHI Entertainment Inc. Executive Producer: Robert Halmi, Sr.
Producer: J. Boyce Harman, Jr. Director: Gene Saks. Shown on
ABC December 3, 1995.
*Cast: Jason Alexander, Vanessa Williams, Chynna Phillips,
George Wendt, Marc Kudisch, Tyne Daly, Jason Gaffney.*

Cafe Society
Cineville, Skyline Entertainment and Daylight Productions.
Executive Producers: Carl-Jan Colpaert, Frederic Bouin, Jim
Steele. Co-executive Producers: Robert Strauss, Christoph
Henkel. Producers: Steve Alexander, Elan Sassoon. Writer-
Director-Music: Raymond De Felitta. Shown on Showtime
February 11, 1996.
*Cast: Peter Gallagher, Frank Whaley, Lara Flynn Boyle,
John Spencer, Anna Thomson, Christopher Murney, Paul
Guilfoyle.*

The Canterville Ghost
Anasazi Prods. Inc. in association with Signboard Hill Prods.
Executive Producer: Richard Welsh. Producer-Writer: Robert
Benedetti. Director: Syd Macartney. Based on the short story
by Oscar Wilde. Shown on ABC January 27, 1996.
*Cast: Patrick Stewart, Neve Campbell, Donald Sinden,
Cherie Lunghi, Edward Wiley, Leslie Phillips, Daniel Betts.*

The Cape
The Cape Prods. MTM Enterprises Inc., ZM Prods. Executive
Producers: Gil Grant, George Zaloom, Les Mayfield, Mary
Antholias, Paris Quailles. Producer: David Blake Hartley.
Director: Jan Toynton. Shown on CBS Aug. 7, 1996
*Cast: Corbin Bernsen, Adam Baldwin, Cameron Bancroft,
Bobby Hosea*

Captains Courageous
Hallmark Entertainment. Executive Producer: Robert Halmi, Sr.
Director: Michael Anderson. Shown on the Family Channel
April 21, 1996.
Cast: Robert Urich, Ken Vadas, Kaj-Erik Eriksen.

Captive Heart: The James Mink Story
Dorothea G. Petrie Prods. and Jaylar Prods. in association with
J.M. Story Prods. and Hallmark Entertainment. Executive
Producers: Dorothea G. Petrie, Michael Spivak. Producer:
Wendy Grean. Director: Bruce Pittman. Shown on CBS
April 14, 1996.
*Cast: Louis Gossett, Jr., Kate Nelligan, Ruby Dee, Peter
Outerbridge, Michael Jai White, Winston Rekert.*

A Case for Life
ABC Productions. Shown on ABC February 18, 1996.
Cast: Mel Harris, Valerie Bertinelli.

Chasing the Dragon
Director: Ian Sander. Shown on Lifetime June 19, 1996.
*Cast: Markie Post, Noah Fleiss, Dennis Boutsikaris, Peter
Frechette, Deirdre O'Connell, Michael Dolan, Bruce Norris.*

The Christmas Box
Co-Producers: Beth Polson, Mauree O'Hara. Shown on UPN
December 17, 1996.
*Cast: Richard Thomas, Annette O'Toole, Maureen O'Hara,
Kelsey Mulrooney.*

Closer and Closer
Director: Fred Gerber. Shown on Lifetime in 1996.
*Cast: Kim Delaney, Anthony Sherwood, Peter MacNeill,
Scott Kraft.*

Co-Ed Call Girl
The Kaufman Co. in association with Citadel Entertainment.
Director: Michael Rhodes. Shown on CBS February 6, 1996.
Cast: Tori Spelling.

The Cold Heart of a Killer
Executive Producer: Kate Jackson. Director: Paul Schneider.
Shown on CBS January 9, 1996.
Cast: Kate Jackson, Corbin Bernsen, Michael Damian.

The Colony
Director: Tim Hunter. Shown on ABC July 13, 1996.
*Cast: Brian Bloom, Michael Pare, Jennifer Guthrie, Alison
Moir.*

The Colony
USA Pictures Original. Director: Rob Hedden. Shown on USA
Network September 13, 1995.
*Cast: John Ritter, Mary Page Keller, Marshall Teague,
Alexandra Picatto.*

Conundrum
Director: Douglas Barr. Shown on Showtime March 1-3, 1996.
*Cast: Marg Helgenberger, Michael Biehn, Ron White, Peter
MacNeill.*

Cracker: Best Boys
Granada Television in association with A&E. Executive
Producer: Gub Neal. Producer: Hilary Bevan Jones. Director:
Charles McDougall. Shown August 6, 1996.
*Cast: Robbie Coltrane, Geraldine Somerville, Liam
Cunningham, John Simm, Ricky Tomlinson, Barbara Flynn,
Kiernan O'Brien.*

Crazy Horse
Von Zerneck-Sertner Films. Executive Producers: Robert M.
Sertner, Frank Von Zerneck. Producers: Salli Newman, Cleve
Landsberg, Hanay Geiogamah, Randy Sutter, Stacy
Mandelberg. Director: John Irvin. Shown on TNT July 7, 1996.
*Cast: Michael Greyeyes, Wes Studi, Irene Bedard, Lorne
Cardinal, August Schellenberg, Ned Beatty, Peter Horton,
Buffalochild C. Koopepequanicit.*

Cyberjack
Director: Robert Lee. Shown on the Sci-Fi Channel May 16,
1996.
Cast: Michael Dudikoff, Suki Kaiser, Brion James.

Daisies in December
HTV Intl. in association with Flextech Plc for Signboard Hill
Prods. Producers: Huw Davies, Alan Clayton. Director: Mark
Haber. Shown on Showtime December 3, 1995.
*Cast: Jean Simmons, Joss Ackland, Pippa Guard, Judith
Barker, Barbara Lott, Muriel Pavlow.*

Dalva
Director: Ken Cameron. Shown on ABC March 3, 1996.
Cast: Farrah Fawcett, Powers Booth, Peter Coyote.

Dalziel and Pascoe: A Clubbable Woman
An A&E Mystery Movie. Shown July 15, 1996.
Cast: Warren Clarke, Colin Buchanan, Ralph Brown.

Danielle Steel's Zoya
Director: Richard Colla. Shown on NBC September 17, 1996
*Cast: Bruce Boxleitner, Philip Casnoff, Diana Rigg, Melissa
Gilbert.*

Daniel Steel's Full Circle
Executive Producer: Douglas S. Cramer. Shown on NBC
September 9, 1996.
Cast: Teri Polo, Corbin Bernsen, Reed Diamond, Eric Lutes.

Dare to Love
Director: Armand Mastroianni. Shown on ABC December 17,
1995.
*Cast: Josie Bissett, Jason Gedrick, Jill Eikenberry,
James B. Sikking, Lorri Lindberg, Terry Loughlin.*

Dark Angel
Spelling Productions. Director: Robert Iscove. Shown on Fox
September 10, 1996.
Cast: Eric Roberts, Ashley Crow.

Dead Ahead
A USA Pictures Original. Director: Stuart Cooper. Shown on
The USA Network April 17, 1996.
*Cast: Stephanie Zimbalist, Sarah Chalke, Brendan Fletcher,
Andrew Airlie.*

Dead By Sunset
Craig Anderson Productions in association with TriStar
Television. Executive Producers: Craig Anderson, Ann Rule.
Producer: Larry Rapaport. Director: Karen Arthur. Shown on
NBC November 19 & 20, 1995.
*Cast: Ken Olin, Lindsay Frost, Annette O'Toole, John Terry,
Sally Murphy, Titan Crawford.*

Deadly Family Secrets
Director: Richard T. Heffron. Shown on NBC December 4, 1995.
Cast: Loni Anderson, Gigi Rice, Greg Evigan.

Deadly Games
Shaken Not Stirred Prods. and Rumbleseat Prods. in association with Viacom Prods. Executive Producers: Paul Bernbaum,

Leonard Nimoy. Producer: Don Gold. Director: Nimoy. Shown on UPN September 5, 1995.

Cast: Cynthia Gibb, James Calvert, Stephen T. Kay, Christopher Lloyd, Tom Rathman, Tony Carreiro.

Deadly Pursuits

Director: Felix Enriquez Alcala. Shown on NBC January 8, 1996.

Cast: Tori Spelling, Patrick Muldoon.

Deadly Voyage

Union Pictures, Viva Film Productions, HBO NYC and BBC. Executive Producers: Danny Glover, George Faber, Franc Roddam. Producers: Bradley Adams, John Goldschmidt. Director: John MacKenzie. Shown on HBO June 15, 1996.

Cast: Omar Epps, Sean Pertwee, Joss Ackland, David Suchet, Jean-Claude LaMarre, Andrew Divoff.

Deadly Web

Chuck Fries Prods. and Hallmark Entertainment. Executive Producer: Charles W. Fries. Producer: Christopher J. Fries. Director: Jorge Montesi. Shown on NBC April 15, 1996.

Cast: Gigi Rice, Ed Marinaro, John Wesley Shipp, Andrew Lawrence, Ted McGinley, Raphael Sbarge, Carlton Wilborn.

Death Benefit

A USA Picture. Shown on March 31, 1996.

Cast: Peter Horton, Carrie Snodgress, Wendy Makkena.

The Deliverance of Elaine

Shown on April 10, 1996.

Cast: Mare Winningham, Lloyd Bridges, Ron Lea, Chris Cooper.

Devil's Food

Pebblehut Prods in association with Jaffe/Braunstein Films, Spectator Films and Victor TV. Director: George Kaczender. Shown on Lifetime September 2, 1996.

Cast: Suzanne Somers, Dabney Coleman, William Katt, Charles R. Frank.

Divas

Director: Thomas Carter. Shown on Fox September 19, 1996

Cast: Khalil Kain, Nicole Parker, Tammy Townsend, Fatima Lowe.

Doctor Who

Universal Productions, Canada. Executive Producers: Alex Beaton, Phillip David Segal. Executive Producer for the BBC: Joe Wright. Producer: Peter V. Ware. Director: Geoffrey Sax. Shown on Fox May 14, 1996.

Cast: Paul McGann, Eric Roberts, Daphne Ashbrook, Sylvester McCoy, Yee Jee Tso, John Novak, Michael David Simms.

Double Jeopardy

Power Pictures in association with Wilshire Court Prods. Executive Producer: Julian Marks. Producer: Robert Baker. Co-producer/Writer/Director: Deborah Dalton. Shown on CBS January 30, 1996.

Cast: Brittany Murphy, Joe Penny, Teri Garr, Shawn Hatosy, Rutanya Alda, Ken James, Frederic Forrest, Mark Donato.

Down Came a Blackbird

Viacom Pictures and Chanticleer Films. Executive Producers: Jana Sue Memel, Thomas Colwell, Laura Dern. Producer: Patrick Whitley. Director: Jonathan Sanger. Shown on Showtime October 22, 1996.

Cast: Raul Julia, Laura Dern, Vanessa Redgrave, Cliff Gorman, Sarita Choudhur, Jay O. Sanders, Jeffrey DeMunn, L. Scott Caldwell.

Ed McBain's 87th Precinct: Ice

Diana Kerew Productions, Inc. in association with Hearst Entertainment, Inc. Executive Producer: Diana Kerew. Director: Bradford May. Shown on NBC February 18, 1996.

Cast: Dale Midkiff, Joe Pantoliano, Paul Johansson, Andrea Parker, Dean McDermott, Andrea Ferrell, Diane Douglas, Nigel Bennett, Michael Gross.

Evil Has a Face

Shown on USA Network March 20, 1996.

Cast: Sean Young, William Moses.

Evolver

Trimark Pictures in association with Blue Rider Pictures. Executive Producer: Mark Amin. Producers: Jeff Geoffray, Walter Josten, Henry Seggerman. Director: Mark Rosman. Shown on the Sci-Fi Channel February 10, 1996.

Cast: John de Lancie, Ethan Randall, Cassidy Rae, Paul Dooley, Cindy Pickett.

Eye of the Stalker: A Moment of Truth Movie

Director: Reza Badiyi. Shown on NBC December 18, 1995.

Cast: Brooke Langton, Jere Burns, Joanna Cassidy.

Face of Evil

Larry Thompson Entertainment. Executive Producer: Larry Thompson. Co-Producers: Robert Kosberg, Arvin Kaufman. Producer: Daniel Schneider. Director: Mary Lambert. Shown on CBS April 9, 1996.

Cast: Tracy Gold, Perry King, Shawnee Smith.

A Face To Die For

Director: Jack Bender. Shown on NBC March 11, 1996.

Cast: Yasmine Bleeth, Robin Givens, James Wilder, Chandra West, Mary Ellen Trainor, Ricky Paull Goldin.

The Final Cut

A BBC production in association with WGBH Boston. Executive Producer: Michael Wearing. Series Executive Producer: Rebecca Eaton. Producer: Ken Riddington. Director: Mike Vardy. Shown on PBS February 4 & 5, 1996.

Cast: Ian Richardson, Diane Fletcher, Nick Brimble, Tom Easley, Erika Hoffman, Nickolas Grace, Andrew Seear, Glyn Grain, William Scott Mason.

For Better or Worse

Castle Rock Entertainment and Columbia Pictures. Executive Producer-Writer: Jeff Nathanson. Producer: David Rotman. Director: Jason Alexander. Shown on TNT February 18, 1996.

Cast: Jason Alexander, Lolita Davidovich, James Woods, Joe Mantegna, Jay Mohr, Robert Costanzo, Beatrice Arthur, Rob Reiner.

For Love Alone

Shown on CBS January 5 & 7, 1996.

Cast: Stephen Collins, Sanna Vraa, Trevor Eve, Brigitte Pacquette, Tom Rack, Madeline Kahn.

For the Future: The Irvine Fertility Scandal

Director: David Jones. Shown on Lifetime.

Cast: Marily Henner, Linda Lavin, Alicia Coppola.

Forgotten Sins

World International Netowrk. Producer: Ken Kaufman. Director: Dick Lowry. Shown on ABC March 7, 1996.

Cast: John Shea, Bess Armstrong, William Devane.

Frequent Flyer

Shown on ABC March 10, 1996.

Cast: Jack Wagner, Shelley Hack, Nicole Eggert, Joan Severance, Kalen Mills, Elizabeth Ruscio, Mark Nutter.

A Friend's Betrayal

Director: Christopher Leitch. Shown on NBC May 19, 1996.

Cast: Brian Austin Green, Sharon Lawrence, Harley Jane Kozak, John Getz, Kataie Wright.

Full Body Massage

Showtime in association with Littman-Gurskis-Nolan Prods. Executive Producer: Robert Littman. Producers: Michael Nolin, Julie Ahlberg. Director: Nicolas Roeg. Shown on November 5, 1995.

Cast: Mimi Rogers, Bryan Brown, Gareth Williams, Elizabeth Barondes, Christopher Burgard, Heather Gunn, Patrick Neil Quinn.

Gallowglass

A BBC production in association with PBS. Producer: Phillippa Giles. Director: Tim Fywell. Shown on PBS October 5, 12 & 19, 1995.

Cast: Michael Sheen, Paul Rhys, John McArdle, Arkie Whitely, Gary Waldhorn, Claire Hackett, Harriet Owen.

Generation X

MT2 Services, Inc. in association with Marvel Films/Entertainment Group Inc. Executive Producers: Avi Arad, Stan Lee, Brue Sallan, Erick Blackeney. Producer: David Roessell. Director: Jack Sholder. Shown on Fox February 20, 1996.

Cast: Matt Frewer, Finola Hughes, Jeremy Ratchford, Heather McComb, Agustin Rodriguez.

Golden Will: The Silken Laumann Story

Producer: Carol Reynolds, Director: Eric Till. Shown on The Disney Channel.

Cast: Nancy Anne Sakovich.

Gone in the Night

Hill/Field Entertainment. Executive Producers: Leonard Hill, Joel Fields. Producers: Ardythe Goergens, Bernie Caulfield. Director: Bill L. Norton. Shown on CBS February 25 & 27, 1996.

Cast: Shannen Doherty, Edward Asner, Dixie Carter, Kevin Dillon, Michael Brandon.

The Good Doctor: The Paul Fleiss Story
Shown on CBS Feb. 21, 1996.
Cast: Michael Gross, Tricia Leigh Fisher, George Segal.

Gotti
HBO Pictures. Executive Producer: Gary Lucchesi. Producer: David Coatsworth. Director: Robert Harmon. Shown on HBO August 17, 1996.
Cast: Armand Assante, Anthony Quinn, William Forsythe, Richard S. Sarafian, Vincent Pastore, Robert Miranda.

Grand Avenue
Wildwood Enterprises and Elsboy Entertainment. Executive Producers: Robert Redford, Paul Aaron, Rachel Pfeffer. Co-Executive Producer-Writer: Greg Sarris. Associate Producer: Janace Tashjian. Producer: Tony To. Director: Daniel Sackheim. Shown on HBO June 30, 1996.
Cast: A. Martinez, Irene Bedard, Tantoo Cardinal, Dianne Debassige, Sheila Tousey, Deeny Dakota.

Gridlock
Shown on NBC January 14, 1996.
Cast: David Hasselhoff, Kathy Ireland, Marc Strange, Miguel Fernandes, Tony Desantis.

Gulliver's Travels
Hallmark Entertainment in association with Channel Four Television Corp. and Jim Henson Productions. Executive Producers: Robert Halmi, Sr., Brian Henson. Producer: Duncan Kenworthy. Director: Charles Sturridge. Shown on NBC February 4, 1996.
Cast: Ted Danson, Mary Steenburgen, James Fox, Ceraldine Chaplin, Edward Fox, John Gielgud, Robert Hardy, Alfre Woodard, Peter O'Toole, Edward Woodward, Omar Sharif.

The Halfback of Notre Dame
A Showtime Production in association with Sugar Entertainment Production. Producer: Larry Sugar. Director: Rene Bonniere. Shown on Showtime January 21, 1996.
Cast: Gabriel Hogan, Emmanuelle Vaugier, Allen Cutler, Scott Hylands, Sandra Nelson, Nicole Parker.

Harrison: Cry of the City
Crescendo Productions, Michael Gleason Productions, Paramount. Executive Producers: William Sackheim, Michael Gleason. Producer: Marilyn Stonehouse. Director: James Frawley. Shown on UPN February 27, 1996.
Cast: Edward Woodward, Jeffrey Nordling, Elizabeth Hurley, Cynthia Harris, Jude Ciccolella, Felicity Huffman, Robert Montano, Elva Mai Hoover.

Harts in High Season
Shown on The Family Channel Mar. 24, 1996.
Cast: Robert Wagner, Stefanie Powers, James Brolin.

Harvest of Fire
Hallmark Hall of Fame. Co-Executive Producer: Brent Shields. Executive Producers: Bernard Sofronski, Richard Welsh. Director: Arthur Allan Seidelman. Shown on CBS April 21, 1996.
Cast: Lolita Davidovich, J.A. Preston, Jean Louisa Kelly, Tom Aldredge, James Read, Craig Wasson, Patty Duke.

The Haunting of Lisa
Shown on Lifetime April 10, 1996.
Cast: Cherly Ladd, Duncan Regehr.

Have You Seen My Son?
Shown on ABC January 8, 1996.
Cast: Lisa Hartman-Black, William Russ, Anne Francis.

Hearts Adrift
Director: Vic Sarin. Shown on The USA Network August 7, 1996.
Cast: Ron McGee, Kathleen Noone, Nicholas Coster, Don Murray, Scott Reeves, Sydney Penny, Rodney Rowland.

Heavy Weather
Shown on PBS Feb. 18, 1996.
Cast: Judy Parfitt, Richard Briers, Benjamin Soames, Richard Johnson.

Heck's Way Home
Showtime Original Pictures for Kids. Shown on March 8 & 10, 1996.
Cast: Alan Arkin, Chad Krowchuck, Michael Riley, Shannon Lawson, Don Francks, Gabe Khouth.

The Heidi Chronicles
A TNT production. Executive Producer: Michael Brandman. Producer-Production Manager: Leanne Moore. Director: Paul Bogart. Shown on TNT October 15, 1995.
Cast: Jamie Lee Curtis, Tom Hulce, Peter Friedman, Kim Cattrall, Eve Gordon, Sharon Lawrence, Julie White, Shari Belafonte.

Her Deadly Rival
Rysher Entertainment. Producers: Judith A. Polone, Judy Cairo. Director: Jim Hayman. Shown on CBS on September 19, 1996.
Cast: Harry Hamlin, Annie Potts, Lisa Zane, D.L. Anderson.

Her Last Chance
Director: Richard Colla. Shown on NBC April 8, 1996.
Cast: Kellie Martin, Patti Lupone, Devon Odessa, Jonathan Brandis, Jenna Elfman.

Hidden in Silence
A Lifetime Original Movie. Director: Richard Colla. Shown on March 6, 1996.
Cast: Kellie Martin, Gemma Coughlan, Marion Ross, Tom Radcliffe, Joss Ackland.

High Incident
DreamWorks Television L.L.C. Executive Producers: Eric Bogosian, Michael Pavone, Dave Alan Johnson. Producer: Ralph Winter. Director: Charles Haid. Shown on ABC March 4, 1996.
Cast: Matthew Beck, Matt Craven, Cole Hauser, Catherine Kellner, Julio Oscar Mechoso.

Hijacked: Flight 285
Shown on ABC February 4, 1996.
Cast: Anthony Michael Hall, James Brolin, Ally Sheedy, Michael Gross.

A Holiday to Remember
Shown on CBS Dec 12, 1995.
Cast: Connie Sellecca, Rue McClanahan.

Homecoming
Shown Showtime April 14, 1996.
Cast: Kimberlee Peterson, Trever O'Brien, Hanna Hall.

Hostile Advances: The Kerry Ellison Story
Director: Allan Kroeker. Shown on Lifetime May 27, 1996.
Cast: Rena Sofer, Victor Garber, Karen Allen.

A Husband, A Wife and A Lover
Shown on CBS Mar. 17, 1996.
Cast: Judith Light, Jay Thomas, William Russo.

Innocent Victims
Kushner-Locke Productions in association with Cates/Doty Productions. Executive Producers: Gilbert Cates, Dennis E. Doty. Producer: Dennis E. Doty. Director: Gilbert Cates. Shown on ABC January 21 & 22, 1996.
Cast: Rick Schroder, Hal Holbrook, Tom Irwin, Rue McClanahan, Howard Hesseman, Ari Myers, John Corbett, Liza Snyder.

Inside
Showtime presents in association with Hallmark Entertainment presents an Elkins Entertainment and Logo Entertainment production. Director: Arthur Penn. Shown on Showtime Aug. 25, 1996
Cast: Eric Stolz, Nigel Hawthorne, Louis Gossett Jr, Ian Roberts, Ross Preller.

In the Blink of an Eye
Hamdon Entertainment. Shown on ABC March 24, 1996.
Cast: Veronica Hamil, Mimi Rogers, Piper Laurie, Polly Bergen.

In the Lake of the Woods
Director: Carl Schenkel. Shown on Fox March 5, 1996.
Cast: Peter Strauss, Peter Boyle, Kathleen Quinlan.

In the Line of Duty: Smoke Jumpers
World International Network. Producer-Director: Dick Lowry. Shown on NBC February 11, 1996.
Cast: Adam Baldwin, Lindsay Frost.

In the Name of Love: A Texas Tragedy
Shown on Fox September 12, 1995.
Cast: Michael Hayden, Richard Crenna, Bonnie Bartlett, Laura Leighton.

The Invaders
Papazian-Hirsch Entertainment in association with Spelling Entertainment Group Inc. Executive Producers: Robert Papazian, James Hirsch, James D. Parriott. Director: Paul Shapiro. Shown on Fox November 12, 1995.
Cast: Scott Bakula, Elizabeth Pena, Richard Thomas, DeLane Matthews, Terence Knox, Richard Belzer, Roy Thinnes.

It Was Him Or Us
Director: Robert Iscove. Shown on CBS November 21, 1995.
Cast: Ann Jillian.

Jack Higgins' On Dangerous Ground
Visionview/Carousel/Telescene Prods. Co-Executive Producers: Romain Schroeder, David Elstein, Robin Spry, Jim Howell, Paul Painter. Producer: Jim Reeve. Director: Lawrence Gordon-Clark. Shown on Showtime May 12, 1996.
Cast: Rob Lowe, Kenneth Cranham, Deborah Moore, Jurgen Prochnow, Ingeborka Dapkunaite.

Jack Reed: A Killer Amongst Us
Kushner-Locke Entertainment and Patricia Clifford Prods. in association with NBC. Executive Producer: Brian Dennehy. Producer: Patricia Clifford. Director: Dennehy. Shown on NBC January 7, 1996.
Cast: Brian Dennehy, Charles S. Dutton, Susan Ruttan, Kevin Dunn, Suki Kaiser, Michael Talbott, C.C.H. Pounder.

Journey
Hallmark Hall of Fame Prods. Executive Producers: Glenn Close, Richard Welsh. Producer: Brent Shields. Director: Tom McLoughlin. Shown on CBS December 10, 1995.
Cast: Max Pomeranc, Jason Robards, Brenda Fricker, Meg Tilly, Eliza Dushku, Sal Lopez, Jason Dohring, Claude Earl Jones.

Justice for Annie: A Moment of Truth Movie
Executive Producers: Michael O'Hara and Lawrence Horowitz. Shown on NBC January 15, 1996.
Cast: Peggy Lipton, Danica McKellar, Susan Ruttan, Bruce Weitz, Terry David Mulligan, Gwynyth Walsh, Teryl Rothery.

A Kidnapping in the Family
Shown on ABC Feb. 26, 1996.
Cast: Tracey Gold, Kate Jackson, Robert Bishop.

Kidz in the Wood
Green/Epstein Prods. Executive Producers: Neal Israel, Robert Klane. Director: Israel. Shown on NBC May 25, 1996.
Cast: Dave Thomas, Julia Duffy, Tatyana M. Ali, Darius McCrary, Candace Cameron.

Kindred: The Embraced
John Leekley Prods. in assciation with Spelling Television. Executive Producers: John Leekley, Aaron Spelling, E. Duke Vincent. Producer: Llewellyn Wells. Director: Peter Medak. Shown on Fox April 2, 1996.
Cast: E. Thomas Howell, Mark Frankel, Kate Vernon, Stacy Haiduk, Jeff Kober, Kelly Rutherford.

Kiss and Tell
New Amsterdam Entertainment in association with the Wilshire/Hauser Co. Executive Producers: Richard p. Rubinstein, Mitchell Galin. Producer: David Kappes. Director: Andy Wolk. Shown on ABC January 15, 1996.
Cast: Cheryl Ladd, John Terry, Francie Swift, Barry Corbin, John Bedford Lloyd, Jack Gilpin, Caitlin Clarke.

Kissinger and Nixon
Paragon Entertainment Corp. Executive Producer: Daniel H. Blatt, Jon Slan, Judith James, Lionel Chetwynd. Producer: Richard Borchiver. Director: Daniel Petrie. Shown on TNT December 10, 1995.
Cast: Ron Silver, Beau Bridges, Matt Frewer, Ron White, George Takei.

Land's End
Fred Dryer Productions, Skyvision Entertainment and Walt Disney Television. Executive Producers: Brian K. Ross, Jim Reid, Fred Dryer, Victor A. Schiro. Producer: Ron Frazier. Director: James Bruce. Shown on KCOP September 22, 1996.
Cast: Fred Dryer, Geoffrey Lewis, Bryan Cranston, Rena Fiffel, Tim Thomerson, Pamela Bowen.

Larry McMurtry's Dead Man's Walk
Saria Co. Inc., de passe Entertainment & Larry Levinson Productions in association with Hallmark Entertainment Inc. Executive Producers: Robert Halmi, Jr., Larry Levinson, Larry McMurtry, Diana Ossana, Suzanne de Passe. Co-Producer: Frank Q. Dobbs. Director: Yves Simoneau. Shown on ABC May 12 & 13, 1996.

Cast: F. Murray Abraham, David Arquette, Keith Carradine, Patricia Childress, Joaquim De Almeida, Brian Dennehy, Harry Dean Stanton, Edward James Olmos.

Larry McMurtry's Streets of Laredo
de Passe Entertainment, Levinson Prods. and RHI Entertainment Inc. Executive Producers: Robert Halmi, Jr., Larry Levinson, Suzanne de Passe, Larry McMurtry, Diana Ossana. Director: Joseph Sargent. Shown on CBS November 12, 1995.
Cast: James Garner, Sissy Spacek, Sam Shepard, Ned Beatty, Randy Quaid, Wes Studi, George Carlin, Kenvin Conway, Sonia Braga.

The Last Frontier
HBO Independent Prods. in association with 20th Century Fox Television. Executive Producer: Howard Meyers. Producers: Leo J. Clarke, Vic Kaplan. Director: Arlene Sanford. Shown on Fox June 3, 1996.
Cast: Anthony Starke, John Terlesky, Patrick Labyorteaux, David Kriegel, Jessica Tuck, Leigh-Allyn Baker, Renee Parent.

The Late Shift
Northern Lights Entertainment. Executive Producer: Ivan Reitman. Co-Executive Producers: Joe Medjuck, Daniel Goldberg. Producer: Don Carmody. Director: Betty Thomas. Shown on HBO February 24, 1996.
Cast: Kathy Bates, John Michael Higgins, Daniel Roebuck, Bob Balaban, Ed Begley, Jr., Sandra Bernhard, Treat Williams, Rich Little.

Lavyrle Spencer's Home Song
Director: Nancy Malone. Shown on CBS March 20, 1996.
Cast: Lee Horsley, Polly Draper, Deborah Raffin, Ari Meyers, Chris Martin, Stan Kirsch.

The Lazarus Man
Ogiens/Kane co. in association with Castle Rock Entertainment and Turner Program Services. Executive Producers: Michael Ogiens, Norman S. Powell. Producer: Harvey Frand. Director: Johnny E. Jensen. Shown on CBS January 1, 1996.
Cast: Robert Urich, Elizabeth Dennehy, David Marshall Grant, John Diehl, John Christian Graas.

The Legend of Gator Face
Showtime Original Pictures for Kids. Shown on Showtime May 19, 1996.
Cast: Paul Winfield, John White, Dan Warry-Smith, Charlotte Sullivan, Matt Evans.

Legend of the Ruby Silver
ABC Productions. Director: Charles Wilkinson. Shown on ABC January 13, 1996.
Cast: Bruce Weitz, Rebecca Jenkins, Jonathan Jackson, John Schneider.

Lifeline
Shown on USA Network May 15, 1996.
Cast: Lorraine Bracco, Jean-Marc Barr.

Lightning in a Bottle
Shown on Lifetime March 20, 1996.
Cast: Lynda Carter, Dee Wallace Stone, Martin Cove, Matt McCoy, Stuart Whitman.

Lily Dale
Producers Entertainment Group and Hallmark Entertainment. Executive Producers: Irwin Meyer, Peter Crane, Linda Curran Wexelblatt. Producer: John Thomas Lenox. Director: Peter Masterson. Adapted from a play by Horton Foote. Shown on SHO June 9, 1996.
Cast: Tim Guinee, Stockard Channing, Mary Stuart Masterson, Sam Shepard, Jean Stapleton, John Slattery.

The Limbic Region
Showtime in association with MGM Television. Executive Proudcer: Frank Mancuso, Jr. Producers: Tom Rowe, George Horie. Director: Michael Pattinson. Shown June 30, 1996.
Cast: Edward James Olmos, George Dzundza, Roger R. Cross, Gwynyth Walsh, Don S. Davis.

Little Riders
Director: Kevin Connor. Shown on The Disney Channel March 24, 1996.
Cast: Paul Scofield, Rosemary Harris, Noley Thornton, Malcolm McDowell, Benedick Blythe.

Live Shot
Rysher Entertainment in association with United Paramount Network. Executive Producers: Steve Marshall, Dan Guentzelman, Scott Brazil. Director: Colin Bucksey. Shown on UPN August 29, 1995.

Cast: Sam Anderson, David Birney, Wanda De Jesus, Hill Harper, Spencer Klein, Burce McGill, Cheryl Pollak.

Losing Chase
Showtime presents in association with Hallmark Entertainment; Director: Kevin Bacon. Shown on Showtime Aug. 18, 1996.
Cast: Helen Mirren, Kyra Sedgwick, Beau Bridges.

Lucifer's Child
ICAP Prods. and Random Entertainment in association with A&E Network and TV2/Danmark. Executive Producers: Iris Caplan, Robert Norton. Director: Tony Abatemarco. Shown on A&E September 21, 1995.
Cast: Julie Harris.

The Man Next Door
Shown on ABC January 18, 1996.
Cast: Michael Ontkean, Pamela Reed, Annette O'Toole, Sam Anderson, Richard Gilliland.

Maternal Instincts
Shooting Star Entertainment in association with Wilshire Court Productions. Executive Producers: Lisa Friedman Bloch, Delta Burke. Producer: Mary Eilts. Director: George Kaczender. Shown on USA Network January 17, 1996.
Cast: Delta Burke, Beth Broderick, Tom Mason, Garwin Sanford, Sandra Nelson, Gillian Barber.

Miami Hustle
Showtime in association with The Private Movie Co. Executive Producers: Dan Dimbort, Avi Lerner, Trevor Short. Producer: R. Ben Efraim. Director: Lawrence Lanoff. Shown July 21, 1996.
Cast: Kathy Ireland, Jon Enos, Audie England, Allan Rich, Richard Sarafian, Eduardo Yanez.

Mr. and Mrs. Loving
Daniel L. Paulson Prods. for Showtime in association with Hallmark Entertainment. Executive Producers: Timothy Hutton, Susan Rose. Producer: Dan Paulson. Director: Richard Friedenberg. Shown March 31, 1996.
Cast: Timothy Hutton, Lela Rochon, Ruby Dee, BillNunn, Corey Parker, Isaiah Washington.

Mrs. Munck
A Diane Ladd Inc. Production. Producers: Barbara Boyle, Michael Taylor. Director: Diane Ladd. Shown on Showtime January 28, 1996.
Cast: Diane Ladd, Bruce Dern, Kelly Preston, Shelley Winters, Scott Fisher, Jim Walton.

Mr. Stitch
Director: Roger Avary. Shown on Sci-Fi Channel Aug. 17, 1996
Cast: Wil Wheaton, Rutger Hauer, Nia Peeples, Michael Harris.

Mixed Blessings
The Cramer Co. in association with NBC Productions Inc. Executive Producer: Douglas S. Cramer. Supervising Producer: Dennis Hammer. Director: Bethany Rooney. Shown December 11, 1995.
Cast: Gabrielle Carteris, Scott Baio, Bess Armstrong, Bruce Greenwood, James Naughton, Alexandra Paul, Bruce Weitz, Julie Condra.

Moonshine Highway
A Showtime Original Picture. Director: Andy Armstrong. Shown on Showtime May 5, 1996.
Cast: Kyle MacLachlan, Randy Quaid, Maria Del Mar.

Moses
Turner and Lube Prods., in association with LUX, BetaTaurus and RAI. Executive Producer: Gerald Rafshoon. Producer: Lorenzo Minoli. Director: Roger Young. Shown on TNT April 7-8, 1996.
Cast: Ben Kingsley, David Suchet, Frank Langella, Christopher Lee, Anna Galiena, Enrico Lo Verso, Geraldine McEwan.

A Mother's Instinct
Director: Sam Pillsbury. Shown on CBS March 13, 1996.
Cast: Lindsay Wagner, Debrah Farentino, John Terry, Barbara Babcock, Lynn Thigpen, Alana Austin.

Murder One: Chapters 20 and 21
Steven Bochco Productions and 20th Century Fox. Executive Producers: Steven Bochco, William M. Finkelstein, Charles H. Eglee. Co-Executive Producer: Michael Fresco. Producers: Geoffrey Neigher, Marc Buckland. Director: Marc Buckland. Shown on ABC April 22, 1996.
Cast: Daniel Benzali, Jason Gedrick, Barbara Bosson, Stnaley Tucci, Mary McCormack, Michael Hayden, Joe Spano, Donna Murphy.

My Son is Innocent
Shown on ABC May 6, 1996.
Cast: Marilu Henner, Nick Stahl, Matt McCoy, Barry Corbin, John O'Hurley.

My Very Best Friend
Shown on CBS Mar. 27, 1996.
Cast: Jill Eikenberry, Tom Irwin, Kim Wamat.

Neil Simon's Jake's Women
RHI Entertainment Inc. in association with Hallmark Entertainment. Executive Producer: Robert Halmi, Sr., Producer-Director: Glenn Jordan. Shown on CBS March 3, 1996.
Cast: Alan Alda, Anne Archer, Lolita Davidovich, Julie Kavner, Mora Sorvino, Joyce Van Patten, Kimberly Williams, Ashley Peldon.

Neil Simon's London Suite
Producer: Greg Smith. Executive Producer: Robert Halmi Sr. Shown on NBC September 15, 1996.
Cast: Michael Richards, Julie Hagerty, Jonathan Silverman, Julia Louis-Dreyfuss.

Never Give Up: The Jimmy V Story
Shown on CBS April 2, 1996.
Cast: Anthony LaPaglia, Ashley Crow.

Night of the Twisters
Director: Tim Bond. Shown on The Family Channel February 14, 1996.
Cast: John Schneider, Devon Sawa, Amos Crawley, Laurie Betram, Helen Hughes.

Nightjohn
Shown on The Disney Channel June 1, 1996.
Cast: Carl Lumbly, Allison Jones, Beau Bridges.

No Greater Love
Executive Producer: Douglas S. Cramer. Director: Richard Heffrom. Shown on NBC December 29-31, 1995.
Cast: Kelly Rutherford, Michael Landes, Simon MacCorkindale, Chris Sarandon, Gina Philips, Nicholas Campbell.

No One Could Protect Her
Director: Larry Shaw. Shown on ABC February 11, 1996.
Cast: Anthony John Denison, Dan Lauria, Joanna Kerns, Lori Hallier.

No One Would Tell
Shown on NBC May 6, 1996.
Cast: Fred Savage, Candace Cameron, Michelle Phillips, Heather McComb.

Norma Jean and Marilyn
HBO in association with Marvin Worth Productions. Executive Producer: Marvin Worth. Producer: Guy Riedel. Director: Tim Fywell. Shown on May 18, 1996.
Cast: Mira Sorvino, Ashley Judd, Josh Charles, Ron Rifkin, Peter Dobson, Lindsay Crouse, David Dukes.

On Seventh Avenue
Pilot for series. Shown on NBC June 10, 1996.
Cast: Wendy Makkena, Stephen Collins, Damian Chapa, Gene Saks, Alan Rosenberg, Liz Coke, Lara Harris.

Our Son, The Matchmaker
Alexander/Enright and Associates. Executive Producers: Les Alexander, Don Enright. Producer: Susan Jeter. Director: Lorraine Senna. Shown on CBS May 8, 1996.
Cast: Ann Jillian, Ellen Burstyn, Drew Ebersole, David Andrews, Linda Larkin.

Out There
An I.R.S. Media production. Executive Producers: Paul Colichman, Miles Copeland III. Producer: Larry Estes. Director: Sam Irvin. Shown on Showtime November 19, 1995.
Cast: Bill Campbell, Wendy Schaal, Rod Steiger, Jill St. John, Bill Cobbs, Leslie Bevis, Paul Dooley, David Rasche.

The Peacock Spring
Mobil Masterpiece Theatre in association with ZED Ltd. for the BBC. Executive Producer: Phillippa Giles. Producers: Sophie Balhetchet, Glenn Wilhide. Director: Christopher Morahan. Shown on PBS May 19 and 26, 1996.
Cast: Peter Egan, Hattie Morahan, Laura Barneby, Jennifer Hall, Naveen Andrews, Madhur Jaffrey, Ravi Kapoor.

The Perfect Daughter
Director: Harry Longstreet. Shown on USA on Aug. 21, 1996.
Cast: Bess Armstrong, Mark Joy.

Peter Benchley's 'The Beast'
Michael R. Joyce Prods. and Dan Wigutow Prods. Executive Producers: Dan Wigutow, Peter Benchley. Producer: Tana Nugent. Director: Jeff Bleckner. Shown on NBC April 28, 1996.
Cast: William Petersen, Karen Sillas, Charles Martin Smith, Ronald Guttman, Missy Crider, Sterling Macer Jr., Denis Arndt.

Pharoah's Army
Shown on PBS September 4, 1996.
Cast: Chris Cooper, Kris Kristofferson.

Pie in the Sky
Director: Bryan Gordon. Shown on HBO Aug. 23 & 25, 1996.
Cast: Anne Heche, Josh Charles.

The Politician's Wife
Producers Films Ltd. for Channel 4. Producers: Jenny Edwards, Jeanna Plley, Neal Weisman. Series Executive Producer: Rebecca Eaton. Director: Graham Theakston. Shown on PBS January 7, 14, 1996.

Poltergeist: The Legacy
Trilogy Entertainment Group in association with Metro Goldwyn Mayer Television and Showtime Networks Inc. Executive Producers: Richard B. Lewis, Pen Densham, John K. Watson. Producer: N. John Smith. Director: Stuart Gillard. Shown April 21, 1996.
Cast: Derek de Lint, Helen Shaver, Robbi Chong, Martin Cummins, Patrick Fitzgerald.

The Price of Love
Gerber Co. in association with PolyGram Filmed Entertainment. Executive Producer: David Gerber. Director: David Burton Morris. Shown on Fox November 28, 1995.
Cast: Peter Facinelli, Jay R. Ferguson, Laurel Holloman, Steven Martini, Alexis Cruz, John Posey, Ben Gould, Harvey Silver.

Pride and Prejudice
A&E in association with the BBC. Executive Producer: Michael Wearing. Producer: Sue Birtwistle. Director: Simon Langton. Shown on A&E January 14-16, 1996.
Cast: Colin Firth, Jennifer Ehle, Alison Steadman, Julia Sawalha, Crispin Bonham-Carter, Susannah Harker, Benjamin Whitrow.

Prime Suspect: Inner Circles
Mobil Masterpiece Theatre in association with Granada Television and PBS. Executive Producer: Sally Head. Producer: Paul Marcus. Director: Sarah Pia Anderson. Shown on PBS February 11, 1996.
Cast: Helen Mirren, Jill Baker, James Laurenson, Helene Kvale, Anthony Bate, Kelly Reilly.

Prime Suspect: The Scent of Darkness
Mobil Masterpiece Theatre in association with Granada Television and PBS. Executive Producer: Sally Head. Producer: Paul Marcus. Shown on PBS May 5, 1996.
Cast: Hellen Mirren, Tim Woodward, Stuart Wilson.

Princess in Love
Director: David Greene. Shown on CBS March 15, 1996.
Cast: Julie Cox, Christopher Bowen, Julia St. John.

Project: Alf
A World International Network production. Producer: Ken Kaufman. Director: Dick Lowry. Shown on ABC in 1996.
Cast: Martin Sheen, Jensen Daggett, William O'Leary, Paul Fusco, John Schuck.

A Promise to Carolyn
The Kaufman Co. in association with Citadel Entertainment. Executive Producers: Paul A. Kaufman, Scott Swanton. Producer: Michael O. Gallant. Director: Jerry London. Shown on CBS January 16, 1996.
Cast: Delta Burke, Swoosie Kurtz, Shirely Knight, Grace Zabriskie, Casey Biggs, Lawrence Monoson, Bill McKinney.

Race Against Time: The Search for Sarah
Director: Fred Gerber. Shown on CBS March 19, 1996.
Cast: Richard Crenna, Patty Duke, Katy Boyer, Jon Gries.

Radiant City
A Witt-Thomas production in association with Warner Bros. Television. Executive Producers: Jeff Weiss, Paul Witt, Tony Thomas. Producer: Timothy Marx. Director: Robert Allan Ackerman. Shown on ABC March 31, 1996.

Cast: Kirstie Alley, Clancy Brown, Gil Bellows, Laraine Newman, Adam Lamberg.

Rasputin
Rysher/Citadel Entertainment Prods. Executive Producers: David Kirkpatrick, David T. Ginsburg. Producer: Nick Gillott. Director: Uli Edel. Shown on HBO March 23, 1996.
Cast: Alan Rickman, Greta Scacchi, Ian McKellen, David Warner, John Wood, James Frain, Diana Quick, Ian Hogg.

Rattled
A USA Pictures Original. Director: Tony Randel. Shown on The USA Network February 14, 1996.
Cast: William Katt, Shanna Reed.

Reasons of the Heart
USA in association with Boardwalk Entertainment. Producers: Perry Husman, Ron McGee. Executive Producers: Fred B. Tarter, Allen Wagner, Stu Segall. Director: Rick Jacobson. Shown on USA Oct. 2, 1996.
Cast: Terry Farrell, Jim Davidson, Mimi Kennedy, Leon Russom, Gloria Dorson.

Remember Me
Shown on CBS November 19, 1995.
Cast: Kelly McGillis, Cotter Smith.

The Return of the Borrowers
Working Title Television for BBC-TV in association with Turner Net TV, BBC Children's International, the Children's Film and Television Foundation and the deFaria Co. Executive Producers: Walt deFaria, Tim Bevan, Angela Beeching. Producer: Grainne Marmion. Director: John Henderson. Shown on TNT June 4, 1996.
Cast: Ian Holm, Penelope Wilton, Rebecca Callard, Sian Phillips, Paul Cross, Ben Chaplin, Ross McCall, Tony Haygarth.

The Right to Remain Silent
Chanticleer Films, Tongue River Productions. Executive Producers: Jana Sue Memel, John McTiernan. Producers: Thom Colwell, Donna Dubrow, Debbie Robins. Director: Hubert de la Bouillerie. Shown on Showtime January 7, 1996.
Cast: Lea Thompson, Robert Loggia, Larry Joshua, Joyce Sylvester, Mary Pat Gleason, Geoffrey Rivas, Christopher Lloyd, Patrick Dempsey.

The Road to Galveston
Wilshire Court Prod. Producer: Bob Roe. Director: Michael Toshiyuki Uno.
Cast: Cicely Tyson, Tess Harper, Piper Laurie, James McDaniel, Starletta DuPois, Penny Johnson.

Ruby Jean and Joe
Viacom Pictures presents a Walter Shenson production in association with TWS productions II, Inc. a Geoffrey Sax film. Director: Geoffrey Sax. Shown on Showtime Aug. 11, 1996.
Cast: Tom Selleck, Jobeth Williams, Ben Johnson.

Riders of the Purple Sage
Rosemont Productions International in association with Zeke Prods. and Amer Prods. Executive Producers: Ed Harris, Amy Madigan, David A. Rosemont. Producer: Thomas Kane. Director: Charles Haid. From the novel by Zane Grey. Shown on TNT January 21, 1996.
Cast: Ed Harris, Amy Madigan, Henry Thomas, Robin Tunney, Norbert Weisser, G.S. Spradlin.

Robin Cook's Terminal
Hallmark Entertainment and Von Zerneck/Sertner Films. Executive Producer: Robert M. Sertner, Frank von Zerneck. Producers: Stacy mandelberg, Michael G. Larkin, Randy Sutter. Associate Producers: Ted Babcock, Richard D. Arredondo. Director: Larry Elikann. Shown on NBC February 12, 1996.

The Rockford Files: Friends and Foul Play
Shown on CBS April 25, 1996.
Cast: James Garner, Wendy Phillips, James Luisi, David Proval, Joe Santos, Gretchen Corbett, Stuart Margolin, Marcia Strassman.

The Rockford Files: Godfather Knows Best
Director: Tony Wharmby. Shown on NBC February 18, 1996.
Cast: James Garner, Damian Chapa, Joe Santos, Barbara Carrera, Stuart Margolin, Al Mancini.

The Rockford Files: If the Frame Fits
Shown on CBS January 14, 1996.
Cast: James Garner, Dyan Cannon, Joe Santos, Stuart Margolin, Gretchen Corbett, James Luisi, Tom Atkins.

478

The Rockford Files: Punishment and Crime
Shown on CBS September 18, 1996.
Cast: James Garner, Richard Kiley, Bryan Cranston.

Ruby Ridge: An American Tragedy
Edgar J. Scherick Associates in association with Regan Co.
and Victor Television Productions. Executive Producers: Edgar
J. Scherick, Judith Regan. Producer: Robert E. Phillips.
Director: Roger Young. Shown on CBS May 19, 21, 1996.
*Cast: Laura Dern, Randy Quaid, Diane Ladd, Kirsten Dunst,
Darren Burrows, G.W. Bailey, Joe Don Baker, Bob Gunton.*

Run for the Dream: The Gail Devers Story
Director: Neema Barnette. Shown on Showtime June 16, 1996.
*Cast: Charlayne Woodard, Louis Gossett, Jr., Robert
Guillaume, Jeffrey Sams.*

Salt Water Moose
A Showtime Original Pictures for Kids production. Producer:
Peter Simpson. Director: Stuart Margolin. Shown on Showtime
June 2, 1996.
*Cast: Timothy Dalton, Lolita Davidovich, Johnny Morina,
Katharine Isobel.*

Saved by the Light
Shown on Fox Dec. 12, 1995.
Cast: Eric Roberts, Lynette Walden, Don McManus

A Season in Purgatory
David Brown Prods. and Spelling TV Inc. Executive Producers:
Aaron Spelling, E. Duke Vincent, David Brown, Richard P.
Rubinstein, Mitchell Galin. Producer: Robert Buzz Berger.
Director: David Greene. Shown on CBS March 5,7, 1996.
*Cast: Patrick Dempsey, Sherilyn Fenn, Craig Sheffer,
Edward Herrmann, Bonnie Bedelia, Blair Brown, Brian
Dennehy.*

A Secret Between Friends
Shown on NBC February 15, 1996.
Cast: Katie Wright, Marley Shelton, Lynda Carter.

The Secretary
Director: Andrew Lane. Shown on CBS September 12, 1996.
Cast: Sheila Kelley, Mel Harris, Rod McCary.

Seduced by Madness, The Diane Borchardt Story
Ann-Margret Productions/Brian Pike Productions in association
with NBC Studios. Executive Producers: Brian Pike, Roger
Smith, Alan Margulies. Director: John Patterson. Shown on
NBC February 26, 1996.
Cast: Ann-Margret, Peter Coyote.

Shadow of a Doubt
Executive Producers: Michele Brustin, Brian Dennehy, David
Percelay. Producer: Richard Brams. Director: Brian Dennehy.
Shown on NBC.
*Cast: Brian Dennehy, Bonnie Bedelia, Fairuza Balk, Kevin
Dunn.*

Shadow-Ops
Shown on UPN December 23, 1995.
Cast: Adam Baldwin.

Shattered Mind
Director: Stephen Gyllenhaal. Shown on NBC May 27, 1996.
*Cast: Heather Locklear, Brett Cullen, Kevin Dunn, Richard
Herd.*

She Woke Up Pregnant
Director: James Contner. Shown on ABC April 28, 1996.
*Cast: Michele Greene, William R. Moses, Joe Penny,
Theresa Saldana, Lynda Carter.*

Sidney Sheldon's Nothing Lasts Forever
Gerber/ITC Entertainment Group. Executive Producer: David
Gerber. Producer: Vanessa Greene. Director: Jack Bender.
Shown on CBS November 5 and 7, 1995.
*Cast: Gail O'Grady, Brooke Shields, Chris Noth, Vanessa
Williams, Lloyd Bridges, Gerald McRaney, Stephen Caffrey,
Gregory Harrison.*

Signs and Wonders
A BBC Production for Mobil Masterpiece Theatre. Director:
Maurice Phillips. Shown on PBS May 12-13, 1996.
*Cast: James Earl Jones, Jodhi May, David Warner, Prunella
Scales, Michael Maloney.*

Silent Witness
Shown on A&E Aug. 20, 1996.
Cast: Amanda Burton.

Sins of Silence
Director: Sam Pillsbury. Shown on CBS February 2, 1996.
Cast: Holly Marie Combs, Lindsay Wagner, Brian Kerwin.

Six Characters in Search of an Author
Bravo in association with BBC Scotland. Producer: Simon
Curtis. Director: Bill Bryden. From the play by Luigi Pirandello.
Shown on Bravo April 2, 1996.
*Cast: Brian Cox, John Hurt, Tara Fitzgerald, Susan
Fleetwood, Rachel Robertson, Steven Mackintosh, Patricia
Hayes.*

Slave of Dreams
A Dino and Martha De Laurentiis Production. Director:
Robert M. Young. Shown on Showtime December 10, 1995.
*Cast: Edward James Olmos, Sherilyn Fenn, Adrian Pasdar,
Orso Maria Guerrini.*

Sophie and the Moonhanger
Berger-Queen Productions in association with ABC
Productions. Executive Producer: Ilene Amy Berg. Producer:
Robert F. Phillips. Director: David Jones. Shown on Lifetime
January 15, 1996.
*Cast: Patricia Richardson, Lynn Whitfield, Jason Bernard,
Ja'net DuBois, David Andrews.*

Soul of the Game
HBO Pictures and Mike Medavoy Prods. in association with
Gary Hoffman Prods. Executive Producers: Gary Hoffman,
Kevin Kelly Brown. Producer: Robert A. Papazian. Director:
Kevin Rodney Sullivan. Shown on HBO April 20, 1996.
*Cast: Delroy Lindo, Mykelti Williamson, Edward Herrmann,
Blair Underwood. R. Lee Ermey, Gina Ravera.*

Space: Above and Beyond
20th Century Fox Television in association with Village
Roadshow Pictures. Creators-Executive Producers: Glen
Morgan, James Wong. Producer: Michael Lake. Director: David
Nutter. Shown on Fox September 24, 1995.
*Cast: Morgan Weisser, Kristen Cloke, Rodney Rowland,
Lanei Chapman, Joel de la Fuente.*

Space Marines
Director: John Weidner. Shown on Showtime July 26 and 28,
1996.
*Cast: Billy Wirth, Cady Huffman, Meg Foster, Edward
Albert.*

Star Command
Shown on The Sci-Fi Channel March 11, 1996.
*Cast: Chad Everett, Morgan Fairchild, Jay Underwood,
Tembi Locke, Chris Conrad, Jennifer Bransford.*

Star Command
High Command Productions, Ltd. in association with UFA
Babelsberg GmbH in association with Wilshire Court
Productions. Executive Producer: Melinda Snodgrass.
Producer: Arti Mandelberg. Director: Jim Johnston. Shown on
UPN March 11, 1996.
*Cast: Chad Everett, Morgan Fairchild, Jay Underwood,
Tembi Locke, Chris Conrad, Jennifer Bransford.*

The Stepford Husbands
Edgar J. Scherick Associates. Director: Fred Walton. Shown on
CBS May 14, 1996.
*Cast: Donna Mills, Michael Ontkean, Cindy williams, Louise
Fletcher, Sara Douglas, Jeffrey Pillars, Joe Inscoe, Caitlin
Clarke.*

Stolen Memories: Secrets From the Rose Garden
Lavin Entertainment Group in association with MTM
Entertainment and The Family Channel. Executive Producer:
Linda Lavin. Producer: Jack Lorenz. Director: Bob Clark.
Shown on January 7, 1996.
*Cast: Nathan Watt, Mary Tyler Moore, Linda Lavin, Shirely
Knight, Paul Winfield, Allison Mack, Martin Hundley,
Christopher Jones.*

The Stranger Beside Me
Shown on ABC September 17, 1996.
*Cast: Tiffani-Amber Thiessen, Eric Close, Gerald
McRaney.*

Sugartime
Pacific Western Productions. Executive Producer: Gale Anne
Hurd. Co-executive Producer: Martyn Burke. Producer: David
Coatsworth. Co-producer: David Gale. Director: John N. Smith.
Shown on HBO November 25, 1995.
*Cast: John Turturro, Mary-Louise Parker, Maury Chaykin,
Elias Koteas, Louis Del Grande.*

Summer of Fear
Shown on CBS April 3, 1996.
Cast: Gregory Harrison, Corin Nemec.

Sweet Temptation
Director: Ron Lagomarsino. Shown on CBS March 6, 1996.
Cast: Jenny Lewis, Beverly D'Angelo, Rob Estes.

Terror in the Family
Shown on Fox April 16, 1996.
Cast: Joanna Kerns, Hilary Swank, Dan Luria.

The Thorn Birds: The Missing Years
The Wolper Organization and Village Roadshow Pictures. Executive Producers: David L. Wolper, Jeffrey M. Hayes, Mark M. Wolper. Producer: Darryl Sheen. Director: Kevin James Dobson. Shown on CBS February 11 & 13, 1996.
Cast: Richard Chamberlain, Amanda Donohoe, Simon West-away, Julia Blake, Olivia Burnette, Maximilian Schell, Zach English, Robert Taylor.

Thrill
Shown on NBC May 20, 1996.
Cast: Antonio Sabato, Jr., Stepfanie Kramer, Christine Hamos, Ted Marcoux, Bill Cobbs, Maxxe Sternbaum.

To Sir With Love II
Verdon-Cedric Productions and Adelson/Baumgarten Productions in association with Tri-Star Television. Executive Producers: Craig Baumgarten, Cedric Scott, Gary Adelson. Producer: Richard Stenta. Director: Peter Bogdanovitch. Shown on CBS April 7, 1996.
Cast: Sidney Poitier, Daniel J. Travanti, Lulu, Judy Geeson, Christian Payton, Dana Eskelson.

Tornado
Shown on Fox May 7, 1996.
Cast: Bruce Campbell, Ernie Hudson, L.Q. Jones, Bo Easton.

Twisted Desire
Director: Craig Baxley. Shown on NBC May 13, 1996.
Cast: Melissa Joan Hart, Daniel Baldwin, Isabella Hofmann, Jeremy Jordan, Meadow Sisto, David Lascher, Kurt Fuller, Eric Laneuville.

The Ultimate Lie
Director: Larry Shaw. Shown on NBC March 18, 1996.
Cast: Michael Murphy, Blair Brown, George Eads, Kristin Davis, John Pennell.

Undue Influence
Shown on CBS September 15 and 17, 1996.
Cast: Brian Dennehy, Patricia Richardson, Jean Smart.

An Unfinished Affair
ABC Productions. Shown on ABC May 5, 1996.
Cast: Jennie Garth, Tim Matheson, Peter Facinelli.

Unforgivable
A Hamdon Entertainment Production. Shown on CBS April 30, 1996.
Cast: John Ritter, Harley Jane Kozak, Susan Gibney.

West Side Waltz
Von Zerneck/Sertner Films in association with CBS Entertainment. Executive Producers: Frank von Zerneck, Robert M. Sertner, Nicole Sequin, Lynn Danielson, Steve Bedell. Co-executive Producer: David Rosemont. Producer: Randy Sutter. Director-Writer: Ernest Thompson. Shown on CBS November 23, 1995.
Cast: Shirley MacLaine, Liza Minelli, Jennifer Grey, Robert Pastorelli, August Schellenberg, Kathy Bates, Richard Gilliland.

Where's the Money, Noreen?
A Power Pictures Production in association with Wilshire Court Productions. Producer: Julian Marks. Director: Artie Mandelberg. Shown on USA Network December 6, 1996.
Cast: Julianne Philips, A. Martinez.

Wiseguy
Stephen J. Cannell Productions in association with Stu Segall Productions. Executive Producers: Kim LeMasters, Stephen J. Cannell, Joel Surnow. Supervising Producer: Stu Segall. Director: James Whitmore, Jr. Shown on ABC May 2, 1996.
Cast: Ken Wahl, Jonathan Banks, Jim Byrnes, Debrah Farentino, Ted Levine.

Woman Undone
A Mace Neufeld/Robert Rehme Production in association with David Lancaster Prods. Executive Producers: Mace Neufeld, Robert Rehme. Producer: David Lancaster. Director: Evelyn Purcell. Shown on Showtime February 4, 1996.
Cast: Mary McDonnell, Randy Quaid, Sam Elliott, Jim Mercer, Charles Noland, Cheryl Anderson.

The Wrong Woman
Shown on CBS March 26, 1996.
Cast: Nancy McKeon, Chelsea Field, Michele Scarbelli.

Young Indiana Jones: Travels with Father
Producer: George Lucas. Director: Michael Schultz. Shown on The Family Channel June 16, 1996.
Cast: Corey Carrier, Michael Gough, George Jackos, Lloyd Owen, George Yiasoumi.

TV Movies and Mini-Series

In the following listings, the network on which the movie first aired is followed by the original airdate, the director (in parentheses) and cast. With the exception of movies shown on premium cable services, all running times include commercials. (For movies and mini-series prior to 1990, see the 1996 Television & Video Almanac.)

ABANDONED AND DECEIVED
ABC 3/20/95. (Joseph Dougherty), Lori Loughlin, Gordon Clapp, Brian Kerwin (2 hrs.).

ABOVE SUSPICION
HBO 5/21/95. (Steven Schachter), Christopher Reeve, Joe Mantegna, Kim Cattrall (90 mins.)

ABRAHAM
TNT 4/3 & 4/94. (Joseph Sargent), Richard Harris, Barbara Hershey, Maximilian Schell (4 hrs.)

ABSOLUTE STRANGERS
CBS 4/14/91. (Gilbert Cates), Henry Winkler, Patty Duke, Richard Kiley (2 hrs.)

ACCIDENTAL MEETING
USA 3/17/94. (Michael Zinberg), Linda Gray, Linda Purl, Leigh J. McCloskey, Ernie Lively (2 hrs.)

ACTING ON IMPULSE
SHO 7/10/93. (Sam Irvin), Linda Fiorentino, C. Thomas Howell, Nancy Allen (2 hrs.)

ADRIFT
CBS 4/13/93. (Christian Duguay), Kate Jackson, Kenneth Welsh, Bruce Greenwood (2 hrs.)

AFTER THE SHOCK
USA 9/12/90. (Ross Gary Sherman), Rue McClanahan, Scott Valentine, Jack Scalia, Yaphet Kotto (2 hrs.)

AFTERBURN
HBO 5/30/92. (Robert Markowitz), Laura Dern, Robert Loggia, Vincent Spano, Michael Rooker (2 hrs.)

AFTERMATH: A TEST OF LOVE
CBS 3/10/91. (Glenn Jordan), Richard Chamberlain, Michael Learned, Zeljko Ivanek (2 hrs.)

AGAINST HER WILL: AN INCIDENT IN BALTIMORE
CBS 1/19/92. (Delbert Mann), Walter Matthau, Susan Blakely, Harry Morgan, Brian Kerwin (2 hrs.).

AGAINST HER WILL: THE CARRIE BUCK STORY
LIF 10/5/94. (John Coles), Marlee Matlin, Melissa Gilbert, Peter Frechette (2 hrs.)

AGAINST THE WALL
HBO 3/26/94. (John Frankenheimer), Kyle MacLachlan, Samuel L. Jackson, Clarence Williams III (2 hrs.).

AGAINST THEIR WILL: WOMEN IN PRISON
ABC 10/30/94. (Karen Arthur), Judith Light, Stacy Keach, Kay Lenz (2 hrs.).

ALIEN NATION: DARK HORIZON
FOX 10/25/94. (Kenneth Johnson), Gary Graham, Eric Pierpoint, Michelle Scarabelli (2 hrs.).

ALIEN WITHIN, THE
SHO 8/20/95. (Scott Levy), Roddy McDowall, Alex Hyde-White, Melanie Shatner (90 mins.).

ALWAYS REMEMBER I LOVE YOU
CBS 12/23/90. (Michael L. Miller), Patty Duke, Stephen Dorff, David Birney (2 hrs.)

AMANDA & THE ALIEN
SHO 8/20/95. (Jon Kroll), Nicole Eggert, Stacy Keach, Michael Bendetti (95 mins.).

AMELIA EARHART: THE FINAL FLIGHT
TNT 6/12/94. (Yves Simoneau), Diane Keaton, Rutger Hauer, Bruce Dern (2 hrs.).

AMERICAN CLOCK, THE
TNT 8/23/93. (Bob Clark), Loren Dean, Mary McDonnell, Eddie Bracken, Darren McGavin (90 mins.).

AMERICAN STORY, AN
CBS 11/29/92. (John Gray), Brad Johnson, Kathleen Quinlan, Tom Sizemore (2 hrs.).

AMY FISHER: MY STORY
NBC 12/28/92. (Bradford May), Ed Marinaro, Noelle Parker, Boyd Kestner (2 hrs.).

AMY FISHER STORY, THE
ABC 1/3/93. (Andy Tennant), Drew Barrymore, Anthony John Denison, Laurie Paton (2 hrs.).

ANDROID AFFAIR, THE
USA 4/12/95. (Richard Kletter), Harley Jane Kozak, Griffin Dunne, Ossie Davis, Saul Rubinek (2 hrs.)

AND THE BAND PLAYED ON
HBO 9/11/93. (Roger Spottiswoode), Matthew Modine, Alan Alda, Lily Tomlin, Ian McKellen, Saul Rubinek (141 mins.).

AND THE SEA WILL TELL
CBS 2/24 & 26/91. (Tommy Lee Wallace), Richard Crenna, Rachel Ward, Hart Bochner, James Brolin (4 hrs.).

... AND THEN SHE WAS GONE
NBC 9/29/91. (David Green), Robert Urich, Megan Gallagher, Brett Cullen, Vondi Curtis-Hall (2 hrs.).

AND THEN THERE WAS ONE
LIF 3/9/94. (David Jones), Amy Madigan, Dennis Boutsikaris, Jane Daly, Steven Flynn (2 hrs.).

ANGEL OF DEATH
CBS 10/2/90. (Bill L. Norton), Gregory Harrison, Jane Seymour, Brian Bonsall (2 hrs.).

ANNA LEE: DIVERSION
A&E 1/3/95. (Christopher King), Imogen Stubbs, Brian Glover, John Bird (2 hrs).

ANOTHER PAIR OF ACES: THREE OF A KIND
CBS 4/9/91. (Bill Bixby), Willie Nelson, Kris Kristofferson, Joan Severance (2 hrs.).

ANOTHER WOMAN
CBS 10/2/94. (Allan Smythe), Justine Bateman, Peter Outerbridge, Ken Holcross (2 hrs.)

ANYTHING TO SURVIVE
ABC 2/5/90. (Zale Dalen), Robert Conrad, Emily Perkins, Matthew LeBlanc (2 hrs.).

APPEARANCES
NBC 6/17/90. (Win Phelps), Scott Paulin, Wendy Phillips, Ernest Borgnine, Matt McGrath (2 hrs.).

ARCHIE: TO RIVERDALE AND BACK AGAIN
NBC 5/6/90. (Dick Lowry), Christopher Rich, Lauren Holly, Karin Kopins (2 hrs.).

ARE YOU LONESOME TONIGHT?
USA 1/22/92. (E.W. Swackhamer), Jane Seymour, Parker Stevenson, Beth Broderick, Joel Brooks (2 hrs.).

ARMED AND INNOCENT
CBS 1/4/94. (Jack Bender), Gerald McRaney, Kate Jackson, Cotter Smith, Andrew Starnes (2 hrs.).

AS GOOD AS DEAD
USA 5/10/95. (Larry Cohen), Judge Reinhold, Crystal Bernard, Traci Lords (2 hrs).

ASSAULT AT WEST POINT
SHO 2/27/94. (Harry Moses), Samuel L. Jackson, Sam Waterston, Seth Gilliam, John Glover, Anthony Rapp (2 hrs.).

ATTACK OF THE 50 FT. WOMAN
HBO 12/11/93. (Christopher Guest), Daryl Hannah, Daniel Baldwin, William Windom, Frances Fisher (2 hrs.).

AVALANCHE
FOX 11/1/94. (Paul Shapiro), Michael Gross, David Hasselhoff, Deanna Milligan, Myles Ferguson (2 hrs.).

AVENGING ANGEL, THE
TNT 1/22/95. (Craig Baxley), Tom Berenger, James Coburn, Charlton Heston (2 hrs).

AWAKE TO DANGER
NBC 3/13/95. (Michael Tuchner), Tori Spelling, Reed Diamond, Michael Gross (2 hrs).

B

BABE RUTH
NBC 10/6/91. (Mark Tinker), Stephen Lang, Bruce Weitz, Donald Moffat, Lisa Zane (2 hrs.).

BABIES
NBC 9/17/90. (Michael Rhodes), Lindsay Wagner, Dinah Manoff, Marcy Walker, Adam Arkin (2 hrs.).

BABY BROKERS
NBC 2/21/94. (Mimi Leder), Cybill Shepherd, Nina Siemaszko, Tom O'Brien, Jeffrey Nordling (2 hrs.).

BABYLON 5
SYND 2/24/93. (Richard Compton), Michael O'Hare, Tamlyn Tomita, Jerry Doyle, Mira Furlan (2 hrs.).

BABYMAKER: THE DR. CECIL JACOBSON STORY
CBS 2/8/94. (Arlene Sanford), Melissa Gilbert, George Dzundza, Shanna Reed (2 hrs.).

BACK TO HANNIBAL: THE RETURN OF TOM SAWYER AND HUCKLEBERRY FINN
DIS 10/21/90. (Paul Krasny), Raphael Sbarge, Mitchell Anderson, William Windom, Paul Winfield (2 hrs.).

BACK TO THE STREETS OF SAN FRANCISCO
NBC 1/27/92. (Mel Damski), Karl Malden, Debrah Farentino, Conor O'Farrell, Carl Lumbly (2 hrs.).

BACKFIELD IN MOTION
ABC 11/13/91. (Richard Michaels), Roseanne Arnold, Tom Arnold, Colleen Camp, Conchata Ferrell (2 hrs.).

BACKSTAB
WPIX 3/26/91. (Jim Kaufman), James Brolin, Meg Foster, Dorothee Berryman (2 hrs.).

BACKTRACK
SHO 12/14/91. (Dennis Hopper), Dennis Hopper, Jodie Foster, Dean Stockwell, Fred Ward (2 hrs.).

BAD ATTITUDES
FOX 9/16/91. (Alan Myerson), Richard Gilliland, Maryedith Burrell, Ethan Randall (2 hrs.).

BANGKOK HILTON
TBS 10/9 & 10/91. (Ken Cameron), Nicole Kidman, Denholm Elliott, Hugo Weaving (6 hrs.).

BARBARIANS AT THE GATE
HBO 3/20/93. (Glenn Jordan), James Garner, Jonathan Pryce, Peter Riegert, Joanna Cassidy (2 hrs.).

BARBARA TAYLOR BRADFORD'S "REMEMBER"
NBC 10/24 & 25/93. (John Herzfeld), Donna Mills, Stephen Collins, Derek De Lint, Ian Richardson (4 hrs.).

BARCELONA '92: 16 DAYS OF GLORY
DIS 8/15/93. (Bud Greenspan), Documentary (135 mins.).

BARE ESSENTIALS
CBS 1/8/91. (Martha Coolidge), Gregory Harrison, Mark Linn-Baker, Lisa Hartman (2 hrs.).

BASED ON AN UNTRUE STORY
FOX 9/20/93. (Jim Drake), Morgan Fairchild, Dyan Cannon, Robert Goulet, Harvey Korman, Ricki Lake (2 hrs.).

BATTLING FOR BABY
CBS 1/12/92. (Art Wolff), Suzanne Pleshette, Debbie Reynolds, Courteney Cox, Doug McClure (2 hrs.).

BEAUTY AND THE BANDIT
SYND 3/30/94. (Brian Bloom), Brian Bloom, Brian Krause, Henry Cho, Joe Cortese, Kathy Ireland (2 hrs.).

BECAUSE MOMMY WORKS
NBC 11/21/94. (Robert Markowitz), Anne Archer, John Heard, Ashley Crow (2 hrs.)

BED OF LIES
ABC 1/20/92. (William A. Graham), Susan Dey, Chris Cooper, G.W. Bailey, Mary Kay Place (2 hrs.)

BEFORE THE STORM
ABC 7/13/91. (Michael Fresco), Linda Purl, Anthony John Denison, Josef Sommer (2 hrs.).

BERMUDA GRACE
NBC 1/7/94. (Mark Sobel), Bill Sadler, David Harewood, Seran Scott Thomas. (2 hrs.).

BETRAYAL OF TRUST
NBC 1/3/94. (George Kaczender), Judith Light, Judd Hirsch, Betty Buckley, Jeffrey DeMunn (2 hrs.).

BETRAYED: THE STORY OF THREE WOMEN
ABC 3/19/95. (William Graham), Meredith Baxter, Swoosie Kurtz, Clare Carey (2 hrs.)

BETRAYED BY LOVE
ABC 1/17/94. (John Power), Mare Winningham, Steven Weber, Patricia Arquette, Perry Lang (2 hrs.)

BETTER OFF DEAD
LIF 1/12/93. (Neema Barnette), Mare Winningham, Tyra Ferrell, Kevin Tighe, Don Harvey (2 hrs.).

BETWEEN LOVE AND HATE
ABC 2/22/93. (Ron Hardy), Susan Lucci, Patrick Van Horn, Raymond J. Barry, Barry Bostwick (2 hrs.).

BETWEEN LOVE AND HONOR
CBS 2/14/95. (Sam Pillsbury), Grant Show, Robert Loggia, Maria Pitillo. (2 hrs.)

BEYOND BETRAYAL
CBS 10/11/94. (Carl Schenkel), Susan Dey, Richard Dean Anderson, Dennis Boutsikaris.(2 hrs.)

BEYOND OBSESSION
ABC 4/4/94. (David Greene), Emily Warfield, Victoria Principal, Henry Thomas (2 hrs.)

BEYOND SUSPICION
NBC 11/22/93. (William A. Graham), Markie Post, Corbin Bernsen, Kelsey Grammer, Don Swayze (2 hrs.).

BEYOND THE LAW
HBO 5/5/94. (Larry Ferguson), Charlie Sheen, Linda Fiorentino, Michael Madsen, Courtney Vance (2 hrs.)

BIG DREAMS AND BROKEN HEARTS: THE DOTTIE WEST STORY
CBS 1/22/95. (Bill D'Elia), Michele Lee, Kenny Rogers, Larry Gatlin. (2 hrs.)

BIG ONE: THE GREAT LOS ANGELES EARTHQUAKE
NBC 11/11 & 12/90. (Larry Elikann), Joanna Kerns, Dan Lauria, Bonnie Bartlett, Ed Begley Jr. (4 hrs.).

BIONIC EVER AFTER
CBS 11/29/94. (Steve Stafford), Lindsay Wagner, Lee Majors, Richard Anderson. (2 hrs.)

BIRDS II: LAND'S END, THE
SHO 3/19/94. (Alan Smithee), Brad Johnson, Chelsea Field, James Naughton, Tippi Hedren (2 hrs.).

BITTER VENGEANCE
USA 7/28/94. (Stuart Cooper), Virginia Madsen, Bruce Greenwood, Kristen Hocking (2 hrs.)

BLACK FOX
CBS 7/28/95. (Steven H. Stern), Chistopher Reeve, Tony Todd, Leon Goodstrike (2 hrs.)

BLACK FOX: GOOD MEN AND BAD MEN
CBS 8/11/95. (Steven H. Stern), Christopher Reeve, Tony Todd, Kim Coates.(2 hrs.)

BLACK FOX: THE PRICE OF PEACE
CBS 8/4/95. (Steven H. Stern), Christopher Reeve, Tony Todd, Raoul Trujillo (2 hrs.)

BLACK MAGIC
SHO 3/21/92. (Daniel Taplitz), Judge Reinhold, Rachel Ward, Anthony LaPaglia, Brion James (2 hrs.).

BLACK RAINBOW
SHO 8/17/91. (Mike Hodges), Rosanna Arquette, Jason Robards, Tom Hulce (2 hrs.).

BLACK SCORPION
SHO 8/22/95. (Jonathan Winfrey), Joan Severance, Bruce Abbott, Garrett Morris (90 mins.).

BLACK WIDOW MURDERS:
THE BLANCHE TAYLOR MOORE STORY
NBC 5/3/93. (Alan Metzger), Elizabeth Montgomery, David Clennon, John M. Jackson (2 hrs.).

BLACKMAIL
USA 10/23/91. (Ruben Preuss), Dale Midkiff, Susan Blakely, Beth Toussaint, Mac Davis (2 hrs.).

BLIND MAN'S BLUFF
USA 2/19/92. (James Quinn), Robert Urich, Lisa Eilbacher, Patricia Clarkson, Ron Perlman (2 hrs.).

BLIND FAITH
NBC 2/11 & 13/90. (Paul Wendkos), Robert Urich, Joanna Kerns, Jay Underwood, Dennis Farina (4 hrs.).

BLIND SIDE
HBO 1/30/93. (Geoff Murphy), Rutger Hauer, Rebecca DeMornay, Ron Silver (2 hrs.).

BLIND SPOT
CBS 5/2/93. (Michael Uno), Joanne Woodward, Laura Linney, Fritz Weaver, Reed Diamond (2 hrs.).

BLIND VENGEANCE
USA 8/22/90. (Lee Philips), Gerald McRaney, Lane Smith, Don Hood, Marg Helgenberger (2 hrs.).

BLINDFOLD: ACTS OF OBSESSION
USA 5/20/94. (Lawrence L. Simeone), Judd Nelson, Shannen Doherty, Kristian Alfonso (2 hrs.).

BLINDSIDED
USA 1/20/93. (Tom Donnelly), Jeff Fahey, Mia Sara, Ben Gazzara, Jack Kehler (2 hrs.).

BLOOD RIVER
CBS 3/17/91. (Mel Damski), Rick Schroder, Wilford Brimley, John P. Ryan, Adrienne Barbeau (2 hrs.).

BLOOD TIES
FOX 5/27/91. (Jim McBride), Harley Venton, Patrick Bauchau, Michelle Johnson (2 hrs.).

BLOODLINES: MURDER IN THE FAMILY
NBC 3/1 & 2/93. (Paul Wendkos), Mimi Rogers, Elliott Gould, Clancy Brown, Kim Hunter (4 hrs.).

BLUE BAYOU
NBC 1/15/90. (Karen Arthur), Alfre Woodard, Mario Van Peebles, Roy Thinnes (2 hrs.).

BODY LANGUAGE
USA 7/15/92. (Arthur Allan Seidelman), Heather Locklear, Linda Purl, Edward Albert (2 hrs.).

BODY LANGUAGE
HBO 7/29/95. (George Case), Tom Berenger, Nancy Travis, Heidi Schanz (100 mins.).

BONANZA: THE RETURN
NBC 11/28/93. (Jerry Jameson), Ben Johnson, Richard Roundtree, Michael Landon Jr., Jack Elam (2 hrs.).

BONANZA: UNDER ATTACK
NBC 1/15/95. (Mark Tinker), Leonard Nimoy, Dirk Blocker, Dennis Farina (2 hrs.).

BONDS OF LOVE
CBS 1/24/93. (Larry Elikann), Treat Williams, Kelly McGillis, Steve Railsback, Hal Holbrook (2 hrs.).

BONNIE AND CLYDE: THE TRUE STORY
FOX 8/17/92. (Gary Hoffman), Tracey Needham, Dana Ashbrook, Doug Savant, Betty Buckley (2 hrs.).

BORIS AND NATASHA
SHO 4/17/92. (Charles Martin Smith), Sally Kellerman, Dave Thomas, Andrea Martin, Alex Rocco (100 mins.).

BORN TO RUN
FOX 8/2/93. (Albert Magnoli), Richard Grieco, Jay Acovone, Joe Cortese, Shelli Lether (2 hrs.).

BORN TOO SOON
NBC 4/24/93. (Noel Nosseck), Pamela Reed, Michael Moriarty, Terry O'Quinn, Joanna Gleason (2 hrs.).

BOYS, THE
ABC 4/15/91. (Glenn Jordan), James Woods, John Lithgow, Joanna Gleason (2 hrs.).

BREAKING THE SILENCE
CBS 1/14/92. (Robert Iscove), Gregory Harrison, Stephanie Zimbalist, Chris Young, Kevin Conway (2 hrs.).

BRAM STOKER'S "BURIAL OF THE RATS"
SHO 8/8/95. (Dan Golden), Adrienne Barbeau, Maria Ford, Kevin Alber (90 mins.).

BREACH OF CONDUCT
USA 12/1/94. (Tim Matheson), Peter Coyote, Courtney Thorne-Smith, Tom Verica. (2 hrs.).

BREATHING LESSONS
CBS 2/6/94. (John Erman), James Garner, Joanne Woodward, Kathryn Erbe, Joyce Van Patten, Eileen Heckart (2 hrs.).

BRIDE IN BLACK, THE
ABC 10/21/90. (James Goldstone), Susan Lucci, Reginald Vel Johnson, David Soul (2 hrs.).

BROKEN CHAIN, THE
TNT 12/12/93. (Lamont Johnson), Eric Schweig, J. C. White Shirt, Wes Studi (2 hrs.).

BROKEN CORD, THE
ABC 2/3/92. (Ken Olin), Jimmy Smits, Kim Delaney, Michael Spears, Raoul Trujillo (2 hrs.).

BROKEN PROMISES
CBS 12/26/93. (Donald Wrye), Cheryl Ladd, Robert Desiderio, Polly Draper (2 hrs.).

BROKEN TRUST
TNT 8/6/95 (Geoffrey Sax), Tom Selleck, Elizabeth McGovern, William Atherton (95 mins.).

BROTHERHOOD OF THE GUN
CBS 10/5/91. (Vern Gillum), Brian Bloom, Jamie Rose, David Carradine, Jorge Cervera Jr. (2 hrs.).

BUFFALO GIRLS
CBS 4/30 & 5/1/95 (Rod Hardy), Anjelica Huston, Melanie Griffith, Gabriel Byrne (4 hrs.).

BUMP IN THE NIGHT
CBS 1/6/91. (Karen Arthur), Meredith Baxter-Birney, Christopher Reeve, Wings Hauser, Shirley Knight (2 hrs.).

BURDEN OF PROOF, THE
ABC 2/9 & 10/92. (Mike Robe), Hector Elizondo, Brian Dennehy, Mel Harris, Stefanie Powers (4 hrs.).

BURIED ALIVE
USA 5/9/90. (Frank Darabont), Tim Matheson, Jennifer Jason Leigh, William Atherton (2 hrs.).

BURNING BRIDGES
ABC 5/6/90. (Sheldon Larry), Meredith Baxter-Birney, Nick Mancuso, Derek de Lint (2 hrs.).

A BURNING PASSION:
THE MARGARET MITCHELL STORY
NBC 11/7/94 (Larry Peerce), Shannen Doherty, Rue McClanahan, Dale Midkiff (2 hrs.).

BURNING SEASON, THE
HBO 9/17/94 (John Frankenheimer), Raul Julia, Sonia Braga, Kamala Dawson. (2 hrs.).

BY DAWN'S EARLY LIGHT
HBO 5/19/90. (Jack Sholder), Powers Boothe, Rebecca De Mornay, James Earl Jones (2 hrs.).

CAGNEY & LACEY: THE RETURN
CBS 11/6/94. (James Frawley), Tyne Daly, Sharon Gless, James Naughton (2 hrs.).

CAGNEY & LACEY: TOGETHER AGAIN
CBS 5/2/95. (Reza Badiyi), Sharon Gless, Tyne Daly, James Naughton. (2 hrs.).

CALENDAR GIRL, COP KILLER?
THE BAMBI BEMBENEK STORY
ABC 5/18/92. (Jerry London), Timothy Busfield, Lindsay Frost, Linda Blair, John Karlen (2 hrs.).

CALL ME ANNA
ABC 11/11/90. (Gilbert Cates), Patty Duke, Timothy Carhart, Howard Hesseman, Karl Malden (2 hrs.).

CALL OF THE WILD
CBS 4/25/93. (Alan Smithee), Rick Schroder, Gordon Tootoosis, Duncan Fraser, Mia Sara (2 hrs.).

CAMP CUCAMONGA
NBC 9/23/90. (Roger Duchowny), John Ratzenberger, Danica McKellar, Sherman Hemsley (2 hrs.).

CANDLES IN THE DARK
FAM 12/3/93. (Maximilian Schell), Chad Lowe, Alyssa Milano, Maximilian Schell (2 hrs.).

CAPTIVE
ABC 10/13/91. (Michael Tuchner), Joanna Kerns, Chad Lowe, John Stamos, Barry Bostwick (2 hrs.).

CAROLINA SKELETONS
NBC 9/30/91. (John Erman), Louis Gossett Jr., Bruce Dern, Melissa Leo, G.D. Spradlin (2 hrs.).

CAROLINE?
CBS 4/29/90. (Joseph Sargent), Stephanie Zimbalist, Pamela Reed, George Grizzard, Patricia Neal (2 hrs.).

CASE FOR MURDER, A
USA 5/19/93. (Duncan Gibbins), Peter Berg, Jennifer Grey, Belinda Bauer, Samantha Eggar (2 hrs.).

CAST A DEADLY SPELL
HBO 9/7/91. (Martin Campbell), Fred Ward, David Warner, Clancy Brown, Julianne Moore (2 hrs.).

CASUALTIES OF LOVE:
THE "LONG ISLAND LOLITA" STORY
CBS 1/3/93. (John Herzfeld), Alyssa Milano, Jack Scalia, Phyllis Lyons, Leo Rossi (2 hrs.).

CASUALTY OF WAR, A
USA 3/14/90. (Tom Clegg), Shelley Hack, David Threlfall, Alan Howard (2 hrs.).

CAUGHT IN THE ACT
USA 7/22/93. (Deborah Reinisch), Gregory Harrison, Leslie Hope, Patricia Clarkson, Kimberly Scott (2 hrs.).

CAUTION:
MURDER CAN BE HAZARDOUS TO YOUR HEALTH
ABC 2/20/91. (Daryl Duke), Peter Falk, George Hamilton, Peter Haskell (2 hrs.).

CHALLENGER
ABC 2/25/90. (Glenn Jordan), Karen Allen, Barry Bostwick, Brian Kerwin, Joe Morton (3 hrs.).

CHANCE OF A LIFETIME
NBC 11/18/91. (Jonathan Sanger), Betty White, Leslie Nielsen, Ed Begley Jr., William Windom (2 hrs.).

A CHANGE OF PLACE
CBS 10/9/94 (Donna Deitch), Andrea Roth, Rick Springfield, Stephanie Beacham, Ian Richardson (2 hrs.).

CHANTILLY LACE
SHO 7/18/93. (Linda Yellen), Lindsay Crouse, Jill Eikenberry, Ally Sheedy, JoBeth Williams, Talia Shire (102 mins.).

CHARLES AND DIANA: UNHAPPILY EVER AFTER
ABC 12/13/92. (John Power), Catherine Oxenberg, Roger Rees, Benedict Taylor (2 hrs.).

CHARLES DICKENS' "DAVID COPPERFIELD"
NBC 12/10/93. (Don Arioli), Animated (2 hrs.).

CHASE, THE
NBC 2/10/91. (Paul Wendkos), Casey Siemaszko, Ben Johnson, Gerry Bamman, Ricki Lake (2 hrs.).

CHERNOBYL: THE FINAL WARNING
TNT 4/22/91. (Anthony Page), Jon Voight, Jason Robards, Sammi Davis (2 hrs.).

CHILD IN THE NIGHT
CBS 5/1/90. (Mike Robe), JoBeth Williams, Tom Skerritt, Elijah Wood (2 hrs.).

CHILD LOST FOREVER, A
NBC 11/16/92. (Claudia Weill), Beverly D'Angelo, Dana Ivey, Michael McGrady, Max Gail (2 hrs.).

CHILD OF DARKNESS, CHILD OF LIGHT
USA 5/1/91. (Marina Sargenti), Anthony John Denison, Sela Ward, Paxton Whitehead, Brad Davis (2 hrs.).

CHILD OF RAGE
CBS 9/29/92. (Larry Peerce), Mel Harris, Dwight Schultz, Ashley Peldon, Rosana DeSoto (2 hrs.).

CHILDREN OF THE BRIDE
CBS 10/5/90. (Jonathan Sanger), Rue McClanahan, Kristy McNichol, Patrick Duffy (2 hrs.).

CHILDREN OF THE DARK
CBS 4/17/94. (Michael Switzer), Peter Horton, Tracy Pollan, Roy Dotrice (2 hrs.).

CHILDREN OF THE DUST
CBS 2/26 & 28/95 (David Greene), Sidney Poitier, Michael Moriarty, Joanne Going. (4 hrs.).

CHILD'S CRY FOR HELP, A
NBC 11/14/94. (Sandor Stern), Veronica Hamel, Pam Dawber, Daniel Hugh Kelly (2 hrs.).

CHINA LAKE MURDERS, THE
USA 1/31/90. (Alan Metzger), Tom Skerritt, Michael Parks, Nancy Everhard (2 hrs.).

CHOICES OF THE HEART:
THE MARGARET SANGER STORY
LIF 3/8/95 (Paul Shapiro), Dana Delany, Henry Czerny, Rod Steiger. (2 hrs.).

CHRISTMAS IN CONNECTICUT
TNT 4/13/92. (Arnold Schwarzenegger), Dyan Cannon, Kris Kristofferson, Tony Curtis (2 hrs.).

CHRISTMAS ON DIVISION STREET
CBS 12/15/91. (George Kaczender), Fred Savage, Hume Cronyn, Badja Djola, Casey Ellison (2 hrs.).

CHRISTMAS ROMANCE, A
CBS 12/18/94. (Sheldon Larry), Olivia Newton-John, Gregory Harrison, Chloe Lattanzi. (2 hrs.).

CHROME SOLDIERS
USA 5/6/92. (Thomas J. Wright), Gary Busey, Ray Sharkey, William Atherton, Yaphet Kotto (2 hrs.).

CISCO KID, THE
TNT 2/6/94. (Luis Valdez), Jimmy Smits, Cheech Marin, Sadie Frost, Bruce Payne (2 hrs.).

CITIZEN COHN
HBO 8/22/92. (Frank Pierson), James Woods, Joe Don Baker, Lee Grant, Tovah Feldshuh (2 hrs.).

CITIZEN X
HBO 2/25/95. (Chris Gerolmo), Stephen Rea, Donald Sutherland, Jeffrey DeMunn, Joss Ackland, Max von Sydow. (2 hrs.).

CLARENCE
FAM 11/22/90. (Eric Till), Robert Carradine, Kate Trotter, Nicholas van Burek (2 hrs.).

CLASS OF '61
ABC 4/12/93. (Gregory Hoblit), Dan Futterman, Clive Owen, Joshua Lucas, Andre Braugher (2 hrs.).

CLOSE RELATIONS
A&E 11/1/90. (Adrian Shergold), James Hazeldine, Clare Holman, Rosalind March (2 hrs.).

COINS IN THE FOUNTAIN
CBS 9/28/90. (Tony Wharmby), Loni Anderson, Stephanie Kramer, Shanna Reed (2 hrs.).

COLUMBO: A BIRD IN THE HAND
ABC 11/22/92. (Vince McEveety), Peter Falk, Tyne Daly, Greg Evigan, Frank McRae (2 hrs.).

COLUMBO AND THE MURDER OF A ROCK STAR
NBC 4/29/91. (Alan J. Levi), Peter Falk, Dabney Coleman, Shera Danese (2 hrs.).

COLUMBO: BUTTERFLY IN SHADES OF GREY
ABC 1/10/94. (Dennis Dugan), Peter Falk, William Shatner, Molly Hagan (2 hrs.).

COLUMBO GOES TO COLLEGE
ABC 12/9/90. (E.W. Swackhamer), Peter Falk, Stephen Caffrey, Gary Hershberger (2 hrs.).

COLUMBO: IT'S ALL IN THE GAME
ABC 10/31/93. (Vincent McEveety), Peter Falk, Faye Dunaway, Claudia Christian (2 hrs.).

COLUMBO: NO TIME TO DIE
ABC 3/15/92. (Alan Levi), Peter Falk, Joanna Going, Thomas Calabro, Juliet Mills (2 hrs.).

COLUMBO: STRANGE BEDFELLOWS
ABC 5/8/95. (Vincent McEveety), Peter Falk, George Wendt, Jeff Yagher (2 hrs.).

COLUMBO: UNDERCOVER
ABC 4/2/94. (Vincent McEveety), Peter Falk, Ed Begley Jr., Burt Young (2 hrs.).

COME DIE WITH ME:
A MICKEY SPILLANE'S MIKE HAMMER MYSTERY
CBS 12/6/94. (Armand Mastroianni), Rob Estes, Pamela Anderson, Randi Interman, Darlanne Fluegel (2 hrs.).

COMMON GROUND
CBS 3/25 & 27/90. (Mike Newell), Jane Curtin, Richard Thomas, C.C.H. Pounder (4 hrs.).

COMPANION, THE
USA 10/13/94 (Gary Fleder), Kathryn Harrold, Bruce Greenwood, Brion James (2 hrs.).

COMPLEX OF FEAR
CBS 1/12/93. (Brian Grant), Hart Bochner, Joe Don Baker, Chelsea Field, Brett Cullen (2 hrs.).

COMPUTER WORE TENNIS SHOES, THE
ABC 2/18/95. (Peyton Reed), Kirk Cameron, Larry Miller, Jason Bernard, Jeff Maynard, Anne Marie Tremko (2 hrs.).

COMRADES OF SUMMER, THE
HBO 7/11/92. (Tommy Lee Wallace), Joe Mantegna, Natalya Negoda, Michael Lerner (2 hrs.).

CONAGHER
TNT 7/1/91. (Reynaldo Villalobos), Sam Elliott, Katharine Ross, Barry Corbin (150 mins.).

CONDITION: CRITICAL
NBC 12/20/92. (Jerry Friedman), Christina Haag, Kevin Sorbo, Mark Blum, Joanna Pacula (2 hrs.).

CONFESSIONS OF A SORORITY GIRL
SHO 7/29/94. (Uli Edel), Jamie Luner, Alyssa Milano, Dani Wheeler, Brian Bloom (90 mins.).

CONFESSIONS: TWO FACES OF EVIL
NBC 1/17/94. (Gilbert Cates), Jason Bateman, James Wilder, James Earl Jones, Arye Gross (2 hrs.).

CONSPIRACY OF SILENCE
CBS 7/26 & 28/92. (Francis Makiewicz), Michael Mahonen, Stephen Quimette, Carl Marotte (4 hrs.).

CONVICT COWBOY
SHO 7/16/95. (Rod Holcomb), Jon Voight, Kyle Chandler, Marcia Gay Harden, Glenn Plummer, Ben Gazzara (2 hrs.).

CONVICTION: THE KITTY DODDS STORY
CBS 11/2/93. (Michael Tuchner), Veronica Hamel, Kevin Dobson, Lee Garlington (2 hrs.).

COOPERSMITH
CBS 7/31/92. (Peter Crane), Grant Show, Colleen Coffey, Clark Johnson (2 hrs.).

CORPSE HAD A FAMILIAR FACE, THE
CBS 3/27/94. (Joyce Chopra), Elizabeth Montgomery, Dennis Farina, Lee Horsley, Yaphet Kotto (2 hrs.).

COSBY MYSTERIES, THE
NBC 1/31/94. (Jerry London), Bill Cosby, James Naughton, Alice Playten, Richard Kiley (2 hrs.).

COUNTERFEIT CONTESSA, THE
FOX 4/4/94. (Ron Lagomarsino), Tea Leoni, D.W. Moffett, David Beecroft (2 hrs.).

COUNTERFORCE
SYND 1/17/91. (J. Anthony Loma), George Rivero, George Kennedy, Andrew Stevens (2 hrs.).

COURT-MARTIAL OF JACKIE ROBINSON, THE
TNT 10/15/90. (Larry Peerce), Andre Braugher, Ruby Dee, Stan Shaw, Daniel Stern (2 hrs.).

COVER GIRL MURDERS, THE
USA 10/28/93. (James A. Contner), Lee Majors, Jennifer O'Neill, Beverly Johnson (2 hrs.).

CRASH LANDING: THE RESCUE OF FLIGHT 232
ABC 2/24/92. (Lamont Johnson), Charlton Heston, Richard Thomas, James Coburn, Leon Russom (2 hrs.).

CRASH: THE MYSTERY OF FLIGHT 1501
NBC 11/18/90. (Philip Saville), Cheryl Ladd, Doug Sheehan, Jeffrey DeMunn (2 hrs.).

CRAZY FROM THE HEART
TNT 8/19/91. (Thomas Schlamme), Christine Lahti, Ruben Blades, William Russ (2 hrs.).

CRAZY IN LOVE
TNT 8/10/92. (Martha Coolidge), Holly Hunter, Gena Rowlands, Frances McDormand, Bill Pullman (2 hrs.).

CRIES FROM THE HEART
CBS 10/16/94. (Michael Switzer), Patty Duke, Melissa Gilbert, Bradley Pierce, Marcus Flanagan (2 hrs.).

CRIES UNHEARD:
THE DONNA YAKLICH STORY
CBS 2/1/94. (Armand Mastroianni), Jaclyn Smith, Brad Johnson, Hilary Swank, David Lascher (2 hrs.).

CRIMINAL BEHAVIOR
ABC 5/11/92. (Michael Miller), Farrah Fawcett, A. Martinez, Morgan Stevens, Dakin Matthews (2 hrs.).

CRIMINAL JUSTICE
HBO 9/8/90. (Andy Wolk), Forest Whitaker, Anthony LaPaglia, Jennifer Grey, Rosie Perez (90 mins.).

CROSSING TO FREEDOM
CBS 4/8/90. (Norman Stone), Peter O'Toole, Mare Winningham, Susan Woodridge (2 hrs.).

CROWFOOT
CBS 6/7/95. (James Whitmore Jr.), Jim Davidson, Tsai Chin, Kate Hodge, Bruce Locke, Larry Manetti, Charles Ka'upu (2 hrs.).

CRUCIFER OF BLOOD, THE
TNT 11/4/91. (Fraser C. Heston), Charlton Heston, Richard Johnson, Susannah Harker, Edward Fox (2-1/2 hrs.).

CRUEL DOUBT
NBC 5/17 & 19/92. (Yves Simoneau), Blythe Danner, Matt McGrath, Gwyneth Paltrow, Ed Asner (4 hrs.).

CRY IN THE WILD:
THE TAKING OF PEGGY ANN
NBC 5/6/91. (Charles Correll), David Morse, Megan Follows, David Soul (2 hrs.).

CURACAO
SHO 6/27/93. (Cark Schultz), George C. Scott, William Petersen, Julie Carmen, Dennis Christopher (2 hrs.).

CURIOSITY KILLS
USA 6/27/90. (Colin Bucksey), C. Thomas Howell, Rae Dawn Chong, Courteney Cox, Jeff Fahey (2 hrs.).

CURSE OF THE STARVING CLASS
SHO 2/4/95. (J. Michael McClary), James Woods, Kathy Bates, Henry Thomas, Louis Gossett Jr., Randy Quaid (2 hrs.).

D

DAD, THE ANGEL AND ME
FAM 3/12/95. (Rick Wallace), Judge Reinhold, Stephi Lineburg, Alan King, Carol Kane (2 hrs.).

DAN TURNER, HOLLYWOOD DETECTIVE
SYND 8/22/90. (Christopher Lewis), Marc Singer, Tracy Scoggins, Nicholas Worth (2 hrs.).

DANCING IN THE DARK
LIF 7/5/95. (Bill Corcoran), Victoria Principal, Nicholas Campbell, Robert Vaughn, Dawn Greenhalgh, Geraint Wyn Davies (2 hrs.).

DANCING WITH DANGER
USA 4/22/94. (Stuart Cooper), Cheryl Ladd, Ed Marinaro, Miguel Sandoval (2 hrs.).

DANGER ISLAND
NBC 9/20/92. (Tommy Lee Wallace), Richard Beymer, June Lockhart, Kathy Ireland (2 hrs.).

DANGER OF LOVE, THE
CBS 10/4/92. (Joyce Chopra), Jenny Robertson, Joe Penny, Richard Lewis, Joseph Bologna (2 hrs.).

DANGEROUS AFFAIR, A
ABC 1/1/95. (Alan Metzger), Connie Sellecca, Gregory Harrison, Christopher Meloni, Rosalind Cash (2 hrs.).

DANGEROUS INTENTIONS
CBS 1/3/95. (Michael Toshiyuki Uno), Donna Mills, Corbin Bernsen, Allison Hossack, Sheila Larken, Ken Pogue, (2 hrs.).

DANGEROUS PASSION
ABC 3/25/90. (Michael Miller), Carl Weathers, Lonette McKee, Billy Dee Williams (2 hrs.).

DANGEROUS PURSUIT
USA 2/14/90. (Sandor Stern), Gregory Harrison, Alexandra Powers, Brian Wimmer (2 hrs.).

DANIELLE STEEL'S "CHANGES"
NBC 4/1/91. (Charles Jarrott), Cheryl Ladd, Michael Nouri, Christie Clark (2 hrs.).

DANIELLE STEEL'S "DADDY"
NBC 10/23/91. (Michael Miller), Patrick Duffy, Kate Mulgrew, Lynda Carter, John Anderson (2 hrs.).

DANIELLE STEEL'S "FAMILY ALBUM"
NBC 10/23/94. (Jack Bender), Jaclyn Smith, Michael Ontkean, Joe Flanigan, Kristin Minter, Leslie Horan, Tom Mason (2 hrs.).

DANIELLE STEEL'S "FINE THINGS"
NBC 10/16/90. (Tom Moore), D.W. Moffett, Tracy Pollan, Cloris Leachman (2 hrs.).

DANIELLE STEEL'S "HEARTBEAT"
NBC 2/8/93. (Michael Miller), Polly Draper, John Ritter, Nancy Morgan (2 hrs.).

DANIELLE STEEL'S "JEWELS"
NBC 10/18 & 20/92. (Roger Young), Annette O'Toole, Anthony Andrews, Jurgen Prochnow (4 hrs.).

DANIELLE STEEL'S "KALEIDOSCOPE"
NBC 10/15/90. (Jud Taylor), Jaclyn Smith, Perry King, Colleen Dewhurst (2 hrs.).

DANIELLE STEEL'S "MESSAGE FROM NAM"
NBC 10/17 & 19/93. (Paul Wendkos), Jenny Robertson, Billy Dee Williams, Rue McClanahan, Esther Rolle (4 hrs.).

DANIELLE STEEL'S "ONCE IN A LIFETIME"
NBC 2/15/94. (Michael Miller), Lindsay Wagner, Barry Bostwick, Duncan Regehr, Rex Smith (2 hrs.).

DANIELLE STEEL'S "PALOMINO"
NBC 10/21/91. (Michael Miller), Lindsay Frost, Lee Horsley, Eva Marie Saint, Rod Taylor (2 hrs.).

DANIELLE STEEL'S "A PERFECT STRANGER"
NBC 9/12/94. (Michael L. Miller), Robert Urich, Stacy Haiduk, Darren McGavin, Susan Sullivan, Holly Marie Combs (2 hrs.).

DANIELLE STEEL'S "SECRETS"
NBC 4/6/92. (Peter H. Hunt), Christopher Plummer, Stephanie Beacham, Linda Purl, Gary Collins (2 hrs.).

DANIELLE STEEL'S "STAR"
NBC 9/30/93. (Michael Miller), Jennie Garth, Craig Bierko, Terry Farrell (2 hrs.).

DANIELLE STEEL'S "VANISHED"
NBC 4/3/95. (George Kaczender), George Hamilton, Lisa Rinna, Robert Hays, Maurice Godin, Alex D. Linz (2 hrs.).

DARK AVENGER
CBS 10/11/90. (Guy Magyar), Leigh Lawson, Maggie Han, Robert Vaughn (2 hrs.).

DARK REFLECTION
FOX 1/10/94. (Jack Sholder), C. Thomas Howell, Lisa Zane, Miko Hughes, Ethan Phillips (2 hrs.).

DARKNESS BEFORE DAWN
NBC 2/15/93. (John Patterson), Meredith Baxter, Stephen Lang, Gwynyth Walsh, L. Scott Caldwell (2 hrs.).

DAUGHTER OF DARKNESS
CBS 1/26/90. (Stuart Gordon), Anthony Perkins, Mia Sara, Jack Coleman (2 hrs.).

DAUGHTER OF THE STREETS
ABC 2/26/90. (Ed Sherin), Jane Alexander, Roxana Zal, John Stamos (2 hrs.).

DAUGHTERS OF PRIVILEGE
NBC 3/17/91. (Michael Fresco), Dick Van Dyke, Daphne Ashbrook, Kate Vernon (2 hrs.).

DAVID'S MOTHER
CBS 4/10/94. (Robert Allan Ackerman), Kirstie Alley, Sam Waterston, Michael Goorjian (2 hrs.).

DAY MY PARENTS RAN AWAY, THE
FOX 12/13/93. (Martin Nicholson), Bobby Jacoby, Brigid Conley Walsh, Matt Frewer, Blair Brown (2 hrs.).

DAY OF RECKONING
NBC 3/7/94. (Brian Grant), Fred Dryer, Geoffrey Lewis, Patrick Bauchau (2 hrs.).

DAY-O
NBC 5/3/92. (Michael Schultz), Delta Burke, Elijah Wood, Carlin Glynn, Charles Shaughnessy (2 hrs.).

DAYBREAK
HBO 5/8/93. (Stephen Tolkin), Cuba Gooding Jr., Moira Kelly, John Cameron Mitchell, John Savage (90 mins.).

DEAD AHEAD:
THE EXXON VALDEZ DISASTER
HBO 12/12/92. (Paul Seed), John Heard, Christopher Lloyd, Ron Frazier, David Morse, Bob Gunton (90 mins.).

DEAD AIR
USA 10/6/94. (Fred Walton), Gregory Hines, Deborah Farentino, Beau Starr, Gloria Reuben, Laura Harrington (2 hrs.).

DEAD AND ALIVE
ABC 11/24/91. (Peter Markle), Tony Danza, Ted Levine, Dan Lauria, Caroline Aaron (2 hrs.).

DEAD BEFORE DAWN
ABC 1/10/93. (Charles Correll), Cheryl Ladd, Jameson Parker, Hope Lange, Kim Coates (2 hrs.).

DEAD IN THE WATER
USA 12/4/91. (Bill Condon), Bryan Brown, Teri Hatcher, Veronica Cartwright, Anne DeSalvo (2 hrs.).

DEAD MAN'S REVENGE
USA 4/15/94. (Alan J. Levi), Bruce Dern, Michael Ironside, Keith Coulouris, Doug McClure (2 hrs.).

DEAD ON THE MONEY
TNT 6/17/91. (Mark Culllingham), Corbin Bernsen, Amanda Pays, John Glover (2 hrs.).

DEAD RECKONING
USA 5/23/90. (Robert Lewis), Cliff Robertson, Rick Springfield, Susan Blakely (2 hrs.).

DEAD SILENCE
FOX 8/26/91. (Peter O'Fallon), Renee Estevez, Lisanne Falk, Carrie Mitchum (2 hrs.).

DEADLINE FOR MURDER:
FROM THE FILES OF EDNA BUCHANAN
CBS 5/9/95. (Joyce Chopra), Elizabeth Montgomery, Yaphet Kotto, Audra Lindley, Dean Stockwell, Evelyn Bakerges (2 hrs.).

DEADLOCK
HBO 9/28/91. (Lewis Teague), Rutger Hauer, Mimi Rogers, Joan Chen, Stephen Tobolowsky (2 hrs.).

DEADLOCKED: ESCAPE FROM ZONE 14
FOX 5/9/95. (Graeme Campbell), Esai Morales, Stephen McHattie, Jon Cuthbert, Sarah Strange, Douglas Arthurs, Nia Peeples (2 hrs.).

DEADLY BETRAYAL: THE BRUCE CURTIS STORY
NBC 2/2/92. (Graeme Campbell), Simon Reynolds, Jaimz Woolvett, Kenneth Welsh, Bruce Boa (2 hrs.).

DEADLY DESIRE
USA 1/29/91. (Charles Correll), Jack Scalia, Kathryn Harrold, Will Patton (2 hrs.).

DEADLY GAME
USA 7/10/91. (Thomas J. Wright), Roddy McDowall, Marc Singer, Michael Beck (2 hrs.).

DEADLY INTENTIONS... AGAIN?
ABC 2/11/91. (James Steven Sadwith), Harry Hamlin, Joanna Kerns, Conchata Ferrell (2 hrs.).

DEADLY INVASION: THE KILLER BEE NIGHTMARE
FOX 3/7/95. (Rockne S. O'Bannon), Robert Hays, Nancy Stafford, Dennis Christopher, Ryan Phillippe, Gina Philips (2 hrs.).

DEADLY MATRIMONY
NBC 11/22 & 23/92. (John Korty), Brian Dennehy, Treat Williams, Embeth Davidtz, Susan Ruttan (4 hrs.).

DEADLY MEDICINE
NBC 11/11/91. (Richard Colla), Veronica Hamel, Susan Ruttan, Stephen Tobolowsky, Scott Paulin (2 hrs.).

DEADLY RELATIONS
ABC 5/22/93. (Bill Condon), Robert Urich, Shelley Fabares, Gwyneth Paltrow, Georgia Emelin (2 hrs.).

DEADLY SURVEILLANCE
SHO 9/6/91. (Paul Ziller), Michael Ironside, Christopher Bondy, Susan Almgren, David Carradine (2 hrs.).

DEADLY VOWS
FOX 9/13/94. (Alan Metzger), Gerald McRaney, Peggy Lipton, Josie Bissett, Ric Reid, Michael MacRae, P. Lynn Johnson (2 hrs.).

DEADLY WHISPERS
CBS 5/10/95. (Bill Norton), Tony Danza, Pamela Reed, Ving Rhames, Heather Tom, Sean Haberle (2 hrs.).

DEAN R. KOONTZ'S "SERVANTS OF TWILIGHT"
SHO 10/14/91. (Jeffrey Obrow), Bruce Greenwood, Belinda Bauer, Grace Zabriskie, Jarrett Lennon.

DEATH DREAMS
LIF 6/25/91. (Martin Donovan), Christopher Reeve, Marg Helgenberger, Fionnula Flanagan (2 hrs.).

DEATH HITS THE JACKPOT
ABC 12/15/91. (Vince McEveety), Peter Falk, Rip Torn, Jamie Rose, Gary Kroeger (2 hrs.).

DEATH IN SMALL DOSES
ABC 11/6/94. (Sondra Locke), Richard Thomas, Tess Harper, Glynnis O'Connor, Shawn Elliott, Gary Frank, (2 hrs.).

DEATH OF THE INCREDIBLE HULK, THE
NBC 2/18/90. (Bill Bixby), Bill Bixby, Lou Ferrigno, Elizabeth Gracen (2 hrs.).

DEATH TRAIN
SHO 4/14/93. (David Jackson), Pierce Brosnan, Patrick Stewart, Christopher Lee, Alexandra Paul (2 hrs.).

DECEPTION: A MOTHER'S SECRET
NBC 11/24/91. (Sandor Stern), Steven Weber, Katharine Helmond, Robert Hy Gorman, Mary Page Keller (2 hrs.).

DECEPTIONS
SHO 6/10/90. (Ruben Preuss), Harry Hamlin, Robert Davi, Nicollette Sheridan (2 hrs.).

DECONSTRUCTING SARAH
USA 6/17/94. (Craig R. Baxley), Sheila Kelley, Rachel Ticotin, A. Martinez, David Andrews (2 hrs.).

DECORATION DAY
NBC 12/2/90. (Robert Markowitz), James Garner, Bill Cobbs, Ruby Dee, Judith Ivey (2 hrs.).

DEEP TROUBLE
USA 7/8/93. (Armand Mastroianni), Robert Wagner, Ben Cross, Isabelle Pasco (2 hrs.).

DELIVER THEM FROM EVIL: THE TAKING OF ALTA VIEW
CBS 4/28/92. (Peter Levin), Harry Hamlin, Teri Garr, Terry O'Quinn, Gary Frank (2 hrs.).

DERBY
ABC 6/17/95. (Bob Clark), Joanne Vannicola, David Charvet, Leon Cariou, Darren McGavin, Felton Perry (2 hrs.).

DESCENDING ANGEL
HBO 11/25/90. (Jeremy Kagan), George C. Scott, Diane Lane, Eric Roberts (2 hrs.).

DESPERATE CHOICES: TO SAVE MY CHILD
NBC 10/5/92. (Andy Tennant), Joanna Kerns, Bruce Davidson, Joe Mazzello, Reese Witherspoon (2 hrs.).

DESPERATE JOURNEY: THE ALLISON WILCOX STORY
ABC 12/5/91. (Dan Lerner), Mel Harris, John Schneider, Dana Ashbrook (2 hrs.).

DESPERATE RESCUE: THE CATHY MAHONE STORY
NBC 1/11/93. (Richard Colla), Mariel Hemingway, Clancy Brown, Jeff Korber, James Russo (2 hrs.).

DESPERATE TRAIL, THE
TNT 7/9/95. (P.J. Pesce), Sam Elliott, Linda Fiorentino, Craig Sheffer, Frank Whaley (2 hrs.).

DEVLIN
SHO 9/12/92. (Rick Rosenthal), Bryan Brown, Roma Downey, Lloyd Bridges, Whip Hubley (2 hrs.).

DIAGNOSIS OF MURDER
CBS 1/5/92. (Chris Hilber), Dick Van Dyke, Mariette Hartley, Ken Kercheval, Bill Bixby (2 hrs.).

DIAMOND FLEECE, THE
USA 6/1/92. (Al Waxman), Ben Cross, Kate Nelligan, Brian Dennehy, Tony Rosato (2 hrs.).

DIANA: HER TRUE STORY
NBC 4/4 & 5/93. (Kevin Connor), Serena Scott Thomas, David Threlfall, Elizabeth Garvie (4 hrs.).

DILLINGER
ABC 1/6/91. (Rupert Wainwright), Mark Harmon, Sherilyn Fenn, Will Patton, Patricia Arquette (2 hrs.).

DIRTY WORK
USA 7/22/92. (John McPherson), Kevin Dobson, John Ashton (2 hrs.).

DISAPPEARANCE OF CHRISTINA, THE
USA 11/4/93. (Karen Arthur), John Stamos, Robert Carradine, Kim Delaney, C.C.H. Pounder (2 hrs.).

DISAPPEARANCE OF NORA, THE
CBS 5/7/93. (Joyce Chopra), Veronica Hamel, Dennis Farina, Stephen Collins (2 hrs.).

DISAPPEARANCE OF VONNIE, THE
CBS 9/27/94. (Graeme Campbell), Ann Jillian, Joe Penny, Kim Zimmer, Robert Wisden, Graham Beckel, Alexandra Purvis (2 hrs.).

DISASTER IN TIME
SHO 5/9/92. (David H. Twohy), Jeff Daniels, Ariana Richards, Emilia Crow, Jim Haynie (2 hrs.).

DOING TIME ON MAPLE DRIVE
FOX 3/16/92. (Ken Olin), William McNamara, James B. Sikking, Bibi Besch, James Carrey (2 hrs.).

DON'T DRINK THE WATER
ABC 12/18/94. (Woody Allen), Woody Allen, Michael J. Fox, Mayim Bialik, Julie Kavner, Dom DeLuise (2 hrs.).

DON'T TALK TO STRANGERS
USA 8/11/94. (Robert Lewis), Pierce Brosnan, Shanna Reed, Terry O'Quinn, Keegan Macintosh (2 hrs.).

DON'T TOUCH MY DAUGHTER
NBC 4/7/91. (John Pasquin), Victoria Principal, Paul Sorvino, Jonathan Banks (2 hrs.).

DONATO AND DAUGHTER
CBS 9/21/93. (Rod Holcomb), Charles Bronson, Dana Delany, Xander Berkeley (2 hrs.).

DONOR
CBS 12/9/90. (Larry Shaw), Melissa Gilbert-Brinkman, Jack Scalia, Wendy Hughes (2 hrs.).

DOOMSDAY GUN
HBO 7/23/94. (Robert Young), Frank Langella, Kevin Spacey, Alan Arkin, Tony Goldwyn, Rupert Graves (2 hrs.).

DOUBLE DECEPTION
NBC 6/21/93. (Jan Egelson), James Russo, Alice Krige, Sally Kirkland, Burt Young (2 hrs.).

DOUBLE DOUBLE TOIL AND TROUBLE
ABC 10/30/93. (Stuart Margolin), Mary-Kate Olsen, Ashley Olsen, Cloris Leachman (2 hrs.).

DOUBLE EDGE
CBS 3/22/92. (Stephen Stafford), Susan Lucci, Robert Urich, Robert Prosky, Michael Woods (2 hrs.).

DOUBLE JEOPARDY
SHO 11/21/92. (Lawrence Schiller), Bruce Boxleitner, Rachel Ward, Sela Ward, Sally Kirkland (2 hrs.).

DOUBLECROSSED
HBO 7/20/91. (Roger Young), Dennis Hopper, Robert Carradine, Adrienne Barbeau (2 hrs.).

DOWN, OUT AND DANGEROUS
USA 8/23/95. (Noel Nosseck), Richard Thomas, Bruce Davison, Cynthia Ettinger, George DiCenzo, Jason Bernard (2 hrs.).

DRAGSTRIP GIRL
SHO 9/2/94. (Mary Lambert), Mark Dacascos, Natasha Gregson Wagner, Maria Celedonio, Raymond Cruz, Traci Lords (90 mins.).

DREAMER OF OZ, THE
NBC 12/10/90. (Jack Bender), John Ritter, Annette O'Toole, Rue McClanahan, John Cameron Mitchell (2 hrs.).

DRIVE LIKE LIGHTNING
USA 1/8/92. (Bradford May), Steven Bauer, Cynthia Gibb, William Russ, Paul Koslo (2 hrs.).

DROP DEAD GORGEOUS
USA 8/7/91. (Paul Lynch), Jennifer Rubin, Peter Outerbridge, Sally Kellerman (2 hrs.).

DRUG WARS: THE COCAINE CARTEL
NBC 1/19 & 20/92. (Paul Krasny), Alex McArthur, Dennis Farina, Julie Carmen, John Glover (4 hrs.).

DRUGS WARS: THE CAMARENA STORY
NBC 1/7, 8 & 9/90. (Brian Gibson), Steven Bauer, Elizabeth Pena, Craig T. Nelson (6 hrs.).

DUE SOUTH
CBS 4/23/94. (Fred Gerber), Paul Gross, David Marciano, Wendel Meldrum (2 hrs.).

DUEL OF HEARTS
TNT 2/24/92. (John Hough), Alison Doody, Michael York, Geraldine Chaplin, Billie Whitelaw (2 hrs.).

DUPLICATES
USA 3/18/92. (Sandor Stern), Gregory Harrison, Kim Griest, Cicely Tyson, Kevin McCarthy (2 hrs.).

DYING TO LOVE YOU
CBS 3/16/93. (Robert Iscove), Tim Matheson, Tracy Pollan, Christine Ebersole (2 hrs.).

DYING TO REMEMBER
USA 10/2/93. (Arthur Allan Seidelman), Melissa Gilbert, Ted Shackelford, Scott Plank (2 hrs.).

DYNASTY: THE REUNION
ABC 10/20 & 22/91. (Irving J. Moore), John Forsythe, Linda Evans, Joan Collins, Jeroen Krabbe (4 hrs.).

EARTH ANGEL
NBC 3/4/91. (Joe Napolitano), Cindy Williams, Cathy Podewell, Mark Hamill (2 hrs.).

ED MCBAIN'S 87TH PRECINCT
NBC 3/19/95. (Bruce Paltrow), Randy Quaid, Alex McArthur, Ving Rhames, Deanne Bray, Eddie Jones (2 hrs.).

EDEN
USA 6/27/93. (Victor Lobl), Barbara Alyn Woods, Steve Chase, Jack Armstrong (2 hrs.).

83 HOURS 'TIL DAWN
CBS 11/11/90. (Donald Wrye), Peter Strauss, Robert Urich, Paul Winfield, Samantha Mathis (2 hrs.).

EL DIABLO
HBO 7/22/90. (Peter Markle), Anthony Edwards, Louis Gossett Jr., John Glover (2 hrs.).

ELVIS AND THE COLONEL
NBC 1/10/93. (William A. Graham), Beau Bridges, Rob Youngblood, Dan Shor, Scott Wilson (2 hrs.).

EMPTY CRADLE
ABC 10/3/93. (Paul Schneider), Kate Jackson, Lori Loughlin, Eric LaSalle, David Lansbury (2 hrs.).

ENDLESS GAME
SHO 1/21/90. (Bryan Forbes), Albert Finney, George Segal, Kristin Scott Thomas, Ian Holm (2 hrs.).

ENTERTAINERS, THE
ABC 11/21/91. (Paul Schneider), Bob Newhart, Linda Gray, Richard Romanus, Bernie White (2 hrs.).

ERNEST GREEN STORY, THE
DIS 1/17/93. (Eric Laneuville), Morris Chestnut, Ossie Davis, C.C.H. Pounder, Avery Brooks (2 hrs.).

ESCAPE FROM TERROR: THE TERESA STAMPER STORY
NBC 1/23/95. (Michael Scott), Maria Pitillo, Adam Storke, Cindy Williams, Tony Becker, Brad Dourif (2 hrs.).

ESCAPE TO WITCH MOUNTAIN
ABC 4/29/95. (Peter Rader), Robert Vaughn, Erik von Detten, Elisabeth Moss, Brad Dourif, Lynne Moody, Lauren Tom (2 hrs.).

EXCLUSIVE
ABC 10/4/92. (Alan Metzger), Suzanne Somers, Michael Nouri, Ed Begley Jr., Joe Cortese (2 hrs.).

EXTREME CLOSE-UP
NBC 10/22/90. (Peter Horton), Craig T. Nelson, Blair Brown, Morgan Weisser, Samantha Mathis (2 hrs.).

EXTREME JUSTICE
HBO 6/26/93. (Mark L. Lester), Lou Diamond Phillips, Scott Glenn, Chelsea Field, Yaphett Kotto (2 hrs.).

EYES OF A WITNESS
CBS 3/31/91. (Peter Hunt), Daniel J. Travanti, Jennifer Grey, Carl Lumbly (2 hrs.).

EYES OF TERROR
NBC 3/18/94. (Sam Pillsbury), Barbara Eden, Michael Nouri, Ted Marcoux (2 hrs.).

F

FACE OF A STRANGER
CBS 12/29/91. (Claudia Weill), Gena Rowlands, Tyne Daly, Cynthia Nixon, Harris Yulin (2 hrs.).

FACE OF FEAR, THE
CBS 9/30/90. (Farhad Mann), Lee Horsley, Pam Dawber, Kevin Conroy (2 hrs.).

FACE ON THE MILK CARTON, THE
CBS 5/24/95. (Waris Hussein), Kellie Martin, Sharon Lawrence, Jill Clayburgh, Edward Herrmann, Michael Rasur (2 hrs.).

FACE TO FACE
CBS 1/24/90. (Lou Antonio), Elizabeth Montgomery, Robert Foxworth, Lou Antonio (2 hrs.).

FADE TO BLACK
USA 2/10/93. (John McPherson), Timothy Busfield, Heather Locklear, Cloris Leachman, Michael Beck (2 hrs.).

FALL FROM GRACE
NBC 4/29/90. (Karen Arthur), Bernadette Peters, Kevin Spacey, Richard Herd (2 hrs.).

FALL FROM GRACE
CBS 6/2 & 3/94. (Waris Hussein), Michael York, Gary Cole, Tara Fitzgerald, James Fox (4 hrs.).

FALLEN CHAMP: THE UNTOLD STORY OF MIKE TYSON
NBC 2/12/93. (Barbara Kopple), Documentary.

FALLING FOR YOU
CBS 2/21/95. (Eric Till), Jennie Garth, Costas Mandylor, Billy Dee Williams, Peter Outerbridge, Helen Shaver (2 hrs.).

FALLING FROM THE SKY!: FLIGHT 174
ABC 2/20/95. (Jorge Montessi), William Devane, Shelley Hack, Scott Hylands, Mariette Hartley, Nicholas Turturro (2 hrs.).

FALSE ARREST
ABC 11/3 & 6/91. (Bill L. Norton), Donna Mills, Robert Wagner, Steven Bauer, Dennis Christopher (4 hrs.).

FAMILY DIVIDED, A
NBC 1/22/95. (Donald Wrye), Faye Dunaway, Stephen Collins, Cameron Bancroft, Judson Mills, Aidan Pendleton, (2 hrs.).

FAMILY FOR JOE, A
NBC 2/25/90. (Jeffrey Melman), Robert Mitchum, Chris Furrh, Maia Brewton (2 hrs.).

FAMILY OF SPIES
CBS 2/4 & 6/90. (Stephen Gyllenhaal), Powers Boothe, Lesley Ann Warren, Lili Taylor (5 hrs.).

FAMILY PICTURES
ABC 3/21 & 22/93. (Philip Saville), Anjelica Huston, Sam Neill, Kyra Sedgwick, Dermot Mulroney (4 hrs.).

FAMILY REUNION: A RELATIVE NIGHTMARE
ABC 4/1/95. (Neal Israel), Jason Marsden, Melissa Joan Hart, Susan French, David L. Lander, Joe Flaherty (2 hrs.).

FAMILY TORN APART, A
NBC 11/21/93. (Craig R. Baxley), Neil Patrick Harris, Gregory Harrison, Johnny Galecki (2 hrs.).

FAST COMPANY
NBC 8/14/95. (Gary Nelson), Ann Jillian, Tim Matheson, Geoffrey Blake, Dex Elliott Sanders, Wendy Phillips (2 hrs.).

FATAL CHARM
SHO 2/22/92. (Fritz Kiersch), Christopher Atkins, Amanda Peterson, James Remar, Andrew Lowery (2 hrs.).

FATAL DECEPTION: MRS. LEE HARVEY OSWALD
NBC 11/15/93. (Robert Dornhelm), Helena Bonham Carter, Frank Whaley, Robert Picardo (2 hrs.).

FATAL EXPOSURE
USA 2/6/91. (Alan Metzger), Mare Winningham, Nick Mancuso, Christopher McDonald (2 hrs.).

FATAL FRIENDSHIP
NBC 12/1/91. (Bradford May), Kevin Dobson, Gerald McRaney, Kate Mulgrew, Patti Yasutake (2 hrs.).

FATAL IMAGE, THE
CBS 12/2/90. (Thomas J. Wright), Michele Lee, Justine Bateman, Jean-Pierre Cassel (2 hrs.).

FATAL MEMORIES
NBC 11/9/92. (Daryl Duke), Shelley Long, Helen Shaver, Dean Stockwell (2 hrs.).

FATAL VOWS: THE ALEXANDRA O'HARA STORY
CBS 10/25/94. (John Power), John Stamos, Cynthia Gibb, David Faustino, Ben Gazzara, Sean McCann (2 hrs.).

FATHER AND SCOUT
ABC 10/15/95. (Richard Michaels), Bob Saget, Brian Bonsall, Troy Evans, Stuart Pankin, David Graf, Heidi Swedberg (2 hrs.).

FATHER & SON: DANGEROUS RELATIONS
NBC 4/19/93. (Georg Stanford Brown), Louis Gossett Jr., Blair Underwood, Rae Dawn Chong (2 hrs.).

FATHER FOR CHARLIE, A
CBS 1/1/95. (Jeff Bleckner), Louis Gossett Jr., Joseph Mazzello, James Greene, Don Swayze, David Hart (2 hrs.).

FATHERLAND
HBO 11/26/94. (Christopher Menaul), Rutger Hauer, Miranda Richardson, Jean Marsh, Peter Vaughan, Michael Kitchen (2 hrs.).

FEAR
SHO 7/15/90. (Rockne S. O'Bannon), Ally Sheedy, Lauren Hutton, Michael O'Keefe (90 mins.).

FEAR INSIDE, THE
SHO 8/9/92. (Leon Ichaso), Christine Lahti, Dylan McDermott, Jennifer Rubin, David Ackroyd (2 hrs.).

FELLOW TRAVELER
HBO 3/4/90. (Philip Saville), Ron Silver, Hart Bochner, Imogen Stubbs (90 mins.).

FERGIE AND ANDREW: BEHIND CLOSED DOORS
NBC 9/28/92. (Michael Switzer), Pippa Hinchley, Sam Miller, Harold Innocent (2 hrs.).

FEVER
HBO 5/11/91. (Larry Elikann), Armand Assante, Sam Neill, Marcia Gay Harden (2 hrs.).

FIGHTING FOR MY DAUGHTER
ABC 1/9/95. (Peter Levin), Lindsay Wagner, Chad Lowe, Piper Laurie, Kirk Baltz, Deirdre O'Connell (2 hrs.).

FINAL APPEAL
NBC 9/26/93. (Eric Till), Brian Dennehy, JoBeth Williams, Tom Mason, Lindsay Crouse (2 hrs.).

FINAL SHOT: THE HANK GATHERS STORY
SYND 4/1/92. (Chuck Braverman), Victor Love, Nell Carter, George Kennedy, Duane Davis (2 hrs.).

FINAL VERDICT
TNT 9/9/91. (Jack Fisk), Treat Williams, Glenn Ford, Olivia Burnette, Gretchen Corbett (2 hrs.).

FINDING THE WAY HOME
ABC 8/26/91. (Rod Holcomb), George C. Scott, Hector Elizondo, Julie Carmen (2 hrs.).

FIRE IN THE DARK
CBS 10/6/91. (David Jones), Olympia Dukakis, Lindsay Wagner, Jean Stapleton, Ray Wise (2 hrs.).

FIRE NEXT TIME, THE
CBS 4/18 & 20/93. (Tom McLoughlin), Craig T. Nelson, Bonnie Bedelia, Richard Farnsworth, Jurgen Prochnow (4 hrs.).

FIRE! TRAPPED ON THE 37TH FLOOR
ABC 2/18/91. (Robert Day), Lisa Hartman, Peter Scolari, Lee Majors (2 hrs.).

FIRESTORM: 72 HOURS IN OAKLAND
ABC 2/7/93. (Michael Tuckner), Jill Clayburgh, LeVar Burton, Michael Gross, Keith Coulouris (2 hrs.).

FIRST DEGREE
HBO 8/20/95. (Jeff Woolnough), Rob Lowe, Leslie Hope, Tom McCamus, Joseph Griffin, Nadia Capone (100 mins.).

FLIGHT OF BLACK ANGEL
SHO 2/23/91. (Jonathan Mostow), Peter Strauss, William O'Leary, James O'Sullivan (2 hrs.).

FLOOD: WHO WILL SAVE OUR CHILDREN?, THE
NBC 10/10/93. (Chris Thomson), Joe Spano, David Lascher, Michael Goorjian (2 hrs.).

FLYING BLIND
NBC 7/30/90. (Vince DiPersio), Richard Panebianco, Emily Longstreth, Frank Whaley (2 hrs.).

FOLLOW THE RIVER
ABC 4/22/95. (Martin Davidson), Sheryl Lee, Ellen Burstyn, Eric Schweig, Tim Guinee, Renee O'Connor (2 hrs.).

FOLLOW YOUR HEART
NBC 4/2/90. (Noel Nosseck), Patrick Cassidy, Catherine Mary Stewart, Jane Alexander (2 hrs.).

FOLLOWING HER HEART
NBC 11/28/94. (Lee Grant), Ann-Margret, Morgan Sheppard, Brenda Vaccaro, George Segal (2 hrs.).

FOR LOVE AND GLORY
CBS 9/11/93. (Roger Young), Daniel Markel, Tracy Griffith, Zach Galligan, Kate Mulgrew (2 hrs.).

FOR RICHER, FOR POORER
HBO 2/29/92. (Jay Sandrich), Jack Lemmon, Talia Shire, Jonathan Silverman, Madeline Kahn (2 hrs.).

FOR THE LOVE OF AARON
CBS 1/1/94. (John Kent Harrison), Meredith Baxter, Keegan Macintosh, Joanna Gleason (2 hrs.).

**FOR THE LOVE OF MY CHILD:
THE ANISSA AYALA STORY**
NBC 5/10/93. (Waris Hussein), Priscilla Lopez, Teresa Dispina, Tony Perez, Robin Thomas (2 hrs.).

FOR THE LOVE OF NANCY
ABC 10/2/94. (Paul Schneider), Tracey Gold, Jill Clayburgh, Cameron Bancroft, Mark-Paul Gosselaar (2 hrs.).

FOR THE VERY FIRST TIME
NBC 4/22/91. (Michael Zinberg), Corin Nemec, Cheryl Pollak, Madchen Amick (2 hrs.).

FOR THEIR OWN GOOD
ABC 4/5/93. (Ed Kaplan), Elizabeth Perkins, Laura San Giacomo, Charles Haid, C.C.H. Pounder (2 hrs.).

FORBIDDEN NIGHTS
CBS 4/10/90. (Waris Hussein), Melissa Gilbert, Robin Shou, Victor K. Wong (2 hrs.).

FOREIGN AFFAIRS
TNT 3/17/93. (Jim O'Brien), Joanne Woodward, Brian Dennehy, Eric Stoltz, Stephanie Beacham (2 hrs.).

**FORGOTTEN PRISONERS:
THE AMNESTY FILES**
TNT 11/19/90. (Robert Greenwald), Ron Silver, Hector Elizondo, Roger Daltrey (2 hrs.).

FOUR DIAMONDS, THE
DIS 8/12/95. (Peter Werner), Thomas Guiry, Christine Lahti, Kevin Dunn, Jayne Brook, Sarah Rose Karr, Michael Bacall (2 hrs.).

FOUR EYES AND SIX-GUNS
TNT 12/7/92. (Piers Haggard), Judge Reinhold, Fred Ward, Patricia Clarkson, Dan Hedaya (2 hrs.).

FOURTH STORY
SHO 1/19/91. (Ivan Passer), Mark Harmon, Mimi Rogers, Paul Gleason, Cliff De Young (2 hrs.).

FRAMED
A&E 9/19 & 20/93. (Geoff Sax), Timothy Dalton, Timothy West, David Morrissey (4 hrs.).

FRANK AND JESSE
HBO 4/22/95. (Robert Boris), Rob Lowe, Bill Paxton, Randy Travis, William Atherton, Dana Wheeler-Nicholson (110 minutes).

FRANKENSTEIN: THE COLLEGE YEARS
FOX 10/28/91. (Tom Shadyac), William Ragsdale, Vincent Hammond, Christopher Daniel Barnes (2 hrs.).

FREAKY FRIDAY
ABC 5/6/95. (Melanie Mayron), Shelley Long, Gaby Hoffmann, Alan Rosenberg, Sandra Bernhard, Carol Kane (2 hrs.).

FRENCH SILK
ABC 1/23/94. (Noel Nosseck), Susan Lucci, Lee Horsley, Shari Belafonte, R. Lee Ermey (2 hrs.).

FRIEND TO DIE FOR, A
ABC 9/26/94. (William A. Graham), Kellie Martin, Tori Spelling, Valerie Harper, Terry O'Quinn, James Avery, Eugene Roche (2 hrs.).

FRIENDS AT LAST
CBS 4/2/95. (John Coles), Kathleen Turner, Colm Feore, Faith Prince, Julie Khaner, Krista Marie Bonura (2 hrs.).

**FROM THE FILES OF JOSEPH WAMBAUGH:
A JURY OF ONE**
NBC 11/29/92. (Alan Metzger), John Spencer, Eddie Velez, Dan Lauria, Rachel Ticotin (2 hrs.).

**FROM THE MIXED-UP FILES OF
MRS. BASIL E. FRANKWEILER**
ABC 6/3/95. (Marcus Cole), Lauren Bacall, Jean Marie Barnwell, Jesse Lee, Miriam Flynn, Mark Taylor, M. Emmett Walsh (2 hrs.).

FUDGE-A-MANIA
ABC 1/7/95. (Anson Williams), Luke Tarsitano, Jake Richardson, Eve Plumb, Forrest Witt, Florence Henderson (2 hrs.).

FUGITIVE AMONG US
CBS 2/4/92. (Michael Toshiyuki Uno), Peter Strauss, Eric Roberts, Elizabeth Pena, Guy Body (2 hrs.).

FUGITIVE NIGHTS: DANGER IN THE DESERT
NBC 11/19/93. (Gary Nelson), Teri Garr, Sam Elliott, Thomas Haden Church (2 hrs.).

G

GAMBLER RETURNS: THE LUCK OF THE DRAW, THE
NBC 11/3 & 4/91. (Dick Lowry), Kenny Rogers, Reba McIntire, Rick Rossovich, David Carradine (4 hrs.).

GAMBLER V: PLAYING FOR KEEPS
CBS 10/2/94. (Jack Bender), Kenny Rogers, Dixie Carter, Loni Anderson, Scott Paulin, Brett Cullen, Kris Kamm (2 hrs.).

GENGHIS COHN
A&E 11/4/94. (Elijah Moshinsky), Robert Lindsay, Diana Rigg, Antony Sher, John Wells (90 mins.).

GERONIMO
TNT 12/5/93. (Roger Young), Joseph Running Fox, Nick Ramus, Michelle St. John (2 hrs.).

GETTING OUT
ABC 4/25/94. (John Korty), Rebecca De Mornay, Ellen Burstyn, Robert Knepper (2 hrs.).

GETTING UP AND GOING HOME
LIF 7/21/92. (Steven Schachter), Tom Skerritt, Blythe Danner, Roma Downey, Julianne Phillips (2 hrs.).

GHOST IN MONTE CARLO, A
TNT 4/2/90. (John Hough), Sarah Miles, Oliver Reed, Christopher Plummer (2 hrs.).

GHOST MOM
FOX 11/1/93. (Dave Thomas), Jean Stapleton, Geraint Wyn Davies, Shae D'Lyn (2 hrs.).

GIFT OF LOVE, THE
CBS 9/25/94. (Paul Bogart), Andy Griffith, Blair Brown, Olivia Burnette, Will Friedle, Joyce Van Patten (2 hrs.).

GIRL FROM MARS, THE
FAM 3/16/91. (Neill Fearnley), Sarah Sawatsky, Edward Albert, Eddie Albert (2 hrs.).

GIRL FROM TOMORROW, THE
DIS 10/23/91. (Kathy Muller), Katharine Cullen, Melissa Marshall, James Findlay (105 mins.).

GIRL WHO CAME BETWEEN THEM, THE
NBC 4/1/90. (Mel Darnski), Cheryl Ladd, Anthony John Denison, Melissa Chan (2 hrs.).

GIRLS IN PRISON
SHO 8/19/94. (John McNaughton), Missy Crider, Ione Skye, Bahni Turpin, Anne Heche (90 mins.).

GOOD COPS, BAD COPS
NBC 12/9/90. (Paul Wendkos), Edward Asner, Ray Sharkey, Steve Railsback (2 hrs.).

GOOD FIGHT, THE
LIF 12/15/92. (John David Coles), Christine Lahti, Terry O'Quinn, Jonathan Crombie (2 hrs.).

GOOD KING WENCESLAS
FAM 11/26/94. (Michael Tuchner), Stefanie Powers, Perry King, Jonathan Brandis, Joan Fontaine, Leo McKern, (2 hrs.).

GOOD NIGHT, SWEET WIFE: A MURDER IN BOSTON
CBS 9/25/90. (Jerrold Freedman), Ken Olin, Margaret Colin, Annabella Price (2 hrs.).

GOOD OLD BOYS, THE
TNT 3/5/95. (Tommy Lee Jones), Tommy Lee Jones, Terry Kinney, Frances McDormand, Sissy Spacek, Sam Shepard, Wilford Brimley (2 hrs.).

GRAMPS
NBC 5/20/95. (Bradford May), Andy Griffith, John Ritter, Mary-Margaret Humes, Casey Moses Wurzbach (2 hrs.).

GRAND ISLE
TNT 7/14/92. (Mary Lambert), Kelly McGillis, Adrian Pasdar, Julian Sands, Glenne Headly (2 hrs.).

GRASS ROOTS
NBC 2/24 & 25/92. (Jerry London), Corbin Bernsen, Mel Harris, John Glover, Reginald Vel Johnson (4 hrs.).

GRAVE SECRETS: THE LEGACY OF HILLTOP DRIVE
CBS 3/2/92. (John Patterson), Patty Duke, David Selby, Blake Clark, David Soul (2 hrs.).

GREAT ELEPHANT ESCAPE, THE
ABC 3/25/95. (George Miller), Stephanie Zimbalist, Joseph Gordon-Levitt, Leo Burmester, Julian Sands (2 hrs.).

GREAT PRETENDER, THE
NBC 4/14/91. (Gus Trikonis), Bruce Greenwood, Jessica Steen, Gregg Henry (2 hrs.).

GREGORY K
ABC 2/8/93. (Linda Otto), Joseph Gordon-Levitt, Bill Smitrovich, Kathleen York, Robert Joy (2 hrs.).

GREEN DOLPHIN BEAT
FOX 6/27/94. (Tommy Lee Wallace), John Wesley Shipp, Jeffrey Sams, Miguel Sandoval (2 hrs.).

GREEN MAN, THE
A&E 6/2/91. (Elijah Moshinsky), Albert Finney, Linda Marlowe, Sarah Berger (3 hrs.).

GREYHOUNDS
CBS 6/24/94. (Kim Manners), James Coburn, Robert Guillaume, Pat Morita, Dennis Weaver (2 hrs.).

GUESS WHO'S COMING FOR CHRISTMAS?
NBC 12/23/90. (Paul Schneider), Richard Mulligan, Barbara Barrie, Paul Dooley (2 hrs.).

GUILTY UNTIL PROVEN INNOCENT
NBC 9/22/91. (Paul Wendkos), Martin Sheen, Brendan Fraser, Caroline Kava, Zachary Mott (2 hrs.).

GUINEVERE
LIF 5/7/94. (Jud Taylor), Sheryl Lee, Sean Patrick Flannery, Noah Wyle, Brid Brennan (2 hrs.).

GUNCRAZY
SHO 10/17/92. (Tamra Davis), Drew Barrymore, James LeGros, Michael Ironside, Ione Skye (95 mins.).

GUNSMOKE: ONE MAN'S JUSTICE
CBS 2/10/94. (Jerry Jameson), James Arness, Bruce Boxleitner, Kelly Morgan (2 hrs.).

GUNSMOKE: THE LAST APACHE
CBS 3/18/90. (Charles Correll), James Arness, Richard Kiley, Michael Learned (2 hrs.).

GUNSMOKE: THE LAST RIDE
CBS 5/8/93. (Jerry Jameson), James Arness, James Brolin, Ali MacGraw, Amy Stock-Paynton (2 hrs.).

GUNSMOKE: TO THE LAST MAN
CBS 1/10/92. (Jerry Jameson), James Arness, Pat Hingle, Amy Stock-Poynton, Matt Mulhern (2 hrs.).

GYPSY
CBS 12/12/93. (Emile Ardolino), Bette Midler, Cynthia Gibb, Peter Riegert, Edward Asner (3 hrs.).

H

HABITATION OF DRAGONS, THE
TNT 9/8/92. (Michael Lindsay-Hogg), Frederic Forrest, Brad Davis, Jean Stapleton, Pat Hingle (2 hrs.).

HANDS OF A MURDERER
CBS 5/16/90. (Stuart Orme), Edward Woodward, John Hillerman, Anthony Andrews (2 hrs.).

HART TO HART: CRIMES OF THE HART
NBC 3/25/94. (Peter Hunt), Robert Wagner, Stefanie Powers, Lionel Stander, John Stockwell (2 hrs.).

HART TO HART: HOME IS WHERE THE HART IS
NBC 2/18/94. (Peter Hunt), Robert Wagner, Stefanie Powers, Maureen O'Sullivan, Howard Keel (2 hrs.).

HART TO HART: OLD FRIENDS NEVER DIE
NBC 5/16/94. (Peter Hunt), Robert Wagner, Stefanie Powers, Mike Farrell, David Rasche (2 hrs.).

HART TO HART RETURNS
NBC 11/5/93. (Peter Hunt), Robert Wagner, Stefanie Powers, Lionel Stander, Mike Connors (2 hrs.).

HART TO HART: SECRETS OF THE HEART
NBC 3/6/95. (Kevin Connor), Robert Wagner, Stefanie Powers, Jason Bateman, Marion Ross, Wendie Malick (2 hrs.).

HARVEST FOR THE HEART
FAM 4/16/94. (Michael Scott), Ted Shackelford, Ron White, Rebecca Jenkins (2 hrs.).

HAUNTED, THE
FOX 5/6/91. (Robert Mandel), Sally Kirkland, Jeffrey DeMunn, Louise Latham (2 hrs.).

HEADS
SHO 1/29/94. (Paul Shapiro), Jon Cryer, Edward Asner, Jennifer Tilly, Roddy McDowall (105 mins.).

HEART OF DARKNESS
TNT 3/13/94. (Nicolas Roeg), John Malkovich, Tim Roth, Isaach de Bankole, James Fox (2 hrs.).

HEART OF JUSTICE, THE
TNT 2/20/93. (Bruno Barreto), Eric Stoltz, Jennifer Connelly, Dermot Mulroney, Vincent Price, Keith Reddin (2 hrs.).

HEAT WAVE
TNT 8/13/90. (Kevin Hooks), Cicely Tyson, Blair Underwood, James Earl Jones (2 hrs.).

HEIDI
DIS 7/18 & 19/93. (Michael Rhodes), Jason Robards, Jane Seymour, Noley Thornton, Patricia Neal (190 mins.).

HELD HOSTAGE: THE SIS AND JERRY LEVIN STORY
ABC 1/13/91. (Roger Young), Marlo Thomas, David Dukes, G.W. Bailey (2 hrs.).

HELL HATH NO FURY
NBC 3/4/91. (Thomas J. Wright), Barbara Eden, Loretta Swit, David Ackroyd (2 hrs.).

HER FINAL FURY:
BETTY BRODERICK—THE LAST CHAPTER
CBS 11/1/92. (Dick Lowry), Meredith Baxter, Judith Ivey, Ray Baker, Kelli Williams (2 hrs.).

HER WICKED WAYS
CBS 1/1/91. (Richard Michaels), Barbara Eden, Tess O'Brien, Heather Locklear (2 hrs.).

HERCULES AND THE AMAZON WOMEN
SYND 4/30/94. (Christian Williams), Kevin Sorbo, Anthony Quinn, Roma Downey (2 hrs.).

HEROES OF DESERT STORM, THE
ABC 10/6/91. (Don Ohlmeyer), Angela Bassett, Daniel Baldwin, Michael Allen Brooks, Kris Kamm (2 hrs.).

HI HONEY—I'M DEAD
FOX 4/22/91. (Alan Myerson), Curtis Armstrong, Catherine Hicks, Kevin Conroy (2 hrs.).

HIDDEN VIEW
WPIX 9/10/90. (Jag Mundhra), Andrew Stevens, Tanya Roberts, Warwick Sims (2 hrs.).

HIGHWAY HEARTBREAKER
CBS 3/29/92. (Paul Schneider), John Schneider, Linda Gray, Heather Locklear, Tracy Nelson (2 hrs.).

HIROSHIMA
SHO 8/6/95. (Roger Spottiswoode, Koreyoshi Kurahara), Kenneth Welsh, Wesley Addy, David Gow, Hisashi Igawa, Ken Jenkins, Saul Rubinek (195 mins.).

HIROSHIMA: OUT OF THE ASHES
NBC 8/6/90. (Peter Werner), Max von Sydow, Judd Nelson, Mako, Pat Morita (2 hrs.).

HIT LIST, THE
SHO 1/17/93. (William Webb), Jeff Fahey, Yancy Butler, James Coburn (2 hrs.).

HIT MAN, THE
ABC 6/29/91. (Gary Nelson), Dennis Boutsikaris, Daryl Anderson, Eagle Eye Cherry (2 hrs.).

HITLER'S DAUGHTER
USA 9/26/90. (James A. Contner), Patrick Cassidy, Melody Anderson, Veronica Cartwright (2 hrs.).

HOLLYROCK–A–BYE BABY
ABC 12/5/93. (William Hanna), Animated. (2 hrs.)

HOME FOR CHRISTMAS
LIF 12/6/90. (Peter McCubbin), Mickey Rooney, Simon Richards, Lesley Kelly (2 hrs.).

HOMETOWN BOY MAKES GOOD
HBO 8/2/90. (David Burton Morris), Anthony Edwards, Cynthia Bain, Grace Zabriskie (90 mins.).

HOMEWRECKER
USA 12/17/92. (Fred Walton), Robby Benson, Sydney Walsh, Sarah Rose Karr, Kate Jackson (voice) (2 hrs.).

HONOR THY FATHER AND MOTHER:
THE TRUE STORY OF THE MENENDEZ MURDERS
FOX 4/18/94. (Paul Schneider), James Farentino, Jill Clayburgh, Billy Warlock, David Beron (2 hrs.).

HONOR THY MOTHER
CBS 4/26/92. (David Greene), Sharon Gless, William McNamara, Paul Scherrer, Brian Wimmer (2 hrs.).

HORSE FOR DANNY, A
ABC 4/8/95. (Dick Lowry), Robert Urich, Ron Brice, Gary Basaraba, Eric Jensen, Leelee Sobieski (2 hrs.).

HOSTAGE FOR A DAY
FOX 4/25/94. (John Candy), George Wendt, John Vernon, Robin Duke, Peter Torkovei (2 hrs.).

HOSTAGES
HBO 2/19/93. (David Wheatley), Colin Firth, Ciaran Hinds, Natasha Richardson, Harry Dean Stanton, Kathy Bates (105 mins.).

HOUSE OF SECRETS
NBC 11/1/93. (Mimi Leder), Melissa Gilbert, Bruce Boxleitner, Cicely Tyson, Kate Vernon (2 hrs.).

HOUSE OF SECRETS AND LIES, A
CBS 9/27/92. (Paul Schneider), Connie Sellecca, Kevin Dobson, Grace Zibriskie, Georgann Johnson (2 hrs.).

HOUSE ON SYCAMORE STREET, THE
CBS 5/1/92. (Christian I. Nyby II), Dick Van Dyke, Cynthia Gibb, Stephen Caffrey, Barry Van Dyke (2 hrs.).

HOW THE WEST WAS FUN
ABC 11/19/94. (Stuart Margolin), Mary-Kate Olsen, Ashley Olsen, Martin Mull, Michele Green, Patrick Cassidy (2 hrs.).

HOW TO MURDER A MILLIONAIRE
CBS 5/23/90. (Paul Schneider), Joan Rivers, Alex Rocco, Morgan Fairchild (2 hrs.).

HUCK AND THE KING OF HEARTS
SHO 10/7/94. (Michael Keusch), John Astin, Joe Piscopo, Dee Wallace Stone (2 hrs.).

HUSH LITTLE BABY
USA 1/6/94. (Jorge Montesi), Diane Ladd, Wendel Meldrum, Geraint Wyn Davies (2 hrs.).

I

I CAN MAKE YOU LOVE ME:
THE STALKING OF LAURA BLACK
CBS 2/9/93. (Michael Switzer), Richard Thomas, Brooke Shields, Viveka Davis, William Allen (2 hrs.).

I KNOW MY SON IS ALIVE
NBC 2/20/94. (Bill Corcoran), Corbin Bernsen, Amanda Pays, Albert Schultz (2 hrs.).

I SPY RETURNS
CBS 2/3/94. (Jerry London), Robert Culp, Bill Cosby, George Newbern, Salli Richardson (2 hrs.).

I STILL DREAM OF JEANNIE
NBC 10/20/91. (Joseph Scanlan), Barbara Eden, Christopher Bolton, Bill Daly, Al Waxman (2 hrs.).

I YABBA DABBA DO!
ABC 2/7/93. (William Hanna), Animated. (2 hrs.).

IF SOMEONE HAD KNOWN
NBC 5/1/95. (Eric Laneuville), Kellie Martin, Kevin Dobson, Linda Kelsey, Ivan Sergei, Kristin Dattilo-Hayward (2 hrs.).

I'LL FLY AWAY: THEN AND NOW
PBS 10/11/93. (Ian Sander), Sam Waterston, Regina Taylor, Jason London (2 hrs.).

I'LL TAKE ROMANCE
ABC 11/25/90. (Piers Haggard), Linda Evans, Larry Poindexter, Tom Skerritt (2 hrs.).

ILLICIT BEHAVIOR
USA 12/9/92. (Worth Keeter), Robert Davi, Joan Severance, Jack Scalia, James Russo (2 hrs.).

I'M DANGEROUS TONIGHT
USA 8/8/90. (Tobe Hooper), Madchen Amick, Corey Parker, Anthony Perkins (2 hrs.).

IMAGE, THE
HBO 1/27/90. (Peter Werner), Albert Finney, John Mahoney, Kathy Baker, Marsha Mason (2 hrs.).

IN A CHILD'S NAME
CBS 11/17 & 19/91. (Tom McLoughlin), Valerie Bertinelli, Michael Ontkean, Louise Fletcher, Timothy Carhart (4 hrs.).

IN BROAD DAYLIGHT
NBC 2/3/91. (James Steven Sadwith), Brian Dennehy, Cloris Leachman, Marcia Gay Harden (2 hrs.).

IN DEFENSE OF A MARRIED MAN
ABC 10/14/90. (Joel Oliansky), Judith Light, Michael Ontkean, Jerry Orbach (2 hrs.).

IN MY DAUGHTER'S NAME
CBS 5/10/92. (Jud Taylor), Donna Mills, Lee Grant, John Rubinstein, John Getz (2 hrs.).

IN PURSUIT OF HONOR
HBO 3/18/95. (Ken Olin), Don Johnson, Craig Sheffer, Gabrielle Anwar, Bob Gunton, Rod Steiger (2 hrs.).

IN SICKNESS AND IN HEALTH
CBS 3/8/92. (Jeff Bleckner), Lesley Ann Warren, Tom Skerritt, Marg Helgenberger, Ray Baker (2 hrs.)

IN THE ARMS OF A KILLER
NBC 1/5/92. (Robert Collins), Jaclyn Smith, John Spencer, Michael Nouri, Nina Foch (2 hrs.).

IN THE BEST INTEREST OF THE CHILD
CBS 5/20/90. (David Greene), Meg Tilly, Ed Begley, Jr., Michael O'Keefe (2 hrs.).

IN THE BEST INTEREST OF THE CHILDREN
NBC 2/16/92. (Michael Ray Rhodes), Sarah Jessica Parker, Sally Struthers, Elizabeth Ashley, Lexi Randall (2 hrs.).

IN THE BEST OF FAMILIES:
MARRIAGE, PRIDE AND MADNESS
CBS 1/16 & 18/94. (Jeff Beckner), Kelly McGillis, Harry Hamlin, Keith Carradine, Holland Taylor (4 hrs.).

IN THE COMPANY OF DARKNESS
CBS 1/5/93. (David Anspaugh), Helen Hunt, Steven Weber, Jeff Fahey, Juan Ramirez (2 hrs.).

IN THE DEEP WOODS
NBC 10/26/92. (Charles Correll), Rosanna Arquette, Anthony Perkins, Will Patton, D.W. Moffet (2 hrs.).

IN THE EYES OF A STRANGER
CBS 4/7/92. (Michael Toshiyuki Uno), Justine Bateman, Richard Dean Anderson, Cynthia Dale, Colin Fox (2 hrs.).

IN THE HEAT OF THE NIGHT: A MATTER OF JUSTICE
CBS 10/21/94. (Reza Badiyi), Carroll O'Connor, George C. Scott, Carl Weathers, Joshua Lucas, Alan Autry, David Hart (2 hrs.).

IN THE HEAT OF THE NIGHT: BY DUTY BOUND
CBS 2/17/95. (Harry Harris), Carroll O'Connor, Carl Weathers, Corbin Bernsen, John Calvin, Denise Nicholas (2 hrs.).

IN THE HEAT OF THE NIGHT: GROW OLD WITH ME
CBS 5/16/95. (Winrich Kolbe), Carroll O'Connor, Carl Weathers, Alan Autry, David Hart, Hugh O'Connor, Crystal Fox (2 hrs.).

IN THE HEAT OF THE NIGHT: WHO WAS GELI BENDL?
CBS 12/9/94. (Larry Hagman), Carroll O'Connor, Carl Weathers, Sydney Rome, Richard T. Jones, Arienne Battiste (2 hrs.).

IN THE LINE OF DUTY: A COP FOR THE KILLING
NBC 11/25/90. (Dick Lowry), James Farentino, Steven Weber, Susan Walters (2 hrs.).

IN THE LINE OF DUTY: AMBUSH IN WACO
NBC 5/23/93. (Dick Lowry), Tim Daly, Dan Lauria, William O'Leary, Clu Gulager (2 hrs.).

IN THE LINE OF DUTY: KIDNAPPED
NBC 3/12/95. (Bobby Roth), Dabney Coleman, Timothy Busfield, Lauren Tom, Tracey Walter, Barbara Williams (2 hrs.).

IN THE LINE OF DUTY: MANHUNT IN THE DAKOTAS
NBC 5/12/91. (Dick Lowry), Rod Steiger, Michael Gross, Gary Basaraba (2 hrs.).

IN THE LINE OF DUTY: STANDOFF AT MARION
NBC 2/10/92. (Charles Haid), Kyle Secor, Dennis Franz, Paul Le Mat, Tess Harper (2 hrs.).

IN THE LINE OF DUTY: STREET WAR
NBC 10/25/92. (Dick Lowry), Ray Sharkey, Peter Boyle, Mario Van Peebles, Courtney B. Vance (2 hrs.).

IN THE LINE OF DUTY: THE PRICE OF VENGEANCE
NBC 1/23/94. (Dick Lowry), Dean Stockwell, Michael Gross, Mary Kay Place (2 hrs.).

IN THE NICK OF TIME
NBC 12/16/91. (George Miller), Lloyd Bridges, Michael Tucker, Alison La Placa, Cleavon Little (2 hrs.).

IN THE SHADOW OF A KILLER
NBC 4/27/92. (Alan Metzger), Scott Bakula, Lindsay Frost, Miguel Ferrer, Robert Clohessey (2 hrs.).

IN THE SHADOW OF EVIL
CBS 2/7/95. (Daniel Sackheim), Treat Williams, Margaret Colin, Joe Morton, William H. Macy, Timothy Busfield. (2 hrs.).

IN THE SHADOWS, SOMEONE'S WATCHING
NBC 10/4/93. (Richard Friedman), Joan Van Ark, Daniel Travanti, Christopher Noth, Rick Springfield (2 hrs.).

INCIDENT, THE
CBS 3/4/90. (Joseph Sargent), Walter Matthau, Susan Blakely, Robert Carradine, Harry Morgan (2 hrs.).

INCIDENT AT DECEPTION RIDGE
USA 9/15/94. (John McPherson), Michael O'Keefe, Ed Begley Jr., Linda Purl, Miguel Ferrer, Michele Johnson (2 hrs.).

INCIDENT IN A SMALL TOWN
CBS 1/23/94. (Delbert Mann), Walter Matthau, Harry Morgan, Stephanie Zimbalist, Nick Stahl (2 hrs.).

INCONVENIENT WOMAN, AN
ABC 5/12 & 13/91. (Larry Elikann), Jason Robards, Jill Eikenberry, Rebecca DeMornay, Chad Lowe (4 hrs.).

INDECENCY
USA 9/16/92. (Marisa Silver), Jennifer Beals, Sammi Davis-Voss, James Remar, Barbara Williams (2 hrs.).

INDICTMENT: THE MCMARTIN TRIAL
HBO 5/20/95. (Mick Jackson), James Woods, Mercedes Ruehl, Henry Thomas, Sada Thompson, Lolita Davidovich, Shirley Knight (2 hrs.).

INFILTRATOR, THE
HBO 6/24/95. (John Mackenzie), Oliver Platt, Arliss Howard, Tony Haygarth, Michael Byrne, Julian Glover, George Jackos (2 hrs.).

INNOCENT, THE
NBC 9/25/94. (Mimi Leder), Kelsey Grammer, Keegan Macintosh, Polly Draper, Dean Stockwell, Jeff Kober (2 hrs.).

INSPECTOR ALLEYN: HAND IN GLOVE
A&E 1/11/94. (Martyn Friend), Patrick Malahide, Belinda Lang, John Gielgud (2 hrs.).

INTO THE BADLANDS
USA 7/24/91. (Sam Pillsbury), Bruce Dern, Mariel Hemingway, Dylan McDermott (2 hrs.).

INTRUDERS
CBS 5/17 & 19/92. (Dan Curtis), Richard Crenna, Mare Winningham, Susan Blakely, Daphne Ashbrook (4 hrs.).

INVASION OF PRIVACY
USA 10/7/92. (Kevin Meyer), Robby Benson, Jennifer O'Neill, Lydie Denier, Ian Ogilvy (2 hrs.).

INVESTIGATION: INSIDE A TERRORIST BOMBING
HBO 4/22/90. (Mike Beckham), John Hurt, Martin Shaw, Roger Allam (140 mins.).

IRAN: DAYS OF CRISIS
TNT 6/9/92. (Kevin Connor), Arliss Howard, Jeff Fahey, Alice Krige, Valerie Kaprisky (2 hrs.).

IRONCLADS
TNT 3/11/91. (Delbert Mann), Virginia Madsen, Alex Hyde-White, Reed Edward Diamond (2 hrs.).

IS THERE LIFE OUT THERE?
CBS 10/9/94. (David Jones), Reba McEntire, Keith Carradine, Genia Michaela, Mitchell Anderson (2 hrs.).

IT'S NOTHING PERSONAL
NBC 2/1/93. (Brandford May), Amanda Donohoe, Bruce Dern, Yaphet Kotto, Veronica Cartwright (2 hrs.).

J

JFK: RECKLESS YOUTH
ABC 11/21 & 23/93. (Harry Winer), Patrick Dempsey, Terry Kinney, Loren Dean, Andrew Lowery (4 hrs.).

JACK REED: A SEARCH FOR JUSTICE
NBC 10/2/94. (Brian Dennehy), Brian Dennehy, Charles Dutton, Susan Ruttan, Joe Grifasi, Rex Linn, Miguel Ferrer (2 hrs.).

JACK REED: BADGE OF HONOR
NBC 11/12/93. (Kevin Connor), Brian Dennehy, Susan Ruttan, Alice Krige, R.D. Call (2 hrs.).

JACKIE COLLINS' "LADY BOSS"
NBC 10/11 & 12/92. (Charles Jarrott), Kim Delaney, Jack Scalia, David Selby, Vanity (4 hrs.).

JACKIE COLLINS' "LUCKY/CHANCES"
NBC 10/7, 8 & 9/90. (Buzz Kulik), Nicollette Sheridan, Vincent Irizarry, Michael Nader (6 hrs.).

JACKSONS: AN AMERICAN DREAM, THE
ABC 11/15 & 18/92. (Karen Arthur), Lawrence Hilton-Jacobs, Angela Bassett, Holly Robinson, Vannessa Williams (5 hrs.).

JACOB
TNT 12/4/94. (Peter Hall), Matthew Modine, Lara Flynn Boyle, Sean Bean, Joss Ackland, Juliet Aubrey, Irene Papas, Giancarlo Giannini (2 hrs.).

JAILBIRDS
CBS 5/16/91. (Burt Brinckerhoff), Dyan Cannon, Phylicia Rashad, David Knell (2 hrs.).

JAILBREAKERS
SHO 9/9/94. (William Friedkin), Shannen Doherty, Antonio Sabato Jr., Vince Edwards, Adrienne Barbeau, Adrien Brody (90 mins.).

JAKE LASSITER: JUSTICE ON THE BAYOU
NBC 1/9/95. (Peter Markle), Gerald McRaney, Robert Loggia, Tracy Scoggins, Daphne Ashbrook, James B. Sikking (2 hrs.).

JAMES A. MICHENER'S "TEXAS"
ABC 4/16 & 17/95. (Richard Lang), Stacy Keach, Patrick Duffy, Rick Schroder, Chelsea Field, Anthony Michael Hall (4 hrs.).

JANEK: A SILENT BETRAYAL
CBS 12/20/94. (Robert Iscove), Richard Crenna, Helen Shaver, Cliff Gorman, Philip Bosco, Gordon Currie, William Shatner (2 hrs.).

JANEK: THE FORGET-ME-NOT MURDERS
CBS 3/29/94. (Robert Iscove), Richard Crenna, Tyne Daly, Helen Shaver, Cliff Gorman (2 hrs.).

JANE'S HOUSE
CBS 1/2/94. (Glenn Jordan), James Woods, Anne Archer, Missy Crider, Keegan MacIntosh (2 hrs.).

JEKYLL & HYDE
ABC 1/21/90. (David Wickes), Michael Caine, Cheryl Ladd, Joss Ackland (2 hrs.).

JOHN CARPENTER PRESENTS "BODY BAGS"
SHO 8/8/93. (John Carpenter, Tobe Hooper), Robert Carradine, Stacy Keach, Mark Hamill, Twiggy (90 mins.).

JOHN JAKES' HEAVEN AND HELL: NORTH AND SOUTH PART III
ABC 2/27, 28 & 3/2/94. (Larry Peerce), Lesley-Anne Down, James Read, Philip Casnoff, Peter O'Toole (6 hrs.).

JOHNNY & CLYDE
SHO 8/13/95. (Bill Bindley), John White, Michael Rooker, Diana Reis, Sam Malkin, Diane Douglass (2 hrs.).

JOHNNY RYAN
NBC 7/29/90. (Robert Collins), Clancy Brown, Bruce Abbott, Teri Austin (2 hrs.).

JONATHAN: THE BOY NOBODY WANTED
NBC 10/19/92. (George Kaczender), JoBeth Williams, Chris Burke, Madge Sinclair, Jeffrey DeMunn (2 hrs.).

JONNY'S GOLDEN QUEST
USA 4/4/93. (Mario Piluso, prod.), Animated.

JOSEPH
TNT 4/16 & 17/95. (Roger Young), Ben Kingsley, Paul Mercurio, Lesley Ann Warren, Martin Landau, Warren Clarke (4 hrs.).

JOSEPHINE BAKER STORY, THE
HBO 3/16/91. (Brian Gibson), Lynn Whitfield, Ruben Blades, David Dukes, Louis Gossett Jr. (135 mins.).

JOSHUA'S HEART
NBC 9/10/90. (Michael Pressman), Melissa Gilbert, Tim Matheson, Matthew Lawrence (2 hrs.).

JOURNEY TO THE CENTER OF THE EARTH
NBC 2/28/93. (Bill Dear), Jeffrey Nordling, Farrah Forke, John Neville, F. Murray Abraham (2 hrs.).

JUDGMENT
HBO 10/13/90. (Tom Topor), Keith Carradine, Blythe Danner, David Strathairn, Dylan Baker (90 mins.).

JUDGMENT DAY: THE JOHN LIST STORY
CBS 2/23/93. (Bobby Roth), Robert Blake, Carroll Baker, Beverly D'Angelo, David Caruso (2 hrs.).

JUDICIAL CONSENT
HBO 3/12/95. (William Bindley), Bonnie Bedelia, Dabney Coleman, Billy Wirth, Lisa Blount, Will Patton (2 hrs.).

JURY DUTY: THE COMEDY
ABC 1/14/90. (Michael Schultz), Bronson Pinchot, Lynn Redgrave, Heather Locklear (2 hrs.).

JUST ONE OF THE GIRLS
FOX 9/13/93. (Michael Keusch), Corey Haim, Nicole Eggert, Cameron Bancroft (2 hrs.).

JUSTICE IN A SMALL TOWN
NBC 9/23/94. (Jan Egleson), Kate Jackson, John Shea, Dean Stockwell, Rand Courtney, Terry O'Quinn (2 hrs.)

K

K-9000
FOX 7/1/91. (Kim Manners), Chris Mulkey, Catherine Oxenberg, Dennis Haysbert (2 hrs.).

KANSAS
ABC 7/27/95. (Bob Mandel), Patricia Wettig, Jenny Robertson, Dierdre O'Connell, Scott Paulin, Luke Rossi (2 hrs.).

KEEP THE CHANGE
TNT 6/9/92. (Andy Tennant), William Petersen, Lolita Davidovich, Rachel Ticotin, Jack Palance (2 hrs.).

KEEPER OF THE CITY
SHO 1/25/92. (Bobby Roth), Louis Gossett Jr., Anthony LaPaglia, Peter Coyote, Renee Soutendijk (2 hrs.).

KEEPING SECRETS
ABC 9/29/91. (John Korty), Suzanne Somers, Ken Kercheval, Michael Learned, David Birney (2 hrs.).

KENNEDYS OF MASSACHUSETTS, THE
ABC 2/18, 19 & 21/90. (Lamont Johnson), William Petersen, Charles Durning, Campbell Scott (6 hrs.).

KEYS, THE
NBC 4/12/92. (Richard Compton), Ben Masters, Brian Bloom, Scott Bloom, Barry Corbin (2 hrs.).

KID WHO LOVED CHRISTMAS, THE
WPIX 12/14/90. (Arthur Allan Seidelman), Michael Warren, Cicely Tyson, Sammy Davis, Jr., Trent Cameron (2 hrs.).

KILLER AMONG FRIENDS, A
CBS 12/8/92. (Charles Robert Carner), Patty Duke, Margaret Welsh, Loretta Swit (2 hrs.).

KILLER AMONG US, A
NBC 10/29/90. (Peter Levin), Jasmine Guy, Anna Maria Horsford, Dwight Schultz (2 hrs.).

KILLER RULES
NBC 1/24/93. (Robert Ellis Miller), Jamey Sheridan, Sela Ward, Peter Dobson, Sam Wanamaker (2 hrs.).

KILLING IN A SMALL TOWN
CBS 5/22/90. (Stephen Gyllenhaal), Barbara Hershey, Brian Dennehy, Hal Holbrook (2 hrs.).

KILLING MIND, THE
LIF 4/23/91. (Michael Ray Rhodes), Stephanie Zimbalist, Tony Bill, Daniel Roebuck (2 hrs.).

KINGFISH: A STORY OF HUEY P. LONG
TNT 3/19/95. (Thomas Schlamme), John Goodman, Matt Craven, Anne Heche, Jeff Perry, Ann Dowd, Bob Gunton (2 hrs.).

KISS OF A KILLER
ABC 2/1/93. (Larry Elikann), Annette O'Toole, Eva Marie Saint, Brian Wimmer, Gregg Henry (2 hrs.).

KISS TO DIE FOR, A
NBC 12/6/93. (Leon Ichaso), Tim Matheson, Mimi Rogers, William Forsythe, Carroll Baker (2 hrs.).

KISSING PLACE, THE
USA 4/11/90. (Tony Wharmby), Meredith Baxter-Birney, David Ogden Stiers, Nathaniel Moreau (2 hrs.).

KNIGHT RIDER 2010
SYND 2/9/94. (Sam Pillsbury), Richard Joseph Paul, Heidi Peick, Michael Beach (2 hrs.).

KURT VONNEGUT'S "HARRISON BERGERON"
SHO 8/13/95. (Bruce Pittman), Sean Astin, Miranda DePencier, Christopher Plummer, Buck Henry, Howie Mandel (90 mins.).

L

LABOR OF LOVE: THE ARLETTE SCHWEITZER STORY
CBS 5/9/93. (Jerry London), Ann Jillian, Tracey Gold, Bill Smitrovich, Diana Scarwid (2 hrs.).

LADY AGAINST THE ODDS
NBC 4/20/92. (Bradford May), Crystal Bernard, Annabeth Gish, Rob Estes, Kevin Kilner, Roy Thinnes (2 hrs.).

LADY KILLER
CBS 4/5/95. (Steven Schachter), Judith Light, Tracey Gold, Jack Wagner, Ben Masters, Diana LeBlanc, J.R. Zimmerman (2 hrs.).

LADYKILLER
USA 8/19/92. (Michael Scott), Mimi Rogers, John Shea, Alice Krige, Bob Gunton (2 hrs.).

LAKE CONSEQUENCE
SHO 2/28/93. (Rafael Eisenman), Billy Zane, Joan Severance, Mary Karasun, Whip Hubley (2 hrs.).

LAKER GIRLS
CBS 4/3/90. (Bruce Seth Green), Tina Yothers, Paris Vaughan, Jean Simmons (2 hrs.).

LAKOTA WOMAN: SIEGE AT WOUNDED KNEE
TNT 10/16/94. (Frank Pierson), Irene Bedard, August Schellenberg, Joseph Runningfox, Floyd Red Crow Westerman, Tantoo Cardinal (2 hrs.).

LANTERN HILL
DIS 1/27/90. (Kevin Sullivan), Sam Waterston, Marion Bennett, Sarah Polley (2 hrs.).

LAST BEST YEAR, THE
ABC 11/4/90. (John Erman), Mary Tyler Moore, Bernadette Peters, Brian Bedford, Dorothy McGuire (2 hrs.).

LAST ELEPHANT, THE
TNT 8/20/90. (Joseph Sargent), John Lithgow, Isabella Rosellini, James Earl Jones (2 hrs.).

LAST FLIGHT OUT
NBC 5/22/90. (Larry Elikann), Richard Crenna, James Earl Jones, Eric Bogosian (2 hrs.).

LAST HIT, THE
USA 3/31/94. (Jan Egelson), Bryan Brown, Brooke Adams, Harris Yulin (2 hrs.).

LAST LIGHT
SHO 8/22/93. (Kiefer Sutherland), Forest Whitaker, Kiefer Sutherland, Amanda Plummer (2 hrs.).

LAST OF HIS TRIBE, THE
HBO 3/28/92. (Harry Hook), Jon Voight, Graham Greene, David Ogden Stiers, Anne Archer (90 mins.).

LAST OUTLAW, THE
HBO 10/30/93. (Geoff Murphy), Mickey Rourke, Dermot Mulroney, Steve Buscemi (2 hrs.).

LAST PROSTITUTE, THE
LIF 9/11/91. (Lou Antonio), Wil Wheaton, Sonia Braga, Cotter Smith, David Kaufman (2 hrs.).

LAST TO GO, THE
ABC 1/21/91. (John Erman), Tyne Daly, Terry O'Quinn, Annabeth Gish (2 hrs.).

LAST TRAIN HOME
FAM 3/2/90. (Randy Bradshaw), Noam Zylberman, Nick Mancuso, Ned Beatty (2 hrs.).

LAST WISH
ABC 1/12/92. (Jeff Bleckner), Patty Duke, Maureen Stapleton, Dwight Schultz, Lee Wallace (2 hrs.).

LAST WORD, THE
SHO 8/27/95. (Tony Spiridakis), Timothy Hutton, Joe Pantoliano, Michelle Burke, Chazz Palminteri, Tony Goldwyn, Cybill Shepherd, Richard Dreyfus, Jimmy Smits (90 mins.).

LAUREL AVENUE
HBO 7/10 & 11/93. (Carl Franklin), Mary Alice, Jay Brooks, Juanita Jennings, Dan Martin (3 hrs.).

LEAVE OF ABSENCE
NBC 5/11/94. (Tom McLoughlin), Brian Dennehy, Jacqueline Bisset, Blythe Danner, Polly Bergen (2 hrs.).

LEGACY OF LIES
USA 4/22/92. (Bradford May), Michael Ontkean, Martin Landau, Eli Wallach, Joe Morton (2 hrs.).

LEONA HELMSLEY: THE QUEEN OF MEAN
CBS 9/23/90. (Richard Michaels), Suzanne Pleshette, Lloyd Bridges, Joe Regalbuto (2 hrs.).

LETHAL EXPOSURE
NBC 3/28/93. (Kevin O'Connor), Ally Sheedy, Francois Eric Gendron, Carmela Valente (2 hrs.).

LETTER TO MY KILLER
USA 8/9/95. (Janet Meyers), Mare Winningham, Nick Chinlund, Rip Torn, Josef Sommer, Eddie Jones (2 hrs.).

LIAR, LIAR
CBS 6/22/93. (Jorge Montesi), Art Hindle, Rosemary Dunsmore, Kate Nelligan (2 hrs.).

LIAR'S EDGE
SHO 12/4/92. (Ron Oliver), Nicholas Shields, David Keith, Joseph Bottoms, Shannon Tweed (2 hrs.).

LIE DOWN WITH LIONS
LIF 6/12/94. (Jim Goddard), Timothy Dalton, Marg Helgenberger, Nigel Havers (2 hrs.).

LIES AND LULLABIES
ABC 3/14/93. (Ron Hardy), Susan Dey, Lorraine Toussaint, D.W. Moffett, Piper Laurie (2 hrs.).

LIES BEFORE KISSES
CBS 3/3/91. (Lou Antonio), Jaclyn Smith, Ben Gazzara, Nick Mancuso (2 hrs.).

LIES OF THE HEART:
THE STORY OF LAURIE KELLOGG
ABC 1/31/94. (Michael Uno), Jennie Garth, Gregory Harrison, Steven Keats (2 hrs.).

LIES OF THE TWINS
USA 8/21/91. (Tim Hunter), Aidan Quinn, Isabella Rossellini, Iman (2 hrs.).

LIFE IN THE THEATRE, A
TNT 10/9/93. (Gregory Mosher), Jack Lemmon, Matthew Broderick (70 mins.).

LIFEFORCE EXPERIMENT, THE
SCI 4/16/94. (Piers Haggard), Donald Sutherland, Corin Nemec, Mimi Kuzyk (2 hrs.).

LIFEPOD
FOX 6/28/93. (Ron Silver), Ron Silver, Robert Loggia, Jessica Tuck, C.C.H. Pounder (2 hrs.).

LIGHTNING FIELD
USA 9/11/91. (Michael Switzer), Nancy McKeon, Polly Bergen, Elpidia Carrillo, Miriam Colon (2 hrs.).

LILY IN WINTER
USA 12/8/94. (Delbert Mann), Natalie Cole, Brian Bonsall, Marla Gibbs, Dwier Brown, Cecil Hoffman, Monte Russell (2 hrs.).

LINDA
USA 10/8/93. (Nathaniel Gutman), Virginia Madsen, Richard Thomas, Ted McGinley (2 hrs.).

LINE OF FIRE: THE MORRIS DEES STORY
NBC 1/21/91. (John Korty), Corbin Bernsen, Jenny Lewis, Sandy Bull (2 hrs.).

LITTLE KIDNAPPERS, THE
DIS 8/17/90. (Donald Shebib), Charlton Heston, Bruce Greenwood, Leo Wheatley (95 mins.).

LITTLE LORD FAUNTLEROY
DIS 7/14/95. (Andrew Morgan), George Baker, Michael Benz, Betsy Brantly, John Castle, Bernice Stegers, Helen Lindsay (2 hrs.).

LITTLE PIECE OF HEAVEN, A
NBC 12/2/91. (Mimi Leder), Kirk Cameron, Cloris Leachman, Jenny Robertson, Chelsea Noble (2 hrs.).

LIVE! FROM DEATH ROW
FOX 4/3/92. (Patrick Duncan), Bruce Davison, Joanna Cassidy, Jason Tomlins, Calvin Levels (2 hrs.).

LIVING A LIE
NBC 9/16/91. (Larry Shaw), Jill Eikenberry, Peter Coyote, Roxanne Hart, Jarred Blanchard (2 hrs.).

LIZ: THE ELIZABETH TAYLOR STORY
NBC 5/21 & 22/95 (Kevin Conner), Sherilyn Fenn, Angus MacFadyen, William McNamara, Nigel Havers, Katherine Helmond (4 hrs.).

LOCKED UP: A MOTHER'S RAGE
CBS 10/29/91. (Bethany Rooney), Cheryl Ladd, Jean Smart, Angela Bassett, Joshua Harris.

LONG ROAD HOME
NBC 2/25/91. (John Korty), Mark Harmon, Lee Purcell, Morgan Weisser (2 hrs.).

LOOKALIKE, THE
USA 12/12/90. (Gary Nelson), Melissa Gilbert-Brinkman, Thaao Penghlis, Diane Ladd (2 hrs.).

LOST CAPONE, THE
TNT 9/10/90. (John Gray), Adrian Pasdar, Ally Sheedy, Eric Roberts (2 hrs.).

LOVE AND BETRAYAL: THE MIA FARROW STORY
FOX 2/28 & 3/2/95. (Karen Arthur), Patsy Kensit, Dennis Boutsikaris, Robert LuPone, Grace Una, Tovah Feldshuh (4 hrs.).

LOVE AND CURSES... AND ALL THAT JAZZ
CBS 9/21/91. (Gerald McRaney), Gerald McRaney, Delta Burke, Elizabeth Ashley, Harold Sylvester (2 hrs.).

LOVE AND HATE: A MARRIAGE MADE IN HELL
NBC 7/15 & 16/90. (Francis Mankiewicz), Kate Nelligan, Kenneth Welsh, Leon Pownall (4 hrs.).

LOVE AND LIES
ABC 3/18/90. (Roger Young), Mare Winningham, Peter Gallagher, Tom O'Brien (2 hrs.).

LOVE BOAT: A VALENTINE VOYAGE, THE
CBS 2/12/90. (Ron Satlof), Gavin McLeod, Tom Bosley, "Rowdy" Roddy Piper, Julia Duffy (2 hrs.).

LOVE CAN BE MURDER
NBC 12/14/92. (Jack Bender), Jaclyn Smith, Corbin Bernsen, Cliff DeYoung, Anne Francis (2 hrs.).

LOVE, CHEAT AND STEAL
SHO 12/5/93. (William Curran), John Lithgow, Eric Roberts, Madchen Amick, Richard Edson (95 mins.).

LOVE, HONOR & OBEY:
THE LAST MAFIA MARRIAGE
CBS 5/23 & 25/93. (John Patterson), Eric Roberts, Nancy McKeon, Ben Gazzara, Dylan Baker (4 hrs.).

LOVE KILLS
USA 11/13/91. (Brian Grant), Virginia Madsen, Lenny Van Dohlen, Jim Metzler, Erich Anderson (2 hrs.).

LOVE, LIES & MURDER
NBC 2/17 & 18/91. (Robert Markowitz), Clancy Brown, Sheryl Lee, Moira Kelly (4 hrs.).

LOVE MATTERS
SHO 10/3/93. (Eb Lottimer), Griffin Dunne, Tony Goldwyn, Annette O'Toole, Kate Burton (96 mins.).

LOVE SHE SOUGHT, THE
NBC 10/21/90. (Joseph Sargent), Angela Lansbury, Denholm Elliott, Cynthia Nixon (2 hrs.).

LUCKY DAY
ABC 3/11/91. (Donald Wrye), Amy Madigan, Olympia Dukakis, Chloe Webb (2 hrs.).

LUCY & DESI: BEFORE THE LAUGHTER
CBS 2/10/91. (Charles Jarrott), Frances Fisher, Maurice Bernard, Robin Pearson Rose (2 hrs.).

LUSH LIFE
SHO 5/20/94. (Michael Elias), Jeff Goldblum, Forest Whitaker, Kathy Baker (105 mins.).

M

MACGYVER: LOST TREASURE OF ATLANTIS
ABC 5/14/94. (Michael Vegar), Richard Dean Anderson, Brian Blessed, Sophie Ward (2 hrs.).

MACGYVER: TRAIL TO DOOMSDAY
ABC 11/24/94. (Charles Correll), Richard Dean Anderson, Beatie Edney, Peter Egan, Alan Armstrong, Bob Sherman (2 hrs.).

MACSHAYNE: THE FINAL ROLL OF THE DICE
NBC 4/29/94. (E.W. Swackhamer), Kenny Rogers, Maria Conchita Alonso, Wendy Phillips (2 hrs.).

MACSHAYNE: WINNER TAKES ALL
NBC 4/11/94. (E.W. Swackhamer), Kenny Rogers, Ann Jillian, John Karlen, Terry O'Quinn (2 hrs.).

MADONNA: INNOCENCE LOST
FOX 11/29/94. (Bradford May), Terumi Matthews, Wendie Malick, Jeff Yagher, Diana Leblanc, Dean Stockwell (2 hrs.).

MAID FOR EACH OTHER
NBC 1/13/92. (Paul Schneider), Nell Carter, Dinah Manoff, Joyce Van Patten, Garrett Morris (2 hrs.).

MAJORITY RULE
LIF 10/27/92. (Gwen Arner), Blair Brown, John Getz, Jensen Daggett, Donald Moffat (2 hrs.).

MAN FROM LEFT FIELD, THE
CBS 10/15/93. (Burt Reynolds), Burt Reynolds, Reba McEntire, Joe Theismann (2 hrs.).

MAN UPSTAIRS, THE
CBS 12/6/92. (George Schaefer), Katharine Hepburn, Ryan O'Neal, Helena Carroll (2 hrs.).

MAN WHO WOULDN'T DIE, THE
ABC 5/29/95. (Bill Condon), Roger Moore, Malcolm McDowell, Nancy Allen, Michael Puttonen, Wendy Van Riesen (2 hrs.).

MAN WITH 3 WIVES, THE
CBS 3/28/93. (Peter Levin), Beau Bridges, Pam Dawber, Joanna Kerns, Kathleen Lloyd (2 hrs.).

MANTIS
FOX 1/24/94. (Eric Laneuville), Carl Lumbly, Bobby Hosea, Gina Torres, Steve James (2 hrs.).

MARILYN AND BOBBY: HER FINAL AFFAIR
USA 8/4/93. (Bradford May), Melody Anderson, James F. Kelly, Thomas Wagner, Richard Dysart (2 hrs.).

MARILYN AND ME
ABC 9/22/91. (John Patterson), Susan Griffiths, Jesse Dabson, Joel Grey, Sal Landi (2 hrs.).

MARK TWAIN AND ME
DIS 11/22/91. (Daniel Petrie), Jason Robards, Amy Stewart, Talia Shire, Fiona Reid (2 hrs.).

MARKED FOR MURDER
NBC 1/17/93. (Mimi Leder), Powers Boothe, Billy Dee Williams, Laura Johnson, Michael Ironside (2 hrs.).

MARLA HANSON STORY, THE
NBC 2/4/91. (John Gray), Cheryl Pollak, Dale Midkiff, Kirk Baltz (2 hrs.).

MATLOCK: THE VACATION
ABC 11/5/92. (Christopher Hillber), Andy Griffith, Brynn Thayer, Warren Frost (2 hrs.).

MATTER OF JUSTICE, A
NBC 11/7 & 8/93. (Michael Switzer), Patty Duke, Martin Sheen, Alexandra Powers, Jason London (2 hrs.).

MATTERS OF THE HEART
USA 12/26/90. (Michael Rhodes), Jane Seymour, Chris Gartin, James Stacy (2 hrs.).

MAX AND HELEN
TNT 1/8/90. (Philip Saville), Treat Williams, Alice Krige, Martin Landau (2 hrs.).

MEMORIES OF MURDER
LIF 7/31/90. (Robert Lewis), Nancy Allen, Robin Thomas, Vanity (2 hrs.).

MEMPHIS
TNT 1/27/92. (Yves Simoneau), Cybill Shepherd, John Laughlin, J.E. Freeman, Moses Gunn (2 hrs.).

MEN DON'T TELL
CBS 3/14/93. (Harry Winer), Peter Strauss, Judith Light, Ashley Johnson, Michael Rand (2 hrs.).

MENENDEZ: A KILLING IN BEVERLY HILLS
CBS 5/22 & 24/94. (Larry Elikann), Edward James Olmos, Beverly D'Angelo, Damian Chapa (4 hrs.).

**MENU FOR MURDER
(FORMERLY "MURDER AT THE PTA LUNCHEON")**
CBS 12/90. (Larry Peerce), Julia Duffy, Morgan Fairchild, Marla Gibbs (2 hrs.).

MERCY MISSION: THE RESCUE OF FLIGHT 771
NBC 12/13/93. (Roger Young), Scott Bakula, Robert Loggia, Alan Fletcher (2 hrs.).

MESSAGE FROM HOLLY, A
CBS 12/13/92. (Rod Holcomb), Lindsay Wagner, Shelley Long, Cotter Smith, MacDonald Carey (2 hrs.).

MIDNIGHT'S CHILD
LIF 4/21/92. (Colin Bucksey), Marcy Walker, Cotter Smith, Olivia D'Abo, Elissabeth Moss.

MILES FROM NOWHERE
CBS 1/7/92. (Buzz Kulik), Rick Schroder, James Farentino, Shawn Phelan, Melora Hardin (2 hrs.).

MILLION DOLLAR BABIES
CBS 11/20 & 22/94. (Christian Duguay), Beau Bridges, Kate Nelligan, Roy Dupuis, Celine Bonnier, Samantha Gilliland (4 hrs.).

MIRACLE CHILD
NBC 4/6/93. (Michael Pressman), Crystal Bernard, Cloris Leachman, John Terry (2 hrs.).

MIRACLE IN THE WILDERNESS
TNT 12/9/91. (Kevin James Dobson), Kris Kristofferson, Kim Cattrall, John Dennis Johnston (2 hrs.).

MIRACLE LANDING
CBS 2/11/90. (Dick Lowry), Connie Sellecca, Wayne Rogers, Nancy Kwan (2 hrs.).

MIRACLE ON I-880
NBC 2/22/93. (Robert Iscove), Ruben Blades, David Morse, Len Cariou, Sandy Duncan (2 hrs.).

MISS AMERICA: BEHIND THE CROWN
NBC 9/21/92. (Richard Michaels), Carolyn Sapp, Ray Bumatai, Jack Blessing, Gedde Watanabe (2 hrs.).

MISS ROSE WHITE
NBC 4/26/92. (Joseph Sargent), Kyra Sedgwick, Maximilian Schell, Amanda Plummer, D.B. Sweeney (2 hrs.).

MISSION OF THE SHARK
CBS 9/29/91. (Robert Iscove), Stacy Keach, Richard Thomas, Don Harvey, David Caruso (2 hrs.).

MODEL BY DAY
FOX 3/21/94. (Christian Duguay), Famke Janssen, Stephen Shellen, Clark Johnson, Shannon Tweed (2 hrs.).

MOM FOR CHRISTMAS, A
NBC 12/17/90. (George Miller), Olivia Newton-John, Juliet Sorcey, Doug Sheehan (2 hrs.).

MOMENT OF TRUTH: A CHILD TOO MANY
NBC 10/11/93. (Jorge Montesai), Michelle Green, Conor O'Farrell, Nancy Stafford (2 hrs.).

MOMENT OF TRUTH: A MOTHER'S DECEPTION
NBC 10/17/94. (Chuck Bowman), Joan Van Ark, Stephen Macht, Daniel Hugh Kelly, Tom Kurlander, Brooke Langton (2 hrs.).

MOMENT OF TRUTH: BROKEN PLEDGES
NBC 4/11/94. (Jorge Montesai), Linda Gray, Leon Russom, David Lipper, Jane Galloway (2 hrs.).

MOMENT OF TRUTH: CAUGHT IN THE CROSSFIRE
NBC 9/14/94. (Chuck Bowman), Dennis Franz, Alley Mills, Daniel Roebuck, Anna Gunn, Ray McKinnon (2 hrs.).

**MOMENT OF TRUTH:
CRADLE OF CONSPIRACY**
NBC 5/2/94. (Gabrielle Beaumont), Dee Wallace Stone, Danica McKellar, Kurt Deutsch (2 hrs.).

**MOMENT OF TRUTH:
MURDER OR MEMORY?**
NBC 12/12/94. (Christopher Leitch), Leigh Taylor-Young, Karl David-Djerf, Michael Brandon, Louis Giambalvo (2 hrs.).

MOMENT OF TRUTH: STALKING BACK
NBC 10/18/93. (Corey Allen), Luanne Ponce, Shanna Reed, John Martin (2 hrs.).

MOMENT OF TRUTH: TO WALK AGAIN
NBC 2/16/94. (Randall Zisk), Blair Brown, Ken Howard, Cameron Bancroft (2 hrs.).

MOMENT OF TRUTH: WHY MY DAUGHTER?
NBC 4/28/93. (Chuck Bowman), Linda Gray, Jaimie Luner, Antonio Sabato Jr. (2 hrs.).

MONTANA
TNT 2/19/90. (William A. Graham), Gena Rowlands, Richard Crenna, Lea Thompson, Scott Coffey (2 hrs.).

MORTAL SINS
USA 11/4/92. (Bradford May), Christopher Reeve, Roxanne Biggs, Francis Guinan (2 hrs.).

MOTHER OF THE BRIDE
CBS 2/27/93. (Charles Correll), Rue McClanahan, Kristy McNichol, Paul Dooley, Ted Shackelford (2 hrs.).

MOTHER'S GIFT, A
CBS 4/16/95. (Jerry London), Nancy McKeon, Adrian Pasdar, Adam Storke, Dan Brook, Helen Cates, Gail Cronauer (2 hrs.).

MOTHER'S JUSTICE, A
NBC 11/25/91. (Noel Nosseck), Meredith Baxter, G.W. Bailey, Carrie Hamilton, Blu Mankuma (2 hrs.).

MOTHER'S PRAYER, A
USA 8/2/95. (Larry Elikann), Linda Hamilton, Noah Fleiss, Bruce Dern, Kate Nelligan, RuPaul, S. Epatha Merkerson (2 hrs.).

MOTHER'S REVENGE, A
ABC 11/14/93. (Armand Mastroianni), Lesley Ann Warren, Bruce Davison, Missy Crider (2 hrs.).

MOTHER'S RIGHT: THE ELIZABETH MORGAN STORY, A
ABC 11/29/93. (Linda Otto), Bonnie Bedelia, Terence Knox, Kenneth Welsh, Pam Grier (2 hrs.).

MOTORCYCLE GANG
SHO 8/5/94. (John Milius), Gerald McRaney, Elan Oberon, Carla Gugino (2 hrs.).

MRS. 'ARRIS GOES TO PARIS
CBS 12/27/92. (Allan King), Angela Lansbury, Diana Rigg, Omar Sharif, Lothaire Bluteau (2 hrs.).

MRS. LAMBERT REMEMBERS LOVE
CBS 5/12/91. (Charles Matthau), Ellen Burstyn, Walter Matthau, Ryan Todd (2 hrs.).

MURDER BETWEEN FRIENDS
NBC 1/10/94. (Waris Hussein), Timothy Busfield, Stephen Lang, Martin Kemp, Lisa Blount (2 hrs.).

MURDER C.O.D.
NBC 9/21/90. (Alan Metzger), Patrick Duffy, Chelsea Field, William Devane (2 hrs.).

MURDER IN BLACK AND WHITE
CBS 1/7/90. (Robert Iscove), Richard Crenna, Diahann Carroll, Cliff Gorman, Fred Gwynne (2 hrs.).

MURDER IN HIGH PLACES
NBC 6/2/91. (John Byrum), Ted Levine, Adam Baldwin, Judith Hoag (2 hrs.).

MURDER IN MISSISSIPPI
NBC 2/5/90. (Roger Young), Tom Hulce, Jennifer Gray, Blair Underwood, Josh Charles (2 hrs.).

MURDER IN NEW HAMPSHIRE: THE PAMELA SMART STORY
CBS 9/24/91. (Joyce Chopra), Helen Hunt, Chad Allen, Ken Howard, Michael Learned (2 hrs.).

MURDER IN PARADISE
NBC 1/19/90. (Fred Walton), Kevin Kilner, Maggie Han, Mako (2 hrs.).

MURDER IN THE HEARTLAND
ABC 5/3 & 4/93. (Robert Markowitz), Tim Roth, Fairuza Balk, Kate Reid, Milo O'Shea (4 hrs.).

MURDER OF INNOCENCE
CBS 11/30/93. (Tom McLaughlin), Valerie Bertinelli, Stephen Caffrey, Graham Beckel (2 hrs.).

MURDER 101
USA 3/20/91. (Bill Condon), Pierce Brosnan, Dey Young, Raphael Sbarge (2 hrs.).

MURDER TIMES SEVEN
CBS 10/14/90. (Jud Taylor), Richard Crenna, Susan Blakely, Cliff Gorman (2 hrs.).

MURDER WITHOUT MOTIVE: THE EDMUND PERRY STORY
NBC 1/6/92. (Kevin Hooks), Curtis McClarin, Anna Maria Horsford, Carla Gugino, Guy Killum (2 hrs.).

MURDEROUS AFFAIR: THE CAROLYN WARMUS STORY
ABC 9/13/92. (Martin Davidson), Virginia Madsen, Chris Sarandon, Ned Eisenberg (2 hrs.).

MURDEROUS VISION
USA 2/20/91. (Gary Sherman), Bruce Boxleitner, Laura Johnson, Joseph d'Angerio (2 hrs.).

MY ANTONIA
USA 3/29/95. (Joseph Sargent), Jason Robards, Eva Marie Saint, Neil Patrick Harris, Elina Lowensohn, Jan Triska (2 hrs.)

MY BREAST
CBS 5/15/94. (Betty Thomas), Meredith Baxter, Jamey Sheridan, James Sutorius (2 hrs.).

MY BROTHER'S KEEPER
CBS 3/19/95. (Glenn Jordan), John Lithgow, Ellen Burstyn, Annette O'Toole, Veronica Cartwright, Richard Masur (2 hrs.).

MY NAME IS KATE
ABC 1/24/94. (Rod Hardy), Donna Mills, Daniel J. Travanti, Nia Peeples, Eileen Brennan (2 hrs.).

MY SON JOHNNY
CBS 11/10/91. (Peter Levin), Michele Lee, Rick Schroder, Corin Nemec, Rip Torn (2 hrs.).

N

NYPD MOUNTED
CBS 8/3/91. (Mark Tinker), Dennis Franz, Dan Gautier, Cliff De Young (2 hrs.).

NAILS
SHO 7/25/92. (John Flynn), Dennis Hopper, Anne Archer, Tomas Milian, Cliff De Young (97 mins.).

NAOMI & WYNONA: LOVE CAN BUILD A BRIDGE
NBC 5/14 & 15/95. (Bobby Roth), Kathleen York, Viveka Davis, Megan Ward, Cari Shayne, Melinda Dillon (4 hrs.).

NED BLESSING: THE TRUE STORY OF MY LIFE
CBS 4/14/92. (Peter Werner), Daniel Baldwin, Chris Cooper, Luis Avalos, Rene Auberjonois (2 hrs.).

NEIL SIMON'S "BROADWAY BOUND"
ABC 3/23/92. (Paul Bogart), Anne Bancroft, Corey Parker, Jonathan Silverman, Hume Cronyn (2 hrs.).

NEVER FORGET
TNT 4/8/91. (Joseph Sargent), Leonard Nimoy, Dabney Coleman, Blythe Danner (2 hrs.).

NEXT DOOR
SHO 9/4/94. (Tony Bill), James Woods, Randy Quaid, Kate Capshaw, Lucinda Jenney, Miles Feulner (95 mins.).

NIGHT OF THE FOX
SYND 11/26 & 27/90. (Charles Jarrott), George Peppard, Deborah Raffin, Michael York (4 hrs.).

NIGHT OF THE HUNTER
ABC 5/5/91. (David Greene), Richard Chamberlain, Diana Scarwid, Reid Binion (2 hrs.).

NIGHT OWL
LIF 8/19/93. (Matthew Patrick), Jennifer Beals, James Wilder, Allison Hossack (2 hrs.).

NIGHT VISIONS
NBC 11/30/90. (Wes Craven), Loryn Locklin, James Remar, Penny Johnson (2 hrs.).

NIGHTMAN, THE
NBC 3/6/92. (Charles Haid), Jenny Robertson, Joanna Kerns, Ted Marcoux, Latanya Richardson (2 hrs.).

NIGHTMARE IN COLUMBIA COUNTY
CBS 12/10/91. (Roger Young), William Devane, Jeri Lynn Ryan, Michele Abrams, Nick Searcy (2 hrs.).

NIGHTMARE IN THE DAYLIGHT
CBS 11/22/92. (Lou Antonio), Jaclyn Smith, Christopher Reeve, Tom Mason, Eric Bell (2 hrs.).

NIGHTMARE ON THE 13TH FLOOR
USA 10/31/90. (Walter Grauman), Michele Greene, James Brolin, Louise Fletcher (2 hrs.).

NO CHILD OF MINE
CBS 10/31/93. (Michael Katleman), Patty Duke, Tracy Nelson, Susan Blakely (2 hrs.).

NOBODY'S CHILDREN
USA 3/3/94. (David Wheatley), Ann-Margret, Dominique Sanda, Jay O. Sanders (2 hrs.).

NOT A PENNY MORE, NOT A PENNY LESS
USA 4/24 & 25/90. (Clive Donner), Edward Asner, Ed Begley, Jr., Jenny Agutter (4 hrs.).

NOT IN MY FAMILY
ABC 2/28/93. (Linda Otto), Joanna Kerns, Michael Brandon, Shelley Hack, Tony Roberts (2 hrs.).

NOT LIKE US
SHO 8/15/95. (David Payne), Morgan Englund, Rainer Grant, Joanna Pacula, Peter Onorati (90 mins.).

NOT OF THIS WORLD
CBS 2/12/91. (Jon Daniel Hess), Lisa Hartman, A. Martinez, Pat Hingle, Luke Edwards (2 hrs.).

NOT OUR SON
CBS 1/31/95. (Michael Rhodes), Neil Patrick Harris, Gerald McRaney, Tom Verica, Cindy Pickett, Ari Myers (2 hrs.).

NOTHING BUT THE TRUTH
CBS 5/23/95. (Michael Switzer), Patricia Wettig, Ken Olin, Bradley Whitford, Harry Lennix, Katherine LaNasa, Kurt Deutsch (2 hrs.).

NOTORIOUS
LIF 1/28/92. (Colin Bucksey), John Shea, Jenny Robertson, Jean-Pierre Cassel, Marisa Berenson (2 hrs.).

NOWHERE TO HIDE
ABC 10/9/94. (Bobby Roth), Rosanna Arquette, Scott Bakula, Max Pomeranc, Clifton Powell, Robert Wisden, Jenny Gago (2 hrs.).

NURSES ON THE LINE: THE CRASH OF FLIGHT 7
CBS 11/22/93. (Larry Shaw), Lindsay Wagner, Robert Loggia, David Clennon (2 hrs.).

O

O PIONEERS!
CBS 2/2/92. (Glenn Jordan), Jessica Lange, David Strathairn, Tom Aldredge, Reed Diamond (2 hrs.).

OBSESSED
ABC 9/27/92. (Jonathan Sanger), Shannen Doherty, William Devane, Clare Carey (2 hrs.).

ODD COUPLE: TOGETHER AGAIN, THE
CBS 9/24/93. (Robert Klane), Tony Randall, Jack Klugman, Barbara Barrie (2 hrs.).

O.J. SIMPSON STORY, THE
FOX 1/31/95. (Alan Smithee), Bobby Hosea, Jessica Tuck, David Roberson, James Handy, Bruce Weitz (2 hrs.).

OLD CURIOSITY SHOP, THE
DIS 3/19/95. (Kevin Connor), Peter Ustinov, James Fox, Tom Courtenay, Julia McKenzie, Sally Walsh, Adam Blackwood (4 hrs.).

OLD MAN AND THE SEA, THE
NBC 3/25/90. (Jud Taylor), Anthony Quinn, Gary Cole, Patricia Clarkson (2 hrs.).

OLDEST LIVING CONFEDERATE WIDOW TELLS ALL
CBS 5/1 & 3/94. (Ken Cameron), Diane Lane, Donald Sutherland, Cicely Tyson, Anne Bancroft, Blythe Danner (4 hrs.).

OMEN IV: THE AWAKENING
FOX 5/20/91. (Jorge Montesi, Dominique Othenin), Faye Grant, Michael Woods, Michael Lerner (2 hrs.).

ON PROMISED LAND
DIS 4/17/94. (Joan Tewksbury), Carl Lumbly, Joan Plowright, Norman D. Golden II, Judith Ivey (2 hrs.).

ON THIN ICE: THE TAI BABILONIA STORY
NBC 11/5/90. (Zale Dalen), Rachel Crawford, Charlie Stratton, Denise Nicholas (2 hrs.).

ONE AGAINST THE WIND
CBS 12/1/91. (Larry Elikann), Judy Davis, Sam Neill, Denholm Elliott, Christien Anholt (2 hrs.).

ONE CHRISTMAS
NBC 12/19/94. (Tony Bill), Katharine Hepburn, Henry Winkler, Swoosie Kurtz, T.J. Lowther, Tonea Stewart (2 hrs.).

ONE MAN'S WAR
HBO 4/20/91. (Sergio Toledo), Anthony Hopkins, Norma Aleandro, Fernanda Torres (90 mins.).

ONE MORE MOUNTAIN
ABC 3/6/94. (Dick Lowry), Meredith Baxter, Chris Cooper, Larry Drake (2 hrs.).

ONE OF HER OWN
ABC 5/16/94. (Armand Mastroianni), Lori Loughlin, Martin Sheen, Greg Evigan (2 hrs.).

ONE SPECIAL VICTORY
NBC 12/8/91. (Stuart Cooper), John Larroquette, Kathy Baker, Christine Estabrook, Dirk Blocker (2 hrs.).

ONE WOMAN'S COURAGE
NBC 2/28/94. (Charles Robert Carner), Patty Duke, James Farentino, Keith Szarabajka, Dennis Farina (2 hrs.).

ONLY ONE SURVIVED
CBS 10/27/90. (Folco Quilici), Perry King, Michael Beck, Fabio Testi (2 hrs.).

ONLY WAY OUT, THE
ABC 12/19/93. (Ron Hardy), John Ritter, Henry Winkler, Stephanie Faracy, Julianne Phillips (2 hrs.).

OPERATION, THE
CBS 1/21/90. (Thomas J. Wright), Joe Penny, Lisa Hartman, Jason Beghe, Kathleen Quinlan (2 hrs.).

OPPOSITES ATTRACT
NBC 10/17/90. (Noel Nosseck), Barbara Eden, John Forsythe, Ilene Graff, Conchata Ferrell (2 hrs.).

ORANGES ARE NOT THE ONLY FRUIT
A&E 11/29/90. (Beeban Kidron), Geraldine McEwan, Kenneth Cranham, Charlotte Coleman (2 hrs.).

ORDEAL IN THE ARCTIC
ABC 2/15/93. (Mark Sobel), Richard Chamberlain, Melanie Mayron, Catherine Mary Stewart (2 hrs.).

ORIGINAL SINS
CBS 4/12/95. (Jan Egelson), Mark Harmon, Julianne Phillips, Sarah Trigger, David Clennon, Ron Perlman, Gus Johnson (2 hrs.).

ORPHEUS DESCENDING
TNT 9/24/90. (Sir Peter Hall), Vanessa Redgrave, Kevin Anderson, Anne Twomey (2-1/2 hrs.).

OTHER MOTHER, THE
NBC 4/17/95. (Bethany Rooney), Frances Fisher, Deborah May, Corrie Clark, Cameron Bancroft, Gwynth Walsh (2 hrs.).

OTHER WOMAN, THE
CBS 3/26/95. (Gabrielle Beaumont), Jill Eikenberry, Laura Leighton, Rosemary Forsyth, Monica Parker (2 hrs.).

OTHER WOMEN'S CHILDREN
LIF 10/24/93. (Anne Wheeler), Melanie Mayron, Geraint Wyn Davies, Eric Pospisil (2 hrs.).

OUR SONS
ABC 5/19/91. (John Erman), Julie Andrews, Ann-Margret, Zeljko Ivanek, Hugh Grant (2 hrs.).

OUT OF ANNIE'S PAST
USA 3/12/95. (Stuart Cooper), Catherine Mary Stewart, Scott Valentine, Dennis Farina, Carsten Norgaard, Ray Oriel (2 hrs.).

OUT OF DARKNESS
ABC 1/16/94. (Larry Elikann), Diana Ross, Ann Weldon, Rhonda Stubbins White (2 hrs.).

OVEREXPOSED
ABC 10/11/92. (Robert Markowitz), Marcy Walker, Dan Lauria, Terence Knox (2 hrs.).

OVERKILL: THE AILEEN WUORNOS STORY
CBS 11/17/92. (Peter Levin), Jean Smart, Park Overall, Ernie Lively, Brion James (2 hrs.).

P

PAIR OF ACES
1/14/90. (Aaron Lipstadt), Willie Nelson, Kris Kristofferson, Helen Shaver, Rip Torn (2 hrs.).

PARALLEL LIVES
SHO 8/14/94. (Linda Yellen), James Belushi, Jill Eikenberry, Liza Minnelli, Ben Gazzara, JoBeth Williams (105 mins.)

PARIS TROUT
SHO 4/20/91. (Stephen Gyllenhaal), Dennis Hopper, Barbara Hershey, Ed Harris (100 mins.).

PARKER KANE
NBC 8/5/90. (Steve Perry), Jeff Fahey, Marisa Tomei, Drew Snyder, Amanda Pays (2 hrs.).

PART OF THE FAMILY, A
LIF 7/6/94. (David Madden), Robert Carradine, Elizabeth Arlen, Ronny Cox (2 hrs.).

PARTNERS IN LOVE
FAM 11/27/92. (Eugene Levy), Eugene Levy, Linda Kash, John James (2 hrs.).

**PASSION FOR JUSTICE, A:
THE HAZEL BRANNON SMITH STORY**
ABC 4/17/94. (James Keach), Jane Seymour, D.W. Moffett, Richard Kiley, Lou Walker (2 hrs.).

PASSPORT TO MURDER
NBC 3/7/93. (David Hemmings), Connie Sellecca, Ed Marinaro, Pavel Douglas (2 hrs.).

PAST TENSE
SHO 6/12/94. (Graeme Clifford), Scott Glenn, Anthony LaPaglia, Lara Flynn Boyle (2 hrs.).

PAST THE BLEACHERS
ABC 6/22/95. (Michael Switzer), Richard Dean Anderson, Barnard Hughes, Glynnis O'Connor, Ken Jenkins, Grayson Fricke (2 hrs.).

PAYOFF
SHO 6/22/91. (Stuart Cooper), Keith Carradine, Harry Dean Stanton, Kim Greist (2 hrs.).

PERCY & THUNDER
TNT 9/7/93. (Ivan Dixon), James Earl Jones, Courtney B. Vance, Gloria Reuben, Gloria Foster (2 hrs.).

PERFECT BRIDE, THE
USA 6/26/91. (Terrence O'Hara), Sammi Davis, Kelly Preston, Linden Ashby (2 hrs.).

PERFECT FAMILY
USA 11/11/92. (E.W. Swackhamer), Bruce Boxleitner, Jennifer O'Neill, Joanna Cassidy (2 hrs.).

PERFECT HARMONY
DIS 3/31/91. (Will MacKenzie), Peter Scolari, Darren McGavin, Catherine Mary Stewart (2 hrs.).

PERFECT TRIBUTE, THE
ABC 4/21/91. (Jack Bender), Jason Robards, Lukas Haas, Campbell Scott, Katherine Helmond (2 hrs.).

PERRY MASON: THE CASE OF THE DEFIANT DAUGHTER
NBC 9/30/90. (Christian I. Nyby II), Raymond Burr, Robert Culp, Robert Vaughn, Jere Burns (2 hrs.).

PERRY MASON:
THE CASE OF THE DESPERATE DECEPTION
NBC 3/11/90. (Christian I. Nyby II), Raymond Burr, Ian Bannen, Yvette Mimieux, Teresa Wright (2 hrs.).

PERRY MASON: THE CASE OF THE FATAL FASHION
NBC 9/24/91. (Christian I. Nyby II), Raymond Burr, Valerie Harper, Diana Muldaur, Scott Baio (2 hrs.).

PERRY MASON: THE CASE OF THE FATAL FRAMING
NBC 3/1/92. (Christian I. Nyby II), Raymond Burr, Barbara Hale, David Soul, John Rhys-Davies (2 hrs.).

PERRY MASON: THE CASE OF THE GLASS COFFIN
NBC 5/14/91. (Christian I. Nyby II), Raymond Burr, William R. Moses, Peter Scolari (2 hrs.).

PERRY MASON:
THE CASE OF THE HEARTBROKEN BRIDE
NBC 10/30/92. (Christian I. Nyby II), Raymond Burr, Ronny Cox, Linda Blair, Paul Dooley (2 hrs.).

PERRY MASON: THE CASE OF THE KILLER KISS
NBC 11/29/93. (Christian I. Nyby II), Raymond Burr, Barbara Hale, William R. Moses, Stuart Damon (2 hrs.).

PERRY MASON:
THE CASE OF THE MALIGNED MOBSTER
NBC 2/11/91. (Ron Satlof), Raymond Burr, Barbara Hale, Paul Anka, Howard McGillin (2 hrs.).

PERRY MASON: THE CASE OF THE MURDERED MADAM
NBC 10/4/87. (Ron Satlof), Raymond Burr, Daphne Ashbrook, Anthony Geary, Ann Jillian (2 hrs.).

PERRY MASON: THE CASE OF THE POISONED PEN
NBC 1/21/90. (Christian I. Nyby II), Raymond Burr, David Warner, William R. Moses, Cindy Williams (2 hrs.).

PERRY MASON: THE CASE OF THE RECKLESS ROMEO
NBC 5/5/92. (Christian I. Nyby II), Raymond Burr, Tracy Nelson, Geraldo Rivera, William R. Moses (2 hrs.).

PERRY MASON:
THE CASE OF THE RUTHLESS REPORTER
NBC 1/6/91. (Christian I. Nyby II), Raymond Burr, John James, Jerry Orbach, Mary Page Keller (2 hrs.).

PERRY MASON: THE CASE OF THE SILENCED SINGER
NBC 5/20/90. (Ron Satlof), Raymond Burr, Tim Reid, Vanessa Williams, Nia Peeples (2 hrs.).

PERRY MASON:
THE CASE OF THE SKIN-DEEP SCANDAL
NBC 2/19/93. (Christian I. Nyby II), Raymond Burr, Morgan Fairchild, Polly Bergen, David Warner (2 hrs.).

PERRY MASON MYSTERY, A:
THE CASE OF THE GRIMACING GOVERNOR
NBC 11/9/94. (Max Tash), Hal Holbrook, Barbara Hale, William R. Moses, Deborah Raffin, James Brolin (2 hrs.).

PERRY MASON MYSTERY, A:
THE CASE OF THE JEALOUS JOKESTER
NBC 4/10/95. (Vince McEveety), Hal Holbrook, Dyan Cannon, Tony Roberts, Victoria Jackson, David Rasche, Tina Yothers (2 hrs.).

PERRY MASON MYSTERY, A:
THE CASE OF THE LETHAL LIFESTYLE
NBC 5/10/94. (Helaine Head), Hal Holbrook, Barbara Hale, William R. Moses, Dixie Carter (2 hrs.).

PERRY MASON MYSTERY, A:
THE CASE OF THE WICKED WIVES
NBC 12/17/93. (Christian I. Nyby II), Paul Sorvino, Barbara Hale, Maud Adams, Eric Braeden (2 hrs.).

PERSONALS
USA 2/28/90. (Steven H. Stern), Stephanie Zimbalist, Jennifer O'Neill, Robin Thomas (2 hrs.).

PHANTOM OF THE OPERA, THE
NBC 3/18 & 19/90. (Tony Richardson), Burt Lancaster, Charles Dance, Teri Polo, Adam Storke (4 hrs.).

PIANO LESSON, THE
CBS 2/5/95. (Lloyd Richards), Charles Dutton, Alfre Woodard, Carl Gordon, Courtney B. Vance, Lou Myers, Tommy Hollis (2 hrs.).

PINK LIGHTNING
FOX 7/8/91. (Carol Monpere), Sarah Buxton, Martha Byrne, Jennifer Blanc (2 hrs.).

PLACE FOR ANNIE, A
ABC 5/1/94. (John Gray), Sissy Spacek, Mary-Louise Parker, S. Epatha Merkerson, Jack Noseworthy (2 hrs.).

PLACE TO BE LOVED, A
CBS 4/4/93. (Sandy Smolan), Tom Guiry, Richard Crenna, Rhea Perlman, Linda Kelsey (2 hrs.).

PLOT TO KILL HITLER, THE
CBS 1/30/90. (Lawrence Schiller), Brad Davis, Madolyn Smith, Ian Richardson (2 hrs.).

PLYMOUTH
ABC 5/26/91. (Lee David Zlotoff), Cindy Pickett, Dale Midkiff, Richard Hamilton (2 hrs.).

POISONED BY LOVE: THE KERN COUNTY MURDERS
CBS 2/2/93. (Larry Peerce), Harry Hamlin, Helen Shaver, K.T. Oslin, Ed Lauter (2 hrs.).

POLLY-COMIN' HOME
NBC 11/18/90. (Debbie Allen), Keshia Knight Pulliam, Phylicia Rashad, Anthony Newley (2 hrs.).

PORTRAIT, THE
TNT 2/13/93. (Arthur Penn), Gregory Peck, Lauren Bacall, Cecilia Peck, Paul McCrane (2 hrs.).

POSING: INSPIRED BY THREE REAL STORIES
CBS 11/5/91. (Stephen Stafford), Lynda Carter, Michele Greene, Amanda Peterson, Josie Bissett (2 hrs.).

POSITIVELY TRUE ADVENTURES OF THE ALLEGED TEXAS CHEERLEADER-MURDERING MOM, THE
HBO 4/10/93. (Michael Ritchie), Holly Hunter, Beau Bridges, Swoosie Kurtz, Matt Frewer (2 hrs.).

POSSESSION OF MICHAEL D., THE
FOX 5/2/95. (Michael Kennedy), Stephen Lang, Sheila McCarthy, Michael Riley, Roger Rees, Phylicia Rashad (2 hrs.).

PRAYING MANTIS
USA 8/11/93. (James Keach), Jane Seymour, Barry Bostwick, Frances Fisher (2 hrs.).

PRECIOUS VICTIMS
CBS 9/28/93. (Peter Levin), Park Overall, Robby Benson, Richard Thomas, Frederic Forrest (2 hrs.).

PRESIDENT'S CHILD, THE
CBS 10/27/92. (Sam Pillsbury), Donna Mills, William Devane, James Read (2 hrs.).

PREY OF THE CHAMELEON
SHO 2/7/92. (Fleming B. Fuller), Daphne Zuniga, James Wilder, Alexandra Paul, Don Harvey (90 mins.).

PRICE SHE PAID, THE
CBS 3/31/92. (Fred Walton), Loni Anderson, Anthony John Denison, Stephen Meadows, Candy Clark (2 hrs.).

PRIDE AND EXTREME PREJUDICE
USA 1/17/90. (Ian Sharp), Brian Dennehy, Alan Howard, Lisa Eichhorn (2 hrs.).

PRISON STORIES: WOMEN ON THE INSIDE
HBO 10/15/91. (Penelope Spheeris, Donna Deitch, Joan Micklin Silver), Rae Dawn Chong, Annabella Sciorra, Lolita Davidovich (2 hrs.).

PRISONER OF HONOR
HBO 11/2/91. (Ken Russell), Richard Dreyfuss, Oliver Reed, Peter Firth, Jeremy Kemp (2 hrs.).

PRIVATE MATTER, A
HBO 6/20/92. (Joan Micklin Silver), Sissy Spacek, Aidan Quinn, Estelle Parsons, Sheila McCarthy (90 mins.).

PROBABLE CAUSE
SHO 11/20/94. (Paul Ziller), Michael Ironside, Kate Vernon, James Downing, David Sivertsen, David McNally (95 mins.).

PROBLEM CHILD 3: JUNIOR IN LOVE
NBC 5/13/95. (Greg Beeman), William Katt, Jack Warden, Justin Chapman, Jennifer Ogletree, Gilbert Gottfried (2 hrs.).

PROMISE KEPT, A: THE OKSANA BAIUL STORY
CBS 11/13/94. (Charles Jarrott), Miguel Ferrer, Monica Keena, Sonja Lanzener, Oksana Baiul, Susanna Thompson (2 hrs.).

PROMISE TO KEEP, A
NBC 10/1/90. (Rod Holcomb), Dana Delany, William Russ, Adam Arkin, Frances Fisher (2 hrs.).

PROPHET OF EVIL: THE ERVIL LEBARON STORY
CBS 5/4/93. (Jud Taylor), Brian Dennehy, William Devane, Tracey Needham, Danny Cooksey (2 hrs.).

PSYCHIC
USA 5/20/92. (George Mihalka), Zach Galligan, Catherine Mary Stewart, Michael Nouri, Albert Schultz (2 hrs.).

PSYCHO IV: THE BEGINNING
SHO 11/10/90. (Mick Garris), Anthony Perkins, Henry Thomas, Olivia Hussey (96 mins.).

Q

QUEEN
CBS 2/14, 16 & 18/93. (John Erman), Ann-Margret, Jasmine Guy, Danny Glover, Madge Sinclair, Martin Sheen (6 hrs.).

QUICKSAND: NO ESCAPE
USA 3/4/92. (Michael Pressman), Donald Sutherland, Tim Matheson, Jay Acovone, Timothy Carhart (2 hrs.).

QUIET KILLER
CBS 3/24/92. (Sheldon Larry), Kate Jackson, Howard Hesseman, Jeffrey Nordling, Chip Zien (2 hrs.).

QUIET LITTLE NEIGHBORHOOD, A PERFECT LITTLE MURDER, A
NBC 10/14/90. (Anson Williams), Teri Garr, Robert Urich, Susan Ruttan, Tom Poston (2 hrs.).

R

RACE TO FREEDOM: THE UNDERGROUND RAILROAD
FAM 2/19/94. (Don McBrearty), Janet Bailey, Courtney Vance, Dawn Lewis, Tim Reid (2 hrs.).

RADIO INSIDE
SHO 10/21/94. (Jeffrey Bell), Elisabeth Shue, William McNamara, Dylan Walsh (2 hrs.).

RAILWAY STATION MAN, THE
TNT 10/18/92. (Michael Whyte), Donald Sutherland, Julie Christie, John Lynch (2 hrs.).

RAINBOW DRIVE
SHO 9/8/90. (Bobby Roth), Peter Weller, Sela Ward, Henry Sanders, David Caruso (2 hrs.).

RANGER, THE COOK AND A HOLE IN THE SKY, THE
ABC 6/15/95. (John Kent Harrison), Sam Elliott, Jerry O'Connell, Ricky Jay (2 hrs.).

RAPE OF DR. WILLIS, THE
CBS 11/3/91. (Lou Antonio), Jaclyn Smith, Robin Thomas, Lisa Jakub, Holland Taylor (2 hrs.).

RAY ALEXANDER: A MENU FOR MURDER
NBC 3/20/95. (Gary Nelson), Louis Gossett Jr., James Coburn, Tracy Nelson, Tony Colitti, Ossie Davis, Beverly Johnson (2 hrs.).

RAY ALEXANDER: A TASTE FOR JUSTICE
NBC 5/13/94. (Gary Nelson), Louis Gossett Jr., James Coburn, Ossie Davis, Tracy Nelson, Ray Charles (2 hrs.).

REASON FOR LIVING: THE JILL IRELAND STORY
NBC 5/20/91. (Michael Rhodes), Jill Clayburgh, Lance Henriksen, Elizabeth Ashley (2 hrs.).

RED SHOE DIARIES
SHO 5/16/92. (Zalman King), David Duchovny, Brigitte Bako, Billy Wirth, Brenda Vaccaro (90 mins.).

RED WIND
USA 5/15/91. (Alan Metzger), Lisa Hartman, Philip Casnoff, Christopher McDonald (2 hrs.).

REDWOOD CURTAIN
ABC 4/23/95. (John Korty), Jeff Daniels, Lea Salonga, John Lithgow, Catherine Hicks, Debra Monk, Vilma Silva (2 hrs.).

RELENTLESS: MIND OF A KILLER
NBC 1/11/93. (John Patterson), Tim Matheson, Alberta Watson, Giancarlo Esposito (2 hrs.).

RETURN OF ELIOT NESS, THE
NBC 11/10/91. (James Contner), Robert Stack, Jack Coleman, Lisa Hartman, Philip Bosco (2 hrs.).

RETURN OF HUNTER, THE : EVERYONE WALKS IN L.A.
NBC 4/30/95. (Bradford May), Fred Dryer, Barry Bostwick, Lisa Eilbacher, John C. McGinley, Beth Toussaint, Miguel Ferrer (2 hrs.).

RETURN OF IRONSIDE, THE
NBC 5/4/93. (Gary Nelson), Raymond Burr, Don Galloway, Perrey Reeves, Cliff Gorman (2 hrs.).

RETURN OF THE MUSKETEERS, THE
USA 4/3/91. (Richard Lester), Oliver Reed, Michael York, C. Thomas Howell (2 hrs.).

RETURN OF THE NATIVE, THE
CBS 12/4/94. (Jack Gold), Catherine Zeta Jones, Ray Stevenson, Clive Owen, Joan Plowright, Steven Mackintosh (2 hrs.).

RETURN TO GREEN ACRES
CBS 5/18/90. (William Asher), Eddie Albert, Eva Gabor, Frank Cady, Henry Gibson (2 hrs.).

RETURN TO LONESOME DOVE
CBS 11/14, 16 & 18/93. (Mike Robe), Jon Voight, Barbara Hershey, Rick Schroder, Louis Gossett Jr., Oliver Reed (7 hrs.).

REUNION
CBS 12/11/94. (Lee Grant), Marlo Thomas, Peter Strauss, Frances Sternhagen, Leelee Sobiesky, Courtney Chase (2 hrs.).

REVEALING EVIDENCE
NBC 6/3/90. (Michael Switzer), Stanley Tucci, Mary Page Keller, Finn Carter (2 hrs.).

REVENGE OF THE NERDS III: THE NEXT GENERATION
FOX 7/13/92. (Roland Mesa), Robert Carradine, Curtis Armstrong, Ted McGinley, Morton Downey, Jr. (2 hrs.).

REVENGE OF THE NERDS IV: NERDS IN LOVE
FOX 5/9/94. (Steve Zacharias), Robert Carradine, Curtis Armstrong, Julia Montgomery (2 hrs.).

REVENGE ON THE HIGHWAY
NBC 12/6/92. (Craig R. Baxley), Stacy Keach, Tom Bower, Lisa Banes, Sandahl Bergman (2 hrs.).

REVOLVER
NBC 4/19/92. (Gary Nelson), Robert Urich, Dakin Matthews, Steve Williams, David Ryall (2 hrs.).

RICH MEN, SINGLE WOMEN
ABC 1/29/90. (Elliot Silverstein), Suzanne Somers, Heather Locklear, Joel Higgins, Larry Wilcox (2 hrs.).

RIDE WITH THE WIND
ABC 4/18/94. (Bobby Roth), Craig T. Nelson, Helen Shaver, Bradley Pierce, Max Gail (2 hrs.).

RING OF SCORPIO
USA 4/24 & 25/91. (Ian Barry), Catherine Oxenberg, Jack Scalia, Caroline Goodall (4 hrs.).

RIO SHANNON
ABC 8/14/93. (Mimi Leder), Blair Brown, Patrick Van Horn, Michael DeLuise, Jay O. Snaders (2 hrs.).

RISE AND WALK: THE DENNIS BYRD STORY
FOX 2/28/94. (Michael Dinner), Peter Berg, Kathy Morris, Johann Carlo (2 hrs.).

RISING SON
TNT 7/23/90. (John David), Brian Dennehy, Matt Damon, Piper Laurie (2 hrs.).

RIVER OF RAGE: THE TAKING OF MAGGIE KEENE
CBS 10/3/93. (Robert Iscove), Victoria Principal, Peter Onorati, Sean Murray (2 hrs.).

ROADRACERS
SHO 7/22/94. (Robert Rodriguez), David Arquette, Salma Hayek, John Hawkes (90 mins.)

ROBIN COOK'S "HARMFUL INTENT"
CBS 12/14/93. (John Patterson), Tim Matheson, Emma Samms, Robert Pastorelli, Alex Rocco (2 hrs.).

ROBIN COOK'S "MORTAL FEAR"
NBC 11/20/94. (Larry Shaw), Joanna Kerns, Gregory Harrison, Max Gail, Tobin Bell, Katherine LaNasa, Judith Chapman (2 hrs.).

ROBIN COOK'S "VIRUS"
NBC 5/8/95. (Armand Mastrioanni), Nicollette Sheridan, William Devane, Stephen Caffrey, Kurt Fuller, William Atherton (2 hrs.).

ROBIN HOOD
FOX 5/13/91. (John Irvin), Patrick Bergin, Uma Thurman, Jurgen Prochnow, Edward Fox (2-1/2 hrs.).

ROCK HUDSON
ABC 1/8/90. (John Nicolella), Thomas Ian Griffith, William R. Moses, Diane Ladd (2 hrs.).

ROCKFORD FILES, THE: A BLESSING IN DISGUISE
CBS 5/14/95. (Jeannot Swarcz), James Garner, Richard Romanus, Joe Santos, Renee O'Connor, Ahron Ipale (2 hrs.).

ROCKFORD FILES, THE: I STILL LOVE L.A.
CBS 11/27/94. (James Whitmore Jr.), James Garner, Stuart Margolin, Joe Santos, Joanna Cassidy, Geoffrey Nauffts (2 hrs.).

ROOMMATES
NBC 5/30/94. (Alan Metzger), Randy Quaid, Eric Stoltz, Charles Durning, Elizabeth Pena (2 hrs.).

ROSE AND THE JACKAL, THE
TNT 4/16/90. (Jack Gold), Christopher Reeve, Madolyn Smith Osborne, Carrie Snodgress (2 hrs.).

ROSEANNE: AN UNAUTHORIZED BIOGRAPHY
FOX 10/11/94. (Paul Schneider), Denny Dillon, David Graf, John Karlen, John Walcutt, Judith Scarpone (2 hrs.).

ROSEANNE AND TOM: BEHIND THE SCENES
NBC 10/31/94. (Richard Colla), Patrika Darbo, Stephen Lee, Jan Hoag, Nancy Youngblut, Robert Neches (2 hrs.).

ROSWELL
SHO 7/31/94. (Jeremy Kagan), Kyle MacLachlan, J.D. Daniels, Doug Wert, Kim Griest, Martin Sheen (105 mins.).

ROYCE
SHO 4/3/94. (Rod Holcomb), Jim Belushi, Peter Boyle, Miguel Ferrer, Chelsea Field (100 mins.).

RUGGED GOLD
12/10/95. (Michael Anderson), Jill Eikenberry, Art Hindle, Graham Greene, Ari Madger (2 hrs.).

RUNAWAY DAUGHTERS
SHO 8/12/94. (Joe Dante), Julie Bowen, Holly Fields, Jenny Lewis, Paul Rudd (90 mins.).

RUNAWAY FATHER
CBS 4/19/92. (John Nicolella), Donna Mills, Jack Scalia, Chris Mulkey, Jenny Lewis (2 hrs.).

RUNNING AGAINST TIME
USA 11/21/90. (Bruce Seth Green), Robert Hays, Catherine Hicks, Sam Wanamaker (2 hrs.).

RUNNING DELILAH
ABC 8/29/94. (Richard Franklin), Kim Cattrall, Billy Zane, Yorgo Voyagis, Diana Rigg (2 hrs.).

RUNNING MATES
HBO 10/4/92. (Michael Lindsay-Hogg), Diane Keaton, Ed Harris, Ed Begley Jr., Ben Masters (90 mins.).

SARAH: PLAIN AND TALL
CBS 2/3/91. (Glenn Jordan), Glenn Close, Christopher Walken, Lexi Randall, Margaret Sophie Stein (2 hrs.).

SAVED BY THE BELL—HAWAIIAN STYLE
NBC 11/27/92. (Don Barnhart), Mark-Paul Gosselaar, Dustin Diamond, Tiffani-Amber Thiessen (2 hrs.).

SAVED BY THE BELL: WEDDING IN LAS VEGAS
NBC 10/7/94. (Jeff Melman), Mark-Paul Gosselaar, Tiffani-Amber Thiessen, Mario Lopez, Dustin Diamond, Elizabeth Berkley (2 hrs.).

SAWBONES
SHO 7/25/95. (Catherine Cyran), Nicholas Sadler, Nina Siemaszko, Barbara Carrera, Don Harvey, Adam Baldwin (90 mins.).

SCAM
SHO 5/22/93. (John Flynn), Christopher Walken, Lorraine Bracco, Miguel Ferrer (2 hrs.).

SCARLETT
CBS 11/13, 15, 16 & 17/94. (John Erman), Joanne Whalley-Kilmer, Timothy Dalton, Barbara Barrie, Ann-Margret, Sean Bean (8 hrs.).

**SCATTERED DREAMS:
THE KATHRYN MESSENGER STORY**
CBS 12/19/93. (Neema Barnette), Tyne Daly, Gerald McRaney, Alicia Silverstone (2 hrs.).

SEA WOLF, THE
TNT 4/18/93. (Michael Anderson), Charles Bronson, Christopher Reeve, Catherine Mary Stewart, Marc Singer (2 hrs.).

SEARCH AND RESCUE
NBC 3/27/94. (Paul Krasny), Robert Conrad, Dee Wallace Stone, Chad McQueen (2 hrs.).

SEARCH FOR GRACE
CBS 5/17/94. (Sam Pillsbury), Lisa Hartman Black, Ken Wahl, Richard Masur, Don Michael Paul (2 hrs.).

SEASON OF GIANTS, A
TNT 3/17 & 18/91. (Jerry London), F. Murray Abraham, Steven Berkoff, Juliette Caton (4 hrs.).

SEASON OF HOPE, A
CBS 1/8/95. (Marcus Cole), JoBeth Williams, Stephen Lang, Stephen Meadows, Jeremy London, Erik Von Detten (2 hrs.).

SEASONS OF THE HEART
NBC 5/22/94. (Lee Grant), Carol Burnett, George Segal, Malcolm McDowell, Eric Lloyd (2 hrs.).

SECOND CHANCES
CBS 12/2/93. (Sharron Miller), Connie Sellecca, Matt Salinger, Ronny Cox (2 hrs.).

SECRET, THE
CBS 4/19/92. (Karen Arthur), Kirk Douglas, Bruce Boxleitner, Brock Peters, Laura Harrington (2 hrs.).

SECRET LIFE OF ARCHIE'S WIFE, THE
CBS 10/28/90. (James Frawley), Michael Tucker, Jill Eikenberry, Ray Wise, Elaine Stritch (2 hrs.).

SECRET LIFE OF IAN FLEMING, THE
TNT 3/5/90. (Ferdinand Fairfax), Jason Connery, Kristin Scott Thomas, Joss Ackland (2 hrs.).

SECRET PASSION OF ROBERT CLAYTON, THE
USA 6/3/92. (E. W. Swackhamer), John Mahoney, Scott Valentine, Eve Gordon, Kevin Conroy (2 hrs.).

SECRET SINS OF THE FATHER
NBC 1/9/94. (Beau Bridges), Beau Bridges, Lloyd Bridges, Lee Purcell, Frederick Coffin (2 hrs.).

SECRET WEAPON
TNT 3/20/90. (Ian Sharp), Griffin Dunne, Karen Allen, Jeroen Krabbe, Brian Cox (2 hrs.).

SECRETS
ABC 5/25/95. (Jud Taylor), Veronica Hamel, Richard Kiley, Shae D'Lyn, Thomas Gibson, Reed Diamond, Jessica Bowman (2 hrs.).

SEDUCED AND BETRAYED
NBC 4/24/95. (Felix Alcala), Susan Lucci, David Charvet, Gabrielle Carteris, Zach Glucksman, Peter Donat (2 hrs.).

SEDUCED BY EVIL
USA 8/25/95. (Tony Wharmby), Suzanne Sommers, John Vargas, James B. Sikking, Julie Carmen (2 hrs.).

SEDUCTION IN TRAVIS COUNTY, A
CBS 5/19/91. (George Kaczender), Lesley Ann Warren, Peter Coyote, Jean Smart (2 hrs.).

SEDUCTION: THREE TALES FROM THE INNER SANCTUM
ABC 4/5/92. (Michael Ray Rhodes), Victoria Principal, John Terry, John O'Hurley, W. Morgan Sheppard (2 hrs.).

SEE JANE RUN
ABC 1/8/95. (John Patterson), Joanna Kerns, John Shea, Katy Boyer, Tiffany Taubman, Lee Garlington, Blaire Baron (2 hrs.).

SEPARATE BUT EQUAL
ABC 4/7 & 8/91. (George Stevens, Jr.), Sidney Poitier, Burt Lancaster, Richard Kiley, Lynne Thigpen (4 hrs.).

SEPARATED BY MURDER
CBS 4/12/94. (Donald Wrye), Sharon Gless, Steve Railsback, Ed Bruce (2 hrs.).

**SERVING IN SILENCE:
THE MARGARETHE CAMMERMEYER STORY**
NBC 2/6/95. (Jeff Bleckner), Glenn Close, Judy Davis, Jan Rubes, Wendy Wakkena, Susan Barnes, Colleen Flynn (2 hrs.).

SET UP, THE
SHO 7/23/95. (Strathford Hamilton), Billy Zane, Mia Sara, James Russo, James Coburn (90 mins.).

SEX, LOVE AND COLD HARD CASH
USA 5/12/93. (Harry S. Longstreet), JoBeth Williams, Anthony John Denison, Richard Sarafian (2 hrs.).

SEXUAL ADVANCES
ABC 5/10/92. (Donna Deitch), Stephanie Zimbalist, William Russ, Terry O'Quinn, Patrick James Clarke (2 hrs.).

SHADOW OF A DOUBT
CBS 4/28/91. (Karen Arthur), Mark Harmon, Margaret Welsh, Diane Ladd (2 hrs.).

SHADOW OF A STRANGER
NBC 12/7/92. (Richard Friedman), Emma Samms, Parker Stevenson, Michael Easton, Joan Chen (2 hrs.).

SHADOW OF OBSESSION
NBC 4/10/94. (Kevin Connor), Veronica Hamel, Jack Scalia, Kim Miyori (2 hrs.).

SHADOWHUNTER
SHO 2/10/93. (J.S. Cardone), Scott Glenn, Angela Alvarado, Robert Beltran (107 mins.).

SHAGGY DOG, THE
ABC 11/12/94. (Dennis Dugan), Ed Begley Jr., Scott Weinger, Sharon Lawrence, Jon Polito, James Cromwell (2 hrs.).

SHAKE, RATTLE AND ROCK
SHO 8/26/94. (Allan Arkush), Renee Zellweger, Jenifer Lewis, Max Perlich, John Doe (90 mins.)

SHAME
LIF 8/18/92. (Dan Lerner), Amanda Donohoe, Dean Stockwell, Fairuza Balk, Shelley Owens (2 hrs.).

SHAME II: THE SECRET
LIF 6/7/95. (Dan Lerner), Amanda Donohoe, Kay Lenz, George Wendt, Geoffrey Blake, David Andrews, Talia Balsam (2 hrs.).

SHAMEFUL SECRETS
ABC 10/10/93. (David Carson), Joanna Kerns, Tim Matheson, LaTanya Richardson, Ashley Peldon (2 hrs.).

SHAMROCK CONSPIRACY, THE
UPN 3/7/95. (James Frawley), Edward Woodward, Jeffrey Nordling, Elizabeth Hurley, Nigel Bennett, Kim Coates (2 hrs.).

SHATTERED DREAMS
ABC 5/13/90. (Robert Iscove), Lindsay Wagner, Michael Nouri, Georgeann Johnson (2 hrs.).

SHATTERED IMAGE
USA 1/21/94. (Fritz Kiersch), Jack Scalia, Bo Derek, John Savage, David McCallum (2 hrs.).

**SHATTERED TRUST:
THE SHARI KARNEY STORY**
NBC 9/27/93. (Bill Corcoran), Melissa Gilbert, Kate Nelligan, Ellen Burstyn (2 hrs.).

SHE LED TWO LIVES
NBC 11/27/94. (Bill Corcoran), Connie Sellecca, Perry King, A. Martinez, Patricia Clarkson, J. Smith Cameron (2 hrs.).

SHE SAID NO
NBC 9/23/90. (John Patterson), Veronica Hamel, Judd Hirsch, Lee Grant, Ray Baker (2 hrs.).

SHE SAYS SHE'S INNOCENT
NBC 10/28/91. (Charles Correll), Katey Sagal, Charlotte Ross, Jameson Parker, Alan Rachins (2 hrs.).

SHE STOOD ALONE
NBC 4/15/91. (Jack Gold), Mare Winningham, Ben Cross, Taurean Blacque (2 hrs.).

SHE STOOD ALONE: THE TAILHOOK SCANDAL
ABC 5/22/95. (Larry Shaw), Gail O'Grady, Hal Holbrook, Rip Torn, Robert Urich, Bess Armstrong, James Marshall (2 hrs.).

SHE WOKE UP
NBC 1/19/92. (Waris Hussein), Lindsay Wagner, David Dukes, Frances Sternhagen, Maureen Mueller (2 hrs.).

SHERLOCK HOLMES RETURNS
CBS 9/12/93. (Kenneth Johnson), Anthony Higgins, Debrah Farentino, Mark Adair Rios (2 hrs.).

SHIMMER
PBS 4/10/95. (John Hanson), Marcus Klemp, Elijah Shepard, Tom Bower, Clem Tucker Jr., Jake Busey, Mary Beth Hurt (90 mins.).

SHOOT FIRST: A COP'S VENGEANCE
NBC 3/24/91. (Mel Damski), Alex McArthur, Dale Midkiff, Terry O'Quinn (2 hrs.).

SIDNEY SHELDON'S "MEMORIES OF MIDNIGHT"
SYND 11/25 & 26/91. (Gary Nelson), Jane Seymour, Omar Sharif, Tato Penghlis, Stephen Macht (4 hrs.).

SIDNEY SHELDON'S "THE SANDS OF TIME"
SYND 11/23 & 24/92. (Gary Nelson), Deborah Raffin, Michael Nouri, Ramy Zada, Amanda Plummer (4 hrs.).

SIGHT UNSEEN
WPIX 4/18/91. (Greydon Clark), Susan Blakely, Edward Albert, Wings Hauser (2 hrs.).

SILENCE OF ADULTERY
LIF 8/9/95. (Stephen Stern), Kate Jackson, Robert Desiderio, Art Hindle, Patricia Gage, Kristin Fairlie, Tori McPetrie (2 hrs.).

SILENT CRIES
NBC 3/8/93. (Anthony Page), Gena Rowlands, Annabeth Gish, Chloe Webb, Clyde Kusatsu (2 hrs.).

SILENT MOTIVE
LIF 10/16/92. (Lee Philips), Patricia Wettig, Mike Farrell, Edward Asner, Rick Springfield (2 hrs.).

SILENT WITNESS: WHAT A CHILD SAW
USA 7/14/94. (Bruce Pittman), Mia Korf, Bill Nunn, Clark Johnson (2 hrs.).

SILHOUETTE
USA 11/28/90. (Carl Schenkel), Faye Dunaway, David Rasche, John Terry, Talisa Soto (2 hrs.).

SIMON & SIMON: IN TROUBLE AGAIN
CBS 2/23/95. (John McPherson), Gerald McRaney, Jameson Parker, Tim Reid, Jeannie Wilson (2 hrs.).

SIN AND REDEMPTION
CBS 3/15/94. (Neema Burnette), Richard Grieco, Cynthia Gibb, Ralph Waite, Cheryl Pollack (2 hrs.).

SINATRA
CBS 11/8 & 10/92. (James Sadwith), Philip Casnoff, Olympia Dukakis, Rod Steiger, Marcia Gay Harden (5 hrs.).

SINS OF THE MOTHER
CBS 2/19/91. (John Patterson), Dale Midkiff, Heather Fairchild, Elizabeth Montgomery (2 hrs.).

SISTER-IN-LAW, THE
USA 7/12/95. (Noel Nosseck), Shanna Reed, Kate Vernon, Craig Wasson, Kent Williams, Kevin McCarthy, Tonea Stewart (2 hrs.).

SITTER, THE
FOX 6/10/91. (Rick Berger), Kim Myers, Brett Cullen, Susan Barnes, Kimberly Cullum (2 hrs.).

SKETCH ARTIST
SHO 6/27/91. (Phedon Papamichael), Jeff Fahey, Sean Young, Drew Barrymore (90 mins.).

SKETCH ARTIST II: HANDS THAT SEE
SHO 1/28/95. (Jack Sholder), Jeff Fahey, Courteney Cox, Michael Beach, Brion James, James Tolkan, Leilani Ferrer (2 hrs.).

SKYLARK
CBS 2/7/93. (Joseph Sargent), Glenn Close, Christopher Walken, Lexi Randall, Christopher Bell (2 hrs.).

SLEEP, BABY, SLEEP
ABC 3/26/95. (Armand Mastroianni), Tracey Gold, Kyle Chandler, Missy Crider, Joe Minjares, Karla Tamburrelli (2 hrs.).

SNAPDRAGON
USA 7/20/94. (Worth Keeter), Steven Bauer, Pamela Sue Anderson (2 hrs.).

SNOW KILL
USA 7/25/90. (Thomas J. Wright), Terence Knox, Patti D'Arbanville, David Dukes (2 hrs.).

SNOWBOUND: THE JIM AND JENNIFER STOLPA STORY
CBS 1/9/94. (Christian Duguay), Neil Patrick Harris, Kelli Williams, Susan Clark, Michael Gross (2 hrs.).

SO PROUDLY WE HAIL
CBS 1/23/90. (Lionel Chetwynd), Edward Herrmann, David Soul, Chad Lowe, Raphael Sbarge (2 hrs.).

SODBUSTER
SHO 7/17/94. (Eugene Levy), Kris Kristofferson, John Vernon, Fred Willard (2 hrs.).

SOLOMON AND SHEBA
SHO 2/26/95. (Robert M. Young), Halle Berry, Jimmy Smits, Nicolas Grace, Kenneth Colley, Ruben Santiago Hudson (90 mins.)

SOMEBODY HAS TO SHOOT THE PICTURE
HBO 9/9/90. (Frank Pierson), Roy Scheider, Bonnie Bedelia, Robert Carradine, Andre Braugher (90 mins.).

SOMEBODY'S DAUGHTER
ABC 9/20/92. (Joseph Sargent), Nicollette Sheridan, Nick Mancuso, Boyd Kestner, Max Gail (2 hrs.).

SOMEONE ELSE'S CHILD
ABC 12/4/94. (John Power), Lisa Hartman Black, Bruce Davison, Whip Hubley, Ken Pogue, Glynn Turman (2 hrs.).

SOMEONE SHE KNOWS
NBC 10/3/94. (Eric Laneuville), Markie Post, Gerald McRaney, Jeffrey Nordling, Sharon Lawrence, Shawn Modrell (2 hrs.).

SOMETHING TO LIVE FOR: THE ALISON GERTZ STORY
ABC 3/29/92. (Tom McLaughlin), Molly Ringwald, Lee Grant, Martin Landau, Perry King (2 hrs.).

SON OF THE MORNING STAR
ABC 2/3 & 4/91. (Mike Robe), Gary Cole, Rosanne Arquette, Rodney A. Grant, David Strathairn (4 hrs.).

SON'S PROMISE, A
ABC 3/5/90. (John Korty), Rick Schroder, Veronica Cartwright, Donald Moffat, Stephen Dorff (2 hrs.).

SOUND AND THE SILENCE, THE
TNT 7/18 & 19/93. (John Kent Harrison), John Bach, Brenda Fricker, Ian Bannen, Vanessa Vaughan (4 hrs.).

SPARKS: THE PRICE OF PASSION
CBS 2/25/90. (Richard Colla), Victoria Principal, Ted Wass, Ralph Waite, Hector Elizondo (2 hrs.).

SPENSER: CEREMONY
LIF 7/22/93. (Andrew Wild), Robert Urich, Avery Brooks, Barbara Williams (2 hrs.).

SPENSER: PALE KINGS AND PRINCES
LIF 2/2/94. (Vic Sarin), Robert Urich, Avery Brooks, Barbara Williams (2 hrs.).

SPENSER: THE JUDAS GOAT
LIF 12/12/94. (Jonas L. Scanlon), Robert Urich, Avery Brooks (2 hrs.).

SPIDER AND THE FLY, THE
USA 5/13/94. (Michael Katleman), Mel Harris, Ted Shackleford, Peggy Lipton (2 hrs.).

SPOILS OF WAR
ABC 4/9/94. (David Greene), Kate Nelligan, John Heard, Tobey Maguire (2 hrs.).

SPRING AWAKENING
CBS 11/6/94. (Jack Gold), Sherilyn Fenn, Jamey Sheridan, Elizabeth Wilson, Sammi Davis, Philip Abbott, Fritz Weaver (2 hrs.).

SPRING FLING!
ABC 4/15/95. (Chuck Bowman), James Eckhouse, Joyce DeWitt, Justin Burnette, Pat Harrington Jr., Billy Jayne (2 hrs.).

SPY GAMES
ABC 7/20/91. (Michael Fresco, Christopher Leitch), Linda Purl, Anthony John Denison, Josef Sommer (2 hrs.).

STALIN
HBO 11/21/92. (Ivan Passer), Robert Duvall, Julia Ormond, Maximilian Schell, Joan Plowright (3 hrs.).

STAR STRUCK
CBS 10/30/94. (Jim Drake), Kirk Cameron, Chelsea Noble, D.W. Moffett, J.T. Walsh, Ned Eisenberg, Desiree Marie (2 hrs.).

STATE OF EMERGENCY
HBO 2/12/94. (Lesli Linka Glatter), Joe Mantegna, Lynn Whitfield, Melinda Dillon (2 hrs.).

STAY THE NIGHT
ABC 4/26 & 7/92. (Harry Winer), Barbara Hershey, Jane Alexander, Morgan Weisser, Fred Dalton Thompson (4 hrs.).

STAYING AFLOAT
NBC 11/26/93. (Eric Launeville), Larry Hagman, Dakin Matthews, Gregg Henry (2 hrs.).

STEEL JUSTICE
NBC 4/5/92. (Christopher Crowe), Robert Taylor, J.A. Preston, Season Hubley, Roy Brocksmith (2 hrs.).

STEPFATHER III
HBO 6/4/92. (Guy Mager), Robert Wightman, Priscilla Barnes, David Tom, Season Hubley (2 hrs.).

STEPHEN KING'S "IT"
ABC 11/18 & 20/90. (Tommy Lee Wallace), Dennis Christopher, Richard Thomas, John Ritter, Tim Reid (4 hrs.).

STEPHEN KING'S "SOMETIMES THEY COME BACK"
CBS 5/7/91. (Tom McLoughlin), Tim Matheson, Brooke Adams, Robert Rusler (2 hrs.).

STEPHEN KING'S "THE LANGOLIERS"
ABC 5/14 & 15/95. (Tom Holland), Dean Stockwell, Patricia Wettig, Mark Lindsay Chapman, Bronson Pinchot (4 hrs.).

STEPHEN KING'S "THE STAND"
ABC 5/8, 9, 11 & 12/94. (Mick Garris), Gary Sinise, Molly Ringwald, Jamey Sheridan, Rob Lowe, Corin Nemec, Ruby Dee (8 hrs.).

STILL NOT QUITE HUMAN
DIS 5/31/92. (Guy Mager), Alan Thicke, Jay Underwood, Betsy Palmer, Christopher Neame (2 hrs.).

STOLEN BABIES
LIF 3/25/93. (Eric Laneuville), Lea Thompson, Mary Tyler Moore, Kathleen Quinlan (2 hrs.).

STOLEN: ONE HUSBAND
CBS 2/27/90. (Catlin Adams), Valerie Harper, Elliott Gould, Brenda Vaccaro, Bruce Davison (2 hrs.).

STOMPIN' AT THE SAVOY
CBS 4/12/92. (Debbie Allen), Lynn Whitfield, Vanessa Williams, Jasmine Guy, Mario Van Peebles (2 hrs.).

STOP AT NOTHING
LIF 3/12/91. (Chris Thomson), Veronica Hamel, Lindsay Frost, David Ackroyd (2 hrs.).

STORM AND SORROW
LIF 11/22/90. (Richard Colla), Lori Singer, Todd Allen, Steven Anderson (2 hrs.).

STORMY WEATHERS
ABC 5/4/92. (Will Mackenzie), Cybill Shepherd, Tony LoBianco, Charlie Schlatter, Robert Beltran (2 hrs.).

STORY LADY, THE
NBC 12/9/91. (Larry Elikann), Jessica Tandy, Lisa Jakub, Stephanie Zimbalist, Tandy Cronyn (2 hrs.).

STORY OF THE BEACH BOYS: SUMMER DREAMS, THE
ABC 4/29/90. (Michael Switzer), Bruce Greenwood, Greg Kean, Arlen Dean Snyder (2 hrs.).

STRANGER AT MY DOOR
CBS 9/27/91. (Vincent McEveety), Robert Urich, Markie Post, Michael Beck, Ken Swofford (2 hrs.).

STRANGER IN THE FAMILY
ABC 10/27/91. (Donald Wrye), Teri Garr, Neil Patrick Harris, Randle Mell, Sierra Samuel (2 hrs.).

STRANGER IN THE MIRROR, A
ABC 10/24/93. (Charles Jarrott), Perry King, Lori Laughlin, Christopher Plummer (2 hrs.).

STRANGER IN TOWN. A
CBS 3/29/95. (Peter Levin), Jean Smart, Gregory Hines, Jeffrey Nordling, Lucinda Jenney, Dave Florek (2 hrs.).

STRANGER WITHIN, THE
CBS 11/27/90. (Tom Holland), Rick Schroder, Kate Jackson, Chris Sarandon (2 hrs.).

STRAPPED
HBO 8/21/93. (Forest Whitaker), Bokeem Woodbine, Michael Biehn, Kia Joy Goodwin (2 hrs.).

STRAYS
USA 12/18/91. (John McPherson), Timothy Busfield, Kathleen Quinlan, Heather Lilley, Jessica Lilley (2 hrs.).

STREET JUSTICE
SYND 9/18/91. (Bill Corcoran), Carl Weathers, Bryan Genesse, Michael A. Jackson, Kimberly Sheppard (2 hrs.).

SUBSTITUTE, THE
USA 9/22/93. (Martin Donovan), Amanda Donohoe, Dalton James, Marky Mark, Natasha Gregson Wagner (2 hrs.).

SUBSTITUTE WIFE
NBC 5/23/94. (Peter Werner), Farrah Fawcett, Lea Thompson, Peter Weller (2 hrs.).

SUDIE AND SIMPSON
LIF 9/11/90. (Joan Tewkesbury), Louis Gossett, Jr., Sara Gilbert, John Jackson, Frances Fisher (2 hrs.).

SUMMER MY FATHER GREW UP, THE
NBC 3/3/91. (Michael Tuchner), John Ritter, Margaret Whitton, Karen Young, Joe Spano (2 hrs.).

SUMMERTIME SWITCH
ABC 10/8/94. (Alan Metter), Rider Strong, Jason Weaver, Richard Moll, Teresa Ganzel, Soleil Moon Frye, Barry Williams (2 hrs.).

SUNSTROKE
USA 9/23/92. (James Keach), Jane Seymour, Stephen Meadows, Steve Railsback, Ray Wise (2 hrs.).

SURVIVE THE NIGHT
USA 1/13/93. (Bill Corcoran), Stefanie Powers, Helen Shaver, Kathleen Robertson (2 hrs.).

SURVIVE THE SAVAGE SEA
ABC 1/6/92. (Kevin James Dobson), Robert Urich, Ali MacGraw, Danielle von Zerneck, Mark Ballou (2 hrs.).

SUSPECT DEVICE
SHO 7/11/95. (Rick Jacobson), C. Thomas Howell, Stacey Travis, Jed Allen, John Beck, Marcus Aurelius, Jonathan Fuller (90 mins.).

SWEET POISON
USA 6/12/91. (Brian Grant), Steven Bauer, Edward Herrmann, Patricia Healy (2 hrs.).

SWEET REVENGE
TNT 7/9/90. (Charlotte Brandstrom), Carrie Fisher, Rosanna Arquette, John Sessions (2 hrs.).

SWITCH, THE
CBS 1/17/93. (Bobby Roth), Gary Cole, Craig T. Nelson, Kathleen Nolan, Beverly D'Angelo (2 hrs.).

SWITCHED AT BIRTH
NBC 4/28 & 29/91. (Waris Hussein), Bonnie Bedelia, Brian Kerwin, Edward Asner, Caroline McWilliams (4 hrs.).

SWORN TO VENGEANCE
CBS 3/23/93. (Peter H. Hunt), Robert Conrad, William McNamara, Gary Bayer (2 hrs.).

T

T BONE N WEASEL
TNT 11/2/92. (Lewis Teague), Christopher Lloyd, Gregory Hines, Ned Beatty, Rip Torn (2 hrs.).

TAD
FAM 2/12/95. (Rob Thompson), Kris Kristofferson, Jane Curtin, Jean Louisa Kelly, Kieran Mulroney, Tyler Long (2 hrs.).

TAGGET
USA 2/14/91. (Richard T. Heffron), Daniel J. Travanti, William Sadler, Roxanne Hart (2 hrs.).

TAINTED BLOOD
USA 3/3/93. (Mathew Patrick), Raquel Welch, Joan Van Ark, Natasha Wagner (2 hrs.).

TAKE, THE
USA 3/28/90. (Leon Ichaso), Ray Sharkey, R. Lee Ermey, Larry Manetti, Lisa Hartman (2 hrs.).

TAKE ME HOME AGAIN
NBC 12/18/94. (Thomas McLoughlin), Kirk Douglas, Craig T. Nelson, Bess Armstrong, Bonnie Bartlett, Richard Gilliland (2 hrs.).

TAKING BACK MY LIFE: THE NANCY ZIEGENMEYER STORY
CBS 3/15/92. (Harry Winer), Patricia Wettig, Stephen Lang, Shelley Hack, Ellen Burstyn (2 hrs.).

TAKING THE HEAT
SHO 6/6/93. (Tom Mankiewicz), Tony Goldwyn, Lynn Whitfield, Alan Arkin, George Segal (2 hrs.).

TALL, DARK AND DEADLY
USA 1/24/95. (Kenneth Fink), Jack Scalia, Kim Delaney, Todd Allen, Gina Mastrogiacomo, Ely Pouget (2 hrs.).

TARGET OF SUSPICION
USA 6/9/94. (Bob Swaim), Tim Matheson, Lysette Anthony, Agnes Soral (2 hrs.).

TASTE FOR KILLING, A
USA 8/12/92. (Lou Antonio), Jason Bateman, Henry Thomas, Michael Biehn, Blue Deckert (2 hrs.).

TEAMSTER BOSS: THE JACKIE PRESSER STORY
HBO 9/12/92. (Alastair Reid), Brian Dennehy, Jeff Daniels, Maria Conchita Alonso, Eli Wallach (2 hrs.).

TEARS AND LAUGHTER: THE JOAN AND MELISSA RIVERS STORY
NBC 5/15/94. (Oz Scott), Joan Rivers, Melissa Rivers, Dorothy Lyman (2 hrs.).

TECUMSEH: THE LAST WARRIOR
TNT 6/4/95. (Larry Elikann), Jesse Borrego, David Morse, David Clennon, Tantoo Cardinal, Jeri Arredondo (2 hrs.).

TEKWAR
SYND 1/18/94. (William Shatner), Greg Evigan, Eugene Clark, Torri Higginson (2 hrs.).

TELLING SECRETS
ABC 1/17 & 18/93. (Marvin J. Chomsky), Cybill Shepherd, Ken Olin, Christopher McDonald, G.D. Spradlin (4 hrs.).

TEN MILLION DOLLAR GETAWAY, THE
USA 3/6/91. (Christopher Canaan), John Mahoney, Karen Young, Tony LoBianco (2 hrs.).

TERROR IN THE NIGHT
CBS 1/11/94. (Colin Bucksey), Joe Penny, Justine Bateman, Matt Mulhern (2 hrs.).

TERROR ON TRACK 9
CBS 9/20/92. (Robert Iscove), Richard Crenna, Swoosie Kurtz, Joan Van Ark, Cliff Gorman (2 hrs.).

TERROR STRIKES THE CLASS REUNION
SYND 5/27/92. (Clive Donner), Kate Nelligan, Jennifer Beals, Geraint Wyn Davies, Manfred Lehmann (2 hrs.).

TEXAS JUSTICE
ABC 2/12 & 13/95. (Dick Lowry), Peter Strauss, Heather Locklear, Dennis Franz, Lewis Smith, Susan Walters, Chris Mulkey (4 hrs.).

THANKSGIVING DAY
NBC 11/19/90. (Gino Tanasescu), Mary Tyler Moore, Jonathan Brandmeir, Tony Curtis (2 hrs.).

THERE ARE NO CHILDREN HERE
ABC 11/28/93. (Anita W. Addison), Oprah Winfrey, Mark Lane, Norman Golden II, Maya Angelou (2 hrs.).

THERE WAS A LITTLE BOY
CBS 5/16/93. (Mimi Leder), Cybill Shepherd, John Heard, Scott Bairstow (2 hrs.).

THEY
SHO 11/14/93. (John Korty), Vanessa Redgrave, Patrick Bergin, Valerie Mahaffey (2 hrs.).

THEY'VE TAKEN OUR CHILDREN: THE CHOWCHILLA KIDNAPPING
ABC 3/1/93. (Vern Gillum), Karl Malden, Tim Ransom, Travis Fine, Julie Harris (2 hrs.).

THICKER THAN BLOOD
CBS 3/6/94. (Michael Dinner), Peter Strauss, Rachel Ticotin, Bob Dishy (2 hrs.).

THICKER THAN WATER
A&E 4/10/94. (Mark Evans), Theresa Russell, Jonathan Pryce, Robert Pugh (3 hrs.).

THIS CAN'T BE LOVE
CBS 3/13/94. (Anthony Harvey), Katharine Hepburn, Anthony Quinn, Jason Bateman, Jami Gertz (2 hrs.).

THIS GUN FOR HIRE
USA 1/9/91. (Lou Antonio), Robert Wagner, Nancy Everhard, John Harkins (2 hrs.).

THOSE SECRETS
ABC 3/16/92. (David Manson), Blair Brown, Arliss Howard, Mare Winningham, Paul Guilfoyle (2 hrs.).

THROUGH THE EYES OF A KILLER
CBS 12/15/92. (Peter Markle), Marg Helgenberger, Richard Dean Anderson, David Marshall Grant (2 hrs.).

TIME TO HEAL, A
NBC 4/18/94. (Michael Toshiyuki Uno), Nicollette Sheridan, Gary Cole, Mara Wilson, Annie Corley (2 hrs.).

TIN SOLDIER, THE
SHO 3/22/95. (Jon Voight), Trenton Knight, Jon Voight, Ally Sheedy, Dom DeLuise, Bethay Richards, Aeryk Egan (2 hrs.).

TO BE THE BEST
CBS 8/2 & 4/92. (Tony Wharmby), Lindsay Wagner, Anthony Hopkins, Stephanie Beacham, Christopher Cazenove (4 hrs.).

TO CATCH A KILLER
SYND 5/13 & 14/92. (Eric Till), Brian Dennehy, Michael Riley, Meg Foster, Margot Kidder (4 hrs.).

TO DANCE WITH THE WHITE DOG
CBS 12/5/93. (Glenn Jordan), Hume Cronyn, Jessica Tandy, Christine Baranski, Amy Wright, Frank Whaley (2 hrs.).

TO GRANDMOTHER'S HOUSE WE GO
ABC 12/6/92. (Jeff Franklin), Ashley Olsen, Mary-Kate Olsen, Rhea Perlman, Jerry Van Dyke (2 hrs.).

TO MY DAUGHTER
NBC 11/26/90. (Larry Shaw), Rue McClanahan, Michele Greene, Ty Miller (2 hrs.).

TO MY DAUGHTER WITH LOVE
NBC 1/24/94. (Kevin Hooks), Rick Schroder, Linda Gray, Lawrence Pressman (2 hrs.).

TO SAVE A CHILD
ABC 4/8/92. (Robert Lieberman), Marita Geraghy, Shirley Knight, Anthony Zerbe, Peter Kowanko (2 hrs.).

TO SAVE THE CHILDREN
CBS 4/5/94. (Steven Stern), Richard Thomas, Robert Urich, Wendy Crewson (2 hrs.).

TOM CLANCY'S "OP CENTER"
NBC 2/26 & 27/95. (Lewis Teague), Harry Hamlin, Wilford Brimley, Rod Steiger, Carl Weathers, Patrick Bauachau (4 hrs.).

TOMMYKNOCKERS, THE
ABC 5/9 & 10/93. (John Power), Jimmy Smits, Marg Helgenberger, Joanna Cassidy, John Ashton (4 hrs.).

TONYA & NANCY: THE INSIDE STORY
NBC 4/30/94. (Larry Shaw), Alexandra Powers, James Wilder, Heather Langenkamp, Susan Clark (2 hrs.).

TOO YOUNG TO DIE
NBC 2/26/90. (Robert Markowitz), Juliette Lewis, Michael Tucker, Brad Pitt, Michael O'Keefe (2 hrs.).

TORCH SONG
ABC 5/23/93. (Michael Miller), Raquel Welch, Jack Scalia, Alicia Silverstone, George Newbern (2 hrs.).

TOWER, THE
FOX 8/16/93. (Richard Kletter), Paul Reiser, Susan Norman, Richard Grant, Roger Rees (2 hrs.).

TOWN TORN APART, A
NBC 11/30/92. (Daniel Petrie), Michael Tucker, Carole Galloway, Linda Griffiths, Jill Eikenberry (2 hrs.).

TRAGEDY OF FLIGHT 103: THE INSIDE STORY, THE
HBO 12/9/90. (Leslie Woodhead), Ned Beatty, Peter Boyle, Vincent Gardenia, Michael Wincott (90 mins.).

TREACHEROUS BEAUTIES
CBS 9/25/94. (Charles Jarrot), Emma Samms, Bruce Greenwood, Catherine Oxenberg, Tippi Hedren (2 hrs.).

TREACHEROUS CROSSING
USA 4/8/92. (Tony Wharmby), Lindsay Wagner, Angie Dickinson, Jeffrey DeMunn, Joseph Bottoms (2 hrs.).

TREASURE ISLAND
TNT 1/22/90. (Fraser C. Heston), Charlton Heston, Christian Bale, Oliver Reed, Christopher Lee (3 hrs.).

TRIAL & ERROR
USA 2/24/93. (Mark Sobel), Tim Matheson, Helen Shaver, Eugene Clark, Sean McCann (2 hrs.).

TRIAL: THE PRICE OF PASSION
NBC 5/3 & 4/92. (Paul Wendkos), Peter Strauss, Beverly D'Angelo, Ned Beatty, Jill Clayburgh (4 hrs.).

TRICK OF THE EYE
CBS 10/23/94. (Ed Kaplan), Ellen Burstyn, Meg Tilly, Barnard Hughes, Paxton Whitehead, Alastair Duncan (2 hrs.).

TRIPLECROSS
SHO 5/28/95. (Jeno Hodi), Patrick Bergin, Michael Pare, Ashley Laurence, Billy Dee Williams, Zachary Bogatz (2 hrs.).

TRIUMPH OF THE HEART: THE RICKY BELL STORY
CBS 4/2/91. (Richard Michaels), Mario Van Peebles, Lane Davis, Susan Ruttan (2 hrs.).

TRIUMPH OVER DISASTER:
THE HURRICANE ANDREW STORY
NBC 5/24/93. (Marvin J. Chomsky), Ted Wass, Brynn Thayer, Brian McNamara, Arnetia Walker (2 hrs.).

TROUBLESHOOTERS: TRAPPED BENEATH THE EARTH
NBC 10/3/93. (Bradford May), Kris Kristofferson, David Newsom, Leigh J. McCloskey (2 hrs.).

TUSKEGEE AIRMEN, THE
HBO 8/26/95. (Robert Markowitz), Laurence Fishburne, Cuba Gooding Jr., Allen Payne, Malcolm Jamal Warner (2 hrs.).

12:01
FOX 7/5/93. (Jack Sholder), Jonathan Silverman, Helen Slater, Nicolas Survoy, Robin Barlett (2 hrs.).

TWIST OF THE KNIFE, A
CBS 2/13/93. (Jerry London), Dick Van Dyke, Suzanne Pleshette, Cynthia Gibb (2 hrs.).

TWO FATHERS: JUSTICE FOR THE INNOCENT
NBC 1/14/94. (Paul Krasny), Robert Conrad, George Hamilton, Danny Goldring (2 hrs.).

TYSON
HBO 4/29/95. (Uli Edel), Michael Jai White, George C. Scott, Paul Winfield, Malcolm Jamal Warner, Tony LoBianco (2 hrs.).

ULTIMATE BETRAYAL
CBS 3/20/94. (Donald Wrye), Marlo Thomas, Mel Harris, Eileen Heckart, Ally Sheedy (2 hrs.).

UNNATURAL PURSUITS
A&E 1/23/94. (Christopher Morahan), Alan Bates, Paul Guilfoyle, Bob Balaban, Keith Szarabajka (2 hrs.).

UNTAMED LOVE
LIF 8/3/94. (Paul Aaron), Cathy Lee Crosby, Ashlee Lauren, John Getz, Gary Frank (2 hrs.).

US
CBS 9/20/91. (Michael Landon), Michael Landon, Casey Peterson, Barney Martin, Meg Wittner (2 hrs.).

VANISHING SON
SYND 3/2/94. (John Nicolella), Russell Wong, Chi Muoi Lo, Rebecca Gayheart (2 hrs.).

VENDETTA: SECRETS OF A MAFIA BRIDE
SYND 5/20 & 21/91. (Stuart Margolin), Eric Roberts, Carol Alt, Eli Wallach, Burt Young (4 hrs.).

VENDETTA 2: THE NEW MAFIA
SYND 12/6 & 7/93. (Ralph Thomas), Carol Alt, Michael Ontkean, Eli Wallach (4 hrs.).

VERNON JOHNS STORY, THE
SYND 1/17/94. (Kenneth Fink), James Earl Jones, Mary Alice, Cissy Houston (2 hrs.).

VESTIGE OF HONOR
CBS 12/30/90. (Jerry London), Gerald McRaney, Michael Gross, Season Hubley (2 hrs.).

VICTIM OF LOVE
CBS 5/5/91. (Jerry London), Pierce Brosnan, JoBeth Williams, Virginia Madsen (2 hrs.).

VICTIM OF LOVE: THE SHANNON MOHR STORY
NBC 11/9/93. (John Cosgrove), Sally Murphy, Dwight Schultz, Bonnie Bartlett, Andy Romano (2 hrs.).

VIRTUAL SEDUCTION
SHO 8/1/95. (Paul Ziller), Jeff Fahey, Ami Dolenz, Carrie Genzel, Emile Levisetti, Meshach Taylor, Rick Dean (90 mins.).

VISIONS OF MURDER
NBC 5/7/93. (Michael Rhodes), Barbara Eden, James Brolin, Terry O'Quinn (2 hrs.).

VOICE OF THE HEART
SYND 4/18 & 19/90. (Tony Whamby), Lindsay Wagner, James Brolin, Victoria Tennant (4 hrs.).

VOICES FROM WITHIN
NBC 10/10/94. (Eric Till), JoBeth Williams, Corbin Bernsen, Stephanie Zimbalist, Winston Rekert, Justin Louis (2 hrs.).

VOICES WITHIN: THE LIVES OF TRUDDI CHASE
ABC 5/20 & 21/90. (Lamont Johnson), Shelley Long, Tom Conti, John Rubinstein (4 hrs.).

VOYAGE
USA 6/2/93. (John Mackenzie), Eric Roberts, Rutger Hauer, Karen Allen, Connie Nelson (2 hrs.).

VOYAGE OF TERROR: THE ACHILLE LAURO AFFAIR
SYND 5/1/90. (Alberto Negrin), Burt Lancaster, Eva Marie Saint, Robert Culp (4 hrs.).

WALTON WEDDING, A
CBS 2/12/95. (Robert Ellis Miller), Richard Thomas, Ralph Waite, Michael Learned, Kate McNiel, Jon Walmsley, Judy Norton (2 hrs.).

WALTONS THANKSGIVING REUNION, A
CBS 11/21/93. (Harry Harris), Richard Thomas, Ralph Waite, Michael Learned, Kate McNeil (2 hrs.).

WASP WOMAN
SHO 8/29/95. (Jim Wynorski), Jennifer Rubin, Doug Wert, Daniel J. Travanti (90 mins.).

WATER ENGINE, THE
TNT 8/24/92. (Steven Schachter), W.H. Macy, John Mahoney, Joe Mantegna, Patti LuPone (2 hrs.).

WEB OF DECEIT
USA 10/17/90. (Sandor Stern), Linda Purl, James Read, Paul de Souza, Barbara Rush (2 hrs.).

WEB OF DECEPTION
NBC 4/25/94. (Richard Colla), Powers Boothe, Pam Dawber, Lisa Collins, Bradley Whitford (2 hrs.).

WHAT EVER HAPPENED TO BABY JANE?
ABC 2/17/91. (David Greene), Vanessa Redgrave, Lynn Redgrave, John Glover (2 hrs.).

WHAT SHE DOESN'T KNOW
NBC 2/23/92. (Kevin James Dobson), Valerie Bertinelli, George Dzundza, Peter Dobson, David Marshall Grant (2 hrs.).

WHEELS OF TERROR
USA 7/11/90. (Chris Cain), Joanna Cassidy, Marcie Leeds, Arlen Dean Snyder (2 hrs.).

WHEN A STRANGER CALLS BACK
SHO 4/4/93. (Fred Walton), Jill Schoelen, Carol Kane, Charles Durning (96 mins.).

WHEN LOVE KILLS:
THE SEDUCTION OF JOHN HEARN
CBS 5/18/93. (Larry Elikann), Gary Cole, Marg Helgenberger, Julie Harris, Charles Hallahan (2 hrs.).

WHEN NO ONE WOULD LISTEN
CBS 11/15/92. (Armand Mastroianni), Michele Lee, James Farentino, Cicely Tyson (2 hrs.).

WHEN THE DARK MAN CALLS
USA 6/14/95. (Nathaniel Gutman), Joan Van Ark, James Read, Geoffrey Lewis, Chris Sarandon, Frances Hyland (2 hrs.).

WHEN WILL I BE LOVED?
NBC 12/3/90. (Michael Tuchner), Stefanie Powers, Katherine Helmond, Crystal Bernard (2 hrs.).

WHEN YOU REMEMBER ME
ABC 10/7/90. (Harry Winer), Fred Savage, Kevin Spacey, Ellen Burstyn, Dwier Brown (2 hrs.).

WHERE ARE MY CHILDREN?
ABC 9/18/94. (George Kaczender), Marg Helgenberger, Christopher Noth, Bonnie Bartlett, Corbin Bernsen, Cynthia Martells (2 hrs.).

WHERE PIGEONS GO TO DIE
NBC 1/29/90. (Michael Landon), Art Carney, Cliff De Young, Michael Landon (2 hrs.).

WHEREABOUTS OF JENNY, THE
ABC 1/14/91. (Gene Reynolds), Ed O'Neill, Debrah Farentino, Eve Gordon, Mike Farrell (2 hrs.).

WHICH WAY HOME
TNT 1/28/91. (Carl Schultz), Cybill Shepherd, John Waters, Peta Toppana (3 hrs.).

WHILE JUSTICE SLEEPS
NBC 12/5/94. (Ivan Passer), Cybill Shepherd, Tim Matheson, Karis Bryant, Dion Anderson, Kurtwood Smith (2 hrs.).

WHITE DWARF
FOX 5/23/95. (Peter Markle), Beverly Mitchell, Roy Brocksmith, C.C.H. Pounder. (2 hrs.).

WHITE HOT:
THE MYSTERIOUS DEATH OF THELMA TODD
NBC 5/5/91. (Paul Wendkos), Loni Anderson, Robert Davi, Paul Dooley, Scott Paulin (2 hrs.).

WHITE LIE
USA 9/25/91. (Bill Condon), Gregory Hines, Annette O'Toole, Bill Nunn, Gregg Henry (2 hrs.).

WHITE MILE
HBO 5/21/94. (Robert Butler), Alan Alda, Peter Gallagher, Robert Loggia, Bruce Altman (2 hrs.).

WHOSE CHILD IS THIS? THE WAR FOR BABY JESSICA
ABC 9/26/93. (John Kent Harrison), Susan Dey, Michael Ontkean, Amanda Plummer, David Keith (2 hrs.).

WIFE, MOTHER, MURDERER
ABC 11/10/91. (Mel Damski), Judith Light, David Ogden Stiers, Kellie Overby, David Dukes (2 hrs.).

WILD CARD
USA 10/28/92. (Mel Damski), Powers Boothe, Cindy Pickett, Rene Auberjonois, Terry O'Quinn (2 hrs.).

WILD JUSTICE
SYND 5/12 & 13/93. (Paul Madigan), Roy Scheider, Ted McGinley, Patricia Millardet, Sam Wanamaker (4 hrs.).

WILD PALMS
ABC 5/16 & 19/93. (Peter Hewitt, Keith Gordon, Kathryn Bigelow, Phil Joanou), James Belushi, Dana Delany, Angie Dickinson, Robert Loggia, Kim Cattrall (8 hrs.).

WILD TEXAS WIND
NBC 9/23/91. (Joan Tewkesbury), Dolly Parton, Gary Busey, Ray Benson, Dennis Letts (2 hrs.).

WILDFLOWER
LIF 12/3/91. (Diane Keaton), Patricia Arquette, William McNamara, Beau Bridges, Reese Witherspoon (2 hrs.).

WILLING TO KILL: THE TEXAS CHEERLEADER STORY
ABC 11/8/92. (David Greene), Lesley Ann Warren, Tess Harper, Dennis Christopher, William Forsythe (2 hrs.).

WITCH HUNT
HBO 12/10/94. (Paul Schrader), Dennis Hopper, Penelope Ann Miller, Eric Bogosian, Sheryl Lee Ralph, Julian Sands (2 hrs.)

WITH A VENGEANCE
CBS 9/22/92. (Michael Switzer), Melissa Gilbert-Brinkman, Michael Gross, Jack Scalia (2 hrs.).

WITH HOSTILE INTENT
CBS 5/11/93. (Paul Schneider), Melissa Gilbert, Mel Harris, Peter Onorati, Cotter Smith (2 hrs.).

WITH MURDER IN MIND
CBS 5/12/91. (Michael Tuchner), Elizabeth Montgomery, Robert Foxworth, Howard Rollins Jr. (2 hrs.).

WITHOUT A KISS GOODBYE
CBS 3/21/93. (Noel Nosseck), Lisa Hartman Black, Chris Meloni, Cloris Leachman (2 hrs.).

WITHOUT CONSENT
ABC 10/16/94. (Robert Iscove), Jennie Garth, Johnny Galecki, Jill Eikenberry, Tom Irwin, Gene Lythgow, Helen Shaver (2 hrs.)

WITHOUT HER CONSENT
NBC 1/14/90. (Sandor Stern), Melissa Gilbert, Scott Valentine, Barry Tubb (2 hrs.).

WITHOUT WARNING
CBS 10/30/94. Sander Vanocur, Jane Kaczmarek, Bree Walker-Lampley, Ernie Anastos, Warren Olney (2 hrs.).

WITHOUT WARNING: THE JAMES BRADY STORY
HBO 6/16/91. (Michael Toshiyuki Uno), Beau Bridges, Joan Allen, Bryan Clark, Steve Flynn (90 mins.).

WITHOUT WARNING: TERROR IN THE TOWERS
NBC 5/26/93. (Alan Levi), George Clooney, Scott Plank, John Karlen, Susan Ruttan (2 hrs.).

WITNESS TO THE EXECUTION
NBC 2/13/94. (Tommy Lee Wallace), Tim Daly, Sean Young, Len Cariou, George Newbern (2 hrs.).

WOMAN NAMED JACKIE, A
NBC 10/13 & 15/91. (Larry Peerce), Roma Downey, Stephen Collins, William Devane, Rosemary Murphy (6 hrs.).

WOMAN OF INDEPENDENT MEANS, A
NBC 2/19, 20 & 22/95. (Preston Fischer), Sally Field, Ron Silver, Tony Goldwyn, Jack Thompson, Sheila McCarthy (6 hrs.).

WOMAN ON A LEDGE
NBC 3/15/93. (Chris Thomson), Leslie Charleston, Deidre Hall, Colleen Zenk Pinter (2 hrs.).

WOMAN ON THE RUN:
THE LAWRENCIA BEMBENEK STORY
NBC 5/16 & 17/93. (Sandor Stern), Tatum O'Neal, Bruce Greenwood, Peggy McCay, Colin Fox (4 hrs.).

WOMAN SCORNED: THE BETTY BRODERICK STORY, A
CBS 3/1/92. (Dick Lowry), Meredith Baxter, Stephen Collins, Michelle Johnson, Kelli Williams (2 hrs.).

WOMAN WHO LOVED ELVIS, THE
ABC 4/18/93. (Bill Bixby), Roseanne Arnold, Tom Arnold, Sally Kirkland, Cynthia Gibb (2 hrs.).

WOMAN WHO SINNED, THE
ABC 11/17/91. (Michael Switzer), Susan Lucci, Tim Matheson, Michael Dudikoff, John Vernon (2 hrs.).

WOMAN WITH A PAST
NBC 3/2/92. (Mimi Leder), Pamela Reed, Dwight Schultz, Richard Lineback, Carrie Snodgress (2 hrs.).

WOMEN & MEN: STORIES OF SEDUCTION
HBO 8/19/90. (Frederic Raphael, Ken Russell, Tony Richardson), Elizabeth McGovern, Peter Weller, James Woods (90 mins.).

WOMEN & MEN 2: IN LOVE THERE ARE NO RULES
HBO 8/18/91. (Walter Bernstein, Kristi Zea, Mike Figgis), Matt Dillon, Andie MacDowell, Scott Glenn (90 mins.).

WOMEN OF SPRING BREAK, THE
CBS 1/10/95. (Bill Norton), Shelley Long, Mel Harris, DeLane Matthews, Ian Ziering, Francois-Eric Gendorn (2 hrs.).

WOMEN OF WINDSOR, THE
CBS 10/23/92. (Steven H. Stern), Sallyanne Law, Nicola Formby, James Piddock (2 hrs.).

WOOF RETURNS! A KID'S BEST FRIEND
DIS 3/30/95. (David Cobham), Edward Fidoe, Thomas Aldwinkle, John Ringham (2 hrs.).

WORKING TRASH
FOX 11/26/90. (Alan Metter), George Carlin, Ben Stiller, Buddy Ebsen (2 hrs.).

WORLD WAR II: WHEN LIONS ROARED
NBC 4/19 & 20/94. (Joseph Sargent), Michael Caine, Bob Hoskins, John Lithgow, Ed Begley Jr. (4 hrs.).

WORLD'S OLDEST LIVING BRIDESMAID, THE
CBS 9/21/90. (Joseph L. Scanlon), Donna Mills, Brian Wimmer, Art Hindle, Beverly Garland (2 hrs.).

WOUNDED HEART
USA 8/16/95. (Vic Sarin), Paula DeVicq, Jon Hensley, Hank Stratton, Anita Barone, William Newman, Scott Stevens (2 hrs.).

WRITER'S BLOCK
USA 10/9/91. (Charles Correll), Morgan Fairchild, Michael Praed, Joe Regalbuto, Douglas Rowe (2 hrs.).

WRONG MAN, THE
SHO 9/5/93. (Jim McBride), John Lithgow, Kevin Anderson, Rosanna Arquette (2 hrs.).

X Y Z

XXX'S AND OOO'S
CBS 6/21/94. (Allan Arkush), Debrah Farentino, Andrea Parker, Nia Peeples (2 hrs.).

YARN PRINCESS, THE
ABC 3/27/94. (Tom McLoughlin), Jean Smart, Robert Pastorelli, Dennis Boutsikaris (2 hrs.).

YEARLING, THE
CBS 4/24/94. (Rod Hardy), Peter Strauss, Jean Smart, Wil Horneff, Philip Seymour (2 hrs.).

YES VIRGINIA, THERE IS A SANTA CLAUS
ABC 12/8/91. (Charles Jarrott), Richard Thomas, Charles Bronson, Katharine Isobel, Edward Asner (2 hrs.).

YOUNG AT HEART
CBS 3/12/95. (Allan Arkush), Olympia Dukakis, Joe Penny, Philip Bosco, Yannick Bisson, Louis Zorich, Audrey Landers (2 hrs.).

YOUNG CATHERINE
TNT 2/17 & 18/91. (Michael Anderson), Vanessa Redgrave, Julia Ormond, Christopher Plummer (4 hrs.).

YOUNG INDIANA JONES AND THE HOLLYWOOD FOLLIES
FAM 10/15/94. (Michael Schultz), Sean Patrick Flanery, Dana Gladstone, Allison Smith, Stephen Caffery, Bill Cusack (2 hrs.).

ZELDA
TNT 11/7/93. (Pat O'Connor), Natasha Richardson, Timothy Hutton, Jon De Vries, Daniel Gerroll (2 hrs.).

ZOOMAN
SHO 3/19/95. (Leon Ichaso), Louis Gossett Jr., Charles S. Dutton, Cynthia Martells, C.C.H. Pounder, Khalil Kain (105 mins.).

TELEVISION COMPANIES

CORPORATE HISTORIES OF THE NETWORKS

TELEVISION CORPORATIONS

PRODUCERS & DISTRIBUTORS

CORPORATE HISTORIES
OF THE NETWORKS

ABC, INC.

ABC's predecessor, the Radio Corporation of America (RCA) owned two radio networks, the Blue and the Red. In 1941, the FCC decreed that the same company could not own two networks, so RCA incorporated the Blue under the name of American Broadcasting System and established it as an independent subsidiary. RCA then sold this network to Edward J. Noble, and in 1944, the name was changed to the American Broadcasting Company. ABC's first television broadcast was on April 19, 1948 with "On the Corner". Later in the year, ABC scored two "firsts": the live broadcast of an opera (Verdi's "Otello") from the Metropolitan Opera House in New York and a TV documentary, "The Marshall Plan." ABC merged with United Paramount Theatres in 1952. This merger was engineered by Leonard H. Goldenson, then the president of UPT. The new company was called American Broadcasting-Paramount Theatres, Inc. During the 1950's, ABC began to operate at a profit although it had to struggle fiercely to acquire new affiliates. In 1954, ABC made a deal with Walt Disney to acquire a 35% interest in Disneyland and all TV programs produced by Disney. The following year, ABC signed an exclusive rights contract with Warner Bros. for TV programming.

In the Fall of 1962, ABC introduced color programming for the fall season which was expanded in 1966 to include full color broadcasting. In 1965, AB-PT's name was changed to American Broadcasting Companies, Inc. The 1960's also introduced blockbuster theatrical movies to TV with spectacular rating results when "The Bridge on the River Kwai" was viewed (in 1966) by 60 million Americans. In 1967, the ABC evening news was expanded from 15 minutes to a half-hour, and Joey Bishop inaugurated ABC's late-night talk show programming.

In 1972, ABC was able to operate at a profit for the first time in ten years. In the 1976-77 season, ABC took first place in the ratings race for the first time. In 1976, Barbara Walters joined ABC, becoming the first anchorwoman in television history. The mini-series "Roots" appeared on ABC in 1977 and became the highest-rated program of all time. This helped immensely in the ratings race, and credit must go in large part to Fred Silverman who, two years before, had joined the company as president of ABC International. He left in 1978 to go to NBC.

The decade of the Eighties was a turbulent one for the networks as cable and home video began whittling away their audiences. In 1985, ABC agreed to be purchased by Capital Cities Communications. The merged company's name was changed to Capital Cities/ABC, Inc. ABC held second place in the ratings from 1979 to 1983 when it dropped to third position. It was unable to rise from third until 1987-88 when it displaced CBS in second place, primarily because of the World Series and the Superbowl. It remained second in 1988-89 and 1989-90. In the latter season, ABC had the distinction of broadcasting the most talked-about new series of the period, "Twin Peaks," and the highest-rated new series, "America's Funniest Home Videos." Daniel B. Burke replaced Frederick J. Pierce as president and chief operating officer. There were also sweeping reductions in personnel in the interests of economy and streamlining. Budget cuts notwithstanding, Capital Cities/ABC chairman Thomas Murphy pledged ABC would not scrimp on programming.

Profits at the end of 1990 rose about $70 million. Of the three networks, ABC won the ratings battle in news coverage of the war in the Persian Gulf. For two seasons in a row the network could boast having the only new series in the top ten: "America's Funniest People" (1990-91) and "Home Improvement" (1991-92). Capital Cities/ABC is a partner in ESPN, the highly successful cable TV sports channel and two other cable TV services—Arts & Entertainment and Lifetime. ABC was the only network in the 1992-93 season to gain ground, moving into second place behind CBS, from its previous third place standing. During the season, Robert A. Iger became the new network president. The network was the first to sign a deal with a cable operator (in this case Continental Cablevision) allowing its stations to be carried on cable without paying a fee. In 1994, the company signed an affiliation deal with E.W.Scripps Company to switch several of their stations over to ABC. The big event of 1995 was the $19 billion acquisition of Capital Cities/ABC by the Walt Disney Company, said to be the second largest corporate takeover in history.

RECENT ABC SERIES

1990-91: America's Funniest People, Dinosaurs.
1991-92:The Commish, Home Improvement, The Young Indiana Jones Chronicles
1992-93: Day One, Hangin' With Mr. Cooper.
1993-94: Grace Under Fire, Lois and Clark, NYPD Blue.
1994-95: My So-Called Life.
1995-96: Champs, Naked Truth.
1996-97: Spin City, Dangerous Minds.

COLUMBIA BROADCASTING SYSTEM, INC.

CBS began in 1927 as a radio network with 16 stations, United Independent Broadcasters, Inc., founded by Arthur Judson, a concert tour manager and backed by Louis Sterling, president of the Columbia Phonograph Company. Later other investors were invited in, the most prominent of whom was William S. Paley. On September 26, 1928, at the age of 27, Paley became president of the firm whose name was changed to the Columbia Broadcasting System. Paley introduced many innovations to radio broadcasting, the most significant of which was the signing of an agreement in 1931 with Paramount Pictures whereby film stars were heard on radio for the first time. This laid the groundwork for the CBS policy in television from the outset to feature shows built around stars (Ed Sullivan, Lucille Ball, Arthur Godfrey, Jack Benny, Burns & Allen, Garry Moore, etc.).

CBS was in TV as early as 1931 when it began regularly scheduled TV programming over experimental station W2XAB in New York City. In 1941, CBS began weekly broadcasts of black-and-white TV programming over WCBS-TV in New York. By 1948, it had 30 affiliated stations.

In 1951, CBS broadcast the first live coast-to-coast TV transmission between New York and San Francisco. 1951 was also the year that Bill Gordon designed the CBS Eye which was destined to become one of the most famous logos in the world.

In 1952, CBS opened Television City in Hollywood—the industry's first self-contained TV production facility. "Playhouse 90" made its debut in 1956, but the big event of the decade was the 1951 debut of "I Love Lucy", a series regarded as the progenitor of the situation-comedy. In the field of soap operas, CBS was both leader and winner, virtually monopolizing that market from 1951 to 1956. In 1951, it introduced "Search for Tomorrow," which was to become the longest-running show in that genre. This was followed by "Love of Life" (1951) and "The Guiding Light" (1952), both overnight hits.

In the late '50s and through the 60's and 70's, CBS reigned as king of prime time ratings, maintaining its long-running lead with such successes as "Gunsmoke" (1957), "The Defenders" (1961), "The Beverly Hillbillies" (1962), "All in the Family" (1972) and "Dallas" (1978). Also helping was "60 Minutes" the news-oriented show which, by 1995, had remained in the Top Ten prime time shows for 18 consecutive seasons.

CBS began the turbulent Eighties with a new president, Thomas Wyman (replacing John D. Backe). In 1985, Ted Turner made an unfriendly bid for CBS, forcing the network to buy up 21% of its own stock to thwart the takeover. Laurence A. Tisch, a former theatre chain executive, had become the major stockholder in CBS when, in 1986, he instigated sweeping changes in the interests of cost-cutting and efficiency. 700 jobs were eliminated at the CBS Broadcast Group. Tisch also removed Wyman as president, named himself chief executive officer and induced founder William Paley to return to active duty as acting chairman of the board. It was quite a jolt to the company when, in 1985-86, it slipped to second place and stayed there through the following season. In 1987-88, CBS came in third for the first time in TV history. In 1988, Tisch shuffled executive ranks again, naming Howard Stringer, previously president of CBS News, president of the Broadcasting Group. The networks new management team sought to devise a strategy to pull the network out of its decline in the prime-time ratings. Jeff Sagansky, former head of Tri-Star Pictures, was brought in as president of the entertainment division in 1990.

Starting in 1991-92, CBS became the number one network for three years in a row based on the success of such shows as "60 Minutes" (the number one show for both '91-'92 and '92-'93), "Murphy Brown," "Murder She Wrote," and "Northern Exposure." CBS was hit hard by Fox's 1994 purchase of twelve stations from New World Communications, losing eight affiliates. However, the following summer, Westinghouse Electric Corp. aquired the final independent network for $5.4 billion creating the largest collection of tv and radio stations in America. The 1994-95 season was a low point for the network as it plunged from number one to number three. By season's end, CBS had the dubious distinction of being the first of the three majors to fall into 4th place, coming in below Fox for the last week before the debut of the 1995-96 season. In late 1995, the venerable news program "60 Minutes" and CBS came under fire for refusing to air a controversial segment on the tobacco industry. Critics of CBS alleged that the network capitulated to the threat of legal action, rather than actual litigation. During this season the network placed third again.

RECENT CBS SERIES

1990-91: Evening Shade, The Trials of Rosie O'Neill.
1991-92: Brooklyn Bridge, Street Stories.
1992-93: Dr. Quinn: Medicine Woman, Picket Fences.
1993-94: Dave's World, Diagnosis Murder,
 The Nanny
1994-95: Chicago Hope, Cybill.
1995-96: Can't Hurry Love, If Not For You.
1996-97: Cosby, Pearl, Ink.

FOX BROADCASTING COMPANY

Fox Broadcasting, a subsidiary of Rupert Murdoch's News Company and owner of Twentieth Century-Fox, began broadcasting with the late night "Late Show with Joan Rivers" on October 9, 1986. The next year, on April 5, 1987, the fledgling network began prime-time broadcasts on Sunday nights only. The initial line-up consisted of "Married With Children" and "The Tracey Ullman Show", which featured animated interludes of a dysfunctional cartoon family named the Simpsons. Three new shows were added in the following weeks, including "21 Jump Street", which helped launch the career of actor Johnny Depp. In July of that year, Fox launched a Saturday night prime time line up. From 1989 to 1993, the network steadily added programming and expanded its prime time coverage to a full seven nights a week. Originally the network aimed its programming at a young urban demographic. Particular attention was given to African-American oriented programming, with comedy series such as "Roc", Martin", "Living Single" and "In Living Color" (a weekly comedy-variety show which showcased not only the talents of Keenan Ivory Wayans and his brother Damon Wayans, but also comedian Jim Carrey). The youth market was provided with its first soap opera with "Beverly Hills 90210", and its succesful spin-off "Melrose Place". Fox consistently programmed "risky" shows, even in the face of boycotts, most notably aimed at "Married With Children" and "Beverly Hills 90210". The network, feeling strong about its programming, slotted "The Simpsons" against NBC's top-rated sitcom "The Cosby Show" in 1991.

The network was also actively pursuing sports' programming. In 1993, Fox won the rights to NFL football for four years, including the rights to 1997's Super Bowl XXXI. In 1994, Fox acquired the rights to broadcast NHL hockey and in 1995, Fox signed an agreement with Major League Baseball to broadcast weekly games, the 1996, 1998 and 2000 World Series, and 1997 and 1999 All Star Games.

Also in 1994, Fox premiered "The X-Files", a fiction series dedicated to exploring the bizarre, the unusual and the paranormal, all with a slant aimed at conspiracy buffs. It took a season to achieve ratings success, but "The X-Files" has become one of the most popular series on Fox and is fast becoming the most imitated series on television (in 1996, the networks have scheduled at least four new series that are very similar in areas of content). All of these programming decisions and experiments have paid off. In the 1994-95 broadcast season Nielsen ratings, Fox finished ahead of pioneer network CBS. Fox beat CBS yet again in November 1995. On October 7, 1996, Fox launched the new Fox News Channel on cable.

RECENT FOX SERIES

1991-92: Melrose Place, Roc
1992-93: Martin
1993-94: Living Single, The X-Files
1994-95: New York Undercover, Party of Five
1995-96: Space: Above and Beyond
1996-97: Millenium, Party Girl, Come Fly With Me.

NATIONAL BROADCASTING COMPANY

NBC was an outgrowth of radio operations. Radio Corp. of America, General Electric and Westinghouse jointly launched a network in 1926 with 31 stations; 25 in a network called Red and 6 in a network called Blue. A year later, it was forced to sell the Blue network to ABC (see history of that network), keeping for itself the one known as Red. Television began for NBC in 1928, when on April 4, it acquired from the Federal Communications Commission a permit to operate an experimental station, W2XBS. Actual transmission from the Empire State Building did not begin until October 30, 1931. Eight years later, the network began broadcasting on a regular basis, beginning with the opening of the New York World's Fair on April 30, 1939.

NBC became a TV network on January 12, 1940, when two stations, WNBC-TV, New York, and WRGB-TV, Schenectady, New York, carried the first network programming. In June, 1941, the FCC granted NBC the first commercial TV license and a month later it had four advertisers signed up. After World War II, NBC scored two big "firsts." On June 19, 1946, Gillette became the first advertiser to sponsor a TV network show, the Joe Louis-Billy Conn boxing match. That same year, Bristol-Myers became the first sponsor of a network TV series, "Geographically Speaking."

NBC can also claim to be the first to introduce coast-to-coast network TV coverage. On September 4, 1951, when the U.S.—Japanese peace treaty was signed in San Francisco, NBC cameras were on hand. In 1952, NBC pioneered early morning programming when it introduced "The Today Show." NBC can also claim the first regularly scheduled network color series "The Marriage," launched in 1954. That same year it achieved the first west-to-east TV transmission with the telecast of the Tournament of Roses Parade in color.

At the start of the 1965-66 season, NBC declared it was the "only all-color network." In 1968, NBC introduced new forms of TV programming with "The Name of the Game," a series that incorporated feature-film elements into a 90-minute show. This then spawned the "NBC Mystery Movie."

In 1972, NBC broke new ground again when it introduced "The Tomorrow Show" shown from 1:00 a.m. to 2:00 a.m. This was a talk program and it demonstrated that in the early hours of the morning something more than re-runs and old movies could be shown. In 1974, another late-night show called "Weekend" was begun. The 1976 NBC telecast of "Gone with the Wind" drew the largest audience to that date for an entertainment program. In 1978, "Holocaust" attracted 107 million viewers and won 21 major awards. Such programs helped NBC in the ratings, but in 1976-77 it fell to third place, where it stayed until 1983-84.

Along with the other networks, NBC moved into a period of turmoil during the decade of the Eighties, fighting off rising costs and competition from cable TV and home video. In 1986, General Electric Corporation purchased RCA (NBC's parent) for $6.28 billion; GE, it will be remembered, helped launch the radio network in 1926 which led to the development of NBC-TV. This brought personnel changes led by the replacement of Grant A. Tinker as NBC chief executive officer by Robert Wright, although Wright was not given Tinker's chairman title, that being taken by John F. Welch of GE. Instead, Wright was named president as well as chief executive officer. Along with its competition, NBC started cutting staff and budgets in 1986. In 1984-85, NBC edged up to second place, and the following year it was ranked number one in prime-time viewing for the first time in the three decades of Nielsen ratings.

NBC held on to its first place standing for the following five seasons, through 1990-91. Long-time hit series in the five-year period included "The Golden Girls," "Cheers," and "The Cosby Show." Despite the network's number one standing, figures showed a steady decline in viewers. In May of 1991, Brandon Tartikoff, credited with pulling the network up from third place 11 years earlier, departed from NBC to become head of Paramount Pictures. When "The Cosby Show" ran its final first run episode on April 30, 1992, it became

NBC's highest-rated series finale episode ever. The 1992 Summer Olympics also gave the network its widest ratings margin of all time. The 1994-95 season found NBC on top with its popular sitcom "Seinfeld" and the two most highly rated new series, "ER" and "Friends," both placing in the top ten. During the 1995-96 season, NBC was again ranked the number one network, with four of its Thursday night shows ranking in the overall top five. In the summer of 1996, NBC, in association with software giant Microsoft, launched a 24 hour cable and Internet news channel.

RECENT NBC SERIES

1990-91: Fresh Prince of Bel Air, Law & Order.
1991-92: I'll Fly Away.
1992-93: Homicide, Mad About You
1993-94: Frasier, The John Larroquette Show.
1994-95: Amazing Grace, ER, Friends.
1995-96: Caroline in the City, Third Rock From the Sun.
1996-97: Men Behaving Badly, Suddenly Susan.

PUBLIC BROADCASTING SERVICE

In 1948, the FCC stopped issuing new television station licenses. American educators, fearful of the impact of unrestricted commercial broadcasting, pushed for the Commission to hold open channel slots for non-commercial, educational television broadcasts. In 1952, when the FCC freeze was lifted, 242 channels were reserved for educational television. America's first non-commercial educational television station was KUHT in Houston, started in 1953. By 1962, 75 educational stations were broadcasting around the country. As these stations shared roughly the same programming interests, a loose distribution network evolved, allowing locally-produced programs like "Children's Corner" to be circulated among these stations. Most of the programming was produced on a shoestring budget. In 1962, the federal government authorized $32 million in matching funds for the construction of new educational television broadcasting facilities. In 1967, a blue ribbon panel urged local and state governments to increase their financial support of "public television" and recommended that the federal government participate in the production of programming. To this end, the first Public Broadcasting Act was enacted. This law also created the Corporation for Public Broadcasting, a non-profit "steward" of the public funds committed to public broadcasting, and, not incidentally, a barrier against government interference in programming decisions. In 1969, the Public Broadcasting Service's charter was signed, with its main intent the establishment of a nation-wide program distribution service. 1969 saw the premiere of an hour long, daily children's variety show, named "Sesame Street," which targeted pre-schoolers with fast-paced educational programming and featured live performers, cartoons and Muppets developed exclusively for the show by Jim Henson.

In 1970, PBS' first year as a "network", its programming included series as widely varied as "Washington Week in Review", "Civilisation", "The French Chef" and "Soul!" By 1973, PBS had more than 1 million individual subscribers. PBS and its member stations were responsible for bringing to U.S. audiences critically acclaimed BBC programming under the flag of "Masterpiece Theatre", which included such classics of television as "Upstairs Downstairs" and "I, Claudius". In 1976, PBS began broadcasting closed-captioned programming for the hearing impaired. In 1978, PBS became the first American network to distribute its programs by satellite.

Although some portion of PBS and its member

stations' budgets are provided by federal and state government funding and corporate gifts, PBS and its member stations have continued to rely upon the contributions of individual viewers to stay afloat. In the late 1980's and early 1990's, PBS and the CPB suffered an enormous amount of criticism by government officials for an alleged "liberal" bias, and later in the 90's, for not being "self sufficient". Although a notable few PBS series have achieved some financial success in other areas (primarily childrens' programming in the home video and product licensing fields), it is important to note that the production of most of the all-important local educational and public affairs programming never breaks even. In the face of continuing cuts in government funding, PBS programmers have accepted what may have been inevitable, the inclusion of commercial sponsorship (and actual commercials) in programming. In response to continuing attacks on the alleged "liberal bias" of PBS, an animated series, "Tales from the Book of Virtues", based on conservative William Bennett's writings was aired in September of 1996.

UPN (UNITED PARAMOUNT NETWORKS)

UPN began broadcasting on January 16, 1995 as a joint venture between United Television/Chris Craft Industries, Inc. and Paramount Television/Viacom Inc. The fledgling network's first official hit was the newest entry in the long-lived Star Trek franchise, "Star Trek: Voyager." Paramount TV executive Lucy Salhany was named president of the network. UPN currently broadcasts two nights of prime-time programming weekly, a Saturday afternoon movie, and plans to add an afternoon children's programming block. In the 1995-96 season, UPN debuted 8 new prime time series.

RECENT UPN SERIES

1994-95: Star Trek: Voyager.
1995-96: Moesha, Nowhere Man, Paranormal Borderline.
1996-97: Goode Behavior, An American Family, Homeboys in Outer Space.

COMPANIES

See also, Index: Producers & Distributors, Services, Cable Networks, Cable Program Suppliers, Direct Broadcast Satellite & Wireless System Broadcasters.

ABC, INC.
77 W. 66th St., New York, NY 10023. (212) 456-7777.
2040 Avenue of the Stars, Century City, CA 90067. (213) 557-7777.
PRESIDENT
Robert A. Iger
PRESIDENT, TELEVISION CREATIVE SERVICES
Stuart Bloomberg
PRESIDENT & CEO, ESPN
Steven Bornstein
SENIOR V.P. & GENERAL COUNSEL
Alan N. Braverman
EXECUTIVE V.P.
Stephen B. Burke
PRESIDENT, ABC RADIO
Robert F. Callahan
SENIOR V.P. & CFO
Ronald H. Doerfler
CHAIRMAN, DISNEY/ABC INTERNATIONAL TELEVISION
Herbert A. Granath
PRESIDENT, DISNEY/ABC CABLE NETWORKS
Geraldine Laybourne
V.P., CORPORATE COMMUNICATIONS
Patricia J. Matson
PRESIDENT, PUBLISHING GROUP
Phillip J. Meek
PRESIDENT, ABC TELEVISION STATIONS
Lawrence J. Pollock

ABC TELEVISION NETWORK GROUP
PRESIDENT
David Westin
EXECUTIVE V.P.
Alex Wallau
EXECUTIVE V.P., MARKETING
Alan Cohen
EXECUTIVE V.P., FINANCE
John J. Wolters
CHAIRMAN, ABC ENTERTAINMENT
Ted Harbert
PRESIDENT, ABC ENTERTAINMENT
Jamie Tarses
EXECUTIVE V.P., BUSINESS AFFAIRS & CONTRACTS
Ronald B. Sunderland
PRESIDENT, ABC DAYTIME
Pat Fili-Krushel
V.P., ABC CHILDREN'S ENTERTAINMENT
Linda M. Steiner
EXECUTIVE V.P., PRODUCTION
Brain McAndrews
PRESIDENT, ABC/KANE PRODUCTIONS INTERNATIONAL
J. Nicoll Durrie
PRESIDENT, ABC NEWS
Roone Arledge
EXECUTIVE V.P., ABC NEWS
Paul Friedman
EXECUTIVE V.P., NETWORK COMMUNICATIONS
Sherrie Sandy Rollings
PRESIDENT, BROADCAST OPERATIONS & ENGINEERING
Preston A. Davis
SENIOR V.P., ADMINISTRATION
Richard E. Hockman
SENIOR V.P., PROGRAMMING, ABC SPORTS
David Downs

AFFILIATE RELATIONS
SENIOR V.P., AFFILIATE RELATIONS
John L. Rouse
V.P. & DIRECTOR OF AFFILIATE OPERATIONS
William (Buzz) Mathesius
V.P., AFFILIATE MARKETING & RESEARCH SERVICES
Mike Nissenblatt

TELEVISION NETWORK SALES
PRESIDENT, SALES & MARKETING
Marvin F. Goldsmith
EXECUTIVE V.P., NATIONAL SALES MANAGER
Robert Cagliero

EXECUTIVE V.P., GENERAL SALES MANAGER
Lawrence S. Fried
SENIOR V.P., FINANCE & ADMINISTRATION
Robert S. Wallen
SENIOR V.P., PRIME TIME SALES
Roger L. Sverdlik
V.P., EASTERN SALES
Mark C. Mitchell
V.P., PRIMETIME SALES PROPOSAL
Peter Scanlon
V.P., CENTRAL SALES
Edward J. Wollock
V.P. & DIRECTOR, CENTRAL DIVISION
Michael R. Rubin
V.P., DETROIT SALES MANAGER
Mary Ellen Holahan
V.P., WESTERN DIVISION SALES
Charles W. Clark
V.P., SALES DEVELOPMENT & MARKETING SERVICES
Charles A. Gabelmann
V.P., SALES MARKETING
Madeline C. Nagel
V.P., PROMOTIONAL SALES & ACCOUNT DEVELOPMENT
Harry H. Factor
V.P., SPORTS SALES
Brian C. Sikorski
V.P. & DIRECTOR, SPORTS SALES
Ronald H. Furman
V.P. SPORTS SALES ADMINISTRATION
Michael Kay
V.P., DAYTIME SALES
Daniel Barnathan
V.P. & DIRECTOR, DAYTIME SALES
Gail A. Sullivan
V.P., NEWS & EARLY MORNING SALES
Cynthia Ponce Abrams
V.P. & DIRECTOR, NEWS, EARLY MORNING & LATE NIGHT SALES
Patrick J. McGovern
V.P., REVENUE PLANNING & ADMINISTRATION
John J. Abbattista

NETWORK COMMUNICATIONS
SENIOR V.P., NETWORK COMMUNICATIONS
Sherrie S. Rollins
V.P., MEDIA RELATIONS
Janice Gretemeyer
V.P., NETWORK COMMUNICATIONS
Mark R. Johnson
V.P., PHOTOGRAPHY
Peter Murray

ABC ENTERTAINMENT
CHAIRMAN
Ted Harbert
PRESIDENT
Jamie Tarses
EXECUTIVE V.P., PRIME TIME
Stuart Bloomberg
SENIOR V.P., TALENT & CASTING
Donna L. Rosenstein
V.P., COMEDY SERIES DEVELOPMENT
Kim Fleary
V.P., DRAMATIC SERIES DEVELOPMENT
Greer Shepherd
SENIOR V.P., PROGRAM PLANNING & SCHEDULING
Alan Sternfeld
SENIOR V.P., VARIETY & SPECIAL EVENTS
John Hamlin
V.P., CURRENT SERIES PROGRAMS
Jeffrey D. Bader
SENIOR V.P., MOTION PICTURES FOR TELEVISION
Judd Parkin
V.P., MOTION PICTURES FOR TV & MINI-SERIES
Barbara Lieberman
SENIOR V.P., CONCEPT SPECIALS
Mark C. Zakarin

V.P., ON-AIR PROMOTION
Stuart L. Brower
V.P., SPECIAL PROJECTS
Geoffrey S. Calnan
V.P., MARKETING
Chris Carlisle
V.P., ON-AIR GRAPHICS
Barbara Eddy
SENIOR V.P., FINANCE & ADMINISTRATION
P. Thomas Van Schaick
V.P., FINANCE & ADMINISTRATION, WEST COAST
Eric Beattie

BUSINESS AFFAIRS
EXECUTIVE V.P., BUSINESS AFFAIRS & CONTRACTS
Ronald V. Sunderland
V.P., BUSINESS AFFAIRS, WEST COAST
Barry Gordon
V.P., BUSINESS AFFAIRS ADMINISTRATION, WEST COAST
Ronald Pratz
V.P., MUSIC & BUSINESS AFFAIRS
David L. Sherman
V.P., BUSINESS AFFAIRS, EAST COAST
Anthony S. Farinacci

DAYTIME, CHILDREN'S & LATE NIGHT ENTERTAINMENT
PRESIDENT, ABC DAYTIME
Pat Fili-Krushel
SENIOR V.P., DAYTIME PROGRAMMING
Maxine Levinson
V.P., DAYTIME PROGRAMMING, WEST COAST
Tom Campbell
SENIOR V.P., MARKETING & PROMOTION, ABC DAYTIME
Angela Shapiro
V.P., PRODUCTION, EAST COAST
Dominick J. Nuzzi
V.P., PRODUCTION, WEST COAST
Edgar Hirst
V.P., ABC CHILDREN'S ENTERTAINMENT
Linda H. Steiner

ABC SPORTS, INC.
PRESIDENT, SPORTS
Dennis Swanson
SENIOR V.P., PRODUCTION
Dennis Lewin
EXECUTIVE PRODUCER OF ABC SPORTS
Jack O'Hara
SENIOR V.P., PROGRAMMING
David Downs
SENIOR V.P., FINANCIAL & ADMINISTRATION
Robert H. Apter
V.P., PRODUCTION PLANNING
Jonathan Leess
V.P., MARKETING
Keith Ritter
V.P., ADVERTISING & PROMOTION
Tom Remiszewski
V.P., PROGRAMMING
Lydia Stephans
V.P., PROGRAMMING
Tony Petitti

ABC NEWS
PRESIDENT, ABC NEWS
Roone Arledge
EXECUTIVE V.P.
Paul Friedman
SENIOR V.P. FOR HARD NEWS
Robert J. Murphy
SENIOR V.P., FINANCE
William N. Temple
SENIOR V.P. OF EDITORIAL QUALITY
Richard Wald
SENIOR V.P. NEWS MAGAZINE, LONG FORM PROGRAM-
MING & EARLY MORNING PROGRAMMING
Alan Wurtzel
V.P. FOR BUSINESS DEVELOPMENT & MARKETING
William Abrams
V.P., OPERATIONS
Michael Duffy
V.P., NEWS OPERATIONS, WASHINGTON
Glenwood Branche
V.P., BUSINESS AFFAIRS
Stevan Sadicurio
V.P., AFFILIATE NEWS SERVICE
Donald Dunphy
V.P. & WASHINGTON BUREAU CHIEF
Robin Sproul
EXECUTIVE PRODUCER, "20/20"
Victor Neufeld

EXECUTIVE PRODUCER, "PRIME TIME LIVE"
Phyllis McGrady
V.P., PRODUCTION CONTROL
William Nagy
V.P. & ASSISTANT TO THE PRESIDENT
Joanna E. Bistany
V.P., TALENT RECRUITMENT & DEVELOPMENT
Amy Entelis
V.P. OF NEW COVERAGE
Mimi Gurbst
EXECUTIVE PRODUCER OF "WORLD NEWS TONIGHT
WITH PETER JENNINGS"
Richard N. Kaplan
EXECUTIVE PRODUCER
Eleanor Prescott
SENIOR BROADCAST PRODUCER "WORLD NEWS TONIGHT
WITH PETER JENNINGS"
Robert Roy
EXECUTIVE PRODUCER "NIGHTLINE"
Tom Bettag

BROADCAST OPERATIONS & ENGINEERING
PRESIDENT
Preston A. Davis
SENIOR V.P., BUSINESS AFFAIRS
Michael Lang
V.P., ENGINEERING SERVICES, EAST COAST
David Elliott
V.P. & DIRECTOR, PROGRAM ADMINISTRATION
Maureen P. Domal
V.P., TELEVISION OPERATIONS, EAST COAST
Diane M. Tryneski
V.P., PROGRAM OPERATIONS
Stephen K. Nenno
V.P., POST PRODUCTION & SPECIAL PROGRAMS
Elliott Reed

ABC BROADCAST GROUP
PRESIDENT
Michael P. Mallardi
PRESIDENT, CABLE & INTERNATIONAL BROADCAST
GROUP
Herbert A. Granath
PRESIDENT, ABC DISTRIBUTION CO.
Joseph Y. Abrams
PRESIDENT, CAPITAL CITIES/ABC OWNED TELEVISION
STATIONS
Lawrence J. Pollock
PRESIDENT, CAPITAL CITIES/ABC NATIONAL TELEVISION
SALES
John B. Watkins
PRESIDENT, CAPITAL CITIES/ABC RADIO
James B. Arcara
PRESIDENT, CAPITAL CITIES/ABC OWNED RADIO STA-
TIONS—GROUP I
Don P. Bouloukos
PRESIDENT, CAPITAL CITIES/ABC OWNED RADIO
STATION—GROUP II
Norman S. Schrutt
PRESIDENT, ABC RADIO NETWORKS
Robert Callahan, Jr.

ABC NATIONAL TELEVISION SALES
PRESIDENT
John B. Watkins

ABC-OWNED TELEVISION STATIONS
PRESIDENT
Lawrence J. Pollock
V.P.
Robert O. Niles

DISNEY/ABC CABLE & INTERNATIONAL TELEVISION
PRESIDENT
Herbert A. Granath
PRESIDENT, ABC INTERNATIONAL OPERATIONS & EXECU-
TIVE V.P., ABC CABLE BROADCAST/EUROPEAN OPERA-
TIONS
John T. Healy
PRESIDENT, ABC EUROPEAN OPERATIONS
Richard F. Spinner
V.P., ABC CABLE INTERNATIONAL BROADCAST/EURO-
PEAN OPERATIONS
Emon Amselem
SENIOR V.P., FINANCE & ADMINISTRATION
Jeremiah G. Sullivan
V.P., FINANCIAL CONTROLS & ACCOUNTING
James R. Waltz

ABC DISTRIBUTION CO.
PRESIDENT
Joseph Y. Abrams

V.P., INTERNATIONAL TELEVISION SALES
Maria D. Komodikis
V.P., THEATRICAL/HOME VIDEO MARKETING
Michael J. Dragotto
V.P., SALES ADMINISTRATION & OPERATIONS
Carol Brokaw

ABC MULTIMEDIA GROUP
PRESIDENT
Stephen A. Weiswasser
EXECUTIVE V.P.
Bruce Maggin
V.P., FINANCE & ADMINISTRATION
Robert J. Ackley
V.P., PRODUCTION & TECHNOLOGY
Katherine Dillon

ABC VIDEO PUBLISHING
PRESIDENT
Jon R. Peisinger
V.P., PROGRAMMING & ACQUISITIONS
Cindy Bressler
V.P., FINANCE & OPERATIONS
Peter Fifield
V.P., SALES & MARKETING
Mark Gilula

BUENA VISTA TELEVISION

(see the Walt Disney Company)

CBS INC.

51 W. 52 St., New York, NY 10019. (212) 975-4321.
CBS Television City, 7800 Beverly Blvd., Los Angeles, CA 90036. (310) 852-2345.
BOARD OF DIRECTORS
Laurence A. Tisch, Michel C. Bergerac, Harold Brown, Ellen V. Futter, Henry A. Kissinger, Henry B. Schacht, Edson W. Spencer, Franklin A. Thomas, Preston R. Tisch, James D. Wolfensohn, Daniel Yankelovich.
PRESIDENT & CEO
Peter A. Lund
CFO
Fred Reynolds
SENIOR V.P., FINANCE, CBS NETWORK TELEVISION
Dennis Ganzak
V.P., MIS OPERATIONS
John Lalli
V.P., TELECOMMUNICATIONS
Thomas Maile
V.P., APPLICATIONS DEVELOPMENT
John Difronzo
V.P., MIS WEST COAST
Michael Vinyard
V.P., FINANCE
Jay Gold
V.P., FINANCE WEST COAST
Gary McCarthy
V.P., FACILITIES OPERATIONS
Kenneth Cooper
SENIOR V.P., FINANCE
Peter Keegan
SENIOR V.P., NEW VENTURES & BUSINESS DEVELOPMENT
Derek Zimmerman
V.P., FINANCIAL PLANNING
Bruce Taub
SENIOR V.P., HUMAN RESOURCES
Joan Showalter
V.P., COMPENSATION & POLICY, PERSONNEL
Karen Beldegreen
V.P., PERSONNEL BENEFITS
Anthony Ambrosio
V.P., HUMAN RESOURCES, WEST COAST
Nan Tepper
SENIOR V.P.
Martin Franks
V.P., FEDERAL POLICY, WASHINGTON
Cecilia Cole McInturff
SENIOR V.P., TECHNOLOGY
Joseph Flaherty
SENIOR V.P., COMMUNICATIONS
Gil Schwartz
V.P., CORPORATE COMMUNICATIONS
Lisa Caputo
V.P., COMMUNICATIONS, CBS ENTERTAINMENT
Christopher Ender
EXECUTIVE V.P., INDUSTRIAL RELATIONS
James F. Sirmons
V.P., INDUSTRIAL RELATIONS
Ed Yergeau

V.P., INDUSTRIAL RELATIONS, EAST COAST
Leon Schulzinger
V.P., INDUSTRIAL RELATIONS, WEST COAST
John M. McLean
EXECUTIVE V.P., GENERAL COUNSEL & SECRETARY
Ellen O. Kaden
SENIOR V.P., DEPUTY GENERAL COUNSEL
Martin P. Messinger
SENIOR V.P., DEPUTY GENERAL COUNSEL
Susan Holliday
ASSOCIATE GENERAL COUNSEL, BROADCAST
Howard Jaeckel
ASSOCIATE GENERAL COUNSEL, LITIGATION
Susanna Lowy
ASSOCIATE GENERAL COUNSEL, LABOR
Mark Engstrom
ASSOCIATE GENERAL COUNSEL, BROADCAST
Sanford Kryle
ASSOCIATE GENERAL COUNSEL
Steve Hildebrandt
ASSOCIATE GENERAL COUNSEL
Mark Johnson
ASSOCIATE GENERAL COUNSEL
Jane Cottrell
V.P., GENERAL MANAGER, EAST COAST BROADCAST OPERATIONS
Jay Fine
V.P., PRODUCTION SERVICES, EAST COAST OPERATIONS
Andrew Barry
V.P., BROADCAST DISTRIBUTION
Brent Stranathan
V.P., TECHNICAL OPERATIONS
Darcy Antonellis
V.P., FIELD OPERATIONS
Raymond W. Potter
V.P., ENGINEERING
Robert Seidel
V.P., SYSTEMS ENGINEERING
Richard Streeter
SENIOR V.P., OPERATIONS TELEVISION CITY
Charles Cappleman
V.P., PROGRAM PRODUCTION SERVICES
Stephen Schifrin
V.P., STAGE OPERATIONS
Harvey Holt
PRESIDENT, STUDIO CENTER
Michael Klausman

CBS ENTERTAINMENT DIVISION
PRESIDENT, ENTERTAINMENT & EXECUTIVE V.P., CBS INC.
Leslie Moonves
EXECUTIVE V.P., CED
Billy Campbell
V.P., PROGRAMMING, EAST COAST
Mitchell Semel
V.P., MOTION PICTURES FOR TELEVISION
Sunta Izzicupo
V.P., MINI-SERIES
Joan Harrison
SENIOR V.P., PROGRAM PLANNING & SPECIALS
Steve Warner
V.P., CURRENT PROGRAMMING
Madalene Horne
V.P., SPECIALS
Terry Botwick
V.P., TALENT & CASTING
Peter Golden
V.P., CREATIVE SERVICES/ARTIST RELATIONS
Madeline Peerce
V.P., COMEDY DEVELOPMENT
Gene Stein
V.P., DRAMA DEVELOPMENT
Anita Addison
V.P., NON-TRADITIONAL PROGRAMMING & DIRECTOR, DRAMA SERIES DEVELOPMENT
William Coveny III
SENIOR V.P., DAYTIME, CHILDREN'S PROGRAMMING & SPECIAL PROJECTS
Lucy Johnson
SENIOR V.P., BUSINESS AFFAIRS
William B. Klein
V.P., BUSINESS AFFAIRS
Layne Britton
V.P., TALENT & GUILD NEGOTIATIONS
Leola Gorius
V.P., BUSINESS AFFAIRS, LONG FORM NEGOTIATIONS & ACQUISITIONS
Sidney Lyons
V.P., BUSINESS AFFAIRS, PROGRAM RIGHTS NEGOTIATIONS
Martin Garcia

PRESIDENT, CBS ENTERTAINMENT PRODUCTIONS
Andy Hill
V.P., SERIES DEVELOPMENT
Kelly Goode
V.P., SERIES DEVELOPMENT
Glenn Adilman
V.P., MOVIES & MINISERIES
Pat Saphier

CBS NEWS DIVISION
PRESIDENT
Andrew Heyward
EXECUTIVE V.P.
Jonathan C. Klein
V.P., HARD NEWS & SPECIAL EVENTS
Lane Venardos
V.P., BUREAU MANAGER, CBS NEWS WASHINGTON
Alberto Ortiz
V.P., CBS NEWS RADIO
Larry D. Cooper
V.P., EUROPE & LONDON BUREAU CHIEF
Marcy McGinnis
V.P., NEWS SERVICES
John Frazee
V.P., FINANCE & ADMINISTRATION
James M. McKenna
V.P., BUSINESS AFFAIRS
Josie Thomas

CBS SPORTS DIVISION
PRESIDENT
David Kenin
SENIOR V.P.,
Rick Gentile
V.P., PROGRAMMING
Michael L. Aresco
V.P., PROGRAMMING
Robert Correa
V.P., BUSINESS PLANNING
Raymond Harmon
V.P., PRODUCTION SERVICES & ADMINISTRATION
James F. Harrington
V.P., BUSINESS DEVELOPMENT
Douglas P. Jacobs
V.P., BUSINESS AFFAIRS
Noel B. Berman
V.P., BUSINESS AFFAIRS
Brian Fielding

CBS TELEVISION NETWORK
PRESIDENT
James Warner
V.P., PROGRAM PRACTICES, NEW YORK
Matthew Margo
V.P., PROGRAM PRACTICES, HOLLYWOOD
Carol A. Altieri
V.P., ADMINISTRATION
Mary Lou Jennerjahn
EXECUTIVE V.P., PLANNING & RESEARCH
David Poltrack
V.P., TELEVISION AUDIENCE MEASUREMENT
Gregory Kasparian
V.P., TELEVISION RESEARCH, LOS ANGELES
Adam Gold
EXECUTIVE V.P., MARKETING & COMMUNICATIONS
George F. Schweitzer
V.P., CREATIVE DIRECTOR, ADVERTISING & PROMOTION
Jeff Kreiner
V.P., ADVERTISING & CREATIVE SERVICES
Ileene H. Mittleman
SENIOR V.P., ADVERTISING & PROMOTION
Michael Mischler
V.P., WEST COAST AFFILIATE PROMOTION
Brad Crum
V.P., MEDIA & PLANNING
Kathy Culleton
V.P., ON-AIR PROMOTION
Steven Jacobson
V.P., PROMOTION MARKETING
Anne O'Grady

CBS SALES
PRESIDENT
Joseph D. Abruzzese
V.P., BUSINESS DEVELOPMENT & MEDIA PLANNING
Elizabeth Rockwood-Fulton
V.P., NATIONAL SALES MANAGER
Daniel J. Koby
V.P., DIRECTOR, SALES & MARKETING
W. Scott McGraw
V.P., DIRECTOR, SALES & MARKETING
John P. O'Sullivan

V.P., DIRECTOR, SALES & MARKETING
Duncan E. Ryder
V.P., DIRECTOR, SALES & MARKETING
Christopher R. Simon
V.P., DIRECTOR, SALES & MARKETING
Martin B. Daly
V.P., PRIME TIME & LATE NIGHT
John Kelly
V.P., DIRECTOR, PRIME TIME & LATE NIGHT SALES
Linda Rene
V.P., DAYTIME & CHILDREN'S SALES
Michael J. Nowacki
V.P., OLYMPIC SALES & SPORTS MARKETING
Jo Ann Ross
V.P., OLYMPIC SALES
Dean Kaplan
V.P., WEST COAST SALES
John H. Gray
V.P., DETROIT SALES
Richard E. Masilotti
V.P., CENTRAL SALES
John F. Lee
V.P., SPORTS SALES
Michael A. Guariglia
V.P. & DIRECTOR, SPORTS SALES
John K. Brooks
V.P., NEWS SALES
Kenneth J. Wachtel
V.P. & GROUP HEAD, PLANNING
Dorothy S. Schwartz
V.P., MARKETING RESOURCES
Serge Del Grosso
V.P., SALES PLANNING
Russ Behrman
V.P., SALES SERVICES
Anne E. Harkins
V.P., PROGRAM SALES
William G. Cecil
V.P., PRIMETIME CENTRAL SALES
Marc Tupper

CBS AFFILIATE RELATIONS DIVISION
SENIOR V.P., AFFILIATE RELATIONS
Peter K. Scruth
V.P., DIRECTOR, AFFILIATE RELATIONS
Preston Farr
V.P., DIRECTOR, AFFILIATE RELATIONS
Frances Eigendorff
V.P., MARKETING, AFFILIATE RELATIONS
Jeffrey McIntyre

CBS ENTERPRISES
PRESIDENT, CBS ENTERPRISES & PRESIDENT, EYEMARK ENTERTAINMENT
Bob Cook
SENIOR V.P., MARKET DEVELOPMENT
Nancy Widmann
PRESIDENT, MEDIA SALES
Dan Cosgrove
V.P., MEDIA SALES, EAST COAST
Elizabeth Koman
V.P., MEDIA SALES, WEST COAST & MIDWEST
Patricia Bailey
SENIOR V.P., CREATIVE SERVICES
Owen Simon
V.P., MARKETING SERVICES
Mary Beth McAdaragh
V.P. COMMUNICATIONS
Andi Sporkin
EXECUTIVE V.P.
Marvin Shirley
V.P., FINANCE
Robert Finkel
SENIOR V.P.
Sam Cue
V.P. & GENERAL MANAGER
George Kieffer
SENIOR V.P., BUSINESS AFFAIRS
Jon Hookstratten
EXECUTIVE V.P., SYNDICATION
Barry Wallach
SENIOR V.P., SALES
William Kunkel
V.P., EASTERN SALES
Sidney Beighley
V.P., EASTERN SALES
Peter Gimber
V.P., MIDWESTERN SALES
Sean O'Boyle
V.P., SOUTHEASTERN SALES
Bradley Liedel

V.P., SOUTHWESTERN SALES
Nancy Cook
V.P., WESTERN SALES
Peter Preis
V.P., SALES SERVICES
Sunilyn Deskin
V.P., RESEARCH
Peggy Burkhardt
SENIOR V.P., PROGRAM & BUSINESS DEVELOPMENT, NY
Jim Dauphinee
SENIOR V.P., PROGRAM & BUSINESS DEVELOPMENT, LA
Robb Dalton

CBS BROADCAST INTERNATIONAL
PRESIDENT
Rainier Siek
V.P., SALES & MARKETING
Scott Michaels
V.P., MARKETING & GENERAL MANAGER, CBS VIDEO
Kenneth Ross
V.P., BUSINESS AFFAIRS & OPERATIONS
Judith Bass
V.P., RISK MANAGEMENT
Dennis D'Oca
V.P., DIRECTOR, REAL ESTATE
Elliott Matz

CBS STATIONS GROUP
PRESIDENT, CBS STATIONS GROUP & EXECUTIVE V.P.,
CBS INC.
Bill Korn
V.P., PERSONNEL
John Moran
V.P., LABOR RELATIONS
Chuck Gidel

CBS TELEVISION STATIONS
PRESIDENT
Jonathan Klein
EXECUTIVE VICE PRESIDENT
Tony Vinciquerra
V.P., FINANCE & PLANNING
Anton Guitano
V.P., CONTROLLERS
Dennis Farrell
C.P., MARKETING
Licia Hahn

CBS TELEVISION STATIONS SALES
PRESIDENT
Joseph Berwanger
V.P. & GENERAL SALES MANAGER
Greg Schaeffer
EXECUTIVE V.P.
Richard Sheingold

CBS RADIO DIVISION
PRESIDENT
Dan Mason
V.P., AM STATIONS
Ed Goldman
V.P., GENERAL MANAGER, CBS RADIO NETWORKS
Robert P. Kipperman

CHILDREN'S TELEVISION WORKSHOP
1 Lincoln Plaza, New York, NY 10023. (212) 595-3456.
CHAIRMAN—EXECUTIVE COMMITTEE
Joan Ganz Cooney
PRESIDENT—CEO
David V. B. Britt
EXECUTIVE V.P., CHIEF OPERATING OFFICER
Emily Swenson
SENIOR V.P., PRODUCTION/PROGRAMMING
Majorie Kalins
V.P., CFO
Ann Sardini
SENIOR V.P. FOR CORPORATE AFFAIRS
Gary Knell
PRESIDENT, COMMUNITY EDUCATION SERVICES
Digna Sanchez
SENIOR V.P., MARKETING & COMMUNICATIONS
Allyson Kossow Felix
SENIOR V.P. & PUBLISHER, CTW PUBLISHING GROUP
Nina B. Link
V.P. & TREASURER
Wayne W. Luteran
V.P., INTERACTIVE TECHNOLOGY
Robert L. Madell, Phd.
V.P., RESEARCH
Josephine Holz, Phd.
V.P., HUMAN RESOURCES
Lavera Johnson

SENIOR V.P., CTW INTERNATIONAL PRODUCT LICENSING &
TELEVISION GROUP
J. Baxter Urist

COLUMBIA PICTURES TELEVISION
(see Sony Pictures Entertainment TV Group)

THE WALT DISNEY COMPANY
500 South Buena Vista Street, Burbank, California 91521.
(818) 560-1000.
CHAIRMAN OF THE BOARD, PRESIDENT & CEO
Michael D. Eisner
PRESIDENT
Michael Ovitz
VICE CHAIRMAN OF THE BOARD
Roy E. Disney
EXECUTIVE V.P. & CHIEF STRATEGIC OFFICER
Lawrence P. Murphy
EXECUTIVE V.P., LAW & HUMAN RESOURCES/ CHIEF OF
CORPORATE OPERATIONS
Sanford Litvack
EXECUTIVE V.P., CORPORATE AFFAIRS
John F. Cooke
SENIOR V.P. & CFO
Richard Nanula
V.P., PLANNING & CONTROL
John Garand
CORPORATE SECRETARY
Marsha L. Reed

WALT DISNEY TELEVISION & TOUCHSTONE TELEVISION
500 South Buena Vista St., Burbank, CA 91521. (818) 560-
5000.
CHAIRMAN
Walter C. Liss, Jr.
PRESIDENT, NETWORK TELEVISION
Dean Valentine
SENIOR V.P., TELEVISION PRODUCTION
Mitch Ackerman
SENIOR V.P., TELEVISION CASTING
Eugene Blythe
SENIOR V.P., NETWORK TELEVISION
John Litvack
SENIOR V.P., WALT DISNEY TELEVISION & TELECOMMUNI-
CATIONS
Laurie Younger
V.P., WRITER, DEVELOPMENT & SPECIAL PROJECTS
Janet Blake
V.P., MOVIES & MINISERIES, NETWORK TELEVISION
Ricka Fisher
V.P., VIDEOTAPE PRODUCTION
Ted Kaye
V.P., DEVELOPMENT, NETWORK TELEVISION
David Kissinger
V.P., CURRENT PROGRAMS, NETWORK TELEVISION
Jan Nash
V.P., TV PRODUCTION FINANCE
Walter O'Neal
V.P., POST PRODUCTION, TELEVISION
Grady Jones
V.P., ADVERTISING/PUBLICITY/PROMOTION
Marian Effinger
V.P., NETWORK TELEVISION BUSINESS AFFAIRS
Scottye Hedstrom
V.P., NETWORK TV BUSINESS AFFAIRS
Rosalind Marks
V.P., NETWORK TELEVISION LEGAL AFFAIRS
Michael Moloney
V.P., NETWORK TV FINANCE
Joanna Spak
V.P., RESEARCH
Joanne Burns
V.P., LABOR RELATIONS
Robert W. Johnson
V.P., PARTICIPATION & RESIDUALS
William Clark
V.P., PAY TELEVISION SALES & ADMINISTRATION
Wendy Ferren

WALT DISNEY TELEVISION ANIMATION
500 South Buena Vista St., Burbank, CA 91521. (818) 560-5000.
PRESIDENT
Gary Krisel
SENIOR V.P., DEVELOPMENT
Bruce Cranston
SENIOR V.P., DOMESTIC PRODUCTION
Tom Ruzicka
V.P., INTERNATIONAL PRODUCTION
Lenora Hume

V.P., ANIMATION TECHNOLOGY
Rob Hummel
V.P., BUSINESS AFFAIRS
Mark Kenchelian
V.P., FINANCE
Fred Paccone
VICE PRESIDENT, SERIES DEVELOPMENT
Barry Blumberg
VICE PRESIDENT, MUSIC
Bambi Moe
VICE PRESIDENT, CURRENT PROGRAMMING
Jat Fukuto
VICE PRESIDENT, DIRECT-TO-VIDEO
Sharon Morill

BUENA VISTA TELEVISION
500 South Buena Vista St., Burbank, CA 91521. (818) 560-5000.
CHIARMAN
Walter C. Liss, Jr.
PRESIDENT
Mort Marcus
SENIOR V.P., SALES
Janice Marinelli-Mazza
V.P./GENERAL SALES MANAGER—EAST COAST
Tom Cerio
V.P./GENERAL SALES MANAGER—WEST COAST
Jim Packer
V.P./SOUTHEAST REGIONAL MANAGER
John Bryan
V.P./EASTERN REGIONAL MANAGER
Lloyd Komesar
V.P., MIDWEST REGIONAL MANAGER
John Rouse
V.P., OPERATIONS & SALES DEVELOPMENT
Helen Faust
SENIOR V.P., AD SALES
Mike Shaw
V.P., AD SALES—MIDWEST
Jim Engleman
V.P., AD SALES
Norman Lesser
V.P., AD SALES
Howard Levy
V.P., RESEARCH—AD SALES
Noreen McGrath
V.P., OPERATIONS—AD SALES
Eddie Meister
SENIOR V.P./BUSINESS AFFAIRS
Kenneth D. Werner
V.P., FINANCE, PLANNING & DISTRIBUTION
Andrew Lewis
V.P., ADVERTISING & CREATIVE SERVICES
Sal Sardo
V.P., MARKETING
Mark Workman
V.P., PUBLICITY
Marian Effinger
V.P., RESEARCH
Joanne Burns

WALT DISNEY INTERNATIONAL TELEVISION
Beaumont House, Kensington Village, Avonmore Road,
London W14 8TS ENGL& (171) 605-2400.
PRESIDENT
Etienne de Villiers
SENIOR V.P. & MANAGING DIRECTOR/ASIA PACIFIC
Ed Borgerding
SENIOR V.P. & MANAGING DIRECTOR/ BROADCASTING
David Simon
V.P. MARKETING
Selby Hall
V.P. TELEVISION/CANADA
Orest Olijnyk
V.P. LEGAL & BUSINESS AFFAIRS
Sally Davies
V.P., SALES
Simon Kenny

THE DISNEY CHANNEL
3800 West Alameda Avenue, Burbank, CA 91505. (818) 569-7500.
PRESIDENT
Anne Sweeney
SENIOR V.P., BUSINESS & LEGAL AFFAIRS
Frederick Kuperberg
SENIOR V.P., FINANCE & ADMINISTRATION
Patrick Lopker
SENIOR V.P., MARKETING
Eleanor Hensleigh

SENIOR V.P., ORIGINAL SPECIALS & PROGRAM
ACQUISITIONS
Douglas Zwick
SENIOR V.P., PROGRAMMING & PRODUCTION
Richard Ross
SENIOR V.P., SALES & MARKETING
Charles Nooney

BUENA VISTA PAY TELEVISION
350 South Buena Vista Street, Burbank, CA 91521. (818) 560-1000.
CHAIRMAN
Walter C. Liss, Jr.
SENIOR V.P., BUSINESS & LEGAL AFFAIRS
John J. Reagan
V.P., BUSINESS & LEGAL AFFAIRS
Dennis Dort
V.P., PAY TV
Wendy Ferren
V.P., SALES & OPERATIONS, PAY TV
Julie Jenkins

EASTMAN KODAK COMPANY

343 State St., Rochester, NY 14650-0310. (716) 724-4000.
6700 Santa Monica Blvd., Hollywood, CA 90038. (213) 464-6131.
360 W. 31 St., New York, NY 10001. (212) 631-3450.
1901 W. 22nd St., Oakbrook, IL 60521-1283. (708) 218-5175.
4 Concourse Parkway, Suite 300, Atlanta, GA 30328. (800) 800-8398.
2800 Forest Lane, Dallas, TX 75234. (214) 919-3444.
CHAIRMAN, PRESIDENT & CEO
George M.C. Fisher
PRESIDENT, ENTERTAINMENT IMAGING
Joerg D. Agin
COO, PROFESSIONAL MOTION IMAGING
Richard P. Aschman
GENERAL MANAGER, DIGITAL MOTION IMAGING
Aidan P. Foley

FOX INC.

(A subsidiary of the News Corporation) P.O. Box 900, Beverly
Hills, CA 90213. (310) 277-2211. Fox Inc. is the parent company
of Fox Broadcasting Co., Fox Television Stations Inc., Twentieth
Century Fox Film Corporation.
CHAIRMAN & CEO, THE NEWS CORPORATION
Rupert Murdoch

FOX BROACASTING COMPANY
P.O. Box 900, Beverly Hills, CA 90213-0900. (310) 369-1000.
New York office: 1211 Avenue of the Americas, 3rd fl., New
York, NY 10036. (212) 556-2400.
Chicago office: 444 N. Michigan Ave., Chicago, IL 60611. (312) 494-2800.
CHAIRMAN & CEO, FOX TELEVISION
Chase Carey
CHAIRMAN & CEO, FOX NEWS
Roger Ailes
PRESIDENT & COO, FOX TV
David Hill
PRESIDENT, FOX ENTERTAINMENT GROUP
Peter Roth
PRESIDENT, SALES
Jon Nesvig
EXECUTIVE V.P., STORYMAKER, FOX CHILDREN'S
NETWORK
Karen Barnes
EXECUTIVE V.P., ON-AIR PROMOTIONS & PRINT
ADVERTISING
Geoff Calnan
EXECUTIVE V.P., NETWORK DISTRIBUTION
Lana Corbi
EXECUTIVE V.P., COMEDY/DRAMA DEVELOPMENT
Robert Greenblatt
EXECUTIVE V.P. & CFO
Larry Jacobson
EXECUTIVE V.P., BUSINESS AFFAIRS
Ira Kurgan
EXECUTIVE V.P., MARKETING
Stacey Marks-Bronner
EXECUTIVE V.P., LEGAL
Eric Yeldell
SENIOR V.P., GOVERNMENT RELATIONS
Peggy Binzell
SENIOR V.P., ON-AIR PROMOTIONS
Robert Bourknight
SENIOR V.P., TALENT & CASTING
Bob Harbin

SENIOR V.P., PRINT ADS & SPECIAL PROJECTS
Cindy Hauser
SENIOR V.P.,SENIOR V.P., PUBLICITY/PUBLIC RELATIONS
Richard Licata
SENIOR V.P., RESEARCH & MARKETING
Giles Lundberg
SENIOR V.P., CREATIVE SERVICES
George Oswald
SENIOR V.P., NETWORK DISTRIBUTION
Victoria Quoss
SENIOR V.P., SALES
Jean Rossi
SENIOR V.P., NATIONAL PROMOTIONS
Mark Stroman
SENIOR V.P., BUSINESS AFFAIRS
Rich Vokulich
SENIOR V.P., SALES PROPOSALS & ADMINISTRATION
Susan Wachter
SENIOR V.P., LONG-FORM PROGRAMMING
Trevor Walton

FOX SPORTS
PRESIDENT & COO, FOX TV, PRESIDENT FOX SPORTS,
CEO FOX SPORTS NET
David Hill
EXEC. V.P., MARKETING & PROMOTIONS, FOX SPORTS
Traci Dolgin
EXEC. V.P., PRODUCTIONS, EXEC. PROD. FOX SPORTS
Edward Goren
EXECUTIVE V.P., BUSINESS OPERATIONS, FOX SPORTS
Larry Jones
EXECUTIVE V.P., FOX SPORTS
George Krieger
SENIOR V.P., SPORTS SALES
James Burnette
SENIOR V.P., FOX SPORTS
George Greenberg

FOX TELEVISION STATIONS INC.
5746 Sunset Blvd., Los Angeles, CA 90028. (213) 856-1000.
PRESIDENT & CHIEF OPERATING OFFICER
Mitchell Stern
EXECUTIVE V.P., NEWS
Ian Rae
SENIOR V.P., LEGAL AFFAIRS
Gerald Friedman
V.P., PERSONNEL
Jean Fuentes
V.P., BUSINESS & LEGAL AFFAIRS
Daphne Gronich
V.P., PROGRAMMING/PROMOTIONS
Suzanne Horenstein
V.P., CONTROLLER
Kathy Maloney
V.P., FINANCE
Betsy Swanson

TWENTIETH CENTURY FOX TELEVISION
P.O. Box 900, Beverly Hills, CA 90213. (310) 277-2211. A divi-
sion of Fox Film Corp.
PRESIDENT
Peter Roth
EXECUTIVE V.P., PRODUCTION & FINANCE
Charlie Goldstein
EXECUTIVE V.P., TELEVISION BUSINESS & LEGAL AFFAIRS
Gary Newman
SENIOR V.P., TELEVISION PRODUCTION
Joel Hornstock
SENIOR V.P., CURRENT PROGRAMMING
Ken Horton
SENIOR V.P., FINANCE
Robert Barron
SENIOR V.P., TELEVISION POST-PRODUCTION
Edward Nassour
SENIOR V.P., TALENT & CASTING
Randy Stone
SENIOR V.P., CREATIVE AFFAIRS
Dawn Tarnofsky

INTERNATIONAL
PRESIDENT, INTERNATIONAL TV
Mark Kaner
EXECUTIVE V.P., INTERNATIONAL TV
Marion Edwards
EXECUTIVE V.P., INTERNATIONAL SALES & DISTRIBUTION
Julian Levin
SENIOR V.P., INTERNATIONAL MARKETING
Scott Neeson
SENIOR V.P., EUROPEAN/NEAR EAST & AFRICA
Jorge Canizares
SENIOR V.P., INTERNATIONAL TV
Ken Bettsteller

**GOLDWYN ENTERTAINMENT COMPANY
(A METROMEDIA ENTERTAINMENT GROUP
COMPANY)**
10203 Santa Monica Blvd., Suite 500, Los Angeles, CA 90067.
(310) 552-2255. FAX: (310) 284-8493.
CHAIRMAN & CEO
Samuel Goldwyn, Jr.
PRESIDENT & CEO
Meyer Gottlieb
SENIOR V.P., BUSINESS AFFAIRS
Norman Flicker
SENIOR V.P., TREASURER & CFO
Hans W. Turner
V.P., TV PRODUCTION & DEVELOPMENT
Dan Smith
V.P., ACQUISITIONS
Rosanne Korenberg

MCA TV
100 Universal Plaza, Universal City, CA 91608. (818) 777-
1000. FAX: (818) 777-8221. (Distributor. A subsidiary of MCA,
Inc. as is Universal Television, the production arm. See sepa-
rate listing.)
CHAIRMAN, MCA TV GROUP
Greg Meidel
EXECUTUVE V.P., & CFO
Bob Fleming
SENIOR V.P., MEDIA RELATIONS
Libby Gill
PRESIDENT, MCA WORLDWIDE TV DISTRIBUTION
Jim McNamara
EXECUTIVE V.P., FIRST RUN PROGRAMMING
Ned Nalle
SENIOR V.P., FIRST RUN & NETWORK REALITY
PROGRAMMING
Arthur Smith
SENIOR V.P., DRAMA DEVELOPMENT
Dan Filie
SENIOR V.P., ADVERTISING & PROMOTION
Susan Kantor
SENIOR V.P., LEGAL & BUSINESS AFFAIRS
Sara Rutenberg
SENIOR V.P., RESEARCH
Lonnie Burstein
SENIOR V.P., SYNDICATION DISTRIBUTION
Bill Vrbanic
V.P., SALES, WESTERN REGION
Bill Trotter
V.P., AFFILIATE RELATIONS
Georgia Scott
V.P., MEDiA RELATIONS
Jim Benson
MANAGER, WESTER REGION
Barbara Zaneri

BRANCH OFFICES

EASTERN
1755 Broadway, 6th Fl., New York, NY 10019. (212) 841-8200.
FAX: (212) 841-8087.
EXECUTIVE V.P.,, SALES, MCA TV
Steve Rosenberg
SENIOR V.P., EASTERN SALES
Arthur Hasson

SOUTHWESTERN
12740 Hillcrest Rd., Suite 115, Dallas, TX 75230. (214) 386-
6400. FAX: (214) 386-5906.
V.P., SOUTHWEST REGION
Cameron Hutton
SOUTHWEST REGION SALES EXECUTIVE
Dennis Grandolas

SOUTHEASTERN
5901-C Peachtree Dunwoody Rd., N.E., Suite 440, Atlanta,
GA 30328. (404) 698-8330. FAX: (404) 698-8411.
V.P., SOUTHEAST REGION
Tony Fasola
Michael Howard

CENTRAL-MIDWEST
435 N. Michigan Ave., Suite 515, Chicago, IL 60611. (312)
337-1100. FAX: (312) 822-9703.
V.P., MIDWEST REGION
Mark Forgea
MIDWEST REGION MANAGERS
Kristine Orr
Gene McGuire

UNIVERSAL TELEVISION

(A division of Universal City Studios Inc, a subsidiary of MCA Inc.)
100 Universal City Plaza, Universal City, CA 91608. (818) 777-1000.
PRESIDENT, UNIVERSAL TELEVISION
Tom Thayer
EXECUTIVE V.P., BUSINESS AFFAIRS & ADMINISTRATION
Susan Workman
EXECUTIVE V.P., PRODUCTION
Jim Watters
SENIOR V.P., BUSINESS AFFAIRS
Dave Mayer
SENIOR V.P., MUSIC
Derek Platt
SENIOR V.P., LEGAL AFFAIRS
Dick Silliman
SENIOR V.P., DRAmATIC DEVELOPMENT
William Hamm
SENIOR V.P., CURRENT PROGRAMMING
Cheryl Bloch
V.P., TV CASTING
Nancy Perkins
V.P., UNIVERSAL TELEVISION
Charles Engel
V.P., BUSINESS AFFAIRS
James Brock
V.P., COMEDY DEVELOPMENT
Maria Grasso
V.P., PUBLICITY
Neil Schubert
V.P., DRAMATIC DEVELOPMENT
Pat Wells
V.P., POST PRODUCTION
Bruce Sandzimier

MCA TELEVISION ENTERTAINMENT

100 Universal City Plaza, Universal City, CA 91608. (818) 777-1000.
PRESIDENT
Barbara Fisher
EXECUTIVE V.P.
Bob Kelley

MCA INTERNATIONAL

100 Universal City Plaza, Universal City, CA 91608. (818) 777-1000.
PRESIDENT, MCA WORLDWIDE TV DISTRIBUTION
Jim McNamara
EXECUTIVE V.P.
Peter Hughes
V.P., AUSTRALIA & FAR EAST
Pal Cleary
V.P. & GENERAL MANAGER, CANADA
Ron Suter
V.P., ENGLAND & FRANCE
Roger Cordjohn
V.P., FRANCE
Hendrik Van Daalen

MTM ENTERTAINMENT, INC.

12700 Ventura Blvd., Suite 200, Studio City, CA 91604. (818) 755-2400. Organized 1970. (TV program production)
CHAIRMAN PRESIDENT & CEO
Anthony Thomopoulos
PRESIDENT, DISTRIBUTION
Charles Larsen
PRESIDENT, TELEVISION
Michael Ogiens

METRO-GOLDWYN-MAYER INC.

2500 Broadway St., Santa Monica, CA 90404-3061. (310) 449-3000. FAX: (310) 449-3100.
1350 Avenue of the Americas, New York, NY 10019-4870. (212) 708-0300. FAX: (212) 708-0337.
CHAIRMAN OF THE BOARD & CEO
Frank G. Mancuso
PRESIDENT OF WORLDWIDE THEATRICAL DISTRIBUTION
Larry Gleason
PRESIDENT OF MGM DOMESTIC TELEVISION DISTRIBUTION
Sid Cohen
PRESIDENT, WORLDWIDE MARKETING—THEATRICAL
Gerry Rich
EXECUTIVE V.P.
Michael S. Hope
EXECUTIVE V.P.
A. Robert Pisano
EXECUTIVE V.P., STRATEGY & DEVELOPMENT
Alan Cole-Ford

EXECUTIVE V.P., CORPORATE AFFAIRS
William A. Jones
EXECUTIVE V.P., GENERAL COUNSEL
David G. Johnson
EXECUTIVE V.P., WORLDWIDE PUBLICITY
Susan Pile
SENIOR V.P., LABOR RELATIONS
Benjamin B. Kahane
SENIOR V.P. & DEPUTY GENERAL COUNSEL
Robert Brada
SENIOR V.P. & DEPUTY GENERAL COUNSEL
Rebecca Laurie Ford
SENIOR V.P. & DEPUTY GENERAL COUNSEL
Mark Fleischer
SENIOR V.P. & FINANCIAL OPERATIONS
Daniel J. Rosett
V.P., INFORMATION SERVICES
Kim Spenchian
V.P., CORPORATE AFFAIRS
Maria C. Angeletti
V.P., TAXES
Deborah J. Arvesen
V.P., CORPORATE COMMUNICATIONS
Anne Corley
V.P., LABOR RELATIONS
Mark Crowley
V.P., LABOR RELATIONS
Patty F. Mayer

MGM/UA TELECOMMUNICATIONS GROUP

PRESIDENT, MGM/UA TELECOMMUNICATIONS GROUP
Gary Marenzi
SENIOR V.P., SALES & BUSINESS DEVELOPMENT
William Lee
SENIOR V.P., CREATIVE & BUSINESS AFFAIRS
Marcia Spielholz
SENIOR V.P., SALES & CO-PRODUCTIONS, EUROPE, MIDDLE EAST & AFRICA
Gilbert de Turenne

MGM WORLDWIDE TELEVISION INC.

2500 Broadway St., Santa Monica, CA 90404-3061. (310) 449-3000.
PRESIDENT, WORLDWIDE TELEVISION
John P. Symes
PRESIDENT, MGM DOMESTIC TELEVISION DISTRIBUTION
Sid Cohen
EXECUTIVE V.P., MGM ANIMATION
Donald Mirisch
EXECUTIVE V.P., DOMESTIC TELEVISION DISTRIBUTION
Noranne Frisby
SENIOR V.P., BUSINESS AFFAIRS
Cecelia Andrews
SENIOR V.P., CREATIVE AFFAIRS
Hank Cohen
SENIOR V.P., TELEVISION FINANCE & ADMINISTRATION
Thomas Malanga
SENIOR V.P.,PRODUCTION
Mel Swope
SENIOR V.P., TELEVISION SALES, CANADA
Tony Leadman
SENIOR V.P., EASTERN DIVISION, DOMESTIC TELEVISION
Jacqueline E. Comeau
SENIOR V.P., CENTRAL DIVISION, DOMESTIC TELEVISION
Steven Hodder
SENIOR V.P., WESTERN SALES DIVISION—DOMESTIC TELEVISION DISTRIBUTION
Donald Golden
SENIOR V.P, ADVERTISING & PROMOTIONS
Dea Shandera
V.P., SOUTHWESTERN DIVISION,DOMESTIC TELEVISION DISTRIBUTION
Frank Hussey

MOTION PICTURE CORPORATION OF AMERICA (A METROMEDIA ENTERTAINMNT GROUP COMPANY)

1401 Ocean Ave., #301, Santa Monica, CA 90401. (310) 319-9500. FAX: (310) 319-9501.
CO-PRESIDENT & TREASURER
Brad Krevoy
CO-PRESIDENT & TREASURER
Steven B. Stabler
EXECUTIVE V.P.
Jeffrey Ivers
SENIOR V.P. & ASSISTANT SECRETARY
John W. Hester
EXECUTIVE V.P., TELEVISION
Paul Frank

NATIONAL BROADCASTING CO., INC.
30 Rockefeller Plaza, New York, NY 10112. (212) 664- 4444.
Registered Telegraphic Address: NAT-BROCAST, NY.
3000 W. Alameda Blvd., Burbank, CA 91523. (818) 840-4444.
4001 Nebraska Ave., NW, Washington, DC 20001. (202) 885-4000.
Government Relations & Law Offices: 1299 Pennsylvania Ave.
N.W., 11th fl., Washington, DC 20004. (202) 833-3600.
PRESIDENT & CEO
Robert Wright
PRESIDENT, NBC ENTERPRISES & EXECUTIVE V.P.,
NBC PRODUCTIONS
John Agoglia
SENIOR V.P. & CFO
Warren C. Jenson
EXECUTIVE V.P. & GENERAL COUNSEL
Richard Cotton
PRESIDENT, NBC SPORTS
Dick Ebersol
PRESIDENT, NBC NEWS
Andrew Lack
SENIOR V.P., CORPORATE COMMUNICATIONS
Judy Smith
PRESIDENT, NBC TELEVISION STATIONS
John Rohrbeck
EXECUTIVE V.P., TECHNOLOGY
Michael Sherlock
PRESIDENT, NBC ENTERTAINMENT
Warren Littlefield
PRESIDENT, NBC TELEVISION NETWORK
Neil Braun
PRESIDENT, CABLE BUSINESS DEVELOPMENT
& EXECUTIVE V.P.
Thomas Rogers
EXECUTIVE V.P., EMPLOYEE RELATIONS
Edward L. Scanlon
PRESIDENT, BROADCAST/NETWORK OPERATIONS
Randall Falco

NBC ENTERTAINMENT
PRESIDENT, NBC WEST COAST
Don Ohlmeyer
PRESIDENT, NBC ENTERTAINMENT
Warren Littlefield
EXECUTIVE V.P., ADVERTISING & PROMOTION & EVENT
PROGRAMMING
John Miller
SENIOR V.P., PROGRAM PLANNING & SCHEDULING
Preston Beckman
SENIOR V.P., MINI-SERIES & MOTION PICTURES FOR TV
Lindy DeKoven
SENIOR V.P., SPECIALS, VARIETY PROGRAMS, & LATE
NIGHT PROGRAMS
Richard Ludwin
SENIOR V.P., ADVERTISING & PROMOTION
Vince Manze
SENIOR V.P., TALENT & CASTING
Lori Openden
V.P., PRINT ADVERTISING
Jenness Brewer
V.P., MOVIES & MINISERIES FOR TV
Jody Brockway
V.P., PRIME TIME SERIES
Karey Burke
V.P., PRIME TIME SERIES
Edward Frank
V.P., AFFILIATE ADVERTISING & PROMOTION SERVICES
Deborah Hamberlin
V.P., SPECIAL PROJECTS ON-AIR PROMOTION
Ron Hayes
V.P., ADVERTISING & PROMOTION, EAST COAST
Jeff Kreiner
V.P., PRIME TIME SERIES
John Landgraf
V.P., PRIME TIME SERIES
Linda Mancuso
V.P., PRIME TIME SERIES
Charisse McGhee-Lazarou
V.P., PRIME TIME SERIES
Stephen McPherson
V.P., PRIME TIME SERIES
David Nevins
V.P., ON-AIR PROMOTION
Jim Vescera

NBC CABLE & BUSINESS DEVELOPMENT
PRESIDENT & EXECUTIVE V.P.
Thomas Rogers
PRESIDENT, CNBC
Albert Barber

NBC TV NETWORK
PRESIDENT
Neil Braun
PRESIDENT, NETWORK SALES
Larry Hoffner
V.P., EASTERN SALES
Mel Berning
V.P./GENERAL MANAGER, EASTERN SALES
Mike Mandelker
SENIOR V.P., MARKETING
Andrew Capone
SENIOR V.P., NETWORK DEVELOPMENT
Robert Niles
V.P., NETWORK SALES PLANNING & PRICING
William Caulfield
V.P., AFFILIATE RELATIONS EAST & MARKETING
Jean Dietz
V.P., TV NETWORK OPERATIONS
John Dewald
SENIOR V.P., BROADCAST ST&ARDS & PRACTICES
Rosalyn Weinman
V.P., CENTRAL NATIONAL SALES
Richard Schade
V.P., DETROIT SALES
J. Nicholls Spain Jr.
SENIOR V.P., AFFILIATE RELATIONS
John Damiano
V.P., AFFILIATE RELATIONS (MOUNTAIN & PACIFIC),
ENTERTAINMENT
William Fouch
SENIOR V.P., RESEARCH
Nicholas Schiavone
V.P., SPORTS SALES
Keith Turner
V.P., AFFILIATE RELATIONS (CENTRAL), SPORTS
Carl Schweinler
V.P., NETWORK MARKETING
Barry Goodman
V.P., WEST COAST SALES
Steve Agase
V.P., SALES DEVELOPMENT
James Hicks

NBC WASHINGTON GOVERNMENT RELATIONS
V.P. WASHINGTON
James H. Rowe III
V.P. GOVERNMENT RELATIONS
Terence P. Mahony

LEGAL
EXECUTIVE V.P. & GENERAL COUNSEL
Richard Cotton
V.P., LEGAL POLICY & PLANNING
Ellen Agress
SENIOR V.P., LAW, NEW YORK
Steve Stander
V.P., LAW, WEST COAST
Anne Egerton

NEWS DIVISION
PRESIDENT, NBC NEWS
Andrew Lack
V.P.S, NBC NEWS
Bill Wheatley
Cheryl Gould
David Corvo
PRESIDENT, NBC NEWS CHANNEL
Robert Horner
SENIOR V.P. & WASHINGTON BUREAU CHIEF
Timothy J. Russert
DIRECTOR, SPECIAL PROJECTS
Lloyd Siegal
V.P., TALENT DEVELOPMENT
Elena Nachmanoff

BROADCAST & NETWORK OPERATIONS
PRESIDENT, BROADCAST & NETWORK OPERATIONS
Randall Falco
V.P., BROADCAST & ENTERTAINMENT OPERATIONS
Frank Accarrino
V.P., NETWORK NEWS FIELD OPERATIONS
Stacy Brady
V.P., BROADCAST & NETWORK ENGINEERING
Charles Jablonski
V.P., BROADCAST & NETWORK FACILITIES PLANNING
Crawford McGill
V.P., SPORTS OPERATIONS & NETWORK TRANSMISSION
Michael Meehan
V.P., ENTERTAINMENT PRODUCTION OPERATIONS,
WEST COAST
James Powell

V.P., PRODUCTION & NETWORK SYSTEMS
David Rabinowitz
V.P., NEWS PRODUCTION OPERATIONS
David Schmerler

TECHNOLOGY DIVISION
EXECUTIVE V.P., SOURCING, REAL ESTATE & FACILITIES
Michael Sherlock
V.P., TECHNOLOGY
Peter Smith

PERSONNEL & LABOR RELATIONS
EXECUTIVE V.P., EMPLOYEE RELATIONS, NBC
Edward Scanlon
V.P., EMPLOYEE RELATIONS, WEST COAST
Wayne Rickert
V.P., LABOR RELATIONS, WEST COAST
Bernard Gehan
V.P., ORGANIZATION & MANAGEMENT RESOURCES PLANNING
Jeffrey Trullinger
V.P., LABOR RELATIONS
Day Krolik, III
V.P., EMPLOYEE RELATIONS, CNBC
Adria Alpert Romm

CORPORATE COMMUNICATIONS
SENIOR V.P., CORPORATE COMMUNICATIONS
Judy Smith
V.P., TALENT RELATIONS & MEDIA SERVICES, WEST COAST
Kathleen Tucci
V.P., CORPORATE & MEDIA RELATIONS, WEST COAST
Pat Schultz

SPORTS
PRESIDENT
Dick Ebersol
V.P.
Gary Zenkel
V.P., OLYMPIC PROGRAMMING
Peter Diamond
SENIOR V.P.
Jonathan Miller
V.P., SPORTS NEGOTIATIONS
John Ertmann
V.P., AFFILIATE SERVICES & PROGRAMMING
Mike Meehan
V.P., AFFILIATE SERVICES & PROGRAM PLANNING
Richard Hussey

TELEVISION STATIONS
PRESIDENT, NBC TELEVISION STATIONS
John Rohrbeck
V.P., FINANCE & OPERATIONS
Robert Finnerty
PRESIDENT & GENERAL MANAGER, WMAQ-TV, CHICAGO
Lyle Banks
GENERAL MANAGER, WCAU-TV, PHILADELPHIA
Pat Wallace
PRESIDENT & GENERAL MANAGER, KNBC-TV, LOS ANGELES
Carole Black
PRESIDENT & GENERAL MANAGER, WNBC-TV, NEW YORK
Dennis Swanson
PRESIDENT & GENERAL MANAGER, WRC-TV, WASHINGTON DC
Allan Horlick
PRESIDENT & GENERAL MANAGER, WTVJ, MIAMI
Don Brown
PRESIDENT & GENERAL MANAGER, KCNC, DENVER
Roger Ogden
V.P., TVSD RESEARCH
Barbara Tenney

NBC PRODUCTIONS
PRESIDENT, CREATIVE AFFAIRS
Michael Zinberg
EXECUTIVE V.P., CREATIVE AFFAIRS
Gary Considine
V.P., CURRENT SERIES
Joann Alfano
V.P., PRODUCTION BUSINESS AFFAIRS
Lorna Bitensky
V.P., CREATIVE AFFAIRS
Michael Browne
V.P., POST PRODUCTION
Joe Dervin
V.P., MOVIES & MINISERIES
Laurie Goldstein
V.P., TAPE PRODUCTION
Nina Lederman

V.P., PRODUCTION & MARKETING BUSINESS AFFAIRS
Albert Spevak
V.P., FILM PRODUCTION
Jim McGee
V.P., FILM PRODUCTION
Johanna Persons
V.P., PRODUCTION & MARKETING BUSINESS
Albert Spevak

NBC ENTERPRISES
PRESIDENT NBC ENTERPRISES
John Agoglia
SENIOR V.P., NBC ENTERPRISES, EAST COAST
Susan Beckett
SENIOR V.P., BUSINESS AFFAIRS & ADMINISTRATION
Harold Brook
SENIOR V.P., BUSINESS AFFAIRS
Joe Bures
V.P., BUSINESS AFFAIRS
Donald Gadsden
V.P., PROGRAM & TALENT CONTRACTS
Richard Nathan
V.P., BUSINESS AFFAIRS
Marjorie Neufeld

FINANCE
SENIOR V.P. & CFO
Warren C. Jenson
PRESIDENT, TREASURY & ADMINISTRATION
Arthur Angstreich
V.P., CORPORATE EVENTS & TRAVEL SERVICES
Victor Garvey
V.P., FORECASTING
Edward Swindler
V.P. NEWS & FINANCE
Daniel J. Renaldo
CFO, NBC INTERNATIONAL
John W. Eck
V.P., CORPORATE FINANCE
Lawrence R. Rutkowski
V.P., BROADCAST & NETWORK OPERATIONS
Peter J. Haas

NEW LINE TELEVISION
888 Seventh Ave., New York, NY 10106. (212) 649-4900. FAX: (212) 649-4966.
PRESIDENT, NEW LINE TELEVISION
Robert Friedman
EXECUTIVE V.P., PRODUCTION/DEVELOPMENT
Sasha Emerson
EXECUTIVE V.P., DOMESTIC TELEVISION DISTRIBUTION
David Spiegelman
EXECUTIVE V.P., INTERNATIONAL TELEVISION
Diane Keating
SENIOR V.P., TELEVISION PRODUCTION
Cindy Hornickel
SENIOR V.P., MARKETING
Christopher Russo
SENIOR V.P., MERCHANDISING & LICENSING
David Imhoff
SENIOR V.P., SALES ADMINISTRATION
Vicky Gregorian
V.P., TELEVISION & ANCILLARY ACCOUNTING
Frank Buquicchio
V.P., PRODUCTION & DEVELOPMENT
Laura Armstrong

NEW WORLD ENTERTAINMENT
(Please see Fox, Inc.)
1440 S. Sepulveda Blvd., Los Angeles, 90025. (310) 444-8100. FAX: (310) 444-8101.

ORION PICTURES CORPORATION (A METROMEDIA ENTERTAINMENT GROUP COMPANY)
1888 Century Park East, Los Angeles, CA 90067. (310) 282-0550. FAX: (310) 201-0798
CHAIRMAN OF THE BOARD
John W. Kluge
VICE CHAIRMAN
Stuart Sobotnick
PRESIDENT & CEO
Leonard White

ORION HOME ENTERTAINMENT CORPORATION
CHAIRMAN OF THE BOARD & CEO
Leonard White
EXECUTIVE V.P.
Herbert N. Dorfman

EXECUTIVE V.P., GENERAL COUNSEL & SECRETARY
John W. Hester
SENIOR V.P. & CFO
Cynthia Friedman
SENIOR V.P., MARKETING
Susan Blodgett
SENIOR V.P., ADMINISTRATION
Gerald Sobczak
V.P., BUSINESS DEVELOPMENT
Nancy Jones

ORION HOME VIDEO
PRESIDENT
Herbert N. Dorfman
V.P., SALES
Michael Katchman

ORION TELEVISION ENTERTAINMENT
EXECUTIVE V.P.
Joseph D. Indelli
V.P., DOMESTIC TELEVISION DISTRIBUTION
Mike Davis

ORION PICTURES INTERNATIONAL
PRESIDENT
Kathryn Cass
V.P., TELEVISION SALES & ADMINISTRATION
Rovert Davie
V.P., SALES & CONTRACT ADMINISTRATION
Rene Soraggi
V.P., INTERNATIONAL SALES
Dean Shapiro

PARAMOUNT TELEVISION GROUP

(See Viacom, Inc.)

PUBLIC BROADCASTING SERVICE

1320 Braddock Place, Alexandria, VA 22314-1698. (703) 739-5000.
1790 Broadway, 16th floor, New York, NY 10019-1412. (212) 708-3000.
5757 Wilshire Blvd., Suite 639, Los Angeles, CA 90036. (213) 965-5265.
PRESIDENT & CEO
Ervin S. Duggan
EXECUTIVE V.P, PBS SYSTEM SERVICE & COO
Robert Ottenhoff
EXECUTIVE V.P., PBS LEARNING VENTURES
John Hollar
EXECUTIVE V.P., PROGRAMMING & CHIEF PROGRAMMING
EXECUTIVE
Kathy Quattrone
EXECUTIVE V.P., LEARNING SERVICES
Sandra H. Welch
SENIOR V.P., DEVELOPMENT & CORPORATE RELATIONS
Jonathan C. Abbott
SENIOR V.P., PROGRAM BUSINESS AFFAIRS
M. Peter Downey
SENIOR V.P., ADVERTISING, PROMOTION & CORPORATE
INFORMATION
Carole Feld
SENIOR V.P., LEARNING SERVICES
Jinny Goldstein
SENIOR V.P., GENERAL COUNSEL & CORPORATE
SECRETARY
Paula A. Jameson
SENIOR V.P., PBS LEARNING MEDIA
Eric L Sass
SENIOR V.P., CFO & TREASURER, FINANCE &
ADMINISTRATION
Elizabeth A. Wolfe
V.P., FINANCE & ASSISTANT TREASURER
Nanette Dudar
SENIOR V.P., BROADCAST & TECHNICAL SERVICES
Bruce Miller
V.P., FUNDRAISING PROGRAMMING
Jim Scalem
V.P., DEPUTY GENERAL COUNSEL & ASSISTANT
SECRETARY
Sherri N. Blount

SONY TELEVISION ENTERTAINMENT

(A Sony Pictures Entertainment company)
10202 West. Washington,.Culver City, CA 90232. (310) 280-8000.

SONY PICTURES ENTERTAINMENT
PRESIDENT & COO
John Calley

CO-PRESIDENT
Jeff Sagansky
EXECUTIVE VICE PRESIDENT
Yuki Nozoe
EXECUTIVE VICE PRESIDENT
Robert Wynne

SONY TELEVISION ENTERTAINMENT
PRESIDENT
Jon Feltheimer
EXECUTIVE VICE PRESIDENT
Andy Kaplan
PRESIDENT—INTERNATIONAL
Nick Bingham
SENIOR V.P, MEDIA RELATIONS
Justin Pierce

COLUMBIA TRISTAR TELEVISION
9336 W. Washington Blvd., Culver City, CA 90232. (310) 202-1234.
PRESIDENT
Eric Tannenbaum
EXECUTIVE V.P.
Helene Michaels
EXECUTIVE V.P., PRODUCTION
Edward Lammi
EXECUTIVE V.P., BUSINESS AFFAIRS
Sandra Stern
EXECUTIVE V.P., MOVIES & MINISERIES
Helen Verno
SENIOR V.P., PROGRAMMING
Jeanie Bradley
SENIOR V.P., BUSINESS AFFAIRS
Bob Chasin
SENIOR V.P., INTERACTIVE PROGRAMMING
Richard Glosser
SENIOR V.P., TALENT
Ruth-Ann Huvane
SENIOR V.P., SERIES DEVELOPMENT
Russ Krasnoff
SENIOR V.P., BUSINESS AFFAIRS
Beverly Nix
SENIOR V.P., CHILDREN'S PROGRAMMING
Sander Schwartz
SENIOR V.P., DRAMA DEVELOPMENT
Sarah Timberman
V.P., MEDIA RELATIONS/PROMOTIONS
Paula Askanas
V.P., POST PRODUCTION
Christina Friedgen
V.P., INT'L PROGRAM DEV. & FORMAT SALES
Paul Gilbert
V.P., COMEDY DEVELOPMENT
Kim Haswell
V.P., PRODUCTION OPERATIONS
David Holman
V.P., PRODUCTION
Andy House
V.P., TELEVISION MUSIC
Robert Hunka
V.P., BUSINESS AFFAIRS
Joanne Mazzu
V.P., FILM PRODUCTION
John Morrissey
V.P., TECHNICAL OPERATIONS
Phil Squyres
V.P., MOVIES & MINISERIES
Winifred White Neisser

COLUMBIA TRISTAR TELEVISION DISTRIBUTION
10202 W. Washington Blvd., Culver City, CA 90232. (310) 280-8000.
PRESIDENT
Barry Thurston
EXECUTIVE V.P., PLANNING & OPERATIONS
David Mumford
SENIOR V.P., BUSINESS AFFAIRS
Richard Frankie
SENIOR V.P., MARKETING
John Moczulski
SENIOR V.P., SYNDICATION
Steve Mosko
SENIOR V.P., FIRST-RUN PROGRAMMING
Alan Perris
V.P., DISTRIBUTION OPERATIONS, DOMESTIC
SYNDICATION
Francine Beougher
V.P., MEDIA RELATIONS
Steve Coe
V.P., DEVELOPMENT
Melanie Chilek

522

V.P., CREATIVE SERVICES
Alan Daniels
V.P., RESEARCH
Doug Roth

COLUMBIA TRISTAR TELEVISION DISTRIBUTION REGIONAL OFFICES

ATLANTA
One Atlantic Center, 1201 W. Peachtree St., No. 4820, Atlanta, GA 30309. (404) 892-2725, FAX (404) 892-1063.
V.P., SOUTHERN REGION
Joe Kissack
V.P., SOUTHEASTERN REGION
Steve Maddox

CHICAGO
445 N. Cityfront Plaza Drive, Suite 3120, Chicago, IL 60611. (312) 644-0770, FAX (312) 644-0781.
V.P., MIDWESTERN REGION
Stuart Walker

DALLAS
8117 Preston Rd., Suite 510, Dallas, TX 75225. (214) 987-3671. FAX (214) 987-3675,
V.P., SOUTHWESTERN REGION
Dirk Johnston

LOS ANGELES
10202 West Washington Blvd., Culver City, CA 90232. (310) 280-8550, FAX (310) 280-1798.
V.P. WESTERN REGION
John Weiser

NEW YORK
550 Madison Ave., 8th Fl., New York, NY 10022. (212) 833-8350. FAX (212) 833-8360.
SENIOR V.P., EASTERN REGION MANAGER
John Rohrs, Jr.
V.P., AD SALES & MARKETING
Chris Kager
V.P., EASTERN REGION
Barbara Baugher
V.P., EASTERN REGION, AD SALES
David Ozer
V.P., NORTHEASTERN REGION
Jeff Wolf

COLUMBIA TRISTAR INTERNATIONAL TELEVISION
10202 W. Washington Blvd., Culver City, CA 90232. (310) 280-8000.
PRESIDENT—INTERNATIONAL, SONY TELEVISION ENTERTAINMENT
Nicholas Bingham
PRESIDENT, CTIT
Michael Grindon
PRESIDENT, SPEJ—JAPAN
Yoshiyuki (Jack) Isomura
PRESIDENT, COLUMBIA TRISTAR FILMS OF KOREA
Hyuk-Jo Kwon
SENIOR V.P., INTERNATIONAL PRODUCTION (BERLIN)
John Barber
SENIOR V.P., INTERNATIONAL NETWORKS
Lauren Cole
SENIOR V.P. & MANAGING MANAGER, EUROPE
Florent Gaignault
SENIOR V.P., INTERNATIONAL NETWORKS
George Leitner
SENIOR V.P.,SALES PLANNING
John McMahon
SENIOR V.P. & MANAGING DIRECTOR, ASIA
William Pfeiffer
SENIOR V.P., INTERNATIONAL PRODUCTION (MUNCHEN)
Ludwig Salm
SENIOR V.P., WORLDWIDE PAY TV
Lawrence Smith
DIVISION MANAGER, JAPAN
Kunikazu Sogabe
SENIOR V.P. & GENERAL MANAGER, LATIN AMERICA
Dorien Sutherland
SENIOR V.P., MARKETING & SALES SUPPORT
Rachel Wells
V.P. & MANAGING DIRECTOR, AUSTRALIA
Jack Ford
V.P., INTERNATIONAL PAY TV
Peter Iacono
V.P. & MANAGING DIRECTOR, INDIA
Sujit Kumar
V.P., SALES, NORTHERN EUROPE
Marck O'Connell
V.P., SALES
Simon Pollock
V.P., NEW BUSINESS DEVELOPMENT
Patrice Van De Walle

COLUMBIA TRISTAR INTERNATIONAL TELEVISION

ARGENTINA
Columbia TriStar Films of Argentina, Inc., Ayacucho 533, (1026) Buenos Aires, Argentina, Tel: (541) 954 3820. FAX: (541) 954 3819.

AUSTRALIA
Columbia TriStar Television Pty., Ltd., 42-46 Longueville Road, Lane Cove, N.S.W. 2066, Australia. Tel: (612) 911 3300. FAX: (612) 418 3548.

BRAZIL
Columbia Tri-Star Films of Brazil, Inc., Rua Santa Isabel 160, 7 Andar, 01221 Sao Paolo, Brazil. Tel: (5511) 220 5200, FAX: (5511) 224 0809.

CANADA
Columbia Tristar Media Group International, 365 Bloor St. East, Suite 1602, Toronto, Ontario, M4W 3L4, Tel: (416) 962 5490, FAX: (416) 962 5496.

CHINA
Sony Pictures Entertainment (China), Inc., Beijing Representative Office, Beijing Asia Jinjiang Hotel, Suite 1819, No. 8 Xin Zhong Xi Jie, Gong Ti Bei Lu, Beijing 100027, People's Republic of China. Tel: (86) 1508 9869, FAX: (86) 1508 0922.

ENGLAND
Columbia Tristar International Television and Corporate Development Group–Europe, 19 Wells St., London W1P 3FP England. Tel: (4471) 637 8444, FAX: (4471) 528 8596.

FRANCE
Columbia Tristar International Television, 131 Avenue de Wagram, 75017 Paris, France, Tel: (331) 4440 6300. FAX: (331) 4440 6301.

GERMANY
Columbia Tristar Film-Und Fernseh Produktion, Richard-Byrd Str. 6, D-50829 Cologne, Germany. Tel: (49221) 915 0600. FAX: (49221) 915 0609.

HONG KONG
Columbia Tristar International Television, 35/F Central Plaza, 18 Harbour Road, Hong Kong. Tel: (852) 593 1118. FAX: (852) 593 1222. Telex: 816-26CE-BCHX.

JAPAN
Sony Pictures Entertainment (Japan) Inc., Columbia Tristar Television Division, Hamamatsucho TS Build., 5th Floor, 8-14, Hamamatsucho, 2-Chome Minato-Ku Tokyo 105, Japan. Tel: (813) 3431 1372. FAX: (813) 3438 2970.

KOREA
Columbia TriStar Films of Korea, Inc., 1st Floor, Songpa Bldg., 505 Shinsa-Dong, Kangnam-Gu, Seoul, Korea. Tel: (822) 545 0101. FAX: (822) 546 0020.

MEXICO
Columbia TriStar International Television, Rio Mississippi No. 57-402, Col. Cuauhtemoc, 06500 Mexico D. F. Tel: (525) 511 0643.

TRISTAR TELEVISION

(See Sony Pictures Entertainment TV Group)

TURNER TELEVISION

(A division of Time-Warner)
One CNN Center, P.O. Box 105366, Atlanta, GA 30348-5366.
CHAIRMAN
Ted Turner

TURNER INTERNATIONAL
One CNN Center, P.O. Box 105366, Atlanta, GA 30348-5366. (404) 827-5639. FAX: (404) 827-3224.
CORPORATE V.P., WORLDWIDE DISTRIBUTION
William H. Grumbles
SENIOR V.P., SYNDICATE SALES
Michael Byrd

TURNER PROGRAM SERVICES
One CNN Center, 12th floor, P.O. Box 105366, Atlanta, GA 30348-5366. (404) 827-2085. FAX: (404) 827-2373.
CHAIRMAN
Russ Barry
PRESIDENT
Susan Grant
SENIOR V.P., CNN TELEVISION
Gary Anderson
SENIOR V.P. MARKETING & SALES STRATEGY
Meade Camp
V.P., WORLDWIDE DUSTRIBUTION, TBS INC.
William Grumbles, Jr.

V.P., PROGRAM PRODUCTION & DISTRIBUTION
Jackie Jusko
V.P., ADVERTISING & PROMOTION
Diane McCauley

TWENTIETH CENTURY FOX TELEVISION

(See Fox, Inc.)

UNIVERSAL TV

(See MCA TV)

UNIVISION COMMUNICATIONS, INC.

605 Third Ave., 12th floor, New York, NY 10158-0180. (212)
455-5200. FAX: (212) 867-6710.
CHAIRMAN & CEO
A. Jerrold Perenchio
PRESIDENT & COO
Ray Rodriguez
EXECUTIVE V.P.
Andrew Hobson
V.P., DIRECTOR OF RESEARCH
Doug Darfield
PRESIDENT, NETWORK SALES
Raul Torano
V.P., NATIONAL SALES
Carlos Deschapelles
DIRECTOR OF RESEARCH
Milagros Carrasquillo
V.P., DIRECTOR OF OPERATIONS
Tony Oquendo
V.P./NEWS DIRECTOR
Alina Falcon

UNIVISION REGIONAL SALES OFFICES

WEST
6701 Centre Drive West, 15th floor, Los Angeles, CA 90095,
(310) 338-0700. FAX: (310) 348-3619.
2030 Main St., Suite 235, Irvine, CA 92714. (714) 474-8585.
FAX: (714) 474-8385.
WEST COAST SALES MANAGER
Steve Mandala
870 Market Street, Suite 654, San Francisco, CA 94102. (415)
677-8730. FAX: (415) 772-9113.
SPOT SALES MANAGER
Doreen Rapelli

MIDWEST
541 N. Fairbanks Court, 11th Floor, Chicago, IL 60611. (312)
494-5100. FAX: (312) 494-5115.
SALES MANAGER
Trisha Pray
3155 West Big Beaver Rd., Suite 105, Troy, MI 48084. (810)
643-1921. FAX: (810) 643-7993.
SALES MANAGER
Mark Brown

SOUTH
9405 N.W. 41st St., Miami, FL 33178. (305) 471-3900. FAX:
(305) 471-4027.
V.P., DIRECTOR, NETWORK OPERATIONS
Tony Oquendo
SALES MANAGER
Evelyn Castillo
1 Buckhead Plaza, Suite 1340, 3060 Peachtree Rd. NW,
Atlanta, GA 30305. (404) 264-8660. FAX: (404) 264-8661.
SPOT SALES MANAGER
Tammy Heinen
600 E. Las Colinas Blvd., Suite 566, Irving, TX 75039. (972)
869-0202. FAX: (972) 869-2635.
SALES MANAGER
Jack Hobbs

VIACOM INC.

1515 Broadway, New York, NY 10036. (212) 258-6000.
SENIOR OFFICERS & MANAGEMENT
CHAIRMAN OF THE BOARD & CEO
Sumner M. Redstone
CEO, SHOWTIME NETWORKS, INC.
Matthew Blank
SENIOR V.P. & TREASURER
Vaughn A. Clarke
PRESIDENT, PARAMOUNT PARKS
Jane Cooper
DEPUTY CHAIRMAN, EXECUTIVE V.P., GENERAL
COUNSEL & CHIEF ADMINISTRATIVE OFFICER
Philippe P. Dauman
CHAIRMAN & CEO, VIACOM ENTERTAINMENT GROUP
Jonathan L. Dolgen

DEPUTY CHAIRMAN, EXECUTIVE V.P., FINANCE,
CORPORATE DEVELOPMENT & COMMUNICATIONS
Thomas E. Dooley
CHAIRMAN & CEO, BLOCKBUSTER ENTERTAINMENT
GROUP
Bill Fields
SENIOR V.P., CORPORATE RELATIONS
Carl D. Folta
CHAIRMAN & CEO/MTV NETWORKS
Thomas E. Freston
SENIOR V.P., LEGAL & DEPUTY COUNSEL GENERAL
Michael D. Fricklas
SENIOR V.P., CORPORATE DEVELOPMENT
Rudolph L. Hertlein
SENIOR V.P., TECHNOLOGY, & CHAIRMAN & CEO,
VIACOM INTERACTIVE MEDIA
Edward D. Horowitz
CHAIRMAN, MOTION PICTURE GROUP, PARAMOUNT
PICTURES
Sherry Lansing
PRESIDENT, NICKELODEON/NICK AT NITE
Herb Scannell
CHAIRMAN, TELEVISION GROUP, VIACOM
ENTERTAINMENT GROUP
Kerry McCluggage
PRESIDENT & CEO, SIMON & SCHUSTER
Jonathan Newcomb
SENIOR V.P., HUMAN RESOURCES & ADMINISTRATION
William A. Roskin
SENIOR V.P. & CFO
George S. Smith, Jr.
SENIOR V.P., GOVERNMENT AFFAIRS
Mark M. Weinstein
PRESIDENT & CEO/VIACOM CABLE
John W. Goddard

PARAMOUNT TELEVISION GROUP

(A division of Paramount Pictures)
5555 Melrose, Hollywood, CA 90038-3197. (213) 956-5000.
CHAIRMAN, PARAMOUNT TELEVISION GROUP
Kerry Mc Cluggage
EXECUTIVE V.P., TELEVISION GROUP
Richard Lindheim
PRESIDENT, DOMESTIC TELEVISION & EEXUTIVE V.P.,
TELEVISION GROUP
Steve Goldman
PRESIDENT, INTERNATIONAL TELEVISION
Bruce Gordon
PRESIDENT, CREATIVE AFFAIRS
Frank Kelly
PRESIDENT, NETWORK TELEVISION
Gary Hart
PRESIDENT, DOMESTIC TELEVISION DISTRIBUTION
Joel Berman
PRESIDENT, DOMESTIC TELEVISION MARKETING
Meryl Cohen
EXECUTIVE V.P., MEDIA RELATIONS
John A. Wentworth
EXECUTIVE V.P., CURRENT PROGRAMS & STRATEGIC
PLANNING
Tom Mazza
EXECUTIVE V.P., BUSINESS AFFAIRS & FINANCE,
DOMESTIC TELEVISION
Robert Sheehan
SENIOR V.P., BUSINESS AFFAIRS
Jake Jacobson
SENIOR V.P., FINANCE & LONG FORM PRODUCTION,
NETWORK TELEVISION
Gerald Goldman
V.P., PROGRAMMING
Lawrence Forsdick
SENIOR V.P., DRAMA DEVELOPMENT, NETWORK
TELEVISION
Kathy Lingg
SENIOR V.P., LEGAL, NETWORK TELEVISION
Melinda McNeely
SENIOR V.P., RESEARCH
Mike Mellon
SENIOR V.P. & GENERAL SALES MANAGER, DOMESTIC
TELEVISION
John Nogawski
SENIOR V.P., BUSINESS AFFAIRS & LEGAL
Bruce Pottash
SENIOR V.P., CREATIVE SERVICES, DOMESTIC
TELEVISION
Tom Connor
SENIOR V.P., OFF-NETWORK SALES, DOMESTIC TELEVISION
Dennis Emerson

SENIOR V.P., DEVELOPMENT, NETWORK TELEVISION
Dan Fauci
SENIOR V.P., TALENT & CASTING, NETWORK TELEVISION
Helen Mossler
SENIOR V.P., BUSINESS AFFAIRS & LEGAL
Tzvi Small
V.P., CURRENT PROGRAMS
Steve Stark

INTERNATIONAL TELEVISION DIVISION
PRESIDENT, INTERNATIONAL TELEVISION
Bruce Gordon
SENIOR V.P., SALES & ADMINISTRATION
Joseph Lucas
V.P., LATIN AMERICA SALES
Susan Bender
V.P., SALES & ADMINISTRATION
Julie Wineberg
ASSOCIATE DIRECTOR, PUBLICITY & PROMOTION
Kristin Torgen

INTERNATIONAL SALES OFFICES
ENGLAND
Paramount TV Ltd., 49 Charles St., London, W1X 8LV, England.
V.P., EUROPEAN SALES
Patrick Stambaugh
DIRECTOR OF SALES, U.K. & EUROPE
Stephen Tague
MANAGER, EUROPE & MIDDLE EAST SALES
David Coombes

AUSTRALIA
Paramount Pictures Pty., Ltd., Suite 3209, Australia Square, Box 4272 GPO, Sydney, 2001, N.S.W. Australia.
V.P., FAR EAST SALES
Stephen Carey

CANADA
Paramount Pictures Corp. Ltd., 146 Bloor Street W., Toronto, Ontario M5S 1M4, Canada.
V.P., TELEVISION SALES, CANADA
Malcolm Orme
V.P., MANAGING DIRECTOR, CANADA
Alaastair Banks
DIRECTOR, SYNDICATED SALES, CANADA
Kevin Keeley

WARNER BROS. TELEVISION

4000 Warner Blvd., Burbank CA 91522. (818) 954-6000. FAX: (818) 954-4539. Telex: 4720389.
75 Rockefeller Plaza, New York, NY 10019. (212) 484-8000.

TELEVISION PROGRAMMING
PRESIDENT
Tony Jonas
EXECUTIVE V.P., CREATIVE AFFAIRS
David Janollari
EXECUTIVE V.P., BUSINESS & FINANCIAL AFFAIRS
Nancy Tellem
SENIOR V.P., PRODUCTION
Andrew Ackerman
SENIOR V.P., DRAMA DEVELOPMENT
Nina Tassler
SENIOR V.P., COMEDY DEVELOPMENT
Maria Rastatter
SENIOR V.P., MOVIES & MINI-SERIES
Gregg Maday
SENIOR V.P., TALENT & CASTING
Barbara Miller
SENIOR V.P., CURRENT PROGRAMS
Steve Pearlman
SENIOR V.P., CURRENT PROGRAMMING
David Sacks
SENIOR V.P., LABOR RELATIONS
Hank Lachmund
SENIOR V.P., STUDIO GENERAL COUNSEL
Paul Stager
SENIOR V.P., COMEDY & DRAMA PRODUCTION
Judith Zaylor
V.P., TELEVISION MUSIC
Tim Bocci
V.P., BUSINESS AFFAIRS
Karen Cease
V.P., BUSINESS AFFAIRS
Donald Feldgreber
V.P., LEGAL AFFAIRS
Jay Gendron
V.P., BUSINESS AFFAIRS
Wilt Haff
V.P., CURRENT PROGRAMMING
Andy Horne

V.P., NETWORK PRODUCTION
Henry Johnson
V.P., CASTING
John Levey
V.P., POST-PRODUCTION
Lisa Lewis
V.P., TALENT & CASTING
Irene Mariano
V.P., BUSINESS AFFAIRS
Roni Mueller
V.P., NETWORK PRODUCTION
Patrick Newcomb
V.P., LEGAL AFFAIRS
Sarah Noddings
V.P., BUSINESS AFFAIRS
Brett Paul
V.P., PRODUCTION CONTROL/ESTIMATING
Dorothy Relyea
V.P., CASTING
Mark Saks
V.P., CASTING
Tony Sepulveda
V.P., PUBLICITY
David Stapf
V.P., DRAMA DEVELOPMENT
David Zucker
V.P., LEGAL AFFAIRS
Barbara Zuckerman
DIRECTOR, CURRENT PROGRAMS
Andrew Barret Weiss
DIRECTOR, CASTING
Deedee Bradley
DIRECTOR, BUSINESS AFFAIRS
Tracy Burnett
DIRECTOR, COMEDY DEVELOPMENT
Keith Cox
DIRECTOR, CURRENT PROGRAMS
Melinda Hage
DIRECTOR, CASTING
Ted Hann
DIRECTOR, CASTING
Lorna Johnson
DIRECTOR, CASTING
Joanne Koehler
DIRECTOR, CASTING
Geraldine Leder
DIRECTOR, ESTIMATING
Mike McKnight
DIRECTOR, NETWORK RESEARCH
Tom O'Connor
DIRECTOR, BUSINESS AFFAIRS
Shirley Sadanga
DIRECTOR, BUSINESS AFFAIRS
Doug Schaeffer
DIRECTOR, CURRENT PROGRAMS
Jane Segal
DIRECTOR, PRODUCTION CONTROL/ESTIMATING
Christina Smith
DIRECTOR, CASTING
Elayne Teitelbaum
DIRECTOR, CURRENT PROGRAMS
Pam Williams
DIRECTOR, LABOR RELATIONS
Samuel Wolfson

WARNER BROS. DOMESTIC TELEVISION DISTRIBUTION
WEST
4001 N. Olive Ave., Burbank, CA 91522. (818) 954-5652. FAX: (818) 954-5694.
PRESIDENT
Dick Robertson
EXECUTICE V.P.
Scott Carlin
SENIOR V.P./GENERAL SALES MANAGER, STATION SALES
Dan Greenblatt
SENIOR V.P., ADMINISTRATION
Leonard Bart
V.P., CONTRACT ADMINISTRATION
Dan McCrae
V.P., FINANCIAL OPERATIONS
David Cooper
V.P., WESTERN SALES
Mark O'Brien
SALES ADMINISTRATION
Lisa Corricello

EAST
New York: 1325 Avenue of the Americas, New York, NY 10019. (212) 636-5300.

V.P.S/EASTERN SALES
Andrew Weir
Chris Smith
Eric Strong
ACCOUNT EXECUTIVE, EASTERN SALES
Joel Lewin
SENIOR V.P., MEDIA SALES
Clark Morehouse
V.P./GENERAL SALES MANAGER, MEDIA SALES
Julie Kantrowitz
DIRECTORS, MEDIA SALES
Diane Rinaldo
Paul Montoya
ACCOUNT EXECUTIVES
Roseann Cacciola
Clifford Brown
DIRECTOR, MEDIA MARKETING & RESEARCH, MEDIA SALES
Jean Goldberg
DIRECTOR,MEDIA FINANCE
Patty Coletti
V.P., CHICAGO MEDIA SALES
Jean Medd

MIDWEST
645 N. Michigan Ave., Chicago, IL 60611. (312) 440-9696.
V.P./GENERAL SALES MANAGER
Mark Robbins
V.P., CENTRAL SALES
Jeff Hufford
MANAGER, CENTRAL SALES
James Knopf
V.P., MEDIA SALES
Jean Medd

SOUTHEAST
Atlanta: 4751 Best Road, Suite 170, Atlanta, GA 30337. (404) 761- 6010.
V.P., SOUTHEASTERN SALES
Mary Voll
MANAGER, SOUTHEASTERN SALES
Marlynda Salas Lecate

SOUTH
Dallas: 8144 Walnut Hill Lane, Suite 500, Dallas, TX 75231-4316.
V.P., SOUTHWESTERN SALES
Jacqueline Hartley
MANAGER, SOUTHWESTERN SALES
Jim Kramer

WARNER BROS. MEDIA SALES
1325 Ave. of the Americas, New York, NY 10019. (212) 636-5102.
SENIOR V.P.
Jim Moloshok
V.P., MARKETING
Yelena Lazovich
DIRECTOR, CREATIVE SERVICES
Wendy Ehrlich
DIRECTORS, CREATIVE SERVICES
Joel Kaplan
Claire Lee
MANAGER, VIDEO PRODUCTION
Michelle Jacoba
ASSISTANT ART DIRECTOR
Perry Raso

WARNER BROS. CORPORATE MEDIA RESEARCH
SENIOR V.P.
Bruce Rosenblum
V.P. & SENIOR RESEARCH ADVISOR
Wayne Neiman
V.P., RESEARCH & NEW MEDIA DEVELOPMENT
Robert Jennings
V.P.
Liz Huszarik
EXECUTIVE DIRECTOR
Kurt Bensmiller
MANAGERS
Karen Barcheski
Keith Friedenberg

TELEPICTURES PRODUCTIONS
3500 W. Olive Ave., Suite 1000, Burbank, CA 91505. (818) 972-0777. (818) 972-0864.
PRESIDENT
Jim Paratore
SENIOR V.P., BUSINESS AFFAIRS
Joe Reilly
V.P., PRODUCTION
Kevin Fortson

V.P.S, DEVELOPMENT
Hilary Estey McLoughlin
David Auerbach
VICE PRESIDENT, CURRENT PROGRAMMING
Wendy Hildebrand
MANAGER, DEVELOPMENT
Lisa Hackner
CONTROLLER
Alan Soloman
(Located at "Jenny Jones," NBC Tower, 454 N. Columbus Dr., 4th Floor, Chicago, IL 60611. (312) 836-9400. FAX: 836-9473.
V.P., CURRENT PROGRAMMING
Wendy Bernier Hildebrand

TELEPICTURES DISTRIBUTION
4001 N. Olive Ave., Burbank, CA 91522. (818) 954-5652. FAX: (818) 954-5694.
SENIOR V.P.S
Vince Messina
Damian Riordan
SENIOR V.P., CENTRAL SALES MANAGER
Bill Hague

PAY TV, CABLE & NETWORK FEATURES
75 Rockefeller Center, New York, NY 10020. (212) 484-8000. FAX: (212) 397-0728.
PRESIDENT
Edward Bleier
V.P., MARKETING
Eric Frankel
V.P.
Jeffrey Calman

WARNER BROS. ANIMATION
15503 Ventura Blvd., Sherman Oaks, CA 91403.
SENIOR V.P. & GENERAL MANAGER
Jean MacCurdy
V.P., PRODUCTION
Kathleen Helppie
DIRECTOR, CLASSIC ANIMATION
Lorri Bond

WARNER BROS. INTERNATIONAL TELEVISION DISTRIBUTION
4000 Warner Blvd., Bldg. 118, Burbank, CA 91522. (818) 954-5491. FAX: (818) 954-4040.
PRESIDENT
Jeffrey R. Schlesinger
SENIOR V.P., INTERNATIONAL PAY TV & ADMINISTRATIVE OPERATIONS
Mauro Sardi
SENIOR V.P., TELEVISION SALES
James P. Marrinan
V.P. INTERNATIONAL TELEVISION PRODUCTION
Catherine Malatesta
V.P., INTERNATIONAL RESEARCH & MARKETING
Lisa Gregorian
V.P., INTERNATIONAL TV OPERATIONS
Annette Bouso
V.P., LEGAL & BUSINESS AFFAIRS
Ron Miele
SENIOR V.P., INTERNATIONAL CHANNELS, NEW BUSINESS DEVELOPMENT
Malcolm Dudley-Smith
SENIOR V.P., INTERNATIONAL CHANNELS, PROGRAMMING & OPERATIONS
Susan Kroll

FOREIGN SALES OFFICES

AUSTRALIA & FAR EAST
Warner Bros. Int'l, Level 22, 8-20 Napier St., N. Sydney, NSW 2060, Australia. Tel: (6102) 957-3899. FAX: (6102) 956-7788.
V.P., MANAGING DIRECTOR, AUSTRALIA/ ASIA PACIFIC
Wayne Broun
V.P., ASIA
Greg Robertson

CHINA
100 Canton Road, 7th Floor, Tsimshatsui, Kowloon, Hong Kong. Tel: (852) 376 3963. FAX: (852) 376 1302.
DIRECTOR, BUSINESS DEVELOPMENT, ASIA
Robert Wood

FRANCE
67 Avenue de Wagram, 75017 Paris, France. Tel: (331) 4401 4999. FAX: (331) 4401 4968.
V.P.
Michel LeCourt

CANADA
Warner Bros. TV, 4576 Yonge St., 2nd floor, North York, Ontario, Canada, M2N 6P1. (416) 250-8384. FAX: (416) 250-8930.
V.P., OPERATIONS
Kevin Byles

mins.), Danger Bay (123 x 30 mins.), Gift To Last (22 x 60 mins.), Home Fires (13 x 60 mins.), The King of Kensington (55 x 30 mins.), Material World (32 x 30 mins.), Moments In Time (15 x 60 mins.), 9B–The Series (5 x 45 mins.), Side Effects: Season 1 (13 x 60 mins.), Season 2 (16 x 60 mins.), Street Legal: Season 1 (6 x 60 mins.), Season 2 (13 x 60 mins.), Season 3 (19 x 60 mins.), Season 4 (16 x 60 mins.), Season 5 (16 x 60 mins.), Season 6 (18 x 60 mins.), Season 7 (18 x 60 mins.), Season 8 (18 x 60 mins. & Last Rights–Finale 93 mins.).

Comedy/Music/Variety: AIDScare (60 mins.), Anne Murray In Nove Scotia (60 mins.), Back To The Beanstalk (60 mins.), Brian Orser: Blame It On The Blues (60 mins.), Bryan Adams: Waking Up The World (60 mins.), Colin James Presents The Blues Masters (60 mins.), Kurt Browning: You Must Remember This (60 mins.), Michelle (60 mins.), Rita McNeil: Once Upon A Christmas (60 mins.), Speak Low, Swing Hard (31 mins.), The Trial Of Red Riding Hood (60 mins.), Wayne & Shuster (80 x 30 mins.), Wayne & Shuster: Once Upon A Giant (90 mins.), The Wayne & Shuster Years (90 mins.).

Cultural Programming: Adrienne Clarkson Presents: All About Yves (23 mins.), Artemisia (48 mins.), Attila Richard Lukacs (30 mins.), The Boundless Sea (15 mins.), Children of Terezin (45 mins.), Evergon: Making Homo Roccoco (43 mins.), Freeman Patterson Up Close (22 mins.), The Gift of Messiah (44 mins.), Jessye Norman (21 mins.), Kokoro Dance (19 mins.), La La Lock (18 mins.), The Lust of His Eye–Vision of J.W. Morrice (36 mins.), Mark Morris Choreographer (45 mins.), Mastersinger Paul Frey (45 mins.), Moxy Früvous World (23 mins.), Mump & Smoot (24 mins.), Nigel Kennedy (9 mins.), Noranda Man (21 mins.), Pavarotti (11 mins.), Piano Man–John Kimura Parker (46 mins.), Pinteresque (29 mins.), Robertson Davies (24 mins.), Ronnie Burkett–Hands On (35 mins.), Sir Yehudi Menuhin (13 mins.), Sophia Loren (9 mins.), Squeeze Box Stories (23 mins.), A Star In The Making–Remy Boucher (13 mins.), Travels With Germaine (22 mins.), Views Of A Room (19 mins.), The World of Janina Fialkowska (46 mins.).

Arts: Alarmel Valli (30 mins.), Anton Kuerti & Yo-Yo Ma (30 mins.), Birds In Art (30 mins.), Degas (60 mins.), Figure Of A Spirit: Kimiko Koyanagi (30 mins.), Giselle (90 mins.), Glenn Gould Plays Beethoven (60 mins.), Grand Piano (60 mins.), Grizzly Kingdom: An Artist's Encounter (60 mins.), Hand & Eye (7 x 60 mins.), Homage To Chagall (90 mins.), Karsch: The Searching Eye (90 mins.), Keewatin Arts & Crafts Festival (34 mins.), Lucy Maud Montgomery: The Road To Green Gables (90 mins.), To Mend The World (87 mins.), The Mystery of Henry Moore (90 mins.), The Quilt As Art (30 mins.), Scented Treasures (18 mins.), The Sleeping Beauty (90 mins.), Tennessee Williams' South (80 mins.), Vivaldi (2 x 53 mins.).

The Stratford Festival: As You Like It (150 mins.), The Gondoliers (154 mins.), H.M.S. Pinafore (90 mins.), The Mikado (150 mins.), Romeo And Juliet (180 mins.), The Taming Of The Shrew (163 mins.).

Continuing Series: Fashion File (52 per year x 30 mins.), The Fifth Estate, 50/Up (72 x 30 mins.), The Health Show (19 x 30 mins.), Market Place (15-30 mins.), The National (15-30 mins.), On The Road Again (30 mins.), Spilled Milk (30 mins.), Undercurrents (13 x 30 mins.), Venture (15-30 mins.), Witness (weekly x 60 mins.).

Children's Series: Degrassi Between Takes (30 mins.), Fred Penner's Place (15 mins.), The Friendly Giant (123 x 15 mins.), Mr. Dressup (65 x 30 mins.), Wonderstruck (52 x 30 mins.).

Documentary: Amazonia (2 hrs.), Battle Diary: A Day In The Life of Charlie Martin (60 mins.), A Bright Idea (17 mins.), A Climate For Change (2 hrs.), The Damned (2 hrs.), Dealing With Drugs (2 hrs.), Drums (2 hrs.), E.T. Abductions (14 mins.), Food or Famine (2 hrs.), Gulf War Syndrome (26 mins.), Indonesia (6 x 30 mins.), Mah Jong Orphan (60 mins.), Man Alive (42 x 30 mins.), Marconi (60 mins.), The Man Who Hid Anne Frank (60 mins.), The Most Dangerous Con Game (30 mins), Mr. Yao & The Crocodiles (30 mins.), The National Dream (6 x 60 mins.), The Nature Of Things (83 x 60 mins., & 45 x 30 mins.), Not My Home (60 mins.), The Other White Powder (17 mins.), Prophecy (90 mins.), Return To Saigon: Two Viet Kieu (60 mins.), Sea of Slaughter (95 mins.), A Secret Underground (30 mins.), The Seeds Of Terror (60 mins.), The Shadow & The Spirit (60 mins.), Temples of Glory (30 mins.), That Perfect Smile (30 mins.), The Third Angel (60 mins.), Timelines (30 x 60 mins.), Trading Futures: Living In The Global Economy (2 hrs.), A Transsexual Journey: Katherine Elizabeth Cohen (60 mins.), The Trouble With Evan (90 mins.), The Ultimate Response (30 mins.), Voices In The Forest (2 hrs.), The War Against The Indians (143 mins.), Water: To The Last Drop (2 hrs.), When The Bough Breaks (90 mins.).

CBS ENTERTAINMENT PRODUCTIONS
7800 Beverly Blvd., Los Angeles, CA 90036. (213) 852-2345.
PRESIDENT, CBS ENTERTAINMENT
Leslie Moonves

S.V.P., PROGRAMMING
Steve Warner
V.P., SERIES DEVELOPMENT
Kelly Goode
V.P., CURRENT PROGRAMS
Maddy Horne
Series: Can't Hurry Love, Central Park West, Dave's World, Dr. Quinn–Medicine Woman, Early Edition, The Gordon Elliott Show, Moloney, Promised Land, Rescue 911, Touched by an Angel, Walker–Texas Ranger.

CBS NEWS
524 W. 57 St., New York, NY 10019. (212) 975-4321.
Series: 48 Hours, 60 Minutes.

CNBC: CONSUMER NEWS & BUSINESS CHANNEL
2200 Fletcher Ave., Ft. Lee, NJ 07024. (201) 585-2622.
Series: Business Insiders, The Dick Cavett Show, Equal Time, Money Tonight, Rivera Live, Talk Live.

CEL COMMUNICATIONS, INC.
460 Park Ave. So., New York, NY 10016. (212) 953-4650.
CHAIRMAN & CEO
Peter Collins
Series: America the Way We Were: The Home Front, 1940-45 (Discovery Channel), Animal Express (syndicated by 20th Century Fox), Biography–Hosted by Peter Graves (A&E Network), Class of the 20th Century–Hosted by Richard Dreyfuss (A&E), Creativity with Bill Moyers (PBS), Dining in France (13 x 30 mins.), John F. Kennedy: A Celebration of His Life & Times (Discovery Channel), Legends in Love (Lifetime), The Magic Years in Sports (ESPN), A Walk Thru the 20th Century with Bill Moyers (PBS), World War II: A Personal Journey– Hosted/Narrated by Glenn Ford (Disney Channel).

CAMELOT ENTERTAINMENT SALES
1700 Broadway, New York, NY 10019. (212) 315-4747.
PRESIDENT
Steve Hirsch
Series: American Journal, Inside Edition, Jeopardy!, The Oprah Winfrey Show, The Rolanda Watts Show, Showtime at the Apollo, Wheel of Fortune.

CANDID CAMERA, INC.
P.O. Box 827, Monterey, CA 93942. (408) 625-3788.
Candid Camera: All-Time Funniest Moments, Candid Camera (385 x 30 mins.), Candid Camera (35 x 30 mins. "adult"), Candid Camera Specials.

STEPHEN J. CANNELL PRODS.
7083 Hollywood Blvd., Hollywood, CA 90028. (213) 465-5800. FAX: (213) 856-7454.
Products: The A-Team (NBC), Booker (FBC), Broken Badges (CBS), The Commish (synd.), Hardcastle & McCormick (ABC), Hat Squad (CBS), Hawkeye, Hunter (NBC), J.J. Starbuck (NBC), The Last Precinct (NBC), Missing Persons, Personals (CBS), Renegade (Synd.), Riptide (NBC), Scene of the Crime (CBS), Silk Stalkings (CBS), Sonny Spoon (NBC), Stingray (NBC), Street Justice (Synd.), Thunder Boat Row (ABC), Top of the Hill (CBS), 21 Jump Street (FBC), Unsub (NBC), Wiseguy (CBS).

CANNELL DISTRIBUTION COMPANY
7083 Hollywood Blvd., 4th fl., Hollywood, CA 90028. (213) 465-5800. FAX: (213) 856-7987.
PRESIDENT
Patrick J. Kenney
V.P. RESEARCH
Richard Zimmer
PRESIDENT, INTERNATIONAL
Herb Lazarus
DIRECTOR, DISTRIBUTION
Jerry Leifer
V.P. SALES
Ed Youngmark

CAROLINE FILM PRODUCTIONS
12711 Ventura Blvd., #210, Los Angeles, CA 91604. (818) 508-3420. FAX: (818) 508-3464.
Series: Touched by an Angel

CARSEY-WERNER PRODUCTIONS
4024 Radford Ave., Bldg. 3, Studio City, CA 91604. (818) 760-5598. FAX: (818) 760-6236.
OWNERS/EXECUTIVE PRODUCERS
Marcy Carsey, Tom Werner
PRESIDENT
Caryn Mandabach
Series: Bill Cosby Project, Cybill, Grace Under Fire, Men Behaving Badly, Roseanne, 3rd Rock From the Sun, Townies.

CARSON PRODUCTIONS
3110 Main St., #200, Santa Monica, CA 90405. (310) 314-8784. FAX: (310) 314-8797.
Series: The Tonight Show (1980–1994).

CASTLE HILL TELEVISION
1414 Ave. of the Americas, New York, NY 10019. (212) 888-0080. FAX: (212) 644-0956.
CEO
Julian Schlossberg
PRESIDENT, MARKETING & DISTRIBUTION
Mel Maron
VICE PRESIDENT
Milly Sherman
V.P., SALES
Barbara Karmel
DIRECTOR, ADVERTISING & CLIENT SERVICES
David Wright
DIRECTOR, DISTRIBUTION
Ivory Harris
Volume III (package of feature films): An American Summer, Control, Defense Play, Double Edge, A Fine Romance, The Imagemaker, Innocent Victim, In the Spirit, Iron Maze, Julia & Julia, Paper Mask, Prayer of the Roller Boys, Primary Motive, Voyager, White Light.
Volume IV (package of feature films): Alan & Naomi, A Climate for Killing, Desire & Hell at Sunset Motel, Honor Among Thieves, Matewan, Rider on the Rain, The Secret Rapture, The Seventh Coin, Sweet Justice, Tim.
Volume V (package of feature films, current and future availability): Andy Warhol Presents Dracula, A Business Affair, Cannibal Women In The Avocado Jungle of Death, Concrete War, A Day In October, Deadly Advice, Hell's Angles On Wheels, The Lost Honor Of Kathryn Beck, Puppetmaster, A Reason To Believe, The Sailor Who Fell From Grace With The Sea.
Made in Hollywood (package of films): Blockade, The Crystal Ball, 52nd Street, Foreign Correspondent, History Is Made at Night, The House Across the Bay, I Married a Witch, The Long Voyage Home, A Night in Casablanca, Stagecoach, To Be or Not to Be, Vogues of 1938, You Only Live Once.

CASTLE ROCK ENTERTAINMENT
335 N. Maple Dr., Beverly Hills, CA 90210. (310) 285-2300.
Series: Boston Common, Lazarus Man, Seinfeld, The Single Guy.

CHICAGO PRODUCTION CENTER, THE
5400 N. Saint Louis Ave., Chicago, IL 60625. (312) 583-5000. FAX: (312) 583-3046.
Series: The McLaughlin Group, McLaughlin One on One, The New Explorers, Sneak Previews.

CINAR FILMS, INC.
1055 Rene Levesque Blvd. East. Montreal, Quebec H2L 4S5, Canada. (514) 843-7070. FAX: (514) 843-7080.
CHAIRMAN & CEO
Micheline Charest
PRESIDENT
Ronald A. Weinberg
V.P. & GENERAL COUNSEL
Marie Josee Corbeil
V.P., FINANCE
Hasanain Panju
V.P., ANIMATION PRODUCTION & DEVELOPMENT
Cassandra Schafhausen
V.P., CINAR ANIMATION
Lesley Taylor
V.P., LIVE-ACTION PRODUCTION & DEVELOPMENT
Patricia Laroie
V.P., CINAR STUDIOS
Francois Deschamps
V.P., DISTRIBUTION & MARKETING
Louis Fournier
New Products: Animal Crackers (13 x 30 mins.), Arthur (30 x 30 mins.), Babalous (65 5 mins.), Bonjour Timothy (90 minutes), Cat Tales (15 x 30 mins.), Emily (13 hours), Ivanhoe (26 x 30 mins.), Lassie (56 x 30 mins.), Million Dollar Babies (2 x 2 hrs.), NightHood (26 x 30 mins.), Papa Beaver's Story Time (52 x 13 mins.), Rinko: The Best Bad Thing (90 mins.), Robinson Sucroe (26 x 30 mins.), Space Cases (26 x 30 mins.), The Country Mouse and the City Mouse Adventures (26 x 30 mins.), The Little Lulu Show (26 x 30 mins.), The Whole of the Moon (90 mins.), Wimzie's House (56 x 30 mins.).
Other Series: Albert the 5th Musketeer (26 x 30 mins.), Are You Afraid of the Dark? (39 x 30 mins.), A Bunch of Munsch (7 x 30 mins.), The Busy World of Richard Scarry (13 x 30 mins.), Chris Cross (13 x 30 mins.), C.L.Y.D.E. (26 x 30

mins.), Happy Castle (13 x 30 mins.), Legend of White Fang (26 x 30 mins.), Madeline (6 x 30 mins.), The Real Story (13 x 30 mins.), Smoggies (52 x 30 mins.), Stand-In for Danger, Wonderful Wizard of Oz (52 x 30 mins., 4 x 90 min. features), Young Robin Hood (26 x 30 mins.).
Features: Adventures in Odyssey (6 x 30 mins.), Clown White (60 mins.), Hockey Night (77 mins.), Peter and the Wolf (85 mins.).

CINETEL PRODUCTIONS
9701 Madison Ave., Knoxville, TN 37932. (423) 690-9950. FAX: (423) 693-6576.
EXECUTIVE V.P. & GENERAL MANAGER
Stephen Land
Series: Club Dance, Crafts & Co., Easy Does It, Remodeling & Decorating Today, Shadetree Mechanic.
Specials: America's Castles, Circus, Freeze Frame.

CITADEL ENTERTAINMENT
11340 W. Olympic Blvd., Suite 100, Los Angeles, CA 90064-1611. (310) 477-5112. FAX: (310) 312-9781.
PRESIDENT
David Ginsburg

DICK CLARK PRODUCTIONS, INC.
3003 W. Olive Ave., Burbank, CA 91510. (818) 841-3003.
CHAIRMAN & CEO
Dick Clark
PRESIDENT & COO
Francis La Maina
Products: Academy of Country Music Awards, American Music Awards, Golden Globe Awards, Rockin' New Years Eve, Tempestt Bledsoe Show, TV's All-Star Censored Bloopers.

COLUMBIA PICTURES TV
10202 W. Washington Blvd., Culver City, CA 90232-3195, (310) 280-8000.
Series: Courthouse, Days of Our Lives, First Time Out, Married ... With Children, NewsRadio, Party of Five, Walker–Texas Ranger, The Young and the Restless.

COLUMBIA TRISTAR INTERNATIONAL TELEVISION
Sony Pictures Plaza, 10202 W. Washington Blvd., 7th floor, Culver City, CA 90232. (310) 280-8000. FAX: (310) 280-1514.
550 Madison Ave., 8th fl., 10022. (212) 833-8350. FAX: (212) 833-8360.
EXECUTIVE V.P., SONY PICTURES ENTERTAINMENT
Dennis Miller
EXECUTIVE V.P., SONY PICTURES ENTERTAINMENT
Ken Lemberger
PRESIDENT, PRESIDENT SONY TV ENTERTAINMENT
Jon Feltheimer
PRESIDENT, INT'L SONY TV ENTERTAINMENT
Nicholas Bingham
EXECUTIVE V.P., COLUMBIA PICTURES TV
Jeff Wachtel
PRESIDENT, COLUMBIA TRISTAR INT'L TV
Michael Grindon
S.V.P., INTERNATIONAL PRODUCTIONS
John Barber
S.V.P., MARKETING & SALES SUPPORT
Rachel Wells
V.P., SALES
Simon Pollock
International Offices & Sales Contacts:
Buenos Aires, Argentina. (54-1-954) 3820-23-24. Armando Cortez.
Sydney Australia. (61-2_ 911-3300. Jack Ford.
Sao Paulo, Brazil. (55-11) 220-5200. Dorien Sutherland.
Toronto, Canada. (416) 962-5490. John Migicovsky.
Beijing, China. (86-10) 500-7788. Mishka Chen.
Paris, France. (33-1-44) 40 63 00. Florent Gaignault.
Cologne, Germany. (49-221) 915-0600. John Barber.
Hong Kong. (852) 2913-3788. Todd Miller.
Tokyo, Japan. (81-333) 311 372. Kunikazi Sogabe.
Seoul, Korea. (822) 545-0101. Katherine Kim.
Mexico City, Mexico. (525) 5207-5433. Beatriz Zavaleta.
London, England. (44-171) 637-8444. Nicholas Bingham.
New Series: Come Fly With Me, Dark Skies, The Dating/Newlywed Hour, Early Edition, Hightower 411, Just Shoot Me, Malcolm and Eddie, Maloney.
Series/First Run: Boston Common, Days of Our Lives, High Tide,. Hudson Street, The Jeff Foxworthy Show, The Larry Sanders How, Mad About You, Married...With Children, The Naked Truth, The Nanny, Ned and Stacey, News Radio, Party of Five, Ricki Lake, Seinfeld, The Single Guy, The Young & The Restless.

Children's Programming: Beakman's World, Jumanji: The Animated Series, Project Geeker, Super Ghostbusters.

TV Movies: Born Free: A New Adventure, Cadillac Desert, To Sir With Love II.

Syndication Feature Film Packages: Columbia Gems I (6 titles), Columbia Gold (24 titles), Columbia Gold II (34 titles), Columbia Night at the Movies (ad hoc quarterly barter network), Columbia Showcase I (22 titles), Columbia Showcase II (25 titles), Embassy II (20 titles), Embassy III (20 titles), Entertainer of the Year (4 titles), TV I (20 titles), TV 20 (20 titles), Volume IV (9 titles), Volume V (16 titles), Volume VI (18 titles), Pegasus I (20 titles), Pegasus II (21 titles), Pegasus III (24 titles), Showcase III (26 titles), Tri-Star Showcase (ad hoc monthly barter network).

Syndication Off-Network Comedy Series: All in the Family (207 x 30 mins.), Archie Bunker's Place (97 x 30 mins.), Barney Miller (170 x 30 mins.), Benson (158 x 30 mins.), Carson's Comedy Classics (130 x 30 mins.), Carter Country (44 x 30 mins.), Designing Women (164 x 30 mins.), Diff'rent Strokes (189 x 30 mins.), The Facts of Life (209 x 30 mins.), Fish (35 x 30 mins.), Good Times (133 x 30 mins.), The Jeffersons (253 x 30 mins.), Married . . . With Children (131 x 30 mins.), Maude (141 x 30 mins.), My Two Dads (60 x 30 mins.), One Day at a Time (209 x 30 mins.), Parker Lewis (73 x 30 mins.), Punky Brewster (88 x 30 mins.), Sanford & Son (136 x 30 mins.), Seinfeld (108 x 30 mins.), Silver Spoons (116 x 30 mins.), Soap (93 x 30 mins.), That's My Mama (39 x 30 mins.), The Three Stooges (190 x 30 mins.), 227 (116 x 30 mins.), Who's the Boss? (196 x 30 mins.).

Syndication Off-Network Drama Series: Charlie's Angels (115 x 60 mins.), Fantasy Island (200 x 30 mins., 152 x 60 mins.), Hart to Hart (112 x 60 mins.), Hunter (129 x 60 mins.), Police Story (105 x 30 mins.), Police Woman (91 x 60 mins.), S.W.A.T. (37 x 60 mins.), Starsky and Hutch (92 x 60 mins.), T.J. Hooker (90 x 60 mins.).

COMMUNICATION COMMISSION OF THE NATIONAL COUNCIL OF THE CHURCHES OF CHRIST IN THE USA
475 Riverside Dr., New York, NY 10115-0050. (212) 870-2574. FAX: (212) 870-2030.
UNIT DIRECTOR OF COMMUNICATION
Betty Thompson
DIRECTOR, ELECTRONIC MEDIA
David W. Pomeroy

COPRODUCERS CORPORATION
2670 N.E. 24th St., Pompano Beach, FL 33064. (954) 781-2627. FAX: (954) 781-2627.
PRESIDENT
John F. Rickert
SECRETARY/TREASURER
Ildiko M. Rickert
25 Theatrical Features.

COSGROVE-MEURER PRODUCTIONS, INC.
4303 W. Verdugo Ave., Burbank, CA 91505. (818) 843-5600.
Series: Unsolved Mysteries.

THE CRAMER CO.
4605 Lankershim Blvd., Suite 617, North Hollywood, CA 91602. (213) 877-0150. FAX: (213) 877-0159.
PRESIDENT
Douglas S. Cramer
DIRECTOR OF DEVELOPMENT
Grady Hall
Features: Danielle Steel's "The Ring," Danielle Steel's "Vanished," Danielle Steel's "Zoya," Family of Cops.

BING CROSBY PRODUCTIONS, INC.
3400 Riverside Dr., Suite 600, Burbank, CA 91505. (818) 557-3775. FAX: (818) 557-3766.
PRESIDENT
Nicholas D. Trigony
VICE PRESIDENTS
J. Randall Stargel, Preston B. Barnett
Series: Ben Casey, Bing Crosby Show, Breaking Point, Hogan's Heroes, The Queen and I, Slattery's People.

CRYSTAL PICTURES, INC.
1560 Broadway, Suite 503, New York, NY 10036-1525. (212) 840-6181. FAX: (212) 840-6182.
Branch Office: 9 SW Park Sq., Asheville, NC 28801. (704) 285-9996. FAX: (704) 285-9997.
PRESIDENT
Joshua Tager
SALES DIRECTOR
S. Tager

D

DIC ENTERPRISES, INC.
303 N. Glenoaks Blvd., Burbank, CA 91505. (818) 955-5400. FAX: (818) 955-5696.
PRESIDENT
Andy Heyard
S.V.P., DEVELOPMENT
Michael Maliani
Series: Adventures of the Sonic Hedgehog, Dennis the Menace, Double Dragon, Gadget Boy's Adventures in History, Hurricane, Inspector Gadget's Field Trip, Madeline, Mummies, Tex Avery Theater.

D. L. T. ENTERTAINMENT
31 W. 56 St., New York, NY 10019. (212) 245-4680. FAX: (212) 315-1132.
PRESIDENT
Donald L. Taffner
CEO
John P. Fitzgerald
EXECUTIVE V.P. & MANAGING DIRECTOR, DOMESTIC
Bob Peyton
V.P., INTERNTIONAL SALES
Gilliam Rose
Series: As Time Goes By (50 x 30 mins), Homestyle (120 x 30 mins.), The Lonely Chef (130 x 30 mins.).

Comedy: About Face (13 x 30 mins.), After Henry (19 x 30 mins.), A Kind of Living (13 x 30 mins.), All at #20 (12 x 30 mins.), Benny Hill (111 x 30 mins.), Chances in a Million (18 x 30 mins.), Executive Stress (19 x 30 mins.), Ffizz (12 x 30 mins.), French Fields (27 x 30 mins.), Fresh Fields (27 x 30 mins.), Never the Twain (42 x 30 mins.), No Job for a Lady (12 x 30 mins.), The Russ Abbot Show (45 x 30 mins.), Shelley (58 x 30 mins.), Thames Comedy Originals (156 x 30 mins.).

Animated: Count Duckula (65 x 30 mins.), Animated Family Classics (29 hours).

Series/Off Network: Check It Out (66 x 30 mins.), Three's Company (222 x 30 mins.), Too Close for Comfort (129 x 30 mins.), The Ropers (26 x 30 mins.), Three's a Crowd (22 x 30 mins.).

Children's Programs: Wind in the Willows (65 x 30 mins.).

Features/Packages: Dick Francis Mysteries (2 hrs. each), The Saint (6 films, 2 hrs. each), Selling Hitler (5 one-hrs.).

Specials: Benny Hill Specials (18 hrs.), The Heat is On, Miss Saigon (60 or 90 mins.).

Game Shows: Talkabout (260 x 30 mins.), 5-4-3-2 Run (34 x 30 mins.).

Drama: The Bill (65 x 30 mins.), Capitol City (23 hrs.), Danger: UXB (13 hrs.), Hannay (13 hrs.), London Embassy (6 hrs.), Lytton's Diary (13 hrs.), Mr. Palfrey of Westminister (10 hrs.), Minder (13 hrs.), The One Game (4 hrs.), Reilly: Ace of Spies (11 hrs. and 1 x 90 mins.), Rock Follies (12 hrs.), Unnatural Causes (7 hrs.).

Documentaries: Black Museum (60 mins.), Cambodia Year Ten (60 mins.), Destination America (9 hrs.), Holiday World (52 x 30 mins.), Hollywood (13 hrs.), Killiam Collection (13 five-mins.), Nature Watch (27 x 30 mins.), Revival at the Desert (45 mins.), The World at War (36 hrs.).

DE PASSE ENTERTAINMENT
5750 Wilshire Blvd., Suite 640, Los Angeles, CA 90036. (213) 965-2580. FAX: (213) 965-2598.
CHAIRMAN & CEO
Suzanne de Passe
RPESIDENT
Suzanne Coston
Series: Lonesome Dove: The Outlaw Years, Lupe Solano, Nite Time, Sister Sister, The Smart Guy.
Specials: Motown 25: Yesterday Today Forever, Motown Goes To The Apollo, Motown 30: What's Goin' On.
Movies: Someone Else's Child.
Miniseries: Buffalo Girls, Dead Man's Walk, The Jacksons: An American Dream, Lonesome Dove, Return To Lonesome Dove, Small Sacrifices, Streets of Laredo.
Upcoming Products: Courage of Conviction: The Martha Bethel Story, Five Smooth Stones, The Kindness of Strangers, Motown Presents, The Ronnie Spector Story, Without A Choice.

VIN DI BONA PRODUCTIONS
12233 W. Olympic Blvd., Suite 170, Los Angeles, CA 90064. (310) 442-5600. FAX: (310) 442-5604.
Series: America's Funniest Home Videos, Sherman Oaks.

DISCOVERY COMMUNICATIONS
7700 Wisconsin Ave., Bethesda, MD 20814. (301) 986-7080.
FAX: (301) 986-4826.
PRESIDENT, CEO & CREATIVE OFFICER
Grey Moyer
V.P., INT'L OPERATIONS & PROGRAM SALES
Lesley Turner
New Products: Eyes In The Sky, Harlem Diary, Last Of The
Czars, Royal Secrets.

WALT DISNEY TELEVISION ANIMATION
5200 Lankershim Blvd., N. Hollywood, CA 91601. (818) 754-7100.
Series: Disney's Aladdin, Duck Daze, Gargoyles, The Lion
King's Timon & Pumbaa.

E

E! ENTERTAINMENT TELEVISION
5670 Wilshire Blvd., Los Angeles, CA 90036. (213) 954-2400.
FAX: (213) 954-2620. URL: http://www.eonline.com
PRESIDENT & CEO
Lee Masters
S.V.P., ADVERTISING SALES
David T. Cassaro
S.V.P. INTERNATIONAL DEVELOPMENT
Christopher B. Fager
S.V.P., AFFILIATE RELATIONS
Debra Green
S.V.P., MARKETING
Dale Hopkins
S.V.P., PROGRAMMING
Fran Shea
Series: Behind the Scenes, Coming Attractions, E! News
Daily, Fashion File, The Gossip Show, Howard Stern, Melrose
Place, On E! Specials, Q & E!, Talk Soup, ThE! Movie, Uncut.

RALPH EDWARDS/STU BILLETT PRODUCTIONS
6922 Hollywood Blvd., #415, Hollywood, CA 90028. (213)
851-1500.
OWNER
Ralph Edwards
Syndication: Family Medical Center, Love Stories, The
People's Court, Superior Court, This is Your Life, Truth or
Consequences.

ENTERTAINMENT PRODUCTIONS, INC.
2118 Wilshire Blvd., Room 744, Santa Monica, CA 90403.
(310) 456-3143. FAX: (310) 828-0427.
PRESIDENT & PRODUCER
Edward Coe
Series: Bankruptcy Fever, Las Vegas Shows, That's Lawyer
Talk.
Specials: Alien Kid, Bankruptcy Exposed, Kidsville, Mama
Hanukkah and Santa Claus–A Joint Adventure.

EYEMARK ENTERTAINMENT
(a unit of CBS Enterprises)
10877 Wilshire Blvd., 9th floor, Los Angeles, CA 90024. (310)
446-6000. FAX: (310) 446-6066.
51 W. 52nd. St., New York, NY 10019. (212) 975-4321. FAX:
(212) 975-9174.
PRESIDENT
Ed Wilson
EXECUTIVE VICE PRESIDENTS
Robert A. Cook, Marvin A. Shirley
EXECUTIVE V.P., SYNDICATION
Barry Wallach
S.V.P., BUSINESS AND PROGRAM DEVELOPMENT
Robb E. Dalton
Series: Bob Vila's Home Again, Day & Date, The Extremists,
George Michael Sports Machine, Haven, Hearts Afire, Martha
Stewart Living, News for Kids, Premier I, Psi Factor:
Chronicles of the Paranormal, Treasury IV, World of Nature.

F

FILM ROMAN INC.
12020 Chandler Blvd., #200, N. Hollywood, CA 91607. (818)
761-2544. FAX: (818) 985-2973.
PRESIDENT
Phil Roman
EXECUTIVE VICE PRESIDENT
Bill Schultz
PRODUCER
Carol Corwin

Series: Bobby's World, Klutter, The Mask, New Adventures of
Felix the Cat.

FILMROOS, INC.
8899 Beverly Blvd., 6th fl., Los Angeles, CA 90048. (310) 205-
5490. FAX: (310) 205-0217.
PRESIDENT & EXECUTIVE PRODUCER
Bram Roos
DIRECTOR, DEVELOPMENT
Sylvia A. Ruiz
Series: Ancient Mysteries, Biography, Intimate Portraits.

FINNEGAN-PINCHUK CO.
4225 Coldwater Canyon, Studio City, CA 91604. (818) 508-
5614.

44 BLUE PRODUCTIONS, INC.
4040 Vineland Ave., Suite 205, Studio City, CA 91604. (818)
760-4442. FAX: (818) 760-1509.
PRESIDENT & CEO
Rasha Drachkovitch
Series: World of Valor, Nash & Zullo's Offbeat Sports Beat,
Champions.
Features: Aspire Higher, Bob Uecker's Wacky World of Sports,
Concours Automotive Series, Death Row: The Only Fitting
Punishment?, Discovery Sport, An Evening with Edward
TellerFootball/Basketball, Future Stars in Sport, Great
Moments in College Bowl History, History of College Football
(also Part II), Legends of College Super Sports Follies,
Legends of Rock 'n' Roll Scrapbook, Secrets of Winning Sweep-
stakes, Serbian Tradition, Showtime Earthquake Relief Benefit.

FOUR POINT ENTERTAINMENT, INC.
3575 Cahuenga Blvd. W., #600, Los Angeles, CA 90068. (213)
850-1600. FAX: (213) 850-6709.
PRESIDENT
Ron Ziskin
CHAIRMAN
Shukri Ghalayini
Series: Amazing America, American Gladiators, Gladiators
2000, Great Drives, Guilty Pleasures, The Other Side.

FOUR STAR INTERNATIONAL, INC.
1440 S. Sepulveda, Los Angeles, CA 90025. (310) 444-8400.
PRESIDENT
Lennart Ringquist
Series: Big Valley, Detectives, Honey West, Rouges.
Movies: Cisco Kid Features (13 features), Dick Tracy (8 fea-
tures), No Restrictions (13 new films), Star One (15 new
films), Star Two (15 new films).

FOX BROADCASTING CO.
P.O. Box 900, Beverly Hills, CA 90213, (310) 277-2211.
(For officers and personnel see listing under Companies.)
Series/First Run: Chicago Hope, Cleghorne!, The Crew, A
Current Affair (daily live 30 mins.), NYPD Blue, Picket Fences,
The Preston Episodes, The Simpsons, Space: Above and
Beyond, The X-Files.
Series/Off-Network: Circus (52 x 30 mins.), That's Hollywood
(74 x 30 mins.).
Series/Off-Network: Adventures in Paradise (91 x 60 mins.),
Animal Express (130 x 30 mins.), The Ann Sothern Show (93
x 30 mins.), Audubon Wildlife Theater (78 x 30 mins.), Batman
(120 x 30 mins.), Bracken's World (41 x 60 mins.), Broken
Arrow (72 x 60 mins. b&w), Circus (52 x 30 mins.), Daniel
Boone (20 x 60 mins.), Dobie Gillis (147 x 60 mins. b&w),
Dynasty (198 hours), Expedition Danger (26 x 30 mins.), Fall
Guy (112 hours), The Ghost and Mrs. Muir (50 x 30 mins.),
Green Hornet (26 x 30 mins.), Incredible World of Adventure
(31 x 30 mins.), Jackie Gleason Show (100 x 30 mins.), Judd
for the Defense (50 x 60 mins.), Julia (86 x 30 mins.), Lancer
(51 x 60 mins.), Land of the Giants (51 x 60 mins.), Lost in
Space (83 x 50 mins., 54 color), M*A*S*H (255 x 30 mins.),
Miller's Court (52 x 30 mins.), The Monroes (26 x 60 mins.),
Movin' On (44 x 60 mins.), Mr. Belvedere (95 x 30 mins.), 9 to
5 (85 x 30 mins.), Nanny and the Professor (54 x 30 mins.),
Peyton Place (247 x 30 mins. color & 267 x 30 mins., b&w),
Private Secretary (104 x 30 mins.), Room 222 (113 x 60
mins.), Small Wonder (96 x 30 mins.), That's Hollywood (74 x
30 mins.), Trapper John (151 x 60 mins.), 12 O'Clock High (78
x 60 mins., 17 color, 61 b&w), The Untamed World (156 x 30
mins.), Vegas (68 x 60 mins.), Voyage to the Bottom of the
Sea (111 x 60 mins., 78 color, 32 b&w).
Specials: Anatomy of a Crime (1 hr.), Assassins Among Us (1
hr.), Blind Alley (1 hr.), The Cancer Confrontation (1 hr.),
Charles Dickens' Classics (8 hrs.), Divorce, Kids in the Middle
(1 hr.), Fox Movietone News (520 newsreels), Future Shock (1
hr.), Gudonov - The World to Dance In (1 hr.), Hollywood: The

Gift of Laughter (3 hrs.), Inside Russia (1 hr.), Jane Goodall and the World of Animal Behavior (4 hrs.), The Making of M*A*S*H (1), The President's Command Performance (2 hrs.), Sex, Teenage Style (1 hr.), Summer Solstice (1 hr.), Time of Man (1 hr.), The Undersea World of Jacques Cousteau (36 hrs.), War to End all Wars (1 hr.).

Features/Packages: Big 36 (36 titles, 5 color, 29 b&w), Carry On (11 titles), Century 5, 6, 7, 8, 9, 20, 22, 23 (total of 220 titles, 212 color and 8 b&w), Century 13 (26 titles), Century 14 (20 titles, includes Aliens, Black Widow, Cocoon, The Fly, The Jewel of the Nile, The Name of the Rose), Fox Premiere Movies (9 titles, includes: Enemy Mine, The Name of the Rose, Project X), Fox Mini-Series I (4 titles: Tender Is the Night, Jamaica Inn, Little Gloria, Evergreen), Fox IV, V & VI (102 color, 102 b&w), Fox Mystery Theatre (13 titles, 90-min. specials), Fox Hollywood Theatre '89 - 90 (7 titles including: Miracle on 34th Street, Almost You, Eating Raoul, Kidco), Golden Century (49 titles b&w), Special 41 (41 titles, 26 color, 15 b&w), Mark I (10 titles), Mark II (16 titles), Mark III (25 titles), MPC-20 (20 titles), Planet of the Apes (5 hrs.), Premiere I (20 titles), Premium Plus (28 titles), Premiere II (22 titles), Premiere III (20 titles), Super 65 (48 color, 17 b&w), Time Tunnel (5 hrs.).

Domestic Late-Night Network: The New Avengers (26 hours).

Domestic Miniseries: Empire, Inc. (6 hrs.), The Far Pavilions (6 hrs.), Mussolini and I (4 hrs.), Roughnecks (4 hrs.), Sara Dane (8 hrs.), Spearfield's Daughter (6 hrs.), Wild Times (4 hrs.).

Domestic Cartoons: Crusader Rabbit (13 color hrs., 260 x 4 mins, 195 x 4 mins. b & w), Doctor Doolittle (17 x 30 mins.), Fantastic Voyage (17 x 30 mins.), Groovie Goolies & Friends (104 x 30 mins.), The Hardy Boys (17 x 30 mins.), Journey to the Center of the Earth (17 x 30 mins.), Return to the Planet of the Apes (13 x 30 mins.).

FOX LORBER ASSOCIATES, INC.
419 Park Ave. South, 20th Floor, New York, NY 10016. (212) 686-6777. FAX: (212) 685-2625.
PRESIDENT & CEO
Richard Lorber
V.P., WORLDWIDE PROGRAM SALES
Sherri Levine
V.P., INTERNATIONAL SALES
Mickie Steinmann
New Entertainment Series: Circus Around the World, Life on the Digital Edge, Models Profiles and Fantasies, Out of Control, Tilt 23 1/2.
Documentary Series: The Directors, Space Tech.

FOXLAB
5746 Sunset Blvd., Los Angeles, CA 90028-8588. (213) 856-1000.
Series: America's Most Wanted, Cops, Final Justice, Liars, Manhunter, Not Just News.

THE FREMANTLE CORPORATION
660 Madison Ave., 21st floor, New York, NY 10021. (212) 421-4530. FAX: (212) 207-8357.
Fremantle of Canada, Ltd., 23 Lesmill Rd., Suite 201, Don Mills, Ontario M3B 3P6. (416) 443-9204. FAX: (416) 443-8685.
The Fremantle Corporation Ltd., Unit 2, Water Lane, Kentish Town Rd., London, England NW1 8NZS. (44-171) 284-0880. FAX: (44-171) 209-2294.
Fremantle Productions Pty., Ltd., 2nd floor, 486 Pacific Highway, St. Leonards, Autralia NSW 2065. (61-2) 428-3377. FAX: (61-2) 439-1827.
Fremantle de Espana, Ltd., Sacedilla 13-13, Bajahonda, Madrid, Spain 28220. (341) 639-2688. FAX: (341) 639-4025.
PRESIDENT & CEO
Paul Talbot
SECRETARY & TREASURER
Fannie Mack
SENIOR VICE PRESIDENT
Josh Talbot
V.P., INT'L SALES, LATIN AMERICA, HOME VIDEO
Julie Zuleta-Corbo
V.P., CHINA SALES
Dianbo Xie
DIRECTOR, NEW PROGRAM DEVELOPMENT
Keith Talbot
V.P., SALES, CANADA
Frank Braun
MANAGING DIRECTOR, UK
Tony Gruner
DIRECTOR OF PROGRAM SALES, UK
Veronique Heim
CHAIRMAN, AUSTRALIA
Russell Becker
MANAGING DIRECTOR, AUSTRALIA
Richard Becker

SALES AGENT, SPAIN
Antoinetta Brughera
Series: The Anti-Gravity Room (26 x 30 mins.), Baywatch (155 hrs. & 7 2 hr. movies), The Baywatch Summerfest Special (1 hr.), The Best of Baywatch Special (1 hr.), The Campbells (100 x 30 mins., Years I, II, III, IV), Candid Camera (385 x 30 mins., 7 hr. specials, 7 30 mins. specials, 35 30 mins. "Adult" versions), The City (30 mins. strip), The Conspiracy Tapes (12 hrs.), Davis Rules (29 x 30 mins.), Family Theater (31 hrs.), Fire Rescue (24 x 30 mins.), Frannie's Turn (6 x 30 mins.), Funny People (6 hrs.), The Galloping Gourmet (595 x 30 mins.), Grace Under Fire (123 x 30 mins.), Loving (30 min. strip), Makin 8 (27 x 30 mins./25 hrs. & 1 hr. special), Mysterious Island (22 hrs./44 x 30 mins.), Raising Miranda (9 x 30 mins.), Save Our Streets (46 hrs.), She TV (6 hrs.), Swiss Family Robinson (26 x 30 mins.), Take Herr (155 5 mins.), TV 101 (17 hrs.), The Tripods (25 x 30 mins.) 3rd Rock From The Sun (19 x 30 mins.), The Van Dyke Show (9 x 30 mins.), Warriors Of Wrestling (52 hrs.), You Bet Your Life (195 x 30 mins.).
Animated Series: The Happy Circus (Le Cirque Bonheur) (10 x 8 mins.), In The Beginning: Stories From The Bible (26 x 30 mins.), Miss Peach: "Career Day At The Kelly School" (1 hr.).
Animated Specials: Family Circus (3 x 30 mins.), Little Orphan Annie's A Very Animated Christmas (1 half hr.), The Mousehole Cat (1 half hr.), On Christmas Eve (1 half hr.), Snowman (1 half hr.).
TV Movies: Can You Feel Me Dancing (2 hrs., NBC), Cat On A Hot Tin Roof (150 mins.), A Fight For Jenny (2 hrs., NBC), Half Slave, Half Free (2 hrs., PBS), The Killing Floor (2 hrs. PBS), The Last Days Of Frank And Jesse James (2 hrs., ABC), Loving (2 hrs., ABC), Manhunt For Claude Dallas (2 hrs., CBS), On Fire (2 hrs., ABC), Special People (2 hrs., CBS), Still Watch (2 hrs., CBS), Strange Possession Of Mrs. Oliver (2 hrs., ABC), Vanishing Act (2 hrs., ABC), We Are The Children (2 hrs., ABC).
Specials: American Comedy Awards (2 hrs.), An All-Star Tribute To Rosemary Clooney (90 mins.), An All-Star Word From Our Sponsor (1 hr.), The All-Star Christmas Concert (1 hr.), Celebrity First Loves (2 hrs.), Comedy Hall Of Fame (2 hrs.), Country Comes Home 1 & 2 (2 hrs. each), Daredevils (2 hrs.), Jazz In America, The Kennedy Center Honors (2 hrs.), Las Vegas 75th Anniversary (2 hrs.), Magic With The Stars (2 hrs.), Muhammad Ali's 50th Birthday Celebration (2 hrs.), A Party For Richard Pryor (2 hrs.), Penn & Teller: Don't Try This At Home (1 hr.), Roy Acuff: The King Of Country Music (2 hrs.), Rowan & Martin's Laugh-In: 25th Anniversary (2 hrs.), Past Christmas Present (1 hr.), Romance, Love Sex And Marriage (1 hr.), Sammy Davis Jr's 60th Anniversary Celebration (2.5 hrs.), Seven Wonders Of The Circus World (1 hr.), The 75th Anniversary Of Beverly Hills (1 hr.), Tony Awards (2 hrs.), A Word From Our Sponsor I & II (1 hr. each),
Documentaries: Erich Von Stroheim–The Man You Loved To Hate (90 mins.), Russia's War: Blood Upon The Snow (10 hrs.), Wild Westerns (9 hrs.), Wildlife International I & II (34 x 30 mins.).

CHUCK FRIES PRODUCTIONS INC.
6922 Hollywood Blvd., Los Angeles, CA 90028. (213) 466-2266. Fax: (213) 465-7835.

G

GGP/GGP SPORTS
400 Tamal Plaza, Corte Madera, CA 9492.5 (415) 924-7500. FAX: (415) 924-0264.
CHAIRMAN & CEO
Corey Busch
PRESIDENT
Robert C. Horowitz
DIRECTOR, OPERATIONS
Robert Boeri
V.P., ACQUISITIONS & DISTRIBUTION
Hillary Mandel
Features: College Bowl Preview, College Football Special, Cool Picks, Escape From Alcatraz Triathlon, NFL Pre-Season Special, Nothin But Net, Olympic Century Series, TV.COM.

GRB ENTERTAINMENT
12001 Ventura Pl., #600, Studio City, CA 91604, (818) 753-3400.
Series: Hollywood's Greatest Stunts, Movie Magic, World of Wonder.

GTG ENTERTAINMENT
9336 W. Washington Blvd., Culver City, CA 90230. (310) 885-2600.
PRESIDENT
Grant Tinker
Series: Baywatch, USA Today on TV.

GENESIS ENTERTAINMENT
1440 South Sepulveda Blvd., Los Angeles, CA 90025. (310)
444-8344. FAX: (310) 231-1633.
625 Madison Ave., 11th fl., New York, NY 10022. (212) 527-
6400. FAX: (212) 527-6401.
PRESIDENT & CEO
Wayne Lepoff
S.V.P., WEST COAST SALES
Ed Wasserman
EXECUTIVE V.P., NEW YORK.
Phil Oldham
S.V.P., DOMESTIC SALES, NEW YORK
Barry Wallach
Series: Biker Mice from Mars (65 x 30 mins.), Emergency Call
(104 x 30 mins.), Fantastic Four (26 x 30 mins.), Juvenile
Justice (210 x 30 mins.), Marvel Action Universe—Iron Man
(26 x 30 mins.), The Mark Walberg Show (195 hours), Real
Stories of the Highway Patrol (325 x 30 mins.).
Syndicated: Tales From The Crypt, Top Cops.

SAMUEL GOLDWYN TELEVISION
10203 Santa Monica Blvd., Los Angeles, CA 90067. (310)
552-2255. FAX: (310) 284-8493.
888 Seventh Ave., #2901, New York, NY 10106. (212) 315-3030.
625 Center St., Elgin, IL 60120. (708) 468-0468.
760 S. Waukegan Rd., Lake Forest, IL 60045. (708) 735-9041.
PRESIDENT, TV
Dick Askin

MARK GOODSON PRODUCTIONS
5750 Wilshire Blvd., Los Angeles, CA 90036. (213) 965-6500.
FAX: (212) 965-6527.
PRESIDENT & CEO
Jonathan Goodson
SENIOR VICE PRESIDENT
Michael S. Brockman
COO
Harris Katleman
CFO
Alan R. Sandler
Products: Beat the Clock, Blockbusters, Body Language, Card
Sharks, Child's Play, Classic Concentration, I've Got A Secret
(all tape), Match Game, Mind Readers, New Family Feud,
Password, The Price Is Right, The Rebel (film), The Richard
Boone Show, Super Password, Tattletales, To Tell The Truth,
Trivia Trap, What's My Line.

GOTHIC RENAISSANCE PRODS.
1223 N. 23rd St., Wilmington, NC 28404. (910) 251-2211.
Series: American Gothic.

GRACIE FILMS
c/o Sony Film Corp., 10202 W. Washington Blvd., Culver City,
CA 90232. (310) 280-4222. FAX: (310) 280-1530.
Current Series: The Simpsons.

GRAY-SCHWARTZ ENTERPRISES, INC.
Teleflix Division, 4507 Park Allegra, Calabasas, CA 91302-
1759. (818) 222-6500. FAX: (818) 222-6501.
PRESIDENT
Marv Gray
Series: Cimarron Strip, I Married Joan, Make Room For
Daddy, My Little Margie.

GREYSTONE COMMUNICATIONS, INC.
4705 Laurel Canyon Blvd., 5th floor, Valley Village, CA 91607-
3960. (818) 762-2900. FAX: (818) 762-1626.
PRESIDENT
Craig A. Haffner
EXECUTIVE VICE PRESIDENTS
Steven Lewis, Donna E. Lusitana
Series: Ancient Mysteries, Biography, The Life and Times of...

MERV GRIFFIN ENTERPRISES
Beverly Hilton Hotel, 9860 Wilshire Blvd., Beverly Hills, CA
90210. (310) 859-0188.
CHAIRMAN & CEO
Merv Griffin
PRESIDENT & COO
Robert J. Murphy
Series: Jeopardy!, Wheel of Fortune.

GRUB STREET PRODS.
c/o Paramount TV, 5555 Melrose Ave., Wilder #101, Los
Angeles, CA 90038-3197. (213) 956-4657. FAX: (213) 956-0064.
Series: Almost Perfect, Frasier, Pursuit of Happiness, Wings.

REG GRUNDY PRODUCTIONS, INC.
9911 W. Pico Blvd., Suite 1200, Los Angeles, CA 90035-2703.
(310) 557-3555. FAX: (310) 277-1687.
CHAIRMAN
Reg Grundy
CEO
Richard Barovick
V.P., DEVELOPMENT
Robert Noah
Syndication: Bony (series), Dangerous Women (series),
Embassy (series), Neighbors (series), The Other Side of
Paradise (mini-series), Sale of the Century (game show),
Scattergories (game show), Scrabble (game show),
Tanamera–Lion of Singapore (mini-series).

H

HBO DOWNTOWN PRODS.
120 E. 23 St., New York, NY 10010. (212) 512-8900. FAX:
(212) 512-8968.
Series: Dr. Katz: Professional Therapist, Exit 57, Mystery
Science Theater 3000, Politically Incorrect.

HBO INDEPENDENT PRODS., INC.
2049 Century Park E., Los Angeles, CA 90067. (310) 201-
9200.
Series: Martin.

HALLMARK ENTERTAINMENT
1325 Avenue of the Americas, 21st floor, New York, NY 10019.
(212) 977-9001. FAX: (212) 977-9049.
9 Cork St., 2nd floor, London W1X 1PD, U.K. (44-171) 439-
0633. FAX: (44-171) 439-0644.
100 Walker St., Suite 9, N. Sydney, NSW 2060, Australia. (02)
9957 2999. FAX: (02) 9957 2247.
Hallmark Home Entertainment: 6100 Wilshire Blvd., Suite 1400,
Los Angeles, CA 90048. (213) 634-3000. FAX: (213) 549-3760.
Hallmark Entertainment Network: 5670 Greenwood Plaza Blvd.,
Penthouse, Englewood, CO 80111. (303) 220-7990. FAX: 9303)
220-7660.
CHAIRMAN
Robert Halmi, Sr.
PRESIDENT & CEO
Robert Halmi, Jr.
EXECUTIVE V.P., & COO
Peter von Gal
PRESIDENT, HALLMARK ENTERTAINMENT PRODUCTIONS
& EXECUTIVE V.P. CREATIVE AFFAIRS
Steve Hewitt
PRESIDENT & CEO HALLMARK ENTERTAINMENT NETWORK
George Stein
S.V.P., MANAGING DIRECTOR INT'L SALES
Joel Denton
Products: Barefoot In The Park (ABC 2 hrs.), Beyond The Call
(Showtime, 2 hrs.), Dean Man's Walk (ABC, 6 hrs.), End of
Summer (Showtime, 2 hrs.), Gulliver's Travels (NBC, 4 hrs.),
Harvey (CBS, 2 hrs.), Homer's Odyssey (NBC, 4 hrs.), In Cold
Blood (CBS, 4 hrs.), Inside (Showtime, 2 hrs.), Jake's Women
(CBS, 2 hrs.), Lily Dale (Showtome, 2 hrs.), London Suite (NBC,
2 hrs.), Lonesome Dove, Losing Chase (Showtime, 2 hrs.),
Money Plays (Showtime, 2 hrs.), National Geographic Night At
The Movies (6 x 2 hrs.), The Ransom of Red Chief (ABC, 2
hrs.), Scarlett, Streets of Laredo.

HAMDON ENTERTAINMENT
12711 Ventura Blvd., Suite 300, Studio City, CA 91604. (818)
753-6363. FAX: (818) 753-6388.
V.P., WORLDWIDE SALES
Michael Appleby
TV Movies: 40 films including: Family Rescue, Here Comes
The Sun, Hunt For Justice, In The Blink Of An Eye, Race
Against Time, Unforgivable.

HANNA-BARBERA CARTOONS, INC.
(A subsidiary of Turner Broadcasting System, Inc.)
3400 Cahuenga Blvd., Hollywood, CA 90068. (213) 851-5000.
FAX: (213) 969-1201.
CO-CHAIRMAN & FOUNDER
Joseph Barbera
CO-CHAIRMAN & FOUNDER
William Hanna
PRESIDENT
Fred Seibert
EXECUTIVE PRODUCER, TV
Buzz Potamkin

V.P., DEVELOPMENT & PROGRAMMING
Jeff Holder
Animated Series: Dumb & Dumber, The New Adventures of Captain Planet, The Real Adventures of Jonny Quest.
Animated Specials: Babe He Calls Me, Bloo's Gang, Boid 'n' Woim, Cow and Chicken, Dexter's Laboratory, Dino: The Great Egg-scape, Help?, Hillbilly Blue, Johnny Bravo and the Amazon Women, Mina and the Count, Pfish and Chip II, Pizza Boy, Podunk Possom, Strange Things, Tales of Worm Paranoia.

DEAN HARGROVE PRODUCTIONS
(Producer in assoc. with Fred Silverman Co. & Viacom Prods.)
100 Universal City Plaza, #507-3E, Universal City, CA 91608. (818) 777-8305
Series/TV Movies: Diagnosis Murder, Matlock, Perry Mason Movies.

HARMONY GOLD U.S.A.
7655 Sunset Blvd., Los Angeles, CA 90046. (213) 851-4900. FAX: (213) 851-5599.
CHAIRMAN & CEO
Frank Agrama
EXECUTIVE V.P., CREATIVE AFFAIRS
Norman Siderow
V.P., BUSINESS & LEGAL AFFAIRS
Robert Cohen
V.P., SALES
Alan Letz
Animation: Animation Adventure Theatre (3 features), Captain Harlock (65 x 30 mins.), Robotech (85 x 30 mins.).
Mini-series: Around the World in 80 Days (6 hrs.), Confessional (4 hrs.), Heidi (4 hrs.), The King of the Olympics (4 hrs.), The Man Who Lived at the Ritz (4 hrs.), Shaka Zulu (10 hrs.), Sherlock Holmes & the Leading Lady (4 hrs.), Sherlock Holmes: Incident at Victoria Falls (4 hrs.).
Series: Animals of Africa (52 x 30 mins.), Stephen King's World of Horror (11 x 60 mins.), World of Horses (26 x 30 mins.).
Features/Specials: Cannibals (1 hr.), Fire Attack (1 hr.), The Lost World (2 hrs.), Return to the Lost World (2 hrs.), The Secret Identity of Jack the Ripper (live special event).

HARPO ENTERTAINMENT GROUP
110 N. Carpenter St., Chicago, IL 60607. (312) 633-1000.
CHAIRMAN & CEO
Oprah Winfrey
PRESIDENT & COO
Jeffrey Jacobs
EXECUTIVE PRODUCER
Danne Atkinson Hudson
Series: The Oprah Winfrey Show.

HEARST ENTERTAINMENT, INC.
235 E. 45 St., New York, NY 10017. (212) 455-4000. FAX: (212) 983-6379. Telex: 7105812391.
PRESIDENT, HEARST ENT. INC.
Bruce L. Paisner
PRESIDENT, DISTRIBUTION & HEARST ANIMATION
William E. Miller
V.P., INTERNATIONAL SALES
Michael Doury
Series: Our Home.

ARTHUR HENLEY PRODUCTIONS
175 Fifth Ave., Suite 2462, New York, NY 10010. (718) 263-0136.
PRESIDENT
Arthur Henley
Products: Lily & Joel, Make Up Your Mind.

JIM HENSON PRODUCTIONS
117 E. 69th St., New York, NY 10021. (212) 794-2400. FAX: (212) 570-1147.
c/o Raleigh Studios, 5358 Melrose Ave., West Office Building, 3rd Floor, Hollywood, CA 90038. (213) 960-4096. FAX: (213) 960-4935.
1(B) Downshire Hill, Hampstead, London NW3 1NR, England. (44-171) 431-2818. FAX: (44-171) 431-3737.
Product: Jim Henson's Animal Show with Stinky and Jake.

WALTER HILL PRODUCTIONS
4500 Wilshire Blvd., Los Angeles, CA 90038. (213) 956-8083. FAX: (213) 954-4550.
EXECUTIVE PRODUCERS
Leonard Hill, Joel Fields
V.P., PRODUCTION
Ardythe Goergens

I

IFEX INTERNATIONAL
159 W. 53 St., Suite 19-B, New York, NY 10019-6050. (212) 582-4318. FAX: (212) 956-2257.
EXECUTIVE OFFICERS
Gerald J. Rappoport, Beulah Rappoport, Dorothy Clarke

INI ENTERTAINMENT GROUP, INC.
11845 W. Olympic Blvd., Suite 1145, Los Angeles, CA 90064. (310) 479-6755. FAX: (310) 479-3475.
CEO
Irv Holender
PRESIDENT & COO
Michael Ricci
EXECUTIVE V.P., SALES & DISTRIBUTION
Sy Samuels
MANAGER, INTERNATIONAL SALES
Tara Spencer
Animated Features: The Adventures of Pinocchio, Alice Through The Looking Glass, International Family Classics (14 x 60 & 90 min. features), The Lollipop Dragon, The New Adventures Of Oliver Twist, Sparky's Magic Piano.
Features: Face Of The Enemy, Operation, Take No Prisoners, Regina, The Return Of Superfly, Tunnels.
Sports Packages: Gorgeous Ladies Of Wrestling (104 hrs.), Universal Wrestling Federation (72 hrs.).

ITC ENTERTAINMENT GROUP
6100 Wilshire Blvd., Suite 600, Beverly Hills, CA 90210. (310) 724-8100. FAX: (310) 274-7849.
115 E. 57 St., New York, NY 10022. (212) 371-6660. FAX: (212) 308-6713.
PRESIDENT & CEO
Jules Haimovitz
SENIOR VICE PRESIDENT
Michael Birnbaum
EXECUTIVE V.P., ITC DISTRIBUTION
Les Haber
V.P. & GENERAL SALES MANAGER, DOMESTIC TV
Mike Russo
Feature Films: Volume 10 (32 features including: Young Doctors in Love, Stepfather 2, Sex Lies and Videotape), Movie of the Month Network 4 (12 features including: Doppelganger, Whispers, David Hardware, Rage in Harlem and Trouble Bound), Volume 9 (8 features including: Better Off Dead, Jacknife and Without a Clue).
Series: Motorweek, Madison's Adventures: Growing Up Wild.
Mini-Series: Night of the Fox, People Like Us, Touch and Die.

IMAGE ORGANIZATION, INC.
9000 Sunset Blvd., Suite 915, Los Angeles, CA 90069. (310) 278-8751. FAX: (310) 278-3967.
CHAIRMAN & CEO
Pierre David
S.V.P., WORLDWIDE DISTRIBUTION
Erik Saltzbrger
DIRECTOR, ACQUISITIONS & MARKETING
Carol Crowe
TV-Movies: Daddy's Girl, The Nurse, The Secretary, Stranger In The House, The Wrong Woman.

INDEPENDENT-INTERNATIONAL PICTURES CORP.
400 Perrine Rd., Old Bridge, NJ 08857. (908) 727-8500. FAX: (908) 727-8881.
PRESIDENT
Samuel M. Sherman
CHAIRMAN
Daniel Q. Kennis
EXECUTIVE VICE PRESIDENT
Jeffrey C. Hogue, J.D., L.L.M.
Feature packages:
Action Group: The Gun Riders, Mission to Death, The Fakers, Queen of Sheba, The Barbarians, Submarine Attack, Fighting Rats of Tobruk, Money.
Scream Showcase: Beyond the Living, Demons of the Dead, Doctor Dracula, Exorcism at Midnight, In Search of Dracula, Man with the Synthetic Brain, Ship of Zombies, Terror of Frankenstein, Vampire Men of the Lost Planet, Hand of Power, Night Fiend, Horror of the Werewolf, Voice from the Grave.
Drive In Theatre: The Murder Gang, Intrigue in the Orient, Blazing Stewardesses, The Naughty Stewardesses, Trapped in the Desert, The Smiling Maniacs, Syndicate Sadists.

J

JEF FILMS, INC.
Film House, 143 Hickory Hill Circle, Osterville, MA 02655-1322. (508) 428-7198. FAX: (508) 428-7198. Organized 1973. Branches: Los Angeles (Film Classic Exchange), Australia, New Zealand, England, France, Spain, Portugal, Greece, Canada, Fiji, Switzerland, Austria, West Germany, Italy, Monaco, Ireland, Denmark, Finland, Sweden, Norway, Belgium, Luxembourg, Algeria, Morocco, Tunisia, South Korea.
CEO
Jeffrey H. Aikman
VICE PRESIDENT
Elsie Aikman
SALES MANAGER
Jo-Ann Pollack
Product: A library of over 30,000 films from the following libraries: Film Classic Exchange, XTC Video, WHAM! Video!, VIP Video, JEF Video line, JEF Films International, PHD Video, The Stock Exchange.

MICHAEL JACOBS PRODS.
c/o Walt Disney Studios, 500 S. Buena Vista St., Animation 2A, Burbank, CA 91521. (818) 560-2160. FAX: (818) 567-0415.
CEO
Michael Jacobs
Series: Boy Meets World.

QUINCY JONES/DAVID SALZMAN ENTERTAINMENT
3800 Barham Blvd., #503, Los Angeles, CA 90068. (213) 874-2009. FAX: (213) 874-3363.
CEO
Quincy Jones, David Salzman
EXECUTIVE PRODUCER
Jerry Gottlieb
V.P., TV DEVELOPMENT
Debra Langford
Series: Fresh Prince of Bel Air, In the House, Jenny Jones.

K

DAVID E. KELLEY PRODS.
c/o Twentieth Century Fox, 10201 W. Pico Blvd., Bldg. 80, Los Angeles, CA 90035-2651. (310) 369-4570.
PRESIDENT
Jeffrey Kramer
WRITER/EXECUTIVE PRODUCER
David E. Kelley
Series: Picket Fences.

KENNEVIK MEDIA PROPERTIES, LTD.
153 E. 53 St., Suite 5900, New York, NY 10022. (212) 755-4742. FAX: (212) 755-4628.
PRESIDENT
Joseph E. Kovacs
Over 150 theatrical motion pictures, including Dirty Dancing, Earth Girls Are Easy, 8 Million Ways to Die, Return of the Secaucus Seven, Steel Dawn, etc.
Made for TV movies including Disaster in Time, Double Jeopardy, Fourth Story, O'Hara's Wife, Past Tense, St. Helen's, Taking the Heat, etc.

KING WORLD PRODUCTIONS, INC.
1700 Broadway, New York, NY 10010. (212) 315-4000.
12400 Wilshire Blvd., Suite 1200, Los Angeles, CA 90025. (213) 826-1108.
455 N. City Front Plaza Dr., Suite 2910, Chicago IL 60611 (312) 644-7500.
CHAIRMAN
Roger M. King
PRESIDENT & CEO
Michael G. King
EXECUTIVE V.P. & COO
Steve Palley
PRESIDENT, INTERNATIONAL SALES
Fred Cohen
EXECUTIVE V.P., PROGRAMMING & PRODUCTION
Andy Friendly
Half Hour Strips: American Journal, C.O.W.Boys of MooMesa, Inside Edition, Jeopardy!, Wheel of Fortune, Wild West.
Movie Packages: Classic Detectives (34), Epics (5), Popcorn Theatre (15), Spotlight 10 (10).
Off-net: Branded, Guns of Will Sonnett, Topper.
One Hour Strips: The Oprah Winfrey Show, Rolonda.

THE KONIGSBERG COMPANY
7919 Sunset Blvd., 2nd floor, Los Angeles, CA 90046. (213) 845-1000. FAX: (213) 845-1020.
EXECUTIVE PRODUCER
Frank Konigsberg
Mini-series: Titanic (4 hrs.).

STEVE KRANTZ PRODUCTIONS
166 Groverton Pl., Los Angeles, CA 90077. (213) 549-6940. FAX: (213) 937-3161.
PRESIDENT
Steve Krantz
Animated Features: Fritz The Cat (75 minutes), Heavy Traffic (75 minutes).

SID & MARTY KROFFT PICTURES CORP.
419 N. Larchmont Blvd., Suite 11, Los Angeles, CA 90004. (213) 467-3125. FAX: (213) 932-6332.
PRESIDENT
Marty Krofft
EXECUTIVE VICE PRESIDENT
Sid Krofft
Series: Land of the Lost (69 episodes).

THE KUSHNER-LOCKE CO.
11601 Wilshire Blvd., 21st floor, Los Angeles, CA 90025, (310) 445-1111. FAX: (310) 445-1191.
CO-CHAIRMEN
Peter Locke, Donald Kushner
1996-1997 TV Movies: Echo (ABC), Every Woman's Dream (CBS), Gun (CBS), Innocent Victims (ABC), Jack Reed: One of Our Own (NBC), Jack Reed 5 (NBC), Princess In Love (CBS), A Strange Affair (CBS).
Past Products: Brave Little Toaster (animated movie), Carolina Skeletons (NBC movie), Cops Are Robbers (NBC movie), Father & Son (NBC), Fire in the Dark (CBS), 1st & Ten (HBO), Getting Gotti (NBC movie), Harts of the West (CBS), Murder C.O.D. (NBC movie), Night Games (CBS), Sweating Bullets (CBS), Sweet Bird of Youth (NBC), To Save the Children (CBS), Your Mother Wears Combat Boots (NBC).

L

THE LANDSBURG CO., INC.
11811 W. Olympic Blvd., Los Angeles, CA 90064. (310) 478-7878. FAX: (310) 477-7166, (310) 473-6776. e-mail: telvideo@ix.netcom.com
CHAIRMAN
Alan Landsburg
PRESIDENT
Howard Lipstone
V.P., DEVELOPMENT
Leslie Lipton
MANAGER, DEVELOPMENT
David Schiff
TV Movies: Adam: His Song Continues, Coalminer's Granddaughter, In Defense Of A Married Man, The Diamond Fleece, The George McKenna Story, If Someone Had Known, Long Gone, A Mother's Right: The Elizabeth Morgan Story, Nightmare In Columbia County, The Parent Trap II, Quiet Victory: The Charlie Wedemeyer Story, The Ryan White Story, A Stoning In Fulham County, Strange Voices, Terror In The Night, Too Young The Hero, Triumph Of The Heart: The Ricky Bell Story, Unspeakable Acts.
Series: High Risk.
Specials: Destined To Live, Maggie's Secret, A Place At The Table, To Protect The Children, The Secret Of..., Wanted: A Room With Love.

LANGLEY PRODUCTIONS
2225 Colorado Ave., Santa Monica, CA 90404. (310) 449-5300. FAX: (310) 449-5330.
EXECUTIVE PRODUCER
John Langley
Series: Code 3, Cops, Cop Files.

LEACH ENTERTAINMENT ENTERPRISES
c/o 885 Second Ave., 25th Floor, New York, NY 10017. (212) 759-8787. FAX: (212) 838-4364.
EXECUTIVE PRODUCER
Robin Leach
PRODUCER
Rob Hess
Series: Gourmet Getaways, Heroes America, Lifestyles of the Rich & Famous (synd.), Miracles, Modern Cuisine, Runaway With the Rich and Famous (synd.), Travel Secrets.

HERBERT B. LEONARD PRODUCTIONS

2240 Manzanita Lane, Reno, NV 89509-7004. (702) 829-0192.
FAX: (702) 829-7099.
PRESIDENT
Herbert B. Leonard
SECRETARY
James P. Tierney
Series: Naked City (138 x 30 mins.), Rin Tin Tin (164 x 30
mins.), Route 66 (116 x 30 mins.).
Features: Going Home, Rin Tin Tin–The Movie, Route 66
(remake).

LEVINSON ENTERTAINMENT VENTURES INTERNATIONAL

1440 Veteran Ave., Suite 650, Los Angeles, CA 90024. (213)
460-4545. FAX: (213) 663-2820.
PRESIDENT
Robert S. Levinson
VICE PRESIDENT
Sandra S. Levinson
DIRECTOR OF DEVELOPMENT
Jed Leland, Jr.
Products: The Hollywood Press Club Awards, A Tribute To The
Institute Of The American Musical
Longbow Prods.
4181 Sunswept Dr., Suite 100, Studio City, CA 91604-2335.
(818) 762-6600.
CHAIRMAN
Richard Kughn
PRESIDENTS
Ronnie D. Clemmer, Bill Pace
V.P., DEVELOPMENT
Sharon Cicero
TV Movies: Dream Of Murder, Journey Of Heart.

M

MCA TV

100 Universal Plaza, Universal City, CA 91608. (818) 777-
1000. FAX: (818) 777-1100.
1755 Broadway, 6th fl., New York, NY 10019. (212) 841-8200.
(For officers see listing under Companies)
Series/First Run: Coach (152 x 30 mins.), Hercules (35 x 60
mins.), Vanishing Son (35 x 60 mins.), Xena: Warrior Princess
(22 x 60 mins.).
One-hour Series/Off-Network: Airwolf (80), Alfred Hitchcock
Hour (93), Alias Smith And Jones (43), The A-Team (98),
B.J./Lobo (85 x 30 mins. or 80 hours), Baretta (82), The Bionic
Woman (58), Black Sheep Squadron (35), The Bold Ones
(98), Buck Rogers (37), Emergency (136), The Equalizer (88),
Five Star Mystery: Delvecchio/Ellery Queen/Mrs.
Columbo/O'Hara (87), The Incredible Hulk (85), Ironside
(198), It Takes A Thief (65), Knight Rider (90), Kojak (118),
Magnum P.I. (162), Marcus Welby M.D. (172), Miami Vice
(114), Northern Exposure (85), Quincy (148), Rockford Files
(125), Run For Your Life (85), Simon & Simon (156), The Six
Million Dollar Man (108), Thriller (67).
Half-hour Series: Alfred Hitchcock Presents (268), Amen
(110), Bachelor Father (157), Charles in Charge (126), The
Deputy (76), Gimme a Break (137), Harper Valley PTA (29),
Harry and The Hendersons (72), House Calls (57), The Jack
Benny Show (104), Kate and Allie (122), Leave It To Beaver
(234), Love That Bob (173), Major Dad (96), McHale's Navy
(138), Mickey Spillane's Mike Hammer (78), The Munsters
Today (72), The Munsters (70), My Secret Identity (72), The
New Dragnet (52), New Leave It To Beaver (105), The New
Adam 12 (52), The New Lassie (48), Operation Petticoat (32),
Out Of This World (94), Rod Serling's Night Gallery (97),
That's Incredible (165), What A Dummy (24).
90 Min. Series: Banacek (16), Men From Shiloh (23), Mystery
Movie: Columbo/McCloud/McMillan (124), The Name of The
Game (76), The Virginian (225), Wagon Train (32).
Features/Packages: Abbott and Costello (29), Comedy
Festival I (26), Dead End Kids Movies, Diabolic Dozen (12),
List of a Lifetime I, List of a Lifetime II, Ninety Minute Movies
(49 Made-For-TV), Paramount Pre'48 (196), Paramount Select
(100), Reserve (169), Universal 53 (50), Universal 123 (114),
Universal Color 100 (99), Universal Grand 50 (48 features),
Universal Marvelous 10 (10 TV movies), Universal Network
Movies 85 (52-2 hours, 33-90 minutes), Universal Pictures
Debut Network (33 features), Universal Pictures Debut
Network II (35 features), Universal Pictures Debut Network III
(29 features), Universal Pictures Debut Network IV (19 fea-
tures), Universal Pictures Debut Network V (19 features),
Universal Pictures Debut Network VI (24 titles).

MCA TELEVISION INTERNATIONAL

100 Universal City Plaza, Universal City, CA 91608. (818)
777-4275. FAX: (818) 733-1554. TWX: 67-7053.
PRESIDENT
Colin P. Davis
EXECUTIVE VICE PRESIDENT
Peter Hughes
V.P., PRODUCT SERVICES
Albert Bartee
V.P., PUBLICITY & PROMOTION
Katarina McMahon
V.P., LEGAL
Ernie Goodman
SALES OFFICES:
Rua Said Aiach, 305, Sao Paulo, CEP04003, Brazil. 884-0166.
VICE PRESIDENT
Wanderley Fucciolo
SALES EXECUTIVE
Edenir Arnadio
Universal House, Poplar & Pelican St., Sydney, NSW,
Australia 2000. 267-9844.
VICE PRESIDENT
Pat Cleary
Maison Hirakawa Bldg., 2-5-2 Hirakawa-cho, Chiyoda-ku,
Tokyo, Japan. 265-5726.
PRESIDENT
Itaru Kurebayashi
2450 Victoria Park Ave., Willowdale, Toronto, Ontario M2J
4A2, Canada. (416) 491-3000.
VICE PRESIDENT & GENERAL MANAGER
Ron Suter
Mutran Attallah St., Chahwan Bldg., Fassouh Achrafleh, P.O.
Box 16-6342, Beirut, Lebanon. (961-1) 200762.
VICE PRESIDENT
Kamal Sayegh
8 Rue La Boetie, Paris 75008, France. (44) 94-8350.
VICE PRESIDENTS
Roger Cordjohn, Hendrik van Daalen
1 Hamilton Mews, London W1V 9FF, England. (71) 491-4666.
VICE PRESIDENT
Roger Cordjohn
SALES EXECUTIVE
Penny Craig

MGM/UA TELEVISION DISTRIBUTION

1350 Ave. of the Americas, New York, NY 10019. (212) 708-
0300. FAX: (212) 708-0397.
2500 Broadway St., Santa Monica, CA 90404-3061. Domestic
TV: (310) 449-3763. Int'l TV: (310) 449-3767.
(For officers see listing under Companies.)
One-hr. Series: Against The Law (17), The Aquanauts (32),
The Bradshaw Difference (195), Cutter To Houston (9), Dark
Shadows (11 & 2 hr. pilot), The Dirty Dozen (11 & 2 hr. pilot),
Dream Street (5 & 90 min. pilot), East Side/West Side (24),
Fame (135), For Love And Honor (11 & 2hr. pilot), Freshman
Dorm (5), In The Heat Of The Night (137 & 8 2 hr. & 2 hr.
pilot), Jack And Mike (17 & 90 min. pilot), Knightwatch (9),
Lady Blue (13 & 2 hr. pilot), Nightmare Cafe (6), The Outer
Limits–New (47), The Outer Limits–Original (49), Paper Dolls
(12 & 2 hr. pilot), Poltergeist: The Legacy (44), Seven
Brides...Seven Brothers (21 & 90 min. pilot), Stoney Burke
(32), Thirtysomething (85), The Young Riders (68).
Half-hr. Series: Adventures At Scott Island (26), All Dogs Go
To Heaven (13), Baby Boom (13), Bat Masterson (108), Bold
Venture (39), Boson Blackie (58), Case Of The Dangerous
Robin (38), Cesar's World (39), Circus Parade (26), Dial 999
(39), Doctor Christian (39), The Edge (3), The Everglades
(38), Favorite Story (78), Group One Medical (130), Harbor
Command (39), Hello Kitty: Furry Tale Theatre (13), Hey,
Landlord (31), Highway Patrol (156), Hollywood & The Stars
(31), Home Run Derby (26), Hudson's Bay (39), I Led Three
Lives (117), It's About Time (26), James Bond, Jr. (65),
Karen's Song (13), Keyhole (38), Kids, Inc. (149), King Of
Diamonds (38), LAPD (365), Lee Marvin Presents Lawbreaker
(32), Lock-Up 1 (78), Love Me, Love Me Not (130), Love
Mackenzie's Raiders (39), Man And The Challenge (36), The
Man Called X (39), Men Into Space (38), Men Of Annapolis
(39), Mona McClusky (26), Mr. District Attorney (78), My
Mother, The Car (30), The New Adventures of Martin Kane
(39), The New Phil Silvers Show (30), The New Pink Panter
Show (60), The Patty Duke Show (104), Pink Panther & Sons
(13), Rat Patrol (58), Ripcord (76), Rough Riders (39),
Science Ficion Theatre (39), Sea Hunt (155), Sea Hunt–1987
(22), The Story Of... (38), Straight To The Heart (50), Super
President (15), The Super Six (20), Target (38), This Man
Dawson (39), Tombstone Territory (91), The Twilight Zone (94),
The Unexpected (39), We Got It Made (24).

TV Movies: Broken Angel, Convict Cowboy, Cry For The Strangers, The Defiant Ones, The Dirty Dozen: Deadly Mission, The Dirty Dozen: Fatal Mission, The Escape, Escape Clause, Extreme Close-Up, Fatal Memories, Finding The Way Home, Have You Seen My Son?, Hot Paint, I Take These Men, I Want To Live, If It's Tuesday It Still..., In The Arms Of A Killer, Inherit The Wind, Johnny Ryan, The King Of Love, Lady Against The Odds, The Limbic Region, The Man Who Fell To Earth, Marian Rose White, Marshal Law, Mercy Or Murder?, Miss America: Behind The Crown, Moving Target, My Father My Son, Police Story: The Freeway Killings, Prime Target, Red River, Separate Tables, The Setup, She Knows Too Much, The Silver Strand, Sketch Artists II: Hands That See, The Tenth Man, Those Secrets, Trenchcoat In Paradise, Witness For The Prosecution, Women Of San Quentin.
Miniseries: George Washington I (8 hrs.), George Washington II (4 hrs.), Studs Lonigan (6 hrs.).
Specials: Happy Anniversary 007 (60 mins.), A Funny Thing Happened... (90 mins.), The Insider (60 mins.), Iron Men (60 mins.), James Cagney: Yankee Doodle (75 mins.), James Stewart: Wonderful Life (98 mins.), The Joy Of Socks (104 mins.), The Kids From Fame (60 mins.), The Making Of A President–1964 (90 mins.), Minnelli On Minnelli (70 mins.), The Olympinks (30 mins.), Pink At First Sight (30 mins.), A Pink Christmas (30 mins.), Reckless Valor (2 rs.), Shari Lewis: Have I Got A Story For You (60 mins.), Shari Lewis: Kooky Classics (54 mins.), Shari Lewis: You Can Do It (60 mins.), That's Panthertainment (60 mins.), A Thousand Days (90 mins.), 7 Days...Life Of The President (90 mins.).

MG/PERIN
104 E. 40 St., New York, NY 10016. (212) 697-8687. FAX: (212) 949-8140.
Specials: Hispanic Americans The New Frontier.

MTM ENTERTAINMENT, INC.
12700 Ventura Blvd., Suite 200, Studio City CA 91604. (818) 755-2400. FAX: (818) 755-2448.
CEO
Anthony Thomopoulos
PRESIDENT, WORLDWIDE DISTRIBUTION
Charles Larsen
PRESIDENT, MTM TV
Michael Ogiens
Syndication: America's Funniest Home Videos, Dr. Quinn–Medicine Woman, Rescue 911.

MTV
1515 Broadway, New York, NY 10036. (212) 258-8000. FAX: (818) 505-7800.
CHAIRMAN & CEO, MTV NETWORKS
Thomas E. Freston
Series: Beavis and Butt Head, The Grind, House of Style, MTV Beach House, MTV Oddities, MTV Unplugged, The Real World, Road Rules, Sandblast, Singled Out, Yo! MTV Raps.
Specials: Freaks Nerds and Weirdos, MTV Music Video Awards, Movie Awards, NBA's Slam N' Jam, Rock n' Jock.

MADISON SQUARE GARDEN NETWORK
2 Pennsylvania Plaza, New York, NY 10121. (212) 465-6000. FAX: (212) 465-6024.
PRESIDENT
Doug Moss
S.V.P., PROGRAMMING & PRODUCTION
Martin Brooks
V.P., PUBLIC RELATIONS/MARKETING
Barry Watkins
Live Events: College football and basketball, pro wrestling, pro boxing, track and field, tennis, Metro Stars soccer, New York Knickerbockers basketball, New York Rangers hockey, New York Yankees baseball.

MALIBU DISTRIBUTION WORLDWIDE
2644 30th St., Santa Monica, CA 90405. (310) 452-9100. FAX: (310) 452-1771.
Series: Could It Be A Miracle (24 x 1 hr.), Hot Blood (13 x 30 mins.), Mowgli (13 x 30 mins.), Samsom (24 x 1 hr.).
Animated series: The Black Stallion (26 x 30 mins.), The Voyages of Doctor Dolittle (65 x 30 mins.).

JEFF MARGOLIS PRODS.
11726 San Vicente Blvd., Suite 360, Los Angeles, CA 90049. (310) 474-5434. FAX: (310) 474-5251.
Productions: Country Fest (CBS), Concert For Humanity (ABC), Ebony's Anniversary (ABC), The Miss America Pageant (NBC).

MARVEL FILMS
(In association with New World Entertainment)
1440 S. Sepulveda Blvd., Suite 114, Los Angeles, CA 90025-3400. (310) 444-8632. FAX: (310) 444-8646.

PRESIDENT & CEO
Avi Arad
Series: Spider-Man.

MEDALLION TV ENTERPRISES, INC.
8831 Sunset Blvd., W. Hollywood, CA 90069. (310) 652-8100. FAX: (310) 659-8512.
PRODUCTION
Lise H. Ettlinger
FINANCE
Linda L. Brooks

MILLER/BOYETT PRODS.
c/o Warner Bros., 4000 Warner Blvd., Bldg. #1, Burbank, CA 90048. (818) 954-7700. FAX: (818) 954-7712.
Series: Angie, Bosom Buddies, The Family Man, Family Matters, Full House, Getting By On Our Own, Going Places, Goodtime Girls, Happy Days, The Hogan Family, Joanie Loves Chachi, Laverne & Shirley, Perfect Strangers, Petrocelli, Step by Step.

MODERN TALKING PICTURE SERVICE, INC.
381 Park Ave. S., Suite 713, New York, NY, 10016. (212) 696-5050. FAX: (212) 696-9065.
PRESIDENT
David A. Conway
MANAGER, TV PROGRAMMING
Sarah Ruszczyk

MOFFITT-LEE PRODUCTIONS
1438 N. Gower St., Suite 250, Hollywood, CA 90028. (213) 463-6646. FAX: (213) 467-2946.
CO-OWNERS/EXECUTIVE PRODUCERS/DIRECTORS
John Moffitt, Pat Tourk Lee
SUPERVISING PRODUCER
Nancy Kurshner
New Products: Thirty Seconds Over Washington (HBO), Not Neccessarily The Election (HBO).

MULLER MEDIA
23 E. 39 St., New York, NY 10016. (212) 683-8220. FAX: (212) 661-0572.
Series: Scratch (65 x 30 mins.).
Feature Packages: Coming Attractions I (18), Godzilla All-Stars (12), Night Raiders I (15), Night Raiders II (12), Prime Targets (15 titles), Smoke Screens (10), Wild Ones (10), Weapons (6).

MULTIMEDIA ENTERTAINMENT
45 Rockefeller Plaza, 35th Floor, New York, NY 10111. (212) 332-2000. FAX: (212) 332-2010.
Multimedia Television Production, 8439 Sunset Blvd., Suite 200, Los Angeles, CA 90069. (213) 656-9756. FAX: (213) 656-1693.
PRESIDENT
Robert L. Turner
S.V.P. & DIRECTOR, STATION SALES
Thomas F. Shannon
EXECUTIVE VICE PRESIDENT
Richard C. Coveny
V.P., BUSINESS AFFAIRS & GENERAL COUNSEL
Elizabeth Allen
S.V.P., INTERNATIONAL SALES
John Ranck
S.V.P., PROGRAMMING
Richard C. Thrall, Jr.
Series: Donahue, Rush Limbaugh, Jerry Springer, Sally Jessy Raphael, Susan Powter, Dennis Prager, Inside the Vatican with Sir Peter Ustinov, Mysteries of the Ancient World.
Specials: Children's Plus Network (67 x 30 mins. & 1 x 60 min. special).

N

NBC INTERNATIONAL, LTD.
30 Rockefeller Plaza, New York, NY 10112. (212) 664-3546. FAX: (212) 333-7546.
(For officers, see listing under Companies)
S.V.P., NBC ENTERPRISES
Susan Beckett
V.P., INTERNATIONAL SALES
Matthew Ody
V.P., INTERNATIONAL SALES & DEVELOPMENT
Sergio Getzel
Hour Series: Amazing Grace (4 hrs.), Father Murphy (35 hrs.), I Witness Video (54 hrs.), Mancuso FBI (20 hrs.), Profiler (13+ hrs.), Secret Service (22 hrs.), Shannon's Deal (16 hrs.).

Half Hour Series: A Family For Joe (13 x 30 mins.), Generations (470 x 30 mins.), Here & Now (13 x 30 mins.), Hot Pursuit (13 x 30 mins.), Man Of The People (12 x 30 mins.), Mr. Rhodes (13+ x 30 mins.), Out All Night (20 x 30 mins.), Sara (8 x 30 mins.), Saved By The Bell: College Years (19 x 30 mins.), Supertrain (10 x 30 mins.), True Blue (13 x 30 mins.).

Childrens' Series: Brains & Brawn (15 x 30 mins.), California Dreams (78 x 30 mins.), Go Show (28 x 30 mins.), Gravedale High (13 x 30 mins.), The Guys Next Door (13 x 30 mins.), Hang Time (26 x 30 mins.), Kissyfur (26 x 30 mins.), Name Your Adventure (40 x 30 mins.), Punky Animated (21 x 30 mins.), Punky Brewster (88 x 30 mins.), Running The Halls (13 x 30 mins.), Saved By The Bell (86 x 30 mins.), Saved By The Bell: The New Class (91 x 30 mins.).

Movies Of The Week: A Burning Passion: The Margaret Mitchell Story, The Abduction of Kari Swenson, Assault & Matrimony, Awake To Danger, Bermuda Grace, Blue Deville, Bonanza: The Return, Bonanza: Under Attack, CAT Squad I: Stalking Danger, CAT Squad II: Python Wolf, Chameleons, Charm, Childsaver, Convicted: A Mother's Story, Christmas Eve, Danger Island, Double Deception, An Early Frost, Express To Terror, Fall From Grace, A Family For Joe, Father's Homecoming, Fight For Justice, Flying Blind, Follow Your Heart, Forget Me Not, The Gifted One, A Good Family, Her Hidden Truth, Her Last Chance, Hot Pursuit, How I Spent The Summer, Hurricane Andrew, I'll Be Home For Christmas, In The Best Interests Of The Children, The Keys To The Kingdom, The Last Flight Out, The Last Ride Of The Dalton Gang, The Little Match Girl, Loneliest Runner, Love On The Run, Marked For Murder, Mothers, Daughter & Lovers, Mrs. R.'s Daughter, Murder In High Places, One Special Victory, One Woman's Courage, Poison Ivy, Roe vs. Wade, Roseanne & Tom: A Hollywood Marriage, Saved By The Bell: Hawaiian Syle, Saved By The Bell: A Wedding In Vegas, Shadow Of A Killer, Shadow Of A Stranger, Shannon's Deal I, Shannon's Deal II, She Fought Alone, The Story Lady, Take My Daughters–Please, Those She Left Behind, Thrill, A Time To Heal, Tonya & Nancy: The Inside Story, Turn Back The Clock, While Justice Sleeps, Winnie.

Danielle Steel Movies: Changes (2 hrs.), Daddy (2 hrs.), Family Album (4 hrs.), Fin Things (3 hrs.), Full Circle (2 hrs.), Heartbeat (2 hrs.), Kaleidoscope (2 hrs.), Message From Nam (4 hrs.), Mixed Blessings (2 hrs.), Once In A Lifetime (2 hrs.), Palomino (2 hrs.), Perfect Stranger (2hrs.), Remembrance (2 hrs.), The Ring (4 hrs.), Secrets (2 hrs.), Star (2 hrs.), Vanished (2 hrs.), Zoya (4 hrs.).

Mini-Series: Blind Faith (4 hrs.), The Brotherhood Of The Rose (4 hrs.), Chances (6 hrs.), Celebrity (6 hrs.), Cruel Doubt (4 hrs.), Devil's Cargo (4 hrs.), Fatal Vision (4 hrs.), The Favorite Son (6 hrs.), Lucky (6 hrs.), Pandora's Clock (4 hrs.), Princess Daisy (4 hrs.), Sidney Sheldon's Rage Of Angels I (4 hrs.), Sidney Sheldon's Rage Of Angels II (4 hrs.), Remember (4 hrs.), The Secret Of Lake Success (6 hrs.), Seduced By Madness (4 hrs.), Tradewinds (6 hrs.), A Woman On The Run (4 hrs.).

Specials: Abbot & Costello (1 hr.), Bonanza: A Retrospective (1 hr.), Life In The Fast Lane II (1 hr.), The Martin Short Show (9 1hrs.), Too Good To Be True (2 hrs.).

NBC NEWS VIDEO ARCHIVES

30 Rockefeller Plaza, New York, NY 10112. (212) 664-3797. FAX: (212) 957-8917.

Complete archives of NBC News.

NBC PRODUCTIONS

330 Bob Hope Dr., Burbank, CA 91523. (818) 840-7500. (For officers, see listing under Companies.)
PRESIDENT, NBC ENTERPRISES
John Agoglia
S.V.P., PRIMETIME SERIES PROGRAMS
Tom Nunan
V.P., PRIMETIME SERIES PROGRAMS
JoAnn Alfano
Series: Friday Night, Hang Time, Homicide: Life on the Street, In the House, Jag, Late Night With Conan O'Brien, Profiler, Saved by the Bell: The New Class, The Single Guy, The Tonight Show With Jay Leno.

NELVANA COMMUNICATIONS, INC.

4500 Wilshire Blvd., Los Angeles, CA 90067. (213) 549-4222. FAX: (213) 549-4232.
c/o 32 Atlantic Ave., Toronto, Ontario, Canada M6K 1X8. (416) 588-5571. FAX: (416) 588-5588.
PRESIDENT
Patrick Loubert
VICE PRESIDENT & CFO
Michael Hirsch
Animated Series: Cadillacs & Dinosaurs, Eek and the Terrible Thunderlizards, Jim Henson's Dog City, Tales From the Cryptkeeper.
Animated Feature: Babar–The Movie.

NEW WORLD ENTERTAINMENT

(a subsidiary of News, Inc.)
1440 S. Sepulveda Blvd., Los Angeles, CA 90025. (310) 444-8100. FAX: (310) 444-8101.
625 Madison Ave., 11th fl., New York, NY 10022. (212) 527-4800.
PRESIDENT
Brandon Tartikoff (outgoing, 1997)
EXECUTIVE VICE PRESIDENT/C.O.O.
William Kerstetter
PRESIDENT, NEW WORLD INTERNATIONAL
Armand Nunez, Jr.
S.V.P., MARKETING
Jerry Zanitsch
Hour Series: Profit, Second Noah, Strange Luck, Tales From the Crypt, U.S. Customs Classified.
Half Hour Series: The Clinic, Cops, Emergency Call, Real Stories of Highway Patrol, Reality Check, Weekly World News.
Animated Series: The Incredible Hulk, Marvel Action Universe, Spider-Man.
INTERNATIONAL TELEVISION PRODUCT:
Hour Series: The Bold and the Beautiful (or 1/2 hrs.), Booker, Crime Story, Customs Classified, Extraordinary, A Fine Romance, Greatest American Hero, The Grudge Match, Hardcastle and McCormick, Hawkeye, High Mountain Rangers, Mariah, Marker, Marvel's Generation X: The Movie, Murphy's Law, Once a Hero, Riptide, Profit, Rags to Riches, Santa Barbara (or 1/2 hrs.), Second Noah, Strange Luck, Tales From the Crypt, Tour of Duty, 21 Jump Street, Two, The Whoopi Goldberg Show (also 1/2 hrs.), Wiseguy.
Half Hour Series: Bagdad Cafe, Caesar's Challenge, Elvis, Emergency Call, The Great Escape, Infatuation, Jacqueline Susann's Valley of the Dolls, The Judge, Judith Krantz's Secrets, Juvenile Justice, Pacific Drive, Paradise Beach, Real Stories of Highway Patrol, Reality Check, The Robert Guillaume Show, The Wonder Years, Zorro.
Mini-Series: Beryl Markham: A Shadow in the Sun (4 hrs.), Courage (3 hrs.), Echoes in the Darkness (5 hrs.), Elvis & Me (4 hrs.), Harem (4 hrs.), In a Child's Name (4 hrs.), Monte Carlo (4 hrs.), Murder in the Heartland (4 hrs.), Queenie (5 hrs.), Sins (7 hrs.), Stay the Night (4 hrs.), Tom Clancy's Op Center (4 hrs.), Voices Within (4 hrs.).
Movies of the Week: Across Five Aprils, After the Promise, Blind Judgment, The Bride in Black, Broken Pledges, Checkered Flag, A Child Too Many, Conspiracy of Love, Cradle of Conspiracy, Cult Rescue, Dangerous Affection, Death of the Incredible Hulk, Deceived by Trust, Easy Prey, Generation X, Gladiator, Hunter, In Broad Daylight, Lassiter, Little White Lies, Men Who Hate Women and the Women Who Love Them, Miles From Nowhere, Murder or Memory?, The Other Mother, Penalty Phase, Poker Alice, The Return of the Incredible Hulk, She'll Take Romance, Something in Common, Stalking Back, The Stranger Within, To Walk Again, Trial of the Incredible Hulk, Why My Daughter?, The Woman He Loved, XXX's & OOO's.
Half Hour Animation: Biker Mice From Mars, Captain America, Dinoriders, Dungeons and Dragons, The Incredible Hulk, Little Wizards, Mighty Thor, Robocop, Rude Dog and the Dweebs, Spider-Man, Spider-Woman, Submariner.
Hour Animation: Marvel Action Hour.

NICKELODEON/NICK AT NITE

1515 Broadway, New York, NY 10036. (212) 258-7500.
PRESIDENT
Geraldine Laybourne
Nickelodeon: AAAHH!! Real Monsters, The Adventures of Pete & Pete, The Adventures of Tin Tin, All That, The Alvin Show, Alvin & the Chipmunks, Allegra's Window, Are You Afraid of the Dark?, Beetlejuice, Bullwinkle's Moose-a-Rama, Cable in the Classroom, Clarissa Explains It All, Doug, Eureeka's Castle, Flipper, Gullah Gullah Island, Gumby, Hey Dude, Lassie, Launch Box, Legends of the Hidden Temple, Looney Tunes, Jim Henson's Muppet Babies, Mr. Wizard's World, The Muppet Show, My Brother & Me, Nick Arcade, Nick News, Nickelodeon Guts U to U, Nickelodeon Special Edition, Nickelodeon Weinerville, Nickelodeon Wild Side Show, Ren & Stimpy Show, Rocko's Modern Life, Roundhouse, Rugrats, Salute Your Shorts, The Secret World of Alex Mack, Welcome Freshmen, What Would You Do?, Wild & Crazy Kids, The World of David the Gnome.
Nick at Nite: The Adventures of Superman, Bewitched, The Bob Newhart Show, The Dick Van Dyke Show, Dragnet, F Troop, Get Smart, I Dream of Jeannie, I Love Lucy, The Lucy & Desi Comedy Hour, The Lucy Show, The Mary Tyler Moore Show, Mork & Mindy, The Munsters, Taxi, Welcome Back Kotter, The White Shadow.

FIMA NOVECK PRODUCTIONS

161 E. 61 St., New York, NY 10021. (212) 751-2329.
432 N. Palm Dr., Beverly Hills, CA 90210. (310) 273-1933.
FAX: (310) 273-1933.
PRESIDENT
Fima Noveck
Productions: Blood Feud, Committed, Joshua Tree, Love and Anarchy, Men of War, No Way Out, Save Me, Swept Away ..., Trouble With Spies, Viper.

O

O'HARA-HOROWITZ PRODUCTIONS

16633 Ventura Blvd., Suite 1330, Encino, CA 91436-1840.
(818) 986-7150. FAX: (818) 986-8226.
EXECUTIVE PRODUCERS
Michael O'Hara, Lawrence Horowitz
TV Movies: A Child's Wish, Crimes of Passion Series, Moment of Truth Series.

ORION TELEVISION ENTERTAINMENT

1888 Century Park E., Los Angeles, CA 90067. (310) 282-0550.
EXECUTIVE V.P., DOMESTIC DISTRIBUTION
Joseph D. Indelli
Off-Network Series: Adderly (44 x 60 mins.), Cagney & Lacey (125 x 60 mins.), The Addams Family (64 x 30 mins.), Green Acres (170 x 30 mins.), Mr. Ed (143 x 30 mins.).
Mini-Series: Blood of Others (4 hrs.), Kennedys of Massachusetts (6 hrs.), King (6 hrs.), Secret of the Black Dragon (5 hrs.).
Features/Packages: Action 16 (16 Features), Beach Blanket Biggies/Young Adult Theater (12 Features), Born Wild (11 Features), Chrome and Hot Leather (12 Features), Ghoul-A-Rama (17 Features), Monsters on the Prowl (9 Features), Orion VI (17 features including Dances with Wolves, Silence of the Lambs, Robocop, etc.), Orion VII (15 features including Bull Durham, Married to the Mob, Dirty Rotten Scoundrels, etc.), Sci-Fi Adventures (51 Features), Winning Hand (16 Titles), World of the Macabre (8 Features).

P

PACIFIC INTERNATIONAL ENTERPRISES, INC.

1133 S. Riverside Ave., Suite #1, P.O. Box 1727, Medford, OR 97501. (541) 779-0990. FAX: (541) 779-8880.
PRESIDENT & PRODUCER
Arthur R. Dubs
V.P. SALES & ACQUISITIONS
Arn S. Wihtol
SECRETARY & TREASURER
Barbara J. Brown
Features: Across the Great Divide, The Adventures of the Wilderness Family, American Wilderness, Aravaipa Desert Bighorn, Blue Fin, Challenge To Be Free, Cold River, The Dream Chasers, The Fourth Wish, Great Adventure, Land of Kilimanjaro, Mountain Family Robinson, Mystery Mansion, Sacred Ground, Vanishing Wilderness, Wilderness Family Part 2, Windwalker, Wonder of It All, Young and Free.

PAPAZIAN-HIRSCH ENTERTAINMENT

500 S. Sepulveda Blvd., Suite 660, Los Angeles, CA 90049.
(310) 471-2332. FAX: (310) 471-3352.
EXECUTIVE PRODUCERS
Robert Papazian, Jim Hirsch
TV Movies: Dead Man's Island (CBS), Empty Cradle (ABC), Hart to Hart (NBC, 5 x 2 hr. features), The Invaders (Fox, 4 hr. miniseries).

PARAGON ENTERTAINMENT

11400 W. Olympic Blvd., #1600, Los Angeles, CA 90064.
(310) 478-7272. FAX: (310) 479-2314.
CHAIRMAN & CEO
Jon Slan
PRESIDENT & COO
Richard Borchiver
PRESIDENT, PARAGON PRODUCTIONS
Gary Randall
V.P., PRODUCTION
Janet Cuddy
V.P., FAMILY ENTERTAINMENT PROGRAMMING
Ken Katsumoto

V.P., MOVIES & MINISERIES

Joey Plager
Animated Series & Features: The Admiral And The Princess (30 mins.), Aliens First Christmas (30 mins.), Aliens Next Door (30 mins.), The Birthday Dragon (30 mins.), Bluetoes–The Christmas Elf (30 mins.), The Christmas Racoons (30 mins.), Easter Egg Mornin' (30 mins.), For Better Or For Worse (6 x 30 mins.), Freaky Stories (30 mins.), Happy Birthday Bunnykins (30 mins.), Johann's Gift To Cristmas (30 mins.), Katie & Orbie (39 x 30 mins.), The Little Crooked Christmas Tree (30 mins.), Peter & Din (26 5 mins.), The Raccoons (60 x 30 mins.), The Raccoons On Ice (30 mins.), The Railway Dragon (30 mins.), The Raccoons–Let's Dance (30 mins.), Teddy Bears' Christmas (30 mins.), Teddy Bears' Picnic (30 mins.), Tooth Fairy, Where Are You? (30 mins.), Up On The Housetop (30 mins.), The Woman Who Raised A Bear As Her Son (30 mins.).
Children's Series & Features: The Argon Quest (100 mins.), The Biggest Little Ticket (1 hr.), Blizzard Island (12 x 30 mins.), Deke Wilson's Mini-Mysteries (13 x 30 mins.), Kingdom Adventure (22 x 30 mins.), Kratts' Creatures (50 x 30 mins.), Lamb Chop's Play-Along (85 x 30 mins.), Lamb Chop's Play-Along Specials (2 1hrs.), Once Upon A Hamster (52 x 30 mins.), Ready Or Not (65 x 30 mins.), The Tin Soldier (1 hr.), Under The Umbrella Tree (200 15 mins.), Under The Umbrella Tree Specials (14 x 30 mins.).
Youth Series & Features: Dog House (26 x 30 mins.), Hamilton's Quest (10 x 30 mins.), Hidden City (26 x 30 mins.), Hillside (13 x 30 mins.), Street Noise (26 x 30 mins.).
Drama Series: Beyond Reality (44 x 30 mins.), Philip Marlowe: Private Eye (6 1hrs.), The Rez, Tracks Of Glory (2 120 mins., & 100 mins.), Urban Angel (15 1hrs.).
Documentary: C'mon Geese (30 mins.), Debbie Travis' Painted House (52 x 30 mins.), Guerilla Gardener (120 30 mins.), Heart Of Courage (40 x 30 mins.), Homeworks (78 x 30 mins.), Lynette Jennings Home (52 x 30 mins.), Mysterious Forces Beyond (26 x 30 mins.), Pet Connection (65 x 30 mins.), Tourist Trap (26 x 30 mins.).
TV Movies/Features: The Big Game (100 mins.), Frequent Flyer (ABC, 2 hrs.), Guitarman (93 mins.), Held Hostage: The Sis & Jerry Levin Story (ABC, 2 hrs.), Improper Channels (90 mins.), Lives Of Girls And Women (90 mins.), Jim's Gift (100 mins.), Kissinger & Nixon (2 hrs.), Off Your Rocker (90 mins.), Romantic Undertaking (100 mins.), Shepherd On The Rock (100 mins.), Sherlock Holmes Returns (90 mins.), Tracks Of Glory (90 mins.).
Specials: A Tribute To Sam Kinison (1 hr.).
Other Features: The HandMade Film Library: Bellman & True, Bullshot, Checking Out, Cold Dog Soup, Five Corners, How To Get Ahead In Advertising, The Lonely Passion Of Judith Hearne, Mona Lisa, Monty Python's Life Of Brian, Nuns On The Run, Powwow Highway, Privates On Parade, The Raggedy Rawney, Scrubbers, A Sense of Freedom, Shanghai Surprise, Time Bandits, Track 29, Water, Withnail And I.

PARAMOUNT NETWORK TELEVISION PRODS.

5555 Melrose Ave., Hollywood, CA 90038. (213) 956-5000.
Series: Almost Perfect, Frasier, The Home Court, JAG, Leeza, The Marshal, Sister, Sister, Star Trek: Deep Space Nine, Star Trek: Voyager, Wings.

PARAMOUNT TELEVISION

5555 Melrose St., Hollywood, CA 90038. (213) 956-5000.
(For officers and personnel, see listing under Companies.)
Series/First Run: Entertainment Tonight (5 x 30 mins., weekend hr., 2 x 60 mins./week), Geraldo (5 x 60 mins./week), Hard Copy (5 x 30 mins./week), Maury, Montel, Nick News, Sightings, This Morning's Business.
Hour Series: The Complete Star Trek (127+ hrs.), Mannix (130 hrs.), Mission: Impossible (171 hrs.), The Untouchables (114 hrs.).
Half Hour Series: Brothers (116 x 30 mins.), Cheers (146+ x 30 mins.), Family Ties (154+ x 30 mins.), Happy Days (255 x 30 mins.), Love American Style (224 x 30 mins.), The Lucy Show (156 x 30 mins.), Taxi (114 x 30 mins.), Webster (150 x 30 mins.).
Features/Packages: Marquee II (17), Marquee III (18), Portfolio XI (22), Portfolio XII (26), Portfolio XIII (27), Preview II (16), Preview III (20), Preview IV (18), Special Edition I (50), Special Edition II (40), Special Edition III (55), The Untouchables (3).
Mini-Series: Shogun (12-hrs.), Space (10 hrs.), Wallenburg (4 hrs.), Winds of War (10-hrs.).

PATCHETT KAUFMAN ENTERTAINMENT

8621 Hayden Pl., Culver City, CA 90232. (310) 838-7000.
FAX: (310) 838-8430.

CHAIRMAN
Tom Patchett
PRESIDENT
Kenneth Kaufman

PATHE PICTURES, INC.
270 Madison Ave., New York, NY 10016. (212) 696-0392. FAX: (212) 213-5498.
CHAIRMAN
Joseph P. Smith
VICE PRESIDENT
Charles J. Gegen
VICE PREIDENT & GENERAL COUNSEL
James J. Harrington
TREASURER
James A. Griffith
Products: Arthur Murray Dance Instructional Programs (14), Captain David Grief (39), Men of Destiny (130), Milestones of the Century (365), Musical Parade of Stars (1100), Pathe Educational Shorts (103), Showtime (39), Showtime at the Apollo (13).

PLAYBOY ENTERTAINMENT GROUP
9242 Beverly Blvd., Beverly Hills, CA 90210. (310) 246-4000.
PRESIDENT
Anthony J. Lynn
Products: Directors Showcase, Hot Rocks, Newsfront, Night Call, Playboy's Really Naked Truth, Take Five, Women of Color, World of Playboy.

POLYGRAM TELEVISION INTERNATIONAL
10 Livonia St., London, England W1V 3PH. (44-171) 800-1339. FAX: (44-171) 800-1337.
Series: The Big Easy–The Series (22 x 60 mins.), Charlotte Sophie Bentinick (6 x 52 mins.).

PROGRAM SYNDICATION SERVICES, INC. /PROGRAM EXCHANGE
(A Division of Saatchi & Saatchi North America, Inc.)
375 Hudson St., New York, NY 10014-3620. (212) 463-3900. FAX: (212) 463-2662.
PRESIDENT
Allen Banks
EXECUTIVE V.P. & DIRECTOR, MEDIA OPERATIONS
Jack Irving
MANAGING DIRECTOR
Christopher Hallowell
V.P., DIRECTOR, STATION RELATIONS
Beth Kempner
Childrens' Series: The Beary Family (13 x 30 mins.), The Berenstain Bears (26 x 30 mins.), The Bullwinkle Show (98 x 30 mins.), Dennis The Menace (78 x 30 mins.), Dinky Dog (16 x 30 mins.), Dinobabies (26 x 30 mins.), The Drak Pack (16 x 30 mins.), Dudley Do-Right And Friends (38 x 30 mins.), Garfield And Friends (73 x 30 mins.), King Leonardo (38 x 30 mins.), The Pink Panther (60 x 30 mins.), Rocky And His Friends (156 x 30 mins.), Space Kidettes (20 x 30 mins.), Tennessee Tuxedo And His Tales (140 x 30 mins.), Uncle Waldo's Cartoon Show (52 x 30 mins.), The Underdog Show (62 x 30 mins./124 x 15 mins.), The Woody Woodpecker Show (91 x 30 mins.), Yogi & Friends (65 x 30 mins.), Young Samson (20 x 30 mins.).
Series/Off Network: Abbot & Costello (52 x 30 mins.), Bewitched (180 x 30 mins.), The Brady Bunch (117 x 30 mins.), I Dream Of Jeannie (109 x 30 mins.), Laverne & Shirley (178 x 30 mins.), The Odd Couple (114 x 30 mins.), The Partridge Family (96 x 30 mins.).

R

MARIAN REES ASSOCS.
4125 Radford Ave., Studio City, CA 91604. (818) 508-5599. FAX: (818) 508-8012.
PRODUCER/PRESIDENT
Marian Rees

REPUBLIC PICTURES CORPORATION
5700 Wilshire Blvd., Los Angeles, CA 90036. (213) 463-2141.
(For officers, see listing under Companies.)
Series/Off Network: Beauty & the Beast (56 hours), Bonanza (260 hours), Car 54 Where Are You? (60 half hours), Get Smart (138 half hours), High Chaparral (98 hours), My World and Welcome To It (26 half hours).

Film Packages: Action-Packed Package (28 features), All Nite Movies (5 nights per week), Animated Features (5 features), Cartoons (15), Christmas Features (4 features), Classic Comedy (13 features), Color movies (quarterly), Hollywood Stars (16 features), Hollywood 1-2-3 (89 features), Home of the Cowboys (22 features), The John Wayne Collection (16 features), Republic Premiere Four (12), Serial Movies (26 features), Showcase One (8), Take 3 (6).

RUBY-SPEARS PRODUCTIONS, INC.
710 S. Victory Blvd., #201, Burbank, CA 91502-2425. (818) 840-1234. FAX: (818) 840-1258.
Series: Mega Man, Skysurfer: Strike Force.

RYSHER ENTERTAINMENT
3400 Riverside Drive, Suite 600, Burbank, CA 91505. (818) 846-003. FAX: (818) 846-1136.
1 Dag Hammarskjold Plaza, 885 Second Ave., New York, NY 10017. (212) 750-9190. FAX: (212) 752-2759.
CEO
Keith Samples
PRESIDENT
Tim Helfet
SENIOR V.P., INTERNATIONAL SALES
Meggan Kimberley
Series: Fire House (13 x 1 hr.), FX The Series (20 x 1hr.), Highlander The Series (110 x 1 hr.), Live Shot (13 x 1 hr.), Nash Bridges (13 x 1 hr.), Soldier of Fortune (19 x 1 hr.), Strange Universe (195 x 30 mins.), Strangers (13 x 30 mins.).
TV Movies: Body Language (2 hrs.), Citizen X (2 hrs.), Gunfiter's Moon (2 hrs.), Her Deadly Rival (2 hrs.), A Kidnapping In The Family (2 hrs.), The Prosecutor (2 hrs.), Sugartime (2 hrs.), Urban Legend (2 hrs.).

S

SFM ENTERTAINMENT
1180 Ave. of the Americas, New York, NY 10036. (212) 790-4800. FAX: (212) 790-4897.
PRESIDENT
Stanley Moger
Products: Alice Through the Looking Glass, America's Dance Honors, America's Hope Awards, The American Craftsman, AFI Life Achievement Award to Jack Nicholson, Steven Spielberg, Clint Eastwood, Believe You Can...and You Can from Fantasyland at Disneyland, Benny Carter: Symphony in Riffs, Breaking The Screen Barrier: The Making of Terminator 2 In 3-D, Country Music Hall of Fame 25th Anniversary Special, Crusade in Europe, Dead as a Doormat, Deal, Dennis the Menace: Mayday for Mother, Dione Lucas Cooking Show, Farm Aid IV, Fear: A Universal Monster, 50 Years of Music-Making with Ray Charles, The First 100 Years of American Cinema, The Flip Wilson Show, George Stevens: D-Day to Berlin, Here Comes the Grump, Hollywood Gets M.A.D.D., The Indomitable Teddy Roosevelt, Industry on Parade, Instant Love, Jaws, The Last Dragon, Joey Bishop Show, K-Nite Color Radio, The Love Chef, Made-for-TV Election, The Making of Jurassic Park–The Ride, Marriage Counselor, Memories 1970-1991*, The Monte Carlo Circus, Moshe Dayan, A Part of the Family, Pillar of Fire, Playback, Sea World Specials, Sleep Dreams & Other Mysteries of the Night, Sports Pros & Cons, Texas, Think Fast Celebrity Auto Race Series, A Time to Remember, Tribute to the Singing Cowboy, Unclaimed Fortunes, Universal Studios Summer Blast, Visions of Light, Wichita Town, Yum Yums, Zoobilee Zoo.
*To Be Reacquired.

SABAN ENTERTAINMENT, INC.
10960 Wilshire Blvd., Los Angeles,. CA 90024. (310) 235-5100. FAX: (310) 235-5102.
CHAIRMAN & CEO
Haim Saban
PRESIDENT
Stan Golden
Branch Offices: Sydney, Toronto, London, Paris, Cologne, Zurich and Tel Aviv.
Live-action series: Mad Scientist Toon Club (synd.), Saban's Masked Rider (Fox), Saban's Mighty Morphin Power Rangers (Fox), Saban's VR Troopers (synd.), Sweet Valley High (synd.), Unsolved Mysteries.
Features/2-hour movies: Addicted to Love, Baby Face Nelson, Behind Closed Doors, Blindfold: Acts of Obsession, Brothers' Destiny, Cadillac Girls, Chantilly Lace, Cheyenne Warrior, Criminal Hearts, Deadly Sins, Edge of Deception, Falling for You, Guns of Honor, Hard Evidence, Honor Thy Father and Mother: The Menendez Killings, Hostile Intentions, Midnight Heat, No Dessert Dad, 'Til You Mow the Lawn, Not Like Us, Not of This Earth, Parallel Lives, Prescription for Murder, Quest for Justice, Samurai Cowboy, Shadow of Obsession,

Someone to Die For, Someone's Watching, Suspicious Agenda, Terminal Voyage, To Catch a Killer, Trapped and Deceived, Two Much Trouble, Unlawful Intent, With Harmful Intent.
Animated Series: Battletech (synd.), Camp Candy (NBC), Captain N: The Game Master (NBC), Creepy Crawlers (synd.), Eagle Riders, Grimm's Fairy Tales (Nick.), Honey Bee Hutch, Iznogoud, Jin Jin and the Panda Patrol, Journey to the Heart of the World, Little Shop (synd.), Noozles, Saban's Adventures of Oliver Twist, Saban's Adventures of the Little Mermaid (synd.), Saban's Around the World in 80 Dreams (synd.), Saban's Gulliver's Travels (synd.), Saban's Little Mouse on the Prairie, Samurai Pizza Cats (synd.), Space Strikers—changed from 20,000 Leagues Into Space (UPN), Teknoman (UPN), Tenko and the Guardians of the Magic (synd.), Video Power (synd.), X-Men (Fox).

EDGAR J. SCHERICK ASSOCS.
1950 Sawtelle Blvd., Suite 282, Los Angeles, CA 90025. (310) 996- 2376. FAX: (310) 996-2392.
EXECUTIVE PRODUCER/PRESIDENT
Edgar J. Scherick

GEORGE SCHLATTER PRODUCTIONS
8321 Beverly Blvd., Los Angeles, CA 90048. (213) 655-1400. FAX: (213) 852-1640.
PRESIDENT
George H. Schlatter
VICE PRESIDENT
Jolene B. Schlatter
Products: American Comedy Awards–Years 1-11, American Television Awards, Ceaser's Palace 30th Anniversary Celebration, Comedy Hall of Fame–Years 1-3, Frank Liza & Sammy: The Ultimate Event, Laugh-In, Meaning of Life, Muhammad Ali's 50th Birthday, People's Choice Awards, Real People, Sammy Davis Jr.'s 60th Anniversary Celebration, She TV, Sinatra 80 Years My Way, Sinatra Duets, USO 50th Anniversary, Welcome Home America.

ARNOLD SHAPIRO PRODUCTIONS
100 Wilshire Blvd., #1800, Santa Monica, CA 90401. (310) 451-6270. FAX: (310) 451-4634.
PRESIDENT
Arnold Shapiro
Series: Rescue 911.

SHUKOVSKY ENGLISH ENTERTAINMENT
CBS Studio Center, 4024 Redford Ave., Studio City, CA 91604. (818) 760-6100.
EXECUTIVE PRODUCERS
Diane English, Joel Shukovsky
Series: Double Rush, The Louie Show, Love and War, Murphy Brown.

SILVERBACH-LAZARUS GROUP, THE
9911 W. Pico Blvd., Suite PH-M, Los Angeles, CA 90035. (310) 552-2660. FAX: (310) 552-9039.
CHAIRMAN
Alan Silverbach
PRESIDENT
Herb Lazarus
DIRECTOR, DOMESTIC SYNDICATION
Jane Metz
DIRECTOR, FOREIGN DISTRIBUTION
Nicole Wonica
Features: The Best Christmas Pageant Ever, The Video History of the Civil War: Gettysburg.

FRED SILVERMAN COMPANY, THE
12400 Wilshire Blvd., Suite 920, Los Angeles, CA 90025. (310) 826-6050.
PRESIDENT
Fred Silverman
Products: Bedtime, Bone Chillers, Diagnosis Murder, In the Heat of the Night, Matlock, Perry Mason movies.

RICK SPALLA VIDEO PRODUCTIONS
Subsidiaries: Hollywood Newsreel Syndicate, Inc., & Rick Spalla Production, Inc.
1622 North Gower St., Hollywood, CA 90028. (213) 469-7307. FAX: (213) 469-8251.
301 W. 45 St., New York, NY 10036. (212) 765-4646.
PRESIDENT
Rick Spalla
VICE PRESIDENT
Anthony J. Spalla
PRODUCTION SUPERVISOR
Richard Spalla
TV Products: Century of Fashion, Century of Fashion...in Motion Pictures, The Great Getaway, High Road to Danger, Hobby Nobbing...with the Stars, Holiday on Wheels, Hollywood Backstage... The Sensational Sixties (104 x 30 mins.),

Hollywood Backstage: Today & Yesterday, Hollywood's Fantastic Artists' and Models' Ball, Hollywood Guest Shot, Hollywood Star Newsreel, Kay Crawford's Pep Arts Training Series (14 hrs.), Miss California International Beauty Pageant (2 hours) (Annual Competition in April.), The Open Road, Portrait: The New Breed, Portrait of a Star, The Wild...Wild...World of Spirit.

SPECTACOR FILMS
9000 Sunset Blvd., Suite 1550, Los Angeles, CA 90069. (310) 271-9990. FAX: (310) 247-0412.
PARTNER
Ed Snider
EXECUTIVE VICE PRESIDENT
David Newlon
TV Movies: Person Unknown, Terminal Jusice.

SPELLING TELEVISION, INC.
5700 Wilshire Blvd., 5th fl., Suite 575, Los Angeles, CA 90036. (213) 965-5800. (213) 965-5895.
CHAIRMAN & CEO
Aaron Spelling
S.V.P. & BUSINESS & LEGAL AFFAIRS
Peter Bachman
S.V.P., PRODUCTION
Gail Patterson
Series: Beverly Hills 90210, Melrose Place, Savannah.

DARREN STAR PRODS.
41 E. 11th St., 6th fl., New York, NY 10003. (212) 529-7970. FAX: (212) 529-9118.
Series: Central Park West.

SANDE STEWART TELEVISION, INC.
20335 Ventura Blvd., #208, Woodland Hills, CA 91364. (818) 313-9394.
PRESIDENT
Sande Stewart

THE SULLIVAN COMPANY
4024 Radford Ave., Studio City, CA 90212. (818) 991-7564. FAX: (818) 991-7619.
EXECUTIVE PRODUCER
Beth Sullivan
Series: Dr. Quinn–Medicine Woman.

SUNBOW ENTERTAINMENT
100 Fifth Ave., New York, NY 10011. (212) 886-4900. FAX: (212) 366-4242.
CO-CHAIRMEN
Thomas L. Griffin, Joe Bacal
PRESIDENT & C.O.O.
C.J. Kettler
C.F.O.
Andrew Karpen
S.V.P., PRODUCTION
Carole Weitzman
S.V.P., SALES
Jane Smith
S.V.P., DEVELOPMENT
Nina Hahn
Series: Bigfoot (9 x 7 mins.), Bucky O'Hare (13 x 30 mins.), Cartoon Capers (17 x 30 mins.), Conan & The Young Warriors (13 x 30 mins.), Conan The Adventurer (65 x 30 mins.), G.I. Joe: Extreme (26 x 30 mins.), G.I. Joe: Original (95 x 30 mins.), G.I. Joe (199 & 300 series, 44 x 30 mins.), Glofriends (26 x 10 mins.), Great Space Coaster (52 x 30 mins.), Inhumanoids (13 x 30 mins.), Jem (65 x 30 mins.), Littlest Pet Shop (40 x 30 mins.), Moondreamers (16 x 10 mins.), My Little Pony N'Friends (65 x 30 mins.), My Little Pony: Original (32 x 30 mins.), My Little Pony Tales (13 x 30 mins.), The Nudnik Show (13 x 30 mins.), The Puzzle Place (65 x 30 mins.), Robotix (15 x 7 mins.), Transformers Generation 2 (52 x 30 mins.), Transformers Takara (115 x 30 mins.), Transformers: Original (98 x 30 mins.), Visionaries (13 x 30 mins.).
Family Features: A Matter of Conscience (60 mins.), All That Glitters (60 mins.), Flour Babies (60 mins.), Private Affairs (60 mins.).

T

TAFFNER ENTERTAINMENT, LTD.
1888 Century Park East, 19th fl., Los Angeles, CA 90067. (213) 937-1144. FAX: (310) 284-3176.
EXECUTIVE VICE PRESIDENT
Don Taffner Jr.

Products: Cinema Europe: The Other Hollywood (6 hrs.), Rumpole of the Bailey, Three's Company, Too Close for Comfort.

TELEPICTURES PRODS.
3500 W. Olive Ave., #1000, Burbank, CA 91505. (818) 972-0777.
Series: Carnie, Jenny Jones.

TELEWORLD, INC.
245 W. 55 St., New York, NY 10019. (212) 489-9310. FAX: (212) 262-9395.
PRESIDENT
Robert Seidelman
Mini-Series: Kennedy (7 hrs.), Mistral's Daughter (8 hrs.).
Features/Packages: Spiderman movie specials (7 live-action features), Teleworld's Top 50 (chiller & action features), 17 AIP Science Fiction Classics.

TOUCHSTONE TELEVISION
500 S. Buena Vista St., Burbank, CA 91521. (818) 560-1000.
Current Series: Boy Meets World, Brotherly Love, Buddies, Ellen, Home Improvement, If Not for You, Maybe This Time, Misery Loves Company, Nowhere Man, Unhappily Ever After.

TRANS WORLD INTERNATIONAL
(A division of IMG, Inc.)
22 E. 71st St., New York, NY 10021. (212) 772-8900. FAX: (212) 772-2617.
Branch offices in Auckland, Barcelona, Budapest, Hamburg, Hong Kong, Johannesburg, London, Milan, Paris, Stockholm, Sydney, Tokyo, Toronto.
CHAIRMAN, PRESIDENT & CEO, IMG
Mark H. McCormack
SENIOR EXECUTIVE VICE PRESIDENT, IMG
Alastair J. Johnson
PROGRAM COORDINATOR, TWI
Katie Boes
Series: Futbol Mundial (26 mins. wkly, ongoing), Transworld Sport (52 mins./wk.).
Features: The Greatest Moments In Sports–Vol 1 (108 mins.), High Five Series Three (13 x 26 mins.)
Athletics: Chemical Bank Millrose Games (1 hr.), Mobil Invitational (1 hr.), New York City Marathon (1996, 1997, 1998), Reno Indoor Games (1 hr.), Uncle Toby's Ironman & Devondale Ironwoman Super Series, USA Indoor Track & Field Championships (2 hrs.), Weetabix New Zealand Ironman Triathlon (52 mins.).
Badminton: Ciba Asia Cup Badminton, Seiko Asian Badminton Championships, Thomas Uber Cup Qualifier & Finals, World Cup Badminton Championships.
Cricket: India vs. South Africa, Indian Domestic Cricket, Pakistan Domestic Cricket, West Indies vs. New Zealand Cricket.
Figure Skating: Canadian Pro Figure Skating Championships, European Speed Skating Championships (2 x 26 mins.), European Figure Skating Championships, Junior World Figure Skating Championships (5 x 28 mins.), Stars On Ice (1 hr.), World Junior Speed Skating Championships, World Junior Track Speed Skating (2 x 26 mins.), World Pro Figure Skating, World Short Track Speed Skating Championships, World Single Distance Championships, World Speed Skating Championships (2 x 26 mins.), World Sprint Speed Skating Championships (2 x 26 mins.).
Men's Golf: Alfred Dunhill Cup, Alfred Dunhill Masters, Alfred Dunhill South African PGA Championship, Anderson Consulting World Championship, AT&T Australian Skins Game, Australian Masters, Benson & Hedges International Open, BMW International Open, Canons Open, Canon European Masters, Chemapol Trophy Czech Open, Collingtree British Masters, Deutsche Bank Open TPC of Europe, Dubai Desert Classic, Dutch Open, English Open, Epson Singapore Open (2 x 52 mins.), FNB Players Championship, German Masters, Heineken Classic, Hohe Brucke Open, Italian Open Golf Championship, Johnnie Walker Asian Classic, Loch Lomond World Invitational, Madeira Island Open, Moroccan Open, Murphy's Irish Open, The 125th British Open Golf Championships–1996, The 126th British Open Golf Championships–1997, 127th British Open Golf Champion-ships–1997, Peugeot Open de Espana, Peugeot Open de France, Portugese Open, The Ryder Cup–1997 (52 mins.), The Scottish Open, The Senior British Open Golf Championship–1996, Smurfit European Open, Toyota World Match Play, Trophée Lancôme, Turespana Masters, Turespana Open Mediterrania, US Open Golf Championship–1996, US PGA Championship–1996, US PGA Championship–1997, Volvo German Open, Volvo PGA Championship, Volvo MastersVolvo Scandinavian Masters, World Championship of Golf, YPF Argentine Republic Open Golf Championship (4 x 60 mins.).

Women's Golf: Chich-fil-A Charity Championship, Chrysler-Plymouth Tournament of Champions, Compaq Open, Fieldcrest Cannon Classic, Healthsouth Inaugural, JAL Big Apple Classic, Jamie Farr Kroger Classic, Ping/AT&T Wireless Services, Ping/Welch's Championship, Rochester International, SAFECO Classic, Sara Lee Classic, ShopRite LPGA Classic, Spint Titleholders Championship, Star Bank LPGA Classic, State Farm Rail Classic, Trygg-Hansa Ladies Open, US Women's Open Golf Championship, Women's British Open Golf Championship – 1996, 1997, 1998, 1999, 2000, Youngstown-Warren LPGA Classic.
Motor Sports: Brickyard 400, Daytona 500, Die Hard 500 (Talladega), Indy Racing League: Indy 200 at Walt Disney World, Indianapolis 500, Las Vegas 200, New England 200, Phoenix 200, Trans Am Racing (includes 12 different venues/races).
Olympic Programming: 1996 Olympic Trials (includes Men's Marathon, Swimming, Boxing, Track & Field, Basketball, Gymnastics), The Olympic Century — Program One: The Olympic Spirit (52 mins.), Program Two: The Pursuit of Excellence (52 mins.), Program Three: The Future of The Games (52 mins.), The Olympic Series — Volume I: Golden Moments of The Olympic Games (10 x 26 mins.), Volume II: Road To Glory (10 x 52 mins.), Volume III: The Dream Team 1992 (1 x 52mins.), Volume IV: The Olympic Spirit (2 x 26 mins.).
Rugby: European Rugby Club Championships for the Heineken Cup (6 x 26 mins.), World Rugby Cup Championships.
Sports Series: Coca-Cola World of Cricket (10 x 26 mins.), Finish Line (32 x 26 mins.), Ian Botham's Dream Team, Survival of The Fittest (15 x 30 mins.).
Snooker: B&H Irish Masters, British Open Snooker, International Open Snooker, Regal Welsh Open Snooker, Thailand Open Snooker.
Soccer: Chinese Soccer, Indian Soccer.
Tennis: Australian Open Tennis–1996 & 1997, Colonial Classic, Peters International, Wimbledon Lawn Tennis Championships–1996 & 1997, WTA Tour 1996 (Acura Classic, Advanta Championships, Ameritech, Bank of The West Classic, Bausch & Lomb, Citizen Cup, Direct Line Insurance Championships, German Open, Italian Open, Lipton Championships, Nicherei International Ladies Championships, Open Ford International Championships, Open Gaz de France, State Farm Evert Cup, Toshiba Tennis Classic, WTA Tour Championships).
Other Programming: Chinese Basketball, Indian Hockey (Field Hockey), Thai Kickboxing, Nobel Prize Awards Ceremony, Rodeo Showdown, World Bull Riding Championships, Whitbread Around the World Race (Sailing), World's Strongest Man, Qatar Table Tennis.

TRANSVUE TV INTERNATIONAL CO.
5131 Colbath Ave., Sherman Oaks, CA 91423. (818) 990-5600.
PRESIDENT
Herbert B. Schlosberg
Assorted features including Disco Godfather, Petey Wheatstraw, Seven Wonders of the West.

TRIBUNE ENTERTAINMENT
435 N. Michigan Ave., Suite 1800, Chicago, IL 60611. (312) 222-4441. FAX: (312) 222-9065.
PRESIDENT & CEO
Rick Jacobson
S.V.P., ADVERTISING & SALES
Marcy Abelow
S.V.P., GENERAL SALES MANAGER
Steve Mulderrig
Talk: Geraldo, The Charles Perez Show.
Series/First Run: Out of the Blue, Soul Train, U.S. Farm Report.
Movies/Mini-Series: To Catch a Killer, Final Shot: The Hank Gathers Story, Sidney Sheldon's Sands of Time, Vendetta II, The Vernon Johns Story, Wild Justice.
Specials: Hollywood Christmas Parade, Macy's Fourth of July Fireworks Spectacular.
Variety/Music/Comedy: Soul Train Lady of Soul Awards, Soul Train Music Awards.
Sports: Chicago Cubs TV Network.

TRISTAR TELEVISION
9336 W. Washington Blvd., Culver City, CA 90232. (310) 202-1234.
EXECUTIVE VICE PRESIDENT
Eric Tannenbaum
V.P., SERIES DEVELOPMENT
Jill Holwager
V.P., PRODUCTION
Andy House

SERIES PROGRAMMING
Steve Tann
Series: Can't Hurry Love, Hudson Street, Mad About You, The Nanny, Ned and Stacy, Simon, TV Nation.

TURNER INTERNATIONAL
One CNN Center, P.O. Box 105366, Atlanta, GA 30348-5366. (404) 827-5639. FAX: (404) 827-3224.
CORPORATE V.P., WORLDWIDE DISTRIBUTION
William H. Grumbles
S.V.P., SYNDICATE SALES
Michael Byrd

TURNER PROGRAM SERVICES
One CNN Center, 12th floor, P.O. Box 105366, Atlanta, GA 30348-5366. (404) 827-2085. FAX: (404) 827-2373.
CHAIRMAN
Russ Barry
PRESIDENT
Susan Grant
S.V.P., CNN TELEVISION
Gary Anderson
S.V.P. MARKETING & SALES STRATEGY
Meade Camp
V.P., WORLDWIDE DISTRIBUTION, TBS INC.
William Grumbles, Jr.
V.P., PROGRAM PRODUCTION & DISTRIBUTION
Jackie Jusko
V.P., ADVERTISING & PROMOTION
Diane McCauley
Children's Programming: Feed Your Mind (52 x 30 mins.), The Flintstones (100+ strips), The Flintstones & The Jetsons (26 each), The New Adventures Of Captain Planet (52 x 30 mins.), Tom And Jerry (100 x 30 mins.), Warner Bros. Cartoons (301 segments).
Hanna-Barbera Specials: Arabian Nights (90 mins.), A Flintstones Christmas Carol (90 mins.), The Halloween Tree (90 mins.), I Yabba-Dabba Do! (120 mins.), Johnny's Golden Quest (120 mins.), Tom And Jerry–The Movie (120 mins.), Yogi, The Easter Bear (60 mins.).
Series/Off Network: Chips (138 one hr.), Gilligan's Island (98 x 30 mins.), The Wonder Years (115 x 30 mins.).
Series/First-Run: Lauren Hutton And... (260 x 30 mins.), The Lazarus Man (22 x 1 hr.), National Geographic On Assignment (12 x 1 hr.), WCW Wrestling, Wild! Life Adventures (12 x 1 hr.).
Features/Packages: Turner Pictures III—The Legends (24 movies), Turner Pictures IV—The Legends (24 mvies), New World I-IV (76 titles), New World: TV Gold (10 titles), New World: Pretty Smart (10 titles).
CNN Television: Headline News Programs, Syndicated News Service, Turner Entertainment Report.

U

UPA PRODUCTIONS OF AMERICA
14101 Valleyheart Dr., Suite 200, Sherman Oaks, CA 91423. (818) 990-3800. FAX: (800) 990-4854.
PRESIDENT
Henry G. Saperstein
Series: Dick Tracy, Gerald McBoing-Boing, Godzilla, Mr. Magoo, Rodan.

UNIVERSAL TELEVISION
A Division of Universal City Studios, Inc., 100 Universal City Plaza, Universal City, CA 91608. (818) 777-1000.
(For officers see listing under Companies.)
Series: Coach, Law and Order, Murder She Wrote, New York Undercover, Partners, seaQuest 2032 (w/Amblin).

V

VH-1
1515 Broadway, New York, NY 10036. (212) 258-7800.
Products: Big Eighties, Crossroads, Flix, Four on the Floor, Top 21 Countdown, VH-1 Archives, VH-1 Video Hall of Fame.

VIACOM INTERNATIONAL, INC.
1515 Broadway, New York, NY 10036. (212) 258-6000. FAX: (212) 258-6627.
(For officers see listing under Companies.)
First Run Programs: Montel Williams Show (daily x 60 mins.), Nick News (wkly x 30 mins.).

Series/Off-Network: The Adventures of Superboy (100 x 30 mins.), All in the Family (207 x 30 mins.), The Andy Griffith Show (249 x 30 mins.), The Beverly Hillbillies (274 x 30 mins.), Cannon (122 x 60 mins.), Clint Eastwood in Rawhide (144 x 60 mins.), The Cosby Show (200 x 30 mins.), A Different World (144 x 30 mins.), Family Affair (138 x 30 mins.), Gomer Pyle U.S.M.C. (150 x 30 mins.), Gunsmoke (402 x 60 mins.), Hawaii Five-O (282 x 60 mins.), Hogan's Heroes (168 x 30 mins.), The Honeymooners (107 x 30 mins.), I Love Lucy (179 x 30 mins., & 26 x 30 mins. of We Love Lucy), The Life and Times of Grizzly Adams (35 hours, 2 x 90 min. specials), Marshall Dillon (233 x 30 mins.), Matlock (177 hours), My Three Sons (160 x 30 mins.), Perry Mason (271 hours), Petticoat Junction (148 x 30 mins.), The Phil Silvers Show, Rawhide (73 x 60 mins.), The Rookies (90 x 60 mins.), Roseanne (147 x 30 mins.), The Twilight Zone (136 x 30 mins. & 18 x 60 mins.), The Wild, Wild West (104 x 60 mins.).
Animated: The Alvin Show (26 x 30 mins.), Harlem Globetrotters (22 x 30 mins.), Terrytoons (689 cartoon units).
Feature Packages: Black Magic, Exploitables, Exploitables III, Exploitables IV, Family Entertainment, Gasp Horror, Gasp Science Fiction, Guts and Glory, The Legend Group, Perry Mason Features, Thematics: TV Net (Tonight Only), Thematics 2: Stories for Men, Stories for Women, Viacom Features I through 14, Viacom Movie Greats, Young and Reckless.

VIACOM PRODS.
c/o Colossal Pictures, 10 Universal City Plaza, Universal City, CA 91608-1002. (818) 505-7500. FAX: (818) 505-7599.
Current Series: Deadly Games.

W

JEFF WALD ENTERTAINMENT
12424 Wilshire Blvd., Suite 840, Los Angeles, CA 90025. (310) 820-9897.
PRESIDENT
Jeff Wald

WARNER BROS. ANIMATION
15303 Ventura Blvd., #1200, Sherman Oaks, CA 91403. (818) 379-9401.
Series: The Adventures of Batman and Robin, Animaniacs, The Bugs Bunny & Tweety Show, Freakazoid, Pinky and the Brain, The Sylvester & Tweety Mysteries, That's Warner Bros.

WARNER BROS. DOMESTIC TELEVISION DISTRIBUTION
4000 Warner Blvd., Burbank, CA 91522. (818) 954-6000.
(For officers and personnel, see listing under Companies.)
Series/First Run: Alvin & the Chipmunks (65 x 30 mins.), Carnie, EXTRA, Getting Even (260 x 30 mins.), History of Rock & Roll, Island City, Jenny Jones (170 x 60 mins.), The Jesse Jackson Show (40 x 60 mins.), Love Connection (195 x 30 mins.), Love Stories (170 x 60 mins.), Merrie Melodies Starring Bugs Bunny & Friends (65 x 30 mins.), P-TEN (Kung Fu: The Legend Continues, Time Trax, Pointman and Babylon 5), The People's Court (195 x 30 mins.), Tiny Toon Adventures (65 x 30 mins.), Trump Card (170 x 30 mins.).
Miniseries: Bare Essence (4 x 60 mins. or 4 x 30 mins.), Hollywood Wives (6 hrs.), The Thorn Birds (10 hrs.), "V" (10 hrs.).
Series/Off-Network: ALF, Alice (202 x 30 mins.), Batman/Superman/Aquaman (69 animated x 30 mins.), The Blue Knight (23 x 60 mins.), Chico and the Man (88 x 30 mins.), Dallas (330 x 60 mins.), The Dukes of Hazzard (147 x 60 mins.), Eight is Enough (112 x 30 mins.), Family Matters, The FBI (234 x 60 mins.), The Fresh Prince of Bel-Air, F-Troop (65 x 30 mins.), Full House, Growing Pains, Harry-O (44 x 60 mins.), Head of the Class, Here's Lucy (144 x 30 mins.), The Hogan Family, It's a Living, Knots Landing (276 x 60 mins.), Kung Fu (62 x 60 mins.), Mama's Family, Matt Houston (68 x 60 mins.), Maverick (124 x 60 mins.), More Real People, Murphy Brown, My Favorite Martian (107 x 30 mins.), The New Dick Van Dyke/Mayberry R.F.D., Night Court, Perfect Strangers, Private Benjamin (39 x 30 mins.), Scarecrow and Mrs. King (88 x 60 mins.), Superman (104 x 30 mins.), Tarzan (57 x 60 mins.), The Waltons (221 x 60 mins.), Welcome Back, Kotter (95 x 30 mins.), Wonder Woman (61 x 60 mins.).
Features/Packages: Bomba the Jungle Boy (13 features), The Bowery Boys (48 features), Classic Thrillers (13 features), Classic Thrillers II (13 features), Cowboys and Indians (32 westerns from Allied Artists), Easy Eight (8 features), Encore One (53 features), The FBI Story (4 features), Lorimar I (21 features), Lorimar II (22 features), Masters of Fury (15 martial arts films), Mint Edition (23 features), Power Package I (13 titles), Premiere Edition (15 titles), Premiere Edition (10 titles),

Premiere Edition 2 (25 made-for-TV movies), Sci-Fi Horror (33 features), Starlite 3 (30 features, 19 in color), Starlite 4 (30 features, 16 in color), Starlite 5 (28 features, 18 in color), Starlite 6 (26 features, 12 in color), Tarzan Features (32 features, 9 in color), Telepictures 1 (14 features), Telepictures 2 (27 made-for-TV movies), Telepictures 3 (24 features), TVI (13 features), TV2 (13 features), TV3 (13 features), TV4 (13 features), 22 Karat (24 features), Ultra 4 (30 features), Volume 1-A (24 features, 17 in color), Volume 13 (25 features, 17 in color), Volume 14-15 (13 features, 12 in color), Volume 16 (18 features, 16 in color), Volume 17 (23 features, 21 in color), Volume 18 (28 features, 25 in color), Volume 19 (29 features, 28 in color), Volume 20 (30 features), Volume 21 (26 features), Volume 22 (38 features), Volume 23 (20 features), Volume 24 (18 features), Volume 25 (24 features), Volume 26 (24 features), Volume 27 (18 features), Volume 28 (28 features), Volume 29 (20 features), Volume 30 (39 titles), Volume 31 (53 titles), Volume 2-A (22 features, 13 in color).

Cartoons: Bugs Bunny & Friends (100 cartoons), Porky Pig & Friends (156 cartoons).

WARNER BROS. INTERNATIONAL TELEVISION
400 Warner Blvd., Tower 14th fl., Burbank, CA 91522. (818) 954-5491. FAX: (818) 954-4040.

(For officers and personnel, see listing under Companies.)

Animated Series: ALF (26 x 30 mins.), ALF Tales (21 x 30 mins.), Alvin and the Chipmunks (65 x 30 mins.), Aquaman (18 x 30 mins.), Batman (17 x 30 mins.), Batman: The Animated Series (85 x 30 mins.), Beetlejuice (94 x 30 mins.), Beverly Hills Teens (65 x 30 mins.), The Botts (65 x 30 mins.), Bugs Bunny and Tweety Show (26 x 30 mins.), Bugs Bunny Show (78 x 30 mins.), Bumpety Boo (43 x 30 mins.), C.O.P.S. (65 x 30 mins.), Camp Candy (39 x 30 mins.), Captain N (26 x 30 mins.), Care Bears (36 x 30 mins.), Cats & Company (86 x 30 mins.), Challenge of Superfriends (16 x 30 mins.), Comic Strip-Karate Kat (13 x 30 mins.), Comic Strip-Monsters (13 x 30 mins.), Comic Strip-Street Frogs (13 x 30 mins.), Comic Strip-Tiger Sharks (26 x 30 mins.), Dennis the Menace (65 x 30 mins.), The Dukes (20 x 30 mins.), Fairy Tale Favorites (5 x 30 mins.), Fat Albert and the Cosby Kids (60 x 30 mins.), Gepetto's Music Shop (13 x 30 mins.), Get Along Gang (13 x 30 mins.), Grendizier Raids (52 x 30 mins.), Gumby (32 x 30 mins.), Inspector Gadget (21 x 30 mins.), Jayce and the Wheeled Warriors (65 x 30 mins.), Kid 'n Play (13 x 30 mins.), Lassie's Rescue Rangers (17 x 30 mins.), Little Women (48 x 30 mins.), Marine Boy (78 x 30 mins.), Mask (75 x 30 mins.), Maxie's World (16 x 30 mins.), Merrie Melodies (24 x 30 mins.), New Adventures of Batman (16 x 30 mins.), New Adventures of Superman (34 x 30 mins.), The New Archies (13 x 30 mins.), The New Gumby (33 x 30 mins.), Photon (26 x 30 mins.), Pole Position (13 x 30 mins.), Police Academy: The Animated Series (65 x 30 mins.), Popples (23 x 30 mins.), Porky Pig Show (26 x 30 mins.), Rainbow Brite (13 x 30 mins.), Roadrunner Show (26 x 30 mins.), Rubik: The Amazing Cube (13 x 30 mins.), Sanybelle (47 x 30 mins.), Silverhawks (65 x 30 mins.), Spiral Zone (65 x 30 mins.), Starcom (24 x 30 mins.), Steven Spielberg Presents Animaniacs (65 x 30 mins.), Tiny Toon Adventures (96 x 30 mins.), Super Mario Brothers (65 x 30 mins.), Superfriends (77 x 30 mins.), Superman Animated (13 x 30 mins.), Sylvanians (13 x 30 mins.), Tarzan: Lord of the Jungle (34 x 30 mins.), Taz-Mania (65 x 30 mins.), Thundercats (130 x 30 mins.), Tiny Toons Adventures–The Looney Beginning (1 x 30 mins.), TV Funnies (16 x 30 mins.), Wolfrock TV (13 x 30 mins.), Zoobilee Zoo (65 x 30 mins.).

Miniseries: A.D. (12 hrs.), Alcatraz: The True Story (4 hrs.), The Awakening Land (7 hrs.), Bare Essence (4 hrs.), Blind Ambition (8), Blood & Orchids (4), Blood Red Roses (4), Bloodlines: Murder in the Family (4 hrs.), Born to the Wind (4 hrs.), The Bourne Identity (4 hrs.), Casanova (4 hrs.), Christopher Columbus (6 hrs.), Common Ground (4 hrs.), Crossings (6 hrs.), Deadly Intentions (4 hrs.), A Death in California (4 hrs.), The Deliberate Stranger (4 hrs.), Dream West (7 hrs.), Dress Gray (4 hrs.), Eleanor and Franklin (4 hrs.), Ellis Island (7 hrs.), Eureka Stockade (4 hrs.), For Those I Loved (8 hrs.), Golden Moment: Olympic Love Story (4 hrs.), Guyana Tragedy (4 hrs.), Hanging by a Thread (4 hrs.), Haywire (4 hrs.), Heaven and Hell (6 hrs.), Hollywood Wives (6 hrs.), I Know My First Name Is Steven (4 hrs.), IT (4 hrs.), Jack the Ripper (4 hrs.), Lace (5 hrs.), Lace II (4 hrs.), Liberty (4 hrs.), A Man Called Intrepid (6 hrs.), Maria Chapdelaine (4 hrs.), Mino (6 hrs.), Moviola (6 hrs.), Mr. Horn (4 hrs.), Murder in Texas (4 hrs.), The Mystic Warrior (5 hrs.), Napoleon and Josephine: A Love Story (6 hrs.), Night the Bridge Fell Down (4 hrs.), North and South - I (12 hrs.), North and South - II (12 hrs.), Nutcracker: Money, Madness and Murder (6 hrs.), Pearl (6 hrs.), Pirate (4 hrs.), Queen (6 hrs.), Race for the Bomb (6 hrs.), Roots (12 hrs.), Roots: The Next Generation (14 hrs.), Roses Are for the Rich (4 hrs.), The Sacketts (4 hrs.), Salem's Lot (4 hrs.), Sands of Time (4 hrs.), Scruples (6 hrs.), Sinatra (5 hrs.), The Sophisticated Gents (4 hrs.), Stalin (4 hrs.), Strong Medicine (4 hrs.), Studs Lonigan (6 hrs.), The Thorn Birds (10 hrs.), Thornbirds: The Missing Years (6 hrs.), The Two Mrs. Grenvilles (4 hrs.), "V" (10 hrs.), The Wild West (10 hrs.), World War III (4 hrs.).

One-Hour Series: Aaron's Way (14), The Adventures of Brisco County Jr. (26), Against the Grain (8), The Alaskans (36), American Detective (14), Angel Street (6), Babylon 5 (22), Banyon (15), Bare Essence (11), Berrenger's (13), The Best Times (6), Big Shamus Little Shamus (10), Billy Crystal Show (6), Bodies of Evidence (16), Booker (13), Boone (13), Bourbon Street Beat (39), Bourbon Street Parade (26), Bridges to Cross (6), Bronco (68), California Fever (10), Casablanca (5), Cheyenne (107), China Beach (62), Cobra (22), Code R (13), The Colbys (49), Crossroads (12), D.E.A. (11), The Dakotas (19), Dark Justice (66), Delphi Bureau (8), Detective in the House (6), Dial M for Murder (13), Diamonds (44), Divine Obsession (122), Double Dare (6), Dramas I & II (42), Dukes of Hazard (147), Enos (17), Eye to Eye (6), Falcon Crest (209), The F.B.I. (238), Finder of Lost Loves (23), Fitzpatricks (13), The Flash (21), Freddy's Nightmares (22), Freebie and the Bean (9), Gabriel's Fire (22), Gallant Men (25), Games People Play (25), Glitter (13), Going to Extremes (17), Guns of Paradise (13), Harry O (44), Hawaiian Eye (134), Heartbeat (17), Hearts Are Wild (7), High Performance (4), Hollywood Beat (14), Homefront (42), Hot House/The Clinic (6), Hotel (124), How'd They Do That? (23), Hulk Hogan's Rock and Wrestling (13), Human Target (7), Hunter (153), I Had Three Wives (6), I'll Fly Away (37), In Concert (78), Island Son (18), Jenny Jones III (170), Jesse Jackson Show/Voices of America (40), Knots Landing (303), Kung Fu (62), Kung Fu: The Legend Continues (42), Life Goes On (61), Life on Earth (13), Lois & Clark: The New Adventures of Superman (20), MacGruder and Loud (13), A Man Called Hawk (13), Maria Maria (198), Matt Houston (66), Maverick (124), Max Headroom (14), Midnight Caller (61), The Mississippi (23), Morningstar/Eveningstar (6), New Adventures of Wonder Woman (46), The New Land (13), Nichols (24), Nightingales (12), Ohara (28), Our Family Honor (12), Our House (46), Paradise (44), Pros and Cons (13), Rafferty (13), Real People (105), Reasonable Doubts (44), Renegade (44), Roaring 20's (45), Scarecrow and Mrs. King (88), Search (23), Secrets of Midland Heights (10), 77 Sunset Strip (205), Shadow Chasers (12), Shell Game (6), Sisters (75), Skag (5), Sonny Spoon (15), Spenser: For Hire (64), Spies (6), Studio 5-B (10), Sugarfoot (69), Surfside Six (74), Tarzan (57), Three Kingdoms (26), Time Express (4), Time Trax (42), Top of the Hill (12), The Tribal Eye (7), Two Marriages (6), Under Cover (12), Unsub (8), "V" (19), The Waltons (219), Wizards and Warriors (8), Wonder Woman (13), Wonderworks (21), World Entertainment (156), The Yeagers (4), The Yellow Rose (22), Young Maverick (6).

Half-Hour Series: Love, Sidney (44), Off the Rack (7), A.E.S Hudson Street (5), ALF (100), All New Let's Make a Deal (170), American Detective (43), Another Day (13), At Ease (14), B.C. Archaelogy of Bible Lands (12), Beetlejuice (21), Behind the Screen (13), Best of the Worst (14), Better Days (12), Bill & Ted's Excellent Adventures (7), Billy/Immediate Family (13), Bourbon Street Parade (26), Brian Keith Show (22), Buffalo Bill (26), Cafe Americain (18), Caribbean Nights (13), Catch Phrase (65), The Challengers (9), Chicago Teddy Bears (13), Chico and the Man (88), College Madhouse (26), Colt .45 (67), The Cowboys (12), Dave Thomas Comedy Show (6), Days and Nights of Molly Dodd (65), Detective School (13), Dorothy (4), Down the Shore (29), Dreams (13), F Troop (65), Family Album (13), Family Man (22), Family Matters (144), Family Medical Center (170), Fantasy Theatre (39), Flatbush (7), Flo (29), Fresh Prince of Bel Air (98), Frontier Adventures (63), Full House (168), Fun House (331), Game of the Century World Cup (6), George Carlin (14), Getting By (31), Gigi (52), Going Places (19), Good Sports (15), Goodnight Beantown (18), Growing Pains (176), Hail to the Chief (7), Hangin' With Mr. Cooper (44), Head of the Class (90), Heavenly Days (4), Here's Lucy (144), Hitchhiker (65), Hogan Family (110), In Concert III (26), It Had to Be You (9), It's a Living (93), Jackie Thomas Show (18), Jimmy Stewart Show (24), John Larroquette Show (22), Just in Time (6), Just Our Luck (13), Just the Ten of Us (47), Last Frontier (100), Laugh-In (130), Lawman (156), Life With Lucy (13), Little Kids Dynamite All-Star Band (13), Little People (24), Little Women (48), Living Single (49), Look at Us (24), Lorne Greene's Wild Wilderness (94), Love Connection (2,118), Love Stories (85), Love Sidney (44), Lulabelle (52), Maggie Briggs (6), Magic Star Traveler (39), Mama's Family (95), Martin (54), Mayberry RFD (78), Me and Maxx (10), Mednews and Family News (170), Mednews II (312), Memories of a Fairy Godmother (13), Molloy (13), More Real People (130), Mr. Moon's Magic Circus (13), Mr. Roberts (30), Murphy Brown (175), My Favorite Martian (107), My Kind of Town (7), My Pet Monster

(13), My Sister Sam (44), Mysteries of the Indigo Depths (39), Nearly Departed (6), New Dick Van Dyke Show (72), Night Court (180), No Time for Sergeants (34), Oceanquest (5), Off the Rack (7), One Big Family (25), $1,000,000 Chance of a Lifetime (285), Parenting Network (312), Park Place (5), People Next Door (10), People's Court (over 2,000 episodes), Perfect Couples (80), Perfect Strangers (144), Private Benjamin (39), The Professionals (13), The Redd Foxx Show (13), Roc (72), Rollergirls (4), Room for One More (26), Room for Two (26), Scorch (6), Shaky Ground (17), Shazam! (28), She's the Sheriff (44), Six O'Clock Follies (6), Slap Maxwell (22), Step by Step (69), Sugar Time (13), Superior Court (510), Tales From the Crypt (21), Tales From the Darkside (90), Tall Hopes (6), Television Parts (8), Third Degree (170), Tom (12), The Trouble With Larry (6), Waverly Wonders (9), Welcome Back Kotter (95).

90 minute series: King's Crossing (10).

One-Hour Specials: Abracadabra: It's Magic, ALF's Christmas Special, All-Star Tribute to Jazz, All-Star Toast to Improv, Andrew Dice Clay: For Ladies Only, Annual Young Comedians Specials (13 episodes), Bernstein at 70, Bill Hicks: Revelations, Blockheads, Boo, Brotherhood, Carly Simon: Coming Around Again, Cinemax Sessions (12), Concert of the World, Damon Wayans, Debby Boone Special, Dennis Miller: Live From Washington D.C., Different Worlds, Dionne Warwick in Concert, Dummies: Third Annual Adult Ventriloquism Show, Entertainment Weekly (91), Evening With Alan King, Garry Shandling: Stand-Up, Garry Trudeau Rap Master, George Burns in Concert, Grammy Hall of Fame, HBO Comedy Hour (3), HBO Magic Show, HBO Presents EMO, International Emmy Awards, Karmon Israeli Dancers, Larry Miller: Just Words, Little River Band in Australia, Loretta Lynn Special, Louie Anderson: Comedy on Canvas, Luciano Pavarotti at Via Reggio, Made in Italy With Irene Cara, Made in Italy With Lola Falana, Manhattan Transfer Special, Martin Mull on Location, Mumbo Jumbo: It's Magic, Pat Benetar, Paul Reiser: Out on a Whim, Paul Shaffer: Viva Shaf Vegas, Paula Poundstone: Cats Cops and Stuff, Pee-wee Herman Show, People Magazine (3), People of the Year I, Presto Chango: It's Magic, Richard Lewis: I'm Exhausted, Rita Rudner: Born to Be Mild, Robert Townsend & His Partners in Crime, Robin Williams on Location, Sinbad: Brain Dead, Sports Illustrated Swimsuit (4), Stand Up at 40, Superman's 50th Anniversary Special, A Very Special Christmas, Whoopi Goldberg: Fontaine...Why Am I Straight?, Women of the Night (3), Woodstock: Return to the Planet of the 60's, World Entertainment: Road to the 1992 Academy Awards, World Figure Skating Champions Salute Dorothy Hamill, A Year Without Santa Claus, 15th Annual Young Comedians Show.

Half-Hour Specials: Alexander and the Terrible No Good Very Bad Year, Ann Magnuson's Vandemonium, Bat Cat and the Penguin, Big Apple Circus, Braingames, Earthday Birthday, Hardcore IV, Hollywood Dog, Jackie Bison Show, Kids on Kids on Kids, Little Drummer Boy Book II, New Home Owner's Guide to Happiness, Norman's Corner, One-Night Stand (38), Paula Poundstone Show, Rock the House, The Wickedest Witch.

Long-form Specials: Barbara Walters 50th Anniversary Special, Boxing Event: Mancini vs. Camacho, Billy Crystal: Midnight Train to Moscow, Diana Ross in Concert, Exploring the Unknown (74 mins.), Gladys Knight and the Pips, Guilt or Innocence: The Trial of James Earl Ray, Here's Looking at You Warner Bros., Presidential Inaugural Gala, Special Olympics, St. Mark's Gospel, Earth Day Special, You Can't Take It With You.

WARNER BROS. TV PRODS.
4000 Warner Blvd., Burbank, CA 901522-0001. (818) 954-7875. FAX: (818) 954-7367.
Current Series: Bless This House, Charlie Grace, The Drew Carey Show, Dweebs, ER, Family Matters, Friends, Hangin' With Mr. Cooper, Hope and Gloria, John Grisham's The Client, Kirk, Living Single, Lois & Clark: The New Adventures of Superman, The Monroes, Murphy Brown, The Parent 'Hood, Sisters, Step by Step, Too Something, The Wayans Bros.

WEISS GLOBAL ENTERPRISES
2055 S. Saviers Rd., Suite 12, Oxnard, CA 93033-3693. (805) 486-4495. FAX: (805) 487-3330
PRESIDENT/TREASURER
Adrian Weiss
VICE PRESIDENT
Karen R. Engelhardt
SECRETARY
Ethel L. Weiss
INFORMATION SERVICES
Alex Gordon
Features: Galaxy "15" (15 features including Ginger in the Morning, Lovers Like Us, Molly and Lawless John), Impact "120" (120 features prod. by Robert L. Lippert incl. Baron of Arizona, I Shot Jesse James, King Dinosaur, Sins of Jezebel, Steel Helmet), Bride & The Beast, Westerns: (60 action features starring Johnny Mack Brown, Harry Carey, Fred Kohler, Jr., Rex Lease, Buddy Roosevelt and Bob Steele), Vintage Flicks (24 features from the 30's and 40's).
Serials: The Black Coin (15 episodes), The Clutching Hand (15 episodes), Custer's Last Stand (15 episodes).
Series: Kids Say the Darndest Things (500 x 5 min. each), The Stan Kann Show (52 x 30 mins.).
Off-Network Series: The Adventures of Jim Bowie (76 x 30 mins.), Craig Kennedy, Criminologist (26 x 30 mins.), I Married Joan (98 x 30 mins.), Make Room For Daddy (161 x 30 mins.), My Little Margie (126 x 30 mins.), Rocky Jones–Space Ranger (39 x 30 mins.), Thrill of Your Life (13 x 30 mins.), Waterfront (78 x 30 mins.).
Comedy Shorts: The Chuckle Heads (150 x 5 mins.).
Cartoons: Alice by Walt Disney (10 Alice cartoons), Krazy Kid Kartunes (4 x 6 mins.), Nursery Rhymes (6 x 1.5 mins.).

WILSHIRE COURT PRODS.
1840 Century Park East, Suite 400, Los Angeles, CA 90067. (310) 557-2444. FAX: (310) 557-0017.
PRESIDENT
John J. McMahon
S.V.P., OPERATIONS
Paul Marquez
V.P., PRODUCTION
Ed Milkovich

WIND DANCER PROD. GROUP
500 S. Buena Vista, Prod. Bldg., 3rd floor, Burbank, CA 91521-2215. (818) 560-5715. FAX: (818) 953-7401.
EXECUTIVE PRODUCERS
Matt Williams, David McFadzean, Carmen Finestra
Series: Home Improvement.

WITT-THOMAS PRODUCTIONS
c/o Sunset-Gower Studios, 1438 N. Gower St., Bldg. 35, 4th fl., Hollywood, CA 90028. (213) 464-1333. FAX: (23) 957-9886.
PARTNERS
Paul Junger Witt, Tony Thomas
Series: Brotherly Love, The John Larroquette Show, Pearl, Common Law.

FRED WOLF FILMS.
4222 W. Burbank Blvd., Burbank, CA 91505. (818) 846-0611.
Animated Series: Teenage Mutant Ninja Turtles, Dino Babies.

WOLF FILMS INC.
c/o Universal TV, 100 Universal City Plaza, Bldg. 69, Universal City, CA 91608-1085. (818) 777-3131.
EXECUTIVE PRODUCER, PRESIDENT
Dick Wolf
DIRECTOR, DEVELOPMENT, TV
Adam Borstein
Series: Law & Order, New York Undercover.

WOLPER ORGANIZATION, THE,
4000 Warner Blvd., Bldg. 14, #X, Burbank, CA 91522-0001. (818) 954-1421. FAX: (818) 954-1593.

WORLDVISION ENTERPRISES, INC.
(A Unit of Spelling Entertainment, Inc.)
1700 Broadway, New York, NY 10019-5992. (212) 261-2700. FAX: (212) 261-2788.
PRESIDENT & CEO
John D. Ryan
EXECUTIVE V.P. & COO
Bert Cohen
S.V.P., FINANCE & CFO
Tony Colabraro
S.V.P., LEGAL & BUSINESS AFFAIRS
Philip Marella
S.V.P., PROGRAMMING
Louis Dennig
S.V.P., MARKETING
Gary G. Montanus
S.V.P., OPERATIONS
Charles Quinones
S.V.P., DOMESTIC SALES
Robert E. Raleigh
V.P., ADVERTISER SALES
Robert Chernoff
EASTERN: 1700 Broadway, New York, NY 10019. (212) 261-2700. FAX: (212) 261-2724.

V.P., CABLE/NEW TECHNOLOGIES
Bill Baffi
V.P., EASTERN DIVISION MANAGER
Frank L. Browne
V.P., EASTERN DIVISION
Brian O'Sullivan
CENTRAL: 515 No. State St., Suite 2305, Chicago, IL 60610.
(312) 527-0461. FAX: (312) 527-0688.
V.P., CENTRAL DIVISION MANAGER
Tony Bauer
ACCOUNT EXECUTIVE, CENTRAL DIVISION
Damon Zaleski
SOUTHERN: 400 Perimeter Center Terrace, Atlanta, GA
30346. (770) 394-7444. FAX: (770) 396-8996.
VICE PRESIDENT, SOUTHERN DIVISION MANAGER
John Barrett
WESTERN: 5700 Wilshire Blvd., 5th fl., Beverly Hills, CA
90036. (213) 965-5910. FAX: (213) 965-5915.
VICE PRESIDENT, WESTERN DIVISION MANAGER
David McNaney
ACCOUNT EXECUTIVE, WESTERN DIVISION
Ed O'Brien

Domestic Product:

First Run Series: Hot Bench, Jim J. & Ann, Night Stand.

First Run Theatrical Features: Carolco III (20 theatrical releases), Carolco IV (20 theatrical releases), Fantastic Fantasies (4
family-oriented features), Showcase Network II (15 theatrical
releases), Worldvision 1 (18 theatrical films), Worldvision 2
(18 theatrical films), Worldvision 3 (26 theatrical films).

Off-Network Hour Series: Barnaby Jones (177), Ben Casey
(153), Beverly Hills 90210 (108), Combat (152), The Invaders
(43), Little House on the Prairie (216.5), Love Boat (140),
Love Boat II (115), Mod Squad (124), Night Heat (96), Streets
of San Francisco (119).

Half-Hour Series: Adventures of Champion (26), After Hours
(120), Almost Alive (65), Annie Oakley (80), Buffalo Bill, Jr.
(40), Come Along (13), Dark Shadows (1,245), Dickens &
Fenster (32), Doris Day Show (128), Douglas Fairbanks
Presents (115), Emergency (6), F.D.R. (27), Flying "A" Series
(222), High Road (36), It Pays to Be Ignorant (39), Love Boat
II (115), Man With Camera (29), Mickey Rooney (17), Next
Step Beyond (24), N.Y.P.D. (49), On the Mat (52), One Step
Beyond (94), People's Choice (104), Range Rider (76), The
Rebel (76), Starring the Actors (13), Starting From Scratch
(22), Take My Word for It (130), Tales From the Dark Side
(90), Tarzan (25), That Girl (136), Throb (48), Wendy and Me
(34), You Again? (26).

Mini-Series: Double Take (4 hrs.), Four Minute Mile (4 hrs.),
Hands Of A Stranger (4 hrs.), Holocaust (10 hrs.), Internal
Affairs (4 hrs.), Key to Rebecca (4 hrs.), Love, Lies & Murder
(4 hrs.), On Wings of Eagles (5 hrs.), Return to Eden (6 hrs.),
Separate But Equal (4 hrs.), Son of the Morning Star (4 hrs.),
Sword of Honor (6 hrs.), Voice of the Heart (4 hrs.).

Features: Prime VIII (20 color features), Prime Time All the
Time (16 theatricals and made-for-tv), Shark's Paradise (2 hr.
movie), Star Performers (12 made-for-tv movies).

Children's Programs: Camp Candy (40 x 30 mins.), The
Jackson Five (23 x 30 mins.), The Jerry Lewis Show (17 x 30
mins.), King Kong (26 x 30 mins. & 78 6–8 mins.), Lancelot
Link (17 x 30 mins.), Milton the Monster (78 6–8 min. & 26 x
30 mins.), Professor Kitzel (104 4 1/2 mins.), The Reluctant
Dragon & Mr. Toad (17 x 30 mins.), Smokey the Bear (51 6–8
min. & 17 x 30 mins.), George of the Jungle (17 x 30 mins. &
51 6–8 mins.), Discovery (103 x 30 mins.).

Specials: Amahl & the Night Visitors (1 hr.), Baseball Our Way
(90 mins.), The Bay City Rollers (1 hr.), The Bobby Vinton
Show (1 hr.), Candid Camera Specials (5 x 60 mins.),
Children of the Gael (1 hr.), Chris Evert Specials (1 hr.),
Christmas Memory (90 mins.), A Christmas Carol (30 mins.),
Cliffhanger Serial Specials (4 x 60 mins.)Dick Smith: Master of
Make-Up (30 mins.), Echo 1 (17 x 60 mins.), An Evening with
Irish Television (1 hr.), The Fabulous Sixties (10 x 60 mins.),
Frankenstein (1 hr.), Greatest American Film (2 hrs.), Herbie
Mann/Roland Kirk (30 mins.), Hollywood Mavericks (2 hrs.),
Irish Rovers Special (1 hr.), Is It Christ? (1 hr.), Jack Nicklaus
at the Home of Golf (3 x 90 mins.), The Last Nazi (1 hr.), The
Musical Ambassadors (1 hr.), The New Fangled Wandering
Minstrel Show (1 hr.), The Night the Animals Talked (30
mins.), Raphael (30 mins.), Roberta Flack/Donny Hathaway
(30 mins.), Ron Luciano's Lighter Side of Sports (30 mins.),
Russian Festival of Music and Dance (1 hr.), Sunshine
Specials (8 x 60 mins.), Tennis Our Way (90 mins.), Thank You
Mr. President (90 mins.), Wedding Planner—Marion Ross (1
hr.), The World of Miss World (1 hr.)

Additional Feature Packages: Animated Features (5), Animated
Cartoons (500), Champions (152), Color Movies 3 (11), Color
Movies 4 (6), Color Movies 5 (13), Hollywood Stars (17), John
Wayne Collection (16), Prime I (10), Prime II (16), Prime III

(16), Prime IV (26), Prime V (26), Prime VI (19), Prime VII (18),
Prime VIII (20), Republic Premiere One (12), Republic Premiere
Two (12), Republic Premiere Three (12), Republic Premiere Four
(12), Showcase One (8), Take 3 (6), Theatrical Cartoons (100).

Additional Hour Series/Specials/Mini-Series: American
Chronicles (13), Cowboy in Africa (26), Dan August (26), The
Fugitive (120), The Heights (13), Momentous Events (6), Most
Deadly Game (12), The Round Table (15), Twin Peaks (30),
2000 Malibu Road (6), Urban Anxiety (6).

WORLDVISION INTERNATIONAL:

AUSTRALIA: Worldvision Enterprises of Australia Pty. Ltd., 5-
13 Northcliff St., Milsons Point 2061, Sydney. (61-2) 922-4722.
FAX: (011-61-2) 955-8207. Brian Rhys-Jones, Debbie Warren,
Karen Zylstra.

BRAZIL: Worldvision Filmes do Brasil Ltd., Rua Macedo
Sobrinho 50, Botafogo, CEP 22271, Rio de Janeiro. (55-21)
286-8992. FAX: (55-21) 266-4737. Raymundo Rodriguez,
Maria Alice Freire.

CANADA: Worldvision Enterprises of Canada, 1200 Bay St.,
Suite 203, Toronto M5R 2A5, Ontario. (416) 967-1200. FAX:
(416) 967-0521. Bruce Swanson, Suzanne Lisi.

U.K: Worldvision Enterprises, U.K. Ltd., 54 Pont St., London,
SW 1X OAE, England. (44-71) 584-5357. FAX: (44-71) 581-
3483. William Peck, Janice Wilson, Zsuzsanna Jung.

FRANCE: Worldvision Enterprises S.A.R.L., 28 rue Bayard
75008, Paris. (33-1) 4723-3995. FAX: (33-1) 4070-9269. Mary
Jane Fourniel, Catherine Molinier, John Hernan.

ITALY: Worldvision Enterprises, Inc., Adalia Anstalt, Via Del
Corso, 22/Interno 10, 00186, Rome. Michael Kiwe, Andrea
Migliori, Dorthy Shaw.

JAPAN: Worldvision Enterprises, Inc., Tsukiji Hamarikyu Bldg.,
7th Floor, 5-3-3, Tsukiji, Chou-ku, Tokyo 104. (81-3) 3545-
3978. FAX: (81-3) 3545-3964. Mie Horasawa, Yukie Kumagai.

LATIN AMERICA (Atlanta Office): Worldvision Enterprises,
Inc., 400 Perimeter Center Terrace, Suite 150, Atlanta, GA
30346. (404) 394-3967. FAX: (404) 394-9002. Mary Ann
Pasante, Leticia Estrada, Carla Araya.

International Product

Series: The Addams Family (64 x 30 mins, b&w), All My
Children, American Chronicle (13 x 30 mins.), The Andros
Targets (13 x 60 mins.), Barnaby Jones (177 x 60 mins.),
Beverly Hills 90210 (Years 1-6, 177 x 60 mins.), Beauty & The
Beast (56 x 60 mins.), Bellevue Emergency (6 x 30 mins.), Ben
Casey (153 x 60 mins, b&w), Burke's Law (27 x 60 mins.),
Charles Perez (260 x 60 mins.), Combat (152 x 60 mins.),
Cowboy In Africa (26 x 60 mins.), Dallas (357 x 60 mins.), Dan
August (26 x 60 mins.), The Doris Day Show (128 x 30 mins.),
Eight Is Enough (112 x 60 mins.), The Fugitive (120 x 60 mins.),
Garrison's Gorrilas (26 hrs.), General Hospital, Geraldo (260 x
60 mins./yr.), Heaven Help Us (13 x 60 mins.), The Heights (13 x
60 mins.), Highway To Heaven (111 x 60 mins.), Hunter (13 x 60
mins.), The Invaders (43 x 60 mins.), Kaz (22 x 60 mins.),
Kindred: The Embraced, The Love Boat (255 x 60 mins.), The
Lucie Arnaz Show (6 x 30 mins.), Malibu Shores, Madman of
The People (16 x 30 mins.), Little House On The Prairie (216 x
60 mins.), Married: The First Year (4 x 60 mins.), Melrose Place
(Years 1-4, 131 x 60 mins.), Mod Squad (124 x 60 mins.),
Models Inc. (29 x 60 mins.), Moesha, Monsters (72 x 30 mins.),
Most Wanted (22 x 60 mins.), The Next Step Beyond (24 x 30
mins.), Night Stand (26 x 60 mins.), On The Air (7 x 30 mins.),
One Life To Live, Project UFO (26 x 60 mins.), Pruitts of
Southhampton (30 x 30 mins.), Return To Eden (22 x 60 mins.),
The Road (21 x 60 mins.), Robin's Hoods (22 x 60 mins.), The
Round Table (8 x 60 mins.), Savannah, Sidney (13 x 30 mins.),
Spencer's Pilots (11 x 60 mins.), Starring The Actors (13 x 30
mins.), Starting From Scratch (22 x 30 mins.), Streets of San
Francisco (119 x 60 mins.), That Girl (136 x 30 mins.), Throb (48
x 30 mins.), Thunder (12 x 30 mins.), Twin Peaks (32 x 60 mins.),
University Hospital (9 x 60 mins.), Urban Anxiety (7 x 30 mins.),
Winnetka Road (6 x 60 mins.), You Again? (26 x 30 mins.).

Republic International Series: Over 3,000 hrs. of off-network
programming including: The Bill Cosby Show (52 x 30 mins.),
Bonanza (430 x 60 mins.), Dr. Kildare (58 x 30 mins, 142 x 60
mins.), Get Smart (117 x 30 mins.), The High Chaparral (98 x
60 mins.).

TV Movies (2 hrs.): Angel In Green, Armed And Innocent,
Back To The Streets of San Francisco, Conviction of Kitty
Dodd, David Lynch's Hotel Room, A Deadly Business, Fatal
Vows: The Alexandra O'Hara Story, Final Appeal, Forget-Me-
Not-Murders, Green Dolphin Beat, The High Price of Passion,
Jailbirds, Jane's House, Kids Like These, Kiss And Tell, The
Love Boat–Valentine Voyage, Love On The Run, Murder In
Black & White, Murder Times Seven, My Two Loves, Night of
Courage, Precious Victims, Rich Men, Sam's Son, Single
Women, Sexual Advances, Shark's Paradise, Sidney
Sheldon's A Stranger In The Mirror, A Silent Betrayal, The
Stepford Children, The Stone Fox, Stones For Ibarra, Stranger

In My Bed, Stranger On My Land, Terror on Track 29, Unholy Matrimony, The Vernon Johns Story, Welcome Home Bobby, When The Bough Breaks, Wild Texas Wind.

Mini-series: Doubletake (4 hrs.), Dynasty: The Reunion (4 hrs.), Grass Roots (4 hrs.), Hands Of A Stranger (4 hrs.), Home Fires (4 hrs.), Internal Affairs (4 hrs.), The Invaders (4 hrs.), Key To Rebecca (4 hrs.), Love, Lies and Murder (4 hrs.), On Wings Of Eagles (5 hrs.), A Season In Purgatory (4 hrs.), Separate But Equal (4 hrs.), Son Of The Morning Star (4 hrs.), Stephen King's Golden Years (8 hrs.), Stephen King's The Langoliers (4 hrs.), Stephen King's The Stand (8 hrs.), Texas (4 hrs.), 2000 Malibu Road (6 hrs.).

Specials: AFI Lifetime Acheivement Awards: Kirk Douglas (90 mins.), Clint Eastwood (2 hrs.), David Lean (90 mins.), Jack Nicholson (2 hrs.), Gregory Peck (90 mins.), Sidney Poitier (90 mins.), Steven Spielberg (2 hrs.), Elizabeth Taylor (90 mins.), Dick Smith: Master of Make-Up (30 mins.), Dracula: Fact or Fiction (1 hr.), Halloween With the Addams Family (90 mins.), Hollywood Mavericks (2 hrs.), Momentous Events: Russia In The 90's (5 x 60 mins.), 1995 Hollywood Christmas Parade (2 hrs.), 1995 Soul Train Lady of Soul Awards (2 hrs.), 1995 Soul Train Music Awards (2 hrs.), Pope John Paul II (3 hrs.), Soul Train 25th Anniversay Hall of Fame Special (2 hrs.),

Special Presentation Programming: An Act of Love: The Patricia Neal Story (2 hrs.), Candid Camera Specials (5 x 60 mins.), Freedom Road (4 hrs.), The Holocaust (9 x 30 mins.), The Last Nazi (90 mins.), Little House on the Prairie (Three Special Presentations: Bless All the Dear Children, Look Back to Yesterday & The Last Farewell, 2 hrs. each), Little Mo (3 hrs.), The Ordeal of Patty Hearst (3 hrs.), Reincarnation (2 hrs.), Russian Festival of Music and Dance (1 hr.), The Trial of Lee Harvey Oswald (4 hrs.), Worldvision Dramatic Specials (7 x 60 mins.).

Paragon Features: Over 90 color features. Stars include Robert Preston, Patty Duke, Valerie Perrine, Dom DeLuise, Patricia Elliott, Gary Coleman, Mickey Rooney, George C. Scott, Henry Fonda, James Whitmore, Dennis Weaver, David Janssen, James Woods, Lee Majors, James Earl Jones, Ed Asner, Suzanne Pleshette, William Devane.

ABC Pictures: includes "Cabaret," "They Shoot Horses, Don't They?," "Charly," "Take the Money and Run," "Straw Dogs," "For Love of Ivy," "Song of Norway," "The Killing of Sister George," and "Krakatoa, East of Java" (all in color).

Prestige Features: 21 features in color including: "I Will, I Will ... For Now," "Night Watch," "A Touch of Class," "Hedda," "Baker's Hawk," "Black Market Baby," "Breakthrough," "Book of Numbers," "Fingers," "Cry For Me Billy," "Sweet Hostage," "Nasty Habits," and "Thieves."

Prestige II Features: 10 features including "A Killing Affair," "Bad Guys," "Dirt Bike Kid," " Vasectomy," "Wizards of the Lost Kingdom," and "Hurry Up or I'll Be 30."

Selznick Classics: 22 films including "Intermezzo," "Duel in the Sun," "Notorious," "Spellbound," "Rebecca," "The Spiral Staircase," "Portrait of Jenny," "The Farmer's Daughter," "The Garden of Allah," "Bill of Divorcement," "Made For Each Other," and "The Wild Heart."

Republic Pictures, over 1,000 Feature Films including, "It's A Wonderful Life," "The Quiet Man," "High Noon," "The Bells of St. Mary's," "Sands of Iwojima," "Father Goose," "Indiscrete,"

"That Touch of Mink." The Republic Library also includes 47 John Wayne films, plus features starring Cary Grant, Marlon Brando, James Cagney, Gary Cooper, Grace Kelly, Ingrid Bergman, Kirk Douglas, James Stewart, Bing Crosby, Gene Kelly, Natalie Wood, and many others.

Children's Programming: Alvin & The Chipmunks (52 x 30 mins.), Bugaloos (17 x 30 mins.), George of The Jungle (17 x 30 mins.), Hot Wheels (17 x 30 mins.), Hugo The Hippo (90 mins.), Jackson 5 (23 x 30 minsw.), The Jerry Lewis Show (17 x 30 mins.), King Kong (26 x 30 mins.), Krofft Superstar Hour Starring The Bay City Rollers (13 x 60 mins.), Lancelot Link (17 x 30 mins.), Land Of The Lost (69 x 30 mins.), Lidsville (17 x 30 mins.), Milton The Monster (26 x 30 mins.), The Point (90 mins.), Professor Kitzel (104 x 4.5 mins.), Reluctant Dragon & Mr. Toad (17 x 30 mins.), Sigmund & The Sea Monster (29 x 30 mins.), Skyhawks (17 x 30 mins.), Smokey The Bear (17 x 30 mins.).

Holiday Specials: Alvin & The Chipmunks Reunion (30 mins.), Amahl and the Night Visitors (1 hr.), A Christmas Memory (1 hr.), A Christmas Carol (30 mins.), I Love the Chipmunks Valentine Special (30 mins.), The Night the Animals Talked (30 mins.).

WORLDWIDE PANTS, INC.
1697 Broadway, New York, NY 10019. (212) 975-5300. FAX: (212) 975-4760.
7716 Beverly Blvd., #25B, Los Angeles, CA 90036. (213) 852-4475. FAX: (213) 852-2885.
Series: Late Show With David Letterman, The Bonnie Hunt Show.

WORLDWIDE TELEVISION NEWS
(A division of ABC in the U.S.)
1995 Broadway, New York, NY 10023. (212) 362-4440. FAX: (212) 496-1269.
The Interchange, Oval Road, Camden Lock, London NW1 7EP. (44) 171 410-5200. FAX: (44) 171 413-8302.
PRESIDENT
Robert Burke
VICE PRESIDENT, AMERICAS
Terry O'Reilly
BUREAU CHIEF, NY
Robert Sullivan
SALES, NORTH AMERICA
Scott Michaeloff
SALES, SOUTH AMERICA
Luiz Carlos Sa
MANAGER, BROADCAST SERVICES
Dolores Wilson

Z

ZM ENTERTAINMENT
c/o Universal Studios, 100 Universal City Plaza, MT #27, Universal City, CA 91608-1085. (818) 777-4664. FAX: (818) 733-1567.

BROADCASTERS

TELEVISION STATIONS
NETWORK AFFILIATES
STATION REPRESENTATIVES
STATE BROADCAST ASSOCIATIONS

———————————

TELEVISION STATIONS

Stations are listed by state and market in which they broadcast. Station ownership is followed by a contact person. Stations marked with an asterisk (*) are not on the air.

ALABAMA

WJSU-TV, Channel 40, CBS
Radio Bldg., 1330 Noble St., Anniston, AL 36202-0040. (205) 237-8651. FAX: (205) 236-7336. Osborn Communications Corp. Phil Cox.

WABM, Channel 68, IND
(see WBRC, Birmingham). Birmingham, AL. Glencairn Ltd.

WBIQ, Channel 10, PBS
2112 11th Ave., Suite 400, Birmingham, AL 35205. (205) 328-8756. FAX: (205) 251-2192. Alabama Educational Television Commission. Judy Stone.

WBMG, Channel 42, CBS
2075 Goldencrest Dr., Birmingham, AL 35209. (205) 322-4200. FAX: (205) 320-2713. Birmingham TV Corp. Tom Thomas.

WBRC-TV, Channel 6, ABC
1720 Valleyview Dr., Birmingham, AL 35201. (205) 322-6666. FAX: (205) 583-4386. Fox Television Stations Inc. Stan Knott.

WTTO, Channel 21, FOX
651 Beacon Pkwy. W., Suite 105, Birmingham, AL 35209. (205) 290-2100. FAX: (205) 290-2114. WTTO Licensee. David Amy.

WVTM-TV, Channel 13, NBC
1732 Valley View Dr., Birmingham, AL 35209. (205) 933-1313. FAX: (205) 933-7389. New World. Chuck Wing.

WIIQ, Channel 41, PBS
(see WBIQ, Birmingham). Demopolis, AL. Alabama Educational Television Commisson.

WDHN, Channel 18, ABC
P. O. Box 6237, Dothan, AL 36302-6237. (334) 793-1818. FAX: (334) 793-2623. Morris Network Inc. H. Dean Hinson.

WTVY, Channel 4, CBS
285 N. Foster St., Dothan, AL 36303. (334) 792-3195. FAX: (334) 793-3947. Benedek Broadcasting. Tom Wall.

WDIQ, Channel 2, PBS
(see WBIQ, Birmingham). Dozier, AL. Alabama Educational Television Commission.

WFIQ, Channel 36, PBS
(see WBIQ, Birmingham). Florence, AL. Alabama Educational Television Commission.

WOWL-TV, Channel 15, NBC
P. O .Box 2220, Florence, AL 35630-0220. (205) 767-1515. FAX: (205) 764-7750. Rick Biddle.

WYLE, Channel 26, IND
4150 Underwood Mountain Rd., Florence, AL 35674. (205) 381-2600. FAX: (205) 383-3157. ETC Communications. Les White.

WNAL-TV, Channel 44, NBC
PO Box 8249, Gadsden, AL 35902-8249. (205) 547-4444. FAX: (205) 547-1789. Anthony Jay Fant.

WTJP, Channel 60, IND
313 Rosedale St., Gadsden, AL 35901-5361. (205) 546-8860, All American TV Inc. Sonny Arguinzoni.

WAAY-TV, Channel 31, ABC
1000 Monte Sano Blvd S.E., Huntsville, AL 35801-6137. (205) 553-3131. FAX: (205) 533-6616. Smith Broadcasting Inc. M.D. Smith IV.

WAFF, Channel 48, NBC
Box 2116, Huntsville, AL 35804. (205) 533-4848. FAX: (205) 533-1337. American Family Broadcast Group. Leroy Paul.

WHIQ, Channel 25, PBS
(see WBIQ, Burmingham). Huntsville, AL. Alabama Educational Television Commission.

WHNT-TV, Channel 19, CBS
200 Holmes Ave., Huntsville, AL 35801. (205) 533-1919. FAX: (205) 539-4503. New York Times Co. Linda Spalla.

WZDX, Channel 54, IND
PO Box 3889, Huntsville, AL 35810-0889. (205) 859-5454. FAX: (205) 859-2194. Grant Communications. Milton Grant.

WGIQ, Channel 43, PBS
(see WBIQ, Birmingham). Louisville, AL. Alabama Educational Television Commission.

WALA-TV, Channel 10, NBC
PO Box 1548, Mobile, AL 36633. (334) 434-1010. FAX: (334) 434-1073. SF Broadcasting. Joseph Cook.

WEAR-TV (Mobile), Channel 3, ABC
P. O. Box 12278, Pensacola, FL 32581. (904) 456-3333. FAX: (904) 455-0159. Heritage Media Corp. Carl Leahy.

WEIQ, Channel 42, PBS
(see WBIQ, Birmingham). Mobile, AL. Alabama Educational Television Commission.

WKRG-TV, Channel 5, CBS
555 Broadcast Dr., Mobile, AL 36606-2936. (205) 479-5555. FAX: (205) 473-8130. Ansley G. Green. D.H. Buck Long Jr.

WMPV-TV, Channel 21, TBN
120 Zeigler Circle E., Mobile, AL 36608-4829. (334) 633-2100. FAX: (334) 633-2174. Jay A. Sekulow. Stuart J. Roth.

WPMI, Channel 15, FOX
PO Box 9038, Mobile, AL 36691-0038. (334) 602-1500. FAX: (334) 602-1515. Clear Channels Licenses, Inc. Dan Sullivan.

WAIQ, Channel 26, PBS
(see WBIQ, Birmingham). Montgomery, AL. Alabama Educational Television Commission.

WCOV-TV., Channel 20, FOX
1 WCOV Ave., Montgomery, AL 36111-2099. (205) 288-7020. FAX: (205) 288-5414. David D. Woods.

WHOA-TV, Channel 32, ABC
P. O. Box 3236, Montgomery, AL 36109. (334) 272-5331. FAX: (334) 271-6348. Montgomery AL Channel 32 Operating L.L.C. Michael R. Brooks.

WMCF-TV, Channel 45, TBN
300 Mendel Pkwy. W., Montgomery, AL 36117. (334) 277-4545. FAX: (334) 277-6635. Sonlight Broadcasting System. Stuart Roth.

WSFA, Channel 12, NBC
12 E. Delano Ave., Montgomery, AL 36105-2506. (334) 288-1212. FAX: (334) 613-8302. Cosmos Broadcasting Corp. James Keelor.

WCIQ, Channel 7, PBS
(see WBIQ, Birmingham). Mount Cheaha State Park, AL. Alabama Educational Television Commission.

WSWS-TV, Channel 66, IND
P. O. Box 870, Opelika, AL 36803-0870. (334) 749-5766. FAX: (334) 749-5583. Genesis Broadcasting. R.C. Hilton.

WDFX-TV, Channel 34, FOX
318 El Palacio Plaza, Ozark, AL 36360. (334) 774-8000. FAX: (334) 774-1118. Woods Television Co. David Woods.

WRJM*, Channel 67, IND
409 E. Broad St., Ozark, AL 36360. (205) 774-9323. FAX: (205) 774-6450. Shelley Broadcasting Co. Jack Mizell.

WAKA, Channel 8, CBS
3020 East Blvd., Selma, AL 36116. (334) 271-8888. FAX: (334) 271-6444. Alabama Broadcasting Partners. Cy N. Bahakel.

WCFT-TV, Channel 33, CBS
4000 37th St E., Tuscaloosa, AL 35405-3543. (205) 553-1333. FAX: (205) 556-4814. Federal Broadcasting Co. W. Tommy Ray.

WDBB, Channel 17, FOX
5455 Jug Factory Rd., Tuscaloosa, AL 35403. (205) 345-1117. FAX: (205) 345-1173. H. Carl Parmer. David R. Ross.

ALASKA

KAKM, Channel 7, PBS
3877 University Dr., Anchorage, AK 99508. (907) 563-7070. FAX: (907) 273-9192. Alaska Public Telecommunications. Susan Reed.

KDMD, Channel 33, IND
6921 Brayton Dr., Suite 220, Anchorage, AK 99507. (907) 344-7817. FAX: (907) 344-7817. GREENTV Corp. Frank Marlin.

KIMO, Channel 13, NBC
2700 E. Tudor Rd., Anchorage, AK 99507-1136. (907) 561-1313. FAX: (907) 561-1377. The Alaska 13 Corp. Mark Chassman.

KTBY, Channel 4, FOX
1840 S. Bragaw St., Suite 101, Anchorage, AK 99508-3439. (907) 274-0404. FAX: (907) 264-5180. Ronald K. Bradley.

KTUU-TV, Channel 2, NBC
Tudor Park, Suite 220, 701 E. Tudor Rd., Anchorage, AK 99510-2880. (907) 762-9260. FAX: (907) 563-3318. Zaser & Longston Inc. Jessica L. Longston

KTVA, Channel 11, CBS
1007 W. 32nd Ave., Anchorage, AK 99503-3728. (907) 562-3456. FAX: (907) 562-0953. Northern TV Inc. A.G. Hiebert.

KYES, Channel 5, IND
3700 Woodland Dr., Anchorage, AK 99517-2555. (907) 248-5937. FAX: (907) 243-0709. Jeremy Lansman & Carol Schatz. Jeremy Lansman.

KZXC*, Channel 9, IND
3211 Providence Rd., Anchorage, AK 99508. (907) 786-1626. FAX: (907) 786-1027. University of Alaska.

KYUK-TV, Channel 4, PBS
Pouch 468, Bethel, AK 99559. (907) 543-3131. FAX: (907) 543-3130. Bethel Broadcasting Inc. Andrew Guy.

KATN, Channel 2, ABC
516 2nd Ave., #400, Fairbanks, AK 99701. (907) 452-2125. FAX: (907) 456-8225. Alaska Broadcasting Network. Bob Underwood.

KFXF, Channel 7, FOX
3650 Braddock St., Fairbanks, AK 99701. (907) 452-2125. FAX: (907) 456-3428. Tanana Valley Television Co. William St. Pierre.

KTVF, Channel 11, CBS
3528 International St., Fairbanks, AK 99701-7382. (907) 452-5121. FAX: (907) 452-5120. Northern Television Inc. Henry H. Hove.

KUAC-TV, Channel 9, PBS
PO Box 755620, University of Alaska-Fairbanks, Fairbanks, AK 99775-5620. (907) 474-7491. FAX: (907) 474-5064. University of Alaska. Joan K. Wadlow.

KJUD, Channel 8, ABC
1107 W. 8th St., Juneau, AK 99801. (907) 586-3145. FAX: (907) 463-3041. Desert Communications, Inc. Elizabeth Arnett.

KTOO-TV, Channel 3, PBS
360 Egan Dr., Juneau, AK 99801. (907) 586-1670. FAX: (907) 586-3612. Capital Community Broadcasting Inc. Bill Legere.

KJNP-TV, Channel 4, NFP
P.O.Box 56359, North Pole, AK 99705. (907) 488-2216. FAX: (907) 488-5246. Alaska Missionary Fellowship. Donald L. Nelson.

KTNL, Channel 13, CBS
PO Box 1309, Sitka, AK 99835-1309. (907) 747-6002. FAX: (907) 747-6003. Wright Home Inc. Bill Wright.

ARIZONA

KMOH (Kingman), Channel 6, IND
2160 S. Hwy. 95, Bullhead City, AZ 86442. (520) 758-7333. FAX: (520) 758-8139. Grand Canyon Television Corp. Dan Robbins.

KNAZ-TV, Channel 2, NBC
2201 N. Vickey St., Flagstaff, AZ 86004. (602) 526-2232. FAX: (602) 526-8110. Grand Canyon Television Co. Dan Robbins.

KWBF, Channel 13, IND
2158 N. 4th St., Flagstaff, AZ 86004. (520) 527-1300. FAX: (520) 527-1394. Dr. Michael Gelfand.

KZJC, Channel 4, IND
(see WTVA, Tupelo, MS). Flagstaff, AZ. WTVA Inc.

KAET, Channel 8, PBS
Arizona State University, Stauffer Hall B-wing, Phoenix, AZ 85287-1405. (602) 965-3506. FAX: (602) 965-1000. Arizona Board of Regents. Charles R. Allen.

KAJW* (Tolleson), Channel 61, IND
11 W. Medlock, Phoenix, AZ 85013. (602) 277-8938. FAX: (602) 957-1354. Hector G. Salvatierra.

KASW, Channel 61, IND
(see KTVK, Phoenix). Phoenix, AZ. Brooks Broadcasting.

KNXV-TV, Channel 15, ABC
4625 S. 33rd Place, Phoenix, AZ 85040-2861. (602) 243-4151. FAX: (602) 304-3000. Scripps Howard Broadcasting Co. Brad Nilsen.

KPAZ-TV, Channel 21, IND
3551 E.McDowell Rd., Phoenix, AZ 85008-3847. (602) 273-1477. FAX: (602) 267-9427. Trinity Broadcasting Networks. Paul F. Crouch.

KPHO-TV, Channel 5, CBS
4016 N. Black Canyon, Phoenix, AZ 85017. (602) 264-1000. FAX: (602) 263-8818. Meredith Corp. Patrick North.

KPNX, Channel 12, NBC
1101 N. Central Ave., P. O. BOX 711, Phoenix, AZ 85004-1818. (602) 257-1212. FAX: (602) 258-8186. Gannett Co. Colleen Brown.

KSAZ-TV, Channel 10, FOX
511 W. Adams St., Phoenix, AZ 85003-1608. (602) 257-1234. FAX: (602) 262-0177. New World Commmunications Group Inc. Dan Berkery.

KTVK, Channel 3, IND
3435 N. 16th St., Phoenix, AZ 85016. (602) 263-3333. FAX: (602) 263-3377. Media America Corp. Jewell M. Lewis.

KTVW-TV, Channel 33, UNI
3019 E. Southern Ave., Phoenix, AZ 85040. (602) 243-3333. FAX: (602) 276-8658. Perenchio Television Inc. Ruben R. Luera.

KUTP, Channel 45, IND
4630 S. 33rd St., Phoenix, AZ 85040-2812. (602) 268-4500. FAX: (602) 276-8482. United Television Inc. Bob Furlong.

KUSK, Channel 7, IND
3211 Tower Rd., Prescott, AZ 86301-3734. (602) 778-6770. FAX: (602) 445-5210. William H. Sauro.

KGUN, Channel 9, ABC
P. O. Box 17990, Tucson, AZ 85731-7990. (602) 722-5486. FAX: (602) 290-7642. Lee Enterprises Inc. Karen Lee Rice.

KHRR, Channel 40, TEL
2919 Broadway, Garden Level, Tucson, AZ 85716. (602) 322-6888. FAX: (602) 881-7926. Jay S. Zucker.

KMSB-TV, Channel 11, FOX
1885 N. 6th Ave., Tucson, AZ 85705-5061. (520) 770-1123. FAX: (520) 629-7185. Providence Journal Broadcasting. Jack Clifford.

KOLD-TV, Channel 13, PBS
7831 N. Business Park Drive, Tucson, AZ 85743. (602) 744-1313. FAX: (520) 744-5233. Ellis Communications. V.P. & GM: Jeff Sales.

KTTU-TV, Channel 18, IND
1855 N. 6th Ave., Tucson, AZ 85705. (602) 624-0180. FAX: (602) 629-7185. Clear Channel Television License. Dan Sullivan.

KUAS, Channel 27, PBS
University of Arizona, Tucson, AZ 85721. (520) 621-5828. FAX: (520) 621-9105. Arizona Board of Regents. GM: Donald Burgess.

KUAT-TV, Channel 6, PBS
(see KUAS-TV). Tucson, AZ. Arizona Board of Regents.

KVOA-TV, Channel 4, NBC
209 W. Elm St., Tucson, AZ 85703. (520) 792-2270. FAX: (520) 620-1309. Evening Post Publishing Co. Jon F. Ruby.

KSWT, Channel 13, CBS
P. O. Box 592, Yuma, AZ 85366-0592. (602) 782-5113. FAX: (602) 782-0320. KB Media Inc. John Radeck.

KYMA Channel 11, NBC
1385 S. Pacific Ave., Yuma, AZ 85365-1725. (602) 782-1111. FAX: (602) 782-5401. Yuma Broadcasting Co. Jim Rogers.

ARKANSAS

KETG, Channel 9, PBS
(see KETS, Little Rock). Arkadelphia, AR. Arkansas Educational TV Commission.

KTVE (El Dorado), Channel 10, NBC
2909 Kilpatrick Blvd., Monroe, LA 71201-5120. (318) 323-1300. FAX: (318) 322-9718. GOCOM Television. Matt James.

KAFT, Channel 13, PBS
(see KETS, Little Rock). Fayetteville, AR. Arkansas Educational TV Commission.

KFSM-TV, Channel 5, CBS
PO Box 369, Fort Smith, AR 72902-0369. (501) 783-3131. FAX: (501) 783-3295. The New York Times Co. Tim Morrissey.

KHBS, Channel 40, ABC
2415 N. Albert Pike Ave., Fort Smith, AR 72904-5617. (501) 783-4040. FAX: (505) 783-0550. Robert Hernreich. Darrel E. Cunningham.

KPOM-TV, Channel 24, NBC
P. O. Box 4610, Fort Smith, AR 72914-4610. (501) 785-2400.
Griffin Entities. John Griffin.

KAIT-TV, Channel 8, ABC
P. O. Box 790, Jonesboro, AR 72403-0790. (501) 931-8888.
FAX: (501) 933-8058. Cosmos Broadcasting Corp. Clyde
Anderson.

KTEJ, Channel 19, PBS
(see KETS, Little Rock). Jonesboro, AR. Arkansas Educational
TV Commission.

KARK-TV, Channel 19, NBC
P. O. Box 748, Little Rock, AR 72203-0748. (501) 376-4444.
FAX: (501) 376-1852. Morris Network Inc. H. Dean Hinson.

KATV, Channel 7, ABC
P. O. Box 77, Little Rock, AR 72203-0077. (501) 324-7777. FAX:
(501) 324-7566. Allbritton Comunications Co. Dale Nicholson.

KETS, Channel 2, PBS
350 N. Donaghey, Little Rock, AR 72033. (501) 682-2388. FAX:
(602) 682-4122. Arkansas Educational TV Commission. Susan
J. Howarth.

KLRT, Channel 16, FOX
11711 W. Markham, Little Rock, AR 72221. (501) 225-0016.
FAX: (501) 225-0428. Clear Channel Television. Jerry Whitener.

KTHV, Channel 11, CBS
P. O. Box 269, Little Rock, AR 72203-0269. (501) 376-1111.
FAX: (501) 376-3719. Gannett Broadcasting. Paul Trelstead.

KTVN (Pine Bluff), Channel 25, IND
701 Napa Valley, Little Rock, AR 72221. (501) 223-2525. FAX:
(501) 225-3837. Agape Church Inc. H. L. Caldwell.

KVUT* (Little Rock), Channel 42, IND
102 Fairmont Ctr., Daphne, AL 36526. (205) 626-3339.
Leininger-Geddes Partnership.

KEMV, Channel 6, PBS
(see KETS, Little Rock). Mountain View, AR. Arkansas
Educational TV Commission.

KASN, Channel 38, UPN
(see KLRT, Little Rock). Pine Bluff, AR. Mercury Broadcasting Co.

KFAA, Channel 51, NBC
1821 S. 8th St., Rogers, AR 72756. (501) 631-8851. FAX: (501)
631-1853. J.D.G. Television. John Griffin.

KSBN*, Channel 57, IND
P. O. Box 6968, Springdale, AR 72766-6968. (501) 361-2900.
Total Life Community Educational Foundation. Carlos
Pardeiro.

CALIFORNIA

KBAK-TV, Channel 29, ABC
P. O. Box 2929, Bakersfield, CA 93303-2929. (805) 327-7955.
Burnham Broadcasting Co. Philip Nye.

KERO-TV, Channel 23, CBS
321 21st St., Bakersfield, CA 93301-4120. (805) 637-2323.
FAX: (805) 322-1701. McGraw-Hill Broadcasting Co. Chris
Westerkamp.

KGET, Channel 17, NBC
2831 Eye St., Bakersfield, CA 93301. (805) 327-7511. FAX:
(805) 327-7576. Ackerly Communications. Raymond A. Watson.

KUZZ-TV, Channel 45, IND
3223 Sillect Ave., Bakersfield, CA 93308. (805) 326-1011. FAX:
(805) 328-7576. Buck Owens Productions. CEO: Mel Owens, Jr.

KTSF (San Francisco), Channel 26, IND
100 Valley Dr., Brisbane, CA 94005-1350. (415) 468-2626. FAX:
(415) 467-7559. Lincoln Broadcasting Co. Lillian L. Howell.

KNBC, Channel 4, NBC
3000 W. Alameda St., Burbank, CA 91523. (818) 840-4444.
FAX: (310) 840-3535. NBC TV Stations. Pres. & GM: Carole
Black.

KRCA (Riverside), Channel 62, IND
1813 Victory Place, Burbank, CA 91504. (818) 563-5722. FAX:
(818) 972-2694. Fouce Amusement Enterprises. Frank L.
Fouce.

KCPM, Channel 24, NBC
180 E. 4th St., Chico, CA 95928. (916) 893-2424. FAX: (916)
893-1033. Cottonwood Communications. Station Mgr.: Ralph
Green.

KCVU (Paradise), Channel 30, FOX
587 Country Dr., Chico, CA 95926. (916) 893-1234. FAX: (916)
893-1266. Sainte Ltd. Chester Smith.

KAIL (Fresno), Channel 53, UPN
1590 Alluvial Ave., Clovis, CA 93611. (209) 299-9753. FAX: (209)
299-9753. Trans-America Broadcasting. Albert J. Williams.

KFCB, Channel 42, IND
5101 Port Chicago Hwy., Concord, CA 94524. (510) 686-4242.
FAX: (510) 825-4242. Pappas Telecasting. Harry Pappas.

KECY-TV, Channel 9, FOX
646 Main St., El Centro, CA 92243. (619) 353-9990. FAX: (619)
352-5471. Pacific Media Corp. Peter G. Sieler.

KAEF, Channel 29, FOX
540 E. St., Eureka, CA 95501. (707) 444-2323. FAX: (707)
445-9451. Lamco Communications. Marshall R. Noecker.

KBVU, Channel 29, FOX
730 7th St., Suite 201, Eureka, CA 95501. (209) 442-2999.

KEET, Channel 13, PBS
7246 Humboldt Hill Rd., Eureka, CA 95503. (707) 445-0813.
Redwood Empire Public TV. Sid Anderson.

KIEM-TV, Channel 3, NBC
5650 S. Broadway, Eureka, CA 95503. (707) 443-3123. FAX:
(707) 442-6084, Pollock/Belz Broadcasting. GM: Thomas J.
Spain, Jr.

KVIQ, Channel 6, CBS
1800 Broadway, Eureka, CA 95501. (707) 443-3061. FAX: (707)
443-4435. Miller Broadcasting Co. Ronald W. Miller.

KFWU, Channel 8, ABC
300B N. Main St., Fort Bragg, CA 95437. (916) 243-7777. FAX:
(916) 243-0217. Lamco Communications. Marshal R. Noecker.

KFSN-TV, Channel 30, ABC
1777 G. St., Fresno, CA 93706. (209) 442-1170. FAX: (209)
233-5844. Capital Cities/ABC. Marc Edwards.

KFTV, Channel 21, UNI
3239 W. Ashlan Ave., Fresno, CA 93722. (209) 584-1800. FAX:
(209) 222-2890. Perenchio Television Inc. Bram J. Watkins.

KGMC, Channel 43, WB
706 W. Herndon Ave., Fresno, CA 93650. (209) 432-4300. FAX:
(209) 435-3201. Owner: Gary Cocola.

KJEO, Channel 47, CBS
4880 N. First, Fresno, CA 93726. (209) 222-2411. FAX: (209)
221-6938. Retlaw Broadcasting Co. Benjamin Tucker.

KMPH, Channel 26, FOX
5111 E. McKinley Ave., Fresno, CA 93727-2033. (209)
255-2600. FAX: (209) 255-0275. Pappas Telecasting
Companies. Harry J. Pappas.

KMSG-TV, Channel 59, TEL
706 W. Herndon Ave., Fresno, CA 93650-1033. (209) 435-5900.
FAX: (209) 435-1448. Diane D. Dostinich. GM: Lisa J. Nilmeier.

KNXT (Visalia market), Channel 49, NFP
1550 N. Fresno St., Fresno, CA 93703. (209) 488-7440. FAX:
(209) 488-7444. Diocese of Fresno Education Corp. Bishop
John T. Steinback.

KSEE, Channel 24, NBC
5035 E. McKinley Ave., Fresno, CA 93727-1964. (209)
454-2424. FAX: (209) 454-2487. Granite Broadcasting Corp.
Marty Edelman.

KVPT, Channel 18, PBS
1544 Van Ness, Fresno, CA 93721. (209) 266-1800. FAX: (209)
443-5433. Valley Public Television. Colin Dougherty.

KVEA (Los Angeles), Channel 52, TEL
1130A Air Way, Glendale, CA 91201. (818) 502-5700. FAX:
(818) 502-0029. Telemundo Group. Roland Hernandez.

KHCV* (Seattle WA), Channel 45, IND
17221 Lido Lane, Huntington Beach, CA 92647. North Pacific
International TV Inc. Allan E. Horn.

KOCE-TV, Channel 50, PBS
15751 Gothard St., Huntington Beach, CA 92647. (714)
895-5623. FAX: (714) 895-0852. Coast Community College.
William A. Furniss.

KDOC-TV (Anaheim), Channel 56, IND
18021 Cowan, Irvine, CA 92714-6023. (714) 442-9800. FAX:
(714) 261-5956. Golden Orange Broadcasting. Calvin Brack.

KABC, Channel 7, ABC
4151 Prospect Ave., Los Angeles, CA 90027. (310) 557-7777.
FAX: (310) 557-5036. Capital Cities/ABC. John Riedl.

KCAL, Channel 9, IND
5515 Melrose Ave., Los Angeles, CA 90038-3149. (213)
467-9999. FAX: (213) 460-6265. The Walt Disney Co. David J.
Woodcock.

KCBS-TV, Channel 2, CBS
6121 Sunset Blvd., Los Angeles, CA 90028. (213) 460-3431.
FAX: (213) 460-3294. CBS Station Group. Program Services:
Marilyn Wills.

KCET, Channel 28, PBS
4401 Sunset Blvd., Los Angeles, CA 90027. (213) 666-6500.
FAX: (213) 665-6067. Community TV of Southern California.
Donald G. Youpa.

KCOP, Channel 13, IND
915 N. La Brea Ave., Los Angeles, CA 90038. (213) 851-1001.
FAX: (213) 851-5197. Chris Craft Industries Inc. Richard Feldman.

KLCS, Channel 58, PBS
1061 Temple St., Los Angeles, CA 90012. (213) 625-6958. Los
Angeles Unified School District. Tom Mossman.

KMEX-TV, Channel 34, UNI
6701 Center Dr. West, Los Angeles, CA 90045-5073. (310)
216-3434. FAX: (310) 348-3459. Univision Television Group.
Pres. & CEO: A. Jerrold Perenchio.

KTLA, Channel 5, IND
5800 Sunset Blvd., Los Angeles, CA 90028. (213) 460-5500.
FAX: (213) 460-5405. Tribune Broadcasting Co. Greg Nathanson.

KTTV, Channel 11, FOX
5746 W. Sunset Blvd., Los Angeles, CA 90028-8588. (213)
856-1000. Fox Television Stations Inc. Michael Stern.

KYHY, Channel 22, IND
5545 Sunset Blvd., Los Angeles, CA 90028. (213) 993-2200.
FAX: (213) 466-3613. Harriscope of Los Angeles. Buzz Harris,
Jr.

KPST-TV (Vallejo), Channel 66, IND
Suite 308, 475 El Camino Real, Millbrae, CA 94030. (415)
697-6682. FAX: (415) 697-1268. Pan Pacific Television Inc.
David Li.

KCSO (Sacramento), Channel 19, Uni
P. O. Box 3689, Modesto, CA 95352. (209) 578-1900. FAX:
(209) 527-2129. Sainte Limited. Sharon Sepulveda.

KNSO* (Merced), Channel 51, IND
P. O. Box 4159, Modesto, CA 95352. (209) 523-0777. FAX:
(209) 523-0898. Sainte Ltd.

KCCN-TV (Salinas), Channel 46, CBS
P. O. Box 1938, Garden Rd., Monterey, CA 93940. (408)
649-0460. FAX: (408) 646-1973. Harron Television of Monterey.
Robert F. Herbst.

KSMS-TV (Salinas), Channel 67, UNI
67 Garden Court, Monterey, CA 93940-5302. (408) 373-6767.
FAX: (408) 373-6700. KSMS-TV L.P. Daniel D. Villanueva.

KTVU, Channel 2, FOX
P. O. Box 22222, Oakland, CA 94623-2222. (510) 834-1212.
FAX: (510) 272-9957. Cox Enterprises. Kevin P. O'Brien.

KHSC-TV, Channel 46, IND
3833 Ebony St., Ontario, CA 91761-1500. (909) 390-8846.
FAX: (909) 390-8857. Silver King Communications Inc. James
Lawless.

KADY-TV, Channel 63, UPN
663 Maulhardt Ave., Oxnard, CA 93030. (805) 983-0444. FAX:
(805) 485-6057. Roklis Broadcasting Corp. John Huddy.

KESQ-TV (Palm Springs), Channel 42, ABC
42-650 Melanie Pl., Palm Desert, CA 92211. (619) 773-0342.
FAX: (619) 773-5107. EGF Broadcasting. Grant Fitts.

KMIR-TV (Palm Springs), Channel 36, NBC
72920 Parkview Dr., Palm Desert, CA 92260. (619) 568-3636.
FAX: (619) 568-1176. Desert Empire TV Corp. John Conte.

KKAG, Channel 61, IND
1077 W. Morton Ave., Porterville, CA 93257. (209) 781-6100.
FAX: (209) 782-0364. Kralowec Children's Family Trust. Art
Kralowec.

KZKI (San Bernardino), Channel 30, IND
Suite 155, 9229 Utica Ave., Rancho Cucamonga CA 91730.
(909) 483-3030. FAX: (909) 483-0333. Paxson Communications
Corp. Terry Crosby.

KIXE, Channel 9, PBS
P. O. Box 9, Redding, CA 96099. (916) 243-5493. FAX: (916)
243-7443. Northern California Educational TV. Myron A. Tisdel.

KRCR-TV, Channel 7, ABC
755 Auditorium Dr., Redding, CA 96001-0920. (916) 243-7777.
FAX: (916) 243-0217. Lamco Communications Inc. Marshall R.
Noecker.

KRCB (Cotati), Channel 22, PBS
5850 Labath Ave., Rohnert Park, CA 94928. (707) 585-8522.
Rural California Broadcasting. Nancy Dobbs.

KCMY, Channel 29, IND
1029 Hook St., Suite 23, Sacramento, CA 95814-3815. (916)
443-2929. FAX: (916) 442-6414. Ponce-Nicasio Broadcasting.
Carmen Briggs.

KCRA-TV, Channel 3, NBC
3 Television Cir., Sacramento, CA 95814-0794. (916) 446-3333.
FAX: (916) 325-3731. Kelly Broadcasting Co. Greg Kelly.

KPWB-TV, Channel 31, IND
500 Media Pl., Sacramento, CA 95815. (916) 925-3100. FAX:
(916) 920-1078. Pappas Telecasting Companies. Elliott
Troshinsky.

KQCA, Channel 58, IND
58 Television Cir., Sacramento, CA 95814. (916) 447-5858.
FAX: (916) 554-4658. Channel 58 Inc. Wing Fat.

KTXL, Channel 40, FOX
4655 Fruitridge Rd., Sacramento, CA 95820. (916) 454-4422.
FAX: (916) 739-1079. Renaissance Communications Group.
Michael Fisher.

KVIE, Channel 6, PBS
Box 6, Sacramento, CA 95812. (916) 929-5843. FAX: (916)
929-7215. KVIE Inc. Don Julian.

KXTV, Channel 10, ABC
400 Broadway, Sacramento, CA 95818. (916) 441-2345. FAX:
(916) 441-3054. A.H. Belo Corp., Broadcast Division. Jim
Saunders.

KCAH (Watsonville), Channel 25, IND
Suite 106, 559 E. Alisal, Salinas, CA 93905. (408) 754-1540.
California Community TV Network. Arlene Kimata.

KCBA, Channel 35, FOX
P. O. Box 3560, Salinas, CA 93912-3560. (408) 422-3500. FAX:
(408) 754-1120. Ackerley Communications Group, Inc. V.P. &
GM: Mark Faylor.

KSBW, Channel 8, NBC
238 John St., Salinas, CA 93901-3339. (408) 758-8888.
FAX: (408) 424-3750. KSBW Licensee Inc. Pres. & GM: Bob
Rice.

KVCR-TV, Channel 24, PBS
701 S. Mt. Vernon Ave., San Bernardino, CA 92410. (909)
888-6511. FAX: (909) 885-2116. San Bernardino Community
College District. GM: Thomas Little.

KFMB-TV, Channel 8, CBS
7677 Engineer Rd., San Diego, CA 92111. (619) 571-8888.
FAX: (619) 569-4203. Midwest Television Inc. Pres. & GM: Ed
Trimble.

KGTV, Channel 10, ABC
Box 85347, San Diego, CA 92186. (619) 237-1010. FAX: (619)
262-1302. McGraw-Hill Broadcasting Co. Ed Quinn.

KNSD, Channel 39, NBC
8330 Engineer Rd., San Diego, CA 92111. (619) 279-3939.
FAX: (619) 279-1076. New World Communications Group Inc.
Neil E. Derrough.

KPBS, Channel 15, PBS
5200 Camponile Rd., San Diego State University, San Diego,
CA 92182-5400. (619) 594-1515. FAX: (619) 265-6417. Board
of Trustees, CSU for SDSU. Doug Myrland.

KTTY, Channel 69, IND
P. O. Box 121569, San Diego, CA 92112-5569. (619) 575-6969.
FAX: (619) 575-6951. San Diego Television Inc. James M.
Harmon.

KUSI-TV, Channel 51, IND
4575 Viewridge Ave., San Diego, CA 92123. (619) 571-5151.
McKinnon Broadcasting Co. Michael D. KcKinnon.

WAOM* (Morehead, KY), Channel 67, IND
c/o Garcia Communications, 1562 Oro Vista Rd., #282, San
Diego, CA 92154-4043. Garcia Communications.

XETV (Tijuana, Mexico), Channel 6, FOX
8253 Ronson Rd., San Diego, CA 92111. (619) 279-6666. FAX:
(619) 268-9388. Bay City Television. V.P. & GM: Joanie
O'Laughlin.

XEWT-TV (Tijuana, Mexico), Channel 12, IND
P. O. Box 434537, San Diego, CA 92143. (619) 528-1212. FAX:
(619) 280-9398. Televisa S.A. Jose Luis Gausch.

BAY-TV, Channel 35, NBC
(see KRON, San Francisco). San Francisco, CA. Chronicle
Broadcasting Inc.

KBHK-TV, Channel 44, IND
650 California St., San Francisco, CA 94108. (415) 249-4444.
FAX: (415) 397-1924. Chris Craft Industries. John C. Siegel.

KCNS, Channel 38, IND
1550 Bryant St., Ste 850, San Francisco, CA 94103-4832. (415) 863-3800. FAX: (415) 863-3998. West Coast United Broadcasting Co. Carson Chen.

KDTV, Channel 14, UNI
2200 Palou Ave., San Francisco, CA 94124. (415) 641-1400. FAX: (415) 641-8677, Perenchio Television Inc. Marcela Medina.

KGO-TV, Channel 7, ABC
900 Front St., San Francisco, CA 94111-1427. (415) 954-7777. FAX: (415) 954-7294. Capital Cities/ABC Broadcast Group. Jim Topping.

KMTP-TV, Channel 32, PBS
211 Brannan St., San Francisco, CA 94107. (415) 777-3232. FAX: (415) 512-4379. Minority Television Project. Otis McGee, Jr.

KOFY-TV, Channel 20, IND
2500 Marin St., San Francisco, CA 94124. (415) 821-2020. Pacific FM Inc. Jim Gabbert.

KPIX TV, Channel 5, CBS
855 Battery St., San Francisco, CA 94111-1503. (415) 362-5550. FAX: (415) 765-8844. CBS Station Group. Henry Fuller.

KQED, Channel 9, PBS
2601 Mariposa St., San Francisco, CA 94110-1400. (415) 864-2000. FAX: (415) 553-2380. KQED Inc. Mary G.F. Bitterman.

KRON-TV, Channel 4, NBC
1001 Van Ness Ave., San Francisco, CA 94109. (415) 441-4444. FAX: (415) 561-8136. Chronicle Broadcasting Inc. Pres. & CEO: Amy S. McCombs.

KICU-TV, Channel 36, IND
1585 Schallenberger Rd., San Jose, CA 95131-2434. (408) 298-3636. FAX: (408) 298-1353. KICU Inc. James H. Evers.

KLXV-TV, Channel 65, IND
2315 Canoas Garden Rd., San Jose, CA 95125. (408) 264-6565. FAX: (408) 723-1670. Paxson Communications Group. Tim Crosby.

KNTV, Channel 11, ABC
645 Park Ave., San Jose, CA 95110-2613. (408) 286-1111. FAX: (408) 295-5461. Granite Broadcasting Corp. Steward Park.

KSTS, Channel 48, TEL
2349 Bering Dr., San Jose, CA 95131-1125. (408) 435-8848. FAX: (408) 433-5921. Telemundo Group Inc. Enrique Perez.

KTEH, Channel 54, PBS
100 Skyport Dr., San Jose, CA 95110-1301. (408) 437-5454. FAX: (408) 437-5469. KTEH-TV Foundation. Tom Fanella.

KFTL (Stockton), Channel 64, IND
403 McCormick St., San Leandro, CA 94577. (510) 632-5835. FAX: (510) 632-8943, Family Stations Inc. Pres. & CEO: Harold Camping.

KSBY, Channel 6, NBC
467 Hill St., San Luis Obispo, CA 93405. (805) 541-6666. FAX: (805) 541-5142. E.P. Communications Inc. Elisabeth Murdoch.

KCSM-TV, Channel 60, PBS
1700 W. Hillsdale Blvd., San Mateo, CA 94402. (415) 574-6586. FAX: (415) 574-6675. San Mateo Community College District. David Hosley.

KTBN-TV, Channel 40, IND
P. O. Box A, Santa Ana, CA 92711. (714) 832-2950. Trinity Broadcasting Co. Paul F. Crouch.

KEYT-TV, Channel 3, ABC
P. O. Box 729, Santa Barbara, CA 93102-0729. (805) 965-8533. FAX: (805) 962-2342. Smith Broadcasting Group Inc. Byron Elton.

KCOY-TV, Channel 12, CBS
1211 W. McCoy Ln., Santa Maria, CA 93455. (805) 925-1200. FAX: (805) 922-9830. Stauffer Communications Inc. Charles S. Stauffer.

KFTY, Channel 50, IND
P. O. Box 1150, Santa Rosa, CA 95402-1150. (707) 526-5050. FAX: (707) 526-7929. KFTY Broadcasting Inc. Gary Heck.

KSTV-TV, Channel 57, IND
Suite A, 6020 Nicolle Ave., Ventura, CA 93003. (805) 650-8857. FAX: (805) 650-8875. Costa de Oro Television Inc. Walter Ulloa.

KHIZ (Barstow), Channel 64, IND
P. O. Box 6464, Victorville, CA 92393. (619) 241-5888. FAX: (619) 241-0056. Sunbelt Television. Margaret Jackson.

KSCI (San Bernardino), Channel 18, IND
12401 W. Olympic, West Los Angeles, CA 90064. (310) 478-1818. FAX: (310) 479-8118. KSCI Inc. Ray Beindorf.

KOVR, Channel 13, CBS
2713 KOVR Dr., West Sacramento, CA 95605. (916) 374-1313. FAX: (916) 374-1459. Sinclair Broadcasting. Steve Gigliotti.

COLORADO

KRMT (Denver), Channel 41, IND
12014 W. 64th Ave., Arvada, CO 80004. (303) 423-4141. FAX: (303) 423-4314. Faith Bible Chapel. George Morrison.

KKTV, Channel 11, CBS
P. O. Box 2110, Colorado Springs, CO 80901-2110. (719) 634-2844. FAX: (719) 634-3741. Ackerley Communications Inc. Jim Lucas.

KRDO-TV, Channel 13, ABC
P. O. Box 1457, Colorado Springs, CO 80901-1457. (719) 632-1515. FAX: (719) 475-0815. Harry W. Hoth Jr. Patti L. Hoth.

KXRM-TV, Channel 21, FOX
P. O. Box 15789, Colorado Springs, CO 80935-5789. (719) 596-2100. FAX: (719) 591-4180. Edison Media Inc. & Z/L Media Inc. Larry W. Douglas.

KBDI-TV, Channel 12, PBS
2900 Welton St., 1st floor, Denver, CO 80205. (303) 296-1212. FAX: (303) 296-6650. Front Range Educational Media Corp. Ted Krichels.

KCEC, Channel 50, UNI
Suite 110, 777 Grant St., Denver, CO 80203. (303) 832-0050. FAX: (303) 832-3410. Golden Hills Broadcasting Corp. Walter Ulloa.

KCNC-TV, Channel 4, CBS
P. O. Box 5012, Denver, CO 80217. (303) 861-4444. FAX: (303) 830-6380. CBS Station Group. Mary Rockford.

KDVR, Channel 31, FOX
501 Wazee St., Denver, CO 80204-1858. (303) 595-3131. FAX: (303) 595-8312. Fox Television Stations Inc. Glenn P. Dyer.

KMGH-TV, Channel 7, ABC
123 Speer Blvd., Denver, CO 80203. (303) 832-7777. FAX: (303) 832-0138. McGraw-Hill Broadcasting Co. V.P. & GM: John Proffitt.

KRMA-TV, Channel 6, PBS
1089 Bannock St., Denver, CO 80204. (303) 892-6666. FAX: (303) 620-5600. Council for Public TV, Ch. 6 Inc. James N. Morgese.

KTVJ (Boulder), Channel 20, IND
2100 Downing St., Denver, CO 80205. (303) 832-1414. Roberts Broadcasting of Denver Inc. Mike Roberts.

KUBD, Channel 59, TEL
9805 E. Iliff, Denver, CO 80231. (303) 751-5959. FAX: (303) 751-5993. UHF Channel 59 Corp. Bud Paxson.

KUSA-TV, Channel 9, NBC
500 Speer Blvd., Denver, CO 80203. (303) 871-9999. FAX: (303) 871-1819. Gannett Broadcasting. Joe Franzgrote.

KFCT, Channel 22, FOX
(see KDVR, Denver). Durango, CO. Fox Television Stations Inc.

KREZ-TV, Channel 6, IND
P. O. Box 2508, Durango, CO 81302. (303) 259-6666. FAX: (303) 247-8472. Lee Enterprises Inc. Dave Brown

KTVD (Denver), Channel 20, UPN
P. O. Box 6522, 11203 E. Peakview, Englewood, CO 80111. (303) 792-2020. FAX: (303) 790-4633. Channel 20 TV Company. V.P. & GM: Terence J. Brown.

KWGN-TV, Channel 2, IND
6160 S. Wabash Way, Englewood, CO 80111-5108. (303) 740-2222. FAX: (303) 740-2847. Tribune Broadcasting Co. James C. Dawdle.

KWHD (Denver/Castle Rock), Channel 53, IND
5450 S. Syracuse St., Englewood, CO 80111. (303) 773-9953. FAX: (303) 773-9960. LeSea Broadcasting. Lester Sumrall.

KJCT, Channel 8, ABC
P. O. Box 3788, Grand Junction, CO 81502-3788. (970) 245-8880. FAX: (970) 245-8249. Pikes Peak Broadcasting Co. Patti Hoth.

KREG-TV (Glenwood Springs), Channel 3, IND
P. O. Box 789, Grand Junction, CO 81502. (303) 963-3333.
FAX: (303) 242-0886. Withers Broadcasting Co. Don Bona.

KREX-TV, Channel 5, CBS
P. O. Box 789, Grand Junction, CO 81502-0789. (303)
242-5000. FAX: (303) 242-0886. Withers Broadcasting Co. Don
Bona.

KZJG* (Longmont, CO), Channel 25, IND
P. O. Box 984, Little Rock, AR, 72203. (501) 753-5338.
Colorado Broadcasters.

KREY-TV, Channel 10, IND
614 N. First, Montrose, CO 71401. (303) 249-9601. FAX: (303)
249-9610. Withers Broadcasting Co. Don Bona.

KJWA* (Grand Junction), Channel 4, IND
P. O. Box 10, 800 Gold Creek Rd., Ohio City, CO 81237. John
Harvey Reese.

KOAA-TV, Channel 5, IND
P. O. Box 195, Pueblo, CO 81002-0195. (719) 544-5781. FAX:
(719) 544-7733. Evening Post Publishing Co. John O. Gilbert.

KTSC, Channel 8, PBS
2200 Bonforte Blvd., Pueblo, CO 81001-4901. (719) 543-8800.
FAX: (719) 549-2208. University of Southern Colorado. Gregory
B. Sinn.

KSBS-TV, Channel 24, IND
P. O. Box 582445, Steamboat Springs, CO 80488. (970)
870-6110. FAX: (970) 870-6210. Green TV Corp. David Drucker.

KTVS, Channel 3, CBS
P. O. Box 432, 9841 County Rd. 59, Sterling, CO 80751. (970)
522-5743. FAX: (970) 522-7813. Morris Communications Inc.
GM: Cathy Doherty.

CONNECTICUT

WEDH, Channel 24, PBS
P. O. Box 6240, 240 New Britain Ave., Hartford, CT 06106-0240.
(203) 278-5310. FAX: (203) 278-2157. Connecticut Public
Broadcasting. Jerry Franklin.

WFSB, Channel 3, CBS
3 Constitution Plz., Hartford, CT 06103-1807. (860) 728-3333.
FAX: (860) 247-8940. Post Newsweek Stations. Christopher J.
Rohrs.

WHCT-TV, Channel 18, IND
c/o Opul Business Systems, 18 Garden St., Hartford, CT
06105. (860) 547-1481. Astroline Communications Co. L.P. Mike
Lupo.

WTIC-TV, Channel 61, FOX
One Corporate Ctr., Hartford, CT 06103. (203) 527-6161.
Renaissance Communications. Edward T. Karlik.

WBNE, Channel 59, WB
8 Elm St., New Haven, CT 06510. (203) 782-5900. FAX: (203)
782-5995. K-W TV Inc. David Katz.

WEDY, Channel 65, PBS
(see WEDH, Hartford). New Haven, CT. Connecticut Public
Broadcasting.

WTNH-TV, Channel 8, ABC
P. O. Box 1859, 8 Elm St., New Haven, CT 06510. (203)
784-8888. FAX: (203) 784-2010. LIN Television Corp. Henry K.
Yaggi.

WTWS, Channel 26, IND
Suite 226, 3 Shaws Cove, New London, CT 06320. (203)
444-2626. Paxson Communications Corp. Bruce Fox.

WEDN, Channel 53, PBS
(see WEDH, Hartford). Norwich, CT. Connecticut Public
Broadcasting.

WTXX, Channel 20, IND
15 Peach Orchard Rd., Prospect, CT 06712-1052. (203)
575-2020. FAX: (203) 758-3908. Counterpoint Communications
Inc. David Brewer.

WHAI-TV (Bridgeport), Channel 43, IND
80 Great Hill Rd., Seymour, CT 06483. (203) 734-6182. FAX:
(203) 795-0061. ValueVision International Inc. Michael K.
Vlock.

WEDW (Bridgeport), Channel 49, PBS
307 Atlantic St., Stamford, CT 06901. (203) 965-0440. FAX:
(203) 965-0447. Connecticut Public Broadcasting. Jay Millard.

WVIT, Channel 30, NBC
1422 New Britain Ave., West Hartford, CT 06110-1632. (860)
521-3030. FAX: (860) 521-4860. Paramount Stations Group. Al
Bova.

DELAWARE

WDPB, Channel 64, PBS
(see WHYY, Wilmington). Seaford, DE. WHYY Inc.

WHYY-TV, Channel 12, PBS
625 Orange St., Wilmington, DE 19801. (302) 888-1200. FAX:
(215) 351-0398. WHYY Inc. Frederick Breitenfeld.

DISTRICT OF COLUMBIA

WBDC-TV, Channel 50, WB
Suite 350, 2121 Wisconsin Ave NW, Washington, DC 20007.
(202) 965-5050. FAX: (202) 965-0050. JASAS Corp. V.P. & GM:
Michael Nurse.

WDCA (Washington), Channel 20, IND
5202 River Rd., Bethesda, MD 20816. (301) 986-9322. FAX:
(301) 654-3517. Paramount Communications Inc. Richard H.
Williams.

WETA-TV, Channel 26, PBS
P. O. Box 2626, Washington, DC 20013. (703) 998-2600. FAX:
(703) 998-3401. Greater Washington Educational
Telecommunications. Daniel Lloyd.

WHMM, Channel 32, PBS
2222 4th St. NW, Washington, DC 20059. (202) 806-3200. FAX:
(202) 806-3300. Howard University. Marva Fletcher.

WJLA-TV, Channel 7, ABC
3007 Tilden St. NW, Washington, DC 20008. (202) 364-7777.
FAX: (202) 364-7922. Allbritton Communications Co. Terry
Connelly.

WRC-TV, Channel 4, NBC
4001 Nebraska Ave. NW, Washington, DC 20016. (202)
885-4000. FAX: (202) 885-5022. NBC TV Stations Division.
Allan Horlick.

WTTG, Channel 5, FOX
5151 Wisconsin Ave. NW, Washington, DC 20016. (202)
244-5151. FAX: (202) 244-1745. Fox Television Stations Inc.
Gene McHugh.

WUSA, Channel 9, CBS
4100 Wisconsin Ave. NW, Washington, DC 20016. (202)
895-5999. FAX: (202) 966-7948. Gannett Broadcasting. Robert
J. Sullivan.

FLORIDA

WGCU-TV (Fort Myers), Channel 30, PBS
Channel 30 Dr., Bonita Springs, FL 33923. (941) 598-9737.
FAX: (941) 598-2598. State Board of Regents, Florida. Station
Manager: Kirk Lethomaa.

WTVK (Fort Myers), Channel 46, IND
3451 Bonita Bay Blvd., Bonita Springs, FL 33923. (941)
498-4600. FAX: (941) 498-0146. Second Generation of Florida
Ltd. Jon Pinch.

WZVN-TV (Naples), Channel 26, ABC
3451 Bonita Bay Blvd., Bonita Springs, FL 33923. (813) 495-
9388. FAX: (813) 947-1722. Ellis Communications. Robert White.

WXEL-TV (West Palm Beach), Channel 42, PBS
3401 S. Congress Ave., Boynton Beach, FL 33426. (407)
737-8000. FAX: (407) 369-3067. South Florida Public
Telecommunications, Inc. Mary Souder.

WFCT, Channel 66, IND
Lakewood Business Park, Suite E18, 4301 32nd St. W.,
Bradenton, FL 34205. (941) 739-2686. FAX: (813) 746-5053.
Bradenton Broadcast Television Co. General Partner: Anita
Rogers.

WGOX* (Inverness), Channel 64, IND
P. O. Box 1000, Bushnell, FL 33513. West Florida Television Ltd.
Peggy R. Prendergrass.

WFTX (Fort Myers), Channel 36, FOX
621 S.W. Pine Island Rd., Cape Coral, FL 33991. (813)
574-3636. FAX: (813) 574-4803. Hulman & Co. Chris Duffy.

WCLF, Channel 22, IND
P. O. Box 6922, Clearwater, FL 34618-6922. (813) 535-5622.
Christian Television Corp. Robert R. D'Andrea.

WBCC, Channel 68, IND
1519 Clearlake Rd., Cocoa, FL 32922. (407) 632-1111. FAX:
(407) 634-3724. Brevard Community College. Dr. Maxwell King.

WCEU (New Smyrna Beach), Channel 15, PBS
1200 W. International Speedway Blvd., Daytona Beach, FL
32124. (904) 254-4415. FAX: (904) 254-4427. Coastal
Educational Broadcasters. Don A. Thigpen.

WBBH-TV, Channel 20, NBC
P. O. Box 7578, Fort Myers, FL 33911-7578. (813) 939-2020.
FAX: (813) 936-7771. Waterman Broadcasting Corp. Steve
Pontius.

WINK-TV, Channel 11, CBS
2824 Palm Beach Blvd., Fort Myers, FL 33916-1503. (941)
334-1111. FAX: (941) 334-0744. Fort Myers Broadcasting Co.
Joe Schwartzel.

WTCE, Channel 21, IND
1040 S. 37th St., Fort Pierce, FL 34947. (407) 489-2701. FAX:
(407) 489-6833. Jacksonville Educators Broadcasting. Bob
Constantino.

WFGX, Channel 35, IND
105 Beach Dr., Fort Walton Beach, FL 32547-2560. (904) 863-
3235. FAX: (904) 862-7659. Bowers Network Inc. Carl Scarlata.

WCJB, Channel 20, ABC
6220 N.W. 43rd St., Gainesville, FL 32653-3334. (352)
377-2020. FAX: (352) 373-6516. Diversified Communications.
Carolyn Catlin.

WGFL* (High Springs), Channel 53, IND
930 N.W. 8th Ave., Gainesville, FL 32601. (352) 371-7772. FAX:
(352) 375-6111. Harvey & Ilene S. Budd.

WUFT, Channel 5, PBS
2200 Weimer, University of Florida, Gainesville, FL 32611. (352)
392-5551. FAX: (352) 392-5731. Florida Board of Regents.
Richard Lehner.

WPAN, Channel 53, IND
P. O. Box 18126, Pensacola, FL 32523. (904) 934-8772. FAX:
(904) 932-7452. John Franklin Ministries Inc. John Franklin.

WBFS-TV, Channel 33, IND
16550 N.W. 52nd Ave., Hialeah, FL 33014-6214. (305)
621-3333. FAX: (305) 628-3448. Viacom Stations Group. Albert
Krivin.

WSCV (Ft. Lauderdale), Channel 51, IND
2340 W. 8th Ave., Hialeah, FL 33010. (305) 888-5151. FAX:
(305) 889-7651. Telemundo Group Inc. Roland Hernandez.

WDZL, Channel 39, IND
2055 Lee St., Hollywood, FL 33020-2410. (305) 925-3939. FAX:
(305) 949-3900. Renaissance Communications Corp. Harvey E.
Cohen.

WHFT (Miami), Channel 45, IND
3324 Pembroke Rd., Hollywood, FL 33021-8320. (305)
962-1700. FAX: (305) 962-2817. Trinity Broadcasting Network.
Paul F. Crouch.

WAWS, Channel 30, FOX
8675 Hogan Rd., Jacksonville, FL 32216-4650. (904) 642-3030.
FAX: (904) 646-0115. Clear Channel Television. Josh McGraw.

WJCT, Channel 7, PBS
100 Festival Park Ave., Jacksonville, FL 32202. (904)
353-7770. FAX: (904) 354-6846. WJCT Inc. Bill Dresser

WJEB-TV, Channel 59, IND
3101 Emerson Expwy., Jacksonville, FL 32207. (904) 399-8413.
FAX: (904) 399-8423. Jacksonville Educators Broadcasting. H.J.
Clarey.

WJKS, Channel 17, ABC
9117 Hogan Rd., Jacksonville, FL 32216-4647. (904) 641-1700.
FAX: (904) 641-0306. Media General Broadcast Group. Jim
Matthews.

WJXT, Channel 4, CBS
P. O. Box 5270, Jacksonville, FL 32247-5270. (904) 399-4400.
FAX: (904) 399-1828. Post-Newsweek Stations Inc. Sherry Burns.

WNFT, Channel 47, IND
1 Independent Dr., Ste 204, Jacksonville, FL 32202-5060. (904)
355-4747. FAX: (904) 353-8400. RDS Broadcasting Inc. Elvin
Feltner.

WTLV, Channel 12, NBC
1070 E. Adams St., Jacksonville, FL 32202. (904) 354-1212.
FAX: (904) 633-8899. Gannett Broadcasting. Ken Tonning.

WEYS, Channel 22, IND
525 Southard St., Key West, FL 33040. (305) 296-4969. FAX:
(305) 296-1669. WEYS Television Corp. Penny Drucker.

WWFD, Channel 8, IND
909 Fleming St., Key West, FL 33040. (305) 296-8212. FAX: (305)
296-8781. Hispanic Keys Broadcasting Corp. Charles P. Curry.

WOFL (Orlando), Channel 35, FOX
35 Skyline Dr., Lake Mary, FL 32746. (407) 644-3535. FAX:
(407) 333-3535. Meredith Broadcasting Group. Norris Reichel.

WIRB (Melbourne), Channel 56, IND
6525 Babcock St., Malabar, FL 32950. (407) 725-0056. FAX:
(407) 951-2669. The Christian Network. Frank Tenore.

WBSF, Channel 33, IND
4450 Enterprise Ct., Suite L, Melbourne, FL 32934-9203. (407)
254-4343. FAX: (407) 242-0863. Blackstar Communications Inc.
John Oxendine.

WCTD, Channel 35, IND
One Datran Ctr., Suite 1804, 9100 S. Dadeland Blvd., Miami,
FL 33156. (305) 670-3535. FAX: (305) 670-0135. Worship
Network. GM: Les Haber.

WFOR-TV, Channel 4, CBS
8900 N.W. Terr., Miami, FL 33172. (305) 591-4444. FAX: (305)
639-4444. CBS Station Group. Allen Shaklan.

WLRN-TV, Channel 17, IND
172 N.E. 15th St., Miami, FL 33132. (305) 995-2204. FAX:
(305) 995-2299. School Board of Dade County. Don MacCullough.

WLTV, Channel 23, UNI
9405 N.W. 41st St., Miami, FL 33178. (305) 470-2323. FAX:
(305) 471-4236. Perenchio Television Inc. Judith Whittaker.

WPBT, Channel 2, PBS
14901 N.E. 20th Ave., Miami, FL 33181. (305) 949-8321. FAX:
(305) 944-4211. Community TV Foundation of Southern Florida.
George Dooley.

WPLG, Channel 2, ABC
3900 Biscayne Blvd., Miami, FL 33137-3721. (305) 576-1010.
FAX: (305) 325-2480. Post-Newsweek Stations, Inc. John G.
Garwood.

WSVN, Channel 7, FOX
1401 79th Street Causeway, Miami, FL 33141-4104. (305)
751-6692. FAX: (305) 795-2746. Edmund N. Ansin.

WTVJ, Channel 6, NBC
316 N. Miami Ave., Miami, FL 33128. (305) 379-6666. NBC TV
Stations Division. Donald V. Browne.

WVOZ-TV, Channel 48, IND
7425 S.W. 42nd St., Miami, FL 33155. International
Broadcasting Corp. Pedro Roman Callozio.

WYHS-TV (Hollywood), Channel 69, IND
10306 USA Today Way, Miramar, FL 33025. (305) 435-6900.
FAX: (305) 435-7406. Silver King Communications Inc. Jim
Lawless.

WAWD*, Channel 58, IND
5080 75th Ave. N.W., Ocala, FL 34482. (904) 622-7550.
Wendell M. Rowans Ministries Inc. Wendell M. Rowans

WOGX, Channel 51, FOX
P. O. Box 3985, Ocala, FL 34478-3985. (352) 873-6951. FAX:
(352) 237-5423. Hulman & Co. Robert Salat.

W47AL, Channel 47, NFP
(see WUJA, Carolina, PR). Orlando, FL. New Conscience
Network.

WAYQ*, Channel 26, IND
c/o George E. Mills Jr., 9334 Bay Vista Estates Blvd., Orlando,
FL 32836. (407) 352-0405. Trustee: George E. Mills Jr.

WCPX-TV, Channel 6, CBS
4466 John Young Pkwy., Orlando, FL 32804. (407) 291-6000.
FAX: (407) 298-2122. First Media Television. Brooke Spectorsky.

WFTV, Channel 9, ABC
P. O. Box 999, Orlando, FL 32802-0999. (407) 841-9000. FAX:
(407) 244-8302. Cox Broadcasting. David B. Lippoff.

WKCF, Channel 18, IND
Suite 200, 602 Courtlandt St., Orlando, FL 32804. (407)
645-1818. FAX: (407) 647-4163. Press Broadcasting Inc. Robert
E. McAllan.

WMFE-TV, Channel 24, PBS
11510 E. Colonial Dr., Orlando, FL 32817-4699. (407)
273-3200. FAX: (407) 273-3613. Community Communications
Inc. Stephen McKenney Steck.

WRBW, Channel 65, IND
Suite 200, 2000 Universal Studios Plaza, Orlando, FL 32819.
(407) 248-6500. FAX: (407) 248-6520. Rainbow Broadcasting
Ltd. Joseph Rey.

WTGL-TV (Cocoa), Channel 52, IND
653 W. Michigan St., Orlando, FL 32805. (407) 423-5200. FAX:
(407) 422-0120. Good Life Broadcasting Inc. Don L. Collins.

WTVX (Fort Pierce), Channel 34, IND
Suite 7007, 3970 RCA Blvd., Palm Beach Garden, FL 33410.
(407) 694-2525. FAX: (407) 627-6738. Whitehead Media Inc.
Eddie Whitehead.

558

WPBF (Tequesta), Channel 25, ABC
Suite 7007, 3970 RCA Blvd., Palm Beach Gardens, FL 33410. (407) 694-2525. FAX: (407) 627-6738. Paxson Communications Corp. Douglas C. Barker.

WFSG, Channel 56, PBS
(see WFSU, Tallahassee). Panama City, FL. Florida Board of Regents, Florida State University.

WJHG-TV, Channel 7, NBC
8195 Front Beach Rd., Panama City, FL 32407. (904) 234-2125. FAX: (904) 233-6647. Gray Communications Systems Inc. John Ray.

WMBB, Channel 13, ABC
P. O. Box 1340, 613 Harrison Ave., Panama City, FL 32402. (904) 769-2313. FAX: (904) 769-8231. Spartan Communications Inc. Nick Evans.

WPGX, Channel 28, FOX
P. O. Box 16028, 637 Luverne Ave., Panama City, FL 32406. (904) 784-0028. FAX: (904) 784-1773. Ashling Broadcasting Group Inc. Elizabeth Wilde Mooney.

WPCT*, Channel 46, IND
P. O. Box 9556, Panama City Beach, FL 32417. (904) 234-2773. FAX: (904) 234-1179. Beach TV Properties Inc. Jud Colley.

WHBR, Channel 33, IND
P. O. Box 2633, Pensacola, FL 32513-2633. (904) 433-8633. FAX: (904) 433-8633. Christian TV of Pensacola/Mobile. Don McCallister.

WJTC (Pensacola), Channel 44, IND
661 Azalea Rd., Mobile, AL 36609. (334) 602-1544. FAX: (334) 602-1547. Mercury Broadcasting Co., Inc. David L. Herbstreith.

WSRE, Channel 23, PBS
1000 College Blvd., Pensacola, FL 32504-8998. (904) 484-1200. FAX: (904) 484-1255. Pensacola Jr. College Board of Trustees. Allan Pizzato.

WRXY-TV (Tice), Channel 49, IND
40000 Horseshoe Rd., Punta Gorda, FL 33955. (941) 543-4173. FAX: (941) 543-6800. Christian Television Network Inc. Robert R. D'Andrea.

WBSV-TV (Venice), Channel 62, IND
2065 Cantu Ct., Sarasota, FL 34232. (813) 379-0062. FAX: (813) 378-9224. DeSoto Broadcasting Inc. Danford L. Sawyer.

WWSB, Channel 40, ABC
5725 Lawton Dr., Sarasota, FL 34233-2419. (941) 923-8840. FAX: (941) 924-3971. Calkins Newspapers, Inc. Carolyn Calkins.

WBHS-TV (Tampa), Channel 50, IND
Suite 301, 12425 28th St. N., St. Petersburg, FL 33716. (813) 573-5550. FAX: (813) 571-1931. Silver King Communications Inc. Cheryl Barron.

WTOG, Channel 44, IND
365 15th Terr. N.E., St. Petersburg, FL 33716. (813) 576-4444. FAX: (813) 577-1806. Hubbard Broadcasting Inc. Stanley S. Hubbard.

WCTV, Channel 6, CBS
P. O. Box 3048, Tallahassee, FL 32315-3048. (904) 893-6666. FAX: (904) 893-5193. John H. Phipps Inc. Dennis O. Boyle.

WFSU-TV, Channel 11, PBS
1600 Red Barber Plaza, Tallahassee, FL 32310. (904) 487-3170. FAX: (904) 487-3093. Florida Board of Regents/Florida State University. Pres.: Patrick Keating.

WTLH, Channel 49, FOX
Suite 501, 1203 Governors Square Blvd., Tallahassee, FL 32301. (904) 942-4900. FAX: (904) 942-0062, Pegasus Broadcast TV Inc. Paul Lansat

WTWC, Channel 40, NBC
8440 Deerlake Road, Tallahassee, FL 32312. (904) 893-4140. FAX: (904) 893-6974. Soundview Media Investments Inc. Thomas M. Duddy.

WTXL-TV, Channel 27, ABC
8927 Thomasville Rd., Tallahassee, FL 32312-9761. (904) 893-3127. FAX: (904) 668-1460. Brian E. Cobb.

WEDU (Tampa), Channel 3, PBS
1300 North Blvd., Tampa, FL 33607. (813) 254-9338. FAX: (813) 253-0826. FL West Coast Pub. Broadcasting Inc. Stephen L. Rogers.

WFLA-TV, Channel 8, NBC
905 E. Jackson St., Tampa, FL 33602-4117. (813) 228-8888. FAX: (813) 221-5787. Media General Broadcast Group. Jim Zimmerman.

WFTS, Channel 28, ABC
4501 E. Columbus Dr., Tampa, FL 33605-3234. (813) 623-2828. FAX: (813) 744-2828. Scripps Howard Broadcasting Co. Jim Major.

WTMV (Lakeland), Channel 32, IND
7201 E. Hillsborough Ave., Tampa, FL 33610. (813) 626-3232. FAX: (813) 622-7732. Public Interest Corp. Dan L. Johnson.

WTSP, Channel 10, CBS
11450 Gandy Blvd., Tampa, FL 33702. (813) 577-1010. FAX: (813) 578-7637. Citicasters Inc. Steve Mauldin.

WTTA, Channel 38, FOX
Suite 38, 5510 W. Gray St., Tampa, FL 33609. (813) 289-3838. FAX: (813) 289-0000. Bay Television Inc. GM: Tom Watson.

WTVT, Channel 13, FOX
P. O. Box 31113, Tampa, FL 33631-3113. (813) 876-1313. FAX: (813) 875-8329. New World Communications Group Inc. Bob W. Franklin.

WUSF-TV, Channel 16, PBS
Univ. of Southern FL, WRB 219, 4202 Fowler Ave., Tampa, FL 33620. (813) 974-4000. FAX: (813) 974-4806. State Board of Regents, Florida. James B. Heck.

WFGC (Palm Beach), Channel 61, IND
Suite 2, 2406 S. Congress Ave., W. Palm Beach, FL 33406. (407) 642-3361. FAX: (407) 967-5961. Christian TV of Palm Beach County. Robert R. D'Andrea.

WHBI, Channel 67, IND
Centurion Tower, Suite 1200, 1601 Forum Place Blvd., W. Palm Beach, FL 33401. (561) 478-9111. FAX: (561) 287-0512. Hispanic Broadcasting Inc. GM: Guenter Marksteiner.

WFLX, Channel 29, FOX
4119 W. Blue Heron Blvd., West Palm Beach, FL 33404-4854. (407) 845-2929. FAX: (407) 863-1238. Malrite Communications Group Inc. V.P. & GM: Murray J. Green.

WPEC, Channel 12, CBS
P. O. Box 24612, West Palm Beach, FL 33416-4612. (407) 844-1212. FAX: (407) 842-1212. Photo Electronics Corp. Alex Dreyfoos.

WPTV, Channel 5, NBC
622 N. Flagler Dr., West Palm Beach, FL 33401. (407) 655-5455. FAX: (407) 655-8947. Scripps Howard Broadcasting. Lawrence A. Leser.

WESH (Orlando), Channel 2, NBC
1021 N. Wymore Rd., Winter Park, FL 32789. (407) 645-222. FAX: (407) 539-7812. Pulitzer Broadcasting Co. Jeffrey H. Lee.

GEORGIA

WALB, Channel 10, NBC
P. O. Box 3130, Albany, GA 31706-3130. (912) 883-0154. FAX: (912) 434-8768. Gray Communications Systems, Inc. James Wilcox.

WFXL, Channel 31, FOX
P. O. Box 4050, Albany, GA 31706-4050. (912) 435-3100. FAX: (912) 435-0485. P. Eppley, A. Kemp, Doug Oliver.

WAGA-TV, Channel 5, FOX
1551 Briarcliff Rd N.E., Atlanta, GA 30306-2217. (404) 875-5555. FAX: (404) 898-0277. New World Communications Group. Jack Sander.

WATL (WB36), Channel 36, WB
1 Monroe Pl. N.E., Atlanta, GA 30324-4836. (404) 881-3600. FAX: (404) 881-3635. Quest Broadcasting, LLC. Station Mgr.: Mike Gehring.

WGNX, Channel 46, CBS
P. O. Box 98097, Atlanta, GA 30359-1797. (404) 325-4646. FAX: (404) 633-8358. Tribune Broadcasting Co. Herman Ramsey.

WGTV (Athens), Channel 8, PBS
1540 Stewart Ave. S.W., Atlanta, GA 30310. (404) 756-2400. FAX: (404) 756-4476. GA Public Television Network. Marcia Killingsworth.

WPBA, Channel 30, PBS
740 Bismark Rd. N.E., Atlanta, GA 30324. (404) 827-8900. FAX: (404) 827-8956. Board of Ed., City of Atlanta. Pres. & COO: Milton Klipper.

WSB-TV, Channel 2, ABC
1601 W. Peachtree St. N.E., Atlanta, GA 30309-2641. (404) 897-7000. FAX: (404) 897-7525. Cox Broadcasting. James C. Kennedy.

WTBS, Channel 17, IND
1050 Techwood Dr. N.W., Atlanta, GA 30318. (404) 827-1717. FAX: (404) 885-4947. Superstation Inc. Turner Broadcasting. Scott Sassa.

WUPA Channel 69, UPN
Suite A., 2700 Northeast Expwy., Atlanta, GA 30345. (404) 325-6969. FAX: (404) 633-4567. Paramount Stations Group. Linda Danna.

WXIA-TV, Channel 11, NBC
1611 W. Peachtree St. N.E., Atlanta, GA 30309. (404) 892-1611. FAX: (404) 892-0182. Gannett Broadcasting. Craig A. Dubow.

WAGT, Channel 26, NBC
P. O. Box 1526, Augusta, GA 30903-1526. (706) 826-0026. Schurz Communications Inc. Hal Edwards.

WFXG, Channel 54, FOX
3933 Washington Rd., Augusta, GA 30907. (706) 650-5400. FAX: (706) 650-8411. Pezold Broadcasting. Mike Reed.

WJBF, Channel 6, ABC
1001 Reynolds St., Augusta, GA 30901. (706) 722-6664. Spartan Radiocasting Company Inc. Walter J. Brown.

WRDW-TV (Augusta), Channel 12, CBS
1301 Georgia Ave., N. Augusta, SC 29841. (803) 278-1212. FAX: (803) 279-8316. Gray Communications Systems Inc. William G. Evans.

WUBI, Channel 34, IND
P. O. Box 1080, E. Jekyll Rd., Baxley, GA 31513. (912) 367-3434. FAX: (912) 367-5299. Upchurch Broadcasting Inc. Jimmy Upchurch.

WNGM-TV (Athens), Channel 34, IND
185 Ben Burton Cir., Bogart, GA 30622. (706) 353-3400. FAX: (706) 549-5844. NGM TV Partners. S. Lanierfinch.

WSBG-TV, Channel 21, IND
7434 Blythe Island Hwy., Brunswick, GA 31525. (912) 267-0021. FAX: (912) 267-9583. Coastal Communications Inc. J.R. Wright.

WCLP-TV, Channel 18, PBS
2765 Ft. Mountain State Park Rd., Chatsworth, GA 30705. (706) 695-2422. GA Public Telecomm. Commission. Frank Bugg.

WDCO-TV, Channel 29, PBS
P. O. Box 269, Cochran, GA 31014. (912) 934-2220. FAX: (912) 934-3646. GA Public Telecomm. Commission. Mell Bland.

WLTZ, Channel 38, NBC
P. O. Box 12289, Columbus, GA 31917-2289. (706) 561-3838. FAX: (706) 563-8467. Lewis Broadcasting Corp. J. Curtis Lewis, Jr.

WRBL, Channel 3, CBS
P. O. Box 270, Columbus, GA 31902-0270. (706) 323-3333. FAX: (706) 327-6655. ML Media and Commonwealth. Jim Caruthers.

WTVM, Channel 9, ABC
P. O. Box 1848, Columbus, GA 31902-1848. (706) 324-6471. FAX: (706) 322-7527. AFLAC Broadcast Division. GM: Lee Brantley.

WXTX, Channel 54, FOX
P. O. Box 12188, Columbus, GA 31907-0865. (706) 561-5400. FAX: (706) 561-6505. John D. Pezold.

WSST-TV, Channel 55, IND
P. O. Box 917, Cordele, GA 31015-0917. (912) 273-0001. FAX: (912) 273-8894. P.A Streetman, William B. Goodson.

KMPX (Decatur), Channel 29, NFP
P. O. Box 612066, Dallas, TX 75261. (214) 432-0029. FAX: (214) 432-0650. Word of God Fellowship Inc. Marcus D. Lamb.

WHSG (Monroe), Channel 63, IND
1550 Agape Way, Decatur, GA 30035. (404) 288-1156. FAX: (404) 288-5613. Trinity Broadcasting Network Inc. Diane Lawson.

WELF (Dalton), Channel 23, IND
Rt. 1, P. O. Box 390, Lookout Mountain, GA 30750. (706) 820-1663. FAX: (706) 820-1735. Sonlight Broadcasting Systems Inc. Stuart J. Roth.

WGNM, Channel 64, UPN
2525 Beech Ave., Macon, GA 31204. (912) 746-6464. FAX: (912) 745-2367. Good News Television. Donald R. Wood.

WGXA, Channel 24, FOX
P. O. Box 340, 599 Martin Luther King Blvd., Macon, GA 31297. (912) 745-2424. FAX: (912) 750-4347. GOCOM Television. GM: Keith True.

WMAZ-TV, Channel 13, CBS
P. O. Box 5008, Macon, GA 31213-8099. (912) 752-1313. FAX: (912) 752-1331. Multimedia Broadcasting Co. Don McGouirk.

WMGT, Channel 41, NBC
P. O. Box 4328, Macon, GA 31213-7799. (912) 745-4141. FAX: (912) 742-2626. Morris Network Inc. L.A. Sturdivant.

WPGA-TV (Perry), Channel 58, FOX
P. O. Box 980, 535 Coliseum Dr., Macon, GA 31201. (912) 745-5858. FAX: (912) 745-5800. Radio Perry Inc. Lowell L. Register.

WTLK-TV (Rome), Channel 14, IND
Suite 114, 200 N. Cobb Pkwy., Marietta, GA 30062. (770) 528-1400. FAX: (770) 528-1422. Paxson Communications Corp. Lowell Paxson.

WATC-TV (Atlanta), Channel 57, IND
1862 Enterprise Drive, Norcross, GA 30093. (770) 244-1616. FAX: (770) 300-9838. Community Television Inc. Pres.: James H. Thompson.

WACS-TV (Dawson), Channel 25, PBS
Rt. 1, P. O. Box 75A, Parrott, GA 31777. (404) 756-2400. FAX: (404) 756-2617. GA Public Telecomm. Commission. Lewis C. Rickerson.

WABW-TV, Channel 14, IND
P. O. Box 249, Pelham, GA 31779. (912) 294-8313. GA Public Telecomm. Commission. Don Mitchell.

WVAN-TV (Savannah), Channel 9, PBS
P. O. Box 367, 86 Vandiver St., Pembroke, GA 31321-0367. (912) 653-4996. FAX: (800) 222-6006. GA Public Telecomm. Commission. Werner Rogers.

WJCL, Channel 22, ABC
10001 Abercorn St., Savannah, GA 31406. (912) 925-0022. FAX: (912) 925-8621. Lewis Broadcasting Corp. J.C. Lewis.

WSAV-TV, Channel 3, NBC
1430 E. Victory Dr., Savannah, GA 31404. (912) 651-0300. FAX: (912) 651-0304. Ellis Communications. Bert Ellis.

WTGS (Hardeeville, SC), Channel 28, FOX
214 Television Circle, Savannah, GA 31406. (912) 925-2287. FAX: (912) 925-7026. American Communications & TV Inc. Coy Eckland.

WTOC-TV, Channel 11, CBS
P. O. Box 8086, Savannah, GA 31412-8086. (912) 234-1111. FAX: (912) 238-5133. AFLAC Broadcast Division. William Cathcart.

WNEG-TV, Channel 32, IND
P. O. Box 907, 100 Blvd., Toccoa, GA 30577. (770) 886-0032. Stephens County Broadcasting Co. Roy E. Gaines.

WGVP-TV, Channel 44, WB
1202 B.W. Gordon St., Valdosta, GA 31602. (912) 253-9487. FAX: (912) 241-0432. Hutchens Communications Inc. Gary L. Hutchens.

WJSP-TV (Columbus), Channel 28, PBS
609 White House Pkwy., Warm Springs, GA 31830. (706) 655-2145. GA Public Telecomm. Commission. Station Mgr.: John H. Davis.

WXGA-TV, Channel 8, PBS
P. O. Box 842, Waycross, GA 31501. (912) 283-4838. FAX: (912) 283-4838. GA Public Telecomm. Commission. Werner Rodgers.

WCES-TV, Channel 20, PBS
P. O. Box 525, Wrens, GA 30833-0525. (706) 547-2104. FAX: (706) 547-7290. GA Public Telecomm. Commission. William A. Newsome.

HAWAII

KGMD-TV, Channel 9, CBS
(see KGMB, Honolulu). Hilo HI. Lee Enterprises Inc.

KHVO, Channel 13, ABC
(see KITV, Honolulu). Hilo, HI. Argyle Television Inc.

KAII-TV (Wailuku), Channel 7, NBC
1116 Auhi St., Honolulu, HI 96814. (808) 591-2222. FAX: (808) 591-9085. S.F. Broadcasting L.L.C. Michael A. Rosenberg.

KBFD, Channel 32, IND
1188 Bishop St., # PH-1, Honolulu, HI 96813-3301. (808) 521-8066. FAX: (808) 521-5233. Kea Sung Chung, O. Chung & J. Chung.

KFVE, Channel 5, IND
150-B Puuhale Rd., Honolulu, HI 96819-2282. (808) 842-5555. FAX: (808) 842-4594. KFVE Joint Venture. Lee M. Holmes.

KGMB, Channel 9, CBS
1534 Kapiolani Blvd., Honolulu, HI 96814. (808) 973-5462. FAX: (808) 941-8153. Lee Enterprises Inc. Richard T. Grimm.

KHAW-TV, Channel 11, NBC
1116 Auahi St., Honolulu, HI 96814-4907. (808) 591-2222. FAX: (808) 593-2418. SF Broadcasting L.L.C.

KHBC-TV, Channel 2, IND
(see KFVE, Honolulu). Honolulu, HI (808) 847-3246. FAX: (808) 845-3616. King Holding Corp.

KHET, Channel 11, PBS
2350 Dole St., Honolulu, HI 96822. (808) 955-7878. FAX: (808) 949-7289. Hawaii Public Broadcasting Auth. Don Robbs.

KHNL, Channel 13, UNI
(see KFVE, Honolulu). Honolulu, HI. King Holding Corp.

KIKU, Channel 20, IND
Suite 2021, 197 Sand Island Access Rd., Honolulu, HI 96819. (808) 847-2021. FAX: (808) 841-3326. KHAI Inc. Joanne Ninomiya.

KITV, Channel 4, ABC
1290 Ala Moana Blvd., Honolulu, HI 96814. (808) 593-4444. FAX: (808) 593-9446. Argyle Television Inc. Richard F. Schaller.

KMEB (Wailuku), Channel 10, PBS
2350 Dole St., Honolulu, HI 69822. (808) 955-7878. FAX: (808) 949-7289. Hawaii Public Broadcasting Authority.

KOBN, Channel 26, IND
Suite 626, 875 Waimanu St., Honolulu, HI 96813. (808) 262-2000. FAX: (808) 254-1313. Christopher J. Racine.

KWHE/KWHH, Channel 14, IND
Century Sq., Suite 502, 1188 Bishop St., Honolulu, HI 96813. (808) 538-1414. FAX: (808) 526-0326. LeSea Broadcasting Corp. Steve Sumrall.

WHON-TV, Channel 2, NBC
1116 Auahi St., Honolulu, HI 36814. (808) 591-2222. FAX: (808) 591-9085. S.F. Broadcasting L.L.C. Michael A. Rosenberg.

KLEI (Kailua-Kona), Channel 6, IND
(see KOBN, Honolulu). Kailua-Kona, HI. Aina'e Co. Ltd.

KGMV (Wailuku), Channel 3, IND
(see KGMB, Honolulu). Wailuku, HI. Lee Enterprises Inc.

KMAU, Channel 12, ABC
(see KITV, Honolulu). Wailuku, HI. Argyle Television Inc.

KOGG, Channel 15, IND
(see KFVE, Honolulu). Wailuku, HI. King Holding Corp.

KWHM, Channel 21, IND
(see KWHE/KWHH, Honolulu). Wailuku, HI. LeSea Broadcasting Corp.

IDAHO

KAID, Channel 4, PBS
1455 N. Orchard, Boise, ID 83706. (208) 373-7220. FAX: (208) 373-7245. Idaho State Board of Education. Jerold A. Garber.

KBCI-TV, Channel 2, CBS
140 N. 16th St., Boise, ID 83702. (208) 336-5222. FAX: (208) 336-9183. Retlaw Broadcasting. Ben Tucker.

KHDT-TV, Channel 9, IND
Suite 402, 816 W. Bannock St., Boise, ID 83702. (208) 331-0900. FAX: (208) 344-0119. Boise Broadcasting Corp. Pres: Michael J. Lambert.

KTVB, Channel 7, NBC
P. O. Box 7, Boise, ID 83707-0007. (208) 375-7277. FAX: (208) 378-1762. King Broadcasting Co. Robert E. Krueger.

KCDT, Channel 26, PBS
Suite 201, 408 Sherman, Coeur d'Alene, ID 83814. (208) 765-9193. FAX: (208) 667-4689. Idaho State Board of Education. Jerold A. Garber.

KIDK, Channel 3, IND
P. O. Box 2008, Idaho Falls, ID 83403. (208) 522-1500. FAX: (208) 522-5103. Retlaw Enterprises Inc. Ben Tucker.

KIFI-TV, Channel 8, NBC
P. O. Box 2148, Idaho Falls, ID 83403-2148. (208) 525-8888. FAX: (208) 522-1930. The Post Company. Jerry M. Brady.

KLEW, Channel 3, CBS
P. O. Box 615, 2626 17th St., Lewiston, ID 83501. (208) 746-2636. FAX: (208) 746-4819. Retlaw Enterprises Inc. Fred Fickenwirth.

WUID-TV, Channel 12, PBS
Radio-TV Ctr., Univ. of Idaho, Moscow, ID 83844-3101. (208) 885-1226. Idaho State Board of Education. Jerold A. Garber.

KIVI (Nampa), Channel 6, ABC
1866 E. Chisholm Dr., Nampa, ID 83687. (208) 336-0500. FAX: (208) 465-5417. Cordillera Communications Inc. Larry J. Chase.

KTRV, Channel 12, FOX
679 6th St S., Nampa, ID 83651-4155. (208) 466-1200. FAX: (208) 467-6958. Blade Communications Inc. Allan Block.

KISU-TV, Channel 10, PBS
P. O. Box 8111, Idaho State University, Pocatello, ID 83209-0009. (208) 236-2857. FAX: (208) 236-2848. Idaho State Board of Education. Jerold A. Garber.

KPVI (Idaho Falls), Channel 6, NBC
425 E. Center, Pocatello, ID 83201. (208) 232-6666. FAX: (208) 233-6678. Oregon Trail Broadcasting. V.P. & GM: Bruce Franzen.

KBGH*, Channel 19, IND
315 Falls Ave., Twin Falls, ID 83301. (208) 733-9554. FAX: (208) 736-3015. College of Southern Idaho. Bon Mauldin.

KIPT, Channel 13, PBS
(see KAID Boise). Twin Falls, ID. Idaho State Board of Education.

KMVT, Channel 11, CBS
1100 Blue Lakes Blvd N., Twin Falls, ID 83301-3305. (208) 733-1100. FAX: (208) 733-4649. Root Communications Inc. Lee Wagner.

KXTF, Channel 35, FOX
1061 Blue Lakes Blvd. N., Twin Falls, ID 83301. (208) 733-0035. FAX: (208) 733-0160. Falls Broadcasting Corp. Station Mgr.: Ted Meirs.

ILLINOIS

WYZZ-TV, Channel 43, FOX
2714 E. Lincoln St., Bloomington, IL 61704-6010. (309) 662-4373. FAX: (309) 663-6943. R. Group Communication. G. J. Robinson.

WSIU-TV, Channel 8, PBS
1048 Communications Bldg., Southern Illinois University, Carbondale, IL 62901-6602. (618) 453-4343. FAX: (618) 453-6186. Board of Trustess, Southern IL U. Lee D. O'Brien.

KPOB-TV, Channel 15, ABC
Rt. 13, Carterville, IL 62918. (618) 985-2333. FAX: (618) 985-9709. Mel Wheeler Inc. Mel Wheeler.

WCFN (Springfield), Channel 49, CBS
P. O. Box 20, 509 S. Neil St., Champaign, IL 61824-0020. (217) 356-8333. Midwest Television Inc. Robb Gray, Jr.

WCIA, Channel 3, CBS
509 S. Neil St., Champaign, IL 61820-5219. (217) 356-8333. FAX: (217) 373-3648. Midwest Television, Inc. Pres.: August C. Meyer, Jr.

WICD, Channel 15, NBC
250 County Fair Drive, Champaign, IL 61821. (217) 351-8500. FAX: (217) 351-6056. Guy Gannett Communications. Les Vann.

WEIU-TV, Channel 51, PBS
Radio & TV Ctr., 139 Buzzard, Eastern Illinois University, Charleston, IL 61920. (217) 581-5956. Eastern Illinois University. John L. Beabout.

WBBM-TV, Channel 2, CBS
630 N. McClurg Ct., Chicago, IL 60611-3007. (312) 944-6000. FAX: (312) 440-0591. CBS Station Group. Robert McGann.

WCFC-TV, Channel 38, IND
38 S. Peoria St., Chicago, IL 60607. (312) 433-3838. FAX: (312) 433-3839. Christian Comm. of Chicagoland. Jerry Rose.

WCIU-TV, Channel 26, IND
26 N. Halsted St., Chicago, IL 60661. (312) 705-2600. FAX: (312) 705-2656. Howard Shapiro. Howard Shapiro.

WEHS-TV (Aurora), Channel 60, IND
100 S. Sanagamon, Chicago, IL 60607. (312) 829-8860. FAX: (312) 829-1059. Silver King Communications Inc. Jim Lawless.

WFLD, Channel 32, FOX
205 N. Michigan Ave., Chicago, IL 60601-5925. (312) 565-5532. FAX: (312) 819-0420. Fox Television Stations Inc. Stacey Marks-Bronner.

WGBO-TV (Joliet), Channel 66, UNI
Suite 1100, 541 N. Fairbanks Ct., Chicago, IL 60611. (312) 670-1000. FAX: (312) 494-6492. Perenchio Television Inc. Jerrold Perenchio.

WGN-TV, Channel 9, WB
2501 W. Bradley Pl., Chicago, IL 60618-4701. (312) 528-2311. FAX: (312) 528-6857. Tribune Broadcasting Co. Peter Walker.

561

WLS-TV, Channel 7, ABC
190 N. State St., Chicago, IL 60601-3302. (312) 750-7777.
FAX: (312) 750-7015. Capital Cities/ABC Inc. Joseph A. Ahern.

WMAQ-TV, Channel 5, NBC
454 N. Columbus Dr., Chicago, IL 60611. (312) 836-5555. FAX:
(312) 527-9072. NBC TV Stations Division. Lyle Banks.

WPWR-TV, Channel 50, IND
2151 N. Elston Ave., Chicago, IL 60614-3903. (312) 276-5050.
FAX: (312) 276-6477. Newsweb Corp. Fred Eychaner.

WSNS, Channel 44, SYN
430 W. Grant Pl., Chicago, IL 60614-3807. (312) 929-1200.
FAX: (312) 929-8153. Harriscope Corp. Jose Francisco.

WYCC, Channel 20, PBS
7500 S. Pulaski St., Chicago, IL 60652. (312) 838-7878. FAX:
(312) 581-2071. College Dist. #508, Cook County. Carole B.
Wright.

WAND, Channel 17, ABC
904 W. South Side Dr., Decatur, IL 62521-4022. (217) 424-2500.
FAX: (217) 422-8203. LIN Television Corp. T.J. Vaughan.

WFHL, Channel 23, IND
2510 Pkwy. Ct., Decatur, IL 62526. (217) 428-2323. FAX: (217)
428-6455. Decatur Foursquare Broadcasting Inc. Mark
Dreistadt.

WSIL-TV, Channel 3, ABC
(see KPOB, Carterville). Harrisburg, IL. Mel Wheeler Inc.

WSEC, Channel 14, PBS
(see Western IL Educational Television, Springfield).
Jacksonville, IL. W. Central IL Edu. Telecomm. Corp.

WMEC, Channel 22, PBS
(see Western IL Educational Television, Springfield). Macomb,
IL. W. Central IL Edu. Telecomm. Corp.

WTCT, Channel 27, IND
P. O. Box 1010 Rt. 37 N., Marion, IL 62959. (618) 997-9333.
FAX: (618) 997-1859. Tri-State Christian T. Garth Coonce.

WQAD-TV, Channel 8, ABC
3003 Park 16th St., Moline, IL 61265. (309) 764-8888. FAX:
(309) 764-5763. The New York Times Co. Perry Chester.

WQPT-TV, Channel 24, PBS
6600 34th Ave., Moline, IL 61265. (309) 796-2424. FAX: (309)
796-2484. Black Hawk College. Charles Law.

WCEE, Channel 13, IND
125 N. 11th St., Mount Vernon, IL 62864. (618) 242-8813. FAX:
(618) 242-8643. McEntree Broadcasting Inc. Dee Rose.

WUSI-TV, Channel 16, PBS
P. O. Box 430, Olney, IL 62450. (618) 754-3335. FAX: (618) 754-
3330. Board of Trustees Southern IL Univ. Dr. Kenneth J. Garry.

WWTO-TV (LaSalle), Channel 35, IND
420 E. Stevenson Rd., Ottawa, IL 61350. (815) 434-2700. FAX:
(815) 434-2458. All American TV Inc. Cruz S. Arguinzoni.

WEEK-TV, Channel 25, NBC
2907 Springfield Rd., Peoria, IL 61611-4878. (309) 698-2525.
FAX: (309) 698-9663. Granite Broadcasting Corp. John
Deushane.

WHOI, Channel 19, ABC
500 N. Stewart St., Peoria, IL 61610-3297. (309) 698-1919.
FAX: (309) 698-4819. Benedek Broadcasting Corp. Station
Mgr.: Sheryl Jonsson.

WMBD-TV, Channel 31, CBS
3131 N. University St., Peoria, IL 61604-1316. (309) 688-3131.
FAX: (309) 686-8650. Midwest Television, Inc. General Mgr.:
Gene Robinson.

WTVP, Channel 47, PBS
1501 W. Bradley Ave., Peoria, IL 61625. (309) 677-4747. IL
Valley Public Telecomm. Corp. Elwin L. Basquin.

KHQA-TV, Channel 7, CBS
510 Maine St., Quincy, IL 62301-3941. (217) 222-6200. FAX:
(217) 228-3164. Benedek Broadcasting Co. K. James Yager.

WGEM-TV, Channel 20, NBC
P. O. Box 80, Quincy, IL 62306-0080. (217) 228-6600. FAX:
(217) 228-6670. Quincy Newspapers Inc. T.A. Oakley.

WQEC, Channel 27, PBS
(see Western IL Educational Television, Springfield). Quincy, IL.
W. Central IL Edu. Telecomm. Corp.

WTJR, Channel 16, IND
P. O. Box 1189, 222 N. 6th St., Quincy, IL 62306. (217)
228-1616. FAX: (217) 228-0966. Believers Broadcasting Corp.
Carl Geisendorfer.

WHBF-TV, Channel 4, CBS
231 18th St., Rock Island, IL 61201-8706. (309) 786-5441.
FAX: (309) 788-4975. Citadel Communications Co. Ltd. Philip J.
Lombardo.

WIFR (Freeport), Channel 23, CBS
Suite 210, 308 W. State St., Rockford, IL 61101. (815)
987-5300. FAX: (815) 965-0985. Benedek Broadcasting Co.
Bruce R. Miller.

WQRF-TV, Channel 39, FOX
401 S. Main St., Rockford, IL 61101-1319. (815) 987-3950.
FAX: (815) 964-9974, Petracom Inc. Henry A. Ash.

WREX-TV, Channel 13, NBC
P. O. Box 530, Rockford, IL 61105-0530. (815) 335-2213. FAX:
(815) 335-2055. Quincy Newspapers Inc. Larry Manne.

WTVO, Channel 17, ABC
1917 N. Meridian Rd., Rockford, IL 61101-9215. (815) 963-5413.
FAX: (815) 963-0201. Young Broadcasting Inc. Bill Snider.

WICS, Channel 20, NBC
P. O. Box 3920, 2680 E. Cook St., Springfield, IL 62703. (217)
753-5620. FAX: (217) 753-8177. Guy Gannett Communications.
Station Mgr.: Jack Conners.

WRSP-TV, Channel 55, FOX
3003 Old Rochester Rd., Springfield, IL 62703. (217) 523-8855.
FAX: (217) 523-4410. Bahakel Communications. Cy N. Bahakel.

Western Illinois Educational Television, PBS
P. O. Box 6248, Springfield, IL 62708. (217) 786-6647. FAX:
(217) 786-7267. W. Central IL Edu. Telecomm. Corp. Jerold A.
Garber.

WCCU, Channel 27, FOX
712 W. Killarney St., Urbana, IL 61801-1015. (217) 367-8827.
FAX: (217) 367-8839. Bahakel Communications. Tom
MacArthur.

WILL-TV, Channel 12, PBS
1110 W. Main St., Urbana, IL 61801. (217) 333-1070. FAX:
(217) 244-6386. Board of Trustees, Univ. of Illinois. Donald P.
Mullally.

WTTW, Channel 11, PBS
5400 N. St. Louis Ave., Chicago, IL 60625. (312) 583-5000.
FAX: (312) 583-3046. Window to the World Communications.
William McCarter.

INDIANA

WINM (Angola), Channel 63, IND
R.R. 1 State Line Rd., Edgerton, OH 43517. (419) 298-3703.
FAX: (419) 298-3704. Tri-State Christian Television. Garth
Coonce.

WTIU, Channel 30, PBS
Radio-TV Bldg., Indiana University, Bloomington, IN 47405.
(812) 855-5900. FAX: (812) 855-0729. Trustees of Indiana
University. Don Agostino.

WNIT-TV (South Bend), Channel 34, PBS
P. O. Box 3434, 2300 Charger Blvd., Elkhart, IN 46514. (219)
674-5961. FAX: (219) 262-8497. Michiana Public Broadcasting
Corp. James Shea Jr.

WSJV, Channel 28, FOX
58096 CR N. 7 South, Elkhart, IN 46517. (219) 679-9758. FAX:
(219) 294-1324. Quincy Newspapers Inc. Thomas A. Oakley.

WEHT, Channel 25, ABC
P. O. Box 25, Evansville, IN 47701-0025. (812) 424-9215. FAX:
(502) 826-6823. James S. Gilmore Stations. Jim Gilmore Jr.

WEVV, Channel 44, CBS
44 Main St., Evansville, IN 47708-1450. (812) 464-4444. FAX:
(812) 465-4559. WEVV Inc. GM: J. A. Simms.

WFIE-TV, Channel 14, NBC
P. O. Box 1414, 1115 Mt. Auburn Rd., Evansville, IN 47720.
(812) 426-1414. FAX: (812) 426-1945. Cosmos Broadcasting
Group. John R. Cottingham.

WNIN, Channel 9, PBS
405 Carpenter St., Evansville, IN 47708. (812) 423-2973. FAX:
(812) 428-7548. Tri-State Public Teleplex Inc. David Dial.

WTVW, Channel 7, ABC
477 Carpenter St., Evansville, IN 47708-1027. (812) 422-1121.
FAX: (812) 421-4040. Petracom Broadcasting of MO Inc. Hank
Ash.

WFTE (Salem), Channel 58, IND
5257 S. Skyline Dr., Floyds Knobs, IN 47119. (812) 948-5841.
FAX: (812) 949-9365. Kentuckiana Broadcasting Inc. James T.
Ledford.

WANE-TV, Channel 15, CBS
P. O. Box 1515, Fort Wayne, IN 46801-1515. (219) 424-1515.
FAX: (219) 424-1428. LIN Television Corp. Frank N. Moore.

WFFT-TV, Channel 55, FOX
3707 Hillegas Rd., Fort Wayne, IN 46808-1351. (219)
471-5555. FAX: (219) 484-4331. Great Trails Broadcasting
Corp. Alexander Williams.

WFWA, Channel 39, PBS
3632 Butler Rd., Fort Wayne, IN 46808. (219) 484-8839. FAX:
(219) 482-3632. Fort Wayne Public Television. Roger Rhodes.

WKJG-TV, Channel 33, NBC
2633 W. State Blvd., Fort Wayne, IN 46808. (219) 422-7474.
The Joseph R. Cloutier Trust. Joseph Cloutier.

WPTA, Channel 21, ABC
3401 Butler Rd., Fort Wayne, IN 46808. (219) 483-0584. FAX:
(219) 483-1835. Granite Broadcasting Corp. Tim Gilbert.

WCLJ (Bloomington), Channel 42, IND
2528 U.S. 31 S., Greenwood, IN 46143. (317) 535-5542.
FAX: (317) 535-8584. Trinity Broadcasting Network. Randall
Lohr.

WYIN (Hammond), Channel 62, IND
18600 S. Oak Park Ave., Tinley Park, IL 60477. (708)
633-0001. FAX: (708) 633-0040. Jovon Broadcasting Group.
Joseph Stroud.

WFYI, Channel 20, PBS
1401 N. Meridian, Indianapolis, IN 46202. (317) 636-2020. FAX:
(317) 633-7418. Metro Indianapolis Public B'casting. Lloyd Wright.

WISH-TV, Channel 8, CBS
P. O. Box 7008, 1950 N. Meridian St., Indianapolis, IN 46207.
(317) 923-8888. FAX: (317) 926-1144. LIN Television Corp.
John Dawson.

WNDY-TV, Channel 23, IND
4555 West 16th St., Indianapolis, IN 46268. (317) 241-2388.
FAX: (317) 381-6975. Wabash Valley Broadcasting Corp. G.
Christopher Duffy.

WRTV, Channel 6, ABC
1330 N. Meridian St., Indianapolis, IN 46202-2303. (317)
635-9788. FAX: (317) 269-1400. McGraw-Hill Broadcasting Co.
Edward T. Reilly.

WTBU, Channel 69, IND
2835 N. Illinois, Indianapolis, IN 46208. (317) 940-9828. FAX:
(317) 940-5971. Butler Universit. Station Mgr.: Kenneth Creech.

WTHR, Channel 13, NBC
1000 N. Meridian St., Indianapolis, IN 46204. (317) 636-1313.
FAX: (317) 636-3717. Dispatch Broadcast Group. Michael J.
Fiorile.

WTTK (Kokomo), Channel 29, IND
3490 Bluff Rd., Indianapolis, IN 46217. (317) 782-4444. FAX:
(317) 780-5464. River City Broadcasting. Mike Granados.

WTTV, Channel 4, IND
3490 Bluff Rd., Indianapolis, IN 46217-3204. (317) 782-4444.
FAX: (317) 780-5464. River City Broadcasting. Michael
Granados.

WXIN, Channel 59, FOX
1440 N. Meridian St., Indianapolis, IN 46202-2305. (317)
632-5900. FAX: (317) 687-6531. Renaissance
Communications. Michael Finkelstein.

WIPB (also production facility), Channel 49, PBS
Edmund F. Ball Bldg., Ball State University Teleplex, Muncie, IN
47306. (317) 285-1249. FAX: (317) 285-5548. Ball State
University. General Mgr.: Alice Cheney.

WHMB-TV (Indianapolis), Channel 40, IND
10511 Greenfield Ave., Noblesville, IN 46060. (317) 773-5050.
FAX: (317) 776-4051. LeSea Broadcasting Corp. V.P.: Peter
Sumrall.

WKOI, Channel 43, IND
1702 S. 9th St., Richmond, IN 47374-7203. (317) 935-2390.
Trinity Broadcasting Network. Paul Crouch.

WHME-TV, Channel 46, IND
P. O. Box 12, South Bend, IN 46624-0012. (219) 291-8200.
FAX: (219) 291-9043. LeSea Broadcasting. Lester Sumrall.

WNDU-TV, Channel 16, NBC
P. O. Box 1616, South Bend, IN 46634-1616. (219) 631-1616.
FAX: (219) 631-1600. Univ. of Notre Dame du Lac. Jim
Behling.

WSBT-TV, Channel 22, CBS
300 W. Jefferson Blvd., South Bend, IN 46601-1513. (219)
233-3141. FAX: (219) 288-6630. Schurz Communications Inc.
James D. Freeman.

WBAK-TV, Channel 38, FOX
P. O. Box 719, Terre Haute, IN 47808-0719. (812) 238-1515.
FAX: (812) 235-3854. Bahakel Communications. Cy N. Bahakel.

WTHI-TV, Channel 10, CBS
P. O. Box 1486, 918 Ohio St., Terre Haute, IN 47808. (812)
232-9481. FAX: (812) 232-8953. Wabash Valley Broadcasting
Corp. G. Christopher Duffy.

WTWO, Channel 2, NBC
P. O. Box 299, Terre Haute, IN 47808. (812) 696-2121. FAX:
(812) 696-2755. RP Companies Inc. I. Martin Pompadur.

WIIB (Bloomington), Channel 63, IND
Rt. 1, P. O. Box 516A, Trafalgar, IN 46181. (317) 878-5407.
FAX: (317) 878-4458. Channel 63 Inc. Barbara Kerr.

WVUT, Channel 22, PBS
David Hall, 1200 N. 2nd St., Vincennes, IN 47951. (812)
885-4345. FAX: (812) 882-2237. Vincennes University Trustees.
Al Rerko.

WLFI-TV, Channel 18, CBS
P. O. Box 2618, West Lafayette, IN 47906-0618. (317) 463-1800.
FAX: (319) 463-7979. The Block Family. Robert A. Ford.

IOWA

KTVC, Channel 48, IND
1404 5th Ave S.E., Altoona, IA 50009-2027. (515) 967-6228.
Jerry D. Montgomery.

KJMH (Burlington), Channel 26, FOX
(see KLJB, Davenport). Burlington, IA 52807. Burlington TV
Acquisition Corp.

KCRG-TV, Channel 9, ABC
P. O. Box 816, Cedar Rapids, IA 52406-0816. (319) 398-8422.
FAX: (319) 398-8378. The Gazette Co. Station Mgr.: Bob Allen.

KFXA, Channel 28, FOX
605 Boyson Rd. N.E., Cedar Rapids, IA 52402-7209. (319)
393-2800. FAX: (319) 395-7028. Second Generation of Iowa.
Larry Blum.

KFXB, Channel 40, FOX
(see KFXA, Cedar Rapids). Cedar Rapids, IA. Second
Generation Iowa.

KGAN, Channel 2, CBS
P. O. Box 3131, Cedar Rapids, IA 52406-3131. (319) 395-9060.
FAX: (319) 395-0987. Guy Gannett Broadcasting Svc. Inc.
Russell Hamilton.

KBIN, Channel 32, PBS
(see Iowa Public Television, Johnston). Council Bluffs, IA. Iowa
Public Broadcasting Board.

KLJB-TV, Channel 18, FOX
937 E. 53rd St., Ste D, Davenport, IA 52807-2614. (319)
386-1818. FAX: (319) 386-8543. Quad Cities. Milton Grant.

KQCT, Channel 36, IND
(see WQPT, Moline, IL). Davenport, IA. Black Hawk College.

KWQC-TV, Channel 6, NBC
805 Brady St., Davenport, IA 52803-5211. (319) 383-7000.
FAX: (319) 383-7165. R. Geismar, A. Adler & F. Walker. Russell
Hamilton.

KCCI, Channel 8, CBS
888 9th St., Des Moines, IA 50309. (515) 247-8888. FAX: (515)
243-4931. Pulitzer Broadcasting Co. Paul Fredericksen.

KDIN-TV, Channel 11, PBS
(see Iowa Public Television, Johnston). Des Moines, IA. Iowa
Public Broadcasting.

KDSM-TV, Channel 17, FOX
4023 Fleur Dr., Des Moines, IA 50321-2321. (515) 287-1717.
FAX: (515) 287-0064. Sinclair Broadcasting. Station Mgr.: Ted
Stephens.

WHO-TV, Channel 13, NBC
1801 Grand Ave., Des Moines, IA 50309. (515) 242-3500. FAX:
(515) 242-3797. New York Times, Inc. Joe Lentz.

WOI-TV, Channel 5, ABC
300 E. Locust St., Des Moines, IA 50309. (515) 282-5555. FAX:
(515) 282-0716. Citadel Communications Company Ltd. Philip
J. Lombardo.

KFXB, Channel 40, FOX
P. O. Box 1090, Towns Clock Plaza, 744 Main St., Dubuque, IA
52001. (319) 556-4040. FAX: (319) 557-7101. Dubuque TV L.P.
Thomas Bond.

KTIN, Channel 21, PBS
(see Iowa Public Television, Johnston). Fort Dodge, IA. Iowa
Public Broadcasting Board.

KIIN-TV, Channel 12, PBS
(see Iowa Public Television, Johnston). Iowa City, IA. Iowa Public Broadcasting Board.

Iowa Public Television, PBS
P. O. Box 6540, Johnston, IA 50131. (515) 242-3100. Iowa Public Broadcasting Board. CEO: C. David Bolender.

KIMT, Channel 3, CBS
P. O. Box 620, Mason City, IA 50402-0620. (515) 423-2540. FAX: (515) 423-7960. Spartan Radiocasting Co., Inc. John Shine.

KYIN, Channel 24, PBS
(see Iowa Public Television, Johnston). Mason City, IA. Iowa Public Broadcasting Board.

KYOU-TV, Channel 15, FOX
820 W. 2nd St., Ottumwa, IA 52501-2212. (515) 684-5415. FAX: (515) 682-5173. Public Interest Broadcast Group Inc. Dirk Engstrom.

KHIN, Channel 36, PBS
(see Iowa Public Television, Johnston). Red Oak, IA. Iowa Public Broadcasting Board.

KCAU-TV, Channel 9, ABC
625 Douglas St., Sioux City, IA 51101. (712) 277-2345. FAX: (712) 277-3733. Citadel Comm. Co./Coronet Comm. Co. Jim Rupert.

KMEG, Channel 14, FOX
P. O. Box 657, Sioux City, IA 51102-0657. (712) 277-3554. FAX: (712) 277-4732. KMEG Television, Inc. Lew Colby.

KSIN, Channel 27, PBS
(see Iowa Public Television, Johnston). Sioux City, IA. Iowa Public Broadcasting Board.

KTIV, Channel 4, NBC
3135 Floyd Blvd., Sioux City, IA 51105. (712) 239-4100. FAX: (712) 239-2621. Quincy Newspapers Inc. James De Schepper.

KRIN, Channel 32, PBS
(see Iowa Public Television, Johnston). Waterloo, IA. Iowa Public Broadcasting Board.

KWWL, Channel 7, NBC
500 E. 4th St., Waterloos, IA 50703. (319) 291-1200. FAX: (319) 291-1255. AFLAC Broadcasting Division. James B. Waterbury.

KANSAS

KOOD (Hays), Channel 9, PBS
P. O. Box 9, 604 Elm St., Bunker Hill, KS 67626. (913) 483-6990. FAX: (913) 483-4650. Smoky Hills Public Television Corp. Dave Wilson.

KSWK (Lakin), Channel 3, IND
P. O. Box 9, 604 Elm St., Bunker Hill, KS 67626. (913) 483-6990. FAX: (913) 483-4605, Smoky Hills Public Television Corp. Dave Wilson.

KLBY, Channel 4, IND
990 S. Range, Colby, KS 67701. (913) 462-8644. FAX: (913) 462-3522. Chronicle Broadcasting Co. Rich Epp.

KBSD-TV (Ensign), Channel 6, CBS
P. O. Box 157, Dodge City, KS 67801. (316) 227-3121. FAX: (316) 225-1675. Spartan Radiocasting Company Inc. Ron Collins.

KSNG, Channel 11, NBC
204 E. Fulton Terrace, Garden City, KS 67846-6151. (316) 276-2311. FAX: (316) 275-5076. Lee Enterprises. Sharolyn Funk.

WUPK-TV, Channel 13, ABC
2900 E. Schulman Ave., Garden City, KS 37846-2649. (316) 275-1560. FAX: (316) 275-1572. Chronicle Broadcasting Co. Jan McDaniel.

KBSL-TV, Channel 10, CBS
P. O. Box 569, Broadcast Plaza, Goodland, KS 67735. (913) 899-2321. FAX: (913) 899-3138. Spartan Radiocasting Company Inc. Wayne Roberts.

KSNC, Channel 2, NBC
P. O. Box 262, Great Bend, KS 67530. (316) 793-7868. FAX: (316) 793-3079. Lee Enterprises Inc. Mark Nichols.

KWNB, Channel 6, ABC
(see KHGI, Kearney). Hayes Center, KS Fant Broadcasting Co. of Nebraska.

KBSH-TV, Channel 7, CBS
2300 Hall St., Hays, KS 67601. (913) 625-5277. FAX: (913) 625-1161. Spartan Radiocasting Company Inc. Nick Evans.

KMCI, Channel 38, IND
2951 Four Wheel Dr., Lawrence, KS 66046. (913) 749-3388. FAX: (913) 749-3377. Miller Broadcasting Inc. Monte M. Miller.

KOAM-TV, Channel 7, CBS
P. O. Box 659, Pittsburg, KS 66762-0659. (417) 624-0233. FAX: (417) 623-6111. Saga Communications Inc. Danny Thomas.

KAAS-TV, Channel 18, FOX
(see KSAS, Wichita). Salina, KS. Clear Channel Television.

KAKE-TV, Channel 10, ABC
1500 N. West, Topeka, KS 67203. (316) 943-4221. FAX: (316) 943-5160. Chronicle Publishing Co. Jan McDaniel.

KSNT, Channel 27, NBC
P. O. Box 2700, Topeka, KS 66601-2700. (913) 582-4000. FAX: (913) 582-5283. Lee Enterprises Inc. Gary W. Sotir.

KTKA-TV, Channel 49, ABC
101 S.E. Monroe St., Topeka, KS 66603-3626. (913) 234-4949. FAX: (913) 234-5256. Marion Brechner, Berl Brechner.

KTWU, Channel 11, PBS
1700 College Ave., Topeka, KS 66621-1100. (913) 231-1111. FAX: (913) 231-1112. Washburn University of Topeka.Station. Mgr.: Dr. Dale Anderson.

WIBW-TV, Channel 13, CBS
5600 W. 6th St., Topeka, KS 66606. (913) 272-3456. FAX: (913) 272-0117. Stauffer Communications Inc. Jerry Holley.

KPTS (Hutchinson), Channel 8, PBS
320 W. 21st. N., Wichita, KS 67203. (316) 838-3090, Kansas Public Telecomm. Service Inc. Zoel Parenteau.

KSAS-TV, Channel 24, FOX
316 N. West St., Wichita, KS 67203-1205. (316) 942-2424. FAX: (316) 942-8927. Clear Channel Television. Steve Spendlove.

KSNW, Channel 3, NBC
P. O. Box 333, Wichita, KS 67201-0333. (316) 265-3333. FAX: (316) 292-1197. Lee Enterprises Inc. Al Buch.

KWCH-TV, Channel 12, CBS
P. O. Box 12, Wichita, KS 67201-0012. (316) 838-1212. FAX: (316) 838-3524. Spartan Radiocasting Co., Inc. Nick Evans.

KWCV* (Wichita), Channel 33, IND
R.R. 1, Box 203, Stockton, IA 52769. Wichita Communications.

KENTUCKY

WKAS, Channel 25, PBS
(see WKLE, Lexington). Ashland, KY. Kentucky Auth. for Educational TV.

WTSF, Channel 61, IND
P. O. Box 2320, 3100 Bath Ave., Ashland, KY 41105-2320. (606) 329-2700. FAX: (606) 324-9256. Tri-State Family Broadcasting Inc. Claude H. Messinger.

WLJC-TV, Channel 65, IND
Rte. 36, P. O. Box 50, Beattyville, KY 41311. (606) 464-3600. FAX: (606) 464-5021. Hour of Harvest, Inc. Forest Drake.

WBKO, Channel 13, ABC
P. O. Box 13000, Bowling Green, KY 42102-9800. (502) 781-1313. FAX: (502) 781-1814. Benedek Broadcasting Group. Richard Benedek.

WKGB-TV, Channel 53, PBS
(see WKLE, Lexington). Bowling Green, KY. Kentucky Auth. for Educational TV.

WKNT, Channel 40, FOX
810 Chestnut St., Bowling Green, KY 42101. (502) 781-2140. FAX: (502) 842-7140. Southeastern Communications Inc. William B. Ewing.

WKYU-TV, Channel 24, PBS
Academic Complex 153, Western Kentucky University, Bowling Green, KY 42101. (502) 745-2400. FAX: (502) 745-2084. Western Kentucky University. Dr. Thomas C. Meredith.

WGRB, Channel 34, FOX
P. O. Box 400, Campbellsville, KY 42719-0400. (502) 465-2223. FAX: (502) 384-6864. Billy Speer, Carol Lafever.

WCVN, Channel 54, PBS
(see WKLE, Lexington). Covington, KY. Kentucky Auth. for Educational TV.

WKZT-TV, Channel 23, PBS
(see WKLE, Lexington). Elizabethtown, KY. Kentucky Auth. for Educational TV.

WAGV, Channel 44, NFP
(see Living Faith Ministries, Vansant, VA). Harlan, KY. Living Faith Ministries Inc.

WKHA, Channel 36, PBS
(see WKLE, Lexington). Hazard, KY. Kentucky Auth. for Educational TV.

WYMT-TV, Channel 57, CBS
P. O. Box 1299, Hazard, KY 41702-1299. (606) 436-5757. Gray Communications Systems. Station Mgr.: Ernestine Cornett.

WDKY-TV, Channel 56, FOX
836 Euclid Ave., Chevy Chase Plaza, Lexington, KY 40502-1509. (606) 269-5656. FAX: (606) 269-3774. Superior Communications of KY Inc. Albert Holtz.

WKLE, Channel 46, IND
600 Cooper Dr., Lexington, KY 40502. (606) 258-7000. FAX: (606) 258-7399. Kentucky Auth. for Educational TV. Virginia G. Fox.

WKMJ, Channel 68, PBS
(see WKLE, Lexington). Lexington, KY Kentucky Auth. for Educational TV.

WKYT-TV, Channel 27, CBS
P. O. Box 55037, Lexington, KY 40555-5037. (606) 299- 0411. FAX: (606) 299-2494. Gray Communications Systems Inc. Pres. & GM: Wayne Martin.

WLEX-TV, Channel 18, NBC
P. O. Box 1457, Lexington, KY 40591-1457. (606) 255-4404. FAX: (606) 255-2418. WLEX-TV Inc. Pres. & GM: John A. Duvall.

WTVQ-TV, Channel 36, ABC
P. O. Box 5590, Lexington, KY 40555. (606) 233-3800. FAX: (606) 293-5002. Park Communications, Inc. Gary B. Knapp.

WAVE, Channel 3, NBC
725 S. Floyd St., Louisville, KY 40203-2337. (502) 585-2201. FAX: (502) 561-4115. Cosmos Broadcasting Corp. Guy Hempel.

WBNA, Channel 21, IND
3701 Fern Valley Rd., Louisville, KY 40219-1918. (502) 964-2121. FAX: (502) 966-9692. Word Broadcasting Network Inc. Robert W. Rodgers.

WDRB-TV, Channel 41, FOX
One Independence Square, Louisville, KY 40203. (502) 584-6441. FAX: (502) 589-5559. Blade Communications Inc. John Dorkin.

WHAS-TV, Channel 11, ABC
P. O. Box 1100, Louisville, KY 40201-1100. (502) 582-7840. Providence Journal Broadcasting Corp. Jack C. Clifford.

WKPC-TV, Channel 15, PBS
4309 Bishop Lane, Louisville, KY 40218. (502) 459-9572. FAX: (502) 452-1500. Fifteen Telecommunications Inc. John-Robert Curtin.

WLKY, Channel 32, CBS
P. O. Box 6205, Louisville, KY 40206-0205. (502) 893-3671. FAX: (502) 897-2384. Pulitzer Broadcasting Co. A. Rabun Matthews.

WKMA (Madisonville), Channel 35, PBS
(see WKLE, Lexington). Madisonville, KY. Kentucky Auth. for Educational TV.

WLCN, Channel 19, IND
P. O. Box 1087, Madisonville, KY 42431-1087. (502) 821-5433. FAX: (502) 821-5343. Life Anew Ministries, Inc. John Stalls.

WKMR, Channel 38, PBS
(see WKLE, Lexington). Morehead, KY. Kentucky Auth. for Educational TV.

WKMU, Channel 21, PBS
(see WKLE, Lexington). Murray, KY. Kentucky Auth. for Educational TV.

WXIX-TV (Newport), Channel 19, FOX
635 W. 7th St., Cincinnati, OH 45203. (513) 421-1919. FAX: (513) 421-3105. Malrite Communications Group, Inc. Pres.: John Chaffee.

WKOH, Channel 31, PBS
(see WKLE, Lexington). Owensboro, KY. Kentucky Auth. for Educational TV.

WKON, Channel 52, PBS
(see WKLE, Lexington). Owenton, KY. Kentucky Auth. for Educational TV.

WKPD, Channel 29, PBS
(see WKLE, Lexington). Paducah, KY. Kentucky Auth. for Educational TV.

WDKA* (Paducah), Channel 49, IND
c/o Sudbrink Broadcasting, 400 Executive Ctr. Dr., Suite 210, West Palm Beach, FL 33401. (407) 640-3585. FAX: (407) 640-7699. MacPherson Broadcasting of KY Inc.

WPSD-TV, Channel 6, NBC
100 Television Lane, Paducah, KY 42003-5098. (502) 442-8214. FAX: (502) 442-2096. Paxton Media Group Inc. Richard Paxton.

WKPI, Channel 22, PBS
(see WKLE, Lexington). Pikeville, KY. Kentucky Auth. for Educational TV.

WKSO-TV, Channel 29, PBS
(see WKLE, Lexington). Somerset, KY. Kentucky Auth. for Educational TV.

LOUISIANA

KALB-TV, Channel 5, NBC
605 Washington St., Alexandria, LA 71301-8028. (318) 445-2458. FAX: (318) 442-7427. Park Comm. Inc. Les Golmon.

KLAX-TV, Channel 31, ABC
P. O. Box 8818, Alexandria, LA 71303-1818. (318) 473-0031. FAX: (318) 442-4646. Pollack-Belz Communications Inc. William H. Pollack.

KLPA-TV, Channel 25, PBS
(see WLPB, Baton Rouge). Alexandria, LA. Louisiana Educational TV Authority.

WAFB, Channel 9, CBS
844 Government St., Baton Rouge, LA 70802-6030. (504) 383-9999. FAX: (504) 379-7891. AFLAC Broadcast Division. Ronald Winders.

WBRZ, Channel 2, ABC
1650 Highland Rd., Baton Rouge, LA 70802. (504) 387-2222. FAX: (504) 336-2246. Louisiana Television Broadcasting. Richard Manship, Sr.

WCCL (New Orleans), Channel 49, IND
c/o Flinn Broadcasting Corp., 6080 Mount Moriah, Memphis, TN 38115. (901) 375-9324. FAX: (901) 795-4454. George S. Flinn, Jr.

WGMB, Channel 44, FOX
5800 Florida Blvd., Baton Rouge, LA 70806. (504) 926-4444. FAX: (504) 826-9462. Com Corp. of Baton Rouge. Tom R. Galloway, Sr.

WLPB-TV, Channel 27, PBS
7860 Anselmo Ln., Baton Rouge, LA 70810. (504) 767-5660. FAX: (504) 767-4277. Louisiana Educational TV Authority. Beth Courtney.

WVLA, Channel 33, NBC
5220 Essen Ln., Baton Rouge, LA 70809-3542. (504) 766-3233. FAX: (504) 768-9191. Cryil Vetter.

KADN, Channel 15, FOX
1500 Eraste Landry Rd., Lafayette, LA 70506-1925. (318) 237-1500. FAX: (318) 237-2237. KADN Broadcasting Inc. Charles Chatelain.

KATC, Channel 3, ABC
P. O. Box 93133, Lafayette, LA 70509-3133. (318) 235-3333. FAX: (318) 235-9363. Cordillera Communications Inc. Richard Harbinson.

KLFY-TV, Channel 10, CBS
2410 Eraste Landry Rd., Lafayette, LA 70509. (318) 981-4823. FAX: (318) 984-8323. Young Broadcasting Inc. Vincent Young.

KLPB-TV, Channel 24, PBS
(see WLPB, Baton Rouge). Lafayette, LA. Louisiana Educational TV Authority.

KLTL-TV, Channel 18, PBS
(see WLPB, Baton Rouge). Lake Charles, LA. Louisiana Educational TV Authority.

KPLC-TV, Channel 7, NBC
320 Division St., Lake Charles, LA 70601-4228. (318) 439-9071. FAX: (318) 437-7600. Cosmos Broadcasting Corp. Jim Serra.

KVHP, Channel 29, FOX
129 W. Prien Lake Rd., Lake Charles, LA 70601-8570. (318) 474-1316. FAX: (318) 477-6795. KVHP-TV Partners. Gary D. Hardesty.

WUPL (Slidell), Channel 54, IND
Suite 454, 3850 N. Causeway Blvd., Metairie, LA 70002. (504) 828-5454. Cornerstone Inc. Larry Safir.

KLTM-TV, Channel 13, PBS
(see WLPB, Baton Rouge). Monroe, LA. Louisiana Educational TV Authority.

KNOE-TV, Channel 8, CBS
1400 Oliver Rd., Monroe, LA 71201. (318) 388-8888. FAX: (318) 388-0070. Noe Enterprises Inc. James A. Noe.

WDSU, Channel 6, NBC
846 Howard Ave., New Orleans, LA 70113. (504) 679-0600. FAX: (504) 679-0745. Pulitzer Broadcasting Co. V.P. & GM: Wayne Barnett.

WGNO, Channel 26, ABC
2 Canal St., Ste 2800, New Orleans, LA 70130-1408. (504) 581-2600. FAX: (504) 522-1885. Tribune Broadcasting Co. James Dowdle.

WHNO, Channel 20, IND
1100 S. Jefferson Davis Pkwy., New Orleans, LA 70125. (504) 822-1920. FAX: (504) 822-2060. LeSea Broadcasting. Steve Sumrall.

WLAE-TV, Channel 32, PBS
2929 S. Carrolton Ave., New Orleans, LA 70118. (504) 866-7411. FAX: (504) 861-5186. Educational Broadcasting Fdn. Inc. Archbishop Phillip M. Hannan.

WNOL-TV, Channel 38, WB
1661 Canal St., New Orleans, LA 70112-2861. (504) 525-3838. FAX: (504) 569-0908. Qwest Broadcasting. Quincy Jones.

WVUE, Channel 8, ABC
1025 S. Jefferson Davis, Pkwy., New Orleans, LA 70125-1218. (504) 486-6161. FAX: (504) 483-1212. SF Broadcasting L.L.C. Thomas Herwitz.

WWL-TV, Channel 4, CBS
1024 N. Rampart St., New Orleans, LA 70116-2406. (504) 529-4444. FAX: (504) 592-1949. A.H. Belo Corp. J. Michael Early.

WYES-TV, Channel 12, PBS
916 Navarre Ave., New Orleans, LA 70124. (504) 486-5511. FAX: (504) 483-8408. Greater New Orleans Edu. TV Fdn. Randall Feldman.

KMSS, Channel 33, FOX
P. O. Box 30033, Shreveport, LA 71130-0033. (318) 631-5677. FAX: (318) 631-4195. Associated Broadcasters Inc. Phyliss Phillips.

KSHV, Channel 45, IND
3519 Jewella Ave., Shreveport, LA 71109. (318) 631-4545. FAX: (318) 431-4195. White Knight Bcstng. of Shreveport. Sheldon Galloway.

KSLA-TV, Channel 12, CBS
P. O. Box 41812, Shreveport, LA 71134-1812. (318) 222-1212. FAX: (318) 677-6703. Ellis Communications. Ed Bradley.

KTAL-TV (Texarkana TX), Channel 6, NBC
3150 N. Market St., Shreveport, LA 71107-4005. (318) 425-2422. FAX: (318) 425-2488. KTAL-TV Inc. Walter E. Hussman.

KTBS, Channel 3, ABC
312 E. Kings Hwy., Shreveport, LA 71104-3504. (318) 861-5800. FAX: (318) 862-9434. KTBS Inc. CEO: George D. Wray Jr.

KLTS-TV (Shreveport), Channel 24, PBS
(see WLPB, Baton Rouge). Shreveport, LA. Louisiana Educational TV Authority.

KARD, Channel 14, ABC
Suite 400, 102 Thomas Rd., West Monroe, LA 71291. (318) 323-1972. FAX: (318) 322-0926. Petracom Broadcasting of Missouri. Hank Ash.

KMCT-TV, Channel 39, IND
701 Parkwood Dr., West Monroe, LA 71291-5435. (318) 322-1399. FAX: (318) 323-3783. LA Christian Broadcasting Inc. Charles Reed.

MAINE

WCBB, Channel 10, PBS
(see Maine Public TV, Lewiston). Augusta, ME. Maine Public Broadcasting Corp.

WABI-TV, Channel 5, CBS
35 Hildreth St., Bangor, ME 04401-5740. (207) 947-8321. FAX: (207) 941-9378. Diversified Communications Service. Carolyn Caltin.

WLBZ-TV, Channel 2, NBC
P. O. Box 315, Bangor, ME 04402-0315. (207) 942-4822. FAX: (207) 945-6816. Maine Broadcasting Co. Lew Colby.

WVII-TV, Channel 7, ABC
371 Target Industrial Cir., Bangor, ME 04401. (207) 945-6457. FAX: (207) 942-0511. Seaway Communications. Dr. James Buckner.

WMEA-TV, Channel 26, PBS
(see Maine Public TV, Lewiston). Biddeford, ME. Maine Public Broadcasting Corp.

WMED-TV, Channel 13, PBS
(see Maine Public TV, Lewiston). Calais, ME. Maine Public Broadcasting Corp.

Maine Public Television, PBS
1450 Lisbon St., Lewiston, ME 04240. (207) 783-9101. FAX: (207) 783-5193. Maine Public Broadcasting Corp. Robert H. Gardiner.

WMEB-TV, Channel 12, PBS
(see Maine Public TV, Lewiston). Orono, ME. Maine Public Broadcasting Corp.

WCSH-TV, Channel 6, NBC
1 Congress Sq., Portland, ME 04101-3801. (207) 828-6666. FAX: (207) 828-6620. Maine Radio and Television Co. Lew Colby.

WGME-TV, Channel 13, CBS
P. O. Box 1731, Portland, ME 04104-5013. (207) 797-9330. FAX: (207) 878-3505. Guy Gannett Communications Group. William B. Stough.

WMTW-TV (Poland Spring), Channel 8, ABC
P. O. Box 9501 D.T.S., 475 Congress St., Portland, ME 04112-9501. (207) 782-1800. FAX: (207) 783-7371. Harron Communications Corp. Paul Harron.

WPXT, Channel 51, FOX
2320 Congress St., Portland, ME 04102. (207) 774-0051. FAX: (207) 774-6849. Pegasus Broadcast TV. GM: Doug Finck.

WAGM-TV, Channel 8, ABC
P. O. Box 1149, Presque Isle, ME 04769-1149. (207) 764-4461. FAX: (207) 764-5329. Peter P. Kosloski.

WMEM-TV, Channel 10, PBS
(see Maine Public TV, Lewiston). Presque Isle, ME. Maine Public Broadcasting Corp.

WWLA* (Lewiston), Channel 35, IND
10 Common St., Waterville, ME 04901. (207) 873-4546. Kennebec Valley TV Inc. V. Wilson Hickam.

MARYLAND

WMPT, Channel 22, PBS
(see WFPT, Owings Mills). Annapolis, MD. MD Public Broadcasting Commission.

WBAL-TV, Channel 11, NBC
11 TV Hill, Baltimore, MD 21211. (410) 467-3000. FAX: (410) 338-6460. Hearst Broadcasting Group. Phil Stolz.

WBFF, Channel 45, FOX
2000 W. 41st St., Baltimore, MD 21211. (410) 467-4545. FAX: (410) 467-5090. Sinclair Broadcasting Group Inc. David D. Smith.

WHSW-TV, Channel 24, IND
4820 Seton Dr., Ste M-N, Baltimore, MD 21215-3210. (410) 358-2400. FAX: (410) 764-7232. Silver King Communications Inc. James Lawless.

WJZ-TV, Channel 13, CBS
TV Hill, Baltimore, MD 21211. (410) 466-0013. FAX: (410) 578-7502. Westinghouse Broadcasting Co., Inc. Marcellus Alexander.

WMAR-TV, Channel 2, ABC
6400 York Rd., Baltimore, MD 21212-2111. (410) 377-2222. Scripps-Howard Broadcasting Co. H. Joseph Lewin.

WMPB, Channel 67, PBS
(see WFPT, Owings Mills). Baltimore, MD. MD Public Broadcasting Commission.

WNUV-TV, Channel 54, IND
3001 Druid Park Dr., Baltimore, MD 21215-7861. (410) 467-8854. FAX: (410) 235-8450. ABRY Communications Inc. Robert Epstein.

WHAG-TV, Channel 25, NBC
13 E. Washington St., Hagerstown, MD 21740. (301) 797-4400. FAX: (301) 733-1735. Great Trails Broadcasting Corp. Hugh J. Breslin.

WWPB, Channel 31, PBS
(see WFPT, Owings Mills). Hagerstown, MD. MD Public Broadcasting Commission.

WGPT, Channel 36, PBS
(see WFPT, Owings Mills). Oakland, MD. MD Public Broadcasting Commission.

WFPT, Channel 62, PBS
11767 Owings Mills Blvd., Owings Mills, MD 21117. (410) 356-5600. FAX: (410) 581-6579. MD Public Broadcasting Commission. Raymond K.K. Ho.

WBOC-TV, Channel 16, CBS
P. O. Box 2057, Salisbury, MD 21802-2057. (410) 749-1111. FAX: (410) 749-2361. Draper Communications Inc. Thomas Draper.

WCPB, Channel 28, PBS
(see WFPT, Owings Mills). Salisbury, MD. MD Public Broadcasting Commission.

WMDT, Channel 47, IND
202 Downtown Plaza, Salisbury, MD 21801. (410) 742-4747. FAX: (410) 742-5767. Delmarva Broadcasting Service G.P. Frank Pilgrim.

MASSACHUSETTS

WCDC Channel 19, ABC
(See WTEN, Albany, NY). Adams, MA. Young Broadcasting of Albany, Inc.

WABU, Channel 68, IND
1660 Soldiers Field Rd., Boston, MA 02135. (617) 787-6868. FAX: (617) 562-4280. BUCI Television. Robert D. Gordon.

WBZ-TV, Channel 4, CBS
1170 Soldiers Field Rd., Boston, MA 02134-1092. (617) 787-7000. FAX: (617) 787-5969. CBS Station Group. Bill Korn.

WCVB-TV, Channel 5, ABC
5 TV Pl., Boston, MA 02194. (617) 449-0400. FAX: (617) 433-4752. Hearst Broadcasting Group. Paul La Camera.

WGBH-TV, Channel 2, PBS
125 Western Ave., Boston, MA 02134. (617) 492-2777. FAX: (617) 787-0714. WGBH Educational Foundation. Henry P. Becton, Jr.

WGBX-TV, Channel 44, PBS
(see WGBH, Boston). Boston, MA. WGBH Educational Foundation.

WHDH-TV, Channel 7, NBC
7 Bulfinch Pl., Boston, MA 02114-2904. (617) 725-0777. Sunbeam Television Corp. Edmund Ansin.

WLVI-TV, Channel 56, WB
75 Morrissey Blvd., Boston, MA 02125. (617) 265-5656. FAX: (617) 265-2538. Tribune Broadcasting Co. V.P. & GM:John Vitanovec.

WLWC (New Bedford), Channel 28, IND
76 Ashford St., Boston, MA 02134. (617) 782-6072. BAF Enterprises.

WMFP (Lawrence), Channel 62, NBC
Suite 1402, 89 Broad St., Boston, MA 02110. (617) 292-0062. FAX: (617) 292-1877. MFP Inc. Avi Nelson.

WSBK-TV, Channel 38, IND
83 Leo Birmingham Pkwy., Boston, MA 02135. (617) 783-3838. FAX: (617) 783-1875. Paramount Stations Group. Stuart P. Tauber.

WFXT, Channel 25, FOX
P. O. Box 9125, 25 Fox Dr., Dedham, MA 02027-9125. (617) 326-8825. FAX: (617) 326-9826. Fox Television Stations Inc. Kathy Saunders.

WHSH-TV (Marlborough), Channel 66, IND
71 Parmenter Rd., Hudson, MA 01749. (508) 562-0660. FAX: (508) 562-1166. Silver King Communications Inc. Merril Buchhalter.

WUNI, Channel 27, UNI
33 Fourth Ave., Needham, MA 02194. (617) 433-2727. FAX: (617) 433-2750. JASAS Corp. Barbara Foster.

WHRC* (Norwell), Channel 46, IND
c/o TV Stn. WTVE, 1729 N. 11th St., Reading, PA 19604. (610) 921-9181. Mass Channel 46 Corp. Michael Parker.

WGBY-TV, Channel 57, PBS
44 Hampden St., Springfield, MA 01103. (413) 781-2801. FAX: (413) 731-5093. WGBH Educational Foundation. Deborah Onslow.

WGGB-TV, Channel 40, ABC
P. O. Box 40, Springfield, MA 01102-0040. (413) 733-4040. FAX: (413) 781-1363. Guy Gannett Communications Inc. Kevin P. LeRoux.

WWLP, Channel 22, NBC
P. O. Box 2210, Springfield, MA 01102-2210. (413) 786-2200. Brissette Broadcasting Corp. William M. Pepin.

WZBU, Channel 58, IND
(see WABU, Boston). Vineyard Haven, MA. BUCI Television.

WYDN* (Worcester), Channel 48, IND
P. O. Box 1975, San Benito, TX 78586. Worcester Educational Corp. Inc.

MICHIGAN

WTLJ (Muskegon MI), Channel 54, IND
10294 48th Ave., Allendale, MI 49401. (616) 895-4154. FAX: (616) 892-4401. Tri-State Christian TV Inc. Garth W. Coonce.

WBKB-TV, Channel 11, CBS
1390 N. Bagley St., Alpena, MI 49707-8101. (517) 356-3434. FAX: (517) 356-4188. Thunder Bay Broadcasting Corp. Stephen A. Marks.

WCML, Channel 6, PBS
(see WCMU, Mt. Pleasant). Alpena, MI. Central Michigan University.

WBSX, Channel 31, IND
3975 Varsity Dr., Ann Arbor, MI 48108. (313) 973-7900. FAX: (313) 973-7906. Blackstar Communications of MI Inc. John Oxendine.

WOTV, Channel 41, ABC
5200 W. Dickman Rd., Battle Creek, MI 49015-1033. (616) 968-9341. FAX: (616) 966-6837. Channel 41 Inc. Jerry P. Colvin.

WCMV, Channel 27, PBS
(see WCMU, Mt. Pleasant). Cadillac, MI. Central Michigan University.

WGKI, Channel 33, FOX
7669 S. 45 Rd., Cadillac, MI 49601. (616) 775-9813. FAX: (616) 775-1898. GRK Production Inc. Gary Knapp.

WWTV, Channel 9, CBS
P. O. Box 627, Cadillac, MI 49601-0627. (616) 775-3478. FAX: (616) 775-3671. Heritage Broadcasting Co. of MI. Mario F. Iacobelli.

WTOM-TV, Channel 4, NBC
(see WBPN, Traverse City). Cheboygan, MI. Federal Broadcasting Co.

WADL (Mount Clemens), Channel 38, IND
22590 15 Mile Rd., Clinton Twp., MI 48035-2841. (810) 790-3838. FAX: (810) 790-3841. Adell Broadcasting Corp. Franklin Z. Adell.

WDIV, Channel 4, NBC
550 W. Lafayette Blvd., Detroit, MI 48226-3123. (313) 222-0444. FAX: (313) 222-0471. Post-Newsweek Stations Inc. Alan W. Frank.

WTVS, Channel 56, IND
7441 Second Blvd., Detroit, MI 48202. (313) 873-7200. FAX: (313) 876-8118. Detroit Educational TV Foundation. Steve Antoniotti.

WWJ-TV, Channel 62, CBS
300 River Place, Detroit, MI 48207. (313) 259-6288. FAX: (313) 259-8215. CBS Station Group. Jay Newman.

WKAR-TV, Channel 23, PBS
212 Communication Arts Bldg., East Lansing, MI 48824-1212. (517) 355-2300. FAX: (517) 353-7124. Michigan State University. Steven K. Meuche.

WJMN-TV, Channel 3, CBS
(see WFRV, Green Bay, WI). Escanaba, MI (906) 786-7767. FAX: (906) 474-6619. CBS Station Group.

WFUM, Channel 28, PBS
U. of Michigan-Flint, 1321 E. Court St., Flint, MI 48502-2186. (810) 762-3028. FAX: (810) 233-6017. Board of Regents, U. of MI. Jim Gaver.

WJRT-TV, Channel 12, ABC
2302 Lapeer Rd., Flint, MI 48503. (810) 233-3130. FAX: (810) 257-2834. Cap Cities/ABC Video Enterprises. Larry Pollock.

WSMH, Channel 66, FOX
G-3463 W. Pierson Rd., Flint, MI 48504. (810) 785-8866. FAX: (810) 785-8963. R Group Communication. G.J. Robinson.

WGVU-TV, Channel 35, PBS
301 W. Fulton St., Grand Rapids, MI 49504-6492. (616) 771-6666. FAX: (616) 771-6625. Board of Control, Grand Valley U. Michael T. Walenta.

WOOD-TV, Channel 8, NBC
P. O. Box B, Grand Rapids, MI 49501-4902. (616) 456-8888. FAX: (616) 771-9676. LCH Communications, Inc. Scott Blumenthal.

WXMI Channel 17, FOX
3117 Plaza Dr N.E., Grand Rapids, MI 49505-2901. (616) 364-8722. FAX: (616) 364-8506. Dudley Communications Corp. Patrick J. Mullen.

WZZM-TV, Channel 13, ABC
P. O. Box Z, Grand Rapids, MI 49501-4926. (616) 785-7373.
FAX: (616) 785-1301. Argyle Television Inc. Bob Marbut.

WJUE* (Battle Creek), Channel 43, IND
P. O. Box 907, Jenison, MI 49429-0907. (616) 457-7010. FAX:
(616) 457-6949. Western MI Christian Broadcasting. William B.
Popjes.

WGVK, Channel 52, PBS
(see WGVU, Grand Rapids). Kalamazoo, MI. Grand Valley
State University.

WLLA, Channel 64, IND
P. O. Box 3157, Kalamazoo, MI 49003-3157. (616) 345-6421.
Christian Faith Broadcasting Inc. Shelby Gillam.

WWMT Channel 3, CBS
590 W. Maple St., Kalamazoo, MI 49008-1926. (616) 388-3333.
FAX: (616) 388-8228. Granite Broadcasting Corp. Gil Buettner.

WDHS (Iron Mountain), Channel 8, IND
P. O. Box 2130, Kingford, MI 49802. (906) 779-5213. FAX:
(906) 779-5257. Danny Hood Evangelistic Assoc. Danny Hood.

WILX-TV, Channel 10, NBC
500 American Rd., Lansing, MI 48911. (517) 393-0110. FAX:
(517) 393-8555. Benedek Broadcasting Corp. Station Mgr.:
Grant Santimore.

WLAJ, Channel 53, ABC
P. O. Box 27307, 5815 S. Pennsylvania Ave., Lansing, MI
48909-7307. (517) 394-5300. FAX: (517) 887-0077. Lansing 53
Inc. Joel Ferguson.

WLNS-TV, Channel 6, CBS
2820 E. Saginaw St., Lansing, MI 48912-4240. (517) 372-8282.
FAX: (517) 374-7610. Young Broadcasting Inc. Ronald J.
Kwasnick.

WSYM-TV, Channel 47, FOX
600 W. St. Joseph St., Lansing, MI 48933. (517) 484-7747. FAX:
(517) 484-3144. Journal Broadcast Group Inc. Douglas Kiel.

WCMW, Channel 21, PBS
(see WCMU, Mt. Pleasant). Manistee, MI. Central Michigan
University.

WNMU-TV, Channel 13, PBS
Northern Michigan University, Marquette, MI 49855. (906)
227-1300. Fax: (906) 227-2905. Board of Control, N. Michigan U.
GM: Scott K. Seaman.

WCMU-TV, Channel 14, PBS
Central Michigan University, 3965 E. Broomfield Rd., Mt.
Pleasant, MI 48859. (517) 774-3105. FAX: (517) 774-4427.
Central Michigan University. William J. Grigaliunas.

WLUC-TV (Marquette), Channel 6, IND
177 U.S. Hwy. 41 E., Negaunee, MI 49866. (906) 475-4161.
FAX: (906) 475-4824. Federal Broadcasting Co. Brad Van
Sluyters.

WAQP, Channel 49, IND
2865 Trautner Dr., Saginaw, MI 48604. (517) 249-5964. Tri-
State Christian TV. Garth W. Coonce.

WNEM-TV (Flint/Bay City), Channel 5, CBS
107 N. Frankling St., Saginaw, MI 48606. (517) 755-8191.
FAX: (517) 758-2110. Meredith Broadcasting Group. Paul
Virciglio.

WWUP-TV (Sault Ste. Marie), Channel 10, CBS
(see WWTV, Cadillac). Sault St. Marie, MI. Heritage
Broadcasting Co. of MI.

WGTQ, Channel 8, ABC
300 Court St., Sault Ste. Marie, MI 49783. (616) 946-2900.
FAX: (616) 946-1600. Scanlan Communications Inc. Thomas
Scanlan.

WJBK-TV, Channel 2, FOX
P. O. Box 2000, Southfield, MI 48037-2000. (810) 557-2000.
FAX: (810) 552-0280. New World Television Inc. John
Spinola.

WKBD (Detroit), Channel 50, UPN
P. O. Box 50, 26905 W. 11 Mile Rd., Southfield, MI 48037-0050.
(810) 350-5050. FAX: (810) 355-2692. Paramount Stations
Group. GM: Mike Dunlop.

WXON (Detroit), Channel 20, WB
Suite 1220, 27777 Franklin Rd., Southfield, MI 48034. (810)
355-2020. FAX: (810) 355-0368. WXON-TV Inc. V.P. & GM:
Doug Johnson.

WXYZ-TV, Channel 7, ABC
P. O. Box 789, Southfield, MI 48037-0789. (810) 827-7777.
FAX: (810) 827-4454. Scripps Howard Broadcasting Co. Grace
Gilchrist.

WGTU, Channel 29, ABC
201 E. Front St., Traverse City, MI 49684-2525. (616)
946-2900. FAX: (616) 946-1600. Scanlan Communications Inc.
Tom Scanlan.

WPBN-TV, Channel 7, NBC
P. O. Box 546, Traverse City, MI 49685-0546. (616) 947-7770.
FAX: (616) 947-0354. Federal Broadcasting Co. Dale Rands.

WUCM-TV, Channel 19, PBS
Delta College Public Broadcasting, Delta and Mackinac Rds.,
University Center, MI 48710. (517) 686-9350. FAX: (517)
686-0155. Delta College. Dr. Peter Boyse.

WUCX-TV, Channel 35, PBS
(see WUCM, University Center). University Center, MI. Delta
College.

WGKU, Channel 45, FOX
(see WGKI, Cadillac). Vanderbilt, MI. GRK Production Joint
Venture.

MINNESOTA

KCCO-TV, Channel 7, CBS
720 Hawthorne St., Alexandria, MN 56308-1841. (612)
763-1736. CBS Station Group. Ken Rees.

KRWF (Redwood Falls), Channel 43, ABC
P. O. Box 189, 415 Filmore, Alexandria, MN 56308. (612)
763-5729. FAX: (612) 763-4627. Hubbard Broadcasting Inc.
Robert Hubbard.

KWCM-TV/KSMN-TV, Channel 10, PBS
120 W. Schlieman, Appleton, MN 56208. (320) 289-2622. FAX:
(320) 289-2634. W. Central MN Educational TV Co. Thomas
Connolly.

KAAL Channel 6, ABC
P. O. Box 577, Austin, MN 55912-0577. (507) 437-6666. FAX:
(507) 433-9560. Eastern Broadcasting Corp. David Tillery.

KSMQ-TV, Channel 15, IND
2000 8th Ave N.W., Austin, MN 55912. (507) 433-0678. FAX:
(507) 433-0670. Independent School District 492. Barry G.
Baker.

KAWE, Channel 9, PBS
P. O. Box 9, BSU, 1400 Birchmont Dr., Bemidji, MN 56601.
(218) 751-3393. Fax: (218) 751-3142. Northen MN Public TV
Inc. Mary Kay Klein.

KXLI (St. Cloud), Channel 41, IND
P. O. Box 407, 22601 176th St., Big Lake, MN 55309. (612)
263-8666. FAX: (612) 263-6600. K.X. Acquisition L.P. Dale W.
Lang.

KXLT-TV (Rochester), Channel 47, IND
P. O. Box 407, 22601 176th St., Big Lake, MN 55309. (612)
263-8666. FAX: (612) 263-6600. K.X. Acquisition L.P. Dale W.
Lang.

KAWB, Channel 22, PBS
(see KAWE, Bemidji). Brainerd, MN. Northern MN Public TV Inc.

KBJR-TV, Channel 6, NBC
KBJR Building, Duluth, MN 55802. (218) 727-8484. FAX: (218)
720-9699. Granite Broadcasting Corp. Robert J. Wilmers.

KDLH, Channel 3, CBS
425 W. Superior St., Duluth, MN 55802-1511. (218) 733-0303.
FAX: (218) 727-7515. Benedek Broadcasting Corp. GM: Gil
Buettner.

KNLD, Channel 21, IND
Suite 711, 301 W. 1st St., Duluth, MN 55802. (218) 727-0483.
FAX: (218) 727-0562. Fant Broadcasting Companies. Anthony
Fant.

WDIO-TV, Channel 10, ABC
10 Observation Rd., Duluth, MN 55811-3506. (218) 727-6864.
FAX: (218) 727-4415. Hubbard Broadcasting Inc. George
Couture.

WDSE-TV, Channel 8, PBS
1202 E. University Cir., Duluth, MN 55811-2420. (218)
724-8567. FAX: (218) 724-4269. Duluth Superior Area Educ.
TV Corp. Mark Melhus.

KMSP-TV (Minneapolis) Channel 9, UPN
11358 Viking Dr., Eden Prairie, MN 55344-7258. (612)
944-9999. FAX: (612) 942-0286. United TV Inc. Evan C.
Thompson.

WIRT (Hibbing), Channel 13, ABC
(see WDIO, Duluth). Hibbing, MN. Hubbard Broadcasting Inc.

WXOW-TV (La Crosse, WI), Channel 19, ABC
3705 County Hwy., La Crescent, MN 55947, 507-895-9969.
FAX: 507-895-8124. Tak Communications Inc. Chuck Roth.

KEYC-TV, Channel 12, CBS
P. O. Box 128, Mankato, MN 56002-0128. (507) 625-7905. FAX: (507) 626-5745. United Communications Corp. Station Mgr.: Dennis M. Wahlstrom.

KARE, Channel 11, NBC
8811 Olson Memorial Hwy., Minneapolis, MN 55427-4762. (612) 546-1111. FAX: (612) 546-8590. Gannett Broadcasting. Henry Hank Price.

KVBM-TV, Channel 45, IND
Suite 210, 89 S. 10th St., Minneapolis, MN 55403. (612) 673-9610. FAX: (612) 673-9620. KVBM Television Inc. Daniel Peters.

WCCO-TV, Channel 4, CBS
90 S. 11th St., Minneapolis, MN 55403. (612) 339-4444. FAX: (612) 330-2603. CBS Station Group. John Culliton.

WFTC, Channel 29, FOX
1701 Broadway St. N.W., Minneapolis, MN 55414. (612) 379-2929. FAX: (612) 379-2900. Clear Channel Television, Inc. Rip Riordan.

KTTC, Channel 10, NBC
601 1st Ave SW, Rochester, MN 55902-3334. (507) 288-4444. FAX: (507) 288-6324. Quincy Newspapers Inc. Jerry Watson.

KLGT-TV, Channel 23, WB
1640 Como Ave., St. Paul, MN 55108. (612) 646-2300. FAX: (612) 646-1220. Lakeland Group Television Inc. Linda Rios Brook.

KSTP-TV, Channel 5, ABC
3415 University Ave., St. Paul, MN 55114. (612) 646-5555. FAX: (612) 642-4172. Hubbard Broadcasting Inc. Stanley S. Hubbard.

KTCA-TV, Channel 2, PBS
172 E. 4th St., St. Paul, MN 55101. (612) 229-1717. FAX: (612) 229-1282. Twin Cities Public TV Inc. Jack Willis.

KTCI-TV, Channel 17, PBS
(see KTCA St. Paul). St. Paul, MN. (612) 229-1717. FAX: (612) 229-1282. Twin Cities Public TV Inc.

KBRR, Channel 10, FOX
(see KVRR, Fargo, ND). Thief River Falls, MN. Red River Broadcast Corp.

KCCW, Channel 12, CBS
(see KCCO Alexandria). Walker, MN 56308. CBS Station Group.

MISSISSIPPI

WLOX Television, Inc. Channel 13, ABC
P. O. Box 4596, Biloxi, MS 39535-4596. (601) 896-1313. FAX: (601) 896-0749. Cosmos Broadcasting Corp. Leon Long.

WMAH-TV, Channel 19, PBS
(see WMAB, Jackson). Biloxi, MS. MS Authority for Educational TV.

WMAE-TV, Channel 12, PBS
(see WMAB, Jackson). Booneville, MS. MS Authority for Educational TV.

WMAU-TV, Channel 17, PBS
(see WMAB, Jackson). Bude, MS. MS Authority for Educational TV.

WBUY, Channel 40, IND
4240 Hwy. 309 N., Byhalia, MS 38611. (901) 521-9289. Sonlight Broadcasting Systems Inc. Stuart J. Roth.

WCBI-TV, Channel 4, CBS
P. O. Box 271, Columbus, MS 39703-0271. (601) 327-4444. FAX: (601) 329-1004. Imes Communication. Frank Imes.

WXVT, Channel 15, CBS
3015 E. Reed Rd., Greenville, MS 38703-9452. (601) 334-1500. FAX: (601) 378-8122. Greenville Television Inc. John Hash.

WABG-TV, Channel 6, ABC
P. O. Box 720, 2001 Garrard Ave., Greenwood, MS 38930. (601) 332-0949. FAX: (601) 334-6420. MS Broadcasting Partners. Cy N. Bahakel.

WMAO-TV, Channel 23, PBS
(see WMAB, Jackson). Greenwood, MS. MS Authority for Educational TV.

WXXV-TV, Channel 25, FOX
14351 Hwy. 49 N., Gulfport, MS 39503. (601) 832-2525. FAX: (601) 832-4442. Prime Cities Broadcasting Co. of MS. Station Mgr.: Bill Ritchie.

WDAM-TV, Channel 7, NBC
P. O. Box 16269, Hattiesburg, MS 39404-6269. (601) 544-4730. FAX: (601) 584-9302. Federal Broadcasting Co. Jim Cameron.

WAPT, Channel 16, ABC
P. O. Box 10297, Jackson, MS 39289-0297. (601) 922-1607. FAX: (601) 922-1663. Argyle Television Inc. Pres. & GM: Stuart Kellogg.

WDBD, Channel 40, FOX
P. O. Box 10888, Jackson, MS 39289-0888. (601) 922-1234. FAX: (601) 922-6752. Pegasus Broadcast Television Inc. D. Guyon Turner.

WJTV, Channel 12, CBS
P. O. Box 8887, Jackson, MS 39284-8887. (601) 372-6311. FAX: (601) 372-8798. Ellis Communications. Bert Ellis.

WLBT, Channel 3, NBC
715 S. Jefferson St., Jackson, MS 39201-5622. (601) 948-3333. FAX: (601) 960-4412. Civic Communication Corp. Frank Melton.

WMAB-TV, Channel 2, PBS
3825 Ridgewood Rd., Jackson, MS 39211. (601) 982-6565. FAX: (601) 982-6746. Mississippi Authority for Ed. TV. Larry Miller.

WMPN-TV, Channel 29, PBS
(see WMAB, Jackson). Jackson, MS. MS Authority for Educational TV.

WGBC, Channel 30, NBC
(see WTOK, Meridian). Meridian, MS. (601) 485-3030. FAX: (601) 693-9889. Global Communications. Alex H. Shields.

WMAW-TV, Channel 14, PBS
(see WMAB, Jackson). Meridian, MS. Mississippi Authority for Ed. TV.

WMDN, Channel 24, IND
(see WTOK, Meridian). Meridian, MS. (601) 693-2424. FAX: (601) 693-7126. WMDN Inc. Marc Grossman.

WTOK-TV, Channel 11, ABC
P. O. Box 2424, Meridian, MS 39302. (601) 693-1441. FAX: (601) 483-3266. Benedek Broadcasting Co. Tracey Jones.

WNTZ, Channel 48, IND
P. O. Box 1836, Natchez, MS 39121. (601) 442-4800. FAX: (601) 446-7019. Charles H. Chatelain, Daniel Penny.

WMAV-TV, Channel 18, PBS
(see WMAB, Jackson). Oxford, MS. Mississippi Authority for Ed. TV.

WTVA, Channel 9, NBC
P. O. Box 350, Tupelo, MS 38801. (601) 842-7620. FAX: (601) 844-7061. WTVA Inc. Frank K. Spain.

WLOV-TV, Channel 27, FOX
(see WTVA, Tupelo). West Point, MS. Love Communications Co.

MISSOURI

KBSI, Channel 23, FOX
806 Enterprise St., Cape Girardeau, MO 63703-7516. (314) 334-1223. FAX: (314) 334-1208. Engles Communications Inc. John Trinder.

KFVS-TV, Channel 12, CBS
310 Broadway, Cape Girardeau, MO 63701. (314) 335-1212. FAX: (314) 335-6303. AFLAC Broadcast Division. Howard Meagle.

KMIZ, Channel 17, ABC
501 Business Loop 70 E., Columbia, MO 65201. (314) 449-0917. FAX: (314) 875-7078. Stauffer Communications Inc. Pat Dalbery.

KOMU-TV, Channel 8, NBC
Hwy 63 S., Columbia, MO 65201. (573) 882-8888. FAX: (573) 884-8888. The Curators of the Univ of MO. Thomas R. Gray.

KRCG, Channel 13, CBS
P. O. Box 659, Jefferson City, MO 65102. (573) 896-5144. FAX: (573) 896-5193. Mel Wheeler. M.J. Bob Groothand.

KODE-TV, Channel 12, ABC
1928 W. 13th St., Joplin, MO 64801-3839. (417) 623-7260. FAX: (417) 623-3736. Eastern Broadcasting Corp. Roger Neuhoff.

KOZJ, Channel 26, PBS
P. O. Box 1226, Joplin, MO 64802. (417) 782-1226. FAX: (414) 782-7222. Ozark Public Telecommunications. Pres. & GM: Sarah White.

KSNF, Channel 16, NBC
P. O. Box 1393, Joplin, MO 64802-1393. (417) 781-2345, US Broadcast Group, LLC, Wayne Bettoney, GM

KCPT, Channel 19, PBS
125 E. 31st Street, Kansas City, MO 64108. (816) 756-3580. FAX: (816) 931-2500. Public TV 19 Inc. William T. Reed.

KCTV, Channel 5, CBS
P. O. Box 5555, Kansas City, MO 64109. (913) 677-5555. FAX: (913) 677-7284. Meredith Corp. Broadcast Group. Jack Rehm.

KMBC, Channel 9, ABC
1049 Central St., Kansas City, MO 64105-1619. (816) 221-9999. FAX: (816) 760-9245. Hearst Broadcasting Corp. Paul Dinovitz.

KSHB-TV, Channel 41, FOX
4720 Oak St., Kansas City, MO 64112-2236. (816) 753-4141. FAX: (816) 932-4122. Scripps-Howard Broadcasting Co. Charlotte Moore English.

KSMO-TV, Channel 62, IND
10 E. Cambridge Cir.Dr., Suite 300, Kansas City, MO 66103. (913) 621-6262. FAX: (913) 621-4703. ABRY Communications. Jim MacDonald.

KYFC, Channel 50, IND
P. O. Box 10150, Kansas City, MO 64111. (913) 262-1700. FAX: (913) 262-1782. Kansas City Youth for Christ Inc. Ronnie Metsker.

WDAF-TV, Channel 4, FOX
3030 Summit, Kansas City, MO 64108. (816) 753-4567. FAX: (816) 932-3984. New World Communications of KC. Ed Piette.

KTVO, Channel 3, ABC
P. O. Box 949, Kirksville, MO 63501-0949. (816) 627-3333. FAX: (816) 627-1885. Federal Broadcasting Co. Dale Rands.

KNLJ, Channel 25, IND
P. O. Box 2525, New Bloomfield, MO 65603. (573) 896-5105. FAX: (573) 896-4376. New Life Evangelistic Center, Inc. Larry Rice.

KDEB, Channel 27, FOX
3000 Cherry St., Springfield, MO 65802. (417) 862-2727. FAX: (414) 831-4209. Petracom Broadcasting of MO. Inc. Kemp Nichol.

KOLR-TV, Channel 10, CBS
P. O. Box 1716, Springfield, MO 65801. (417) 862-1010. FAX: (417) 862-6439. Independent Broadcasting Co. J.H. Cooper.

KOZK, Channel 21, PBS
P. O. Box 21, 821 N. Washington Ave., Springfield, MO 65801. (417) 865-2100. FAX: (417) 863-1599. Ozark Public Telecommunications Inc. Sarah White.

KSPR Channel 33, ABC
1359 St. Louis St., Springfield, MO 65802. (417) 831-1333. FAX: (417) 831-4125. Cottonwood Communications L.L.C. Al Seethaler.

KYTV, Channel 3, NBC
999 W. Sunshine, Springfield, MO 65807. (417) 868-3800. FAX: (417) 868-3894. Schurz Communications Inc. Pres. & GM: Gary DeHaven.

KQTV, Channel 2, ABC
P. O. Box 6247, 4oth & Faraon Sts., St. Joseph, MO 64506. (816) 364-2222. FAX: (816) 364-3787. Fabri Developmement Corp. Jerry Condra.

KTAJ, Channel 16, IND
4410-B S. 40th St., St. Joseph, MO 64503. (816) 364-1616. FAX: (816) 364-6729. All-American TV. Sonny Argbinzoni.

KDNL-TV, Channel 30, ABC
1215 Cole St., St. Louis, MO 63106. (314) 436-3030. FAX: (314) 259-5763. River City Broadcasting L.P. Barry Baker.

KETC, Channel 9, PBS
6996 Millbrook Blve., St. Louis, MO 63130. (314) 512-9000. FAX: (314) 512-9005. St. Louis Regional Ed. & Pub. TV. Michael Hardgrove.

KMOV, Channel 4, CBS
One Memorial Dr., St. Louis, MO 63102. (314) 621-4444. FAX: (314) 444-3367. Paramount Stations Group. V.P. & GM: Allan Cohen.

KNLC, Channel 24, NFP
P. O. Box 924, St. Louis, MO 63188. (314) 436-2424. FAX: (314) 436-2434. New Life Evangelistic Center. Larry Rice.

KPLR-TV, Channel 11, IND
4935 Lindell Blvd., St. Louis, MO 63108-1587. (314) 367-7211. FAX: (314) 454-6488. Edward Koplar.

KSDK, Channel 5, NBC
TV Plaza, 1000 Market St., St. Louis, MO 63101. (314) 421-5055. FAX: (314) 444-5289. Multimedia Broadcasting Co. Don Sbarra.

KTVI, Channel 2, FOX
5915 Berthold Ave., St. Louis, MO 63110. (314) 647-2222. FAX: (314) 644-7419. New World Communications Group Inc. Spencer Koch.

WHSL, Channel 46, IND
Suite 300, 1408 N. King's Hwy. Blvd., St. Louis, MO 63113. (314) 367-3600. FAX: (314) 367-0174. Home Shopping Network. Steven C. Roberts.

KTVI, Channel 2, PBS
Central Mo. State Univ., Wood 11, Warrenburg, MO 64093. (816) 543-4155. FAX: (816) 543-8863. Central Missouri State University. Dr. Donald W. Peterson.

MONTANA

KSVI, Channel 6, ABC
P. O. Box 23309, 445 S. 24th St. W. Billings, MT 59104-3309. (406) 652-4743. FAX: (406) 652-6963. Big Horn Communications Inc. Thomas Hendrickson.

KTVQ, Channel 2, CBA
P. O. Box 2557, Billings, MT 59103. (406) 252-5611. FAX: (406) 252-9938. Cordillera Communications Inc. Kelly Sugai.

KULR-TV, Channel 8, NBC
P. O. Box 80810, Billings, MT 59108-0810. (406) 656-8000. FAX: (406) 652-8207. Dix Communications. Pres. & CEO: Stan Whitman.

KUSM, Channel 9, PBS
Visual Communication Bldg, Mt. St. Univ., Rm 172, Bozeman, MT 59717. (406) 994-3437. FAX: (406) 994-6221. Montana State University. Jack Hyyppa.

KCTZ (Bozeman), Channel 7, CBS
P. O. Box 3500, c/o KXLF-TV, Butte, MT 59701. (406) 782-0444. FAX: (406) 782-8906. Cordillera Communications Inc. Ron Cass.

KTVM, Channel 6, NBC
P. O. Box 3118, Suite One, 750 Dewey Blvd., Butte, MT 59701. (406) 494-7603. FAX: (406) 721-2083. Eagle Communications Inc. Robert Precht.

KXLF-TV, Channel 4, CBS
P. O. Box 3500, Butte, MT 59701. (406) 782-0444. FAX: 406) 782-8906. Cordilliera Communications Inc. Pres.: Ron Cass.

KXGN-TV, Channel 5, CBS
210 S. Douglas, Glendive, MT 59330. (406) 365-3377. FAX: (406) 365-2181. Stephen A. Marks.

KFBB-TV, Channel 5, ABC
P. O. Box 1139, Great Falls, MT 59403. (406) 453-4377. FAX: (406) 727-9703. Dix Communications. Stan Whitman.

KRTV, Channel 3, CBS
P. O. Box 2989, Great Falls, MT 59403. (406) 791-5400. FAX: (406) 791-5479. Cordillera Communications Inc. William Preston.

KWYB (Butte), Channel 18, ABC
118 Sixth St. S., Great Falls, MT 59405. (406) 761-8816. FAX: (406) 454-3484. Continental Television Network Inc. James M. Colla.

KHMT, Channel 4, FOX
(see KSVI, Billings). Hardin, MT. National Indian Media Foundation.

KTVH, Channel 12, NBC
P. O. Box 6125, Helena, MT 59601. (406) 443-5050. FAX: (406) 442-5106. Big Sky Broadcasting. John Radeck.

KCFW-TV, Channel 9, NBC
P. O. Box 857, Kalispell, MT 59901. (406) 755-5239. FAX: (406) 752-8002. Eagle Communications. Robert Precht.

KYUS-TV, Channel 3, ABC
(see KXGN-TV, Glendive). Miles City, MT. Glendive Broadcasting Corp.

KECI-TV, Channel 13, NBC
340 W. Main, Missoula, MT 59802. (406) 721-2063. FAX: (406) 721-2083. Eagle Communications Inc. Robert Precht.

KPAX-TV, Channel 8, CBS
P. O. Box 4827, 2204 Regent St., Missoula, MT 59801. (406) 542-4400. FAX: (406) 543-7111. Cordillera Communications Inc. William F. Sullivan.

KTMF, Channel 23, ABC
2200 Stephens Ave., Missoula, MT 59801. (406) 542-8900. FAX: (406) 728-4800. Continental Television Network Inc. James M. Colla.

NEBRASKA

KCAN (Albion), Channel 8, ABC
c/o KCAU-TV, 825 Douglas St., Sioux City, IA 51101. (712) 277-2345. FAX: (712) 277-3733. Citadel Communications Co. Ltd. Philip J. Lombardo.

KMNE-TV, Channel 7, PBS
(see Nebraska Educ. Tele., Lincoln). Bassett, NE Nebraska Educ. Telecommunications.

KSTF (Scottsbluff), Channel 10, CBS
3385 N. 10th St., Gering, NE 69341. (308) 743-2494. FAX: (308) 743-2644. Stauffer Communications Inc. Bill Yost.

KGIN Channel 11, CBS
P. O. Box 1069, Grand Island, NE 68801. (308) 382-6100. FAX: (308) 382-3216. Busse Broadcasting Corp. Frank Jonas.

KTVG, Channel 17, FOX
P. O. Box 717, Grand Island, NE 68802-0717. (308) 384-1717. FAX: (308) 384-1986. Hill Broadcasting Inc. Robert Hill.

KHAS-TV, Channel 5, NBC
P. O. Box 578, Hastings, NE 68901. (402) 463-1321. FAX: (402) 463-6551. Seaton Stations. John T. Benson.

KHNE-TV, Channel 29, PBS
(see Nebraska Educ. Tele., Lincoln). Hastings, NE. Nebraska Educ. Telecommunications.

KHGI-TV, Channel 13, ABC
P. O. Box 220, 13 S. Hwy 44, Kearney, NE 68848. (308) 743-2494. FAX: (308) 743-2644. Fant Broadcasting Co of Nebraska. Pres.: Anthony Fant.

KLNE-TV, Channel 3, PBS
(see Nebraska Educ. Tele., Lincoln). Lexington, NE. Nebraska Educ. Telecommunications.

KOLN, Channel 10, CBS
P. O. Box 30350, Lincoln, NE 68503. (402) 467-4321. FAX: (402) 467-9210. Busse Broadcasting Corp. Frank Jonas.

Nebraska Educational Telecommunications, PBS
P. O. Box, Lincoln, NE 68501. (402) 472-3611. FAX: (402) 472-1785. Jack McBride.

KSNK, Channel 8, PBS
(see Nebraska Educ. Tele., Lincoln). McCook, NE. Nebraska Educ. Telecommunications.

KXNE-TV, Channel 19, PBS
(see Nebraska Educ. Tele., Lincoln). Norfolk, NE. Nebraska Educ. Telecommunications.

KSNK (McCook), Channel 8, NBC
P. O. Box 238, McCook, KS 67749. (913) 475-2248. FAX: (913) 475-3944. Lee Enterprises Inc. Al Buch.

KNOP-TV, Channel 2, NBC
P. O. Box 749, North Platte, NE 69103. (308) 532-2222. FAX: (308) 532-9579. Shively Communications. Richard F. Shively.

KPNE-TV, Channel 9, PBS
(see Nebraska Educ. Tele., Lincoln). North Platte, NE. Nebraska Educ. Telecommunications.

KETV, Channel 7, ABC
2665 Douglas St., Omaha, NE 68131-2699. (402) 978-8922. FAX: (402) 978-8931. Pulitzer Broadcasting Co. Ken Elkins.

KMTV, Channel 3, CBS
10714 Mockingbird Dr., Omaha, NE 68127. (402) 592-3333. FAX: (402) 592-4406. Lee Entrerprises Inc. Howard Kennedy.

KPTM, Channel 42, FOX
4625 Farnam St., Omaha, NE 38132. (402) 558-4200. FAX: (402) 554-4290. Pappas Telecasting Companies. Harry J. Pappas.

KXVO, Channel 15, IND
4625 Farnam St., Omaha, NE 68132. (402) 554-1500. Cocola Broadcasting Co. Gary M. Cocola.

KYNE-TV, Channel 26, PBS
P. O. Box 83111, Omaha, NE. Nebraska Educ. Telecomm.

WOWT, Channel 6, NBC
3501 Farnam St., Omaha, NE 68131. (402) 346-6666. FAX: (402) 233-7888. Chronicle Broadcasting Co. D.R. Oswald.

KDUH-TV, Channel 4, ABC
P. O. Box 1529, Scottsbluff, NE 69363-1529. (308) 632-3071. FAX: (308) 632-3596. Duhamel Broadcasting Enterprises. William F. Duhamel.

KSNB-TV (Superior), Channel 4, ABC
(see KHGI, Kearney). Superior, NE. Fant Broadcasting Co of Nebraska.

NEVADA

KVVU-TV (Henderson), Channel 5, FOX
25 TV-5 Dr., Henderson, NV 89014. (702) 435-5555. FAX: (702) 451-4220. Meredith Broadcasting Group. Phil Jones.

KBLR (Paradise), Channel 39, TEL
5000 W. Oakey, #B-2, Las Vegas, NV 89102. (702) 258-0039. FAX: (702) 258-0556. Summit Media Limited Partnership. Pres. & GM: Scott Gentry.

KFBT, Channel 33, IND
3840 S. Jones Blvd., Las Vegas, NV 89103. (702) 873-0033. FAX: (702) 873-6192. Channel 33 Inc. Dan Koker.

KLAS-TV, Channel 8, CBS
P. O. Box 15047, Las Vegas, NV 89114. (702) 792-8888. FAX: (702) 734-7437. Landmark Communications Inc. Dick Fraim.

KLVX, Channel 10, PBS
4210 Channel 10 Dr., Las Vegas, NV 89119. (703) 799-1010. FAX: (702) 799-5586. Clark City School District Bd. of Trustees. Thomas Axtell.

KTNV Channel 13, ABC
3355 S. Valley View Blvd., Las Vegas, NV 89102. (702) 878-1313. FAX: (702) 876-2237. Journal Broadcast Group Inc. Peter Bannister.

KUPN, Channel 21, UPN
920 S. Commerce, Las Vegas, NV 89106. (702) 382-2121. FAX: (702) 382-1351. Las Vegas Channel 21 Inc. Michael Lambert.

KVBC, Channel 3, NBC
1500 Foremaster Ln., Las Vegas, NV 89701. (702) 642-3333. FAX: (702) 657-3208. Valley Broadcasting Co. James E. Rogers.

KAME-TV, Channel 21, FOX
P. O. Box 11129, Reno, NV 89511. (702) 856-2121. FAX: (702) 856-9146. Ellis Communications Inc. Kevin O'Brien.

KNPB, Channel 5, PBS
1670 N. Virginia St., Reno, NV 89503. (702) 784-4555. FAX: (702) 784-1438. Channel 5 Public Broadcasting Inc. James R. Pagliarini.

KOLO-TV, Channel 8, ABC
P. O. Box 10000, Reno, NV 89510. (702) 858-8880. FAX: (702) 858-8855. Stephens Group Inc. Emmett Jones.

KREN-TV, Channel 27, SYN
961 Matley Ln., Suite 130, Reno, NV 89502. (702) 333-2727. FAX: (702) 333-5264. Pappas Telecasting Companies. Harry Pappas.

KRNV Channel 4, NBC
P. O. Box 7160, Reno, NV 89510. (702) 322-4444. FAX: (702) 785-1200. Sierra Broadcasting Co. James E. Rogers.

KTVN, Channel 2, CBS
P. O. Box 7220, Reno, NV 89510. (702) 858-2222. FAX: (702) 858-2345. Sarkes Tarzian Inc. Lawson Fox.

NEW HAMPSHIRE

WNBU, Channel 21, IND
(see WABU, Boston, MA). Concord, NH. BUCI Television.

WNDS, Channel 50, IND
50 TV Place, Derry, NH 03038. (603) 434-8850. FAX: (603) 434-8627. CTV of Derry Inc. Donna Cole.

WENH-TV, Channel 11, PBS
P. O. Box 1100, Durham, NH 03824. (603) 868-1100. FAX: (603) 868-7552. University of New Hampshire. GM: Peter A. Frid.

W15BK-TV, Channel 15, PBS
(see WENH Durham). Hanover, NH. University of New Hampshire.

WEKW-TV, Channel 52, PBS
(see WENH Durham). Keene, NH University of New Hampshire.

WLED-TV, Channel 49, PBS
(see WENH Durham). Littleton, NH. University of New Hampshire.

WGOT (Merrimack), Channel 60, IND
One Sundial Ave., Suite 501, Manchester, NH 03103. (603) 647-6060. FAX: (603) 644-0060. Paxson Communications Corp. Lon Mirolli.

WMUR-TV, Channel 9, ABC
P. O. Box 9, 100 S. Commercial St., Manchester, NH 03105. (603) 669-9999. FAX: (603) 641-9065. Imes Communications. Frank Imes Jr.

571

W18BO-TV, Channel 18, PBS
(see WENH Durham). Pittsburg, NH. University of New Hampshire.

NEW JERSEY

WGTW (Burlington), Channel 48, IND
3900 Main St., Philadelphia, PA 19127. (215) 930-0482. FAX: (215) 930-0496. Brunson Commmunications, Inc. Pres. & CEO: Dorothy Brunson.

WNJS, Channel 23, PBS
(see WNJT, Trenton). Camden, NJ. New Jersey Public Broadcasting.

WMBC-TV (Newton), Channel 63, IND
P. O. Box 156, Lake Hopatcong, NJ 07849-0156. (201) 697-0063. FAX: (201) 697-5515. Mountain Broadcasting Corp. Sun Young Joo.

WMGM-TV (Wildwood), Channel 40, NBC
1601 New Rd., Linwood, NJ 08221. (609) 927-4440. FAX: (609) 927-7014. The Green Group. Howard L. Green.

WNJN, Channel 50, PBS
(see WNJT, Trenton). Montclair, NJ. New Jersey Public Broadcasting.

WNJB, Channel 58, PBS
(see WNJT, Trenton). New Brunswick, NJ. New Jersey Public Broadcasting.

WHSE-TV, Channel 68, IND
390 W. Market St., Newark, NJ 07105. (201) 643-6800. FAX: (201) 643-1903. Silver King Communications, Inc. Barry Diller.

WNET (Newark), Channel 13, PBS
356 W. 58th St., New York, NY 10019. (212) 560-2000. FAX: (212) 560-3191. Educational Broadcasting Corp. Dr. William F. Baker.

WHSP-TV (Vineland), Channel 65, IND
4449 N. Delsea Dr., Newfield, NJ 08344. (609) 691-6965. FAX: (609) 691-2483. Silver King Communications, Inc. Barry Diller.

WWOR-TV, Channel 9, UPN
9 Broadcast Plaza, Secaucus, NJ 07096. (201) 349-0009. FAX: (201) 330-2488. Chris Craft Industries, Inc. Robert Qudeen.

WXTV (Paterson), Channel 41, IND
24 Meadowlands Pkwy., Secaucus, NJ 07094. (201) 348-4141. FAX: (201) 348-4104. Perenchio Television Inc. Christine Schwarz.

WNJU (Linden), Channel 47
Syn, 47 Industrial Ave., Teterboro, NJ 07608. (201) 288-5550. FAX: (201) 288-5166. Telemundo Group, Inc. Manuel Martinez-Lorian.

WNJT, Channel 52, PBS
25 S. Stockton St., Trenton, NJ 08611. (609) 777-5000. FAX: (609) 633-2920. New Jersey Public Broadcasting. William Jobes.

NEW MEXICO

KCHF (Santa Fe), Channel 11, IND
P. O. Box 4338, Albuquerque, NM 87107. (505) 883-1111. FAX: (505) 473-1111. Son Broadcasting Inc. Belarmino R. Gonzales.

KASA-TV (Santa Fe), Channel 2, FOX
P. O. Box 25200, Albuquerque, NM 87125. (505) 246-2222. FAX: (505) 242-1355. Journal Broadcasting of New Mexico Inc. Erick B. Steffens.

KASY-TV, Channel 50, IND
P. O. Box 30068, Albuquerque, NM 87190. (505) 881-2000. Ramar Communications, Inc. Ray Moran.

KASY-TV (Albuquerque), Channel 50, IND
4501 Montgomery N.E., Albuquerque, NM 87109. (505) 884-8355. FAX: (505) 883-1229. Alpha-Omega Broadcasting of Albuquerque. Raymond L. Franks.

KLUZ-TV, Channel 41, SYN
2725 F Broadbent Pkwy N.E. Albuquerque, NM 87107. (505) 344-5589. FAX: (505) 344-0891. Perenchio Television Inc. Marcela Medina.

KNAT, Channel 23, IND
1510 Coors Rd. N.W., Albuquerque, NM 87121. (505) 836-6585. All American Network Inc. Linda Hernandez.

KNME-TV, Channel 5, PBS
1130 University Blvd. N.E. Albuquerque, NM 87102. (505) 277-2121. FAX: (505) 277-6904. Regents of U of NM & Bd of Educ. Jon Cooper.

KOAT-TV, Channel 7, ABC
P. O. Box 25982, Albuquerque, NM 87125. (505) 884-7777. FAX: (505) 884-6282. Pulitzer Broadcasting Co. Ken J. Elkins.

KOB-TV, Channel 4, NBC
P. O. Box 1351, Albuquerque, NM 87103. (505) 243-4411. FAX: (505) 764-2522. Hubbard Broadcasting Inc. Mike Burgess.

KRQE, Channel 13, CBS
P. O. Box 1294, Albuquerque, NM 87103. (505) 243-2285. FAX: (505) 842-8483. Lee Enterprises Inc. Jim Thompson.

KOCT Channel 6, ABC
(see KOAT, Albuquerque). Carlsbad, NM. Pulitzer Broadcasting Co.

KVIH-TV, Channel 12, ABC
(see KVII, Amarillo, TX). Clovis, NM. Marsh Media Inc.

KZIA (Las Cruces), Channel 48, UPN
10033 Carnegie, El Paso, NM 79925. (915) 591-9595. FAX: (915) 591-9896. Lee Enterprises Inc. Station Mgr.: Ray Depa.

KOBF, Channel 12, NBC
P. O. Box 1620, Farmington, NM 87499. (505) 326-1141. FAX: (505) 327-5196. Hubbard Broadcasting Inc. Steve Henderson.

KHFT, Channel 29, IND
420 N. Turner, Hobbs, NM 88240. (505) 393-0944. FAX: (505) 393-6208. Warren Electronic Systems. Porter Vine.

KRWG-TV, Channel 22, PBS
P. O. Box 30001, Dept. 3TV22, Las Cruces, NM 88003. (505) 646-2222. FAX: (505) 646-1924. Regents of New Mexico State Univ. Ronald K. Salak.

KENW, Channel 3, PBS
52 Broadcast Ctr, Portales, NM 88130. (505) 562-2112. FAX: (505) 562-2590. Regents of Eastern New Mexico Univ. Everett L. Frost.

KBIM-TV, Channel 10, CBS
P. O. Box 910, Roswell, NM 88201. (505) 622-2120. FAX: (505) 623-6606. Lee Enterprises Inc. Richard Gotlieb.

KOBR, Channel 8, NBV
124 E. 4th St., Roswell, NM 88201. (505) 625-8888. FAX: (505) 625-8866. Hubbard Broadcasting Inc. Stanley S. Hubbard.

KRPV, Channel 27, NFP
P. O. Box 967, Roswell, NM 88201. (505) 622-5778. Prime Time Christian Broadcasting. Al Cooper.

KOVT, Channel 10, ABC
(see KOAT, Albuquerque). Silver City, NM. Pulitzer Broadcasting Co.

NEW YORK

WIVB-TV (Buffalo), Channel 4, CBS
2077 Elmwood Ave., Albany, NY 14207. (716) 874-4410. FAX: (716) 879-4896. LIN Television Corp. Anthony K. Kiernan.

WNYT, Channel 13, NBC
P. O. Box 4035, Albany, NY 12204. (518) 436-4791. FAX: (516) 436-8723. Paramount Stations Group. Donald D. Perry.

WTEN, Channel 10, ABC
341 Northern Blvd., Albany, NY 12204. (518) 436-4822. FAX: (518) 462-6065. Young Broadcasting Inc. Vincent Young.

WXXA-TV, Channel 23, FOX
815 Central Ave., Albany, NY 12206-1502. (518) 438-8700. FAX: (518) 438-0090. Clear Channel Communications Inc. David M. McDonald.

WMGC-TV, Channel 34, ABC
203 Ingraham Hill Rd., Binghamton, NY 13903. (607) 723-7464. FAX: (607) 723-1034. U.S. Broadcast Group.

WNYE-TV, Channel 25, PBS
112 Tillary St., Brooklyn, NY 11201. (718) 250-5800. FAX: (718) 855-8865. Bd. of Edcuation of the City of NY. Frank Sobrino.

WGRZ-TV, Channel 2, NBC
259 Delaware Ave., Buffalo, NY 14202. (716) 856-1414. FAX: (716) 849-5703. Tak Communications Inc. Eric S. Land.

WKBW-TV, Channel 7, ABC
7 Broadcast Plaza, Buffalo, NY 14202. (716) 845-6100. FAX: (716) 842-1855. Granite Broadcasting Corp. Pres. & CEO: W. Don Cornwell.

WNED-TV, Channel 17, PBS
P. O. Box 1263, Buffalo, NY 14240. (716) 845-7000. FAX: (716) 845-7036. Western NY Public Broadcasting Assoc. J. Michael Collings.

WNEQ-TV, Channel 23, PBS
(see WNED, Buffalo). Buffalo, NY. Western NY Public Broadcasting Assoc.

WNYB-TV, Channel 49, NFP
699 Hertel Ave., Suite 100, Buffalo, NY 14207. (716) 875-4919. In-State Christian TV. Garth Coonce.

WYDC Channel 48, IND
33 E. Market St., Corning, NY 14830. (607) 937-6144. FAX: (607) 937-6144. Standfast Broadcasting Corp. David Grant.

WENY-TV, Channel 36, ABC
P. O. Box 208, Elmira, NY 14902. (607) 739-3636. The Green Group. Howard L. Green.

WETM-TV, Channel 18, NBC
101 E. Water St., Elmira, NY 14901. (607) 733-5518. FAX: (607) 734-1176. Smith Television Investment Co. Robert N. Smith.

WUTV (Buffalo), Channel 29, FOX
951 Whitehaven Rd., Grand Island, NY 14072. (716) 773-7531. FAX: (716) 773-5753. Sullivan Broadcasting of Buffalo. V.P. & GM: Donald Moran.

WBNG-TV (Binghamton), Channel 12, CBS
P. O. Box 12, 12 Gateway Plz., Johnson City, NY 13790. (607) 729-8812. FAX: (607) 797-6211. Gateway Communications Inc. Viki Regan.

WRNN-TV, Channel 62, IND
P. O. Box 1609, Kingston, NY 12401. (914) 339-6200. FAX: (914) 339-6264. Richard French Jr. Greg Floyd.

WTBY (Poughkeepsie), Channel 54, IND
P. O. Box 1355, Melville, NY 11747. (516) 777-8855. FAX: (516) 777-8180. Trinity Broadcasting Network. Paul Crouch.

WABC-TV, Channel 7, ABC
7 Lincoln Sq., New York, NY 10023. (212) 456-7777. FAX: (212) 456-2290. Capital Cities/ABC Broadcast Group. Walter C. Liss, Jr.

WCBS-TV, Channel 2, CBS
524 W. 57 St., New York, NY 10019. (212) 975-7609. FAX: (212) 975-5656. CBS Station Group. Bud Carey.

WNBC, Channel 4, NBC
30 Rockefeller Plaza, New York, NY 10112. (212) 664-4444. FAX: (212) 664-6449. NBC TV Station Division. William L. Bolster.

WBIS-TV, Channel 31, IND
One Centre St., New York, NY 10007. (212) 669-7800. FAX: (212) 669-3585.

WNYW, Channel 5, FOX
205 E. 67th St., New York, NY 10021. (212) 452-5555. FAX: (212) 249-1182. Fox Television Stations Inc. Mitchell Stern.

WPIX, Channel 11, IND
220 E. 42nd St., New York, NY 10017. (212) 949-1100. FAX: (212) 986-1032. Tribune Broadcasting Co. Michael Eigner.

WNPI-TV, Channel 18, PBS
(see WNPE, Watertown). Norwood, NY. St. Lawrence Valley Educational Television Council.

WLIW (Garden City), Channel 21, PBS
Channel 21 Dr., Plainview, NY 11803. (516) 692-7629. FAX: (516) 454-8924. Long Island Educational Television Council Inc. Terrel L. Cass.

WCFE-TV, Channel 57, PBS
One Sesame St., Plattsburgh, NY 12901. (518) 563-9770. FAX: (518) 561-1928. Mountain Lake Public Telecomm. Council. George Sherwin.

WHEC-TV, Channel 10, NBC
191 East Ave., Rochester, NY 14604. (716) 546-5670. FAX: (716) 454-7433. Paramount Stations Group. Arnold Klinsky.

WOKR, Channel 13, ABC
4225 W. Henrietta Rd., Rochester, NY 14602-0555. (716) 334-8700. FAX: (716) 359-1570. Guy Gannett Comm. Gary Nielsen.

WROC-TV, Channel 8, CBS
201 Humboldt St., Rochester, NY 14610. (716) 288-8400. FAX: (716) 288-7679. Smith Broadcating Group Inc. Gary R. Bolton.

WUHF, Channel 31, FOX
360 East Avenue, Rochester, NY 14604. (716) 232-3700. FAX: (716) 546-4774. Act III Broadcasting of Rochester. Heather Farnsworth.

WXXI-TV, Channel 21, PBS
P. O. Box 21, Rochester, NY 14601. (716) 325-7500. FAX: (716) 258-0338. WXXI Public Broadcasting Council. Pres. & CEO: Norm Silverstein.

WRGB, Channel 6, CBS
1400 Balltown Rd., Schenectady, NY 12309. (518) 346-6666. FAX: (518) 381-3721. Freedom Communications Inc. David M. Lynch.

WOCD (Amsterdam), Channel 55, IND
165 Freeman's Bridge Rd., Scotia, NY 12302. (518) 372-8855. FAX: (518) 372-8874. Cornerstone Television Inc. Olean Eagle.

WCNY-TV, Channel 24, PBS
P. O. Box 2400, Syracuse, NY 13220-2400. (315) 453-2424. FAX: (315) 451-8824. Public Brdcstng Cncl of Central NY. Richard W. Russell.

WIXT, Channel 9, ABC
P. O. Box 699, Syracuse, NY 13057. (315) 446-4780. FAX: (315) 446-0045. Ackerley Communications Inc. Barry Ackerley.

WNYS-TV, Channel 43, IND
401 W. Kirkpatrick St., Syracuse, NY 13204. (315) 471-4343. Metro TV Inc. Craig Fox.

WSTM-TV, Channel 3, NBC
1030 James St., Syracuse, NY 13203. (315) 477-9400. FAX: (315) 474-5082. Federal Braodcasting Co. Dale G. Rands.

WSYT, Channel 68, FOX
1000 James St., Syracuse, NY 13203. (315) 472-6800. FAX: (315) 471-8889. Max Television of Syracuse L.P. Charles A. McFadden.

WTJA (Jamestown), Channel 26, IND
401 W. Kirkpatrick St., Syracuse, NY 13204. (315) 468-0908. Jamestown TV Assoc. Craig L. Fox.

WTVH, Channel 5, CBS
980 James St., Syracuse, NY 13203. (315) 425-5555. FAX: (315) 425-5513. Granite Broadcasting Corp. Maria Moore.

WFXV, Channel 33, FOX
33 Greenfield Rd., Utica NY 13440. (315) 337-3300. FAX: (315) 337-1862. Kevin O'Kane.

WKTV, Channel 2, NBC
P. O. Box 2, Utica NY 13503. (315) 733-0404. FAX: (315) 793-3498. Smith Television of NY. V.P. & GM: Stephen Merren.

WUTR, Channel 20, ABC
P. O. Box 20, Utica, NY 13503. (315) 797-5220. Park Communications Inc. Wright M. Thomas.

WICZ-TV (Binghamton), Channel 40, FOX
P. O. Box 40, VestaL NY 13850. (607) 770-4040. FAX: (607) 798-7950. Stainless Broadcasting Co. Nora L. Guzewicz.

WSKG-TV & Radio (Binghamton), Channel 46, PBS
P. O. Box 3000, VestaL NY 13902. (607) 729-0100. FAX: (607) 729-7328. WSKG Public Telecommuncations Council. Michael Ziegler.

WNPE-TV, Channel 16, PBS
1056 Arsenal St., Watertown, NY 13601. (315) 782-3142. FAX: (315) 782-2491. St. Lawrence Valley Educational Television Council. William J. Saiff, Jr.

WWNY-TV (Carthage), Channel 7, CBS
120 Arcade St., Watertown, NY 13601. (315) 788-3800. FAX: (315) 782-7468. United Communications Corp. Howard J. Brown.

WWTI, Channel 50, ABC
1222 Arsenal St., Watertown, NY 13601. (315) 785-8850. FAX: (315) 785-0127. Smith Broadcasting of Watertown. Nicklaos Darling.

NORTH CAROLINA

WASV-TV, Channel 62, IND
225 Summit St-Asheville, NC 28803. (704) 227-8167. Video Marketing Network Inc. Robert J. Murley.

WHNS (Asheville), Channel 21, FOX
21 Interstate Ct., Greenville, SC 29615. (864) 288-2100. FAX: (864) 297-0728. First Media Television. William A. Schwartz.

WUNF-TV, Channel 33, PBS
(see University of NC, Research, Triangle Park). Asheville, NC. University of North Carolina.

WUNC-TV, Channel 4, PBS
(see University of NC, Research, Triangle Park). Chapel Hill, NC. University of North Carolina.

WBTV, Channel 3, CBS
One Julian Price Pl., Charlotte, NC 28208. (704) 374-3500. FAX: (704) 374-3885. Jefferson-Pilot Communication Co. John H. Hutchinson.

WCCB, Channel 18, FOX
One TV Pl., Charlotte, NC 28205. (704) 372-1800. FAX: (704) 376-3415. North Carolina Broadcasting Prtnrs. Cy N. Bahakel.

WCNC-TV, Channel 36, NBC
1001 Wood Ridge Center Dr., Charlotte, NC 28217-1901. (704) 329-3636. FAX: (704) 357-4980. Providence Journal Bcstg Corp. John Llewellyn.

WJZY (Belmont), Channel 46, IND
P. O. Box 668400, Charlotte, NC 28266-8400. (704) 393-0046. FAX: (704) 393-8407. Capitol Croadcasting Co., Inc. James Goodmon.

WSOC-TV, Channel 9, ABC
P. O. Box 34665, Charlotte, NC 28234. (704) 335-4999. FAX: (704) 335-4968. Cox Broadcasting. Nicholas D. Trigony.

WTVI, Channel 42, PBS
3242 Commonwealth Ave., Charlotte, NC 28205. (704) 372-2442. FAX: (704) 335-1358. Charlotte-Mecklenburg Public Broadcasting. Wes Sturgis.

WUND-TV, Channel 2, PBS
(see University of NC, Research, Triangle Park). Columbia, NC. University of North Carolina.

WUNG-TV, Channel 58, PBS
(see University of NC, Research, Triangle Park). Concord, NC. University of North Carolina.

WRDC Channel 28, IND
(see WLFL Raleigh). Durham, NC. Glencairn Ltd.

WTVD, Channel 11, ABC
P. O. Box 2009, Durham, NC 27702. (919) 683-1111. FAX: (919) 682-7225. Capital Cities/ABC Broadcast Group. Emily L. Barr.

WKFT, Channel 40, IND
P. O. Box 2509, Fayetteville, NC 28302-2509. (910) 323-4040. FAX: (910) 323-3924. Robert P. Holding III.

WAAP (Burlington), Channel 16, IND
P. O. Box 16106, Greensboro, NC 27416. (910) 376-6016. FAX: (910) 376-6018. Jack Rehburg.

WEJC (Lexington), Channel 20, IND
622-G Guilford College Rd., Greensboro, NC 27409. (910) 547-0020. Pappas Telecasting Companies. William P. Register.

WFMY-TV (High Point), Channel 2, CBS
P. O. Box TV2, Greensboro, NC 27420. (910) 379-9369. FAX: (910) 273-3444. Gannett Broadcasting. Debra Hooper.

WGGT, Channel 48, ABC
P. O. Box 1618, Greensboro, NC 27402. (910) 274-4848. FAX: (910) 230-1315. Robinson O. Everett. James Thrash.

WLXI-TV, Channel 61, IND
2109 Patterson St., Greensboro, NC 27407. (910) 855-5610. FAX: (910) 855-3645. Garth W. Coonce, Larry Patton.

WNCT-TV, Channel 9, CBS
P. O. Box 898, Greenville, NC 27835-0898. (919) 355-8500. FAX: (919) 355-8568. Park Communications Inc. Edward J. Adams.

WUNK-TV, Channel 25, PBS
(see University of NC, Research, Triangle Park). Greenville, NC. University of North Carolina.

WYDO, Channel 14, FOX
P. O. Box 2044, Greenville, NC 27836. (919) 746-8014. FAX: (919) 746-2555. Frederick J. McCune. Hamp Ferguson.

WHKY-TV, Channel 14, IND
P. O. Box 1059, Hickory, NC 28603. (704) 322-5115. FAX: (704) 322-8256. The Long Family Partnership. Thomas E. Long.

WGHP-TV, Channel 8, FOX
2005 Francis St., High Point, NC 27263. (910) 841-8888. FAX: (910) 841-8050. Fox TV Stations. David Boylan.

WUNM-TV, Channel 19, PBS
(see University of NC, Research, Triangle Park). Jacksonville, NC. University of North Carolina.

WKAY, Channel 64, IND
910 Fairview St., Kannapolis, NC 28083. (704) 933-9529. FAX: (704) 932-3880. Kannapolis Television Co. Station Mgr.: Mark Russell.

WUNE-TV, Channel 17, PBS
(see University of NC, Research, Triangle Park). Linville, NC. University of North Carolina.

WFAY (Fayetteville), Channel 62, FOX
Drawer 62, Lumber Bridge, NC 28357. (910) 843-3884. FAX: (910) 843-2873. Robinson O. Everett, James Thrash.

WRAY-TV (Wilson), Channel 30, IND
Drawer 62, Lumber Bridge, NC 28357. (910) 843-3884. Channel 30 Telecasters L.P. James Thrash.

WUNU, Channel 31, IND
(see University of NC, Research, Triangle Park). Lumberton, NC. University of North Carolina.

WRMY (Rocky Mount), Channel 47, IND
P. O. Box 280, Macclesfield, NC 27852. (919) 827-2800. FAX: (919) 827-2713. Family Broadcasting Enterprises. Dr. Robert J. Pelletier.

WFXI, Channel 8, FOX
P. O. Box 2069, 5441 Highway 70, Morehead City, NC 28557. (919) 240-0888. FAX: (919) 240-2028. COCOM Television, L.P. Ric Gorman.

WCTI, Channel 12, ABC
P. O. Box 12325, New Bern, NC 28561. (919) 638-1212. FAX: (919) 637-4141. Lamco Communications Inc. Clay Millstead.

WLFL, Channel 22, FOX
3012 Highwoods Blvd., Raleigh, NC 27604. (919) 872-9535. Sinclair Broadcast Group. Jim Lapiano.

WNCN (Goldsboro), Channel 17, NBC
1205 Front St., Raleigh, NC 27609. (919) 836-1717. FAX: (919) 836-1747. NBC Television Stations. Pres.: Bud Polacek.

WRAL-TV, Channel 5, CBS
P. O. Box 12000, Raleigh, NC 27605. (919) 821-8555. FAX: (919) 821-8566. Capitol Broadcasting Co. Inc. James F. Goodman.

University of North Carolina, PBS
P.O.P. O. Box 14900, Reseach Triangle Pk, NC 27709-4900. (919) 549-7000. FAX: (919) 549-7201. Tom Howe.

WUNP-TV, Channel 36, PBS
(see University of NC, Research, Triangle Park). Roanoke Rapids, NC. University of North Carolina.

WITN-TV, Channel 7, NBC
P. O. Box 468, Hwy 17 S, Washington, NC 27889. (919) 946-3131. FAX: (919) 946-9265. AFLAC Broadcast Division. Michael D. Weeks.

WECT Channel 6, NBC
P. O. Box 4029, Wilmington, NC 28406. (910) 791-8070. FAX: (910) 392-1509. Ellis Communications. Pres. & CEO: Bert Ellis.

WUNJ-TV, Channel 39, PBS
(see University of NC, Research, Triangle Park). Wilmington, NC. University of North Carolina.

WWAY, Channel 3, ABC
P. O. Box 2068, Wilmington, NC 28402. (910) 762-8581. FAX: (910) 762-8367. Hillside Broadcasting of N.C. Gina H. Teague.

WUNL-TV, Channel 26, PBS
(see University of NC, Research, Triangle Park). Winston-Salem, NC. University of North Carolina.

WXII, Channel 12, NBC
P. O. Box 11847, Winston-Salem, NC 27116. (910) 721-9944. FAX: (910) 722-7685. Pulitzer Broadcasting Co. Ken J. Elkins.

WXLV-TV, Channel 45, ABC
3500 Myer-Lee Dr., Winston-Salem, NC 27101. (910) 722-4545. FAX: (910) 723-8217. Sullivan Broadcasting Inc. Joe Koff.

NORTH DAKOTA

KBME Channel 3, PBS
(see KFME Fargo). Bismarck, ND Prairie Public Broadcasting Inc.

KBMY, Channel 17, ABC
P. O. Box 7277, Bismarck, ND 58507. (701) 223-1700. FAX: (701) 258-0886. Forum Publishing Co. Marc Prather.

KFYR-TV, Channel 5, NBC
P. O. Box 1738, Bismarck, ND 58502. (701) 255-5757. FAX: (701) 255-8220. Meyer Broadcasting Co. Judith Ekberg Johnson.

KQCD-TV (Dickinson), Channel 7, NBC
P. O. Box 1577, Bismarck, ND 58601. (701) 225-6843. FAX: (701) 225-8231. Meyer Broadcasting Co. Judith Ekberg Johnson.

KXMA-TV (Dickinson), Channel 2, CBS
Drawer B, Bismarck, ND 58602. (701) 227-1400. FAX: (701) 227-8896. Chester Reiten & Family. Charles Tibor.

KXMB-TV, Channel 12, CBS
P. O. Box 1617, Bismarck, ND 58501. (701) 223-9197. FAX: (701) 223-3320. Reiten Television Inc. David Reiten.

KDSE, Channel 9, PBS
(see KFME Fargo). Dickinson, ND. Prairie Public Broadcasting Inc.

KJRE, Channel 19, PBS
(see KFME Fargo). Ellendale, ND. Prairie Public Broadcasting Inc.

KFME Channel 13, PBS
P. O. Box 3240, Fargo, ND 58108-3240. (701) 241-6900. FAX: (701) 239-7650. Prairie Public Broadcasting Inc. Bruce Jacobs.

KVLY-TV, Channel 11, NBC
P. O. Box 1878, Fargo, ND 58107. (701) 237-5211. FAX: (701) 232-0493. Meyer Broadcasting Co. Wayne Sanders.

KVRR, Channel 15, IND
4015 9th Ave. SW, P. O. Box 9115, Fargo, ND 58106. (701) 277-1515. FAX: (701) 277-1830. Red River Broadcast Group. Pres.: Ron Grignon.

KXJB-TV (Valley City), Channel 4, CBS
P. O. Box 10399, Fargo, ND 58106. (701) 282-0444. FAX: (701) 282-9331. North American Commmuniation Corp. Bruce E. Barnes.

WDAY-TV, Channel 6, ABC
P. O. Box 2466, Fargo, ND 58108. (701) 237-6500. FAX: (701) 241-5368. Forum Communications Co. William Marcil.

KGFE, Channel 2, PBS
(see KFME Fargo). Grand Forks, ND. Prairie Public Broadcasting Inc.

WDAZ-TV (Devils Lake), Channel 8, ABC
P. O. Box 12639, Grand Forks, ND. 58208, Forum Communications Co., Robert Kerr.

KJRR, Channel 7, IND
(see KVRR, Fargo). Jamestown, ND. Red River Broadcast Corp.

KMCY, Channel 14, ABC
P. O. Box 2276, Minot, ND 58702. (701) 838-6614. FAX: (701) 852-9315. Forum Publishing Co. Marc Prather.

KMOT, Channel 10, NBC
P. O. Box 1120, Minot, ND 58702. (701) 852-4101. FAX: (701) 838-8195. Meyer Broadcasting Co. Judith Ekberg Johnson.

KSRE, Channel 6, PBS
(see KFME Fargo). Minot, ND Prairie Public Broadcasting.

KXMC-TV, Channel 13, CBS
P. O. Box 1686, Minot, ND 58701. (701) 852-2104. FAX: (701) 838-9360. Chester Reiten, David Reiten.

KNRR, Channel 12, FOX
(see KVRR, Fargo). Pembina, ND Red River Braodcast Group.

KUMV-TV, Channel 8, NBC
P. O. Box 1287, Williston, ND 58801. (701) 572-4676. FAX: (701) 572-0118. Meyer Broadcasting Co. Judith Ekberg Johnson.

KWSE, Channel 4, PBS
(see KFME, Fargo). Williston, ND. Prairie Public Broadcasting Inc.

KXMD-TV, Channel 11, CBS
P. O. Box 790, Williston, ND 58801. (701) 572-2345. FAX: (701) 572-0658. Reiten Television Inc. Chester Reiten.

OHIO

WAKC-TV, Channel 23, ABC
853 Copley Rd., Akron, OH 44320. (216) 535-7831. FAX: (216) 535-5370. Paxon Communications. GM: Glenn Schiller.

WNEO, Channel 45, PBS
(see WEAO, Kent). Alliance, OH. Northeastern Educ. TV of Ohio Inc.

WOUB, Channel 20, PBS
9 S. College St., Athens, OH 45701. (614) 593-1771. FAX: (614) 593-0240. Ohio University. Assoc. Dir.: Paul Witkowski.

WOUC-TV, Channel 44, PBS
(see WOUB, Athens). Cambridge, OH. Ohio University.

WOAC, Channel 67, IND
P. O. Box 35367, Canton, OH 44735-5367. (216) 492-5267. FAX: (216) 492-8487. Whitehead Media Inc. Eddie Whitehead.

WGGN-TV (Sandusky) Channel 52, NFP
P. O. Box 247, 3809 Maple Ave., Castalia, OH 44824. (419) 684-5311. FAX: (419) 684-5378. Christian Faith Broadcasting Inc. Shelby Gillam.

WWHO, Channel 53, IND
10 S. Paint St., Chillicothe, OH 45601. (614) 775-3578. FAX: (614) 775-5300. Anthony J. Fant.

WCET, Channel 48, PBS
1223 Central Pkwy., Cincinnati, OH 45214-2890. (513) 381-4033. FAX: (513) 381-7520. Greater Cincinnati TV Educ. Foundation. W. Wayne Godwin.

WCPO-TV, Channel 9, CBS
500 Central Ave., Cincinnati, OH 45202. (513) 721-9900. Scripps Howard Broadcasting Co. J.B. Chase.

WKRC-TV, Channel 12, ABC
1906 Highland Ave., Cincinnati, OH 45219. (513) 763-5500. FAX: (513) 651-0704. Citicasters. William Moll.

WLWT, Channel 5, NBC
140 W. Ninth St., Cincinnati, OH 45202. (513) 352-5000. FAX: (513) 352-5028. Gannett Broadcasting. GM: James Clayton.

WSTR-TV, Channel 64, IND
5177 Fishwick Dr., Cincinnati, OH 45216. (513) 641-4400. FAX: (513) 242-2633. ABRY Communications. Joe Koff.

WEWS, Channel 5, ABC
3001 Euclid Ave., Cleveland, OH 44115. (216) 431-5555. FAX: (216) 361-1762. Scripps Howard Broadcasting Co. Gary R. Robinson.

WJW-TV, Channel 8, FOX
5800 S. Marginal Rd., Cleveland, OH 44103. (216) 431-8888. FAX: (216) 391-9559. New World Communications. Robert Rowe.

WKYC-TV, Channel 3, NBC
1403 E. 6th St., Cleveland, OH 44114. (216) 344-3333. FAX: (216) 344-3326. Gannett Broadcasting. V.P. & GM: Bill Scaffide.

WOIO (Shaker Heights), Channel 19, CBS
1717 E. 12th St., Cleveland, OH 44114. (216) 771-1943. FAX: (216) 515-7152. Malrite Communications Group. Tom Griesdorn.

WUAB (Lorain), Channel 43, IND
1717 E.12th St., Cleveland, OH 44114. (216) 771-1943. FAX: (216) 515-7152. Cannell Communications L.P. GM: Tom Griesdorn.

WVIZ-TV, Channel 25, PBS
4300 Brookpark Rd., Cleveland, OH 44134. (216) 398-2800. FAX: (216) 749-2560. Ed. TV Assoc. of Metro Cleveland. Jerry Wareham.

WBNS, Channel 10, CBS
770 Twin Rivers Dr., Columbus, OH 43215. (614) 460-3700. FAX: (614) 460-2812. Dispatch Printing Co. Michael Fiorile.

WCMH, Channel 4, NBC
P. O. Box 4, Columbus, OH 43216. (614) 263-4444. FAX: (614) 447-9107. Outlet Communications Inc. James G. Babb.

WOSU, Channel 34, PBS
2400 Olentangy River Rd., Columbus, OH 43210. (614) 292-9678. FAX: (614) 688-3343. Ohio State University. Dale K. Ouzts.

WSYX, Channel 6, ABC
1216 Dublin Rd., Columbus, OH 43215. (614) 481-6666. FAX: (614) 481-6624. River City Broadcasting. Barry Baker.

WTTE, Channel 28, FOX
P. O. Box 280, Columbus, OH 43216-0280. (614) 895-2800. FAX: (614) 895-3159. Sinclair Broadcasting Group Inc. David Smith.

WBNX, Channel 55, IND
2690 State Rd., Cuyahoga Falls, OH 44223. (216) 843-5555. FAX: (216) 929-2410. Winston Broadcasting Network Inc. Pres.: Lou Spangler.

WDTN, Channel 2, ABC
P. O. Box 741, Dayton, OH 45401. (513) 293-2101. FAX: (513) 294-6542. Hearst Broadcasting Group. Cheryl A. Craigie.

WHIO-TV, Channel 7, CBS
P. O. Box 1206, Dayton, OH 45401. (513) 259-2111. FAX: (513) 259-2024. Cox Broadcasting. Don Kemper.

WKEF, Channel 22, NBC
1731 Soldiers Home Rd., Dayton, OH 45418. (513) 263-2662. FAX: (513) 268-2332. Max Television Co. V.P. & GM: Jeff Cash.

WPTD, Channel 16, PBS
110 S. Jefferson St., Dayton, OH 45402-2415. (513) 220-1600. FAX: (513) 220-1642. Greater Dayton Public TV Inc. David Fogarty.

WRGT-TV, Channel 45, FOX
45 Broadcast Plaza, Dayton, OH 45408. (513) 263-4500. FAX: (513) 268-5265, Sullivan Broadcasting of Dayton. V.P. & GM: Dave Miller.

WEAO (Akron), Channel 49, PBS
P. O. Box 5191, Kent, OH 44240-5191. (330) 677-4549. FAX: (330) 678-1656. Northeastern Educ. TV of Ohio Inc.

WLIO, Channel 35, NBC
1424 Rice Ave., Lima, OH 45805. (419) 228-8835. FAX: (419) 229-7091. Blade Communications Inc. Station Mgr.: Bruce Opperman.

WTLW, Channel 44, NFP
1844 Baty Rd., Lima, OH 45807. (419) 339-4444. FAX: (419) 339-6812. American Christian Television Svcs. Robert Placie.

WDLI (Canton), Channel 17, IND
6600 Atlantic Blvd., Louisville, OH 44641. (330) 875-5542. Trinity Broadcasting Network. Pres.: Paul F. Crouch.

WMFD-TV, Channel 68, IND
2900 Park Ave. W., Mansfield, OH 44906. (419) 529-5900. FAX: (419) 529-2319. Mid-State Television Inc. Gunther Meisse.

WSFJ, Channel 51, NFP
P. O. Box 770, 10077 Jacksontown Rd S.E., Newark, OH 43076. (614) 833-0771. FAX: (614) 323-3242. Christian Television of Ohio. Larry Maley.

WQHS-TV, Channel 61, IND
2861 W. Ridgewood Dr., Parma, OH 44134. (216) 888-0061. FAX: (216) 888-6551. Silver King Communications Inc. Jim Lawless.

WPBO-TV, Channel 42, PBS
(see WOSU, Columbus). Portsmouth, OH. Ohio State University.

WTJC, Channel 26, IND
2675 Dayton Rd., Springfield, OH 45506. (513) 323-0026. Video Mall Communications Inc. Marvin D. Sparks.

WTOV-TV, Channel 9, NBC
P. O. Box 9999, Altamont Hill, Steubenville, OH 43952. (304) 232-6933. FAX: (614) 282-0439. Smith Broadcasting Partners L.P. Tim McCoy.

WGTE-TV, Channel 30, PBS
P. O. Box 30, 136 Huron St., Toledo, OH 43697. (419) 243-3091. FAX: (419) 243-9711. Public Broadcasting Foundation of N.W. Ohio. Shirley E. Timonere.

WLMB, Channel 40, IND
2757 Monroe St., Toledo, OH 43606. (419) 243-7005. FAX: (419) 243-5340. Dominion Broadcasting Inc. Larry Whatley.

WNWO-TV, Channel 24, ABC
300 S. Byrne Rd., Toledo, OH 43615. (419) 535-0024. FAX: (419) 535-0202. Toledo Television Investors. Brett D. Cornwell.

WTOL-TV, Channel 11, CBS
P. O. Box 1111, Toledo, OH 43699-1111. (419) 248-1111. FAX: (419) 248-1177. Cosmos Broadcasting Corp. Melbourne Stebbins.

WTVG, Channel 13, NBC
4247 Dorr St., Toledo, OH 43607. (419) 531-1313. FAX: (419) 531-1399. Capital Cities/ABC Video Entrprs. David Zamichow.

WUPW, Channel 36, FOX
Four SeaGate, Toledo, OH 43601. (419) 244-3600. FAX: (419) 244-8842. Ellis Communications. Shelia J. Oliver.

WFMJ-TV, Channel 21, NBC
P. O. Box 6230, Youngstown, OH 44501-6230. (216) 744-8611. FAX: (216) 744-3402. WFMJ Television Inc. Betty Brown.

WKBN-TV, Channel 27, CBS
3930 Sunset Blvd., Youngstown, OH 44512. (330) 782-1144. FAX: (330) 782-3504. WKBN Broadcasting Corp. J.D. Williamson II.

WYTV, Channel 33, ABC
3800 Shady Run Rd., Youngstown, OH 44502. (216) 783-2930. FAX: (216) 782-8154. Benedek Broadcasting Corp. A. Richard Benedek.

WHIZ-TV, Channel 18, NBC
629 Downard Rd., Zanesville, OH 43701. (614) 452-5431. FAX: (614) 452-6553. Southeastern Ohio TV System. Pres.: Allan Land.

OKLAHOMA

KDOR (Bartlesville/Tulsa), Channel 17, IND
2120 N. Yellowood, Broken Arrow, OK 74012. (918) 250-0777. All American TV Inc. Pres.: Sonny Arguinzoni.

KWET, Channel 12, PBS
(see KETA, Oklahoma City). Cheyenne, OK Oklahoma Educational TV Authority.

KRSC-TV, Channel 35, NFP
College Hill, Claremore, OK, 74017. (918) 343-7772. FAX: (918) 343-7952. Rogers State College. Station Mgr.: Virgle L. Smith.

KOET, Channel 3, PBS
(see KETA, Oklahoma City). Eufaula, OK. Oklahoma Educational TV Authority.

KSWO-TV, Channel 7, ABC
P. O. Box 708 Hwy 7, Lawton, OK 73502. (405) 355-7000, R.H. Drewry Group. R.H. Drewry.

KETA, Channel 13, PBS
P. O. Box 14190, Oklahoma City, OK 73113. (405) 848-8501. FAX: (405) 841-9282. Oklahoma Educational TV Authority. Robert L. Allen.

KFOR-TV, Channel 4, NBC
P. O. Box 14068, Oklahoma City, OK 73113. (405) 424-4444. FAX: (405) 478-6206. The New York Times Company. Wiliam J. Katsafanas.

KOCB, Channel 34, UPN
P. O. Box 13034, Oklahoma City, OK, 73113. (405) 478-3434. FAX: (405) 478-1027. Sinclair Communications, Inc. Station Mgr.: Joe Muller

KOCO-TV, Channel 5, ABC
P. O. Box 14555, Oklahoma City, OK, 73113. (405) 478-3000. FAX: (405) 478-6675. Gannett Broadcasting. V.P. & GM: Lawrence Herbster.

KOKH-TV, Channel 25, FOX
P. O. Box 14925, Oklahoma City, OK, 73113. (405) 843-2525. FAX: (405) 478-4343. Heritage Media Services Inc. Steve Herman.

KSBI, Channel 52, IND
P. O. Box 26404, Oklahoma City, OK, 73126. (405) 631-7335. FAX: (405) 631-7367. Locke Supply Co. Don J. Locke.

KTBO-TV, Channel 14, IND
3705 N.W. 63rd St., Oklahoma City, OK, 73116. (405) 848-1414. Trinity Broadcasting Network. Paul F. Crouch.

KTLC, Channel 43, PBS
(see KETA, Oklahoma City). Oklahoma City, OK. Oklahoma Educational TV Authority.

KWTV, Channel 9, CBS
P. O. Box 14159, Oklahoma City, OK 73113. (405) 843-6641. FAX: (405) 841-9135. Griffin Television Inc. David F. Griffin.

KJRH, Channel 2, NBC
P. O. Box 2, Tulsa, OK, 74105-3263. (918) 743-2222. FAX: (918) 748-1460. Scripps Howard Stations. Lawrence Leser.

KOED-TV, Channel 11, PBS
811 N. Sheridan, Tulsa, OK, 74115. (918) 838-7611. FAX: (918) 838-1807. Oklahoma Educational TV Authority. GM: Loren Farr.

KOKI-TV, Channel 23, FOX
5416 S. Yale Ave., Suite 500, Tulsa, OK 74135. (918) 491-0023. FAX: (918) 491-6650. Clear Channel TV Licenses Inc. Dan Sullivan.

KOTV, Channel 6, CBS
P. O. Box 6, Tulsa, OK 74101. (918) 582-6666, A.H. Belo. Ward Huey.

KTFO, Channel 41, UPN
5416 S. Yale, Suite 500, Tulsa, OK, 74135. (918) 491-6141. FAX: (918) 491-6049. RDS Broadcasting Inc. Robert Rosenheim.

KTUL, Channel 8, ABC
P. O. Box 8, Tulsa, OK, 74101. (918) 445-8888. FAX: (918) 445-9316. Allbritton Communications Co. Dan Bates.

KWHB, Channel 47, IND
11414 E. 58th Street, Tulsa, OK, 74146. (918) 250-9402. FAX: (918) 254-5614. LeSea Broadcasting. Peter Sumrall.

OREGON

KEBN/KWBP (Salem), Channel 32, IND
10255 S.W. Artic Dr., Beaverton, OR 97005. (503) 644-3232. FAX: (503) 626-3576. Channel 32 Inc. Victor Ives.

KOAB-TV, Channel 3, PBS
7140 S.W. Madam Ave., Bend, OR 97709. (503) 244-9900. FAX: (503) 293-1919. Charles J. Swindells. Charles Swindells.

KTVZ, Channel 21, NBC
P. O. Box 149, Bend, OR 97709. (541) 383-2121. FAX: (541) 382-1616. Stainless Broadcasting Co. John Larkin.

KCBY-TV, Channel 11, CBS
P. O. Box 1156, Coos Bay, OR. 97420. (503) 269-1111. FAX: (503) 269-7464. Northwest Television Inc. Donald E. Tykeson.

KMTZ, Channel 23, NBC
(see KMTR, Springfield). Coos Bay, OR. Wicks Broadcast Group.

KOAC-TV, Channel 7, PBS
(see KOPB, Portland). Corvallis, OR. Charles J. Swindells.

KEPB-TV, Channel 28, PBS
(see KOPB, Portland). Eugene, OR Charles J. Swindells.

KEVU, Channel 34, IND
P. O. Box 10185, Eugene, OR 97401. (541) 342-3435. FAX: (541) 342-2818. California Oregon Broadcasting Inc. Mark Metzger.

KEZI, Channel 9, ABC
P. O. Box 7009, Eugene, OR 97401. (503) 485-5611. Carolyn S. Chambers.

KROZ (Roseburg), Channel 36, IND
888 Goodpasture Island Rd., Eugene, OR 97401. (503) 683-2525. Johanna Broadcasting Inc. Mark Metzger.

KVAL-TV, Channel 13, CBS
P. O. Box 1313, Eugene, OR 97440. (541) 342-4961. FAX: (541) 342-2635. Northwest Television Inc. Donald E. Tykeson.

KDKF, Channel 31, ABC
4509 S. 6th St., Suite 308, Klamath Falls, OR 97603. (503) 883-3131. FAX: (503) 883-8931. Soda Mountain Broadcasting Inc. Carolyn S. Chambers.

KFTS, Channel 22, PBS
(see KSYS, Medford). Klamath Falls, OR. Southern Oregon Public TV Inc.

KOTI, Channel 2, NBC
P. O. Box 2K, Klamath Falls, OR 97601. (503) 882-2222. California Oregon Broadcasting Inc. Patricia C. Smullin.

KTVR, Channel 13, PBS
(see KOPB, Portland). La Grande OR. Charles J. Swindells.

KDRV, Channel 12, ABC
1090 Knutson Ave., Medford, OR 97504. (503) 773-1212. FAX: (503) 779-9261. Chambers Communications Corp. Carolyn Chambers.

KMVU, Channel 26, FOX
820 Crater Lake Ave., Medford, OR 97504. (503) 772-2600. FAX: (503) 772-7364. 914 Broadcasting Inc. Robert Hamacher.

KOBI, Channel 5, NBC
P. O. Box 5M, Medford, OR 97501. (503) 779-5555. FAX: (503) 779-5564. California Oregon Broadcasting Inc. Patricia C. Smullin.

KSYS, Channel 8, PBS
34 S. Fir St., Medford, OR 97501. (503) 779-0808. FAX: (503) 779-2178. Southern Oregon Public TV Inc. William R. Campbell.

KTVL, Channel 10, CBS
P. O. Box 10, Medford, OR 97501. (541) 773-7373. FAX: (541) 779-0451. Freedom Communications, Inc. V.P. & GM: Thomas Long.

KATU, Channel 2, ABC
P. O. Box 2, Portland, OR 97207. (503) 231-4222. FAX: (503) 231-4233. Fisher Broadcasting Inc. Patrick Scott.

KGW, Channel 8, NBC
1501 S.W. Jefferson St., Portland, OR 97201. (503) 226-5000. FAX: (503) 226-4448. Providence Journal Brdcstg Corp. Dennis Williamson.

KNMT, Channel 24, IND
432 N.E. 74Th Ave., Portland, OR 97213. (503) 252-0792. FAX: (503) 256-4205. National Minority TV Inc. Jane P. Duff.

KOIN, Channel 6, CBS
222 S.W. Columbia St., Portland, OR 97201. (503) 464-0600. FAX: (503) 464-0717. Lee Enterprises Inc. Greg R. Veon.

KOPB-TV, Channel 10, PBS
7140 S.W. Macadam Ave., Portland, OR 97219. (503) 244-9900. FAX: (503) 293-1919. Charles J. Swindells. Maynard E. Orme.

KPTV, Channel 12, IND
P. O. Box 3401, Portland, OR 97203. (503) 222-9921. Chris Craft Industries, Inc. Martin Brantley.

KMTX-TV, Channel 46, NBC
(see KMTR, Springfield). Rosebug, OR. Wicks Broadcast Group.

KPIC, Channel 4, CBS
P. O. Box 1345, Rosebug, OR 97470. (503) 672-4481. FAX: (503) 672-4482. California Oregon Broadcasting Inc. Don Clithero.

KBSP-TV, Channel 22, IND
4923 Indian School Rd. N.E. Salem, OR 97305. (503) 390-2202. FAX: (503) 390-6829. Blackstar Communications Inc. Judith Koenig.

KMTR (Eugene), Channel 16, NBC
3825 International Court, Springfield, OR 97401. (503) 746-1600. FAX: (503) 747-0866. Wicks Broadcast Group. GM: Brian Benschoter.

PENNSYLVANIA

WFMZ-TV, Channel 69, IND
300 E. Rock Rd., Allentown, PA 18103. (610) 797-4530. FAX: (610) 791-2288, Richard C. Dean.

WATM-TV (Altoona), Channel 23, ABC
(see WWCP, Johnstown). Altoona, PA. Smith Broadcasting Group Inc. Marty Ostrow.

WKBS-TV, Channel 47, IND
1813 Valley View Blvd., Altoona, PA 16602. (814) 942-3400. FAX: (814) 942-3400. Cornerstone Television Inc. R. Russell Bixler.

WTAJ-TV, Channel 10, CBS
P. O. Box 10, Commerce Park, Altoona, PA 16603. (814) 944-2031. FAX: (814) 946-8746. Macromedia. Lamont T. Pinker.

WBPH-TV, Channel 60, IND
Suite 407, 2 Bethlehem Plaza, Bethlehem, PA 18018. (610) 691-3000. FAX: (610) 954-7505. Sonshine Family TV Inc. Patricia Huber.

WLVT-TV (Allentown), Channel 39, PBS
1525 Mountain Drive N., Bethlehem, PA 18015. (610) 867-4677. FAX: (610) 867-3544. Lehigh Valley Public Telecomm. James Baum.

WJAL Channel 68, WB
P. O. Box 229, 262 Swamp Fox Rd., Chambersburg, PA 17201. (719) 375-4000. FAX: (719) 375-4052. Channel 68 Broadcasting Corp. Pres.& CEO: Jerold Jacobs.

WSWB-TV (Scranton), Channel 64, IND
P. O. Box 764, Clarks Summit, PA 18411.(717) 586-1744. Ehrhardt Broadcasting. Ted. H. Ehrhardt.

WFXP, Channel 66, FOX
Suite 102, 155 West 8th Street, Erie, PA 16501. (814) 451-1066. FAX: (814) 451-0483. Erie Broadcasting Inc. Art Arkelian.

WICU-TV, Channel 12, NBC
3514 State St., Erie, PA 16508. (814) 454-5201. FAX: (814) 455-0703. Lamb Enterprises. Priscilla Lamb Schwier.

WJET-TV, Channel 24, ABC
8455 Peach St., Erie, PA 16509. (814) 864-2400. FAX: (814) 868-3041. The Jet Broadcasting Company. John Kanzius.

WQLN, Channel 54, PBS
8425 Peach St., Erie, PA 16509. (814) 864-3001. FAX: (814) 864-4077. Public Broadcasting of N.W. PA. Ronald Daugherty.

WSEE-TV, Channel 35, CBS
1220 Peach St., Erie, PA 16501. (814) 455-7575. FAX: (814) 454-5541. Northstar Television Group, Inc. Robert Hoffman.

WHP-TV, Channel 21, CBS
3300 N. Sixth St., Harrisburg, PA 17110. (717) 238-2100. FAX: (717) 236-0198. Clear Channel Communications. John F. Feeser III.

WHTM-TV, Channel 27, ABC
P. O. Box 5860, 3235 Hoffman St., Harrisburg, PA 17110-5860. (717) 236-2727. FAX: (717) 232-5272. Allbritton Communication Corp. Robert Allbritton.

WITF-TV, Channel 33, PBS
P. O. Box 2954, Harrisburg, PA 17105. (717) 236-6000. FAX: (717) 236-4628. Eastern Education. Dr. Jane D. Coleman.

WWLF-TV, Channel 56, FOX
(see WOLF, Scranton). Hazleton, PA. Pegasus Broadcast Television Inc.

WJAC-TV, Channel 6, NBC
1949 Hickory Lane, Johnstown, PA 15905. (814) 255-7600. FAX: (814) 255-3958. Anderson H. Walters Estate. James M. Edwards, Sr.

WTWB-TV (Johnstown), Channel 38, IND
6611 Santa Monica Blvd., Los Angeles, CA 90038. (213) 469-5696. FAX: 213-469-2193. Leon A. Crosby. Larry Rogow.

WWCP-TV, Channel 8, FOX
1450 Scalp Ave., Johnstown, PA 15904. (814) 266-8088. FAX: (814) 266-7749. U.S. Broadcast Group. V.P. & GM: Sharon Moloney.

WGAL Channel 8, NBC
1300 Columbia Ave., Lancaster, PA 17603. (717) 393-5851. FAX: (717) 383-9484. Pulitzer Broadcasting Co. Paul Quinn.

WLYH-TV (Lancaster), Channel 15, CBS
P. O. Box 1283, Lebanon, PA 17042. (717) 228-1500. FAX: (717) 270-0901. Gateway Communications Inc. David F. Metz.

WNEP-TV (Scranton), Channel 16, ABC
16 Montage Mountain Rd., Moosic, PA 18507. (717) 346-7474. FAX: (717) 347-0359. The New York Times Co. Warren A. Reed.

KYW-TV, Channel 3, CBS
101 S. Independence Mall E., Philadelphia, PA 19106. (215) 238-4700. FAX: (215) 238-4545. CBS Station Group. Jonathan Klein.

WACI (Atlantic City), Channel 62, IND
400 W. Hortter, Philadelphia, PA 19123. (215) 848-5815. FAX: (215) 848-9471. Garden State Communications. Gloria Penn Easton.

WCAU, Channel 10, NBC
City Ave. & Monument Rd., Philadelphia, PA 19131. (610) 668-5510. FAX: (610) 668-7039. NBC TV Station Division. GM: Pat Wallace.

WGBS-TV, Channel 57, IND
420 N. 20th St., Philadelphia, PA 19130. (215) 563-5757. FAX: (215) 563-5786. Paramount Stations Group. Walter DeHaven.

WPHL-TV, Channel 17, IND
5001 Wynnefield Ave., Philadelphia, PA 19131. (215) 878-1700. Fax: (215) 879-3665. Tribune Broadcasting Group. Randall E. Smith.

WPVI-TV, Channel 6, ABC
4100 City Line Ave., Philadelphia, PA 19131. (215) 878-9700. FAX: (215) 581-4515. Capital Cities/ABC Broadcasting. Thomas Kane.

WTGI-TV, Channel 61, IND
520 N. Delaware Ave., Philadelphia, PA 19123. (215) 923-2661. Fax: (215) 923-2677. Paxson Communications Corp. Bob Backman.

WTXF-TV, Channel 29, FOX
330 Market St., Philadelphia, PA 19106. (215) 925-2929. FAX: (215) 592-1535. Fox Television Stations Inc. Mike Conway.

WWAC-TV (Atlantic City), Channel 53, IND
844N. 4th St., Philadelphia, PA 19123. (609) 344-6800. FAX: (609) 347-4758. Cellular Phone Centers, Inc. David W. Allen.

WYBE, Channel 35, PBS
P. O. Box 11896, Philadelphia, PA 19128-1604. (215) 483-3900. FAX: (215) 483-6908. Independence Public Media of Phil. Fran McElroy.

KDKA-TV, Channel 2, CBS
One Gateway Ctr., Pittsburgh, PA 15222. (412) 575-2200. FAX: (412) 575-3207. CBS Station Group. V.P. & GM: Gary Cozen.

WPGH-TV, Channel 53, FOX
750 Ivory Ave., Pittsburgh, PA 15214. (412) 931-5300. FAX: (412) 931-8029. Sinclair Broadcast Group Inc. Alan Frank.

WPTT-TV, Channel 22, IND
P. O. Box 2809, Pittsburgh, PA 15230. (412) 856-9010. FAX: (412) 856-0633. WPTT Inc. Eddie Edwards.

WPXI, Channel 11, NBC
11 Television Hill, Pittsburgh, PA 15214. (412) 237-1100. FAX: (412) 323-8097. Cox Broadcasting. John A. Howell III.

WQED, Channel 13, PBS
4802 Fifth Ave., Pittsburgh, PA 15213. (412) 622-1300. FAX: (412) 622-1488. Metro Pittsburgh Publice Broadcasting. Michael Fields.

WQEX, Channel 16, PBS
(see WQED, Pittsburgh). Pittsburgh, PA. QED Communications Inc. George Miles.

WTAE-TV, Channel 4, ABC
400 Ardmore Blvd., Pittsburgh, PA 15221. (412) 242-4300. FAX: (412) 244-4512. Hearst Broadcasting Group. James R. Heffner III.

WVIA-TV, Channel 44, PBS
70 Old Boston Rd., Pittston, PA 18640. (717) 826-6144. FAX: (717) 655-1180. Northeastern PA Education TV Assoc. A. William Kelly.

WTVE, Channel 51, IND
1729 N. 11th St., Reading, PA 19604. (610) 921-9181. FAX: (610) 921-9139. Partel Inc. Michael Parker.

WGCB-TV, Channel 49, IND
P. O. Box 88, Red Lion, PA 17356. (717) 246-1681. FAX: (717) 244-9316. Red Lion Broadcasting Co. John H. Norris.

WOLF-TV, Channel 38, FOX
916 Oak St., Scranton, PA 18508. (717) 347-9653. FAX: (717) 347-3141. Pegasus Broadcast Television Inc. Guyon W. Turner.

WYOU, Channel 22, CBS
415 Lackawanna Ave., Scranton, PA 18503. (717) 961-2222. FAX: (717) 342-1254. Diversified Communications. Bill Christian.

WPSX-TV, Channel 3, PBS
Wagner Annex, University Park, PA 16802-3899. (814) 865-3333. FAX: (814) 865-3145. Pennsylvania State University. Mark Erstling.

WPCB-TV (Greensburg), Channel 40, IND
Signal Hill Dr., Wall, PA 15148-1499. (412) 824-3930. FAX: (412) 824-5442. Cornerstone Television Inc. Pres. & CEO: R. Russell Bixler.

WBRE-TV, Channel 28, NBC
62 S. Franklin St., Wilkes-Barre, PA 18773. (717) 823-2828. FAX: (717) 823-4523. RP Companies. I. Martin Pompadur.

WILF, Channel 53, FOX
(see WOLF, Scranton). Williamsport, PA. Pegasus Broadcast Television Inc.

WPMT, Channel 43, FOX
2005 S. Queen St., York, PA 17403. (717) 843-0043. FAX: (717) 843-9741. Renaissance Communication Corp. Michael Filkenstein.

RHODE ISLAND

WJAR, Channel 10, NBC
23 Kenney Rd., Cranston, RI 02920. (401) 455-9100. FAX: (401) 455-9168. Outlet Communications Inc. James G. Babb.

WPRI-TV, Channel 12, CBS
25 Catamore Blvd., E. Providence, RI 02914-1203. (401) 438-7200. FAX: (401) 434-3761. Clear Channel Communications. Deborah Sinay.

WOST-TV (Block Island), Channel 69, IND
P. O. Box 515, Pocasset, RI 02559. (508) 563-2585. FAX: (401) 466-5222. Raymond Yorke.

WLNE Channel 6, ABC
10 Orms St., Providence, RI 02904. (401) 453-8000. FAX: (401) 453-8088. Freedom Communications Inc. V.P. & GM: Doreen Dawson.

WNAC-TV (Providence), Channel 64, FOX
33 Pine St., Rehoboth, MA 02769. (508) 252-9711. FAX: (508) 252-6210. Argyle Television Inc. Blake Byrne.

WSBE-TV, Channel 36, PBS
50 Park Ln., Providence, RI 02907. (401) 277-3636. FAX: (401) 277-3407. Rhode Island Public Telecomm. Susan L. Farmer.

SOUTH CAROLINA

WFBC-TV, Channel 40, IND
(see WLOS, Asheville). Anderson, SC. (864) 297-1313. FAX: (864) 297-8085. River City Broadcasting L.P. Barry Baker.

WLOS, Channel 13, ABC
288 Macon Ave., Asheville, SC 28804. (704) 255-0013. FAX: (704) 255-4612. River City Broadcasting L.P. Barry Baker.

WEBA-TV (Allendale), Channel 14, IND
Rt. 3, P. O. Box 380, Barnwell, SC 29812. (803) 259-3245. South Carolina Educational Television Commission. Charles E. Cortez.

WJWJ-TV, Channel 16, PBS
P. O. Box 1165, Beaufort, SC 29901. (803) 524-0808. FAX: (803) 524-1016. South Carolina Educational Television Commission. Station Mgr.: Michael Brannen.

WCBD-TV, Channel 2, ABC
P. O. Box 879, Charleston, SC 29402. (803) 884-2222. FAX: (803) 881-3410. Media General Broadcast Group. J. William Evans III.

WCSC-TV, Channel 5, CBS
P. O. Box 186, 485 E. Bay St., Charleston, SC 29402. (803) 723-8371. FAX: (803) 723-0074. William E. Blackwell. James H. Smith.

WITV, Channel 7, PBS
(see South Carolina Educational Television Commission, Columbia). Charleston, SC. South Carolina Educational TV Comm.

WTAT-TV, Channel 24, FOX
4301 Arco Ln., Charleston, SC 29418. (803) 744-2424. FAX: (703) 554-9649. Sullivan Broadcasting. P.J. Ryal.

South Carolina Educational Television Commission, PBS
P. O. Box 11000, Columbia, SC 29211. (803) 737-3200. FAX: (803) 737-5000. Henry J. Cauthen.

WACH, Channel 57, FOX
1400 Pickens St., Columbia, SC 29201. (803) 252-5757. FAX: (803) 212-7270. Ellis Communications. C. Joseph Tonsing.

WIS, Channel 10, NBC
1111 Bull St., Columbia, SC 29201. (803) 799-1010. FAX: (803) 758-1278. Cosmos Broadcasting Corp. Ron Loewen.

WLTX, Channel 19, CBS
6027 DeVine St., Columbia, SC 29209. (803) 776-3600. FAX: (803) 783-2971. Lewis Broadcasting Corp. J. Curtis Lewis.

WOLO-TV, Channel 25, ABC
5807 Shakespeare Rd., Columbia, SC 29240. (803) 754-7525. FAX: (803) 754-6147. South Carolina Broadcasting Partners. Cy N. Bahakel.

WRLK-TV, Channel 35, PBS
1101 George Rogers Blvd., Columbia, SC 29209. (803) 737-3200. FAX: (803) 737-3500. South Carolina Educational Television Commission. Henry J. Cauthen.

WHMC, Channel 23, PBS
(see South Carolina Educational Television Commission, Columbia). Conway, SC. South Carolina Educational TV Comm.

WBTW, Channel 13, CBS
3430 N. TV Rd., Florence, SC 29501-0013. (803) 662-1565. FAX: (803) 678-4253. Spartan Radiocasting. Miss Lou Kirchen.

WJPM-TV, Channel 33, PBS
(see South Carolina Educational Television Commission, Columbia). Florence, SC. South Carolina Educational Television Commission.

WPDE-TV, Channel 15, ABC
3215 S. Cashua Dr., Florence, SC 29501. (803) 665-1515. FAX: (803) 679-2723. Diversified Communications. Peter Owens.

WWMB, Channel 21, IND
3215 S. Cashua Dr., Florence, SC 29501. (803) 679-5487. FAX: (803) 665-4907. C. Lenoir Sturkie. Al Irving.

WGGS-TV, Channel 16, IND
P.O.P. O. Box 1616, Greenville, SC 29602. (864) 244-1616. FAX: (864) 292-8481. Carolina Christian Broadcasting Inc. James H. Thompson.

WNTV, Channel 29, PBS
(see South Carolina Educational Television Commission, Columbia). Greenville, SC. South Carolina Educational Television Commission.

WSPA-TV (Spartanburg), Channel 7, CBS
250 International Dr., Greenville, SC 29304. (864) 576-7777. Spartan Radiocasting Co. Nick Evans.

WYFF, Channel 4, NBC
505 Rutherford St., Greenville, SC 29602. (864) 242-4404. FAX: (864) 240-5329. Pulitzer Broadcasting Co. David McAtee.

WNEH, Channel 38, PBS
(see South Carolina Educational Television Commission, Columbia). Greenwood, SC. South Carolina Educational Television Commission.

WBNU (Charleston), Channel 36, IND
1558 Ben Sawyer Blvd., Mt. Pleasant, SC 29464. (803) 884-3185. FAX: (803) 849-1434. Caro Broadcasting Ltd. Arnold Baynard.

WCIV (Charleston), Channel 4, NBC
888 Allbritton Blvd., Mt. Pleasant, SC 29464. (803) 881-4444. FAX: (803) 849-2507. Allbritton Communications Co. Joe L. Allbritton.

WGSE, Channel 43, NFP
P. O. Box 1243, 803 A Seaboard St., Myrtle Beach, SC 29577. (803) 626-4300. FAX: (803) 448-8654. Carolina Christian Broadcasting Inc. James Thompson.

WFVT (Rock Hill), Channel 55, IND
3501 Performance Rd., Charlotte, NC 28214. (704) 398-0046. Family Fifty-Five Inc. Dave Turner.

WNSC-TV, Channel 30, PBS
P. O. Box 11766, Rock Hill, SC 29731. (803) 324-3184. FAX: (803) 324-0580. South Carolina Educational Television Commission. Henry J. Cauthen.

WRET-TV, Channel 49, PBS
P. O. Box 4069, Media Bldg., UCSC Spartanburg, SC 29305-4069. (864) 599-0201. FAX: (864) 578-6957. South Carolina Educational Television Commission. William S. Hart.

WRJA-TV, Channel 27, PBS
18 N. Marvin St., Sumter, SC 29150. (803) 773-5546. FAX: (803) 775-1059. South Carolina Educational Television Commission. James L. Barnard.

SOUTH DAKOTA

KABY-TV, Channel 9, ABC
P. O. Box 1520, Aberdeen, SD 57401. (605) 225-9200. FAX: (605) 225-9226. Ellis Communications. Mike Brunette.

KDSD-TV, Channel 16, PBS
(see KUSD, Vermillion). Aberdeen, SD. SD Board of Directors for Educational Television.

KESD-TV, Channel 8, PBS
(see KUSD, Vermillion). Brookings, SD. SD Board of Directors for Educational Television.

KPSD-TV, Channel 13, PBS
(see KUSD, Vermillion). Eagle Butte, SD. SD Board of Directors for Educational Television.

KDLO-TV, Channel 3, CBS
(see KELO, Sioux Falls). Florence, SD. Young Broadcasting.

KHSD-TV, Channel 11, ABC
(see KOTA, Rapid City). Lead, SD. Duhamel Broadcasting Enterprises.

KIVV-TV, Channel 5, NBC
(see KEVN, Rapid City)., Lead, SD. Heritage Media Corp.

KQSD-TV, Channel 11, PBS
(see KUSD, Vermillion). Lowry, SD. SD Board of Directors for Educational Television.

KZSD-TV, Channel 8, PBS
(see KUSD, Vermillion). Martin, SD. SD Board of Directors for Educational Television.

KPRY-TV, Channel 4, ABC
(see KFSY, Sioux Falls). Pierre, SD. Ellis Communications.

KTSD-TV, Channel 10, PBS
(see KUSD Vermillion). Pierre, SD. SD Board of Directors for Educational Television.

KBHE-TV, Channel 9, PBS
(see KUSD, Vermillion). Rapid City, SD. SD Board of Directors for Educational Television.

KCLO-TV, Channel 15, CBS
2497 W. Chicago St., Rapid City, SD 57702. (605) 341-1500. FAX: (605) 348-5518. Midcontinent Media Inc. Mike Braker.

KEVN-TV, Channel 7, NBC
P. O. Box 677, Rapid City, SD 57709. (605) 394-7777. FAX: (605) 348-9128. Heritage Media Corp. Gerry Fenske.

KOTA-TV, Channel 3, ABC
P. O. Box 1760, Rapid City, SD 57709-1760. (605) 342-2000. FAX: (605) 342-7305. Duhamel Broadcasting Enterprises, William F. Duhamel.

KPLO-TV, Channel 6, CBS
(see KELO, Sioux Falls). Reliance, SD. Young Broadcasting.

KCSD-TV, Channel 23, PBS
(see KUSD Vermillion). Sioux Falls, SD. SD Board of Directors for Educational Television.

KDLT (Mitchell), Channel 5, NBC
3600 S. Westport Ave., Sioux Falls, SD 57116-0196. (605) 361-5555. FAX: (605) 361-3982. Red River Broadcast Corp. Earl Beall.

KELO-TV, Channel 11, CBS
501 S. Phillips, Sioux Falls, SD 57102. (605) 336-1100. FAX: (605) 334-3447. Young Broadcasting.

KSFY-TV, Channel 13, ABC
300 N. Dakota Ave., Sioux Falls, SD 57102. (605) 336-1300. FAX: (605) 336-3468. Ellis Communications. Bert Ellis.

KTTW, Channel 17, FOX
P. O. Box 5103, Sioux Falls, SD 57117-5103. (605) 338-0017. FAX: (605) 338-7173. Independent Communications Inc. Charles Poppen.

KTTW, Channel 12, FOX
P. O. Box 5103, Sioux Falls, SD 57117-5103. (605) 338-0017. FAX: (605) 338-7173. Independent Communications Inc. Charles Poppen.

KUSD-TV, Channel 2, PBS
P. O. Box 5000, Cherry & Dakota Sts., Vermillion, SD 57069-5000. (605) 677-5861. FAX: (605) 677-5010. SD Board of Directors for Educational Television. Don Checots.

TENNESSEE

WDEF-TV, Channel 12, CBS
3300 Broad St., Chattanooga TN 37408. (423) 785-1200. FAX: (423) 785-1271. Park Communications Inc. Station Mgr.: Gary Andrich.

WDSI-TV, Channel 61, FOX
1101 E. Main St., Chattanooga, TN 37408. (615) 265-0061. FAX: (615) 265-3636. Pegasus Broadcast TV Inc. Jim Wright.

WRCB-TV, Channel 3, NBC
900 Whitehall Rd., Chattanooga, TN 37405-3247. (423) 267-5412. FAX: (423) 267-6840. Sarkes Tarzian Inc. Chairman: Tom Tarzian.

WTCI, Channel 45, PBS
4411 Amnicola Hwy., Chattanooga, TN 37406. (615) 629-0045. FAX: (615) 698-8557. The Greater Chattanooga PTV Corp. Victor A. Hogstrom.

WTVC, Channel 9, ABC
P. O. Box 1150, Chattanooga, TN 37401. (615) 756-5500. FAX: (615) 757-7400. Freedom Communications Inc. Jim Rosse.

WFLI-TV (Cleveland), Channel 53, IND
P. O. Box 302, 4654 Cohutta-Varnell Rd., Cohutta, GA 30710, 706-694-3337. FAX: 706-694-4112. William E. & Ying Hau Benns.

WCTE, Channel 22, PBS
P. O. Box 2040, Cookeville, TN 38502. (615) 528-2222. FAX: (615) 372-6284. Upper Cumberland Broadcast Council.

WKZX, Channel 28, IND
P. O. Box 2628, 404 E. Broad, Cookeville, TN 38501. (615) 520-0228. FAX: (615) 839-6172. Invavision Broadcasting Inc. Ed Gilgenbach.

WINT-TV, Channel 20, IND
P. O. Box 608, Crossville, TN 38555. (615) 484-6508. Larry D. Hudson, John A. Cunnigham.

WPGD, Channel 50, IND
36 Music Village Blvd., Hendersonville, TN 37075. (615) 822-1243. FAX: (615) 822-1642. Sonlight Broadcasting System Inc. Stuart J. Roth.

WBBJ-TV, Channel 7, IND
346 Muse St., Jackson, TN 38301. (901) 424-4515. FAX: (901) 424-9299. Tennessee Broadcasting Partners. Cy N. Bahakel.

WMTU, Channel 16, FOX
Jackson, TN. Chesapeake Bay Holding Co. Jack Peck.

WPMC, Channel 54, NFP
P. O. Box 54, 1 Huddleston Cemetary Rd. Jellico TN 37762. (615) 784-7854. FAX: (615) 784-9536. Pine Mountain Christian Broadcasting. Rev. Wayne Marler.

WEMT (Greeneville), Channel 39, FOX
3206 Hanover Rd., Johnson City, TN 37604. (615) 283-3900. FAX: (615) 283-4938. John Trinder. Ed Groves.

WJHL-TV, Channel 11, CBS
P. O. Box 1130, Johnson City, TN 37605. (615) 926-2151. FAX: (615) 434-4537. Park Communications Inc. Roy H. Park.

WKPT-TV, Channel 19, ABC
222 Commerce St., Kingsport, TN 37660. (423) 246-9578. FAX: (423) 246-6261. Glenwood Communications Corp. George E. DeVault, Jr.

WATE-TV, Channel 6, ABC
P. O. Box 2349-37901, 1306 N.E. Broadway, Knoxville, TN 37917. (615) 637-6666. FAX: (615) 525-4091. Young Broadcasting Inc. Jan Wade.

WBIR-TV, Channel 10, NBC
1513 Hutchison Ave., Knoxville, TN 37917. (615) 637-1010. FAX: (615) 637-6280. Multimedia Broadcasting Co. Chris Gallu.

WKOP-TV, Channel 15, PBS
1661 E. Magnolia Ave., Knoxville, TN 37917. (615) 595-0220. FAX: (615) 595-0300. E. Tennessee Public Comm. Corp. E. Almer Curtis, Jr.

WKXT-TV, Channel 8, CBS
P. O. Box 59088, Knoxville, TN 37950. (423) 450-8888. FAX: (423) 450-8869. Phipps Television of Tennessee Inc. Lewis F. Cosby III.

WTNZ, Channel 43, FOX
Bldg. D, Suite 300, 9000 Executive Park Dr., Knoxville, TN 37923. (615) 693-4343. FAX: (615) 691-6904. Ellis Communications. Bert Ellis.

WJFB, Channel 66, IND
200 E. Spring St., Lebanon, TN 37087. (615) 444-8206. FAX: (615) 444-7592. Bryant Communications Inc. Pres.: Joe F. Bryant.

WLJT-TV (Lexington), Channel 11, PBS
U.T.-Martin, Clement Hall, Martin, TN 38238. (901) 587-7561. FAX: (901) 587-7566. W. Tennessee Public TV Council Inc. Alice Houff.

WFBI, Channel 50, IND
6080 Mt. Mariah, Memphis, TN 38115. (901) 375-9324. FAX: (901) 795-4454. Flinn Broadcasting Corp. George S. Flinn.

WHBQ-TV, Channel 13, FOX
P. O. Box 11407, 405 S. Highland St., Memphis, TN 38111. (901) 320-1313. FAX: (901) 323-0092. Fox Television Stations Inc. Mitchell Stern.

WKNO-TV, Channel 10, PBS
900 Getwell Rd., Memphis, TN 38111. (901) 458-2521. FAX: (901) 452-2221. Mid-South Public Communications. Michael LaBonia.

WLMT Channel 30, IND
P. O. Box 30030, Memphis, TN 38130. (901) 346-3030. FAX: (901) 346-1451. Chesapeake Bay Holding Co. Jack Peck.

WMC-TV, Channel 5, NBC
1960 Union Ave., Memphis, TN 38104. (901) 726-0555. FAX: (901) 276-6851. Ellis Communications. U. Bertram Ellis, Jr.

WPTY-TV, Channel 24, ABC1
P. O. Box 42424, 2225 Union Ave., Memphis, TN 38104. (901) 278-2424. FAX: (901) 272-8759. Clear Channel Communications Inc. Dan Sullivan.

WREG-TV, Channel 3, CBS
803 Channel 3 Drive, Memphis, TN 38103. (901) 577-0100. FAX: (901) 577-0198. The New York Times Co. Bob Eoff.

WDCN, Channel 8, PBS
P. O. Box 120609, Nashville, TN 37212-0609. (615) 259-9325. FAX: (615) 248-6120. Metropolitan Board of Public Ed. Robert L. Shephard.

WKRN-TV, Channel 2, ABC
441 Murfreesboro Rd., Nashville, TN 37210. (615) 259-2200. FAX: (615) 248-7298. Young Broadcasting Inc. Vincent Young.

WNAB, Channel 58, WB
3201 Dickerson Pike, Nashville, TN 37207. (615) 650-5858. FAX: (615) 650-5859. WNAB Limited Partners. Pres. & CEO: Vince Barresi.

WSMV-TV, Channel 4, NBC
5700 Knob Rd., Nashville, TN 37209. (615) 353-4444. FAX: (615) 353-2343. Meredith Broadcasting Group. GM: Francis DeTillio.

WTVF, Channel 5, CBS
474 James Robertson Pkwy., Nashville, TN 37219. (615) 244-5000. FAX: (615) 248-5353. Landmark Communications Inc. Lem Lewis.

WXMT Channel 30, IND
300 Peabody St., Nashville, TN 37210. (615) 256-3030. FAX: (615) 244-7442. MT Communications. Michael Thompson.

WZTV, Channel 17, FOX
631 Mainstream Dr., Nashville, TN 37228. (615) 244-1717. FAX: (615) 259-3962. Act III Broadcasting Inc. Richard Ballinger.

WHTN (Murfreesboro), Channel 39, IND
14346 Lebanon Rd., Old Hickory, TN 37138. (615) 754-0037. FAX: (615) 754-0047. Christian Television Network. Bob D'Andrea.

WSJK-TV, Channel 2, PBS
(see WKOP, Knoxville). Sneedville, TN. E. Tennessse Public Communications.

TEXAS

KRBC-TV, Channel 9, NBC
P. O. Box 178, Abilene, TX 79604. (915) 692-4242. FAX: (915) 692-8265. Abilene Radio & TV Stations. Ken Knox.

KTAB-TV, Channel 32, CBS
5401 S. 14th St., Abilene, TX 79606. (915) 695-2777. FAX: (915) 695-9922. Shamrock Broadcasting Inc. Wayne Roy.

KTXS-TV (Sweetwater), Channel 12, ABC
P. O. Box 2997, Abilene, TX 79604. (915) 677-2281. Lamco Communications. Jackie Rutledge.

KHSH-TV, Channel 67, IND
2522 Highland Square Mall, Alvin, TX 77511. (713) 331-8867, Silver King Communications Inc. Barry Diller

KACV-TV, Channel 2, PBS
2408 S. Jackson, Amarillo, TX 79109. (806) 371-5222. FAX:
(806) 371-5258. Amarillo Junior College District. Station Mgr.:
Joyce Herring.

KAMR-TV, Channel 4, NBC
P. O. Box 751, Amarillo, TX 79189. (806) 383-3321. FAX: (806)
381-2943. Darrold Cannan Communications Inc. Darrold A.
Cannan.

KCIT, Channel 14, FOX
P. O. Box 1414, 1015 S. Fillmore, Amarillo, TX 79105. (806)
374-1414. FAX: (806) 371-0408. WBG License Co., LLC.
President: Pete D'Acosta.

KFDA-TV, Channel 10, CBS
P. O. Box 10, Amarillo, TX 79105-0010. (806) 383-1010. FAX:
(806) 383-6397. R.H. Drewry Group. Robert Drewry.

KVII-TV, Channel 7, ABC
One Broadcast Center, Amarillo, TX 79101. (806) 373-1787. FAX:
(806) 371-7329. Marsh Media Inc. Station Mgr.: Mac Douglas.

KEYE-TV, Channel 42, CBS
10700 Metric Blvd., Austin, TX 78758. (512) 835-0042. FAX:
(512) 837-6753. Granite Broadcasting Corp. Pres. & GM:
Dennis Upah.

KLRU-TV, Channel 18, PBS
P. O. Box 7158, Austin, TX 78713. (512) 471-4811. FAX: (512)
475-9090. Capital of TX Public Broadcasting. Bill Arhos.

KNVA, Channel 54, IND
P. O. Box 684647, Austin, TX 78768. (512) 478-5400. FAX:
(512) 476-1520. 54 Broadcasting Inc. Mark Goldberg.

KTBC-TV, Channel 7, FOX
119 E. 10th St., Austin, TX 78701. (512) 476-7777. FAX: (512)
495-7001. New World Communications Group Inc. Craig Millar.

KVUE-TV, Channel 24, ABC
3201 Steck Ave., Austin, TX 78757. (512) 459-6521. FAX: (512)
467-7503. Gannett Broadcasting. Sam Rosenwasser.

KXAN-TV, Channel 36, NBC
908 W. Martin Luther King Blvd., Austin, TX 78701. (512)
476-3636. FAX: (512) 476-1520. LIN Television Corp. Jane
Wallace.

KBMT, Channel 12, ABC
P. O. Box 1550, 525 I-10 S. Beaumont, TX 77704. (409)
833-7512. FAX: (409) 833-4007. McKinnon Broadcasting Co.
Michael McKinnon.

KFDM-TV, Channel 6, CBS
P. O. Box 7128, 2955 I-10 E., Beaumont, TX 77726-7128. (409)
892-6622. FAX: (409) 892-6665. Freedom Communications Inc.
Alan Bell.

KWAB, Channel 4, IND
2500 Kentucky Way, Big Spring, TX 79720. (915) 263-4901.
FAX: (915) 263-4901. Midessa Television. John Foster.

KVEO, Channel 23, NBC
394 N. Expressway, Brownsville, TX 78521. (210) 544-2323.
FAX: (210) 544-4636. Tom Galloway. Patti C. Smith.

KAMU-TV (College Station), Channel 15, PBS
Texas A & M University, Bryan, TX 77843. (409) 845-5611.
Texas A&M University. Rodney L. Zent.

KBTX-TV, Channel 3, CBS
Drawer 3730, Bryan, TX 77805. (409) 846-7777. FAX: (409)
846-1490. KWTX Broadcasting Co. Thomas Pears.

KYLE, Channel 28, IND
Suite 100, 820 Industrial Blvd., Bryan, TX 77803. (409)
823-2828. FAX: (409) 822-5511. Silent Minority Group Inc.
Roger B. Watkins.

KTRG (Del Rio), Channel 10, IND
P. O. Box 276, River Road 1120, Concan, TX 78838. (210)
232-6700. FAX: (210) 232-6700. Thomas Gilchrist, Robert
Gilchrist.

NEW-TV, Channel 55, IND
200 Ave. J, Conroe, TX 77301. Imagists.

KEDT, Channel 16, PBS
Suite 38, 4455 S. Padre Island Dr., Corpus Christi, TX 78411.
(512) 855-2213. FAX: (512) 855-3877. South Texas Public
Broadcasting. Robert Valarius.

KIII, Channel 3, ABC
P. O. Box 6669, Corpus Christi, TX 78466. (512) 854-4733.
FAX: (512) 855-8419. McKinnon Broadcasting Co. Pres.:
Michael D. McKinnon.

KORO, Channel 28, UNI
102 N. Mesquite, Corpus Christi, TX 78401. (512) 883-2823.
FAX: (512) 883-2931. Telecorpus Inc. Jose R. De Leon.

KRIS-TV, Channel 6, NBC
P. O. Box 840, Corpus Christi, TX 78403. (512) 886-6100. FAX:
(512) 887-6666. T. Frank Smith, Jr.

KZTV, Channel 10, CBS
P. O. Box TV-10, 301 Artesian, Corpus Christi, TX 78403. (512)
883-7070. FAX: (512) 882-8553. Corpus Christi Broadcasting
Inc. Vann M. Kennedy.

KDAF, Channel 33, IND
8001 Carpenter Fwy., Dallas, TX 75247. (214) 640-3300. FAX:
(214) 640-3409. Renaissance Communications Corp. Joseph
A. Young.

KDFI-TV, Channel 27, IND
400 N. Griffin St., Dallas, TX 75202. (214) 720-3849. FAX:
(214) 720-3263. Dallas Media Investors Corp. Ray Lucky.

KDFW-TV, Channel 4, FOX
400 N. Griffin St., Dallas, TX 75202. (214) 720-4444. FAX:
(214) 720-3177. New World Communications Group, Inc. C.
David Whitaker.

KERA-TV, Channel 13, PBS
3000 Harry Hines Blvd., Dallas, TX 75201. (214) 871-1390.
FAX: (214) 754-0635. Texas Public Broadcasting Inc. Richard J.
Meyer.

KTXA (Arlington), Channel 21, IND
Suite 700, 601 Pacific Ave., Dallas, TX 75202. (214) 743-2100.
FAX: (214) 763-2121. Paramount Communications Inc. Rick
Mills.

KXTX-TV, Channel 39, IND
P. O. Box 190307, 3900 Harry Hines Blvd., Dallas, TX 75219.
(214) 521-3900. FAX: (214) 533-5946. U.S. Media Corp. Nancy
Dervin.

WFAA-TV, Channel 8, ABC
Communication Ctr., 606 Young St., Dallas, TX 75202-4810.
(214) 748-9631. FAX: (214) 977-6268. A.H. Belo Corp. Cathy
Creany.

KTEN, Channel 10, ABC
101 E. Main St., Denison, TX 75020. (903) 465-5836. FAX:
(903) 465-5859. Tom L. Johnson.

KDTN, Channel 2, PBS
(see KERA, Dallas). Denton, TX. Community Board of
Directors.

KTFH, Channel 49, IND
Suite 49, 256 N. Sam Pkwy., E. Houston, TX 77060. (713)
820-4900. FAX: (713) 820-4048. Paxson Communications
Corp. Roger Ramirez.

KVAW, Channel 16, IND
P. O. Box 788, Eagle Pass, TX 78852. (210) 757-0316. Juan
Wheeler, Jr.

KCOS, Channel 13, PBS
Rm. 105 Education Bldg., Univ of Texas-El Paso, El Paso, TX
79902. (915) 747-6500. FAX: (915) 747-6605. El Paso Public
TV Foundation. Maria Lelena.

KDBC-TV, Channel 4, CBS
2201 Wyoming, El Paso, TX 79903. (915) 532-6551. FAX: (915)
544-2591. Imes Communications. Jim Grimes.

KFOX-TV, Channel 14, FOX
6004 N. Mesa, El Paso, TX 79912. (915) 833-8585. FAX: (915)
833-8942. KCIK-TV Inc. Don Caparis.

KINT-TV, Channel 26, UNI
5426 N. Mesa, El Paso, TX 79912. (915) 581-1126. FAX: (915)
581-1393. Paso Del Norte Broadcasting Corp. Martino Silva.

KJLF-TV, Channel 65, IND
5925 Cromo Dr., El Paso, TX 79912. (915) 833-0065. FAX:
(915) 584-8005. UN2JC Communications. Sara Diaz Warren.

KSCE, Channel 38, NFP
6400 Escondido Dr., El Paso, TX 79912. (915) 585-8838. FAX:
(915) 533-7403. Channel 38 Christian Television. Andrew
Paschall.

KTSM-TV, Channel 9, NBC
801 N. Oregon St., El Paso, TX 79902. (915) 532-5421. FAX:
(915) 532-6793. El Paso Community Foundation. Richard
Pearson.

KVIA-TV, Channel 7, NBC
4140 Rio Bravo, El Paso, TX 79902. (915) 532-7777. FAX:
(915) 532-0070. NPG of Texas L.P. Art Olivas.

XHIJ (Ciudad Juarez, Mex), Channel 44, TEL
Suite 200, 1790 Lee Trevino, El Paso, TX 79936. (915)
598-0440. FAX: (915) 598-1485. Arnoldo Cabada De la O.
Sergio Cabada.

KTVT, Channel 11, IND
5233 Bridge St., Fort Worth, TX 76103. (817) 451-1111. FAX: (817) 457-1897. Gaylord Broadcasting Co. Ed Trimble.

KXAS-TV, Channel 5, NBC
3900 Barnett, Fort Worth, TX 76103. (214) 745-5555. FAX: (817) 654-6362. LIN Television Corp. Douglas Adams.

KUVN, Channel 23, UNI
3720 Marquis Dr., Garland, TX 75042. (214) 485-2323. Perenchio Television Inc. Mario M. Carrera.

KTAQ, Channel 47, IND
P. O. Box 8383, Greeneville, TX 75404. (903) 455-8847. FAX: (903) 455-8891. Mike Simons.

KGBT-TV, Channel 4, CBS
9201 W. Expressway 83, Harlingen, TX 78552. (210) 421-4444. FAX: (210) 421-2318. Draper Communications Inc. Thomas H. Draper.

KLUJ, Channel 44, IND
1920 AL Coneway Dr., Harlingen, TX 78550. (210) 425-4225. FAX: (210) 412-1740. Community Educational TV Inc. Dr. Reginald Cherry.

KMBH, Channel 60, PBS
1701 Tennessee St., Harlingen, TX 78550. (210) 421-4111. FAX: (210) 421-4150. RGV Educational Broadcasting Inc. John E. Harris III.

KETH, Channel 14, IND
10902 S. Wilcrest Dr., Houston, TX 77099. (713) 561-5828. FAX: (713) 561-9793. Community Educational TV of Houston. Velma Marlin.

KHOU-TV, Channel 11, CBS
9145 Allen Pkwy., Houston, TX 77019. (713) 526-1111. FAX: (713) 521-4326. A.H. Belo Corp. Broadcast Division. Allan E. Howard.

KHTV, Channel 39, WB
7700 Westpark Dr., Houston, TX 77063. (713) 781-3939. FAX: (713) 781-3441. Tribune Broadcasting Co. GM: David Tynan.

KLTJ (Galveston), Channel 22, IND
1050 Gemini, Houston, TX 77058. (713) 212-1077. FAX: (713) 212-1022. GO Inc. Eldred Thomas.

KNWS-TV (Katy), Channel 51, IND
8440 Westpark, Houston, TX 77063. (713) 974-5151. FAX: (713) 975-6397. Douglas R. Johnson.

KPRC-TV, Channel 2, NBC
8181 Southwest Fwy., Houston, TX 77074. (713) 222-2222. FAX: (713) 270-9334. Post-Newsweek Stations Inc. Steve Wasserman.

KRIV, Channel 26, FOX
3935 Westheimer Rd., Houston, TX 77027. (713) 626-2610. FAX: (713) 625-1809. Fox Television Stations Inc. Jerry Marcus.

KTMD (Galveston), Channel 48, TEL
3903 Stoney Brook, Houston, TX 77063. (713) 974-4848. FAX: (713) 974-5875. Telemundo Group Inc. Station Mgr.: Luis Fernandez-Roch.

KTRK-TV, Channel 13, ABC
3310 Bissonnet Rd., Houston, TX 77005. (713) 666-0713. FAX: (713) 668-0024. Cap Cities/ABC Broadcast Group. James Masucci.

KTXH, Channel 20, IND
8950 Kirby Dr., Houston, TX 77054. (713) 661-2020. FAX: (713) 665-3909. Paramount Communications Inc. Mike Dunlop.

KUHT, Channel 8, PBS
4513 Cullen Blvd., Houston, TX 77004. (713) 748-8888. FAX: (713) 749-8216. U of Houston, Board of Regents. Jeff Clarke.

KVVV (Baytown), Channel 57, IND
1044 Hercules Ln., Houston, TX 77058. (713) 286-4245. FAX: (713) 286-4541. VVI Baytown Inc. Bob Johander.

KXLN-TV (Rosenberg), Channel 45, UNI
9440 Kirby Dr., Houston, TX 77054. (713) 662-4545. FAX: (713) 668-9054. Perenchio Television Inc. Jose A. Trevino.

KDTX-TV (Dallas), Channel 58, IND
2823 W. Irving Blvd., Irving, TX 75061-4236. (214) 313-1333. FAX: (214) 790-5853. Trinity Broadcasting of Texas Inc. Paul F. Crouch.

KFWD (Fort Worth), Channel 52, TEL
3000 W. Story Rd., Irving, TX 75038. (214) 255-5200. FAX: (214) 258-1770. Interspan Communications L.P. Wayne Casa.

KHSX-TV, Channel 49, IND
1957 E. Irving Blvd., Irving, TX 75060. (214) 579-4900. FAX: (214) 579-1105. Silver King Communications Inc. Jim Lawless.

KRRT, Channel 35, IND
(see KABB, San Antonio). Kerrville, TX. The Jet Broadcasting Co. David Boaz.

KNCT (Belton), Channel 46, PBS
P. O. Box 1800, Killeen, TX 76540-1800. (817) 526-1176. FAX: (817) 526-4000. Central Texas College. Jose Fajardo.

KGNS-TV, Channel 8, NBC
P. O. Box 2829, 120 W. Del Mar Blvd., Laredo, TX 78045. (210) 727-8888. FAX: (210) 727-5336. Century Development Inc. Malcolm Glazer.

KLDO-TV, Channel 27, TEL
Riverdrive Mall, 1600 Water St., Laredo, TX 78040. (210) 727-0027. FAX: (210) 727-2673. Panorama Broadcasting Co. Oscar M. Laurel.

KVTV, Channel 13, CBS
P. O. Box 2039, 2600 Shea & Ana, Laredo, TX 78041. (210) 723-2923. FAX: (210) 723-0474. K-SIX TV Inc. Vann M. Kennedy.

KLDT (Lake Dallas), Channel 55, IND
2450 Rockbrook, Lewisville, TX 75067. (214) 316-7000. KLDT-TV 55 Inc. Opal Thornton.

KXAM-TV, Channel 14, NBC
(see KXAN, Austin). Llano, TX. KXAN Inc.

KFXK, Channel 51, FOX
701 N. Access Rd., Longview, TX 75602. (903) 236-0051. FAX: (903) 753-6637. Warwick Communications, Inc. Ed Stanton.

KAMC, Channel 28, ABC
1201 84th St., Lubbock, TX 79423. (806) 745-2828. FAX: (806) 748-1080. McAlister TV Enterprises Inc. Pres. & GM: Greg McAlister.

KCBD-TV, Channel 11, NBC
5600 Avenue A, Lubbock, TX 79404. (806) 744-1414. FAX: (806) 744-0449. Holsum Inc. V.P. & GM: Bill de Tournillon.

KJTV, Channel 34, FOX
9800 University Ave., Lubbock, TX 79423. (806) 745-3434. FAX: (806) 748-1949. Raymar Communications Inc. Ray Moran.

KLBK-TV, Channel 13, CBS
7403 S. University Ave., Lubbock, TX 79423. (806) 745-2345. FAX: (806) 748-2250. Petracom Broadcasting of TX, Inc. GM: Rick Lipps

KMZN (Farwell), Channel 18, IND
P. O. Box 3757, Lubbock, TX 79452. Ramar Communications Inc. Troy Ray Moran.

KTXT-TV, Channel 5, PBS
P. O. Box 42161, Tech Stn., 17th St. & Indiana Ave., Lubbock, TX 79409-2161. (806) 742-2209. FAX: (806) 742-1274. Texas Tech University. John Henson.

KTRE, Channel 9, ABC
P. O. Box 729, Lufkin, TX 75902. (409) 853-5873. FAX: (409) 853-3084. Civic Communication Corp. Frank Melton.

KITU (Beaumont), Channel 34, IND
P. O. Box 158, Mauriceville, TX 77626. (409) 745-3434. FAX: (409) 745-4752. Community Educational TV Inc. Dr. Reginal Cherry.

KNVO, Channel 48, UNI
Suite 850, 1800 S. Main St., McAllen, TX 78503. (210) 687-4848. FAX: (210) 687-7784. Rosalie Goldberg, Larry Safir.

KMID, Channel 2, ABC
P. O. Box 60230, 3200 Laforce Blvd., Midland, TX 79711. (915) 563-2222. FAX: (915) 563-5819. Cottonwood Communications L.L.C. Don Hale.

KPTB* (Lubbock), Channel 16, NFP
P. O. Box 61000, Midland, TX 79711. Primetime Christian Broadcasting. Albert Fuentes.

KLSB-TV, Channel 19, NBC
204 W. Main St., Nacogdoches, TX 75961. (409) 564-1911. FAX: (409) 569-1595. Region 56 Television Network Inc. Eva Brown.

KMLM, Channel 42, NFP
P. O. Box 61000, 3719 S. CR 1305, Odessa, TX 79765. (915) 563-0420. FAX: (915) 563-1736. Prime Time Christian Broadcasting. Al Cooper.

KOCV-TV, Channel 36, PBS
201 W. University, Odessa, TX 79764. (915) 335-6336. FAX: (915) 339-0529. Odessa Junior College District. John McCarroll.

KOSA-TV, Channel 7, CBS
1211 N. Whitaker, Odessa, TX 79760. (915) 580-5672. FAX: (915) 580-8010. Brissette Broadcasting Corp. Paul Brissette.

KPEJ, Channel 24, FOX
1550 W. I-20, Odessa, TX 79763. (915) 337-2424. FAX: (915) 337-3707. Associated Broadcasters Inc. James Beeghley.

KWES-TV, Channel 9, NBC
P. O. Box 60150, 11320 County Rd., 127 W. Midland, Odessa, TX 79711-0150. (915) 567-9999. FAX: (915) 567-9992. R.H. Drewry Group. John L. Foster.

KJAC-TV, Channel 4, NBC
P. O. Box 3257, Port Arthur, TX 77643. (409) 985-5557. FAX: (409) 832-2444. U.S.Broadcast Group LLC. V.P. & GM: Ron Kelly.

KACB-TV, Channel 3, NBC
(see KRBC, Abilene). San Angelo, TX.

KIDY, Channel 6, FOX
406 S. Irving, San Angelo, TX 76903. (915) 655-6006. FAX: (915) 655-8461. Raymond Schindler. Bill Carter.

KLST, Channel 8, CBS
2800 Armstrong, San Angelo, TX 76903. (915) 949-8800. FAX: (915) 658-4006. Jewell Television Corp. Tedford Kimbell.

KABB, Channel 29, FOX
4335 N.W. Loop 410, San Antonio, TX 78229-5168. (210) 366-1129. FAX: (210) 377-4758. River City Broadcasting. Barry Baker.

KENS-TV, Channel 5, CBS
5400 Fredericksburg Rd., San Antonio, TX 78229. (210) 366-5000. FAX: (210) 377-0740. Harte-Hanks Communications. Michael J. Conly.

KHCE, Channel 23, IND
326 Sterling Browning Dr., San Antonio, TX 78232. (210) 496-2323. Hispanic Community Educational Television Inc. Delfino F. Sanchez.

KLRN, Channel 9, PBS
501 Broadway, San Antonio, TX 78215. (210) 270-9000. FAX: (210) 270-9078. Alamo Public Telecomm. Council. Joanne Winik.

KMOL-TV, Channel 4, NBC
1031 Navarro, San Antonio, TX 78205. (210) 226-4444. FAX: (210) 223-5693. Chris Craft Industries Inc. Robert P. Donohue.

KSAT-TV, Channel 12, ABC
1408 N. St. Mary's St., San Antonio, TX 78215. (210) 351-1200. FAX: (210) 351-1297. Post-Newsweek Stations Inc. James Joslyn.

KVDA, Channel 60, TEL
6234 San Pedro, San Antonio, TX 78216. (210) 340-8860. FAX: (210) 341-3962. Telemundo Group Inc. Arthur Emerson.

KWEX-TV, Channel 41, UNI
411 E. Durango Blvd., San Antonio, TX 78204. (210) 227-4141. FAX: (210) 227-0469. Perenchio Television Inc. Steve Giust.

KXII, Channel 12, CBS
P. O. Box 1175, 4201 Texoma Pkwy., Sherman, TX 75090. (903) 892-8123. FAX: (903) 893-7858. KXII Broadcasters Inc. M.N. Bostick.

KCEN-TV, Channel 6, NBC
17 S. Third, Temple, TX 76503-6103. (817) 773-6868. FAX: (817) 770-0204. Anyse Sue Mayborn, Gayle Kiger.

KETK-TV, Channel 56, NBC
4300 Richmond Rd., Tyler, TX 75703. (903) 581-5656. FAX: (903) 561-1648. Lone Star Broadcasting Inc. Station Mgr.: Philip H. Hurley.

KLTV, Channel 7, ABC
105 West Ferguson, Tyler, TX 75702. (903) 597-5588. FAX: (903) 510-7847. Civic Communication Corp. Brad Streit.

KAVU-TV, Channel 25, ABC
3808 N. Navarro, Victoria, TX 77901. (512) 575-2500. FAX: (512) 575-2255. Withers Broadcasting Co. W. Russell Withers, Jr.

KCTF, Channel 34, PBS
Sid Richardson Biology Bldg., Baylor Univ., Waco TX 76798. (817) 755-3472. FAX: (817) 755-3874. Brazos Valley Pub. Broadcasting. Sylvia Avey.

KWKT, Channel 44, FOX
8803 Woodway Dr., Waco TX 76712. (817) 776-3844. FAX: (817) 776-8032. Associated Broadcasters Inc. Ron Crowder.

KWTX-TV, Channel 10, CBS
6700 American Plaza, Waco TX 76712. (817) 776-1330. FAX: (817) 751-1088. KWTX Broadcasting Co. Thomas G. Pears.

KXXV, Channel 25, ABC
1909 S. New Rd., Waco TX 76711. (817) 754-2525. R.H. Drewry Group. Jeff Cook.

KRGV-TV, Channel 5, ABC
900 E. Expwy., Weslaco TX 78599. (210) 968-5555. FAX: (210) 973-5001. Manship Stations. Douglas Manship.

KAUZ-TV, Channel 6, CBS
One Broadcast Ave., Wichita Falls, TX 76307. (817) 322-6957. FAX: (817) 761-3331. Benedek Broadcasting Corp. Mark Cummings.

KFDX-TV, Channel 3, NBC
4500 Seymour Hwy., Wichita Falls, TX 76309. (817) 692-4530. FAX: (817) 691-4384. U.S.Broadcast Group. V.P. & GM: Andy Lee.

KJTL, Channel 18, FOX
P. O. Box 4865, 3800 Call Field Rd., Wichita Falls, TX 76308. (817) 691-1808. FAX: (817) 696-5766. BSP Broadcasting Inc. Peter D'Acosta.

KVCT (Victoria), Channel 19, FOX
980 FM 1746, Woodville, TX 75979-9609. (409) 429-3679. FAX: (409) 429-5257. Gerald R. Proctor.

UTAH

KOOG-TV, Channel 30, IND
1209 16th St., Ogden, UT 84404. (801) 621-3030. FAX: (801) 394-1451. Alpha & Omega Communications L.L.C. Vicky Bojanski.

KULC, Channel 9, PBS
(see KUED, Salt Lake City). Ogden. UT. (801) 581-4194. FAX: (801) 585-6105. Utah State Board of Regents. Helen Lacy.

KBYU-TV, Channel 11, PBS
2000 E. Ironto Blvd., Provo, UT 84606. (801) 378-8450. FAX: (801) 378-8478. Brigham Young University. John Reim.

KZAR-TV, Channel 16, IND
(see WHSL, St. Louis, MO). Provo. UT. Royal Television of Utah Inc.

KJZZ-TV, Channel 14, UPN
5181 Amelia Earhart Dr., Salt Lake City, UT 84116. (801) 537-1414. FAX: (801) 238-6414. Larry H. Miller. V.P. & GM: Randy Rigby.

KSL-TV, Channel 5, NBC
P. O. Box 1160, KSL-TV, Broadcast House, Salt Lake City, UT 84110-1160. (801) 575-5500. FAX: (801) 575-5830. Bonneville International Corp. Pres.: Allan Henderson.

KSTU, Channel 13, FOX
5020 W. Amelia Earhart Dr., Salt Lake City, UT 84116. (801) 532-1300. FAX: (801) 537-5335. Fox Television Stations Inc. Steve Carlston.

KTVX, Channel 4, ABC
1760 Fremont Dr., Salt Lake City, UT 84104. (801) 975-4444. FAX: (801) 975-4442. Chris Craft Industries Inc. Evan C. Thompson.

KUED, Channel 7, PBS
101 Wasatch Dr., Salt Lake City, UT 84112. (801) 581-7777. FAX: (801) 581-5620. University of Utah. Fred Esplin.

KUTV, Channel 2, CBS
2185 S. 3600 W., Salt Lake City, UT 84119. (801) 973-3000. FAX: (801) 973-3369. KUTV Associates. V.P. & Station Mgr.: David Phillips.

KSGI-TV, Channel 4, IND
P. O. Box 1450, 210 N. 1000 E., St. George, UT 84771. (801) 628-1000. FAX: (801) 628-6636. Seagull Communications Corp. Owner & GM: E. Morgan Skinner, Jr.

KUSG, Channel 12, CBS
(see KUTV, Salt Lake City). St. George. UT. (801) 973-3115. FAX: (801) 973-3387. KUTV L.P.

VERMONT

WCAX-TV, Channel 3, CBS
P. O. Box 608, Burlington, VT 05402. (802) 658-6300. FAX: (802) 658-0529. S.T. Martin & Family. Stuart T. Martin.

WETK, Channel 33, PBS
(see Vermont Educational Television, Colchester). Burlington, VT. Vermont Educational Television Inc.

WVNY, Channel 22, ABC
P. O. Box 22, 100 Market Square, Burlington, VT 05401. (802) 658-8022. FAX: (802) 865-9976. U.S. Broadcast Group. Pres.: Raymond Schonback.

Vermont Educational Television, PBS
88 Ethan Allen Ave., Colchester, VT 05446-3129. (802) 655-4800. Hope S. Green.

WFFF-TV (Burlington), Channel 44, IND
29 Orchard Dr., Colchester, VT 05446. (802) 872-2839. Champlain Valley Telecasting Inc. John Nichols.

WVER, Channel 28, PBS
(see Vermont Educational Television, Colchester). Rutland, VT. Vermont Educational Television Inc.

WVTB, Channel 20, PBS
(see Vermont Educational Television, Colchester). St. Johnsbury, VT. Vermont Educational Television Inc.

WNNE-TV, Channel 31, NBC
P. O. Box 1310, White River Junction, VT 05001. (802) 295-3100. FAX: (802) 295-9056. Heritage Media Corp. Robert Shields.

WVTA, Channel 41, PBS
(see Vermont Educational Television, Colchester). Windsor, VT. Vermont Educational Television Inc.

VIRGINIA

WTMW, Channel 14, IND
3565 Lee Hwy., Arlington, VA 22207. (703) 528-0051. FAX: (703) 528-2956. Theodore White.

WCYB-TV, Channel 5, NBC
101 Lee St., Bristol, VA 24201. (703) 645-1555. FAX: (703) 645-1553. Appalachian Broadcasting Corp. Exec V.P. & GM: Joe Macione Jr.

WHTJ, Channel 41, PBS
P. O. Box 2021, 300 Preston Ave., 4th Fl., Charlottesville, VA 22902. (804) 320-1301. FAX: (804) 320-8729. Central Virginia Educational TV Communications. Dr. Charles W. Sydnor Jr.

WVIR-TV, Channel 29, NBC
P. O. Box 769, 503 E. Market St., Charlottesville, VA 22902. (804) 977-7082. FAX: (804) 971-2800. Waterman Broadcasting Corp. Harold B. Wright Jr.

WDRG, Channel 24, IND
713 Piney Forest Rd., Danville, VA 24541. (804) 791-2424. FAX: (804) 791-1056. Danville Television Partnership. Mel Eleazer.

WNVC, Channel 56, IND
8101A Lee Hwy., Falls Church, VA 22042. (703) 698-9682. FAX: (703) 849-9796. Central Virginia Educational Television Communications. Dr. Charles W. Sydnor Jr.

WNVT Channel 53, PBS
8101A Lee Hwy., Falls Church, VA 22042. (703) 698-9682. FAX: (703) 849-9796. Central Virginia Educational Television Communications. Dr. Charles W. Sydnor Jr.

WLFG, Channel 68, NFP
(see Living Faith Ministries, Vansant). Grundy, VA. Tookland Pentecostal Church.

WJCB (Norfolk), Channel 49, NFP
Suite 2C, 910 W. Mercury Blvd., Hampton, VA 23666. (804) 838-4949. FAX: (804) 838-4840. Tidewater Christian Communications. Hugo A. Owens Sr.

WHSV-TV, Channel 3, ABC
P. O. Box TV 3, Hwy. 33 W., Harrisonburg, VA 22801-0030. (540) 433-9191. FAX: (540) 433-4028. Benedek Broadcasting Co. Robert Smith.

WVPT (Staunton), Channel 51, PBS
298 Port Republic Rd., Harrisonburg, VA 22801. (540) 434-5391. Shenandoah Valley Educational Television Corp. Arthur E. Albrecht.

WJPR, Channel 21, FOX
(see WFXR, Roanoke). Lynchburg, VA. Grant Broadcasting System II Inc.

WSET-TV, Channel 13, ABC
2320 Langhorne Rd., Lynchburg, VA 24501. (804) 528-1313. FAX: (804) 847-0458. Allbritton Communications Co. Jerry Heilman.

WVVI, Channel 66, IND
9008 Center St., Manassas, VA 22110. (703) 631-2310. FAX: (703) 361-0795. Robert L. Johander, Mike Jones.

WHRO-TV (Hampton-Norfolk), Channel 15, PBS
5200 Hampton Blvd., Norfolk, VA 23508. (804) 889-9400. FAX: (804) 489-0007. Hampton Roads Educ. Telecomm. Assn. John Morison.

WTKR, Channel 3, CBS
720 Boush St., Norfolk, VA 23510. (804) 446-1000. FAX: (804) 622-1113. The New York Times Co. Elden A. Hale, Jr.

WTVZ, Channel 33, FOX
900 Granby St., Norfolk, VA 23510. (804) 622-3333. FAX: (804) 623-1541. Sinclair Broadcast Group Inc. Steves Markes.

WVEC-TV (Hampton), Channel 13, ABC
613 Woodis Ave., Norfolk, VA 23510. (804) 625-1313. FAX: (804) 628-6220, A.H. Belo Corp. Broadcast Division. V.P. & GM: Rick Keith.

WAVY-TV, Channel 10, NBC
300 Wavy St., Portsmouth, VA 23704. (804) 393-1010. FAX: (804) 399-7628. LIN Television Corp. Edward L. Munson Jr.

WGNT, Channel 27, IND
1318 Spratley St., Portsmouth, VA 23704.(804) 393-2501. FAX: (804) 399-3303. Centennial Communications Inc. Raymond Bottom.

WAWB (Ashland), Channel 65, IND
4120 E. Parham Rd., Richmond, VA 23228. (804) 672-6565. FAX: (804) 672-6571. Christel Broadcasting Inc. Jim Campana.

WCVE-TV, Channel 23, PBS
23 Sesame St., Richmond, VA 23235. (804) 320-1301. FAX: (804) 320-8729. Central VA Educational Telcomm Corp. Dr. Charles W. Sydnor Jr.

WRIC-TV, Channel 8, ABC
301 Arboretum Pl., Richmond, VA 23236-3464. (804) 330-8888. FAX: (804) 330-8882. Young Broadcasting Inc. Tom Best.

WRLH-TV, Channel 35, FOX
1925 Westmoreland St., Richmond, VA 23230. (804) 358-3535. FAX: (804) 359-3510. Act III Broadcasting Inc. Don Richards.

WTVR-TV, Channel 6, CBS
3301 W. Broad St., Richmond, VA 23230. (804) 254-3600. FAX: (804) 254-3699. Park Communications Inc. Mark Keown.

WWBT, Channel 12, NBC
5710 Midlothian Tpke., Richmond, VA 23225. (804) 230-1212. FAX: (804) 230-2500. Jefferson-Pilot Communications Co. GM: John R. Shreves, Jr.

WBRA-TV, Channel 15, PBS
1215 McNeil Dr. S.W., Roanoke, VA 24015. (540) 344-0994. FAX: (540) 344-2148. Blue Ridge Public Television Inc. Donald Piedmont.

WDBJ, Channel 7, CBS
2001 Colonial Ave., Roanoke, VA 24015. (540) 344-7000. FAX: (540) 344-5097. Schurz Communications Inc. Robert G. Lee.

WEFC, Channel 38, IND
612 Bullitt Ave. S.E., Roanoke, VA 24013. (540) 982-3696. FAX: (540) 345-8568. Vine & Branch Inc. C. Kenneth Wright.

WFXR-TV, Channel 27, FOX
2618 Colonial Ave. SW, Roanoke, VA 24015. (540) 344-2127. FAX: (540) 345-1912. Grant Broadcasting System II Inc. Pres.: Milt Grant.

WMSY-TV (Marion), Channel 52, PBS
P. O. Box 13246, 1215 McNeil Dr., Roanoke, VA 24032. (540) 344-0991. FAX: (540) 344-2148. Blue Ridge Public Television Inc. Donald Piedmont.

WSBN-TV (Norton), Channel 47, PBS
P. O. Box 13246, Roanoke, VA 24032. (540) 344-0991. FAX: (540) 344-2148. Blue Ridge Public Television Inc. Donald Piedmont.

WSLS-TV, Channel 10, NBC
401 3rd St. N.W., Roanoke, VA 24011. (703) 981-9110. FAX: (703) 343-3157. Park Communications Inc. Don Tomlin.

WASHINGTON

WBEH*, Channel 51, IND
P. O. Box 3765, Bellevue, WA 98009-3765. Darlene C. McHenry.

KBCB (Bellingham), Channel 64, IND
c/o Frank Washington, Suite 211, 601 University Ave., Sacramento, CA 95825. (916) 921-2290. FAX: 916-921-2085. Prism Broadcasting Corp. Larry Rogow.

KVOS-TV, Channel 12, IND
1151 Ellis St., Bellingham, WA 98225. (360) 671-1212. FAX: (604) 647-0824. Ackerly Communications Inc. David Reid.

KCKA, Channel 15, PBS
(see KBTC, Tacoma). Centralia, WA. State Board, Community & Tech Coll.

KNDU (Richland), Channel 25, NBC
3312 W. Kennewick Ave., Kennewick, WA 99336. (809) 783-6151. FAX: (509) 783-3746. Farragut Communications Inc. Marvin L. Shapiro.

KVEW, Channel 42, ABC
601 N. Edison, Kennewick, WA 99336. (509) 735-8369. FAX: (509) 735-8369. Morgan Murphy Stations. Darrell Blue.

KEPR-TV, Channel 19, CBS
2807 W. Lewis, Pasco WA 99301. (509) 547-0547. FAX: (509) 547-2845. Retlaw Broadcasting Co. Ben Tucker.

KWSU-TV, Channel 10, PBS
Murrow Communications Ctr., Washington State Univ., Pullman, WA 99164-2530. (509) 335-6511. FAX: (509) 335-3772. Washington State University. Dennis Haarsager.

KTNW, Channel 31, PBS
(see KWSU, Pullman). Richland, WA. Washington State University.

KCTS-TV, Channel 9, PBS
401 Mercer, Seattle, WA 98109. (206) 728-6463. FAX: (206) 443-6691. KCTS Television. Burnill Clark.

KING-TV, Channel 5, NBC
333 Dexter Ave. N., Seattle, WA 98109. (206) 448-5555. FAX: (206) 448-3936. Providence Journal Broadcasting Co. Tony Twibell.

KIRO-TV, Channel 7, IND
P. O. Box C 21326, 2807 3rd Ave., Seattle, WA 98111-7000. (206) 728-7777. FAX: (206) 441-4840. A.H. Belo Corp. Station Mgr.: Glenn Wright.

KOMO-TV, Channel 4, ABC
100 Fourth Ave. N., Seattle, WA 98109. (206) 443-4000. FAX: (206) 443-4014. Fisher Broadcasting Inc. Pres. & CEO: Patrick Scott.

KSTW (Tacoma), Channel 11, CBS
2320 S. 19th St., Seattle, WA 98405. (206) 572-5789. FAX: (206) 272-7581. Gaylord Broadcasting Co. V.P. & GM: Kevin Hale.

KTZZ-TV, Channel 22, WB
945 Dexter Ave. N., Seattle, WA 98109. (206) 282-2202. FAX: (206) 281-0207. Dudley Communications Corp. Richard Dudley.

WBGE (Bellevue), Channel 33, IND
9620 Rainer Ave. S., Seattle, WA 98118. Robert Gill Communications L.P.

KAYU-TV, Channel 28, FOX
P. O. Box 30028, S. 4600 Regal St., Spokane, WA 99223. (509) 448-2828. FAX: (509) 448-3815. Salmon River Communcations L.P. Robert J. Hamacher.

KHQ-TV, Channel 6, NBC
4202 S. Regal Spokane, WA 99223-7738. (509) 448-6000. FAX: (509) 448-4694. James P. & William Stacey Cowles. Betsey Cowles

KREM-TV, Channel 2, CBS
4103 S. Regal Spokane, WA 99223. (509) 448-2000. FAX: (509) 448-2969. Providence Journal Broadcasting Co. Jack Clifford.

KSKN, Channel 22, IND
6213 N. Normandy, Spokane, WA 99205. (509) 535-8040. KSKN Inc. Steve Whitehead.

KSPS-TV, Channel 7, PBS
3911 S. Regal, Spokane, WA 99223. (509) 353-5777. Spokane School District No. 81. Claude Kistler.

KXLY-TV, Channel 4, ABC
500 W. Boone Ave., Spokane, WA 99201. (509) 324-4000. FAX: (509) 328-5274. Morgan Murphy Stations. V.P. & GM: Stephen R. Herling.

KBTC-TV, Channel 28, PBS
1101 S. Yakima, Tacoma, WA 98405. (206) 596-1528. FAX: (206) 596-1623. State Board, Community & Tech Coll. Debbie Emond.

KCPQ, Channel 13, FOX
400 Steilacoom Blvd., Tacoma, WA 98449. (206) 625-1313. FAX: (206) 383-9551. Kelly Broadcasting Co. GM: Roger Ottenbach.

KTBW-TV, Channel 20, IND
1909 S. 341st Pl., Federal Way, Tacoma, WA 98003. (206) 927-7000. FAX: (206) 874-7420. Trinity Broadcasting Network. Paul F. Crouch.

KWDK* (Tacoma), Channel 56, NFP
Suite 571, 2166 W. Broadway, Anaheim, CA 92804. Korean-American Missions Inc.

KPDX (Vancouver), Channel 49, FOX
910 N.E. M.L. King Blvd., Portland, OR 97232. (503) 239-4949. FAX: (503) 239-6184. First Media Television. William A. Schwartz.

KAPP, Channel 35, ABC
1610 S. 24th Ave., Yakima, WA 98902. (509) 453-0351. FAX: (509) 453-3623. Apple Valley Broadcasting. Elizabeth M. Burns.

KIMA-TV, Channel 29, CBS
2801 Terrace Heights Dr., Yakima, WA 98901. (509) 575-0029. FAX: (509) 248-1218. Retlaw Broadcasting Corp. Ben Tucker.

KNDO, Channel 23, NBC
1608 S. 24th Ave., Yakima, WA 98902. (509) 248-2300. FAX: (509) 575-0266. Farragut Communications Inc. Marvin L. Shapiro.

KYVE, Channel 47, PBS
1105 S. 15th Ave., Yakima, WA 98902. (509) 452-4700. FAX: (509) 452-4704. KCTS Television. Nancy Leahy.

WEST VIRGINIA

WSWP-TV (Grandview), Channel 9, PBS
P. O. Box A.H., Airport Rd., Beckley, WV 25802. (304) 255-1501. FAX: (304) 252-9797. WV Educational B'casting Authority. Ann Brotherton.

WLF, Channel 40, NFP
(see Living Faith Ministries, Vansant, VA). Bluefield, WV. Living Faith Ministries Inc.

WVVA Channel 6, NBC
P. O. Box 1930, Rt. 460 Bypass, Bluefield, WV 24701. (304) 325-5487. FAX: (304) 327-5586. Quincy Newspapers Inc. Tomas A. Oakley.

WDTV (Weston), Channel 5, CBS
5 Television Dr., Bridgeport, WV 26330. (304) 623-5555. FAX: (304) 842-7501. Withers Broadcasting Co. W. Russell Withers Jr.

WCHS-TV, Channel 8, ABC
1301 Piedmont Rd., Charleston, WV 25301. (304) 346-5358. FAX: (304) 346-4765. Heritage Media Corp. Dennis Adkins.

WBOY-TV, Channel 12, NBC
904 W. Pike St., Clarksburg, WV 26301. (304) 632-3311. FAX: (304) 624-6152. Imes Communications. Birney Imes.

WLYJ, Channel 46, NFP
P. O. Box 2544, 775 W. Pike St., Clarksburg, WV 26302. (304) 623-5784. Christian Communication Center Inc. Arthur Armstrong.

WOWK-TV, Channel 13, CBS
TV Center, 555 Fifth Ave., Huntington, WV 25701. (304) 525-1313. FAX: (304) 529-4910. Gateway Communications Inc. Lamont T. Pinker.

WPBY-TV, Channel 33, PBS
1615 Third Ave., Huntington, WV 25701. (304) 696-6630. FAX: (304) 696-4343. WV Educational Broadcasting Authority. Thomas K. Holleron.

WSAZ-TV, Channel 3, NBC
P. O. Box 2115, 645 Fifth Ave., Huntington, WV 25721. (304) 697-4780. FAX: (304) 697-4325. Lee Enterprises Inc. Richard D. Gottlieb.

WVAH-TV (Charleston), Channel 11, FOX
11 Broadcast Plaza, Hurricane, WV 25526. (304) 757-0011. FAX: (304) 757-7533. Act III Broadcasting Inc. Richard Ballinger.

WVGV-TV, Channel 59, IND
Rt. 2, P. O. Box 365, Houfnagle Rd., Lewisburg, WV 24901. (304) 645-5173. FAX: (304) 645-5177. WVGV-TV Corp. Sid Shumate.

WYVN, Channel 60, IND
One Discovery Pl., Martinsburg, WV 25401. (304) 264-9960. FAX: (304) 264-4618. Paxson Communications. CEO: Lowell Paxson.

WNPB-TV, Channel 24, PBS
191 Scott Ave., Morgantown, WV 26505. (304) 293-6511. FAX: (304) 293-2642. WV Educational Broadcasting Authority. Carolyn Bailey Lewis.

WOAY-TV, Channel 4, ABC
P. O. Box 251, Rte. 16 S., Oak Hill, WV 25901. (304) 469-3361. FAX: (304) 465-1420. Thomas Broadcasting Co. Robert R. THomas III.

WTAP-TV, Channel 15, NBC
One Television Plaza, Parkersburg, WV 26101. (304) 485-4588. FAX: (304) 422-3920. Benedek Broadcasting Corp. Keith Bland.

WTRF-TV, Channel 7, CBS
96 16th St., Wheeling, WV 26003. (304) 232-7777. FAX: (304) 232-4975. Benedek Broadcasting Corp. Pres. & GM: Jim Squibb Jr.

WISCONSIN

WEAU-TV, Channel 13, NBC
1907 S. Hastings Way, Eau Claire, WI 54701. (715) 835-1313.
FAX: (715) 832-0246. Busse Broadcasting Corp. Cheri Weinke.

WEUX (Chippewa Falls), Channel 48, FOX
1324 W. Clairemont Ave., Eau Claire, WI 54701. (715)
831-2548. Aries Telecommunication Corp. Nancy Martinson.

WQOW-TV, Channel 18, ABC
2881 S. Hastings Way, Eau Claire, WI 54701. (715) 835-1881.
FAX: (715) 835-8009. Tak Communications Inc. Chuck Ross.

WMMF-TV* (Fond du Lac), Channel 68, IND
500 S. Chinowth Rd., Visalia, CA 93277. 209-733-7800. FAX:
209-627-5363. Harry J. & Stella A. Pappas. Jarry J. Pappas

WACY (Appleton), Channel 32, UPN
P. O. Box 12328, Green Bay, WI 54307-2328. (414) 490-0320.
FAX: (414) 494-7071. Ace TV Inc. GM: Robert Cox

WBAY-TV, Channel 2, ABC
115 S. Jefferson, Green Bay, WI 54301. (414) 432-3331. FAX:
(414) 432-7808. Young Broadcasting Inc. Don Carmichael.

WFRV-TV, Channel 5, CBS
1181 E. Mason St., Green Bay, WI 54307-9055. (414)
437-5411. FAX: (414) 437-4576. CBS Station Group. R. Perry
Kidder.

WGBA, Channel 26, NBC
P. O. Box 19099, 1391 North Rd., Green Bay, WI 54307-9099.
(414) 494-2626. FAX: (414) 494-7071. Aries Telecommunication
Corp. GM: James L. Tomlin.

WLUK-TV, Channel 11, NBC
P. O. Box 19011, 787 Lombardi Ave., Green Bay, WI 54307-
9011. (414) 494-8711. FAX: (414) 494-8782. SF Broadcasting
L.L.C. James Schuessler.

WPNE Channel 38, PBS
(see WI Educ. Comm. Bd., Madison). Green Bay, WI.
Wisconsin Educational Communications Board.

WJNW* (Janesville), Channel 57, IND
483 N. Mulford Rd., Rockford, IL 61107. (815) 229-3600.
Harish Puri.

vWHKE, Channel 55, IND
4300 43rd Ave., Kenosha, WI 53144. (414) 657-9453. FAX:
(414) 656-7664. LeSea Broadcasting Inc. Lester Sumrall.

WKBT, Channel 8, CBS
141 S. 6th St., La Crosse, WI 54601. (608) 782-4678. FAX:
(608) 782-2892. Young Broadcasting Inc. Ronald J. Kwasnick.

WLAX, Channel 25, FOX
1305 Interchange Pl., La Crosse, WI 54603. (608) 781-0025.
FAX: (608) 781-1456. Aries Telecommunications Corp. Nancy
Martinsen.

WHLA-TV, Channel 31, PBS
(see WI Educ. Comm. Bd., Madison). Lacrosse, WI. Wisconsin
Educational Communications Board.

WWRS-TV (Mayville), Channel 52, IND
1750 W. Freedom Rd., Little Chute, WI 51540. (414) 687-0722.
TV-52 Inc. Lyle R. Evans.

WHA-TV, Channel 21, PBS
821 University Ave., Madison, WI 53706. (608) 263-2121. FAX:
(608) 263-9763. U. of Wisconsin Board of Regents. Byron
Knight.

WISC-TV, Channel 3, CBS
7025 Raymond Rd., Madison WI 53744-4965. (608) 271-4321,
Morgan Murphy Stations. Elizabeth Murphy Burns.

WKOW-TV, Channel 27, ABC
5727 Tokay Blvd., Madison, WI 53719. (608) 274-1234. FAX:
(608) 274-9514. Shockly Communications. GM: Robert
Miller

WMSN-TV, Channel 47, FOX
7847 Big Sky Dr., Madison, WI 53719. (608) 833-0047. FAX:
(608) 833-5055. Channel 47 L.P. GM: Jim Arnold.

WMTV, Channel 15, NBC
615 Forward Dr., Madison, WI 53711. (608) 274-1515. FAX:
(608) 271-5193. Brissette Broadcasting Corp. David Trabert.

Wisconsin Educational Communications Bd., PBS
3319 W. Beltline Hwy., Madison, WI 53713. (608) 264-9600.
FAX: (608) 264-9622. WI Educational Communications Board.
Byron Knight.

WHWC-TV, Channel 28, PBS
(see WI Educ. Comm. Bd., Madison). Menomonie, WI.
Wisconsin Educational Communications Board.

WCGV-TV, Channel 24, IND
4041 N. 35th St., Milwaukee, WI 53216. (414) 442-7050. FAX:
(414) 874-1899. Sinclair Broadcast Group. Alan Frank.

WDJT-TV, Channel 58, CBS
Suite 2500, 509 W. Wisconsin Ave., Milwaukee, WI 53203.
(414) 271-5800. FAX: (414) 272-1368. Weigel Broadcasting.
Irwin Starr.

WISN-TV, Channel 12, ABC
P. O. Box 402, Milwaukee, WI 53201. (414) 342-8812. FAX:
(414) 342-6490. Hearst Broadcasting Group. Howard Ritchie.

WITI-TV, Channel 6, FOX
P. O. Box 17600, 9001 N. Green Bay Rd., Milwaukee, WI
53217-0600. (414) 355-6666. FAX: (414) 362-2141. New World
Television. Andrew P. Potos.

WMVS, Channel 10, NFP
1036 N. 8th St., Milwaukee, WI 53233-1400. (414) 271-1036.
FAX: (414) 297-7536. Milwaukee Area Technical College.
William Bryce Combs.

WMVT, Channel 36, NFP
(see WMVS, Milwaukee). Milwaukee, WI. Milwaukee Area
Technical College.

WTMJ-TV, Channel 4, NBC
720 E. Capitol Dr., Milwaukee, WI 53212. (414) 332-9611. FAX:
(414) 223-5255. Journal Broadcast Group Inc. Douglas G. Kiel.

WVCY, Channel 30, IND
3434 W. Kilbourn Ave., Milwaukee, WI 53208. (414) 935-3000.
FAX: (414) 935-3015. VCY/America Inc. Randall Melchert.

WVTV, Channel 18, IND
4041 N. 35th St., Milwaukee, WI 53216. (414) 442-7050. FAX:
(414) 874-1899. Glencairn Ltd. Alan Frank.

WJJA (Racine), Channel 49, IND
P. O. Box 92, 4311 E. Oakwood Rd., Oak Creek, WI 53154.
(414) 764-4953. FAX: (414) 764-5190. TV-49 Inc. Joel Kinlow.

WLEF-TV, Channel 36, PBS
(see WI Educ. Comm. Bd., Madison). Park Falls, WI. Wisconsin
Educational Communications Board.

WFJW-TV, Channel 12, NBC
P. O. Box 858, S. Onieda Ave., Rhinelander, WI 54501. (715)
369-4700. FAX: (715) 369-1910. Seaway Communications Inc.
GM: Marie Fields.

WSCO, Channel 14, IND
(see WVCY, Milwaukee). Suring, WI 53208. VCY/America Inc.

WAOW-TV, Channel 9, ABC
1908 Grand Ave., Wausau, WI 54403-6897. (715) 842-2251.
FAX: (715) 848-0195. Shockley Communications Corp. Pres &
GM: Laurin Jorstad.

WHRM-TV, Channel 20, PBS
(see WI Educ. Comm. Bd., Madison). Wausau, WI. Wisconsin
Educational Communications Board.

WSAW-TV, Channel 7, CBS
1114 Grand Ave., Wausau, WI 54403. (715) 845-4211. FAX:
(715) 845-2649. Benedek Broadcasting Corp. Scott Chorski.

WYOMING

KFNB-TV, Channel 20, ABC
7075 Salt Creek Rd., Hwy. #1, Casper, WY 82601. (307)
577-5923. FAX: (307) 577-5928. WyoMedia Corp. Mark
Nalbone.

KGWC-TV, Channel 14, IND
304 N. Center, Casper, WY 82601. (307) 234-1111. FAX: (307)
234-2835. Stauffer Communications Inc. John H. Stauffer.

KGWC-TV, Channel 14, CBS
304 N. Center, Casper, WY 86201. (307) 234-1111. FAX: (307)
234-2835. Stauffer Communications Inc. John H. Stauffer.

KTWO-TV, Channel 2, NBC
4200 E. 2nd St., Casper, WY 82602. (307) 237-3711. FAX:
(307) 234-9866. Eastern Broadcasting Corp. GM: Al
Parsons.

KGWN-TV, Channel 5, IND
2923 E. Lincolnway, Cheyenne, WY 82001. (307) 634-7755.
FAX: (307) 637-8604. Stauffer Communications Inc. Billie
Morris.

KKTU, Channel 33, NBC
612 W. 17th Street, Cheyenne, WY 82001. (307) 632-2662.
FAX: (307) 632-8556. Eastern Broadcasting Corp. GM: Al
Parsons.

KLWY Channel 27, IND
(see KFNB, Casper). Cheyenne, WY. WyoMedia Corp.

KJVI, Channel 2, NBC
P. O. Box 7454, 970 N. Broadway, Jackson, WY 83002. (307) 733-2066. FAX: (307) 733-4834. Ambassador Media Group. Bill Armstrong.

KGWL-TV, Channel 5, CBS
(see KGWC, Casper). Lander, WY. Stauffer Communications Inc.

KFNR, Channel 11, ABC
(see KFNB, Casper). Rawlins, WY. First National Broadcasting Corp.

KCWC-TV (Lander), Channel 4, PBS
Central Wyoming College, 2660 Peck Ave., Riverton, WY 82501. (307) 856-9291. FAX: (307) 856-3893. Central Wyoming College. Gregory T. Ray.

KFNE, Channel 10, ABC
(see KFNB, Casper). Riverton, WY. First National Broadcasting Corp.

KSGW-TV, Channel 12, IND
(see KOTA, Rapid City SD). Sheridan, WY. Duhamel Broadcasting Enterprises.

U.S. TERRITORIES & POSSESSIONS

AMERICAN SAMOA

KVZK-2, Channel 2, PBS
KVZK-TV, American Samoa, 96799. (684) 633-4191. FAX: (684) 633-1044. The Govt. of American Samoa. Vaoita Savali.

KVZK-4, Channel 4, IND
(see KVZK-TV 2). American Samoa. The Govt. of American Samoa.

KVZK-5, Channel 5, IND
(see KVZK-TV 2). American Samoa. The Govt. of American Samoa.

GUAM

KGTF, Channel 12, PBS
P. O. Box 21449, Agana, GU 96921 (671) 734-2207. FAX: (671) 734-5483. Guam Educational Telecomm. Corp. Station Mgr.: Mrs. Ginger Underwood.

KUAM-LP, Channel 20, CBS
(see KUAM-TV, Agana). Agana, GU. Pacific Telestations, Inc.

KUAM-TV, Channel 8, IND
P. O. Box 368, Agana, GU 96910. (671) 637-5826. FAX: (671) 637-9865, Pacific Telestations, Inc. Jonathan M. DeKnight

KTGM, Channel 14, IND
Suite 308, 692 N. Marine Dr., Tamuning, GU 96911. (671) 646-4873. FAX: (671) 649-0371. Island Broadcasting Inc. David M. Larson.

PUERTO RICO

WQHA, Channel 50, NFP
(see WUJA, Carolina). Aguada, PR. New Conscience Network.

WELU* (Aguadilla), Channel 32, NFP
P. O. Box 530777, Harlingen, TX 78553. (210) 412 5600. FAX: (210) 428-7556. Healthy Christian Family Media, Inc. Rene Hinojosa.

WIRS, Channel 42, NFP
P. O. Box 635, Bayamon, PR 00960. (809) 799-6400. FAX: (809) 797-2450. Maranatha Christian Network. Rafael Torres.

WRWR-TV* (San Juan), Channel 30, IND
Calle No. One, No. 364 Hnas. Cavila, Bayamon, PR 00629. La Fe Del Progreso B'casting Corp. Ramon Rodriguez-Nieves.

WTIN* (Ponce), Channel 14, IND
AS-15 Rio Orocovis St., Bayamon, PR 00961. (809) 795-4010. Hector Nicolau.

WECN, Channel 64, NFP
P. O. Box 310, Bayanon, PR 00960. (809) 799-6400. FAX: (809) 797-2450. Encuentro Christian Net. Rafael Torres Ortega.

WMEI-TV (Arecibo), Channel 60, IND
G.P. O. 7017, Caguas, PR 00726. Hector Negroni Cartagena.

WCCV-TV (Arecibo), Channel 54, IND
P. O. Box 949, Kilo 92.6 Bo Membrillo, Carr. #2, Camuy, PR 00627. (809) 898-5120. FAX: (809) 262-0541. Asociacion Evan. Cristo Viene Inc. Francisco Valazquez.

WDZE, Channel 52, IND
P. O. Box 1833, Carolina, PR 00984-1833. (809) 762-5500. FAX: (809) 752-1825. Enrique A. & Blanche Vidal Sanchez.

WSJU (San Juan), Channel 18, IND
Call P. O. Box 18, Carolina, PR 00984. (809) 752-1800. FAX: (809) 257-9271. International Broadcasting Corp. Pedro Roman-Collazo.

WUJA (Caguas), Channel 58, IND
P. O. Box 4039, Carolina, PR 00984. (787) 750-5858. FAX: (787) 757-1500. Community TV of Caguas. Luz Villanueva.

WIDP (Guayama), Channel 46, IND
P. O. Box 501, Cidra, PR 00661. Bocanegra/Girlad Broadcasting Group.

WRUA, Channel 34, IND
101-1 107th St., Villa Carolina, Fajardo, PR 00630. Damarys de Jesus.

WIPR-TV, Channel 6, PBS
P. O. Box 909, Hostos Ave. #570, Baldrich, Hato Rey, PR 00919-0909. (787) 766-0505. FAX: (787) 753-9846. PR Public Broadcasting Corp. GM: Jorge M. Eserne.

WKAQ-TV, Channel 2, TEL
383 Roosevelt Ave., Hato Rey, PR 00918. (809) 758-2222. FAX: (809) 759-9575. Telemundo Group Inc. Joe Ramos.

WDWL, Channel 36, NFP
P. O. Box 50615, Levittown, PR 00950. (809) 795-8181. Bayamon Christian Network. Jesus Velez.

WIPM-TV, Channel 3, PBS
Post St. 502 S., Mayaguez, PR 00680. (809) 834-0164. PR Public Broadcasting Corp. Alberto Acedevo.

WNJX-TV, Channel 22, IND
P. O. Box 1030, Mayaguez, PR 00681-1030. (809) 831-2222. FAX: (809) 834-2222. WJNX-TV. Ana J. Plaza.

WOLE-TV, Channel 12, IND
P. O. Box 1200, Mayaguez, PR 00709-1200. (809) 833-1200. FAX: (809) 831-6330. Western Broadcasting Corp. of PR. Irwin Young.

WORA-TV, Channel 5, IND
P. O. Box 43, Mayaguez, PR 00681. (809) 831-5555. FAX: (809) 833-0075. Alfredo R. deArellano Jr. & Family. Pres. & CEO: Alfredo R. deArellano.

WTRA, Channel 16, IND
P. O. Box 980, Quebradillas, PR 00678. (809) 895-2725. Jose Arzuaga

WMTJ, Channel 40, IND
P. O. Box 21345, Road 176, Kilometer 3, Isoro Color, Cupey Bajo, Rio Piedras, PR 00928. (809) 766-2600. FAX: (809) 250-8546. Ana G. Mendez Educational Foundation. Jose F. Mendez.

WQTO, Channel 26, IND
P. O. Box 21345, Rio Piedras, PR 00928. (809) 766-2600. FAX: (809) 250-8546. Fundacion Educativa Ana G. Mendez. Jose F. Mendez.

WAPA-TV, Channel 4, IND
State Rd. 19, San Juan, PR 00657. (809) 792-4444. FAX: (809) 782-4420. Pegasus Broadcasting of San Juan. John R. Bennett.

WJWN-TV*, Channel 38, IND
P. O. Box 4522, San Juan, PR 00936. S&E Network Inc.

WLII (Caguas), Channel 11, NBC
Small Wood Bldg., Street 3 Stop 8, Tuerta de Tierra, San Juan, PR 00903. (809) 724-1111. FAX: (809) 724-7071. Estrella Brilliante Ltd. David E. Murphy.

WSTE, Channel 7, IND
P. O. Box A, Old San Juan Station, San Juan, PR 00902. (809) 724-7777. FAX: (809) 725-5870. Jerry B. & Esther M. Hartman. Wanda Costanzo.

WSUR-TV, Channel 9, IND
P. O. Box 10000, Santurce, PR 00901. (809) 724-1111. FAX: (809) 721-0777. Malrite Communications Group Inc. Dave Murphy.

U.S. VIRGIN ISLANDS

WTJX-TV, Channel 12, PBS
P. O. Box 7879, Barbel Plaza S., Charlotte Amalie, VI 00801. (809) 774-6255. FAX: (809) 774-7092. Virgin Islands Public Television. Richard P. Bourne-Vanneck.

WSVI, Channel 8, ABC
P. O. Box 8ABC, Sunny Isle Shopping Ctr., Christiansted, VI 00823. (809) 778-5008. FAX: (809) 778-5011. Alpha Broadcasting Corp.. Michael A. Wach.

WVXF* (U.S.V.I.), Channel 17, IND
P. O. Box 1605, Milwaukee, WI 53201. Atlantic Broadcasting Corp.

NETWORK AFFILIATES

ABC AFFILIATES

ALABAMA

WBRC-TV 6 ....Birmingham
WDHN 18 ....Dothan
WAAY-TV 31 ....Huntsville
WEAR-TV 3 ....Mobile
WHOA-TV 32 ....Montgomery

ALASKA

KATN 2 ....Fairbanks
KJUD 8 ....Juneau

ARIZONA

KNXV-TV 15 ....Phoenix
KGUN 9 ....Tucson

ARKANSAS

KHBS 40...................................Fort Smith
KAIT-TV 8 ....Jonesboro
KATV 7 ....Little Rock

CALIFORNIA

KBAK-TV 29 ....Bakersfield
KFWU 8 ....Fort Bragg
KFSN-TV 30...................................Fresno
KABC 7 ....Los Angeles
KESQ-TV 42 ....Palm Springs
KRCR-TV 7..................................Redding
KXTV 10 ....Sacramento
KGTV 10 ....San Diego
KGO-TV 7 ....San Francisco
KNTV 11 ....San Jose
KEYT-TV 3 ....Santa Barbara

COLORADO

KRDO-TV 13 ....Colorado Springs
KMGH-TV 7 ....Denver
KJCT 8.............................Grand Junction

CONNECTICUT

WTNH-TV 8 ....New Haven

DISTRICT OF COLUMBIA

WJLA-TV 7 ....Washington

FLORIDA

WCJB 20 ....Gainesville
WJKS 17.................................Jacksonville
WPLG 2 ....Miami
WZVN-TV 26.................................Naples
WFTV 9 ....Orlando
WMBB 13 ....Panama City
WWSB 40 ....Sarasota
WTXL-TV 27 ....Tallahassee
WFTS 28 ....Tampa
WPBF 25 ....Tequesta

GEORGIA

WSB-TV 2 ....Atlanta
WJBF 6 ....Augusta
WTVM 9 ....Columbus
WJCL 22 ....Savannah

HAWAII

KHVO 13..Hilo
KITV 4...................................Honolulu
KMAU 12 ....Wailuku

IDAHO

KIVI 6..Nampa

ILLINOIS

KPOB-TV 15 ....Carterville
WLS-TV 7 ....Chicago

WAND 17....................................Decatur
WSIL-TV 3................................Harrisburg
WQAD-TV 8.................................Moline
WHOI 19 ....Peoria
WTVO 17 ....Rockford

INDIANA

WEHT 25 ....Evansville
WTVW 7....................................Evansville
WPTA 21 ....Fort Wayne
WRTV 6 ....Indianapolis

IOWA

KCRG-TV 9.........................Cedar Rapids
WOI-TV 5 ....Des Moines
KCAU-TV 9 ....Sioux City

KANSAS

WUPK-TV 13 ....Garden City
KWNB 6 ....Hayes Center
KAKE-TV 10 ....Topeka
KTKA-TV 49 ....Topeka

KENTUCKY

WBKO 13..........................Bowling Green
WTVQ-TV 36 ....Lexington
WHAS-TV 11...........................Louisville

LOUISIANA

KLAX-TV 31 ....Alexandria
WBRZ 2 ....Baton Rouge
KATC 3 ....Lafayette
WGNO 26..........................New Orleans
WVUE 8 ....New Orleans
KTBS 3 ....Shreveport
KARD 14...........................West Monroe

MAINE

WVII-TV 7 ....Bangor
WMTW-TV 8 ....Poland Springs
WAGM-TV 8 ....Presque Isle

MARYLAND

WMAR-TV 2...............................Baltimore

MASSACHUSSETTS

WCDC 19.......................................Adams
WCVB-TV 5 ....Boston
WGGB-TV 40 ....Springfield

MICHIGAN

WOTV 41..............................Battle Creek
WJRT-TV 12...Flint
WZZM-TV 13 ....Grand Rapids
WLAJ 53 ....Lansing
WGTQ 8 ....S. Ste. Marie
WXYZ-TV 7...............................Southfield
WGTU 29 ....Traverse City

MINNESOTA

KAAL 6 ....Austin
WDIO-TV 10 ....Duluth
WIRT 13.......................................Hibbing
KRWF 43.......................Redwood Falls
KSTP-TV 5...................................St. Paul

MISSISSIPPI

WLOX 13...Biloxi
WABG-TV 6 ....Greenwood
WAPT 16.....................................Jackson
WTOK-TV 11 ....Meridian

MISSOURI

KMIZ 17 ....Columbia

KODE-TV 12 ....Joplin
KMBC 9 ....Kansas City
KTVO 3 ....Kirksville
KQTV 2 ....St. Joseph
KDNL-TV 30 ....St. Louis
KSPR 33 ....Springfield

MONTANA

KSVI 6...Billings
KWYB 18 ....Butte
KFBB-TV 5 ....Great Falls
KYUS-TV 3...............................Miles City
KTMF 23 ....Missoula

NEBRASKA

KCAN 8 ....Albion
KHGI-TV 13 ....Kearney
KETV 7 ....Omaha
KDUH-TV 4 ....Scottsbluff
KSNB-TV 4 ....Superior

NEVADA

KTNV 13 ....Las Vegas
KOLO-TV 8 ....Reno

NEW HAMPSHIRE

WMUR-TV 9 ....Manchester

NEW MEXICO

KOAT-TV 7 ....Albuquerque
KOCT 6..................................Carlsbad
KVIH-TV 12 ....Clovis
KOVT 10 ....Silver City

NEW YORK

WTEN 10...Albany
WMGC-TV 34 ....Binghamton
WKBW-TV 7...................................Buffalo
WENY-TV 36 ....Elmira
WABC-TV 7.............................New York
WOKR 13.................................Rochester
WIXT 9 ....Syracuse
WUTR 20 ....Utica
WWTI 50 ....Watertown

NORTH CAROLINA

WSOC-TV 9 ....Charlotte
WTVD 11.......................................Durham
WGGT 48 ....Greensboro
WCTI 12.....................................New Bern
WWAY 3 ....Wilmington
WXLV-TV 45 ....Winston-Salem

NORTH DAKOTA

KBMY 17 ....Bismarck
WDAZ-TV 8 ....Devils Lake
WDAY-TV 6 ....Fargo
KMCY 14 ....Minot

OHIO

WAKC-TV 23 ....Akron
WKRC-TV 12...........................Cincinnati
WEWS 5..Cleveland
WSYX 6 ....Columbus
WDTN 2 ....Dayton
WNWO-TV 24.................................Toledo
WYTV 33 ....Youngstown

OKLAHOMA

KSWO-TV 7...................................Lawton
KOCO-TV 5 ....Oklahoma City
KTUL 8..Tulsa

OREGON

KEZI 9...Eugene
KDKF 31.............................Klamath Falls
KDRV 12.......................................Medford
KATU 2...Portland

PENNSYLVANIA

WATM-TV 23................................Altoona
WJET-TV 24...Erie
WHTM-TV 27.........................Harrisburg
WPVI-TV 6................................Philadelphia
WTAE-TV 4.................................Pittsburgh
WNEP-TV16 ....Scranton

RHODE ISLAND

WLNE 6...................................Providence

SOUTH CAROLINA

WLOS 13.....................................Asheville
WCBD-TV 2..............................Charleston
WOLO-TV 25 ....Columbia
WPDE-TV 15............................Florence

SOUTH DAKOTA

KABY-TV 9...............................Aberdeen
KHSD-TV 11 ....Lead
KPRY-TV 4...Pierre
KOTA-TV 3..............................Rapid City
KSFY-TV 13 ....Sioux Falls

TENNESSEE

WTVC 9..............................Chattanooga
WKPT-TV 19 ....Kingsport

WATE-TV 6 ....Knoxville
WPTY-TV 24.............................Memphis
WKRN-TV 2................................Nashville

TEXAS

KVII-TV 7 ....Amarillo
KVUE-TV 24....................................Austin
KBMT 12.......................................Beaumont
KIII 3.................................Corpus Christi
WFAA-TV 8..Dallas
KTEN 10 ....Denison
KTRK-TV 13 ....Houston
KAMC 28 ....Lubbock
KTRE 9...Lufkin
KMID 2...Midland
KSAT-TV 12 ....San Antonio
KTXS-TV 12 ....Sweetwater
KLTV 7..Tyler
KAVU-TV 25...................................Victoria
KXXV 25 ....Waco
KRGV-TV 5..................................Weslaco

UTAH

KTVX 4 ....Salt Lake City

VERMONT

WVNY 22 ....Burlington

VIRGINIA

WVEC-TV 13...........................Hampton
WHSV-TV 3 ....Harrisonburg
WSET-TV 13..........................Lynchburg
WRIC-TV 8..............................Richmond

WASHINGTON

KVEW 42 ....Kennewick
KOMO-TV 4 ....Seattle
KXLY-TV 4 ....Spokane
KAPP 35 ....Yakima

WEST VIRGINIA

WCHS-TV 8.............................Charleston
WOAY-TV 4................................Oak Hill

WISCONSIN

WQOW-TV 18 ....Eau Claire
WBAY-TV 2 ....Green Bay
WXOW-TV 19 ....La Crosse
WKOW-TV 27 ....Madison
WISN-TV 12 ....Milwaukee
WAOW-TV 9...............................Wausau

WYOMING

KFNB-TV 20 ....Casper
KFNR 11...Rawlins
KFNE 10 ....Riverton

U.S. TERRITORIES AND POSSESSIONS

U.S. VIRGIN ISLANDS

WSVI 8................................Christiansted

CBS Affiliates

ALABAMA

WJSU-TV 40..............................Anniston
WBMG 42.............................Birmingham
WTVY 4...Dothan
WHNT-TV 19...........................Huntsville
WKRG-TV 5................................Mobile
WAKA 8 ....Selma
WCFT-TV 33........................Tuscaloosa

ALASKA

KTVA 11 ....Anchorage
KTVF 11....................................Fairbanks
KTNL 13 ....Sitka

ARIZONA

KPHO-TV 5................................Phoenix
KSWT 13 ....Yuma

ARKANSAS

KFSM-TV 5 ....Fort Smith
KTHV 11 ....Little Rock

CALIFORNIA

KERO-TV 23.........................Bakersfield
KVIQ 6...Eureka
KJEO 47 ....Fresno
KCBS-TV 2 ....Los Angeles
KCCN-TV 46................................Salinas
KFMB-TV 8.............................San Diego
KPIX-TV 5......................San Francisco
KCOY-TV 12.....................Santa Maria
KOVR 13 ....W. Sacramento

COLORADO

KKTV 11 ....Colorado Springs
KCNC-TV 4 ....Denver
KREX-TV 5....................Grand Junction
KTVS 3..Sterling

CONNECTICUT

WFSB ....Hartford

DISTRICT OF COLUMBIA

WUSA ....Washington

FLORIDA

WINK-TV 11 ....Fort Myers
WJXT 4................................Jacksonville
WFOR-TV 4 ....Miami
WCPX-TV 6 ....Orlando
WCTV 6...............................Tallahassee
WTSP 10 ....Tampa
WPEC 12 ....West Palm Beach

GEORGIA

WGNX 46 ....Atlanta
WRDW-TV 12..............................Augusta
WRBL 3....................................Columbus
WMAZ-TV 13..................................Macon
WTOC-TV 11 ....Savannah

HAWAII

KGMD-TV 9......................................Hilo
KGMB 9....................................Honolulu

IDAHO

KBCI-TV 2 ....Boise
KLEW 3 ....Lewiston
KMVT 11 ....Twin Falls

ILLINOIS

WCIA 3...................................Champaign
WBBM-TV 2 ....Chicago
WIFR 23...Freeport
WMBD-TV 31 ....Peoria
KHQA-TV 7 ....Quincy
WHBF-TV 4 ....Rock Island
WCFN 49.........................Springfield IL

INDIANA

WEVV 44...................................Evansville
WANE-TV 15........................Fort Wayne
WISH-TV 8 ....Indianapolis
WSBT-TV 22 ....South Bend

WTHI-TV 10...........................Terre Haute
WLFI-TV 18........................W. Lafayette

IOWA

KGAN 2 ....Cedar Rapids
KCCI 8.....................................Des Moines
KIMT 3....................................Mason City

KANSAS

KBSD-TV 6.....................................Ensign
KBSL-TV 10.............................Goodland
KBSH-TV 7...Hays
KOAM-TV 7....................................Pittsburg
WIBW-TV 13.................................Topeka
KWCH-TV 12 ....Wichita

KENTUCKY

WYMT-TV 57.............................Hazard
WKYT-TV 27 ....Lexington
WLKY 32....................................Louisville

LOUISIANA

WAFB 9 ....Baton Rouge
KLFY-TV 10..............................Lafayette
KNOE-TV 8 ....Monroe
WWL-TV 4 ....New Orleans
KSLA-TV 12 ....Shreveport

MAINE

WABI-TV 5 ....Bangor
WGME-TV 13...............................Portland

MARYLAND

WJZ-TV 13 ....Baltimore
WBOC-TV 16..........................Salisbury

MASSACHUSSETTS

WBZ-TV 4..Boston

MICHIGAN

WBKB-TV 11 ....Alpena
WWTV 9 ....Cadillac

589

WWJ-TV 62....................................Detroit	WFMY-TV 2............................High Point	**TEXAS**
WJMN-TV 3................................Escanaba	WRAL-TV 5 ....Raleigh	
WNEM-TV 5 ....Flint/Bay City		KTAB-TV 32................................Abilene
WWMT 3..................................Kalamazoo	**NORTH DAKOTA**	KFDA-TV 10 ....Amarillo
WLNS-TV 9 ....Lansing		KEYE-TV 42 ....Austin
WWUP-TV 10 ....S. St. Marie	KXMB-TV 12..............................Bismarck	KFDM-TV 6 ....Beaumont
	KXMA-TV 2 ....Dickinson	KBTX-TV 3.....................................Bryan
MINNESOTA	KXMC-TV 13................................Minot	KZTV 10 ....Corpus Christi
	KXJB-TV 4 ....Valley City	KDBC-TV 4 ....El Paso
KCCO-TV 7 ....Alexandria	KXMD-TV 11 ....Williston	KGBT-TV 4 ....Harlingen
KDLH 3...Duluth		KHOU-TV 11.............................Houston
KEYC-TV 12................................Mankato	**OHIO**	KVTV 13.......................................Laredo
WCCO-TV 4 ....Minneapolis		KLBK-TV 13................................Lubbock
KCCW 12.......................................Walker	WCPO-TV 9............................Cincinnati	KOSA-TV 7..................................Odessa
	WBNS 10...............................Columbus	KLST 8.................................San Angelo
MISSISSIPPI	WHIO-TV 7..................................Dayton	KENS-TV 5 ....San Antonio
	WOIO 19............................Shaker Hts.	KXII 12.......................................Sherman
WCBI-TV 4 ....Columbus	WTOL-TV 11 ....Toledo	KWTX-TV 10 ....Waco
WXVT 15..................................Greenville	WKBN-TV 2 ....Youngstown	KAUZ-TV 6 ....Wichita Falls
WJTV 12.......................................Jackson		
	OKLAHOMA	**UTAH**
MISSOURI		
	KWTV 9 ....Oklahoma City	KUTV 2................................Salt Lake City
KFVS-TV 12 ....Cp. Girardeau	KOTV 6...Tulsa	KUSG 12 ....St. George
KRCG 13 ....Jefferson City		
KCTV 5..............................Kansas City	**OREGON**	**VIRGINIA**
KOLR-TV 10 ....Springfield		
KMOV 4.......................................St. Louis	KCBY-TV 11 ....Coos Bay	WTKR 3......................................Norfolk
	KVAL-TV 13 ....Eugene	WTVR-TV 6 ....Richmond
MONTANA	KTVL 10 ....Medford	WDBJ 7 ....Roanoke
	KOIN 6.......................................Portland	WCAX-TV 3...............................Burlington
KCTZ 7 ....Bozeman	KPIC 4.......................................Roseburg	
KXLF-TV 4 ....Butte		**WASHINGTON**
KXGN-TV 5 ....Glendive	**PENNSYLVANIA**	
KRTV 3 ....Great Falls		KEPR-TV 19 ....Pasco
KPAX-TV 8 ....Missoula	WTAJ-TV 10 ....Altoona	KSTW 11...................................Tacoma
	WSEE-TV 35....................................Erie	KREM-TV 2 ....Spokane
NEBRASKA	WHP-TV 21............................Harrisburg	KIMA-TV 29 ....Yakima
	WLYH-TV 15............................Lancaster	
KGIN 11 ....Grand Island	KYW-TV 3 ....Philadelphia	**WEST VIRGINIA**
KOLN 10.......................................Lincoln	KDKA-TV 2................................Pittsburgh	
KMTV 3...Omaha	WYOU 22 ....Scranton	WOWK-TV 13...........................Huntington
KSTF 10...................................Scottsbluff		WDTV 5.....................................Weston
	RHODE ISLAND	WTRF-TV 7 ....Wheeling
NEVADA		
	WPRI-TV 12 ....E. Providence	**WISCONSIN**
KLAS-TV 8 ....Las Vegas		
KTVN 2 ....Reno	**SOUTH CAROLINA**	WFRV-TV 5 ....Green Bay
		WKBT 8..................................La Crosse
NEW MEXICO	WCSC-TV 5 ....Charleston	WISC-TV 3..................................Madison
	WLTX 19...................................Columbia	WDJT-TV 58 ....Milwaukee
KRQE 13 ....Albuquerque	WBTW 13 ....Florence	WSAW-TV 7 ....Wausau
KBIM-TV 10 ....Roswell	WSPA-TV 7..........................Spartanburg	
		WYOMING
NEW YORK	**SOUTH DAKOTA**	
		KGWC-TV 14............................Casper
WBNG-TV 12 ....Binghamton	KDLO-TV 3..................................Florence	KGWL-TV 5 ....Lander
WIVB-TV 4 ....Buffalo	KCLO-TV 15 ....Rapid City	
WWNY-TV 7...............................Carthage	KPLO-TV 6 ....Reliance	**U.S. TERRITORIES AND**
WCBS-TV 2 ....New York	KELO-TV 11 ....Sioux Falls	**POSSESSIONS**
WROC-TV 8 ....Rochester		
WRGB 6..............................Schenectady	**TENNESSEE**	**GUAM**
WTVH 5.....................................Syracuse		
	WDEF-TV 12....................Chattanooga	KUAM-LP 20 ....Agana
NORTH CAROLINA	WJHL-TV 11.................Johnson City	
	WKXT-TV 8.................................Knoxville	
WBTV 3 ....Charlotte	WREG-TV 3............................Memphis	
WNCT-TV 9 ....Greenville	WTVF 5.......................................Nashville	

FOX AFFILIATES

ALABAMA	**CALIFORNIA**	**DISTRICT OF COLUMBIA**
WTTO 21 ....Birmingham	KECY-TV 9..................................El Centro	WTTG 5 ....Washington
WPMI 15 ....Mobile	KAEF 29.......................................Eureka	
WCOV-TV 20 ....Montgomery	KBVU 29......................................Eureka	**FLORIDA**
WDFX-TV 34 ....Ozark	KMPH 26 ....Fresno	
WDBB 17 ....Tuscaloosa	KTTV 11...............................Los Angeles	WFTX 36 ....Fort Myers
	KTVU 2......................................Oakland	WAWS 30 ....Jacksonville
ALASKA	KCVU 30.....................................Paradise	WOFL 35......................................Orlando
	KTXL 40 ....Sacramento	WSVN 7 ....Miami
KTBY 4 ....Anchorage	KCBA 35.......................................Salinas	WOGX 51 ....Ocala
KFXF 7 ....Fairbanks	XETV 6 ....San Diego	WPGX 28 ....Panama City
		WTLH 49....................................Tallahassee
ARIZONA	**COLORADO**	WTTA 38 ....Tampa
		WTVT 13.......................................Tampa
KSAZ-TV 10................................Phoenix	KXRM-TV 21................Colorado Springs	WFLX 29 ....West Palm Beach
KMSB-TV 11 ....Tucson	KDVR 31......................................Denver	
	KFCT 22....................................Durango	**GEORGIA**
ARKANSAS		
	CONNECTICUT	WFXL 31......................................Albany
KLRT 16..................................Little Rock		
	WTIC-TV 61..............................Hartford	

WAGA-TV 5 ....Atlanta
WFXG 54 ....Augusta
WXTX 54 ....Columbus
WGXA 24 ....Macon
WPGA-TV 58 ....Perry

IDAHO

KTRV 12 ....Nampa
KXTF 35 ....Twin Falls

ILLINOIS

WYZZ-TV 43 ....Bloomington
WFLD 32 ....Chicago
WQRF-TV 39 ....Rockford
WRSP-TV 55 ....Springfield

INDIANA

WSJV 28 ....Elkhart
WFFT-TV 55 ....Fort Wayne
WXIN 59 ....Indianapolis
WBAK-TV 38 ....Terre Haute

IOWA

KJMH 26 ....Burlington
KFXA 28 ....Cedar Rapids
KFXB 40 ....Cedar Rapids
KLJB-TV 18 ....Davenport
KDSM-TV 17 ....Des Moines
KFXB 40 ....Dubuque
KYOU-TV 15 ....Ottumwa
KMEG 14 ....Sioux City

KANSAS

KAAS-TV 18 ....Salina
KSAS-TV 24 ....Wichita

KENTUCKY

WKNT 40 ....Bowling Green
WGRB 34 ....Campbellsville
WDKY-TV 56 ....Lexington
WDRB-TV 41 ....Louisville
WXIX-TV 19 ....Newport

LOUISIANA

WGMB 44 ....Baton Rouge
KADN 15 ....Lafayette
KVHP 29 ....Lake Charles
KMSS 33 ....Shreveport

MAINE

WPXT 51 ....Portland

MARYLAND

WBFF 45 ....Baltimore

MASSACHUSSETTS

WFXT 25 ....Dedham

MICHIGAN

WGKI 33 ....Cadillac
WSMH 66...Flint
WXMI 17............................Grand Rapids
WSYM-TV 47 ....Lansing
WJBK-TV 2 ....Southfield
WGKU 45.................................Vanderbilt

MINNESOTA

WFTC 29 ....Minneapolis
KBRR 10....................Thief River Falls

MISSISSIPPI

WXXV-TV 25 ....Gulfport
WDBD 40.....................................Jackson
WLOV-TV 27........................West Point

MISSOURI

KBSI 23 ....Cape Girardeau
KSHB-TV 41 ....Kansas City
WDAF-TV 4 ....Kansas City
KDEB 27..............................Springfield
KTVI 2 ....St. Louis

MONTANA

KHMT 4 ....Hardin

NEBRASKA

KTVG 17 ....Grand Island
KPTM 42 ....Omaha

NEVADA

KVVU-TV 5.............................Henderson
KAME-TV 21 ....Reno

NEW MEXICO

KASA-TV 2 ....Santa Fe

NEW YORK

WXXA-TV 23 ....Albany
WICZ-TV 40.........................Binghamton
WUTV 29..Buffalo
WNYW 5......................................New York
WUHF 31......................................Rochester
WSYT 68 ....Syracuse
WFXV 33 ....Utica

NORTH CAROLINA

WHNS 21 ....Asheville
WCCB 18 ....Charlotte
WFAY 62 ....Fayetteville
WYDO 14 ....Greenville
WGHP-TV 8 ....High Point
WFXI 8 ....Morehead City
WLFL 22................................Raleigh

NORTH DAKOTA

KNRR 12....................................Pembina

OHIO

WJW-TV 8................................Cleveland
WTTE 28 ....Columbus
WRGT-TV 45 ....Dayton
WUPW 36 ....Toledo

OKLAHOMA

KOKH-TV 25 ....Oklahoma City
KOKI-TV 23 ....Tulsa

OREGON

KMVU 26 ....Medford

PENNSYLVANIA

WFXP 66 ....Erie

WWLF-TV 56...........................Hazleton
WWCP-TV 8............................Johnstown
WTXF-TV 29 ....Philadelphia
WPGH-TV 53...........................Pittsburgh
WOLF-TV 38 ....Scranton
WILF 53 ....Williamsport
WPMT 43 ....York

RHODE ISLAND

WNAC-TV 64 ....Providence

SOUTH CAROLINA

WTAT-TV 24.........................Charleston
WACH 57.................................Columbia
WTGS 28 ....Hardeeville

SOUTH DAKOTA

KTTW 17 ....Sioux Falls
KTTW 12 ....Sioux Falls

TENNESSEE

WDSI-TV 61 ....Chattanooga
WEMT 39...............................Greeneville
WMTU 16.....................................Jackson
WTNZ 43 ....Knoxville
WHBQ-TV 13 ....Memphis
WZTV 17..................................Nashville

TEXAS

KCIT 14......................................Amarillo
KTBC-TV 7 ....Austin
KDFW-TV 4.....................................Dallas
KFOX-TV 14 ....El Paso
KRIV 26.....................................Houston
KFXK 51 ....Longview
KJTV 34 ....Lubbock
KPEJ 24 ....Odessa
KIDY 6 ....San Angelo
KABB 29 ....San Antonio
KWKT 44 ....Waco
KJTL 18 ....Wichita Falls
KVCT 19 ....Victoria

UTAH

KSTU 13............................Salt Lake City

VIRGINIA

WJPR 21 ....Lynchburg
WTVZ 33 ....Norfolk
WRLH-TV 35 ....Richmond
WFXR-TV 27 ....Roanoke

WASHINGTON

KAYU-TV 28 ....Spokane
KCPQ 13.......................................Tacoma
KPDX 49 ....Vancouver

WEST VIRGINIA

WVAH-TV 11 ....Charleston

WISCONSIN

WEUX 48........................Chippewa Falls
WLAX 25................................La Crosse
WMSN-TV 47 ....Madison
WITI-TV 6 ....Milwaukee

NBC AFFILIATES

ALABAMA

WVTM-TV13.........................Birmingham
WOWL-TV 15.............................Florence
WNAL-TV 44 ....Gadsden
WAFF 48 ....Huntsville
WALA-TV 10 ....Mobile
WSFA 12.................................Montgomery

ALASKA

KIMO 13 ....Anchorage

KTUU-TV 2 ....Anchorage

ARIZONA

KNAZ-TV 2................................Flagstaff
KPNX 12....................................Phoenix
KVOA-TV 4..................................Tucson
KYMA 11......................................Yuma

ARKANSAS

KPOM-TV 24...........................Fort Smith

KARK-TV 19 ....Little Rock
KFAA 51 ....Rogers

CALIFORNIA

KGET 17 ....Bakersfield
KNBC 4...............................Los Angeles
KCPM 24 ....Chico
KIEM-TV 3.....................................Eureka
KSEE 24 ....Fresno
KMIR-TV 36........................Palm Springs

591

KCRA-TV 3..............................Sacramento
KSBW 8..Salinas
KNSD 39...................................San Diego
BAY-TV 35............................San Francisco
KRON-TV 4............................San Francisco
KSBY 6.............................San Luis Obispo

COLORADO

KUSA-TV 9.....................................Denver

CONNECTICUT

WVIT 30..................................W. Hartford

DISTRICT OF COLUMBIA

WRC-TV 4...............................Washington

FLORIDA

WBBH-TV 20 ....Fort Myers
WTLV 12................................Jacksonville
WTVJ 6...Miami
WESH 2......................................Orlando
WJHG-TV 7.........................Panama City
WTWC 40 ....Tallahassee
WFLA-TV 8 ....Tampa
WPTV 5...................West Palm Beach

GEORGIA

WALB 10.......................................Albany
WXIA-TV 11...................................Atlanta
WAGT 26....................................Augusta
WLTZ 38..................................Columbus
WMGT 41.......................................Macon
WSAV-TV 3..............................Savannah

HAWAII

KHAW-TV 11 ....Honolulu
WHON-TV 2 ....Honolulu
KAII-TV 7...................................Wailuku

IDAHO

KTVB 7...Boise
KIFI-TV 8...............................Idaho Falls
KPVI 6...................................Idaho Falls

ILLINOIS

WICD 15................................Champaign
WMAQ-TV 5 ....Chicago
WEEK-TV 25 ....Peoria
WGEM-TV 20 ....Quincy
WREX-TV 13.............................Rockford
WICS 20 ....Springfield

INDIANA

WFIE-TV 14 ....Evansville
WKJG-TV 33 ....Fort Wayne
WTHR 13.............................Indianapolis
WNDU-TV 16...........................South Bend
WTWO 2 ....Terre Haute

IOWA

KWQC-TV 6 ....Davenport
WHO-TV 13 ....Des Moines
KTIV 4 ....Sioux City
KWWL 7 ....Waterloo

KANSAS

KSNG 11 ....Garden City
KSNC 2 ....Great Bend
KSNT 27.......................................Topeka
KSNW 3 ....Wichita

KENTUCKY

WLEX-TV 18 ....Lexington
WAVE 3......................................Louisville
WPSD-TV 6 ....Paducah

LOUISIANA

KALB-TV 5..............................Alexandria
WVLA 33 ....Baton Rouge
KPLC-TV 7 ....Lake Charles
KTVE 10......................................Monroe
WDSU 6.............................New Orleans

MAINE

WLBZ-TV 2 ....Bangor
WCSH-TV 6...............................Portland

MARYLAND

WBAL-TV 11.............................Baltimore
WHAG-TV 25...........................Hagerstown

MASSACHUSSETTS

WHDH-TV 7.................................Boston
WMFP 62 ....Lawrence
WWLP 22...................................Springfield

MICHIGAN

WTOM-TV 4 ....Cheboygan
WDIV 4..Detroit
WOOD-TV 8 ....Grand Rapids
WILX-TV 10...............................Lansing
WPBN-TV 7 ....Traverse City

MINNESOTA

KBJR-TV 6 ....Duluth
KARE 11...............................Minneapolis
KTTC 10..................................Rochester

MISSISSIPPI

WDAM-TV 7 ....Hattiesburg
WLBT 3.......................................Jackson
WGBC 30...................................Meridian
WTVA 9 ....Tupelo

MISSOURI

KOMU-TV 8 ....Columbia
KSNF 16...Joplin
KYTV 3 ....Springfield
KSDK 5 ....St. Louis

MONTANA

KULR-TV 8 ....Billings
KTVM 6..Butte
KTVH 12...Helena
KCFW-TV 9 ....Kalispell
KECI-TV 13 ....Missoula

NEBRASKA

KHAS-TV 5 ....Hastings
KSNK 8.......................................McCook
KNOP-TV 2...........................North Platte
WOWT 6 ....Omaha

NEVADA

KVBC 3.................................Las Vegas
KRNV 4 ....Reno

NEW JERSEY

WMGM-TV 40 ....Wildwood

NEW MEXICO

KOB-TV 4 ....Albuquerque
KOBF 12 ....Farmington

NEW YORK

WNYT 13.......................................Albany
WGRZ-TV 2.....................................Buffalo
WETM-TV 18.................................Elmira
WNBC 4.................................New York
WHEC-TV 10..........................Rochester
WSTM-TV 3..............................Syracuse
WKTV 2 ....Utica

NORTH CAROLINA

WCNC-TV 36 ....Charlotte
WNCN 17................................Goldsboro
WITN-TV 7 ....Washington
WECT 6 ....Wilmington
WXII 12..........................Winston-Salem

NORTH DAKOTA

KFYR-TV 5.................................Bismarck
KQCD-TV 7 ....Dickinson
KVLY-TV 11...................................Fargo
KMOT 10.......................................Minot
KUMV-TV 8 ....Williston

OHIO

WLWT 5 ....Cincinnati
WKYC-TV 3 ....Cleveland

WCMH 4

WCMH 4 ....Columbus
WKEF 22 ....Dayton
WLIO 35...Lima
WTOV-TV 9 ....Steubenville
WTVG 13...Toledo
WFMJ-TV 21 ....Youngstown
WHIZ-TV 18................................Zanesville

OKLAHOMA

KFOR-TV 4 ....Oklahoma City
KJRH 2 ....Tulsa

OREGON

KTVZ 21 ....Bend
KMTZ 23 ....Coos Bay
KOTI 2 ....Klamath Falls
KOBI 5 ....Medford
KGW 8.......................................Portland
KMTX-TV 46.............................Rosebug
KMTR 16 ....Eugene

PENNSYLVANIA

WICU-TV 12.......................................Erie
WJAC-TV 6.............................Johnstown
WGAL 8 ....Lancaster
WCAU 10 ....Philadelphia
WPXI 11 ....Pittsburgh
WBRE-TV 28...................Wilkes-Barre

RHODE ISLAND

WJAR 10 ....Cranston

SOUTH CAROLINA

WCIV 4 ....Charleston
WIS 10......................................Columbia
WYFF 4 ....Greenville

SOUTH DAKOTA

KIVV-TV 5...Lead
KDLT 5...Mitchell
KEVN-TV 7 ....Rapid City

TENNESSEE

WRCB-TV 3 ....Chattanooga
WBIR-TV 10 ....Knoxville
WMC-TV 5 ....Memphis
WSMV-TV 4 ....Nashville

TEXAS

KRBC-TV 9 ....Abilene
KAMR-TV 4....................................Amarillo
KXAN-TV 36 ....Austin
KVEO 23..............................Brownsville
KRIS-TV 6.........................Corpus Christi
KTSM-TV 9......................................El Paso
KVIA-TV 7 ....El Paso
KXAS-TV 5 ....Fort Worth
KPRC-TV 2.....................................Houston
KGNS-TV 8.....................................Laredo
KXAM-TV 14......................................Llano
KCBD-TV 11 ....Lubbock
KLSB-TV 19......................Nacogdoches
KWES-TV 9 ....Odessa
KJAC-TV 4 ....Port Arthur
KACB-TV 3................................San Angelo
KMOL-TV 4 ....San Antonio
KCEN-TV 6 ....Temple
KTAL-TV 6...............................Texarkana
KETK-TV 56...................................Tyler
KFDX-TV 3 ....Wichita Falls

UTAH

KSL-TV 5.............................Salt Lake City

VERMONT

WNNE-TV 31 ....White River Junction

VIRGINIA

WCYB-TV 5 ....Bristol
WVIR-TV 29.....................Charlottesville
WAVY-TV 10...........................Portsmouth
WWBT 12 ....Richmond
WSLS-TV 10 ....Roanoke

WASHINGTON

KNDU 25.......................................Richland
KING-TV 5......................................Seattle

KHQ-TV 6 ....Spokane
KNDO 23 ....Yakima

WEST VIRGINIA

WVVA 6 ....Bluefield
WBOY-TV 12 ....Clarksburg
WSAZ-TV 3 ....Huntington
WTAP-TV 15 ....Parkersburg

WISCONSIN

WEAU-TV 13 ....Eau Claire
WGBA 26 ....Green Bay
WLUK-TV 11 ....Green Bay
WMTV 15 ....Madison
WTMJ-TV 4 ....Milwaukee
WFJW-TV 12 ....Rhinelander

WYOMING

KTWO-TV 2 ....Casper
KKTU 33 ....Cheyenne
KJVI 2 ....Jackson

U.S TERRITORIES AND POSSESSIONS

PUERTO RICO

WLII 11 ....Caguas

PBS AFFILIATES

ALABAMA

WBIQ 10 ....Birmingham
WIIQ 41 ....Demopolis
WDIQ 2 ....Dozier
WFIQ 36 ....Florence
WHIQ 25 ....Huntsville
WGIQ 43 ....Louisville
WEIQ 42 ....Mobile
WAIQ 26 ....Montgomery
WCIQ 7 ....Mt. Cheaha St. Park

ALASKA

KAKM 7 ....Anchorage
KYUK-TV 4 ....Bethel
KUAC-TV 9 ....Fairbanks
KTOO-TV 3 ....Juneau

ARIZONA

KAET 8 ....Phoenix
KOLD-TV 13 ....Tucson
KUAS 27 ....Tucson
KUAT-TV 6 ....Tucson

ARKANSAS

KETG 9 ....Arkadelphia
KAFT 13 ....Fayetteville
KTEJ 19 ....Jonesboro
KETS 2 ....Little Rock
KEMV 6 ....Mountain View

CALIFORNIA

KRCB 22 ....Cotati
KEET 13 ....Eureka
KVPT 18 ....Fresno
KOCE-TV 50 ....Huntington Beach
KCET 28 ....Los Angeles
KLCS 58 ....Los Angeles
KIXE 9 ....Redding
KVIE 6 ....Sacramento
KVCR-TV 24 ....San Bernardino
KPBS 15 ....San Diego
KMTP-TV 32 ....San Francisco
KQED 9 ....San Francisco
KTEH 54 ....San Jose
KCSM-TV 60 ....San Mateo

COLORADO

KBDI-TV 12 ....Denver
KRMA-TV 6 ....Denver
KTSC 8 ....Pueblo

CONNECTICUT

WEDW 49 ....Bridgeport
WEDH 24 ....Hartford
WEDY 65 ....New Haven
WEDN 53....................................Norwich

DISTRICT OF COLUMBIA

WETA-TV 26 ....Washington
WHMM 32 ....Washington

DELAWARE

WDPB 64 ....Seaford
WHYY-TV 12 ....Wilmington

FLORIDA

WGCU-TV 30 ....Fort Myers
WUFT 5.................................Gainesville

WJCT 7.................................Jacksonville
WPBT 2...Miami
WCEU 15...................New Smyrna Beach
WMFE-TV 24 ....Orlando
WFSG 56 ....Panama City
WSRE 23 ....Pensacola
WFSU-TV 11 ....Tallahassee
WEDU 3 ....Tampa
WUSF-TV 16...................................Tampa
WXEL-TV 42 ....West Palm Beach

GEORGIA

WGTV 8...Athens
WPBA 30......................................Atlanta
WCLP-TV 18 ....Chatsworth
WDCO-TV 29 ....Cochran
WJSP-TV 28 ....Columbus
WACS-TV 25..................................Dawson
WVAN-TV 9 ....Savannah
WXGA-TV 8 ....Waycross
WCES-TV 20 ....Wrens

HAWAII

KHET 11 ....Honolulu
KMEB 10 ....Wailuku

IDAHO

KAID 4 ....Boise
KCDT 26 ....Coeur d'Alene
WUID-TV 12 ....Moscow
KISU-TV 10 ....Pocatello
KIPT 13 ....Twin Falls

ILLINOIS

WSIU-TV 8 ....Carbondale
WEIU-TV 51 ....Charleston
WTTW 11 ....Chicago
WYCC 20....................................Chicago
WSEC 14................................Jacksonville
WMEC 22.....................................Macomb
WQPT-TV 24 ....Moline
WUSI-TV 16 ....Olney
WTVP 47 ....Peoria
WQEC 27 ....Quincy
WILL-TV 12 ....Urbana

INDIANA

WTIU 30.................................Bloomington
WNIN 9..Evansville
WFWA 39 ....Fort Wayne
WFYI 20.................................Indianapolis
WIPB 49 ....Muncie
WNIT-TV 34 ....South Bend
WVUT 22 ....Vincennes

IOWA

KBIN 32 ....Council Bluffs
KDIN-TV 11 ....Des Moines
KTIN 21 ....Fort Dodge
KIIN-TV 12 ....Iowa City
KYIN 24 ....Mason City
KHIN 36..Red Oak
KSIN 27 ....Sioux City
KRIN 32..Waterloo

KANSAS

KOOD 9 ....Hays
KPTS 8 ....Hutchinson
KTWU 11...................................Topeka

KENTUCKY

WKAS 25 ....Ashland
WKGB-TV 53 ....Bowling Green
WKYU-TV 24.....................Bowling Green
WCVN 54.................................Covington
WKZT-TV 23 ....Elizabethtown
WKHA 36 ....Hazard
WKMJ 68......................................Lexington
WKPC-TV 15 ....Louisville
WKMA 35..............................Madisonville
WKMR 38....................................Morehead
WKMU 21 ....Murray
WKOH 31 ....Owensboro
WKON 52 ....Owenton
WKPD 29.......................................Paducah
WKPI 22...Pikeville
WKSO-TV 29..............................Somerset

LOUISIANA

KLPA-TV 25 ....Alexandria
WLPB-TV 27......................Baton Rouge
KLPB-TV 24 ....Lafayette
KLTL-TV 18 ....Lake Charles
KLTM-TV 13...................................Monroe
WLAE-TV 32 ....New Orleans
WYES-TV 12 ....New Orleans
KLTS-TV 24 ....Shreveport

MAINE

WCBB 10.......................................Augusta
WMEA-TV 26 ....Biddeford
WMED-TV 13..................................Calais
WMEB-TV 12.................................Orono
WMEM-TV 10 ....Presque Isle

MARYLAND

WMPT 22 ....Annapolis
WMPB 67 ....Baltimore
WWPB 31 ....Hagerstown
WGPT 36....................................Oakland
WFPT 62 ....Owings Mills
WCPB 28 ....Salisbury

MASSACHUSETTS

WGBH-TV 2.....................................Boston
WGBX-TV 44...................................Boston
WGBY-TV 57 ....Springfield

MICHIGAN

WCML 6...Alpena
WCMV 27......................................Cadillac
WKAR-TV 23 ....East Lansing
WFUM 28...Flint
WGVU-TV 35........................Grand Rapids
WGVK 52....................................Kalamazoo
WCMW 21 ....Manistee
WNMU-TV 13 ....Marquette
WCMU-TV 14 ....Mt. Pleasant
WUCM-TV 19.................University Center
WUCX-TV 35 ....University Center

MINNESOTA

KWCM-TV/KSMN-TV 10 ....Appleton
KAWE 9...Bemidji
KAWB 22..Brainerd
WDSE-TV 8................................Duluth
KTCA-TV 2 ....St. Paul
KTCI-TV 17 ....St. Paul

MISSISSIPPI

WMAH-TV 19 ....Biloxi

593

WMAE-TV 12 ....Booneville
WMAU-TV 17 ....Bude
WMAO-TV 23 ....Greenwood
WMAB-TV 2 ....Jackson
WMPN-TV 29...........................Jackson
WMAW-TV 14 ....Meridian
WMAV-TV 18................................Oxford

MISSOURI

KOZJ 26 ....Joplin
KCPT 19.............................Kansas City
KOZK 21 ....Springfield
KETC 9 ....St. Louis
KTVI 2 ....Warrenburg

MONTANA

KUSM 9 ....Bozeman

NEBRASKA

KMNE-TV 7................................Bassett
KHNE-TV 29 ....Hastings
KLNE-TV 3 ....Lexington
KSNK 8......................................McCook
KXNE-TV 19 ....Norfolk
KPNE-TV 9 ....North Platte
KYNE-TV 26 ....Omaha

NEVADA

KLVX 10 ....Las Vegas
KNPB 5 ....Reno

NEW HAMPSHIRE

WENH-TV 11 ....Durham
WBK-TV 15 ....Hanover
WEKW-TV 52 ....Keene
WLED-TV 49 ....Littleton
W18BO-TV 18 ....Pittsburg

NEW JERSEY

WNJS 23....................................Camden
WNJN 50...................................Montclair
WNJB 58 ....New Brunswick
WNJT 52....................................Trenton

NEW MEXICO

KNME-TV 5 ....Albuquerque
KRWG-TV 22.........................Las Cruces
KENW 3...................................Portales

NEW YORK

WSKG-TV 46.......................Binghamton
WNYE-TV 25 ....Brooklyn
WNED-TV 17.............................Buffalo
WNEQ-TV 23..............................Buffalo
WLIW 21 ....Garden City
WNET 13 ....New York
WNPI-TV 18 ....Norwood
WCFE-TV 57 ....Plattsburgh
WXXI-TV 21 ....Rochester
WCNY-TV 24..........................Syracuse
WNPE-TV 16........................Watertown

NORTH CAROLINA

WUNF-TV 33 ....Asheville
WUNC-TV 4 ....Chapel Hill
WTVI 42 ....Charlotte
WUND-TV 2..............................Columbia
WUNG-TV 58 ....Concord
WUNK-TV 25..........................Greenville
WUNM-TV 19 ....Jacksonville
WUNE-TV 17............................Linville
WUNP-TV 36 ....Roanoke Rapids
WUNJ-TV 39........................Wilmington
WUNL-TV 26 ....Winston-Salem

NORTH DAKOTA

KBME 3....................................Bismarck
KDSE 9 ....Dickinson

KJRE 19....................................Ellendale
KFME 13...Fargo
KGFE 2...............................Grand Forks
KSRE 6...Minot
KWSE 4...................................Williston

OHIO

WEAO 49 ....Akron
WNEO 45 ....Alliance
WOUB 20 ....Athens
WOUC-TV 44 ....Cambridge
WCET 48 ....Cincinnati
WVIZ-TV 25 ....Cleveland
WOSU 34....................................Columbus
WPTD 16.......................................Dayton
WPBO-TV 42......................Portsmouth
WGTE-TV 30..............................Toledo

OKLAHOMA

KWET 12 ....Cheyenne
KOET 3....................................Eufaula
KETA 13 ....Oklahoma City
KTLC 43 ....Oklahoma City
KOED-TV 11.................................Tulsa

OREGON

KOAB-TV 3.....................................Bend
KOAC-TV 7 ....Corvallis
KEPB-TV 28 ....Eugene
KFTS 22...........................Klamath Falls
KTVR 13 ....La Grande
KSYS 8 ....Medford
KOPB-TV 10.............................Portland

PENNSYLVANIA

WLVT-TV 39 ....Allentown
WQLN 54...Erie
WITF-TV 33 ....Harrisburg
WYBE 35..............................Philadelphia
WQED 13 ....Pittsburgh
WQEX 16...............................Pittsburgh
WVIA-TV 44 ....Pittston
WPSX-TV 3 ....University Park

RHODE ISLAND

WSBE-TV 36 ....Providence

SOUTH CAROLINA

WJWJ-TV 16 ....Beaufort
WITV 7 ....Charleston
WRLK-TV 35 ....Columbia
WHMC 23 ....Conway
WJPM-TV 33 ....Florence
WNTV 29 ....Greenville
WNEH 38 ....Greenwood
WNSC-TV 30............................Rock Hill
WRET-TV 49 ....Spartanburg
WRJA-TV 27 ....Sumter

SOUTH DAKOTA

KDSD-TV 16 ....Aberdeen
KESD-TV 8 ....Brookings
KPSD-TV 13 ....Eagle Butte
KQSD-TV 11 ....Lowry
KZSD-TV 8 ....Martin
KTSD-TV 10 ....Pierre
KBHE-TV 9 ....Rapid City
KCSD-TV 23 ....Sioux Falls
KUSD-TV 2 ....Vermillion

TENNESSEE

WTCI 45...........................Chattanooga
WCTE 22...................................Cookeville
WKOP-TV 15........................Knoxville
WLJT-TV 11..............................Lexington
WKNO-TV 10.............................Memphis
WDCN 8 ....Nashville
WSJK-TV 2 ....Sneedville

TEXAS

KACV-TV 2...............................Amarillo
KLRU-TV 18...............................Austin
KNCT 46.......................................Belton
KAMU-TV 15 ....College Station
KEDT 16 ....Corpus Christi
KERA-TV 13 ....Dallas
KDTN 2 ....Denton
KCOS 13 ....El Paso
KMBH 60 ....Harlingen
KUHT 8..Houston
KTXT-TV 5..................................Lubbock
KOCV-TV 36..............................Odessa
KLRN 9 ....San Antonio
KCTF 34 ....Waco

UTAH

KULC 9 ....Ogden
KBYU-TV 11 ....Provo
KUED 7 ....Salt Lake City

VERMONT

WETK 33 ....Burlington
WVER 28....................................Rutland
WVTB 20 ....St. Johnsbury
WVTA 41...................................Windsor

VIRGINIA

WHTJ 41 ....Charlottesville
WNVT 53..........................Falls Church
WHRO-TV 15..............Hampton-Norfolk
WMSY-TV 52 ....Marion
WSBN-TV 47 ....Norton
WCVE-TV 23..........................Richmond
WBRA-TV 15..............................Roanoke
WVPT 51 ....Staunton

WASHINGTON

KCKA 15....................................Centralia
KWSU-TV 10 ....Pullman
KTNW 31 ....Richland
KCTS-TV 9 ....Seattle
KSPS-TV 7 ....Spokane
KBTC-TV 28...............................Tacoma
KYVE 47......................................Yakima

WEST VIRGINIA

WSWP-TV 9 ....Grandview
WPBY-TV 33 ....Huntington
WNPB-TV 24 ....Morgantown

WISCONSIN

WPNE 38................................Green Bay
WHLA-TV 31 ....Lacrosse
WHA-TV 21 ....Madison
WHWC-TV 28 ....Menomonie
WLEF-TV 36 ....Park Falls
WHRM-TV 20 ....Wausau

WYOMING

KCWC-TV 4..................................Lander

U.S. TERRITORIES AND POSSESSIONS

AMERICAN SAMOA

KVZK-2 2 ....American Samoa

GUAM

KGTF 12..Agana

PUERTO RICO

WIPR-TV 6...............................Hato Rey
WIPM-TV 3..............................Mayaguez

U.S. VIRGIN ISLANDS

WTJX-TV 12 ....Charlotte Amalie

Station Representatives

JOHN BLAIR COMMUNICATIONS INC.
1290 Ave. of the Americas, New York, NY 10104. (212) 603-5000. FAX: (212) 603-5453.
CHAIRMAN & CEO
Timothy M. McAuliff
PRESIDENT, BLAIR AMERICA
Floyd J. Gelini
PRESIDENT, BLAIR USA
Leo M. MacCourtney Jr.,
SENIOR V.P.
John B. Poor
SR. V.P. & DIRECTOR, CLIENT SERVICES
James R. Kelly
V.P., ADVERTISING & COMMUNICATION
Kenneth P. Donnellon
REGIONAL OFFICES
Atlanta, Boston, Charlotte, Chicago, Dallas, Denver, Detroit, Houston, Los Angeles, Miami, Minneapolis, Philadelphia, Portland, St. Louis, San Francisco, Seattle, Tampa.

CBS/GROUP W TELEVISION SALES
51 W. 52 St., New York, NY 10019. (212) 975-4321.
V.P , GEN. MGR., SLS. & MARKETING
Philip Press
BRANCH OFFICES
11 Piedmont Center, Atlanta, GA 30305. (404) 261-2227.
MANAGER
Gene McHugh
218 Newbury St., 3rd Fl.,Boston, MA 02116. (617) 262-7337.
MANAGER
Diane Ciproani
630 N. McClurg Ct., Chicago, IL 60611. (312) 944-6000.
MANAGER
Terry Dunning
545 E. John Carpenter Fwy., Suite 1540, Dallas, TX 75062. (214) 556-1245.
MANAGER
Sandy Delauney
26877 Northwestern Hwy., Southfield, MI 48034. (313) 351-2170.
MANAGER
Elaine Carpenter
6121 Sunset Blvd., Los Angeles, CA 90028. (310) 460-3010.
MANAGER
Julie Ballard
One Embarcadero Center, San Francisco, CA 94111. (415) 765-4155.
MANAGER
Frank Wheeler
One Farragut Sq., 1634 One St. NW, Suite 100, Washington, DC 20006. (202) 457-4509.
MANAGER
Sonja Miller

CC/ABC NATIONAL TELEVISION SALES
77 W. 66 St., New York, NY 10023-6298. (212) 456-7777. FAX: (212) 456-7607.
PRESIDENT
John B. Watkins
VICE PRESIDENT
Phillip J. Sweenie
V.P., GENERAL SALES MANAGER
Ed Pearson
BRANCH OFFICES
190 N. State St., Chicago, IL 60601. (312) 899-4200.
SALES MANAGER
Scott Thomas
2020 Ave. of Stars, Los Angeles, CA 90067. (213) 557-6241.
SALES
Michael Jack
900 Front St., San Francisco, CA 94111. (415) 954-7810.
SALES
Gill Fitts
3000 Town Center, Southfield, MI 48075. (313) 355-4490.
SALES
Hyla Griesdorn
12222 Merit Dr., Dallas, TX 75251. (214) 960-7981.
SALES
Michael Irvine
3060 Peachtree Rd. N.W., Atlanta, GA 30305. (404) 266-1750.
SALES
Paul Courtney
One Exeter Plaza, Boston, MA 02116. (617) 262-8989.
SALES
Stewart Scott
6525 Morrison Blvd., Charlotte, NC 28211. (704) 364-6767.
SALES
Scott Dempsey
4100 City Line Ave., Philadelphia, PA 19131. (215) 879-3100.

SALES
Kristin Long
10 South Broadway, St. Louis, MO 63102. (314) 231-6050.
SALES
Gene Reinhardt

CABALLERO SPANISH MEDIA
261 Madison Ave., 18th fl., New York, NY 10016. (212) 697-4120. FAX: (212) 697-9151.
CEO
Eduardo Caballero
SENIOR V.P., NATIONAL SALES
Manny Ballastero
V.P., NEW YORK SALES
George Ortiz
ACCOUNT EXECUTIVES
Eric Bench, Rafael Cabrera, Anne-Marie Diaz, Lisa Rodriguez, Deborah Sackman, Marisol Vega
BRANCH OFFICES
205 N. Michigan Ave., Sutie 2015, Chicago, IL 60601. (312) 616-7251. FAX: (312) 819-8371.
SALES DIRECTOR
Kevin Jenkins
3500 Maple Ave., Suite 1320, Dallas, TX 75219. (214) 522-1888. FAX: (214) 522-7406.
V.P., SOUTHERN REGIONAL SALES
Charles Crawford
1156 W. 103rd St., Suite 215, St. Louis, MO 64114. (816) 471-5502. FAX: (816) 471-5502.
SALES
Gene Gray
3530 Wilshire Blvd., Suite 1260, Los Angeles, CA 90010. (213) 365-1222. FAX: (213) 365 1560.
V.P., WESTERN REGIONAL SALES
Leopoldo Ramos
Texas Bank Bldg., 13750 U.S. Hwy. 281 N., Suite 220, San Antonio, TX 78232. (210) 496-9262. FAX: (210) 496-6381.
750 Battery St., Suite 340, San Francisco, CA 94111. (415) 772-2740. FAX: (415) 772-2757.
SALES DIRECTOR
Janet Emmelman-Zablah

CABLE NETWORKS INC.
530 5th Ave., 6th floor, New York, NY 10036. (212) 382-5000. FAX: (212) 382-5055.
PRESIDENT & COO
Kathryn Lazar Sinnes
SENIOR V.P.
Stacey M. Colbeth
DIRECTOR, EASTERN DIVISION
Michael Labriola
BRANCH OFFICES
7 Piedmont Ctr., Suite 420, Atlanta, GA 30305. (404) 266-3885. FAX: (404) 266-3938.
NATIONAL SALES MANAGER
Jenny Harris
Prudential Tower, 800 Boylston St., 11th floor, Boston, MA 02199. (617) 266-7711. FAX: (617) 266-7853.
NATIONAL SALES MANAGER
Bill Wayland
625 N. Michigan Ave., Suite 1701, Chicago, IL 60611. (312) 335-0870. FAX: (312) 335-5466.
DIRECTOR, CENTRAL DIVISION
Gerry Himmel
8150 Brookriver Dr., Suite S-608, Dallas, TX 75247. (214) 905-9966. FAX: (214) 688-7472.
NATIONAL SALES MANAGER
Ray Gaskin
2000 Town Center, Suite 1390, Southfield, MI 48075. (810) 356-0580. FAX: (810) 356-2018.
NATIONAL SALES MANAGER
Laura Blake
2425 W. Olympic Blvd., Suite 5050, Santa Monica, CA 90404. (310) 828-1142. FAX: (310) 828-1232.
DIRECTOR, WESTERN DIVISION
Ilise Welter
(Cleveland Office), 6500 Rockside Rd., Suite 140, Independence, OH 44161. (216) 328-1214. FAX: (216) 328-1337.
NATIONAL SALES MANAGER
Tom Byrnes
353 Sacramento St., Suite 600, San Francisco, CA 94111. (415) 296-8222. FAX: (415) 296-9049.
NATIONAL SALES MANAGER
Ed Wocher
(Washington, DC Office), 1100 Wilson Blvd., Suite 1712, Arlington, VA 22209. (703) 276-1108. FAX: (703) 276-8398.
NATIONAL SALES MANAGER
Robert Ware

COMMERCIAL MEDIA SALES INC.
1439 Denniston Ave., Pittsburgh, PA 15217. (412) 421-2600.
FAX: (412) 421-6001.
PRESIDENT
Roger Rafson
DORA-CLAYTON AGENCY INC.
Box 33100, Decatur, GA 30033. (404) 373-2662. FAX: (404)
373-4658.
PRESIDENT
Daniel A. Haight
GROUP W TELEVISION SALES
565 Fifth Ave., New York, NY 10017. (212) 856-8000. FAX:
(212) 856-8144.
PRESIDENT
Joseph Berwanger
NY SALES MANAGER
Greg Schaefer
NY GROUP SALES MANAGER
Bob Kaplan
DIRECTOR, RESEARCH
Joseph Piccirillo
BRANCH OFFICES
1170 Soldiers Field Rd., Boston, MA 02134. (617) 787-7220.
SALES
Scott Brady
NBC Tower, 455 Cityfront Plaza, Chicago, IL 60611. (312) 245-
4830.
SALES
Greg Kess
31000 Telegraph Rd., Suite 200, Birmingham, MI 48010. (313)
647-8960.
SALES
Patricia Curry
6500 Wilshire Blvd., Suite 1150, Los Angeles, CA 90048. (213)
655-3556.
SALES
David Morris
Independence Mall East, Philadelphia, PA 19106. (215) 238-
4966.
SALES
Gary Herman
HARRINGTON, RIGHTER & PARSONS INC.
805 Third Ave., New York, NY 10022. (212) 756-3600. FAX:
(212) 756-3688.
CHAIRMAN
John J. Walters, Jr.
PRESIDENT
Peter F. Ryan
KATZ AMERICAN TELEVISION
125 W. 55 St., New York, NY 10019. (212) 424-6330. FAX:
(212) 424-6489.
PRESIDENT
Michael F. Hugger
V.P. & GENERAL SALES MANAGER
Swain Weiner
KATZ TELEVISION GROUP
PRESIDENT
Jim Beloyianis
KATZ CONTINENTAL TELEVISION
PRESIDENT
Jack Higgins
V.P., NATIONAL SALES MANAGER (EAST)
Chris Jordan
V.P., NATIONAL SALES MANAGER (SOUTHEAST)
Neil Davis
V.P., NATIONAL SALES MANAGER (EAST CENTRAL)
Bob Swan
V.P., NATIONAL SALES MANAGER (WEST CENTRAL)
Ardie Bialek
V.P., MANAGER (SOUTHEAST)
Paul Bowlin
KATZ NATIONAL TELEVISION
PRESIDENT
Marty Ozer
KATZ MEDIA GROUP
CHAIRMAN
Thompson Dean
PRESIDENT & CEO
Thomas F. Olson
HISPANIC MEDIA
V.P., MARKETING
Laura Hagan
V.P., GENERAL SALES MANAGER
Jeff Hodge
BRANCH OFFICES
6 Piedmont Center, Suite 710, Atlanta, GA 30305-1579. (404)
365-3100. FAX: (404) 816-5548.
MANAGER
Michael Panthere
Statler Office Bldg., Suite 220, Boston, MA 02116-4396. (617)
542-5466. FAX: (617) 357-1677.
MANAGER
Ruth Robertson
5821 Fairview Rd., Suite 407, Charlotte, NC 28209-3514. (704)
553-0220. FAX: (704) 553-1547.

MANAGER
Mark Turner
455 N. Cityfront Plaza Dr., Suite 1700, Chicago, IL 60611.
(312) 755-3800. FAX: (312) 755-1547.
MANAGER
Tom Morrissey
Keith Bldg., 1621 Euclid Ave., Suite 1718, Cleveland, OH
44115-5197. (216) 621-7924. FAX: (216) 623-8363.
MANAGER
Ray Mendelsohn
300 Crescent Ct., Suite 400, Dallas, TX 75201-1817. (214)
999-2014. FAX: (214) 855-78010.
MANAGER
Don Adams
(Detroit Office), 3310 W. Big Beaver Rd., Suite 501, Troy, MI
48084-2870. (313) 649-6390. FAX: (313) 649-2086.
MANAGER
Karen Nielsen
2900 Wesleyan, Suite 62, Houston, TX 77027-5150. (713) 961-
5195. FAX: (713) 961-5814.
MANAGER
Roger Ashley
6500 Wilshire Blvd., Suite 200, Los Angeles, CA 90048-4922.
(213) 966-5000. FAX: (213) 658-6901.
MANAGER
Shelly Adrian
Piper Jaffray Tower, Suite 2885, Minneapolis, MN 55402. (612)
339-4405. FAX: (612) 339-1335.
MANAGER
Deborah Ryan
1880 J.F. Kennedy Blvd., Phildelphia, PA 19103-2113. (215)
567-7590. FAX: (215) 567-3668.
MANAGER
Joe Eisenberg
10 S. Broadway. Suite 550, St. Louis, MO 63102-1795. (314)
231-1868. FAX: (314) 231-3620.
MANAGER
Gina Richardson
100 Spear St., Suite 1900, San Francisco, CA 94105-1575.
(415) 777-3377. FAX: (415) 978-9657.
MANAGER
Sandy York
3131 Elliot Ave., Suite 620, Seattle, WA (206) 284-3088. FAX:
(206) 284-5733.
MANAGER
Kevin Cahill
Suite 450, 7650 W. Courtney Campbell Causeway, Tampa, FL
33607-1462. (813) 287-8686. FAX: (813) 287-0953.
MANAGER
Greg Goldman
1233 20th St. NW, Suite 203, Washington, DC 20036-2304.
(202) 872-5880. FAX: (202) 872-0263.
MANAGER
Cliff McKinney
MMT SALES, INC.
150 E. 52 St., New York, NY 10022. (212) 319-8008.
CHAIRMAN & PRESIDENT
Jack Oken
EXECUTIVE V.P.
Charles Lizzo
SENIOR V.P., DIRECTOR
Don Gorman
SENIOR V.P., DIRECTOR OF SALES
Ted Van Erk
CORPORATE V.P., DIRECTOR OF RESEARCH
Al Cannarella
ART MOORE INC.
2200 Sixth Ave., Suite 707, Seattle, WA 98121-1823. (206)
443-9991. FAX: (206) 443-9998.
PRESIDENT
Greg Smith
MANAGER
Sandy Runnion
COO & SENIOR V.P.
Ruth Hallett
BRANCH OFFICES
4800 S.W. Macadam Ave., Suite 200, Portland, OR 97201.
(503) 228-0016. FAX: (503) 228-0556
V.P., MANAGER
Teddy Jones
222 Milwaukee St., Suite 209, Denver, CO 80206. (303) 321-
2354. FAX: (303) 321-1087.
SALES
Adriana Vernon
575 E. 4500 S., Salt Lake City, UT 84107. (801) 266-3576.
(801) 266-2365.
SENIOR V.P., MANAGER
Kathy Bingham
NBC SPOT TELEVISION SALES
30 Rockefeller Plaza, Rm. 5159, New York, NY 10128. (212)
664-3688. FAX: (212) 582-7452.
EXECUTIVE V.P., SALES & MARKETING
Monte Newman
DIRECTOR, SALES
Andrew Carone

PETRY TELEVISION, INC.
3 E. 54th St., New York, NY 10022. (212) 688-0200.
CHAIRMAN EMERITUS
David S. Allen
CHAIRMAN & CEO
Thomas F. Burchill
EXECUTIVE V.P. & CFO
James R.Ganley
EXECUTIVE V.P. & PRESIDENT
John Heise
V.P. & GENERAL SALES MANAGER
Jerry Linehan Sr.
V.P. & SALES DIRECTOR
Donald O'Toole

RAINBOW ADVERTISING SALES CORP.
260 Madison Ave., New York, NY 10016. (212) 889-3380. FAX:
(212) 725-6949.
PRESIDENT & COO
Thom McKinney
SENIOR V.P., ADVERTISING DIRECTOR
Phil De Cabia

RILEY REPRESENTATIVES
14330 Midway Rd., Suite 216, Dallas, TX 75244. (214) 788-
1630. FAX: (214) 490-6438.
OWNER
Jack Riley

SAVALLI BROADCAST SALES
11 Penn Plaza, Suite 962, New York, NY 10001. (212) 239-
3288. FAX: (212) 563-1301.
OWNER
Howard Weiss
SALES ACCOUNT EXECUTIVE
Joseph Savalli

SELTEL, INC.
40 West 57 St., New York, NY 10019. (212) 476-9400. FAX:
(212) 476-9630.
PRESIDENT & CEO
L. Donald Robinson
SENIOR V.P. & TREASURER
Maria Busi
SENIOR V.P., DOMESTIC SALES
David Schwartz
SENIOR V.P., CLIENT RELATIONS
Carl Mathis
BRANCH OFFICES
3490 Piedmont Rd., N.E., Suite 1206, Atlanta, GA 30309.
(404) 233-3906. FAX: (404) 233-5440.
GENERAL MANAGER
Dan Griffin
38 Newbury St., Suite 603, Boston, MA 02116. (617) 236-
8666. FAX: (617) 236-4927.
GENERAL MANAGER
Rose Ferarra
5821 Fairview Rd., Suite 308, Charlotte, NC 28209. (704) 554-
7124. FAX: (704) 553-7320.
V.P. & GENERAL MANAGER
Suzy Plettner
211 E. Ontario, Suite 700, Chicago, IL 60611. (312) 642-2450.
FAX: (312) 642-1631.
V.P. & GENERAL MANAGER
Mike Custardo
3131 McKinney Ave., Suite 240, Dallas, TX 75204. (214) 720-
0070. FAX: (214) 720-0111.
GENERAL MANAGER
Mike Girocco
222 Milwaukee St., Suite 210, Denver, CO 80206. (303) 333-
4845. FAX: (303) 321-1087.
GENERAL MANAGER
Gerriann Sullivan-Ward
4848 Loop Central Dr., Suite 710, Houston, TX 77081. (713)
660-8881. FAX: (713) 666-9586.
GENERAL MANAGER
Mike Thomas
6300 Wilshire Blvd., Suite #1700, Los Angeles, CA 90048.
(213) 658-5022. FAX: (213) 658-5312.
GENERAL MANAGER
David Ware
6101 Blue Lagoon Dr., Suite 340, Miami, FL 33126. (305) 266-
4066. FAX: (305) 266-7713.
GENERAL MANAGER
Enid Bluestone
120 S. 6th St., Suite 2005, Minneapolis, MN 55402. (612) 338-
7017. FAX: (612) 349-6261.
GENERAL MANAGER
Essie Dalton
1760 Market St., 7th fl., Philadelphia, PA 19103. (215) 563-
5400. FAX: (215) 563-2974.
GENERAL MANAGER
Rickie Roberts
1512 S.W. 18th Ave., Portland, OR 97201. (503) 226-2911.
FAX: (503) 226-6596.

GENERAL MANAGER
Richard Gohlman
St. Louis Place, 200 N. Broadway, Suite 1125, St. Louis, MO
63102. (314) 241-4193. FAX: (314) 241-9849.
V.P., GENERAL MANAGER
Richard J. Quigley III
444 Market, Suite 1520, San Francisco, CA 94133. (415) 391-
8890. FAX: (415) 391-8890.
GENERAL MANAGER
Steve Jones
211 6th Ave. N., Suite 200, Seattle, WA 98109. (206) 285-
1913. FAX: (206) 281-4178.
GENERAL MANAGER
Bob Tacher
3507 Frontage Rd., Suite 130, Tampa, FL 33607. (813) 286-
9686. FAX: (813) 282-3234.
V.P., GENERAL MANAGER
Steve Henderson

TCI CABLE ADVERTISING, INC.
2940 Limited Ln. N.W., Olympia, WA 98502. (360) 754-7081.
FAX: (360) 943-5911.
GENERAL MANAGER
Darrin Struckman
AREA SALES MANAGER
Linda Boysen

TV-REP INC.
Box 708, Bloomfield Hills, MI 48303-0708. (810) 355-2020.
FAX: (810) 355-0368.
PRESIDENT
Douglas Johnson

TELEREP, INC.
1 Dag Hammarskjold Plaza, New York, NY 10017-2296. (212)
759-8787.
PRESIDENT & GENERAL MANAGER
Steven Herson
V.P., & GENERAL SALES MANAGER
Larry Goldberg
V.P. & GENERAL SALES MANAGER (COUGAR & WILDCAT
STATIONS)
Lisa Brown
V.P. & SALES DIRECTOR (TIGER STATIONS)
Thomas Tilson
V.P. & GENERAL SALES MANAGER (TIGER STATIONS)
Andy Feinstein
V.P. & GENERAL SALES MANAGER (LION STATIONS)
John Dewan

ADAM YOUNG, INC.
599 Lexington Ave., New York, NY 10022. (212) 688-5100.
FAX: (212) 758-5090.
CHAIRMAN
Vincent J. Young
VICE CHAIRMAN & TREASURER
Adam Young
PRESIDENT
Arthur W. Scott, Jr.
BRANCH OFFICES
4 Piedmont Center, Suite 711, Atlanta, GA 30305. (404) 261-
8800. FAX: (404) 261-8800.
MANAGER
Tom Durr
31 St. James Ave., 9th fl., Boston, MA 02116. (617) 423-4987.
FAX: (617) 423-4604.
MANAGER
John D. Ketell
444 N. Michigan Ave., Suite 920, Chicago, IL 60611. (312)
744-1313. FAX: (312) 744-0196.
V.P. & MANAGER
Lois Hamelin
3232 McKinney Ave., Suite 670, Dallas, TX 75204. (214) 871-
2988. FAX: (214) 871-2900.
MANAGER
Lynda Showtell
2855 Coolidge, Suite 222, Detroit, MI 48084. (313) 649-3999.
FAX: (313) 649-6455.
MANAGER
Allan Baur
6100 Wilshire Blvd., Suite 320, Los Angeles, CA 90048. (213)
938-2081. FAX: (213) 938-1483.
WEST COAST MANAGER
Thomas Camarada
706 2nd Ave. S., Minneapolis, MN 55402. (612) 339-3397.
FAX: (612) 339-7182.
MANAGER
James O. Ramsland
Box 411186, St. Louis, MO 63147. (314) 991-5249. FAX: (314)
991-2268.
MANAGER
Bruce Schneider
155 Montgomery St., Suite 406, San Francisco, CA 94104.
(415) 986-5366. FAX: (415) 986-0224.
ACCOUNT EXECUTIVE
Andrew Rosenfeld

State Broadcast Associations

ALABAMA BROADCASTERS ASSOCIATION
1316 Alford Ave., Suite 201, Birmingham AL 35226. (205) 979-1690. FAX: (205) 979-9981.
EXECUTIVE DIRECTOR
Ben K. McKinnon

ALASKA BROADCASTERS ASSOCIATION
Box 102424, Anchorage, AK 99510. (907) 258-2424. FAX: (907) 258-2414.
EXECUTIVE DIRECTOR
Robin Kornfield

ARIZONA BROADCASTERS ASSOCIATION
3101 N. Central Ave., Suite 560, Phoenix, AZ 85012. (602) 274-1418. FAX: (602) 631-9853.
EXECUTIVE DIRECTOR
Art Brooks

ARKANSAS BROADCASTERS ASSOCIATION
2024 Arkansas Valley Drive, Suite 201, Little Rock, AR 72212. (501) 227-7564. FAX: (501) 223-9798.
PRESIDENT
Elvis Moody

CALIFORNIA BROADCASTERS ASSOCIATION
1127 11th St., Suite 730, Sacramento, CA 95814. (916) 444-2237. FAX: (916) 444-2043.
EXECUTIVE DIRECTOR
Victor J. Biondi

COLORADO BROADCASTERS ASSOCIATION
1660 Lincoln, #2202, Denver, CO 80264. (303) 894-0911. FAX: (303) 830-8326.
EXECUTIVE DIRECTOR
Cliff Dodge

CONNECTICUT BROADCASTERS ASSOCIATION
Box 678, Glastonbury, CT 06033. (203) 633-5031. FAX: (203) 657-2491.
PRESIDENT
Paul K. Taff

FLORIDA ASSOCIATION OF BROADCASTERS, INC.
109 E. College Ave., Tallahassee, FL 32301. (904) 681-6444. FAX: (904) 222-3957.
PRESIDENT
C. Patrick Roberts

GEORGIA ASSOCIATION OF BROADCASTERS, INC.
8010 Roswell Rd.. Suite 260, Atlanta, GA 30350. (404) 395-7200. FAX: (404) 395-7235.
EXECUTIVE DIRECTOR
William G. Sanders

HAWAII ASSOCIATION OF BROADCASTERS
Box 91049, Honolulu, HI 96835. (808) 591-9349.
PRESIDENT
Bernie Armstrong

IDAHO STATE BROADCASTERS ASSOCIATION
405 S. Eighth St., #365, Boise, ID 83702-7100. (208) 345-3072. FAX: (208) 343-8046.
PRESIDENT
Connie Searles

ILLINOIS BROADCASTERS ASSOCIATION
1125 S. 5th St., Springfield, IL 62704. (217) 753-2636. FAX: (217) 753-8443.
EXECUTIVE DIRECTOR
Wally Gair

INDIANA BROADCASTERS ASSOCIATION, INC.
11595 Meridian St., Carmel, IN 46032. (317) 573-2995. FAX: (317) 573-2994.
EXECUTIVE DIRECTOR
Linda Compton

IOWA BROADCASTERS ASSOCIATION
Box 71186, Des Moines, IA 50325. (515) 224-7237. FAX: (515) 224-6560.
EXECUTIVE DIRECTOR
Sue Toma

KANSAS ASSOCIATION OF BROADCASTERS
800 S.W. Jackson St., Suite 818, Topeka, 66612-1216. (913) 235-1307. FAX: (913) 233-3052.
EXECUTIVE DIRECTOR
Harriet J. Lange

KENTUCKY BROADCASTERS ASSOCIATION
Box 680, Lebanon, KY 40033. (502) 692-6888. FAX: (502) 692-6003.
EXECUTIVE DIRECTOR & TREASURER
J.T. Whitlock

LOUISIANA ASSOCIATION OF BROADCASTERS
8762 Quarters Lake Rd., Baton Rouge, LA 70809. (504) 922-9150. FAX: (504) 922-7750.
EXECUTIVE DIRECTOR
Louise Lowman

MAINE ASSOCIATION OF BROADCASTERS
128 State St., Augusta, ME 04330. (207) 623-3870. FAX: (207) 621-0585.
EXECUTIVE DIRECTOR
Suzanne Goucher

MARYLAND-DISTRICT OF COLUMBIA-DELAWARE BROADCASTERS ASSOCIATION, INC.
1 E. Chase St., Suite 1129, Baltimore, MD 21202. (410) 385-0224. FAX: (410) 783-1875.
PRESIDENT
Chip Weinman

MASSACHUSETTS BROADCASTERS ASSOCIATION INC.
446 Boston Rd., Suite 351, Billerica, MA 01821. (800) 471-1875. FAX: (800) 471-1876.
EXECUTIVE DIRECTOR
B. Allan Sprague

MICHIGAN ASSOCIATION OF BROADCASTERS
819 N. Washington Ave., Lansing, MI 48906. (517) 484-7444. FAX: (517) 484-5810.
EXECUTIVE DIRECTOR
Karole White

MINNESOTA BROADCASTERS ASSOCIATION
3517 Raleigh Ave. S., Box 16030, St. Louis Park, MN 55416-0030. (612) 926-8123. FAX: (612) 926-9761.
EXECUTIVE DIRECTOR
James J. Wychor

MISSISSIPPI ASSOCIATION OF BROADCASTERS
15 Northtown Dr., Suite A, Jackson, MS 39211. (601) 957-9121. FAX: (601) 957-9121.
EXECUTIVE DIRECTOR
Jackie Lett

MISSOURI BROADCASTERS ASSOCIATION
P.O. Box 104445, 1803 Sun Valley Dr., Jefferson City, MO 65110-4445. (314) 636-6692. FAX: (314) 634-8258.
EXECUTIVE V.P.
Don Hicks

MONTANA BROADCASTERS ASSOCIATION
Box 503, Helena, MT 59624. (406) 442-3961. FAX: (406) 442-3987.
EXECUTIVE DIRECTOR
Bob Hoehne

NEBRASKA BROADCASTERS ASSOCIATION
12020 Shamrock Pl., Suite 200, Omaha, NE 68154. (402) 333-3034. FAX: (402) 333-1762.
EXECUTIVE DIRECTOR
Richard Palmquist

NEVADA BROADCASTERS ASSOCIATION
2255-A Renaissance Dr., Suite 28, Las Vegas, NV 89119. (702) 891-0177. FAX: (702) 891-0203.
PRESIDENT
Robert D. Fisher

NEW HAMPSHIRE ASSOCIATION OF BROADCASTERS
10 Chestnut Dr., Bedford, NH 03110. (603) 472-9800. FAX: (603) 472-9803.
PRESIDENT
B. Allan Sprague

NEW JERSEY BROADCASTERS ASSOCIATION
7 Centre Dr., Suite One, Jamesburg, NJ 08331. (609) 860-0111. FAX: (609) 860-0110.
PRESIDENT
Phil Roberts

NEW MEXICO BROADCASTERS ASSOCIATION
790-9D Tramway Lane N.E., Albuquerque, NM 87122. (505) 856-6748. FAX: (505) 856-6748.
EXECUTIVE DIRECTOR
Dee Schelling

NEW YORK STATE BROADCASTERS ASSOCIATION, INC.
115A Great Oaks Office Park, Albany, NY 12203. (518) 456-8888. FAX: (518) 456-8943.
PRESIDENT
Joseph A. Reilly

NORTH CAROLINA ASSOCIATION OF BROADCASTERS
Box 627, Raleigh, NC 27602. (919) 821-7300. FAX: (919) 829-1583.
EXECUTIVE MANAGER
Laura Ridgeway

NORTH DAKOTA BROADCASTERS ASSOCIATION
Box 5324, Grand Forks, ND 58206. (701) 775-3537. FAX: (701) 775-3537.
EXECUTIVE DIRECTOR
Chuck Bundlie

OHIO ASSOCIATION OF BROADCASTERS, INC.
88 E. Broad St., Suite 1780, Columbus, OH 43215. (614) 228-4052. FAX: (614) 228-8133.
EXECUTIVE V.P.
Dale V. Bring

OKLAHOMA ASSOCIATION OF BROADCASTERS
6520 N. Western, Suite 104, Oklahoma City, OK 73116. (405) 848-0771. FAX: (405) 848-0772.
EXECUTIVE DIRECTOR
Carl C. Smith

OREGON ASSOCIATION OF BROADCASTERS
Box 20037, Portland, OR 97220. (503) 257-3041. FAX: (503) 257-3041.
EXECUTIVE DIRECTOR
Gordon Bussey

PENNSYLVANIA ASSOCIATION OF BROADCASTERS
P.O. Box 4669, Harrisburg, PA 17111-0669. (717) 534-2504. FAX: (717) 533-1119.
PRESIDENT
Richard Wyckoff

RHODE ISLAND BROADCASTERS ASSOCIATION
c/o WNRI Radio, 786 Diamond Hill Rd., Woonsocket, RI 02895. (401) 769-6925.
PRESIDENT
William Campbell

SOUTH CAROLINA BROADCASTERS ASSOCIATION
College of Journalism & Mass Communications, Univ. of South Carolina, Columbia, SC 29208. (803) 777-6783. FAX: (803) 777-4103.
EXECUTIVE MANAGER
Dr. Richard M. Uray

SOUTH DAKOTA BROADCASTERS ASSOCIATION
1018 S. Lyndale, Sioux Falls, SD 57105. (605) 334-2682.
PRESIDENT
Joe Cooper

TENNESSEE ASSOCIATION OF BROADCASTERS
Box 101015, Nashville, TN 37224-1015. (615) 399-3791. FAX: (615) 361-3488.
VICE PRESIDENT
Whit Adamson

TEXAS ASSOCIATION OF BROADCASTERS
1907 N. Lamar, Suite 300, Austin, TX 78705. (512) 322-9944. FAX: (512) 322-0522.
EXECUTIVE DIRECTOR
Ann Arnold

UTAH BROADCASTERS ASSOCIATION
1600 S. Main St., Salt Lake City, UT 84115. (801) 486-9521. FAX: (801) 484-7294.
EXECUTIVE DIRECTOR
Dale O. Zabriskie

VERMONT ASSOCIATION OF BROADCASTERS
15 W. Patterson St., Barre, VT 05641. (802) 476-8789. FAX: (802) 479-5893.
EXECUTIVE DIRECTOR
Alan H. Noyes

VIRGINIA ASSOCIATION OF BROADCASTERS
630 County Green Lane, Charlottesville, VA 22902. (804) 977-3716. FAX: (804) 979-2439.
EXECUTIVE DIRECTOR
Peter Easter

WASHINGTON STATE ASSOCIATION OF BROADCASTERS
924 Capitol Way S., Suite 104, Olympia, WA 98501. (206) 705-0774. FAX: (206) 705-0873.
EXECUTIVE DIRECTOR
Mark Allen

WEST VIRGINIA BROADCASTERS ASSOCIATION
2120 Weberwood Dr., South Charleston, WV 25303-3099. (304) 744-2143. FAX: (304) 345-3798.
PRESIDENT
Marilyn Fletcher

WISCONSIN BROADCASTERS ASSOCIATION
44 E. Mifflin St., Suite 900, Madison, WI 53703. (608) 255-2600. FAX: (608) 256-3986.
PRESIDENT
M. John Laabs

WYOMING ASSOCIATION OF BROADCASTERS
1807 Capitol Ave., Cheyenne, WY 82003. (307) 632-7622. FAX: (307) 638-3469.
EXECUTIVE DIRECTOR
Ray Lansing

THE CABLE INDUSTRY

CABLE NETWORKS

CABLE SYSTEM OPERATORS

DIRECT BROADCAST SATELLITE
& WIRELESS BROADCASTERS

CABLE NETWORKS

Premium cable services and pay-per-view services are designated as such. All others are basic cable services. Regional news and sports programming is excluded. Most programming is also available on selected satellite broadcasting services.

A & E TELEVISION NETWORK/THE HISTORY CHANNEL
(A joint venture of Hearst Corp., ABC and NBC)
235 E. 45 St., New York, NY 10017.(212) 210-1328. FAX: (212) 949-7147.
PRESIDENT & CEO
Nickolas Davatzes
SENIOR V.P., PROGRAMMING & PRODUCTION
Brooke Baily Johnson
EXECUTIVE V.P., SALES & MARKETING
Whitney Goit II
EXECUTIVE V.P./CHIEF FINANCIAL OFFICER/ADMIN. OFFICER
Seymour H. Lesser

AMERICAN MOVIE CLASSICS (AMC)
Rainbow Programming Service Holdings Inc., 150 Crossways Park West, Woodbury, NY 11797. (516) 364-2222. FAX: (516) 364-8929.
PRESIDENT, NATIONAL SERVICES
Joshua Sapan
V.P./GENERAL MANAGER
Kate McEnroe

BLACK ENTERTAINMENT TELEVISION (BET)
One Bet Plaza, 1900 W. Place NE, Washington, D.C. 20018-1211. (202) 608-2000.
CHAIRMAN & CEO
Robert L. Johnson
PRESIDENT & COO
Debra Lee, Legal
PRESIDENT, BET NETWORKS
Jeffers K. Lee
CFO
William T. Gordon III

THE BOX
12000 Biscayne Blvd., #600, Miami, FL 33181-2742. (305) 899-9000. FAX: (305) 892-3600.
CHIEF FINANCIAL OFFICER
Luann Simpson

BRAVO
Rainbow Programming Holdings Inc., 150 Crossways Park West, Woodbury, NY 11797. (516) 364-2222. FAX: (516) 364-7638.
PRESIDENT, NATIONAL SERVICES
Joshua Sapan
V.P./GENERAL MANAGER
Kathleen Dore
V.P., PROGRAMMING
Jonathan Sehring

CONSUMER NEWS & BUSINESS CHANNEL (CNBC)
(A subsidiary of NBC)
2200 Fletcher Ave., Ft. Lee, NJ 07024. (201) 585-2622. FAX: (201) 585-6482.

C-SPAN CABLE SATELLITE PUBLIC AFFAIRS NETWORK (C-SPAN/C-SPAN 2)
400 N. Capitol St., N.W., Suite 650, Washington, DC 20001. (202) 737-3220. FAX: (202) 737-3323.
CHAIRMAN AND CEO
Brian P. Lamb
SENIOR V.P.
Robert Kennedy
SENIOR V.P.
Susan Swain
V.P. OF PROGRAMMING
Terence Murphy

CABLE NEWS NETWORK (CNN) & HEADLINE NEWS
Turner Broadcasting System, One CNN Center, P.O. Box 105366, Atlanta, GA 30348-5366. (404) 827-1700. FAX: (404) 523-8517. Headline News: (404) 827-1500.
BOARD CHAIRMAN, CEO & PRESIDENT OF TBS, INC.
R. E. (Ted) Turner
PRESIDENT
Tom Johnson
VICE CHAIRMAN
Burt Reinhardt
EXECUTIVE V.P., NEWS GATHERING
Ed Turner

EXECUTIVE V.P., HEADLINE NEWS
John Petrovich

CABLE VIDEO STORE
532 Broadway, 7th fl., New York, NY 10012. (212) 941-1434. FAX: (212) 941-4746.
V.P., PROGRAMMING
Barry Teiman

CARTOON NETWORK
(A subsidiary of TBS)
1050 Techwood Dr. N.W., Atlanta, GA 30318. (404) 885-2263. FAX: (404) 885-4301.
PRESIDENT
Betty Cohen
GENERAL MANAGER
Rob Sorcher
SENIOR V.P., MARKETING
Craig McAnsh
SENIOR V.P., PROGRAMMING
Mike Lazzo
SENIOR V.P., CREATIVE SERVICES
Stephen Croncota
V.P., PUBLIC RELATIONS
Shirley Powell

CHRISTIAN BROADCASTING NETWORK
977 Centerville Tpke., Virginia Beach, VA 23463-0001. (804) 579-7000. FAX: (804) 579-2017.
FOUNDER & CHIEF EXECUTIVE OFFICER
M.G. (Pat) Robertson

CINEMAX
(See Home Box Office Listing)

COMEDY CENTRAL
1775 Broadway, New York, NY 10019. (212) 767-8600. FAX: (212) 767-8582.
PRESIDENT & CEO
Bob Kreek
SENIOR V.P., AD SALES
Larry Divney
SENIOR V.P., PROGRAMMING
Vinny Faelle
V.P., MEDIA RELATIONS
Tony Fox

COUNTRY MUSIC TELEVISION
2806 Opreyland Dr., Nashville, TN 37214. (615) 871-5830. FAX: (615) 871-6698.
PRESIDENT
David Hall

THE DISCOVERY CHANNEL
7700 Wisconsin Ave., Bethesda, MD 20814. (301) 986-1999. FAX: (301) 986-4826.
CHAIRMAN & CEO
John S. Hendricks
PRESIDENT & CEO
Gregory Moyer
CHIEF FINANCIAL OFFICER
Greg Durig
SENIOR V.P., PROGRAMMING
Chuck Gingold
SENIOR V.P., PRODUCTION
Tim Cowling
SENIOR V.P., ADVERTISING SALES
Bill McGowan

THE DISNEY CHANNEL
(A premium cable service of the Walt Disney Company)
3800 West Alameda Ave., Burbank, CA 91505. (818) 569-7500. FAX: (818) 588-1241.

E! ENTERTAINMENT TELEVISION
5670 Wilshire Blvd., Los Angeles, CA 90036-3709. (213) 954-2400. FAX: (213) 954-2661.
PRESIDENT & CEO
Lee Masters
SENIOR V.P. & CFO
Bill Keenan

SENIOR V.P., INTERNATIONAL DEVELOPMENT
Chris Fager
SENIOR V.P., PROGRAMMING
Fran Shea
SENIOR V.P., MARKETING
Dale Hopkins
SENIOR V.P., AFFILIATE RELATIONS
Debra Green
SENIOR V.P., HUMAN RESOURCES
Patti Robinson
SENIOR V.P., ADVERTISING SALES
Dave Cassaro
SENIOR V.P., LEGAL & BUSINESS AFFAIRS
Mark Feldman

ENTERTAINMENT & SPORTS PROGRAMMING NETWORK, INC. (ESPN)
ESPN Plaza, Bristol, CT 06010. (203) 585-2000. FAX: (203) 585-2213: and 605 Third Ave., New York, NY 10158-0180. (212) 916-9200.
PRESIDENT & CEO (NY)
Steve Bornstein
SENIOR V.P., COMMUNICATIONS (CT)
Rose M. Gatti
EXECUTIVE V.P., MARKETING & GENERAL COUNSEL (NY)
Ed Durso

ENCORE
(A premium cable service)
5445 Denver Tech. Center Parkway, #600, Engelwood, CO 80111-3051. (303) 771-7700. FAX: (303) 741-3067.
CHAIRMAN & CEO
John J. Sie

FAITH & VISION (F & V)
74 Trinity Pl., Suite 915, New York, NY 10006. (212) 964-1663. FAX: (212) 964-5966.
CEO
Nelson Price

FAMILY CHANNEL
2877 Guardian Lane, Virginia Beach, VA 23452. (804) 459-6000. FAX: (804) 459-6425.
CEO & PRESIDENT
Timothy B. Robertson
CEO, MTM ENTERTAINMENT
Tony Thomopoulos

FOX NEWS CHANNEL
(A subsidiary of Fox, Inc.)
Box 900, Beverly Hills, CA 90213. (310) 369-1000. FAX: (310) 369-3779.

FX NETWORKS INC.
(A subsidiary of Fox, Inc.)
Box 900, Beverly Hills, CA 90213. (310) 369-1000. FAX: (310) 369-3779.
CHAIRMAN & CEO
Anne Sweeney

GALAVISION
(Spanish language)
605 Third Ave., 12th Floor, New York, NY 10158. (212) 455-5200.
PRESIDENT & COO
Javier Saralegui

HOME BOX OFFICE, INC.
(A premium service and subsidiary of Time Warner, Inc.)
1100 Ave. Of the Americas, New York, NY 10036. (212) 512-1000. FAX: (212) 512-5517.
PRESIDENT & CEO
Jeff Bewkes
EXECUTIVE V.P., SALES & MARKETING
John Billock
SENIOR V.P., CORPORATE COMMUNICATIONS
Richard Plepler

HOME SHOPPING NETWORK INC.
P.O. Box 9090, Clearwater, FL 34618-9090. (813) 572-8585. FAX: (813) 539-8137.
PRESIDENT & CEO
Gerald Hogan
EXECUTIVE V.P.
Nory Le Brun

INDEPENDENT FILM CHANNEL
(A premium cable service.)
Rainbow Programming Holdings Inc., 150 Crossways Park West, Woodbury, NY 11797. (516) 364-2222. FAX: (516) 364-7638.
EXECUTIVE V.P. & GENERAL MANAGER
Kathleen Dore
V.P., PROGRAMMING
Jonathan Sehring

KTLA
(United Video Television)
7140 S. Lewis Ave., Tulsa, OK 74136-5422. (800) 331-4806. FAX: (918) 488-4928.

PRESIDENT
Jeff Treeman

KALEIDOSCOPE TELEVISION (KTV)
(Programming for Americans with disabilities.)
1777 N.E. Loop 410, Suite 300, San Antonio, TX 78217. (210) 824-7446. (210) 824-1666. FAX: (210) 829-1388.
PRESIDENT & CEO
Dr. Bill Nichols
EXECUTIVE V.P., PROGRAMMING & PRODUCTION
Ron Dixon

THE LEARNING CHANNEL, THE
Discovery Communications Inc., 7700 Wisconsin Ave., Bethesda, MD 20814. (301) 986-1999.
CHAIRMAN & CEO
Harold E. Morse
PRESIDENT & CHIEF OPERATING OFFICER
Robert J. Shuman

LIFETIME
(Lifetime Entertainment Services)
Worldwide Plaza, 309 W. 49th St., New York, NY 10019. (212) 424-7000. FAX: (212) 424-4264.
PRESIDENT & CEO
Douglas W. McCormick
SENIOR V.P., PROGRAMMING & PRODUCTION
Judy Girard
EXECUTIVE V.P.
Jane Tollinger

MSNBC
(A joint venture of NBC and Microsoft, also providing service on the Internet.)
2200 Fletcher Ave., Ft. Lee, NJ 07024. (201) 583-5010. Internet programming and e-mail: http://www.msnbc.com
PRESIDENT, NBC NEWS
Andrew Lack
V.P. & GENERAL MANAGER, MSNBC
Mark Harrington
PRESIDENT, NBC CABLE & BUSINESS DEVELOPMENT
Tom Rogers
V.P., STATEGIC PARTNERSHIPS, INTERACTIVE MEDIA DIVISION, MICROSOFT
Peter Neupert
V.P., MSNBC MEDIA RELATIONS
Lauren Leff

MTV NETWORKS, INC.
(A subsidiary of Viacom, Inc.)
1515 Broadway, New York, NY 10036. (212) 258-7800. FAX: (212) 258- 8358.
CHAIRMAN & CEO
Thomas E. Freston

MOVIES FROM FOX (FXM)
(See FX Networks listing.)

NICKELODEON
(See MTV Network listing)

NOSTALGIA TELEVISION
650 Massachusetts Ave. NW, Washington, DC 20001. (202) 289-6633. FAX: (202) 289-6632. e-mail: http://www.nostalgiatv.com
PRESIDENT & CEO
Squire Rushnell

PREVUE NETWORK
(Program listings for cable.)
One Technology Plaza, 7140 S. Lewis Ave., Tulsa, OK 74136-5422. (918) 488-4450. FAX: (918) 488-4638.
PRESIDENT
Joe Batson

PRISM
(A premium cable service)
225 City Line Ave., Bala Cynwyd, PA 19004. (215) 668-2210. FAX: (215) 668-9499.
V.P. & GENERAL MANAGER
Dennis E. Patton
DIRECTOR OF ENTERTAINMENT & PROGRAMMING
Lynn Lonker

PLAYBOY TV
(A pay-per-view cable service)
9242 Beverly Blvd., Beverly Hills, CA 90210. (310) 246-4000. FAX: (310) 246-4050.
PRESIDENT
Tony Lynn

QVC
Goshen Corporate Park, 1365 Enterprise Dr., West Chester, PA 19380. (610) 701-1000. FAX: (610) 701-8170.

PRESIDENT
Doug Briggs

REQUEST TELEVISION
(A pay-per-view cable service)
5619 DTC Pkwy., Suite 800, 9th fl., Denver, CO 80111. (303) 267-6100. FAX: (303) 267-6195.
PRESIDENT & CEO
Hugh Panero
V.P., MARKETING & PROGRAMMING
Jeffrey Bernstein

THE SCI-FI CHANNEL
(See USA Network)

SHOWTIME NETWORKS, INC.
(A premium cable service and a subsidiary of Viacom, Inc.)
1633 Broadway, New York, NY 10019. (212) 708-1600. FAX: (212) 708-1530.
CHAIRMAN & CHIEF EXECUTIVE OFFICER
Winston H. (Tony) Cox
PRESIDENT & COO
Matthew Blank
EXECUTIVE V.P., PROGRAMMING
Jim Miller
EXECUTIVE V.P.&GENERAL COUNSEL
Gregory J. Ricca
EXEC. V.P. & G. M., SHOWTIME SATELLITE NETWORKS
Susan Denison

SPICE
(A pay-per-view cable service)
536 Broadway, 7th fl., New York, NY 10012. (212) 941-1434. FAX: (212) 941-4746.
PRESIDENT
Mark Graff

TBS
Turner Broadcasting System, 1050 Techwood Drive, N.W., Atlanta, GA 30318. (404) 827-1700. FAX: (404) 827-1947.
CHAIRMAN
R.E. (Ted) Turner

THE NASHVILLE NETWORK (TNN)
(A service of Opryland USA, Inc. and Group W Satellite Communications.)
Box 10210, 250 Harbor Plaza Dr., Stamford, CT 06904-2210. (203) 965-6000.
Production Center address: 2806 Opryland Dr., Nashville, TN 37214. (615) 889-6840. FAX (615) 871-6944.
PRESIDENT
Don Mitzner
EXECUTIVE V.P.
Lloyd Werner

TURNER NETWORK TELEVISION (TNT)
1050 Techwood Dr., N.W., P.O. Box 105366, One CNN Center, Atlanta, GA 30318. (404) 885-4538. FAX: (404) 885-4947.
1888 Century Park East, 14th Fl., Los Angeles, CA 90067 (310) 551-6341. FAX (310) 551-6634.
EXECUTIVE V.P. ORIGINAL PROGRAMMING
Allen Sabinson
EXECUTIVE V.P., TURNER PICTURE GROUP
Robert Osher
SENIOR V.P., BUSINESS AFFAIRS
Susan Oman Gross
V.P., PROGRAM DEVELOPMENT
Howard Cohen
Betsy Newman

THE TRAVEL CHANNEL
2690 Cumberland Pkwy., Suite 500, Atlanta, GA 30339. (770) 801-2400. FAX: (770) 801-2441.
PRESIDENT & CEO
Kevin D. Senie
SENIOR V.P., ADVERTSING SALES
William C. Wiehe
VICE PRESIDENT, NEW MEDIA
Mike Carey
V.P., PROGRAMMING & PRODUCTION
Gail Gleeson
V.P., PROGRAMMING & PRODUCTION
Karen Hanley
V.P., MARKETING
Thomas Lucas
V.P., AFFILIATE SALES
Dana Michaelis
V.P., BUSINESS DEVELOPMENT
T. Bahnson
V.P., PUBLIC RELATIONS
Gillian Renault

TRINITY BROADCASTING NETWORK
2900 Airport Fwy., Irving, TX 75062. (214) 313-1333.
PRESIDENT
Paul F. Crouch
DIRECTOR, NATIONAL CABLE MARKETING
Bob Higley

USA NETWORKS
1230 Ave. of the Americas, New York, NY 10020. (212) 408-9100. FAX: (212) 408-3606.
FOUNDER, CHAIRMAN & CEO
Kay Koplovitz
CFO & SENIOR V.P., ADMINISTRATION
Doug Hamilton
SENIOR V.P., RESEARCH
Tim Brooks
SENIOR V.P., MARKETING
Andrew Besch
EXEC. V.P., BUSINESS AFFAIRS, OPERATIONS & GENERAL COUNSEL
Stephen Brenner
EXECUTIVE V.P., AFFILIATE RELATIONS
Douglas Holloway
EXECUTIVE V.P., PROGRAMMING & PRESIDENT, USA NETWORKS ENTERTAINMENT
Rhoderic Perth
EXECUTIVE V.P., AD SALES
John Silvestri

UNITED VIDEO TELEVISION
A UVSG Company, 7140 S. Lewis Ave., Tulsa, OK 74136-5422. (800) 331-4806. FAX: (918) 488-4928.
PRESIDENT
Jeff Treeman

UNIVISION
Univision Holdings, Inc., 605 Third Ave., 12th fl., New York, NY 10158-0180. (212) 455-5200.
V.P & DIRECTOR, AFFILIATE RELATIONS
Stuart Livingston

VH-1
(See MTV Network listing)

VIEWER'S CHOICE
(A pay-per-view cable service.)
909 Third Ave., 21st floor, New York, NY 10022. (212) 486-6600. FAX: (212) 688-9497.
PRESIDENT
James O. Heyworth
EXECUTIVE V.P., SALES & MARKETING
J. Robert Bedell
SENIOR V.P., FINANCE & ADMINISTRATION
Samuel Yates
V.P. OF TECHNOLOGY & OPERATIONS
John Vartanian
V.P., PROGRAMMING
Michael Klein
V.P. & GENERAL COUNSEL
Sandra E. Landau, Esq.
V.P. AFFILIATE RELATIONS
Terry Taylor
V.P.VIDEO PROMOTION
Leigh Bolton

WPIX
United Video, Inc., A UVSG Company, 7140 S. Lewis Ave., Tulsa, OK 74136-5422. (918) 488-4000. FAX: (918) 488-4250.
CONTACT
Jeff Treeman

WWOR TV
Advance Entertainment Corporation, 5015 Campuswood Dr., E., Syracuse, NY 13057 (315) 455-5955. (800) 448-3322. FAX: (315) 433-2342.
MARKETING MANAGER
Betsy Bianco

THE WEATHER CHANNEL
2600 Cumberland Parkway, Atlanta, GA 30039. (404) 434-6800. FAX: (404) 801-2130.
CHIEF EXECUTIVE OFFICER
Michael J. Eckert
SENIOR V.P., PROGRAMMING & OPERATIONS
Stan Hunter
SENIOR V.P., ADVERTISING SALES
William Wiehe
V.P., AFFILIATE SALES
Rebecca Ruthuen

ADELPHIA COMMUNICATIONS CORP.
Box 472, 5 West Third St., Coudersport, PA 16915. (814) 274-9830. FAX: (814) 274-8631.
PRESIDENT, CHAIRMAN & CEO
John Rigas
CHIEF FINANCIAL OFFICER
Timothy J. Rigas

AMERICAN CABLE ENTERTAINMENT
4 Landmark Sq., Suite 302, Stamford, CT 06901. (203) 323-1100. FAX: (203) 325-3110.

ARMSTRONG GROUP OF COLORADO
One Armstrong Pl., Butler, PA 16001. (412) 283-0925. FAX: (412) 283-2602.

BLADE COMMUNICATIONS
541 N. Superior St., Toledo, OH 43660. (419) 245-6000. FAX: (419) 245-6167.

BOOTH AMERICAN CO.
333 W. Fort St., Detroit, MI 48226. (313) 202-3360. FAX: (313) 202-3390.

BRESNAN COMMUNICATIONS
709 Westchester Ave., White Plains, NY 10604. (914) 993-6600. FAX: (914) 993-6601.

C-TEC CABLE SYSTEMS
150 Carnegie Center, Princeton, NJ 08540. (609) 734-3700. FAX: (609) 734-3717.
EXECUTIVE VICE PRESIDENT
Stephen J. Rabbitt
CHIEF FINANCIAL OFFICER
Loraine Reddington

CABLEVISION INDUSTRIES INC.
One Cablevision Ctr., Liberty, NY 12754. (914) 292-7550. FAX: (914) 295-2761.
CHAIRMAN & CEO
Alan Gerry
V.P., OPERATIONS
Fred H. Schulte

CABLEVISION SYSTEMS CORPORATION
Box 311, One Media Crossways, Woodbury, NY 11797. (516) 364-8450. FAX: (516) 496-1780.
CHAIRMAN & CEO
Charles F. Dolan
CHIEF FINANCIAL OFFICER & V.P., SALES
William J. Bell
V.P., OPERATIONS
William J. Quinn

CENTURY COMMUNICATIONS CORP.
50 Locust Ave., New Canaan, CT 06840. (203) 972-2000. FAX: (203) 966-9228.
CHAIRMAN & CEO
Leonard Tow
PRESIDENT
Bernard P. Gallagher

CHARTER COMMUNICATIONS
12444 Powerscourt Dr., Suite 400, St. Louis, MO 63131. (314) 965-0555. FAX: (314) 965-8793. 1 million subscribers.
CHAIRMAN
Barry L. Babcock
PRESIDENT
Jerald L. Kent

COMCAST CABLE COMMUNICATIONS, INC.
1500 Market St., Philadelphia, PA 19102. (215) 665-1700. FAX: (215) 981-7790.
PRESIDENT
Thomas G. Baxter

CONTINENTAL CABLEVISION, INC.
The Pilot House, Lewis Wharf, Boston, MA 02110. (617) 742-9500. FAX: (617) 742-0530.
CHAIRMAN & CEO
Amos B. Hostetter, Jr.
PRESIDENT
Michael J. Ritter
CHIEF FINANCIAL OFFICER
Nancy Hawthorne
V.P., MARKETING
Frederick C. Livingston
V.P., PROGRAMMING
Robert A. Stengel

VICE PRESIDENTS
Robert J. Sachs, Richard A. Hoffstein

COX CABLE COMMUNICATIONS
(A division of Cox Enterprises, Inc.)
1400 Lake Hearn Dr., Atlanta, GA 30319. (404) 843-5000. FAX: (404) 843-5777.
PRESIDENT & CEO
James O. Robbins
EXECUTIVE V.P., OPERATIONS
Barry R. Elson
SENIOR V.P., MARKETING & PROGRAMMING
Ajit M. Dalvi
CFO & SENIOR V.P., FINANCE
Jimmy W. Hayes
V.P., ADVERTISING SALES
Patrick J. Esser

DOUGLAS COMMUNICATION
600 Liberty, Rantoul, IL 61866. (217) 892-9333. FAX: (217) 893-1036.
PRESIDENT & CEO
Douglas K. Dittrick
CHAIRMAN
Jay E. Ricks

FALCON CABLE TV
(Owned by Falcon Holding Group, Inc.)
10900 Wilshire Blvd., 15th floor, Los Angeles, CA 90024. (310) 824-9990. FAX: (310) 208-3635.
PRESIDENT & CEO
Mark Nathanson

FANCH COMMUNICATIONS INC.
1873 S. Bellaire St., Suite 1550, Denver, CO 80222. (303) 756-5600. FAX: (303) 756-5774.

GARDEN STATE CABLE TV
1250 Haddonfield-Berlin Rd., Cherry Hill, NJ 08034. (609) 354-1880. FAX: (609) 354-1459. 202, 000 subscribers.

GEORGIA CABLE TV & COMMUNICATIONS
1018 W. Peachtree St., Atlanta, GA 30309. (404) 874-8000. FAX: (404) 873-5216.

GRASSROOTS CABLE SYSTEM
Box 280, Exeter, NH 03833. (603) 772-4600. FAX: (603) 772-4650.
PRESIDENT
W. Robert Felder
V.P., OPERATIONS
Marsha B. Felder

GREATER MEDIA INC.
2 Kennedy Blvd., Box 1059, East Brunswick, NJ 08816. (908) 247-5161. FAX: (908) 247-0215.

HARMON CABLE COMMUNICATIONS
8480 E. Orchard Rd., Suite 6900, Englewood, CO 80111. (303) 773-3821. FAX: (303) 773-0839.
EXECUTIVE VICE PRESIDENT
James Jackson
CHIEF FINANCIAL OFFICER
Robert M. Fukumoto

HARRON COMMUNICATIONS CORP.
70 E. Lancaster Ave., Frazer, PA 19355. (610) 644-7500. FAX: (610) 644-2790.
PRESIDENT & CEO
Paul F. Harron
EXECUTIVE VICE PRESIDENT, COO & CFO
Joel C. Cohen

INSIGHT COMMUNICATIONS CO.
126 E. 56 St., New York, NY 10022. (212) 371-2266. 170,000 subscribers.
CHAIRMAN
Sidney R. Knafel
PRESIDENT
Michael S. Willner

INTERMEDIA PARTNERS
235 Montgomery St., San Francisco, CA 94104. (415) 616-4600. FAX: (415) 397-3406. 620,000 subscribers.
CEO
Leo J. Hindery Jr.
DIRECTOR, MARKETING
Donna Young

JONES INTERCABLE, INC.
9697 East Mineral Ave., Englewood, CO 80112. (303) 792-3111. FAX: (303) 790-0533. 1,430,000 subscribers.
CHAIRMAN & CEO
Glenn R. Jones
PRESIDENT
James B. O'Brien

LENFEST GROUP
200 Cresson Blvd., P.O. Box 989, Oaks, PA 19456. (610) 650-3600. FAX: (610) 650-3011. 920,000 subscribers.
CHAIRMAN, CEO & PRESIDENT
H. F. Lenfest

MARCUS CABLE PARTNERS L.P.
2911 Turtle Creek Blvd., Suite 1300, Dallas, TX 75219. (214) 521-7898. FAX: (214) 526-2154.
PRESIDENT & CEO
Jeffrey A. Marcus

MEDIA GENERAL INC.
Box 85333, Richmond, VA 23293. (804) 649-6000. FAX: (804) 649-6898

MIDCONTINENT CABLE CO.
Box 910, 24 First Ave. N.E., Aberdeen, SD 57402. (605) 229-1775. FAX: (605) 229-0478.
CHAIRMAN & CEO
Joe H. Floyd
PRESIDENT
N. L. Bentson

MOFFAT COMMUNICATIONS LTD.
Box 220, Station L, Winnipeg, Manitoba, Canada R3H 0Z5. (204) 788-2440. FAX: (204) 956-2710.

MULTIMEDIA CABLEVISION
701 E. Douglas, Box 3027, Wichita, KS 67201. (316) 262-4270.
CEO
Mike Burrus

NEW HERITAGE ASSOCIATES
2600 Grand Ave., Suite 301, Des Moines, IA 50312. (515) 246-1750.
CHAIRMAN
James Cownie

NEWCHANNELS CORP.
(A subsidiary of Newhouse Broadcasting Corp.)
Box 4872, 5015 Campuswood Dr., Syracuse, NY 13221. (315) 463-2288. FAX: (315) 463-6584.
PRESIDENT
Leo A. Calistri
VICE PRESIDENTS
Mary Cotter, William Doolittle, Joseph Majczak
V.P., MARKETING
Thomas Kirkwood
V.P., PROGRAMMING
Dan Cavallo
V.P., ADVERTISING SALES
Susan Basile

NORTHLAND COMMUNICATIONS CORP.
1201 Third Ave., Suite 3600, Seattle, WA 98101. (206) 621-1351. FAX: (206) 623-9015.

NOVA CABLE MANAGEMENT INC.
Box 793, 228-1/2 Washington Ave., Grand Haven, MI 49417. (616) 847-0072. FAX: (616) 847-9409.
PRESIDENT
Gary Van Volkenburg

OMEGA COMMUNICATIONS, INC.
Box 1766, 29 E. Maryland St., Indianapolis, IN 46206. (317) 264-4000. FAX: (317) 264-4020.
PRESIDENT & CEO
Robert E. Schloss

PENCOR SERVICES
471 Delaware Ave., Box 215, Palmerton, PA 18071. (610) 826-2551. FAX: (610) 826-7626.

POST-NEWSWEEK CABLE
(A subsidiary of The Washington Post Co.)
4742 N. 24th St., Suite 270, Phoenix, AZ 85016. (602) 468-1177. FAX: (602) 468-9216.
CHAIRMAN & CEO
Howard E. Wall
PRESIDENT
Thomas O. Might

PREMIERE CABLE II, LTD.
1104 Ironwood Dr., Coeur d'Alene, ID 83814. (208) 664-3370. FAX: (208) 664-5888.
CFO
Sharon Shull

PRIME CABLE
One American Center, Suite 3000, 600 Congress Ave., Austin, TX 78701. (512) 476-7888. FAX: (512) 476-4869.
CHAIRMAN & CEO
Robert W. Hughes
PRESIDENT
Gregory Marchbanks
VICE PRESIDENTS
Allan Barnes, Jerry Lindauer, William Glasgow

RIFKIN & ASSOCIATES
360 S. Monroe St., Suite 600, Denver, CO 80209. (303) 333-1215. FAX: (303) 322-3553.
CHAIRMAN & CEO
Monroe M. Rifkin
PRESIDENT
Jeffrey D. Bennis

ROGERS CABLESYSTEMS LIMITED
One Valleybrook Dr., 5th fl., Toronto, Ontario, M3B 2S7, Canada. (416) 447-5500. FAX: (416) 391-7247.
PRESIDENT & CEO
E.S. Rogers

SRW INC.
71 Cedar Ave., Hershey, PA 17033. (717) 533-3322. FAX: (717) 533-3344.
PRESIDENT
Richard Snyder

SAMMONS COMMUNICATIONS, INC.
3010 LBJ Fwy., #800, Dallas, TX 75234. (214) 484-8888. FAX: (214) 919-5799.
PRESIDENT
Mark S. Weber
V.P., OPERATIONS
Don Amick
V.P., MARKETING
Sherry Wilson

SCRIPPS HOWARD CABLE
Box 5380, #2800, Cincinnati, OH 45201. (513) 977-3000. FAX: (513) 977-3768.
PRESIDENT & CEO
Larry Leser

SERVICE ELECTRIC CABLEVISION
1259 S. Cedar Crest Blvd., Suite 255, Allentown, PA 18103-6206. (610) 432-2210. FAX: (610) 432-8262.
CHAIRPERSON
Margaret Walson
PRESIDENT
Hoyt D. Walter

SHAW COMMUNICATIONS
630 Third Ave. SW, 9th Fl, Calgary, Alberta, Canada T2P 4L4. (403) 269-5200. FAX: (403) 750-4501. 1.2 million subscribers.

SUBURBAN CABLE TV CO., INC.
202 Shoemaker Rd., Pottstown, PA 19464. (610) 327-0965. FAX: (610) 327-6340.

SUMMIT COMMUNICATIONS GROUP INC.
115 Perimeter Ctr., Pl., Atlanta, GA 30346. (404) 394-0707. FAX: (404) 394-9778.
CHAIRMAN, PRESIDENT & CEO
James Wesly, Jr.

TCA CABLE TV
Box 130489, 3015 E.S.E. Loop 323, Tyler, TX 75713-0489. (903) 595-3701. FAX: (903) 595-1929.
CHIEF EXECUTIVE OFFICER
Robert M. Rogers
PRESIDENT
Fred Nichols

TKR CABLE CO.
67-B Mountain Blvd., Warren, NJ 07060. (908) 356-1010. FAX: (908) 356-9087.
PRESIDENT
Paul Freas

TELE-COMMUNICATIONS, INC.
5619 DTC Parkway, Englewood, CO 80111-3000. Mailing: P.O. Box 5630, Denver, CO 80217.
VICE CHAIRMAN & CEO
Fred A. Vierra
PRESIDENT & COO
Adam Singer
SENIOR VICE PRESIDENT
Miranda Curtis

TELE-MEDIA CORPORATION
320 West College Ave., P.O. Box 5301, Pleasant Gap, PA 16823-5301. (814) 359-3481. FAX: (814) 359-5391.
CEO & CHAIRMAN
Robert E. Tudek

TIME WARNER CABLE-ATLANTA NATIONAL DIVISION
(Partnership between Time Warner Entertainment and Advance/Newhouse.)
115 Perimeter Center Pl., Suite 550, Atlanta, GA 30346. (770) 394-8837. FAX (770) 698-0228. 680,000 subscribers.
DIVISION PRESIDENT
Henry Harris

TIME WARNER CABLE GROUP
(A subsidiary of Time Inc.)
300 First Stamford Place, Stamford, CT 06902. (203) 328-0600. FAX: (203) 328-4887.
CHAIRMAN & CEO
Joseph J. Collins
PRESIDENT
James H. Doolittle
CHIEF FINANCIAL OFFICER
Tom Harris

TRIAX COMMUNICATIONS CORP.
100 Fillmore St., Suite 600, Denver, CO 80206. (303) 333-2424. FAX: (303) 333-1110.

US CABLE CORPORATION
28 W. Grand Ave., Montvale, NJ 07645. (201) 930-9000. FAX: (201) 930-9232. 238,000 subscribers.
CHAIRMAN
Stephen E. Myers
PRESIDENT
James D. Pearson

EXECUTIVE VICE PRESIDENT
Michael C. Anderson

UNITED VIDEO CABLEVISION INC.
100 1st Stamford Pl., Box 420, Stamford, CT 06904. (203) 363-0200. FAX: (203) 363-0349.

VIACOM CABLE
(A division of Viacom International.)
P.O. Box 13, 5924 Stoneridge Dr., Pleasanton, CA 94566. (510) 463-0870. FAX: (510) 463-3241.
CEO & PRESIDENT
John W. Goddard
CHIEF FINANCIAL OFFICER
John Kopchik

VISION CABLE COMMUNICATIONS, INC.
(A division of Newhouse Broadcasting)
One Coliseum Centre, 2300 Yorkmont Rd., Charlotte, NC 28217. (704) 357-6900. FAX: (704) 329-7580.
PRESIDENT
Mitchell Roberts

WESTERN COMMUNICATIONS, INC.
(Owned by Chronicle Publishing Co.)
2 Rincon Center, 121 Spear St., Suite 203, San Francisco, CA 94105. (415) 896-5000. FAX: (415) 896-0236.
PRESIDENT
Christopher J. Lammers
CEO
John B. Sias

DIRECT BROADCAST SATELLITE SYSTEMS OPERATORS

Satellite broadcasters provide direct broadcasts to consumers of various programming. A satellite dish and descrambler are usually required for reception.

ACCESS AMERICA
3200 Chartres St., New Orleans, LA 70117. (504)942-9204. FAX: (504) 942-9204.
PRESIDENT
Barbara Lamont

ALPHASTAR DIGITAL TELEVISON
208 Harbor Dr., Stamford, CT 06907. (203) 359-8077. FAX: (203) 359-8281. URL: http://www.Alphastar/TV.com
2,000 subscribers.
PRESIDENT AND CEO
Murray Klippenstein

CANADIAN SATELLITE COMMUNICATIONS, INC. (CAN-COM)
50 Burnhamthorpe Rd. West, 10th Floor, Mississauga, Ontario, CANADA, L5B 3C2. (905) 272-4960. FAX: (905) 272-3399.
PRESIDENT AND CEO
Alain Gourd

DIRECTV INC.
(A subsidiary of Hughes Electronics Corp.)
2230 E. Imperial Highway, El Segundo, CA 90245. (310) 535-5113. FAX: (310) 535-5225. 1.65 million subscribers.
PRESIDENT
Eddy Hartenstein

DOMINION VIDEO SATELLITE, INC.
5551 Ridgewood Dr., Suite 505, Naples, FL 33963. (941) 597-3320. FAX: (941) 597-6478.
CHAIRMAN AND CEO
Robert W. Johnson

EXPRESSVU INC.
1290 Central Pkwy. W., Suite 1008, Mississauga, Ontario, Canada, L5C 4R3. (905) 272-9171. FAX: (905) 272-5514.
PRESIDENT AND CEO
J. E. Boyle

FORT WAYNE TELSAT (DBA CHOICE TV)
1909 Production Rd., Fort Wayne, IN 46808. (219) 471-2324. FAX: (219) 471-5406.
V.P. & GENERAL MANAGER
William A. Millett

PRIMESTAR PARTNERS
3 Bala Plaza W., Suite 700, Bala Cynwyd, PA 19004. (610) 617-5300. FAX: (610) 617-5312.
CHAIRMAN AND CEO
James Gray

UNITED STATES SATELLITE BROADCASTING CO., INC.
3415 University Ave., St. Paul, MN 55114. (612) 645-4500. FAX: (612) 642-4578. URL: http://www.USSBTV.com
791,469 subscribers.
PRESIDENT AND CEO
Stanley E. Hubbard

WIRELESS CABLE SYSTEMS

AMERICAN TELECASTING INC.
4065 N. Sinton Rd., Suite 201, Colorado Springs, CO 80907. (719) 632-5544. FAX: (719) 632-5549
PRESIDENT & CEO
Brian Gast

AMERICAN WIRELESS SYSTEMS INC.
7426 E. Stetson Dr., Suite 220, Scottsdale, AZ 85251-3544. (602) 994-4301. FAX: (602) 994-4325.
PRESIDENT & CEO
Steven G. Johnson

CAI WIRELESS
2510 Metropolitan Dr., Trevose, PA 19053. (215) 369-9400. FAX: (215) 369-9550.
PRESIDENT
Alan Sonnenberg

FORT WAYNE TELSAT, INC. (DBA CHOICE TV)
1909 Production Rd., Fort Wayne, IN 46808. (219) 471-2324. FAX: (219) 471-5406.
V.P. & GENERAL MANAGER
William A. Millett

GEAR WIRELESS CABLE
Box 28404, Providence, RI 02908. (401) 331-6072.
PRESIDENT & CEO
Jack G. Thayer

HEARTLAND WIRELESS COMMUNICATIONS, INC.
200 Chiselm Place, Suite 200, Plano, TX 75075. (214) 633-4000. FAXL (214) 423-0819.
PRESIDENT
David Webb

LIBERTY CABLE TELEVISION
575 Madison Ave., New York, NY 10022. (212) 891-7701. FAX: (212) 891-7790.
PRESIDENT
P. Price

NEW YORK CHOICE TELEVISION
286 Eldridge Rd., Fairfield, NJ 07004. (201) 808-3700. FAX: (201) 227-2612.
GENERAL MANAGER & CONTROLLER
Robert Bauman

POPVISION
3115 N. Sillect Ave., Bakersfield, CA 93308-6339. (805) 638-2222. FAX: (805) 638-2223.

TV COMMUNICATIONS NETWORK
10020 Girard Ave., Denver, CO 80231. (303) 751-2900. FAX: (303) 751-1081. 490 subscribers.
CHAIRMAN OF THE BOARD, PRESIDENT & CEO
Omar A. Duwalk

VIDEO TEL
13-15 Fairlawn Ave., Fairlawn, NJ 07410. (201) 794-1506. FAX: (201) 794-1970. 3,000 subscribers.
PRESIDENT
Scott Lagrosa

WIRELESS ADVANTAGE
2155 Main St., Sarasota, FL 34237. (941) 955-0065. FAX: (941) 955-6586.
PRESIDENT
David Bednarsh

WIRELESS CABLE INTERNATIONAL, INC.
67-A Mountain Blvd., Warren, NJ 07059. (908) 271-4880. FAX: (908) 469-8778.
PRESIDENT & CEO
George M. Ring

WIRELESS CABLE OF FLORIDA, INC.
1950 Landings Blvd., Suite 110, Sarasota, FL 34231-3310. (941) 924-2400. FAX: (941) 924-1650.
CHAIRMAN
Jim Hall

THE VIDEO INDUSTRY

HOME VIDEO COMPANIES

CONSUMER ELECTRONICS

VIDEO SERVICES

HOME VIDEO COMPANIES

A & E HOME VIDEO/HISTORY CHANNEL HOME VIDEO
235 E. 45th St., New York, NY 10017. (212) 210-1319. FAX: (212) 210-1326.

A & M VIDEO
1416 N. La Brea Ave., Hollywood, CA 90028. (213) 856-2767. FAX: (213) 856-2778.
V.P., BUSINESS DEVELOPMENT
Milton E. Olin, Jr.
SENIOR DIRECTOR OF VIDEO PROMOTIONS
Emily Wittman
NATIONAL MANAGER OF VIDEO PROMOTIONS
Sergio Silva

ACTIVE HOME VIDEO
12121 Wilshire Blvd., Suite 200, Los Angeles, CA 90025. (310) 447-6131. FAX: (310) 207-0411.
GENERAL MANAGER
Ron Levanson
CREATIVE SERVICES DIRECTOR
Juanita Weber
SALES
Alice de Buhr

ADMIT ONE VIDEO PRESENTATIONS
P.O. Box 66 Station "O", Toronto, Ontario, Canada M4A 2M8. (416) 463-5714.

A-PIX ENTERTAINMENT
500 Fifth Ave., New York, NY 10110. (212) 764-7171. FAX: (212) 575- 6578.
PRESIDENT
Robert Baruch

ASTRAL HOME ENTERTAINMENT
(A division of Astral Communications) 7215 Trans Canada Highway, Montreal, Quebec H4T 1A2. Canada. (514) 333-7555. FAX: (514) 333-7309.
PRESIDENT
Sidney Greenberg
NATIONAL SALES MANAGER
Barry Brooker
DIRECTOR OF PURCHASING
Joel Greenberg

BFS LIMITED
350 Newkirk Road North, Richmond Hill, Ontario, L4C 3G7, CANADA. (905) 884-2323

BMG VIDEO
1540 Broadway, New York, NY 10036. (212) 930-4607. FAX: (212) 930- 7043.
GENERAL MANAGER
Joe Shults
V.P., SALES
Gene Fink
V.P., ACQUISITIONS
Susan Rosenberg

BUENA VISTA HOME VIDEO
350 S. Buena Vista St., Burbank, CA 91521. (818) 560-1000. (Distributor of Walt Disney, Touchstone, Hollywood Pictures, Jim Henson, DIC Toon-Time, Miramax, Dimension and Buena Vista Home Video lines.)
PRESIDENT, DOMESTIC HOME VIDEO
Ann Daly
PRESIDENT, INTERNATIONAL HOME VIDEO
Michael Orlin Johnson
SENIOR V.P., MARKETING
Dennis Rice
V.P., RETAIL MARKETING
Kelley Avery
SENIOR V.P., SALES
Dennis Maguire
V.P., SALES
Matt Brown
SENIOR V.P., BUSINESS AFFAIRS & ACQUISITIONS
Jere Hausfater

CBS FOX VIDEO
1330 Ave. of the Americas, New York, NY 10019-5402. (212) 373-4800. FAX: (212) 373-4803. (Partnership between CBS, Inc./Fox Film Corp.)
SENIOR V.P., PROGRAM ACQUISITIONS
Steven Poe
V.P., SPORTS & FITNESS MARKETING
Kevin Conroy
V.P., NON-THEATRICAL MARKETING
Mindy Pickard

V.P., PROGRAM ACQUISITIONS
Ken Horowitz
V.P., BUSINESS AFFAIRS/GENERAL COUNSEL
Curtis Roberts
CONTROLLER
Louis Polenta

CC STUDIOS/CHILDREN'S CIRCLE
389 Newtown Turnpike, Weston, CT 06883. (203) 222-0002. (800) 457-0686. FAX: (203) 226-3818.
PRESIDENT & TREASURER
Morton Schindel
V.P.
Linda Lee

CABIN FEVER ENTERTAINMENT
1 Sound Shore Dr., Greenwich, CT 06830. (203) 863-5200. FAX: (203) 863-5258.
PRESIDENT
Tom Molito

CABLE FILMS & VIDEO
7171 County Club Station, Kansas City, MO 64113. (913) 362-2804. FAX: (913) 341-7365. e-mail: jlsoren@sound.net
PRESIDENT
Herb Miller
GENERAL MANAGER
Todd Randall

CAPITOL RECORDS VIDEO
1750 North Vine St., Tower-6, Hollywood, CA 90028. (213) 871-5180. Organized 1940s.
V.P., VIDEO PRODUCTION AND DEVELOPMENT
Michelle Peacock

CENTRAL PARK MEDIA
250 W. 57 St., #317, New York, NY 10107. (212) 977-7456. FAX: (212) 977-8709.

CINEVISTA
1680 Michigan Ave., Suite 1106, Miami Beach, FL 33139. (305) 532-3400. FAX: 532-0047.
PRESIDENT
Rene Fuentes-Chao
EDITOR-IN-CHIEF, CINEVISTANEWS & DIRECTOR, ACQUISTIONS AND SALES
Susan M. Alvarez

COLUMBIA TRISTAR HOME VIDEO
10202 W. Washington Blvd., Culver City, CA 90232. (310) 280-8000.
PRESIDENT
Ben Feingold
EXECUTIVE V.P.
William Chardavoyne
EXECUTIVE V.P., NORTH AMERICA
Paul Culberg
EXECUTIVE V.P., OPERATIONS & EUROPEAN SUPERVISION
Alan Pritchard
SENIOR V.P., CONTROLLER
Robert Houseal
SENIOR V.P., LEGAL
Kim Lynch
SENIOR V.P., BUSINESS AFFAIRS & ACQUISITIONS
Peter Schlessel
SENIOR V.P., SALES, U.S.
Ralph Walin
V.P., LICENSING, FAR EAST
Janet Almroth Robertson
V.P., MANUFACTURING & PRODUCTION
Walt Engler
V.P., SALES, CANADA
Marshall Forster
V.P., WORLDWIDE PUBLICITY
E. Fritz Friedman
V.P., SALES, RENTAL, U.S.
Jeff Rabinowitz
V.P., SALES, RETAIL, U.S.
John Reina
V.P., LICENSING, LATIN AMERICA
Rodolfo Vila
V.P., MARKETING, NORTH AMERICA
Lon Von Hurwitz
V.P., INTERNATIONAL MARKETING
Lexine Wong

CORONET FILM & VIDEO
4350 Equity Dr., P.O. Box 2649, Columbus, OH 43216. (614) 771-7361. (800) 777-8100. FAX: (614) 771-7361.
MARKETING COORDINATOR
Nancy Osman

EPIC HOME VIDEO
4640 Lankershim Blvd., #600, Hollywood, CA 91602. (818) 766-6888.
CHIEF EXECUTIVE OFFICER
John Peters
SENIOR V.P., DOMESTIC SALES & MARKETING
Sandy Lang

FIRST RUN /ICARUS FILMS, INC.
153 Waverly Pl., Sixth floor, New York, NY 10014. (212) 727-1711. E-mail: frif@echonyc.com
PRESIDENT
Jonathan Miller

FOX VIDEO
2121 Avenue of the Stars, #2500, Los Angeles, CA 90067. (310) 203-3900. FAX: (310) 203-3318.
PRESIDENT
Robert DeLellis
SENIOR V.P., ADMINISTRATION & OPERATIONS
David Goldstein
SENIOR V.P., MARKETING
Bruce Psander
SENIOR V.P., SALES
Vince Larinto

FOX/LORBER ASSOCIATES, INC.
419 Park Ave. South, 20th Floor, New York, NY 10016. (212) 686-6777. FAX: (212) 685-2625.
PRESIDENT & CEO
Richard Lorber

FULL MOON HOME VIDEO
3030 Andrita St., Los Angeles, CA 90065. (213) 341-5959. FAX: (213) 341-5960.
DIRECTOR OF VIDEO MARKETING & DISTRIBUTION
Dwight Krizman

GOLDEN BOOK VIDEO
11444 W. Olympic Blvd., 10th fl., Los Angeles, CA 90064. (310) 445-8877.

GOODTIMES HOME VIDEO
16 E. 40 St., New York, NY 10016. (212) 951-3000.
PRESIDENT
Joseph Carey
SENIOR V.P., THEATRICAL ACQUISITIONS
Jeff Baker

HBO VIDEO
1100 Ave. of the Americas, New York, NY 10036. (212) 512-7400. FAX: (212) 512-7458.
PRESIDENT
Henry McGee
DIRECTOR, SALES—RENTAL
Michael Vassen
DIRECTOR, SALES—SELL-THROUGH
Bob Cowan

HEMDALE HOME VIDEO, INC.
7966 Beverly Blvd., Los Angeles, CA 90048. (213) 966-3700. FAX: (213) 653-5492.
CO-CHAIRMAN & CEO
Eric Parkinson
CO-CHAIRMAN & COO
Larry Abramson

JIM HENSON VIDEO
Raleigh Studios, 5358 Melrose Ave., Hollywood, CA 90038. (213) 960-4096. FAX: (213) 960-4935.

HOME VISION
5547 N. Ravenswood, Chicago, IL 60640. (312) 878-2600, ext. 325.
PRESIDENT, PUBLIC MEDIA INC.
Wes Monty
SENIOR V.P., SALES
Jeff McGuire
V.P., NEW BUSINESS
John Hillsman
CHAIRMAN OF PUBLIC MEDIA INC.
Charles Benton

IRS VIDEO
3520 Hayden Ave., Culver City, CA 90232. (310) 841-4100. 594 Broadway, #901, New York, NY 10012. (212) 334-2173.

KINO INTERNATIONAL
333 West 39th St., Suite 503, New York, NY 10018. (212) 629-6880. FAX: (212) 714-0871.

KULTUR INTERNATIONAL FILMS/WHITE STAR VIDEO
195 Highway 36, West Long Branch, NJ 07764. (908) 229-2343. (800) 458-5887. FAX: (908) 229-0066.
PRESIDENT
Dennis M. Hedlund
VICE PRESIDENT
Pearl Lee

CFO
Patricia Checkler
MANAGING DIRECTOR & ACQUISITIONS DIRECTOR
Ronald F. Davis
BUSINESS ADMINISTRATOR
Joe Kennedy
SALES EXECUTIVE
Leslie Cohen Murray

LIVE ENTERTAINMENT
15400 Sherman Way, Suite 500, Van Nuys, CA 91406. (818) 908-0303. FAX: (805) 908-0320.
PRESIDENT & COO
Roger Burlage
CFO
Ron Cushey
EXECUTIVE V.P., DISTRIBUTION & MARKETING
Elliot Slutzky
SENIOR V.P., PRODUCTION & ACQUISITION
Paul Almond
SENIOR V.P., SALES & DISTRIBUTION
Jeffrey Fink
SENIOR V.P. & GENERAL MANAGER INTERNATIONAL
Edwin Friendly

LYONS GROUP
2435 N. Central Expressway, Suite 1600, Richardson, TX 75080-2722. (214) 390-6000. FAX: (214) 390-6190.
V.P., COMMUNICATIONS
Russell Mack

MCA/UNIVERSAL HOME ENTERTAINMENT
70 Universal City Plaza, #435, Universal City, CA 91608. (818) 777-2100. (818) 733-1483. A division of MCA/Universal.
PRESIDENT, MCA HOME VIDEO
Louis Feola
PRESIDENT, DISTRIBUTION
John Burns
V.P., VIDEO DISTRIBUTION
Dan Gant
SENIOR V.P., SALES & ADVERTISING ADMINISTRATION
June Morishita
BRANCHES:
REGIONAL VIDEO DIRECTOR (N.E.)/DIRECTOR OF EAST COAST SALES
Bill Hickman
REGIONAL VIDEO DIRECTOR (SOUTHEAST)
Barbara Schmitt
REGIONAL VIDEO DIRECTOR (SOUTH)
Ron Gibson
REGIONAL VIDEO DIRECTOR (MIDWEST)
Gary Pogachar
REGIONAL VIDEO DIRECTOR (WEST)
Jay Barack

MGM/UA HOME VIDEO, INC.
2500 Broadway St., Santa Monica, CA 90404-3061. (310) 449-3000.
SENIOR V.P., FINANCE
Thomas P. Carson
SENIOR V.P., MARKETING & SALES
George Fettenstein
SENIOR V.P., CORPORATE GENERAL COUNSEL & SECRETARY
William Allen Jones
V.P., SALES
Minda Phillips
V.P. & CONTROLLER
Kathleen Coughlan
V.P., BUSINESS AFFAIRS
Ron Miele
V.P., MARKETING SERVICES
Kimberly Wertz

MPI HOME VIDEO
16101 S. 108th Ave., Orland Park, IL 60462. (708) 460-0555. FAX: (708) 460-0175.
CEO
Waleed B. Ali
PRESIDENT
Malik B. Ali
MARKETING DIRECTORS
Nasser Zegar
Sam Citro
MARKETING DIRECTOR, WEST COAST
Richard Shenson

NATIONAL GEOGRAPHIC SOCIETY
1145 17th St., N.W., Washington, D.C. 20036. (202) 857-7680. FAX: (202) 775-6590.
Explorer Office: 810 Seventh Ave., New York, NY 10019. (212) 841-4400.
Los Angeles TV Office: 4370 Tujunga Ave., #300, Studio City, CA 91604. (818) 506-8300.

SENIOR V.P.
Tim Kelly
BOARD OF TRUSTEES
Gilbert M. Grosvenor (President and Chairman)

NEW LINE HOME VIDEO
888 Seventh Ave., 20th fl., New York, NY 10106. (212) 649-4900.
FAX: (212) 649-4966.
PRESIDENT & COO
Stephen Einhorn

NEW WORLD VIDEO
1440 S. Sepulveda Blvd., Los Angeles, CA 90025. (310) 444-8100. FAX: (310) 444-8101.
SENIOR V.P., SALES AND MARKETING
Rex Bowring
EXECUTIVE DIRECTOR, CREATIVE SERVICES
Jerry Zanitsch

NEW YORKER VIDEO
16 W. 61 St., New York, NY 10023. (212) 247-6117. (800) 447-0196. FAX: (212) 307-7855.
PRESIDENT
Daniel Talbot
V.P. & DIRECTOR OF HOME VIDEO
Jose Lopez

ORION HOME ENTERTAINMENT
1888 Century Park East, Los Angeles, CA 90067. (310) 282-0550. FAX: (310) 201-0798.
CHAIRMAN OF THE BOARD & CEO
Leonard White
PRESIDENT
Herb Dorfman
SENIOR V.P., ADMINISTRATION OPERATIONS
Jerry Sobczak
SENIOR V.P., MARKETING
Susan Blodgett
V.P., BUSINESS DEVELOPMENT
Nancy Jones
V.P., CREDIT
Peter Dunn

PBS HOME VIDEO
1320 Braddock Pl., Alexandria, VA 22314-1698. (703) 739-5380.
(800) 424-7963.

PARAMOUNT HOME VIDEO
5555 Melrose Ave., Los Angeles, CA 90038. (213) 956-5000.
PRESIDENT, WORLDWIDE VIDEO
Eric Doctorow
SENIOR V.P., ADVERTISING & SALES PROMOTION
Hollace Brown
EXECUTIVE V.P., SALES & MARKETING
Jack Kanne
SENIOR V.P., BUSINESS AFFAIRS & LEGAL
Steve Madoff
SENIOR V.P., MARKETING
Alan Perper

POLYGRAM HOME VIDEO
Worldwide Plaza, 825 Fifth Ave., New York, NY 10019. (212) 333-8000. A subsidiary of Polygram.
CORPORATE COMMUNICATIONS
Grace Salafia

PRISM ENTERTAINMENT CORPORATION
1888 Century Park E., Suite 350, Los Angeles, CA 90067. (310) 277-3270. FAX: (310) 203-8036.
PRESIDENT & CEO
Barry Collier
CFO
Earl Rosenstein
PRESIDENT-PRISM PICTURES
Barbara Jamvitz
SENIOR V.P., SALES
Joe Petrone

RANDOM HOUSE, INC.
201 E. 50 St., New York, NY 10022. (212) 751-2600. FAX: (212) 940-7640.
PRESIDENT, JUVENILE DIVISION
Harold Clarke
V.P. & PUBLISHER, CHILDREN'S MEDIA
Sharon Lerner
V.P., SALES & MARKETING, CHILDREN'S MEDIA
Gary Gentel

REGENCY HOME VIDEO
9911 W. Pico Blvd., PH-M, Los Angeles, CA 90035. (310) 552-2660. FAX: (310) 552-9039.
CHAIRMAN
Alan Silverbach
PRESIDENT
Herb Lazarus
GENERAL MANAGER
Betty Jane Metz

REPUBLIC PICTURES HOME VIDEO
(A subsidiary of Spelling Entertainment.) 5700 Wilshire Blvd., #575, Los Angeles, CA 90036. (213) 965-5700.

RHINO HOME VIDEO
10635 Santa Monica Blvd., Los Angeles, CA 90025-4900. (310) 474-4778.
V.P./GENERAL MANAGER
Arny Schorr

TURNER HOME ENTERTAINMENT
P.O. Box 105366, Atlanta, GA 30348-5366. (404) 827-3261.

VIDMARK, INC.
2644 30th St., Santa Monica, CA 90405-2906. (310) 399-8877, (800) 424-7070, (CA). (800) 351-7070. FAX: (310) 392-0252.
CHAIRMAN
Mark Amin
PRESIDENT, CEO
Roger Burlage

WEA CORP. (WARNER/ELEKTRA/ATLANTIC)
(A subsidiary of Warner Bros. Inc., a Time Warner company.) 111 N. Hollywood Way, Burbank, CA 91505-4356. (818) 843-6311.
FAX: (818) 840-6212.
CHAIRMAN & CEO
Dave Mount
EXECUTIVE VP/MARKETING
George Rossi
SENIOR VP/SALES
Fran Aliberte

WARNER HOME VIDEO INC.
(A subsidiary of Warner Bros. Inc., a Time Warner company.) 3903 W. Olive Ave., Burbank, CA 91522. (818) 954-6000.
PRESIDENT
Warren N. Lieberfarb
EXECUTIVE V.P./GENERAL MANAGER, INTERNATIONAL
Edward J. Byrnes
V.P. WORLDWIDE PLANNING & OPERATIONS
James F. Cardwell
V.P./MARKETING
Barbara O'Sullivan
V.P., U.S. SALES
John Quinn
V.P., WORLDWIDE VIDEO ACQUISITION
Elyse Eisenberg
DIRECTOR OF PUBLICITY & PROMOTION
Donald M. Keefer
DIRECTOR OF PRODUCTION
Lewis Ostrover
DIRECTOR OF MARKETING
Brian Moreno

WEST GLEN COMMUNICATIONS, INC.
1430 Broadway, New York, NY 10018. (212) 921-2800. (800) 325-8677. FAX: (212) 944-9055.
PRESIDENT
Stanley S. Zeitlin
SENIOR VICE PRESIDENT PRODUCTION
John Summerlin

WESTERN PUBLISHING COMPANY
1220 Mound Ave., Racine, WI 53404-3336. (414) 633-2431. FAX: (414) 631-1854. A subsidiary of Western Publishing Group, Inc.
PRESIDENT & CEO
John F. Moore
V.P., CONSUMER PRODUCTS MARKETING
Jim Gonedes
SENIOR V.P., CONSUMER PRODUCTS SALES & MARKETING
Jay Becker

MAJOR VIDEO RETAILERS

BLOCKBUSTER ENTERTAINMENT CORP.
200 S. Andrews Ave., Ft. Lauderdale, FL 33301. (305) 832-3000.
FAX: (305) 832-3901.
PRESIDENT & CEO
Steven R. Berrard

THE MOVIE EXCHANGE
705 General Washington Ave., Suite 300, Norristown PA 19403.
(610) 631-9180. FAX: (610) 631-9359. 175 retail outlets.
CHAIRMAN
Lamont Tibbits
BUYER
Glenn Gasser

MOVIES UNLIMITED
6736 Castor Ave., Philadelphia, PA 19149. (215) 722-8298.
4 outlets and mail order.
CEO
Jery Frebowitz

PALMER VIDEO CORPORATION
1767 Morris Ave., Union, NJ 07083-3598. (908) 686- 3030. FAX: (908) 686-2151. 45 Corporate offices, plus franchises.
CEO
Joe Ciano
BUYER
Paul Rosen

SUNCOAST VIDEO
10400 Yellow Circle Dr., Minnetonka, MN 55343. (612) 932-7700. FAX: (612) 931-8300. A subsidiary of Music Land Group. 403 outlets in the U.S. and Puerto Rico.
CEO
Jack Eugster
BUYER
Peter Busch

TOWER VIDEO
MTS. Inc., 2500 Delmonte, Building C, West Sacramento, CA 95691. (916) 373-2500. 95 outlets in the U.S.. 49 International.
CEO
Russ Solomon
BUYER
John Thrasher

WEST COAST VIDEO ENTERPRISES, INC.
9990 Global Rd., Philadelphia, PA 19115. (215) 677-1000. 350 outlets.
BUYER
Tom Foltz

MAJOR VIDEO WHOLESALERS

BAKER & TAYLOR VIDEO
8140 N. Lehigh Ave., Morton Grove, IL 60053. (708) 965-8060.
PRESIDENT
Jim Warburton

BUDGET VIDEO INC.
9830 Charleville Blvd., Beverly Hills, CA 90212.

THE CINEMA GUILD
1697 Broadway, Suite 506, New York, NY 10019-5904. (212) 246-5522. e-mail: TheCinemaGuild@aol.com
CHAIRMAN
Philip Hobel
CO-CHAIRMAN
Mary-Ann Hobel
PRESIDENT
Gary Crowdus
DISTRIBUTION MANAGER
Tamara Fishman
SALES DIRECTOR
Marlene Graham

ETD ENTERTAINMENT DISTRIBUTING
7171 Grand Blvd., Houston, TX 77054. (713) 748-2520, (800) 892-5055. FAX: (713) 748-2617.
PRESIDENT
Ron Eisenberg
MARKETING & SALES
Julie Cross

FIRST VIDEO EXCHANGE
13722 Harvard Pl., Gardena, CA 902498. (310) 516-6422, (800) 247-2351. FAX: (310) 516-6654.
PRESIDENT
Jeff Leyton

INGRAM ENTERTAINMENT, INC.
2 Ingram Blvd., La Vergne, TN 37086-1986. (615) 287-4000. (800) 759-5000. FAX: (615) 793-3875.
PRESIDENT & CEO
David Ingram
SENIOR V.P., SALES & MARKETING
Vern Fross
V.P., OPERATIONS & PURCHASING
Robert Webb
V.P., MIS & STRATEGIC PLANNING
Mark Ramer

M.S. DISTRIBUTING CO.
6405 Muirfield Dr., Hanover Park, IL 60103. (708) 582-2888. FAX: (708) 582-8448.
PRESIDENT
Tony Dalesandro
EXECUTIVE V.P.
John Salstone
MARKETING & SALES
Rick Chrzan

RENTRAK HOME ENTERTAINMENT
7227 NE 55th Avenue, Portland, OR 97218-0888. (503) 284-7581. FAX: (503) 288-1563.
PRESIDENT
Ron Berger
V.P., SALES
Chris Roberts
SENIOR V.P./MARKETING
Michael R. Lightbourne

SIGHT AND SOUND DISTRIBUTORS
2055 Walton Rd., St. Louis, MO 63114. (314) 426-2388. (800) 388-6601. FAX: (314) 426-1307.
CHIEF EXECUTIVE OFFICER
John Mandelker

VIDEO DIMENSIONS
322 Eighth Ave., New York, NY 10011. (212) 929-6135. FAX: (212) 929-6135.
GENERAL MANAGER
Allan Greenfield

VIDEO MARKETING & DISTRIBUTING INC.
4301 Hwy. 7, St. Louis Park, MN 55416. (612) 920-8400. FAX: (612) 920-8474.
PRESIDENT
Mark Saliterman

WAX WORKS/VIDEO WORKS
325 E. 3rd St., Owensboro, KY 42301. (800) 825-8558. (502) 683-1585. FAX: (502) 685-0563.
BRANCHES
4011 Winchester Rd., Memphis, TN 38118. (800) 331-0993, (901) 366-4088.
3258 Ruckriegel Pkwy., Louisville, KY 40299. (800) 866-6557. (502) 266-6555. FAX: (502) 266-9073.
530 Lakeview Plaza Blvd., Worthington, OH 43085. (800) 816-6843. (614) 848-6440.
PRESIDENT
Terry Woodward
V.P.
Noel Clayton
SALES MANAGER
Kirk Kirkpatrick
CREDIT MANAGER
Ann Fiorella
BUYER
Andrew Goetz

MAJOR VIDEO DIRECT MARKETERS

BOOK-OF-THE-MONTH CLUB, INC.
1271 Avenue of the Americas, 3rd fl., New York, NY 10020. (212) 522-4200.
V.P., NEW BUSINESS DEVELOPMENT
Steve Frary

COLUMBIA HOUSE VIDEO
1400 N. Fruitridge Ave., Terre Haute, IN 47811. (800) 457-0866. Executive offices: 1221 Avenue of the Americas, New York, NY 10020-1090. (212) 596-2691. FAX: (212) 596-2740.
EXECUTIVE V.P., COLUMBIA HOUSE VIDEO
Brian Wood
V.P., COLUMBIA HOUSE VIDEO LIBRARY
Harry Elias

DISCOUNT VIDEO TAPES, INC.
P.O. Box 7122, Burbank, CA 91510. (818) 843-3366. FAX: (818) 843-3821. Mail-order.
BUYER
Woody Wise

PBS DIRECT
2800 28th St., Suite 310, Santa Monica, CA 90405. (310) 581-3700. FAX: (310) 581-3707.
SALES MANAGER
Harry Haber

SPECIAL INTEREST VIDEO
1717 Darby Rd., Sebastopol, CA 95472. (707) 829-0127. FAX: (707) 829-9542.
PRESIDENT
Michael Heumann

TIME-LIFE HOME VIDEO/TIME-LIFE KIDS
777 Duke St., Alexandria, VA 22314. (703) 838-7000.
DIRECTOR OF PROMOTIONS
Hope Berschler

CONSUMER ELECTRONICS

APPLE COMPUTER
1 Infinite Loop, Mail 35MM, Cupertino, CA 95014. (408) 996-1010. FAX (408) 974-0866.

ATARI CORPORATION
1196 Borregas St., Sunnyvale, CA 94089. (408) 745-2000.

FUJI PHOTO FILM USA, INC.,
MAGNETIC PRODUCTS DIVISION
555 Taxter Rd., Elmsford, NY 10523. (914) 789-8100. FAX: (914) 789-8490.

GENERAL INSTRUMENT CORP.
Gerrold Communications Division, 2200 Byberry Rd., Hatboro, PA 19040. (215) 674-4800.

HITACHI DENSHI AMERICA, LTD.
150 Crossways Park Dr., Woodbury, NY 11797. (516) 921-7200. FAX: (516) 496-3718.

IBM COMPUTERS
Rt. 100, Mail Drop 1197, Somers, NY 10589. (914) 766-1855.

IKEGAMI ELECTRONICS (U.S.A.), INC.
37 Brook Ave., Maywood, NJ 07607. (201) 368-9171.

JVC PROFESSIONAL PRODUCTS COMPANY
41 Slater Dr., Elmwood Park, NJ 07407. (201) 794-3900. FAX: (201) 523-2077.

MATSUSHITA ELECTRIC OF CANADA LTD.
5770 Ambler Dr., Mississauga, Ont., L4W 2T3 Canada. (416) 624-5010. FAX: (416) 238-2362.

MAXELL CORP. OF AMERICA
22-08 Route 208, Fair Lawn, NJ 07410. (201) 794-5900. FAX: (201) 796-8790.
CORPORATE PRESIDENT
Tsutomu Fukushima

NINTENDO OF AMERICA
4820 150th Ave. N.E., Redmond, WA 98052. (206) 882-2040.

PANASONIC
(Subsidiary of Matsushita Electric Corp. of America.)
One Panasonic Way, Secaucus, NJ 07094. (201) 348-7000.
PRESIDENT
Steve Bonica

PHILIPS MEDIA INC.
10960 Wilshire Blvd., Los Angeles, CA 90024. (310) 444-6500.

QUASAR COMPANY
(Division of Matsushita Electric Corp. of America)
1707 N. Randall Rd., Elgin, IL 60123-7847. (708) 468-5600.

SANYO FISHER CORP.
21350 Lassen St., Chatsworth, CA 91311. (818) 998-7322.

SEGA OF AMERICA
255 Shoreline Dr., Redwood City, CA 94605. (415) 508-2800.

SHARP ELECTRONICS CORPORATION
P.O. Box 650, Sharp Plaza, Mahwah, NJ 07430. (201) 529-8200.

SONY CORPORATION
15 Essex Rd., Box 919, Paramus, NJ 07653. (201) 368-5000. FAX (201) 368-3514.

TDK ELECTRONICS CORP.
12 Harbor Park Dr., Port Washington, NY 11050. (516) 625-0100. Telex 144535.

TEKTRONIX, INC.
P.O. Box 500, Beaverton, OR 97077. (503) 627-7111.

3DO CORPORATION
600 Galveston Dr., Redwood City, CA 94063. (415) 261-3000. FAX (415) 261-3120.
CEO
Trip Hawkins

3M/CONSUMER VIDEO & AUDIO PRODUCTS DIVISION
223-5S-01, 3M Center, St. Paul, MN 55125. (612) 733-1110.

TOSHIBA AMERICA, INC.
Corporate Headquarters: 1251 Ave. of the Americas, 41st fl., New York, NY 10020. (212) 596-0600. FAX: (212) 593-3875. Consumer Products Division: 82 Totowa Rd., Wayne, NJ 07470. (201) 628-8000. FAX: (201) 628-1875.

ZENITH ELECTRONICS CORPORATION
1000 Milwaukee Ave., Glenview, IL 60025-2493. (312) 391-7000.

VIDEO SERVICES

CALIFORNIA

ADVANCE RECORDING PRODUCTS
7190 Clairemont Mesa Blvd., San Diego, CA 92111. (619) 277-2540.

CAL IMAGE
3034 Gold Canal Dr., #B, Rancho Cordova, CA 95670. (916) 638-8383.

CARROL FILM & VIDEO, INC.
3535 Ross Ave., Bldg. II, Suite 205, San Jose, CA 91524. (408) 978-2784.

FESTIVAL PRODUCTIONS
849 E. Charleston Rd., Palo Alto, CA 94303. (415) 494-9366.

INTERFACE PRODUCTIONS
1534 Vallejo St., San Francisco, CA 94109. (415) 673-5946.

KTEH VIDEOSERVICES
100 Skyport Dr. San Jose, CA 95115. (408) 437-5454.

ONE PASS FILM & VIDEO
One China Basin Building, San Francisco, CA 94107. (415) 777-5777.

RUSSIAN HILL RECORDING
1520 Pacific Ave., San Francisco, CA 94109. (415) 474-4520.

TELEVISION ASSOCIATES, INC.
2410 Charleston Rd., Mountain View, CA. (415) 967-6040.

VARITEL VIDEO
350 Townsend St., San Francisco, CA 94107. (415) 495-3328.

VIDICOPY
650 Vaqueros Ave., Sunnyvale, CA 94086. (408) 739-7390.

WEST COAST DUPLICATING, INC.
385 Valley Dr., Brisbane, CA 94005. (415) 468-7330.

DISTRICT OF COLUMBIA

HENNINGER CAPITOL
2121 Wisconsin Ave., N.W., Suite 110, Washington, DC 20007. (202) 965-7800.

PUBLIC PRODUCTION GROUP
900 Second St., N.E., Suite 4, Washington D.C. 20002. (202) 898-1808. FAX: (202) 898-1811.

VOX-CAM ASSOCIATES
813 Silver Springs Ave., Silver Springs, MD 20910. (301) 589-5377.

ILLINOIS

CINEMA VIDEO CENTER, INC.
211 E. Grand Ave., Chicago, IL 60611. (312) 644-1650.

MEDIATECH INC.
110 W. Hubbard St., Chicago, IL 60610. (312) 828-1146. FAX: (312) 828-0982.

POLYCOM TELEPRODUCTIONS
142 E. Ontario, Chicago, IL 60611. (312) 337-6000.

TAPE FILM INDUSTRIES
640 N. LaSalle St., #275, Chicago, IL 60610. (312) 951-6700.

LOS ANGELES

ABC TELEVISION CENTER
4151 Prospect Ave., Los Angeles, CA 90027. (310) 557-7777. (310) 557-5707.

A.M.E. INC.
1133 N. Hollywood Way, Burbank, CA 91505. (818) 841-7440. FAX: (818) 845-0791.

AT&T RECORDING
501 N. Larchmont Blvd., Los Angeles, CA 90004. (213) 466-7756.

AARON & LE DUC VIDEO PRODUCTION
2002 21 St., Suite A, Santa Monica, CA 90404. (310) 450-8275. FAX: (310) 396-8265.

ABBEY TAPE DUPLICATORS INC.
9525 Vassar Ave., Chatsworth, CA 91311. (818) 882-5210. FAX: (818) 407-5900.

ABERDEEN POST DUPLICATION
3349 Cahuenga Blvd. W., Suite 1A, Los Angeles, CA 90068. (213) 874-3050.

ABSOLUTE POST
2911 W. Olive Ave., Burbank, CA 91505. (818) 953-4820. FAX: (818) 845-9179.

ACTION VIDEO, INC.
6616 Lexington Ave., Hollywood, CA 90038. (213) 461-3611. FAX: 460-4023.

ACTORS CENTER
11969 Ventura Blvd., Studio City, CA 91604. (818) 505-9400.

ADVANCED VIDEO INC.
6753 Santa Monica Blvd., Los Angeles, CA 90038. (213) 469-0707.

ADVENTURES IN FILM & TAPE
1034 N. Seward, Hollywood, CA 90038. (213) 460-4557.

ALL SEASONS ENTERTAINMENT
18121 Napa St., Northridge, CA 91325. (818) 886-8680. (800) 423-5599.

ALPHA CINE LABORATORY, INC.
5724 W. Third St., Suite 311, Los Angeles, CA 90036. (213) 934-7793. FAX: (213) 934-6307.

ALPHA STUDIOS VIDEO INC.
4720 W. Magnolia Blvd., Burbank, CA 91505. (818) 506-7443. FAX: (818) 506-4369.

ALTER IMAGE
1818 S. Victory Blvd., Glendale, CA 91201. (818) 244-6030. FAX: (818) 244-5824.

AMERICAN VIDEOGRAM INC.
12020 W. Pico Blvd., Los Angeles, CA 90064-1504. (310) 477-1535. (310) 477-5299.

AMETRON AUDIO VISUALS
1200 N. Vine St., Hollywood, CA 90038. (213) 466-4321.

ANDERSON VIDEO
100 Universal Plaza, Bldg. 153, Universal City, CA 91608. (818) 777-7999. FAX: (818) 777-7998.

APRICOT ENTERTAINMENT
940 N. Orange Dr., Hollywood, CA 90038. (213) 469-4000. FAX: (213) 469-5809.

APPLEGATE ENTERTAINMENT
15229 Fonthill Ave., Lawndale, CA 90260. (310) 676-3262.

ASHFIELD FILM LAB
747 N. Seward St., Hollywood, CA 90038. (213) 462-3231.

ATLAS VIDEO
8113 State S Gt., Los Angeles, CA. (213) 569-1393.

AUDIO ARTS PUBLISHING CO.
5617 Melrose Ave., Los Angeles, CA 90038. (213) 461-3507.

AUDIO GRAPHICS FILMS AND VIDEO
14932 Delano Ave., Van Nuys, CA 91411. (818) 780-7400. FAX: (213) 467-1234.

AUDIO RENTS INC.
7237 Santa Monica Blvd., Hollywood, CA 90046-6724. (213) 874-1000, (213) 265-4400. FAX: (213) 851-9586.

AUDIO SERVICES CORPORATION
10639 Riverside Dr., N. Hollywood, CA 91602. (818) 980-9891. (800) 228-4429. FAX: (818) 980-9911.

AUDIO VISUAL HEADQUARTERS CORP.
2300 Gladwick St., Rancho Dominguez, CA 90220. (310) 419-4040.

AUDIO-VIDEO CRAFT, INC.
6753 Santa Monica Blvd., Los Angeles, CA 90038. (213) 655-3511.

AUTOGRAPHICS
6335 Homewood Ave., Hollywood, CA 90028. (213) 464-2244.

B & J STUDIO
3575 Cahuenga Blvd. W., Los Angeles, CA 90068. (213) 876-1130.

BCS BROADCAST STORE, INC.
1840 Flower St., Glendale, CA 91201. (818) 845-7000. FAX: (818) 845-9483.

BABYLON POST
901 N. Seward St., Hollywood, CA 90038. (213) 460-4088. FAX: (213) 460-6312.

BACKGROUND ENGINEERS INC.
1213 Flower St., P.O. Box 3217, Glendale, CA 91221-0217. (818) 500-0454. FAX: (818) 500-8913.

BERC/BROADCAST EQUIPMENT RENTAL COMPANY
4545 Chermak St., Burbank, CA 91505-9930. (818) 841-3000. FAX: (818) 841-7919.

BETACAM SPECIALISTS
719 S. Victory, Burbank, CA 91502. (818) 845-6480. FAX: (818) 848-0955.

BEXEL CORPORATION
801 S. Main St., Burbank, CA 91506. (818) 841-5051. FAX: (818) 841-0428.

BEVERLY HILLS VIDEOCENTRE
145 S. Beverly Dr., Beverly Hills, CA 90212-3002. (310) 550-1092. FAX: (310) 550-4512.

BOULEVARD VIDEO PRODUCTIONS
15016 Ventura Blvd., Suite 4, Sherman Oaks, CA 91403. (818) 501-7369. FAX: (818) 501-7370.

BOWEN VIDEO FACILITIES
4406 Deseret Dr., Woodland Hills, CA 91364. (818) 342-8106. FAX: (818) 591-8605.

BROADCAST STANDARDS, INC.
2044 Cotner Ave., Los Angeles, CA 90025. (310) 312-9060. FAX: (310) 479-5771.

BRYAN WORLD PRODUCTIONS
P.O. Box 74033, Los Angeles, CA 90004. (213) 856-9256. FAX: (213) 856-0855.

BURBANK PRODUCTION PLAZA
801 S. Main St., Burbank, CA 91506. (818) 846-7677. (818) 958-8842. FAX: (818) 841-1572.

WALLY BURR RECORDING
1126 Hollywood Way, Suite 203, Burbank, CA 91505. (818) 845-0500.

BUZZY'S RECORDING
6900 Melrose Ave., Los Angeles, CA 90038. (213) 931-1867. FAX: (213) 931-9681.

CAHUENGA WEST VIDEO
3255 Cahuenga Blvd. West, Suite 100, Hollywood, CA 90068. (213) 850-1789.

CAL VISTA INTERNATIONAL LTD.
6649 Odessa Ave., Van Nuys, CA 91406. (818) 780-9000, (818) 780-7100. FAX: (818) 997-3064.

CALIFORNIA COMMUNICATIONS, INC.
6900 Santa Monica Blvd., Los Angeles, CA 90038. (213) 466-8511. FAX: (213) 466-2392.

CALIFORNIA VIDEO CENTER
5432 W. 102 St., Los Angeles, CA 90045. (310) 216-5400. FAX: (310) 216-5498.

CARMAN PRODUCTIONS, INC.
15456 Cabrito Rd., Van Nuys, CA 91406. (213) 873-7370. (818) 787-6436. FAX: (818) 787-3981.

CENTRE FILMS INC.
1103 N. El Centro Ave., Los Angeles, CA 90038. (213) 466-5123.

CENTURY SOUTHWEST PRODUCTION SERVICES
2939 Nebraska Ave., Santa Monica, CA 90404. (310) 315-4400.

CHOICE TELEVISION
800 S. Date Ave., Alhambra, CA 91803. (818) 576-2906. FAX: (818) 289-7719.

CINE VIDEO
948 N. Cahuenga Blvd., Hollywood, CA 90038. (213) 464-6200. FAX: (213) 469-8566.

CINEMA PRODUCTS CORPORATION
2037 Granville Ave., West Los Angeles, CA 90025. (310) 478-0711.

CINETYP INC.
843 Seward St., Hollywood, CA 90038. (213) 463- 8569. FAX: (213) 463-4129.

CLARASOL PRODUCTION CO.
3334 Oak Glen Dr., Hollywood, CA 90038. (213) 969-0583.

COMPACT VIDEO SERVICES INC.
2813 W. Alameda Ave., Burbank, CA 91505. (818) 840-7000. (800) 423-2277.

COMPLETE POST, INC.
6087 Sunset Blvd., Hollywood, CA 90028. (213) 467-1244. FAX: (213) 467-0278.

COMPOSITE IMAGE SYSTEMS
1144 N. Las Palmas Ave., Hollywood, CA 90038. (213) 463-8811.

COMPREHENSIVE SERVICE CORPORATION
P.O. Box 38339, Los Angeles, CA 90038. (213) 462-0969.

COMTEL
140 S. Victory Blvd., Burbank, CA 91502. (818) 840-0108.

CONRAD FILM DUPLICATING CO.
6750 Santa Monica Blvd., Hollywood, CA 90038. (213) 463-5614. FAX: (213) 463-4436.

CONSOLIDATED FILM INDUSTRIES
959 Seward St., Los Angeles, CA 90038. (213) 960-7444. FAX: (2123) 962-8746.

CONTINENTAL CAMERA SYSTEMS, INC.
7240 Valjean Ave., Van Nuys, CA 91406. (818) 989-5222. FAX: (818) 994-8405.

THE CREATIVE PARTNERSHIP, INC.
7525 Fountain Ave., Hollywood, CA 90046. (213) 850-5551. FAX: (213) 850-0391.

CREATIVE SOUND CORPORATION
P.O. Box 755, Malibu, CA 90265. (310) 456-5482. (800) 323-PACK. FAX: (310) 456-7886.

CREST NATIONAL FILM & VIDEOTAPE LABS
1000 N. Highland Ave., Hollywood, CA 90038. (213) 466-0624. FAX: (213) 461-8901.

CREST NATIONAL FILM & VIDEOTAPE LABS
1141 N. Seward St., Los Angeles, CA 90038. (213) 466-0624, (213) 462-6696. FAX: (213) 461-8901.

CRYSTAL SOUND RECORDING
1014 N. Vine St., Los Angeles, CA 90038. (213) 466-6452.

CUSTOM DUPLICATION INC.
3404 Century Blvd., Inglewood, CA 90303. (310) 776-4810.

CUSTOM VIDEO
3900 E. Whiteside St., Los Angeles, CA 90063. (213) 267-1146.

DSR PRODUCTIONS
607 North Avenue 64, Los Angeles, CA 90042. (213) 258-6741.

DAUGHERTY AUDIO/VIDEO DESIGN
2172 Ridgemont, Los Angeles, CA 90046. (213) 626-7001.

WALT DAVIS ENTERPRISES, INC.
931 N. Cole Ave., Hollywood, CA 90038. (213) 461-0700. FAX: (213) 461-0946.

DELTA PRODUCTIONS
3333 Glendale Blvd., Suite 3, Los Angeles, CA 90039. (213) 663-8754.

DELUXE LABORATORIES, INC.
1377 N. Serrano Ave., Hollywood, CA 90027. (213) 461-0608. FAX: (213) 462-6171.

DEVONSHIRE AUDIO/VIDEO STUDIOS
10729 Magnolia Blvd., N. Hollywood, CA 91601. (818) 985-1945. FAX: (818) 985-9915.

DIGITAL SOUND & PICTURE
2700 La Cienega, Los Angeles, CA 90034. (310) 836-7688. FAX: (310) 836-7499.

DUBS, INC.
1220 N. Highland, Hollywood, CA 90038. (213) 461-3726. FAX: (213) 466-7406.

DUPLITAPE
15016 Ventura Blvd., Suite 4, Sherman Oaks, CA 91403. (818) 501-7370. FAX: (818) 501-7370.

EFX SYSTEMS
1117 Isabell St. Burbank, CA 91506-1405. (818) 843-4762. FAX: (818) 848-0706.

ECHO FILM SERVICES INC.
4119 Burbank Blvd., Burbank, CA 91505. (818) 841-4114.

EDIT POINT
P.O. Box 55760, Valencia, CA 91355. (818) 841-7336. (805) 254-2108. FAX: (805) 259-1269.

EDITEL-LOS ANGELES
729 N. Highland Ave., Hollywood, CA 90038-3437. (213) 931-1821. FAX: (213) 931-7771.

THE EDITING COMPANY
8300 Beverly Blvd., Los Angeles, CA 90048. (213) 653-3570. FAX: (213) 931-7771.

ELECTRONIC ARTS & TECHNOLOGY
3655 Motor Ave., Los Angeles, CA 90034. (310) 836-2556.
ELECTRONIC SERVICE CENTER
4774 W. Adams Blvd., Los Angeles, CA 90016. (213) 731-5611. (213) 931-1178.
ENCORE VIDEO INC.
6344 Fountain Ave., Hollywood, CA 90028. (213) 466-7663. FAX: (213) 467-5539.
RAY ENGEL PRODUCTIONS
1730 Camino Palmero, Suite 206, Los Angeles, CA 90046. (213) 850-5411.
EYE ON VIDEO
224 N. Juanita Ave., Los Angeles, CA 90004. (213) 465-7777.
FACE BROADCAST PRODUCTIONS
115 N. Hollywood Way, Suite 102, Burbank, CA 91505. (818) 842-9081. FAX: (818) 842-3708.
FIDELITY RECORDING STUDIO
4412 Whitsett Ave., Studio City, CA 91604. (818) 508-3263. FAX: (818) 508-3267.
FILM TECHNOLOGY CO.
726 N. Cole Ave., Hollywood, CA 90038. (213) 464-3456.
FILMCORE PRINT AND TAPE
849 N. Seward St., Los Angeles, CA 90038. (213) 464-7303. (213) 464-8600.
FILMSERVICE LABORATORIES, INC.
6325 Santa Monica Blvd., Los Angeles, CA 90038. (213) 464-5141. FAX: (213) 469-9703.
FILMUSIK INC.
1229 N. Sycamore Ave., Suite 415, Los Angeles, CA 90038. (213) 259-6576.
525 POST PRODUCTION
6424 Santa Monica Blvd., Hollywood, CA 90038. (213) 466-3348. FAX: (213) 467-1589.
FOTO-KEM/FOTO TRONICS FILM-VIDEO LAB
2800 W. Olive Ave., Burbank, CA 91505. (818) 846-3101. FAX: (818) 841-2130.
SYLVIA FRANKS: THE CREATIVE RESOURCE
12056 Summit Circle, Beverly Hills, CA 90210. (310) 276-5282. FAX: (310) 276-9793.
G & B VIDEO LAB
255 E. Colorado Blvd., Pasadena, CA 91101. (818) 440-1909. (818) 440-9853.
GLENDALE POST PRODUCTION
1239 S. Glendale Ave., Glendale, CA 91205. (818) 502-5300. FAX: (818) 502-5311.
GLENDALE STUDIOS
1239 S. Glendale Ave., Glendale, CA 91205. (818) 502-5300. FAX: (818) 502-5311.
GLOBAL VISION CORPORATION
3255 Cahuenga Blvd., Hollywood, CA 90068. (213) 851-1190.
ALAN GORDON ENTERPRISES, INC.
1430 Cahuenga Blvd., Hollywood, CA 90028. (213) 466-3561. (818) 985-5500.
GREENE, COWE & CO.
1101 Isabel St., Burbank, CA 91506. (818) 841-7821. FAX: (818) 841-7916.
GROUP IV RECORDING
1541 N. Wilcox Ave., Los Angeles, CA 90028. (213) 466-6444. FAX: (213) 466-6714.
GROUP W VIDEOSERVICES
One Lakeside Pl., 3801 Barham Blvd., Los Angeles, CA 90068. (213) 850-3800. (800) 232-8872. FAX: (213) 850-3889.
HARMONEY HOUSE
1915 W. Glenoaks Blvd., Suite 200, Glendale, CA 91201. (818) 500-0100.
STAN HARRISON
39039 Willowvale Rd., Palmdale, CA 93551. (818) 569-4528.
HIT CITY, WEST
6146 W. Pico Blvd., Los Angeles, CA 90035. (213) 852-0186.
HOFFMAN VIDEO SYSTEMS
1945 S. Figueroa, Los Angeles, CA 90007. (213) 749-3311.
HOLLYWOOD HOME THEATRE
1540 N. Highland Ave., Suite 110, Los Angeles, CA 90028. (213) 466-0121. FAX: (213) 466-0121.
HOLLYWOOD NATIONAL STUDIOS
6605 Eleanor Ave., Los Angeles, CA 90038. (213) 467-6272.
HOLLYWOOD NEWSREEL SYNDICATE INC.
1622 N. Gower St., Los Angeles, CA 90028. (213) 469-7307. FAX: (213) 469-8251.

HOLLYWOOD VAULTS
742 N. Seward St., Los Angeles, CA 90038. (213) 461-6464. (805) 569-5336. FAX: (805) 569-1675.
HOMER & ASSOCIATES, INC.
Sunset Gower Studios, 1420 N. Beachwood Dr., Hollywood, CA 90028. (213) 462-4710.
HUCHINGSON MARTIN
3169 Barbara Court, Suite A, Los Angeles, CA 90068. (213) 876-4001.
IMAGE TRANSFORM INC.
4142 Lankershim Blvd., North Hollywood, CA 91602-2987. (818) 985-7566. FAX: (818) 980-4268.
IMAGE TRANSFORM LABORATORY
3611 N. San Fernando Rd., Burbank, CA 91505. (818) 841-3812. FAX: (818) 841-3999.
IPS/INDEPENDENT PRODUCERS
1741 N. Ivar Ave., Suite 109, Hollywood, CA 90028. (213) 461-6966. FAX: (213) 461-6966.
INTER VIDEO/TRITRONICS, INC.
10623 Riverside Dr., Toluca Lake, CA 91602. (818) 843-3633. (818) 569-4000. FAX: (818) 843-6884.
INTERLOK STUDIOS
1550 Crossroads of the World, Hollywood, CA 90028. (213) 469-3986.
INTERMIX, INC.
2505 S. Robertson Blvd., Los Angeles, CA 90034. (213) 870-2121.
INTERNATIONAL VIDEO CONVERSIONS
840 N. Hollywood Way, Burbank, CA 91505. (818) 569-3784. FAX: (818) 569-3659.
INTERSOUND
8746 Sunset Blvd., Los Angeles, CA 90069. (213) 652-3741. FAX: (310) 854-7290.
INSTITUTE OF AUDIO/VIDEO ENGINEERING
1831 Hyperion Ave., Hollywood, CA 90027. (213) 666-2380.
J & R FILM CO./MOVIOLA
6820 Romaine, Los Angeles, CA 90038. (213) 467-3107. FAX: (818) 505-9261.
JKR PRODUCTIONS, INC.
12140 W. Olympic Blvd., Suite 21, Los Angeles, CA 90064. (310) 826-3666.
JONES, TYLIE & ASSOCIATES
3519 W. Pacific Ave., Burbank, CA 91505. (818) 955-7600. (212) 972-3800. FAX: (818) 955-8542.
KCET
4401 Sunset Blvd., Los Angeles, CA 90027. (213) 666-6500. (213) 953-5258. FAX: (213) 953-5496.
KCOP TELEVISION INC.
915 N. La Brea Ave., Los Angeles, CA 90038. (213) 851-1000. (213) 850-2232.
KNBC
3000 W. Alameda St., Burbank, CA 91523. (818) 840-4444.
KTEH VIDEOSERVICES
100 Skyport Dr., San Jose, CA 95115. (408) 437-5454.
KWHY-TV, CHANNEL 22
5545 Sunset Blvd., Los Angeles, CA 90028. (213) 466-5441.
KAPPA VIDEO
1117 Isabel St., Burbank, CA 91506. (818) 843-3400. FAX: (818) 559-2418.
KEY WEST/VERITE POST
7223 Beverly Blvd., #200, Los Angeles, CA 90036. (213) 937-7528.
KLASKY/CSUPO
1258 N. Highland Ave., Hollywood, CA 90038. (213) 957-4010.
LP PRODUCTIONS
223 Strand St., Suite K, Santa Monica, CA 90405-6103. (310) 399-1101. FAX: (310) 392-6103
LA BREA STUDIOS
3334 Oak Glen Dr., Hollywood, CA 90038. (213) 876-5113.
LAJON PRODUCTIONS INC.
705 S. Victory Blvd., Burbank, CA 91505. (818) 841-1440. FAX: (818) 841-4659.
LASER PACIFIC MEDIA CORP.
809 N. Cahuenga Blvd., Hollywood, CA 90038. (213) 462-6266.
LASEREDIT, INC.
540 N. Hollywood Way, Burbank, CA 91505. (818) 842-0777. FAX: (818) 566-9834.

616

KARL M. LEVIN
20959 Elkwood St., Canoga Park, CA 91304. (818) 882-7262.
FAX: (818) 882-4122.

LIMELITE VIDEO WEST
6464 Sunset Blvd., #1110, Hollywood, CA 90028. (213) 856-
8606. (800) 634-5024.

LIONEL TELEVISION PRODUCTIONS
3329 Brookside Dr., Malibu, CA 90265. (310) 456-5809. FAX:
(310) 456-5800.

LUCAS ARTS ENTERTAINMENT
P.O. Box 2009, San Raphael, CA 94912. (415) 662-1800. FAX:
(415) 662-2460.

M.A.T.E. VIDEOTAPE
1653 18th St., Suite 3, Santa Monica, CA 90404. (310) 828-
8807.

M.F.I. VIDEO CENTER
1905 Grace Ave., Hollywood, CA 90068. (213) 851-0373.

MGS SERVICES
10507 Burbank Blvd., North Hollywood, CA 91601. (818) 508-
5488. FAX: (818) 508-5493.

MAGNASYNC MOVIOLA
5539 Riverton Ave., North Hollywood, CA 91601. (818) 763-
8441. FAX: (818) 505-9261.

MAJESTIC DUPLICATION & VIDEO SERVICE
1208 W. Isabel St., Burbank, CA 91506. (213) 849-1535. (818)
843-1806.

MANSFIELD STUDIOS
1041 N. Mansfield Ave., Hollywood, CA 90038. (213) 461-
9457. (213) 461-3393.

MARKET STREET SCREENING ROOM
73 Market St., Venice, CA 90291. (310) 396-5937.

MASTER DIGITAL INC.
1749 14th St., Santa Monica, CA 90404. (310) 452-1511.

MASTERWORDS
1512 Eleventh Street, Santa Monica, CA 90401. (310) 394-
7998.

CAMERON MCKAY PRODUCTIONS
6311 Romaine, Los Angeles, CA 90038. (213) 463-6073.

MEDIA HOME ENTERTAINMENT INC.
5730 Buckingham Pkway, Culver City, CA 90230. (310) 216-
7900. FAX: (310) 216-9305.

MEDIATECH WEST
1640 N. Gower St., Hollywood, CA 90028. (213) 466-6442.
FAX: (213) 466-2376.

MEGA PRODUCTIONS INC.
1714 North Wilton Place, Hollywood, CA 90028. (213) 462-
6342.

METAVISION
350 N. Glenoaks Blvd., Suite 208, Burbank, CA 91502. (818)
848-5929. FAX: (818) 848-2120.

METROPOLITAN ENTERTAINMENT
11946 Ashdale Lane, Studio City, CA 91604. (310) 657-9265.

MIDLAND STUDIOS
1615 Rancho Ave., Glendale, CA 91202. (818) 507-7982.

MIDTOWN VIDEO
8489 W. Third St., Suite 1066, Los Angeles, CA 90048. (213)
651-2420. FAX: (213) 651-1240.

MILES & COMPANY
1418 Dodson Ave., San Pedro, CA 90732. (310) 548-0462.

MOBILE IMAGE
2944 W. Mountain Pine Dr., La Crescenta, CA 91214. (213)
873-5203, (818) 248-6905.

MOBILE TRANSFERS, INC.
5417 N. Cahuenga Blvd., Suite A, N. Hollywood, CA 91601.
(213) 466-2044.

MODERN TALKING PICTURE SERVICE INC.
6735 San Fernando Rd., Glendale, CA 91201. (818) 240-0519.
(813) 541-7571. FAX: (813) 544-4624.

MODERN VIDEOFILM
7165 Sunset Blvd., Hollywood, CA 90046. (213) 851-8070.
FAX: (213) 851-0704.

MULTI-MEDIA WORKS
7227 Beverly Blvd., Los Angeles, CA 90036. (213) 939-1185.

MUSIC LAB INC.
1831 Hyperion Ave., Hollywood, CA 90027. (213) 666-3003.

NATIONAL TELEVISION NEWS INC.
23480 Park Sorrento, Suite 201A, Calabasas Park, CA 91302.
(818) 883-6121.

ORION ENTERPRISES, INC.
1811 W. Burbank Blvd., Burbank, CA 91506. (818) 954-8943.
FAX: (818) 846-6563.

P.D.S. VIDEO PRODUCTIONS
1102 W. Chestnut St., Burbank, CA 91506. (818) 841-4711.

PACIFIC OCEAN POST
730 Arizona Ave., Santa Monica, CA 90401. (310) 458-3300.
(213) 394-6852.

PACIFIC TITLE & ART STUDIO
6350 Santa Monica, Hollywood, CA 90038. (213) 464-0121.

PACIFIC VIDEO
809 N. Cahuenga Blvd., Los Angeles, CA 90038. (213) 462-
6266. FAX: (213) 464-3233.

PAL VIDEO
19061 Tina Pl., Tarzana, CA 91356. (818) 344-1603. FAX:
(818) 344-2852.

PARALLAX PRODUCTIONS
P.O. Box 2413, Beverly Hills, CA 90213. (310) 840-4513.

POLYCOM GROUP INC.
2911 W. Olive, Burbank, CA 91504. (818) 845-1917.

THE POST GROUP
6335 Homewood Ave., Los Angeles, CA 90028. (213) 462-
2300. FAX: (213) 462-0836.

THE POST HOUSE
1311 N. Highland Ave., Hollywood, CA 90028. (213) 464-0116.
FAX: (213) 464-0139.

POST LOGIC
1800 N. Vine, Hollywood, CA 90028. (213) 461-7887.

POST MODERN PICTURES
937 N. Cole Ave., Suite 3, Hollywood, CA 90038. (213) 464-
2823. FAX: (213) 464-2610.

POST TIME VIDEOTAPE
7551 Sunset Blvd., #103, Hollywood, CA 90046. (213) 876-
2440.

POWERHOUSE AUDIO/VIDEO
19347 Londelius St., Northridge, CA 91324. (818) 993-4778.

PREMORE INC.
5130 Klump Ave., N. Hollywood, CA 91601. (818) 506-7714.

PRO VIDEO
801 N. La Brea Ave., Los Angeles, CA 90038. (213) 934-8836.
(213) 934-8840. FAX: (213) 939-8837.

PRODUCERS ASSOCIATES
7243 Santa Monica Blvd., Hollywood, CA 90046. (213) 851-
4123. FAX: (213) 851-9959.

THE PRODUCTION GROUP
1330 N. Vine St., Hollywood, CA 90028. (213) 469-8111. FAX:
(213) 462-0836.

PROFESSIONAL ARTISTS GROUP
845 N. Highland Ave., Hollywood, CA 90038. (213) 871-2222.

PROJECT ONE
6669 Sunset Blvd., Hollywood, CA 90028. (213) 464-2285.
FAX: (213) 464-1858.

PROVIDEO
10635 Van Owen St., Burbank, CA 91505. (818) 762-9671.

QUIK VIDEO COPIES
11394 Ventura Blvd., Studio City, CA 91604. (818) 509-9316.

R. PRODUCTIONS & VIDEO EVENTS
6255 W. Sunset Blvd., Hollywood, CA 90028. (213) 465-4197.
FAX: (213) 465-6549.

RVS-TAPE TO FILM TRANSFER SERVICES
2408 W. Olive Ave., Burbank, CA 91506. (818) 954-8621.

RALEIGH STUDIOS
5300 Melrose Ave., Hollywood, CA 90038. (213) 466-3111.
FAX: (213) 871-4428.

RANK CINTEL, INC.
25358 Avenue Stanford, Valencia, CA 91355. (805) 294-2310.
FAX: (805) 294-1019.

RANK VIDEO
11150 Santa Monica Blvd., Suite 700, Los Angeles, CA 90025.
(310) 477-7755. FAX: (310) 477-7088.

RAZ VIDEO PRODUCTIONS
1828 E. Walnut St., Pasadena, CA 91107. (818) 449-1175.
FAX: (818) 854-0973.

RED CAR
1040 N. Las Palmas Ave., Bldg. 9, Los Angeles, CA 90038.
(213) 466-4467. FAX: (213) 466-4925.

THE REEL THING OF CALIFORNIA, INC.
1253 N. Vine St., Hollywood, CA 90038. (213) 466-8588. FAX:
(213) 466-0603.

REN-MAR STUDIOS
846 Cahuenga Blvd., Los Angeles, CA 90038. (213) 463-0808.

RENCHER'S JOY EDITORIAL SERVICE
738 N. Cahuenga Blvd., Hollywood, CA 90038. (213) 463-9836.

RINGER VIDEO SERVICES
2408 W. Olive Ave., Burbank, CA 91506. (818) 954-8621.

GLENN ROLAND FILMS
P.O. Box 341408, Los Angeles, CA 90034. (310) 475-0937. FAX: (310) 475-0939.

NEIL ROSS
261 S. Robertson Blvd., Beverly Hills, CA 90211. (310) 855-1700.

RUBBER DUBBERS, INC.
626 Justin Ave., Glendale, CA 91201-2327. (818) 241-5600. FAX: (818) 902-9284.

RUSK SOUND STUDIO
1556 N. La Brea Ave., Hollywood, CA 90028. (213) 462-6477. FAX: (213) 462-5684.

RYDER SOUND SERVICES, INC.
1611 N. Vine St., Los Angeles, CA 90038. (213) 469-3511.

SAR PRODUCTIONS
3575 Cahuenga Blvd. W., PH, Los Angeles, CA 90068. (213) 969-8081.

SABAN ENTERTAINMENT
4000 W. Alameda Ave., Burbank, CA 91505. (818) 972-4800.

SIM SADLER POST PRODUCTION
6602 Lexington Ave., Hollywood, CA 90028. (213) 962-9877.

SCOTTSOUND INC.
6110 Santa Monica Blvd., Los Angeles, CA 90038. (213) 464-6007.

SCREENMUSIC STUDIOS
11700 Ventura Blvd., Studio City, CA 91604. (818) 877-0300. (818) 985-0900. FAX: (818) 508-4870.

SCHULMAN VIDEO CENTER
861 Seward St., Hollywood, CA 90038-3601. (213) 465-8110. FAX: (213) 465-1874.

SELL ENTERTAINMENT
9701 Wilshire Blvd., Beverly Hills, CA 90212. (310) 874-5402.

SHORELINE PROFESSIONAL VIDEO SYSTEMS
1622 N. Highland Ave., Hollywood, CA 90028. (213) 461-9800. FAX: (213) 461-1450.

SIERRA VIDEO
4216 N. Maxon Ave., El Monte, CA 91732. (818) 579-7023. FAX: (818) 579-7045.

SKYLINE PRODUCTIONS
1041 N. Orange Dr., Hollywood, CA 90038-2317. (213) 856-0033. FAX: (213) 856-9845.

SKYLIGHT PRODUCTIONS INC.
6815 W. Willoughby, Suite 201, Los Angeles, CA 90038. (213) 464-4500. FAX: (213) 464-1225.

SOUND CHAMBER
27 S. El Molino Ave., Pasadena, CA 91101. (818) 449-8133.

SOUND IMAGE STUDIO INC.
6556 Wilkinson Ave., North Hollywood, CA 91606-2320. (818) 762-8881.

SOUND MASTER AUDIO/VIDEO
10747 Magnolia Blvd., North Hollywood, CA 91601. (213) 650-8000.

SOUND SERVICES INC.
7155 Santa Monica Blvd., Los Angeles, CA 90046. (213) 874-9344. (213) 986-3255. FAX: (213) 850-7189.

THE SOUND SURGEON
11712 Moorpark St., #104, Studio City, CA 91604. (818) 763-7746.

SOUND WEST, INC.
12166 Olympic Blvd., Los Angeles, CA 90064. (310) 826-6560.

LEONARD SOUTH PRODUCTIONS
4883 Lankershim Blvd., N. Hollywood, CA 91601-2746. (818) 760-8383. FAX: (818) 766-8301.

SOUTHLAND VIDEO
3255 Cahuenga Blvd., Hollywood, CA 90068. (213) 851-1190.

RICK VIDEO SPALLA PRODUCTIONS
1622 N. Gower St., Hollywood, CA 90028. (213) 469-7307.

SPECTRA SYSTEMS INC.
540 N. Hollywood Way, Burbank, CA 91505. (818) 842-1111.

SPLIT REEL RECORDING
943 Cole Ave., Hollywood, CA 90038. (213) 466-3817.

SPRINGBOARD STUDIOS
12229 Montague St., Arleta, CA 91331. (818) 896-4321.

SQUARE WHEEL PRODUCTIONS/THE CONSULTANCY
P.O. Box 675, Van Nuys, CA 91408-0675. (818) 508-0332.

STARFAX
8300 Beverly Blvd., Los Angeles, CA 90048. (213) 653-3570. FAX: (818) 244-3600.

STEENBECK INC.
9554 Vassar Ave., Chatsworth, CA 91311. (818) 998-4033.

KRIS STEVENS ENTERPRISES INC.
14241 Ventura Blvd., Suite 204, Sherman Oaks, CA 91423. (818) 981-8255. FAX: (818) 990-4350.

SHADOE STEVENS INC.
3575 Cahuenga Blvd. W., Los Angeles, CA 90069. (310) 274-1244.

STUDIO FILM & TAPE INC.
6670 Santa Monica Blvd., Los Angeles, CA 90038. (213) 466-8101. (800) 824-3130.

STUDIO PRODUCTIONS, INC.
5358 Melrose Ave., Hollywood, CA 90004. (213) 856-8048. FAX: (213) 461-4202.

STUDIO SPECTRUM INC.
1056 N. Lake St., Burbank, CA 91502. (818) 843-1610. FAX: (818) 843-1145.

SUNRISE CANYON VIDEO
P.O. Box 10968, Burbank, CA 91510. (818) 845-7473.

SUNSET POST INC.
1817 Victory Blvd., Glendale, CA 91201. (818) 956-7912. FAX: (818) 545-7586.

SUNSHINE COMMUNICATIONS
565 N. Gower St., Hollywood, CA 90004. (213) 464-6652.

SUPERCINE INC.
2214 W. Olive Ave., Burbank, CA 91506. (818) 843-8260.

SUPERCOLOSSAL PICTURES CORP.
7793 Skyhill Dr., Los Angeles, CA 90032. (213) 874-0303.

SYNC, INC.
931 N. Gardner St., W. Hollywood, CA 90046. (213) 851-6624.

TAJ SOUNDWORKS
8207 W. 3rd St., Los Angeles, CA 90048. (213) 655-2775.

TAV/AME, INC.
1541 N. Vine St., Hollywood, CA 90028. (213) 466-2141. FAX: (213) 464-4636.

TAPE-FILM INDUSTRIES (TFI)
941 N. Highland Ave., Hollywood, CA 90038. (213) 461-3361.

TELEPRINT OF LOS ANGELES
3779 Cahuenga Blvd. West, Studio City, CA 91604. (818) 760-3191. FAX: (818) 760-3194.

THIRD STREET SOUND INC.
6200 W. 3rd St., Los Angeles, CA 90038. (213) 937-2460. FAX: (213) 935-3719.

TODD-AO/GLEN GLENN STUDIOS
900 N. Seward St., Hollywood, CA 90038. (213) 962-4000.

TOP VIDEO SERVICES INC.
10153 Riverside Dr., Suite 1B, Toluca Lake, CA 91602. (818) 763-1295.

TRANS-AMERICAN VIDEO INC.
1541 N. Vine St., Los Angeles, CA 90028. (213) 466-2141.

TRANSWORLD VIDEO LAB INC.
1811 W. Magnolia Blvd., Burbank, CA 91506. (818) 841-2416.

2M PRODUCTIONS
3518 Cahuenga Blvd. W., Suite 202, Los Angeles, CA 90068. (213) 850-5656. FAX: (213) 850-5656.

U P A PRODUCTIONS OF AMERICA
14101 Valleyheart Dr., Sherman Oaks, CA 91423. (818) 990-3800.

USA PRODUCTIONS
1645 Vine St., Suite 350, Hollywood, CA 90028. (213) 465-6320.

U.T. PHOTO SERVICE INC.
4121 Vanowen Pl., Burbank, CA 91505. (213) 556-6066.

BILL UDELL PRODUCTIONS
6006 Vantage Ave., North Hollywood, CA 91606. (818) 985-6867.

UNITED TELEPRODUCTION SERVICES
15055 Oxnard St., Van Nuys, CA 91411. (818) 997-0100.

UNITEL VIDEO
3330 Cahuenga Blvd. West, Los Angeles, CA 90068. (213) 878-5800. FAX: (213) 878-5999.

UNIVERSAL FACILITIES RENTAL DIVISION
100 Universal City Plaza, Universal City, CA 91608. (818) 777-3000.

VCC TELEVISION PRODUCTION SERVICES (VENTURA COUNTRY CABLEVISION)
30901 Agoura Rd., Westlake Village, CA 91361. (818) 879-5993. FAX: (818) 879-5999.

VRA TELEPLAY PICTURES
P.O. Box 8471, Universal Plaza Station, Universal City, CA 91608. (213) 462-1099. FAX: (818) 795-8436.

VTE MOBILE TELEVISION PRODUCTIONS INC.
21041 S. Western Ave., Suite 220, Torrance, CA 90501. (310) 328-1353. FAX: (310) 328-0681.

VTR SERVICE COMPANY
3169 Barbara Ct., Suite D, Hollywood, CA 90068. (213) 851-9700.

THE VALENCIA STUDIOS
28343 Avenue Crocker, Valencia, CA 91355. (800) STA-GEIT. (805) 257-1202. FAX: (805) 257-1002.

VALLEY PRODUCTION CENTER
6633 Van Nuys Blvd., Van Nuys, CA 91405-4689. (818) 988-6601.

VARITEL VIDEO
3575 Cahuenga Blvd. West, Suite 675, Los Angeles, CA 90068. (213) 850-1165. FAX: (213) 850-6151.

VECTOR PRODUCTIONS INC.
P.O. Box 7000-645, Redondo Beach, CA 90277. (213) 757-0520. (310) 316-6031.

GREG VENABLE ENTERPRISES
10220 Riverside Dr., Suite B, Toluca Lake, CA 91602. (818) 985-3339.

VIDCOM POST
2600 W. Olive Ave., Suite 100, Burbank, CA 91505. (818) 841-1199. FAX: (818) 841-2350.

VIDCOM ENTERTAINMENT, INC.
P.O. Box 2926, Hollywood, CA 90078. (310) 301-8433.

VIDCOM PRODUCTION FACILITY
2426 Townsgate Rd., Suite K, Westlake Village, CA 91361. (818) 991-1974.

VIDEO ADVENTURES
1015 Cahuenga Blvd., Hollywood, CA 90038. (213) 461-3288.

VIDEO CRAFTSMEN INC.
6311 Romaine St., Los Angeles, CA 90038. (213) 464-4351.

VIDEO DIMENSIONS
330 Washington St., Suite 400, Marina del Rey, CA 90292. (310) 578-1300. (310) 578-1301. FAX: (310) 578-6070.

VIDEO EQUIPMENT RENTALS
450 S. Central Ave., Glendale, CA 91204. (818) 956-0212.

VIDEO EVENTS INC.
1741 Ivar Ave., Los Angeles, CA 90038. (213) 465-4197.

VIDEO GENERAL
1200 E. 2 St., Long Beach, CA 90802. (310) 437-7569. (310) 436-4525.

VIDEO IMAGE
5333 Mc Connell Ave., Los Angeles, CA 90066. (310) 822-8872. FAX: (310) 821-1012.

VIDEO IMAGE
4121 Redwood Ave., Suite 215, Los Angeles, CA 90066. (310) 822-8872.

VIDEO MASTERS
4146 Lankershim Blvd., N. Hollywood, CA 91602. (213) 877-1511. (818) 761-4484.

VIDEO SUPPORT SERVICES INC.
3473-1/2 Cahuenga Blvd. W., Los Angeles, CA 90068. (213) 469-9000.

THE VIDEO TAPE CO.
10523 Burbank Blvd., North Hollywood, CA 91601. (818) 985-1666. (818) 753-3000. FAX: (818) 985-0614.

VIDEO TAPE TRANSFER LABS
450 S. Central Ave., Glendale, CA 91204. (818) 956-1669.

VIDEO WEST
805 Larrabee St., W. Hollywood, CA 90069. (310) 659-5762

VIDEOASIS
317 S. Verdugo Rd., Glendale, CA 91205. (818) 507-1037.

VIDEO-IT INC.
5000 Overland Ave., Suite 6, Culver City, CA 90232. (310) 280-0505. (818) VID-EOIT.

VIDEO-PAC SYSTEMS LTD.
800 Seward St., Hollywood, CA 90038. (213) 464-2551

VIDEOTAPE PRODUCTS INC.
320 N. Madison Ave., Los Angeles, CA 90004. (213) 664-1144. (800) 422-2444. FAX: (213) 661-2177.

VIDEOWERKS
1316 Third St., Suite 102, Santa Monica, CA 90401. (310) 393-8754. FAX: (310) 458-7802.

VIDE-U PRODUCTIONS
1034 Shenandoah St., Los Angeles, CA 90035. (310) 657-4385. FAX: (310) 657-4385.

VILLAGE POST
1616 Butler Ave., Los Angeles, CA 90025-3098. (310) 478-8227. FAX: (310) 478-2414.

VOICE OVER L.A. INC.
1717 N. Highland Ave., Suite 620, Hollywood, CA 90028. (213) 463-8652. FAX: (213) 463-5443.

WARNER BROS. STUDIOS
4000 Warner Blvd., Burbank, CA 91522. (818) 954-6000.

WAVES SOUND RECORDERS
1956 N. Cahuenga Blvd., Hollywood, CA 90068. (213) 466-6141. FAX: (213) 466-3751.

WEBSTER COMMUNICATIONS
607 N. Ave. 64, Los Angeles, CA 90042. (213) 258-6741.

WEST PRODUCTIONS, INC.
2921 W. Olive Ave., Burbank, CA 91505. (818) 841-4500.

WESTERN FILM INDUSTRIES
30941 W. Agoura Rd., Suite 302, Westlake Village, CA 91361. (818) 889-7350. FAX: (818) 707-3937.

WEXLER VIDEO, INC.
800 N. Victory Blvd., Burbank, CA 91502. (818) 846-9381. (800) 800-9383.

WHIDBEY VIDEO
12117 Moorpark, Studio City, CA 91604. (818) 766-9855. FAX: (818) 766-3950.

THE WILD SIDE THEATRE
10945 Camarillo St., N. Hollywood, CA 91602. (818) 506-8838.

WILDER BROTHERS VIDEO
10327 Santa Monica Blvd., Los Angeles, CA 90025. (310) 557-3500.

WILDWOOD FILM SERVICE
6855 Santa Monica Blvd., Suite 400, Los Angeles, CA 90038. (213) 462-6388.

WILLIAM SOUND SERVICE
1343 N. Highland Ave., Los Angeles, CA 90028. (213) 461-5321. FAX: (213) 465-8888.

GLENN WINTERS PRODUCTIONS, INC.
P.O. Box 920, Montrose, CA 91020. (818) 790-4201.

WOLLIN PRODUCTION SERVICES INC.
666 N. Robertson Blvd., Los Angeles, CA 90069. (310) 659-0175. FAX: (310) 659-2946.

YALE LABS
1509 N. Gordon, Los Angeles, CA 90028. (213) 464-6181.

Z & A SERVICE
9707 W. Washington Blvd., Culver City, CA 90232. (310) 836-3194.

MICHIGAN

PREMIERE VIDEO, INC.
35687 Industrial Rd., Livonia, MI 48150. (313) 464-4650.

PRODUCERS COLOR SERVICE INC.
24242 Northwestern Highway, Southfield, MI 48075. (313) 352-5353. (800) 727-8700.

NEW JERSEY

COLOR LEASING STUDIO
330 Rt. 46, Fairfield, NJ 07006. (201) 575-1118.

VIDEO RESOURCE
140 Centennial Ave., Piscataway, NJ 08854. (908) 457-7400.

VIDEOCENTER OF NJ INC.
228 Park Ave. E., Rutherford, NJ 07073. (201) 935-0900.

NEW YORK

ANS INTERNATIONAL VIDEO LTD.
35 E. 21 St., New York, NY 10010. (212) 366-1733.

ACE AUDIO VISUAL CO.
13 E. 31 St., New York, NY 10016. (212) 685-3344. 33-49 55th St., Woodside, NY 11377. (718) 458-3800.

ADVISORY TV & RADIO LABORATORY OF AMERICA
175 Seventh Ave., New York, NY 10011. (212) 243-0786.

DOM ALBI ASSOCIATES, INC.
121 W. 27 St., New York, NY 10001. (212) 727-2256.
ALL MOBILE VIDEO
221 W. 26th St., New York, NY 10001. (212) 727-1234.
AMERICAN VIDEO SERVICE DEPT.
516 Amsterdam Ave., New York, NY 10024. (212) 724-4870.
AMERICAN VIDEO-CHANNELS INC.
321 W. 44 St., New York, NY 10036. (212) 765-6324.
AMERICAN VIDEO STUDIOS INC.
717 Lexington Ave., New York, NY 10022. (212) 888-0888.
ANIMATED PRODUCTIONS, INC.
1600 Broadway, New York, NY 10019. (212) 265- 2942.
APEX VIDEO ELECTRONICS
352 E. 76 St., New York, NY 10021. (212) 517-4300.
ARTEL VIDEO, INC.
1600 Broadway, New York, NY 10019. (212) 315-5665.
AUDIO PLUS VIDEO INTERNATIONAL, INC.
25 W. 45 St., New York, NY 10036. (212) 704-4000.
UDIO SERVICES CORPORATION
326 W. 48 St., New York, NY 10036. (212) 977-5150.
AUDIOVISIONS
1221 Second Ave., New York, NY 10021. (212) 593-3326.
AUTHORIZED FACTORY SERVICE CO.
460 W. 34 St., New York, NY 10001. (212) 290-4800.
BETELGEUSE PRODUCTIONS
44 E. 32 St., New York, NY 10016. (212) 251-8600.
BROADWAY VIDEO
1619 Broadway, New York, NY 10019. (212) 265-7600.
TONY BROWN PRODUCTIONS
1501 Broadway, Rm. 412, New York, NY 10036. (212) 575-0876.
C&C VISUAL
1500 Broadway, 4th floor, New York, NY 10036. (212) 869-4900.
CAMERA SERVICE CENTER, INC.
625 W. 54 St., New York, NY 10019. (212) 757-0906.
CAROB VIDEO
250 W. 57 St., New York, NY 10019. (212) 957-9525.
CENTER LIGHT TV
245 W. 19 St., New York, NY 10011. (212) 929-4745.
CHARLEX
2 W. 45 St., New York, NY 10036. (212) 719-4600.
CINE-MAGNETICS FILM & VIDEO
298 Fifth Ave., New York, NY 10016. (212) 564-6737.
650 Halstead Ave., Mamaroneck, NY 10543. (914) 698-3434, (800) 431-1102. FAX: (914) 698-0680.
CINERGY COMMUNICATIONS CORP.
321 W. 44 St., New York, NY 10036. (212) 582-2900.
CITICAM VIDEO SERVICES
630 Ninth Ave., Suite 910, New York, NY 10036. (212) 315-4855.
COMMUNICATIONS PLUS
102 Madison Ave., New York, NY 10016. (212) 686-9570.
COMP ART PLUS
49 W. 45th St., 4th floor, New York, NY 10036. (212) 921-1199.
COMPREHENSIVE SERVICE A-V INC.
432 W. 45 St., New York, NY 10036. (212) 586-6161.
COMTECH VIDEO PRODUCTIONS
770 Lexington Ave., New York, NY 10021. (212) 826-2935.
CREATIVE WAYS, INC.
305 E. 46 St., New York, NY 10017. (212) 935-0145.
DJM FILMS INC.
4 E. 46 St., New York, NY 10017. (212) 687-0111.
DEVLIN VIDEOSERVICE
1501 Broadway, Suite 401, New York, NY 10036. (212) 391-1313. FAX: (212) 391-2744.
DU ART VIDEO
245 W. 55 St., New York, NY 10019. (212) 757-3681.
E C ELECTRONICS
253 W. 51 St., New York, NY 10019. (212) 586-6156.
EDIT DECISIONS, LTD.
311 W. 43 St., New York, NY Rm. 701, 10036. (212) 757-4742.
EDITEL, NEW YORK
222 E. 44 St., New York, NY 10017. (212) 867-4600.
EDITING CONCEPTS INC.
214 E. 50 St., New York, NY 10022. (212) 980-3340.

86TH ST. PHOTO
1525 Third Ave., New York, NY 10028. (212) 737-2265.
ELECTRIC FILM
87 Lafayette St., New York, NY 10013. (212) 925-3429.
EMPIRE STAGES OF NY
50-2025 St., Long Island City, NY 11101. (718) 392-4747.
EMPIRE VIDEO
216 E. 45 St., New York, NY 10017. (212) 687-2060.
EQUITABLE PRODUCTION GROUP
787 Seventh Ave., New York, NY 10019. (212) 554-1389.
EVEN TIME INC.
62 W. 45 St., New York, NY 10036. (212) 764-4700.
FEATURE SYSTEMS
512 W. 36 St., New York, NY 10018. (212) 736-0447.
FRAMERUNNER INC.
1995 Broadway, Suite 1100, New York, NY 10023. (212) 874-1730.
GLOBE VIDEO SERVICES
286 Fifth Ave., New York, NY 10001. (212) 695-6868.
GRAMERCY BROADCAST CENTER
230 Park Ave. S., New York, NY 10003. (212) 614-4088.
HBO STUDIO PRODUCTIONS
120A E. 23 St., New York, NY 10010. (212) 512-7800.
HORN/EISENBERG FILM & TAPE EDITING
16 W. 46 St., New York, NY 10036. (212) 391-8166.
INTERCONTINENTAL TELEVIDEO INC.
29 W. 38 St., New York, NY 10018. (212) 719-0202.
INTERNATIONAL DUPLICATION CENTRE, INC.
321 West 44 Street, Suite 908, New York, NY 10036. (212) 581-3940. FAX: (212) 581-3979.
INTERNATIONAL VIDEO MARKET
926 Second Ave., New York, NY 10022. (212) 826-1996.
INTERNATIONAL VIDEO SERVICES
1501 Broadway, Suite 1300, New York, NY 10036. (212) 730-1411.
JPC VISUALS INC.
11 E. 47 St., 4th floor, New York, NY 10017. (212) 223-0555.
K. V. L. AUDIO VISUALS INC.
6 Executive Plaza, Yonkers, NY 10701. (212) 581-8050.
KAUFMAN ASTORIA STUDIOS
34-12 36th St., Astoria, NY 11106. (718) 392-5600.
LAUMIC CO.
306 E. 39 St., New York, NY 10016. (212) 889-3300.
LEE PRODUCTIONS, INC.
137 E. 25 St., New York, NY 10010. (212) 213-4110.
LUNAR VIDEO LTD.
138 E. 26 St., New York, NY 10010. (212) 686-4802.
MGS SERVICES
619 W. 54 St., New York, NY 10019. (212) 765-4500.
MAGNO SOUND, INC.
729 Seventh Ave., New York, NY 10019. (212) 302-2505. FAX: (212) 819-1282.
MANHATTAN TRANSFER EDIT
545 Fifth Ave., New York, NY 10017. (212) 687-4000.
WILLIAM MARKLE ASSOCIATES INC.
455 W. 43 St., New York, NY 10018. (212) 246-8642.
MODERN TELECOMMUNICATIONS INC.
1 Dag Hammarskjold Plaza, Level C, New York, NY 10017. (212) 355-0510.
MULTI VIDEO GROUP LTD.
50 E. 42 St., New York, NY 10017. (212) 986-1577.
NAPOLEON VIDEOGRAPHICS
460 W. 42 St., New York, NY 10036. (212) 967-6655.
NATIONAL RECORDING STUDIOS
460 W. 42 St., New York, NY 10036. (212) 279-2000.
NATIONAL VIDEO CENTER
460 W. 42 St., New York, NY 10036. (212) 279-2000.
NATIONAL VIDEO INDUSTRIES, INC.
15 W. 17 St., New York, NY 10011. (212) 691-1300.
NEW BREED STUDIOS
251 W. 30 St., Suite 7RW, New York, NY 10001. (212) 714-9379.
NEXUS PRODUCTIONS, INC.
10 E. 40 St., New York, NY 10016. (212) 679-2180.
OCCASIONAL VIDEO
534 E. 84 St., New York, NY 10028. (212) 737-3058.

OLDEN CAMERA VIDEO & COMPUTER STORE
1265 Broadway, New York, NY 10001. (212) 725-1234.
OMNI VIDEO SERVICES, LTD.
511 W. 33 St., New York, NY 10001. (212) 629-4303.
OTTERSON TV VIDEO INC.
251 W. 30 St., Suite 14 W, New York, NY 10001. (212) 695-7417.
P.A.T. FILM SERVICES
630 Ninth Ave., New York, NY 10036. (212) 247-0900.
PDR PRODUCTIONS, INC.
219 E. 44 St., New York, NY 10017. (212) 986-2020.
PARTNERS & AGOSTINELLI PRODUCTIONS, INC.
1123 Bdwy., New York, NY 10010. (212) 255-2000.
PELCO EDITORIAL INC.
757 Third Ave., New York, NY 10017. (212) 319-3348.
PICSONIC PRODUCTIONS CORP.
25 W. 45 St., #703, New York, NY 10036. (212) 575-1910.
POST EXPRESSIONS
5 E. 47 St., New York, NY 10017. (212) 838-5130.
POST PERFECT
220 E. 42 St., New York, NY 10017. (212) 972-3400.
PREMIERE POST
630 Ninth Ave., PH, New York, NY 10036. (212) 757-1711.
PRIMALUX VIDEO PRODUCTION
30 W. 26 St., New York, NY 10010. (212) 206-1402.
PRINCZKO PRODUCTIONS
9 E. 38 St., New York, NY 10016. (212) 683-1300.
R.G. VIDEO
21 W. 46 St., New York, NY 10036. (212) 997-1464. FAX: (212) 827-0726.
RAFIK FILM & VIDEOTAPE COMPANY
814 Broadway, New York, NY 10001. (212) 475-7884.
REBO HIGH DEFINITION STUDIO
530 W. 25 St., New York, NY 10001. (212) 989-9466. FAX: (212) 627-9083.
REEVES AV SYSTEMS INC.
227 E. 45 St., New York, NY 10017. (212) 573-8652. FAX: (212) 986-3591.
REILLY VIDEO COMMUNICATIONS
508 W. 26 St., New York, NY 10001. (212) 924-4880.
RELIANCE AUDIO-VISUAL CORP.
1600 Broadway, New York, NY 10019. (212) 586- 5000.
ROSS-GAFFNEY
21 W. 46 St., New York, NY 10036. (212) 719-2744.
SALAMANDRA IMAGES, INC.
6 E. 39 St., New York, NY 10016. (212) 779-0707.
HOWARD M. SCHWARTZ RECORDING, INC.
420 Lexington Ave., New York, NY 10017. (212) 687-4180.
SILVER CUP STUDIOS
42-25 21st St., Long Island City, NY 11101. (718) 784-3390.
SOUND ONE CORP.
1619 Broadway, New York, NY 10019. (212) 765-4757.
RICK SPALLA VIDEO PRODUCTIONS
301 W. 45 St., New York, NY 10036. (212) 765-4646.
SPLICE IS NICE LTD.
141 E. 44 St., New York, NY 10017. (212) 599-1711.
STREETVISIONS REMOTE INC.
34 Gansevoort St., New York, NY 10014. (212) 242- 4324.
SYNC SOUND INC.
450 W. 56 St., New York, NY 10019. (212) 246-5580.
TAPE FILM INDUSTRIES
619 W. 54 St., New York, NY 10019. (212) 708-0500.
TAPE HOUSE INC.
216 E. 45 St., New York, NY 10017. (212) 557-4949.
THE TAPE PLACE
4 E. 46 St., New York, NY 10017. (212) 986-5970.
TAPESTRY PRODUCTIONS LTD.
920 Broadway, New York, NY 10010. (212) 677-6007.
TEATOWN VIDEO EDITING
165 W. 46 St., New York, NY 10036. (212) 302-0722.
TECHNETRON ELECTRONICS INC.
39 E. 29 St., New York, NY 10016. (212) 725-8778, (212) 725-8779.
TECHNISPHERE
29 E. 19 St., New York, NY 10003. (212) 777-5100.
TELETECHNIQUES
1 W. 19 St., New York, NY 10011. (212) 206-1475.

TELSTAR EDITING, INC.
29 W. 38 St., New York, NY 10018. (212) 730-1000.
TODAY VIDEO, INC.
475 Tenth Ave., New York, NY 10018. (212) 391-1020. FAX: (212) 768-1302.
TULCHIN PRODS.
240 E. 45 St., New York, NY 10017. (212) 986-8270.
UNITEL VIDEO SERVICES
515 W. 57 St., New York, NY 10019. (212) 265-3600. FAX: (212) 765-5801.
VALKHN FILMS, INC.
1650 Broadway, Suite 404, New York, NY 10019. (212) 586-1603.
VIDEO CASSETTE TRANSFERS
8 W. 19 St., New York, NY 10011. (212) 206-1642.
VIDEO CENTRAL INC.
20 E. 49 St., New York, NY 10017. (212) 688-5110.
VIDEO CONNECTION
2240 Broadway, New York, NY 10024. (212) 724-2727.
VIDEO DUB, INC.
423 W. 55 St., New York, NY 10019. (212) 757-3300.
VIDEO INSTALLATIONS PLUS INC.
360 S. Broadway, Yonkers, NY 10705. (914) 968-3636.
VIDEO OVERSEAS INC.
249 W. 23 St., New York, NY 10011. (212) 645-0797.
VIDEO PLANNING INC.
250 W. 57 St., New York, NY 10019. (212) 582-5066.
VIDEO PRODUCTIONS
333 W. 52 St., New York, NY 10019. (212) 581-7312.
VIDEO RESOURCES NEW YORK, INC.
220 W. 71 St., New York, NY 10023. (212) 724-7055, (800) 442-7055.
VIDEO STOP, INC.
367 Third Ave., New York, NY 10016. (212) 685-6199.
VIDEO STORYBOARD TESTS
107 E. 31 St., New York, NY 10016. (212) 689-0207.
VIDEO 35
552 W. 43 St., New York, NY 10036. (212) 629-5686.
VIDEO WORLD
138 W. Houston, 10012. (212) 673-2435.
VIDEOGENIX OF NY INC.
594 Broadway, New York, NY 10012. (212) 925-0445.
VIDLO VIDEO
40 E. 21 St., New York, NY 10010. (212) 475-4140.
VISUAL CREATIONS, INC.
305 E. 46 St., New York, NY 10017. (212) 935-0145.
VISUAL WORD SYSTEMS INC.
17 E. 45 St., New York, NY 10017. (212) 661-3366.
WILLOUGHBY'S
110 W. 32 St., New York, NY 10001. (212) 564-1600.
WINDSOR VIDEO
8 W. 38 St., New York, NY 10018. (212) 944-9090.
WINKLER VIDEO ASSOCIATES INC.
248 E. 48 St., New York, NY 10017-1598. (212) 753-9300.
5801 Westside Ave., N. Bergen, NJ 07047. (201) 861-6500.
YK VIDEO
418 Park Ave. S., New York, NY 10037. (212) 686-8515.

PENNSYLVANIA

CENTER CITY FILMS & VIDEO
1503 Walnut St., Philadelphia, PA 19102. (215) 568-4134.
FILMMAKERS OF PHILADELPHIA
725 N. 24 St., Philadelphia, PA 19130. (215) 763-3400.
GROUP W VIDEOSERVICES
310 Parkway View Dr., Pittsburgh, PA 15205. (412) 747-4700. FAX: (412) 747-4726.
INSTANT REPLAY
2839 Tyson Ave., Philadelphia, PA 19149. (215) 624-2666.
LAIRD PRODUCTIONS, INC.
2153 Market St., Camp Hill, PA 17011. (717) 737-1556.
MEDIA CONCEPTS
331 N. Broad St., Philadelphia, PA 19107. (215) 923-2545.
E. J. STEWART
525 Mildred Ave., Primos, PA 19018. (215) 626-6500.
VIDEOSMITH, INC.
2006 Chancellor St., Philadelphia, PA 19103. (215) 665-3690.

THE INDUSTRY IN GREAT BRITAIN

TELEVISION & HOME VIDEO YEARS IN REVIEW

COMMERCIAL, GOVERNMENT, CABLE &
SATELLITE BROADCASTERS

TELEVISION PRODUCERS & DISTRIBUTORS

SERVICES FOR TELEVISION

HOME VIDEO DISTRIBUTORS

BRITISH TELEVISION YEAR IN REVIEW

The major development in the U.K. television industry in 1996 was the awarding by the ITC (Independent Television Commission) of the Channel 5 license to Channel 5 Broadcasting Ltd. The company bid £22 million to secure the contract. It plans a nightly hospital soap, 14 hours per week of children's programs and hourly news bulletins in association with ITN (Independent Television News). Initially, it will cover some 79% of the U.K. population, or 16.4 million of the 22.5 million homes that have television.

In addition to Channel 5, expansion of the commercial television industry has continued apace. ITC maintained the momentum of local delivery service licensing and issued 96 new cable and satellite program licenses. Revenues increased but the pace of growth on advertising revenue was outstripped by that of subscription income, the main source of funding for cable and satellite services. The cable industry passed a major milestone reaching its one millionth subscriber.

The new cable and satellite channels of the last two years include: European Business News, SelecTV and LiveTV, the Disney Channel, the Sci-Fi Channel, the History Channel, Sky Sports Gold and the Racing Channel. An ITC survey of viewing in cable homes indicated that 40% were watching ITV and BBC1. This compared to 35% the previous year. In homes which subscribe to the film channels, those channels were the most watched of cable and satellite channels. The balance of children's viewing is in the other direction: over half the viewing time of 12-15 year olds was devoted to cable and satellite with the Cartoon Network beating BBC1 into second place in share of viewing.

BSkyB remains the dominant satellite player with a record 66% increase in profits to £257 million. The total number of subscribers jumped 16% to 5.5 million while overall turnover increased 30% to £1 billion. At the same time, the group is pressing ahead with a move to digital technology that will allow it to offer up to 500 channels. Commenting on this, Sam Chisolm, Chairman and Chief Executive of BSkyB, said the new digital service will be launched in the second half of 1997 initially with 200 channels. This increase in capacity will allow it to schedule movies at a variety of times and will increase the scope for 'pay-per-view' television.

At the same time as the commercial networks report their success, the British Broadcasting Corporation (BBC) with its new charter claims it has had a "golden" period of programs, is ready to face the digital era, and its attention would now be turned to improving the quality and appeal of early evening entertainment and morning schedules. 95% of households still tune into the BBC for at least two hours every week. A typical home turns to the BBC Television and Radio for over 44 hours each week, maintaining its 45% share of all U.K. viewing and listening. The BBC's annual report shows it to be not only creatively strong, but effectively and professionally managed. Borrowings have been reduced and should be eliminated by the end of 1997. A further £100 million was saved through more efficient working practices and most of this was, in turn, invested in new programs. Net benefit to the BBC from its commercial arm, BBC Worldwide Ltd., rose from £53 million to £77 million.

Revenue from licensing of television programs such as "People's Century" and "Pride and Prejudice" to other channels showed a 15% increase, excluding sales to the United States. BBC World, the international news and information channel, is now available in more than 40 million homes globally while BBC Prime, the European entertainment channel has four million subscribers. The next challenge for Worldwide Television is to develop its business in the USA. BBC Video's top best-seller was "Pride and Prejudice" with sales of £4 million.

The BBC is the public broadcaster funded by the government imposed license fee on owners of TV sets. Its income has shown a modest growth and now stands at more than £2.4 billion, assisted by reduced license fee evasion and increased revenue from BBC's commercial activities. Sales of licenses have risen to a record 21 million. The license cost is currently £89.50.

The majority of overseas material on the networks still originates in the USA although in recent years, there has been a fall-off in the popularity of bulk American imports such as "Dallas" and "Dynasty" which used to attract audiences of 15 million. Such programs today are bringing about half that audience. This is despite the fact that 80% of money spent by British broadcasters on imports still goes to American shows, they occupy only a small proportion of the peak-time schedules on BBC1 and ITV. Also, Australian series and films continue to succeed in Great Britain.

Furthermore, the government is to relax the rules on ITV ownership. Companies will no longer be limited to holding only 2 ITV licenses. Instead, ownership will be limited to 15% of the total television audience. National newspaper groups will also enjoy greater freedom to enter the TV market since the rule restricting their investment to 20% of a single television license will be abolished. So, as we have repeatedly reported, the British television markets can only become more lucrative, especially with a record 22.5 million television license holders.

— WILLIAM PAY

Home Entertainment Equipment

	All Homes	Homes w/Children
Video recorder	83%	94%
Teletext	55%	63%
Compact disc player	35%	47%
Home computer	29%	45%
Video games	11%	45%
Satellite TV dish	14%	19%
Video camera	11%	17%
Nicam digital stereo TV	10%	12%
Cable TV	7%	10%
Cable telephone	5%	7%
Widescreen TV	7%	7%
Video disc player	4%	3%

Overseas Transactions of the Television Industry
In £ million

	1987	1988	1989	1990	1991	1992	1993	1994
Total Receipts [1]	117	128	194	128	133	131	278	370
Total Payments	130	121	186	207	233	254	251	296
Net Receipts	(13)	7	8	(79)	(100)	(123)	27	74

[1] Includes transactions of BBC & ITN
Source: Governmental Statistical Service

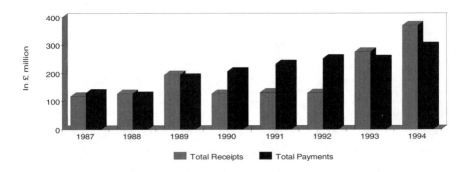

Total Receipts Total Payments

Overseas Transactions of the BBC, IBA and Satellite and Cable Television Companies by Area
In £ million

	1987	1988	1989	1990	1991	1992	1993	1994
Receipts [1]								
EC	28	30	68	46	45	51	119	142
Other Western Europe	7	7	8	12	15	11	26	31
North America	54	64	77	41	35	35	69	94
Other Developed Countries	21	21	26	21	23	20	38	50
Rest of the World	8	6	14	8	16	14	26	53
Total	117	128	194	128	133	131	276	370
Payments [2]								
EC	20	24	33	50	35	47	21	45
Other Western Europe	11	7	10	7	6	21	20	20
North America	82	73	117	126	166	168	196	207
Other Developed Countries	9	9	13	17	16	8	10	13
Rest of the World	8	8	12	7	10	10	14	12
Total	130	121	186	207	233	254	251	296

[1] Sums receivable from overseas residents/companies
[2] Sums payable to overseas residents/companies
Source: Governmental Statistical Service

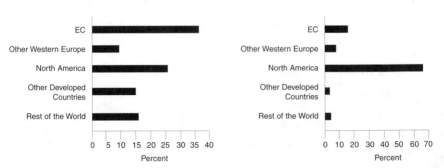

Television Companies: 1994 Receipts

Television Companies: 1994 Payments

BRITISH HOME VIDEO YEAR IN REVIEW

Both the renting and sales of pre-recorded video cassettes continue to grow apace in the British market. With the rental sales (up 4%) and retail (up 11%), the total retail value has been estimated at £1.2 billion. 81.5%of the population have a video recorder and 26% of households have two or more. It has also been estimated that video revenues produce 50% of the total investment in films. "Th Lion King" was the best selling video of 1995 which means that Buena Vista has topped the chart every year this decade. They would have taken the top three places had it not been for the remarkable success of "Riverdance." The most successful British film of all time in both the cinemas and on video rental became the best selling film of 1995. "Four Weddings and a Funeral" was released for a limited period at Easter and sold enough to withstand the challenges of the blockbusters, the strongest of which was "Batman Forever." "Jungle Book" remains at the top of the all time chart.

Just over 460 titles were released as rentals in 1995, fewer than in 1994. A quarter of these were dramas. In contrast, comedy accounted for a much higher share of rentals than of releases and was the most rented genre of all, helped by the success of films like "Forrest Gump," "The Mask" and "Dumb and Dumber." According to a BVA (British Videogram Association) survey, Warner Home Entertainment had seven titles in the year's top twenty which helped them to lead the company ranking for the third consecutive year. CIC had been in the lead for most of the year but had to settle for second place when "Batman Forever" propelled Warner back to the top. CIC did gain significantly over prior years as did Buena Vista, Polygram and First Independent. BBC Video's top-seller was "Pride and Prejudice," with sales of almost £4 million. BVA members had a combined share of 90%. The average price paid by the consumer for a video is £10.99.

The Rank Organisation is a leading supplier of products and services to the film and television industries, with exclusive supply contracts with a number of Hollywood studios. Major businesses include video duplication, film processing and cinema exhibition. Over 80 million US households own a video cassette recorder, for which Americans purchased some 730 million cassettes in 1995. Rank reports that demand for pre-recorded videos continues to grow and the group's volume increased by a quarter. It is investing $70 million in expansion of its duplication facilities in North Little Rock, Arkansas.

The Federation Against Copyright Theft (FACT) campaign against video piracy gathered momentum last year with the seizure of illicit VCRs and TVs, rather than just quantities of cassettes. Intelligence is improving and the heavier penalties imposed for piracy by the new Proceeds of Crime Act will be a further deterrent. This new law means that convicted pirates could have their possessions seized by the courts. The number of searches conducted by FACT is leveling off at about 1,400 per year, but the figures for fines and costs, up 30% in 1994, show that searches are becoming increasingly effective.

At the same time, the BBFC (British Board of Film Classification) reported that the number of videos cut due to content has been slightly down despite more strict regulations. The main fall was in '18' category reflecting the recent tendency of British distributors to steer away from the kind of violence that has given rise to so much criticism in recent years.

Top 20 Video Rentals of 1995

The Lion King	1
Riverdance—The Show	2
The Aristocats	3
The Fox and the Hound	4
Four Weddings and a Funeral	5
Pinocchio	6
Coronation Street Special	7
Batman Forever	8
The Mask	9
Star Wars	10
The Return of Jafar	11
Pulp Fiction	12
Robson and Jerome	13
Return of the Jedi	14
Power Rangers—The Movie	15
The Empire Strikes Back	16
Bottom Live—The Big No. 2 Tour	17
Miracle on 34th Street	18
Roy Chubby Brown—Clitoris Allsorts	19
Forrest Gump	20

Top 20 Video Rentals of All-Time

The Jungle Book	1
The Lion King	2
Fantasia	3
Snow White and the Seven Dwarfs	4
Beauty and the Beast	5
Aladdin	6
Bambi	7
Riverdance—The Show	8
Peter Pan	9
The Aristocats	10
Jurassic Park	11
Ghost	12
The Fox and the Hound	13
Lady and the Tramp	14
Mrs Doubtfire	15
The Little Mermaid	16
Cinderella	17
The Muppet Christmas Carol	18
Dirty Dancing	19
Pretty Woman	20

COMMERCIAL BROADCASTERS AND GOVERNMENT UNITS

BRITISH BROADCASTING CORPORATION TELEVISION SERVICE
Television Centre, Wood Lane, London W.12 7RJ. Tel: (0181) 743 8000. FAX: (0181) 576 1865.
CHAIRMAN
Sir Christopher Bland
DIRECTOR-GENERAL
John Birt
DEPUTY DIRECTOR-GENERAL
Bob Phillis
MANAGING DIRECTOR, NETWORK TELEVISION
Will Wyatt
CONTROLLER BBC-1
Alan Yentob
CONTROLLER BBC-2
Michael Jackson
CONTROLLER, PUBLICITY AND PUBLIC RELATIONS
Keith Samuel
ACTING HEAD OF DRAMA GROUP
Ruth Caleb
HEAD OF DRAMA SERIALS
Michael Wearing
HEAD OF DRAMA SERIES
Chris Parr
HEAD OF SINGLE DRAMA
George Faber
HEAD OF BBC FILMS
Mark Shivas
HEAD OF ENTERTAINMENT GROUP
Chris Pye
HEAD OF LIGHT ENTERTAINMENT
Michael Leggo
HEAD OF COMEDY
Geoffrey Perkins
HEAD OF COMEDY ENTERTAINMENT
Jon Plowman
HEAD OF INDEPENDENT COMMISSIONS
Kevin Lygo
HEAD OF SPORT AND EVENTS GROUP
Jonathan Martin
HEAD OF DEVELOPMENT, SPORTS
Brian Barwick
HEAD OF FACTUAL GROUP
Mark Thompson
HEAD OF DOCUMENTARIES
Paul Hamann
HEAD OF SCIENCE
Jana Bennett
HEAD OF DEVELOPMENT, SCIENCE
Susan Spindler
HEAD OF FEATURES
Anne Morrison
DEPUTY HEAD OF FEATURES
Jane Lush
HEAD OF MUSIC AND ARTS
Kim Evans
HEAD OF MUSIC
Avril McRory
HEAD OF CHILDREN'S PROGRAMMES
Anna Home
HEAD OF PROGRAMME ACQUISITION GROUP
Alan Howden
HEAD OF PURCHASED PROGRAMMES
June Dromgoole
CONTROLLER, BROADCASTING & PRESENTATION
Pam Masters
HEAD OF YOUTH AND ENTERTAINMENT FEATURES
John Whiston
HEAD OF RELIGIOUS PROGRAMMES
Ernest Rea
DIRECTOR OF EDUCATION
Jane Drabble
MEMBERS OF THE BBC'S BOARD OF MANAGEMENT
DIRECTOR-GENERAL
John Birt
DEPUTY DIRECTOR-GENERAL & CHAIRMAN, BBC WORLDWIDE
Bob Phillis
MANAGING DIRECTOR, NETWORK TELEVISION
Will Wyatt
ACTING MANAGING DIRECTOR, NETWORK RADIO
Michael Green

MANAGING DIRECTOR, REGIONAL BROADCASTING
Ronald Neil
MANAGING DIRECTOR, NEWS AND CURRENT AFFAIRS
Tony Hall
MANAGING DIRECTOR, WORLD SERVICE
Sam Younger
DIRECTOR OF EDUCATION
Jane Drabble
MANAGING DIRECTOR, RESOURCES
Rod Lynch
DIRECTOR OF POLICY & PLANNING
Patricia Hodgson, CBE
DIRECTOR OF FINANCE & INFORMATION TECHNOLOGY
Rodney Baker-Bates
DIRECTOR OF CORPORATE AFFAIRS
Colin Browne
MANAGING DIRECTOR, BBC WORLDWIDE TELEVISION
Dick Emery
MANAGING DIRECTOR, BBC WORLDWIDE PUBLISHING
Nick Chapman
MANAGING DIRECTOR, BBC WORLDWIDE LEARNING
Dr. John Thomas
DIRECTOR OF PERSONNEL
Margaret Salmon

BRITISH SKY BROADCASTING
6 Centaurs Business Park, Grant Way, Isleworth, Middx; TW7 5QD. Tel: (0171) 705 3000. FAX: (0171) 705 3030.
CHIEF EXECUTIVE AND MANAGING DIRECTOR
Sam Chisolm
DEPUTY MANAGING DIRECTOR PROGRAMME DIRECTOR
Gary Davey
EXECUTIVE DIRECTOR OF MARKETING & DISTRIBUTION
David Chance
GROUP SALES & MARKETING DIRECTOR
Tony Vickers

INDEPENDENT TELEVISION COMMISSION (ITC)
33 Foley Street, London, WIP 7LB. Tel: (0171) 255 3000. FAX: (0171) 306 7800.
Founded in 1991, the ITC was created by Parliament under the terms of the Broadcasting Act 1990 to license and regulate all commercially-funded television in the United Kingdom, whether delivered terrestrially (i.e., ITV, Channel 4 and Channel 5) or by cable or satellite, public teletext and certain other text and data services. The ITC regulates these services through license conditions and through its various codes on program content, advertising, sponsorship and technical standards.
CHAIRMAN
Sir George Russell, CBE.
CHIEF EXECUTIVE
Peter Rogers
DIRECTOR OF PROGRAMMES
Clare Mulholland
DIRECTOR OF CABLE AND SATELLITE
Jon Davey
DIRECTOR OF ADVERTISING AND SPONSORSHIP
Frank Willis
DIRECTOR OF PUBLIC AFFAIRS
Sarah Thane
Director of Engineering
Gary Tonge

DEPARTMENT OF NATIONAL HERITAGE
Broadcasting and Media Division, 4th Floor, 2-4 Cockspur Street, London, SWIY 5DH. Tel: (0171) 211 6000. FAX: (0171) 211 6210. Paul Wright.

COMMERCIAL BROADCASTERS
(Appointed by the Independent Television Commission (ITC)).

ANGLIA TELEVISION LTD.
Registered office: Anglia House, Norwich, NR1 3JG. Tel: (01603) 615151. Telex: 97424. FAX: (01603) 631032.
London Office: 48 Leicester Square, London, WC2H 7FB. Tel: (0171) 389 8555. FAX: (0171) 930 8499.
EAST OF ENGLAND LICENCE
DIRECTORS
CHAIRMAN
D. S. McCall, CBE
MANAGING DIRECTORS
M. Wall

M.J. Hughes
Lord Hollick
Sir David Puttnam, CBE
P. G. Sharman
P. Hickson
R. Laughton
Lord Eatwell
SECRETARY
Jan Rowland
ANGLIA TELEVISION BROADCASTING DIVISION
DIRECTOR OF PROGRAMMES
Graham Creelman
DEPUTY DIRECTOR OF PROGRAMMES
Malcolm Allsop
DIRECTOR OF FINANCE
Brian Bolt
DIRECTOR OF FACILITIES
Debbie Hills
DIRECTOR OF PERSONNEL & ADMINISTRATION
Peter Meier
CONTROLLER OF PROGRAMME PLANNING
Steve West
CONTROLLER, NEWS
Mike Read
EDITOR OF ANGLIA NEWS EAST
David Jennings
EDITOR OF ANGLIA NEWS WEST
Guy Adams
SPORT EDITOR
Kevin Piper
HEAD OF PRESS & PR
Martin Morrall
TECHNICAL CONTROLLER
Tim Dye
PRODUCTION CONTROL MANAGER
Chris Wilden
POST PRODUCTION MANAGER
David Brackenbury
NEWS OPERATIONS MANAGER
Roger Beavis
ADMINISTRATION MANAGER
Gina Boltwood
BUSINESS AFFAIRS & PROGRAMME CONTRACTS MGR.
Paddy Burns
DATA PROCESSING MANAGER
Alan Hough
COMMUNITY EDUCATION OFFICER
Cathy Mason
ANGLIA TELEVISION ENTERTAINMENT LTD.
CHAIRMAN
David McCall, CBE
MANAGING DIRECTOR
Sarah Lawson
CONTROLLER OF PRODUCTION & PROGRAMME FINANCE
David Fitzgerald
SURVIVAL ANGLIA LTD.
CHAIRMAN
David McCalle CBE
EXECUTIVE PRODUCERS
Graham Creelman
Sir David Puttnam
Roger Laughton
Alan Root
Petra Regent
PRODUCTION CONTROLLER
Peter Schofield

BORDER TELEVISION
(Borders and Isle of Man Licence). The Television Centre, Carlisle, CA1 3NT, Cumbria. Tel: (01228) 25101. FAX: (01228) 41384.
CHAIRMAN
James L. Graham
MANAGING DIRECTOR
P. Brownlow
DIRECTORS
Mrs. K. Worrall
M. Sutherland
M. Hartley
Dr. June Paterson-Brown
Sir David Steel
Robin Burgess
CONTROLLER OF PROGRAMMES
N. Robinson

CARLTON UK TELEVISION
(London and South East Weekday Licence). 101 St. Martin's Lane, London, WC2N 4AZ. Tel: (0171) 240 4000. FAX: (0171) 240 4171.
CHAIRMAN
Nigel Walmsley
CHIEF EXECUTIVE
Clive Jones

DIRECTOR OF PROGRAMMES
Andy Allan
MANAGING DIRECTOR, CARLTON UK SALES
Martin Bowley
FINANCE DIRECTOR
Mike Green
COMMERCIAL DIRECTOR
Paul Phayer
BUSINESS AFFAIRS DIRECTOR
John Egan
CONTROLLER OF PUBLIC AFFAIRS
L. Hardeep Karsi
CONTROLLER OF PRESS AND P.R.
John Palmer
HEAD OF PERSONNEL
Alan Pankhurst
SALES DIRECTOR OF CARLTON UK SALES
Steve Platt

CENTRAL BROADCASTING
(Operated by Carlton UK Television)
(East, West and South Midlands Licence). Central House, Broad Street, Birmingham B1 2JP. Tel: (0121) 643 9898. FAX: (0121) 643 4897.
CHAIRMAN
Leslie Hill
MANAGING DIRECTOR
Ron Henwood

CHANNEL FOUR TELEVISION
124 Horseferry Road, London, SW1P 2TX. Tel: (0171) 396 4444. FAX: (0171) 306 8353.
CHAIRMAN
Sir Michael Bishop, CBE
CHIEF EXECUTIVE
Michael Grade
DIRECTOR OF PROGRAMS
John Willis
DIRECTOR OF FINANCE
David Scott
DIRECTOR OF ACQUISITION
Colin Leventhal
DIRECTOR AND GENERAL MANAGER
Frank McGettigan

CHANNEL FIVE BROADCASTING LTD.
(National Network). 22 Long Acre, London, WC2E 9LY. Tel: (0171) 497 5225. FAX: (0171) 497 5222.
CHIEF EXECUTIVE
Ian Ritchie
DIRECTOR OF PROGRAMMES
Dawn Airey
CONTROLLER OF ENGINEERING OPERATIONS
Chris Collingham
DIRECTOR OF MARKETING & COMMUNICATIONS
David Brook

CHANNEL TELEVISION CHANNEL ISLANDS.
(Serves the Bailiwicks of Jersey and Guernsey as well as several smaller islands). The Television Centre, St. Helier, Jersey, JE1 3ZD, Channel Islands. Tel: (01534) 816816. FAX: (01534) 816817.
The Television Centre, St. George's Place, St. Peter Port, Guernsey, GY2 4LA, Channel Islands. Tel: (01481) 723451. FAX: (01481) 710739.
CHAIRMAN
John Riley
MANAGING DIRECTOR
John Henwood
DIRECTOR OF SALES & MARKETING
Bob Jones
DIRECTOR OF FINANCE
Charles Day
DIRECTOR OF TELEVISION
Michael Lucas
DIRECTOR OF OPERATIONS
Roy Manning
DIRECTOR OF TELEVISION
Michael Lucas
GUERNSEY OFFICE MANAGER
Roger Bowns
HEAD OF PROGRAMME DEVELOPMENT
Frank Hayes

DATA BROADCASTING INTERNATIONAL LTD.
(Commercial Additional Services Licence). Allen House, Station Road, Egham, Surrey, TW20 9NT. Tel: (01784) 471515. FAX: (01784) 438732.
CHIEF EXECUTIVE
P. W. H. Mason
CHAIRMAN
G. J. P. Cadbury

GMTV LTD.
(National breakfast-time licence. 7 days weekly, 6:00-9:25 am.).
The London Television Centre, Upper Ground, London, SE1
9TT. Tel: (0171) 827 7000. FAX: (0171) 827 7001.
MANAGING DIRECTOR
Christopher Stoddart
CHAIRMAN
Nigel Walmsley
DIRECTOR OF PROGRAMMING
Peter McHugh
MANAGING EDITOR REUTERS
Henry Clark
MANAGING EDITOR, GMTV
John Scammell
EDITOR
David Hannion
FINANCE DIRECTOR
Simon Davey

GRAMPIAN TELEVISION PLC.
Queen's Cross, Aberdeen, AB9 2XJ, Scotland. Tel: (01224)
846846. FAX: (01224) 846800.
Albany House, 68 Albany Road, West Ferry, Dundee DD5
1NW, Scotland. Tel: (01382) 739363. FAX: (01382) 480230.
23-25 Huntly Street, Inverness IV3 5PR, Scotland. Tel:
(01463) 242624. FAX: (01463) 242624.
Seaforth House, Stornoway, HS1 25D, Scotland. Tel: (01851)
704433. FAX: (01851) 706406.
NORTH SCOTLAND LICENSEE
NON-EXECUTIVE DIRECTORS
Dr. Catum A. Maleod, CBE, MA, LLB, CC (Chairman)
Fiona Lyall, M.B., Ch.B., D.P.H.
Alistair Mair, M.B.E., B.Sc.
Angus Stewart Macdonald, CBE
DEPUTY CHAIRMAN AND CHIEF EXECUTIVE
Donald H. Waters, C.A., O.B.E.
DIRECTOR OF TELEVISION
Robert Christie
DIRECTOR OF FINANCE/CO. SECRETARY
Graham Good, C.A.
DIRECTOR OF PROGRAMS
George W. Mitchell
HEAD OF DOCUMENTARIES AND FEATURES
Ted Brocklebank
HEAD OF NEWS AND CURRENT AFFAIRS
Alistair Gracie
HEAD OF GAELIC
Bob Kenyon
HEAD OF PUBLIC RELATIONS
Michael J. McLintock, M.A., D.I.P. C.A.M.
PRODUCTION SERVICES EXECUTIVE
Eric M. Johnstone
CHIEF ENGINEER
John Robertson

GRANADA TELEVISION LTD.
(Northwest England Licence). Granada TV Centre, Quay Street,
Manchester M60 9EA. Tel: (0161) 832 7211. FAX: (0161) 832
7211.
36 Golden Square, London W1R 4AH. Tel: (0171) 734 8080.
News Centre, Albert Dock, Liverpool L3 4BA.
News Centre, White Cross, Lancaster LA1 4XQ.
News Centre, Bridgegate House, Chester and Daisyfield
Business Centre, Blackburn BB1 3BL.
CHAIRMAN
Gerry Robinson
CHIEF EXECUTIVE
Charles L. Allen
MANAGING DIRECTOR
Steve Morrison
COMMERCIAL DIRECTOR
Kate Stross
DIRECTOR OF PROGRAMMES
Andrea Wonfor
DIRECTOR OF PROGRAM & MANAGEMENT SERVICES
Jules Burns
DIRECTOR OF SALES
Michael Desmond
DIRECTOR OF RESOURCES
Brenda Smith
DIRECTOR OF BROADCASTING
Julia Lamaison
HEAD OF DRAMA
Sally Head
CONTROLLER OF ENTERTAINMENT & COMEDY
Andy Harries
CONTROLLER OF FACTUAL PROGRAMMES
Dianne Nelmes
HEAD OF SPORT
Paul Doherty
CONTROLLER OF PROGRAMME SERVICES
& PERSONNEL
David Fraser

HEAD OF PROGRAMME PUBLICITY
Ian Haworth
DIRECTOR OF PUBLIC AFFAIRS
Chris Hopson
HEAD OF COMEDY
Tony Wood
HEAD OF CHILDREN'S PROGRAMMES
Ed Pugh
HEAD OF CURRENT AFFAIRS AND DOCUMENTARIES
Charles Tremayne
HEAD OF REGIONAL PROGRAMMES
Mike Spencer
HEAD OF FEATURES
James Hunt
HEAD OF GRANADA TV FACTUAL DRAMA
Ian McBride

HTV GROUP PLC.
(Wales and West of England Licence). Television Centre,
Culverhouse Cross, Cardiff CF5 6XJ, Wales. Tel: (01222)
590590. FAX: (01222) 597183.
HTV West Ltd., Television Centre, Bath Road, Bristol BS4 3HG.
Tel: (01179) 778366.
CHAIRMAN HTV GROUP PLC
Louis Sherwood
CHIEF EXECUTIVE, HTV GROUP PLC
Christopher Rowlands
GROUP DIRECTOR OF BROADCASTING
Ted George

ITN LTD.
200 Gray's Inn Rd., London WC1X 8XZ. Tel: (0171) 833 3000.
FAX: (0171) 430 4016. Telex: 22101.
CHAIRMAN
Gerry Robinson
CHIEF EXECUTIVE
Stewart Purvis
EDITOR-IN-CHIEF
Richard Tait

LWT (LONDON WEEKEND TELEVISION)
(London Licence—Friday 5:15 p.m. to Monday 6:00 a.m.).
The London Television Centre, Upper Ground, London SE1 9LT.
Tel: (0171) 620 1620. FAX: (0171) 261 1290.
BOARD OF DIRECTORS
CHAIRMAN
Gerry Robinson
CHIEF OPERATING OFFICER, GRANADA MEDIA GROUP
Steve Morrison
DEPUTY MANAGING DIRECTOR & PROGRAMME DIRECTOR
Steve Liddiment
MANAGING DIRECTOR OF BROADCASTING
Eileen Gallagher
DIRECTOR OF PROGRAMME MANAGEMENT
John Howard
CHIEF EXECUTIVE, GRANADA MEDIA GROUP
Duncan Lewis
GENERAL MGR. & BUSINESS DEVELOPMENT DIRECTOR
Tom Sheriff
COMMERICAL DIRECTOR
Kate Stross
MANAGING DIRECTOR OF LONDON STUDIOS
Harry Urquhart
DIRECTOR OF FINANCE
Janet Walker
EXECUTIVES OF LWT GROUP
HEAD OF CURRENT AFFAIRS, LWT PRODUCTIONS LTD.
Jim Allen
HEAD OF PRODUCTION MANAGEMENT, ENTERTAINMENT,
LWT PRODUCTIONS LTD.
Vijay Amarnani
HEAD OF DRAMA, LWT PRODUCTIONS LTD.
Gwenda Bagshaw
CONTROLLER OF COMEDY, LWT PRODUCTIONS LTD.
Humphrey Barclay
CONTROLLER OF ARTS, LWT PRODUCTIONS LTD.
Melvyn Bragg
SENIOR CLIENT LIAISON MANAGER, THE LONDON STU-
DIOS LTD.
Susanna Burleigh
DRAMA PRODUCTION EXECUTIVE, LWT PRODUCTIONS LTD.
Julie Burnell
HEAD OF LICENSING & MARKETING, LWT
Richard Cox
HEAD OF ENTERTAINMENT FEATURES, LWT PRODS., LTD.
Lorna Dickinson
HEAD OF ARTS, LWT PRODUCTIONS LTD.
Nigel Wattis
HEAD OF FACTUAL DRAMA, LWT PRODUCTIONS, LTD.
Jeff Pope
HEAD OF COMMERCIAL DEVELOPMENT (PROGRAMMES),
GRANADA TELEVISION & LWT
Sarah Doole

CONTROLLER OF BROADCAST FINANCE
Anne Dundas
HEAD OF REGIONAL & PUBLIC AFFAIRS, LWT
Sue Elliott
FINANCIAL CONTROLLERS, LWT
Carolyn Foxhall
HEAD OF PRODUCTION FINANCE, LWT
Paul Green
DIRECTOR OF BROADCASTING, LWT
Liam Hamilton
CONTROLLER OF BROADCAST RESEARCH, LWT
Suzanne Hatley
CONTROLLER OF PRODUCTION MANAGEMENT,
LWT PRODUCTIONS LTD.
Terri Jones
CONTROLLER OF ENTERTAINMENT,
LWT PRODUCTIONS LTD.
Nigel Lythgoe
CONTROLLER OF DRAMA, LWT PRODUCTIONS LTD.
Sally Head
DIRECTOR OF PUBLIC AFFAIRS, LTW/GTV
Chris Hopson
DIRECTOR OF OPERATIONS, THE LONDON STUDIOS LTD.
Kate Hynes
DIRECTOR OF SALES, MARKETING & DEVELOPMENT,
THE LONDON STUDIOS LTD.
Penny Lent

MERIDIAN BROADCASTING LTD
(South, Southeast England Licence). Television Centre,
Northam, Southampton S014 OPZ. Tel: (01703) 222555. FAX:
(01703) 335050.
CHAIRMAN
Lord Hollick
CHIEF EXECUTIVE
Roger Laughton
FINANCE DIRECTOR
John Cresswell
DIRECTOR OF RESOURCES
Peter Booth
CONTROLLER OF CHILDREN'S & DAYTIME PROGRAMMES
Richard Mass
CONTROLLER OF DRAMA
Simon Lewis
DIRECTOR OF PROGRAMMING
Richard Platt
DIRECTOR OF PROGRAMMES & PRODUCTION
Mary McAnally
CONTROLLER OF NEWS, SPORT & CURRENT AFFAIRS
Jim Raven
HEAD OF PRESS & REGIONAL AFFAIRS
Allan Robertson

RADIO TELEFIS EIREANN
(National Network of the Republic of Ireland). Donnybrook,
Dublin 4, Ireland. Tel: (3531) 2083111.
Ireland House, 150 New Bond Street, London, W1Y OHD. Tel:
(0171) 233 3382.
CHAIRMAN
Farrel Corcoran
DIRECTOR-GENERAL
Joe Barry
ASST. DIRECTOR-GENERAL
Bob Collins
DIRECTOR OF TELEVISION PROGRAMMES
Liam Miller
DIRECTOR OF RADIO PROGRAMMES
Kevin Healy
DIRECTOR OF NEWS
Joe Mulholland

SS4C
Parc Ty Glas, Llanishen, Cardiff CF4 5DU, Wales. Tel: (01222)
747444. Telex: 94017032 SIAN G. FAX: (01222) 741457.
THE WELSH FOURTH CHANNEL AUTHORITY
CHAIRMEN
Prys Edwards
Dr. Gywn Jones
Janet Lewis-Jones
Janice Rowlands
Peter Davies, CBE
Dr. Gwenllian Awbery
Dyfrig John
CHIEF EXECUTIVE
Huw Jones
DIRECTOR OF PROGRAMMES
Deryk Williams
DIRECTOR OF BROADCASTING
Dafydd Rhys
DIRECTOR OF CORPORATE POLICY
Emyr Byron Hughes
CHIEF ENGINEER
Rodger Fuse

DIRECTOR OF ANIMATION
Christopher Grace
HEAD OF FINANCE
Kathryn Morris
HEAD OF MARKETING
Menna Lewis
HEAD OF PRESS AND PUBLIC RELATIONS
David Meredith
CONTROLLER OF S4C INTERNATIONAL
Ian Jones

SCOTTISH TELEVISION, PLC
(Central Scotland Licence). Cowcaddens, Glasgow, G2 3PR,
Scotland. Tel: (0141) 300 3000. Telex 77388. FAX: (0141) 300
3030.
The Gateway, Edinburgh EH7 4AH, Scotland. Tel: (0131) 557
4020. FAX: (0131) 557 9199.
CHAIRMAN
Gus Macdonald
DIRECTOR OF BROADCASTING
Blair Jenkins
MANAGING DIRECTORS
Andrew Flanagan
CHIEF EXECUTIVE OF SCOTTISH TV ENTERPRISES
Alistair Moffat
FINANCE DIRECTOR
Gary Hughes
COMPANY SECRETARY/HEAD OF LEGAL
& BUSINESS AFFAIRS
Sheelagh Lawrie
HEAD OF NEWS, SPORT & CURRENT AFFAIRS
Scott Ferguson
HEAD OF PUBLIC AFFAIRS
Bob Timlinson
HEAD OF PERSONNEL
Christine Walsh
HEAD OF SERVICES
Lesley White
CONTROLLER OF PRODUCTION
Ron Ferguson
HEAD OF TECHNICAL OPERATIONS
Tom Gallagher
BROADCAST SERVICES MANAGER
Carol Sinclair
PRODUCTION MANAGER, TECHNICAL OPERATIONS
Steve Dunlop
COMMERCIAL DIRECTOR
Donald Emslie
SCOTTISH TELEVISION ENTERPRISES
DEPUTY CHIEF EXECUTIVE
Sandy Ross
GENERAL MANAGER
Liz Moriarty
DIRECTOR OF BUSINESS DEVELOPMENT
Darrel James
CONTROLLER OF DRAMA
Robert Love
HEAD OF PROGRAMME SALES
Anita Cox
HEAD OF CHILDREN'S PROGRAMMING
Elizabeth Partyka

TELETEXT UK LTD.
(Holder of the public service licence for Teletext on ITV and
Channel 4). 101 Farm Lane, London, SW6 1QJ. Tel: (0171) 386
5000; FAX: (0171) 386 5002.
MANAGING DIRECTOR
Peter van Gelder
EDITOR
Graham Lovelace
SALES & MARKETING DIRECTOR
Lawrence Lawson
FINANCIAL DIRECTOR
Julian Staniforth

TYNE TEES TELEVISION LTD.
(North East England Licence). The Television Centre, City Road,
Newcastle upon Tyne, NE1 2AL. Tel: (0191) 261 0181. FAX:
(0191) 261 2302.
15 Bloomsbury Square, London, WC1A 2LJ. Tel: (0171) 312
3700. FAX: (0171) 242 2441.
MANAGING DIRECTOR
John Calvert
DIRECTORS
Sir Ralph Carr-Ellison, T.D.
R. H. Dickinson
Sir Paul Nicholson, D.L., F.C.A.
DIRECTOR OF RESOURCES
Margaret Fay
DIRECTOR OF FINANCE
Nick Castro
SECRETARY
Simon Carlton

ULSTER TELEVISION PLC
(Northern Ireland Licence). Havelock House, Ormeau Road, Belfast BT7 1EB, Ireland. Tel: (01232) 328122. Telex: 74654. FAX: (01232) 246695.
CHAIRMAN
J. B. McGuckian B.Sc. (Econ.)
MANAGING DIRECTOR
J.D. Smyth, B.Sc, F.C.A.
VICE CHAIRMAN
H. R. C. Catherwood
DIRECTORS
R.E. Benner, O.B.E.
Lord Dunluce, F.R.S.A.
Captain O.W.J. Henderson, O.B.E., D.L., F.B.I.M.,
G.C. Hutchinson
Lady McCollum
E. J. O'Driscoll
GENERAL MANAGER
J. McCann
COMPANY SECRETARY
J. Rooney

WESTCOUNTRY TELEVISION LTD.
(South-West England Licence). Western Wood Way, Language Science Park, Plymouth, PL7 5BG. Tel: (01752) 333333. FAX: (01752) 333444.
CHAIRMAN
Sir John Banham
CHIEF EXECUTIVE
Stephen Redfarn
MANAGING DIRECTOR
John Prescott Thomas
HEAD OF FINANCE
Mark Haskell
DIRECTOR OF NEWS AND SPORT
Richard Myers
DIRECTOR OF BROADCAST
Steve Ellis
CONTROLLER OF PRESS & PUBLICITY
Mark Clare

YORKSHIRE TELEVISION LTD.
(Yorksire Contractor). The Television Centre, Leeds, LS3 1JS. Tel: (01132) 438283. FAX: (01132) 445107.
Television House, 15 Bloomsbury Square, London WC1A 2LJ. Tel: (0171) 312 3700. FAX: (0171) 242 2441.
Charter Square, Sheffield, S1 3EJ. Tel: (01142) 723262.
88 Bailgate, Lincoln, LN1 3AR. Tel: (01522) 530738.
8 Bullring Lane, Grimsby, DN31 1DY. Tel: (01472) 357026.
8 Coppergate, York Y01 1NR. Tel: (01904) 610066.

GROUP CHAIRMAN & CHIEF EXECUTIVE
G.E. Ward Thomas, CBE, D.F.C., CdG
NON-EXECUTIVE CHAIRMAN
Victor Watson
GROUP MANAGING DIRECTOR & CHIEF EXEC.,
YORKSHIRE TELEVISION
Bruce Gyngell
GROUP DIRECTOR OF RESOURCES
Tony Brill
GROUP FINANCIAL DIRECTOR
Nick Castro
NON-EXECUTIVE DIRECTOR
Kenneth Dixon, DL
DIRECTOR OF BROADCASTING
Richard Gregory
GROUP CONTROLLER OF COMMERCIAL AFFAIRS
David Holdgate
CONTROLLER, PLANNING AND PRESENTATION
Bob Bairstow
DIRECTOR, GROUP CORPORATE AFFAIRS
Geoff Brownlee
CONTROLLER OF DOCUMENTARIES
& CURRENT AFFAIRS
Chris Bryer
HEAD OF SPORT
Robert Charles
DEPUTY GROUP CONTROLLER OF COMMERCIAL AFFAIRS
Filip Cieslik
HEAD OF RELIGION
Pauline Duffy
CONTROLLER OF PROPERTY MANAGEMENT
Peter Fox
HEAD OF TRANSMISSION
John Hastings
CONTROLLER OF EDUCATION
Chris Jelley
DIRECTOR OF SPECIAL PROJECTS
David Lowen
HEAD OF NEWS & CURRENT AFFAIRS
Ali Rashid
CONTROLLER, ENTERTAINMENT
David Reynolds
CONTROLLER, DRAMA
Keith Richardson
CHIEF ENGINEER
John Nichol
CONTROLLER OF PRODUCTION RESOURCES
Peter Rogers
HEAD OF CHILDREN'S PROGRAMMES
Patrick Titley

SATELLITE-CABLE
BROADCASTERS & PROGRAMMERS

ABERDEEN CABLE SERVICES
303 King Street, Aberdeen, AB2 3AP. Tel: (01224) 649444. FAX: (01224) 645372.

ANGLIA CABLE
17-19 Rayntham Rd., Bishops Stortford, Hertf., CM23 5PB. Tel: (01279) 867000. FAX: (01279) 866000.

BELL CABLEMEDIA EASTERN REGION, NORWICH
31 King St., Norwich NR3 2AZ. Tel: (01603) 445000. FAX: (01603) 448900.

BELL CABLEMEDIA NORTHEAST REGION
Ring Rd., Seacroft, Leeds LS14 1NH. Tel: (01132) 932000. FAX: (01132) 932111.

BELL CABLEMEDIA SOUTHERN REGION
Bell Cablemedia House, 5 Limeharbour, London. E14 9TY. Tel: (0171) 363 2000. FAX: (0171) 363 3500.

BIRMINGHAM CABLE LTD.
CablePhone House, Small Heath Business Park, Talbot Way, Small Heath, Birmingham B10 0HJ. Tel: (0121) 628 1234. FAX: (0121) 628 4321.

BT NEW TOWNS SYSTEMS (IRVINE)
15 Mackintosh Place South, Newmoor, Irvine KA11 1BR. Tel: (01294) 218218. FAX: (01294) 216631.

BT NEW TOWNS SYSTEMS (MILTON KEYNES)
51 Alston Dr., Bradwell Abbey, Milton Keynes MK13 9HB. Tel: (01908) 322522. FAX: (01908) 319802.

BT NEW TOWNS SYSTEMS (WASHINGTON)
Suite 10, Coniston House, Washington NE38 7RN. Tel: (0191) 415 0604. FAX: (0191) 417 7763.

CABLECOM INVESTMENTS LTD.
Surtees House, The Market Pl., Maidenhall, Suffolk 1P28 7EF. Tel: (01638) 711345. FAX: (01638) 711074.

CABLE CORPORATION LTD.
Cable House, Waterside Dr., Langley, Berkshire SL3 6EZ. Tel: (01753) 810810. FAX: (01753) 810818.

CABLE LONDON PLC.
2 Stephen St., London W1 1PL. Tel: (0171) 911 0555. FAX: (0171) 209 8459.

CABLE & TELECOM UK LTD.
P.O. Box 319, whipsnade, Dunstable, LU6 2LT. Tel: (01582) 873006. FAX: (01582) 873003.

CABLETEL BEDFORDSHIRE LTD.
CableTel House, 2-8 Laporte Way, Luton, Befdordshire LU4 8RJ. Tel: (01582) 610000. FAX: (01582) 610100.

CABLETEL GLASGOW
40 Anderson Quay, Glasgow G3 8DA. Tel: (0141) 564 0000. FAX: (0141) 564 0100.

CABLETEL KIRKLEES
CableTel House, Market St., Huddersfield, Yorkshire HD1 2EH. Tel: (01484) 438700. FAX: (01484) 438777.

CABLETEL PORT TALBOT
Network House, Baglan Industrial Park, Baglan, Port Talbot SA12 7DJ. Tel: (01639) 899999. FAX: (01639) 891100.

CABLETEL SOUTH WALES LTD.
Colchester House, Colchester Ave., Cardiff CF3 7RR. Tel: (01222) 456644. FAX: (01222) 456645.

CABLETEL SURREY LTD.
CableTel House, Reading North Rd., Fleet, Hants, GU13 8XR. Tel: (01252) 652000. FAX: (01252) 652100.

CABLEVISION (WELLINGBOROUGH OFFICE LTD.)
c/o Mobile Radio Services Ltd., Centre Hall Buildings, Wellingborough, NN8 4HT. Tel: (01933) 222078. FAX: (01933) 223890.

CAMBRIDGE CABLE GROUP OF COMPANIES
1st floor, Block D, Westbrook Centre, Cambridge CB4 1YG. Tel: (01223) 567200. FAX: (01223) 567200.

COMCAST—TEESSIDE
Roberts House, DeHavilland Ave., Preston Farm Business Park, Stockton-on-Tees, TS18 3TH. Tel: (01642) 642600. FAX: (01642) 626648.

COMTEL ANDOVER
284 Wethill Rd., Andover, Hants, SP10 1YB. Tel: (01264) 401402. FAX: (01264) 401403.

COVENTRY CABLE
Whitley Village, London Road, Coventry, West Midlands CV3 4HL. Tel: (01203) 505345. FAX: (01203) 505445.

DIAMOND CABLE LTD.
Regency House, 2a Sherwood Rise, Nottingham NG7 6JN. Tel: (01159) 522240. FAX: (01159) 522211.

EUROBELL (SOUTH WEST) LTD.
Multimedia House, Abbey Court, Eagle Way, Sowton Industrial Estate, Exeter, EX2 7HY. Tel: (01392) 200222. FAX: (01392) 200220.

HARRIS OF SALTCOATS
104-106 Dockhead St., Saltcoats, Strathclyde KA21 5EL. Tel: (01294) 646330. FAX: (01294) 466665.

JERSEY CABLE LTD.
2 Colomberie, St. Hellier, Jersey JE2 4QB. Tel: (01534) 66555. FAX: (01534) 66681.

MEDWAY CABLEVISION LTD.
2-4 William St., Sittingbourne, Kent ME10 1HR. Tel: (01795) 429711. FAX: (01795) 422807.

METRO CABLE TELEVISION.
Unit 12, Park Royal Road, London, NW10 7JH. Tel: (0181) 961 6776. FAX: (0181) 961 6776.

METRO CABLE TELEVISION (ENGLAND)
Unit 17 Weltech Centre, Ridgeway, Welwyn Garden City, Hertf. AL7 2AA. Tel: (01707) 372631. FAX: (01707) 325621.

METRO CABLE TELEVISION (MID GLAMMORGAN)
Patridge Rd., Llwynpia, Rhondda, Mid Glammorgan CF40 2SH. Tel: (01443) 440270. FAX: (01443) 435700.

METRO CABLE TELEVISION (NORTH MIDLANDS)
Unit 1, 40 Commercial Square, Freemans Common, Leicester LE2 7SR. Tel: (01162) 550824. FAX: (01162) 546351.

METRO CABLE TELEVISION (OXFORD)
Nuttfield Press Site, Hollow Way, Coweley, Oxford OX4 2PH. Tel: (01865) 711108. FAX: (01865) 77159.

METRO CABLE TELEVISION (SE REGION)
Bentalls, Basildon, Essex SS14 3BY. Tel: (01268) 526841. FAX: (01268) 527797.

METRO CABLE TELEVISION (WALES)
5 Penrice Court, Fendrod Business Park, Enterprise Park, Morriston, Swansea SA6 8QW. Tel: (01792) 701601. FAX: (01792) 702510.

METRO CABLE TELEVISION (WALES/DYFED OFFICE)
Unit 64, Honeyborough Industrial Estate, Dyfed. Tel: (01646) 601494. FAX: (01646) 600804.

METRO CABLE TELEVISION (WALES—GWENT)
Bridge Terrace, Newbridge, Gwent NP1 5FE. Tel: (01495) 247595. FAX: (01495) 246095.

MULTICHANNEL TELEVISION LTD. (NORTHERN)
Reservoir Rd., Clough Rd., Hull HU6 7QD. Tel: (01482) 470805. FAX: (01482) 470806.

MULTICHANNEL TELEVISION LTD. (SOUTHERN)
Summerland St., Exeter EX1 2AT. Tel: (01224) 646644.

NYNEX CABLECOMMS (BROMLEY OFFICE)
NYNEX House, 2a Farwig Lane, Bromley, Kent BR1 3QS. Tel: (0181) 402 2000. FAX: (0181) 402 9090.

NYNEX CABLECOMMS (MIDLAND REGION)
Kedleston House, Prime Business Centre, Aspen Dr., Raynesway, Derby DE21 7SG. Tel: (01332) 380038. FAX: (01332) 661431.

NYNEX CABLECOMMS (N.W. BOLTON OFFICE)
25-30 Queensbrook, Bolton Technology Exchange, Spa Rd., Bolton BL1 4AY. Tel: (01204) 365111. FAX: (01204) 365417.

NYNEX CABLECOMMS (N.W. MANCHESTER OFFICE)
NYNEX House, Timpson Rd., off Southmoor Rd., Baguley, Manchester M23 9WX. Tel: (0161) 946 0388. FAX: (0161) 945 6932.

NYNEX CABLECOMMS (SOLENT)
Unit c, Wellington Gate, Silverthorne Way, Waterlooville, Hampshire P07 7XY. Tel: (01705) 610061. FAX: (01705) 230548.

NYNEX CABLECOMMS (SOUTHERN REGION)
Langbourne House, Randalls Way, Leatherhead, Surrey KT22 7TW. Tel: (01372) 360844. FAX: (01372) 360605.

NYNEX CABLECOMMS (SUSSEX HEAD-END)
South Wharf House, Basin Road South, Aldrington Basin, Hove BN41 1WF. Tel: (01273) 413021. FAX: (01273) 416081.

OXFORD CABLE LTD.
c/o IVS Cable Services, 284 Weyhill Rd., Andover, Hampshire SP10 1YB. Tel: (01264) 334697. FAX: (01264) 332071.

SALFORD CABLE TELEVISION
Unit 5, (Shopping Giant) 385 Bolton Rd., Irlam, O'Th Heights, Salford M6 7NL. Tel: (0161) 737 9313. FAX: (0161) 736 9313.

STAFFORD COMMUNICATIONS LTD.
c/o IVS Cable Services, 284 Weyhill Rd., Andover, Hampshire SP10 1YB. Tel: (01264) 334607. FAX: (01264) 332071.

SWINDON CABLE
Newcombe Dr., Hawksworth Estate, Swindon, Wiltshire SN2 1TU. Tel: (01793) 480482. FAX: (01793) 619535.

TAWD VALLEY CABLE LTD.
82 Sandy Lane, Skelmersdale, Lancashire WN8 8LQ. Tel: (01695) 51000. FAX: (01695) 51315.

TELCENTIAL COMMUNICATIONS, NORTHANTS
11 Duncan Close, Moulton Park, Northampton NN3 1WL. Tel: (01604) 451111. FAX: (01604) 451126.

TELECENTIAL COMMUNICATIONS, THAMES VALLEY
Imperial Way, Reading RG2 0BS. Tel: (01734) 544000. FAX: (01734) 544001.

TELECENTIAL COMMUNICATIONS, WEST HERTS.
Unit 1A, Centro, Maxted Rd., Hemel Hempstead, Hertf. HP2 7EF. Tel: (01442) 369111. FAX: (01442) 368100.

THOMSON (RELAY) LTD.
27 Auld Lea Rd., Beith, Ayrshire KA15 2DA. Tel: (01505) 502118.

UNITED ARTISTS COMMUNICATIONS, AVON
700 Waterside Dr., Aztec West, Almondsbury, Bristol BS12 4ST. Tel: (01179) 839000. FAX: (01179) 839966.

UNITED ARTISTS COMMUNICATIONS, COTSWOLDS
The Network Centre, Staverton Technology Park, Staverton, Cheltenham GL51 6TQ. Tel: (01452) 535353. FAX: (01452) 535399.

UNITED ARTISTS COMMUNICATIONS, SCOTLAND WEST
Unit 7, Bothwell Industrial Estate, Uddingston, Glasgow G71 6NX. Tel: (01689) 322322. FAX: (01689) 322213.

UNITED ARTISTS, DUNDEE
Tat Works, Brown St., Dundee DD1 5EF. Tel: (01382) 322220. FAX: (01382) 322225.

UNITED ARTISTS, GLENROTHES
4 Bankhead Ave., Bankhead Industrial Estate, Glenrothes KY7 6JG. Tel: (01592) 595857. FAX: (01592) 590001.

UNITED ARTISTS, LONDON SOUTH
Communications House, 5 Factory Lane, Croydon, CR9 3RA. Tel: (0181) 760 0222. FAX: (0181) 681 2340.

UNITED ARTISTS, NORTHEAST
Communications House, 1 Dukesway West, Team Valley, Gateshead NE11 0PN. Tel: (0191) 420 2000. FAX: (0191) 420 2001.

UNITED ARTISTS, PERTH
13 Canal St., Perth PH2 84Q. Tel: (01763) 838794. FAX: (01763) 36867.

UNITED ARTISTS, SCOTLAND
1 South Gyle Crescent Lane, Edinburgh EH12 9EG. Tel: (0131) 539 0002. FAX: (0131) 539 0003.

631

UNITED ARTISTS, SOUTHEAST
Unit 1, Scimitar Park, Basildon, Essex SS1 1ND. Tel: (01268) 471000. FAX: (01268) 470199.

VIDEOTRON CORPORATION
London Division, Viedoetron House, 76 Hammersmith Rd., London, WI4 8UD. Tel: (0181) 244 1234. FAX: (0181) 244 1232.

VIDEOTRON CORPORATION LTD., SOUTHAMPTON
Hampshire Division, Ocean House, West Quay Rd., Southampton, Hants SO1 OXL. Tel: (01703) 315000. FAX: (01703) 315002.

WESSEX CABLE LTD.
c/o IVS Cable Services, 284 Weyhill Rd., Andover, Hampshire SP10 1YB. Tel: (01264) 334607. FAX: (01264) 332071.

WESTMINSTER CABLE TELEVISION
87-89 Baker Street, London, W1M 1AJ. Tel: (0171) 935 4400. FAX: (0171) 486 9447.

YORKSHIRE CABLE COMMUNICATIONS LTD.
Communications House, Mayfair Business Park, Broad Lane, Bradford BD4 8PW. Tel: (01274) 828282. FAX: (01274) 828400.

MULTIPLE SYSTEM CABLE GROUP OPERATORS

BELL CABLEMEDIA PLC
Bell Cablemedia House, Upton Road, Watford, Hertfordshire, WD1 7EL. Tel: (01923) 444 000. FAX: (01923) 444 004.

BT CABLE TV SERIES
Room 2636, Euston Tower, 286 Euston Road, London, NW1 3DG. Tel: (0171) 728 7145. FAX: (0171) 728 5265.

CABLETEL UK LTD.
CableTel House, Guildford Business Park, Guildford, Surrey, GU2 5AD. Tel: (01483) 254 000; FAX (01483) 254 100.

CAMBRIDGE CABLE GROUP FRANCHISES
Unit 26, The Cambridge Science Park, Milton Road, Cambridge, CB4 4WA. Tel: (01223) 567 200. FAX: (01223) 567 236.

COMCAST EUROPE
Network House, Bradfield Close, Woking, Surrey, GU22 7RE. Tel: (01483) 722 000. FAX: (01483) 763 005.

COMTEL
284 Weyhill Road, Andover, Hampshire, SP10 3LS. Tel: (01264) 401 402. FAX: (01264) 401 403.

DEVANHA GROUP PLC
303 King St., Aberdeen, Scotland, AB2 3AP. Tel: (01224) 646 644. FAX: (01224) 644 601.

DIAMOND CABLE
Diamon Plaza, Daleside Rd., Nottingham, NG2 3GG. Tel: (01159) 522 222. FAX: (01159) 522 211.

EUROBELL LTD.
Multimedia House, Lloyds Court, Manor Royal, Crawley, RH10 2PT. Tel: (01293) 400 444. FAX: (01293) 400 440.

GENERAL CABLE LTD.
37 Old Queen Street, London, SW1H 9JA. Tel: (0171) 393 2828. FAX: (0171) 393 2800.

IVS CABLE HOLDINGS LTD.-JERSEY OFFICE
3 Colomberie, St. Helier, Jersey, Channel Islands, JE2 4QB. Tel: (01534) 66477. FAX: (01534) 66681.

IVS CABLE HOLDINGS LIMITED-LONDON OFFICE
54 Warwick Square, London, SW1V 2AJ. Tel: (0171) 834 6012. FAX: (0171) 630 6270.

LCL COMMUNICATIONS
28-29 Oswin Road, Leicester, LE3 1HR. Tel: (01162) 334 100. FAX: (01162) 334 050.

METRO CABLE TELEVISION-WELWYN OFFICE
Unit 17, Weltech, Ridgeway, Welwyn Garden City, AL7 2AA. Tel: (01707) 372 631. FAX: (01707) 325 621.

METRO CABLE TELEVISION-LONDON OFFICE
Unit 12, 23 Park Royal Road, London, NW10 7JH. Tel: (0181) 961 6776. FAX: (0181) 961 6771.

NYNEX CABLE COMMS.
The Tolworth Tower, Ewell Road, Surbiton, KT6 7EL. Tel: (0181) 873 2000. FAX: (0181) 873 9993.

SBC CABLECOMMS
Hollywood House, Church Street East, Woking, Surrey, GU21 1HJ. Tel: (01483) 751756. FAX: (01483) 740922.

TELECENTIAL COMMUNICATIONS
Imperial Way, Reading, RG2 0BS. Tel: (01734) 544 000. FAX: (01734) 544 001.

TELEWEST COMMUNICATIONS GROUP LTD.
Unit 1, Genesis Business Park, Albert Drive, Woking, Surrey, GU21 5RW. Tel: (01483) 750900. FAX: (01483) 750901/2.

VIDEOTRON HOLDINGS LTD.
Videotron House, 76 Hammersmith Road, London W14 8UD. Tel: (0181) 244 1234. FAX: (0181) 244 1232.

YORKSHIRE CABLE GROUP
Communications House, Mayfair Business Park, Broad Lane, ford, BD4 8PW. Tel: (01274) 828282. FAX: (01274) 828400.

TV PROGRAM MATERIAL — PRODUCERS, DISTRIBUTORS AND SERVICE COMPANIES

AARDMAN ANIMATIONS
Gas Ferry Rd., Bristol BS1 6UN. Tel: (0117) 984 8485. FAX: (0117) 984 8486. Michael Rose.

ABC INTERNATIONAL
54 Portland Place, London, WIN 4DY. Tel: (0171) 636 4225. FAX: (0171) 636 4159. Wendy Hallam.

ABC SPORTS
8 Carburton Street, London, W1P 7DT. Tel: (0171) 636 7366. Telex: 23625 ABC5PT G. FAX: (0171) 323 4986.

ACI INTERNATIONAL
Lee House, 109 Hammersmith Rd., London, WI4 0QH. Tel: (0171) 602 7020. FAX: (0171) 371 3679. Brian Harris.

ADN ASSOCIATES/HOLLYWOOD CLASSICS
8 Cleveland Gardens, London, W2 6HA. Tel: (0171) 262 4646. FAX: (0171) 262 3242. Pano A. Alafouzo, Joe Dreier, John Flynn (USA).

ABACUS PRODUCTIONS LTD.
31 Shelton Street, London, WC2H 9HT. Tel: (0171) 240 1277. FAX: (0171) 836 7014.
DIRECTORS
Abbie Gache
Ron Trainer

ABBEY BROADCAST COMMUNICATIONS
53 Abbey Rd., London, NW8 OAD. Tel: (0171) 372 0752. FAX: (0171) 372 0887.

AEROFILMS
Gate Studios, Station Rd., Boreham Wood, Herts., WD6 1EJ. Tel: (0181) 207 0666. FAX: (0181) 207 5433.

AGRAN BARTON TELEVISION LTD.
The Yacht Club, Chelsea Harbour, London, SW10 OXA. Tel: (0171) 351 7070. FAX: (0171) 352 3528.

ALLIED TELEVISION
The Glassworks, 3-4 Ashland Place, London, W1M 3JH. Tel: (0171) 224 1992. FAX: (0171) 224 1110.
MANAGING DIRECTOR
Peter McRae

ALPHA FILMS LTD.
Unit 1, McKay Trading Estate, Kensal Rd., London, W10 5BX. Tel: (0181) 960 8211. Telex: 291877 Vision G.

ANIMAL ARK
The Studio, 29 Somerset Rd., Brentford, Middlesex TW8 8BT. Tel: (0181) 560 3029. FAX: (0181) 560 5762.

ANIMATION LINK
7 Baron's Gate, 33/35 Rothschild Rd., Chiswick, London, W4 5HT. Tel: (0181) 995 5080. FAX: (0181) 747 9452. Jo Kavanagh.

ANVIL POST PRODUCTION LTD.
Denham Studios, North Orbital Rd., Denham, Nr. Uxbridge, Middx. UB9 5HL. Tel: (01895) 833522. Telex: 934704. FAX: (01895) 835006. Ken Somerville, Alan Snelling.

ANTELOPE FILMS LTD.
2 Bloomsbury Place, London, WC1A 2QA. Tel: (0171) 209 0099. FAX: (0171) 209 0098. Mick Csaky.

ARTS COUNCIL FILMS
14 Great Peter St., London, SW1P 3NQ. Tel: (0171) 973 6443. FAX: (0171) 973 6581.
HEAD OF FILM, VIDEO & BROADCASTING
Rodney Wilson

AUSTRALIAN BROADCASTING CORPORATION
54 Portland Place, London, W1N 4DY. Tel: (0171) 631 4456. Telex: 263897. FAX: (0171) 323 1125 (News), (0171) 323 0059 (Admin).

AUSTRALIAN FILM COMMISSION
2nd Floor, Victory House, 99-101 Regent Street, London, WIR 7HB. Tel: (0171) 734 9383. FAX: (0171) 434 0170.
DIRECTOR OF MARKETING
Sue Murray

AUTOCUE LTD.
Autocue House, 265 Merton Rd., London, SW18 5JS. Tel: (0181) 870 0104. FAX: (0181) 874 3726. Mick Gould, Sarah Lewis.

BBC WORLDWIDE TELEVISION.
Woodlands, 80 Wood Lane, London, W12 0TT. Tel: (0181) 576 2000. FAX: (0181) 749 0538.
MANAGING DIRECTOR
Dr. John Thomas

BFI FILM & VIDEO LIBRARY
21 Stephen St., London, W1P 1PL. Tel: (0171) 255 1444. Telex: 27624. Heather Stewart.

JANE BALFOUR FILMS LTD.
Burghley House, 35 Fortress Rd., London, NW5 1AD. Tel: (0171) 267 5392. FAX: (0171) 267 4241. Mary Barlow.

BLUE DOLPHIN FILM PRODUCTIONS LTD.
40 Langham Street, London, W1N 5RE. Tel: (0171) 255 2494. FAX: (0171) 580 7670. Joseph D'Morais.

BOULTON-HAWKER FILMS LTD.
Hadleigh, Ipswich, Suffolk, 1P7 5BG. Tel: (01473) 822 235. FAX: (01473) 824 519.
DIRECTORS
K.P. Boulton
M.J. Boulton
N.H.L. Rea
D.A. Boulton.

BRAVEWORLD LTD.
Multimedia House, Trading Estate Rd., Park Royal, London NW10 7NA. Tel: (0181) 961 0011. FAX: (0181) 961 1413.
MANAGING DIRECTOR
Colin Bayliss

MARY BREEN-FARRELLY PRODUCTIONS LTD.
Ardmore Studios, Herbert Rd., Bray Co., Wicklow, Ireland. Tel: (3531) 286 2971. FAX: (3531) 286 6637. Mary Breen Farrelly.

BRITE
(The International sales representatives of LWT, Granada TV and Yorkshire Tyne-Tees Television).
The London Television Centre, Upper Ground, London SE1 9LT. Tel: (0171) 737 8603. FAX: (0171) 261 8162.
MANAGING DIRECTOR
Nadine Nohr

BRITISH LION
Pinewood Studios, Pinewood Rd., Iver, Bucks., 5L0 0NH. Tel: (01753) 651 700. Telex: 847505. FAX: (01753) 656 391.
CHAIRMAN AND CHIEF EXECUTIVE
Peter R. E. Snell

BRITISH MOVIETONEWS LTD.
North Orbital Rd., Denham, Uxbridge, Middx., UB9 5HQ. Tel: (01895) 833 071. FAX: (01895) 834 893.
MANAGING DIRECTOR
Barry S. Florin
LIBRARIAN
Barbara Heavens

BRITISH SCREEN FINANCE
14/17 Wells Mews, London, W1P 3FL. Tel: (0171) 323 9080. FAX: (0171) 323 0092.
CHIEF EXECUTIVE
Simon Perry

BRITISH SKY BROADCASTING LTD.
Grant Way, Isleworth, Middx: TW7 5QD. Tel: (0171) 705 3000. FAX: (0171) 705 3030.
CHIEF EXECUTIVE AND MANAGING DIRECTOR
Sam Chisolm
DEPUTY MANAGING DIRECTOR
David Chance

BRITISH UNIVERSITIES FILM & VIDEO COUNCIL
55 Greek St., London, W1V 5LR. Tel: (0171) 734 3687. FAX: (0171) 287 3914.
DIRECTOR
Murray Weston

BROOK PRODUCTIONS LTD.
21-24 Bruges Place, Randolph Street, London NW1 0TF. Tel: (0171) 482 6111. FAX: (0171) 284 0626. Anne Lapping.

BRYON PARKIN ASSOCIATES LTD.
37 Dover Street, London, W1X 3RA. Tel: (0181) 950 5151.

BUENA VISTA PRODUCTIONS LTD.
Beaumont House, Kensington Village, Avonmore Rd., London, WI4 8TS. Tel: (0171) 605 2400. FAX: (0171) 605 2597.
MANAGING DIRECTOR
David Simon

CBS NEWS
100 Brompton Rd., London, S.W.3. Tel: (0171) 584 3366. Telex: 916 319. Cables: Colnews London.

CBC TV PROGRAM SALES
43-51 Great Titchfield Street, London W1P 8DD. Tel: (0171) 580 0336. FAX: (0171) 323 5658. Susan Hewitt Jolley.

C.T.S. STUDIOS LTD.
Engineers Way, Wembley, Middlesex, HA9 0DR. Tel: (0181) 903 4611. FAX: (0181) 903 7130. Adrian Kerridge

CTVC
Hillside Studios, Merry Hill Rd., Bushey, Watford, WD2 1DR. Tel: (0181) 950 4426. FAX: (0181) 950 1437.

CABLE CONNECTIONS TELEVISION LTD.
201 Holland Park Avenue, London, W11 4UN. Tel: (0171) 603 4500. Telex: 8950117 AZITAP G. FAX: (0171) 603 1830.

CANADIAN BROADCASTING CORPORATION
43-51 Great Titchfield Street, London, W1P 8DD. Tel: (0171) 412 9200. FAX: (0171) 323 5658.

CAPITAL GROUP STUDIOS
13 Wandsworth Plain, London, SW18 1ET. Tel: (0181) 874 0131. FAX: (0181) 871 9737. Telex: 929509. Sally Trickett.

CARLTON UK PRODUCTIONS
35-38 Portman Square, London W1H 9FH. Tel: (0171) 486 6688. FAX: (0171) 486 1132.
MANAGING DIRECTOR
Andy Allan

CASTLE COMMUNICATIONS PLC.
(Castle Target International), A29 Barwell Business Park, Leatherhead Rd., Chessington, Surrey KT9 2NY. Tel: (0181) 974 1021. FAX: (0181) 974 2674.
CHAIRMAN
Terry Shand
MANAGING DIRECTOR
Geoff Kempin

CASTLE ROCK INTERNATIONAL
8 Queen Street, Mayfair, London, W1X 7PH. Tel: (0171) 409 3532. FAX: (0171) 499 9885.
PRESIDENT
Mashmo Grabosi
VICE PRESIDENT, MARKETING & PUBLICITY
Lindsey Stride

CBS BROADCAST INTERNATIONAL
1 Red Place, London, W1Y 3RE, Tel: (0171) 355 4422. FAX: (0171) 355 4429.

CENTRAL OFFICE OF INFORMATION
Hercules Rd., London, SE1 7DU. Tel: (0171) 261 8495. FAX: (0171) 261 8874.
DIRECTOR, FILMS, TV AND RADIO DIVISION
Malcolm Nisbet

CHEERLEADER PRODUCTIONS
3rd floor, 141-143 Drury Lane, London WC2B ST8. Tel: (0171) 240 5389. FAX: (0171) 240 5391.
MANAGING DIRECTOR
Charles Thompson

CHANNEL 4 INTERNATIONAL LTD.
124 Horseferry Rd., London, SW1P 2TX. Tel: (0171) 396 4444. FAX: (0171) 306 8363.

CHATSWORTH TELEVISION
97-99 Dean Street, London, W1V 5RA. Tel: (0171) 396 4444. FAX: (0171) 306 8363.
MANAGING DIRECTOR
Colin Leventhal

CHESS VALLEY FILMS AND VIDEO
38 Batchelor Way, Amersham, Bucks. HP7 9AJ. Tel: 01494 725 359. FAX: 01494 725 359.
DIRECTORS
Ronald E. Haddock, F.B.I.P.P., P. M.
Trudi Drayton
Heather M. Davies, MBKSTS

CHILDREN'S CHANNEL
9-13 Grape Street, London, WC2H 8DR. Tel: (0171) 240 3422. FAX: (0171) 497 9113. Ann Cook.

CHRYSALIS GROUP PLC
The Chrysalis Bldg., Bramley Rd., London, W10 6SP. Tel: (0171) 221 2213. FAX: (0171) 221 6341.

CI BY SALES
14 Curzon St., London, W1Y 7FH. Tel: (0171) 333 8877. FAX: (0171) 493 2443. Wendy Palmer.

CINE ELECTRA
National House, 60-66 Wardour Street, London, W1V 3HP. Tel: (0171) 287 1123. FAX: (0171) 722 4251.
INTERNATIONAL COORDINATOR
Anne Billard
MANAGING DIRECTOR
Julia Kennedy

CINE-LINGUAL SOUND STUDIOS LTD.
27-29 Berwick Street, London, W1V 3RF. Tel: (0171) 437 0136. FAX: (0171) 439 2012.
DIRECTORS
A. Anscombe
P.J. Anscombe
M. Anscombe
D.J. Old
D.J. Newman

CINEMA VERITY PRODUCTIONS LTD.
The Mill House, Millers Way, 1A Shepherds Bush Rd., London, W6 7NA. Tel: (0181) 749 8485. FAX: (0181) 743 5062.
EXECUTIVE PRODUCER
Verity Lambert

CINESOUND EFFECTS LIBRARY LTD.
Imperial Studios, Maxwell Rd., Elstree Way, Boreham Wood, Herts., WD6 IWE. Tel: (0181) 953 5837 and 5545, 1587, 4904. FAX: (0181) 207 1728. Mike Rogers, Angela Marshall.

BRIAN CLEMENS ENTERPRISES LTD.
Park Farm Cottage, Ampthill Beds. Tel: (01525) 402215. FAX: (01525) 402954.
DIRECTORS
John Simmons, Cecilia Simmons

CLIP SHOP
47 Dean St., London W1V 5HL. Tel: (0171) 287 1808. FAX: (0171) 287 1454.
DIRECTORS
Helen Bennitt, Jenny Morgan

COLOUR VIDEO SERVICES LTD.
10 Wadsworth Rd., Perivale, Greenford, Middlesex UB6 7JX. Tel: (0181) 998 2731. FAX: (0181) 997 8738.

COLSTAR INTERNATIONAL
11 Wythburn Place, London, WIH 5WL. Tel: (0171) 437 5725. FAX: (0171) 706 1704. Steve Goddard.

COLUMBIA TRISTAR INTERNATIONAL TELEVISION
A Division of Sony Pictures Entertainment, St. Margaret's House, 19/23 Wells Street, London, W1P 4DH. Tel: (0171) 580 2090. FAX: (0171) 436 0323.

CREWS EMPLOYMENT AGENCY
111 Wardour Street, London, W1V 4AY. Tel: (0171) 437 0350. FAX: (0171) 494 4644. Lynda Loakes, Shirley Hinds.

CROWN TELEVISION.
Crown House, 72 Hammersmith Rd., London W14 8YE. Tel: (0171) 371 6060. FAX: (0171) 371 2727. Bruce Todd.

CTE
35-38 Portman Square, London W1H 9FH. Tel: (0171) 224 3339. FAX: (0171) 486 1707.
MANAGING DIRECTOR
Philip Jones

CTVC
Hillside Studios, Merry Hill Rd., Bushey, Watford, WD2 1DR. Tel: (0181) 950 4426. FAX: (0181) 950 1437. Peter Davies.

CYGNET VIDEO & FILM
Communication Business Centre, Blenheim Rd., High Wycombe, Bucks., HP12 3RS. Tel: 01494 450541. FAX: 01494 462154.
MANAGING DIRECTOR
D. N. Plunket
PRODUCER
Philip Lee

DL TAFFNER UK
10 Bedford Square, London WC1B 3RA. Tel: (0171) 631 1184. FAX: (0171) 636 4571.
MANAGING DIRECTOR
John Reynolds

DLT ENTERTAINMENT
10 Bedford Square, London, WC1B 3RA. Tel: (0171) 631 1184. FAX: (0171) 636 4571.

DANDELION DISTRIBUTION LTD.
5 Churchill Court Station Rd., North Harrow, Middx. HA2 7SA. Tel: (0181) 863 1888. FAX: (0181) 863 0463.

DE LANE LEA SOUND CENTRE
75 Dean Street, London, W1V 5HA. Tel: (0171) 439 1721. FAX: (0171) 437 0913. Richard Paynter.

DE WOLFE LTD.
80-88 Wardour Street, London, W1V 3LF. Tel: (0171) 439 8481. FAX: (0171) 437 2744.
DIRECTORS
James de Wolfe
Gordon Chambers
Warren de Wolfe

WALT DISNEY COMPANY LTD.
Beaumont House, Kensington Village, Avonmore Rd., London, WI4 8TS. Tel: (0171) 605 2400. FAX: (0171) 605 2593.
MANAGING DIRECTOR
Etienne de Villiers

DRAKE VIDEO SERVICES
89 St. Fagans Rd., Fairwater, Cardiff CF5 3AE, Wales.
MANAGING DIRECTORS
R. G. Drake
H. Drake

DRUMMER FILMS LTD.
14 Haywood Close, Pinner, Middx., HA5 3LQ. Tel: (0181) 866 9466. FAX: (0181) 866 9466.
MANAGING DIRECTOR
Martin M. Harris (Producer)

DUCK LANE FILM PRODUCTIONS LTD.
8 Duck Lane, London, W1V 1FL Tel: (0171) 439 3912. FAX: (0171) 437 2260.
DIRECTOR
Rigby Andrews

EPA INTERNATIONAL DISTRIBUTORS
31-A Regents Park Rd., London NW1 7TL. Tel: (0171) 267 9198. FAX: (0171) 267 8852.

EATON FILMS LTD.
10 Holbein Mews, London, SW1W 8NN. Tel: (0171) 823 6173. FAX: (0171) 823 6017. Judith Bland, Liz Cook.

EDUCATIONAL & TELEVISION FILMS LTD.
247a Upper Street, London, N1-1RU. Tel: (0171) 226 2298. FAX: (0171) 226 8016.
GENERAL MANAGER
Stanley Forman

ELECTRONIC PUBLISHING CO. LTD.
68-70 Wardour Street, London, W1V 3HP. Tel: (0171) 734 4609. Telex: Peclon 25554. FAX: (0171) 437 1366.

ENTERTAINMENT FILM PRODUCTIONS LTD.
27 Soho Square, London, W1V 5FL. Tel: (0171) 439 1606. FAX: (0171) 734 2483. Telex: 262428 ENT VIF.
DIRECTORS
Michael L. Green
Nigel G. Green
Trevor H. Green

ENTERTAINMENT PRODUCTIONS
3 Fitzroy Square, London, W1P 5AH. Tel: (0171) 388 1234. FAX: (0171) 387 5789. Tony Fitzpatrick.

EUREKA LOCATION MANAGEMENT
51 Tonsley Hill, London, SW18 1BW. Tel: (0181) 870 4569. FAX: (0181) 871 2158.
HEAD OF OPERATIONS
Suzannah Holt

EUSTON FILMS LTD.
Pinewood Studios, Iver Heath, Bucks, SL0 0NH. Tel: 01753 650222. FAX: 01753 650222. John Hambley.

EYELINE FILM AND VIDEO LTD.
77 Dean Street, London, W.1. Tel: (0171) 734 3391. Telex: 265351. FAX: (0171) 437 2095.
DIRECTORS
Harold Orton
Jacki Roblin

F.I.L.M.S. LTD.
2 Savile Row, London W1X 1AF. Tel: (0171) 434 0340. FAX: (0171) 434 0442.

FTS BONDED
Heston Industrial Estate, Aerodrome Way, Cranford Lane, Hounslow, Middx., TW5 9QB. Tel: (0181) 897 7973. Telex: 21747 FILM BO G. FAX: (0181) 897 7979.
SALES DIRECTOR
John Reeves

FILM AND GENERAL PRODUCTIONS LTD.
10 Pembridge Place, London, W2 4XB. Tel: (0171) 221 1141. FAX: (0171) 792 1167.
DIRECTORS
Clive Parsons
Davina Belling
Richard Whatmore

FILM FAIR LTD.
1-4 Jacobs Wells Mews, London, W1H 5PD. Tel: (0171) 935 1596.
MANAGING DIRECTOR
Lewis Rudd

FILM FOUR INTERNATIONAL
124 Horseferry Rd., London, SW1P 2TX. Tel: (0171) 396 4444. FAX: (0171) 306 8361.
DIRECTOR OF SALES
Bill Stephens
FILM SALES MANAGER
Heather Playford-Denman

FIRST INDEPENDENT FILMS LTD.
69 New Oxford St., London, WC1A 1DG. Tel: (0171) 528 7767. FAX: (0171) 528 7770.
MANAGING DIRECTOR
Michael Myers

MARK FORSTATER PRODUCTIONS LTD.
Suite 66, Pall Mall Deposit, 124-128 Barlby Rd., London, WI0 6BL. Tel: (0181) 964 1888. FAX: (0181) 960 9819.
DIRECTOR
Mark Forstater

FOWLER-CHAPMAN COMPANY LTD.
28 Saint Mary le Park Court, Albert Bridge Rd., London, SW11 4PJ. Tel: (0171) 223 0034. FAX: 0892 784023.
MANAGING DIRECTOR
Roy Fowler

FOX VIDEO
31-32 Soho Square, London, WIV 6AP. Tel: (0171) 753 8686.

FRIDAY PRODUCTIONS LTD.
23a St. Leonards Terrace, London SW3 40G. Tel: (0171) 730 0608. FAX: (0171) 730 0608.

G.H.W. PRODUCTIONS LTD.
52 Queen Anne Street, London, W1M 9LA. Tel: (0171) 935 1186.
DIRECTORS
Peter Rogers
Betty E. Box, O.B.E.
D.G. Truscott.

GAINSBOROUGH (FILM & TV) PICTURES LTD.
8 Queen Street, Mayfair, London, W17 XPH. Tel: (0171) 409 1925. FAX: (0171) 408 2042.

GANNET FILMS LTD.
88 Gresham Rd., Staines, Middx., TW18 2AE. Tel: (01784) 453912.
DIRECTORS
Bob Kellett
Anne Kellett

JAMES GARRETT & PARTNERS LTD.
25 Bruton Street, London, W1X 7DB. Tel: (0171) 499 6452. Telex: 261163. FAX: (0171) 409 1797.
DIRECTORS
J. L. M. P. Garrett
M. Gilmour
D. T. Cromwell
M. Garrett

GATEWAY AUDIOVISUAL/VIDEO
470-472 Green Lanes, Palmers Green, London, N13 5XF. Tel: (0181) 882 0177. Telex: 896462. FAX: (0181) 882 4161.
DIRECTOR
G.L. Smart, A.R.P.S., M.B.K.S.

JOHN GAU PRODUCTIONS LTD.
Burston House, 1 Burston Rd., Putney, London, SW15 6AR. Tel: (0181) 788 8811. FAX: (0181) 789 0903.

NOEL GAY TELEVISION
6th Floor, 76 Oxford Street, London, W1N 0AT. Tel: (0171) 412 0400. FAX: (0171) 402 0300. Charles Armitage, Alex Armitage.

GENERAL SCREEN ENTERPRISES
Highbridge Estate, Oxford Rd., Uxbridge, Middx., UB8 1LX. Tel: (01895) 231931. FAX: (01895) 235335.
DIRECTOR & GENERAL MANAGER
Fred Chandler

GFD COMMUNICATIONS LTD
Unit 15A, Parkmore Industrial Estate, Longmile Rd., Dublin 12, Ireland. Tel: (3531) 569500. FAX: (3531) 569342.

WILLIAM GILBERT ASSOCIATES LTD.
16 Brook Mews North, London, W2 3BW. Tel: (0171) 258 3620. Telex: 264826 RKOINT. FAX: (0171) 723 5100. William Gilbert.

GINGER FILM PRODUCTIONS LTD.
39-41 Hanover Steps, St. George's Fields, Albion St., London, W2 2YG. Tel: (0171) 402 7543. Telex: 896559 Gecoms G. FAX: (0171) 262 5736. Brian Jackson.

GLOBAL ENTERTAINMENT MANAGEMENT LTD.
22 Wadsworth Rd., Perivale, Middx. UB6 7JD. Tel: (0181) 991 5051. FAX: (0181) 998 3521.
CHIEF EXECUTIVE
Claude Heilman
DIRECTOR
P. Kotak

GLOBO INTERNATIONAL (LONDON) LTD.
29 Princes St., London, W1R 7RG. Tel: (0171) 409 1712. FAX: (0171) 491 3167. Roberto Filippelli.

BOB GODFREY FILMS LTD
55 Neal Street, London, W.C.2 Tel: (0171) 240 1793/1889.

GOLDCREST FILMS AND TELEVISION LTD.
65-66 Dean Street, London, WIV 6PL. Tel: (0171) 437 8696. Telex: 267458 Goldcr. FAX: (0171) 437 4448.
CHIEF EXECUTIVE
John Quested

SAMUEL GOLDWYN COMPANY
St. George's House, 14-17 Wells Street, London, W1P 3FP. Tel: (0171) 436 5105. FAX: (0171) 580 6520.
VICE PRESIDENT, WORLDWIDE MARKETING
Richard Bornstein

THE GRADE COMPANY
34 Grosvenor St., Mayfair, London, W1X 9FG. Tel: (0171) 409 1925. FAX: (0171) 408 2042. Lord Grade.

GRANADA LWT INTERNATIONAL LTD.
The London Television Centre, Upper Ground, London, SE1 9LT. Tel: (0171) 620 1620. FAX: (0171) 928 8476.
HEAD OF SALES
Nadine Nohr

GREEN & HEATON LTD.
37 Goldhwak Rd., London W12 8QQ. Tel: (0181) 749 0315. FAX: (0181) 749 0318.
DIRECTORS
Carol Heaton
Timothy Webb

GRUNDY WORLDWIDE LTD.
Grundy House/Barge House CRESCENT, 34 Upper Ground, London, SE1 9PD. Tel: (0171) 928 8942. FAX: (0171) 928 8417.

HALLIFORD STUDIOS LTD
Manygate Lane, Shepperton, Middx., TW17 9EG. Tel: (01932) 226341. FAX: (01932) 246336.
STUDIO MANAGER
Allan d'Aguiar

HAMMER FILM PRODUCTIONS LTD.
Millenium Studios, Elstree Way, Boreham Wood, Herts. WD6 1SF. WD6 1UG. Tel: (0181) 207 4011. FAX: (0181) 905 1127.
DIRECTORS
Roy Skeggs
Andrew Mitchell

HAMPDEN GURNEY STUDIOS, LTD.
39-41 Hanover Steps, St. George's Fields, Albion Street, London, W2 2YG. Tel: (0171) 402 7543. FAX: (0171) 262 5736. Telex: 896559 GECOMS G.

635

STEWART HARDY FILMS LTD.
2-4 Wigton Gardens, Stanmore, Middx., HA7 18G. Tel: (0181) 204 4153.
DIRECTOR
J. R. Williams

HAT TRICK PRODUCTIONS
10 Livonia Street, London, W1V 3PH. Tel: (0171) 434 2451. FAX: (0171) 437 0773. Denise O'Donoghue.

HEMDALE HOLDINGS
21 Albion Street, London, W2 2AS. Tel: (0171) 724 1010. Telex: 25558. FAX: (0171) 724 9168.
DIRECTORS
J. Daly
A.D. Kerman
D. Gibson

JIM HENSON PRODUCTIONS
1(B) Downshire Hill, Hampstead, London, NW3 1NR. Tel: (0171) 431 2818. FAX: (0171) 431 3737.

HIGH POINT FILM AND TV
25 Elizabeth Mews, London, NW3 4UH. Tel: (0171) 586 3686. FAX: (0171) 586 3117.

HIT ENTERTAINMENT PLC
The Pump House, 13-16 Jacobs Well Mews, London, W1H 5PD. Tel: (0171) 224 1717. FAX: (0171) 224 1719.
MANAGING DIRECTOR
Peter Orton

GERARD HOLDSWORTH PRODUCTIONS LTD.
140 Buckingham Palace Rd., London, SW1W 95A. Tel: (0171) 824 8770. FAX: (0171) 824 8762.
DIRECTORS
P. H. Filmer-Sankey
A.M.V. Brunker

MICHAEL HURLL TELEVISION
8-12 Broadwick Street, London, W1V 1PH. Tel: (0171) 2874314. FAX: (0171) 287 4315.

ITC ENTERTAINMENT GROUP LTD.
33 Foley St., London, W1. Tel: (0171) 255 3000. Telex: 912121. FAX: (0171) 306 7800.
SENIOR VICE PRESIDENT, INTERNATIONAL
Lynden Parry

ITC HOME VIDEO (UK)
161-167 Oxford St., London W1R 1TA. Tel: (0171) 439 3000. FAX: (0171) 437 4370.

ITN LTD.
200 Gray's Inn Rd., London, WC1X 8XZ. Tel: (0171) 833 3000. FAX: (0171) 430 4016.
CHAIRMAN
Gerry Robinson
CHIEF EXECUTIVE
Stewart Purvis
EDITOR-IN-CHIEF
Richad Tait

IVS ENTERPRISES LTD.
54 Warwick Square, London, SW1V 2AJ. Tel: (0171) 834 6012. Telex: 27151. FAX: (0171) 630 6270.

ITV NETWORK ACQUISITIONS
ITV Network Centre, 200 Gray's Inn Rd., London, WCIX 8X2. Tel: (0171) 843 8120. Telex: 262988. FAX: (0171) 843 8160.
CONTROLLER OF ACQUISITIONS
Pat Mahoney

INDEPENDENT COMMUNICATIONS ASSOCIATES (INCA)
20-28 Dalling Rd., London, W6 0JB. Tel: (0181) 748 0160. FAX: (0181) 748 0160. Richard Melman.

INIMITABLE LTD.
Greenman, Highmoor, Henley-on-Thames, Oxfordshire, RG9 5DH. Tel: 01491 641140. FAX: 01491 641080.
Contact: Gerry Anderson

INITIAL FILM & TV LTD.
74 Black Lion Lane, Hammersmith, London, W6 9BF. Tel: (0181) 741 4500. FAX: (0181) 741 9416. Malcolm Gerrie.

ISLAND WORLD PRODUCTIONS
12-14 Argyll St., London, W1V 1AB. Tel: (0171) 734 3536. FAX: (0171) 734 3585.

ITEL
48 Leicester Square, London, WC2H 7FB. Tel: (0171) 491 1441. FAX: (0171) 493 7677.
MANAGING DIRECTOR
Andrew MacBean

J & M ENTERTAINMENT
2 Dorset Square, London, NW1 6PU Tel: (0171) 723 6544. Telex: 298538 FILMIN G. FAX: (0171) 724 7541. Cables: Filming London NW1. Julia Palau, Michael Ryan.

BRIAN JACKSON FILMS LTD.
39-41 Hanover Steps, St. Georges Fields, Albion Street, London, W2 2YG. Tel: (0171) 402 7543 and (0171) 262 5736. FAX: (0171) 262 5736. Telex: 896559 GECOMS-G.

JARAS ENTERTAINMENTS LTD.
Broughton House, 3rd fl., 6-8 Sackville St., London, W1X 1DD. Tel: (0171) 287 4601. FAX: (0171) 287 9652.

CYRIL JENKINS PRODUCTIONS LTD.
7 Coniston Court, Carlton Drive, London, SW15 2BZ. Tel: (0181) 788 2733.
DIRECTORS
Cyril G. Jenkins
J.M. Jenkins

KAVUR PRODUCTIONS LTD.
14 Lownes Square, London, SW1X 9HB. Tel: (0171) 235 4602. FAX: (0171) 235 5215.

KILROY TELEVISION COMPANY LTD.
Teddington Studios, Teddington, Middx., TW11 9NT. Tel: (0181) 943 3555. FAX: (0181) 943 3646. Robert Strange.

LWT INTERNATIONAL
London Television Centre, London, SE1 9LT. Tel: (0171) 620 1620. FAX: (0171) 430 4016.

LITTLE KING PRODUCTIONS LTD.
Greek Court, 14a Old Compton St., London W1V 5PE. Tel: (0171) 437 1772. FAX: (0171) 437 1782.

LONDON FILM PRODUCTIONS LTD
Kent House, 14-17 Market Place, Great Titchfield Street, London, W1N 8AR. Tel:(0171) 323 5251. FAX: (0171) 436 2834.

LUCIDA PRODUCTIONS LTD.
53 Greek Street, London, WIV 5LR. Tel: (0171) 437 1140. FAX: (0171) 287 5335.
DIRECTORS
Paul Joyce
Chris Rodley

MCA TV INTERNATIONAL
1 Hamilton Mews, London, W1V 9FF. Tel: (0171) 491 4666. FAX: (0171) 493 4702.

M.C.E.G. VIRGIN VISION
Atlantic House, 1 Rockley Rd., Shepherd's Bush, London, W14 0DB. Tel: (0181) 740 5500. FAX: (0181) 967 1360.
DIRECTORS
Bill Tennant
Julian Portman
Angus Margerison
Peter Coles

MGM/UA HOME VIDEO (UK) LTD
84-86 Regent Street, London, W1R 5PF. Tel: (0171) 915 1717. FAX: (0171) 734 8411. Jonathan Cocker.

MTM INTERNATIONAL
84 Buckingham Gate, London SW1E 6PD. Tel: (0171) 233 0901. FAX: (0171) 233 1134. Greg Phillips.

MTV EUROPE
Hawley Crescent, London, NW1 8TT. Tel: (0171) 284 7777. FAX: (0171) 284 7788.
DIRECTOR OF CORPORATE COMMUNICATIONS
Monique Amaudry

MCCANN INTERNATIONAL PROGRAMME MARKETING LTD.
88-94 Tottenham Court Rd., London, W1P 9HE. Tel: (0171) 323 4641. Telex: 297957.

MAJESTIC FILMS AND TELEVISION INTERNATIONAL
P.O. Box 13, Gloucester Mansions, Cambridge Circus, London, WC2H 8XD. Tel: (0171) 836 8630. FAX: (0171) 836 5819. Telex: 46601 BTGKAG.
CHIEF EXECUTIVE
Guy East

MIKE MANSFIELD TELEVISION LTD.
5-7 Carnaby Street, London, W1V 1PG. Tel: (0171) 494 3061. FAX: (0171) 494 3057.

MARK I PRODUCTIONS LTD.
Lee International Studios, 128 Wembley Park Drive, Wembley, Middlesex, HA9 8JE. Tel: (0181) 902 1262.

MECCA INTERNATIONAL PRODUCTIONS LTD
14 Oxford Street, London, W1N 0HL. Tel: (0171) 637 9401.

MEDIA RELEASING DISTRIBUTORS LTD.
27 Soho Square, London, W1V 5FL. Tel: (0171) 437 2341. Telex: 943763 CROCOM G(MRD). FAX: (0171) 734 2483.
DIRECTORS
Trevor H. Green
J. Green

MEDUSA COMMUNICATIONS LTD.
Regal Chambers, 51 Bancroft, Hitchin, Herts., SG5 1LL. Tel: 01462 421818. FAX: 01462 420393.
CHAIRMAN
David Hodgins
EXECUTIVE DIRECTOR
Stephen Rivers

MENTORN FILMS
Mentorn House, 140 Wardour Street, London, W1V 3AV. Tel: (0171) 287 4545. FAX: (0171) 287 3728. Tom Gutteridge, John Needham.

MERIT TELEVISION LTD.
48 Boscombe Rd., London, W12 9HU. Tel: (0181) 749 1175. FAX: (0181) 749 8662.

MIRACLE COMMUNICATIONS LTD.
69 New Oxford St., London, W1A 1DG. Tel: (0171) 379 5006. FAX: (0171) 528 7772. Michael Myers.

THE MOVING PICTURE COMPANY
25 Noel Street, London, W1V 3RD. Tel: (0171) 434 3100. FAX: (0171) 287 5187.
MANAGING DIRECTOR
David Jeffers

MUSEUM OF THE MOVING IMAGE
South Bank, Waterloo, London, SE1 8XT. Tel: (0171) 928 3535. FAX: (0171) 815 1378.
CONTROLLER
Adrian Wootton
CURATOR
Leslie Hardcastle, OBE

MUSIC BOX
247-257 Euston Rd., London NW1 2HY. Tel: (0171) 387 9808. FAX: (0171) 387 9106.
MANAGING DIRECTOR
John Leach

NBC EUROPE
3 Shortlands, Hammersmith, London, W6 8BX. Tel: (0181) 846 8704. FAX: (0181) 846 8768.
MANAGING DIRECTOR
Patrick Cox

NBD TELEVISION
Unit 2, Royalty Studios, 105 Lancaster Rd., London, WII 1QF. Tel: (0171) 243 3646. FAX: (0171) 243 3656.

N.F.H. LTD.
37 Ovington Square, London SW3 1LJ. Tel: (0171) 584 7561. FAX: (0171) 589 1863.
MANAGING DIRECTOR
Norma Heyman

NVC ARTS
The Forum, 74-80 Camden Street, London, NW1 0JL. Tel: (0171) 388 3833. FAX: (0171) 383 5332. Telex: 893045 NVCG.

NAMARA LTD.
51 Beak Street, London, W1R 3LF. Tel: (0171) 437 9524. FAX: (0171) 734 1844.
EXECUTIVE PRODUCER
Naim Attaliah

NATIONAL FILM AND TELEVISION SCHOOL
Beaconsfield Studios, Station Rd., Beaconsfield, Bucks. HP9 1LG. Tel: (01494) 671234. FAX: (01494) 674042.
DIRECTOR
Henning Camre

NATIONAL SCREEN
Wedgwood Mews, Greek Street London, W1V 6BH. Tel: (0171) 437 4851. FAX: (0171) 287 0328.
Studios: 15 Wadsworth Rd., Greenford, Middx., UB6 7JN. Tel: (0181) 998 2851. FAX: (0181) 997 0840.
DIRECTORS
John Mahony
Norman Darkins
Brian McIlmail

NELSON TELEVISION
8 Queen Street, London, W1X 7PH. Tel: (0171) 493 3362. FAX: (0171) 409 0503 Ian Scorer.

NETWORK TELEVISION LTD.
47 Poland Street, London, W1V 3DF. Tel: (0171) 734 0496.

NEW CENTRAL FILM SERVICES LTD.
97-99 Dean Street, London, W.1. Tel.: (0171) 734 5827-8.

NEW WORLD/TRANS ATLANTIC PICTURES (UK) LTD.
27 Soho Square, London, W1V 5FL. Tel: (0171) 434 0497. FAX: (0171) 434 0490.

NIXPARGO ANIMATIONS
Maidensgrove, Nr. Henley-on-Thames, Oxon., RG9 6EZ. Tel: (0149) 163 286.
PRODUCERS
Nicholas Spargo
Mary Spargo

OPEN MEDIA
9 Leamington Rd., Villas, W11 1HS. Tel: (0171) 229 5416. FAX: (0171) 221 4842.

OPTICAL FILM EFFECTS LTD.
Pinewood Studios, Iver Heath, Bucks. 5L0 0NH. Tel: (01753) 655486. Telex: 847505 G. FAX: (01753) 656844.
DIRECTORS
R. W. Field
R. A. Dimbleby

OVERVIEW FILMS LTD.
16 Brook Mews North, London, W2 3BW. Tel: (0171) 258 3620. FAX: (0171) 723 5100. Telex: 264826 RKOINT G. William G. Gilbert.

OXFORD SCIENTIFIC FILMS
Lower Rd., Long Hanborough, Oxon, OX8 8LL. Tel: 01993 881881. FAX: 01993 882808. 10 Poland Street, London W1V 3DE. Tel: (0171) 494 0720. FAX: (0171) 4287 9125.

PACIFIC TELEVISION ENTERPRISES LTD.
4th fl., Century House, 100 Oxford St., London, W1N 9FB. Tel: (0171) 437 9314. FAX: (0171) 631 3049.

DAVID PARADINE PRODUCTIONS LTD.
5 St. Mary Abbots Place, Kensington, London, W8 6L5. Tel: (0171) 371 3111. FAX: (0171) 602 0411.

PAVILION INTERNATIONAL
60-62 Margaret Street, London W1N 7FJ. Tel: (0171) 636 9421. FAX: (0171) 436 7426.

PEARL & DEAN LTD.
Woolverstone House, 61-62 Berners Street, London, WIP 3AE. Tel: (0171) 636 5252. FAX: (0171) 637 3191.
MANAGING DIRECTOR
Peter Howard Williams

PETROFILMS UK LTD
8 West Street, London W.C.2. Tel: (0171) 836 2112.

PHOENIX FILMS LTD.
6 Flitcroft Street, London, WC2 8DJ. Tel: (0171) 836 5000. FAX: (0171) 836 3060.
DIRECTORS
Lewis More O'Ferrall
Alan Taylor

PIZAZZ PICTURES
S30 Berwick Street, London, W1V 3RF. Tel: (0171) 434 3581. FAX: (0171) 437 2309.
PRODUCER
Pamela Dennis
DIRECTORS
Eric Goldberg
Mario Cavalli

PLANET 24 LTD.
Norex Court, Thames Quay, 195 Marsh Wall, London, E14 9SG. Tel: (0171) 712 9300. FAX: (0171) 712 9400.
DIRECTORS
Waheed Alli
Bob Geldof
Charlie Parsons

PLATO FILMS LTD.
247A Upper Street, London, N1 1RU. Tel: (0171) 226 2298.
MANAGING DIRECTOR
Stanley Forman

POLYGRAM FILM INTERNATIONAL
76 Oxford St., London W1N 0HQ. Tel: (0171) 307 1300. FAX: (0171) 307 1355.
PRESIDENT
Aline Perry

POLYMUSE INTERNATIONAL TELEVISION
22 Cleveland Square, London, W2. Tel: (0171) 402 9066.

PORTMAN INTERNATIONAL
Advance House, 95 Ladbroke Grove, London W11 1PG. Tel: (0171) 468 3400. FAX: (0171) 468 3499. Victor Glynn.

PORTMAN ZENITH GROUP LTD.
43-45 Dorset Street, London, W1H 4AB. Tel: (0171) 224 3344. FAX: (0171) 224 1057.
DIRECTORS
Victor Glynn
John Hall
John Sivers
Simon Cox
Andrew Warren
Scott Meek
Dorothy Berwin
Ivan Rendall
Richard Leworthy

PORTOBELLO PICTURES
42 Tavistock Rd., London, W11 1AW. Tel: (0171) 379 5566. FAX: (0171) 379 5599. Telex: 268388 PORTO G.
EXECUTIVE PRODUCER & DIRECTOR
Eric Abraham

POST OFFICE FILM & VIDEO UNIT
(Archival Material) 130 Old Street, London, EC1V 9PQ. Tel: (0171) 320 7125. FAX: (0171) 320 7209. Alma Headland.

RICHARD PRICE TELEVISION ASSOCIATES LTD
Seymour Mews House, Seymour Mews, Wigmore Street, London, W1H 9PE. Tel: (0171) 935 9000. FAX: (0171) 935 1992.
DIRECTORS
Richard Price
Richard Leworthy
Simon Willock

PRIMROSE FILM PRODUCTIONS LTD.
61 Regents Park Rd., London, N.W.1. Tel: (0171) 722 7475.
DIRECTORS
Louis Hagen
Anne Hagen

PRIMETIME TELEVISION LTD.
Seymour Mews House, Seymour Mews, Wigmore Street, London, W1H 9PE. Tel: (0171) 935 9000. FAX: (0171) 935 1992.
Richard Price, Ian Gordon.

PROSPECT PICTURES
30-32 Mortimer St., London, W1N 7RA. Tel: (0171) 636 1236.
MANAGING DIRECTOR
Tony McAvoy

QUADRANT TELEVISION
17 West Hill, Wandsworth, London SW18 1RB. Tel: (0181) 870 9930. FAX: (0181) 870 7172.

RADIO LUXEMBOURG (LONDON) LTD.
38 Hertford Street, London, W1V 8BA. Tel: (0171) 493 5961.
DIRECTOR OF SALES AND MARKETING
Brian Mellor

RADIUS TELEVISION PRODUCTION
Glenageary Office Park, Dun Laoghaire Co., Dublin, Ireland. Tel: (3531) 285 6511. FAX: (3531) 285 6831.

RANDOM FILM PRODUCTIONS LTD.
Unit 2, Cornwall Works, Cornwall Avenue, Finchley, London, N3 1LD. Tel: (0181) 349 9155.
DIRECTORS
F.G. Woosnam-Mills
M.R. Woosnam-Mills
M.P. Molloy

RANK FILM DISTRIBUTORS LTD.
127 Wardour Street, London, WIV 4AD. Tel: (0171) 437 9020. Telex: 262556. FAX: (0171) 434 3689.
MANAGING DIRECTOR
F. P. Turner
HEAD OF INTERNATIONAL SALES
Nicole MacKey

RANK VIDEO SERVICES LTD.
Phoenix Park, Great West Rd., Brentford, Middlesex, TW8 9PL. Tel: (0181) 568 4311. Telex: 22345. FAX: (0181) 847 4032.
MANAGING DIRECTOR
Peter Pacitt

RAVENSDALE FILM & TELEVISION LTD
34-35 Dean Street, London, W.1. Tel: (0171) 734 4686.

RECORDED PICTURE CO. LTD.
24 Hanway St., London, W1P 9DD. Tel: (0171) 636 2251. FAX: (0171) 636 2261.
DIRECTORS
Jeremy Thomas
Hercules Bellville
Chris Auty

REDIFFUSION FILMS LTD
P.O. Box 451, Buchanan House, 3 St. James's Square, London, SW1Y 4LS. Tel: (0171) 925 0550. Telex: 919673. Cables: Rediffuse. FAX: (0171) 839 7135.
PRODUCTION EXECUTIVE
Jelte Bonnevie

RED ROOSTER FILM & TELEVISION ENTERTAINMENT LTD.
29 Floral Street, London, WC2E 9DP. Tel: (0171) 379 7727. FAX: (0171) 379 5756.
CHIEF EXECUTIVE
Linda James

REGENT PRODUCTIONS
The Mews, 6 Putney Common, London, SW15 1HL. Tel: (0181) 789 5350. William G. Stewart.

REUTERS TELEVISION LTD.
40 Cumberland Avenue, London, NW10 7EH. Tel: (0171) 542 6444. FAX: (0171) 542 8568.

DIRECTOR
Enrique Jara
HEAD OF NEWS
Stephen Claypole
MANAGER, FACILITIES
Howard Barrow

REVELATION FILM GROUP
5-6 Parkside, Ravenscourt Park, Hammersmith, London. Tel: (0181) 741 2203. FAX: (0181) 741 2204.

REX ROBERTS STUDIOS LTD.
22, Glasthule Rd., Dun Laoghaire, Co. Dublin, Ireland. Tel: (3531) 808305.

RIGHT ANGLE PRODUCTIONS LTD.
31 Ransome's Dock, 35 Parkgate Rd., London, SW11 4NP. Tel: (0171) 228 9968. FAX: (0171) 223 8116. Anise Driessen.

PETER ROGER PRODUCTIONS LTD.
Pinewood Studios, Iver Heath, Bucks. 5CO ONH. Tel: (01753) 651700. FAX: (01753) 656844.
DIRECTORS
Peter Rogers
B.E. Rogers
G.E. Malyon

ROYAL SOCIETY FOR THE PROTECTION OF BIRDS (RSPB)
Film and Video Unit, The Lodge, Sandy, Beds., SG19 2DL. Tel: 01767 680551. Telex: 82469 RSPB. FAX: 01767 692365.
FILM AND VIDEO MANAGER
Colin Skevington

SR PROGRAMS INTERNATIONAL LTD.
Broadfield House, 22 Wilton Rd., Beaconsfield, Bucks. HP9 2DE. Tel: (01494) 670 100. FAX: (01494) 670 101.

SAGITTA PRODUCTIONS LTD.
c/o Pamela Gillis Management, 46 Sheldon Avenue, London, N6 4JR. Tel: (0181) 340 7868.
MANAGING DIRECTOR
John Hawkesworth

SAMUELSON FILM SERVICE LTD.
21 Derby Rd., Metropolitan Centre, Greenford, Middx., UB6 8US. Tel: (0181) 578 7887. FAX: (0181) 575 2733.
MANAGING DIRECTOR
Barry Measure

SCORES FILM & TELEVISION
44 Great Marlborough St., London, W1V 1DB. Tel: (0171) 439 0225. FAX: (0171) 734 5288.

CINEMA SEVEN PRODUCTIONS LTD.
Pinewood Studios, Iver Heath, Bucks, SL0 0NH. Tel: (01753) 651700. FAX: (01753) 652525.
DIRECTORS
Cassian Elwes
George Pappas
CONTACT
Chantal Ribeiro

SILVERBACH LAZARUS LTD.
South Bank TV Centre, Upper Ground, London, SE1 9LT. Tel: (0171) 261 1284. FAX: (0171) 633 0412. George Blaug.

SETANA STUDIOS LTD.
Ardmore Studios, Herbert Rd., Bray Co. Wicklow, Ireland. Tel: (3531) 286 2971. FAX: (3531) 286 1894. Tracey Richardson.

SKREBA FILMS LTD.
5a Noel St., London, W1V 3RB. Tel: (0171) 437 6492. FAX: (0171) 437 0644.
PRODUCERS
Ann Skinner
Simon Relph

SOVEREIGN PICTURES INC.
10 Greek Street, London, W1V 5LE. Tel: (0171) 494 1010. FAX: (0171) 494 3949. Telex: 261564 SOVE G.

SPITTING IMAGE PRODUCTIONS
4 Nice St., London, N1. Tel: (0171) 251 2626. FAX: (0171) 251 2066.
MANAGING DIRECTOR
Joanna Beresford

STRAIGHT FORWARD FILM AND TELEVISION PRODUCTIONS LTD.
Crescent Studios, 18 High Street, Holywood Co. Down BT18 9AD. Northern Ireland. Tel: 01232 427697. FAX: 01232 422289. Moya Neeson.

SUMMIT ENTERTAINMENT
18 Broadway St., London W1V 1FG. Tel: (0171) 494 1724. FAX: (0171) 494 1725. David Garrett.

SUNSET & VINE PLC
30 Sackville Street, London, WIX 1DB. Tel: (0171) 287 5700. FAX: (0171) 287 6524. Colin Frewin.

SURVIVAL ANGLIA LTD.
Anglia House, Norwich, NR1 3JG. Tel: (01603) 615151.
EXECUTIVE PRODUCER
Graham Creelman

SWIFT FILM PRODUCTIONS
1 Wool Rd., Wimbledon, London, S.W.20. Tel: (0181) 946 2040.
DIRECTOR
T. Peter Hadingham, M.B.K.S.

SWINDON CABLE LTD.
Newcome Drive, Hawksworth Estate, Swindon, SN2 1TU. Tel:
01793 615601.

TKO FILM & TELEVISION LTD.
P.O. Box 130, Hove, East Sussex, BN3 6QU. Tel: (01273)
550088. Telex: 877050. FAX: (01273) 540969.
DIRECTOR
J.S. Kruger
R. Kruger

TV CARTOONS
39 Grafton Way, London, W1P 5LA. Tel: (0171) 388 2222. FAX:
(0171) 383 4192. John Coates.

TV SALES COMPANY
3 Derby Street, Mayfair, London, WIY 7HD. Tel: (0171) 355 2868.
FAX: (0171) 495 3310. Nick Witkowski.

TVI LTD.
142 Wardour Street, London, W1V 3AU. Tel: (0171) 434 2141.
Telex: 268208. FAX: (0171) 439 3984.
MANAGING DIRECTOR
Debbie Hills

D. L. TAFFNER LTD.
10 Bedford Square, London, WC1B 3RA. Tel: (0171) 631 1184.
FAX: (0171) 636 4571.
MANAGING DIRECTOR
John Reynolds

TALBOT TELEVISION LTD.
57 Jamestown Rd., London, NWI 7DB. Tel: (0171) 284 0880.
FAX: (0171) 916 5511.
MANAGING DIRECTOR & CHIEF EXECUTIVE
David Champtaloup
CHAIRMAN
Anthony Gruner
EXECUTIVE PRODUCER
Howard Huntridge
CHIEF OF FINANCE
Susan Sharples

TELECINE
Video House, 48 Charlotte Street, London, W1P 1LX. Tel: (0171)
916 3711. FAX: (0171) 916 3700. Sian Morgan.

TELEFILM CANADA
22 Kingly Court, London, W1R 5LE. Tel: (0171) 437 8308. FAX:
(0171) 734 8586.
INTERIM DIRECTOR
Bill Niven

TELEVENTURES
19/23 Wells Street, London, W1P 3FP. Tel: (0171) 436 5720. Ray
Lewis.

THAMES TELEVISION INTERNATIONAL
Broom Rd., Teddington Lock, Teddington, Mddx TW11 9NT. Tel:
(0181) 614 2800. FAX: (0181) 943 0344.

TIGER FILM
65 Portland Rd., London W11 4LQ. Tel: (0171) 727 9810. FAX:
(0171) 243 2940.
DIRECTORS
Angela Cheyne
Carole Rousseau

TRANSATLANTIC FILMS
100 Blythe Rd., London, W14 0HE. Tel: (0171) 727 0132. FAX:
(0171) 603 5049.
MANAGING DIRECTOR
Revel Guest

TRANSWORLD INTERNATIONAL (UK) INC.
TWI House, 23 Eyot Gardens, London W6 9TR. Tel: (0181) 846
8070. FAX: (0181) 746 5334.

TURNER INTERNATIONAL
CNN House, 19-22 Rathbone Place, London, W1P 1DF. Tel:
(0171) 637 6900. FAX: (0171) 637 6713.

TWICKENHAM FILM STUDIOS LTD.
St. Margarets, Twickenham, Middlesex, TW1 2AW. Tel: (0181)
892 4477. FAX: (0181) 891 0168.
DIRECTORS
G. Humphreys
M. Landserger
N. Daou
S. J. Mullens
R. O'Donoghue

TYNE TEES ENTERPRISES LTD.
15 Bloomsbury Square, London, WC1A 2LJ. Tel: (0171) 405
8474. FAX: (0171) 242 2441.
INTERNATIONAL SALES MANAGER
Ann Gillham

UNICORN PICTURES LTD.
65 Corringway, London, W5 3HB. Tel: (0181) 998 2611.
DIRECTOR
John Simmons

UNION PICTURES
36 Marshall Street, London, W1V 1LL. Tel: (0171) 287 5100.
FAX: (0171) 287 3770.
DIRECTORS
Brad Adams
Franc Roddam
Geoff Deeham

UNITED ARTISTS PROGRAMMING
Twyman House, 16 Bonny Street, London, NW1 9PG. Tel:
(0171) 482 4824. FAX: (0171) 284 2042.
DIRECTORS
Trevor Fetter
Brian Yell
CONTACT
Paul Hudson

UNITED INTERNATIONAL PICTURES
(A subsidiary of United International Pictures B.V., Postbus
9255, 1006 AG Amsterdam, The Netherlands).
UIP House, 45 Beacon Rd., Hammersmith, London, W6 0EG.
Tel: (0181) 741 9041. Telex: 8956521. FAX: (0181) 748 8990.
PRESIDENT & CHIEF EXECUTIVE OFFICER
Michael Williams-Jones
SENIOR V.P., FINANCE & ADMINISTRATION
Peter Charles
SENIOR V.P. & GENERAL COUNSEL
Brian Reilly
SENIOR V.P., MARKETING
Hy Smith
SENIOR V.P., INTERNATIONAL SALES
Andrew Cripps
V.P., PUBLICITY
Anne Bennett
V.P., PROMOTIONS
Mark De Quervain
V.P., SALES, SPECIAL MARKETS
Michael Macclesfield
V.P. SALES, LATIN AMERICA
Michael Murphy
V.P., SALES, EUROPE
Tony Themistocleous
SENIOR EXECUTIVE/GENERAL MANAGER-PAY-TV GROUP
Andrew Kaza

UNITED TELEVISION ARTISTS LTD.
12-14 Argyll Street, London, W1V 1AB. Tel: (0171) 287 2727.
FAX: (0171) 287 5053. David Rowley.

UNITED VIDEO INTERNATIONAL
54 Warwick Square, London, SW1V 2AJ. Tel: (0171) 834 6012.

UNIVERSAL PICTURES LTD.
c/o U1P House 45 Beadon Rd., Hammersmith, London, W6
OEG. Tel: (0181) 563 4329. FAX: (0181) 563 4331.

VATV LTD.
60-62 Margaret St., London, W1N 7FJ. Tel: (0171) 636 9421.
FAX: (0171) 436 7426.

VCI PROGRAMME SALES LTD.
36-38 Caxton Way, Watford, Herts., WD1 8UF. Tel: (01923) 255
558. FAX: (01923) 817 969. Karen Chillery.

VISUAL PROGRAMME SYSTEMS LTD.
Sardinia House, 52 Lincoln's Inn Fields, London, WC2A 2LZ. Tel:
(0171) 405 0438. FAX: (0171) 831 9668. Bernard Gilinsky.

VOICE OF LONDON LTD.
245 Old Marylebone Rd., London, NW1 5RT. Tel: (0171) 402 8385.
STUDIO MANAGER
Miss Pat Smith

WALPORT INTERNATIONAL LTD.
(Subsidiary of Novo Communications), 15 Park Rd., London,
NW1 6XH. Tel: (0171) 258 3477. FAX: (0171) 723 9568.
DIRECTORS
C. Preuster
S. Campion

WARNER HOME VIDEO
135 Wardour Street, London, W1V 4AP. Tel: (0171) 494 3441.
FAX: (0171) 494 3297. Mike Heap.

WATERLOO PRODUCTIONS
1 Lower James Street, London, W1. Tel: (0171) 734 8311.

WESTCOUNTRY TELEVISION LTD.
Western Wood Way, Langage Science Park, Plymouth PL7 5BG.
Tel: (01752) 333333. FAX: (01752) 333444.

WITZEND PRODUCTIONS LTD.
6 Derby Street, Mayfair, London, W1Y 7HD. Tel: (0171) 355 2868. FAX: (0171) 629 1604.

WORLD AUDIO VISUAL ENTERTAINMENT PLC
18 Great Marlborough Street, London, W1V 1AF. Tel: (0171) 439 9596. Telex: 264036 WAVE G.

WORLDMARK PRODUCTIONS LTD.
The Old Studio, 18 Middle Row, London, W10 5AT. Tel: (0181) 960 3251. FAX: (0181) 960 6150.
DIRECTORS
Drummond Challis
David Wooster

WORLD WIDE GROUP
21-25 St. Anne's Court, London, W1V 3AW. Tel: (0171) 434 1121. FAX: (0171) 734 0619. R. King, M. Rosenbaum, C. Courtenay-Taylor.

WORLDWIDE TELEVISION NEWS
The Interchange, Oval Rd., Camden Lock, London, NW1 7EP. Tel: (0171) 410 5200. Telex: 23915. FAX: (0171) 413 8302.
MARKETING MANAGER
Lorrie Graham Morgan

WYATT CATTANEO PRODUCTIONS LTD.
Charing Cross Rd., London, WC 2. Tel: (0171) 379 6444.

YO YO FILMS LTD.
173a New Camberwell Rd., London, SE5 0TJ. Tel: (0171) 735 3711. FAX: (0171) 735 0795. Lauren C. Postma, Phillip Bartlett.

ZENITH PRODUCTIONS LTD.
43-45 Dorset Street, London, W1H 4AB. Tel: (0171) 224 2440. FAX: (0171) 224 2440.
DIRECTOR OF PRODUCTION
Scott Meek

ZOOM PRODUCTION COMPANY
102 Dean Street, London, W1V 5RA. Tel: (0171) 434 3895. FAX: (0171) 734 2751. Geraldine Flinn.

SERVICES FOR TV PRODUCERS/DISTRIBUTORS

PRODUCTION, EQUIPMENT & SUPPLIES

AGFA-GEVAERT (MOTION PICTURE DIVISION)
27 Great West Road, Brentford, Middlesex, TW8 9AX. Tel: (0181) 231 4310. FAX: ((0181)) 231 4315.
DIVISIONAL MANAGER
Ken Biggins

ACMADE INTERNATIONAL
Studio 64, Shepperton Studios, Studios Road, Shepperton, Middlesex, TW17 QD. Tel: (01932) 562 611. FAX: (01932) 568 414.

ADVANCED VIDEO HIRE LTD.
51 The Cut, London, SE1 8LF. Tel: (0171) 928 1963.

AMPEX MEDIA EUROPA
Unit 3, Commerce Park, Brunel Road, Reading, Berks, RG7 4AB. Tel: (01734) 302 208. FAX: (01734) 800 521 773.

AMSTRAD PLC
Brentwood House, 169 Kings Road, Brentwood, Essex, CM14 4EF. Tel:(01277) 228888.

AUTOCUE LTD.
265 Merton Road, London, SW18 5JS. Tel: (0181) 870 0104. FAX: (0181) 874 3726. Telex: Autocue Telexir 885039 Autocu G. Sarah Lewis, Mick Gould.

F. W. O. BAUCH LTD.
49 Theobald Street, Boreham Wood, Herts., WD6 4RZ. Tel: (0181) 953 0091. Telex: 27502. FAX: (0181) 207 5970.

R. R. BEARD LTD.
110 Trafalgar Avenue, London, SE15 6NR. Tel: (0171) 703 3136.

STUART BELL & PARTNERS LTD.
40 Frith Street, London, W1V 5TF. Tel: (0171) 439 2700.

BETTER SOUND LTD.
35 Endell Street, London, WC2. Tel: (0171) 836 0033.

CFS EQUIPMENT HIRE LTD.
10 Wadsworth Road, Perivale, Greenford, Middx., UB6 7JX. Tel: (0181) 998 2731. FAX: (0181) 997 8738.

CINESOUND INTERNATIONAL LTD.
Imperial Studios, Maxwell Road, Boreham Wood, Herts., LWD6 1WE. Tel: (0181) 953 5387. FAX: (0181) 207 1728.
DIRECTORS
Mike Rogers
Angela Marshall

CINETECHNIC LTD.
169 Oldfield Lane, Greenford, Middlesex. Tel: (0181) 578 1011. 35 Briardale Gardens, London, NW3 7PN. Tel: (0171) 435 2289.

CINEVIDEO LTD.
7 Silver Road, White City Industrial Park, Wood Lane, London, W12 7SG. Tel: (0181) 743 3839. FAX: (0181) 743 8417. Telex: 915 282 CINEGP G.

DOLBY LABORATORIES INC.
Interface Park, Wootton Bassett, Wiltshire, SN4 8QJ. Tel: (01793) 842100. FAX: (01793) 842101. Catherine Unwin.

JOE DUNTON CAMERAS LTD.
Wycombe Road, Wembley, Middlesex, HA0 1QN. Tel: (0181) 903 7933. Telex: 291843.

EDRIC AUDIO VISUAL LTD.
34-36 Oak End Way, Gerrard's Cross, Bucks, SL9 8BR. Tel: (01753) 884 646.

ENGLISH ELECTRIC VALVE COMPANY LTD.
Waterhouse Lane, Chelmsford, Essex. Tel: (01245) 493493. Telegrams: Enelectico, Chelmsford. Telex: 99103.

FAMILY CHANNEL STUDIOS
Vinters Park, Maidstone, ME14 5NZ. Tel: (01622) 691111. FAX: (01622) 684 456.

FUJI PHOTO FILM (UK) LTD.
Fuji Film House, 125 Finchley Road, London, NW3 6JH. Tel: (0171) 586 5900. FAX: (0171) 722 4259, Telex: 8812995.
DIVISIONAL MANAGER
E. J. Mould

HARKNESS HALL LTD.
Gate Studios, Station Road, Boreham Wood, Herts., WD6 1DQ. Tel: (0181) 953 3611. FAX: (0181) 207 3657.

HAYDEN LABORATORIES LTD.
Hayden House, Chiltem Hill, Chalfont St. Peter, Gerrards Cross, Bucks., SL9 9UG. Tel: (01753) 888 447. FAX: (01753) 880 109.

HENDON STUDIO
2 Victoria Road, London, NW4 2BE. Tel: (0181) 203 4206. FAX: (0181) 203 7377.

HITACHI DENSHI (UK) LTD.
13-14 Garrick Ind. Centre, Irving Way, Hendon, London, NW9 6AZ. Tel: (0181) 202 4311. FAX: (0181) 202 2451.

INTERNATIONAL VIDEO CORPORATION
10 Portman Road, Reading, Berks., RG3 1JR. Tel: (01734) 585421. Telex: 847579.

ITN LTD.
200 Gray's Inn Road, London, WC1X 8XZ. Tel: (0171) 833 3000. FAX: (0171) 430 4016. Telex: 22101.
CHIEF EXECUTIVE
Stewart Purvis

KEM ELECTRONIC LTD
24 Vivian Avenue, Hendon Central, London, NW4 3XP. Tel: (0181) 202 0244. Telex: 28303.

KODAK LTD.
Professional Motion Imaging, P.O. Box 66, Kodak House, Station Road, Hemel Hempstead, Herts., HP1 1JU. Tel: (01442) 61122. FAX: (01442) 844458.
DIRECTOR & GENERAL MANAGER
John Parsons-Smith
NATIONAL SALES MANAGER
Denis Kelly

LEE COLORTRAN LTD.
Ladbroke Hall, Barlby Rd., London, W10 5HH. Tel: (0181) 968 7000.

LEE LIGHTING
Wycombe Road, Wembley, Middlesex, HA0 1QD. Tel: (0181) 900 2900. FAX: (0181) 902 5500.

LEE FILTERS LTD.
Central Way, Walworth Industrial Estate, Andover, Hants., SP10 5AN. Tel: (01264) 66245. Telex: 477259.

LIGHTHOUSE EDITING SYSTEMS LTD.
38 Soho Square, London, W1V GLE. Tel: (0171) 494 3084. FAX: (0171) 437 3570.

LIMEHOUSE TELEVISION LTD.
The Trocadero, 19 Rupert Street, London, W1V 7FS. Tel: (0171) 287 3333. FAX: (0171) 287 1998.
Contact: A. Goddard

MARCONI COMMUNICATION SYSTEMS LTD.
Marconi House, Chelmsford, Essex, CM1 1PL. Tel: (01245) 353221.

NEILSON-HORDELL LTD.
Unit 18, Central Trading Estate, Staines, Middlesex, TW18 4XE. Tel: (01784) 456 456. FAX: (01784) 459 657.

PANASONIC BROADCAST EUROPE
117-119 Whitby Road, Slough, Berks, SL1 3DR. Tel: (01753) 692 442. FAX: (01753) 512 705.

PHOENIX VIDEO
Unit 4, Denham Way, Maple Cross, Herts., WD3 2AS. Tel: (01923) 777 782. FAX: (01923) 772 163.

RADAMEC EPO LTD.
Bridge Road, Chertsey, Surrey, KT16 8LJ. Tel: (01932) 561 181. FAX: (01932) 568 775. Telex: 929945 RADEPOG.

RANK CINTEL
Watton Road, Ware, Herts, SG12 0AE. Tel: (01895) 463 939. Telex: 81415. FAX: (01895) 460 803.
MANAGING DIRECTOR
Jack R. Brittain

RANK TAYLOR HOBSON LTD.
P.O. Box 36, 2 New Star Road, Leicester, LE4 7JQ. Tel: (01533) 763 771. Telex: 342338. Cables: Metrology Lestr. FAX: (01533) 740167.
MANAGING DIRECTOR
Richard Freeman

RECORDING & PRODUCTION SERVICES LTD.
10 Giltway, Giltbrook, Nottingham, NG16 2GN. Tel: (01602) 384 103.

PHILIP RIGBY & SONS LTD.
14 Creighton Avenue, Muswell Hill, London, N10 1NU. Tel: (0181) 883 3703. FAX: (0181) 444 3620.

RONFORD-BAKER
Braziers, Oxhey Lane, Watford, Herts., WD1 4RJ. Tel: (0181) 428 5941. FAX: (0181) 428 4743.

RONFORD LTD.
Shepperton Film Studios, P. O. 30, Studio Road, Shepperton, Middlesex, TW17 0QD. Tel: (01932) 564 111. FAX: (01932) 561 423.

SAMUELSON FILM SERVICE LONDON LTD.
21 Derby Road, Metropolitan Centre, Greenford, Middx., UB6 8UQ. Tel: (0181) 578 7887. FAX: (0181) 578 2733.

MICHAEL SAMUELSON LIGHTING LTD.
Pinewood Studios, Iver Heath, Bucks. 8LO 0NH. Tel: (01753) 631 133. FAX: (01753) 630 485.

SET PARTNERS
13 D'Arblay Street, London, W1V 3FP. Tel: (0171) 734 1067. FAX: (0171) 494 0197.

SHURE ELECTRONICS LTD.
Eccleston Road, Maidstone, Kent, ME15 6AU. Tel: (01622) 59881.

SIGMA FILM EQUIPMENT LTD.
Unit K, Chantry Lane, Industrial Estate, Storrington, West Sussex, RH20 4AD. Tel: (019066) 3382.

SONY BROADCAST LTD.
Jay Close, Viables, Basingstoke, Hants, RG22 4SB. Tel: (01256) 474 011. FAX: (01256) 474 585.

SOHO IMAGES GROUP LTD.
8-14 Meard Street, London, W1V 3HR. Tel: (0171) 437 0831. FAX: (0171) 734 9471.
MANAGING DIRECTOR
Ray Adams

STRAND LIGHTING
Grant Way, Off Syon Lane, Isleworth, Middx. TW9 5QD. Tel: (0181) 560 3171. FAX: (0181) 490 0002.

TECHNOVISION CAMERAS LTD.
Unit 4, St. Margaret's Business Centre, Drummond Place, Twickenham, Middlesex, TW1 1JN. Tel: (0181) 891 5961. Telex: 917408 TECNOV G. FAX: (0181) 744 1154.

VARIAN TUT LTD.
P.O. Box 41, Coldhams Lane, Cambridge, CB1 3JU. Tel: (01223) 245 115. Telex: 81342. VARTUT G.. FAX: (01223) 214 632.

VIDEO TIME
22/24 Greek Street, London, W1V 5LG. Tel: (0171) 439 1211. Telex: 27256. FAX: (0171) 439 7336.

VIEWPLAN
1 Syon Gateway, Great West Road, Brentford, Middx., TW8 9DD. Tel: (0181) 847 5771.

VINTEN BROADCAST
Western Way, Bury St. Edmunds, Suffolk, IP33 3TB. Tel: (01284) 752 121. Telex: 81176 VINTEN G. FAX: (01284) 750 560.

WESTAR SALES & SERVICES LTD.
Unit 7, Cowley Mill Trading Estate, Longbridge Way, Uxbridge, Middx., UB8 2YG. Tel: (01895) 34429. Telex: 8954169.

ZONAL LTD.
Holmethorpe Avenue, Redhill, Surrey, RH1 2NX. Tel: (01737) 767 171. FAX: (01737) 767 610.

MUSIC LIBRARIES-FACILITIES

ABBEY ROAD STUDIOS
3 Abbey Road, St. John's Wood, London NW8 9AY. Tel: (0171) 286 1161. FAX: (0171) 289 7527.

BOOSEY & HAWKES MUSIC PUBLISHERS LIMITED
295 Regent Street, London, W1R 8JH. Tel: (0171) 580 2060. Telex: 8954613 Boosey G.

BOURNE MUSIC LTD.
34/36 Maddox Street, London, W1R 9PD. Tel: (0171) 493 6412 and 6583.

C.T.S. STUDIOS LTD.
Engineers Way, Wembley, Middlesex, HA9 0DR. Tel: (0181) 903 4611. FAX: (0181) 903 7130.

DE WOLFE LTD.
80-88 Wardour Street, London, W1V 3LF. Tel: (0171) 439 8481.

EMI MUSIC LTD.
30 Gloucester Place, London, W1A 1ES.

FILM BOOKING OFFICES, LTD.
(Film Library Ltd.)
211 The Chambers, Chelsea Harbour, London, SW10 0XF. Tel: (0171) 437 1572.

MOZART EDITION (GREAT BRITAIN) LTD.
c/o Somerset and Co., 19 Woburn Place, London, WC1H 0LV. Tel: (0171) 278 3615.

MUSIC SALES LTD.
8-9 Frith Street, London, W1V 5TZ. Tel: (0171) 434 0066.

PEER INTERNATIONAL LIBRARY LTD.
8 Denmark Street, London, WC2H 8LT. Tel: (0171) 836 4524.

POLYGRAM MUSIC VIDEO
Unit 6, Castle Row, Horticultural Place, Chiswick, London, W4 4JQ. Tel: (0181) 994 6840.

PORTLAND RECORDING STUDIOS LTD.
35 Portland Place, London, W1N 3AG. Tel: (0171) 637 2111/4.

REUTERS TELEVISION LTD.
40 Cumberland Avenue, London, NW10 7EH. Tel: (0171) 510 4978. FAX: (0171) 510 4978.

SOUTHERN LIBRARY OF RECORDED MUSIC LTD.
8 Denmark Street, London, WC2H 8LT. Tel: (0171) 836 4524.

SOHO IMAGES GROUP LTD.
8-14 Meard Street, London, W1V 3HR. Tel: (0171) 437 0831. FAX: (0171) 734 9471.

THAMES TELEVISION
(Library Sales)
Teddington Studios, Teddington Lock, Teddington, Middlesex, TW11 9NT. Tel: (0181) 614 2800. FAX: (0181) 614 2964.

JOSEF WEINBERGER LTD.
12-14 Mortimer Street, London, W1N 8EL. Tel: (0171) 580 2827. (Representing Telemusic Library, France.)

JOHN WOOD SOUND LTD.
St. Martin's Studios, Greenbank Road, Ashton-upon-Mersey Sale, Cheshire, M33 5PN. Tel: (0161) 905 2077. FAX: (0161) 905 2382.

ZOMBA MUSIC SERVICES
Zomba House, 165-167 High Road, Willesden, London, NW10 2SG. Tel: (0181) 459 8899. Telex: 919884. FAX: (0181) 451 3900.

FILM LABORATORIES & VIDEO SERVICES

BUCKS MOTION PICTURE LABORATORIES LTD.
714 Banbury Avenue, Slough, Berks., SL1 4LH. Tel: (01753) 576 611. FAX: (01753) 691 762. Harry Rushton, Mike Bianchi.

COLOUR FILM SERVICES LTD.
22-25 Portman Close, Baker Street, London, W1A 4BE. Tel: (0171) 486 2881. Telex: 24672. and 10 Wadsworth Road, Perivale, Greenford, Middx., UB6 7JX. Tel: (0181) 998 2731.

FILMATIC LABORATORIES LTD.
16 Colville Road, London, W11 2BS. Tel: (0171) 221 60181. FAX: (0171) 229 2718.
CHAIRMAN & MANAGING DIRECTOR
D. L. Gibbs
ASSISTANT MANAGING DIRECTOR
I. Magowan

HALLIFORD STUDIOS
Manygate Lane, Shepperton, Middlesex. Tel: (01932) 226 341. FAX: (01932) 246 336.
STUDIO MANAGER
Allan d'Aguiar

METROCOLOR LONDON LTD.
22 Soho Square, London, W1V 5FL. Tel: (0171) 437 7811. 91/95 Gillespie Road, Highbury, London, N.5 1LS. Tel: (0171) 226 4422. FAX: (0171) 359 2353.
MANAGING DIRECTOR
K. B. Fraser

PORTLAND RECORDING STUDIOS LTD.
35 Portland Place, London, W1N 3AG. Tel: (0171) 637 2111.

RANK FILM LABORATORIES LTD.
Denham, Uxbridge, Middlesex, UB9 5HQ. Tel: (01895) 832 323. Telex: 934704. FAX: (01895) 833 617.
MANAGING DIRECTOR
T. A. McCurdie
DIRECTOR OF SALES
David Dowler

SOHO IMAGES GROUP LTD.
8-14 Meard Street, London, W1V 3HR. Tel: (0171) 437 0831. FAX: (0171) 734 9471.
MANAGING DIRECTOR
Ray Adams

TECHNICOLOR LTD.
Bath Road, West Drayton, Middx., UB7 0DB. Tel: (0181) 759 5432. FAX: (0181) 897 2666.
MANAGING DIRECTOR
Ashley Hopkins

TWICKENHAM FILM STUDIOS, LTD.
St. Margarets, Twickenham, Middlesex, TW1 2AW. Tel: (0181) 892 4477. FAX: (0181) 891 0168.

UNITED MOTION PICTURES (LONDON) LTD.
3 and 36/38 Fitzroy Square, London, W.1. Tel: (0171) 580 1171 and (0171) 388 1234.

WORLD WIDE GROUP
21-25, St. Anne's Court, London, W1V 3AW. Tel: (0171) 434 1121. Telex: 269271. FAX: (0171) 734 0619.

RECORDING STUDIOS

ABBEY ROAD STUDIOS
3 Abbey Road, St. John's Wood, London, NW8 9AY. Tel: (0171) 286 1161. FAX: (0171) 289 7527.

ADVISION SOUND STUDIOS
23 Gosfield Street, London, W1P 7HB. Tel: (0171) 580 5707. Telex: 28668. FAX: (0171) 631 1457.

AIR STUDIOS
214 Oxford Street, London, W.1. Tel: (0171) 637 2758.

EAMONN ANDREWS STUDIOS LTD.
The Television Club, 46/48 Harcourt Street, Dublin, Ireland. Tel: (3531) 758891.

ANVIL FILM & RECORDING GROUP LTD.
Denham Studios, North Orbital Road, Denham, Nr. Uxbridge, Middx., UB9 5HL. Tel: (01895) 833 522. Telex: 934704. FAX: (01895) 835 006. R. W. Keen, K. Somerville, Alan Snelling.

AUDIO INTERNATIONAL RECORDING STUDIOS LTD.
18 Rodmarton Street, London, W1H 3FW. Tel: (0171) 486 6466.

CBS RECORDING STUDIOS
CBS Records, 31-37 Whitfield Street, London, W1P 5RE. Tel: (0171) 636 3434.

CINE-LINGUAL SOUND STUDIOS LTD.
27-27 Berwick Street, London, W1V 3RF. Tel: (0171) 437 0136. FAX: (0171) 439 2012.

CINESOUND EFFECTS LIBRARY LTD.
Imperial Studios, Maxwell Road, Elstree Way, Boreham Wood, Herts., WD6 IWE. Tel: (0181) 953 5837 and 5545, 4904, 1587. FAX: (0181) 207 1728. Mike Rogers or Angela Marshall.

C.T.S. STUDIOS LTD.
Engineer's Way, Wembley, Middlesex, HA9 0DR. Tel: (0181) 903 4611. FAX: (0181) 903 7130. Adrian Kerridge.

DE LANE LEA SOUND CENTRE
75 Dean Street, London, W1V 5HA. Tel: (0171) 439 0913. FAX: (0171) 437 0913. Richard Paynter.

DELTA SOUND SERVICES LTD.
Shepperton Studio Centre, Squires Bridge Road, Shepperton, Middx., TW17 0QD. Tel: (019328) 62045.

MOTIVATION SOUND LTD.
(Voice-over Recording Studios)
35a Broadhurst Gardens, London, NW6 3QT. Tel: (0171) 624 7785.

NATIONAL SCREEN
15 Wadsworth Road, Greenford, Middlesex. Tel: (0181) 998 2851. 2 Wedgwood Mews, 12-13 Greek Street, London, W1V 5LE. Tel: (0171) 437 4851-6.

NEW CENTRAL FILM SERVICES LTD.
97-99 Dean Street, London W.1. Tel: (0171) 734 5827-8.

PORTLAND RECORDING STUDIOS LTD.
35 Portland Place, London, W1N 3AG. Tel: (0171) 637 2111.

RANK FILM LABORATORIES LTD.
Denham, Uxbridge, Middlesex, UB9 5HQ. Tel: (01895) 832 323. FAX: (01895) 833 617
MANAGING DIRECTOR
T. A. McCurdie
DIRECTOR OF SALES
David Dowler

SHEPPERTON STUDIO CENTRE
Studios Road, Shepperton, Middx., TW17 0QD. Tel: (01932) 562 611. FAX: (01932) 568 989. Telex: 929416 MOVIES G. Paul Olliver.

SOHO IMAGES GROUP LTD.
8-14 Meard Street, London, W1V 3HR. Tel: (0171) 437 0831. FAX: (0171) 734 9471.
MANAGING DIRECTOR
Ray Adams

UNITED MOTION PICTURES (LONDON) LTD.
Boston House, 36/38 Fitzroy Square, London, W.1. Tel: (0171) 580 1171.

W.F.S. (FILM FACILITIES) LTD.
153 Wardour Street, London, W1V 3TB. Tel: (0171) 437 5532.

JOHN WOOD SOUND LTD.
St. Martin's Studios, Greenbank Road, Ashton-upon-Mersey, Sale, Cheshire, M33 5PN. Tel: (0161) 905 2077. FAX: (0161) 905 2383. John Wood.

WORLD WIDE GROUP
21-25 St. Anne's Court, London, W1V 3AW. Tel: (0171) 434 1121. FAX: (0171) 734 0619.

PRODUCTION SERVICES/FACILITIES

AKA FILM SERVICES LTD.
60 Farringdon Road, London EC1R 3BP. Tel: (0171) 251 3885.

ANVIL POST PRODUCTION LTD.
Denham Studios, North Orbital Road, Denham, Uxbridge, Middx., UB9 5HL. Tel: (01895) 833522. Telex: 934704. FAX: (01895) 835006.

PRODUCTION
R. W. Keen
SOUND, POST PRODUCTION
Ken Somerville
C. Eng. M.I.E.R.E.
Alan Snelling

BARRY WESTWOOD PRODUCTIONS
231 West Street, Fareham, Hants., PO16 0HZ. Tel: (01329) 285 941.

CAMERA EFFECTS
8-11 Bateman Street, London W.1. Tel: (0171) 437 9377.

CENTRAL TELEVISION FACILITIES
Central House Broad Street, Birmingham, B1 2JP. Tel: (0121) 643 9898. FAX: (0121) 633 4473.

CHERRILL, ROGER LTD.
65-66 Dean Street, London, W1V 6PL. Tel: (0171) 437 7972. FAX: (0171) 437 6411.

CINEBUILD LTD.
1 Wheatsheaf Hall, Wheatsheaf Lane, London S.W.8. Tel: (0171) 582 8750. Telex: 943763 Crocom G Cinebuild.

CINEVIDEO LTD.
7 Silver Road, White City Industrial Park, Wood Lane, London, W12 7SG. Tel: (0181) 743 3839. Telex: 915 282 CINEGP G. FAX: (0181) 749 3501.

CLAPP, NIKKI
18 Cresswell Road, East Twickenham, Middx., TW1 2DZ. Tel: (0181) 891 0054.

COLOUR FILM SERVICES LTD.
22-25 Portman Close, Baker Street, London, W1A 4BE. Tel: (0171) 486 2881. Telex: 24672. FAX: (0171) 486 4152.

COMBINED PRINTS & PRODUCTION SERVICE LTD.
65-66 Dean Street, London, W1V 5HD. Tel: (0171) 437 7972. FAX: (0171) 437 6411.

COMPLETE VIDEO
3 Slingsby Place, London, WC2E 9AB. Tel: (0171) 379 7739.

COMPONENT GROUP
1 Newman Passage, London, W1P 3PF. Tel: (0171) 631 4400. FAX: (0171) 580 2890.

CROW FILM & TV SERVICES LTD.
12 Wendell Road, London, W12 9RT. Tel: (0181) 749 6171. FAX: (0181) 740 0785.

DIGITAL FILM
5 D'Arblay Street, London, W1V 3FD. Tel: (0171) 434 3100. FAX: (0171) 287 3191. Matthew Holben.

EDINBURGH FILM & TV STUDIOS
Nine Mile Burn, by Penicuik, Midlothian, EH 26 9LT. Tel: Penicuik 01968 72131.

EDIT ART POST PRODUCTION
86 Wardour Street, London, W1V 3LF. Tel: (0171) 734 8966.

EDIT 142
5th Floor, 142 Wardour Street, London W.1. Tel: (0171) 439 7934.

THE FRAME SHOP
33 Great Pulteney Street, London, W1R 3DE. Tel: (0171) 439 1267. FAX: (0171) 439 0129.

FRONTLINE TELEVISION SERVICES
44 Earlham Street Covent Garden, London, WC2H 9LA. Tel: (0171) 836 0411. FAX: (0171) 379 5210.

FOUNTAIN TELEVISION
Cocks Crescent, New Malden, Surrey, KT3 4TA. Tel: (0181) 942 6633. FAX: (0181) 949 7911.

CHARLES H. FOX LTD.
22 Tavistock Street, Covent Garden, London WC2E 7PY. Tel: (0171) 240 3111.

GENERAL SCREEN ENTERPRIZES
Highbridge Estate, Oxford Road, Uxbridge, Middlesex, UB8 1LX. Tel: (01895) 231 931. FAX: (01895) 235 335.

HAMLET TELEVISION LTD.
28 Denmark Street, London, WC2H 8NJ. Tel: (0171) 240 9(0181). FAX: (0171) 836 5358.

INFOVISION LTD.
Bradley Close, White Lion Street, London, N1 9PN. Tel: (0171) 837 0012. Telex: 299800 ACTION.

ISLAND FILMS/EDITING
22 St. Peter's Square, London, W6 9NW. Tel: (0181) 741 1511.

KAUFMAN, MIKE (POST PRODUCTIONS) LTD.
80-82 Wardour Street, London, W1V 3LF. Tel: (0171) 734 8335. Telex: 264864 Answerback MKPPLN G.

LWT PRODUCTION FACILITIES
South Bank TV Centre, London, SE1 9LT. Tel: (0171) 261 3683. Telex: 91823. Derek Chason.

LEGEND TELEVISION
Pinewood Studios, Pinewood Road, Iver Heath. Bucks. SL0 0NH. Tel: (01753) 656 027. FAX: (01753) 656 028.

LIMEHOUSE TELEVISION LTD.
The Trocadero, 19 Rupert Street, London, W1V 7FS. Tel: (0171) 287 3333. FAX: (0171) 287 1998.
Contact: A. Goddard

LOUIS ELMAN + LEAH INTERNATIONAL PRODUCTIONS LTD.
Denham Studios, Denham, Nr. Uxbridge, Middlesex. Tel: (01895) 833 036, (01895) 853 522. Telex: 934704.

METRO VIDEO
The Old Bacon Factory, 57-59 Great Suffolk Street, London, SE1 0BS. Tel: (0171) 929 2088.

MILLS, PETER FILM EDITING LTD.
75 Dean Street, London, W1V 5HA. Tel: (0171) 437 3003 & (0171) 439 1721.

MOLINARE
34 Fouberts Place, London, W1V 2BH. Tel: (0171) 439 2244. FAX: (0171) 734 6813. Telex: 299200 MOLI G.

NORWOOD STUDIOS LTD.
147 Victoria Road, Leeds, LS6 1DU. Tel: (01532) 787539. (For rushes-35mm and 16mm optical and mags.)

N S & H CREATIVE PARTNERSHIP
13 John Street, London, W.C.1. Tel: (0171) 405 2324.

OASIS TELEVISION LTD.
76a Wardour Street, London, W1V 3LF. Tel: (0171) 434 4133. FAX: (0171) 494 2843.

ONE INCH VIDEO COMPANY
11/13 Neal's Yard, Covent Garden, London, WC2H 9LZ. Tel: (0171) 831 1900. FAX: (0171) 836 0914. Telex: 22125 VIDEO G.

PMPP FACILITIES
(Formerly Paul Miller Post Production)
69 Dean Street (Entrance Meard Street), London, W1V 5HB. Tel: (0171) 437 0979.

PEERLESS CAMERA CO.
15 Neals Yard, London, WC2H 9DP. Tel: (0171) 836 3367.

PLATYPUS FILMS LTD.
9 Grape Street, London, WC2H 8DR. Tel: (0171) 240 0351.

POST HOUSE (POST PRODUCTIONS) LTD.
12 D'Arblay Street, London, W1V 3FP. Tel: (0171) 439 1705/6/7.

PRATER AUDIO VISUAL LTD.
7A College Approach, Greenwich, London, SE10 9HY. Tel: (0181) 858 8939. FAX: (0181) 305 1537.

RANK VIDEO SERVICES LTD.
Phoenix Park, Great West Road, Brentford, Middlesex, TW8 9PL. Tel: (0181) 568 4311. Telex: 22345. FAX: 091 847 4032.
MANAGING DIRECTOR
Peter Pacitt

REALITY POST PRODUCTION LTD.
15 Kingly Court, London, W1R 5LE. Tel: (0171) 287 3812. FAX: (0171) 734 1592.

REUTERS TELEVISION LTD.
40 Cumberland Avenue, London, NW10 7EN. Tel: (0181) 965 7733. FAX: (0181) 965 0620.
DIRECTOR
Enrique Jara

RUSHES
66 Old Compton Street, London, W1V 5PH. Tel: (0171) 437 8676. FAX: (0171) 734 2519.

SVC TELEVISION
142 Wardour Street, London, W1V 5PH. Tel: (0171) 734 1600. FAX: (0171) 437 1854.

SAMUELSON COMMUNICATIONS BROADCAST
Unit 20, Fairway Drive, Fairway Industrial Estate, Greenford, Middx., UB6 8PW. Tel: (0181) 566 6444. FAX: (0181) 566 6365.

SET PARTNERS
13 D'Arblay Street, London, W1V 3FP. Tel: (0171) 734 1067. FAX: (0171) 494 0197.

SOLUS ENTERPRISES
35 Marshall Street, London, W1V 1LL. Tel: (0171) 734 0645 and (0171) 734 3384/5.

SPITFIRE TELEVISION PLC
19 Hatton Street, London, NW8 8PR. Tel: (0171) 724 7544. FAX: (0171) 724 2058.

TABS
63 Stirling Court, Marshall Street, London W.1. Tel: (0171) 734 3356/7. Janet Easton.
(Specialities: Technicians answering and booking service.)

TATTOOIST INTERNATIONAL LTD.
9 Lyme Steet, London N.W.1. Tel: (0171) 267 0242/3.

TELEVISUAL LTD.
58 Kew Road, Richmond, Surrey, TW9 2PQ. Tel: (0181) 940 1155.

THAMES TELEVISION PLC
Broon Road, Teddington Lock, Teddington, Middx.: TW11 9NT. Tel: (0181) 614 2800.

VIDEO EUROPE
31 Ransome's Dock, Parkgate Road, Battersea, London, SW11 4NP. Tel: (0171) 585 0555.

VIDEO ROOM
155-157 Oxford Street, London, W1R 1TB. Tel: (0171) 434 0724.

WSTV PRODUCTION LTD.
159-163 Great Portland Street, London, W1N 5FD. Tel: (0171) 580 5896. (Video tape and TV production, TV commercials).

WEST 1 TELEVISION
10 Bateman Street, London, W1V 5TT. Tel: (0171) 437 5533. FAX: (0171) 287 8621.

WETFORD FILMS LTD.
Wetford Lodge, 163 Nightingale Lane, London S.W.12. Tel: (0181) 675 1333.

WOLFF PRODUCTIONS
6a Noel Street, London, W1V 3RB. Tel: (0171) 439 1838.

WOOD, PATRICK FILM SERVICES
13 South Road, Amersham, Bucks. Tel: (01494) 724 941.

WORLD WIDE GROUP
21-25 St. Anne's Court, London, W1V 3AV. Tel: (0171) 434 1121. Telex: 269271. FAX: (0171) 734 0619.

TITLING-SPECIAL EFFECTS

CASEY'S FILM AND VIDEO
Unit 9, Mitre Bridge, Industrial Park, Mitre Way, (Off Scrubs Lane) London, W10 6AV. Tel: (0181) 960 0123. FAX: (0181) 969 3714.

CINE-SOUND EFFECTS LTD.
(Soundefex Ltd., Lansdowne Vaults Ltd.) Imperial Studios, Maxwell Road Elstree Way, Boreham Wood, Herts. Tel: (0181) 953 5837. FAX: (0181) 207 1728.

ELECTROCRAFT CONSULTANTS LTD.
Sales Office and Works: Liss Mill, Mill Road, Liss, Hants. Tel: (01730) 893 444.

FILMTEXT LTD.
37 Kew Road, Richmond Surrey, TW9 2NQ. Tel: (0181) 940 5034.

GENERAL SCREEN ENTERPRISES
97 Oxford Road, Uxbridge, Middx. Tel: (01895) 31931. FAX: (01895) 35335.

METROCOLOR LONDON LTD.
91/95 Gillespie Road, Highbury, London, N5 1LS. Tel: (0171) 226 4422.
22 Soho Square, London, W1V 5FL. Tel: (0171) 437 7811. FAX: (0171) 359 2353.

NATIONAL SCREEN
15 Wadsworth Road, Greenford, Middlesex, UB6 7JN. Tel: (0181) 998 2851.
2 Wedgwood Mews, Greek Street, London, W1V 5LE. Tel: (0171) 437 4851. FAX: (0181) 997 0840.

RANK FILM LABORATORIES LTD.
North Orbital Road, Denham Uxbridge, Middlesex, UB9 5HQ. Tel: (01895) 832 323. Telex: 832323. FAX: (01895) 833 617.
MANAGING DIRECTOR
T. A. McCurdie
DIRECTOR OF SALES
David Dowler

SOHO IMAGES GROUP LTD.
8-14 Meard Street London, W1V 3HR. Tel: (0171) 437 0831. FAX: (0171) 734 9471.
MANAGING DIRECTOR
Ray Adams

TECHNICOLOR LTD.
(Subsidiary of Carlton Communications Plc.) Bath Road, West Drayton, Middlesex, UB7 0DB5. Tel: (0181) 759 5432. Telegraphic and Cable Address: Technicolor, West Drayton. FAX: (0181) 897 2666.

UNIVERSAL FILM LABORATORY LTD.
Braintree Road, Ruislip, Middlesex. Tel: (0181) 841 5101.

STUDIOS

ARDMORE STUDIOS LTD.
Herbert Road, Bray, Co. Wicklow, Ireland. Tel: (0404) 416 2971. Telex: 91504 PAI I E1. FAX: (0404) 416 1894.

BRAY STUDIOS
Windsor Road, Windsor, Berks SL4. Tel: (01628) 22111. FAX: (01628) 770381. (4 stages, total 23,600 sq. ft. All depts. theatre, workshops, bar and catering.)

CAPITAL GROUP STUDIOS
13 Wandsworth Plain, London, SW18 1ET. Tel: (0181) 874 0131. FAX: (0181) 871 9737. (Central London, fully-equipped broadcast standard TV studio. Post-production. B.T.Line. Telecine.)

CENTRAL TELEVISION STUDIOS
Lenton Lane, Nottingham NG7 2NA. Tel: (01602) 863 322. FAX: (01602) 435 142. Nic Beeby, Cynthia Jones.

EALING STUDIOS
Ealing Green, Ealing, London, W5 5EP. Tel: (0181) 567 6655. FAX: (0181) 758 8579. Bernie Pearson.

FOUNTAIN TELEVISION
128 Wembley Park Drive, Wembley, Middlesex HA9 8HQ. Tel: (0181) 900 1188. FAX: (0181) 900 2860. Brianan Dolan.

HALLIFORD FILM STUDIOS LTD.
Manygate Lane, Shepperton, Middlesex, TW17 9EG. Tel: (01932) 226 341. FAX: (01932) 246 336.
STUDIO MANAGER
Allan d'Aguiar

HAMPDEN GURNEY STUDIOS LTD.
39/41 Hanover Steps, St. George's Fields, Albion Street, London, W2 2YG. Tel: (0171) 402 7543. FAX: (0171) 262 5736. Telex: 896559 GECOMS G.

HILLSIDE STUDIOS
Merry Hill Road, Bushey, Watford WD2 1DR. Tel: (0181) 950 7919. FAX: (0181) 950 1437. Dave Hillier.

LIMEHOUSE STUDIOS
The Trocadero, 19 Rupert Street, London, W1V 7FS. Tel: (0171) 287 3333. FAX: (0171) 287 1998. A. Goddard.

THE LONDON STUDIOS
The London Television Centre, Upper Ground, London SE1 9LT. Tel: (0171) 737 8888. FAX: (0171) 928 8405.

PARAMOUNT CITY TV THEATRE
Great Windmill Street, London, W1V 7PH. Tel: (0171) 722 8111. FAX: (0171) 483 4264. Andrew Jones.

PINEWOOD STUDIOS
Iver Bucks., SL0 0NH. Tel: (01753) 651 700. FAX: (01753) 656 844. (18 stages, exterior lot and largest outdoor tank in Europe. sound and projection department. 5 theatres, 60 cutting rooms.)
MANAGING DIRECTOR
Steve Jaggs

PROSPECT STUDIOS LTD.
High Street, Barnes, London, S.W.13. Tel: (0181) 876 6284/5.

REEL TV STUDIOS
19 Derry's Cross, Plymouth, PL1 2SP. Tel: (01752) 255529. FAX: (01752) 255531. Tim Watson.

SHEPPERTON STUDIOS
Studios Road, Shepperton, Middlesex, TW17 0QD. Tel: (01932) 562611. FAX: (01932) 568989. Paul Olliver.

TEDDINGTON STUDIOS
Broom Road, Teddington Lock, Middx., TW11 9NT. Tel: (0181) 977 3252. FAX: (0181) 943 4050. Steve Gunn.

TWICKENHAM
(Owned by Twickenham Film Studios, Ltd.), St. Margaret's, Twickenham, Middlesex, TW1 2AW. Tel: (0181) 892 4477. FAX: (0181) 891 0168. (Three stages, two dubbing theatres, one ADR/Foley theatre, 40 cutting rooms. Lightworks-Avid-35/16mm.)
EXECUTIVE DIRECTOR
G. Humphreys

JOHN WOOD SOUND LTD.
St. Martin's Studios, Greenbank Road, Ashton-upon-Mersey, Sale, Cheshire, M33 5PN. Tel: (0161) 905 2077. FAX: (0161) 905 2383. John Wood.

WORLD WIDE GROUP
21-25 St. Anne's Court, London, W1V 3AW. Tel: (0171) 434 1121. FAX: (0171) 734 0619.

NEWS FILM SERVICE

BRITISH MOVIETONEWS LTD.
North Orbital Road, Denham, Nr. Uxbridge, Middx. UB9 5HQ.
Tel: (01895) 833 0171. FAX: (01895) 834893.
MANAGING DIRECTOR
Barry S. Florin
LIBRARIAN
Barbara Heavens

CBS NEWS
100 Brompton Road, London S.W.3. Tel: (0171) 584 3366.

CCL NEWS & FEATURES
87 Charlotte Street, London, W1P 1LB. Tel: (0171) 631 5424.
Telex: 266685 CCLLDN.

CNN INTERNATIONAL
19-22 Rathbone Place, London, W1P 1DF. Tel: (0171) 637 6800.
FAX: (0171) 637 6868.
MANAGING DIRECTOR
Mark Rudolph

CHANNEL NINE AUSTRALIA INC.
(Television New Zealand News)
31-36 Foley Street, London, W1P 7LB. Tel: (0171) 636 0036.
FAX: (0171) 636 9041.

ITN LTD.
200 Gray's Inn Road, London, WC1X 8XZ. Tel: (0171) 833 3000.
FAX: (0171) 430 4016. Telex: 22101.
CHIEF EXECUTIVE
Stewart Purvis
EDITOR-IN-CHIEF
Richard Tait

NBC NEWS WORLDWIDE INC.
8 Bedford Avenue, London W.C.1. Tel: (0171) 637 8655.

REUTERS TELEVISION LTD.
40 Cumberland Avenue, London, NW10 7EH. Tel: (0181) 965
7733. FAX: (0181) 965 0620.
DIRECTOR
Enrique Jara

WORLDWIDE ENTERTAINMENT NEWS
140 Wardour Street, London, W1V 3AV. Tel: (0171) 287 4545.
FAX: (0171) 287 3728. Tom Gutteridge, John Needham.

WORLDWIDE TELEVISION NEWS
The Interchange, Oval Road, Camden Lock, London, NW1 7EP.
Tel: (0171) 413 8302. Telex: 23915. FAX: (0171) 413 8302.
MARKETING MANAGER
Lorrie Grabham Morgan

COSTUME SUPPLIERS

ANGELS & BERMANS
119 Shaftesbury Avenue, London, WC2H 8AE. Tel: (0171) 836
5678. FAX: (0171) 240 9527.
40 Camden Street, London, NW1 0EN. Tel: (0171) 387 0999.
FAX: (0171) 383 5603. Tim Angel, Ron Mawbey, Richard Green.

ARMS & ARCHERY
The Coach House, London Road, Ware Herts, SG12 9QV. Tel:
(01920) 460335. FAX: (01920) 461044. Terry Gouldon.

COSPROP LTD.
26-28 Rochester Place, London, NW1 9JR. Tel: (0171) 485
6731. FAX: (0171) 485 5942. Bernie Chapman.

THE COSTUME STUDIO
6 Penton Grove, Off White Lion Street, London, N1 9HS. Tel:
(0171) 388 4481. FAX: (0171) 837 5326. Rupert Clive, Richard
Dudley.

CARLO MANZI RENTALS
32-33 Liddell Road, London, NW6 2EW. Tel: (0171) 625 6391.
FAX: (0171) 625 5386.

LEADING ADVERTISING AGENCIES

Source: Campaign

ABBOT MEAD VICKERS BBDO
191 Old Marylebone Road, London, NW1 5DW. Tel: (0171) 402
4100.

AMMIRATI & PURIS/LINTAS
84 Eccleston Sq., London SW1V 1PX. Tel: (0171) 932 8888.

BATES DORLAND
121-141 Westbourne Terrace, London, W2 6JR. Tel: (0171) 262
5077.

BMP DDB NEEDHAM
12 Bishop's Bridge Rd., London W2 6AA. Tel: (0171) 258 3979.

D M B & B
123 Buckingham Palace Rd., London SW1W 9D2. Tel: (0171)
630 0000.

GREY ADVERTISING
215-227 Great Portland St., Lodnon W1N 5HD. Tel: (0171) 636
3399.

LOWE HOWARD-SPINK
Bowater House, Knightsbridge, London, SW1X 7LT. Tel: (0171)
584 5033.

OGILVY AND MATHER
10 Cabot Square, Canary Wharf, London, E14 4QB. Tel: (0171)
345 3000.

SAATCHI AND SAATCHI
80 Charlotte Street, London, W1A 1AQ. Tel: (0171) 636 5060.

J WALTER THOMPSON
40 Berkeley Square, London W1X 6AD. Tel: (0171) 499 4040

FINANCIAL SERVICES AND FUNDING

BARCLAYS BANK PLC
The Media Section, Barclays Business Centre, 27 Soho Square,
London, W1A 4WA. Tel: (0171) 439 6851. FAX: (0171) 434 9035.

BRITISH SCREEN FINANCE LTD.
14-17 Wells Street, London, W1P 3FL. Tel: (0171) 323 9080.
Telex: 888694 BRISCR G. FAX: (0171) 323 0092.

COMPLETION BOND COMPANY INC.
Pinewood Studios, Iver Heath, Bucks., SL0 0NH. Tel: (01753)
652 433. Telex: 849003 CPLBND G. FAX: (01753) 655 697.

CONSOLIDATED ARTISTS
Strachans Somerville, Phillips Street, St. Helier, Jersey, Channel
Islands. Tel: (01534) 71505. FAX: (01534) 23902.

CONTRACTS INTERNATIONAL LTD.
13-14 Golden Square, London, W1R 3AG. Tel: (0171) 287 5800.
FAX: (0171) 287 3779. Telex: 295835.

DISTANT HORIZON
4th Floor, 17 Great Cumberland Place, London, W1H 7LA. Tel:
(0171) 724 3440. Telex: 917354 PROTAC G.

ERNST & YOUNG
Beckett House, 1 Lambeth Palace Road, London, SE1 7EU. Tel:
(0171) 928 2000. FAX: (0171) 401 2136.

EUROPEAN SCRIPT FUND
39c Highbury Place, London, N5 1QP. Tel: (0171) 226 9903.

FILM FINANCES LTD.
1/11 Hay Hill, Berkeley Square, London, W1X 7LF. Tel: (0171)
629 6557. FAX: (0171) 491 7530.

FILM TRUSTEES LTD.
Swan House, 52 Poland Street, London, W1V 3DF. Tel: (0171)
439 8541. FAX: (0171) 495 3223. Telex: 23788.

GENERAL ENTERTAINMENT INVESTMENTS
65-67 Ledbury Road, London, W11 2AD. Tel: (0171) 221 3512.
Telex: 28604. FAX: (0932) 868 989.

GUARANTORS INTERNATIONAL INC.
5 Carlton Gardens, Pall Mall, London, SW1Y 5AD. Tel: (0171)
839 9355. FAX: (0171) 839 1774.

GUINNESS MAHON & CO. LTD.
32 St. Mary at Hill, London, EC3P 3AJ. Tel: (0171) 623 9333.
FAX: (0171) 283 4811.

INTERNATIONAL COMPLETION INC.
Pinewood Studios, Pinewood Road, Iver Heath, Bucks SL0
0NH. Tel: (01753) 651 700. FAX: (01753) 656 564.

J & M ENTERTAINMENT
2 Dorset Square, London, NW1 6PU. Tel: (0171) 723 6544. FAX:
(0171) 724 7541.

KMPG PEAT MARWICK
1 Puddle Dock, Blackfriars, London, EC4V 3PD. Tel: (0171) 236
8000. FAX: (0171) 248 6552.

PARMEAD INSURANCE BROKERS LTD.
Lyon House, 160-166 Borough High Street, London, SE1 1JR.
Tel: (0181) 467 8656. FAX: (0181) 295 1659.

PERFORMANCE GUARANTEES LTD.
66 Munster Road, London, SW6 4EP. Tel: (0181) 731 7314. FAX:
(0181) 736 2462.

PIERSON, BELDRING & PIERSON
99 Gresham Street, London, EC2V 7PH. Tel: (0171) 696 0500.
FAX: (0171) 600 1732. Telex: 885119.

PRODUCTION PROJECTS FUND
BFI, 29 Rathbone Place, London, WIP 1AG. Tel: (0171) 636 5587. FAX: (0171) 780 9456.

ROLLINS BURDICK HUNTER (INTERNATIONAL) LTD.
Braintree House, Braintree Road, Ruislip, Middx., HA4 0YA. Tel: (0181) 841 4461. Telex: 935792 HOWINS G. FAX: (0181) 842 2124.

RUBEN SEDGWICK INSURANCE SERVICES
Pinewood Studios, Pinewood Road, Iver, Bucks., SL0 0NH. Tel: (01753) 654 555. Telex: 851 848708 SEDFOR G. FAX: (01753) 653 152

SAMUEL MONTAGU & CO. LTD.
10 Lower Thames Street, London, EC3 R6AE. Tel: (0171) 260 9000. FAX: (0171) 488 1630.

SARGENT-DISC LTD.
Pinewood Studios, Pinewood Road, Iver, Bucks. Tel: (01753) 656 631. FAX: (01753) 655 881.

SPECTRUM ENTERTAINMENT GROUP PLC
The Pines, 11 Putney Hill, London, SW15 6BA. Tel: (0181) 780 2525. FAX: (0181) 780 1671. Telex: 262433.

STOY HAYWARD
8 Baker Street, London, WIM 1DA. Tel: (0171) 486 5888. FAX: (0171) 487 3686.
Contact: Carl Williams

TOUCHE ROSS
Hill House, 1 Little New Street, London, EC4A 3TR. Tel: (0171) 936 3000. FAX: (0171) 583 8517.

UBA LTD.
Pinewood Studios, Pinewood Road, Iver Heath, Bucks SL0 0NH. Tel: (01753) 656 699. FAX: (01753) 656844.

WILLIS WRIGHTSON LONDON LTD.
Willis Wrightson House, Wood Street, Surrey KT1 1UG. Tel: (0171) 860 6000. Telex: 929606. FAX: (0181) 943 4297.

PROFESSIONAL, TRADE AND GOVERNMENT UNITS

THE ADVERTISING ASSOCIATION
(The Advertising Association is the federated organisation representing the shared advertising interests of advertisers, agencies and the media. It is the central spokesman for the UK advertising business at national and international levels, and as such, maintains a continuing programme of research and information retrieval. It is responsible for the collection and dissemination of the UK statistics on advertising expenditure, and runs an annual programme of seminars and courses for people in the communications business.)
Abford House, 15 Wilton Road, London SW1V 1NJ. Tel: (0171) 828 2771. FAX: (0171)-931 0376.
DIRECTOR GENERAL
Richard L. Wade

THE ADVERTISING STANDARDS AUTHORITY
Brook House, 2-16 Torrington Place, London, WC1E 7HN. Tel: (0171) 580 5555. FAX: (0171) 631 3051.

AMALGAMATED ENGINEERING & ELECTRICAL UNION
(The Union represents electrical lighting operatives engaged in production.)
Hayes Court, West Common Road, Bromley, BR2 7AU. Tel: (0181) 462 7755. FAX: (0181) 462 4959.
GENERAL SECRETARY
Paul Gallagher

ARTS COUNCIL OF ENGLAND
14 Great Peter Street, London, SW1P 3NQ. Tel: (0171) 973 6443. FAX: (0171) 973 6581.
HEAD OF FILM, VIDEO & BROADCASTING DEPARTMENT
Rodney Wilson

ASSOCIATION OF PROFESSIONAL RECORDING SERVICES LTD.
2 Windsor Square, Silver Street, Reading, Berks. RG1 2TH. Tel: (01734) 756 218. FAX: (01734) 756 216.
CHIEF EXECUTIVE
Philip Vaughan

ASSOCIATION OF PROFESSIONAL VIDEO DEALERS LTD.
P.O. Box 25, Godalming, Surrey, GU7 1PL. Tel: (014868) 23429.
DIRECTOR AND SECRETARY
Charles Potter, M.B.E.

AUSTRALIAN FILM COMMISSION
2nd Floor, Victory House, 99-101 Regent Street, London, WIR 7HB. Tel: (0171) 734 9383. FAX: (0171) 434 0170.

BRITISH ACADEMY OF FILM AND TELEVISION ARTS
(The British Academy of Film and Television Arts exists in order to promote, improve and advance original and creative work amongst people engaged in film and television production.)
195 Piccadilly, London, W1V 9LG. Tel: (0171) 734 0022. FAX: (0171) 734 1792.
PRESIDENT
H.R.H. The Princess Royal
VICE PRESIDENT
Sir David Puttnam, CBE
CHAIRMAN
Edward Mirzoeff CVO
HON. TREASURER
John Chambers
CHIEF EXECUTIVE
Harry Manley

BRITISH ACTORS' EQUITY ASSOCIATION
(Incorporating the Variety Artistes Fed.), Guild House, Upper St. Martins Lane, London, WC2 9EG. Tel: (0171) 379 6000. FAX: (0171) 379 7001.
GENERAL SECRETARY
Ian McGarry

BRITISH BOARD OF FILM CLASSIFICATION
3 Soho Square, London, W1V 5DE. Tel: (0171) 439 7961. FAX: (0171) 287 0141.
PRESIDENT
Earl of Harewood, KBE
DIRECTOR
James Ferman

BRITISH FILM COMMISSION
70 Baker Street, London, W1M 1DJ. Tel: (0171) 224 5000. FAX: (0171) 224 1013.
COMMISSIONER
Sir Sydney Samuelson
CHIEF EXECUTIVE
Andrew Patrick

BRITISH COUNCIL
Events Section, Films, Television and Video Department, 11 Portland Place, London, W1N 4EJ. Tel: (0171) 389 3063/4. Telex: 8952201 BRICON G. FAX: (0171) 389 3041.
FESTIVALS OFFICERS
Kevin Franklin
Satwant Gill
OTHER EVENT COORDINATORS
Geraldine Higgins
Jo Maurice

BRITISH FILM DESIGNERS GUILD
9 Elgin Mews South, London, W9 1JZ. Tel: (0171) 286 6716. FAX: (0171) 286 6716.
EXECUTIVE CONSULTANT
John French

BRITISH FILM INSTITUTE
(The BFI exists to encourage the development of film, television and video in the UK and to promote knowledge, understanding and enjoyment of the culture of the moving image. The Board of Governors is appointed by the Minister for National Heritage. Two are selected by a poll of the membership. The BFI's divisions include BFI South Bank (National Film Theatre Museum of the Moving Image), and London Film Festival Research, Exhibition & Distribution, the National Film Archive, Publishing including Sight & Sound, Library and Information Services, Planning and Production.)
21 Stephen Street, London, W1P 1PL. Tel: (0171) 255 1444. Telex: 27624 BFILDNG. FAX: (0171) 436 7950.
CHAIRMAN
Jeremy Thomas
DIRECTOR
Wilf Stevenson

BRITISH KINEMATOGRAPH SOUND AND TELEVISION SOCIETY
(Founded in 1931, the Society was incorporated in 1946 to service the industries of its title, encouraging technical and scientific progress. To further these aims, the Society disseminates to its Members information on technical developments within these industries, arranges technical lectures, international conferences, and demonstrations, and encourages the exchange of ideas. The broad nature of its purpose is made possible by the subscriptions of its members and by its freedom from political or commercial bias. The BKSTS Journal, Image Technology, is published and sent free to all members.)
M6-M14 Victoria House, Vernon Place, London, WC1B 4DF. Tel: (0171) 242 8400. FAX: (0171) 405 3560.
EXECUTIVE DIRECTOR
Anne Fenton

BRITISH MUSIC INFORMATION CENTRE
(Reference library of works by 20th Century British composers.)
10 Stratford Place, London, W1N 9AE. Tel: (0171) 499 8567. FAX: (0171) 499 4795.

THE BRITISH RADIO AND ELECTRONIC EQUIPMENT MANUFACTURERS' ASSOCIATION
Landseer House, 19 Charing Cross Road, London, WC2H 0ES. Tel: (0171) 930 3206. Telex: 296215 BREMA G.
DIRECTOR
O.P. Sutton, C.B.E.
SECRETARY
R.B. S. Purdy, O.B.E.

BRITISH SOCIETY OF CINEMATOGRAPHERS LTD.
(To promote and encourage the pursuit of the highest standards in the craft of motion picture photography.)
Tree Tops, 11 Croft Road, Chalfont St. Peter, Gerrards Cross, Bucks., SL9 9AE. Tel: (01753) 888 052. FAX: (01753) 891 486.
PRESIDENT
Robin Vidgeon
SECRETARY AND TREASURER
Frances Russell

BRITISH VIDEO ASSOCIATION LTD.
167 Great Portland Street, London, W1M 5FD. Tel: (0171) 436 0041. FAX: (0171) 436 0043.
DIRECTOR GENERAL
Mrs. Lavinia Carey

BROADCASTING ENTERTAIMENT CINEMATOGRAPH AND THEATRE UNION
111 Wardour Street, London, W1V 4AX. Tel: (0171) 437 8506. FAX: (0171) 437 8268.

BROADCASTING STANDARDS COUNCIL
7 The Sanctuary, London, SW1P 3JS. Tel: (0171) 233 0544. FAX: (0171) 233 0397.
CHAIRMAN
The Lady Howe

CABLE COMMUNICATIONS ASSOCIATION
(The Cable Television Association is the trade body representing the interests of companies with an interest in the provision of cable communications in the United Kingdom.
Fifth Floor, Artillery House, Artillery Row, London, SW1P 1RT. Tel: (0171) 222 2900. FAX: (0171) 799 1471.
CHIEF EXECUTIVE
Bob Frost
CONTACT
Simone Wright

CENTRAL CASTING LTD.
(Licensed annually by the Dept. of Employment.)
162-170 Wardour Street, London, W1V 3AT. Tel: (0171) 437 1881. FAX: (0171) 437 2614.
MANAGING DIRECTOR
B. T. Yeoman

CHILDREN'S FILM & TELEVISION FOUNDATION LTD.
Elstree Studios, Boreham Wood, Herts., WD6 1JG. Tel: (0181) 953 0844. FAX: (0181) 207 0860.
CHIEF EXECUTIVE
Stanley T. Taylor

CINEMA AND TELEVISION BENEVOLENT FUND
(The Fund gives relief by financial grants and allowances to needy members or ex-members of the film industry or independent TV, and their widows. Convalescence is available to assist in recovery after illness or operations at "Glebelands," Wokingham, Berks.)
22 Golden Square, London, WIR 4AD. Tel: (0171) 437 6567. FAX: (0171) 437 7186.
EXECUTIVE DIRECTOR
P. J. C. Ratcliffe, O.B.E.
APPEALS & PR OFFICER
Sandra Bradley

CINEMA AND TELEVISION VETERANS
166 The Rocks Road, East Malling, Kent, ME19 6AX. Tel: (01732) 843 291.
PRESIDENT
Roger Bennett
SECRETARY
K. M. Morgan

COMPOSERS' GUILD OF GREAT BRITAIN
34 Hanway Street, London, W1P 9DE. Tel: (0171) 436 0007. FAX: (0171) 436 1913.
GENERAL SECRETARY
Heather Rosenblatt

DEPARTMENT NATIONAL HERITAGE BROADCASTING AND MEDIA DIVISION
Room 203, 2-4 Cockspur Street, London, SW1Y 5DH. Tel: (0171) 211 6000. FAX: (0171) 211 6210. Paul Wright.

DIRECTORS GUILD OF GREAT BRITAIN
15-19 Great Titchfield Street, London, W1P 7FB. Tel: (0171) 436 8626. FAX: (0171) 436 8646. David Litchfield.

ELECTRONIC ENGINEERING ASSOCIATION
Leicester House, 8 Leicester Street, London WC2H 7BN. Tel: (0171) 437 0678. Telex: 263536.

THE ENTERTAINMENT AGENTS' ASSOCIATION (GREAT BRITAIN)
54 Keyes House, Dolphin Square, London, SW1V 3NA. Tel: (0171) 834 0515. FAX: (0171) 821 0261.
PRESIDENT
Kenneth Earle
SECRETARY
Ivan Birchall

FEDERATION AGAINST COPYRIGHT THEFT (FACT)
7 Victory Business Centre, Worton Road, Isleworth, Middlesex, TW7 6ER. Tel: (0181) 568 6646. FAX: (0181) 560 6364.
DIRECTOR GENERAL
R. Dixon

FILM ARTISTES' ASSOCIATION
F.A.A. House, 61 Marloes Road, London W8 6LE. Tel: (0171) 937 4567. FAX: (0171) 937 0790.
GENERAL SECRETARY
George Avory

FILM INSTITUTE OF IRELAND
Irish Film Centre, 6 Eustace Street, Dublin 2, Republic of Ireland. Tel: (3531) 679 5744. FAX: (3531) 677 8755.
DIRECTOR
Sheila Pratschke

GENERAL MUNICIPAL BOILERMAKERS & ALLIED TRADES UNION
Thorne House, Ruxley Ridge, Claygate, Esher, Surrey. Tel: (01372) 620 181. Telex: 27428.
GENERAL SECRETARY
John Edmonds

GUILD OF BRITISH CAMERA TECHNICIANS
5-11 Taunton Road, Metropolitan Centre, Greenford, Middx., UB6 8UQ. Tel: (0181) 578 9243. FAX: (0181) 575 5972. Maureen O'Grady.

GUILD OF FILM PRODUCTION ACCOUNTANTS AND FINANCIAL ADMINISTRATORS (GFPA)
Pinewood Studios, Pinewood Road, Iver. Bucks. SL0 0NH. Tel: (01753) 656 473. FAX: (01753) 656 023.
PRESIDENT
Mike Smith
HON. SECRETARY
Robin Busby

GUILD OF FILM PRODUCTION EXECUTIVES
Pinewood Studios, Iver Heath, Bucks. Tel: (01753) 651700.
PRESIDENT
Stuart Lyons

ITV NETWORK CENTRE
(The ITV Network Centre, wholly owned by the ITV companies, independently commissions and schedules the television programmes which are shown across the ITV network.)
200 Gray's Inn Road, London, WC1X 8HF. Tel: (0171) 843 8000. FAX: (0171) 843 8158.
CHIEF EXECUTIVE
Andrew Quinn
NETWORK DIRECTOR
Marcus Plantin

THE INCORPORATED SOCIETY OF BRITISH ADVERTISERS LTD.
44 Hertford Street, London W1Y 8AE. Tel: (0171) 499 7502.
DIRECTOR
K. N. Miles

INSTITUTE OF PRACTITIONERS IN ADVERTISING
44 Belgrave Square, London, SW1X 8QS. Tel: (0171) 235 7020. FAX: (0171) 245 9904.

INTERNATIONAL ANIMATED FILM ASSOCIATION
(The promotion of animation in all its aspects. economics, creativity and the expansion of its scope and uses. It provides patronage to many festivals including major international film festivals in Europe, N. America and Asia.)
61 Railwayside, Barnes, London, SW13 0PQ. Tel: (0181) 878 4040. FAX: (0181) 675 8499.
VICE PRESIDENT
Pat Raine Webb

INTERNATIONAL ASSOCIATION OF BROADCASTING MANUFACTURERS
(The IABM was formed in 1976 with the purpose of fostering and co-ordinating the wide common interests of manufacturers of broadcast and television equipment and associated products worldwide.)
4-B, High Street, Burnham, Slough, SL1 7JH. Tel: (01628) 667 633. FAX: (01628) 665 882.

CHAIRMAN
Tom McGann
SECRETARY
Claude Guillaume
TREASURER
Dan Anco
ADMINISTRATOR
Alan Hirst
SECRETARIAT
Ken Walker

INTERNATIONAL VISUAL COMMUNICATION ASSOCIATION (IVCA)
(The International Visual Communications Association represents the interests of the suppliers and users of visual communications in the form of film, video and business events.)
Bolsover House, 5-6 Clipstone Street, London, W1P 7EB. Tel: (0171) 580 0962. FAX: (0171) 436 2606.
CHIEF EXECUTIVE
Jamie Neil

IRISH ACTORS EQUITY GROUP
Liberty Hall, Dublin 1, Rep. of Ireland. Tel: (3531) 874 0181. FAX: (3531) 874 3691.
GROUP SECRETARY
Gerard Browne

LONDON FILM COMMISSION
c/o Carnival Films, 12 Raddington Rd., Ladbroke Grove, London W10 5TG. Tel: (0181) 968 0968 FAX: (0181) 968 0177.
DIRECTOR
Christabel Albery

MECHANICAL COPYRIGHT PROTECTION SOCIETY LTD.(MCPS)
Elgar House, 41 Streatham High Road, London, SW16 1ER. Tel: (0181) 769 4400. Telex: 946792. FAX: (0181) 769 8792.
CUSTOMER SERVICES ADVISOR
Malcolm Carruthers

MUSICIANS' UNION
60-62, Clapham Road, London, SW9 0JJ. Tel: (0171) 582 5566. FAX: (0171) 582 9805.
GENERAL SECRETARY
Dennis Scard

NATIONAL FILM AND TELEVISION SCHOOL
Beaconsfield Studios, Station Road, Beaconsfield, Bucks., HP9 1LG. Tel: (01494) 671 234. FAX: (01494) 674 042.
DIRECTOR
Henning Camre

PACT LTD.
(Producers Alliance for Cinema and Television)
Gordon House, Greencoat Place, London, SW1P 1PH. Tel: (0171) 233 6000. FAX: (0171) 233 8935.
CHIEF EXECUTIVE
John Woodward
MEMBERSHIP OFFICER
Martin Hart

THE PERFORMING RIGHT SOCIETY LTD. (PRS)
(Representing the composers and publishers of music.)
29-33 Berners Street, London, W1P 4AA. Tel: (0171) 580 5544. Telex: 892678 PRSLONG. FAX: (0171) 631 4138.
GENERAL MANAGER
John Axon
PUBLIC AFFAIRS CONTROLLER
Terri Anderson

THE PERSONAL MANAGERS' ASSOCIATION LTD.
Rivercroft, One Summer Road, East Molesey, Surrey, KT8 9LX. Tel: (0181) 398 9796.
SECRETARY
Angela Adler

PHONOGRAPHIC PERFORMANCE LTD.
(A company founded by the British recording industry to own and exercise the public performance and broadcasting rights in sound recordings in the U.K. and to issue licences for public performances and broadcasting.)
Ganton House, 14/22 Ganton Street, London, W1V 1LB. Tel: (0171) 437 0311.
CHAIRMAN
J. A. Brooks
MANAGING DIRECTOR
J. V. Love

THE RADIO, ELECTRICAL AND TELEVISION RETAILERS' ASSOCIATION (RETRA) LTD.
RETRA House, St. Johns' Terrace, 1 Ampthill Street, Bedford, MK42 9EY. Tel: (01234) 269 110. FAX: (01234) 269 609.
CHIEF EXECUTIVE
J. Scott

THE RADIO INDUSTRY COUNCIL
Landseer House, 19 Charing Cross Road, London, WC2H 0ES. Tel: (0171) 930 3206. Telex: 296215 BREMAG.
Director: O. P. Sutton, C.B.E.
Secretary: R. B. S. Purdy, O.B.E.

RADIO SOCIETY OF GREAT BRITAIN
Lambda House, Cranborne Road, Potters Bar, Herts., EN6 3JE.
CHIEF EXECUTIVE/SECRETARY
David A. Evans

ROYAL TELEVISION SOCIETY
Holborn Hall, 100 Gray's Inn Road, London, WC1X 8AL. Tel: (0171) 430 1000. FAX: (0171) 430 0924.
EXECUTIVE DIRECTOR
Michael Bunce

SCREEN ADVERTISING WORLD ASSOCIATION LTD.
103A Oxford Street, London, W1R 1TF. Tel: (0171) 734 7621.
SECRETARY GENERAL
Charles Sciberras

SOCIETY OF AUTHORS BROADCASTING GROUP
84 Drayton Gardens, London, SW10 9SB. Tel: (0181) 363 6642.

SOUND AND COMMUNICATIONS INDUSTRIES FEDERATION
4-B, High Street, Burnham, Slough, SL1 7JH. Tel: (01628) 667 633. FAX: (01628) 665 882.
CHIEF EXECUTIVE
Ken Walker, M.B.E.

VARIETY CLUB OF GT. BRITAIN (TENT NO. 36)
326 High Holbron, London WC1V 7AN. Tel: (0171) 611 3888. FAX: (0171) 611 3892.
PRESS GUY
Bill Hagerty

VIDEO STANDARDS COUNCIL
Research House, Fraser Rd., Perivale, Middlesex UB6 7AQ. Tel: (0181) 566 8272. FAX: (0181) 991 2653.
SECRETARY GENERAL
Laurie Hall

THE WRITERS GUILD OF GREAT BRITAIN
(The Writers Guild of Great Britain is the Trades Union Council-affiliated union which is the recognised representative body for negotiating agreements for writers in film, television, and radio as well as in the theatre and publishing.)
430 Edgware Road, London, W2 1EH. Tel: (0171) 723 8074. FAX: (0171) 706 2413.
PRESIDENT
Rosemary Anne Sigson
HONORARY TREASURER
Cecil Howard
GENERAL SECRETARY
Gary Hopkins

Home Video Distributors

ABBEY HOME ENTERTAINMENTS
106 Harrow Road, London, W12 4XD. Tel: (0171) 262 1012.

BBC VIDEO
Woodland, 80 Wood Land, London, W12 0TT. Tel: (0181) 743 5588

BMG RECORDS (UK) LTD.
69-79 Fulham High Street, London, SW6 3JW. Tel: (0171) 973 0011.

BUENA VISTA HOME ENTERTAINMENT
Beaumont House, Kensington Village, Avonmore Road, London, W14 8TS. Tel: (0171) 605 2400.

CARLTON HOME ENTERTAINMENT LTD
The Water Front, Elstree Road, Elstree, Herts WD6 3EE. Tel: (0181) 207 6207.

CIC VIDEO
Glenthorne House, 5-17 Hammersmith Grove, London. W6 0ND. Tel (0181) 846 9433.

CHANNEL FOUR VIDEO
124 Horseferry Road, London SW1P ZTX. Tel: (0171) 306 8687.

CTE (CARLTON)
35-38 Portian Square, London, W1H 9FH. Tel: (0171) 224 3399.

COLUMBIA TRISTAR HOME VIDEO
Horatio House. 77-85 Fulham Palace Road, London W6 8JA. Tel: (0181) 748 6000. Cees Zwaard.

EMAP PLC
2nd Floor, Mappin House, 4 Winsley Street, London, W1N 7AR. Tel: (0171) 636 5447.

ENTERTAINMENT UK
Blyth Road, Hayes. Middx., UB4 1DN. Tel: (0181) 848 7511.

FIRST INDEPENDENT FILMS LTD.
69 New Oxford Street, London WC1 1DG. Tel: (0171) 528 7767.

GMH ENTERTAINMENTS
22 Manasty Road, Orton Southgate. Peterborough. PE2 6UP Tel: (0173) 3223 3464. Iain Muspratt.

GUILD ENTERTAINMENT
Kent House, 14-17 Market Place Great Tilchfield Street, London, W1N 8AR. Tel: (0171) 323 5751.

MANGA ENTERTAINMENT LTS.
40 St. Peters Road, London, W6 9BD. Tel: (0181) 748 9000.

MOSAIC MOVIES
22 Manasty Road, Orton Southgate, Peterborough PE2 6UP. Tel: (0173) 323 3464.

ODYSSEY VIDEO
15 Dufours Place, London, W1V IFE. Tel: (0171) 437 8251.

PEARSON NEW VIDEO
536 Kings Road, London, SW10 0TE. Tel: (0171) 331 3920.

PICKWICK GROUP LTD.
The Water Front, Elstree Road, Elstree. Herts., WD66 3EE. Tel: (0181) 207 6207. Contact: Gary LeCount.

POLYGRAM VIDEO LTD.
P.O. Box 1425, Chancellors House, 72 Chancellors Road, Hammersmith, London, W6 9QB. Tel: (0181) 910 5000.

SCREEN MULTIMEDIA
P.O. Box 161 Radlett. Herts. WD7 8ED. Tel: (0192) 385 8043.

SONY MUSIC U.K. LTD.
Rabans Lane, Aylesbury, Bucks, HP19 3BX. Tel: (01296) 26151.

TELSTAR VIDEO ENTERTAINMENT
The Studio, 5 King Edwards Mews, Byfield Gardens, Barnes, London SW13 9HP. Tel: (0181) 846 9946.

THAMES VIDEO LTD.
Broom Road, Teddington Lock, Middx., TW11 9NT. Tel: (0181) 977 3252.

TWENTIETH CENTURY FOX HOME ENTERTAINMENT
31-32 Soho Square, London, W1V 6AP. Tel: (0171) 753 8686.

VIDEO COLLECTION INTERNATIONAL.
Royalty House, 72-74 Dean St., London, W1V 5HB. Tel: (0171) 470 6666.

VISION VIDEO LTD.
P.O. Box 1425. 72 Chancellors Road, Hammersmith, London, W6 9QB. Tel: (0181) 910 5000.

WARNER HOME VIDEO
135 Wardour Street, London, W1V 4AP. Tel: (0171) 494 3441.

WARNER VISION
35-38 Portman Sq., London W1H 0EU. Tel: (0171) 467 2524.

THE WORLD MARKET

ASSOCIATIONS, ORGANIZATIONS, BROADCASTERS, CABLE SYSTEMS & SATELLITE BROADCASTERS, PROGRAM SUPPLIERS AND HOME VIDEO COMPANIES BY COUNTRY

TV & VIDEO WORLD MARKET

The following is a list of companies, associations and organizations by category of service and in alphabetical order by country. All country code and city code numbers appear within parenthesis before the telephone numbers. Estimates of television sets, VCRs cable service and satellite service, when available, are for 1995.

AFRICA

Africa is financially the poorest of all of the continents and the least served by television broadcasters of all sorts (except in notable examples such as South Africa and the Arab nations of the Middle East). Most television stations are state-controlled and subject to government censorship. In addition, many of the states in Africa are predominantly Moslem, and Moslem traditions and customs must be honored by broadcasters.

ASIA

Asia's start-up media companies often begin broadcasting and cable operations without government approval, and with disregard for existing copyright laws, occasionally retransmitting Western satellite broadcasts without consent. Many countries will not allow foreign companies to own media companies. The U.S. threatened to hold off any agreement regulating international telecommunications if it was not allowed access to Asian markets. With the transition of Hong Kong's governance to mainland Chinese control scheduled for 1997, other "Young Lions" nations such as Malaysia are poised to enter the lucrative satellite broadcasting market.

THE EUROPEAN UNION

The European television market is growing at a faster pace than any other market in the world. Pay-TV revenues grew to a reported $4.75 billion, while cable revenues rose to $4.6 billion. 98 new channels started up in Europe in 1995.
Citing the need for a fair share of the marketplace and the necessity of preserving "cultural and linguistic diversity", the European Union is standing firm in its stand that at least 51% of all TV programming must be of European production and extended those protective quotas to emerging technologies for the next ten years. However, Britain, Germany and the Netherlands oppose the quotas. This stance is most probably in response to the fact that American programming may control as much as 70% of the European Union's market.
The "Europe Without Frontiers" project continues apace, with German media conglomerate Bertelsmann, CLT of Luxembourg, BSkyB of Britain, Canal Plus of France and other companies attempting to reach an agreement on technical standards to provide digital pay-TV services via satellite, although such negotiations have been subject to much tension and vacillation between the parties, and by the early Fall of 1996, the German end of the alliance appeared to be falling apart. EU antitrust specialists will most likely be scrutinizing any such agreements. The European pay-TV market is expected to grow by 25% in the next decade. Europe stands to be the first market for digital TV in the world, and such steps will place Europe at least a decade ahead of the United States.
American companies like Viacom's MTV and CNBC are finding that the European market is demanding that services be more customized to local tastes. For example, CNBC has formed an alliance with The Financial Times to provide European business news.
While video piracy still remains a problem, particularly in the former Soviet bloc nations, most European nations have seen an increase in video sales in the past couple of years. This growth seems to be at the expense of the video rental business, which showed an average market-wide decline in the European Union over the past several years. EU technical standards groups are arguing the introduction of the DVD in Europe, citing the maze of differing video standards across the continent.

LATIN AMERICA

American companies, from cable providers and satellite services to programmers and producers, have set their sights on the expanding Latin American market, with the added benefit of being able to offer the same services to America's growing Spanish-speaking population. Westinghouse has purchased Spanish language news service, Telenoticias. TCI has plans to expand into Argentina and the Hearst Group plans to start up a cartoon channel based on some of its popular newspaper comic strip characters.

A consortium of investors intends to supply Latin America with a 192 channel satellite broadcast service, to be named Galaxy Latin America. Dick Clark International Cable Ventures plan to build fiber optic cable networks

THE MIDDLE EAST

Three major companies have been formed to provide satellite broadcasts to the Arab world, Middle Eastern Broadcasting Center (MBC), Arab Radio and Television, and the Saudi-backed Orbit Radio and Television Network. These commercial broadcasters will compete with traditional government broadcasters, such as the Egyptian Satellite Channel (ESC). The News Corporations STARTV signed a last minute agreement with Orbit to provide multichannel services to the Middle East.

AFGHANISTAN

Population: 17.8 million.
TV Sets: 100,000.
Video Standard: PAL & SECAM.
PEOPLE'S RADIO & TELEVISION AFGHANISTAN
Post Office Box 544, Kabul. 9 stations. Tel: (93) 25460.

ALBANIA

Population: 3.4 million.
Video Standard: PAL.
RADIOTELEVISIONE SHQIPTAR
Rruga Ismail Qemali 11, Tirana.

ALGERIA

Population: 27.9 million.
Video Standard: PAL.
ENTERPRISE NATIONALE DE TELEVISION
21 Boulevard des Martyrs, Algiers 16000.

ANGOLA

Population: 11.2 million.
Video Standard: PAL.
TELEVISAO POPULAR DE ANGOLA
Avenida Ho-Chi-Minh, P.O. Box 2604, Luanda. Tel: (2442) 320025. FAX: (2442) 391091.

ARGENTINA

Population: 33.1 million.
TV Homes: 9.1 million.
Pay TV Homes: 4.2 million.
Estimated Piracy Level: 40%
Video Standard: PAL.
American media giant TCI has stated plans to invest in Argentina's telecommunications industry when the country eases state sponsored monopolies in 1997.
A new law was passed levying a 10% tax on video sales and rentals. As Argentina's video industry is in a battle against piracy, this law will help solve problems with the six-month window between theatrical and video release.
BROADCASTERS
ASOCIACION DE TELERADIODIFUSORAS (ATV)
Av. Cordoba 323, 6to., 1054 Buenos Aires. Tel: (541) 312 4208. FAX: (541) 312 4208.
ARGENTINA TELEVISORA COLOR (ATC) LS 82 CANAL 7
Avda. Figueroa Alcorta 2977, 1425 Buenos Aires. Tel: (541) 802 6001/6. Telex: 22916 TVCOL AR.
CANAL 2 DE LA PLATA (LS 86)
Calle 36 entre 2 y 3, 1900 La Plata, Prov. Buenos Aires. Tel: (54 21) 24 4270. Telex: 23517 TVPLA AR.
CANAL 2 DE LA PLATA (LS 86)
Cerrito 1266, Piso 11, 1010 Buenos Aires. Tel: (541) 313 6879, 393 9186, 393 9270, 393 9388, 393 9430.
CANAL 5 DE ROSARIO (LT 84)
Belgrano 1055, 2000 Rosario, Prov. Santa Fe. Tel: (5441) 4 4638. Telex: 41810.

CANAL 8 DE MAR DEL PLATA (LRI 486)
Avda. Pedro Luro 2907, 7600 Mar del Plata, Prov. Buenos Aires. Tel: (5423) 232 3046/8.

CANAL 9 (BUENOS AIRES) LS 83
Pasaje Gelly 3378, 1425 Buenos Aires. Tel: (541) 801 3065, 801 3072, 801 3075. Telex: 22132 LIBER AR.

CANAL 9 DE BAHIA BLANCA (LU 80)
Sarmiento 54, 8000 Bahia Blanca, Prov. Buenos Aires. Telex: 81826 CANUEVE AR.

CANAL 11 (BUENOS AIRES) LS 84
Pavon 2444, 1248 Buenos Aires. Tel: (541) 941 2448, 941 9231, 948 9351. Telex: 22780 DICON AR.

PROARTEL (CANAL 13 LS 85)
Avda. San Juan 1170, 1147 Buenos Aires. Tel: (541) 27 0321, 27 3601, 27 3605. Telex: 21762 PATEL AR.

CABLE AND SATELLITE
AVELLANEDA TELEVISION SA
España 130, 1870 Avellaneda, Prov. Buenos Aires. Tel: (541) 201 0134, 201 3432, 201 4331, 201 4718.

CABLEVISION
Bonpland 1773, 1414 Buenos Aires. Tel: (541) 771 6021, 775 3090, 775 3190, 775 3290, 775 3390, 775 3490, 775 3590. Telex: 18390 UZAL AR.

OESTE CABLE COLOR SRL
French 187, 1704 La Matanza, Prov. Buenos Aires. Tel: (541) 654 0416, 654 7893.

VIDEO CABLE COMUNICACION SA
Cuba 2370, 1428 Buenos Aires. Tel: (541) 782 0237, 782 0364, 782 0413, 783 0465, 782 0565. Telex: 26284 AR.

VIDEO ORGANIZATIONS
ASSOCIATION OF ARGENTINEAN INDEPENDENT VIDEO EDITORS
Ayacucho 457, Piso 2/21, 1026 Buenos Aires. Tel: (541) 953 7336.

ARGENTINEAN VIDEO UNION
Planta baja, Viamonte 2095, 1056 Buenos Aires. Tel: (541) 46 8248.

VIDEO DISTRIBUTORS
FILMARTE
Ayacucho 595, Buenos Aires, Tel: (541) 459945. FAX: (541) 403662.

FILMEX
Lavalle 17-18 9 A, Buenos Aires. Tel: (541) 814 3048. FAX: (541) 9533654.

GRECIAN FILMS
Lavalle 2047, Buenos Aires, Tel: (541) 954 0850. FAX: (541) 9540850.

MUNDIAL FILMS
Lavalle 2024 piso 8, Buenos Aires. Tel: (541) 953 1793.

TRANSEUROPA
Ayacucho 586, Buenos Aires, Tel: (541) 492653.

UNITED INTERNATIONAL PICTURES
Ayacucho 520, Buenos Aires, Tel: (541) 490261. FAX: (541) 490261.

WARNER BROS.
Tucuman 1938, Buenos Aires. Tel: (541) 456094.

AUSTRALIA

Population: 7.8 million.
VCR Homes: 6 million.
Video Standard: PAL-B
Nine Network averaged 38.9% of the national audience in 1995. Seven Network, with a 35.8% share, has completely restructured its management, naming Kerry Stokes as chairman, and overhauled its news programming in the hopes of capturing the lead. Seven also purchased Golden West Network. Seven's profits were up 18% in the last 6 months of 1995. Ten Network showed a solid 13% increase in net profits in the last quarter of 1995 and the first quarter of 1996, but came in third in audience with 25.3%
Foxtel, Australia's largest cable system, won a landmark case allowing it to retransmit broadcast signals. Galaxy, Australia's first pay-TV service more than doubled its subscriber base in 1995 to 82,000.

BROADCASTERS
ABD DARWIN
1st Floor, Australian Airlines Building, Bennet Street, Darwin 0801, Northern Territory. Tel: (6189) 823222.

ABN 2 SYDNEY
221 Pacific Highway, Gore Hill 2065, New South Wales. Tel: (612) 4378000. FAX: (612) 950 3546.

ABQ 2 BRISBANE
600-612 Coronation Drive, Toowong 4066, Queensland. Tel: (617) 377 5222. FAX: (617) 377 5307.

ABS 2 ADELAIDE
85 North East Rd., Collinswood 5081, South Australia. Tel: (618) 343 4000. FAX: (618) 343 4027.

ABT 2 HOBART
5-7 Sandy Bay Rd., Hobart 7000, Tasmania. Tel: (6102) 353 661.

ABV 2 MELBOURNE
8 Gordon St., Elsternwick 3185, Victoria. Tel: (612) 528 4444. FAX: (612) 5242504.

ABW 2 PERTH
GPO Box 9994, Perth 6001, Western Australia. Tel: (619) 326 0222.

ADS 10 ADELAIDE
125 Strangways Terrace, Adelaide 5006, South Australia. Tel: (618) 877 7777. FAX: (618) 877 7888.

ATN 7 SYDNEY
TV Centre, Mobbs Lane, Epping 2121, New South Wales. Tel: (612) 858 7777. FAX: (612) 877 7888.

AUSTRALIAN BROADCASTING CORPORATION
GPO Box 9994, Sydney 2001, New South Wales. Tel: (612) 950 3177. FAX: (612) 950 3169.

AUSTRALIAN CAPITAL TELEVISION
Aspinall St., Watson 2602, ACT. Tel: (616) 242 2400. FAX: (616) 241 7230.

BTQ 7 BRISBANE
Sir Samuel Griffiths Drive, Mount Coot-tha 4000, Queensland. Tel: (617) 369 7777. FAX: (617) 368 4024.

GOLDEN WEST NETWORK
30 Kings Park Rd., West Perth 6005, Western Australia. Tel: (619)481 0050. FAX: (619) 321 2470.

HSV 7 MELBOURNE
119 Wells St., South Melbourne 3205, Victoria. Tel: (613) 697 7777. FAX: (613) 687 7888.

IMPARJA TELEVISION PTY LTD.
14 Leichhardt Terrace, NT 0871, Alice Springs. Tel: (6189) 530 300. FAX: (6189) 530 322.

NBN 3 NEWCASTLE
11-17 Mosbri Crescent, Newcastle 2300, New South Wales. Tel: (6149) 292 933. FAX: (6149) 263 629.

NETWORK TEN AUSTRALIA
Northern Star Holdings, GPO Box 10, Sydney 2007, New South Wales. Tel: (612) 844 1010. FAX: (612) 844 1364.

NEW 10 PERTH
Cottonwood Crescent, Dianella Heights 6062, Western Australia. Tel: (619) 345 1010. FAX: (619) 345 2210.

NINE NETWORK AUSTRALIA
24 Artarmon Rd., Willoughby 2068, New South Wales. Tel: (612) 906 9999.

NTD 8 DARWIN
Blake St., Gardens Hill, Darwin 0820, Northern Territory. Tel: (6189) 818 888. FAX: (6189) 816 802.

NWS 9 ADELAIDE
202-208 Tynte St., North Adelaide 5006, South Australia. Tel: (618) 267 0111. FAX: (618) 267 3996.

PRIME TELEVISION ORANGE
P.O. Box 465, Orange 2800, New South Wales. Tel: (6163) 622 288. FAX: (6163) 631889.

QTQ 9 BRISBANE
Sir Samuel Griffith Drive, Mount Coot-tha 4066, Queensland. Tel: (617) 369 9999. FAX: (617) 369 3512.

QTV ROCKHAMPTON
Acquatic Place, North Rockhampton 4700, Queensland. Tel: (6179) 261 155. FAX: (6179) 261 931.

QTV TOWNSVILLE
Telecasters North Queensland, 12 The Strand, Townsville 4810, Queensland. Tel: (6177) 213 377. FAX: (6177) 211 705.

SAS 7 ADELAIDE
45 Park Terrace, Gilberton 5081, South Australia. Tel: (618) 342 7777. FAX: (618) 342 7717.

SEVEN NETWORK
Television Centre, Mobbs Lane, New South Wales 2121. Tel: (612) 858 7777. FAX: (612) 967 7770.

SOUTHERN CROSS TELEVISION (TNT 9)
37 Watchorn St., Launceston 7250, Tasmania. Tel: (6103) 440 202. FAX: (6103) 430 340.

SPECIAL BROADCASTING SERVICE
Cnr Herbert & Fredrick Sts., Artarmon 2064, New South Wales. Tel: (612) 964 2828. FAX: (612) 957 3571.

SUNSHINE TELEVISION
78 Mulgrave Rd., Cairns 4870, Queensland. Tel: (6170) 312 777. FAX: (6170) 315 235.

TASMANIAN TELEVISION
48-52 New Town Rd., New Town 7008, Tasmania. Tel: (6102) 780 612. FAX: (6102) 281 825.

TEN 10 SYDNEY
44 Bay Street, Sydney 2001, New South Wales. Tel: (612) 844 1010. FAX: (612) 844 1368.

TVQ 10 BRISBANE
Sir Samuel Griffith Drive, Mt. Coot-tha 4066, Queensland. Tel: (617) 368 1010. FAX: (617) 369 3786.

VIDEO ORGANIZATION
VIDEO INDUSTRY DISTRIBUTORS ASSOCIATION
302 Pitt St., Sydney 2000, New South Wales. (612) 264 3411.
FAX: (612) 267 9581.

VIDEO DISTRIBUTORS
AAV AUSTRALIA
180 Bank St., South Melbourne 3205, Victoria. Tel: (613) 699
1844. FAX: (613) 690 3734.

ABC ENTERPRISES
PO Box 9994, Sydney 2001, New South Wales. Tel: (612) 950
3999. FAX: (612) 950 3888.

ALL MEDIA INTERNATIONAL
643 Chapel St., South Yarra 3141, Victoria. Tel: (613) 926
3637. FAX: (613) 824 0370.

ANJOHN INTERNATIONAL
19/151 Bayswater Rd., Rushcutters Bay 2011, New South
Wales. Tel: (612) 361 6536. FAX: (612) 361 6521.

ATLANTIS RELEASING
Suite 4, 65 Military Rd., Neutral Bay 2089, New South Wales.
Tel: (612) 953 2999. FAX: (612) 953 3248.

AUSTRALIAN BROADCASTING AUTHORITY
1st Floor, 76 Berry St., North Sydney 2060, New South Wales.
Tel: (612) 959 7811. FAX: (612) 954 4328.

AUSTRALIAN FILM INSTITUTE DISTRIBUTION
49 Eastern Rd., South Melbourne 3205, Victoria. Tel: (613) 696
1844. FAX: (613) 696 7972.

AUSTRALIAN VISUAL PRODUCTIONS
Unit 1, 17 Grosvenor St., Neutral Bay 2096, New South Wales.
Tel: (612) 953 8877. FAX: (612) 953 6221.

AUSTRALIAN WORLD ENTERTAINMENT
202 Tynte St., North Adelaide 5006, South Australia. Tel: (618)
267 3644. FAX: (618) 267 3996.

BUSINESS FILMS
43 Davey St., Frankston 3199, Victoria. Tel: (613) 866 8735.
FAX: (613) 770 1650.

COLIN MCCLENNAN AND ASSOCIATES
13 Napier St., North Sydney 2060, New South Wales. Tel:
(612) 955 5122. FAX: (612) 957 3550.

COLUMBIA TRISTAR HOYTS HOME VIDEO
42-46 Longueville Rd., Lane Cove 2066, New South Wales. Tel:
(612) 911 3300. FAX: (612) 911 3333.

D. L. TAFFNER AUSTRALIA
Unit 20, Greenwich Square, 130-134 Pacific Highway,
Greenwich 2065, New South Wales. Tel: (612) 439 5699. FAX:
(612) 439 4501.

DENDY FILMS
34 Louisa Rd., Birchgrove 2041, New South Wales. Tel: (612)
810 8733. FAX: (612) 810 3228.

DISCOVERY COMMUNICATIONS
PO Box 550, Malvern 3144, Victoria. Tel: (613) 563 9344. FAX:
(613) 563 9885.

FIELD ASSOCIATES (AUSTRALIA)
Suite 4, 2nd Floor, 118 Willoughby Rd., Crows Nest 2065, New
South Wales. Tel: (612) 439 4730. FAX: (612) 439 3103.

FIRST RELEASE HOME ENTERTAINMENT
9th Fl., 42-46 Longueville Rd., Lane Cove 2066, New South
Wales. Tel: (612) 911 3300. FAX: (612) 911 3333.

FOX VIDEO
22 Thorogood St., Victoria Park 6100, Western Australia. Tel:
(619) 361 8144. FAX: (619) 348 1054.

HOYTS FOX COLUMBIA TRI-STAR FILMS
490 Kent St., Sydney 2000, New South Wales. Tel: (612) 261
7800. FAX: (612) 283 2191.

M.C. STUART AND ASSOCIATES
88 Highett Street, Richmond 3121, Victoria. Tel: (613) 429
8666. FAX: (613) 429 1839.

MCA
1st Fl., MCA Universal House, 23 Pelican Street, Sydney 2010,
New South Wales. Tel: (612) 267 9844. FAX: (612) 264 1742.

MCMAHON AND LAKE
Warner Roadshow Movie World Studio, Pacific Highway,
Oxenford 4210, Queensland. Tel: (617) 588 6666. FAX: (617)
553 3698.

NETWORK ENTERTAINMENT
2B Woodcock Place, Lane Cove, 2066 New South Wales. Tel:
(612) 418 8099. FAX: (612) 418 8598.

NEW VISION FILM DISTRIBUTORS
2nd Floor, 254 Bay Street, Port Melbourne 3207, Victoria. Tel:
(613) 646 5555. FAX: (613) 646 2411.

OPEN EYE (FILM & TV)
1/87 Bent St., North Sydney 2060, New South Wales. Tel: (612)
954 3626. FAX: (612) 959 3253.

OTHER FILM DISTRIBUTION
89 High St., Northcote 3070, Victoria. Tel: (613) 489 1741.
FAX: (613) 481 5618.

PACIFIC LINK COMMUNICATIONS
2A Eltham St., Gladesville 2111, New South Wales. Tel: (612)
817 5055. FAX: (612) 879 7297.

**R A BECKER AND CO./FREEMANTLE INTERNATIONAL
PRODUCTIONS**
4/21 Chandos St., St. Leonards 2065, New South Wales. Tel:
(612) 438 3377. FAX: (612) 439 1827.

REID AND PUSKAR
44 Moruben Rd., Mosman 2088, New South Wales. Tel: (612)
969 2077. FAX: (612) 960 4971.

RONIN FILMS
PO Box 1005, Civic Square 2068, ACT. Tel: (616) 248 0851.
FAX: (616) 249 1640.

SHARMILL FILMS
Suite 4, 200 Toorak Rd., South Yarra 3141, Victoria. Tel: (613)
826 9077. FAX: (613) 826 1935.

SHOWBIZ VIDEO
183 Harris St., Pyrmont 2009, New South Wales. Tel: (612) 660
8999. FAX: (612) 660 7916.

SMART ST. FILMS
3/30 Lamrock Ave., Bondi Beach 2026, New South Wales. Tel:
(612) 360 8429. FAX: (612) 365 3195. Contacts: Cai Steele,
Haydn Keenan.

SOUTH AUSTRALIAN FILM AND VIDEO CENTRE
113 Tapley's Hill Rd., Hendon 5014, South Australia. Tel: (618)
348 9355. FAX: (618) 347 0385.

SOUTHERN STAR INTERNATIONAL
10th Floor, 8 West St., North Sydney 2060, New South Wales.
Tel: (612) 957 2788. FAX: (612) 956 6918.

VIRGIN VISION AUSTRALIA
99 Victoria St., Potts Point 2011, New South Wales. Tel: (612)
368 1700.

WARNER HOME VIDEO
Level 7, 116 Military Rd., Neutral Bay 2089, New South Wales.
Tel: (612) 908 3088. FAX: (612) 909 8494.

WORLD VISION ENTERPRISES
2nd Floor, 5-13 Northcliff Street, Milsons Point 2061, New
South Wales. Tel: (612) 922 4722. FAX: (612) 955 8207.

ARMENIA

Population: 3.6 million
Video Standard: SECAM.
Relays of Russian OK-1 and RTV are also carried in Armenia.
ARMENIAN TELEVISION
Alek Manukyan 5, 375025 Yerevan. Tel: (3742) 552 502. FAX:
(3742) 551 513.

AUSTRIA

Population: 8 million.
TV Sets: 2.7 million.
VCR Homes: 1.9 million.
Home Cable Service : 34%
Home Satellite Service: 31%
Video Standard: PAL B & G.
Broadcasting and advertising monies were in short supply in
Austria, most probably due to economic adversities encoun-
tered in joining the EU. ORF's budget has been cut by nearly
70% in the past 3 years.

STATE BROADCASTER
OSTERREICHISCHER RANDFUNK—ORF-ZENTRUM WIEN
Wurzburggasse 30, Vienna A-1136. Tel: (431) 878 780. FAX:
(431) 878 2250. 24 stations.

CABLE SERVICES
BKS BERGENLANDSCHERS KABELFERNSEHEN
Kasernenstrasse 9, Eisenstadt A-7001. Tel: (432682) 170
1471. FAX: (432682) 170 1480.

KABLE TV VIENNA
Hofzeile Strasse 3, Vienna. Tel: (431) 363 4240

PREMIERE
Neubaugasse 25, Vienna A-1070. Tel: (431) 52127. FAX: (431)
523 8253.

TELESYSTEM
Salurnerstrasse 11, Innsbruck A-6020. Tel: (43512) 599 330.

HOME VIDEO DISTRIBUTORS
BMG ARIOLA
Erlachgasse 134-8, Vienna A-1010. Tel: (431) 60154. FAX:
(431) 60154 139.

CCS MEDIENPRODUKTION
Stolzenthalergasse 14, Vienna A-1080. Tel: (431) 408 6198.

COLUMBIA TRISTAR
Wallgasse 21, Vienna A-1080. Tel: (431) 597 1515. FAX: (431)
597 1516.

EMI AUSTRIA
Webgasse 43, Vienna A-1060. Tel: (431) 599 890. FAX: (431)
596 9336.

**MEDIENWERKSTAT (STUDIO FOR UNABHANGIGE
VIDEOARBEIT)**
Neubaugasse 40A, Vienna A-1070. Tel: (431) 5263 667. FAX:
(431) 5267 168.

PAUKER
Ortsstrasse 18, Voesendorf A-2331. Tel: (431) 881 149.
POLYGRAM
Edelsinnstrasse 4, Vienna A-1120. Tel: (431) 811 210. FAX: (431) 813 1300.
PREISER
Fischerstiege 9, Vienna A-1010. Tel: (431) 533 6228.
RAINBOW VIDEO
Tetmajergasse 5A, Vienna. Tel: (431) 2701 8230. FAX: (431) 270 6278.
VIDEO MARKET
Ortsstrasse 18, Vosendorf A-2331. Tel: (431) 692 593. FAX: (431) 6295 9315.
VIDEO VERTRIEB
Webgasse 43, Vienna A-1060. Tel: (431) 597 9795. FAX: (431) 596 8111.
WARNER BROS.
Zieglergasse 10, Vienna A-1072. Tel. (431) 523 8626. FAX: (431) 523 8626 31.

AZERBAIDZHAN

Population: 7.8 million.
Video Standard: SECAM
AZERBAYCAN RESPUBIKASI RABITA NAZIRLIYI
Azebaidzhan pr. 33, Bake 370139. Tel: (99412) 930 004. FAX: (99412) 983 325.
AZERBAIDZHAN TELEVISION
Medhi Huseyn kucasi 1, Bake 370000. Tel: (78922) 398 585. FAX: (99412) 395 452.

BAHAMAS

Population: 257,000
TV Sets: 50,000.
Video Standard: NTSC
BAHAMAS TELEVISION
Broadcasting Corp. of the Bahamas, P.O.Box N-1347, Nassau. Tel: (809) 322 4623. FAX: (809) 322 3924.

BAHRAIN

Population: 600,000.
TV Sets: 260,000.
Video Standard: PAL.
BAHRAIN TV
P.O. Box 1075, Manama, Bahrain. Tel: (973) 781 888.

BANGLADESH

Population: 116.6 million.
TV Sets: 600,000.
Video Standard: PAL.
BANGLADESH TV
Television Bhaban, P.O. Box 456, Rampura, Dhaka 1219. Tel: (8802) 400 131. FAX: (8802) 832 927.

BARBADOS

Population: 260,000.
TV Sets: 65,000.
Video Standard: NTSC.
CARIBBEAN BROADCASTING CORP.
P.O.Box 900, Bridgetown. Tel: (809) 429 2041. FAX: (809) 429 4795.

BELARUS

TV Sets: 10,000.
Video Standard: SECAM.
Belarussian television stations also retransmit programming from Russia's OK-1 (16 stations), RTV (7 stations) and TV-P (4 stations).
BELARUSKAE TELEBACHANNE
Makaenka 9, Miensk, 220807. Tel: (375172) 649 286. FAX: (375172) 648182.
VIDEO DISTRIBUTOR
FOBOS S
P/B 490, Minsk 220050, Belarus. Tel: (375172) 393 383. FAX: (375172) 393 383.

BELGIUM

Population: 10.2 million.
TV Sets: 4.2 million.
VCR Homes: 2.28 million.
Home Cable Service : 3.5 million.
Home Satellite Service: 13,000.
Video Standard: PAL.
French TV giant Canal Plus plans to offer digital TV services via cable to the French speaking population of Belgium in 1997. Canal Plus already serves nearly 200,000 Belgian

households with its standard format broadcasts. TRL-TV added a second channel in 1995. The Cartoon Network was effectively granted permission to provide its programming when a Belgian appellate court ruled that its programming was within the EU standards for European content. Belgian cable systems were also allowed to carry pay-per-view services and home shopping services.
TELEVISION BROADCASTERS
ARBELTSGEMELNSCHAFT DER OFFENTIICHEN RUND-FUNKANSTALTEN DER BUNDESREPUBLIK DEUTSCH-LAND (ARD)
Wetstraat 223-225, B-1040 Brussels. Tel: (322) 230 48 77.
BELGISCHE RADIO EN TELEVISIE (BRT)
Boulevard August Reyerslaan 52, B-1043 Brussels. Tel: (322) 742 5215. FAX: (322) 734 9351.
BRITISH BROADCASTING CORPORATION (BBC)
Karel de Grotelaan 1, Box 50, B-1040 Brussels. Tel: (322) 230 2120.
CANAL PLUS
Chaussee de Lauvain 656, 1050 Brussels. Tel: (322) 7300 211. FAX: (322) 732 1848.
RADIO TELEVISION LUXEMBOURGEOISE-TELEVISION INDEPENDANTE (RTL-TVI)
1 Ave. Ariane, 1210 Brussels. Tel: (322) 640 5150. FAX: (322) 737 4357.
RADIO-TELEVISION BELGE DE LA COMMUNAUTE FRANCAISE (RTBF)
Boulevard August Reyerslaan 52, B-1040 Brussels. Tel: (322) 737 2111. FAX: (322) 733 4020.
RADIOTELEVISIONE ITALIANA UNO (RAI-1) & DUE (RAI-2)
Karel de Grotelaan 1, Box 13, B-1040 Brussels. Tel: (RAI-1) (322) 238 09 30; (RAI-2) (322) 238 08 14.
TV5
(See RTBF listing above.)
VLAAMSE TELEVISIE MAATSCHAPPIJ (VTM)
1 Medialaan, B-1800 Vilvoorde. Tel: (322) 255 3211. Fax: (322) 252 5141.
ZWEITES DEUTSCHES FERNSEHEN (ZDF)
Wetstraat 223, Box 5, B-1040 Brussels. Tel: (322) 230 0814.
CABLE SERVICES
ANTENNE CENTRE TELEVISION
Rue de la Tombelle 92, B-7110 Houdeng-Aimeries. Tel: (3264) 281 542, 281 106. FAX: (3264) 285 644.
ASSOC. OF PRIVATE EUROPEAN CABLE OPERATORS
1 Boulevard Anspach, Box 25, B-1000 Brussels. Tel: (322) 229 2885. FAX: (322) 229 2889
ASSOC. INTERCOMMUNALE
(Pour Le Developpement Economique Et L'Amenagement Des Regions Du Centre Et Du Borinage-Idea)
74 Rue de Paturages, B-7300 Quaregnon. Tel: (3265) 665 701. FAX: (3265) 665 769.
ASSOCIATION LIEGOISE D'ELECTRICITE-ALE
95 Rue Louvrez, B-4000 Liege. Tel: (3241) 201 211. FAX: (3241) 201 363.
BRUTELE
29-31 Rue de Naples, B-1050 Brussels. Tel: (322) 511 6543.
CANAL C
Rue Froidebise 1, 5000 Namur. Tel: (3281) 741 000. FAX: (3281) 740 946.
CANAL PLUS BELGIUM
656 Chaussee de Louvain, B-1030 Brussels. Tel: (322) 732 0211. FAX: (322) 732 1848.
CANAL ZOOM
5 Place Du Sablon, 5030 Gembloux. Tel: (3281) 610 017. FAX: (3281) 612 999.
CODITEL BRABANT
26 Tweerkerkenstraat, B-1040 Brussels. Tel: (322) 226 5211.
ELECTRABEL
271 Mechelsesteenweg, 2018 Antwerp. Tel: (323) 280 0211. FAX: (323) 218 7788.
GASELWEST
57 Ryselstraat, 8500 Kotrijk. Tel: (3256) 369 211. FAX: (3256) 369 360.
HAVI TV
10 Noordkustlaan, 1702 Groot-Bijgaarden. Tel: (322) 466 2222. FAX: (322) 466 4202.
INTERELECTRA
8 Trichterheideweg, 3500 Hasselt. Tel: (3211) 221 171. FAX: (3211) 266 910.
NO TELE
2 Blvd. des Freres Rimbaut, 7500 Tournai. Tel: (3269) 210 691. FAX: (3269) 215 383.
RADIO PUBLIC
140 Ave. Chazel, B-1030 Brussels. Tel: (322) 240 0800. FAX: (322) 240 0801.
RTC TELE LIEGE
Rue de Rotterdam 33, 4000 Liege. Tel: (3241) 524 077. FAX: (3241) 520 353.

TELE BRUXELLES
Ave. Louise 166, B-1050 Brussels. Tel: (322) 640 6645. FAX: (322) 640 8583.
TELE MONS BORINAGE
8 Rue des Arbalestriers, 7000 Mons. Tel: (3265) 353 552. FAX: (3265) 346 241.
TELESAMBRE
Espace Sud, Route de Philipeville, 6010 Charleroi. Tel: (3271) 473 737. FAX: (3271) 473 838.
TELEVESDRE
Rue Neufmoulin 3, 4820 Dison. Tel: (3287) 337 625. FAX: (3287) 338 263.
TEVE WEST
56 Scheepsdalelaan, 8000 Brugge. Tel: (3250) 440 811. FAX: (3250) 440 905.
TV-5
(See TV-5 listing under Broadcasters.)
TV COM
7 Chaussee de la Croix, 1340 Ottignies. Tel: (3210) 410 196. FAX: (3210) 414 168.
VIDEOSCOPE
1 Place de la Gare, 5580 Rochefort. Tel: (3284) 211 572. FAX: (3284) 221 102.
VTM
(See VTM listing under Broadcasters.)
WOLU-TV
399 Avenue Georges Henri, 1200 Brussels. Tel: (322) 736 8733. FAX: (322) 733 7881.
SATELLITE BROADCASTERS
EURATEL BRUSSELS
12 Ave. Ariane, B-1200 Brussels. Tel: (322) 736 1795. FAX: (322) 773 4895.
FILMNET BELGIUM
Tollaan 97, St. Stevens Woluwe, B-1932 Brussels. Tel: (322) 714 1818. FAX: (322) 714 1814.
VIDEO ORGANIZATIONS
BELGIAN VIDEO FEDERATION
Jozef Mertensstraat 46, B-1702 Groot-Bijgaarden. Tel: (322) 463 1812. FAX: (322) 46 31481.
VIDEO DISTRIBUTORS
BAETEN & DE MUNCK-BDM
Box 12, 70 Barklaan, 9100 St Nicholas. Tel: (323) 766 4800. FAX: (323) 766 1004.
BELGIAN PRODUCTION VIDEO-BPV
5 Rue de College, 6000 Charleroi. Tel: (3271) 322 733. FAX: (3271) 325 012.
BMG ARIOLA
Square F, Riga 30, B-1030 Brussels. Tel: (322) 240 2863. (322) 737 1750.
BUENA VISTA INTERNATIONAL
Romeinsesteenweg 486, B-1853 Grimbergen. Tel: (322) 263 1711. FAX: (322) 263 1797.
C.T.V. CENTRE D'ACTION ET DE DOCUMENTATION POUR LA TELEVISION
Ave. des Nerviens 3, B-1040 Brussels. Tel: (322) 735 22 77.
CANEL C
1 Rue Res des Relis Namurees, 5000 Namur. Tel: (3281) 741 000. FAX: (3281) 740 946.
CINELIBRE
Chaussee de Haecht, 270, B-1030 Brussels. Tel: (322) 245 8700. FAX: (322) 216 2575.
CNR VIDEO
Box 3, 17 De Vunt, 3220 Holsbeek. Tel: (3216) 441 111. FAX: (3216) 441 119.
COLUMBIA TRISTAR HOME VIDEO
38 Rue Souveraine, B-1050 Brussels. Tel: (322) 513 8684. FAX: (322) 502 3575.
CONCORDE VIDEO
130 Hulpa, 1050 Brussels. Tel: (322) 675 2050. FAX: (322) 675 3076.
ECVD
7 Rue de Chatelet, 6030 Marchienne-au-Pont. Tel: (3271) 517 984. FAX: (3271) 519 410.
METEOR HOME VIDEO
Box 40, 1 Doornveld, 1731 Zellik. Tel: (322) 463 1775. FAX: (322) 466 5456.
OCIC
Rue de L'Orme 8, B-1040 Brussels. Tel: (322) 734 4294. FAX: (322) 734 3207.
PAULINE PICTURES
159 Berkendaelstraat, 1060 Brussels. Tel: (322) 347 5846. FAX: (322) 347 2462.
POLYGRAM VIDEO
34 Blvd. de la Woluwe, Woluwedal, B-1200 Brussels. Tel: (322) 775 8140. FAX: (322) 770 7691.
RCA/COLUMBIA PICTURES VIDEO
38 Opperstraat, 1050 Brussels. Tel: (322) 512 5872. FAX: (322) 733 4020.

SUPER CLUB
110 Van Kerckhovenstraat, 2880 Bornem. Tel: (323) 890 4811. FAX: (323) 890 4800.
SUPER PRODUCTION VIDEO BELGIUM
241 Rue Royale, 1210 Brussels. Tel: (322) 218 7280.
VDM VIDEO
Box 12, 70 Parklaan, 9100 Sint-Niklaas. Tel: (323) 766 4800. FAX: (323) 766 1004.
VIDEO PLAY
14 Rue de la Neuville, 6000 Charleroi. Tel: (3271) 330 701. FAX: (3271) 332 224.
VIDEOPOOL
Inquisitiestraat 21, B-1040 Brussels. Tel: (322) 736 11 85. FAX: (322) 736 8200.
WARNER HOME VIDEO
42-44 Boulevard Brand Whitlock, B-1200 Brussels. Tel: (322) 735 1791. FAX: (322) 736 2318.

BELIZE

Population: 214,000.
TV Sets: 24,000.
TROPICAL VISION
48 Albert Cattouse Bldg., Regent St., Belize City. Tel: (5012) 772 46. FAX: (5012) 750 40.

BENIN

Population: 5.5 million.
TV Sets: 20,000.
OFFICE DE RADIODIFFUZION ET TV DE BENIN (ORTB)
P.O.Box 366, Cotonou. (229) 301 0628.

BERMUDA

Population: 61,600.
TV Sets: 50,000.
Video Standard: NTSC.
ZBM-ZFB RADIO & TELEVISION
P.O. Box HM 452, Hamilton. Tel: (809) 295 2828.

BOLIVIA

Population: 8 million.
TV Sets: 50,000.
Video Standard: NTSC.
MAJOR BROADCASTERS
TV POPULAR
Calle Juan de la Riva 1527, Casilla 8704, La Paz.
GALAVISION
Cas. 495, Santa Cruz.
AMERICA TV
Cas. 10076, Santa Cruz.
EMPRESA NACIONAL DE TV
Cas. 900, La Paz.
REDE ATB
Ave. 6 de Agnosto 2972, La Paz.
TELEANDINA
Cas. 1665, La Paz.
TV UNIVERSTARIA
Cas. 21982, La Paz.
SONOMAC
Cas. 21375, La Paz.
TECNITRON
Cas. 4410, La Paz.

BOPHUTHATSWANA

Population: 1.4 million.
Video Standard:PAL.
BOP-TV MMABATHO
P.O. Bag X 2150, Mmabatho. Tel: (27140) 289 111. FAX: (27140) 260 09.

BOSNIA HERZEGOVINIA

Population: 3.2 million.
TV Sets: 1.1 million.
Video Standard: PAL
TELEVIZIJA SARAJEVO
VI Prolerterske Brigade 4, 71000 Sarajevo. Tel: (3871) 522333.

BRAZIL

Population: 160.7 million.
TV Sets: 32 million.
Video Standard: PAL-M.
NETWORKS
REDE GLOBO DE TELEVISTAO
Rua Lopes Quintas 303, 22463 Rio de Janeiro. Tel. (5521) 294 7732. Telex: 21-22795.

REDE MANCHETE DE TELEVISTAO
Rua do Russel 766, 22210 Rio de Janeiro. Tel: (5521) 285
0033. Telex: 21 21525.
REDE BANDEIRANTES DE TELEVISTAO
Rua Radiantes 13, 05699 Sao Paulo. Tel: (5511) 842 3011.
Telex 11 81680.
SISTEMA BRASILEIRO DE TELEVISTAO
Rua Dona Sta Veloso 575, 02050 Sao Paulo. Tel: (5511) 292
9044. Telex: 11 63892.
TV CULTURA (SAO PAULO)
Rua Ceno Sbrighi 378, 05099 Sao Paulo. Tel: (5511) 263 9111.
Telex :11 82052.
TV EDUCATIVA (FEDERAL)
Av. Gomes Freire 474, 20231 Rio de Janeiro. Tel: (5521) 221
2227. Telex: 21 22609
TV GAZETA
Av Paulista 900, 01310 Sao Paulo. Tel:. (5511) 287 4322. Telex:
11 35914.
TV RECORD
Av. Miruna 713, 04084 Sao Paulo. Tel:. (5511) 240 1633. Telex:
11 22245.
TV RIO
Rua Miguel de Frias 57, 20211 Rio de Janeiro. Tel:. (5521) 293
0012. Telex: 21 38183.
VIDEO ORGANIZATIONS
BRAZILIAN VIDEO TRADE ASSOCIATION
Ave. Reboucas 1206, Sao Paulo. Tel: (5511) 881 8111.
BRAZIL VIDEO UNION
Rua Mexico 31/603, Rio de Janeiro. Tel: (5521) 240 2326.

BRUNEI DARUSSALAM

Population: 300,000.
TV Sets: 100,000.
Video Standard: PAL.
RADIO TV BRUNEI
Bander Seri Begawan, 2042 Brunei, Negara Brunei
Darussalam. Two channels.

BULGARIA

Population: 8.4 million.
TV Sets: 3.2 million.
Video Standard: SECAM.
Bulgarian television also retransmits programming from
Russian OK-1 and European TV-5.
BULGARIAN TELEVISION
Ul, San Stefano Str 29, 1504 Sofia. Tel. (3592) 652 870. FAX:
(3592) 871 871.

BURKINA FASO

Population: 10.4 million.
TV Sets: 75,000.
Video Standard: SECAM.
TÉLÉVISION NATIONALE BURKINA
B.P. 1 2530, Ougadougou. Tel: (226) 354 773.

BURUNDI

Population: 6.3 million.
Video Standard: SECAM.
TELEVISION NATIONALE DU BURUNDI
B.P. 1900, Bujumbura. Tel: (257) 2247 60.

CAMBODIA

Population: 10.3 million.
TV Sets: 70,000.
Video Standard: PAL
CAMBODIAN TV
19, Street 242, Chaktomuk, Daun Penh, Phnom Penh.

CAMEROON

TV Sets: 15,000.
Video Standard: PAL.
CAMEROON RADIO AND TELEVISION
P.O. Box 1634, Yaoundé. Tel: (237) 42 6060. FAX: (237) 203 340.

CANADA

Population: 28.4 million.
TV Sets: 17 million.
Video Standard: NTSC.
TELEVISION STATISTICS
Latest information published by Statistics Canada (StatsCan), a
federal government agency. All figures are in Canadian dollars.
TV REVENUES
The total revenue of the broadcasting industry (television and
radio) in 1994, including the Canadian Broadcasting

Corporation (CBC), was $2.61 billion, an increase of 2.6%
since 1993. Privately owned television broadcasting reported a
$38.4 million profit in 1994 compared to $58.5 million in 1993.
Excluding the CBC, there were 110 licensed TV stations, with
108 in operation in 1994.
In 1994, total program expenses of private television broadcasters totalled $821 million, and net profit after tax for private
stations declined with a profit of $7.1 million in 1994 compared
to $10.3 million in 1993.
The television operating revenues of the Canadian
Broadcasting Corporation (CBC) were $348.476 million in
1993, and the net cost of CBC operations increased from
$1,069 million to $1,122.8 million.
NUMBER OF TV SETS
In 1995 colour televisions were in 11.076 million households,
with 5.593 million homes having two or more colour sets. In
1995 the province of Ontario again led with estimates of 2.023
million households owning one television and 2.060 million
owning two or more (compared to 1.634 million with one and
2.153 million with two or more in 1994). The province of
Québec followed with estimates of 1.398 million owning one
television and 1.505 with two or more (compared to 1.178 million owning one television and 1.518 million with two or more
in 1994).
TELEVISION VIEWING:
The following data was collected from Canadians two years
and over, during a seven-day period, by means of a diary-type
questionnaire, recorded at quarter-hour intervals during three
separate weeks in November/95.
In 1995 more time was spent watching TV, bringing to a halt
the modest decline from 24.2 hours weekly in 1986 to 22.7
hours weekly in 1994. 1995 stats showed an average of 23.2
hours weekly spent watching TV across Canada, up 30 minutes more than the previous year. Much of this increase was
due in part to new cable specialty services becoming available
in 1995. Viewing by teenagers (12-17) and children (2-11)
increased slightly with teens spending 17.5 hours weekly viewing TV in 1995 and children averaging 17.8 hours. Young men
(18-24) watched only 15.1 hours a week, and young women in
the same age group 19.0 hours a week. Individuals over 50
watched the most television: men (50-59) 24.1 hours a week,
(over 60) 33.0 hours a week, with women tuning in more than
men - (50-59) 29.4 hours a week, (over 60) 37.2 hours a week.
In Québec francophone viewers spent more time in front of the
television set than anglophones (26.7 hours vs. 23.0 hours),
and viewing among age and sex francophone groups in
Québec was usually higher than corresponding groups of citizens across the country. TV viewing increased countrywide in
the age groups 50-59 and 60+.
CABLE TV REVENUES/SUBSCRIBERS
[Data based on annual returns from cable television licensees
and used to generate information on basic tier services and
discretionary and other services of the cable television indus-
try] In 1995 revenues for the entire cable television industry
totalled $2,532.3 million, an 8.7% increase over 1994, and
basic tier cable revenues were $1,759.1 up 4.9% from 1994.
Total revenue from discretionary and other services was
$686.2 million, an increase of 20.3% from 1994.
Expenses for the industry were $2,352.3 million in 1995, a
17.6% increase over 1994. Net profit after income taxes for the
entire cable television industry was $325.9 million, an increase
of 25.6% over 1994. There were 7,231,028 direct subscribers
and 560,078 indirect subscribers in 1995 compared to
7,087,013 and 746,178 in 1994, representing an overall
decrease of 0.5% from the previous year.
CABLE LICENSEES
In 1995 there were 2,050 cable television systems licensed by
the Canadian Radio-Television and Telecommunications
Commission (CRTC) across all the provinces, with 50 of these
under development and not operating.
VIDEO
Latest information published by Statistics Canada (StatsCan),
a federal government agency.
VCRS
Out of a total of 11.243 million responding households sam-
pled in 1995 an estimated 7.423 million owned one VCR, and
1.809 million owned two or more. The province of Ontario led
with an estimated 2.775 million households owning one VCR
and 716,000 households with two or more, out of 4.143 million
reponding. Québec followed with an estimated 1.887 million
households owning one VCR and 395,000 households with two
or more, out of 2.937 million responding.
VIDEO MARKET
The 1994-95 sales revenue from the home entertainment distribution market rose to $132.9 million from $121.5 million in
1993-94. Videocassette wholesalers recorded $717.0 million in
videocassette sales in 1994-95, a 39% increase from 1993-94
and the highest level of sales ever. The Canadian content
share of the home entertainment market was estimated to be
minimal—less than 0.5%.

—PATRICIA THOMPSON

CANADIAN RADIO-TELEVISION AND TELECOMMUNICATIONS COMMISSION (CRTC)
Ottawa, ON, K1A 0N2. (819) 997-0313. Chairman: Keith Spicer, Vice-Chairman, Broadcasting: Fernand Belisle, Vice-Chairman, Telecommunications: David Colville
The CRTC is an independent authority responsible for regulating (under the Broadcasting Act) all broadcasting in Canada, including AM and FM radio, television, cable television, specialty services and pay-television.
The CRTC is also responsible for the regulation, mainly with respect to rates and terms of service, of Canada's federally-regulated telecommunications carriers.

TV CORPORATIONS
ACCESS—THE EDUCATION STATION
3720 76 Ave., Edmonton, AB, T6B 2N9. (403) 440-7777. FAX: (403) 440-8899.

CANADIAN BROADCASTING CORPORATION
1500 Bronson Ave., P.O.Box 8478, Ottawa, ON, K1G 3J5. (613) 724-1200.
English Networks: P.O.Box 500, Stn. A, Toronto, ON, M5W 1E6. (416) 205-3311.
French Networks: 1400 René Lévesque Blvd. E., P.O.Box 6000, Montréal, QC. H3C 3A8. (514) 597-5970.

CFMT INTERNATIONAL
(A multilingual station serving 21 ethnic communities), 545 Lakeshore Blvd.W., Toronto, ON. M5V 1A3. (416) 260-0047. FAX: (416) 260-3621.

CITY-TV
299 Queen St. W., Toronto, ON, M5V 2Z5. (416) 591-5757. FAX/News: (416) 593-NEWS, FAX/Sales: (416) 591-7792, FAX/Executive offices: (416) 340-7005.

CTV TELEVISION NETWORK LTD.
250 Yonge St., Ste. 1800, Toronto, ON, M5B 2N8. (416) 595-4100. FAX: (416) 595-1203.

GLOBAL COMMUNICATIONS LIMITED/ GLOBAL TELE-VISION NETWORK/ CANWEST GLOBAL SYSTEM
81 Barber Greene Rd., Don Mills, ON, M3C 2A2. (416) 446-5311. FAX: (416) 446-5543.

KNOWLEDGE NETWORK/OPEN LEARNING AGENCY
(Educational- adults & children), 4355 Mathissi Place, Burnaby, BC, V5G 4S8. (604) 431-3000. FAX: (604) 431-3333.

SASKATCHEWAN COMMUNICATIONS NETWORK (SCN)
(Educational), 800—1920 Broad St., Regina, SK, S4P 3V7. (306) 787-0490. FAX: (306) 787-0496.

TV ONTARIO
(Educational), 2180 Yonge St., Toronto, ON, M4S 2B9. (416) 484-2600, (800) INFO-TVO. FAX: (416) 484-6285.

PAY TV
ALLARCOM PAY TELEVISION LTD.
5324 Calgary Trail S., Ste. 200, Edmonton, AB, T6H 5B8. (403) 430-2800. FAX: (403) 437-3188.

THE FAMILY CHANNEL INC.
BCE Place, 181 Bay St., P.O.Box 787, Toronto, ON, M5J 2T3. (416) 956-2030. FAX: 9416) 956-2035.

MOVIEPIX
(An Astral Communications Company), BCE Place, 181 Bay St., P.O.Box 787, Toronto, ON, M5J 2T3. (416) 956-2010. FAX: (416) 956-2012.

PREMIER CHOIX: CANAL D/CANAL FAMILLE/SUPER ECRAN
(Astral Communications Companies), 2100 rue Ste-Catherine ouest, bur. 800, Montréal, QC. H3H 2T3. (514) 939-3150. FAX: (514) 939-3151.

TMN - THE MOVIE NETWORK
(an Astral Communications Company), BCE Place, 181 Bay St., P.O.Box 787, Toronto, ON, M5J 2T3. (416) 956-2010. FAX: (416) 956-2011.

VIEWER'S CHOICE CANADA
(an Astral Communications Company) BCE Place, 181 Bay St., P. O. Box 787, Toronto, ON, M5J 2T3. (416) 956-2010. FAX: (416) 956-2055.

SPECIALTY CHANNELS
BRAVO
299 Queen St. W., Toronto, ON, M5V 2Z5. (416) 591-5757. FAX: (416) 591-8497.

CBC NEWSWORLD
P.O.Box 500, Stn. A., Toronto, ON, M5W 1E6. (416) 205-2950. FAX: (416) 205-6080.

THE DISCOVERY CHANNEL
2225 Sheppard Ave. E., Ste. 100, North York, ON, M2J 5C2. (416) 494-2929. FAX: (416) 490-7067.

FAIRCHILD TV
Production: 494 W. 39th Ave., Ste. B8, Vancouver, BC, V6X 3R8. (604) 708-1313. FAX: (604) 708-1300.

LIFE NETWORK
1155 Leslie St., Toronto, ON, M3C 2J6. (416) 444-9494, FAX (416) 444-0018.

MUCHMUSIC NETWORK
299 Queen St.W., Toronto, ON, M5V 2Z5. (416) 591-5757. FAX/Studio: (416) 591-6824, FAX/Executive offices: (416) 340-7005.

NCN—NEW COUNTRY NETWORK
49 Ontario St., Toronto, ON, M5A 2V1. (416) 360-4626. FAX: (416) 360-6263.

SHOWCASE
160 Bloor St.E., Ste. 1000, Toronto, ON, M4W 1B9. (416) 967-0022. FAX: (416) 967-0044.

TELELATINO NETWORK INC.
5125 Steeles Ave. W., Weston, ON, M9L 1R5. (416) 744-8200. FAX: (416) 744-0966 (approx. 100 hours weekly of Spanish & Italian programming).

VISION TV
90 Bond St., Toronto, ON, M5B 1X2. (416) 368-3194. FAX: (416) 368-9774 (Alternative, multicultural, multi-faith - national satellite to cable).

WTN (WOMEN'S TELEVISION NETWORK)
1661 Portage Ave., Ste. 300, Winnipeg, MB, R3J 3T7. (204) 783-5116. FAX: (204) 774-3227.

YTV CANADA INC.
64 Jefferson Ave., Unit 18, Toronto, ON, M6K 3H3. (416) 534-1191. FAX: (416) 533-0346.

INDUSTRY ORGANIZATIONS:
ACADEMY OF CANADIAN CINEMA AND TELEVISION
158 Pearl St., Toronto, ON, M5H 1L3. (416) 591-2040. FAX: (416) 591-2157.
3375 boul. St-Laurent, bur. 709 Montréal, QC, H2X 2T7. (514) 849-7448. FAX: (514) 849-5069.
1385 Homer St., Vancouver, BC, V6B 2S2. (604) 684-4528. FAX: (604) 684-4574.
1652 Barrington St., Halifax, NS, B3J 2A2. (902) 425-0489. FAX: (902) 425-8851.
Los Angeles Division: (800) 644-5194.

ACTRA PERFORMERS GUILD (CLC, FIA)
National Office, 2239 Yonge St., Toronto, ON, M4S 2B5. (416) 489-1311. FAX: (416) 489-8076.

ASSOCIATION DES PRODUCTEURS DE FILMS ET DE T ÉL ÉVISION DU QU ÉBEC (APFTQ)
740 St-Maurice, Bur. 201, Montréal, QC, H3C 1L5. (514) 397-8600. FAX: (514) 392-0232.

ASSOCIATION QUÉBECOISE DES REALISATEURS ET REALISATRICES DE CINÉMA ET DE TÉLÉVISION
1600 De Lorimier, Bur.122, Montréal, QC, H2K 3W5. (514) 527-2197/521-1984 Poste 436. FAX: (514) 527-7699.

CANADIAN CABLE TELEVISION ASSOCIATION
360 Albert St., Ste. 1010, Ottawa, ON, K1R 7X7. (613) 232-7800. FAX: (232) 2137.

CANADIAN FILM & TELEVISION PRODUCTION ASSOCIATION (CFTPA)
171 Bloor St. E., North Tower, Ste. 806, Toronto, ON, M4W 3R8. (416) 927-8942, (800) 267-8208. FAX: (416) 922-4038.

VIDEO TRADE ASSOCIATION
VIDEO SOFTWARE DEALERS ASSOCIATION (VSDA)
Canadian office: 40 Sheppard Ave. W., 8th.Fl., North York, ON, M2N 6K9. (416) 733-2294. FAX: (416) 730-8591.

VIDEO DISTRIBUTORS
FIDELITY HOME ENTERTAINMENT
5600 Ambler Dr., Mississauga, ON, L4W 2K9. (905) 625-7333. FAX: (905) 625-0541.
#215 - 2550 Boundary Rd., Burnaby, BC, V5M 3Z3. (604) 438-4336. FAX: (604) 438-4337.

VIDEO ONE CANADA, LTD.
5600 Ambler Dr., Mississauga, ON, L4W 2K9. (905) 624-7337. FAX: (905) 624-7310.
Branches: 105 2250 Boundary Rd., Burnaby, BC, V5M 3Z3. (604) 437-4473, (800) 242-0648. FAX: (604) 432-6926.
6023 4th St.S.E., Calgary, AB, T2H 2A5,. (403) 258-3880, (800) 352-8245. FAX: (403) 252-3176.
11133 156th St., Edmonton, AB T5M 1X9,. (403) 451-9060, (800) 661-9635. FAX: (403) 452-1763.
Bay D, 2220 Northridge Dr., Saskatoon, SK, S7L 6X8. (306) 933-4930. FAX: (306) 933-4139.
1821 King Edward, Unit 12, Winnipeg, MB, R2R 0N1. (204) 694-6007. FAX: (204) 694-0928.
647 Wilton Grove Rd. W., Units 1 & 2, London, ON, N6A 4C2. (519) 685-1502, (800) 265-6054. FAX: (519) 668-2059.
5600 Ambler Dr., Mississauga, ON, L4W 2K9. (905) 624-4330. FAX: (905) 624-9077.
105 Scarsdale Rd., Toronto, ON, M3B 2R2. (416) 447-9600, (800) 387-0184. FAX: (416) 447-7775.
380 Terminal Rd., Ottawa, ON, K1G 0Z3. (613) 244-0000. FAX: (613) 244-1230.
10 Morris Dr., Unit 40, Dartmouth, NS, B3B 1K8. (902) 468-6661. FAX: (902) 468-2260.
21 Mews Pl., St. John's, NF, A1B 3V8,. (709) 754-3437. FAX: (709) 754-3230.

VIDEO GLOBE 1
398 Isabey, Ville St-Laurent, QC, H4T 1V3. (514) 738-6665, (800) 361-7151. FAX: (514) 738-3923

ASTRAL HOME ENTERTAINMENT
(An Astral Communications Company)
Head Office: 7215 route Trans-Canadienne, Montréal, QC, H4T
1A2. (514) 333-7555. FAX: (514) 333-7309.
Branches: 96 Orfus Rd., North York, ON, M6A 1C9. (416)
785-5580, (800) 263-2974. FAX: (416) 785-1219.
7215 route Trans-Canadienne, Montréal, QC, H4T 1A2. (514)
333-7555, (800) 361-3320. FAX: (514) 333-7309.
2058 Alpha St., Burnaby, BC, V6K 5K7. (604) 299-8484, (800)
663-4559. FAX: (604) 299-8494.
11472 149th St., Edmonton, AB, T5M 1W8. (403) 453-3007,
(800) 252-7907. FAX: (403) 452-8026.
6143 4th St.S.E., Unit 9, Calgary, AB, T2H 2H9. (403) 258-
2131, (800) 661-1545. FAX: (403) 253-3455.
76 1313 Border St., Winnipeg, MB, R3H 0X4. (204) 694-4421,
(800) 665-8012. FAX: (204) 694-7177.
201 Brownlow Ave., #15, Dartmouth, NS, B3B 1W2. (902)
468-3393, (800) 565-1778 (Newfoundland only). FAX: (902)
468-3197.

R.O.W. ENTERTAINMENT
255 Shields Ct., Markham, ON, L3R 8V2. (905) 475-3550.
FAX: (905) 475-4163.

THE SHANNOCK CORPORATION
4222 Manor St., Burnaby, BC V5G 1B2. (604) 433-3331, (800)
665-9767. FAX: (604) 433-4815.
10-6120 3rd St. S.E., Calgary, AB T2H 1K4. (403) 253-2113,
(800) 661-1636, FAX (403) 255-3359.
14944 121 Ave., Edmonton, AB T5V 1A3. (403) 453-1986,
(800) 661-6969. FAX: (403) 451-0401.
2228 Ave. C North, Saskatoon, SK S7L 6C4. (306) 652-3553.
FAX: (306) 652-2726.
1692 Dublin Ave., Unit 2, Winnipeg, MB R3H 0H1. (204) 632-
0581. FAX: (204) 632-7855.
5582 Ambler Dr., Mississauga, ON, L4W 2K9. (905) 602-5922,
(800) 665-9417. FAX: (905) 602-5925.
109 Ilsley Ave., Unit 15, Dartmouth, NS B3B 1S8. (902) 468-
2868, (800) 565-0668. FAX: (902) 468-2814.

SMA DISTRIBUTION
(a division of the Shannock Corporation) 45 Colewater Rd.,
Don Mills, ON, M3B 1Y8. (416) 441-0699, (800) 267-1216.
FAX: (416) 441-4563.

SHANNOK QUEBEC AUDIO & VIDEO
8569 Dalton Rd., Ville-Mont-Royal, QC H4T 1V5. (514) 344-
4424, (800) 567-4424. FAX: (514) 344-4461.

VIDEO DISTRIBUTION

ALLIANCE RELEASING
Home Video Division, 5 Place Ville-Marie, Ste. 1435, Montréal,
QC H3G 2G2. (515) 878-2282. FAX: (514) 878-2419.

ASTRAL DISTRIBUTION
(An Astral Communications Company) 33 Yonge St., Ste. 1020,
Toronto, Ont. M5E 1S9. 416-956-2000. FAX: (416) 956-2020.

BBS PRODUCTIONS, INC.
9 Channel Nine Court, Scarborough, ON, M1S 4B5. (416) 299-
2000. FAX: (416) 299-2067.

BVA VIDEO LTD.
(A Joint Venture between Buena Vista Home Video and Astral
Bellevue Pathé Inc.)
BCE Place, 181 Bay St., Ste. 100, Toronto, ON, M5J 2T3. (416)
956-5387. FAX: (416) 956-2024.

CYCLOPS COMMUNICATION CORP.
44 Gibson Ave., Toronto, ON, M5R 1T5. (416) 926-8981. FAX:
(416) 926-9878.

FRANCE FILM COMPANY/ COMPGNIE FRANCE FILM
505 Sherbrooke St. E., Ste. 2401, Montréal, QC H2L 4N3.
(514) 844-0680.

MALOFILM DISTRIBUTION INC.
(Video Division) 3575 Boul. St-Laurent, bur. 650, Montréal, QC
H2X 2T7 (514) 844-4555. FAX:. (514) 844-1471.
2221 Yonge St., Ste. 400, Toronto, ON, M4S 2B4. (416) 480-
0453. FAX: (416) 480-0501.

NORSTAR RELEASING
86 Boor St. W., 4th Fl., Toronto, ON, M5S 1M5. (416) 961-
6278. FAX: (416) 961-5608.

NORTH AMERICAN RELEASING, INC.
808 Nelson St., Ste.2105, Vancouver, BC V6Z 2H2. (604) 681-
2165. FAX: (604) 681-5538.

POLYGRAM FILMED ENTERTAINMENT
80 Citizen Court, Unit 1, Markham, ON, L6G 1A7. (905) 940-
9700. FAX: (905) 940-9556.

TELEGENIC VIDEO DISTRIBUTORS, INC.
20 Holly St., Ste. 300, Toronto, ON, M4S 3B1. (416) 484-8000.
FAX: (416) 484-8001.

VIDEOVILLE SHOWTIME INC.
4610 Côte Vertu, Ville St.-Laurent, QC H4S 1C7. (514)
336-0038. FAX: (514) 745-4274.

CENTRAL AFRICAN REPUBLIC

Population: 3.2 million.
Video Standard: SECAM.

RADIODIFFUSION TELEVISION CENTRAFIQUE
P.O.Box 940, Bagui. (236) 613 342.

CHAD

Population: 5.6 million.
TV Sets: 50,000.
Video Standard: SECAM.
TÉLÉCHAD
B.P. 74, N'Djamena. Tel: (235) 512 923.

CHILE

Population: 14.2 million.
Percentage of Homes with TV: 99.
Number of VCRs: 1.1 million.
Retail Price Per Video: US$19.00.
Rental Price Per Video: US$2.00.
Blank Tape: US$5.00.
Video Standard: NTSC.
As real wages increase and the middle class has more and
more access to consumer credit, the rate of VCR ownership
will continue to increase, particularly in the Regions. Renting a
video cassette is the cheapest and easiest form of entertainment. Video stores are in every barrio, no matter how poor the
district may be. The duty rate on the importation of VCRs is a
20% surtax on top of the basic duty rate of 11% on all import-
ed goods. Piracy is estimated at 30% of legitmate sales. The
Association of Video Distributors has been very successful in
exposing video bootleggers.

BROADCASTERS

**UNIVERSIDAD CATÓLICA DE CHILE TELEVISIÓN,
CHANNEL 13**
Ines Matte Urrejola 0848, Santiago. Tel: (562) 251-4000.

TELEVISIÓN NACIONAL DE CHILE, CHANNEL 7
Bellavista 0990, Santiago. Fax: 735-3000.

**MEGAVISIÓN (TELEVISA - MEXICO/RICARDO CLARO
GROUP), CHANNEL 9**
Av. Vicuna Mackenna 1348, Santiago. Tel: (562) 555-5400.

**LA RED (GLOBAL CAN-WEST, CANADA/COPESA-
BANCOSORNO), CHANNEL 4**
Av. Maquehue Sur 1201, Las Condes, Santiago. Tel: (562) 212-
1111.

UNIVERSIDAD CATÓLICA DE VALPARAISO, CHANNEL 5
Aqua Santa 2455, Via del Mar. Tel: (Santiago) (562) 231-8950.

ROCK & POP (RADIO COOPERATIVA), CHANNEL 2
Antonio Bellet 223, Providencia, Santiago. Tel/FAX: (562) 236
0066.

CABLE & PAY TV

CABLEXPRESS
Salesianos 1140, Santiago. Tel: (562) 554 4500. FAX: (562)
551 9050.

METROPOLIS
Irarrazaval 4760 Vicuna. Tel: (562) 237 1010.

INTERCOM
Manquehue Sur 520, Las Condes. Tel: (562) 224 5150. FAX:
224 5830.

CABLE HOGAR
Pajaritos 5717, Maipe. Tel/FAX: (562) 743 1998.

ALPHACOMM
Apoquindo 6415, of. 92, Las Condes. Tel: (562) 229 7735.

KUHN LTDA.
Marin 097, Santiago. Tel: (562) 222 6451. FAX: (562) 634 4631.

MARKET RESEARCH AND RATINGS

HERNANDO DE AGUIRRE
111, Providencia. Tel: (562) 231 5064; FAX: (562) 233 5599.

REGULATORY BODY

CONSEJO NACIONAL DE TELEVISION
Moneda 1020, Santiago.

VIDEO RETAILERS

BLOCKBUSTER CHILE
Colon 3494, Las Condes. Tel: (562) 207 1427. FAX: (562) 208
7698

VIDEO DISTRIBUTORS

VIDEO CHILE
Colon 3494, Las Condes, Tel: (562) 207 1427. FAX: (562) 208
7698. (rep. for Cinea International, Paramount, Warner Bros.,
Touchstone and Walt Disney).

VIDEO LKTEL
Alameda 1146, 3rd Flr., sector B, Santiago, Tel: (562) 696
9814. FAX: (562) 698 7100. (rep. for Columbia, Orion and Tri
Star)

TRANSANDIA
Rancagua 0226, Santiago, Tel: (562) 699 1239. FAX: (562) 698
9692. (rep. for Twentieth-Century Fox)

TRANSEUROPA
General del Canto 10, 3rd flr., Providencia. Tel: (562) 235
5683. FAX: (562) 235 2399. (rep. for New Line)

CHINA

Population: 1.2 billion.
TV Sets: 228 million.
Video Standard: PAL.
Home Cable Service: 7 million TV sets linked to nearly 9,000 cable systems.
Cable: CGTV Beijing.
Columbia TriStar International Television plans to offer 400 hours of Mandarin programming for the Chinese market.The Chinese aerospace industry suffered a setback in its program of providing launch services for commercial telecommunication satellites when a Long March rocket exploded on take-off. China's thriving piracy industry in videos, CDs and computer software forced American trade negotiators to reconsider China's Most Favored Nation trade status, and nearly impose sanctions against $2 billion in Chinese imports (with Chinese retaliations also threatened). The crisis was averted in mid-Summer 1996, with the Chinese government agreeing to begin policing manufacturers better. Although the Chinese government has made some efforts to stem the illegal practices, it has failed to stop the piracy. Some 31 factories are allegedly engaged in the piracy of copyrighted materials. However, Warner Bros. Home Video and MGM have signed a deal to allow a Chinese company to manufacture licensed copies of movies.

GOVERNMENT BROADCASTER
CHINA CENTRAL TELEVISION (CCTV)
11 Fuxing Lu Road, Beijing 100859. Tel: (8610) 850 0144. FAX: (8610) 851 2010.

COLOMBIA

Population: 36.2 million.
TV Sets: 5.5 million.
VCR Ownership level: 24%.
Estimated Piracy Level: 40%
Video Standard: NTSC.
TELEVISION COMPANIES
AMD TELEVISION
Cra 30 No 90-54, Bogota. Tel: (571) 610 1155. FAX: (571) 236 1601.
AUDIOVISUALES
Edificio Murillo Toro, Piso 4, Bogota. Tel: (571) 283 4325.
JORGE BARON TELEVISION
Centro Jorge Baron, Ave. 15 No 123-31, Torre A, Bogota. Tel: (571) 215 0211.
CARACOL TELEVISION
Calle 19 No 3-16, Piso 3, PO Box 26484, Bogota. Tel: (571) 281 7900. FAX: (571) 286 3160. Telex: 41480.
COESTRELLAS SA
Tr 6 No 51A-25, Bogota. Tel: (571) 288 7154. FAX: (571) 288 5443. Telex: 45611.
COLOMBIANA DE TELEVISION
Calle 92 No 9-17, PO Box 7661, Bogota. Tel: (571) 236 9267. FAX: (571) 218 1775. Telex: 45614.
INSTITUTO NACIONAL DE RADIO Y TELEVISION (INRAVISION)
National Radio and Television Institute, Centro Administrativo Nacional CAN, Bogota. Tel: (571) 222 0700. Telex: 43311.
PREGO TELEVISION
Cra 6 No 35-37, Bogota. Tel: (571) 285 0211.
PRODUCCIONES JES
Calle 21 No 42A-10, PO Box 28508, Bogota. Tel: (571) 268 5500. FAX: (571) 269 9473. Telex: 42072.
PRODUCCIONES PUNCH
Calle 43 No 27-47, Bogota. Tel: (571) 269 4711. FAX: (571) 269 3539.
PRODUCCIONES TEVECINE LTDA
Cra 18 No 80-15, Bogota. Tel: (571) 218 4799. FAX: (571) 211 1924.
RCN TELEVISION
Ave. de la Americas No 65-82, PO Box 35800, Bogota. Tel: (571) 290 6088. FAX: (571) 260 0924. Telex: 45470.
RTI
Calle 19 No 4-56, Piso 2, PO Box 7808, Bogota. Tel: (571) 282 7700. FAX: (571) 284 9012. Telex: 43294.
TELEANTIOQUIA
Calle 41 NO 25-28 (Piso 3), Medellin. Tel: (574) 262 0311.
TELECARIBE
Cra 54 No 72-142, Piso 10, Barranquilla. Tel: (5753) 582 297. FAX: (58) 560 924.
TELEPACIFICO
Calle 5 No 38A-14. Of 308, Centro Comercial Imbanaco, Cali. Tel: (5723) 575 014.
VIDEO DISTRIBUTORS
VIDEO IMPACTO
Carrera 13, 77-31, Bogota. Tel: (571) 623 7083. FAX: (571) 610 3692.
ALFA VIDEO
Carrera 28 bis, 50-25, Bogota. Tel: (571) 310 0077. FAX: (571) 2117470.

BATI VIDEOS DE COLOMBIA
Calle 91, 8-69, Bogota. Tel: (571) 218 9800. FAX: (571) 218 8841.
MAGNUM VIDEO
Transversal 42B, 99-A66, Bogota. Tel: (571) 245 3060. FAX: (571) 287 7795.

CONGO

Population: 2.5 million.
TV sets: 8,500.
Video Standard: SECAM.
RADIODIFFUSION TELEVISION CONGOLAISE
B.P. 2241, Brazzaville. Tel: (242) 814 574.

COSTA RICA

Population: 3.42 million.
TV Sets: 340,000.
Video Standard: NTSC.
BROADCASTERS
CORP. COSTARICENSE DE TELEVISION
P.O. Box 2860, San Jose 1000. Tel: (506) 312 222.
MULTIVISION
Apt 4666, San Jose 1000. Tel: (506) 334 444.
TELEVISORA DE COSTA RICA
Apt. 3786, San Jose 1000. Tel: (506) 322 222.
REDE NACIONAL DE TELEVISION
Apt. 7-1980, San Jose 1000. Tel: (506) 200 071.
UNIVERSIDAD DE COSTA RICA
San Pedro, Montes de Doa, San Jose 1000.Tel.: (506) 340 463. FAX: (506) 256 950.

CROATIA

Population: 4.8 million.
TV Sets: 750,000.
Video Standard: PAL.
BROADCASTERS
HRVATSKA TELEVIZIJA (HTV)
Prisavlke 3, Zagreb 10000. Tel: (3851) 616 3366. FAX: (3851) 510 093.
OTV
Teslina 7, Zagreb 10000. Tel: (3851) 424 124. FAX: (3851) 455 1386.
SLAVONSKA TELEVISIJA OSIJEK
Hrvatske Republike 20, Osijek 31000. Tel: (38531) 124 666. FAX: (38531) 124 111.
TBV MARJAN
Savska bb, Split 21000. Tel: (38521) 364 525. FAX: (38521) 523 455.
VINOVACKA TELEVIZIJA
Genschera 2, Vinkovci 32000. Tel: (38532) 331 990. FAX: (38532) 331 985.
ZADARSKA TELEVISIJA
Molotska bb, Zadar 23000. Tel: (38523) 311 791. FAX: (38523) 314 749.
VIDEO DISTRIBUTORS
BLITZ FILM & VIDEO
Sv Mateja 121-04, Zagreb 10000. Tel: (3851) 687 541. FAX: (3851) 692 814.
CONTINENTAL FILM
Sostariceva 10, Zagreb 10000. Tel: (3851) 421 312. FAX: (3851) 428 247.
JADRAN FILM DD
Oporovecka 12, Zagreb 10000. Tel: (3851) 298 7222. FAX: (3851) 251 394.
MOVIE PRODUCTION
Frankopanska 3, Osijek 31000. Tel: (38531) 559 704. FAX: (38531) 559 730.
ORLANDO FILM
Nasicka 14, Zagreb 10000. Tel: (2851) 334 587. FAX: (3851) 170 167.
POLYBROS
Draganicka 19, Zagreb 10000. Tel: (3851) 563 236. FAX: (3851) 563 236.
ZAUDER FILM
Jablanicka 1, Zagreb 10040. Tel: (3851) 245 724. FAX: (3851) 245 973.

CUBA

Population: 11 million.
TV Sets: 2.5 million.
Video Standard: NTSC.
BROADCASTERS
INSTITUTO CUBANO DE RADIODIFUSION (TV NACIONAL/CUBA VISION)
Calle M, No. 313, Vedado, Havana.
TELE REBELDE
Mazon # 52, Vedado, Havana. Tel: (53732) 3369.

CYPRUS

Population: 740,000.
TV Sets: 148,000.
Video Standard: PAL.

PIK CYBC
P.O. Box 4824, Nicosia. Tel: (3572) 422 231. FAX: (3572) 314 055.

CZECH REPUBLIC

Population: 10.4 million (1.5 million in Prague).
TV Homes: 4 million.
VCR Homes: 400,000.
Home Cable Service : 15.3%.
Home Satellite Service: 1.5%.
Video Standard: SECAM.
Premiera TV, the Czech Republic's second largest broadcaster, announced plans to revitalize its programming in order to gain a larger market share by producing more local programming. Video rentals fell 7.6% in 1994.

ASSOCIATIONS & ORGANIZATIONS

CZECH CABLE TV ASSOCIATION
Novodvorska 994, 14000 Prague 4. Tel: (422) 373 690. FAX: (422) 381 157.

CZECH PRODUCERS ASSOCIATION
Krizeneckeho Nam 322, Prague 5. Tel: (422) 6709 1111.

CZECH TELEVISION COUNCIL
Kavcihory, 14070 Prague 4. Tel: (422) 6113 1111. FAX: (422) 420 997.

FITES-UNION OF TV AND FILM
Pod Nuselskymi Schody 3, 12000 Prague 2. Tel: (422) 691 0310. FAX: (422) 691 1375.

MINISTRY OF CULTURE
Valdstejnske Nam 4, 11000 Prague 1. Tel: (422) 513 1111. FAX: (422) 536 322.

RADA CESKE TELEVIZE
Na Hrebenech 2, 14070 Prague 4. Tel: (422) 420997. FAX: (422) 420997.

BROADCASTERS

CZECH TELEVISION
Kavcihory, 140 70 Prague 4. Tel: (422) 6113 1111. FAX: (422) 421 562.

NOVA
Vladislavova 20, 11313 Prague 1. Tel: (422) 110 0111. FAX: (422) 2110 0182.

PREMIERA TV
Dukelskych Hrdinu 47, Prague 7. Tel: (422) 430 1147. FAX: (422) 430 1115.

LOCAL CABLE OPERATORS

CABLE PLUS
28 Rijna 124, 70924 Ostrava. Tel: (4269) 217 4202. FAX: (4269) 644 5441.

CODIS
Novodvorska 994, 14221 Prague 4. Tel: (422) 354 893. FAX: (422) 356 734.

HBO
Pod Visnovicou 21, 14000 Prague 4. Tel: (422) 472 1347. FAX: (422) 472 2749.

KABEL NET
Pod Visnovkou, 14000 Prague 4. Tel: (422) 425 145. FAX: (422) 472 2242.

VIDEO ORGANIZATIONS

UNION OF VIDEO DISTRIBUTORS (ANTI-PIRACY SECTION)
Thamova 7, 11000 Prague 8. Tel: (422) 2426 0340.

VIDEO DISTRIBUTORS

ARTEMIS
Horova 6, 40001 Usti nad Labem. Tel: (4247) 521 4254. FAX: (4247) 521 4261.

BONTON HOME VIDEO
Ostrov Stvanice 858, 17021 Prague 7. Tel: (422) 377 019. FAX: (422) 376 457.

FILM VIDEO STUDIO PRAGUE
Vycpalkova 368, 14000 Prague 4. Tel: (422) 793 1317.

FILMEXPORT HOME VIDEO
Na Morani 5, 12800 Prague. Tel: (422) 295 820. FAX: (422) 293 275.

HOLLYWOOD CLASSIC ENTERTAINMENT
Baarova 1, 14000 Prague 4. Tel: (422) 464 135. FAX: (422) 464 395.

LUCERNA FILM VIDEO
Narodni Trida 28, 11000 Prague 1. Tel: (422) 2422 7644. FAX: (422) 2422 5263.

TRANSPRESS
Starochodovska 1098, PO Box 62, 14900 Prague 4. Tel: (422) 763 161. FAX: (422) 766 995.

WARNER HOME VIDEO
Na Porici 30, 11000 Prague 1. Tel: (422) 282 2401. FAX: (422) 282 2501.

DENMARK

Population: 5.2 million.
TV Sets: 2.7 million.
VCR Homes: 1.5 million.
Home Cable Service: 59%
Home Satellite Service: 11%
Video Standard: PAL.
Danmarks Radio Television plans to program required public service broadcasts on its new cable channel, and concentrate on entertainment programming for its traditional broadcast service, competing with commercial television networks.

BROADCASTERS

DANMARKS RADIO
TV-Byen, DK-2860 Soborg. Tel: (45) 3520 3040. FAX: (45) 3520 2644.

KANAL 2 PRIME TIME
Mileparken 20A, Skovlunde DK-2740. Tel: (45) 4291 6699. FAX: (45) 4284 1360.

TELECOM A/S
Telegade 2, DK-2630 Taastrup. Tel: (45) 4252 9111. FAX: (45) 4255 29331.

TV 2/DANMARK
Rugaardsvej 25, Odense C DK-5100. Tel: (45) 6591 1244. FAX: (45) 6591 3322.

TV3 A/S
Overgaden Oven Vandet 10, Copenhagen K DK-1415. Tel: (45) 3157 3080. FAX: (45) 3157 8081.

TV MIDT-VEST
Sovej 2, Box 1460, Holstebro DK-7500. Tel: (45) 9740 3300. FAX: (45) 9740 1444.

TV NORD
Soparken 2, Aabybro DK-9440. Tel: (45) 9824 4600. FAX: (45) 9824 4698.

TV SYD A/S
Laurids Skausgade 12, Haderslev DK-6100. Tel: (45) 7453 0 511. FAX: (45) 7453 2316.

CABLE SERVICES

TELE DANMARK
Kannikegade 16, Aarhus DK-8000. Tel: (45) 8080 8080. FAX: (45) 8933 7719.

TELE DENMARK
Norregarde 21, Copenhagen DK-0900. Tel: (45) 8080 8080. FAX: (45) 3311 8050.

TELE DENMARK KTAS
Rosenbaengets Alle 11, Copenhagen DK-2100. Tel: (45) 3399 3399.

SATELLITE

TV3
Indiakaj 6, Copenhagen DK-2100. Tel. (45) 3543 9600. FAX: (45) 3543 9606.

VIDEO DISTRIBUTORS

BMG ARIOLA
Overgaden Neden, Vandat 17, Copenhagen DK 1414. Tel: (45) 3157 922.

BUENA VISTA INTERNATIONAL
Ostergade 24B, 3rd Floor, Copenhagen DK-1100. Tel: (45) 3312 0800. FAX: (45) 3312 4332.

DANSK MANAGEMENT CENTER (DMC)
Kristianiagade 7, Copenhagen DK-2100. Tel: (45) 3527 7777. FAX: (45) 3527 7779.

IRISH VIDEO
Haandvaerkerbyen 7, Greve DK-2670. Tel: (45) 4290 2700. FAX: (45) 4290 0053.

KRAK VIDEO
Virumsgardvej 21, Virum DJ-2830. Tel: (45) 4583 6600. FAX: (45) 4583 1011.

METRONOME VIDEO
Sondermarksvej 16, Copenhagen DK-2500. Tel: (45) 3646 7755. FAX: (45) 3644 0969.

NORDSIK FILM ACQUISITION
Skelbaekgade 1, Copenhagen DK-1717. Tel: (45) 3123 2488. FAX: (45) 3123 0488. email: nikki@inet.uni-c.dk

POLYGRAM
Emdrupvej 115A, Copenhagen NK-2400. Tel: (45) 3969 2522. FAX: (45) 3969 4616.

REGINA FILM IMPORT
Bregnegaardsvej 7, Charlottenlund DK-2920. Tel: (45) 3962 9640.

SAGA FILM INTERNATIONAL
Soendergada 5, Hjorring DK-9800. Tel: (45) 9892 2199. FAX: (45) 9890 0439.

SATURN FILMS
Maerum Husvej 9, Naerum DK-2850. Tel: (45) 4280 0869.

SCANBOX DANMARK
Hirsemarken 3, Farum DK-3520. Tel: (45) 4499 6200. FAX: (45) 4295 1786.

SFC
Vestergade 27, Copenhagen P DK-1456. Tel: (45) 3313 2686.
FAX: (45) 3313 0203.
SONET/DANSK FILM APS
Sndermarksvej 16, Valby DK-2500. Tel: (45) 36 467755. FAX:
(45) 36 440969.
UNITED INTERNATIONAL PICTURES
Haunchvej 13, Frederiksberg C DK-1825. Tel: (45) 3131 2330.
FAX: (45) 3123 3420.
WARNER BROS. INTERNATIONAL
(see Metronome Film listing.)

DJIBOUTI

Population: 421,320.
TV Sets: 17,000.
RADIO TELEVISION DE DJIBOUTI
Malabo Bioko Norte, Djibouti.

DOMINICAN REPUBLIC

Population: 8 million.
TV Sets: 728,000.
Video Standard: NTSC.
BROADCASTERS
CANAL 6
Circuito Independencia C-A, Mariano Cestero esq. Enrique
Henriquez, Santo Domingo. Tel: (809) 689 8151.
COLOR VISION
(Corp. Dominicana de Radio & Television) Emilio Morel esq.
Lulu Perez, Ens. La Fe, Santo Domingo. Tel: (809) 556 5876.
RADIOTELEVISION DOMINICA
Dr. Tejeda Florentino 8, Santo Domingo. Tel: (809) 689 2120.
RAHINTEL
Av. Independencia, Centro de los Heroes, Santo Domingo. Tel:
(809) 532 2531.
CANAL 7 CIBAO
Edificio Banco Universal, Calle de Sol, Santiago. Tel: (809) 583
0421.
TELEANTILLAS
Autopista Duarte Km. 7, Santo Domingo. Tel: (809) 567 7751.
TELESISTEMA
27 de Febrero, Santo Domingo. Tel: (809) 567 1251.
TV 13
Av. Pasteur esq., Santiago, Santo Domingo. Tel: (809) 687
9161.

ECUADOR

Population: 11 million.
TV Sets: 900,000.
Video Standard: NTSC.
BROADCASTERS
CANAL 2 QUITO
Murgeon 732, Quito. Tel: (5932) 540 877.
CANAL 4 GUAYAQUIL S.A.
9 de Octobure 1200, Guayaquil. (5934) 308 914.
CANAL 8 ESMERELDAS
Cas. 108, Esmeraldas. Tel: (5932) 710 090.
CANAL 10
Casilla 673, Guayaquil. Tel: (5934) 391-555.
CANAL 13 QUITO
Rumipampa 1039, Quito. Tel: (5932) 242 758.
CORPORACION ECUATORIANA DE TELEVISION
Casilla 1239, Guayaquil. Tel: (5934) 300 150. FAX: (5934) 303
677.
MANAVISION S.A.
Apt. 50, Portoviejo.
TELECUENCA
Canal Universidad Catolica, Casilla 400, Cuenca. (593) 827
862.
TELEAMAZONAS
Av. Diguja 529 y Brazil, Quito. Tel: (5932) 430 313.
TELEVISORA NACIONAL
Bosmediano 447 y Jose Carb, Quito.

EGYPT

Population: 62.4 million.
TV sets: 7 million.
Video Standard: PAL.
National channels: Channel One: The national channel.
Channel Two: local and world events in Arabic, English and
French.
Local Channels: Channel Three: Greater Cairc's channel, serv-
ing Cairo, Giza and El-Qaliubia. Channel Four: Suez Canal
Zone channel, serving Port Said, Ismailia and Suez. Channel
Five: Alexandria channel, serving Alexandria and El-Beheira.
Channel Six: The Nile Delta channel. Channel Seven: Upper
Egypt. The Information Channel: Teletext

SATELLITE BROADCASTERS
News exchange via satellites is through B/Y PAL/system transmission and reception, through B/Y US and Japanese agencies transmission/reception and through Arabsat transmission/
reception.
The Egyptian Space Channel (ESC) transmits its programs
through the Higher Power Transponder S-Band, ARABSAT,
covering all Arab countries besides Europe, Africa and West
Asia. Down Link Frequency: 2560-5 MHZ.
The Egyptian News Company (C.N.E.). An Egyptian joint-stock
company with CNN: by subscription only.
Canal France International (CFI). Under a protocol of coopera-
tion between ERTU and CFI, ERTU receives six hours trans-
mission of CFI programs per day. CFI items are subject to cen-
sorship.
BROADCASTER
EGYPTIAN RADIO AND TV UNION
TV Building, Cornish El-Nil, Maspero, Cairo. (202) 757 155.
SATELLITE BROADCASTER
EGYPTIAN SPACE CHANNEL
P.O. Box 1886, Cairo. Tel: (202) 574 6881. FAX: (202) 749 310.

EL SALVADOR

Population: 5.9 million.
TV Sets: 500,000.
Video Standard: NTSC.
BROADCASTERS
CANAL DOS SA
Ap. Postal 720, San Salvador. Tel: (503) 236 744.
CANAL CUATRO
(See Canal Dos above). Tel: (503) 244 633.
CANAL SEIS
Km. 6, Carretera Panamericana a Santa Tecla, San Savador.
Tel: (503) 235 122.
TELEVISION CULTURAL EDUCATIVA
Ap. Postal 4, Santa Tecla. Tel: (503) 280 499.

ESTONIA

Population: 1.6 million.
TV Sets: 600,000.
Video Standard: PAL/SECAM.
TALLINN EESTI TELEVISIOON
12 Faehlmanni St., Tallinn EE 0100. Tel. (372014) 2434 113.

ETHIOPIA

Population: 55.2 million.
TV Sets: 100,000.
Video Standard: PAL.
ETHIOPIA TELEVISION
Post Office Box 5544, Addis Ababa. Tel: (251) 116 701.

FINLAND

Population: 5.1 million.
TV Sets: 2 million.
VCR Homes: 1.4 million.
Home Cable Service : 868,000.
Home Satellite Service: 20,000.
Video Standard: PAL.
As in the rest of Europe, video sales overtook rentals in
Finland in 1995.
BROADCASTERS
THE FINNISH BROADCASTING COMPANY
Head Office, P.O. Box 99,Yliesradio, Helsinki 0024. Tel: (3580)
148 01. FAX: (3580) 1480 3391.
Radio and TV Centre: Pasilankatu 39, SF-0240 Helsinki, Tel:
(3580)-150 01.
MTV3
Ilmalantori 2, SF-00240 Helsinki 24. Tel: (3580) 150 01. FAX:
(3580) 150 0572
KOLMOSTELEVISIOIY AB-CHANNEL THREE FINLAND
Ilmalanakatu 2 C, Helsinki. 00240. Tel: (3580)-150 01. FAX
(3580)-150 0707.
TV 2
Yleisradio, Tohloppinrata 31, Tampere 33270. Tel: (35831) 345
6111. FAX: (35831) 345 6891.
CABLE
HAMEEN PUHELIN
P.O. Box 94, Hameenlinna SF-13101. Tel: (35817) 614 4204.
FAX: (35817) 6121 005.
HTV PRODUCTION
Raramasgarinkata 11, Helsinki SF-00520. Tel: (3580) 156 51.
FAX: (3580) 140 487.
KAJAANI TV
Pohgolakatu 20, Kajaani, SF-87100. Tel: (35886) 613 0070.
FAX: (35886) 617 7255.

CABLE SYSTEMS

HAMEEN PUHELIN
P.O. Box 94, Hameenlinna 13101. Tel: (35817) 6144 204. FAX: (35817) 6121 005.

KAJAANI TV
Pohgolakatu 20, Kajaani 87100. Tel: (35886) 6130 070. fax: (35886) 6177 255.

HTV PRODUKTION
Asemapaalilikonkatu 3, Helsinki 00290. Tel: (3580) 156 51. FAX: (3580) 140 487.

SATELLITE

FINNISH BROADCASTING AUTHORITY
(see Finnish Broadcasting listing under Broadcasters.)

VIDEO DISTRIBUTORS

BMG ARIOLA
P.O. Box 173, Helsinki 00211. Tel: (3580) 613 201. FAX: (3580) 6132 0299.

DOUBLECHECK
Askoukatou 5, Lahti SF-15100. Tel: (35818) 783 2077. FAX: (35818) 752 1958.

EL-KO FILMS
Kavallvagen 23A, Grankulla SF-02700. Tel: (3580) 505 2600.

ERIKSSON ENTERTAINMENT
Kaisaniemenkatu 2B, Helsinki SF-00100. Tel: (3580) 1311 9377. FAX: (3580) 1311 9444.

EUROPA VISON
Koivuvaarakuja 2, Vantaa 01640. Tel: (3580) 852 711. FAX: (3580) 853 2183.

FINNKINO
Kaisaniemenkatu 2B, Helsinki SF-0100. Tel: (3580) 131 191. FAX: (3580) 1311 9300.

VIPVISION FINLAND
Kapytie 6A, Tampere SF-33180. Tel: (35831) 253 4466. FAX: (35831) 253 3366.

WARNER HOME VIDEO
Kaisaniemenkatu 1b A 73, Helsinki SF-00100. Tel: (3580) 638 192. FAX: (3580) 638 289.

FRANCE

Population: 58.1 million.
TV Sets: 29.3 million.
VCR Households: 15 million.
Home Satellite Service: 750,000.
Home Cable Service : 1.6 million.
Television advertising increased by 7% with over $3 billion in revenues in 1995. Domestic French television production has also increased in 1995 and French broadcaster TF1 showed ratings increases for domestically-produced shows, directly competing with U.S. productions.
Cable and satellite broadcasting have been gradually eroding the market shares of the major French broadcasters. Satellite broadcasting revenue was up 30% in 1995, and with the growth of the European digital satellite broadcasting industry is expected to service over 1.25 million French homes by the end of 1996.
Sales now dominate the video market, with some estimates showing that sell-through now exceeds rental income by 500%.

ASSOCIATIONS & ORGANIZATIONS

CONSEIL SUPERIEURE DE L'AUDIOVISUEL
39 Quai Andre Citroen, Paris 75015. Tel: (331) 4058 3800. FAX: (331) 4579 0006.

OBSERVATOIRE DE L'AUDIOVISUEL
76 allee de la Robertsan, Strasbourg 67000. Tel: (3388) 1444 00. FAX: (3388) 1444 19.

PRODUCTEURS DE FILM ET DE PROGRAMMES AUDIOVISUELLES
50 Ave. Marcel, Paris 75008. Tel: (331) 4723 7910. FAX: (331) 4723 9157.

SYNDICAT FRANCAIS DES ARTISTES
21 bis rue Victor Masse, Paris 75009. Tel: (331) 4285 8811. FAX: (331) 4526 4721.

BROADCASTERS

ARTE
50 Ave. Theophile Gautier, Paris 75016. Tel: (331) 4414 7777. FAX: (331) 4414 7700.

ARTE GEIE
2 Rue de le Fonderie, Strasbourg 6700. Tel: (3388) 522 47.

CANAL J
91 Rue de Cherche Midi, Paris 75286. Tel: (331) 4954 5454. FAX: (331) 4222 8717.

CANAL PLUS
85/89 Quai Andre Citroen, Paris Cedex 75015. Tel: (331) 4425 1000. FAX: (331) 4425 1234.

EUROSPORT
1 quai du Point du Jour, Boulogne 92100. Tel: (331) 4141 2820. FAX: (331) 4141 1953.

FRANCE 2
22 Ave. Montaigne, Paris 75008. Tel: (331) 4421 4242. FAX: (331) 4421 5145.

FRANCE 3
116 Ave. du Res. Kennedy, Paris 75790. Tel: (331) 4230 2222. FAX: (331) 4224 6366.

FRANCE TELEVISION
42 Ave. d'Iena, Paris 75008. Tel: (331) 4431 6000. FAX: (331) 4720 2454.

LA CINQUIEME
10 Rue Horace-Vesnet, Paris 92136. Tel: (331) 4146 5555. FAX: (331) 4108 0222.

METROPOLE TELEVISION (M6)
16 cours Albert Premier, Paris 75008. Tel: (331) 4421 6853. FAX: (331) 4421 6568.

TF1
11 quai de Pont du Jour, Boulogne 92100. Tel: (331) 4141 1234. FAX: (331) 4141 3400.

CABLE

ALCATEL
30 Rue des Chassees, P.O. Box 309, Clichy 92111. Tel: (331) 4756 6900.

CANAL J
(See Canal J listing under Broadcasters.)

CANAL PLUS
(See Canal Plus listing under Broadcasters.)

LA CHAINE INFO
33 Rue Vaugelas, Paris 75015. Tel: (331) 4045 2345. FAX: (331) 4045 2362.

LYONNAISE COMMUNICATIONS
6 Villa Thoreton, Paris 75015. Tel: (331) 4425 8181. FAX: (331) 4425 8140.

TDF
21-27 rue d'Oradour-sur-Glane, Paris 75732. Tel: (331) 4095 4000. FAX: (331) 4663 3203.

TDF CABLE
21-27 rue Barbes BP-518, Montrouge 92524. Tel: (331) 4965 1000. FAX: (331) 4965 2046.

TELE SHOPPING
30-32 Rue Proudhon, La Plaine Street, Denis 93214. Tel: (331) 4917 7600. FAX: (331) 4917 0395.

TV5
174 Rue de la Universite, Paris 75007. Tel: (331) 4556 0080. FAX: (331) 4556 0004.

SATELLITE BROADCASTERS

CANAL COURSES
83 rue de la Boutie, Paris 75008. Tel: (331) 4953 3900. FAX: (331) 4289 0895.

CANAL FRANCE INTERNATIONALE
59 Boulevard Exelmans, Paris 75016. Tel: (331) 4067 1177. FAX: (331) 4071 1171.

CANAL JEUNESSE
(See Canal J listing under Broadcasters.)

CANAL JIMMY
305 Rue le jour se leve, Boulogne-Cedex 92654. Tel: (331) 4425 1129.

CANAL PLUS SATELLITE
(See Canal Plus listing under Broadcasters.)

EUTELSAT
Tour Maine Montparnasee, 33 Ave. du Maine, Paris 75755. Tel: (331) 4538) 4747. FAX: (331) 4538 3700.

LA CHAINE INFO
33 Rue Vaugelas, Paris 75015. Tel: (331) 4045 2345. FAX: (331) 4045 2362.

TV-5 EUROPE
174 rue de l'Universite, Paris 7507. Tel: (331) 4556 0080. FAX: (331) 4556 0004.

CABLE AND SATELLITE PROGRAM SUPPLIERS

ARTE GEIE
(See Arte Geie listing under Broadcasters.)

EURONEWS
60 Chemin des Monilles, ecully 69130. Tel: (3372) 1881 06. FAX: (3372) 1893 71.

EUROSPORT
54 avenue de la Voie Lactee, Boulogne 92100. Tel: (331) 4141 1234. FAX: (331) 4141 2485.

FRANCE SUPERVISION
22 Ave. Montaigne, Paris 75008. Tel: (331) 4421 4514. FAX: (331) 4421 4481.

MCM EUROMUSIQUE
109 Rue de Fauborg Ste. Honore, Paris 75008. Tel: (331) 4495 9100. FAX: (331) 4495 9125.

MULTIVISION
6 Villa Thorepon, Paris 75015. Tel: (331) 4425 8181. FAX: (331) 4425 8940.

RFO
5 Ave.du Recteur Poincare, Paris 75016. Tel: (331) 4524 7100. FAX: (331) 4524 9596.

SERIE CLUB
16 Cours Albert, Paris 75008. Tel: (331) 4256 7666. FAX: (331) 4256 9666.

TELE MONTE CARLO
16 Blvd. Princesse Charlotte, Monte Carlo 98000. Tel: (3393) 151 415.

TV-SPORT
305 Avenue Le Jour se Leve, Boulogne-Billancourt 92657. Tel: (331) 4694 6100. FAX: (331) 4761 0030.

VIDEO DISTRIBUTORS
ALPHA VIDEO
126 Rue la Boetie, Paris 75008. Tel: (331) 4563 4411.

ATOLL VIDEO
18-20 Rue Borrego, Paris 75003. Tel: (331) 4366 6922. FAX: (331) 4366 5221.

CENTRE NATIONALE DE DOCUMENTATION PEDA-GOGIQUE
29 Rue D'IUlm, Paris 75230 Cedex 5. Tel: (331) 4634 9000. FAX: (331) 4634 5544.

CIC VIDEO
1 bis Rue du Petit Clamart, P.O. Box 13, Velizy 78149. Tel: (331) 4094 1020. FAX: (331) 4094 1004.

CINEMADIS FILMS
78 Ave. des Champs Elysees, Paris 75008. Tel: (331) 4562 8287. FAX: (331) 4289 2198.

COLMAX PRODUCTIONS
46 Rue de la Comete, Asnaires 75008. Tel: (331) 4790 6570. FAX: (331) 4733 6585.

CONCORDE
276 Rue des Pyrenees, Paris 75020. Tel: (331) 4797 3374. FAX: (331) 4797 7259.

DCX
31 Rue Rennequin, Paris 75017. Tel: (331) 4267 3037. FAX: (331) 4267 0278.

EMI FRANCE
43 rue camille Desmoulins, Issy-les-Moulineaux 92130. Tel: (331) 4629 2020. FAX: (331) 4629 2121.

FFCM VIDEO
126 Rue la Boetie, Paris 75008. Tel: (331) 4256 1642.

FILM OFFICE
63 Champs-Elysees, Paris 75008. Tel: (331) 5377 1800. FAX: (331) 4256 0375.

LES FILMS ARIANE/REVCOM INTERNATIONAL
62 Rue Louis Bleriot, Boulogne Billancourt 92641 Tel: (331) 4110 5000. FAX: (331) 4110 5025.

LES FILMS VERTS
La Tissote, Mondragon 84430. Tel: (3390) 406 211. FAX: (3390) 406 639.

FRANCE TELEVISION DISTRIBUTION
(See France 2 listing under Broadcasters.)

GAUMONT COLUMBIA TRISTAR HOME VIDEO
31 rue Louis Pasteur, Boulogne-Billancourt, 92100. Tel: (331) 4684 1919. FAX: (331) 4604 2818.

HEURE EXQUISE
Rue de Normandie Le Fort BP 113, Mons en Bareuil 59370. Tel: (3320) 432 432. FAX: (3320) 432 433.

IMPEX FILMS
102 Ave. des Champs Elysees, Paris 75008. Tel: (331) 4562 2060. FAX: (331) 4289 3362.

JOHNSON TVI
Zone Industrielle Les Joncaux, Hendaye 64700. Tel: (3359) 200 580. FAX: (3359) 201 836.

K-FILMS
15 Rue Saintonges, Paris 75003. Tel: (331) 4274 7014. FAX: (331) 4274 7024.

LA MEDIATHEUE DES TROIS MONDES
63 bis Rue due Cardinal Lemoine, Paris 75005. Tel: (331) 4354 3338. FAX: (331) 4634 7019.

LAURA VIDEO PRODUCTION
64 Blvd. Voltaire, Paris 75011. Tel: (331) 4355 8805. FAX; (331) 4355 0190.

POLYGRAM VIDEO
107 Blvd Periere, Paris 75017. Tel: (331) 4415 6615. FAX: (331) 4415 9588.

RENE CHATEAU VIDEO
72 Rue Lariston, Paris 75116. Tel: (331) 4727 9968. FAX: (331) 4704 5980.

SONY MUSIC
131 Avenue de Wagram, Paris 75017. Tel: (331) 4440 6905. FAX: (331) 4440 6666.

TF1 VIDEO
1 quai de Point du Jour, Boulogne Cedex 92656. Tel: (331) 4141 2416. FAX: (331) 4141 2929.

TWENTIETH CENTURY FOX
8 Rue Bellini, Paris 75116. Tel: (331) 4434 6000. FAX: (331) 4434 6105.

VAUBAN PRODUCTIONS
9 Avenue Franklin D. Roosevelt, Paris 75008. Tel: (331) 4225 6604. FAX: (331) 4953 0491.

WARNER BROS.
67 Ave. de Wagram, Paris 75017. Tel: (331) 4401 4999. FAX: (331) 40547193.

GABON

Population: 1.16 million.
TV sets: 40,000.
Video Standard: PAL-B.
RTG TV GABON
P.O. Box 150, Libreville. Tel: (241) 732 152. FAX: (241) 732 153.

GAMBIA

Population :990,000
TV sets: 6000.
Video Standard: PAL-B.
INFORMATION AND BROADCASTING SERVICE
19 Hagan St. Banjul. (220) 272 30.
RADIO GAMBIA
Mile 7, Banjul. (220) 495 101. FAX: (220) 495 102.

GERMANY

Population: 81.3 million.
TV Sets: 30.5 million.
Home Cable Service : 14.7 million.
VCR Homes: 46 million.
Home Satellite Service: 7 million.
Video Standard: PAL

Germany is the world's third largest industrial superpower and Germany's share of Western Europe's television business is 20.5%, and expected to grow to over 25% in the next decade. TV revenues from all sectors are estimated at $1.7 billion for 1996. Bertelsman's Ufa and CLT proposed a merger that may take years to clear EU courts. After much discussion, major German satellite broadcasters Kirch, Bertelsmann, Deutsche Telekom, CLT, the two government broadcasters and French pay-TV company Canal Plus have agreed on a single standard for digital television. However, due to disputes regarding the manufacturing rights and formats for home digital decoders, by early October the digital alliance had nearly splintered. The start-up costs for the proposed digital broadcast project are expected to exceed $700 million. The Kirch Group signed a deal with Viacom and MCA for television programming and films, following Kirch's earlier agreement (rumored to be nearly $1 billion) with Columbia TriStar Television. The Kirch Group has co-produced the Fall '96 television series "Dark Skies" with Columbia TriStar. Meanwhile, The News Corp. was forging a deal with CLT to provide digital TV services to Germany. ARD, Germany's oldest public broadcaster, was spared possible termination when the 11 regional stations who make up ARD's loose network agreed to distribute ARD's programming for at least another year. Despite decreased profits in 1995, RTL, Europes largest TV network, planned major expansions in the upcoming years, including the launch of satellite broadcasting. RTL planned to cut costs by cutting the number of programs it imports—mostly from American suppliers. This did not stop RTL from agreeing to distribute MCA's products in Germany for 10 years. ZDF signed a deal with Microsoft to offer online programming.

Nickelodeon Germany filed a suit claiming that the German cable industry regulatory board preferentially reserved a cable slot for ARD and ZDF's joint venture children's channel, in accordance with Germany's "must carry" law.

BROADCASTERS
ARD
Arnulfstrasse 42, 80335 Munich. (4989) 590 001. FAX: (4989) 5900 3249.

BAYERISCHER RUNDFUNK FERNSEHEN
Rundfunkplatz 1, 80300 Munich. Tel: (4989) 590 001. FAX: (4989) 590 80714.

DEUTSCHE WELLE TV
Voltastrasse 5, Berlin 13355. Tel: (4930) 469 90. FAX: (4930) 4631 998.

DEUTSCHES SPORTFERNSEHEN
Bahnhofstrasse 27, 8774 Unterfohring. (4989) 950 020. FAX: (4989) 950 02392.

HR2 KULTUR
Bertramstrasse 8, Frankfurt am Main 60320. (4969) 155 1. FAX: (4969) 155 2900.

DER KABELKANAL-DKK
Bahnhofstrasse 28, Unterfohring 85774. Tel: (4989) 950 8070. FAX: (4989) 950 80714.

MDR MITTELDEUTSCHER RUNDFUNK
Springerstrasse 22-24, Leipzig 04105. Tel: (49341) 559 50. FAX: (49341) 559 55 44.

NDR
Ruetersbank 46 22529 Hamburg. Tel: (4940) 415 60. FAX: (4940) 4156 5336.

NORDOSTDEUTSCHE VERLAGSGESSELSCHAFT
Domhof 24, 31139 Hildesheim. Tel: (495121) 169 253. FAX: (495121) 169 259.

OSTDEUTSCHER RUNDFUNK BRANDENBURG
August-Bebelstrasse 26-53, 14482 Postdam. Tel: (49331) 965 10. FAX: (49331) 965 35 76.

PRIVATE BAYRISCHE AV UND TV GESELLSCHAFT (PRIBAG)
Binsberg 28, 85658 Egmating. Tel: (4980) 957 51. FAX: (4980) 957 53.

PRO-7
Bahnhofstrasse 27a, Unterfohring 85774. Tel: (4989) 95001 0. FAX: (4989) 95001 230.

RTL 2
Bavaria Filmplatz, 82031 Gruunewald. Tel: (4989) 6418 5210. FAX: (4989) 6418 5209.

RTL FERNSEHEN
Aachenerstrasse 1036, 50858 Cologne. (49221) 456 0. FAX: (49221) 456 4290.

SAT EINS
Martin Luther Strasse 1, 10777 Berlin. (4930) 212 410. FAX: (4930) 212 4140.

VOX
Richard Byrd Strasse 6, D-50829 Cologne. (49221) 915 50. FAX: (49221) 915 5404.

SUPER RTL
Bavaria Filmplatz, 82031 Gruunewald. Tel: (4989) 6419 3840. FAX: (4989) 6419 3849.

VOX
Richard Byrd Strasse 6, D-50829 Cologne. (49221) 953 40. FAX: (49221) 953 4440.

ZWEITES DEUTSCHES FERNSEHEN (ZDF)
P.O. Box 4040, 55030 Mainz. Tel: (496131) 702. FAX: (496131) 702 157.

CABLE SERVICES

DER KABELKANAL-DKK
Bahnhofstrasse 28, 85774 Unterfohring. Tel: (4989) 950 8070. FAX: (4989)950 80714.

DEUTSCHE TELEKOM
Postfach 2000, 33105 Bonn. Tel: (49228) 181 4949. FAX: (49228) 181 8941.

ENGELS TELEVISION
Berlinstrasse 12, 36270 Niederaula. Tel: (49662) 592 130. FAX: (49662) 570 60.

KOMMUNAL BAU RHEINLAND-PFALZ
Hindenburgplatz 7, 55188 Mainz. Tel: (49613) 123 490. FAX: (49 613) 123 4949.

PREMIERE PAY-TV
Bahnhofstrasse 27a, 85774 Hamburg. Tel: (4989) 6680 1261. FAX: (4989) 6680 1287.

PREMIERE MEDIEN
Tonndorfer Haupt Strasse 90, 22045 Hamburg. Tel: (4940) 6680 1261. FAX: (4940) 6680 1199.

SATELLITE

AFN-TELEVISION EUROPE
Bertramstrasse 6, 60320 Frankfurt am Main. Tel: (4969) 1568 8262. FAX: (4969) 1568 3800.

ARD
(See ARD listing under Broadcasters.)

DEUTSCHE BUNDEPOST TELEKOM
Heinrich-von-Stephan Strasse, 53175 Bonn. Tel: (49228) 140. FAX: (49228) 148 872.

DEUTSCHES SPORTFERNSEHEN
(See Deutsches Sportfernsehen listing under Broadcasters.)

DEUTSCHE WELLE
Raderberggurtel 50, 50968 Cologne. Tel: (49 221 3890 FAX: (49 221 3893 000.

KABAL 1
Bahnhofstrasse 28, 85774 Unterfohring. Tel: (4989) 9508 070 FAX: (4989) 9508 8044.

N-TV
Taubenstrasse 1, 10117 Berlin. Tel: (4930) 231 25500. FAX: (4930) 231 25505.

RTL-FERNSEHEN
(see RTL listing under Broadcasters.)

RTL NORD
Jenfelder Allee 80, 22045 Hamburg. Tel: (4940) 6688 4350. FAX: (4940) 6688 4400.

SAT EINS FERNSEHEN
Martin Luther Strasse 1, 10777 Berlin. Tel: (4930) 212 410. FAX: (4930) 212 4140.

SWF
Hans Bredow Strasse, P.O. Box 820, 76522 Baden Baden. (497221) 920. FAX: (497221) 922 010.

VOX
Richard Byrd Strasse 6, D-50829 Cologne. (49221) 953 40. FAX: (49221) 953 4440.

WDR-3 KOLN
Appellhofplatz 1, 50667 Cologne. Tel: (49221) 1602 132. FAX: (49221) 1602 135.

VIDEO DISTRIBUTORS

ATLAS FILM UND AV GMBH & CO. KG
Ludgeristrasse 14-16, 47057 Duisburg. Tel: (49203) 378 6201. FAX: (49203) 378 6200.

BAVARIA FILM
Bavariafilmplatz 7, 82031 Geiselgasteig. Tel: (4989) 64990. FAX: (4989) 6492507.

BUENA VISTA
Kastenbauer Strasse 2, 81677 Munich. Tel: (4989) 9934 0270. FAX: 9934 0139.

BMG VIDEO
Kastenbauer Strasse 2, 81677 Munich. Tel: (4989) 413 6687. FAX: (4989) 413 6130.

COLUMBIA TRISTAR HOME VIDEO
Ickstatt Strass 1, 80469 Munich. Tel: (4989) 230 370. FAX: (4989) 2303 7400.

CONCORDE-CASTLE ROCK-TURNER VIDEO
Rosenheimer Strasse 143b, 90600 Frankfurt. Tel: (4969) 450 6100. FAX: (4969) 4506 1092.

CONCORDE VIDEO
Stefan-George-Ring 23, 81929 Munich. Tel: (4989) 930 950. FAX: (4989) 930 9575.

CONSTANTIN VIDEO
Kaiserstrasse 39, 80801 Munich 80801. Tel: (4989) 386 090. FAX: (4989) 3860 9242.

EMI ELECTROLA
Maarweg 149, 50825 Cologne. Tel: (49221) 490 20. FAX: (49221) 497 2335.

EUROVIDEO BILDPROGRAM
Oskar Messterstrasse 15, Ismaning 85737. Tel: (4989) 9624 4432. FAX: (4989) 9642 4450.

FIPRO/VMP
Taunusstrasse 51, Munich 80807. Tel: (4989) 350940. FAX: (4989) 35094101.

FOX VIDEO
Am Forsthaus Gravenbruh 7, Neue Isenberg. Tel: (496102) 500 40. FAX: (496102) 5550.

HIGHLIGHT FILMVERLEIH
Herkomerplatz 2, 82131 Stockdorf. Tel: (4989) 895 6170. FAX: (4989) 8956 1730.

HVW FOCUS FILMVERTRIEBS
Industrie Strasse 49, 41564 Kaarst. Tel: (4921) 3160 4041. FAX: (4921) 316 3290.

INTER-PATHE GMBH & CO. KG
Bolongarostrasse 141, 65929 Frankfurt am Main. Tel: (4969) 304 043. FAX: (4969) 311 091.

KIRCHGRUPPE
2 Robert Buerkle Strasse, 85737 Munich. Tel: (4989) 9956 2422. FAX: (4989) 9956 2640.

MERKUR FILM AGENCY
Isarstrasse 6, 82065 Baierbrunn. Tel: (4989) 793 7879. FAX: (4989) 793 7970.

PHILIPS MEDIA
Alexander Strasse 1, 20099 Hamburg. Tel: (4940) 2852 1401. FAX: (4940) 2852 1402.

POLYGRAM VIDEO
Glockengiesserwalle 2, 20095 Hamburg. Tel: (4940) 308 7740. FAX: (4940) 308 7436.

ROTAVISION FILMHANDEI
Postfach 1701, Koblenz 56015. Tel: (49261) 188 88. FAX: (49261) 188 68.

SONY MUSIC ENTERTAINMENT
Stephan Strasse 15, 60313 Frankfurt. Tel: (4969) 138 880. FAX: (4969) 1388 8440.

SPRINGER-VERLAG GMBH & CO. KG
Heidelbergerplatz 3, 14197 Berlin. Tel: (4930) 820 71. FAX: (4930) 820 7821.

UNIVERSUM FILM GMBH (UFA)
Kastenbauer Strasse 2, 81677 Munich. Tel: (4989) 413 6671. FAX: (4989) 413 6870.

VESTISCHER MEDIEN VERLAG (VMV)
Postfach 1464, Hertener Mark 7, 45672 Herten. Tel: (492366) 80 80. FAX: (492366) 808 291.

VIPRO VIDEO VERTRIEBS UND PRODUKTIONS
Taunusstrasse 51, 80807 Munich. Tel: (4989) 350 940. FAX: (4989) 3509 4101.

VPS FILM-ENTERTAINMENT
Waldmeisterstrasse 72, 80935 Munich. Tel: (4989) 3548 4154. FAX: (4989) 3548 4160.

GHANA

Population: 17.7 million.
TV Sets: 250,000.
Video Standard: PAL-B.
GHANA BROADCASTING CORPORATION
Broadcast House, P.O. Box 1633, Accra. (23321) 221 161.
FAX: (23321) 773 227.

GREECE

Population: 10.5 million.
TV homes: 2.2 million.
VCR Households:1.1 million
VCR Penetration: 40%.
Video Prices: $2.00—$4.00
Video Standard: PAL and SECAM
The number of TV viewers dropped by 25% in 1996, due to the bad quality of the local TV serials, TV films and many talk shows. In addition, a great number of advertising spots interrupt programming. Fines are levied by the National AudioVisual Council to stations violating the lawful ad time restrictions. Consequently, the total ad income dropped by 20.3% and some channels are in the red. Besides the State Channels, O Hellejiki Teleorassi (ET I, II & III), there are 220 other private channels operating all over the county, of which only 12 are operating legally.
Video piracy is epidemic. It is estimated that American companies are losing about $59 million annually to pirates in Greece. Many TV regional channels are prosecuted every year by the Society of Protection of AudioVisual Works and violators pay heavy fines.

BROADCASTERS
ANTENNA I
10-12 Kifissias Str., Athens 151 29. Tel: (301) 685 3770. FAX: (301) 681 0128.
CHANNEL 5
31 Demetros Str., Tavrow Athens. Tel: (301) 342 4090. FAX: (301) 341 2608.
ET I/ET II
431 Messoguion Str, Athens 153 42.Tel.: (301) 638 0390. FAX: (301) 639 0652.
ET 3
20 Evangueki Str. 632 26, Tgessakibuju. Tel: (3031) 264 800. FAX: (3031) 236 466.
FILMNET CABLE CHANNEL
144 Kifissias Str., 7 Katachaki 76, Athens. Tel: (301) 672 3110. FAX: (301) 671 9926.
MEGA CHANNEL
Alamanaas—Delphi Str., Athens 104 41. Tel: (301) 618 1207. FAX: (301) 689 9016.
NEW CHANNEL
9-11 Pireas Str., Athens 105 52. Tel: (301) 523 8230. FAX: (301) 524 4514.
SEVEN X CHANNEL
27 Demetros Str., Tavrow, Athens 151 25. Tel: (301) 689 7604. FAX: (301) 689 7608.
SKY CHANNEL
6 Philellinon Str., Athens 105 57. Tel: (301) 422 2002. FAX: (301) 412 7628.
STAR CHANNEL
22 Ometros Str., Tavrow, Athens 177 78. Tel: (301) 342 1201. FAX: (301) 342 7816.
TELECITY CHANNEL
22 Vassileos Kons Str., Athens 116 35. Tel: (301) 937 6400. FAX: (301) 956 3545.
TELETORA CHANNEL
15 Elia Eliou m/ Kosmos, Athens.
TV 100
1 Nikolaou Germanou Str., Thessalonki 546 21. Tel: (3031) 265 828.

CABLE AND SATELLITE
ANTENNA TV
(See listing for Antenna under Broadcasters)
FILMNET CABLE TV
(See listing for Filmnet under Broadcasters)
ET 5 AND ET 6
(See listing for ET I under Broadcasters)
VIDEO DISTRIBUTORS
AUDIOVISUAL ENTERPRISES
32 Sochou Str, Athens 115 25. Tel: (301) 666 8824. FAX: (301) 666 6996.
CBS-FOX VIDEO
311 Mesogion Str., Chalandri, Athens 15 231. Tel: (301) 647 7727. FAX: (301) 672 7728.
HOME VIDEO HELLAS
276 Messoguion Str, Athens 152 31. Tel: (301) 647 7727. FAX: (301) 647 7728.

KEY VIDEO
14-16 Skalidi Str, Athens 116 26. Tel: (301) 671 7297. FAX: (301) 671 8764.
VIDEOSONIC
1 Evrydamantos Str, Athens 117 34. Tel. (301) 924 2200. FAX: (301) 924 7388.

—RENA VELISSARIOU

GUADALOUPE

Population: 430,000.
TV Sets: 150,000.
Video Standard: NTSC.
BROADCASTERS
RFO GUADALOUPE
P.O. Box 402, F-97163, Point-a-Pitre. Tel: (590) 939 696. FAX: (590) 939 682.
ARCHIPEL 4
ResidenceLes Palmiers, Gabarre 2, 97110. Tel: (590) 836 350.
CANAL ANTILLES (PAY TV)
2 lot. Les Jardins de Houelbourg, 97122 Baie Mahault. (590) 268 179.
TCI GUADALOUPE
Montaubon, 97190 Gosier.

GUATEMALA

Population: 11 million.
TV Sets: 475,000.
Video Standard: NTSC.
BROADCASTERS
RADIO TELEVISON GUATEMALA
Apt. 1367, Guatemala. Tel: (5022) 922 491.
TELEVISION CULTURAL EDUCATIVA
4a Calle 18-38, Zona 1, Guatemala. Tel: (5022) 531 913.
TELEVISIETE
Apt. Postal 1242., Guatemala. Tel: (5022) 622 16.
TELEONCE
Ca. 20, 5-02, Zona 10, Guatemala. Tel: (5022) 682 165.
TRECEVISION
3a Calle 10-70, Zona 10, Guatemala. Tel: (5022) 632 66.

GUINEA

Population: 6.4 million.
TV Sets: 65,000.
TV Standard: PAL.
RADIO-DIFFUSION GUINIEENNE
B.P. 391, Conraky.

GUYANA

Population: 724,000
TV Sets: 15,000.
Video Standard: NTSC.
GUYANA TELEVISION
68 Hadfield St., Lodge Georgetown. Tel: (5922) 692 31.

HAITI

Population: 6.5 million.
TV Sets: 25,000.
Video Standard: NTSC.
BROADCASTERS
TELEVISON NATIONALE D'HAITI
P.O. Box 13400 Delmas 33, Port-au-Prince. (5091) 633 24.
TELE HAITI
P.O. Box 1126, Port-au-Prince. (5091) 230 00.

HONDURAS

Population: 5.5 million.
TV Sets: 160,000.
Video Standard: NTSC.
BROADCASTERS
COMPANIA BROADCASTING
Apt. Postal 882, Bariio Rio Pedras.
COMPANIA CENTROAMERICANA DE TV
Apt. Postal 68, Tegucigalpa.
CORP. CENTROAMERICANA DE COMMUNICACIONES, S.A.
Apt. Postal 120, San Pedro Sula.
CRUCENA DE TELEVISON
Casilla 3424, Tegucigalpa.
TELESISTEMA HONDURENO
Apt. Postal 734, Tegucigalpa. Tel: (50432) 78 35.

HONG KONG

Population: 6.3 million.
TV sets: 1.75 million.
Cable Homes: 200,000.
Satellite dish homes: 360,000.
VCR Homes: 1.25 million.
Hong Kong reverts to mainland China's control in 1997. Although the mainland government is aware of Hong Kong's pre-eminence as a provider of broadcast media and programming to the Chinese-speaking population of Southeast Asia, no firm assurances have been given that business will be allowed to continue as before. Public programmer Radio Television Hong Kong (which leases time on TVA & TVB) refused the mainland Chinese government's request for free air-time prior to the reversion. NBC International launched a new English-language channel for the Asian market in April.
Deregulation of Hong Kong's pay TV market was delayed until at least 1998, freezing out many companies who wished entry into the profitable market, including STAR-TV. As a compromise, two video-on-demand channels are expected to be added in 1997. Editor's note: In future editions on the Almanac, Hong Kong will be covered in the China section.
Main broadcasters: TVB Jade (Cantonese), ATV Home (Cantonese), TVB Pearl (English), ATV World (English),

BROADCASTERS

ASIA TELEVISION LTD.
81 Broadcast Dr., Kowloon, Tel: (852) 2338 7123. FAX: (852) 2338 4347.

RADIO TELEVISION HONG KONG
Broadcasting House, 30 Broadcast Drive, Kowloon. (852) 2339 3600. FAX (852) 2338 0279.

TELEVISION BROADCASTS LTD.
TV City, Clear Water Bay Rd., Kowloon. (852) 2719 4828.

CABLE & SATELLITE

RCP-TV/CHINA CABLEVISION LTD.
1 Suffolk Rd., Kowloon Tong. Tel: (852) 338 3641.

STAR TV (SATELLITE TELEVISION ASIAN REGION LTD.)
12th floor, Hutchison House, 10 Harcourt Road. Tel: (852) 524 4093.

HUNGARY

Population: 10.3 million.
TV Sets: 4.26 million.
VCR Homes: 1.3 million.
Cable Service: 950,000.
Satellite Service: 150,000.
Video Standard: PAL.
HBO Hungary has begun a program of investment in local Hungarian TV and motion picture production. State broadcaster Magyar TV is required by law to broadcast 50% Hungarian programming, with Magyar TV 2 required to broadcast 20%. No quotas have been imposed on the commercial networks. Magyar TV will be privatized in 1997.

ORGANIZATIONS

ASSOCIATION OF FILM & TV MAKERS
Gorkij Fasor 38, H-1068 Budapest. Tel: (361) 142 5756.
HUNGARIAN VIDEO DISTRIBUTORS ASSOCIATION
Farogato Ut-24, H-1068 Budapest. Tel: (361) 176 7291.

BROADCASTERS

MAGYAR TELEVIZLO (MTV 1 & 2)
Szabadsag Ter 17, H-1810 Budapest. Tel: (361) 153 3200. FAX: (361) 1113 7875.
NAP-TV
Angol Ut 13, H-11141 Budapest. Tel: (361) 251 0490. FAX: (361) 251 3371.

CABLE

GLOBAL KABELTELEVISIO
P.O. Box 25, H-1506 Budapest. Tel: (361) 173 6250. FAX: (361) 173 6252.
HBO HUNGARY/KABELKOM
Budafoki Ut 59, H-1111 Budapest. Tel: (361) 165 2466. FAX: (361) 181 2377
KABELKOM (KFT)
(See HBO Hungary listing.)

SATELLITE BROADCASTERS

ALFA TV
Vadrosligeti Fusor 38, H-1068 Budapest. Tel. (361) 351 7762. FAX: (361) 351 7768.
DUNA-TV
Rona Ut 174, H-1145 Budapest. Tel: (361) 562 449. FAX: (361) 558 458.

VIDEO DISTRIBUTORS

BEST HOLLYWOOD
P.O. Box 1167, H6701 Szeged. Tel: (3662) 202 4697.
CINE-ART LTD
CINEMAGYAR KFT (HUNGAROFILM EX)
Batori u 10, H-1054 Budapest. (361) 111 4614. FAX: (361) 153 1317.

DUNA/UIP DANUBE
Tarogato u 24, H-1021 Budapest. Tel: (361) 174 7291. FAX: (361) 176 7291.
FLAMEX
Labanc u 22B, Budapest H-1021. Tel: (361) 176 1543. FAX: (361) 176 0596.
INTERCOM
Rona Ut 174, H-1145 Budapest. Tel: (361) 467 1400. FAX: (361) 252 2736.
MOKEP
Bathori u 10, Budapest H-1054. Tel: (361) 111 2097. FAX: (361) 153 1613.
VIDEO RENT
Szepvigyi Ut 128, H-1025 Budapest. Tel: (361) 250 4523. FAX: (361) 250 4106.

ICELAND

Population: 266,000.
TV sets: 92,800.
Video households: 53,000.
Cable households: 28,000.
Video Standard: PAL.
Iceland's first pay cable channel, ICE-TV, debuted in 1995.

BROADCASTERS

ICELANDIC BROADCASTING CORPORATION
Lynghalsi 5, Reykjavik 110. Tel: (3541) 563 3600. FAX: (3541) 567 3011.
Channel Two:. Tel: (3541) 515 6000. FAX: (3541) 515 6820. TV Syn: Tel: (3541) 567 2255. FAX: (3541) 567 3684.
ICELANDIC NATIONAL BROADCASTING SERVICE TELEVISION
Laugavegi 176, Reykjavik 105. Tel: (3541) 169 3900. FAX: (3541) 169 3843.
Icelandic National Broadcasting Service Television (RUV):. Tel: (3541) 515 6000. FAX: (3541) 515 6800.

CABLE

ICE-TV CHANNEL 3
Laufey Gudjonsdottir, Kringlan 7, Reykjavik 103. (3541) 533 5633. FAX: (3541) 533 5699.

INDIA

Population: 950 million.
TV Homes: 50 million.
VCR Homes: 12 million.
Average Video Price: Rs.250.
Rental: 40 cents (overnight rental).
Legal Home Video Distributors: 2000.
Estimated Piracy level: 60%
Video Standard: PAL.
India's state controlled television is known as Doordarshan and has 34 program production centers and as many as 656 TV transmitters of varying power covering over 85% of the population. Viewership surveys have shown that feature films, film based programs and sponsored serials are popular all over the country across regional and linguistic barriers, bringing in sizeable advertising revenues to Doordarshan. Cable TV reaches 16 million households.

BROADCASTERS

ATN
Jal Building, Nehru Rd, Off Western Express Highway, Ville Parle (E), Bombay 400057; Tel: (9122) 610 4617; FAX: (9122) 287 2753
ASIANET
Center Plaza, Vezhutacaud, Trivandrum 14 (kerala). Tel: (91471) 085 03; FAX: (91471) 685 63.
BBC WORLD LTD
AIFACS Bldg, 1 Rafi Marg, New Delhi 110001. Tel: (9111) 335 5751. FAX: (9111) 3355673.
CNN
Taj Mahal Hotel, Suite 1112, 1 Mansingh Road, New Delhi. Tel: (9111) 601 6162. FAX: (9111) 301 9480.
DOORDARSHAN
Mandi House, Copernicus Marg, New Delhi-110001
Tel: (9111) 338 3396. FAX: (9111) 338 6507.
ESPN
Modi Entertainment Network: c-44/32 Okhla Industrial Area-Phase!!, New Delhi 20. Tel: (9111) 683 3409. FAX: (9111) 684 7605.
JAIN SATELLITE TELEVISION
Jain Studio Campus, Scindia Villa, Ring Rd, New Delhi 23.
NEPC COMMUNICATIONS
GR Coplex Annex, 3rd floor, 407-408 Anna Salai, Nandanam, Madras 400 035. Tel: (9144) 433 0489. FAX: (9144) 433 1029.
SONY TV
Plot 23, Shah Industrial Estate, Off Veera Desai Road, Andheri (West) Bombay 400 058. Tel: (9122) 633 1729. FAX: (9122) 731 7836

STAR TV
News TV India Ltd, 3rd Floor, Sanghrajka House, 431 Lamington Road, Bombay 400 004. Tel: (9122) 382 7878. FAX: (9122) 3827979
SUN TV
268/269, 3rd floor, Anna Salai, Teynampeh, Madras 600018. Tel: (9144) 457 424. FAX: (9144) 825 1266.
WHAT'S IN MUMBAI (HINDUJAS)
Sind Mercantile Bldg., Hindujas College Compound, Charni Road (E), Bombay 400 004. Tel: (9122) 386 0404. FAX: (9122) 383 3232.
ZEE TV
Continental Bldg, 135 dr.a.B.Rd, Worli, Bombay 400 018. Tel: (9122) 492 5723. FAX: (9122) 493 1938.

—B.D. GARGA

INDONESIA

Population: 203.6 million.
TV sets: 11 million.
Decoder Homes: 30,000.
Satellite Dish Homes: 300,000.
Video Standard: PAL-B.
Program suppliers were angered over STAR-TV's demands that they pay start-up fees to help finance STAR-TV's new digital TV service to the Indonesian market.

BROADCASTERS
PT RAJAWALI CITRA TELEVISI INDONESIA (RCTI)
J1 Raya Perjuangan, No. 3, Jeruk, Jakarta 11000. (6221) 5303 540. FAX: (6221) 5493 852.
PT SURYA CITRA TELEVISI (SCTV)
JL Raya Darma Permai III, Surabaya 60189. (6231) 714 567. FAX: (6231) 717 723.
PT CIPTA TELEVISI PENDIDKAN INDONESIA (TPI)
Jalan Pintu II, Taman Mini Indonesian Indah, Podok Gede, Jakarta Timur 13810. (6221) 8412 473. FAX: (6221) 8412 740.
TELEVISI REPUBLIK INDONESIA (TVRI)
J1 Gerbang Pemuda-Senayan, Jakarta. Tel: (6221) 5704 720. FAX: (6221) 5821 40.

IRAN

Population: 64.6 million.
TV Sets: 7 million.
Number of VCRs: 2.5 million.
Video Standard: SECAM-B.
ISLAMIC REPUBLIC OF IRAN BROADCASTING
Post Office Box 19395, 1774 Tehran. Tel: (9821) 298 053. FAX: (9821) 295 056.

IRAQ

Population: 20.6 million.
TV sets: 1 million.
Video Standard: SECAM B.
IRAQI BROADCASTING AND TV ESTABLISHMENT
Salihiya Blvd., Karkh, Baghdad. Tel: (9641) 884 4412. FAX: (9641) 541 0480.

ISRAEL

Population: 5.14 million.
TV sets: 1.5 million.
Cable homes: 1.2 million.
Video Standard: PAL.
BROADCASTERS
CHANNEL 2
97 Jaffa St., Jerusalem 94340. (9722) 242 776. FAX: (9722) 242 720.
ISRAEL BROADCASTING AUTHORITY (IBA)
P.O. Box 7139, Jerusalem 91071. (9722) 291 888. FAX: (9722) 292 944.
ISRAEL EDUCATIONAL TV
14 Klausner St., Tel Aviv 690011. (9723) 543 4343.
ISRAEL BROADCASTING AUTHORITY TELEVISION ROMENA
P.O. Box 7139, Jerusalem 91905. Telephone: (9722) 557 111.
PALESTINIAN BROADCASTING CORP.
Police Headquarters, Jericho. Tel: (9722) 921 220.
CABLE/TV STUDIO
JERUSALEM CAPITAL STUDIOS LTD.
P.O. Box 13172, 206 Jaffa Rd., Jerusalem 91131. (9722) 701 711.

VIDEO DISTRIBUTORS
ARGO FILMS
43 Ben-Yehuda St., Tel Aviv 63341. (9723) 522 8251. FAX: (9723) 524 6910.

FORUM FILM
11 Pinsker St., Tel Aviv 63421. Tel: (9723) 528 6211. FAX: (9723) 528 0313.
SHAPIRA FILMS
34 Allenby Rd., P.O. Box 4842, Tel Aviv 63325.
TAMUZ FILMS
5 Pinsker St., Tel Aviv. FAX: (9723) 528 1564.

ITALY

Population: 58.3 million.
TV sets: 17 million.
Video households: 9.9 million.
Satellite households: 80,000.
Video Standard: PAL
RAI announced that it would allot more than half of its annual $300 million budget to new Italian productions, reversing a trend of increased acquisitions in recent years. RAI has been thwarted in its attempt to enter the pay TV market by the Italian government. Former Prime Minister Silvio Berlusconi's media holding took serious damage in 1995 and 1996, with critics charging that laws were written to Mediaset's benefit, including a law allowing cable carriers to enter the telephone business. Mediaset, achieving ratings success with Hollywood programming, was threatened by quotas being raised to a proposed 51%. Mediaset and RAI will be subject to legislation forcing each to turn over a land broadcast channel to public broadcasting. TCI, Canal Plus, Bertelsman, BSkyB, and Generale d'Images announced plans to set up an Italian digital pay television service.
The Italian government has set up a new anti-piracy task force to deal with home video counterfeitors who have made Italy the piracy capitol of Western Europe (and who have made an estimated $324 million in 1995). Bootleg videos are estimated to do better than their legitimate counterparts in Italy.

BROADCASTERS
CANALE 5
Viale Europa 48, Cologno Monzese, Milan 20093. Tel: (392) 251 41. FAX: (392) 2162 8951.
CINQUESTELLE/GBR
Passeggiata di Ripetta 11, Rome 00186. Tel: (396) 324 2408. FAX: (396) 320 3642.
ITALIA 1
Viale Europa 48, Cologno Monzese, Milan 20093. Tel: (392) 251 41. FAX: (392) 2514 6599.
ITALIA 7
Via Turati 3, Milan 20121. Tel: (392) 659 8238.
ITALIA 3
Consorzio Televisivo Italiano, Via Velletri 30, Rome 00198. Tel: (396) 844 2873.
ITALIA NOVE NETWORK
Via Settala 57, Milan 20124. Tel: (392) 221 964.
JUNIOR TV
Corso Garibaldi 3, Milan 20122. Tel: (392) 805 5820. FAX: (392) 864 2343.
R.T.I.
Viale Europa 48, Cologno Monzese, Milan 20093. Tel: (392) 2102 8460.
RAI-RADIO TELEVISIONE ITALIANA (RAI UNO, DUE & TRE)
Viale Mazzini 14, Rome 00195. Tel: (396) 3686 9831. FAX: (396) 372 8824.
RETE A
Viale Morelli 165, Milan 20099. Tel: (392) 247 7241. FAX: (392) 240 1630.
RETECAPRI
Via Li Campi 19, Capri 80073. Tel: (3981) 837 0144. FAX: (3981) 837 0421.
RETEQUATTRO
Viale Europa 48, Cologno Monzese, Milan 20093. Tel: (392) 251 41. FAX: (392) 2162 8951.
SUPER SIX
Via Andrea Appiani 2, Milan 20121. Tel: (392) 2900 2040. FAX: (392) 2900 1047.
TELEMONTECARLO-TV INTERNAZIONALE
Piazza della Balduina 49, Rome 00136. Tel: (396) 355 841. FAX: (396) 3558 4227.
TELEVENEZIA
Via Piraghetto 86, Mestre (VE) 30173. Tel: (3941) 931 183. FAX: (3941) 932 326.
TIVUITALIA
Via S. Senatore 6/1, Milan 20122. Tel: (392) 8901 0772. FAX: (392) 890 0987.
TV ELEFANTE
Via Villa Nuova 38, Rocandelle, Brescia 25030. Tel: (3930) 258 2611. FAX: (3930) 258 3341.
TVA
Via de Gasperi 77, Trento 38100. Tel: (39461) 911 000. FAX: (39461) 934 880.

TVA VICENZA
Via del Commercio 17, Vicenza 36100. Tel: (39444) 562 355. FAX: (39444) 960 883.

TVRS
Via Politi 27, Recanati (MC) 65019. Tel: (3971) 757 0002. FAX: (3971) 982 463.

VCO
Via S. Antonio 11, Domodossola 28037. Tel: (39324) 454 54. FAX: (39324) 454 57.

VIDEO BOX
Via F. Bazzaro 6, Milan 20128. Tel: (392) 257 1688.

VIDEOMUSIC
Via Englen 25, Rome 00165. Tel: (396) 6641 6820. FAX: (396) 6641 6598.

CABLE
TELEPIU PRIMA TV
Via Piranesi 46, Milan 20124. Tel: (392) 70097387.

SATELLITE BROADCASTERS
CINQUESTELLE
Via del Garivaggio 4, Milan 20144. Tel: (392) 433 889. FAX: (392) 498 5514.

ORBIT COMMUNICATIONS
Sapienza Network Centre, Via Raffaele, Costi 60, Rome. Tel: (396) 2254 3615. FAX: (396) 225 4639.

R.T.I. SPA
Palazzo del Cigni, Segrate 20090, Milan 2. Tel: (392) 216 001. FAX: (392) 213 8090.

RAI INTERNATIONAL
Saxa Ruba, L'Go Villy De Luca, Rome 00188. Tel: (396) 3317 2270. FAX: (396) 3317 1885.

RAISAT
via del Babuino 9, Rome 00187. Tel: (396) 368 62276. FAX: (396) 322 0390.

SILVIO BERLUSCONI COMMUNICATIONS
Palazzo Michelangelo, Via Cassanese 224, Segrate 20090. Tel: (392) 216 21. FAX: (392) 2162 8724.

TELESPACIO/ITALSAT
Via Alberto Bergamini 50, Rome 00159. Tel: (396) 406 931.

VIDEO DISTRIBUTORS
A B FILM DISTRIBUTORS
Via Monte Zebio 28, Rome 00195. Tel: (396) 321 9554. FAX: (396) 361 3641.

AVO FILM
Via C. Ravizza 20, Milan 20149. Tel: (392) 4801 2727. FAX: (392) 4801 2737.

BMG
Via S Alessandro 7, Rome 00131. Tel: (396) 4199 51. FAX: (396) 4199 5235.

BLACK HORSE
C. so Rosmini 8, Rovereto 38068. Tel: (3946) 443 1313. FAX: (3946) 443 1314.

BUENA VISTA HOME VIDEO
Via Sandro Sandri, Milan 20121. Tel: (392) 290 851. FAX: 2908 5650.

CECCHI GORI EDITORIA ELETTRONICA
Via Tornabuoni 17, Florence 50123. Tel: (3955) 218 131. FAX: (3955) 217 543.

CINEHOLLYWOOD EDUCATIONAL VIDEO
Via Reguzzoni 15, Milan 20125. Tel: (392) 643 9042. FAX: (392) 6610 3899.

COLUMBIA TRISTAR HOME VIDEO
Via Flaminia, 872, Rome 00191. Tel: (396) 3330 180. FAX: (396) 3330 174.

EAGLE PICTURES
Via M Buonarroti 5, Milan 20149. Tel: (392) 481 4169. FAX: (392) 481 3389.

EMI
Via Bergamo 315, Caronno Pertusella 21042. Tel: (39322) 965 11. FAX: (39322) 965 6002.

FOX HOME VIDEO
Piazza Fontana 6, Milan 20123. Tel: (392) 723 251. FAX: (392) 805 1371.

IMPACT FILM GROUP
Via Bertoloni 41, Rome 00197. Tel: (396) 803 2235. FAX: (396) 808 8166.

MCA
Corso Matteotti 3, Milan 20121. Tel: (392) 760 321. FAX: (392) 7603 2502.

MONDADORI VIDEO
Via Mondadori 1, Segrate MI 75421. Tel: (392) 7542 2060. FAX: (392) 7542 3230.

PENTA VIDEO/SILVIO BERLUSCONI COMMUNICATIONS
Palazzo Michelangelo, Via Cassanese 224, Segrate 20090. Tel: (392) 2162 8882. FAX: (392) 2162 8880.

POLYGRAM
Via Carlo Tenca 2, Milan 20124. Tel: (392) 679 61. FAX: (392) 679 6471.

RCS HOME VIDEO
Via Mecenate 91, Milan 20138. Tel: (392) 509 51. FAX: (392) 5095 5576.

SONY MUSIC VIDEO
Via Amedei 9, Milan 20161. Tel: (392) 853 61. FAX: (392) 860 175.

STARLIGHT
Via Bellerio 30, Milan 20161. Tel: (392) 646 6441. FAX: (392) 6620 4483.

VIDEO DIRECT MARKETING
Via P. Amedeo 25, Bari 70121. Tel: (3980) 524 5325. FAX: (3980) 524 3216.

VIDEOEVENT
Via Zamenhoff 21, Milan 20136. Tel: (392) 837 3551. FAX: (392) 837 5852.

WARNER HOME VIDEO
Via U. Foscolo 1, Milan 20121. Tel: (392) 721 281. FAX: (392) 7212 8200.

IVORY COAST

Population: 14.8 million.
TV sets: 810,000.
Video Standard: SECAM.
TELEVISION IVOIRIENNE
08 B.P. 883, Abidjan 08. Tel: (225) 439 039. FAX: (225) 222 297.

JAMAICA

Population: 2.57 million.
TV sets: 484,000.
Number of VCRs: 235,000.
Video Standard: NTSC.
JAMAICA BROADCASTING CORP.
P.O. Box 100, Kingston 10. Tel: (809) 926-5620. FAX: (809) 929 1069.

JAPAN

Population: 125.5 million.
TV Sets: 100 million.
Video Standard: NTSC.
The head of the Tokyo Broadcast System was replaced after a scandal erupted over an unaired documentary about the Aum Shinryku cult.
A Japanese plan to begin 40-channel digital satellite broadcasts in September 1996 was bolstered when major broadcasters and movie distributors joined in the venture. Japanese hardware manufacturers plan to begin offering an entire line of high-quality digital home entertainment machines to take advantage of the new technology.
JVC introduced a digital VCR able to digitize and record digitize analog video broadcasts on a standard VHS cassette.

ASSOCIATION
THE NATIONAL ASSOCIATION OF COMMERCIAL BROADCASTERS IN JAPAN
3-23, Kioi-Cho, Chiyodaku, Tokyo 102. (813) 5213 7700. FAX: (813) 5213 7701.

BROADCASTERS
ASAHI NATIONAL BROADCASTING (TV ASAHI OR ANB)
1-1-1, Roppongi, 1-chome, Minato-ku, Tokyo 106. Tel: (813) 3587 5416 (Intl Dept.). FAX: (813) 3585 3539 (Int'l Dept.).

FUJI NEWS NETWORK/FUJI TELEVISION NETWORK
3-1, Kawada-cho, Shinjuku-ku, Tokyo 106. (813) 3353-1111. FAX: (813) 3358-1747.

NHK (JAPAN BROADCASTING CORPORATION)
2-2-1 Jinnan, Shibuya-ku, Tokyo 105-01. Tel: (813) 3485 6517. FAX: (813) 3481 1576.

NIPPON TELEVISION NETWORK CORPORATION
14, Niban-cho, Chiyoda-ku, Tokyo 102 40. Tel: (813) 5275 1111. FAX: (813) 5275 4008.

TOKYO BROADCASTING SYSTEM/JAPAN NEWS NETWORK
5-3-6 Akasaka 5-chome, Minato-ku, Tokyo 107 06. Tel: (813) 3746 1111. FAX: (813) 3588 6378.

TXN NETWORK/TELEVISION TOKYO
3-12, Toranomon 4-chome, Minato-ku, Tokyo 105-12. (813) 5473 3447. FAX: (813) 5473 3447.

SATELLITE
CNN
2-23, Roppongi 6-Chome, Minato-ku, Tokyo. Tel: (813) 3405 3186. FAX: (813) 3405 5454.

JCTV
2-23, Roppongi 6-Chome, Minato-ku, Tokyo. Tel: (813) 3405 3186. FAX: (813) 3405 5454.

JAPAN SATELLITE BROADCASTING, INC. (JSB)
No. 6 Central Building, 1-19-10, Toranomon, Minato-ku, Tokyo.

NHK (JAPAN BROADCASTING CORPORATION)
(see Japan Broadcasting Corp. listing under Broadcasters.)

STAR CHANNEL
4-17-7 Akasaka, Mianto-ku 107, Tokyo. Tel: (813) 5563 0438.
FAX: (813) 5563 0440.
STUDIOS
AVACO CREATIVE STUDIOS
2-3-18 Nishi-Waseda Shinjuku-ku, Tokyo 169. Tel: (813) 3203
4181. FAX: (813) 3207 1398.
IMAGICA CORPORATION
2-14-1, Higashigotanda, Shinagawa-ku, Tokyo 141. Tel: (813)
3280 1280. FAX: (813) 3280 1364.
NATIONAL PANASONIC
National No. 1 Bldg., 1-2, 1-Chome, Shiba-Koen, Minato-ku
105, Tokyo. Tel: (813) 578 1237. FAX: (813) 437 2776.
NIKKATSU CORPORATION
3-28-12, Hongou, Bunkyo-ku, Tokyo. Tel: (813) 5689 1019.
FAX: (813) 5689 1043.
SONY CORPORATION
6-7-35, Kitashinagawa, Shinagawa-ku 141, Tokyo. Tel: (815)
448 2200. FAX: (815) 448 3061.
VIDEO DISTRIBUTORS
20TH CENTURY FOX (FAR EAST)
Fukide Bldg. 4-1-13 Toranomon, Minato-ku, Tokyo. Tel: (813)
3436 3421. FAX: (813) 3433 5322.
ASCII PICTURES
12 Mori Bldg. SF, 1-17-3 Toranomon, Minato-ku, Tokyo 105. Tel:
(813)581 9501. FAX: (813) 3581 9510.
BUENA VISTA JAPAN
DK Bldg., 7-18-23 Roppongi 106, Minato-ku, Tokyo. Tel: (813)
3746 5069. FAX: (813) 3746 0009.
CHANNEL COMMUNICATIONS
Osakaya Bldg., 3-1-9 Mita, Minato-ku 108, Tokyo. Tel: (813)
798 3304. FAX: (813) 798 5072.
DISC CENTER
C.P.O. Box 874, Osaka 530-91. Tel: 81 6 323 6350. FAX: 81 6
323 0249.
GAGA COMMUNICATIONS
Step Roppongi Bldg., 6-8-10 Rappongi, Minato-ku, Tokyo 106.
Tel: (813) 5410 3507. FAX: (813) 5410 3558.
MITSUBISHI CORPORATION
3-1, Marunouchi 2-Chome, Chiytoda-ku, Tokyo 100-86. Tel:
(813) 3210 7795. FAX: (813) 3210 7397.
NEW SELECT
Nakamura Bldg., 7th Floor, 5-9-13 Ginza, Ghuo-ku. Tel: (813)
3573 7571. FAX: (813) 3572 0139.
PONY CANYON
4-3-31 Kudan Kita, Chiyoda ku 102, Tokyo. Tel: (813) 3221
3155. FAX: (813) 3221 3168.
TIME WARNER ENTERTAINMENT
1-2-4 Hama matsu-Cho, Minato-ku 105, Tokyo. Tel: (813) 5472
8000. FAX: (813) 5472 8029.
TOEI COMPANY
2-17, 3-Chome, GinzaJapan, Chuo-ku 104, Tokyo. Tel: (813)
535 4641.
TOHO INTERNATIONAL
(A Division of Toho) 1-8-1, Yurakucho, Chiyoda-ku, Tokyo 100.
Tel: (813) 3213 6821. FAX: (813) 3213 6825.
TOHO TOWA COMPANY
6-4, Ginza 2-Chome, Chuo-ku, Tokyo 104. Tel: (813) 3562
0109. FAX: (813) 3535 3656.
UNITED INTERNATIONAL PICTURES (FAR EAST)
Riccar Kaikan Bldg. 6-2-1 Ginza, Choo-ku 104, Tokyo. Tel:
(813) 3248 1771. FAX: (813) 3248 6274.
VICTOR CO. OF JAPAN
4-8-14 Nihon Bashi-Honcho, Chuo-ku 103, Tokyo. Tel: (813)
3246 1254. FAX: (813) 3246 1254.

JORDAN

Population: 4.2 million.
TV Sets: 250,000.
Video Standard: PAL-B
JORDAN RADIO & TELEVISION CORPORATION
Post Office Box 1041, Amman. Tel: (9626) 773 111. FAX:
(9626) 751 503.

KAZHAKHASTAN

Population: 17.4 million.
Video Standard: SECAM.
KAZHAKHSTAN TELEVISION
Jeltoksan kosesi 175, Alma Ata 480013. Tel: (73272) 695 188.
FAX: (73272) 631 207.
VIDEO DISTRIBUTORS
GRANIT
Khaji Mukan St, Alma-Ala 480099, Kazakhstan. Tel: (73272)
650515. FAX: (73272) 650 515.
ORKEN-FILM
Abai St. 10, Apartment 213, Alma-Ata 480000, Kazakhstan.
Tel: (73272) 691 697. FAX: (73272) 632 249.

KENYA

Population: 28.8 million.
TV Sets: 500,000.
Video Standard: PAL B.
KENYA BROADCASTING CORP.
P.O. Box 30456, Nairobi, Tel: (2542) 334 567. FAX: (2542) 220
675.

NORTH KOREA

Population: 23.5 million.
TV Sets: 2 million reported.
Video Standard: PAL/NTSC.
**RADIO AND TELEVISION BROADCASTING OF
THE REPUBLIC OF KOREA.**
Chonsung-dong, Moranbong District, Pyongyang. Tel. (8502)
816 035. FAX: (8502) 812 100.

SOUTH KOREA

Population: 45.6 million.
TV Sets: 11 million.
Video Standard: NTSC.
KOREAN BROADCASTING SYSTEM
18, Yoido-dong, Youngdupo-gu, Seoul 150-790. Tel: (822)
781 2001. FAX: (822) 781 2099.
EDUCATION BROADCASTING SYSTEM
92-6, Umyeon-dong, Seocho-gu, Seoul 137-791. Tel: (822) 521
1586. FAX: (822) 521 0241.
MUNHWA TV-RADIO BROADCASTING CORP.
31, Yoido-dong, Youngdungpo-gu, Seoul, 150-728. Tel: (822)
789 2851. FAX: (822) 782 3094.
SEOUL BROADCASTING SYSTEM
10-2, Yoido-dong, Youngdungpo-gu, Seoul 150-010. Tel: (822)
786 0792. FAX: (822) 785 0006.

KUWAIT

Population: 1.8 million.
TV Sets: 800,000.
Video Standard: PAL B & G.
KUWAIT TELEVISION
P.O. Box 193, 13007 Safat, Kuwait. Tel: (96524) 150 301. FAX:
(96524) 345 11.

LAOS

Population: 4.8 million.
TV Sets: 80,000.
Video Standard: PAL-B.
LAO NATIONAL TELEVISION
P.O. Box 310, Vientiane. (856) 4475.

LATVIA

Population: 2.75 million.
TV Sets: 1.2 million.
Video Standard: SECAM/PAL.
Regional and commercial stations serving the Latvian popula-
tion now number around 100.
LATVIJAS TELEVIZIJA
Zakusalas krastmala 3, Riga LV-1509. Tel: (3712) 200 314.
FAX: (3712) 200 0025.

LEBANON

Population: 3.7 million.
TV Sets: 1.1 million.
Video Standard: SECAM.
BROADCASTERS
TELE-LIBAN
B.P. 115054, Hazmieh, Beirut. Tel: (961) 450 100.
LEBANESE BROADCASTING CORP.
P.O. Box 16-5853, Beirut. Tel: (961) 938 938.

LIBERIA

Population: 3.1 million.
TV Sets: 45,000.
Video Standard: PAL.
LIBERIAN BROADCASTING CORPORATION
Post Office Box 594, Monrovia. Tel: (231) 271 250.

LIBYA

Population: 5.25 million.
TV Sets: 550,000.
Video Standard: PAL.
LIBYAN TV
P.O. Box 333, Tripoli 1.

LITHUANIA

Population: 3.9 million.
TV Sets: 1.75 million.
Video Standard: PAL.
BROADCASTERS
BALTIJOS TELEVIZIJA
Laisves pr.60, LT-2044 Vilnius. Tel: (3702) 417134. FAX: (3702) 428 907
LIETUVOS RADIJAS IR TELEVIZIJA
Konarskio 43, IT-2674, Vilnius. Tel: (3702) 633 182. FAX: (3702) 261 166.
TELES-3
Kalvariju 35, LT-2000 Vilnius. Tel: (3702) 752 533. FAX: (3702) 355 032.
VILNIAUS TV
Vivulskio 25, LT-2000 Kedainiai. Tel: (3702) 661 560.
5 KANALAS
Vanagupes 20, LT-5720 Palanga. Tel: (37036) 511 31. FAX: (37036) 528 78.

LUXEMBOURG

Population: 404,000.
TV Sets: 100,000
Video Standard: PAL/SECAM.
BROADCASTERS
CLT MULTI MEDIA
45 Blvd. Pierre Frieden, Luxembourg-Kirchberg L-1543. Tel: (352) 42142 3930. FAX: (352) 42142 3771.
RTL LUXEMBOURG
Villa Louvigny, Alle Marconi, Luxembourg 2850. Tel: (352) 4766 2933. FAX: (352) 4766 2730.
CABLE
ASTRA/SOCIETE EUROPEENNE DES SATELLITES (SES)
Chateau Betzdorf, Betzdorf 6815. Tel: (352) 7172 51. FAX: (352) 7172 5324.
ELTRONA
4-6 Rue de l'Acierie L-1010. Tel: (352) 499 4661. FAX: (352) 499 4661.
MEDIAPORT LUXEMBOURG
5 Rue Large, Luxembourg L-1917. Tel. (352) 478 2160. FAX: (352) 475 662.
SATELLITE BROADCASTERS
ASTRA
(See Astra listing under Cable.)
RTL-4
Villa Louvigny, Allee Marconi, Luxembourg L-2850. Tel: (352) 4766 2933. FAX: (352) 4766 2744.
VIDEO DISTRIBUTORS
CINE UTOPIA
16 Ave.de Faiencerie, Luxembourg L-1510. Tel: (352) 464 902.
PAUL THILTGES DIST.
1 Rue de Nassau, Luxembourg L1510. Tel. (352) 442 429.

MACAU

Population: 491,000.
TV Sets: 70,000.
Video Standard: PAL.
Macau, currently a Portugese possession, will revert to Chinese control in 1999.
TELEDIFUSAO MACAU
P.O. Box 446, Macau. Tel: (853) 520 204. FAX: (853) 520 208.

MACEDONIA

Population: 2.16 million.
TV Sets: 400,000.
Video Standard: PAL.
TELEVIZIJA MAKEDONIJE
Dolno Nerezi bb, 9100 Skopje. (3891) 258 230.

MADAGASCAR

Population: 13.9 million.
TV Sets: 130,000.
Video Standard: SECAM K.
TELEVISION MADAGASCAR
P.O. Box 442, Antananarivo. Tel. (2612) 217 84.

MALAYSIA

Population: 19.7 million.
TV Sets: 13 million.
Home Satellite Service: 0.15% (another 20,000 illegal)
Video Standard: SECAM K.
Malaysian censorship rules may be eased, allowing "adult-oriented" programming to be shown after 10 p.m. Strict Muslim censorship standards forced either the cutting or outright banning of programming that did not meet local standards. Malaysia debuted Mega TV, a five-channel pay TV system, in late 1995. The Malaysian government announced plans to build a satellite center in Kuala Lumpur, positioning Malaysia as a major force in Southeast Asian telecommunications.
BROADCASTERS
MALAYSIAN TELEVISION SYSTEM BERHAD (TV3)
Sri Pentas, Ground Floor, South Wing, No. 3, Persiaan Benjar Urama, 47800 Petaling Jaya Selangor Darul Ehsan. (603) 716 6333. FAX: (603) 716 133.
RADIO TELEVISION MALAYSIA (RTM)
Department of Broadcasting, Angkasapuri, Kuala Lumpur 50614. Tel: (603) 2825 333. FAX: (603) 2824 375.
TV MALAYSIA SABAH AND SARAWAK
P.O. Box 1016, 88614 Kota Kinabalu. (6088) 52711.

MALI

Population: 9.4 million.
TV Sets: 10,000.
Video Standard: SECAM K.
RADIODIFFUSION TELEVISION DU MALI
P.O. Box 171, Bamako. Tel: (22322) 2019 224308.

MAURITANIA

Population: 2.3 million.
Video Standard: SECAM.
TV NATIONALE MAURITAINE
B.P. 2000, Nouakchott.

MAURITIUS

Population: 1.13 million.
TV Sets: 150,000.
Video Standard: SECAM
MAURITIUS BROADCASTING CORP.
1 Louis Pasteur St., Forest Side. Tel: (230) 675 5001. FAX: (230) 675 7332.

MEXICO

Population: 94 million.
TV Sets: 15.7 million.
VCR Homes: 6 million.
Home Satellite Service: 500,000 (mostly pirated signals).
Home Cable Service : 1.7 million.
Video Standard: NTSC.
TELEVISION BROADCASTERS
CANAL ONCE
Carpio 475, Col. Casco de Santos Tomas, 11340 Mexico, DF. Tel: (525) 396 8177. Telex: 1777554.
DIRECCION GENERAL DE TELEVISION UNIVERSITARIA
Circuito Mario de la Cueva sin numero, Ciudad Universitaria, 04510 Mexico, DF. Tel: (525) 622 6461.
DOS PRODUCCIONES
Amores 809, Col. del Valle, 03100 Mexico. Tel: (525) 523 3117, 523 6652.
IMAGEN OCHO
Av Mzexico 51, Col. Hipodromo Condesa, 06100 Mexico, DF. Tel: (525) 286 3581.
IMEVISION
Periferico Sur 4121, 01420 Mexico, DF. Tel: (525) 652 0973. FAX: (525) 652 0803.
MEDIOS PRODUCCION DE COMUNICACION
Sacramento 121, Col. Del Valle, 03100 Mexico, DF. Tel: (525) 543 6780.
TELEMEDIA
Romulo O'Farril 535, Col. Las Aguilas, 01720 Mexico, DF. Tel: (525) 680 4399. FAX: (525) 680 0984. Telex: 1777202 MTSA ME.
TELEREY
Blvd Puerto Aereo 486, Col. Moctezuma, 15500 Mexico, DF. Tel: (525) 762 9030.
TELEVISA
Av Chapultepec 28, Col. Doctores, 06724 Mexico, DF. Tel: (525) 709 3333. FAX: (525) 709 3021.
VIDEO OMEGA
Monte Elbruz 145, Col. Lomas de Chapultepec, 11000 Mexico, DF. Tel: (525) 202 0936. FAX: (525) 540 2157.
XEIPN (CANAL 11)
Prolongiacion Carpio 475, Colonio Santo Toomas, Mexico DF 11340.
XHDF (CANAL 13)
Av. Periferico Sur 4121, Mexico City 12 DF.
CABLE AND SATELLITE
CABLEVISION
Dr Rio de la Loza 190, Colonia Doctores, 06720 Mexico, DF. Tel: (525) 588 2200. FAX: (525) 588 1474.

MULTIVISION
Blvd Puerto Aereo 486, Col Moctezuma, 15500 Mexico, DF.
Tel: (525) 785 4230.

MONGOLIA

Population: 2.5 million.
TV Sets: 135,000.
Video Standard: SECAM.
RADIO-TV MONGOLIA
Mongolian TV Centre, Huvisgalyn Zalm 3, P.O. Box, Ulan Bator.
Tel: (9761) 328 939. FAX: (9671) 237 234.

MOLDAVA

Population: 4.5 million.
Video Standard: SECAM.
VTV
Str. Hinncesti 61, Chisinau 277028.

MOROCCO

Population: 28.6 million.
TV Sets: 1.2 million.
Video Standard: SECAM.
BROADCASTERS
RADIODIFFUSION TELEVISION MAROCAINE
1 rue Al Brihi, Rabat. Tel. (2127) 649 51.
2M INTERNATIONAL
52 Ave. Hassan II, Casablanca. (21235) 4444.

MOZAMBIQUE

Population: 18 million.
TV Sets: 35,000.
Video Standard: PAL.
TELEVISAO DE MOCAMBIQUE TVM
P.O. Box 2675, Mabuto. Tel: (258) 744 788.

MYANMAR (BURMA)

Population: 45.1 million.
TV Sets: 900,000.
Video Standard: NTSC.
TV MYANMAR
P.O. Box 1432, Yangon. Tel: (951) 31 355. FAX: (951) 30 211.

NAMIBIA

Population: 1.65 million.
TV Sets: 41,000.
Video Standard: PAL.
NAMIBIA BROADCASTING CORP.
P.O. Box 321, Windhoek 9000. Tel: (26461) 215 811. FAX:
(26461) 2912 291.

NEPAL

Population: 21.56 million.
TV Sets: 250,000.
Video Standard: PAL.
NEPAL TELEVISION CORPORATION
P.O. Box 3826, Singha Durbar, Kathmandu. Tel: (9771) 227
290. FAX: (9771) 228 312.

THE NETHERLANDS

Population: 15.4 million
TV Sets: 6.2 million
VCR homes: 3.8 million
Home Satellite Service: 220,000
Home Cable Service: 5.8 million
BROADCASTERS
AVRO
P.O. Box 2, 1200 JA Hilversum. Tel: (3135) 671 7911. FAX:
(3135) 671 7517.
E.O.
P.O. Box 21000, 1202 BB Hilversum. Tel: (3135) 647 4592.
FAX: (3135) 647 4617.
HOLLAND MEDIA GROUP
P.O. Box 15016, 1200 GV Hilversum. Tel: (3135) 671 8718.
FAX: (3135) 623 6463.
IKON TELEVISION
P.O. Box 10009, 1201 DA Hilversum. Tel: (3135) 623 3841.
FAX: (3135) 621 5100. Telex: 43974 IKON NL.
KRO TELEVISION
P.O. Box 23000, 1202 EA Hilversum. Tel: (3135) 671 3911.
FAX: (3135) 623 7345. Telex: 43534.
NCRV
P.O. Box 25000, 1202 HB Hilversum. Tel: (3135) 671 9911.
FAX: (3135) 671 9445.

NCVR
P.O. Box 121, 1200 JE Hilversum. Tel: (3135) 671 9325. FAX:
(3135) 671 9445.
NPS
Sumatralaan 45, P.O. Box 29000, 1202 MA Hilversum. Tel:
(3135) 677 9222. FAX: (3135) 677 2649.
NEDERLANDSE OMROEPPROGRAMMA STICHTING (NOS)
P.O. Box 26444, 1200 JJ Hilversum. Tel: (3135) 677 8037. FAX:
(3135) 677 5318.
NETHERLANDS BROADCASTING SERVICE
P.O. Box 10, 1200 JB Hilversum. Tel: (3135) 677 5445.
TROS
P.O. Box 450, 1202 LL Hilversum. Tel: (3135) 671 5715. FAX:
(3135) 671 5236.
TV PLUS
P.O. Box 427, 1200 AK Hilversum. Tel: (3135) 677 3840. FAX:
(3135) 677 3770.
TV PLUS SELECT
P.O. Box 427, 1200 AK Hilversum. Tel: 06 300 180.
TV 10 GOLD
Sumatralaan 45, P.O. Box 45, 1217 GP Hilversum. Tel: (3135)
677 2700. FAX: (3135) 677 2872.
VARA
P.O. Box 175, 1200 AD Hilversum. Tel: (3135) 671 1370. FAX:
(3135) 671 1378.
VERONICA
Laapersveld 75 1213 VB Hilversum. Tel: (3135) 671 6716. FAX:
(3135) 624 9771.
VPRO
P.O. Box 11, 1200 JC Hilversum. Tel: (3135) 671 2911.
CABLE
CNN INTERNATIONAL SALES
Kolfweg 10, 3255 BK Oude Tonge. Tel: (3118) 741 522.
ENECO
P.O. Bax 1313, 3000 DE Rotterdam. Tel: (3110) 457 5157. FAX:
(3110) 457 5281.
E.O.
(See E.O. listing under Broadcasters.)
KABEL TV AMSTERDAM
Willem de Zwygerlaan 350, 1055 RD Amsterdam. Tel: (3120)
584 8801. FAX: (3120) 400 3025.
KPN Kabel:. Tel: (3120) 584 8888. FAX: (3120) 682 0992.
KTA Amsterdam:. Tel: (3120) 686 8691.
NETHOLD
Neptuusstraat 41, 2132 JA Hoofddorp. Tel: (3123) 568 1500.
FAX: (3123) 561 4952.
NOS
(See NOS listing under Broadcasters.)
NUON
Paramariboweg 65, 7333 BR Appeldorn. Tel: (3155) 265 173.
REMU
P.O. Box 8888, 3503 SG Utrecht. Tel: (3130) 297 5911. FAX:
(3130) 294 1631.
TELESELECT
Karlseldrees 19, 1102 BB Amsterdam. Tel: (3120) 691 9192.
FAX: (3120) 696 9507.
SATELLITE
EURO 7
Lorentzweg 46, 1221 EH Hilversum. Tel: (3135) 646 4646. FAX:
(3135) 646 4600.
FILMNET NEDERLAND
Hoge Naarderweg 1, 1217 AB Hilversum. Tel: (3130) 605 0120.
FAX: (3130) 605 0005.
KINDERNET
Joan Muyskenweg 42, 1099 CK Amsterdam. Tel: (3120) 665
9576. FAX: (3120) 692 8772.
RTL 4 AND 5
Franciscusweg 219, 1216 SE Hilversum. Tel: (3135) 671 8709.
FAX: (3135) 621 0942. Telex: 43079.
SKY CHANNEL
Amstel 62, 1017 AC Amsterdam. Tel: (3120) 555 9911. FAX:
(3120) 620 3348.
VIDEO DISTRIBUTORS
BUENA VISTA HOME ENTERTAINMENT
Postbus 891, 1170 AH Badhoevedorp. Tel: (3120) 658 0300.
FAX: (3120) 659 3836.
CIC VIDEO BV
Ampereweg 13, 3442 AB Woerden. Tel: (313480) 66 900. FAX:
(313480) 10 576.
CINEMA INTERNATIONAL
P.O. Box 9228, 1006 AE Amsterdam. Tel: (3120) 617 7575.
FAX: (3120) 617 7434.
CINEMIEN FILM AND VIDEO DISTRIBUTORS
Entrepotdok 66, 1018 AD Amsterdam. Tel: (3120) 625 8857.
FAX: (3120) 620 9857.
CNR FILM RELEASING
Amstellandlaan 78 P.O. Box 237, 1380 AE Weesp. Tel: (3129)
446 1800.

COLUMBIA TRISTAR HOME VIDEO
Vreelandseweg 428, 1216 CH Hilversum. Tel: (3135) 625 0750.
FAX: (3135) 625 0777.
CONCORDE FILM BENELUX
Lange Voorhout 35, 2514 EC Den Haag. Tel: (3170) 360 5810.
FAX: (3170) 360 4925.
FOX VIDEO
P.O. Box 1213, 1200 NL Hilversum. Tel. (3135) 222 111. FAX:
(3135) 222 190.
POLYGRAM
Mozartlaan 27, 1200 CM Hilversum. Tel: (3135) 261 740. FAX:
(3135) 281 474.
20TH CENTURY FOX VIDEO
Mozartlaan 27, 1200 CM Hilversum. Tel: (3135) 622 2111. FAX:
(3135) 622 2190.
WARNER BROS. HOLLAND
De Boelelaan 16 3H, 1083 HJ Amsterdam. Tel: (3120) 541
1211. FAX: (3120) 644 9001.

NEW ZEALAND

Population: 3.4 million.
TV Sets: 1.1 million.
Video Standard: PAL-B.
ORGANIZATION
INTERNATIONAL TV ASSOCIATION OF NEW ZEALAND
P.O. Box 10092, Wellington. Tel: (644) 385 8055. FAX: (644)
385 8055.
BROADCASTERS
ACTION TV
P.O. Box 388-99 ,Wellington. Tel. (644) 576 6999. FAX: (644)
576 6942.
CANTERBURY TELEVISION
P.O. Box 3741, 196 Gloucester St., Christchurch.
SKY NETWORK TV (PAY-TV)
P.O. Box 9059, New Market, Auckland. Tel: (649) 525 5555.
FAX: (649) 555 5725.
TELEVISION NEW ZEALAND
P.O. Box 3819, Auckland. Tel: (649) 377 0630. FAX: (649) 375
0918.
TV3 NETWORK (AUCKLAND)
Private Bag 92624, Symonds St., Auckland. Tel: (649) 377
9730. FAX: (649) 366 7029.
VIDEO ORGANIZATION
VIDEO ASSOCIATION
125 Vincent St., Auckland. Tel: (649) 308 9421.
VIDEO DISTRIBUTORS
EVERARD FILMS
P.O. Box 3664, Auckland 1. Tel: (649) 302 1193. FAX: (649) 302
1192.
HOYTS CORPORATION (NZ)
P.O. Box 6445, Auckland. Tel: (649) 303 2739. FAX: (649) 307
0011.
KONTACT VIDEO SERVICES
P.O. Box 25156, Auckland. Tel: (649) 575 8238.
UNITED INTERNATIONAL PICTURES
P.O. Box 105263, Auckland. Tel: (649) 379 6269. FAX: (649)
379 6271.
WARNER BROS. (NZ)
P.O. Box 8687, Mt. Eden, Auckland. Tel: (649) 377 5223. FAX:
(649) 309 2795.

NICARAUGUA

Population: 4.2 million.
TV Sets: 2 million.
Video Standard: NTSC.
SISTEMA SANDINISTA DE TELEVIAION (GOV.)
Km 31/2 Carretera Sur, Contigo Shell, Las Palmas, Managua.
Tel: (5052) 660 028. FAX: (5052) 662 411.

NIGER

Population: 9.3 million.
TV Sets: 25,000.
Video Standard: SECAM.
ORTV NIGER
P.O. Box 309, Niamey. Tel: (227) 723 155. FAX: (227) 723
548.

NIGERIA

Population: 101.2 million.
TV Sets: 4.1 million.
Video Standard: PAL-B.
NIGERIAN TELEVISION AUTHORITY
Television House, PMB 12036, Victoria Island, Lagos.

NORWAY

Population: 4.3 million.
TV Sets: 1.8 million.
VCR Homes: 54,000.
Home Satellite Service: 123,000.
Home Cable Service : 755,000.
Norway is the fastest growing TV market in Europe, and the
main target group driving the buying at MIP is Norwegian
women. Video sales were up.
BROADCASTERS
NORSK RIKSKRINGKARTING (NRK)
Bjrnstjerne Bjrnsons Plass 1, N-0340 Oslo 1. Tel: (47) 2245
9090. FAX: (47) 2245 7252.
TV2 AS
P.O. Box 2, Verfsgt 2c, N-5002. Tel: (47) 5590 8070. FAX: (47)
5590 8137.
TV3
Karl Johansgt 12J, N-0154 Oslo. Tel: (47) 2242 3030. FAX: (47)
2242 5029.
TV4 NORDISK TELEVISJON AS
Sandakervn 24 c, N-0473 Oslo. Tel: (47) 2235 5080.FAX: (47)
2232 5180.
ZTV
Maridalsvn 139 A, N-0406. Tel: (47) 2271 4000. FAX: (47) 2271
6550.
CABLE
FREDRIKSTAD NAERINGKASTIG
P.O. Box 444, N-1601, Fredrikstad. Tel: (47) 6931 9030. FAX:
(47) 6931 9280.
TV 1000 NORGE AS
Nedre Slottsgt 8, N-0157 Oslo. Tel: (47) 2241 1000. FAX: (47)
2242 2715.
TV HALDEN
Os Alle P.O. Box 623 Busterud, N-1754 Halden. Tel: (47) 6917
5310. FAX: (47) 6918 7913.
TV HEDMARK
Elvarheimgt 10, N-2400 Elverum. Tel: (47) 6241 3555. FAX:
(47) 6241 3375.
TV NORDMORE
Idustivn 18, N-6500 Kristiansund. Tel: (47) 7158 4922. FAX:
(47) 7158 3755.
TV3
(See TV3 listing under Broadcasters.)
TV PLUS
Grensen 15, P.O. Box 289, Sentrum, N-0103 Oslo. Tel: (47)
2286 4150. FAX: (47) 2286 4430.
SATELLITE
SCANSAT BROADCASTING TV3
Bogstadveien 8, N-0355 Oslo. Tel: (47) 2260 1860. FAX: (47)
2260 1310.
TV 1000 NORGE AS
(See TV 100 listing under Cable.)
TV2 AS
(See TV2 listing under Broadcasters.)
TV3
(See TV3 listing under Broadcasters.)
TVNORGE AS
Sagveien 17, N-0458 Oslo. Tel: (47) 2235 3379. FAX: (47) 2235
4374.
TV PLUS
(See TV Plus listing under Cable.)
VIDEO DISTRIBUTORS
ACTION FILM
Valerenggata 47, PO Box 9343,Valerenga, Oslo N-0610. Tel:
(47) 2267 3131. FAX: (47) 2267 3005.
BUENA VISTA HOME VIDEO
PO Box 164, Stabekk N-1320. Tel: (47) 6756 3609. FAX: (47)
6758 3709.
BV FILM INTERNATIONAL
PO Box 17, Avaldnsnes, Oslo N-4262. Tel: (47) 5284 3544.
FAX: (47) 5284 3575.
CCC VIDEO
PO Box 95, Alnabru, Oslo N-0614. Tel: (47) 2264 7770. FAX:
(47) 2264 2122.
CIC VIDEO NORWAY
Gjerdrumsvel 21, PO Box 38, Tasen, Oslo N-0801. Tel: (47)
2223 2500. FAX: (47) 2223 2599.
EGMONT FILM
PO Box 417, Asker N-1370. Tel: (47) 6690 4121. FAX: (47)
6690 4175.
FILMCO
Profdaohlsegt 8, Oslo N-03554262. Tel: (47) 2646 4000.
HOLLYWOOD FILM
Baneviksgt 7, Stavanger N-4014. Tel: (47) 5153 4045. FAX:
(475152) 7398.

NORSK FILM DISTRIBUTION
Stortingsgt 12, Oslo N-0161. Tel: (47) 2242 3600. FAX: (47) 2242 2313.
NOVIO
Nes Terrasse 45, Nesbru N-1360. Tel: (47) 6684 9160. FAX: (47) 6698 0342.
POLYGRAM
Drammensvn 88B, Oslo N-4262. Tel: (47) 2243 6060. FAX: (47) 2243 4430.
SF NORGE
Box 6868, St Olavs Plass, Oslo N-0614. Tel: (47) 2233 4750. FAX: (47) 2242 4430.
TOUR DE FORCE
Georgemes V 3, Bergen N-5011. Tel: (47) 5532 2590. FAX: (47) 5532 3740.
WARNER HOME VIDEO
Oscargate 55, Oslo N-0258. Tel: (47) 2243 1800. FAX: (47) 2255 4683.

OMAN

Population: 2.12 million.
TV sets: 1.5 million
Video Standard: PAL-B & G.
OMAN TELEVISION
P.O. Box 600, Muscat 113.

PAKISTAN

Population: 129.91 million
TV Sets: 3 million
Licensed TV Sets: 1.2 million
VCRs/VCPs: 2 million
VCR Households: 60% approximately
VCR Prices: $330—$400
VCP Prices: $150 and $200
Estimated Piracy level: 70% (Video is an illegal business under Pakistani laws.)
Video Standard: PAL.
All of the five centers of Pakistan Television Corporation Ltd. (PTV) produce and transmit color programs, including foreign films around the clock. Three centers of Shalimar Television Co., (which is a state-controlled network) are leased out to a private company, NTM, for five hours from 7 to 12 pm. The remaining time is fed by CNN live. One more channel, Shaheen PTV, has started its transmission recently. PTV also exports a good number of its programs to other countries, particularly to those where large numbers of Pakistanis and Indians live.
The main source of income for PTV are commercials and license fees of Rs.250 per year for domestic and Rs.500 per year for commecial sets. All PTV programs are now broadcast via satellite in 38 neighboring countries. The second channel project went on the air in 1995. It is being used mostly for educational purposes and is described as ETC or PTV 2. There are at present two studios for ETC at Islamabad for recording purposes, and an Academy for the training of artists and technicians.
Dish antennas have strongly affected the VCR/VCP business, as the prices of dish technology have gone down considerably—between Rs. 8,000 and Rs.15000 (the more expesive dishes cover a much larger area). A registration fee of Rs.1000 and Rs.2000 is imposed annually on dish antennae, but few pay. Cable operators charge between Rs. 30 and Rs. 100 per month.
There are two kinds of video shops—one deals in sales, the other in rentals only. The number of video distributors is countless, but there are about a dozen big ones, who 'import' video films from all countries except India. Their main business is Indian films and sexy pictures. Video viewers love to see films full of sex, violence and thrills. Because of strict censorship, moviegoers cannot see such films in cinemas. Therefore pirated, uncensored videos are popular.
BROADCASTERS
PAKISTAN TELEVISION CORPORATION LTD.
Aga Khan Road, Islamabad. Tel: (9251) 8124 6165. Cable: Telecast, ISLAMABAD.
PTV-LAHORE
21 Mehmood Ghaznavi Road, Lahore. Tel: (9242) 3059 4549. Cable: Telecast, LAHORE.
PTV-KARACHI
Stadium Road, Karachi. Tel: (9221) 4930 0109. Telex: 2767 PTVCS PAK.
PTV-QUETTA
Sahra-e-Hali, Quetta. Tel: (9281) 7013 039. Cable: Telecast, QUETTA.
PTV-PESHAWAR
58 Shahrah-e-Quaide Azam m, Peshawar. Tel: (9291) 7910 009. Cable: Telecast, PESHAWAR.
SHALIMAR TELEVISION CO.
PTV Center, Islamabad. Tel: (9251) 827-119.

NETWORK TELEVISION MARKETING (PVT) LTD.
44 Nazimuddin Road, Sector F-7/4, Islamabad. Tel: (9251) 2211 9003. FAX: (9251) 221 193.
NETWORK TELEVISION MARKETING (PVT) LTD.
43/15 F Block 6, P.E.C.H.S., Karachi. Tel: (9221) 4541 170. FAX: (9221) 4545 538.

—A.R. SLOTE

PANAMA

Population: 2.7 million.
TV Sets: 223,000.
Video Standard: NTSC.
TELEVISION NACIONAL
Apr. 6-3092, El Dorado, Panama.
RPC TELEVISION
Apt. 1795, Panama 1.
PANAVISION
Apt. 6-2605, El Dorado, Panama 1.
SISTEMA DE TV EDUCATIVA
Estafeta Universitaria, Universidad de Panama.
TELEMETRO
P.O. Box 8-116, Panama 8.

PAPUA NEW GUINEA

Population: 4.3 million.
TV Sets: 100,000.
Video Standard: PAL.
EMTV
P.O. Box 443 Boroko. Tel: (675) 3257 322. FAX: (675) 3254 450.

PARAGUAY

Population: 5.6 million.
TV Sets:350,000.
Video Standard: PAL.
TELEVISION ITAPUA
Avda. Irrazabal 25 de Mayo, Encarnacion.
TELEVISORA DEL ESTE
Area 5, Cd. Puerto Stroessner.
CANAL 9 TV CERRO CORA S.A.,
Avenida Carlos Antonio Lopez 572, Asuncion. Tel: (59584) 222 26. Tel: (59584) 498 911.
TELEDIFUSORA PARAGUAYA S.A.
8 Proy Lambare, Asuncion. Tel: (59521) 443 093.

PERU

Population: 22.9 million.
TV Sets: 2 million.
Video Standard: NTSC.
ANDINA DE TELEVISION/CANAL 9
Arequipa 3570, San Isidro, Apartado 270077, Lima.
CANAL 4
Montero Rosas 1099, Santa Beatriz, Lima.
CANAL 11
Avenido Manca Capac 333, La Victoria, Lima.
CANAL 13
Jiron Huarez 1098, Pueblo Libre, Lima.
COMPANIA LATINOAMERICANA DE RADIODIFUSION S.A/CANAL 2
San Felipe 968, Jesus Maria, Lima 11. Tel: (51 (14) 707272. FAX: (51 (14) 712688
COMPANIA PERUANA DE RADIODIFUSION
Cas. 1192, Lima.
DIFUSORA UNIVERSAL DE TELEVISION
Paseo de la Republica 6099, San Antonio, Miraflores, Lima.
EMPRESA DE CINE, RADIO Y TELEVISION PERUANA/CANAL 7
Jose Galvez 1040, Lima.
EMPRESA RADIODIFUSORA 1160 TV
Apt. Postal 2355, Lima.
PANAMERICANA DE TELEVISION/CANAL 5
Av Arequipa 1110, Lima.
RBC TELEVISION
Juan de la Fuente 453, Miraflores, Lima.

PHILIPPINES

Population: 68.7 million.
TV Sets: 8 million.
Video Standard: NTSC.
Cable Homes: 200,000.
NATIONAL TELECOMMUNICATIONS COMMISSION
865 Vibal Bldg., Esda Corner Times Str., Quezon City.

ABS-CBN BROADCASTING CORP. (CH. 12)
Mother Ignacia Street, Queson City.
PEOPLE'S TELEVISION NETWORK, INC.
Broadcast Complex, Visayas, Avenue Quezson City 1100. Tel:
(632) 921 2344. FAX: (632) 921 1777.

POLAND

Population: 38.8 million.
TV Sets: 10 million.
Video Standard: PAL.
BROADCASTERS
POLISH TELEVISION
JP Woronicza 17, Warsaw 00950. Tel: (4822) 478 100. FAX:
(4822) 430 141.
POLSAT
Zjednoc Zonych 53, Warsaw 04028. Tel: (4822) 104 001. FAX:
(4822) 134 295.
TV WROCLAW
Ul Karkonoska 8/10, Wroclaw 53/015. Tel: (4871) 684 300.
FAX: (4871) 679 454.
TVN
Powsinska Str 4, Warsaw 02920. Tel: (4822) 640 4446. FAX:
(4822) 640 4456.
CABLE
HBO POLSKA
Wilcza Str 8/3, Warsaw. Tel: (4822) 622 1034. FAX: (4822) 622
1035.
MULTICHOICE/FILMNET
Domaniewska Str 39A, Warsaw 04028. Tel: (4822) 222 909.
FAX: (4822) 222 929.
SATELLITE
CANAL & POLSKA
Kawaleri 5, Warsaw 00468. Tel: (4826) 570 748. FAX: (4826)
570 710.
TV POLONIA
Woronicza 17, Warsaw 00950. Tel: (4822) 476 013. FAX:
(4822) 434 833.
VIDEO DISTRIBUTORS
ANWA FILM INTERNATIONAL
Smolensk 27/3, Krakow 30960. Tel: (4812) 215 634.
ARATHOS
Lakowa Str 29, Lodz 90554. Tel: (4842) 362 592. FAX: (4842)
360 487.
ARTVISION
Smocza 18, Warsaw 01034. Tel: (4822) 382 407. Tel: (4822)
382 407.
BEST FILM
Ul Twarda 16a, Warsaw 00105. Tel: (4826) 201 207. FAX:
(4826) 201 203.
BOOM-FILM
Os Plastow 12C, Krakow 31410. Tel: 48 12 486 802. FAX: 48
12 486 802.
DEMEL
Al Stanow Zjednoczonych, Pawilon, C3, Warsaw 04028. Tel:
(4826) 101 854. FAX: 48 23 103 074.
DG FILM
Jelinka 2, Warsaw 01645. Tel: (4822) 338 559. Tel: (4822) 338
559.
EUROKADR
Potocka Str 14, Warsaw 01639. Tel: (4822) 332 491. FAX:
(4822) 332 491.
EUROPOL
Chelmzynska 180, Warsaw 01639. Tel: (4822) 611 1140. FAX:
(4822) 610 8717.
FILM STUDIO HELIOS.
Przybyszewskiego 167, Lodz 93120. Tel: (4842) 417 510. FAX:
(4842) 417 367.
IFDF MAX
Jagelionska Str 26, Warsaw 03719. Tel: (4826) 190 481. Tel:
(4826) 191 209.
IMP
Ul Hoza 66, Warsaw 00950. Tel: (4826) 226 819. FAX: (4826)
226 821.
IMPERIAL ENTERTAINMENT
Przasnysla 9, Warsaw 01756. Tel: (4822) 637 871. FAX: (4822)
637 884.
ITI HOME VIDEO
Klobucka 23, Warsaw 02699. Tel: (4822) 430 506. FAX: (4822)
430 506.
MARIANNE
Al Lotnikow 1, Warsaw 02668. Tel: (4822) 431 406. Tel: (4822)
434 492.
MUVI ENTERTAINMENT GROUP
Rovbrat St 44, Warsaw 00-419. Tel: (4822) 629 2664. FAX:
(4822) 629 5911.

NEPTUN VIDEO CENTER
Sapiezynska 10, Warsaw 00131. Tel: (4826) 359 276. FAX:
(4826) 359 276.
PELOGRAF
Pl Mirowski 14, Warsaw 00135. Tel: (4822) 2051260. FAX:
(4822) 208 342.
SILESIA-FILM
Kosciuszki 88, Katowice 40041. Tel: (4832) 512 248. Tel: (4832)
512 284.
SALOPAN
Ul Krakowskie Przedmiescie 21/23, Warsaw 00071. Tel: (4822)
226 3335. FAX: (4822) 635 0044.
STARCUT FILM-POLAND
Beniowskiego 7A, Gdynia 81226. Tel: (4858) 206 646. FAX:
(4858) 209 676.
STUDIO KINEO
Ul Zlota 7/9, Warsaw 00019. Tel: (4822) 272 906. FAX: (4822)
266 468.
SYRENA ENTERTAINMENT GROUP
Marszalkowska 115, Warsaw 00950. Tel: (4822) 275 204. Tel:
(4822) 275 648.
TOP VIDEO
Ul Frankuska 11, Warsaw 03906. Tel: (4826) 174 082. FAX:
(4822) 241 762.
VIM
Ul Wspolna 30a, Warsaw 00930. Tel: (4822) 623 2155. FAX:
(4822) 623 2157.
WARNER HOME VIDEO
Ks J Popieluszki Str 16, Warsaw 01-590. Tel: (4822) 339 808.
FAX: (4822) 335 497.

PORTUGAL

Population: 10.6 million.
TV sets: 1.9 million.
Video Standard: PAL.
BROADCASTERS
RTP (PORTUGUESE RADIOTELEVISION)
Av 5 de Outubro, 197, Lisboa 1050. Tel: (3511) 793 1774. FAX:
(3511) 797 1045.
SIC (SOCIEDADE INDEPENDENTE DE COMMUNICACAO)
Estrada da Outurela, Camaxide, Linda-A-Velha. Tel: (3511) 417
3138. FAX: (3511) 417 3119.
TVI (INDEPENDENT TELEVISION)
Edificio Altejo, rua 3 da Martinha, 6 piso, sala 609, Lisbon
1900. Tel: (3511) 868 7970. FAX: (3511) 868 8013.
VIDEO DISTRIBUTORS
ACTUAL-VIDEO
Campo Grande 30, 3 F, Lisbon 1700. Tel: (3511) 793 6726.
FAX: (3511) 797 8816.
ATALANA FILMS
Av Joao Crisostomo, 38C-1, Escrittorio 3, Lisbon 1000. Tel:
(3511) 353 1616. FAX: (3511) 353 1636.
BMG ARIOLA
Rua Joao Chagas, N-53-1, Alges 1495. Tel: (3511) 414 8020.
FAX: (3511) 414 2959.
CASTELO LOPES
Rua de St Amaro Estrela, 17A, Lisbon 1200. Tel: (3511) 395
5955. FAX: (3511) 395 5924/5.
COMPETIVIDEO
Rua da Trinidad, 12-2, Lisbon 1000. Tel: (3511) 346 6971. FAX:
(3511) 346 6967.
DEVA VIDEO
Av Duque de Loule 75 8 dto 1000. Tel: (3511) 573 698.
ECOVIDEO EDICOES VIDEO
Estrada de Benifica 407 1 dto, Lisbon 1500. Tel: (3511) 778
1921.
EDIVIDEO
Rua Manual Ferreira Andrade, B, Lisbon 1500. Tel: (3511) 778
3158. FAX: (3511) 778 0661.
EMI-VALENTIM DE CARVALHO
Rua Cruz dos Polais 111, Lisbon 1200. Tel: (3511) 600 111.
FAX: (3511) 395 7074.
FANTAS VIDEO
Rua Diogo Brandao 87, Porto 4000. Tel: 351 2 32 07 59. FAX:
351 2 38 36 79.
FILMAYER ALFA
Praca de Alegria 22-1, Lisbon 1250. Tel: (3511) 347 4561. FAX:
(3511) 346 5349.
FILITALUS
Rua Alexandre Herculano 2, Lisbon 1150. Tel: (3511) 547 988.
Tel: (3511) 524 674.
LUSOMUNDO
Praca de Alegria 22, Lisbon 1250. Tel: (3511) 347 4561. FAX:
(3511) 346 5349.
MEDUSA FILMS
Rua Washington 37 R/C, Lisbon 1100. Tel: (3511) 815 1185.
FAX: (3511) 813 7614.

MUNDIAL VIDEO
Rua Luciano Cordeiro 113 7 Esq, Lisbon 1100. Tel: (3511) 315 0860.
POLYGRAM DISCO
Rua Prof Reinaldo dos Santos 12, Lisbon 1200. Tel: (3511) 778 7101. FAX: (3511) 778 0212.
PRISVIDEO EDICOES VIDEOGRAF
Durbalino Neves, Rua Bartolomeu Dias, PO Box 207, S Joao Madeira Codex 3701. Tel: 351 56 881 992. FAX: 351 56 881 923.
ROMALUSA
Rua Alexandre Herculano 2 Lisbon 1150. Tel: (3511) 354 7142. FAX: (3511) 352 4674.
TRANSVIDEO
Rua dos Soeiros 317 A, Lisbon 1500. Tel: (3511) 726 2510. Tel: (3511) 726 9579.
UNITED KING VIDEO
E. N. 2494, Km 7, 4, Abobada, Parede 2775. Tel: (35144) 443 24. FAX: (35144) 438 92.
VERA VIDEO
Alameda das Linhas de Torres, 104, 1 Esq, Lisbon 1700. Tel: (3511) 759 0591. FAX: (3511) 353 5630.
VISAO VIDEO
Rua de Santa Marta21, 1 dto, Lisbon 1100. Tel: (3511) 353 0736. FAX: (3511) 315 5630.

QATAR

Population: 534,000.
TV sets: 300,000.
Video Standard: PAL.
QATAR TELEVISION SERVICE
Min. of Information and Culture, QTV, P.O. Box 1944, Doha. Tel: (974 89 4444. FAX: (974 86 4511.

ROMANIA

Population: 23.2 million.
Number of TV Sets: 4 million.
Video Standard: PAL.
A new national channel, Pro TV, was introduced in Romania in December 1995. The station, owned by American investor Ronald Lauder, earned a 70% share of viewers against the state-owned broadcaster.
RADIO TELIVIZIUNEA ROMANA
Str. General Berthelot 69/62, 79756 Bucaresti, P.O. Box 111, Tel: (90) 503055.

RUSSIAN FEDERATION

Population: 149 million.
TV sets: 55 million.
Video Standard: SECAM.
A regional broadcaster, CINV, that started out as an illegal pirate operation has become one of Russia's top broadcasters, with an audience of nearly 100 million. Lower advertising rates than major Russian broadcasters have helped the station grow. Turner International set up a distribution deal with TV Network ORT for movies and current Turner programming.
Video piracy is still a major problem in Russia. Editor's note: The listings for companies in the former member states of the USSR have been moved to their individual country's listing.
BROADCASTERS
6TR PETERSBURG - CHANNEL 5
6 Chapygina Str., St Petersburg 198022. Tel: (7812) 234 3763. FAX: (7812) 234 1416.
AS BAIKAL TV - TV & RADIO
6 Shelehov, Shelehov 666020. Tel: (7395) 109 3303. FAX: (7395) 103 1917
ARKHANGELSKAYA TV COMPANY
Levachov St. 17, Cor 2, Arkhangelsk 163020, Russia. Tel: (7818) 0027 777.
BRYANSK STATE TV
Stanice Dmitrov Propsect 77, Bryansk 241033, Russia. Tel: (7832) 212 661.
EVRASIA TV
Lesvaya St. 63/43, Moscow 103055, Russia. Tel: (7095) 250 1248. FAX: (7095) 973 1216.
INDEPENDENT BROADCASTING SYSTEM (MVS)
Suite 303, 8A, Suvoroysky Blvd., Moscow 121019. Tel: (7095) 291 1787. FAX: (7095) 291 4174.
KALININGRAD STATE TV & RADIO
19 Klinicheskaja Str., Kaliningrad 136016. Tel: (70112) 452 700. FAX: (70112) 452 233.
LENINGRAD REGION TV
Uritskogo Str 2, St Petersburg 188350. Tel: (7812) 274 3536. FAX: (7812) 274 4470.
MOSCOW TV
12 Akademika Korolyova Str., Moscow. Tel: (7095) 217 5298. FAX: (7095) 216 5401.

MOSCOW TV 6
Ilyinka 15, Moscow. Tel: (7095) 206 8423. FAX: (7095) 206 8423.
NTV
Novyi Arbat Str 36, Moscow 121102. Tel: (7095) 290 7077. FAX: (7095) 290 9757.
ORT/OSTANKINO
12 Akademika Korolyova St., Moscow 127000. (7095) 217 9838. FAX: (7095) 215 9356.
REGIONAL TELEVISION
Akademika Pavlova Str 3, St Petersburg 197022. Tel: 7 812 238 6073. FAX: 7 812 238 5807.
RTR NETWORK
5YA Yamskogo Polya 19/21, Moscow 125124. Tel: (7095) 213 4052. FAX: (7095) 213 6081.
RUSSIAN INSTITUTE FOR CULTURAL RESEARCH
20 Bersenevskaya Nab, Moscow 109072. Tel: (7095) 230 0177. FAX: (7095) 230 0822.
RUSSIAN UNIVERSITY CHANNEL
5 Yamskogo Polya 19/21, Moscow 125124. Tel: (7095) 213 1754. FAX: (7095) 213 1436.
RUSSKOYE VIDEO—CHANNEL 11
Malaya Nevka 4, St Petersburg 197022. Tel: 7 812 234 4207. FAX: (7095) 234 0088.
STATE NATIONAL TV COMPANY OF SAKHA REPUBLIC
Ordjokinidze St. 48, Yakutsk 677892, Russia. Tel: 7 41122 53176.
TELEXPRESS—CHANNEL 31
Korolyova Str. 12, Moscow 127000. Tel: (7095) 282 4260. FAX: (7095) 276 8892.
TV CHANNEL 2X2
Korolyova St 12, Moscow 127000. Tel: (7095) 217 7094. FAX: (7095) 215 2063.
TV 6 MOSCOW
Lubovsky Boulevard 4, Moscow 119847, Russia. Tel: (7095) 290 8885. FAX: (7095) 202 4634.
TV COMP FOURTH CHANNEL
PO Box 751, Yekaterinburgh 620069. Tel: (73432) 232 041. FAX: (73432) 235 033.
VGTRK
Jamskogo polja 5-ja ul. 19/12, Moskow 124124. (7095) 217 9981. FAX: (7095) 250 0506.
SATELLITE
KOSMOS TV
Akademika Kovoleva UL 15, Moscow. Tel: (7095) 282 3360. FAX: (7095) 286 2631
OSTANKINO TV-1
Piatickaia 25, Moscow 113326. Tel: (7095) 217 7260. FAX: (7095) 215 1324
RTR NETWORK
5YA Yamskogo Polya 19/21, Moscow 125124. Tel: (7095) 213 4052. FAX: (7095) 213 6081
RUSSIA TV-2
12 Korolyov Street, Moscow 127000. Tel: (7095) 2177 898. FAX: (7095) 2889 508.
CABLE
TELESET
Soretskaya st 80, P/B55, Moscow 105037. Tel: (7095) 166 9763. FAX: (7095) 166 1436.
VIDEO DISTRIBUTORS
ATLANT CO
9A Kirovogradskaya St, Moscow 113587. Tel: (7095) 312 5203. FAX: (7095) 312 8127.
EKATERINBURG ART
Chebyshev Str., 5th Fl., Ekaterinburg 620062. Tel: (73432) 442 1120. FAX: (73432) 442 343.
GEMINI FILM
Bldg 6, 40 Myasnitskaya Str., Moscow 101000. Tel: (7095) 921 0854. FAX: (7095) 921 2394.
KINOTON
16 Okruzhnoy Proyezd, Moscow 101000. Tel: (7095) 290 3412. FAX: (7095) 200 5612.
KREDO-ASPEK
Novy Arbat St 11, Moscow 121019. Tel: (7095) 291 7269. FAX: (7095) 219 6880.
MOST MEDIA
Maly Gnezdnikovsky, Moscow 103877. Tel: (7095) 229 1172. FAX: (7095) 229 1274.
PARADISE LTD AGENCY
12a Christoprudny Blvd, Suite 601, Moscow, 101000. Tel: (7095) 916 9220. FAX: (7095) 924 1331.
SKIP CENTRE FILM
2 Filevskaya Str 7/19, Moscow 121096. Tel: (7095) 145 2459. FAX: (7095) 145 3355.
SOVEXPORTFILM
14 Kalashny Pereulok, Moscow 103009. Tel: (7095) 290 2053. FAX: (7095) 200 1256.

STUDIO PYRAMID
8 K-1, Ak Koroleva Str., Moscow. Tel: (7095) 216 4778. FAX: (7095) 216 4778.
VARUS VIDEO
1-st Veshnyakovsky Proezd 1, Moscow 109 456. Tel: (7095) 170 9629. FAX: (7095) 170 5738.

SAUDI ARABIA

Population: 18 million.
TV sets: 4.8 million.
Video Standard: SECAM & PAL.
Saudi-backed Orbit-TV, a satellite broadcaster, became the newest entrant into the Mideast satellite industry, signing a deal to retransmit the News Corp.'s STAR-TV programming in October. As the religious center of the Islamic world, Saudi Arabia will have an enormous amount of influence in programming, and will compete directly with Egypt's giant programming ventures.
BROADCASTERS
ARABSAT
P.O. Box 1038, Riyadh. Tel: (9661) 464 6666. FAX: (9661) 465 6983.
BSKSA SAUDI ARABIA
P.O. Box 57137, Riyadh 11574. Tel: (9661) 4010 40. FAX: (9661) 4044 192.
CHANNEL 3TV
Bldg. 3030, LIP, Dhahran, Saudi Arabia.
SAUDI ARABIAN TELEVISION
Ministry of Information, P.O. Box 570, Riyadh, Saudi Arabia, 11421.

SENEGAL

Population: 9 million.
TV sets: 69,000.
Video Standard: SECAM.
SENEGAL TELEVISION
Radiodiffision Television Senegalaise (RTS), Triangle Sud - B.P. 1765 Dakar. Tel: (221) 2178 7801. FAX: (221) 2234 90.

SIERRA LEONE

Population: 4.6 million.
Video Standard: PAL-B.
TV Sets: 25,000.
SIERRA LEONE TV SERVICE
New England, Private Mail Bag, Freetown

SINGAPORE

Population: 3 million.
TV Sets: 601,000.
Video Standard:
Pay TV Subscribers: 26,000.
VCR Homes: 90%.
BROADCASTERS
SINGAPORE BROADCASTING CORP.
Caldecott Mill, Andrew Rd., 1129. Tel: (65) 256 0401.
TELEVISION TWELVE (TV-12)
12 Price Edward Road, #05-00 Bestway Bldg., Singapore 0207. Tel: (65) 225 8133. FAX: (65) 220 388.
SINGAPORE CABLEVISION (SCV)
150 Beach Road, #30-00, Singapore 0718. Tel: (65) 299 8500. FAX: (65) 299 6313

SLOVAKIA

Population: 5.4 million.
TV sets: 10,000.
Video Standard: SECAM.
BROADCASTERS
DANUBIUS TV
Brectanova 1, Bratislava 830 07. Tel: (427) 371 801. FAX: (427) 371 801.
SATELLITE
DANUBIUS CABLE TV
(See Danubius listing under Broadcasters)
MARKYZA
Palisady 39, Bratislava 81106. Tel: (427) 531 6610. FAX: (427) 531 4061.
VIDEO DISTRIBUTORS
ATRAKT
Prepostska Str 4, Bratislava 81101. Tel: (427) 533 5911.
DAVAY
Trnavska 67, PO Box 15, Bratislava 82101. Tel: (427) 294 645. FAX: (427) 294 677.
INTERSONIC TAUNUS PRODUCTIONS
Stare Grunty 36, Bratislava 84225. Tel: (427) 571 1176. FAX: (427) 571 1181.

SLOVENIA

Population: 2 million.
Video Standard: PAL.
TELEVIZJA SLOVENIJA
Tavcarjeva 17, 6100 Ljubljana. Tel: (3861) 311 922.

SOMALIA

Population: 7.3 million.
Video Standard: PAL.
MINISTRY OF INFORMATION
P.O. Box 1748, Mogadishu.

SOUTH AFRICA

Population: 41.2 million.
TV sets: 3.5 million.
Video Standard: PAL.
Australia's Nine Network has agreed to help start up South Africa's first black-owned broadcaster in partnership with a consortium of local investors.
ASSOCIATIONS & ORGANIZATIONS
ASSOCIATION OF ADVERTISING AGENCIES
5 Tyrwhitt Ave., AAA House, Rosebank, P.O. Box 2302, Parklands 2121. Tel: (2711) 880 3908. FAX: (2711) 447 1147.
AFRICAN FILM AND TELEVISION COLLECTIVE
P.O. Box 42723, Fordsbury 2033. Tel: (2711) 804 5186. FAX: (2711) 838 3034.
SOUTH AFRICAN FILM AND TELEVISION INSTITUTE
P.O. Box 3512, Halfway House 1685. Tel: (2711) 315 0140. FAX: (2711) 315 0146.
BROADCASTERS
CCV-TV
P.O. Box 2491, Johannesberg 2000.
M-NET TELEVISION
P.O. Box 4950, Randburg 2125. Tel: (2711) 889 1251. FAX: (2711) 789 4447.
SOUTH AFRICA BROADCASTING CORPORATION
Broadcasting Centre, Auckland Park, Johannesberg 2092. Tel: (2711) 714 9111. FAX: (2711) 714 5055.
CABLE
FRAMEWORK TELEVISION
P.O. Box 5200, Horizon 1730. Tel: (2711) 475 4220. FAX: (2711) 475 5333.
STUDIOS: FILM & TV
FRAMEWORK TELEVISION
P.O. Box 5200, Horizon 1730. Tel: (2711) 475 4220. FAX: (2711) 475 5333.
SONNEBLOM FILM PRODUCTIONS
P.O. Box 3940, Honeydew 2040. Tel: (2711) 794 2100. FAX: (2711) 794 2061.
SONOVISION STUDIOS
P.O. Box 783133, Sandton 2146. Tel: (2711) 783 1100. FAX: (2711) 883 3834.
TELENEWS VIDEO STUDIO
13-2nd Ave., Houghton. Tel: (2711) 728 4450.
TORON INTERNATIONAL
P.O. Box 89271, Lyndhurst 2106. Tel: (2711) 786 2360. FAX: (2711) 440 5132.

SPAIN

Population: 39.2 million.
TV sets: 17 million.
Cable households: 750,000.
Video households: 6.5 million.
Video retailers: 4,200 (down from a high of 11,000).
Satellite households: 500,000.
Video Standard: PAL.
The Spanish opposition party Partido Popular plans to privatise the financially troubled public television network RTVE, which has accumulated debt in excess of $3 billion.
The major multimedia conglomerate, Timon, owner of Canal Plus-Spain, film company Sogetel and the Prisa group, received criticism from EU broadcasting officials regarding its cable television deal with the state-controlled telecommunications company, Telefonica. Critics charge that the Spanish government is showing favoritism to Prisa in exchange for preferential editorial treatment by the conglomerate's media holdings. Prisa also plans to offer digital satellite and cable broadcasts by the beginning of 1997. Antena 3 will launch a 20 channel digital satellite service through its subsidiary Cable Antena. The Spanish government has loosened the regulations allowing regional cable companies to be established. Cable television serves only 6% of Spain's 11.5 million television households, and is expected to become an extremely lucrative market. Telefonica, the state-owned telephone company, was ordered by a Spanish court to suspend cable broadcasting by its subsidiary cable service, Cablevision, pending the resolution of a suit charging unfair competition by Cableuropa.

Video sales increased 22.5% in 1995 to nearly $172 million, while rental income fell to $40 million. Illegal transmission of videos over cable television "communities" and low power television stations reportedly cost the legitimate Spanish video industry nearly $48 million.

BROADCASTERS

ANTENA 3 TV
Avda. Isla Graciosa s/n, San Sebastian de los Reyes, Madrid 18013. Tel: (341) 623 0500

CANAL PLUS
Gran Via, 32/3a planta, Madrid 28013. Tel: (341) 396 5500. FAX: (341) 396 5600.

CANAL PLUS SOCIEDAD ESPANOLA DE TELEVISION
Torre Picasso Pl., Complejo Azca, Madrid 28020. Tel: (341) 396 5500. FAX: (341) 556 4253.

EUSKAL TELEBISTA (ETB)
Municipio Irrueta, Vizcaya 48200. Tel: (344) 620 3000

RADIO TELEVISION ESPANOLA SA (RTVE)
Prado del Rey, Pozuelo, Madrid 28023. Tel: (341) 346 4000.

RETEVISION
Paseo de La Castellana 83-85, Madrid 28046. Tel: (341) 556 0214. FAX: (341) 555 5892.

TELECINCO
Plaza Pablo Ruiz Picasso s/n, Torre Picasso, Plantz 36, Madrid 28020. Tel: (341) 396 6100. FAX: (341) 555 0044.

TELECONCO
Carretera Irun KM 11, 700, Madrid 28049. Tel: (341) 396 6100. FAX: (341) 555 0044.

TELEMADRID (TM-3)
Zurbano 70, Madrid 28010 Madrid. Tel: (341) 308 3188. FAX: (341) 308 3811.

TELETRES MURCIA
Plateria 44 2 C, Murcia 300001 Murcia. Tel: (3468) 212 270. FAX: (3468) 212224.

TELEVISION ANDALUCIA (RTVA/CANAL SUR)
Ctra San Juan de Aznalfarache a Tomares, Km 1.3 San Jaun de AzwalFarache, Seville 41920. Tel: (345) 560 7600. FAX: (345) 560 7663.

TELEVISIO DE CATALUNYA
PO Box 30300, Barcelona 08080. Tel: (343) 499 9333. FAX: (343) 473 2714.

TELEVISION DE GALICIA (TVG)
Apto de Corrces 707, San Marcos, Santiago de Compostela, 15080. Tel: (3481) 564 400. FAX: (3481) 586 577.

TELEVISIO VALENCIANA (CANAL 9)
Poligono de acceso a Ademuz s/n, Burjassot 46100 Burjassot (Valencia). Tel: (346) 364 1100. FAX: (346) 363 4355.

TV 3
Televisio de Catalunya, Independent Network, Mossen Jacint, Verdeguer, s/n, Sant Joan Despi, Barcelona 08970. Tel: (343) 473 0333. FAX: (343) 473 1563.

CABLE

CABLE DEVELOPMENT & SYSTEMS
Vincente Blasco Ibanez 27, Elche 03201. Tel: (346) 546 1850. FAX: (346) 667 3874

CABLEDIS
Guipozo Kalea 15, Zarautz 20800. Tel: (3443) 131 650. FAX: (3443) 133 079.

CABLEVISION
Gral Marinez Campos 53, Madrid 28010. Tel: (341) 310 2008. Tel: (341) 310 4789.

CALVIA 2000
Lisboa 6, Santa Fonca 07180. Tel: (3471) 693 652. FAX: (3471) 693 507.

CARTAGENA DE COMUNICACIONES
Carmen Conde 4, Cartagena 30204. Tel: (3468) 310 304. FAX: (3468) 310 204.

CREVISIO
Rey Jamie 11, Crevillente 03330. Tel: (346) 540 4634. FAX: (346) 540 1649.

DTC
Antonio Machado 5, Arnedo 26580. Tel: (3441) 381 677. FAX: (3441) 384 070.

EUROPEAN CANAL & TV
Paseo de la Castellan 9, Madrid 28046. Tel: (341) 308 1819. FAX: (341) 308 2023.

GALAVISION TELEVICINE ESPANA
Arrastaria s/n Ctra de Barcelona Km, 11.300, Poligono de Las Mercedes, Madrid 28022. Tel: (341) 329 0369. FAX: (341) 747 6463.

GENERAL DE SERVICIOS DE COMMUNICATION
Consell de Cent 303 pral, Barcelona 08007. Tel: (343) 323 5654. FAX: (343) 323 7596

HISPASAT
Gobelas 41-45 2, La Florida, Madrid 28023. Tel: (341) 372 9000. FAX: (341) 307 6683.

MULTIMEDIA TELECOM SERVICES
Graal Peron 38 pl 11, Madrid 28020. Tel: (341) 584 8125. FAX: (341) 584 8127.

MULTITEL
Marques de Cubas 21, Madrid 28014. Tel: (341) 429 1222. FAX: (341) 420 3755.

MUNDICABLE
San Valeriano 1, Torrent 46900. Tel: (346) 155 6050. FAX: (346) 156 3524.

OPERADORA CABLE SISTEMAS
Llacuna 93, Barcelona 08018. Tel: (343) 300 8480. Tel: (343) 300 8529.

TDC SANLUCAR
Infanta Beatriz 24, Sanlucar de Barrameda 11540. Tel: (3456) 365 077. FAX: (3456) 367 771.

TELECABLE MENORCA
Deya 2 Bajo, Mahon 07701. Tel: (3471 365 065. FAX: (3471 354 839.

TELECABLE SALAMANCA
Aliso 2 Jajo, Salamanca 37004. Tel: (3423) 121 455. FAX: (3423) 121 466.

TELEON
Covadonga 4, Bajo D, Leon 24004. Tel: (3487) 212 200. FAX: (3487) 261 184.

TELEVIDEO COSTA BLANCA
San Policarpo 41, Torrevieja 03180. Tel: (346) 571 5392. FAX: (346) 571 5392.

UIH
Marques de la Ensenada 16, Apartamentos Colon no 211, Madrid 28046. Tel: (341) 319 7566. FAX: (341) 308 3305.

VICOSAT
Plaza de las Farolas, 1 Bajo, Mula 30170. Tel: (3468) 662 411. FAX: (3468) 662 160.

SATELLITE

ANTENA TRES TV/RADIO
Carretera San Sebastian de los Reyes, Madrid 28700. Tel: (341) 632 0500. FAX: (341) 632 7144

CANAL PLUS ESPANA
Gran Via 32, 3rd floor, Madrid 28103. Tel: (341) 396 5500. FAX: (341) 396 5600

COTELSAT
Desengano 9, 6th Flr izq, Madrid 2844. Tel: (341) 521 0729. FAX: (341) 521 7846.

DOCUMANIA SOGECABALE
Gran Via 32 3 Piso, Madrid 28103. Tel: (341) 396 5687. FAX: (341) 396 5484

GALAVISION
(See Galavision listing under Cable.)

HISPASAT
P.O. Box 95000, Madrid 28080. Tel: (341) 372 9000. FAX: (341) 307 6683

SOGECABALE
Torre Picasso, Plaza Ruiz Picasse, Madrid E-28020. Tel: (341) 3965 514.

VIDEO DISTRIBUTORS

BMG ARIOLA
Corazon de Maria 13, Madrid 28002. Tel: (341) 413 3999. FAX: (341) 413 5561.

BMG VIDEO SPAIN
27 Avda. de los Madronos, Parqu Conde Orgaz, Madrid 28043. Tel: (341) 388 0002. FAX: (341) 759 0135.

BUENA VISTA HOME VIDEO
Jose Berdasamo Baos 9, Madrid 28016. Tel: (341) 383 0312. FAX: (341) 308 3152.

CHESTER INTERNATIONAL
Industria 26-Enio 1, Barcelona E-08037. Tel: (343) 257 9402. Tel: (343) 207 1378.

CIC VIDEO Y CIA
Albacete 5 3, Planta, Edificio AGF, Madrid 28027. Tel: (341) 326 0120. FAX: (341) 326 5823.

CINE COMPANY
Zurbano 4, Madrid 28010. Tel: (341) 442 2944. FAX: (341) 441 0098.

COLUMBIA TRISTAR VIDEO
Albacete 5 4, Madrid 28027. Tel: (341) 326 4362. FAX: (341) 409 9458.

CROWN FILMS HOME VIDEO
Maldonado 56, Madrid. Tel: (341) 445 3112.

CYB VIDEO
Mn Cinto Verdaguer 185, Sant Vincent Vicena dels Horts, Barcelona 08620. Tel: (343) 656 3361. FAX: (343) 656 1817.

DIFUSION VIDEO INTERNATIONAL
Gran Via 42, Madrid. Tel: (341) 222 5140.

DISTER GROUP
Caidos de la Division Azul, 22-B, Madrid 28016. Tel: (341) 250 3900. FAX: (341) 250 3904.

DOBLE A FILMS AND TAPES
Quinonnes 2, Madrid 28015. Tel: (341) 594 2059. FAX: (341) 594 2709.

EDITMEDIA TV
Rosellon 205, Barcelona. Tel: (343) 414 1331. FAX: (343) 414 0676.

ESPACIO P
Nunezde Arce 11, Madrid 28012. Tel: (341) 531 3111.

EUROVENTANILLA
Plaza de la Constitucion 9, Malaga 29008. Tel: (345) 222 0959. FAX: (345) 222 0936.

EX LIBRIS VIDEO
C Rossello 17, 1er 1a, Barcelona 08029. Tel: (343) 410 0556. FAX: (343) 419 0262.

FILM INTERNATIONAL
Arda Burgos, 8-A planta 10-1, Madrid 28036. Tel: (341) 383 0265. FAX: (341) 383 0845.

FOREM
Longares 6-8, Madrid 28002. Tel: (341) 324 0119. FAX: (341) 306 9193.

FOX VIDEO ESPANOLA
Avida de Burgos 8a Pllz 11, Madrid 28036. Tel: (341) 343 4640. Tel: (341) 343 4655.

FRAN-EL
Villa Tibidado, Colonia Tibidado 14, Barcelona 08023. Tel: (343) 212 5965. FAX: (341) 212 7503.

FURA DELS BAUS
Diputacio 291-2n, Barcelona 08009. Tel: (343) 487 5982. FAX: (343) 487 6776.

G & CM INTERNACIONAL
Sagasta 15.5 Izq, Madrid 28004. Tel: (341) 447 7100. FAX: (341) 593 3886.

GESTMUSIC
Santa Elionor 3, Barcelona 08024. Tel: (343) 210 5666. Tel: (343) 219 4797.

GRUP CONTINENTAL
Victor Chavarri 19-1, Ovideo 33001. Tel: (3485) 222 971. FAX: (3485) 227 952.

INTEGRA MULTIMEDIA
Parque Tecnologico 103-2 Planta, Samupio 48016. Tel: (344) 420 9812. Tel: (344) 420 9813.

INTERACCION
c/o Enrique Granados, 125 Entio 1, Barcelona 08008. Tel: (343) 415 3204. FAX: (343) 415 3215.

INTERNATIONAL FILM GROUP
Gran Via de las Cortes Catalanas 1176, Barcelona. Tel: (343) 305 3605. FAX: (341) 305 3259.

JMM INVEST (WANDA FILMS)
Avda. de Europa 9, Portal 3 Bajoc, Madrid 28224. Tel: (341) 352 8466. FAX: (341) 352 8371.

KALENDER VIDEO
Pintor Juan Gris 5 1B, Madrid 28020. Tel: (341) 555 4477. Tel: (341) 597 3807.

LAUREN FILMS VIDEO HAGAR
Balmes 87, Barcelona 08008. Tel: (343) 451 7189. FAX: (343) 323 6155.

METROMEDIA ESPANOLA
Rio Tormes, Nave 6, Poligorno Industrial de Algete, Madrid 28110. Tel: (341) 803 2142. Tel: (341) 803 6158.

MGM UA
Doce de Octubre 28, Madrid 28009. Tel: (341) 574 9008. FAX: (341) 574 9005.

MUNDOGRAFICO
Marin Baldo 1-Bajo, Murcia 30001. Tel: (34968) 210 561. Tel: (34968) 221 271.

MUSIDORA FILMS
Calle Princess 17, Madrid 30001. Tel: (341) 541 6869. FAX: (341) 541 5482.

POLYGRAM IBERICA
Suero de Quinnones 38, Madrid 28002. Tel: (341) 564 3310. FAX: (341) 564 3235.

PRIME FILMS
Padre Xitre 5-7C, Madrid 28002. Tel: (341) 519 0181. Tel: (341) 413 0772.

PROFILMAR
Rambla Cataluna 50-1, Barcelona 08007. Tel: (343) 488 0180.

SELECTA VISION
Calle Roma 4-Bajos, Barcelona 08023. Tel: (343) 418 5300. FAX: (343) 418 8811.

TRI PICTURES
Doce de Octubre 28, Madrid 28009. Tel: (341) 574 9008. FAX: (341) 574 9005.

TRIPICTURES
Doce de Octubre 28, Madrid 28009. Tel: (341) 574 9008. FAX: (341) 574 9005.

VIDEO COLLECTION
Crta Boadilla a, 28220. Tel: (341) 639 5562. FAX: (341) 639 5456.

VIDEO MERCURY FILMS
Fernan Gonzalez 28, Madrid 28009. Tel: (341) 431 4790. FAX: (341) 431 7555.

VIDEOMAN INTERNATIONAL
Doce de Octubre 28, Madrid 28009. Tel: (341) 574 9008. FAX: (341) 574 9005.

VISUAL EDICIONES
Paravincinos 16-1 Planta, Madrid 28039. Tel: (341) 450 0750. FAX: (341) 450 0877.

WARNER HOME VIDEO ESPANOLA
Angel Munoz 14-16, Entreplanta, Madrid 28043. Tel: (341) 413 0543. FAX: (341) 519 5759.

SRI LANKA

Population: 18.3 million.
TV sets: 1.7 million.
Video Standard: PAL-B
BRPOADCASTERS
INDEPENDENT TELEVISION NETWORK (ITN)
Wickremasinghepura, Battaramulla. Tel: (941) 864 491. FAX: (941) 864 591

MAHARAJA ORGANIZATION LTD. (MTV)
146 Dawson St, Colombo 2, Tel: (941) 448 375.

RUPAVAHINI CORPORATION
Torrington Square, Colombo 7. Tel: (941) 580 131.

SRI LANKA BROADCASTING CORPORATION
P.O. Box 574, Colombo 7. Tel: (941) 696 140.

TELESHAN TV NETWORK CHANNEL 21
1st Floor, Vogue Building, 528 Galle Road, Colombo 3. Tel: 575436.

PRODUCERS
TELECINE LTD.
43 Hyde Park Corner, Colombo 2, Sri Lanka. Tel: (941) 239 09.

TELESHAN LTD.
1st Floor, Vogue Buiding, 528 Galle Road, Colombo 3. Tel: (941) 575 436.

SELACINE
2 Gregory's Avenue, Colombo 7. Tel: (941) 596 926.

FILMTEL
81/3 Isipathana Mawatha, Colombo 5. Tel: (941) 585 573.

WORLDVIEW FOUNDATION
8 Kinross Avenue, Colombo 4. Tel: (941) 589 225.

SUDAN

Population: 30.1 million.
TV sets: 250,000.
Video Standard: PAL.
SUDAN TELEVISION
P.O. Box 1094, Omdurman. Tel: (24911) 550 22.

SURINAME

Population: 430,000.
TV sets: 44,,000.
Video Standard: NTSC.
BROADCASTERS
SURINAAMSE TELEVISIE STICHTING (STVS)
P.O. Box 535, Paramaribo. Tel: (597) 473 100. FAX: (597) 477 216.

ALTERNATIEVE TELEVISIE VERZORGING
Adrianusstraat 1, Paramaribo. Tel: (597) 410027. FAX: (597) 470 425.

SWAZILAND

Population: 966,000.
TV sets: 12,500
Video Standard: PAL.
BROADCASTING AUTHORITY OF SWAZILAND
Swazi TV, P.O. Box A146, Mbabane. Tel: (268) 430 36. FAX: (268) 420 93.

SWEDEN

Population: 8.8 million.
TV sets: 3.8 million.
VCRs: 2.41 million.
Cable Service: 1.87 million
Satellite Service: 328,000.
Video Standard: PAL.
The Modern Times Group launched two PPV channels. Cable channel TV-Fenman blocked programs with violent content before 9 PM. Video sales were up for the second straight year.
ASSOCIATION
NORDISK FILM/TV UNION, SVERIGE
Stig Palm, Swedish Television-Training, Centre, Stockholm S-10510. Tel: (468) 784 44 03. FAX: (468) 667 44 66.

BROADCASTERS
SVERIGES TELEVISION
Karlavalgen 112, Stockholm S-105 10. Tel: (468) 784 6001.
FAX: (468) 784 6010
SVERIGES TV—GOTHENBURG
Gothenburg S-405 13. Tel: (4631) 837 000. FAX: (4631) 401
741
SVERIGES TV—MALMO
Malmo S-212 01. Tel: (4640) 227 000. FAX: (4640) 227 020
TV4 NORDISK TELEVISION
Tegeluddsvegen 3-5, Stockholm S-115 79. Tel: (468) 459 400.
FAX: (468) 459 444
TERRACOM SVENSK RUNDRADIO
PO Box 17666, Stockholm S-118 92. Tel: (468) 671 2000. FAX:
(468) 671 2401.

CABLE
FILM NET TV
PO Box 5165, Stockholm S-102 44. Tel: (468) 660 2700. FAX:
(468) 660 9218.

SATELLITE
FILMMAX
P.O. Box 2133, Stockholm 10314. Tel: (468) 1000 19. FAX:
(468) 2438 40.
FILMNET SCANDINAVIA
Hornsgatan 166, Box 9006, Stockholm 10271. Tel: (468) 772
2500. FAX: (468) 669 9098.
TV-1000 SUCCE KANALEN (SCANSAT)
Skeppsbron 44, P.O. Box 2133, Stockholm 10314. Tel: (468)
100 019. FAX: (468) 243 840.
TV-3 (SCANSAT)
P.O. Box 2094, Stockholm 10313. Tel: (468) 403 333. FAX:
(468) 216 564.
TV-4 NORDISK TELEVISION
Storangskroken 10, Stockholm 11479. Tel: (468) 644 4400.
FAX: (468) 644 4440.
TV-5 (FEMMAN) NORDIC
Stockholmsvagen 30, Stocksund 18281. Tel: (468) 624 4400.
FAX: (468) 85 15 18.
TERRACOM SVENSK RUNDRADIO
PO Box 17666, Stockholm S-118 92. Tel: (468) 671 2000. FAX:
(468) 671 2401.

VIDEO ORGANIZATION
**FILM-OCH VIDEOBRANCHENS SAMAR, FILM AND VIDEO
JOINT INDUSTRY**
P.O. Box 49084, Stockholm S-100 28. Tel: (468) 785 04 00.
FAX: (468) 653 24 25.

VIDEO DISTRIBUTORS
ATLANTIC FILM
Norra Stationsgatan, PO Box 21112, Stockholm S-100 86. Tel:
(468) 305 230. FAX: (468) 305 280.
BUENA VISTA HOME ENTERTAINMENT
PO Box 5631, Stockholm S-114 86. Tel: (468) 679 1550. FAX:
(468) 678 0728.
BUENA VISTA INTERNATIONAL
PO Box 5631, Stockholm S-114 86. Tel: (468) 679 1550. FAX:
(468) 678 0728.
CIC
Lilla Bommen, Gothenborg 411 04. Tel: (4631) 771 2450. FAX:
(4631) 152 455.
EGMONT FILM
PO Box 507, Taby S-183 25. Tel: (468) 510 100 50. FAX: (468)
510 120 46.
FILM AB CORONA
Brantingsgatan 35, Stockholm S-115 35. Tel: (468) 661 0509.
FAX: (468) 663 3595.
FILMCO
PO Box 11128, Bromma S-161 11. Tel: (468) 285 111. FAX:
(468) 284 111.
FILMGORLAGET
PO Box 27066, Stockholm S-102 52. Tel: (468) 665 1100. FAX:
(468) 661 1053.
FILMO
Skulptorvagen 25, Stockholm S-121 43. Tel: (468) 772 9510.
FAX: (468) 772 9966.
FILMPARTNER
Lilla Verkstadsgaten 7, Kungsbacka S-434 42. Tel: (46) 300
70010. FAX: (46) 300 70241.
FOX FILM
Box 9501, Stockholm S-102 74. Tel: (468) 658 1144. FAX:
(468) 841 204.
LUDAVDELNINGEN
Kummelnasvagen 74, Saltsjo-Boo S-132 37. Tel: (468) 747
9367. FAX: (468) 747 9367.
NORDISK FILM & TV DISTRIBUTION
PO Box 45437, Stockholm S-104 31. Tel: (468) 440 9070. FAX:
(468) 440 9080.

PICKWICK
PO Box 1150, Boras S-501 11. Tel: (4633) 116 800. FAX:
(4633) 100 588.
POLYGRAM
PO Box 20510, Bromma S-161 02. Tel: (468) 629 5300. FAX:
(468) 764 5688.
SANDREW FILM & TEATER
Box 5612, Stockholm S-114 86. Tel: (468) 234 700. FAX: (468)
103 850.
SF VIDEO
Soder Malarstrand 27, Stockholm S-117 88. Tel: (468) 658
7500. FAX: (468) 658 3705
SONET FILM
PO Box 20105, Bromma S-161 20. Tel: (468) 799 7700. FAX:
(468) 285 834.
SVENSK FILMINDUSTRI
Suder Malerstrand 27, Stockholm S-127 83. Tel: (468) 680
3500. FAX: (468) 710 4460.
WARNER HOME VIDEO SWEDEN
Hornsbruksgatan 19, Stockholm S-117 34. Tel: (468) 616 7240.
FAX: (468) 844 078.
WENDROS
PO Box 5100, Huddinge S-141 05. Tel: (468) 774 0425. FAX:
(468) 779 8316.

SWITZERLAND

Population: 6.9 million.
Number of TV Sets: 2.52 million.
Number of TV Stations: 4 German, French, Italian.
Video Standard: PAL.

BROADCASTERS
SWISS BROADCASTING CORPORATION (SBC)
Giacomettistrasse 3, Postfach, CH-3000 Bern 15. Tel: (4131)
350 9111. FAX: (4131) 350 9256.
SCHWEIZER FERNSEHEN DRS
Fernsehstrasse 1-4, Postfach, CH-8052 Zurich. Tel: (411) 305
6611. FAX: (411) 305 5660.
TELEVISION DE LA SUISSE ROMANDE (TSR)
20, quai Ernest-Ansermet, Case postale 234, CH-1211 Geneve
8. Tel: (4122) 708 99 11. FAX: (4122) 329 41144.
TELEVISIONE DELLA SVIZZERA ITALIANA (TSI)
Casella postale, CH-6903 Lugano. Tel: (4191) 585 111. FAX:
(4191) 58 53 55.

CABLE
022 TELEGENEVE
Quai Ernest Ansermet 20, CH-1211 Geneva. Tel: (4122) 781
1222. FAX: (4122) 329 8804.
ASCOM TELEMATIC
Raugistr 71, CH-8048 Zurich. Tel: (411) 631 2111. FAX: (411)
405 2103.
BALLCAB
Postfach, CH-4058 Basel. Tel: (4161) 691 9151. FAX: (4161)
691 9147.
LOKALFERNSEHEN DIESSENHOFEN
Gabenstr 26, CH-8253 Dissenhofen. Tel: (4153) 373 890.
REDIFFUSION
Postfach, CH-8021 Zurich. Tel: (411) 277 9111. FAX: (411) 272
8184.
SERVICE DE L'ELECTRICITE DE LA VILLE DE LAUSANNE
Case Postale 836, CH-1000 Lausanne. Tel: (4121) 315 8111.
FAX: (4121) 315 8456.
TELE M1
Stadtturmstrasse 19, CH-5401 Baden. Tel: (411) 209 410. FAX:
(411) 209 409.

VIDEO DISTRIBUTORS
ADO FILM
Stollenraen 4, CH-4144 Arlesheim. Tel: (4161) 701 3756. Tel:
(4161) 701 3711.
ALPHA FILMS
4 Pl du Cirque, PO Box 5311, Geneva. Tel: (4122) 328 0204.
FAX: (4122) 781 0676.
ATLANTIC FILM
Munchhaldenstrasse 10, PO Box 322, CH-8034 Zurich. Tel:
(411) 422 3832. FAX: (411) 422 3793.
ATLAS
Munchhaldenstrasse 10, Postfach 322, CH-8034 Zurich. Tel:
(411) 422 3833. FAX: (411) 422 3383.
BERNARD LANG
Dorf Str 14D, Freienstein, CH-8427 Zurich. Tel: (411) 865 6627.
Tel: (411) 865 6629.
BUENA VISTA INTERNATIONAL
Am Schanzengraben 27, CH-8427 Zurich. Tel: (411) 201 6655.
FAX: (411) 201 7770.
EFFECTRONIC
Schindellegistrasse 57, CH-8808 Pfaffikon. Tel: (4155) 415
4550. FAX: (4155) 415 4051.

ELITE FILM
Molkenstrasse 21, CH-8026 Zurich. Tel: (411) 242 8822. FAX: (411) 241 2123.

LES FILMS ROGER WEIL
Ave.Leon Gaud 5, CH-1206 Geneva. Tel: (4122) 346 9532. Tel: (4122) 781 0676.

FOX VIDEO
Rte des Acacias 52, CH-1211 Geneva. Tel: (4122) 343 3315. FAX: (4122) 343 9255.

HIGHLIGHT COMMUNICATIONS
Schindellegistrasse 3, Neffenbach, CH-8413 Zurich. Tel: (4155) 487 170. FAX: (4155) 486 960.

HOME MOVIES
Stegackerstrasse 6, CH-8409 Winterthur. Tel: (4152) 233 6822. FAX: (4152) 233 6830

IMPULS VIDEO & HANDELS
Sumpf Str 28, 6302. Zug Tel: (4142) 417 171. Tel: (4142) 417 174

PRIMEFILMS
Via Tamporiva 3, CH-6976 Castagnola-Lugano. Tel: (4191) 972 9630. FAX: (4191) 972 9632

LES PRODUCTIONS JMH
Ave.de Beaumont 70, CH-1010 Lausanne. Tel: (4121) 653 6550. FAX: (4121) 653 6553

RAINBOW VIDEO
Netziboden Str 23B, 2133 Prattein. Tel: (4161) 811 4480. FAX: (4161) 811 4490

REGINA FILM
4 Rue de Rive, CH-1204 Geneva. Tel: (4122) 310 8136. FAX: (4122) 310 9476

RIALTO VIDEO
Munchalden Str 10, 8048 Zurich. Tel: (411) 422 3831. FAX: (411) 422 3793

SCHMALFILM
Badenstrasse 342, PO Box 182, CH-8040 Zurich. Tel: (411) 491 2727. Tel: (411) 492 4046

STELLA VIDEO
Munchhalden Str 10, PO Box 322, CH-8034 Zurich. Tel: (411) 422 3831. FAX: (411) 422 3793

SWISS FILM INSTITUTE
Erlachstrasse 21, CH-3000 Berne. Tel: (4131) 301 0831. FAX: (4131) 301 2860

VIDEO-T-RONIC
Allmend Str 29, 8320 Fehraltori. Tel: (411) 955 1020. FAX: (411) 955 0010

VIDEOPHON
Badner Str 555, CH-8048 Zurich. Tel: (411) 491 3545. FAX: (411) 401 4420

WARNER HOME VIDEO
Studerweg 3, CH-8802 Kilchberg. Tel: (411) 715 5752. FAX: (411) 715 3451

SYRIA

Population:15.5 million.
TV sets: 780,000.
Video Standard: PAL.
SYRIAN ARAB TELEVISION (GOV.)
Ommayyad Square, Damascus. Tel: (96311) 720 700.

TAIWAN

Population: 21.1 million.
TV sets: 7 million
Home Cable Service : 59%
Video Standard: NTSC.
The Taiwan government maintains a ceiling of 30% foreign pro-gramming on terrestrial channels.
BROADCASTERS
CHINA TELEVISION COMPANY
No. 120 Chung Yang Rd., Nankang Dist., Taipei. (8862) 783 8308. FAX: (8862) 782 6007.

CHINESE TELEVISION SERVICE
100 Kuang Fu South Rd., Taipei. (8862) 751 0321. FAX: (8862) 751 6019.

TAIWAN TELEVISION ENTERPRISE
No. 120, Pa Te Rd., Section 3, Taipei 10560. (8862) 771 1515. FAX: (8862) 741 3626.

TAJIKISTAN

Population: 6.2 million.
TV sets: 970,000.
Video Standard: SECAM.
TAJIK TELEVISION
Behzod kuca 7, 734013 Dushanbe. Tel: (73772) 224 357.

TANZANIA

Population: 28.7 million.
TV sets:80,000.
Video Standard: PAL.
TELEVISION ZANZIBAR TVZ
P.O. Box 314, Zanzibar. Tel: (25554) 328 16.

THAILAND

Population: 60.3 million.
Number of TV Sets: 3.6 million.
Cable Homes: 150,000.
Video Standard: PAL.
The Thai National Broadcasting Board has mandated that all foreign language programming must carry subtitles in Thai. Bangkok Entertainment Company and Hong Kong-based Television Broadcasts Ltd. have signed an agreement to create TVB-3 and Thai-language Asia Entertainment Network, to be distributed in Thailand via cable and worldwide by satellite. The Thai government has given notice to cable licensees to begin wiring the country or forfeit their $800,000 license fees.
BROADCASTERS
BANGKOK BROADCASTING & TV CO (BBTV)
998/1 Phaholyothjn Rd., P.O. Box 4-56, Bangkok. Tel: (662) 278 1255. FAX: (662) 270 1976.

BANGKOK ENTERTAINMENT CO. (CHANNEL 3)
Vanit Bldg., 1126/1 New Petchburi Rd., Phayathal, Bangkok 10400. Tel: (662) 253 9970.

THE MASS COMMUNICATION ORGANIZATION OF THAILAND (CHANNEL 9)
222 Asok-Dindang Rd., Bangkok 10310. Tel: (662) 245 0700. Telex: 84577.

TELEVISION OF THAILAND
Ratchadamoen Rd., Bangkok 10200. Tel: (662) 222 8821.

TELEVISION OF THAILAND (CHANNEL 11)
New Petchburi Rd., Phayathal, Bangkok 1030. Tel: (662) 318 3330. FAX: (662) 318 2991.

TOGO

Population: 4.4 million.
TV sets: 26,730.
Video Standard: SECAM.
TELEVISION TOGOLAISE
B.P. 3286, Lome. Tel: (228) 215 357. FAX: (228) 215 786

TUNISIA

Population: 8.9 million.
TV sets: 680,000.
Video Standard: SECAM.
BROADCASTERS
ARAB STATES BROADCASTING UNION (ASBU)
17 rue el-Mansoura, el-Mennsah 4, Tunis 1014. Tel: (2161) 23 8044. FAX: (2161) 766 551.

RADIODIFFUSION TELEVISION TUNISIENNE
71 Ave. de la Liberte, 1002 Tunis.

RTT TUNISIA
71 Avenue de la Liberte, Tunis 1002. Tel: (2161) 287 300. FAX: (2161) 781 058.

TURKEY

Population: 63.4 million.
TV sets: 10.5 million.
Video Standard: PAL-B.
It remains to be seen whether the new coalition government and the rise of fundamentalist Islam in Turkey will affect the television and video industries, whose traditionally less stri-nent.
TURKISH RADIO & TELEVISION CORP.
TRT TV Dept., TRT Sitesi Katib Ablok Oran 06450, Ankara. (90312) 4904 983. FAX: (90313) 4904 985.

TRT, THE TURKISH RADIO-TV CORP.
Oran Sitesi, Oran, Ankara. Tel: (90312) 490 3884. FAX: (90312) 490 4985.

KANAL 6, ARTI YAYINCILIK & FILMCILIK
Imam Cesme Caddesi, G 48 Sok. No. 12, Seyrantepe, Levent 4, Istanbul. Tel: (901) 285 1250. FAX: (901) 286 0073.

ATV, SATEL TELEVIZYON PRODUKSIYON
Basin Express Yolu, Media Plaza, Gunesli, Istanbul. Tel: (901) 550 4900. FAX: (901) 502 8468, (901) 502 8233.

DTV HABER & GORSEL YAYINCILIK
Yuzyil Mahallesi, Mahmutbey Viyadugu Alti, Milliyet Tesisleri, 4. Kat Ikitelli, Istanbul. Tel: (901) 512 1107, 513 6100. FAX: (901) 505 6509.

TGRT, IHLAS FILM PRODUKSIYON
Sanayi Caddesi No. 17, Yenibosna, Istanbul. Tel: (901) 652 2560. FAX: (901) 652 2592.

INTERSTAR
Basin Expres Yolu, Medya Print Binasi No. 2, Gunesli 34540, Istanbul. Tel: (901) 698 4901. FAX: (901) 698 4957, (901) 698 4934.

SHOW TV, AKS TELEVIZYON REKLAMCILIK & FILMCILIK
Hurriyet Medya Towers, 34540 Gunesli, Istanbul. Tel: (901) 655 1111. FAX: (901) 515 5128.

HAS BILGI BIRIKIM TELEVIZYON
Yeni Bosna Asfalti, Bahcelievler, Isanbul. Tel: (901) 281 4800. FAX: (901) 281 4808.

CINE 5, CINE 5 FILMCILIK & YAPIMCILIK
Hurriyet Medya Towers, 34540 Gunesli, Istanbul. Tel: (901) 655 8822, (901) 655 9860. FAX: (901) 655 9867.

EKO RADIO & TELEVISION
Nakkastepe Azizbey Sokak No. 1, 81207 Kuzguncuk, Istanbul. Tel: (901) 341 8523. FAX: (901) 343 1944.

VIDEO DISTRIBUTORS
BARLIK FILM
Ahududu Cad 32/3, Beyoglu, Istanbul 80060. Tel: (901) 2441542. FAX: (901) 2510386.

KILIC FILM
Yesilcam SK 26/2, Beyoglu, Istanbul 80070. Tel: (901) 2495804. FAX: (901) 2441612.

TOPKAPI MUZIK VIDEO
Mesrutiyet Cad 113, Ece Han Kat 2, Tepebasi 80050, Istanbul. Tel: (901) 2524235. FAX: (901) 2526274.

ATV
Medya Plaza Basin Express Yolu, Gunesli 34540. Tel: (901) 603 9006. FAX: (901) 502 8802.

HBB TV
Buyukdere Cad 187, Levent, Istanbul. Tel: (90212) 281 4800. FAX: (90212) 281 4808.

INTERSTAR (AKK)
Divan Yolu Turbedar Sok 2, Iketelli Gunesli, Istanbul. Tel: (90212) 698 4901. FAX: (90212) 698 4970.

SHOW TV
Halaskargazi Cad 180, Istanbul. Tel: (901) 246 1260. FAX: (901) 247 5778.

TELEON
Divanyolu, Turbedar Sok 22, Cagaloglu, Istanbul 34410.

TRT INTERNATIONAL
Nevzat Tandogan Cad No. 2, Kavaklidare, Ankara. Tel: (904) 1280 456. FAX: (904) 1680 420.

TURKMENISTAN

Population: 4 million.
Video Standard: SECAM.
TURKMEN TELEVISION
Machtumkuli 89, 744000 Asgabat. Tel: (73632) 251515. FAX: (73632) 251 412.

UGANDA

Population: 19.6 million.
TV sets: 127,000.
Video Standard: PAL.
UGANDA TELEVISION
P.O. Box 7142, Kampla. Tel: (2564) 254 461.

UKRAINE

Population: 52 million.
TV Sets: 20 million.
Video Standard: SECAM.
Nova and Central European Media Enterprises obtained licensing to start broadcasting in 16 of the Ukraine's largest cities.
BROADCASTER
UKRAJINSKA TELEBACENNJA
vul. Chrescatik 26, 252001 Kiev. (38044) 229 0638.

VIDEO DISTRIBUTORS
ADONIS
40 Letiya Oktyabrya Prospect 116, Kiev 252127.
ALAN
Sevastopolskaya St 8, Simeropol 333005.
FILMMARKET
Krasnopresueuskaya Nab. 19, Kiev 252004.

UNITED ARAB EMIRATES

Population: 2.9 million.
TV sets: 170,000.
Video Standard: PAL.
EDTV/UAE RADIO & TELEVISION
P.O. Box 1695, Dubai. Tel: (9714) 470 255. FAX: (9714) 371 079.

SHARJAH TV
P.O. Box 111, Sharjah. Tel: (9716) 547 755.

UNITED ARAB EMIRATES TELEVISION SERVICE
P.O. Box 637, Abu Dhabi. Tel: (9712) 452 000. FAX: (9712) 461 823.

URUGUAY

Population: 3.2 million.
TV sets: 620,000.
Video Standard: PAL.
BROADCASTERS

CANAL 5 S.O.D.R.E.
Bulevar Artigas 2552, Montevideo.
CANAL 8 TV MELO
18 de Julio 572, 37000 Melo, Cerro Largo.
CANAL 9 DEL ESTES TV COLOR
Av. Artigas 879, 20000 Maldonado.
CANAL 11 PUNTADEL ESTE
Cantegril Country Club, 20100 Punta del Este, Maldonado.
CANAL 12 RIO URUGUAY
Cno, San Salvador s/n 65000 Fray Bentos, Rio Negro.
MELO TV
Castellanos 723, 37000 Melo, Cerro Largo.
MONTE CARLO TV COLOR
Paraguay 2253, 11800 Montevideo.
RADIOTELEVISION "ZORILLA DE SAN MARTIN"
18 de Julio 302, 45000 Tucuarenbo.
RIO DE LOS PAJAROS TV
Av. Espana 1629, 6000 Paysandu.
S.O.D.R.E.
Bul Artigas 2552, 11600 Montevideo.
SAETA TV CANAL 10
Dr. Lorenzo Carnelli 1234, 11200 Montevideo.
TELE-ARTIGAS
Lecueder 291, 55000 Artigas.
TELEDIEZ
General Rivera s/n 55100 Bela Union Artigas.
TELEVISORA COLONIA
W. Barbot 172, 70000 Colonia.
TELIVISORA SALTO GRANDE
Av Vieta 1280, 50000 Salto.
TELEVISORA TREINTA Y TRES
Pablo Zufriategui 226, Treinta y Tres, 9700 Durazno.
TELEDOCE TELEVISION COLOR
Enriqueta Compte y Rique 1276, 11800 Montevideo.
TV CERRO DEL VERDUN
Treinta y Tres 632, 30000 Minas Lavalleja.

UZBEKISTAN

Population: 23 million.
TV sets: 3.7 million.
Video Standard: SECAM.
UZBEK TELEVISION
Navoii kucasi 69, 700011. Tel: (73712) 495214.
VIDEO DISTRIBUTOR
VOLZHSKY KINOTSENTR
Molodogvardeyskaya St. 53, Samara 443099, Uzbekistan. Tel: (78462) 333 18.

VENEZUELA

Population: 21.3 million.
TV Sets: 3.9 million.
Home Cable Service: 150,000.
Venezuela, South America's third largest TV market, is worth about $400 million, even under the country's credit crunch and depressed ad sales.
STATIONS
AMAVISION
Calle Selesiano, Colegio Pio XI, Puerto Ayacucho.
CAMARA VENEZOLANA DE LA TELEVISION
Ap. 60423, Chacao, Caracas 1010-A. Tel: (582) 7814608.
CANAL 10
Av. Francisco de Miranda, con Principal de los Ruices, Centro Empresaria Miranda PHD, Caracas. Tel: (582) 239 8697. FAX: (582) 239 7757.
CANAL METROPOLITANO DE TELEVISION
Av. Circumvalacion El Sol, Centro Professional Santa Paula, Torre B. Piso 4, Santa Paula, Caracas. Tel: (582) 987 6190. FAX: (582) 985 4856.
NCTV
Urv. La Paz, Avenida 57 y Maracaibo, Maracaibo. Tel: (5861) 512 662. FAX: (5861) 512 729.
OMNIVISION
Calle Milan, Edif. Omnivision, Los Ruices Sur, Caracas. Tel: (582) 256 3586. Tel: (582) 256 4482.

RADIO CARACAS TELEVISION RCTV
Ap. 2057, Caracas. Tel: (582) 256 3696. FAX: (582) 256 1812.
TELE BOCONO
Calle 3, Qta. Caleuche, El Saman, Bocono. Tel: (5872) 521 27.
FAX: (5872) 524 85.
TELECARIBE
Centro Banaven (Cubo Negro), Torre C, Piso 1, of C-12,
Chuao, Caracas. Tel: (582) 911 964.
TELECENTRO
Avenida Pedro Leon Torres, Esquina de la Calle 47, Edificio
Telecentro, Barquisimeto.
TELESOL
Calle Sucre no 15, Cuman, Sucre. Tel: (5893) 662 059. FAX:
(5893) 662 775.
TELEVEN
C.C. Los Chaguaramos, Caracas. Tel: (582) 6617 511. Tel:
(582) 662 5300.
TELEVISORA ANDINA DE MERIDA
Av. Bolivar, Calle 23 entre Av. 4-5, Merida 5101. Tel: (5874) 525
785. FAX: (5874) 520 098.
TELIVISORA DE ORIENTE, TVO
Puerto la Cruz, Anzoategui. Tel: (5882) 662 163.
TELEVISORA NACIONAL-CHANNEL 5 & 8
Apt. 3979, Caracas.
TELEVISORA REGIONAL DEL TACHIRA
Av. Libertador, edif. Servicios Unidos, Piso 3, San Cristobal,
Tachira. Tel: (5876) 447 366. Tel: (5876) 465 277.
TV GUAYANA
Puerto Ordaz, Bolivar Caracas. Tel: (5886) 229 908.
VENEVISION
Av. La Salle, Edificio Venevision, Colinas de Los Caobos,
Caracas. Tel: (582) 782 0111.
VENEZOLANA DE TELEVISION 5
Ap. 2739, Caracas 1010-A. Tel: (582) 239 9811. FAX: (582)
35734.
VENEZOLANA DE TELEVISION 8
Ap. 2739, Caracas 1010-A. Tel: (582) 349 571.
VIDEO DISTRIBUTORS
3M DE VENEZUELA
Puente Brion a Luis Razetti, Edificio 3M, Caracas. Tel: (582)
572 8074.
ABD VIDEO
Calle Los Cerritos Edo ADB, Urb Bello Monte, Caracas. Tel:
(582) 762 9572.
AUDIO VIDEO MISION
Av Varsovia, Casa Parroquial, La California Sur, Caracas. Tel:
(582) 214 117.
BOLIVAR FILMS VIDEO
Av Luis Guillermo Villegas B, Edificio Bolivar Films, Santa
Euvigis, Caracas. Tel: (582) 283 5177.
DISTRIBUIDORA SONIA
Marron a Cuji, Edificio Aldomar, Caracas. Tel: (582) 561 9359.
ELINCHRON
4a Av, Quinta Emy, n-24, Campo Alegre, Caracas. Tel: (582)
331 912. FAX: (582) 316 852.
GRAN VIDEO/VIDEO DE VENEZUELA
Centro Comercial Concresa, Pisa 2, 422 Prados del Este, Apt
80926, Caracas 1080. Tel: (582) 979 6111. FAX: (582) 979 3590.
PRODUCCIONES VIDEO LASER
Av La Salle, Edif Mengal, piso 4, Ofic, 4-C, los Caobos,
Caracas. Tel: (582) 781 8107.
RENT-A-EQUIPO
Av San Marino, Quinta Pena Fiel, Country, Club, Caracas. Tel:
(582) 323 380. FAX: (582) 284 7801.
VIDEO HOME
Calle Madrid, entre New York y Trinidad, Qta Maremi, Local B,
Las Mercedes, Caracas. Tel: (582) 910 101. FAX: (582) 962
7319.
VIDEO RODVEN
Centro Comercial Concresa, piso 2, Ofic 422, Prados del Este,
Caracas. Tel: (582) 979 5742.
VIDEOMAX
Av Urdaneta, Esquina Urapal, Edificio, Centro Urapal, Piso 17,
Oficina 17-10, Caracas. Tel: (582) 573 4020. FAX: (582) 575
2309.
VIDEO GRABACIONES MERVIN
Professional La Urbina, Calle 3-A, Caracas. Tel: (582) 241
9015. FAX: (582) 241 3475.

VIETNAM

Population: 73.1 million.
TV Sets: 2.5 million.
Video Standard: NTSC/SECAM.
Satellite receivers are still illegal in Vietnam. The Ministry of
Culture explains that the dishes spoil the architectural beauty
of Vietnamese cities. Hanoi-based MMDS cable now boasts
1000 subscribers.
TELEVISION VIETNAM
59 Giang Vo St., Hanoi. (8443) 431 88. FAX: (8443) 553 32.

YEMEN

Population: 14.7 million.
TV sets: 433,000.
Video Standard: PAL & NTSC.
YEMEN RADIO & TV CORP.
Tel.: (9672) 231 181

YUGOSLAVIA

Population: 11.1 million.
TV sets: 1.73 million.
Video Standard: PAL.

BROADCASTERS

NTV STUDIO B
Masarikova 5, 11000 Belgrade.
TELEVIZIJA SRBIJE TELEVIZIJIA BEOGRAD
Takovrska 10, 100 Belgrade. Tel: (3811) 342 001.
TELEVIZIJA SRBIJE NOVI SAD
Kamenicki put 45,2100 Novi Sad. Tel: (38121) 56 855
TELEVIZIJA SRBIJE PRISTINA
Beograd 66m 38000 Pristina. Tel: (38138) 31 211.
TELEVIZIJA CRNE GORE
Cetinski put bb. 81000 Podgorica. Tel: (38181) 41 529.
TV ART CHANNEL
VI Kovacevica6, 1000 Belgrade.
TV PALMA
Banijska 2, 11080 Belgrade.
TV POLITIKA
Makedonska, 1100 Belgrade.
**UDRYZEBE HUGOSLOVENSKIH RADIOTELEVIZIJA D.O.O.
(JRFT)**
JRT Permanent Series—Television Department Hartvigova
70/I, 11000 Beograd. Tel: (3811) 434 910.

ZAIRE

Population: 44 million.
TV sets: 22,000.
Video Standard: SECAM
BROADCASTERS
OZRT ZAIRE TV
P.O. Box 3171, Kinshasa, Gombe. Tel: (243) 12 231 71.
ANTENNE A
Av. du Port 4, Building Forescom, 2nd Floor, Kishasa, Gombe.
Tel: (243) 217 36.
CANAL Z
P.O. Box 613, Kinshasa. Tel: (243) 202 39.

ZAMBIA

Population: 9.5 million.
TV sets: 200,000
Video Standard: PAL-B.
TELEVISION ZAMBIA
Broadcasting House, P.O.Box 50015, Lusaka 229648. Tel:
(2601) 220 864.

ZIMBABWE

Population: 11.2 million.
TV sets: 137,000.
Video Standard: PAL-B.
ZIMBABWE BROADCASTING CORP.
P.O. Box H.G. 444, Highlands, Harare. Tel: (2634) 498 659.

ON MICROFILM

MOTION PICTURE HERALD

MOTION PICTURE DAILY

These historically invaluable trade journals of the Motion Picture industry published by Quigley Publishing Company from 1915 to 1972 have been recorded on microfilm by Brookhaven Press and are now available for immediate delivery.

MOTION PICTURE HERALD
1915-1972 (77 reels)

MOTION PICTURE DAILY
1930-1972 (39 reels)

For price and further information
call (608) 781-0850
or order from:

BROOKHAVEN PRESS
Box 2287
La Crosse, WI 54602

SPECIFICATIONS: 35mm positive microfilm, silver halide at a reduction of approximately 17X (meeting ANSI/NMA standards).